THE
CHAMBERS
THESAURUS

Edited by
Martin H Manser

CHAMBERS

CHAMBERS
An imprint of Chambers Harrap Publishers Ltd
7 Hopetoun Crescent, Edinburgh, EH7 4AY

Previous edition published 1996
This edition published by Chambers Harrap Publishers Ltd 2004

A CIP catalogue record for this book is available from the British Library.

ISBN 0550 10067 9

Designed and typeset by Chambers Harrap Publishers Ltd, Edinburgh
Printed and bound in Great Britain by William Clowes, Beccles, Suffolk

Preface

A thesaurus is a dictionary that provides alternatives to a particular word or phrase. It is the essential companion for anyone who wants to create something satisfying out of words – a quick, convenient source of synonyms and related terms that will help users express themselves in as precise, succinct and yet varied a manner as possible.

It was in 1852 that Peter Mark Roget published his *Thesaurus*. Its full original title was *The Thesaurus of English Words and Phrases Classified and Arranged so as to Facilitate the Expression of Ideas and Assist in Literary Composition*. His purpose was to provide readers not only with synonyms for a word, but, more generally, with a wide choice of expressions relevant to a particular concept. His method was to classify these within a framework of ideas on 17th-century philosophical and scientific principles. This meant that a very full alphabetical index was needed to open up the classified lists to the user. It was probably the complications of this system that ensured the continued popularity of the more 'user-friendly' type of word-finding book already in production in Roget's time – the simple alphabetical list of words, each followed by its own group of synonyms. More recently there has emerged the type of thesaurus that, while preserving the alphabetical arrangement, acknowledges the value of Roget's approach by supplying related words within each entry on a rather broader, more comprehensive basis than that of mere synonymity.

The Chambers Thesaurus belongs to this last type – it lists the commonest, most synonym-rich words in the language, arranged alphabetically, each with a plentiful supply of alternative and connected expressions. Selected antonyms have also been added wherever appropriate. It has all the recognized usefulness of any thesaurus – but its special advantage is that it draws on the rich resources of *The Chambers Dictionary*, known to dictionary connoisseurs and wordgame enthusiasts alike as a mine of useful, interesting and diverting items of vocabulary.

In this second edition, the text has been enlarged by 20 per cent, with many entries revised, and over 1500 new entries. Over 70,000 new synonyms and antonyms have been added, including many spellings and words from varieties of English around the world, old (obsolete, archaic or literary) words, and technical terms and expressions. It is recommended that *The Chambers Thesaurus* should be used in conjunction with *The Chambers Dictionary*, to which it is the perfect companion volume, since the words listed are only rarely completely interchangeable alternatives.

A thesaurus jogs the memory – it offers help to the person struggling to encapsulate a meaning in a forgotten *mot juste* that might remain tantalizingly on the tip of the tongue. It is indispensable to the student, writer or reporter. A thesaurus is fun to use, and with the fun comes the opportunity to enhance a personal command of words and increase general knowledge. Words that may not be well known to the reader will trigger off investigations in a dictionary, leading to an exploration of the remoter corners of the language. Finally, a thesaurus is a tool that the word-gamester – player, solver or compiler – cannot do without.

It is hoped that readers will enjoy using this thesaurus not only to discover the exact word or phrase for an appropriate context but also to appreciate more fully the rich diversity of the English language.

Martin H Manser
Aylesbury 2004

Contributors

Editor
Martin H Manser

Project Editor
Mary O'Neill

Assistant Editor
Elaine O'Donoghue

Synonym Nuance Panels
Sheila Ferguson

Editorial Assistance
Helen Bleck
Kay Cullen
Carolyn Fox

Publishing Manager
Patrick White

Prepress
Clair Cameron
Sharon McTeir

Acknowledgements

For the second edition, the editor wishes to thank Rosalind Desmond for her careful keyboarding of the text and Mary O'Neill, Siri Hansen, and Patrick White for their encouragement during the editorial work on this book.

Features of the thesaurus

The following features are shown in context on pages vi–vii.

Clear distinction of senses

Senses within an entry are distinguished by numbered sections and by either a key synonym in SMALL CAPITALS or an example in *bold italics*, eg

sad *adj*
1 UNHAPPY, sorrowful...
2 *sad news*
upsetting, distressing...

Example phrases or sentences are based on citations from the British National Corpus.

Synonyms grouped by register

Synonyms are listed by range of context ('register') to show the appropriate styles within which words are used.

TECHNICAL
indicates a word that is restricted to a certain subject area such as music, philosophy, medicine or law, eg **codicil** (a supplement to a will) at **supplement**

OLD
indicates a word that is no longer in common use, be it obsolete, archaic or literary, eg **spoffish** at **fussy**

Shakesp and *Spenser* are extra labels used to annotate words featured in the works of Shakespeare and Spenser.

FORMAL
indicates a formal word, eg **discourse** and **colloquium** at **discussion**

COLLOQ.
indicates an informal word, eg **powwow** at **discussion**

SLANG
indicates a word used only very informally, eg **dough** and **dosh** at **money**

derog, offensive, vulgar and *taboo* are extra labels used to annotate words considered particularly vulgar or which may give offence.

Countrywide and worldwide English

Terms from varieties of English from around Britain and around the world are included (eg North American **ornery** at **stubborn**), and labelled as

dialect (usually indicates Northern English dialects)
Scot (Scottish)
Welsh
Irish
N Am (used mainly in the United States and, sometimes, Canada)

Can (used mainly in Canada, rather than the United States)
Aust (Australian)
NZ (New Zealand)
S Afr (South African)

Related adjectives

Where a headword has an adjective related to it, a note is included. For example, the entry **meaning** gives the related adjective **semantic**.

Confusable words

Where a headword is sometimes confused with another word, eg **censor** or **censure**, **fatal** or **fateful**, concise explanatory notes are included to distinguish them.

The explanations are backed up by example phrases and sentences based on citations from the British National Corpus.

Hyponym panels

Around 500 special panels show word families ('hyponyms'), and give lists of related words presenting:

- different types of, eg **film**, **food** and **sport**

- parts of, eg the **brain**, a **flower** and a **motor vehicle**

- the terminology used in particular subject areas, eg **cookery**, **football** and **medicine**

- informative encyclopedic information, eg **longest rivers**, **highest mountains** and **active volcanoes**

Synonym nuance panels

Synonym nuance panels distinguish shades of meaning among synonyms in over 300 entries, identifying and exemplifying words that:

- have particular associations or convey certain suggestions:

  unworldly suggests a vulnerability arising from lack of experience: *a schoolgirl who was unworldly in the extreme.*

- have a particular tone or convey an attitude on the part of the speaker:

  both **gullible** and **credulous** further imply a tendency to be duped and are rather more contemptuous in tone: *he treated her as a credulous imbecile.*

- usually have a specific referent or context:

  consort is a formal term which tends to be reserved for a spouse: *the queen's consort.*

Structure of thesaurus entries

Headwords in bold type at the beginning of each entry

brain *n*
1 *damage to the brain*
cerebrum
TECHNICAL encephalon, sensorium
OLD (*Shakesp*) pia mater
SLANG upper storey
Related adjectives: cerebral, encephalic
2 MIND, head, intellect, intelligence, wit, reason, sense, common sense, shrewdness, understanding
FORMAL acumen, sagacity
COLLOQ. grey matter, brains, nous, savvy

Register labels in bold small capitals

3 *the real brain in the family*
mastermind, intellectual, scholar, expert, pundit, highbrow, genius, prodigy
COLLOQ. egghead, boffin, brainbox, cleverclogs
E**3** 3 simpleton, idiot

Antonyms, indicated by E**3**, in numbered sections corresponding to those of the synonyms

Parts of the brain include:

brainstem	forebrain	optic thalamus
Broca's area	frontal lobe	parietal lobe
cerebellum	hindbrain	pineal body
cerebral cortex	hypothalamus	pituitary gland
cerebral	medulla	pons
hemisphere	oblongata	spinal cord
cerebrum	meninges	temporal lobe
cinerea (grey	mesencephalon	thalamus
matter)	midbrain	Wernicke's area
corpus callosum	occipital lobe	

Hyponym panels

Synonyms or alternative words listed after the headword, and arranged according to shades of meaning

brainless *adj*
silly, stupid, crazy, daft, foolish, incompetent, half-witted, simple-minded, idiotic, inept, mindless, thoughtless, senseless
E**3** sensible, shrewd, wise

brainteaser *n*
riddle, puzzle, problem, conundrum, mind-bender, poser; *N Am* brain-twister

Geographical information in italic labels

brainwashing *n*
indoctrination, conditioning, pressurizing, re-education, grilling, intellectual suicide, mind-bending, persuasion
FORMAL menticide

brainy *adj*
intellectual, intelligent, clever, gifted, smart, bright, brilliant, wise
FORMAL sapient
E**3** dull, stupid

Parts of speech listed after the headword and treated in order within the entry

brake *n, v*
♦ *n*
check, curb, rein, restraint, control, restriction, constraint, drag
FORMAL retardment
♦ *v*
slow (down), decelerate, reduce speed, drag, slacken, moderate, check, halt, stop, pull up
FORMAL retard
E**3** accelerate

branch *n, v*

♦ *n*

1 BOUGH, limb, sprig, shoot, stem, offshoot, arm, leg, lobe, loop, wing, prong, whip, withy; *Scot* cow, scrog
TECHNICAL ramus, axis, cladode, phylloclade
OLD braunch, rice
Related adjectives: ramal, rameal, rameous, ramous

2 *a different branch of the company*
department, office, local/regional office, agency, bureau, part, section, division, subsidiary, subsection, subdivision, affiliate, corps, wing, discipline
FORMAL succursal, ramification

3 *the branch of a river*
tributary, fork, division

■ **branch off**
divide, fork, diverge, deviate, separate
FORMAL bifurcate, furcate

■ **branch out**
diversify, subdivide, vary, develop, expand, enlarge, spread out, extend, add to, broaden out, increase, multiply, proliferate
FORMAL ramify

brand *n, v*

♦ *n*

1 *different brands of soap*
make, brand-name, tradename, trademark, line, logo, symbol, sign, emblem, label, stamp, hallmark, marque

2 KIND, quality, class, type, sort, line, variety, species

3 MARK, tag, identification, identifying mark

♦ *v*

1 *branded as a troublemaker*
mark, stamp, label, typecast, stigmatize, stain, taint, disgrace, discredit, denounce, censure
FORMAL besmirch

2 *brand cattle*
mark, stamp, burn (in), sear

brandish *v*
wave, flourish, shake, raise, swing, wield, flash, flaunt, exhibit, display, parade
OLD wag, wampish; (*Spenser*) bless, hurtle

bravery *n*
courage, pluck, fearlessness, boldness, courageousness, daring, stalwartness, hardiness, fortitude, resolution, tenacity, stout-heartedness, valour, gallantry, chivalry, heroism, indomitability, mettle, spirit, dauntlessness, audacity, bravado, prowess
FORMAL intrepidity, valiance
COLLOQ. guts, grit, spunk
F3 cowardice, fearfulness, faint-heartedness, timidity

⚠ bravery or **bravado**?
Bravery is courage: *soldiers decorated for bravery.*
Bravado is a boastful act of bravery intended to impress or intimidate or a boastful pretence of bravery aimed at concealing cowardice: *She felt her defiant bravado disintegrate like shattered glass.*

Synonym nuances
Courage is used in general contexts, whereas **pluck** has a very positive aspect of spiritedness, and is often

Related adjective notes

Idioms and phrasal verbs highlighted separately at the end of entries

Different meanings in numbered sections

Key synonyms in small capitals

Example phrases in bold italics

Additional information in bracketed italic labels

Notes on words easily confused indicated by ⚠

Synonym nuances panels

Abbreviations used in the thesaurus

adj	adjective	*N Am*	North American English
adv	adverb	*NZ*	New Zealand English
Aust	Australian English	*prep*	preposition
Can	Canadian English	*pron*	pronoun
colloq.	colloquial	®	trademark
conj	conjunction	*S*	south, southern
derog	derogatory	*S Afr*	South African English
E	east, eastern	*Scot*	Scottish English
interj	interjection	*Shakesp*	found in Shakespeare's works
N	north, northern	*v*	verb
n	noun	*W*	west, western

A

aback
■ **take aback**
surprise, astonish, astound, startle, stagger, stun, shock, disconcert, bewilder, dumbfound, dismay, upset
COLLOQ. knock out, flabbergast

abandon *v, n*
♦ *v*
1 *abandon a baby*
desert, leave (behind), maroon, strand, walk out on; *Scot* forhow
FORMAL forsake
COLLOQ. run out on, jilt, ditch, chuck, dump, leave in the lurch, leave for dead, give the elbow to, break (it) off with, leave high and dry
2 *abandon the boat*
vacate, evacuate, leave, depart from, withdraw from, go away from, bail out, escape, get out, break free from, break away from, break loose, jump ship
COLLOQ. quit
3 *abandon an activity/your responsibilities*
give up, stop (doing), cease, let go, leave, abort, resign (from), jettison, surrender, waive, sacrifice
FORMAL renounce, part with, desist, discontinue, for(e)go, forswear, dispense with, relinquish, abdicate, yield, cede
COLLOQ. drop, scrap, ditch, leave it at that, quit, jack in, pack in, kick the habit
4 *abandon yourself to despair*
give way to, give yourself up to, yield to, lose yourself in, be overcome by
E3 **1** support, maintain, stay (with), remain (with) **3** start, begin, continue
♦ *n*
carelessness, recklessness, unrestraint, uninhibitedness, wildness, impetuosity, impulsiveness, thoughtlessness
E3 restraint, caution, inhibition(s), moderation, care, carefulness

---

Synonym nuances
verb sense 1
To **desert** or **walk out on** someone or something implies abandonment of a duty or obligation: *deserting his regiment*; *walked out on his wife*. A quality that you are dependent on can also **desert** you: *his energy was deserting him*. **Maroon** and **strand** have the more specific meaning of abandoning someone or something in an isolated place with no means of leaving, or in a difficult situation with no help.

Similarly, to **leave someone in the lurch** or **leave someone high and dry** is to leave them helpless in a difficult situation. **Leave behind** carries connotations of permanence and sometimes reluctance: *leaving behind my childhood*. Likewise, **forsake** is used of something that has been valued or enjoyed: *forced to forsake his country*; *forsook photography for film-making*.

The colloquial terms **run out on**, **jilt**, **ditch**, **chuck**, **dump**, **give the elbow to**, or **break (it) off with** are usually used of a partner or lover. However, you can **ditch** any person or thing that is no longer useful: *ditched their manager*; *ditched plans*.

---

abandoned *adj*
1 *abandoned buildings*
deserted, unoccupied, unused, disused, empty, vacant, derelict, neglected, forlorn, desolate
FORMAL forsaken
2 *abandoned young people*
dissolute, wild, crazy, uninhibited, unrestrained, reckless, mad, wanton, wicked, debauched, immoral, corrupt
FORMAL reprobate, profligate
E3 **1** (well-)kept, occupied **2** restrained, (self-)controlled

abandonment *n*
1 DESERTION, leaving (behind), neglect, marooning, stranding
FORMAL forsaking, decampment, dereliction
COLLOQ. running out on, jilting, ditching
2 *abandonment of an activity*
giving-up, stopping, resignation (from), surrender, waiving, sacrifice
FORMAL renunciation, relinquishment, cessation, discontinuation, discontinuance, abdication, cession
COLLOQ. dropping, scrapping, ditching

abase *v*
humble, humiliate, kowtow
FORMAL debase, demean, mortify, belittle, malign, disparage
COLLOQ. crawl, suck up to
E3 elevate, honour, raise

abasement *n*
humbleness, humility, humiliation
FORMAL debasement, demeaning, mortification, disparagement
COLLOQ. crawling, sucking up to

abashed *adj*
ashamed, shamefaced, embarrassed, mortified, remorseful, humiliated, humbled, affronted, confused, taken aback, bewildered, nonplussed, confounded, dumbfounded, discomposed
FORMAL perturbed, disconcerted, discomfited, discountenanced
COLLOQ. floored
E3 composed, at ease; *formal* audacious

abate *v*
1 *the storm abated*
decrease, subside, reduce, lessen, sink, dwindle, die down, ease, moderate, drop off, taper off, peter out, fall off, wane
FORMAL diminish, decline, attenuate
COLLOQ. let up
2 *abate anger/pain*
moderate, ease, relieve, lessen, decrease, reduce, alleviate, soothe, mitigate, pacify, quell, subside, weaken, wane, slacken, slow, fade
FORMAL remit
COLLOQ. let up
E3 **1** increase, strengthen

abatement *n*
1 *the abatement of the storm; noise abatement*
reduction, lessening, subsidence, dying-down,

dwindling, easing, lowering, dropping-off
FORMAL decline, diminution, attenuation
2 *abatement of anger*
moderation, easing, relief, lessening, decrease, alleviation, mitigation, weakening, wane, slackening
FORMAL remission, assuagement, palliation

abattoir *n*
slaughterhouse, butchery, shambles

abbey *n*
monastery, priory, friary, seminary, convent, nunnery, cloister, minster, cathedral

abbreviate *v*
shorten, cut (down), trim, clip, abridge, summarize, précis, abstract, digest, condense, compress, reduce, lessen, shrink, contract
FORMAL truncate, curtail, constrict
E3 extend, lengthen, expand, amplify

abbreviated *adj*
shortened, short, cut, abridged, contracted, reduced, condensed, clipped, truncated, summary, compact
E3 lengthened, long, extended

abbreviation *n*
shortening, short form, shortened form, contraction, acronym, initialism, clipping, curtailment, abridgement, summary, synopsis, résumé, précis, abstract, digest, compression, reduction
FORMAL truncated form, summarization, truncation
E3 long form, extension, expansion, amplification

abdicate *v*
1 *the king abdicated*
resign, resign from the throne, stand down, step down, give up, give up the throne
FORMAL retire, relinquish/renounce the throne
COLLOQ. quit
2 *abdicate responsibility*
abandon, give up, reject, refuse to accept any longer, surrender, disown
FORMAL renounce, relinquish, cede, yield, forsake, for(e)go, abjure, abnegate, repudiate
COLLOQ. shirk, quit, turn your back on, wash your hands of

abdication *n*
1 *the abdication of the king*
resignation, retirement, standing-down, stepping-down, giving up of the throne
FORMAL renunciation/relinquishment of the throne
2 *abdication of responsibilities*
abandonment, rejection, refusal, surrender, giving-up, disowning
FORMAL renunciation, relinquishment, abjuration, abnegation, repudiation

abdomen *n*
belly, stomach, midriff, middle, maw
OLD ventricle, heart, little Mary
COLLOQ. guts, tummy, tum, insides, paunch, pot belly, corporation; *Aust* bingy
SLANG bread-basket
Related adjectives: coeliac, abdominal

abdominal *adj*
coeliac, ventral, intestinal, visceral, ventricular, gastric

abduct *v*
kidnap, seize, take (away) by force, capture, carry off, make off with, snatch, shanghai, take as hostage, hold to ransom, spirit away, lay hold of
FORMAL appropriate
COLLOQ. run away/off with

abduction *n*
kidnapping, kidnap, seizure, capture, snatching, taking as hostage, carrying off, ravishing, seduction, rape

aberrant *adj*
deviant, deviating, divergent, different, irregular, abnormal, anomalous, odd, peculiar, eccentric, rogue, defective, corrupt
FORMAL incongruous, atypical
COLLOQ. freakish, quirky
E3 regular, normal, typical

aberration *n*
1 *an aberration in behaviour*
deviation, straying, wandering, divergence, instability, irregularity, abnormality, nonconformity, oversight, anomaly, oddity, peculiarity, eccentricity, lapse, delusion
2 *scientific aberrations*
deviation, divergence, irregularity, abnormality, variation, anomaly, oddity, peculiarity, mistake
E3 1 conformity, regularity, normality

abet *v*
help, aid, assist, support, encourage, lend a hand, endorse, promote, sanction, spur, condone, collude with
FORMAL succour
COLLOQ. egg on
E3 prevent, hinder, discourage

abeyance
■ **in abeyance**
no longer in use, cancelled temporarily, postponed, not in operation, disused, suspended, in (a state of) suspension, pending
FORMAL dormant
COLLOQ. hanging fire, on ice, shelved
E3 in use, in operation, continued

abhor *v*
hate, detest, loathe, recoil from, spurn, despise, have an aversion to, cannot abide/bear, shudder at, shrink from
FORMAL abominate, execrate
COLLOQ. hate someone's guts, can't stand
E3 love, adore

abhorrence *n*
hate, hatred, aversion, loathing, horror, revulsion, disgust, distaste, contempt
FORMAL abomination, repugnance, execration, detestation, animosity, enmity, malice, odium
E3 love, adoration

abhorrent *adj*
repugnant, detestable, loathsome, abominable, obnoxious, hated, hateful, horrible, horrid, offensive, repellent, repulsive, revolting, nauseating, disgusting, distasteful
FORMAL execrable, heinous, odious, absonant
E3 delightful, attractive, lovable

abide *v*
1 BEAR, put up with, tolerate, accept, take, brook, endure; *Scot* thole
COLLOQ. stand, stomach, hack
2 REMAIN, last, endure, continue, survive, live on, persist
■ **abide by**
obey, observe, follow, go along with, carry out, discharge, stand by, hold to, keep to, agree to, comply with, adhere to, conform to, submit to, accept, respect, uphold, fulfil
COLLOQ. go by the book, stick to the rules, toe the line
E3 ignore, reject; *colloq.* flout

abiding *adj*
lasting, enduring, constant, continual, continuous, long-lasting, long-term, long-running, lifelong, persistent, persisting, unchanging, unchangeable, eternal, everlasting, immortal, unending, chronic, permanent, stable, standing, fixed, firm, durable
FORMAL immutable
E3 short-lived, short-term; *formal* ephemeral, transient

ability *n*
1 *the ability to teach*
capability, capacity, faculty, facility, power(s), means, resources
FORMAL potentiality, potential, propensity, wherewithal
2 *someone of great ability*
skill, competence, proficiency, qualification, talent, gift, calibre, endowment, expertise, forte, strength, dexterity, aptitude, deftness, adeptness, adroitness, prowess, motivation
FORMAL competency
COLLOQ. knack, flair, touch, knowhow, genius, the hang, the knack, what it takes, savoir-faire, savvy
1 inability **2** incompetence, weakness

ⓘ ability or **capability**?
Ability is the more general term, referring to the possession of particular skills, knowledge, powers, etc or the simple fact of something being possible: *his ability to write a catchy tune; our ability to work together. Capability* may refer to the possession of an aptitude, especially one that derives from a person's character: *my mother's organizational capabilities.*

---

ab initio *adv*
from the beginning, from the start, at first, at the beginning, at the start, to begin with, to start with, initially, primarily, originally, firstly

abject *adj*
1 *abject poverty*
miserable, wretched, forlorn, hopeless, woeful, awful, shameful, humiliating, pitiable, pitiful, pathetic, outcast, degraded
FORMAL execrable
2 *an abject coward*
contemptible, worthless, base, low, mean, dishonourable, deplorable, despicable, vile, sordid, debased, degenerate, submissive, servile, slavish, grovelling, ingratiating
FORMAL ignoble, ignominious
2 proud, exalted

abjure *v*
abandon, disown, deny, reject
FORMAL renounce, relinquish, retract, forswear, abdicate, dispense with, forsake, abnegate, disavow, disclaim, renege on
agree, assent, support

ablaze *adj*
1 BURNING, alight, blazing, flaming, in flames, on fire, ignited, lighted, alight, incandescent
OLD afire
FORMAL aflame
2 *a house ablaze with lights*
illuminated, luminous, glowing, aglow, alight, radiant, flashing, gleaming, sparkling, shimmering, brilliant, lit up
FORMAL incandescent
3 *eyes ablaze with passion*
impassioned, passionate, fervent, ardent, fiery, intense, enthusiastic, excited, exhilarated, stimulated, aroused, angry, furious, fuming, raging, incensed, frenzied

able *adj*
capable, competent, fit, fitted, dexterous, adroit, deft, adept, proficient, qualified, practised, experienced, skilled, accomplished, clever, intelligent, expert, masterly, skilful, ingenious, talented, gifted, strong, powerful, effective, efficient
COLLOQ. all there, on the ball, up to it, clued up, cut out for
unable, incapable, incompetent, ineffective

■ **able to**
capable of, competent to, qualified to, fit to, prepared to, allowed to, free to

---

Synonym nuances
The words **capable**, **competent** and **proficient** are used of someone with sufficient ability or skill for a particular task, while **fit** and **fitted**, and the more colloquial **cut out for**, can be used to imply suitability in general.
 While someone can be said to be **skilful** if they demonstrate skill in undertaking an action, **skilled** is more often used of someone who possesses specific skills and training. **Qualified** is used where someone has official recognition of having the necessary competency, while **practised**, **experienced** and **accomplished** are used of someone whose expertise has been honed by familiarity; **expert** and **masterly** can be used of someone who demonstrates complete mastery as a result. On the other hand, someone with a special innate skill or natural ability can be described by the words **talented** and **gifted**.
 Clever, **intelligent** and **ingenious** suggest the use of highly developed mental ability, while **dexterous**, **adroit**, **deft** and **adept** may be used to suggest either physical or mental agility. **Strong**, **powerful** and **effective** can be used where stamina or technique are used to achieve a successful conclusion: *the most powerful lever for peace.* **Efficient**, however, suggests the ability to achieve satisfactory results with economy of effort.
 Up to it suggests being able, although little more, and is usually used in the negative: *she wasn't up to it.*

---

able-bodied *adj*
fit, healthy, sound, in good health, strong, robust, hardy, tough, vigorous, powerful, hale, hearty, hale and hearty, fine, lusty, sturdy, rugged, strapping, stout, burly, stalwart, staunch
COLLOQ. as fit as a fiddle
disabled, handicapped, infirm, delicate

ablution *n*
washing, cleaning, cleansing, bathing, showering, scrubbing, soaking, rinsing

abnegate *v*
give up, abstain, reject, refuse, abandon, surrender
FORMAL renounce, relinquish, forbear, abjure, forswear, disavow, repudiate, eschew

abnegation *n*
abstinence, self-denial, surrender, self-sacrifice, giving-up, temperance
FORMAL renunciation, relinquishment, forbearance, abjuration, repudiation, eschewal

abnormal *adj*
odd, strange, peculiar, curious, queer, weird, eccentric, idiosyncratic, paranormal, unnatural, uncanny, extraordinary, exceptional, unusual, uncommon, unexpected, irregular, erratic, wayward, deviant, divergent, different
FORMAL singular, anomalous, aberrant, atypical, outré, preternatural
COLLOQ. oddball
normal, regular, typical

abnormality *n*
oddity, peculiarity, eccentricity, strangeness, bizarreness, unnaturalness, unusualness, uncommonness, irregularity, exception, anomaly, deformity, flaw, malformation, dysfunction, deviation, divergence, difference
FORMAL singularity, aberration, atypicality
normality, regularity

aboard *adv, prep*
on, onto, in, into, on board, on board ship

abode *n*
home, lodgings, habitat
FORMAL dwelling, dwelling-place, residence,

place of residence, domicile, habitation
COLLOQ. pad

abolish v
cancel, end, stop, do away with, quash, repeal, revoke,
annul, invalidate, rescind, suppress, destroy, eliminate, put
an end to, exterminate, annihilate, obliterate, sink,
eradicate, overthrow, blot out, wipe out, get rid of, scrap,
stamp out, subvert, overturn
FORMAL terminate, discontinue, nullify, vitiate, abrogate,
expunge
COLLOQ. axe, chop, dump
☞ create, introduce, establish, institute, retain, authorize,
continue

> **Synonym nuances**
> The fairly neutral term **cancel** is to abolish something not
> yet in place, but **end**, **stop** or **discontinue** are used of
> something currently happening. You can use **put an end
> to**, **scrap**, **get rid of** or **do away with** as general terms for
> removing something, although the latter two carry
> connotations of a welcome riddance.
>   **Eliminate**, **eradicate** and **stamp out** suggest complete
> and permanent removal, often as a result of strong
> measures. The words **destroy, exterminate, annihilate,
> obliterate, sink** and **wipe out** imply destruction with
> force. **Overthrow** is usually used for the toppling of
> regimes, but you can subvert or overturn a corrupt
> system or a decision.
>   You can also talk of someone in authority **quashing** a
> ruling or decision, while **repeal, revoke, annul, rescind**
> and **abrogate** are only used of legal or official measures;
> similarly **annul** and **terminate** describe the abolition of
> laws or contracts. **Axe, chop** and **dump** are very emotive
> informal terms to describe getting rid of someone or
> something; the first usually relates to jobs or services:
> *1220 jobs axed*. **Nullify** and **vitiate** are used where the
> results of an action are negated rather than abolished:
> *the costs would nullify any tax relief.*
>   To describe the removal of thoughts from the mind, you
> can use **expunge** or **blot out**: *to blot out the horror.*

abolition n
cancellation, annulment, ending, stopping, doing-away
with, repeal, suppression, destruction, elimination,
scrapping, annihilation, extinction, overthrow, blotting-
out, quashing, withdrawal
FORMAL termination, invalidation, nullification, voiding,
rescindment, revocation, vitiation, abrogation, rescission,
obliteration, extermination, eradication, extirpation,
dissolution, subversion
COLLOQ. axe, chop, chopping, dumping
☞ creation, introduction, retention, authorization,
continuation

abominable adj
loathsome, detestable, hateful, horrid, horrible, abhorrent,
offensive, repulsive, repellent, disgusting, revolting,
repugnant, obnoxious, nauseating, foul, base, vile,
atrocious, appalling, dreadful, terrible, contemptible,
despicable, wretched, cursed, damnable
FORMAL execrable, odious, heinous, reprehensible
COLLOQ. god-awful
☞ delightful, pleasant, desirable

abominably adv
horribly, disgustingly, obnoxiously, appallingly, terribly,
dreadfully
FORMAL odiously, reprehensibly, execrably

abominate v
abhor, hate, loathe, detest, despise, have an aversion to,
condemn
FORMAL execrate
☞ love, adore

abomination n
1 *murder is an abomination*
outrage, offence, disgrace, horror, atrocity, evil, curse,
plague, torment
FORMAL anathema
2 HATE, hatred, detestation, loathing, abhorrence,
revulsion, disgust, distaste, aversion, hostility
FORMAL execration, repugnance, odium
☞ **2** adoration, delight

aboriginal adj
native, indigenous, original, earliest, initial, first, primal,
primitive, ancient, local
FORMAL autochthonous, prim(a)eval

aborigine n
native, indigene, original inhabitant, earliest inhabitant,
first inhabitant

abort v
1 *abort a pregnancy*
terminate, miscarry, have a miscarriage
2 *abort a plan*
end, bring/come to an end, stop, suspend, discontinue,
halt, call off, cut short, check, frustrate, thwart, fail
FORMAL nullify
COLLOQ. axe, pull the plug on
☞ **2** continue, start, begin

abortion n
termination, miscarriage
FORMAL aborticide, foeticide

abortive adj
failed, unsuccessful, fruitless, unproductive, barren,
sterile, vain, idle, futile, useless, ineffective,
thwarted
OLD bootless
FORMAL unavailing, ineffectual, inefficacious
☞ successful, fruitful

abound v
be plentiful, flourish, swell, increase, swarm, teem,
crowd, be full, be abundant, bristle, brim over,
overflow
FORMAL proliferate, thrive, superabound, exuberate,
luxuriate

about prep, adv
♦ *prep*
1 *write about a subject*
regarding, on, on the subject of, concerning, relating to,
connected with, concerned with, as regards, referring
to, with regard to, with respect to, with reference to,
on the subject of, in the matter of, re, dealing with; *Scot*
anent
FORMAL apropos of
2 *somewhere about the house*
close to, near, nearby, beside, adjacent to, in the vicinity of,
around
3 *walk about the town*
round, around, surrounding, throughout, all over
FORMAL encircling, encompassing
♦ *adv*
1 *about twenty*
around, approximately, roughly, in the region of, in the
neighbourhood of, more or less, almost, nearly,
approaching, nearing
FORMAL circa
2 *run about*
to and fro, here and there, from place to place
OLD hither and thither
3 *Is there anyone about?*
near, nearby, close, close by, around, within reach
■ **about to**
going to, on the point of, on the verge of, all but, ready to,
soon to, intending to, preparing to, all set to

about-turn n

about-face, volte-face, (complete) reversal, turnabout, turnaround
FORMAL enantiodromia
COLLOQ. U-turn

above prep, adv, adj

♦ prep
1 above the clouds
over, higher than, upon, on top of
FORMAL atop
2 above the rank of sergeant
superior to, senior to, higher than, over
3 temperatures above the average
in excess of, exceeding, beyond, higher than, greater than
FORMAL surpassing
4 above suspicion
beyond, not liable to, not open to, not exposed to, immune to, exempt from, superior to
F∃ 1 below, under 2 below
♦ adv
1 noise from above
overhead, high up, higher
FORMAL aloft, on high
2 as mentioned above
earlier, before, previously
F∃ 1 below, underneath 2 below
♦ adj
above-mentioned, previous, earlier, preceding
OLD prevenient
FORMAL above-stated, foregoing, prior, aforementioned, aforesaid
■ **above all**
primarily, firstly, first of all, most importantly, chiefly, most of all
■ **above yourself**
conceited, vain, proud, arrogant, haughty, boastful, swollen-headed, immodest, egotistical, narcissistic, self-important, full of yourself, puffed-up, supercilious, self-satisfied, complacent, smug
FORMAL vainglorious
COLLOQ. cocky, bigheaded, stuck-up, toffee-nosed, too big for your boots

above-board adj

honest, legitimate, straight, true, open, frank, candid, straightforward, forthright, truthful, trustworthy, honourable, reputable, upright
FORMAL guileless, veracious
COLLOQ. on the level, legit, kosher, fair and square, square
F∃ dishonest, underhand, shady

abracadabra n

magic word, spell, open sesame, gibberish, hocus pocus
COLLOQ. mumbo-jumbo

abrade v

rub, graze, scratch, scrape, scrape away, scour, grate, grind, chafe, erode, wear away/down

abrasion n

graze, scratch, cut, scrape, scratching, scraping, scouring, grating, grinding, abrading, chafing, chafe, friction, rubbing, erosion, wearing-away, wearing-down
FORMAL excoriation

abrasive adj

1 abrasive material
rough, scratching, scraping, grating, grinding, harsh, chafing, corrosive
FORMAL erosive, frictional, attritional, erodent
2 an abrasive person
harsh, brusque, caustic, sharp, biting, grating, hurtful, nasty, unpleasant, irritating, annoying
F∃ 1 smooth 2 pleasant, kind

abreast adj

1 walk abreast
side by side, shoulder to shoulder, level, beside/alongside each other, next to each other, cheek by jowl
2 keep abreast of the news
acquainted, informed, knowledgeable, au courant, up to date, in touch, au fait, familiar, well up
FORMAL conversant
COLLOQ. in the picture, on the ball, with your finger on the pulse
F∃ 2 unaware, out of touch, unfamiliar

abridge v

shorten, cut (down), prune, curtail, abbreviate, cut short, contract, reduce, decrease, lessen, summarize, précis, abstract, digest, condense, compress, truncate, concentrate
FORMAL synopsize
COLLOQ. clip, lop
F∃ expand, amplify; colloq. pad out

abridged adj

short, shorter, cut down, abbreviated, cut short, contracted, reduced, digested, summarized
COLLOQ. clipped, potted

abridgement n

1 the abridgement of the story
shortening, cutting, reduction, decrease, diminishing, concentration, contraction, restriction
FORMAL diminution, truncation
2 an abridgement of a report
summary, synopsis, résumé, short version, shortened version, outline, précis, abstract, digest, epitome
FORMAL conspectus, abrégé
F∃ 1 expansion; colloq. padding (out)

abroad adv

1 OVERSEAS, in/to a foreign country, in/to foreign parts, out of the country, far and wide, widely
2 news spread abroad
at large, widely, publicly, around, about, circulating, extensively, far and wide, current
F∃ 1 at home

abrogate v

abolish, cancel, annul, end, stop, repeal, revoke, do away with, invalidate, reverse
TECHNICAL disaffirm
FORMAL countermand, rescind, retract, dissolve, repudiate, disenact, vitiate
COLLOQ. axe, scrap, chop, dump
F∃ establish, institute, introduce

abrogation n

abolition, cancellation, annulment, repealing, revocation, invalidation, reversal, overruling
TECHNICAL disaffirmation
FORMAL countermanding, rescinding, rescindment, recision, dissolution, repudiation, vitiation
COLLOQ. axe, scrapping, chop, dumping

abrupt adj

1 come to an abrupt end
sudden, unexpected, unforeseen, unannounced, unceremonious, surprising, startling, dramatic, quick, rapid, swift, hasty, hurried, immediate, instant, instantaneous
FORMAL precipitate
COLLOQ. snap
2 BRUSQUE, curt, terse, brisk, gruff, rough, rude, offhand, dismissive, discourteous, impolite, unfriendly, blunt, direct, uncivil
COLLOQ. short, off, snappy, snappish
3 an abrupt slope
sheer, steep, sharp, vertical
FORMAL precipitous, declivitous

⊟1 gradual, slow, leisurely **2** friendly, expansive, ceremonious, polite

abruptly adv
1 the phone call ended abruptly
suddenly, unexpectedly, unceremoniously, quickly, rapidly, swiftly, hastily, hurriedly, immediately, instantly, instantaneously
FORMAL precipitately
2 BRUSQUELY, curtly, tersely, briskly, gruffly, roughly, rudely, offhand, dismissively, discourteously, impolitely, bluntly, directly
COLLOQ. shortly, snappily, snappishly
⊟1 gradually, slowly **2** expansively, courteously, politely

abscess n
swelling, ulcer, ulceration, boil, sore, infection, inflammation, canker, noma
OLD impostume
COLLOQ. gathering

abscond v
run away, run off, make off, decamp, flee, fly, escape, disappear, vanish, bolt, take French leave
COLLOQ. quit, scram, skedaddle, vamoose, scarper, clear off/out, make a quick getaway, beat it, run for it, do a runner, do a bunk, do a moonlight flit

absence n
1 absence from school
non-attendance, non-appearance, truancy; N Am playing hookey; absenteeism, non-existence
COLLOQ. skiving, bunking off
2 LACK, need, deficiency, scarcity, unavailability, default, omission, vacancy
FORMAL want, dearth, privation, paucity, vacuity
⊟1 presence, attendance, appearance **2** presence

absent adj, v
◆ adj
1 absent from the meeting
missing, not present, not here, not there, not around, away, out, off, unavailable, gone, lacking, truant, AWOL
FORMAL in absentia
COLLOQ. when someone's back is turned
2 INATTENTIVE, daydreaming, dreamy, faraway, elsewhere, absent-minded, blank, preoccupied, unaware, oblivious, unheeding
FORMAL vacant, distracted
COLLOQ. miles away, in a world of your own
⊟1 present, here, there **2** attentive, alert, aware
▪ **absent yourself**
take your leave, withdraw, retire, depart, exit, back out, retreat, slip away

absentee n
non-attender, no-show, truant

absently adv
absent-mindedly, inattentively, blankly, abstractedly
COLLOQ. in a world of your own, with your head in the clouds

absent-minded adj
forgetful, scatterbrained, having a bad memory, absent, withdrawn, faraway, distracted, preoccupied, absorbed, engrossed, musing, dreaming, dreamy, wool-gathering, inattentive, unaware, oblivious, unconscious, heedless, unheeding, unthinking, impractical, abstracted, pensive
FORMAL distrait(e)
COLLOQ. with a memory like a sieve, not all there, somewhere else, dead to the world, miles away, in a world of your own, scatty
⊟ attentive

absent-mindedly adv
absently, inattentively, blankly, abstractedly
COLLOQ. in a world of your own, with your head in the clouds

absolute adj
1 in absolute confidence
utter, total, complete, entire, full, thorough, exhaustive, supreme, definitive, conclusive, final, definite, unquestionable, indubitable, unambiguous, undivided, unlimited, categorical, decided, decisive, positive, sure, certain, genuine, pure, perfect, sheer, unmixed, unadulterated, unqualified, unconditional, unmitigated, unrestrained, unequivocal, unrestricted, downright, rank, out-and-out, outright
FORMAL consummate, peremptory
2 absolute power
totalitarian, unlimited, unrestricted, unrestrained, boundless
3 an absolute ruler
supreme, totalitarian, autocratic, tyrannical, despotic, dictatorial, sovereign, authoritarian, high-handed, almighty
FORMAL omnipotent, autarchic, autarchical
4 absolute truth
fixed, non-variable, unalterable, non-negotiable, set, established, settled, firm, rigid, universal

absolutely adv
1 I agree with you absolutely
utterly, totally, completely, entirely, fully, wholly, thoroughly, exhaustively, perfectly, supremely, unconditionally, finally, categorically, definitely, positively, in every way/respect, wholeheartedly, conclusively, unequivocally, unambiguously, unquestionably, decidedly, decisively, surely, certainly, infallibly, genuinely, truly, purely, exactly, precisely
COLLOQ. dead
2 the despot ruled absolutely
tyrannically, autocratically, despotically, dictatorially, high-handedly
3 'He really ought to take more rest.' 'Absolutely.'
certainly, of course, yes, surely, naturally, obviously, clearly, plainly, definitely, for sure, undoubtedly, without a doubt, no doubt, undeniably, unquestionably, by all means, doubtless, doubtlessly, assuredly, positively
COLLOQ. quite (so)

absolution n
forgiveness, pardon, pardoning, deliverance, freedom, liberation, release, mercy, redemption, acquittal, discharge, amnesty, emancipation
OLD shrift
FORMAL exoneration, remission, vindication, exculpation, purgation
COLLOQ. letting off

absolve v
excuse, clear, forgive, pardon, deliver, free, set free, discharge, liberate, release, loose, have mercy on, show mercy towards, emancipate
FORMAL exonerate, vindicate, justify, acquit, exculpate, remit
COLLOQ. let off

absorb v
1 absorb liquid/heat
take in, draw in, soak up, drink in, suck up, blot up, sponge up, assimilate, engulf
FORMAL ingest, imbibe, consume
COLLOQ. devour
2 absorb facts
take in, digest, assimilate, understand, receive, drink in, hold, retain
3 absorb your attention
engross, involve, fascinate, enthral, captivate, engage, hold, preoccupy, occupy, use up, fill (up), monopolize
COLLOQ. not be able to put down
4 absorbed into a bigger company
incorporate, integrate, assimilate

COLLOQ. swallow up
⊡ **1** give out; *formal* exude

absorbed *adj*
engrossed, involved, fascinated, interested, enthralled, captivated, preoccupied, occupied, taken up with, spellbound, riveted

absorbent *adj*
receptive, porous, permeable, pervious, spongy, soaking, blotting, retentive
TECHNICAL sorbefacient
FORMAL absorptive, assimilative, spongiform, resorbent
⊡ water-repellent, waterproof

absorbing *adj*
interesting, amusing, entertaining, enjoyable, diverting, engrossing, preoccupying, intriguing, fascinating, captivating, enthralling, spellbinding, gripping, riveting, compelling, compulsive
COLLOQ. unputdownable
⊡ boring, off-putting

absorption *n*
1 *the absorption of liquid/heat*
taking-in, drawing-in, soaking-up, assimilation
TECHNICAL osmosis
FORMAL ingestion, consumption
COLLOQ. devouring
2 *absorption of your attention*
engrossing, involvement, captivating, riveting, engagement, holding, preoccupation, occupation, immersion, raptness, attentiveness, concentration, intentness, monopoly

abstain *v*
1 *abstain from food*
refuse, reject, resist, shun, avoid, keep from, give up, do/go without, stop, stop short of, hold back, keep from
FORMAL refrain, decline, renounce, forbear, for(e)go, desist, deny yourself, eschew
COLLOQ. quit, cut out, jack in, think twice before doing something
2 *abstain in an election*
not vote, refuse to vote, be neutral
COLLOQ. sit on the fence
⊡ **1** indulge

abstemious *adj*
temperate, moderate, abstinent, self-denying, self-disciplined, disciplined, sober, sparing, frugal, austere, ascetic, restrained
FORMAL self-abnegating
⊡ intemperate, gluttonous, luxurious

abstention *n*
not voting, refusal to vote, declining to vote, neutrality
COLLOQ. sitting on the fence

abstinence *n*
1 *abstinence from sensual desires*
abstaining, self-denial, non-indulgence, avoidance, fasting, refusal, giving-up, going-without, restraint, self-restraint, self-control, self-discipline
FORMAL abstemiousness, continence, forbearance, refraining, declension, renunciation, desistance, eschewal, abjuration
2 TEETOTALISM, temperance, moderation, frugality, asceticism
FORMAL sobriety, nephalism
⊡ **1** indulgence, self-indulgence

abstinent *adj*
abstaining, self-denying, non-indulgent, restrained, self-restrained, self-controlled, self-disciplined, temperate, moderate, frugal, ascetic, teetotal, sober
FORMAL abstemious, continent, forbearing
⊡ self-indulgent

abstract *adj, n, v*
♦ *adj*
1 *abstract nouns*
non-concrete, conceptual, notional
2 *abstract reasoning*
theoretical, conceptual, notional, intellectual, hypothetical, unpractical, unrealistic, general, generalized, indefinite, philosophical, academic, complex, deep, profound, subtle
TECHNICAL metaphysical, ideational, ideative
FORMAL abstruse, arcane, recondite, suppositional, suppositive
3 *abstract paintings*
non-realistic, non-representational, symbolic, contrived
⊡ **1** concrete **2** concrete, real, actual, practical
3 representational, realistic, figurative
♦ *n*
synopsis, outline, summary, recapitulation, résumé, précis, digest, abridgement, compression, compendium, syllabus
FORMAL epitome, conspectus
♦ *v*
1 *abstract a report*
summarize, outline, précis, digest, condense, compress, abridge, abbreviate, shorten, cut (down)
2 *abstract coal from the ground*
extract, remove, take away/out, withdraw, draw off, isolate, detach, tap, separate
FORMAL dissociate, prescind, subduce
⊡ **1** expand, lengthen **2** insert, put in
▪ **in the abstract**
theoretically, hypothetically, conceptually, notionally, generally, philosophically, *in abstracto*
COLLOQ. on paper

abstracted *adj*
preoccupied, absent-minded, distracted, forgetful, scatterbrained, absent, withdrawn, absorbed, engrossed, pensive, musing, dreaming, dreamy, bemused, wool-gathering, inattentive, unaware, oblivious, unconscious, heedless, unheeding, unthinking, impractical
COLLOQ. scatty, miles away
⊡ attentive, alert; *colloq.* on the ball

abstractedly *adv*
absently, absent-mindedly, inattentively, blankly
COLLOQ. in a world of your own, with your head in the clouds

abstraction *n*
1 IDEA, notion, concept, thought, conception, theory, hypothesis, theorem, conjecture, formula, generalization, generality
2 INATTENTION, dream, dreaminess, absent-mindedness, preoccupation, remoteness, withdrawal
FORMAL distraction, pensiveness, absorption, bemusedness
3 EXTRACTION, withdrawal, removal, isolation, separation

abstruse *adj*
obscure, difficult to understand, deep, profound, complex, mysterious, cryptic, unfathomable, incomprehensible, high, long, Delphic, subtle, perplexing, puzzling
OLD exquisite
FORMAL arcane, esoteric, inscrutable, enigmatic, recherché, hermetic, recondite
⊡ simple, obvious

absurd *adj*
ridiculous, ludicrous, preposterous, fantastic, illogical, paradoxical, unreasonable, irrational, nonsensical, meaningless, senseless, foolish, silly, stupid, idiotic, crazy, farcical, inane, comical, funny, humorous, harebrained, laughable, derisory, grotesque, priceless, unearthly
OLD Laputan
FORMAL incongruous, implausible, untenable, risible, asinine

COLLOQ. daft
SLANG *N Am* gonzo
⊟ reasonable, logical, rational, sensible

absurdity *n*
ridiculousness, ludicrousness, preposterousness, illogicality, unreasonableness, meaninglessness, senselessness, foolishness, folly, silliness, fatuousness, idiocy, stupidity, craziness, inanity, paradox, humour, farce, charade, travesty, joke, caricature, nonsense, rubbish
FORMAL incongruity, irrationality, implausibility
COLLOQ. daftness, craziness, twaddle, gibberish, drivel, claptrap, balderdash, malarkey
⊟ reasonableness, logicality, rationality, (good) sense

absurdly *adv*
ridiculously, ludicrously, preposterously, fantastically, paradoxically, unreasonably, irrationally, nonsensically, meaninglessly, senselessly, foolishly, stupidly, idiotically, crazily, farcically, inanely, comically, funnily, humorously, laughably
FORMAL incongruously, implausibly, untenably
⊟ reasonably, logically, rationally, sensibly

abundance *n*
plenty, fullness, great supply, wealth, generosity, richness, riches, lavishness, overflow, land of milk and honey, glut, extravagance, excess, bonanza, fortune
FORMAL amplitude, bounty, plethora, copiousness, profusion, exuberance, luxuriance, munificence, plenitude, prodigality, opulence, affluence, plentifulness
COLLOQ. bags, heaps, masses, piles, loads, stacks, lashings, oodles, lots; *N Am* scads
⊟ shortage, scarcity; *formal* dearth, paucity

abundant *adj*
plentiful, in plenty, full, filled, ample, copious, profuse, bountiful, exuberant, more than enough, well-supplied, ample, generous, rich, affluent, lavish, teeming, overflowing, galore
OLD plenteous, bounteous
FORMAL luxuriant, opulent
⊟ scarce, sparse, scant, insufficient

abundantly *adv*
1 *abundantly clear*
extremely, exceedingly, excessively, very, really, exceptionally, extraordinarily, intensely, thoroughly, remarkably, utterly, greatly, highly, unusually, unreasonably, immoderately, uncommonly, inordinately, acutely, severely, decidedly
OLD jolly
COLLOQ. awfully, terribly, dreadfully, frightfully, terrifically
2 *mushrooms found abundantly in early autumn*
in abundance, plentifully, copiously, profusely, in profusion, exuberantly, amply, extensively, prolifically

abuse *n, v*
♦ *n*
1 *the abuse of drugs/power*
misuse, exploitation, imposition, oppression, wrong
FORMAL misapplication, misemployment
2 *child abuse*
mistreatment, maltreatment, ill-treatment, cruelty, hurt, injury, interference, sexual assault, molestation, damage, harm, beating, torture
3 *shout abuse*
insult(s), swearing, swear-word, cursing, curse, offence, defamation, libel, slander, reproach, censure, scolding, billingsgate; *Scot* snash
FORMAL affront, upbraiding, invective, castigation, malediction, vilification, vituperation, calumniation, calumny, contumely, denigration, derision, disparagement, tirade, diatribe, vitriol
COLLOQ. mud-slinging
SLANG jawing

⊟ **2** care, attention **3** compliment(s), praise
♦ *v*
1 *abuse authority*
misuse, exploit, take advantage of
FORMAL misapply, misemploy
2 *abuse children*
ill-treat, maltreat, mistreat, hurt, injure, damage, harm, beat, hit, batter, oppress, exploit, wrong, torture, molest, interfere with, rape, assault/harass sexually
3 INSULT, swear at, curse, hurl abuse at, call names, be rude to, defame, libel, slander, pick on, bully, smear, scold, rail, victimize, bullyrag
FORMAL malign, revile, slate, upbraid, calumniate, impugn, vituperate, castigate, denigrate, disparage, oppugn
COLLOQ. treat like dirt
SLANG slag off; *Aust & NZ* chuck off at
⊟ **2** cherish, care for, look after **3** compliment, praise

> **! abuse** or **misuse**?
> *Abuse* refers to the use of something for the wrong purposes: *substance abuse*, eg glue-sniffing. *Misuse* refers to the use of substances or objects in an incorrect way: *Bacteria may acquire resistance to a particular antibiotic by its overuse or misuse.*

abusive *adj*
insulting, offensive, rude, scathing, scornful, hurtful, harmful, injurious, cruel, brutal, destructive, defamatory, libellous, slanderous, derogatory, disparaging, pejorative, maligning, reviling, reproachful, scolding, scurrilous, blasphemous
OLD opprobrious
FORMAL vilifying, censorious, upbraiding, railing, vituperative, castigating, calumniating, contumelious, denigrating
COLLOQ. bitchy
⊟ complimentary, polite

abusively *adv*
insultingly, offensively, rudely, scathingly, scornfully, injuriously, cruelly, brutally, disparagingly, pejoratively, revilingly, reproachfully, scoldingly, scurrilously, blasphemously
OLD opprobriously
FORMAL censoriously, upbraidingly, vituperatively, calumniously, contumeliously, denigratingly
COLLOQ. bitchily
⊟ complimentarily, politely

abut *v*
border, be next to, verge on, join, touch, impinge
FORMAL adjoin, conjoin, be contiguous with

abysmal *adj*
dismal, shocking, disgraceful, dreadful, appalling, awful, terrible, frightful, complete, utter

abysmally *adv*
awfully, disgracefully, dreadfully, appallingly, terribly, frightfully

abyss *n*
fall into an abyss; the abyss of war
gulf, chasm, crevasse, fissure, gorge, canyon, ravine, crater, pit, bottomless pit, depth(s), void, swallow
OLD profound, Avernus Tartarus
FORMAL barathrum

academic *adj, n*
♦ *adj*
1 *academic qualifications*
educational, instructional, scholastic
FORMAL pedagogical
2 *she's very academic*
scholarly, intellectual, educated, well-educated, learned, well-read, studious, bookish, literary, highbrow, serious, donnish

FORMAL erudite
COLLOQ. brainy, smart
3 *an academic, not practical, approach*
theoretical, hypothetical, speculative, abstract,
conceptual, impractical, irrelevant, ivory-tower
FORMAL conjectural, notional, suppositional
E3 3 practical, relevant, applied
◆ *n*
teacher, professor, don, master, fellow, lecturer, tutor,
educator, instructor, trainer, student, scholar, man/woman
of letters, pedant, bookworm
FORMAL pedagogue

academy *n*
college, school, university, institute, seminary, educational
institution, training institute
OLD academe

accede *v*
1 *accede to a request*
accept, comply with, bow to, agree to, consent to, admit,
give in, back down
FORMAL assent to, acquiesce, concur
2 *accede to the throne*
come to, take over, inherit
FORMAL assume, attain, succeed (to)

accelerate *v*
1 *the car/driver accelerated*
quicken, speed, speed up, drive faster, go faster, pick up/
gather speed, gain momentum
COLLOQ. open up, put your foot down, step on it/the gas/
the juice, put on a spurt
2 *accelerate a process*
speed up, hurry, step up, stimulate, facilitate, advance,
further, promote, spur on, forward
TECHNICAL festinate
FORMAL hasten, expedite, precipitate
E3 1, 2 decelerate, slow down, delay

acceleration *n*
1 *the acceleration of a car*
speeding-up, rate of increase, gathering speed,
momentum
2 *acceleration of a process*
speeding-up, stepping-up, stimulation, promotion,
forwarding, furtherance
FORMAL advancement, hastening, expedition
E3 1, 2 deceleration, slowing-down, delay

accent *n*
1 *speak with a strong Irish accent*
pronunciation, articulation, brogue, tone, pitch,
intonation, inflection, accentuation, stress, emphasis,
intensity, force, rhythm, beat, pulse
TECHNICAL cadence, timbre, modulation, enunciation
FORMAL diction, pulsation
COLLOQ. twang
2 *the accent comes on the second syllable*
stress, emphasis, accentuation, beat, force
TECHNICAL ictus
3 *the accent is on ease of use*
emphasis, prominence, importance, priority, stress,
underlining, highlighting
4 *with an acute accent*
diacritic, diacritical mark

accentuate *v*
accent, stress, emphasize, put the emphasis on, underline,
underscore, highlight, give prominence to, heighten,
intensify, strengthen, spotlight, deepen
COLLOQ. point up, drive the point home, make great play
of, show up
E3 weaken; *colloq.* play down

accept *v*
1 *accept a job/an offer*

take, take up, receive, obtain, acquire, gain, welcome,
grasp, pocket, secure, get, come by, say yes to, not say no
to
FORMAL reply in the affirmative
COLLOQ. jump at
2 *accept advice*
take, welcome
FORMAL embrace
COLLOQ. take on board, take someone's point
3 *accept a decision*
acknowledge, recognize, admit, allow, approve, agree to,
consent to, take on, adopt, bow to, honour, comply with,
go along with, give in, back down
TECHNICAL *Scot* approbate
FORMAL abide by, accede to, acquiesce in, concur
with
4 *accept responsibility/blame*
take on, undertake, bear, be responsible for, admit,
acknowledge, face up to
5 *accept an explanation*
believe (in), trust, credit, take, be certain of
COLLOQ. buy, swallow, fall for, wear
6 *accept into the family*
welcome, receive, receive warmly, embrace, integrate
7 *accept ill-treatment*
tolerate, stand, bear, abide, face up to, take, endure, suffer,
put up with, yield to, resign yourself to, be resigned to,
come to terms with, let go of
COLLOQ. stomach, swallow, make the best of
E3 1 refuse, turn down **2, 3, 4, 5, 6** reject

acceptable *adj*
1 *homework that is just acceptable*
satisfactory, tolerable, moderate, passable, adequate,
reasonable, all right, unexceptionable
COLLOQ. OK, so-so
2 *acceptable not to smoke*
admissible, allowable, permissible, tolerable, agreeable,
appropriate, desirable
COLLOQ. the done thing
3 *a most acceptable present*
welcome, delightful, pleasant, pleasing, agreeable,
desirable, gratifying, appreciated
E3 1 unacceptable, unsatisfactory **2** unacceptable

acceptably *adv*
agreeably, desirably, appropriately, suitably, tolerably,
moderately, passably, adequately, satisfactorily, reasonably
E3 1 unacceptably

acceptance *n*
1 *acceptance of a job/an offer*
taking (-up), accepting, receipt, receiving, obtaining,
getting, acquiring, gaining, securing
FORMAL affirmative reply
2 *acceptance of advice*
taking, welcoming
FORMAL embracing
COLLOQ. taking on board, taking someone's point
3 *acceptance of the decision*
acknowledgement, admission, recognition, approval,
consent, affirmation, agreement, taking on, adoption,
going along with, compliance, giving-in, backing-down
FORMAL assent, accession, acquiescence, concurrence,
endorsement, ratification
COLLOQ. seal/stamp of approval, OK
4 *acceptance of responsibility/blame*
taking on, undertaking, assumption, admission,
acknowledgement
5 *the idea gained acceptance*
credence, belief, trust, faith
COLLOQ. buying, falling for
6 *acceptance into the family*
welcome, welcoming, receiving, recognition, integration

7 *acceptance of your situation*
tolerance, bearing, facing up to, endurance, resignation, putting up with
COLLOQ. making the best of
⊟ 1 refusal **2, 3, 4, 5, 6** rejection

accepted *adj*
recognized, established, authorized, approved, ratified, sanctioned, agreed, acknowledged, admitted, confirmed, acceptable, correct, appropriate, conventional, orthodox, traditional, customary, time-honoured, received, universal, regular, standard, normal, usual, common
⊟ unconventional, unorthodox, controversial

access *n, v*
• *n*
1 *gain access to the building*
means of approach/entry, entry, entering, entrance, gateway, door, way in, key, approach, passage, road, path, drive, driveway, course
2 *deny access to the prisoner*
admission, admittance, right of entry, permission to enter/see, accessibility
FORMAL entrée, ingress
⊟ 1 exit, outlet; *formal* egress
• *v*
locate, use, retrieve, read, gain access to

accessibility *n*
1 *easy accessibility to the site*
approachability, ease of access
OLD attainability
2 *the accessibility of affordable health care*
availability, convenience, obtainability, ease of access
3 *the programme's accessibility to ordinary people*
intelligibility, comprehensibility, approachability
⊟ 1 inaccessibility **2** unavailability **3** incomprehensibility

accessible *adj*
1 *accessible from the motorway*
reachable, attainable, approachable, open, achievable
OLD patent
COLLOQ. get-at-able
2 *financial help that is accessible to everyone*
obtainable, available, on hand, ready, handy, convenient, near, nearby
FORMAL procurable
3 *an accessible book/painting*
understandable, intelligible, comprehensible, easy to understand, easy to read, easy to follow
COLLOQ. user-friendly
⊟ 1 inaccessible, remote; *colloq.* out of the way, off the beaten track **3** incomprehensible, unintelligible

accession *n*
1 *accession to the throne*
taking over, inheritance
FORMAL assumption, attaining, succession
2 *accessions to the library*
addition, acquisition, increase, possession, gain, purchase, gift

accessorize *v*
add to, enhance, set off, contrast, complement, round off, supplement, augment, decorate, adorn, trim
OLD bedizen, bedaub

accessory *n, adj*
• *n*
1 *computer accessories*
extra, supplement, addition, attachment, extension, component, fitting
TECHNICAL peripheral, add-in, add-on
FORMAL appendage, adjunct
2 *accessories to match an outfit*
decoration, adornment, ornament, frill, trimming,

supplement, complement, gloves, hat, belt, shoes, handbag, jewellery
FORMAL embellishment
3 *an accessory to a crime*
accomplice, partner, associate, colleague, confederate, assistant, helper, help, aid
TECHNICAL accessory before the fact, accessory after the fact, *particeps criminis*
FORMAL abettor, conniver
• *adj*
additional, extra, supplementary, subsidiary, contributory, incidental, secondary, ancillary, auxiliary, subordinate
FORMAL supplemental

accident *n*
1 *an accident with boiling water*
mishap, casualty, calamity, disaster, tragedy
FORMAL misfortune, mischance, misadventure
COLLOQ. blow
2 *a car accident*
collision, crash, fatality, RTA, road traffic accident
FORMAL contretemps
COLLOQ. pile-up, smash-up; *N Am* wreck
SLANG shunt, prang
3 *happen by accident*
chance, hazard, luck, good luck, fortune, good fortune, fate, freak, coincidence
OLD upcast
FORMAL fortuity, serendipity, contingency, hap, happenstance
COLLOQ. fluke

accidental *adj*
unintentional, unintended, inadvertent, unplanned, uncalculated, unpremeditated, unwitting, unexpected, unanticipated, unforeseen, unlooked-for, chance, uncertain, haphazard, random, casual, incidental
FORMAL fortuitous, adventitious, serendipitous, contingent, aleatory
COLLOQ. fluky
⊟ intentional, deliberate, calculated, premeditated

> **Synonym nuances**
> The words **unintentional**, **unintended**, **unplanned** and **inadvertent** tend to be used of unwanted accidental events: *unintentional injuries; unplanned pregnancies; the leaks caused unplanned shutdowns*. Actions can also be described as **inadvertent**, **uncalculated** and **unpremeditated** if they have not been thought through, as can their generally negative results: *inadvertent use of an incorrect word*.
> **Unforeseen** and **unanticipated** events also tend to come as an unpleasant surprise: *unanticipated allergic reactions*. **Unexpected**, **chance** and **unlooked-for** are more neutral, and are used to describe both pleasant and unpleasant events: *an unexpected windfall*. To say that something is **uncertain** is to suggest unreliability: *the uncertain economic climate*.
> If you want to suggest that there is an element of human carelessness involved in accidental events, you might use **haphazard**, whereas **random** is a more neutral term to describe disordered events. To describe something as **casual** or **incidental** has the added implication that it is of relatively little importance: *a casual encounter*.
> **Fortuitous** and **serendipitous** and the colloquial **fluky** express a good accidental outcome. **Adventitious** is now often used in scientific contexts; **aleatory** is only used in the context of music and poetry.

accidentally *adv*
unintentionally, inadvertently, unexpectedly, by chance, by accident, as luck would have it, by mistake, unwittingly, haphazardly, randomly, incidentally

FORMAL fortuitously, bechance, adventitiously, serendipitously

E3 intentionally, deliberately

acclaim *v, n*

◆ *v*

praise, commend, extol, exalt, honour, hail, salute, welcome, applaud, clap, cheer, celebrate, fanfare, toast

FORMAL laud, eulogize

COLLOQ. rave about, give rave reviews to, give a good press to

E3 condemn, criticize; *colloq.* give a bad press to

◆ *n*

praise, commendation, homage, tribute, exaltation, honour, welcome, approval, bouquets, applause, ovation, clapping, fanfare, cheers, cheering, shouting, celebration

FORMAL acclamation, approbation, eulogy, eulogium, extolment, laudation, plaudits

E3 criticism, disapproval, condemnation; *formal* vituperation; *colloq.* brickbats, bad press

acclaimed *adj*

famous, famed, renowned, illustrious, celebrated, eminent, distinguished, admired, honoured, exalted, revered, great, noted, notable, prominent, outstanding, legendary

E3 unknown, unsung, forgotten, obscure

acclamation *n*

praise, commendation, homage, tribute, exaltation, honour, welcome, approval, congratulations, applause, ovation, clapping, fanfare, cheering, bravos, shouting, celebration, enthusiasm

FORMAL approbation, eulogy, laudations, felicitations, paean, panegyric

E3 criticism, disapproval, condemnation

acclimatization *n*

adjustment, adaptation, accommodation, familiarization, orientation, naturalization; *N Am* acclimation

FORMAL habituation, acculturation

acclimatize *v*

adjust, adapt, accustom, get used to, find your way around, accommodate, familiarize, attune, conform, naturalize; *N Am* acclimate

FORMAL habituate, acculturate, inure

COLLOQ. find/get your bearings, find your feet

accolade *n*

award, honour, recognition, homage, tribute, testimonial, praise

COLLOQ. pat on the back

accommodate *v*

1 *accommodate someone in a hotel*

put up, take in, house, shelter, provide shelter for, cater for, lodge, board, billet, quarter

OLD bestow

FORMAL domicile

COLLOQ. put a roof over someone's head

2 *the hall accommodates 400*

take, hold, seat, have room/space for

3 *accommodate customers*

help, be helpful to, oblige, assist, aid, serve, provide, supply, comply, conform, fit in with

COLLOQ. give/lend a (helping) hand to

4 *accommodate yourself to new developments*

adapt, accustom, acclimatize, adjust, modify, fit, attune, harmonize, reconcile, settle, compose

FORMAL habituate

accommodating *adj*

obliging, indulgent, helpful, co-operative, agreeable, willing, compliant, kind, considerate, unselfish, sympathetic, friendly, hospitable

FORMAL complaisant

E3 disobliging, selfish

accommodation *n*

1 *find accommodation*

housing, shelter, board, rooms, quarter(s), lodging(s)

FORMAL dwelling, residence, abode

COLLOQ. a roof over someone's head, digs, pad, place

SLANG crashpad, gaff

2 *reach an accommodation*

agreement, compromise, understanding, negotiation(s), reconciliation, settlement, harmony, conformity

---

Types of accommodation include:

apartment	flat	*N Am* room and
barracks	guest house	board
bed and board	halls of residence	rooms
bed and breakfast	hostel	self-catering
bedsit	hotel	shelter
bedsitter	inn	squat
billet	loft conversion	studio
board	married quarters	timeshare
boarding-house	motel	villa
digs	pension	youth hostel
N Am dormitory	penthouse	

See also **house**; **room**.

---

accompaniment *n*

1 *a musical accompaniment*

support, background, backing, backup

TECHNICAL obbligato, vamp

2 *wine as an accompaniment to food*

complement, accessory, supplement, addition

FORMAL concomitant, adjunct, coexistence

accompanist *n*

instrumentalist, accompanier, backing group

COLLOQ. comp

accompany *v*

1 *accompany someone on holiday*

escort, attend, go (along) with, travel with, walk with, associate with, come (along) with, tag along with, partner, chaperon(e), squire, usher, conduct, follow

FORMAL consort, convoy, wait upon

COLLOQ. hang around with

2 *a book accompanied by a study guide*

complement, supplement, belong to, go with, go together with, occur with

FORMAL coexist, coincide

3 *accompany someone on the guitar*

play with, back, support, provide backing/support for

Synonym nuances

sense 1

To **escort** or **squire** someone is to accompany them in a rather formal manner, the suggestion being that you are protecting or guarding them; **squire** is used where a man accompanies a woman, with the added suggestion of sexual relations. **Chaperon(e)** is only used where you accompany someone with the specific purpose of being responsible for them. **Attend** is archaic and rarely used, but always in the context of accompanying someone as an inferior with the intention of serving them, as is the more familiar **wait upon**.

To **partner**, **go (along) with** or **come (along) with** someone, however, is to join them on equal terms, but to **tag along with** them makes the implication that you are uninvited. To **associate with** someone suggests keeping more regular company, as does the colloquial **hang around with**. To **consort** with someone has negative connotations: *consort with the enemy*.

To **conduct** or **usher** someone would only be used of leading them or guiding them in a particular direction, with **usher** having the connotation of brusqueness, whereas **follow** specifically indicates that you are at the rear. **Convoy** is generally confined to military contexts, describing the accompanying of vehicles.

accomplice *n*

assistant, helper, abettor, mate, henchman, conspirator, collaborator, ally, confederate, partner, associate, colleague, aide, participator, accessory, right-hand man/woman
OLD complice, copesmate, fedarie, stale
COLLOQ. sidekick
SLANG swagsman; *N Am* shill
OLD SLANG button

accomplish *v*

achieve, attain, do, perform, carry out, manage, execute, fulfil, discharge, finish, complete, conclude, realize, bring about, bring off, engineer, produce, obtain, compass
OLD complish
FORMAL consummate, effect, carry into effect, effectuate
COLLOQ. hack it, pull it off, wangle, deliver the goods, bring home the bacon

accomplished *adj*

skilled, professional, practised, proficient, gifted, talented, skilful, experienced, adroit, adept, expert, masterly, polished, cultivated, learned, savant
OLD compleat
FORMAL consummate
COLLOQ. ace
SLANG wicked, shit-hot
E3 unskilled, inexpert, incapable

accomplishment *n*

1 *no mean accomplishment*
feat, achievement, deed, act, performance, operation, triumph, exploit, stroke of genius
OLD qualification, virtue
COLLOQ. stroke, feather in your cap
2 SKILL, talent, ability, capability, proficiency, gift, quality, knack, forte, art
FORMAL aptitude, faculty
3 *the accomplishment of a task*
achievement, attainment, doing, performance, carrying-out, execution, discharge, fulfilment, finishing, completion, management, conclusion, perfection, realization, fruition, production
FORMAL consummation, effecting, futurition

accord *v, n*

♦ *v*
1 *not accord with the truth*
correspond, agree, square, harmonize, be in agreement/harmony, match, conform, suit
FORMAL concur
2 *accord someone recognition*
grant, give, tender, allow, endow, confer, present
FORMAL bestow, vouchsafe
E3 1 disagree **2** deny
♦ *n*
1 *sign an accord*
treaty, agreement, pact, settlement, convention, deal, contract
FORMAL compact, concordat
2 *to reach accord*
agreement, assent, unanimity, unity, correspondence, conformity, harmony, sympathy
FORMAL congruence, congruity, concurrence, consensus, accordance, concert
E3 2 conflict, discord, disharmony
■ **of your own accord**
voluntarily, of your own free will, freely, willingly, without being asked/forced, of your own volition
■ **with one accord**
unanimously, of one mind, in complete agreement

accordance

■ **in accordance with**
in agreement with, consistent with, in keeping with, obedient to, in conformity with, in line with, in proportion to, in relation to, after, in the light of, in the manner of
FORMAL commensurate with, in concert with, in consonance with

according

■ **according to**
1 *according to this book*
as said/claimed/stated by, on the report of
2 *play according to the rules*
in accordance with, in keeping with, obedient to, in conformity with, in line with, consistent with, after, in the light of, in the manner of, after the manner of, as per
3 *be paid according to experience*
in proportion to, in relation to, depending on, as per
FORMAL commensurate with

accordingly *adv*

1 *he was dishonest and was distrusted accordingly*
correspondingly, so, as a result, for that reason, consequently, in consequence, therefore
OLD hence
FORMAL thus, ergo
2 *act accordingly*
appropriately, properly, suitably, duly, fitly, consistently

accost *v*

approach, confront, address, waylay, stop, halt, detain, importune, solicit, attack, molest
COLLOQ. nobble, buttonhole

account *n, v*

♦ *n*
1 *an account of what happened*
story, tale, commentary, narrative, chronicle, history, memoir, record, statement, report, communiqué write-up, version, narration, portrayal, sketch, description, presentation, explanation, detail(s)
2 *pay an account*
bill, statement, invoice, tab, charges
3 *the accounts of a business*
ledger, books, journal, register, inventory
4 *a matter of no account*
importance, significance, consequence, regard
FORMAL distinction, esteem, import, moment
♦ *v*
consider, assess, believe, count, hold, reckon, look upon, regard as, view as, value, esteem
FORMAL adjudge, appraise, deem
■ **account for**
1 *account for the missing money*
explain, give reasons for, come up with an explanation, illuminate, clear up, rationalize, justify, answer for, say why
FORMAL elucidate, vindicate
2 *exports account for half our income*
make up, comprise, be responsible for, represent, supply, provide, give
FORMAL constitute
3 *account for an enemy*
defeat, destroy, kill, eliminate
■ **on account of**
because of, owing to, through, in view of, the reason is
■ **on no account**
under no circumstances, certainly not
COLLOQ. never, no way

accountability *n*

responsibility, answerability, liability, amenability, reporting, obligation

accountable *adj*

responsible, answerable, liable, amenable, obliged, bound, charged with, chargeable
FORMAL obligated

accoutrements *n*

paraphernalia, gear, equipment, decorations, fittings, fixtures, furnishings, appointments, kit,

outfit, trimmings, adornments, things
FORMAL appurtenances, caparison
COLLOQ. stuff, gear, clobber, bits and pieces, odds and
ends

accredit v
endorse, recognize, authorize, approve, certify, license,
commission, warrant
FORMAL depute, certificate

accredited adj
recognized, official, authorized, qualified, endorsed,
appointed, approved, certified, licensed, commissioned
FORMAL certificated, deputed

accretion n
1 the accretions of self-respect
addition, growth, supplement, increment, add-on
2 the accretion of fat
collecting, accumulation, gathering, build-up, growth,
increase
FORMAL cumulation, augmentation

accrue v
accumulate, increase, mount (up), be added, build up,
collect, amass
FORMAL augment

accumulate v
gather, build up, assemble, collect, amass, accrue, grow,
increase, multiply, pile up, hoard, stockpile, store, gain,
acquire
FORMAL aggregate, augment, cumulate
COLLOQ. stash, tot up, snowball
F3 formal disseminate, diffuse

accumulation n
1 small accumulations of mail
hoard, mass, pile, stockpile, store, stack, stock, reserve,
gain
2 the gradual accumulation of blood
gathering, build-up, building-up, collection, growth, gain,
increase, multiplication, conglomeration, accrual,
assembly, acquisition
FORMAL aggregate, augmentation, cumulation, accretion
F3 2 formal dissemination

accumulative adj
increasing, growing, mounting, multiplying, enlarging,
growing
COLLOQ. snowballing

accuracy n
correctness, precision, exactness, authenticity, truth,
truthfulness, closeness, faithfulness, carefulness,
meticulousness
FORMAL veracity, fidelity, exactitude, scrupulosity, verity,
veridicality
F3 inaccuracy

accurate adj
1 an accurate report/translation
faithful, true, factual, correct, exact, strict, literal, word-for-
word, word-perfect, close, sound, truthful, valid,
authentic, unerring, faultless, perfect, fair
FORMAL veracious, letter-perfect, veridical
2 accurate calculations
exact, correct, precise, right, valid, rigorous, meticulous
COLLOQ. spot-on, bang on
3 an accurate gun/throw
well-aimed, well-directed, precise, on target, on the mark
F3 1, 3 inaccurate 2 inaccurate, imprecise, inexact

accurately adv
faithfully, truly, correctly, precisely, exactly, strictly, literally,
closely, truthfully, unerringly, rigorously, meticulously,
faultlessly, perfectly
FORMAL veraciously, veridically
F3 inaccurately, imprecisely, inexactly

accursed adj
damned, wretched, hateful, despicable, abominable,
detestable, loathsome, condemned, doomed,
bewitched
FORMAL execrable, anathematized, bedevilled
F3 blessed

accusation n
charge, allegation, denunciation, impeachment,
recrimination, complaint, incrimination, blame,
indictment, prosecution, information; dialect threap
OLD tax
FORMAL imputation, arraignment, inculpation, citation,
crimination, gravamen, delation

accuse v
1 accused of murder
make accusations, bring/press charges, charge, lay to
someone's charge, blame, prosecute, put on trial, allege,
make allegations, denounce, impeach, confront,
challenge, attribute, indict, incriminate, criminate,
implicate, inform against
OLD attaint, detect; (Shakesp & Spenser) appeal; (Shakesp)
peach, appeach
FORMAL impugn, impute, arraign, cite, criminate
OLD SLANG COLLOQ. frame, book
2 accuse someone of cheating
blame, hold responsible
FORMAL censure, recriminate
COLLOQ. point the finger at, throw the book at

accustom v
familiarize, adjust, adapt, accommodate, get used to, get
familiar with, get acquainted with, conform
FORMAL habituate, inure, attune

accustomed adj
1 accustomed to the dark
used, in the habit of, given, acclimatized, acquainted
FORMAL habituated, inured, wont
COLLOQ. at home
2 sitting in her accustomed chair
normal, usual, ordinary, familiar, everyday, conventional,
routine, regular, customary, habitual, traditional,
established, fixed, prevailing, general
FORMAL wonted, consuetudinary
F3 1 unaccustomed, unused

ace n, adj
♦ n
champion, expert, genius, master, maestro, winner,
virtuoso
COLLOQ. dab hand, hotshot, whizz
♦ adj
brilliant, excellent, first-class, superb, outstanding, great,
very good, perfect
COLLOQ. top-notch, terrific, brill
SLANG cool, wicked

acerbic adj
sharp, harsh, biting, stinging, abrasive, sarcastic, caustic,
acrimonious, spiky, rancorous
FORMAL astringent, vitriolic, mordant, trenchant
F3 mild, friendly, kind

ache v, n
♦ v
1 HURT, be sore, pain, be painful, suffer, be in agony,
agonize, throb, pound, twinge, smart, sting
COLLOQ. play up, kill
2 aching to tell her
long, yearn, pine, hanker, desire, crave, hunger, thirst,
itch
COLLOQ. yen
♦ n
1 PAIN, hurt, soreness, suffering, anguish, agony, throb,
throbbing, pounding, pang, twinge, smarting, stinging

2 *an ache for the past*
longing, desire, hankering, yearning, craving, itch
COLLOQ. yen

achieve *v*
accomplish, attain, reach, get, obtain, acquire, gain, earn, win, succeed, manage, do, perform, carry out, execute, fulfil, finish, complete, bring about, realize, produce
FORMAL procure, consummate, effect, effectuate
COLLOQ. polish off, wrap up
Ⅻ miss, fail

Synonym nuances

Whilst **do** is an unmarked neutral term, **accomplish**, **attain** and **reach** suggest achieving through effort. **Get**, **obtain** and **acquire** are again neutral terms with no connotations of effort, and are appropriate where possession of something has been achieved; **gain** is similar, but has the added suggestion that something has been obtained to your advantage. Using the words **earn** and **win** suggest that labour or effort was involved, while **procure** has an undertone of disapproval, suggesting contrivance.

  Succeed is quite positive in tone, with an undercurrent of admiration for someone's efforts – similarly **manage**, though less so. **Perform**, **carry out** and **execute**, **finish** and **complete**, as well as **bring about**, **produce**, **effect** and **effectuate** are again all unmarked terms with few positive or negative implications. However, to hint at the sense of satisfaction in achieving, **fulfil** and **realize** could be used.

  To emphasize the speed with which something has been achieved, you might use the colloquial term **polish off**, and if you want to stress completeness of an achievement, you could talk of **wrapping it up**. **Consummate** is nowadays usually associated with marriage.

---

achievement *n*
1 *the achievement of our aims*
accomplishment, attainment, performance, execution, fulfilment, completion, success, realization, fruition
OLD chevisance
FORMAL procurement, consummation, acquirement, fruition, effectuation
2 *great achievements*
accomplishment, act, action, activity, deed, performance, exploit, feat, stroke, stroke of genius, triumph, effort
COLLOQ. feather in your cap

achiever *n*
doer, performer, succeeder
COLLOQ. high-flyer, go-getter, live wire, success story, whizz kid

Achilles' heel *n*
weakness, weak point, weak spot, vulnerable point, fault, failing, imperfection
COLLOQ. chink in your armour

acid *adj*
1 *an acid taste*
acidic, sour, bitter, tart, vinegary, unsweetened, sharp, pungent, acerbic, caustic, corrosive
FORMAL acetic, acetous, acidulous
2 *an acid remark*
bitter, unkind, critical, sarcastic, stinging, biting, caustic, cutting, incisive, harsh, morose, hurtful
FORMAL acerbic, astringent, mordant, trenchant, vitriolic
COLLOQ. catty
Ⅻ **1** alkaline **2** kind, complimentary
See also panel below

acknowledge *v*
1 *acknowledge a fact/an error*
admit, recognize, accept, agree to, declare, affirm, grant, allow, confess, own up to, concede
OLD agnize, avouch
FORMAL acquiesce, accede
2 *acknowledge him with a nod*
greet, wave to, signal to, address, notice, recognize
FORMAL salute, hail
3 *acknowledge a letter*
answer, write back to, reply to, respond to, react to, confirm
4 *acknowledge someone's help*
thank, say thank you, express/show your appreciation, be grateful, give thanks for, express your thanks/gratitude, honour, celebrate, mark, recognize
Ⅻ **1** deny, disagree with **2** ignore

acknowledged *adj*
recognized, accepted, approved, declared, professed, confirmed
FORMAL accredited, attested, avowed

acknowledgement *n*
1 *an acknowledgement of defeat*
recognition, admission, confession, declaration, profession, acceptance, granting, appreciation
2 *a gesture of acknowledgement*
greeting, notice, recognition, welcome, nod, smile, wave
FORMAL salutation
3 *an acknowledgement of a letter*
answer, reply, response, reaction
COLLOQ. comeback
4 *an acknowledgement of assistance*
gratitude, appreciation, thanks, praise, expression of gratitude/appreciation/thanks, gratefulness, tribute, credit
COLLOQ. bouquets

acme *n*
high point, highest point, height, peak, pinnacle, apex, zenith, apogee, climax, culmination, crown, optimum, summit
Ⅻ low point, nadir

acolyte *n*
follower, assistant, helper, attendant, adherent
COLLOQ. hanger-on, sidekick

Types of acid include:

acetic (ethanoic)	boric	folic	malic	pectic	salicylic
acetylsalicylic	butanoic	formic	nicotinic	phenol	spirits of salt
acrylic	butyric	(methanoic)	nitric	phosphoric	stearic
amino	carbolic	glutamic	nitrohydrochloric	propanoic	sulphuric
aqua fortis	chloric	hydrochloric	nitrous	prussic	sulphurous
aqua regia	citric	hydrocyanic	nucleic	pteroic	tannic
ascorbic	DNA (deoxy-	lactic	oxalic	pyruvic	tartaric
aspartic	ribonucleic)	linoleic	palmitic	RNA	uric
benzoic	fatty	linolenic	pantothenic	(ribonucleic)	

See also **amino acid**.

acoustic *adj*
hearing, sound
FORMAL auditory, aural, audile

acquaint *v*
familiarize, let know, accustom, tell, notify, advise, inform, make aware of, brief, enlighten, divulge, disclose, reveal, announce
FORMAL make conversant, apprise
COLLOQ. put in the picture, give someone the lowdown, bring someone up to speed

acquaintance *n*
1 *friends and acquaintances*
associate, companion, colleague, friend, contact, connection
FORMAL confrère
2 *my acquaintance with them*
familiarity, association, relationship, intimacy, social contact, contact, fellowship, companionship
3 *some acquaintance with art*
familiarity, awareness, knowledge, understanding, experience
FORMAL cognizance, conversance

acquainted *adj*
1 *acquainted with him*
friendly, on friendly terms, on good terms
2 *acquainted with that book*
familiar, well-versed, knowledgeable, aware, abreast, au fait, *au courant*
FORMAL conversant, cognizant, apprised
COLLOQ. in the know, up to speed
E3 2 unfamiliar, unaware, ignorant

acquiesce *v*
consent, submit, agree, accept, allow, permit, approve, defer
FORMAL concur, accede
COLLOQ. give in, give the go-ahead to, give the green light to, give the thumbs-up to, give the nod to
E3 disagree, object, resist

acquiescence *n*
consent, agreement, acceptance, approval, compliance, submission, yielding, deference
FORMAL concurrence, assent
COLLOQ. go-ahead, green-light, thumbs-up, nod, say-so
E3 disagreement, resistance

acquiescent *adj*
consenting, agreeable, agreeing, accepting, approving, amenable, obedient, compliant, submissive, yielding, deferential, servile
FORMAL acceding, concurring, complaisant

acquire *v*
buy, purchase, obtain, get, come by, receive, collect, gather, amass, accumulate, net, gain, secure, earn, take on, win, achieve, attain, realize
FORMAL procure, appropriate
COLLOQ. grab, pick up, snap up, splash out on
SLANG bag, cop, collar
E3 relinquish, forfeit, sell

acquisition *n*
1 *his latest acquisition*
purchase, buy, gain, possession, accession, investment, takeover, property
2 *the acquisition of a skill*
securing, gaining, obtaining, achievement, attainment
FORMAL procurement, appropriation

acquisitive *adj*
greedy, covetous, hoarding, grasping
FORMAL avaricious, avid, predatory, rapacious, voracious

acquisitiveness *n*
greed, covetousness, cupidity, graspingness
FORMAL avarice, avidity, predatoriness, rapacity, voracity

acquit *v*
1 *acquitted of the crime*
clear, reprieve, excuse, free, set free, liberate, deliver, relieve, release, dismiss, discharge, settle, satisfy, repay
FORMAL absolve, exonerate, exculpate, vindicate
COLLOQ. let off, let off the hook
2 *acquit yourself well*
perform, behave, act, do, conduct
FORMAL comport, bear
COLLOQ. make a good/bad job
E3 1 convict, condemn

acquittal *n*
clearance, clearing, reprieve, excusing, freeing, liberation, deliverance, relief, release, dismissal, discharge
FORMAL absolution, exoneration, exculpation, vindication, compurgation
E3 conviction, condemnation

acrid *adj*
1 *an acrid smell*
pungent, sharp, stinging, acid, sour, bitter, tart, harsh, burning, caustic, acerbic
2 *an acrid comment*
caustic, biting, cutting, incisive, sarcastic, sardonic, bitter, acrimonious, harsh, nasty, malicious, venomous
FORMAL acerbic, astringent, mordant, trenchant, virulent, vitriolic

acrimonious *adj*
bitter, biting, cutting, caustic, sharp, virulent, severe, spiteful, censorious, abusive, ill-tempered, waspish, venomous, rancorous, splenetic, petulant
OLD atrabilious
FORMAL acerbic, astringent, trenchant, vitriolic, irascible
COLLOQ. crabbed, bitchy
E3 peaceable, kindly; *formal* irenic

acrimony *n*
bitterness, resentment, spite, ill will, gall, ill temper, ill feeling, sarcasm, harshness, venom
FORMAL causticity, rancour, petulance, irascibility, mordancy, trenchancy, vitriol, spleen, astringency, acerbity, asperity, acridity, virulence

acrobat *n*
gymnast, tumbler, balancer, somersaulter, contortionist, trapeze artist, tightrope-walker, rope-walker, rope-dancer, stuntman, stuntwoman
OLD *Scot* speel
FORMAL funambulist, aerialist, equilibrist

acrobatics *n*
gymnastics, balancing, somersaulting, tightrope-walking, rope-walking, wire-walking, stunts
FORMAL funambulism, equilibrity

act *v, n*
♦ *v*
1 *act fast*
be, move, do, take action, take steps, take measures, be active, be busy, go about, react
2 BEHAVE, perform, respond, react, function
FORMAL conduct yourself, acquit yourself, exert yourself, comport yourself
3 *the drug will act soon*
take effect, have an effect, work, operate, function
FORMAL be efficacious
4 *the gear acts as a brake*
work, function, serve, operate, do, do the job of
5 *act upset*
pretend, fake, put on, simulate
FORMAL feign, affect, assume, dissemble, dissimulate
COLLOQ. kid, sham
6 *act in a play*
perform, go on the stage, play, portray, represent, mime, characterize, enact, mimic, imitate, impersonate

◆ *n*

1 *acts of bravery*

deed, action, undertaking, enterprise, operation, manoeuvre, move, step, doing, execution, accomplishment, achievement, exploit, feat, stroke

2 *the second act of the play*

part, division, section, subsection, episode

3 *put on an act*

pretence, make-believe, counterfeit, fake

FORMAL feigning, dissimulation, dissemblance, affectation

COLLOQ. sham, show, put-up job, front

4 *an act of parliament*

law, statute, ordinance, canon, edict, decree, resolution, measure, ruling, bill

5 *a juggler's act*

turn, item, routine, sketch, performance, number

COLLOQ. skit, gig

■ **act on**

1 *act on orders*

carry out, fulfil, comply with, conform to, obey, follow, heed, take

2 AFFECT, work on, influence, alter, modify, change, transform

■ **act up**

1 MISBEHAVE, behave badly, cause trouble, give bother

COLLOQ. play up, carry on, mess about, muck around

2 MALFUNCTION, break down, go wrong, fail, stop working

COLLOQ. play up, go kaput, pack up

SLANG conk out

acting *adj, n*

◆ *adj*

temporary, provisional, interim, stopgap, short-term, supply, stand-by, stand-in, standing in for, in place of, covering, deputy, substitute, reserve, fill-in, relief, pro tem, surrogate

◆ *n*

theatre, drama, performing, performing arts, stagecraft, artistry, performance, play-acting, show business, melodrama, dramatics, theatricals, histrionics, footlights, portrayal, characterization, impersonation, imitating

FORMAL Thespianism

COLLOQ. showbiz

SLANG luvviedom

action *n*

1 *his prompt action*

act, move, deed, exploit, step, measure, course of action, feat, accomplishment, achievement, performance, effort, endeavour, enterprise, undertaking, proceeding, process, move, activity

2 *put an idea into action*

operation, practice, effect, force, functioning, doing, performance, exercise, exertion, work, mechanism, movement, motion

3 *the action of a chemical on metal*

effect, operation, power, result, work, influence

4 *people of action*

vitality, liveliness, spirit, energy, vigour, power, force, forcefulness, activity

COLLOQ. get-up-and-go, pizzazz

5 *killed in action*

warfare, battle, conflict, combat, fight, fighting, fray, engagement, encounter, skirmish, clash, hostilities

FORMAL affray

6 *a legal action*

litigation, lawsuit, suit, case, prosecution, proceedings

7 *where the action is*

excitement, exhilaration, stimulation, activity, activities, events, happenings

COLLOQ. goings-on

activate *v*

start, start working, set off, fire, switch/turn/put on, set in

motion, mobilize, propel, move, stir, rouse, arouse, get going, set going, trigger (off), trip, stimulate, initiate, motivate, prompt, energize, excite, galvanize

OLD bestir

FORMAL actuate, animate, impel

COLLOQ. push/press the button, throw the switch, kick-start

◪ deactivate, stop, arrest

active *adj*

1 *an active person*

busy, occupied, industrious, diligent, hard-working, forceful, spirited, vital, vibrant, forward, hyperactive, manic, frenetic; *Scot* birkie; *Irish* stirabout

FORMAL indefatigable, astir

COLLOQ. on the go

2 *active for his age*

agile, nimble, spry, sprightly, light-footed, quick, alert, animated, lively, energetic, mobile, vigorous; *Scot* yauld

OLD springe; (*Shakesp*) quiver; (*Spenser*) wimble

COLLOQ. zippy, bright-eyed and bushy-tailed

3 *active members*

devoted, engaged, involved, committed, contributing, militant, activist, enterprising, enthusiastic

4 *the system is active*

in operation, operational, functioning, working, operative, running, in force

OLD practive

FORMAL effectual

◪ **1** passive **3** inactive

Synonym nuances

sense 1

Busy, occupied and the more literary **astir** are fairly neutral in tone, and can be used of any active person or situation. The words **industrious**, **diligent**, **hard-working** and indefatigable suggest approbation of someone's untiring thoroughness: *a diligent search*.

  Spirited, **vital**, **vibrant** and the colloquial **on the go** are also positive terms to use, with the emphasis this time on animation and vigour: *a vibrant democracy*. **Forceful** and **forward** emphasize the energy and power something or someone has, but are not necessarily suggesting you are regarding it with favour.

  To describe an activity that is undesirably out of control, you might use the terms **manic** or **frenetic**: *a grin of manic glee*. **Hyperactive** is used in the field of medicine to describe abnormal activity: *hyperactive children*, but it can also be used figuratively without implying an opinion on the speaker's part: *hyperactive charm*.

---

activist *n*

militant, agitator, troublemaker, subversive, revolutionary, inciter, firebrand, incendiary, fomenter, henchman

COLLOQ. stirrer

activity *n*

1 *the office is full of activity*

business, liveliness, life, activeness, action, motion, movement, commotion, bustle, hustle and bustle, industry, labour, exertion, exercise

COLLOQ. hurly-burly, a hive of activity/industry, comings and goings, toing and froing

2 *holiday activities*

pursuit, hobby, pastime, interest, diversion, distraction, something to do, occupation, job, work, act, deed, project, scheme, task, venture, enterprise, endeavour, undertaking

FORMAL avocation

◪ **1** inactivity, passivity

actor, actress *n*

play actor, film actor, movie actor, film star, movie star, comedian, tragedian, player, performer, stage performer,

artist, dramatic artist, trouper, artiste, character actor, leading lady, leading man, understudy, extra, walk-on, impersonator, mime, mime artist, mummer
FORMAL Thespian, Roscius
COLLOQ. ham, luvvie, thesp

actual *adj*

real, existent, substantial, tangible, material, physical, concrete, positive, definite, absolute, certain, unquestionable, indisputable, confirmed, verified, factual, truthful, true, genuine, legitimate, bona fide, authentic, realistic
FORMAL de facto
COLLOQ. real live
Ea theoretical, apparent, imaginary

actuality *n*

reality, fact, substance, existence, truth
TECHNICAL ens
FORMAL factuality, historicity, corporeality, materiality, substantiality

actually *adv*

1 *Did you actually see him fall?*
in fact, as a matter of fact, as it happens, in truth, in reality, really, truly, indeed, absolutely
OLD insooth, soothly
FORMAL de facto
2 *she took her degree eventually and actually got a first class*
even, though it may seem strange, surprisingly, believe it or not, as it happens

actuate *v*

move, stir, stimulate, activate, motivate, instigate, prompt, rouse, arouse, kindle, start, start working, set off, set going, trigger (off), switch/turn on, set in motion

acumen *n*

astuteness, shrewdness, sharpness, keenness, quickness, penetration, insight, intuition, discrimination, discernment, judgement, perception, sense, wit, wisdom, intelligence, cleverness, ingenuity
FORMAL judiciousness, percipience, perspicacity, perspicuity, sagacity, sapience
COLLOQ. smartness, gumption

acute *adj*

1 *an acute shortage*
severe, intense, extreme, violent, critical, dangerous, serious, grave, urgent, crucial, drastic, dire, vital, decisive, sharp, cutting, poignant, distressing, unbearable
2 *an acute mind*
sharp, sharp-witted, keen, incisive, penetrating, astute, shrewd, canny, judicious, discerning, clever, observant, perceptive, insightful, sensitive
FORMAL percipient, perspicacious, sapient
COLLOQ. smart
3 *an acute illness*
severe, serious, intense, dangerous, critical, grave
TECHNICAL peracute
Ea 1 mild, slight **3** mild, chronic, persistent

acutely *adv*

very, intensely, extremely, strongly, seriously, severely, gravely, sharply, keenly, markedly

adage *n*

maxim, saying, axiom, proverb, byword, precept, saw
FORMAL aphorism, apophthegm, gnome, paroemia

adamant *adj*

hard, resolute, determined, set, firm, insistent, rigid, stiff, inflexible, unbending, unrelenting, unyielding, stubborn, unwavering, uncompromising, tough, fixed, immovable, unshak(e)able
FORMAL intransigent, obdurate
Ea hesitant, flexible, yielding

adapt *v*

1 *adapt to a new environment*
adjust, acclimatize yourself, familiarize yourself, orientate yourself, accommodate yourself, get used/accustomed
FORMAL habituate yourself
2 *adapt a building*
alter, change, qualify, modify, adjust, convert, remodel, customize, fit, tailor, fashion, shape, harmonize, match, suit, conform, comply, prepare
OLD attemper, contemper

adaptable *adj*

flexible, compliant, amenable, easy-going, versatile, plastic, malleable, pliable, alterable, changeable, variable, modifiable, adjustable, convertible, open-ended, conformable
Ea inflexible; *formal* refractory

adaptation *n*

1 *adaptation to a different situation*
adjustment, acclimatization, familiarization, accommodation, getting used/accustomed
FORMAL habituation
2 *adaptation of a novel for TV*
alteration, change, modification, shift, transformation, revision, variation, adjustment, conversion, remodelling, customization, fitting, refitting, fashioning, refashioning, reworking, shaping, reshaping, harmonization, matching, conformity, preparation

add *v*

1 *add an introduction to the book*
put on, put in, include, complete, improve, attach, supplement, combine, build on
FORMAL adjoin, affix, append, annex, augment
COLLOQ. throw in
2 *add numbers*
count (up), total, work out/calculate the total
COLLOQ. tot up
3 *the rain added to her misery*
increase, raise, boost, intensify, deepen, heighten, extend
FORMAL augment
COLLOQ. hike up, aggravate
4 *'Thanks,' I added*
tack on, continue, go on, go on to say, carry on
Ea 1 take away, remove, reduce, decrease **2** subtract, take (away), deduct, remove

■ add up

1 *add up numbers*
add, sum up, add together, total, tally, count (up), reckon, calculate, compute, figure up
COLLOQ. tot up
2 *the total adds up to 100*
amount, make, come to, run to, include, spell
FORMAL constitute
3 *it doesn't add up*
be consistent, hang together, fit, be plausible, be reasonable, stand to reason, make sense, mean, signify, indicate, ring true
Ea 1 subtract

added *adj*

additional, supplementary, extra, more, another, fresh, further, new, spare
FORMAL adjunct

addendum *n*

appendix, addition, postscript, supplement; *N Am* annex
FORMAL codicil, adjunct, appendage, augmentation, attachment, endorsement, allonge

addict *n*

1 *a drug addict*
drug taker, drug user
COLLOQ. junkie, druggie, user, dope-fiend
SLANG freak, head, coke-head, crackhead, tripper,

mainliner, hop-head, hype, snowbird
2 *a chess addict*
enthusiast, fan, devotee, follower, adherent, fanatic, hound
COLLOQ. buff, fiend, freak

addicted *adj*
1 *addicted to drugs*
dependent, drug-dependent
COLLOQ. hooked, strung out
2 *addicted to TV*
obsessed, absorbed, devoted, dedicated, fond, inclined, fanatical
COLLOQ. hooked, wild, crazy, daft, nuts, potty

addiction *n*
1 *alcohol addiction*
dependence, dependency, compulsion, craving, habit
SLANG monkey
2 *addiction to chocolate*
craving, habit, obsession, compulsive behaviour, mania
COLLOQ. thing

addictive *adj*
habit-forming, compulsive, irresistible, uncontrollable, obsessive

addition *n*
1 *the index is a welcome addition*
supplement, attachment, extra, increment, additive, rider, afterthought, postscript, annexe, addendum, appendix, accessory
FORMAL adjunct, appendage, augmentation, appurtenance
2 *the addition of a separate phone line*
adding, extension, enlargement, increasing, increase, gain, inclusion
FORMAL annexation, accession, accretion
3 *addition of numbers*
summing-up, totalling, counting, reckoning, inclusion, computation
COLLOQ. totting-up
F3 **2** removal, taking-away **3** subtraction, deduction
■ **in addition**
additionally, too, also, as well, besides, moreover, further, furthermore, over and above, not to mention; *Scot* forby
OLD to boot, withal
COLLOQ. into the bargain, for good measure

additional *adj*
added, extra, supplementary, spare, more, further, increased, other, new, fresh, another
FORMAL supplemental, adscititious, adventitious, supervenient, excrescent

additionally *adv*
in addition, too, also, as well, besides, moreover, further, furthermore, over and above; *Scot* forby
OLD to boot, withal
COLLOQ. into the bargain, for good measure

additive *n*
supplement, addition, extra, preservative

addle *v*
confuse, befuddle, bewilder, fluster, muddle, perplex, daze
COLLOQ. faze

addled *adj*
confused, befuddled, bewildered, lost, flustered, muddled, mixed-up, perplexed
COLLOQ. fazed
F3 clear

address *n, v*
 ◆ *n*
1 *write down an address and phone number*
home, house, flat, apartment, lodging, directions,

inscription, whereabouts, location, situation, place, poste restante, dwelling
FORMAL (place of) residence, abode
2 SPEECH, talk, lecture, sermon, oration, harangue, discourse, monologue, soliloquy, dissertation
FORMAL diatribe, philippic, apostrophe, allocution, disquisition
COLLOQ. spiel
3 *forms of address*
greeting, welcome
FORMAL salutation, invocation
 ◆ *v*
1 *address a letter*
direct, label, send, post, mail
FORMAL superscribe
2 *address an audience*
lecture, speak to, talk to, give a talk/speech to, make/deliver a speech, preach to, harangue
FORMAL sermonize, orate
3 *address a remark to someone*
communicate, direct, convey, send, intend for
FORMAL remit
4 *How should I address a duke?*
call, speak/write to, greet, designate
■ **address (yourself) to**
deal with, give your attention to, apply yourself to, devote yourself to, attend to, undertake, concentrate on, focus on, tackle, buckle down to, engage in, take care of

adduce *v*
cite, mention, allude to, refer to, name, quote, put forward, point out, present
FORMAL proffer, evidence

adept *adj, n*
 ◆ *adj*
skilled, accomplished, expert, masterly, experienced, versed, practised, polished, proficient, competent, capable, good, clever, able, adroit, deft, nimble
COLLOQ. ace, sharp, hot stuff, no flies on someone
SLANG wicked
F3 bungling, incompetent, inept
 ◆ *n*
expert, genius, master, maestro, veteran
COLLOQ. dab hand, hot stuff, nobody's fool, wizard
F3 bungler, incompetent

adequacy *n*
sufficiency, suitability, fitness, ability, competence, capability, serviceability, acceptability, satisfactoriness, reasonableness, passability, tolerability, tolerableness, fairness, indifference, mediocrity
FORMAL commensurateness, requisiteness
F3 inadequacy, insufficiency

adequate *adj*
1 *adequate amounts of food*
enough, sufficient, suitable, appropriate
FORMAL commensurate, requisite
2 *adequate work*
acceptable, satisfactory, passable, reasonable, tolerable, unexceptional, indifferent, undistinguished, average, suitable, fit, able, competent, capable, serviceable
COLLOQ. all right, OK, will do, could be better/worse, no great shakes, patchy, fair to middling, ho-hum, run of the mill, nothing (much) to write home about, nothing (much) to shout about, not set the Thames on fire
F3 **1** insufficient **2** inadequate

adequately *adv*
sufficiently, suitably, appropriately, satisfactorily, acceptably, passably, reasonably, tolerably
F3 inadequately, insufficiently

adhere *v*
1 STICK, stick together, glue, paste, cement, grip, fix, fasten,

attach, join, link, combine, coalesce, cohere, hold, hold fast, cling
FORMAL cleave to, accrete

2 *adhere to the agreement*
observe, follow, abide by, comply with, fulfil, obey, keep, heed, respect, stand by, go along with
COLLOQ. stick

3 *adhere to an opinion*
support, hold, defend, stand by, go along with, stick up for
FORMAL espouse

adherence *n*
support, advocacy, observance, compliance, fulfilment, respect, defence

adherent *n*
supporter, upholder, advocate, partisan, follower, disciple, satellite, henchman, devotee, admirer, fan, enthusiast
FORMAL votary, aficionado, sectary
COLLOQ. hanger-on, buff, freak, nut

adhesion *n*
adherence, adhesiveness, holding together, sticking (together), bond, attachment, grip, purchase, cohesion

adhesive *adj, n*
♦ *adj*
sticky, stick-on, tacky, self-adhesive, gummed, adhering, sticking, clinging, holding, attaching, cohesive
FORMAL adherent, glutinous, mucilaginous, emplastic
COLLOQ. gummy, gluey
♦ *n*
glue, gum, fixative, paste, cement, tape, sticky tape, Sellotape®, passe-partout, Elastoplast®, Band-aid®, Cow Gum®, Superglue®, Blu-tak®
FORMAL mucilage

ad hoc *adj, adv*
♦ *adj*
makeshift, improvised, extempore, ad-lib, unscripted, unrehearsed, unprepared, spontaneous
COLLOQ. off-the-cuff
E3 rehearsed
♦ *adv*
without preparation, extempore, ad lib, spontaneously
COLLOQ. on the spur of the moment, off the top of your head, off the cuff

adieu *n, interj*
♦ *n*
goodbye, farewell, leave-taking, *au revoir*
FORMAL valediction, valedictory
♦ *interj*
goodbye, farewell, *au revoir, auf Wiedersehen, ciao, adios, arrivederci*
COLLOQ. cheerio, bye, bye-bye, cheers, see you (later), see you around, be seeing you, all the best, mind how you go, take care, have a nice day, ta-ta, so long

ad infinitum *adv*
for ever, evermore, perpetually, permanently, constantly, at all times, continually, incessantly, endlessly, eternally, until the end of time, till doomsday, till your dying day
OLD aye
COLLOQ. till the cows come home

adjacent *adj*
adjoining, touching, bordering, alongside, beside, next-door, neighbouring, next, closest, nearest, close, near
FORMAL abutting, contiguous, juxtaposed, conterminant, conterminate, conterminous, proximate, vicinal
E3 remote, distant

adjoin *v*
touch, meet, border, verge, neighbour, be next, interconnect, link, connect, join, combine, unite, couple, attach, add, annex
FORMAL abut, append, juxtapose

adjoining *adj*
adjacent, touching, bordering, near, neighbouring, next, next door, verging, interconnecting, linking, connecting, joining, combining, uniting
FORMAL contiguous, impinging, abutting, proximate, juxtaposed, conjoining, vicinal

adjourn *v*
1 *adjourn a meeting*
stop temporarily, interrupt, suspend, break off, delay, stay, defer, postpone, put off, pause
FORMAL discontinue, prorogue
COLLOQ. put on the back burner
2 *adjourn to the lounge*
withdraw, retreat
OLD betake yourself
FORMAL retire, repair
E3 1 assemble, convene

adjournment *n*
interruption, suspension, break, pause, interval, recess, intermission, delay, stay, postponement, putting-off
TECHNICAL moratorium
FORMAL discontinuation, deferment, deferral, dissolution, prorogation
COLLOQ. let-up

adjudge *v*
decree, judge, consider, regard, deem, determine, reckon

adjudicate *v*
judge, arbitrate, umpire, referee, settle, determine, decide, pronounce, pass
FORMAL adjudge

adjudication *n*
judgement, arbitration, settlement, ruling, determination, decree, decision, conclusion, pronouncement, verdict

adjudicator *n*
judge, arbitrator, umpire, referee, arbiter, mediator

adjunct *n*
addition, supplement, accompaniment, complement, accessory
FORMAL appendage, concomitant

adjust *v*
1 *adjust to new circumstances*
become/grow accustomed, adapt, acclimatize yourself, become acclimatized, orientate yourself, accommodate yourself, reconcile yourself, harmonize, conform
FORMAL habituate yourself
COLLOQ. get used to
2 MODIFY, change, adapt, alter, convert, dispose, shape, remodel, fit, accommodate, suit, measure, amend, revise, make adjustments, rectify, regulate, balance, repair, reshape, refashion, temper, tune, modulate, fix, set, arrange, align, compose, settle, shape, square
FORMAL coapt
COLLOQ. fine-tune, tweak
E3 2 upset; *formal* disarrange

adjustable *adj*
adaptable, modifiable, convertible, flexible, alterable, versatile, movable
E3 fixed, immovable

adjustment *n*
1 *minor adjustments to the engine*
modification, change, adaptation, alteration, conversion, remodelling, shaping, fitting, accommodation, amendment, revision, rectification, regulation, tuning, fixing, setting, arranging, rearranging, arrangement, rearrangement, ordering, settlement
COLLOQ. fine-tuning, tweaking
2 *adjustment to a new job*
orientation, adaptation, acclimatization, accommodation, naturalization, reconciliation, harmonization,

conforming, settling down/in, getting used to
FORMAL habituation

ad-lib *v, adj, adv*
* *v*

improvise, make up, invent
FORMAL extemporize
COLLOQ. play it by ear, speak off the cuff/off the top of your head, wing it
* *adj*

impromptu, improvised, unprepared, without preparation, unpremeditated, unrehearsed, spontaneous, made-up
FORMAL extempore, extemporaneous, extemporized
COLLOQ. off-the-cuff, off the top of your head
E3 prepared
* *adv*

impromptu, spontaneously, impulsively
FORMAL extempore, extemporaneously
COLLOQ. off the cuff, off the top of your head

administer *v*

1 *administer a country/law/project*
organize, direct, conduct, manage, run, control, regulate, superintend, supervise, oversee, govern, rule, lead, head, guide, preside over, officiate
2 *administer a drug*
give, provide, supply, distribute, give out, measure out, mete out, deliver, execute, impose, apply
FORMAL discharge, dispense, disburse, adhibit
COLLOQ. dole out

administration *n*

1 *reduce the cost of administration*
administering, management, running, paperwork, organization, direction, control, superintendence, supervision, overseeing, governing, ruling, command, leadership, execution
COLLOQ. red tape
2 *a country's administration*
government, governing body, regime, ministry, cabinet, leadership, directorship, management, parliament, council, senate, congress, executive, term of office
COLLOQ. powers that be, corridors of power
3 *the administration of a law/drug*
provision, supplying, execution, application, imposition
FORMAL dispensation, discharge

administrative *adj*
management, managerial, governmental, legislative, authoritative, executive, organizational, regulatory, supervisory
FORMAL directorial, gubernatorial

Administrative areas include:

area	enclave	state
borough	municipality	territory
city	parish	town
constituency	precinct	village
conurbation	province	ward
county	region	zone
district	sector	
division	shire	

administrator *n*
manager, organizer, director, controller, superintendent, supervisor, overseer, governor, ruler, leader, president, chairman, chief executive, executive, managing director, head, chief
FORMAL custodian, guardian, trustee
COLLOQ. boss, top dog, bigwig, big noise, big cheese

admirable *adj*
praiseworthy, commendable, creditable, deserving, worthy, respected, fine, excellent, magnificent,

exceptional, superior, wonderful, exquisite, choice, rare, masterly, valuable
FORMAL estimable, laudable, meritorious
COLLOQ. cool, terrific, brill, out of this world, second to none
SLANG wicked, shit-hot
E3 contemptible, despicable, deplorable

admirably *adv*
commendably, deservingly, excellently, magnificently, exceptionally, wonderfully, eminently, supremely

admiration *n*
respect, (high) regard, (high) esteem, reverence, worship, idolism, adoration, affection, adulation, approval, praise, appreciation, kudos, pleasure, delight, wonder, astonishment, amazement, surprise, acclaim, commendation
FORMAL approbation, veneration, *fureur*
COLLOQ. yen
E3 contempt, disrespect, scorn

admire *v*

1 *admire his honesty*
respect, think highly of, have a high opinion of, hold in high regard, hold in high esteem, esteem (highly), look up to, like very much, revere, worship, idolize, adore, approve, praise, applaud
FORMAL venerate, laud, prize, iconize
COLLOQ. think the world of, hero-worship, put on a pedestal, take your hat off to
SLANG (*vulgar*) think the sun shines out of someone's arse
2 *admire a car*
appreciate, value, like, approve of
E3 1 despise, censure

> **Synonym nuances**
> *sense 1*
> **Respect** and **like very much** and **approve** are fairly restrained terms for admire; to suggest a higher level of admiration you might use **think highly of** or **have a high opinion of**, **hold in high esteem** or **regard** (**highly**), the rather colloquial **think the world of** or the more vulgar **think the sun shines out of someone's arse**. When you **prize** someone or something you also value them, but to use this term suggests you are doing so from a superior or possessive position.
> To say you **look up to** someone implies humility on the part of the speaker, and hints at emulation. This can be even more strongly conveyed with **hero-worship** or **put on a pedestal**. To express an extreme level of admiration, there are many other words you could use, for example **revere**, **worship**, **idolize**, **venerate**, **iconize** and **adore**. Although many of these terms are associated with admiration of deities, they can be used with a more light-hearted tone: *I adore cats; he worships his wife.*
> If you are talking of admiring someone for a particular achievement, you **take your hat off to** them; similarly **laud**, **praise** or **applaud** are usually used in the context of expressing your admiration: *I applaud your calmness in this situation.*

admirer *n*

1 *a great admirer of classical music*
follower, disciple, adherent, supporter, fan, enthusiast, devotee, worshipper, idolizer, idolater
FORMAL aficionado
COLLOQ. buff, fiend, freak
2 *a woman's admirers*
suitor, boyfriend, girlfriend, sweetheart, lover, beloved
FORMAL beau, wooer, gallant
E3 1 critic, opponent

admissible *adj*
acceptable, allowable, permissible, allowed, permitted,
lawful, legitimate, justifiable, tolerable, tolerated, passable
FORMAL licit
COLLOQ. legit, OK
🖃 inadmissible, illegitimate

admission *n*
1 *refuse admission*
permission, entrance, access, right of access, right of entry,
entrée
FORMAL ingress
2 *admission is £5*
admission fee, entrance, entrance fee, entry charge
3 *an admission of guilt*
confession, granting, acknowledgement, recognition,
acceptance, allowance, concession, affirmation,
declaration, profession, disclosure, divulgence, revelation,
exposé
FORMAL avowal, *mea culpa*, *peccavi*, asseveration
🖃 **1** exclusion, prohibition **3** denial, contradiction

🛘 admission or **admittance**?
Each word means 'the act of entering' or 'permission to
enter', but *admittance* is used in more formal styles:
*Admission by ticket only; gain admittance to the palace of
the President.*

---

admit *v*
1 CONFESS, own up, grant, acknowledge, recognize,
accept, allow, concede, agree, declare, affirm,
profess, own, yield, disclose, unburden yourself,
divulge, reveal
COLLOQ. blurt out, eat your words, come clean
SLANG fess up
2 LET IN, allow to enter, allow entry, give access, give
admission, accept, receive, take in, welcome, adopt,
introduce, initiate
OLD adhibit
FORMAL intromit
🖃 **1** deny, hide **2** shut out, exclude, let out

Synonym nuances
sense 1
To **confess** or **own up** are widely used synonyms of
admit, both used in the context of admitting some
wrongdoing. **Grant**, **acknowledge** and **recognize** are
also common synonyms, but used in the context of
admitting that something is true or exists. **Accept** is a
fairly straightforward term for simply complying or
agreeing with something; but **allow** implies agreement
with far less conviction: *he allowed that legislation could
restrict liberty*. Similarly, if you **agree** with someone
about something then you concur, and there is no
implication of prior dissent; but to **concede**, **own** or
yield suggests you admit something you previously
opposed or denied.
  To describe a public admission you could use **declare**,
affirm or **profess**, with the latter having the added
implication that the claims may be false: *they declared
their opposition*; *she thrived on the publicity she
professed to loathe*. **Disclose**, **divulge** and **reveal** would
suggest publicly and willingly bringing secrets to light,
while **unburden yourself** gives a strong sense of the
relief felt on doing so. **Come clean** again suggests a
deliberate act, with more emphasis on admitting all that
you know. However, **blurt out** carries the distinct
impression of an admission accidentally or unadvisedly
made: *he blurted out his drugs secret*.

---

admittance *n*
admitting, admission, letting in, (right of) access,
entrance, (right of) entry, entrée, acceptance,

reception, introduction, initiation
FORMAL ingress
🖃 exclusion

admitted *adj*
confessed, acknowledged, recognized, accepted,
declared, professed, confirmed, affirmed

admittedly *adv*
confessedly, allowedly, avowedly, granted, certainly

admixture *n*
mixture, compound, combination, blend, amalgamation,
mix, fusion, amalgam, alloy
FORMAL commixture, intermixture, tincture

admonish *v*
scold, rebuke, reprimand, discipline, correct, reprove,
warn, upbraid, chide, censure, exhort, counsel
FORMAL berate
COLLOQ. tell off, give someone a dressing-down, give
someone an earful, tear a strip off, rap over the knuckles

admonition *n*
rebuke, reprimand, reproof, scolding, correction, warning,
censure, exhortation, counsel
FORMAL berating, reprehension
COLLOQ. telling-off, ticking-off, dressing-down, earful,
wigging

ad nauseam *adv*
endlessly, interminably, boringly, monotonously,
perpetually, constantly, continually, continuously

ado *n*
fuss, bother, bustle, to-do, commotion
COLLOQ. hurly-burly, hassle, flap, tizzy, hoo-ha, song and
dance

adolescence *n*
teens, teenage years, puberty, youth, young adulthood,
minority, boyhood, girlhood, development, immaturity,
youthfulness, boyishness, girlishness
FORMAL pubescence, juvenescence, juvenility
Related adjective: neanic

adolescent *adj, n*
 ♦ *adj*
1 *an adolescent son*
teenage, young, youthful, juvenile, boyish, girlish,
growing, developing
FORMAL pubescent, juvenescent
2 *adolescent behaviour*
immature, puerile, childish, infantile
 ♦ *n*
teenager, youth, young person, young adult, juvenile, minor

adopt *v*
1 *adopt children*
take in, take as your own, foster
2 *adopt a policy*
take up, take on, accept, assume, follow, choose, select,
support, maintain, back, endorse, ratify, approve
FORMAL appropriate, embrace, espouse, arrogate
3 *adopt a candidate*
select, choose, decide on, settle on, nominate, appoint,
vote, elect
🖃 **1** disown **2** reject

adoption *n*
1 *the adoption of children*
taking as your own, taking-in, (long-term) fostering
2 *the adoption of a suggestion*
taking-on, acceptance, taking-up, choice, selection,
support, backing, endorsement, ratification, approval
FORMAL appropriation, approbation, embracement,
embracing, espousal
3 *adoption of a candidate*
selection, choice, vote, election, nomination,
appointment

adorable *adj*
lovable, dear, darling, precious, appealing, sweet, winsome, charming, enchanting, captivating, winning, delightful, pleasing, attractive, wonderful, fetching, bewitching
E3 hateful, abominable

adoration *n*
1 *adoration for someone*
love, admiration, devotion, cherishing, doting on, (high) regard, esteem
2 *adoration of God*
worship, praise, reverence, homage, idolization, exaltation, magnification, glorification, thanksgiving
FORMAL laudation, veneration
E3 2 abhorrence, detestation

adore *v*
1 *adore your parents*
love, cherish, be devoted to, dote on, hold dear, be fond of, admire, esteem (highly), honour, revere, worship
FORMAL venerate
COLLOQ. think the world of
2 *adore apricots*
love, like very much, enjoy greatly, be fond of, enjoy, savour, relish, be partial to
COLLOQ. have a weakness for, not be able to resist
E3 1, 2 hate, abhor

adorn *v*
decorate, deck, ornament, crown, trim, garnish, gild, enhance, embellish, enrich, grace
OLD bedeck, bedight, bedizen, begem, bejewel, bestick, bespangle, aguise, dight; (*Spenser*) attrap
FORMAL festoon, emblazon, furbish, adonize, apparel, array, attire, beautify, impearl, miniate
COLLOQ. do up, doll up, tart up

adornment *n*
1 *bodily adornment*
beautification, decorating, ornamentation, ornateness, enrichment, embellishment
OLD bedizenment
FORMAL garniture
2 *gold adornments*
accessory, ornament, decoration, jewellery, frill, trappings, trimmings, garnish, flounce, frippery
FORMAL falbala, fallal, fallalery, fandangle, figgery, furbelow, garnishry, gilding

adrift *adj*
1 *the boat had been cut adrift*
at sea, drifting, off course, unanchored, anchorless
2 *feel adrift and lonely*
aimless, rootless, directionless, disorientated, disoriented, having lost your bearings, goalless, insecure, lost, unsettled
E3 1 anchored **2** stable, secure, settled

adroit *adj*
skilful, adept, able, clever, expert, resourceful, masterful, proficient, deft, dexterous
OLD habile
E3 clumsy, inept, maladroit

adroitly *adv*
skilfully, ably, cleverly, expertly, resourcefully, masterfully, proficiently, deftly, dexterously
E3 clumsily, ineptly

adroitness *n*
skill, skilfulness, adeptness, ability, cleverness, expertise, resourcefulness, mastery, facility, finesse, proficiency, competence, deftness, dexterity
E3 clumsiness, ineptitude

adulation *n*
flattery, idolization, personality cult, hero worship, admiration, praise, sycophancy, bootlicking, fawning
FORMAL blandishment
COLLOQ. pats on the back

adulatory *adj*
flattering, praising, complimentary, bootlicking, fawning, servile, sycophantic
FORMAL blandishing, fulsome, obsequious, unctuous
E3 unflattering

adult *adj, n*
◆ *adj*
1 *adult responsibilities*
grown-up, of age, full-grown, fully-grown, fully-fledged, developed, mature, ripe, ripened
2 *adult magazines*
sexually explicit, pornographic, obscene, indecent, hard-core
COLLOQ. blue, X-rated, raunchy, fruity, sleazy, near the knuckle/bone
E3 1 immature
◆ *n*
grown person, grown-up, man, woman
Related adjective: ephebic

adulterate *v*
contaminate, pollute, taint, corrupt, defile, debase, degrade, dilute, water down, weaken, devalue, deteriorate, make impure
FORMAL attenuate, bastardize, vitiate
OLD (*Shakesp*) card
E3 purify, refine

adulteration *n*
contamination, pollution, corruption, defilement, debasement, dilution, weakening, deterioration
FORMAL vitiation

adulterer *n*
libertine, lecher, profligate, rake, roué, playboy, philanderer, womanizer, ladies' man, flirt, Casanova, Don Juan, deceiver, cad
OLD avouterer
COLLOQ. lady-killer, stud, wolf

adulterous *adj*
unfaithful, deceitful, false, disloyal, inconstant
COLLOQ. two-timing, cheating

adultery *n*
unfaithfulness, infidelity, affair, liaison, extramarital relations/ relationship, extramarital sex, entanglement, flirtation, unchastity
OLD avoutry, fornication
COLLOQ. two-timing, cheating, a bit on the side
SLANG playing around, playing the field
E3 faithfulness, fidelity

advance *v, n, adj*
◆ *v*
1 PROCEED, go forward, move on, move forward, come forward, surge forward, go ahead
2 *advance the date of the wedding*
bring forward, move forward, make earlier
3 PROGRESS, make progress, make headway, forge ahead, develop, grow, improve, better, prosper, thrive, flourish
COLLOQ. make great strides, come on in leaps and bounds
4 FURTHER, promote, upgrade, foster, support, assist, help, benefit, facilitate, increase, grow
5 *advance an idea*
present, submit, put forward, suggest, allege, cite, bring forward, offer, provide, supply, furnish
FORMAL proffer, adduce
6 *advance a sum of money*
lend, loan, pay, pay beforehand, pay in advance, give
COLLOQ. sub
E3 1 retreat **2** put back **4** impede, hinder
◆ *n*

1 *the army's advance*
progress, forward movement, onward movement, moving forward, going forward, marching forward
2 *recent advances in medicine*
breakthrough, step, step forward, development, furtherance, progression, headway, growth, increase, improvement
FORMAL advancement, betterment, amelioration
3 *an advance of £500*
deposit, down payment, prepayment, credit, loan, retainer
F3 1 retreat, recession
♦ *adj*
1 *advance booking*
early, prior, forward, preliminary
2 *an advance party*
expeditionary, forward, leading, preliminary, vanguard
■ **in advance**
beforehand, previously, early, earlier, sooner, ahead of time, ahead, in front, in the lead, in the forefront
COLLOQ. up front
F3 later, behind

advanced *adj*
1 *an advanced design*
up-to-date, leading, foremost, ahead, forward, precocious, progressive, forward-looking, high-tech, state-of-the art, avant-garde, ultra-modern, ahead of the times, sophisticated, complex, higher, at the cutting/leading edge
2 *an advanced course of studies*
high-level, complex
F3 1 backward, retarded **2** elementary

Synonym nuances
sense 1
While something **up-to-date** has followed all the latest developments, the terms **leading** and **foremost**, and **at the cutting/leading edge** are reserved for something showing the way. To describe someone or something as **ahead**, **forward** or **higher** also places them in front of others: *forward thinking*; *a higher mind*. Someone who is **precocious** is strikingly advanced for their age or time, but this term often has the implication they are irksomely so: *a precocious young debater*.
  Progressive and **forward-looking** would appropriately describe something enlightened, having regard to the future: *progressive moves towards full employment*. **High-tech** and **state-of-the-art** are usually used to describe something advanced in a specialist field such as electronics. Technology with the most up-to-date devices could also be described as **sophisticated**, while **complex** things have evolved beyond the knowledge of many. **Ultra-modern**, although describing something entirely up-to-date, is ironically rather old-fashioned in tone.
  Avant-garde is often used in the context of art and literature, and carries connotations of unconventionality and daring innovation; if you want to express an unconventionality that society may not be ready for you could use **ahead of the times**.

---

advancement *n*
1 *advancement in a career*
promotion, furtherance, betterment, upgrading, upward step
FORMAL preferment
COLLOQ. kick upstairs
2 *the advancement of science*
improvement, development, growth, evolution, rise, gain, advance, progress, headway
F3 1 demotion **2** retardation

advances *n*
overtures, addresses, approach(es), attentions, moves, proposition, offer, suggestion

advantage *n*
1 *the advantages of electric light*
asset, blessing, benefit, value, reward, good, good point, plus, plus point, virtue, pro, boon, fruit, welfare, interest, service, help, aid, assistance, use, convenience, helpfulness, usefulness, utility, profit, gain
OLD vantage, boot, obvention; (*Shakesp*) prize
FORMAL perquisite, avail
COLLOQ. beauty, pay-off
2 *an advantage over other candidates*
edge, lead, upper hand, head, superiority, precedence, dominance, pre-eminence, sway, leverage
COLLOQ. head start, whip hand; *Aust* box-seat; everything going for you, the odds in your favour
F3 1 disadvantage, drawback, hindrance

advantageous *adj*
beneficial, favourable, convenient, helpful, of assistance, of service, useful, worthwhile, valuable, profitable, gainful, remunerative, rewarding
FORMAL opportune, propitious, furthersome
F3 disadvantageous, adverse, damaging

advent *n*
coming, appearance, approach, arrival, entrance, introduction, occurrence, emergence, looming, onset, dawn, birth, beginning
FORMAL accession, inception

adventitious *adj*
unplanned, unintended, accidental, uncalculated, unexpected, unforeseen
FORMAL fortuitous

adventure *n*
1 *exciting adventures*
exploit, venture, undertaking, enterprise, quest, escapade, risk, hazard, chance, speculation, experience, incident, happening, occurrence
OLD aunter
2 *a life of adventure*
excitement, enterprise, risk, danger, peril, romance, thrill
COLLOQ. kick(s)

Synonym nuances
sense 1
The words **occurrence**, **happening** and **experience** are generally neutral in tone: they can be used of any event that happens to someone without implying either approval or disapproval, or that the person has any control over what happens: *his experiences in the Peruvian jungle*; *some occurrences in her younger life*. The word **incident** also implies that a person has no control over events, but can be more disapproving: *that unsavoury incident last Thursday*.
  When you want to express approval, **exploit** is more appropriate: *heroic exploits*. On the other hand, **escapade** suggests something done with daring, but with comic or disreputable elements: *drunken escapades in Manchester*. The words **quest** and **undertaking** are only appropriate when there is something that a person deliberately sets out to achieve, **quest** having a more romantic tone: *a quest in search of lost civilizations*. When someone decides to do something requiring initiative or imagination, you can use **enterprise** or **venture**.
  When you want to emphasize uncertainty about whether the person will be successful, you can use **speculation**, **hazard**, **risk** and **chance**. The words **undertaking**, **enterprise**, **venture** and **speculation** are often used in the context of business and finance.

adventurer *n*

opportunist, hero, heroine, traveller, venturer, voyager, wanderer, daredevil, pirate, filibuster, swashbuckler, *chevalier d'industrie*
OLD bandeirante, Odysseus, Ulysses, Argonaut

adventurous *adj*

1 *an adventurous person*
daring, intrepid, bold, headstrong, audacious, impetuous, reckless, rash, risky, venturesome, enterprising, daredevil
COLLOQ. spunky, gutsy
2 *an adventurous life*
exciting, enterprising, risky, dangerous, perilous, precarious, hazardous, romantic
F3 1, 2 unadventurous **1** cautious, chary, prudent

adversary *n*

enemy, opponent, antagonist, assailant, attacker, competitor, contestant, foe, opposer, rival
F3 ally, supporter, friend

adverse *adj*

unfavourable, disadvantageous, hostile, antagonistic, opposing, opposite, counter, contrary, conflicting, counter-productive, negative, unfortunate, unlucky, detrimental, harmful, injurious, hurtful, unfriendly, uncongenial, inexpedient
OLD perverse
FORMAL inauspicious, inopportune, unpropitious, untoward
F3 advantageous, favourable

⚠ adverse or **averse**?
Adverse means 'unfavourable, hostile, harmful': *adverse criticism*. *Averse* means 'having a dislike, disinclined': *She's not averse to walking all over people to get what she wants.*

---

adversely *adv*

unfavourably, negatively, unfortunately, unluckily, harmfully, detrimentally
FORMAL inauspiciously, unpropitiously
F3 favourably

adversity *n*

misfortune, ill fortune, bad luck, ill luck, reverse, hardship, hard times, misery, wretchedness, affliction, suffering, distress, sorrow, woe, trouble, trial, cross, calamity, disaster, catastrophe, traverse
FORMAL tribulation
COLLOQ. hell, living hell
SLANG the pits
F3 prosperity

advertise *v*

1 *advertise a product*
publicize, promote, market, merchandize, sell, praise, talk up, tout
COLLOQ. push, plug, hype
2 *advertise the time of a performance*
announce, declare, proclaim, broadcast, publish, display, make known, make public, inform, notify
FORMAL promulgate

advertisement *n*

commercial, publicity, promotion, marketing, jingle, display, blurb, announcement, notice, poster, bill, placard, leaflet, handbill, circular, handout, propaganda, trailer, bulletin
COLLOQ. advert, ad, promo, plug, hype

advice *n*

1 *give someone advice*
warning, caution, dos and don'ts, injunction, instruction, counsel, counselling, help, guidance, direction, suggestion, recommendation, opinion, view, tip, wisdom, word, constructive criticism, encouragement
2 *a remittance advice*
notification, notice, memorandum, communication, information

Synonym nuances
sense 1

The words **guidance** and **direction** can be used widely in situations where a person is looking to be told what they should do: *we give you guidance to make the right decision*. **Suggestion**, **recommendation** and **tip** are likely to be used where a specific course of action is being proposed: *the recommendation was made that Smith be appointed chairman.*

Opinion, **view** and **word**, on the other hand, are appropriate words to use when only a personal angle is called for, without the expectation that it will be acted upon.

However, with **dos and don'ts** and **instruction**, the tone is authoritative, and these terms carry the expectation that a proposed action is carried out. **Injunction** makes the most compelling demand for action, and is used mainly in legal contexts. A **warning** or a **caution** describes a type of advice that usually has not been sought, and suggests that there is danger in taking a particular course. It can also imply that the person giving it may take punitive action themselves.

Other words are more positive in tone: **wisdom** and **counsel** suggest advice given by someone with knowledge and experience, with the implication that it should be respected on those grounds. **Counselling** is typically used in the more specific sense of professional advice, given to assist people with particular problems. Also conveying the idea of advice given to counter possible difficulties are **help**, **constructive criticism** and **encouragement**: *ask your solicitor for help in writing your will.*

---

advisability *n*

desirability, suitability, appropriateness, aptness, preferability, wisdom, judiciousness, prudence, soundness
FORMAL expediency
F3 inadvisability, folly

advisable *adj*

suggested, recommended, sensible, wise, wisest, prudent, expedient, judicious, sound, profitable, beneficial, best, desirable, preferable, suitable, appropriate, apt, fitting, fit, proper, correct
FORMAL politic
F3 inadvisable, foolish

advise *v*

1 COUNSEL, give counsel, guide, give guidance, warn, forewarn, caution, instruct, teach, tutor, suggest, give/offer/make suggestions, recommend, give/offer/make recommendations, commend, urge
FORMAL enjoin, forewarn
2 NOTIFY, inform, tell, acquaint, make known, report, give notice
FORMAL apprise
COLLOQ. fill in on, give the low-down

advisedly *adv*

cautiously, carefully, prudently, judiciously, after careful consideration

adviser *n*

counsellor, consultant, authority, guide, teacher, tutor, instructor, coach, mentor, helper, aide, right-hand man/woman, therapist, guru, confidant(e), counsel, lawyer

advisory *adj*

advising, consultative, consulting, counselling, helping, recommending
FORMAL consultatory

advocacy *n*

support, backing, adoption, campaigning, promotion,

championing, defence, encouragement, patronage, proposal, recommendation, justification, upholding, propagation
FORMAL espousal, advancement, promulgation
COLLOQ. pushing

advocate v, n
♦ v
defend, champion, campaign for, press for, argue for, preach, plead for, justify, urge, encourage, advise, recommend, propose, prescribe, promote, endorse, back (up), support, uphold, patronize, adopt, subscribe to, favour, believe in, sympathize with, lobby
FORMAL espouse, countenance
COLLOQ. plug, push for, be behind, be pro, throw your weight behind
E3 *formal* impugn, disparage, deprecate
♦ n
1 *an advocate of an idea*
defender, supporter, upholder, champion, campaigner, pleader, vindicator, proponent, exponent, promoter, evangelist, speaker, spokesperson, spokesman, spokeswoman
2 *the advocate in a court of law*
lawyer, solicitor, barrister, counsel, attorney, paraclete; *Scot* peat
E3 **1** opponent, critic

aegis n
support, backing, auspices, guardianship, patronage, sponsorship, wing, advocacy, championship, favour

aeon n
age, era, epoch, span, time, duration, generation, year(s)

aerate v
oxygenate, put air into, charge with air, charge with gas, gasify, refresh, ventilate, lighten

aerial adj, n
♦ adj
aerial combat
above the ground, in the air, midair, air-to-air
OLD aery
FORMAL aeolian
♦ n
antenna, booster, receiver, satellite dish
TECHNICAL dipole, duplex

aeroplane n
See panel at **aircraft**.

aesthetic adj
decorative, ornamental, adorning, embellishing, fine, elegant, stylish, tasteful, artistic
FORMAL beautifying

afar adv
a long distance, a long way, far off, far away, distantly

affability n
friendliness, amiability, approachability, openness, geniality, good humour, good nature, mildness, benevolence, kindliness, graciousness, obligingness, courtesy, amicability, congeniality, cordiality, warmth, sociability, pleasantness
FORMAL benignity, conversableness
COLLOQ. chumminess, matiness, palliness
E3 unfriendliness, reserve, reticence, coolness

affable adj
friendly, amiable, approachable, open, expansive, genial, good-humoured, good-natured, mild, benevolent, kindly, gracious, obliging, courteous, amicable, congenial, cordial, warm, sociable, pleasant, agreeable
OLD facile

COLLOQ. chummy, mat(e)y, pally
E3 unfriendly, reserved, reticent, cool

affair n
1 BUSINESS, transaction, operation, proceeding, undertaking, activity, project, responsibility, interest, concern, matter, question, issue, subject, topic, circumstance, happening, occurrence, incident, episode, event, thing, ploy; *Scot* effeir, hypothec
OLD gear
COLLOQ. show, pigeon, funeral, shebang
OLD COLLOQ. go
2 *have an affair*
relationship, liaison, intrigue, love affair, romance, *affaire, affaire d'amour, affaire de coeur, grande passion,* amour
COLLOQ. fling, carry-on

affect v
1 *changes that affect the schedule*
have an effect/influence on, concern, regard, involve, relate to, apply to, do to, bear upon, impinge upon, act on, change, transform, alter, modify, influence, sway, prevail over, impact
2 *deeply affected by the poverty*
move, touch, impress, interest, stir, upset, disturb, trouble, overcome
FORMAL perturb
COLLOQ. faze, throw
3 *a disease affects the body*
attack, strike, take hold of
4 *affect an attitude*
adopt, simulate, imitate, fake, counterfeit, sham, pretend, profess
FORMAL feign, assume
COLLOQ. put on

⚠ affect or **effect**?
Affect is usually a verb. Its most common meaning is 'to have an influence on; change the circumstances, etc of': *The accident affected his eyesight. Effect* is used as a noun or a verb: as a noun it means 'result or consequence': *recover from the effects of his illness.* As a verb it is used in formal styles to mean 'to cause or bring about': *effect a reconciliation with his parents.*

Synonym nuances
sense 2
To say you are **moved** or **touched** suggests something has aroused your sentiments, especially pity. The term **impress** might be used instead to describe a profound effect on the intellect rather than emotion, whereas to **interest** is far less significant of any deep emotional involvement.
 To convey excitement, you could use **stir**: *a cause which stirred the electorate,* but **upset** would only be appropriate where a degree of distress has been caused. **Disturb**, **trouble** and **perturb** are similar to upset, though they have the added suggestion of agitation. To express a more extreme effect, **overcome** suggests your feelings have got the better of you: *overcome by grief.* When something **fazes** you it worries, confuses or unsettles you, and the similarly colloquial term **throw** denotes much the same.

affectation n
airs, pretentiousness, mannerism, pose, act, show, appearance, façade, pretence, charade, sham, false display, simulation, imitation, artificiality, insincerity, theatricism, airs and graces
E3 artlessness, ingenuousness

Synonym nuances

Many of these synonyms have a tone of disapproval; to say someone has put on **airs** or **airs and graces** is to accuse them of affecting superiority or refined behaviour; **pretentiousness** goes further by suggesting someone acting in a foolishly grandiose way. A **mannerism** is a more neutral term to denote a marked peculiarity or a trick of style or manner, whereas striking a **pose** is again more marked by the suggestion of a false act and a desire to impress.

Act and **show** also suggest a pretence, this time with the aim to deceive: *I put on a show of contrition.* An **appearance** similarly denotes an outward look or show, and is not a particularly marked term; **façade**, too, can be used to describe an outward display, but it is usually showier and with little behind it: *the façade of respectability.* **Pretence** also signifies an act put on deliberately to mislead, while **false display** and **sham** are even more strongly uncomplimentary terms intimating an imposture or fraud.

Simulation and **imitation** can again be used as more neutral terms to describe insincere acts, but **artificiality** and **insincerity** again imply criticism, the latter carrying a strong suggestion of hypocrisy. If you want to emphasize the exaggerated nature of the affectation, you might choose the word **theatricism**.

---

affected *adj*
pretentious, pompous, stiff, unnatural, insincere, twee, simulated, artificial, fake, counterfeit, sham, contrived, studied, precious, mannered, contrived
FORMAL assumed, feigned, literose, minikin
COLLOQ. put-on, la-di-da, hoity-toity, phoney
F3 genuine, natural

affecting *adj*
moving, touching, impressive, powerful, piteous, pitiable, pitiful, poignant, heartbreaking, heart-rending, pathetic, sad, stirring, troubling

affection *n*
fondness, attachment, devotion, love, tenderness, care, caring, warmth, feeling, kindness, friendliness, endearment, goodwill, favour, liking, partiality, inclination, passion, desire
FORMAL amity, penchant, predilection, predisposition, proclivity, propensity
F3 dislike, antipathy

affectionate *adj*
fond, attached, devoted, doting, loving, adoring, tender, caring, warm, warm-hearted, kind, friendly, amiable, cordial
F3 cold, undemonstrative

affectionately *adv*
fondly, lovingly, devotedly, adoringly, tenderly, kindly, warmly, amiably, cordially
F3 coldly

affiliate *v*
join, associate, ally, amalgamate, unite, annex, combine, connect, incorporate, merge, team up, syndicate, band together
OLD filiate
FORMAL confederate, conjoin

affiliated *adj*
associated, allied, in partnership, in league, connected, related, incorporated, amalgamated, integrated
F3 independent

affiliation *n*
connection, relationship, link, tie, bond, alliance, union, amalgamation, association, coalition, combination, confederation, federation, incorporation, membership, joining, league, merger
OLD filiation

affinity *n*
1 RAPPORT, attraction, compatibility, empathy, sympathy, fondness, liking, good terms, bond, partiality
OLD affiance
FORMAL predisposition, propensity
COLLOQ. chemistry
2 RESEMBLANCE, similarity, likeness, relationship, correspondence, analogy, comparability, kin, kinship
FORMAL similitude
F3 1 hatred 2 dissimilarity

affirm *v*
confirm, corroborate, endorse, ratify, uphold, support, certify, witness, testify, swear, maintain, state, assert, declare, pronounce
FORMAL asseverate, attest, aver, avouch, avow
F3 refute, deny

affirmation *n*
yes, assertion, statement, declaration, attestation, certification, confirmation, corroboration, endorsement, ratification, oath, pronouncement, protest, testimony, witness
FORMAL affirmance, asseveration, averment, deposition, avouchment, avowal

affirmative *adj, n*
◆ *adj*
agreeing, concurring, approving, assenting, consenting, positive, confirming, corroborative, emphatic
FORMAL concurring, assertory
F3 negative, dissenting
◆ *n*
yes, agreement, confirmation, acceptance, ratification
FORMAL concurrence, acquiescence
COLLOQ. OK
F3 negative

affix *v*
stick, glue, paste, adhere, pin on, tack, attach, add, annex, append, bind, connect, fasten, join, tag
FORMAL adjoin, subjoin
F3 detach

afflict *v*
strike, visit, trouble, burden, oppress, distress, strain, stress, bother, bear hard upon, grieve, pain, hurt, ail, wound, harm, try, harass, plague, anguish, curse, gripe, torment, torture
OLD smite, visit; (*Spenser*) assay
FORMAL beset
F3 comfort; *formal* solace

🛈 **afflict** or **inflict**?
Afflict means 'to cause pain or distress to': *Pre-fight nerves afflict almost everyone.* *Inflict* means 'to impose something unpleasant or unwanted': *They inflicted heavy casualties on the enemy.*

affliction *n*
distress, grief, sorrow, misery, depression, suffering, pain, torment, disease, illness, sickness, plague, curse, scourge, sore, night, cross, ordeal, trial, trouble, hardship, adversity, misfortune, calamity, disaster, woe, furnace, wretchedness
OLD languor, teen; (*Spenser*) tine; unweal, visitation
FORMAL tribulation
F3 comfort, blessing; *formal* consolation, solace

affluence *n*
wealthiness, wealth, riches, fortune, substance, property, prosperity, abundance, profusion, plenty
FORMAL opulence
COLLOQ. tidy sum, easy street
SLANG megabucks
F3 poverty

affluent *adj*
wealthy, rich, moneyed, well-off, prosperous, well-to-do, comfortable

FORMAL opulent
COLLOQ. well-heeled, flush, in the money, on easy street, rolling in it
SLANG loaded
E poor, impoverished

afford v
1 *afford school fees*
have enough for, pay for, have the money for, be able to pay, spare, allow, stretch to, manage, sustain, bear
2 *privileges afforded by the membership*
provide, supply, furnish, give, grant, offer, impart, present, produce, yield, generate

affordable adj
inexpensive, cheap, low-priced, low-cost, budget, economical, moderate, reasonable, manageable, sustainable

affray n
brawl, brush, contest, disturbance, fight, quarrel, riot, row, feud, fracas, fray, mêlée, scuffle, set-to, skirmish, squabble, tussle, wrangle
COLLOQ. punch-up, fisticuffs, scrap, free-for-all

affront v, n
♦ v
offend, insult, abuse, snub, slight, provoke, displease, irritate, annoy, anger, vex, incense, outrage, pique
E compliment, appease
♦ n
offence, insult, slur, rudeness, discourtesy, disrespect, indignity, snub, slight, wrong, injury, abuse, provocation, vexation, outrage
FORMAL aspersion
COLLOQ. facer, slap in the face, kick in the teeth
E compliment, pat on the back

affronted adj
injured, offended, insulted, slighted, displeased, irritated, annoyed, angry, vexed, incensed, outraged, piqued

aficionado n
devotee, fan, enthusiast, admirer, connoisseur, authority, expert, specialist
COLLOQ. buff, fiend, freak, nut

aflame adj
1 ALIGHT, burning, ablaze, on fire, ignited, lighted
2 AGLOW, lit up, illuminated, bright, radiant, shining

afloat adv
1 FLOATING, buoyant, unsinkable, swimming, drifting
COLLOQ. with your head above water
2 *keep business afloat*
solvent, viable, sound, out of debt
COLLOQ. in the black, with your head above water
E 1 sinking 2 *colloq.* in the red

afoot adv
about, around, circulating, current, going on, going about, in the air, in the wind, brewing
FORMAL abroad
COLLOQ. in the pipeline

aforementioned adj
already mentioned, previously mentioned
OLD aforesaid, aforenamed

afraid adj
1 FRIGHTENED, scared, alarmed, terrified, petrified, panic-stricken, fearful, timorous, daunted, intimidated, faint-hearted, cowardly, craven, reluctant, apprehensive, anxious, nervous, timid, distrustful, suspicious; *dialect* nesh; *Scot* rad
OLD affrayed, effraide, afear, adred; (*Spenser*) adrad
FORMAL tremulous, aghast
COLLOQ. scared out of your wits, scared to death, having kittens, in a cold sweat, in a blue funk, shaking in your shoes, shaking like a leaf, with your heart in your mouth

2 *I'm afraid she's badly hurt*
sorry, concerned, regretful, apologetic
E 1 unafraid, brave, bold, confident

Synonym nuances
sense 1
The words **frightened**, **scared** and **alarmed** are fairly straightforward synonyms of afraid; **terrified** and **petrified** might be used of more extreme fear, with the implication of being almost fixed in fear.
 Panic-stricken likewise indicates being struck by a panic or fear resulting in mental inaction. **Daunted** is a less extreme term, which more often nowadays suggests discouragement rather than fear. If you want to emphasize that something in particular is striking fear into someone and making them less able to act, you could say they are **intimidated**.
 To describe someone as **timid**, **faint-hearted**, **cowardly** or **craven** says they lack courage generally, often without good cause, and these terms are rather contemptuous; **craven** has a literary, old-fashioned tone. **Reluctant** is a fairly mild term suggesting only unwillingness.
 To convey an unwillingness or fear caused by the anticipation of something adverse, you could use **apprehensive**, **anxious** or **nervous**. **Tremulous** can be used to suggest a physical manifestation of fear or apprehensiveness. To describe someone as **aghast** would be appropriate where something in particular has struck them with horror, and they are showing signs of it: *they stood aghast at the news.*

---

afresh adv
anew, again, once again, once more, newly, over again

after prep
1 *life after death*
following, subsequent to
FORMAL posterior
2 *run after a thief*
in pursuit of, following, chasing
3 *be after the manager's job*
wanting, trying to get
4 *ask after someone*
about, regarding, with regard to, concerning
5 *named after his mother*
in honour of, given the same name as; *N Am* for
6 *after the way I've been treated*
because of, owing to, in consequence of, as a result of, on account of
E 1 before
■ after all
1 *it's only a game after all*
in spite of what was expected, despite what was expected
2 *you can't expect to learn English in a few days; after all it is a difficult language*
it must be remembered that, primarily, first of all, most importantly, most of all

after-effect n
result, consequence, repercussion, upshot, aftermath, spin-off

aftermath n
after-effects, effects, results, outcome, consequences, end, repercussions, upshot, wake

afterwards adv
next, later (on), subsequently, after that, then
OLD thereupon

again adv
once more, once again, yet again, one more time, another time, over again, afresh, anew, encore
■ again and again

repeatedly, continually, constantly, frequently, often, over and over again, time and time again, time and again

against prep
1 *against the wall*
adjacent to, close up to, touching, in contact with, on
FORMAL abutting
2 *against corporal punishment*
opposing, versus, opposed to, in opposition to, antagonistic to, hostile to, resisting, in defiance of, opposite to, facing, fronting, in the face of, confronting, in contrast to
COLLOQ. anti
3 *insure against fire*
in case of, as a protection from
4 *his youth is against him*
disadvantageous, unfavourable, harmful, detrimental, prejudicial
Ea 2 in favour of, for; *colloq.* pro

age n, v
♦ n
1 *the Ice Age*
era, epoch, day, days, generation, date, time, period, duration, span, years, aeon
2 *the experience of age*
old age, maturity, elderliness, seniority, dotage, senility, decline, advancing/declining years
FORMAL senescence, decrepitude
Ea 2 youth; *colloq.* salad days
♦ v
grow old/up, become old, come of age, mature, ripen, mellow, season, decline, deteriorate, degenerate, wither

aged adj
old, elderly, advanced (in years), ag(e)ing, mature, senior, geriatric, grey, hoary, patriarchal, superannuated
FORMAL senescent
COLLOQ. getting on, past it, over the hill, have seen better days, no spring chicken, not as young as you were, not getting any younger, with one foot in the grave, ancient
Ea young, youthful

agency n
1 *a recruitment agency*
bureau, office, department, organization, business, firm, company, work
2 MEANS, medium, instrumentality, vehicle, power, force, influence, effect, intervention, action, activity, involvement, operation, mechanism, workings

agenda n
list, plan, programme, schedule, calendar, diary, timetable, to-do list, scheme, scheme of work, menu

agent n
1 *a travel agent*
representative, broker, middleman, go-between, liaison, intermediary, negotiator, substitute, deputy, delegate, envoy, emissary, minister, proxy, trustee, assignee, mover, doer, performer, operator, operative, functionary, worker, factor
COLLOQ. rep
2 *a secret agent*
spy, double agent, shadow, setter, emissary, sleeper, *mouchard* ; *N Am* operative
OLD beagle, wait, spial, spie
COLLOQ. mole
SLANG nark, plant, spook
3 *water-purifying agents*
instrument, vehicle, channel, means, medium, agency, cause, force
4 *an agent of change*
instrument, vehicle, engine, medium, factor, channel, route, way, means, root, source, performer

age-old adj
ancient, old, very old, aged, time-worn, antique, long-lived
FORMAL prim(a)eval
Ea new

agglomeration n
accumulation, build-up, collection, gathering, mass, stockpile, increase, store, aggregate
FORMAL augmentation, aggregation
COLLOQ. stash

aggrandize v
make richer, make more powerful, advance, dignify, elevate, enhance, enlarge, ennoble, enrich, exaggerate, exalt, glamorize, glorify, inflate, amplify, magnify, promote, upgrade, widen
Ea belittle, debase

aggrandizement n
advancement, elevation, enlargement, enhancement, exaggeration, exaltation, promotion, magnification

aggravate v
1 *aggravate the problem*
worsen, make worse, compound, inflame, increase, intensify, heighten, magnify, exaggerate
FORMAL exacerbate
COLLOQ. add fuel to the fire/flames, add insult to injury, rub salt in the wound
2 ANNOY, irritate, vex, irk, exasperate, incense, provoke, tease, pester, harass
COLLOQ. wind up, get at, get on someone's nerves, get up someone's nose, get under someone's skin, rub up the wrong way, needle
Ea 1 improve, alleviate **2** soothe, appease, mollify

aggravation n
annoyance, exasperation, irritation, provocation, teasing, vexation, irksomeness
COLLOQ. aggro, hassle, thorn in the flesh

aggregate n, adj
♦ n
total, sum, sum total, grand total, amount, total/whole amount, whole, totality, entirety, generality, combination, collection, accumulation
♦ adj
total, entire, complete, whole, full, combined, gross, inclusive, comprehensive, accumulated

aggression n
1 ANTAGONISM, provocation, offence, injury, attack, offensive, assault, onslaught, raid, incursion, strike, encroachment, infringement, invasion, intrusion
2 AGGRESSIVENESS, militancy, belligerence, combativeness, hostility, forcefulness
FORMAL pugnacity, bellicosity
Ea 1 peace, resistance **2** passivity, gentleness

aggressive adj
1 *an aggressive person*
argumentative, quarrelsome, contentious, belligerent, hostile, offensive, provocative, intrusive, invasive, ruthless, brutal, savage, ferocious, destructive
FORMAL pugnacious, bellicose
COLLOQ. cut-throat; *Can* chippy
SLANG *N Am* bad-ass
2 *an aggressive sales rep*
bold, assertive, pushy, go-ahead, competitive, forceful, vigorous, zealous
COLLOQ. feisty, full-on
SLANG in-your-face
Ea 1 peaceable, friendly **2** submissive, unassertive, timid

aggressor n
invader, attacker, assailant, assaulter, intruder, offender, provoker, instigator
Ea victim

aggrieved *adj*
bitter, resentful, pained, distressed, saddened, unhappy, upset, angry, annoyed, wronged, offended, hurt, injured, insulted, maltreated, ill-used
COLLOQ. disgruntled, miffed, peeved
SLANG pissed off
⊟ pleased, happy

aghast *adj*
shocked, appalled, horrified, horror-struck, thunderstruck, stunned, stupefied, amazed, astonished, astounded, startled, confounded, dismayed

agile *adj*
1 *an agile person*
active, lively, nimble, spry, sprightly, mobile, deft, dexterous, athletic, flexible, limber, lithe, fleet, quick, swift, brisk; *Scot* swank
COLLOQ. nifty
2 *an agile mind*
astute, sharp, acute, alert, quick-witted, clever
⊟ 1 clumsy, stiff **2** slow

agility *n*
1 *agility of movement*
activeness, liveliness, nimbleness, mobility, flexibility, deftness, quickness, swiftness, briskness
2 *agility of thought*
astuteness, sharpness, alertness, quick-wittedness
⊟ 1 clumsiness, stiffness **2** slowness

agitate *v*
1 *the news agitated them*
worry, trouble, upset, alarm, disturb, unsettle, disquiet, discompose, fluster, ruffle, flurry, unnerve, confuse, distract, disconcert, work up
OLD (*Shakesp*) betoss
FORMAL perturb
COLLOQ. faze, rattle
2 *agitate for reform*
campaign, argue, fight, battle, rouse, arouse, stir up, excite, stimulate, incite, inflame, ferment, work up
3 *agitate the mixture*
shake, rattle, convulse, rock, stir, beat, churn, toss, whisk, blend; *dialect* poss
OLD commove
⊟ 1 calm, tranquillize

agitated *adj*
worried, troubled, upset, disturbed, anxious, unsettled, flustered, ruffled, distraught, unnerved, disconcerted, nervous, wrought up
COLLOQ. in a lather, in a tizzy
⊟ calm, composed

agitation *n*
1 ANXIETY, worry, concern, distress, trouble, alarm, disquiet, restlessness, tension
FORMAL perturbation
2 *periods of political agitation*
fighting, striving, struggle, battle, campaigning, crusade
3 *agitation of the particles*
shaking, moving, movement, stirring, whisking, beating, tossing, turning, blending
⊟ 1 calmness

agitator *n*
troublemaker, activist, subversive, rabble-rouser, revolutionary, *agent provocateur*, inciter, instigator, firebrand, fomenter
COLLOQ. stirrer

agnostic *n, adj*
♦ *n*
unbeliever, sceptic, doubter, questioner
COLLOQ. doubting Thomas
♦ *adj*
unbelieving, sceptical, doubting, questioning, disbelieving

ago *adv*
from that time, gone, past, in the past, before, since, previously, earlier

agog *adj*
eager, excited, curious, enthralled, enthusiastic, impatient, in suspense, keen, anxious, avid
COLLOQ. on the edge of your seat, on tenterhooks
⊟ incurious

agonize *v*
worry, labour, strain, strive, struggle, fret, trouble, wrestle

agonizing *adj*
distressing, excruciating, harrowing, painful, tormenting, torturous, worrying, piercing, racking

agony *n*
anguish, torment, torture, pain, spasm, throes, suffering, affliction, distress, hurt, woe, misery, wretchedness
FORMAL tribulation

agrarian *adj*
agricultural, agronomic, farming, cultivated
OLD georgic
FORMAL bucolic, geoponic, praedial

agree *v*
1 *agree with someone*
concur, get on, settle, be of one mind, be of the same opinion, share the view, be at one, come to/reach an agreement, compromise, make concessions
OLD gree, fadge
FORMAL accord
COLLOQ. fall in with, get on, see eye to eye, go along with, go with, meet halfway
2 *agree to your request*
consent, allow, permit, accept, grant, admit, concede, yield, comply, say yes to
OLD gree, underwrite
FORMAL assent, accede, acquiesce in
COLLOQ. give the go-ahead, give the green light, give the thumbs-up, rubber-stamp
3 *agree on a schedule*
decide, settle, make up your mind about, determine, reach an agreement on, strike a bargain
COLLOQ. clinch
4 *the reports do not agree*
match, suit, fit, tally, correspond, conform, be consistent, coincide, square, chime
OLD gree, congree, comport; (*Shakesp*) congrue, atone
FORMAL accord
⊟ 1 disagree **2** refuse **4** disagree, differ, conflict

Synonym nuances
sense 4
To say two things **match**, **tally**, **correspond** or **coincide** is simply to say they are exactly or nearly alike: *a manager with the credentials to match the club's aspirations*, but to say they **suit** or **fit** each other is to suggest that one has an effect on the outcome of the other: *the darkness suited his evil purpose.*
  However, **conform** would be used where an effort has to be made to make something agree. To **square** one thing with another suggests that you have to bring them into accord or reconcile them: *such optimism is hard to square with history*, but if they **chime** or **accord** then they already agree: *his poem chimes with our experience of loss.*

---

agreeable *adj*
1 *agreeable weather*
pleasant, enjoyable, delightful, fine, nice, acceptable
2 *an agreeable person*
pleasant, congenial, lik(e)able, nice, attractive, delightful, charming, friendly, good-natured, amicable, sympathetic

3 *agreeable to a suggestion*
willing, amenable, compliant
FORMAL complaisant
E3 1 disagreeable, nasty **2** unpleasant **3** unwilling, reluctant to accept

agreeably *adv*
acceptably, pleasantly, pleasingly, enjoyably, delightfully, attractively

agreement *n*
1 *a trade agreement*
settlement, covenant, treaty, pact, contract, deed, deal, bargain, arrangement, understanding
FORMAL concordat, compact, indenture
2 *be in agreement*
unanimity, union, harmony, sympathy, consensus, affinity
FORMAL assent, complaisance
3 *the agreement of the reports*
matching, fitting, tally, correspondence, consistency, conformity, compatibility, similarity
FORMAL concurrence, accord, concord, consonance
E3 2 disagreement **3** inconsistency

agricultural *adj*
agronomic, agrarian, farming, farmed, cultivated, rural, countryside, pastoral
OLD georgic
FORMAL bucolic, geoponic, praedial

Types of agricultural implement and machinery include:

all-terrain vehicle (ATV)	fork	reversible plough
axe	fork-lift truck	rotary hoe
baler	front end loader	Rotovator®
bale wrapper	harrow	saw
broadcaster	harvester	scarifier
chainsaw	hayfork	scythe
clover fertilizer	hayrake	seed drill
distributor	hedgecutter	shovel
combine	hoe	sickle
harvester	irrigator	slurry sprayer
combination	mattock	spade
seed-harrow	milking machine	tanker
corn drill	mower	tedder
cultivator	muckspreader	tractor
disc harrow	pitchfork	trailer
drill	plough	wheelbarrow
fertilizer spreader	potato planter	wheel plough
field sprinkler	power lift	whetstone
flail mower	rake	
	reaping hook	

---

agriculture *n*
farming, husbandry, cultivation, tilling, tillage
TECHNICAL agribusiness, agronomics, agronomy, agroscience, geoponics
Related adjective: geoponic

aground *adj, adv*
ashore, beached, foundered, grounded, high and dry, marooned, stranded, stuck, wrecked, on the rocks
E3 afloat

ahead *adv*
1 *glance ahead*
forward(s), onward(s), leading, at the head, in front
2 *go on ahead*
in advance, in front, in the lead, in the vanguard
3 *ahead on points*
in the lead, leading, winning, at an advantage, advanced, superior, to the fore, in the forefront
4 *plan ahead*
in advance, before, earlier on
E3 1 behind

aid *v, n*
◆ *v*
1 *aid an invalid*
help, assist, rally round, relieve, support, subsidize, sustain, second, serve, favour, co-operate with
FORMAL succour, oblige, accommodate
2 *aid a process*
promote, boost, encourage, facilitate, speed up, ease
FORMAL expedite, hasten
E3 1 *colloq.* not lift a finger **2** hinder, impede, obstruct
◆ *n*
1 *aid for refugees*
relief, benefit, (financial) assistance, (financial) support, (financial) backing, subsidy, donation, gift, contribution, funding, grant, sponsorship, patronage, favour, encouragement, service
FORMAL subvention
2 *turn to someone for aid*
help, assistance, prop, support, backup, boost
FORMAL succour
COLLOQ. (helping) hand, a shot in the arm, a leg up
E3 2 hindrance, impediment, obstruction

aide *n*
adviser, assistant, right-hand man/woman, supporter, adjutant, advocate, aide-de-camp, attaché, confidant(e), disciple, follower

ail *v*
afflict, trouble, upset, bother, distress, fail, irritate, pain, sicken, weaken, worry
E3 comfort, flourish

ailing *adj*
1 UNWELL, ill, sick, poorly, suffering, languishing, sickly, diseased, invalid, infirm, unsound, unfit, frail, weak, feeble, failing, indisposed, debilitated
COLLOQ. out of sorts, under the weather, off-colour
2 *an ailing business*
failing, weak, foundering, insolvent, inadequate, poor, deficient
E3 1 healthy, fit **2** thriving, flourishing

ailment *n*
illness, sickness, complaint, malady, disease, infection, disorder, affliction, infirmity, disability, weakness
FORMAL indisposition
COLLOQ. *Aust* dog's disease

aim *v, n*
◆ *v*
1 POINT, direct, take aim, shoot at, level, line up, train, sight, target
COLLOQ. zero in on
2 *aim to achieve*
plan, aspire, want, wish, seek, resolve, purpose, intend, propose, mean, design, strive, try, attempt, endeavour, work towards, set your sights on
◆ *n*
purpose, motive, end, intention, object, objective, target, mark, goal, direction, course, plan, design, scheme, aspiration, mission, mission statement, ambition, hope, dream, desire, wish

aimless *adj*
pointless, purposeless, goalless, futile, unmotivated, irresolute, directionless, rambling, drifting, wandering, undirected, unguided, unsettled, stray, chance, random, haphazard, erratic, unpredictable, wayward
E3 purposeful, positive, determined

air *n, v*
◆ *n*
1 *birds flying in the air*
atmosphere, oxygen, sky, heavens
FORMAL ether
Related adjective: aerial

2 *the air we breathe*
breath, fresh air, puff, waft, whiff, draught, breeze, wind, blast
FORMAL zephyr
Related adjective: pneumatic
3 APPEARANCE, look, aspect, aura, bearing, manner, mien, character, effect, impression, feeling, expression, carriage
FORMAL ambience, demeanour
◆ *v*
1 *air a room*
ventilate, aerate, freshen
2 *air an opinion*
utter, voice, express, give vent to, make known, communicate, tell, declare, state, reveal, disclose, divulge, expose, make public, broadcast, publish, ventilate, circulate, publicize
FORMAL disseminate
COLLOQ. speak your mind, have your say

airborne *adj*
flying, in the air, in flight, hovering, winging

aircraft

Types of aircraft include:

aeroplane	glider	skiplane
air-ambulance	hang-glider	spitfire
Airbus	helicopter	spy plane
airship	hot-air balloon	swing-wing
all-wing	jet	taildragger
amphibian	jump jet	triplane
aquaplane	jumbo	troop carrier
biplane	*colloq.* kite	turbojet
bomber	microlight	turboprop
slang chopper	monoplane	two-seater
Concorde	multiplane	VTOL (vertical
delta-wing	intercepter	take-off and
dive-bomber	plane	landing)
fighter	rocket plane	warplane
fixed-wing	seaplane	zeppelin
freighter	single-seater	

airily *adv*
casually, breezily, lightly, readily, flippantly, nonchalantly, light-heartedly, jauntily

airing *n*
1 *give clothes an airing*
ventilation, aeration, freshening, refreshing
2 *the airing of opinions*
expression, making known, communication, declaration, statement, revelation, disclosure, divulgence, exposure, uttering, voicing, venting, broadcast, publication, circulation
FORMAL dissemination

airless *adj*
unventilated, badly/poorly ventilated, stuffy, musty, stale, suffocating, stifling, sultry, muggy, close, heavy, oppressive
E3 airy, fresh

airs *n*
arrogance, artificiality, haughtiness, posing, pretensions, pretentiousness, superciliousness
FORMAL affectation, affectedness, hauteur, pomposity
COLLOQ. swank, snootiness

airtight *adj*
1 *an airtight container*
closed, sealed, impenetrable, impermeable, tight-fitting
2 *a simple airtight explanation*
indisputable, unquestionable, incontrovertible, indubitable, irrefutable, incontestable, conclusive, beyond question, beyond dispute, flawless

airy *adj*
1 *an airy room*

roomy, spacious, open, well-ventilated, draughty, fresh, breezy, blowy, windy, gusty
2 ETHEREAL, unsubstantial, immaterial, intangible, incorporeal, spirit-like, spiritual
3 CASUAL, cheerful, happy, light-hearted, high-spirited, sprightly, lively, jaunty, nonchalant, breezy, flippant, offhand
E3 1 airless, stuffy, close, heavy, oppressive

aisle *n*
gangway, corridor, passage, passageway, alleyway, walkway, path, lane

ajar *adj*
open, unclosed, half open, slightly open, unfastened, unbolted, unlocked, unlatched
E3 closed, shut, fastened, locked

akin *adj*
similar, like, close, related, near, corresponding, equivalent, comparable

alacrity *n*
promptness, briskness, eagerness, keenness, readiness, willingness, enthusiasm, fervour, ardour, impatience

alarm *n, v*
◆ *n*
1 FRIGHT, scare, fear, terror, panic, horror, shock, consternation, dismay, distress, anxiety, nervousness, apprehension, trepidation, uneasiness
OLD tirrit
FORMAL perturbation
2 *a burglar alarm*
danger signal, alert, warning, distress signal, siren, horn, whistle, bell, alarm-bell
OLD larum
FORMAL tocsin
E3 1 calmness, composure
◆ *v*
frighten, scare, startle, terrify, panic, make afraid, unnerve, daunt, dismay, distress, agitate
FORMAL perturb, affright
COLLOQ. put the wind up, rattle
E3 reassure, calm, soothe

alarming *adj*
frightening, startling, terrifying, unnerving, daunting, ominous, worrying, threatening, dismaying, disturbing, distressing, shocking, dreadful
FORMAL perturbing
COLLOQ. scary
E3 reassuring

alarmist *n*
scaremonger, pessimist, doomwatcher, doomsayer
COLLOQ. doom-merchant, prophet of doom
E3 optimist

alcohol *n*
drink, liquor, spirits, strong drink, intoxicant, grog, liqueur, stimulus, slug; *Scot* skink, strunt
OLD fuddle; (*Shakesp*) tickle-brain
COLLOQ. hard stuff, the bottle, Dutch courage, firewater, the creature, jar, tipple, tiddly, tinct, sauce
SLANG booze, jungle juice; *N Am* juice

alcoholic *adj, n*
◆ *adj*
intoxicating, inebriating, brewed, fermented, distilled, strong, hard, ardent
◆ *n*
drunk, drunkard, inebriate, drinker, hard drinker, heavy drinker, dipsomaniac, wine-bibber, Bacchus, bloat, habitual; *N Am* souse
COLLOQ. tippler
SLANG boozer, wino, lush, alkie, dipso, soak, piss artist, pisshead, toper, tosspot, sot, sponge

alcove n

niche, nook, recess, bay, corner, cubbyhole, opening, compartment, cubicle, booth, carrel

alert adj, v, n

◆ adj

attentive, awake, wide-awake, watchful, vigilant, on the lookout, sharp-eyed, observant, perceptive, sharp-witted, active, lively, spirited, quick, brisk, agile, nimble, ready, prepared, careful, heedful, circumspect, wary, on the qui vive
COLLOQ. with your eyes open/peeled, on the ball, on your toes
E3 slow, listless, unprepared

◆ v

warn, forewarn, notify, inform, tip off, signal, alarm
FORMAL apprise

◆ n

warning, notice, notification, alarm, caution, signal
COLLOQ. tip-off, wake-up call

alertness n

attentivenenss, watchfulness, vigilance, wariness, observance, perceptiveness, sharp-wittedness

algae

Types of algae and lichen include:

anabaena	fucoid	redware
badderlocks	fucus	reindeer moss
bladderwrack	gulfweed	rock tripe
bull kelp	Irish moss	rockweed
carrageen	kelp	sargassum
Ceylon moss	laminaria	sea lace
chlorella	laver	sea lettuce
conferva	lecanora	sea tangle
desmid	nostoc	sea wrack
diatom	nullipore	Spanish moss
dinaflagellate	oak moss	spirogyra
dulse	oarweed	stonewort
euglena	peacock's tail	wrack

---

alias n, adv

◆ n

pseudonym, false name, assumed name, nom de guerre, nom de plume, pen name, stage name, nickname
FORMAL so(u)briquet, allonym, anonym
SLANG monicker

◆ adv

also known as, also called, otherwise, otherwise known as, under the name of, formerly, née
COLLOQ. aka

alibi n

defence, justification, story, explanation, vindication, excuse, cover-up, pretext, reason

alien adj, n

◆ adj

1 an alien culture
foreign, exotic, extraterrestrial, extraneous, remote
OLD forinsec
2 alien surroundings
strange, unfamiliar, outlandish, odd, peculiar, incongruous
3 alien to her nature
opposed, contrary, conflicting, unusual, antagonistic, incompatible, repugnant
FORMAL inimical

◆ n

1 FOREIGNER, immigrant, newcomer, incomer, stranger, outsider, non-native
2 EXTRATERRESTRIAL, ET, Martian
COLLOQ. LGM, little green man
E3 1 native, resident

alienate v

antagonize, set against, turn away, turn off, cut off, sever, make hostile, separate, divorce
FORMAL estrange, disaffect
E3 unite

alienation n

antagonization, turning away, indifference, remoteness, rupture, separation, detachment, isolation, severance, divorce, disunion, diversion
FORMAL estrangement, disaffection
E3 endearment

alight[1] adj

1 set the rubbish alight
lighted, lit, ignited, on fire, burning, blazing, ablaze, aflame, flaming, fiery
2 eyes alight with excitement
lit up, illuminated, bright, radiant, shining, gleaming, brilliant, lively, alive

alight[2] v

passengers alighting from buses
descend, get down, get off, land, touch down, come down, come to rest, settle, light, perch, pitch
OLD avale
FORMAL dismount, disembark, debark, detrain, disentrain
COLLOQ. pop
E3 ascend, board, get on, get on to, rise

align v

1 align yourself with a political party
ally, side, sympathize, associate, affiliate, join, co-operate, agree, join forces, combine, unite
2 align two pieces of wood
arrange, straighten, range, line up, make parallel, even (up), adjust, regulate, regularize, order, co-ordinate

alignment n

1 alignment with a political party
affiliation, association, alliance, co-operation, agreement, sympathy, siding
2 alignment of the pieces
arrangement, straightening, line, lining up, order, ranging

alike adj, adv

◆ adj

similar, resembling, comparable, akin, corresponding, equivalent, equal, the same, much the same, identical, indistinguishable, duplicate, parallel, even, uniform
FORMAL analogous, cognate
COLLOQ. like two peas in a pod
E3 different, dissimilar, unlike

◆ adv

similarly, in the same way, the same, analogously, correspondingly, equally, in common

alimony n

maintenance, support, upkeep, allowance, palimony, child support; Scot aliment

alive adj

1 LIVING, having life, live, animate, breathing, existent, in existence
OLD quick
FORMAL extant
COLLOQ. (still) going strong, in the land of the living, on the hoof
2 LIVELY, animated, spirited, awake, alert, active, brisk, energetic, full of life, vigorous, zestful, vivacious, vibrant, vital; Scot vive
COLLOQ. chirpy, bright-eyed and bushy-tailed
3 keep a tradition alive
active, surviving, carrying on, in existence, in force, in operation, functioning, running, working
FORMAL extant
4 alive with tourists

full of, teeming with, abounding in, overflowing with, thronged with
COLLOQ. crawling with, swarming with
5 *alive to the danger*
aware of, conscious of, heedful of, alert to, awake to, sensitive to
FORMAL cognizant of
F3 1 dead, extinct **2** lifeless, apathetic **3** dead **5** unaware of, blind to, deaf to

all *adj, pron, adv*
 ◆ *adj*
1 *all people are equal*
each, every, each and every, every single, every one of, the whole of, every bit of, in its entirety, from start to finish
2 *run with all speed*
complete, entire, full, total, utter, outright, perfect, greatest
F3 1 no, none
 ◆ *pron*
everything, everyone, everybody, sum, total, aggregate, total amount, whole amount, whole, entirety, utmost, comprehensiveness, universality
COLLOQ. the lot
F3 nothing, none
 ◆ *adv*
completely, entirely, wholly, fully, totally, utterly, without exception, altogether, wholesale

allay *v*
alleviate, relieve, soothe, ease, smooth(e), calm, tranquillize, compose, quiet, quell, pacify, mollify, soften, blunt, lessen, reduce, decrease, diminish, check, moderate
OLD allege
F3 exacerbate, intensify

allegation *n*
accusation, charge, claim, profession, assertion, affirmation, declaration, statement, testimony, plea
FORMAL avowal, deposition, asseveration

allege *v*
assert, affirm, declare, state, maintain, insist, urge, hold, put forward, contend, claim, profess, plead
OLD obtend, trump
FORMAL attest, asseverate

alleged *adj*
supposed, reputed, inferred, so-called, professed, declared, stated, claimed, described, designated, doubtful, dubious, suspect
FORMAL ostensible, purported, putative

allegedly *adv*
supposedly, apparently, reportedly, by all accounts, doubtfully, dubiously
FORMAL ostensibly, purportedly, putatively

allegiance *n*
loyalty, fidelity, faithfulness, constancy, duty, obligation, obedience, devotion, support, adherence, solidarity, friendship
OLD (*Spenser*) foy
FORMAL fealty, liegedom
F3 disloyalty, enmity

allegorical *adj*
figurative, representative, symbolic, metaphorical, symbolizing, typical
FORMAL parabolic, emblematic, significative

allegory *n*
analogy, comparison, metaphor, symbol, parable, story, fable, myth, legend, tale, symbolism
FORMAL emblem, apologue

allergic *adj*
1 *allergic to shellfish*
sensitive, hypersensitive, susceptible, affected

2 *allergic to Mondays*
averse, disinclined, opposed, hostile, antagonistic
FORMAL dyspathetic

allergy *n*
1 *an allergy to dogs*
sensitivity, hypersensitivity, susceptibility
2 *an allergy to work*
opposition, hostility, antagonism, aversion, disinclination
FORMAL antipathy, dyspathy

alleviate *v*
relieve, soothe, ease, mitigate, soften, cushion, dull, deaden, allay, abate, lessen, assuage, reduce, diminish, check, moderate, mollify, temper, take the edge off, subdue
OLD allege
FORMAL palliate
COLLOQ. kill
F3 aggravate

alleviation *n*
relief, soothing, easing, mitigation, dulling, deadening, abatement, lessening, assuagement, reduction, moderation, mollification
FORMAL palliation, diminution
F3 aggravation

alley *n*
alleyway, back street, lane, street, road, mall, passage, passageway, pathway, close, gate, walk; *dialect* ginnel; *Scot* wynd, vennel

alliance *n*
partnership, confederation, federation, association, affiliation, coalition, league, bloc, cartel, conglomerate, consortium, syndicate, guild, union, marriage, agreement, bond, pact, treaty, axis, combination, connection
FORMAL compact, concordat
F3 separation, divorce, estrangement, enmity, hostility

allied *adj*
associated, connected, linked, bound, combined, in league, joined, joint, kindred, related, affiliated, amalgamated, federated, confederated, coupled, unified, united, married, wed
COLLOQ. hand in glove, in cahoots
F3 estranged

allocate *v*
assign, designate, budget, allow, earmark, set aside, issue, task, allot, apportion, share out, distribute, deal out, dispense, divide, parcel out, mete (out), ration
FORMAL admeasure
COLLOQ. dole out

allocation *n*
1 *the allocation of funds*
apportionment, distribution, giving-out, sharing-out, allotment
2 *an allocation of tickets*
share, measure, lot, portion, stint, ration, quota, budget, allowance, grant
COLLOQ. cut, whack, slice of the cake

allot *v*
divide, ration, apportion, share out, distribute, dispense, mete (out), allocate, assign, designate, budget, apportion, allow, grant, earmark, set aside
OLD stint; (*Shakesp*) rate, sort
FORMAL admeasure
COLLOQ. dole out

allotment *n*
1 *dig an allotment*
land, plot of land
2 *an allotment of funds*
division, partition, allocation, apportionment, distribution, measure, percentage, lot, portion, share,

stint, ration, quota, allowance, grant
FORMAL apportionment
COLLOQ. cut, whack, slice of the cake

all-out *adj, adv*
• *adj*
complete, full, total, undivided, comprehensive,
exhaustive, thorough, intensive, thoroughgoing,
wholesale, vigorous, energetic, powerful, full-scale,
maximum, utmost, unlimited, unrestrained, unremitting,
unstinted, resolute, determined, forceful
COLLOQ. no-holds-barred
E3 perfunctory, half-hearted
• *adv*
exhaustively, thoroughly, intensively, vigorously,
energetically, powerfully, unremittingly, resolutely,
determinedly, forcefully
E3 half-heartedly

allow *v*
1 PERMIT, let, enable, authorize, sanction, warrant, approve,
say yes to, give your consent (to), consent (to), agree to,
give leave, tolerate, put up with, endure, suffer
COLLOQ. OK, okay, give the go-ahead to, give the green
light to
2 ADMIT, confess, own, acknowledge, concede, grant, agree
OLD (*Shakesp & Spenser*) beteem
3 *allow two hours for the journey*
allot, allocate, assign, earmark, apportion, afford, give,
provide, set aside, spare
E3 1 forbid, prevent **2** deny
■ **allow for**
take into account, make provision for, make allowances for,
provide for, foresee, plan for, arrange for, bear/keep in mind,
consider, include
E3 discount

allowable *adj*
permissible, acceptable, admissible, justifiable, all right,
appropriate, approved, legal, legitimate, lawful
FORMAL licit, sanctionable
COLLOQ. legit
E3 unacceptable

allowance *n*
1 PAYMENT, remittance, pocket money, grant, bursary,
income, maintenance, subsistence allowance, exhibition,
budget, capitation grant, table money, expenses, expense
allowance, contribution, benefit, child benefit, stipend,
pension, annuity, assistance, alimony, corrody, privy purse;
Scot aliment
COLLOQ. *N Am* baby bonus
2 REBATE, reduction, deduction, discount, concession,
subsidy, weighting
TECHNICAL cloff
3 ALLOCATION, lot, amount, portion, share, ration, quota,
feed
TECHNICAL tare
OLD diet, provand, livery, ratio, tret
■ **make allowances**
1 TAKE INTO ACCOUNT, take into consideration, bear/keep in
mind, consider, make concessions for
2 *make allowances for her inexperience*
excuse, bear with, pardon, forgive, overlook, condone

allowed *adj*
permitted, accepted, authorized, approved, tolerated
E3 disallowed

alloy *n*
blend, compound, composite, amalgam, combination,
mixture, fusion, coalescence
FORMAL admixture, composite

all-powerful *adj*
almighty, supreme, pre-eminent, absolute, great,
totalitarian

FORMAL omnipotent
E3 powerless

all-purpose *adj*
versatile, adaptable, flexible, all-round, multi-purpose,
general-purpose
E3 inflexible

all right *adj, adv, interj*
• *adj*
1 SATISFACTORY, passable, unobjectionable, acceptable,
reasonable, good enough, allowable, adequate, fair,
average
COLLOQ. OK; *N Am* A-OK; *Aust* sweet
2 *Are you all right?*
well, healthy, unhurt, uninjured, unharmed, unimpaired,
whole, sound, safe, secure
COLLOQ. OK, right as rain
E3 1 unacceptable, inadequate, unsatisfactory
• *adv*
1 SATISFACTORILY, well enough, passably, unobjectionably,
acceptably, suitably, appropriately, adequately, reasonably
COLLOQ. OK
2 *it's true all right*
definitely, no doubt, certainly, absolutely, without
question, indeed
E3 1 unsatisfactorily, unacceptably
• *interj*
OK, fine, right, agreed, okay, very well

allude *v*
mention, refer, remark, speak of, hint, imply, infer,
insinuate, intimate, suggest, touch on/upon
FORMAL adumbrate

⚠ allude or **elude**?
If you *allude* to something, you refer to it; if something
eludes you, you cannot remember it or understand it.

allure *v, n*
• *v*
lure, entice, seduce, lead on, tempt, coax, cajole, persuade,
win over, disarm, charm, enchant, attract, interest, fascinate,
captivate, entrance, beguile, decoy, sirenize
OLD train, troll
COLLOQ. give the come-on, work on
E3 repel
• *n*
lure, enticement, seduction, temptation, appeal, attraction,
magnetism, draw, pull, fascination, glamour, captivation,
charm, enchantment

alluring *adj*
attractive, fascinating, intriguing, interesting, captivating,
winning, enchanting, engaging, enticing, arousing,
beguiling, bewitching, fetching, seductive, sensuous, sexy,
desirable, tempting
COLLOQ. come-hither
E3 repellent, unattractive

allusion *n*
mention, reference, citation, quotation, remark, comment,
observation, suggestion, hint, intimation, implication,
insinuation

⚠ allusion or **illusion**?
An *allusion* to something is an indirect reference to it; an
illusion is a false belief or appearance.

ally *n, v*
• *n*
supporter, associate, consort, confederate, partner,
colleague, co-worker, collaborator, helper, accomplice,
accessory, friend
COLLOQ. sidekick
E3 enemy, antagonist
• *v*

associate, collaborate, join forces, band together, team up, go into partnership, fraternize, confederate, affiliate, league, side, join, connect, link, marry, unite, unify, amalgamate, combine
E3 estrange, separate

almanac *n*
yearbook, annual, calendar, register, ephemeris

almighty *adj*
1 *almighty God*
all-powerful, supreme, absolute, great, invincible
FORMAL omnipotent, plenipotent
2 ENORMOUS, severe, intense, very great, immense, huge, overwhelming, overpowering, terrible, awful, desperate
E3 1 impotent, weak

almost *adv*
nearly, practically, virtually, just about, as good as, all but, well-nigh, more or less, to all intents and purposes, close to/on, not far from, approaching, nearing, not quite, about, approximately
FORMAL quasi-
COLLOQ. pretty much/well

alms *n*
gifts, donations, handouts, contributions, charity, endowment, largesse

aloft *adv*
in the air, in the sky, off the ground, high, high up

alone *adv, adj*
♦ *adv*
1 *go for walks alone*
on your own, by yourself, singly, unaccompanied, unescorted, unattended, companionless
COLLOQ. on your tod
2 *left to cope alone*
by yourself, on your own, without help, unaided, unassisted, independently
COLLOQ. off your own bat
E3 1 together, accompanied, escorted
♦ *adj*
1 LONELY, isolated, lonesome, deserted, forsaken, forlorn, desolate, rejected, unhappy, miserable, sad
2 *you alone can put things right*
only, just, solely, exclusively, uniquely

Synonym nuances
adjective sense 1
Lonely and **lonesome** carry a strong impression of sadness caused by being alone. The term **isolated** suggests a detached or secluded place, either physical or mental; **desolate** conveys this idea even more stongly, with a sense of insurmountable or frightening aloneness.
The terms **deserted**, **forsaken** and **forlorn** would be used where something or someone has been abandoned or left behind, and again have connotations of sadness and pity: *I looked back at his forlorn figure.*
Rejected would be used specifically where others have refused to accept you. However, to clearly and simply express sorrow as a result of being alone, you may choose to use the explicit terms **unhappy**, **miserable** or **sad**.

---

along *prep, adv*
♦ *prep*
1 *walk along a road*
down, up, in the same direction as
2 *trees growing along the river bank*
beside, at the side of, next to, alongside, adjacent to, close to, near
♦ *adv*
1 *driving along*
on, onwards, ahead, further

2 *bring a friend along*
with you, as a partner, as company
■ **along with**
together with, in addition to, including, over and above, not to mention, to say nothing of
■ **all along**
all the time, continually, constantly, always, for ever

aloof *adj*
distant, remote, offish, standoffish, haughty, supercilious, unapproachable, inaccessible, detached, forbidding, cool, chilly, cold, unsympathetic, unresponsive, indifferent, uninterested, reserved, unforthcoming, unfriendly, insular, unsociable, antisocial, formal, chill; *Scot* abeigh, skeigh
E3 sociable, friendly, concerned

aloud *adv*
out loud, audibly, intelligibly, clearly, plainly, distinctly, for all to hear, loudly, resoundingly, sonorously, noisily, vociferously, *à haute voix*
E3 silently

alphabet

Alphabets and writing systems include:

Arabic	Greek	Kufic
Braille	Gurmukhi	linear A
Byzantine	Hebrew	linear B
Chalcidian	hieroglyphs	logograph
alphabet	hiragana	nagari
cuneiform	ideograph	naskhi
Cyrillic	Initial Teaching	ogam
devanagari	Alphabet (ITA)	pictograph
estrangelo	International	romaji
finger-alphabet	Phonetic	Roman
futhark	Alphabet (IPA)	runic
Georgian	kana	syllabary
Glagol	kanji	
Glossic	katakana	

---

already *adv*
1 *I've read the book already*
before now, beforehand, just now, previously
OLD heretofore, hitherto
2 *he can already count*
even now, even then, so soon (as this), so early by now, by that time, by then, by this time
FORMAL thus far

also *adv*
too, as well, and, plus, along with, including, as well as, additionally, in addition, besides, further, furthermore, moreover

alter *v*
change, vary, diversify, modify, qualify, shift, transpose, make different, adjust, adapt, convert, turn, transform, reform, reshape, rework, remodel, recast, revise, improve, amend, tweak
FORMAL emend, metamorphose, transmute
See Synonym nuances panel at **change**.
E3 fix

alteration *n*
change, variation, variance, difference, diversification, shift, transposition, modification, adjustment, adaptation, conversion, transformation, transfiguration, reformation, reshaping, reworking, remodelling, revision, amendment, tweak
FORMAL emendation, metamorphosis, transmutation, vicissitude
E3 fixity

altercation *n*
argument, dispute, clash, disagreement, difference, difficulty, bicker, breach, ruffle, discord, dissension, fracas,

quarrel, row, squabble, wrangle, beef; *dialect* fratch, whid; *Scot* brattle, wap
OLD dependence, square
FORMAL logomachy
COLLOQ. set-to, dust-up, row, scrap, barney, breeze, broil, miff, bust-up, slanging match, punch-up; *Aust* yike

alternate *v, adj*
◆ *v*
interchange, reciprocate, rotate, take turns, take it in turns, follow one another, replace each other, substitute, change, alter, vary, oscillate, fluctuate, intersperse
COLLOQ. chop and change
◆ *adj*
1 *alternate weekends*
alternating, every other, every second
2 *alternate bouts of depression and happiness*
(repeated) one after the other, in turns, consecutive, interchanging, reciprocal, rotating

---

⚠ alternate or **alternative**?
Alternate refers to something happening or coming every second day, week, etc or in turns: *He visits them on alternate Tuesdays; alternate bursts of hot and cold water. Alternative* refers to the choice of two possibilities: *If that doesn't work, we'll have to think of an alternative plan.*

---

alternative *n, adj*
◆ *n*
option, choice, selection, preference, other, recourse, substitute, back-up
◆ *adj*
1 *an alternative possibility*
substitute, second, another, other, different, substitute, surrogate
2 *alternative medicine*
unorthodox, unconventional, uncommon, unusual, fringe, nontraditional
COLLOQ. wacky, oddball
F3 **2** conventional, traditional, orthodox, standard, regular

alternatively *adv*
otherwise, instead, on the other hand, as another option, as a substitute

although *conj*
though, even though, despite/in spite of the fact that, while, even if, even supposing, granted that
OLD howbeit
FORMAL albeit, whilst, notwithstanding

altitude *n*
height, elevation, loftiness, tallness, stature, depth

altogether *adv*
1 *altogether more efficient*
totally, completely, entirely, wholly, fully, utterly, absolutely, quite, perfectly, thoroughly
2 *the meal came to £60 altogether*
in total, in all, all told, *in toto*, all in all

altruism *n*
selflessness, unselfishness, disinterest, self-sacrifice, public-spiritedness, benevolence, generosity, considerateness
FORMAL magnanimity
F3 selfishness

altruistic *adj*
selfless, unselfish, self-sacrificing, disinterested, public-spirited, philanthropic, charitable, humanitarian, benevolent, generous, considerate, humane
FORMAL magnanimous
F3 selfish

always *adv*
1 *always be home by 6 o'clock*
every time, all the time, consistently, invariably, without exception, habitually, unfailingly, regularly, on every

occasion, on each occasion, perpetually, *in perpetuum*, evermore
2 *always criticizing others*
again and again, continually, constantly, repeatedly, forever, endlessly, unceasingly, eternally
F3 **1** never

amalgam *n*
mixture, blend, fusion, alloy, compound, merger, coalescence, synthesis, combination, union
TECHNICAL admixture, aggregate, commixture

amalgamate *v*
merge, blend, mingle, intermix, incorporate, alloy, integrate, compound, fuse, coalesce, synthesize, combine, unite, unify, ally
TECHNICAL commingle, homogenize
F3 separate

amalgamation *n*
merger, blend, incorporation, integration, joining, compound, fusion, coalescence, synthesis, combination, unity, union, unification, alliance
TECHNICAL admixture, commingling, homogenization
F3 separation

amass *v*
accumulate, accrue, assemble, collect, gather, heap (up), hoard, pile (up), store (up), gain, acquire
OLD foregather, garner
FORMAL agglomerate, agglutinate, aggregate

amateur *n*
non-professional, layman, lay person, dilettante, dabbler, enthusiast, fancier
COLLOQ. ham, buff
F3 professional, specialist

amateurish *adj*
non-professional, lay, unpaid, unqualified, untrained, unskilful, inexpert, unprofessional, clumsy, crude, incompetent, bungling, blundering, inept
F3 professional, expert, skilled

amatory *adj*
amorous, passionate, loving, affectionate, tender, fond, erotic, sexual, impassioned
COLLOQ. randy

amaze *v*
surprise, startle, astonish, astound, stun, stupefy, daze, stagger, dumbfound, shock, dismay, disconcert, confound, bewilder, flatten
OLD (*Spenser*) awhape
COLLOQ. floor, flabbergast, bowl over, gobsmack, wow, kill, blow your mind, knock for six, knock you down with a feather, strike dumb

amazed *adj*
surprised, startled, astonished, astounded, stunned, dazed, dumbfounded, bewildered, speechless
OLD (*Shakesp*) agazed
COLLOQ. floored, flabbergasted, gobsmacked, thunderstruck

amazement *n*
surprise, astonishment, shock, dismay, confusion, perplexity, bewilderment, admiration, wonder, marvel; *dialect* maze
FORMAL consternation, stupefaction, wonderment

amazing *adj*
surprising, astonishing, astounding, wonderful, magnificent, marvellous, impressive, dazzling, spectacular, formidable, awe-inspiring, exciting, thrilling, stunning, bewildering, overwhelming, staggering, disconcerting
COLLOQ. fabulous, incredible, jaw-dropping
SLANG far-out, unreal

ambassador *n*

1 *a country's ambassador*
envoy, diplomat, consul, nuncio, elchi
OLD ledger, leaguer
FORMAL emissary, legate, plenipotentiary
2 *an ambassador of peace*
representative, agent, deputy, delegate, minister,
campaigner, advocate, supporter, backer

ambience *n*

atmosphere, air, aura, climate, milieu, mood, spirit,
surroundings, environment, character, feel, feeling,
flavour, impression, tenor, tone
COLLOQ. vibes, vibrations

ambiguity *n*

double meaning, double entendre, ambivalence, double-
talk, double-speak, polysemy, equivocality, equivocation,
confusion, obscurity, unclearness, vagueness, woolliness,
imprecision, indeterminateness, dubiousness, doubt,
doubtfulness, uncertainty, enigma, puzzle, paradox
FORMAL dubiety
E3 clarity

ambiguous *adj*

double-meaning, equivocal, multivocal, double-edged,
two-edged, back-handed, cryptic, enigmatic,
paradoxical, puzzling, confusing, obscure, unclear, vague,
indefinite, imprecise, woolly, confused, dubious, doubtful,
uncertain, inconclusive, indeterminate
E3 clear, definite, unambiguous

Synonym nuances

If a statement is of **double-meaning** then you might
simply be saying that there is more than one way to
interpret it; however, you might also use this term to
suggest that the second meaning has a risqué element. If
you say something is **equivocal** you mean it is capable of
meaning two or more things, usually with the implication
that this makes it vague and is a weakness. The more
neutral **multivocal** can be used of a word or other item
that can have many meanings.

However, when something is described as being
double-edged or **two-edged** the suggestion is that it
has two very different aspects, both positive and
negative, and that it can be deceiving. **Back-handed**
would usually be used of compliments, implying that the
apparent meaning could have a different spin put on it:
her exclusion can be read as a back-handed compliment.

If you say something is **cryptic** or **obscure**, you are
emphasizing that it is mysterious or difficult to
understand, whilst if you claim it is **enigmatic** you are
suggesting it has a hidden meaning to be guessed at:
cryptic symbols; *his reaction was enigmatic*. However,
paradoxical is only appropriate when describing
something of a self-contradictory nature. If you are
perplexed by something ambiguous, you may describe it
as **puzzling** or **confusing**.

Unclear, **vague**, **indefinite**, **imprecise**, and **woolly** are
negative in tone, all emphasizing a lack of clarity, whilst
confused suggests an undesirable lack of order. To stress
the element of doubt you might use **dubious**, **doubtful**
or **uncertain**: *doubtful authenticity*. Similarly
inconclusive and **indeterminate** express an element of
doubt; the former in the context of something that has
not been settled, and the latter of something that remains
unfixed or undefined.

---

ambit *n*

scope, extent, range, area, sphere, realm, sweep, breadth,
compass, confines, bounds

ambition *n*

1 ASPIRATION, aim, goal, target, objective, intent, purpose,
design, object, ideal, dream, holy grail, hope, wish, desire,
yearning, longing, hankering, craving, hunger
2 *a woman of ambition*
enterprise, drive, determination, push, thrust, striving,
eagerness, commitment, initiative, zeal
COLLOQ. get-up-and-go, fire in your belly, what it takes
E3 2 apathy, diffidence

ambitious *adj*

1 ASPIRING, hopeful, desirous, intent, purposeful, bold,
assertive, pushy, go-ahead, enterprising, driving,
energetic, enthusiastic, eager, keen, striving, industrious,
zealous, determined
OLD (*Shakesp*) emulate
COLLOQ. power-hungry, full of go, go-getting, not
backward in coming forward
2 FORMIDABLE, hard, difficult, arduous, strenuous,
demanding, challenging, bold, exacting, impressive,
grandiose, elaborate
E3 1 lazy, unassuming **2** modest, uninspiring

ambivalence *n*

contradiction, conflict, clash, opposition, inconsistency,
confusion, fluctuation, wavering, equivocation, hesitation,
irresoluteness, unsureness, uncertainty, doubt,
inconclusiveness
FORMAL vacillation
E3 certainty

ambivalent *adj*

contradictory, conflicting, clashing, warring, opposed,
inconsistent, mixed, confused, fluctuating, wavering,
hesitant, irresolute, equivocal, undecided, unresolved,
unsettled, uncertain, unsure, doubtful, debatable,
inconclusive
FORMAL vacillating
E3 unequivocal

amble *v*

walk, saunter, stroll, dawdle, wander, drift, meander,
ramble
FORMAL perambulate, promenade
COLLOQ. mosey along, toddle
E3 stride, march

ambush *n, v*

◆ *n*
waylaying, surprise attack, trap, snare
OLD ambuscade, lurch; (*Spenser*) await
◆ *v*
lie in wait, waylay, lay a trap for, surprise, trap, entrap,
attack, ensnare; *N Am* bushwhack
OLD ambuscade, wait, lay wait, forelay, lie perdu(e)
COLLOQ. turn on, pounce on, jump

ameliorate *v*

alleviate, improve, better, make better, amend, benefit,
ease, elevate, enhance, mend, rectify, mitigate, promote,
relieve
E3 exacerbate, worsen

amelioration *n*

alleviation, improvement, amendment, enhancement,
benefit, refinement, help, rectification, mitigation
E3 exacerbation, worsening

amenable *adj*

accommodating, flexible, willing, open, agreeable,
biddable, persuadable, compliant, submissive, responsive,
susceptible, liable, responsible
FORMAL tractable, acquiescent, complaisant
E3 unwilling, intractable

amend *v*

revise, correct, rectify, fix, repair, mend, remedy, heal,
redress, reform, change, alter, adjust, modify, qualify,
enhance, improve, better
FORMAL emend, emendate, ameliorate
E3 impair, worsen

⚠ amend or emend?

If you *amend* a document, you alter or improve it; if you *emend* a text, you correct errors in it.

amendment *n*

revision, correction, remedy, reform, change, alteration, adjustment, modification, improvement, qualification, enhancement, clarification, addition, attachment, adjunct
FORMAL corrigendum, rectification, emendation, addendum
EA impairment, deterioration

amends *n*

atonement, expiation, requital, satisfaction, recompense, compensation, indemnification, indemnity, reparation, redress, restoration, restitution

amenity *n*

facility, advantage, convenience, opportunity, arrangement, service, utility, resource

amiability *n*

friendliness, warmth, warm-heartedness, cheerfulness, cordiality, kindness, lik(e)ability, pleasantness

amiable *adj*

affable, friendly, approachable, genial, warm, warm-hearted, cordial, cheerful, good-tempered, good-natured, kind, easy to get along/on with, gentle, obliging, charming, engaging, lik(e)able, lov(e)able, sweet, pleasant, agreeable, congenial, companionable, clubbable, sociable, *gemütlich*
COLLOQ. mat(e)y, pally, chummy
EA unfriendly, curt, hostile

⚠ amiable or amicable?

Amiable is used to describe a person who is friendly, good-tempered and pleasant; *amicable* is used to describe relationships or agreements that are conducted in a friendly way without anger.

amicable *adj*

friendly, cordial, good-natured, civil, harmonious, civilized, peaceful
EA hostile

amicably *adv*

cordially, good-naturedly, civilly, harmoniously, peaceably

amid *prep*

amidst, midst, in the midst of, in the thick of, among, amongst, in the middle of, surrounded by

amino acid

Amino acids include:

alanine	glycine	proline
arginine	histidine	serine
asparagine	isoleucine	threonine
aspartic acid	leucine	trytophan
cysteine	lysine	tyrosine
glutamic acid	methionine	valine
glutamine	phenylalanine	

amiss *adj*

wrong, awry, defective, false, faulty, improper, out of order, inaccurate, inappropriate, incorrect, unsuitable, untoward, imperfect, out of kilter
COLLOQ. wonky
EA right, well

amity *n*

peace, peacefulness, understanding, accord, concord, cordiality, fellowship, fraternity, brotherliness, friendliness, friendship, goodwill, harmony, kindness, sympathy
FORMAL comity
EA discord, hostility

ammunition *n*

missiles, bullets, shells, rockets, projectiles, cartridges, explosives, slugs, grenades, bombs, shot, mine, gunpowder
COLLOQ. ammo
See panel at **weapon**.

amnesty *n*

pardon, forgiveness, absolution, mercy, lenience, indulgence, reprieve, remission, dispensation, immunity, release, discharge, freedom, liberty

amok *adv*

berserk, crazy, in a frenzy, frenzied, insanely, like a lunatic, madly, wildly, out of control, uncontrollably, violently, on the rampage

among *prep*

amongst, between, in the middle of, surrounded by, in the midst of, with, together with, in the company of, in the thick of
OLD amid, amidst, midst

amorous *adj*

passionate, loving, affectionate, tender, fond, erotic, sexual, impassioned, in love, lovesick, lustful
FORMAL amatory
COLLOQ. randy, kissy
EA cold, indifferent

amorphous *adj*

formless, nebulous, shapeless, featureless, indeterminate, indistinct, irregular, undefined, unformed, unshapen, unstructured, vague
FORMAL inchoate
EA definite, distinctive, shapely

amount *n, v*

quantity, number, sum, total, sum total, whole, entirety, lot, quota, supply, volume, mass, bulk, measure, magnitude, extent, expanse
TECHNICAL quantum
FORMAL aggregate
■ amount to
1 *amount to a total*
add up to, total, come to, make, equal, run into, run to
FORMAL aggregate
COLLOQ. tot up, tot up to
2 *giving presents to potential customers amounts to bribery*
mean, be tantamount to, be equivalent to, correspond to, come down to, boil down to

amphibian

Amphibians include:

axolotl	bullfrog	natterjack toad
eft	tree frog	newt
eel	toad	salamander
conger eel	horned toad	
frog	midwife toad	

ample *adj*

1 *ample opportunity/space*
(more than) enough, sufficient, adequate, considerable, substantial, plentiful, plenty, abundant, unrestricted, profuse, spacious, rich, good, handsome, great, copious
OLD plenteous
FORMAL commodious
2 *of ample proportions*
large, big, extensive, expansive, broad, wide, full, roomy, spacious, liberal, generous, substantial; *Scot* wally
FORMAL voluminous
EA 1 insufficient, inadequate, meagre **2** small, thin, narrow

amplification n
1 *amplification of sound*
making louder, loudening, increase, boosting, intensification, strengthening, raising
2 *amplification of a statement*
enlargement, expansion, addition, supplement, development, elaboration
FORMAL augmentation

amplify v
1 *amplify sound*
make louder, louden, increase, heighten, enhance, boost, intensify, strengthen, deepen, raise
2 *amplify a statement*
enlarge on, expand, fill out, bulk out, add to, supplement, increase, extend, lengthen, widen, broaden, develop, elaborate on, go into details, flesh out
FORMAL augment, expatiate on
F3 1 reduce, decrease, soften

amplitude n
expanse, vastness, volume, bulk, capacity, extent, size, fullness, greatness, largeness, magnitude, mass, profusion, spaciousness, width
FORMAL copiousness, plenitude, capaciousness

amputate v
cut off, remove, sever, dissever, separate, dock, chop off, hack off, lop off, curtail, truncate

amulet n
charm, talisman, mascot, fetish, juju, lucky charm, churinga, grisgris
OLD periapt
FORMAL braxas, pentacle, phylactery

amuse v
1 *the joke amused them*
make laugh, cheer (up), gladden, entertain, charm, delight, please, enthral
COLLOQ. tickle, crease, crack, tickle your funny bone
2 *amuse yourselves while I'm away*
occupy, entertain, divert, regale, engross, absorb, engage, interest, recreate, relax
FORMAL disport
F3 1 displease **2** bore

amusement n
1 *a look of amusement at the joke*
fun, enjoyment, light-heartedness, pleasure, delight, hilarity, laughter
OLD merriment, mirth
2 *to the amusement of the onlookers*
entertainment, diversion, distraction, pleasure
3 PASTIME, game, sport, recreation, hobby, interest
COLLOQ. R & R

amusing adj
funny, humorous, hilarious, comical, laughable, ludicrous, droll, drôle, quizzical, witty, facetious, jocular, jolly, waggish, enjoyable, pleasant, charming, light, delightful, entertaining, interesting
COLLOQ. zany, killing, a scream, a hoot
See Synonym nuances panel at **funny**.
F3 dull, boring

amusingly adv
humorously, hilariously, comically, wittily, enjoyably, pleasantly, delightfully, entertainingly, interestingly
F3 dully, boringly

anaemic adj
1 *a pale anaemic-looking girl*
bloodless, ashen, chalky, livid, pasty, pallid, sallow, whey-faced, pale, wan, colourless, insipid, weak, feeble, ineffectual, enervated, frail, infirm, sickly
TECHNICAL exsanguinous
2 *the most anaemic cup final for years*
weak, ineffective, feeble, insipid, poor, lame, unimaginative, uninspired, unoriginal, hackneyed, bland, stale, tame
F3 1 ruddy, sanguine, full-blooded **2** strong, powerful

anaesthetic n
painkiller, sedative, analgesic, anodyne, narcotic, opiate, palliative, soporific, epidural, stupefacient, stupefactive, premedication, local/general anaesthetic

anaesthetize v
desensitize, numb, deaden, dull, drug, dope, stupefy

analogous adj
comparable, similar, like, resembling, matching, kindred, parallel, corresponding, equivalent, relative, correlative, agreeing
F3 disparate

analogy n
comparison, simile, metaphor, likeness, resemblance, similarity, parallel, correspondence, equivalence, relation, correlation, agreement
FORMAL similitude, semblance

analyse v
break down, separate, divide, take apart, dissect, reduce, resolve, construe, sift, investigate, inquire, study, examine, scrutinize, review, interpret, test, judge, evaluate, estimate, consider, process, critique, calendar
FORMAL anatomize, assay

analysis n
breakdown, separation, division, dissection, reduction, resolution, sifting, investigation, inquiry, study, examination, inspection, scrutiny, review, check, check-up, exposition, explication, explanation, interpretation, test, judgement, opinion, evaluation, estimation, reasoning, anatomy
FORMAL anatomization, assay

analyst n
analyser, dissector, inquirer, researcher, experimenter, experimentalist, tester, prober, chemist
FORMAL assayer

analytical adj
analytic, detailed, in-depth, searching, critical, questioning, inquiring, inquisitive, investigative, dissecting, diagnostic, systematic, methodical, logical, rational, interpretative, explanatory, expository, studious

anarchic adj
lawless, ungoverned, anarchistic, libertarian, nihilist, revolutionary, rebellious, mutinous, riotous, chaotic, disordered, confused, disorganized
F3 submissive, orderly

anarchism n
lawlessness, disorder, chaos, insurgency, insurrection, rebellion, revolution, sedition, mob-rule, racketeering
FORMAL ochlocracy
COLLOQ. mobocracy, rent-a-mob

anarchist n
revolutionary, rebel, insurgent, Bolshevik, libertarian, nihilist, terrorist

anarchy n
lawlessness, unrule, misrule, anarchism, revolution, rebellion, insurrection, mutiny, riot, pandemonium, chaos, disorder, confusion
F3 rule, control, order

anathema n
aversion, abhorrence, abomination, curse, object of loathing, bête noire, bugbear, bane, proscription, taboo

anatomy n
1 *the study of anatomy*
dissection, vivisection, zootomy
See panel on next page

Anatomical terms include:

aural	dental	gastric	laryngal	neural	renal
cardiac	diaphragmal (or	genital	ligamental	ocular	spinal
cartilaginous	diaphragmatic)	gingival	lumbar	oesophagal	tendinous
cerebral	dorsal	hepatic	mammary	optical	umbilical
cervical	duodenal	intercostal	membral	pectoral	uterine
cranial	epidermal	jugular	muscular	pedal	uvular
crural	epiglottal	lachrymal	nasal	pulmonary	

See also **bone; brain; ear; eye; gland; heart; mouth; muscle; tooth; vein**.

2 *an anatomy of contemporary life*
analysis, make-up, composition, constitution, construction, frame, framework, build, structure

ancestor *n*
forebear, forefather, progenitor, predecessor, forerunner, precursor, antecedent
FORMAL primogenitor
E3 descendant

ancestral *adj*
inherited, familial, parental, genealogical, hereditary, genetic
FORMAL lineal

ancestry *n*
ancestors, forebears, forefathers, progenitors, parentage, family, family tree, lineage, line, descent, blood, race, stock, stirps, roots, pedigree, genealogy, extraction, derivation, origin, heritage, heredity

anchor *n, v*
◆ *n*
1 HOOK, mooring
2 *trust in God as an anchor in life*
support, mainstay, bulwark, linchpin, backbone, foundation
COLLOQ. tower of strength
3 PRESENTER, anchorman/woman, announcer, newsreader, host, compère
◆ *v*
moor, berth, tie up, make fast, fasten, attach, affix, fix

Types of anchor include:

car	kedge	sea
double fluked	killick	stocked
drogue	mushroom	stockless
grapnel	navy	yachtsman

anchorite *n*
anchoress, recluse, ascetic, hermit, solitary, loner, monk, eremite, stylite, solitarian
OLD anchor

ancient *adj*
1 *ancient history*
early, earliest, first, antediluvian, prehistoric, fossilized, immemorial, old, aged, time-worn, age-old, antique
FORMAL pristine, prim(a)eval, primordial
COLLOQ. as old as the hills
2 OLD-FASHIONED, out-of-date, antiquated, archaic, outmoded, passé, *démodé*, obsolete, bygone, early, original
FORMAL superannuated, atavistic
COLLOQ. past its sell-by date
E3 1 recent, contemporary **2** modern, up-to-date, original

ancillary *adj*
auxiliary, supporting, helping, accessory, contributory, extra, secondary, subordinate, additional, subsidiary, supplementary
FORMAL adjuvant, adminicular

and *conj*
also, too, together (with), besides, as well (as), with, along with, in addition (to), plus, including, furthermore, moreover, by the way, then
COLLOQ. what's more

androgynous *adj*
hermaphrodite, bisexual, male and female, polygamic
TECHNICAL androdioecious, gynodioecious, heterogamous, monoclinous, monoecious, protogynous

anecdotal *adj*
1 *anecdotal evidence*
informal, unofficial, everyday, unscientific
2 *anecdotal writing*
narrative, storytelling, reminiscing

anecdote *n*
story, tale, yarn, sketch, narrative, reminiscence

anew *adv*
afresh, again, once again, once more

angel *n*
1 *an angel of God*
divine messenger, messenger of God, heavenly messenger, heavenly being, principality, power
2 DARLING, treasure, saint, paragon, gem, ideal, nonpareil
E3 1 devil, fiend

angelic *adj*
cherubic, seraphic, celestial, heavenly, divine, holy, pious, saintly, pure, innocent, unworldly, virtuous, lovely, beautiful, adorable
FORMAL beatific, ethereal, empyrean
E3 devilish, fiendish

The nine orders of angels are:

angel	principality
archangel	seraph
cherub	throne
domination/dominion	virtue
power	

anger *n, v*
◆ *n*
annoyance, irritation, antagonism, displeasure, irritability, temper, pique, vexation, ire, rage, fury, wrath, exasperation, chagrin, outrage, indignation, gall, bitterness, rancour, resentment, fit of anger, boiling-point, bluster, pelt, blood, bad blood, paroxysm; *Scot* fuff, kippage
OLD mood, face, gram, teen
FORMAL choler, dudgeon
COLLOQ. huff, wax; *N Am* conniption
SLANG monkey, flake
E3 forgiveness, forbearance
◆ *v*
annoy, irritate, irk, vex, rile, make angry, bother, ruffle, provoke, antagonize, offend, affront, gall, madden, enrage, incense, infuriate, inflame, exasperate, outrage
OLD emboil, move
COLLOQ. aggravate, wind up, get at, bug, drive mad, drive crazy, drive bananas, drive up the wall, drive round the

bend/twist, miff, needle, nettle, make your blood boil, make someone see red, rattle someone's cage, ruffle someone's feathers, raise someone's dander, make someone's hackles rise, make sparks fly, get under someone's skin, get up someone's nose, get on someone's wick
SLANG nark, piss off
OLD SLANG get someone's shirt out
F3 please, appease, calm

Synonym nuances
noun
Annoyance, **irritation** and **chagrin** suggest something which troubles you a little; **vexation** and **exasperation** are stronger terms, and suggest a greater degree of annoyance. **Displeasure**, however, would only be appropriate for very mild anger or annoyance. If you want to express a feeling of vexation arising from injured pride, you could use **pique**. **Indignation** is again used more specifically, for a feeling or display of justified anger, with the implication it is mingled with scorn.

 Antagonism would be used where hostility is involved; **gall** and **bitterness** on the other hand could be used to put the emphasis on feelings of resentment. **Irritability** would be used more of the quality of being easily angered, while **temper** would appropriately describe a demonstration of uncontrolled anger. **Ire** is a fairly straightforward synonym of anger, but **rage**, **outrage**, **fury** and **wrath** are all indicative of overpowering, even violent anger. The term **boiling-point** also suggests that you have reached the point at which you lose control of your anger. **Bluster** and **pelt** likewise imply loss of control, sharing the notion of a storm of rage. **Paroxysm** is similar, but is more suggestive of a fit of passion. **Blood** is generally used in the expression 'someone's blood being up': *Tabitha's blood was up.*

---

angle¹ *n, v*
♦ *n*
1 CORNER, intersection, projection, nook, bend, flexure, hook, crook, elbow, knee, crotch, edge, point, slant, gradient, inclination
2 ASPECT, outlook, facet, side, approach, direction, position, standpoint, viewpoint, point of view, slant, perspective
COLLOQ. spin, take
♦ *v*
face, point, turn, aim, direct, slant, tilt

angle²
■ **angle for**
seek, seek to obtain, aim, try to get, go for, shoot for, make a bid for
COLLOQ. fish for

angler *n*
fisherman, rod
OLD fisher, Waltonian
FORMAL piscator, piscatrix

angrily *adv*
crossly, irately, wrathfully, furiously, passionately, hotly, warmly, indignantly, bitterly, resentfully, rancorously
COLLOQ. stroppily
F3 calmly

angry *adj*
annoyed, cross, in a temper, irritated, displeased, irate, enraged, incensed, livid, seething, infuriated, furious, raging, passionate, heated, hot, warm, exasperated, outraged, high, beside yourself, black, evil, sullen, sultry, up in the air, wrathful, choleric, splenetic; *Scot* radge; indignant, bitter, resentful, rancorous, on the rampage
OLD moody; (*Shakesp*) moody-mad; foribund, wrath, stomachful; (*Spenser*) yond

COLLOQ. aggravated, ratty, uptight, mad, hopping mad, raving mad, seeing red, in a lather, disgruntled, up in arms, hot under the collar, stroppy, choked, fit to be tied, on the warpath, in a paddy; *N Am* ticked off; *Aust* spewy, ropable; *Aust & NZ* crooked
SLANG pissed off, hairless; *N Am* burned up
F3 content, happy, calm

Colloquial ways of expressing becoming angry and losing your temper include:

be fizzing	foam at the mouth	have your
blow a fuse	freak out	monkey up
blow a gasket	get all steamed	hit the ceiling
blow up	up	hit the roof
blow your cool	go ape	let off steam
blow your stack	go ballistic	lose your cool
blow your top	go berserk	lose your
boil over	*Aust* go crook	patience
burst a blood	go mad	lose your rag
vessel	go nuts	*Aust* perform
Aust & NZ do your	go off the deep	raise Cain
block	end	raise hell
do your nut	*Aust* go to market	see red
explode	go up the wall	sizzle
flip your lid	have a fit	throw a tantrum
fly into a rage	have kittens	throw a wobbly
fly off the handle		

---

angst *n*
anxiety, worry, distress, apprehension, dread, anguish, foreboding, uneasiness, tension, stress
FORMAL disquietude, worriment

anguish *n*
agony, anxiety, desolation, distress, suffering, torment, torture, grief, heartache, heartbreak, misery, pain, pang, rack, sorrow, tribulation, woe, wretchedness, affliction
OLD dole, dolour
F3 happiness, solace

anguished *adj*
afflicted, tormented, stressed, distressed, harrowed, miserable, stricken, suffering, tortured, wretched
OLD dolorous

angular *adj*
bony, thin, gaunt, gawky, lank, lanky, lean, sharp-pointed, rawboned, scrawny, skinny, spare

animal *n, adj*
♦ *n*
1 *wild animals*
creature, mammal, beast
COLLOQ. furry friend; *N Am* critter
Related adjective: zoic
See panel on next page
2 *that man is an animal*
beast, brute, barbarian, savage, monster
COLLOQ. swine, pig
♦ *adj*
1 *animal fats*
FORMAL animalic, zoic
TECHNICAL theriomorphic
2 *animal instincts*
bestial, brutish, inhuman, savage, wild, instinctive, bodily, physical, carnal, fleshly, sensual

animate *adj, v*
♦ *adj*
alive, living, live, breathing, conscious
OLD quick
F3 inanimate
♦ *v*
activate, enliven, arouse, instigate, invigorate, galvanize,

Animals include:

aardvark	cat	fox	hippopotamus	mouse	puma	walrus
antelope	cheetah	gazelle	horse	lemur	rabbit	weasel
ape	chimpanzee	gerbil	hyena	lion	racoon	whale
armadillo	cougar	giant panda	impala	moose	rat	wolf
baboon	cow	gibbon	jaguar	ocelot	reindeer	wolverine
badger	deer	giraffe	kangaroo	orang-utan	rhinoceros	wombat
bear	dog	gnu	koala	otter	seal	zebra
beaver	dolphin	goat	leopard	panda	sealion	
bison	eland	gorilla	llama	panther	sheep	
buffalo	elephant	grizzly bear	mink	pig	skunk	
bull	elk	hamster	mole	platypus	squirrel	
camel	ermine	hare	mongoose	polar bear	tiger	
caribou	ferret	hedgehog	monkey	polecat	wallaby	

See also **amphibian; bird; butterfly; cat; cattle; dog; fish; horse; insect; invertebrate; mammal; marsupial; mollusc; monkey; moth; reptile; rodent**.

See also **animal sounds** at **sound**[1].

See also **collective nouns**.

goad, spur, impel, stimulate, incite, energize, excite, fire, kindle, move, quicken, reactivate, revive, rouse, spark, stir, urge, vitalize, bring to life, encourage, inspire
FORMAL embolden, vivify, inspirit
COLLOQ. buck up
E3 dull, inhibit

animated *adj*
lively, spirited, buoyant, vibrant, ebullient, vivacious, alive, vital, quick, brisk, vigorous, energetic, active, passionate, impassioned, sparkling, vehement, ardent, fervent, glowing, radiant, excited, enthusiastic, eager, instinct
COLLOQ. peppy, chipper, chirpy, zappy, full of beans, bright and breezy, bright-eyed and bushy-tailed
E3 lethargic, sluggish, inert

animatedly *adv*
excitedly, enthusiastically, eagerly, vibrantly, vivaciously, briskly, vigorously, energetically, actively, passionately, vehemently, ardently, fervently, radiantly
E3 sluggishly, inertly

animation *n*
liveliness, spirit, action, activity, ebullience, passion, elation, energy, enthusiasm, excitement, exhilaration, fervour, high spirits, life, radiance, sparkle, sprightliness, verve, vibrancy, vigour, vitality, zeal, zest
COLLOQ. pep, zing, go
E3 dullness, inertia

animosity *n*
ill feeling, ill will, acrimony, bitterness, rancour, resentment, spite, malice, malignity, malevolence, hate, hatred, loathing, abhorrence, antagonism, hostility, enmity, friction, feud
FORMAL odium, animus
E3 goodwill

annals *n*
archives, chronicles, records, registers, history, journals, accounts, memoirs, reports

annex *v*
1 ADD, append, affix, attach, fasten, join, connect, unite, incorporate
FORMAL adjoin
2 SEIZE, appropriate, acquire, usurp, occupy, conquer, take over
FORMAL arrogate

⚠ annex or **annexe**?
Annex, stressed on the second syllable, is a verb meaning to add or acquire: *The USSR annexed Latvia in World War II.* The noun, stressed on the first syllable, may be spelt *annex* or *annexe*, but the form with *-e* is more common.

---

annexation *n*
seizure, appropriation, acquisition, usurping,

occupation, conquest, takeover
FORMAL arrogation

annexe *n*
wing, extension, attachment, addition, supplement, expansion

annihilate *v*
eliminate, eradicate, obliterate, erase, wipe out, murder, assassinate, exterminate, extinguish, raze, destroy, abolish, conquer, defeat, rout
FORMAL extirpate
COLLOQ. liquidate, rub out, take out, thrash, trounce, bring to their knees

annihilation *n*
elimination, eradication, obliteration, erasure, murder, assassination, extermination, extinction, destruction, abolition, defeat
FORMAL extirpation
COLLOQ. liquidation

anniversary

Traditional names of wedding anniversary include:

1st paper	9th pottery/ willow	25th silver
2nd cotton	10th tin/ aluminium	30th pearl
3rd leather		35th coral
4th flowers/fruit	11th steel	40th ruby
5th wood	12th silk/linen	45th sapphire
6th iron/sugar	13th lace	50th gold
7th copper/wool	14th ivory	55th emerald
8th bronze/ pottery	15th crystal	60th diamond
	20th china	70th platinum

Modern names of wedding anniversary include:

1st clocks	10th diamond jewellery	25th silver
2nd china		30th diamond
3rd crystal/glass	11th fashion jewellery	35th jade
4th appliances		40th ruby
5th silverware	12th pearl	45th sapphire
6th wood	13th textiles/fur	50th gold
7th desk sets	14th gold jewellery	55th emerald
8th linen/lace		60th diamond
9th leather	15th watches	70th platinum
	20th platinum	

annotate *v*
note, add notes to, gloss, comment, explain, interpret, elucidate
FORMAL marginalize, explicate

annotation n
note, footnote, gloss, comment, commentary, exegesis, explanation, elucidation
FORMAL explication

announce v
declare, proclaim, report, state, make/issue a statement, reveal, disclose, divulge, make known/public, notify, intimate, give out, publish, broadcast, advertise, publicize
OLD blazon (abroad), betoken
FORMAL promulgate, propound, preconize
F3 suppress

announcement n
1 make an announcement
statement, declaration, proclamation, release, report, communiqué, dispatch, bulletin, message, information, notification, intimation, revelation, disclosure, divulgence, publication, broadcast, advertisement, publicity
FORMAL pronunciamento, *ipse dixit*, promulgation
2 the announcement of the news
declaration, proclamation, reporting, revelation, disclosure, divulgence, making known/public, notification, intimation, giving-out, release, publication, publicizing

announcer n
broadcaster, newscaster, newsreader, commentator, compère, host, master of ceremonies, MC, presenter, anchor, anchorman, anchorwoman, town crier, herald, messenger

annoy v
irritate, rile, displease, anger, vex, irk, madden, exasperate, tease, provoke, ruffle, gall, trouble, nag, disturb, bother, pester, plague, harass, molest; *Scot* fash
COLLOQ. aggravate, bug, hassle, rub up the wrong way, wind up, get your blood up, make your blood boil, get on your nerves, get up your nose, get under your skin, get your goat, get on your wick, drive crazy/nuts/bananas, drive up the wall, drive round the bend/twist, get your back up, brass off, cheese off, make your hackles rise, make sparks fly, give you the hump, get your dander up; *N Am* tick/hack off
SLANG piss someone off
F3 please, gratify, comfort

Synonym nuances
The terms **irritate** and **displease**, **vex**, **gall** and **irk** are fairly mild terms for annoy: *you sound a trifle irked*; *it galled him to have to sit in silence*. **Ruffle** would be used of slight annoyance, but to **rile** suggests making someone rather more angry (for which you could also use the very direct **anger**). **Madden** is similar, but more suggestive of constant mental derangement: *maddened with pain*; **exasperate** is the term to use if you want to convey feelings of frustration.
  Provoke indicates deliberate intent to annoy or anger. To use **tease** would imply annoying someone deliberately but in a playful, mischievous or unkind way. **Trouble**, **disturb** and **bother** suggest a more active annoyance: *stop bothering me with your questions*. To say something **nags** suggests it is continually worrying and upsetting. **Pester**, **plague** and **harass** also convey the idea of persistent annoyance, but again suggest more deliberate annoyance: *children often pester you to buy them things*. **Molest** is similar, but carries more connotation of evil intent.

---

annoyance n
1 NUISANCE, pest, disturbance, bother, trouble, bore, tease, provocation, irritant, bugbear, bête noire
COLLOQ. bind, drag, headache, thorn in the side, pain (in the neck)
SLANG bugger, pain in the backside/arse; *N Am* pain in the ass/butt

2 express your annoyance
irritation, displeasure, anger, vexation, exasperation, harassment; *Scot* sturt, fash
OLD (*Shakesp & Spenser*) noyance
FORMAL chagrin
COLLOQ. aggravation
F3 2 pleasure, satisfaction, contentment

annoyed adj
irritated, cross, upset, displeased, angry, vexed, piqued, exasperated, provoked, indignant, harassed
OLD hipped
COLLOQ. peeved, miffed, narked, bugged, stroppy, shirty, hassled, driven crazy, driven nuts, cheesed off, brassed off, got the hump, in a huff, in a paddy, hot under the collar; *N Am* ticked off
SLANG pissed off, chocker
F3 pleased

annoying adj
irritating, vexatious, irksome, troublesome, bothersome, tiresome, trying, maddening, infuriating, exasperating, galling, offensive, teasing, provoking, disturbing, intrusive, unwelcome, harassing
COLLOQ. aggravating, infernal, pesky
F3 pleasing, welcome

annual n, adj
♦ n
yearbook, almanac, calendar, register
♦ adj
yearly, every twelve months

annul v
nullify, invalidate, void, rescind, suspend, set aside, cancel, abolish, quash, repeal, revoke, countermand, negate, declare null and void, retract, recall, reverse, dissolve, disannul
OLD vacate, vacuate
FORMAL abrogate
F3 enact, restore

annulment n
invalidation, voiding, rescindment, abrogation, suspension, cancellation, abolition, quashing, repeal, countermand, negation, nullification, recall, reverse
FORMAL revocation, rescission
F3 enactment, restoration

anodyne adj
bland, inoffensive, neutral, dull, innocuous, deadening

anoint v
1 OIL, grease, lubricate, apply oil/lubrication to, rub, smear, daub
OLD anele
FORMAL embrocate
2 BLESS, consecrate, sanctify, set apart, hallow, dedicate, ordain

anomalous adj
abnormal, atypical, exceptional, irregular, inconsistent, incongruous, deviant, freakish, eccentric, peculiar, odd, unusual, singular, rare
COLLOQ. freak
F3 normal, regular, ordinary

anomaly n
abnormality, exception, irregularity, inconsistency, incongruity, aberration, deviation, divergence, departure, freak, misfit, eccentricity, peculiarity, oddity, rarity

anon adv
soon, quite soon, shortly, before long, in the near future, in a little while, by and by

anonymous adj
1 an anonymous poem
unnamed, nameless, unsigned, unacknowledged, unspecified, unidentified, unknown, unsigned, unattributed, incognito

FORMAL unattested, innominate
2 *a row of anonymous-looking houses*
faceless, impersonal, nondescript, unremarkable,
unexceptional
F3 1 named, signed, identifiable **2** distinctive

Synonym nuances

sense 1

The terms **unknown** and **unidentified** are fairly neutral;
unnamed however implies that an identity is being kept
secret deliberately: *the unnamed source of the story*. If
something is **nameless** or **innominate**, then the
implication is that it is not possible to be named: *nameless
terrors*. **Unsigned** is used in fairly specific contexts where
an author has not wished to make their identity known.
To say something is **unacknowledged** suggests that it
has gone unrecognized or unnoticed, whether the
originator wanted it or not.

To indicate that it is not known exactly what something
is, **unspecified** is used: *some unspecified crime*. The
unmarked term **unattributed** simply suggests that we do
not know an origin or source: *unattributed stories*; while
unattested only tells you that there have been no
witnesses to it. **Incognito**, however, again would be used
to refer to a deliberate attempt by someone to remain
unidentified or even in disguise: *travelling incognito*.

---

another *adj*
1 ADDITIONAL, further, extra, more, added, spare,
second
2 DIFFERENT, other, some other, alternative, not the same,
variant

answer *n, v*
♦ *n*
1 REPLY, acknowledgement, response, reaction, rejoinder,
retort, riposte, retaliation, rebuttal
FORMAL replication
COLLOQ. comeback
2 SOLUTION, explanation, result, key, resolution, unravelling
COLLOQ. quick fix
F3 1 question
♦ *v*
1 REPLY, acknowledge, respond, write back, react, refute,
retaliate
COLLOQ. get/come back to
2 *answer a need*
fulfil, fill, meet, satisfy, match up to
3 *answer (to) a description*
fit, correspond to, match, correlate, conform, agree, suit,
serve, pass
■ **answer back**
talk back, be cheeky to, retort, riposte, retaliate,
contradict, disagree, argue, dispute, rebut
COLLOQ. *N Am* sass
■ **answer for**
1 *answer for her loyalty*
vouch for, be responsible for, be accountable for, be liable
for, speak for
2 *answer for the crimes*
pay for, be punished for, suffer for
■ **answer to**
report to, be responsible to, be accountable to, work under

answerable *adj*
liable, responsible, accountable, chargeable,
blameworthy, to blame

antagonism *n*
hostility, opposition, enmity, rivalry, antipathy, ill feeling/
will, animosity, friction, discord, dissension, contention,
conflict
OLD (*Shakesp*) oppugnancy
F3 rapport, sympathy, agreement

antagonist *n*
opponent, adversary, enemy, foe, rival, competitor,
contestant, contender
F3 ally, supporter

antagonistic *adj*
conflicting, opposed, adverse, at variance, incompatible,
hostile, belligerent, contentious, unfriendly, ill-disposed,
averse
F3 sympathetic, friendly

antagonize *v*
alienate, estrange, disaffect, repel, embitter, offend, insult,
provoke, annoy, irritate, anger, rile, incense
FORMAL disaffect
COLLOQ. aggravate, wind up, get at, bug, drive mad, drive
crazy, drive bananas, drive up the wall, drive round the
bend/twist, miff, needle, nettle, make someone's blood
boil, make someone see red, rattle someone's cage, ruffle
someone's feathers, make sparks fly, get under someone's
skin, get up someone's nose, get on someone's wick, make
someone's hackles rise
F3 disarm

antecedent *n*
1 *antecedents of the aeroplane*
precursor, forerunner, precedent
2 *with Welsh antecedents*
ancestors, forebears, forefathers, progenitors, blood, race,
stock, stirps, roots, extraction, genealogy

antedate *v*
precede, come before, go before
FORMAL antecede, prevene

antediluvian *adj*
old, early, antiquated, archaic, outmoded, passé, bygone
COLLOQ. as old as the hills, old hat
F3 modern, recent

anteroom *n*
antechamber, vestibule, foyer, hall, entrance hall, lobby,
porch, waiting-room

anthem *n*
hymn, song, chorale, psalm, song of praise, canticle, chant
TECHNICAL motet
FORMAL paean

anthology *n*
selection, collection, compilation, compendium, digest,
treasury, miscellany, omnibus
FORMAL spicilege, chrestomathy, florilegium

Antichrist *n*
the Beast, lawless one, man of sin, man of lawlessness

anticipate *v*
1 FORESTALL, pre-empt, intercept, prevent, second-guess
OLD prevent, prevene
FORMAL obviate, preclude
COLLOQ. second-guess, beat to it
2 EXPECT, foresee, predict, forecast, think likely, look for,
await, look forward to, hope for, bank on, count on/upon,
reckon on, prepare for; *N Am* figure on

anticipation *n*
1 *in anticipation of the shortage*
expectation, preparation, prediction, forecast
2 *eager anticipation*
excitement, expectancy, hope
COLLOQ. bated breath

anticlimax *n*
comedown, let-down, disappointment, fiasco
FORMAL bathos
COLLOQ. non-event, damp squib, not all that it was cracked
up to be

antics *n*
foolery, tomfoolery, silliness, buffoonery, clowning,

horseplay, frolics, capers, skylarking, playfulness, mischief, tricks, monkey-tricks, pranks, stunts, doings

antidote n
1 an antidote to a sting
cure, counter-agent, antitoxin, neutralizer, neutralizing agent, countermeasure, serum
TECHNICAL antivenin, mithridate, alexipharmic, alexipharmakon, naloxone
OLD treacle, Venice treacle, theriac
2 an antidote to depression
remedy, cure, corrective

antipathy n
aversion, dislike, hate, hatred, loathing, abhorrence, distaste, disgust, repulsion, antagonism, animosity, ill will, bad blood, enmity, hostility, opposition, incompatibility
FORMAL animus, odium
Fⁿ sympathy, affection, rapport

antiquated adj
obsolete, old-fashioned, outdated, outmoded, out-of-date, dated, bygone, anachronistic, ancient, antediluvian, archaic, démodé, fossilized, outworn, passé
COLLOQ. on the way out, old hat
Fⁿ forward-looking, modern

antique adj, n
◆ adj
antiquarian, ancient, old, veteran, vintage, quaint, antiquated, old-fashioned, outdated, archaic, obsolete
◆ n
antiquity, relic, bygone, period piece, heirloom, curio, museum piece, collector's item, curiosity, rarity, object of virtu

antiquity n
1 the great civilizations of antiquity
ancient times, time immemorial, distant past, olden days
OLD days of yore
2 of great antiquity
age, old age, oldness, ancientness, agedness
Fⁿ 1 modernity, novelty

antiseptic adj, n
◆ adj
disinfectant, medicated, aseptic, germ-free, clean, pure, unpolluted, uncontaminated, sterile, sterilized, sanitized, sanitary, hygienic
◆ n
disinfectant, germicide, bactericide, purifier, cleanser

antisocial adj
1 an antisocial person
unfriendly, unsociable, uncommunicative, reserved, retiring, withdrawn, alienated, unapproachable, unforthcoming
2 antisocial behaviour
asocial, unacceptable, disruptive, disorderly, rebellious, lawless, belligerent, antagonistic, hostile, anarchic
Fⁿ 1 sociable, gregarious 2 acceptable, orderly

antithesis n
1 OPPOSITE, converse, reverse, opposite extreme
2 OPPOSITION, contrast, contradiction, reversal

antithetical adj
opposed, opposing, in opposition, contrary, conflicting, clashing, contradictory, incompatible, irreconcilable

anxiety n
worry, concern, care, distress, nervousness, apprehension, disquiet, dread, anguish, foreboding, misgiving, uneasiness, restlessness, fretfulness, impatience, suspense, tension, stress, strain, rack
TECHNICAL dysthymia
OLD cark
FORMAL disquietude, solicitousness, solicitude, worriment
COLLOQ. tizzy, tiz, stew, hang-up, jitters, butterflies (in your

stomach), collywobbles, heebie-jeebies, willies, fantods, fantigue
Fⁿ calm, composure, serenity

> **Synonym nuances**
> **Worry**, **concern** and **care** are straightforward terms for troubled feeling: *inflation is causing worry.* **Distress** and **anguish**, on the other hand, are appropriate for extreme mental or emotional suffering. **Nervousness**, **apprehension**, **suspense** and **tension** all suggest uneasiness in anticipation of a future event. Similarly **dread** has a sense of something yet to happen, but suggests a great fear of it: *a dread of death.* Again looking to the future, **foreboding** can be used to describe an apprehension of coming evil. **Disquiet**, **misgiving** and **uneasiness** would appropriately describe a constant feeling that all is not well; **restlessness**, **fretfulness** and **impatience** all convey an image of a state of uneasy activity arising from such anxiety. **Stress**, **strain** and **rack** would all be used in the context of constant and often specific emotional or mental pressure, though the latter to a more extreme degree: *the rack of rejection.* The formal terms **disquietude**, **solicitousness**, **solicitude** and **worriment** all suggest a constant uneasiness of mind.

anxious adj
1 APPREHENSIVE, worried, concerned, nervous, afraid, fearful, upset, uneasy, restless, fretful, impatient, in suspense, on tenterhooks, tense, taut, distressed, dismayed, disturbed, troubled, tormented, overwrought, tortured
FORMAL solicitous
COLLOQ. uptight, jittery, het up, in a stew/tizzy, having butterflies in your stomach/tummy, tearing your hair out, with your knickers in a twist, a bundle of nerves
SLANG Aust toey
2 EAGER, keen, longing, enthusiastic, yearning, desirous, expectant
COLLOQ. desperate
Fⁿ 1 calm, composed

anxiously adv
apprehensively, nervously, fearfully, uneasily, restlessly, fretfully, impatiently, tensely, tormentedly
FORMAL solicitously

any adj, pron, adv
◆ adj
some, a few, a bit of, whichever
◆ pron
one, a single one
◆ adv
to some extent, to any extent, at all, in the least, the least bit

anyhow adv
1 it's too late to go and anyhow we've run out of petrol
anyway, in any event, in any case, no matter what
2 the books are arranged anyhow
untidily, not in order, at random, haphazardly

apace adv
speedily, swiftly, double-quick, fast, hastily, quickly, rapidly, at full/top speed, without delay

apart adv
1 stand apart from the others
aside, to one side, away, afar, distant, aloof, excluded, isolated, cut off, separated, separate, distinct, piecemeal
2 live apart
separately, independently, separated, divorced, not together, not living together, individually, singly, alone, on your own, by yourself, privately
3 tear apart
to pieces, to bits, into parts, in pieces, in bits, piecemeal
OLD asunder
Fⁿ 2, 3 together

■ **apart from**
except (for), not counting, excepted, aside from, excluding, with the exception of, but for, save

apartment n
1 FLAT; *N Am* condominium, duplex apartment; *Scot* tenement; *Aust & NZ* home unit
OLD mansion, paradise
COLLOQ. pad; *N Am* condo
SLANG gaff
2 the state apartments
room, chamber, accommodation
OLD bower

apathetic adj
uninterested, uninvolved, indifferent, blasé, cool, unemotional, emotionless, impassive, unmoved, unconcerned, cold, unfeeling, numb, unresponsive, passive, listless, lethargic, unambitious, lukewarm, half-hearted
FORMAL insouciant
COLLOQ. ho-hum
E3 enthusiastic, involved, concerned, feeling, responsive

apathy n
uninterestedness, indifference, coolness, impassivity, unconcern, lack of interest, lack of concern/enthusiasm, coldness, insensibility, passivity, listlessness, lethargy, sluggishness, torpor, inertia
FORMAL languor, acedia, accidie
E3 enthusiasm, interest, concern

ape v, n
♦ v
copy, imitate, echo, mirror, parrot, mimic, caricature, parody, mock, counterfeit, affect
COLLOQ. take off, send up
♦ n
monkey, chimpanzee, gibbon, gorilla, baboon, orang-utan, magot
OLD jackanapes
Related adjective: simian

aperture n
gap, hole, opening, passage, perforation, breach, chink, cleft, crack, eye, fissure, rent, slit, slot, space, vent, mouth
TECHNICAL orifice, foramen, punctum
FORMAL interstice

apex n
top, high point, peak, pinnacle, point, summit, tip, climax, consummation, crest, crown, crowning point, culmination, height, acme, apogee, vertex, zenith
TECHNICAL fastigium
FORMAL apotheosis
E3 nadir

aphorism n
maxim, adage, axiom, dictum, precept, proverb, saw, saying, witticism
FORMAL apophthegm, epigram, gnome

aphrodisiac n, adj
♦ n
love potion, stimulant
♦ adj
stimulant, stimulative, erogenous, erotic
FORMAL amative, amatory, erotogenous, venerous

apiece adv
each, individually, per person, per head, per capita, respectively, separately, singly

aplomb n
poise, assurance, calmness, composure, confidence, coolness, equanimity, sang-froid, savoir-faire, self-assurance, self-confidence, self-possession
COLLOQ. unflappability
E3 discomposure

apocryphal adj
unauthenticated, unverified, unsubstantiated, unsupported, questionable, spurious, equivocal, doubtful, dubious, fabricated, concocted, fictitious, made-up, imaginary, legendary, mythical
E3 authentic, true

apologetic adj
sorry, repentant, penitent, contrite, remorseful, conscience-stricken, regretful, rueful
E3 unrepentant, impenitent, defiant

apologetically adv
penitently, repentantly, contritely, remorsefully, regretfully, ruefully
E3 unrepentantly, defiantly

apologia n
defence, vindication, explanation, argument
FORMAL explication

apologist n
defender, vindicator, supporter, advocate, backer, endorser, upholder

apologize v
say you are sorry, say sorry, regret, be apologetic, ask forgiveness, ask pardon, beg someone's pardon, acknowledge, confess, explain, justify, plead
COLLOQ. swallow your pride, eat your words, eat humble pie

apology n
1 he accepted my apology
saying sorry, acknowledgement, confession, excuse, regrets, explanation, justification, vindication, defence, plea
FORMAL palliation
2 he has an apology for a brain
mockery, travesty, caricature, corruption, distortion, excuse, poor substitute, poor specimen
E3 1 defiance

apoplectic adj
incensed, furious, very angry, annoyed, cross, in a temper, irritated, irate, enraged, incensed, livid, seething, infuriated, furious, raging, passionate, exasperated, outraged, high, beside yourself, sullen, sultry, up in the air, wrathful, wroth, rancorous, choleric, splenetic; *Scot* radge; indignant, bitter, resentful, on the rampage
OLD moody, foribund, wrath
COLLOQ. cross, ratty, uptight, mad, hopping mad, raving mad, seeing red, in a lather, disgruntled, up in arms, hot under the collar, stroppy, choked, fit to be tied, on the warpath, in a paddy; *N Am* ticked off; *Aust* spewy, ropable; *Aust & NZ* crooked
SLANG pissed off, hairless; *N Am* burned up

apostasy n
defection, desertion, disloyalty, faithlessness, falseness, treachery, unfaithfulness, heresy, rattery, ratting
FORMAL perfidy, recreance, recreancy, renegation, renunciation
E3 loyalty, orthodoxy

apostate n
renegade, defector, deserter, traitor, turncoat, heretic, runagate
OLD recreant
FORMAL recidivist, tergiversator
E3 follower

apostle n
1 Jesus Christ's apostles
disciple, messenger, preacher, evangelist, missionary, teacher, reformer, proselytizer
2 apostles of a united Europe
advocate, champion, supporter, crusader, pioneer, proponent
FORMAL apologist

apotheosis n
high point, peak, apex, pinnacle, point, summit, tip, climax, consummation, crest, crown, crowning point, culmination, height, acme, apogee, vertex, zenith
TECHNICAL fastigium

appal v
horrify, shock, outrage, disgust, dismay, disconcert, daunt, intimidate, unnerve, alarm, scare, frighten, terrify
E3 reassure, encourage

appalling adj
1 work in appalling conditions
horrifying, horrific, harrowing, shocking, outrageous, atrocious, disgusting, awful, dreadful, frightful, terrible, dire, grim, hideous, ghastly, horrible, horrid, loathsome, daunting, intimidating, unnerving, alarming, frightening, terrifying, nightmarish
2 appalling handwriting
terrible, awful, frightful, very bad, very disappointing, dreadful, poor, atrocious, inadequate, unsatisfactory, inferior, unacceptable, hopeless
COLLOQ. pathetic, lousy, rop(e)y
SLANG pants, the pits, naff
E3 1 reassuring, encouraging **2** excellent

appallingly adv
1 an appallingly disfigured face
horrifically, shockingly, frightfully, hideously, horribly
2 behave appallingly
awfully, terribly, frightfully, dreadfully, unsatisfactorily, unacceptably, hopelessly
COLLOQ. pathetically

apparatus n
1 gym apparatus
appliance, gadget, device, contraption, equipment, rig, gear, tackle, outfit, tools, implements, utensils, materials, machine, machinery
2 the apparatus of government
system, structure, network, set-up, mechanism, framework, means

apparel n
clothing, clothes, garments, dress, costume, garb, outfit, wardrobe
OLD raiment, habiliments, vesture
FORMAL attire
COLLOQ. gear, clobber, togs, get-up, kit

apparent adj
1 his distrust was all too apparent
visible, evident, noticeable, perceptible, plain, clear, distinct, marked, unmistakable, conspicuous, be standing out, obvious, manifest, patent, open, declared
2 their apparent calmness
seeming, superficial, outward, visible, ostensible
E3 1 hidden, obscure

apparently adv
seemingly, ostensibly, outwardly, on the face of it, to all appearances, superficially, on the surface, reputedly, plainly, clearly, obviously, manifestly, patently, evidently

apparition n
ghost, spectre, phantom, phantasm, semblance, wraith, spirit, vision, manifestation, manifest, illusion, shape, materialization, presence, fetch, hobgoblin, doppelgänger, double; *dialect* gytrash; *Scot* taisch
FORMAL eidolon, chimera, visitant
COLLOQ. spook

appeal n, v
♦ n
1 REQUEST, application, claim, approach, petition, suit, solicitation, plea, entreaty, supplication, prayer, invocation
OLD conjuration
FORMAL imploration, adjuration, orison

2 ATTRACTION, allure, interest, fascination, enchantment, charm, attractiveness, winsomeness, beauty, charisma, magnetism
3 an appeal in a lawcourt
retrial, reconsideration, review, re-evaluation, re-examination
TECHNICAL recusation
♦ v
1 appeal for help
ask (for), request, call, call on, apply, claim, address, petition, solicit, plead, beg, beseech, implore, entreat, pray, invoke, call upon
TECHNICAL *Scot* reclaim
OLD TECHNICAL avouch, provoke
OLD (*Spenser*) peal
FORMAL supplicate, sue
2 ATTRACT, draw, allure, lure, tempt, entice, invite, interest, engage, fascinate, charm, please

appealing adj
pleasing, attractive, tempting, enticing, inviting, alluring, interesting, fascinating, engaging, winning, enchanting, charming, winsome, charismatic, magnetic

appear v
1 ARRIVE, enter, turn up, attend, be present, materialize, develop, show (up), come into sight/view, become visible, come along, loom, rise, surface, arise, occur, crop up, come to light, come out, emerge, issue, be published
COLLOQ. show up
2 SEEM, look, give the impression of being, come across as, show signs of, take the guise of, turn out
COLLOQ. pop up
3 appear in a show
act, perform, play, take part, be a guest in, be on stage
4 his book appeared in the shops
be published, come out, become available
E3 1 disappear, vanish

appearance n
1 APPEARING, arrival, advent, coming, coming into view, rise, emergence, debut, introduction, attendance, presence
2 LOOK, expression, face, aspect, air, bearing, manner, looks, figure, (outward) form, complexion, image
FORMAL mien, visage, demeanour
3 keep up an appearance
pretence, show, front, guise, illusion, impression, outward impression, façade, image
OLD (*Shakesp*) ostent, outward
FORMAL semblance
E3 1 disappearance

appease v
placate, pacify, reconcile, satisfy, mitigate, make peace with, conciliate
FORMAL propitiate
E3 aggravate

appeasement n
reconciliation, conciliation, peacemaking, placation, pacification, satisfaction

appellation n
epithet, name, nickname, title, designation, description
FORMAL so(u)briquet, denomination
SLANG monicker

append v
add, affix, attach, fasten, join, tack on
FORMAL adjoin, annex, conjoin, subjoin

appendage n
addendum, appendix, addition, supplement, adjunct, tailpiece

appendix n
addition, appendage, adjunct, addendum, supplement, epilogue, codicil, postscript, rider

appertain v
pertain, relate, apply, be relevant, bear on, have a bearing on, concern, refer, regard

appetite n
1 *a good appetite*
hunger, stomach, relish, zest, taste, desire, tooth
TECHNICAL malacia, orexis
COLLOQ. inner man, inner woman
SLANG twist
2 *appetite for sensation*
hunger, taste, thirst, inclination, liking, desire, longing, urge, propensity, yearning, craving, lust, eagerness, passion, zeal
OLD maw
COLLOQ. yen

appetizer n
starter, first course, canapé, *hors d'œuvre*, meze, apéritif, cocktail, tapas, bhajee, whet, relish
OLD antepast

appetizing adj
mouthwatering, tempting, inviting, appealing, palatable, tasty, delicious, succulent, piquant, savoury
COLLOQ. scrumptious, mor(e)ish, yummy
⊟ disgusting, distasteful

applaud v
1 *the audience applauded*
clap, cheer, put your hands together for, give an ovation/a standing ovation to, give a round of applause, show your appreciation to
COLLOQ. give a big hand to
2 *applaud the government's efforts*
acclaim, compliment, congratulate, approve, commend, praise
FORMAL laud, eulogize, extol

applause n
ovation, standing ovation, clapping, cheering, cheers, bravos, acclaim, acclamation, accolade, congratulation, approval, commendation, praise
FORMAL encomium
COLLOQ. a big hand
⊟ criticism, censure

appliance n
1 *domestic appliance*
machine, device, contrivance, contraption, gadget, tool, implement, instrument, apparatus, mechanism, waldo
COLLOQ. gizmo
2 APPLICATION, use, value, relevance, function, carrying-out
TECHNICAL praxis

applicable adj
relevant, apt, appropriate, fitting, suited, useful, suitable, fit, proper, valid, legitimate
FORMAL pertinent, apposite
⊟ inapplicable, inappropriate

applicant n
candidate, interviewee, claimant, contestant, competitor, aspirant, suitor, petitioner, inquirer
TECHNICAL postulant

application n
1 REQUEST, appeal, petition, suit, claim, inquiry, demand
2 RELEVANCE, function, purpose, use, value, bearing, significance, aptness, germaneness
TECHNICAL praxis
FORMAL pertinence
3 DILIGENCE, hard work, industry, industriousness, effort, commitment, dedication, perseverance, keenness, attentiveness
FORMAL assiduity, sedulousness
4 *computer applications*
program, software

5 *the application of ointment*
putting on, smearing, spreading, rubbing, treatment, anointing

applied adj
practical, real, useful, functional, relevant, actual, hands-on
⊟ pure, theoretical

apply v
1 REQUEST, ask for, requisition, put in for, put in an application for, fill in a form for, order, write away/off for, appeal, petition, solicit, sue, claim, inquire
2 *apply yourself to a task*
address, buckle down, settle down, commit, devote, dedicate, give, direct, concentrate, study, persevere, be diligent, be industrious, work hard, make an effort, commit/devote yourself
COLLOQ. buckle down, knuckle down
3 USE, exercise, utilize, employ, bring into play, put into practice/operation, draw on, engage, harness, ply, wield, administer, execute, implement, assign, direct, bring to bear, exert, practise, resort to
4 REFER, relate, be relevant, be significant, fit, suit, affect, involve
FORMAL pertain, appertain
5 *apply ointment*
put on, spread on, lay on, cover with, paint, anoint, smear, rub, treat with
OLD appose
FORMAL adhibit

appoint v
1 NAME, nominate, be shortlisted, elect, install, choose, select, pick, engage, employ, take on, hire, recruit, commission, co-opt, delegate, assign, allot, designate, command, direct, charge, detail
2 DECIDE, determine, arrange, settle, fix, set, specify, assign, establish, ordain, decree, destine, designate, allot
⊟ **1** reject, dismiss, discharge

appointed adj
determined, decided, scheduled, chosen, assigned, arranged, pre-arranged, settled, fixed, set, established, ordained, decreed, destined, preordained, designated, allotted

appointment n
1 ARRANGEMENT, engagement, date, meeting, arrangement to meet, interview, consultation, rendezvous
OLD tryst, assignation
2 JOB, position, situation, post, office, place
3 NAMING, nomination, election, choosing, choice, selection, commissioning, delegation

apportion v
assign, allocate, allot, distribute, divide, dispense, deal (out), hand out, grant, measure out, mete (out), ration (out), share (out), carve
OLD stint
FORMAL admeasure
COLLOQ. dole out

apportionment n
allocation, allotment, distribution, division, dispensation, assignment, dealing, grant, ration(ing), sharing, share
COLLOQ. handout

apposite adj
relevant, applicable, appropriate, apt, germane, suitable, suited, to the point, to the purpose
FORMAL pertinent, apropos, befitting
⊟ inapposite

appraisal n
evaluation, assessment, survey, inspection, review, examination, estimate, estimation, judgement, reckoning,

opinion, appreciation, valuation, rating
FORMAL assay
COLLOQ. once-over

appraise v
evaluate, assess, survey, inspect, review, examine,
estimate, sum up, judge, value, rate; *N Am* valuate
FORMAL assay
COLLOQ. size up, once-over

⚠ **appraise** or **apprise**?
If you *appraise* someone or something, you form an
opinion about their quality, value, etc. If you are *apprised* of
something, you are told about it.

---

appreciable adj
noticeable, significant, considerable, substantial, definite,
perceptible, discernible, recognizable
⊟ insignificant, imperceptible, negligible

appreciably adv
noticeably, significantly, considerably, substantially,
definitely, markedly, perceptibly

appreciate v
1 ENJOY, relish, savour, prize, treasure, value, cherish,
admire, respect, regard, like, welcome, take kindly to, think
highly of, relish, esteem
OLD apprize
2 UNDERSTAND, comprehend, perceive, realize, recognize,
grasp, be aware of, be conscious of, be sensitive to,
acknowledge, sympathize with, know, see, sense
3 *I appreciate your help*
be grateful for, express your gratitude/appreciation, thank,
give thanks for, be appreciative, be indebted to
4 *appreciate in value*
grow, increase, rise, mount, go up, inflate, gain, strengthen,
improve, enhance
⊟ 1 despise, hate **2** overlook, ignore **4** depreciate, go
down

Synonym nuances
sense 1
The word **enjoy** is a straightforward one to use for taking
pleasure or delight in something. To express a deeper,
more conscious appreciation and increased sensation,
you could use **relish** and **savour**: *he savoured life to the
full; she relished the experience.* The terms **prize**,
treasure or **value** appropriately describe appreciation
from the point of view of placing a high value on it, while
cherish suggests doing the same but with more
affection involved.
  Respect and **regard** are restrained terms, having more
to do with treating with consideration, although **regard**
in some contexts carries more implication of kindly
feelings. To **think highly of** or **esteem** someone or
something returns to the notion of highly respecting and
appreciating their merits or qualities: *poets were highly
esteemed*, whereas **like** is a far more mild, not
particularly demonstrative term.
  To **take kindly to** is very similar, though its usage is
generally in the negative: *she does not take kindly to
criticism.* **Welcome** is used specifically of receiving
something with pleasure: *Britain welcomes foreign
investment.*

---

appreciation n
1 ENJOYMENT, relish, admiration, liking, respect, respecting,
regard, high opinion, esteem, valuing
2 *send a present to show your appreciation*
gratitude, gratefulness, thankfulness, thanks,
indebtedness, obligation
3 UNDERSTANDING, comprehension, perception,
awareness, realization, recognition, grasp,
acknowledgement, sympathy, sensitivity, responsiveness,

valuation, assessment, estimation, judgement, knowledge
FORMAL cognizance
4 REVIEW, critique, evaluation, analysis, assessment,
commentary, notice, praise
5 GROWTH, increase, rise, inflation, gain, improvement,
escalation, enhancement
⊟ 2 ingratitude **5** depreciation

appreciative adj
1 GRATEFUL, thankful, obliged, indebted, pleased
FORMAL beholden
2 ADMIRING, encouraging, enthusiastic, respectful,
sensitive, responsive, supportive, perceptive,
knowledgeable, conscious, mindful
⊟ 1 ungrateful **2** ignorant, insensitive

apprehend v
1 CATCH, arrest, capture, detain, seize
COLLOQ. pick up, bust, nick, collar, grab, nab, run in, pull in
2 UNDERSTAND, comprehend, grasp, believe, conceive,
perceive, realize, recognize, see
COLLOQ. twig

apprehension n
1 ANXIETY, dread, foreboding, misgiving, qualm, unease,
uneasiness, worry, concern, disquiet, concern,
nervousness, alarm, fear, trepidation, doubt, suspicion,
mistrust
FORMAL perturbation
COLLOQ. jitters, butterflies, butterflies in your stomach,
collywobbles, heebie-jeebies, willies
2 ARREST, capture, detention, seizure, taking
3 UNDERSTANDING, comprehension, grasp, belief,
conception, perception, discernment, realization,
recognition, uptake
TECHNICAL noesis
FORMAL cognizance

apprehensive adj
nervous, anxious, worried, concerned, uneasy, doubtful,
suspicious, mistrustful, distrustful, bothered, alarmed,
afraid, fearful
COLLOQ. on tenterhooks, having the jitters, having
butterflies in your stomach, having the collywobbles,
having the willies
SLANG *Aust* toey
⊟ assured, confident

apprehensively adv
nervously, anxiously, uneasily, doubtfully, suspiciously,
mistrustfully, distrustfully, fearfully
⊟ assuredly, confidently

apprentice n
trainee, probationer, student, pupil, learner, novice,
beginner, starter, recruit, newcomer, tyro, cadet, prentice,
intern
OLD *Scot* servitor
COLLOQ. *N Am* rookie
⊟ expert

apprenticeship n
training period, traineeship, studentship, trial period,
probationary period, novitiate

apprise v
inform, notify, acquaint, advise, brief, communicate,
enlighten, intimate, tell, warn
COLLOQ. tip off

⚠ **apprise** or **appraise**?
See panel at **appraise**.

---

approach v, n
♦ v
1 GET CLOSER TO, come nearer/closer, advance towards,
move towards, proceed towards, go near(er), draw near,
near, gain on, catch up, reach, meet, arrive

2 SPEAK TO, talk to, address, make conversation with, greet, accost
3 TACKLE, deal with, begin, commence, set about, embark on, launch into, undertake, introduce, mention, treat
4 APPLY TO, appeal to, sound out, contact, get in touch with, get onto, invite, make advances, make overtures, broach
COLLOQ. buttonhole
5 *a speed approaching 200 km/h*
reach, come close to, border on, come near to, compare with, approximate
♦ *n*
1 *the approach of winter*
advance, coming, coming near/close, arrival
FORMAL advent
2 ATTITUDE, point of view, viewpoint, opinion, position, perspective, slant, standpoint, stance, angle
3 APPLICATION, appeal, overture(s), advances, suggestion(s), invitation, proposition, proposal, request, plea
4 METHOD, manner, style, technique, procedure, means, modus operandi, strategy, system, tactics, course of action
5 ACCESS, road, avenue, drive, driveway, way, passage, entrance, doorway, threshold

approachable *adj*
1 FRIENDLY, easy to get on/along with, sociable, congenial, warm, affable, agreeable, open, informal, pleasant, welcoming
2 ACCESSIBLE, attainable, reachable
COLLOQ. get-at-able
E3 1 aloof, unapproachable **2** inaccessible, remote

approbation *n*
approval, good opinion, praise, respect, acceptance, favour, commendation, endorsement, encouragement, recognition, esteem
FORMAL laudation

appropriate *adj, v*
♦ *adj*
suitable, applicable, relevant, to the point, well-chosen, apt, fitting, fit, befitting, germane, seemly, becoming, proper, right, correct, accepted, well-timed, timely, seasonable, opportune
OLD seemly, meet
FORMAL pertinent, appurtenant, apropos, felicitous
COLLOQ. spot-on
E3 inappropriate, irrelevant, unsuitable
♦ *v*
1 SEIZE, take, take possession of, commandeer, requisition, confiscate, impound, assume, usurp
FORMAL expropriate, arrogate
2 STEAL, pocket, pilfer, embezzle, misappropriate, thieve, make off with
FORMAL purloin, peculate
COLLOQ. nick, pinch, swipe, nab, lift, filch, knock off

appropriately *adv*
suitably, fittingly, correctly, properly, relevantly
FORMAL felicitously

approval *n*
1 ADMIRATION, regard, respect, good opinion, esteem, liking, appreciation, acceptance, favour, recommendation, praise, commendation, acclaim, acclamation, honour, applause
OLD approof
FORMAL approbation
2 AGREEMENT, acceptance, assent, consent, permission, leave, sanction, authorization, licence, mandate, endorsement, blessing, certification, ratification, validation, confirmation, support
FORMAL approbation, concurrence, imprimatur
COLLOQ. go-ahead, green light, OK, rubber stamp, nod, wink, thumbs-up
E3 1 disapproval, condemnation

Synonym nuances
sense 2
The general term **agreement** suggests approval given with accord, but **acceptance** does not carry the same implication of accord. **Assent** implies a degree of compliance whereas **consent** has more to do with accordance. Both **permission** and **leave** are general terms that might be used of any act of permitting or authorization. **Sanction** suggests more official approval, even more so **authorization**, which indicates being established by some form of authority: *authorization to carry a weapon.*
  Meanwhile a **licence** can be used both of an official document and a more abstract permission: *licence to own a gun*; *his words gave me licence to act*; but a **mandate** again is an indication of legal authorization, usually to carry out an action. **Certification** is only used in the context of granting of a written declaration, and **ratification** also denotes approval that has been signed. **Validation** is especially appropriate where some checking has taken place before approval is granted.
  If you talk of giving something your **endorsement** or the less formal **blessing** it implies that you are expressing personal agreement of it as well; **support** suggests an even more active backing: *his support for devolution*. **Approbation** can be used of a formal act of approval while **concurrence** leans more towards agreement and co-operation. An **imprimatur** refers specifically to permission to print: *now it has the imprimatur of the Pope, the Catechism will be sent for translation.*

approve *v*
1 ADMIRE, regard, like, think well/highly of, hold in high regard, be pleased with, appreciate, favour, recommend, praise, commend, acclaim, applaud, esteem
OLD countenance
2 *approve a proposal*
agree to, assent to, consent to, accede to, allow, permit, pass, sanction, authorize, mandate, bless, countenance, ratify, validate, endorse, support, hold with, uphold, second, back, accept, adopt, carry, confirm
FORMAL concur, homologate
COLLOQ. give the go-ahead to, give the green light to, OK, rubber-stamp, give the nod to, give the thumbs-up to, buy
OLD SLANG dig
E3 1 disapprove, condemn **2** reject

approved *adj*
accepted, authorized, orthodox, official, recommended, sanctioned, correct, favoured, permissible, permitted, preferred, proper, recognized
E3 unauthorized, unorthodox

approving *adj*
admiring, appreciative, favourable, praising, respectful, supportive, commendatory
FORMAL laudatory

approvingly *adj*
admiringly, appreciatively, with pleasure, favourably

approximate *adj, v*
♦ *adj*
estimated, guessed, rough, inexact, imprecise, loose, close, near, like, similar, relative
COLLOQ. ballpark
E3 exact, precise
♦ *v*
approach, come close to, come near to, border on, verge on, be tantamount to, resemble, be similar to

approximately *adv*
roughly, around, about, some, something like, odd, circa, more or less, loosely, round about, or thereabouts,

---

Types of arable crop include:

N Am alfalfa	corn	linseed	oats	potato	soya bean	sweet potato
barley	fodder beet	mangel wurzel	oilseed rape	rice	sugar beet	turnip
bean	kale	millet	pea	rye	swede	wheat
cassava	lucerne	mung bean	popcorn	sorghum	sweetcorn	yam

---

approaching, close to, nearly, just about, not far off, in the region/neighbourhood/vicinity of, somewhere in the region of, in round numbers, rounded up/down
COLLOQ. give or take
E₃ exactly

approximation *n*
1 ESTIMATE, rough calculation, rough idea, guess, estimation, conjecture
COLLOQ. guesstimate, ballpark figure
2 *an approximation to a dress*
likeness, resemblance, similarity, correspondence
FORMAL semblance

appurtenance *n*
accessories, equipment, belongings, trappings, paraphernalia, impedimenta

a priori *adj*
theoretical, deduced, hypothetical, inferred
FORMAL conjectural, suppositional

apron *n*
1 PINAFORE, bib, tablier, tabard, pinnie; *N Am* tier
OLD napron, barm-cloth, brat, placket
2 *the apron of the stage*
edge, fringe, periphery, skirt, rim, border
3 *aeroplanes on the apron*
standing, hard-standing, bay, loading bay, forecourt

apropos *adj, prep*
♦ *adj*
suitable, applicable, relevant, to the point, well-chosen, apt, fitting, befitting, becoming, proper, right, correct, accepted, timely, seasonable, opportune
OLD seemly
FORMAL pertinent, felicitous
E₃ inappropriate
♦ *prep*
with reference to, with regard to, with respect to, in relation to, in respect of, on the subject of, in connection with, re, regarding, respecting

apt *adj*
1 RELEVANT, applicable, appropriate, fitting, acceptable, suitable, fit, germane, seemly, proper, correct, accurate, timely, seasonable
FORMAL apposite
COLLOQ. spot-on
2 *apt to do something*
inclined, liable, prone, given, disposed, tending, likely, given, ready, subject
E₃ 1 inapt, unsuitable

aptitude *n*
ability, natural ability, capability, capacity, faculty, gift, talent, flair, facility, skill, proficiency, cleverness, intelligence, quickness, bent, inclination, leaning, disposition, tendency
E₃ inaptitude

aptly *adv*
suitably, appropriately, fittingly, fitly, relevantly, to the point
FORMAL appositely

aquatic *adj*
water, sea, river, marine, maritime, nautical, watery, fluid, liquid
FORMAL fluvial

arable *adj*
cultivable, ploughable, farmable, tillable, fertile, productive, fruitful
FORMAL fecund
See panel above

arachnid
See panel at **insect**.

arbiter *n*
1 ADJUDICATOR, judge, referee, umpire
2 *an arbiter of style*
authority, expert, pundit, master, governor, judge, controller

arbitrarily *adv*
by chance, randomly, illogically, inconsistently, unreasonably, irrationally, subjectively

arbitrary *adj*
1 RANDOM, chance, capricious, whimsical, inconsistent, discretionary, subjective, personal, instinctive, unreasoned, illogical, irrational, unreasonable
2 DESPOTIC, tyrannical, dictatorial, autocratic, absolute, imperious, magisterial, domineering, overbearing, high-handed, dogmatic
E₃ 1 reasoned, rational, circumspect

arbitrate *v*
judge, adjudicate, pass judgement, sit in judgement, referee, umpire, mediate, settle, decide, determine

arbitration *n*
judgement, adjudication, intervention, mediation, negotiation, settlement, decision, determination
FORMAL arbitrament

arbitrator *n*
judge, adjudicator, arbiter, referee, umpire, moderator, mediator, negotiator, intermediary, go-between

arbour *n*
bower, shelter, alcove, grotto, bay, recess, retreat, sanctuary

arc *n, v*
♦ *n*
curve, curved line, bend, arch, bow, curvature, semicircle
♦ *v*
curve, bend, arch, bow, turn, round, spin, swerve

arcade *n*
gallery, cloister, colonnade, covered way, mall, piazza, portico, precinct, shopping mall, shopping precinct, plaza
TECHNICAL loggia, peristyle, stoa

arcane *adj*
secret, mysterious, concealed, obscure, hidden, abstruse, mystical, cryptic, enigmatic, esoteric, recondite, occult, profound

arch *n, v, adj*
♦ *n*
1 *the arches of a bridge*
archway, bridge, span, dome, vault, concave
See panel on next page
2 ARC, bend, curve, curvature, bow, semicircle
♦ *v*
bend, curve, bow, arc, vault, camber
♦ *adj*
mischievous, playful, mysterious, cunning, sly

Types of arch include:

basket handle	equilateral	horseshoe	Norman	round	skew	trefoil
convex	four-centre	keel	ogee	segmental	stilted	Tudor
corbel	Gothic	lancet	parabolic	shouldered	tented	

archaeology
See panel below

archaic *adj*
antiquated, old-fashioned, outmoded, passé, outdated, out-of-date, obsolete, old, ancient, antique, quaint, bygone, primitive, medi(a)eval, antediluvian, obsolescent
COLLOQ. old hat, out of the ark
E3 modern, recent

archetypal *adj*
model, standard, typical, representative, characteristic, original, classic, ideal, stock
FORMAL exemplary, quintessential, paradigmatic

archetype *n*
pattern, model, standard, form, type, prototype, original, precursor, classic, paradigm, ideal, epitome, stereotype
FORMAL exemplar, quintessence, typification, entity

architect *n*
1 *the architect of the building*
designer, planner, master builder, draughtsman
2 *the architect of modern economics*
creator, author, inventor, engineer, maker, constructor, prime mover, originator, founder, instigator, shaper
COLLOQ. mastermind

architecture *n*
1 *study architecture*
designing, planning, building, construction
TECHNICAL architectonics
See panel on next page
2 *Victorian architecture*
style, design, composition, structure, arrangement, make-up, framework
3 *the architecture of a software program*
structure, framework, frame, construction, form, make-up, arrangement, organization, composition, constitution, system, set-up
FORMAL configuration, conformation

archives *n*
records, annals, chronicles, memorials, papers, documents, deeds, ledgers, registers, memorabilia, roll

arctic *adj*
1 *the Arctic Ocean*
polar, far northern
FORMAL boreal, hyperborean
2 *arctic weather*
freezing, freezing cold, bitterly cold, frozen, frosty, Siberian, glacial, subzero
E3 1 Antarctic **2** tropical

ardent *adj*
fervent, fiery, warm, passionate, impassioned, fierce, avid, vehement, intense, strong, spirited, enthusiastic, eager, keen, dedicated, devoted, zealous, evangelical, hot, burning, fervid, sanguine, mettled, mettlesome, spiritous
OLD perfervid
E3 apathetic, unenthusiastic

ardently *adv*
fervently, warmly, passionately, strongly, avidly, vehemently, intensely, hotly, enthusiastically, eagerly, devotedly, zealously
E3 unenthusiastically

ardour *n*
fervour, passion, fire, flame, heat, warmth, avidity, vehemence, intensity, spirit, enthusiasm, eagerness, animation, zest, keenness, dedication, devotion, zeal, lust, rage, *duende*
OLD covetise; (*Shakesp*) wrath
FORMAL empressement
E3 apathy, coolness, indifference

arduous *adj*
hard, difficult, tough, onerous, burdensome, heavy, rigorous, severe, harsh, formidable, strenuous, tiring, taxing, fatiguing, wearying, daunting, exhausting, backbreaking, punishing, gruelling, uphill, stiff, laborious
COLLOQ. be a slog, be murder
E3 easy

area *n*
1 *the Muslim areas of the city*
locality, neighbourhood, quarter, environment, environs, patch, terrain, district, region, parish, zone, sector, department, precinct, province, enclave, catchment area, reserve area
2 *an area of land*
expanse, width, breadth, stretch, extent, part, portion, section, tract
3 *an area of activity/knowledge*
field, sphere, domain, world, realm, territory, department, province, branch, sector, range, scope, compass, size, extent

arena *n*
1 STADIUM, field, ground, bowl, ring, area, amphitheatre, theatre, coliseum, hippodrome
2 *the political arena*
sphere, scene, domain, world, realm, department, province, battlefield, battleground, area of conflict

argot *n*
jargon, cant, slang, idiom, specialist language, parlance

arguable *adj*
debatable, open to question, questionable, disputable,

Archaeological terms include:

agger	cairn	flint	kitchen-midden	obelisk	stele
amphitheatre	cartouche	handaxe	kurgan	palmette	stone circle
amphora	cave art/rock art	henge	ley lines	palstave	tell
artefact	cist	hieroglyph	loom weight	papyrus	tumulus
barrow	cromlech	hill fort	lynchet	potassium-argon	urn
beaker	cup	hoard	megalith	dating	vallum
blade	dolmen	hypocaust	microlith	radiocarbon	whorl
bogman	earthwork	incised	mosaic	dating	
bowl	eolith	decoration	mound	rock shelter	
bracteate	flake	jar	mummy	sondage	
burin	flask	jug	neolith	spindle	

Architectural and building terms include:

alcove	cornice	Edwardian	frieze	Norman	rotunda
annexe	coving	elevation	frontispiece	pagoda	roughcast
architrave	dado	Elizabethan	gable	pantile	sacristy
baluster	decorated	façade	gargoyle	parapet	scroll
barge-board	dogtooth	fanlight	gatehouse	pinnacle	soffit
baroque	dome	fascia	Georgian	plinth	stucco
bas-relief	Doric	festoon	Gothic	Queen Anne	terrazzo
capstone	dormer	fillet	groin	rafters	Tudor
casement	double glazing	finial	groundplan	Regency	Tuscan
window	drawbridge	flamboyant	half-timbered	reveal	wainscot
classical	dry-stone	Flemish bond	Ionic	ridge	weathering
coping stone	duplex	fletton	jamb	rococo	
Corinthian	Early English	fluting	lintel	Romanesque	
cornerstone	eaves	French window	mullion	roof	

See also **arch**; **roof**; **tower**; **wall**; **window**.

open to doubt, contentious, uncertain, undecided, moot
FORMAL controvertible
◆ incontrovertible, indisputable, certain

arguably *adv*
probably, maybe, possibly, in all likelihood, most likely

argue *v*
1 QUARREL, squabble, bicker, row, have a row, wrangle, haggle, wrestle, remonstrate, take/join issue, fight, feud, fall out, disagree, dispute, quibble, rag, spar; *Scot* cangle
FORMAL altercate, moot
COLLOQ. be at each other's throats, be at loggerheads, fall out, hassle, have it out (with), have words, cross swords, have a bone to pick
2 REASON, assert, contend, hold, hold a brief, declare, maintain, claim, plead
FORMAL expostulate, logicize
3 *argue the point*
question, debate, discuss, reason
4 *argued them out of leaving*
persuade, dissuade, talk out of, convince
5 BE EVIDENCE FOR, exhibit, display, show, manifest, demonstrate, indicate, denote, prove, suggest, imply

argument *n*
1 QUARREL, squabble, row, wrangle, controversy, polemic, debate, discussion, dispute, disagreement, clash, difference of opinion, heated exchange, conflict, fight, feud, rumpus, ruckus, spat
OLD controverse
FORMAL altercation
COLLOQ. tiff, barney, argy-bargy, running battle, shouting-match, slanging-match, set-to, dust-up, ding-dong, bust-up; *Aust* yike
SLANG *Aust & NZ* blue
2 REASONING, reason, logic, rationale, assertion, declaration, contention, claim, demonstration, evidence, argumentation, debate, defence, case, justification
FORMAL expostulation
Related adjective: elenctic
3 *the argument of the book*
synopsis, summary, theme, topic, outline, plot, thesis

Synonym nuances
sense 1
Quarrel, **squabble** and **wrangle** are synonyms which suggest a personal argument with distinct viewpoints involved. **Row** is similar, but is often associated with domestic disagreements: *she had a row with her husband*. However, both **row** and **controversy** can suggest a more general argument, and one that it is within the public domain: *political controversy*.
  Debate and **discussion** are the terms to use when talking is the main expression of the dispute, especially where it has been deliberately organized; **dispute**, likewise, indicates a contest with words but with no

---

formalization behind it.
  The word **disagreement** is a general one with no strong associations, whereas **clash** implies noisy opposition or contradiction. Likewise, **difference of opinion** would describe a fairly tame argument on a matter on which two or more groups disagree, but **altercation** or **heated exchange** describe dialogue that has become angry. Both **conflict** and **fight** suggest a very passionate and intense struggle, often with a physical element implied, and **rumpus** puts the emphasis on noisiness or uproar: *a mighty rumpus*. **Feud** is used particularly of a persistent state of private enmity.

---

argumentation *n*
reasoning, debate, argument, rationale, logic, contention, claim, justification, evidence, case, defence
FORMAL expostulation

argumentative *adj*
quarrelsome, contentious, polemical, opinionated, belligerent, perverse, contrary, cantankerous
FORMAL captious, disputatious, litigious, dissentious, truculent
COLLOQ. stroppy; *Can* chippy
◆ complaisant

arid *adj*
1 *an arid landscape*
dry, parched, waterless, moistureless, desiccated, torrid, dehydrated, baked, shrivelled up, barren, infertile, unproductive, desert, waste
FORMAL torrefied
2 DULL, uninteresting, boring, monotonous, tedious, dry, sterile, dreary, drab, flat, colourless, lifeless, spiritless, uninspired, vapid, jejune
◆ **1** fertile **2** lively, exciting

aright *adv*
rightly, accurately, exactly, properly, correctly, truly, fitly, suitably, aptly
COLLOQ. OK

arise *v*
1 OCCUR, emerge, issue, appear, come to light, come up, present itself, happen, begin, start, commence, come into being/existence
COLLOQ. crop up
2 *points that arose from the report*
result, be a result of, be caused by, ensue, follow, derive, stem, come, spring, proceed, flow
3 RISE, get up, stand up, get to your feet, straighten up, rise up, go up, ascend, climb, mount, lift, soar, tower

aristocracy *n*
upper class, privileged class, gentry, aristocrats, lords, ladies, nobility, noblemen, noblewomen, peers, peerage, ruling class, gentility, high society, élite, rank

Terms used in armour:

HEAD AND NECK:	nosepiece	faulds	LEGS:	FOR HORSES:	lame
armet	sallet (or salade)	hauberk	cuisse	barding	palette
aventail	ventail	pectoral	culet	chamfrain (or	plate armour
basinet (or	visor (or vizor)	**SHOULDERS AND**	greave	chamfron)	rondel
bascinet)	**TORSO:**	**ARMS:**	poleyn	crinet	splint armour
beaver	backpiece (or	ailette	sabaton	pectoral	suit
casque	backplate)	brassard	shynbald	poitrel	surcoat
gorget	body armour	couter	solleret	**MISCELLANEOUS:**	
grille	breastplate	gauntlet	spur	cap-à-pie	
helmet	corslet (or	pauldron (or	tasse	chain mail	
mentonnière	corselet)	pouldron)	tonlet	coat-armour	
morion (or	cuirass	rerebrace	tuille	gusset	
morrion)		vambrace			

FORMAL patriciate, patricians, optimates, *haute monde*
COLLOQ. toffs, nobs, top drawer, upper crust
◢◣ common people, lower classes, working class, proletariat, hoi polloi, riff-raff; *colloq.* plebs, proles

aristocrat *n*
noble, nobleman, noblewoman, peer, peeress, lord, lady, patrician, *grande dame*, *grand seigneur*
FORMAL grandee, eupatrid, optimate
COLLOQ. toff, nob
◢◣ commoner

aristocratic *adj*
upper-class, highborn, well-born, noble, patrician, blue-blooded, titled, lordly, courtly, élite, dignified, elegant, refined, thoroughbred
COLLOQ. upper-crust, born with a silver spoon in your mouth
◢◣ plebeian, vulgar

arm[1] *n*
1 *with folded arms*
limb, upper limb, appendage
TECHNICAL brachium
Related adjective: brachial
2 *the air arm of the fighting forces*
wing, section, division, detachment, department, branch, offshoot, extension, projection
3 *an arm of the sea*
inlet, estuary, bay, channel, firth, passage, cove, creek
4 *the arm of the law*
authority, power, force, strength
FORMAL might

arm[2] *v*
arm someone with weapons/information
provide, supply, issue, equip, rig, outfit, prime, prepare, forearm, rearm, gird, steel, brace, reinforce, strengthen, protect
FORMAL array, furnish, fortify, accoutre

armada *n*
fleet, flotilla, navy, naval force, squadron

armaments *n*
weapons, arms, artillery, guns, cannon, munitions, ammunition, ordnance, weaponry

armed services
See panel below

armistice *n*
ceasefire, truce, peace, peace treaty, pact, agreement to end/cease/suspend hostilities

armour *n*
protective covering, panoply, shield, mail, chain mail, iron-cladding, armature, garniture
See panel above

armoured *adj*
armour-plated, steel-plated, iron-clad, toughened, reinforced, protected, bullet-proof, bomb-proof

armoury *n*
arsenal, ordnance depot, ammunition dump, magazine, (arms) depot, repository, stock, stockpile, garderobe

arms *n*
1 WEAPONS, weaponry, firearms, guns, cannon, missiles, projectiles, artillery, instruments of war, armaments, ordnance, munitions, ammunition
2 COAT-OF-ARMS, armorial bearings, shield, crest, insignia, emblem, heraldic device, escutcheon, heraldry, blazonry

army *n*
1 *a captain in the army*
armed force, military, militia, land forces, soldiers, soldiery, troops, infantry
Related adjective: military
2 *an army of workers*
legions, cohorts, multitude, throng, host, horde, pack, mob, crowd, swarm

aroma *n*
smell, odour, scent, perfume, fragrance, bouquet, savour, nose
FORMAL fumet(te), redolence

aromatic *adj*
perfumed, fragrant, sweet-smelling, sweet-scented, fresh, scented, balmy, savoury, spicy, pungent
FORMAL redolent, odoriferous
◢◣ acrid, foul-smelling

around *prep, adv*
◆ *prep*
1 SURROUNDING, round, encircling, encompassing, enclosing, on all sides of, on every side of, about, framed by
FORMAL circumambient, circumjacent
2 EVERYWHERE IN, to all parts of, about, all over
3 *around a dozen*
approximately, roughly, about, circa, more or less, close to, nearly
◆ *adv*
1 EVERYWHERE, all over, in all directions, on all sides,

Units in the armed services include:

garrison	squadron	brigade	regiment	Royal Marines	squadron
militia	wing	company	squad	**NAVY:**	
task force	**ARMY:**	corps	troop	convoy	
AIR FORCE:	battalion	patrol	**MARINES:**	fleet	
flight	battery	platoon	commandos	flotilla	

throughout, about, here and there, to and fro
2 CLOSE, close by, near, nearby, at hand, within reach

arousal *n*

1 SEXUAL STIMULATION, excitement, titillation
COLLOQ. getting going
2 *arousal to anger*
provocation, agitation, excitement, stirring, evocation, firing

arouse *v*

1 *arouse suspicion*
cause, instigate, induce, summon up, call forth, spark, kindle, inflame, whet, sharpen, quicken, animate, excite, prompt, provoke, stimulate, trigger, incur
2 *arouse someone to anger*
provoke, incite, agitate, stir up, excite, evoke, rouse, fire, startle, galvanize, goad, spur, whip up, get going
OLD upraise
FORMAL suscitate
3 *arouse from sleep*
wake up, waken, awaken, disentrance
OLD bestir
COLLOQ. knock up
4 *arouse sexually*
stimulate, excite, get going, titillate
COLLOQ. turn on
F3 2 calm, lull, quieten

arraign *v*

accuse, call to account, charge, impeach, indict, prosecute, impugn, incriminate, bring an action against

arraignment *n*

accusation, charge, trial, legal action, case, impeachment, incrimination, indictment, summons

arrange *v*

1 *arrange a meeting*
decide, settle on, agree, plan, organize, set up, make (an appointment)
COLLOQ. fix (up), pencil in, ink in
2 ORGANIZE, co-ordinate, prepare, fix, plan, project, design, devise, contrive, determine, settle
3 ORDER, put in order, tidy, range, marshal, dispose, distribute, position, set out, lay out, align, line up, group, class, classify, categorize, sort (out), sift, grade, list, file, systematize, catalogue, codify, methodize, regulate, adjust
FORMAL array
4 *arrange music*
adapt, set, score, orchestrate, instrument, harmonize
F3 3 untidy, disorganize, muddle

arrangement *n*

1 *make arrangements*
plan(s), preparation(s), detail(s), planning, preparing, groundwork
2 AGREEMENT, settlement, contract, terms, compromise, *modus vivendi*
3 ORDER, display, disposition, layout, line-up, positioning, grouping, classification, structure, system, method, set-up, organization, preparation, planning, plan, scheme, design, format, schedule
FORMAL array
4 ADAPTATION, version, interpretation, setting, score, orchestration, instrumentation, harmonization

arrant *adj*

absolute, complete, utter, downright, extreme, out-and-out, outright, rank, thorough, thoroughgoing, brazen, flagrant, gross, blatant, unmitigated, incorrigible, infamous, notorious, barefaced, vile
FORMAL egregious

array *n, v*

♦ *n*
arrangement, display, show, exhibition, exposition, assortment, collection, muster, order, formation, line-up, parade, disposition, marshalling
FORMAL assemblage
♦ *v*
1 ARRANGE, order, range, dispose, position, group, lay out, line up, align, draw up, marshal, assemble, muster, parade, display, show, exhibit
2 CLOTHE, dress, robe, deck, adorn, decorate
OLD bedizen, accoutre
FORMAL attire, apparel, habilitate

arrears *n*

debt(s), liabilities, outstanding payment/amount, sum of money owed, amount owed, money owing, liabilities, balance, deficit
■ **in arrears**
owing, outstanding, behind(hand), in debt, overdue, late

arrest *v, n*

♦ *v*
1 *arrest a criminal*
capture, catch, seize, apprehend, detain, take into custody
COLLOQ. bust, nick, collar, grab, nab, book, run in, pick up, pull in, do, nail
2 STOP, stem, check, restrain, inhibit, halt, interrupt, stall, delay, slow (down), retard, block, obstruct, impede, hinder
COLLOQ. nip in the bud
3 *arrest your attention*
capture, attract, catch, grip, hold, engage, absorb, engross, rivet, fascinate, intrigue
♦ *n*
capture, apprehension, detention, taking into custody, seizure
■ **under arrest**
in custody, helping police with their inquiries, in captivity

arresting *adj*

striking, amazing, surprising, stunning, extraordinary, impressive, remarkable, engaging, notable, noteworthy, conspicuous, noticeable, eye-catching, outstanding
F3 inconspicuous, unremarkable

arrival *n*

1 *the arrival of the president/fresh supplies*
appearance, entrance, entry, coming, approach, emergence
FORMAL advent
2 *welcome new arrivals*
newcomer, incomer, comer, visitor, guest, entrant, debutant(e), fresher; *N Am* freshman
FORMAL visitant
3 *the arrival of credit cards*
invention, appearance, coming, start, development, emergence, occurrence, origin, birth, dawn
F3 1 departure **2** leaver **3** death

arrive *v*

1 *arrive at the airport*
come, reach, get to, get there, get here, be present, reach your destination, appear, put in an appearance, fetch, land, touch down, dock, pull in, come in, check in, clock in, materialize, enter, come on the scene, occur, happen
FORMAL accede
COLLOQ. show (up), turn up, make it, drop in, blow in, swan in, roll up, pitch up, surface
2 APPEAR, become available, come on the market, be produced
3 *arrive at a decision*
reach, come to, get, obtain, gain, achieve, accomplish, attain, hammer out, thrash out
4 *he thinks he's really arrived*
succeed, be a success, become famous
COLLOQ. make it, get to the top
F3 1 depart, leave

arrogance n

pride, conceit, boasting, haughtiness, vanity, superciliousness, disdain, scorn, contempt, superiority, egotism, condescension, lordiness, pomposity, high-handedness, imperiousness, self-importance, snobbishness, presumption, insolence
OLD surquedry; (*Shakesp*) opinion
FORMAL hauteur, hubris, contumely
COLLOQ. nerve
SLANG side
▰ humility, unassumingness, bashfulness

arrogant adj

proud, conceited, boastful, full of yourself, haughty, supercilious, disdainful, scornful, contemptuous, superior, egotistic, condescending, patronizing, imperious, lordly, overbearing, overweening, high-handed, self-important, snobbish, presumptuous, assuming, insolent, on the high ropes; *dialect* cobby; *N Am* topping
OLD dangerous, stout, wanton
FORMAL hubristic
COLLOQ. bigheaded, stuck-up, high and mighty, uppity, toffee-nosed, hoity-toity
▰ humble, unassuming, bashful

arrogantly adv

proudly, conceitedly, boastfully, haughtily, superciliously, disdainfully, scornfully, contemptuously, condescendingly, patronizingly, imperiously, overbearingly, overweeningly, high-handedly, self-importantly, snobbishly, presumptuously, insolently
FORMAL hubristically
▰ humbly, bashfully

arrogate v

seize, usurp, assume, presume, take over, commandeer, misappropriate
FORMAL appropriate, possess yourself of

arrogation n

seizure, assumption, taking over, commandeering, possession
FORMAL appropriation

arrow n

1 *shoot with an arrow*
shaft, bolt, dart, flight
OLD quarrel, quar'le; (*Shakesp*) butt-shaft
Related adjective: sagittal
2 *follow the arrows*
marker, indicator, pointer

arsenal n

armoury, ordnance depot, ammunition dump, weapons, weaponry, magazine, (arms) depot, repository, stock, stockpile, garderobe

arson n

fire-raising, incendiarism, pyromania, firebombing

arsonist n

fire-raiser, incendiary, pyromaniac, firebomber
COLLOQ. firebug
SLANG *N Am* torch

art n

1 FINE ART, painting, sculpture, drawing, artwork, design, visual arts, craft, creative work, artistry, draughtsmanship, craftsmanship
2 SKILL, knack, technique, craft, method, aptitude, facility, talent, flair, gift, dexterity, finesse, ingenuity, mastery, expertise, virtuosity, adroitness, profession, trade
COLLOQ. knowhow
3 ARTFULNESS, cunning, craftiness, slyness, guile, deceit, trickery, astuteness, shrewdness, wiliness, sleight, daubery

---

Arts and crafts include:

animation	graphics	photography
animatronics	film	portraiture
architecture	fresco	pottery
batik	illustration	screenprinting
calligraphy	jewellery	sculpture
caricature	knitting	silk-screen
ceramics	lithography	printing
cloisonne	marquetry	sketching
collage	metalwork	spinning
crochet	modelling	stained glass
digital design	mosaic	tapestry
drawing	needlework	video
embroidery	oil painting	watercolour
enamelling	origami	weaving
engraving	painting	woodcarving
etching	patchwork	woodcraft

See also **embroidery**.

---

artefact n

thing, something, object, item, tool, piece of jewellery

artery n

See panel at **vein**.

artful adj

cunning, crafty, sly, foxy, wily, tricky, scheming, designing, deceitful, devious, subtle, sharp, shrewd, smart, clever, masterly, ingenious, resourceful, skilful, dexterous
OLD (*Shakesp*) cautel
FORMAL vulpine
▰ artless, naive, ingenuous

artfully adv

cunningly, craftily, slyly, deceitfully, deviously, shrewdly, cleverly, skilfully, ingeniously
▰ naively

article n

1 *articles in a magazine*
feature, report, story, account, piece, item, review, commentary, write-up, composition, essay,

---

Schools of art include:

abstract	classicism	The Glasgow	Naturalism	Pointillism	Rococo
action painting	Conceptual Art	Boys	the Nazarenes	Pop Art	Romanesque
Aestheticism	concrete art	Gothic	Neoclassicism	Post-	Romanticism
Art Brut	Constructivism	Hellenistic	Neo-	Impressionism	socialist realism
Art Deco	Cubism	Impressionism	expressionism	Post-Modernism	social realism
Art Nouveau	Dadaism	junk art	Neohellenism	Preraphaelite	Superrealism
Bauhaus	Etruscan art	Kinetic Art	Neo-	Brotherhood	Suprematism
Barbizon	Expressionism	Mannerism	impressionism	Primitivism	Surrealism
Baroque	Fauvism	magic realism	Neo-Plasticism	Purism	Symbolism
Bohemian	Florentine	medi(a)eval art	New Realism	quattrocento	tenebrism
Brit art	folk art	Minimal Art	Op Art	Rayonism	Venetian
Byzantine	Futurism	Modernism	Orphism	Realism	Vorticism
classical revival		the Nabis	plastic art	renaissance	

See also **painting; picture; sculpture**.

paper, monograph, offprint
2 ITEM, thing, something, object, commodity, unit, artefact, part, constituent, piece, portion
COLLOQ. thingummy, thingummyjig, thingummybob, what-d'you-call-it, whatsit
3 *article 25 of the contract*
paragraph, section, subsection, clause, point

articulate *adj, v*
♦ *adj*
distinct, well-spoken, eloquent, clear, lucid, intelligible, comprehensible, understandable, communicative, coherent, fluent, vocal, expressive, meaningful
F3 inarticulate, incoherent
♦ *v*
say, utter, speak, talk, express, give expression to, voice, vocalize, verbalize, state, frame, pronounce, enunciate, enounce, breathe

---

Synonym nuances
adjective
Distinct and **clear** are the most general and neutral terms to describe articulacy in expression, whereas to describe someone as **well-spoken** suggests approval of the grace and courtesy in their speech. **Eloquent** is also very admiring, this time of someone's expressive and fluent language. **Lucid** puts the focus on content and suggests that what you say is easily understood: *a beautifully lucid narrative*; likewise **intelligible**, **comprehensible** and **understandable** all simply suggest that something is capable of being understood, without any particular suggestion of approval.

The terms **communicative** and **vocal** are properly used of a person's willingness to put their views across, although you would be more likely to use **vocal** if you did not particularly approve of it. **Coherent** and **fluent** tend to be interpreted as terms of praise; likewise **expressive** and **meaningful**, although these would put the emphasis again on the content of what is being said, rather than the delivery.

---

articulated *adj*
coupled, linked, hinged, interlocked, joined, attached, connected, fastened, segmented, fitted together, joint, jointed

articulately *adv*
distinctly, clearly, eloquently, lucidly, intelligibly, comprehensibly, coherently, fluently, expressively
F3 inarticulately, incoherently

articulation *n*
1 *a speaker with clear articulation*
saying, utterance, speaking, talking, expression, voicing, vocalization, verbalization, pronunciation, enunciation, diction, delivery
2 CONNECTION, junction, coupling
TECHNICAL arthrosis, diarthrosis, schindylesis, clavation

artifice *n*
1 TRICK, device, dodge, ruse, scheme, stratagem, strategy, subterfuge, tactic, wile, contrivance
COLLOQ. set-up, scam, con
2 DECEIT, trickery, artfulness, deception, deceit, deviousness, fraud, guile, craft, craftiness, cunning, slyness, subtlety, chicanery, cleverness

artificial *adj*
1 *artificial flowers*
synthetic, imitation, mock, faux, plastic, man-made, manufactured, simulated, non-natural, unnatural, processed
2 *an artificial smile*
false, fake, bogus, counterfeit, spurious, specious, sham, insincere, assumed, affected, mannered, studied, forced, contrived, made-up, feigned, pretended, simulated
COLLOQ. phoney, pseudo, pseud
F3 1 natural, real **2** genuine

Synonym nuances
sense 1
All the synonyms for artificial can be negative in tone, depending on the context; **synthetic** and **simulated** are perhaps the least inherently marked: *a simulated coal fire*. **Imitation**, **mock** and **faux**, on the other hand, while they may be used without implication, can also be suggestive of cheap imitations of more luxurious fabrics, and so hint at bad taste. Similarly, if you describe something as **plastic**, it may well be made of plastic, or you may wish to imply that is unattractively artificial. **Man-made** tends to be used widely and neutrally of materials that have been developed by man; whereas **manufactured** can also be used in various contexts to suggest undesirable artificiality: *manufactured pop bands and their manufactured songs*.

Describing something as **non-natural** unavoidably conveys the powerful, negative suggestion that it is not produced by or according to nature: *the non-natural use of land*; **unnatural** is even more marked in that it suggests being totally at odds with nature: *how unnatural our lifestyles have become*. The term **processed** is most commonly used of foodstuffs; while not particularly marked in itself, again the context may lend it a negative connotation.

---

artificiality *n*
1 UNNATURALNESS, simulation
2 FALSITY, spuriousness, insincerity, pretence, sham, speciousness

artificially *adv*
1 SYNTHETICALLY, unnaturally
2 FALSELY, spuriously, insincerely, speciously

artillery *n*
heavy guns, heavy weapons, guns, weapons, ordnance, cannons, munitions

artisan *n*
craftsperson, craftsman, craftswoman, artificer, journeyman, expert, skilled worker, mechanic, technician, operative
Related adjective: banausic

artist *n*
1 CREATOR, maker, inventor, designer, architect, founder, author, writer, poet, originator, composer, musician, actor, dancer, painter, sculptor
2 EXPERT, specialist, authority, professional, maestro; *N Am* maven, mavin
COLLOQ. dab hand, pro, ace

! **artist** or **artiste**?
An *artist* is someone who paints pictures or is skilled in one of the fine arts. An *artiste*, or *artist*, is a performer in a theatre or circus or on television; *artiste* is now regarded as old-fashioned or affected.

Types of artist include:

animator	draughtswoman	painter
architect	engraver	photographer
blacksmith	etcher	portraitist
caricaturist	goldsmith	potter
carpenter	graphic artist	printer
cartoonist	graphic designer	screenprinter
craftsman	illustrator	sculptor
craftswoman	lithographer	silversmith
designer	master	watercolourist
draughtsman	oil painter	weaver

---

artiste *n*
performer, entertainer, variety artist, vaudevillian, comic, comedian, comedienne, player, trouper, actor, actress, dancer, musician, singer

artistic *adj*
1 *an artistic person*
creative, sensitive, refined, cultured, original, expressive, gifted, cultivated, skilled, talented, imaginative
2 *an artistic design*
aesthetic, ornamental, decorative, beautiful, attractive, fine, exquisite, elegant, stylish, tasteful, graceful, harmonious
F3 2 inelegant

artistry *n*
craftsmanship, workmanship, skill, craft, talent, flair, ability, brilliance, genius, finesse, style, mastery, expertise, proficiency, accomplishment, deftness, touch, sensitivity, creativity
F3 ineptitude

artless *adj*
simple, natural, unpretentious, genuine, guileless, honest, ingenuous, sincere, straightforward, open, plain, pure, childlike, innocent, naive, direct, frank, candid, true, trusting, unsophisticated, unwary, unworldly
F3 artful, cunning

artlessly *adv*
simply, naturally, unpretentiously, purely, innocently, naively, ingenuously, sincerely, straightforwardly, directly, frankly, openly, plainly, candidly, truly
F3 artfully, cunningly

as *conj, prep*
♦ *conj*
1 WHILE, when, just as, whilst, at the same time (that/as), simultaneously
2 SUCH AS, for example, for instance, like
3 IN THE SAME MANNER THAT, in the same way that, like
4 BECAUSE, since, seeing that, considering that, inasmuch as, being, the reason is …, through, on account of, as a result of, owing to
OLD forasmuch
♦ *prep*
1 *work as a taxi-driver*
in the role of, with the part of, functioning as
2 *dressed as a man*
like, similar to, with the appearance of, in the guise of
▪ **as for**
with reference to, as regards, with regard to, on the subject of, in connection with, in relation to, with relation to, concerning, respecting, with respect to, apropos
▪ **as it were**
so to speak, in a manner of speaking, in a way, in some way, so to say, as it might be
▪ **as yet**
so far, up to now, up to this point, up to the present moment, till now
OLD hitherto
FORMAL thus far

ascend *v*
rise, take off, lift off, go up, come up, move up, gain height, slope upwards, climb, scale, mount, tower, float up, fly up, soar, arise
F3 descend, go down

ascendancy *n*
dominance, domination, authority, command, control, power, dominion, superiority, lordship, mastery, supremacy, edge, predominance, pre-eminence, influence, prevalence, sway
FORMAL hegemony
COLLOQ. upper hand
F3 decline, subordination

ascendant *adj*
dominant, powerful, rising in power, superior, predominant, prevalent, growing, developing
COLLOQ. on the up and up

ascent *n*
1 ASCENDING, ascension, climb, climbing, scaling, escalation, rise, rising, mounting
2 SLOPE, gradient, incline, ramp, hill, elevation, rise
FORMAL acclivity
3 *their rapid ascent to power*
rise, advance, progress
FORMAL advancement
F3 1 descent

ascertain *v*
find out, learn, discover, get to know, come to know, determine, fix, establish, settle, locate, detect, identify, verify, confirm, make certain
COLLOQ. suss out, twig, pin down

ascetic *adj, n*
♦ *adj*
self-denying, self-disciplined, austere, abstemious, abstinent, self-controlled, stern, strict, severe, rigorous, harsh, plain, puritanical, spartan
♦ *n*
hermit, recluse, solitary, anchorite, abstainer, celibate, monk, nun, puritan, stylite, pillarist, Nazarite, fakir, dervish, yogi, sadhu, sannyasi, Jainist, Montanist

asceticism *n*
self-denial, self-discipline, austerity, severity, harshness, self-control, abstinence, monasticism, ascesis

ascribe *v*
attribute, credit, give credit to, put down, assign, charge
FORMAL accredit, impute

ash *n*
embers, cinders, charcoal, residue
Related adjectives: cinereal, cinerary

ashamed *adj*
1 *ashamed of your behaviour*
sorry, apologetic, remorseful, contrite, guilty, conscience-stricken, sheepish, embarrassed, blushing, red-faced, mortified, humiliated, discomfited, abashed, humbled, crestfallen, distressed, discomposed, shamefaced, penitent
COLLOQ. not able to look someone in the face, having your tail between your legs, on a guilt trip
2 *ashamed to admit his mistakes*
reluctant, hesitant, unwilling, loath, self-conscious, bashful, modest
F3 1 shameless, proud, defiant **2** proud

Synonym nuances
sense 1
The words **sorry** and **apologetic** imply an acknowledgement of guilt, and are used where regret is being expressed. **Guilty** suggests shame that is felt rather than expressed, as do the more intense terms **remorseful**, **penitent** and **conscience-stricken**, which are appropriate to describe a deep, burdensome guilt: *police found the remorseful robber desperate to give himself up.* When you want to emphasize someone's embarrassment, you are more likely to use words such as **sheepish**, **embarrassed** or **abashed**; and **blushing** and **red-faced** could also be used of comparatively mild embarrassment. The stronger terms **shame-faced** and **crestfallen** again suggest physical displays of embarrassment, but with connotations of a deeper, moral ashamedness, while **mortified** and **humiliated** are stronger again, and can be used of a crippling embarrassment. **Humbled**, on the other hand, would be used in a context where you have been made to feel low by your shame, but can learn moral lessons from it: *he was humbled in the face of their selflessness*. If shame has led to a loss of composure, the words **discomfited** and **discomposed** could be used. **Distressed**, however, would be reserved to describe someone whose shame is causing mental pain.

ashen *adj*
pallid, pale, pale-faced, pasty, wan, white, anaemic,
blanched, bleached, colourless, ghastly, grey, leaden, livid,
pallid
F∃ ruddy

ashore *adv*
onto the shore, onto the beach, onto the land, towards the
shore

aside *adv, n*
• *adv*
1 *move aside*
to one side, on one side, alongside, apart, away, out of the
way, separately, in isolation, alone, privately, secretly
2 *his money aside*
apart
FORMAL notwithstanding
• *n*
digression, parenthesis, incidental remark, cursory remark,
departure, soliloquy, monologue, stage whisper, whisper
FORMAL apostrophe, *obiter dictum*

asinine *adj*
silly, stupid, foolish, senseless, nonsensical, idiotic,
ludicrous, moronic, imbecilic, absurd, half-witted, fatuous,
inane
COLLOQ. crazy, daft, potty, gormless
F∃ intelligent, sensible

ask *v*
1 *ask a question*
inquire, enquire, query, question, put a question to, pose,
put forward, propose, want to know the answer to,
interrogate, propose, suggest, cross-examine, cross-
question, poll, canvass, interview, press; *Scot* speir
OLD yearn
FORMAL posit, postulate, propound
COLLOQ. grill, give a grilling to, fire off, give someone the
third degree, pump, quiz, put on the spot
2 *ask for advice*
request, appeal, petition, sue, plead, beg, entreat, implore,
clamour, pray, crave, demand, order, bid, require, seek,
approach, solicit, invite, summon, requisition; *Aust* put the
hard word on
OLD beseech, bespeak
FORMAL supplicate
3 *ask them to dinner*
invite, have round/over, entertain

Synonym nuances
sense 1
The word **inquire** is a fairly formal but neutral term to use in
situations where someone is asking for, or seeking,
information. **Question** can be used of someone asking
questions but, like **query**, it can also imply that they are in
some doubt about information they have already received:
he queried Miller's description. You would use the terms
pose, put forward or **propose** when someone has a
specific question to ask or proposal to advance. If you use
suggest, this also implies putting some proposition before
people but with, perhaps, less assurance.
  The term **press** has a tone of urgency, and suggests that
you are urgently entreating someone for their response,
before they are really willing to give it: *when pressed upon
the issue he admitted the deal.* Generally **interrogate,
cross-examine** and **cross-question** would be used in
official contexts, but they may also be used more widely to
suggest any thorough and intense questioning, particularly
with an air of intimidation.
  Interview, while still with an element of formality and used
in official contexts, is less threatening in tone. **Poll** and
canvass are generally confined to a process of questioning
a group of people for their views: *an obvious and
frequently canvassed solution.*

---

askance *adv*
suspiciously, disapprovingly, contemptuously, scornfully,
disdainfully, distrustfully, doubtfully, dubiously,
mistrustfully, sceptically, indirectly, sideways, obliquely
OLD asconce

askew *adv, adj*
crooked(ly), lopsided(ly), sideways, oblique(ly), at an
oblique angle, off-centre, out of line, asymmetrical(ly),
squint, tipsy; *Scot* agley
OLD *Scot* skivie
COLLOQ. skew, skew-whiff
F∃ straight, level

asleep *adj*
sleeping, napping, snoozing, fast asleep, sound asleep,
resting, inactive, inert, unconscious, numb, dozing
FORMAL dormant, reposing
COLLOQ. flaked out, nodded off, popped off, crashed out,
conked out, comatose, dead to the world, out like a light,
out for the count, having forty winks, in the land of Nod
SLANG sparked out

aspect *n*
1 *many aspects of life*
angle, direction, side, facet, feature, point, factor,
dimension, position, standpoint, point of view, view,
outlook, light
2 *take on a more promising aspect*
appearance, look, air, manner, bearing, face, expression,
countenance
3 *a house with a northern aspect*
direction, position, standpoint, point of view, view,
outlook

asperity *n*
sharpness, acerbity, harshness, roughness, severity,
acrimony, astringency, abrasiveness, bitterness,
churlishness, crabbedness, crossness, irascibility,
irritability, peevishness, sourness
FORMAL causticity
F∃ mildness

aspersion
▪ **cast aspersions on**
make critical comments about, criticize, slate, censure,
defame, reproach, run down, slander
FORMAL disparage, denigrate, deprecate, vilify, calumniate
COLLOQ. throw/sling mud at, slur, smear, knock, haul over
the coals
F∃ commend, compliment

asphyxiate *v*
suffocate, choke, smother, stifle, strangle, strangulate,
throttle

asphyxiation *n*
suffocation, strangulation, choking, smothering, stifling

aspiration *n*
aim, intent, purpose, endeavour, object, objective, goal,
ambition, hope, dream, ideal, wish, desire, yearning,
longing, craving, hankering
COLLOQ. yen

aspire *v*
aim, intend, purpose, seek, pursue, hope, dream, wish,
have as an ambition/aim/goal, desire, yearn, long, crave,
hanker
COLLOQ. yen

aspiring *adj*
would-be, aspirant, striving, endeavouring, ambitious,
enterprising, budding, keen, eager, intending, hopeful,
optimistic, wishful, longing

ass *n*
1 *ride an ass*
donkey, mule, burro, hinny, jackass, pony, neddy; *Scot*
cuddy

COLLOQ. moke
2 *call someone an ass*
fool, idiot, imbecile, halfwit, oaf, innocent, buffoon, clot, gull, lemming, neddy, jackass, muggins, soft, want-wit, mooncalf, Tom-noddy; *dialect* mumchance; *Scot* gowk, sumph, coof, dottle, numpty; *N Am* cluck, dumb-cluck, yap
OLD capocchia, cony, natural, nidget, fon, fondling, lack-brain, patch, snipe, sot, wigeon
COLLOQ. blockhead, nincompoop, ninny, nitwit, nit, mug, numskull, twerp, twit, dimwit, cretin, knuckle-head, lame brain, proper Charlie, dope, gubbins, saphead; *Scot* bampot; *N Am* lunkhead; *Aust* dill
SLANG wally, dipstick, nerd, plonker, dork, geek, git, prat, goop, berk, nerk, dickhead, airhead, dweeb, joss, nana, nig-nog, sawney, schlemiel, turkey, yo-yo; *Irish* omadhaun; *N Am* klutz, jughead, schmo, flathead; *Aust* galah, drongo; *Aust & NZ* nong
OLD SLANG cake
Related adjective: asinine

assail *v*
1 *assailed by the newspapers/foreign army*
attack, criticize, slate, lay into, set about, set upon, run down, malign, maltreat, strike, invade, bombard
COLLOQ. tear into, slam, rubbish, badmouth, slag off
2 *assailed by doubts*
beset, plague, worry, trouble, torment, disturb, bedevil, perplex

assailant *n*
attacker, invader, opponent, adversary, enemy, aggressor, assailer, assaulter, abuser, reviler
COLLOQ. mugger

assassin *n*
murderer, killer, slayer, cut-throat, executioner, gunman
COLLOQ. hatchet man, liquidator, contract man, hit-man

assassinate *v*
murder, kill, slay, slaughter, execute, dispatch, take someone's life
COLLOQ. eliminate, liquidate, hit, bump off, do in

assassination *n*
murder, killing, slaughter, execution, termination

assault *n, v*
♦ *n*
1 ATTACK, offensive, onslaught, blitz, strike, raid, invasion, incursion, storm, storming, charge, act of aggression
2 *charged with assault*
battery, violent act, grievous bodily harm, rape, abuse, molestation
COLLOQ. GBH, mugging
♦ *v*
attack, charge, invade, strike, hit, set upon, fall on, rape, molest, interfere with, abuse, bombard
OLD smite
COLLOQ. go for, lay into, beat up, do over, mug

assay *n*
test, evaluation, assessment, analysis, check, examination, inspection, judgement
FORMAL appraisal

assemblage *n*
accumulation, collection, gathering, group, mass, multitude, rally, crowd, flock, throng

assemble *v*
1 GATHER, congregate, muster, summon(s), rally, convene, meet, join up, flock, group, collect, accumulate, amass, bring/come together, get together, rendezvous, round up, marshal, mobilize, mass
OLD relide, troop
FORMAL convoke
2 CONSTRUCT, build, put together, piece together, fit

together, compose, make, connect, join, fabricate, manufacture, set up, collate
E3 1 scatter, disperse **2** dismantle

assembly *n*
1 GATHERING, rally, meeting, convention, conference, congress, council, audience, chamber, court, plenum, group, body, body of people, company, congregation, flock, crowd, multitude, throng, collection
TECHNICAL synod, chapter, synagogue, synedrion, diet, Majlis, volksraad, gorsedd, indaba, kgotla
OLD agora, consistory, divan, ecclesia, moot, folkmoot, presence, frequence, gemot, thing
FORMAL convocation, panegyry, assemblage, concourse
See panel at **parliaments and political assemblies**.
2 CONSTRUCTION, building, fabrication, manufacture, putting together, piecing together

assent *v, n*
♦ *v*
agree, approve, accept, comply, allow, consent, grant, permit, sanction, submit, subscribe, yield
FORMAL accede, acquiesce, concede, concur
COLLOQ. buy, give the thumbs-up, give the go-ahead, give the green light
E3 disagree
♦ *n*
agreement, approval, acceptance, capitulation, concession, consent, permission, sanction, submission, compliance
FORMAL accord, acquiescence, concurrence, approbation
COLLOQ. thumbs-up, go-ahead, green light

Synonym nuances
verb
You can use **agree** as a general term to show that two parties share the same opinion; **concur** is a more formal word to express the same. The word **approve**, however, intimates that you are in a position of some power and your decision has an important part to play: *the acquisition of the stores was approved by the shareholders*. Similarly, **consent**, **permit** and **sanction** imply that others await your authorization before proceeding, with the latter used in more official contexts. **Accept** also indicates affirmation but with an element of reluctance suggested.
  If you use **allow** you go further by giving the impression of surrender: *he allowed that legislation could restrict liberty*, whereas the term **grant** implies an element of equanimity in the decision. The word **submit** could be used to imply deference to the decision of another, while **yield** gives a stronger suggestion of defeat. On the other hand, **subscribe** suggests not only agreement but also support, although it is often used in the negative: *few engineers subscribe to this theory*.
  Meanwhile, **accede**, **acquiesce**, **comply** and **concede** all return to the idea of reluctance to assent to something, or succumbing to the will of another.

---

assert *v*
1 *assert a fact*
declare, state, pronounce, profess, affirm, confirm, attest, argue, swear, testify to
FORMAL predicate
2 *assert your rights*
maintain, insist on, establish, stress, protest, defend, vindicate, uphold, claim, stand up for, contend, pose, lay down
OLD avouch
COLLOQ. crack the whip
E3 1 deny, refute
■ **assert yourself**
behave confidently, put yourself forward, make your

presence felt, make your voice heard, make people sit up and take notice, make people sit up and listen

assertion *n*
affirmation, attestation, word, allegation, claim, contention, insistence, vindication, declaration, profession, statement, pronouncement; *Scot* threap
FORMAL averment, avowal, predication, constatation
F⅃ denial

assertive *adj*
bold, confident, self-confident, self-assured, sure of yourself, positive, forward, insistent, emphatic, forceful, firm, decided, strong-willed, determined, dogmatic, opinionated, presumptuous, assuming, overbearing, domineering, dominant, aggressive, pushy
COLLOQ. not backward in coming forward; *N Am* feeling your oats
F⅃ timid, diffident

Synonym nuances
Bold can be used to suggest assertiveness but is also imbued with a hint of risk-taking: *his bold, almost visionary, ideas*. **Confident**, however, along with **self-confident** and **self-assured**, is widely used to describe someone who is sure of their capabilities, as does **sure of yourself**, although this also hints at cockiness. The word **positive** can be generally used to describe someone who exhibits certainty, but if their certainty progresses to impudence, you could use the term **forward**.

  Insistent, **emphatic** or **forceful** are more typically used to describe the way someone imparts their ideas and opinions, if they display no doubts that they are correct. The words **firm**, **decided**, **strong-willed** and **determined** are used slightly differently, usually to describe someone who is convinced of their opinions and will not be moved from them, rather than someone who wants to inflict them on others. **Dogmatic** and **opinionated** again imply certainty of opinion, but with the inference that there is an unreasonable element to their assertions. You would generally use the terms **presumptuous** and **assuming** when you wish to suggest that someone's certainty has to do with their expectations of others: *isn't it rather presumptuous to decide what he needs?*

  On the other hand, to use the descriptions **overbearing**, **domineering** or **dominant** would suggest that someone uses the sheer force of their personality, to get the consensus they seek: *she was intimidated by his overbearing attitude*. **Aggressive**, meanwhile, although similar, goes further by implying that a more menacing approach could be deployed.

---

assertively *adv*
boldly, confidently, self-confidently, positively, insistently, firmly, forcefully, presumptuously, dominantly, aggressively
F⅃ timidly

assess *v*
1 *assess a situation*
evaluate, gauge, estimate, appraise, review, judge, consider, weigh, size up, sum up
OLD cense
COLLOQ. check out
2 *assess the value of something*
compute, calculate, determine, estimate, fix, value, rate, tax, levy, impose, demand, teind; *Scot* stent
OLD assize, affeer

assessment *n*
1 *the assessment of a situation*
evaluation, estimation, appraisal, review, testing, judgement, consideration, opinion
COLLOQ. recce

2 *a tax assessment*
levy, computation, valuation, rate, toll, tariff, imposition, demand

assessor *n*
1 VALUER, estimator, measurer, gauger, valuator, appraiser
2 JUDGE, reviewer, examiner, inspector, arbitrator, arbiter, adjudicator, umpire, referee, estimator, recorder, expert, adviser, consultant, counsellor

asset *n*
1 *an asset to the school*
strength, strong point, resource, virtue, benefit, advantage, blessing, boon, help, aid, liability
COLLOQ. plus, plus point
2 *the assets of a company*
estate, property, possessions, goods, holdings, securities, money, wealth, capital, funds, reserves, savings, valuables, resources, means

asseverate *v*
declare, affirm, assert, claim, profess, maintain, state, confirm
FORMAL aver, avow, attest

assiduous *adj*
industrious, diligent, hard-working, careful, meticulous, conscientious, constant, dedicated, devoted, attentive, persevering, persistent, steady, studious, thorough, unflagging, indefatigable, untiring
FORMAL sedulous
F⅃ negligent

assiduity *n*
diligence, industry, industriousness, meticulousness, hard work, conscientiousness, dedication, devotion, constancy, perseverance, persistence, indefatigability
FORMAL sedulity
F⅃ laziness

assign *v*
1 ALLOCATE, grant, give, dispense, distribute, allot, hive off
OLD aret; (*Shakesp*) sort
FORMAL apportion
2 *a social worker is assigned to each family*
detail, delegate, name, nominate, designate, appoint, choose, select, commission, install, determine, set, fix, specify, stipulate, range, rank, station
FORMAL consign, adjudge
3 ATTRIBUTE, ascribe, put down
FORMAL accredit, impute, arrogate
COLLOQ. chalk up to
4 TRANSFER, grant, make over, hand over, consign, transmit
TECHNICAL convey

assignation *n*
secret meeting, appointment, arrangement, date, engagement, rendezvous
OLD tryst

assignment *n*
1 *written assignments*
task, project, job, position, post, duty, responsibility, obligation, commission, errand, charge
2 *his assignment to the job*
appointment, delegation, designation, nomination, selection, allocation, consignment, grant, distribution
3 TRANSFER, grant, consignment
TECHNICAL conveyance, disposition

assimilate *v*
1 *assimilate new ideas*
ABSORB, take in, pick up, incorporate, imbibe, internalize, learn, grasp
2 INTEGRATE, absorb, blend, mix, mingle, unite, accustom, adapt, adjust, acclimatize
FORMAL accommodate
F⅃ 1, 2 reject

assimilation *n*
1 INTEGRATION, blending, mixing in, adaptation, adjustment, acclimatization
FORMAL accommodation
2 ABSORPTION, learning, grasping, taking in, internalization, incorporation
TECHNICAL osmosis, resorption

assist *v*
1 *assist with someone's work/expenses*
help, aid, give/lend a hand, lend a helping hand, abet, rally round, co-operate, collaborate, back (up), second, support, reinforce, sustain, relieve
FORMAL succour
COLLOQ. do your bit, give a leg up to, pitch in
2 *assist in the operation of a task*
facilitate, make easier, expedite, benefit, encourage, serve, aid, enable, further, advance
F3 1 hinder **2** thwart

assistance *n*
help, aid, co-operation, collaboration, backing, support, reinforcement, relief, benefit, service, boost, furtherance
COLLOQ. a helping hand, a leg up
FORMAL succour
F3 hindrance, resistance

assistant *n*
1 DEPUTY, subordinate, right-hand man, auxiliary, ancillary, backer, second, second-in-command, supporter, driving force
2 *a personal assistant*
helper, aide, accomplice, accessory, abettor, collaborator, colleague, partner, ally, confederate, associate, acolyte
TECHNICAL amanuensis, suffragan
3 *a shop assistant*
salesperson, salesman, saleswoman, checkout person; *N Am* sales clerk

associate *v, n*
♦ *v*
1 CONNECT, link, think of together, couple, pair, identify
OLD mell
FORMAL correlate, consociate
COLLOQ. speak of in the same breath, go hand in hand
2 *associate with bad company*
socialize, mingle, mix, keep company, fraternize, haunt, be involved
FORMAL consort
COLLOQ. hang around/about, pal, hobnob, rub shoulders
3 AFFILIATE, confederate, ally, league, join, amalgamate, combine, unite, link, connect, relate, couple, attach, band together, syndicate, yoke
♦ *n*
partner, ally, confederate, affiliate, collaborator, co-worker, mate, colleague, peer, compeer, fellow, comrade, companion, friend, assistant, helper, follower, confrère, yokefellow
COLLOQ. sidekick, mate, pal, crony

associated *adj*
1 CONNECTED, linked, coupled, related, corresponding, similar, alike
FORMAL correlated
2 AFFILIATED, allied, amalgamated, confederated, combined, linked, in league, in partnership, related, syndicated

association *n*
1 ORGANIZATION, corporation, company, partnership, league, alliance, coalition, confederation, confederacy, federation, affiliation, consortium, cartel, syndicate, union, society, club, fraternity, fellowship, guild, clique, group, band
FORMAL sodality
2 BOND, tie, connection, link, correlation, relation, relationship, interrelation, involvement, intimacy, friendship, companionship, familiarity, identification

assorted *adj*
miscellaneous, mixed, varied, different, differing, diverse, sundry, motley, various, several, manifold, sortable
OLD divers, farraginous
FORMAL variegated, heterogeneous, multifarious

assortment *n*
miscellany, medley, potpourri, jumble, mix, mixture, variety, diversity, collection, selection, choice, arrangement, group(ing), lot, bunch, salmagundi, olla-podrida, smörgåsbord, farrago
FORMAL array

assuage *v*
1 *assuage grief/pain*
relieve, ease, lessen, reduce, soften, allay, alleviate, calm, lighten, lower, lull, mitigate, moderate, soothe, mollify, pacify, palliate
2 *assuage your thirst*
alleviate, quench, satisfy, appease
FORMAL slake
F3 1 exacerbate, worsen

assume *v*
1 PRESUME, accept, take for granted, take as read, expect, understand, deduce, infer, guess, suppose, presuppose, think, believe, imagine, fancy
FORMAL surmise, postulate
COLLOQ. take it ..., take someone's word for it
2 AFFECT, take on, feign, counterfeit, simulate, put on, pretend
3 *assume great importance*
take on, adopt, come to have, acquire
4 *assume command*
undertake, adopt, enter upon, take upon yourself, accept, bear, shoulder, embrace, seize, arrogate, commandeer, appropriate, usurp, pre-empt, take over

---

Synonym nuances
sense 1
You could use **presume** to imply that a supposition has been formed without any proof: *one man missing, presumed dead*. Similarly the terms **accept**, **take for granted**, **take as read** and **expect** all suggest an element of presumption but with a more passive or unconscious aspect: *she had always taken for granted that unemployment was an evil*.
However, if you use the terms **understand**, **deduce** and **infer** you are suggesting that any assumptions made have been reached by assessment of facts: *the occupational structure of the town can be deduced from the registers*. The opposite may be said of **guess** and **believe**, which imply conjecture or instinct rather than reason; similarly **imagine** and **fancy** eschew reason completely in favour of imagination: *sometimes he fancied a ghost in the room*.
When you use **suppose** you may suggest that something has been assumed provisionally, for argument's sake whilst **presuppose**, although similar in meaning, tends to be used in philosophical or theoretical contexts: *the principle of non-discrimination presupposed the existence of the concept of nationality*.

---

assumed *adj*
false, bogus, counterfeit, fake, sham, affected, feigned, simulated, pretended, made-up, fictitious, hypothetical
FORMAL supposititious, putative, pseudonymous
COLLOQ. phoney
F3 true, real, actual

assumption *n*
1 *make an assumption*
presumption, surmise, inference, conclusion, supposition,

presupposition, guess, conjecture, theory, hypothesis, premise, postulate, idea, notion, axiom, belief, expectation, fancy
FORMAL postulation
2 *her assumption of power*
undertaking, adoption, taking upon yourself, embarkation, acceptance, shouldering, embrace, seizure, commandeering, takeover
FORMAL arrogation, appropriation, usurpation, pre-emption

assurance *n*
1 GUARANTEE, pledge, promise, security, vow, declaration, affirmation, assertion, word, certainty, undertaking, oath
OLD (*Shakesp*) surance
FORMAL positivism
2 CONFIDENCE, self-confidence, self-assurance, assuredness, aplomb, boldness, self-reliance, belief in yourself, audacity, courage, nerve, conviction, sureness, certainty, nerve, gall
COLLOQ. unflappability
E3 2 shyness, doubt, uncertainty

assure *v*
1 *assured me he would be safe*
convince, persuade, encourage, hearten, reassure, soothe, comfort, tell
OLD resolve
2 *success is assured*
guarantee, warrant, pledge, promise, seal, secure, ensure, confirm, affirm, vow, swear, certify; *Scot* hight
OLD avouch
FORMAL attest

assured *adj*
1 SURE, certain, indisputable, irrefutable, confirmed, promised, positive, definite, settled, fixed, ensured, guaranteed, secure
COLLOQ. cut and dried
2 SELF-ASSURED, confident, calm, self-confident, self-possessed, sure of yourself, bold, audacious, assertive
E3 1 uncertain **2** shy, bashful

assuredly *adv*
certainly, definitely, surely, indisputably, without doubt, without question, unquestionably
OLD (*Shakesp & Spenser*) perdie

astonish *v*
surprise, startle, amaze, astound, stun, stupefy, daze, stagger, dumbfound, take aback, take your breath away, shock, confound, bewilder
OLD stony
COLLOQ. floor, flabbergast, flummox, bowl over, gobsmack, blow your mind, knock for six, wow, make someone's hair stand on end, set back on your heels

astonished *adj*
surprised, startled, amazed, astounded, stunned, dazed, staggered, dumbfounded, taken aback, shocked, confounded, bewildered, open-eyed, wide-eyed
COLLOQ. lost for words, knocked for six, bowled over, flabbergasted, gobsmacked, thunderstruck

astonishing *adj*
surprising, startling, amazing, astounding, stunning, breathtaking, impressive, striking, staggering, shocking, bewildering
COLLOQ. mind-boggling

astonishment *n*
surprise, amazement, shock, disbelief, dismay, consternation, confusion, bewilderment, wonder
FORMAL stupefaction, wonderment

astound *v*
surprise, startle, amaze, astonish, stun, take your breath away, stupefy, overwhelm, shock, bewilder
COLLOQ. knock for six, floor, flummox, bowl over

astounding *adj*
surprising, startling, amazing, astonishing, stunning, breathtaking, stupefying, overwhelming, staggering, shocking, bewildering

astray *adv*
1 *lead someone astray*
into bad/foolish/wrong behaviour, off the straight and narrow
COLLOQ. off the rails
2 ADRIFT, off course, lost, missing, miss, amiss, wrong, awry, off the mark
OLD abroad, agate; (*Spenser*) miswandred

astringent *adj*
1 *an astringent liquid*
acerbic, acid, caustic
TECHNICAL styptic
2 *astringent criticism*
caustic, biting, trenchant, scathing, hard, harsh, critical, severe, stern
FORMAL mordant
E3 1, 2 bland

astronaut *n*
spaceman, spacewoman, space traveller, cosmonaut

astronomical *adj*
1 *the cost is astronomical*
enormous, huge, immense, vast, substantial, considerable, gigantic, massive, colossal, mammoth, tremendous, immeasurable, infinite
COLLOQ. whopping, thumping
2 *astronomical observations*
cosmological, cosmic, celestial, heavenly, stellar, interstellar, planetary

astute *adj*
shrewd, prudent, wise, canny, knowing, intelligent, sharp, sharp-witted, penetrating, keen, perceptive, discerning, subtle, clever, crafty, cunning, cute, sly, wily
FORMAL perspicacious, sagacious
SLANG wide
E3 stupid, slow

astutely *adv*
shrewdly, wisely, intelligently, keenly, sharp-wittedly, perceptively, craftily

asunder *adv*
in two, in pieces, to pieces, up

asylum *n*
1 *seek political asylum*
haven, sanctuary, refuge, shelter, retreat, place of safety
OLD frithsoken, grith
COLLOQ. port in a storm
2 *an asylum for the mentally ill*
mental hospital, psychiatric hospital, institution, Magdalen
OLD bedlam; (*Shakesp*) dark-house
SLANG funny farm, loony bin, bin, madhouse, nuthouse

asymmetrical *adj*
unsymmetrical, unbalanced, uneven, lopsided, crooked, awry, unequal, disproportionate, irregular, distorted, malformed
TECHNICAL anaxial
E3 symmetrical

asymmetry *n*
imbalance, unevenness, unsymmetry, crookedness, lopsidedness, inequality, disproportionateness, irregularity, distortion, malformation
E3 symmetry

atheism *n*
unbelief, non-belief, disbelief, scepticism, irreligion, ungodliness, godlessness, impiety, infidelity, paganism,

heathenism, freethinking, rationalism
TECHNICAL nihilism

atheist *n*
unbeliever, non-believer, humanist, rationalist, disbeliever, sceptic, infidel, heretic, pagan, heathen, freethinker
TECHNICAL nihilist
FORMAL nullifidian

athlete *n*
sportsman, sportswoman, runner, gymnast, competitor, contestant, contender, player

athletic *adj*
1 *an athletic person*
fit, energetic, vigorous, active, sporty, muscular, muscly, sinewy, brawny, strapping, robust, sturdy, strong, powerful, well-knit, well-proportioned, wiry
2 *athletic events*
sports, sporting, gymnastic, games
🔁 **1** puny

athletics *n*
sports, games, matches, races, track events, field events, exercises, gymnastics
TECHNICAL aerobics, callisthenics

Athletic events include:

TRACK EVENTS:		ROAD EVENTS:
sprint (100m, 200m and 400m)	relay	half-marathon
	steeplechase	marathon
	FIELD EVENTS:	race walking
middle-distance running (800m and 1500m)	high jump	COMBINED EVENTS:
	long jump	triathlon
	triple jump	heptathlon
long-distance running (3000m, 5000m and 10000m)	pole vault	decathlon
	discus	MISCELLANEOUS:
	hammer	cross-country running
hurdles	javelin	
	shot put	

---

atmosphere *n*
1 AIR, sky, aerospace, heavens, ether
OLD firmament, empyrean, welkin
FORMAL vault of heaven
Related adjective: epedaphic
2 AMBIENCE, environment, surroundings, setting, milieu, background, air, aura, feel, feeling, mood, climate, spirit, tone, tenor, character, quality, flavour
COLLOQ. vibes

The different layers of the atmosphere are:

troposphere	mesosphere	ionosphere
stratosphere	thermosphere	exosphere

---

atom *n*
molecule, particle, bit, morsel, crumb, fragment, grain, spot, speck, mite, shred, scrap, hint, trace, scintilla, jot, iota, whit

---

Subatomic particles include:

anti-neutrino	lambda particle	positron
anti-neutron	lepton	proton
anti-proton	meson (X particle)	psi particle
baryon		quark
B-meson	muon	sigma particle
boson	neutrino	tau
electron	neutron	W particle
gluon	omega particle	Z particle
hadron	photon	
kaon	pion	

---

atone *v*
make amends, pay for, remedy, indemnify, reconcile, repent, compensate, recompense, make up for, make right, make good, make reparation, offset, redeem, redress, appease, satisfy, propitiate, expiate
OLD aby

atonement *n*
amends, reparation, repayment, reimbursement, ransom, redemption, requital, restitution, restoration, satisfaction, compensation, indemnity, payment, penance, recompense, redress, appeasement, propitiation, expiation
TECHNICAL acceptilation
COLLOQ. eye for an eye

atrocious *adj*
1 *atrocious behaviour*
shocking, appalling, abominable, dreadful, terrible, horrible, horrendous, hideous, ghastly, grievous, diabolical, savage, vicious, monstrous, fiendish, wicked, brutal, cruel, ruthless, merciless
FORMAL heinous, nefarious, flagitious
2 *atrocious weather*
dreadful, terrible, appalling, awful, frightful, disgusting
🔁 **1** admirable **2** fine

atrociously *adv*
shockingly, appallingly, abominably, dreadfully, terribly, horribly, monstrously, fiendishly, wickedly, brutally, cruelly, ruthlessly
FORMAL heinously

atrocity *n*
outrage, abomination, enormity, horror, monstrosity, savagery, barbarity, brutality, cruelty, viciousness, evil, villainy, wickedness, violation, vileness, hideousness, atrociousness
FORMAL heinousness, flagitiousness

atrophy *n, v*
♦ *n*
withering, shrivelling, wasting (away), emaciation, decay, decline, degeneration, deterioration, diminution, involution
TECHNICAL marasmus, tabefaction, amyotrophy
♦ *v*
wither, shrivel, waste (away), emaciate, decay, decline, degenerate, deteriorate, diminish, dwindle, fade, shrink
TECHNICAL tabefy

attach *v*
1 *attach a label*
affix, stick, adhere, fasten, fix, secure, tie, bind, pin, nail, weld, join, unite, connect, link, couple, add (on), annex, make secure, tack, harness
OLD adhibit
2 *attach yourself to a group*
join, affiliate with, associate with, combine with, align with, ally, unite
COLLOQ. latch onto
3 ASCRIBE, attribute, assign, put, place, lay, associate, relate to, belong
FORMAL impute
4 *a centre attached to the university*
link, affiliate, associate, connect, assign, allocate, detail, send, second
🔁 **1** detach, unfasten

attached *adj*
1 *very attached to her family*
affectionate, fond, loving, tender, liking, friendly, devoted
2 *Is she attached?*
married, engaged, spoken for, in a relationship, involved with someone
FORMAL affianced
COLLOQ. going steady

⊞ 1 unloving, indifferent **2** single, unattached, on your own

attachment n

1 ACCESSORY, fitting, fixture, fitment, extension, extra, supplement, supplementary part, addition, adjunct, codicil
FORMAL appendage, appurtenance, accoutrement
2 FONDNESS, affection, tenderness, love, liking, partiality, loyalty, devotion, friendship, affinity, attraction, bond, tie, link, closeness

attack v, n

• v

1 *attack a country/person*
raid, strike, storm, rush, charge, assail, assault, besiege, set about, set upon, fall on, lay into, go for, fly at, weight into, pounce on, ambush, sandbag
OLD aggress
COLLOQ. beat up, do over, mug, make a dead set at, jump, duff up, light into, get stuck into, leave for dead
SLANG knock into the middle of next week, have your guts for garters, take to the cleaners
2 CRITICIZE, find fault with, slate, censure, blame, denounce, revile, malign, abuse, run down, reprove, rebuke
FORMAL berate, impugn, revile, fulminate against, vilify, inveigh, lampoon, oppugn, calumniate, decry
COLLOQ. slam, knock, blast, rubbish, clobber, pan, tear/pull to pieces, tear to shreds, pick holes in, pull apart, have a go at, bitch about
SLANG slag off; *Aust & NZ* chuck off at
3 *the disease attacks the nerves*
destroy, affect, infect, strike at
4 *attack a task*
tackle, deal with, address, attend to, focus on, begin, start, get started on, commence, set about, embark on, undertake, apply yourself to
⊞ **1** defend, protect

• n

1 OFFENSIVE, blitz, bombardment, invasion, incursion, foray, raid, strike, charge, storming, rush, onslaught, assault, sortie, push, sally, act of aggression, battery, *coup de main*, strafe
OLD (*Spenser*) bodrag
FORMAL irruption
2 *an attack on his reputation*
criticism, censure, abuse, broadside, snipe
FORMAL invective, impugnment, revilement, vilification
COLLOQ. slating, slamming, roasting, hatchet job, knocking, flak
3 SEIZURE, fit, convulsion, bout, paroxysm, spasm, stroke
TECHNICAL ictus
OLD *dialect* brash
FORMAL access

Synonym nuances

noun sense 1
The word **offensive** is generally used to talk about the course of action taken by an attacking party, whereas **blitz** has the more specific element of an attack or bombing from the air, although nowadays it may also be used of any overwhelming attack: *the book was launched with a marketing blitz*. Likewise the term **bombardment** has come to suggest any succession of blows; *the artillery bombardment*; *the constant press bombardment*.
 Invasion, on the other hand, refers to an attack that makes inroads into another's territory; **incursion**, while similar, often suggests a degree of suddenness; *commercial groups are paying dearly for their rash incursion into property*. **Foray** and **raid** are similar manoeuvres implying a sudden swift inroad, generally undertaken for assault or seizure, whilst a **strike** is most

---

commonly used of an attack by aircraft. The terms **charge**, **storming**, **rush**, and **onslaught** all suggest a swift, sometimes violent, impetuous forward movement, though onslaught is nowadays often used figuratively; *the storming of the Golden Temple*; *the cultural onslaught*. **Assault** similarly implies a sudden violent attack and it too has a spreading figurative usage: *Leeds are about to mount an assault on the European Cup*. **Sortie** and **sally** both suggest a sudden rush forward by a besieged party, whilst **push** is more generally connected with a concentrated, ongoing offensive: *the three main parties are prepared for a big push over the last weekend of the campaign*.
 Generally you would use **act of aggression** to suggest an initial act of hostility, but **battery** would be more likely used (especially by legal practitioners) to describe a violent beating. **Strafe** was originally used of a machine-gun attack from the air, though nowadays the origin of the attack is less specific. If the attackers burst in they could be accused of **irruption**.

---

attacker n

assailant, aggressor, invader, raider, assaulter, striker, critic, detractor, reviler, abuser, persecutor
COLLOQ. mugger
⊞ defender, supporter

attain v

accomplish, achieve, fulfil, complete, effect, realize, earn, reach, touch, arrive at, hit, grasp, find, get, acquire, obtain, procure, secure, gain, win, net

attainable adj

achievable, feasible, viable, manageable, obtainable, possible, potential, practicable, probable, reachable, realistic, within reach, at hand, accessible, imaginable, conceivable
COLLOQ. doable
⊞ unattainable

attainment n

1 *artistic attainments*
accomplishment, achievement, feat, success, ability, capability, competence, proficiency, skill, art, talent, gift, aptitude, facility
2 *the attainment of his ambitions*
fulfilment, completion, consummation, realization, accomplishment, mastery
FORMAL procurement, acquirement

attempt v, n

• v

try, have a try, endeavour, aspire, set out, seek, strive, undertake, tackle, venture, aim, experiment, see if you can do, try your hand; *Scot* mint
OLD fand
FORMAL essay
COLLOQ. have a go/shot/crack/stab, give it a go/try/whirl, try your hand at, do your level best, bend over backwards, give it your best shot

• n

try, endeavour, go, push, effort, struggle, bid, undertaking, venture, trial, experiment, foray, shy, whack; *Scot* mint
FORMAL essay
COLLOQ. shot, stab, bash, crack; *Aust & NZ* burl

attend v

1 *attend a meeting*
be present at, take part in, be here, be there, go/come along, appear, put in/make an appearance at, go to, frequent, visit
COLLOQ. turn up, show (up)
2 PAY ATTENTION, concentrate, listen, hear, heed, mind, mark, watch, note, notice, take note/notice, follow, observe

3 ESCORT, chaperon(e), accompany, usher, follow, guard, squire
4 *attend the sick*
look after, take care of, care for, nurse, tend, minister to, help, serve, wait upon
■ **attend to**
deal with, see to, take care of, look after, cope with, manage, handle, process, direct, control, oversee, supervise, follow up (on), heed

attendance *n*
presence, appearance, appearing, audience, house, crowd, gate, turnout; *Aust* roll-up
COLLOQ. showing (up)

attendant *n, adj*
♦ *n*
assistant, aide, helper, auxiliary, steward, waiter, waitress, servant, page, retainer, guide, marshal, usher, escort, companion, follower, guard, custodian, chaperon(e)
♦ *adj*
accompanying, attached, associated, related, incidental, resultant, consequent, subsequent
FORMAL concomitant

attention *n*
1 *let your attention wander*
alertness, vigilance, concentration, heed, notice, observation, regard, mind, mindfulness, awareness, recognition, thought, focus of your thoughts, contemplation, consideration, preoccupation
FORMAL advertence, advertency
2 *attract great public attention*
notice, observation, regard, awareness, recognition, scrutiny, thought, contemplation, consideration, heed, concern
COLLOQ. limelight, high profile
3 *receive medical attention*
care, treatment, therapy, help, service
4 *flattered by his attentions*
respect, courtesy, politeness, civility, compliments, gallantry
E3 1 inattention, disregard, daydreaming **2** inattention, disregard **3** carelessness
■ **pay attention to**
concentrate on, focus your mind/thoughts on, focus on, heed, devote your attention to, take notice, listen/watch carefully

attentive *adj*
1 ALERT, awake, vigilant, aware, watchful, watching, observant, noticing, concentrating, heedful, mindful, careful, conscientious, on the qui vive, listening
OLD whist
FORMAL advertent
COLLOQ. all ears, on the ball
2 CONSIDERATE, thoughtful, kind, obliging, accommodating, civil, polite, courteous, devoted, gracious, conscientious, chivalrous, gallant, punctilious
E3 1 inattentive, heedless **2** inconsiderate

attentively *adv*
watchfully, observantly, mindfully, carefully, conscientiously
E3 inattentively

attenuated *adj*
thin, narrow, slender, slim, fine, slight, skinny, bony, scraggy, scrawny
E3 broad, fat

attest *v*
prove, confirm, corroborate, demonstrate, show, display, manifest, endorse, certify, affirm, assert, declare, demonstrate, vouch for, bear witness to, verify
FORMAL adjure, aver, asseverate, evince, evidence

attic *n*
loft, garret, mansard
OLD COLLOQ. sky parlour

attire *n*
dress, clothes, clothing, wear, garments, outfit, garb, costume, finery
OLD habilements
FORMAL habit, apparel, accoutrements
COLLOQ. gear, togs, clobber, rig-out

attired *adj*
clothed, dressed, adorned, turned out
FORMAL arrayed, habilitated
COLLOQ. decked out, rigged out

attitude *n*
1 OPINION, feeling, disposition, sentiment, mood, aspect, manner, position, point of view, view, viewpoint, approach, outlook, perspective, approach, way of thinking, mentality, mindset, world-view, *Weltanschauung, Anschauung*
2 POSTURE, bearing, pose, stance, stand
FORMAL deportment, carriage

attorney *n*
lawyer, solicitor, barrister, advocate, counsel, QC, legal adviser, legal representative
COLLOQ. brief

attract *v*
pull, draw, lure, allure, entice, seduce, tempt, invite, induce, incline, appeal to, bring in, pull in, hook, rivet, magnetize, interest, engage, fascinate, enchant, charm, bewitch, captivate, excite
COLLOQ. tickle someone's fancy
E3 repel, disgust

attraction *n*
1 *the attraction of an exotic lifestyle*
pull, draw, magnetism, lure, allure, bait, hook, enticement, inducement, seduction, temptation, invitation, appeal, affinity, interest, fascination, enchantment, charm, glamour, captivation
2 *tourist attractions*
sight, feature, building, activity, entertainment, diversion
E3 1 repulsion

attractive *adj*
1 *an attractive person*
pretty, fair, fetching, good-looking, handsome, beautiful, gorgeous, striking, stunning, glamorous, elegant, lovely, pleasant, charismatic, picturesque, photogenic, personable, pleasing, cute, engaging, prepossessing, winsome, luscious, nubile, nymphic, desirable, sexy; *Scot* bonny
OLD comely, dashing
COLLOQ. all right, terrific, dishy, fanciable, hunky, hot stuff, knockout; *N Am* foxy
OLD COLLOQ. taky
SLANG beddable; *N Am* bad
2 *an attractive suggestion*
agreeable, appealing, winsome, winning, enticing, seductive, tempting, inviting, interesting, pleasant, agreeable, toothsome, engaging, fascinating, charming, captivating, irresistible, catchy, magnetic

---

Synonym nuances
sense 1
The words **pretty** and **fair** are rather mild terms of praise generally used of women and girls, suggesting an element of daintiness. **Fetching** is more likely to be used of a garment or outfit, though it is possible for a person to look fetching: *a very fetching hat; she looked fetching in her uniform.*
  Good-looking, **handsome** and **beautiful** are stronger adjectives, and all imply being blessed with regular facial

features – **handsome** is generally used of men, although distinguished older women can also be described thus; similarly **beautiful**, although traditionally associated with women, may now sometimes be used to describe an attractive man.

Gorgeous, **striking** and **stunning** suggest attractiveness that is impossible to miss; **glamorous** has the added implication that the appeal is aided by clothes or artificial enhancements: *he seemed less glamorous out of uniform*. **Elegant**, on the other hand, conveys dignity combined with good taste.

The words **winsome**, **luscious**, **nubile** and **nymphic** are used specifically of sexually appealing females, but **desirable** and **sexy** are commonly used of either sex. The words **picturesque** and **photogenic** have more specific usages – the first to describe an exceedingly attractive place, the latter generally used of someone who is bound to photograph well: *the picturesque little French town*; *her photogenic face*.

Cute, on the other hand, is used of attractiveness that appeals to protective or nurturing instincts: *cute puppy dogs*. **Lovely**, **pleasant**, **personable**, **pleasing** and **engaging** are fairly restrained compliments, referring to attractive personal rather than physical qualities: *the chaplain was a pleasant gentleman*. The word **charismatic**, however, conjures up someone with a strong, indefinable quality that draws people: *a fiery, charismatic man*. The term **prepossessing**, however, is generally used in the negative, often implying a degree of distaste: *none of them were even slightly prepossessing*.

attribute *v, n*

◆ *v*
ascribe, credit, assign, put down, blame, charge, refer, apply
FORMAL accredit, impute
◆ *n*
property, quality, virtue, point, aspect, facet, feature, trait, characteristic, idiosyncrasy, peculiarity, quirk, note, mark, side, streak, sign, indicator, symbol

attrition *n*

1 FRICTION, abrasion, rubbing, scraping, chafing, erosion
FORMAL detrition
2 *a war of attrition*
wearing away, wearing down, weakening, grinding, harassment
FORMAL attenuation

attuned *adj*

acclimatized, assimilated, accustomed, familiarized, adapted, adjusted, regulated, co-ordinated, harmonized, set, tuned

atypical *adj*

uncharacteristic, unusual, exceptional, untypical, aberrant, abnormal, uncommon, anomalous, deviant, divergent, unconventional, eccentric, extraordinary, freakish
🔁 typical

auburn *adj*

reddish-brown, dark-red, chestnut, tawny, russet, copper, rust, henna, Titian

audacious *adj*

adventurous, daring, enterprising, courageous, rash, reckless, risky, assuming, assured, unabashed, bold, brave, fearless, intrepid, dauntless, valiant, plucky, devil-may-care, disrespectful, impertinent, forward, presumptuous, impudent, insolent, cheeky, pert, brazen, rude, shameless
FORMAL venturesome
COLLOQ. fresh, lippy; *N Am* nervy
🔁 cautious, reserved, timid

audacity *n*

adventurousness, daring, enterprise, courage, rashness, recklessness, risk, boldness, bravery, fearlessness, intrepidity, dauntlessness, valour, pluck, disrespectfulness, impertinence, forwardness, presumption, impudence, insolence, cheek, pertness, brazenness, effrontery, defiance, rudeness, shamelessness
COLLOQ. bottle, guts, grit
🔁 caution, reserve, timidity

audible *adj*

clear, distinct, recognizable, perceptible, discernible, detectable, appreciable, hearable, heard
🔁 inaudible, silent, unclear

audience *n*

1 *members of the audience*
spectators, onlookers, house, auditorium, listeners, viewers, crowd, turnout, gathering, assembly, congregation, fans, devotees, followers, regulars, following, patrons, public, ratings
COLLOQ. *Brit & Aust* bums on seats
2 MEETING, interview, hearing, consultation, discussion, reception, conference

audit *n, v*

◆ *n*
examination, inspection, check, verification, investigation, scrutiny, analysis, review, survey, statement, balancing
◆ *v*
examine, inspect, check, verify, investigate, scrutinize, analyse, review, go over, go through, work through, balance

auditorium *n*

concert hall, hall, chamber, conference hall, theatre, playhouse, opera house, assembly room

au fait *adj*

up to date, familiar, aware, abreast, in touch, knowledgeable, versed, conversant, *au courant*

augment *v*

add to, amplify, boost, enlarge, build up, put on, expand, extend, grow, increase, make greater, magnify, multiply, raise, inflate, enhance, heighten, intensify, reinforce, strengthen, swell
OLD (*Shakesp*) eche
🔁 decrease

augmentation *n*

enlargement, increase, build-up, amplification, expansion, extension, growth, strengthening, magnification, intensification, boost
🔁 decrease

augur *v*

herald, prophesy, foretell, predict, promise, be a sign of, signify; *Scot* spae
OLD betoken
FORMAL forebode, harbinger, bode, presage, portend

augury *n*

omen, herald, prophecy, prediction, foreboding, prognostication, forerunner, forewarning, token, warning, portent, promise, sign
TECHNICAL ornithoscopy
OLD sooth
FORMAL harbinger, haruspication, prodrome

august *adj*

dignified, exalted, distinguished, respected, solemn, noble, impressive, imposing, glorious, grand, lofty, magnificent, majestic, stately, awe-inspiring

aura *n*

air, ambience, atmosphere, mood, quality, emanation, feel, feeling, hint, suggestion, vibrations
FORMAL nimbus
COLLOQ. vibes

auspices

■ **under the auspices of**

under the aegis of, under the authority of, with the patronage/sponsorship of, with the backing/support/ approval of, under the supervision/control/influence/ guidance of, in the charge/care of

auspicious *adj*

favourable, encouraging, cheerful, bright, rosy, promising, hopeful, optimistic, fortunate, lucky, opportune, timely, happy, prosperous
FORMAL propitious, felicitous
F3 unfavourable, inauspicious, ominous

austere *adj*

1 STARK, bleak, plain, simple, basic, functional, unadorned, unornamented, grim, forbidding, sombre
2 SEVERE, stern, strict, cold, formal, distant, rigid, rigorous, stringent, exacting, hard, harsh, spartan, grave, serious, solemn, sober, abstemious, astringent, killjoy, unfeeling, unbending, inflexible, self-denying, restrained, economical, frugal, ascetic, self-disciplined, stoic, Dantean, puritanical, Waldensian, chaste
OLD stoor
FORMAL self-abnegating
F3 **1** ornate, elaborate **2** genial

austerity *n*

plainness, simplicity, severity, coldness, formality, hardness, harshness, solemnity, abstemiousness, abstinence, economy, asceticism, self-denial, self-discipline, inflexibility, rigour, puritanism
F3 elaborateness, extravagance, materialism

authentic *adj*

1 *an authentic signature*
genuine, real, actual, certain, attested, undisputed, bona fide, lawful, legal, legitimate, valid, sterling, *echt*
COLLOQ. the real thing, the genuine article, the real McCoy
2 *an authentic description*
accurate, factual, true, true-to-life, historical, correct, faithful, reliable, dependable, trustworthy, honest, credible
COLLOQ. kosher
F3 **1** false, fake, counterfeit, spurious **2** inaccurate, unfaithful

authentically *adv*

1 GENUINELY, really, actually, legitimately, lawfully
2 ACCURATELY, faithfully, reliably, historically, credibly
F3 **1** falsely **2** inaccurately

authenticate *v*

verify, validate, certify, endorse, confirm, ratify, corroborate, guarantee, warrant, vouch for, authorize, prove, substantiate
FORMAL accredit, attest

authentication *n*

verification, validation, endorsement, confirmation, authorization, ratification, corroboration, substantiation
FORMAL attestation, accreditation

authenticity *n*

genuineness, certainty, authoritativeness, validity, truth, veracity, truthfulness, honesty, accuracy, correctness, faithfulness, fidelity, reliability, dependability, credibility, trustworthiness, legality, legitimacy
F3 spuriousness, invalidity

author *n*

1 WRITER, novelist, man of letters, woman of letters, biographer, dramatist, playwright, poet, essayist, composer, contributor, screenwriter, librettist, lyricist, songwriter, reporter, journalist, pen, penman, penwoman
Related adjective: auctorial
2 CREATOR, founder, originator, initiator, parent, prime mover, mover, inventor, designer, architect, planner, maker, producer

authoritarian *adj, n*

♦ *adj*
strict, disciplinarian, severe, harsh, rigid, tough, inflexible, unyielding, dogmatic, doctrinaire, absolute, autocratic, dictatorial, totalitarian, Orwellian, magisterial, despotic, tyrannical, oppressive, domineering, imperious
F3 liberal

♦ *n*
autocrat, absolutist, totalitarian, dictator, despot, tyrant

⚠ authoritarian or **authoritative**?
You describe a person or government as *authoritarian* if they try to control people instead of letting them have the freedom to make their own decisions. An *authoritative* account of something is one that is reliable; an *authoritative* person is one who inspires attention and obedience from others.

---

authoritarianism *n*

autocracy, despotism, totalitarianism, dictatorship, absolutism, oppression, repression, Fascism, Nazism
F3 democracy, liberalism

authoritative *adj*

1 *an authoritative study*
definitive, decisive, authentic, factual, true, truthful, accurate, faithful, convincing, sound, reliable, dependable, trustworthy, scholarly, learned, official, authorized, legitimate, valid, approved, sanctioned, accepted
FORMAL cathedratic
2 *an authoritative person*
self-confident, confident, self-assured, self-possessed, decisive, sure of yourself, bold, audacious, assertive, imposing, commanding, magisterial, masterful
F3 **1** unofficial, unreliable

authoritatively *adv*

1 RELIABLY, dependably, definitively, decisively, factually, authentically, accurately, faithfully, convincingly
2 SELF-CONFIDENTLY, confidently, boldly, audaciously, assertively

authority *n*

1 GOVERNMENT, administration, establishment, management, officialdom, state, council, bureaucracy
COLLOQ. they, the powers that be
2 SOVEREIGNTY, supremacy, rule, sway, control, dominion, influence, command, power, force, jurisdiction
COLLOQ. clout, muscle
3 AUTHORIZATION, permission, sanction, permit, warrant, licence, credentials, right, power, prerogative, consent, leave, carte blanche
COLLOQ. go-ahead, green light, thumbs-up
4 *an authority on antiques*
expert, pundit, connoisseur, specialist, professional, master, scholar, sage, adept
COLLOQ. buff

authorization *n*

authority, permission, consent, sanction, approval, mandate, validation, ratification, confirmation, licence, entitlement, empowering, commission, warranty, permit, leave, credentials, passport, stamp, retainer
FORMAL accreditation
COLLOQ. OK, okay, go-ahead, green light, thumbs-up

authorize *v*

legalize, make legal, validate, ratify, confirm, license, entitle, empower, give authority to, enable, commission, warrant, permit, give permission to, allow, let, consent to, sanction, approve, mandate
FORMAL accredit
COLLOQ. OK, okay, give the go-ahead to, give the green light to, give the thumbs-up to

authorized *adj*

licensed, under licence, commissioned, permitted,

warranted, official, approved, recognized, legal, lawful
FORMAL accredited

autobiography *n*
memoirs, life story, story of your life, diary, journal

autocracy *n*
absolutism, totalitarianism, dictatorship, despotism, tyranny, authoritarianism, fascism
Fa democracy

autocrat *n*
absolutist, totalitarian, dictator, despot, tyrant, authoritarian, panjandrum
COLLOQ. (little) Hitler

autocratic *adj*
absolute, all-powerful, totalitarian, despotic, tyrannical, authoritarian, dictatorial, domineering, overbearing, imperious
FORMAL autarchic
Fa democratic, liberal

autograph *n, v*
◆ *n*
signature, name, initials, countersignature, inscription, endorsement, mark
SLANG monicker
◆ *v*
sign, write your name, initial, countersign, endorse, put your mark

automatic *adj*
1 AUTOMATED, self-activating, mechanical, mechanized, programmed, self-regulating, computerized, push-button, robotic, self-propelling, unmanned
2 SPONTANEOUS, reflex, involuntary, mechanical, unwilled, unconscious, unthinking, natural, instinctive, routine, necessary, certain, inevitable, unavoidable, inescapable, uncontrollable
COLLOQ. knee-jerk

automatically *adj*
1 MECHANICALLY, robotically
2 INVOLUNTARILY, spontaneously, mechanically, unconsciously, unthinkingly, naturally, instinctively, routinely, necessarily, certainly, inevitably, unavoidably, inescapably, uncontrollably

automobile *n*
car, motor car, motor vehicle, motor, vehicle
See panel at **car**.

autonomous *adj*
self-governing, self-directing, self-determining, independent, free, sovereign
Fa dependent

autonomy *n*
self-government, self-rule, home rule, sovereignty, independence, self-determination, self-sufficiency, freedom, free will
FORMAL autarky
Fa subjection, compulsion

autopsy *n*
post-mortem, dissection, necropsy

auxiliary *n, adj*
◆ *n*
ancillary, subordinate, helper, partner, supporter, right-hand man/woman, backer, second, second-in-command
◆ *adj*
ancillary, assistant, subsidiary, accessory, secondary, supporting, supportive, helping, assisting, aiding, extra, supplementary, additional, spare, reserve, back-up, emergency, substitute

avail *v*
make use of, use, utilize, exercise, accept, resort to, draw on, take advantage of

■ **to no avail**
without success, in vain, unsuccessfully, fruitlessly, vainly
FORMAL ineffectually

available *adj*
1 *have rooms available*
free, vacant, unoccupied, untaken, to hand, within reach, at hand, accessible, handy, convenient, on hand, at your disposal, disposable, ready, obtainable, usable, forthcoming
FORMAL procurable
COLLOQ. on tap, up your sleeve, up for grabs, yours for the asking/taking
2 *not available for comment*
free, not busy, contactable, at liberty
Fa 1 unavailable, taken **2** unavailable

avalanche *n*
1 *an avalanche in the Alps*
landslide, landslip
2 *an avalanche of letters*
deluge, flood, cascade, torrent, inundation, wave, barrage

avant-garde *adj*
innovative, innovatory, pioneering, ground-breaking, experimental, unconventional, original, progressive, advanced, forward-looking, futuristic, enterprising, go-ahead, inventive, modern, contemporary
SLANG far-out, way-out
Fa conservative

avarice *n*
covetousness, acquisitiveness, avidity, greed, greediness, meanness, miserliness, selfishness, materialism
OLD gourmandise; (*Shakesp*) misery
FORMAL pleonexia
SLANG *N Am* the gimmes
Fa generosity, liberality

avaricious *adj*
covetous, grasping, acquisitive, greedy, griping, mercenary, mean, miserly, avid; *Scot* gare, grippy
OLD gripple
FORMAL rapacious, pleonectic
Fa generous, liberal

avenge *v*
take revenge for, take vengeance for, punish, requite, repay, pay back, retaliate
OLD wreak; (*Shakesp*) venge
COLLOQ. get even with, get back at, get your own back

avenue *n*
1 ROAD, street, drive, way, thoroughfare, boulevard, broadway, passage
2 *an avenue for his missionary zeal*
way, method, line, approach, course of action, scheme, modus operandi

aver *v*
state, declare, maintain, confirm, affirm, make known
FORMAL avow, attest

average *n, adj*
◆ *n*
mean, mid-point, median, norm, mode, standard, centre, rule, par, medium, run
Fa extreme, exception
◆ *adj*
1 *the average age*
mean, medial, median, middle, intermediate, medium
2 *the average reader*
ordinary, everyday, common, usual, normal, regular, standard, typical, routine, unexceptional
3 *an average performance*
mediocre, moderate, satisfactory, fair, middling, fair to

middling, indifferent, passable, tolerable, undistinguished, unexceptional, nothing special
COLLOQ. run-of-the-mill, so-so, common-or-garden, not up to much, nothing much to write home about, not much cop, no great shakes
E3 1 extreme **3** exceptional, remarkable

■ **on average**
normally, usually, generally, mainly, chiefly, mostly, ordinarily, typically, routinely, as a rule, by and large, on the whole, in the main

averse *adj*
reluctant, unwilling, loath, disinclined, ill-disposed, hostile, opposed, antagonistic, unfavourable
FORMAL antipathetic
E3 willing, keen, sympathetic

⚠ averse or **adverse**?
See panel at **adverse**.

---

aversion *n*
dislike, hate, hatred, loathing, abhorrence, abomination, horror, phobia, reluctance, unwillingness, disinclination, distaste, disgust, revulsion, repulsion, hostility, opposition, antagonism
FORMAL detestation, repugnance
E3 liking, sympathy, desire

avert *v*
turn away, deflect, turn aside, parry, head off, fend off, ward off, stave off, forestall, frustrate, prevent, avoid, evade, stop
FORMAL obviate, preclude

aviation *n*
aeronautics, flying, flight, aircraft industry

Aviation terms include:

aeronautics	flight	nose dive
aeroplane	flight crew	overshoot
aerospace	flight deck	parachute
aileron	flight recorder	pilot
aircraft	fly-by	plane
airfield	fly-by-wire	pressurized cabin
airline	fly-past	*slang* prang
air miss	fuselage	propeller
NAm airplane	*slang* George	rotor blade
airport	glider	rudder
airship	ground control	runway
airspace	ground speed	solo flight
air station	hangar	sonic boom
air steward	helicopter	sound barrier
airstrip	holding pattern	spoiler
air traffic control	hop	subsonic
airway	hot-air balloon	supersonic
altitude	jet	swing-wing
automatic pilot	jet engine	take-off
biplane	jet propulsion	taxi
black box	jetstream	test flight
captain	joystick	test pilot
colloq. chocks	jumbo jet	thrust
away	landing	touchdown
cockpit	landing gear	undercarriage
console	landing strip	undershoot
control tower	lift-off	vapour trail
crash dive	loop-the-loop	vertical take-off
crash-landing	Mach number	and landing
dive	maiden flight	(VTOL)
drag	mid-air collision	windsock
fixed-wing	monoplane	wingspan
flap	night-flying	

See also **aircraft**.

---

aviator *n*
pilot, flyer, airman, airwoman, aircraftsman, aircraftswoman

avid *adj*
eager, earnest, keen, enthusiastic, fanatical, devoted, dedicated, zealous, ardent, fervent, intense, great, passionate, insatiable, ravenous, hungry, thirsty, athirst, greedy, grasping, covetous
COLLOQ. crazy, mad
E3 indifferent

avidly *adv*
eagerly, earnestly, keenly, enthusiastically, fanatically, devotedly, zealously, ardently, fervently, intensely, passionately, insatiably, ravenously, hungrily, thirstily, greedily, covetously
COLLOQ. madly
E3 indifferently

avoid *v*
evade, stay/keep away from, elude, sidestep, escape, run away from, get out of, bypass, get round, balk, decline, prevent, avert, shun, abstain from, hold back from, shy away from, steer clear of, make a detour, keep your distance from
OLD evite, evitate
FORMAL eschew, circumvent, refrain from, forbear
COLLOQ. hedge, duck, dodge, shirk, wriggle/worm your way out of, give a miss, give a wide berth to

---

Synonym nuances
Unlike the straightforward **stay** or **keep away from**, **evade** suggests an element of furtiveness: *I managed to evade detection*, and when something **eludes** someone it takes on an almost ethereal quality: *happiness has eluded him*. The word **sidestep** may be used to imply that someone has dodged something, either literally or figuratively: *he neatly sidestepped the questions*. Similarly **bypass** also suggests avoidance, through finding another route: *this leap of faith bypasses the truth*, whereas **escape** is suggestive of a more dramatic avoidance: *the thieves escaped detection*.
  You can use the phrase **get out of** when talking about getting free of an unpleasant situation or responsibility, whilst **get round** implies that an alternative solution has been found: *the student got round the question in such an ingenious way*. **Balk** suggests a real aversion to doing something: *the banks have balked at new lending*, unlike **decline**, which describes a more restrained, less instinctive reaction.
  Prevent, on the other hand, has more to do with stopping something from taking place, as does **avert**, although it is usually used of avoiding undesirable consequences: *the disaster was averted*. The word **shun** implies ignoring that which is to be avoided, whereas **abstain from** has more to do with not taking part. The phrases **shy away from** and **steer clear of** are similar in sense but differ in degree, the latter being used to emphasize a more determined avoidance.

---

avoidable *adj*
escapable, preventable, stoppable
OLD evitable
FORMAL avertible, eludible
E3 inevitable, inescapable

avow *v*
declare, admit, assert, maintain, state, profess, confess, acknowledge, swear, vow
OLD avouch
FORMAL attest, aver

avowed *adj*
sworn, declared, professed, self-proclaimed, self-confessed, confessed, admitted, acknowledged, open, overt
OLD (*Shakesp*) barefaced

await v
1 *await his return*
wait for, expect, hope for, anticipate, look forward to, look for
OLD bide, tarry
2 *troubles that await us*
be in store for, lie in wait for

awake adj, v
♦ *adj*
1 *stay awake*
wakeful, wide awake, stirring, aroused, alert, vigilant, watchful, observant, attentive, conscious
COLLOQ. tossing and turning, not sleeping a wink
2 *awake to the possibilities*
aware, sensitive, conscious, alive, appreciative, mindful
F3 **1** asleep, sleeping **2** unaware
♦ *v*
awaken, waken, wake, wake up, rouse, stir, arouse
OLD abraid

awaken v
1 *awakened to the danger*
cause to realize, generate, stir, rouse, stimulate, inspire, excite, engender
2 *awakened by the alarm*
awake, waken, wake, wake up, rouse, stir
OLD abraid

awakening n
awaking, wakening, waking, rousing, arousal, stimulation, animating, enlivening, activation, revival, birth
FORMAL vivification

award n, v
♦ *n*
1 *an award for bravery*
prize, trophy, decoration, medal, honours, reward, accolade, certificate, presentation, commendation, citation
COLLOQ. gong
See panel at **honour**.
2 *an award for compensation*
endowment, gift, grant, scholarship, bursary, allotment, allowance, settlement, payment, dispensation, bestowal, conferral, adjudication, judgement, decision, order
FORMAL subvention
♦ *v*
give, present, distribute, dispense, bestow, confer, decorate, accord, endow, gift, grant, allot, allocate, assign, allow, determine
OLD addeem; (*Spenser*) addoom; adward, aret
FORMAL apportion, adjudge

aware adj
1 *aware of the problem*
conscious, alive to, sensitive, acquainted, appreciative, mindful, heedful, attentive, observant, sharp, alert, vigilant
FORMAL sentient, sensible, recognizant
2 *politically aware*
familiar, conversant, acquainted, informed, enlightened, *au courant*, knowing, knowledgeable, shrewd
FORMAL cognizant, apprised
COLLOQ. clued up, in the know, on the ball, sussed
F3 **1** unaware, oblivious, insensitive

Synonym nuances
sense 1
Conscious may be used to show that something is continually present in your thoughts: *we were conscious of the insecurity of our situation*, whilst the term **alive to** is more suggestive of being actively receptive: *teachers need to be alive to cultural differences*. **Sensitive** again suggests being open but further implies a highly tuned awareness: *the profession must be sensitive to change*. The term **acquainted**, however, suggests only a

---

previous introduction to something: *pilgrimage acquainted men with the spiritual treasure in the world*; whereas **appreciative**, **mindful** and **heedful** imply that something is not only known of, but is also an active consideration: *mindful of the danger of tropical storms*. **Attentive** similarly suggests paying constant heed to something in particular, whilst **observant** implies a more inherent quality of watchfulness. If you describe someone as **sharp** or **alert** you again suggest that their lively minds would instantly pick up on something, whereas **vigilant** implies a degree of conscientious awareness of potential danger or wrongdoing: *the burglars were spotted by vigilant neighbours*.

---

awareness n
consciousness, appreciation, recognition, sensitivity, familiarity, knowledge, understanding, grasp, perception, acquaintance
FORMAL cognizance

awash adj
1 FLOODED, inundated, soaked, drenched, saturated, submerged
2 *awash with reporters*
crawling, teeming, swarming, alive, full, packed, inundated
FORMAL replete

away adv
1 *move away*
from here, from there, off, elsewhere, apart, aside
2 *I've been away in France*
not at home, not at work, absent, on holiday, on vacation, abroad
3 *live away from the city*
at a distance, far

awe n
wonder, reverence, respect, honour, admiration, amazement, astonishment, fear, terror, dread, apprehension
FORMAL wonderment, veneration, stupefaction
F3 contempt

awed adj
awe-struck, amazed, astonished, stunned, reverential, fearful
COLLOQ. lost for words

awe-inspiring adj
wonderful, sublime, magnificent, stupendous, overwhelming, breathtaking, striking, spectacular, stupefying, stunning, astonishing, amazing, impressive, dazzling, imposing, majestic, solemn, exalted, sublime, moving, awesome, formidable, daunting, intimidating, fearsome
FORMAL numinous
COLLOQ. mind-boggling
F3 contemptible, tame

awesome adj
impressive, formidable, extraordinary, overwhelming, breathtaking, spectacular, amazing, astonishing, stunning, daunting, intimidating
COLLOQ. mind-boggling, jaw-dropping

awestruck adj
amazed, astonished, impressed, awed, awe-struck
COLLOQ. lost for words

awful adj
1 *an awful accident*
horrific, terrible, dreadful, fearful, frightful, ghastly, unpleasant, nasty, horrible, horrid, gruesome, dire, atrocious, horrifying, shocking, appalling, alarming, disgusting, distressing
FORMAL heinous

2 *the film was awful*
unsatisfactory, very poor, abysmal, inferior, dreadful, inadequate, second-rate, third-rate
COLLOQ. terrible, lousy, pathetic, crummy, a load of rubbish
SLANG pants, naff, the pits; (*vulgar*) shit, crap; *Aust* spewy
3 *I feel awful*
ill, unwell, sick, poorly, in pain, washed out
COLLOQ. terrible, rough, seedy, under the weather
E3 1 wonderful **2** excellent **3** well

awfully *adv*
very, extremely, greatly, deeply, really, immensely, particularly, remarkably, absolutely, unbelievably
COLLOQ. terribly, dreadfully, tremendously

awhile *adv*
for a short time, for some time, for a moment

awkward *adj*
1 CLUMSY, gauche, inept, inexpert, unskilful, bungling, ham-fisted, handless, heavy-handed, left-handed, unco-ordinated, ungainly, graceless, ungraceful, ungainly, gawky, inelegant, cumbersome, unwieldy, lubberly, chuckle-headed
FORMAL maladroit
COLLOQ. all thumbs, thumby, having two left feet
2 *feeling awkward in their presence*
uncomfortable, ill at ease, embarrassed, shy, bashful; *Scot* blate
3 *put me in an awkward position*
difficult, tricky, embarrassing, uncomfortable, delicate, troublesome, perplexing, problematic, annoying, inconvenient, fiddly
4 OBSTINATE, stubborn, unco-operative, obstructive, disobliging, troublesome, unaccommodating, irritable, touchy, prickly, oversensitive, rude, unpleasant, boorish, loutish, rustic, cubbish
COLLOQ. stroppy, bloody-minded
E3 1 graceful, elegant, convenient, handy **2** comfortable, relaxed, at ease **3** straightforward, easy **4** amenable, pleasant

awkwardly *adv*
1 CLUMSILY, gracelessly, ungracefully, inelegantly, ineptly, inexpertly, unskilfully, ham-fistedly, heavy-handedly
FORMAL maladroitly
2 UNCOMFORTABLY, uneasily, shyly, bashfully
E3 1 gracefully, elegantly **2** comfortably, confidently

awkwardness
1 EMBARRASSMENT, self-consciousness, confusion, bashfulness, uneasiness

FORMAL discomfiture
2 CLUMSINESS, ungainliness, gracelessness, inelegance, gawkiness, heavy-handedness, lack of co-ordination
E3 1 ease **2** grace, elegance

awning *n*
canopy, cover, covering, shade, shelter, sunshade

awry *adv, adj*
1 *clothing left awry*
askew, asymmetrical, cockeyed, crooked, misaligned, oblique, off-centre, skew-whiff, twisted, uneven; *Scot* agley
OLD skivie; (*Shakesp*) kam
COLLOQ. wonky
2 *plans gone awry*
wrong, amiss
E3 1 straight, symmetrical

axe *n, v*
◆ *n*
hatchet, chopper, cleaver, tomahawk, battle-axe
◆ *v*
1 CUT DOWN, fell, hew, chop, cleave, split
2 CANCEL, terminate, discontinue, remove, withdraw, eliminate, get rid of, throw out, dismiss, discharge
COLLOQ. cut, sack, fire, give someone the sack, give someone their marching orders, give someone their cards
■ **get the axe**
be cancelled
COLLOQ. get the boot, get the chop

axiom *n*
principle, fundamental, truth, truism, precept, dictum, byword, maxim, adage, aphorism
TECHNICAL postulate

axiomatic *adj*
manifest, assumed, certain, given, granted, self-evident, understood, unquestioned, unquestionable, indubitable, presupposed, fundamental, accepted, proverbial
FORMAL aphoristic, apophthegmatic, gnomic

axis *n*
centre-line, vertical, horizontal, pivot, hinge

axle *n*
shaft, spindle, rod, pin, pivot
TECHNICAL mandrel

azure *adj*
sky-blue, light blue, pale blue, Cambridge blue, Saxe
OLD cerulean

B

babble *v, n*

♦ *v*

1 CHATTER, gabble, jabber, gibber, cackle, prate, mutter, mumble, murmur, prattle, twaddle, twattle
COLLOQ. rabbit on, waffle, gab, blabber, jaw, witter

2 *the stream babbled*
burble, gurgle, murmur

♦ *n*

chatter, gabble, prattle, clamour, hubbub, babel, gibberish, burble, murmur, twaddle, twattle, tongue-work
OLD bibble-babble
COLLOQ. waffle, gab, blabber, jawing, wittering

babe *n*

baby, child, infant, newborn, newborn baby, suckling, tot, tiny tot, babe in arms

babel *n*

babble, hubbub, clamour, bedlam, hullabaloo, chaos, commotion, confusion, din, disorder, pandemonium, tumult, turmoil, uproar

baby *n, adj*

♦ *n*

1 *she's expecting a baby*
babe, infant, newborn, newborn baby, suckling, child, tiny, toddler, tot, tiny tot; *Scot* bairn
TECHNICAL neonate
COLLOQ. *Aust & NZ* bub, bubby
SLANG sprog

2 *take it easy, baby*
darling, sweetheart, love, dear, dearest
COLLOQ. sweetie, honey

♦ *adj*

miniature, small-scale, midget, small, little, tiny, minute, diminutive, dwarf; *Scot.* wee
COLLOQ. mini, teeny, pint-size(d)

babyish *adj*

childish, juvenile, puerile, infantile, silly, foolish, baby, young, immature, naive
COLLOQ. soft, sissy
🖃 mature, precocious

back *n, v, adj, adv*

♦ *n*

1 *lie on your back*
backbone, spine
TECHNICAL dorsum, rachis, tergum
Related adjective: dorsal

2 *the back of an envelope*
rear, stern, end, rear end, tail, tail end, far end, hind part, hindquarters, posterior, backside, reverse, reverse side, other side
🖃 front, face

♦ *v*

1 GO BACKWARDS, move backwards, reverse, recede, backtrack, retreat, retire, withdraw, back away, recoil
FORMAL regress

2 SUPPORT, sustain, assist, help, aid, abet, side with, champion, advocate, encourage, promote, boost, favour, confirm, bolster, give countenance to, sanction, countenance, endorse, second, countersign, sponsor,

finance, put up the money for, subsidize, underwrite
COLLOQ. throw your weight behind, get/be behind

3 BET, wager, gamble, speculate, risk, chance, venture, bid, stake
🖃 **1** advance, approach **2** discourage, weaken

♦ *adj*

1 *the back door*
rear, end, tail, posterior, hind, hindmost, reverse, other

2 *back copies*
past, previous, earlier, former, outdated, elapsed, bygone, out of date, obsolete
🖃 **1** front

♦ *adv*

1 BACKWARDS, to the rear, behind, off, away

2 *it happened several years back*
ago, past, previously, before, earlier
🖃 **1** forwards

■ **back away**
retreat, withdraw, draw back, fall back, move back, give ground, recoil, step back, recede

■ **back down**
abandon, yield, submit, surrender, concede, give in, retreat, withdraw, back-pedal, backtrack, climb down

■ **back out**
abandon, give up, withdraw, retreat, resign, recant, go back on, cancel
COLLOQ. pull out, get cold feet, chicken out

■ **back up**
support, confirm, corroborate, bear out, stand by, validate, substantiate, endorse, second, champion, reinforce, bolster, assist, aid

■ **behind your back**
secretly, without your knowledge, deceitfully, slyly, furtively, covertly, sneakily, surreptitiously

■ **turn your back on**
reject, exclude, ignore, repudiate, abandon, leave, throw out
COLLOQ. quit, wash your hands of, not touch with a bargepole

Synonym nuances
verb sense 2
The word **support** has positive connotations of actively and wholeheartedly backing, whereas **sustain** suggests merely keeping something going: *illegal trafficking is sustained by increasing demand.* **Assist**, **help** and **aid** all return to the positive aspect of active involvement; similarly **abet**, although it has a further implication of being associated with something illegal or undesirable: *politicians who have abetted our national decline.*
  The term **side with** may be used of a dispute between rival parties, but **champion** supplies a dashing image of bringing a cause or ideology to people's attention: *he championed the cause of the poor.* **Advocate**, **promote**, **boost** and **bolster** similarly suggest an active role in the advancement of something: *the movement promoted single-issue politics*; whilst **encourage** has more to do with attracting people to it: *the children are encouraged to express themselves freely.* To **favour** something

suggests having it as a preference over others, but to **confirm** it goes further by implying validation.

The words **sanction** and **countenance** also convey differing aspects; the first suggests a more positive commitment, the latter incorporates a degree of tolerance rather than committed backing: *this is widely sanctioned socially; such concessions could not be countenanced.* The terms **endorse**, **second**, and **countersign** all describe a public action whereby you are happy for your name to be linked with a cause, whilst **sponsor**, **finance**, **subsidize** and **underwrite** are used only when you are willing to put your money where your mouth is, and give financial backing.

backbiting *n, adj*

♦ *n*

criticism, slander, libel, defamation, abuse, insults, slurs, gossip, malice, scandalmongering, spite, spitefulness
FORMAL aspersion, calumny, disparagement, denigration, revilement, detraction, vilification, vituperation
COLLOQ. bitchiness, cattiness, slagging off, mud-slinging, rubbishing
E3 praise

♦ *adj*

abusive, spiteful, malicious, slanderous, libellous, disparaging, scandalmongering
OLD (*Shakesp*) back-wounding
FORMAL vilifying
COLLOQ. bitchy, catty, cattish

backbone *n*

1 SPINE, spinal column, vertebrae, vertebral column
OLD chine
Related adjective: vertebrate, vertebrated
2 *the backbone of an organization*
mainstay, support, core, cornerstone, foundation, basis, nucleus
3 COURAGE, mettle, pluck, nerve, grit, determination, resolution, resolve, (strength of) character, firmness, tenacity, steadfastness, willpower, toughness, stamina, strength, power, vertebration
COLLOQ. bottle, grit, guts
E3 3 spinelessness, weakness

backbreaking *adj*

arduous, exhausting, gruelling, strenuous, onerous, hard, heavy, crushing, laborious, punishing
COLLOQ. killing
E3 easy

backchat *n*

impudence, impertinence, insolence, rudeness, cross-talk; *Scot* snash; *N Am* back talk
COLLOQ. cheek, nerve, sauciness, lip, face, mouth, brass neck

backer *n*

advocate, benefactor, promoter, second, seconder, sponsor, subscriber, supporter, underwriter, investor, subsidizer, funder, champion, patron, well-wisher, friend, bottle-holder
OLD stickler
COLLOQ. angel

backfire *v*

1 *the engine backfired*
misfire, explode, discharge, blow up, detonate
2 *the plans backfired*
recoil, rebound, ricochet, boomerang, strike back, miscarry, fail, defeat itself, be self-defeating, be counterproductive
COLLOQ. flop, come home to roost, score an own goal, blow up in your face

background *n*

1 SETTING, backdrop, backcloth, scene, surroundings,
surround, environment, milieu, context, framework, circumstances, influences, factors
2 HISTORY, record, credentials, experience, qualifications, grounding, preparation, education, upbringing, family, (family) circumstances, breeding, social standing, status, origins, culture, tradition

back-handed *adj*

ambiguous, double-edged, two-edged, indirect, oblique, dubious, equivocal, ironic, sarcastic, sardonic
E3 sincere, wholehearted

backing *n*

1 *financial backing*
support, accompaniment, aid, assistance, help, co-operation, helpers, championing, advocacy, encouragement, moral support, commendation, favour, approval, sanction, promotion, endorsement, seconding, patronage, sponsorship, finance, funds, grant, subsidy
2 *a plastic backing*
lining, padding, facing, interlining, stiffening, reinforcement
3 *musical backing*
accompaniment, support, backup
TECHNICAL obbligato, vamp

backlash *n*

reaction, response, repercussion, reprisal, retaliation, counteraction, recoil, kickback, backfire, boomerang

backlog *n*

accumulation, stock, supply, resources, reserve, reserves, heap, pile, excess, hoard
COLLOQ. mountain

back-pedal *v*

take back, retract, change your mind, about-face, about-turn, have second thoughts, abandon, yield, submit, surrender, concede, give in, retreat, withdraw, backtrack, go back on, climb down
FORMAL renege, tergiversate
COLLOQ. do a U-turn

backslide *v*

lapse, relapse, default, defect, turn away, turn your back, fall from grace, renege, desert, revert, go back, regress, sin, slip, stray, go astray
FORMAL apostatize, tergiversate
COLLOQ. leave the straight and narrow
E3 persevere

backslider *n*

apostate, defaulter, defector, deserter, renegade, reneger, turncoat
OLD recreant
FORMAL recidivist, tergiversator

backsliding *n*

lapse, relapse, regression, apostasy, defection, desertion, defaulting
FORMAL tergiversation

backtrack *v*

back-pedal, climb down, go back on, withdraw, change your mind, have second thoughts
FORMAL renege, tergiversate
COLLOQ. do a U-turn

backup *n*

support, help, assistance, aid, encouragement, confirmation, endorsement, reinforcement, additional equipment/resources

backward *adj*

1 *a backward step*
rearward, reverse, to the back, retrograde, retrogressive, regressive
2 *a backward country/society*
undeveloped, underdeveloped, unsophisticated
3 SHY, bashful, retiring, reticent, reluctant, unwilling,

hesitant, hesitating, shrinking, timid, wavering
4 *a backward child*
slow, immature, retarded, having learning difficulties,
subnormal
E3 1 forward **2** advanced, developed **3** bold, confident **4**
precocious

backwards *adv*
rearwards, to the back, retrogressively, regressively

backwash *n*
1 *the backwash of a ship*
wash, flow, swell, waves, wake, path
2 REPERCUSSIONS, aftermath, after effect(s), result(s),
consequence(s), reverberations

backwater *n*
isolated place, remote place
COLLOQ. *Aust* scrub, Woop Woop

backwoods *n*
isolated place, remote place, back of beyond, backwater,
bush, outback; *Aust & NZ* back-blocks; *S Afr* backveld
COLLOQ. middle of nowhere, the sticks; *N Am* the
boondocks, the boonies; *Aust & NZ* beyond the black
stump

bacteria *n*
germs, viruses, microbes, micro-organisms, parasites,
bacilli
COLLOQ. bugs

bad *adj*
1 UNPLEASANT, disagreeable, nasty, dreadful, appalling,
atrocious, undesirable, unfortunate, distressing, adverse,
detrimental, harmful, damaging, hurtful, dangerous,
injurious, unhealthy, unwholesome, destructive, ruinous
FORMAL deleterious
2 EVIL, wicked, sinful, criminal, corrupt, dishonest,
shameful, immoral, vile, offensive, degenerate,
outrageous, deplorable
FORMAL reprehensible, reprobate
3 *bad workmanship; bad at speaking French*
poor, inferior, inadequate, weak, mediocre, substandard,
shoddy, imperfect, faulty, defective, deficient,
unsatisfactory, unacceptable, second-rate, third-rate,
hopeless, incompetent, mismanaged, ineffective
FORMAL ineffectual
COLLOQ. awful, terrible, botched, lousy, crummy, pathetic,
ropy, useless; *Aust* onkus; a load of rubbish, a load of
garbage
SLANG the pits, pants, poxy, naff, crappy; (*vulgar*) a load of
crap/shit
4 *feel bad today*
unwell, sick, ill, poorly, diseased, painful, in pain, aching,
unhappy, despondent, gloomy
COLLOQ. under the weather
5 ROTTEN, mouldy, decayed, spoilt, putrid, rancid, sour, off,
tainted, contaminated, high
FORMAL putrefactive, putrescent
6 *a bad child*
naughty, mischievous, badly-behaved, ill-behaved,
disobedient, unruly, uncontrollable, wayward; *Scot* gallus
FORMAL refractory
COLLOQ. stroppy, bolshie
7 *have a bad cold*
serious, grave, severe, intense, critical, acute, harsh
8 *a bad time to call*
inconvenient, difficult, adverse, unfortunate,
unfavourable, unsuitable, inappropriate
FORMAL inauspicious
9 *have a bad back*
injured, hurt, diseased, wounded, weak, impaired
COLLOQ. gammy
10 *in a bad mood*
angry, bad-tempered, irritable, cross, snappy, quick-

tempered, grumpy, tetchy, testy, mean, foul, filthy, black,
gnarled, peppery, thin-skinned, prickly, fractious, narky,
petulant, impatient, choleric, bilious, splenetic, dyspeptic;
dialect stingy; *Scot* capernoity; *Scot & Irish* carnaptious
FORMAL irascible, querulous, cantankerous
COLLOQ. stroppy, in a huff, in a sulk, having got out of bed
on the wrong side, having a short fuse, cross as a bear with
a sore head, crotchety, crabbed, crabby, grouchy, shirty,
ratty, edgy, feisty, humpy
11 *feel bad about letting you down*
guilty, sorry, ashamed, shamefaced, apologetic,
conscience-stricken, remorseful, contrite
12 *bad language*
rude, offensive, abusive, insulting, blasphemous, profane,
discourteous, impolite, crude, coarse, vulgar, indecent,
obscene, gross, dirty, smutty
COLLOQ. raunchy, blue, hot, juicy
E3 1 good, pleasant, mild **2** virtuous **3** skilled, skilful **4** well,
happy **5** fresh **6** well-behaved, obedient **7** good,
convenient, favourable; *formal* auspicious **10** good, good-
tempered, equable **12** polite
▪ **not bad**
quite good, all right, tolerable, passable, acceptable, fair,
average, adequate, reasonable, satisfactory
COLLOQ. OK, so-so

Synonym nuances
sense 1
Unpleasant and **disagreeable** are both suggestive of
bad behaviour (towards someone), though they are less
intensive than **nasty**, which implies an inherent cruelty.
The terms **dreadful**, **appalling** and **atrocious** were
initially used to denote something truly horrific, but the
sense has weakened and can be used of many things:
that dreadful child; atrocious weather. **Undesirable** is
used more specifically, to describe something that falls
below accepted levels or standards: *undesirable
practices*.
 If something is described as **unfortunate** or
distressing you can infer that its failure to measure up is
a source of regret: *her unfortunate gaffe*. However the
terms **adverse**, **detrimental**, **harmful**, **damaging** and
hurtful are only used of something with definite
negative effects. **Dangerous**, **injurious**, **destructive**
and **ruinous** all suggest even more devastating effects,
whilst **unhealthy** and **unwholesome** are terms you can
use when your physical wellbeing or moral fibre is at risk:
an unhealthy obsession.

---

badge *n*
1 *a school badge*
identification, emblem, device, insignia, crest, shield,
escutcheon, rondel, sign, mark, token, stamp, brand,
trademark, logo, ensign
TECHNICAL episemon
2 *a badge of power*
sign, mark, token, symbol, indicator, indication

badger *v*
pester, plague, torment, harass, bait, bully, chivvy, go on at,
keep at, goad, harry, hound, nag, ride, bullyrag
FORMAL importune
COLLOQ. hassle

badinage *n*
banter, repartee, wordplay, jocularity, teasing, waggery,
chaff, drollery, give and take, humour, mockery, raillery
OLD dicacity
FORMAL persiflage
COLLOQ. ribbing
SLANG *Aust & NZ* borak

badly *adv*
1 *a badly directed play*

poorly, inadequately, imperfectly, defectively, unsatisfactorily, unacceptably, uselessly, incompetently, wrongly, incorrectly, improperly, faultily, negligently, carelessly, ineptly
FORMAL ineffectually
COLLOQ. awfully, terribly, pathetically, appallingly
2 badly hurt
seriously, acutely, bitterly, painfully, desperately, severely, critically, dangerously, gravely, crucially
3 WICKEDLY, cruelly, criminally, immorally, shamefully, dishonestly, sinfully, evilly, offensively, unfairly
4 UNFAVOURABLY, adversely, critically, unfortunately, unsuccessfully, unhappily
5 want something badly
very much, greatly, exceedingly, enormously, tremendously, desperately, intensely, extremely, deeply
E3 1 well **2** slightly, mildly **3** well **4** favourably, fortunately

---

Synonym nuances
sense 1
Poorly can be used as a general term to suggest that something has failed to reach an acceptable standard, likewise if it is done **inadequately**. However, something done **imperfectly** implies that it has not been fully completed: *a new challenge, as yet imperfectly understood*. **Defectively** is rarely used and only in the context of an inherent fault, whilst **unsatisfactorily** and **unacceptably** both imply that the outcome of an action is fit only for rejection.
  The word **uselessly** describes an ineffective action: *she peered uselessly into the dark corners*; whereas **incompetently** suggests one not done well. **Wrongly** and **incorrectly** are used of something done erroneously: *the paper incorrectly identified the former cricket player*. **Improperly** has to do with the manner of doing something and suggests that the correct procedures have not been followed. Another term rarely used is **faultily**, which suggests an inherent flaw.
  If, however, you say that something has been done **negligently** or **carelessly**, it implies that it was not accorded the correct level of care or responsibility: *the fire had been started negligently*; whilst to use **ineptly** would suggest it was not done with the correct level of skill: *the game was ineptly refereed*.

---

badness *n*
wickedness, evil, dishonesty, corruption, depravity, vileness, immorality, sin, foulness, shamefulness, nastiness, unpleasantness, cruelty
E3 goodness

bad-tempered *adj*
irritable, cross, snappy, quick-tempered, grumpy, tetchy, testy, mean, black, gnarled, peppery, thin-skinned, prickly, fractious, in a (bad) mood, petulant, narky, impatient, choleric, bilious, splenetic, dyspeptic; *dialect* stingy; *Scot & Irish* carnaptious; *Scot* capernoity
FORMAL irascible, querulous, cantankerous
COLLOQ. stroppy, in a huff, in a sulk, having got out of bed on the wrong side, having a short fuse, cross as a bear with a sore head, crotchety, crabbed, crabby, grouchy, shirty, ratty, edgy, feisty, humpy
E3 good-tempered, genial, equable

baffle *v*
puzzle, perplex, nonplus, mystify, bemuse, bewilder, confuse, mystify, confound, dumbfound, daze, upset, fox, disconcert, foil, thwart, frustrate, hinder, block, bar, check, defeat; *Scot* bumbaze, fickle
OLD mate, bring to naught
COLLOQ. bamboozle, flummox, stump, throw, get, faze
E3 enlighten, help

baffling *adj*
puzzling, perplexing, mysterious, bewildering, cryptic, enigmatic, confusing, stupefying, perplexing, disconcerting, surprising, amazing, astounding, bemusing, extraordinary, unfathomable
E3 enlightening, explanatory

bag *v, n*
♦ *v*
1 CATCH, capture, trap, land, net, kill, shoot
2 OBTAIN, acquire, get, gain, come by, secure, net, corner, take, grab, appropriate, commandeer, reserve
♦ *n*
container, receptacle; *dialect* poke; *Scot* pock, pouch

Types of bag include:

attaché-case	flight bag	rucksack
backpack	Gladstone bag	sack
briefcase	grip	saddlebag
bumbag	handbag	satchel
carpetbag	haversack	shoulder bag
carrier bag	holdall	suitcase
N Am carry-all	kitbag	tote bag
case	knapsack	*Aust* tuckerbag
clutch bag	money bag	valise
ditty bag	moneybelt	vanity bag
duffel bag	pack	
N Am fanny pack	reticule	

---

baggage *n*
luggage, suitcases, cases, bags, belongings, things, equipment, gear, paraphernalia, effects
FORMAL impedimenta, accoutrements
COLLOQ. clobber

baggy *adj*
loose, loose-fitting, slack, roomy, ill-fitting, billowing, bulging, ballooning, floppy, shapeless, sagging, droopy, oversize, extra large
E3 tight, firm

bail *n, v*
♦ *n*
security, surety, pledge, bond, guarantee, warranty, collateral
TECHNICAL *Scot* caution
OLD replevy
■ **bail out**
1 HELP, aid, assist, relieve, rescue, save, finance
2 (*also* **bale out**) withdraw, retreat, quit, back out, escape, eject, get out, get clear

bait *n, v*
♦ *n*
lure, incentive, inducement, bribe, temptation, snare, enticement, decoy, allurement, incitement, attraction
E3 disincentive
♦ *v*
tease, provoke, goad, irritate, annoy, hound, taunt, irk, harass, persecute, torment, badger, plague, harry
COLLOQ. needle, hassle, give a hard time to

bake *v*
1 COOK, roast, oven-roast, pot-roast, spit-roast, brown
2 clay baked in the sun
dry, parch, harden, heat, fire, scorch, burn, wither, shrivel

balance *v, n*
♦ *v*
1 STEADY, poise, stabilize, level, square, equalize, even out, even up, equate, match
OLD (*Shakesp*) weigh; (*Shakesp & Spenser*) peise
2 balance the cost against the benefits
equalize, equate, match, correspond, agree, tally, counterbalance, counteract, counterweigh, neutralize,

offset, set, adjust, juggle, compensate for
3 COMPARE, consider, weigh, weigh up, estimate, evaluate, appraise, review
E3 1 unbalance, overbalance
♦ *n*
1 EQUILIBRIUM, steadiness, stability, evenness, symmetry, equality, parity, equity, equivalence, correspondence, uniformity
TECHNICAL stasis
FORMAL equipoise
2 COMPOSURE, calmness, self-possession, self-control, poise, assurance, aplomb, level-headedness, cool-headedness, equanimity
FORMAL sangfroid
COLLOQ. unflappability
3 REMAINDER, rest, residue, surplus, excess, difference
E3 1 imbalance, instability
■ **in the balance**
uncertain, unsure, unknown, undetermined, indefinite, unpredictable;
COLLOQ. iffy, in the air, touch and go
■ **on balance**
in conclusion, all in all, overall, generally, taking everything into consideration

balanced *adj*
1 *a balanced report*
objective, fair, impartial, unbiased, unprejudiced, equitable
2 *a balanced diet*
well-rounded, healthy, sound, complete
3 *a balanced person*
calm, self-possessed, assured, level-headed, cool-headed, dispassionate, equitable, even-handed, sensible
E3 1 prejudiced, biased

balcony *n*
terrace, veranda, portico, loggia, gallery, upper circle, gods

bald *adj*
1 BALD-HEADED, hairless, smooth, uncovered, tonsured, peeled, pollard
TECHNICAL glabrous, glabrate
FORMAL depilated
COLLOQ. bald as a coot
2 BARE, naked, unadorned, plain, simple, severe, stark, barren, exposed, treeless, unsheltered, bleak
3 *a bald statement*
forthright, direct, straight, blunt, outright, downright, straightforward, outspoken, simple, plain, unambiguous, unadorned
E3 1 hairy, hirsute **2** adorned, covered **3** veiled, equivocal

balderdash *n*
rubbish, nonsense, drivel, gibberish, trash, tripe, twaddle, blague, doggerel; *dialect* faddle; havers; *Scot* blethers, clamjamphrie
OLD galimatias
COLLOQ. bunk, bunkum, claptrap, piffle, bilge, cock, poppycock, hot air, cobblers, rot, tommyrot, codswallop, baloney, blah, bosh, eyewash, hogwash, rhubarb, guff, hooey, malarkey, moonshine, stuff and nonsense; *Aust & NZ* bulldust; *Aust* bull's wool
SLANG bull; (*vulgar*) balls, bollocks, crap, shit, bullshit; *N Am* jazz; *Aust & NZ* borak

balding *adj*
receding, losing your hair, thin on top, bald

baldness *n*
bald-headedness, bareness, hair loss, hairlessness, starkness
TECHNICAL calvities, calvousness, glabrousness, psilosis, madarosis
FORMAL alopecia
E3 hirsuteness

bale *n, v*
♦ *n*
bundle, truss, pack, package, parcel
■ **bale out**
see **bail out** [2].

baleful *adj*
deadly, harmful, threatening, destructive, evil, hurtful, injurious, malevolent, malignant, menacing, mournful, noxious, ominous, pernicious, ruinous, sinister, venomous
E3 favourable

balefully *adv*
harmfully, hurtfully, destructively, menacingly, threateningly, dangerously, destructively, detrimentally

balk, baulk *v*
1 FLINCH, recoil, shrink, jib, boggle, hesitate, refuse, resist, dodge, evade, shirk
FORMAL eschew
2 THWART, frustrate, foil, forestall, disconcert, baffle, hinder, obstruct, check, stall, bar, prevent, impede, defeat, counteract

ball[1] *n*
a golf ball
sphere, globe, orb, globule, drop, conglomeration, projectile, pellet, pill, shot, bullet
COLLOQ. slug
■ **play ball**
co-operate, collaborate, go along, play along, show willing, respond, reciprocate

ball[2] *n*
an invitation to a ball
dance, dinner-dance, party, soirée, masquerade, carnival, assembly

ballad *n*
poem, song, folk-song, singsong, shanty, carol, ditty, calypso, cantilena, mento, romance, forebitter; *Scot* ballant

ballet *n*
ballet-dancing, dancing
SLANG leg-business

Terms used in ballet include:

à pointe	coryphée	pas de seul
arabesque	dégagé	pirouette
attitude	divertissement	plié
balancé	écarté	ports de bras
ballerina	échappé	premier danseur
prima ballerina	élévation	première
ballon	en l'air	danseuse
barre	en pointe	prima ballerina
battement	entrechat	assoluta
batterie	figurant	principal male
battu	fish dive	dancer
bourrée	five positions	régisseur
brisé	foudroyant	sur les pointes
brisé volé	fouetté	sur place
cabriole	fouetté en	répétiteur
capriole	tournant	ballet shoe
chassé	glissade	point shoe
choreography	jeté	splits
ciseaux	grande jeté	tutu
company	leotard	
corps de ballet	pas de deux	

---

balloon *v*
1 *his cheeks ballooned*
bag, belly, billow, blow up, bulge, dilate, enlarge, expand, inflate, puff out, swell
FORMAL distend
2 *the deficit ballooned to 4 billion dollars*
soar, rocket, increase rapidly, snowball, grow rapidly, escalate, skyrocket

ballot *n*
poll, polling, vote, voting, election, referendum, plebiscite

ballyhoo n
fuss, hubbub, to-do, hullabaloo, clamour, commotion, excitement, disturbance, noise, racket, tumult, hue and cry, agitation, build-up, promotion, propaganda, publicity, advertising, hype
COLLOQ. kerfuffle

balm n
1 soothing balm for the skin
cream, lotion, salve, sedative, unguent, balsam, bromide, calmative, curative, embrocation, emollient, lenitive, ointment, palliative, restorative, anodyne, opobalsam
2 balm for a troubled spirit
comfort, consolation, relief
⊟ 1 irritant, vexation

balmy adj
warm, summery, gentle, mild, pleasant, soft, temperate, clement, soothing
⊟ inclement

bamboozle v
confound, dumbfound, daze, upset, disconcert, trick, cheat, dupe, deceive, hoodwink, fool, swindle, puzzle, perplex, nonplus, mystify, bemuse, bewilder, confuse, mystify; Scot bumbaze
COLLOQ. con, gull, rook, diddle, lead up the garden path, pull a fast one on

ban v, n
♦ v
forbid, prohibit, disallow, bar, exclude, ostracize, outlaw, banish, suppress, veto, restrict, censor, disqualify
OLD (Spenser) band
FORMAL proscribe
⊟ allow, permit, authorize
♦ n
prohibition, embargo, injunction, sanctions, veto, moratorium, boycott, stoppage, restriction, suppression, censorship, outlawry, bar, disqualification, banishment, condemnation, denunciation, curse, taboo
FORMAL interdiction, proscription
⊟ permission, dispensation

Synonym nuances
noun
The word **prohibition** often has legal connotations: *the Sunday trading prohibition*; while **embargo** is usually used of government orders banning trade: *the US arms embargo.* **Sanctions** are more in use on the international stage, when penalties have been imposed: *China must open its markets or face sanctions.* **Injunction** is used in the legal world, usually in the context of making someone refrain from certain actions. The term **veto**, although again often legal, can be used more widely to describe a ban on certain actions. Similarly **moratorium**, although it usually has a legal aspect, may also be used to talk about any enforced postponement: *a moratorium on commercial whaling.*
The term **boycott** usually suggests a pointed refusal to deal with someone; **stoppage** implies something organized, usually a cessation of labour. **Restriction** and **suppression** both suggest a ban that involves inhibiting development; the former through limiting it, the latter by more forceful means, quashing it completely. **Censorship** is an appropriate word to refer to stifling expression such as writing or speech. The word **outlawry** is suggestive of a legal act of banning, but its use is rare nowadays, unlike the common **bar**, a more general term for the forbidding of something.
The word **curse** is a powerful term with supernatural overtones, implying an almost otherworldly preventative force; the unofficial but powerful restraining influence suggested by the word **taboo**, however, is more likely to be the conventions of this world: *the use of violence must remain a taboo in our society.*

---

banal adj
trite, commonplace, ordinary, everyday, mundane, humdrum, boring, dull, unimaginative, nondescript, bland, hackneyed, clichéd, stock, stereotyped, stale, overused, threadbare, tired, unoriginal, inane, wearing thin, empty, vapid
COLLOQ. corny, old hat
⊟ original, fresh, imaginative

banality n
triteness, ordinariness, dullness, unimaginativeness, staleness, tiredness, unoriginality, inaneness, emptiness, vapidity, fatuity, cliché, commonplace, bromide, platitude, prosaicism, triviality, truism, old chestnut; N Am cornball, glittering generality
⊟ originality

band¹ n
1 a metal band
strip, belt, ribbon, sash, girdle, tape, bandage, binding, tie, ligature, bond, strap, cord, chain, connection, link, shackle, manacle, fetter
2 STRIP, stripe, line, belt, bar, streak, swathe

band² n, v
♦ n
1 bands of looters
gang, crew, group, troop, herd, flock, party, body, gathering, crowd, throng, horde, contingent, association, company, society, club, clique
2 the band played on
group, music/musical group, pop group, orchestra, ensemble
♦ v
group, gather, join, unite, join forces, team up, close ranks, stand together, pull together, club together, ally, collaborate, consolidate, amalgamate, merge, affiliate, federate
COLLOQ. stick together
⊟ disband, disperse

bandage n, v
♦ n
dressing, plaster, gauze, compress, lint, ligature, tourniquet, swathe, swaddle, Tubigrip®, Elastoplast®, Band-aid®
TECHNICAL capeline, spica
♦ v
bind (up), dress, wrap, cover, swathe, swaddle

bandit n
robber, thief, brigand, marauder, plunderer, outlaw, highwayman, pirate, buccaneer, hijacker, cowboy, gunman, desperado, gangster, crook, criminal, racketeer, raider
COLLOQ. mugger

bandy¹ v
bandy words about
exchange, swap, trade, barter, interchange, reciprocate, spread, pass, toss, throw, fling

bandy² adj
bandy-legged
bow-legged, curved, bowed, bent, misshapen, crooked

bane n
ruin, adversity, destruction, scourge, affliction, torment, trial, trouble, vexation, woe, annoyance, bête noire, blight, burden, calamity, curse, disaster, distress, downfall, evil, irritation, misery, misfortune, nuisance, ordeal, plague, pest, pestilence
COLLOQ. thorn in the flesh/side
⊟ blessing

baneful adj
destructive, ruinous, troublesome, distressing, painful, harmful, noxious, annoying, disastrous, posionous, pernicious

bang *n, v, adv*
* *n*

1 *a loud bang*
explosion, detonation, pop, boom, crack, clap, peal, clang, clash, thud, thump, thwack, slam, noise, report, shot
FORMAL report

2 *a nasty bang on the head*
blow, hit, knock, bump, crash, collision, crack, smack, punch, thump, stroke, bash
COLLOQ. wallop, whack, sock

* *v*

1 STRIKE, hit, bump into, crash into, bash, knock, bump, rap, drum, hammer, pound, wham, thump, stamp

2 EXPLODE, burst, detonate, crack, blow up, boom, echo, resound, crash, slam, clatter, clang, peal, thunder

* *adv*

straight, directly, headlong, right, exactly, precisely, absolutely, slap, slap-bang, smack, hard, noisily, suddenly, abruptly
COLLOQ. dead

bangle *n*
bracelet, band, circlet, wristlet, anklet

banish *v*

1 *banish someone from their country*
expel, eject, evict, deport, transport, drive away, cast out, throw out, exile, outlaw, ban, bar, debar, exclude, shut out, ostracize, excommunicate, expatriate, repatriate, extradite
OLD (*Spenser*) band, forsay
FORMAL rusticate

2 *banish thoughts from your mind*
dismiss, oust, dislodge, remove, get rid of, drive away, send away, shut out, discard, dispel, dislodge, eliminate, eradicate
FORMAL disimagine
E3 1 recall, welcome

Synonym nuances
sense 1

The words **expel**, **eject** and **evict** can all be used for the forcible removal of someone, though the first two imply greater force. **Deport** is used in the context of someone being removed from their land of residency: *many Madeirans were deported to the Azores*; while **transport** can be used when the destination is specified: *convicts transported to Australia*. The term **exile** could be used to intimate estrangement from one's native land or home. **Drive away** should be used if someone has been pressurized into choosing to leave a place, whereas the terms **cast out** and **throw out** return to the idea of a more physical enforcement.

The word **outlaw** has a narrower sense of being placed outside the law: *computer hacking should be outlawed*. The words **ban**, **bar** and **debar** are more generally used when admission has been refused.

Exclude and **shut out** similarly have to do with keeping someone out, and **ostracize** has the further suggestion of punishment or disapproval: *the new Federal Republic was internationally ostracized*. **Excommunicate** is only appropriate for exclusion from the church. The words **expatriate** and **repatriate** should also be used in specific contexts: the former of being forced from your native land, the latter of being sent back to it. **Extradite** similarly is used in the specific context of returning someone to a country, particularly for trial.

---

banishment *n*
expulsion, eviction, deportation, expatriation, transportation, exile, exclusion, ostracism, excommunication, extradition
FORMAL outlawry
E3 return, recall, welcome

banisters *n*
railing, rail, handrail, balustrade

bank¹ *n, v*
* *n*

1 *a bank account*
financial institution, high-street bank, clearing bank, merchant bank, savings bank, building society, finance company/house

2 *a blood bank*
accumulation, fund, pool, reservoir, depository, repository, treasury, savings, reserve, store, stock, stockpile, hoard, cache

* *v*

deposit, save (up), keep, store, accumulate, stockpile, lay by, put aside
COLLOQ. stash away, save for a rainy day
E3 spend

■ **bank on**
depend on, rely on, count on, bet on, trust, believe in
COLLOQ. bargain on, pin your hopes on

bank² *n, v*
* *n*

1 *the banks of a river*
side, embankment, slope, tilt, edge, shore, margin
Related adjective: riparian

2 *a bank of ground*
mound, earthwork, ridge, hillock, knoll, rampart, levee, parados, slope, rise, incline, heap, pile, mass

* *v*

1 SLOPE, incline, pitch, slant, tilt, tip

2 HEAP, heap up, pile, pile up, stack, stack up, mass, amass, accumulate, put together, mound, drift

bank³ *n*

a bank of switches
row, series, array, panel, bench, group, tier, rank, line, succession, sequence, train

banknote *n*
bill, note, paper money, treasury note; *N Am* greenback
SLANG flimsy

bankrupt *adj, v, n*
* *adj*

1 *the company went bankrupt*
insolvent, in liquidation, ruined, failed, folded, in administration, beggared, destitute, impoverished, spent
FORMAL penurious, impecunious
COLLOQ. bust, broke, broken, stony broke, hard up, gone to the wall, gone under, in the red, on the rocks, on your uppers; *Aust* bung

2 *bankrupt philosophies of life*
deficient, lacking, wanting, deprived, exhausted, depleted, without, bereft
E3 1 solvent, wealthy, flourishing, prospering, rich; *colloq.* in the black

* *v*

ruin, impoverish, break, bankrupt, cripple; *Scot* sequester

* *n*

insolvent, debtor, pauper, beggar, duck
OLD *Scot* dyvour

bankruptcy *n*
insolvency, (financial) ruin, liquidation, disaster, exhaustion, failure, indebtedness, lack, smash; *Scot* sequestration
OLD *Scot* dyvoury
FORMAL penury, beggary, ruination
COLLOQ. Carey Street
SLANG stumer
E3 solvency, wealth

banner *n*
flag, standard, colours, ensign, pennant, streamer, placard,

sign, banderol, burgee, fanion, pennon, gonfalon, vexillum, oriflamme, labarum
OLD *Scot* gumphion

banquet *n*
feast, dinner, dinner party, meal, party, treat, spread

banter *n, v*
◆ *n*
joking, jesting, pleasantry, badinage, repartee, word play, chaff, chaffing, derision, mockery, ridicule, raillery, quiz
OLD dicacity
FORMAL persiflage
COLLOQ. kidding, ribbing
SLANG *Aust & NZ* borak
◆ *v*
joke, jest, chaff, deride, mock, ridicule, pun, make fun of
COLLOQ. kid, rib, rag, pull someone's leg
SLANG josh

baptism *n*
1 *the child's baptism*
christening, immersion, sprinkling, affusion, aspersion, purification, naming, dedication
TECHNICAL paedobaptism, parabaptism
OLD mersion
2 *a baptism of fire*
beginning, initiation, introduction, debut, launch, launching, inauguration

baptize *v*
christen, immerse, sprinkle, dip, purify, cleanse, name, call, term, style, title, introduce, initiate, admit, enrol, recruit

bar *n, v, prep*
◆ *n*
1 PUBLIC HOUSE, inn, tavern, saloon, taproom, lounge, lounge bar, grill, brasserie, counter, table; *Scot* howf; *Can* beer-parlor, beverage room
COLLOQ. pub, hostelry, watering-hole
SLANG boozer
2 ROD, stick, shaft, pole, stake, stanchion, batten, crosspiece, rail, railing, paling, barricade
3 SLAB, cake, block, lump, chunk, hunk, wedge, ingot, nugget
4 OBSTACLE, impediment, hindrance, obstruction, barrier, stop, check, deterrent, drawback
5 *called to the Bar*
barristers, lawyers, counsel, advocates, court, tribunal
◆ *v*
1 EXCLUDE, debar, ban, forbid, prohibit, prevent, hinder, obstruct, block, blockade, restrain, check, stop, disqualify, suspend
FORMAL preclude
2 *bar the door*
barricade, lock, bolt, latch, fasten, secure, padlock
◆ *prep*
except (for), with the exception of, excepting, apart from, aside from, save, but for, excluding, omitting

barb *n*
1 *the barb on a fish hook*
arrow, point, spike, prong, needle, thorn, prickle, bristle, beard, tang
TECHNICAL harl, ramus, fluke, killick
2 *critical barbs at leaders*
gibe, insult, affront, sneer, rebuff, scorn
COLLOQ. dig

barbarian *n, adj*
◆ *n*
savage, brute, wild person, ruffian, hooligan, vandal, lout, oaf, boor, philistine, ignoramus, illiterate
◆ *adj*
savage, brute, wild, rough, brutish, coarse, crude, uncivilized, uncouth, uncultivated, uncultured,

unsophisticated, vulgar, loutish, hooligan
FORMAL tramontane
COLLOQ. Neanderthal

barbaric *adj*
barbarous, primitive, wild, savage, fierce, ferocious, vicious, cruel, inhuman, brutal, brutish, bestial, murderous, ruthless, uncivilized, uncouth, vulgar, coarse, crude, rude
F3 humane, civilized, gracious

barbarism *n*
wildness, savagery, fierceness, ferocity, viciousness, cruelty, inhumanness, brutality, brutishness, bestiality, murderousness, ruthlessness, uncivilizedness, corruption, enormity, uncouthness, vulgarity, coarseness, crudeness, rudeness

barbarity *n*
barbarousness, wildness, savagery, ferocity, viciousness, cruelty, inhumanity, brutality, ruthlessness, brutishness, atrocity, outrage, enormity
F3 civilization, humanity, civility

barbarous *adj*
1 *barbarous behaviour*
wild, savage, fierce, ferocious, vicious, cruel, inhuman, barbarian, barbaric, brutal, brutish, bestial, murderous, ruthless, heartless
2 *barbarous by modern standards*
primitive, ignorant, uncivilized, unrefined, unsophisticated, uncultured, unlettered, vulgar, rough, rude, crude
F3 **2** civilized, cultured, educated

barbecue *n, v*
◆ *n*
N Am cookout; *S Afr* braaivleis
COLLOQ. BBQ; *Aust* barbie
◆ *v*
cook, grill, griddle, bake, brown, roast, spit-roast, stir-fry

barbed *adj*
1 PRICKLY, spiny, thorny, spiked, spiky, pronged, hooked, jagged, toothed, pointed; *Scot* jaggy
2 *a barbed remark*
sarcastic, cutting, caustic, acid, hurtful, unkind, wounding, nasty, snide, hostile, critical
COLLOQ. catty, bitchy

bare *adj, v*
◆ *adj*
1 NAKED, nude, in the nude, unclothed, undressed, with nothing on, stripped, denuded, uncovered, exposed
COLLOQ. in your birthday suit, in the raw, in the buff; *Scot* in the scud; *Irish* in the nip
2 *bare shelves/rooms*
empty, vacant, clear, unfurnished
3 *a bare tree/landscape*
barren, denuded, exposed, bleak, desolate, stark, unsheltered, treeless, unforested, unwooded, woodless
FORMAL defoliated
4 *the bare facts*
simple, plain, unadorned, barren, bald, stark, basic, essential, straightforward, cold, hard, sheer, absolute, mere
5 *the bare minimum*
mere, very least, very, sheer, no more than, utter, pure, absolute, complete
F3 **1** clothed **2** full, decorated **3** wooded, sheltered, forested **4** detailed
◆ *v*
uncover, lay bare, unveil, strip, expose, unmask, peel, undress, unclothe, display, reveal

barefaced *adj*
brazen, shameless, blatant, bold, brash, flagrant, glaring, arrant, impudent, insolent, unabashed, undisguised, unconcealed, audacious, naked, manifest, open, palpable, patent, obvious, transparent, bald, bald-faced

barefooted *adj*
barefoot, shoeless, unshod
FORMAL discalced
🔁 shod

barely *adv*
hardly, scarcely, no sooner, only just, just, almost, none too, by a short head
OLD scrimp
COLLOQ. be a near/close thing, by the skin of your teeth, by a whisker

bargain *n, v*
♦ *n*
1 DEAL, transaction, contract, treaty, pact, pledge, promise, covenant, agreement, understanding, arrangement, negotiation
FORMAL concordat
2 DISCOUNT, reduction, special offer, good buy, cheap buy, value for money, *bon marché*; *Scot* wanworth
COLLOQ. snip, giveaway, steal
SLANG *N Am* whizz
♦ *v*
negotiate, haggle, beat down, deal, trade, traffic, broke; *N Am* broker; barter, buy, sell, transact, settle, clinch
OLD chaffer, indent
■ **bargain for**
expect, anticipate, plan for, be prepared for, include, reckon on, take into account, look for, foresee, imagine, contemplate, consider, figure on
■ **into the bargain**
as well, besides, additionally, also, furthermore

bargaining *n*
negotiation, haggling, dealing(s), trade, trafficking, barter(ing), buying, selling, transaction, horsetrading, wheeling and dealing, wheeler-dealing

barge *n, v*
♦ *n*
canal-boat, flatboat, narrowboat, houseboat, lighter, wherry, pontoon, pram, scow, keel, keelboat, *barca*, budgerow, casco, piragua
OLD birlinn, Bucentaur, galley; *dialect* butty; *Scot* gabbart
♦ *v*
push (in), push your way, force your way, shove, rush, bump, hit, collide, press, jostle, elbow, smash, plough
■ **barge in**
interrupt, butt in, burst in, break in, cut in, gatecrash, intrude, interfere

bark¹ *v, n*
♦ *v*
1 *the dog barked*
yap, woof, yelp, snap, snarl, growl, bay, howl
2 *bark orders at someone*
yell, shout, cry, bawl, thunder, bellow, snap, snarl
♦ *n*
yap, woof, yelp, snap, snarl, growl, bay, howl

bark² *n*
the bark of a tree
covering, casing, crust, husk, rind, peel, skin, hide, shell
TECHNICAL cortex, integument

barmy *adj*
crazy, foolish, idiotic, insane, mad, odd, silly, stupid
COLLOQ. daft, batty, dippy, dotty, loony, loopy, nuts, crackers, nutty, off your head/rocker/nutter, need your head examining, round the bend/twist, off your trolley, out to lunch
🔁 rational, sane, sensible, of sound mind

baron *n*
1 NOBLEMAN, peer, aristocrat, lord
2 *press barons*
magnate, tycoon, captain of industry, industrialist, mogul, entrepreneur, executive
COLLOQ. fat cat, bigwig, big shot
OLD SLANG big cheese

baroness *n*
noblewoman, peer, aristocrat, lady

baroque *adj*
elaborate, ornate, rococo, florid, flowery, flamboyant, embellished, exuberant, vigorous, bold, decorated, overelaborate, overdecorated, overwrought, extravagant, showy, fanciful, fantastic, whimsical, grotesque
TECHNICAL churrigueresque
FORMAL convoluted
🔁 plain, simple, unadorned, austere

barrack *v*
heckle, jeer, taunt, hiss, boo, shout down, interrupt

barracking *n*
heckling, jeering, hissing, boos, interruption(s)

barracks *n*
garrison, camp, encampment, fort, guardhouse, quarters, billet, lodging, accommodation, casern, gendarmerie
SLANG glasshouse

barrage *n*
1 *a barrage of fire/criticism*
bombardment, shelling, gunfire, cannonade, battery, volley, salvo, burst, broadside, fusillade, assault, attack, onset, onslaught, deluge, torrent, flood, stream, storm, hail, rain, shower, mass, abundance, profusion
2 DAM, barrier, enbankment, wall, dyke, barricade, obstruction

barrel *n*
cask, keg, tun, butt, water-butt, firkin, hogshead, *pièce*, wood, tierce, rundlet

barren *adj*
1 *barren land/activity*
dry, arid, desert, desolate, waste, uncultivable, empty, addle
OLD effete, teemless; *Scot* hirstie
2 INFERTILE, sterile, childless, unprolific, unbearing; *Scot* yeld
FORMAL infecund
3 DULL, flat, vapid, uninteresting, uninspiring, uninformative, uninstructive, unrewarding, unbearing, unproductive, profitless, unfruitful, fruitless, pointless, useless, valueless, purposeless
🔁 1 fertile, productive 2 fertile 3 fruitful, useful

barrenness *n*
1 DRYNESS, aridity, emptiness, dullness, unfruitfulness, pointlessness, uselessness
2 INFERTILITY, sterility, unfruitfulness
TECHNICAL infecundity

barricade *n, v*
♦ *n*
blockade, obstruction, obstacle, barrier, bar, fence, stockade, bulwark, rampart, palisade, protection, defence
♦ *v*
block, obstruct, bar, blockade, close (up), shut (off), fortify, strengthen, defend, protect

barrier *n*
1 WALL, fence, railing, ha-ha, barricade, bar, gate, blockade, stockade, obstacle, roadblock, boom, rampart, fortification, ditch, frontier, boundary, bar, check
2 *a barrier to success*
obstacle, hurdle, stumbling-block, impediment, obstruction, hindrance, handicap, limitation, restriction, drawback, check, restraint, difficulty

barring *prep*
except (for), except (in the event of), if, unless, bar

barrister *n*
lawyer, solicitor, advocate, counsel, QC; *N Am* attorney, counsellor
COLLOQ. brief

bartender *n*
barman, barmaid, barkeeper, publican, mixologist; *N Am* barkeep

barter *v, n*
♦ *v*
trade, exchange, bargain, swap, traffic, deal, truck, haggle, negotiate, sell, chop; *Scot* coup, niffer; *dialect* cope
♦ *n*
trade, trading, exchange, bargaining, swapping, truck, trafficking, dealing, haggling, negotiation; *N Am* dicker
OLD permutation

base¹ *n, v*
♦ *n*
1 *the base of the statue*
BOTTOM, foot, pedestal, plinth, stand, stay, rest, support, prop, foundation, foundation stone, keystone, underneath, substructure, understructure, bed, groundwork
TECHNICAL fundus
2 BASIS, foundation, fundamental, essential, component, principal, key, heart, core, essence, backbone, bedrock, root, origin, source
3 HEADQUARTERS, HQ, centre, post, station, camp, settlement, depot, home, starting-point
4 *a biscuit base*
layer, thickness, bed, coating, covering
♦ *v*
1 *research based on fact*
found, establish, ground, build, construct, derive, have as a basis, depend, rest, hinge
2 *based in Edinburgh*
locate, station, position, situate, site, install

base² *adj*
base behaviour
abject, contemptible, despicable, wicked, corrupt, immoral, evil, vile, reprobate, vulgar, shameful, sordid, depraved, unprincipled, disgraceful, disreputable, wretched, worthless, ignominious, infamous, scandalous, low, lowly, low-minded, mean, miserable, pitiful, poor, valueless

baseless *adj*
groundless, unfounded, unsupported, unsubstantiated, unauthenticated, unconfirmed, unjustified, uncalled-for, unattested, untrue, fabricated, gratuitous
E3 justifiable, substantiated

basement *n*
cellar, crypt, vault
COLLOQ. *Scot* dunny

bash *v, n*
♦ *v*
hit, strike, knock, punch, belt, smash, smack, thump, slug, break, crash
COLLOQ. wallop, whack, clobber, biff, sock
♦ *n*
1 *a bash on the head*
knock, blow, bump, bang, box, thump, clip
2 *have a bash at something*
attempt, go, try
COLLOQ. crack, whirl, shot, stab
3 *throw a bash*
party, celebration
COLLOQ. thrash, blast, rave-up, rave

bashful *adj*
shy, coy, retiring, backward, reticent, reserved, unforthcoming, hesitant, shrinking, nervous, timid, timorous, diffident, modest, self-effacing, inhibited, self-conscious, embarrassed, blushing, abashed,

shamefaced, sheepish; *Scot* laithfu', blate
E3 bold, confident, aggressive, assertive

bashfully *adv*
shyly, reticently, hesitantly, nervously, timidly, diffidently, modestly, self-effacingly, self-consciously, sheepishly
E3 boldly, aggressively

bashfulness *n*
shyness, coyness, reticence, reserve, hesitancy, nervousness, timidity, diffidence, modesty, self-effacement, inhibition, self-consciousness, embarrassment, blushes, shamefacedness, sheepishness
E3 boldness, confidence, assertiveness

basic *adj*
1 FUNDAMENTAL, elementary, primary, rudimentary, radical, root, underlying, key, central, inherent, intrinsic, essential, indispensable, vital, necessary, important, first, preparatory
2 *basic rate of pay*
standard, minimum, lowest level, starting
3 *basic accommodation*
primitive, elementary, plain, simple, minimal, staple, unadorned, spartan, stark, austere, crude, unsophisticated
COLLOQ. *N Am* down-and-dirty
E3 1 inessential, minor, peripheral **2** with commission, premium **3** elaborate, sophisticated

basically *adv*
fundamentally, essentially, in essence, at bottom, at heart, inherently, radically, intrinsically, principally, primarily, substantially, mainly, in the main, when it comes down to it

basics *n*
fundamentals, essentials, rudiments, (first) principles, introduction, facts, necessaries, practicalities, ABC, alphabet, realities, bedrock, rock bottom, core
COLLOQ. brass tacks, nitty-gritty, nuts and bolts

basin *n*
1 *a pudding basin*
bowl, dish, pot, pan, sink
TECHNICAL lavabo
2 *the basin of a river*
bed, crater, cavity, hollow, gully, valley, depression, channel, dip
TECHNICAL playa

basis *n*
1 *research that forms the basis of the book*
foundation, support, base, bottom, footing, ground(s), groundwork, cornerstone, bedrock, key, keynote, reason(s), rationale, fundamental(s), fundamental point, starting-point, premise, principle, first principles, main ingredient, alpha and omega, essential(s), essence, heart, core, thrust
FORMAL quintessence, hypostasis
2 *on a particular basis*
arrangement, procedure, method, system, principle, condition(s), terms, status, footing, way, approach

---

Synonym nuances
sense 1
Foundation, **support**, **base** and **footing** share wide usage and imply the necessary first steps in establishing any process: *basic research is an essential foundation for applied research*; while **bottom** might also be used of any fundamental aspect. **Groundwork** can also be used of essential preparatory work: *the groundwork of the veterinary art was medical science*. **Grounds**, however, more appropriately describes a reason or excuse: *their refusal was on religious grounds*.

The terms **cornerstone** and **bedrock**, although they convey a physical image, are also widely used figuratively, with connotations of strength and immutability: *a cornerstone of government policy*; *the bedrock of* *democracy.* **Key** and **keystone** may be used of any factor considered crucial or central to a system or policy, whereas **reason**(**s**) and **rationale** are appropriate to describe a more intellectual explanation. Likewise **principle** and **premise** tend to present a primary assumption: *he starts with the premise that safety is impossible.*

Essentials is a fairly unmarked term for necessary things, but **essence**, **heart** or **core** have a more spiritual tone, suggesting something's essential nature. **Thrust** is rather different, in that it is suggestive of future direction: *economic reform will be the thrust of his plan.*

bask *v*
1 *bask in the sun*
sunbathe, bathe, lie, lounge, relax, laze, loll, sprawl
OLD apricate
2 *bask in someone's approval*
revel, delight in, enjoy, take pleasure in, relish, savour, lap up, wallow
FORMAL luxuriate

basket *n*
hamper, container, bin, box, holder, receptacle, case, trolley, creel, pannier, punnet, bassinet, coop, skep, trug, scull, scuttle, van, chip, corbeil, crib, cabas, pottle, corf, frail, gabion, seedlip, petara; *dialect* cob, kipe, leap, maund, rip, willy, wisket; *Scot* murlain
OLD flasket

bass *adj*
deep, deep-pitched, deep-toned, low, low-pitched, low-toned, grave, full, full-toned, rich, resonant, sonorous

bastard *n*
illegitimate, illegitimate child, love child, natural child, misfortune, slink, by-blow, come-o'-will, come-by-chance, mamzer, *filius nullius*
OLD whoreson, sideslip
COLLOQ. basket, lucky-piece

bastardize *v*
adulterate, pervert, defile, contaminate, corrupt, debase, degrade, demean, depreciate, devalue, cheapen, distort
FORMAL vitiate

bastion *n*
stronghold, citadel, fortress, defence, bulwark, mainstay, support, prop, pillar, rock, protection, defence
TECHNICAL lunette, moineau
FORMAL redoubt

batch *n*
lot, consignment, parcel, pack, bunch, set, assortment, collection, assemblage, cluster, accumulation, mass, group, conglomeration, contingent, amount, quantity, aggregate, crowd

bath *n, v*
♦ *n*
1 *be in the bath*
bathtub, tub, sauna, steam bath, hot tub, Jacuzzi®, whirlpool, bath, slipper bath, Turkish bath, steam room, spa, hamman, thermae
FORMAL balneary
Related adjective: balneal
2 *have/take a bath*
wash, scrub, soak, shower, douche, tub, dip
♦ *v*
bathe, have/take a bath, wash, clean, dip, soak, shower, freshen up

bathe *v, n*
♦ *v*
1 *bathe in the sea*
swim, bath, take a dip, surf, tub; *Scot* dook
2 *bathe a wound*

wet, moisten, immerse, wash, clean, cleanse, rinse, soak, steep, flood, cover
OLD embathe, lave, stew; (*Spenser*) beath, embay
3 *bathed in light*
suffuse, permeate, cover, saturate, steep
♦ *n*
swim, dip, paddle, wash, rinse, soak

bathos *n*
anticlimax, comedown, disappointment, let-down

baton *n*
stick, rod, staff, truncheon, cudgel
OLD warder

battalion *n*
1 *an infantry battalion*
army, force, garrison, brigade, regiment, squadron, company, platoon, division, detachment, section, contingent, legion, troops, unit
2 *a battalion of people*
crowd, mob, horde, multitude, throng, army, host, mass, herd

batten *n, v*
♦ *n*
strip, bar, bolt, board
♦ *v*
barricade, board up, clamp down, fasten, fix, nail down, secure, tighten

batter *v*
1 *waves battering the pier*
beat, pound, pummel, buffet, smash, dash, pelt, lash, bombard, damage, demolish, destroy, wear down, wear out, erode, mangle
2 *battering his wife*
abuse, maltreat, ill-treat, hit, strike, knock about, club, bash, beat, assault, hurt, injure, bruise, disfigure, maul
COLLOQ. lay into, wallop, thrash, whack, rough up
SLANG *NAm* lam
■ **batter down**
break down, smash, demolish, destroy, ruin, wreck

battered *adj*
1 *a battered child*
beaten, abused, hit, maltreated, ill-treated, injured, bruised
2 *a battered old shed*
weather-beaten, dilapidated, tumbledown, run-down, damaged, ramshackle, shabby, crumbling, damaged, crushed

battery *n*
1 *a battery of tests*
sequence, series, set, cycle, succession
2 *a battery of cameras*
set, row, bank, group
FORMAL array
3 *assault and battery*
attack, assault, beating, grievous bodily harm, force, striking, thrashing, violence
COLLOQ. mugging
4 *the military battery*
artillery, cannon, cannonry, emplacements, guns, ordnance

battle *n, v*
♦ *n*
war, warfare, hostilities, action, conflict, armed conflict, strife, combat, fight, engagement, final battle, Armageddon, field, encounter, attack, fray, skirmish, brawl, clash, struggle, free-for-all, contest, tournament, campaign, drive, race, competition, crusade, row, disagreement, confrontation, dispute, debate, controversy, stour; *Aust & NZ* stoush
FORMAL altercation
COLLOQ. scrap, set-to
♦ *v*

fight, combat, war, feud, contend, struggle, strive, combat, campaign, crusade, agitate, clamour, contest, encounter, engage, argue, quarrel, disagree, dispute
OLD darraign

battle-axe n
1 POLEAXE, axe, bill
OLD gisarme, Jeddart staff, wifel
2 *his battle-axe of a wife*
dragon, disciplinarian, harridan, hag, shrew, fury, witch, martinet, Tartar, termagant, virago

battle-cry n
1 WAR CRY, war song, rallying cry/call, banzai
2 SLOGAN, motto, watchword, catchword, catchphrase

battlefield n
battleground, field of battle, field, front, front line, war/combat zone, theatre of operations, arena, Armageddon

batty adj
crazy, foolish, idiotic, insane, mad, demented, odd, eccentric, peculiar, silly, stupid
COLLOQ. daft, barmy, bats, bonkers, dippy, dotty, loony, loopy, nuts, crackers, nutty, off your head/rocker/nut, need your head examining, round the bend/twist, out to lunch
F3 rational, sane, sensible

bauble n
knick-knack, trinket, toy, plaything, trifle, ornament, bagatelle, bibelot, gewgaw, gimcrack, kickshaw, tinsel
OLD flamflew

baulk
see **balk**.

bawd n
brothel-keeper, madam, panderess, pimp, procuress, procurer

bawdy adj
lewd, adult, pornographic, coarse, dirty, rude, vulgar, erotic, obscene, X-rated, gross, improper, indecent, indecorous, indelicate, lecherous, lascivious, licentious, lustful, ribald, risqué, smutty, suggestive; *Scot* sculduddry
FORMAL libidinous, prurient, salacious
COLLOQ. blue, raunchy, near the knuckle
F3 chaste, clean

bawl v
1 *the baby bawled*
cry, weep, sob, blubber, wail, snivel, squall
2 *bawl loudly at someone*
yell, shout, cry (out), bellow, howl, roar, call (out), scream, screech, yowl
OLD (*Shakesp*) gape
FORMAL vociferate
COLLOQ. holler
■ **bawl out**
scold, rebuke, reprimand, yell at
COLLOQ. tell off, give someone a telling-off, dress down, give someone a dressing-down, give someone a piece of your mind, tear someone off a strip, give someone an earful

bay[1] n
moor the ship in a bay
gulf, bight, arm, sound, firth, inlet, indentation, fleet, embayment, cove, lagoon, estuary; *Scot* loch, voe
OLD reach

bay[2] n
a bay in the lounge
recess, alcove, niche, nook, opening, compartment, cubicle, cubbyhole, booth, stall, carrel
OLD classis

bay[3] v
baying for blood

howl, clamour, roar, bellow, bell, bawl, cry, bark, yelp
COLLOQ. holler

bayonet n, v
♦ *n*
knife, blade, sword, pike, spear, dagger, poniard, white arm
SLANG spike
♦ *v*
stab, impale, knife, pierce, spear, stick

bazaar n
1 MARKET, , marketplace, mart, souk, alcaicería, alcázar, exchange
2 *a school bazaar*
sale, fair, fête, bring-and-buy, jumble sale, nearly-new sale

be v
1 EXIST, breathe, live, be alive, inhabit, be present, be situated, be located, stand, lie, reside, dwell
2 STAY, remain, last, endure, persist, continue, survive, stand, prevail, obtain
FORMAL abide
3 HAPPEN, occur, arise, come about, take place, come to pass, develop, transpire
FORMAL befall
4 REPRESENT, constitute, make (up), form, amount to, add up to, account for

beach n, v
♦ *n*
sand, sands, shingle, shore, seashore, seaside, water's edge, coast, coastline, seaboard, machair, lido, plage
OLD strand
FORMAL littoral
Related adjective: littoral
♦ *v*
go ashore, run ashore, run aground, land, ground, strand, be grounded, be stranded

beachcomber n
forager, loafer, loiterer, scavenger, wayfarer

beacon n
signal, fire, watch fire, bonfire, light, beam, lighthouse, watchtower, flare, rocket, sign, warning light, danger signal, needfire
OLD fanal
FORMAL pharos

bead n
1 *a string of beads*
ball, pearl, jewel, pellet, globule, spheroid, tear, bugle
TECHNICAL paternoster, knurl, ojime, spacer plate
OLD bede, gaud
2 *beads of sweat*
drop, droplet, drip, blob, dot, bubble
COLLOQ. glob

beak n
bill, mandibles, nib, neb, rostrum, nose, proboscis, snout, rostellum
OLD becke

beaker n
glass, tumbler, jar, cup, mug, tankard

beam n, v
♦ *n*
1 *a beam of light*
ray, shaft, gleam, stream, flash, flare, glint, glimmer, glow, streak, bar
2 PLANK, board, timber, rafter, joist, girder, spar, boom, bar, support, stanchion, strut, transom, lintel, cantilever, stringer, summer, lath, scantling
TECHNICAL purlin
3 SMILE, grin, laugh, smirk
♦ *v*
1 *beam a TV signal*
transmit, emit, broadcast, send, aim, direct, relay

2 *sunlight beaming through the window*
shine, emit, radiate, glare, gleam, glitter, glow, glimmer, flash, sparkle
FORMAL effulge
3 SMILE, grin, laugh, smirk
■ **off beam**
wrong, mistaken, inaccurate, incorrect
COLLOQ. wide of the mark, off target

bean *n*
Related adjectives: fabaceous, leguminous

Varieties of bean and pulse include:

ad(z)uki bean	pea)	sugar pea)
alfalfa	dwarf runner	marrowfat pea
bean sprout	bean	mung bean
black bean	fava bean	*N Am* navy bean
black-eye(d)	flageolet bean	pea
bean (or	French bean	pinto bean
cowpea)	gram	puy lentil
black gram	golden gram	red kidney bean
borlotti bean	green bean	red lentil
broad bean	green gram	runner bean
butter bean	green lentil	scarlet runner
cannellini bean	haricot bean	*N Am* snap bean
(or fasolia)	kidney bean	soy (or soya)
carob (or locust)	legume	bean
bean	lentil	split pea
chickpea (or	*N Am* lima (or	string bean
garbanzo)	sugar) bean	tonka bean
chilli bean	mangetout (or	wax bean
d(h)al (or pigeon	snow pea or	

See also **legumes and pulses** *at* **vegetable**.

---

bear *v*
1 CARRY, convey, transport, move, take, bring, fetch
COLLOQ. hump, tote
2 SUPPORT, hold (up), keep (up), carry, shoulder, uphold, sustain
3 *bear children*
give birth to, breed, deliver, give up
OLD beget
FORMAL engender
4 TOLERATE, stand, put up with, endure, abide, suffer, like, permit, allow, admit, endorse, accept, take, live with, brook; *Scot* thole
OLD (*Shakesp*) abrooke
COLLOQ. stomach, hack, grin and bear it
5 *bear signs of a struggle*
carry, show, display, exhibit, have
6 *bear the cost*
pay, accept, support, carry, shoulder, sustain
7 *bear someone malice*
hold, have, maintain, entertain, harbour, foster, cherish
8 *bear fruit*
propagate, produce, generate, develop, yield, bring forth
FORMAL fructify
9 *bear yourself well*
carry, behave, act, conduct, acquit, move
OLD abear
FORMAL comport
10 *bear left at the junction*
veer, turn, move, go, drive, diverge, deviate, bend, curve, swerve
■ **bear down on**
advance on, approach, move in on, close in on, move threateningly towards, move menacingly towards
■ **bear in mind**
keep in, mind, remember, be mindful of, consider, note, take into account, make a mental note
■ **bear out**
confirm, endorse, support, back up, uphold, prove,

demonstrate, corroborate, substantiate, validate, warrant, ratify, vindicate, justify, verify
■ **bear up**
persevere, cope, soldier on, carry on, suffer, endure, survive, withstand
COLLOQ. grin and bear it, keep your pecker up
■ **bear with**
tolerate, put up with, endure, suffer, forbear, be patient with, make allowances for

---

Synonym nuances
sense 4
Tolerate, **stand** and **put up with** are fairly neutral terms in general use, while **endure** would imply a stronger test of one's stoicism: *she endured years of abuse*. The word **abide** is again more marked, and is invariably used in the negative to convey strong feeling: *I can't abide that man*. **Suffer** can also be used in the negative in a similar way: *he did not suffer fools gladly*. However, if it is not used in the negative, the suggestion is that great pain or distress is being borne. If you use **like**, however, the tone is positive.
Unlike all the aforementioned words, **permit**, **allow**, **admit** and **accept** are not emotive, and they hint at an element of concession, whilst **endorse** implies collusion: *the plan endorses private ownership of land*. Both **take** and **live with** are again less intense terms referring to inaction and resignation, whilst **brook** is another generally found in negative usage and in more formal contexts: *he will brook no dissent*.

---

bearable *adj*
tolerable, endurable, sufferable, supportable, sustainable, passable, acceptable, admissible, manageable, liv(e)able
OLD (*Shakesp*) portable
F∃ unbearable, intolerable

beard *n, v*
♦ *n*
facial hair, stubble, bristle, goatee, imperial, vandyke, moustache, whiskers, five o'clock shadow, mutton chops, sideburns, sideboards, tuft, peak, Charlie, imperial, Newgate frill, vandyke, kesh, pappus
SLANG beaver; *Aust* ziff
♦ *v*
brave, challenge, confront, dare, defy, face, oppose, stand up against

bearded *adj*
unshaven, bristly, stubbly, whiskered, bewhiskered, tufted, hairy, hirsute, shaggy, bushy
TECHNICAL pogoniate
F∃ beardless, clean-shaven, smooth

bearer *n*
1 *the bearer of bad news*
conveyor, courier, messenger, runner, agent
2 *the bearers of a coffin*
carrier, conveyor, porter, transporter
3 *the bearer of a document*
holder, possessor, owner, beneficiary, consignee, payee

bearing *n*
1 *have no bearing on the matter*
influence, relevance, significance, connection, relation, concern, reference
FORMAL pertinence
2 MANNER, air, aspect, attitude, behaviour, poise, carriage, gait, posture, stature
OLD (*Shakesp & Spenser*) portance
FORMAL demeanour, comportment, deportment, mien
3 *find your bearings*
orientation, sense of direction, position, situation, location, whereabouts, course, track, way, direction, aim

beast n
1 *birds and beasts*
animal, creature, brute
2 *You selfish beast!*
brute, monster, savage, barbarian, pig, swine, devil, ogre, fiend
Related adjectives: bestial, theriomorphous

beastly adj
horrible, horrid, terrible, unpleasant, disagreeable, awful, nasty, rotten, foul, repulsive, mean, brutal, cruel, swinish

beat v, n, adj
♦ v
1 HIT, flog, lash, whip, flay, cane, birch, strap, thrash, lay into, punch, strike, swipe, knock, clout, bang, wham, club, bash, slap, smack, pound, hammer, batter, thump, drub, welt, thwack, buffet, pelt, bruise, box, cudgel, lambast, pummel
OLD contuse, knubble, knout, vapulate; (*Shakesp*) firk
COLLOQ. tan, wallop, whack, belt, clobber, knock about, biff, fill in
SLANG *N Am* lam
2 PULSATE, pulse, throb, thump, pound, race, palpitate, flutter, vibrate, quiver, tremble, shake, quake
3 *waves beating against the rocks*
pound, strike, dash, batter, lash
4 *beat a drum*
hit, strike, bang, tap, pound
5 *a bird's wings beating*
flap, flutter, shake, swing, quiver, thresh, thrash, vibrate
6 *beat the eggs*
stir, mix, whisk, blend, combine
7 *beat metal*
hammer, forge, knock, fashion, form, shape, mould, work, stamp
FORMAL malleate
8 CONQUER, beat, overcome, overpower, best, get the better of, have the edge on, be more than a match for, outscore, outplay, outwit, outsmart, eclipse, excel, surpass, outmatch, subdue, overthrow, worst, repel, drub, trounce, overwhelm, rout, ruin, crush, conquer, quell, pulverize, bring someone to their knees, reject, throw out; *Scot* granny
OLD put to the worse
FORMAL subjugate, vanquish, discomfit
COLLOQ. thrash, lick, hammer, thump, trounce, clobber, annihilate, smash, devastate, slaughter, make mincemeat (out) of, run rings round, wipe the floor with, paste, marmelize; *Scot* gub
SLANG *N Am* lam
*See Synonym nuances panel at **defeat**.*
9 *beat the record*
surpass, excel, exceed, outdo, outstrip, outrun, transcend
♦ n
1 *the beat of a drum*
hit, stroke, strike, striking, bang, banging, blow, knocking, pounding
2 PULSATION, pulse, stroke, throb, pounding, thump, palpitation, vibration, flutter
3 RHYTHM, time, tempo, metre, measure, rhyme, pulse, stress, accent
FORMAL cadence
4 *a police officer's beat*
round, rounds, territory, circuit, course, journey, way, path, route, walk
♦ adj
exhausted, fatigued, tired, dog-tired, tired out, wearied, worn out, zonked
COLLOQ. jiggered, dead-beat, all in, done in, whacked,
knackered, bushed, clapped-out, zonked (out); *N Am* pooped (out), tuckered out
■ **beat off**
repel, drive back, repulse, fight off, hold off, ward off, force back, beat back, push back, keep at bay
■ **beat up**
attack, assault, knock about, knock around, batter
COLLOQ. do over, mug, rough up, clobber, knock about, knock someone's block off, beat the living daylights out of, knock into the middle of next week, batter; *S Afr* donder

beaten adj
1 *beaten metal*
hammered, stamped, forged, wrought, worked, moulded, formed, shaped, fashioned
2 *beaten paths*
trampled, trodden, well-trodden, well-worn, well-used
3 WHISKED, whipped, mixed, blended, stirred, frothy, foamy
■ **off the beaten track**
remote, isolated, secluded, unfrequented, private, god-forsaken, outlying, out-of-the-way
COLLOQ. in the sticks

beatific adj
blissful, blessed, divine, exalted, sublime, glorious, heavenly, joyful, ecstatic, rapturous, angelic, seraphic

beatification n
canonization, sanctification, exaltation, glorification

beatify v
canonize, sanctify, bless, exalt, glorify
FORMAL macarize

beating n
1 CORPORAL PUNISHMENT, hitting, whipping, flogging, caning, the cane/birch/strap, thrashing, lashing, drubbing, punching, clubbing, slapping, smacking, battering, thumping, bruising, chastisement
COLLOQ. tanning, whacking, walloping, hiding, doing-over, belting, clobbering
2 DEFEAT, conquest, loss, rout, ruin, downfall, overthrow, trouncing, overwhelming, overpowering, annihilation, outwitting, outsmarting
FORMAL vanquishing
COLLOQ. hammering, slaughter, clobbering, thrashing

beatitude n
happiness, blessedness, ecstasy, rapture, contentedness, delight, elation

beau n
1 BOYFRIEND, admirer, suitor, sweetheart, lover, escort, fiancé
OLD spark
COLLOQ. guy
2 FOP, dandy, coxcomb, popinjay, Adonis
OLD muscadin

beautician n
beauty specialist, cosmetician, hairdresser, friseur
FORMAL visagiste

beautiful adj
attractive, fair, pretty, lovely, good-looking, handsome, gorgeous, radiant, ravishing, voluptuous, striking, stunning, pleasing, appealing, alluring, charming, delightful, fine, graceful, exquisite, becoming, magnificent; *Scot* bonny
OLD comely, seemly
FORMAL pulchritudinous
COLLOQ. smashing, out of this world
SLANG drop-dead gorgeous
E3 ugly, plain, hideous

Synonym nuances
Attractive and **lovely** can be used fairly generally to describe someone or something pleasing to look at, but **fair** and **pretty** are fairly mild terms usually reserved for females, though the latter may also be used of clothes and the like. **Good-looking** and **handsome**, on the other hand, are traditionally used of males, though both may also be applied to middle-aged women with distinguished features.

The term **voluptuous** is more usually reserved to conjure up the charms of more buxom women. You might use **radiant**, again usually of a woman, to suggest a more ethereal beauty that seems to shine from within, whilst **ravishing** carries a sense of being stunned by someone's or something's charms: *a ravishing smile*. Both **striking** and **stunning** may be used of both sexes, as well as scenery, and again suggest a breathtaking element. **Pleasing**, however, presents a much more restrained description.

You can use **appealing** to conjure up aspects of cuteness, whereas **alluring** suggests a more sensual aspect. **Charming** and **delightful** are now rather old-fashioned terms suggestive of a more quaint beauty: *a charming cottage*; whilst **fine**, along with **graceful** and **exquisite**, can be used to convey strongly an elegance of form or manner, the latter being generally used of things: *exquisite watercolours*. **Becoming** has an element of approval of something's suitability: *a few soft curls over each ear are very becoming*; whereas **magnificent** expresses extreme admiration of anything or anyone impressive.

---

beautifully *adv*
attractively, radiantly, strikingly, stunningly, pleasingly, pleasantly, charmingly, delightfully, gracefully

beautify *v*
embellish, smarten (up), enhance, improve, grace, gild, garnish, decorate, ornament, deck, adorn, array, glamorize, spruce up
OLD bedeck; (*Shakesp*) flourish
COLLOQ. titivate, tart up, doll up
E3 disfigure, spoil

beauty *n*
1 *the beauty of a woman/poem*
attractiveness, prettiness, loveliness, (good) looks, handsomeness, gorgeousness, radiance, appeal, allure, charm, delight, grace, gracefulness, exquisiteness, seemliness, excellence, harmony, symmetry
FORMAL pulchritude
Related adjective: pulchritudinous
2 *think her a real beauty*
belle, charmer, siren, Venus, *femme fatale*
COLLOQ. good-looker, smasher, corker, cracker, knockout, stunner, peach; *N Am* doozy, doozer
3 *the beauties of the plan*
attraction, advantage, benefit, good thing, plus point, good point, virtue, merit, glory, boon, blessing, strength, asset, bonus, dividend
E3 **1** ugliness, repulsiveness **2** frump **3** disadvantage

beaver
■ **beaver away**
work hard, work at, put a lot of effort in, persist, persevere
COLLOQ. slog, plug away, slave away

becalmed *adj*
at a standstill, at a halt, idle, motionless, still, stranded, marooned, stuck

because *conj*
as, for, for the reason that, since, owing to, due to, on account of, as a result of, the reason is ..., through, thanks to, in view of the fact that, in consideration of

FORMAL by reason of, by virtue of, forasmuch
COLLOQ. seeing as, 'cos

beckon *v*
1 *beckon to someone*
summon, motion, gesture, signal, nod, wave, waft, gesticulate
2 *fame beckons*
call, invite, attract, pull, draw, lure, allure, entice, tempt, induce, persuade, coax

become *v*
1 *become old-fashioned*
turn, grow (into), get, change into, be changed into, be transformed into, develop into, mature into, pass into, come to be, turn out to be, wax
2 SUIT, befit, flatter, look good on, enhance, grace, embellish, ornament, set off, harmonize
OLD (*Shakesp*) besort
■ **become of**
happen to, be the fate of
OLD befall

becoming *adj*
1 *a hat in a more becoming style*
attractive, charming, flattering, graceful, elegant, tasteful, fetching, pretty
OLD comely
2 *becoming behaviour*
appropriate, suitable, fit, fitting, befitting, consistent, congruous, compatible
E3 **1, 2** unbecoming

becomingly *adv*
attractively, charmingly, fetchingly, gracefully, elegantly, tastefully

bed *n, v*
♦ *n*
1 *get out of bed*
divan, couch, bunk, berth
SLANG sack, hay, kip
2 LAYER, stratum, substratum, matrix, base, basis, bottom, floor, foundation, groundwork, watercourse, channel
3 *bed of flowers*
garden, border, patch, area, space, strip, row, plot
♦ *v*
base, embed, establish, fix, set, found, ground, implant, inlay, insert, bury, plant, settle
■ **bed down**
sleep, go to bed, settle down, call it a day, turn in
COLLOQ. doss down, hit the hay/sack, kip, kip down, get some kip
■ **go to bed with**
sleep with, have sex with, have sexual intercourse with, make love to
SLANG bed, have it off with, bonk; (*taboo*) fuck, screw, shag

---

Kinds of bed include:

adjustable bed	foldaway bed	put-you-up
bassinet	folding bed	queen-size(d)
bed settee	four-poster	shakedown
berth	futon	single bed
box bed	hammock	sleigh bed
bunk bed	high sleeper	sofa bed
camp-bed	mid sleeper	trestle bed
chaise longue	king-size(d)	truckle bed
cot	lit bateau (or boat	trundle bed
couchette	bed)	twin bed
cradle	mattress	water-bed
crib	pallet	Z-bed
day bed	palliasse	
divan bed	platform bed	
double bed	Put-u-up®	

Kinds of bedclothes include:

bed canopy	candlewick	coverlet	electric blanket	pillow sham	sleeping bag
bedroll	bedspread	*Aust* doona	mattress cover	pillowslip	throwover
bedspread	cellular blanket	duvet	patchwork quilt	quilt	valance
blanket	*N Am* comforter	duvet cover	pillow	quilt cover	valanced sheet
bolster	counterpane	eiderdown	pillowcase	sheet	

bedclothes *n*
bedding, bed-linen, covers
See panel above

bedeck *v*
beautify, decorate, deck, adorn, embellish, festoon, garnish, ornament, array, trick out, trim; *N Am* trick up

bedevil *v*
afflict, torment, confound, frustrate, harass, irk, pester, plague, tease, annoy, besiege, torture, trouble, distress, vex, fret, worry, irritate
FORMAL beset

bedfellow *n*
associate, colleague, partner, ally, fellow, companion, friend, partner

bedlam *n*
chaos, pandemonium, madhouse, commotion, confusion, furore, clamour, hubbub, hullabaloo, noise, tumult, turmoil, uproar, babel, anarchy
E3 calm

bedraggled *adj*
untidy, unkempt, dishevelled, disordered, scruffy, slovenly, messy, dirty, muddy, muddied, soiled, wet, soaked, soaking (wet), sodden, dripping, drenched
COLLOQ. like something the cat brought in
E3 neat, tidy, clean

bedridden *adj*
confined to bed, incapacitated, housebound; *N Am* bedrid
COLLOQ. laid up, flat on your back

bedrock *n*
the bedrock of a building/your life
foundation, support, basis, base, bottom, footing, reason(s), rationale, fundamentals, basics, essentials, fundamental point, starting-point, premise, first principles, essence, heart, core

beef *v*
complain, criticize, grumble, moan, grouse, object, dispute, disagree
COLLOQ. gripe
E3 approve
■ **beef up**
strengthen, consolidate, give new energy to, toughen (up),

invigorate, build up, establish, reinforce, substantiate, flesh out
E3 weaken

beefy *adj*
brawny, muscular, bulky, burly, fat, fleshy, heavy, hefty, hulking, stalwart, stocky, robust, sturdy
FORMAL corpulent
COLLOQ. tubby
E3 slight

beer *n*
ale, brew, liquor
COLLOQ. *Aust & NZ* grog; *N Am* brewski; *Aust* amber liquid
See panel below

beetle *v*
dash, hurry, nip, run, rush, scamper, scurry, bustle, tear, zip
COLLOQ. scoot

beetling *adj*
overhanging, protruding, poking out, projecting, jutting, leaning over, sticking out
FORMAL pendent

befall *v*
1 HAPPEN TO, come upon, overwhelm, strike, fall upon
2 TAKE PLACE, happen, occur, arrive, chance, result, ensue, fall, follow, materialize
OLD bechance
FORMAL betide, supervene

befit *v*
become, suit, sit, harmonize with, match, complement; *Scot* set
OLD seem, befall, sort; (*Shakesp*) besort
FORMAL behove

befitting *adj*
appropriate, suitable, becoming, apt, correct, decent, fit, fitting, proper, right
OLD meet, seemly
E3 unbecoming

before *prep, adv*
♦ *prep*
1 *before breakfast*
earlier than, previous to, prior to, not later than, sooner than, in preparation for, in anticipation of, on the eve of
2 *perform before the king*

Types of beer include:

abbey beer	ale	Guinness®	Kristall-Weizen	Pils	*N Am* steam beer
ale	Christmas ale	guest beer	kvass	Pilsener (or	stone beer
Altbier	cream ale	harvest ale	lager	Pilsner)	sweet stout
amber ale	draught	*Scot* heavy	lambic	porter	stout
barley wine	dry beer	Hefeweizen (or	light ale	Rauchbier	Trappist
Berliner Weisse	Dunkel	Hefe-Weissbier)	low-alcohol	real ale	Vienna
bière de garde	*Scot* eighty	Helles	*N Am* malt liquor	red ale	Weizenbier (or
bitter	(shilling)	honey beer	March (or	rice beer	Weissbier)
black-and-tan	Eisbock	ice beer	Märzen) beer	sahti	wheat beer
black beer	export	India Pale Ale	microbrew	*Scot* seventy	winter ale
black lager	Framboise (or	(IPA)	mild	(shilling)	
bock	frambozen)	Irish ale	milk stout	shandy	
bottled beer	fruit beer	keg beer	oatmeal stout	*Scot* sixty	
brown ale	green beer	Kölsch	old ale	(shilling)	
cask-conditioned	gueuze	Kriek	pale ale	snakebite	

See also **drink**.

in front of, in the presence of, in the sight of
3 *all of his life before him*
in front of, ahead of
F3 **1** after **3** behind
♦ *adv*
1 *have been here before*
earlier, formerly, previously, already
2 *go on before*
ahead, in front, in advance
F3 **1** later **2** behind

beforehand *adv*
in advance, preliminarily, already, before, previously,
earlier, sooner, ahead of time

befriend *v*
help, aid, assist, succour, back, support, protect, defend,
look after, stand by, uphold, sustain, comfort, encourage,
welcome, favour, benefit, take under your wing, keep an
eye on, make friends with, make a friend of, get to know, fall
in with, stick up for
FORMAL succour
F3 neglect, oppose

befuddle *v*
confuse, muddle, baffle, bewilder, daze, disorient,
perplex, nonplus, puzzle, stupefy
COLLOQ. faze

beg *v*
1 *beg someone to do something*
ask for, request, require, desire, crave, plead, appeal, turn
to, entreat, implore, pray, supplicate, petition, solicit,
importune; *Scot* fleech
OLD beseech
2 *beg for money*
ask for money, cadge, stand pad, skelder; *Scot* thig; *N Am*
panhandle
OLD prog
COLLOQ. bum, scrounge, touch for money, sponge; *N Am*
mooch (off)
SLANG *N Am* schnorr
OLD SLANG maund, maunder

Synonym nuances
sense 1
Ask for and **request** are in general use in situations where
someone wishes to obtain something, whereas **require**
implies an element of need. The word **desire**, on the other
hand, expresses a wish for something, while **crave** and
plead are appropriate words for making a more heartfelt
request: *I must crave your indulgence*. If an approach is
aimed directly at someone, often someone in a position of
power, then **appeal** is used: *Amnesty appealed to the king
to stop the torture*; whereas the term **turn to** hints at a
request for help or advice. Both **entreat** and **implore**,
however, are more urgent in tone, suggesting an earnest,
even piteous, application to someone: *his friends
entreated him not to go*.
  To convey an element of humility in begging, you could
use **pray** or the rarer **supplicate**: *I pray you forgive me!*
Solicit is less marked in tone and can be used of applying
for something of a more abstract nature: *solicited support*;
they solicited his intervention. For official approaches, the
terms **petition** and **importune** can be used; these also
suggest repetition and persistence: *I bombarded the War
Office and importuned the Red Cross to protest.*

---

beget *v*
1 CAUSE, bring about, create, breed, give rise to, lead to,
occasion, result in, engender
FORMAL effect
2 *beget a child*
breed, father, generate, produce, propagate, sire, spawn
FORMAL procreate

beggar *n, v*
♦ *n*
mendicant, supplicant, pauper, down-and-out, tramp, vagrant,
vagabond, craver, besognio, lazzarone, canter, whipjack;
dialect randy; *Scot* beadsman, bedesman, gaberlunzie, hallan-
shaker; *N Am* panhandler, down-and-outer
OLD blowze, palliard, ruffler; (*Shakesp*) bezonian
COLLOQ. cadger, scrounger, sponger, freeloader, bum; *N Am*
moocher
SLANG bludger, blighter, toerag; *N Am* schnorrer
OLD SLANG maunder, mumper, upright-man, jarkman
Related adjective: mendicant
♦ *v*
defy, baffle, challenge, exceed, surpass, transcend

beggarly *adj*
stingy, abject, meagre, mean, miserly, contemptible,
despicable, inadequate, low, needy, niggardly, paltry,
slight, insubstantial, modest, pathetic, pitiful, wretched
F3 affluent, generous

begin *v*
start, commence, set about, embark on, set in motion, get
going, launch into, do first, activate, actuate, set off,
originate, initiate, introduce, found, institute, open,
instigate, arise, spring, emerge, appear, crop up
COLLOQ. kick off, get cracking, set the ball rolling, take the
plunge
F3 end, stop, finish, cease, conclude

Synonym nuances
Start and **commence** are general terms to describe the
initial action or operation of someone or something. **Set
about** hints at preparation: *he set about ordering his life*.
Embark on is used to imply that someone is at the
beginning of a more lengthy undertaking: *He'd
embarked on a thorough analysis of the historical data*.
Set in motion could describe the actions of someone
with responsibility for the initial stages of a process: *the
Home Secretary set in motion a review of the law*. If
something or someone **gets going** a sense of moving
into a phase of productive activity is conveyed: *the film
was slow to start but when it got going it was outstanding*.
  The term **launch into** can also be used to suggest great
activity and enthusiasm, sometimes to the point of
naivety, while **activate**, **actuate** and **set off** are also
suggestive of moving something into action. On the
other hand, **originate** and **initiate**, along with the terms
found and **institute**, are more suggestive of creating
something from scratch: *the alarm is activated when
oxygen levels fall; psychological studies initiated by
Freud*. **Instigate** is another word suggestive of providing
the means for existence. **Introduce**, however,
emphasizes bringing something to people's attention
rather than creating it. **Open** may be used of abstracts,
such as discussions, but equally of more tangible things:
they opened their first hotel.
  Arise and **spring** appropriately describe coming
suddenly into being, and while **emerge** and **appear** are
also used of something coming to light, it is at a more
gradual pace. The informal term **crop up** would only be
used to indicate something happening unexpectedly: *a
problem had just cropped up*.

---

beginner *n*
novice, tiro, starter, learner, trainee, apprentice, student,
probationer, initiate, freshman, fresher, pupil, recruit, raw
recruit, cub, tenderfoot, fledgling, neophyte, Johnny-raw
OLD abecedarian
COLLOQ. greenhorn, rookie, newbie
SLANG *Aust* new chum
F3 veteran, old hand, expert

beginning *n*
start, commencement, onset, outset, first part, opening

part, opening, preface, prelude, introduction, initiation, establishment, inauguration, institution, launch, inception, starting-point, birth, dawn, origin, source, fountainhead, root, seed, conception, genesis, emergence, rise, fresh start, new beginnings, pastures new
FORMAL inchoation, incipience
COLLOQ. the word go, day one, square one, first base, kick-off, intro, new leaf
E3 end, finish, conclusion

begrudge v
resent, be resentful of, grudge, mind, object to, envy, covet, be jealous of, stint
E3 allow

beguile v
1 CHARM, enchant, bewitch, captivate, delight, attract, amuse, entertain, divert, distract, occupy, engross
2 DECEIVE, fool, hoodwink, dupe, trick, cheat, delude, mislead, seduce, cozen, wile
OLD blend; (*Spenser*) guile
COLLOQ. lead up the garden path, pull the wool over someone's eyes

beguiling adj
alluring, appealing, attractive, bewitching, captivating, charming, delightful, diverting, enchanting, entertaining, interesting, intriguing, enticing, seductive
E3 offensive, repulsive

behalf
■ **on behalf of**
for, representing, as a representative of, acting for, for the benefit/good of, for the sake of, in the name/authority of, for the good of, in the interests of, to the advantage/profit of, for account of, in support of

behave v
1 *behave aggressively*
act, conduct yourself, be, acquit yourself, respond, react, perform
FORMAL comport yourself
2 *tell the children to behave themselves*
be good, be well-behaved, act properly/politely, be on your best behaviour, mind your manners, stay out of trouble
COLLOQ. act your age, keep your nose clean, not mess about/muck about, stop fooling around, mind your p's and q's, not put a foot wrong
3 *electrons behave like this*
function, operate, work, act, perform, react
E3 2 misbehave, get into trouble; *colloq.* act up, be up to no good

behaviour n
1 *the child's behaviour*
conduct, manner, manners, ways, habits, dealings, way of acting, response, reaction, attitudes
FORMAL demeanour, comportment, deportment
2 *the behaviour of chemical elements*
operation, performance, functioning, action, reaction

Synonym nuances
sense 1
Conduct is a general term used to describe the way a person acts, and **manner** may also be used in this way; **manners**, however, is used of behaviour in relation to expected social conventions: *he didn't have the manners to write*. **Ways**, on the other hand, would be used of the usual mannerisms peculiar to an individual: *he'd become set in his ways*; whilst **habits** may be used more narrowly to imply certain instilled traits. To talk of the way someone conducts their affairs, particularly in business, you might use the word **dealings**.
The idea of **attitudes** returns us to the notion of generally held opinions within society, and their effect on behaviour: *puritanical attitudes in sexual matters*. **Response** and **reaction** are only appropriate where a person's actions are the result of something that has previously taken place.

---

behead v
decapitate, execute, kill, put to death, guillotine
OLD decollate, head

behest
■ **at the behest of**
with the authority of, at the bidding of, at the order/command of, at the request of, on the instruction(s) of, on the wishes of
OLD at the hest of

behind prep, adv, n
♦ *prep*
1 *a shed behind the garage*
at the back of, at the rear of, on the other side of; *N Am* in back of
2 *walk behind the others*
after, following, at the back of, at the rear of, close on
3 *behind schedule*
late, later than, running late, overdue, slow, slower than usual
4 *we are behind you in your decision*
supporting, backing, endorsing, for, on the side of
5 *the reasons behind the change in policy*
responsible for, explaining, accounting for, instigating, causing, initiating, giving rise to, at the bottom of
E3 1 in front of **2** ahead of **3** in advance of
♦ *adv*
1 *with a garden behind*
at the back/rear, in the rear
2 *with the stragglers following behind*
after, following, at the back, next, subsequently
3 *be behind with work/payments*
behindhand, late, delayed, overdue, in arrears, in debt
♦ *n*
bottom, buttocks, backside, rump
COLLOQ. bum, posterior; *N Am* ass, butt, heinie
SLANG (*vulgar*) arse

behindhand adv
delayed, late, behind, behind schedule, remiss, slow, tardy, backward
FORMAL dilatory

behold v, interj
♦ *v*
consider, contemplate, descry, discern, espy, look at, see, watch, note, observe, mark, perceive, regard, scan, gaze at, survey, view, witness
♦ *interj*
look, mark, observe, see, watch, *voici, voila, ecce*, la
OLD lo

beholden adj
indebted, obligated, obliged, under (an) obligation, bound, grateful, owing, thankful, appreciative; *Scot* addebted

behove v
be proper, be to your advantage, benefit, profit, be advantageous, be necessary, be essential, be suitable for, be appropriate for
OLD be seemly
FORMAL befit

beige adj
buff, fawn, mushroom, camel, sandy, khaki, coffee, oatmeal, oyster, suede, tan, ecru, greige, taupe, neutral

being n
1 EXISTENCE, reality, life, living, animation, essence, substance, nature, soul, spirit
TECHNICAL haecceity, esse
FORMAL actuality
2 CREATURE, animal, beast, human being, human, man, woman, mortal, person, individual, thing, entity
3 *deep in my being*
soul, spirit, inner being, inner self, nature, psyche,

heart, emotions, will, personality
COLLOQ. heart of hearts

belabour v
1 HIT, attack, beat, flog, thrash, strike, whip, belt, flay, pummel
OLD sauce, lay on load
2 *belabour the point*
harp on about, keep talking about, dwell on, reiterate
COLLOQ. go on and on about, flog to death

belated adj
late, tardy, overdue, delayed, behindhand, behind schedule, unpunctual
F3 punctual, on time, timely

belatedly adv
behind schedule, unpunctually, tardily
F3 punctually, on time

belch v, n
♦ v
1 *the baby belched*
burp, hiccup, bring up wind; *dialect* boke; *Scot* rift, yex, yesk
FORMAL eruct, eructate
2 *chimneys belching out smoke*
emit, give out, give off, discharge, issue, gush, vent, eject, disgorge, spew
♦ n
burp, hiccup
FORMAL eructation

beleaguered adj
1 *a beleaguered person*
harassed, pestered, troubled, tormented, badgered, bothered, worried, vexed, plagued, persecuted, beset
2 *a beleaguered city*
besieged, under siege, surrounded, blockaded

belie v
1 *the statistics belie the theory*
disprove, contradict, deny, refute, negate, run counter to
FORMAL gainsay, confute
2 *her looks belie her age*
conceal, disguise, misrepresent, falsify, mislead, deceive, cover up

belief n
1 OPINION, persuasion, feeling, intuition, impression, notion, theory, view, viewpoint, point of view, conviction, judgement
2 CONFIDENCE, reliance, trust, faith, credit, assurance, certainty, sureness, presumption, expectation
3 IDEOLOGY, faith, creed, doctrine, teaching, dogma, theory, ism, tenet, principle, ethic, ideal
F3 2 disbelief, doubt

believable adj
credible, imaginable, conceivable, acceptable, plausible, possible, likely, probable, authoritative, reliable, trustworthy, (well) within the bounds of possibility, not beyond the realms of possibility, with a ring of truth
F3 unbelievable, incredible, inconceivable, implausible, unconvincing

believe v
1 *I believe she's a professor*
think, be of the opinion that, accept, suppose, gather, reckon, assume, consider, hold, maintain, understand, speculate, conjecture, guess, imagine, judge; *N Am* figure
OLD ween, wis, wist
FORMAL deem, postulate, opine
2 *believe him/that he is telling the truth*
accept, trust, be convinced by, be persuaded by, have confidence in, be certain of, take someone's word for it
OLD trow
COLLOQ. take on board, swallow, fall for, buy, wear,

fall for/swallow hook line and sinker
F3 2 disbelieve, doubt, question
■ **believe in**
1 *believe in God*
be sure of the existence/reality of, be convinced of
2 *believe in hard work*
approve of, favour, be in favour of, recommend, encourage, swear by, trust, be persuaded by, value highly, depend on, rely on, have confidence in, trust, accept the importance of
FORMAL set great store by
COLLOQ. rate

believer n
convert, proselyte, disciple, follower, adherent, devotee, zealot, supporter, upholder
F3 unbeliever, sceptic

belittle v
demean, minimize, play down, trivialize, dismiss, underrate, understate, undervalue, underestimate, downgrade, deprecate, lessen, diminish, detract from, decry, slate, sell short, deride, scorn, ridicule
FORMAL deprecate, disparage
COLLOQ. slam, knock, run down, rubbish, pick holes in, pull to pieces, tear to shreds, do a hatchet job on
SLANG slag (off); *N Am* dump on
F3 exaggerate, praise

bell n
gong, ring, chime, peal, knell, warning, signal, siren, horn, hooter, bleep, bleeper
OLD alarum

belle n
beauty, charmer, siren, Venus, *femme fatale*
COLLOQ. good-looker, smasher, corker, cracker, knockout, stunner, peach

bellicose adj
aggressive, militant, argumentative, quarrelsome, contentious, belligerent, combative, violent, bullying, antagonistic, warring, warlike
FORMAL pugnacious
F3 peaceable

belligerence n
aggression, militancy, argumentativeness, provocation, quarrelsomeness, unfriendliness, contentiousness, combativeness, violence, bullying, antagonism, war, warmongering, sabre-rattling
FORMAL pugnacity
F3 complaisance

belligerent adj
aggressive, militant, argumentative, provocative, hostile, quarrelsome, contentious, combative, violent, bullying, antagonistic, warring, warlike, warmongering, sabre-rattling
FORMAL pugnacious, disputatious, truculent
COLLOQ. scrappy; *Can* chippy
F3 peaceable

bellow v, n
♦ v
roar, yell, shout, bawl, cry, scream, shriek, howl, clamour, thunder, raise your voice, troat; *dialect* rout; *Scot* buller
COLLOQ. holler
♦ n
roar, yell, shout, bawl, cry, scream, shriek, howl, troat; *Scot* buller
COLLOQ. holler

belly n
stomach, abdomen, gut, guts, insides, intestines, paunch, pot-belly, beer belly; *dialect* wame
TECHNICAL venter
COLLOQ. tummy, corporation

SLANG bread basket
Related adjective: alvine

belong *v*
1 *this book belongs to me*
be owned by, be the possession of, be the property of, be under the ownership of, be yours
2 *belong to a rugby club*
be a member of, be affiliated to, be connected with, be associated with, be in, be an adherent of
3 *this lid belongs to that pan*
fit, go with, be part of, attach to, link up with, tie up with, be connected with, relate to
4 *Where do these toys belong?*
have as its place/home, go, be situated, be found, fit in, be sorted, be categorized, be classified, be included

belonging *n*
rapport, closeness, acceptance, affinity, association, attachment, compatibility, fellow-feeling, fellowship, affiliation, kinship, link(s), loyalty, relationship
F3 antipathy

belongings *n*
possessions, property, chattels, goods, (personal) paraphernalia
FORMAL effects, appurtenances, accoutrements
COLLOQ. gear, stuff, tackle, kit, clobber, things

beloved *adj, n*
♦ *adj*
loved, much loved, adored, cherished, endeared, treasured, prized, precious, pet, favourite, dearest, dear, darling, admired, revered, worshipped
OLD lief, alder-liefest; (*Shakesp*) tender
♦ *n*
sweetheart, darling, dear, dearest, love, loved one, true-love, fiancé, fiancée, betrothed, boyfriend, girlfriend, special friend, partner, spouse, husband, wife, favourite, lover, pet, precious, sweet, lady-love, joy; *Scot* jo
OLD (*Spenser*) belamoure; liking
FORMAL inamorata, inamorato
COLLOQ. angel, baby, sweetie, honey, bird, fella

below *adv, prep*
♦ *adv*
1 *the flat below mine*
beneath, under, underneath, down, lower, lower down
2 *see below for details*
later, at a later place, further on, underneath
F3 1, 2 above
♦ *prep*
1 UNDER, underneath, beneath, lower than
2 INFERIOR TO, lower (in rank) than, lesser than, subordinate to, subject to
F3 1, 2 above

belt *n, v*
♦ *n*
1 SASH, girdle, waistband, girth, strap, baldric, cingulum, bandoleer, zona
OLD cestus, mitre
FORMAL cummerbund, ceinture, cincture
2 *a conveyor belt*
strip, band, strap, cord, chain, loop
3 STRIP, area, region, district, sector, zone, swathe, stretch, tract, extent, layer
4 THUMP, hit, punch, strike, swipe, knock, clout, bang, blow, bashing, slap, smack, pelt, bruise, box
COLLOQ. tan, wallop, whack, biff, slosh
♦ *v*
1 HIT, strap, flog, lash, whip, flay, cane, birch, punch, strike, swipe, knock, clout, bang, slap, smack, thump, thwack, pelt, bruise, box
COLLOQ. bash, clobber, tan, wallop, whack, biff, give someone a good hiding

2 *belt along the road*
dash, tear, fly, rush, career, zip, charge, speed
▪ **belt up**
shut up, be quiet
COLLOQ. pipe down, cut it out
SLANG put a sock in it, keep your trap shut, shut your mouth/face
▪ **below the belt**
unfair, unjust, uncalled-for, unjustified, dishonest, underhand, unscrupulous, unethical
COLLOQ. dirty, out of order

bemoan *v*
lament, mourn, bewail, wail, deplore, grieve for, regret, rue, sigh for, sorrow over, weep for
F3 gloat

bemuse *v*
confuse, bewilder, puzzle, baffle, perplex, daze, muddle, befuddle, stupefy
COLLOQ. bamboozle, throw, faze, floor
F3 enlighten, illuminate

bemused *adj*
bewildered, confused, puzzled, perplexed, baffled, disconcerted, dazed, overwhelmed, muddled, befuddled, stupefied, astounded, astonished, mused; *N Am* pixilated
COLLOQ. bamboozled, fazed, floored
F3 clear-headed, clear, lucid

bemusement *n*
confusion, puzzlement, bewilderment, perplexity, daze, bafflement, disorientation, stupefaction

bench *n*
1 SEAT, form, settle, pew, ledge
TECHNICAL thwart
OLD bink
2 *work at a bench*
counter, table, stall, board, workbench, worktable
3 COURT, courtroom, tribunal, judiciary, judicature, judge, magistrate, tribune, bank
TECHNICAL banc

benchmark *n*
criterion, example, level, model, norm, pattern, reference, reference-point, point of reference, guideline(s), standard, basis, gauge, scale, touchstone, yardstick

bend *v, n*
♦ *v*
1 *bend down to pick up a pin*
stoop, crouch, lean, incline, bow, kneel, squat
2 *bend the wire*
curve, make curved, turn, deflect, twist, contort, flex, crook, shape, mould, arch, bow, loop, contort, buckle, warp
3 *the road bends*
curve, turn, deflect, veer, diverge, twist, wind, meander, zigzag, swerve, deviate
FORMAL incurve
4 *bend to their will*
mould, shape, persuade, influence, affect, sway, direct, manipulate, compel
F3 2 straighten
♦ *n*
curvature, curve, arc, bow, loop, hook, crook, elbow, angle, corner, hairpin bend, dog-leg, turn, twist, kink, zigzag, divergence, deflection
TECHNICAL flexure
FORMAL incurvation
▪ **bend over backwards**
try very hard, exert yourself, go all out, do your best, put yourself out, trouble yourself
COLLOQ. leave no stone unturned, move heaven and earth, pull out all the stops

beneath *adv, prep*
♦ *adv*

below, under, underneath, lower, lower down
⊟ above
◆ *prep*
1 UNDER, underneath, below, lower than
2 UNWORTHY OF, unbefitting, unbecoming
⊟ **1** above

benediction *n*
blessing, prayer, thanksgiving, consecration, favour, grace, invocation
FORMAL benison
⊟ anathema, curse; *formal* execration

benefactor *n*
patron, sponsor, backer, supporter, promoter, donor, contributor, subscriber, provider, subsidizer, philanthropist, helper, friend, well-wisher, giver
COLLOQ. angel, fairy godmother
⊟ opponent, persecutor

beneficent *adj*
altruistic, liberal, benevolent, benign, bountiful, charitable, compassionate, generous, helpful, kind, unselfish, Grandisonian, benefic
FORMAL munificent
⊟ mean

beneficial *adj*
advantageous, favourable, useful, helpful, good, worthwhile, promising, profitable, serviceable, rewarding, valuable, improving, edifying, wholesome, salutary
FORMAL propitious
⊟ harmful, detrimental, useless

beneficiary *n*
payee, receiver, recipient, inheritor, legatee, heir, heiress, successor, the assured

benefit *n, v*
◆ *n*
1 *the benefits of exercise*
advantage, good, good point, gain, profit, asset, reward, merit, blessing, boon, interest, favour, bonus, benefaction, dividend, fringe benefit
OLD behoof
FORMAL perquisite
COLLOQ. pay-off, perk
2 *of benefit to children*
good, help, aid, assistance, service, use, sake, interest, behalf, welfare
OLD behoof
FORMAL avail
3 *child benefit; unemployment benefit*
income, allowance, pension, sick pay, payment, social security, credit, support, Job Seekers Allowance (JSA), unemployment benefit, income support; *Scot & Irish* buroo
COLLOQ. dole; *N Am* welfare
⊟ **1** disadvantage **2** harm, damage
◆ *v*
help, aid, assist, serve, be of service to, be advantageous to, be of advantage to, do good to, profit, gain, improve, enhance, better, further, advance, promote
FORMAL avail
⊟ hinder, harm, undermine

benevolence *n*
philanthropy, humanitarianism, charitableness, generosity, liberality, magnanimity, altruism, humaneness, goodness, goodwill, kindness, kind-heartedness, friendliness, compassion, pity, mercy, grace, tolerance, care, considerateness
FORMAL munificence
⊟ meanness

benevolent *adj*
philanthropic, humanitarian, charitable, generous, liberal,
magnanimous, altruistic, benign, humane, kind, kind-hearted, soft-hearted, friendly, kindly, well-disposed, compassionate, merciful, gracious, tolerant, caring, considerate
FORMAL munificent
⊟ mean, selfish, malevolent

benevolently *adv*
philanthropically, charitably, generously, liberally, magnanimously, altruistically, benignly, humanely, kindly, kind-heartedly, soft-heartedly, compassionately, mercifully, graciously, tolerantly, considerately
⊟ selfishly, malevolently

benighted *adj*
ignorant, unenlightened, inexperienced, unknowing, uneducated, unschooled, uncultured, backward, illiterate, unlettered, unfortunate, nighted
OLD belated

benign *adj*
1 BENEVOLENT, charitable, good, gracious, gentle, kind, kindly, warm-hearted, obliging, friendly, amiable, affable, genial, avuncular, sweet, cordial, generous, liberal, sympathetic
OLD benefic
2 *benign conditions/climate*
favourable, advantageous, opportune, providential, beneficial, agreeable, temperate, mild, gentle, warm, refreshing, healthy, restorative, wholesome
OLD benedict
FORMAL auspicious, propitious, salubrious
3 *a benign tumour*
curable, harmless, non-malignant, treatable, innocent
⊟ **1** hostile **2** harmful, unpleasant **3** malignant, cancerous, dangerous

benignly *adv*
benevolently, charitably, graciously, generously, sympathetically, kindly, obligingly, genially, amiably, affably

bent *adj, n*
◆ *adj*
1 ANGLED, curved, bowed, arched, crooked, folded, doubled, twisted, hunched, stooped, warped, contorted
2 DISHONEST, illegal, criminal, corrupt, fraudulent, swindling, untrustworthy
COLLOQ. dodgy, crooked
3 HOMOSEXUAL, gay, lesbian
COLLOQ. camp, butch
SLANG (*offensive*) queer, dykey
⊟ **1** straight, upright **2** honest, trustworthy
◆ *n*
tendency, inclination, disposition, leaning, preference, ability, capacity, faculty, aptitude, facility, gift, talent, fondness, knack, flair, forte
FORMAL predisposition, predilecton, penchant, proclivity, propensity
COLLOQ. cup of tea
■ **bent on**
determined to, resolved to, set on, fixed on, insistent on, intent on, inclined to, disposed to

bequeath *v*
1 *bequeathed in her will*
leave, bestow, will, make over, give, endow, grant, consign, transfer, assign, entrust, commit
FORMAL demise, devise
2 *social problems bequeathed by past generations*
hand down, pass on, impart, transmit

bequest *n*
legacy, inheritance, heritage, trust, endowment, gift, donation, estate, settlement
FORMAL devisal, bestowal, bequeathal

berate v

scold, chide, reprimand, rebuke, tell off, reproach, reprove, censure, chastise, chide, criticize, slate, rail at, revile, upbraid

FORMAL castigate, fulminate, vituperate

COLLOQ. blast, read the riot act to, dress down, tear a strip off, give a rocket to, rap over the knuckles, give hell, *N Am* chew out

⊟ praise

bereaved adj

deprived, grieving, lost, dispossessed, divested, robbed, orphaned, widowed

bereavement n

loss, death, passing, passing-away, deprivation, dispossession, sadness, sorrow, grief

OLD orbity

bereft

■ **bereft of**

deprived of, robbed of, stripped of, destitute of, devoid of, lacking, wanting, parted from, cut off from, minus

berserk adj

mad, crazy, demented, insane, deranged, frantic, frenzied, crazed, wild, raging, furious, violent, rabid, manic, maniacal, raving, hysterical, uncontrollable, beside yourself

COLLOQ. barmy, batty, nuts, out of your mind, off your head, off the deep end

⊟ sane, calm

berth n, v

♦ n

1 BED, bunk, hammock, billet

2 MOORING, anchorage, quay, wharf, dock, harbour, port

♦ v

anchor, dock, drop/cast anchor, land, moor, tie up

⊟ weigh anchor, up anchor

■ **give a wide berth to**

avoid, evade, shun, steer clear of, keep your distance from, keep at arm's length

FORMAL eschew

COLLOQ. dodge, give a miss

beseech v

beg, call on, entreat, implore, ask, petition, plead, pray, solicit, appeal to, supplicate, crave, desire

FORMAL adjure, importune, obsecrate, sue, exhort

beset v

assail, attack, harass, entangle, worry, pester, plague, press, torment, bedevil, hem in, surround, besiege

OLD bego, belay; (*Shakesp*) lay; obsess

COLLOQ. hassle

besetting adj

compulsive, habitual, persistent, dominant, inveterate, irresistible, uncontrollable, obsessive, prevalent, constant, recurring, troublesome, harassing

beside prep

next to, by, alongside, by the side of, abreast of, adjacent, abutting, bordering, neighbouring, next door to, close to, near, overlooking

■ **beside yourself**

berserk, insane, mad, crazy, crazed, delirious, demented, deranged, overcome, out of your mind, frantic, frenetic, frenzied, distraught, unbalanced, unhinged

besides adv, prep

♦ adv

also, as well, too, in addition, additionally, further, furthermore, moreover

OLD forby, withal

COLLOQ. what's more

♦ prep

apart from, other than, aside from, in addition to, over and above, as well as, excluding

besiege v

1 LAY SIEGE TO, blockade, surround, encircle, encompass, confine, beleaguer

OLD (*Spenser*) assiege; belay, besit, obsess

2 *besieged by reporters*

surround, encircle, encompass, confine, shut in, hem in, overwhelm

3 TROUBLE, worry, bother, oppress, torment, importune, assail, beset, beleaguer, harass, pester, badger, nag, hound, plague

besmirch v

defame, defile, dishonour, slander, smear, soil, dirty, blacken, damage, stain, sully, tarnish, besmear; *dialect* slur

OLD besmutch

⊟ enhance

besotted adj

infatuated, doting, obsessed, smitten, hypnotized, spellbound, stupefied, bewitched, intoxicated, bedazzled, sotted

COLLOQ. crazy, wild, mad, potty, bowled over, swept off your feet

⊟ indifferent, disenchanted

bespatter v

spatter, splatter, splash, splodge, spray, sprinkle, shower, scatter, dirty, soil, stain, smear

bespeak v

demonstrate, indicate, reveal, show, speak for, signify, denote, display, exhibit, attest, proclaim, suggest, imply, engage

FORMAL evince, evidence, betoken

best adj, adv, n, v

♦ adj

optimum, optimal, first, foremost, leading, top, ultimate, prime, record-breaking, unequalled, unsurpassed, unrivalled, unbeatable, matchless, peerless, incomparable, supreme, pre-eminent, premium, of highest quality, greatest, highest, largest, finest, worthiest, excellent, outstanding, superlative, first-rate, first-class, ideal, perfect, top-drawer

FORMAL nonpareil

COLLOQ. ace, star, number one, (the) tops, plum, second to none, the pick of the bunch, one in a million, a cut above the rest

⊟ worst

♦ adv

greatly, extremely, exceptionally, excellently, outstandingly, superlatively, unsurpassedly, matchlessly, incomparably, supremely, most, to the greatest/highest degree

⊟ worst, least

♦ n

1 *students who are the best in their year*

finest, cream, prime, élite, top, first, pick, choice, flower, jewel, favourite, star, highlight, *crème de la crème*, *pièce de résistance*

COLLOQ. the pick of the bunch

2 *do your best*

hardest, utmost, greatest effort

COLLOQ. damnedest

⊟ 1 worst

♦ v

defeat, conquer, overcome, beat, get the better of, overwhelm, overpower, subdue, rout, annihilate, outplay, outwit, outsmart, worst, trounce, be more than a match for, have the edge on

FORMAL vanquish

COLLOQ. hammer, slaughter, clobber, lick, thrash

Synonym nuances
adjective

Optimum and **optimal** are interchangeable and convey the sense of something advantageous: *the optimum conditions for growth.* On the other hand, **first**, **foremost**, **leading** and **pre-eminent** are suitable terms to describe the position held by someone or something in relation to their peers: *the foremost authority on the subject*; *the pre-eminent players in the global market.* **Top** is similar, but possibly more suggestive of an underlying hierarchy. **Worthiest** is applicable to something outstanding in terms of merit: *the worthiest of causes.*

If you wish to emphasize thoroughly the outstanding nature of something, you could use **unequalled**, **unsurpassed**, **unrivalled**, **unbeatable**, **matchless**, **peerless**, **incomparable** and **outstanding**, which suggest that everyone or everything else is infinitely inferior: *a place of matchless beauty.* The terms **ultimate** or **supreme** go further by suggesting it cannot be bettered: *the ultimate weapon against crime; he was the supreme all-rounder.*

Fine and **prime** are more restrained adjectives to use, but can convey an impression of quality: *one of the finest poets; a prime tourist attraction.* Similarly, you can use **superlative** and **excellent** to suggest that something is extraordinarily good, but **ideal** and **perfect** applied literally suggest the aspirational rather than achievable, though their everyday usage implies perfection is now more easily reached: *the perfect pint.*

bestial *adj*
cruel, savage, brutal, animal, barbaric, barbarous, beastly, inhuman, brutish, carnal, depraved, degraded, gross, sensual, sordid, vile
FORMAL feral
E3 civilized, humane

bestiality *n*
cruelty, savagery, animal behaviour, barbarism, sordidness, inhumanity

bestir *v*
arouse, exert, awaken, stimulate, energize, galvanize, incite, motivate, activate, actuate, animate
E3 calm, lull, quell

bestow *v*
award, present, grant, confer, endow, bequeath, communicate, dispose, commit, entrust, impart, transmit, allot, apportion, accord, give, donate, lavish, wreak
OLD estate
E3 withhold, deprive

bestride *v*
1 DOMINATE, command, overshadow
2 BESTRADDLE, cross, sit astride, stand astride, straddle

bestseller *n*
blockbuster, hit, smash hit, success, triumph, brand leader

bestselling *adj*
famous, popular, leading, top, unbeaten

bet *v, n*
♦ *v*
1 *bet money on a horse*
wager, gamble, punt, speculate, risk, hazard, chance, venture, lay, stake, bid, pledge, back, put, place, play for money
COLLOQ. have a flutter
2 *I bet she did it on purpose*
be certain, be sure, be convinced, expect, not be surprised
♦ *n*
1 *place a bet*
wager, gamble, speculation, risk, venture, stake, ante, bid, pledge, lottery, sweepstake, accumulator, triple, perfecta; *N Am* superfecta; *Aust* trifecta
COLLOQ. flutter, punt
2 *my bet is that he'll stay*
opinion, feeling, intuition, impression, notion, theory, view, viewpoint, point of view, conviction, judgement, forecast, prediction
3 *your best bet*
choice, option, course of action, alternative

bête noire *n*
bugbear, bane, abomination, anathema, aversion, curse, pet hate, pet aversion
COLLOQ. thorn in the flesh/side
E3 favourite

betide *v*
chance, develop, ensue, happen, occur, take place, overtake
OLD befall
FORMAL supervene

betoken *v*
signal, indicate, signify, suggest, token, bode, forebode, presage, declare, denote, represent, manifest, mark, promise
OLD bespeak
FORMAL augur, portend, evidence, prognosticate

betray *v*
1 *betray a friend*
inform on, double-cross, cross, desert, abandon, turn traitor, be disloyal to, be unfaithful to, break faith with, go back on, break your promise to, renege on, abuse, let down, play false, deceive, delude, mislead, dupe
OLD bewray
FORMAL forsake
COLLOQ. tell on, rat on, sell (out), sell down the river, stab in the back, squeal on, blow the whistle on, shop, walk out on, split on; *Aust* dob
SLANG grass, rumble, peach; *N Am* stool on
2 DISCLOSE, give away, tell, divulge, expose, reveal, show, manifest, let slip, bring to light, unmask
E3 1 defend, protect, be loyal to **2** conceal, hide

Synonym nuances
sense 1

Most of the terms to describe the action of betraying carry a tone of disapproval. **Inform on** is used generally for the verbal identification of someone or their deeds, whereas **double-cross** suggests a pretence of aiding someone while actually working against them, and carries a strong tone of disapprobation.

Desert, **abandon** and **forsake** all share the idea of leaving something or someone behind because it is no longer of use: *politicians are willing to forsake their principles*; whilst **go back on**, and **renege on** have more to do with acting contrary to a promise: *the country reneged on its pledge.* **Abuse** implies an improper treatment of trust, and again carries a rather strong note of criticism: *you abused your position as police officer.* You might use **let down** to place more emphasis on the disappointment felt by the betrayed person. **Deceive** and **mislead** are the words to use when false information has been given; likewise **dupe**, which further implies trickery has been involved. **Delude** also suggests a trick, but more likely one played on the mind: *ideas which delude people into thinking they are safe.*

betrayal *n*
treachery, treason, sell-out, disloyalty, unfaithfulness, double-dealing, double-crossing, duplicity, deception, trickery, duping, falseness, breaking faith
FORMAL perfidy
COLLOQ. sell-out, stab in the back
E3 loyalty, faithfulness, protection

betrayer n
traitor, Judas, informer, stool pigeon, double-crosser, deceiver, conspirator, renegade, apostate
OLD traditor, treacher
COLLOQ. whistle-blower, backstabber
SLANG grass, supergrass; N Am stoolie
E3 protector, supporter

betrothal n
engagement, proposal of marriage, promise, vow(s), contract
OLD affiance, assurance, handfast, plighting of your troth, troth
FORMAL espousal, fiançailles

betrothed adj
engaged, engaged to be married, contracted, promised, pledged
OLD affianced, troth; (Shakesp) trothplight, combinate
FORMAL espoused

better adj, v
♦ adj
1 SUPERIOR, bigger, larger, longer, greater, worthier, of higher quality, finer, surpassing, preferable, more acceptable, more fitting, more advantageous, more valuable
COLLOQ. a cut above
2 IMPROVING, progressing, on the mend, recovering, fitter, healthier, stronger, (fully) recovered, restored, cured, healed, well
COLLOQ. on the mend
E3 1 inferior **2** worse
♦ v
1 IMPROVE, enhance, raise, make better, further, promote, forward, reform, mend, correct, rectify, enrich
FORMAL ameliorate
2 SURPASS, top, beat, outdo, exceed, improve on, outstrip, overtake, cap, go one better than
E3 1 worsen, deteriorate

betterment n
improvement, furtherance, advancement, edification, enhancement, enrichment
FORMAL amelioration, melioration
E3 deterioration, impairment

between prep
in the middle (of), in the space between, among, halfway, mid, amid, amidst, amongst

bevel n, v
♦ n
oblique, slant, slope, tilt, angle, bias, splay, diagonal, mitre, basil, bezel, cant
TECHNICAL chamfer
♦ v
slant, slope, tilt, angle, mitre, bias, cant
TECHNICAL chamfer

beverage n
drink, draught, liquor, liquid, refreshment
OLD potation, potable

bevy n
gathering, group, band, gang, company, assembly, collection, troop, troupe, flock, gaggle, pack, bunch, crowd, throng

bewail v
grieve over, sorrow over, lament, bemoan, cry over, moan, mourn, regret, repent, rue, sigh over, beat your breast, deplore, keen
E3 gloat, glory, vaunt

beware v
watch out, look out, mind (out), be careful, be cautious, be wary, take heed, steer clear of, avoid, shun, guard

against, be on your guard, be on the lookout for
OLD ware
SLANG cave

bewilder v
confuse, muddle, mix up, disconcert, confound, baffle, puzzle, perplex, nonplus, mystify, daze, maze, stupefy, bemuse, disorient; Scot bumbaze, fickle
OLD wilder
COLLOQ. bamboozle, stump, flummox, faze, floor, wander, tie up in knots; N Am buffalo
SLANG take to town

bewildered adj
confused, muddled, uncertain, disoriented, distracted, baffled, puzzled, perplexed, mystified, taken aback, bemused, surprised, speechless, stunned, wandered, mixed up, muzzy, dizzy, fogged, pixy-led; Scot tavert, will, wull
OLD bemazed
COLLOQ. bamboozled, nonplussed, flummoxed, fazed, floored, jiggered; N Am pixilated; (all) at sea
E3 unperturbed, collected

bewildering adj
puzzling, perplexing, baffling, confusing, mystifying, mysterious, surprising, amazing, astounding, dizzy, unfathomable, cryptic, enigmatic

bewilderment n
perplexity, confusion, uncertainty, daze, disconcertion, disorientation, mystification, puzzlement, stupefaction, surprise, awe, muddle, fog, mizmaze, égarement; dialect maze
OLD amaze
E3 composure, confidence

bewitch v
charm, enchant, allure, beguile, spellbind, possess, enthral, captivate, enrapture, delight, obsess, fascinate, intrigue, tantalize, seduce, entrance, mesmerize, hypnotize, transfix, strike, take, witch, sirenize, overlook, hex, voodoo, hoodoo, obi; dialect wish; Scot forspeak
OLD ensorcell
E3 disenchant, repel

beyond prep
1 *the fields beyond the house*
on the far side of, on the other side of, further than, away from, remote from, apart from
2 *beyond the age of 16*
after, past, later than, above, over, greater than, upwards of
3 *beyond me/my understanding*
out of reach of, out of range of, further than the limitations of

bias n, v
♦ n
1 *racial bias*
prejudice, partiality, favouritism, one-sidedness, unfairness, bigotry, intolerance, stereotyping, distortion, bent, leaning, inclination, tendency
FORMAL propensity, proclivity, predilection
2 *cut on the bias*
diagonal, angle, slant, oblique, cross
E3 1 impartiality, fairness
♦ v
prejudice, influence, sway, predispose, distort, colour, jaundice, twist, angle, load, slant, warp, weight
OLD earwig; (Shakesp) partialize
FORMAL prejudicate
COLLOQ. load the dice

biased adj
prejudiced, one-sided, unfair, bigoted, blinkered, jaundiced, influenced, swayed, partial, predisposed, discriminatory, interested, subjective, partisan, slanted, angled, skewed, distorted, warped, twisted, loaded, weighted

The books of the Bible are:

THE OLD TESTAMENT:	Psalms	Zephaniah	2 Thessalonians	Tobit
Genesis	Proverbs	Haggai	1 Timothy	Judith
Exodus	Ecclesiastes	Zechariah	2 Timothy	Additions to Esther
Leviticus	Song of Solomon	Malachi	Titus	Wisdom of Solomon
Numbers	(Song of Songs)	**THE NEW TESTAMENT:**	Philemon	Ecclesiasticus
Deuteronomy	Isaiah	Matthew	Hebrews	Letter of Jeremiah
Joshua	Jeremiah	Mark	James	Baruch
Judges	Lamentations	Luke	1 Peter	Prayer of Azariah
Ruth	Ezekiel	John	2 Peter	Song of the Three
1 Samuel	Daniel	Acts of the Apostles	1 John	Young Men
2 Samuel	Hosea	Romans	2 John	History of Susanna
1 Kings	Joel	1 Corinthians	3 John	Bel and the Dragon
2 Kings	Amos	2 Corinthians	Jude	Prayer of Manasseh
1 Chronicles	Obadiah	Galatians	Revelation	1 Maccabees
2 Chronicles	Jonah	Ephesians	**THE APOCRYPHA**	2 Maccabees
Ezra	Micah	Philippians	**(DEUTERO-CANONICAL**	
Nehemiah	Nahum	Colossians	**BOOKS):**	
Esther	Habakkuk	1 Thessalonians	1 Esdras	
Job			2 Esdras	

FORMAL prejudicate, tendentious
F3 impartial, fair, objective

> **Synonym nuances**
> The word **prejudiced** is a fairly general term to describe a person with unfounded preconceived opinions, while **bigoted** is more emphatic, and can be used of someone displaying irrational dislike as a consequence of these opinions. **Discriminatory** also carries a negative aspect, implying unjustifiable exclusion: *discriminatory employment practices.*
> **One-sided** is more likely to be used to suggest a lack of balance in an article or approach, especially in a narrative account: *one-sided reporting*; while **subjective** may be used to suggest the influence of personal taste or opinion. **Slanted**, **angled** and **skewed** all imply that a particular spin has been applied to present something in a particular way, and if you want to express that your distaste for this you might use **distorted**, **warped** or **twisted**, which imply deliberate misrepresentation. The terms **loaded** and **weighted** also imply being altered, but in order to achieve a specific outcome: *the arbitration must be independent, not loaded in their favour.*
> **Blinkered** may be used if you wish to suggest a narrow viewpoint, unlike **jaundiced**, which implies a viewpoint adversely affected by experience: *a jaundiced view of the world*. Both these terms carry implicit criticism.
> **Influenced** can be used with more positive connotations, having more to do with being unduly in favour of something, and **swayed**, **partial** and **predisposed** echo this suggestion. **Partisan** is less likely to suggest approval of this favour: *his partisan commitment is foolish.*
> **Tendentious** is used of a more intentional bias, one causing controversy: *the tendentious terms of their father's will.* To express disapproval of bias in any form, you might say it is **unfair**.

Bible *n*
1 *study the Christian Bible*
Scriptures, holy Scriptures, Holy Bible, holy writ, Old Testament, New Testament, Apocrypha, writings, canon, revelation, Pentateuch, law, prophets, Gospels, epistles, letters
COLLOQ. good book
See panel above
2 *the gardener's bible; the cyclist's bible*
manual, handbook, authority, reference book, ABC, encyclopedia, dictionary, lexicon, guidebook, directory, companion, textbook, primer

bibliography *n*
book list, list of books, list of references, record, catalogue

bicker *v*
squabble, row, quarrel, wrangle, argue, spar, fight, clash, disagree, dispute, fall out
FORMAL altercate
COLLOQ. scrap, spat
F3 agree, make up

bickering *adj*
squabbling, quarrelling, arguing, clashing, disagreeing, at odds, at one another's throats
COLLOQ. at loggerheads, scrapping, like cats and dogs

bicycle *n*
cycle, two-wheeler, pedal cycle, racer, mountain bike, all-terrain bike, tandem, unicycle
COLLOQ. bike, pushbike

Parts of a bicycle include:

aero bars	down tube	rim brake
bar ends	drive train	rim tape
bell	drop handlebars	rod brake
bottom bracket	drum brake	roller chain
brake	dynamo	saddle
brake block	*N Am* fender	Schrader® valve
brake cable	fork	seat pillar (or
brake caliper	frame	post)
brake lever	freewheel unit	seat stays
brake shoe	gear	seat tube
cable braking	gear cable	shock absorber
system	gear lever	side-pull brakes
carrier	gear shifter	speedometer
cassette	gearwheel	spokes
centre-pull	handlebars	spoke nipples
brakes	handlebar stem	sprocket (wheel)
chain	hanger	stabilizer
chain guide	headset	steering head
chain guard	head tube	steering tube
chain link	hub	stirrup guide
chain ring	hub gear	toe clip
chainset	inner tube	tool bag
chain stays	kickstand	top tube
chain wheel	lamp	tyre (or *N Am* tire)
clipless pedal	lamp bracket	tyre valve
coaster brake	mudguard	wheel bearing
crank	pannier	wheel lock
crank lever	pedal	wheel nut
crankset	Presta® valve	wheel rim
crossbar	prop stand	wheel spindle
derailleur	pulley	Woods® valve
diamond frame	pump	
disc brake	reflector	

bid *v, n*

♦ *v*

1 *bid for a painting*
offer, tender, submit, put up, put forward, advance, propose
FORMAL proffer

2 ASK, request, desire, instruct, direct, command, order, require, charge, call (for), demand, tell, summon, invite, solicit
FORMAL enjoin

3 *bid them farewell*
wish, greet, say, call, tell, wave

♦ *n*

1 OFFER, tender, sum, amount, price, advance, submission, proposal; *Scot* bode
OLD vie

2 ATTEMPT, effort, try, endeavour, venture
COLLOQ. go

biddable *adj*
amenable, submitting, obedient, subservient, tractable, malleable, easy-going, meek, compliant
COLLOQ. under someone's thumb

bidding *n*
request, desire, instruction, direction, command, order, charge, call, demand, summons, requirement, invitation, injunction
FORMAL behest

big *adj*

1 *a big house*
large, great, siz(e)able, considerable, substantial, huge, enormous, immense, vast, massive, colossal, gigantic, giant, mammoth, extensive, spacious, cavernous, extra large
FORMAL voluminous
COLLOQ. whopping, jumbo, bumper, ginormous, humungous
SLANG mega

2 *a big person*
well-built, large, burly, tall, huge, enormous, bulky, hulking, massive, beefy, brawny, muscular, fat, stout, obese
FORMAL corpulent
COLLOQ. hefty

3 *love your big brother*
older, elder, grown-up, adult, mature

4 *a big decision*
important, significant, momentous, major, serious, weighty, salient, critical, radical, fundamental

5 *a big name in the fashion world*
important, significant, well-known, famous, leading, main, principal, eminent, distinguished, prominent, influential, outstanding, noteworthy, valued, powerful

6 *that's big of you*
generous, gracious, kind-hearted, benevolent, unselfish
FORMAL magnanimous, munificent
E3 **1, 2** small, little **3** younger, little **4** insignificant, unimportant **5** insignificant, unknown **6** mean, miserly, selfish

---

Synonym nuances
sense 1

Large and **great** can be widely used to describe greatness of size, in relation to others: *a large population*; *a great portion of the foreground*. Similarly **sizable** can be used when something is above the average size, though perhaps less impressively so: *a sizable workforce*. Both **considerable** and **substantial** and **extensive** also suggest something worthy of attention, but you might tend to use them more of abstract ideas: *considerable success*; *a substantial increase*.

Immense and vast would tend to convey the extent of

---

something: *vast plains*. **Huge, enormous, massive, colossal, gigantic, giant** and **mammoth** would be used to describe something of extraordinary size: *huge monuments; the colossal Ionic columns; a problem of mammoth proportions*. **Spacious** and **cavernous** are appropriate only when talking about space or capacity, with the latter having the association with darkness too: *cavernous tunnels*.

---

bigheaded *adj*
conceited, vain, arrogant, haughty, swollen-headed, self-important, full of yourself, self-satisfied, cocky; *N Am* swell-headed
FORMAL vainglorious
COLLOQ. stuck-up, too big for your boots

bigot *n*
sectarian, dogmatist, fanatic, zealot, partisan, chauvinist, racist, sexist, male chauvinist pig (MCP), religionist
E3 liberal, humanitarian

bigoted *adj*
prejudiced, biased, intolerant, one-sided, fanatical, illiberal, narrow-minded, narrow, blinkered, closed, dogmatic, hidebound, opinionated, obstinate, jaundiced, influenced, swayed, partial, warped, twisted
E3 tolerant, liberal, broad-minded, enlightened

bigotry *n*
prejudice, discrimination, bias, injustice, unfairness, intolerance, partiality, narrow-mindedness, dogmatism, fanaticism, chauvinism, jingoism, sectarianism, racism, racialism, sexism
E3 tolerance

bigwig *n*
celebrity, dignitary, personage, somebody, VIP, notable, mogul, panjandrum
COLLOQ. big gun, big noise, big shot, big cheese, heavyweight, nob; *N Am* honcho
E3 nobody, nonentity

bijou *adj*
small, little, tiny, minute, petite, diminutive, compact, pocket; *Scot* wee

bile *n*
anger, bitterness, bad temper, short temper, ill-humour, irascibility, irritability, testiness, peevishness, rancour, choler, gall, spleen

bilge *n*
rubbish, nonsense, drivel, gibberish, trash, tripe, twaddle; *dialect* faddle; *Scot* blethers, clamjamphrie
COLLOQ. claptrap, piffle, codswallop, poppycock, hot air, cobblers, rot, tommyrot, stuff and nonsense
SLANG (*vulgar*) balls, bollocks, crap, shit, bullshit

bilious *adj*

1 IRRITABLE, bad-tempered, short-tempered, ill-tempered, ill-humoured, choleric, cross, grumpy, testy, peevish
COLLOQ. crotchety, grouchy, crabby, edgy

2 SICK, queasy, nauseated, sickly
COLLOQ. out of sorts

3 *bilious colours*
sickly, disgusting, nauseating, garish, lurid

bilk *v*
cheat, deceive, defraud, trick, fleece, swindle
COLLOQ. con, do, do out of, diddle, bamboozle, pull a fast one
SLANG sting

bill¹ *n, v*

♦ *n*

1 INVOICE, statement, account, charges, reckoning, tally, score; *N Am* check
COLLOQ. *N Am* tab

2 CIRCULAR, leaflet, handout, bulletin, handbill, broadsheet,

Biological terms include:

amino acid	conservation	evolution	germ	natural selection	reproduction
anatomy	corpuscle	excretion	Golgi apparatus	nuclear	respiration
animal behaviour	cultivar	extinction	hereditary factor	membrane	reticulum
animal kingdom	cytoplasm	flora and fauna	homeostasis	nucleus	ribonucleic acid
bacillus	deoxyribonucleic	food chain	living world	nutrition	(RNA)
bacteria	acid (DNA)	fossil	meiosis	order	ribosome
biologist	diffusion	gene	membrane	organism	secretion
botanist	ecosystem	genetic	metabolism	osmosis	survival of the
cell	ectoplasm	engineering	micro-organism	parasitism	fittest
chromosome	embryo	genetic	microbe	photosynthesis	symbiosis
class	endoplasmic	fingerprinting	mitosis	pollution	virus
clone	reticulum (ER)	genetically	molecule	protein	
coccus	enzyme	modified (GM)	mutation	protoplasm	

advertisement, notice, announcement, poster, flyer, placard, playbill, programme
COLLOQ. advert, ad
3 parliamentary bill
proposal, measure, (piece of) legislation, statute, act
♦ *v*
1 bill you at the end of the month
invoice, charge, debit, list costs, send a statement, send an account/invoice
2 be billed to appear in a show
advertise, announce, give notice, promote, post

**bill² ** *n*
a bird's bill
beak, mandible, neb, nib, rostrum

billet *n, v*
♦ *n*
1 ACCOMMODATION, quarters, living quarters, rooms, barracks, lodging, housing, berth
OLD casern
2 EMPLOYMENT, post, job, post, position, situation, office, occupation
♦ *v*
accommodate, lodge, put up, quarter, station

billow *v, n*
♦ *v*
swell, expand, bulge, puff out, fill out, balloon, rise, heave, surge, roll, undulate; *dialect & N Am* roil
♦ *n*
cloud, mass, surge, rush, wave, flood, breaker

billowy *adj*
billowing, swelling, surging, heaving, rippling, rolling, tossing, swirling, undulating, waving

bin *n*
container, receptacle, box, holder, basket, chest

bind *v, n*
♦ *v*
1 FASTEN, tie (up), attach, fasten, secure, clamp, stick, join, lash, truss, rope, strap, fetter, tether, shackle, chain, bandage, cover, dress, wrap, tape, embale; *Scot* oup
OLD enfetter, wap
2 OBLIGE, force, compel, constrain, impel, require, necessitate, restrict, confine, restrain, hamper, yoke
OLD gage, objure, thirl
3 bound together by a common grief
unite, join, tie, unify, bond, stand together, knit together, pull together, close ranks
♦ *n*
1 BORE, difficulty, inconvenience, irritation, impasse, nuisance
COLLOQ. pain, pain in the neck
2 PREDICAMENT, dilemma, embarrassment, quandary
COLLOQ. hole, spot, tight spot

binding *adj, n*
♦ *adj*

obligatory, compulsory, mandatory, necessary, permanent, conclusive, irrevocable, unalterable, indissoluble, unbreakable, strict, stringent, rigorous, tight, valid
FORMAL requisite
♦ *n*
cover, covering, wrapping, border, edging, trimming, tape, bandage

binge *n*
spree, bout, fling, session, orgy, jag, guzzle
COLLOQ. do, beano, bender, blind, sesh
SLANG blow-out; *N Am* toot
⟨⟩ fast

biography *n*
life story, life, history, autobiography, memoir(s), journal(s), diary, diaries, letter(s), recollection(s), profile, curriculum vitae, CV, account, record, biopic, hagiography
FORMAL prosopography

biology *n*
See also panel above

Fields of biology include:

aerobiology	conservation	marine biology
agrobiology	biology	Mendelism
bacteriology	cryobiology	microbiology
biochemistry	cybernetics	molecular
biodynamics	cytogenetics	biology
biogeochemisty	cytology	morphology
biogeography	Darwinism	natural history
bioinformatics	developmental	organography
biomathematics	biology	palaeontology
biometeorology	neo-Darwinism	parasitology
biometrics (or	ecology	pathology
biometry)	embryology	photobiology
bionics	endocrinology	phycology
bionomics	enzymology	physiology
biophysics	evolution	population
biopsychology	evolutionary	genetics
biorhymics	biology	radiobiology
bioscience	genetics	sociobiology
biosystematics	Haeckel's law	stoichology
biotechnology	histology	systematics
botany	human biology	taxonomy
cellular biology	hydrobiology	teratology
chronobiology	immunology	toxicology
computational	Lamarckism	virology
biology	macroecology	zoology

bird *n*
Related adjectives: avian, avine, volucrine, ornithoid
See panel on next page

birth *n*
1 CHILDBIRTH, labour, confinement, delivery, arrival, nativity
FORMAL parturition
COLLOQ. patter of tiny feet
Related adjective: natal

Birds include:

bee-eater	prunella	bittern	kingfisher	condor	ptarmigan
blackbird	raven	boatbill	knot	eagle	quail
bluetit	robin	chough	lapwing	falcon	turkey
brambling	rook	cormorant	mallard	harrier	**TROPICAL BIRDS**:
bullfinch	sedge warbler	coot	moorhen	hawk	ani
chaffinch	shrike	crane	oyster-catcher	kestrel	barbet
crow	skylark	curlew	peewit	kite	bird of paradise
cuckoo	sparrow	darter	pelican	osprey	budgerigar
dove	starling	dipper	petrel	owl	*colloq.* budgie
dunnock	swallow	duck	plover	sparrowhawk	canary
goldcrest	swift	dunlin	puffin	vulture	cockatiel
greenfinch	thrush	eider	rail	**FLIGHTLESS BIRDS**:	cockatoo
hedge sparrow	tit	flamingo	roller	dodo	kookaburra
hoopoe	titlark	frigate bird	seagull	emu	lovebird
jackdaw	tree sparrow	fulmar	snipe	kiwi	macaw
jay	wagtail	gallinule	stilt	ostrich	mockingbird
lark	warbler	gannet	stork	peacock	myna bird
linnet	woodpecker	godwit	swan	penguin	parakeet
magpie	wren	golden eye	teal	**FOWL**:	parrot
martin	yellowhammer	goose	tern	chicken	plume-bird
nightingale	**WATER BIRDS**:	grebe	turnstone	francolin	toucan
nutcracker	albatross	guillemot	whimbrel	grouse	
pigeon	auk	heron	**BIRDS OF PREY**:	partridge	
pipit	avocet	ibis	buzzard	pheasant	

2 *of noble birth*
ancestry, family, parentage, origin(s), descent, line, lineage, genealogy, derivation, pedigree, blood, stock, race, strain, house, extraction, background, breeding
3 BEGINNING, rise, emergence, arrival, appearance, origin(s), start, starting-point, commencement, source, dawn, derivation, fountainhead, root, seed
FORMAL advent, genesis
E3 1 death 3 end, finish, conclusion
■ **give birth to**
cause to exist, bring into existence, give rise to, initiate, create, found, establish, inaugurate

birthday *n*
anniversary, day of birth
Related adjectives: natalitial, genethliac

birthmark *n*
blemish, discoloration, mole, patch, naevus, strawberry mark
Related adjective: naevoid

birthplace *n*
place of origin, place of birth, native town, native country, fatherland, mother country, home, home town, root(s), provenance, source, fount, cradle

birthright *n*
privilege, prerogative, due, inheritance, legacy
OLD (*Shakesp*) birthdom

biscuit *n*
cake; *N Am* cookie; cracker, cracknel, pretzel, rusk, wafer, hardtack
COLLOQ. biccy

bisect *v*
halve, cut in half, divide, divide into two, cut in two, separate, split, intersect, cross, fork
FORMAL bifurcate

bisexual *adj*
androgynous, hermaphrodite
TECHNICAL gynandromorphic, gynandromorphous, monoclinous, epicene
COLLOQ. AC/DC, ambidextrous, bi, swinging both ways
E3 heterosexual, homosexual

bishop *n*
prelate, archbishop, primate, diocesan, metropolitan, patriarch, suffragan
OLD episcopant
Related adjective: episcopal

bishopric *n*
diocese, episcopacy, see

bit *n*
fragment, part, segment, portion, piece, small piece, small portion, slice, crumb, grain, morsel, mouthful, drop, dash, chunk, lump, scrap, particle, atom, mite, whit, jot, iota, tittle, shred, grain, flake, chip, sliver, speck, touch, tad, hint, trace, scintilla, soupçon, vestige
■ **a bit**
1 *a bit boring*
slightly, fairly, rather, a little, not much, not very
2 *wait a bit*
a while, a little while, a moment, a short time, minute, few minutes, moment, few moments
COLLOQ. jiffy, tick
■ **bit by bit**
gradually, little by little, in stages, step by step, slowly, piecemeal
E3 all at once, wholesale

bitch *n, v*
♦ *n*
1 *a bitch and her puppies*
female dog
2 *that woman's a bitch*
vixen, shrew, harpy, virago
COLLOQ. cat
SLANG (*offensive*) cow
3 ORDEAL, trial, torment, nightmare
COLLOQ. pig, swine
♦ *v*
complain, moan, grumble, criticize, find fault with, be spiteful about, talk about behind their back
COLLOQ. gripe, whinge, whine, badmouth

bitchiness *n*
nastiness, meanness, maliciousness, malice, cruelty, spite, venom
COLLOQ. cattiness
E3 kindness

bitchy *adj*
snide, nasty, mean, spiteful, malicious, vindictive, cutting, backbiting, venomous, rancorous, shrewish, vixenish, cruel, vicious
COLLOQ. catty
E3 kind, loving

bite *v, n*

♦ *v*

1 CHEW, eat, munch, gnaw, nibble, peck, chomp, champ, crunch, crush
OLD begnaw, pinch
FORMAL masticate
2 *the dog bit her hand*
nip, snap, pierce, wound, tear, rend, sink/get your teeth into
3 SMART, sting, tingle
4 *the rise in costs was beginning to bite*
grip, take effect, work, grip, hold, seize, pinch

♦ *n*

1 NIP, snap, wound, sting, smarting, pinch, prick, puncture, lesion
Related adjective: morsal
2 *have a bite to eat*
snack, light meal, refreshment, mouthful, morsel, taste, piece, bit
3 POWER, force, effect, impact, impression, strength, influence
OLD (*Spenser*) remorse
4 PUNGENCY, piquancy, spiciness, spice, sharpness
COLLOQ. kick, punch

biting *adj*

1 COLD, freezing, sharp, bitter, harsh, severe, keen, penetrating, piercing, nipping, stinging
2 CUTTING, incisive, bitter, piercing, penetrating, acid, pointed, pungent, acrid, raw, stinging, sharp, tart, caustic, sarcastic, scathing, harsh, vicious, vitriolic, cynical, hurtful
OLD shrewd
FORMAL trenchant, mordant, mordacious, astringe
F∃ 1 mild **2** bland

bitter *adj*

1 ACID, tart, sharp, sour, vinegary, unsweetened, pungent, tangy; *Scot* wersh
FORMAL acrid, astringent, acerb, acerbic
2 RESENTFUL, embittered, begrudging, indignant, aggrieved, angry, disgruntled, sour, morose, jaundiced, cynical, sullen, hostile, acrimonious, rancorous, malevolent, spiteful, vindictive, venomous, scathing, caustic, sardonic, wry
FORMAL acerbic, vitriolic, vituperative, virulent
COLLOQ. with a chip on your shoulder
3 INTENSE, severe, harsh, fierce, cruel, savage, merciless, painful, sad, unhappy, disappointing, tragic, distressing, harrowing, heartbreaking, heart-rending, gut-wrenching
4 *bitter winds*
stinging, biting, sharp, freezing, freezing cold, arctic, raw, harsh, piercing, penetrating
COLLOQ. nippy, parky
F∃ 1 sweet **2** contented **3** mild, happy **4** warm, mild

bitterly *adv*

1 *bitterly cold*
bitingly, piercingly, penetratingly
2 *bitterly disappointed*
intensely, severely, cruelly, savagely, grievously, painfully
3 RESENTFULLY, embitteredly, grudgingly, begrudgingly, indignantly, angrily, sourly, morosely, cynically, sullenly, hostilely, spitefully, acrimoniously, rancorously, malevolently, vindictively, venomously, scathingly, caustically, sardonically, wryly
FORMAL acerbically, vituperatively, with vitriol

bitterness *n*

1 ACIDITY, tartness, sharpness, sourness, vinegar, pungency, tanginess
2 RESENTMENT, embitterment, grudge, indignation, anger, sourness, moroseness, jaundice, cynicism, sullenness, spleen, hostility, antagonism, acrimony, malevolence, rancour, enmity, spite, vindictiveness, venom
OLD gall, wormwood; (*Spenser*) fell

FORMAL acerbity, virulence
COLLOQ. chip on your shoulder
3 INTENSITY, severity, harshness, ferocity, cruelty, pain, painfulness, sadness, unhappiness, disappointment, tragedy, distress, heartbreaking, heart-rending
OLD marah
4 *the bitterness of the winter*
sharpness, coldness, iciness, chilliness, frostiness, rawness, harshness, penetration, bite

bitty *adj*

disconnected, disjointed, fragmented, broken, fitful, incoherent, scrappy, piecemeal

bizarre *adj*

strange, odd, queer, curious, weird, peculiar, funny, eccentric, outlandish, ludicrous, ridiculous, fantastic, comical, extravagant, grotesque, freakish, abnormal, deviant, unusual, uncommon, unconventional, extraordinary
COLLOQ. left-field, offbeat, oddball, wacky, Pythonesque
SLANG way-out; *N Am* gonzo, off the wall
F∃ normal, ordinary, standard

bizarrely *adv*

strangely, oddly, curiously, weirdly, unusually, peculiarly, outlandishly, ludicrously, freakishly, abnormally, unconventionally, ridiculously, comically, extravagantly
F∃ normally

blab *v*

blurt out, tell, reveal, disclose, divulge, let slip, gossip, tattle; *N Am* blat
COLLOQ. squeal, leak, give the game away, let the cat out of the bag, blow the gaff
F∃ hide, hush up

blabber *v*

chat, chatter, prattle, gabble, twitter, twattle, gossip, jabber, babble, witter; *Scot* blether; *dialect & N Am* blather

black *adj, v*

♦ *adj*

1 JET-BLACK, coal-black, pitch-black, jet, ebony, raven, sable, inky, sooty, dusky, swarthy
OLD (*Shakesp*) hell-black
FORMAL nigrescent
COLLOQ. black as coal
2 *black people*
dark-skinned, coloured; (*offensive*) Negro, Negroid, nigger; swarthy
TECHNICAL melanistic
3 DARK, unlit, unilluminated, moonless, starless, overcast, dingy, dusky, dim, gloomy, overcast, sombre, funereal, pitch-black
FORMAL crepuscular, tenebrous, fuliginous, subfusc, Cimmerian, Stygian
4 FILTHY, dirty, soiled, stained, grimy, sooty, grubby, muddy, unclean
COLLOQ. grotty, gungy
5 *the future looks black*
bleak, gloomy, sad, depressing, distressing, melancholy, dismal, hopeless, sombre, mournful, funereal, awful, tragic
6 *in a black mood*
miserable, sad, unhappy, depressed, resentful, bitter, sullen, angry, threatening, menacing
FORMAL lugubrious
7 *black humour*
cruel, sick, cynical, tasteless, vulgar, gross, in bad taste
8 EVIL, wicked, bad, vile, cruel, malicious, malevolent, wrong, immoral, odious, devilish, satanic, demonic, diabolical
FORMAL nefarious, heinous
F∃ 1, 2 white **3** bright, light **4** clean, spotless **5** bright

▪ **black out**

1 FAINT, pass out, lose consciousness, keel over, collapse

COLLOQ. flake out
2 DARKEN, eclipse, cover up
3 CENSOR, conceal, suppress, withhold, gag
■ **black and white**
1 *a black and white issue*
definite, clear-cut, well-defined, unambiguous, plain,
distinct, unequivocal, categorical
2 *I've seen it in black and white*
printed, written, written down, on paper, on record
■ **in the black**
in credit, without debt, out of debt, solvent
COLLOQ. with your head above water
♦ *v*
1 *black someone's eye*
bruise, blacken, punch, hit, injure
2 *they blacked the imported goods*
boycott, embargo, blacklist, ban, bar, taboo

blackball *v*
vote against, ban, bar, blacklist, debar, ostracize, shut out,
drum out, throw out, exclude, expel, oust, reject,
repudiate, snub, veto, pill
COLLOQ. give the cold shoulder to

blacken *v*
1 DARKEN, black, nigrify, dirty, make dirty, soil, smudge,
cloud, smoke
OLD besmut
2 DEFAME, malign, slander, libel, revile, detract, smear,
besmirch, sully, stain, tarnish, taint, defile, denigrate,
discredit, dishonour
FORMAL impugn, calumniate, vilify, decry
COLLOQ. run down
F3 **2** praise, enhance

blackguard *n*
scoundrel, rascal, rogue, villain, devil, knave, miscreant,
reprobate, wretch
COLLOQ. bleeder, blighter, bounder, rotter, stinker, crook,
swine, scumbag
OLD SLANG sweep

blacklist *v*
debar, disallow, exclude, ban, outlaw, bar, boycott, expel,
ostracize, reject, shut out, repudiate, snub, taboo, veto
FORMAL preclude, proscribe
F3 accept, allow

blackmail *n, v*
♦ *n*
extortion, intimidation, exaction, bribery, ransom,
greenmail, chout
FORMAL chantage
COLLOQ. hush money
SLANG shakedown
OLD SLANG *N Am* strike
♦ *v*
extort, exact, hold to ransom, threaten, force, pressurize,
compel, coerce, demand
COLLOQ. bleed, milk, squeeze, lean on, put the screws on
SLANG black

blackmailer *n*
bloodsucker, extortioner, extortionist, vampire, hijacker;
N Am highbinder

blackout *n*
1 POWER FAILURE, power cut, electricity failure; *N Am*
brownout
2 FAINT, coma, unconsciousness, passing out, loss of
consciousness, swoon, oblivion
TECHNICAL syncope
COLLOQ. flaking-out
3 *a news blackout*
suppression, embargo, censorship, withholding,
concealment, secrecy, silence
COLLOQ. cover-up

blade *n*
edge, cutting edge, knife, dagger, sword, scalpel, razor,
vane

blame *v, n*
♦ *v*
hold responsible, say something is someone's fault, hold
accountable, hold liable, accuse, charge, tax, reprimand,
chide, reprove, upbraid, reprehend, admonish, rebuke,
reproach, censure, attribute liability, thank, criticize, find
fault with, fault, find guilty, disapprove, condemn,
scapegoat
OLD wite
FORMAL berate, inculpate, discommend, dispraise
COLLOQ. tear into, point the finger at, lay at someone's
door, pin it on, name names, name and shame
F3 exonerate, vindicate
♦ *n*
censure, criticism, reprimand, reproof, reproach,
recrimination, condemnation, accusation, charge,
incrimination, guilt, fault, responsibility, accountability,
liability, onus; *dialect* wite; *Scot* dirdum
FORMAL culpability, berating, dispraise, odium
SLANG stick, rap

blameless *adj*
innocent, guiltless, clear, faultless, without fault, perfect,
lily-white, unblemished, stainless, virtuous, sinless,
upright, above reproach, irreproachable, irreprovable,
unblamable, unimpeachable; *dialect* witeless
OLD (*Shakesp & Spenser*) unreproved
FORMAL irreprehensible, inculpable
F3 guilty, blameworthy

blameworthy *adj*
at fault, guilty, discreditable, disreputable, shameful,
unworthy, indefensible, inexcusable, reprehensible,
responsible, reproachable
FORMAL culpable, flagitious
F3 blameless

blanch *v*
1 *blanch at the sight*
grow/become/turn pale, go/become/turn white, whiten,
lighten, grow/become pallid, blench
TECHNICAL etiolate
2 *blanch vegetables*
boil, scald
F3 **1** colour, blush, redden

bland *adv*
1 *a bland person/statement*
boring, monotonous, humdrum, tedious, dull, uninspiring,
uninteresting, unexciting, nondescript, characterless,
ordinary, mundane, inoffensive, flat, anodyne, smooth,
suave, weak
COLLOQ. spammy
2 TASTELESS, insipid, flavourless, weak, mild
COLLOQ. vanilla
F3 **1** exciting, lively, stimulating **2** tasty, piquant, rich

blandishments *n*
flattery, compliments, enticements, fawning,
inducements, ingratiation, blarney, cajolery, coaxing,
persuasiveness, sycophancy, wheedling, treacle, lipsalve,
agréments
OLD sooth
FORMAL inveiglement
COLLOQ. soft soap, flannel, spiel, sweet talk

blank *adj, n*
♦ *adj*
1 *a blank page*
empty, unfilled, void, clear, bare, unmarked, unwritten,
plain, clean, white
2 EXPRESSIONLESS, deadpan, poker-faced, impassive,
emotionless, without feeling, lifeless, apathetic,

uninterested, indifferent, glazed, empty, vacant, vacuous, inscrutable, uncomprehending

◆ *n*

space, gap, break, void, emptiness, empty space, vacancy, vacuity, nothingness, vacuum

blanket *n, v, adj*

◆ *n*

1 *blankets on a bed*

cover, covering, bedcover, coverlet, bedspread, quilt, eiderdown, underblanket, manta; *dialect* whittle
OLD stroud

2 *a blanket of snow*

covering, coating, coat, layer, film, carpet, cloak, mantle, cover, sheet, film, envelope, overlay, wrapper, wrapping

◆ *v*

cover, coat, carpet, overlay, eclipse, hide, conceal, mask, cloak, surround, muffle, deaden, obscure, suppress, cloud

◆ *adj*

across-the-board, all-embracing, all-inclusive, comprehensive, inclusive, overall, global, total, wholesale, indiscriminate, sweeping, wide-ranging

blankly *adv*

expressionlessly, impassively, lifelessly, apathetically, uninterestedly, indifferently, vacantly, vacuously, emotionlessly, without feeling

blare *v, n*

◆ *v*

trumpet, clamour, roar, blast (out), boom (out), resound, sound loudly, thunder, ring, peal, clang, hoot, toot, honk

◆ *n*

clamour, roar, blast, boom, thunder, ring, peal, clang, hoot

blarney *n*

blandishments, cajolery, coaxing, flattery, persuasiveness, wheedling, soft sawder; *N Am* taffy
COLLOQ. soft soap, flannel, spiel, sweet talk

blasé *adj*

nonchalant, offhand, unimpressed, unmoved, unexcited, jaded, weary, bored, uninterested, uninspired, apathetic, indifferent, impassive, cool, lukewarm, unconcerned
FORMAL phlegmatic
E3 excited, enthusiastic, responsive

blaspheme *v*

swear, curse, profane, utter profanities, utter oaths, take the Lord's name in vain, desecrate, damn, revile, abuse
FORMAL execrate, imprecate, anathematize
OLD SLANG cuss

blasphemous *adj*

profane, impious, sacrilegious, godless, ungodly, irreligious, irreverent
OLD sulphurous
FORMAL imprecatory

blasphemously *adv*

profanely, sacrilegiously, irreverently, disrespectfully

blasphemy *n*

profanity, profaneness, curse, expletive, cursing, swearing, oaths, impiety, impiousness, ungodliness, irreverence, unholiness, sacrilege, desecration, violation, outrage
FORMAL execration, imprecation

blast *n, v*

◆ *n*

1 EXPLOSION, blow-up, detonation, shot, bang, crash, clap, crack, volley, burst, outburst, discharge

2 *a blast of cold air*

draught, gust, rush, gale, squall, storm, tempest, flurry, bluster, puff; *dialect* wuther; *Scot* waff, wap
TECHNICAL flatus
OLD sideration

3 SOUND, blow, blare, blaring, roar, roaring, boom, booming, thunder, clamour, bellow, peal, hoot, toot,

honk, wail, scream, shriek, clang, tantara; *dialect* wuther
OLD trump
COLLOQ. parp

◆ *v*

1 EXPLODE, blow up, blow to pieces, burst, shatter, destroy, demolish, ruin, assail, attack, strike, bomb, shoot/gun down

2 SOUND, blare (out), boom (out), roar, thunder, peal, bellow, hoot, toot, honk, wail, scream, shriek, clang
COLLOQ. parp

3 CRITICIZE, slate, reprimand, rebuke, tell off, reprove, upbraid, scathe
OLD siderate
FORMAL berate
COLLOQ. slam, come down heavily on

■ **blast off**
take off, lift off, be launched

blasted *adj*

damned, cursed, confounded, infernal, flaming, annoying, unpleasant
COLLOQ. blooming, flipping, darned, ruddy, dratting
SLANG (*taboo*) fucking

blatant *adj*

flagrant, brazen, barefaced, bald, blad-faced, shameless, unashamed, naked, arrant, open, overt, undisguised, ostentatious, glaring, conspicuous, manifest, patent, obtrusive, prominent, pronounced, hard-core, obvious, sheer, outright, unmitigated, out-and-out
COLLOQ. full-on

⚠ blatant or flagrant?
Blatant means 'glaringly or shamelessly obvious': *a blatant lie/liar*. *Flagrant* implies a greater degree of condemnation and means 'scandalous, very obvious and wicked': *a flagrant misuse of his powers*.

---

blatantly *adv*

flagrantly, brazenly, unashamedly, shamelessly, openly, glaringly, conspicuously, obviously, patently, manifestly, out-and-out

blaze *n, v*

◆ *n*

1 FIRE, flames, inferno, bonfire, flare-up, explosion, blast; *Scot* lunt
FORMAL conflagration

2 *a blaze of colour*

radiance, brilliance, beam, glare, flash, gleam, glitter, glow, light, burst, outburst

◆ *v*

1 *the fire was blazing*

burn, flame, flare (up), be on fire, be alight, ignite, catch fire, burst into flames

2 *blazing with light*

shine, beam, glare, flash, flare, gleam, glitter, glow, light, burst, be radiant, be brilliant

3 *eyes blazing with anger*

blow up, explode, erupt, burst, burn, fire, flash, rage, boil, seethe
COLLOQ. see red

4 *guns blazing away*

shoot, fire, blast, discharge, let off, let fly, set off

blazon *v*

proclaim, publicize, announce, make known, broadcast, celebrate, flourish, trumpet, herald, flaunt, vaunt
E3 deprecate, hush up

bleach *v*

whiten, make/turn white, blanch, decolour, decolorize, fade, pale, make/turn pale, lighten
TECHNICAL etiolate, peroxide

bleak *adj*

1 GLOOMY, sombre, leaden, grim, dreary, dismal, dark, drab,

depressing, miserable, wretched, desperate, joyless, cheerless, comfortless, hopeless, discouraging, disheartening, unfavourable, unpromising
2 *a bleak landscape*
unsheltered, windy, windswept, exposed, open, barren, bare, empty, arid, soulless, spartan, desolate, chilly, cold
3 COLD, chilly, harsh, raw; *Scot* blae; weather-beaten, dreary, dull
E3 1 bright, cheerful **3** bright, fine, pleasant

bleakly *adv*
gloomily, sombrely, grimly, dismally, drearily, miserably, wretchedly, joylessly, cheerlessly, unfavourably, unpromisingly

bleary *adj*
bleary-eyed, blurred, blurry, cloudy, dim, tired, watery, rheumy, unfocused

bleat *v*
1 *sheep bleating*
baa, bray, maa, cry, call; *dialect* whicker; *N Am* blat
2 *bleating about price increases*
complain, grumble, moan, kvetch
COLLOQ. whine, whinge, beef, grouse, gripe

bleed *v*
1 HAEMORRHAGE, lose blood, shed blood, let blood, blood, gush, spurt, flow, flood, run, exude, weep, ooze, seep, trickle
TECHNICAL exsanguinate, phlebotomize, extravasate
2 DRAIN, suck dry, exhaust, squeeze, milk, sap, reduce, bleed white
FORMAL deplete
3 *bleed money*
extort, extract
COLLOQ. milk, squeeze
4 *the stain has bled into the wood*
run, merge, flow, glide, melt

blemish *n, v*
♦ *n*
1 *a blemish on her skin*
deformity, disfigurement, mark, speck, smudge, blotch, botch, blot, stain, discoloration
OLD mote
2 *a blemish on his character*
flaw, imperfection, defect, fault, stain, taint, disgrace, dishonour
OLD want, mote
♦ *v*
tarnish, flaw, deface, disfigure, spoil, mar, damage, impair, spot, mark, blot, stain, sully, taint, compromise; *Scot* tash

---

Kinds of blemish include:

acne	chilblain	scar
birthmark	corn	spot
blackhead	freckle	strawberry mark
blister	mole	verruca
boil	naevus	wart
bump	pimple	whitehead
bunion	pockmark	*slang* zit
callus	pustule	
carbuncle	scab	

---

blench *v*
falter, hesitate, recoil, flinch, shrink, pull back, draw back, shudder, cower, shy, start, wince, quail, quake, quiver

blend *v, n*
♦ *v*
1 MERGE, combine, mix, mingle, amalgamate, coalesce, compound, synthesize, fuse, unite, homogenize, alloy, interweave, intertwine, stir, beat, whisk; *N Am* meld
FORMAL intermix, admix, commix, commingle, contemper
2 HARMONIZE, complement, fit, match, go (well) with, go together, suit, set off

E3 1 separate, divide **2** clash, jar
♦ *n*
compound, composite, alloy, amalgam, amalgamation, merging, synthesis, fusion, combination, union, uniting, mix, mixture, cross between two things, concoction
FORMAL admixture, commixture

bless *v*
1 ANOINT, sanctify, consecrate, hallow, dedicate, ordain, lay hands on
2 PRAISE, worship, extol, magnify, glorify, exalt, honour, thank
FORMAL laud
3 *the priest blessed the congregation*
ask God's favour for, ask God's protection for
4 *I bless the day I bought this washing machine*
give thanks for, be thankful for, be grateful for, favour
E3 1 curse **2** condemn

blessed *adj*
1 HOLY, sacred, hallowed, consecrated, sanctified, revered, adored, divine
2 HAPPY, contented, glad, joyful, joyous, lucky, fortunate, prosperous
3 *blessed with a good memory*
favoured, endowed, graced, provided
E3 1 cursed **2** unhappy, sad

blessing *n*
1 CONSECRATION, dedication, benediction, grace, thanksgiving, commendation
TECHNICAL darshan, kiddush
FORMAL invocation, benison
2 BENEFIT, advantage, favour, godsend, windfall, gift, gain, profit, help, service, bounty, boon, good thing, good fortune
3 *give a proposal your blessing*
approval, backing, support, agreement, authority, sanction, consent, permission, leave
FORMAL approbation, concurrence
COLLOQ. go-ahead, green light, OK, thumbs-up
E3 2 curse, blight **3** condemnation

blight *n, v*
♦ *n*
1 *affected by planning blight*
curse, misfortune, woe, trouble, calamity, bane, evil, scourge, blast, affliction, decay, pollution, contamination, corruption
OLD sideration
2 *potato blight*
disease, fungus, mildew, rot, infestation, cancer, canker
E3 1 blessing, boon
♦ *v*
spoil, mar, injure, undermine, ruin, wreck, crush, dash, shatter, destroy, damage, kill, annihilate, blast, wither, shrivel, frustrate, disappoint; *Scot* scouther
OLD strike
E3 bless

blind *adj, v, n*
♦ *adj*
1 SIGHTLESS, visually impaired, unsighted, unseeing, visionless, eyeless
See panel on next page
2 *blind to their needs*
unaware, ignorant, oblivious, unconscious, unobservant, imperceptive, slow, inattentive, neglectful, unmindful, indifferent, insensitive, thoughtless, inconsiderate
3 *love is blind*
unreasoning, uncritical, unthinking, irrational, injudicious, indiscriminate, heedless, mindless, impulsive, hasty, rash, impetuous, reckless, wild, mad, careless
4 CLOSED, obstructed, hidden, concealed, out of sight, obscured
E3 1 sighted **2** aware, sensitive **3** careful, cautious

Ways of describing sight impairment include:

amaurotic	far-sighted	long-sighted	partially-sighted	snow-blind
astigmatic	glaucomatous	myopic	presbyopic	stone-blind
colloq. blind as a bat	half-blind	near-sighted	purblind	trachomatous
(having) cataracts	hemeralopic	night-blind	sand-blind	visually handicapped
colour-blind	hypermetropic	nyctalopic	short-sighted	visually impaired

♦ *v*

1 *blinded in the accident*
make blind, cause to lose your vision, deprive of sight, deprive of vision, put the eyes out of, gouge the eyes out of

2 *blinded by the car's headlights*
dazzle, block your vision, obscure your vision

3 *tolerance blinds you to faults*
cause to lose reason/sense, deceive, mislead, intimidate, trick, trap, confuse

♦ *n*

1 *a window blind*
screen, cover, curtain, (window) shade, shutter, roller blind, Austrian blind, Venetian blind, festoon blind

2 *operate as a blind for illegal activities*
cloak, mask, camouflage, masquerade, front, façade, distraction, screen, smokescreen, cover
COLLOQ. cover-up

blindly *adv*

1 *feel your way blindly*
without vision, without sight, sightlessly, unseeingly

2 UNCRITICALLY, unthinkingly, irrationally, indiscriminately, mindlessly, senselessly, thoughtlessly, impulsively, rashly, impetuously, recklessly, wildly, madly, carelessly, incautiously
F3 2 critically, cautiously

blink *v*

1 *his eyes blinked*
wink, twinkle, twink, flicker, flutter
FORMAL nictate, nictitate

2 *the light blinked*
flash, flicker, twinkle, shine, gleam, glimmer, glitter, sparkle, scintillate

blip *n*

1 BLEEP, pip, buzz, squeal, screech

2 *a blip in the economy's recovery*
COLLOQ. glitch, hiccup, fly in the ointment, spanner in the works

bliss *n*
blissfulness, ecstasy, euphoria, rapture, joy, elation, happiness, gladness, blessedness, paradise, heaven, seventh heaven, utopia, nirvana
F3 misery, hell, damnation

blissful *adj*
ecstatic, euphoric, elated, enraptured, idyllic, rapturous, delighted, enchanted, joyful, joyous, happy
F3 miserable, wretched

blister *n*
sore, blain, swelling, cyst, boil, abscess, ulcer, pustule, pimple, canker, carbuncle
TECHNICAL bleb, bulla, furuncle, papilla, papula, phlyctaena, pompholyx, vesicle, vesicula, wen
OLD blab
Related adjective: vesicant

blistering *adj*

1 *blistering heat*
hot, scorching, withering, intense, extreme, fierce, ferocious

2 *blistering criticism*
cruel, vicious, savage, virulent, fierce, caustic, scathing, sarcastic

blithe *adj*

1 CASUAL, unthinking, thoughtless, careless, heedless, uncaring, unconcerned, carefree, untroubled

2 CHEERFUL, cheery, happy, light-hearted
F3 1 serious **2** morose

blithely *adv*
casually, thoughtlessly, carelessly, unthinkingly

blitz *n*

1 *the blitz during the war*
bombardment, attack, offensive, raid, strike, campaign, onslaught, blitzkrieg

2 *have a blitz on the garden*
effort, all-out effort, attack, exertion, attempt, endeavour, campaign

blizzard *n*
snowstorm, squall, storm, tempest, buran

bloated *adj*
swollen, puffy, puffed out, puffed up, blown up, inflated, dilated, expanded, enlarged, full, stuffed
FORMAL distended
F3 thin, shrunken, shrivelled

blob *n*
drop, droplet, globule, bead, pearl, bubble, dab, spot, splash, gob, lump, mass, ball, tear, pellet, pill
COLLOQ. glob

bloc *n*
alliance, group, league, coalition, federation, union, association, ring, syndicate, entente, axis, cabal, cartel, clique, faction

block *n, v*

♦ *n*

1 *a block of offices*
building, development, structure, complex

2 *a block of stone*
piece, lump, mass, slab, chunk, hunk, square, cube, wedge, cake, brick, bar

3 *a block of seats/tickets*
batch, cluster, quantity, group, series, section

4 OBSTACLE, barrier, bar, jam, blockage, stoppage, resistance, obstruction, impediment, hindrance, drawback, deterrent, stumbling-block, let, delay

♦ *v*

block a pipe/progress
choke, clog (up), plug, stop up, dam up, close, seal, bar, obstruct, be in the way, impede, hamper, hinder, stonewall, stop, check, arrest, halt, thwart, frustrate, scotch, deter
FORMAL occlude
COLLOQ. bung up

■ **block off**
shut off, seal, close (up), stop (up)

■ **block out**

1 *block out light*
hide, conceal, screen, blot out, obliterate, eclipse, obscure

2 *block out memories*
shut out, blank out, mask, screen, veil, suppress, repress

blockade *n, v*

♦ *n*
barrier, barricade, siege, obstruction, restriction, obstacle, block, stoppage, closure, encirclement
TECHNICAL investment

♦ *v*
keep from, prevent, hinder, stop, check, obstruct, prevent entering/reaching, prevent using, besiege, barricade, encircle, surround

blockage *n*
obstruction, blocking, stoppage, block, clot, jam, log jam, bottleneck, congestion, hindrance, impediment
FORMAL occlusion

blockhead *n*
fool, idiot, imbecile, dunce
COLLOQ. nincompoop, ninny, nitwit, numskull, twerp, dope, twit, dimwit; *N Am* bufflehead
SLANG wally, jerk, plonker, git, prat, dipstick, nerd, dork, geek
F3 brain, genius

bloke *n*
man, boy, fellow, male, individual, character
COLLOQ. chap, guy

blond, blonde *adj*
fair, flaxen, golden, fair-haired, golden-haired, light, light-coloured, tow-coloured, bleached

blood *n*
1 *lose blood*
lifeblood, vital fluid, gore
Related adjectives: haemal, haemic, haematic, sanguineous
2 *of aristocratic blood*
extraction, birth, descent, lineage, family, kindred, relations, ancestry, descendants, kinship, relationship

bloodcurdling *adj*
horrifying, chilling, spine-chilling, hair-raising, terrifying, frightening, scary, dreadful, fearful, appalling, horrific, horrible, horrid, horrendous

bloodless *adj*
1 *a bloodless coup*
peaceful, non-violent, strife-free, unwarlike
2 *her bloodless face*
ashen, anaemic, colourless, pale, pallid, pasty, sallow, white, sickly, wan, chalky, cold, drained, feeble, insipid, languid, lifeless, listless, unfeeling, unemotional, passionless, spiritless, torpid
F3 **1** bloody, violent **2** bloody, ruddy, vigorous

bloodshed *n*
killing, murder, slaughter, slaying, massacre, bloodbath, butchery, carnage, pogrom, gore, bloodletting, decimation

bloodsucker *n*
blackmailer, extortioner, extortionist
COLLOQ. leech, parasite, sponger

bloodthirsty *adj*
murderous, homicidal, warlike, savage, barbaric, barbarous, brutal, ferocious, vicious, cruel, inhuman, ruthless
FORMAL sanguinary

bloody *adj*
bleeding, bloodstained, gory, murderous, bloodthirsty, savage, brutal, ferocious, fierce, cruel
FORMAL sanguinary, sanguine, sanguineous, sanguinolent, ensanguinated

bloody-minded *adj*
awkward, difficult, obstinate, stubborn, unhelpful, unco-operative, obstructive, irritable, touchy
COLLOQ. stroppy

bloom *n, v*
♦ *n*
1 BLOSSOM, flower, bud
TECHNICAL efflorescence, florescence
2 PRIME, heyday, perfection, blush, flush, glow, rosiness, beauty, radiance, lustre, health, vigour, strength, freshness
♦ *v*
1 *the flowers were blooming*
bud, sprout, blossom, flower, open

2 *the children are blooming*
flourish, develop, mature, grow, blossom, prosper, thrive, glow
F3 **1** fade, wither

blooming *adj*
blossoming, healthy, flowering, rosy, ruddy, bonny
TECHNICAL florescent
OLD (*Shakesp*) primy
F3 ailing

blossom *n, v*
♦ *n*
bloom, flower, bud
TECHNICAL efflorescence, florescence, pruina
OLD bloosme
♦ *v*
1 *the trees were blossoming*
bloom, flower
OLD bloosme
FORMAL burgeon
2 *blossom into a beautiful young woman*
develop, mature, grow, progress, bloom, flourish, thrive, prosper, succeed
FORMAL burgeon
F3 **2** fade, wither

blot *n, v*
♦ *n*
1 *an ink blot*
spot, stain, smudge, blotch, smear, mark, dot, splodge, speck, blemish
2 *a blot on his reputation*
blemish, flaw, fault, defect, imperfection, taint, stain, disgrace, tarnishing, black mark
♦ *v*
1 *blot a surface*
spot, mark, stain, smudge, blur, dry (up), soak (up), absorb
2 *blotted his character*
sully, taint, tarnish, stain, blacken, spoil, mar, disfigure, disgrace
■ **blot out**
obliterate, cancel, delete, erase, darken, black out, obscure, hide, conceal, screen, shadow, eclipse
FORMAL efface, expunge

blotch *n*
patch, splodge, splotch, splash, smudge, blot, spot, mark, stain, blemish, monk

blotched *adj*
marked, spotted, spotty, stained, blemished, blotchy, scarred, pimply, freckly, scratched

blotchy *adj*
spotty, spotted, patchy, uneven, smeary, blemished, reddened, inflamed

blow[1] *v, n*
♦ *v*
1 *the wind was blowing*
gust, blast, flurry, puff
2 *blow leaves along the road*
waft, fan, flutter, float, flow, stream, drift, rush, whirl, whisk, sweep, carry, fling, buffet, drive, blast
3 BREATHE, breathe out, pant, puff (out)
TECHNICAL insufflate, exsufflate
FORMAL inhale, exhale
4 *blow a horn*
play, sound, pipe, trumpet, toot, blare, blast
5 *blow a lot of money*
fritter away, misspend, spend freely, squander
FORMAL dissipate
COLLOQ. spend like water, pour down the drain
6 *blow a chance/opportunity*
waste, spoil, ruin, wreck, bungle, make a mess of, miss out on

COLLOQ. botch, fluff, miss the boat; *N Am* flub
SLANG cock up, screw up
7 *the car blew a tyre*
blow out, burst, puncture, rupture, tear, split
8 *the fuse blew*
short-circuit, break, fuse, melt

■ **blow out**
1 EXTINGUISH, put out, smother, snuff out
2 BURST, puncture, rupture, tear, split

■ **blow over**
die down, subside, end, finish, cease, pass, vanish,
disappear, be forgotten, settle down, fizzle out, peter out
FORMAL abate, dissipate

■ **blow up**
1 EXPLODE, go off, go up, detonate, burst, blast, bomb
2 INFLATE, pump up, swell, fill (out), puff up, balloon, bloat,
dilate, expand, enlarge, magnify, exaggerate, overstate
FORMAL distend
3 LOSE YOUR TEMPER, become angry, get into a rage, take
leave of your senses
COLLOQ. blow your top, hit the roof, fly off the handle, go
mad, flip (your lid)
SLANG go ape, go ballistic
♦ *n*
puff, draught, flurry, gust, blast, wind, gale, storm, squall,
tempest
OLD blore

blow² *n*
1 *a blow on the head*
hit, concussion, box, cuff, clip, swipe, bash, slap, smack,
buffet, butt, bang, clap, clout, knock, rap, stroke, thump,
punch, hook, yank, souse, swat, thwack, wap, whang,
whop, wuther, pelt, plug; *dialect* scat; *Scot* devvel,
lounder, paik, skiff, spang, stot, waff, whample
TECHNICAL appel
OLD buff, dint, whirret; (*Spenser*) peise
COLLOQ. whack, wallop, belt
SLANG biff, sock, bop, conk
2 MISFORTUNE, affliction, reverse, setback, comedown,
disappointment, upset, jolt, shock, surprise, bombshell,
calamity, catastrophe, disaster
COLLOQ. shocker, bolt from the blue, rude awakening,
whammy

blow-out *n*
1 PUNCTURE, flat tyre, burst tyre
COLLOQ. flat
2 PARTY, celebration, feast
COLLOQ. binge, bash, knees-up, rave, rave-up, beanfeast

blowy *adj*
breezy, windy, fresh, blustery, gusty, squally, stormy

blowzy *adj*
sloppy, slovenly, unkempt, untidy, bedraggled, dishevelled,
ungroomed, tousled, messy, slipshod
F∃ neat, smart

blubber *v*
cry, weep, blub, sob, snivel, sniffle, whimper

bludgeon *v, n*
♦ *v*
1 BEAT, strike, club, batter, hit, beat, cudgel
COLLOQ. clobber, cosh
2 FORCE, coerce, compel, intimidate, bulldoze, badger,
hector, harass, browbeat, bully, dragoon, pressurize,
terrorize
♦ *n*
club, baton, cosh, cudgel, truncheon

blue *adj*
1 AZURE, sky-blue, royal blue, ice-blue, sapphire, cobalt,
ultramarine, navy blue, navy, indigo, aquamarine,
turquoise, cyan, cerulean, jacinth, dumortierite, haüyne
2 DEPRESSED, low, dejected, downcast, dispirited,

downhearted, despondent, gloomy, glum, dismal, sad,
unhappy, miserable, melancholy, morose
COLLOQ. fed up, down in the dumps
3 *a blue joke*
obscene, offensive, indecent, improper, rude, coarse,
vulgar, lewd, dirty, pornographic, X-rated, erotic, bawdy,
fruity, saucy, smutty, risqué, adult
COLLOQ. raunchy, steamy, near the knuckle/bone
F∃ 2 cheerful, happy **3** decent, clean

blueprint *n*
design, outline, draft, sketch, pilot, guide, plan, scheme,
strategy, project, programme, archetype, prototype,
representation, model, pattern

blues *n*
depression, despondency, unhappiness, sadness, gloom,
gloominess, moodiness, glumness, melancholy, miseries,
dejection, doldrums
COLLOQ. dumps
F∃ euphoria

bluff¹ *v, n*
♦ *v*
was only bluffing
lie, pretend, feign, sham, fake, deceive, delude, mislead,
hoodwink, blind, fool
COLLOQ. bamboozle
♦ *n*
lie, idle boast, bravado, humbug, pretence, show, sham,
fake, fraud, trick, subterfuge, deceit, deception, feint
FORMAL braggadocio

bluff² *adj, n*
♦ *adj*
a bluff man
blunt, candid, direct, downright, open, outspoken, plain-
spoken, straightforward, frank, genial, good-natured,
hearty, affable
F∃ diplomatic, refined
♦ *n*
cliff, crag, escarpment, peak, precipice, promontory,
foreland, bank, brow, headland, height, ridge, scarp,
escarp

blunder *n, v*
♦ *n*
mistake, error, inaccuracy, misjudgement, slip,
indiscretion, gaffe, faux pas, oversight, fault, break, bevue,
bêtise
FORMAL solecism
COLLOQ. howler, bloomer, clanger, boob, booboo, slip-up,
bish, clanger, goof; *N Am* flub
SLANG cock-up, boner, floater; *N Am* pratfall
♦ *v*
make a mistake, stumble, flounder, bumble, err,
miscalculate, misjudge, mess up, get wrong, go wrong,
bungle, mismanage
COLLOQ. muck up, botch, slip up, fluff, drop a clanger;
N Am flub
SLANG goof (up), cock up, screw up

blunt *adj, v*
♦ *adj*
1 UNSHARPENED, not sharp, dull, worn, pointless, edgeless,
rounded, stubbed
2 FRANK, candid, direct, forthright, unceremonious,
explicit, plain-spoken, honest, straightforward, downright,
outspoken, tactless, insensitive, rude, impolite, uncivil,
brusque, curt, stark, abrupt
COLLOQ. calling a spade a spade, speaking your mind, not
beating about the bush, not mincing your words
F∃ 1 sharp, pointed **2** subtle, tactful
♦ *v*
dull, take the edge off, dampen, soften, deaden, numb,
anaesthetize, alleviate, allay, weaken

FORMAL abate, hebetate
E3 sharpen, intensify

bluntly *adv*
frankly, candidly, directly, forthrightly, unceremoniously, explicitly, brusquely, rudely, impolitely, insensitively, tactlessly
E3 subtly, tactfully

blur *v, n*
◆ *v*
1 *the windscreen blurred*
smear, smudge, spot, blotch, stain, blear
2 *blurred memories/views*
obscure, make vague/indistinct, mask, conceal, mist, fog, befog, cloud, becloud, veil, dim, dull, darken, confuse, soften
COLLOQ. mudge
◆ *n*
1 *a blur on the picture*
smear, smudge, spot, blotch, stain, slur
TECHNICAL mackle
2 *my memories are a blur*
haze, mist, fog, cloudiness, fuzziness, indistinctness, obscurity, muddle, confusion, dimness

blurb *n*
advertisement, commendation, copy, puff
COLLOQ. hype, spiel

blurred *adj*
out of focus, fuzzy, unclear, indistinct, vague, ill-defined, lacking definition, faint, hazy, misty, foggy, cloudy, clouded, bleary, dim, obscure, confused
E3 clear, distinct

blurt *v*
▪ **blurt out**
exclaim, cry (out), call out, come out with, gush, spout, utter, tell, reveal, disclose, divulge, let out, leak, let slip, plump; *NAm* blat
FORMAL ejaculate
COLLOQ. blab, let the cat out of the bag, give the game away, spill the beans
E3 bottle up, hush up

blush *v, n*
◆ *v*
flush, redden, go red, turn red, crimson, scarlet, colour (up), glow, rouge
OLD mantle
◆ *n*
flush, reddening, rosiness, ruddiness, colour, glow

blushing *adj*
flushed, red, rosy, glowing, apple-cheeked, confused, embarrassed, ashamed, modest
FORMAL erubescent
E3 pale, white, composed

bluster *v, n*
◆ *v*
boast, brag, crow, swagger, strut, vaunt, show off, rant, roar, storm, bully, harangue, hector, huff, roister
OLD ruffle
FORMAL rodomontade
COLLOQ. talk big
◆ *n*
boasting, crowing, bravado, bluff, swagger, domineering
OLD huff
FORMAL braggadocio, rodomontade

blustery *adj*
windy, gusty, squally, stormy, tempestuous, violent, wild, boisterous
E3 calm

board *n, v*
◆ *n*

1 *a wooden board*
sheet, panel, slab, plank, beam, timber, slat
2 COMMITTEE, council, panel, jury, commission, directorate, directors, trustees, governors, advisers, advisory group, working party, management, head office
3 MEALS, food, sustenance, provisions, rations
FORMAL victuals
SLANG grub, nosh
◆ *v*
get on, get in/into, embark, mount, step aboard, enter, catch
FORMAL embus, emplane, entrain
▪ **board up**
close (up), cover (up), shut (up), seal

boast *v, n*
◆ *v*
1 *boasts about his qualifications*
brag, crow, claim, exaggerate, overstate, bluster, trumpet, vaunt, strut, swagger, prate, show off, sing your own praises; *dialect* crake
OLD yelp, gasconade, cry roast-meat
FORMAL rodomontade
COLLOQ. swank, talk big, loudmouth, blow your own trumpet; *NAm* blow your own horn; *Aust* big-note, skite
2 *boasts a new sauna*
exhibit, have, possess, enjoy, pride yourself on
E3 1 *formal* belittle, deprecate
◆ *n*
brag, crowing, blustering, self-praise, overstatement, claim, vaunt, pride, joy, gem, treasure
OLD gab
FORMAL fanfaronade, gasconade, gasconism, rodomontade, jactation
COLLOQ. hot air, swank

Synonym nuances
verb sense 1
Many of the synonyms are disapproving in tone; **brag** suggests arrogance in talking of one's achievements, whilst **crow** expresses a degree of gloating. **Claim**, however, hints that those achievements may not in fact be true, while **exaggerate** and **overstate** probably allow of their existence but imply they are less significant than projected: *I think you exaggerate your influence.*
  Bluster could be used to describe voluble but perhaps unsubstantiated boasting; likewise **trumpet**. **Vaunt** has a narrower usage, generally of a public declaration of pride: *Canada's much vaunted multiculturalism.* **Prate** might be used of boastful speaking containing little of consequence; its usage is, surprisingly, rare. Both **strut** and **swagger** have connotations of a physical manner of carrying oneself, and can be used to emphasize this aspect: *he swaggered around in his new uniform.*

---

boastful *adj*
proud, conceited, vain, puffed up, bragging, crowing, cocky, swaggering, arrogant, self-flattering, egotistical, bigheaded, swollen-headed; *NAm* swell-headed
FORMAL vainglorious
COLLOQ. swanky
E3 modest, self-effacing, humble

boastfully *adv*
proudly, conceitedly, crowingly, cockily, arrogantly, egotistically
FORMAL vaingloriously
E3 modestly, self-effacingly, humbly

boat
See panel on next page

boatman *n*
ferryman, oarsman/woman, rower, sailor, yachtsman/woman, waterman, bargee, gondolier, voyageur

Types of boat or ship include:

airboat	coracle	dugout	junk	packet	square-rigger
aircraft-carrier	corvette	ferry	kayak	paddle steamer	submarine
barge	cruiser	freighter	ketch	pedalo	swamp boat
battleship	currach (or	frigate	lifeboat	punt	tanker
brig	curragh)	galleon	liner	rowing-boat	trawler
cabin-cruiser	cutter	gondola	lugger	sampan	trimaran
canoe	destroyer	gulet	man-of-war	schooner	tug
catamaran	dhow	houseboat	minesweeper	scow	U-boat
clipper	dinghy	hovercraft	motor-boat	skiff	yacht
coble or cobble	dreadnought	hydrofoil	motor-launch	smack	warship
container-ship	dredger	NZ jet boat	narrow boat	speedboat	

See also **sail; ship.**

---

bob v

1 *a raft bobbing up and down*
bounce, float, move up and down shake, quiver, wobble, bobble, popple; *Scot* hod
FORMAL oscillate

2 *bobbed back into the house*
leap, spring, jump, jerk, jolt, twitch, nod, bow, curtsy, hop, skip

■ **bob up**
appear, emerge, arrive, materialize, rise, surface, pop up, spring up, crop up, arise
COLLOQ. show up

bode v
predict, foretell, prophesy, indicate, signify, intimate, herald, threaten, warn
OLD sign
FORMAL augur, adumbrate, forebode, foreshadow, foreshow, foretoken, forewarn, presage, betoken, portend, prognosticate, purport

bodge v
botch, bungle, mess (up), blunder, ruin, spoil
COLLOQ. muck up, foul up, fluff, make a hash of; *N Am* flub
SLANG goof (up), screw up, louse up

bodily adj, adv
♦ *adj*
physical, carnal, fleshly, real, actual, tangible, substantial, concrete, material
FORMAL corporeal
E3 spiritual
♦ *adv*
altogether, en masse, collectively, as a whole, as one, completely, fully, wholly, entirely, totally, in toto
E3 piecemeal

body n

1 *his whole body was aching*
physique, build, form, frame, figure, anatomy, skeleton, trunk, torso
Related adjective: corporal

2 CORPSE, cadaver, carcase, dead body
SLANG stiff

3 *sit in the body of the church*
main part, central part, largest part, bulk, heart, core, nub, kernel

4 ORGANIZATION, association, society, corporation, company, confederation, council, authority, bloc, cartel, syndicate, congress, collection, group, band, crowd, throng, multitude, mob, mass, phalanx

5 *the body of a car*
shell, framework, frame, chassis, structure, casing, skeleton

6 *a body of water*
expanse, area, range, stretch, extent, area

7 *a body of information*
quantity, amount, mass, lot, volume, weight, bulk

8 CONSISTENCY, density, solidity, firmness, bulk, mass, substance, essence, fullness, richness

bodyguard n
guard, protector, defender, guardian
SLANG minder

boffin n
scientist, expert, engineer, designer, planner, inventor, mastermind, genius, brain, intellect, intellectual, thinker
COLLOQ. egghead, wizard, backroom-boy

bog n, v
♦ *n*
marsh, swamp, fen, mire, quagmire, quag, slough, morass, quicksands, marshland, swampland, wetlands; *dialect* sump; *Can* muskeg

■ **bog down**
encumber, hinder, overwhelm, deluge, sink, stick, trap, slow down, slow up, delay, halt, hold up, set back, stall
FORMAL impede, retard, mire

boggle v
astound, startle, amaze, surprise, wonder, marvel, overwhelm, stagger, alarm, confuse
COLLOQ. bowl over, flabbergast

boggy adj
marshy, miry, swampy, muddy, oozy, morassy, quaggy, soft, spongy, waterlogged, fenny
FORMAL paludal
E3 arid

bogus adj
false, fake, counterfeit, forged, fraudulent, spurious, sham, make-believe, artificial, imitation, dummy
COLLOQ. spoof, phoney, pseudo, pseud
E3 genuine, true, real, valid

bohemian adj, n
♦ *adj*
artistic, unconventional, unorthodox, nonconformist, alternative, original, avant-garde, eccentric, offbeat, bizarre, exotic
COLLOQ. boho, arty, oddball, off-the-wall
SLANG way-out
E3 bourgeois, conventional, orthodox
♦ *n*
beatnik, hippie, drop-out, nonconformist
COLLOQ. boho
E3 conformist

boil[1] v

1 *boil water*
simmer, stew, cook, heat, seethe, bring/come to the boil, brew, gurgle, bubble, fizz, effervesce, froth, foam, steam, parboil, decoct, wallop; *dialect* leep

2 *boil with anger*
erupt, explode, rage, rave, storm, fume, seethe
FORMAL fulminate
COLLOQ. blow your top, fly off the handle, fly into a rage, go

off the deep end, blow a fuse, see red, hit the roof
- **boil down**
amount, reduce, concentrate, distil, condense, digest, abstract, summarize, abridge

boil² n
a boil on the skin
pustule, abscess, gumboil, ulcer, sore, tumour, growth, ganglion, bunion, pimple, carbuncle, blister, inflammation, swelling, blain, furuncle
OLD botch
COLLOQ. gathering

boiling adj
1 boiling water
turbulent, gurgling, bubbling, steaming, scalding
2 HOT, baking, roasting, scorching, sweltering, blistering, torrid; N Am broiling
3 ANGRY, indignant, incensed, infuriated, enraged, furious, fuming, flaming

boisterous adj
exuberant, rollicking, romping, bouncy, active, hyperactive, lively, spirited, turbulent, energetic, animated, tumultuous, loud, noisy, clamorous, rowdy, rough, disorderly, riotous, wild, unrestrained, unruly, obstreperous, roisting; dialect randy; Scot goustrous
TECHNICAL strepitoso
OLD dithyrambic
COLLOQ. rumbustious, rambunctious
Fa quiet, calm, restrained, docile

boisterously adv
exuberantly, actively, hyperactively, spiritedly, turbulently, energetically, animatedly, tumultuously, loudly, noisily, clamorously, rowdily, roughly, riotously, wildly, unrestrainedly, obstreperously
Fa quietly, calmly, restrainedly

bold adj
1 BRAVE, dauntless, daring, audacious, fearless, undaunted, courageous, valiant, intrepid, heroic, gallant, adventurous, venturesome, enterprising, plucky, spirited, confident, outgoing
OLD haughty
FORMAL valorous
COLLOQ. bold as a lion
2 BRAZEN, brash, forward, shameless, unabashed, impudent, insolent, barefaced, bald-faced
COLLOQ. cheeky, saucy, brassy, pert, bold as brass
SLANG in-your-face
3 EYE-CATCHING, striking, conspicuous, prominent, strong, pronounced, distinct, definite, bright, vivid, colourful, loud, flashy, showy, flamboyant
4 in bold print
heavy, thick, pronounced
Fa **1** cowardly, nervous, cautious, timid, shy **2** timid, modest, shy, diffident **3** faint, restrained **4** light

boldly adv
1 BRAVELY, daringly, courageously, confidently,

fearlessly, audaciously, valiantly, intrepidly, heroically, adventurously, pluckily
2 VIVIDLY, strikingly, strongly, brightly, prominently, distinctly, definitely
Fa **1** cowardly, cautiously, timidly **2** faintly

bolshie adj
awkward, obstinate, unhelpful, difficult, stubborn, unco-operative, irritable, touchy, prickly, oversensitive, rude, unpleasant, problem
COLLOQ. stroppy, bloody-minded
Fa amenable, pleasant, co-operative, helpful

bolster v, n
♦ v
boost, aid, assist, help, maintain, prop, reinforce, strengthen, supplement, support, brace, buoy up, buttress, firm up, shore up, stay, stiffen, revitalize, invigorate
FORMAL augment
Fa undermine
♦ n
pillow, support, cushion, Dutch wife

bolt n, v
♦ n
1 a bolt on a door
bar, rod, shaft, fastener, latch, catch, lock; Scot snib
2 nuts and bolts
screw, pin, peg, rivet
TECHNICAL pintle
3 a bolt of lightning
flash, shaft, burst, streak, ray, spark, blaze, flare
♦ v
1 FASTEN, secure, bar, latch, lock, rivet, pin, screw
OLD (Spenser) sperre
2 bolt for the door
escape, flee, fly, run (away), run off, sprint, rush, dash, dart, hurtle
FORMAL abscond
COLLOQ. scarper
3 bolt your food down
gulp, wolf (down), gobble, gorge, guzzle, devour, cram, stuff
COLLOQ. scoff

bomb n, v
♦ n
bombshell, explosive, projectile, device
COLLOQ. pineapple
SLANG egg
See panel below
♦ v
bombard, shell, torpedo, attack, blow up, destroy

bombard v
1 bombard the airport
attack, assail, pelt, pound, strafe, blast, bomb, shell, torpedo, stone, blitz, raid, besiege
2 bombard with criticism

Types of bomb include:

aerobomb	colloq. daisy-cutter	general purpose	Molotov cocktail	shell
atom bomb	depth charge	bomb	nail bomb	smart bomb
Bangalore torpedo	dirty bomb	grenade	neutron bomb	smoke bomb
binary bomb	old slang doodlebug	hydrogen bomb	nuclear bomb	stink bomb
blockbuster	drogue bomb	incendiary	parcel bomb	stun grenade
bomblet	colloq. dumb bomb	landmine	penetration bomb	thermobaric bomb
bouncing bomb	E-bomb	letter bomb	petrol bomb	thermonuclear bomb
colloq. bunker buster	firebomb	massive ordnance air	pipe bomb	time bomb
buzz bomb	fission bomb	burst (MOAB)	plastic bomb	torpedo
candle bomb	flying bomb	megaton bomb	radium bomb	V-1
cluster bomb	fragmentation bomb	Mills bomb	rifle grenade	V-2
car bomb	fusion bomb	mine	rocket	
cobalt bomb		missile	sensor fuzed bomb	

Human bones include:

carpal	incus (anvil)	patella (kneecap)	skull
clavicle (collarbone)	innominate bone (hip bone)	pelvis	sternum (breastbone)
coccyx	ischium	phalange	stapes (stirrup-bone)
cranium	malleus (hammer)	pubis	tarsal
femur (thigh bone)	mandible (lower jawbone)	radius	temporal
fibula	maxilla (upper jawbone)	rib	tibia
humerus (funny bone)	metacarpal	sacrum	ulna
ilium	metatarsal	scapula (shoulder-blade)	vertebra

attack, hound, bother, harass, pester, flood, deluge, inundate, swamp

bombardment n
1 *aerial bombardment*
attack, assault, air raid, bombing, shelling, pounding, blitz, barrage, cannonade, fusillade, salvo, fire, flak, hail
SLANG stonker
2 *bombardment of questions*
attack, onslaught, besieging, hounding, bothering, harassing, pestering

bombast n
pomposity, pretentiousness, bluster, wordiness, heroics, rant, verbosity, turgidity; N Am sophomoric
OLD ampullosity, dithyramb
FORMAL grandiloquence, magniloquence, fustian, euphuism
COLLOQ. hot air

bombastic adj
pompous, pretentious, grandiose, verbose, wordy, turgid, ostentatious, affected, high-flown, inflated, bloated, windy
FORMAL grandiloquent, magniloquent, portentous, euphuistic, fustian
F3 reserved, restrained

bon mot n
witticism, quip, riposte, repartee, pleasantry, wisecrack
COLLOQ. one-liner

bona fide adj
genuine, real, valid, true, actual, authentic, lawful, legal, legitimate, kosher, honest
COLLOQ. the real McCoy
F3 bogus

bonanza n
windfall, sudden wealth, godsend, stroke of luck, blessing, boon

bond n, v
♦ n
1 *bonds of friendship*
connection, relation, relationship, link, tie(s), binding, union, yoke, affiliation, attachment, rapport, friendship, affinity, chemistry
TECHNICAL nexus, ligament, valence

FORMAL vinculum
2 CONTRACT, covenant, agreement, pledge, promise, vow, pact, transaction, deal, treaty, word, obligation
3 FETTER, shackle, manacle, chain, cord, band, binding
♦ v
connect, fasten, bind, unite, fuse, join, stick, attach, glue, gum, paste, weld, seal

bondage n
imprisonment, captivity, confinement, restraint, slavery, enslavement, serfdom, servitude, subservience, subjection, subjugation, yoke
OLD thrall
FORMAL incarceration, thraldom, vassalage
F3 freedom, independence

bone n
Related adjectives: osseous, osteal
See panel above

bonhomie n
warm-heartedness, kind-heartedness, friendliness, conviviality, geniality, sympathy, tenderness, good nature, affability, amiability

bonny adj
attractive, lovely, beautiful, pretty, fine, fair, blooming, handsome, bouncing, cheerful, cheery, joyful, merry
F3 ugly

bonus n
1 *pay a bonus*
commission, dividend, premium, prize, reward, honorarium, tip, gratuity, gift, fringe benefits, handout
FORMAL lagniappe
2 *the good weather is a bonus*
advantage, benefit, gain, extra
FORMAL perquisite
COLLOQ. plus, perk
F3 **2** disadvantage, disincentive

bony adj
thin, lean, angular, lanky, gawky, gangling, skinny, scrawny, scraggy, emaciated, skeletal, rawboned, gaunt, drawn
FORMAL osseous
F3 fat, plump

book n, v
♦ n

Types of book include:

album	concordance	lexicon	romantic novel	journal	prayer book
almanac	cookbook	libretto	story	ledger	psalter
annual	copybook	manual	thesaurus	notebook	**FORMATS**:
anthology	detective	manuscript	thriller	pad	audio book
atlas	dictionary	novel	yearbook	scrapbook	e-book
A to Z	directory	omnibus	**WRITING BOOKS**:	sketchbook	hardback
bestseller	encyclopedia	penny dreadful	album	textbook	paperback
catalogue	fiction	phrase book	book of days	workbook	softback
children's book	gazetteer	picture book	chapbook	**CHURCH BOOKS**:	
coffee-table book	gradus	pocket companion	diary	hymnal	
comic book	grimoire	primer	exercise book	hymn-book	
compendium	guidebook	reference book	Filofax®	lectionary	
	handbook		jotter	missal	

See also **literature**; **story**.

Terms used in bookbinding include:

adhesive binding	book block	fore edge	lining	rounding and	tail
all edges gilt (aeg)	buckram	front board	Linson®	backing	tailband
backboard	case	full bound	loose-leaf	saddle-stitch	thermal tape
backbone	casebound	gather	mechanical	sewing	binding
back cornering	casing-in	half bound	binding	shoulder	thermoplastic
back lining	cloth-lined board	hardback	millboard	side-stitch	binding
N Am binder's	comb binding	head	morocco	signature	thread sewing
board	debossing	headband	notch binding	smashing	unsewn binding
binder's brass	doublure	headcap	open-flat	soft-cover	varnishing
binder's die	drawn-on	hinge	paperback	spine	velo binding
binding	drilling	hot foil stamping	pasteboard	spiral binding	whole bound
blind blocking	dust cover	jacket	perfect binding	square back	wire binding
blocking	embossing	laminating	quarter bound	stab-stitch	wire stitching
boards	· endpaper	library binding	raised band	stamping	wiro binding
bolts	flyleaf	limp	ring binding	strawboard	yapp

volume, tome, publication, work, booklet, tract

♦ *v*

1 *book a ticket*
arrange (in advance), reserve, make a reservation for, prearrange, engage, charter, procure, order, organize, schedule, programme
COLLOQ. bag
2 *booked for assault*
charge, accuse (of), blame
F3 1 cancel
■ **book in**
register, enrol, check in, record your arrival

bookbinding
See panel above

booking *n*
reservation, arrangement, appointment, prior arrangement

bookish *adj*
studious, well-read, academic, scholarly, cultured, erudite, highbrow, intellectual, learned, literary, scholastic, lettered, donnish, bluestocking, pedantic
F3 lowbrow, unlettered

booklet *n*
leaflet, pamphlet, folder, circular, handout, notice

books *n*
accounts, ledgers, records, financial statement, balance sheet

boom *v, n*
♦ *v*
1 BANG, crash, roar, blare, thunder, roll, bellow, rumble, resound, reverberate, blast, explode, bombilate
2 FLOURISH, thrive, prosper, succeed, develop, grow, do well, increase, gain, progress, expand, swell, surge, leap, escalate, skyrocket, intensify, strengthen, go from strength to strength, mushroom, snowball, explode
FORMAL burgeon
F3 2 fail, collapse, slump
♦ *n*
1 BANG, clap, crash, roar, thunder, rumble, reverberation, blast, blare, bellow, roll, resonance, explosion, burst, loud noise
2 INCREASE, growth, expansion, gain, upsurge, jump, surge, leap, spurt, boost, upturn, upswing, improvement, advance, progress, success, development, escalation, explosion
F3 2 failure, collapse, slump, recession, depression

boomerang *v*
rebound, bounce back, spring back, recoil, ricochet, reverse, backfire

boon¹ *n*
a great boon to the elderly
blessing, advantage, benefit, bonus, help, godsend,

windfall, favour, kindness, gift, present, grant, gratuity
OLD bene
COLLOQ. plus
F3 disadvantage, blight

boon²
■ **boon companion**
close friend, dear friend, special friend, best friend, bosom friend, confidant(e)
OLD cupman, franion, Trojan

boor *n*
oaf, lout, barbarian, philistine, vulgarian, rustic, yahoo, hog, plebeian, clown, Grobian; *dialect* chuff; *Scot* keelie
OLD kern, Jack
COLLOQ. peasant, country bumpkin, clod, clodhopper, yokel, pleb, oik
SLANG yob, yobbo, slob

boorish *adj*
uncouth, oafish, loutish, ill-mannered, ill-bred, rude, coarse, rough, crude, vulgar, unrefined, uncivilized, gruff, impolite, rustic, uneducated, ignorant, crass, gross, lumpen, clodhopping; *Aust* ocker
OLD borrel, swain
F3 polite, refined, cultured, genteel

boost *v, n*
♦ *v*
1 *boost confidence*
bolster, lift, encourage, inspire, uplift, foster, support, stimulate; *Aust* rap
TECHNICAL potentiate
2 *boost sales*
increase, raise, put up, improve, enhance, develop, enlarge, expand, supplement, amplify, advance, help, aid, assist, maximize, promote, encourage, further, heighten
FORMAL augment
3 *boost a product*
advertise, promote, publicize, praise
COLLOQ. plug, hype, talk up
F3 1 undermine **2** lower, deteriorate, hinder
♦ *n*
1 *a boost to morale*
lift, uplift, fillip, encouragement, inspiration, stimulus, spur, support; *Aust* rap
COLLOQ. shot in the arm, ego-trip
2 *a boost to sales*
increase, rise, improvement, enhancement, development, enlargement, expansion, increment, addition, supplement, amplification, advance, help, aid, assistance, furtherance
FORMAL augmentation
3 *a boost for a product*
advertisement, promotion, publicity, praise
COLLOQ. plug, hype
F3 1 setback, blow **2** setback, deterioration

boot¹ v
kick, shove
- **boot out**
  dismiss, eject, expel, lay off, suspend, shed, give notice, make redundant
  COLLOQ. kick out, fire, sack, give someone their cards, give the heave

boot²
- **to boot**
  as well, in addition, besides, too
  COLLOQ. into the bargain

Types of boot include:

ankle boot	football boot	muckluck
balmoral	galosh	overshoe
bootee	gambado	platform boot
bottine	gumboot	riding boot
old buskin	half-boot	rugby boot
Chelsea boot	Hessian boot	*colloq.* scarpetto
chukka boot	high shoe	skating boot
climbing-boot	jemima	snowboot
clodhopper	kamik	top-boot
old crow boot	kid	wader
derby	lace-boot	walking-boot
Doc Marten®	larrigan	wellington
finnesko	moon boot	*colloq.* welly

---

booth n
cubicle, compartment, carrel, stall, stand, kiosk, hut, box; *Scot* bothan, crame, luckenbooth

bootleg adj
illegal, unlawful, illicit, criminal, wrong, forbidden, prohibited, banned, outlawed, barred, unauthorized, under-the-counter, black-market
FORMAL proscribed, interdicted
🖪 legal

bootless adj
fruitless, futile, vain, ineffective, useless, pointless, profitless, sterile, unavailing, unsuccessful, worthless unproductive, barren
🖪 profitable, useful

booty n
loot, plunder, pillage, spoil(s), haul, gains, takings, pickings, prize, profits, takings, winnings; *Scot* creagh
OLD purchase
SLANG swag

booze n, v
- *n*
  alcohol, drink, liquor, spirits, strong drink, intoxicant, grog, liqueur, stimulus, slug; *Scot* skink, strunt
  OLD fuddle
  COLLOQ. hard stuff, the bottle, Dutch courage, firewater, the creature; *Scot & Irish* the cratur; jar, tipple, tiddly, tinct
  SLANG jungle juice; *N Am* juice
- *v*
  drink, indulge, have a drink, be a hard drinker, be a heavy drinker
  COLLOQ. tipple, hit the bottle, drink like a fish
  SLANG get pissed

boozer n
1 PUB, bar, saloon, public house, tavern, inn, lounge, lounge bar; *Scot* howf
COLLOQ. local, hostelry, watering-hole
2 DRINKER, alcoholic, drunk, drunkard, inebriate, hard drinker, heavy drinker, dipsomaniac, wine-bibber, Bacchus, bloat, habitual; *N Am* souse
COLLOQ. tippler
SLANG wino, lush, alkie, dipso, soak, piss artist, pisshead, toper, tosspot, sot, sponge

bop n, v
- *n*
  dance, hop, twist, jive, stomp
  COLLOQ. boogie
- *v*
  dance, leap, jump, move to music, rock, spin, sway, gyrate, twirl, pirouette, whirl, trip the light fantastic
  COLLOQ. hoof it, hop, jig, shake a leg

border n, v
- *n*
  1 BOUNDARY, frontier, line, state line, marchlands, marches
  2 *herbaceous borders*
  bed, edge, rim, brim, verge, margin, fringe, periphery, surround, perimeter, circumference, bound, bounds, confine, confines, limit, demarcation, borderline, brink
  3 HEM, frill, valance, skirt, trimming, frieze, selvage, list, rand, welt
  TECHNICAL limb, mat, bordure, orle, cartouche, dado, guilloche, furbelow, purfle
  OLD swage
- *v*
  1 *Sweden borders Norway*
  lie/be next to, be adjacent to, join, touch, connect, trench
  FORMAL adjoin, abut, impinge, be contiguous with
  2 *streets bordered with trees*
  edge, bound, skirt, flank, fringe, rim, surround, enclose, trim, selvage, hem
  OLD emborder, engrail
  FORMAL circumscribe
- **border on**
  verge on, be almost, be nearly, resemble, approximate to, be tantamount to, approach

borderline n, adj
- *n*
  demarcation line, boundary, differentiation, line, dividing-line, divide, division, limit
- *adj*
  marginal, problematic, indefinite, doubtful, uncertain, indecisive, indeterminate, ambivalent
  COLLOQ. iffy
  🖪 certain, definite, clear-cut

bore¹ v, n
- *v*
  the speech bored them
  tire, make tired, weary, wear out, fatigue, exhaust, pall on, be tedious to, jade, trouble, bother, worry, irritate, annoy, vex, irk
  COLLOQ. turn off, send to sleep, bore the pants off
  🖪 interest, excite
- *n*
  nuisance, bother
  COLLOQ. bind, drag, turn-off, headache, pain, pain in the neck
  🖪 pleasure, delight

bore² v
bore a hole
drill, mine, pierce, perforate, penetrate, puncture, sink, dig (out), burrow, hollow (out), tap, tunnel, undermine, sap

bored adj
uninterested, unexcited, tired, wearied, exhausted
FORMAL ennuied, ennuyé
COLLOQ. bored to tears, bored stiff, bored out of your mind, cheesed off, fed up, turned off, sick and tired, in a rut, brassed off, browned off
🖪 interested, excited

boredom n
tedium, tediousness, monotony, humdrum, dullness, sameness, flatness, apathy, listlessness, weariness, world-weariness, frustration

FORMAL ennui, malaise, acedia
◨ interest, excitement

boring adj
tedious, dull, monotonous, routine, repetitious,
uninteresting, unexciting, uneventful, mundane, dreary,
humdrum, tiring, tiresome, unvaried, commonplace, trite,
unimaginative, uninspired, uninspiring, dry, stale, flat,
insipid, prosaic, long-winded
OLD stultifying, jejune
COLLOQ. samey, dull as ditchwater, soul-destroying, with
the novelty worn off, ho-hum
◨ interesting, exciting, stimulating, original

boring adj
tediously, dully, monotonously, repetitiously,
uninterestingly, unexcitingly, uneventfully, drearily,
tiresomely, tritely, unimaginatively, flatly, insipidly,
prosaically, long-windedly
OLD stultifyingly
◨ interestingly, excitingly

Synonym nuances
Tedious may be used to imply the cause of boredom
could well be excessive length: *reasons too tedious to
relate*. The words **monotonous**, **routine** and
repetitious, point to the same thing happening over and
over: *her life is a monotonous routine*. **Dull**,
uninteresting, **unexciting**, **uneventful** and **unvaried**,
on the other hand, express a lack of anything new or
stimulating. **Dreary** and **humdrum** are similar,
suggesting a lack of variety, but with more emotional
effect: *she was sick of her humdrum existence*. **Tiring** can
be used to suggest something so boring that is physically
or mentally draining: *a tiring journey*; whilst **tiresome**
suggests it is irritating: *a truly tiresome and boring movie*.
 Commonplace, **unimaginative** and **uninspired** can
be used of boring speech or writing to indicate there it
contains nothing of distinction. Both **flat** and **insipid** also
point to a lack of inspiration, while **prosaic** similarly is
lacking in imagination: *news reports are commonly
prosaic and patronising*. The word **dry**, while also
generally used of the written or spoken word,
appropriately describes a heaviness of style with little in
the way of light relief; whereas **stale** has more of a
suggestion that it has already been experienced many
times before: *stale jokes*.
 Long-winded, however, is appropriate when many
more words have been used than are actually required.
Trite tends to be used more narrowly of over-used words
or phrases: *trite accolades*.

---

borough n
town, district, area, community, constituency, parish; *Scot*
burgh

borrow v
1 *borrow a friend's car*
have the use of, take/have on loan, use temporarily, take
out a loan, rent, hire, charter, lease; *dialect* scunge
TECHNICAL lever
COLLOQ. scrounge, cadge, sponge
2 *borrow words/ideas*
adopt, take (over), draw, derive, obtain, use, acquire
FORMAL appropriate
◨ **1** lend

borrowing n
1 *borrowing of money*
use, temporary use, loan, rental, hire, charter, leasing
2 *English borrowings in German*
loan, loan-translation, loan-word, adoption, takeover,
derivation, use, acquisition
TECHNICAL calque
◨ **1** lending

bosom n, adj
◆ n
1 BUST, breasts, chest, breast; *dialect* pap, diddy
COLLOQ. boob, booby
SLANG bristol, knocker, tit, titty; *Aust* nork
2 *in the bosom of the family*
heart, core, centre, midst, protection, shelter, sanctuary
◆ adj
close, intimate, dear, devoted, loving, faithful, confidential,
boon

boss n, v
◆ n
employer, master, owner, captain, head, chief, leader, top
man, top woman, supremo, administrator, executive,
director, chairman, chairperson, chairwoman, manager,
superior, foreman, superintendent, overseer, governor,
supervisor; *S Afr* oubaas
COLLOQ. gaffer, gov, guv, bigwig, big cheese, top dog, top
banana; *N Am* honcho
◆ v
order around, order about, domineer, tyrannize, bully,
bulldoze, browbeat, give orders to, dominate
COLLOQ. push around, throw your weight about, lay down
the law

bossiness n
authoritarianism, high-handedness, imperiousness,
assertiveness, autocracy, tyranny, despotism
◨ unassertiveness

bossy adj
authoritarian, autocratic, tyrannical, despotic, dictatorial,
domineering, overbearing, oppressive, lordly, high-
handed, dominating, imperious, insistent, assertive,
demanding, exacting
◨ unassertive

botch v, n
◆ v
bungle, mess (up), make a mess of, blunder, mar,
mismanage, ruin, spoil, patch; *N Am* mux
COLLOQ. foul up, fluff, muck up, muff, make a hash of, make
a bad job of, bodge; *N Am* flub
SLANG goof (up), louse up, screw up, cock up, balls up;
(taboo) fuck up
◨ accomplish, succeed
◆ n
blunder, bungle, failure, muddle, mess, miscarriage
COLLOQ. flop, farce, shambles, hash
SLANG cock-up, balls-up
◨ success

both adj
the two, each, the pair, the one and the other

bother v, n
◆ v
1 *not bother to reply*
concern yourself, trouble, make the/an effort, think
necessary
2 *the heat bothered us*
worry, upset, trouble, concern, annoy, dismay, alarm,
distress, vex; *Scot* fash, deave
COLLOQ. bug
3 *don't bother her*
disturb, inconvenience, put out, trouble, pester, plague,
harass, nag, annoy, irritate, molest
FORMAL incommode
COLLOQ. hassle
◆ n
1 *not worth the bother*
trouble, inconvenience, effort, problem, difficulty, fuss,
exertion, pains, bustle, flurry
COLLOQ. hassle
SLANG shtook

2 *office paperwork is a real bother*
nuisance, annoyance, irritation, problem, difficulty, vexation, worry, strain
COLLOQ. aggravation, pest, pain in the neck
3 *a spot of bother in the pub*
trouble, fighting, disturbance, disorder, unrest, rumpus
COLLOQ. aggro
SLANG bovver

bothersome *adj*
troublesome, annoying, irksome, irritating, infuriating, vexatious, vexing, inconvenient, distressing, exasperating, laborious, boring, tedious, tiresome, wearisome; *Scot* fashious
OLD brickle
COLLOQ. aggravating, pesky

bottle *n, v*
♦ *n*
1 container
2 COURAGE, bravery, boldness, daring, valour, intrepidity
COLLOQ. guts, nerve, spunk, grit
■ **bottle up**
hide, conceal, restrain, curb, keep back, hold back, keep in check, suppress, repress, inhibit, restrict, shut in, enclose, contain, disguise
▬ unbosom, unburden

Types of bottle include:

ampulla	feeding bottle	poison bottle
apothecary	flacon	scent bottle
bottle	flagon	screwtop
beer bottle	flask	snuff bottle
calabash	gourd	*Aust* stubby
carafe	hip flask	Thermos® flask
carboy	hot-water bottle	torpedo bottle
codd bottle	jack	vial
cruet	lagena	vinegar bottle
decanter	milk bottle	wine bottle
demijohn	phial	
dumpy	pitcher	

See also **wine bottle sizes**.

---

bottleneck *n*
hold-up, traffic jam, snarl-up, congestion, gridlock, clogging, blockage, obstruction, block, obstacle, restriction, constriction, narrowing

bottom *n, adj*
♦ *n*
1 UNDERSIDE, underneath, sole, base, foot, plinth, pedestal, support, foundation, substructure, basis, underpinning, ground, nadir
2 *at the bottom of the sea*
floor, bed, depths
3 *at the bottom of the garden*
end, far end, furthest end, farthest end
4 *children at the bottom of the class*
lowest level, least important position
5 *sitting on his bottom*
rear, behind, buttocks, seat, rump
COLLOQ. posterior, backside, tail, bum; *NAm* butt, heinie, booty
SLANG (*vulgar*) arse; *NAm* ass, tush; *Aust* coit, quoit
▬ **1** top **2** surface **4** top
♦ *adj*
lowest, lower, underside, undermost

bottomless *adj*
a bottomless pit/supply of funds
deep, profound, fathomless, unfathomed, unplumbed, unbottomed, immeasurable, unfathomable, measureless, infinite, boundless, limitless, unlimited, inexhaustible
TECHNICAL subjacent

OLD unfounded
FORMAL abysmal, abyssal
▬ shallow, limited

bough *n*
branch, limb

boulder *n*
rock, stone, niggerhead; *Aust* gibber
OLD bowlder

boulevard *n*
avenue, mall, parade, promenade, drive, road, street, prospect, thoroughfare

bounce *v, n*
♦ *v*
1 *bounce a ball*
rebound, spring back, bob, ricochet, recoil, throw, dap; *Scot* stoit, stot
2 *children bouncing about*
spring, jump, leap, bound
♦ *n*
1 *allowed one bounce of the ball*
rebound, bound, spring, jump, leap; *Scot* stot
2 SPRING, springiness, elasticity, give, resilience, rebound, recoil
3 EBULLIENCE, exuberance, vitality, vivacity, energy, vigour, animation, dynamism, spiritedness, liveliness
COLLOQ. go, get-up-and-go, zip
■ **bounce back**
recover, get better, get back to normal, improve, make a comeback

bouncing *adj*
healthy, lively, robust, strong, vigorous, thriving, blooming, bonny

bouncy *adj*
1 SPRINGY, resilient, flexible, elastic, stretchy, rubbery, spongy
2 LIVELY, active, energetic, alive, spirited, dynamic, vivacious, vigorous, sprightly
COLLOQ. full of beans

bound[1] *adj*
1 *bound to go wrong*
sure, certain, definite, fated, destined, doomed
2 LIABLE, committed, duty-bound, pledged, obliged, required, forced, compelled, constrained
FORMAL beholden
3 FASTENED, secured, fixed, tied (up), chained, roped, fettered, tethered, held, attached, clamped, lashed, trussed, strapped, shackled, restricted, bandaged
■ **bound up with**
tied up with, connected with, linked with, related to, associated with, dependent on
COLLOQ. (going) hand in hand with

bound[2] *adj*
be bound for Norway
heading, headed, off (to), on your way to, travelling, going, coming, proceeding

bound[3] *v, n*
♦ *v*
she bounded down the stairs
jump, leap, vault, hurdle, spring, bounce, bob, hop, skip, dance, frisk, gambol, frolic, caper, prance, cavort, lollop, galumph; *Scot* scoup, skelp, spang, stend
♦ *n*
jump, leap, vault, spring, bounce, bob, hop, skip, gambol, frolic, caper, dance, prance; *Scot* spang, stend
TECHNICAL gambado

bound[4] *n, v*
♦ *n*
1 BORDER, line, limit(s), borderline, demarcation, confine(s), margin, verge, brink, edge, perimeter,

circumference, extremity, termination
2 LIMITATION, limit, restriction, check, curb, restraint
◆ v
1 BORDER, outline, limit, enclose, edge, skirt, flank, fringe, surround; *dialect* mere
2 RESTRICT, regulate, control, limit, moderate, restrain, contain
FORMAL circumscribe

boundary *n*
border, frontier, barrier, line, borderline, demarcation, bounds, confine(s), limit(s), margin, fringe, verge, brink, edge, perimeter, extremity, termination, point of no return, Rubicon, score; *dialect* mere; *Scot* meith
OLD bourn, limes, list, mark
Related adjectives: perimetric, peripheral

bounded *adj*
enclosed, surrounded, bordered, edged, encircled, encompassed, limited, restrained, restricted, confined, walled in, hemmed in, controlled, defined, demarcated
FORMAL circumscribed, delimited

bounder *n*
cad, cheat, blackguard, rogue, miscreant, cur, dastard, knave
COLLOQ. blighter, rotter, pig, swine, rat, dirty dog

boundless *adj*
unbounded, limitless, unlimited, illimitable, unconfined, countless, incalculable, numberless, innumerable, untold, incalculable, vast, immense, measureless, immeasurable, infinite, endless, unending, never-ending, interminable, everlasting, inexhaustible, unflagging, indefatigable
🖙 limited, restricted

bounds *n*
restrictions, confines, limits, borders, marches, demarcations, margins, fringes, boundaries, periphery, circumference, perimeter, edges, extremities, parameters, scope
▪ **out of bounds**
off limits, prohibited, forbidden, not allowed

bountiful *adj*
abundant, plentiful, exuberant, profuse, ample, prolific, overflowing, ungrudging, unstinting, boundless, copious, generous, lavish, liberal, open-handed, princely
FORMAL magnanimous, munificent, bounteous, plenteous, luxuriant
🖙 meagre, mean, sparse

bounty *n*
1 REWARD, recompense, premium, bonus, gratuity, tip, gift, present, donation, grant, allowance
2 GENEROSITY, liberality, largesse, almsgiving, charity, philanthropy, kindness
FORMAL munificence, beneficence, magnanimity

bouquet *n*
1 *a bouquet of flowers*
bunch, posy, nosegay, spray, corsage, buttonhole, boutonnière, wreath, garland
2 AROMA, smell, odour, scent, perfume, fragrance, nose
FORMAL redolence, odoriferousness
3 COMPLIMENT, favour, approval, honour, congratulations, praise, commendation, accolade, tribute
FORMAL eulogy, felicitation
COLLOQ. pat on the back

bourgeois *adj*
middle-class, materialistic, money-orientated, conservative, traditional, conformist, conventional, hidebound, unadventurous, ordinary, dull, humdrum, banal, commonplace, trite, pedestrian, uninspired, unoriginal, uncreative, unimaginative, *Biedermeier*, uncultured
🖙 bohemian, unconventional, original

bout *n*
1 PERIOD, spell, time, stint, turn, term, stretch, run, course, session, spree, jag
COLLOQ. go, binge, splurge, sesh
2 *a bout of illness*
attack, fit, spasm, touch
3 FIGHT, battle, engagement, encounter, struggle, wrestle, set-to, match, contest, competition, round, heat

bovine *adj*
1 *bovine animals*
cattlelike, cowlike
2 *his bovine response*
stupid, slow, dull, slow-witted
COLLOQ. dense, dumb, thick, doltish, dim-witted
🖙 **2** quick

bow¹ *v, n*
◆ v
1 *bow your head*
incline, bend, nod, bob, curtsy, kowtow, salaam, stoop, curve, arch, crook, crouch; *Scot* jouk
FORMAL genuflect, make obeisance
2 YIELD, give in, give way to, consent, surrender, capitulate, submit, succumb, concede, accept, comply, defer
FORMAL accede, acquiesce
3 SUBDUE, overpower, conquer, crush, humble, humiliate
FORMAL subjugate, vanquish
◆ n
inclination, bending, nod, bob, curtsy, arc, kowtow, salaam, salutation, acknowledgement; *Scot* beck, jouk
FORMAL genuflexion, obeisance, prostration
▪ **bow out**
withdraw, pull out, desert, abandon, defect, back out, retire, resign, leave, stand down, step down, give up
COLLOQ. chicken out, quit

bow² *n*
the bow of a ship
front, beak, head, prow, stem, forepart, rostrum
🖙 stern

bow³ *n*
tie a bow
loop, ring, circle, knot, lavallière

bowdlerize *v*
censor, cut, edit, excise, expunge, expurgate, purge, clean up, purify, modify, blue-pencil

bowels *n*
1 INTESTINES, entrails, guts, colon
TECHNICAL viscera
COLLOQ. insides, innards
2 *in the bowels of the earth*
depths, interior, inside, middle, centre, core, heart, belly, cavity

bower *n*
arbour, shelter, alcove, grotto, bay, recess, retreat, sanctuary

bowl¹ *n*
a washing-up bowl
receptacle, container, vessel, dish, basin, sink, pan, piggin, tazza, pottinger, porringer; *Scot* coggie
OLD monteith

bowl² *v*
1 *bowl a ball*
throw, hurl, fling, pitch, propel, roll, spin, whirl, rotate, revolve
2 *bowl along in a car*
move steadily, motor, speed, race, career, rush, hurry
▪ **bowl over**
1 *bowled over by the news*
overwhelm, affect deeply, impress greatly, surprise, amaze,

box 117 **bracket**

Types of box include:

ballot-box	cigarette box	knife box	punnet	tin
bin	coffer	locker	safe	toolbox
black box	coffin	matchbox	sarcophagus	trinket box
box-file	collection-box	pack	sewing box	trunk
caddy	coolbox	package	shoebox	*Aust* tuckerbox
canister	crate	pencilbox	snuffbox	vesta
cardboard box	dispatch box	pillar box	strongbox	writing-slope
cartridge	hatbox	pillbox	suggestion box	
casket	jewellery box	postbox	tea chest	

astound, astonish, shock, startle, stagger, stun, dumbfound
COLLOQ. flabbergast, floor, wow
2 *bowl over a person*
knock down, fell, topple, unbalance, push into

box¹ *n, v*
• *n*
boxes of books
container, receptacle, case, carton, packet, present, bijou, casket, pyxis, pyx, chest, coffret
• *v*
package, pack, wrap, parcel, case, encase
■ **box in**
enclose, surround, block in, cordon off, hem in, shut in, fence in, corner, trap, confine, restrain, coop up, restrict, imprison, cage, contain
FORMAL circumscribe

box² *v, n*
• *v*
1 *learn to box*
fight, spar, engage in fisticuffs
2 *box someone's ears*
punch, hit, strike, slap, batter, thump, buffet, clout, cuff
COLLOQ. wallop, whack, slug
SLANG sock
• *n*
punch, hit, strike, slap, batter, thump, buffet, clout, cuff
COLLOQ. wallop, whack, slug
SLANG sock

boxer *n*
fighter, prizefighter, sparring partner
FORMAL pugilist
COLLOQ. ham

boxing *n*
prizefighting, fighting, fisticuffs, sparring
FORMAL pugilism
Related adjective: pugilistic

Weight divisions in professional boxing:

heavyweight	junior-lightweight/super- featherweight
cruiserweight/junior- heavyweight	featherweight
light-heavyweight	super-bantamweight/ junior-featherweight
super-middleweight	bantamweight
middleweight	super-flyweight/junior- bantamweight
light-middleweight/junior- middleweight	flyweight
welterweight	light-flyweight/junior- flyweight
light-welterweight/junior- welterweight	mini-flyweight/straw- weight/minimum weight
lightweight	

boy *n*
son, lad, youngster, stripling, youth, junior, schoolboy, fellow, child, adolescent, teenager, young man, male, garçon, groom, hokra; *Scot* gilpy, loon, chield, knave-bairn, nickum; *Irish* gossoon, spalpeen; *N Am* bub

OLD dandiprat, galopin, kinchin-cove; (*Shakesp*) Jack-a-Lent
COLLOQ. kid, nipper, whippersnapper, guttersnipe, sprog, shaver; *Irish* bucko
SLANG boyo

boycott *v, n*
• *v*
refuse, reject, embargo, black, ban, prohibit, disallow, bar, exclude, blacklist, outlaw, ostracize, ignore, avoid, spurn, snub
FORMAL eschew, proscribe
COLLOQ. cold-shoulder, send to Coventry
E3 encourage, support, advocate, defend, champion, patronize
• *n*
refusal, rejection, embargo, ban, prohibition, spurning, snub, exclusion, ostracism
FORMAL proscription

boyfriend *n*
young man, man, admirer, sweetheart, lover, suitor, best boy, fiancé, beau, date, steady, partner, cohabitee, live-in lover, common-law spouse
COLLOQ. fellow, fella, guy, bloke, toyboy, significant other, squeeze

boyish *adj*
youthful, childlike, adolescent, childish, immature, innocent, juvenile, puerile, tomboy, unfeminine, unmaidenly, young
COLLOQ. green

brace¹ *n, v*
• *n*
fit braces to strengthen a wall
support, stay, strap, prop, clamp, fastener, vice, beam, strut, reinforcement, truss, buttress, shoring
FORMAL stanchion
• *v*
1 STRENGTHEN, reinforce, bolster, buttress, prop (up), shore (up), support, hold up, steady, secure, tighten, fasten, tie, strap, bind, bandage
FORMAL fortify
2 *brace yourself for bad news*
prepare, get ready, compose, nerve, steel
FORMAL fortify
COLLOQ. gear up, psych up

brace² *n*
a brace of pheasant
pair, couple, twosome, duo

bracelet *n*
bangle, band, circlet, wristlet
OLD armilla
Related adjective: armillary

bracing *adj*
fresh, crisp, refreshing, reviving, strengthening, fortifying, tonic, rousing, stimulating, exhilarating, invigorating, enlivening, energizing, brisk, energetic, vigorous
E3 weakening, draining, debilitating; *formal* enervating

bracket *n*
1 SUPPORT, stay, prop, frame, rest, holder

2 CLASSIFICATION, group, grouping, class, category, batch, lot, cohort

brackish *adj*
bitter, briny, saline, salt, saltish, salty; *S Afr* brak
FORMAL salsuginous
E3 fresh, clean, clear

brag *v*
bluster, boast, show off, swagger, vaunt, vapour
OLD gab, cry roast-meat
FORMAL hyperbolize
COLLOQ. blow your own trumpet; *N Am* blow your own horn; crow, talk big, lay it on thick/with a trowel; *Aust* big-note
SLANG bull
E3 be modest

braggart *n*
boaster, bluffer, blusterer, show-off, braggadocio, fanfaron, gascon, rodomontader, swaggerer, swashbuckler
OLD puckfist; (*Shakesp*) swasher
COLLOQ. big mouth, windbag, loud-mouth

bragging *n*
showing-off, bluster, boastfulness, boasting, bravado, exaggeration
FORMAL vauntery
COLLOQ. hot air
E3 modesty, unobtrusiveness

braid *n, v*
♦ *n*
cord, thread, yarn, twine, plait; *dialect* pleat; tress, caddis, sennit, soutache, passement
♦ *v*
plait, interweave, interlace, intertwine, weave, lace, twine, entwine, ravel, twist, wind
OLD embraid
E3 undo, unravel

brain *n*
1 *damage to the brain*
cerebrum
TECHNICAL encephalon, sensorium
OLD (*Shakesp*) pia mater
SLANG upper storey
Related adjectives: cerebral, encephalic
2 MIND, head, intellect, intelligence, wit, reason, sense, common sense, shrewdness, understanding
FORMAL acumen, sagacity
COLLOQ. grey matter, brains, nous, savvy
3 *the real brain in the family*
mastermind, intellectual, scholar, expert, pundit, highbrow, genius, prodigy
COLLOQ. egghead, boffin, brainbox, cleverclogs
E3 2 simpleton, idiot

Parts of the brain include:

brainstem	forebrain	optic thalamus
Broca's area	frontal lobe	parietal lobe
cerebellum	hindbrain	pineal body
cerebral cortex	hypothalamus	pituitary gland
cerebral	medulla	pons
hemisphere	oblongata	spinal cord
cerebrum	meninges	temporal lobe
cinerea (grey	mesencephalon	thalamus
matter)	midbrain	Wernicke's area
corpus callosum	occipital lobe	

---

brainless *adj*
silly, stupid, crazy, daft, foolish, incompetent, half-witted, simple-minded, idiotic, inept, mindless, thoughtless, senseless
E3 sensible, shrewd, wise

brainteaser *n*
riddle, puzzle, problem, conundrum, mind-bender, poser; *N Am* brain-twister

brainwashing *n*
indoctrination, conditioning, pressurizing, re-education, grilling, intellectual suicide, mind-bending, persuasion
FORMAL menticide

brainy *adj*
intellectual, intelligent, clever, gifted, smart, bright, brilliant, wise
FORMAL sapient
E3 dull, stupid

brake *n, v*
♦ *n*
check, curb, rein, restraint, control, restriction, constraint, drag
FORMAL retardment
♦ *v*
slow (down), decelerate, reduce speed, retard, drag, slacken, moderate, check, halt, stop, pull up
FORMAL retard
E3 accelerate

branch *n, v*
♦ *n*
1 BOUGH, limb, sprig, shoot, stem, offshoot, arm, leg, lobe, loop, wing, prong, whip, withy; *Scot* cow, scrog
TECHNICAL ramus, axis, cladode, phylloclade
OLD braunch, rice
Related adjectives: ramal, rameal, rameous, ramous
2 *a different branch of the company*
department, office, local/regional office, agency, bureau, part, section, division, subsidiary, subsection, subdivision, affiliate, corps, wing, discipline
FORMAL succursal, ramification
3 *the branch of a river*
tributary, fork, division
▪ **branch off**
divide, fork, diverge, deviate, separate
FORMAL bifurcate, furcate
▪ **branch out**
diversify, subdivide, vary, develop, expand, enlarge, spread out, extend, add to, broaden out, increase, multiply, proliferate
FORMAL ramify

brand *n, v*
♦ *n*
1 *different brands of soap*
make, brand-name, tradename, trademark, line, logo, symbol, sign, emblem, label, stamp, hallmark, marque
2 KIND, quality, class, kind, type, sort, line, variety, species
3 MARK, tag, identification, identifying mark
♦ *v*
1 *branded as a troublemaker*
mark, stamp, label, typecast, stigmatize, stain, taint, disgrace, discredit, denounce, censure
FORMAL besmirch
2 *brand cattle*
mark, stamp, burn (in), sear

brandish *v*
wave, flourish, shake, raise, swing, wield, flash, flaunt, exhibit, display, parade
OLD wag, wampish; (*Spenser*) bless, hurtle

brash *adj*
1 BRAZEN, forward, impertinent, impudent, insolent, rude, cocky, self-confident, assertive, assured, bold, audacious
COLLOQ. pushy
2 RECKLESS, rash, impetuous, impulsive, hasty, foolhardy, incautious, indiscreet
FORMAL precipitate
E3 1 reserved, unassuming, modest, unobtrusive **2** cautious, wary, prudent

brashly adv

1 BRAZENLY, forwardly, impertinently, impudently, insolently, rudely, cockily, self-confidently, assertively, assuredly, boldly, audaciously
COLLOQ. pushily
2 RECKLESSLY, rashly, impetuously, impulsively, hastily, foolhardily, incautiously, indiscreetly
FORMAL precipitately
1 reserved, unassuming, modest, unobtrusive **2** cautious, wary, prudent

brashness n

1 BRAZENNESS, impertinence, impudence, insolence, rudeness, self-confidence, assertiveness, boldness, audacity
COLLOQ. pushiness
2 RECKLESSNESS, rashness, hastiness, foolhardiness, incaution
1 modesty **2** caution

brass n

brazenness, impertinence, impudence, insolence, gall, rudeness, presumption, audacity
FORMAL effrontery, temerity
COLLOQ. cheek, nerve, chutzpah, brass neck, brass nerve; N Am sass
timidity; formal circumspection

brassy adj

1 *brassy music*
noisy, loud, blaring, dissonant, grating, hard, harsh, jangling, jarring, piercing, raucous, strident
2 *a brassy blonde*
shameless, forward, brash, insolent, cocky, bold, loud, brazen
COLLOQ. pushy, loud-mouthed, saucy; N Am sassy

brat n

kid, youngster, rascal, brach; *Scot* get, gyte
OLD bantling
COLLOQ. nipper, guttersnipe, jackanapes, puppy, whippersnapper

bravado n

swagger, boasting, bragging, bluster, talk, boast, showing-off, parade, show, pretence
FORMAL vaunting, bombast, braggadocio, fanfaronade, rodomontade
modesty, restraint

brave adj, v

• *adj*
courageous, plucky, unafraid, fearless, undaunted, unflinching, bold, daring, intrepid, stalwart, hardy, stoical, resolute, stout-hearted, lion-hearted, valiant, gallant, heroic, indomitable, manly, yeomanly
FORMAL dauntless, audacious, valorous, doughty
COLLOQ. gutsy, spunky, gritty, feisty
cowardly, afraid, timid, craven, faint-hearted; *colloq.* yellow, spineless, wimpish, chicken
• *v*
face, confront, defy, challenge, dare, stand up to, put up with, face up to, suffer, endure, bear, withstand
COLLOQ. put up with, face the music, keep a stiff upper lip, put a bold/brave face on it, not turn a hair, keep your chin up
yield, capitulate, give in; *colloq.* get cold feet, chicken out

bravely adv

courageously, pluckily, fearlessly, undauntedly, unflinchingly, boldly, daringly, intrepidly, stalwartly, hardily, stoically, resolutely, stout-heartedly, valiantly, gallantly, heroically, indomitably
FORMAL dauntlessly, audaciously, valorously, doughtily

bravery n

courage, pluck, fearlessness, boldness, courageousness, daring, stalwartness, hardiness, fortitude, resolution, tenacity, stout-heartedness, valour, gallantry, chivalry, heroism, indomitability, mettle, spirit, dauntlessness, audacity, bravado, prowess
FORMAL intrepidity, valiance
COLLOQ. guts, grit, spunk
cowardice, fearfulness, faint-heartedness, timidity

> **▌ bravery** or **bravado**?
> *Bravery* is courage: *soldiers decorated for bravery. Bravado* is a boastful act of bravery intended to impress or intimidate or a boastful pretence of bravery aimed at concealing cowardice: *She felt her defiant bravado disintegrate like shattered glass.*

Synonym nuances

Courage is used in general contexts, whereas **pluck** has a very positive aspect of spiritedness, and is often used of facing up to difficulties rather than overt danger: *few people had the pluck to stand up to her.* **Fearlessness** suggests bravery that has more to do with an inability to experience fear than to confront it: *the fearlessness that only fanaticism confers.* **Indomitability** and **dauntlessness** are also suggestive of an inability to be conquered or frightened, whereas **mettle** and **spirit** more appropriately describe an inborn intrepid nature: *these crises will test his mettle.*

The terms **boldness**, **daring**, **audacity** and **bravado** strongly suggest the idea of taking risks and perhaps even showing off: *the audacity of criminals;* in contrast to the uncommon **stalwartness**, which suggests a more down-to-earth dependability in the face of difficulty. **Hardiness**, **fortitude** and **stout-heartedness** also imply innate strength of spirit and an ability to persevere, whereas **resolution** and **tenacity** emphasize more intellectual determination: *a tenacity of purpose.*

Heroism is a word generally reserved for those responsible for acts that endanger themselves whilst safeguarding others: *the heroism of the firefighters.* **Valour** is usually used in the context of the battlefield: *he received a medal for valour.* **Gallantry** and **chivalry** are more romantic in tone, and suggest the qualities associated with dashing warriors from the past, though still recognized today: *his gallantry in action.*

---

bravura n

spirit, dash, sparkle, brilliance, magnificence, élan

brawl n, v

• *n*
fight, scuffle, mêlée, free-for-all, fray, affray, broil, skirmish, fracas, rumpus, disorder, row, argument, quarrel, squabble, dispute, clash, fisticuffs, Donnybrook, *bagarre*; *dialect* fratch; *Aust & NZ* stoush
OLD brangle; (*Shakesp*) brabble; *Scot* tuilyie
FORMAL altercation
COLLOQ. punch-up, bust-up, dust-up, scrap, ruckus
• *v*
fight, scuffle, wrestle, tussle, argue, quarrel, squabble, wrangle, dispute; *Scot* flyte; *Aust & NZ* stoush
FORMAL altercate
OLD brabble
COLLOQ. scrap, row

brawn n

strength, might, muscle, muscles, bulk, bulkiness, muscularity, power, robustness, sinews; N Am headcheese
COLLOQ. beef, beefiness

brawny adj

muscular, sinewy, meaty, athletic, well-built, burly, hefty, solid, bulky, hulking, massive, strapping, strong, powerful, vigorous, sturdy, robust, hardy, stalwart

COLLOQ. beefy, husky, hunky
⊟ slight, frail, skinny, weak, weedy

bray v
neigh, whinny, heehaw, blare, hoot, roar, screech, trumpet, bell, bellow

brazen adj, v adj
bold, forward, barefaced, bald-faced, impudent, insolent, defiant, shameless, unashamed, unabashed, immodest, blatant, flagrant, brash, pert
FORMAL audacious
COLLOQ. pushy, brassy, saucy, hard-boiled
SLANG in-your-face
⊟ shy, shamefaced, modest, cautious
■ **brazen it out**
be unashamed, defy, be defiant, be impenitent
COLLOQ. put a brave/bold face on it

brazenly adv
boldly, impudently, insolently, defiantly, shamelessly, unashamedly, immodestly, blatantly, flagrantly
FORMAL audaciously
⊟ modestly, cautiously

breach n, v
♦ n
1 *a breach of the rules*
breaking, violation, contravention, infringement, trespass, disobedience, offence, lapse, disruption
FORMAL infraction, transgression
2 *a breach in international relations*
quarrel, disagreement, dissension, difference, variance, schism, rift, rupture, split, division, gulf, chasm, separation, parting, severance, alienation, dissociation
FORMAL disaffection, estrangement
3 *a breach in the defences*
break, crack, rift, rupture, split, fissure, cleft, crevice, opening, aperture, gap, space, hole, gulf, chasm
♦ v
1 *breach an agreement*
violate, break, contravene, infringe
2 *breach the sea wall*
rupture, break (open), open up, break through, burst through, split

---

Synonym nuances
noun sense 1
Breaking, **violation**, **infringement** and **contravention** are widely used in instances where official specifications have not been adhered to: *a clear violation of international law*; *his persistent infringement of school laws*; *each side made repeated raids in contravention of treaty terms*. You would probably use the word **trespass** primarily of illegal entry, and **disobedience** to describe orchestrated action, taken usually to get a certain change in the law: *civil disobedience by peace protesters*.
Disruption is more usually associated with creating conditions to make it difficult for a rule or law to function.
  Other terms are less forceful in tone. **Offence** is often qualified to convey a degree of severity: *a minor offence*; while **transgression** nowadays is perhaps more appropriate for an act at odds with social mores. The word **lapse** also suggests a failure to follow social or personal rules: *I gave up smoking, then had a lapse*.

---

bread n
1 *bread and jam*
crusts, roll, loaf, bap, plait, cob, sandwich
Related adjective: panary
See panel below
2 *our daily bread*
food, provisions, diet, fare, nourishment, necessities
FORMAL nutriment, sustenance, subsistence, victuals
3 CASH, money, funds
COLLOQ. the necessary
SLANG dough, dosh, lolly, spondulicks

breadth n
1 *the breadth of the garden*
width, broadness, wideness, latitude, thickness, size, magnitude, measure
2 *a great breadth of interests*
range, scale, reach, scope, compass, span, sweep, extent, expanse, spread, comprehensiveness, extensiveness, vastness
FORMAL amplitude

break v, n
♦ v
1 *break a plate*
fracture, crack, snap, split, sever, separate, divide, rend, smash, disintegrate, splinter, shiver, shatter, ruin, destroy, demolish
2 *break the law*
violate, contravene, infringe, breach, disobey, flout, dishonour
3 *the television has broken*
stop working, fail
FORMAL malfunction
COLLOQ. go on the blink, pack up, conk out, go kaput, go phut, crash, cut out
4 *break for lunch*
pause, halt, stop, interrupt, suspend, rest
FORMAL discontinue
5 *break a silence*
interrupt, suspend, disturb, interfere with, bring to an end
FORMAL discontinue
COLLOQ. cut off
6 *the news broke his spirit*
destroy, crush, overcome, subdue, tame, weaken, enfeeble, impair, undermine, demoralize
7 *the injury broke her skin*
pierce, perforate, puncture, open (up)
8 *break the news*
tell, inform, impart, divulge, disclose, reveal, announce
9 *break a record*
exceed, beat, better, excel, surpass, outdo, outstrip
10 *the weather broke*
change (for the better/worse), vary, improve, worsen
11 *the branches broke his fall*
weaken, soften, lessen, reduce, cushion, diminish
12 *break a habit*
give up, stop, abandon
FORMAL discontinue, relinquish
COLLOQ. quit, kick, shake off
13 *as day broke*
dawn, lighten, begin, appear, emerge, rise, be born
14 *waves breaking against the raised bank*
dash, pound, smash, strike, lash, beat, crash

Kinds of bread include:

bagel	challah	focaccia	naan	pumpernickel	tortilla
baguette	chapati	French stick	paratha	roti	wholemeal
bara brith	ciabatta	granary	pitta	rye bread	wholewheat
barmbrack	croissant	matzo	poori	soda bread	
brioche	farl	milk bread	pretzel	sourdough	

15 *his voice broke*
falter, stammer, stutter, stumble
16 *break a code*
crack, decipher, decode, decrypt, unravel, solve, work/
figure out
E3 1 mend, put together **2** keep, obey, observe, abide by **3**
mend, fix **4** start again, resume **6** encourage, strengthen **12**
start, take up **13** end

• *n*
1 *a break in the defences/diplomatic relations*
fracture, crack, split, rift, rupture, schism, separation, tear,
gash, fissure, cleft, crevice, opening, gap, hole, breach
FORMAL estrangement
2 *have a break for coffee*
interval, intermission, interlude, interruption, stop, pause,
halt, lull, respite, rest; *Aust* smoke-ho
COLLOQ. let-up, breather, time-out
3 *go away for a short break*
time off, holiday; *N Am* vacation
COLLOQ. vac
4 *a lucky break*
opportunity, chance, advantage, fortune, (stroke of) luck,
opening
■ **break away**
separate, split (off), part company, detach, secede, leave,
depart, quit, run away, escape, flee, fly
COLLOQ. make a run for it
■ **break down**
1 *the van broke down*
fail, stop, stop working, give way, collapse
COLLOQ. pack up, conk out, go phut, seize up
2 *negotiations broke down*
fail, collapse, come to nothing, founder
COLLOQ. fall through
3 *break down in tears*
lose control, be overcome, collapse
COLLOQ. go to pieces, crack up
4 *break down a door*
knock down, smash, demolish, destroy
5 *break down the figures*
analyse, dissect, separate, itemize, categorize, detail
■ **break in**
1 *break in with unhelpful remarks*
interrupt, butt in, cut in, interject, intervene, intrude,
encroach, impinge
FORMAL interpose
2 *break in and steal the money*
burgle, rob, raid, enter illegally
3 *break in a horse/pair of walking boots*
train, condition, wear, accustom, prime, get used to
■ **break off**
1 DETACH, separate, part, divide, disconnect, sever
FORMAL dissever
COLLOQ. snap off
2 *break off as the phone rang; break off a relationship*
pause, interrupt, suspend, halt, stop, cease, end, finish,
bring to an end
FORMAL discontinue, terminate
■ **break out**
1 *war broke out in 1939*
begin (suddenly), start, arise, emerge, happen, occur,
erupt
FORMAL commence
COLLOQ. blow up, flare up, burst out
2 *break out of prison*
escape, bolt, flee
FORMAL abscond
3 *'Just a minute,' she broke out*
exclaim, shout, interject
COLLOQ. burst out
4 *break out into a rash*
erupt, come out in, flare up

■ **break through**
emerge, gain ground, leap forward, make headway, pass,
penetrate, progress, succeed, overcome
■ **break up**
1 *break up a monopoly*
dismantle, take apart, demolish, destroy, disintegrate,
splinter, sever, divide, split (up), part, separate
2 *the couple broke up*
separate, part, part company, divorce, finish
COLLOQ. split up
3 *the meeting broke up*
disband, disperse, dissolve, adjourn, suspend, stop, finish,
bring/come to an end
FORMAL discontinue, terminate
■ **break with**
finish with, part with, reject, separate from
FORMAL renounce, repudiate
COLLOQ. drop, jilt, ditch

breakable *adj*
brittle, fragile, delicate, flimsy, insubstantial, frail, easily
broken
FORMAL friable, frangible
COLLOQ. jerry-built
E3 unbreakable, durable, sturdy, long-lasting, shatterproof

breakaway *adj*
rebel, dissenting, separatist, renegade, heretical
FORMAL apostate, schismatic, seceding, secessionist

breakdown *n*
1 *the breakdown of the talks/car*
failure, collapse, disintegration, interruption, stoppage
FORMAL malfunction
2 *a nervous breakdown*
collapse
COLLOQ. going to pieces, cracking-up
3 ANALYSIS, dissection, itemization, classification,
categorization

breaker *n*
wave, roller, billow, white horses

break-in *n*
burglary, house-breaking, robbery, raid, invasion,
intrusion, trespass, larceny

breakneck *adj*
very fast, very quick, rapid, swift, speedy, express, headlong
FORMAL precipitate
COLLOQ. like lightning

breakthrough *n*
discovery, find, finding, invention, innovation, advance,
progress, headway, step, gain, leap, step/leap forward,
quantum leap (forward), development, improvement,
milestone

break-up *n*
divorce, separation, parting, split, rift, finish, end, dispersal,
disintegration, crumbling, dissolution, debacle, upbreak
FORMAL dissolution, termination
COLLOQ. splitting-up

breakwater *n*
groyne, mole, bulwark, sea wall, jetty, pier, quay, spur,
wharf, dock

breast *n*
1 *beat your breast in sorrow*
bosom, bust, chest, front, heart, thorax
2 *a woman's breasts*
bust, nipple, teat; *dialect* diddy
TECHNICAL mamma
COLLOQ. boob, booby
SLANG bristol, knocker, tit, titty; *Aust* nork
Related adjective: mammary

breath *n*
1 *take deep breaths to relax*

air, breathing, respiration, sigh, gasp, pant, gulp
FORMAL flatus, inhalation, inspiration, exhalation
Related adjectives: respiratory, aspiratory
2 *a breath of fresh air*
breeze, puff, waft, gust
FORMAL pneuma
3 *a breath of autumn in the air*
aroma, smell, odour, whiff
4 *a breath of scandal*
hint, suggestion, suspicion, undertone, whisper, murmur

breathe *v*
1 *breathe deeply*
sigh, gasp, pant, puff, snore
OLD embreathe, suspire
FORMAL inhale, inbreathe, exhale, respire, expire, insufflate
2 *not breathe a word to anyone*
express, voice, murmur, whisper, tell, articulate, utter, impart
3 *breathe new life into a project*
instil, imbue, infuse, inject, inspire
FORMAL transfuse

breather *n*
break, rest, constitutional, pause, halt, recess, relaxation, rest, walk
FORMAL respite
COLLOQ. breathing space

breathless *adj*
1 *breathless from climbing*
short-winded, out of breath, panting, puffing, puffed (out), exhausted, winded, gasping, wheezing, choking
COLLOQ. *N Am* pooped (out), tuckered out
2 *breathless anticipation*
expectant, impatient, in suspense, eager, agog, excited, open-mouthed, feverish, anxious

breathtaking *adj*
awe-inspiring, impressive, magnificent, spectacular, overwhelming, amazing, astonishing, stunning, stupendous, exciting, thrilling, stirring, moving
COLLOQ. drop-dead

breathtakingly *adv*
overwhelmingly, amazingly, astonishingly, stunningly, spectacularly, stupendously, excitingly, thrillingly, stirringly, awe-inspiringly, impressively

breed *v, n*
♦ *v*
1 *breed dogs*
reproduce, procreate, multiply, hatch, bear, give birth to, rear, raise, bring up, bring forth
FORMAL propagate, pullulate
2 *breed suspicion*
produce, create, originate, arouse, cause, occasion, bring about, give rise to, generate, make, foster, nurture, nourish, cultivate, develop
FORMAL engender
♦ *n*
1 *breeds of cattle*
species, strain, variety, family, stamp, stock, race, line, lineage, pedigree, hybrid
FORMAL progeny
2 *the new breed of leader*
kind, type, sort, variety, calibre, class

breeding *n*
1 *the breeding of cattle*
reproduction, nurture, development, rearing, raising, upbringing, ancestry, lineage, stock, genetic engineering
FORMAL procreation
2 *have breeding*
(good) manners, politeness, gentility, refinement, cultivation, culture, polish, education, training
FORMAL civility, urbanity
E∃ 2 vulgarity, bad manners

breeding-ground *n*
nest, nursery, school, training ground, cradle, hothouse
COLLOQ. hotbed

breeze *n, v*
♦ *n*
wind, gust, flurry, waft, puff, breath, draught, air, snift, cat's paw
OLD zephyr
♦ *v*
glide, sail, hurry, sweep, trip, wander, saunter
COLLOQ. flit, sally

breezy *adj*
1 WINDY, blowing, blowy, fresh, airy, gusty, brisk, blustery, squally
2 LIVELY, confident, animated, jaunty, buoyant, debonair, carefree, cheerful, casual, informal, relaxed, easy-going, light-hearted, light, bright, exhilarating, vivacious
OLD blithe
E∃ 1 still, calm, windless **2** staid, serious, quiet, sad

brevity *n*
1 *the brevity of the speech*
briefness, shortness, conciseness, compactness, succinctness, pithiness, economy, economy of language, crispness, incisiveness, abruptness, curtness
FORMAL terseness, concision, laconism
2 *the brevity of life*
briefness, shortness
FORMAL impermanence, ephemerality, transience, transitoriness
E∃ 1 long-windedness, wordiness; *formal* verbosity, prolixity **2** permanence; *formal* longevity

brew *v, n*
♦ *v*
1 *brew tea*
stew, boil, prepare, soak, steep, cook, make
FORMAL infuse, seethe, ferment, prepare
2 *the tea is still brewing*
infuse, be in preparation, mash
3 *brew beer*
ferment, make
4 *trouble/a storm is brewing*
build up, gather, develop, loom, be in the offing, be on its way
5 *brew a scheme*
plot, scheme, plan, project, devise, contrive, concoct, hatch, excite, foment
♦ *n*
1 *boil up a hot brew*
drink, liquor, potion
FORMAL beverage, infusion
2 *a powerful brew of sex and violence*
mixture, blend, compound, combination, preparation, fermentation, distillation
FORMAL concoction

bribe *n, v*
♦ *n*
incentive, inducement, allurement, enticement, bonus, dash, kickback, douceur, palm-grease, palm-oil, pension
OLD gift, gratification, vail
COLLOQ. carrot, back-hander, refresher, sweetener, hush money, pay-off, kickback, slush fund, protection money; *N Am* payola, boodle
SLANG bung, the drink
♦ *v*
corrupt, reward, suborn, square, hamper
COLLOQ. buy/pay off, grease, grease someone's palm, fix, take care of, keep sweet, fix
SLANG nobble, bung

bribery *n*
corruption, inducement, protection, malversation,

suborneration, embracery
COLLOQ. palm-greasing, graft

bric-à-brac n
knick-knacks, ornaments, curios, antiques, trinkets, baubles, trumpery, gewgaws, bibelots, gimcracks, bits and pieces, odds and ends

brick n
1 *bricks and mortar*
breeze block, adobe, firebrick, block, briquette, header, klinker, stretcher, rock, stone
2 *a huge brick of fresh butter*
block, piece, lump, mass, slab, wedge, bar
3 *be a real brick for helping*
mate, pal, real friend, chum; *N Am* buddy

bridal adj
wedding, nuptial, marriage, marital
FORMAL conjugal, matrimonial, connubial

bride n
honeymooner, newly-wed, wife, wife-to-be, bride-to-be, spouse, marriage partner, war bride, GI bride

bridegroom n
honeymooner, newly-wed, husband, husband-to-be, spouse, marriage partner, groom

bridge n, v
◆ n
1 *a bridge over the river*
arch, span, causeway, link
2 *act as a bridge between the different factions*
link, connection, bond, tie
◆ v
span, cross, go over, reach across, fill, link, connect, couple, join, unite, bind
FORMAL traverse

Types of bridge include:

aqueduct	cantilever bridge	railway bridge
arch bridge	drawbridge	rope bridge
Bailey bridge	flying bridge	suspension
bascule bridge	flyover	bridge
beam bridge (or	footbridge	swing bridge
girder bridge)	humpback bridge	toll bridge
box girder bridge	overbridge	viaduct
cable-stayed	overpass	
bridge	pontoon bridge	

---

bridle v, n
◆ v
1 *bridle your temper*
check, curb, restrain, control, govern, master, subdue, moderate, repress, hold back, contain
2 *bridle at someone's anger*
bristle, become indignant, be offended by
◆ n
check, halter, control, curb, restraint, hackamore; *Scot* branks

brief adj, n, v
◆ adj
1 *a brief report*
short, terse, succinct, concise, pithy, crisp, compressed, condensed, abridged, thumbnail
FORMAL aphoristic
2 *a brief manner*
abrupt, sharp, short, brusque, blunt, curt, surly
FORMAL laconic
3 *a brief visit; this brief life*
short-lived, momentary, transient, fleeting, passing, transitory, temporary, limited, cursory, hasty, quick, swift
FORMAL fugacious, ephemeral, evanescent
F3 1 lengthy, long-winded, extensive, verbose, protracted
◆ n

1 *with a brief to reduce crime*
responsibility, orders, instructions, directions, remit, mandate, directive, advice, briefing, data, information
2 *a brief of the day's events*
outline, summary, précis, abstract, abridgement, digest
3 *a legal brief*
dossier, case, defence, argument, evidence, data
TECHNICAL breviate
◆ v
instruct, direct, explain, guide, advise, prepare, prime, inform, tell, bring up to date
COLLOQ. fill in, gen up, give someone the run-down/low-down, put someone in the picture

---

Synonym nuances
adjective sense 1
Short is a neutral term to describe something that is limited in length or duration, whereas **terse** is more usually applied to speech or text with no extraneous material, with the added suggestion of an unwelcome abruptness: *an economical, even terse, style*. **Succinct** and **concise**, however, are more expressive of favour, suggesting that a lack of unnecessary material leads to a more satisfactory outcome: *our goal is a set of succinct definitions*. To use **pithy** likewise would suggest that you approve of this economy with words: *pithy, punchy posters*; while **crisp** is another positive term to speak about words, with overtones of clarity and neatness.
  Condensed and **compressed** are not necessarily positive, both terms suggestive of squeezing an abundance into less or limited space: *patterns stored in the memory are compressed*. **Abridged** is a neutral term describing something has been cut in order to fit. **Thumbnail** is usually reserved for shortened representations: *a thumbnail sketch of the scene*.

---

briefing n
meeting, conference, preparation, priming, information, advice, guidance, directions, instructions, orders
FORMAL intimation
COLLOQ. filling-in, gen, run-down, low-down

briefly adv
1 *speak briefly*
concisely, succinctly, cursorily, precisely, quickly, summarily, tersely, to the point
2 *briefly, the answer is no*
in brief, in a word, in a few words
COLLOQ. in a nutshell
F3 1 at length, fully

brigade n
group, band, body, company, unit, corps, crew, force, party, squad, team, troop, contingent

brigand n
bandit, robber, desperado, gangster, outlaw, marauder, plunderer, ruffian, highwayman, freebooter, haiduk
OLD cateran, trailbaston

bright adj
1 *bright lights/colours*
brilliant, luminous, illuminated, light, radiant, shining, beaming, flashing, gleaming, glistening, glittering, sparkling, twinkling, shimmering, glowing, glorious, splendid, dazzling, blinding, glaring, blazing, intense, vivid
FORMAL resplendent, effulgent, refulgent, lustrous, incandescent
2 HAPPY, cheerful, glad, joyful, merry, jolly, lively, genial
FORMAL vivacious
3 *the future looks bright*
promising, favourable, rosy, optimistic, hopeful, encouraging
FORMAL propitious, auspicious
4 CLEVER, smart, intelligent, quick-witted, quick, sharp,

acute, keen, astute, perceptive
COLLOQ. brainy, bright as a button
5 a bright day
fine, sunny, cloudless, unclouded, pleasant
E3 1 dull, drab, colourless, pale, dim, soft **2** sad, gloomy, depressed; *colloq.* down **3** depressing, gloomy; *formal* inauspicious **4** stupid; *colloq.* thick **5** dark, overcast, cloudy

brighten v
1 brighten up a room
light up, illuminate, lighten, make bright, smarten up, enhance, refurbish
FORMAL irradiate
2 brighten up the silver
polish, burnish, rub (up), shine, gleam, glow
3 brighten at the prospect
cheer up, gladden, hearten, encourage, liven up, buoy up
FORMAL enliven
COLLOQ. buck up, perk up, pep up
E3 1 darken, shadow **2** dull, tarnish

brightly adv
1 a light shining brightly
brilliantly, radiantly, intensely, splendidly, glowingly, dazzlingly, blindingly, glaringly, ablaze
2 smile brightly
happily, cheerfully, gladly, joyfully
FORMAL vivaciously

brilliance n
1 brilliance at the piano
talent, virtuosity, genius, greatness, distinction, excellence, aptitude, cleverness, prowess, distinction, bravura
2 the brilliance of the sun
radiance, brightness, sparkle, dazzle, intensity, vividness, gloss, lustre, sheen, tone, glamour, glory, magnificence, splendour
FORMAL resplendence, effulgence, refulgence, fulgency, coruscation

brilliant adj
1 a brilliant flautist
gifted, talented, accomplished, expert, skilful, masterly, exceptional, outstanding, superb, illustrious, famous, celebrated
2 a brilliant light/show
sparkling, glittering, scintillating, dazzling, glaring, blazing, intense, vivid, bright, shining, glossy, showy, glorious, magnificent, splendid
OLD splendent
FORMAL resplendent, effulgent, refulgent, fulgent, l ambent
3 a brilliant mind
clever, bright, intelligent, quick, astute
FORMAL erudite
COLLOQ. brainy
4 a brilliant performance
clever, skilful, masterly, remarkable, magnificent, superb, resourceful, enterprising
5 What a brilliant game!
great, excellent, fantastic, superb, wonderful, magnificent
COLLOQ. brill, cool, top-notch, smashing, terrific, neat, ace, out of this world, second to none
SLANG mega, wicked, radical, crucial
E3 1 undistinguished, untalented **2** dull, dim **3** stupid, slow **4** ordinary; *colloq.* run-of-the-mill **5** awful, bad

brilliantly adv
1 a brilliantly acted play
superbly, magnificently, wonderfully, masterfully, skilfully, cleverly
2 brilliantly coloured
dazzlingly, intensely, vividly, brightly, gloriously, magnificently, splendidly
FORMAL resplendently

brim n, v
♦ n
rim, perimeter, circumference, lip, edge, margin, border, brink, verge, top, limit
♦ v
be full with, be (packed) full with, be filled with, overflow with, be overflowing with

brimful adj
full, filled, filled to capacity, abrim, overflowing, bulging, crammed, stuffed, jammed
COLLOQ. chock-a-block, packed out

brindled adj
dappled, streaked, speckled, mottled, stippled, dotted, flecked, variegated, piebald, pied

bring v
1 bring a drink; bring you home later
take, carry, transport, fetch, deliver, escort, accompany, usher, guide, conduct, lead, convey
FORMAL bear
2 bring misery
cause, produce, result in, create, make happen, prompt, provoke, force
FORMAL engender
3 bring a charge
present, put forward, initiate, lay, submit
■ **bring about**
cause, occasion, create, produce, generate, accomplish, achieve, fulfil, realize, manage
FORMAL effect
■ **bring back**
suggest, call up, evoke, remind, take you back to, make you think of
■ **bring down**
1 bring down the government
overthrow, unseat, depose, oust, defeat, destroy
FORMAL vanquish
COLLOQ. topple, knock down, shoot down
2 REDUCE, decrease, lower, cause to fall/drop
■ **bring forward**
1 ADVANCE, put forward, make earlier
2 PROPOSE, suggest, present, raise, put forward
E3 1 postpone, put back
■ **bring in**
1 bring in new laws
introduce, initiate, originate, pioneer, set up, launch, usher in
FORMAL inaugurate
2 bring in £30,000
earn, net, gross, produce, make, fetch, return, yield
FORMAL accrue, realize
■ **bring off**
succeed in, achieve, fulfil, perform, accomplish, discharge
FORMAL execute, consummate
COLLOQ. pull off
■ **bring on**
1 bring on a headache
cause, lead to, give rise to, generate, inspire, prompt, make happen, provoke
FORMAL occasion, induce, precipitate
2 bring on the plant's growth
advance, accelerate, foster, nurture, improve
FORMAL expedite, precipitate
■ **bring out**
1 bring out a point in a story
emphasize, stress, highlight, enhance, draw out, accentuate, make someone aware of
2 bring out a book
publish, print, issue, launch, introduce, produce
■ **bring round**
1 REVIVE, resuscitate, bring to, rouse, wake up, awaken
2 bring someone round to your way of thinking
persuade, convince, win over, convert, coax, cajole

■ **bring up**
1 bring up children
care for, raise, rear, foster, nurture, educate, teach, train, form
2 bring up a matter for discussion
raise, introduce, broach, mention, touch on, submit, propose
3 bring up food
vomit, regurgitate
COLLOQ. throw up, puke

brink n
verge, threshold, edge, margin, fringe, border, boundary, limit, extremity, lip, rim, brim, bank
OLD marge

brio n
vigour, energy, liveliness, spirit, verve, gusto, animation, force, dash, dynamism
FORMAL vivacity
COLLOQ. zip, oomph, pep

brisk adj
1 go for a brisk walk
energetic, vigorous, quick, rapid, snappy, lively, spirited, active, busy, bustling, agile, nimble, alert
2 a brisk manner
lively, quick, businesslike, no-nonsense
3 brisk business
busy, active, lively, bustling, rapid, good
4 brisk weather
invigorating, exhilarating, stimulating, bracing, refreshing, cold, fresh, crisp
☒ 1 unenergetic, slow 2 slow, lethargic 3 slow, sluggish

briskly adv
1 walk briskly
quickly, rapidly, energetically, vigorously, nimbly
TECHNICAL con moto
2 products selling briskly
rapidly, quickly, well, busily
3 work briskly
quickly, decisively, sharply, abruptly, brusquely

bristle n, v
♦ n
1 shave off bristles
hair, whisker, stubble
2 bristles on an animal's back
spine, prickle, barb, quill, thorn, awn; Scot birse
TECHNICAL seta, setule, striga, vibrissa
♦ v
1 the hairs on the back of my head bristled
stand on end, rise
2 bristling with anger
seethe (with), draw yourself up, bridle at, be incensed at, bridle, make someone's hackles rise
TECHNICAL horripilate
3 bristling with police
teem with, swarm with
FORMAL abound in
COLLOQ. be thick with, hum with

bristly adj
hairy, whiskered, bearded, unshaven, stubbly, rough, spiny, prickly, spiky, thorny
TECHNICAL hispid, barbellate, echinate
FORMAL hirsute
☒ clean-shaven, smooth

brittle adj
1 BREAKABLE, easily broken, fragile, delicate, frail, hard, crisp, crackly, crumbly, crumbling, shattery, spall; dialect frowy; Scot birsy, bruckle, frush; N Am brash
FORMAL friable, frangible
2 a brittle situation
unstable, fragile, delicate

3 a brittle manner
tense, curt, irritable, harsh, nervous
COLLOQ. edgy, nervy
4 a brittle laugh
short hard, sharp, harsh, grating
☒ 1 durable, resilient, sturdy 2 stable, secure, constant

broach v
1 INTRODUCE, raise, mention, propose, suggest, bring up, allude to, refer to, hint at
2 broach a cask
tap, pierce, open
OLD (Shakesp) strike

broad adj
1 broad avenues/valleys
wide, large, vast, roomy, spacious, ample, extensive, widespread
FORMAL capacious, latitudinous
2 a broad education
wide-ranging, far-reaching, encyclopedic, extensive, all-embracing, inclusive, comprehensive, general, sweeping, universal, unlimited
FORMAL catholic, eclectic, compendious
3 the broad meaning of the term
general, vague, not detailed
4 broad support
widespread, extensive, general
5 a broad hint
obvious, clear, plain, direct, undisguised, unconcealed
6 a broad accent
strong, marked, noticeable, obvious, evident
☒ 1 narrow 2 limited, restricted 3 narrow, detailed, specific, precise 4 limited 5 veiled, disguised 6 slight

❗ broad or **wide**?
Broad refers to the extent across something and often has the connotation of spaciousness or ampleness, whereas _wide_ refers to the distance separating, or the gap between, sides or edges: _a person's broad back; broad shoulders; wide sleeves; a wide doorway._

broadcast v, n
♦ v
1 broadcast TV programmes
transmit, air, show, beam, relay, televise, cable, radiate
2 broadcast the decision widely
make known, report, announce, publicize, advertise, publish, circulate, spread, scatter
FORMAL promulgate, disseminate
♦ n
transmission, programme, show, access broadcast, community broadcast, simulcast, simultaneous transmission, television première, teletext, satellite programme, telebridge, webcast

broaden v
widen, spread, enlarge, expand, extend, stretch, increase, develop, open up, branch out, diversify
FORMAL augment
☒ narrow, reduce, restrict

broadly adv
1 GENERALLY, usually, normally, mostly, in most cases, commonly, mainly, largely, as a rule, more or less, by and large, on the whole, for the most part
2 EXTENSIVELY, widely, generally, thoroughly, fully, comprehensively

broad-minded adj
liberal, tolerant, permissive, forbearing, enlightened, free-thinking, progressive, indulgent, impartial, open-minded, receptive, unbiased, unprejudiced, dispassionate
☒ narrow-minded, intolerant, biased, prejudiced

broadside n
1 fire a broadside at a ship

attack, assault, volley, salvo, battering, cannonade, blast, bombardment, counterblast, tire
2 *verbal broadsides*
criticism, denunciation, censure
FORMAL philippic, diatribe, fulmination, harangue, invective
COLLOQ. brickbat, stick

brochure *n*
leaflet, booklet, pamphlet, prospectus, broadsheet, handbill, circular, handout, folder, flyer; *N Am* throwaway

broil *v*
grill, cook, fry, toast, barbecue, roast

broiling *adj*
sweltering, boiling, hot, baking, roasting, scorching, blistering

broke *adj*
penniless, bankrupt, ruined, poor, impoverished, poverty-stricken, destitute
FORMAL insolvent, impecunious, penurious, indigent
COLLOQ. bust, skint, stony-broke, strapped (for cash), cleaned out, on your uppers, on your beam ends, not having two pennies to rub together
E3 rich, affluent, solvent

broken *adj*
1 *a broken pipe*
fractured, burst, ruptured, severed, separated, shattered, smashed, damaged, destroyed, demolished
COLLOQ. broken to smithereens
2 *broken machinery*
faulty, damaged, defective, out of order/action, not working, gone wrong
FORMAL malfunctioning, inoperative
COLLOQ. bust, kaput, duff, on the blink, wonky; *N Am* on the fritz
3 *broken sleep*
disjointed, disconnected, fragmentary, interrupted, disturbed, fitful, intermittent, spasmodic, erratic
FORMAL discontinuous
4 *a broken marriage*
failed, ended, divorced
5 *speak broken German*
hesitating, stammering, halting, faltering, imperfect, disjointed
6 *a broken man*
beaten, defeated, crushed, demoralized, dispirited, weak, feeble, exhausted, tamed, subdued, oppressed
FORMAL vanquished
COLLOQ. down, knackered
E3 1 mended, intact, whole **2** mended, in order/action, working **3** continuous, uninterrupted **5** fluent, perfect

broken-down *adj*
1 *a broken-down machine*
faulty, damaged, defective, broken, out of order
FORMAL inoperative
COLLOQ. on the blink, bust, kaput, duff; *N Am* on the fritz
2 *a broken-down old house*
dilapidated, in disrepair, decrepit, ramshackle, rickety, ruined, decayed, collapsed

broken-hearted *adj*
heartbroken, inconsolable, devastated, grief-stricken, desolate, despairing, miserable, wretched, mournful, sorrowful, sad, unhappy, dejected, despondent, crestfallen, disappointed
FORMAL dolorous, forlorn, wretched, disconsolate, prostrated
COLLOQ. down, down in the dumps

broker *n, v*
♦ *n*
agent, middleman, dealer, factor, handler, intermediary, negotiator, go-between, stockbroker, jobber, stockjobber
TECHNICAL arbitrageur
♦ *v*

negotiate, deal, mediate, arbitrate, bargain, arrange, settle, organize, settle, complete, agree, job
FORMAL conclude, execute
COLLOQ. clinch

bromide *n*
1 PLATITUDE, banality, cliché, commonplace, stereotype, truism
FORMAL anodyne
2 TRANQUILLIZER, sedative, calmative, sleeping pill, opiate, narcotic, barbiturate
COLLOQ. downer

bronze *adj*
copper, copper-coloured, auburn, chestnut, reddish-brown, rust, tan, Titian
OLD brass

bronzed *adj*
bronze, tanned, suntanned, brown, browned, sunburnt

brooch *n*
badge, pin, clip, clasp, breastpin, lapel pin, tiepin, fibula
OLD broch, ouch
SLANG prop

brood *v, n*
♦ *v*
1 *brood over lost opportunities*
ponder, meditate, muse, mull over, go over, dwell on, worry about, fret about, sulk, agonize
FORMAL , rehearse, ruminate
COLLOQ. fret, mope
2 *hens brood*
incubate, sit, cover; *Scot* clock; hatch
♦ *n*
1 *a brood of birds*
clutch, chicks, hatch, litter, young, offspring, issue, progeny, nest, nid, spawn; *Scot* cleck
OLD kindle, sperm, team
2 *a brood of children*
children, family, household, clan; *Scot* bairn-team, bairn-time
COLLOQ. tribe

brook¹ *n*
a brook running by the cottage
stream, rivulet, beck, watercourse, channel, inlet, gill, runnel, fleet, rill; *Scot* burn; *N Am* branch, kill; *N Am, Aust & NZ* creek
OLD purl

brook² *v*
will brook no interference
tolerate, allow, accept, allow, permit, bear, endure, stand, put up with, support, withstand
OLD abrooke
FORMAL countenance
COLLOQ. stomach

brothel *n*
bordello, bawdy-house, house of ill fame, house of ill repute, whorehouse, bagnio, disorderly house; *Irish* kip; *N Am* sporting house
OLD bordel, flash-house, stew, vaulting-house, Corinth; (*Shakesp*) hothouse, leaping-house
COLLOQ. red light
SLANG knocking-shop, crib; *N Am* cathouse

brother *n*
1 *brothers and sisters*
sibling, blood-brother, full brother, twin-brother, half-brother, relation, relative, sib; *N Am* brer
OLD german, brother-german
COLLOQ. bro
Related adjective: fraternal
2 *brothers in the struggle against injustice*
comrade, friend, mate, partner, colleague, associate, fellow, companion

COLLOQ. chum, mate, pal, buddy
3 *brothers in a monastery*
monk, friar, *fra*

brotherhood *n*
1 *feelings of brotherhood*
fellowship, comradeship, friendship, friendliness,
fraternalism, camaraderie
2 *a brotherhood of monks*
fraternity, association, society, league, confederation,
confederacy, alliance, union, guild, fellowship,
confraternity, confrère, community, clique

brotherly *adj*
fraternal, loyal, affectionate, amicable, caring,
sympathetic, friendly, kind, loving, benevolent,
philanthropic
E3 callous, unbrotherly

brow *n*
1 *sweat on your brow*
forehead, temples
2 *the brow of the hill*
summit, ridge, top, tip, peak, verge, brink, cliff

browbeat *v*
bully, coerce, force, intimidate, threaten, tyrannize, hector,
hound, dragoon, domineer, overbear, oppress
COLLOQ. bulldoze
E3 coax, flatter; *colloq.* sweet-talk

brown *adj, v*
♦ *adj*
1 *brown in colour*
mahogany, chocolate, coffee, *café au lait*, Mocha, hazel,
bay, chestnut, auburn, umber, burnt umber, raw umber,
sepia, ginger, beige, fawn, tan, tawny, honey, biscuit, bistre,
cinnamon, earth-tone, nut-brown, walnut, oatmeal, pine,
teak, vandyke brown, fuscous, infuscate, russet, rust, rusty,
brunette, dark, dusky
OLD burnet, orange-tawny
2 *brown from lying in the sun*
sunburnt, tanned, bronze, bronzed, browned
♦ *v*
cook, seal, fry, grill, toast, singe, embrown

browned off *adj*
bored, fed up, discontented, discouraged, disheartened,
annoyed, irritated, exasperated, weary
COLLOQ. bored stiff, brassed off, cheesed off, hacked off,
disgruntled
SLANG pissed off
E3 fascinated, interested, intrigued

browse *v, n*
♦ *v*
1 *browse through a book*
survey, scan, leaf through, flick through, dip into, skim
FORMAL peruse
2 *sheep browsing in the fields*
graze, pasture, feed, eat, nibble
♦ *n*
scan, skim, quick read, look, flick-through

bruise *v, n*
♦ *v*
1 *bruise your leg*
discolour, blacken, mark, blemish, injure, wound, pound,
stun
OLD beat, surbate, to-bruise; (*Shakesp*) frush
FORMAL contuse
2 *bruise someone's feelings*
hurt, injure, insult, offend, grieve, upset, crush
3 *bruise fruit*
damage, mark, spoil, blemish, crush, discolour, break
♦ *n*
discoloration, mark, blemish, injury, lesion; *Scot* clour
TECHNICAL ecchymosis

OLD intuse
FORMAL contusion
COLLOQ. black eye, shiner
SLANG rainbow

bruiser *n*
ruffian, thug, tough, rough, roughneck, hoodlum, bully,
bully boy
COLLOQ. bovver boy

brunt *n*
burden, thrust, (main) force, impact, impetus, pressure,
(full) weight, shock, strain

brush[1] *n, v*
♦ *n*
1 *sweep the room with a brush*
broom, sweeper, besom, whisk
2 *give the room a good brush*
sweep, clean, clear, dust, wipe
♦ *v*
1 *brush the room*
clean, clean, sweep, flick, burnish, polish, shine
2 *brush against the table*
touch, contact, graze, kiss, stroke, caress, rub, scrape, scuff
■ **brush aside**
dismiss, ignore, flout, disregard, dismiss, override
FORMAL belittle
COLLOQ. pooh-pooh
■ **brush off**
disregard, ignore, slight, snub, rebuff, dismiss, spurn, reject,
repulse, disown
FORMAL repudiate
COLLOQ. cold-shoulder
■ **brush up**
1 *brush up your Spanish*
revise, relearn, improve, polish up, study, go over, read up
COLLOQ. swot, bone up on, cram
2 *go and brush up*
refresh (yourself), freshen up, clean (yourself up), tidy
(up)

brush[2] *n*
a ball lost in the brush
bush, scrub, thicket, bushes, shrubs, brushwood,
undergrowth, underwood, ground cover, frith

brush[3] *n*
a brush with the police
confrontation, encounter, disagreement, argument, clash,
conflict, fight, skirmish, tussle, fracas
COLLOQ. dust-up, set-to, scrap

brush-off *n*
discouragement, dismissal, rebuff, refusal, rejection,
repudiation, repulse, slight, snub
FORMAL repudiation
COLLOQ. cold shoulder
SLANG *N Am* kiss-off
E3 encouragement

brusque *adj*
abrupt, sharp, short, terse, curt, blunt, downright, gruff,
surly, discourteous, impolite, uncivil, blunt, tactless,
uncivil, undiplomatic
E3 courteous, polite, tactful

brutal *adj*
1 *a brutal murder/attacker*
savage, bloodthirsty, vicious, ferocious, cruel, inhumane,
animal, inhuman, beastly, barbarous, boarish, doggish,
Rottweiler, ruffian, brutish, remorseless, pitiless, merciless,
ruthless, callous
FORMAL bestial
2 *brutal frankness*
harsh, insensitive, unfeeling, heartless, iron-hearted,
unsparing, plain, straightforward, frank, severe, tough
E3 1 kindly, humane, civilized **2** kind, gentle, sensitive

brutality n

savagery, bloodthirstiness, viciousness, ferocity, cruelty, inhumanity, violence, atrocity, ruthlessness, callousness, roughness, coarseness, barbarism, barbarity, brutishness
FORMAL callosity
F3 gentleness, kindness

brutalize v

1 HARDEN, deaden, desensitize, inure, dehumanize
2 ATTACK, assault, beat, pound, batter, thrash, pound, hit, flog

brutally adv

1 *brutally honest*
harshly, insensitively, unfeelingly, heartlessly, straightforwardly, frankly, severely
2 SAVAGELY, viciously, ferociously, cruelly, inhumanely, barbarously, brutishly, pitilessly, mercilessly, ruthlessly, callously
F3 1 gently, sensitively **2** humanely, kindly

brute n, adj

♦ n
animal, beast, swine, creature, monster, ogre, devil, fiend, savage, sadist, bully, lout, yahoo, ruffian, *bête*, Rottweiler, Caliban
♦ adj
physical, senseless, unthinking, bodily, carnal, coarse, depraved, fleshly, gross, instinctive, mindless, sensual

brutish adj

brutal, uncivilized, barbarian, barbaric, barbarous, animal, coarse, crass, crude, cruel, gross, loutish, savage, stupid, uncouth, vulgar
FORMAL bestial, feral, ferine
F3 refined, civilized, polite

bubble n, v

♦ n
1 *soap bubbles*
ball (of air), air-bell, drop, droplet, bead, blister, fizz, foam, froth, head, lather, suds, effervescence, globule, spume, bleb, bell, air-lock
OLD (*Spenser*) rowndell
FORMAL vesicle
2 *a bubble in glass*
dimple, depression, blister, blowhole, seed
3 *the bubble of all their dreams burst*
delusion, fantasy, fraud, illusion, trifle, vanity
♦ v
1 SPARKLE, froth, foam, seethe, boil, burble, gurgle, effervesce, gloop; *Scot* wallop
OLD mantle
COLLOQ. fizz
2 *bubble with enthusiasm*
be filled, be excited, sparkle, be elated
COLLOQ. bounce

bubbly adj

1 SPARKLING, carbonated, frothy, foaming, sudsy, effervescent
COLLOQ. fizzy
2 LIVELY, happy, merry, elated, excited, exuberant, vivacious
FORMAL animated, ebullient
COLLOQ. bouncy
F3 1 flat, still **2** lethargic

buccaneer n

pirate, corsair, filibuster, freebooter, privateer, sea robber, sea rover, sea wolf

buck v

1 *buck the trend*
resist, ignore, oppose, break the rules, contradict
2 *feel very bucked*
encourage, cheer, hearten, reassure, buoy up
■ **buck up**
1 *buck someone up*
cheer (up), encourage, improve, rally, stimulate, take heart,

hearten, enliven
FORMAL inspirit
COLLOQ. perk up
2 *Buck up or we'll be late!*
hurry (up)
FORMAL hasten
COLLOQ. get a move on, get your skates on, step on it
F3 1 discourage **2** slow down

bucket n, v

♦ n
pail, can, bail, scuttle, pitcher, vessel, tub, ladle, dip, kibble
OLD situla, stoup, stoop
■ **bucket down**
pour (down), rain heavily, pelt down
COLLOQ. rain cats and dogs, come down in buckets/stair rods/torrents

buckle n, v

♦ n
1 *a buckle on a belt*
clasp, clip, catch, fastener, hasp
2 *a buckle in metal*
bulge, warp, distortion, twist, kink
FORMAL contortion
♦ v
1 FASTEN, clasp, catch, hook, hitch, connect, close, secure
2 *the metal buckled*
bend, warp, twist, distort, bulge, fold, wrinkle, crumple, collapse
COLLOQ. cave in
■ **buckle down**
knuckle down, start to work hard, get down to it
COLLOQ. pull your finger out, go all out, pull out all the stops

bucolic adj

pastoral, rural, agrarian, agricultural, country
FORMAL rustic
COLLOQ. countrified
F3 industrial, urban

bud n, v

♦ n
shoot, sprout, sprig, germ, embryo, button, knot
TECHNICAL bulbil, gemma, knosp, turion
OLD knop
FORMAL plumule
♦ v
shoot, sprout, develop, grow
FORMAL burgeon, pullulate
F3 wither, waste away

budding adj

potential, promising, embryonic, developing, growing, up-and-coming, flowering, fledgling
FORMAL incipient, nascent, burgeoning
F3 experienced, mature

buddy n

friend, good friend, companion, comrade
COLLOQ. buddy-buddy, pal, mate, chum, crony

budge v

1 *the door won't budge*
move, stir, shift, remove, dislodge, push, roll, slide; *Scot* jee
OLD bouge, bodge
2 *not budge from your position*
change, bend, yield, give (way), give in, change your mind, not compromise, sway, influence, persuade, convince

budget n, v

♦ n
finances, funds, resources, economics, means, allowance, allotment, quota, allocation, (financial) plan, (financial) estimate, what you can afford

OLD bouget, bowget
* v

plan, estimate, schedule, allow, allot, allocate, set aside, ration, afford
FORMAL apportion

buff¹ *adj, v*
* *adj*

buff-coloured envelopes
yellowish-brown, yellowish, straw, sandy, fawn, khaki, beige, natural, nankeen, tan
* v

polish, burnish, shine, smooth, rub (up), brush

■ **in the buff**
naked, nude, bare, with nothing on, undressed, unclothed, uncovered, stripped, stark-naked
COLLOQ. in the altogether, in the raw, starkers, not a stitch on

buff² *n*

a computer buff
expert, connoisseur, enthusiast, fan, fanatic, admirer, devotee, addict; *N Am* maven
FORMAL aficionado
COLLOQ. freak, fiend

buffer *n, v*
* *n*

shock absorber, bumper, fender, pad, cushion, pillow, intermediary, screen, shield, bulwark
* v

cushion, soften, deaden, absorb, suppress, lessen, reduce, diminish, mitigate, protect

buffet¹ *n*

1 *a railway buffet*
snackbar, counter, café, cafeteria
2 *a buffet supper*
self-service, cold meal, smorgasbord, cold table
COLLOQ. help yourself

buffet² *v, n*
* v

1 *buffeted by the storm*
batter, hit, strike, knock, bang, bump, push, pound, pummel, beat, shove, thump, box, cuff, clout, slap
2 *a government buffeted by corruption*
trouble, afflict, disturb, weigh (down), burden, distress, harm, oppress, tax, blight
* *n*

blow, knock, bang, bump, jar, jolt, push, thump, box, cuff, clout, slap, smack, shove
OLD buff

buffoon *n*

clown, comedian, comic, fool, harlequin, jester, joker, wag, droll, tomfool, zany, *farceur*, mime, mountebank
OLD antic, Jack-pudding, merry-andrew, mome, Punchinello, Scoggin, Scaramouch, Vice, Iniquity

buffoonery *n*

clowning, jesting, pantomime, tomfoolery, waggishness, drollery, nonsense, silliness, farce, pantaloonery, Pantagruelism

bug *n, v*
* *n*

1 INSECT, flea, mite
COLLOQ. creepy-crawly
2 *a stomach bug*
virus, bacterium, germ, microbe, micro-organism, infection, illness, disease
COLLOQ. *Aust* wog
SLANG *N Am* cootie
3 *a bug in a computer program*
fault, defect, flaw, blemish, imperfection, failing, error
COLLOQ. gremlin
4 *bitten by the decorating bug*
craze, fad, obsession, mania
COLLOQ. thing

5 *put a bug in a room*
hidden microphone, listening device
COLLOQ. wire-tap, phone-tap
* v

1 *their attitude bugs me*
annoy, irritate, vex, irk, bother, disturb, harass
COLLOQ. aggravate, needle, wind up
2 *bug an office*
tap, listen in (on/to), monitor
FORMAL eavesdrop (on)
COLLOQ. wiretap, phone-tap

bugbear *n*

anathema, bane, bête noire, pet hate, dread, fiend, horror, nightmare, bogle, bogy, poker, rawhead
OLD bug

build *v, n*
* v

1 *build a new hotel*
construct, put up, erect, raise, fabricate, make, form, constitute, assemble, put together, knock together, shape, fashion, rear, mason, substruct, throw out, overbuild, upbuild; *Scot* big
OLD edify
2 *build a fairer society*
inaugurate, initiate, institute, begin, start, develop, enlarge, extend, increase, escalate, intensify
FORMAL augment
🖙 1 destroy, demolish; *colloq.* knock down **2** lessen
* *n*

physique, figure, body, form, shape, size, frame, structure; *dialect* set

■ **build up**
1 *build up a navy*
assemble, put together, piece together, extend, enlarge, set up, establish
2 *build up your strength*
reinforce, extend, expand, develop, grow, amplify, increase, escalate, intensify, heighten, strengthen, boost, improve, enhance
FORMAL fortify
3 *build a person up as important*
publicize, advertise, promote
COLLOQ. plug, hype
4 ACCUMULATE, increase, mount (up), add, gather, collect, amass, snowball
FORMAL augment

Synonym nuances
verb sense 1
Construct may be used generally to talk about creating something, whereas **erect** and **raise** would be used starting from the lowest level and elevating into position: *barriers erected to prevent trespassing.* **Put up** can cover both nuances: *they put up very inferior dwellings; they put up statues of him.*

Fabricate and, especially, **make** are widely used to mean creating something, while **form**, **shape** and **fashion** convey an idea of giving something shape: *the attic, formed by the steep-sided pitched roof; the scoured branches, fashioned by the weather.*

Constitute is used of the parts making up the whole: *a trolley of books constituted the hospital library*; whereas **assemble** and **put together** is used of making something from those parts: *sculptures assembled from pieces of scrap iron.* While the preceding terms are neutral in tone, the terms **knock together** and **throw out** may be taken as pejorative in that they carry the suggestion of carelessness.

Rear revisits the idea of elevating, and its tone tends to the poetic, and so is fairly uncommon.

Usually **mason** has the narrower application of building stonework, whilst **substruct**, with its sole application to foundation work, is rarely used.

Types of building include:

abbey	church	hotel	observatory	*Aust* skillion (or
NAm apartment	cinema	house	office block	skilling)
building (or	college	inn	outhouse	skyscraper
apartment house)	*NAm* condominium	library	pagoda	*NAm* sliver building
arena	cottage	lighthouse	palace	sports hall
barn	dovecote	low-rise	pavilion	stable
barracks	exhibition centre	maisonette	pier	store
beach hut	factory	mandir	power station	summerhouse
block of flats	farmhouse	mansion	prison	synagogue
boathouse	fort	mausoleum	*colloq.* pub	temple
bungalow	fortress	mews	public house	theatre
cabin	garage	mill	restaurant	tower block
café	gazebo	monastery	school	university
castle	gurdwara	monument	shed	villa
cathedral	gymnasium	mosque	shop	warehouse
chapel	high-rise	multiplex	showroom	windmill
chateau	hospital	museum	silo	

See also **house; restaurant; shop**.

builder *n*

construction worker, labourer, manual worker, mason, craftsman, craftsperson, craftswoman, skilled worker

building *n*

construction, development, fabrication, structure, erection, architecture
FORMAL edifice, dwelling
Related adjective: tectonic
See also panel above

Types of building material include:

aggregate	gravel	plastic
aluminium	granite	plywood
asbestos	grout	reinforced
ashlar	gypsum	concrete
asphalt	hardboard	roofing felt
bitumen	hard core	roof tile
breeze block	insulation	sand
brick	foam insulation	sandstone
building block	loose fill	*Scot & NZ* sarking
cast iron	insulation	shingle
cement	lagging	*NAm* siding
chipboard	lintel	slate
cladding	*NAm* lumber	stainless steel
clapboard	marble	steel
clay	mastic	steel beam
concrete	matchboard	stone
decking	medium density	tarmac
NAm drywall	fibreboard	thatch
fixings	(MDF)	tile
flagstone	mortar	timber
floor tile	paving stone	wall tile
girder	pavior	wattle and daub
glass	plaster	wood
glass fibre	plasterboard	

build-up *n*

1 *a build-up of fat*
enlargement, expansion, development, increase, gain, growth, accumulation, escalation
FORMAL accretion
2 *build-up of nuclear weapons*
accumulation, mass, load, heap, stack, drift, store, stockpile
3 *build-up to the competition*
publicity, promotion, advertising, marketing
COLLOQ. plug, hype, puff
F∃ **1** reduction, decrease, contraction

built-in *adj*

1 *built-in wardrobes*
fitted, integral, in-built, fixed, included

2 *built-in safeguards*
inherent, included, incorporated, implicit, in-built, inseparable, integral, intrinsic, essential, fundamental, necessary

bulb

Plants grown from bulbs and corms include:

acidanthera	crown imperial	jonquil
allium	cyclamen	lily
amarylis	daffodil	montbretia
anemone	fritallary	narcissus
autumn crocus	galtonia	nerine
(colchicum)	garlic	ranunculus
bluebell	gladioli	scilla
(endymion)	grape hyacinth	snowdrop
chincherinchee	(muscari)	(galanthus)
chionodoxa	hyacinth	sparaxis
crocosmia	iris	tulip
crocus	ixia	winter aconite

bulbous *adj*

rounded, swollen, swelling, bulging, convex, bloated, puffed (out)
TECHNICAL pulvinate(d), tuberous
FORMAL distended

bulge *n, v*

♦ *n*
1 *a bulge on the wall*
swelling, bump, lump, hump, bias, blister, shoulder, pouch
FORMAL projection, protuberance, distension
2 *a bulge in the production figures*
rise, increase, surge, upsurge, intensification
♦ *v*
swell, hump, expand, enlarge, bulb, project, protrude, bag, belly, billow; *dialect* strout
OLD strut
FORMAL dilate, distend
COLLOQ. puff out, sag; *NAm* bug

bulk *n, v*

♦ *n*
1 *the vast bulk of the ship*
size, magnitude, dimensions, extent, bigness, largeness, immensity, volume, mass, weight, substance, body, quantity; *Scot* bouk
OLD great
FORMAL amplitude
2 MAJORITY, most, nearly all, preponderance, weight, gross; *Scot* feck
COLLOQ. lion's share
■ **bulk out/up**

expand, extend, make bigger, increase, pad out, fill out, fill (up)

bulky *adj*
substantial, big, large, huge, enormous, immense, ample, volumed, gross, lusty, mammoth, massive, colossal, hulking, hefty, heavy, weighty, unmanageable, unwieldy, awkward, cumbersome, lofty
FORMAL voluminous
Ea insubstantial, small, handy

bulldoze *v*
1 *bulldoze buildings*
clear, flatten, demolish, level, raze
COLLOQ. knock down
2 *bulldoze someone into buying; bulldoze plans through a committee*
force, push (through), intimidate, browbeat
FORMAL coerce
COLLOQ. bully, steamroller

bullet *n*
shot, pellet, ball, missile, propellant, cartridge, cartouche, shot, dumdum
OLD Biscayan
FORMAL projectile
COLLOQ. slug
OLD SLANG lead towel

bulletin *n*
1 *televison news bulletins*
report, newsflash, dispatch, communiqué, statement, announcement, notification, communication, message, update, release
2 *an office bulletin*
news sheet, newspaper, newsletter, leaflet, update

bullish *adj*
optimistic, confident, hopeful, positive, cheeful, buoyant
FORMAL sanguine
COLLOQ. upbeat

bully *n, v*
♦ *n*
persecutor, tormentor, browbeater, intimidator, tyrant, bully-boy, ruffian, thug, bouncer, hoodlum, swashbuckler, bucko
OLD brave, cuttle, huff, killcow, Drawcansir
COLLOQ. heavy, tough
♦ *v*
persecute, torment, terrorize, bulldoze, coerce, browbeat, bullyrag, intimidate, cow, tyrannize, prey, bluster, hector, haze, pick on, victimize, domineer, overbear, oppress
COLLOQ. push around
Ea coax, persuade, encourage

bulwark *n*
bastion, buttress, defence, wall, guard, safeguard, security, protection, support, mainstay, outwork, buffer, embankment, fortification, partition, rampart
TECHNICAL redoubt

bum[1] *n*
sitting on his bum
bottom, buttocks, behind, rear, seat, rump
COLLOQ. backside, tail; *NAm* butt, booty
SLANG arse; *NAm* ass

bum[2] *n, v, adj*
♦ *n*
end up as a drunken bum
tramp, vagrant, hobo, vagabond; *Scot* gangrel
SLANG dosser
♦ *v*
cadge, scrounge, beg, borrow
COLLOQ. sponge
♦ *adj*
poor, bad, worthless, low, useless, unpleasant,

disagreeable, adverse, inadequate, imperfect, unsatisfactory, unacceptable
COLLOQ. awful, terrible, rubbish, duff, crummy
SLANG naff, crappy

bumble *v*
blunder, stumble, falter, stagger, lurch, totter, teeter

bumbling *adj*
bungling, awkward, inept, blundering, botching, clumsy, inefficient, incompetent, lumbering, muddled, stumbling
FORMAL maladroit
Ea competent, efficient

bump *v, n*
♦ *v*
1 *bump into the wall/against the table*
hit, strike, knock, bang, crash, collide (with), barge; *dialect* jowl; *Scot* dunch
COLLOQ. slam, prang
2 *bump along a track*
jolt, jerk, jar, jostle, rattle, shake, bounce, jounce
♦ *n*
1 *hear a bump*
blow, hit, knock, bang, thump, thud, smash, crash, collision, impact, jolt, jar, shock, whop
2 *a bump on your head*
lump, swelling, bulge, injury, hump, irregularity
TECHNICAL papilla, knur, nodule
FORMAL protrusion, protuberance, tumescence
3 *a bump on a road*
lump, bulge, hump, protuberance, speed bump, sleeping policeman
■ **bump into**
come across, meet (unexpectedly), meet by chance, encounter
FORMAL chance upon, happen upon, light upon
COLLOQ. run into
■ **bump off**
kill, murder, assassinate, remove
COLLOQ. eliminate, liquidate, do in, rub out, blow away, top

bumper *adj*
plentiful, abundant, rich, large, great, enormous, massive, excellent, exceptional
COLLOQ. whopping, jumbo, ginormous
Ea small, tiny

bumpkin *n*
country bumpkin, country yokel, boor, lout, clodhopper, clodpoll, rustic, oaf, peasant, provincial, hawbuck; *NAm* yap; *NAm & Aust* bushwhacker
OLD putt
COLLOQ. hillbilly, hick, hayseed
SLANG *NAm* rube

bumptious *adj*
self-important, pompous, officious, overbearing, pushy, assertive, over-confident, presumptuous, forward, full of yourself, impudent, arrogant, cocky, brash, conceited, swaggering, boastful, egotistic
COLLOQ. too big for your boots
Ea humble, modest, unassertive

bumpy *adj*
1 *a bumpy road*
rough, lumpy, pot-holed, knobbly, knobby, uneven, irregular
2 *a bumpy ride*
rough, uneven, jerky, jolting, bouncy, choppy
Ea 1 smooth, level **2** smooth, even, uncomfortable

bunch *n, v*
♦ *n*
1 *a bunch of grapes*
bundle, sheaf, tuft, club, clump, cluster, string, racemation; *dialect* bob

2 *a bunch of keys/papers*
batch, lot, wad, heap, pile, stack, mass, number, quantity, collection, assortment
FORMAL agglomeration, fascicle, fascicule
3 *a bunch of flowers*
bouquet, posy, spray, nosegay, corsage, tussie mussie
OLD boughpot
4 *a bunch of people*
gang, band, troop, crew, team, party, gathering, flock, swarm, crowd, mob, multitude

♦ *v*

group, bundle, cluster, collect, gather, flock, herd, crowd, mass, pack, huddle
FORMAL assemble, congregate
E3 disperse, scatter, spread out

bundle *n, v*

♦ *n*

1 *a bundle of hay/sticks*
bunch, sheaf, shook, roll, bale, truss, faggot, wad, wisp, woolpack, bavin, bottle; *dialect* knitch, wap, yelm; *Scot* dorlach
OLD fasces
FORMAL fascicle, fascine, fascicule
2 *carry bundles of clothes*
pack, batch, parcel, package, packet, carton, box, bag; *Aust* swag, bluey, drum
OLD *Aust* shiralee
FORMAL consignment
3 *a bundle of books/paper*
group, set, collection, assortment, quantity, mass, accumulation, pile, stack, heap, skein
OLD trousseau

♦ *v*

1 *bundle papers together*
pack, wrap, bale, truss, cluster, gather, parcel, bind, tie, fasten, huddle
2 *bundle someone into a van*
rush, hurry, push roughly, shove, tumble

bung *n*
stopper, plug, cork, seal, spigot

bungle *v*
mismanage, make a mess of, botch, ruin, spoil, mar, fudge, blunder, mishandle, muddle, fluff, bumble, duff, mangle, mull; *Scot* bauchle, blunk, misguggle; *N Am* bobble
COLLOQ. foul up, mess up, louse up, bodge, boob, muck up, foozle, muff; *N Am* flub
SLANG goof (up), cock up, screw up

bungler *n*
incompetent, blunderer, bumbler, tinker; *Scot* blunk
COLLOQ. botcher, butterfingers, duffer, muff
SLANG schlemiel

bungling *adj*
awkward, clumsy, incompetent, inept, unskilful, messy, amateurish
FORMAL maladroit
COLLOQ. blundering, botching, cack-handed, ham-fisted, ham-handed

bunkum *n*
nonsense, rubbish
COLLOQ. balderdash, baloney, bilge, bosh, bunk, blah, garbage, cobblers, hooey, piffle, malarkey, codswallop, poppycock, rot, stuff and nonsense, tommyrot, trash, tripe, twaddle; *N Am* hogwash, horsefeathers, BS; *Aust & NZ* bulldust
SLANG bull; (*vulgar*) balls, bollocks, bullshit

buoy *n, v*

♦ *n*

float, marker, signal, beacon, mooring, dan, dolphin
■ **buoy up**

support, sustain, raise, lift, boost, encourage, cheer (up), hearten
E3 depress, discourage

buoyancy *n*
1 LIGHTNESS, floatability
2 CHEERFULNESS, happiness, gladness, joy, light-heartedness, enthusiasm, geniality, jolliness, brightness, confidence, optimism, good spirits
COLLOQ. bounce, pep
3 *the buoyancy of the economy*
strength, vigour, toughness, resilience, growth, development

buoyant *adj*
1 *a buoyant mood*
light-hearted, carefree, bright, cheerful, optimistic, happy, joyful, lively, blithe, bullish, debonair, animated, vivacious, youthful
COLLOQ. bouncy, peppy
2 *a buoyant raft*
floatable, floating, afloat, light, weightless
3 *a buoyant economy*
strong, tough, resilient, hardy, adaptable, growing, developing, thriving
E3 1 depressed, despairing **2** heavy

burble *v*
babble, gurgle, lap, murmur, purl

burden *n, v*

♦ *n*

1 *put down a heavy burden*
cargo, load, weight, dead-weight
OLD burthen; (*Shakesp*) carriage
2 *the burdens of office*
obligation, responsibility, duty, onus, imposition, millstone, pressure, strain, stress, worry, anxiety, weight, care, trouble, trial, affliction, cross, grievance, sorrow, overburden, yoke
FORMAL encumbrance, cumbrance
SLANG monkey

♦ *v*

burdened with a heavy load/worldly cares
weigh down, lade, handicap, bother, worry, tax, strain, charge, land with, lumber, saddle, overload, overburden, overstress, overextend, lie heavy/hard on, oppress, overwhelm, crush, task
OLD cark; (*Shakesp*) overbulk
FORMAL encumber
E3 unburden, relieve

burdensome *adj*
onerous, crushing, difficult, weighty, exacting, heavy, irksome, oppressive, taxing, troublesome, trying, wearisome, grievous
OLD chargeable, importune
E3 easy, light

bureau *n*
1 *the Federal Bureau of Investigation*
office, service, agency, branch, department, division, counter
2 *sit at a bureau*
desk, writing-desk

bureaucracy *n*
1 *a bureaucracy of thousands of civil servants*
administration, government, ministry, civil service, the authorities, the system; *N Am* city hall
2 *try to reduce bureaucracy*
administration, rules and regulations, paperwork, officialdom, officiousness, beadledom
COLLOQ. red tape

bureaucrat *n*
officer, official, office-holder, administrator, civil servant, functionary, (government) minister, committee member,

mandarin, apparatchik, Eurocrat, chinovnik
SLANG suit

bureaucratic adj
official, administrative, governmental, ministerial,
complicated, procedural, inflexible, rigid

burgeon v
grow, develop, increase, expand, extend, enlarge, swell,
escalate, proliferate, snowball

burglar n
housebreaker, robber, thief, pilferer, trespasser, cat-
burglar, cracksman; N Am yegg

burglary n
housebreaking, break-in, robbery, theft, stealing, trespass,
pilferage, larceny
COLLOQ. heist

burgle v
break into, rob, steal from, burst into, force your way into;
N Am burglarize

burial n
burying, funeral, committal
FORMAL interment, entombment, obsequies, exequies,
inhumation, sepulchre

burial place n
graveyard, cemetery, churchyard, God's acre, vault, crypt,
catacomb, mausoleum, necropolis, tumulus
OLD charnel, kurgan

burlesque n, adj
♦ n
caricature, mock, mockery, parody, ridicule, satire,
travesty, Pantagruelism
COLLOQ. take-off, send-up, spoof, mickey-taking
♦ adj
comic, derisive, farcical, mocking, parodying, satirical,
heroi-comic
FORMAL caricatural, hudibrastic
F∃ serious

burly adj
well-built, thickset, hulking, hefty, heavy, stocky, big,
sturdy, brawny, beefy, muscular, athletic, strapping, strong,
powerful; Scot buirdly
F∃ small, puny, thin, slim

burn v
1 *the fire's burning*
be on/catch fire, be in flames, burst into flames, blaze, be/
catch ablaze, go up in smoke, flame, inflame, flare (up),
flash, glow, flicker, smoulder, smoke
OLD bren, brenne
2 *burn rubbish*
ignite, light, set fire to, put a match to, set alight, kindle,
incinerate, cremate, consume, corrode, burn down,
destroy, go up in flames, gut, put to the torch, combust,
chark
TECHNICAL cense
OLD incremate, conflagrate
FORMAL deflagrate
3 *burn your hand on the oven; burn a hole in a cardigan*
scald, scorch, parch, shrivel, singe, char, toast, fry, grill,
brand, sear, inure; dialect plot, sweal; Scot scouther
FORMAL cauterize
4 *make your throat burn*
smart, sting, bite, hurt, tingle
5 *burn with anger*
fume, simmer, seethe
OLD emboil
6 *burn to be with someone*
long, desire, yearn, itch, be eager, be consumed by

burning adj
1 *a burning building*
ablaze, aflame, afire, fiery, flaming, blazing, flashing,
gleaming, glowing, smouldering, alight, lit, illuminated,
quick
OLD conflagrant, flagrant, swealing
2 *a burning forehead; a burning hot day*
hot, scalding, scorching
OLD swealing
3 *a burning sensation*
searing, piercing, acute, smarting, stinging, prickling,
tingling, biting, caustic, pungent, urent
FORMAL acrid
4 *burning desire*
passionate, ardent, fervent, eager, earnest, intense, fiery,
vehement, impassioned, frantic, frenzied, consuming
OLD inburning
FORMAL fervid
5 *a burning issue*
urgent, pressing, important, significant, crucial, essential,
vital, live
F∃ **2** cold **4** apathetic **5** unimportant

burnish v
polish (up), brighten, buff, glaze, shine

burp v, n
♦ v
belch, bring up wind
FORMAL eructate
♦ n
belch
FORMAL eructation

burrow n, v
♦ n
warren, hole, earth, set, den, lair, retreat, shelter, tunnel;
dialect bury
♦ v
1 TUNNEL, dig, delve, excavate, mine, undermine, gopher;
Scot howk
2 *burrow for the keys*
rummage, delve, search, root

bursar n
treasurer, cashier, purser

bursary n
scholarship, grant, award, endowment, fellowship,
exhibition

burst v, n
♦ v
1 *the tyre burst*
puncture, rupture, tear, split (open), blow, crack, break
(open), fragment, shatter, shiver, disintegrate, spring,
disrupt, part, pull apart
OLD (Spenser) distrain
2 *the dam burst*
gush, spout, rush, erupt
3 *burst into a room*
rush, run, hurry, race, dart, fly, bounce, plump, break in on
COLLOQ. barge, push your way
4 *the bomb burst*
explode, blow up, go off
COLLOQ. go pop, go bang
♦ n
1 *have a burst on the motorway*
puncture
COLLOQ. blow-out
2 *a burst of gunfire; a sudden burst of activity*
discharge, volley, salvo, gush, spurt, surge, rush, spate,
torrent, outpouring, outburst, outbreak, fit, bang, clap,
flash, blaze, blitz, start, gust
FORMAL fusillade
■ **burst out**
1 *burst out crying*
begin, start
FORMAL commence

2 EXCLAIM, cry (out), call out, utter
COLLOQ. blurt out

bury v
1 *bury the dead*
lay to rest, shroud; *Scot* yird
OLD earth, grave; (*Shakesp*) inhearse
FORMAL inter, entomb, tomb, sepulchre, inhume, inearth
COLLOQ. put six feet under
SLANG plant
2 *bury your face in your hands; bury a memory*
sink, submerge, plant, implant, embed, conceal, hide,
cover, engulf, immerse, enclose
FORMAL enshroud
3 *buried yourself in work*
immerse, engross, occupy, engage, absorb
🔁 **1** *formal* disinter, exhume **2** uncover, discover, expose

bush n
1 *a rose bush*
shrub, hedge, plant, thicket; *dialect* scrog
OLD tod, todde; (*Spenser*) busket
2 *go camping in the bush*
scrub, brush, scrubland, backwoods, brush, wilds, outback
▪ **not beat about the bush**
speak plainly/openly, come to the point, commit yourself
COLLOQ. call a spade a spade

bushy adj
shaggy, thick, bristling, bristly, fluffy, fuzzy, luxuriant,
woody, spreading, stiff, unruly, rough, wiry
TECHNICAL dasyphyllous, dumose, dumous
🔁 thin, neat, tidy, trim, well-kept

busily adv
actively, diligently, assiduously, earnestly, energetically,
hard, industriously, purposefully, briskly, speedily,
strenuously

business n
1 *do business*
trade, commerce, industry, manufacturing, dealings,
transactions, bargaining, trading, buying, selling,
merchandizing
2 *set up a new business*
company, firm, industry, corporation, establishment,
organization, concern, operation, franchise, enterprise,
private enterprise, flagship, industry, venture, management
buyout, consortium, syndicate, holding company,
parent/subsidiary company, conglomerate,
multinational
3 *a line of business*
job, occupation, work, employment, trade, profession,
line, calling, career, vocation, duty, task, responsibility,
métier
4 *none of your business*
affair, concern, matter, issue, subject, topic, question,
problem, point
COLLOQ. baby, pigeon
5 *the business of the meeting*
topic, subject, issue, question, matter

businesslike adj
professional, efficient, thorough, systematic, methodical,
organized, orderly, well-ordered, slick, painstaking,
practical, pragmatic, matter-of-fact, precise, correct,
formal, impersonal
🔁 inefficient, wasteful, disorganized; *colloq.* sloppy

businessman, businesswoman n
executive, entrepreneur, industrialist, trader, merchant,
tycoon, magnate, capitalist, financier, employer,
manufacturer, Babbitt
COLLOQ. city gent

busker n
street-entertainer, street-musician

bust[1] n
1 *a bust of the President*
sculpture, head, torso, statue
TECHNICAL herm, term, terminus
2 *a woman's bust*
bosom, breasts, chest, breast
COLLOQ. boobs
SLANG bristols, knockers, tits

bust[2] v, adj
◆ v
someone's bust the television
break, damage, shatter, crack, smash, destroy
◆ adj
broken, faulty, defective, out of order/action
COLLOQ. on the blink, wonky, phut, kaput, duff; *N Am* on
the fritz
▪ **go bust**
become bankrupt, become insolvent, fail, collapse,
founder, crash, close down
COLLOQ. fold, flop, go to the wall, *Aust* go bung

bustle v, n
◆ v
hurry, dash, rush, scamper, scurry, rush to and fro,
scramble, fuss, bumble, fluster, trot; *dialect* whew
FORMAL hasten, bestir
COLLOQ. tear, belt, to and fro
SLANG buzz
◆ n
activity, stir, commotion, to-do, tumult, agitation,
excitement, fuss, scramble, flurry, hurry, hurly-burly, hustle
and bustle, rush hour, the rush, hurry-scurry; *Irish*
stirabout; *N Am* rustle
OLD (*Shakesp*) ruffle
FORMAL haste, pother, ado
COLLOQ. a hive of activity, comings and goings

bustling adj
lively, active, energetic, busy, hectic, buzzing, rushing,
crowded, eventful, full, humming, restless, stirring,
swarming, teeming
FORMAL astir, abustle, thronged
COLLOQ. on the trot
🔁 quiet, sleepy, restful

busy adj, v
◆ adj
1 *be busy at the moment*
occupied, engaged, otherwise engaged, employed,
unavailable, working, having a previous engagement/prior
appointment
FORMAL in conference
COLLOQ. tied up, hard at it, on the job, in the thick of it, busy
as a bee
2 *a very busy day*
active, lively, energetic, strenuous, tiring, full, crowded,
swarming, vibrant, teeming, bustling, hectic, frantic,
eventful
3 *busy preparing for the meeting*
occupied, involved, engrossed, working
4 *a busy person*
active, having a lot to do, energetic, lively, diligent,
industrious, assiduous, restless, tireless; *Scot* eident; *Irish*
stirabout
FORMAL sedulous
COLLOQ. on the go, having a lot on, having your hands full,
fully stretched, rushed off your feet, under pressure,
snowed under, up to your eyes in something, on the trot
🔁 **1** free, available **2** quiet, leisured, empty, slack **3**
unoccupied **4** lazy, idle; *colloq.* at a loose end
◆ v
occupy, involve, engage, employ, engross, absorb,
immerse, interest, concern, go about, bustle
OLD embusy

Synonym nuances

adjective sense 2
The words **active**, **lively**, **energetic** and **vibrant** are positive in tone, with the suggestion that the activity is enjoyable: *an active campaign*; *lively discussion*; *vibrant Rhodes*. However, **strenuous** and **tiring** put a negative slant on any activity: *strenuous manual work*.

Full and **eventful** would usually be applied to a time characterized by numerous incidents, and are fairly neutral in tone, although **eventful** is sometimes used facetiously when a day has been too packed with incident for your liking: *the car broke down and the toaster blew up – you could call it an eventful day.* **Crowded** carries the negative implication that too much has been packed into a time or place, whilst **swarming** and **teeming** have the restricted use of describing too many animate things in a confined area, although **swarming** has a far more pejorative feel than **teeming**: *the beach was swarming with people*; *hillsides teeming with deer*.

The term **bustling** may be applied to crowded places as well as busy people, but implies a favourable view of the underlying excitement: *bustling waiters*. Both **hectic** and **frantic**, on the other hand, would appropriately describe stressful activity.

---

busybody *n*
meddler, interferer, intruder, pry, gossip, eavesdropper, snoop, snooper, troublemaker, mischief-maker, scandalmonger
OLD pragmatic
FORMAL pantopragmatic, quidnunc
COLLOQ. Nosey Parker

but *conj, prep, adv*
♦ *conj*
however, nevertheless, nonetheless, anyway, even so, all/ just the same, for all that
FORMAL notwithstanding
♦ *prep*
except, excepting, apart from, other than, with the exception of, aside from, save, omitting, leaving out, excluding, besides, bar, barring
♦ *adv*
only, just, at most, merely, simply, purely, no more than

butch *adj*
masculine, male, manlike, mannish, virile
COLLOQ. macho

butcher *n, v*
♦ *n*
1 *buy meat from the butcher's*
meat counter, meat retailer, meat trader, supermarket; *Scot* flesher
2 SLAUGHTERER, destroyer, killer, (mass) murderer, slayer
♦ *v*
slaughter, massacre, assassinate, exterminate, kill, liquidate, mutilate, slay, destroy

butchery *n*
1 SLAUGHTER, massacre, (mass) murder, carnage, killing, mass destruction, blood-letting, bloodshed
2 MEAT-SELLING, meat trade, meat retailing, butcher's

butt¹ *n*
1 *the butt of a gun/tool*
end, butt end, base, foot, shaft, stock, handle, haft
2 *the butt of a cigarette*
stub, tip, end, tail end
COLLOQ. fag end, dog-end; *Scot* dout, nip; *Aust* bumper
SLANG *NAm* snipe, roach
3 *sit on your butt*
bottom, buttocks
COLLOQ. bum, posterior
SLANG (*vulgar*) arse

butt² *n*
the butt of jokes
target, mark, object, subject, victim, laughing-stock, dupe, scapegoat
OLD stooge, jesting-stock, table-sport

butt³ *v*
butt someone with its horns
hit, bump, knock, buffet, push, ram, thrust, shove, punch, jab, prod, poke, bunt, horn; *Scot* box, dunch, dunsh
SLANG nut
■ **butt in**
interrupt, cut in, break in, intrude, meddle, interfere
FORMAL interpose, interject
COLLOQ. stick your nose in, put your oar in

butt⁴ *n*
a water-butt
cask, barrel, keg, tun, tierce, rundlet, firkin, hogshead

butter
■ **butter up**
flatter, praise, blarney, cajole, coax, pander to, wheedle, kowtow to
FORMAL be obsequious to
COLLOQ. suck up to, soft-soap

butterfly *n*
Related adjectives: papilionaceous, rhopaloceral, rhopalocerous

---

Types of butterfly include:

apollo	grayling	Queen of Spain
black hairstreak	green hairstreak	fritillary
brimstone	green-veined	red admiral
brown argus	white	ringlet
brown hairstreak	grizzled skipper	Scotch argus
cabbage white	hairstreak	silver-spotted
Camberwell	heath fritillary	skipper
beauty	hermit	silver-studded
chalkhill blue	holly blue	blue
chequered	large copper	silver-washed
skipper	Lulworth skipper	fritillary
Cleopatra	map	small copper
clouded yellow	marbled white	swallowtail
comma	marsh fritillary	tortoiseshell
common blue	meadow brown	wall
dingy skipper	monarch	white admiral
Duke of Burgundy	orange-tip	white letter
fritillary	painted lady	hairstreak
Essex skipper	peacock	wood white
fritillary	purple emperor	
gatekeeper	purple hairstreak	
Glanville fritillary		

See also **moth**.

---

buttocks *n*
bottom, rump, hindquarters, rear, behind, seat, breech, haunches, *derrière*; *Scot* doup, fud, hinderlings, hurdies
TECHNICAL gluteus, nates
OLD crouper
COLLOQ. backside, bum, posterior, fundament, tail; *NAm* butt, heinie, booty
SLANG duff, prat; (*vulgar*) arse; *NAm* ass, can, fanny, keister, tush; *Aust* coit, quoit
Related adjective: gluteal

button *n*
1 *buttons on a shirt*
fastener, fastening, catch, clasp, link, stud, frog, olivet
2 *press the button*
knob, disc, switch, lever

buttonhole *v*
accost, waylay, catch, take aside, detain

FORMAL importune
COLLOQ. grab, nab, corner, collar

buttress *n, v*
♦ *n*

support, prop, shore, stay, brace, pier, strut, mainstay, reinforcement
TECHNICAL counterfort, tambour
FORMAL abutment, stanchion

♦ *v*

support, prop up, shore up, hold up, back up, brace, underpin, strengthen, reinforce, bolster up, sustain
E3 undermine, weaken

buxom *adj*

plump, ample, large-breasted, full-breasted, bosomy, busty, chesty, well-endowed, well-rounded, full-figured, Junoesque, Rubenesque, zaftig; *Scot* sonse
OLD bucksom
FORMAL voluptuous, comely
COLLOQ. busty
SLANG well-stacked, pneumatic
E3 petite, slim, small

buy *v, n*
♦ *v*
1 *buy a car*

pay for, acquire, obtain, get, go shopping, do the shopping, shop around, shop for, stock up on, invest in, speculate, take, hedge, job, market, trade, merchandize, underbuy, overbuy, panic-buy, redeem, subsidize; *Scot* coff
TECHNICAL engross
OLD chop
FORMAL purchase, procure
COLLOQ. snap up, pick up, splash out on; *N Am* scalp
2 *buy the tax man*
bribe, buy off, suborn
COLLOQ. fix, grease someone's palm
SLANG nobble
E3 1 sell

♦ *n*
purchase, acquisition, bargain, deal
FORMAL emption
E3 selling

buyer *n*

purchaser, shopper, consumer, customer, client, patron, broker, dealer
FORMAL vendee, emptor
E3 seller; *formal* vendor

buzz *v, n*
♦ *v*
1 *bees buzzing round*
hum, whirr, drone, murmur
FORMAL bombilate, bombinate, susurrate
2 *the clock buzzed*
ring, purr, reverberate, resound, resonate
3 *buzz with excitement*
hum, throb, pulse, bustle, race
♦ *n*
1 *the buzz of bees*
hum, whirr, buzzing, drone, murmur, purr
TECHNICAL tinnitus
FORMAL bombilation, bombination, susurration, susurrus

2 *give someone a buzz*
ring, (phone) call
3 *the latest buzz*
rumour, gossip, scandal, latest, hearsay
COLLOQ. word on the street
4 THRILL, excitement, stimulation
COLLOQ. kick(s), high

by *prep, adv*
♦ *prep*
1 *a low table by the chair*
near, next to, close to, beside, alongside
2 *enter by the window*
along, over, through, via
3 *earn money by working hard*
by means of, through the agency of, through, using
FORMAL under the aegis of
4 *get home by noon*
before, no later than, at
5 *by any standard*
according to, in relation to
♦ *adv*
near, close (by), handy, at hand, past, beyond, away, aside
OLD forby

bygone *adj*

past, ancient, departed, forgotten, former, previous, lost, olden, one-time, antiquated, antique, dinosauric
OLD forepast
FORMAL erstwhile, forepast
E3 modern, recent, future, forthcoming

bypass *v, n*
♦ *v*
avoid, find a way round, sidestep, ignore, neglect, evade, steer clear of, omit, sidetrack, shunt
FORMAL circumvent
COLLOQ. dodge, skirt
♦ *n*
ring road, slip road, alternative route, detour, diversion

by-product *n*
1 *cattle feed is a by-product of whisky*
derivative, spin-off
2 *by-products of modern life*
consequence, result, side effect, repercussion, after-effect, spin-off, knock-on effect
FORMAL concomitant, entailment, epiphenomenon
COLLOQ. fallout

bystander *n*

spectator, onlooker, looker-on, watcher, observer, witness, eyewitness, passer-by
COLLOQ. rubberneck
E3 participant

byword *n*
1 *a byword for efficiency*
model, example, standard, ideal, paragon, perfect example, embodiment
FORMAL exemplar, epitome
2 SLOGAN, catchword, watchword, dictum, maxim, proverb, motto, saw, saying, precept, adage, aphorism
OLD nayword; (*Shakesp*) ayword
FORMAL apophthegm

C

cab *n*
1 *hire a cab*
taxi, taxicab, minicab, hackney carriage, four-wheeler, droshky, vettura
OLD fiacre, hansom, two-wheeler
OLD SLANG growler
2 *the cab in a lorry*
compartment, driver's compartment, cabin, quarters

cabal *n*
clique, faction, party, plotters, coalition, league, set, coterie, conclave junta, junto, camarilla

cabaret *n*
1 ENTERTAINMENT, show, performance, dancing, singing, comedy, acts, turns, variety
2 NIGHT CLUB, club, restaurant

cabin *n*
1 *a log cabin*
HUT, shack, shanty, lodge, chalet, cottage, shed, shelter; *Scot* bothy; refuge; *N Am* cabana
2 BERTH, quarters, sleeping quarters, compartment, room, stateroom, saloon, coach, cuddy, roundhouse

cabinet *n*
1 *a medicine cabinet*
cupboard, closet, dresser, case, store, chest, locker, console, secretaire, shrine, almirah, bahut, chiffonier, encoignure, varguño
2 *Cabinet ministers*
government, ministers, leadership, senate, administration, executive, Privy Council

cable *n, v*
♦ *n*
1 *tie with cable*
line, rope, cord, chain, guy, stay, hawser
2 *electric cable*
wire, flex, lead, coaxial, co-ax
3 *send a message by cable*
telegram, telegraph, Telemessage®, wire, fax, facsimile, e-mail
♦ *v*
send a telegram/telemessage/wire, send by telegraph, telegraph, wire, transmit, radio, fax, e-mail

cache *n*
store, accumulation, collection, fund, hoard, reserve, stock, stockpile, storehouse, supply, garner, treasure-store, hidden treasure
FORMAL repository
COLLOQ. stash

cachet *n*
estimation, prestige, reputation, approval, favour, esteem, distinction, eminence, status
COLLOQ. street cred

cack-handed *adj*
clumsy, awkward, unco-ordinated, ham-fisted, heavy-handed, unskilful, inept, bungling, blundering, ungraceful
COLLOQ. gawky, all thumbs

cackle *v, n*
♦ *v*
laugh loudly, laugh unpleasantly, chortle, chuckle, clack, gabble, gaggle, crow, giggle, snigger, titter; *Scot* keckle
♦ *n*
loud laugh, unpleasant laugh, chortle, chuckle, clack, gabble, crow, giggle, snigger, titter

cacophonous *adj*
raucous, loud, strident, grating, harsh, discordant, dissonant, inharmonious, jarring
FORMAL horrisonant
E3 harmonious, pleasant

cacophony *n*
raucousness, stridency, harshness, racket, din, discord, dissonance, disharmony, jarring, caterwauling, charivari
FORMAL horrisonance
E3 harmony

cad *n*
blackguard, scoundrel, rascal, rogue, villain, devil, knave, deceiver, miscreant, reprobate, wretch
COLLOQ. bleeder, blighter, bounder, rotter, stinker, rat, oik, swine, scumbag

cadaver *n*
dead body, body, corpse, remains, carcase
SLANG stiff

cadaverous *adj*
corpse-like, death-like, pale, ashen, wan, ghostly, gaunt, haggard, thin, emaciated, skeletal
COLLOQ. like death warmed up

cadence *n*
intonation, lilt, modulation, inflection, accent, rhythm, beat, stress, tempo, measure, metre, pattern, swing, pulse, throb, rate, fall, close

cadge *v*
scrounge, beg
COLLOQ. sponge, bum, mooch; *Aust* bot

cadre *n*
team, small group, squad, crew, corps, gang, band, set

café *n*
coffee shop, tea shop, tea room, coffee bar, cybercafé, cafeteria, snackbar, buffet, bistro, wine bar, brasserie, restaurant
SLANG caff, greasy spoon

cafeteria *n*
self-service café, self-service restaurant, self-service canteen, café, canteen, restaurant, buffet
SLANG caff

cage *n*
aviary, coop, hutch, enclosure, pen, pound, lock-up, corral, grate, corf, tumbler, mew; *Scot* cavie, keavie

caged *adj*
encaged, cooped up, shut up, confined, restrained, fenced in, imprisoned, impounded, locked up, mewed
OLD encaged
FORMAL incarcerated
E3 released, let out, free

cagey *adj*

careful, chary, cautious, discreet, guarded, non-committal, secretive, shrewd, wary, wily

FORMAL circumspect

COLLOQ. playing your cards close to your chest

E3 frank, indiscreet, open

cahoots

▪ **in cahoots**

colluding, in collusion, in league, in alliance, collaborating, conspiring

COLLOQ. hand in glove

cajole *v*

coax, persuade, get round, wheedle, flatter, blandish, blarney, tempt, lure, seduce, entice, beguile, mislead, dupe, wile, soothe, humbug, diddle; *Scot* cuittle, whilly, whillywha

OLD beflum

FORMAL inveigle

COLLOQ. sweet-talk, butter up, soft-soap, work yourself, chat up

SLANG moody

E3 bully, force, compel

cajolery *n*

cajolement, coaxing, persuasion, wheedling, flattery, blarney, enticement, inducement(s), beguilement, misleading, duping, wiles; *Scot* whillywha

FORMAL blandishments, inveiglement, inveigling

COLLOQ. sweet talk, soft soap

E3 bullying, force, compulsion

cake *n, v*

♦ *n*

1 *tea and cakes*

gateau, fancy, pastry, bun, pie, tart, flan

2 LUMP, mass, bar, slab, block, tablet, cube, chunk, loaf

♦ *v*

coat, cover, encrust, plaster, dry, harden, solidify, consolidate, coagulate, congeal, thicken

---

Kinds of cake and pastry include:

angel food cake	Danish pastry	Sachertorte
apple pie	drop scone	saffron cake
Bakewell tart	Dundee cake	Sally Lunn
banana cake	doughnut	sandwich cake
banana-nut cake	Eccles cake	savarin
Banbury cake	éclair	scone
bannock	flan	*N Am* shoofly pie
banoffee pie	fruitcake	simnel cake
Battenburg cake	gateau	sponge cake
birthday cake	Genoa cake	stollen
black bun	gingerbread	strawberry
Black Forest	hot-cross-bun	shortcake
gateau	lady's finger	strudel
brownie	*Aust* lamington	sultana cake
N Am bundt cake	lardy cake	Swiss roll
carrot cake	Madeira cake	tarte tatin
cheesecake	madeleine	teacake
Chelsea bun	marble cake	tipsy cake
cherry-pie	meringue	turnover
chocolate cake	mince pie	upside-down
Christmas cake	muffin	cake
coffee cake	pancake	Victoria sponge
cream cake	panettone	waffle
cream horn	plum-cake	wedding cake
cream puff	pound cake	yeast cake
crêpe	profiterole	Yule log
crumpet	queen cake	
custard slice	rock cake	

See also **dessert**.

---

calamitous *adj*

disastrous, catastrophic, ruinous, devastating, deadly, fatal, cataclysmic, dire, ghastly, dreadful, wretched, tragic, woeful, grievous

E3 good, fortunate, happy

calamity *n*

disaster, catastrophe, mishap, misadventure, mischance, misfortune, blow, adversity, scourge, reverse, trial, tribulation, affliction, distress, tragedy, ruin, downfall, trouble, woes, sword of Damocles

OLD ruth

E3 blessing, godsend

calculate *v*

1 WORK OUT, compute, count, enumerate, reckon (up), figure, determine, make, derive, measure, weigh, assess, rate, value, estimate, gauge; *N Am* work

OLD cast, cipher

2 *a plan calculated to make him jealous*

judge, consider, plan, intend, aim, design

Synonym nuances

sense 1

Work out is a general, widely used term to suggest going through something systematically to reach a solution: *how is holiday pay worked out?*; whereas **compute**, **count** and **enumerate** would all be used for the involvement of figures: *the index is computed from actual prices.* **Reckon** is more generally used to imply an addition based on estimates: *he reckoned he had spent £30,000*; while the less common **reckon up** suggests a more accurate totalling. The words **figure** and **make** also suggest a less exact calculation and that there might be an element of inaccuracy in the conclusions: *I make it ten pounds; what do you make it?*

Determine and **derive**, however, appropriately describe a more methodical approach and conclusions reached from what is already known: *interest rates are to be politically determined*; *he derived that this must indeed be the murder weapon.* **Rate**, **value**, **estimate**, **assess** and **gauge** share the idea of a calculation involving prediction and guesswork: *the significance of the market can be gauged from these tables.*

---

calculated *adj*

considered, deliberate, intended, intentional, planned, measured, well-judged, tactical, purposeful, wilful, premeditated

FORMAL purposed

E3 unintended, unplanned

calculating *adj*

crafty, cunning, sly, devious, scheming, designing, contriving, manipulative, sharp, shrewd, wily, Machiavellian

E3 artless, naive

calculation *n*

sum, computation, working-out, answer, result, arithmetic, figurework, reckoning, figuring, estimate, estimation, forecast, assessment, judgement, planning, deliberation

TECHNICAL mensuration, alligation, evolution, logistic

calibre *n*

1 DIAMETER, bore, gauge, size, measure

2 *candidates of the right calibre*

talent, gifts, strength, worth, merit, quality, character, ability, capacity, faculty, league, excellence, competence, endowments, stature, distinction

call *v, n*

♦ *v*

1 NAME, christen, baptize, title, entitle, dub, style, term, label, brand, describe as, designate, rename

FORMAL denominate

2 SHOUT, yell, exclaim, cry (out), scream, shriek, bellow, roar, bawl

3 TELEPHONE, phone (up), ring (up), contact, give someone a ring
COLLOQ. buzz, give someone a buzz, give someone a tinkle
4 call a doctor
ask to come in/round, ask for, send for, contact, order
FORMAL summon
5 call to collect the money
call in/round, drop in, pay a visit, stop by, come by
COLLOQ. pop in
6 call a meeting
invite, bid, assemble
FORMAL convene, summon
♦ n
1 CRY, exclamation, shout, yell, scream, shriek
2 VISIT, ring, summons, invitation
3 a telephone call
ring
COLLOQ. buzz, tinkle, bell
4 calls for his resignation
APPEAL, request, plea, order, command, claim, announcement, signal
5 there's no call for it
demand, market, need, occasion, cause, excuse, justification, reason, grounds, right, run
■ **call for**
1 FETCH, collect, pick up, go for
2 DEMAND, require, need, make necessary, necessitate, justify, involve, occasion, suggest, press for, push for
FORMAL entail, warrant
■ **call off**
cancel, drop, abandon, discontinue, break off, withdraw
FORMAL rescind, revoke
COLLOQ. scrub, shelve
■ **call on**
1 call on a friend
pay someone a (short) visit, visit, look in on, go and see
2 call on the government to resign
appeal, appeal to, ask, bid, ask, demand, urge, request, plead, press for
FORMAL request, summon, supplicate, entreat
■ **call up**
1 TELEPHONE, phone (up), ring (up), contact, give someone a ring
COLLOQ. buzz, give someone a buzz, give someone a tinkle
2 ENLIST, sign up, recruit, conscript, take on
3 CHOOSE, select, pick, settle on, invite
■ **on call**
ready, on standby, standing by, on duty

call girl n
prostitute, whore, harlot, loose woman, woman of the streets, street-walker, lady of the night
COLLOQ. hooker, hustler
SLANG tart

calling n
mission, vocation, career, profession, occupation, job, trade, business, line, line of business/work, work, employment, field, province, pursuit, métier

callous adj
heartless, hard-hearted, cold, cold-hearted, cold-blooded, harsh, tough, indifferent, uncaring, unsympathetic, unfeeling, insensitive, hardened, case-hardened, hard-bitten, hard as nails, stony, stony-hearted, iron-headed, thick-skinned, horny, seared
FORMAL obdurate, indurate, insensate, insensible
COLLOQ. hard-boiled
F3 kind, caring, sympathetic, sensitive
See Synonym nuances panel at **cold**.

callously adv
heartlessly, hard-heartedly, coldly, cold-bloodedly, harshly,

unsympathetically, unfeelingly, insensitively
F3 sympathetically, sensitively

callow adj
inexperienced, immature, naive, innocent, guileless, juvenile, puerile, raw, fledgling, uninitiated, unsophisticated, unfledged, untried
FORMAL jejune
COLLOQ. green, rookie
F3 experienced

calm adj, v, n
♦ adj
1 COMPOSED, self-possessed, self-controlled, collected, quiet, serene, cool, cool-headed, dispassionate, unemotional, impassive, unmoved, placid, sedate, poised, imperturbable, nerveless, phlegmatic, unexcitable, unpassionate, relaxed, unexcited, unruffled, unflustered, unperturbed, undisturbed, untroubled, unapprehensive, steady, even, on an even keel
FORMAL reposed
COLLOQ. laid-back, unflappable, cool as a cucumber; N Am supercool
2 calm waters/weather
smooth, still, waveless, windless, unclouded, mild, tranquil, serene, peaceful, quiet, undisturbed, restful, unclouded; Scot lown
F3 1 excitable, worried, anxious, upset **2** rough, wild, windy, stormy
♦ v
compose, soothe, relax, sedate, tranquillize, hush, lull, quieten, still, settle (down), allay, pacify, ease
FORMAL mollify, placate, appease, assuage, smooth, becalm, sleek
COLLOQ. cool down, simmer down, keep your head, lighten up, pour oil on troubled waters
F3 excite, worry, upset
♦ n
calmness, stillness, tranquillity, restfulness, composure, contentment, serenity, equanimity, peacefulness, peace, quiet, hush, lull, impassiveness, impassivity, presence of mind
FORMAL quietude, repose, placidity, sangfroid, ataraxia
COLLOQ. unflappability, cool
F3 storminess, restlessness, trouble, excitement

Synonym nuances
adjective sense 1
Composed and **collected** may be used quite widely of someone who is in control of their emotions, while **quiet** and, especially, **serene** and **sedate** go further by suggesting an inner peace. **Cool**, **unemotional**, **impassive** and **unmoved**, on the other hand, more accurately describe someone completely unaffected by emotion in a given circumstance, perhaps with the implication that it is an unnatural reaction; **dispassionate** further suggests a consequent lack of prejudice: his admirable dispassionate analysis of the issues.
Unexcitable, **unpassionate**, **imperturbable** and **nerveless**, however, are stronger terms to use, suggesting that someone is never likely to be upset or anxious. The term **phlegmatic** may be used appropriately of resignation or a lack of reaction: he is phlegmatic enough to accept his lot. **Steady** and **even** have the positive connotation of a calmness that is constant and dependable: his steady honesty.

---

calmly adv
steadily, on an even keel, unemotionally, phlegmatically, dispassionately, impassively

calumny n
slander, abuse, attack, backbiting, defamation, insult, libel, lying, misrepresentation, mud pie

FORMAL aspersion, denigration, obloquy, revilement, derogation, detraction, disparagement, vilification, vituperation, smear
SLANG slagging-off

camaraderie n

brotherhood, brotherliness, companionship, comradeship, *esprit de corps*, fellowship, friendship, fraternization, good fellowship, sociability, closeness, affinity, intimacy, togetherness

camera

Types of camera include:

advanced photo system (APS)	film	single-lens reflex (SLR)
automatic	folding reflex	sliding box
bellows	half-plate	sound
binocular	Instamatic®	Steadicam®
box Brownie®	large-format	still
camcorder	miniature	stereo
camera obscura	subminiature	Super 8®
cine	panoramic	surveillance
cinematographic	pinhole	twin-lens reflex (TLR)
compact	plate	TV
daguerreotype	quarter-plate	video
digital	point-and-press	view
disc	Polaroid®	Webcam
disposable	press	wet-plate
dry-plate	reflex	
	security	

See also **photographic**.

Parts of a camera include:

accessory shoe	flash setting	program card
AF lenses	focal plane shutter	program reset button
aperture	focus control/ setting	rangefinder window
aperture setting control	focusing hood	reflex viewer
autofocus (AF)	focusing ring	registration pin
autofocus sensor	frame counter	release button
automatic focusing system	function adjustment button	rewind handle/ crank
battery chamber	function selector key	shutter
blind		shutter release
cable release	iris diaphragm	shutter speed control
card door	leaf shutter	shutter/film speed indicator
card on/off key	lens	
card window	lens cap	spool
compact lens	lens release	spool knob
compound lens	light control	take-up reel/ spool
data panel/ display	long-focus lens	telephoto lens
diaphragm	magazine	viewfinder eyepiece
exposure meter	medium focal-length lens	viewfinder
exposure mode button	meter cell	viewing lens
film advance/ transport	mirror	wide-angle lens
film gate	mirror lens	zoom lens
film holder	mirror shutter	
fisheye lens	object lens	
flash contact	pentaprism	

camouflage n, v

♦ *n*

disguise, guise, masquerade, mask, cloak, screen, blind, front, cover, cover-up, protective colouring, concealment, deception, façade, maskirovka

♦ *v*

disguise, mask, cloak, veil, screen, cover, cover up, conceal, hide, obscure
Ƹ uncover, reveal

camp¹ n, v

♦ *n*

1 *a Scout camp*
campsite, camping-site, camping-ground, encampment, tents, bivouac
OLD leaguer
2 *the union camp*
side, faction, group, party, section, set, crowd, caucus, clique
♦ *v*
pitch tents, pitch camp, set up camp, sleep outdoors, bivouac, tent
OLD gypsy, outlie
FORMAL encamp
COLLOQ. rough it
Ƹ break camp, strike camp, decamp, rise

camp² adj

camp behaviour
affected, artificial, campy, exaggerated, mannered, ostentatious, posturing, theatrical, effeminate, homosexual
COLLOQ. over the top, poncy
SLANG (*offensive*) queer, queeny

campaign n, v

♦ *n*
crusade, movement, promotion, drive, push, course of action, strategy, offensive, attack, battle, expedition, operation, war
OLD journey
COLLOQ. blitz
♦ *v*
crusade, promote, push, drive, advocate, lobby, canvass, work, fight, strive, struggle, battle, attack

campaigner n

crusader, advocate, champion, promoter, activist, enthusiast, reformer, zealot, fighter

camp-follower n

hanger-on, henchman, lackey, toady

can n

tin, container, receptacle, canister, jar, jerrycan, pail

canal n

1 *the Grand Union canal*
waterway, watercourse, navigation, channel, ditch, trench, moat, foss, zanja
2 *the alimentary canal*
tube, channel, passage, duct

cancel v

1 *cancel a concert*
call off, abort, abandon, drop, postpone
COLLOQ. scrap, scrub, shelve, axe, wash out, wipe, kill
2 *cancel a reservation/debt*
abolish, annul, quash, stop, break off, repeal, delete, erase, obliterate, undo, write off, cross out, red-line, eliminate, dissolve, override, strike out, withdraw, declare off
TECHNICAL adeem
FORMAL discontinue, countermand, rescind, revoke, nullify, invalidate, retract, abrogate, vitiate
SLANG nix
▪ **cancel out**
offset, compensate, make up for, redeem, counterbalance, balance, neutralize, counteract, nullify

cancellation n

calling-off, abandoning, abandonment, abolition, dropping, stopping, deletion, elimination, neutralization, quashing, repeal
FORMAL annulment, revocation, invalidation, nullifying
COLLOQ. shelving, scrubbing

cancer n

1 TUMOUR, growth, malignancy, malignant growth
TECHNICAL carcinoma
COLLOQ. Big C

2 EVIL, blight, canker, pestilence, sickness, disease, plague, scourge, corruption, rot

candelabrum *n*
candlestick, menorah, lampadary

candid *adj*
frank, open, truthful, honest, sincere, forthright, straightforward, ingenuous, guileless, simple, plain, plain-spoken, clear, unequivocal, blunt, outspoken, round, liberal, heart-to-heart
F3 guarded, evasive, devious

candidate *n*
1 *candidates for a job*
applicant, aspirant, contender, contestant, competitor, seeker, runner, possibility, nominee
2 *candidates for an exam*
entrant

candidly *adv*
frankly, openly, truthfully, honestly, sincerely, forthrightly, straightforwardly, ingenuously, guilelessly, simply, plainly, clearly, unequivocally, bluntly, outspokenly, roundly, liberally
F3 guardedly, evasively

candle *n*
taper, tallow candle, cerge, wax light, torch, dip, amandine, bougie, shammes

candour *n*
frankness, openness, truthfulness, honesty, plain-dealing, sincerity, forthrightness, straightforwardness, directness, brusqueness, ingenuousness, guilelessness, naivety, artlessness, simplicity, plainness, unequivocalness, bluntness, outspokenness, liberality, *franchise*
F3 guardedness, evasiveness, deviousness

candy *n*
sweets, confectionery, chocolates, toffees

cane *n*
stick, staff, crook, rod, walking-stick, switch, swish, tickler, alpenstock, rattan, supplejack, whangee, swagger-stick
OLD jambee

canker *n*
1 EVIL, blight, cancer, pestilence, sickness, disease, plague, scourge, bane, corrosion, corruption, rot
2 *canker in an animal's ear*
sore, ulcer, boil, infection, lesion

cannabis *n*
marijuana, hemp, hashish, bhang
COLLOQ. dope, ganja, grass, hash, pot, spliff, puff, tea, kef, wacky baccy
SLANG blow, weed, skunk, punk, leaf

cannibal *n*
people-eater, man-eater
TECHNICAL anthropophagite
OLD (*Shakesp*) anthropophaginian

cannibalism *n*
man-eating, people-eating
TECHNICAL anthropophagy, endophagy, exophagy

cannibalistic *adj*
man-eating, people-eating, Thyestean
TECHNICAL anthropophagous, endophagous, exophagous

cannily *adv*
shrewdly, acutely, sharply, astutely, cleverly, knowingly, skilfully, subtly

cannon *n*
gun, mortar, field gun, howitzer, artillery, battery, ordnance, falcon
OLD basilisk, bombard, carronade, chamber, culverin, demi-culverin, monkey, murderer, Quaker, saker, serpentine, stern-chaser, zumbooruk
COLLOQ. big gun
OLD SLANG barker

⚠ cannon or **canon**?
A *cannon* is a large gun. A *canon* is a Christian priest who helps to run the work of a cathedral, and also a general rule or belief: *the canons of literary taste*.

cannonade *n*
barrage, bombardment, shelling, volley, broadside, pounding, salvo

canny *adj*
shrewd, acute, sharp, astute, careful, cautious, prudent, clever, knowing, skilful, sly, subtle, wise, worldly-wise, artful; *Scot* pawky, wice
FORMAL circumspect, perspicacious, judicious, sagacious
COLLOQ. no flies on someone
F3 foolish, imprudent

canoe *n*
dugout, kayak, monoxylon, montaria, piragua, woodskin

canon *n*
1 *a cathedral canon*
prebendary, clergyman, vicar, priest, minister, reverend, residentiary, vice-dean
2 *the canons of literary taste*
principle, rule, regulation, statute, criterion, standard, law, precept, dictate, yardstick, line, brocard
OLD square, squire

canonical *adj*
authorized, recognized, accepted, sanctioned, approved, authoritative, orthodox, regular

---

Names of canonical hours include:

matins	terce	vespers
lauds	sext	compline
prime	none	

---

canonize *v*
beatify, saint, declare to be a saint, sanctify, bless
OLD besaint

canopy *n*
awning, cover, covering, shade, shelter, sunshade, umbrella, tester, tilt, baldachin, tabernacle, dais, chuppah, cloth of state, marquise
OLD estate, state, pavilion, hearse

cant *n*
1 *insincere cant*
insincerity, hypocrisy, pretentiousness, sanctimoniousness, snivel, snuffle
2 *underworld cant*
argot, jargon, lingo, slang, vernacular, rogues'/thieves' Latin

cantankerous *adj*
irritable, irascible, grumpy, crusty, testy, bad-tempered, quick-tempered, ill-humoured, cross, peevish, difficult, perverse, contrary, quarrelsome; *Scot & Irish* carnaptious; *N Am* ornery
COLLOQ. crabbed, crabby, crotchety, grouchy
F3 good-natured, pleasant, easy-going

canteen *n*
cafeteria, restaurant, snackbar, café, buffet, refectory, commissary

canter *n, v*
◆ *n*
amble, trot, jog, jogtrot, lope, gallop, run, tittup; *S Afr* tripple
OLD false gallop
◆ *v*
amble, trot, jog, jogtrot, lope, gallop, run; *S Afr* tripple

canvass v
1 ELECTIONEER, agitate, campaign, solicit votes, ask for votes, seek votes, poll, drum up support
2 EXAMINE, inspect, find out, scrutinize, study, scan, investigate, explore, survey, examine, inquire into, analyse, sift, evaluate, poll, discuss, debate

canyon n
gorge, ravine, gully, valley, chasm, abyss; N Am cañada

cap n, v
◆ n
1 HAT, bonnet; Scot bunnet
See panel at **hat**.
2 LID, top, cover, stopper, plug, bung, ferrule
◆ v
1 *cap someone's story*
exceed, excel, surpass, transcend, better, beat, outdo, outstrip, outshine, eclipse, go one better than
2 *mountains capped with snow*
crown, top, cover, coat
3 *cap council spending*
limit, restrict, curb, restrain, control

capability n
ability, capacity, faculty, power, potential, means, facility, competence, qualification, skill, skilfulness, accomplishment, proficiency, talent, aptitude, efficiency
☒ inability, incompetence

🛈 **capability** or **ability**?
See panel at **ability**.

---

capable adj
1 *a capable person*
able, competent, efficient, qualified, experienced, accomplished, skilful, adept, proficient, gifted, talented, masterly, clever, intelligent, smart, businesslike
2 *capable of winning*
fitted, suited, apt to, liable to, disposed to, inclined to, tending to, having the inclination/tendency to, allowing, needing
☒ 1 incompetent, useless 2 incapable

capably adv
competently, ably, efficiently, skilfully, proficiently, cleverly, intelligently, adeptly
☒ incompetently

capacious adj
ample, big, vast, wide, broad, huge, large, roomy, sizable, spacious, comfortable, comprehensive, expansive, extensive, generous, liberal, substantial, elephantine
OLD (Shakesp) womby
FORMAL commodious, voluminous
☒ cramped, small

capacity n
1 CAPABILITY, ability, faculty, power, potential, competence, proficiency, efficiency, skill, gift, talent, genius, cleverness, intelligence, aptitude, resources, readiness
2 VOLUME, space, room, size, dimensions, proportions, magnitude, extent, largeness, compass, range, scope
3 *in her capacity as president*
role, function, position, office, post, appointment, job

cape[1] n
wear a cape
cloak, shawl, wrap, mantle, robe, poncho, pelisse, pelerine, coat

cape[2] n
the Cape of Good Hope
headland, head, promontory, point, ness, neck, tongue, peninsula

caper v, n
◆ v
cavort, frisk, frolic, gambol, bounce, bound, dance, hop, jump, leap, romp, skip, spring
◆ n
antic, escapade, high jinks, jest, lark, mischief, prank, stunt, jape, affair, business
COLLOQ. N Am dido

capital n, adj
◆ n
1 *need capital to expand the business*
funds, finance, principal, money, cash, savings, investment(s), wealth, means, wherewithal, resources, assets, liquid assets, property, stock, reserves
2 *the capital of France*
main city, most important city, administrative centre, seat of government
3 *write in capitals*
block letter, block capital, capital letter, upper-case letter
FORMAL majuscule, uncial
◆ adj
1 PRINCIPAL, important, leading, primary, prime, main, major, cardinal, central, chief, first, foremost
2 *a capital offence*
serious, punishable by death
☒ 1 minor, unimportant 2 minor

capitalism n
private enterprise, free enterprise, private ownership, laissez-faire

capitalist n
banker, financier, investor, moneyman, tycoon, magnate, mogul, person of means, plutocrat
OLD moneyer
COLLOQ. moneybags, money-spinner
SLANG fat cat

capitalize
■ **capitalize on**
take advantage of, profit from, make the most of, exploit
COLLOQ. cash in on

capitulate v
surrender, yield, give in, give up, relent, back down, submit, succumb
COLLOQ. throw in the towel/sponge

capitulation n
surrender, yielding, giving-in, giving-up, relenting, backing-down, submission, succumbing

caprice n
whim, fad, fancy, impulse, whimsy, fantasy, notion, quirk, vagary, vapour, fickleness, fitfulness, inconstancy, humour, freak
OLD megrim, spleen

capricious adj
changeable, inconstant, mercurial, erratic, arbitrary, wayward, fickle, uncertain, unpredictable, variable, fitful, petulant, perverse, fanciful, fantastic, whimsical, freakish, impulsive, odd, queer, quirky; Scot capernoity, kittle
OLD humorous, wanton
☒ sensible, steady

capsize v
overturn, turn over, turn turtle, invert, keel over, tip over, roll over, upset, purl; dialect whemmle

capsule n
1 *a capsule of medicine*
pill, tablet, caplet, lozenge, receptacle, container

2 *a seed capsule*
shell, sheath, pod
3 *a space capsule*
craft, module, probe

captain *n, v*
♦ *n*
officer, commander, master, skipper, pilot, head, chief, leader, commodore, shipmaster, master-mariner, patron, patroon, old man, cid
OLD (*Spenser*) capitayn; ritt-master, protospatharius
COLLOQ. boss
SLANG owner
♦ *v*
lead, command, skipper, control, direct, manage, supervise, be in charge of

caption *n*
heading, note, title, legend, wording, inscription, underline

captious *adj*
carping, critical, quibbling, nit-picking, hypercritical, niggling, hair-splitting, peevish

captivate *v*
charm, enchant, bewitch, beguile, fascinate, delight, enthral, hypnotize, mesmerize, lure, allure, seduce, win, get, attract, enamour, infatuate, enrapture, enthral, take by storm, dazzle
E3 repel, disgust, appal

captivating *adj*
attractive, charming, fascinating, beautiful, enchanting, bewitching, beguiling, delightful, catching, taking, enthralling, alluring, seductive, winsome, dazzling
E3 ugly, unattractive

captive *n, adj*
♦ *n*
prisoner, hostage, slave, detainee, internee, convict, jailbird
♦ *adj*
imprisoned, caged, confined, restricted, secure, locked up/away, shut up, interned, detained, held in custody, restrained, enchained, enslaved, ensnared, in bondage, subject
OLD (*Spenser*) caitive
FORMAL incarcerated
E3 free, liberated

captivity *n*
custody, detention, imprisonment, internment, confinement, restraint, constraint, bondage, duress, slavery, enslavement, exile
OLD endurance
FORMAL incarceration, servitude
E3 freedom, liberation

captor *n*
guard, custodian, warder, keeper, jailor, incarcerator

capture *v, n*
♦ *v*
1 *capture a prisoner*
catch, trap, entrap, hunt down, snare, ensnare, net, land, occupy, take, take possession of, seize, arrest, apprehend, imprison, take prisoner, recapture, pick up, carry, run down, rush, secure, win, mop up
COLLOQ. nab, collar, nick, cop
SLANG snaffle, snabble
2 *capture a mood*
encapsulate, represent, record, express, reproduce, embrace
♦ *n*
catching, trapping, taking, taking captive, taking prisoner, seizure, arrest, imprisonment
COLLOQ. nabbing, collaring, nicking

Synonym nuances
verb sense 1
Trap and **entrap** contain a suggestion that a plan or even trickery has been involved in capture; **snare** and **ensnare** are similar, but with the added notion of getting caught up in something restrictive: *they were snared in a police sting; they became ensnared in the rush-hour traffic.* The word **net** has literal associations: *netted fish*; along with **land**, it is also often used in the context of a total taken, or getting something worthwhile despite competition: *the raid netted him £500 million; he landed a part in the musical.*

The terms **occupy, take** and **seize** are appropriate when an element of force has been used; **rush** would suggest greater force and speed.

The term **pick up** has an element of casualness about it: *the railways picked up some custom from the bus strike.* **Hunt down** and **run down**, however, would be used when capture has involved a lengthy pursuit or an exhaustive chase.

The term **secure** implies that possession is assured: *the team secured victory early in the game*, whereas **win** is usually used to suggest that something has been gained against the odds or in competition: *human rights can be won.*

---

car *n*
automobile, motor car, motor vehicle, motor, vehicle
OLD horseless carriage

Types of car include:

all-roader	jeep	saloon
banger	Land Rover®	*N Am & Aust*
Beetle	*colloq.* limo	sedan
bubble-car	limousine	shooting brake
buggy	Mini®	sports car
cab	minivan	sports-utility
cabriolet	multi-purpose	vehicle (SUV)
convertible	vehicle (or MPV	*N Am, Aust & NZ*
coupé	or people	station wagon
estate	carrier)	taxi
fastback	off-roader	veteran car
four-wheel drive	panda car	vintage car
hatchback	patrol car	
jalopy	Range Rover®	

See also **motor vehicle**.

---

carafe *n*
bottle, decanter, flagon, flask, jug, pitcher

caravan *n*
1 MOBILE HOME, van, camper van, Dormobile®; *N Am* trailer, motor home, recreational vehicle, RV, Winnebago®
2 *a caravan of traders crossing the desert*
convoy, line, group, train, cafila

carbuncle *n*
boil, inflammation, bunion, lump, bump, pimple, sore, blister, anthrax

carcase *n*
1 *the carcase of an animal*
body, dead body, corpse, cadaver, remains
2 *the carcase of a building*
shell, structure, framework, hulk, skeleton

card
▪ **on the cards**
likely, probable, possible, being a strong possibility, looking like, looking as if
COLLOQ. the chances are

cardinal *adj*

chief, main, principal, fundamental, basic, greatest, highest, important, key, leading, paramount, pre-eminent, primary, prime, central, essential, first, foremost, capital

care *n, v*

♦ *n*

1 *handle with care*

carefulness, caution, prudence, forethought, watchfulness, vigilance, pains, meticulousness, accuracy, consideration

OLD attendance

FORMAL circumspection

2 *children need care*

looking-after, concern, attention, tending, minding, protection, watching-over, heed, regard, consideration, interest

3 *in their care*

keeping, safekeeping, custody, guardianship, protection, ward, charge, responsibility, control, supervision, tutelage

4 WORRY, anxiety, stress, strain, pressure, responsibility, burden, concern, trouble, distress, affliction, fear, disquiet

FORMAL tribulation, vexation

COLLOQ. hang-up

E₃ 1 carelessness, recklessness **2** carelessness, thoughtlessness, inattention, neglect

♦ *v*

worry, mind, bother, be concerned, be interested

COLLOQ. give a damn

E₃ neglect, ignore, be indifferent; *slang* not give a hoot/hang/damn/toss, not give a monkey's, not give a tinker's cuss/brass farthing

■ **care for**

1 LOOK AFTER, take care of, nurse, tend, mind, watch over, protect, provide for, minister to, attend, tend, maintain

2 BE FOND OF, feel affection for, love, be in love with, be keen on, be close to, enjoy, delight in, cherish

3 *Would you care for a cup of tea?*

like, want, desire

career *n, v*

♦ *n*

vocation, calling, life-work, life, occupation, pursuit, profession, trade, job, employment, métier, livelihood

♦ *v*

rush, dash, tear, hurtle, race, run, gallop, speed, shoot, bolt, whang

carefree *adj*

unworried, untroubled, unconcerned, easy-going, blithe, breezy, happy-go-lucky, cheery, light-hearted, cheerful, happy, halcyon, rollicking, fancy-free, thoughtless, irresponsible, debonair

FORMAL insouciant, nonchalant

COLLOQ. laid-back

E₃ worried, anxious, troubled, distressed, despondent

careful *adj*

1 CAUTIOUS, aware, wary, chary, vigilant, watchful, alert, attentive, mindful, heedful, prudent, discreet, tactful, guarded, softly-softly

OLD (*Spenser*) heedy

FORMAL circumspect, judicious

2 METICULOUS, painstaking, conscientious, diligent, assiduous, scrupulous, fastidious, rigorous, thorough, detailed, showing great attention to detail, close, deliberate, methodical, systematic, particular, accurate, precise, thoughtful; *dialect* eyeful

FORMAL punctilious, solicitous

3 *careful with money*

prudent, thrifty, economical, sensible, wise, penny-wise, frugal, sparing, mean, miserly, niggardly, close-fisted, close-handed, fast-handed

FORMAL parsimonious

COLLOQ. tight, tight-fisted, hard-fisted, stingy, penny-pinching

E₃ 1 careless, inattentive, thoughtless, reckless **2** careless **3** extravagant, wasteful

---

Synonym nuances
sense 2

Many of the synonyms are approving in tone. **Meticulous** is a fairly positive term to describe an extreme attention to detail; **painstaking** is similar in meaning but perhaps a little more neutral in tone: *painstaking precision.* The terms **conscientious**, **diligent**, **assiduous** and **scrupulous** all describe thoroughness, often where it arises from a sense of duty, and again would suggest a favourable view: *assiduous planning brings results.* **Fastidious**, **rigorous** and **thorough** also describe an exacting application, but more neutrally: *you must fold it with fastidious care.*

   Detailed and **close** have the emphasis on taking note of minutiae: *detailed analysis of the facts.* To emphasize that something is carried out in a rational sequence you might prefer to use **deliberate**, **methodical** and **systematic**: *you should record the findings on a more methodical basis.* **Particular** has connotations of fussiness, but **precise** and **accurate** are more suggestive of a desirable level of correctness: *precise in detail.*

   To use **thoughtful** would shift the emphasis back to attentiveness in practice, rather than the accuracy of the results: *a clear, thoughtful exploration of the theory.*

---

carefully *adv*

1 METICULOUSLY, painstakingly, conscientiously, diligently, assiduously, scrupulously, fastidiously, rigorously, thoroughly, with great attention to detail, closely, deliberately, methodically, systematically, accurately, precisely, thoughtfully

FORMAL punctilious, solicitous

2 CAUTIOUSLY, warily, charily, vigilantly, watchfully, attentively, mindfully, heedfully, prudently, discreetly, tactfully, guardedly

FORMAL circumspectly, judiciously

E₃ 1 carelessly **2** carelessly, thoughtlessly, recklessly

careless *adj*

1 UNTHINKING, thoughtless, inattentive, inconsiderate, uncaring, unconcerned, heedless, incautious, unmindful, forgetful, remiss, negligent, absent-minded, irresponsible, reckless, indiscreet, tactless, unguarded, regardless; *Scot* untenty

OLD secure

2 *careless work*

inaccurate, messy, untidy, disorganized, disorderly, neglectful, slack, lax, slipshod, slapdash, hasty, perfunctory, cursory, superficial, offhand, casual, shoddy

COLLOQ. sloppy

3 *careless charm*

casual, easy-going, carefree, unworried, untroubled, simple, artless, breezy, light-hearted, cheerful, happy-go-lucky

FORMAL insouciant, nonchalant

COLLOQ. laid-back, happy as a sandboy; *N Am* happy as a clam

E₃ 1 thoughtful, careful **2** careful, accurate, meticulous

Synonym nuances
sense 2

Inaccurate describes the introduction of error through carelessness, although it is not strongly critical; on the other hand, **messy** and **untidy**, along with **disorganized** and **disorderly**, are marked by disapproval. Other inherently critical terms are **slack**, **lax** and **slipshod**, which strongly suggest a lack of care and precision: *he was becoming slipshod in his editing;* whilst both slapdash and hasty could be used of something that has been done too quickly: *the book is full of slapdash theories*. Less marked terms to use include **perfunctory** or **cursory**, which suggest that something has been completed with the minimum effort. **Superficial** similarly implies lack of depth or exertion, while **offhand** and **casual** also suggest something undertaken without due consideration: *an offhand reply*. More critical, however, is **shoddy**, which is very strongly marked by disapproval of something badly done: *we will not tolerate shoddy service*.

carelessly *adv*
1 *a carelessly planned project*
hastily, perfunctorily, cursorily, superficially, offhandedly, casually, shoddily
COLLOQ. sloppily
2 *he spoke carelessly*
unthinkingly, thoughtlessly, inattentively, inconsiderately, uncaringly, unconcernedly, heedlessly, incautiously, unmindfully, forgetfully, remissly, negligently, absent-mindedly, irresponsibly, recklessly, indiscreetly, tactlessly, unguardedly
1 careful, accurately, meticulously **2** thoughtfully, carefully

caress *v, n*
♦ *v*
stroke, pet, fondle, cuddle, hug, embrace, kiss, touch, rub, nuzzle, bill
COLLOQ. canoodle, grope; *N Am* lallygag
SLANG feel up, touch up
♦ *n*
stroke, touch, pat, fondle, cuddle, hug, embrace, kiss, petting, butterfly kiss, endearment
COLLOQ. slap and tickle

caretaker *n, adj*
♦ *n*
janitor, porter, watchman, keeper, custodian, curator, warden, superintendent, concierge, steward, ostiary, doorkeeper, verger, sexton, dvornik, shammes
♦ *adj*
acting, temporary, provisional, substitute, short-term, fill-in, stand-in, pro tem
permanent

careworn *adj*
tired, weary, worn, worn-out, exhausted, fatigued, gaunt, haggard, anxious, worried
lively, sprightly

cargo *n*
freight, load, payload, haul, lading, tonnage, shipment, consignment, contents, goods, merchandise, baggage

caricature *n, v*
♦ *n*
cartoon, parody, lampoon, burlesque, satire, mimicry, imitation, representation, distortion, travesty
COLLOQ. send-up, take-off
♦ *v*
parody, mock, ridicule, satirize, mimic, distort, exaggerate
COLLOQ. send up, take off

caring *adj*
kind, kind-hearted, good-natured, helpful, thoughtful, compassionate, sympathetic, warm, tender-hearted, tender, benevolent, friendly, loving, affectionate, devoted, fond, philanthropic, altruistic
uncaring, inconsiderate

carnage *n*
bloodshed, bloodbath, butchery, slaughter, killing, murder, mass murder, massacre, genocide, ethnic cleansing, holocaust

carnal *adj*
sensual, sexual, erotic, fleshly, physical, human, natural, animal, bodily, impure, lascivious, lecherous, lewd, licentious, lustful
TECHNICAL belly
FORMAL corporeal, libidinous
chaste, pure, spiritual

carnival *n*
festival, fiesta, gala, jamboree, fête, fair, holiday, jubilee, celebration, merrymaking, revelry, *Mardi Gras, Fasching*
SLANG *N Am* carny

carnivorous *adj*
meat-eating
TECHNICAL creophagous, zoophagous

carol *n*
Christmas song, noel, song, hymn, strain, wassail, chorus, noel
OLD carrel

carouse *v*
make merry, revel, drink, drink freely, party, celebrate, quaff, roister, wassail, spree; *dialect* birl
FORMAL imbibe
SLANG booze

carousing *n*
celebrating, drinking, merrymaking, partying, compotation
OLD mallemaroking

carp *v*
complain, criticize, censure, reproach, find faults, nag, quibble, go on at; *Aust* have a shot at
OLD yerk, pinch
FORMAL ultracrepidate
COLLOQ. knock, nit-pick
praise, compliment

carpenter *n*
woodworker, joiner, cabinet-maker; *Scot* wright
SLANG chips, chippy

carpet *n, v*
♦ *n*
1 *fit a new carpet*
floor-covering, covering, mat, rug, matting, Axminster, Aubusson, Wilton, Kidderminster, kali, kilim, Persian carpet, moquette, Bessarabian, Kirman, Brussels
2 *a carpet of leaves*
layer, blanket, covering, bed
♦ *v*
cover, spread, blanket, dress, clothe, coat, wrap, overlay, encase, cake

carping *n*
complaining, criticizing, fault-finding, nagging, quibbling
COLLOQ. nit-picking

carriage *n*
1 COACH, wagon, cab, car, vehicle, turnout, equipage, trap, buggy, hackney, stagecoach; *Scot* hurly-hacket, clatch; *vettura, voiture*
OLD diligent, dilly, job
See panel on next page
2 POSTURE, bearing, air, manner, attitude, stance, presence, guise, behaviour, conduct, poise, set, tenue
OLD (*Shakesp & Spenser*) portance
FORMAL deportment, demeanour, mien, port
3 CARRYING, conveyance, transport, transportation, delivery, freight, truckage, postage, porterage

carrier *n*
bearer, conveyor, delivery-person, roundsperson, messenger, porter, runner, transmitter, transporter, vehicle, vector; *dialect* tranter

---

Types of carriage include:

barouche	caroche	dogcart	hansom	ricksha	T-cart
berlin	carryall	drag	herdic	rockaway	tilbury
britzka	chaise	dray	jump-seat	sociable	victoria
brougham	chariot	droshky	landau	spider phaeton	vis-à-vis
cabriolet	clarence	ekka	phaeton	stanhope	wagonette
calash	coupé	four-in hand	pillbox	sulky	
cariole	désobligeante	gig	post chaise	surrey	

---

carry *v*

1 BRING, convey, transport, haul, move, transfer, relay, release, take, drive, fetch, shift, conduct, pipe, deliver, hand over
COLLOQ. lug, cart, hump, tote
2 BEAR, shoulder, support, underpin, maintain, hold (up), uphold, sustain, suffer, stand, take someone's weight
3 *carry a disease*
transmit, pass on, be infected with
4 *the proposal was carried*
pass, vote for, vote in favour, accept, approve, adopt, authorize, ratify, sanction
5 *she carries herself well*
bear, behave, hold, acquit, act
FORMAL comport
6 *drug-smuggling carries a risk*
bear, involve, have (as a consequence), lead to, mean
FORMAL entail
7 *the newspaper carried the story*
cover, contain, display, show, present, communicate, print, publish, release, broadcast
FORMAL disseminate
8 *carry several brands*
stock, keep in stock, sell, retail, have, have for sale
9 *the crime carries a year's imprisonment*
have, lead to, result in, present, show
10 *her voice carried far*
be heard, be audible, reach, travel

■ **carry off**
1 *carry a project off*
achieve, complete, succeed in
COLLOQ. crack
2 *carry off a prize*
win, gain, secure, pick up
COLLOQ. come away with, land, net

■ **carry on**
1 CONTINUE, proceed, last, endure, maintain, go on, keep (on), keep up, persist, persevere, progress, return to, resume, restart
2 *carry on a business*
operate, run, manage, conduct, engage in, administer
3 *children carrying on*
misbehave, behave foolishly
COLLOQ. mess around, play up
4 *carrying on with a colleague at work*
have an affair, be involved
COLLOQ. play around
E3 **1** stop, finish **3** behave (well)

■ **carry out**
do, perform, undertake, discharge, conduct, execute, implement, fulfil, accomplish, achieve, realize, bring off, put into effect/operation/practice
FORMAL effect
COLLOQ. deliver (the goods)

■ **get carried away**
become excited, become overexcited, lose your self-control
COLLOQ. lose it

carry-on *n*
fuss, bother, trouble, commotion, stir
COLLOQ. hassle, to-do, hoo-ha, flap, kerfuffle

cart *n, v*
♦ *n*
barrow, handcart, wheelbarrow, wagon, truck, dray, float, cariole, gill, jill, hackery, pram, tumbrel; *dialect* shandry; *Welsh* gambo; *N Am* gurney; *Aust* furby
OLD car; *N Am* democrat
♦ *v*
move, convey, transport, haul, bear, carry, transfer, shift; *dialect* jag, lead
COLLOQ. lug, hump, tote

carton *n*
box, packet, pack, case, container, package, parcel, tub

cartoon *n*
1 *newspaper cartoons*
sketch, drawing, picture, bubble, balloon, caricature, strip cartoon, parody, lampoon, burlesque
COLLOQ. send-up, take-off
2 *watch cartoons on TV*
comic strip, animation, animated film, *fumetto*

cartridge *n*
cassette, canister, cylinder, tube, container, case, capsule, shell, torpedo, magazine, round, charge

carve *v*
1 *carve meat*
cut (up), slice, chop, hack, unlace, truncheon
OLD dismember, kerve
2 *carve stone*
sculpt, sculpture, shape, form, fashion, mould, hew, cut, whittle, chisel, chip
OLD entail
3 *carve a design*
etch, engrave, write, incise, notch, indent
OLD sculp, insculp

■ **carve up**
divide, share (out), separate, partition, parcel out, distribute, split (up)

carving *n*
bust, incision, sculpture, statue, statuette, model, cut, knotwork
TECHNICAL dendroglyph, lithoglyph, petroglyph, mezzo-relievo, tondo
Related adjective: glyptic

cascade *n, v*
♦ *n*
rush, gush, outpouring, flood, deluge, torrent, avalanche, cataract, waterfall, fall, falls, fountain, chute, shower, trickle
♦ *v*
rush, gush, surge, flood, overflow, spill, tumble, fall, descend, shower, pour, plunge, pitch

case[1] *n*
1 OCCURRENCE, circumstances, context, state, condition, position, situation, occasion, event, specimen, example, instance, illustration, point
FORMAL contingency
2 LAWSUIT, suit, trial, proceedings, action, process, cause, argument, dispute
3 *a doctor's case*
patient, invalid, victim, client
4 *a murder case*
crime, investigation, inquiry, incident, affair

5 *argue the case against the death penalty*
evidence, reasoning, argument, grounds, defence

case² *n*

1 CONTAINER, receptacle, holder, trunk, crate, box, carton, casket, chest, cabinet, showcase, casing, canister, cartridge, shell, capsule, sheath, cover, jacket, wrapper
2 SUITCASE, briefcase, vanity-case, bag, holdall, portmanteau, valise, overnight bag, flight bag, hand luggage, travel bag, attaché case, portfolio, trunk

cash *n, v*

♦ *n*
1 *pay by cash*
money, hard money, ready money, banknotes, notes, coins, change, legal tender, currency, hard currency, bullion
2 *have no cash for a holiday*
funds, resources, capital, finance, wherewithal
SLANG loot, readies, ready, megabucks, dough, dosh, bread, lolly, spondulicks, brass, loot, gravy, greens, shekels, moolah, greenies, scratch, smash, stumpy; *Aust & NZ* Oscar
OLD SLANG blunt, rhino
♦ *v*
exchange, realize, liquidate, change, turn into cash, encash

cashier¹ *n*

a bank cashier
clerk, bank clerk, teller, treasurer, bursar, purser, banker, accountant, financial controller, checker

cashier² *v*

be cashiered from the army
discharge, dismiss, drum out, expel, break, discard, throw out, get rid of
COLLOQ. sack, give someone the boot, unfrock

casing *n*

cover, covering, wrapping, jacket, envelope, shell, sheath, sheathing, trunking, protection, housing, core
TECHNICAL cowling, binnacle

cask *n*

barrel, tun, keg, firkin, vat, tub, butt, casket, barrico, octave, pin, pipe, tierce, wood
OLD hogshead, kilderkin, leaguer, puncheon

casket *n*

1 *keep jewels in a casket*
box, case, chest, coffer, jewel-box, kist, pyxis, cassette
2 COFFIN, box, sarcophagus, shell; *Scot* kist
OLD larnax
SLANG *N Am* pine overcoat, wooden overcoat, wooden kimono

cast *v, n*

♦ *v*
1 THROW, hurl, lob, pitch, fling, toss, sling, heave, shy, launch, impel, drive
2 *cast light*
direct, project, shed, emit, give out, give off, radiate, diffuse, spread, scatter
3 *cast your eyes/a glance*
look (at), glimpse, glance, see, view, catch sight, turn, throw
4 *cast doubt/suspicion*
place, put, throw, put in jeopardy
COLLOQ. put a question mark over
5 *cast your vote*
vote, register, record, mark with a cross
6 MOULD, shape, form, model, fashion, found
♦ *n*
1 COMPANY, troupe, actors, players, performers, entertainers, characters, dramatis personae
2 CASTING, mould, shape, form, die, model, covering

■ **cast aside**
reject, discard, turn down, say no to

FORMAL dispense with
COLLOQ. get rid of

■ **cast down**
depress, discourage, dishearten, deject, sadden, crush, desolate
🗲 cheer up, encourage

caste *n*

class, social class, social standing, order, group, position, rank, station, status, grade, lineage, background, degree, estate, stratum, race

castigate *v*

criticize, reprimand, chasten, chastise, rebuke, scold, discipline, punish, correct, censure, chide, reprove, upbraid, berate
FORMAL admonish
COLLOQ. dress down, haul over the coals, rap on the knuckles, tear a strip off, give someone hell

castle *n*

stronghold, fort, fortress, fastness, citadel, keep, tower, château, palace, mansion, stately home, country house, *schloss*, villa

---

Parts of a castle include:

approach	curtain wall	outer bailey
arrow-slit	ditch	parados
bailey	donjon	parapet
barbican	drawbridge	portcullis
bartizan	dungeon	postern
bastion	embrasure	rampart
battlements	enclosure wall	scarp
berm	fosse	stockade
brattice	gatehouse	tower
buttress	inner wall	lookout tower
chapel	keep	turret
corbel	loophole	wall walk
courtyard	merlon	ward
crenel	moat	watchtower
crenellation	motte	
crosslet	mound	

---

castrate *v*

emasculate, geld, neuter, unman, unsex, cut, knacker, swig
OLD alter; (*Shakesp*) glib
FORMAL evirate
COLLOQ. doctor

casual *adj*

1 UNCONCERNED, nonchalant, blasé, lackadaisical, lukewarm, negligent, apathetic, indifferent, informal, offhand, relaxed, easy-going
FORMAL insouciant
COLLOQ. couldn't-care-less, laid-back, happy-go-lucky, free-and-easy
2 *casual clothes*
informal, comfortable, relaxed, leisure
3 *casual work*
temporary, irregular, intermittent, occasional, part-time, short-term, provisional
4 *a casual meeting*
chance, accidental, spontaneous, unintentional, unpremeditated, unexpected, unforeseen, irregular, random, occasional, incidental, superficial, cursory
FORMAL fortuitous, serendipitous
🗲 **1** worried, concerned **2** formal **3** permanent, regular, full-time **4** deliberate, planned

casually *adv*

1 *'I'm sorry,' I added casually*
spontaneously, parenthetically, on the spur of the moment
COLLOQ. off the cuff, off the top of your head
2 *dress casually*

Breeds of cat include:

Abyssinian	British shorthair	domestic tabby	Havana	Persian	Singapura
American	Burmese	Egyptian Mau	Himalayan	rag-doll	Somali
shorthair	Carthusian	Exotic shorthair	Japanese Bobtail	rex	Tiffany
Balinese	chinchilla	Foreign Blue	Korat	Russian Blue	Tonkinese
Birman	Cornish rex	Foreign spotted	Maine Coon	Scottish Fold	Tortoiseshell
Bombay	Cymric	shorthair	Manx	Siamese	Turkish Angora
British longhair	Devon rex	Foreign White	Norwegian Forest	silver tabby	Turkish Van

informally, comfortably, sportily
E3 2 formally, smartly

casualty *n*
injury, loss, death, fatality, victim, sufferer, injured, injured person, wounded, dead person, missing

casuistry *n*
chicanery, sophism, sophistry, speciousness, equivocation

cat *n*
tabby, kitten, mouser, tomcat
COLLOQ. puss, pussy, pussy cat, mog, moggy
OLD grimalkin
Related adjective: feline
See panel above

cataclysm *n*
disaster, calamity, catastrophe, debacle, devastation, upheaval, blow, collapse, convulsion

cataclysmic *adj*
catastrophe, disastrous, tragic, fatal, calamitous, devastating, terrible, dreadful, awful

catacomb *n*
underground passages, underground rooms, underground tunnels, underground cemetery, burial-vault, vault, tomb, crypt, mausoleum
FORMAL ossuary

catalogue *n, v*
• *n*
list, inventory, roll, register, roster, schedule, checklist, record, table, classification, index, directory, gazetteer, brochure, guide, prospectus, manifest, calendar, bulletin, specialogue, litany
TECHNICAL iconography, notitia
OLD catelog, ragman
COLLOQ. magalog
• *v*
list, compile/make a list, register, record, index, classify, alphabetize, file, categorize

catapult *n, v*
• *n*
1 sling; *N Am* slingshot; *Aust & NZ* shanghai
OLD bricole
• *v*
propel, hurl, fling, throw, pitch, toss, sling, hurtle, launch, shoot, fire

cataract *n*
waterfall, falls, rapids, force, cascade, overfall, downpour, torrent, deluge

catastrophe *n*
disaster, calamity, debacle, fiasco, failure, ruin, devastation, tragedy, blow, reverse, mischance, misfortune, adversity, trouble, doom, upheaval
FORMAL cataclysm, affliction

catastrophic *adj*
disastrous, tragic, fatal, calamitous, devastating, terrible, dreadful, awful, of the first magnitude
FORMAL cataclysmic

catcall *n*
jeer, boo, gibe, hiss, whistle, barracking; *N Am* Bronx cheer
COLLOQ. raspberry

catch *v, n*
• *v*
1 *catch a ball*
hold, grab, take, seize, grasp, snatch, grip, clutch
2 *catch an animal/a prisoner*
capture, trap, entrap, hunt down, snare, ensnare, hook, net, seize, lay hold of, arrest, apprehend, corner, round up, recapture
COLLOQ. nab, collar, nick
3 *catch a train*
get, get on, make, board, be in time for
4 *catch what someone says*
hear, make out, perceive, recognize, understand, follow, take in, fathom, grasp
FORMAL comprehend
COLLOQ. get the hang of, twig, get it
5 *catch someone doing something wrong*
surprise, catch red-handed/in the act, expose, unmask, startle, find (out), discover, detect, discern
OLD (*Shakesp*) watch
6 *catch a cold*
get, develop, go down with, pick up, become infected with, become ill with
FORMAL contract, succumb to
7 *catch someone's attention*
attract, draw, grasp, hold, capture, engage
E3 1 drop **2** release, free **3, 4** miss
• *n*
1 FASTENER, clip, hook, clasp, hasp, latch, lock, bolt; *dialect* sneck
2 *herring catches*
haul, net, bag
3 DISADVANTAGE, drawback, snag, hitch, obstacle, problem, difficulty
COLLOQ. fly in the ointment
▪ **catch on**
1 *the new style is catching on quickly*
become popular, become fashionable
COLLOQ. become all the rage
2 *catch on to what she said*
understand, follow, take in, fathom, grasp, comprehend
▪ **catch up**
draw level, gain on, overtake

catching *adj*
infectious, contagious, communicable, transmittable, transmissible

catchphrase *n*
saying, slogan, motto, jingle, watchword, byword, catchword, formula, password, parrot-cry
SLANG wheeze

catchy *adj*
memorable, unforgettable, haunting, popular, melodic, tuneful, attractive, captivating, appealing
E3 dull, boring, instantly forgettable

catechize *v*
instruct, interrogate, question, cross-examine, examine, test, drill
COLLOQ. grill, give the third degree

categorical *adj*
absolute, total, utter, unqualified, unreserved, unconditional, downright, positive, definite, emphatic,

unequivocal, clear, conclusive, explicit, express, direct
◨ tentative, qualified, vague

categorically *adv*
absolutely, utterly, unconditionally, emphatically, unequivocally, unreservedly, definitely, clearly, directly, positively, explicitly, expressly

categorization *n*
classification, grouping, sorting, ranking, ordering, arrangement, listing

categorize *v*
class, classify, group, sort, grade, rank, order, arrange, list, tabulate, stereotype, pigeonhole

category *n*
class, classification, group, grouping, kind, sort, type, variety, genre, section, division, department, chapter, head, heading, title, rubric, grade, rank, order, list, listing, bracket, chapter
TECHNICAL superclass, superorder, superphylum, taxon, stirps

cater *v*
1 *cater for people's needs/interests*
provide, supply, furnish, serve
FORMAL provision, victual
2 *cater to someone's desires*
indulge, pander, satisfy

caterwaul *v*
wail, scream, cry, screech, shriek, bawl, howl, miaow, squall, yowl
OLD (*Spenser*) wrawl

catharsis *n*
cleansing, purging, purification, purifying, release
TECHNICAL abreaction, abstersion, epuration, lustration

cathartic *adj*
cleansing, purging, purgative, purifying, release
TECHNICAL abreactive, abstersive, lustral, eccoprotic

cathedral *n*
minster, duomo, procathedral
OLD dome

catholic *adj*
broad, broad-based, diverse, wide, wide-ranging, widespread, varied, universal, global, general, comprehensive, inclusive, all-inclusive, all-embracing, all-encompassing, liberal, tolerant, open-minded, broad-minded
FORMAL eclectic
◨ narrow, limited, narrow-minded, bigoted

cattle *n*
cows, bulls, oxen, livestock, stock, beasts
Related adjective: bovine

Breeds of cattle include:

Aberdeen Angus	Chillingham	Longhorn
Africander	Devon	Luing
Alderney	dexter	Red Poll
Ankole	Durham	Romagnola
Ayrshire	Friesian	Santa Gertrudis
Belgian Blue	Galloway	Shetland
Blonde	Guernsey	Shorthorn
d'Aquitaine	Hereford	Simmenthaler
Brahman	Highland	South Deven
Brown Swiss	Holstein	Teeswater
cattabu	Jersey	Ukrainian
cattalo	Latvian	Welsh Black
Charolais	Limousin	(British) White

---

catty *adj*
bitchy, malicious, spiteful, venomous, vicious, mean, ill-

natured, malevolent, rancorous, backbiting
◨ kind, pleasant

caucus *n*
assembly, meeting, session, convention, gathering, conclave, get-together, parley, set, clique

causative *adj*
causing, root
TECHNICAL factitive, factive

cause *n, v*
◆ *n*
1 SOURCE, origin, beginning, root, basis, factor, spring, mainspring, originator, creator, producer, maker, author, mover, prime mover, agent, agency
2 REASON, motive, grounds, justification, explanation, basis, motivation, stimulus, incentive, inducement, impulse
3 *a worthy cause*
object, purpose, end, aim, ideal, principle, belief, conviction, movement, undertaking, enterprise
◨ **1** effect, result, consequence
◆ *v*
begin, give rise to, be the cause of, be at the root of, lead to, result in, occasion, bring about, make, make happen, produce, generate, originate, create, breed, precipitate, trigger (off), motivate, stimulate, provoke, incite, induce, prompt, force, compel
FORMAL effect, render
◨ stop, prevent

Synonym nuances
verb
Begin, **give rise to**, **lead to** and **result in** are fairly general and neutral terms: *his pioneering work began a new era*; *the delay gave rise to suspicion*. **Bring about** and **make happen** are similar, but suggest a more active involvement: *his speech brought about a change of heart*. **Breed** and **occasion** often have the narrower use of providing the correct conditions, though the former is often used of negative consequences: *oppression breeds violence*, and the latter is rather more formal sounding: *the marches occasioned violent encounters with the police*. **Precipitate** should be used of causing something to happen quickly: *the surge of nationalism which precipitated the end of the colonial era*. **Trigger** (**off**) could be used of sudden, unavoidable consequences, very often negative: *the economic downturn has triggered a rash of redundancies*. **Motivate**, **stimulate** and **prompt** might be used to convey positive aspects of encouraging, but **provoke** and **incite** tend to be used of actions with less favourable developments: *the violence, incited by propaganda*. The words **force** and **compel** are confined to circumstances in which no other outcome would be allowed, or even possible.

---

caustic *adj*
1 *caustic chemicals*
corrosive, acid, destructive, burning, stinging, erodent, escharotic
2 *a caustic remark*
biting, cutting, stinging, keen, pungent, bitter, acid, sarcastic, scathing, virulent, severe, acrimonious, vitriolic, snide
FORMAL astringent, mordant, trenchant
◨ **1** soothing **2** mild, kind

caustically *adv*
bitterly, scathingly, sarcastically, severely, acrimoniously, vitriolically, virulently
FORMAL trenchantly

cauterize *v*
burn, sterilize, disinfect, scorch, sear, singe, carbonize
TECHNICAL fire

caution *n, v*

♦ *n*

1 CARE, carefulness, watchfulness, vigilance, alertness, guard, mindfulness, heed, heedfulness, discretion, prudence, forethought, deliberation, wariness
FORMAL circumspection
OLD cautel

2 WARNING, injunction, reprimand, advice, counsel
FORMAL admonition, caveat
COLLOQ. tip-off
F3 1 carelessness, recklessness

♦ *v*

warn, advise, counsel, urge, alert, deter
FORMAL admonish
COLLOQ. tip off

cautious *adj*

careful, watchful, vigilant, alert, heedful, shrewd, prudent, discreet, tactful, defensive, chary, wary, guarded, heedful, safe, tentative, conservative, deliberate, Fabian, unadventurous
OLD cautelous
FORMAL circumspect, judicious
COLLOQ. cagey, softly-softly, gingerly
F3 reckless, rash, foolhardy

cautiously *adv*

carefully, prudently, discreetly, tactfully, defensively, tentatively, deliberately, conservatively
FORMAL circumspectly, judiciously
COLLOQ. gingerly
F3 recklessly, rashly

cavalcade *n*

procession, parade, march-past, troop, array, retinue, cortège, train, sowarry, motorcade

cavalier *n, adj*

♦ *n*

1 HORSEMAN, equestrian, horse soldier, cavalryman, knight, chevalier, Bashi-Bazouk, chasseur, Ironside, spahi
2 GENTLEMAN, gallant, escort, partner

♦ *adj*

supercilious, patronizing, condescending, lordly, haughty, lofty, arrogant, swaggering, insolent, scornful, disdainful, curt, offhand, casual, free-and-easy

cavalry *n*

horsemen, equestrians, horse soldiers, cavalrymen, horse, light-horse, mounted troops, troopers, dragoons, hussars, lancers, sabreurs, chasseurs, risaldars, the heavies
OLD reiters, ritt-masters

cave *n, v*

♦ *n*

cavern, grotto, hole, pothole, tunnel, dugout, underground chamber, hollow, cavity
OLD antre, delve; (*Shakesp*) antar
Related adjective: speleological

■ **cave in**

collapse, subside, give way, yield, fall (in), slip

caveat *n*

caution, warning, proviso, alarm
FORMAL admonition

cavern *n*

cave, cavity, den, grotto, hollow, pothole, vault, vaultage, tunnel, dugout, underground chamber, cove, Erebus

cavernous *adj*

hollow, concave, gaping, yawning, echoing, resonant, deep, unfathomable, bottomless, large, huge, immense, vast, spacious, dark, gloomy, sunken, depressed

cavil *v*

complain, carp, criticize, censure, reproach, quarrel, find faults, nag, quibble, haggle

COLLOQ. nit-pick
F3 praise, compliment

cavity *n*

hole, gap, dent, hollow, excavation, crater, pit, well, bore, chamber, pocket, vein, tear, sinus, womb; *dialect* vug; *N Am & Aust* thunder-egg
TECHNICAL antrum, atrium, cell, orifice, ventricle, aperture, lacuna, camera, sac, vesicle, acetabulum, blastocoel, cochlea, concha, eardrum, coelom, vestibule, splanchnocele, cotyle, crypt, druse, geode, haematocele, lumen, mediastinum, neuroblastoma, pelvis, rhynchocoel, vacuole, vitta
OLD TECHNICAL conceptacle, purse
OLD mine

cavort *v*

caper, frolic, gambol, prance, skip, dance, frisk, sport, romp

cease *v*

stop, refrain, halt, call a halt, come/bring to a halt, break off, leave (off), finish, end, come/bring to an end, conclude, terminate, suspend, let up, peter out, fail, die; *Scot* devall
OLD surcease, unbe; (*Spenser*) cesse, blin, lin
FORMAL abate, discontinue, desist
COLLOQ. fizzle out, pack in, quit; *N Am* poop (out)
F3 begin, start, commence

ceaseless *adj*

endless, unending, never-ending, eternal, everlasting, continuous, non-stop, incessant, unceasing, interminable, constant, perpetual, continual, persistent, untiring, uninterrupted, unremitting
F3 occasional, irregular

ceaselessly *adv*

endlessly, unendingly, eternally, everlastingly, for ever, for ever and ever, uninterruptedly, continuously, incessantly, unremittingly, constantly, unceasingly, interminably, day in day out
COLLOQ. till the cows come home

cede *v*

surrender, give up, resign, abandon, yield, relinquish, convey, transfer, hand over, turn over, grant, deliver, allow, concede
FORMAL abdicate, renounce

ceiling *n*

1 *a decorated ceiling*
vault, plafond, roof, overhead, overhead covering, rafters, beams, awning, canopy, plafond
TECHNICAL laquearia
OLD seeling, soffit; (*Spenser*) loft
2 LIMIT, upper limit, maximum, most, cut-off point

celebrate *v*

1 *celebrate a birthday*
commemorate, remember, observe, keep, mark, hold, record, honour, do something in someone's honour, have/throw a party, rejoice, enjoy yourself, have fun, go out, toast, drink to, extol, revel, sonnet, sound, trumpet, sing, hymn, carol, chant
OLD besing, emblaze, maffick
FORMAL laud, tune, emblazon, renown, repeat, procession
COLLOQ. rave, binge, have a ball, live it up, whoop it up, go out on the town, go on the razzle, paint the town red, kill the fatted calf, put the flags out, push the boat out
SLANG wet
2 *the priest celebrated Communion*
bless, perform, observe, solemnize, concelebrate

celebrated *adj*

famous, well-known, famed, renowned, illustrious, glorious, eminent, distinguished, great, notable, noted, prominent, outstanding, legendary, popular, acclaimed, admired, exalted, revered

Celebrations include:

anniversary	centenary	festival	harvest-home	marriage	retirement
banquet	christening	fête	homecoming	May Day	reunion
baptism	coming-of-age	gala	Independence	name-day	saint's day
bar mitzvah	commemoration	graduation	Day	party	thanksgiving
bat mitzvah	Confirmation	harvest festival	jubilee	reception	tribute
birthday	feast	First Communion	Labour Day	remembrance	wedding

See also **anniversary**; **party**.

See also **church services** *at* **church**; **religious festivals** *at* **religious**.

COLLOQ. with your name in lights
E3 unknown, obscure, forgotten

celebration *n*
observance, merrymaking, jollification, revelry, orgy, festivity, feast, festival, occasion
COLLOQ. rave, rave-up, binge, spree, do, shindig; *Irish* hooley
SLANG *S Afr* jol
See panel above

celebrity *n*
1 STAR, personality, name, dignitary, famous person, superstar, legend, legend in their own lifetime, living legend, household name
FORMAL personage, notable, luminary, worthy
COLLOQ. celeb, VIP, big name, bigwig, big shot
2 FAME, renown, stardom, distinction, prominence, eminence, esteem, greatness, notability, note, reputation, illustriousness
E3 1 nobody, unknown, nonentity

celerity *n*
rapidity, fastness, quickness, speed, swiftness, velocity, dispatch, expedition, fleetness, haste, promptness
E3 slowness

celestial *adj*
heavenly, divine, godlike, spiritual, angelic, seraphic, elysian, empyrean, ethereal, paradisaic, eternal, immortal, sublime, supernatural, transcendental, astral, starry
E3 earthly, mundane

celestially *adv*
divinely, spiritually, angelically, eternally, immortally, sublimely, supernaturally, transcendentally
E3 mundanely

celibacy *n*
singleness, bachelorhood, spinsterhood, maidenhood, virginity, chastity, purity, self-denial, self-restraint, abstinence, continence
FORMAL abnegation

celibate *adj*
chaste, pure, abstinent, virgin, single, unmarried, unwed, bachelor, spinster

cell *n*
1 *a prison cell*
prison, jail, dungeon, lock-up, room, cubicle, chamber, compartment, enclosure
2 *living cells*
unit, organism
TECHNICAL protoplasm, cytoplasm, protoplast, gamete, zygote, spore, nucleus, matrix
Related adjective: cytoid
3 *a political cell*
faction, nucleus, group, party, unit, section, set, crowd, caucus, clique

cellar *n*
basement, crypt, vault, storeroom, wine cellar; *Scot* dunny

cement *n, v*
♦ *n*

plaster, mortar, concrete, screed, compo, putty, pointing, grout, grouting, gunite, lute, mastic, fixative, matrix, bonding, adhesive, glue, paste
TECHNICAL ciment fondu
OLD maltha
♦ *v*
stick, bond, weld, solder, join, fasten, fix, cohere, unite, combine, bind, affix, attach, glue, gum, solution; *dialect* lime

cemetery *n*
burial ground, burial place, burial site, graveyard, churchyard, necropolis, charnel house, God's acre, graves, tombs, urnfield, *campo santo*
SLANG boneyard

censor *v, n*
♦ *v*
cut, make cuts, ban, edit, delete, blue-pencil, bowdlerize, expurgate
♦ *n*
inspector, examiner, editor, bowdlerizer, expurgater

⚠ censor or **censure**?
To *censor* books, films, etc is to examine them, deleting parts of them or forbidding publication: *His letters home were censored*. To *censure* someone is to criticize them severely: *The President was severely censured for abusing his powers.*

censorious *adj*
condemnatory, disapproving, disparaging, fault-finding, carping, cavilling, critical, hypercritical, overcritical, severe
FORMAL captious
E3 complimentary, approving

censoriously *adv*
disapprovingly, disparagingly, critically, hypercritically, overcritically, severely
FORMAL captiously
E3 approvingly

censure *v, n*
♦ *v*
condemn, denounce, blame, criticize, disapprove of, reprehend, reprove, reproach, rebuke, reprimand, scold
FORMAL castigate, admonish, remonstrate, upbraid
COLLOQ. tell off, haul over the coals, come down heavy on, pull to pieces
E3 praise, compliment, approve
♦ *n*
condemnation, blame, disapproval, criticism, denunciation, reprehension, reproof, reproach, rebuke, reprimand, scolding
FORMAL admonition, admonishment, castigation, upbraiding, remonstrance, obloquy, vituperation
COLLOQ. telling-off
E3 praise, compliments, approval

central *adj*
1 MIDDLE, centre, mid, inner, interior, medial, median
2 PRINCIPAL, main, major, most important, chief, key,

primary, fundamental, foremost, dominant, vital, crucial, significant, focal, pivotal, basic, essential, core, prime
🢂 1 peripheral **2** minor, secondary

centralization n
concentration, convergence, consolidation, incorporation, rationalization, amalgamation, unification, focusing, streamlining

centralize v
concentrate, converge, bring/gather together, consolidate, incorporate, rationalize, focus, streamline, amalgamate, compact, condense, unify
🢂 decentralize

centre n, v
◆ n
middle, midpoint, heart, core, nucleus, kernel, pivot, hub, focus, focal point, crux, linchpin, arena
COLLOQ. bull's-eye
🢂 edge, periphery, outskirts
◆ v
focus, concentrate, converge, gravitate, revolve, pivot, hinge

centrepiece n
most significant feature, focus of attention, highlight, high point, high spot, most interesting part, best, peak, climax, cream

ceramics n
pottery, earthenware, ware, bisque, faience, ironstone, porcelain, raku
See panel at **pottery**.

cereal n
1 *cereal crops*
barley, grain, corn, wheat, maize, millet, oats, rye, sorghum, rice, amarant
2 *breakfast cereal*
cornflakes, muesli, porridge, oatmeal; *N Am* granola
Related adjective: farinaceous

ceremonial adj, n
◆ adj
formal, official, stately, state, solemn, dignified, ritual, ritualistic
🢂 informal, casual
◆ n
ceremony, formality, protocol, custom, solemnity, ritual, rite

⚠ ceremonial or ceremonious?
Ceremonial means 'relating to or appropriate for a ceremony': *ceremonial dress; a ceremonial occasion.*
Ceremonious means 'very formal or polite': *He ushered her through with a ceremonious bow.*

ceremonially adv
formally, officially, solemnly, ritually
🢂 informally, casually

ceremonious adj
stately, dignified, grand, imposing, solemn, ritual, civil, official, majestic, polite, courteous, deferential, courtly, formal, stiff, starchy, exact, precise, scrupulous
FORMAL punctilious
🢂 unceremonious, informal, relaxed

ceremoniously adv
grandly, solemnly, ritualistically, civilly, officially, politely, courteously, deferentially, formally, stiffly, starchily, exactly, precisely, scrupulously
FORMAL punctiliously
🢂 unceremoniously, informally

ceremony n
1 *wedding ceremony*
service, rite, sacrament, ordinance, liturgy, commemoration, occasion, observance, festival,

celebration, formality, solemnity, function, custom, tradition, parade, anniversary, inauguration, dedication, induction, initiation, graduation, coronation, investiture, unveiling; *N Am* exercise, commencement
2 ETIQUETTE, formality, protocol, form, order, circumstance, niceties, ceremonial, ritual, pomp, pageantry, show, gaud
FORMAL decorum, propriety, punctilio
COLLOQ. spit and polish

Ceremonies include:

amrit	chuppah	matrimony
baptism	committal	matsuri
bar mitzvah	confirmation	maundy
bat mitzvah	doseh	nipter
colloq. capping	fire-walking	nuptials
chanoyu	graduation	tangi
christening	marriage	wedding

---

certain adj
1 *I'm certain he's telling the truth*
sure, positive, assured, confident, convinced, persuaded
2 *it's certain that she left yesterday*
indisputable, unquestionable, undeniable, undoubted, indubitable, incontrovertible, irrefutable, evident, obvious, clear, plain, sure, conclusive, absolute, convincing, true
COLLOQ. no two ways about it, no ifs and buts, sure as eggs is eggs; *Aust* dead set
3 *success is certain*
inevitable, unavoidable, inescapable, bound, bound to happen, meant to happen, assured, destined, fated, doomed
FORMAL inexorable, ineluctable
COLLOQ. cut and dried, open-and-shut, home and dry, in the bag
4 *below a certain income*
specific, special, particular, individual, precise, express, fixed, established, settled, decided, definite, determined
5 *to a certain extent*
some, partial, small, limited
🢂 1 uncertain, unsure, hesitant, doubtful **3** unlikely

certainly adv
surely, of course, naturally, obviously, clearly, plainly, definitely, for sure, undoubtedly, without a doubt, no doubt, undeniably, unquestionably, beyond question, absolutely, by all means, doubtlessly, assuredly, positively

certainty n
1 *identify someone with certainty*
sureness, positiveness, assurance, confidence, conviction, faith, trust, assurance, assuredness
2 *it's a certainty that she'll get the job*
inevitability, foregone conclusion, matter of course, truth, validity, fact, reality
COLLOQ. sure thing, safe bet, dead cert
SLANG *Aust* moral
🢂 1 uncertainty, doubt, hesitation

certificate n
document, award, diploma, qualification, credentials, testimonial, guarantee, endorsement, proof, warrant, licence, authorization, register, pass, voucher
TECHNICAL lines, marriage-lines, patent, aegrotat, testamur, bill of health, clearance, navicert, cocket, docket, debenture, scrip, securities, title; *N Am* land-scrip
OLD TECHNICAL smart-ticket, Tyburn-ticket
FORMAL certificatory
SLANG ticket

certify v
declare, assure, guarantee, endorse, confirm, pronounce, vouch, testify, witness, bear witness to, substantiate, verify,

authenticate, validate, warrant, ratify, authorize, recognize, license
FORMAL attest, aver, corroborate, accredit

certitude n
(full) assurance, assuredness, certainty, confidence, conviction, sureness, positiveness
FORMAL plerophoria, plerophory
⊟ doubt

cessation n
halt, halting, ceasing, discontinuation, discontinuing, end, ending, remission, respite, rest, standstill, stay, stoppage, stopping, conclusion, suspension, termination, pause, recess, break, let-up, interruption, intermission, interval
FORMAL abeyance, desistance, discontinuance, hiatus
⊟ beginning, start, commencement

chafe v
1 *chafe someone's skin*
rub, grate, irritate, rasp, scrape, fret, bind, inflame, scratch, wear (away), wear down
OLD chauf, chauff
FORMAL abrade, excoriate
2 *chafing at the rules*
anger, annoy, enrage, exasperate, incense, provoke, inflame, vex, be angry
COLLOQ. peeve, get on someone's nerves, get on someone's wick

chaff n, v
♦ n
1 HUSKS, shells, pods, cases
Related adjective: paleaceous
2 BANTER, teasing, joking, jesting, badinage, repartee
COLLOQ. kidding, ribbing, have-on
♦ v
tease, joke, jest, banter, mock, make fun of
COLLOQ. kid, rib, rag, pull someone's leg, chip
SLANG josh, rot

chagrin n, v
♦ n
annoyance, exasperation, indignation, disappointment, displeasure, irritation, vexation, disquiet, dissatisfaction, discomposure, embarrassment, mortification, humiliation, shame, fretfulness
FORMAL discomfiture
⊟ delight, pleasure
♦ v
annoy, exasperate, disappoint, displease, irritate, vex, irk, disquiet, dissatisfy, embarrass, humiliate, mortify
COLLOQ. peeve

chain n, v
♦ n
1 FETTER, manacle, restraint, bond, shackle, trammel, link, coupling, union
Related adjective: catenary
2 *a hotel chain*
group, company, firm
3 *a chain of islands*
string, line, row, range, train, set
FORMAL concatenation
4 *a chain of events*
series, sequence, succession, progression, string
♦ v
fasten, secure, bind, tie, hitch, restrain, tether, confine, fetter, shackle, manacle, handcuff, enslave
⊟ free, release, liberate

chair n, v
♦ n
1 SEAT, armchair, recliner, swivel-chair, stool, bench, form
2 *Sally is the new chair*
chairperson, chairman, chairwoman, president, convenor, organizer, director, master of ceremonies,

MC, toastmaster, speaker
♦ v
lead, act as chairperson/chairman/ chairwoman, convene, direct, supervise, preside over, moderate

---

Chairs include:

armchair	fauteuil	prie-dieu
beanbag	fiddle-back	recliner
bench	form	rocker
bergère	guérite	rocking chair
carver	high chair	sedan
commode	jampan	stool
Cromwellian	kitchen chair	swivel-chair
dining chair	ladder-back	throne
easy chair	lounger	
estate	pouffe	

See also **stool**.

---

chairman, chairwoman n
chairperson, president, convenor, organizer, director, spokesman, spokeswoman, spokesperson, master of ceremonies, MC

chalk
■ **chalk up**
1 ACHIEVE, attain, gain, log, score, tally, register, record, accumulate
2 ASCRIBE, attribute, charge, credit, put down

chalky adj
1 ASHEN, pale, pallid, white, wan, colourless
2 POWDERY, dusty, ground, crushed, granulated
FORMAL calcareous, cretaceous

challenge v, n
♦ v
1 DARE, defy, confront, brave, summon, invite, accost, tackle; *Scot* hen
OLD provoke, champion, darraign, defy; (*Shakesp*) assay
COLLOQ. throw down the gauntlet, throw your hat into the ring
2 *challenged his authority*
question, dispute, query, protest, disagree with, object to, take exception to, call in(to) question
FORMAL demur
3 *challenged my ability*
test, tax, try, stretch, strain
♦ n
1 *the new job is a real challenge*
test, trial, hurdle, obstacle, problem, risk, hazard, opportunity
2 *take up the challenge to fight*
dare, defiance, confrontation, provocation, call, summons, bidding, defiance
OLD vie
3 *a challenge to their powers*
dispute, protest, opposition, defiance, disagreement, objection, calling into question, questioning, interrogation, stand, confrontation, ultimatum

challenging adj
exciting, exacting, demanding, testing, taxing, stretching
⊟ undemanding

chamber n
1 HALL, assembly room, auditorium, meeting-place, moot-hall
2 ROOM, apartment, compartment, bedroom, boudoir
3 *the chambers of the heart*
cavity, ventricle, compartment, hollow
4 *the upper chamber of parliament*
assembly, legislature, parliament, council, house

champion n, v
♦ n

1 *the school chess champion*
winner, victor, conqueror, title-holder, hero, ace, expert
OLD kemp, kemper
COLLOQ. champ; *Aust & NZ* gun
2 *a champion of animal rights*
guardian, protector, defender, vindicator, patron, backer, supporter, upholder, advocate, tribune, protagonist, messiah, saviour, asserter, deliverer, apostle
TECHNICAL promachos
FORMAL proponent
COLLOQ. angel
◆ *v*
defend, stand up for, stand for, back, support, protect, maintain, uphold, advocate, promote, hold a brief for
FORMAL espouse

chance *n, v, adj*
◆ *n*
1 *meet someone by chance*
accident, coincidence, luck, fortune, providence, fate, destiny, risk, gamble, speculation
FORMAL fortuity, serendipity
COLLOQ. fluke
2 *there's a chance that I'll be late*
possibility, prospect, probability, likelihood, odds
3 *a second chance*
opportunity, opening, occasion, time; *N Am, Aust & NZ* show
COLLOQ. break, golden opportunity, chance of a lifetime, your best shot
F3 **1** certainty
◆ *v*
1 RISK, hazard, take a chance, gamble, wager, stake, try, speculate, venture
FORMAL essay
COLLOQ. chance your luck, push your luck, play a hunch, bet your boots/life, bet your bottom dollar
2 HAPPEN, occur, come about, take place, arise, crop up, develop, result, follow
▪ **chance on/upon**
meet, meet unexpectedly, find by chance, discover, come across, run across, stumble on
COLLOQ. run into, bump into
◆ *adj*
casual, accidental, inadvertent, unintentional, unintended, unforeseen, unexpected, unanticipated, unlooked-for, random, arbitrary, haphazard, incidental
FORMAL fortuitous, serendipitous
COLLOQ. flukey
F3 deliberate, intentional, foreseen, certain
▪ **by chance**
 accidentally, unintentionally, inadvertently, unexpectedly, by accident, as luck would have it, by mistake, unwittingly, haphazardly, randomly, incidentally
OLD bechance
FORMAL fortuitously, adventitiously, serendipitously

Synonym nuances
noun sense 1
Accident is widely used to suggest any unplanned incident, whereas a **coincidence** more specifically refers to the unlikely occurrence of two related events. **Luck** refers to circumstances over which you have no control, as does **fortune**, although when used without any qualification the implication is usually of something beneficial: *an adventitious stroke of fortune.* **Providence** connotes a benevolent divine contribution, and **fate** and **destiny** an element of preordination: *his heroic struggle against his destiny.*
 The terms **risk** and **gamble** are suggestive of possible unhappy consequences: *a risk of thundery showers;* whilst **speculation** would be an appropriate term for chance based on theories or unfounded conclusions.

---

chancy *adj*
risky, speculative, tricky, uncertain, unpredictable, fraught, hazardous, dangerous, problematical
COLLOQ. dicey, dodgy
F3 safe, secure

change *v, n*
◆ *v*
1 *water changes into ice; prices keep changing*
make/become different, alter, vary, convert, turn, go, become, develop, modify, reorganize, reform, restructure, remodel, revise, renew, amend, adapt, customize, adjust, transform, evolve, transfer, move, shift, fluctuate, vacillate, be in a state of flux
TECHNICAL mutate, transmutate, metamorphose, transfigure
COLLOQ. do a U-turn
2 *change one thing for another*
substitute, replace, alternate, interchange, rotate, transpose, exchange, swap, trade, switch, barter
COLLOQ. chop and change
3 *change buses*
transfer, connect, make a connection
◆ *n*
1 *a change in the weather*
difference, alteration, variation, conversion, modification, reorganization, shake-up, transition, trend, movement, diversion, novelty, innovation, variety, revolution, upheaval, development, reform, restructuring, remodelling, reconstruction, revision, renewal, amendment, adaptation, customization, adjustment, transformation, evolution, transfer, move, shift, fluctuation, vacillation, state of flux, reversal, about-turn, about-face, volte-face, turnabout, ebb and flow
TECHNICAL mutation, transmutation, metamorphosis, transfiguration
FORMAL vicissitude
COLLOQ. U-turn
2 *a change of government*
exchange, transposition, interchange, substitution, substitute, replacement, alternation, rotation, swap, trade, switch, barter
3 *Have you got any change?*
coins, cash, silver, coppers

Synonym nuances
noun sense 1
Conversion is suggestive of a complete change, or can be used of being turned to a different purpose, while **modification, amendment, adaptation, customization** and **adjustment** all suggest more minor interference to make something better suited for its purpose.
 Shake-up, revolution and **upheaval**, on the other hand, are appropriate words to use where there has been a dramatic process of change: *a radical shake-up of commercial TV.* **Transition, movement, development, evolution, move** and **shift** all suggest something more gradual. The term **trend** is usually used in the context of changing fashions or current influences: *the trend towards early retirement.*
 Both **novelty** and **innovation** suggest the introduction of something new and unlike anything else, whilst **reform, revision** and **renewal** all have to do with new approaches to something current.
 Transformation returns to the idea of something being turned into something else, often with the implication that it is a postive change: *aim for self-improvement and personal transformation.* **Fluctuation** and **vacillation** appropriately describe constant moving between states, whereas **reversal** and **turnabout** are often used of a single, dramatic change in thought or action: *a rapid turnabout in attitudes.*

changeable *adj*
variable, varying, fluctuating, fluid, kaleidoscopic, versatile, shifting, mobile, movable, unsettled, unstable, uncertain, unpredictable, unreliable, changeful, erratic, irregular, inconstant, inconsistent, fickle, flighty, whimsy, capricious, volatile, skittish, windy, unstable, unsteady, wavering, vacillating, mercurial, labile, chameleonic, chamelion-like, Protean; *dialect* wankle
OLD various, voluble
FORMAL mutable, vicissitudinous
⊟ constant, settled, reliable
See Synonym nuances panel at **variable**.

changeless *adj*
unchangeable, unalterable, unchanging, invariable, static, permanent, fixed, final, eternal, timeless
FORMAL immutable

channel *n, v*
• *n*
1 *a channel for rainwater; irrigation channels*
passage, duct, conduit, main, groove, furrow, trough, bed, way, ditch, gutter, gully, canal, flume, course, trunk, culvert, watercourse, waterway, strait, narrows, cut-off, offtake, hollow, siphon, aqueduct, chamfer, gut, grough, artery, drain, sewer, sluice, overflow, spill-stream, fairway, feed, lead, level, tube, gate, lane, neck, sound; *dialect* ea, eau, gullet; *Scot* sheuch, stank; *N Am* kill, snye; *Aust* wash-away; *S Afr* sluit, sloot
TECHNICAL chime, glyph, race, headrace, millrace, tailrace, limbers
OLD lake, falaj
2 *channels of communication*
route, course, path, avenue, way, means, medium, use, approach, passage, agent, agency
• *v*
direct, guide, conduct, convey, send, transmit, force, concentrate, focus, major

chant *n, v*
• *n*
1 *the football supporters' chants*
shout, cry, slogan, warcry
2 *a religious chant*
plainsong, psalm, song, melody, chorus, refrain, ditty, incantation, recitation, intonation, mantra
• *v*
sing, chorus, recite
FORMAL intone, incant

chaos *n*
disorder, confusion, disorganization, disarray, anarchy, lawlessness, tumult, upheaval, disruption, pandemonium, uproar, riot, bedlam, madhouse, mess
FORMAL tohu bohu
COLLOQ. pig's breakfast, dog's dinner, shambles
SLANG *N Am* snafu
⊟ order

chaotic *adj*
disordered, confused, disorganized, topsy-turvy, disorderly, deranged, anarchic, lawless, orderless, riotous, tumultuous, unruly, uncontrolled, disrupted
COLLOQ. shambolic, at sixes and sevens, all over the place/ shop, higgledy-piggledy
SLANG *N Am* snafu
⊟ ordered, organized

chap *n*
fellow, man, boy, male person, individual, character, sort, type, codger; *dialect* cod
COLLOQ. bloke, guy, shaver; *Irish* bucko; *Aust* cove
SLANG sod, bastard, cat, Johnny, boyo, oik

chaperon, chaperone *n, v*
• *n*
companion, escort, duenna

• *v*
escort, accompany, attend, guard, protect, safeguard, shepherd, take care of, look after, mind, watch over

chapped *adj*
sore, chafed, cracked, raw, cracked, sprayed

chapter *n*
1 *read chapter 3*
section, division, part, clause, portion, topic
2 *a new chapter in my life*
episode, period, phase, stage, time
3 *the local chapter of a club*
branch, division, section, department

char *v*
burn, cauterize, scorch, sear, singe, carbonize, blacken, brown, coal

character *n*
1 *the cruel side of his character; the character of the countryside*
nature, essential quality, essence, ethos, personality, disposition, temperament, temper, constitution, make-up, individuality, identity, peculiarity, feature, attributes, characteristics, quality, property, type, stamp, calibre, reputation, psyche, status, position, trait, image
FORMAL persona
COLLOQ. what makes someone tick
2 *he has character; this house has character*
strength, strength of purpose, backbone, determination, courage, honesty, integrity, uprightness, honour, moral fibre, charm, appeal, attractiveness, attractive features, distinctive features, arresting qualities, specialness, style, interest
3 ECCENTRIC, eccentric person, original, oddity
COLLOQ. oddball, case
4 *the characters in a play*
individual, person, human being, role, part, sort, type
5 LETTER, figure, symbol, sign, mark, type, device, logo, emblem, cipher, rune, hieroglyph, ideograph

---

Synonym nuances
sense 1
Nature and **essence** are both used of the innate qualities that contribute to identity, while **ethos** is more likely to be used of the beliefs or credo that distinguishes a particular group: *the public ethos of the health service*. The word **psyche** is generally used of mental character: *Scotland's footballing psyche*.
  Personality is associated more with the way people project their character, while **disposition**, **temperament** and **temper** emphasize their dominant emotions and the way they are affected by them. Terms such as **constitution** and **make-up**, which convey a picture of various elements making up the whole, and **feature**, **attributes**, **characteristics**, **quality**, **property** and **trait** are all neutral terms to use when describing any aspect of character: *physical attributes; personality traits*.
  The terms **individuality**, **identity** and **peculiarity** are more suggestive of something unique: *litigation was a peculiarity of modern America*. Both **stamp** and **calibre** may be used positively to suggest quality: *mathematicians of the finest calibre*; whereas **reputation**, **status**, **position** and **image** would more appropriately be used in contexts describing how the character of something is perceived or ranked.

---

characteristic *n, adj*
• *n*
feature, trait, attribute, property, quality, essential quality, mark, hallmark, factor, peculiarity, idiosyncrasy, mannerism, symptom
• *adj*

distinctive, distinguishing, individual, idiosyncratic, peculiar, specific, special, typical, representative, symbolic, symptomatic

E3 uncharacteristic, untypical

characteristically *adv*
typically, distinctively, individually, peculiarly, idiosyncratically

characterization *n*
description, representation, presentation, depiction, portrayal

characterize *v*
1 *materialism that characterizes life*
typify, mark, stamp, brand, identify, distinguish, indicate, specify, designate
2 DESCRIBE, represent, portray, present, depict

charade *n*
farce, mockery, parody, pretence, fake, travesty, sham, pantomime

charge *v, n*
♦ *v*
1 *charge a high price*
ask, ask for, ask someone to pay, demand, demand in payment, set/fix a price, levy, exact, debit, bill, put down to
2 ACCUSE, indict, impeach, incriminate, blame
FORMAL arraign, impute
3 ATTACK, assail, assault, storm, rush (forward), tear
4 FILL, pervade, affect, imbue, infuse, suffuse, burden, saturate, overwhelm
♦ *n*
1 PRICE, cost, fee, rate, amount, expense, expenditure, outlay, payment, rent, rental, dues, toll, levy, tax, tariff
2 ACCUSATION, indictment, allegation, impeachment, blame, incrimination
FORMAL arraignment, imputation
3 ATTACK, assault, onslaught, sortie, incursion, offensive, storming, rush, onrush
4 *in your charge*
custody, keeping, care, safekeeping, guardianship, ward, protection, trust, responsibility, duty, burden, obligation
■ *in charge of*
responsible for, managing, leading, controlling, directing, supervising, overseeing, heading up, looking after, taking care of

charisma *n*
charm, appeal, lure, allure, attraction, magnetism, drawing-power, draw, pull

charismatic *adj*
charming, magnetic, attractive, glamorous, appealing, fascinating, captivating, irresistible

charitable *adj*
philanthropic, humanitarian, benevolent, benign, kind, compassionate, sympathetic, understanding, considerate, generous, open-handed, liberal, tolerant, broad-minded,

kindly, lenient, forgiving, indulgent, gracious
FORMAL magnanimous, beneficent, bounteous, eleemosynary
E3 uncharitable, inconsiderate, unforgiving

charitably *adv*
kindly, compassionately, sympathetically, considerately, generously, tolerantly, open-mindedly, liberally, graciously
FORMAL bounteously

charity *n*
1 fund, trust, foundation, caritas, voluntary organization, non-profit-making organization, not-for-profit organization, mission, institution, confraternity
OLD hospital
2 *live on charity*
gift, donation, handout, aid, relief, contribution, funding, (financial) assistance, alms
3 GENEROSITY, goodwill, bountifulness, almsgiving, philanthropy, unselfishness, altruism, benevolence, benignness, kindness, goodness, humanity, compassion, considerateness, thoughtfulness, tender-heartedness, love, affection, tolerance, clemency, indulgence
FORMAL beneficence, munificence
4 *show some charity*
compassion, kindness, sympathy, kind-heartedness, graciousness, consideration, concern, tolerance, leniency
E3 **3** selfishness, malice

charlatan *n*
impostor, cheat, fake, fraud, confidence, trickster, pretender, bogus caller/official, quack, sham, swindler, mountebank
COLLOQ. phoney, con man

charm *n, v*
♦ *n*
1 ATTRACTION, allure, allurement, magnetism, appeal, delightfulness, attractiveness, desirability, fascination, enchantment, captivation, glamour, prestige, aroma; *dialect* comether
COLLOQ. it, what it takes
2 *a lucky charm*
trinket, ornament, talisman, medicine, phylactery, mascot, amulet, fetish, idol, grisgris, ju-ju, obi, periapt, *porte-bonheur*, hand of glory
SLANG *NAm* mojo
3 *the magician's charm*
spell, sorcery, magic, abracadabra, abraxas
OLD *Scot* weird
♦ *v*
please, delight, enrapture, captivate, fascinate, beguile, enchant, bewitch, mesmerize, attract, draw, take, allure, intrigue, cajole, win, enamour, seduce
OLD becharm, encharm
E3 repel, disgust

charming *adj*
pleasing, delightful, pleasant, lovely, captivating, enchanting, attractive, fetching, appealing, tasteful, sweet,

---

Charities in the UK with the largest income include:

Wellcome Trust	Save the Children (UK)	Comic Relief
Cancer Research UK	Salvation Army Trust	ActionAid
National Trust	Scope	Women's Royal Voluntary Service
Charities Aid Foundation	National Society for the Prevention of	(WRVS)
Oxfam	Cruelty to Children (NSPCC)	Royal Society for the Protection of
British Red Cross Society	Royal National Institute for the Blind	Birds (RSPB)
Barnardo's	(RNIB)	People's Dispensary for Sick Animals
Royal National Lifeboat Institution	Marie Curie Cancer Care	(PDSA)
(RNLI)	British Refugee Council	
Royal Mencap Society	Help the Aged	Royal British Legion
British Heart Foundation	Royal Society for the Prevention of	St John Ambulance
NCH	Cruelty to Animals (RSPCA)	Christian Aid
Leonard Cheshire	Macmillan Cancer Relief	

cute, winsome, alluring, engaging, tempting, glamorous, seductive, winning, irresistible
FORMAL delectable
E∃ ugly, unattractive, repulsive

charmingly adv
pleasingly, delightfully, pleasantly, attractively, enchantingly, sweetly, winsomely, alluringly, glamorously, irresistibly
FORMAL delectably
E∃ unattractively, repulsively

chart n, v
♦ n
1 *a chart showing the patient's temperature*
diagram, table, graph, map, plan, blueprint, bar chart, flow chart, pie chart, flow sheet
TECHNICAL nomogram, nomograph
2 *number one in the charts*
hit parade, top twenty, list, league
♦ v
1 *chart an area*
map, map out, sketch, draw, draft, outline, delineate, mark, plot, place
2 MONITOR, document, record, keep a record of, put on record, note, register, observe, follow

charter n, v
♦ n
right, privilege, prerogative, authority, authorization, permit, licence, franchise, concession, contract, covenant, indenture, deed, bond, warrant, sanction, document
TECHNICAL Scot novodamus
OLD charta, carta
FORMAL accreditation
♦ v
hire, rent, lease, commission, engage, employ, authorize, sanction, license

chary adj
careful, prudent, cautious, wary, shy, tender, guarded, heedful, uneasy, unwilling, reluctant, slow, suspicious, leery
FORMAL circumspect
COLLOQ. cagey
E∃ heedless, unwary

chase v, n
♦ v
pursue, follow, hunt, run after, give chase, track, drive, trail, tail, shadow, hound, drive, expel, send away, rush, hurry, course, chivvy, sick
OLD prosecute, scorse
COLLOQ. be hot on someone's heels
♦ n
pursuit, trail, running after, hunt, hunting, coursing, rush
OLD chivvy

chasm n
1 *a chasm in the rocks*
crack, rift, split, cleft, fissure, crevasse, canyon, gorge, ravine, gap, gape, opening, gulf, abyss, void, hollow, cavity, crater, breach, yawn
2 *a chasm between two people*
rift, split, gulf, gap, opening, gulf, breach, divorce, separation, estrangement, alienation, disagreement, quarrel

chassis n
framework, bodywork, frame, fuselage, skeleton, structure, substructure, undercarriage

chaste adj
1 *a chaste person*
pure, virginal, unsullied, undefiled, immaculate, abstinent, continent, celibate, unmarried, single, virtuous, moral, innocent, demure, vestal
OLD graced, honest

2 *a chaste style*
modest, decent, plain, simple, restrained, classic, bare, austere, unadorned, unembellished
E∃ 1 promiscuous, immoral, corrupt **2** unrestrained, decorated

chasten v
humble, humiliate, tame, subdue, repress, curb, restrain, moderate, soften, discipline, punish, correct, reprove
FORMAL chastise, castigate

chastise v
punish, discipline, reprimand, correct, reprove, scold, censure, beat, flog, whip, lash, scourge, smack, spank, strap, cane
OLD disple, swinge; (Spenser) reform
FORMAL admonish, castigate, upbraid, berate
COLLOQ. haul over the coals, dress down, take to task, wallop
SLANG fix
E∃ praise, encourage

chastisement n
punishment, discipline, correction, censure, scolding, beating, flogging, whipping, smacking, spanking
FORMAL admonition, castigation
COLLOQ. dressing-down, walloping

chastity n
purity, virginity, maidenhood, modesty, abstinence, temperateness, continence, continency, celibacy, unmarried state, singleness, virtue, honour, innocence, immaculateness
OLD (Shakesp) honesty
E∃ promiscuity, immorality

chat v, n
♦ v
talk, gossip, chatter, tittle-tattle, chitchat, coze, babble, jabber; *dialect* cosher; *Scot* blether; *Scot & NAm* crack; *Aust* yabber
FORMAL converse
COLLOQ. natter, rabbit (on), gas, waffle, prattle, chinwag, jaw, chew the rag/fat, shoot the breeze; *Aust* wongi
SLANG schmooze
♦ n
talk, conversation, gossip, tête-à-tête, heart-to-heart, cosy chat, small talk, tittle-tattle, causerie, coze; *Scot* blether; *Aust* yabber
COLLOQ. natter, confab, chinwag, rap; *NAm* visit; *Aust* wongi
SLANG schmooze
■ **chat up**
flirt with, try to get off with, make a pass at, make advances to, ogle, leer at, eye
COLLOQ. come on to

chatter v, n
♦ v
chat, chitchat, gossip, tattle, tittle-tattle, tattle, gabble, babble, jabber, rattle (on), cackle, clack, clatter, jargon, palaver; *dialect* chitter, mag; *Scot* blether
COLLOQ. pass the time of day, natter, witter, rabbit (on), gab, gas, waffle, prattle, chinwag, earbash, jaw, talk the hind legs off a donkey, chunter
♦ n
talk, conversation, gossip, tête-à-tête, chitchat, natter, jabber, witter, prattle, babble, tittle-tattle, jaw, tattle, twattle, patter, jargon, clitter-clatter, gibble-gabble, talkee-talkee, tongue-work; *dialect* mag; *Scot* blether, clash, yatter, gabnash, nashgab
COLLOQ. natter, confab, chinwag, yap
SLANG gammon

chatterbox n
chatterer, babbler, gossipper, gossip, talker,

conversationalist, jabberer, tittle-tattler, tattler
COLLOQ. natterer, windbag, gasbag, gasser, gabber, big mouth, blabbermouth, loudmouth

chatty adj

1 *a chatty person*
talkative, gossipy, conversational, communicative, garrulous, gushing, effusive, verbose, long-winded, glib
FORMAL loquacious
COLLOQ. gabby, mouthy
2 *a chatty letter*
newsy, friendly, informal, casual, colloquial, conversational, gossipy, familiar
E3 quiet, taciturn

chauvinism n

jingoism, nationalism, bias, prejudice, partisanship, flag-waving, sexism, male chauvinism

chauvinist adj, n

• *adj*
jingoist, nationalist, biased, prejudiced, flag-waving, sexist, male chauvinist
• *n*
jingoist, nationalist, male chauvinist
COLLOQ. MCP, male chauvinist pig

chauvinistic adj

biased, prejudiced, sexist, jingoistic, nationalistic

cheap adj

1 INEXPENSIVE, reasonable, low-price, low-cost, affordable, bargain, reduced, cut-price, knock-down, marked-down, discounted, slashed, rock-bottom, giveaway, throwaway, budget, economy, sale, economical, no-frills, cheap-rate, reduced-rate, concessional-rate, on special offer, value-for-money, a good buy, bargain-basement, *à bon marché*
OLD good-cheap
COLLOQ. a snip, a steal, going for a song, dirt-cheap, dog-cheap, ten a penny, on a shoestring
2 SHODDY, cheap and nasty, tatty, tawdry, inferior, second-rate, worthless, vulgar, tasteless, common, chintz, gingerbread, sixpenny, improvised, ramshackle, poor, cheapjack, paltry
COLLOQ. cheapo, tacky; *N Am* two-bit, a dime a dozen, jitney
3 *cheap comments*
mean, contemptible, despicable, low, vulgar, sordid
E3 **1** expensive, costly, dear **2** superior, good quality **3** noble, admirable

---

Synonym nuances
sense 1
Reasonable and **affordable** are both positive-sounding terms, suggesting simply that something is not overpriced: *Stilton is an affordable substitute for Roquefort.* **Bargain** is similarly positive, in that it suggests you getting a good deal for your money, as is **giveaway**, which is usually applied to price to create the impression of a virtual gift. Other terms with much the same meaning have different connotations, however; **throwaway**, for instance, connotes something of little value rather than a desirably low price.
Budget and **economy**, although they can be used straightforwardly to describe something cheap because it is the lower end of a scale, may also have associations of poor quality or discomfort: *economy air travel.*
Economical is different again, however, having as it does the positive implication of long-term savings for the buyer: *the development of a more economical car.*

---

cheapen v

devalue, degrade, lower, demean, depreciate, belittle, discredit, downgrade
FORMAL disparage, denigrate, derogate

cheaply adv

inexpensively, affordably, economically, reasonably, at low cost, at an affordable price, on special offer, at a cheap rate, at a reduced/discounted rate, at rock-bottom prices, with no frills, *à bon marché*
E3 expensively

cheat v, n

• *v*
1 *cheat someone*
defraud, swindle, diddle, short-change, double-cross, mislead, deceive, dupe, fool, trick, hoodwink, gull, beguile, cozen, fiddle, fleece, fake, bluff, welsh, cajole, rogue, skelder, hocus, chouse, cog, smouch, fudge, jink; (*offensive*) jew; *Scot* begunk
OLD baffle, colt, cully, fob, mump, slur; (*Shakesp*) cony-catch
COLLOQ. do, do one over on, do the dirty on, con, take, pull the wool over someone's eyes, two-time, bilk, fix, rig, bamboozle, bam, clip, fox; *Aust & NZ* duckshove
SLANG take for a ride, screw, sting, touch, trim, chisel, chizz, swiz, gum, queer, rip off, stiff, take to the cleaners, do a flanker; *N Am* hornswoggle
2 *cheated out of their inheritance*
prevent, deprive, deny, thwart, frustrate, check
OLD (*Shakesp*) bob
COLLOQ. do, have
• *n*
cheater, dodger, crook, fraud, swindler, extortioner, double-crosser, impostor, charlatan, deceiver, trickster, confidence trickster, rogue, cozener, sharper, chouse, picaroon
OLD biter; (*Shakesp*) cony-catcher, gull-catcher
COLLOQ. con man, shark
SLANG chiseller, chizz, intake; *N Am* gyp; *Aust* dingo
OLD SLANG snap

Synonym nuances
verb sense 1
Predictably, many of the synonyms for cheat have strong implications of disapproval. The terms **defraud**, **swindle**, and **diddle** generally suggest cheating someone out of money, as can the word **fiddle**, which can also be used of tampering with something with the aim of deceiving: *he fiddled the statistics in his thesis.* **Short-change**, although used literally of money, can be used in wider contexts: *the victim's family felt short-changed by the sentence.*
Double-cross carries an emotive suggestion of betrayal, and **welsh** is similarly marked, but used in the context of dereliction of an obligation or financial debt. The terms **mislead**, **deceive**, **dupe**, **fool**, **trick**, **hoodwink** and the less common **gull** would usually be used in the context of convincing someone of a falsehood: *don't be hoodwinked into thinking money brings happiness.*
Beguile has strong associations of cheating someone through charm, and **cajole**, through persuasion: *she could not be cajoled into agreeing.* If, however, you imply that something has been made less clear in order to obscure the truth, you could use **fudge**: *the media fudged the events.*

---

check v, n

• *v*
1 EXAMINE, inspect, scrutinize, look at (closely), go through, scan, investigate, probe, inquire into, test, monitor, police, study, research, analyse, compare, cross-check, screen, take stock, make sure, confirm, verify
FORMAL corroborate, substantiate, validate
COLLOQ. give the once-over
2 *check an impulse*

curb, bridle, restrain, control, limit, contain, rein in, repress, inhibit, damp, thwart, hinder, impede, obstruct, bar, delay, slow (down), stop, staunch, stem, arrest, halt, bring to a standstill
FORMAL retard
♦ *n*
1 EXAMINATION, inspection, scrutiny, check-up, investigation, inquiry, audit, test, research, monitoring, analysis, probe, confirmation, verification
COLLOQ. once-over
2 BILL, invoice, statement, account, charges, reckoning, tally; *N Am* tab
■ **check in**
register, book in, enrol, record your arrival, report your arrival
■ **check out**
1 *check out of a hotel*
leave, pay the bill, settle up
2 *check out the procedure*
examine, investigate, test, study, look into
COLLOQ. recce
■ **check up**
investigate, inspect, evaluate, assess, analyse, probe, inquire into, ascertain, make sure, confirm, verify
■ **hold/keep in check**
restrain, hold back, keep back, suppress, repress, curb, bridle, rein in, stop, arrest, prevent, hinder, obstruct, impede

check-up *n*
examination, inspection, scrutiny, investigation, inquiry, audit, test, research, monitoring, analysis, evaluation, appraisal, probe, confirmation, verification

cheek *n*
1 *his cheeks went red*
jowl, jaw, chop, chap, dimple; *Scot* chafts
TECHNICAL gena
OLD wang
Related adjectives: buccal, malar
2 IMPERTINENCE, impudence, insolence, disrespect, brazenness, audacity, gall
FORMAL effrontery, temerity
COLLOQ. nerve, sauce, lip, mouth, attitude, neck, brass neck, chutzpah
SLANG *Aust* arse

cheekily *adv*
impertinently, impudently, insolently, disrespectfully, pertly
🔁 respectfully, politely

cheeky *adj*
impertinent, impudent, insolent, disrespectful, forward, brazen, pert, audacious, overfamiliar
COLLOQ. fresh, saucy, lippy, mouthy; *N Am* sassy
🔁 respectful, polite

cheep *v, n*
chirp, chirrup, tweet, peep, trill, sing, twitter, warble, pipe, whistle

cheer *v, n*
♦ *v*
1 ACCLAIM, hail, clap, applaud, salute, welcome, celebrate, fanfare, shout, support; *Aust & NZ* barrack for
COLLOQ. root for
2 COMFORT, console, brighten, gladden, warm, uplift, raise/lift the spirits of, elate, exhilarate, encourage, hearten, enliven, buoy up
FORMAL solace, inspirit
COLLOQ. buck up, perk up
♦ *n*
1 *the cheers of the crowd*
acclamation, hurrah, bravo, applause, clapping, ovation
FORMAL plaudits

2 CHEERFULNESS, gladness, happiness, hopefulness, joyfulness, high spirits, light-heartedness, merriment, merrymaking, revelry
🔁 criticism
■ **cheer up**
comfort, console, encourage, brighten (up), hearten, liven (up), take heart, rally
COLLOQ. buck up, perk up
🔁 **1** boo, jeer **2** dishearten, discourage

cheerful *adj*
1 *a cheerful person*
happy, glad, contented, joyful, joyous, blithe, carefree, light-hearted, cheery, good-humoured, sunny, optimistic, enthusiastic, hearty, genial, jovial, jolly, gay, merry, lively, animated, exuberant, bright, smiling, laughing, spirited, in good spirits, chirpy, breezy, jaunty, buoyant, sparkling, upbeat
2 *painted in a cheerful yellow*
attractive, pleasing, pleasant, agreeable, delightful, warm, sunny, bright, comforting, encouraging, heartening, inspiring, stirring
🔁 **1** sad, dejected, depressed **2** depressing, disheartening

cheerily *adv*
happily, gladly, light-heartedly, cheerfully, enthusiastically, jovially, brightly
🔁 sadly, unhappily

cheerio *interj*
goodbye, farewell, adieu, *au revoir*
COLLOQ. cheers, so long, bye, bye-bye, see you, see you later, ta-ta; *Aust* hooray

cheerless *adj*
gloomy, dismal, dreary, dull, depressing, dejected, despondent, austere, barren, desolate, forlorn, grim, bleak, cold, sad, unhappy, sombre, sorrowful, comfortless, joyless, lonely, melancholy, miserable, mournful, dank, dark, dingy, drab, sullen, sunless, winterly, uninviting
FORMAL disconsolate, dolorous
🔁 bright, cheerful

cheers *interj*
1 *say cheers as a toast*
bottoms up, here's to you, your good health, here's looking to you, here's mud in your eye, here's to ..., to absent friends, down the hatch, happy landings, all the best, chin-chin, *prosit*, *skol*, *slàinte*
2 THANK YOU, thank you very much, bless you, much obliged
COLLOQ. many thanks, thanks a lot, ta
3 GOODBYE, farewell, adieu, *au revoir*
COLLOQ. so long, bye, bye-bye, see you, see you later, ta-ta

cheery *adj*
happy, glad, contented, joyful, carefree, light-hearted, cheerful, optimistic, enthusiastic, hearty, genial, jovial, jolly, gay, merry, lively, animated, exuberant, bright, smiling, laughing, spirited, in good spirits, chirpy, breezy, jaunty, buoyant, sparkling
🔁 downcast, sad

cheese *n*
Related adjective: caseous
See panel on next page

cheesed off *adj*
fed up, disappointed, bored, depressed, discontented, disgruntled, dissatisfied, annoyed, disgusted
COLLOQ. brassed off, browned off, hacked off, sick and tired
SLANG pissed off; *N Am* pissed
🔁 contented, happy

Varieties of cheese include:

Amsterdam	Cheshire	Double	Gruyère	Neufchâtel	ricotta
Bel Paese	chevreton	Gloucester	Huntsman	Orkney	Roquefort
Bleu d'Auvergne	Churnton	Dunlop	Jarlsberg®	Parmesan	sage Derby
Blue Cheshire	cottage cheese	Edam	Killarney	pecorino	Saint-Paulin
Blue Vinny	cream cheese	Emmental	Lancashire	Petit Suisse	Stilton
Boursin	crottin	Emmentaler	Leicester	Pont-l'Évêque	stracchino
Brie	Crowdie	ewe-cheese	Limburg(er)	Port Salut	Vacherin
Caboc	curd cheese	Feta	Lymeswold	processed cheese	vegetarian cheese
Caerphilly	Danish blue	Fontina	manchego	provolone	Wensleydale
Camembert	Derby	fromage frais	mascarpone	quark	
Cantal	Dolcelatte	Gloucester	Monterey Jack	reblochon	
Carré	Dorset Blue	Gorgonzola	mouse-trap	Red Leicester	
Cheddar		Gouda	mozzarella	Red Windsor	

---

chemical elements

The chemical elements (with their symbols) are:

actinium (Ac)	hahnium (Ha)	praseodymium
aluminium (Al)	helium (He)	(Pr)
americium (Am)	holmium (Ho)	promethium (Pm)
antimony (Sb)	hydrogen (H)	protactinium (Pa)
argon (Ar)	indium (In)	radium (Ra)
arsenic (As)	iodine (I)	radon (Rn)
astatine (At)	iridium (Ir)	rhenium (Re)
barium (Ba)	iron (Fe)	rhodium (Rh)
berkelium (Bk)	krypton (Kr)	rubidium (Rb)
beryllium (Be)	lanthanum (La)	ruthenium (Ru)
bismuth (Bi)	lawrencium (Lr)	rutherfordium
boron (B)	lead (Pb)	(Rf)
bromine (Br)	lithium (Li)	samarium (Sm)
cadmium (Cd)	lutetium (Lu)	scandium (Sc)
caesium (Cs)	magnesium (Mg)	selenium (Se)
calcium (Ca)	manganese (Mn)	silicon (Si)
californium (Cf)	mendelevium	silver (Ag)
carbon (C)	(Md)	sodium (Na)
cerium (Ce)	mercury (Hg)	strontium (Sr)
chlorine (Cl)	molybdenum	sulphur (S)
chromium (Cr)	(Mo)	tantalum (Ta)
cobalt (Co)	neodymium (Nd)	technetium (Tc)
copper (Cu)	neon (Ne)	tellurium (Te)
curium (Cm)	neptunium (Np)	terbium (Tb)
dubnium (Db)	nickel (Ni)	thallium (Tl)
dysprosium (Dy)	niobium (Nb)	thorium (Th)
einsteinium (Es)	nitrogen (N)	thulium (Tm)
erbium (Er)	nobelium (No)	tin (Sn)
europium (Eu)	osmium (Os)	titanium (Ti)
fermium (Fm)	oxygen (O)	tungsten (W)
fluorine (F)	palladium (Pd)	uranium (U)
francium (Fr)	phosphorus (P)	vanadium (V)
gadolinium (Gd)	platinum (Pt)	xenon (Xe)
gallium (Ga)	plutonium (Pu)	ytterbium (Yb)
germanium (Ge)	polonium (Po)	yttrium (Y)
gold (Au)	potassium (K)	zinc (Zn)
hafnium (Hf)		zirconium (Zr)

---

chemistry
See panel on next page

chequered *adj*
1 *a chequered tablecloth*
checked, multicoloured, variegated, particoloured, striped, diced
TECHNICAL checky, chequy
2 VARIED, mixed, diverse, with good and bad parts, with ups and downs, with sad and happy downs, with its fair share of rough and tumble

cherish *v*
1 *cherish someone*
care for, look after, love, take (good) care of, hold dear, have at heart, encourage, make much of, treasure, adore, hug, support, foster, nurture, nourish, nurse, sustain
OLD refocillate, tender

2 *cherish a tradition/privilege*
foster, nurture, sustain, hold dear, value, prize, treasure, enshrine
3 *cherish hopes/memories*
harbour, shelter, entertain, hold dear, value, prize, treasure, nourish, brood on

cherub *n*
angel, seraph

cherubic *adj*
adorable, appealing, cute, sweet, innocent, lov(e)able, lovely, heavenly, angelic, seraphic

chest *n*
1 *a man with a hairy chest*
breast
TECHNICAL sternum, thorax
Related adjective: pectoral, thoracic
2 *a treasure chest*
trunk, crate, box, case, casket, coffer, strongbox, bunker, hutch, ark, chiffonier, commode, tallboy, bahut, *cassone*, cub, slop-chest; *Scot* kist, corn-kist, girnel, meal-ark; *N Am* bureau, dresser
OLD cap-case, larnax, scrine, shrine

chew *v*
bite, gnaw, munch, champ, chomp, crunch, grind, eat, ruminate; *dialect* chaw, chumble
FORMAL masticate, manducate
■ **chew over**
consider, meditate on, mull over, ponder, weigh up, muse on, deliberate upon
FORMAL ruminate on
COLLOQ. put on your thinking cap

chic *adj*
elegant, fashionable, sophisticated, modish, smart, stylish, dapper, à la mode
COLLOQ. snazzy, trendy, with it
E3 outmoded, unfashionable

chicanery *n*
trickery, deception, fraud, deceitfulness, dishonesty, deviousness, cheating, double-dealing, guile, hoodwinking, duplicity, artifice, intrigue, sharp practice, underhandedness, sophistry, subterfuge, wiles
COLLOQ. dodge, jiggery-pokery

chide *v*
scold, tell off, blame, criticize, censure, lecture, rebuke, chastise, reprehend, reprimand, reproach, reprove, row, dress, rate; *Scot* quarrel
OLD shend
FORMAL admonish, berate, upbraid, objurgate
E3 praise

chief *adj, n*
♦ *adj*
leading, foremost, uppermost, highest, supreme, grand, arch, head, premier, principal, main, key, central, prime, prevailing, predominant, dominant, pre-eminent,

Terms used in chemistry include:

acid	chemical	diffusion	hydrolysis	mixture	salt
alkali	compound	dissociation	immiscible	mole	solids
analysis	chemical element	distillation	indicator	molecule	solution
atom	chemical	electrochemical	inert gas	neutron	solvent
atomic number	equation	cell	ion	noble gas	substance
atomic structure	chemical reaction	electrode	ionic bond	nucleus	suspension
subatomic	chemist	electron	isomer	oxidation	symbol
particles	chlorination	electrolysis	isotope	periodic table	synthesis
base	combustion	emulsion	lipid	pH	valency
bond	compound	fermentation	liquid	polymer	zwitterion
buffer	corrosion	fixation	litmus paper	proton	
catalysis	covalent bond	formula	litmus test	radioactivity	
catalyst	crystal	free radical	mass	reaction	
chain reaction	cycle	gas	matter	reduction	
chemical bond	decomposition	halogen	metallic bond	respiration	

See also **acid; chemical elements; gas; minerals**.

outstanding, vital, most important, essential, primary, major, controlling, directing, supervising
F3 minor, unimportant
♦ *n*
ruler, chieftain, lord, overlord, master, supremo, head, principal, leader, commander, captain, governor, boss, director, manager, premier, prime minister, president, suzerain, chair, chairperson, chairman, chairwoman, chief executive, managing director, superintendent, superior, ringleader
COLLOQ. boss, gaffer, top dog, top banana, big cheese, big noise, big gun
SLANG *Scot* head bummer; *N Am* honcho

chiefly *adv*
mainly, mostly, for the most part, in the main, predominantly, principally, primarily, essentially, especially, generally, on the whole, usually

child *n*
youngster, young person, little one, little 'un, young one, young 'un, baby, infant, toddler, minor, juvenile, boy, little boy, girl, little girl, son, daughter, grandchild, stepchild, schoolchild, adolescent, teenager, youth, young adult, descendant, godchild, orphanmite, changeling, innocent, suckling, weanling, tiny, trot, littling, pledge, *enfant*, papoose; (*offensive*) pickaninny; preschooler, underfive, preteen, weeny-bopper, prodigy, wunderkind, ragamuffin, imp, waif, brat, jackanapes, bambino, cherub, elf, chick, chit, guttersnipe, Benjamin, olive branch; *Scot* bairn, wean, tyke, knave-bairn, gyte, smout; *N Am* subteen
OLD bantling, dilling, wanton, wench; (*Shakesp*) eyas-musket; *Scot* gangrel
FORMAL offspring, issue, progeny
COLLOQ. tot, tiny tot, kid, nipper, brat, sprog; *N Am* hellion; *Scot* get
SLANG kinchin, ankle-biter; *N Am* rug rat
OLD SLANG butter-print

childbirth *n*
labour, delivery, confinement, child-bearing, lying-in, pregnancy, maternity
TECHNICAL parturition
FORMAL travail, accouchement, puerperal

childhood *n*
babyhood, infancy, boyhood, girlhood, schooldays, early days, early years, youth, adolescence, minority, immaturity

childish *adj*
babyish, boyish, girlish, infantile, puerile, juvenile, immature, irresponsible, silly, foolish, frivolous
F3 mature, sensible

🛈 **childish** or **childlike**?
You describe someone as *childish* if you think they are behaving in a silly immature way: *Stop being so childish!* *Childlike* is a neutral term: *childlike innocence*.

childishly *adv*
immaturely, irresponsibly, foolishly

childlike *adj*
innocent, naive, ingenuous, artless, guileless, credulous, trusting, trustful, simple, natural, unaffected

chill *n, v, adj*
♦ *n*
1 *a wintry chill in the air*
coolness, cold, coldness, rawness, bite, nip, crispness, iciness
2 *catch a chill*
cold, fever, flu, influenza, virus
3 *a chill ran down my spine*
shiver, fear, anxiety, apprehension, dread
F3 1 warmth
♦ *v*
1 COOL, cool down, refrigerate, make/become cold(er), freeze, ice
2 FRIGHTEN, terrify, dismay, scare, dishearten, petrify, discourage, depress, dampen
F3 1 warm, heat
♦ *adj*
cold, cool, raw, sharp, biting, icy, freezing, wintry, chilly, frigid, depressing, bleak
COLLOQ. nippy, parky
F3 warm, hot
■ **chill out**
calm down, relax, have a rest, unwind
COLLOQ. take it easy

chilly *adj*
1 *chilly weather*
cold, fresh, brisk, crisp, cool, raw, sharp, biting, icy, freezing, frigid, wintry
COLLOQ. nippy, parky
2 *a chilly response*
cool, frigid, unsympathetic, unwelcoming, aloof, stony, distant, unresponsive, unfriendly, unenthusiastic, hostile
F3 1 warm **2** friendly

chime *v, n*
♦ *v*
sound, strike, toll, ring, peal, clang, ding, dong, jingle, tinkle, reverberate, boom, resound
FORMAL tintinnabulate
♦ *n*
toll, ring, peal, clang, ding, dong, tinkle, boom, reverberation
■ **chime in**
1 *chime in when someone is talking*
interrupt
FORMAL interject, interpose

COLLOQ. chip in, butt in, cut in
2 *his analysis chimed in with mine*
fit in, harmonize, correspond, blend, agree, be consistent, be similar

chimera *n*
illusion, fantasy, delusion, dream, fancy, idle fancy, figment of the imagination, hallucination, will-o'-the-wisp, spectre

chimney *n*
shaft, stack, chimney stalk, vent, flue, funnel, cleft, crevice, lum, femerall

china *n*
1 *a vase made of china*
porcelain, ceramic, pottery, earthenware, terracotta
2 *serve the best china*
crockery, plates, dishes, cups and saucers, tableware, dinner service

Chinese calendar

The animals representing the years in which people are born:

rat	dragon	monkey
buffalo	snake	rooster
tiger	horse	dog
rabbit (or hare)	goat (or sheep)	pig

chink *n*
crack, rift, cleft, fissure, crevice, cut, split, slit, slot, cavity, opening, aperture, gap, space

chip *n, v*
♦ *n*
1 *fish and chips*
fried potato, (French) fry
2 NOTCH, nick, crack, scratch, dent, flaw
3 FRAGMENT, bit, piece, scrap, wafer, splinter, sliver, flake, shred, shard, shaving, paring
4 *gambling chips*
counter, disc, token
♦ *v*
chisel, whittle, nick, crack, fragment, break (off), crumble, notch, gash, snick, damage
■ **chip in**
1 CONTRIBUTE, make a donation, donate, club together, have a collection, pay, subscribe
COLLOQ. have a whip-round
2 *chip in when someone is talking*
interrupt
FORMAL interject, interpose
COLLOQ. chime in, butt in, cut in

chirp *v, n*
chirrup, tweet, cheep, peep, trill, twitter, warble, sing, pipe, whistle

chirpy *adj*
cheerful, cheery, bright, happy, glad, jolly, merry, gay, jaunty, blithe
COLLOQ. perky
Ea downcast, sad

chit-chat *n*
chat, chatter, talk, conversation, gossip, idle gossip, tête-à-tête, heart-to-heart, cosy chat, small talk, tittle-tattle
COLLOQ. natter, confab, chinwag

chivalrous *adj*
gentlemanly, polite, courteous, well-mannered, gallant, heroic, valiant, brave, courageous, bold, gracious, noble, honourable, knightly
Ea ungallant, cowardly

chivalry *n*
gentlemanliness, politeness, courtesy, graciousness, good manners, courtliness, gallantry, bravery, courage, boldness, honour, truthfulness, integrity, bushido

chivvy *v*
badger, harass, annoy, hound, goad, nag, urge, pester, plague, pressure, hurry (up), prod, torment
FORMAL importune
COLLOQ. bug, hassle

chock-a-block *adj*
packed, crammed, full, overfull, jammed, crowded, congested, brimful
COLLOQ. jam-packed, packed like sardines, full to bursting
SLANG chocker
Ea empty

choice *n, adj*
♦ *n*
1 *a choice of several dishes; make a choice between two things*
selection, variety, range, choosing, opting, picking, preference, decision, election, discrimination
2 *have no choice but to go*
option, alternative, answer, solution
♦ *adj*
select, best, superior, prime, plum, excellent, first-class, first-rate, fine, finest, exquisite, exclusive, hand-picked, special, prize, valuable, precious
Ea inferior, poor

choke *v*
1 STRANGLE, throttle, asphyxiate, suffocate, stifle, smother, suppress, overpower, overwhelm
OLD worry
2 OBSTRUCT, constrict, congest, clog, block, dam (up), bar, close, stop, plug, glut, silt (up)
OLD (*Spenser*) accloy; stap
FORMAL occlude
3 COUGH, gag, retch
■ **choke back**
suppress, restrain, contain, control, check, curb, repress, inhibit, fight back

choleric *adj*
fiery, hot-tempered, angry, bad-tempered, ill-tempered, quick-tempered, testy, touchy, irascible, irritable, petulant
COLLOQ. crabbed, crabby, crotchety
Ea calm, placid

choose *v*
1 *choose a new dress*
pick (out), select, single out, take, go for, opt for, vote for, decide on, settle on, fix on, designate, adopt, take up, appoint, elect, predestine
FORMAL espouse
COLLOQ. plump for
2 *choose to do something*
decide, prefer, wish, desire, make up your mind, want, favour, see fit

---

Synonym nuances
sense 1
Pick (out), **decide on**, **settle on** and **fix on** are terms that could be used to refer to choosing after some thought.
Select is similar, but with more implication of discrimination in your choice: *he was selected for the England squad*. **Take**, **opt for** or **go for** sometimes imply instinct rather than careful discrimination: *I opted for the quickest route home*.
  Single out might be used where there is an element of drawing special attention to something: *the over-40s are being singled out as potential customers*. To refer to

purposefully marking something out for specific recognition, you may wish to use **designate**: *nursing staff designated specifically for the care of the elderly.* Both **adopt** and **take up** suggest a degree of support or activity is involved: *they took up the theme of citizenship*; whilst **appoint** and **elect** are generally used in the context of deciding on suitable candidates for office, though the latter may also be suggestive of deciding a course of action: *they elected to live together.* The term **predestine** lends itself to a narrower range of uses and specifically suggests a preordained decision: *he was predestined to be black sheep of the family.*

choosy *adj*
selective, discriminating, fussy, particular, finicky, fastidious, exacting, faddy
COLLOQ. picky, pernickety; *N Am* persnickety
F3 undemanding

chop *v*
cut (up), hack, fell, hew, lop, saw, sever, truncate, slice, carve, cleave, divide, dissect, split, slash, axe
■ **chop up**
cut (up), cut into pieces, slice (up), divide, cube, dice, shred, mince, grind, grate

choppy *adj*
rough, turbulent, tempestuous, stormy, squally, blustery, ruffled, wavy, uneven, broken
F3 calm, still, peaceful

chore *n*
task, job, errand, routine, duty, burden, piece of work

chortle *v*
cackle, chuckle, guffaw, laugh, crow, snigger, snort

chorus *n*
1 REFRAIN, response, burden, strain, call, shout
2 CHOIR, choristers, singers, vocalists, ensemble, choral group

Christ *n*
Messiah, Saviour, Son of God, Son of Man, deliverer, Redeemer, I am, Immanuel, Lord, Lord of lords, King of kings, Word of God, Lamb of God, Good Shepherd

christen *v*
1 *christen a baby*
baptize, name, give a name to, sprinkle, immerse
2 *christened it 'the emerald forest'*
name, call, dub, title, style, term, designate
3 *christen the wine glasses*
inaugurate, use for the first time, begin using

Christmas *n*
Xmas, Noel, Christmas-tide, Christmas-time, Nativity, Yule, Yuletide
COLLOQ. Chrissie, Crimbo

chronic *adj*
1 *a chronic illness*
persistent, deep-seated, recurring, incessant, constant, continual, long-lasting, long-standing, long-term, ingrained, deep-rooted
2 *a chronic worrier*
inveterate, confirmed, habitual, hardened, incorrigible
3 *the film was chronic*
awful, terrible, dreadful, appalling, atrocious, frightful, abysmal
COLLOQ. ropy, a load of rubbish
SLANG naff, crappy, the pits, pants
F3 **1** temporary **3** excellent

chronically *adv*
1 *chronically sick*
persistently, recurrently, incessantly, constantly, continually,

long-term, deep-rootedly
2 *chronically disorganized*
inveterately, habitually, incorrigibly

chronicle *n, v*
◆ *n*
account, record, register, annals, archives, diary, calendar, history, journal, narrative, story, saga, epic
◆ *v*
recount, narrate, relate, report, tell, write down, set down, record, put on record, register, enter, list

chronicler *n*
historian, archivist, annalist, diarist, narrator, recorder, reporter, scribe, historiographer, chronographer, chronologer

chronological *adj*
consecutive, sequential, in sequence, progressive, ordered, in order, serial, historical

chubby *adj*
plump, fat, podgy, fleshy, flabby, stout, portly, round, full, tubby, paunchy, roly-poly
FORMAL rotund
F3 slim, skinny

chuck *v*
1 THROW, cast, toss, fling, heave, hurl, jettison, pitch, put, shy, sling
2 *chuck a habit/your boyfriend*
give up, abandon, reject, discard, get rid of, jilt
FORMAL forsake
COLLOQ. quit, dump, pack in, give the brush-off, give the elbow

chuckle *v*
laugh, laugh quietly, giggle, titter, snigger, chortle, snort, cackle, crow

chum *n*
friend, companion, comrade
COLLOQ. mate, pal, crony, buddy
F3 enemy

chummy *adj*
friendly, affectionate, close, intimate, sociable
COLLOQ. mat(e)y, pally, thick

chunk *n*
lump, hunk, mass, wedge, block, slab, piece, dollop, portion
COLLOQ. wodge

chunky *adj*
1 *a chunky man*
heavy, broad, well-built, stocky, solid, thickset, dumpy
2 *a chunky bag*
large, thick, bulky, substantial, weighty, heavy, unwieldy, awkward, cumbersome
F3 **1** tall, skinny **2** small, light

church *n*
1 *go to church*
place of worship, chapel, house of God, Lord's house, house of prayer, house of worship, place of worship, cathedral, minster, abbey, tabernacle, meeting-house, bethel, chantry, shrine, basilica, Bethesda, preaching-house, procathedral, temple; *Scot* kirk
2 *the Methodist Church*
denomination, tradition, grouping, sect, cult
3 CONGREGATION, assembly, fellowship, community, people of God, body of Christ, bride of Christ, flock, fold
TECHNICAL ecclesia
Related adjective: ecclesiastical
See panels on next page

Parts of a church or cathedral include:

adytum	deambulatory	rood
aisle	diaconicon	rood screen
almonry	fenestella	sacellum
altar	font	sacrarium
ambulatory	frithstool	sacristy
antechoir	frontal	sanctuary
apse	gallery	schola cantorum
arcade	keystone	sedile
arch	lectern	sepulchre
atrium	lucarne	shrine
baptistery	misericord	slype
belfry	narthex	spire
bell screen	nave	squint
bell tower	parclose	stall
chancel	parvis	stasidion
chapel	pew	stations of the
chapterhouse	pinnacle	cross
chevet	piscina	steeple
choir	porch	stoup
clerestory	portal	tambour
cloister	predella	tomb
confessional	presbytery	tower
corona	pulpit	transept
credence	reredos	triforium
crossing	retrochoir	vault
crypt	ringing chamber	

See also **places of worship** at **worship**.

Names of church services include:

Advent	Eucharist	morning prayers
Ascension Day	evening service	morning service
Ash Wednesday	evensong	Mothering
baptism	funeral	Sunday
benediction	Good Friday	Nones
christening	High Mass	nuptial Mass
Christingle	Holy Communion	Palm Sunday
Christmas	Holy Matrimony	Pentecost
communion	Lord's Supper	Remembrance
confirmation	marriage	Sunday
dedication	Mass	Requiem Mass
Easter	Midnight Mass	Vigil Mass
Epiphany	memorial service	

See also **canonical**; **celebration**.

churchyard n
graveyard, cemetery, God's acre, burial ground, burial place, burial site, necropolis, charnel, house; Scot kirkyard, kirkyaird
SLANG boneyard

churlish adj
bad-tempered, ill-tempered, harsh, impolite, morose, rough, brusque, rude, sullen, surly, uncivil, unmannerly, ill-mannered, ill-bred, discourteous, unneighbourly, unsociable, loutish, boorish, oafish
COLLOQ. crabbed
≠ polite, urbane

churn v
1 *my stomach is churning*
heave, turn, vomit, be sick, retch
COLLOQ. throw up, puke
2 *churn up mud*
move about violently, agitate, beat, stir, disturb, swirl, toss, writhe, convulse, boil, foam, froth, seethe
■ **churn out**
turn out, produce in great quantities, pump out, throw together, knock up

chute n
channel, incline, slide, slope, ramp, runway, shaft, funnel, gutter, trough

chutzpah n
cheek, impertinence, impudence, gall, insolence, disrespect, brazenness, audacity
COLLOQ. nerve, sauce, lip, mouth, brass neck

cigarette n
cigar, menthol, filter-tip, king-size, high-tar, low-tar, roll-up, roll-your-own, smoke, whiff
OLD paper-cigar
COLLOQ. cig, ciggy, fag, fag end, dog end, gasper, joint, spliff, weed, burn, reefer, tailor-made; N Am roach
SLANG cancer-stick, coffin-nail, snout
See also panel at **tobacco**.

cinch n
COLLOQ. child's play, doddle, piece of cake, snip, scoosh, stroll, walkover, pushover; N Am cakewalk

cinders n
embers, ashes, clinker, charcoal, coke, slag

cinema n
1 FILMS, pictures, movies, motion pictures
OLD flicks; N Am nickelodeon
COLLOQ. big screen, silver screen
2 PICTURE-HOUSE; N Am & Aust theatre; S Afr bioscope; film theatre, movie theatre, movies, entertainment centre, multiplex, picture-palace
COLLOQ. fleapit; S Afr scope

cipher n
1 CODE, secret writing, secret system, coded message, cryptogram, cryptograph
2 NONENTITY, nobody, yes-man

circa adv
about, approximately, roughly, around, some, something like, odd, more or less, loosely, round about, or thereabouts, approaching, close to, nearly, just about, not far off, in the region/neighbourhood/vicinity of, somewhere in the region of
≠ exactly

circle n, v
♦ n
1 RING, hoop, round, annulus, epicycle, disc, discus, ball, sphere, orb, globe, circumference, perimeter, circuit, lap, compass, cordon, girdle, band, belt, orbit, loop, revolution, cycle, rotation, gyration, spiral, coil, curl, halo, circlet, coronet, crown, plate, saucer, turn, tyre, wheel, wreath
Related adjective: circular
2 *circle of friends*
group, band, company, crowd, set, clique, coterie, gang, ring, club, society, assembly, fellowship, fraternity
♦ v
1 RING, loop, encircle, surround, belt, gird, encompass, enclose, envelop, hem in, hedge in
FORMAL circumscribe, circumnavigate
2 ROTATE, revolve, move round, pivot, gyrate, circulate, whirl, turn, swivel, wheel, pivot, coil, wind

circuit n
1 *a racing circuit; run a circuit*
race track, track, running-track, lap, orbit, revolution, course, route, round, beat
FORMAL perambulation
2 *the circuit of the gardens*
circumference, boundary, bounds, limit, range, compass, ambit
3 *a judge's circuit*
tour, district, area, region

circuitous adj
roundabout, indirect, oblique, devious, tortuous, winding, meandering, rambling
FORMAL periphrastic, labyrinthine
≠ direct, straight

circular adj, n
♦ adj

round, annular, ring-shaped, hoop-shaped, disc-shaped, spherical
◆ *n*
handbill, leaflet, pamphlet, notice, announcement, advertisement, letter, flyer

circulate *v*
1 *circulate information*
spread (around), spread about, diffuse, broadcast, transmit, publicize, publish, issue, give out, propagate, pass round, distribute, go/get around, utter
FORMAL disseminate, promulgate
2 GO ROUND, rotate, revolve, gyrate, whirl, swirl, flow

circulation *n*
1 BLOOD-FLOW, flow, motion, movement, rotation, circling, cycle
TECHNICAL cyclosis
2 SPREAD, transmission, currency, issuing, publication, readership, distribution, publicity, propagation
FORMAL dissemination
■ **in circulation**
in use, available, around, published, issued, printed, current, distributed, spread about/around, afloat

circumference *n*
circuit, circle, perimeter, rim, edge, girth, round, outline, boundary, border, bounds, limits, confines, compass, extremity, margin, arc, verge, fringe, periphery

circumlocution *n*
diffuseness, discursiveness, tautology, indirectness, euphemism, redundancy, roundaboutness, wordiness, verbosity
FORMAL convolution, periphrasis, pleonasm, prolixity
COLLOQ. beating about the bush

circumlocutory *adj*
diffuse, discursive, tautological, indirect, euphemistic, redundant, roundabout, wordy, verbose
FORMAL convoluted, periphrastic, pleonastic, prolix

circumscribe *v*
bound, limit, restrain, restrict, confine, curtail, trim, define, delimit, delineate, demarcate, surround, encircle, enclose, encompass, hem in, pen in

circumspect *adj*
careful, cautious, prudent, attentive, deliberate, discreet, guarded, observant, wary, canny, watchful, vigilant, discriminating, wise
FORMAL sagacious, judicious, politic
E3 unguarded, unwary, reckless

circumspection *n*
care, carefulness, caution, deliberation, discretion, prudence, guardedness, canniness, chariness, wariness, vigilance
E3 recklessness

circumstance *n*
1 *died in mysterious circumstances*
condition, fact, factor, situation, position, state, state of affairs, background, environment, arrangement, detail, particular, item, thing, element, event, occurrence, happening, respect, lie of the land, how the land lies
2 *in impoverished circumstances*
situation, means, resources, status, (financial) position, case, lifestyle, plight
3 *a victim of circumstance*
fate, fortune, lot

circumstantial *adj*
conjectural, presumed, deduced, contingent, hearsay, incidental, indirect, provisional, inferred
FORMAL evidential, presumptive, inferential

circumvent *v*
avoid, get round, get out of, get past, evade, bypass, sidestep, steer clear of, dodge, thwart, outwit

circumvention *n*
avoidance, evasion, bypassing, sidestepping, steering clear, thwarting, dodging

cissy
see **sissy**.

cistern *n*
tank, reservoir, sink, basin, vat

citadel *n*
fortress, stronghold, bastion, castle, keep, tower, fort, fortification, acropolis

citation *n*
1 AWARD, commendation, honour
2 QUOTATION, quote, cutting, excerpt, illustration, mention, passage, reference, source, allusion

cite *v*
quote, mention, refer to, name, specify, state, allude to, exemplify, give an example, enumerate, advance, bring up
FORMAL adduce, evidence

citizen *n*
city-dweller, townsman, townswoman, inhabitant, denizen, resident, householder, voter, taxpayer, freeman, burgher, national, subject, urbanite, local
FORMAL denizen, oppidan

city *n*
metropolis, town, urban district, conurbation, megalopolis, metropolitan area, inner city, city centre, downtown, concrete jungle, urban sprawl, precinct, micropolis, cosmopolis, municipality, pentapolis; *N Am* metroplex
COLLOQ. big smoke
Related adjectives: civic, urban

civic *adj*
city, metropolitan, urban, town, municipal, borough, local, public, communal, community

civil *adj*
1 *civil affairs*
domestic, home, national, internal, interior, state, municipal, civic, public, communal, local, community, secular, civilian
2 POLITE, courteous, well-mannered, mannerly, well-bred, cultivated, courtly, refined, civilized, polished, urbane, affable, respectful, complaisant, obliging, accommodating
E3 **1** international, military, religious **2** uncivil, discourteous, rude

civility *n*
politeness, courteousness, courtesy, breeding, refinement, (good) manners, respect, urbanity, tact, graciousness, affability, pleasantness, amenity
FORMAL comity
E3 discourtesy, rudeness, uncouthness

civilization *n*
1 *ancient civilizations*
society, human society, culture, customs, community, people
2 *modern western civilization*
progress, advancement, development, education, enlightenment, cultivation, refinement, sophistication, urbanity
E3 **2** barbarity, primitiveness

civilize *v*
educate, enlighten, educate, instruct, cultivate, refine, edify, polish, sophisticate, socialize, improve, perfect, tame, humanize

civilized *adj*
1 *a civilized society*
advanced, developed, educated, enlightened, cultured, refined, sophisticated, cultivated, urbane, polite, sociable
2 *a polite, civilized manner*

reasonable, sensible, polite, courteous, refined, well-mannered, urbane, cultured, cultivated
E3 1 uncivilized, barbarous, primitive **2** harsh, coarse, unreasonable, unsophisticated

civilly *adv*
politely, courteously, urbanely, respectfully, mannerly, courtly, obligingly
E3 uncivilly, discourteously, rudely

clad *adj*
clothed, wearing, covered, dressed
FORMAL attired

claim *v, n*
♦ *v*
1 MAINTAIN, allege, profess, state, affirm, declare, assert, maintain, contend, hold, insist, pretend, profess
FORMAL avow, aver, postulate, purport, assume
2 *claim a refund*
ask, request, put in for, require, need, demand, exact, take, collect, lay claim to, have a right to, be entitled to, deserve
FORMAL requisition
3 *claimed the lives of three people*
take, cause, kill
♦ *n*
1 ALLEGATION, pretension, affirmation, assertion, contention, declaration, profession, insistence
FORMAL avowal, averment, asseveration
2 APPLICATION, petition, request, requirement, demand, call, right, privilege, entitlement

claimant *n*
applicant, candidate, petitioner, suppliant, supplicant, litigant, pretendant, pretender

clairvoyance *n*
psychic powers, ESP, extrasensory perception, telepathy, second sight, fortune-telling
TECHNICAL cryptaesthesia, hyperaesthesia

clairvoyant *adj, n*
♦ *adj*
psychic, prophetic, visionary, telepathic, extrasensory
♦ *n*
psychic, fortune-teller, prophet, prophetess, visionary, seer, soothsayer, augur, oracle, diviner, telepath

clamber *v*
scramble, claw, climb, scrabble, shin, scale, mount, ascend; *NAm* shinny

clammy *adj*
damp, moist, sweaty, sweating, sticky, slimy, dank, muggy, heavy, close

clamorous *adj*
noisy, blaring, vociferous, vocal, loud, deafening, lusty, riotous, tumultuous, uproarious, vehement, insistent
E3 quiet, silent

clamour *v, n*
♦ *v*
demand, ask for noisily, call for, press for, claim, insist, urge, bark
OLD brabble
♦ *n*
noise, uproar, commotion, shouting, din, racket, blare, agitation, hubbub, cry, outcry, hue and cry, complaints, brouhaha, rout, rumour; *Scot* stramash, reird; *NAm* katzenjammer
OLD (*Spenser*) outrage; (*Shakesp*) utis
FORMAL vociferance, vociferation
E3 quietness, silence

clamp *n, v*
♦ *n*
vice, grip, press, brace, clasp, bracket, fastener, hand-screw, pinchcock, immobilizer
♦ *v*

fasten, secure, fix, clinch, clench, squeeze, press, grip, hold, brace, immobilize
■ **clamp down on**
control, limit, crack down on, come down hard on, restrict, confine, restrain, suppress, stop, put a stop to, prevent

clampdown *n*
control, limit, restriction, restraint, suppression, prevention, stop, crackdown

clan *n*
1 *the Macleod clan*
tribe, family, house, race, name, kindred, line, sept
OLD gens
2 GROUP, circle, society, brotherhood, fraternity, confraternity, sect, faction, band, set, clique, coterie, horde

clandestine *adj*
secret, surreptitious, undercover, underhand, concealed, hidden, covert, fraudulent, sly, sneaky, stealthy, underground, closet, furtive, private
COLLOQ. backroom, behind-door, cloak-and-dagger, under-the-counter
E3 open

clandestinely *adv*
secretly, surreptitiously, covertly, fraudulently, slyly, stealthily, sneakily, privately, furtively
COLLOQ. under the counter
E3 openly

clang *v, n*
♦ *v*
clash, jangle, clank, clink, clunk, clatter, peal, bong, chime, resound, reverberate, ring, toll
♦ *n*
clash, jangle, clank, clink, clunk, clatter, peal, bong, chime, resound, reverberation, ring, toll

clanger *n*
mistake, error, blunder, inaccuracy, misjudgement, slip, indiscretion, gaffe, faux pas, oversight, fault
FORMAL solecism
COLLOQ. howler, bloomer, boob, booboo, slip-up; *NAm* flub
SLANG boner, goof, cock-up

clank *v, n*
♦ *v*
clang, clash, jangle, clink, clunk, clatter, resound, reverberate, ring, toll
♦ *n*
clang, clash, jangle, clink, clunk, clatter, resounding, reverberation, ring, toll

clannish *adj*
cliquey, cliquish, unfriendly, select, exclusive, insular, narrow, parochial, sectarian
E3 friendly, open

clap *v, n*
♦ *v*
1 APPLAUD, acclaim, cheer, put your hands together for
2 SLAP, smack, strike, pat, hit, bang
OLD chop
COLLOQ. wallop, whack
♦ *n*
1 APPLAUSE, round of applause, acclaim, handclap, ovation, standing ovation
2 *a clap of thunder*
bolt, crack, flash, shaft, burst, streak, ray, spark, blaze, flare

claptrap *n*
rubbish, nonsense, drivel, gibberish, trash, tripe, twaddle, blarney; *dialect* faddle; *Scot* blethers
COLLOQ. bunk, bunkum, claptrap, piffle, bilge, baloney, blah, bosh, eyewash, hogwash, rhubarb, guff, poppycock,

hot air, cobblers, codswallop, rot, tommyrot
SLANG bull; (*vulgar*) balls, bollocks, shit, bullshit

clarification *n*
explanation, simplification, interpretation, exposition,
definition, gloss, illumination
FORMAL elucidation
Ea *formal* obfuscation

clarify *v*
1 EXPLAIN, make clear, throw light on, shed light on, simplify,
resolve, spell out, clear up, make plain, define, illuminate, gloss
FORMAL elucidate
2 REFINE, purify, filter, clear
Ea 1 obscure, confuse **2** cloud

clarity *n*
1 *clarity of thought*
lucidity, simplicity, intelligibility, comprehensibility,
plainness, explicitness, unambiguousness, obviousness
2 *clarity of the water/her diction*
clearness, transparency, precision, sharpness, definition,
visibility
Ea 1 vagueness, woolliness **2** cloudiness, obscurity,
imprecision

clash *v, n*
♦ *v*
1 CRASH, bang, strike, collide, fall foul (of), clank, clang,
jangle, clatter, rattle, jar, swash
OLD hurtle
2 CONFLICT, disagree, quarrel, wrangle, grapple, fight,
contend, feud, war
3 *two events clash*
happen at the same time, coincide
FORMAL co-occur
4 *the styles clash*
not match, not go with, not go together, look unpleasant,
be incompatible, be discordant, jar
COLLOQ. scream
Ea 4 match, be compatible, harmonize, go well together
♦ *n*
1 CRASH, striking, bang, clank, clank, jangle, clatter, noise,
snap
2 *a clash with the police*
confrontation, showdown, conflict, disagreement,
argument, fight, brush, collision, warring, fighting, feud,
quarrel, wrangle
FORMAL altercation
3 *a clash of colours*
mismatch, jarring, discordance, incompatibility,
misalliance, irregularity

clasp *n, v*
♦ *n*
1 FASTENER, buckle, clip, pin, hasp, hook, fastening, catch,
hair slide, slide, brooch, safety pin
TECHNICAL agraffe
OLD tach, spang; (*Shakesp*) tassel
2 HOLD, grip, grasp, embrace, hug, cuddle, bosom
♦ *v*
1 HOLD, grip, grasp, clutch, embrace, enfold, hug, squeeze,
press, cling to, embosom, enclasp
2 FASTEN, connect, attach, grapple, hook, clip, pin,
interlock, unite
TECHNICAL infibulate

class *n, v*
♦ *n*
1 *a French class*
lesson, period, lecture, seminar, tutorial, workshop, teach-
in, course, year, form, study group, set, stream; *NAm* grade
2 *a social class*
social order, social status, status, (social) standing,
standing in society, social division, rank, level, (social)
background, caste

COLLOQ. pecking order
3 CATEGORY, classification, group, set, section, division,
department, sphere, grouping, order, league, rank, status,
caste, quality, grade, type, genre, sort, kind, species,
genus, style
TECHNICAL phylum
FORMAL denomination
4 *he has class*
taste, style, stylishness, elegance, sophistication, chic,
distinction
♦ *v*
categorize, classify, group, sort, rank, arrange, order,
grade, rate, pigeonhole, designate, brand

Social classes/groups include:

aristocracy	upper class	bourgeoisie
nobility	*colloq.* Sloane	proletariat
gentry	Ranger	hoi polloi
landed gentry	ruling class	commoners
gentlefolk	jet set	serfs
élite	*colloq.* glitterati	plebeians
colloq. nobs	middle class	*colloq.* plebs
high society	lower class	
top drawer	working class	

See also **nobility**.

---

classic *adj, n*
♦ *adj*
1 *a classic film*
first-class, first-rate, outstanding, brilliant, ideal, best,
finest, definitive, masterly, authoritative, excellent
FORMAL consummate
2 TYPICAL, prime, representative, characteristic,
archetypal, standard, regular, usual, true
FORMAL paradigmatic, quintessential
3 *classic style*
traditional, time-honoured, established, archetypal,
model, exemplary, ageless, timeless, immortal, undying,
lasting, enduring, abiding, simple, understated,
undecorated, unsophisticated, elegant
Ea 1 second-rate **2** unrepresentative
♦ *n*
standard, model, prototype, masterwork, masterpiece,
established work, great, *pièce de résistance*
FORMAL exemplar

classical *adj*
1 *classical style/form*
traditional, elegant, refined, excellent, plain, pure,
simple, restrained, well-proportioned, symmetrical,
harmonious
2 *classical music*
serious, traditional, concert, symphonic
3 *classical studies/languages*
ancient Greek, Grecian, Hellenic, ancient Roman, Latin,
Attic
Ea 1 modern

classically *adv*
1 *a classically trained musician*
traditionally, historically, originally, purely
2 *a classically beautiful profile*
simply, elegantly, traditionally, plainly, purely,
symmetrically, harmoniously
3 *classically the term should only be applied in
technical contexts*
typically, usually, normally, ordinarily, characteristically,
customarily, as a rule
FORMAL quintessentially

classification *n*
categorization, sorting, classing, grading, grouping,

Ways to clean include:

bath	disinfect	groom	refine	shower	sweep
bathe	distil	Hoover®	rinse	soak	swill
bleach	dry-clean	launder	rub	soap	tidy
brush	dust	mop	sandblast	sponge	vacuum
buff	filter	muck out	sanitize	spring-clean	valet
cleanse	floss	pasteurize	scour	spruce	wash
clear	flush	pick	scrape	spruce up	wipe
comb	freshen	polish	scrub	steep	
decontaminate	freshen up	purge	shampoo	sterilize	
deodorize	fumigate	purify	shine	swab	

arrangement, systematization, codification, tabulation, cataloguing
TECHNICAL taxonomy

classify *v*
categorize, class, group, pigeonhole, sort, grade, rank, arrange, order, type, distribute, systematize, codify, tabulate, file, catalogue
FORMAL dispose

classy *adj*
stylish, elegant, sophisticated, up-market, expensive, exclusive, exquisite, fine, grand, high-class, select, superior, gorgeous
COLLOQ. posh, ritzy, swanky
F3 dowdy, plain, unstylish

clatter *n, v*
bang, strike, clank, clunk, clang, jangle, crash, rattle, jar

clause *n*
article, item, part, section, subsection, particle, paragraph, heading, chapter, passage, phrase, condition, proviso, provision, rider, specification, point, loophole
TECHNICAL adjunct, clausula, novodamus, reddendum, salvo, tenendum

claw *n, v*
♦ *n*
talon, nail, pincer, nipper, gripper, pounce; *Scot* claut
TECHNICAL chela, unguis
OLD clutch, fang, griff, sere
♦ *v*
scratch, scrabble, scrape, graze, tear, rip, lacerate, maul, mangle, crab; *Scot* claut
OLD clapperclaw; (*Shakesp*) cloye

clay *n*
earth, loam, ground, soil, kaolin, lute, marl, brick, pottery, ceramics, slip, bole, clunch, gley, pisé, pug; *dialect* cloam; *Scot* cam, caum, calm, till
TECHNICAL illuvium, argil, cimolite, fango, laterite, plastilina, wax

clean *adj, adv*
♦ *adj*
1 WASHED, laundered, sterile, aseptic, antiseptic, hygienic, sanitary, sterilized, sterile, cleansed, laundered, decontaminated, purified, pure, unadulterated, fresh, unpolluted, uncontaminated, immaculate, spotless, unspotted, unstained, unsoiled, unsullied, perfect, speckless, spick and span, faultless, flawless, unblemished
COLLOQ. clean as a new pin
See panel above
2 *a clean life*
innocent, guiltless, virtuous, pure, good, upright, moral, honest, honourable, righteous, reputable, upstanding, respectable, decent, chaste
COLLOQ. squeaky-clean
3 *a clean sheet of paper*
blank, new, fresh, unmarked, unused, empty
4 *a clean joke*
decent, wholesome, proper, modest, appropriate, ethical
5 *a clean game*

fair, just, honest, according to the rules, even-handed, proper
COLLOQ. above board
6 *clean lines*
simple, well-defined, clean-cut, graceful, elegant, smooth, regular, straight, neat, tidy
7 *made a clean break with his past life*
complete, whole, total, utter, perfect, decisive, conclusive, final
F3 1 dirty, polluted **2** dishonourable, indecent **4** dirty; *colloq.* blue **5** dirty, rough **6** ragged
♦ *adv*
completely, straight, directly, entirely, fully, totally, quite

> **Synonym nuances**
> *sense 1*
> **Sterile**, **aseptic**, **antiseptic** and **sterilized** suggest freedom from germs rather than a less defined cleanliness, and so lend a rather clinical tone, especially if they are not used in specifically clinical contexts. **Hygienic** and **sanitary** are similar, though not quite so stark: *the hygienic handling of chemicals*.
> The terms **cleansed**, **purified** and **decontaminated** imply that something harmful has now been removed, the first having the most scientific association: *the instruments are decontaminated after use*. **Pure**, **unadulterated**, **unpolluted** and **uncontaminated** suggest always having been free from anything harmful: *unadulterated essential oils for aromatherapy*; of these, **pure** is the most widely applied and the most suggestive of favour.
> The words **immaculate**, **spotless**, **unspotted**, **unstained** and the less common **speckless** might all be used with regard to appearance; of these, **immaculate** and **spotless** are more approving in tone: *the woodwork was an immaculate white*. **Unsullied** tends to have a narrower implication of having avoiding contact with anything odious or undesirable: *the unsullied emotions of childhood*; whereas **perfect**, **flawless** and **unblemished** could be used to convey admiration of cleanliness, literal or figurative, that is exemplary: *a flawless complexion; an unblemished career*.

clean-cut *adj*
neat, tidy, orderly, smart, fresh, spruce, trim
COLLOQ. natty

cleaner *n*
char, charlady, charwoman, daily, Mrs Mop(p), wiper, orderly

cleanliness *n*
cleanness, purity, freshness, spotlessness, perfection
F3 dirtiness

cleanse *v*
1 *cleanse a wound*
disinfect, sterilize, clean, bathe, wash, rinse
FORMAL deterge
2 *cleansed from sin/cleanse your soul*

absolve, purify, purge, make free from, clear
FORMAL lustrate
⊞ 1 dirty **2** defile

cleanser *n*
soap, soap powder, detergent, cleaner, solvent, scourer, scouring powder, purifier, disinfectant

clear *adj, v*
♦ *adj*
1 PLAIN, distinct, comprehensible, understandable, intelligible, coherent, lucid, explicit, precise, unambiguous, well-defined, apparent, evident, patent, obvious, manifest, conspicuous, unmistakable, unquestionable, explicit, sure, unequivocal, incontrovertible, beyond question, crystal-clear, beyond doubt, certain, positive, definite, convinced
2 *clear thinking*
sharp, keen, perceptive, penetrating, quick, sensible, reasonable, logical
3 *clear water*
transparent, limpid, crystalline, glassy, translucent, see-through, clean, unclouded, colourless
FORMAL pellucid, diaphonous
4 *a clear day*
cloudless, unclouded, fine, fair, bright, sunny, light, luminous, undimmed
5 UNOBSTRUCTED, unblocked, open, free, empty, unhindered, unimpeded
6 *a clear conscience*
guiltless, innocent, blameless, untroubled, having no qualms, in the clear
FORMAL having/feeling no compunction
7 AUDIBLE, perceptible, pronounced, distinct, recognizable
COLLOQ. clear as a bell
⊞ 1 unclear, vague, ambiguous, confusing, unsure **2** muddled, woolly **3** opaque, cloudy **4** dull, cloudy, rainy, misty **5** blocked, jammed **6** guilty, troubled **7** inaudible, indistinct, faint
♦ *v*
1 *clear the dishes/room*
remove, take away, empty, unload, vacate, evacuate, void, move, shift, get rid of, rid, free, clean, fine, filter, tidy, wipe, erase, cleanse, refine, filter
2 UNBLOCK, unclog, unstop, decongest, free, rid, extricate, disentangle, loosen
3 *clear a fence*
jump (over), vault, leap over, go over
4 *the fog cleared*
disappear, vanish, go, evaporate, melt away
FORMAL evanesce
5 ACQUIT, exonerate, absolve, pardon, vindicate, find not guilty, excuse, justify, free, liberate, release, let go
FORMAL exculpate
6 *cleared for publication*
permit, give permission, allow, authorize, approve, pass, sanction
COLLOQ. give the green light, give the go-ahead
7 *clear £1000*
earn, take home, net, make a profit, make, gain, land, bring (in), pocket
⊞ 1 dirty, mess up **2** block, jam **5** condemn, find guilty **6** prohibit, veto
▪ **clear off**
go away, run along
COLLOQ. buzz off, get out, push off, shove off
▪ **clear out**
1 *been told to clear out*
get out, leave, go away, depart, withdraw
COLLOQ. get lost, beat it, clear off, push off, shove off, hop it
SLANG piss off
2 *clear out a cupboard*
tidy (up), empty, sort (out), throw out
▪ **clear up**

1 EXPLAIN, clarify, elucidate, unravel, solve, resolve, answer, straighten (out), sort out, iron out
COLLOQ. crack
2 TIDY, order, sort, rearrange, put in order, straighten (up), remove
3 *the weather cleared up*
clear, become fine, become sunny, stop raining, brighten (up), improve

clearance *n*
1 *clearance of old buildings*
demolition, removal, taking-away, emptying, unloading, vacating, evacuation, clearing, moving, shifting, freeing, cleansing
2 AUTHORIZATION, sanction, endorsement, permission, consent, leave
COLLOQ. OK, go-ahead, green light, say-so
3 SPACE, gap, room, headroom, margin, allowance

clear-cut *adj*
definite, explicit, well-defined, clear, precise, specific, straightforward, unambiguous, unequivocal, distinct, trenchant, plain
COLLOQ. cut and dried, black and white
⊞ ambiguous, vague

clear-headed *adj*
sensible, rational, intelligent, wise, sober, realistic, practical

clearing *n*
space, gap, opening, glade, dell

clearly *adv*
1 *speak clearly*
plainly, distinctly, comprehensibly, intelligibly, coherently, lucidly, explicitly, conspicuously, patently
2 OBVIOUSLY, without doubt, undoubtedly, undeniably, evidently, incontestably, incontrovertibly, indisputably, unmistakably, manifestly, plainly, patently, distinctly, openly, markedly

cleave¹ *v*
cleave the tree in two
split (open), divide, separate, sever, cut, slice, chop, crack (open), disunite, halve, hew, open, part, pierce, rend
FORMAL dissever, sunder
⊞ join, unite

cleave² *v*
cleave to your marriage partner
adhere, cling, cohere, hold, stick, remain, attach, unite

cleft *n*
fissure, opening, gap, fracture, breach, break, chasm, chink, crack, cranny, crevice, crevasse, rent, split, rift; *Scot* cloff, riva, slack
TECHNICAL pharynx, jag, chimney
FORMAL scissure

clemency *n*
mercy, mercifulness, pity, compassion, forbearance, forgiveness, generosity, humanity, indulgence, kindness, sympathy, leniency, mildness, moderation, soft-heartedness, tenderness
FORMAL magnanimity
⊞ harshness, ruthlessness

clench *v*
grip, hold, clasp, close (tightly), squeeze, press (together), seal, fasten, shut, clutch, double, grasp, grit

clergy *n*
clergymen, clergywomen, churchmen, churchwomen, clerics, the church, the cloth, ministry, priesthood, holy orders
OLD spirituality
Related adjectives: clerical, ecclesiastical

Types of clerical vestment include:

alb	clerical collar	ephod	maniple	scapular	tallith
amice	cope	frock	mantle	scarf	tippet
biretta	cotta	Geneva bands	mitre	skullcap	tunicle
cassock	cowl	Geneva gown	mozzetta	soutane	wimple
chasuble	dalmatic	habit	pallium	stole	wimple
chimere	*colloq.* dog-collar	hood	rochet	surplice	yarmulka

clergyman, clergywoman *n*
churchman, churchwoman, cleric, ecclesiastic, divine, man of God, woman of God, man of the cloth, woman of the cloth, minister, priest, reverend, bishop, preacher, vicar, pastor, padre, parson, rector, canon, dean, prebendary, father, mother, deacon, deaconess, chaplain, curate, presbyter, prelate, secular, spintext, squarson, arch-priest, rural dean, diocese, superintendent, clerk, Nonjuror, vartabed; *N Am* dominie; rabbi, imam, muezzin, mullah
SLANG Levite, sky pilot; *Aust* josser

clerical *adj*
1 ADMINISTRATIVE, office, secretarial, white-collar, official, filing, typing, keyboarding
COLLOQ. pen-pushing
2 ECCLESIASTICAL, pastoral, ministerial, priestly, episcopal, canonical, sacerdotal

clerk *n*
account-keeper, record-keeper, book-keeper, assistant, official, administrative officer, administrator, notary, receptionist, secretary, typist, stenographer, shop-assistant, writer, copyist, protocolist
COLLOQ. pen-pusher

clever *adj*
1 *a clever student*
intelligent, bright, brilliant, smart, witty, gifted, talented, expert, knowledgeable, adroit, apt, able, capable, deft, quick, quick-witted, sharp, sharp-witted, keen, shrewd, knowing, perceptive, discerning, cute, cunning; *Scot* gleg, souple
OLD apprehensive, artful, conceited, notable
FORMAL sapient, sagacious
COLLOQ. brainy
2 *a clever plan*
inventive, resourceful, sensible, rational, ingenious, cunning, shrewd, pretty
COLLOQ. natty
F3 **1** foolish, stupid, senseless, ignorant **2** foolish, irrational

Synonym nuances
sense 1
Intelligent, **bright**, and **smart** are fairly broad and straightforward synonyms, whereas **brilliant** would suggest clever to a more extreme degree: *the most brilliant poet of her generation*. **Witty** would more appropriately be used of sharp humour and expression. **Gifted** and **talented**, meanwhile, imply a particularly outstanding aptitude, but one which is instinctive rather than learned: *a gifted painter*. **Expert** and **knowledgeable**, on the other hand, would be appropriate to convey a high degree of learning.
Adroit, **deft**, **quick**, **sharp** and **keen** are also approving terms, highly suggestive of speed and directness of thought: *adroit manipulation of language*; *a keen analytical mind*. The terms **shrewd** and **knowing** describe innate practical judgement, although an element of potential underhandedness may be suggested.
Perceptive is a more positive term, appropriately describing someone with an ability to identify all aspects of a situation, with **discerning** further implying an element of good taste: *readers were becoming more discerning*. To use **cute** and **cunning**, however, implies an underhand element to someone's smartness, and so often sounds unfavourable: *the Minister was cute enough to cultivate the backbenchers*.

cleverly *adj*
1 INTELLIGENTLY, expertly, knowledgeably, ably, capably, discerningly, quick-wittedly
2 INGENIOUSLY, skilfully, astutely, craftily, shrewdly, artfully
F3 **1** foolishly, stupidly **2** foolishly, artlessly

cliché *n*
platitude, hackneyed phrase/expression, commonplace, banality, truism, bromide, (old) chestnut, stereotype; *N Am* glittering generality

click *v, n*
♦ *v*
1 *the machine clicked*
clack, clink, snap, snick, snip, tick, beat
2 *it suddenly clicked*
(begin to) understand, make sense, become clear, fall into place
COLLOQ. twig, cotton on
3 *they clicked and became close friends*
hit it off, get on, get on well, get along, relate well to each other
COLLOQ. get on like a house on fire
♦ *n*
beat, clack, clink, snap, snick, snip, tick

client *n*
customer, patron, regular, buyer, purchaser, shopper, consumer, user, patient, applicant
COLLOQ. punter

clientèle *n*
business, clients, customers, following, market, patronage, patrons, regulars, trade, buyers, purchasers, shoppers, consumers, users

cliff *n*
precipice, overhang, bluff, face, rock-face, scar, scarp, escarpment, crag, tor, promontory

climactic *adj*
decisive, critical, final, crucial, exciting, paramount
F3 trivial

climate *n*
1 *a cold climate*
weather, weather conditions, temperature
2 *a hostile political climate*
atmosphere, feeling, mood, temper, disposition, setting, milieu, environment, spirit, ambience, tendency, trend

climax *n*
culmination, height, high point, highlight, acme, zenith, peak, pinnacle, summit, apex, apogee, top, head
F3 low point, nadir

climb *v, n*
♦ *v*
1 *climb the stairs*
go up, ascend, scale, shin up, clamber, scramble, mount, ramp, surmount; *Scot* speel, sclim
TECHNICAL herringbone, jumar, prusik
OLD scan, sty
2 *climb into the car*
move, stir, shift, clamber, scramble
3 *unemployment is climbing*
increase, go up, rise, soar, shoot up, top
♦ *n*

ascent, going up, clamber, scramble, uphill struggle, upward slope; *Scot* speel
TECHNICAL jumar
⊟ descent
▪ **climb down**
retract, back down, admit that you are wrong, concede, retreat, surrender, yield
COLLOQ. eat your words

Synonym nuances

verb sense 1
Go up is a term that can be widely used for any movement that takes you in an upward direction, similarly **ascend**, although it is more formal sounding and perhaps suggestive of a more dignified or gradual movement.
  Scale, on the other hand, would be used for the physical act of climbing, and is particularly suggestive of height: *the crew scaled the masts barefoot*. **Shin up** is more descriptive of the physical way progress is made: *the animal shinned up his leg*. **Clamber** and **scramble** are equally descriptive, but suggestive of a rather ungainly and desperate manner: *I scrambled up the embankment*.
  Mount could be used of reaching the top after a climb, or often in the more specific context of getting on to a horse or bike. **Surmount** is more often used figuratively to imply overcoming an obstacle: *the challenge could not be surmounted.*

---

climb-down *n*
withdrawal, retraction, retreat, concession, surrender, yielding

clinch *v*
settle, secure, seal, close, conclude, decide, determine, confirm, verify
COLLOQ. land

cling *v*
1 *cling to a branch*
clasp, clutch, grasp, grip, hold on to, stick, adhere, cleave, fasten, embrace, hug
2 *cling to old ideas*
adhere, stick, support, hold, defend, stand by, be faithful, stay true

clinic *n*
medical centre, health centre, hospital, infirmary, sanatorium, doctor's, outpatients' department

clinical *adj*
1 *clinical trials of the drug*
medical, hospital, patient
2 *a clinical design*
simple, plain, austere, stark, basic, unadorned
3 *a clinical attitude*
impersonal, analytic, businesslike, cold, emotionless, unemotional, unfeeling, detached, disinterested, dispassionate, uninvolved, impassive, objective, scientific
⊟ 2 decorated, ornamented **3** warm, biased, subjective

clinically *adv*
clinically proven remedies
medically, scientifically

clip *n, v*
♦ *n*
1 *a paper clip*
fastener, staple, pin
2 *a clip from a newspaper*
cutting, snippet, quotation, citation, passage, section, excerpt, extract
3 *a clip round the ear*
punch, slap, smack, cuff, box, clout, thump
COLLOQ. wallop, whack
♦ *v*

1 *clipped the pen to her pocket*
pin, staple, fasten, attach, fix, hold
2 *clip a bush*
trim, snip, cut, cut short, prune, pare, shear, crop, dock, poll, pollard, truncate, curtail, shorten, abbreviate
3 HIT, strike, graze, tough, collide with, crash into, run into

clipping *n*
cutting, snippet, quotation, citation, passage, section, excerpt, extract, clip

clique *n*
circle, set, coterie, group, circle, bunch, band, pack, gang, crowd, in-crowd, society, fraternity, faction, clan

cloak *n, v*
♦ *n*
1 *wear a cloak*
cape, mantle, robe, wrap, shawl, coat, cover.
2 *a cloak of secrecy*
coat, cover, shield, mask, front, screen, blind, veil, pall, mantle, shroud, pretext
♦ *v*
cover, veil, mask, screen, hide, conceal, obscure, shroud, disguise, shield, camouflage
OLD palliate

Types of cloak include:

abolla	gaberdine	*old* pelisse
amice	gallabea(h)	pilch
buffalo-robe	grego	poncho
capa	himation	rail
capote	manta	*Scot* rokelay
Capuchin	manteel	roquelaure
cardinal	mantilla	sagum
chlamys	mousquetaire	sarafan
cope	paenula	talma
djellaba	pall	visite
domino	paludament	

See also **clothes; coat**.

---

clobber¹ *n*
clothing, equipment, things, garments, belongings, possessions, baggage, tackle, kit, paraphernalia
COLLOQ. gear, togs, stuff, bits and pieces, bits and bobs

clobber² *v*
1 HIT, strike, bash, knock, clout, slap, thrash, punch, thump
COLLOQ. wallop, whack, belt, sock, zap
2 DEFEAT, overwhelm, beat, conquer, crush, rout, ruin
COLLOQ. thrash, wallop, lick, hammer, trounce

clock
▪ **clock up**
reach, record, register, achieve, log, attain, chalk up, notch up
▪ **round the clock**
day and night, all day and all night, continuously, ceaselessly, without stopping, constantly
COLLOQ. twenty-four seven, 24-7

Types of clock or watch include:

CLOCKS:	grandfather clock	travelling clock
alarm clock	grandmother	**WATCHES:**
analogue clock	clock	fob-watch
atomic clock	longcase clock	pendant watch
bracket clock	mantel clock	repeating watch
carriage clock	quartz clock	ring-watch
chronograph	speaking clock	stopwatch
chronometer	sundial	wristwatch
cuckoo-clock	*colloq.* Tim	
digital clock		

clod *n*
lump, clump, chunk, hunk, mass, block, slab, wedge
OLD glebe

clog *v*
block, choke, stop up, bung up, dam (up), congest, jam,
obstruct, impede, hinder, hamper, encumber, burden
FORMAL occlude
F3 unblock, free, clear

cloister *n*
walkway, pavement, corridor, aisle, arcade, portico,
ambulatory

cloistered *adj*
sheltered, secluded, confined, restricted, enclosed,
shielded, withdrawn, insulated, protected, isolated
FORMAL reclusive, sequestered, cloistral, hermitic
F3 open

close[1] *v, n*
* *v*
1 SHUT, shut up, fasten, secure, lock (up), bar, bolt, padlock
2 *close a road/bottle*
obstruct, block (off/up), shut, clog, plug, cork, stop up, fill,
seal
FORMAL occlude
3 END, bring to an end, draw to an end, finish, complete,
conclude, terminate, adjourn, wind up, round off, stop,
cease
FORMAL discontinue
4 *the shop closes at 6 o'clock*
shut, close for the night
5 *the factory closed in March*
close down, close permanently, cease operating, cease
operations, shut down, go bankrupt, fail
COLLOQ. fold, flop, go bust, go to the wall
6 *pursuers closing on you*
catch up with, get closer to, come closer, approach, near,
gain on
7 *close a gap*
join, unite, fuse, seal, narrow, lessen
8 *close a deal*
settle, secure, seal, clinch, conclude, decide, determine,
establish, confirm, verify
F3 **1** open, separate **3** start, begin **4** open, open for
business **7** widen
* *n*
end, finish, completion, conclusion, culmination, ending,
finale, dénouement, termination, adjournment, winding-
up, stop, pause
FORMAL cessation
F3 start, beginning
▪ **close in**
come nearer, draw near, approach, surround, encircle

close[2] *n*
live in a close
courtyard, enclosure, quadrangle, square, place, court,
road, street, row, terrace, lane, mews, cul-de-sac

close[3] *adj*
1 NEAR, close by, nearby, at hand, not far, neighbouring,
adjacent, adjoining, in the vicinity, in close proximity,
impending, imminent
COLLOQ. on your doorstep, in your own backyard, a stone's
throw
2 INTIMATE, dear, familiar, attached, inseparable, devoted,
loving, close-knit, tight, best, good, bosom
3 *close relations*
immediate, direct
4 *a close resemblance*
strong, near, distinct, marked, similar, like, comparable,
corresponding
5 *a close game*
evenly matched, well-matched, hard-fought

COLLOQ. neck and neck
6 *close to tears*
near, on the verge of, on the brink of, approaching
7 HUMID, heavy, stuffy, fuggy, muggy, oppressive, sultry,
sweltering, airless, stifling, suffocating, stuffy, unventilated,
sticky
8 MISERLY, mean, stingy, niggardly, penny-pinching
FORMAL parsimonious
COLLOQ. tight
9 SECRETIVE, uncommunicative, unforthcoming, quiet,
taciturn, reticent, private, secret, confidential
10 *a close translation*
exact, precise, accurate, strict, literal, faithful, true
11 *pay close attention*
fixed, concentrated, thorough, rigorous, painstaking,
detailed, methodical, careful, intense, keen, searching
12 DENSE, compact, condensed, solid, tight, packed,
crowded, cramped
F3 **1** far, distant **2** cool, unfriendly, distant **3** distant **7** fresh,
cool **8** generous, liberal **9** open **10** rough, loose

Synonym nuances
sense 1
Near, **nearby** and **close by** are synonyms with a wide
range of applications for things that are close in space, or
time: *the near future*. **At hand** tends to have a less physical
aspect, and is often used of abstracts: *help was at hand*;
success was at hand. The words **neighbouring**, **adjacent**
and **adjoining** are limited to where two things are side by
side: *neighbouring countries*; *adjacent streets*; *the park
adjoining the palace*.
   The term **in the vicinity** is rather vague as to distance:
there are three villages in the vicinity; whereas **in close
proximity** is more explicit and puts great emphasis on the
physical nearness of something: *The UFO was seen at
close proximity*.
   If you want to say that some event is very near in time, you
might prefer to use **impending** or **imminent**: *impending
motherhood*; *a flu epidemic was imminent*.

---

closet *n, adj, v*
* *n*
cupboard, wardrobe, storage room, recess, press, cabinet
* *adj*
secret, private, unrevealed, hidden, covert, furtive,
underground, surreptitious, undercover
F3 open, having come out
* *v*
cloister, shut away, confine, seclude, isolate

closure *n*
1 *the closure of the factory*
closing-down, permanent closing, shutdown, failure,
bankruptcy, winding-up
FORMAL cessation of operations
COLLOQ. folding
2 *the closure of the road*
obstruction, block, blocking, shutting, stopping-up

clot *n, v*
* *n*
1 *a blood clot*
lump, mass, glob, clump, thrombus, thrombosis, clotting,
obstruction, coagulation; *dialect* lopper; *Scot* lapper; *Scot
& N Am* splatch
TECHNICAL thrombus, embolus, cruor, grume, crassamentum
OLD gobbet
2 FOOL, idiot, imbecile
COLLOQ. nit, mug, blockhead, nincompoop, twit, twerp,
dope; *N Am* bufflehead
SLANG wally, nerd, plonker, dork, git, prat
* *v*
coalesce, curdle, coagulate, congeal, thicken, solidify, set, gel

Clothes include:

DRESSES:
caftan
dinner-gown
evening dress
frock
kimono
sari
shirtwaister
SKIRTS:
culottes
dirndl
divided skirt
kilt
mini skirt
pencil skirt
pinafore skirt
sarong
TOPS:
blouse
boiled shirt
cardigan
crop top
dress shirt
fleece
guernsey
jersey
jumper
polo neck
polo shirt

pullover
shirt
smock
sweater
sweat-shirt
tabard
tank top
tee-shirt
T-shirt
tunic
turtleneck
twinset
waistcoat
TROUSERS:
bell-bottoms
Bermuda shorts
breeches
Capri pants
cargo pants
combat trousers
cords
denims
drainpipes
dungarees
flannels
hipsters
hot pants
jeans

jodhpurs
Levis®
501s®
leggings
palazzo pants
pedal-pushers
plus-fours
shorts
slacks
SUITS:
boiler suit
catsuit
N Am coveralls
double-breasted
dress suit
jumpsuit
leisure suit
lounge suit
morning suit
overall
shell suit
single-breasted
three-piece suit
trouser suit
tracksuit
wet suit
WOMEN'S UNDERWEAR:
basque

body stocking
bra
brassière
briefs
camiknickers
camisole
corset
French knickers
girdle
garter
g-string
hosiery
liberty bodice
lingerie
panties
pantihose
pants
petticoat
shift
slip
stockings
suspender belt
suspenders
teddy
thong
tights

MEN'S UNDERWEAR:
boxer-shorts (or
   boxers)
singlet
string vest
underpants
vest
Y-fronts
SPORTSWEAR:
bathing costume
bikini
cycling shorts
jockstrap
leotard
salopette
swimsuit
swimming
   costume
swimming trunks
NIGHTWEAR:
bed-jacket
bedsocks
dressing-gown
housecoat
negligee
nightdress
colloq. nightie

nightshirt
pyjamas
colloq. jimjams
colloq. PJs
ACCESSORIES:
belt
bow tie
braces
cravat
cummerbund
earmuffs
glove
leg warmers
mitten
muffler
necktie
pashmina
scarf
shahtoosh
shrug
shawl
sock
stole
tie
MISCELLANEOUS:
burka
veil
yashmak

See also **clerical; coat; fabric; footwear; hat**.

---

cloth *n*
1 FABRIC, material, stuff, textile, upholstery
See panel at **fabric**.
2 RAG, facecloth, flannel, dishcloth, floorcloth, duster, towel; *S Afr* lap, lappie
3 THE CLERGY, the church, clergymen, clergywomen, churchmen, churchwomen, the ministry, holy orders

clothe *v*
1 DRESS, put on, robe, deck, outfit, fit out, rig, vest, drape, cover
FORMAL attire, apparel, accoutre, habit, invest, bedizen, caparison
2 *mountains clothed in verdure*
cover, overlay, envelop, blanket, drape, carpet
F3 1 undress, strip, disrobe

clothes *n*
clothing, garments, wear, garb, outfit, dress, costume, uniform, wardrobe, vestments
OLD weed
FORMAL attire, apparel, raiment, habilments, vesture
COLLOQ. gear, clobber, togs, get-up, hand-me-downs, cast-offs
SLANG threads
Related adjectives: sartorial, habilatory
See panel above

cloud *n, v*
♦ *v*
mist, fog, blur, dull, dim, darken, shade, shadow, overshadow, eclipse, cover, veil, shroud, mantle, obscure, muddle, confuse
FORMAL obfuscate
F3 clear
Related adjective: nubiform

Types of cloud include:

altocumulus	cirrus	fractostratus
altostratus	cumulonimbus	nimbostratus
cirrocumulus	cumulus	stratocumulus
cirrostratus	fractocumulus	stratus

cloudless *adj*
unclouded, fine, bright, clear, sunny, fair, dry, pleasant
F3 cloudy, overcast

cloudy *adj*
1 *a cloudy sky*
overcast, dull, dark, murky, gloomy, sombre, grey, leaden, heavy, lowering, dim, sunless, hazy, misty, foggy
2 *a cloudy liquid*
opaque, milky, muddy, murky
3 *cloudy issues*
indistinct, obscure, nebulous, hazy, misty, foggy, blurred, blurry, vague, confused, muddled
F3 1 bright, sunny, cloudless **2** clear **3** clear, distinct, plain

clout *v, n*
♦ *v*
punch, strike, smack, hit, slap, cuff, box
COLLOQ. thump, wallop, whack
SLANG sock, slug
♦ *n*
1 *gave him a clout*
punch, strike, smack, hit, slap, cuff, box
COLLOQ. thump, wallop, whack
SLANG sock, slug
2 *political clout*
influence, weight, authority, power, standing, prestige
COLLOQ. pull, muscle

cloven *adj*
divided, split, bisected, cleft
F3 solid

clown *n, v*
♦ *n*
1 *clowns at a circus*
buffoon, comic, comedian, joker, jester, fool, harlequin, Joey, rustic, bumpkin, merry-andrew, gracioso, Pierrot, august
OLD zany, antic, pickle-herring, Owl-glass
OLD SLANG joskin
2 *some clown has parked in front of the gates*
fool, idiot, blockhead, imbecile

COLLOQ. nincompoop, ninny, nitwit, numskull, twerp, twit, dimwit
SLANG wally, jerk, dipstick, nerd, dork, geek
• *v*
fool around, act foolishly, act/play the fool, jest, joke
COLLOQ. mess around, muck about
SLANG *NAm* goof around

cloying *adj*
disgusting, nauseating, sickening, sickly, excessive, choking, oversweet, fulsome
🔁 pleasing, pleasant

club *n, v*
• *n*
1 ASSOCIATION, society, organization, group, league, guild, order, union, auxiliary, fraternity, federation, company, brotherhood, sisterhood, set, circle, clique, social club, chapter, fasciol, free-and-easy; *NAm* glee club, sorosis
OLD hetairia
2 NIGHTCLUB, discotheque, bar, cabaret
COLLOQ. disco
3 STICK, staff, bat, bludgeon, truncheon, cudgel, mace, life-preserver, knobkerrie; *NAm* blackjack, billy, billystick; *Aust* waddy, nulla-nulla
TECHNICAL bandy, priest, shinty-stick, caman, hurley
OLD bourdon, trunnion, polt
COLLOQ. cosh
See panel at **golf**.
• *v*
hit, strike, beat (up), bash, clout, bludgeon, batter, pummel
COLLOQ. clobber, clout, cosh
▪ **club together**
give money, share the cost, join forces, contribute, chip in
COLLOQ. have a whip-round

clue *n*
hint, tip, suggestion, idea, notion, lead, tip-off, pointer, sign, indication, evidence, trace, suspicion, inkling, intimation

clueless *adj*
ignorant, inexperienced, unschooled, unlearned, uninitiated, uninformed
COLLOQ. dense, thick, not all there; (*offensive*) dumb

clump *n, v*
• *n*
cluster, bundle, bunch, tuft, thicket, mass, accumulation, collection, lot, group
FORMAL agglomeration, agglutination
• *v*
1 *clump around*
tramp, clomp, stamp, stomp, stumble, plod, trudge, lumber, thump, thud
2 *clump together*
group, accumulate, amass, cluster, bunch, bundle

clumsy *adj*
1 *a clumsy person*
awkward, unco-ordinated, ham-fisted, ham, accident-prone, unhandy, heavy-handed, unskilful, inept, bungling, blundering, lumbering, gauche, ungainly, ungraceful, wooden, cack-handed, oafish, squab, banana-fingered, two-fisted, thumby, chuckle, chuckle-headed, hippopotamian, looby
OLD unhandsome
FORMAL maladroit
COLLOQ. gawky, all thumbs, having two left feet
SLANG (*offensive*) spastic
2 *clumsy objects*
awkward, unwieldy, ungainly, heavy, bulky, hulking, unmanageable, cumbersome, ill-made, shapeless, Dutch-built
COLLOQ. clumping, clunky
3 *a clumsy attempt to comfort her*

insensitive, rude, tactless, awkward, uncouth, rough, crude
🔁 **1** co-ordinated, skilful, careful, graceful, natural **2** elegant, dainty **3** sensitive, tactful

---

Synonym nuances
sense 1
Both **awkward** and **unco-ordinated** are fairly mild terms to describe a clumsy manner or movement: *his arms moved in the most unco-ordinated way*; whilst **ham-fisted** is a more disparaging term, with an added implication of incompetence: *the ham-fisted police hunt allowed the criminals to escape detection*. **Heavy-handed, unskilful, inept** and the less common **unhandy** also suggest a lack of the required precision, and are again rather pejorative in tone; the terms **bungling, blundering** and **lumbering** are highly pejorative, and imply that a clumsy approach may prove a distinct liability: *bungling bureaucratic incompetence*.
  Gauche appropriately describes a clumsiness born of being ill at ease and lacking in sophistication: *this imposing woman made her feel gauche*; whereas **ungainly, ungraceful** and **wooden** are fairly straightforward descriptions physical movement: *an ungainly walk*. **Oafish**, on the other hand, is strongly suggestive of an inherent ignorance, and is therefore highly derogatory: *her oafish, idiot son*.

---

cluster *n, v*
• *n*
bunch, clump, batch, group, knot, band, mass, crowd, gathering, huddle, collection, assembly, assortment
TECHNICAL inflorescence, raceme, panicle, truss
FORMAL assemblage, agglomeration
• *v*
bunch, group (together), gather, collect, assemble, congregate, come together, flock

clustered *adj*
bunched, gathered, grouped, assembled, massed
FORMAL glomerate

clutch *v, n*
• *v*
hold, get/take hold of, clasp, grip, hang on to, grasp, cling to, clench, seize, snatch, grab, catch, grapple, embrace
• *n*
1 *in someone's clutches*
control, grasp, grip, power, sway, dominion, possession, hands, keeping, custody, embrace, mercy, claws, jaws
2 *a clutch of eggs*
set, setting, group, hatching, incubation

clutter *n, v*
• *n*
litter, mess, jumble, untidiness, disorder, disarray, muddle, chaos, confusion
• *v*
litter, encumber, fill (untidily), mess (up), make a mess, make untidy, cover, strew, scatter

coach *n, v*
• *n*
1 *travel by coach*
express coach, bus, minibus; *NAm* Greyhound
OLD charabanc, motor-bus, motor-coach
2 *a train of twelve coaches*
carriage, car, wagon
3 *a football coach*
trainer, instructor, tutor, teacher, educator, mentor
4 *a coach and horses*
carriage, wagon, cab, trap, hackney, hansom, gig, landau, brougham, barouche, cabriolet, droshky
• *v*
train, drill, instruct, teach, tutor, prime, cram, prepare

coagulate v
congeal, thicken, solidify, gel, melt, clot, cake, curdle

coagulation n
congealing, thickening, solidifying, clotting

coalesce v
amalgamate, join (together), blend, mix, unite, combine, consolidate, cohere, fuse, incorporate, integrate, merge, affiliate
FORMAL commingle, commix

coalescence n
amalgamation, blending, mixture, combination, consolidation, fusion, incorporation, integration, merger, affiliation
OLD immixture

coalition n
alliance, merger, amalgamation, combination, integration, fusion, joining, league, bloc, compact, federation, confederation, confederacy, association, partnership, affiliation, union
FORMAL conjunction, compact

coarse adj
1 ROUGH, unpolished, unfinished, uneven, lumpy, unpurified, unrefined, unprocessed, rugged, hairy, bristly, scaly, prickly
2 coarse humour
bawdy, ribald, earthy, obscene, smutty, vulgar, crude, offensive, foul-mouthed, boorish, loutish, rude, impolite, ill-mannered, rough, gross, rank, indelicate, improper, indecent, immodest, off-colour
COLLOQ. blue, raunchy
F3 **1** smooth, fine **2** refined, sophisticated, polite, clean

---

Synonym nuances
sense 2
Bawdy, ribald and **earthy** may be used of something with sexually explicit content, suggesting a lack of refinement: *bawdy limericks*; they are fairly neutral in tone and do not suggest disapproval. **Smutty**, on the other hand, implies a degree of disfavour on the speaker's part.
   Obscene, **offensive**, and the more informal **off-colour** put the emphasis on audience sensibilities, clearly implying that they will be upset: *the Obscene Publications Act*. The words **indelicate**, **improper**, and **immodest** suggest a lack of decorum and propriety, and are understated, even rather euphemistic terms: *improper sexual conduct*; **indecent** could be used to be more direct.
   The terms **vulgar**, **crude**, **gross** and **rank** also describe a lack of delicacy, but are very pejorative in tone: *his crude jokes were not funny*. Similarly, **impolite** and **ill-mannered** are fairly mild terms; to suggest unacceptably coarse behaviour you could use **foul-mouthed**, **loutish** or **rude**.

---

coarsen v
roughen, thicken, blunt, deaden, desensitize, dull, harden
FORMAL indurate
F3 sensitize

coarsely adv
1 ROUGHLY, unevenly, ruggedly, irregularly
2 BAWDILY, obscenely, crudely, vulgarly, rudely, impolitely, offensively, roughly, immodestly, indecently, improperly, boorishly, loutishly
F3 **1** smoothly **2** politely

coarseness n
1 OBSCENITY, bawdiness, ribaldry, smut, smuttiness, vulgarity, crassitude, crudity, earthiness, indelicacy, offensiveness, indecency, immodesty

2 ROUGHNESS, unevenness, ruggedness, irregularity, hairiness, prickliness
F3 **1** delicacy, politeness, sophistication **2** smoothness

coast n, v
♦ n
coastline, seaboard, shore, seashore, beach, seaside, strand, foreshore
FORMAL littoral
Related adjectives: littoral, orarian
♦ v
freewheel, glide, slide, sail, cruise, taxi, drift

coat n, v
♦ n
1 FUR, hair, fleece, wool, pelt, hide, skin
2 LAYER, coating, covering, cover, overlay, film, blanket, sheet, mantle, glaze, varnish, finish, veneer, laminate, lamination, cladding
TECHNICAL integument, pellicle
♦ v
cover, paint, spread, layer, smear, daub, apply, put on/over, overlay, plaster, pave, cake, encrust

---

Types of coat include:

Afghan	Eton jacket	raincoat
anorak	frock-coat	redingote
blanket	fur coat	reefer
blazer	greatcoat	tail coat
blouson	hacking-jacket	safari jacket
body-warmer	jacket	shooting-jacket
bomber jacket	jerkin	snorkel
Burberry®	mackintosh	*N Am, Aust & NZ*
cagoul(e)	*colloq.* mac	sports coat
cape	matinee jacket	sports jacket
car-coat	overcoat	trench coat
cloak	parka	tuxedo
dinner jacket	pea-jacket	windcheater
donkey jacket	poncho	
duffel coat	puffa jacket	

---

coating n
covering, layer, dusting, wash, coat, blanket, sheet, membrane, film, skin, finish, overlay, veneer, glaze, varnish, enamel, lamination, crust
FORMAL patina

coax v
persuade, cajole, wheedle, blandish, draw, get round, talk into, win over/round, flatter, beguile, allure, induce, entice, tempt, prevail upon, wile; *dialect* carny; *Scot* cuittle, fleech, whillywha
OLD collogue
FORMAL inveigle
COLLOQ. sweet-talk, soft-soap

cobble
▪ **cobble together**
make/prepare/produce roughly, make/prepare/produce quickly, improvise, knock up, put together
COLLOQ. throw together

cock n, v
♦ n
rooster, capon, cockerel, chicken, chanticleer
♦ v
lift, raise, point, slant, incline, bend, tip, tilt

cockeyed adj
1 CROOKED, lopsided, askew, asymmetrical, awry, skew-whiff
2 SENSELESS, absurd, crazy, ludicrous, nonsensical, preposterous
COLLOQ. daft, barmy, half-baked
F3 **2** sensible, sober

cockily adv

cheekily, impertinently, impudently, insolently, disrespectfully
E3 respectfully, politely

cocksure adj

cocky, arrogant, self-important, conceited, vain, swollen-headed, swell-headed, egotistical, swaggering, brash, self-assured, self-confident, overconfident
E3 humble, modest, shy

cocktail

Cocktails include:

Acapulco	gloom raiser	Pink Lady
American Beauty	G&T	planter's punch
Bellini	Harvey	rickey
Between the	Wallbanger	Rob Roy
Sheets	horse's neck	rusty nail
Black Russian	kir	salty dog
black velvet	Kir Royale	Sazerac®
bloody Mary	long vodka	screwdriver
blue lagoon	Long Island iced	sea breeze
brandy Alexander	tea	sidecar
Bronx	Mai Tai	Singapore sling
Brown Cow	Manhattan	snowball
Buck's fizz	margarita	stinger
caipirinha	Martini®	tequila slammer
Champagne	mojito	tequila sunrise
Cocktail	Molotov cocktail	Tom Collins
Cosmopolitan	Moscow Mule	whisky mac
daiquiri	negroni	whisky sour
eggnog	old-fashioned	white lady
gimlet	piña colada	White Russian
gin-and-tonic	pink gin	

cocky adj

arrogant, self-important, conceited, vain, swollen-headed, egotistical, swaggering, brash, cocksure, self-assured, self-confident, overconfident, bumptious
FORMAL hubristic
E3 humble, modest, shy

cocoon v

protect, overprotect, isolate, preserve, defend, envelop, cushion, insulate, wrap, cover, swathe, cloister

coddle v

pamper, pet, spoil, protect, overprotect, mollycoddle, cosset, humour, indulge, baby

code n

1 ETHICS, rules, regulations, laws, principles, morals, morality, system, custom, convention, etiquette, manners, practice, conduct
2 *written in code*
cipher, secret language, secret writing, secret message, cryptograph, cryptogram, Morse code
3 *a book's code number*
numbers, letters, signs, symbols, bar code, postcode, postal code, zip code, dialling code, local code, national code, international code, machine code

codify v

order, systematize, organize, classify, group, sort out, marshal, catalogue

coerce v

force, use force, drive, compel, constrain, pressurize, pressure, bully, intimidate, browbeat, bludgeon, dragoon, pressgang
COLLOQ. put the screws on, bulldoze, strongarm, twist someone's arm, lean on

coercion n

force, duress, compulsion, constraint, pressure, bullying, intimidation, threats, direct action, browbeating, arm-twisting, duress, strongarm tactics
COLLOQ. heat

coffer n

1 *jewels hidden in a coffer*
casket, case, box, chest, trunk, ark, safe, strongbox, treasury, moneybox, repository
2 *the coffers of an organization*
funds, finance, resources, assets, capital, backing, money, cash, wealth, means

coffee n

COLLOQ. *N Am* joe

Types of coffee include:

COFFEE DRINKS:	mocha	Java
(caffè) americano	mochaccino	Kenyan
black coffee	ristretto	light roast
café au lait	skinny latte	**BEANS AND**
caffè con panna	Turkish coffee	**BLENDS:**
café filtre	white coffee	decaffeinated
café noir	**PREPARATIONS:**	*colloq.* decaf
cappuccino	Arabica	filter
espresso	Blue Mountain	ground
Frappuccino®	Colombian	instant
iced coffee	Costa Rican	percolated
Irish coffee	dark roast	
latte	French roast	
macchiato		

See also **tea**.

coffin n

sarcophagus, shell; *Scot* kist; *N Am* casket
OLD larnax
SLANG *N Am* wooden kimono, wooden overcoat, pine overcoat

cogency n

power, strength, force, potency, forcefulness, influence, weight, plausibility, effectiveness, urgency

cogent adj

convincing, compelling, conclusive, potent, powerful, strong, forceful, forcible, influential, weighty, irresistible, persuasive, unanswerable, effective, urgent
E3 weak, ineffective, unsound

cogently adv

convincingly, compellingly, conclusively, potently, powerfully, strongly, forcefully, forcibly, persuasively, effectively, urgently
E3 weakly, ineffectively

cogitate v

think deeply, consider, contemplate, deliberate, meditate, muse, ponder, reflect, mull over
FORMAL ruminate, cerebrate

cognate adj

related, affiliated, associated, connected, kindred, akin, alike, allied, analogous, corresponding, similar
TECHNICAL agnate, consanguine, congeneric
E3 unrelated, unconnected

cognition n

perception, awareness, consciousness, knowledge, apprehension, learning, discernment, insight, comprehension, understanding, thinking, intelligence, enlightenment, reason, reasoning, rationality

cognizance

■ **take cognizance of**
acknowledge, regard, recognize, take notice of, become aware of, accept

cognizant adj

aware, conscious, conversant, familiar, informed, knowledgeable, acquainted, versed, witting
FORMAL apprised
E3 unaware

cohabit v

live together, live together as man and wife, live with, sleep together
OLD live in sin, occupy, company
COLLOQ. bed
SLANG shack up
OLD SLANG live tally

cohere v

1 STICK, adhere, cling, fuse, unite, bind, combine, coalesce, consolidate
2 *the argument does not cohere*
agree, square, correspond, harmonize, hold, hang together, make sense, be consistent, add up
E3 separate

coherence n

agreement, harmony, consistency, correspondence, connection, sense, logicality, union, unity
FORMAL congruity, consonance, concordance
E3 incoherence

coherent adj

articulate, intelligible, comprehensible, easy to understand, meaningful, lucid, clear, consistent, logical, reasoned, rational, sensible, orderly, systematic, organized, well-structured, well-planned
E3 incoherent, unintelligible, meaningless

cohesion n

union, unity, whole, agreement, harmony, consistency, correspondence, solidarity, connection, sense
COLLOQ. togetherness

cohesive adj

coherent, close, united, joined, continuous, connected, interrelated
COLLOQ. together

cohort n

1 *Roman cohorts*
troop, division, legion, regiment, squadron, band, brigade, squad, body, column, company, contingent, unit
2 GROUP, unit, set, body, lot, batch, combination, class, classification, bracket, category, categorization
3 COMPANION, partner, accomplice, assistant, supporter, associate, follower, myrmidon
COLLOQ. mate, buddy, sidekick

coil v, n

♦ v
wind, spiral, curl, loop, turn, twist, writhe, snake, fake, twirl, writhe, wreathe, twine, entwine
OLD wring
FORMAL convolute
♦ n
roll, curl, loop, turn, ring, spiral, spire, corkscrew, helix, twist, twine, whorl, wreathe, skein, hank, rouleau, bight, fake; *Scot* fank
OLD (*Spenser*) bought
FORMAL convolution, volution

coin n, v

♦ n
piece, bit, money, cash, change, small change, loose change, silver, copper
FORMAL specie
Related adjectives: numismatic, nummulary, nummary
♦ v
1 *coin a new word*
invent, make up, think up, conceive, dream up, devise, formulate, originate, create, fabricate, produce, neologize
2 *coin money*
produce, mint, stamp, cast, strike, forge

Types of coin include:

angel	half-crown	rap
bezant	half guinea	real
colloq. bob	halfpenny	sesterce
copper	half sovereign	shilling
crown	ha'penny	sixpence
dandiprat	krugerrand	solidus
denarius	louis d'or	sou
dime	moidore	sovereign
doubloon	napoleon	spade guinea
ducat	nickel	stater
farthing	noble	*colloq.* tanner
florin	obol	thaler
groat	penny	threepenny bit
guilder	pound	
guinea	*colloq.* quid	

coincide v

1 *the two events coincided*
happen at the same time, happen together, clash, take place simultaneously, coexist, synchronize
FORMAL concur
2 *our opinions coincide*
be the same, agree, correspond, square, tally, harmonize, be consistent with, match
FORMAL concur, accord

coincidence n

1 CHANCE, accident, luck, eventuality
FORMAL fortuity, serendipity
COLLOQ. fluke
2 COEXISTENCE, correspondence, happening at the same time, happening together, clash, clashing, taking place simultaneously, synchronization
FORMAL concurrence, conjunction, correlation

coincident adj

1 SIMULTANEOUS, contemporaneous, coinciding, coexisting
FORMAL concurrent
2 SIMILAR, the same, like, alike, close, related, corresponding, equivalent, comparable, consistent, in agreement, in harmony
FORMAL concurrent

coincidental adj

accidental, chance, casual, unintentional, unplanned, lucky
FORMAL fortuitous, serendipitous
COLLOQ. flukey
E3 deliberate, planned, arranged

coincidentally adv

accidentally, by chance, unintentionally, luckily

coitus n

sexual intercourse, sex, union, intimacy, copulation, coupling, lovemaking, marriage-bed, bed, sleeping with someone, going to bed with someone, mating, relations
OLD commixtion, embraces
FORMAL carnal knowledge, congress, consummation, coition
COLLOQ. how's your father, it, the other; *Aust & NZ* naughty
SLANG lay, bang, bonk, leg-over, wham bam thank you ma'am, greens, jig-a-jig, knee-trembler, quickie, nooky, pussy, rumpy-pumpy, tail; *N Am* jazz, poontang; (*taboo*) fuck, fucking, screw, screwing, shag, shagging

cold adj, n

♦ adj
1 UNHEATED, cool, chilled, ice-cold, chilly, chill, shivery, raw, biting, cutting, bitter, fresh, wintry, bleak, frigid, frosty, icy, rimy, glacial, arctic, Siberian, polar, freezing, frozen, numbed, keen, Decemberish; *Scot* cauld
OLD frore
FORMAL gelid, brumal, brumous

COLLOQ. nippy, parky

2 feel cold
shivery, chilly, freezing, frozen, numb, agued

3 UNFEELING, unmoved, unsympathetic, unemotional, frigid, icy, impersonal, unfriendly, distant, remote, aloof, standoffish, reserved, chilly, clinical, undemonstrative, unresponsive, passionless, unexcitable, indifferent, lukewarm, stony, callous, insensitive, heartless, biting, dead, uncaring, antagonistic, hostile, repulsive; *Scot* fremd
FORMAL phlegmatic

1 hot, warm **2** hot **3** friendly, responsive, warm

◆ *n*
coldness, chill, chilliness, coolness, frigidity, iciness, rawness, winter, frost, snow, ice; *Scot* cauld, jeel
warmth, heat

Synonym nuances
sense 1

Cool is a fairly positive synonym, suggesting a level of coldness that may be desirable: *the evening was pleasantly cool*; *cool drinks*. **Fresh** may be used in a similar way, to imply an invigorating aspect: *fresh, bracing breezes*. **Chilled**, **chilly** and **chill**, however, may be used to suggest a stronger, although not severe coldness, with the strong connotation of a potential effect on the body: *the chilly station foyer*. **Chilled** is often used specifically of foodstuffs and other objects that have been deliberately cooled.

Ice-cold suggests a severely low temperature, again with a connotation of physical sensation: *he fell into the ice-cold lake*. The terms **keen**, **raw**, **biting**, **cutting** and **bitter** are the most strongly suggestive of physical effects, and are appropriately used of the natural elements: *the biting cold penetrated our clothes*; *bitter frosty nights*.

Freezing and **frozen** could be used literally or figuratively to convey severe coldness; however, **glacial**, **arctic**, **Siberian** and **polar** would only be used in the context of extremes of low temperature: *arctic conditions hampered the expedition*. **Wintry** and **bleak** can be used evoke the desolation that cold weather may bestow: *many resorts can be bleak and damp in winter*.

---

cold-blooded *adj*
cruel, inhuman, brutal, savage, barbaric, barbarous, merciless, ruthless, pitiless, callous, unfeeling, heartless, iron-headed
compassionate, merciful

cold-hearted *adj*
unfeeling, unkind, uncaring, insensitive, unsympathetic, uncompassionate, callous, stony-hearted, cold, heartless, indifferent, detached, flinty, inhuman, iron-headed
warm-hearted

coldly *adv*
unfeelingly, unsympathetically, unemotionally, undemonstratively, callously, insensitively, heartlessly, antagonistically
warmly, responsively

collaborate *v*
1 WORK TOGETHER, co-operate, join, join forces, work jointly, work as partners, combine forces, team up, associate with, unite, participate
2 collaborate with the enemy
conspire, collude, fraternize, betray, turn traitor

collaboration *n*
1 in collaboration with local industry
association, alliance, partnership, teamwork, co-operation, participation, union, combined/joint/collective effort
2 collaboration with the enemy
conspiring, collusion, fraternizing

collaborator *n*
1 collaborators in the research
co-worker, associate, partner, teammate, fellow worker, colleague, assistant
2 traitors and collaborators
conspirator, accomplice, traitor, turncoat, betrayer, colluder, fraternizer, quisling, renegade

collapse *v, n*
◆ *v*
1 the bridge collapsed
fall down, fall in, fall to pieces, come apart, fall apart, sink, founder, disintegrate, crumble, subside, give way, cave in
2 the business collapsed
fail, founder, break down, fall through, finish, disintegrate, come to an end, come to nothing, slump, go to the wall
COLLOQ. fold, flop; *Aust* go bung
3 collapse with exhaustion
faint, pass out, lose consciousness, black out, keel over, swoon, crumple
4 collapse in tears
break down, lose control, fall apart, go to pieces, have a (nervous) breakdown
COLLOQ. crack up
◆ *n*
1 the collapse of the roof
falling-down, falling-in, falling to pieces, coming apart, sinking, foundering, disintegration, subsidence, giving way, cave-in
2 the collapse of the talks
failure, foundering, breakdown, falling-through, disintegration, downfall, ruin, debacle
COLLOQ. flop
3 his collapse in the street
fainting, passing-out, loss of consciousness, blackout, keeling-over, swoon
4 BREAKDOWN, nervous breakdown, loss of control, attack

collar *n, v*
◆ *n*
neckband, band, ring, dog-collar, choker, gorget, ruff, bertha, ruche, vandyke, rollcollar, turn-down, ox-bow, jampot
TECHNICAL collet, chevesaile, holderbat
OLD carcanet, mousquetaire, partlet, piccadilly, rebato, whisk, rabatine
◆ *v*
stop, grab, capture, catch, seize, arrest, apprehend
COLLOQ. nab, nick, bust, haul in

collate *v*
gather, collect, sort, arrange, order, put in order, organize, compare, compose, compile, edit, put together

collateral *n*
security, guarantee, pledge, surety, assurance, deposit, funds

collation *n*
gathering, arrangement, ordering, organization, composition, compilation, editing, putting together

colleague *n*
workmate, co-worker, teammate, partner, collaborator, ally, associate, confederate, confrère, comrade, fellow worker, companion, aide, helper, assistant, auxiliary

collect *v*
1 collect firewood
gather, accumulate, amass, heap, hoard, pile up, stockpile
FORMAL aggregate
2 a crowd collected
gather, form, come together, amass, mass, converge, congregate, assemble, convene, muster, rally
3 collect them from the station
fetch, pick up, meet, get, call for, come for, go and get, go and take, go and bring; *Scot & NZ* uplift

Collective nouns (by animal) include:

shrewdness of *apes*	school of *dolphins*	tribe of *goats*	swarm of *locusts*	muster of *penguins*	flock of *sheep*
cete of *badgers*	dole of *doves*	husk of *hares*	tittering of *magpies*	nye of *pheasants*	murmuration of *starlings*
sloth of *bears*	team of *ducks*	cast of *hawks*	troop of *monkeys*	litter of *pigs*	ambush of *tigers*
swarm of *bees*	parade of *elephants*	brood of *hens*	watch of *nightingales*	school of *porpoises*	rafter of *turkeys*
obstinacy of *buffaloes*	busyness of *ferrets*	bloat of *hippopotami*	family of *otters*	bury of *rabbits*	turn of *turtles*
clowder of *cats*	charm of *finches*	string of *horses*	parliament of *owls*	colony of *rats*	descent of *woodpeckers*
drove of *cattle*	shoal of *fish*	pack of *hounds*	pandemonium of *parrots*	unkindness of *ravens*	gam of *whales*
brood of *chickens*	skulk of *foxes*	troop of *kangaroos*	covey of *partridges*	crash of *rhinoceros*	rout of *wolves*
bask of *crocodiles*	army of *frogs*	kindle of *kittens*	muster of *peacocks*	building of *rooks*	zeal of *zebras*
murder of *crows*	gaggle/skein of *geese*	exaltation of *larks*		pod of *seals*	
herd of *deer*		leap of *leopards*			
pack of *dogs*		pride of *lions*			

4 *collect for a charity*
raise money, ask for money, ask people to give, solicit, acquire
5 *collect stamps*
acquire, save, amass, have as a hobby, be interested in
6 *collect your thoughts*
compose, gather (together), assemble, recover, prepare
F3 **2** disperse, scatter **3** drop off, leave

collected *adj*
composed, controlled, self-controlled, self-possessed, placid, serene, calm, unruffled, unshaken, unperturbed, imperturbable, poised, cool
COLLOQ. unflappable, unfazed
F3 anxious, worried, agitated

collection *n*
1 *an art collection; the collection of information*
group, cluster, accumulation, gathering, assembly, conglomeration, mass, heap, pile, hoard, stockpile, store, assortment, job-lot
FORMAL assemblage
2 *a collection of poems*
set, anthology, compilation, collected works, selection, series
3 *a collection for charity*
donation(s), gift(s), contribution(s), subscription, offering, offertory
COLLOQ. whip-round

collective *adj, n*
♦ *adj*
united, combined, concerted, co-operative, collaborative, joint, common, shared, corporate, democratic, composite, aggregate, unanimous, cumulative
F3 individual
♦ *n*
commune, co-operative, community, kibbutz, kolkhoz, moshav

collective nouns
See panel above

collector
See panel below

college *n*
educational institution, educational establishment, university, institute, college of further education, technical college, adult education centre, academy, school, seminary
OLD polytechnic, poly
Related adjective: collegiate

collide *v*
1 *the cars collided*
crash (into), meet head on, smash (into), bump (into), run into, go into, plough into, hit
COLLOQ. prang
2 *their opinions collided*
clash, conflict, be in conflict, disagree, quarrel, wrangle, grapple, fight, contend, feud, war

collision *n*
1 *in collision with a lorry*
crash, impact, bump, smash, accident, pile-up, wreck, disaster
COLLOQ. prang
2 *a collision of interests*
clash, conflict, confrontation, opposition, showdown, disagreement, fight, brush, collision, warring, fighting, feud, quarrel, wrangle

colloquial *adj*
conversational, informal, familiar, everyday, vernacular, casual, idiomatic, chatty, popular
FORMAL demotic
F3 formal

colloquially *adv*
informally, familiarly, popularly, conversationally
F3 formally

collude *v*
conspire, plot, connive, collaborate, scheme, intrigue
FORMAL machinate
COLLOQ. be in cahoots

collusion *n*
complicity, deceit, conspiracy, plot, connivance, collaboration, league, scheme, scheming, intrigue, artifice
FORMAL machination
COLLOQ. cahoots

Names of collectors and enthusiasts include:

zoophile (*animals*)	gamer (*computer games*)	entomologist (*insects*)
antiquary (*antiques*)	conservationist (*countryside*)	phillumenist (*matches/matchboxes*)
tegestologist (*beer mats*)	cruciverbalist (*crosswords*)	monarchist (*the monarchy*)
campanologist (*bell-ringing*)	environmentalist (*the environment*)	deltiologist (*postcards*)
ornithologist (*birds*)	xenophile (*foreigners*)	arachnologist (*spiders/arachnids*)
bibliophile (*books*)	gourmet (*good food*)	philatelist (*stamps*)
audiophile (*broadcast sound*)	gastronome (*good food and wine*)	arctophile (*teddy bears*)
lepidopterist (*butterflies*)	discophile (*gramophone records*)	etymologist (*words*)
cartophilist (*cigarette cards*)	chirographist (*handwriting*)	
numismatist (*coins/medals*)	hippophile (*horses*)	

colonist n
colonial, settler, colonizer, immigrant, emigrant, pioneer

colonize v
settle, occupy, people, pioneer, found, populate

colonnade n
arcade, cloisters, portico, covered walk, stoa
FORMAL columniation, peristyle

colony n
1 *Britain's former colonies*
settlement, outpost, dependency, dominion, protectorate, possession, satellite, satellite state, territory, province, settlement
OLD plantation
2 *a colony of birds*
group, association, community, settlement
TECHNICAL hive, swarm, apery, coenobium, formicarium, polyzoarium

colossal adj
huge, enormous, immense, vast, massive, great, gigantic, mammoth, monstrous, monumental, herculean, gargantuan
FORMAL Brobdingnagian
COLLOQ. whopping, jumbo
E3 tiny, minute

colossus n
giant, titan, Goliath, Hercules, monster, ogre, Cyclops

colour n, v
♦ n
1 HUE, shade, tinge, tone, tincture, tint, dye, paint, wash, pigment, pigmentation, colorant, coloration, complexion
See panel below
2 *the colour of her cheeks*
rosiness, redness, ruddiness, pinkness, glow
3 *regardless of colour or creed*
skin colour, pigmentation, race, racial group, ethnic group, nationality
4 VIVIDNESS, liveliness, life, richness, brilliance, animation
COLLOQ. kick, oomph, pizzazz
5 *a nation's colours*
flag, standard, banner, emblem, ensign, insignia, badge
6 *a team's colours*
strip, kit, tackle, clothing
COLLOQ. get-up
♦ v
1 PAINT, crayon, dye, tint, stain, tinge, wash, highlight
2 BLUSH, flush, redden, go/turn red
3 *colour your judgement*
affect, bias, prejudice, influence, sway, distort, slant, pervert, exaggerate, overstate, misrepresent, falsify, taint
Related adjective: chromatic

colourful adj
1 MULTICOLOURED, kaleidoscopic, variegated, many-coloured, parti-coloured, polychrome, vivid, bright, brilliant, rich, deep, intense, vibrant, gaudy, garish

2 *a colourful description*
vivid, graphic, picturesque, animated, lively, stimulating, exciting, interesting, rich, vibrant
E3 **1** colourless, drab

colourfully adv
brightly, brilliantly, vibrantly, intensely, kaleidoscopically

colourless adj
1 TRANSPARENT, neutral, uncoloured, monochrome, white, in black and white, bleached, washed out, faded, pale, ashen, sickly, anaemic, wan
2 INSIPID, lacklustre, dull, dreary, drab, plain, characterless, unmemorable, boring, uninteresting, tame
E3 **1** colourful, polychrome **2** bright, exciting

column n
1 PILLAR, post, shaft, pole, upright, support, pier, obelisk
TECHNICAL asta, caryatid, telamon, Atlas, pilaster
2 *a column of people*
line, row, rank, file, procession, queue, string, parade, list
3 *a column in a newspaper*
article, item, piece, feature, story
Related adjectives: columnal, columnar

columnist n
journalist, reporter, reviewer, writer, correspondent, contributor, critic, editor

coma n
unconsciousness, hypnosis, insensibility, lethargy, oblivion, stupor, torpor, trance, drowsiness
TECHNICAL PVS, persistent vegetative state, catalepsy, sopor
FORMAL somnolence

comatose adj
unconscious, out, out cold, in a coma, insensible, lethargic, drowsy, sleepy, sluggish, stupefied, stunned, dazed, torpid
TECHNICAL cataleptic, soporose
FORMAL somnolent
E3 conscious

comb v
1 *comb your hair*
groom, neaten, tidy, arrange, dress, untangle, disentangle
2 SEARCH, hunt, scour, sweep, explore, sift, screen, rake, rummage, ransack, go through
COLLOQ. go over with a fine-tooth comb, turn upside down

combat n, v
♦ n
war, warfare, hostilities, action, battle, fight, fighting, skirmish, struggle, conflict, clash, encounter, engagement, contest, bout, duel
♦ v
fight, battle, do battle, war, wage war, take up arms, strive, struggle, contend, contest, oppose, resist, withstand, defy

combatant n
fighter, warrior, soldier, serviceman, servicewoman,

The range of colours includes:

red	coral	chocolate	chartreuse	sapphire	magnolia
crimson	salmon	tan	green	gentian	cream
scarlet	peach	sepia	eau de nil	indigo	ecru
vermillion	amber	taupe	emerald	anil	milky
cherry	brown	beige	jade	navy	white
cerise	chestnut	fawn	bottle	violet	grey
magenta	mahogany	yellow	avocado	purple	silver
maroon	bronze	lemon	sage	mauve	charcoal
burgundy	auburn	canary	khaki	plum	ebony
ruby	rust	ochre	turquoise	lavender	jet
orange	umber	saffron	aquamarine	lilac	black
tangerine	copper	topaz	cobalt	pink	
apricot	cinnamon	gold	blue	rose	

enemy, opponent, adversary, antagonist, belligerent, contender

combative adj

aggressive, antagonistic, belligerent, warring, argumentative, contentious, militant, quarrelsome, warlike, hawkish
FORMAL bellicose, pugnacious, truculent
E3 pacific, peaceful

combination n

1 *in combination with other subjects*
association, co-operation, conjunction, co-ordination, union, amalgamation, coalition, unification, alliance, federation, confederation, confederacy, combine, consortium, syndicate, merger, integration, synergy
2 BLEND, mix, mixture, composite, cross, amalgam, amalgamation, merger, union, fusion, conflation, coalescence, collection, connection, group, synthesis, compound, solution

combine v

merge, amalgamate, bring together, put together, club together, unify, blend, stir, mix, mingle, integrate, incorporate, synthesize, compound, alloy, fuse, bond, bind, conflate, weld, join, join forces, connect, link, marry, unite, pool, ally, associate, team up, co-operate
FORMAL admix, homogenize
E3 divide, separate, detach

combustible adj

1 *combustible gas*
explosive, flammable, incendiary, ignitable, inflammable
2 *a combustible temper*
excitable, sensitive, explosive, stormy, tense, volatile, charged
E3 incombustible, non-flammable, flameproof

combustion n

burning, igniting, ignition, firing

come v

1 *they came to me*
advance, move towards, travel towards, move forward, approach, move nearer, near, draw near
2 *come to the river/party*
reach, attain, arrive, enter, get here, get there, appear, put in an appearance, attend, materialize
COLLOQ. turn up, show up, surface, burst in, barge in
3 *come to power*
reach, attain, achieve, gain, secure, pass into
4 *the time for action has come*
arrive, occur, take place, happen, come about, present itself, come to pass, transpire
5 *she comes from Belgium*
originate, be, be a native of, be ... by birth, have as your home, hail, have as its source/origin
6 *his arrogance comes from his insecurity*
result from, be caused by, follow, issue, develop, arise, stem, evolve
7 *it may come to war*
pass into, become, turn, evolve into, develop into, enter, go as far as
8 *the idea came to me*
think of, remember, strike, occur to, come to the mind of, dawn on
9 *this wallpaper comes in blue or green*
be available, be produced, be on the market, be on offer
10 REACH AN ORGASM, have an orgasm, climax
E3 1 go, retreat **2** depart, leave **3** fall from, lose **8** forget
■ **come about**
happen, occur, come to pass, take place, result, arise, transpire
FORMAL befall
■ **come across**

1 FIND (BY CHANCE), discover, meet by chance, stumble across, encounter, notice
FORMAL chance upon, happen upon
COLLOQ. run into, bump into
2 *his speech came across well*
come over, seem, appear, communicate, give the impression of being
■ **come along**
1 PROGRESS, make progress, develop, get better, improve, show an improvement, make headway, advance, rally, mend, recover, recuperate
2 HURRY UP
COLLOQ. get a move on, get cracking, shake a leg, get your skates on, pull your finger out
■ **come apart**
collapse, disintegrate, fall to bits/pieces, break (up), separate, split, tear, crumble
■ **come back**
1 RETURN, reappear, come home, go back, get back
2 BE REMEMBERED, remind, be recalled, be recollected, be suggested
■ **come between**
separate, part, divide, split up, disunite, alienate, cause a rift between
FORMAL estrange
■ **come by**
acquire, get, get hold of, obtain, secure, come into someone's possession, fall into someone's hands
FORMAL procure
■ **come clean**
acknowledge, admit, confess, own up, reveal, tell all
COLLOQ. make a clean breast of something, spill the beans
SLANG fess up
■ **come down**
decrease, fall, drop, reduce, descend, decline, deteriorate, worsen, degenerate
■ **come down on**
blame, criticize, rebuke, reprimand, find fault with, chide, reprove, upbraid, reprehend, admonish
FORMAL berate
COLLOQ. slate, knock, tear into
■ **come down to**
mean, be tantamount to, be equivalent to, correspond to, amount to, add up to, boil down to
■ **come down with**
catch, become/fall ill with, get, develop, go down with, pick up, become infected with, become ill with
FORMAL contract, succumb to
■ **come forward**
offer (yourself), offer your services, volunteer, step forward
■ **come in**
enter, appear, arrive, finish, receive
COLLOQ. show up
E3 go out
■ **come in for**
receive, get, suffer, endure, bear, undergo, experience, be subjected to, sustain
■ **come into**
inherit, be left, have bequeathed to you, be heir to, acquire, receive
■ **come off**
succeed, be successful, be effective, go well, work (out), happen, occur, take place, end up
COLLOQ. pay off
■ **come on**
begin, appear, advance, proceed, progress, make progress, develop, improve, show an improvement, get better, thrive, succeed rally, mend, recover, recuperate
■ **come out**
1 *it came out that she never liked him*

become known, emerge, leak out, come to light, appear, be revealed, be made public

2 *the magazine comes out monthly*
be published, appear, be produced, be released, become available

3 *everything came out all right in the end*
result, end (up), finish, conclude, terminate

4 *gay people coming out*
come out of the closet, declare yourself to be, declare openly, admit

■ **come out with**
say, state, affirm, declare, utter, exclaim, disclose, divulge, exclaim, blurt out

■ **come round**

1 *come around from the anaesthetic*
come to, recover, recover/regain consciousness, wake, awake

2 YIELD, change your mind, agree, be converted to, be persuaded, be won over, relent, concede, allow, grant, accede

3 *spring comes round again*
occur, happen, take place, recur, reappear
E3 1 pass out

■ **come through**
endure, withstand, survive, ride out, pull through, prevail, triumph, succeed, accomplish, achieve

■ **come to**

1 *come to after the operation*
come round, recover, recover/regain consciousness, wake, awake

2 *come to a total*
add up to, total, aggregate, amount to, make, equal, run to

■ **come up**
rise, arise, happen, occur, present itself, crop up, turn up

■ **come up to**
reach, meet, match up to, measure up to, live up to, make the grade, compare with, approach, bear comparison with

■ **come up with**
suggest, put forward, propose, offer, present, think of, dream up, conceive, devise, advance, produce, submit

comeback *n*
return, reappearance, resurgence, revival, recovery, rally

comedian *n*
comic, clown, humorist, funny man, funny woman, comedienne, entertainer, wit, joker, gagman
COLLOQ. wag, gagster

comedown *n*
anticlimax, let-down, disappointment, deflation, blow, reverse, reversal, decline, descent, demotion, humiliation, degradation
TECHNICAL bathos

comedy *n*

1 *comedy on TV*
farce, entertainment, humour, pantomime, burlesque, vaudeville, slapstick, satire, situation comedy, sitcom, tragicomedy, commedia dell'arte

2 *the comedy of the situation*
humour, hilarity, funniness, fun, drollery, clowning, wit, joking, jesting, facetiousness
E3 1 tragedy

comely *adj*
attractive, beautiful, pretty, lovely, good-looking, blooming, buxom, fair, graceful, pleasing, winsome; *Scot* bonny
FORMAL pulchritudinous

come-on *n*
encouragement, inducement, enticement, lure, allurement, temptation, attraction

comeuppance *n*
deserts, just deserts, what you deserve, dues, merit,

punishment, rebuke, chastening, recompense, requital, retribution

comfort *n, v*
♦ *n*
1 EASE, relaxation, luxury, plenty, snugness, cosiness, wellbeing, satisfaction, contentment, enjoyment, freedom from pain, freedom from worry/unhappiness, freedom from difficulties
FORMAL repose, opulence
COLLOQ. easy street
2 CONSOLATION, compensation, cheer, reassurance, encouragement, condolence, alleviation, relief, help, aid, support
FORMAL solace, succour
E3 1 discomfort **2** distress
♦ *v*
ease, soothe, relieve, alleviate, assuage, console, cheer, gladden, reassure, hearten, encourage, help, support, sympathize, empathize, invigorate, strengthen, enliven, refresh
OLD encheer, stay, speak to the heart, recomfort
FORMAL solace, bring solace to, succour

comfortable *adj*
1 SNUG, cosy, relaxing, restful, easy, convenient, pleasant, agreeable, enjoyable, delightful, warm, homelike, kindly, well, *gemütlich*; *Scot* couthie, bein, tosh
OLD commodious
COLLOQ. comfy
2 *comfortable clothes*
well-fitting, loose-fitting, loose, roomy
3 AFFLUENT, well-off, well-to-do, without financial problems, pleasant, prosperous, luxurious; *Scot* bein
FORMAL opulent
COLLOQ. cushy
4 UNHURRIED, leisurely, slow, relaxed, easy, gentle, carefree, lazy, slow, armchair
COLLOQ. laid-back
5 *feel comfortable talking about it*
relaxed, at ease, unembarrassed, confident, happy, contented, safe, secure
E3 1 uncomfortable, unpleasant **2** uncomfortable, tight **3** poor, hard-up **5** uneasy, awkward, nervous, offended, embarrassed, threatened

---

Synonym nuances
sense 1
Snug and **cosy** and are highly suggestive of security and shelter: *they're snug in their beds; a cosy place by the fire.* **Homelike** would be used to describe a similar place which prompts a feeling of familiarity. **Relaxing** and **restful** suggest the removal of tension, either physical or mental, while **easy** has the added connotation of absence of any discomfort: *he has had an easy life.*
  The word **convenient** perhaps conveys the least feeling, merely suggesting suitability: *convenient working hours.* **Pleasant** and **agreeable** are suggestive of mild pleasure gained from comfort: *an agreeable spot on the beach*; whilst **enjoyable** and **delightful** are similar but more effusive.

---

comforting *adj*
soothing, reassuring, encouraging, heartening, heartwarming, helpful, cheering, consolatory, consoling, encouraging
FORMAL inspiriting
E3 worrying

comic *adj, n*
♦ *adj*
funny, hilarious, side-splitting, comical, droll, humorous, witty, amusing, entertaining, diverting, joking, facetious, jocular, light, farcical, ridiculous,

ludicrous, absurd, laughable, zany, buffo
COLLOQ. priceless, rich, knee-slapping
E3 tragic, serious, straight
• *n*
comedian, clown, humorist, funny man, funny woman,
entertainer, wit, joker, gagman, buffoon, buffo
COLLOQ. wag, gagster

comical *adj*
funny, hilarious, droll, humorous, witty, amusing,
entertaining, diverting, laughable, farcical, absurd,
ridiculous, ludicrous
E3 sad, unamusing

comically *adv*
funnily, hilariously, humorously, wittily, amusingly, absurdly,
ridiculously, ludicrously, farcically
E3 sadly

coming *adj, n*
• *adj*
1 *in the coming months*
next, forthcoming, upcoming, impending, imminent, due,
approaching, advancing, near, nearing, future
2 *the coming man*
aspiring, promising, rising, up-and-coming
• *n*
advent, approach, arrival, nearing, birth, dawn, accession

command *v, n*
• *v*
1 ORDER, bid, give orders to, charge, enjoin, direct, instruct,
require, demand, compel
FORMAL adjure
2 LEAD, head, rule, reign, govern, control, be in charge/
control of, direct, dominate, manage, superintend,
supervise, preside over
3 *command respect*
be given, gain, receive, get, obtain, secure
• *n*
1 COMMANDMENT, decree, edict, precept, mandate, order,
bidding, charge, injunction, dictate, directive, direction,
instruction, requirement
OLD (*Shakesp*) impose; (*Spenser*) hest
FORMAL behest
2 *be in command*
power, authority, leadership, control, charge, domination,
dominion, mastery, rule, sway, government, ascendancy,
management, supervision, superintendence

commandeer *v*
seize, take possession of, take, confiscate, impound,
hijack, usurp
FORMAL appropriate, requisition, expropriate, arrogate,
sequester, sequestrate

commander *n*
leader, head, chief, director, commander-in-chief, general,
admiral, captain, commanding officer, officer, chieftain,
governor, master, superintendent
COLLOQ. boss
SLANG bloke

Types of commander include:

aga	meer	*old* taxiarch
old chiliarch	*old* polemarch	*old* tetrarch
encomendero	*old* phylarch	*old* trierarch
old hipparch	*old* prefect	*old* turcopolier
imperator	privateer	warlord
mir	risaldar	

---

commanding *adj*
1 *in a commanding lead*
powerful, strong, superior, advantageous, dominant,
dominating, controlling, directing

2 *a commanding personality*
authoritative, forceful, powerful, assertive, confident,
autocratic
FORMAL peremptory
3 *the castle's commanding position*
dominating, imposing, impressive, lofty

commemorate *v*
celebrate, solemnize, remember, mark, honour, pay
tribute to, salute, immortalize, observe, keep, recognize
FORMAL memorialize

commemoration *n*
celebration, observance, remembrance, memory, tribute,
honour, honouring, ceremony, salute, recognition,
dedication

commemorative *adj*
memorial, celebratory, remembering, marking,
honouring, saluting, dedicatory, in memory of, in
memoriam, in remembrance of, in honour of, as a tribute
to, in recognition of

commence *v*
begin, make a beginning, start, make a start, embark on,
originate, initiate, inaugurate, open, launch, go ahead
E3 finish, end, cease

commencement *n*
beginning, start, initiation, origin, opening, launch, outset,
onset, initiation
COLLOQ. kick-off
E3 finish, end, conclusion

commend *v*
1 PRAISE, compliment, acclaim, extol, applaud, speak
highly of
FORMAL laud, eulogize
2 *commend this book*
recommend, suggest, approve, propose, advocate, put in
a good word for
3 COMMIT, entrust, trust, confide, consign, hand over, give,
deliver, yield
E3 1 criticize, censure

commendable *adj*
admirable, excellent, noble, praiseworthy, worthy,
creditable, exemplary, deserving, estimable
FORMAL laudable, meritorious
E3 blameworthy, poor

commendation *n*
praise, acclaim, acclamation, accolade, applause,
congratulation, high/good opinion, good word, approval,
credit, recognition, encouragement, recommendation,
seal/stamp of approval, special mention
FORMAL approbation, encomium, panegyric
COLLOQ. brownie points
E3 blame, criticism

commensurate *adj*
proportionate, equivalent, equal, corresponding,
comparable, in proportion to, according to, corresponding
to, consistent with, appropriate to, compatible with,
acceptable, adequate, sufficient, due, fitting

comment *v, n*
• *v*
remark, give an opinion, observe, note, mention, say, point
out, explain, interpret, gloss, speak to
OLD descant, gloze
FORMAL interpose, interject, elucidate, opine
• *n*
opinion, statement, remark, observation, view, note,
annotation, footnote, marginal note, sidenote,
explanation, illustration, exposition, commentary, criticism
FORMAL elucidation, scholion, scholium

commentary *n*
1 *a commentary on a football match*

narration, voice-over, analysis, description, report, account, review
2 *a Bible commentary*
explanation, interpretation, analysis, notes, annotation, treatise, critique
FORMAL elucidation, exegesis, exposition, postil

commentator *n*
1 *a sports commentator*
broadcaster, reporter, correspondent, sportscaster, newscaster, narrator, commenter
2 *a commentator on the text*
annotator, interpreter, critic
FORMAL expositor, exegete

commerce *n*
trade, business, industry, private enterprise, buying and selling, dealings, relations, dealing, traffic, trafficking, exchange, marketing, merchandizing

commercial *adj, n*
• *adj*
1 *buildings for commercial use*
trade, trading, business, industrial
2 *a commercial success*
profitable, profit-making, lucrative, moneymaking, money-spinning, sellable, saleable, popular, monetary, financial, entrepreneurial, profit-orientated, materialistic, mercenary, venal
• *n*
advertisement, publicity, promotion, marketing, jingle, display, blurb, announcement, notice, poster, bill, placard, leaflet, handbill, circular, handout, propaganda
COLLOQ. advert, ad, plug, hype

commiserate *v*
express/offer sympathy, send/offer condolences, sympathize, comfort, feel for, feel sorry for, understand, console, show consideration

commiseration *n*
pity, sympathy, compassion, consolation, comfort, consideration, understanding, condolence(s)
FORMAL solace

commission *n, v*
• *n*
1 ASSIGNMENT, mission, errand, task, job, duty, function, appointment, employment, mandate, work, piece of work, warrant, authority, charge, trust, responsibility
2 COMMITTEE, board, delegation, council, advisory group/ body, deputation, representative
3 *commission on a sale*
percentage, share, royalty, allowance, fee, brokerage, compensation
COLLOQ. cut, rake-off
• *v*
nominate, select, appoint, arrange, contract, engage, employ, assign, authorize, empower, delegate, depute, send, order, place/put in an order for, request, ask for, mandate

commit *v*
1 *commit a crime*
do, carry out, get up to, indulge in, perform, execute, enact
FORMAL effect, perpetrate
2 ENTRUST, trust, confide, commend, consign, deliver, hand over, give, assign, deposit
3 *commit yourself to do something*
promise, pledge, bind, engage, decide, dedicate, bind, covenant, cross the Rubicon
FORMAL obligate
4 *committed to a mental hospital*
admit, send, assign, confine
COLLOQ. put away

commitment *n*
1 DEDICATION, involvement, adherence, devotion, allegiance, loyalty, hard work, effort

2 DUTY, responsibility, undertaking, obligation, engagement, liability, tie
3 *make a commitment*
undertaking, guarantee, assurance, promise, word, covenant, pledge, vow
1 vacillation, wavering

committal *n*
admission, confinement, consignment, sending

committed *adj*
active, dedicated, devoted, loyal, involved, enthusiastic, zealous, fervent, red-hot, evangelical, hardworking, diligent, industrious, studious
FORMAL engagé
COLLOQ. card-carrying, paid up, sold out (on)
apathetic, uncommitted

Synonym nuances
Active and **involved** are neutral terms suggesting participation: *an active campaigner*. **Dedicated** and **devoted** would imply centring your life on someone or something, and any inference is likely to be favourable: *a dedicated priest*; *a devoted husband*. The term **loyal** is similar, this time with the focus on fidelity: *a loyal customer base*.

Enthusiastic implies an intense and lively interest, and there is a note of approval in this term; both **zealous**, **fervent** and **red-hot** are similar, but usually refer to an extreme degree of enthusiasm, and not necessarily with favour: *a zealous evangelist*. The term **evangelical** implies the wish to convert people to the same way of thinking, and again a slightly disapprobatory feeling is likely to come across: *her evangelical attitude to breastfeeding*.

The more approbatory terms **hardworking**, **diligent** and **industrious** appropriately describe a committed application to work, and **studious** could be used to refer to a similar application to learning.

---

committee

Types of committee include:

advisory group/ body	focus group	sub-committee
assembly	group	synod
board	jury	task force
caucus	legation	team
commission	mission	*colloq.* think tank
congress	panel	user group
council	quango	working group
delegation	quorum	working party
deputation	steering	workshop
discussion group	committee	
	steering group	

---

commodious *adj*
roomy, spacious, large, ample, comfortable, expansive, extensive
FORMAL capacious
cramped

commodity *n*
product, thing, article, item, goods, merchandise, material, output, produce, stock, wares

common *adj*
1 *a common response*
frequent, familiar, customary, habitual, usual, daily, everyday, routine, ordinary, normal, regular
COLLOQ. two/ten a penny, dime a dozen
2 *share a common belief*
mutual, shared, joint, collective
3 *common land*
communal, community, public

Members of the British Commonwealth are:

Antigua and	Cameroon	Jamaica	Namibia	St Vincent and the	Trinidad and
Barbuda	Canada	Kenya	Nauru	Grenadines	Tobago
Australia	Cyprus	Kiribati	New Zealand	Seychelles	Tuvalu
the Bahamas	Dominica	Lesotho	Nigeria	Sierra Leone	Uganda
Bangladesh	Fiji Islands	Malawi	Pakistan	Singapore	United Kingdom
Barbados	the Gambia	Malaysia	Papua New	Solomon Islands	United Republic
Belize	Ghana	the Maldives	Guinea	South Africa	of Tanzania
Botswana	Grenada	Malta	Samoa	Sri Lanka	Vanuatu
Brunei	Guyana	Mauritius	St Kitts and Nevis	Swaziland	Zambia
Darussalam	India	Mozambique	St Lucia	Tonga	Zimbabwe

4 common knowledge
widespread, prevalent, general, universal, conventional, accepted, popular, commonplace
5 a common soldier
ordinary, standard, average, plain, simple, workaday, run-of-the-mill, undistinguished, unexceptional
COLLOQ. bog standard
6 VULGAR, coarse, unrefined, crude, inferior, low, ill-bred, uncouth, loutish, plebeian
COLLOQ. common as muck
E3 1 uncommon, unusual, rare, noteworthy **5** different, special **6** tasteful, refined

common sense *n*
good sense, sense, sensibleness, level-headedness, sanity, soundness, reason, pragmatism, hard-headedness, realism, experience, discernment, wisdom, shrewdness, astuteness, judgement, native intelligence, prudence, practicality
FORMAL judiciousness
COLLOQ. gumption, nous, savvy
E3 folly, stupidity

commonly *adv*
generally, normally, usually, often, frequently, regularly, typically, routinely, as a rule, for the most part
E3 rarely

commonplace *adj*
ordinary, unexceptional, everyday, common, routine, humdrum, pedestrian, banal, trite, widespread, frequent, hackneyed, stock, stale, obvious, worn out, boring, uninteresting, threadbare, mundane
E3 memorable, exceptional

common-sense *adj*
commonsensical, matter-of-fact, sensible, level-headed, sane, sound, reasonable, practical, down-to-earth, pragmatic, hard-headed, realistic, experienced, wise, discerning, prudent, shrewd, astute
FORMAL judicious
E3 foolish, unreasonable, unrealistic

commonwealth
See panel above

commotion *n*
agitation, hurly-burly, turmoil, tumult, excitement, ferment, fuss, bustle, ado, uproar, furore, racket, hubbub, rumpus, row, clamour, fracas, upheaval, disturbance, confusion, disorder, disquiet, riot, stir; *Irish* stirabout
COLLOQ. ballyhoo, hullabaloo, to-do, brouhaha, bust-up

communal *adj*
public, community, shared, joint, collective, general, common
E3 private, personal

communally *adv*
collectively, jointly, generally, commonly, community
E3 personally, privately

commune *n, v*
◆ *n*

collective, co-operative, kibbutz, community, fellowship, colony, settlement
◆ *v*
converse, discourse, communicate, make contact, feel/get close to, feel/get in touch, relate spiritually

communicable *adj*
infectious, contagious, transmittable, transmissible, transferable, conveyable, catching, spreadable
FORMAL infective

communicate *v*
1 ANNOUNCE, impart, inform, acquaint, intimate, notify, publish, broadcast, relay, spread, diffuse, pass on, transmit, convey, declare, proclaim, make known, report, reveal, disclose, divulge, unfold, express, get across, get over, put across, put over, deliver, reach, mediate
FORMAL disseminate
2 TALK, speak, converse, commune, correspond, write, phone, telephone, contact, get/be in touch, liaise, keep the lines open

communication *n*
information, intelligence, intimation, disclosure, contact, connection, transmission, message
FORMAL dissemination
See panel on next page

communicative *adj*
talkative, voluble, expansive, informative, chatty, sociable, friendly, forthcoming, outgoing, extrovert, unreserved, free, open, frank, candid
E3 quiet, reserved, reticent, secretive

communion *n*
1 communion with nature
sharing thoughts, sharing feelings, communing, closeness, sympathy, empathy, togetherness, unity, harmony, fellowship, participation, rapport, affinity, community
FORMAL accord, concord, intercourse
2 Holy Communion
Lord's Supper, Eucharist, Mass, Sacrament
TECHNICAL agape
OLD *Scot* occasion

communiqué *n*
announcement, bulletin, (official) communication, press release, dispatch, message, report, statement, newsflash

communism *n*
collectivism, sovietism, revisionism, socialism, totalitarianism, Bolshevism, Leninism, Marxism, Stalinism, Trotskyism, Maoism, Titoism

communist *n*
collectivist, socialist, leftist, soviet, revisionist, Bolshevist, Leninist, Marxist, Stalinist, Trotskyist, Trotskyite, Maoist, Spartakist
COLLOQ. red, tanky; (*derog*) commie, comrade; *Aust* commo

community *n*
1 the local community
district, region, locality, locale, neighbourhood, population, people, populace, public, residents

Forms of communication include:

advertising	correspondence	letter	pager	statement	typewriter
aerogram	data	loud-hailer	pamphlet	tannoy	wireless
announcement	communication	magazine	PDA (Personal	telecom-	video
answering	dialogue	mailshot	Digital Assistant)	munications	video-
machine	dictaphone	mass media	post	telegram	conferencing
bleeper	dispatch	media	postcard	Telemessage®	video-on-
Braille	e-mail (or email)	megaphone	poster	telephone	demand
broadband	facsimile	memo	press	teleprinter	voice mail
broadcasting	fax	message	press release	teletext	walkie-talkie
brochure	gossip	MMS	publicity	television (or TV)	webcast
bulletin	grapevine	(multimedia	radar	access TV	website
cable	information	messaging	radio	cable TV	wire
call-conferencing	technology (IT)	service)	report	digital TV	word
catalogue	intercom	Morse code	semaphore	satellite TV	word processor
chain letter	the Internet (or	news	sign language	subscription TV	World Wide Web
circular	the Net)	newsflash	SMS (short	pay TV	
communiqué	journal	newspaper	message	pay-per-view	
computer	junk mail	note	service)	telex	
conversation	leaflet	notice	speech	text message	

See also **telephone**.

---

2 *the Bangladeshi community*
population, people, populace, public, residents, nation, state, section, group, body, colony, fellowship, brotherhood, fraternity
3 *a religious community*
commune, kibbutz, society, association, fellowship, brotherhood, sisterhood, fraternity
Related adjectives: communal, civil

commute *v*
1 *commute by train*
travel to work, travel to and from work, journey, shuttle
2 *commute the death sentence*
reduce, decrease, shorten, curtail, lighten, soften, lessen, mitigate, remit, adjust, modify

commuter *n*
traveller, passenger
COLLOQ. strap-hanger, suburbanite

compact[1] *adj, v*
 ◆ *adj*
a compact book
small, neat, short, brief, terse, succinct, concise, pithy, condensed, pocket, little, compressed, pressed together, close, close-packed, close-pressed, dense, impenetrable, solid, firm
E3 large, rambling, diffuse
 ◆ *v*
to compact collected refuse
compress, press down, press together, condense, consolidate, pack down, cram, flatten, ram, squeeze, tamp

compact[2] *n*
the compact between the nations
agreement, alliance, pact, treaty, arrangement, transaction, deal, settlement, bargain, understanding, accord, bond, indenture, concordat, contract, covenant, entente

companion *n*
fellow, comrade, friend, intimate, confidant(e), ally, confederate, colleague, associate, partner, consort, escort, chaperon(e), attendant, aide, assistant, accomplice, follower, workmate, compeer, lad, playmate, *bon vivant(e)*, inseparable, shadow, barnacle, compadre, *compagnon de voyage*, compotation, pew-fellow; *dialect* marrow
OLD book-mate, convive, copes-mate, copemate, Trojan, Ephesian, fere, pheere, franion, skaines mate; (*Shakesp*) co-mate; (*Spenser*) beau-pere
COLLOQ. mate, pal, buddy, crony, sidekick, cohort

companionable *adj*
friendly, affable, sympathetic, familiar, genial, amiable, congenial, convivial, sociable, extrovert, outgoing, approachable, gregarious, cordial, informal, neighbourly
E3 unfriendly

companionship *n*
fellowship, comradeship, camaraderie, *esprit de corps*, support, friendship, company, togetherness, closeness, conviviality, association, social intercourse, intimacy, sympathy, rapport
Related adjective: contubernal

company *n*
1 *a manufacturing company*
firm, business, business organization, concern, association, corporation, establishment, house, partnership, syndicate, cartel, trust, consortium, conglomerate, multinational, holding company, subsidiary, public limited company (PLC or plc), private limited company, limited company, limited liability company
2 TROUPE, group, band, ensemble, set, circle, crowd, throng, body, troop, crew, party, assembly, gathering, community, society, team
OLD (*Shakesp*) heap
3 GUESTS, visitors, callers
4 *be glad of company*
friendship, companionship, support, togetherness, closeness, fellowship, comradeship, conviviality, attendance, contact, presence

comparable *adj*
similar, like, alike, related, close, near, akin, corresponding, analogous, equivalent, tantamount, proportional, proportionate, commensurate, parallel, equal
FORMAL cognate
E3 dissimilar, unlike, unequal

❗ comparable or **comparative**?
Comparable means 'of the same kind, to the same degree, etc': *cheaper than any comparable hotel. Comparative* means 'judged by comparing with something else': *After they had stopped playing so noisily there was a period of comparative silence.*

comparably *adv*
similarly, correspondingly, analogously, proportionally, proportionately, equally

comparative *adj*
relative, by/in comparison

comparatively *adv*
relatively, by/in comparison

compare
 ◆ *v*
1 *compare the new edition with the old one*

contrast, juxtapose, balance, weigh, measure, set against, set side by side, note the differences between, correlate
OLD confer, confront, paragon
2 compare her to an angel
liken, equate, link, correlate, regard as the same, show the similarities between, draw analogies with, draw a parallel between; *dialect* even
OLD resemble; (*Shakesp*) like
FORMAL analogize
3 not compare with his predecessor
resemble, match, equal, parallel, bear comparison, be comparable to, be as good as, match, touch
COLLOQ. hold a candle to
■ **beyond compare**
without equal, without parallel, matchless, unmatched, incomparable, unequalled, unrivalled, unsurpassed, brilliant, superb, supreme, superlative, nonpareil, peerless

comparison *n*
juxtaposition, analogy, parallel, correlation, relationship, likeness, resemblance, similarity, comparability, contrast, differences, differentiation, distinction

compartment *n*
section, division, subdivision, part, category, pigeonhole, cubbyhole, niche, alcove, bay, area, stall, booth, cubicle, locker, partition, carrel, cell, chamber, berth, carriage

compartmentalize *v*
categorize, classify, group, sort, file, tag, slot, catalogue, pigeonhole, alphabetize, sectionalize

compass *n*
limit(s), range, scope, stretch, space, extent, sphere, area, reach, field, realm(s), boundary, bounds, circle, circuit, circumference, enclosure, round, scale, zone

compassion *n*
kindness, gentleness, tenderness, tender-heartedness, heart, fellow-feeling, humanity, mercy, pity, leniency, sympathy, commiseration, condolence, sorrow, benevolence, consideration, concern, care, understanding; *S Afr* ubuntu
OLD bowels; (*Spenser*) remorse
E3 cruelty, indifference

compassionate *adj*
kind-hearted, kindly, tender-hearted, tender, gentle, caring, warm-hearted, benign, benevolent, charitable, humanitarian, humane, merciful, clement, lenient, pitying, forgiving, forbearing, feeling, sympathetic, understanding, supportive
OLD bleeding, piteous, remorseful; (*Shakesp*) passionate
E3 cruel, indifferent
See Synonym nuances panel at **kind.**

compatibility *n*
suitability, harmony, consistency, match, adaptability, sympathy, rapport, like-mindedness

compatible *adj*
harmonious, in harmony, consistent, matching, suitable, suited, reconcilable, adaptable, conformable, sympathetic, having rapport, like-minded, well-matched, well-suited, similar
FORMAL congruous, congruent, accordant, consonant
E3 incompatible, antagonistic, contradictory

compatriot *n*
fellow citizen, fellow national, countryman, fellow countryman, countrywoman, fellow countrywoman

compel *v*
force, make, constrain, oblige, necessitate, drive, urge, enforce, impel, insist on, coerce, pressure, pressurize, hustle, browbeat, bully, intimidate, press-gang, dragoon; *Scot* gar
OLD coact, compulse, efforce

COLLOQ. bulldoze, strongarm, twist someone's arm, lean on, put the screws on

compelling *adj*
1 a compelling story
fascinating, gripping, riveting, enthralling, spellbinding, absorbing, mesmeric, irresistible, compulsive
COLLOQ. unputdownable
2 compelling reasons
forceful, imperative, urgent, pressing, overriding, powerful, cogent, persuasive, convincing, weighty, conclusive, incontrovertible, irrefutable
E3 1 boring **2** weak, unconvincing

compendious *adj*
brief, short, concise, succinct, compact, terse, condensed, to the point, crisp, summary, comprehensive, complete, all-embracing

compendium *n*
companion, handbook, manual, collection, anthology, compilation, digest, summary, synopsis, vade-mecum

compensate *v*
1 compensate you for any loss
repay, refund, reimburse, indemnify, recompense, reward, remunerate
2 compensate for doing wrong
make amends, make reparation, make good, make up for, restore, requite, atone, redeem, redress, satisfy
3 COUNTERACT, balance (out), counterbalance, cancel, neutralize, nullify, offset
FORMAL countervail, counterpoise

compensation *n*
1 pay compensation
recompense, reward, payment, remuneration, requital, repayment, refund, reimbursement, indemnification, indemnity, damages, reparation, return
TECHNICAL demurrage, solatium
OLD boot, reprisal
SLANG *Aust* compo
2 make compensation for wrongdoing
amends, redress, satisfaction, restoration, restitution, atonement, consolation, comfort, correction

compère *n*
host, link person, presenter, master of ceremonies, MC, announcer, anchor, anchorman, anchorwoman
COLLOQ. emcee

compete *v*
1 compete against/with other firms
vie, contest, contend, fight, battle, struggle, strive, oppose, challenge, pit yourself, rival, jostle
2 compete in a contest
contend, participate, enter, run, race, take part, go in for

competence *n*
1 ABILITY, proficiency, capability, aptitude, capacity, skill, technique, experience, expertise, facility, fitness
2 challenge the competence of the court
power, authority, jurisdiction, legal capacity
E3 1 incompetence

competent *adj*
1 competent to deal with them
capable, able, adept, efficient, trained, qualified, well-qualified, skilled, skilful, accomplished, experienced, proficient, expert, masterly, equal
2 competent work
satisfactory, acceptable, reasonable, passable, respectable, adequate, sufficient, fit, suitable, appropriate
E3 1 incompetent, incapable, unable, inefficient **2** excellent, outstanding

competition *n*
1 CONTEST, championship, tournament, cup, event, race, match, game, quiz, bout, meet, encounter

2 RIVALRY, opposition, challenge, contest, contention, conflict, struggle, strife, vying, competitiveness, combativeness

3 COMPETITORS, rivals, opponents, opposition, challengers, field

competitive *adj*

1 AMBITIOUS, combative, contentious, antagonistic, aggressive, pushy, keen
COLLOQ. cut-throat, dog-eat-dog

2 *competitive prices*
moderate, reasonable, modest, just, fair, average, inexpensive, low, cut-rate
COLLOQ. bargain-basement

competitively *adv*
competitively priced
moderately, reasonably, modestly, fairly, inexpensively, low

competitiveness *n*
combativeness, contentiousness, antagonism, assertiveness, challenge, aggression, aggressiveness, rivalry, ambition, ambitiousness, keenness
FORMAL pugnacity
COLLOQ. pushiness, rat race, survival of the fittest
🖃 backwardness, sluggishness

competitor *n*
contestant, contender, entrant, candidate, participant, challenger, player, opponent, adversary, antagonist, rival, emulator, competition, opposition

compilation *n*
composition, collection, accumulation, collation, anthology, selection, organization, arrangement, thesaurus, treasury, album, compendium, miscellany, omnibus, potpourri, corpus, opus, work, segue
FORMAL assemblage, amassment, collectanea, florilegium, chrestomathy

compile *v*
compose, put together, collect, gather, garner, cull, accumulate, amass, assemble, collate, marshal, organize, arrange

complacency *n*
smugness, self-satisfaction, gloating, triumph, pleasure, pride, self-righteousness, serenity, self-assurance, gratification, contentment, satisfaction, self-content
🖃 diffidence, discontent

complacent *adj*
smug, self-satisfied, gloating, triumphant, proud, self-righteous, serenity, unconcerned, serene, self-assured, pleased, gratified, contented, self-contented, satisfied
🖃 diffident, concerned, discontented

❗ complacent or **complaisant**?
Complacent means 'smugly pleased with yourself or your own abilities': *One of the dangers of success is that you can become complacent. Complaisant* means 'being cheerfully willing to do what others want': *Franca's complaisant kindness was too much for him.*

complain *v*

1 *complain to the manager; always complaining*
criticize, find fault, file/lodge a complaint, take something up with someone, kick up a fuss, object, protest, air your grievances, grumble, carp, fuss, lament, bemoan, bewail, moan, nag, whine, carry on, groan, growl, kvetch; *dialect* girn; *Scot* mump, mean
OLD plain; (*Spenser*) grutch
FORMAL remonstrate, expostulate, repine
COLLOQ. beef, bellyache, moan and groan, grouse, gripe, grump, bleat, whinge, squawk, squeal, raise a stink, have a bone to pick
SLANG bitch

OLD SLANG bind
2 *complain of an illness*
suffer from, endure, be in pain, feel pain, hurt, ache

Synonym nuances
sense 1
Criticize and **find fault** emphasize the element of dissatisfaction in a complaint, whereas **file/lodge a complaint** or **take up something with someone** are fairly mild, neutral terms for conveying dissatisfaction to someone. **Object**, **protest** and **air your grievances** are appropriate terms for more vehement claims: *the former employees protested at their treatment by the company.* **Kick up a fuss** also suggests less inhibited complaining, creating a disturbance as you do so.
  While these terms do not convey any particular view of the complaining, to use **grumble**, which suggests a less distinct mode of expression, would imply that you think it unconstructive or unnecessary: *he grumbled to himself about the way he was treated.* **Carp**, **kvetch** and **fuss** are similar, and can be used to suggest bothering about trivialities, or even pettiness: *his carping and negative attitude; I can't stand people who fuss about their health.* When someone complains in a sorrowful or pained way, you can use the words **groan**, **lament**, **bemoan** and **bewail**: *she bewailed her ill-fortune;* **moan** and **whine** are similar, but more strongly imply a self-pitying aspect.
  To refer to constant, repetitive complaining, you could use **nag**, but this term will also convey disapproval of this behaviour: *I am ashamed to say I nagged my mother until she gave in.*

---

complainer *n*
grumbler, moaner, niggler, fault-finder
COLLOQ. bellyacher, grouser, fusspot, nit-picker, whiner, whinger; *N Am* fussbudget

complaint *n*

1 PROTEST, objection, grumble, moan, grievance, dissatisfaction, annoyance, fault-finding, criticism, carping, censure, accusation, charge, representation
OLD querimony; (*Shakesp*) plaining
COLLOQ. beefing, bellyaching, grouse, gripe, bleating, whingeing

2 *a chest complaint*
ailment, illness, sickness, disease, disorder, infection, trouble, upset, condition
FORMAL indisposition, affliction, malady, malaise

complaisant *adj*
agreeable, amenable, amiable, accommodating, willing, obliging, solicitous, biddable, compliant, deferential, conciliatory, docile, obedient, conformable
FORMAL tractable
🖃 obstinate, perverse

❗ complaisant or **complacent**?
See panel at **complacent**.

---

complement *n, v*
◆ *n*
1 *wine as a complement to the dinner*
companion, counterpart, addition, accessory, accompaniment, completion
FORMAL consummation
2 *the ship's complement*
allowance, quota, total, totality, aggregate, sum, amount, capacity, entirety
◆ *v*
go well with, go well together, combine well with, accompany, match, set off, contrast, round off, complete, crown

⚠ complement, compliment or supplement?
One thing is a *complement* to another when it makes a pleasant contrast or makes the combination of the two things pleasantly balanced: *Yoghurt can be used as a complement to spicy dishes.* You pay someone a *compliment* when you praise them. A *supplement* is something added to something else that is already complete or to make up for a deficiency: *a magazine supplement; take vitamin supplements.*

complementary *adj*

finishing, completing, perfecting, reciprocal, interdependent, correlative, interrelated, corresponding, matching, twin, fellow, companion, compatible, harmonious, supporting
Ⅰ contradictory, incompatible

⚠ complementary, complimentary or supplementary?
Two things are *complementary* if they complement each other: *use complementary colours in all the furnishings.* You say something *complimentary* to someone as an expression of admiration or praise to them; a *complimentary* ticket is one given free of charge. You use *supplementary* to describe something that is added: *ask a supplementary question.*

complete *adj, v*

◆ *adj*
1 ENTIRE, integral, whole, entire, full, unbroken, undivided, total, intact, plenary, unabbreviated, unabridged, unshortened, unedited, unexpurgated, detailed, comprehensive, exhaustive
2 FINISHED, ended, completed, concluded, over, done, accomplished, finalized, settled, achieved
FORMAL terminated
3 UTTER, total, absolute, outright, downright, out-and-out, thorough, unqualified, unmitigated, unconditional, perfect, consummate
Ⅰ 1 abridged **2** incomplete **3** partial

◆ *v*
1 *complete the work*
finish, end, close, conclude, finalize, settle, perform, discharge, execute, fulfil, realize, accomplish, achieve, make up, crown, cap, round off, wind up, perfect
FORMAL terminate, consummate
COLLOQ. polish off, clinch
2 *complete a form*
fill in, fill out, answer

Synonym nuances
verb sense 1
Conclude, **finalize** and **settle** have a strong element of finality about them and are suggestive of tying up all the relevant loose ends to reach the final state: *the Cabinet finalized the budget for the fiscal year.* **Perform** and **discharge** could be used if you want to put more emphasis on the manner in which tasks have been completed: *she discharged her duties with detached severity.* **Execute** is similar, with strong connotations of efficiency: *brilliantly executed colour illustrations.*
The terms **fulfil** is appropriate in the context of completing duties or aims: *he fulfilled his obligations*, and **realize** in the context of carrying plans through to completion. The positive terms **accomplish** and **achieve** could be used if you want to convey the idea of completing something successfully.
Crown, **cap** and **perfect** are also positive terms to use and again suggest an impressive achievement, surpassing what has gone before: *the striker capped his team's rousing display with his audacious goal; the ancient art of batik has been perfected over the centuries.* **Make up**, on the other hand, has a more restrained tone and merely suggests the provision of something previously lacking: *I was just there to make up the numbers.*

completely *adv*

totally, utterly, wholly, fully, in full, absolutely, perfectly, quite, thoroughly, through and through, altogether, entirely, solidly
COLLOQ. in every respect, lock stock and barrel, from first to last, root and branch, every inch, heart and soul, hook line and sinker

completion *n*

finish, end, close, conclusion, finalization, settlement, discharge, execution, fulfilment, realization, accomplishment, achievement, attainment, fruition, culmination, perfection
FORMAL termination, consummation

complex *adj, n*

◆ *adj*
complicated, intricate, elaborate, involved, difficult, circuitous, tortuous, devious, mixed, varied, diverse, multiple, composite, compound, ramified
FORMAL convoluted, Byzantine
Ⅰ simple, easy

◆ *n*
1 NETWORK, structure, system, scheme, composite, organization, establishment, institute, development
FORMAL aggregation
2 FIXATION, obsession, preoccupation, phobia, disorder, neurosis
COLLOQ. hang-up, thing

Synonym nuances
adjective
Intricate, **elaborate** and **involved** convey fairly straightforwardly the idea of something multi-faceted: *a long and elaborate trial.* **Complicated** is similar, but can be used with the added implication of being difficult to follow or understand. To use **difficult**, however, would make a clear comment that something is too complex to understand or use easily.
Circuitous and **devious** are more likely to be used in the context of an indirect route, or an indirect approach to dealing with a matter, but again have the negative implication that it is unnecessarily or tiresomely complex. **Tortuous** similarly describes a far from straightforward method or route, but is even more suggestive of associated frustration: *six years of tortuous legal battles.*
The terms **mixed**, **varied** and **diverse** are neutral terms conveying the idea of variety of elements, while **multiple**, **composite** and **compound** are similarly neutral, but suggest several components: *a composite remedy of five different flowers.* **Ramified** could be used of situations with a variety of possible or actual consequences: *he was involved in a bitter and ramified dispute.*

complexion *n*

1 SKIN, colour, colouring, tone, texture, pigmentation
2 LOOK, appearance, aspect, attitude, guise, light, character, perspective, nature, cast, type, stamp, kind, sort

complexity *n*

complication, complicatedness, intricacy, elaboration, involvement, circuitousness, tortuousness, deviousness, multifariousness, multiplicity, variety, diverseness, compositeness, entanglement, ramification, repercussion
FORMAL convolution
Ⅰ simplicity

compliance *n*

obedience, submissiveness, submission, agreement, accordance, assent, conformability, deference, passivity, yielding
FORMAL acquiescence, complaisance, concurrence
Ⅰ defiance, disobedience

compliant adj

obedient, submissive, subservient, pliable, accommodating, agreeable, biddable, conformable, amenable, deferential, passive, docile, yielding, indulgent
FORMAL acquiescent, complaisant, tractable
F3 disobedient, intractable

complicate v

compound, elaborate, make difficult, involve, make involved, muddle, mix up, confuse, jumble, tangle, entangle
F3 simplify

complicated adj

complex, intricate, elaborate, involved, tortuous, difficult, puzzling, perplexing, problematic, cryptic, labyrinthine, Byzantine
FORMAL convoluted
COLLOQ. fiddly
F3 simple, easy

complication n

difficulty, problem, drawback, snag, obstacle, problem, ramification, repercussion, complexity, intricacy, elaboration, convolution, tangle, web, confusion, mixture

complicity n

collusion, collaboration, connivance, involvement, agreement, approval, knowledge
FORMAL concurrence, abetment
COLLOQ. being in cahoots
F3 ignorance, innocence

compliment n, v

♦ n
1 pay someone a compliment
flattery, flattering remark, admiration, favour, approval, congratulations, tribute, honour, accolade, commendation, praise, sugarplum
OLD douceur
FORMAL eulogy, homage, felicitation, encomium, laudation
COLLOQ. bouquet
2 sends his compliments
greetings, regards, best wishes, good wishes, congratulations, remembrances, respects
FORMAL salutation, devoirs
F3 1 insult, criticism
♦ v
flatter, admire, commend, speak highly/well of, praise, extol, congratulate, applaud, salute
FORMAL felicitate, laud, eulogize
COLLOQ. pat on the back
F3 insult, condemn

⚠ compliment, complement or supplement?
See panel at **complement**.

complimentary adj

1 FLATTERING, admiring, favourable, approving, appreciative, congratulatory, commendatory
FORMAL eulogistic, panegyrical
2 complimentary ticket
free, gratis, for nothing, honorary, courtesy
COLLOQ. on the house
F3 1 insulting, unflattering, critical

⚠ complimentary or complementary or supplementary?
See panel at **complementary**.

comply v

agree, consent, assent, yield, submit, defer, respect, observe, obey, abide by, all in, conform, follow, perform, discharge, fulfil, satisfy, meet, oblige, accommodate
FORMAL acquiesce, accord, accede
F3 defy, disobey

component n, adj

♦ n
part, constituent, constituent part, integral part, ingredient, element, factor, item, unit, piece, section, module, bit, spare part
♦ adj
constituent, integral, essential, basic, intrinsic, inherent

comport v

acquit, conduct, carry, bear, act, behave, perform
FORMAL demean, deport

compose v

1 the board is composed of four directors
make up, constitute, form, comprise
2 CREATE, write, arrange, produce, make (up), think of/up, devise, form, fashion, build, construct, frame, invent, concoct, put together, assemble
3 CALM, calm down, soothe, quiet, collect, still, settle, steady, tranquillize, quell, assuage, pacify, control

composed adj

calm, calmed down, tranquil, quite, quietened down, serene, relaxed, unworried, unruffled, level-headed, cool, collected, cool and collected, self-possessed, controlled, self-controlled, confident, imperturbable, placid, sedate, at ease
COLLOQ. unflappable, cool as a cucumber
F3 agitated, worried, troubled

composer n

musician, arranger, songwriter, songsmith, tunesmith, melodist, author, writer, creator, maker, master, originator, producer, poet, bard

composite adj, n

♦ adj
compound, conglomerate, complex, blended, combined, fused, mixed, patchwork, synthesized
FORMAL heterogeneous, agglutinate
F3 homogeneous, uniform
♦ n
compound, conglomerate, blend, combination, alloy, amalgam, amalgamation, fusion, conflation, mixture, synthesis, pastiche, patchwork
FORMAL agglutination

composition n

1 CONSTITUTION, make-up, combination, mixture, form, structure, configuration, layout, arrangement, organization, character, harmony, consonance, balance, symmetry
FORMAL conformation
2 a musical composition
creation, work, work of art, opus, piece, arrangement, adaptation, accompaniment, symphony, opera, study, exercise, poem, picture, painting, drawing, story, novel
3 MAKING, production, formation, creation, invention, arranging, devising, putting together, concoction, design, formulation, writing, compilation, proportion
4 ESSAY, paper, article, piece, text, assignment, task, review, dissertation, thesis

compost n

fertilizer, humus, mulch, manure, peat, dressing, leaf-mould, leaf-soil, grow-bag, growing-bag

composure n

calm, tranquillity, serenity, ease, coolness, self-possession, self-control, level-headedness, confidence, assurance, self-assurance, poise, dignity, imperturbability, placidity, equanimity, dispassion, impassivity
FORMAL aplomb
F3 agitation, nervousness, discomposure

Synonym nuances

Calm, **tranquillity** and **serenity**, along with **equanimity** and **placidity**, are suggestive of a naturally peaceful, undisturbed state of mind: *the monk exuded serenity*. If you want to place the emphasis on an ability to keep emotions in check, you might use the terms **coolness**, **self-possession** or **self-control**: *he displays remarkable coolness, in view of his inexperience*.

  Level-headedness suggests composure with common sense at its core. The terms **confidence**, **assurance** and **self-assurance** imply being imbued with a sense of self-belief: *he went about his illegal business with a brazen assurance*; **poise** and **dignity** have positive connotations of a stately demeanour. **Dispassion** or **impassivity** could be used for composure stemming from lack of emotion: *they viewed the scene with worldly dispassion*; *her face was a white mask of impassivity.*

---

compound¹ *n, adj, v*

◆ *n*

a chemical compound

blend, mixture, medley, hybrid, composite, amalgam, alloy, synthesis, fusion, composition, amalgamation, combination, conglomerate
TECHNICAL admixture

◆ *adj*

composite, blended, combined, fused, mixed, synthesized, multiple, complex, complicated, intricate, conglomerate

◆ *v*

1 COMBINE, put together, amalgamate, unite, fuse, coalesce, synthesize, alloy, blend, mix, mingle, intermingle
2 WORSEN, exacerbate, aggravate, make matters worse, complicate, intensify, heighten, magnify, add to, increase
FORMAL augment
COLLOQ. add insult to injury, add fuel to the fire/flames, rub salt in the wound

compound² *n*

a prison compound

enclosure, yard, pen, fold, pound, paddock, stockade, corral, court

comprehend *v*

1 UNDERSTAND, conceive, see, grasp, sense, make sense of, make out, fathom, penetrate, realize, appreciate, know, catch, apprehend, perceive, discern, take in, assimilate, compass, put your finger on; *Aust & NZ* get the strength of
COLLOQ. tumble to, twig, get it
2 INCLUDE, comprise, take in, encompass, involve, contain, embrace, cover, generalize
1 misunderstand, misapprehend

comprehensible *adj*

understandable, easy to understand, intelligible, graspable, discernible, conceivable, coherent, explicit, clear, lucid, plain, simple, accessible, straightforward
incomprehensible, obscure

comprehension *n*

understanding, conception, grasp, realization, appreciation, knowledge, apprehension, perception, discernment, judgement, sense, insight, intelligence
COLLOQ. ken
incomprehension, unawareness

comprehensive *adj*

thorough, exhaustive, full, complete, encyclopedic, compendious, broad, wide, widespread, extensive, sweeping, general, blanket, inclusive, overall, all-inclusive, all-embracing, across-the-board
partial, incomplete, selective

comprehensively *adv*

thoroughly, exhaustively, fully, completely, broadly, widely, widespread, extensively
partially, selectively

compress *v*

1 *compress petrol and air*

press, squeeze, crush, squash, flatten, jam, wedge, cram, tamp, stuff, pack, pinch, pump, compact, condense, constrict, strangulate, strain, consolidate, impact, pressurize, concentrate, crowd, lace, screw, shoehorn
TECHNICAL astringe
OLD astrict
2 *compress an article*

abridge, condense, contract, telescope, shorten, abbreviate, reduce, summarize, synopsize
FORMAL coarctate
2 expand, diffuse

compression *n*

constriction, consolidation, concentration, condensing, pressing, squashing, stuffing, packing, pinching, pumping

comprise *v*

1 *the flat comprises three rooms*

consist of, be composed of, include, contain, take in, incorporate, embody, involve, encompass, cover
FORMAL comprehend, embrace
2 *the countries that comprise Great Britain*

make up, constitute, compose, form

compromise *v, n*

◆ *v*

1 NEGOTIATE, bargain, arbitrate, settle (for), agree, concede, make concessions, meet halfway, come to/reach an understanding, give and take, adapt, adjust
2 *compromise your principles*

weaken, undermine, expose, endanger, imperil, jeopardize, risk, prejudice
3 DISHONOUR, discredit, shame, bring shame to, bring into disrepute, damage, embarrass, involve, implicate

◆ *n*

settlement, agreement, concession, negotiation, mediation, understanding, bargain, deal, co-operation, accommodation, adjustment, trade-off, middle way, give-and-take, balance, composition, *modus vivendi*
OLD temperament
disagreement, intransigence

compulsion *n*

1 *use compulsion to obtain something*

force, coercion, duress, constraint, obligation, pressure, demand, insistence
2 *feel a compulsion to do something*

urge, drive, impulse, desire, longing, need, necessity, temptation, obsession, preoccupation

compulsive *adj*

1 IRRESISTIBLE, overwhelming, overpowering, uncontrollable, obsessive, compelling, driving, besetting, urgent
2 *a compulsive gambler*

obsessive, habitual, addicted, dependent, hardened, inveterate, chronic, incorrigible, irredeemable, incurable, hopeless
COLLOQ. pathological, hooked
3 *compulsive viewing*

compelling, fascinating, gripping, riveting, enthralling, spellbinding, absorbing, mesmeric, irresistible, unavoidable

compulsively *adv*

1 OBSESSIVELY, habitually, chronically, incorrigibly, incurably
COLLOQ. pathologically
2 IRRESISTIBLY, unavoidably, involuntarily, inevitably

compulsory *adj*

obligatory, mandatory, imperative, forced, set, stipulated, binding, contractual, essential, necessary, required
FORMAL requisite, *de rigueur*
optional, voluntary, discretionary

Computer terms include:

TYPES OF COMPUTER:
Apple Mac®
desktop
handheld
iMac®
laptop
Mac (infml)
mainframe
microcomputer
minicomputer
notebook
palmtop
PC (personal computer)

HARDWARE:
bubblejet printer
cable modem
card
chip
circuit board
CPU (central processing unit)
disk drive
dot-matrix printer
floppy drive
graphics card
hard drive
inkjet printer
joystick
joypad
keyboard
laser printer
light pen
microprocessor
modem
monitor
motherboard
mouse
pointer
printer
scanner
screen
silicon chip

sound card
terminal
touchpad
trackball
VDU (visual display unit)
video card

SOFTWARE:
abandonware
application
bot
freeware
program
shareware

MEMORY:
backing storage
CD-R (Compact Disc Recordable)
CD-ROM (Compact Disc Read Only Memory)
CD-RW (Compact Disc Rewritable)
DVD-ROM (Digital Versatile Disc Read Only Memory)
external memory
immediate access memory
internal memory
magnetic tape
read-write memory
RAM (Random Access Memory)
ROM (Read Only Memory)

DISKS:
Compact Disc (CD)
Digital Versatile Disc (DVD)
floppy disk
hard disk
magnetic disk
optical disk
zip disk

PROGRAMMING LANGUAGES:
AWK
BASIC
C
C++
COBOL
Delphi
FORTRAN
HTML
Java
Pascal
Perl
Postscript
Python

MISCELLANEOUS:
access
ASCII
autosave
backup
binary
BIOS (Basic Input/Output System)
bitmap
boot
buffer
bug
bus
byte
cache
character
character code

client-server
cold boot
compression
computer game
computer graphics
computer literate
computer simulation
core dump
cracking
crawler
cursor
data
databank
database
debugging
default
desktop publishing (DTP)
digitizer
directory
DOS (disk operating system)
dump
editor
e-mail (or email)
file
firewall
format
FTP (File Transfer Protocol)
function
gigabyte
grammar checker
graphics
GUI (graphical user interface)
hacking
hit
hyperlink
icon

installation
interface
Internet
interoperable
kilobyte
Linux
login
log off
log on
Mac OS (Macintosh® operating system)
macro
megabyte
menu
message box
metafile
MS-DOS (Microsoft® disk operating system)
mouse mat
multimedia
network
output
P2P (peer-to-peer)
package
parallel port
password
PDF (portable document format)
peripheral
pixel
platform
plug-in
port
protocol
reboot
rewritable
RTF (rich text

format)
script
scripting language
scrolling
serial port
shell
shellscript
spellchecker
spreadsheet
sprite
subdirectory
template
terabyte
toggle
toolbar
Trojan horse
Unicode
uniform resource locator (URL)
Unix®
upgrade
user-friendly
user interface
utilities
video game
virtual reality (VR)
virus
virus checker
warm boot
wide area network (WAN)
window
Windows®
word processing
workstation
World Wide Web (WWW)
worm
WYSIWYG (what you see is what you get)

See also **Internet**.

---

compunction *n*
remorse, regret, repentance, penitence, shame, contrition, sorrow, qualm(s), misgiving(s), guilt, reluctance, hesitation, unease, uneasiness
Ⓕ callousness, defiance

computation *n*
calculation, sum, answer, result, figuring, working-out, reckoning, estimation, forecast, forecasting

compute *v*
calculate, count (up), work out, sum, tally, add up, total, enumerate, reckon, estimate, assess, evaluate, figure, measure, rate

computer
See panel above

comrade *n*
fellow, companion, friend, intimate, confidant(e), ally, confederate, colleague, associate, partner, consort, escort, chaperon(e), attendant, aide, assistant, accomplice, follower, *bon camarade*, frater, tovarish, Achates; *dialect* butty; *Scot* billy
OLD bully-rook
COLLOQ. mate, pal, buddy, crony, sidekick

comradeship *n*
camaraderie, companionship, fellowship, friendship, sociability, closeness, togetherness, affinity, brotherhood, brotherliness, sisterhood, sisterliness, *esprit de corps*

con *v, n*
♦ *v*
trick, cheat, hoax, dupe, deceive, mislead, hoodwink, double-cross, swindle, fleece, defraud, rook
FORMAL inveigle
COLLOQ. do, bamboozle
SLANG rip off
♦ *n*
confidence trick, trick, bluff, deception, swindle, cheating, fraud, racket
COLLOQ. fiddle, scam

concatenation *n*
sequence, series, course, progress, progression, succession, string, chain, connection, interlinking, interlocking, linking, nexus, thread, trail, procession, train

concave *adj*
hollow, hollowed, curved in, bending inwards, cupped, scooped, excavated, sunken, indented, depressed
FORMAL incurvate, incurved
Ⓕ convex

conceal *v*
1 *conceal a body*
hide, obscure, disguise, camouflage, mask, screen, veil, cloak, shroud, cover, bury, submerge, keep hidden, keep out of sight, tuck away
FORMAL secrete
COLLOQ. stash

2 *conceal a secret*
hide, keep dark, keep secret, keep quiet, suppress
FORMAL dissemble
COLLOQ. cover up, hush up, sweep under the carpet, put the lid on, whitewash
E3 1 uncover **2** reveal, disclose

concealed *adj*
hidden, covered, screened, unseen, covert, disguised, inconspicuous, latent, tucked away
E3 clear, plain, visible

concealment *n*
1 *concealment of guns*
hideaway, hideout, hiding, disguise, camouflage, mask, protection, screen, veil, shroud, cloak, cover, secrecy, shelter
FORMAL secretion
2 *concealment of information*
hiding, suppression, keeping dark, keeping secret, secrecy
COLLOQ. cover-up, whitewash, smokescreen
E3 1 uncovering, exposing **2** openness, revelation

concede *v*
1 ADMIT, confess, acknowledge, recognize, own (up), grant, allow, accept
FORMAL accede
2 YIELD, give up, surrender, relinquish, forfeit, sacrifice, hand over
FORMAL cede
E3 1 deny

conceit *n*
1 VANITY, conceitedness, pride, arrogance, haughtiness, immodesty, boastfulness, swagger, egotism, self-love, narcissism, self-importance, self-admiration, superciliousness, cockiness, self-satisfaction, complacency
FORMAL vainglory
COLLOQ. bigheadedness
2 *literary conceits*
image, comparison, simile, metaphor, figurative expression, figure of speech
OLD device
E3 1 modesty, diffidence

conceited *adj*
vain, proud, arrogant, haughty, boastful, swollen-headed, swell-headed, immodest, egotistic, egotistical, narcissistic, self-important, full of yourself, puffed up, supercilious, self-satisfied, complacent, smug, overweening, above yourself, cocky, cat-witted, windy; *Scot* upsetting
OLD flory
FORMAL vainglorious
COLLOQ. bigheaded, stuck-up, toffee-nosed, snotty, too big for your boots; *Aust* having tickets on yourself
E3 modest, self-effacing, diffident, humble

conceivable *adj*
imaginable, credible, believable, thinkable, tenable, possible, likely, probable, plausible
E3 inconceivable, unimaginable

conceivably *adv*
possibly, probably, imaginably, plausibly
E3 inconceivably

conceive *v*
1 IMAGINE, envisage, visualize, see, picture, grasp, understand, perceive, apprehend, comprehend, realize, appreciate, believe, think, fancy, suppose, guess, suppose, get into your head
OLD conceit, contrive, fantasy; (*Shakesp*) brain
FORMAL gestate
2 INVENT, design, devise, formulate, think of/up, come up with, create, originate, form, take, contrive, produce, develop

3 *conceive a baby*
become pregnant, get pregnant, become fertilized, be fertile, become impregnated, become inseminated, reproduce, give birth to, start
OLD enwomb

concentrate *v, n*
♦ *v*
1 FOCUS, converge, centre, direct, centralize, rivet, consolidate, cluster, crowd, congregate, gather, collect, accumulate, amass
2 APPLY YOURSELF, think, give your (undivided) attention, pay/devote attention, attend, put/keep your mind, consider, mind
3 CONDENSE, evaporate, boil down, reduce, compress, distil, thicken, intensify
E3 1 disperse **3** dilute
♦ *n*
essence, extract, distillation, juice
TECHNICAL apozem, decoction, decocture
FORMAL quintessence, elixir

concentrated *adj*
1 *concentrated liquid*
condensed, evaporated, reduced, distilled, thickened, compressed, dense, rich, strong, undiluted
2 INTENSE, intensive, all-out, concerted, vigorous, strenuous, hard, deep
E3 1 diluted **2** half-hearted

concentration *n*
1 ATTENTION, deep/close thought, heed, absorption, application, mind, devotion, single-mindedness, engrossment, intensity
2 CONVERGENCE, centralization, focusing, cluster, mass, crowd, grouping, collection, congregation, accumulation, consolidation, conglomeration
FORMAL agglomeration
3 COMPRESSION, evaporation, boiling-down, distillation, reduction, consolidation, denseness, thickness
E3 1 distraction **2** dispersal **3** dilution

concept *n*
idea, notion, plan, theory, hypothesis, thought, abstraction, conception, conceptualization, visualization, image, view, picture, impression

conception *n*
1 CONCEPT, idea, notion, thought, plan, abstraction, theory, hypothesis, image, view, vision, picture, impression, intention
2 KNOWLEDGE, understanding, comprehension, appreciation, perception, visualization, image, picture, vision, impression, idea, inkling, clue
3 INVENTION, design, birth, beginning, origin, origination, outset, initiation, inauguration, formation, launching
OLD inception, genesis
4 *from conception to birth*
impregnation, insemination, fertilization, conceiving, pregnancy, reproduction
FORMAL fecundation

conceptual *adj*
notional, abstract, theoretical, hypothetical, speculative, thematic, classificatory

concern *v, n*
♦ *v*
1 WORRY, distress, trouble, disturb, bother, upset, alarm, make worried, make anxious, prey on your mind
OLD reck
FORMAL perturb
2 *concern yourself with their problems*
give your attention to, involve, interest, busy, devote, affect, touch, reckon
OLD meddle, cern
3 BE ABOUT, relate to, refer to, regard, deal with, be

connected with, have to do with, involve, cover, apply to, bear on
FORMAL appertain to, pertain to
♦ *n*
1 *a cause for concern*
anxiety, worry, unease, disquiet, care, sorrow, distress, apprehension, disturbance, strain, pressure, anguish
OLD concernment
FORMAL perturbation
2 REGARD, consideration, attention, attentiveness, care, heed, thought
OLD (*Shakesp*) tender
FORMAL solicitude
3 *it's not my concern*
duty, responsibility, charge, job, task, field, business, affair, matter, lookout, problem, interest, part, involvement
OLD concernment
COLLOQ. baby, pidgin, pidgeon, pigeon
4 ISSUE, matter, affair, problem, point, subject, topic, question, debate, argument
OLD concernment
COLLOQ. *S Afr* indaba
5 COMPANY, firm, business, corporation, association, establishment, enterprise, organization, partnership, syndicate
1 joy **2** indifference

concerned *adj*
1 ANXIOUS, worried, uneasy, apprehensive, upset, unhappy, distressed, troubled, disturbed, bothered
FORMAL perturbed
2 *concerned teachers*
attentive, caring, considerate, kind, thoughtful, helpful, charitable, unselfish, altruistic, gracious, sensitive
3 CONNECTED, related, involved, implicated, interested, involved, affected
1 unconcerned, indifferent, apathetic **2** inconsiderate, thoughtless, selfish

concerning *prep*
about, regarding, with regard to, as regards, respecting, with respect to, with reference to, referring to, relating to, relevant to, in the matter of, on the subject of, re
FORMAL apropos

concert *n*
1 *a musical concert*
performance, entertainment, presentation, production, show, recital, appearance, engagement, rendering, rendition, gig, jam session, prom, soirée
COLLOQ. *N Am* hootenanny
2 *work in concert with others*
agreement, harmony, unanimity, union, unison, collaboration, co-operation, partnership
OLD quill
FORMAL accord, concord, concordance, consonance
2 disunity, disharmony, conflict, opposition

concerted *adj*
combined, united, joint, collective, shared, co-operative, collaborative, co-ordinated, interactive, organized, concentrated, prearranged, planned
separate, unco-ordinated, disorganized

concession *n*
1 YIELDING, giving-up, surrender, relinquishment, forfeit, sacrifice, handover, admission, acknowledgement, recognition, grant, allowance, compromise, adjustment, acceptance
FORMAL ceding
COLLOQ. sop
2 *tax concessions*
reduction, decrease, cut, discount, (special) right, (special) privilege, favour, grant, allowance, exception, bending of the rules

conciliate *v*
reconcile, pacify, placate, appease, restore harmony to, satisfy, soften, soothe, disarm, disembitter, mollify, propitiate
antagonize

conciliation *n*
reconciliation, peacemaking, pacification, placation, appeasement, mollification, propitiation
alienation, antagonization

conciliator *n*
reconciler, mediator, negotiator, peacemaker, intermediary, broker, middleman, go-between, intercessor, dove
troublemaker, hawk

conciliatory *adj*
reconciliatory, peacemaking, peaceable, appeasing, disarming, mollifying, pacific, assuaging
FORMAL irenic, pacificatory, placatory, propitiative, propitiatory
antagonistic

concise *adj*
short, brief, terse, curt, succinct, pithy, crisp, compendious, elliptic, compact, compressed, condensed, abridged, abbreviated, summary, to the point, thumbnail, tight, laconic
FORMAL synoptic, compendious, epigrammatic, aphoristic
diffuse, verbose, wordy

concisely *adv*
briefly, tersely, succinctly, curtly, pithily, crisply, laconically, to the point, in brief, in short, in a word
diffusely, verbosely

conclave *n*
assembly, (secret) meeting, council, conference, session, gathering, cabinet, cabal
FORMAL confabulation
COLLOQ. powwow, parley

conclude *v*
1 END, bring/come/draw to an end, cease, close, finish, discontinue, complete, culminate
FORMAL consummate, terminate
COLLOQ. wind up, polish off, top off
2 INFER, deduce, come to the conclusion, assume, reason, gather, suppose, reckon, judge, decide
FORMAL conjecture, surmise
COLLOQ. put two and two together
3 SETTLE, resolve, close, decide, establish, determine, negotiate, accomplish, agree, arrange, work out
FORMAL effect
COLLOQ. wrap up, bring off, pull off, clinch
1 begin, start, commence

conclusion *n*
1 INFERENCE, deduction, assumption, opinion, conviction, judgement, verdict, decision, resolution, settlement, result, consequence, outcome, upshot, issue, answer, solution
OLD consectary
FORMAL illation
2 END, ending, close, finish, completion, culmination, point, finale, epilogue, *finis*, punchline; *Scot* pirlicue
TECHNICAL coda
OLD fine, explicit
FORMAL consummation, cessation, termination, discontinuance, omega, peroration
COLLOQ. come-off
3 SETTLING, resolution, decision, establishment, determination, negotiation, brokering, accomplishment, agreement, arrangement, working-out
FORMAL effecting
COLLOQ. pulling-off, clinching
▪ **in conclusion**

finally, to conclude, in closing, to sum up
OLD in fine

conclusive *adj*
final, ultimate, definitive, decisive, clear, convincing,
definite, undeniable, irrefutable, indisputable,
incontrovertible, unarguable, unanswerable
E3 inconclusive, questionable

conclusively *adv*
definitively, decisively, clearly, convincingly, definitely,
undeniably, irrefutably, indisputably, incontrovertibly,
unarguably, finally, ultimately
E3 inconclusively

concoct *v*
1 *concoct a meal*
put together, mix, prepare, make, develop, blend, cook
(up), brew
COLLOQ. fix, rustle up
2 *concoct a story*
fabricate, invent, make up, think up, devise, contrive,
formulate, plan, plot, hatch, dream up
FORMAL decoct
COLLOQ. cook up

concoction *n*
1 MIXTURE, brew, potion, preparation, blend, combination,
compound, creation
2 FABRICATION, fiction, fable, story, myth, untruth
COLLOQ. cock-and-bull story, fairy story

concomitant *adj, n*
♦ *adj*
complementary, accompanying, associative, attendant,
co-existent, coincidental, incidental, simultaneous,
synchronous, contributing
FORMAL concurrent, contemporaneous, conterminous,
syndromic
E3 accidental, unrelated
♦ *n*
accompaniment, by-product, incidental, secondary,
symptom, side effect
FORMAL epiphenomenon

concord *n*
harmony, accord, agreement, friendship, entente,
consensus, unanimity, unison, union, amicability, peace,
compact, treaty, rapport
FORMAL amity, consonance
E3 discord

concourse *n*
1 *the station concourse*
hall, entrance, foyer, lobby, lounge, piazza, plaza
2 *a concourse of people*
gathering, multitude, crowd, swarm, throng, assembly,
collection, meeting, crush, press

concrete *adj*
1 *concrete objects*
real, actual, solid, physical, material, substantial, tangible,
touchable, perceptible, visible
2 *concrete evidence*
firm, definite, positive, specific, explicit, genuine, factual,
solid
E3 1 abstract, immaterial **2** weak, vague

concubine *n*
mistress, kept woman, paramour, lover, courtesan, leman,
lorette, apple-squire, sultana
OLD madam; (*Shakesp*) guinea-hen

concupiscence *n*
appetite, desire, libido, lasciviousness, lechery, lewdness,
lust, lustfulness, sexual desire
OLD concupy
FORMAL libidinousness, lubricity
COLLOQ. randiness, horniness

concupiscent *adj*
lascivious, lecherous, lewd, lustful
FORMAL libidinous, lubricious
COLLOQ. randy, horny

concur *v*
agree, approve, comply, consent, co-operate, harmonize,
be in harmony
FORMAL accede, assent, accord, acquiesce
E3 disagree

concurrence *n*
1 *concurrence on the decision*
agreement, association, convergence, common ground,
acceptance, approval
FORMAL assent, acquiescence
2 *the concurrence of the two events*
coincidence, coexistence, synchrony
FORMAL contemporaneity, juxtaposition, simultaneity
E3 1 difference, disagreement

concurrent *adj*
simultaneous, synchronous, contemporaneous,
coinciding, coincident, coexisting, coexistent
FORMAL concomitant

concussion *n*
unconsciousness, head injury, brain injury, water hammer

condemn *v*
1 *condemn his actions*
disapprove, criticize, reproach, blame, revile, deplore,
denounce, censure
FORMAL reprehend, reprove, deprecate, berate, upbraid,
castigate, disparage, decry, slate, run down
COLLOQ. slam, knock
2 *condemn a prisoner*
sentence, give/pass a sentence, punish, find guilty,
convict, judge, damn, accurse
3 *condemned to a life of poverty*
doom, compel, coerce, force, consign, ordain, destine
4 *condemn a building*
declare unsafe, declare unfit, demolish, destroy, bar, ban
E3 1 praise, approve **2** acquit, pardon

condemnation *n*
disapproval, criticism, reproof, reproach, blame, censure,
denunciation, damnation, conviction, sentence,
judgement
FORMAL castigation, deprecation, disparagement
COLLOQ. thumbs-down
E3 praise, approval

condemnatory *adj*
critical, judgemental, disapproving, discouraging,
incriminating, unfavourable, accusatory, accusing,
damnatory
FORMAL censorious, denunciatory, deprecatory,
proscriptive, reprobative, reprobatory
E3 approving, complimentary, indulgent; *formal* laudatory

condensation *n*
1 *condensation of liquid*
distillation, liquefaction, precipitation, concentration,
moisture, steam, evaporation, reduction, boiling-down,
consolidation
TECHNICAL deliquescence
2 ABRIDGEMENT, précis, synopsis, digest, summary,
contraction, compression, curtailment

condense *v*
1 *condense a book*
shorten, cut (down), curtail, abbreviate, abridge, précis,
summarize, encapsulate, contract, compress, compact,
capsulize
FORMAL epitomize
2 DISTIL, precipitate, concentrate, evaporate,
reduce, thicken, solidify, coagulate, compress,

boil down, precipitate, intensify
TECHNICAL condensate, deliquesce, inspissate
F3 1 expand **2** dilute

condensed *adj*
1 *a condensed book*
shortened, cut (down), curtailed, abridged abbreviated,
summarized, abstracted, reduced, contracted, compact,
concise
2 *condensed liquid*
concentrated, evaporated, reduced, thickened,
compressed, clotted, coagulated, dense, rich, strong,
undiluted
F3 1 expanded **2** diluted

condescend *v*
1 *condescend to do something*
deign, see fit, stoop, bend, lower yourself, demean
yourself, humble yourself, descend
OLD vouchsafe
FORMAL decline
2 *condescend to people*
patronize, talk down to, treat condescendingly, be
snobbish to

condescending *adj*
patronizing, disdainful, supercilious, snooty, snobbish,
haughty, lofty, superior, lordly, imperious
COLLOQ. stuck-up, toffee-nosed
F3 gracious, humble

condescendingly *adv*
patronizingly, superciliously, imperiously, disdainfully,
snobbishly

condescension *n*
disdain, haughtiness, superciliousness, superiority,
loftiness, snobbishness, lordliness, airs
F3 humility

condition *n, v*
♦ *n*
1 STATE, circumstances, factor(s), case, position, situation,
predicament, plight, quandary
2 *the conditions in which people work*
surroundings, environment, milieu, setting, atmosphere,
climate, background, context, circumstances, factors, way
of life, situation, state, set-up
3 REQUIREMENT, obligation, prerequisite, terms, stipulation,
demand, necessity, essential, precondition, provision,
proviso, qualification, limit, limitation, restriction, rule
4 *out of condition*
fitness, health, state, state of health, shape, form, order,
working order, fettle, kilter
COLLOQ. nick
5 *a heart condition*
disorder, defect, weakness, infirmity, problem, complaint,
disease, illness, ailment
FORMAL malady
♦ *v*
1 *a shampoo that conditions*
tone, make healthy, restore, revive, treat, improve, nourish,
groom
2 *conditioned by experience*
influence, mould, shape, transform, educate, train, teach,
groom, equip, prepare, prime, accustom, familiarize,
season, temper, adapt, adjust, tune, indoctrinate,
brainwash

conditional *adj*
provisional, qualified, limited, restricted, tied, relative,
subject, based, dependent, contingent
F3 unconditional, absolute

conditionally *adv*
provisionally, qualifiedly, with qualification, limitedly,
relatively
F3 unconditionally, absolutely

conditioning *n*
moulding, shaping, transforming, preparation, adaptation,
adjustment, influence

condolence *n*
sympathy, commiseration, compassion, pity, comfort,
consolation, support
F3 congratulation

condom *n*
sheath, contraceptive, female condom, Femidom®; *N Am*
prophylactic, protective
SLANG French letter, johnnie, rubber; *N Am* scumbag, safe

condone *v*
forgive, pardon, excuse, overlook, ignore, disregard,
tolerate, brook, let pass, allow, accept
COLLOQ. turn a blind eye to
F3 condemn, censure

conducive *adj*
leading, tending, contributing, contributory, productive,
promoting, advantageous, beneficial, favourable, helpful,
useful, instrumental, encouraging
F3 detrimental, adverse, unfavourable

conduct *v, n*
♦ *v*
1 CARRY OUT, perform, do, administer, manage, run,
organize, direct, orchestrate, chair, control, be in charge
of, handle, regulate
2 ACCOMPANY, show, take, bring, escort, usher, lead, guide,
direct, pilot, steer
3 *conduct heat*
convey, carry, bear, transmit
4 *conduct yourself*
behave, acquit, act
FORMAL comport
♦ *n*
1 *good conduct*
behaviour, actions, ways, manners, bearing, practice,
attitude
FORMAL comportment, demeanour, deportment
2 ADMINISTRATION, management, direction, running,
organization, operation, control, supervision, leadership,
guidance

conduit *n*
channel, pipe, tunnel, passage, passageway, duct, tube,
drain, gutter, culvert, ditch, flume, chute, watercourse,
waterway, canal, main, trough, trunk, wireway

confectionery *n*
sweets, sweetmeats, chocolates, candy, toffees, bonbons
OLD junkets
COLLOQ. sweeties, goodies

confederacy *n*
union, federation, alliance, coalition, confederation,
league, partnership
FORMAL compact

confederate *n, adj*
♦ *n*
accomplice, ally, assistant, associate, colleague, friend,
partner, supporter, collaborator, abettor, accessory,
conspirator
♦ *adj*
federate, federal, allied, associated, combined, united

confederation *n*
union, federation, alliance, association, coalition,
amalgamation, confederacy, league, partnership
FORMAL compact

confer *v*
1 DISCUSS, debate, deliberate, consult, talk, converse,
exchange views
2 BESTOW, award, present, give (out), grant, accord, impart,
lend

conference n

meeting, convention, congress, summit, symposium, forum, discussion, debate, consultation, dialogue, colloquium, seminar, council of war, diet, palaver, parley, powwow, pourparler; *S Afr* indaba
FORMAL convocation, imparlance
COLLOQ. get-together, huddle

confess v

admit, confide, own (up), accept blame, accept responsibility, grant, concede, acknowledge, recognize, affirm, assert, profess, declare, disclose, reveal, make known, divulge, expose, unbosom, unburden
TECHNICAL shrive
OLD agnize
FORMAL avow
COLLOQ. come clean, make a clean breast of, get off your chest, come out with it, spill the beans, spill your guts, tell all
SLANG cough, fess up
EƎ deny, conceal

confession n

admission, acknowledgement, owning-up, affirmation, assertion, profession, declaration, disclosure, making known, divulgence, exposure, revelation, unbosoming, unburdening, short shrift
OLD (*Shakesp*) submission
FORMAL avowal, *amende honorable*
EƎ denial, concealment

confidant, confidante n

friend, close friend, bosom friend, best friend, intimate, companion
COLLOQ. crony, pal, mate, chum, buddy, bosom buddy

confide v

confess, admit, tell a secret, reveal, disclose, divulge, whisper, breathe, tell, impart, intimate, unburden, unbosom, pour out your heart to
COLLOQ. get off your chest
EƎ hide, suppress, conceal

confidence n

1 have confidence in someone
trust, faith, reliance, dependence, credence, belief, conviction, certainty
2 SELF-ASSURANCE, assurance, composure, calmness, self-possession, self-confidence, self-reliance, self-assurance, belief in yourself, poise, boldness, courage
FORMAL aplomb
3 SECRET, confidential matter, private matter, intimacy
EƎ 1 distrust **2** diffidence
■ **in confidence**
privately, in privacy, in private, confidentially, in secret, personally, between ourselves, *entre nous*, behind closed doors, within these four walls
COLLOQ. between you and me, between you me and the gatepost/bedpost
EƎ openly

confident adj

1 confident that it will happen
sure, certain, positive, convinced, definite, unhesitating, comfortable
2 a confident person
assured, sure of yourself, sure-footed, composed, self-possessed, calm, cool, self-confident, self-reliant, self-assured, unselfconscious, bold, courageous, fearless, secure, hardy, positive, happy, optimistic, sanguine, dauntless, unabashed; *Scot* crouse
COLLOQ. upbeat
EƎ 1 doubtful, unsure **2** diffident, insecure

Synonym nuances

sense 2
Assured suggests a strong element of self-belief, as do **self-possessed**, **self-confident** and **self-assured**: *a self-possessed manner touching on the arrogant*.
Composed, **cool** and **calm** are more passive in tone, suggesting an absence of disturbance or doubt. **Self-reliant** would appropriately describe a confident and independent nature, whilst **unselfconscious** places the emphasis on lack of embarrassment.
The term **bold** suggests a degree of daring: *a bold programme of reforms*, as do **courageous** and **fearless**. The words **dauntless** and **unabashed** would suggest no impediment will be permitted to someone's view: *Dauntless, he set off the climb the mountain*. You could use **positive**, **optimistic** or **sanguine** to describe a hopeful outlook where the best outcome is expected.

confidential adj

secret, top secret, classified, restricted, off-the-record, private, personal, intimate, bosom, sensitive, man-to-man, woman-to-woman, tête-à-tête; *Scot* pack
TECHNICAL a latere
OLD privy, inward
COLLOQ. hush-hush

confidentially adv

privately, in privacy, in private, in confidence, in secret, personally, between ourselves, *entre nous*, behind closed doors, on the quiet, within these four walls
OLD privily
FORMAL in camera
COLLOQ. between you and me, between you me and the gatepost/bedpost
EƎ openly

confidently adv

assuredly, composedly, calmly, coolly, unselfconsciously, unhesitatingly, comfortably, boldly, courageously, fearlessly, positively, optimistically

configuration n

arrangement, composition, figure, form, outline, shape, contour, cast
FORMAL conformation, disposition

confine v, n

♦ *v*
1 confine a disease; confine yourself to something
restrict, limit, keep within limits, bound, bind, constrain, control, fix, regulate, delimit
FORMAL circumscribe
2 confine in prison
imprison, cage, enclose, shut (up), hold prisoner, hold captive, hold in custody, intern, impound, keep in, lock up/away, coop up, bind, shackle, trammel, restrain, repress, inhibit
FORMAL incarcerate, immure
EƎ 1 derestrict **2** free, release
♦ *n*
limit, limitation, restriction, scope, parameter, bound, boundary, frontier, border, circumference, perimeter, edge

confined adj

restricted, limited, narrow, constrained, constricted, cramped, controlled, enclosed, housebound
FORMAL circumscribed
EƎ free, unrestricted

confinement n

1 IMPRISONMENT, internment, custody, detention, captivity, house arrest
FORMAL incarceration
2 CHILDBIRTH, birth, labour, delivery
TECHNICAL parturition
EƎ 1 freedom, liberty

confirm v
1 PROVE, corroborate, substantiate, verify, check, validate, authenticate, give credence to, evidence, demonstrate, endorse, back, support
2 ESTABLISH, fix, settle, ratify, sanction, approve, authorize, warrant, endorse, validate
COLLOQ. clinch
3 *confirm that he will go*
affirm, assert, assure, pledge, promise, guarantee
FORMAL asseverate, aver
4 *confirmed me in my decision*
strengthen, reinforce, harden, support, uphold
FORMAL fortify
Ⅎ **1** refute, deny

confirmation n
affirmation, validation, authentication, corroboration, substantiation, verification, proof, evidence, testimony, ratification, sanction, approval, assent, acceptance, agreement, endorsement, backing, support
FORMAL accreditation
Ⅎ denial

confirmed adj
inveterate, entrenched, dyed-in-the-wool, rooted, firm, fixed, set, established, long-established, long-standing, habitual, chronic, through and through, seasoned, hardened, incorrigible, incurable
FORMAL inured

confiscate v
seize, remove, take away, take possession of, impound, commandeer
TECHNICAL escheat, sequester
OLD forfeit
FORMAL appropriate, expropriate, arrogate
Ⅎ return, restore

confiscation n
seizure, removal, takeover, impounding, commandeering
FORMAL appropriation, distrainment, distraint, escheat, expropriation, sequestration, forfeiture
Ⅎ restoration

conflagration n
blaze, fire, flames, inferno, holocaust
FORMAL deflagration

conflate v
combine, amalgamate, merge, bring/put together, blend, integrate, incorporate, compound, synthesize

conflict n, v
◆ n
1 DISAGREEMENT, quarrel, dissension, dispute, opposition, antagonism, hostility, friction, collision, strife, unrest, confrontation, feud, discord, contention, ill-will, difference of opinion, variance, clash, clashing, incompatibility, row, jar
TECHNICAL antinomy, dissonance
FORMAL antipathy
COLLOQ. bust-up, dust-up
2 BATTLE, war, warfare, combat, fight, contest, struggle, front line, engagement, skirmish, fracas, brawl, quarrel, feud, encounter, row, clash, mêlée
OLD agony, agon, camp, muss; (*Shakesp*) close
COLLOQ. set-to, bust-up, scrap, scrape
Ⅎ **1** agreement, harmony, concord
◆ v
differ, clash, collide, disagree, be at variance, be at loggerheads, be at odds, be inconsistent with, contradict, oppose, be in opposition, contest, go against, fight, combat, battle, war, strive, struggle, contend, thwart
FORMAL be incongruous
Ⅎ agree, harmonize

Synonym nuances
noun sense 1
Disagreement, **dissension** and **variance** may be used of any difference of opinion between two parties, however mild. **Quarrel** and **dispute** are similar, but imply a more heated exchange, and the more informal **row** and **clash** could refer to being violently at odds. Similarly, the term **opposition** can be used to express varying degrees, whereas **antagonism** and **hostility** suggest something more keenly felt and expressed: *French antagonism towards England was still very much alive.*
  Friction could be used of annoyance between two parties: *the incompatible demands of the various departments resulted in friction*; while the terms **strife** and **unrest** could be used in the context of dissatisfaction within a group, especially where knock-on effects are possible: *internecine strife*; *industrial unrest*.
  To refer to a long-term conflict and enmity between two parties, you could use **feud**; for the existence of more general bad feelings towards someone you might use the term **discord**, the more formal term **antipathy**, or, to be more explicit, **ill-will**.

conflicting adj
contradictory, contrary, opposing, clashing, inconsistent, incompatible, at variance, at odds
FORMAL incongruous, antithetical
Ⅎ consistent

confluence n
convergence, junction, meeting, meeting-point, concurrence, union, watersmeet
FORMAL conflux

conform v
1 *conform to a law*
obey, follow, comply (with), fall in with, observe, abide by, adapt, adjust, accommodate
2 *conform in your behaviour*
follow, be conventional, be uniform, do the same thing
COLLOQ. follow the crowd, go with the flow/stream, toe the line
3 *conform to a pattern*
agree, harmonize, match, suit, fit, correspond, tally, square
FORMAL accord
Ⅎ **1** disobey **2** rebel **3** differ, conflict

conformist n
conventionalist, traditionalist
COLLOQ. yes-man, stick-in-the-mud, rubber-stamp
Ⅎ bohemian, nonconformist

conformity n
1 *in conformity with the law*
compliance, observance, obedience, allegiance adaptation, adjustment, accommodation, affinity, agreement, harmony, correspondence, likeness, similarity, resemblance
FORMAL consonance, congruity
2 *conformity in behaviour*
conventionality, orthodoxy, traditionalism, uniformity
Ⅎ **1** disobedience, non-compliance **2** nonconformity, rebellion

confound v
1 CONFUSE, bewilder, baffle, perplex, mystify, puzzle, nonplus, surprise, startle, amaze, astonish, astound, dumbfound, stun, stupefy
FORMAL discomfit
COLLOQ. bamboozle, flabbergast, flummox, throw, floor, faze, stump
2 *confound their plans*
thwart, frustrate, upset, beat, defeat, overwhelm, overthrow, destroy, demolish, ruin

confront v

1 *confront a problem*
face, face up to, brave, tackle, address, deal with, cope with, contend with, reckon with, come to terms with
COLLOQ. come to grips with, meet head on, face the music
2 *confront the enemy*
face, face up to, meet, encounter, stand up to, challenge, oppose, brave, defy, resist, withstand, attack, assault, accost
3 *confront him with the facts*
challenge, present, face, show

confrontation n
encounter, clash, conflict, collision, showdown, disagreement, fight, battle, quarrel, engagement, contest, brush
COLLOQ. set-to

confuse v
1 BEWILDER, baffle, perplex, mystify, confound, dizzy, maze, dither, puzzle, bemuse, disorient, disorientate, disconcert, fluster, discompose, distract, dumbfound, jumble, flurry, surprise, upset, embarrass, mortify; *dialect* moider; *Scot* bumbaze, fickle
OLD embrangle
COLLOQ. throw, flummox, faze, stump, floor, tie in knots, blind with science
2 MUDDLE, mix up, mistake, jumble, disarrange, disorder, tangle, entangle, involve, mingle, fog, fuddle, mudge, mizzle; *Scot* burble
OLD bemuddle, bemud
3 COMPLICATE, make more difficult, compound, elaborate, make difficult, involve, make involved
E3 **1** enlighten, orient **3** simplify, clarify

confused adj
1 BEWILDERED, baffled, perplexed, mystified, confounded, puzzled, bemused, nonplussed, disconcerted, flustered, disorientated, dazed, unbalanced
COLLOQ. flummoxed, floored, not knowing whether you are coming or going, up a gumtree, in a flat spin, in a flap, all at sea, like a headless chicken
2 MUDDLED, jumbled, disarranged, disordered, untidy, disorderly, chaotic, disorganized, mixed-up, out of order
COLLOQ. higgledy-piggledy, at sixes and sevens, having your wires crossed
SLANG with your knickers in a twist
E3 **2** orderly

confusing adj
puzzling, baffling, bewildering, muddling, perplexing, unclear, difficult, ambiguous, complicated, involved, contradictory, inconclusive, inconsistent, misleading, cryptic, tortuous
E3 clear, definite

confusion n
1 DISORDER, disarray, untidiness, mess, clutter, jumble, muddle, mix-up, disorganization, disarrangement, chaos, turmoil, commotion, upheaval
COLLOQ. shambles
2 MISUNDERSTANDING, puzzlement, perplexity, mystification, bewilderment, bafflement, muddle
E3 **1** order, organization **2** clarity, enlightenment

confute v
disprove, refute, contradict, prove false, rebut, discredit
FORMAL negate, controvert
COLLOQ. debunk
E3 confirm, prove

congeal v
clot, curdle, coalesce, coagulate, thicken, stiffen, harden, concentrate, fuse, solidify, set, cake, gel, freeze
E3 dissolve, melt, liquefy

congenial adj
agreeable, pleasant, pleasing, relaxing, delightful,

favourable, friendly, companionable, genial, sympathetic, homely, compatible, complaisant, cosy, like-minded, suitable, well-suited
E3 disagreeable, unpleasant

congenital adj
1 *a congenital disease*
hereditary, inborn, inbred, inherited, innate, inherent, constitutional, natural
TECHNICAL connate
2 *a congenital liar*
inveterate, entrenched, habitual, compulsive, chronic, seasoned, hardened, incorrigible, incurable, complete, thorough, utter
FORMAL inured

congested adj
1 *congested roads*
blocked, clogged, jammed, packed, stuffed, crammed, full, crowded, overcrowded, overflowing, teeming
2 *a congested nose*
blocked, clogged, choked, engorged
E3 **1, 2** clear

congestion n
1 *congestion on the roads*
clogging, blockage, crowding, overcrowding, jam, traffic jam, snarl-up, gridlock, bottleneck, pinchpoint
2 *nasal congestion*
clogging, blockage, blocking, choking

conglomerate n
corporation, multinational, merger, cartel, trust, consortium, combine, group, company, firm, business, business organization, concern, association, partnership, multinational, establishment

conglomeration n
mass, agglomeration, aggregation, accumulation, collection, assemblage, composite, assortment, medley, hotchpotch

congratulate v
praise, compliment, say well done to, wish well, wish happiness to, send/offer good wishes to, send/offer best wishes to
OLD gratulate, greet
FORMAL felicitate
COLLOQ. take your hat off to, pat on the back
E3 commiserate

■ **congratulate yourself**
pride, preen, plume
COLLOQ. give yourself a pat on the back, delight in

congratulations n
compliments, good wishes, best wishes, greetings
FORMAL felicitations
COLLOQ. pat on the back, bouquet(s)
E3 commiserations, condolences

congregate v
gather, assemble, collect, muster, rally, rendezvous, meet, come together, convene, converge, flock, crowd, throng, form, mass, accumulate, cluster, clump
E3 disperse

congregation n
assembly, crowd, group, throng, mass, multitude, host, meeting, flock, fold, parishioners, parish, laity, fellowship

congress n
assembly, conference, convention, council, legislature, meeting, gathering, forum, parliament, synod, diet
FORMAL conclave, convocation

congruence n
correspondence, consistency, agreement, conformity, coincidence, harmony, compatibility, similarity, resemblance, identity, match, parallelism

FORMAL concinnity, concurrence, consonance
▪ incongruity

congruent adj
consistent, compatible, harmonious, similar, parallel, corresponding
FORMAL concurrent, consonant

conical adj
cone-shaped, pyramidal, pyramid-shaped, funnel-shaped, tapering, tapered, pointed
FORMAL infundibular, infundibulate, turbinate

conjectural adj
hypothetical, assumed, surmised, tentative, theoretical, speculative, supposed, academic, suppositional
FORMAL posited, postulated
▪ factual, real

conjecture v, n
◆ v
speculate, theorize, hypothesize, guess, estimate, reckon, fancy, suppose, presuppose, surmise, assume, presume, infer, imagine, suspect
◆ n
speculation, theory, hypothesis, fancy, notion, guesswork, guess, estimate, supposition, presupposition, surmise, suspicion, assumption, presumption, conclusion, inference, extrapolation, projection
COLLOQ. guesstimate

conjoin v
combine, amalgamate, unite, unify, join (together), link, connect, match, synthesize
FORMAL concur

conjugal adv
marital, nuptial, married, wedded, bridal
FORMAL matrimonial, connubial, epithalamic, spousal, hymeneal

conjunction n
coincidence, co-occurrence, coexistence, combination, amalgamation, association, union, unification
FORMAL concurrence, juxtaposition
▪ **in conjunction with**
together with, with, along with, alongside, combined with, in partnership with, in collaboration with, in association with, in company with

conjure v
1 *conjuring at the children's party*
do tricks, perform tricks, do magic, perform magic
2 *conjure handkerchiefs from a hat*
summon, invoke, call up, evoke, make appear, materialize, rouse, raise, bewitch, charm, fascinate, compel
▪ **conjure up**
evoke, create, produce, excite, awaken, recollect, recall, call/bring to mind, summon up

conjurer n
magician, illusionist, miracle-worker, sorcerer, wizard
FORMAL prestidigitator, prestigiator, thaumaturge

conk v
▪ **conk out**
break down, collapse, fail
COLLOQ. pack up, go bust, go on the blink, go haywire, go phut, go kaput

con man n
con artist, confidence trickster, cheat, liar, deceiver, swindler, overcharger, usurer, extortionist
COLLOQ. rip-off artist, crook, hustler; N Am bunco, bunco artist, grifter
SLANG blagger; Aust illy whacker

connect v
1 *connect two objects*
join, link, unite, couple, bridge, combine, fasten,

secure, affix, tie, clamp, fuse, attach
FORMAL concatenate
2 *connected with the murder*
relate (to), correlate, associate, bracket, identify, link, couple, equate, ally
▪ **1** disconnect, cut off, detach

connected adj
joined, linked, united, coupled, tied, combined, fastened, secured, related, akin, associated, affiliated, allied
▪ disconnected, unconnected

connection n
1 *a connection between pipes; a connection between smoking and cancer*
junction, coupling, joint, fastening, attachment, clasp, bond, tie, link, association, alliance, relation, relationship, interrelation, contact, communication, parallel, correlation, analogy, correspondence, relevance, reference
2 *use your connections to get a job*
friend, acquaintance, relation, relative, contact, sponsor, person of influence, person of importance
▪ **1** disconnection
▪ **in connection with**
with regard to, in regard to, as regards, regarding, concerning, with reference to, with respect to, in relation to, re, about, as to, on the subject of
FORMAL apropos

connivance n
collusion, complicity, condoning, consent, abetment, abetting, conspiracy

connive v
1 *connive with someone to commit an offence*
collude, conspire, intrigue, plot, scheme, collaborate
FORMAL complot, cabal, coact
2 *connive at wrongdoing*
overlook, ignore, disregard, condone, tolerate, brook, let go, let pass, pass over, gloss over, allow, wink at
COLLOQ. turn a blind eye to

conniving adj
scheming, colluding, conspiring, plotting, nasty, immoral, unscrupulous, corrupt, manipulative

connoisseur n
authority, specialist, expert, judge, arbiter, pundit, specialist, devotee, cognoscente, gourmet, gastronome, epicure, virtuoso, aesthete
FORMAL aficionado
COLLOQ. buff

connotation n
implication, suggestion, intimation, intent, hint, nuance, allusion, undertone, overtone, insinuation, colouring, association, undercurrent
TECHNICAL comprehension

connote v
imply, suggest, intimate, hint at, allude to, insinuate, signify, indicate, associate
OLD betoken
FORMAL import, purport, connotate

conquer v
1 *conquer an enemy/your fears*
defeat, beat, overthrow, overpower, rout, crush, subdue, quell, overrun, best, get the better of, worst, overcome, surmount, win, succeed, triumph over, prevail over, rise above, master, suppress, humble
OLD debel
FORMAL vanquish, subjugate
COLLOQ. trounce
See Synonym nuances panel at **defeat**.
2 SEIZE, take, annex, occupy, possess, take possession of,

conqueror n
acquire, obtain, win, control
FORMAL appropriate
≠ 1 surrender, yield, give in

conqueror n
victor, winner, champion, hero, master, lord
FORMAL vanquisher, subjugator, conquistador
COLLOQ. champ

conquest n
1 *the conquest of the country*
victory, triumph, win, success, defeat, beating, overthrow,
overpowering, coup, rout, crushing, mastery, subjection,
invasion, overrunning, possession, occupation, capture,
seizing, annexation, acquisition
FORMAL appropriation, subjugation, vanquishment
COLLOQ. trouncing
2 *his latest conquest*
captive, lover, catch, acquisition

conscience n
principles, standards, morals, ethics, sense of right, sense
of right and wrong, moral sense, moral code, still small
voice, voice within, scruples, qualms
TECHNICAL syneidesis, synteresis
OLD inwit

conscience-stricken adj
ashamed, sorry, contrite, guilt-ridden, guilty, penitent,
regretful, remorseful, repentant, disturbed, troubled
FORMAL compunctious
COLLOQ. on a guilt trip
≠ unashamed, unrepentant

conscientious adj
diligent, hard-working, scrupulous, painstaking,
methodical, thorough, meticulous, punctilious,
industrious, dedicated, assiduous, particular, careful,
attentive, responsible, upright, honest, faithful, dutiful
≠ careless, irresponsible, unreliable

conscious adj
1 AWAKE, alive, responsive, sensible, rational, reasoning,
alert
TECHNICAL conscient
FORMAL sentient
2 AWARE, self-conscious, heedful, mindful, alert
FORMAL cognizant, recognizant, percipient, sensible
3 *a conscious effort to be polite*
deliberate, intentional, on purpose, calculated,
premeditated, studied, knowing, wilful, voluntary,
witting
FORMAL volitional
≠ 1 unconscious 2 unaware 3 involuntary, unintentional

consciously adv
deliberately, intentionally, knowingly, wilfully, voluntarily,
on purpose
≠ unintentionally

consciousness n
1 *enter his consciousness*
awareness, mind, knowledge, intuition, perception,
apprehension, realization, recognition, psyche
TECHNICAL coenaesthesis
FORMAL cognizance, sentience, sensibility
2 *lose consciousness*
being awake, wakefulness, awareness, alertness
≠ 2 unconsciousness

conscript v, n
◆ v
recruit, enlist, draft, call up, take on, round up,
muster
≠ volunteer
◆ n
recruit, enlistee, draftee
≠ volunteer

consecrate v
sanctify, bless, anoint, hallow, make holy, dedicate, devote,
vow, ordain, venerate, revere, exalt

consecutive adj
successive, sequential, serial, continuous, unbroken,
uninterrupted, following, succeeding, running, one after
the other, in turn, straight, in a row
FORMAL seriate
COLLOQ. on the trot, back to back
≠ discontinuous

consecutively adv
successively, sequentially, continuously, uninterruptedly,
one after the other, in turn, in a row
COLLOQ. on the trot, back to back

consensus n
agreement, consent, harmony, majority view, unanimity,
unity
FORMAL concord, concurrence, consentience, consension
≠ disagreement

consent v, n
◆ v
agree, accept, approve, permit, allow, authorize, grant,
admit, concede, yield, submit, go along with, comply
OLD afford, condescend
FORMAL concur, assent, accede, acquiesce, homologate
COLLOQ. give the go-ahead, give the green light, give the
thumbs-up
≠ refuse, decline, oppose
◆ n
agreement, acceptance, approval, authorization,
permission, clearance, sanction, concession, compliance
FORMAL concurrence, assent, acquiescence
COLLOQ. go-ahead, green light
≠ disagreement, refusal, opposition
Related adjective: consensual

consequence n
1 RESULT, outcome, issue, end, upshot, effect, side effect,
eventuality, implication, repercussion, reverberation
2 *of no consequence*
importance, significance, concern, value, weight,
substance, note, eminence, prominence, distinction
FORMAL import, moment
≠ 1 cause 2 unimportance, insignificance

consequent adj
resultant, resulting, ensuing, subsequent, following,
successive, sequential

consequential adj
1 RESULTANT, resulting, ensuing, subsequent, following,
successive, sequential
2 IMPORTANT, significant, momentous, noteworthy,
material, relevant, crucial, weighty, valuable, serious, far-
reaching, substantial, vital, key, prominent
≠ 2 unimportant, insignificant

consequently adv
as a result, therefore, with the result that, so that,
accordingly, consequentially, necessarily, subsequently,
then
FORMAL inferentially, ergo, hence, thus

conservation n
keeping, safe-keeping, custody, saving, care, economy,
husbandry, maintenance, upkeep, preservation,
protection, safeguarding, ecology, environmentalism
≠ destruction

conservatism n
conservativeness, conventionalism, orthodoxy,
traditionalism
≠ radicalism

conservative adj, n
◆ adj

1 *conservative politicians*
Tory, right-wing, hidebound, diehard, reactionary, establishmentarian
2 *conservative opinions/estimates*
unprogressive, conventional, traditional, traditionalist, orthodox, inflexible, set in your ways; *NAm* old-line; hidebound, moderate, middle-of-the-road, careful, cautious, guarded, sober
COLLOQ. *NAm* buttoned-down
Ⅲ 1 left-wing, radical **2** innovative, progressive
♦ *n*
Tory, right-winger, diehard, stick-in-the-mud, reactionary, traditionalist, moderate; *NAm* old-liner
Ⅲ left-winger, radical

conservatory *n*
1 *grow plants in the conservatory*
greenhouse, glasshouse, hothouse
2 *study music at the conservatory*
conservatoire, school, college, academy, institute, music school, drama college

conserve *v*
keep, keep back, keep in reserve, save, store up, hoard, maintain, preserve, protect, take care of, guard, safeguard
Ⅲ use, waste, squander

consider *v*
1 PONDER, deliberate, reflect, contemplate, meditate, muse, mull over, examine, study, weigh (up), respect, remember, note, make a mental note of, give thought to, bear/keep in mind, take into account/consideration
FORMAL cogitate, ruminate
COLLOQ. chew over, toy with
2 *consider it an honour*
regard as, think, believe, judge, rate, count, hold, feel
FORMAL deem

considerable *adj*
great, large, big, siz(e)able, substantial, ample, plentiful, abundant, lavish, generous, marked, noticeable, perceptible, appreciable, reasonable, tolerable, respectable, important, significant, noteworthy, distinguished, influential, serious
COLLOQ. tidy
Ⅲ small, slight, insignificant, unremarkable

considerably *adv*
significantly, substantially, greatly, markedly, much, noticeably, remarkably, appreciably, abundantly
Ⅲ slightly

considerate *adj*
kind, thoughtful, caring, attentive, obliging, helpful, charitable, unselfish, concerned, selfless, altruistic, gracious, sympathetic, compassionate, generous, sensitive, tactful, discreet, solicitous
Ⅲ inconsiderate, thoughtless, selfish

consideration *n*
1 THOUGHT, deliberation, reflection, contemplation, meditation, examination, analysis, scrutiny, review, inspection, attention, notice, heed, regard, reckoning, account
FORMAL cogitation, rumination
2 KINDNESS, thoughtfulness, care, attention, regard, respect, helpfulness, unselfishness, concern, selflessness, altruism, graciousness, sympathy, compassion, generosity, sensitivity, tact, discretion
3 *the cost is a major consideration*
fact, circumstance, factor, issue, point, concern
Ⅲ 1 disregard, dismissal **2** thoughtlessness, lack of concern
■ **take into consideration**
take into account, consider, plan for, allow for, make allowances for, bear in mind, keep in mind, give thought to

considering *prep*
1 *considering her age*
taking into account/consideration, bearing in mind, making allowances for, in view of, in the light of
2 *he's very well, considering*
all things considered, all in all

consign *v*
entrust, assign, commend, commit, devote, hand over, give over, transfer, transmit, deliver, send, convey, ship, banish, relegate
OLD recommend

consignment *n*
cargo, shipment, load, batch, delivery, goods

consist *v*
1 *a jury consists of twelve people*
comprise, be composed, be made up, contain, include, incorporate, embody, be formed, embrace, involve, amount to
2 *the poem's beauty consists in its simplicity*
inhere, lie, reside, exist, be contained, have as its main feature
FORMAL subsist

consistency *n*
1 *the consistency of the porridge*
thickness, density, firmness, cohesion, smoothness
TECHNICAL viscosity
2 STEADINESS, regularity, evenness, uniformity, continuity, sameness, identity, constancy, steadfastness, stability, persistence, dependability, reliability, unchangeableness, lack of change
3 AGREEMENT, accordance, correspondence, compatibility, harmony
FORMAL congruity, consonance
Ⅲ 3 inconsistency

consistent *adj*
1 STEADY, stable, regular, uniform, straight, unchanging, undeviating, constant, same, persistent, unfailing, dependable, predictable
2 *not consistent with his colleague's version*
agreeing, compatible, corresponding, coinciding, matching, harmonious, conforming, logical, coherent, hanging together
FORMAL accordant, consonant, congruous, consentaneous
Ⅲ 1 irregular, erratic **2** inconsistent

consistently *adv*
regularly, constantly, persistently, unfailingly, uniformly, dependably, predictably

consolation *n*
comfort, cheer, encouragement, help, support, reassurance, aid, sympathy, commiseration, relief, ease, soothing, alleviation
OLD (*Shakesp*) recomforture
FORMAL solace, succour, assuagement
Ⅲ discouragement

console[1] *v*
console the bereaved
comfort, cheer, hearten, encourage, help, support, reassure, sympathize with, commiserate with, relieve, soothe, calm
FORMAL solace, succour
Ⅲ upset, agitate

console[2] *n*
an instrument console
panel, control panel, board, dashboard, keyboard, instruments, controls, switches, knobs, dials, buttons, levers

consolidate *v*
1 *consolidate power/support*
reinforce, strengthen, make strong(er), secure, make (more) secure, stabilize, make (more) stable, cement

FORMAL fortify

2 *consolidate businesses*
unite, join, combine, amalgamate, merge, unify, fuse

consolidation *n*

1 *consolidation of power*
reinforcement, strengthening, securing, stabilization, cementing
FORMAL fortification

2 *consolidation of businesses*
uniting, joining, combination, amalgamation, merger, unification, affiliation, alliance, association, confederation, federation, fusion

consonance *n*
compatibility, agreement, consistency, conformity, correspondence, harmony, suitability
FORMAL accordance, congruity, concord
🔁 dissonance

consonant *adj*
compatible, consistent, correspondent, conforming, harmonious, in harmony, agreeing, in agreement, suitable, in accordance, according
FORMAL accordant, congruous
🔁 dissonant

consort *n, v*

♦ *n*
partner, companion, associate, escort, spouse, husband, wife

♦ *v*
associate, spend time, keep company, fraternize, mingle, mix

consortium *n*
partnership, confederation, federation, association, affiliation, coalition, league, corporation, company, bloc, cartel, conglomerate, alliance, organization, syndicate, guild, union, marriage, agreement, compact, bond, pact, treaty, combination

conspicuous *adj*
apparent, visible, noticeable, easily seen/noticed, marked, clear, obvious, evident, recognizable, observable, discernible, perceptible, patent, manifest, prominent, eminent, remarkable, shining, striking, blatant, flagrant, glaring, ostentatious, showy, flashy, garish; *dialect* kenspeckle
COLLOQ. standing out a mile
🔁 inconspicuous, concealed, hidden

conspicuously *adv*
noticeably, visibly, markedly, clearly, obviously, evidently, recognizably, observably, discernibly, perceptibly, patently, manifestly, prominently, patently, remarkably, strikingly, blatantly, flagrantly, glaringly, ostentatiously, showilyy, flashily, garishly
🔁 inconspicuously

conspiracy *n*
plot, scheme, intrigue, stratagem, league, cabal, collusion, collaboration, connivance, treason, confederacy
OLD complot, consult, covin
FORMAL machination
COLLOQ. fix, frame-up, set-up

conspirator *n*
conspirer, plotter, schemer, intriguer, colluder, collaborator, traitor; *N Am* highbinder
OLD practisant

conspire *v*

1 *conspire to oust the president*
plot, hatch a plot, scheme, intrigue, manoeuvre, plan, connive, collude, collaborate
FORMAL machinate

2 *events conspiring for their harm*
combine, join, join forces, work/act together, connect, link, unite, ally, associate, co-operate

constancy *n*

1 STABILITY, steadiness, permanence, consistency, unchangeability, firmness, regularity, uniformity
2 LOYALTY, faithfulness, fidelity, devotion, steadfastness, dependability, trustworthiness, firmness, steadiness, persistence, resolution, perseverance, tenacity
🔁 **1** change, irregularity **2** fickleness

constant *adj*

1 *a constant barrage of questions*
continual, unbroken, never-ending, non-stop, endless, ceaseless, interminable, incessant, eternal, everlasting, perpetual, persistent, chronic, continuous, unremitting, uninterrupted, unbroken, without respite, relentless, unflagging, unwavering

2 *his temperature is constant*
stable, steady, unchanging, unvarying, changeless, invariable, unalterable, consistent, permanent, firm, even, regular, uniform
FORMAL immutable

3 *a constant friend*
loyal, faithful, staunch, steadfast, dependable, trustworthy, true, devoted, firm, steady, persistent, resolute, persevering
🔁 **1** fitful, occasional **2** variable, irregular **3** disloyal, fickle

constantly *adv*
always, continually, all the time, for ever, permanently, continuously, endlessly, non-stop, ceaselessly, everlastingly, incessantly, interminably, invariably, perpetually, perennially, daily, relentlessly, ad nauseam, on and on, day in day out; *dialect* aye
OLD still
COLLOQ. twenty-four seven, 24-7
🔁 occasionally

constellation
See panel on next page

consternation *n*
alarm, dismay, anxiety, fear, distress, dread, horror, fright, shock, terror, panic, awe, bewilderment
FORMAL disquietude, perturbation, trepidation
🔁 composure

constituency *n*
area, region, district, borough, zone, division, ward, parish, community, shire, electorate; *Scot* burgh; *N Am* precinct

constituent *n, adj*

♦ *n*

1 *voting by constituents*
elector, voter

2 *the constituents of the mixture*
ingredient, element, factor, principle, component, component part, part, content, bit, section, unit
🔁 **2** whole, total

♦ *adj*
component, integral, essential, basic, intrinsic, inherent

constitute *v*

1 *six counties constitute the province*
comprise, make up, form, compose

2 *his remarks constitute a challenge to the leadership*
be, represent, mean, form, make, be equivalent to, amount to, add up to, be tantamount to, be regarded as

3 *constitute a committee*
form, create, establish, set up, found, inaugurate, initiate, institute, appoint, authorize, commission, charter, empower

constitution *n*

1 *a country's constitution*
laws, rules, statutes, basic principles, code, social code, state, charter, codified law, bill of rights, *fuero*
OLD policy
FORMAL polity

The constellations (with common English names) are:

Andromeda
Antlia (Air Pump)
Apus (Bird of Paradise)
Aquarius (Water Bearer)
Aquila (Eagle)
Ara (Altar)
Aries (Ram)
Auriga (Charioteer)
Boötes (Herdsman)
Caelum (Chisel)
Camelopardalis (Giraffe)
Cancer (Crab)
Canes Venatici (Hunting
  Dogs)
Canis Major (Great Dog)
Canis Minor (Little Dog)
Capricornus (Sea Goat)
Carina (Keel)
Cassiopeia
Centaurus (Centaur)
Cepheus
Cetus (Whale)
Chamaeleon (Chameleon)
Circinus (Compasses)

Columba (Dove)
Coma Berenices (Berenice's
  Hair)
Corona Australis (Southern
  Crown)
Corona Borealis (Northern
  Crown)
Corvus (Crow)
Crater (Cup)
Crux (Southern Cross)
Cygnus (Swan)
Delphinus (Dolphin)
Dorado (Swordfish)
Draco (Dragon)
Equuleus (Little Horse)
Eridanus (River Eridanus)
Fornax (Furnace)
Gemini (Twins)
Grus (Crane)
Hercules
Horologium (Clock)
Hydra (Sea Serpent)
Hydrus (Water Snake)
Indus (Indian)

Lacerta (Lizard)
Leo (Lion)
Leo Minor (Little Lion)
Lepus (Hare)
Libra (Scales)
Lupus (Wolf)
Lynx
Lyra (Harp)
Mensa (Table)
Microscopium
  (Microscope)
Monoceros (Unicorn)
Musca (Fly)
Norma (Level)
Octans (Octant)
Ophiuchus (Serpent Bearer)
Orion
Pavo (Peacock)
Pegasus (Winged Horse)
Perseus
Phoenix
Pictor (Easel)
Pisces (Fishes)
Piscis Austrinus (Southern

Fish)
Puppis (Ship's Stern)
Pyxis (Mariner's Compass)
Reticulum (Net)
Sagitta (Arrow)
Sagittarius (Archer)
Scorpius (Scorpion)
Sculptor
Scutum (Shield)
Serpens (Serpent)
Sextans (Sextant)
Taurus (Bull)
Telescopium (Telescope)
Triangulum (Triangle)
Triangulum Australe
  (Southern Triangle)
Tucana (Toucan)
Ursa Major (Great Bear)
Ursa Minor (Little Bear)
Vela (Sails)
Virgo (Virgin)
Volans (Flying Fish)
Vulpecula (Fox)

See also **star**.

---

2 COMPOSITION, make-up, structure, organization, formation, nature
FORMAL configuration
3 HEALTH, condition, physique, physical condition, make-up, disposition, temperament, temper, temperature, character, nature, habit, idiosyncrasy, upmake

constitutional *adj, n*
♦ *adj*
statutory, by law, according to the law, legal, legitimate, lawful, legislative, governmental, authorized, vested, codified, ratified
♦ *n*
walk, stroll, saunter, amble, promenade, turn, airing

constrain *v*
1 FORCE, compel, coerce, oblige, necessitate, drive, put, impel, pressurize, pressure, urge
OLD strain
2 LIMIT, confine, constrict, restrain, check, curb, bind, restrict, hinder, hold back
OLD perstringe

constrained *adj*
uneasy, embarrassed, inhibited, reticent, reserved, guarded, stiff, forced, unnatural, awkward
◪ relaxed, free

constraint *n*
1 FORCE, duress, compulsion, coercion, pressure, necessity, obligation, demand, insistence, forcedness
2 RESTRICTION, limitation, hindrance, restraint, check, curb, damper, shackle, impediment
3 INHIBITION, restraint, self-control, reticence, guardedness, stiffness, unnaturalness, awkwardness

constrict *v*
1 *constrict an air passage*
squeeze, compress, pinch, cramp, narrow, make narrow, tighten, contract, close, shrink, choke, strangle, strangulate
2 *constricted by lower budgets*
limit, restrict, confine, constrain, check, curb, bind, hinder, impede, hold back, obstruct, hamper, inhibit
◪ **1** expand, widen, open

constriction *n*
1 *feel a constriction in the chest*
squeezing, narrowing, pressure, tightness, tightening, compression, cramp, blockage
TECHNICAL stricture, stenosis

FORMAL constringency
2 *constrictions in the budget*
restriction, constraint, limitation, reduction, check, curb, hindrance, impediment
◪ **1** expansion, widening

construct *v*
1 *construct a building*
build, erect, raise, elevate, make, manufacture, fabricate, assemble, structure, establish, put up, put together, set up, carpenter, craft, patch, weave
OLD fabric
COLLOQ. throw up, throw together, knock up, knock together
2 *construct a theory*
compose, form, put together, shape, fashion, fabricate, model, devise, design, engineer, create, found, establish, formulate
◪ **1** demolish, destroy

construction *n*
1 *houses under construction*
building, erection, fabrication, assembly, elevation, making, manufacture, establishment
2 *the cathedral is a magnificent construction*
structure, building, edifice, assembly, fabric, form, shape, framework, figure, model
3 *the construction put on his remarks*
interpretation, meaning, inference, deduction, reading
4 *the art of sentence construction*
structure, formation, arrangement, order, organization, composition, make-up
FORMAL configuration, disposition
◪ **1** demolition, destruction

constructive *adj*
practical, productive, positive, helpful, useful, valuable, beneficial, advantageous
◪ destructive, negative, unhelpful

constructively *adv*
productively, positively, practically, helpfully, usefully, beneficially, advantageously
◪ destructively, negatively, unhelpfully

construe *v*
interpret, explain, understand, see as, regard as, read, render, take to mean, deduce, infer, analyse
FORMAL expound

consul n

ambassador, envoy, diplomat, representative, agent, delegate, minister, nuncio, elchi
OLD ledger, leaguer
FORMAL emissary, legate, plenipotentiary

consult v

1 *consult an expert*
ask/seek advice, ask/seek information, ask someone's opinion, question, interrogate, turn to, see
COLLOQ. pick someone's brains
2 *consult with business partners*
confer, discuss, debate, talk, deliberate
3 *consult a map*
look up, refer to, turn to

consultant n

adviser, expert, authority, specialist, associate

consultation n

discussion, deliberation, talk, dialogue, conference, meeting, hearing, interview, examination, appointment, forum, session

consultative adj

advisory, advising, consulting, counselling, helping, recommending
FORMAL consultatory

consume v

1 EAT, eat up, drink (up), swallow, devour, dispose of, gobble, take
OLD bezzle
FORMAL ingest
COLLOQ. tuck in, guzzle, scoff, snarf, polish off, touch, shift, discuss, get stuck into, murder, kill, punish
SLANG mainline
2 USE UP, use, absorb, spend, get through, go through, expend, drain, exhaust, squander, waste, fritter away
FORMAL deplete, dissipate, expend, utilize
3 DESTROY, demolish, annihilate, devastate, burn, gut, ravage, lay waste, waste, wear (down), damage
OLD pine
4 *consumed with jealousy*
devour, dominate, absorb, engross, preoccupy, grip, obsess, monopolize, overwhelm, torment
COLLOQ. eat up

consumer n

user, end-user, customer, buyer, purchaser, shopper, patron, client, mouth

consuming adj

dominating, compelling, absorbing, preoccupying, devouring, engrossing, gripping, obsessive, immoderate, monopolizing, overwhelming, tormenting

consummate adj, v

♦ adj
absolute, complete, total, utter, perfect, supreme, superior, ultimate, superb, transcendent, unqualified, skilled, accomplished, finished, gifted, practised, exact, proficient, distinguished, matchless, exemplary, polished
OLD replenished; (*Shakesp*) made up

E3 imperfect
♦ v
perfect, accomplish, fulfil, realize, complete, perform, achieve, crown, cap, end, finish, conclude
FORMAL terminate, execute, effectuate

consummation n

perfection, accomplishment, achievement, fulfilment, realization, completion, performance, achievement, culmination, crowning, capping, end, finish, conclusion
FORMAL termination, execution, actualization, effectuation

consumption n

1 EATING, drinking, swallowing, devouring
FORMAL ingestion
COLLOQ. tucking-in, guzzling, scoffing
2 USING-UP, absorption, spending, getting-through, going-through, draining, exhaustion, squandering, waste
FORMAL depletion, expending, expenditure, utilization

contact n, v

♦ n
1 *in contact with an object*
touching, touch, impact, meeting, junction, union, proximity
FORMAL juxtaposition, contiguity
2 *in contact with old friends*
touch, communication, connection, association
3 *use your contacts to get a job*
friend, acquaintance, relation, relative, connection, sponsor, person of influence, person of importance, network of contacts
♦ v
approach, get onto, apply to, reach, get hold of, get in touch with, get through to, communicate with, notify, write to, speak to, telephone, phone, ring, call, fax, e-mail

contagion n

infection, contamination, pollution, defilement, tainting, poison, corruption

contagious adj

1 *a contagious disease*
infectious, catching, communicable, transmissible, transmittable, spreading, epidemic, pandemic
2 *contagious laughter*
infectious, compelling, irresistible, catching, spreading

contain v

1 INCLUDE, take in, comprise, incorporate, embody, involve, embrace, enclose, have inside, hold, carry, take, accommodate, seat
2 *contain your feelings*
repress, suppress, stifle, restrain, control, keep under, keep back, hold in, check, keep in check, curb, limit, stop, rein in, prevent from spreading
E3 **1** exclude

container n

receptacle, vessel, holder
FORMAL repository
See panel below

Types of container include:

bag	can	crock	kettle	purse	tube
barrel	canister	cup	locker	sack	tumbler
basin	carton	cylinder	mug	suitcase	tureen
basket	case	dish	pack	tank	urn
bath	cask	drum	packet	tea caddy	vase
beaker	casket	dustbin	pail	tea chest	vat
bin	cauldron	glass	pan	teapot	waste bin
bottle	chest	hamper	pannier	tin	wastepaper
bowl	churn	jar	pitcher	trough	basket
box	cistern	jug	pot	trunk	water-butt
bucket	crate	keg	punnet	tub	well

See also **box**[1].

containment *n*
control, restraint, limitation, check, curb, suppression, repression, stifling

contaminate *v*
infect, pollute, decay, adulterate, taint, soil, sully, defile, corrupt, harm, foul, spoil, make impure, deprave, debase, stain, tarnish
FORMAL vitiate
COLLOQ. spike
E∃ purify, decontaminate

contamination *n*
infection, pollution, decay, adulteration, taint, soiling, sullying, defilement, desecration, corruption, harm, foulness, rottenness, spoiling, filth, impurity, debasement, stain, tarnish
FORMAL vitiation
E∃ purification, decontamination

contemplate *v*
1 *contemplate leaving; contemplate the meaning of life*
consider, think about, deliberate, reflect on, ponder, meditate, muse, mull over, give thought to, dwell on, examine, study, weigh (up), turn over in your mind, have in mind/view, expect, foresee, envisage, plan, design, propose, intend
FORMAL cogitate, ruminate
2 *contemplate the view*
look at, regard, view, observe, scrutinize, survey, examine, inspect

contemplation *n*
1 *religious contemplation*
consideration, thought, deliberation, reflection, recollection, pondering, meditation, musing, mulling-over, dwell, examination, study, weighing (up)
FORMAL cogitation, rumination, cerebration
2 *contemplation of the view*
gazing, regard, regarding, view, viewing, observation, scrutiny, survey, examination, inspection
OLD beholding

contemplative *adj*
thoughtful, reflective, meditative, introspective, musing, pensive, rapt, intent, deep in thought
FORMAL cerebral, ruminative
E∃ impulsive, thoughtless

contemporaneous *adj*
simultaneous, coexistent, synchronous
FORMAL concurrent, coetaneous, coeval

contemporary *adj, n*
• *adj*
1 MODERN, current, present, present-day, present-time, today's, topical, recent, latest, up-to-date, fashionable, up-to-the-minute, ultra-modern, avant-garde, futuristic
OLD contemporanean
COLLOQ. trendy, new-fangled, with it, now
2 CONTEMPORANEOUS, coexistent, parallel, synchronous, simultaneous
OLD contemporanean
FORMAL concurrent, coetaneous, coeval
E∃ 1 out-of-date, old-fashioned
• *n*
fellow, partner, associate, peer, equal, colleague, co-worker, confrère, counterpart, collateral
OLD contemporanean
FORMAL coeval

contempt *n*
scorn, disdain, condescension, derision, ridicule, mockery, disrespect, dishonour, disregard, neglect, dislike, loathing, hatred
FORMAL detestation, contumely
E∃ respect, admiration, regard

contemptible *adj*
despicable, shameful, low, mean, vile, base, detestable, lamentable, loathsome, abject, wretched, hateful, degenerate, unworthy, pitiful, paltry, worthless
OLD (*Shakesp*) pelting
FORMAL ignominious
E∃ admirable, honourable

contemptuous *adj*
scornful, disdainful, sneering, supercilious, condescending, disdainful, arrogant, haughty, high and mighty, tossy, cynical, derisive, derisory, insulting, mocking, jeering, disrespectful, insolent, withering
OLD dispiteous
FORMAL contumelious
E∃ respectful, polite, humble

contend *v*
1 *contend with a problem*
deal, cope, grapple, face, face up to, brave, tackle, address, reckon, come to terms
COLLOQ. come to grips, meet head on
2 MAINTAIN, state, hold, argue, allege, assert, declare, affirm, profess, claim
FORMAL aver, asseverate
3 COMPETE, vie, contest, dispute, clash, wrestle, grapple, struggle, strive, tussle, oppose, challenge, fight, battle, combat, war

content[1] *n*
1 *the contents of the package*
constituents, parts, elements, ingredients, components, component parts, load, items, what is contained, things inside
2 *the contents of the book*
chapter, division, section, subject, subject matter, topic, theme
3 SUBSTANCE, matter, material, essence, gist, meaning, significance, text, theme, subject matter, ideas, contents, load, burden, gist
4 AMOUNT, proportion, capacity, volume, size, measure

content[2] *adj, n, v*
• *adj*
content with the arrangements
satisfied, fulfilled, contented, comfortable, unworried, untroubled, pleased, happy, glad, cheerful, willing, at ease
E∃ dissatisfied, troubled
• *n*
comfort, contentment, satisfaction, fulfilment, delight, pleasure, happiness, gladness, cheerfulness, peace, peacefulness, ease, serenity, gratification, equanimity
E∃ discontent
• *v*
satisfy, humour, indulge, gratify, please, be happy, be pleased, be glad, delight, appease, pacify, placate, soothe
E∃ displease

contented *adj*
happy, glad, pleased, cheerful, comfortable, relaxed, content, satisfied, fulfilled, unworried, untroubled
OLD perfect
E∃ discontented, troubled, unhappy, annoyed

contention *n*
1 *it is my contention that ...*
belief, contention, opinion, persuasion, feeling, intuition, impression, notion, theory, view, viewpoint, point of view, thesis, conviction, claim, judgement, plea, stand, position, assertion, argument
2 *a matter of contention*
disagreement, argument, controversy, dispute, debate, discord, dissension, enmity, feuding, hostility, strife, struggle, rivalry, wrangling

contentious adj

1 *a contentious issue*
controversial, polemical, disputed, doubtful, questionable, debatable, disputable
FORMAL tendentious
2 *a contentious person*
argumentative, antagonistic, quarrelsome, hostile, perverse, querulous, bickering, captious
FORMAL pugnacious
E3 1 uncontroversial, straightforward **2** co-operative, peaceable

contentment n

contentedness, happiness, gladness, cheerfulness, pleasure, gratification, comfort, ease, complacency, peace, peacefulness, serenity, equanimity, content, satisfaction, gratification, fulfilment
E3 unhappiness, discontent, dissatisfaction

contest n, v

• *n*
competition, game, match, race, championship, tournament, event, encounter, fight, battle, combat, conflict, struggle, skirmish, combat, dispute, vying, debate, controversy, challenge, bout, *concours*
COLLOQ. set-to
• *v*
1 DISPUTE, debate, question, call into question, doubt, challenge, oppose, argue against, object to, deny, refute
TECHNICAL litigate
2 COMPETE, be in competition with, vie, contend, strive, struggle, fight, battle, try to beat, tussle
E3 1 accept

contestant n

competitor, contender, player, participant, entrant, candidate, aspirant, rival, opponent, adversary, prizer, disputant

context n

background, setting, surroundings, framework, frame of reference, state of affairs, situation, general situation, position, circumstances, factors, conditions, connection

contiguous adj

adjacent, adjoining, touching, beside, bordering, near, close, neighbouring, next, tangential
TECHNICAL vicinal
FORMAL abutting, conjoining, conterminous, juxtaposed, juxtapositional

continent n

mainland, terra firma

The continents of the world are:

Africa	Australia	South America
Antarctica	Europe	
Asia	North America	

---

contingency n

eventuality, possibility, accident, randomness, arbitrariness, chance, chance event, emergency, event, happening, incident, uncertainty
FORMAL fortuity, juncture

contingent n, adj

• *n*
body, company, deputation, delegation, mission, representatives, detachment, section, division, group, band, set, batch, quota, party, complement
• *adj*
dependent, conditional, subject, based, relative

continual adj

constant, perpetual, incessant, interminable, eternal, everlasting, regular, frequent, recurrent, repeated, repetitive, persistent
E3 occasional, intermittent, temporary

⚠ continual or **continuous**?
Continual means 'very frequent, happening again and again': *I've had continual interruptions all morning.*
Continuous means 'without a pause or break': *continuous rain.*

continually adv

constantly, perpetually, incessantly, interminably, ceaselessly, ever, forever, eternally, everlastingly, always, endlessly, on and on, non-stop, regularly, frequently, recurrently, repeatedly, persistently, habitually, all the time
E3 occasionally, intermittently

continuance n

continuation, duration, endurance, period, term, permanence, persistence
FORMAL protraction

continuation n

1 *continuation after a pause*
resumption, recommencement, starting again, carrying-on, renewal, maintenance, development, furtherance, addition, supplement, sequel
2 *the continuation of the road*
prolongation, lengthening, extension
FORMAL protraction
E3 1 *formal* cessation, termination

continue v

1 *continue doing something*
go on, carry on, not stop, keep, keep on (with), proceed, pursue, stay, persist in, persevere in, progress, press on
COLLOQ. stick at, soldier on
2 *the course continues next term*
resume, recommence, renew, proceed (again), start again, begin again, take up again, carry on, go on
COLLOQ. pick up the threads, pick up where you have left off
3 *if the storm continues; continue your training*
last, endure, remain, abide, survive, hold (out), stay, rest, pursue, sustain, maintain, keep up, lengthen, prolong, extend, persist, keep on, project
OLD dure
FORMAL subsist
4 *'I'm not sure,' she continued*
start talking again, resume, go on
5 *continue on your way*
keep going, keep travelling, keep walking, keep moving, move on, keep on, carry on, proceed, press ahead
E3 1, 2, 3, 4 stop

continuity n

flow, progression, succession, sequence, linkage, interrelationship, connection, cohesion, continuousness, uninterruptedness, unchangeableness
E3 discontinuity

continuous adj

unbroken, uninterrupted, consecutive, non-stop, not stopping, without a break, endless, seamless, unending, never-ending, solid, unceasing, ceaseless, interminable, persistent, relentless, constant, unremitting, prolonged, extended, continued, lasting
COLLOQ. with no let-up
E3 discontinuous, broken, sporadic

⚠ continuous or **continual**?
See panel at **continual.**

Contraceptives and other forms of birth control include:

barrier contraceptive	diaphragm	loop	*slang* rubber
barrier method	Dutch cap	minipill	sheath
cervical cap	female condom	morning-after pill	spermicide
coil	Femidom®	oral contraceptive	vaginal ring
coitus interruptus	*slang* French letter	pill	withdrawal method
condom	injectable contraceptive	*N Am* prophylactic	
contraceptive ring	intrauterine device (IUD)	protective	
contraceptive sponge	*slang* johnnie	rhythm method	

> **Synonym nuances**
> **Unbroken**, **uninterrupted**, **solid** and **non-stop** are used quite neutrally of something carrying on without interruption: *the remedy for irritability is uninterrupted sleep*; *three months of non-stop rain*.
> **Unending**, **unceasing**, **unremitting** and **endless** go further by suggesting the feeling that something will carry on forever, and are often used in figurative contexts, either negatively or positively: *endless summer evenings*; *an unremitting battle against prejudice*. **Interminable** again suggests the feeling that it will never end, with a clear implication of monotony: *bogged down in interminable discussions*. **Prolonged** also hints at something gruelling, but is used in the context of unexpected additional time: *prolonged talks on the economy*.
> **Seamless** may be used similarly to suggest the apparent flow of one thing into another, and is often used as a term of approbation: *a professional and seamless show*. You can use **persistent** or **relentless**, however, to describe repeated action and imply a perhaps unwelcome tenacity: *the persistent questions of a newspaper reporter*. **Lasting** would be used with the positive implication that something will endure: *a deep and lasting friendship*.

continuously *adv*
uninterruptedly, consecutively, endlessly, ceaselessly, interminably, persistently, relentlessly, constantly, unremittingly
COLLOQ. twenty-four seven, 24-7
≢ sporadically

contort *v*
twist, distort, warp, wrench, disfigure, deform, misshape, bend out of shape, screw up, gnarl, knot, writhe, squirm, wriggle
FORMAL convolute

contortionist *n*
acrobat, gymnast, tumbler, balancer, somersaulter, trapeze artist, rope-walker, rope-dancer, stuntman, stuntwoman
FORMAL funambulist, aerialist, equilibrist

contour *n*
outline, silhouette, shape, form, figure, curve, lines, relief, profile, character, aspect
TECHNICAL isobase, isobath
FORMAL contorno, tournure

contraband *n*
banned/black-market goods, smuggling, forbidden/illegal traffic, bootlegging, prohibited/unlawful goods
FORMAL proscribed goods
COLLOQ. hot goods

contraceptive
See panel above

contract *v, n*
 ♦ *v*
1 SHRINK, lessen, diminish, reduce, decrease, shorten, make/become shorter, make/become smaller, curtail, abbreviate, abridge, condense, compress, constrict, narrow, tighten, tense, draw in, shrivel, wrinkle
2 *contract pneumonia*
catch, get, go/come down with, develop, pick up, become infected with, become ill with, be taken ill with
FORMAL succumb to
3 PLEDGE, promise, undertake, engage, agree, stipulate, covenant, arrange, agree terms, settle, negotiate, bargain
≢ 1 expand, enlarge, lengthen
 ♦ *n*
agreement, bond, commitment, engagement, covenant, treaty, convention, pact, transaction, deal, bargain, settlement, arrangement, understanding
FORMAL compact, concordat
■ **contract out**
1 SUBCONTRACT, pass/give to others, delegate, farm out, outsource
2 WITHDRAW, get out, drop out

contraction *n*
1 *'Don't' is a contraction of 'do not'*
abbreviation, shortening, shortened form, abridgement
2 *the contraction of muscles*
constriction, compression, narrowing, tightening, tensing, drawing-in, shrivelling, shrinkage, lessening, reduction, curtailment
TECHNICAL astringency
≢ 2 relaxation, expansion, growth

contradict *v*
1 *contradict someone*
deny, challenge, oppose, dispute, rebut, counter, go against, argue with; *dialect* threap
TECHNICAL sublate, traverse
OLD nay, outface
FORMAL disaffirm, confute, refute, impugn, gainsay, contrary
2 *one statement contradicts another*
disagree with, clash with, conflict with, contrast with, go against, be at variance with, be at odds with, be in conflict with, be inconsistent with
FORMAL negate, belie
COLLOQ. fly in the face of
≢ 1 agree **2** agree with, confirm; *formal* corroborate

contradiction *n*
1 *the contradiction between theory and practice*
clash, variance, odds, conflict, inconsistency, disagreement, paradox
FORMAL incongruity, negation, antithesis
2 *contradiction of an earlier report*
denial, challenge, opposition, dispute, rebuttal, counter-argument
FORMAL disaffirmance, disaffirmation, confutation, refutation
≢ 1, 2 agreement

contradictory *adj*
contrary, opposite, opposing, paradoxical, conflicting, clashing, inconsistent, incompatible, antagonistic, irreconcilable, opposed
FORMAL discrepant, dissentient, repugnant, incongruous, antithetical
≢ consistent

Synonym nuances
The word **contrary** suggests going against something established: *contrary to popular belief*. **Opposite** and **opposing** imply being at the furthest extremities of anything: *the stark polarization of these opposing views*. The term **paradoxical** is appropriately used only to describe a contradiction with apparent absurdity: *the paradoxical view of ugliness as a special kind of beauty*.
You might use **incompatible** if two or more things are simply unable to co-exist, or **irreconcilable** where inherent differences mean no area of agreement can be found: *the irreconcilable differences between landowners and conservationists*. **Antagonistic** would be most appropriately used to suggest a more violent disagreement, and to convey this notion further, you could use **conflicting** or **clashing**.

contraption *n*
contrivance, device, gadget, waldo, apparatus, rig, machine, mechanism, invention
COLLOQ. gizmo, widget, doodah; *N Am* doodad; thingamy, thingamybob, thingamyjig, what's-its-name
SLANG doofer

contrary *adj, n*
♦ *adj*
1 OPPOSITE, counter, reverse, conflicting, clashing, inconsistent, incompatible, irreconcilable, antagonistic, opposed, opposing, adverse, hostile
2 PERVERSE, awkward, disobliging, difficult, unco-operative, wayward, obstinate, stubborn, headstrong, intractable, cantankerous
FORMAL refractory
COLLOQ. stroppy
⊟ 1 like **2** obliging
♦ *n*
opposite, converse, reverse
FORMAL antithesis
■ **on the contrary**
conversely, quite/just the reverse, quite/just the opposite, *per contra, au contraire, tout au contraire*
■ **contrary to**
in opposition to, at variance with, at odds with, in conflict with, inconsistent with

contrast *n, v*
♦ *n*
difference, dissimilarity, divergence, distinction, differentiation, comparison, foil, set-off, opposite, opposition, relief
TECHNICAL chiasmus, contraposition, counterchange
FORMAL disparity, dissimilitude, antithesis
⊟ similarity, resemblance
♦ *v*
1 *contrast two people*
compare, differentiate, distinguish, discriminate
2 *her expression contrasted sharply with her dress*
disagree, contradict, clash, conflict, differ, oppose, go against, be at variance, be at odds, be in conflict, be inconsistent with
■ **in contrast to**
as distinguished from, opposed to, in opposition to, rather than, as against

contravene *v*
infringe, violate, break, breach, disobey, defy, flout
FORMAL transgress
⊟ uphold, observe, obey

contravention *n*
infringement, violation, breaking, breach
FORMAL transgression, dereliction
⊟ observance, compliance

contretemps *n*
argument, disagreement, squabble, clash, brush, tiff, difficulty, accident, misadventure, misfortune, mishap, hitch, predicament

contribute *v*
1 *contribute money to charity*
give, donate, give a donation, subscribe, grant, present, endow, provide, supply, furnish
FORMAL bestow
COLLOQ. chip in; *Aust* chuck in
2 *poor design contributed to the disaster*
cause, play a part in, give rise to, lead to, result in, occasion, bring about, make, make happen, produce, generate, originate, create, promote, help, add to, be a factor in, be instrumental in
FORMAL conduce
3 *contribute an article for a magazine*
write, compose, create, compile, prepare, edit, submit, supply, provide

contribution *n*
1 *a contribution of £1000*
donation, subscription, gift, gratuity, handout, grant, levy, tax, mite, present, endowment, superannuation, offering, input, addition, proportion, shot, Peter's pence
FORMAL bestowal
2 *a contribution to a magazine*
article, story, feature, item, piece, column, report, review, paper, feuilleton

contributor *n*
1 DONOR, subscriber, giver, patron, benefactor, sponsor, backer, supporter
2 WRITER, author, journalist, reporter, compiler, correspondent, reviewer, critic, columnist, freelance

contrite *adj*
sorry, regretful, remorseful, repentant, penitent, penitential, guilt-ridden, conscience-stricken, chastened, humble, ashamed, red-faced

contrition *n*
remorse, sorrow, regret, shame, humiliation, penitence, repentance, sackcloth and ashes, self-reproach
FORMAL compunction

contrivance *n*
1 INVENTION, device, contraption, gadget, implement, appliance, machine, mechanism, tool, apparatus, equipment, gear
COLLOQ. gizmo, widget, doodah; *N Am* doodad; thingamy, thingamybob, thingamyjig, what's-its-name
SLANG doofer
2 STRATAGEM, ploy, trick, dodge, ruse, expedient, tactic, plan, design, project, scheme, plot, intrigue
FORMAL machination, artifice

contrive *v*
1 *somehow contrived to blame me*
manage, succeed, arrange, bring about, create, design, devise, find a way
2 *contrive a meeting between them*
engineer, manoeuvre, orchestrate, stage-manage, plan, plot, scheme, fabricate, create, devise, invent, concoct, construct
COLLOQ. set up, wangle

contrived *adj*
unnatural, artificial, false, forced, strained, laboured, mannered, elaborate, overdone
COLLOQ. set-up
⊟ natural, genuine, spontaneous

control *n, v*
♦ *n*
1 POWER, charge, authority, command, mastery, dominance, sway, supremacy, government, rule, reign,

direction, management, oversight, supervision, superintendence, discipline, guidance, influence
FORMAL jurisdiction
2 RESTRAINT, self-restraint, self-control, self-discipline, constraint, check, curb, repression
3 *price controls*
restriction, constraint, limitation, regulation, limit, reduction, brake, check, curb, hindrance, impediment
4 INSTRUMENT, dial, switch, button, knob, lever
♦ *v*
1 LEAD, be in charge of, have authority over, govern, rule, command, direct, manage, run, head, oversee, preside over, dominate, supervise, superintend
COLLOQ. be the boss, be in the driving seat, be in the saddle, pull the strings, rule the roost, run the show, call the tune/shots, wear the trousers
2 *control a machine/the temperature*
run, operate, work, make go, regulate, modulate, adjust, monitor, verify
3 *control wages*
restrict, limit, regulate, constrain, constrict, reduce, check, curb
OLD perstringe
COLLOQ. keep a tight rein on, put the brakes on
4 *control your temper*
restrain, check, curb, subdue, repress, hold back, keep, keep in check, contain

controversial *adj*
contentious, polemical, disputed, doubtful, questionable, debatable, disputable, at issue, moot
FORMAL tendentious, eristic

controversy *n*
debate, discussion, war of words, difference of opinion, dispute, disagreement, argument, quarrel, squabble, wrangle, strife, contention, discord, friction, dissension, *cause célèbre*
OLD debatement
FORMAL polemic, altercation
E3 accord, agreement
Related adjective: eristic

contusion *n*
bruise, bump, discoloration, mark, blemish, injury, knock, lump, swelling
TECHNICAL ecchymosis

conundrum *n*
puzzle, problem, enigma, difficulty, quandary, poser, riddle, word game, anagram
COLLOQ. brainteaser, brain-twister

conurbation *n*
city, metropolitan area, metropolis, megalopolis, inner city, city centre, downtown, concrete jungle, urban sprawl, precinct, ghetto, suburbia, micropolis, cosmopolis, pentapolis, municipality, town, urban area, urban district; *N Am* metroplex
COLLOQ. big smoke

convalesce *v*
recuperate, recover, get better, get well, get stronger, regain your strength, improve, pick up, rally, revive
COLLOQ. pull through

convalescence *n*
recuperation, getting better, improvement, recovery, rehabilitation, restoration

convene *v*
1 *convene a meeting*
call/bring (together), rally, summon
2 *the court convened*
assemble, meet, gather, collect, congregate, muster, come together
FORMAL convoke

convenience *n*
1 ACCESSIBILITY, availability, handiness, usefulness, use, ease of use, usability, utility, serviceability, service, benefit, advantage, advantageousness, help, suitability, fitness, appropriateness, opportuneness
FORMAL expediency, propitiousness, propinquity
2 *all modern conveniences*
facility, amenity, appliance, device, labour-saving device, gadget, service, resource
E3 1 inconvenience

convenient *adj*
nearby, at hand, near/close at hand, within reach, within walking/driving distance, accessible, available, at your disposal, handy, useful, beneficial, helpful, labour-saving, easy, adapted, fitted, suited, suitable, fitting, appropriate, opportune, timely, well-timed, expedient; *dialect* gain
OLD advantageable, commodious, handsome, hend
COLLOQ. just/only round the corner, at your fingertips
E3 inconvenient, awkward

conveniently *adv*
accessibly, helpfully, usefully, suitably, appropriately, nearby, at hand, near/close at hand, within reach, within walking/driving distance
COLLOQ. just/only round the corner, at your fingertips
E3 inconveniently

convent *n*
nunnery, priory, cloister, abbey

convention *n*
1 CUSTOM, tradition, practice, use, usage, fashion, ceremony, protocol, etiquette, formality, matter of form, code, ethos, mores
FORMAL propriety, punctilio
2 ASSEMBLY, congress, conference, meeting, gathering, council, delegates, representatives, synod
FORMAL convocation, conclave
3 *the Geneva convention*
agreement, bond, commitment, engagement, covenant, treaty, pact, contract, transaction, deal, bargain, settlement, arrangement, understanding
FORMAL accord, compact, concordat

conventional *adj*
1 *a conventional person*
traditional, conservative, proper, correct, formal, conformist, hidebound
2 *a conventional approach*
unoriginal, routine, usual, customary, regular, standard, normal, ordinary, mainstream, straight, stereotyped, trite, pedestrian, commonplace, common, traditional, orthodox, formal, prevalent, prevailing, accepted, received, expected, ritual
COLLOQ. common-or-garden, run-of-the-mill
E3 1 unconventional, nonconformist **2** unusual, original, exotic, alternative

Synonym nuances
sense 1
Traditional suggests adherence to, or a liking for, long-established customs, and is often used with a tone of approval: *traditional pubs, lovingly restored*; whereas **conservative** tends more to suggest a reluctance to change, and is not particularly marked by favour or disfavour: *police society's conservative outlook*. The term **formal** suggests an adherence to etiquette, as do **proper** and **correct**, which also imply some agreement with this view.
  Conformist has more to do with adherence to social norms, and, like **conservative**, is likely to take its tone from its context: *scientists tend to be more conformist than artists*. **Hidebound**, however, is more suggestive of being restricted by out-of-date practices, and so is inherently critical in tone: *hidebound attitudes of bureaucracy*.

conventionally *adv*
traditionally, formally, routinely, usually, commonly, regularly, normally, ordinarily
F3 unconventionally, unusually

converge *v*
1 *crowds converged on the car*
approach, move towards, gather, close in, form, mass, focus, concentrate
2 *the roads converge at the bridge*
meet, join, combine, merge, coincide, unite, come together, intersect
F3 1 disperse **2** diverge

convergence *n*
concentration, approach, merging, combination, blending, meeting, coincidence, junction, intersection, union
FORMAL confluence
F3 divergence, separation

conversant
■ **conversant with**
familiar with, acquainted with, experienced in, informed about, knowledgeable about, practised in, proficient in, skilled in, versed in, au fait with
FORMAL apprised of
F3 ignorant of

conversation *n*
talk, chat, gossip, chitchat, discussion, discourse, dialogue, exchange, communication, tête-à-tête, heart-to-heart, cosy chat, table talk, small talk, pillow talk; *Aust* yabber
OLD parlance; (*Shakesp*) question; (*Spenser*) board
FORMAL colloquy, interlocution
COLLOQ. chinwag, natter, confab; *Aust* wongi

conversational *adj*
informal, chatty, colloquial, communicative, talkative, relaxed, casual

converse[1] *v*
converse with people
talk, speak, discuss, confer, communicate, chat, chitchat, gossip, chatter
OLD (*Shakesp*)propose, question, reason, relate
FORMAL commune, discourse
COLLOQ. natter

converse[2] *n, adj*
◆ *n*
the converse is true
opposite, reverse, contrary, obverse
FORMAL antithesis
COLLOQ. other way round, other side of the coin
◆ *adj*
opposite, opposing, reverse, counter, contrary, reversed, transposed, obverse
FORMAL antithetical

conversely *adv*
on the other hand, on the contrary, contrarily, contrariwise, obversely
FORMAL antithetically

conversion *n*
1 *a loft conversion*
alteration, change, transformation, turning, adaptation, modification, remodelling, reshaping, reconstruction, reorganization, customization, adjustment
TECHNICAL metamorphosis, transfiguration, mutation, transmutation
2 *conversion of pounds into francs*
change, exchange, substitution, switch
3 *conversion to Judaism*
persuasion, conviction, reformation, regeneration, rebirth, evangelization, proselytization, preaching

convert *v, n*
◆ *v*
1 *convert the building*
alter, change, turn, transform, make, adapt, customize, adjust, modify, go over to, transfer, switch, reform, restructure, remodel, reshape, refashion, restyle, revise, reorganize, rebuild, reconstruct
TECHNICAL metamorphose, transfigure, mutate, transmute
2 *convert inches into centimetres*
change, exchange, substitute, turn into, switch from
3 WIN OVER, convince, persuade, cause to change beliefs/religion, reform, evangelize, proselytize
4 CHANGE RELIGION, change beliefs, reform, move over, turn
COLLOQ. *Scot* jump/loup the dyke
◆ *n*
disciple, believer, new person, changed person, proselyte, neophyte, adherent

convertible *adj*
adaptable, adjustable, changeable, exchangeable, modifiable, interchangeable
FORMAL permutable

convex *adj*
rounded, curved out, bending outwards, bulging, swelling, protuberant, bow-fronted, gibbous
TECHNICAL nowy
F3 concave, hollow

convey *v*
1 *convey feelings*
communicate, express, tell, relate, reveal, disclose, announce, make known, transmit, hand on, pass on
FORMAL impart
2 TRANSPORT, carry, bear, bring, fetch, move, transport, drive, shift, send, forward, deliver, transfer, conduct, guide, channel, pipe

conveyance *n*
1 VEHICLE, car, taxi, cab, bus, coach, bicycle, motorcycle, lorry, truck, van, wagon, carriage
2 *the conveyance of bicycles*
transport, transportation, movement, carriage, transfer, transference
3 *the conveyance of property*
transfer, transference, granting, transmission, consignment, delivery, bequeathal, ceding

convict *v, n*
◆ *v*
condemn, find guilty, sentence, judge, imprison
TECHNICAL crime
OLD reprove, attaint; (*Shakesp*) approve
◆ *n*
criminal, lawbreaker, felon, culprit, villain, offender, wrongdoer, prisoner, inmate, old hand, *forçat*
OLD emancipist
COLLOQ. crook, jailbird; *N Am* yardbird
SLANG lag, con; *Aust* canary

conviction *n*
1 BELIEF, view, opinion, faith, creed, tenet, principle
2 *speak with conviction*
assurance, confidence, fervour, wholeheartedness, earnestness, certainty, firmness, persuasion
FORMAL certitude
3 *previous convictions*
condemnation, pronouncement of guilt, sentence, judgement, imprisonment

convince *v*
assure, persuade, prove to, sway, talk into, talk over, win over, bring round, bring home, sell, induce, influence, prompt, satisfy
OLD resolve
FORMAL prevail upon

convincing adj

persuasive, powerful, telling, impressive, credible, plausible, likely, probable, conclusive, compelling, forceful, incontrovertible

FORMAL cogent

E= unconvincing, improbable

Synonym nuances

Persuasive implies having the power to influence the mind or passions in a subtle way: *persuasive tax advantages*, whilst **compelling**, **forceful** and **powerful** could be used of stronger, more immediately apparent case: *there is a compelling case for routine cancer screening*; *a powerful argument*.

The term **telling** may be used if you also want to suggest an action or idea has some significance: *the speech is short but very telling*. **Impressive** is the word to use to convey the additional sense of something producing a profound and positive effect: *he has impressive credentials*.

Both **credible** and **plausible** would suggest that some notion is highly believable or possible; to put more emphasis on the idea of it actually being true, you might choose **likely** or **probable**. **Conclusive** and **incontrovertible**, on the other hand, would be reserved for an unquestionable finality: *conclusive evidence*; *the facts were hard and incontrovertible*.

---

convincingly adv

persuasively, powerfully, tellingly, impressively, credibly, plausibly, conclusively, compellingly, forcefully

FORMAL cogently

E= unconvincingly

convivial adj

friendly, sociable, genial, cheerful, cordial, festive, affable, hearty, jolly, jovial, lively, merry, fun-loving

E= taciturn

conviviality n

friendliness, geniality, cheer, cordiality, sociability, gaiety, jollity, joviality, good feeling, bonhomie, liveliness, mirth, festivity, merrymaking, fun

convocation n

congress, convention, forum, council, assembly, conference, congregation, meeting, diet, synod

FORMAL conclave, forgathering, assemblage

convoluted adj

convoluted carvings/ideas

twisting, winding, meandering, tortuous, involved, complicated, complex

E= straight, straightforward

convolution n

1 *convolutions in the design*

coil, twist, whorl, turn, spiral, helix, loop, coiling, winding, sinuousness, sinuosity

TECHNICAL gyrus

FORMAL curlicue

2 *convolutions in relationships*

complexity, intricacy, complication, entanglement, involvement, tortuousness

convoy n

fleet, line, escort, guard, protection, attendance, train, group, company

convulse v

suffer a fit/seizure, shake uncontrollably/violently, jerk, shudder, seize, unsettle, disturb

convulsion n

1 FIT, seizure, attack, paroxysm, spasm, cramp, contraction, tic, tremor

TECHNICAL ictus

2 *major political convulsions*

eruption, outburst, furore, disturbance, unrest, disorder, commotion, tumult, turmoil, agitation, turbulence, upheaval

convulsive adj

jerky, spasmodic, fitful, sporadic, uncontrolled, violent

cook v

prepare, heat, warm, put on, put together, make, improvise, undercook, underdo, overcook, overdo, burn

COLLOQ. rustle up, scare up, throw together

■ **cook up**

concoct, prepare, brew, invent, make up, falsify, fabricate, contrive, devise, plan, plot, scheme

---

Terms used in cookery include:

à la crème	drizzle	oven-roast
à la Grècque	dum	parboil
à la mode	dust	peel
al dente	en cocotte	peppered
au gratin	en croûte	pickle
au naturel	en papillote	plate (up)
au poivre	farci	poach
bake	fillet	pot-roast
bake blind	flambé	potted
balti	flash fry	*colloq.* prep
barbecue	Florentine	preserve
bargar	fold in	prove
baste	freeze	Provençale
bhuna (or	fricassee	purée
bhoona)	fry	reduce
bind	fusion	re-heat
blanch	fu yung	rest
blend	glaze	rise
boil	grate	roast
bone	grind	rogan josh
bonne femme	griddle	roulade
braise	grill	roux
broil	haute cuisine	rub in
brown	ice	sauté
brûlé	jalfrezi	scramble
cacciatore	joint	sear
caramelize	jug	sieve
carve	jus	sift
casserole	knead	simmer
chargrill	knock back	skim
chasseur	korma	smoke
chill	liquidize	souse
chop	Lyonnaise	spit-roast
chop suey	madras	steam
coddle	Marie Rose	stew
cordon bleu	Marengo	stir
core	marinate	stir-fry
cream	masala	strain
crumble	mash	stuff
cure	microwave	sweat
curry	mince	sweet-and-sour
deep-fry	mix	thicken
defrost	mornay	toast
deglaze	mull	truss
devil	Niçoise	whisk
dopiaza	nouvelle cuisine	

See also **kitchen utensils**.

---

cool adj, v, n

♦ adj

1 CHILLY, fresh, breezy, nippy, cold, bracing, crisp, draughty

COLLOQ. parky

2 *a cool drink*

cold, chilled, iced, ice-cold, refreshing

3 CALM, unruffled, unexcited, composed, self-possessed, level-headed, collected, unemotional, dispassionate, quiet, relaxed, impassive, unmoved, placid, sedate, poised, imperturbable, unexcitable, unflustered, unperturbed, undisturbed, untroubled, unapprehensive

COLLOQ. laid-back, unflappable, cool as a cucumber

4 *a cool reception*
unfriendly, unwelcoming, cold, frigid, frosty, lukewarm, tepid, half-hearted, unenthusiastic, apathetic, uninterested, unresponsive, uncommunicative, undemonstrative, reserved, distant, aloof, standoffish
5 *look cool in that outfit*
sophisticated, fashionable, elegant, smart, stylish, chic
COLLOQ. trendy, streetwise
6 *a really cool party*
great, wonderful, excellent, fantastic, marvellous
COLLOQ. smashing, terrific, neat, ace, brill, out of this world, second to none
SLANG mega, wicked
F3 1, 2 warm, hot **3** excited, angry **4** friendly, welcoming
◆ *v*
1 CHILL, refrigerate, ice, freeze, make/become cold, make/ become colder, get/turn cold, get/turn colder, fan, air-condition
2 MODERATE, lessen, temper, dampen, diminish, subside, reduce, quiet, calm, allay
FORMAL abate, assuage
F3 1 warm, heat **2** excite
◆ *n*
1 *keep/lose your cool*
composure, coolness, calmness, collectedness, poise, self-possession, self-discipline, self-control, control, temper
2 *the cool of the early morning*
chill, freshness, breeze, nippiness, cold, coldness, chilliness, crispness, draught
TECHNICAL defervescence, defervescency

coolly *adv*
1 CALMLY, unexcitedly, composedly, level-headedly, collectedly, unemotionally, dispassionately, quietly, impassively, placidly, sedately, imperturbably, unexcitably
2 *coolly received ideas*
half-heartedly, unenthusiastically, apathetically, uninterestedly, unresponsively, reservedly, distantly, standoffishly, coldly, frostily

cooling *n, adj*
◆ *n*
chilling, refrigeration, air-conditioning, ventilation
TECHNICAL defervescence, defervescency
F3 heating, warming
◆ *adj*
freezing, refrigerant, refrigerative, refrigeratory
F3 warming

coop *n, v*
◆ *n*
cage, box, enclosure, pen, hutch, pound, run
■ **coop up**
imprison, cage, enclose, shut (up), confine, impound, shut in, keep in, close in, lock up/away, pen, imprison
FORMAL incarcerate, immure

co-operate *v*
collaborate, work together, pull together, band together, team up, help, assist, aid, contribute, participate, combine, unite, join forces, play along, work side by side, share, pool, pool your resources, put your heads together, pull your weight, conspire
COLLOQ. play ball

co-operation *n*
helpfulness, help, helping hand, assistance, aid, contribution, participation, collaboration, teamwork, working together, unity, co-ordination, joint action, concerted action/effort, give-and-take, team spirit, *esprit de corps*
F3 opposition, rivalry, competition

co-operative *adj*
1 COLLECTIVE, joint, shared, combined, united, concerted,

co-ordinated, collaborative, working together
2 HELPFUL, helping, assisting, supportive, responsive, obliging, accommodating, willing, compliant
FORMAL coactive
F3 2 unco-operative, rebellious

co-ordinate *v*
1 ORGANIZE, arrange, systematize, order, work together, co-operate, collaborate, tabulate, integrate, mesh, synchronize, correlate, regulate
FORMAL ordinate
COLLOQ. join up
2 *co-ordinate colours*
harmonize, match, complement, blend (in), adapt, go, go together, go well, be/make compatible
COLLOQ. mix 'n' match

co-ordination *n*
1 ORGANIZATION, ordering, arrangement, co-operation, collaboration, integration
2 COMPATIBILITY, harmony, matching, complementation, blending

cop *n, v*
◆ *n*
police officer, officer, policeman, policewoman, constable, PC
COLLOQ. copper, bobby, rozzer
SLANG pig, nark, bizzy, flatfoot, bluebottle, bull
■ **cop out**
avoid, evade, stay/keep away from, elude, sidestep, escape, run away from, get out of, bypass, get round, balk, prevent, avert, shun, abstain from, hold back from, shy away from, steer clear of, make a detour, keep your distance from
COLLOQ. hedge, duck, dodge, shirk, wriggle/worm your way out of, give a miss, give a wide berth to

cope *v*
manage, carry on, survive, get by, get through, make do, succeed, take in your stride
FORMAL subsist
■ **cope with**
deal with, encounter, contend with, struggle with, grapple with, wrestle with, handle, manage, treat, weather, endure
F3 *colloq.* not hack it

copious *adj*
abundant, plentiful, inexhaustible, overflowing, profuse, rich, lavish, bountiful, liberal, full, ample, generous, extensive, numerous, great, huge
FORMAL plenteous, bounteous, luxuriant
COLLOQ. bags of
F3 scarce, meagre

cop-out *n*
excuse, dodge, evasion, fraud, pretence, pretext, alibi
COLLOQ. get-out, shirking, passing the buck

copse *n*
coppice, wood, thicket, grove, bush, brush

copulate *v*
mate, make love, have sex, have sexual intercourse, go to bed with, enjoy, horse, line
OLD gender, mell
COLLOQ. fool around, get off with, go all the way
SLANG get your leg over, have, lay, make it with, have it off with, bed, bonk, bang; (*taboo*) screw, hump, shag, stuff, fuck

copulation *n*
sexual intercourse, sex, union, intimacy, coupling, love-making, marriage-bed, bed, sleeping with someone, going to bed with someone, mating, relations
OLD commixtion, embraces
FORMAL consummation, coitus, coition, carnal knowledge, congress

COLLOQ. how's your father, it; *Aust & NZ* naughty
SLANG lay, bang, bonk, leg-over, wham bam thank you
ma'am, greens, jig-a-jig, knee-trembler, quickie; *N Am*
jazz, poontang, nooky, pussy, rumpy-pumpy, tail; (*taboo*)
fuck, fucking, screw, screwing, shag, shagging

copy *n, v*
♦ *n*
1 *copies of the letter*
duplicate, facsimile, fax, carbon copy, photocopy,
Photostat®, Xerox®, reproduction, print, tracing,
transcript, transcription, replica, model, pattern,
archetype, representation, image, likeness, counterfeit,
forgery, fake, imitation, borrowing, plagiarism, crib
COLLOQ. knock-off
2 *buy a copy of the magazine*
issue, sample, example, specimen
E3 **1** original
♦ *v*
duplicate, photocopy, Photostat®, Xerox®, reproduce,
print, trace, transcribe, fax, scan, forge, counterfeit, pirate,
simulate, imitate, impersonate, mimic, ape, parrot, repeat,
echo, mirror, follow, emulate, borrow, plagiarize, crib
FORMAL replicate

Synonym nuances
verb
Duplicate can be used to suggest creating something
identical, but may occasionally further imply
wastefulness: *efforts to eliminate duplicating research
and expenditure*. **Scan** has the specific usage of using
photographic technology for copying purposes.
   Pirate, like **forge** and **counterfeit**, is only used in the
context of illegal activity; **plagiarize** and **crib** also imply
dishonest copying, this time stealing another's ideas. To
convey the idea of copying a person's style, you could
use **imitate** or **mirror**, especially where there is an
element of trying to be like someone admired: *his style
imitated that of Keats*; this is even more strongly
suggested by **follow** and **emulate**.
   However, if you want to convey the idea of assuming
another's character for humour or ridicule, you could use
impersonate or **mimic**: *I mimicked his slow accent*. **Ape**
similarly suggests imitation but further implies that it is
not completely successful: *the bourgeoisie, who aped
aristocratic style*.
   The terms **repeat** and **echo** have more to do with
copying sounds and speech, though the latter may also
be used figuratively: *he echoed the thoughts of many*.
Parrot is similar in sense but tends to be rather
derogatory in tone: *all he does is parrot what his boss
says*.

---

coquettish *adj*
flirtatious, seductive, amorous, provocative, dallying,
flighty, flirty, inviting, teasing
COLLOQ. come-hither, vampish

cord *n*
string, twine, thread, ribbon, lace, rope, line, cable, flex,
connection, link, bond, tie
Related adjective: funicular

cordial *adj*
friendly, amicable, affable, affectionate, agreeable,
cheerful, genial, sociable, pleasant, heartfelt, warm,
warm-hearted, welcoming, wholehearted, earnest,
hearty, stimulating, invigorating
E3 hostile, aloof, cool

cordiality *n*
friendliness, affability, affection, agreeableness,
cheerfulness, geniality, sociability, heartiness, warmth,
welcome, wholeheartedness, earnest, sincerity
E3 coolness, hostility

cordially *adv*
amicably, affably, cheerfully, genially, sociably, pleasantly,
warmly, warm-heartedly, wholeheartedly

cordon *n, v*
♦ *n*
line, ring, barrier, chain, fence, column
■ **cordon off**
close off, fence off, seal off, isolate, separate, encircle,
enclose, surround

core *n, adj*
♦ *n*
kernel, nucleus, heart, centre, middle, interior, nub, crux,
essence, substance, gist
FORMAL quintessence
COLLOQ. nitty-gritty
E3 surface, exterior
♦ *adj*
essential, fundamental, basic, intrinsic, inherent, innate,
underlying, principal, main, key, central, crucial, vital,
characteristic, definitive, typical, constituent
E3 incidental

cork *n*
stopper, plug, bung, seal, stop, cover, lid

corn *n*
arable crop, cereal crop, cereal, wheat, barley, oats, rye,
maize, grain
Related adjective: frumentarious

corner *n, v*
♦ *n*
1 *round the corner*
angle, joint, crook, bend, curve, turning, fork, junction,
intersection
2 NOOK, cranny, niche, recess, crevice, cavity, hole,
hideout, hideaway, retreat
3 *in a tight corner*
predicament, plight, situation, hardship, straits
COLLOQ. tight spot, nowhere to turn, hole, jam, fix, scrape,
pickle
♦ *v*
1 *corner an animal*
force into a place, trap, hunt down, catch, cut off, block off,
run to earth, confine
2 *corner the market*
monopolize, control, dominate, have sole rights in
COLLOQ. hog
■ **round/around the corner**
1 IMMINENT, impending, approaching, coming, near, close,
looming, in the air, about to happen
2 NEAR, nearby, close, close by, within reach, within range,
at hand, accessible, convenient, local, neighbouring
COLLOQ. a stone's throw (away)

cornerstone *n*
basis, support, base, groundwork, bedrock, mainstay, key,
keystone, keyhole, fundamental(s), fundamental point,
starting-point, (basic) principle, first principles, main
ingredient, alpha and omega, essential(s), essence, heart,
core, thrust

corny *adj*
banal, commonplace, hackneyed, stale, overused,
stereotyped, trite, clichéd, sentimental, dull, feeble,
maudlin, mawkish, old-fashioned, platitudinous
E3 new, original

corollary *n*
consequence, conclusion, result, upshot, deduction,
induction, inference
FORMAL illation
TECHNICAL function

coronation *n*
enthronement, crowning, accession to the throne

coronet *n*
crown, diadem, tiara, circlet, wreath, garland

corporal *adj*
anatomical, bodily, fleshly, carnal, material, substantial, concrete, actual, physical, tangible, corporeal
FORMAL somatic
Ea spiritual

corporate *adj*
combined, collective, concerted, joint, common, communal, merged, pooled, shared, united, allied, amalgamated, collaborative

corporation *n*
1 *a business corporation*
firm, company, business, concern, association, organization, establishment, house, partnership, syndicate, cartel, trust, consortium, conglomerate, multinational, industry, holding company
2 *the Corporation of London*
council, authority, authorities, governing body
3 PAUNCH, belly, pot-belly, beer belly

corporeal *adj*
actual, material, physical, substantial, concrete, tangible, bodily, fleshly, human, mortal, carnal, corporal
Ea spiritual

corps *n*
band, body, detachment, unit, squad, team, division, brigade, company, contingent, crew, regiment, squadron

corpse *n*
body, dead body, carcase/carcass, cadaver, skeleton, remains, mummy, zombie; *Scot* like
OLD relics, corse
COLLOQ. deader
SLANG stiff, flatliner

corpulent *adj*
fat, fattish, large, obese, overweight, plump, stout, beefy, bulky, burly, fleshy, portly, pot-bellied, podgy, roly-poly, tubby, well-padded
FORMAL rotund, adipose
Ea thin

corpus *n*
collection, compilation, body, entirety, whole
FORMAL aggregation

corral *n*
enclosure, fold, pound, stall, coop, sty, kraal

correct *adj, v*
♦ *adj*
1 *the correct answer*
right, accurate, precise, exact, strict, true, truthful, actual, real, faithful, word-perfect, faultless, flawless, unerring
COLLOQ. spot-on, bang on
2 PROPER, acceptable, accepted, standard, regular, right, just, appropriate, suitable, fitting, conventional
OLD seemly
COLLOQ. OK
Ea **1** incorrect, wrong, inaccurate
♦ *v*
1 *correct an error*
rectify, put right, right, set right, sort (out), put straight, fix, remedy, cure, debug, redress, adjust, regulate, revise, improve, amend, tweak
FORMAL emend, ameliorate, disabuse
COLLOQ. put the record straight
2 PUNISH, discipline, reprimand, reprove, scold, rebuke, reform, rehabilitate
FORMAL admonish

correction *n*
1 *corrections to the text*
rectification, remedying, adjustment, alteration, modification, amendment, improvement, tweak

FORMAL emendation, amelioration
2 PUNISHMENT, discipline, reprimand, chastisement, reproof, scolding, rebuke, reform, reformation, rehabilitation
FORMAL admonition

corrective *adj*
1 *corrective measures*
remedial, curative, medicinal, palliative, restorative, therapeutic
FORMAL emendatory
2 DISCIPLINARY, disciplinary, penal, punitive, reformatory, rehabilitative

correctly *adv*
1 ACCURATELY, rightly, right, exactly, precisely, actually, faultlessly, flawlessly, unerringly
2 PROPERLY, acceptably, appropriately, suitably, fittingly, conventionally
Ea **1** incorrectly, wrongly, inaccurately

correlate *v*
associate, compare, connect, show a connection/relationship, co-ordinate, correspond, agree, equate, tally, interact, link, parallel, relate, link, tie in

correlation *n*
association, connection, relationship, correspondence, equivalence, interaction, interchange, interdependence, interrelationship, link, reciprocity, fit

correspond *v*
1 MATCH, match up, fit (together), answer, conform, tally, square, agree, be in agreement, be consistent, coincide, harmonize, sympathize, balance, dovetail, complement, be similar, be equivalent, tally, represent
TECHNICAL assonate
FORMAL concur, correlate, accord, be analogous
2 COMMUNICATE, write, pen, exchange letters, keep in touch

correspondence *n*
1 COMMUNICATION, writing, letters, post, mail, e-mail
2 CONFORMITY, agreement, coincidence, relation, analogy, comparison, comparability, similarity, resemblance, equivalence, harmony, match, fit
FORMAL concurrence, correlation, congruity, consonance
Ea **2** divergence, incongruity

correspondent *n*
journalist, reporter, contributor, columnist, writer, letter-writer, pen friend, pen pal

corresponding *adj*
matching, complementary, reciprocal, interrelated, comparable, relative, equivalent, similar, like, matching, agreeing, congruent, parallel, identical
FORMAL commensurate, analogous

corridor *n*
aisle, passageway, passage, gangway, hallway, hall, lobby

corroborate *v*
confirm, prove, bear out, verify, support, back up, endorse, ratify, certify, substantiate, validate, authenticate, document, underpin, uphold, sustain
FORMAL evidence, attest
Ea contradict

corroboration *n*
confirmation, verification, endorsement, ratification, substantiation, authentication, validation
FORMAL attestation
Ea contradiction

corroborative *adj*
confirming, confirmatory, supporting, supportive, verifying, endorsing, substantiating, validating
FORMAL confirmative, evidential, evidentiary, verificatory

corrode v

erode, wear away, eat away, etch, consume, destroy, waste, burn, fret, rust, oxidize, tarnish, impair, deteriorate, rot, crumble, disintegrate
FORMAL abrade

corrosion n

erosion, wasting, burning, rusting, tarnishing, deterioration, rot, rotting, disintegration
FORMAL abrasion

corrosive adj

corroding, acid, caustic, cutting, abrasive, wearing, consuming, destructive, wasting
TECHNICAL erosive

corrugated adj

ridged, fluted, grooved, channelled, furrowed, wrinkled, folded, crinkled, rumpled, creased
TECHNICAL striate

corrupt adj, v

♦ adj

rotten, unscrupulous, unprincipled, unethical, immoral, evil, wicked, fraudulent, dishonest, untrustworthy, bribable, venal, depraved, degenerate, debauched, obscene, abusive, barbarous, dissolute, tainted, contaminated, impure
COLLOQ. shady, bent, crooked
F3 ethical, virtuous, upright, honest, fair, trustworthy

♦ v

1 CONTAMINATE, spoil, pollute, decay, canker, poison, putrefy, rot, adulterate, taint, infect, mar, blight, defile, debase, debauch, pervert, deprave, demoralize, subvert, barbarize, bastardize, warp, be a bad influence, lead astray, lure, seduce, bribe, suborn
OLD empoison, inquinate
COLLOQ. buy (off), grease someone's palm
2 *corrupt a piece of text*
tamper with, adulterate, contaminate, falsify, defile, debase, doctor
FORMAL vitiate
F3 **1** purify

corruption n

1 IMMORALITY, unscrupulousness, impurity, depravity, degeneration, degradation, perversion, debauchery, abuse, distortion, dishonesty, fraud, bribery, subornation, extortion, sharp practice, vice, wickedness, iniquity, evil, criminality, villainy, contamination, pollution, rottenness; N Am graft
COLLOQ. wheeling and dealing, crookedness, shadiness, sleaze
2 *a corruption of a Maori word*
alteration, adaptation, modification
F3 **1** honesty, virtue, fairness, trustworthiness

Synonym nuances
sense 1
Immorality can be widely used to suggest behaviour that is inconsistent with accepted moral standards. **Impurity** implies being tainted in some way, and can be used both of physical and moral corruption: *there was a lethal impurity in the drug.* **Contamination** and **pollution** echo this idea, while **rottenness** suggests the ultimate state of decay or badness, and implies a very unfavourable judgement.
Depravity is a powerful term suggesting a state of complete wickedness, while **degeneration** is only slightly less condemnatory, and suggests heading down that route: *unrivalled degeneration among the young.* **Degradation** is another emotive word, but has elements of disgrace or humiliation: *the degradation of women through pornography.* **Debauchery** is more suggestive of a lewd lifestyle and is strongly censorious in tone. You can use **vice**, **wickedness**, **iniquity** and **evil** to suggest

---

the varying degrees of extreme moral corruption, but all of these make a clear judgement.
The term **sharp practice** describes acts that perhaps just manage to stay just within the law, while **criminality** is specifically used of illegal activity: *the dividing line between sharp practice and criminality is becoming increasingly thin.* **Villainy** is similar but rather old-fashioned or literary in tone.

corset n

girdle, panty girdle, shaper, belt, bodice, corselet, foundation garment, stays, busk, roll-on, waspie

cortège n

procession, retinue, suite, train, column, entourage, cavalcade, parade

cosily adv

snugly, comfortably, warmly, safely, securely, initmately

cosmetic adj

1 *a cosmetic substance*
make-up, beauty, beautifying
2 *cosmetic changes*
superficial, surface, external, shallow, skin-deep, peripheral, minor, slight, trivial
F3 **2** basic, essential

cosmetics

Types of cosmetics include:

blusher	face powder	moisturizer
bronzer	false eyelashes	nail polish
cleanser	foundation	nail varnish
concealer	greasepaint	pancake make-
eyebrow pencil	kohl pencil	up
eyelash dye	lip gloss	panstick
eyeliner	lip liner	pressed powder
eye shadow	lipstick	rouge
face cream	loose powder	toner
face mask	maquillage	
face pack	mascara	

---

cosmic adj

1 *cosmic forces*
worldwide, universal, in/from space, infinite, limitless, measureless
2 *changes of cosmic proportion*
immense, vast, huge, enormous, colossal, massive, grandiose, infinite, limitless, immeasurable, measureless
SLANG mega, seismic

cosmonaut n

astronaut, spaceman, spacewoman, space traveller

cosmopolitan adj

1 *a very cosmopolitan city*
international, universal, multiracial, multicultural
2 *a very cosmopolitan outlook*
worldly, worldly-wise, well-travelled, broad-minded, sophisticated, cultured, urbane
F3 **2** insular, parochial

cosmos n

universe, creation, galaxy, system, worlds

cosset v

coddle, mollycoddle, baby, pamper, indulge, overindulge, spoil, pet, fondle, cuddle, cherish

cost n, v

♦ n

1 EXPENSE, outlay, payment, expenditure, charge, price, selling price, asking price, rate, fee, tariff, levy, toll, quotation, amount, figure, value, valuation, worth
FORMAL disbursement
COLLOQ. damage
2 *cover costs*

budget, expenses, expenditure, spending, outgoings, outlay, overheads
FORMAL disbursements

3 *the cost to her health of smoking*
harm, injury, hurt, loss, suffering, deprivation, detriment, sacrifice, penalty, price

♦ *v*

1 *it costs £500*
pay, charge, be priced at, ask for, sell for, retail at, buy for, be valued at, be worth, fetch, go for, come to, amount to
COLLOQ. set back, knock back

2 *cost a job*
price, estimate, cost out, quote, value, calculate, work out

3 *cost him his life*
cause the loss/sacrifice of, cause harm/injury, destroy, deprive, take, harm, injure, hurt, be a high price to pay

costly *adj*

1 EXPENSIVE, dear, exorbitant, extortionate, excessive, lavish, rich, splendid, valuable, precious, high-cost, high-priced, overpriced, priceless
OLD chargeful
COLLOQ. steep, pricey, posh, sky-high, costing an arm and a leg, costing the earth, costing a bomb, daylight robbery; *N Am* big-ticket
OLD SLANG salt
2 HARMFUL, damaging, destructive, detrimental, disastrous, ruinous, catastrophic, loss-making
FORMAL deleterious
E3 1 cheap, inexpensive

costume *n*

outfit, uniform, livery, ensemble, robes, vestments, suit, dress, style of dress, fashion, clothes, clothing, garments, garb, habit, fancy dress
FORMAL apparel, attire
COLLOQ. get-up, clobber, rig-out
SLANG threads

cosy *adj*

snug, comfortable, warm, sheltered, secure, safe, homely, congenial, intimate
COLLOQ. comfy
E3 uncomfortable, cold

coterie *n*

set, circle, clique, group, club, association, community, faction, camp, caucus, cabal, gang

cottage *n*

lodge, chalet, bungalow, villa, hut, cabin, shack, shanty

couch *n, v*

♦ *n*
sofa, settee, chesterfield, chaise-longue, ottoman, divan, bed, day bed, sofa bed

♦ *v*
express, frame, phrase, word, set, bear, support, utter, cradle

cough *v, n*

♦ *v*
clear your throat, bark, hack, hawk, hem

♦ *n*
bark, hack, rasp, croak, hawking, hem, clearing your throat
TECHNICAL tussis
OLD (*Shakesp*) tisick
COLLOQ. frog in your throat

▪ **cough up**
pay up, pay, pay out, hand over, give; *N Am* ante up
COLLOQ. fork out, shell out, stump up

council *n*

1 *the town council*
local authority, corporation, cabinet, ministry, chamber, parliament, government, governing body, senate, administration, executive

2 *the Arts Council*

advisory body, advisory group, committee, panel, jury, commission, directorate, directors, trustees, governors, advisers, board, working party, focus group, management

3 *a ministerial council*
congress, assembly, convention, conference, forum, gathering, rally, meeting, convocation, group, body, body of people, company, congregation, flock, crowd, multitude, throng
FORMAL convocation
Related adjective: conciliar

⚠ council or **counsel**?
A *council* is 'a body of people who organize, control, advise or take decisions': *a county council. Counsel* is a rather formal word for 'advice': *give wise counsel.*

---

counsel *n, v*

♦ *n*
1 ADVICE, suggestion, recommendation, guidance, direction, information, consultation, conferring, conference, deliberation, consideration, forethought, opinion, viewpoint, suggestion, moralism
OLD (*Spenser*) read
FORMAL exhortation, admonition

2 *counsel for the defence*
lawyer, advocate, solicitor, attorney, barrister, *avocat consultant*

♦ *v*
advise, warn, caution, suggest, recommend, advocate, urge, exhort, guide, give guidance, direct, teach, instruct, give your opinion
OLD aread, rede
FORMAL exhort, admonish

counsellor *n*

consultant, authority, guide, teacher, tutor, instructor, coach, mentor, therapist, guru, confidant(e)

count *v, n*

♦ *v*
1 NUMBER, enumerate, list, include, reckon, calculate, compute, tell, check, add (up), total, score, tally
COLLOQ. tot up
2 MATTER, be important, signify, qualify, carry weight, make a difference, make an impression, mean something
COLLOQ. cut some ice
3 *count yourself lucky*
consider, regard, judge, think, reckon, look upon, hold, feel
FORMAL esteem, deem
4 *if you count children*
include, take account of, take into account, take into consideration, consider, allow for

♦ *n*
numbering, enumeration, poll, reckoning, calculation, computation, sum, total, tally, number, whole, full amount
COLLOQ. totting-up

▪ **count in**
include, involve, let in on, put in, introduce, allow for, allow to take part in
COLLOQ. rope in

▪ **count on**
depend on, rely on, bank on, lean on, reckon on, swear by, expect, believe, trust

▪ **count out**
exclude, eliminate, ignore, leave out, omit, pass over, disregard, include out
E3 include, consider

countenance *n, v*

♦ *n*
face, expression, appearance, features, look
FORMAL mien, physiognomy, visage

♦ *v*
tolerate, agree, allow, permit, approve, brook, stand for, put up with, back, condone, endorse, endure, sanction

counter¹ n

1 *serve at the counter*
worktop, surface, work surface, table, stand, bar
2 *a counter in a game*
disc, token, chip, piece, coin, marker

counter² v, adv, adj

♦ v
counter someone's argument
parry, resist, oppose, combat, dispute, offset,
answer, respond, retaliate, retort, hit back at, return,
meet
♦ adv
against, in opposition, contrary, conversely
♦ adj
contrary, opposite, opposing, conflicting, contradictory,
contrasting, opposed, against, adverse

counteract v

neutralize, counterbalance, offset, act against, oppose,
resist, hinder, check, thwart, frustrate, prevent, foil, defeat,
undo, annul, invalidate
FORMAL negate, countervail
◼ support, assist

counterbalance v

balance, compensate for, make up for, equalize, neutralize,
offset, undo
FORMAL counterpoise, countervail

counterfeit adj, n, v

♦ adj
fake, faked, false, forged, copied, pirate, fraudulent, bogus,
sham, spurious, imitation, artificial, simulated, pretended,
borrowed, queer, base, snide, postiche
FORMAL feigned, simular
COLLOQ. phoney, pseud, pseudo, brummagem
◼ genuine, authentic, real
♦ n
fake, forgery, copy, reproduction, imitation, fraud, sham,
dummy
COLLOQ. dud
♦ v
fake, forge, fabricate, copy, imitate, disguise, phantasm,
reproduce, pirate, impersonate, falsify, pretend, simulate,
sham, camouflage
FORMAL feign
COLLOQ. phoney

countermand v

cancel, reverse, annul, override, overturn, quash,
repeal
FORMAL abrogate, rescind, revoke

counterpart n

equivalent, opposite number, equal, complement,
supplement, parallel, match, fellow, mate, peer, twin,
duplicate, copy, obverse

counterpoint n, v

♦ n
contrast, foil, differentiation, set-off, opposite, relief,
complement
♦ v
contrast, differentiate, set off, foil, enhance, heighten,
intensify, throw into relief

countless adj

innumerable, myriad, numberless, unnumbered, untold,
incalculable, infinite, endless, without end, legion,
immeasurable, measureless, inexhaustible, limitless,
boundless
COLLOQ. umpteen
◼ finite, limited

countrified adj

rural, rustic, pastoral, provincial, idyllic, agricultural,
agrarian, outback

FORMAL bucolic
COLLOQ. hick
◼ urban; *formal* oppidan

country n, adj

♦ n
1 STATE, nation, kingdom, realm, republic, power,
community, principality, inhabitants, people, population,
populace, public, residents, citizens, voters, electors
2 COUNTRYSIDE, green belt, farmland, moorland, rural area,
outback, bush
COLLOQ. provinces, backwater, backwoods, wilds, sticks,
back of beyond, middle of nowhere; *Aust & NZ* beyond
the black stump
Related adjective: rural
3 TERRAIN, land, territory, region, area, district,
neighbourhood, locality
◼**2** town, city
♦ adj
rural, rustic, pastoral, landed, provincial, idyllic,
agricultural, agrarian
FORMAL bucolic
◼ urban

countryman, countrywoman n

1 *fellow countrywomen*
compatriot, fellow citizen, fellow national
2 *local countrymen's skills*
farmer, yokel, boor, clodhopper, rustic, peasant,
provincial, backwoodsman, bushwhacker; *Scot* hind
COLLOQ. bumpkin, hillbilly, hick, hayseed

countryside n

landscape, scenery, country, green belt, farmland,
moorland, rural area, outdoors

county n

shire, province, region, area, state, territory, district,
department
Related adjective: comital

coup n

1 *a military coup*
coup d'état, overthrow, revolution, (military) takeover,
uprising, insurrection, palace revolution, putsch, rebellion,
revolt
2 *a big coup for the company*
feat, success, triumph, masterstroke, stroke,
accomplishment, deed, exploit, stunt, action, manoeuvre,
tour de force

coup de grâce n

death blow, finishing blow
FORMAL quietus
COLLOQ. clincher, kiss of death, kibosh, kill

coup d'état n

coup, overthrow, revolution, (military) takeover, uprising,
insurrection, palace revolution, putsch, rebellion, revolt

couple n, v

♦ n
pair, husband and wife, newlyweds, partners, lovers,
brace, twosome, duo
♦ v
pair, match, marry, wed, unite, join, link, connect,
combine, integrate, ally, associate, attach, fasten, hitch,
clasp, bind, buckle, yoke
FORMAL conjoin

coupon n

voucher, token, slip, check, stub, counterfoil, docket,
ticket, certificate, form

courage n

bravery, pluck, fearlessness, dauntlessness, heroism,
gallantry, valour, boldness, audacity, intrepidity, daring,
determination, resolution, spirit, mettle, backbone, heart,
gumption

FORMAL fortitude
COLLOQ. nerve, guts, bottle, spunk, grit, stomach
SLANG balls; *N Am* cojones, moxie
E3 cowardice, fear
*See Synonym nuances panel at **bravery**.*

courageous *adj*

brave, plucky, fearless, dauntless, indomitable, heroic, gallant, valiant, lion-hearted, stout-hearted, full-hearted, high-hearted, hardy, bold, audacious, daring, intrepid, adventurous, determined, resolute
FORMAL valorous
COLLOQ. gutsy, spunky, feisty
E3 cowardly, afraid

courageously *adv*

bravely, boldly, fearlessly, audaciously, intrepidly, dauntlessly, indomitably, heroically, gallantly, valiantly, resolutely, adventurously
E3 fearfully, timidly

courier *n*

1 *the courier delivered the parcels*
messenger, carrier, dispatch rider, runner, bearer, emissary, envoy, representative, herald, legate, nuncio, estafette, pursuivant
2 *a guided tour by the courier*
guide, travel guide, tour guide, escort, company representative
COLLOQ. rep

course *n, v*

♦ *n*
1 CURRICULUM, syllabus, programme, schedule, classes, lessons, lectures, studies
2 FLOW, movement, advance, march, rise, progress, development, unfolding, furtherance, order, sequence, series, succession, progression
3 DURATION, time, period, lapse, term, spell, span, passing, passage
4 ROUTE, direction, way, passage, path, track, tack, road, lane, run, channel, trail, line, circuit, orbit, ambit, trajectory, flight path
5 *course of action*
plan, schedule, programme, policy, procedure, system, process, manner, method, way, approach, tack
FORMAL mode
6 *the last hole on the course*
golf course, racecourse, racetrack, track, ground, circuit
7 *chicken for main course*
dish, part, stage, remove, starter, *hors d'œuvre*, appetizer, entrée, main course, dessert, sweet, pudding, entremets
8 *a course of medical treatment*
sequence, series, programme, schedule, regimen
♦ *v*
1 *tears coursing down her cheeks*
flow, run, move, pour, gush, stream, surge, race, dash
2 *coursing hares*
chase, hunt, pursue, run after, follow, track, race
■ **in due course**
in time, in due time, sooner or later, in the fullness of time, in the course of time, finally, eventually
■ **of course**
naturally, certainly, surely, by all means, definitely, without a doubt, no doubt, undoubtedly, doubtlessly, needless to say, to be sure
FORMAL indubitably
SLANG natch

court *n, v*

♦ *n*
1 LAWCOURT, bench, bar, judiciary, tribunal, trial, session, assizes, see
2 *tennis courts*
playing area, game area, enclosure, track, ground, arena, ring, alley, green

3 COURTYARD, yard, quadrangle, square, patio, cloister, forecourt, enclosure, plaza, esplanade, piazza
COLLOQ. quad
4 *at the king's court*
palace, castle, royal residence
5 ENTOURAGE, attendants, household, retinue, suite, train, cortège
♦ *v*
1 *court a young lady*
woo, pursue, chase, go out with, go around/round with, go with, date, go steady
2 *court support/publicity*
cultivate, try to win, solicit, flatter, pander to, curry favour with, ingratiate yourself with, attract, prompt, provoke, incite, seek, invite, risk
COLLOQ. *N Am* cozy up with

Types of court include:

Admiralty Division	Court of Exchequer	House of Lords
assizes	court of justice	Industrial tribunals
Central Criminal Court	Court of Protection	International Court of Justice
Chancery Division	Court of Session	juvenile court
children's court	criminal court	Lord Chancellor's Court
circuit court	crown court	magistrates' court
civil court	district court	municipal court
coroner's court	divorce court	Old Bailey
county court	European Court of Justice	police court
court-martial	family court	Privy Council
court of appeals	federal court	sheriff court
court of claims	High Court	small claims court
Court of Common Pleas	High Court of Justiciary	Supreme Court

---

courteous *adj*

polite, civil, respectful, well-mannered, well-bred, deferential, ladylike, gentlemanly, mannerly, gracious, obliging, considerate, kind, diplomatic, tactful, attentive, gallant, chivalrous, courtly, urbane, debonair, refined, polished
E3 discourteous, impolite, rude

courteously *adv*

politely, civilly, respectfully, deferentially, graciously, obligingly, considerately, kindly, diplomatically, tactfully, attentively, gallantly, chivalrously, urbanely, refinedly
E3 discourteously, impolitely, rudely

courtesy *n*

politeness, civility, respect, etiquette, (good) manners, (good) breeding, deference, graciousness, consideration, kindness, favour, generosity, tact, attention, gallantry, chivalry, refinement, urbanity, gentility, devoir
OLD gentilesse; (*Shakesp*) gentry
FORMAL comity
E3 discourtesy, incivility, rudeness

courtier *n*

noble, nobleman, lord, lady, lady-in-waiting, steward, page, attendant, cup-bearer, train-bearer, subject, liegeman, follower, flatterer, sycophant, toady

courtly *adj*

gracious, dignified, polite, refined, obliging, polished, elegant, stately, aristocratic, high-bred, lordly, ceremonious, gallant, chivalrous, civil, formal, decorous, flattering
E3 inelegant, provincial, rough

courtship *n*

wooing, pursuit, suit, courting, chasing, going-out, dating, going steady, romance, affair
OLD (*Shakesp*) love-suit

courtyard *n*
yard, quadrangle, area, enclosure, court, square, cloister, forecourt, plaza, patio, esplanade, atrium, cortile, garth, marae
COLLOQ. quad

cove *n*
bay, bight, inlet, estuary, firth, fiord, creek

covenant *n, v*
● *n*
arrangement, promise, contract, bond, commitment, deed, engagement, pact, pledge, treaty, trust, convention, stipulation, undertaking
OLD warranty
FORMAL testament, indenture, compact, concordat
Related adjective: federal
● *v*
agree, contract, promise, stipulate, undertake, engage, pledge, vow

cover *v, n*
● *v*
1 HIDE, put/place over, conceal, bury, obscure, shroud, veil, wreathe, screen, mask, disguise, camouflage
2 *covered with mud*
be over, coat, spread, overspread, daub, plaster, cake, encase, wrap, envelop, blanket, carpet, swaddle, clothe, dress, overlay
FORMAL attire, accoutre
3 SHELTER, put/place over, protect, shield, guard, safeguard, defend
4 *cover a topic*
deal with, treat, consider, examine, investigate, give details of, review, survey, report, describe, encompass, embrace, incorporate, embody, involve, include, contain, comprise, take in
5 *cover 25 miles*
travel (over), cross, go, go across, journey, go, do
FORMAL traverse
6 *cover for a colleague*
stand in for, fill in for, deputize, relieve, replace, take over from, be a replacement/substitute for
COLLOQ. *N Am* pinch-hit for
7 *the estate covers some 500 acres*
extend over, stretch, continue, stretch, measure
8 *£50 to cover expenses*
pay for, be enough for, recompense, make up for, compensate for, counterbalance, balance out
9 *the insurance will cover it*
protect, insure, underwrite, provide for
FORMAL indemnify
10 *journalists covering an event*
report, describe, give details of, tell, talk/write about, give an account of, narrate, present, investigate, analyse
F3 1 uncover **2** strip **3** expose **4** exclude
● *n*
1 SHELTER, refuge, protection, shield, guard, defence, concealment, hiding-place, sanctuary, refuge, disguise, camouflage
2 COVERING, coating, top, lid, cup, jacket, wrapper, sleeve, binding, case, envelope, package, coat, layer, film, skin, carpet, mantle, clothing, dress, bedclothes, bedding, blankets, duvet, bedspread, throw, canopy
3 *as a cover for illegal activity*
cover-up, concealment, screen, smokescreen, veil, screen, mask, front, façade, pretence, conspiracy, complicity
COLLOQ. whitewash
4 *insurance cover*
protection, insurance, security, compensation, assurance
FORMAL indemnity, indemnification
■ **cover up**
conceal, hide, suppress, keep secret, keep dark, repress, gloss over

FORMAL dissemble
COLLOQ. whitewash, hush up
F3 disclose, reveal

coverage *n*
reporting, report(s), description, account, investigation, analysis, item, story, reportage

covering *n, adj*
● *n*
layer, coat, coating, blanket, carpet, film, veneer, skin, crust, case, shell, casing, housing, wrapping, clothing, protection, shelter, mask, overlay, cover, top, shelter, roof, roofing, awning, tarpaulin
● *adj*
accompanying, explanatory, descriptive, introductory

covert *adj*
hidden, secret, private, clandestine, concealed, disguised, veiled, sneaky, stealthy, furtive, sidelong, surreptitious, unsuspected, ulterior, underhand
FORMAL dissembled, subreptitious
COLLOQ. under the table
F3 open, overt

covertly *adv*
secretly, privately, furtively, surreptitiously
F3 openly, overtly

cover-up *n*
concealment, screen, smokescreen, front, faõcade, pretence, deception, conspiracy, complicity
COLLOQ. whitewash

covet *v*
desire, crave, long for, yearn for, hanker for, want, hunger/thirst for, lust after, envy, begrudge
COLLOQ. fancy

covetous *adj*
yearning, craving, wanting, longing, hankering, hungering, thirsting, acquisitive, grasping, greedy, insatiable, jealous, envious
FORMAL desirous, avaricious, rapacious
F3 generous, temperate

covey *n*
cluster, flight, flock, group, brood, hatch, party, set, band, company, bevy, nid, skein

cow *v*
intimidate, domineer, browbeat, bully, terrorize, frighten, scare, overawe, subdue, unnerve, daunt, dishearten, discourage, dismay
COLLOQ. rattle
F3 encourage

coward *n*
craven, faint-heart, weakling, poltroon, renegade, deserter
OLD cowheard, cowherd, recreant, dastard, nithing, hilding, viliaco, viliago
COLLOQ. chicken, scaredy-cat, yellow-belly, sissy, crybaby, wimp; *Aust* sook
SLANG *N Am* wuss; *Aust* cat, dingo
F3 hero

cowardice *n*
cowardliness, faint-heartedness, weak-spiritedness, fearfulness, spiritlessness, timidity, timorousness, spinelessness
FORMAL pusillanimity
F3 courage, bravery, valour

cowardly *adj*
faint-hearted, craven, fearful, timid, coward, dastardly, timorous, scared, unheroic, unmanly, chicken-hearted, chicken-livered, white-livered, lily-livered, spiritless, spineless, weak, weak-spirited, weak-kneed, soft, jittery; *dialect* mangy, nesh

OLD faint, nithing; (*Shakesp*) cowish, milk-livered, meacock
FORMAL pusillanimous
COLLOQ. chicken, gutless, wimpish, yellow-bellied, yellow, showing the white feather
E3 brave, courageous, bold

Synonym nuances
Faint-hearted, **fearful**, **timid** and **timorous** simply suggest a lack of spirit or mettle: *the mountain pass is a sore trial for a timid car driver*. **Craven** makes a strong statement by further implying total temerity: *craven abdication of his duty*. **Dastardly** is similar but literary in tone, and suggests an underhand element: *a dastardly plan was hatched*.
 Unheroic and **unmanly** suggest a lack of certain expected qualities and are in themselves rather negative, although in particular contexts the tone may not necessarily be unfavourable: *a modest leader with an unheroic attitude to war; American officers consider community policing as 'unmanly'.*
 The terms **chicken-hearted**, **chicken-livered** and **white-livered** are insulting ways to suggest that someone lacks courage; **spiritless**, **spineless** and **soft**, as well as **weak**, **weak-spirited**, **weak-kneed** all suggest a lack of fortitude or resolution, but are similarly derogatory: *the authorities are being spineless.*

---

cowboy *n*
1 *cowboys to look after cattle*
drover, cattleman, cowhand, herdsman, cattleherder, herder, stockman, rancher, ranchero, waddy; *N Am* bronco-buster, buckaroo, cowpoke, cowpuncher, gaucho, vaquero, wrangler
2 *a plumbing firm full of cowboys*
bungler, incompetent, rascal, rogue, cheat, fraudster, scoundrel, swindler
E3 2 professional

cower *v*
crouch, grovel, skulk, shrink, flinch, draw back, recoil, wince, cringe, quail, tremble, quake, shake, shiver

co-worker *n*
colleague, workmate, teammate, partner, collaborator, ally, associate, confederate, confrère, comrade, fellow worker, companion, aide, helper, assistant, auxiliary

coy *adj*
modest, demure, prudish, prim, diffident, shy, bashful, timid, shrinking, backward, retiring, self-effacing, withdrawn, reserved, reticence, evasive, arch, flirtatious, coquettish, skittish, kittenish
E3 bold, forward

coyly *adv*
modestly, bashfully, demurely, primly, prudishly, diffidently, timidly, self-effacingly, evasively, flirtatiously, coquesttishly
E3 boldly, forwardly

crabbed, crabby *adj*
bad-tempered, cross, ill-tempered, irritable, fractious, morose, snappish, cantankerous, petulant, perverse, acrid, acrimonious, awkward, difficult, harsh, tough, sour, captious, churlish, fretful, snappy, surly, tart, testy, prickly, splenetic
FORMAL iracund, iracundulous, irascible, misanthropic
COLLOQ. crotchety, grouchy
E3 calm, placid

crack *v, n, adj*
 ♦ *v*
1 SPLIT, burst, fracture, break, snap, shatter, splinter, fragment, chip
2 EXPLODE, go bang, bang, detonate, boom, burst, pop,

crackle, snap, crash, bash, hit, beat, strike, clap, clout, slap, bump
COLLOQ. whack, wallop
3 *crack under pressure*
lose control, collapse, break down, go to pieces, cave in
4 *crack a code*
decipher, docode, decrypt, work out, solve, resolve, unravel, figure out, find the answer to
COLLOQ. *N Am* dope (out)
 ♦ *n*
1 BREAK, fracture, flaw, chip, split, rift, breach, rupture, gap, crevice, fissure, cleft, cavity, chink, line, cranny
2 EXPLOSION, bang, boom, detonation, burst, pop, snap, crash, clap, clout, blow, smack, slap, hit, bump
FORMAL report
COLLOQ. whack
3 *have a crack at something*
attempt, go, try, effort
COLLOQ. bash, shot, stab, whirl
4 JOKE, quip, witticism, one-liner, wisecrack, gibe, repartee
COLLOQ. gag, dig
 ♦ *adj*
first-class, first-rate, excellent, outstanding, brilliant, superior, choice, hand-picked, expert, skilled, skilful
COLLOQ. top-notch
■ **crack down on**
clamp down on, end, stop, put a stop to, crush, suppress, check, control, limit, restrict, confine, repress, act against
COLLOQ. get tough on
■ **crack up**
1 BREAK DOWN, lose control, go to pieces, fall apart, have a nervous breakdown, collapse, go mad, go crazy
SLANG go ballisitic
2 LAUGH UNCONTROLLABLY, dissolve into laughter
COLLOQ. be rolling in the aisles, fall about, split your sides

crackdown *n*
clampdown, crushing, end, check, stop, repression, suppression

cracked *adj*
1 *a cracked glass*
broken, chipped, damaged, defective, flawed, imperfect, faulty, fissured, split, torn
2 *they're cracked*
crazy, insane, deranged, crazed, foolish, idiotic
COLLOQ. daft, barmy, batty, crackbrained, crackpot, nuts, nutty, round the bend; *Aust & NZ* dingbats
SLANG loony, off your rocker, out of your tree
E3 1 flawless, perfect **2** sane, of sound mind

crackers *adj*
cracked, crazy, mad, foolish, idiotic
COLLOQ. daft, batty, crackbrained, crackpot, nuts, nutty, round the bend
SLANG loony
E3 sane, sound

crackle *v, n*
 ♦ *v*
snap, crack, sizzle, rustle
FORMAL crepitate, decrepitate
 ♦ *n*
snap, crack, sizzle, rustle
FORMAL crepitation, crepitus, decrepitation

crackpot *n*
idiot, fool
COLLOQ. freak, weirdo, oddball, nutter, nutcase
SLANG loony, basket case

cradle *n, v*
 ♦ *n*
1 COT, carry-cot, Moses basket, travel-cot, crib, bassinet, bed, *berceau*
FORMAL cunabula

2 SOURCE, origin, spring, wellspring, fount, fountain-head, birthplace, starting-point, beginning
FORMAL incunabula
3 *put the telephone receiver back on its cradle*
rocker, holder, rest, prop, stand, base, support, mount, mounting, frame, framework
♦ *v*
hold, support, rock, lull, nestle, nurse, shelter, nurture, tend

craft *n*
1 SKILL, expertise, mastery, talent, knack, flair, ability, skilfulness, expertness, aptitude, dexterity, cleverness, artistry, art, handicraft, handiwork, workmanship, technique
2 TRADE, business, calling, vocation, job, occupation, work, employment, line, activity, pursuit
3 VESSEL, boat, ship, aircraft, spacecraft, spaceship, landing craft
4 CUNNING, cunningness, craftiness, slyness, art, artfulness, trickery, deviousness, subtlety, deceit, deceitfulness, guile, wiles, sharpness, shrewdness, astuteness, ingenuity, cleverness, imaginativeness, sleight, inventiveness, resourcefulness, deftness, finesse, adroitness, fiendishness, Machiavellianism
OLD (*Shakesp*) foxship

craftily *adv*
slyly, cunningly, artfully, deviously, deceitfully, guilefully, fraudulently, shrewdly, astutely
🖅 naively

craftsman, craftswoman *n*
artist, artisan, technician, mechanic, expert, master, maker, tradesman, tradeswoman, tradesperson, craftsperson, skilled worker, wright, smith

craftsmanship *n*
artistry, workmanship, skill, skilfulness, technique, dexterity, expertise, mastery

crafty *adj*
sly, cunning, artful, wily, foxy, devious, subtle, scheming, calculating, conniving, designing, deceitful, guileful, fraudulent, sharp, shrewd, astute, canny, tricksy, guileful, knackish, knacky, Machiavellian, versute, slim, subdolous; *Scot* loopy
FORMAL duplicitous, disingenuous
COLLOQ. crooked
🖅 artless, naive, guileless

crag *n*
bluff, cliff, escarpment, scarp, ridge, peak, pinnacle, rock, tor

craggy *adj*
1 *a craggy cliff*
precipitous, rocky, rough, rough-hewn, rugged, cragged, stony, jagged, uneven
2 *a craggy face*
rough, rugged, jagged, uneven, weather-beaten, marked
🖅 **2** smooth

cram *v*
1 *cram sweets into your mouth*
stuff, jam, ram, force, press, squeeze, crush, compress, pack, crowd, overcrowd, fill (up), overfill, glut, gorge
FORMAL compact
2 *cram for an exam*
revise, study hard
COLLOQ. swot, mug up, bone up on, grind

cramp *n, v*
♦ *n*
pain, ache, twinge, pang, contraction, convulsion, spasm, muscular contraction, crick, stitch, pins and needles, stiffness
♦ *v*

hinder, hamper, obstruct, impede, inhibit, handicap, thwart, frustrate, check, restrict, limit, bridle, rein, hamstring, arrest, constrain, restrain, confine, stymie, shackle, tie

cramped *adj*
narrow, tight, small, uncomfortable, poky, restricted, confined, crowded, packed, squashed, squeezed, closed in, hemmed in, overcrowded, full, overfull, jam-packed, congested
COLLOQ. no room to swing a cat
🖅 spacious

crane *n*
derrick, hoist, tackle, winch, block and tackle, davit

crank *n, v*
♦ *n*
eccentric, character, madman, idiot
COLLOQ. freak, weirdo, oddball, nutter, kook, crackpot
SLANG loony
■ **crank up**
increase, intensify, step up, build up, add to, further, strengthen
COLLOQ. hike up

cranky *adj*
1 ECCENTRIC, odd, peculiar, unconventional, strange, bizarre, freakish, fey, queer, idiosyncratic
COLLOQ. wacky, dotty, screwy
2 BAD-TEMPERED, cross, ill-tempered, irritable, cantankerous, awkward, difficult, harsh, snappy, surly, tart, testy, prickly
COLLOQ. crabby, crotchety, grouchy
🖅 **1** normal, sensible **2** calm, placid

cranny *n*
chink, cleft, crack, crevice, fissure, rent, gap, hole, slit, nook, opening, cleavage
FORMAL interstice

crash *n, v, adj*
♦ *n*
1 *a car crash*
accident, collision, bump, pile-up, wreck; *Scot* frush
OLD rack
COLLOQ. smash, smash-up, prang; *Aust* bingle
2 BANG, clash, clatter, clang, clank, thud, thump, boom, explosion, thunder, thunderclap, clap, smash, racket, din
OLD fragor
3 *stock market crash*
collapse, failure, ruin, downfall, fall, bankruptcy, depression, meltdown, black Monday
♦ *v*
1 COLLIDE, hit, knock, bump, bang, run into, go into, drive into, smash into, plough into, ditch
COLLOQ. bash, prang, shunt, wham
2 BREAK, fracture, smash, batter, dash, pound, shatter, splinter, shiver, fragment, disintegrate
3 FALL, topple, pitch, plunge, collapse, fail, fold (up), founder, go under, go into liquidation
COLLOQ. go bust, go to the wall
4 *the computer crashed*
cut out, break down, stop working, fail
FORMAL malfunction
COLLOQ. pack up, go on the blink, go phut, go kaput
♦ *adj*
intensive, rapid, accelerated, concentrated, telescoped, emergency, immediate, round-the-clock, urgent

crass *adj*
stupid, indelicate, tasteless, insensitive, tactless, unrefined, unsophisticated, blundering, rude, crude, coarse, dense, oafish, clumsy, unsubtle, witless
FORMAL obtuse
🖅 refined, sensitive

crassly adv
stupidly, clumsily, indelicately, insensitively, tactlessly, rudely, crudely, coarsely, tastelessly
⊟ sensitively

crate n
container, box, case, chest, tea chest, packing-box, packing-case; dialect & Scot kist

crater n
hollow, depression, hole, basin, bowl, dip, pit, cavity, chasm, abyss

crave v
hunger for, thirst for, long for, yearn for, pine for, sigh for, hanker after, pant for, lust after, desire, covet, want, dream of, wish, need, require
COLLOQ. be dying for, fancy
⊟ dislike

craven adj
cowardly, faint-hearted, fearful, timorous, timid, scared, afraid, unheroic, chicken-hearted, white-livered, chicken-livered, lily-livered, mean-spirited, spineless, spiritless, weak, weak-spirited, weak-kneed, soft
OLD recreant, poltroon
FORMAL pusillanimous
COLLOQ. chicken, gutless, yellow
⊟ brave, courageous, bold

craving n
appetite, hunger, thirst, longing, yearning, pining, sighing, hankering, panting, lust, desire, wish, need, urge
⊟ dislike, distaste

crawl v
1 CREEP, go on all fours, move on your hands and knees, inch, edge, slither, wriggle, squirm, writhe, drag, move/advance slowly
2 GROVEL, cringe, toady, fawn, flatter, bow and scrape, curry favour
FORMAL be obsequious to
COLLOQ. be all over, suck up, creep, kowtow
3 the city centre crawling with police
teem, swarm, seethe, bristle, be full of

craze n
fad, novelty, fashion, vogue, mode, trend, obsession, preoccupation, mania, frenzy, passion, infatuation, whim, enthusiasm
COLLOQ. rage, the latest, thing

crazed adj
mad, insane, lunatic, unbalanced, deranged, demented, crazy, wild, berserk, unhinged, out of your mind
COLLOQ. nuts, round the bend, round the twist
SLANG loony, off your rocker

crazily adv
madly, insanely, wildly, franctically, frenetically, manically

crazy adj
1 MAD, insane, lunatic, unbalanced, disturbed, deranged, demented, crazed, wild, berserk, frantic, unhinged, distracted, distraught, frenetic, maniac, out of your mind, infuriate; Scot gyte
OLD frantic-mad, lymphatic, bestraught
COLLOQ. crazy, demented, nuts, nutty, nutty as a fruitcake, wacky, mad as a hatter, barmy, bonkers, batty, cracked, crackers, dippy, daffy, dotty, loopy, potty, off your nut, off your head, wrong in the head, out of your head, off the wall, out to lunch, round the bend, round the twist, bats, having bats in the belfry, cuckoo, off the rails, screwy, up the wall, raving, not all there; N Am buggy, flaky, fruity; Aust & NZ dingbats
SLANG loony, mental, bananas, barking, wacko, doolally, off your rocker, off your chump, off your trolley, out of your tree, needing your head examined, having lost your marbles, having a screw loose, having a tile loose, having

several cards short of a full deck, with one sandwich short of a picnic, meshuga; N Am gonzo, loco, wiggy
2 What a crazy idea!
silly, foolish, idiotic, stupid, senseless, unwise, imprudent, nonsensical, absurd, odd, peculiar, ludicrous, ridiculous, preposterous, outrageous, impracticable, unrealistic, foolhardy, irresponsible, wild; Aust strange
COLLOQ. daft, barmy, batty, potty, half-baked, hare-brained, crackbrained, crackpot
3 crazy about golf
enthusiastic, fanatical, zealous, devoted, fond, keen, avid, ardent, passionate, infatuated, enamoured, smitten, mad, wild
COLLOQ. daft, nuts, potty
⊟ **1** sane **2** sensible **3** indifferent

Synonym nuances
sense 1
Mad can be widely used to suggest any incomprehensible behaviour or deviation from mental norms, whilst **insane** and **lunatic** may be used to suggest extreme irrationality: a policy of lunatic aggression. Both **distracted**, which is a fairly mild term, and **distraught**, which is rather stronger, could be used where someone's whole attention is taken up by something, usually upsetting: distraught at the separation from her husband. **Unbalanced** and **disturbed** suggest being out of kilter, possibly mildly, while **unhinged**, **deranged** and **demented** imply situations where the mind has undergone more deeply troubling changes, and someone's mental ability has degenerated: demented by grief. **Wild** and **berserk** are appropriately used of outrageous behaviour; **frenetic** and **maniac** of a highly excited manner: a frenetic flurry of activity. The term **frantic** is similar, but hints at a strong element of anxiety: frantic signalling.

---

creak v
squeak, groan, grate, scrape, rasp, scratch, grind, squeal, screech

creaky adj
squeaky, squeaking, groaning, grating, scraping, rasping, scratching, grinding, squealing, screeching, rusty, unoiled

cream n, adj
♦ n
1 PASTE, emulsion, oil, lotion, ointment, preparation, application, salve, cosmetic
TECHNICAL emollient, liniment, unguent
2 BEST, pick, élite, flower, choice/select part, prime, finest, pick of the bunch, crème de la crème
♦ adj
yellowish-white, whitish-yellow, off-white, ivory, pale, pasty, milky

creamy adj
1 CREAM-COLOURED, off-white, ivory, yellowish-white, whitish-yellow, pale, pasty, milky
2 MILKY, buttery, oily, smooth, velvety, rich, thick

crease v, n
♦ v
fold, pleat, wrinkle, pucker, crumple, rumple, crinkle, crimp, tuck, corrugate, groove, furrow, ridge
♦ n
fold, line, pleat, tuck, wrinkle, pucker, ruck, crinkle, corrugation, furrow, ridge, groove
■ **crease up**
make laugh, amuse
COLLOQ. make someone fall about, make someone split their sides, have rolling in the aisles

create v
invent, coin, formulate, compose, design, devise, concoct,

hatch, originate, initiate, found, establish, set up, institute, cause, cause to happen, bring about, occasion, give rise to, produce, bring into being, bring into existence, generate, engender, make, form, shape, mould, develop, build, construct, erect, frame, fabricate, appoint, install, invest, inaugurate, ordain, lead to, result in
F₃ destroy

creation *n*

1 MAKING, formation, constitution, invention, concoction, origination, foundation, establishment, institution, production, generation, origin, conception, initiation, birth, development, design, construction, fabrication
TECHNICAL biopoiesis
FORMAL procreation, genesis

2 *God's creation*
world, universe, cosmos, nature, life, everything

3 INVENTION, innovation, brainchild, concept, product, production, achievement, work, work of art, handiwork, masterpiece, composition, design, *pièce de résistance*, *chef d'oeuvre*
F₃ 1 destruction

creative *adj*

artistic, inventive, original, imaginative, inspired, visionary, full of ideas, innovative, talented, gifted, clever, ingenious, resourceful, fertile, productive, intuitive
F₃ unimaginative

creativity *n*

artistry, inventiveness, originality, imagination, imaginativeness, inspiration, vision, talent, gift, cleverness, ingenuity, resourcefulness, fertility, productiveness
F₃ unimaginativeness

creator *n*

maker, inventor, designer, architect, author, originator, producer, initiator, builder, composer, founder, father, mother, prime mover, first cause

creature *n*

animal, beast, bird, fish, insect, organism, being, living thing, mortal, individual, person, human being, human, man, woman, body, soul, mortal; *Scot & Irish* cratur
COLLOQ. *N Am* critter

credence *n*

belief, confidence, trust, faith, dependence, reliance, acceptance, support, credibility, credit
F₃ distrust

credentials *n*

diploma, certificate, reference, testimonial, recommendation, authorization, warrant, licence, permit, passport, identity card, proof of identity, papers, documents, deed, title
FORMAL accreditation

credibility *n*

integrity, reliability, trustworthiness, plausibility, probability, likelihood, reasonableness
F₃ implausibility

credible *adj*

believable, imaginable, convincing, conceivable, thinkable, tenable, plausible, likely, probable, possible, reasonable, persuasive, convincing, sincere, honest, trustworthy, reliable, dependable
OLD credent
COLLOQ. with a ring of truth
F₃ incredible, unbelievable, implausible, unreliable

! **credible, creditable** or **credulous**?
Credible means 'believable, even if untrue': *a credible theory*. *Creditable* means 'worthy of praise or respect': *a very creditable performance*. *Credulous* means 'too easily convinced; easily fooled': *Only the most credulous of voters would believe all the party's election promises.*

Synonym nuances
Believable, imaginable, conceivable, thinkable, plausible and **tenable** may be widely used, simply to say that something is very possible: *it was conceivable that a foreign investor might be tempted; it appeared to them a tenable meaning to the words.* **Likely** and **probable**, on the other hand, further suggest there is a good chance of something happening: *the probable effects of higher taxation.*

Convincing suggests there may be strong evidence of verity, while the term **reasonable** suggests that judgement grants something may be the case: *a reasonable supposition*, and **persuasive** implies outside forces have been brought to bear on this perception: *influenced by his persuasive argument.*

Sincere and **honest** might be used of people as well as more abstract notions and carry the positive suggestion of inherent believability, similarly **trustworthy, reliable** and **dependable**, which are all approbatory and appropriately describe something inspiring justifiable confidence: *any information system should be reliable.*

---

credibly *adv*

believably, imaginably, convincingly, conceivably, thinkably, plausibly, possibly, reasonably, persuasively, convincingly, sincerely, honestly, trustworthy, reliably, dependably

credit *n, v*

♦ *n*

1 *get the credit for his success*
acknowledgement, recognition, thanks, approval, commendation, praise, acclaim, tribute, plaudits
FORMAL laudation

2 *your loyalty does you credit*
glory, fame, prestige, distinction, honour, reputation, asset, boast, pride, esteem, estimation
COLLOQ. feather in your cap, pride and joy

3 *give someone credit for their ability*
belief, trust, faith, credence, confidence
F₃ 1 blame, discredit, shame

♦ *v*

1 *credited with the invention*
attribute, ascribe, put down, assign, charge
FORMAL accredit, impute

2 *the reports are difficult to credit*
believe, accept, subscribe to, trust, have faith, rely on
COLLOQ. swallow, buy
F₃ 2 disbelieve

■ **in credit**
have money in your bank account, solvent
COLLOQ. in the black

■ **on credit**
on account, by instalments, by deferred payment, on hire purchase
COLLOQ. on tick, on the slate, on the tab, on the never-never

creditable *adj*

honourable, reputable, respectable, estimable, admirable, commendable, praiseworthy, good, excellent, exemplary, worthy, deserving
FORMAL laudable, meritorious
F₃ shameful, blameworthy

creditably *adv*

well, excellently, honourably, respectably, admirably, commendably
F₃ shamefully

creditor *n*

person/business you owe money to, lender, moneylender
FORMAL debtee

COLLOQ. loan shark
🔁 debtor

credulity n
naivety, gullibility, credulousness, dupability, silliness, simplicity, stupidity, uncriticalness
🔁 scepticism

credulous adj
naive, gullible, wide-eyed, trusting, overtrusting, dupable, unsuspecting, uncritical
🔁 sceptical, suspicious

❗ **credulous, credible** or **creditable**?
See panel at **credible**.

creed n
belief, faith, persuasion, credo, catechism, doctrine, teaching, principles, tenets, articles, canon, dogma, ideology

creek n
inlet, estuary, cove, bay, bight, firth, fiord

creep v, n
♦ v
crawl, inch, edge, tiptoe, steal, sneak, slink, move unnoticed, slither, worm, wriggle, squirm, grovel, writhe, snake
♦ n
1 *You little creep!*
sneak, fawner, sycophant, toady
COLLOQ. yes-man, bootlicker
SLANG geek
2 *gave me the creeps*
fear, horror, revulsion, terror, alarm, unease, disquiet

creeper n
climber, climbing plant, trailer, trailing plant, plant, rambler, runner, trailing, vine, liana

creepy adj
eerie, sinister, threatening, frightening, terrifying, hair-raising, bloodcurdling, spine-chilling, nightmarish, macabre, gruesome, horrible, horrifying, horrific, unpleasant, menacing, ominous, disturbing, weird
COLLOQ. scary, spooky

crescent-shaped adj
bow-shaped, sickle-shaped
FORMAL falcate, falcated, falciform, lunate, lunated, lunular

crest n
1 *the crest of the hill*
ridge, crown, top, peak, summit, pinnacle, apex, head, edge, chine, comb, cornice
2 TUFT, tassel, plume, comb, cockscomb, mane, aigrette, caruncle, panache
TECHNICAL crista
OLD copple
3 INSIGNIA, regalia, device, symbol, emblem, badge, coat of arms

crestfallen adj
disappointed, downhearted, dejected, sad, depressed, despondent, discouraged, disheartened, dispirited, downcast
FORMAL disconsolate
COLLOQ. cheesed off, in the doldrums, down in the dumps
🔁 elated

cretin n
fool, blockhead, moron, fathead, dolt, dunce, dimwit, simpleton, halfwit, idiot, imbecile, ignoramus
COLLOQ. nincompoop, ass, chump, ninny, clot, dope, twit, nitwit, nit, sucker, mug, twerp, birdbrain; N Am bufflehead
SLANG wally, jerk, dumbo, pillock, prat, dork, geek, plonker, prick; N Am schmuck, jughead, schmo

crevasse n
abyss, chasm, cleft, crack, fissure, gap, bergschrund

crevice n
crack, fissure, split, rift, cleft, slit, chink, cranny, gap, hole, opening, break
FORMAL interstice

crew n
team, party, squad, troop, corps, company, complement, force, corps, gang, band, pack, group, unit, bunch, crowd, mob, set, lot

crib n, v
♦ n
carry-cot, cot, crib, travel-cot, Moses basket, bassinet, bed
♦ v
copy, cheat, steal, reproduce, pirate, plagiarize
FORMAL purloin
COLLOQ. lift, pinch

crick n
pain, spasm, stiffness, convulsion, cramp, rick, twinge

cricket

Terms used in cricket include:

all-rounder	gully	pull
the Ashes	half-volley	run
bail	hat-trick	run out
ball	hook	scorer
bat	howzat?	seam bowler
batsman	ICC (International	short leg
block	Cricket Council)	short
bouncer	infield	sightscreen
boundary	innings	silly point
bowled	lbw (leg before	single
bowler	wicket)	six
box	leg bye	slip
bye	leg spinner	spin bowler
caught	limited-overs	square
century	match	square cut
chinaman	long hop	square leg
county	long leg	stump
championship	long off	stumped
cover	long on	sweep
crease	maiden	sweeper
cut	mid off	swing bowler
drive	mid on	test match
duck	mid-wicket	thigh pad
Duckworth-	nightwatchman	third man
Lewis method	no ball	twelfth man
extra cover	off spinner	umpire
extras	one-day match	whites
fast bowler	outfield	wicket
fielder	over	wicketkeeper
fine leg	pace bowler	wide
four	pad	wrong 'un
full toss	pavilion	yorker
glance	pitch	
googly	point	

crier n
announcer, proclaimer, messenger, bearer of tidings, herald, town crier

crime n
lawbreaking, lawlessness, delinquency, illegal act, unlawful act, offence, felony, misdemeanour, misdeed, wrongdoing, misconduct, violation, sin, iniquity, vice, villainy, wickedness, atrocity, outrage
OLD (*Shakesp*) malefaction
FORMAL malfeasance, transgression
See panel on next page

criminal n, adj
♦ n
lawbreaker, felon, delinquent, offender, wrongdoer, miscreant, culprit, villain, convict, prisoner
FORMAL malefactor

Crimes include:

arson	counterfeiting	grievous bodily harm	manslaughter	stalking
assassination	cybercrime	hate crime	mugging	terrorism
assault	drink-driving	hijack	murder	theft
battery	drug dealing	homicide	perjury	treason
blackmail	drug smuggling	hooliganism	pilfering	trespassing
breach of the peace	drunk and disorderly	housebreaking	piracy	vandalism
breaking and entering	embezzlement	insider dealing/	poaching	
bribery	extortion	trading	rape	
burglary	forgery	joy-riding	robbery	
computer hacking	fraud	kidnapping	sabotage	
corruption	*colloq.* GBH	larceny	shoplifting	

COLLOQ. crim
See panel below
• *adj*
1 *a criminal offence*
illegal, unlawful, illicit, lawless, lawbreaking, wrong, indictable, dishonest, villainous, corrupt, wicked, evil, iniquitous
FORMAL culpable, felonious, nefarious
COLLOQ. crooked, bent
2 *a criminal waste*
scandalous, deplorable, disgraceful, outrageous, preposterous, infamous, disgusting, shameful, reprehensible
COLLOQ. obscene
E3 1 legal, lawful, honest, upright

crimp *v*
flute, pleat, fold, gather, furrow, ridge, corrugate, groove, wrinkle, pucker, crease, crumple, rumple, crinkle, tuck

cringe *v*
1 *the sight made me cringe*
shrink, recoil, shy, start, flinch, draw back, wince, blench, quail, tremble, quiver, cower, crouch, bend, bow, stoop
2 GROVEL, toady, fawn, flatter, bow and scrape, tug the forelock, curry favour
COLLOQ. crawl, creep, kowtow, be all over, suck up

crinkle *n, v*
• *n*
fold, line, pleat, crease, tuck, ruffle, rumple, twist, wave, wrinkle, pucker, ruck, crinkle, corrugation, furrow, ridge, groove
• *v*
fold, pleat, crease, wrinkle, pucker, curl, twist, crumple, rumple, crinkle, crimp, tuck, corrugate, groove, furrow, ridge

crinkly *adj*
fluted, pleated, folded, gathered, furrowed, ridged, corrugated, grooved, wrinkled, wrinkly, puckered, curly, frizzy, kinky, creased, crimped, crumpled, rumpled, crinkled, tucked
E3 smooth, straight

cripple *v*
crippled by the accident/the tax increase
paralyse, disable, handicap, injure, maim, lame, immobilize, mutilate, damage, impair, spoil, ruin, destroy, sabotage, weaken, debilitate, hamstring, hamper, impede, spoil
FORMAL incapacitate, vitiate

crippled *adj*
lame, paralysed, disabled, handicapped, deformed
FORMAL incapacitated

crisis *n*
emergency, extremity, catastrophe, disaster, calamity, critical situation, crossroads, dilemma, quandary, predicament, difficulty, trouble, problem, turn, turning-point, brunt, crise
TECHNICAL solution
OLD acme, fit
FORMAL exigency
COLLOQ. crunch, mess, scrape, pickle, jam, fix, hole, stew, hot water

crisp *adj*
1 *a crisp biscuit*
crispy, crunchy, brittle, crumbly, breakable, firm, hard
FORMAL friable
2 BRACING, invigorating, refreshing, fresh, brisk, chilly, cool
3 BRIEF, pithy, terse, brief, short, succinct, concise, clear, incisive
COLLOQ. snappy
E3 1 soggy, limp, flabby **2** muggy, humid **3** wordy, vague

criterion *n*
standard, norm, touchstone, benchmark, yardstick, basis, measure, gauge, rule, scale, law, principle, model, canon, test, shibboleth
OLD square
FORMAL exemplar

critic *n*
1 *a music critic*
reviewer, commentator, analyst, pundit, authority, monitor, observer, expert, judge
2 *a critic of the government*
judge, censor, censurer, carper, fault-finder, attacker
OLD find-fault
COLLOQ. backbiter, carper, nit-picker, knocker

Types of criminal include:

armed robber	car-thief	forger	killer	racketeer	strangler
arsonist	cat burglar	gangster	*slang* lag	ram-raider	swindler
assassin	counterfeiter	gunman	larcenist	rapist	terrorist
bandit	cracksman	highwayman	*N Am* mobster	receiver	thief
batterer	crook	hijacker	mugger	robber	thug
bigamist	dope pusher	*slang* hood	murderer	rustler	trespasser
blackmailer	drink-driver	hoodlum	paedophile	saboteur	vandal
bogus caller	drug dealer	housebreaker	pederast	safecracker	war criminal
bootlegger	drug smuggler	*colloq.* jailbird	perjurer	sexual abuser	
brigand	embezzler	joyrider	pickpocket	shoplifter	
buccaneer	extortionist	kerb-crawler	pirate	smuggler	
burglar	fire-raiser	kidnapper	poacher	stalker	

critical adj

1 *at the critical moment*
crucial, vital, essential, important, all-important, significant, momentous, major, deciding, decisive, historic, fateful, pivotal, urgent, serious, compelling, pressing
FORMAL exigent, climacteric
2 *in a critical condition*
dangerous, serious, grave, precarious
FORMAL perilous
3 UNCOMPLIMENTARY, derogatory, disparaging, condemnatory, judgemental, disapproving, disapprobative, censorious, scathing, carping, fault-finding, captious, niggling, quibbling, hypercritical, venomous, vitriolic
FORMAL vituperative
COLLOQ. cavilling, nit-picking
4 ANALYTICAL, diagnostic, penetrating, probing, discerning, evaluative, explanatory, interpretative, perceptive
FORMAL expository
E3 1 unimportant, insignificant **3** complimentary, appreciative

critically adv

1 *critically important*
significantly, vitally, crucially, seriously, decisively, urgently
2 *critically ill*
dangerously, seriously, gravely, acutely
FORMAL perilously
3 *look critically*
disparagingly, disapprovingly, captiously, hypercritically
4 *evaluate critically*
analytically, diagnostically
E3 3 appreciatively

criticism n

1 CONDEMNATION, disapproval, fault-finding, censure, reproof, blame
FORMAL animadversion, disparagement
COLLOQ. brickbat, flak, slating, slamming, nit-picking, niggle, knocking, stick
2 REVIEW, critique, assessment, evaluation, appraisal, judgement, analysis, commentary, write-up, appreciation, explanation, interpretation
FORMAL exposition, explication
COLLOQ. bad press
E3 1 praise, commendation

criticize v

1 CONDEMN, carp, disapprove of, find fault with, pass judgement on, denounce, speak ill of, run down, attack, slate, censure, blame, canvass, niggle, peck at, scarify, slash, snipe at, tilt at; *N Am* score
FORMAL disparage, cast aspersions on, animadvert, excoriate, decry, denigrate, vituperate, castigate, impugn
COLLOQ. nag, slam, hammer, knock, come down on, give someone some stick, go to town on, haul over the coals, pick holes in, pan, take apart, pull/tear apart, pull to pieces, tear to shreds, tear a strip off, nit-pick, do a hatchet job on, badmouth, rubbish, trash, put the boot in, cut up, roast, have a go at, wade into; *N Am & Aust* bag; *Aust* have a shot at
SLANG slag (off), take to the cleaners; *N Am* rip into, zing
2 REVIEW, assess, evaluate, appraise, judge, analyse, explain, interpret
E3 1 praise, commend

Synonym nuances

sense 1
Condemn and **censure** may be used to convey speaking out vehemently against, as can the term **attack**: *the Prime Minister attacked the doom-mongers*; **denounce** has a narrower suggestion of public accusation: *they denounced him as a traitor*. **Disparage** has a strong element of humiliation or belittling: *there are many students who feel disparaged by teachers.*
  Carp, **niggle** and **peck at** could be used of continuous and implicitly irritating fault-finding, whereas **scarify**, though rarely used, suggests the fault-finding is much more severe: *a columnist who scarified our leading politicians*. **Snipe at** and **tilt at** are likely to be used of a fairly mild, possibly veiled verbal assault: *the critic tilted at the art world's honours system.* **Wade into**, on the other hand, could be used of a much more blatant onslaught: *he waded into his father with anger.*

---

critique n

review, essay, assessment, evaluation, appraisal, judgement, analysis, commentary, write-up, appreciation, explanation, interpretation
FORMAL exposition, explication

croak v, n

♦ *n*
rasp, squawk, caw, crow, croup, wheeze, speak harshly, rasp, gasp, grunt; *dialect* crake
♦ *n*
rasp, squawk, caw, wheeze, rasp, gasp, grunt

crock n

jar, pot, urn, vessel

crockery n

dishes, tableware, china, porcelain, earthenware, stoneware, pottery

---

Items of crockery include:

basin	dinner plate	salad bowl
beaker	dinner service	saucer
bowl	dish	side plate
butter dish	gravy boat	soup bowl
cafétière	jug	sugar bowl
cakestand	meat dish	tea cup
cereal bowl	milk jug	teapot
coffee cup	mug	tea set
coffee pot	percolator	tureen
cruet	plate	
cup	pot	

---

croft n

farm, plot, smallholding, farmland

crony n

friend, companion, familiar, intimate, confidant(e), associate, colleague, accomplice, ally, comrade, follower, sidekick
COLLOQ. mate, pal, chum, buddy

crook n, v

♦ *n*
1 CRIMINAL, thief, robber, offender, lawbreaker, swindler, operator, cheat, rogue, fraud, villain
COLLOQ. shark, con man
2 BEND, twist, slant, angle, hook, curve, bow, kink, distortion
♦ *v*
bend, twist, tilt, slant, angle, hook, curve, flex, bow, distort, warp, deform

crooked adj

1 ASKEW, awry, lopsided, asymmetric, irregular, uneven, off-centre, tilted, slanting, bent, angled, hooked, curved, bowed, warped, distorted, misshapen, deformed, contorted, twisted, buckled, tortuous, sinuous, winding, zigzag; *Scot* camsho, thrawn
OLD wrong
FORMAL anfractuous
COLLOQ. skew-whiff
2 CRIMINAL, illegal, unlawful, illicit, criminal, dishonest, deceitful, corrupt, fraudulent, shifty, underhand,

treacherous, unscrupulous, unprincipled, unethical
FORMAL nefarious
COLLOQ. bent, shady
⊟ 1 straight 2 honest

crookedly adv
lopsidedly, askew, awry, asymmetrically, unevenly, off-centre

croon v
sing, hum, warble, lilt, vocalize

crop n, v
♦ n
1 grow crops
growth, yield, produce, fruits, harvest, vintage, gathering, reaping, gleaning
See also **arable crop**.
2 this year's crop of graduates
batch, group, lot, set, collection
♦ v
cut, snip, clip, shear, trim, pare, prune, mow, lop, shorten, reduce, curtail
■ **crop up**
arise, emerge, appear, arrive, occur, happen, come up, turn up, present itself, come to pass, take place

cross n, v, adj
♦ n
1 CRUX, transverse
Related adjective: crucial
2 BURDEN, load, misfortune, trouble, adversity, worry, disaster, catastrophe, trial, grief, misery, pain, suffering, woe
FORMAL affliction, tribulation
3 CROSSBREED, hybrid, mongrel, blend, mix, mixture, mixed breed, amalgam, combination
♦ v
1 cross the river
go across, travel across, pass over, ford, bridge, arch, span
FORMAL traverse
2 INTERSECT, meet, join, converge, criss-cross, lace, interweave, intertwine
3 CROSSBREED, interbreed, mongrelize, hybridize, cross-fertilize, cross-pollinate, blend, mix
4 THWART, frustrate, foil, hinder, hamper, impede, obstruct, block, check, defy, resist, oppose
♦ adj
1 IRRITABLE, annoyed, angry, vexed, bad-tempered, ill-tempered, grumpy, put out, splenetic, irate, short, snappy, snappish, surly, sullen, fractious, cantankerous, awkward, difficult, prickly, harsh, fretful, disagreeable, impatient
FORMAL irascible
COLLOQ. peeved, shirty, crotchety, grouchy, crabby
2 TRANSVERSE, crosswise, oblique, diagonal, intersecting, opposite, reciprocal
⊟ 1 placid, pleasant
■ **cross out**
delete, remove, cancel, rub out, strike out, obliterate, edit out, cut out, blue-pencil

---

Types of cross include:

ankh	fleury	quadrate
Avelian	fylfot	rood
botoné	Geneva	Russian
Calvary	Greek	saltire
capital	Jerusalem	St Andrew's
cardinal	Latin	St Anthony's
Celtic	Lorraine	St George's
Constantinian	Maltese	St Peter's
Cornish	moline	swastika
crosslet	papal	tau
crucifix	patriarchal	Y-cross
encolpion	potent	

---

cross-examination n
interrogation, questioning, cross-questioning, examination, quiz, quizzing
COLLOQ. grilling, the third degree

cross-examine v
interrogate, question, cross-question, quiz, examine
COLLOQ. grill, pump, give someone the third degree

crossing n
1 meet at the crossing
junction, intersection, crossroads
2 a pedestrian crossing
pedestrian crossing, zebra crossing, pelican crossing, Toucan crossing; NAm crosswalk
3 a sea crossing
journey, trip, passage, voyage

crosswise adv
diagonally, crossways, crisscross, across, over, sideways, transversely, aslant, obliquely, athwart, awry
FORMAL catercorner, catercornered

crotch n
crutch, groin, genitals

crotchety adj
grumpy, awkward, bad-tempered, ill-tempered, cross, irritable, difficult, disagreeable, obstreperous, peevish, prickly, surly, testy, petulant, fractious, cantankerous, contrary, crusty
FORMAL irascible, iracund, iracundulous
COLLOQ. crabby, crabbed, grouchy
⊟ calm, placid, pleasant

crouch v
squat, kneel, stoop, bend, bow, hunch, duck, cower, ruck, cringe
OLD dare

crow v
bluster, boast, brag, show off, gloat, rejoice, triumph, exult, flourish, vaunt
OLD cry roast-meat
COLLOQ. blow your own trumpet, talk big; NAm blow your own horn

crowd n, v
♦ n
1 THRONG, multitude, army, host, mob, masses, populace, people, public, riff-raff, rabble, horde, swarm, flock, herd, drove, huddle, pack, press, crush, squash, assembly, collection, company; dialect mong; Scot meinie
OLD (Shakesp) varletry
2 all the college crowd
group, bunch, lot, set, circle, band, clique, fraternity
3 SPECTATORS, viewers, watchers, listeners, gate, attendance, audience, house, turnout; Aust roll-up
♦ v
1 crowd around the pop star
cluster, gather, congregate, muster, converge, huddle, hustle, mass, mob, throng, swarm, flock, surge, stream
2 crowd into a van
push, shove, elbow, jostle, thrust, press, surge, squeeze, bundle, pile, pack, cram, jam, stuff, compress, congest, overflow

crowded adj
full, filled, packed, jammed, congested, crammed, cramped, crushed, overfull, overcrowded, overpopulated, busy, teeming, swarming, overflowing
COLLOQ. full to bursting, jam-packed, packed like sardines, chock-a-block, thick on the ground
SLANG chocker
⊟ empty, deserted

crown n, v
♦ n
1 CORONET, diadem, tiara, circlet, wreath, corona, taj

TECHNICAL aureola
OLD pschent, garland
Related adjective: coronal
2 PRIZE, trophy, reward, honour, award, title, distinction, glory, kudos, garland, laurels, bays
3 SOVEREIGN, monarch, king, queen, emperor, empress, ruler, sovereignty, monarchy, royalty, empire
4 MONARCHY, sovereignty, royalty, empire
TECHNICAL ultimus haeres
5 TOP, tip, crest, summit, pinnacle, peak, acme, apex, climax, height, culmination; *S Afr* krantz
TECHNICAL corona
6 *the crown of the head*
pate; *Scot* cantle
TECHNICAL vertex
OLD sconce, foretop, noll
♦ *v*
1 *crown the king*
enthrone, invest, induct, install, anoint, adorn, festoon, honour, dignify, reward, laureate
2 TOP, cap, complete, perfect, fulfil, finalize, round off, perfect, be the culmination of
FORMAL consummate

crowning *adj, n*
♦ *adj*
culminating, final, perfect, supreme, top, ultimate, unmatched, unsurpassed, paramount, sovereign
FORMAL climactic, consummate
♦ *n*
coronation, enthronement, installation, investiture, inauguration
FORMAL incoronation

crucial *adj*
urgent, pressing, vital, essential, key, pivotal, central, important, momentous, major, deciding, decisive, critical, trying, testing, compelling, searching, historic, pivotal
🖃 unimportant, trivial

crucially *adv*
critically, vitally, essentially, centrally, momentously, importantly, decisively
🖃 unimportantly, trivially

crucify *v*
1 *Christ was crucified*
kill on the cross, execute, put to death
2 *crucified by the critics*
criticize, run down, slate, mock, ridicule, persecute, torment, punish, torture, rack
FORMAL excoriate, denigrate
COLLOQ. slam, rubbish, knock, tear to pieces, tear to shreds, pull to pieces

crude *adj*
1 RAW, unprocessed, unrefined, untreated, rough, coarse, unfinished, unpolished
2 *a crude cabin*
rough, natural, primitive, makeshift, unfinished, undeveloped, simple, basic, rudimentary
FORMAL rude
COLLOQ. *N Am* down-and-dirty
3 *a crude remark*
vulgar, coarse, rude, indecent, obscene, uncouth, risqué, offensive, gross, dirty, lewd, earthy, bawdy, smutty
COLLOQ. raunchy, blue, hot, juicy
🖃 **1** refined, finished **3** polite, decent, tasteful

crudely *adv*
1 *a crudely-painted building*
roughly, simply, basically, primitively
2 RUDELY, coarsely, offensively, indecently, obscenely

cruel *adj*
fierce, ferocious, vicious, savage, barbarous, barbaric, bloodthirsty, murderous, cold-blooded, bloody, butcherly, sadistic, raw, brutal, inhuman, inhumane, unkind, heathenish, nasty, mean, evil, wicked, malevolent, fiendish, spiteful, malicious, callous, heartless, unfeeling, merciless, pitiless, flinty, hard-hearted, stony-hearted, iron-headed, implacable, ruthless, remorseless, blistering, unrelenting, inexorable, grim, hellish, diabolic, Neronian, atrocious, bitter, severe, cutting, painful, excruciating, fell, wanton
OLD felon, immane, marble-breasted, marble-hearted, truculent
FORMAL vengeful, indurate
🖃 kind, compassionate, merciful

Synonym nuances
Fierce, ferocious and **vicious** all imply an unrestrained element, whilst **savage, barbarous** and **barbaric** more strongly suggest cruelty with an uncivilized aspect; **raw, brutal, inhuman** and **inhumane** also convey this idea: *his brutal reign of terror; the inhuman system of slavery*.
The terms **cold-blooded, callous, heartless, unfeeling, merciless, pitiless, ruthless** and **wanton** could all be used to emphasize the idea of absent feeling, while **flinty, hard-hearted** and **stony-hearted** continue this suggestion.
Bloodthirsty and **sadistic**, however, put the emphasis on relish and enjoyment of cruelty. The terms **nasty, mean, spiteful** and **malicious** all conjure up a somewhat underhand malevolence: *spiteful taunts*.
Implacable, however, should be used specifically of an inability to be appeased even by cruelty: *the implacable tyranny of time*; **remorseless, unrelenting** and **inexorable** of a cruelty that is constant: *the war was a bitter and remorseless struggle*.

---

cruelly *adv*
fiercely, ferociously, viciously, savagely, cold-bloodedly, brutally, inhumanly, inhumanely, unkindly, spitefully, maliciously, callously, heartlessly, pitilessly, mercilessly, hard-heartedly, implacably, painfully, ruthlessly, remorselessly
OLD immanely, truculently
🖃 kindly, compassionately, mercifully

cruelty *n*
ferocity, viciousness, savagery, barbarity, bloodthirstiness, murderousness, violence, sadism, abuse, bullying, brutality, bestiality, inhumanity, spite, malice, venom, callousness, heartlessness, hard-heartedness, mercilessness, ruthlessness, tyranny, unkindness, meanness, harshness, severity
🖃 kindness, compassion, mercy

cruise *n, v*
♦ *n*
holiday, voyage, sail, journey, trip
♦ *v*
1 *cruising round the Mediterranean*
sail, travel, journey, voyage
2 *cruising along comfortably*
sail, coast, drift, freewheel, glide, slide, taxi

crumb *n*
piece, scrap, morsel, bit, titbit, particle, grain, atom, fragment, flake, speck, iota, jot, mite, shred, sliver, snippet, soupçon

crumble *v*
1 *the plaster is crumbling*
fragment, break up, come away, decompose, disintegrate, decay, degenerate, deteriorate, collapse, crush, pound, grind, powder, pulverize
2 *the organization began to crumble*
collapse, fail, fall to pieces, fall apart, disintegrate, decay, degenerate, deteriorate, break down, rot

crumbly *adj*
brittle, powdery, short
FORMAL friable, pulverulent

crummy *adj*
inferior, miserable, poor, rotten, shoddy, trashy, cheap, useless, weak, worthless, contemptible, substandard, second-rate, third-rate
COLLOQ. grotty, pathetic, rubbishy, half-baked
SLANG crappy
Ⅎ excellent

crumple *v*
crush, wrinkle, pucker, crinkle, rumple, crease, fold, collapse, fall

crunch *v, n*
◆ *v*
1 *crunch a biscuit*
munch, chomp, champ, chew, bite, grind, crush
FORMAL masticate
2 *snow crunching*
grind, crush, scrunch, smash
◆ *n*
crisis, crux, critical point/situation, emergency, test, moment of truth
COLLOQ. pinch

crusade *n, v*
◆ *n*
1 *the Crusades*
holy war, jihad
2 *the crusade against nuclear power*
campaign, drive, struggle, push, movement, cause, undertaking, expedition, strategy, war, battle, offensive
◆ *v*
campaign, promote, push, drive, advocate, work, fight, strive, struggle, battle, attack

crusader *n*
advocate, campaigner, champion, promoter, enthusiast, reformer, zealot, activist, fighter, battler, missionary

crush *v, n*
◆ *v*
1 SQUASH, compress, squeeze, squelch, pinch, stamp, tread, mash, press, pulp, break (up), smash, mill, pound, pulverize, bruise, mangle, shatter, screw up, grind, crunch, scrunch, champ, crumble, crumple, rumple, crease, crinkle, wrinkle, telescope; *dialect* thrutch
TECHNICAL contuse
OLD oppress; (*Shakesp*) pash
FORMAL comminute, triturate
2 *the rebels were crushed*
conquer, demolish, devastate, defeat, overpower, overwhelm, overcome, quash, quell, suppress, squelch, subdue, step on, put down
FORMAL vanquish
COLLOQ. squabash
3 *crushed by the criticism*
upset, devastate, annihilate, mortify, humiliate, shame, abash; *dialect* mush
COLLOQ. put down
◆ *n*
1 *injured in the crush*
crowd, pack, press, squash, throng, horde, jam
2 *a crush on the French teacher*
infatuation, passion, obsession, love, liking
COLLOQ. pash

crust *n*
surface, exterior, outside, covering, topping, coat, coating, layer, film, casing, mantle, skin, rind, shell, husk, scab, caking
TECHNICAL incrustation, concretion

crusty *adj*
1 *crusty bread*

crispy, crunchy, brittle, crumbly, breakable, firm, hard, well-done, baked, well-baked
FORMAL friable
2 *a crusty old man*
grumpy, awkward, bad-tempered, short-tempered, brusque, gruff, cross, irritable, difficult, disagreeable, obstreperous, peevish, prickly, surly, testy, touchy, petulant, fractious, splenetic, cantankerous, contrary
FORMAL irascible
COLLOQ. crabby, crabbed, grouchy
Ⅎ 1 soft, soggy **2** calm, placid, pleasant

crux *n*
nub, heart, core, essence, centre, kernel, nucleus
COLLOQ. the bottom line

cry *v, n*
◆ *v*
1 WEEP, sob, be in/shed tears, wail, howl, bawl, whimper, whine, snivel; *Scot* greet
COLLOQ. blub, blubber, burst into tears, cry your eyes out, turn on the waterworks; *Scot* bubble
2 SHOUT, call (out), exclaim, roar, bellow, yell, scream, howl, bawl, shriek, screech
◆ *n*
1 WEEP, sob, tears, wail, howl, bawl, whimper, whine, snivel; *Scot* greet
COLLOQ. blubber; *Scot* bubble
2 SHOUT, call, plea, exclamation, roar, bellow, yell, scream, howl, bawl, shriek, screech
■ **cry off**
cancel, withdraw, excuse yourself, back out, decide against, change your mind
■ **cry out for**
need, call for, demand, want, require, necessitate

Synonym nuances
verb sense 1
Weep can be widely used, without any suggestion of disapproval, to refer to the shedding of tears, generally as an expression of grief; **sob** suggests a more dramatic act with a convulsive catching of the breath: *she sobbed, gasping for air*. **Blubber** also suggests the effusive shedding of tears, but carries a further implication of impatience from those witnessing it: *he was blubbering like a child*.
  Wail, **howl** and **bawl**, however, would be appropriate to use of a usually prolonged, loud sound: *the cat wailed to be let out*; *he bawled loudly when getting his hair washed*. For a quieter, almost muffled, low crying sound, you could use **whimper**: *the children whimpered piteously*; **whine**, although similar, often has a further accusation of peevishness: *the babies were whining and fractious*. If you use **snivel**, you are implying contempt for the person doing it: *oh, do stop snivelling!*

---

crypt *n*
tomb, vault, burial chamber, catacomb, mausoleum, undercroft
Related adjective: cryptal

cryptic *adj*
enigmatic, ambiguous, equivocal, puzzling, perplexing, mysterious, strange, bizarre, secret, hidden, veiled, obscure, dark, occult
FORMAL abstruse, esoteric
Ⅎ straightforward, clear, obvious

cryptically *adv*
enigmatically, ambiguously, mysteriously, strangely, secretly, bizarrely, obscurely
Ⅎ clearly, obviously

crystallize *v*
1 *the substance crystallized*
solidify, harden, materialize, form

2 the idea crystallized
make/become clear, make/become definite, clarify, appear, emerge, form

cub n

1 fox cubs
offspring, pup, puppy, whelp, baby, young

2 a cub reporter
beginner, novice, tiro, starter, learner, trainee, apprentice, student, probationer, initiate, freshman, fresher, recruit, raw recruit, tenderfoot, fledgling, neophyte, youngster, youth
COLLOQ. greenhorn, rookie, newbie

cubbyhole n
compartment, niche, pigeonhole, slot, recess, booth, cubicle, den, hideaway, hole, tiny room

cube n
dice, die, solid, block, cuboid, hexahedron

cuddle v, n
◆ v
hug, embrace, clasp, hold, enfold, nurse, nestle, snuggle, pet, fondle, caress
COLLOQ. snog, canoodle, neck, smooch
◆ n
hug, embrace, clasp, hold, snuggle
COLLOQ. snog, canoodle, neck, smooch

cuddly adj
cuddlesome, lov(e)able, huggable, plump, soft, warm, cosy

cudgel n, v
◆ n
club, stick, mace, bludgeon, bat, truncheon; Irish shillelagh, alpeen; bastinado
COLLOQ. cosh
◆ v
hit, strike, beat, club, bash, clout, thwack, pound, bludgeon, batter
COLLOQ. clobber, cosh

cue n
signal, sign, nod, hint, suggestion, intimation, indication, reminder, prompt, incentive, stimulus

cuff v
hit, thump, box, clip, knock, buffet, slap, smack, strike, clout, beat
COLLOQ. biff, clobber, belt, whack

■ **off the cuff**
impromptu, extempore, without preparation, ad lib, spontaneously, improvised, unprepared, unrehearsed, unscripted
COLLOQ. off the top of your head, on the spur of the moment

cuisine n
cooking, cookery, haute cuisine, cordon bleu, nouvelle cuisine

cul-de-sac n
no through road, dead end, blind alley

cull v

1 cull information
collect, gather, choose, pick (out), select, sift, glean, pluck, amass

2 cull wild animals
kill, destroy, slaughter, thin (out)

culminate v
climax, come to a climax, come to a head, end (up), terminate, close, conclude, finish, peak
FORMAL consummate
COLLOQ. wind up
E3 start, begin

culmination n
climax, height, high point, peak, apex, acme, zenith, pinnacle, summit, top, crown, perfection, finale, conclusion, completion
FORMAL consummation
E3 start, beginning

culpability n
responsibility, accountability, liability, answerability, blame, guilt, fault

culpable adj
to blame, wrong, in the wrong, at fault, responsible, guilty, liable, offending, answerable, blam(e)able, blameworthy, censurable, reprehensible, sinful
FORMAL peccant
E3 blameless, innocent

culprit n
guilty party, offender, wrongdoer, miscreant, lawbreaker, criminal, felon, delinquent, convict, villain

cult n

1 SECT, denomination, religion, faith, belief, affiliation, school, movement, party, faction

2 CRAZE, fad, fashion, vogue, obsession, mania, fixation, trend
COLLOQ. in-thing

cultivate v

1 FARM, till, work, plough, dig, prepare, grow, sow, plant, tend, raise, bring on, fertilize, produce, harvest, garden; dialect labour
OLD husband, manure
FORMAL culture

2 FOSTER, nurture, cherish, help, aid, assist, support, back, encourage, promote, further, forward, advance, enhance, work on, pursue, court, woo, develop, train, prepare, polish, refine, improve, enrich, enlighten
E3 2 neglect

cultivated adj
refined, cultured, civilized, sophisticated, polished, genteel, urbane, advanced, enlightened, educated, well-read, well-informed, scholarly, highbrow, discerning, discriminating

cultivation n

1 FARMING, agriculture, growing, sowing, planting, tilling, working, preparation, harvesting

2 FOSTERING, encouragement, nurture, nurturing, cherishing, assistance, support, backing, furthering, forwarding, advancing, development, improvement, refinement

cultural adj

1 cultural events
artistic, aesthetic, liberal, civilizing, humanizing, enlightening, educational, educative, edifying, improving, broadening, developmental, enriching, elevating

2 cultural heritage
communal, national, ethnic, folk, tribal, traditional
TECHNICAL anthropological
FORMAL societal

culture n

1 popular culture
the arts, humanities, painting, philosophy, music, literature, history, learning

2 CIVILIZATION, society, lifestyle, way of life, customs, traditions, heritage, habits, behaviour
FORMAL mores

3 cell culture
growth, production, crop, tendering, nurturing

cultured adj
cultivated, civilized, advanced, enlightened, educated, well-educated, well-read, well-informed, learned, scholarly, highbrow, intellectual, erudite, artistic, well-bred, refined, polite, polished, sophisticated, genteel, tasteful, urbane

COLLOQ. arty; (*derog*) arty-farty
⊞ uncultured, uneducated, ignorant

culvert *n*
channel, conduit, drain, duct, gutter, sewer, watercourse

cumbersome *adj*
1 *a cumbersome machine*
awkward, inconvenient, bulky, unwieldy, unmanageable, burdensome, onerous, heavy, weighty
FORMAL incommodious, cumbrous
2 *a cumbersome process*
complicated, complex, involved, difficult, inefficient, badly organized, wasteful, slow
⊞ **1** convenient, manageable **2** simple, efficient

cumulative *adj*
increasing, growing, mounting, multiplying, enlarging, growing, progressive, collective
COLLOQ. snowballing

cunning *adj, n*
♦ *adj*
1 *a cunning person*
crafty, sly, artful, wily, tricky, devious, subtle, deceitful, arch, sneaky, guileful, manipulative, sharp, shrewd, astute, canny, knowing, deep, insidious, varmint, vulpine, knackish, leery, *rusé*; *dialect* carny; *Scot* sleekit
OLD quaint
COLLOQ. shifty, cunning as a fox
2 *a cunning plan*
clever, imaginative, ingenious, skilful, inventive, resourceful, deft, dexterous, fiendish
⊞ **1** naive, ingenuous, gullible
♦ *n*
cunningness, craftiness, slyness, artfulness, trickery, deviousness, subtlety, deceit, deceitfulness, guile, wiles, sharpness, shrewdness, astuteness, ingenuity, cleverness, imaginativeness, skill, art, craft, policy, sleight, inventiveness, resourcefulness, deftness, finesse, adroitness, fiendishness, Machiavellianism
OLD (*Shakesp*) cautel; (*Spenser*)practic

cup *n*
1 *drink from a cup*
mug, tankard, beaker, goblet, chalice
2 *win a cup*
trophy, award, medal, prize, reward
3 *claret cup*
punch, wine

cupboard *n*
cabinet, locker, closet, wardrobe, pantry, sideboard, tallboy, dresser, Welsh dresser, chest

cupidity *n*
acquisitiveness, greed, greediness, avarice, avariciousness, graspingness, covetousness, eagerness, hunger, hankering, itching, longing, yearning
FORMAL avidity, rapaciousness, rapacity, voracity

curable *adj*
remediable, treatable, operable, medicable, reparable, rectifiable, reformable
⊞ incurable

curative *adj*
healing, healthful, health-giving, therapeutic, tonic, medicinal, remedial, restorative, corrective, salutary
TECHNICAL febrifugal
FORMAL alleviative, vulnerary

curator *n*
keeper, attendant, conservator, custodian, caretaker, steward, warden, warder, guardian

curb *v, n*
♦ *v*
restrain, constrain, restrict, contain, control, keep under control, check, keep in check, rein, moderate, reduce,

bridle, muzzle, keep back, hold back, suppress, subdue, repress, inhibit, hinder, impede, hamper
FORMAL retard
⊞ encourage, foster
♦ *n*
limitation, restriction, check, control, constraint, restraint, brake, rein, bridle, deterrent, damper, holding-back, suppression, repression, hindrance, hamper, impediment
FORMAL retardant

curdle *v*
coagulate, congeal, clot, solidify, thicken, turn, sour, turn sour, ferment
OLD (*Shakesp*) posset; (*Spenser*) cruddle

cure *v, n*
♦ *v*
1 HEAL, remedy, correct, restore, treat, repair, fix, rectify, mend, relieve, ease, alleviate, remedy, help, make better, make well
2 PRESERVE, dry, smoke, salt, pickle, kipper
♦ *n*
remedy, antidote, panacea, cure-all, solution, medicine, corrective, restorative, healing, treatment, therapy, alleviation, recovery
TECHNICAL specific
FORMAL elixir

cure-all *n*
panacea, universal remedy, nostrum
FORMAL elixir, catholicon, diacatholicon, panpharmacon

curio *n*
antique, bygone, curiosity, knick-knack, trinket, bibelot, *objet d'art*, object of virtu, *objet de vertu*

curiosity *n*
1 INQUISITIVENESS, interest, questioning, querying, search, inquiry, prying, snooping, interference
COLLOQ. nosiness
2 CURIO, *objet d'art*, antique, bygone, novelty, trinket, knick-knack
3 ODDITY, rarity, peculiarity, freak, phenomenon, spectacle, wonder, marvel, exotica

curious *adj*
1 INQUISITIVE, questioning, querying, searching, inquiring, interested, intrigued, fascinated, keen to know, wanting to learn, prying, meddling, snooping, agog, meddlesome, interfering
COLLOQ. nos(e)y
2 *a curious sight*
odd, queer, funny, strange, peculiar, bizarre, mysterious, puzzling, extraordinary, out of the ordinary, unusual, remarkable, rare, unique, novel, exotic, unconventional, weird, freakish, unorthodox, quaint
⊞ **1** uninterested, indifferent **2** ordinary, usual, normal

curiously *adv*
1 INQUISITIVELY, questioningly, inquiringly, meddlesomely, interferingly
2 ODDLY, strangely, peculiarly, mysteriously, unusually, remarkably, unconventionally, quaintly, bizarrely, out of the ordinary
⊞ **2** usually, normally

curl *v, n*
♦ *v*
crimp, crimple, frizz, frizzle, wave, roll, crinkle, ripple, kink, bend, curve, meander, loop, turn, twist, wind, wreathe, twirl, twine, coil, spiral, snake, corkscrew, scroll, tong, purl, becurl
OLD frounce
⊞ uncurl
♦ *n*
wave, kink, swirl, twist, roll, ring, ringlet, coil, crimp, crinkle, frizz, frizzle, curlicue, helix, spiral, whorl, dildo,

heartbreaker, kiss-curl, wreath
OLD frounce, earlock, favourite, lovelock, pinch

curly *adj*
curled, crimped, permed, frizzy, fuzzy, wavy, kinky,
curling, looping, turning, twisting, winding, wreathing,
twirling, coiling, spiralled, spiralling, corkscrew
⊟ straight

currency *n*
1 MONEY, legal tender, coinage, coins, notes, cash, bills
2 ACCEPTANCE, publicity, popularity, vogue, circulation,
prevalence, exposure
FORMAL dissemination

Currencies of the world include:

baht (*Thailand*)
bolivar (*Venezuela*)
cent (*EU, USA, Canada,
    Australia, New Zealand,
    South Africa* etc)
centavo (*Brazil, Mexico* etc)
centime (*Algeria, Andorra*
    etc)
centimo (*Costa Rica,
    Venezuela, Paraguay* etc)
Congolese franc
    (*Democratic Republic of
    the Congo*)
dinar (*Bosnia-Hercegovina,
    Yugoslavia, Iraq, Jordan*
    etc)
dirham (*Morocco*)
dollar (*USA, Canada,
    Australia, New Zealand,*
    etc)
dong (*Vietnam*)
dram (*Armenia*)
euro (*European Union*)
fils (*Iraq, Jordan* etc)
franc (*Switzerland* etc)
hyrvnia (*Ukraine*)
kopek (*Russia, Belarus,
    Tajikistan*)
koruna (*Czech Republic,
    Slovakia*)
krona (*Sweden*)
króna (*Iceland*)
krone (*Denmark, Norway*)
kroon (*Estonia*)

kunar (*Croatia*)
kyat (*Myanmar*)
lari (*Georgia*)
lats (*Latvia*)
lek (*Albania*)
leu (*Romania, Moldova*)
lev (*Bulgaria*)
litas (*Lithuania*)
manat (*Azerbaijan,
    Turkmenistan*)
pence (*UK*)
peso (*Mexico, Chile* etc)
piastre (*Egypt, Syria* etc)
pound (*UK, Egypt* etc)
rand (*South Africa*)
real (*Brazil*)
rial (*Iran*)
riyal (*Saudi Arabia*)
rouble (*Russia, Belarus,
    Tajikistan*)
rupee (*India, Pakistan* etc)
shekel (*Israel*)
shilling (*Kenya, Uganda* etc)
som (*Kyrgyzstan*)
sterling (*UK*)
sucre (*Ecuador*)
sum (*Uzbekistan*)
tenge (*Kazakhstan*)
tolar (*Slovenia*)
won (*N Korea, S Korea*)
yen (*Japan*)
yuan (*China*)
zloty (*Poland*)

Former currencies of the world include:

centavo
    (*Portugal*)
centime (*France,
    Belgium,
    Luxembourg*)
drachma
    (*Greece*)
escudo (*Portugal*)

franc (*France,
    Belgium,
    Luxembourg*)
guilder (*The
    Netherlands*)
lira (*Italy*)
mark (*Germany*)
markka (*Finland*)

peseta (*Spain*)
pence (*Ireland*)
pfennig
    (*Germany*)
punt (*Ireland*)
schilling (*Austria*)
zaïre (*Zaire*)

---

current *adj, n*
  • *adj*
1 current events
present, ongoing, existing, contemporary, present-day,
present-time, modern, fashionable, in fashion, up-to-date,
up-to-the-minute, in vogue, popular, topical
FORMAL extant
COLLOQ. trendy, in, now
2 still current in the 1800s
(generally) accepted, widespread, prevalent, common,
popular, general, prevailing, reigning, in circulation,
valid
COLLOQ. going around

⊟ 1 obsolete, old-fashioned
  • *n*
draught, stream, mainstream, jet, flow, swirl, movement,
drift, ebb, tide, course, progress, trend, direction,
tendency, undercurrent, tenor, mood, feeling

currently *adv*
now, at present, at the present time, right now, just now, at
the moment, for the time being, at this time, today, these
days; *N Am* presently

curriculum *n*
syllabus, core curriculum, national curriculum, subjects,
course of studies, discipline, course, course of study,
module, educational programme, timetable

curse *v, n*
  • *v*
1 SWEAR, use bad language, blaspheme, damn
FORMAL imprecate
COLLOQ. damn and blast, blind, eff and blind
SLANG cuss
2 CONDEMN, damn, denounce, blast
OLD ban, shrew; (*Shakesp*) beshrew
FORMAL accurse, execrate, imprecate, anathematize,
fulminate
COLLOQ. put a jinx on
3 BLIGHT, plague, scourge, afflict, harm, ruin, trouble, beset,
torment
⊟ 2 bless
  • *n*
1 SWEAR-WORD, oath, expletive, blasphemy, obscenity,
profanity, bad language; *N Am* curse-word
FORMAL imprecation
COLLOQ. four-letter word
SLANG cuss; *N Am* cussword
2 JINX, spell, anathema, Indian sign, bane, evil, plague,
scourge, blight, affliction, trouble, torment, ordeal,
calamity, misfortune, disaster; *Scot* winze
OLD pox, woe, maugre, vengeance, ban, malison
FORMAL anathema, execration, malediction, tribulation
COLLOQ. *Aust* moz
⊟ 2 blessing, advantage

cursed *adj*
damned, detestable, abominable, hateful, loathsome,
odious, vile, fiendish, annoying, unpleasant, pernicious,
infamous
FORMAL execrable
COLLOQ. blasted, blooming, blinking, flipping, flaming,
darned, dashed, confounded, infernal, dratting
SLANG bloody, cussed; (*taboo*) fucking, frigging

cursory *adj*
brief, slight, summary, superficial, desultory, quick, rapid,
fleeting, hasty, hurried, offhand, dismissive, passing,
perfunctory, careless, casual, slapdash
⊟ painstaking, thorough

curt *adj*
abrupt, blunt, rude, sharp, brusque, gruff, laconic, offhand,
short, short-spoken, tart, terse, snappish, unceremonious,
uncivil, ungracious, brief, pithy, concise, succinct,
summary
⊟ voluble

curtail *v*
reduce, limit, restrict, shorten, truncate, cut, cut down, cut
short, cut back (on), trim, shrink, abridge, abbreviate,
lessen, decrease, pare, pare down/back, prune, slim,
guillotine
⊟ lengthen, extend, increase

curtailment *n*
reduction, limitation, restriction, shortening, truncation,
cut, cutback, trimming, shrinkage, abridgement,
abbreviation, contraction, lessening, decrease, paring,
docking, pruning, slimming, guillotine

FORMAL retrenchment
🠿 extension, lengthening, increase

curtain n
blind, screen, cover, shutter, net curtain, hanging, window hanging, backdrop, portière, drapery, tapestry; N Am drape

curtly adv
abruptly, bluntly, rudely, sharply, brusquely, laconically, gruffly, tersely, unceremoniously, uncivilly, ungraciously, briefly, pithily, concisely, succinctly

curtsy v
bob, bow, kowtow, salaam
FORMAL genuflect

curvaceous adj
shapely, well-proportioned, well-rounded, buxom, comely, curvy, bosomy, voluptuous
SLANG well-stacked
🠿 skinny

curve v, n
♦ v
bend, arch, arc, bow, bulge, swell, hook, crook, turn, wind, twist, round, swerve, loop, spiral, coil
FORMAL incurve
♦ n
bend, turn, bow, loop, arc, arch, circle, crescent, trajectory, helix, spiral, winding, meandering, camber, kink, curvature, flexure

curved adj
bent, arched, bowed, rounded, humped, bulging, swelling, convex, concave, bending, cupped, scooped, crooked, twisted, warped, sweeping, sinuous, tortuous, serpentine
TECHNICAL arcuate, curviform
🠿 straight

cushion n, v
♦ n
pillow, bolster, headrest, squab, beanbag, hassock, kneeler, pad, padding, mat, bum roll, pillion, buffer, protection, shock absorber; Scot cod
TECHNICAL pulvinus
Related adjectives: pulvillar, pulvinar
♦ v
soften, deaden, dampen, absorb, muffle, stifle, suppress, lessen, reduce, diminish, mitigate, protect, bolster, buttress, buffer, prop up, support

cushy adj
comfortable, easy, undemanding
COLLOQ. jammy, soft, plum
🠿 demanding, tough, taxing

custodian n
caretaker, conservator, curator, guard, guardian, warden, warder, keeper, overseer, superintendent, watchdog, watchman, protector, castellan

custody n
1 KEEPING, possession, charge, care, safekeeping, protection, preservation, custodianship, trusteeship, guardianship, wardship, guidance, supervision, responsibility
2 DETENTION, confinement, imprisonment, captivity, arrest
FORMAL incarceration

custom n
1 *national customs*
tradition, usage, use, habit, routine, procedure, practice, policy, way, manner, style, form, fashion, way of behaving, convention, etiquette, ethos, mores, formality, observance, ritual, rite, institution
2 *take my custom elsewhere*
business, trade
FORMAL patronage

Synonym nuances
sense 1
The word **tradition** appropriately describes something that has been passed down through the generations and has positive associations, whereas **usage** and **use** are more neutral, suggesting only the constant use of something until it becomes established. Both **habit** and **routine** can be used of custom that has been established by repetition: *get into the habit of separating recyclable material from the rest of the household rubbish.*

The terms **procedure** and **practice** are the words to use to convey an established way of going about something: *police procedure; accepted hospital practice;* **policy** is appropriate where an official declaration of this has been made: *it's not company policy to allow extra days off.* **Form** also conveys this notion of what is or is not accepted, but might be used with a more social slant: *it's not good form to turn up drunk to a party.*

Convention and **etiquette** also relate to custom conforming to an established set of rules, although convention can have the widest application: *the conventions of the detective story.* **Fashion** is similar, but would most appropriately be used of customs conforming to current trends.

The term **ethos** has connotations of an intrinsic and usually positive distinguishing character: *the American ethos of freedom and liberty.* **Observance**, **rite** and **ritual** are more appropriate where ceremony is involved: *the observance of Remembrance Day.* **Institution**, meanwhile, is again quite positive in tone, referring to something that forms the bedrock of everyday life: *the pub is a great British institution.*

---

customarily adv
traditionally, conventionally, habitually, routinely, regularly, as a rule, usually, normally, ordinarily, commonly, generally, popularly, fashionably
🠿 unusually, occasionally, rarely

customary adj
traditional, conventional, obligatory, accepted, established, set, habitual, routine, regular, usual, normal, ordinary, everyday, familiar, common, general, popular, fashionable, prevailing
🠿 unusual, rare

customer n
client, patron, regular, consumer, shopper, buyer, purchaser, prospect
COLLOQ. punter

customize v
adapt, convert, modify, tailor, alter, adjust, tweak, suit, fit, transform, personalize
COLLOQ. fine-tune

customs n
taxes, duties, dues, tariffs, levies, exise
FORMAL impost

cut v, n
♦ v
1 *cut the paper/your finger; cut a hole*
slit, pierce, slice, sever, chop, hack, hew, carve, split, dock, lop, prune, excise
2 *cut meat*
dissect, divide, carve, slice, chop (up), dice, mince, shred, grate
FORMAL cleave
3 *cut hair/grass*
shorten, trim, clip, crop, snip, shear, mow, shave, pare, prune, dock
4 *cut glass*
engrave, incise, chisel, score
5 *cut someone's throat*

stab, wound, nick, slash, lacerate, gash, slit

6 *cut costs*
reduce, decrease, lower, diminish, lessen, curtail, curb, prune
COLLOQ. slash, axe

7 *cut a story/broadcast*
shorten, make shorter, curtail, abbreviate, abridge, condense, précis, summarize, edit, delete, omit
FORMAL excise, expurgate

8 *cut a supply*
stop, end, bring to an end, halt, suspend, disconnect, break off, block, obstruct, intercept
FORMAL discontinue

9 *cut a recording*
record, make, tape, tape-record, videotape, burn

10 *cut someone dead*
ignore, spurn, avoid, pretend not to see/notice, shun, snub, slight, rebuff, insult, scorn
COLLOQ. cut dead, cold-shoulder, look right through, blank, send to Coventry, not give someone the time of day

◆ *n*

1 INCISION, wound, nick, gash, slit, slash, rip, laceration, notch, score

2 *go for a cut at the barber's*
trim, clip, crop, shave

3 *spending cuts*
reduction, decrease, lowering, cutback, saving, economy, lessening
FORMAL retrenchment

4 *a cut of meat*
joint, section, slice, piece, bit, part

5 *a power cut*
failure, fault, breakdown, breaking-down, cutting-out
FORMAL malfunctioning

6 *a cut of the profits*
share, allocation, proportion, portion, quota, ration
COLLOQ. slice, slice of the cake, rake-off, whack

7 *the cut of a garment*
shape, style, fashion, form, profile, design

■ **cut across**
transcend, surmount, go beyond, rise above, leave behind

■ **cut back**
check, crop, curb, curtail, decrease, economize, lessen, lop, lower, prune, reduce, trim, scale down
FORMAL retrench
COLLOQ. slash, downsize, pull/tighten the purse strings

■ **cut down**

1 *cut down a tree*
fell, chop down, hew, saw, lop, level, raze

2 REDUCE, decrease, lower, lessen, diminish, curtail, curb, prune

■ **cut in**
interrupt, break in, butt in, intervene, intrude
FORMAL interpose, interject
COLLOQ. barge in

■ **cut off**

1 *cut off his head*
remove, sever, detach, amputate, chop off, take off, break off, tear off

2 *feel cut off from friends*
separate, isolate, keep apart, detach, seclude, sever, insulate, shelter

3 *cut off a supply*
stop, end, bring to an end, halt, suspend, disconnect, break off, block, obstruct, intercept
FORMAL discontinue

4 *get cut off on the phone*
disconnect, break off, unhook, separate, detach, intercept, interrupt

■ **cut out**

1 *cut out a coupon*
extract, remove, separate, take out, tear out
FORMAL excise

2 OMIT, cut, exclude, leave out, drop, delete, edit
FORMAL excise

3 stop, refrain, cease
FORMAL desist, discontinue
COLLOQ. quit, leave off, lay off, knock off, pack in

4 *the engine cut out*
stop working, fail, break down, go wrong
FORMAL malfunction
COLLOQ. pack up, go on the blink, go phut, go kaput
SLANG conk out

■ **cut up**
carve, slice(up), chop (up), dice, mince, dissect, dismember, divide, slash

■ **cut out for**
suitable, suited, right, appropriate, qualified, made, good

■ **cut and dried**
clear, definite, certain, settled, decided, fixed, organized, prearranged, automatic, predetermined
COLLOQ. sewn up

■ **cut up**
upset, unhappy, hurt, annoyed, distressed, bothered, saddened, troubled
COLLOQ. put out, het up, worked up

cutback *n*
cut, saving, economy, reduction, decrease, curtailment, lowering, lessening
FORMAL retrenchment
COLLOQ. slashing

cute *adj*
sweet, endearing, lov(e)able, charming, appealing, attractive, pretty, lovely, delightful, adorable
F3 unpleasant, unattractive, nasty

cutlery

Items of cutlery include:

apostle spoon	corn holders	salt spoon
bread knife	dessertspoon	soupspoon
butter knife	fish fork	spoon
caddy spoon	fish knife	steak knife
cake server	fish slice	sugar tongs
canteen of cutlery	fork	tablespoon
carving fork	knife	teaspoon
carving knife	ladle	vegetable knife
cheese knife	pickle fork	
chopsticks	salad servers	

See also **kitchen utensils**.

Types of cutter include:

adze	flick knife	lopper	saw	spokeshave
axe	fretsaw	machete	scalpel	Stanley knife®
billhook	guillotine	mower	scissors	Strimmer®
blade	hacksaw	penknife	scythe	Swiss army knife
chainsaw	hedgetrimmer	pinking shears	secateurs	sword
chisel	jigsaw	plane	shears	
chopper	knife	pocket knife	shredder	
clippers	lawnmower	razor	sickle	

See also **cutlery**; **saw**[1]; **weapon**.

cut-price *adj*
reduced, sale, discount, bargain, cheap, low-priced, cut-rate, marked-down

cutter
See panel on previous page

cut-throat *adj*
ruthless, pitiless, merciless, relentless, fierce, highly/fiercely competitive, keen, keenly contested, cruel, brutal
COLLOQ. dog-eat-dog

cutting *adj, n*
♦ *adj*
1 *a cutting wind*
bitter, raw, chill, sharp, keen, penetrating
2 *a cutting comment*
pointed, incisive, bitter, penetrating, piercing, wounding, hurtful, stinging, biting, caustic, acid, scathing, sarcastic, snide, malicious
FORMAL mordant, trenchant
COLLOQ. bitchy
♦ *n*
clipping, clip, extract, excerpt, piece

cycle *n*
circle, round, rotation, oscillation, rhythm, biorhythm, body clock, revolution, rota, series, sequence, order, pattern, succession, phase, period, era, age, epoch, aeon

cyclical *adj*
cyclic, recurring, recurrent, repeated, repetitive, regular

cyclone *n*
hurricane, monsoon, tempest, tropical storm, storm, tornado, typhoon, whirlwind; *Aust* willy-willy

cylinder *n*
column, barrel, drum, reel, bobbin, spool, spindle

cynic *n*
sceptic, doubter, pessimist, killjoy, scoffer
FORMAL misanthrope
COLLOQ. knocker, spoilsport

cynical *adj*
sceptical, doubtful, doubting, distrustful, disillusioned, disenchanted, pessimistic, negative, critical, scornful, derisive, suspicious, contemptuous, sneering, unsentimental, surly, scoffing, mocking, sarcastic, sardonic, ironic, bitter, embittered, worldly-wise, streetwise
FORMAL Diogenic, Mephistophelean
COLLOQ. hard-boiled, hardnosed

cynically *adv*
sceptically, distrustfully, pessimistically, critically, scornfully, derisively, suspiciously, contemptuously, mockingly, bitterly, negatively

cynicism *n*
scepticism, doubt, disbelief, distrust, disillusionment, disenchantment, pessimism, scorn, suspicion, contempt, sneering, scoffing, mocking, sarcasm, irony
FORMAL misanthropy

Synonym nuances
Scepticism may be used of a general lack of trust, similar to **distrust** and **suspicion**, though perhaps with a more world-weary view: *rising scepticism over politicians' promises*. **Doubt** suggests hesitancy in accepting something, whilst **disbelief** goes further and would only be appropriate to describe a complete lack of faith.
  Both **disillusionment** and **disenchantment**, however, emphasize the idea of being let down by something you did previously believe in: *his growing disenchantment with communism*; while the term **pessimism** is suggestive of a generally bleak outlook, anticipating the worst.
  Contempt and **sneering** could be used of an actively expressed cynicism born of a complete lack of regard: *their total contempt for democracy*. **Scorn**, **scoffing** and **mocking** might be used of vociferous cynicism involving jeering derision. **Sarcasm** is only appropriate where there is an element of cutting verbal expression: *social commentaries, loaded with sarcasm*.

---

cyst *n*
growth, sac, vesicle, blister, wen, abscess, bladder, bleb
TECHNICAL atheroma, utricle, ranula, steatoma, chalazion, dermoid, hydatid

D

dab *v, n*
* *v*
pat, daub, swab, wipe, touch, press, blot, mop, tap
* *n*
1 BIT, drop, dash, speck, spot, trace, trickle, splash, sprinkle, tinge, smear, smudge, fleck
COLLOQ. dollop, tad, smidgen
2 TOUCH, pat, stroke, tap, mop, wipe, press
■ **dab hand**
expert, pastmaster, wizard, ace, adept

dabble *v*
1 TRIFLE, play, tinker, toy, dally, dip, flirt, fiddle, potter; *NAm* putter
2 PADDLE, moisten, wet, dampen, sprinkle, dip, immerse, splash, splatter

dabbler *n*
amateur, lay person, dilettante, trifler, dallier, tinkerer
Ƀ professional, expert

daemon *n*
spirit, good spirit, genius, *genius loci*, force, animus, deva, geist, evil spirit, devil, demon, cacodemon

daft *adj*
1 *a daft idea*
foolish, crazy, silly, stupid, absurd, ridiculous, ludicrous, preposterous, farcical, laughable, outrageous, nonsensical, senseless, unwise, imprudent, odd, peculiar, impracticable, unrealistic, foolhardy, irrational, irresponsible, wild, idiotic, fatuous, inane
COLLOQ. dotty; (*offensive*) dumb; barmy, batty, potty, half-baked, hare-brained, addle-brained, crackbrained, crackpot, wacky; *Aust & NZ* dingbats
2 *a daft boy*
simple, simple-minded, stupid, dim, dull, dense, slow, slow-witted
COLLOQ. thick, thick as a plank/two short planks, dim-witted, dopey, gormless, dumb
3 INSANE, mad, lunatic, crazy, unbalanced, disturbed, deranged, demented, crazed, wild, berserk, touched, unhinged, out of your mind
COLLOQ. loopy, bonkers, nuts, nutty, nutty as a fruitcake, round the bend, round the twist
SLANG mental, loony, off your rocker, needing your head examining
4 INFATUATED, passionate, enamoured, smitten, obsessed, mad, wild, enthusiastic, fanatical, zealous, devoted, fond, keen, avid, ardent
COLLOQ. crazy, wild, nuts, potty, sweet
Ƀ **1** sensible **2** sane **3** indifferent

dagger *n*
knife, blade, poniard
OLD baselard, bodkin, dudgeon, puncheon

Daggers include:

bayonet	kirpan	sai	whinger
dirk	kris	skene	whinyard
handjar	kukri	skene-dhu	yatagan
jambiya	misericord	stiletto	

---

daily *adj, adv*
* *adj*
1 REGULAR, routine, everyday, customary, common, commonplace, ordinary, habitual
2 EVERYDAY
OLD (*Shakesp*) journal; (*Spenser*) adays
FORMAL diurnal, quotidian, circadian
* *adv*
every day, day after day, day by day

dainty *adj, n*
* *adj*
1 DELICATE, elegant, pretty, exquisite, petite, little, small, refined, fine, graceful, neat, trim, charming
2 *a dainty morsel*
tasty, delicious, delightful, enjoyable, appetizing, choice, palatable mouth-watering, luscious, succulent, juicy, savoury
FORMAL delectable
3 FASTIDIOUS, fussy, particular, discriminating, hard to please, finicky, scrupulous
COLLOQ. choosy, faddy
Ƀ **1** gross, clumsy, unwieldy **2** unpalatable
* *n*
delicacy, fancy, titbit, sweetmeat, bonbon, bonne-bouche

dais *n*
platform, stage, rostrum, podium, stand, staging

dale *n*
valley, vale, glen, dell, coomb, cwm; *dialect* griff, grike; *Scot* heuch, strath; *NAm* gulch; dean, den, dene, ria, slade, dingle, gill

dalliance *n*
1 PLAYING, sporting, toying, flirting, trifling
2 DELAY, dawdling, pottering, tarrying, loitering

dally *v*
1 DAWDLE, linger, loiter, delay, take your time
FORMAL procrastinate, tarry
2 *dally with an idea*
toy, play, flirt, trifle, frivol, carry on
Ƀ **1** hasten, hurry

dam *n, v*
* *n*
barrier, barrage, embankment, wall, blockage, barricade, obstruction, hindrance
* *v*
block, confine, restrict, check, barricade, staunch, stem, obstruct

damage *v, n*
* *v*
harm, injure, hurt, spoil, ruin, destroy, impair, mar, abuse, wreck, deface, vandalize, sabotage, desecrate, mutilate, weaken, tamper with, play/wreak havoc with, incapacitate
FORMAL vitiate
Ƀ mend, repair, fix
* *n*
1 *extensive damage after the fire*
harm, injury, hurt, destruction, ruin, devastation, havoc, loss, abuse, suffering, mischief, mutilation, impairment,

detriment, defacement, vandalism, desecration, vandalization, defilement
2 pay damages
compensation, fine, indemnity, indemnification, reimbursement, recompense, reparation, restitution, satisfaction
3 What's the damage?
cost, expense, charge, price
≠ 1 repair

Synonym nuances
verb
Harm is in general use to suggest physical, emotional or moral damage: *motherhood harmed her career*; **hurt** and **injure** may be used in the same way: *the scandal hurt the campaign*. The terms **spoil**, **ruin** and **mar** could be used of the irreparable damaging of a variety of things: *low cloud spoiled our view*; *the mud ruined my shoes*; *the text was marred by careless errors*. **Destroy** and **wreck** are fairly emotive terms conveying the notion of causing the end of something: *his cruelty had wrecked her love for him*; if something or someone has simply been put out of action, you might use **incapacitate**.
Impair and **weaken**, however, is more vague in the level of damage it suggests: *pollution is impairing our health*. **Abuse** could be used of various forms of maltreatment, but **deface** and **vandalize** suggest deliberate and wanton acts of physical damage: *textbooks defaced by doodles*. **Sabotage**, too, could be used of deliberate action, but usually to foil an end purpose: *the massacre sabotaged the resumption of negotiations*. **Tamper with** also suggests ill-intentioned interference: *someone has tampered with the brakes*.
The term **desecrate** is usually reserved to talk about damage to something sacred, while **mutilate** is usually used to refer to bodily maiming, but you may also use it to convey strong distaste for other forms of damage: *I managed to mutilate my life by making these choices*. The phrases **play/wreak havoc on** are very strong terms for creating problems: *the floods wrought havoc on the roads*.

---

damaging *adj*
harmful, hurtful, injurious, unfavourable, bad, detrimental, disadvantageous, pernicious, prejudicial, ruinous, destructive
FORMAL deleterious
≠ favourable, helpful

dame *n*
1 Dame Edith Evans
lady, noblewoman, baroness, dowager, peeress, aristocrat
2 WOMAN, female; (*offensive*) broad

damn *v, n*
♦ *v*
1 CURSE, swear, blast, doom, blaspheme, use bad language, sink
FORMAL accurse, imprecate, execrate, maledict, anathematize, fulminate
2 CONDEMN, revile, denounce, criticize, slate, run down, censure, attack, denunciate
FORMAL berate, castigate, inveigh, excoriate, decry, denigrate
COLLOQ. slam, pan, knock, come down on, pick holes in, pan, pull to pieces, tear to shreds
SLANG slag (off)
≠ 1 bless **2** praise, commend
♦ *n*
iota, jot
COLLOQ. dang, darn, dash
SLANG toss, monkey's, brass farthing, hoot, two hoots, tinker's cuss

damnable *adj*
abominable, atrocious, horrible, unpleasant, disagreeable, objectionable, offensive, despicable, detestable, iniquitous, cursed, infernal, damned, hellish, diabolical, wicked
FORMAL execrable
≠ admirable, praiseworthy

damnation *n*
condemnation, doom, denunciation, hell, hell-fire, perdition, excommunication, anathema
FORMAL proscription

damned *adj*
1 the damned in hell
condemned, doomed, lost, cursed, accursed, reprobate, anathematized
FORMAL execrated
2 a damned disgrace
cursed, detestable, despicable, abominable, confounded, infernal, hateful, loathsome, odious, vile, fiendish, annoying, unpleasant, pernicious
FORMAL execrable
COLLOQ. blasted, blooming, flipping, darned, dashed, dratting, flaming, blinking
SLANG bloody, effing; (*taboo*) fucking, frigging
≠ 1 blessed

damning *adj*
incriminating, condemning, implicating
FORMAL accusatorial, condemnatory, damnatory, implicative, inculpatory

damp *adj, n, v*
♦ *adj*
moist, moistened, wet, wettish, clammy, dank, humid, dewy, muggy, rainy, drizzly, misty, soggy, vaporous, rheumy
OLD moisty
≠ dry, arid
♦ *n*
dampness, moisture, clamminess, dankness, humidity, wet, wetness, dew, rain, drizzle, fog, mist, vapour
≠ dryness
■ **damp down**
calm, dull, deaden, restrain, check, reduce, lessen, moderate, decrease, diminish

dampen *v*
1 MOISTEN, wet, spray, damp
2 DISCOURAGE, dishearten, damp down, deter, dash, dull, deaden, restrain, check, depress, dismay, reduce, lessen, moderate, decrease, diminish, put a damper on, muffle, inhibit, stifle, smother
≠ 1 dry **2** encourage

damper
■ **put a damper on**
discourage, dishearten, damp down, deter, dash, dull, deaden, restrain, check, depress, dismay, reduce, lessen, moderate, decrease, diminish, muffle, inhibit, stifle, smother
≠ encourage

dampness *n*
damp, moisture, clamminess, dankness, humidity, wet, wetness, dew, rain, drizzle, fog, mist, vapour

damsel *n*
maiden, girl, lass, young woman, young lady; *Scot* lassie

dance *v, n*
♦ *v*
1 learn to dance
move to music, rock, spin, sway, gyrate, twirl, pirouette, whirl, trip the light fantastic
COLLOQ. bop, hoof it, hop, jig, shake a leg
2 dance for joy

skip, leap, jump, bounce, frisk, caper, cavort, frolic, gambol, juke, kantikoy, prance, skip, spin, stomp, sway, swing, tread a measure, whirl

3 *lights dancing on the water*
leap, sway, flicker, twinkle, flash, shimmer, sparkle, waver, play, ripple, move lightly

◆ *n*
ball, social
COLLOQ. bop, hop, knees-up, shindig
Related adjectives: orchestic, terpsichorean

Dances include:

beguine	Highland fling	polka
belly-dance	hoe-down	quadrille
black bottom	hokey-cokey	quickstep
bop	hora	reel
bolero	jig	rock 'n' roll
bossanova	jitterbug	rumba
can-can	jive	salsa
ceroc	kazachoc	samba
cha-cha	Lambeth Walk	square dance
Charleston	Lancers	stomp
Circassian circle	macarena	Strip the Willow
clog dance	mambo	tango
conga	mashed potato	turkey trot
dashing white	mazurka	twist
sergeant	merengue	valeta
fandango	military two-step	vogue
flamenco	minuet	waltz
foxtrot	morris-dance	
galliard	one-step	
gavotte	paso doble	
the Gay Gordons	Paul Jones	

Types of dancing include:

ballet	disco	limbo-dancing
ballroom	flamenco	line-dancing
bogling	folk	morris dancing
break-dancing	Highland	old-time
clog-dancing	Irish	robotics
country	Latin-American	tap

See also **ballet**.

Dance functions include:

ball	disco	*N Am* prom
barn dance	fancy dress ball	rave
ceilidh	*colloq.* hop	shindig
charity ball	hunt ball	social
dance	knees-up	tea dance

---

dancer *n*
danseur, danseuse, ballerina, ballet dancer, baladin, coryphee, figurant, comprimario, tap-dancer, morisco, belly-dancer, showgirl
COLLOQ. bopper, hoofer

dandle *v*
jiggle, bounce, dance, toss, cradle, fondle, pet, cuddle; *Scot* doodle

dandy *n, adj*
◆ *n*
fop, coxcomb, beau, man about town, Adonis, beau, blade, dapperling, dude, exquisite, peacock, popinjay, swell, toff
OLD (*Shakesp*) princox
SLANG *Aust* lair
◆ *adj*
fine, capital, excellent, first-rate, great, splendid

danger *n*
1 *in danger of falling*

insecurity, jeopardy, precariousness, perilousness, liability, vulnerability
FORMAL endangerment, imperilment
2 *the dangers of smoking*
risk, threat, peril, hazard, menace, pitfall
F3 **1** safety, security **2** safety

dangerous *adj*
unsafe, insecure, risky, high-risk, fraught with danger, threatening, breakneck, hazardous, chancy, perilous, precarious, reckless, treacherous, vulnerable, defenceless, menacing, ominous, exposed, susceptible, alarming, critical, severe, serious, grave, daring, nasty
FORMAL minacious
COLLOQ. dicey, hairy, dodgy
F3 safe, secure, harmless

Synonym nuances
Unsafe and **insecure** can be widely used to suggest an inherent lack of safety, physical or otherwise: *his job was very insecure*. To describe a situation or condition that has likely pitfalls you could use **perilous** or **precarious**, the latter giving a strong impression of potential failure: *in some areas farming is a precarious business*. Both **risky** and **high-risk**, as well as **chancy**, suggest an element of actively gambling on something.

The term **daring**, meanwhile, would be appropriately used of a bold but dangerous exploit. **Hazardous** can be similarly used to suggest taking a chance: *setting up as an artist is a hazardous undertaking*, although it can also be used of more unavoidable dangers: *hazardous driving conditions*. **Breakneck** is specifically used of high speed, while **reckless** could be used to describe an approach that gives no regard to safety. **Treacherous** implies hidden dangers: *prematurely aged by the treacherous sun*.

The terms **vulnerable**, **defenceless** and **exposed** could be used of a dangerous situation offering no protection; **susceptible** is similar but is even more suggestive of actually being prone to an attack. **Menacing**, on the other hand, emphasizes the intimidating aspect of danger, whereas **ominous** is strongly suggestive of foreboding evil or harm: *the ominous escalation of tension*.

---

dangerously *adv*
perilously, precariously, menacingly, threateningly, seriously, critically, gravely, severely, acutely, alarmingly

dangle *v*
1 HANG, droop, swing, sway, sag, wave, flap, trail
2 TEMPT, entice, flaunt, flourish, offer, seduce, lure, hold out, tantalize

dank *adj*
damp, moist, wet, clammy, sticky, dewy, musty, chilly, slimy, soggy
F3 dry

dapper *adj*
trim, well-dressed, well-turned-out, well-groomed, debonair, chic, dainty, neat, tidy, smart, spruce, stylish, nimble, active, brisk, spry
COLLOQ. natty
F3 dishevelled, dowdy, scruffy, shabby, sloppy

dappled *adj*
speckled, mottled, spotted, blotched, blotchy, streaked, stippled, dotted, flecked, freckled, variegated, bespeckled, piebald, pied, chequered

dare *v, n*
◆ *v*
1 RISK, venture, brave, be brave/bold enough, have the courage, hazard, adventure, endanger, stake, gamble, go so far as

COLLOQ. go out on a limb
2 CHALLENGE, goad, provoke, taunt, defy, invite, throw down the gauntlet
COLLOQ.
3 DEFY, face, brave, confront, resist, flout, stand up to
◆ *n*
challenge, venture, risk, provocation, taunt, goad, ultimatum, gauntlet

daredevil *n, adj*
◆ *n*
adventurer, desperado, madcap, hothead, swashbuckler, stuntman
F∃ coward
◆ *adj*
adventurous, daring, bold, fearless, dauntless, intrepid, brave, plucky, audacious, dauntless, hasty, reckless, rash, impetuous, impulsive, valiant, madcap, hotheaded

daring *adj, n*
◆ *adj*
bold, adventurous, intrepid, courageous, fearless, brave, plucky, audacious, valiant, venturesome, dauntless, undaunted, reckless, wild, rash, impulsive, foolhardy
F∃ cautious, timid, afraid
◆ *n*
boldness, fearlessness, courage, bravery, adventurousness, audacity, intrepidity, valour, defiance, pluck, nerve, spirit, gall, prowess, wildness, recklessness, rashness, foolhardiness
COLLOQ. guts, grit, bottle, spunk
F∃ caution, timidity, cowardice

daringly *adv*
boldly, adventurously, courageously, fearlessly, bravely, audaciously

dark *adj, n*
◆ *adj*
1 *a dark room/day*
unlit, badly/poorly/dimly lit, overcast, black, dim, unilluminated, shady, shadowy, sunless, cloudy, murky, misty, foggy, dusky, gloomy, dingy
FORMAL tenebrous, crepuscular
2 *dark hair*
black, brown, auburn, tawny, chestnut, dark-haired, brunette
3 *dark skin*
dark-skinned, swarthy, Black, dusky, tanned, suntanned, bronzed, olive
4 *a dark manner*
gloomy, grim, sad, cheerless, joyless, drab, dismal, bleak, forbidding, sombre, sinister, dejected, mournful, morose, moody, ominous, menacing
5 *the dark days of war*
unpleasant, tragic, disastrous, awful, worrying, sad, gloomy, distressing, hopeless, frightening, bleak, dismal, black
6 *dark secrets*
hidden, mysterious, obscure, secret, concealed, veiled, inscrutable, unintelligible, puzzling, enigmatic, intricate, cryptic
FORMAL abstruse, arcane, recondite, esoteric
7 *dark deeds*
evil, wicked, bad, wrong, horrible, iniquitous, immoral, base, vile, despicable, foul
COLLOQ. dirty, crooked
F∃ 1 light, bright, clear **2** fair, blond(e) **3** light, pale **4** bright, cheerful **5** happy, joyful **6** comprehensible **7** good
◆ *n*
1 DARKNESS, dimness, night, night-time, nightfall, evening, blackness, gloom, gloominess, dusk, twilight, half-light, shadows, shade, shadiness, murkiness, sunlessness, cloudiness, mist, fog
FORMAL tenebrity, tenebrosity

2 IGNORANCE, secrecy, privacy, concealment, obscurity, mystery
F∃ 1 light, brightness, daylight, lightness **2** enlightenment, openness

---

Synonym nuances
adjective sense 1
Unlit or **unilluminated** simply describe any situation where no light has been introduced, whereas **cloudy** and **overcast** specifically mean clouds are blocking the sun's light, which in itself can create an ominous or gloomy impression: *the sky was growing overcast and threatening.* **Black**, although literally describing the colour, can again sound vaguely threatening when describing something very dark: *black pools of water; the black woods.* **Dim**, however, simply suggests lacking brightness: *dim streetlamps.*
The term **shady** implies pleasant protection from light and heat: *a shady patio;* the less positive **shadowy** suggests a more hostile or threatening darkness: *the empty shadowy corridors.* **Misty** and **foggy** again describe atmospheric conditions: *the misty valley; foggy autumn days.* **Murky**, on the other hand, suggests an unpleasant lack of clarity, possibly exacerbated by the presence of dirt: *the murky waters.* The term **dusky** tends to be more narrowly used to suggest the idea of muted evening light, and the connotations may be quite pleasant. However, to use **gloomy** and **dingy** of a lack of light results in a somewhat depressing impression: *a dingy bedsit.*

---

darken *v*
1 DIM, become/grow darker, obscure, blacken, cloud (over), fog, shadow, overshadow, shade, fade, eclipse
OLD obnubilate
2 DEPRESS, sadden, deject, make gloomy, cast down, weigh down, grow/become angry, look angry, frown
F∃ 1 lighten **2** brighten

darkly *adv*
1 DIMLY, obscurely, blackly, at/by night, in the shadows
2 GLOOMILY, dismally, glumly, sullenly
3 MYSTERIOUSLY, enigmatically, cryptically, inscrutably
F∃ 1 lightly **2** happily

darling *n, adj*
◆ *n*
1 *come here, darling*
beloved, dear, dearest, favourite, sweetheart, love, pet, poppet, treasure, precious; *Irish* mavourneen, acushla, asthore
COLLOQ. angel, honey, sweetie, sugar
2 *the darling of the fashion world*
favourite, pet, celebrity, idol, hero, apple of your eye
COLLOQ. blue-eyed boy, teacher's pet; *N Am* fair-haired boy
◆ *adj*
dear, dearest, beloved, loved, adored, cherished, prized, precious, treasured

darn *v*
mend, repair, stitch, sew (up), patch, cobble

dart *v, n*
◆ *v*
1 DASH, bound, sprint, flit, flash, fly, rush, run, race, spring, leap, tear, bolt, scurry, start, pounce, skit; *Scot* cook, wheech
OLD endart
COLLOQ. scoot
2 THROW, cast, hurl, fling, shoot, toss, sling, strike, launch, project, propel, send, flash, glance
OLD lance
◆ *n*

bolt, arrow, barb, feather, flight, shaft, fléchette, harpoon, banderilla

dash v, n
- v

1 RUSH, fly, hurry, tear, dart, dive, race, sprint, run, speed, bolt, bound, hurtle; *Scot* wheech
COLLOQ. nip, pop
2 *waves dashing against rocks*
smash, strike, lash, pound, beat, break, throw, crash, toss, slam, hurl, fling
OLD (*Shakesp*) pash
3 *dash your hopes*
crush, smash, shatter, disappoint, discourage, dishearten, let down, depress, sadden, dampen, confound, blight, ruin, destroy, spoil, frustrate, thwart, destroy, devastate, ruin, wreck
- n

1 DROP, pinch, grain, touch, flavour, soupçon, spot, speck, trace, suggestion, hint, tinge, bit, little
COLLOQ. tad, smidgen
2 SPRINT, dart, bolt, rush, spurt, race, run
3 *everything she did showed dash and determination*
verve, vitality, vivacity, animation, energy, élan, liveliness, sparkle, vigour, passion, fervour, enthusiasm, gusto, life, relish, spirit, force, brio
COLLOQ. pizzazz, zip
■ **dash off**
scribble, jot down, scrawl

dashing adj
1 LIVELY, vigorous, spirited, energetic, animated, gallant, daring, bold, plucky, exuberant
2 SMART, stylish, fashionable, elegant, debonair, showy, flamboyant, attractive, dapper
F3 1 lethargic 2 dowdy

dastardly adj
wicked, iniquitous, evil, fiendish, diabolical, low, mean, base, contemptible, underhand, vile, cowardly, craven, despicable, faint-hearted, lily-livered
F3 heroic, noble

data n
information, documents, facts, input, statistics, figures, details, material, research, particulars, features

date n, v
- n

1 TIME, age, period, era, stage, epoch, day, week, month, year, decade, century, millennium
2 APPOINTMENT, engagement, meeting, rendezvous
OLD tryst
FORMAL assignation
3 FRIEND, boyfriend, girlfriend, young man, young lady, man friend, woman friend, lady friend, partner, escort
COLLOQ. steady
- v

1 *date back to the 18th century*
originate, go back, come/exist from, belong
2 *buy styles that won't date*
become old-fashioned/obsolete, go out, go out of use, show its age
FORMAL obsolesce
3 *date someone*
go out with, take out, go with, be involved with, be together, go steady with, court
■ **out of date**
old-fashioned, unfashionable, outdated, obsolete, dated, outmoded, antiquated, archaic, passé
F3 fashionable, modern
■ **to date**
so far, until now, as yet, yet, until the present time, up to now, up to the present
■ **up to date**
fashionable, modern, current, contemporary, up-to-the-minute, latest, recent, present-day

COLLOQ. trendy, now, in, cool, with it, hip, all the rage, state-of-the-art
F3 old-fashioned, dated

dated adj
old-fashioned, obsolete, outdated, outmoded, out-of-date, passé, superseded, unfashionable, unstylish, obsolescent, antiquated, archaic
COLLOQ. old hat, square
F3 fashionable, up-to-the-minute

daub v, n
- v

smear, plaster, coat, paint, cover, smirch, bedaub, splash, dab, beplaster, smudge, spatter, bespatter, splatter, stain, sully
- n

smear, splash, splodge, splotch, spot, stain, blot, blotch

daughter n
girl, child, lass, lassie, offspring, descendant, inhabitant, disciple

daunt v
intimidate, unnerve, alarm, scare, dismay, frighten, disconcert, cow, overawe, take aback, discourage, dishearten, demoralize, disillusion, put off, dispirit, abash, shake, ruffle, deter
COLLOQ. faze, rattle
F3 encourage, hearten

daunting adj
intimidating, unnerving, alarming, frightening, disconcerting, discouraging, disheartening, demoralizing, dispiriting
COLLOQ. scary
F3 encouraging, heartening

dauntingly adv
intimidatingly, unnervingly, alarmingly, frighteningly, disconcertingly, discouragingly, dishearteningly, demoralizingly, dispiritingly
COLLOQ. scarily
F3 encouragingly

dauntless adj
fearless, undaunted, resolute, brave, courageous, bold, determined, indomitable, intrepid, daring, plucky, valiant, doughty
F3 discouraged, disheartened

dawdle v
delay, loiter, lag, go slowly, go at a snail's pace, hang about, linger, dally, take your time, take too long, trail, potter; *N Am* putter
FORMAL tarry
COLLOQ. dilly-dally, drag your feet, faff about
F3 hurry

dawn n, v
- n

1 SUNRISE, daybreak, break of day, morning, daylight, first light, crack of dawn, cock-crow, sunrise, sun-up, Aurora
Related adjectives: auroral, aurorean
2 BEGINNING, start, emergence, onset, origin, birth, arrival, rise
FORMAL commencement, advent, inception, genesis
F3 1 dusk 2 end
- v

1 BREAK, brighten, lighten, become/grow light, gleam, glimmer
2 BEGIN, appear, emerge, open, break, arrive, develop, originate, be born, come into being, rise
FORMAL commence
■ **dawn on**
realize, strike, occur to, sink in, register with, come into your mind
COLLOQ. hit, click

day *n*
1 DAYTIME, daylight, daylight hours
2 AGE, period, time, date, era, generation, epoch
3 *he must have been good-looking in his day*
heyday, peak, prime, flush, bloom, golden age
F3 1 night

■ **day after day**
regularly, repeatedly, again and again, time and (time)
again, continually, endlessly, persistently, monotonously,
perpetually, relentlessly

■ **day by day**
gradually, progressively, slowly but surely, steadily

■ **day in, day out**
every day, regularly, repeatedly, again and again, time and
(time) again, continually, endlessly, persistently,
monotonously

■ **have had its day**
be no longer fashionable/popular, be no longer useful/
successful, be out of date
COLLOQ. be past it
Related adjective: diurnal

daybreak *n*
sunrise, dawn, break of day, morning, daylight, first light,
crack of dawn, cock-crow, sun-up, Aurora
F3 sunset, sundown

daydream *n, v*
◆ *n*
fantasy, imagining, reverie, castles in the air, pipe dream,
vision, musing, wish, dream, inattention, figment, trance,
woolgathering
◆ *v*
fantasize, imagine, muse, fancy, dream, be lost in space,
muse, not pay attention, let your thoughts wander, stare
into space, be in a brown study, build castles in the air
COLLOQ. switch off

daydreamer *n*
fantasizer, fantasist, dreamer, romantic, idealist, visionary,
Walter Mitty, Don Quixote

daylight *n*
1 *during daylight hours*
light, natural light, day, daytime, sunlight
2 SUNRISE, dawn, daybreak, break of day, morning, first
light, crack of dawn, cock-crow, sun-up
F3 1 night, dark

daze *v, n*
◆ *v*
1 STUN, stupefy, shock, numb, paralyse, knock out, knock
unconscious
2 DAZZLE, bewilder, blind, confuse, baffle, dumbfound,
amaze, surprise, shock, stun, startle, perplex, astonish,
astound, stagger, take aback
COLLOQ. flabbergast, bowl over, blow away, knock for six
◆ *n*
bewilderment, confusion, stupor, numbness, trance,
shock, distraction, spin, whirl

dazed *adj*
1 STUNNED, stupefied, shocked, numbed, paralysed,
unconscious
COLLOQ. out
2 DAZZLED, bewildered, confused, baffled, dumbfounded,
speechless, amazed, surprised, shocked, stunned,
startled, perplexed, astonished, astounded, staggered,
taken aback
COLLOQ. flabbergasted, bowled over, blown away

dazzle *v, n*
◆ *v*
1 DAZE, blind, confuse, blur
2 SPARKLE, fascinate, impress, strike, overwhelm, awe,
overawe, overpower, scintillate, bedazzle, amaze,
astonish, bewitch, hypnotize, dumbfound, stupefy

COLLOQ. bowl over, knock out, wow
◆ *n*
1 *the dazzle of the headlights*
glare, brightness, blaze, flare, gleam, flash, brilliance
2 *the glamour and dazzle of the theatre*
sparkle, brilliance, brightness, magnificence, splendour,
scintillation, glitter
COLLOQ. razzmatazz

dazzling *adj*
1 *a dazzling light*
bright, glaring, shining, brilliant, blinding
2 *a dazzling performance*
brilliant, splendid, impressive, stunning, awe-inspiring,
breathtaking, spectacular, glaring, glittering, shining,
sparkling, glorious, radiant, ravishing, scintillating,
sensational, grand, superb

dazzlingly *adv*
1 *dazzlingly coloured*
brightly, glaringly, brilliantly, blindingly
2 *dazzlingly talented*
brilliantly, impressively, breathtakingly, spectacularly,
gloriously, radiantly, sensationally, superbly

deactivate *v*
disable, immobilize, paralyse, stop, put out of action
FORMAL render inoperative

dead *adj, adv*
◆ *adj*
1 LIFELESS, inanimate, defunct, departed, passed on, passed
away, perished, extinct, late, gone, no more, asleep
FORMAL deceased, expired
COLLOQ. dead as a dodo, dead as a doornail, pushing up
the daisies, six feet under; *Aust* bung
2 *dead leaves*
inanimate, lifeless, barren, inert
FORMAL insentient, insensate, exanimate
3 *a dead language*
obsolete, extinct, discontinued, disused, defunct, no
longer spoken
4 *that issue is dead*
dated, out of date, passé, no longer of interest
COLLOQ. old hat, dead as a dodo
5 *this town is dead*
boring, dull, humdrum, tedious, uninteresting, unexciting,
with nothing happening, quiet, flat, sleepy
6 *my fingers have gone dead*
numb, unfeeling, not feeling anything, gone to sleep,
paralysed, benumbed
FORMAL insensate
7 UNRESPONSIVE, apathetic, dull, indifferent, insensitive,
numb, cold, emotionless, unemotional, unfeeling, frigid,
lukewarm, unsympathetic, torpid
8 *dead centre*
exact, absolute, perfect, unqualified, utter, outright,
complete, entire, total, downright, thorough
9 EXHAUSTED, tired, tired out, worn out
COLLOQ. knackered, dead beat, ready to drop
10 *the telephone line is dead*
out of order, not working, broken, broken-down, defunct,
ineffective
COLLOQ. kaput, on the blink, conked out, bust; *N Am* on
the fritz
F3 1 alive **3** living **7** lively **9** refreshed **10** working
◆ *adv*
1 *the post office is dead opposite the library*
directly, straight, exactly, immediately
COLLOQ. bang, smack
2 *it's dead easy*
very, absolutely, completely, extremely, exceptionally,
really, terribly, awfully
3 *the train stopped dead*
completely, absolutely, quite, utterly

Synonym nuances

adjective sense 1

Lifeless can be used of any lack of movement or any other sign of life: *his lifeless body*. **Inanimate** would only be used when life was never present: *inanimate objects*. **Defunct**, on the other hand, describes something that was formerly functioning: *the now defunct air-conditioning*.

The terms **departed**, **passed on** and **passed away** are rather euphemistic ways of referring gently to the death of any living creature, especially man: *my dear departed grandmother*. **Gone** and **no more** are also indirect ways of describing a person or animal that has died, as is the even more euphemistic **asleep**.

Perished, though also used of previously living things, is more suggestive of having met an unnatural end: *they perished when their boats capsized*. **Extinct** would be used specifically of an entire group or species ceasing to exist: *the red squirrel is virtually extinct in parts of the country*. **Late** is a more formalized way of referring to someone who has expired: *it was her late grandfather's house*.

deaden *v*

1 *deaden pain*
reduce, blunt, muffle, dull, lessen, quieten, suppress, weaken, numb, diminish, stifle, mitigate, alleviate, soothe, moderate, take the edge off, anaesthetize, desensitize, smother, check, allay, assuage, subdue, dampen, hush, mute, paralyse
FORMAL abate
2 *deaden imagination*
numb, benumb, desensitize, make insensitive, harden
F3 1 heighten

deadline *n*
time limit, target date, time, time up, term

deadlock *n*
standstill, stalemate, checkmate, impasse, dead end, halt, stoppage, log jam; *N Am* stand-off

deadly *adj, adv*
♦ *adj*
1 *deadly poison*
lethal, fatal, dangerous, venomous, toxic, destructive, life-threatening, death-dealing, pernicious, noxious, malignant, murderous, mortal
2 *deadly enemies*
implacable, irreconcilable, mortal, murderous, hated, grim, fierce, savage, bitter
3 *in deadly earnest*
great, serious, marked, intense, extreme
4 *a deadly lecture*
dull, boring, uninteresting, unexciting, tedious, monotonous, humdrum
5 *deadly aim*
unerring, unfailing, precise, accurate, perfect, flawless, sure, effective, true
F3 1 harmless **4** exciting
♦ *adv*
utterly, thoroughly, dreadfully, absolutely, completely, entirely, perfectly, quite, totally, utterly

deadpan *adj*
blank, empty, expressionless, unexpressive, impassive, inexpressive, inscrutable, poker-faced, straight-faced, dispassionate
F3 expressive

deaf *adj*
1 HARD OF HEARING, stone-deaf, with impaired hearing
COLLOQ. deaf as a post
2 UNCONCERNED, indifferent, impervious, unmoved, unaffected, untouched, oblivious, heedless, unmindful
F3 2 aware, conscious

deafening *adj*
piercing, very loud, very noisy, ear-splitting, ear-piercing, booming, resounding, thundering, thunderous, ringing, reverberating, roaring, overwhelming
F3 quiet

deal *v, n*
♦ *v*
1 DISTRIBUTE, give out, share, dole out, divide, allot, dispense, assign, mete out
FORMAL apportion, bestow
2 TRADE, do business, buy and sell, negotiate, traffic, export, bargain, handle, treat, operate, market, stock
OLD (*Shakesp*) mart
FORMAL vend
COLLOQ. flog, push
3 *deal a blow*
deliver, administer, direct, mete, inflict, dispense
♦ *n*
1 QUANTITY, lot, load, amount, extent, degree, portion, share
2 AGREEMENT, contract, understanding, pact, transaction, bargain, buy, arrangement, covenant
3 ROUND, hand, distribution
■ **deal with**
1 *deal with a situation*
attend to, concern, see to, manage, handle, tackle, cope with, get to grips with, take care of, look after, sort out, process
2 *her novel deals with the future*
treat, consider, be about, concern, cover, tackle, have to do with

dealer *n*
trader, seller, salesman, saleswoman, salesperson, merchant, retailer, wholesaler, supplier, distributor, marketer, merchandizer, vendor, trafficker, agent, broker, brinjarry, hawker, pedlar, chapman, coper, monger; *Scot* couper
COLLOQ. pusher, tout

dealing *n*
1 *drug dealing*
trading, business, trade, commerce, transaction, operation, traffic, trafficking, marketing
2 *my dealings with you*
relations, association, connections, communication
FORMAL intercourse
COLLOQ. truck

dean *n*
1 *the dean of the Faculty of Law*
head of faculty, head of department, head, principal, director, doyen
2 *dean of the cathedral*
chapter head, rural dean, cardinal-bishop, vicar-forane

dear *adj, n*
♦ *adj*
1 LOVED, beloved, treasured, valued, cherished, adored, favoured, esteemed, precious, favourite, intimate, respected, close, darling, familiar, endearing
2 EXPENSIVE, high-priced, costly, high-cost, overpriced, excessive, exorbitant, not cheap, extortionate
OLD chargeful
COLLOQ. steep, pricey, posh, sky-high, costing an arm and a leg, costing the earth, costing a bomb, daylight robbery; *N Am* big-ticket
OLD SLANG salt
F3 1 disliked, hated **2** cheap, inexpensive
♦ *n*
beloved, loved one, precious, darling, pet, sweetheart, treasure
COLLOQ. angel, honey, sweetie, sugar

dearly *adv*
1 *he loves her dearly*

fondly, affectionately, with affection, lovingly, devotedly, adoringly, tenderly, intimately, with favour/respect
2 *I wish it dearly*
greatly, extremely, very much, deeply, profoundly, a great deal
3 *pay dearly for something*
at a great cost, at a high price, with great loss, with much suffering

dearth *n*
scarcity, shortage, deficiency, insufficiency, inadequacy, deficiency, lack, absence, scantiness, sparsity, need, poverty, famine, meagreness
FORMAL paucity, want, exiguousness
E3 excess, abundance

death *n*
1 *people in danger of death*
loss, departure, loss of life, fatality, passing, passing away, passing on, perishing, end, finish, the grave
OLD (*Shakesp & Spenser*) funeral; (*Shakesp*) defunction
FORMAL expiration, decease, demise, quietus
COLLOQ. last farewell, curtains
2 *the death of the welfare state*
ruin, destruction, end, finish, undoing, annihilation, downfall, extermination, dissolution, extinction
FORMAL demise, obliteration, eradication, extirpation, termination, cessation
EE **1** life, birth
■ **put to death**
execute, kill, hang, electrocute, shoot, guillotine, behead, decapitate, shoot, gas, send to the electric chair, exterminate, martyr
COLLOQ. do in, take out
SLANG bump off, knock off, rub out, waste, blow away
Related adjective: mortal

deathless *adj*
immortal, imperishable, eternal, everlasting, undying, never-ending, timeless, incorruptible, inextinguishable, memorable, unforgettable

deathly *adj*
1 ASHEN, grim, haggard, pale, pallid, ghastly, wan, white, colourless, cadaverous, ghostly, ghost-like
2 FATAL, deadly, mortal, intense, extreme, terrible, harmful, utmost

debacle *n*
fiasco, catastrophe, failure, collapse, defeat, devastation, disaster, downfall, havoc, cataclysm, overthrow, reversal, rout, turmoil, disintegration, ruin, ruination, stampede, farce
COLLOQ. hash, foul-up, washout
SLANG cock-up, balls-up, screw-up

debar *v*
ban, bar, forbid, prohibit, eject, exclude, shut out, keep out, expel, stop, hamper, hinder, obstruct, prevent, segregate, restrain, deny, blackball
FORMAL preclude, proscribe
EB admit, allow

debase *v*
degrade, demean, devalue, disgrace, dishonour, discredit, shame, humble, humiliate, cheapen, lower, reduce, abase, defile, contaminate, pollute, corrupt, adulterate, bastardize, embase, alloy, dilute, taint
FORMAL vitiate
EE elevate, enhance, purify

debased *adj*
degraded, devalued, disgraced, dishonoured, discredited, shamed, humbled, humiliated, cheapened, abased, defiled, contaminated, impure, polluted, perverted, corrupt, debauched, immoral, sinful, fallen, low, degenerate, adulterated, tainted, base, sordid, vile
EE elevated, pure, honourable

debasement *n*
degradation, devaluation, disgrace, dishonour, shame, humiliation, cheapening, depravation, abasement, defilement, contamination, pollution, perversion, corruption, degeneration, adulteration
EB elevation, purification

debatable *adj*
questionable, arguable, uncertain, unsure, unclear, disputable, contestable, controversial, open to question, doubtful, contentious, undecided, unsettled, problematical, dubious, moot
EB unquestionable, certain, indisputable, incontrovertible

debate *n, v*
♦ *n*
discussion, argument, controversy, deliberation, consideration, forum, exchange of views, contention, dispute, reflection, polemic; *Scot* flyte
FORMAL disputation, altercation
COLLOQ. powwow
♦ *v*
1 DISPUTE, argue, reason, discuss, talk about/over/through, contend, contest, wrangle, thrash out
FORMAL altercate
COLLOQ. kick about/around, knock about/around
2 CONSIDER, think over, deliberate, ponder, reflect, meditate on, mull over, weigh
FORMAL cogitate

debauch *v*
corrupt, lead astray, deprave, over-indulge, pervert, pollute, subvert, ravish, ruin, seduce, violate, whore
FORMAL vitiate
EB cleanse, purge, purify

debauched *adj*
depraved, abandoned, immoral, corrupt, corrupted, debased, perverted, degenerate, degraded, intemperate, overindulgent, dissipated, dissolute, excessive, decadent, promiscuous, wanton, lewd, carousing, riotous
FORMAL licentious
EB decent, pure, virtuous, chaste

debauchery *n*
depravity, immorality, corruption, degeneracy, degradation, intemperance, overindulgence, rakishness, dissoluteness, excess, decadence, wantonness, lewdness, carousal, orgy, revel, lust, riot
FORMAL dissipation, licentiousness, libertinism
EB restraint, temperance, morality

debilitate *v*
weaken, undermine, sap, incapacitate, wear out, exhaust, drain, tire, fatigue, impair, cripple
FORMAL enervate, enfeeble, devitalize
EB strengthen, invigorate, energize

debilitating *adj*
weakening, undermining, incapacitating, wearing out, fatiguing, tiring, exhausting, impairing, crippling
FORMAL enervating, enervative, enfeebling
EB invigorating, strengthening

debility *n*
weakness, infirmity, tiredness, fatigue, weariness, exhaustion, faintness, feebleness, frailty, incapacity, infirmity, lack of energy/vitality
TECHNICAL asthenia, atonicity, atony, myasthenia
FORMAL decrepitude, enervation, enfeeblement, languor, malaise
EB strength, vigour

debonair *adj*
suave, refined, urbane, well-bred, sophisticated, cultured, dignified, stylish, smooth, dashing, elegant, affable, breezy, buoyant, charming, courteous, cheerful, jaunty, light-hearted

debrief v

interview, question, examine, interrogate, cross-examine, cross-question
COLLOQ. grill, give the third degree

debris n

remains, ruins, rubbish, refuse, waste, wreck, wreckage, litter, fragments, rubble, trash, pieces, bits, sweepings, scrap, dross, drift
TECHNICAL eluvium, tephra, pyroclastics
FORMAL detritus

debt n

1 their debts amounted to £10,000
overdraft, money owing/due, due, amount owing/due, arrears, liability, debit, duty, bill, account, hock, claim, score
2 he owed them a debt of gratitude
indebtedness, obligation, commitment, liability
E3 1 credit, asset
■ **in debt**
insolvent, in arrears, in overdraft, owing money
COLLOQ. gone to the wall, gone under, in the red, in Queer Street
■ **in someone's debt**
indebted, obliged, honour-bound, thankful, appreciative
FORMAL beholden

debtor n

borrower, bankrupt, insolvent, defaulter, mortgagor
COLLOQ. N Am deadbeat
E3 creditor

debunk v

expose, deflate, puncture, show up, ridicule, mock, explode, disprove, lampoon
COLLOQ. cut down to size, quash, shoot down in flames

debut n

first appearance, first performance, first night, first recording, first time, introduction, launch, launching, beginning, entrance, presentation, inauguration, première, coming-out, initiation

decadence n

corruption, debasement, debauchery, depravity, dissolution, immorality, degeneracy, degenerateness, degeneration, deterioration, self-indulgence, debasement, decay, decline, fall, perversion
FORMAL dissipation, licentiousness, retrogression
E3 flourishing, rise

decadent adj

1 CORRUPT, debased, debauched, depraved, dissolute, dissipated, immoral, degenerate, degraded, self-indulgent, unprincipled
FORMAL licentious
2 DECAYING, declining, degenerating, deteriorating, debased
E3 1 moral **2** resurgent

decamp v

make off, run away, take off, run off, abscond, bolt, desert, escape, flee, flit, fly
COLLOQ. scarper, skedaddle, vamoose, scrap, split, make tracks, do a runner, do a bunk, do a moonlight flit, hightail it, absquatulate
SLANG N Am lam it, take in on the lam

decant v

pour out, draw off, siphon off, transfer, drain, tap

decapitate v

behead, execute, guillotine, unhead

decay v, n

♦ v
1 ROT, go bad, go off, decompose, spoil, fester, perish, rust, corrode
FORMAL putrefy
2 DECLINE, deteriorate, disintegrate, corrode, crumble,

waste away, degenerate, atrophy, wear away, weaken, dwindle, fail, shrivel, wither, sink
COLLOQ. go downhill, go the the dogs, go to pot
E3 2 flourish, grow
♦ n
1 ROT, rotting, going bad, decomposition, perishing, mould, fungus, mildew
FORMAL putrefaction, putrescence, putridity
2 DECLINE, deterioration, disintegration, degeneration, collapse, crumbling, decadence, debasement, weakening, wasting, failing, atrophy, withering, fading

decayed adj

rotten, rotting, bad, off, stale, sour, rank, addled, carious, decomposed, spoiled, mouldy, mildewed, perished, corroded, carrion, wasted, withered
FORMAL putrefied, putrid, putrescent

decease n

death, dying, demise, departure, end, passing, passing away, passing on, dissolution, rest
FORMAL expiration, demise

deceased adj, n

♦ adj
dead, departed, former, late, lost, defunct, gone, no more, asleep, finished, extinct
FORMAL expired
COLLOQ. dead as a doornail, pushing up the daisies, six feet under
♦ n
dead, departed

deceit n

deception, pretence, cheating, misrepresentation, fraud, trickery, fraudulence, double-dealing, underhandedness, chicanery, fake, guile, subterfuge, swindle, treachery, hypocrisy, artifice, ruse, cunning, slyness, craftiness, wiliness, stratagem, wile, imposition, feint, abuse
OLD barrat, glozing, cozenage; (Spenser) malengine; Aust & NZ slenter
FORMAL duplicity
COLLOQ. sham, con, game, monkey business, dodge; N Am gold brick; Aust & NZ slinter
E3 honesty, openness, frankness

deceitful adj

dishonest, untruthful, lying, deceptive, deceiving, false, insincere, untrustworthy, double-dealing, double, fraudulent, treacherous, guileful, underhand, sneaky, counterfeit, crafty, sly, cunning, hypocritical, designing, illusory, knavish
FORMAL mendacious, duplicitous, dissembling, perfidious
COLLOQ. crooked, two-faced, tricky, foxy, sharp
E3 honest, open

deceitfully adv

dishonestly, untruthfully, deceptively, deceivingly, falsely, insincerely, fraudulently, treacherously, underhandedly, sneakily, craftily, slyly, cunningly, hypocritically
FORMAL mendaciously, duplicitously, perfidiously
E3 honestly, openly

deceive v

mislead, delude, cheat (on), betray, fool, trick, hoax, defraud, bluff, dupe, swindle, outsmart, outwit, impose upon, lead on, misguide, outwit, hoodwink, beguile, set a trap for, entrap, ensnare, camouflage, abuse, seduce, gull; Aust slip up
OLD (Shakesp) misuse
FORMAL dissemble
COLLOQ. con, kid, bamboozle, have on, do, string along, double-cross, two-time, pull someone's leg, pull a fast one on, pull the wool over someone's eyes, put up a smokescreen, lead up the garden path, put one over on; N Am pull/yank someone's chain
SLANG take for a ride

deceiver n

deluder, cheat, betrayer, fake, fraud, hypocrite, trickster, hoaxer, swindler, impostor, charlatan, abuser, seducer, mountebank
OLD guiler, guyler, treacher, tregetour; (*Spenser*) treachetour, falser
FORMAL dissembler, inveigler
COLLOQ. con man, diddler, crook, double-dealer

decelerate v

slow down, slow, go more slowly, brake, put the brakes on, reduce speed

decency n

respectability, uprightness, integrity, civility, correctness, fitness, good taste, etiquette, courtesy, politeness, modesty, helpfulness
OLD seemliness
FORMAL propriety, decorum
Ⓔ impropriety, discourtesy

decent adj

1 *decent behaviour*
respectable, upright, worthy, proper, fitting, dignified, correct, tasteful, chaste, virtuous, ethical, suitable, modest, appropriate, presentable, pure, fit, becoming, befitting, nice
OLD seemly
FORMAL decorous
2 *a decent person*
kind, obliging, courteous, helpful, accommodating, generous, thoughtful, honest, dependable, trustworthy, civil, polite, gracious
3 ADEQUATE, acceptable, satisfactory, reasonable, sufficient, tolerable, fair, competent
COLLOQ. OK
Ⓔ 1 indecent **2** disobliging **3** unsatisfactory

Synonym nuances
sense 1
Respectable and **upright** are fairly restrained terms to describe someone (or the behaviour of someone) who merits the esteem of others, as is **worthy**, although this may be used with a slightly sneering or facetious implication: *the classics teacher was a worthy pedant*. The terms **proper**, **fitting** and **correct**, as well as **fit** and **befitting**, may all be used to approve of something appropriate to the situation: *his fitting tribute*; *a welcome befitting their status*; **suitable** and **appropriate** are similar, but more neutral in tone.
  Dignified puts the emphasis on a degree of stateliness and decorum, while **tasteful** could be used to suggest an element of discernment: *a tasteful joke*. **Chaste**, **pure** and **virtuous** strongly imply approval of moral or sexual decency, and **modest** implies decency born of a sense of propriety. **Ethical** has more to do with adhering to a moral code: *the City's ethical standards seem to have disappeared.*
  Presentable, meanwhile, might be used of a decent appearance, although it may be used to suggest being little more than passable: *give me time to make myself look presentable.*

---

decently adv

1 *act decently*
respectably, properly, correctly, ethically, honestly, suitably, appropriately, presentably, becomingly, nicely, obligingly, courteously, politely, graciously, helpfully, generously, thoughtfully
FORMAL decorously
2 *a decently sized share*
adequately, acceptably, satisfactorily, reasonably, sufficiently, tolerably, fairly

decentralize n

devolve, regionalize, localize, delegate, deconcentrate, spread downwards/outwards
Ⓔ centralize

deception n

deceit, pretence, deceptiveness, insincerity, treachery, hypocrisy, cheating, misrepresentation, trickery, fraudulence, double-dealing, underhandedness, chicanery, trick, cheat, imposture, lie, hoax, fraud, bluff, ruse, snare, guile, sham, subterfuge, artifice, swindle, stratagem, illusion, smoke and mirrors, wile, craftiness, cunning
FORMAL dissembling, duplicity
COLLOQ. con, set-up, scam, put-up job, leg-pull, flim-flam
Ⓔ openness, honesty

deceptive adj

misleading, dishonest, false, fraudulent, cheating, cunning, sly, crafty, underhand, unreliable, illusive, fake, illusory, spurious, specious, mock, bogus, sham, ambiguous
FORMAL fallacious, dissembling, duplicitous
COLLOQ. crooked, foxy, sharp
Ⓔ genuine, artless, open

deceptively adv

misleadingly, illusively, ambiguously, spuriously, speciously, dishonestly, falsely, fraudulently

decide v

1 *decide to do something*
make up your mind, come to/arrive at a decision, reach/make a decision, come to/reach a conclusion, determine, resolve, commit yourself, opt in
2 *decide an issue/a case*
settle, resolve, determine, work out, conclude, fix, establish, adjudicate, arbitrate, judge, rule, give a judgement/ruling
COLLOQ. clinch, wrap up
3 *decide on a new car*
choose, pick, select, opt for, settle
COLLOQ. go for, plump for

decided adj

1 DEFINITE, clear, certain, marked, obvious, undeniable, indisputable, unequivocal, absolute, clear-cut, pronounced, undisputed, unmistakable, unquestionable, positive, unambiguous, categorical, express, absolute, distinct, emphatic
2 RESOLUTE, decisive, determined, purposeful, firm, unhesitating, unswerving, unwavering, deliberate, forthright
Ⓔ 1 inconclusive **2** irresolute

decidedly adv

very, absolutely, certainly, downright, positively, quite, unquestionably, unequivocally, unmistakably, clearly, definitely, distinctly, markedly, noticeably, obviously, decisively

decider n

clincher, *coup de grâce*, determiner

deciding adj

decisive, determining, conclusive, critical, crucial, significant, final, chief, influential, prime, principal, key, supreme
COLLOQ. crunch
Ⓔ insignificant

decimate v

destroy, devastate, obliterate, flatten, annihilate, eliminate, eradicate

decipher v

decode, unscramble, unravel, interpret, translate, make out, work out, solve, make sense of, understand, transliterate

FORMAL construe
COLLOQ. crack, figure out, suss out; N Am dope (out)
⊞ encode

decision n
1 CONCLUSION, result, outcome, verdict, finding, settlement, resolution, recommendation, judgement, arbitration, adjudication, ruling, decree, pronouncement, opinion
2 DETERMINATION, decisiveness, firmness, resolve, forcefulness, purpose, strong-mindedness, single-mindedness

---

Synonym nuances
sense 1
Conclusion is used to refer to a decision arrived at through consideration, although it is often based on inference: *don't jump to the wrong conclusion*. **Result** and **outcome** put less emphasis on the human element, and more on how something turns out: *press reports influenced the outcome of the trial*.
  Judgement may also be used to suggest that everything has been duly considered before coming to a decision, as does **verdict**, which has strong associations with legal judgements and has connotations of finality. Although **finding** is more suggestive of action based on what has been elicited, this word too is often used in a courtroom context: *the tribunal's finding of unfair dismissal*. The terms **settlement** and **resolution** might be used of the agreed end of a dispute, and you may choose the terms **arbitration** or **adjudication** where there has been external mediation: *independent adjudication found in favour of the company*.
  Recommendation would be used specifically where a decision is accompanied by strong advice, often official: *the recommendation of the Law Commission*. The terms **ruling** and **decree** can be used of a decision with the weight of law behind them, but a **pronouncement**, however authoritative, is really just a declaration: *an official pronouncement on terrorism*.

---

decisive adj
1 CONCLUSIVE, deciding, definite, definitive, determining, absolute, final, critical, crucial, key, influential, significant, momentous, prime, principal, fateful
2 *a decisive person*
determined, resolute, decided, positive, firm, forceful, forthright, purposeful, strong, strong-minded, single-minded, unwavering, unswerving
⊞ 1 inconclusive, insignificant 2 indecisive

decisively adv
1 CONCLUSIVELY, definitively, absolutely, critically, crucially, influentially, significantly, momentously, fatefully
2 *act decisively*
determinedly, resolutely, positively, firmly, forcefully, forthrightly, purposefully, strongly, single-mindedly, unwaveringly, unswervingly
⊞ 1 inconclusively 2 indecisively

deck v
decorate, ornament, adorn, beautify, embellish, trim, garnish, garland, festoon, grace, enrich, prettify, beautify, trick out; N Am trick up
FORMAL array, bedeck
COLLOQ. tart up
■ **deck out**
dress, decorate, dress up, clothe, robe, garb
FORMAL array
COLLOQ. do up, rig, tog, tart up, get up, doll up

declaim v
speak boldly/dramatically, proclaim, hold forth, pronounce, lecture, harangue, rant, sermonize
OLD bespout

FORMAL orate, perorate, expostulate
COLLOQ. spiel, spout, sound off

declamation n
speech, address, lecture, oration, sermon, recitation, harangue, tirade, rant, speechifying

declamatory adj
bold, dramatic, rhetorical, bombastic, discursive, grandiloquent, grandiose, high-flown, inflated, oratorical, overblown, pompous, stagy, theatrical, stilted
TECHNICAL parlando
FORMAL magniloquent, orotund, fustian

declaration n
1 ANNOUNCEMENT, notification, communication, pronouncement, statement, proclamation, edict, decree, manifesto, broadcast
FORMAL promulgation
2 AFFIRMATION, acknowledgement, assertion, statement, confession, testimony, confirmation, disclosure, profession, revelation
FORMAL attestation, avowal, affidavit, asseveration, averment

declare v
1 ANNOUNCE, proclaim, make known, reveal, express, communicate, pronounce, decree, publish, broadcast
FORMAL promulgate
2 AFFIRM, assert, claim, profess, maintain, state, certify, pronounce, confess, confirm, disclose, make known, reveal, show, swear, testify, witness, validate
FORMAL aver, avow, attest, asseverate

decline v, n
♦ v
1 DIMINISH, become/get less, go/come down, decrease, de-escalate, dwindle, lessen, fade, fall, sink, subside, reduce, slide, drop, wane, weaken, wither, fade, ebb, flag, plummet, plunge, slump, tail off, peter out
FORMAL abate
2 REFUSE, turn down, say no to, reject, deny, repudiate, for(e)go, avoid, balk
COLLOQ. give the thumbs-down to, give the red light to
3 DECAY, deteriorate, worsen, degenerate, sink, rot, slip, fall off, lapse
FORMAL regress
COLLOQ. go to pot, go to pieces, go downhill
4 DESCEND, sink, slope, dip, slant
⊞ 1 grow, increase 2 accept 3 improve 4 rise
♦ n
1 DECREASE, reduction, lessening, lowering, dwindling, drop, downturn, downswing, slump
2 DETERIORATION, dwindling, lessening, decrease, reduction, de-escalation, decay, degeneration, weakening, worsening, failing, failure, downturn, dwindling, waning, fall, falling-off, recession, slump
FORMAL diminution, abatement
3 DESCENT, dip, declination, hill, slope, incline, divergence, deviation
FORMAL declivity
⊞ 1 increase 2 improvement 3 rise

decode v
decipher, decrypt, interpret, unscramble, unravel, translate, make out, work out, understand, transliterate, uncipher
FORMAL construe
COLLOQ. crack, figure out; N Am dope (out)
⊞ encode

decomposable adj
biodegradable, degradable, destructible, decompoundable

decompose v
disintegrate, rot, decay, go bad, go off, break down, break up, crumble, fragment, spoil, dissolve, separate, fester
FORMAL putrefy

decomposition n
rot, rotting, going bad, going off, decay, rotting, perishing, corruption, disintegration, dissolution
FORMAL putrefaction, putrescence, putridity
🗲 combination, unification

decontaminate v
disinfect, sterilize, fumigate, sanitize, cleanse, purify, purge, clean
🗲 contaminate

décor n
decoration, ornamentation, furnishings, colour scheme, ornamentation, scenery

decorate v
1 ORNAMENT, adorn, beautify, embellish, trim, garnish, deck, garland, festoon, grace, enrich, prettify, trick out; N Am trick up
OLD bedizen, bedaub
FORMAL array
COLLOQ. tart up
2 RENOVATE, paint, paper, wallpaper, colour, smarten, refurbish, furbish
COLLOQ. do up, spruce up, tart up
3 HONOUR, crown, cite, reward, give a medal/honour to, give an award to, garland, bemedal

decoration n
1 ORNAMENT, adornment, ornamentation, trimming, embellishment, beautification, enhancement, décor, furnishings, mural, colour scheme, garnish, flourish, enrichment, elaboration, bunting, frill, scroll, trinket, bauble, knick-knack
2 AWARD, medal, order, badge, garland, crown, colours, ribbon, cross, laurel, wreath, star, emblem, insignia, honour, title

decorative adj
ornamental, fancy, adorning, beautifying, embellishing, non-functional, pretty, prettifying, ornate, elaborate, enhancing, rococo
COLLOQ. flashy
🗲 plain

decorous adj
polite, refined, correct, courtly, decent, dignified, proper, well-behaved, appropriate, suitable, becoming, befitting, comely, comme il faut, fit, mannerly, modest, sedate, staid
OLD seemly
🗲 indecorous

decorum n
good manners, good form, etiquette, respectability, conformity, protocol, behaviour, decency, dignity, restraint, politeness, courtesy, modesty, grace, breeding
OLD seemliness
FORMAL propriety, deportment
🗲 bad manners; formal impropriety

decoy n, v
• n
lure, trap, snare, enticement, inducement, ensnarement, allurement, pretence, attraction, temptation, bait, diversion, pitfall, stall, dummy
OLD roper, trepan; (Shakesp) tame cheater
COLLOQ. red herring
SLANG shill
OLD SLANG button
• v
bait, lure, entrap, entice, ensnare, allure, tempt, deceive, attract, seduce, lead, draw; N Am tole
FORMAL inveigle

decrease v, n
• v
lessen, make/become less, go/come down, lower, diminish, dwindle, decline, de-escalate, fall (off), reduce,
subside, slide, plummet, plunge, cut back/down, contract, drop, ease, shrink, taper (off), wane, slim (down), let up, slacken, peter out, curtail, scale down, trim
FORMAL abate
🗲 increase
• n
lessening, reduction, decline, de-escalation, lowering, drop, fall, falling-off, dwindling, loss, cutback, contraction, downturn, ebb, shrinkage, subsidence, step-down
FORMAL diminution, abatement
🗲 increase

Synonym nuances
verb
Lessen, **lower** and **reduce** are neutral terms with very little inherent association: his comments lessened their fears; the price rise lowered demand. While these terms are often used transitively and suggest an outside influence, both **diminish** and **dwindle** are usually intransitive and suggest a gradual becoming less, often with the implication of negative effects: football attendances are dwindling and revenue is down.
Decline, similarly, implies a gradual deterioration, and can be negative in its implication: declining standards of behaviour. **Drop** and the rather more informal **fall off**, however, could be used to suggest a speedier decrease.
The term **subside** appropriately describes weakened intensity, and can be used in positive contexts: the panic has subsided, whereas **slide** suggests a relentless and undesirable drop: the country was sliding into anarchy. Both **plummet** and **plunge** further convey the idea of a rapid and uncontrollable descent.
Cut back/down are again used transitively, often of decreasing motivated by economy or discipline: many companies are cutting back on training; he cut down on alcohol. The term **scale down** also suggests a deliberate, practical decrease: the police have scaled down their search; **slim** (**down**) and **trim** have the added association of removing excess: the new team managed to trim the business costs. **Contract** and **shrink**, on the other hand, are often intransitive, and you might use them to move the emphasis away from active influences: the contracting labour force.
Ease is suggestive of a slow but usually comforting process: the pressure to do well has eased; **taper** (**off**), **wane** and **peter out** are slightly more negative in tone: interest in traditional games has sadly waned. **Let up** and **slacken**, however, would be the terms to use of a slowing down of something previously brisk: I slackened my pace; business in the shop has slackened since Christmas.

---

decree n, v
• n
order, command, law, ordinance, regulation, ruling, judgement, directive, rule, statute, act, enactment, edict, fiat, proclamation, mandate, manifesto, precept
FORMAL interlocution, indiction, promulgation, ukase, firman, rescript, psephism
Related adjective: decretal
• v
order, command, rule, lay down, dictate, direct, decide, determine, ordain, prescribe, proclaim, pronounce, enact
FORMAL enjoin

decrepit adj
1 a decrepit building
dilapidated, run-down, ramshackle, rickety, broken-down, battered, worn-out, old, in bad condition/shape, tumbledown, crumbling, falling apart/to bits/to pieces
COLLOQ. clapped-out; Aust warby
2 a decrepit person
weak, aged, feeble, enfeebled, frail, worn-out, infirm,

elderly, doddering, tottering
FORMAL senescent
COLLOQ. getting on, past it, over the hill

decrepitude n
ruin, dilapidation, decay, degeneration, deterioration,
ricketiness, disability, debility, weakness, feebleness,
infirmity, incapacity, incapacitation, dotage, old age,
senility
FORMAL senescence
Ea good repair, fitness

decriminalize v
legalize, legitimize, license, permit, sanction, allow,
authorize, warrant, validate, approve, ratify

decry v
criticize, condemn, carp, snipe, disapprove of, find fault
with, denounce, attack, slate, tear to shreds, belittle, run
down, come down on, blame, crab, preach down,
depreciate, devalue, underrate, undervalue
FORMAL censure, disparage, declaim against, animadvert,
excoriate, derogate, inveigh against, denigrate,
traduce
COLLOQ. knock, slam, pan, pull to pieces, tear a strip off, nit-
pick, do a hatchet job on
Ea praise, value

dedicate v
1 DEVOTE, commit, assign, bind, give, give over to, pledge,
present, offer, sacrifice, surrender
2 *dedicate a book*
inscribe, address, name
3 CONSECRATE, bless, sanctify, set apart, hallow, make
holy

dedicated adj
1 *a dedicated teacher*
devoted, committed, enthusiastic, single-minded,
wholehearted, single-hearted, zealous, staunch, dyed-in-
the-wool, given over to, purposeful, hard working,
industrious, diligent
COLLOQ. card-carrying, sold out (on)
2 CUSTOMIZED, custom-built, bespoke
Ea 1 uncommitted, apathetic

dedication n
1 COMMITMENT, devotion, single-mindedness,
wholeheartedness, allegiance, attachment, adherence,
faithfulness, loyalty, enthusiasm, zeal, self-sacrifice
2 INSCRIPTION, address
3 CONSECRATION, hallowing, blessing, benediction,
sanctification, presentation, wake
Ea 1 apathy

deduce v
derive, infer, gather, conclude, come to the
conclusion, work out, reason, surmise, understand,
draw, glean
COLLOQ. figure out, suss; *N Am* dope (out)

deduct v
subtract, take away/off/from, remove, reduce by, decrease
by, withdraw
COLLOQ. knock off, dock
Ea add

deduction n
1 SUBTRACTION, reduction, decrease, taking away/off,
withdrawal, removal, discount, allowance, off-reckoning
OLD reprise
FORMAL diminution, abatement
COLLOQ. dock
2 INFERENCE, reasoning, finding, conclusion, consequence,
corollary, surmising, assumption, presumption, result
OLD consectary
FORMAL hypothesis
Ea 1 addition, increase

deed n
1 ACTION, act, activity, achievement, performance,
accomplishment, undertaking, exploit, feat, attainment,
endeavour, fact, truth, reality
FORMAL actuality
2 DOCUMENT, contract, agreement, record, title,
transaction
FORMAL mortgage, title, indenture, enfeoffment

deem v
judge, believe, suppose, think, conceive, consider,
estimate, hold, imagine, account, esteem, reckon,
regard
FORMAL adjudge

deep adj, adv, n
♦ adj
1 *a deep river/pit*
profound, bottomless, unplumbed, fathomless,
unfathomed, immeasurable, yawning, cavernous, gaping,
uncrossable
2 *a deep sleep/crisis/feeling*
intense, serious, earnest, extreme, profound, very great,
severe, heart-felt, passionate, impassioned, wholehearted,
fervent, ardent, strong, vigorous, grave
3 *a deep person*
perceptive, discerning, profound, wise, learned,
knowledgeable, astute, clever, serious, intellectual, quiet,
reserved
FORMAL sagacious, perspicacious
COLLOQ. deep as a well
4 *deep in thought*
preoccupied, absorbed, engrossed, immersed, intent,
rapt, lost, faraway
5 LOW, low-pitched, bass, resonant, sonorous, resounding,
booming, rich, full, full-toned, strong, powerful
6 *a deep colour*
strong, intense, rich, vivid, brilliant, warm, glowing,
dark
7 OBSCURE, mysterious, difficult
FORMAL abstruse, esoteric, recondite, arcane
Ea 1 shallow, open 2 light 3 superficial, shallow,
frivolous 5 high, high-pitched 6 light, pale 7 clear, plain,
open
♦ adv
far, a long way, a great distance
♦ n
sea, high seas, ocean, main
COLLOQ. briny, the drink

deepen v
1 INTENSIFY, grow, increase, strengthen, reinforce, heighten,
extend, magnify, build up, step up, mushroom, deteriorate,
worsen, get worse
COLLOQ. hike up, bump up
2 EXCAVATE, hollow, dig out, scrape out, scoop out

deeply adv
intensely, seriously, earnestly, extremely, completely,
thoroughly, profoundly, very much, greatly, severely,
passionately, fervently, ardently, movingly, strongly,
vigorously, keenly, sharply, acutely, distressingly, feelingly,
gravely, mournfully, sadly, to the quick
COLLOQ. from the bottom of your heart
Ea slightly

deep-seated adj
ingrained, entrenched, deep-rooted, fixed, confirmed,
deep, profound, fundamental, settled
Ea superficial, eradicable, temporary

deer n
buck, doe, hart, reindeer, roe, stag
Related adjective: cervine

deface v
damage, spoil, disfigure, blemish, impair, mutilate, mar,

sully, tarnish, vandalize, deform, obliterate, ruin, injure, destroy
⊞ repair

de facto *adv, adj*
actually, in effect, really, actual, existing, real, in practice
⊞ de jure

defamation *n*
slander, libel, slur, smear, smear campaign, innuendo, scandal, character assassination, backbiting
FORMAL vilification, disparagement, aspersion, calumny, traducement, denigration, derogation, obloquy, opprobrium, malediction
COLLOQ. mud-slinging, slamming, slagging-off, badmouthing
⊞ commendation, praise

defamatory *adj*
slanderous, libellous, disparaging, pejorative, insulting, injurious, derogatory
FORMAL vilifying, denigrating, contumelious, calumnious, maledictory
COLLOQ. mud-slinging
⊞ complimentary, appreciative

defame *v*
slander, libel, discredit, disgrace, dishonour, libel, malign, blacken, smear, blemish, cloud, speak evil of, run down, stigmatize
OLD disparage, infame, bespatter, besmirch, deface, detract, scandal
FORMAL cast aspersions, denigrate, asperse, calumniate, traduce, vilify, vituperate
COLLOQ. slam, badmouth, drag through the mud, sling/throw mud at
SLANG slag (off)
⊞ compliment, praise

default *v, n*
♦ *v*
fail, evade, defraud, neglect, dodge, swindle, backslide
♦ *n*
failure, absence, neglect, negligence, non-payment, omission, deficiency, lapse, fault, lack, defect
FORMAL want, dereliction

defaulter *n*
non-payer, offender, absentee, non-appearer

defeat *v, n*
♦ *v*
1 CONQUER, beat, overcome, overpower, best, get the better of, have the edge on, pip at the post, inch out, be more than a match for, outscore, outplay, outwit, outsmart, eclipse, excel, surpass, outmatch, subdue, overthrow, worst, repel, drub, trounce, overwhelm, rout, ruin, crush, conquer, quell, pulverize, bring someone to their knees, reject, throw out; *Scot* granny
OLD put to the worse
FORMAL subjugate, vanquish, discomfit
COLLOQ. thrash, lick, hammer, thump, trounce, clobber, annihilate, smash, devastate, slaughter, make mincemeat (out) of, run rings round, wipe the floor with, paste, marmelize; *Scot* gub
SLANG *N Am* lam
2 FRUSTRATE, confound, balk, get the better of, disappoint, foil, thwart, baffle, puzzle, perplex, checkmate, block, obstruct
♦ *n*
1 CONQUEST, beating, overthrow, overcoming, rout, repulsion, ruin, crushing, rejection, loss, debacle
OLD defeasance
FORMAL subjugation, vanquishment
COLLOQ. trouncing, thrashing, pasting
2 FRUSTRATION, failure, setback, reverse, breakdown, downfall, disappointment, thwarting, checkmate

---

Synonym nuances
verb sense 1
Overcome suggests a hard-fought achievement, as does **conquer**, which has an added suggestion of gaining control over someone or something and has a vaguely triumphant tone: *as one disease is conquered, another appears*. **Overpower** and **overwhelm** could be used to emphasize superior strength. **Overthrow**, likewise, suggests using strength, but usually against those in authority: *a conspiracy to overthrow the government*.
  Eclipse implies a very definite defeat, and complete overshadowing: *young tennis players who have eclipsed their more renowned contemporaries*. **Excel** and **surpass** similarly suggest outstanding superiority. The less forceful term **repel** is appropriate for referring to foiling invaders.
  Where defeat has put a total end to opposition, you could use the words **subdue**, **crush** or **quell**, or **rout** or **pulverize**, which are even more strongly suggestive of damage: *the party's left wing was routed; their spokesman was pulverized by her expertise*. **Ruin**, although similar, perhaps does not convey the same sense of relish. In the narrower context of defeating proposals, you might use **reject** or **throw out**: *the appeals court threw out the previous verdict*.

---

defeatist *n, adj*
♦ *n*
pessimist, quitter, yielder, doomwatcher, doomsayer, prophet of doom
⊞ optimist
♦ *adj*
pessimistic, resigned, fatalistic, despondent, helpless, hopeless, despairing, gloomy, negative
⊞ optimistic

defecate *v*
empty/move your bowels, evacuate, excrete, pass a motion, relieve yourself, void excrement, poop; *dialect* mute
OLD scumber, ease yourself, cover the feet
FORMAL egest
COLLOQ. do your business, do number two
SLANG poo, poop, plop; (*vulgar*) shit, crap

defect *n, v*
♦ *n*
imperfection, fault, flaw, deficiency, failing, mistake, error, inadequacy, blemish, taint, deformity, shortcoming, shortfall, weakness, frailty, lack, spot, weak spot, snag, absence, omission
FORMAL want
COLLOQ. bug
♦ *v*
desert, abandon, break faith, change sides, rebel, revolt, turn traitor, abscond
FORMAL renege, apostatize, tergiversate
COLLOQ. *Scot* jump/loup the dyke

Synonym nuances
noun
Imperfection is a fairly mild term for some minor element that makes the whole fall short of perfection: *Nature is full of imperfections*, but both **fault** and **flaw** more decidedly suggest something that is wrong: *there is a fault on the line; there is a basic flaw in that argument*. **Deficiency** or **shortcoming** might be used where something is lacking: *deficiencies common to many secondary schools; a moral shortcoming*, while to refer to a more general falling short of what is required you might use **inadequacy**. **Failing** and **weak spot** usually apply to an area of human vulnerability or relate to a man-made defect: *his old failing – impetuosity*.

Both **mistake** and **error** make a clear suggestion that something has been done wrongly to create a defect. The term **blemish** is suggestive of something that spoils the whole, while the more marked **taint** has undercurrents of contamination: *the taint of corruption*. You may use **deformity** to state clearly that something is physically shaped other than it should be, but it is a word that should be used sensitively of living creatures.

Shortfall should be used specifically of something missing, usually money or items: *a shortfall of several thousand*. **Snag** is usually reserved for a defect in a material.

defection *n*
desertion, abandonment, disloyalty, backsliding, rebellion, revolt, mutiny, betrayal, absconding, treason
FORMAL renegation, apostasy, defalcation, dereliction, perfidy, tergiversation

defective *adj*
faulty, imperfect, out of order, flawed, deficient, broken, in disrepair, abnormal
FORMAL malfunctioning
COLLOQ. bust, duff, on the blink, kaput; *N Am* on the fritz
Ｆ∃ in order, working; *formal* operative

❗ defective or **deficient**?
Defective means 'having a fault or flaw': *The crash was caused by defective wiring in the signalling system.*
Deficient means 'inadequate, lacking in what is needed': *a diet deficient in essential vitamins and minerals.*

---

defector *n*
deserter, traitor, turncoat, betrayer, rebel, Judas, quisling, mutineer, backslider
OLD recreant
FORMAL renegade, apostate, tergiversator
COLLOQ. rat

defence *n*
1 PROTECTION, resistance, security, fortification, cover, safeguard, shelter, guard, shield, screen, deterrence, deterrent, barricade, bastion, keep, fortress, outpost, stronghold, garrison, immunity, bulwark, rampart, buttress
OLD (*Shakesp*) propugnation
2 *a country's defences*
military resources, armed forces, army, navy, air force, troops, soldiers, military, weapons, weaponry, armaments
3 JUSTIFICATION, explanation, excuse, argument, plea, vindication, pleading, testimony, alibi, case
OLD propugnation
FORMAL apologia, apologetic, explication, extenuation, exoneration
Ｆ∃ 1 attack, assault **3** accusation, attack

defenceless *adj*
unprotected, undefended, unarmed, unguarded, vulnerable, exposed, susceptible, open to attack, weak, helpless, powerless, impotent
Ｆ∃ protected, guarded

defend *v*
1 PROTECT, guard, safeguard, watch over, shelter, secure, preserve, shield, screen, cover, resist, withstand, oppose, hold, keep from harm, contest, deter, barricade, garrison, buttress, bulwark
OLD bestride, enguard, fend, warrant
FORMAL fortify
2 SUPPORT, stand up for, stand by, back, uphold, endorse, vindicate, champion, bolster, argue for, speak up for, make a case for, maintain, explain, justify, plead, assert, fight/ stand your corner
FORMAL exonerate
COLLOQ. stick up for
Ｆ∃ 1 attack **2** accuse, attack

Synonym nuances
sense 1
The term **safeguard** is slightly more emotive in tone than **guard**, and suggests keen efforts to look after someone or something that it is worth defending: *regulations designed to safeguard the health of the workforce.*
Watch over is likely to suggest a more personal involvement: *she watched over us as if we were her children*. The term **shelter** might be used of taking someone or something in to a place of safety, whilst **secure** may be used to describe defending a place by making it safe: *secured with a giant lock*.

You would use the word **preserve** of taking action to maintain the existence of someone or something: *peace must be preserved*. **Shield**, **screen** and **cover**, however, all suggest providing some form of barrier against danger, whilst **resist**, **withstand** and **oppose** all convey the idea of encountering dangerous forces by standing firm against them. Similarly, **hold** suggests taking a stand, but in order to keep control of something: *they held the city for fifteen weeks.*

Contest continues the idea of defence through offering resistance, whilst **deter** would only be appropriate of discouraging any possible threat: *an alarm system to deter burglars.*

---

defendant *n*
accused, offender, prisoner
TECHNICAL litigant, appellant, respondent

defender *n*
1 PROTECTOR, guard, bodyguard, keeper
2 SUPPORTER, guardian, advocate, vindicator, backer, endorser, upholder, preserver, champion, patron, sponsor, counsel, apologist
Ｆ∃ 1 attacker **2** accuser, detractor

defensible *adj*
justifiable, tenable, arguable, permissible, plausible, valid, maintainable, safe, secure, unassailable, impregnable, pardonable, vindicable
Ｆ∃ indefensible, insecure

defensive *adj*
1 PROTECTIVE, defending, safeguarding, protecting, wary, opposing, cautious, watchful
2 SELF-JUSTIFYING, apologetic, self-defensive, oversensitive

defer[1] *v*
defer a meeting
delay, postpone, put off, adjourn, hold over, put back, shelve, suspend, waive
FORMAL procrastinate, prorogue, protract
COLLOQ. put on ice, put on the back burner, take a raincheck on
Ｆ∃ bring forward

defer[2] *v*
defer to an expert opinion
yield, give way, comply, submit, surrender, give in, capitulate, respect, bow
FORMAL accede, acquiesce

deference *n*
1 RESPECT, respectfulness, regard, esteem, honour, reverence, courtesy, civility, politeness, attentiveness, consideration, thoughtfulness
2 SUBMISSION, submissiveness, obedience, compliance, yielding
FORMAL acquiescence
Ｆ∃ 1 contempt **2** resistance

deferential *adj*
respectful, reverent, reverential, courteous, civil, dutiful, humble, polite, attentive, ingratiating

FORMAL morigerous, regardful, complaisant, obeisant, obsequious
🔁 arrogant, immodest

deferment n
delay, postponement, deferral, putting-off, adjournment, holding-over, shelving, suspension, stay, moratorium, waiving
FORMAL procrastination, prorogation

defiance n
opposition, confrontation, resistance, challenge, disobedience, rebelliousness, contempt, insubordination, disregard, insolence
FORMAL recalcitrance, truculence, contumacy
🔁 compliance, acquiescence, submissiveness

defiant adj
challenging, resistant, antagonistic, aggressive, rebellious, insubordinate, disobedient, intransigent, bold, insolent, contemptuous, scornful, obstinate, unco-operative, militant, provocative
OLD roisting
FORMAL recalcitrant, refractory, truculent, contumacious
🔁 compliant, acquiescent, submissive

defiantly adv
rebelliously, insubordinately, disobediently, intransigently, obstinately, unco-operatively, militantly, boldly, insolently, contemptuously, scornfully, provocatively, antagonistically, aggressively
FORMAL recalcitrantly, truculently, contumaciously
🔁 compliantly, submissively

deficiency n
1 SHORTAGE, lack, inadequacy, scarcity, insufficiency, dearth, want, scantiness, poverty, absence, deficit
2 IMPERFECTION, shortcoming, weakness, fault, defect, flaw, failing, frailty
🔁 1 excess, surfeit 2 perfection

deficient adj
inadequate, insufficient, scarce, short, low, poor, lacking, meagre, scant, scanty, skimpy, incomplete, unsatisfactory, imperfect, inferior, weak, bankrupt
FORMAL wanting, exiguous, defectible
COLLOQ. minus
🔁 excessive

⚠ **deficient** or **defective**?
See panel at **defective**.

deficit n
shortage, shortfall, deficiency, loss, arrears, lack, default
🔁 excess

defile v, n
♦ v
pollute, violate, contaminate, degrade, dishonour, desecrate, defame, debase, soil, dirty, infect, stain, spoil, sully, tarnish, taint, make impure/unclean, profane, treat sacrilegiously, corrupt, blacken, disgrace
OLD inquinate, defoul, file, moil; (Shakesp) enseam, ray
FORMAL denigrate, vitiate, maculate
🔁 clean, cleanse, purify
♦ n
pass, gorge, valley, gully, passage, ravine, gate; dialect halse
TECHNICAL col

defilement n
contamination, degradation, pollution, impurity, violation, desecration, defamation, debasement, staining, sullying, tarnishing, tainting, profanity
OLD conspurcation
FORMAL denigration
🔁 cleansing, purification

definable adj
ascertainable, definite, identifiable, describable, determinable, perceptible, definite, fixed, specific, exact, precise
FORMAL explicable
🔁 indefinable

define v
1 *define the meaning*
explain, characterize, describe, interpret, determine, designate, specify, spell out, detail, clarify
FORMAL expound, elucidate
2 *define the boundaries*
bound, limit, delimit, establish, determine, demarcate, mark out, fix
FORMAL circumscribe, delineate

definite adj
1 CLEAR, clear-cut, exact, precise, specific, explicit, particular, firm, obvious, marked, noticeable, unmistakable
2 CERTAIN, settled, sure, positive, fixed, decided, determined, assured, guaranteed
🔁 1 vague, unclear 2 indefinite, provisional

⚠ **definite** or **definitive**?
Definite means 'clear' or 'certain': I'll give you a definite answer later. Definitive means 'final, settling things once and for all': a definitive study of Ben Jonson.

definitely adv
positively, surely, unquestionably, without question, absolutely, certainly, categorically, undeniably, clearly, undoubtedly, doubtless, without doubt, no denying, unmistak(e)ably, for sure, plainly, obviously, indeed, easily
FORMAL indubitably

definition n
1 EXPLANATION, meaning, significance, sense, description, interpretation, clarification, determination
TECHNICAL denotation
FORMAL exposition, elucidation
2 DISTINCTNESS, clarity, precision, clearness, focus, sharpness, visibility, contrast

definitive adj
decisive, conclusive, final, authoritative, standard, correct, ultimate, reliable, exhaustive, perfect, classic, exact, absolute, complete, categorical
🔁 interim

definitively adv
decisively, conclusively, finally, authoritatively, absolutely, completely, categorically

deflate v
1 FLATTEN, puncture, collapse, let down, exhaust, squash, empty, contract, void, shrink, squeeze
2 *deflate his opinion of himself*
humiliate, debunk, dash, disappoint, dispirit, subdue, humble, mortify, chasten, disconcert
COLLOQ. put down, burst someone's bubble, rain on someone's parade
3 DEPRECIATE, devalue, reduce, lessen, lower, diminish, decrease, depress, slow (down)
🔁 1 inflate 2 boost 3 inflate, increase

deflect v
deviate, diverge, turn (aside), swerve, veer, change course, sidetrack, drift, twist, avert, head off, wind, glance (off), bend, ricochet, snick
TECHNICAL refract
OLD withdraw

deflection n
deviation, divergence, turning, turning aside, diversion, swerve, veer, changing course, sidetracking, drift, twisting, glancing-off, bend, ricochet
TECHNICAL refraction
FORMAL aberration

deflower v
violate, assault, defile, rape, seduce, spoil, desecrate, force, harm, mar, molest, ruin
FORMAL ravish, despoil

deform v
distort, contort, disfigure, deface, malform, misshape, warp, mar, pervert, ruin, spoil, damage, maim, mutilate, twist, buckle

deformation n
bend, curve, distortion, contortion, disfiguration, defacement, malformation, misshapenness, mutilation, twist, twisting, warp, buckle
TECHNICAL diastrophism

deformed adj
distorted, misshapen, malformed, contorted, disfigured, crippled, crooked, gnarled, bent, twisted, warped, buckled, defaced, mangled, maimed, marred, ruined, mutilated, perverted, corrupted

deformity n
distortion, misshapenness, malformation, disfigurement, defacement, abnormality, irregularity, imperfection, misproportion, defect, ugliness, crookedness, vileness, grossness, monstrosity, corruption, perversion

defraud v
cheat, swindle, dupe, rob, trick, fleece, rook, wrong, deceive, delude, mislead, fool, hoodwink, outwit, embezzle, beguile, nick
OLD lurch
FORMAL cozen
COLLOQ. fiddle, rush, do, diddle, con
SLANG screw, sting, rip off, swiz, take to the cleaners

defray v
reimburse, refund, repay, recompense, discharge, meet, pay, cover, square, settle
E3 incur

deft adj
adept, handy, dexterous, nimble, skilful, adroit, agile, expert, nifty, proficient, able, neat, clever
E3 clumsy, awkward

deftly adv
skilfully, adeptly, nimbly, expertly, ably, cleverly, neatly, proficiently
E3 awkwardly

defunct adj
1 DEAD, deceased, departed, gone, expired, extinct
2 OBSOLETE, disused, unused, invalid, expired, passé, outmoded, bygone
FORMAL inoperative
E3 1 alive, live 2 functioning; formal operative

defuse v
1 defuse a tense situation
calm (down), quieten, relieve, alleviate
COLLOQ. cool (down), clear the air, pour oil on troubled waters
2 defuse a bomb
deactivate, disarm, disable, immobilize
FORMAL render inoperative
E3 1 intensify, make worse 2 activate

defy v
1 defy the authorities
challenge, confront, resist, dare, outdare, brave, face, repel, spurn, beard, flout, slight, withstand, stand up to, disobey, rebel against, disrespect, disregard, ignore, scorn, mock, despise, defeat, beard, provoke, frustrate, thwart, fly in the face of
2 her writings defy categorization
elude, avoid, frustrate, baffle, foil
E3 1 obey, comply 2 permit, allow

degeneracy n
dissoluteness, debauchery, depravation, degradation, debasement, decadence, corruption, fallenness, immorality, vileness, wickedness, sinfulness, degeneration, perversion, deterioration
FORMAL effeteness
E3 morality, uprightness

degenerate adj, v, n
• adj
dissolute, debauched, depraved, degraded, debased, base, low, abandoned, decadent, corrupt, fallen, immoral, mean, ignoble, vile, wicked, sinful, degenerated, perverted, deteriorated
OLD (Shakesp) derogate
FORMAL effete, profligate
COLLOQ. off the rails
E3 moral, upright
• v
decline, deteriorate, sink, decay, rot, fail, slip, worsen, fall off, lapse, decrease, bastardize
OLD degender; (Shakesp) recoil
FORMAL regress
COLLOQ. go downhill, go to pot, go down the tubes
E3 improve
• n
reprobate, miscreant, rake, roué, wrongdoer, criminal, evildoer, sinner, rogue, rascal, scoundrel, scamp, scallywag, villain, vagabond, wretch, mischief-maker, ne'er-do-well, knave, dastard, troublemaker
FORMAL profligate

degeneration n
decline, deterioration, debasement, decay, rot, failure, slip, worsening, falling-off, sinking, drop, slide, lapse, atrophy, decrease
FORMAL regression
E3 improvement

degradation n
1 ABASEMENT, humiliation, mortification, dishonour, disgrace, shame, ignominy, decadence, degeneracy, dissoluteness, debauchery, depravation, debasement, corruption, fallenness, immorality, vileness, wickedness, sinfulness, degeneration, perversion
2 DETERIORATION, degeneration, decline, downgrading, demotion
E3 1 virtue 2 enhancement

degrade v
1 DISHONOUR, disgrace, debase, abase, shame, humiliate, humble, put down, discredit, mortify, demean, belittle, diminish, lower, sink, devalue, weaken, impair, deteriorate, cheapen, adulterate, pervert, sully, defile, corrupt, prostitute, brutalize, embase
2 DEMOTE, depose, downgrade, deprive, cashier, reduce/lower in rank, relegate, unseat, declass, disennoble
COLLOQ. drum out, take down a peg or two
E3 1 exalt, elevate 2 promote

degrading adj
humiliating, dishonourable, disgraceful, debasing, base, shameful, contemptible, discrediting, mortifying, demeaning, belittling, cheapening, ignoble, undignified, unworthy
E3 enhancing

degree n
1 to a great degree
extent, measure, range, stage, step, level, amount, point, intensity, strength, standard
2 GRADE, class, rank, rung, order, position, standing, status, stage, level, limit, unit, point, mark

dehydrate v
dry, dry up, dry out, evaporate, lose water, drain, parch
FORMAL desiccate, exsiccate, effloresce

dehydration *n*
drying, evaporation, parching, dehumidifying
FORMAL desiccation

deification *n*
exaltation, elevation, worship, glorification, idolization, extolling, revering, reverence, immortalization, ennoblement, idealization
FORMAL veneration, apotheosis, divinification, divinization

deify *v*
exalt, elevate, worship, glorify, idolize, extol, revere, immortalize, ennoble, idealize
FORMAL aggrandize, venerate

deign *v*
condescend, stoop, lower yourself, consent, demean yourself

deity *n*
god, goddess, divinity, divine being, supreme being, godhead, idol, demigod, spirit, power, eternal, immortal

dejected *adj*
downcast, despondent, depressed, downhearted, discouraged, disheartened, down, low, melancholy, sad, miserable, cast down, gloomy, glum, crestfallen, crushed, demoralized, dismal, wretched, doleful, morose, spiritless, dispirited
FORMAL disconsolate
COLLOQ. blue, down in the dumps
E3 cheerful, high-spirited, happy

dejectedly *adv*
despondently, sadly, miserably, glumly, gloomily, dismally, wretchedly, morosely
FORMAL disconsolately
E3 cheerfully, happily

dejection *n*
despondency, depression, downheartedness, discouragement, low spirits, despair, melancholy, sadness, sorrow, unhappiness, misery, gloom, gloominess, wretchedness, dolefulness, moroseness, dispiritedness
FORMAL disconsolateness, disconsolation
COLLOQ. blues, dumps
E3 happiness, high spirits

de jure *adv, adj*
legally, rightfully, legal, rightful
E3 de facto

delay *v, n*
♦ *v*
1 OBSTRUCT, hinder, impede, hamper, hold up, check, hold back, set back, slow, stay, stop, halt, detain, stonewall, filibuster, keep, restrain, retard, stave
2 POSTPONE, put off, put back, defer, suspend, shelve, hold over, detain, reprieve, adjourn, stall
OLD (*Shakesp & Spenser*) forslow
FORMAL procrastinate
COLLOQ. sit on, put on ice, put on the back burner
3 DAWDLE, hang on, linger, hesitate, lag (behind), loiter, dither, hold back
FORMAL tarry
COLLOQ. dilly-dally, faff about
E3 **1** accelerate **2** bring forward **3** hurry, keep up
♦ *n*
1 OBSTRUCTION, hindrance, impediment, hold-up, check, setback, stay, stoppage, halt, retardation, interruption, lull, interval, wait
OLD let
2 POSTPONEMENT, deferment, putting-off, adjournment, holding-over, shelving, suspension, detaining, detention, stay, respite, moratorium, waiving, reprieve
TECHNICAL demurrage, mora
OLD frist
FORMAL procrastination, cunctation

3 DAWDLING, lingering, loitering, stalling, hesitance, lag
FORMAL tarrying
COLLOQ. dilly-dallying
E3 **1** hastening, continuation **3** hurry

Synonym nuances
verb sense 1
Both **obstruct** and **impede** may be used to refer to placing something in the way, perhaps deliberately: *UN officials accused the government of obstructing relief operations.* The terms **check**, **stay**, **hold back** and **set back** again suggest preventing progress, although they are perhaps less strong terms: *a tax credit checked the slump.* **Hinder**, **hamper**, and **hold up** are similar, though perhaps more suggestive of action that slows something down rather than stops it temporarily: *failing eyesight which hampered his work;* **detain** could be used where a person has been kept somewhere and so delayed: *unforeseen business detained him.*
    The words **keep** and **restrain** could also be used especially where there is a deliberate effort to keep something in check: *efforts to restrain the lava flows from the volcano.* To refer to delaying development, you might choose **retard**: *the monetary squeeze is already retarding recovery.* **Stave**, however, is more suggestive of delaying something by warding it off: *employers skilfully staved off demands for big wage increases.* Both **stonewall** and **filibuster** are used specifically of delaying tactics used within government.

---

delectable *adj*
1 DELICIOUS, appetizing, palatable, tasty, dainty, luscious, mouthwatering, succulent, flavoursome, savoury
COLLOQ. scrumptious, yummy
2 ATTRACTIVE, pleasant, delightful, adorable, charming, beautiful, lovely, enchanting, engaging, exciting, pleasing, agreeable
E3 **1** unpalatable **2** unpleasant

delectation *n*
enjoyment, delight, happiness, pleasure, comfort, contentment, gratification, refreshment, relish, satisfaction, amusement, diversion, entertainment
E3 distaste

delegate *n, v*
♦ *n*
representative, agent, envoy, messenger, deputy, second, secondary, substitute, ambassador, spokesperson, spokesman, spokeswoman, legate, emissary, proxy, commissioner
TECHNICAL vicar
OLD TECHNICAL syndic
♦ *v*
authorize, appoint, depute, charge, commission, commit, give, pass on/over, assign, empower, entrust, devolve, consign, leave, designate, ordain, nominate, name, hand over

delegation *n*
1 DEPUTATION, representatives, commission, legation, mission, contingent, embassy
2 *delegation of responsibility*
committal, transference, assignment, consignment, entrusting, passing on/over, devolution, empowerment

delete *v*
erase, remove, cross out, cancel, rub out, strike (out), take out, obliterate, edit (out), cut (out), blot out, blue-pencil
FORMAL excise, efface, expunge
E3 add, insert

deleterious *adj*
destructive, detrimental, harmful, hurtful, injurious, bad, damaging, ruinous, pernicious, prejudicial
FORMAL noxious
E3 enhancing, helpful

deliberate *adj, v*

♦ *adj*

1 INTENTIONAL, planned, calculated, prearranged, set, premeditated, preplanned, preconceived, willed, wilful, conscious, witting, designed, considered, advised, *voulu*
TECHNICAL volitive
OLD propense
2 CAREFUL, unhurried, thoughtful, methodical, cautious, studied, studious, prudent, slow, ponderous, steady, leisurely, measured, heedful, resolute, unhesitating, unwavering
FORMAL circumspect
F3 1 unintentional, accidental **2** hasty, casual

♦ *v*

consider, ponder, reflect, think (over), think about, meditate, mull over, muse, debate, discuss, evaluate, weigh (up), consult
OLD advise
FORMAL cogitate, ruminate, excogitate

deliberately *adv*

1 INTENTIONALLY, on purpose, consciously, pointedly, calculatingly, by design, in cold blood, coldbloodedly, knowingly, wittingly, wilfully, with malice aforethought
2 CAREFULLY, unhurriedly, thoughtfully, methodically, cautiously, prudently, slowly, ponderously, steadily, studiously
FORMAL circumspectly
F3 1 unintentionally, by accident, accidentally, by mistake **2** hastily, casually

deliberation *n*

1 CONSIDERATION, reflection, thought, calculation, forethought, meditation, pondering, musing, mulling, brooding, study, evaluation, weighing-up
FORMAL cogitation, rumination, excogitate
2 *secret deliberations*
debate, discussion, consultation, conferring
3 CARE, carefulness, caution, thoughtfulness, unhurriedness, slowness, steadiness, prudence
FORMAL circumspection

delicacy *n*

1 DAINTINESS, fineness, elegance, exquisiteness, lightness, fragility, precision
2 SENSITIVITY, tact, diplomacy, discretion, care, consideration, subtlety, finesse, discrimination, niceness
3 TITBIT, dainty, taste, treat, luxury, sweetmeat, savoury, relish, speciality, bonne-bouche
OLD delice
F3 1 coarseness, roughness **2** tactlessness, insensitivity

delicate *adj*

1 FINE, dainty, exquisite, elegant, slight, graceful
OLD (*Shakesp*) incony
2 FRAIL, sickly, weak, ailing, infirm, unwell, in poor health, faint, debilitated; *dialect* nesh
3 *delicate china*
fragile, breakable, easily damaged/broken, frail, flimsy, brittle, insubstantial, light
4 *a delicate situation*
sensitive, tricky, difficult, problematic, critical, awkward, touchy, controversial
5 *needs delicate handling*
tactful, sensitive, diplomatic, careful, considerate, discreet
COLLOQ. softly-softly, kid-glove
6 SUBTLE, muted, pastel, pale, muted, subdued, soft, faint, mild, bland
7 *a delicate instrument*
precision, sensitive, precise, exact, accurate
F3 1 coarse, clumsy **2** healthy, strong **3** strong, tough **4** easy, straightforward **6** strong, bold

delicately *adv*

1 DAINTILY, finely, exquisitely, elegantly, gracefully
2 SUBTLY, softly, faintly, mildly, blandly, palely

3 SENSITIVELY, critically, carefully, finely, tactfully, gently, diplomatically

delicious *adj*

1 TASTY, palatable, appetizing, mouth-watering, juicy, succulent, toothsome, savoury, good, choice, tempting, melting in the mouth
FORMAL delectable, nectareous, ambrosial
COLLOQ. delish, mor(e)ish, scrumptious, yummy, scrummy, lip-smacking
SLANG goluptious
2 ENJOYABLE, pleasant, agreeable, delightful, charming, enchanting, captivating, pleasurable, pleasing, gratifying, entertaining, fascinating, exquisite
F3 1 unpalatable, tasteless **2** unpleasant

Synonym nuances
sense 1

Tasty is a very widely used and approbatory term to describe something that really appeals to our sense of taste; **toothsome** is similar, though much less common: *toothsome vegetable-based dishes*. **Palatable**, however, is less effusive and simply describes something pleasing, or even merely tolerable: *safe, palatable drinking water*. The terms **appetizing** and **tempting** could be used of something that prompts our desire to eat, whilst **mouth-watering** goes even further by suggesting an ability to provoke salivation: *mouth-watering desserts on offer*.
 The words **juicy** and **succulent** return to the idea of how things taste, as opposed to the response they provoke, and, as both suggest lushness, would be used of more moist foods. **Melting in the mouth** also has more to do with the texture of the food, this time describing something tender. **Savoury** was originally used to suggest having full flavour, but tends nowadays to be used simply as the converse of sweet: *a savoury smell*; *savoury snacks*.

---

delight *n, v*

♦ *n*

happiness, joy, pleasure, contentment, enjoyment, gladness, glee, rapture, transport, bliss, exultation, euphoria, ecstasy, elation, gratification, jubilation, amusement, entertainment
OLD delice, mirth
FORMAL delectation, felicity
F3 disgust, displeasure

♦ *v*

1 *the prospect of being parents delighted them*
please, charm, gratify, cheer, gladden, excite, enchant, captivate, enrapture, entrance, tickle, thrill, ravish, give enjoyment to, amuse, entertain
OLD rape
COLLOQ. bowl over, tickle pink, take your breath away
2 *delight in something*
enjoy, relish, like, love, appreciate, revel in, feast, take pleasure in, take pride in, glory in, boast of, wallow in, savour
OLD (*Spenser*) fain
F3 1 disappoint, displease, dismay **2** dislike, hate

delighted *adj*

happy, pleased, glad, enchanted, captivated, enraptured, entranced, elated, euphoric, ecstatic, thrilled, excited, joyful, overjoyed, gleeful, jubilant, gratified, charmed
FORMAL joyous
COLLOQ. over the moon, tickled pink, happy as Larry/a sandboy, pleased as Punch
F3 disappointed, dismayed

delightful *adj*

charming, enchanting, captivating, enjoyable, pleasant, thrilling, exciting, agreeable, pleasurable, engaging, attractive, beautiful, pleasing, gratifying, appealing,

fascinating, amusing, diverting, entertaining
FORMAL delectable
COLLOQ. out of this world, great, magic, ace, divine, the tops
E3 nasty, unpleasant

delimit v
bound, demarcate, determine, establish, fix, set, mark, define

delineate v
describe, depict, portray, set forth, outline, draw, sketch, trace, design, chart, render, represent, define, mark, bound, determine, establish, fix

delineation n
description, depiction, portrayal, tracing, rendering, representation

delinquency n
crime, offence, misdeed, wrongdoing, misbehaviour, misconduct, lawbreaking, misdemeanour, criminality
FORMAL transgression

delinquent n, adj
• n
offender, criminal, wrongdoer, lawbreaker, hooligan, young offender, culprit, ruffian, vandal, *Halbstarker*
FORMAL miscreant, malefactor
• adj
criminal, offending, lawbreaking, lawless, guilty, negligent
FORMAL remiss, culpable
E3 blameless, careful

delirious adj
1 *delirious because of fever*
demented, raving, incoherent, beside yourself, irrational, deranged, frenzied, light-headed, wild, mad, frantic, frenetic, insane, crazy, unhinged, babbling, rambling, wandering, out of your mind
COLLOQ. gone, spaced out
2 *delirious with excitement*
ecstatic, euphoric, overjoyed, elated, jubilant, rapturous, hysterical, beside yourself, carried away
COLLOQ. over the moon
E3 **1** sane

deliriously adv
ecstatically, jubilantly, rapturously, hysterically

delirium n
1 *feverish delirium*
derangement, raving, incoherence, irrationality, fever, frenzy, passion, wildness, madness, insanity, lunacy, dementia, craziness, hallucination, hysteria
COLLOQ. jimjams
2 *the delirium of first love*
ecstasy, euphoria, joy, elation, rapture, excitement, jubilation, wildness, passion
E3 **1** sanity

deliver v
1 *deliver a parcel*
convey, bring, take, send, give, carry, supply, distribute, give out
FORMAL dispatch
2 SURRENDER, hand over, turn over, render, relinquish, yield, transfer, grant, entrust, commit
FORMAL cede
3 *deliver a speech*
utter, make, speak, give, proclaim, declare, announce, pronounce, express, voice, give voice to
FORMAL enunciate
4 ADMINISTER, deal, give, inflict, launch, direct, aim, strike
5 *deliver the promised benefits*
fulfil, provide, supply, do, carry out, implement, live up to
6 *deliver a baby*
help give birth to, assist in/at the delivery of, bring into the world

7 SET FREE, liberate, save, rescue, release
FORMAL emancipate, ransom, redeem, manumit

deliverance n
rescue, liberation, salvation, freedom, release, escape, extrication
FORMAL emancipation, ransom, redemption

delivery n
1 CONVEYANCE, supply, distribution, transport, transportation, carriage, consignment, transmission, transfer, shipment
FORMAL dispatch
2 CONSIGNMENT, batch, load, shipment
3 ARTICULATION, pronunciation, speech, utterance, intonation, elocution
FORMAL enunciation
4 CHILDBIRTH, birth, labour, confinement
FORMAL parturition, travail

dell n
valley, vale, dale, hollow, dean, dingle, slade

delude v
deceive, mislead, beguile, dupe, fool, take in, lead on, trick, hoodwink, hoax, cheat, cajole, misguide, misinform
OLD blend, put the change on
COLLOQ. bamboozle, have on, kid, take for a ride, double-cross, two-time, pull someone's leg, pull a fast one on, pull the wool over someone's eyes

deluge n, v
• n
1 *a deluge of rain*
flood, inundation, downpour, overflowing, torrent
2 *a deluge of letters*
flood, torrent, avalanche, spate, barrage, rush, wave
• v
1 *deluged by rain*
flood, inundate, drench, drown, soak, engulf, submerge
2 *deluged by queries*
overwhelm, inundate, swamp, flood, snow under

delusion n
illusion, hallucination, fancy, misconception, misapprehension, false belief/impression, deception, misbelief, fallacy, misinformation, tricking

⚠ **delusion** or **illusion**?
A *delusion* is a false belief arising in your own mind, whereas an *illusion* is a false impression coming into your mind from the world outside it.

de luxe, deluxe adj
luxury, luxurious, select, choice, quality, expensive, costly, special, exclusive, grand, lavish, fine, elegant, palatial, rich, splendid, sumptuous, superior
FORMAL opulent
COLLOQ. plush, swish

delve v
burrow, rummage, search, dig into, hunt in/through, poke, scrabble, ransack, root, probe, examine, explore, investigate, go/look into, research

demagogue n
agitator, orator, speaker, public speaker, firebrand, haranguer, rabble-rouser, tub-thumper

demand v, n
• v
1 ASK (FOR), request, tell, call for, insist on, urge, press for, hold out for, order, dictate, stipulate, solicit, claim, clamour, petition, exact, inquire, question, interrogate
2 REQUIRE, need, necessitate, take, call for, involve, cry out for
• n
1 REQUEST, question, claim, petition, call, plea, order, inquiry, desire, pressure, insistence, clamour, interrogation

2 NEED, necessity, call, requirement, want
FORMAL exigency
3 *there's no demand for it*
call, market, need, desire, run
■ **in demand**
popular, fashionable, asked for, requested, desired, sought after
COLLOQ. big, trendy, in, of the moment

demanding *adj*
hard, difficult, challenging, exacting, taxing, tough, exhausting, wearing, back-breaking, insistent, nagging, harassing, pressing, testing, urgent, trying
FORMAL exigent
COLLOQ. a tall order
🖪 easy, undemanding

demarcate *v*
determine, establish, fix, mark (out), mark off, divide, separate, delimit, define, bound

demarcation *n*
boundary, bound, differentiation, distinction, division, separation, enclosure, limit, line, margin, determination, establishment, fixing, marking off/out, delimitation, definition

demean *v*
lower, humble, degrade, belittle, deprecate, humiliate, debase, abase, descend, demote, stoop, condescend
🖪 exalt, enhance

demeaning *adj*
degrading, humiliating, dishonourable, disgraceful, debasing, base, shameful, contemptible, discrediting, mortifying, belittling, cheapening, ignoble, undignified, unworthy
🖪 enhancing

demeanour *n*
manner, conduct, behaviour, air, carriage
FORMAL bearing, deportment, mien, comportment

demented *adj*
mad, insane, lunatic, unbalanced, disturbed, deranged, crazy, crazed, wild, berserk, frantic, unhinged, distracted, distraught, frenetic, maniac, out of your mind, infuriate;
Scot gyte
OLD frantic-mad, lymphatic, bestraught
COLLOQ. crazy, demented, nuts, nutty, nutty as a fruitcake, wacky, mad as a hatter, barmy, bonkers, batty, cracked, crackers, dippy, daffy, dotty, loopy, potty, off your nut, off your head, wrong in the head, out of your head, off the wall, out to lunch, round the bend, round the twist, bats, having bats in the belfry, cuckoo, off the rails, screwy, up the wall, raving, not all there; *N Am* buggy, flaky, fruity;
Aust & NZ dingbats
SLANG loony, mental, bananas, barking, wacko, doolally, off your rocker, off your chump, off your trolley, out of your tree, needing your head examined, having lost your marbles, having a screw loose, having a tile loose, having several cards short of a full deck, with one sandwich short of a picnic, meshuga, ape, apeshit; *N Am* gonzo, loco, wiggy; *Aust* out of your tree
🖪 sane

demise *n*
1 DEATH, decease, end, dying, passing, departure
FORMAL termination, expiration, cessation
2 DOWNFALL, fall, end, collapse, failure, ruin, disintegration

demobilize *v*
disperse, disband, break up, dismiss
COLLOQ. demob
🖪 assemble, conscript

democracy *n*
self-government, commonwealth, autonomy, republic

democratic *adj*
self-governing, representative, elected, egalitarian, autonomous, popular, populist, republican

demolish *v*
1 DESTROY, dismantle, knock down, pull down, take down, ruin, flatten, bulldoze, raze, tear down, break up, pulverize, level, unbuild
OLD abate, ruinate
2 *demolish the opponents*
beat, overcome, overpower, get the better of, conquer, excel, surpass, subdue, overthrow, repel, overwhelm, rout, ruin, crush, quell, break down, bring someone to their knees
FORMAL subjugate, vanquish
COLLOQ. thrash, lick, hammer, annihilate, devastate, massacre, slaughter
3 *demolish an argument*
destroy, ruin, wreck, overturn, undo, tear down
COLLOQ. drive a coach and horses through
🖪 **1** build up, erect, construct

demolition *n*
1 DESTRUCTION, dismantling, knocking-down, pulling-down, flattening, razing, tearing-down, breaking-up, levelling, razing
2 *demolition of the opposing team*
beating, overpowering, surpassing, overthrow, overwhelming, rout
COLLOQ. thrashing, clobbering, licking, hammering, annihilation, massacre, slaughter

demon *n*
1 DEVIL, fiend, evil spirit, fallen angel, imp, ghoul, warlock, familiar, daemon, satyr, cacodemon, afrit, rakshas, incubus, succubus, *duende*
2 VILLAIN, devil, rogue, monster, fiend, beast, ogre, savage, brute
3 *a demon at chess*
addict, fanatic, fiend, buff, wizard
COLLOQ. ace, freak, dab hand

demonic *adj*
fiendish, devilish, diabolical, hellish, infernal, satanic, possessed, mad, maniacal, manic, crazed, frantic, frenetic, frenzied, furious

demonstrable *adj*
verifiable, provable, arguable, attestable, self-evident, obvious, evident, certain, clear, positive
FORMAL evincible
🖪 unverifiable

demonstrate *v*
1 PROVE, determine, show, establish, verify, indicate
FORMAL validate, substantiate
2 SHOW, display, exhibit, express, indicate, register, betray
OLD remonstrate
FORMAL manifest, testify to, bear witness to, evince, betoken, bespeak
3 EXPLAIN, illustrate, describe, show, teach, communicate, make clear
FORMAL expound
4 PROTEST, march, parade, rally, picket, sit in

demonstration *n*
1 DISPLAY, expression, indication, exhibition, proof, confirmation, evidence, testimony, verification, affirmation
FORMAL manifestation, evincement, substantiation, validation
2 EXPLANATION, illustration, description, presentation, communication, test, trial
FORMAL exposition, elucidation
3 PROTEST, march, rally, mass rally, picket, sit-in, parade, picket, civil disobedience
COLLOQ. demo

demonstrative *adj*
affectionate, expressive, extrovert, unreserved, effusive, gushing, expansive, emotional, open, loving, warm
E3 reserved, introvert, cold, restrained

demonstratively *adv*
expressively, openly, emotionally, warmly, affectionately, lovingly
E3 coldly

demoralize *v*
1 DISCOURAGE, dishearten, dispirit, depress, deject, cast down, crush, disconcert, make despondent, daunt, lower, undermine, weaken
2 CORRUPT, deprave, debase, pervert, contaminate, defile
E3 1 encourage, inspire confidence **2** improve

demoralizing *adj*
discouraging, disheartening, depressing, disconcerting, daunting, weakening, dispiriting
E3 encouraging

demote *v*
downgrade, reduce in rank, degrade, relegate, humble, cashier
E3 promote, upgrade

demotion *n*
downgrading, relegation, degrading
E3 promotion

demotic *adj*
popular, vernacular, colloquial, vulgar
FORMAL enchorial, enchoric

demur *v, n*
◆ *v*
disagree, dissent, object, take exception, refuse, protest, dispute, balk, cavil, scruple, doubt, express doubts, hesitate, be unwilling, refuse
◆ *n*
disagreement, dissent, hesitation, objection, protest, misgiving, qualm, reservation, doubt, scruple
FORMAL compunction, demurral

demure *adj*
modest, reserved, unassuming, reticent, coy, shy, timid, quiet, serious, retiring, prissy, grave, prudish, sober, strait-laced, prim, staid
E3 wanton, forward

demurely *adv*
modestly, unassumingly, reticently, quietly, seriously, coyly, shyly, timidily, primly, staidly

den *n*
1 *a wolf's den*
lair, hideout, hole, hollow
2 *a den of forgers*
haunt, meeting-place, patch, pitch, hotbed
COLLOQ. dive, joint
3 *study in his den*
retreat, study, studio, hideaway, shelter, sanctuary

denial *n*
1 CONTRADICTION, opposition, disagreement, dissent, disclaimer, dismissal, renunciation
OLD denay, denegation
FORMAL negation, disavowal, disaffirmation, abjuration, refutation, repudiation
2 REFUSAL, rebuff, rejection, dismissal, prohibition, veto
3 *denial of your parents*
disowning, renunciation, repudiation, forsaking
FORMAL disavowal

denigrate *v*
run down, slander, belittle, abuse, assail, criticize, deprecate
FORMAL disparage, cast aspersions on, revile, defame, malign, vilify, decry, besmirch, impugn, calumniate, vilipend

COLLOQ. fling/sling/throw mud, pick holes in
E3 praise, acclaim

denigration *n*
slander, belittling, abuse, deprecation, degradation
FORMAL disparagement, vilification, calumny
E3 praise

denizen *n*
citizen, dweller, inhabitant, occupant, resident, townsman, townswoman, habitant, habitué

denomination *n*
1 RELIGION, persuasion, Church, sect, religious body/group, belief, faith, creed, communion, cult, school, order, constituency, tradition
2 *the denomination of a banknote*
value, face value, worth, unit, grade, class, kind, sort, designation

denote *v*
indicate, be a sign of, stand for, signify, represent, symbolize, mean, refer to, express, designate, typify, mark, show, imply, suggest
OLD betoken

dénouement *n*
climax, culmination, conclusion, outcome, upshot, finale, resolution, clarification, unravelling, finish, last act, solution, close
COLLOQ. pay-off

denounce *v*
condemn, censure, denunciate, accuse, attack, run down, criticize, inform against, betray, indict, pronounce
FORMAL deplore, revile, decry, castigate, impugn, vilify, arraign, declaim, fulminate, inculpate, execrate, proscribe
COLLOQ. slate, knock, pick holes in, pull/tear to pieces, rubbish, badmouth, put the boot in
SLANG slag (off)
E3 acclaim, praise

dense *adj*
1 *a dense crowd/forest*
solid, packed, crammed, jammed together, close-packed, tightly packed, crowded, thick, compact, compressed, condensed, close, close-knit, heavy; *dialect* rank
2 *dense smoke*
thick, opaque, impenetrable, concentrated
3 STUPID, dim, dull, slow, slow-witted
FORMAL obtuse
COLLOQ. thick, thick as two short planks, dim-witted, dopey, dumb, gormless
E3 1 thin, sparse **3** quick-witted, clever

densely *adv*
solidly, closely, thickly, heavily, firmly, tightly, compactly
E3 sparsely

density *n*
body, mass, bulk, closeness, compactness, consistency, denseness, solidity, solidness, thickness, tightness, impenetrability
E3 sparseness

dent *n, v*
◆ *n*
1 HOLLOW, depression, dip, concavity, indentation, crater, dimple, dint, pit
2 REDUCTION, lessening, deduction, cut, drop, fall
◆ *v*
1 DEPRESS, gouge, push in, indent
2 REDUCE, lessen, diminish, damage, weaken

denude *v*
strip, divest, expose, uncover, bare, clear, deforest, defoliate
E3 cover, clothe

denunciation *n*
condemnation, denouncement, censure, accusation,

incrimination, attack, criticism
FORMAL invective, decrial, castigation, obloquy, fulmination
E3 acclaim, praise

deny v
1 deny the allegations
contradict, oppose, disagree with, disprove, repudiate, rebut, nay
TECHNICAL sublate, traverse
OLD denay, renay
FORMAL refute, disaffirm, negate, abnegate, nullify, abjure, gainsay, forswear, renege
2 deny him access to his children
refuse, turn down, forbid, prohibit, reject, withhold, dismiss, rebuff, veto
FORMAL decline, disallow
3 deny your parents
disown, disclaim, repudiate, turn your back on, unget
FORMAL renounce, disavow, recant
E3 1 admit 2 allow

deodorant n
anti-perspirant, deodorizer, scent, air-freshener, disinfectant, fumigant, fumigator

deodorize v
freshen, purify, refresh, sweeten, disinfect, fumigate, aerate, ventilate

depart v
1 GO, go away, go off, leave, withdraw, exit, make off, part, decamp, take your leave, absent yourself, set off, set out, start out, pull out, get going, remove, retreat, migrate, escape, disappear, retire, vanish, take wing
OLD avaunt
COLLOQ. push along/off, make tracks, quit, scat, scoot, scram, take off, take to your heels, make yourself scarce, shove off, bunk off, clear off, split, scarper, skedaddle, vamoose, skive, do a runner, do a bunk, do a moonlight flit, hit the road/trail, make a bolt/break for it, up sticks, hightail it, sling your hook
SLANG N Am lam it, take it on the lam
2 DEVIATE, digress, differ, diverge, fork, branch off, swerve, turn aside, veer, vary
E3 1 arrive, return 2 keep to

Synonym nuances
sense 1
The terms **withdraw** and **exit** are suggestive of moving out of a specific place: *we exited the aircraft*. You may use **make off** to imply haste, with, perhaps, an element of guilt attached: *two men had made off as the police arrived*. You would use **part** to place emphasis on the idea of moving from a place or person. **Remove** could be used to refer to permanent departure to another place, and **decamp**, although it has the literal use of breaking up camp, is more widely used, sometimes facetiously or with a suggestion of secretiveness, of moving away from one place to another: *fashionable society decamped from London to Bath*.

The phrases **absent yourself** and **take your leave** are suggestive of a somewhat formal departure, the latter sometimes including farewells: *he bowed and took his leave*. If you want to talk about embarking on a journey, you could use **set off**, **set out**, **start out** or **get going**, whereas to use **retreat** would imply an element of running away from something, and **escape**, though similar, would further suggest departing previous restrictions and therefore relief.

Migrate is used of movement from one country to another, whilst **retire** tends towards the idea of taking yourself away to a much closer location: *she retired to her room*. Both **vanish** and **disappear** can be used fairly informally to suggest going away at speed: *his brother had vanished upstairs*, whilst **take wing** similarly suggests speed of departure.

---

departed adj
dead, gone, late, lost, passed away
FORMAL deceased, expired

department n
1 DIVISION, branch, subdivision, section, sector, wing, office, bureau, agency, organization, station, unit, branch, region, district
2 SPHERE, realm, province, domain, field, area, concern, responsibility, interest, function, speciality, line

departure n
1 EXIT, going, going away/off, leaving, leave-taking, removal, withdrawal, retirement, retreat, escape, exodus, setting-off, setting-out
2 DEVIATION, digression, divergence, variation, innovation, branching (out), forking, difference, change, shift, veering
E3 1 arrival, return

depend v
1 the cost depends on the quantity
hinge on, be dependent on, rest on, revolve around, be subject to, hang on, be decided by, be determined by, be based on, ride on
FORMAL turn on, be contingent on
2 depend on her for support
rely on, count on, calculate on, reckon on, build upon, trust in, have confidence in, lean on, need, not manage without, cling to, expect; *Scot* lippen
COLLOQ. bank on

dependable adj
reliable, trustworthy, steady, trusty, responsible, faithful, unfailing, sure, honest, conscientious, steadfast, certain, stable, rock-solid
COLLOQ. tried and tested, a safe pair of hands
E3 unreliable, fickle

dependant n
child, minor, relative, charge, protégé, ward, client, hanger-on, henchman, minion, subordinate, parasite

dependence n
1 RELIANCE, confidence, faith, trust, need, expectation
2 ADDICTION, attachment, dependency, subservience, abuse, helplessness, subordination
E3 1 independence

dependency n
1 COLONY, province, protectorate, dominion, satellite
2 RELIANCE, helplessness, weakness, immaturity, support, subordination
3 ADDICTION, attachment, habit, subservience, abuse

dependent adj
1 RELIANT, helpless, weak, immature, subject, sustained, leaning, supported, subordinate, vulnerable
2 the profit is dependent on the quantity bought
conditional, decided, determined, controlled, dictated, based, influenced, relative, subject, subordinate
FORMAL contingent
E3 1, 2 independent

depict v
1 depicted in a painting
portray, illustrate, sketch, outline, draw, picture, paint, trace, show, represent, describe
2 novels depicting Victorian life
portray, describe, recount, characterize, detail, illustrate, outline, trace, show, represent, render, reproduce, record
FORMAL delineate

depiction n
portrayal, description, characterization, detailing, drawing, illustration, image, likeness, picture, caricature, sketch, outline, representation, rendering
FORMAL delineation

deplete v
empty, drain, exhaust, impoverish, bankrupt, weaken,

evacuate, use up, consume, spend, expend, run down, reduce, lessen, decrease, diminish, eat into, erode, whittle away
FORMAL attenuate
F3 increase; *formal* augment

depletion *n*
exhaustion, impoverishment, weakening, evacuation, consumption, using-up, expenditure, reduction, lessening, decrease, deficiency, dwindling, lowering, shrinkage
FORMAL attenuation, diminution
F3 increase, supply; *formal* augmentation

deplorable *adj*
disgraceful, reprehensible, scandalous, outrageous, shameful, dishonourable, disreputable, blameworthy, abominable, despicable, lamentable, pitiable, grievous, regrettable, unfortunate, wretched, distressing, sad, miserable, heartbreaking, melancholy, disastrous, dire, appalling
F3 excellent, commendable

deplorably *adv*
disgracefully, scandalously, unfortunately, miserably, appallingly, outrageously, shamefully, despicably, abominably, despicably, lamentably
F3 commendably

deplore *v*
1 DISAPPROVE OF, condemn, criticize, reproach, blame, revile, denounce
FORMAL reprehend, reprove, deprecate, berate, upbraid, castigate, disparage, censure, slate
COLLOQ. slam
2 GRIEVE FOR, lament, mourn, regret, bemoan, bewail, pine, rue, weep, cry, shed tears
F3 **1** extol

deploy *v*
arrange, position, station, spread out, scatter, use, make use of, utilize, distribute
FORMAL dispose

depopulate *v*
empty, dispeople, unpeople

deport¹ *v*
deported from a country
expel, banish, exile, extradite, repatriate, transport, oust, ostracize

deport² *v*
deport yourself well
conduct, bear, behave, carry, hold, manage, act, perform
FORMAL acquit, comport

deportation *n*
expulsion, banishment, exile, extradition, repatriation, transportation, ousting, ostracism

deportment *n*
manner, air, appearance, aspect, bearing, behaviour, carriage, conduct, pose, posture, gait, stance, etiquette
FORMAL comportment, demeanour, mien

depose *v*
oust, overthrow, dismiss, fire, remove, unseat, topple, disestablish, displace, demote, dethrone, discharge, downgrade
COLLOQ. sack

deposit *v, n*
◆ *v*
1 LAY, drop, plant, place, put (down), set (down), settle, park, sit, locate, land, ware
TECHNICAL precipitate, depone, sediment, sublime, oviposit
FORMAL reposit
COLLOQ. dump, bung
2 SAVE, store, hoard, bank, amass, consign, entrust, lodge,

file, stow, put away, put by, pay in
◆ *n*
1 SECURITY, stake, down payment, pledge, retainer, instalment, part payment, margin; *S Afr* lay-by
OLD gage
FORMAL earnest
2 SEDIMENT, accumulation, dregs, lees, silt, bed, dew, soot, warp
TECHNICAL alluvium, fall-out, precipitate
FORMAL deposition

Types of deposit include:

amyloid	globigerina ooze	salamander
arcus	hypostasis	Saturn's tree
bergmehl	infiltration	shell-marl
black earth	loess	sinter
bone-bed	moorlog	tar-sand
cave-earth	placer	tartar
coral reef	precipitation	terramara
crag	sublimate	tophus
delta	pteropod ooze	tree of silver
Diana's tree	radiolarian ooze	Zechstein
diatom ooze	red clay	
diluvium	saburra	

---

deposition *n*
1 *the deposition of the ruler*
ousting, overthrow, dismissal, removal, unseating, toppling, displacement, dethronement
2 *the witness's deposition*
affidavit, declaration, statement, testimony, evidence, information
FORMAL attestation

depository *n*
storehouse, store, warehouse, bonded warehouse, depot, repository, arsenal, cache

depot *n*
1 *military depot*
storehouse, store, warehouse, depository, repository, cache, arsenal
2 *bus depot*
station, garage, terminal, terminus

deprave *v*
corrupt, debauch, debase, degrade, pervert, subvert, warp, infect, demoralize, lead astray, seduce, pollute, defile, contaminate
F3 improve, reform

depraved *adj*
corrupt, debauched, degenerate, perverted, debased, warped, reprobate, dissolute, immoral, obscene, base, shameless, wicked, sinful, vile, evil, iniquitous, criminal
FORMAL licentious
F3 moral, upright

depravity *n*
corruption, debauchery, degeneracy, perversion, debasement, reprobacy, dissoluteness, immorality, baseness, wickedness, sinfulness, vileness, evil, iniquity, vice
FORMAL turpitude
F3 uprightness

deprecate *v*
condemn, disapprove of, censure, criticize, object to, protest at, reject, reproach, reprove, berate, upbraid, blame, revile, run down, slate, denounce
FORMAL deplore, reprehend, deprecate, castigate, disparage
COLLOQ. slam, knock, rubbish
F3 approve, commend

⚠ **deprecate** or **depreciate**?
Deprecate is a formal word meaning 'to disapprove of': *The government deprecated the soldiers' actions*. *Depreciate* most commonly means 'to fall or cause to fall in value': *Property shares have depreciated rapidly*. A rarer meaning of *depreciate* is 'to speak of as having little value or importance': *to depreciate your achievements*.

---

deprecatory *adj*
disapproving, censorious, condemnatory, reproachful, dismissive, protesting, apologetic, regretful
🗲 encouraging; *formal* commendatory

depreciate *v*
1 DEVALUE, deflate, downgrade, decrease/fall/go down in value, reduce, lower, drop, fall, lessen, decline, slump
2 BELITTLE, undervalue, underestimate, underrate, slight, run down, make light of
FORMAL disparage, denigrate, revile, defame, malign
🗲 **1** appreciate **2** overrate

depreciation *n*
1 DEVALUATION, deflation, depression, slump, fall, reduction in price/value, mark-down, cheapening
2 BELITTLEMENT, underestimation
FORMAL disparagement, denigration

depredation *n*
desolation, destruction, devastation, laying waste, ravaging, marauding, pillage, looting, plunder, plundering, raiding, ransacking, harrying, robbery, theft
FORMAL despoiling, denudation

depress *v*
1 DEJECT, sadden, make sad, dishearten, discourage, cast down, bring down, weigh down, oppress, upset, daunt, burden, overburden
COLLOQ. get down, break someone's heart
2 WEAKEN, undermine, debilitate, sap, tire, drain, exhaust, weary, impair, reduce, lessen, press, lower, level
FORMAL enervate
3 DEVALUE, bring down, reduce, lower, cut, depreciate, cheapen
COLLOQ. slash
4 *depress a lever*
push, push down, press, press down, lower, hold down
🗲 **1** cheer **2** vitalize, energize; *formal* fortify **3** increase, raise

depressant *n*
sedative, tranquillizer, downer, relaxant, calmant, calmative
COLLOQ. downer
🗲 stimulant

depressed *adj*
1 DEJECTED, low-spirited, melancholy, dispirited, sad, unhappy, low, low in spirits, out of spirits, down, downcast, disheartened, miserable, moody, cast down, discouraged, gloomy, glum, downhearted, moping, broken-hearted, heartsick, cowed, dumpish, distressed, despondent, morose, crestfallen, pessimistic, exanimate, *accablé*
OLD jaw-fallen
COLLOQ. fed up, blue, doomy, a peg too low, down in the dumps
2 POOR, disadvantaged, deprived, needy, run-down, destitute, poverty-stricken, under hatches
3 SUNKEN, recessed, low, concave, hollow, indented, dented, pushed in
TECHNICAL emarginate
🗲 **1** cheerful **2** thriving, affluent **3** convex, protuberant

depressing *adj*
dejecting, dismal, bleak, gloomy, saddening, cheerless, dreary, disheartening, unhappy, sad, melancholy, sombre, grey, black, daunting, discouraging, dispiriting, heartbreaking, distressing, upsetting, hopeless, grave
🗲 cheerful, happy, encouraging

depressingly *adv*
dishearteningly, dauntingly, discouragingly, dispiritingly, heartbreakingly, distressingly, unhappily, sadly, bleakly, gloomily, cheerlessly, drearily
🗲 encouragingly, happily

depression *n*
1 DEJECTION, despair, despondency, melancholy, low spirits, unhappiness, sadness, gloom, gloominess, doldrums, glumness, downheartedness, broken-heartedness, pessimism, hopelessness, desolation, discouragement
TECHNICAL melancholia
COLLOQ. blues, dumps, black dog
2 RECESSION, slump, stagnation, crash, hard times, decline, inactivity, slowdown, standstill
3 INDENTATION, hollow, hole, dip, concavity, dent, dimple, valley, pit, sink, dint, bowl, cavity, basin, impression, dish, excavation
🗲 **1** cheerfulness, happiness, euphoria **2** prosperity, boom **3** convexity; *formal* protuberance

deprivation *n*
1 *deprivation of sleep*
denial, withdrawal, withholding, removal, lack, dispossession
2 *deprivation in inner cities*
hardship, poverty, impoverishment, want, need, disadvantage
FORMAL destitution, privation, penury

deprive *v*
take away, dispossess, strip, divest, rob, confiscate, bereave, deny, withhold, refuse
FORMAL denude, expropriate
🗲 endow, provide

Synonym nuances
Take away may be broadly used of removing something from someone's possession, while **dispossess** tends more usually to relate to having land or property removed: *the dispossessed peasantry of old Ireland*. Both **strip** and **divest** suggest removal of clothing, sometimes the formal trappings of office and often a title or station, and so these terms can carry connotations of indignity: *divested of her robes*.
  If you use **rob** the implication is that something is being removed illegally or at least unfairly, but **confiscate** suggests having the force of law behind it: *the government confiscated all the TV footage*. The terms **deny**, **withhold** and **refuse** are all fairly unmarked terms for having something within your power or possession that you deliberately refuse to pass on to someone else: *he was denied permission to appeal; she was withholding evidence; he was refused the right to call witnesses*.
  Bereave, meanwhile, is more appropriately used of depriving by death: *she was bereaved of two daughters*.

---

deprived *adj*
poor, needy, in need, underprivileged, disadvantaged, impoverished, destitute, lacking, bereft
🗲 prosperous, privileged

depth *n*
1 DEEPNESS, profoundness, extent, measure, drop
FORMAL profundity
2 *depth of feeling*
intensity, strength, thoroughness, seriousness, severity, gravity, earnestness, passion, vigour, fervour
3 *a person of great depth*
wisdom, insight, discernment, perception, penetration, awareness, intuition, astuteness, cleverness, shrewdness, acumen
FORMAL profundity
4 *the depths of their knowledge*
extent, extensiveness, scope, range, amount

FORMAL profundity
5 depth of colour
intensity, strength, richness, vividness, brilliance, warmth, glow, darkness
6 the depths of the sea
remotest area, bed, floor, bottom, abyss, deep, gulf, middle, midst
F∃ 1 shallowness **6** surface
■ in depth
comprehensively, thoroughly, exhaustively, extensively, in detail
F∃ superficially, broadly

deputation n
commission, delegation, embassy, mission, representatives, legation, committee

depute v
appoint, authorize, charge, commission, second, designate, nominate, empower, entrust, mandate, delegate, consign, hand over
FORMAL accredit

deputize n
represent, stand in for, fill in for, take over, substitute, replace, act for, understudy, take the place of, double, relieve, cover
COLLOQ. sub for; NAm pinch-hit for

deputy n, adj
♦ n
representative, agent, delegate, proxy, substitute, stand-in, second-in-command, second, ambassador, envoy, commissioner, lieutenant, legate, surrogate, alternate, subordinate, assistant, locum, locum tenens, spokesperson, vice-president, vice-chairperson, vice-regent, commissary, commis, official
COLLOQ. sidekick, mate
♦ adj
assistant, representative, substitute, stand-in, surrogate, subordinate, vice-; Scot -depute

derail v
derail peace talks; the train was derailed
hold back, obstruct, prevent, impede, upset, displace, disturb, throw off course, disrupt

deranged adj
disordered, demented, crazy, mad, lunatic, insane, of unsound mind, non compos mentis, unbalanced, unstable, unhinged, fey, unsettled, distracted, disturbed, irrational, confused, frantic, frenzied, frenetic, wild, manic, maniac, maniacal, crazed, delirious, distraught, berserk, out of your mind, out of your senses, psychotic
OLD frantic-mad, lymphatic, bestraught
COLLOQ. crazy, nuts, nutty, nutty as a fruitcake, wacky, mad as a hatter, barmy, bonkers, batty, cracked, crackers, dippy, daffy, dotty, loopy, potty, off your nut, off your head, wrong in the head, out of your head, off the wall, out to lunch, round the bend, round the twist, bats, having bats in the belfry, cuckoo, off the rails, screwy, up the wall, raving, not all there; NAm buggy, flaky, fruity; Aust & NZ dingbats
SLANG loony, mental, bananas, barking, wacko, doolally, off your rocker, off your chump, off your trolley, out of your tree, needing your head examined, having lost your marbles, having a screw loose, having a tile loose, having several cards short of a full deck, with one sandwich short of a picnic, meshuga, ape, apeshit; NAm gonzo, loco, wiggy; Aust out of your tree
F∃ sane, calm

derangement n
aberration, agitation, confusion, delirium, dementia, disorder, distraction, disturbance, frenzy, hallucination, mania, insanity, lunacy, madness
F∃ order, sanity

derelict adj, n
♦ adj
abandoned, neglected, deserted, forsaken, desolate, discarded, dilapidated, falling to pieces, ramshackle, tumbledown, run-down, ruined, in disrepair
♦ n
tramp, vagrant, dosser, beggar, wretch, vagabond, down-and-out, drifter, hobo, outcast, no-good, good-for-nothing, no-hoper, ne'er-do-well; NAm down-and-outer
COLLOQ. Scots jakey

dereliction n
1 DILAPIDATION, abandonment, neglect, desertion, forsaking, desolation, ruin(s), disrepair
2 dereliction of duty
neglect, negligence, abdication, abandonment, desertion, evasion, failure, faithlessness, forsaking, betrayal, relinquishment, remissness
FORMAL apostasy, renegation, renunciation
F∃ 2 devotion, faithfulness, fulfilment

deride v
ridicule, laugh at, mock, scoff at, scorn, jeer at, sneer at, make fun of, satirize, gibe, insult, belittle, disdain, taunt, tease, rag
FORMAL disparage
COLLOQ. knock, pooh-pooh; Aust chiack
F∃ respect, praise

de rigueur adj
conventional, fashionable, fitting, necessary, correct, decent, done, proper, expected, required, compulsory, right
FORMAL decorous
COLLOQ. the done thing

derision n
ridicule, mockery, scorn, contempt, scoffing, hissing, satire, sneering, taunting, disrespect, insult, teasing, ragging, disdain
FORMAL disparagement
F∃ respect, praise

derisive adj
mocking, scornful, contemptuous, scoffing, disrespectful, insulting, irreverent, jeering, disdainful, taunting
F∃ respectful, flattering

❗ derisive or derisory?
Derisive means 'mocking; showing derision': derisive laughter. Derisory means 'ridiculous; deserving mockery or derision': The management offered a derisory pay increase.

derisively adv
scornfully, contemptuously, disrespectfully, irreverently, disdainfully
F∃ respectfully

derisory adj
laughable, ludicrous, absurd, ridiculous, contemptible, insulting, outrageous, preposterous, small, tiny, inadequate, insufficient, paltry
FORMAL risible

derivation n
source, origin, root, beginning, etymology, extraction, foundation, genealogy, ancestry, basis, descent, deduction, inference

derivative adj, n
♦ adj
unoriginal, acquired, copied, borrowed, derived, imitative, obtained, second-hand, secondary, plagiarized, hackneyed, trite

COLLOQ. cribbed, rehashed
E3 original, inventive, innovative
• *n*
derivation, offshoot, by-product, development, branch, outgrowth, spin-off, product, descendant

derive *v*
1 *derive pleasure from something*
gain, obtain, get, take, draw, extract, receive, reap, acquire, borrow
FORMAL procure
2 ORIGINATE, arise, spring, flow, have as the source, have its origin/roots in, descend, stem, issue, follow, develop, evolve
FORMAL emanate, proceed

derogatory *adj*
disparaging, insulting, pejorative, belittling, offensive, critical, disapproving, unfavourable, slighting, uncomplimentary, injurious
FORMAL depreciative, defamatory, vilifying, denigratory
E3 flattering, favourable, complimentary

descend *v*
1 GO DOWN, come down, move down, drop, fall, dive, plummet, plunge, tumble, swoop, pitch, parachute, pancake, sink, arrive, alight, dismount, dip, slope, incline, subside, *dégringoler*
2 CONDESCEND, deign, sink, stoop, lower yourself
3 DEGENERATE, deteriorate, decline
COLLOQ. go downhill, go to the dogs, go to pot
4 ORIGINATE, issue, spring, stem, derive
FORMAL proceed, emanate
5 *family descended on us*
invade, arrive suddenly, storm, swoop, take over
E3 1 ascend, rise

descendants *n*
offspring, children, issue, progeny, successors, heirs, lineage, line, scions, posterity
FORMAL seed
E3 ancestors

descent *n*
1 FALL, going-down, drop, plunge, sinking, subsiding, dip, decline, incline, slope, slant, gradient
FORMAL declivity
2 COMEDOWN, debasement, degradation, deterioration, decline, degeneration, degeneracy, decadence
3 ANCESTRY, parentage, heredity, family tree, genealogy, lineage, line, stock, extraction, origin
E3 1 ascent, rise

describe *v*
1 *describe a situation*
portray, depict, illustrate, characterize, specify, draw, define, detail, give details of, explain, express, tell, talk, write, narrate, outline, relate, recount, present, represent, report
FORMAL delineate, elucidate
2 *describe someone as clever*
call, portray, consider, think, style, label, designate, brand, hail
3 *skaters describing circles on the ice*
mark out, draw, sketch, trace, outline
FORMAL delineate

description *n*
1 PORTRAYAL, representation, characterization, account, depiction, sketch, portrait, presentation, report, statement, outline, explanation, narration, commentary, chronicle, profile
FORMAL delineation, exposition, elucidation
2 SORT, type, kind, variety, specification, order, class, designation, category, style, breed, brand, make

---

Synonym nuances
sense 1
Portrayal and **presentation** suggest the use of words, drawings or even performance to show what someone is like: *the portrayal of women in the media*; *one textbook distorted its presentation of the data*; whereas **representation** and **depiction** suggest something more definite, perhaps less subjective: *the representation of movement in drawings*; *the depiction of country life*. **Characterization** is usually limited to suggesting the nature of a particular person or thing.
  Both **sketch** and **portrait** are used in a literal way of drawings, but they may sometimes be used of pictures drawn from words, though **sketch** is usually less clearly defined: *a sketch of the proceedings*. **Outline** and **profile** also suggest a general overview minus details. To describe a continuous vocal description of something that has happened or is happening, the terms **narration** or **commentary** may be used: *narration of past events*; *a running commentary on the match*. **Chronicle** could also be used of the idea of a continuous record, although usually written.

---

descriptive *adj*
illustrative, explanatory, expressive, detailed, graphic, colourful, pictorial, striking, vivid, detailed
FORMAL elucidatory

descry *v*
discern, catch sight of, mark, notice, observe, perceive, recognize, discover, distinguish, glimpse, see, spot, detect
OLD espy

desecrate *v*
defile, violate, pervert, pollute, profane, contaminate, debase, dishallow, dishonour, insult, abuse, blaspheme, vandalize, violate

desecration *n*
defilement, violation, blasphemy, debasement, dishonouring, pollution, profanation, sacrilege, impiety, insult

desegregate *v*
integrate, assimilate, merge, blend, join, incorporate, intermix, harmonize

desert¹ *n, adj*
• *n*
the Sahara desert
wasteland, wilderness, wilds, barrenness, void, dust bowl
Related adjective: eremic
• *adj*
bare, barren, waste, wild, uninhabited, empty, uncultivated, dry, dried up, arid, parched, moistureless, infertile, unproductive, desolate, sterile, lonely, solitary

---

Deserts of the world (with locations) include:

Sahara (*N Africa*)	Great Victoria (*SW Australia*)
Arabian (*SW Asia*)	Thar (*India/Pakistan*)
Gobi (*Mongolia and NE China*)	Sonoran (*SW USA*)
Patagonian (*Argentina*)	Kara Kum (*Turkmenistan*)
Great Basin (*SW USA*)	Kyzyl-Kum (*Kazakhstan*)
Chihuahuan (*Mexico*)	Takla Makan (*N China*)
Great Sandy (*NW Australia*)	Kalahari (*SW Africa*)
Nubian (*Sudan*)	

---

desert² *v*
1 *desert his family*
abandon, leave, maroon, strand, give up, walk out on
FORMAL renounce, forsake, relinquish, cast off, abscond;
Scot forhow
COLLOQ. jilt, quit, throw over, run out on, leave in the lurch,

leave high and dry, rat on, chicken out; *NAm* bug out
2 *the soldier deserted*
decamp, defect, run away, fly, flee, go AWOL
FORMAL abscond, tergiversate
3 *desert a political party*
abandon, give up, turn your back on, deny, betray, defect, change sides
FORMAL forsake, relinquish, renounce, recant, apostasize, tergiversate
Ea 1 stand by, support **3** support

desert[3] *n*
1 DUE, right, reward, deserts, what you deserve, return, retribution, payment, recompense, remuneration
COLLOQ. comeuppance
2 WORTH, merit, virtue
OLD demerit

deserted *adj*
abandoned, empty, derelict, desolate, god-forsaken, forsaken, neglected, underpopulated, stranded, isolated, bereft, left, vacant, betrayed, lonely, solitary, uninhabited, unoccupied
Ea populous

deserter *n*
runaway, absconder, escapee, truant, renegade, defector, traitor, turncoat, fugitive, betrayer, backslider, delinquent
FORMAL apostate
COLLOQ. rat; *NAm* bug-out

desertion *n*
1 *desertion of his family*
abandonment, leaving, give up
FORMAL forsaking, relinquishment, absconding, casting-off, renunciation
COLLOQ. jilting, quitting; *NAm* bug-out
2 *desertions from the armed forces*
defection, decamping, running-away, flight, going AWOL, truancy
FORMAL absconding, dereliction
3 *desertion of a political party*
abandonment, giving-up, denial, betrayal
FORMAL renunciation, forsaking, relinquishment, apostasy, renegation, tergiversation
Ea 3 support

deserve *v*
earn, be worthy of, merit, be entitled to, warrant, justify, have a right to, win, rate, incur
COLLOQ. have it coming (to you)

deserved *adj*
due, earned, merited, justifiable, justified, warranted, right, rightful, well-earned, suitable, proper, fitting, fair, just, appropriate, apt, legitimate
FORMAL meet, apposite, condign
Ea gratuitous, undeserved

deservedly *adv*
justifiably, duly, rightly, rightfully, by rights, justly, fairly, suitably, properly, fittingly, appropriately

deserving *adj*
worthy, estimable, exemplary, praiseworthy, admirable, commendable, upright, righteous, virtuous
FORMAL laudable, meritorious
Ea undeserving, unworthy

desiccated *adj*
dehydrated, drained, dried, dried up, dry, arid, dead, lifeless, parched, powdered, sterile
FORMAL exsiccated

desiccation *n*
dehydration, dryness, aridity, parching, sterility
FORMAL exsiccation, xeransis

desideratum *n*
requirement, requisite, prerequisite, need, want,

necessity, essential, sine qua non
COLLOQ. must

design *v, n*
♦ *v*
1 DRAW, plan, sketch, draw up, draft, outline, plot
FORMAL delineate
2 INVENT, originate, conceive, create, think up, develop, construct, fashion, form, model, fabricate, hatch, make
3 INTEND, plot, plan, devise, purpose, contrive, aim, scheme, shape, project, propose, tailor, mean, gear
♦ *n*
1 BLUEPRINT, draft, pattern, plan, prototype, sketch, drawing, outline, map, diagram, scheme, model, guide
FORMAL delineation
2 MOTIF, style, pattern, logo, shape, form, figure, device, emblem, monogram, cipher, format, structure, organization, arrangement, composition, make-up, construction
3 AIM, intention, goal, purpose, plan, end, object, objective, scheme, plot, project, meaning, target, point, wish, desire, hope, dream, enterprise, undertaking
■ **by design**
intentionally, deliberately, on purpose, consciously, pointedly, calculatingly, knowingly, wittingly, wilfully

designate *v*
1 *designated as a listed building*
call, name, title, entitle, term, dub, style, describe, class, classify, christen
2 *designated to be chairman*
choose, appoint, nominate, select, elect, assign, specify, define, stipulate, earmark, set aside, show, denote, indicate

designation *n*
1 NAME, title, term, label, epithet, nickname, description, style, sobriquet
FORMAL appellation, denomination
COLLOQ. tag
2 SPECIFICATION, description, definition, denoting, marking, classification, category, stipulation, indication
3 NOMINATION, appointment, selection, election

designer *n*
deviser, originator, maker, stylist, inventor, creator, contriver, producer, fashioner, planner, architect, author

designing *adj*
artful, crafty, scheming, conspiring, calculating, devious, intriguing, plotting, tricky, wily, sly, deceitful, cunning, guileful, underhand, sharp, shrewd
Ea artless, naive

desirability *n*
1 *the desirability of qualifications*
advantage, profit, advisability, benefit, preference, usefulness, merit, worth, excellence, popularity
2 *the desirability of the woman*
attractiveness, attraction, allure, seductiveness, appeal
COLLOQ. sexiness
Ea 1 disadvantage, inadvisability, undesirability

desirable *adj*
1 *a desirable qualification*
advantageous, sought-after, profitable, worthwhile, advisable, appropriate, expedient, beneficial, preferable, sensible, eligible, good, pleasing, pleasant, agreeable, popular, in demand
2 *a desirable woman*
attractive, alluring, seductive, fetching, tempting, tantalizing
COLLOQ. sexy
SLANG beddable, hot
Ea 1 undesirable **2** unattractive

desire *v, n*
♦ *v*
1 WANT, wish for, covet, long for, like, need, crave, hunger

for, gasp for, yearn for, set your heart on, fancy, feel like, hanker after, envy
OLD (*Spenser*) fain
FORMAL desiderate
COLLOQ. be dying for, have your eyes on, have designs on, give the world for
2 desire a man
lust after, burn for, take to
COLLOQ. fancy, be crazy about, have a crush on, take a shine to
SLANG have the hots for
• *n*
1 WANT, longing, wish, need, fancy, yearning, craving, hankering, lust, appetite, greed, preference, aspiration, demand, *besoin*
OLD covetise; (*Shakesp*) bosom
FORMAL predilection, predisposition, proclivity, cacoëthes
COLLOQ. itch, yen
2 LUST, passion, sexual attraction, sexuality, sex drive, ardour, libido, sensuality, lasciviousness
TECHNICAL ephebophilia
FORMAL concupiscence
Related adjective: epithymetic

desired *adj*
required, proper, accurate, appropriate, correct, exact, expected, fitting, necessary, particular, right
E3 undesired, unintentional

desirous *adj*
ready, willing, ambitious, aspiring, avid, burning, craving, itching, eager, enthusiastic, fervent, fervid, hopeful, hoping, keen, longing, anxious, wishing, yearning
FORMAL cupidinous
E3 reluctant, unenthusiastic

desist *v*
stop, leave off, end, break off, give up, halt, suspend, pause, peter out, cease
FORMAL abstain, refrain, discontinue, remit, forbear
E3 continue, resume

desk *n*
table, bureau, lectern, reading-desk, davenport, écritoire, secretaire, writing-table, ambo

desolate *adj, v*
• *adj*
1 DESERTED, uninhabited, unoccupied, abandoned, unfrequented, barren, bare, arid, desert, bleak, gloomy, dismal, dreary, lonely, solitary, isolated, god-forsaken, forsaken, waste, wild, depressing; *Scot* gousty
2 MISERABLE, forlorn, bereft, depressed, dejected, forsaken, despondent, distressed, melancholy, gloomy, unhappy, sad, disheartened, dismal, downcast, broken-hearted, heartbroken, wretched, drearisome
E3 1 populous **2** cheerful
• *v*
devastate, upset, disconcert, overwhelm, take aback, confound, nonplus, get down
FORMAL discomfit
COLLOQ. shatter, floor

desolation *n*
1 DESTRUCTION, ruin, devastation, ravages, laying waste
2 BARRENNESS, bleakness, emptiness, forlornness, loneliness, isolation, solitude, remoteness, wildness, wilderness
3 DEJECTION, despair, despondency, gloom, misery, sadness, melancholy, sorrow, unhappiness, broken-heartedness, anguish, depression, grief, distress, wretchedness

despair *v, n*
• *v*
lose heart, lose hope, give up, give in, be despondent, be discouraged, collapse, surrender

COLLOQ. hit rock bottom, throw in the towel
E3 hope
• *n*
despondency, gloom, hopelessness, desperation, dejection, anguish, distress, inconsolableness, melancholy, misery, depression, pessimism, wretchedness
TECHNICAL dysthymia
OLD wanhope
E3 cheerfulness, resilience

despairing *adj*
despondent, distraught, inconsolable, desolate, desperate, heartbroken, suicidal, grief-stricken, hopeless, depressed, discouraged, disheartened, dejected, miserable, anguished, wretched, sorrowful, pessimistic, dismayed, downcast, *au désespoir*
FORMAL disconsolate
E3 cheerful, hopeful

despatch
see **dispatch**.

desperado *n*
bandit, criminal, brigand, terrorist, gangster, gunman, outlaw, ruffian, thug, cut-throat, lawbreaker; *N Am* badman
COLLOQ. hoodlum, mugger

desperate *adj*
1 HOPELESS, inconsolable, wretched, despondent, abandoned, distraught, desolate, heartbroken, suicidal, grief-stricken, depressed, discouraged, disheartened, dejected, miserable, anguished, sorrowful, pessimistic, dismayed, downcast
FORMAL disconsolate
COLLOQ. at rock-bottom
2 RECKLESS, rash, impetuous, bold, audacious, daring, dangerous, do-or-die, foolhardy, risky, hazardous, hasty, wild, violent, lawless, frantic, frenzied, incautious, determined
FORMAL precipitate
3 CRITICAL, dire, acute, crucial, serious, grave, severe, extreme, urgent, compelling, pressing, great, dangerous
4 desperate to leave school
wanting very much, needing very much, crying out for, in great need
COLLOQ. dying
E3 1 hopeful, optimistic **2** cautious, considered

desperately *adv*
dangerously, critically, gravely, acutely, hopelessly, seriously, severely, badly, dangerously, urgently, greatly, extremely, dreadfully, fearfully, frightfully

desperation *n*
despair, despondency, anguish, hopelessness, gloom, misery, agony, distress, pain, wretchedness, sorrow, trouble, worry, anxiety, depression

despicable *adj*
contemptible, vile, worthless, detestable, disgusting, mean, low, degrading, base, wretched, disgraceful, disreputable, shameful, abominable, loathsome, reprobate
OLD dastardly, caitiff
FORMAL reprehensible
COLLOQ. lowdown
E3 admirable, noble

despise *v*
scorn, hold in contempt, look down on, disdain, condemn, spurn, undervalue, slight, dislike, hate, detest, loathe, abhor, shun, mock, sneer
OLD contemn, forhow, set at naught/nought
FORMAL revile, deplore, deride, vilipend
E3 admire

despite *prep*
in spite of, regardless of, in the face of, undeterred by, against, defying
FORMAL notwithstanding

despoil *v*
destroy, devastate, loot, maraud, pillage, plunder, ransack, ravage, deprive, dispossess, divest, rifle, rob, strip, vandalize, wreck
FORMAL denude, depredate, spoliate
E∃ adorn, enrich

despondency *n*
broken-heartedness, dejection, depression, despair, desperation, discouragement, dispiritedness, downheartedness, gloom, glumness, hopelessness, inconsolability, melancholia, melancholy, distress, misery, sadness, sorrow, grief, wretchedness
FORMAL disconsolateness
COLLOQ. blues, heartache
E∃ cheerfulness, hopefulness

despondent *adj*
depressed, dejected, disheartened, downcast, down, low, gloomy, glum, discouraged, distressed, miserable, melancholy, sad, sorrowful, doleful, despairing, heartbroken, heartsick, inconsolable, mournful, wretched
COLLOQ. down in the dumps, blue
E∃ cheerful, heartened, hopeful

despot *n*
autocrat, tyrant, dictator, oppressor, absolute ruler, absolutist, boss, sultan, tsar

despotic *adj*
autocratic, tyrannical, imperious, oppressive, dictatorial, authoritarian, domineering, high-handed, absolute, overbearing, arbitrary, arrogant
E∃ democratic, egalitarian, liberal, tolerant

despotism *n*
autocracy, totalitarianism, tyranny, dictatorship, absolutism, oppression, repression
E∃ democracy, egalitarianism, liberalism, tolerance

dessert *n*
sweet, sweet dish, sweet course, pudding
COLLOQ. afters, pud

Desserts and puddings include:

baked Alaska	crêpe suzette	plum-duff
baklava	egg custard	plum pudding
banana split	Eton mess	profiteroles
banoffee pie	Eve's pudding	queen of
blancmange	frangipane	puddings
bombe	fruit cocktail (or	rice pudding
bread-and-butter	salad)	roly-poly pudding
pudding	fruit crumble	soufflé
N Am Brown	ice cream	spotted dick
Betty	jelly	sticky toffee
charlotte russe	knickerbocker	pudding
cheesecake	glory	sorbet
Christmas	kulfi	summer pudding
pudding	millefeuilles	sundae
clafoutis	milk pudding	syllabub
Scot clootie	mousse	tapioca
dumpling	mud pie	tartufo
cobbler	*N Am* pandowdy	tiramisu
compote	panna cotta	trifle
cranachan	parfait	vacherin
crème brûlée	pavlova	yogurt
crème caramel	peach Melba	zabaglione

---

destination *n*
1 GOAL, aim, objective, object, purpose, target, end, intention, aspiration, design, ambition
2 JOURNEY'S END, terminus, station, stop, final port of call, end of the line, landing place

destined *adj*
1 FATED, doomed, inevitable, certain, meant, unavoidable, inescapable, fatal, born, marked, intended, designed, appointed, predetermined, ordained, preordained, set apart
FORMAL foreordained
2 *passengers destined for Glasgow*
bound, directed, routed, en route, headed, heading, scheduled, assigned, intended, booked

destiny *n*
fate, future, doom, fortune, lot, luck, karma, kismet, Moira
FORMAL portion, predestination, predestiny

destitute *adj*
1 POOR, hard up, badly off, penniless, poverty-stricken, impoverished, distressed, bankrupt
FORMAL impecunious, indigent, penurious
COLLOQ. broke, stony-broke, down-and-out, on the breadline, cleaned out, strapped for cash, with your back to the wall, on your beam-ends, dirt-poor
SLANG skint, rooked
2 LACKING, needy, wanting, innocent of, deprived, deficient, depleted
FORMAL devoid of, bereft
E∃ 1 prosperous, rich

destitution *n*
poverty, pennilessness, impoverishment, distress, bankruptcy, beggary, starvation, straits
FORMAL impecuniousness, indigence, penury, pauperdom
E∃ prosperity, wealth

destroy *v*
1 DEMOLISH, ruin, shatter, wreck, devastate, smash, break, crush, subdue, overthrow, sabotage, undo, stamp out, dismantle, knock down, pull down, tear down, flatten, obliterate, thwart, undermine, waste, lay waste, gut, level, spoil, ravage, raze, ransack, torpedo, unshape
OLD (*Shakesp*) ruinate
FORMAL extirpate
2 KILL, kill off, annihilate, eliminate, extinguish, eradicate, dispatch, slaughter, put down, put to sleep, put out of its misery
FORMAL slay, nullify, vitiate
COLLOQ. decimate
E∃ 1 build up 2 create

Synonym nuances
sense 1
Demolish can be used to suggest knocking down, literally or figuratively: *he demolished the class barrier*, while both **level** and **raze** would be used with the literal sense of reducing to the ground. **Ruin**, **shatter** and **wreck** are descriptive terms all suggestive of action causing irredeemable damage. The even stronger term **devastate** similarly suggests destruction on a huge scale, and **obliterate** further suggests the removal of any trace: *the park was completely obliterated beneath the snow.*
  Smash, **crush** and **break**, however, all have implications of deliberate harm, with the first two possibly implying an element of zeal. **Undo** has gentler associations, more suggestive of reversing what has already been done, while **dismantle** is also less forceful, suggesting a taking apart piece by piece: *after the British and French dismantled their empires.* The term **stamp out** can be used of putting an end to something perceived as undesirable, and again there is an underlying sense of eagerness: *a need to stamp out violence.*
  If you want to convey the destruction of more abstract notions such as plans, systems or feelings, then you might use **thwart** or **undermine**, the latter appropriately describing a severe weakening rather than outright

destruction: *aggressive actions can undermine international stability.*

Lay waste is best used of rendering land desolate, while **gut** may be used of buildings, especially the interior: *the church was gutted by fire.* **Ravage** also conveys images of desolation, and has additional connotations of plunder, as indeed has **ransack. Torpedo**, with its image of a rapid and violent attack, has connotations of complete and irreversible destruction: *the outbreak of fighting torpedoed the peace talks.*

destroyer *n*
wrecker, annihilator, demolisher, desolater, despoiler, ransacker, ravager, vandal, locust, kiss of death
⊟ creator

destruction *n*
1 RUIN, devastation, shattering, smashing, crushing, wreckage, demolition, knocking-down, pulling-down, tearing-down, vandalism, defeat, downfall, overthrow, ruination, desolation, obliteration, undoing, wastage, razing, levelling, dismantling, havoc, ravagement
FORMAL depredation
2 ANNIHILATION, killing, killing-off, extermination, eradication, elimination, extinction, slaughter, murder, massacre, end, liquidation
FORMAL nullification
⊟ 2 creation

destructive *adj*
1 *destructive storms*
devastating, damaging, catastrophic, disastrous, deadly, harmful, fatal, disruptive, lethal, ruinous, injurious, detrimental, hurtful, malignant, pernicious, mischievous
FORMAL noxious, nullifying, deleterious, baneful, slaughterous
2 *destructive criticism*
adverse, hostile, antagonistic, negative, discouraging, unfavourable, unfriendly, disparaging, contrary, derogatory, undermining, subversive, vicious
FORMAL denigrating
⊟ 1 creative **2** constructive, favourable

destructively *adv*
disastrously, catastrophically, harmfully, hurtfully, detrimentally, lethally
⊟ creatively

desultorily *adv*
casually, aimlessly, erratically, half-heartedly, loosely, fitfully
⊟ methodically

desultory *adj*
random, erratic, aimless, casual, disorderly, chaotic, haphazard, irregular, half-hearted, spasmodic, inconsistent, undirected, unco-ordinated, unsystematic, unmethodical, fitful, disconnected, rambling, loose
FORMAL capricious
⊟ systematic, methodical

detach *v*
1 *detach the reply slip*
separate, take/tear off, disconnect, unfasten, disjoin, cut off, disengage, remove, undo, uncouple, unhitch, sever, dissociate, isolate, loosen, free, unfix, unhitch, segregate, divide, disentangle
2 *detach yourself from something*
separate, sever, split, cut off, dissociate, isolate, loosen, free, segregate, divorce
FORMAL estrange
⊟ 1 attach **2** involve

detachable *adj*
remov(e)able, mov(e)able, separable, eradicable, transferable

detached *adj*
1 SEPARATE, disconnected, unfastened, dissociated, severed, free, loose, divided, discrete
2 ALOOF, remote, dispassionate, impersonal, neutral, impartial, independent, indifferent, unconcerned, disinterested, cold, clinical, unemotional, objective
⊟ 1 connected **2** involved

detachment *n*
1 ALOOFNESS, remoteness, coolness, reserve, unconcern, indifference, impassivity, disinterestedness, neutrality, dispassion, dispassionateness, lack of emotion, impartiality, objectivity, lack of bias, fairness
2 SEPARATION, disconnection, unfastening, uncoupling, disengagement, removal, withdrawal, undoing, severance, isolation, loosening, disentangling
FORMAL disunion
3 SQUAD, unit, force, corps, brigade, patrol, task force, detail
⊟ 1 concern, bias, prejudice

detail *n, v*
♦ *n*
1 *personal details*
particular, item, factor, element, aspect, characteristic, component, feature, point, fact, circumstance, respect, specific, specification, ingredient, attribute, respect, technicality, complication, intricacy
2 *attention to detail*
minutiae, triviality, nicety, thoroughness, elaboration, meticulousness, precision, complexity, refinement
COLLOQ. ins and outs, nitty-gritty, nuts and bolts
3 SQUAD, unit, force, corps, brigade, patrol, task force
♦ *v*
1 LIST, set out, enumerate, itemize, specify, catalogue, spell out, tabulate, describe, present, portray, depict, point out, recount, relate
FORMAL delineate, rehearse
2 ASSIGN, appoint, choose, allocate, charge, delegate, commission
▪ **in detail**
point by point, carefully, thoroughly, comprehensively, exhaustively, fully, item by item, at length, in depth

detailed *adj*
comprehensive, exhaustive, complete, full, itemized, thorough, minute, in-depth, exact, precise, specific, particular, itemized, intricate, elaborate, complex, complicated, meticulous, descriptive
FORMAL convoluted
COLLOQ. blow-by-blow
⊟ cursory, general

detain *v*
1 DELAY, hold (up), make late, hold back, keep (back), inhibit, hinder, impede, check, slow, stay, stop
FORMAL retard
2 CONFINE, arrest, intern, hold, restrain, keep, keep/hold in custody, take into custody, lock up, put in prison, imprison
FORMAL incarcerate
⊟ 2 release

detect *v*
1 NOTICE, ascertain, sense, note, observe, perceive, become aware of, make out, recognize, discern, distinguish, identify, sight, catch, spot, spy
2 UNCOVER, catch, discover, disclose, expose, find (out), turn up, track down, uncover, unearth, unmask, reveal, bring to light

detectable *adj*
noticeable, discoverable, perceivable, discernible, perceptible, perceivable, recognizable, identifiable, visible, apparent, clear, distinct, before your eyes

detection *n*
1 NOTICING, ascertaining, note, observation, perception,

recognition, discernment, distinguishing, identification, sighting
2 UNCOVERING, discovery, disclosure, exposé, exposure, tracking-down, smelling-out, sniffing-out, unearthing, unmasking, revelation

detective n
police officer, (private) investigator, thief-catcher, thief-taker, plain-clothes officer, sherlock, plant, Pinkerton, shadow; *N Am* operative
COLLOQ. 'tec, private eye, sleuth, sleuth-hound, bloodhound, gumshoe, shamus, dick, tail, busy, jack, prodnose

detention n
1 DETAINMENT, custody, confinement, imprisonment, captivity, restraint, constraint, internment, quarantine, punishment
FORMAL incarceration
2 DELAY, hindrance, holding-back, slowing-up
E∃ 1 release

deter v
discourage, disincline, put off, talk out of, inhibit, frighten, intimidate, scare off, daunt, check, caution, warn, restrain, hinder, prevent, prohibit, stop
FORMAL dissuade
COLLOQ. turn off
E∃ encourage

detergent n
cleaner, cleanser, soap, washing powder, washing-up liquid
TECHNICAL abstergent

deteriorate v
1 WORSEN, get/become/grow worse, decline, degenerate, depreciate, drop, fail, fall off, lapse, go from bad to worse, slide, relapse, slip, wane, ebb, tail off/away
FORMAL retrograde, retrogress
COLLOQ. go downhill, go down, go to pot, go down the tube, go/run to seed
2 DECAY, disintegrate, decompose, spoil, degrade, degenerate, go bad, break up, fall apart, fall to pieces, weaken, fade
OLD starve
E∃ 1 improve, get better

Synonym nuances
sense 1
Decline is suggestive of becoming less rather than simply getting worse: *his health rapidly declined.*
Degenerate suggests becoming something inferior, and has an element of judgement: *the loan scheme has degenerated into a farce.* The term **depreciate** can be used to convey a straightforward lessening in value: *your car has depreciated since you bought it.* **Drop** and **fall off** similarly suggest a decrease in level or value, but perhaps a sharper one: *audience figures fell off during the second series.*
  Fail has inherently negative connotations, and is appropriate to use where there are unhappy effects: *my eyesight is failing*, whilst **lapse**, **slide** and **slip** simply suggest a quiet or gradual descent into a worse state: *he lapsed into a coma.* **Relapse** would only be used of a return to a worse state. The terms **wane** and **ebb** can both be used of deteriorating very gradually, with the implication that it will happen until nothing remains: *her confidence ebbed away; prosperity waned.*

---

deterioration n
worsening, decline, degeneration, drop, failure, falling-off, downturn, lapse, slide, relapse, slipping, waning, ebb, decay, atrophy, corrosion, debasement, degradation, disintegration
FORMAL retrogression, exacerbation, pejoration
E∃ improvement

determinate adj
fixed, absolute, certain, clear-cut, distinct, explicit, express, conclusive, decided, decisive, defined, settled, specific, specified, definite, definitive, established, positive, precise, quantified
E∃ indeterminate

determination n
1 RESOLUTENESS, tenacity, firmness, willpower, perseverance, persistence, purpose, resolution, resolve, backbone, steadfastness, single-mindedness, will, insistence, conviction, dedication, push, drive, thrust, stamina, strength of character, firmness of purpose
FORMAL fortitude
COLLOQ. guts, grit
2 DECISION, judgement, sentence, settlement, conclusion, ruling, decree, verdict, opinion
TECHNICAL arbitrament, assay, value
FORMAL resolution
E∃ 1 irresolution, indetermination

Colloquial expressions showing determination include:

be hell-bent	go the whole hog	pull out all the
dig your heels in	hang on like grim	stops
do your utmost	death	put your heart
get stuck into	hold your ground	and soul into
give your all	leave no stone	stay the course
go all out	unturned	stick to your guns
go for it	mean business	stop at nothing
go to extremes	move heaven and	strain every nerve
go to great	earth	
lengths		

---

determine v
1 AFFECT, influence, govern, control, condition, dictate, direct, guide, prompt, impel, regulate, ordain
2 DISCOVER, establish, find out, learn, ascertain, identify, check, detect, verify
3 DECIDE, settle, set, make up your mind, choose, conclude, agree on, establish, fix (on), resolve, elect, finish
FORMAL purpose
COLLOQ. clinch

determined adj
resolute, firm, purposeful, strong-willed, single-minded, persevering, persistent, strong, strong-minded, steadfast, tenacious, dogged, insistent, intent, set, resolved, fixed, bent, dedicated, convinced, decided, unflinching, unwavering, uncompromising, stubborn
COLLOQ. hell-bent, dead set, out
E∃ irresolute, wavering

Synonym nuances
Resolute describes someone who has made up their mind and will not be swayed from it, and it is a term with favourable connotations of strength of mind or character.
Fixed, although similar, is associated more with the negative quality of narrow-mindedness than the positive one of conviction: *try not to have too many fixed ideas about the job.*
  Purposeful would suggest someone has a specific aim, whilst **strong-willed** and **single-minded** could be used of those who neither need nor want advice. These three terms can be used without implying any judgement. The term **persevering** may be used of someone who will endure in their pursuit, which may be perceived as admirable: *their persevering efforts to remove oppression*, whereas to describe someone as **persistent** suggests they may be more likely to annoy: *persistent telephone salespeople.* **Strong** and **strong-minded**, however, are again more approving in tone in that they return to the idea of strength of character, and the ability

to see things through; **steadfast** is similarly positive in its connotation of constancy. **Dedicated**, **unflinching** and **unwavering** further suggest positive elements of devotion and strength of purpose.

Uncompromising implies a reluctance to yield in any respect, and might be used with a hint of admiration of this determination: *he is a tough, uncompromising boxer*, while **stubborn**, although similar in meaning, strongly hints at obstinacy rather than conviction and is more disapproving in tone.

determinedly *adv*
resolutely, firmly, strongly, purposefully, single-mindedly, strong-mindedly, persistently, steadfastly, tenaciously, insistently, decidedly, stubbornly, uncompromisingly, unflinchingly
ⓔ irresolutely

deterrence *n*
prevention, hindrance, avoidance, heading-off, warding-off, elimination
FORMAL dissuasion, obviation
ⓔ encouragement

deterrent *n*
hindrance, impediment, obstacle, repellent, check, bar, barrier, block, discouragement, disincentive, obstruction, curb, restraint, difficulty
ⓔ incentive, encouragement

detest *v*
hate, loathe, abhor, dislike, recoil from, deplore, despise
FORMAL abominate, execrate
COLLOQ. can't stand
ⓔ adore, love

detestable *adj*
hateful, loathsome, abhorrent, repellent, obnoxious, despicable, abominable, odious, contemptible, revolting, repulsive, repugnant, offensive, vile, disgusting, distasteful, shocking, sordid
FORMAL execrable, accursed, reprehensible, heinous
ⓔ adorable, admirable

detestation *n*
hate, hatred, loathing, abhorrence, dislike, anathema, animosity, hostility, antipathy, aversion, repugnance, revulsion
FORMAL abomination, execration, odium
ⓔ adoration, approval, love

dethrone *v*
depose, oust, topple, unseat, unthrone, uncrown
ⓔ crown, enthrone

detonate *v*
blow up, discharge, blast, explode, ignite, kindle, set off, let off, go off, spark off, shoot, knock
FORMAL fulminate

detonation *n*
bang, blast, explosion, blow-up, blowing-up, boom, burst, discharge, igniting, ignition
FORMAL fulmination, report

detour *n*
deviation, diversion, indirect route, circuitous route, roundabout route, scenic route, digression, byroad, byway, bypath, bypass

detract *v*
diminish, subtract from, take away from, spoil, mar, reduce, lessen, lower, devaluate, depreciate, belittle
FORMAL disparage
ⓔ add to, enhance, praise

detractor *n*
backbiter, belittler, defamer, slanderer, critic, muck-raker, reviler, scandalmonger, enemy

FORMAL denigrator, disparager, traducer, vilifier
ⓔ flatterer, supporter, defender

detriment *n*
damage, harm, hurt, disadvantage, loss, ill, injury, impairment, disservice, wrong, evil, mischief, prejudice
ⓔ advantage, benefit

detrimental *adj*
damaging, harmful, hurtful, adverse, disadvantageous, prejudicial, mischievous, pernicious, destructive
FORMAL deleterious, injurious, inimical
ⓔ advantageous, favourable, beneficial

detritus *n*
remains, rubbish, debris, rubble, fragments, garbage, junk, litter, scum, waste, wreckage

devalue *v*
1 *devalue someone's work*
make light of, demean, play down, run down, slate, minimize, dismiss, underrate, undervalue
FORMAL disparage
COLLOQ. knock, slam, pull/tear to pieces
SLANG slag (off)
2 *devalue a currency*
deflate, devaluate, lower, reduce, decrease
FORMAL devalorize

devastate *v*
1 DESTROY, desolate, lay waste, demolish, spoil, despoil, wreck, ruin, ravage, waste, ransack, plunder, level, flatten, raze, pillage, sack
2 DISCONCERT, overwhelm, overcome, shock, take aback, confound, nonplus, discompose, traumatize
FORMAL perturb, discomfit
COLLOQ. shatter, floor

devastated *adj*
shocked, overwhelmed, crushed, heartbroken, overcome, taken aback, upset, distressed, desolate, appalled, traumatized, stunned, horrified, in anguish
COLLOQ. gutted, knocked for six

devastating *adj*
1 *devastating storms*
destructive, disastrous, ruinous, damaging, harmful, catastrophic
2 *a devastating blow to his pride*
effective, incisive, overwhelming, crushing, shocking, traumatizing, stunning
COLLOQ. shattering
3 *in devastating form*
stunning, brilliant, striking, impressive, spectacular, extraordinary, remarkable, wonderful, lovely, gorgeous, dazzling, magnificent, marvellous, great, staggering
COLLOQ. smashing, fabulous

devastation *n*
destruction, desolation, waste, havoc, ruin(s), damage, wreckage, ravages, demolition, annihilation, pillage, plunder, spoliation

develop *v*
1 ADVANCE, grow, evolve, expand, enlarge, progress, foster, nurture, flourish, mature, prosper, improve, branch out, spread
2 ELABORATE, amplify, argument, enhance, unfold, work out, expand on, enlarge
FORMAL dilate on
3 ACQUIRE, begin, start, generate, create, invent, produce, originate, establish, set about/off, set in motion, initiate, found, institute
FORMAL contract, commence
4 RESULT, come about, grow, ensue, arise, follow, happen
5 *develop an illness*

catch, get, go down with, pick up, become infected with, become/fall ill with
FORMAL contract, succumb to

development n

1 GROWTH, evolution, advance, blossoming, elaboration, furtherance, progress, progression, unfolding, expansion, enlargement, extension, spread, increase, improvement, maturing, maturity, flourishing, prosperity, promotion, refinement, issue
2 OCCURRENCE, happening, event, turn of events, incident, circumstance, change, outcome, situation, result, phenomenon
3 *a housing development*
complex, centre, block, estate, land, area

Synonym nuances
sense 1
Growth tends to suggest increasing in size, whereas **evolution** suggests changing to a more advanced state: *linguistic evolution.* **Advance** can be used of a positive move forward: *recent advances in technology*; **progress** and **progression** are both similar but suggest a continual move. **Blossoming** could be used of a coming to fruition, with a hint at its inevitability: *the blossoming of your career.*
Elaboration, on the other hand, has more to do with working out the details: *there is no elaboration of the reasoning behind the diagnosis*, whereas **furtherance** implies moving forward with some help: *his personal sacrifices for the furtherance of his son's career.*
Unfolding could be used a gradual disclosure of events: *the unfolding of the plot.* You could use **improvement** to emphasize that something has become better than it was, while **refinement** would be the word to use of development by attending to fine details.
Maturing and **maturity** imply that any benefits have come through age, and again would be used positively: *intellectual maturity.* Both **flourishing** and **prosperity** are very positive terms suggestive of success, usually financial in the latter instance, but **promotion** might simply be used in the context of something being made known or widespread.

deviance n

divergence, aberration, anomaly, abnormality, irregularity, variance, eccentricity, perversion
FORMAL disparity
E∃ normality

deviant adj, n

* *adj*

divergent, aberrant, anomalous, abnormal, irregular, variant, bizarre, eccentric, quirky, freakish, perverse, perverted, twisted, wayward, bent
FORMAL disparate
COLLOQ. kinky, oddball, with a screw loose, with bats in the belfry
E∃ normal

* *n*

freak, oddity, eccentric, nonconformist, misfit, dropout, odd sort, pervert
COLLOQ. oddball, kook, crank, weirdo
SLANG geek, goof
E∃ straight

deviate v

diverge, veer, turn (aside), digress, sheer, swerve, deflect, incline, change, vary, differ, depart, stray, oblique, yaw, wander, err, go astray, drift, part, decline
TECHNICAL sport
OLD prevaricate
FORMAL aberrate
COLLOQ. go off the rails

deviation n

divergence, aberration, departure, abnormality, irregularity, difference, variance, variation, digression, eccentricity, anomaly, deflection, turning-aside, alteration, discrepancy, detour, fluctuation, inconsistency, change, drift, quirk, shift, freak
OLD prevarication
FORMAL disparity
E∃ conformity, regularity

device n

1 TOOL, implement, appliance, gadget, waldo, contrivance, contraption, apparatus, utensil, instrument, machine, mechanism
COLLOQ. gizmo
2 SCHEME, ruse, strategy, stratagem, plan, plot, ploy, tactic, gambit, manoeuvre, wile, trick, artifice, stunt
FORMAL machination
COLLOQ. dodge; *Aust & NZ* slinter
3 EMBLEM, symbol, motif, logo, colophon, design, insignia, crest, badge, shield, seal, token, coat of arms

Synonym nuances
sense 1
Tool is widely used of something created to be of help in accomplishing a manual task, whereas **implement** is more vague, and often used when its actual identity is unknown: *an implement may have been used in the attack.* **Appliance** suggests domestic devices, often electrical: *kitchen appliances such as toasters*, whereas **gadget** generally implies something small but ingenious: *a gadget to remove bobbles from knitwear.*
Both **contrivance** and **contraption** are less approving, and suggestive of something rather complicated.
Apparatus is most appropriately used in technical applications, of a variety of things set up as required, or sometimes even one thing with a specific function: *the laboratory apparatus for this experiment*; *the stinging apparatus of the wasp.* **Utensil**, on the other hand, tends now to be associated with cooking.
The term **instrument** suggests something usually used for precise work: *dental instruments*, whilst **machine** might be used of something larger, which is capable of completing a task: *a sewing machine.* A **mechanism**, on the other hand, is usually a component necessary for such a thing to work, and would generally describe part of a larger device.

devil n

1 SATAN, arch-fiend, Lucifer, Evil One, the wicked one, Prince of Darkness, Adversary, Beelzebub, Mephistopheles, Apollyon, Belial, the Tempter, arch-traitor, bogy, man of sin, ragman, deuce, dickens, sorrow; *Scot* the deil, Hornie, Clootie, Cloots, Mahoun, worricow
OLD (*Shakesp*) goodyear, yoke-devil; Ragamuffin
COLLOQ. Old Nick, Old Harry, Old One, Old Poker, Old Scratch, Davy Jones, mischief, goodman
Related adjective: diabolic
2 DEMON, fiend, evil spirit, imp, incubus, succubus, daemon, cacodemon; *Scot* fient
OLD Ragamuffin
3 BRUTE, rogue, monster, ogre, savage, beast, demon, terror, imp, rascal, wretch

devilish adj, adv

* *adj*

1 DIABOLICAL, diabolic, fiendish, satanic, demonic, hellish, damnable, evil, infernal, wicked, cruel, vile, atrocious, dreadful, outrageous, shocking, disastrous, excruciating, accursed
FORMAL execrable, nefarious
2 *a devilish problem*
tricky, difficult, awkward, problematic, complicated,

knotty, thorny, sensitive, delicate, ticklish
• *adv*
extremely, exceedingly, excessively, very, really,
exceptionally, extraordinarily, intensely, thoroughly,
remarkably, greatly, highly, unusually, unreasonably,
immoderately, uncommonly, severely
OLD jolly
COLLOQ. awfully, terribly, dreadfully, frightfully

devil-may-care *adj*
careless, reckless, rash, casual, cavalier, easy-going,
flippant, frivolous, happy-go-lucky, heedless, nonchalant,
unconcerned, unworried, swaggering, swashbuckling
FORMAL insouciant

devilry *n*
wickedness, evil, depravity, vileness, atrocity,
abomination, corruption, corruptness, foulness,
fiendishness, immorality, shamefulness, sin, sinfulness,
impiety, unrighteousness, enormity, amorality
FORMAL dissoluteness, heinousness, iniquity, reprobacy
F∃ uprightness

devious *adj*
1 UNDERHAND, deceitful, dishonest, double-dealing,
unscrupulous, scheming, insidious, insincere, designing,
calculating, crafty, cunning, evasive, wily, sly, artful,
surreptitious, treacherous, misleading
FORMAL disingenuous
COLLOQ. tricky, slippery, crooked
2 INDIRECT, circuitous, rambling, roundabout, wandering,
winding, deviating, tortuous, erratic
F∃ **1** straightforward **2** direct

devise *v*
invent, contrive, plan, plot, design, conceive, come up
with, work out, think up, dream up, put together, arrange,
formulate, imagine, scheme, construct, originate, create,
concoct, forge, fabricate, hatch, frame, project, shape,
form, compose
COLLOQ. cook up

> **Synonym nuances**
> **Contrive**, though similar, suggests a degree of complexity
> or difficulty rather than creativity: *they contrived an
> ingenious scheme of tunnels.* **Plot** and **scheme** can have
> rather sinister, clandestine undertones: *they plotted his
> downfall*; *he schemed to retain power,* whilst **hatch** also
> generally implies malign intentions: *they hatched a plot to
> subvert the constitution.*
> While **plan**, **design** and **work out** convey the idea of
> lengthy or careful deliberation, **conceive** and **come up
> with** suggest a more spontaneous idea: *they came up with
> an ideal slogan.* **Think up**, **dream up** and **imagine** are
> similar, but suggest that the idea may not be particularly
> practical: *he dreamed up some harebrained plan.* **Put
> together**, **construct** and **compose** are appropriate to
> describe drawing together separate components: *we've
> put together a basic guide*; **formulate**, **shape** and **form**
> emphasizes giving a clear form to: *he formulated their
> education policy*; and **frame** similarly suggests deciding
> what form something should take: *his question was
> framed to elicit a yes or no reply.*
> **Originate** and **create** have an implication of innovation;
> **concoct** and **fabricate**, on the other hand, suggest an
> element of effort or even untruth: *some concocted yarn*;
> *officers fabricated evidence.* **Forge** implies a successful
> beginning, or an element of constancy or unity: *a tradition
> forged over two hundred years ago.*

devoid *adj*
lacking, wanting, without, free, bereft, destitute, deprived,
bare, barren, empty, vacant, void
FORMAL deficient
F∃ endowed

devolution *n*
decentralization, delegation of power, distribution,
transference of power, dispersal
F∃ centralization

devolve *v*
hand down, pass down, delegate, transfer, consign,
convey, deliver, depute, entrust, commission, fall to, rest
with

devote *v*
dedicate, consecrate, commit, give yourself, set apart, set
aside, reserve, consign, apply, allocate, allot, sacrifice,
enshrine, assign, appropriate, surrender, offer, give, put in,
pledge

> **Synonym nuances**
> **Commit** suggests a deep involvement: *a government
> committed to free enterprise*, while **dedicate** can be
> used with the positive implication of being really giving
> of time and effort: *dedicated musicians.* To use the terms
> **give yourself** and **surrender** make a clear statement of
> complete devotion: *he gave himself to God*; **sacrifice** is
> appropriate to refer to devotion at a personal cost.
> The terms **set aside** and **reserve** straightforwardly refer
> to retaining for a specific purpose: *time set aside for
> training*, as do **allocate**, **allot**, and **assign**. **Put in** is
> similar, but more generally implies effort: *he put in a
> strenuous two hours at the gym.*
> **Pledge** would be best used of giving a solemn promise:
> *candidates pledged to unilateral disarmament*, whilst
> **consecrate** most strongly suggests devoting to some
> religious purpose: *the day, consecrated by the Romans to
> the sun.*
> You may use **consign** to suggest entrusting to an
> appropriate place, though this usually implies a
> reduction in status: *consigning to a museum*; *consigned
> to obscurity.*

devoted *adj*
dedicated, ardent, committed, loyal, faithful, devout,
loving, staunch, steadfast, true, constant, fond,
unswerving, tireless, concerned, attentive, caring
F∃ indifferent, disloyal

> **Synonym nuances**
> **Dedicated** suggests being completely given over to a
> cause, whilst **ardent** is more suggestive of strong
> passion: *an ardent fan of opera.* **Committed** also
> suggests deep involvement, whilst **loyal**, **faithful** and
> **steadfast**, along with **unswerving** and **tireless**, are
> positive terms describing continuing support and
> implying approval of this constancy: *faithful customers*;
> *his steadfast character.* **Staunch** is similar in meaning, but
> is less approbatory (although not necessarily negative) in
> tone. **True** and **constant** also suggest unwavering and
> genuine support: *he was a true democrat.*
> **Devout** generally suggests strict religious observance,
> but can be more widely applied to convey depth of
> feeling: *a devout capitalist.* **Loving**, however, would be
> appropriate to describe being enamoured, while the
> term **fond** is less strong, and simply suggestive of a
> partiality. You may use **concerned** to emphasize the
> element of care or worry: *we crept about like concerned
> parents around a sleeping child*, whilst **attentive** and
> **caring** will similarly emphasize involvement with
> another's needs: *attentive service.*

devotedly *adv*
committedly, dedicatedly, ardently, loyally, faithfully,
devoutly, staunchly, steadfastly, unswervingly, tirelessly,
attentively, caringly, fondly, lovingly
F∃ indifferently

devotee n
enthusiast, fan, fanatic, addict, follower, supporter, zealot, adherent, admirer, disciple, hound; *Irish* voteen
FORMAL aficionado
COLLOQ. buff, freak, merchant, fiend

devotion n
1 DEDICATION, commitment, consecration, ardour, loyalty, faithfulness, allegiance, adherence, trueness, staunchness, constancy, solidarity, zeal, support, love, passion, fervour, fondness, attachment, admiration, warmness, closeness, adoration, affection, faithfulness, reverence, steadfastness, regard, earnestness
FORMAL fidelity
2 DEVOUTNESS, piety, godliness, faith, holiness, spirituality, sanctity, religiousness
3 PRAYER, worship, observance
F3 **1** inconstancy **2** irreverence

devotional adj
devout, holy, pietistic, religious, reverential, sacred, solemn, spiritual, dutiful, pious

devour v
1 EAT, eat up, consume, finish off, guzzle, gulp, gorge, gobble, bolt, swallow, stuff, cram, gormandize, feast on, relish, revel in; *Scot* worry
OLD (*Spenser*) engorge; raven
COLLOQ. wolf down, polish off, tuck into, scoff, put away, knock back, snarf; *N Am* scarf
2 DESTROY, devastate, lay waste, consume, absorb, engulf, envelop, ravage, dispatch, deprecate
3 *devour a book*
be engrossed in, take in, drink in, appreciate, enjoy, relish, feast on

devout adj
1 PIOUS, godly, religious, reverent, prayerful, saintly, holy, orthodox, church-going, committed, practising
2 SINCERE, earnest, devoted, fervent, genuine, staunch, steadfast, ardent, passionate, serious, wholehearted, dedicated, committed, constant, faithful, intense, vehement, heartfelt, zealous, unswerving, deep, profound
F3 **1** irreligious **2** insincere

devoutly adv
1 *devoutly religious*
piously, religiously, reverently, prayerfully
2 SINCERELY, deeply, earnestly, fervently, staunchly, steadfastly, ardently, passionately, wholeheartedly, faithfully, zealously

dewy adj
1 *dewy grass*
bedewed, roral, rorid, roric
OLD roscid
2 BLOOMING, innocent, starry-eyed, youthful

dexterity n
deftness, adeptness, address, adroitness, agility, handiness, nimbleness, proficiency, mastery, readiness, skilfulness, ability, skill, expertise, aptitude, art, artistry, expertness, facility, knack, finesse, legerdemain, sleight, ingenuity, effortlessness
F3 clumsiness, awkwardness, ineptitude

dexterous adj
deft, adept, adroit, agile, able, nimble, proficient, skilful, clever, expert, accomplished, nippy, handy, facile, nimble-fingered, neat-handed
COLLOQ. nifty
F3 clumsy, inept, awkward

diabolical adj
devilish, fiendish, demonic, hellish, damnable, evil, infernal, satanic, wicked, vile, sinful, dreadful, outrageous, shocking, appalling, disastrous, monstrous, excruciating, atrocious, nasty
FORMAL execrable

diadem n
circlet, coronet, crown, tiara, headband, mitre, round

diagnose v
identify, determine, recognize, pinpoint, distinguish, analyse, explain, isolate, detect, interpret, investigate

diagnosis n
identification, verdict, explanation, conclusion, answer, interpretation, judgement, analysis, opinion, investigation, recognition, detection, examination, scrutiny

diagnostic adj
analytical, indicative, interpretative, interpretive, recognizable, symptomatic, demonstrative, distinguishing

diagonal adj
oblique, slanting, cross, crossing, crosswise, sloping, crooked, angled, cornerways, catercorner

diagonally adv
obliquely, crossways, crosswise, at an angle, cornerwise, on the cross, on the slant, slantwise, aslant, on the bias

diagram n
plan, sketch; *N Am* plat; chart, bar chart, pie chart, flow chart, run chart, drawing, figure, representation, schema, illustration, outline, draft, graph, picture, exploded view, cutaway, layout, table, floor plan, indicator, key, scheme, tree, family tree
FORMAL delineation

diagrammatic adj
diagrammatical, schematic, graphic, illustrative, representational, tabular
F3 imaginative, impressionistic

dial n, v
◆ n
circle, disc, face, clock, control
◆ v
phone, telephone, ring, call (up)
COLLOQ. give a buzz/a bell

dialect n
idiom, language, regionalism, localism, patois, provincialism, vernacular, variety, argot, jargon, accent, speech, diction
COLLOQ. lingo

dialectic adj, n
◆ adj
dialectical, logical, rational, argumentative, analytical, rationalistic, logistic, polemical, inductive, deductive
FORMAL disputatious
◆ n
dialectics, logic, reasoning, rationale, analysis, debate, argumentation, contention, discussion, polemics, deduction
FORMAL disputation, induction, ratiocination

dialogue n
1 CONVERSATION, communication, talk, chat, tête-à-tête, gossip, exchange, discussion, discourse, conference
FORMAL interchange, converse, debate, colloquy, interlocution
2 LINES, script

diametrically adv
directly, completely, absolutely, utterly
FORMAL antithetically

diaphanous adj
cobwebby, delicate, filmy, fine, gauzy, gossamer, gossamery, chiffony, light, see-through, sheer, thin, translucent, transparent, veily
FORMAL pellucid
F3 heavy, opaque, thick

diarrhoea n
looseness of the bowels, gippy tummy, holiday tummy, dysentery

COLLOQ. the runs, the trots, Spanish tummy, Delhi belly, Montezuma's revenge
SLANG (*vulgar*) the shits
⊟ constipation

diary *n*
journal, day-book, logbook, chronicle, memoir, year-book, appointment book, engagement book, Filofax®

diatribe *n*
tirade, abuse, harangue, attack, onslaught, denunciation, criticism, insult, reviling, upbraiding, reproof, reprimand, rebuke
FORMAL invective, vituperation, philippic
COLLOQ. knocking, slating, slamming, running-down
⊟ praise, eulogy

dicey *adj*
risky, chancy, unpredictable, uncertain, tricky, problematic, dangerous, difficult, dubious
COLLOQ. iffy, hairy, dodgy
⊟ certain

dichotomy *n*
difference, dissimilarity, discrepancy, divergence, variation, variance, conflict, division, opposition, deviation, differentiation
FORMAL disparity

dicky *adj*
unsound, unsteady, weak, ailing, frail, infirm, shaky
⊟ healthy, robust

dictate *v, n*
♦ *v*
1 SAY, read, read aloud, read out, speak, utter, announce, pronounce, transmit
OLD dite, indite
2 COMMAND, lay down, set down, impose, demand, insist, order, give orders to, direct, decree, instruct, rule
OLD dite, indite
FORMAL prescribe, promulgate
♦ *n*
command, decree, precept, principle, rule, direction, charge, injunction, edict, order, ruling, statute, requirement, law, bidding, mandate, ultimatum, word
FORMAL ordinance, behest, promulgation

dictator *n*
despot, absolute ruler, autocrat, tyrant, oppressor, Caesar, Führer, Hitler
FORMAL autarchist
COLLOQ. supremo, Big Brother, little Hitler

dictatorial *adj*
tyrannical, despotic, totalitarian, all powerful, authoritarian, autocratic, oppressive, imperious, domineering, absolute, unlimited, unrestricted, repressive, overbearing, arbitrary, dogmatic
FORMAL omnipotent, peremptory, autarchic
COLLOQ. bossy
⊟ democratic, egalitarian, liberal

dictatorship *n*
tyranny, despotism, totalitarianism, authoritarianism, autocracy, absolute rule, fascism, police state, reign of terror, Hitlerism
⊟ democracy, egalitarianism

diction *n*
speech, articulation, language, elocution, intonation, pronunciation, inflection, fluency, delivery, expression, phrasing
FORMAL enunciation, locution

dictionary *n*
lexicon, glossary, thesaurus, vocabulary, wordbook, encyclopedia, concordance

dictum *n*
1 RULING, pronouncement, direction, proclamation, decree, dictate, edict, precept, command, order
FORMAL fiat
2 SAYING, maxim, axiom, utterance, proverb, aphorism

didactic *adj*
instructive, educational, informative, prescriptive, pedantic, moralizing, moral
FORMAL educative, pedagogic

die *v*
1 *he died in terrible pain*
pass away, pass on, pass, depart, depart this life, breathe your last, draw your last breath, lose your life, perish, fail, go, drown, starve, go west, succumb, close your eyes, go over to the majority
OLD exit, famish, be gathered to your fathers, give up the ghost, go the way of all flesh, go the way of the earth, pip out, sterve, swelt; (*Shakesp*) go off; (*Spenser*) quell
FORMAL expire, decease
COLLOQ. peg out, bite the dust, pop off, give up the ghost, have had it, meet your maker, push up daisies, shuffle off this mortal coil; *Aust* go bung; slip the cable, turn up your toes
SLANG snuff it, cash in your chips, cash/pass in your checks, kick the bucket, kick off, kiss off, spark out, choke, croak, flatline, hop the twig, pop your clogs; *N Am* go belly up; *Aust* cark
2 DWINDLE, fade, pass, ebb, sink, wane, peter out, wilt, wither, decline, decay, decrease, finish, lapse, end, come to an end, disappear, vanish, subside, dissolve, melt away
3 *the machine died*
stop, break down, fail, lose power, cut out
SLANG conk out
4 LONG FOR, pine for, yearn, desire, be desperate
COLLOQ. be crazy, be mad, be nuts, be wild, be raring
▪ **die away**
fade, fall, become weak, become faint, disappear
OLD evanish
▪ **die down**
decrease, subside, decline, quieten, drop, quench, slake, stop, blow over
FORMAL abate
▪ **die out**
become rarer/less common, disappear, vanish, extinguish, peter out
⊟ **1** live

diehard *n, adj*
♦ *n*
reactionary, hardline, ultra-conservative, rightist, fanatic, zealot
COLLOQ. blimp, old fogey, stick-in-the-mud
♦ *adj*
hardline, reactionary, ultra-conservative, rightist, fanatical, traditionalist, conservative, dyed-in-the-wool
FORMAL intransigent
COLLOQ. stick-in-the-mud
⊟ progressive

diet *n, v*
♦ *n*
1 FOOD, nutrition, rations, foodstuffs, fare, subsistence
OLD provisions
FORMAL sustenance, victuals, comestibles, viands
2 FAST, abstinence, regimen, regime
♦ *v*
lose weight, slim, fast, reduce, cut down, abstain
COLLOQ. weight-watch

differ *v*
1 VARY, diverge, deviate (from), depart from, be a departure from, contradict, contrast, be unlike, be dissimilar
2 DISAGREE, argue, conflict, oppose, dispute, be at odds with, be at variance, clash, quarrel, fall out, debate,

contend, not see eye to eye, take issue
FORMAL dissent, altercate
▣ 1 conform 2 agree

difference *n*
1 DISSIMILARITY, unlikeness, discrepancy, divergence, diversity, variation, variance, variety, distinctness, distinction, deviation, differentiation, contrast, singularity, exception
FORMAL dissimilitude, antithesis, incongruity, dichotomy, disparity
2 DISAGREEMENT, clash, dispute, conflict, argument, misunderstanding, quarrel, row, set-to, contention
FORMAL controversy, disputation, altercation
COLLOQ. set-to, spat, tiff
3 REMAINDER, rest, balance, residue
▣ 1 conformity 2 agreement

Synonym nuances
sense 1
Dissimilarity and the less commonly used **unlikeness** may be used generally of a difference between things; to suggest more strongly the idea of things being opposites you can use **contrast**. **Discrepancy**, however, usually suggests that one of two things amounts to less, and can be negative in that it hints at potential problems: *the discrepancy between the actual and the expected rates of inflation*. The term **divergence**, though, has to do with separation out from a single standard: *the divergence of opinion*, while **deviation** has more to do with turning away from an accepted form: *this deviation from the general trend*.
The terms **diversity** and **variety** would refer to the existence of many types, which, especially in the case of **variety**, could be viewed as a positive thing: *cultural diversity*; *a variety of entertainments*. **Variation** straightforwardly suggests a slightly different form of something: *there is appetising variation in the diet*, whereas **variance** can often be suggestive of a negative element of dispute: *ideas at variance with prevailing medical views*.
Singularity is more positively suggestive of uniqueness: *the singularity of a work of art*, like the rarely used **distinctness**, which is unlike, surprisingly, **distinction**, which is more likely to refer simply to the main area where two things differ: *the distinction between punishment and rehabilitation*.

different *adj*
1 DISSIMILAR, unlike, contrasting, divergent, inconsistent, deviating, at odds, at variance, clashing, opposed
COLLOQ. a far cry, poles/worlds apart, different as chalk and cheese
2 VARIED, various, varying, separate, diverse, miscellaneous, assorted, many, numerous, several, sundry, other, another
FORMAL disparate, discrete
COLLOQ. mixed bag
3 UNUSUAL, unconventional, unique, distinct, distinctive, extraordinary, individual, original, special, strange, remarkable, odd, peculiar, rare, bizarre, anomalous, out of the ordinary
4 INCONVENIENT, awkward, unsuitable, unfavourable, unmanageable, ill-timed, untimely, inopportune
▣ 1 similar, identical 2 same 3 conventional, ordinary 4 convenient

differential *n, adj*
◆ *n*
difference, variance, divergence, discrepancy, contrast, gap
FORMAL disparity
◆ *adj*

different, distinctive, separate, divergent, contrasting
FORMAL disparate

differentiate *v*
distinguish, tell apart, discriminate, contrast, separate, mark off, individualize, particularize

differentiation *n*
distinction, distinguishing, discrimination, contrast, separation, demarcation, individualization, particularization, modification
▣ assimilation, association, confusion, connection

differently *adv*
diversely, dissimilarly, contrastingly, inconsistently, incompatibly, at odds, at variance
COLLOQ. a far cry, poles/worlds apart, different as chalk and cheese

difficult *adj*
1 HARD, laborious, demanding, arduous, strenuous, tough, gruelling, tiring, wearisome, exhausting, back-breaking, uphill, formidable, exacting, burdensome, onerous
2 COMPLEX, complicated, intricate, hard, involved, obscure, dark, knotty, thorny, problematical, puzzling, perplexing, abstract, baffling, tricky
FORMAL abstruse, intractable, recondite, arcane, esoteric
3 UNMANAGEABLE, awkward, perverse, troublesome, trying, demanding, hard to please, unco-operative, tiresome, stubborn, obstinate
FORMAL intractable, recalcitrant, refractory
▣ 1 easy 2 straightforward, simple, intelligible 3 manageable, helpful

Synonym nuances
sense 1
The simple synonym **hard** is widely used of something that will take much effort or thought, whilst **laborious** is more suggestive of something being much work, with a further implication that it will take up a lot of time and is possibly unnecessary: *the laborious old-style methods of wheat-grinding*. **Demanding** and **exacting**, however, could be used of an activity that requires much attention or precision, and often a particular skill: *intellectually demanding projects*; *an exacting regimen of exercises*.
The terms **arduous** and **tough** can be used of any activity that can be a problem to accomplish: *a tough assignment*, whereas **strenuous** and the stronger **back-breaking** suggest physical exertion. **Gruelling**, **tiring**, **wearisome** and **exhausting** all have strong associations with using up energy reserves and consequent fatigue: *a gruelling four-month tour*. **Uphill** and **formidable** are fairly gentle terms to use of something that will actually require strength and commitment, but they do also have the implication of something rather daunting: *an uphill struggle*; *a formidable rival*.
To suggest very oppressive difficulty you might use **burdensome** or **onerous**, which have the added implication of being almost too much to bear: *for many elderly people the effort of daily living becomes burdensome*.

difficulty *n*
1 HARDSHIP, trouble, labour, strain, arduousness, strenuousness, painfulness, trial, struggle, struggling, awkwardness
FORMAL tribulation, exigency
2 PROBLEM, predicament, complication, snag, dilemma, quandary, perplexity, embarrassment, plight, distress, hang-up, obstacle, hindrance, hurdle, impediment, objection, opposition, block, barrier, obstruction, pitfall, stumbling-block, cleft stick
COLLOQ. fix, mess, jam, spot, hiccup, hole, stew, dire straits, pickle, tall order, hot/deep water, fly in the ointment, Catch-22, how-d'you-do, devil, tight spot, pretty pass

SLANG bitch, bugger, pain in the arse
FE 1 ease
■ **in difficulties**
having problems, in trouble
COLLOQ. up against it, stumped, at the end of your tether, out of your depth, not knowing which way to turn, in the soup, in a fix/mess/jam/hole, in dire straits, in a scrape, in hot/deep water, in a stew, in a tight spot
SLANG up shit creek (without a paddle)

diffidence *n*
unassertiveness, modesty, shyness, self-consciousness, self-effacement, timidity, insecurity, reserve, bashfulness, humility, inhibition, meekness, self-distrust, self-doubt, hesitancy, reluctance, backwardness
FE confidence

diffident *adj*
unassertive, modest, shy, timid, self-conscious, self-effacing, insecure, nervous, bashful, abashed, meek, reserved, withdrawn, tentative, shrinking, inhibited, hesitant, reluctant, unsure, shamefaced, sheepish
FE assertive, confident

diffuse *v, adj*
• *v*
spread, scatter, disperse, distribute, propagate, send out, dispense, permeate, circulate
FORMAL disseminate, dissipate, promulgate
FE concentrate
• *adj*
1 *diffuse outbreaks of rain*
scattered, unconcentrated, diffused, dispersed, disconnected
2 *a diffuse prose style*
verbose, imprecise, wordy, rambling, long-winded, profuse, vague, discursive
FORMAL prolix, loquacious, periphrastic, circumlocutory
COLLOQ. waffling
FE **1** concentrated **2** succinct

diffusion *n*
spreading, scattering, dispersal, distribution, propagation, permeation, circulation
FORMAL dissemination, dissipation, promulgation

dig *v, n*
• *v*
1 EXCAVATE, penetrate, burrow, make a hole, mine, quarry, scoop, scratch, spade, fork, hollow, channel, tunnel, till, turn over, work, break up, spit, spud, cultivate, harrow, plough, gouge, delve, pierce, grub (up/out), ditch, trench, entrench, disinter, unearth, undermine; *dialect* graft; *Scot* cast, howk; *Aust* fossick
OLD grave
2 POKE, prod, jab, punch
3 INVESTIGATE, probe, go into, research, search, delve
4 UNDERSTAND, grasp, take in, follow, figure out, realize, appreciate
COLLOQ. get, click, twig, get the hang of
• *n*
1 *a dig in the ribs*
poke, prod, jab, punch
2 GIBE, jeer, sneer, taunt, crack, insinuation, insult, wisecrack, compliment
OLD gird
■ **dig up**
discover, unearth, uncover, root out, bring to light, disinter, expose, extricate, find, retrieve, track down
FORMAL exhume
FE bury, obscure

digest *v, n*
• *v*
1 ABSORB, assimilate, incorporate, process, dissolve, break down

FORMAL macerate
2 TAKE IN, absorb, understand, comprehend, assimilate, grasp, study, consider, contemplate, meditate, mull over, ponder
3 SHORTEN, summarize, condense, compress, reduce, abridge
FORMAL comprehend
• *n*
summary, abridgement, abstract, précis, synopsis, résumé, reduction, abbreviation, compression, compendium

digestion *n*
absorption, assimilation, breaking-down, transformation
FORMAL ingestion, eupepsia, maceration

digit *n*
1 FINGER, thumb
2 NUMBER, numeral, figure, integer

dignified *adj*
stately, solemn, imposing, grand, majestic, noble, august, lordly, courtly, ceremonious, lofty, exalted, formal, distinguished, grave, impressive, reserved, honourable
FORMAL decorous
FE undignified, lowly

dignify *v*
honour, distinguish, grace, exalt, enhance, adorn, glorify, advance, elevate, ennoble, promote, raise
FORMAL aggrandize, apotheosize
FE degrade, demean

dignitary *n*
worthy, notable, high-up, personage, grandee, somebody, name
FORMAL luminary
COLLOQ. VIP, bigwig, big name, big gun, big shot, top brass

dignity *n*
stateliness, solemnity, nobleness, courtliness, self-possession, grandeur, loftiness, majesty, honour, eminence, importance, excellence, honourability, nobility, self-respect, self-esteem, self-importance, standing, poise, respectability, greatness, elevation, status, pride
FORMAL propriety, decorum

Synonym nuances
Many of these synonyms are approbatory in tone. **Stateliness** may be used to suggest an elegance of carriage and conduct, while **solemnity** is more suggestive of an observance of ritual, often with a degree of pomposity: *he was laid to rest with great solemnity in Poets' Corner*. Both **nobleness** and **courtliness** have echoes of aristocracy, and consequently imply refinement. **Grandeur** and **majesty** are highly connotative terms, suggesting an elegant and imposing air: *the house has all the grandeur of a small manor*. **Loftiness** has the implication of haughtiness, whilst **self-possession** and **poise** can be used fairly neutrally of dignity through personal composure.
   The terms **respectability**, the stronger **honour** and **honourability**, and the more common **nobility** have more to do with a moral code and suggest a fineness of character. Both **self-respect** and **self-esteem** have the positive implication of valuing yourself, whilst **self-importance** makes the negative suggestion of over-valuing yourself unduly.
   The words **standing** and **status** can be used of dignity acquired from a perceived place within a group: *he held the office with standing for many years*, whilst **greatness** and **elevation** are similar but less reserved. **Pride**, meanwhile, can be suggestive either of a desirable sense of self-worth, or a rather less admirable conceit.

---

digress *v*
diverge, deviate, stray, wander, go off at a tangent, go off

the subject, drift, depart, ramble, turn aside, be sidetracked

digression n
divergence, deviation, straying, wandering, aside, departure, diversion, footnote, parenthesis
FORMAL apostrophe, divagation, *obiter dictum*, excursus

digs n
lodgings, accommodation, quarters, billet, boarding-house, rooms, place
COLLOQ. pad, a roof over your head

dilapidated adj
ramshackle, shabby, broken-down, neglected, tumbledown, uncared-for, rickety, shaky, decrepit, crumbling, run-down, worn-out, beat-up, ruined, in ruins, decayed, decaying, falling apart, in a state of disrepair

dilapidation n
decay, ruin, disrepair, collapse, demolition, destruction, deterioration, disintegration, waste

dilate v
enlarge, expand, spread (out), broaden, widen, increase, extend, stretch, swell, bloat, inflate
FORMAL distend
FⳐ contract, constrict, shorten

dilatory adj
delaying, slow, sluggish, lingering, dawdling, lazy, lackadaisical, slack, snail-like, time-wasting, postponing, stalling
FORMAL procrastinating, tardy, tarrying
FⳐ prompt

dilemma n
quandary, conflict, predicament, problem, vicious circle, difficulty, puzzle, embarrassment, mess, perplexity, plight, cleft stick, *crise de conscience*
TECHNICAL double bind
OLD why-not
COLLOQ. Catch-22, spot, fix, no-win situation, tight corner, the devil and the deep (blue) sea, a rock and a hard place

dilettante n
dabbler, amateur, non-professional, trifler, potterer
FORMAL aesthete, sciolist
FⳐ professional

diligence n
assiduity, assiduousness, industry, conscientiousness, attention, care, thoroughness, dedication, attentiveness, application, constancy, earnestness, intentness, laboriousness, perseverance
FORMAL pertinacity, sedulousness
FⳐ laziness

diligent adj
assiduous, industrious, hard-working, conscientious, painstaking, busy, attentive, tireless, careful, thorough, dedicated, meticulous, persevering, persistent, studious, earnest, constant
FORMAL sedulous
FⳐ negligent, lazy

dilly-dally v
dally, dawdle, delay, falter, hesitate, hover, linger, loiter, dither, potter, vacillate, waver, take your time, waste time
FORMAL procrastinate, tarry
COLLOQ. shilly-shally, faff about

dilute v
adulterate, water down, thin (out), make thinner, weaken, make weaker, diffuse, diminish, decrease, lessen, reduce, temper, moderate, tone down
FORMAL attenuate, mitigate
FⳐ concentrate

diluted adj
watered down, watery, weak, thinned (out)
FⳐ concentrated

dim adj, v
• adj
1 DARK, dull, dusky, cloudy, clouding, overcast, grey, shadowy, gloomy, leaden, sombre, dingy, unlit, lacklustre, feeble
OLD caliginous
FORMAL crepuscular, tenebrous
2 INDISTINCT, blurred, hazy, ill-defined, obscure, misty, unclear, foggy, fuzzy, vague, faint, weak, feeble, pale, confused, imperfect
FORMAL obfuscated
3 STUPID, simple, simple-minded, dense, dull, obtuse, slow, slow-witted, doltish
COLLOQ. thick, dumb, dopey, gormless, dim-witted
4 *dim prospects*
unpromising, unfavourable, gloomy, discouraging, adverse
FORMAL inauspicious
FⳐ 1 bright 2 distinct 3 bright, intelligent 4 hopeful, promising
• v
darken, dull, obscure, cloud, blur, make/become blurred, fade, make/become faint, pale, tarnish, shade, dusk, blear
OLD bedim, appal, becloud
FⳐ brighten, illuminate

dimension n
1 *the dimensions of the room*
extent, measurement, measure, size, length, width, breadth, height, depth, area, proportions, scope, magnitude, largeness, volume, capacity, mass
2 *the dimensions of a problem*
extent, size, scale, range, bulk, importance, magnitude, greatness
3 *add a new dimension to the matter*
aspect, facet, side, factor, element, feature

diminish v
1 DECREASE, lessen, become/grow less, reduce, lower, detract, drop, deactivate, contract, decline, dwindle, shrink, recede, wane, weaken, become/grow weaker, impair, pare (down), fade, peter out, sink, subside, deflate, ebb, slacken, taper off, wear down, whittle (down/away), die away, die out, cut, take the edge off, mince, minify
TECHNICAL damp, rebate
OLD bate, minish
FORMAL abate, retrench
COLLOQ.
2 BELITTLE, devalue, defame
FORMAL disparage, deprecate, denigrate, derogate, vilify
FⳐ 1 increase, grow 2 exaggerate

diminution n
reduction, lessening, contraction, decline, ebb, decrease, cut, cutback, curtailment, deduction, decay, subsidence, weakening, shortening, shrinkage
FORMAL abatement, retrenchment
FⳐ enlargement, increase, growth

diminutive adj
small-scale, tiny, little, undersized, small, miniature, minute, microscopic, infinitesimal, elfin, petite, midget, compact, Lilliputian, pocket(-sized), pygmy, dwarfish; *dialect & Scot* tottie; *Scot* wee
FORMAL homuncular
COLLOQ. mini, teeny, teeny-weeny, dinky, pint-size(d)
FⳐ big, large, oversized

dimly adv
1 DARKLY, dully, sombrely, gloomily, dingily, feebly

2 FAINTLY, weakly, unclearly, indistinctly, obscurely, hazily, mistily
E3 1 brightly **2** clearly, distinctly

dimness *n*
darkness, dullness, dusk, cloudiness, mist, greyness, twilight, half-light, dinginess
TECHNICAL caligo
OLD caliginosity
FORMAL crepuscule

dimple *n*
concavity, depression, dint, hollow, indentation
TECHNICAL fovea, umbilicus

dimwit *n*
idiot, fool, blockhead, nitwit, dunce, dullard, dunderhead, ignoramus, halfwit, clot
COLLOQ. bonehead, numskull, twit, dope, knuckle-head
SLANG plonker, dork, geek, dweeb, berk, git, prat, dickhead

din *n*
noise, loud noise, row, racket, clash, clatter, clamour, clangour, pandemonium, uproar, tumult, commotion, crash, hubbub, brouhaha, outcry, shout, shouting, yelling, babble
COLLOQ. hullabaloo
E3 quiet, calm

dine *v*
eat, have dinner, feast, sup, lunch, banquet, feed

dingy *adj*
dark, drab, grimy, murky, faded, dull, dim, shabby, soiled, discoloured, dirty, dreary, gloomy, dismal, cheerless, seedy, sombre, obscure, run-down, colourless, dusky, worn
E3 bright, clean

dinky *adj*
dainty, fine, small, little, petite, neat, trim, miniature
COLLOQ. natty, mini

dinner *n*
meal, main meal, evening meal, supper, tea, banquet, feast, spread
FORMAL repast, refection
COLLOQ. blow-out
Related adjective: prandial

dinosaur

Dinosaurs include:

Allosaurus	Corythosaurus	Pachycepha-
Ankylosaurus	Deinonychus	losaurus
Apatosaurus	Diplodocus	Parasaurolophus
Barosaurus	Hetero-	Plateosaurus
Brachiosaurus	dontosaurus	Saurischia
Brontosaurus	Iguanodon	Stegosaurus
Camptosaurus	Ophiacodon	Styracosaurus
Coelophysis	Ornithischia	Triceratops
Compsognathus	Ornithomimus	Tyrannosaurus

---

dint *n*
dent, indentation, impression, hollow, depression, blow, concavity, stroke
■ **by dint of**
by means of, by the agency of, through the medium of, with the assistance of
FORMAL by virtue of

dip *v, n*
♦ *v*
1 PLUNGE, immerse, submerge, duck, dunk, dap, dib, dive, nod, lower, bathe, soak, douse, souse, sink, baptize; *dialect* plot

TECHNICAL dibble
OLD dop, immerge, merge
2 DECREASE, go down, decline, drop, fall, descend, subside, slump, sink, lower
3 *the track dips*
slope, descend, go down, decline, drop, fall, sink, delve
♦ *n*
1 HOLLOW, basin, decline, hole, drop, concavity, incline, descent, indentation, dent, depression, fall, slope
2 DECREASE, slump, lowering, lessening, fall, decline, reduction
3 SWIM, bathe, immersion, plunge, soaking, ducking, swim, drenching, dive
FORMAL infusion
4 *an avocado dip*
sauce, cream, dressing, relish
■ **dip into**
1 *dip into a book*
look at, leaf through, look through, run through, flick through, thumb through, skim, browse
2 *dip into your savings*
spend, draw on, use

diplomacy *n*
1 TACT, tactfulness, finesse, sensitivity, delicacy, discretion, prudence, savoir-faire, cleverness, subtlety, skill, craft
FORMAL judiciousness
2 STATECRAFT, statesmanship, international relations, politics, negotiation(s), manoeuvring

diplomat *n*
go-between, mediator, negotiator, ambassador, envoy, emissary, legate, attaché, consul, plenipotentiary, *chargé d'affaires*, conciliator, peacemaker, arbitrator, moderator, politician, statesman

diplomatic *adj*
1 *diplomatic relations*
consular, ambassadorial
2 TACTFUL, prudent, discreet, subtle, sensitive, clever, skilful
FORMAL politic, judicious
E3 tactless

diplomatically *adv*
1 POLITICALLY, by negotiation, conciliatorily, with diplomacy
2 TACTFULLY, discreetly, sensitively, skilfully, prudently
FORMAL judiciously
E3 **2** tactlessly

dipsomaniac *n*
alcoholic, drunk, drunkard, inebriate, drinker, hard drinker, heavy drinker, wine-bibber, Bacchus, bloat, habitual; *N Am* souse
COLLOQ. tippler
SLANG boozer, wino, lush, alkie, dipso, soak, toper, tosspot, sot, sponge, piss artist, pisshead

dire *adj*
1 DISASTROUS, dreadful, terrible, frightful, awful, appalling, calamitous, catastrophic, horrible, atrocious, shocking, alarming, distressing
2 DESPERATE, urgent, grave, drastic, crucial, extreme, vital, pressing, ominous

direct *adj, v, adv*
♦ *adj*
1 STRAIGHT, undeviating, unswerving, through, uninterrupted, non-stop, unbroken
2 STRAIGHTFORWARD, outspoken, blunt, bluff, frank, straight, forthright, plainspoken, unequivocal, sincere, candid, honest, explicit, unambiguous
COLLOQ. up-front
3 IMMEDIATE, first-hand, face-to-face, personal
E3 **1** indirect, circuitous **2** equivocal **3** indirect
♦ *v*
1 CONTROL, be in control of, manage, run, administer, be in charge of, organize, lead, govern, regulate, superintend,

preside over, oversee, supervise, handle, mastermind
COLLOQ. call the shots, be the boss of
2 INSTRUCT, command, order, tell, give orders, issue instructions, charge
FORMAL adjure
3 GUIDE, lead, conduct, point, show, steer, show/point the way, escort, usher
4 AIM, point, focus, turn, intend, mean, level, target, market
• *adv*
directly, straight, right, uninterruptedly, non-stop

direction *n*
1 CONTROL, administration, management, government, running, handling, supervision, guidance, leadership, superintendency, overseeing, regulation
2 ROUTE, way, line, road, course, path, track, bearing, orientation
3 *change the direction of your career*
course, trend, tendency, inclination, drift, tenor, current aim, orientation
4 *give someone directions*
instructions, guidelines, orders, brief, briefing, information, guidance, recommendations, indication, plan, rules, regulations

directive *n*
command, instruction, order, direction, regulation, ruling, imperative, dictate, decree, charge, bidding, mandate, injunction, ordinance, edict, notice
FORMAL fiat

directly *adv*
1 IMMEDIATELY, instantly, at once, promptly, right away, speedily, forthwith, instantaneously, quickly, soon, presently, straightaway, without delay, as soon as possible, straight, right, exactly
COLLOQ. pronto
2 FRANKLY, bluntly, candidly, honestly, straightforwardly, unequivocally, sincerely, clearly, plainly, explicitly, unambiguously
3 SQUARELY, straight, unswervingly, right, dead, just, exactly, precisely
COLLOQ. bang, smack, plumb

directness *n*
1 IMMEDIACY, immediateness, uninterruptedness
2 CANDIDNESS, straightforwardness, outspokenness, bluntness, frankness, forthrightness, plainspokenness, honesty

director *n*
manager, managing director, board of directors, head, boss, chief, controller, executive, chief executive, principal, governor, leader, president, superintendent, organizer, supervisor, overseer, administrator, producer, chairman, chairwoman, chairperson, chair, conductor, régisseur
COLLOQ. top dog, top banana

directory *n*
catalogue, index, list, listing, inventory, guide

dirge *n*
elegy, lament, funeral song, requiem, dead-march, coronach, threnody, monody

dirt *n*
1 EARTH, soil, clay, dust, mud, loam
2 FILTH, grime, soot, pollution, muck, mire, bilge, excrement, stain, smudge, sludge, slime, tarnish; *dialect* clart; *Aust & NZ* scunge
COLLOQ. gunge, yuck, grot
SLANG crud, gunk, grunge, crap
3 INDECENCY, impurity, obscenity, pornography, lewdness, sordidness, salaciousness
COLLOQ. smut, sleaze

dirty *adj, v*
• *adj*
1 FILTHY, grimy, grubby, mucky, soiled, greasy, unclean, unwashed, unhygienic, foul, messy, muddy, dusty, sooty, polluted, slimy, squalid, insanitary, miry, scruffy, shabby, sullied, stained, defiled, tarnished, clouded, cloudy, black, dark, dull, grungy; *dialect* clart, grufted; *Aust & NZ* scungy
COLLOQ. grotty, yucky, flea-bitten, cruddy, manky, skanky; *Aust & NZ* chatty
2 UNPLEASANT, dishonest, unfair, immoral, deceitful, unscrupulous, bad, foul, nasty, contemptible, despicable, undesirable
SLANG cruddy, poxy
3 INDECENT, improper, obscene, coarse, filthy, smutty, sordid, salacious, suggestive, risqué, vulgar, pornographic, X-rated, contaminated, corrupt, lewd, bawdy, ribald
COLLOQ. blue, raunchy, sleazy
E3 1 clean **2** honest **3** decent
• *v*
pollute, soil, stain, foul, mess up, defile, contaminate, adulterate, smear, smirch, spoil, smudge, splash, sully, tarnish, mud, muddy, blacken, discolour, draggle, mess, muck up; *dialect* clart, soss
OLD assoil, bedaggle; (*Shakesp*) ray
FORMAL besmirch, begrime
E3 clean, cleanse

Synonym nuances
adjective sense 1
Whilst **grimy** and **soiled** appropriately describe something superficially unclean, **filthy** and **foul** are more emotive and would generally suggest being disgustingly dirty. **Grubby**, **shabby** and **mucky** possibly fall midway, but can imply disgust at a moral aspect: *his was a grubby little life.* **Messy** is more suggestive of untidiness. **Greasy**, **muddy**, **dusty** and **sooty** are all fairly literal and mild terms, although **greasy** has a tactile element to it; **slimy** again is tactile in its suggestion but has a far more repulsive element: *horrible, slimy worms.*
  Unhygienic and **insanitary** are used only in contexts of carrying germs or dirt posing a threat to health, like **polluted**, which could be used of poisonous dirt caused by a variety of things, often by-products of industry: *polluted by radiation; polluted rivers.* **Squalid** is more suggestive of neglect, and often poverty, but again has highly negative connotations of unhealthiness: *the squalid housing estates.*
  Scruffy returns to the idea of a more superficial untidiness, whereas **sullied** and **stained**, **defiled** and **tarnished** suggest deeper and irreversible marks, and often suggest being tainted in a moral sense.

---

disability *n*
handicap, disablement, disorder, inability, incapability, incapacity, infirmity, defect, unfitness, disqualification, illness, ailment, complaint, weakness
FORMAL impairment, affliction, malady

disable *v*
1 *disable a person*
cripple, lame, damage, handicap, hamstring, make unfit, disqualify, weaken, debilitate, immobilize, invalidate, paralyse, prostrate
FORMAL incapacitate, impair, enfeeble
2 *disable a machine*
immobilize, paralyse, stop, deactivate, defuse, put out of action
FORMAL render inoperative

disabled *adj*
handicapped, infirm, unfit, crippled, lame, immobilized, debilitated, maimed, weak, weakened, out of action, paralysed, bed-ridden, wrecked

FORMAL incapacitated, impaired, indisposed, enfeebled
≡ able, able-bodied

disabuse v
disillusion, disenchant, disappoint, enlighten

disadvantage n
1 DRAWBACK, snag, hindrance, liability, handicap,
impediment, limitation, inconvenience, disamenity, flaw,
defect, nuisance, weakness, weak point, trouble, penalty,
catch; N Am out
OLD disinterest
FORMAL disbenefit, disutility
COLLOQ. downside, minus, hang-up, spanner in the works,
fly in the ointment, weak link in the chain, chink in your
armour, Achilles heel, own goal
2 HARM, damage, detriment, hurt, injury, loss, prejudice,
hardship, lack, disservice
FORMAL privation
≡ 1 advantage, benefit, asset

disadvantaged adj
deprived, underprivileged, poor, poverty-stricken,
handicapped, impoverished, struggling, in need, in
distress, in want
≡ privileged

disadvantageous adj
unfavourable, harmful, detrimental, inopportune,
prejudicial, adverse, unfortunate, unlucky, damaging,
hurtful, injurious, inconvenient, ill-timed, inexpedient
FORMAL hapless, deleterious
≡ advantageous, favourable; formal auspicious

disaffected adj
disloyal, hostile, alienated, antagonistic, rebellious,
mutinous, dissatisfied, disgruntled, discontented,
unfriendly, seditious
FORMAL estranged
≡ loyal, friendly, satisfied

disaffection n
disloyalty, hostility, alienation, discontentment,
resentment, ill-will, dissatisfaction, disgruntlement,
animosity, coolness, unfriendliness, antagonism,
disharmony, discord, disagreement, aversion, dislike
FORMAL estrangement
≡ loyalty, contentment

disagree v
1 *disagree with someone; the two sides disagree*
conflict, clash, contradict, diverge, differ, beg to differ,
agree to differ, vary, not see eye to eye with, be at odds
with, be at loggerheads with, quarrel, argue, bicker,
wrangle, fight, squabble, contend, dispute, contest, take
issue
FORMAL dissent, discord
COLLOQ. fall out
2 *disagree with an idea*
disapprove of, think wrong, oppose, object, contradict,
take issue with, argue against, be against
FORMAL dissent
3 *food disagreeing with you*
upset, make unwell, cause illness, sicken, nauseate
≡ 1 agree **2** approve, accept **3** agree

Synonym nuances
sense 1
Conflict may be used to suggest being in marked or
vociferous opposition: *these proposals conflicted with
official policy*; whilst **contradict** and **be at odds with**
can be used of asserting the opposite in a more
restrained way: *his version was contradicted by
eyewitness accounts*. **Diverge** suggests that elements,
often formerly unified, are going their separate ways: *we
diverged from the original strategy.*
  Clash would suggest only very forceful opposition or

---

highly marked or significant disagreement: *MPs clashed
openly in a chaotic parliament*. **Quarrel** can be used to
refer to any verbal expression of disagreement or discord,
as can **argue**, **bicker**, **wrangle** and **squabble**, although
quarrel is perhaps a more vociferous expression. **Fight** is
similar in that it suggests forceful opposition as well as
disagreement. **Contend** is slightly less forceful, although
it suggests rigorously maintaining something to be the
case, in disagreement with others: *the president
contended the elections were free*. To refer to
questioning the validity of a claim, the terms **dispute** and
contest are appropriate: *officials disputed the need for
nuclear weapons*.

---

disagreeable adj
1 *disagreeable old man*
bad-tempered, ill-humoured, impolite, difficult,
unfriendly, ill-natured, awkward, unhelpful, peevish, rude,
surly, churlish, irritable, nasty, disobliging, contrary, cross,
brusque
COLLOQ. grouchy
2 *a disagreeable taste*
disgusting, unpleasant, offensive, repulsive, repellent,
repugnant, obnoxious, unsavoury, horrible, dreadful,
abominable, objectionable, nasty
≡ 1 amiable, pleasant **2** agreeable, pleasant

disagreeably adv
unpleasantly, horribly, dreadfully, nastily, objectionably,
obnoxiously, offensively, repulsively, disgustingly
≡ pleasantly

disagreement n
1 DISPUTE, argument, difference/variance of opinion,
friction, fight, disharmony, disunion, conflict, quarrel, row,
clash, dissent, dissension, contention, strife, dissension,
misunderstanding, squabble, wrangle
FORMAL altercation, discord, disputation, dissidence,
dissonance
COLLOQ. falling-out, tiff, bust-up, flak
2 DIFFERENCE, variance, unlikeness, discrepancy, deviation,
conformity, dissimilarity, incompatibility, inconsistency,
divergence, diversity
FORMAL disparity, incongruity, dissimilitude
≡ 1 agreement, harmony **2** similarity, conformity

disallow v
ban, cancel, forbid, prohibit, refuse, reject, debar, dismiss,
embargo, disown, rebuff, repudiate, veto, say no to,
exclude
FORMAL abjure, disaffirm, disavow, disclaim, proscribe,
interdict
≡ allow, permit

disappear v
1 VANISH, wane, recede, fade, evaporate, melt away, drop
away, die away, peter out, dissolve, ebb, go out of sight,
pass from sight, get lost, go missing, dematerialize, ghost
FORMAL dissipate, evanesce
COLLOQ. make tracks, walk
2 GO, depart, withdraw, retire, exit, flee, fly, escape, hide,
take flight
COLLOQ. scarper, vamoose, slope
3 END, perish, pass, cease, die out, die away, become
extinct, go cold
FORMAL expire
≡ 1 appear **3** emerge, start, begin

disappearance n
1 VANISHING, fading, passing from sight, evaporation,
melting away, departure, withdrawal, exit, loss, going,
passing, desertion, flight
2 END, passing, dying-out, expiry, extinction
FORMAL expiry, evanescence
≡ 1 appearance, manifestation **2** start, beginning

disappoint v

let down, fail, dissatisfy, disillusion, dismay, discourage, depress, dispirit, disenchant, sadden, thwart, vex, baffle, frustrate, foil, dishearten, disgruntle, disconcert, hamper, hinder, deceive, betray, mock, fail, make a fool of, break someone's heart, defeat, delude, dash someone's hopes; *dialect* mislippen; *Scot* mistryst; *Aust* slip up
OLD deceive
COLLOQ. devastate
F3 satisfy, please, delight

disappointed adj

let-down, frustrated, thwarted, disenchanted, deflated, disillusioned, dissatisfied, upset, vexed, discouraged, disgruntled, disheartened, distressed, downhearted, saddened, cast down, despondent, depressed, disenchanted, betrayed
COLLOQ. miffed, devastated, gutted
F3 pleased, satisfied

disappointing adj

unsatisfactory, inferior, inadequate, insufficient, unworthy, pathetic, sad, sorry, unhappy, discouraging, disconcerting, depressing, disagreeable, anticlimactic
COLLOQ. not all it's cracked up to be, underwhelming
F3 encouraging, pleasant, satisfactory

disappointment n

1 FRUSTRATION, dissatisfaction, failure, disenchantment, disillusionment, displeasure, discouragement, discontent, distress, regret, chagrin, sadness, despondency, dispiritedness
COLLOQ. cold comfort
2 FAILURE, let-down, anticlimax, setback, comedown, non-event, blow, misfortune, fiasco, disaster, calamity
COLLOQ. washout, wipeout, damp squib, swiz, swizzle, bummer, bitter pill (to swallow)
F3 1 pleasure, satisfaction, delight **2** success

disapprobation n

blame, censure, condemnation, criticism, denunciation, disapproval, disfavour, dissatisfaction, dislike, displeasure, objection, exception, reproach, reproof
FORMAL remonstration, disparagement
F3 approval; *formal* approbation

disapproval n

censure, condemnation, criticism, blame, displeasure, reproach, exception, objection, dissatisfaction, denunciation, dislike, rejection, veto, rebuke, reproof
OLD disallowance, misliking
FORMAL disapprobation, remonstration, disparagement
COLLOQ. the thumbs-down
F3 approval; *formal* approbation

disapprove v

censure, condemn, blame, take exception to, be against, object to, find unacceptable, deplore, denounce, dislike, reject, veto, spurn, look down on, think little of, hold in contempt, frown on, take a dim view of, take exception to, think badly of, have a low opinion of, not hold with, harrumph, reprobate
OLD disallow, disprove; (*Spenser*) disproove; mislike
FORMAL disparage, deprecate, discountenance, disallow, disfavour, disesteem, animadvert
COLLOQ. look down your nose at, give the thumbs-down
F3 approve, agree, have a high opinion of

Synonym nuances

Both **censure** and **condemn** involve speaking out strongly against: *a judicial inquiry severely censured police behaviour*; whereas **blame** involves holding someone or something responsible, whether voiced or not. **Deplore** suggests strength of feeling and being appalled by, whilst **denounce** returns to the idea of strongly and publicly vilifying, and the milder **disparage** can be used for talking slightly about: *the art critical*

---

establishment is still sniffily disparaging about his work.
Where disapproval is expressed in a refusal to accept, you could use the terms **reject** and **spurn**, and, in official contexts, **veto**: *their diplomatic overtures were spurned by the French government.*
Meanwhile, the phrases **look down on** and **hold in contempt** suggest a feeling of superiority behind any disapproval; **think little of, frown on, take a dim view of, think badly of** and **have a low opinion of** can be used to refer to varying degrees of disapprobation, from the mild to the severe, and which may be keenly felt but not expressed. **Take exception to** and **not hold with** are also fairly restrained but imply active objection.

---

disapproving adj

censorious, condemnatory, critical, reproachful, reproving, derogatory, pejorative
FORMAL deprecatory, disparaging, disapprobative, disapprobatory, improbative, improbatory

disarm v

1 DISABLE, unarm, demilitarize, demobilize, deactivate, disband, immobilize, lay down arms/weapons, make powerless, put out of action
FORMAL render inoperative
2 APPEASE, conciliate, win over, mollify, placate, persuade, charm
F3 1 arm

disarmament n

demilitarization, demobilization, deactivation, laying-down of arms/weapons, arms control/limitation/reduction

disarming adj

charming, winning, persuasive, conciliatory, irresistible, likeable, mollifying

disarmingly adv

charmingly, pleasantly, persuasively, irresistibly

disarrange v

untidy, disorganize, disorder, confuse, disturb, jumble, mess, dislocate, shuffle, unsettle, put out of place
FORMAL derange
F3 arrange, tidy

disarray n

disorder, confusion, chaos, mess, muddle, disorganization, clutter, untidiness, dishevelment, unruliness, unsettledness, jumble, clutter, indiscipline, tangle, upset
COLLOQ. shambles
F3 order

disassemble v

dismantle, take apart, pull apart, separate, pull/take to pieces
F3 assemble, put together

disassociate v

dissociate, separate, cut off, remove, withdraw, break

disaster n

calamity, catastrophe, misfortune, reverse, reversal, adversity, tragedy, blow, accident, act of God, cataclysm, debacle, mishap, misadventure, setback, failure, fiasco, ruin, stroke, trouble, mischance, ruination, mucker, sticky end; *N Am* providence
OLD shipwreck
COLLOQ. flop, washout, wipeout, holocaust, horror story
SLANG screw-up
F3 success, triumph

disastrous adj

calamitous, catastrophic, cataclysmic, devastating, ravaging, ruinous, tragic, unlucky, unfortunate, adverse, dreadful, dire, terrible, appalling, shocking, destructive, harmful, injurious, ill-fated, ill-starred, fatal, miserable
F3 successful; *formal* auspicious

disavow v

repudiate, deny, disown, contradict, reject
FORMAL renounce, disaffirm, abjure
COLLOQ. wash your hands of

disavowal n

repudiation, denial, contradiction, rejection, dissent
FORMAL renunciation, disaffirmation, abjuration

disband v

disperse, break up, scatter, dismiss, demobilize, part
company, separate, dissolve, go separate ways
COLLOQ. demob
Fa assemble, gather, muster

disbelief n

unbelief, incredulity, doubt, scepticism, questioning,
suspicion, distrust, mistrust, discredit, rejection
FORMAL dubiety
Fa belief, conviction

Colloquial expressions of disbelief include:

a good one!	I ask you!	strike me dead!
a likely story!	I bet!	strike me pink!
come	I don't think	stuff and
come!	I'll eat my hat!	nonsense!
come off it!	I've heard that	tell it to the
do me a favour!	one before!	marines!
don't give me	if you believe that	tell me another!
that!	you'd believe	that's a tall story!
don't make me	anything!	that's news to me!
laugh!	just fancy!	that's rich!
don't tell me!	make me laugh!	the devil you do!
do you mean to	my (giddy) aunt!	the hell you say!
say?	my foot!	what a load of
excuses	my goodness!	cobblers!
excuses!	my hat!	you can't be
fancy that!	no kidding!	serious!
get along (with	oh yeah!	you don't say!
you)!	promises,	you'll be lucky!
get away (with	promises!	you must be
you)!	pull the other one,	joking!
go on!	it's got bells on!	you must be
go on with you!	says who?	kidding!
good heavens!	says you!	you're kidding!
good Lord!	sez who?	you're pulling my
goodness	sez you!	leg!
gracious me!	stone me!	you what!
goodness me!	stone the crows!	
heavens above!	strike a light!	

---

disbelieve v

discount, discredit, repudiate, reject, distrust, mistrust,
suspect, question, doubt, be unconvinced
COLLOQ. take something with a pinch of salt
Fa believe, trust, give credence to, accept

disbeliever n

doubter, agnostic, atheist, unbeliever, non-believer,
questioner, sceptic, scoffer, doubting Thomas
FORMAL nullifidian
Fa believer

disbelieving adj

incredulous, unbelieving, unconvinced, sceptical, cynical,
suspicious, uncertain, doubtful, doubting, distrustful

disburse v

pay out, spend, lay out
FORMAL expend
COLLOQ. fork out, shell out, dish out, cough up

disbursement n

payment, outlay, spending, expenditure
FORMAL disbursal, disposal

disc n

1 CIRCLE, face, plate, ring, round, saucer, counter, discus

2 RECORD, album, LP, CD, vinyl, gramophone record
3 DISK, diskette, hard disk, floppy disk, compact disk, CD-
ROM, microfloppy

discard v

reject, abandon, dispose of, get rid of, throw away, throw
out, jettison, dispense with, cast aside, toss out, drop,
scrap, shed, remove, relinquish, repudiate
FORMAL forsake
COLLOQ. ditch, dump, chuck away/out
Fa retain, adopt

discern v

perceive, make out, observe, detect, recognize, see,
get, tell (from), pick out, ascertain, notice, determine,
discover, spot, distinguish, differentiate, judge,
discriminate
OLD scerne, wit
FORMAL descry

discernible adj

perceptible, noticeable, detectable, appreciable, distinct,
distinguishable, observable, recognizable, visible,
apparent, manifest, clear, obvious, plain, conspicuous,
patent, discoverable
Fa imperceptible

discerning adj

discriminating, perceptive, astute, prudent, clear-sighted,
sensitive, shrewd, wise, ingenious, intelligent, clever,
quick, sharp, subtle, penetrating, acute, piercing, critical,
selective, tasteful, eagle-eyed, sound
FORMAL sagacious, judicious, perspicacious, percipient,
sapient
Fa dull, obtuse

discernment n

judgement, discrimination, perception, perceptiveness,
acuteness, clear-sightedness, shrewdness, wisdom,
sharpness, ingenuity, insight, intelligence, cleverness,
understanding, awareness, acumen, keenness, (good)
taste, penetration
FORMAL ascertainment, percipience, perspicacity,
sagacity

discharge v, n

♦ v
1 LIBERATE, free, set free, let go, pardon, release, clear,
absolve, acquit, relieve, dismiss
FORMAL exonerate, exculpate
2 *discharge from employment*
remove, dismiss, expel, get rid of, discard, oust, eject
COLLOQ. sack, fire, turf out, boot out, give the boot to, give
the elbow, give someone their marching orders, give
someone their cards/jotters, give someone the heave-ho,
axe
3 FULFIL, carry out, perform, do, fulfil
FORMAL dispense
4 FIRE, shoot, let off, detonate, explode, set off
5 *discharge fumes*
emit, let off/out, give off, send out, pour, release, exude,
ooze, leak, disgorge, gush
FORMAL excrete, disembogue
6 *discharge a debt*
settle, pay, clear, honour, satisfy, meet
Fa 1 detain 2 appoint, hire 3 neglect
♦ n
1 LIBERATION, release, acquittal, clearance, absolution
FORMAL exoneration, exculpation
2 *discharge from employment*
dismissal, removal, expulsion, ousting, cashiering
COLLOQ. sacking, the sack, firing, the boot, the elbow, the
heave-ho
3 EMISSION, secretion, ejection, flow, leak, exuding, release,
pus
FORMAL excretion, suppuration

4 FULFILMENT, accomplishment, performance, carrying-out, doing, execution, achievement
5 *discharge of a debt*
settling, payment, repayment, clearance, honouring
EϪ 1 confinement, detention **2** hiring, appointment **3** absorption **4** neglect

disciple *n*
follower, convert, proselyte, adherent, believer, devotee, supporter, upholder, learner, pupil, student, votary

disciplinarian *n*
authoritarian, (hard) taskmaster, autocrat, stickler, despot, tyrant, martinet

discipline *n, v*
♦ *n*
1 TRAINING, direction, control, regulation, exercise, drill, practice, routine, regimen
2 PUNISHMENT, correction
FORMAL chastisement, castigation
3 STRICTNESS, control, self-control, self-discipline, restraint, self-restraint, regulation, orderliness
4 SUBJECT, area of study, field of study, course of study, branch, speciality
EϪ 3 indiscipline
♦ *v*
1 TRAIN, instruct, drill, teach, educate, exercise, break in, ground
FORMAL inculcate, inure
2 CHECK, keep in check, control, keep under control, curb, correct, restrain, govern, regulate, limit, restrict
3 PUNISH, chasten, rebuke, reprove, penalize, correct, reprimand, make an example of, teach someone a lesson
OLD disple
FORMAL chastise, castigate

disclaim *v*
deny, disown, repudiate, abandon, reject, decline, refuse
FORMAL renounce, abjure, disavow
COLLOQ. wash your hands of
EϪ accept, confess

disclaimer *n*
denial, repudiation, rejection, contradiction
FORMAL renunciation, abjuration, abnegation, disavowal, disaffirmation, disownment, retraction

disclose *v*
make known, reveal, tell, confess, let slip, let drop, blurt out, relate, publish, broadcast, communicate, make public, expose, reveal, divulge, impart, betray, tell a tale, show, exhibit, uncover, unfold, lay bare, unveil, bring to light, develop, discover, evolve, open out, unlock, unrip
OLD propale; (*Spenser*) unhele, unheal
COLLOQ. let on, leak, blab, squeal, let the cat out of the bag, spill the beans, blow the gaff, blow the whistle, give the game away, take the wraps off
EϪ conceal

disclosure *n*
revelation, exposure, exposé, uncovering, publication, discovery, admission, confession, acknowledgement, announcement, publication, broadcast, declaration, bringing to light, laying bare
FORMAL divulgence
COLLOQ. leak

discoloration *n*
blemish, stain, spot, streak, mark, patch, blot, blotch, splotch
TECHNICAL dyschroa, ecchymosis

discolour *v*
disfigure, fade, stain, soil, mark, mar, rust, streak, tarnish, tinge, weather

discomfit *v*
embarrass, disconcert, discompose, unsettle, demoralize,

abash, confound, baffle, confuse, perplex, fluster, ruffle, frustrate, thwart, outwit
FORMAL perturb
COLLOQ. faze, rattle

discomfiture *n*
unease, uneasiness, embarrassment, confusion, abashment, discomposure, demoralization, frustration, disappointment, humiliation, chagrin

discomfort *n*
1 ACHE, pain, soreness, tenderness, hurt, twinge, pang, jet lag
TECHNICAL irritation, cardialgia
2 UNEASE, uneasiness, embarrassment, trouble, distress, disquiet, hardship, vexation, irritation, annoyance, misery, worry, apprehension, restlessness
FORMAL malaise
COLLOQ. hell, purgatory
3 INCONVENIENCE, difficulty, trouble, disadvantage, drawback, worry, nuisance, bother, irritation, annoyance
COLLOQ. hassle
EϪ 2 comfort, ease

discomposure *n*
unease, uneasiness, upset, agitation, restlessness, fluster, disturbance, anxiety, irritation, annoyance
FORMAL disquietude, inquietude, perturbation
EϪ *formal* composure

disconcert *v*
unsettle, disturb, confuse, upset, unnerve, put off/out, shake, alarm, startle, take aback, throw off balance, surprise, fluster, ruffle, bewilder, nonplus, embarrass, baffle, perplex, dismay
FORMAL perturb
COLLOQ. faze, rattle, throw, put someone's nose out of joint
SLANG *N Am* discombobulate

disconcerting *adj*
disturbing, confusing, upsetting, unnerving, unsettling, daunting, alarming, bewildering, distracting, embarrassing, awkward, baffling, perplexing, dismaying, bothersome
FORMAL perturbing
COLLOQ. off-putting

disconnect *v*
cut off, disengage, uncouple, sever, separate, detach, de-energize, unplug, undo, unhook, unhitch, part, divide, split
EϪ attach, connect, join, unite

disconnected *adj*
confused, incoherent, garbled, rambling, unco-ordinated, unintelligible, loose, wandering, rambling, irrational, disjointed, illogical, jumbled, mixed-up, abrupt, staccato
EϪ coherent, connected

disconnection *n*
separation, division, detachment, disengagement, uncoupling, severance, unplugging, undoing
EϪ connection, linking

disconsolate *adj*
desolate, dejected, dispirited, sad, melancholy, depressed, unhappy, wretched, miserable, despondent, gloomy, downcast, forlorn, inconsolable, low, low-spirited, down, crushed, heavy-hearted, hopeless, heartbroken, wretched, grief-stricken
COLLOQ. down in the dumps
EϪ cheerful, joyful

disconsolately *adv*
sadly, unhappily, miserably, wretchedly, desolately, dejectedly, despondently, inconsolably, heavy-heartedly
EϪ happily, cheerfully

discontent *n*
uneasiness, dissatisfaction, disquiet, disaffection, restlessness, fretfulness, unrest, impatience, vexation,

regret, displeasure, misery, unhappiness, wretchedness
COLLOQ. fed-upness
☶ content, satisfaction, happiness

discontented *adj*
dissatisfied, disgruntled, unhappy, restless, inpatient,
disaffected, miserable, wretched, exasperated,
displeased, complaining
COLLOQ. fed up, browned off, cheesed off
SLANG pissed off
☶ contented, satisfied, happy

discontinue *v*
stop, come to a stop, end, come to an end, cease, finish,
break off, refrain, do away with, halt, drop, suspend,
abolish, abandon, cancel, interrupt
FORMAL terminate
COLLOQ. quit, scrap
☶ begin, continue, produce

discontinuity *n*
disjointedness, disconnectedness, incoherence,
interruption, breach, break, disconnection, disruption,
disunion, rupture
☶ continuity, coherence

discontinuous *adj*
intermittent, broken, disconnected, fitful, interrupted,
irregular, sporadic, spasmodic, periodic, punctuated
☶ continuous

discord *n*
1 CONFLICT, disagreement, clashing, disunity,
incompatibility, difference, difference of opinion, dispute,
contention, friction, division, opposition, strife, split,
wrangling, argument, row, dissent
FORMAL dissension, discordance
2 DISCORD OF SOUNDS, disharmony, jangle, jangling, jarring,
harshness
TECHNICAL suspension
FORMAL dissonance, cacophony, inharmonicity
☶ 1 concord, agreement 2 harmony

discordant *adj*
1 DISAGREEING, conflicting, at odds, at variance, opposing,
clashing, hostile, contradictory, differing, dissenting,
incompatible, inconsistent
FORMAL incongruous
2 DISSONANT, grating, jangling, jarring, harsh, strident,
sharp, flat
TECHNICAL atonal
FORMAL cacophonous, inharmonious
☶ 1 agreeing 2 harmonious

discount *n, v*
◆ *n*
reduction, rebate, allowance, cut price, cut, concession,
deduction, mark-down
◆ *v*
1 DISREGARD, ignore, overlook, dismiss, disbelieve, pass
over, gloss over
COLLOQ. pooh-pooh
2 REDUCE, deduct, mark down, take off
COLLOQ. knock off, slash
☶ 1 pay attention to, take notice of 2 increase

discourage *v*
1 DISHEARTEN, dampen, damp, dispirit, depress,
demoralize, dismay, unnerve, put off, daunt, deject,
disappoint, cast down, chill, put a damper on
FORMAL discountenance
COLLOQ. pour/throw cold water on
2 DETER, dissuade, hinder, put off, restrain, prevent, hold
back, talk out of, advise against, choke off
☶ 1 encourage, hearten 2 encourage, persuade

discouraged *adj*
disheartened, let down, deflated, dispirited, depressed,

demoralized, dejected, dismayed, downcast, glum,
pessimistic, daunted, dashed, crestfallen
COLLOQ. down in the dumps
☶ encouraged, heartened

discouragement *n*
1 DOWNHEARTEDNESS, despondency, pessimism, dismay,
depression, dejection, despair, disappointment,
hopelessness, gloom
2 DETERRENT, damper, setback, impediment, obstacle,
curb, barrier, disincentive, opposition, hindrance, restraint,
rebuff
☶ 1 encouragement 2 incentive

discouraging *adj*
disheartening, dispiriting, depressing, disappointing,
demoralizing, off-putting, unfavourable, dampening,
daunting
FORMAL dehortatory, dissuasive, dissuasory, inauspicious,
unpropitious
☶ encouraging, heartening

discourse *n, v*
◆ *n*
1 CONVERSATION, dialogue, chat, communication, talk,
discussion
FORMAL converse, colloquy, confabulation
COLLOQ. chit-chat
2 SPEECH, address, lecture, sermon, essay, treatise,
dissertation, homily
FORMAL oration, disquisition
◆ *v*
converse, talk, speak, discuss, debate, confer, lecture,
preach, hold forth

discourteous *adj*
rude, bad-mannered, impolite, boorish,
uncouth, disrespectful, unpleasant, offensive, ill-bred,
uncivil, unmannerly, ungracious, unceremonious,
impertinent, impudent, insolent, offhand, curt, brusque,
abrupt, short, gruff
☶ courteous, polite

discourteously *adv*
rudely, impolitely, disrespectfully, uncivilly, unpleasantly,
offensively, ungraciously, unceremoniously, impertinently,
impudently, insolently, offhandedly, curtly, brusquely,
abruptly, gruffly
☶ courteously, politely

discourtesy *n*
rudeness, bad manners, impoliteness, disrespectfulness,
ill-breeding, unmannerliness, ungraciousness, incivility,
impertinence, insolence, curtness, brusqueness, rebuff,
slight, snub, insult, affront
FORMAL indecorousness, indecorum
☶ courtesy, politeness

discover *v*
1 FIND OUT ABOUT, determine, realize, notice, make out,
recognize, perceive, see, spot, trace, discern, establish,
learn, detect, unmask, spy, come to know, fathom (out),
sound out, analyse
OLD espy
FORMAL ascertain, descry, excogitate
COLLOQ. twig, suss out, get wise to, rumble, get onto, get
wind of, hit on, smoke out
2 FIND, come across, uncover, unearth, dig up, disclose,
reveal, stumble across/on, turn up, come to light, ferret
out, light on, locate
3 ORIGINATE, invent, pioneer, devise, create, work out,
compose
☶ 1 conceal, cover (up) 2 miss

discoverer *n*
explorer, finder, founder, pioneer, initiator, inventor,
originator, author, deviser, creator

discovery n
1 FINDING, determination, realization, recognition, discernment, learning, disclosure, detection, revelation, location
2 BREAKTHROUGH, find, finding(s), origination, introduction, innovation, research, invention, devising, exploration, pioneering

discredit v, n
♦ v
1 *discredit someone*
dishonour, degrade, defame, damage, disgrace, bring into disrepute, give someone a bad name, run down, belittle, slate, slander, slur, smear, tarnish, reproach, reflect (badly) on, put in a bad light
FORMAL disparage, vilify, cast aspersions on
COLLOQ. rubbish, badmouth
SLANG slag (off)
2 *discredit a theory*
disprove, disbelieve, distrust, doubt, question, mistrust, challenge, invalidate, deny, discard, reject, explode, debunk, shake your faith in
FORMAL refute
Ⓔ 1 honour **2** believe
♦ n
dishonour, disrepute, censure, disgrace, blame, shame, reproach, slur, stigma, smear, scandal, infamy, humiliation
FORMAL aspersion, opprobrium, ignominy
Ⓔ honour, respect

discreditable adj
improper, dishonourable, disreputable, disgraceful, scandalous, blameworthy, shameful, infamous, degrading
FORMAL reprehensible
Ⓔ creditable

discreet adj
tactful, careful, diplomatic, cautious, prudent, delicate, reserved, guarded, wary, sensible, wise, considerate
FORMAL politic, judicious, circumspect
Ⓔ tactless, indiscreet

❗ discreet or **discrete**?
Discreet means 'prudent, cautious, not saying or doing anything that might cause trouble': *My secretary won't ask awkward questions; she's very discreet. Discrete* means 'separate, not attached to others': *a suspension of discrete particles in a liquid.*

---

discreetly adv
tactfully, carefully, diplomatically, cautiously, delicately, prudently, sensibly, wisely, considerately
FORMAL judiciously, circumspectly
Ⓔ tactlessly, indiscreetly

discrepancy n
inconsistency, difference, variance, variation, dissimilarity, deviation, divergence, disagreement, conflict, contradiction, inequality
FORMAL disparity, discordance, incongruity

discrete adj
separate, distinct, detached, disconnected, unattached, individual, discontinuous, disjoined
FORMAL disjunct

discretion n
1 TACT, diplomacy, caution, wisdom, discernment, judgement, good sense, care, carefulness, prudence, reserve, consideration, wariness, guardedness
FORMAL judiciousness, circumspection, volition, predilection
2 CHOICE, freedom, preference, will, wish, desire, inclination
Ⓔ 1 indiscretion

discretionary adj
optional, voluntary, elective, open
Ⓔ fixed, mandatory, compulsory, automatic

discriminate v
1 DISTINGUISH, differentiate, discern, tell apart, tell/ recognize the differences, draw/make a distinction, segregate, separate
2 BE PREJUDICED, show prejudice, be biased, victimize, treat differently, treat unfairly, be intolerant
Ⓔ 1 confuse, confound **2** favour

discriminating adj
discerning, fastidious, selective, critical, perceptive, particular, tasteful, keen, astute, shrewd, sensitive, cultivated

discrimination n
1 BIAS, prejudice, intolerance, unfairness, bigotry, favouritism, narrow-mindedness, inequity, segregation, racism, colour bar, sexism, male chauvinism, ageism, homophobia, heterosexism, classism, lookism, siz(e)ism
SLANG N Am Jim Crow
2 DISCERNMENT, judgement, acumen, perception, acuteness, insight, shrewdness, astuteness, penetration, subtlety, keenness, sensitivity, refinement, distinction, taste
OLD skill
FORMAL perspicacity
Ⓔ 1 equal opportunities

discriminatory adj
biased, prejudiced, favouring, inequitable, prejudicial, unfair, unjust, discriminative, partial, partisan, preferential, loaded, weighted, one-sided
Ⓔ fair, impartial, unbiased

discursive adj
rambling, digressing, wandering, wordy, long-winded, meandering, wide-ranging, circuitous, diffuse, verbose
FORMAL prolix
Ⓔ terse

discuss v
debate, talk about/over, confer, argue, consider, go into, weigh up, deliberate, converse, consult, exchange views on, canvass, examine, study, review, analyse, reason, handle, treat, critique, go into detail, deal with, thrash out, speak to, take up, agitate
TECHNICAL interplead
OLD parley; (*Shakesp*) question
FORMAL discourse, confabulate, expostulate, pro and con
COLLOQ. kick about/around, knock about/around, put your heads together

---

Synonym nuances
Debate may be used of a more formal or official method of discussing various aspects, whilst **talk about/over** would be appropriately used of a more informal chat. **Confer** and **consult** might be used of seeking the opinions of others: *she had conferred with her lawyers,* unlike **argue**, which implies pushing personal opinions: *he argued for an increase in hospital funding.*
The terms **consider**, **go into**, **weigh up** and **deliberate**, and the more explicit terms **examine**, **study** and **analyse** might be used where there is a thorough discussion and examination of all the facts. The word **review**, however, is reserved for looking again at a previous decision or practice: *the party will review its industrial relations policy,* while **reason** is best applied to discussion applying logic. Discussing with the aim of finding a solution or answering questions is suggested by the terms **handle**, **treat** and **deal with**: *training strategies should be handled at a local level; other civilizations will be treated in separate studies.* The more informal **thrash out** which also gives the impression of an exhaustive exchange.
Critique and **agitate**, on the other hand, are suggestive of critical questioning with the purpose of raising problematic issues rather than solving them: *they had long been agitating for land reform.*

discussion n
debate, conference, argument, conversation, talk, talks,
dialogue, exchange, consultation, forum, negotiations,
deliberation, consideration, analysis, review, examination,
study, scrutiny, seminar, symposium; *NZ* korero
OLD parley; (*Shakesp*) question
FORMAL discourse, colloquium
COLLOQ. powwow

disdain n, v
◆ n
scorn, contempt, arrogance, haughtiness, derision,
sneering, dislike, snobbishness
FORMAL disparagement, deprecation, contumely
F∃ admiration, respect
◆ v
scorn, look down on, despise, slight, disregard, snub,
ignore, reject, spurn, rebuff, turn down, belittle, sneer at,
undervalue
FORMAL contemn, deride, disavow
COLLOQ. pooh-pooh, cold shoulder
F∃ admire, respect

disdainful adj
scornful, contemptuous, derisive, haughty, aloof, arrogant,
supercilious, sneering, slighting, pompous, superior,
proud, insolent
FORMAL disparaging
F∃ respectful

disease n
illness, sickness, ill-health, infirmity, complaint, disorder,
ailment, condition, disability, infection, contagion,
epidemic
FORMAL indisposition, malady, affliction
COLLOQ. bug, virus
F∃ health
See panel below

diseased adj
sick, ill, unhealthy, unwell, infirm, ailing, unsound,
contaminated, infected, blighted
F∃ healthy, well

disembark v
land, arrive, dismount, leave, get off, step off
FORMAL alight, debark, detrain, deplane
F∃ embark

disembodied adj
bodiless, ghostly, phantom, spiritual, immaterial, intangible
FORMAL incorporeal, discarnate, spectral

disembarkation n
landing, arrival
FORMAL alighting
F∃ embarkation

disembowel v
disbowel, draw, embowel, gut, gralloch, paunch
FORMAL eviscerate, exenterate

disenchanted adj
disillusioned, disappointed, let down, discouraged,
dissatisfied, jaundiced, cynical, soured, blasé, indifferent
COLLOQ. fed up

disenchantment n
disillusionment, disillusion, disillusionment,
disappointment, dissatisfaction, cynicism, revulsion
COLLOQ. fed-upness

disengage v
disconnect, disunite, detach, loosen, free, extricate,
withdraw, undo, unfasten, untie, uncouple, unhitch,
unhook, remove, release, liberate, separate, loosen,
disentangle
F∃ connect, engage, unite

disengaged adj
detached, liberated, loose, released, free(d), disentangled,
separate(d), unattached, unconnected, unhitched
F∃ connected, joined, united

disengagement n
withdrawal, removal, taking away, detachment,
disconnection, loosening, release, disentanglement,
retreat, retirement

disentangle v
1 LOOSE, release, free, extricate, disconnect, untangle,

Diseases and disorders include:

Addison's disease	Creutzfeldt-Jakob disease	impetigo	rheumatic fever
AIDS	(CJD)	influenza	rheumatoid arthritis
alopecia	Crohn's disease	Lassa fever	rickets
Alzheimer's disease	croup	Legionnaires' disease	ringworm
anaemia	cystic fibrosis	leprosy	rubella
angina	deep-vein thrombosis	leukaemia	scabies
anorexia nervosa	(DVT)	lockjaw	scarlet fever
anthrax	diabetes	Lyme disease	schistosomiasis
arthritis	diphtheria	malaria	schizophrenia
asbestosis	dropsy	mastoiditis	scurvy
asthma	dysentery	measles	septicaemia
athlete's foot	eclampsia	meningitis	severe acute respiratory
autism	emphysema	Ménière's disease	syndrome (SARS)
Bell's Palsy	encephalitis	motor neuron disease	shingles
beriberi	endometriosis	multiple sclerosis (MS)	silicosis
Black Death	enteritis	mumps	smallpox
botulism	farmer's lung	muscular dystrophy	syphilis
Bright's disease	*colloq.* flu	myalgic encephalo-myelitis	tapeworm
bronchitis	foot-and-mouth disease	(ME)	tetanus
brucellosis	gangrene	nephritis	thrombosis
bubonic plague	German measles	osteomyelitis	thrush
bulimia	gingivitis	osteoporosis	tinnitus
cancer	glandular fever	Paget's disease	tuberculosis (TB)
cerebral palsy	glaucoma	Parkinson's disease	typhoid
chickenpox	gonorrhoea	peritonitis	typhus
cholera	haemophilia	pneumonia	vertigo
cirrhosis	herpes	poliomyelitis	West Nile virus
coeliac disease	hepatitis	psittacosis	whooping cough
common cold	Hodgkin's disease	psoriasis	yellow fever
consumption	Huntington's chorea	pyorrhoea	
	hydrophobia	rabies	

unwind, unfasten, disengage, detach, unravel, ravel out, unsnarl, untwist, undo, unknot, separate, unfold, straighten (out); *Scot* redd
OLD debarrass
FORMAL disinvolve
2 RESOLVE, clarify, simplify, distinguish, separate, distance
⊞ 1 entangle

disfavour *n*
1 *fall into disfavour*
unpopularity, discredit, disrepute
FORMAL ignominy, opprobrium
2 *look with disfavour at someone*
dislike, disapproval, displeasure, distaste, dissatisfaction, disregard, low opinion
FORMAL disapprobation, disesteem
⊞ 1, 2 favour

disfigure *v*
deface, blemish, mutilate, maim, scar, mar, deform, scar, distort, damage, injure, ruin, spoil, flaw, make ugly
⊞ adorn, embellish

disfigurement *n*
blemish, defacement, defect, deformity, mutilation, scar, spot, blotch, stain, disgrace, impairment, injury, distortion, uglification
OLD (*Shakesp*) defeature
⊞ adornment

disgorge *v*
discharge, empty, eject, expel, vomit, spew, spout, pour out, belch, regurgitate
FORMAL effuse
COLLOQ. throw up

disgrace *n, v*
• *n*
shame, disrepute, disrespect, dishonour, contempt, discredit, disfavour, humiliation, loss of face, defamation, degradation, infamy, indignity, discredit, scandal, reproach, reproof, blot, slur, smear, stain, stigma, black mark
TECHNICAL atimy
OLD TECHNICAL disworship, villainy
FORMAL ignominy, debasement, disapprobation, opprobrium, obloquy, attainder
COLLOQ. skeleton in the cupboard
⊞ honour, esteem
• *v*
shame, bring shame on, put to shame, dishonour, abase, defame, humiliate, cause to lose face, put someone's nose out of joint, blot someone's copybook, disfavour, degrade, debase, belittle, discredit, reproach, blame, slur, sully, taint, stain, stigmatize
OLD attaint, baffle, indignify, scandal, shend
FORMAL disparage, denigrate
COLLOQ. drag through the mud
⊞ honour, respect

disgraced *adj*
discredited, shamed, dishonoured, humiliated, degraded, branded, stigmatized, under a cloud
COLLOQ. in the doghouse, in someone's black books
⊞ honoured, respected

disgraceful *adj*
shameful, dishonourable, disreputable, scandalous, outrageous, despicable, contemptible, blameworthy, infamous, shocking, unworthy, dreadful, terrible, awful, appalling
FORMAL ignominious, culpable, reprehensible
⊞ honourable, respectable

disgracefully *adv*
shamefully, dishonourably, disreputably, scandalously, outrageously, despicably, contemptibly, shockingly, dreadfully, terribly, awfully, appallingly

FORMAL ignominiously, reprehensibly
⊞ honourably, respectably

disgruntled *adj*
discontented, dissatisfied, displeased, annoyed, exasperated, grumpy, irritated, peeved, peevish, resentful, sulky, sullen, testy, vexed, put out, petulant
FORMAL malcontent
COLLOQ. fed up, hacked off, cheesed off, browned off, brassed off
⊞ pleased, satisfied

disguise *n, v*
• *n*
concealment, camouflage, cloak, cover, costume, mask, front, façade, face, masquerade, deception, misrepresentation, false picture, pretence, travesty, screen, veil, shroud
OLD visor
FORMAL coverture
• *v*
1 CONCEAL, cover, cover up, be under cover, camouflage, mask, hide, dress up, impersonate, cloak, screen, veil, shroud, colour, mantle, veneer, suppress, repress
OLD palliate, vizard; (*Shakesp*) immask
FORMAL dissemble, dissimulate
COLLOQ. put on a brave face
2 FALSIFY, deceive, pretend, misrepresent, gloss over, fake, fudge
FORMAL dissemble, feign
COLLOQ. cook the books, whitewash, put up a smokescreen, ring
⊞ 1 reveal, expose

disguised *adj*
camouflaged, cloaked, veiled, hidden, made up, masked, incognito, under cover, unrecognizable, fake, false
FORMAL covert, feigned

disgust *v, n*
• *v*
offend, displease, nauseate, revolt, sicken, repel, shock, outrage, put off, make your gorge rise
COLLOQ. turn off, turn your stomach
⊞ delight, please
• *n*
revulsion, repulsion, repugnance, detestation, distaste, aversion, nausea, loathing, abhorrence, hatred, disapproval, displeasure

---

Synonym nuances
verb
Offend is a fairly mild term for hurting someone's sensibilities, whereas **displease** makes the even more restrained suggestion of doing something with which they are unhappy. The terms **nauseate**, **revolt** and **sicken**, however, are highly marked terms, suggestive of feelings of utmost abhorrence: *the whole country was revolted by the bombing*. **Repel**, while similar in the reaction it conveys, is slightly less emotive: *some were repelled by his reactionary views*. Both **shock** and **outrage** again are strong terms suggestive of profound feelings, this time suggesting disgust at the breaking of moral codes: *outraged by the scale of corruption*.
  Put off is a much milder term to use and suggests being discouraged, often in a physical way: *they were put off the food by the smell of garlic*; whereas **make your gorge rise** returns to the idea of filling with loathing, and is strongly connotative of physical manifestations of disgust.

---

disgusted *adj*
repelled, repulsed, revolted, sickened, offended, appalled, outraged, put off
COLLOQ. up in arms
⊞ attracted, delighted

disgusting adj
repellent, repulsive, revolting, repugnant, offensive, sickening, nauseating, nauseous, off-putting, odious, foul, unappetizing, unpalatable, distasteful, unpleasant, bad, vile, obscene, abominable, detestable, disgraceful, appalling, objectionable, nasty, shocking, outrageous
OLD ugsome
FORMAL rebarbative
COLLOQ. yucky, gross
E3 delightful, pleasant, acceptable

dish n, v
◆ n
plate, bowl, platter, food, fare, recipe, speciality, delicacy, course
■ **dish out**
distribute, give out, share out, hand out, hand round, pass round, dispense, dole out, allocate, mete out, inflict
■ **dish up**
serve, present, ladle, spoon, scoop, dispense, offer, present

disharmony n
conflict, clash, discord, friction, strife, incompatibility
FORMAL disaccord, discordance, dissonance
E3 harmony

dishearten v
discourage, dispirit, dampen, cast down, demoralize, depress, make depressed, dismay, dash, disappoint, deject, weigh down, daunt, crush, deter, put a damper on
E3 encourage, hearten

disheartened adj
discouraged, dispirited, downcast, depressed, disappointed, dismayed, downhearted, dejected, demoralized, daunted, crestfallen, crushed
E3 encouraged, heartened

dishevelled adj
tousled, unkempt, uncombed, untidy, bedraggled, messy, in a mess, ruffled, rumpled, slovenly, scruffy, disordered
FORMAL disarranged
COLLOQ. Aust & NZ daggy
E3 neat, tidy

dishonest adj
untruthful, fraudulent, deceitful, false, lying, deceptive, double-dealing, cheating, treacherous, untrustworthy, unscrupulous, unprincipled, swindling, corrupt, disreputable, dishonourable, crafty, cunning, sly, devious, irregular
FORMAL perfidious, mendacious, duplicitous
COLLOQ. crooked, shady, bent, shifty, fishy, iffy
E3 honest, trustworthy, scrupulous

Synonym nuances
Although many of these synonyms are marked by disapproval, **untruthful** is perhaps the least implicitly judgemental. **Fraudulent** carries strong implications of illegal activity, often with regard to money: *fraudulent benefit claims*. **False, deceptive**, and the more explicit **deceitful**, invariably suggest something deliberately misleading: *false news accounts of the war; the board ruled that the advertisement was deceptive*. The term **lying** makes an explicit accusation to this effect. **Double-dealing** suggests an element of treachery: *double-dealing spies*, whilst **cheating** and **treacherous** are explicit in their suggestion of a breach of trust.
  Swindling is a disapprobatory term used in the context of tricking someone out of money, while **corrupt**, although similarly disapproving, can be used in wider contexts such as being amenable to questionable dealings, often for financial gain: *corrupt city officials allowed the supermarket to be built*. The term **disreputable** is rather milder, appropriately used of something known for unreliability: *a disreputable*

---

opportunist, whilst **dishonourable** is more marked, and implies shameful behaviour: *the government is backing the cause for dishonourable reasons*.
  Crafty, cunning, sly and **devious** would all hint at dishonesty, with an element of a sneaky cleverness which is by no means admirable: *a cunning ploy; devious schemes*, whereas **irregular** is an almost euphemistic term to describe something of questionable legitimacy: *this accounting practice is highly irregular and we will be consulting our lawyers*.

---

dishonestly adv
fraudulently, deceitfully, falsely, deceptively, treacherously, unscrupulously, corruptly, disreputably, dishonourably, deviously
FORMAL perfidiously
E3 honestly, scrupulously

dishonesty n
deceit, falsehood, falsity, fraudulence, fraud, criminality, insincerity, untruthfulness, treachery, cheating, double-dealing, corruption, unscrupulousness, trickery, chicanery, sharp practice, irregularity
FORMAL duplicity, improbity, perfidy
COLLOQ. crookedness, shadiness, dirty trick
E3 honesty, truthfulness

dishonour v, n
◆ v
1 *dishonour the family's name*
disgrace, shame, humiliate, debase, defile, wrong, degrade, defame, discredit, stain, sully, abuse, insult, offend, affront, demean, debauch
2 *dishonour an agreement/a cheque*
refuse, reject, turn down
E3 1 honour **2** honour, accept
◆ n
disgrace, abasement, humiliation, shame, degradation, disrepute, infamy, indignity, reproach, slight, slur, scandal, stigma, insult, offence, outrage, abuse, discourtesy
OLD disworship
FORMAL discredit, ignominy, disfavour, aspersion, debasement, opprobrium
E3 honour

dishonourable adj
disreputable, unprincipled, unscrupulous, untrustworthy, unethical, unworthy, corrupt, discreditable, treacherous, scandalous, shameful, shameless, disgraceful, contemptible, despicable, infamous, ignoble
FORMAL ignominious, perfidious
COLLOQ. shady
E3 honourable

dishy adj
good-looking, attractive, charming, handsome
COLLOQ. gorgeous, hunky, sexy
E3 ugly

disillusion v, n
◆ v
disenchant, disappoint, undeceive
FORMAL disabuse
◆ n
disillusionment, disenchantment, disappointment

disillusioned adj
disenchanted, undeceived, disappointed, let-down
FORMAL disabused

disincentive n
deterrent, barrier, constraint, damper, determent, discouragement, dissuasion, hindrance, impediment, obstacle, repellent, restriction, turn-off
E3 encouragement, incentive

disinclination *n*
reluctance, unwillingness, hesitation, dislike, loathness, objection, opposition, resistance, alienation, averseness, aversion, repugnance
FORMAL antipathy
E3 inclination, enthusiasm

disinclined *adj*
reluctant, unwilling, resistant, indisposed, unenthusiastic, loath, opposed, hesitant
FORMAL averse
E3 inclined, willing, enthusiastic

disinfect *v*
sterilize, fumigate, sanitize, decontaminate, clean, cleanse, purify, purge
E3 contaminate, infect

disinfectant *n*
antiseptic, sterilizer, sanitizer, fumigant, decontaminant, bactericide, germicide

disingenuous *adj*
insincere, deceitful, dishonest, devious, designing, guileful, wily, sly, crafty, artful, cunning, two-faced, shifty, insidious, uncandid
FORMAL duplicitous, feigned
E3 artless, frank, ingenuous, naive

disingenuously *adv*
insincerely, deceitfully, dishonestly, deviously, slyly, cunningly, artfully, insidiously
E3 ingenuously, frankly, naively

disinherit *v*
cut off, reject, abandon, dispossess, impoverish, repudiate, cut someone out of your will
FORMAL renounce
COLLOQ. cut off without a penny, turn your back on

disintegrate *v*
break up, decompose, fall apart, break apart, crumble, rot, decay, moulder, separate, shatter, smash, splinter, fall to pieces

disintegration *n*
breakup, falling-apart, crumbling, decaying, separation, shattering, decomposition

disinter *v*
dig up, unearth, exhume, excavate, disentomb, unbury, uncover, expose, reveal, bring to light
FORMAL disinhume
E3 bury

disinterest *n*
disinterestedness, impartiality, neutrality, detachment, unbiasedness, dispassionateness, fairness

disinterested *adj*
unbiased, neutral, impartial, objective, unprejudiced, dispassionate, detached, uninvolved, open-minded, fair, equitable, just, even-handed, unselfish
E3 biased, prejudiced, concerned

! **disinterested** or **uninterested**?
Disinterested means 'not biased, not influenced by private feelings or selfish motives': *I think we need the opinions of a few disinterested observers.* *Uninterested* means 'not interested, not showing any interest': *uninterested in politics.*

---

disjointed *adj*
1 INCOHERENT, aimless, directionless, confused, disordered, loose, unconnected, bitty, wandering, rambling, spasmodic
2 DISCONNECTED, dislocated, divided, separated, disunited, displaced, broken, fitful, split, disarticulated
COLLOQ. bitty
E3 1 coherent

dislike *n, v*
♦ *n*
aversion, hatred, hostility, distaste, disapproval, disinclination, displeasure, resentment, animosity, antagonism, enmity, detestation, repugnance, disgust, loathing, down
OLD mislike
FORMAL disapprobation, disrelish, dyspathy, disfavour, disesteem, antipathy, animus
COLLOQ. allergy, thing, needle
SLANG *Aust* derry
E3 liking; *formal* predilection
♦ *v*
hate, detest, object to, loathe, abhor, abominate, disapprove, regard with distaste, shun, despise, scorn, lump, take against; *Scot* take a scunner to
OLD defy, distaste, mind, mislike
FORMAL execrate, disfavour, disrelish, disesteem
COLLOQ. hate someone's guts, not stand the sight of, not be someone's cup of tea, be sick to the back teeth of, be no love lost between
SLANG *Aust* have a derry on
E3 like, favour

Synonym nuances
noun
The word **disapproval** is quite restrained and suggests an intellectual or moral dislike, while **distaste** implies a more instinctive element of recoiling: *a distaste for all that is foreign.* The term **aversion** suggests a much stronger disinclination, and **hatred**, **detestation**, **disgust** and **loathing** leave no room for doubt about its intensity: *an abiding loathing of racism.*
  Displeasure has an element of being annoyed at something, and while **resentment** also implies irritable feelings, these have more to do with a perceived injury or affront: *the promotions caused resentment among those who were passed over.*
  The terms **hostility**, **animosity**, **antagonism** and **enmity** all suggest an active expression of strong feelings against someone or something disliked: *public antagonism to the institution runs high.* The more informal **down**, on the other hand, is much less extreme, implying only unkind feelings: *the boy had a down on his school.*

---

dislocate *v*
1 *dislocate a bone*
disjoint, put out of joint/place, displace, misplace, twist, strain, sprain, pull, disengage, put out, disorder, shift, disconnect, disunite
TECHNICAL luxate
COLLOQ. do in
2 *dislocate plans*
disrupt, disturb, disorganize, confuse, throw into confusion

dislocation *n*
disruption, disturbance, disarray, disorder, disorganization
E3 order

dislodge *v*
displace, eject, remove, oust, extricate, force out, shift, move, uproot

disloyal *adj*
treacherous, faithless, false, traitorous, deceitful, double-dealing, two-faced, unfaithful, untrue, unpatriotic
FORMAL apostate, perfidious
E3 loyal, faithful, trustworthy, constant

disloyalty *n*
treachery, unfaithfulness, falseness, falsity, breach of trust, betrayal, treason, double-dealing, deceit, infidelity, adultery

FORMAL apostasy, inconstancy, perfidiousness, perfidy, sedition
⬛ loyalty, faithfulness

dismal *adj*
1 DREARY, gloomy, depressing, bleak, cheerless, dull, dark, dingy, drab, low-spirited, melancholy, desolate, sad, cheerless, sombre, forlorn, despondent, miserable, sorrowful, hopeless, discouraging, glum
FORMAL lugubrious
COLLOQ. long-faced
2 *a dismal failure*
awful, terrible, bad, poor, frightful, dreadful, unsuccessful
COLLOQ. ropy, lousy, crummy, useless
SLANG naff, crappy
⬛ **1** cheerful, bright **2** good, successful

dismally *adv*
1 DREARILY, gloomily, sadly, despondently, miserably, darkly, drably
2 TERRIBLY, badly, frightfully, dreadfully, unsuccessfully
⬛ **1** happily, cheerfully **2** successfully, well

dismantle *v*
demolish, take apart, disassemble, strip (down), pull apart, separate, take to pieces
⬛ assemble, put together

dismay *n, v*
♦ *n*
alarm, distress, agitation, dread, fear, fright, horror, terror, discouragement, disappointment
FORMAL consternation, apprehension, trepidation
⬛ boldness, encouragement
♦ *v*
alarm, daunt, frighten, unnerve, unsettle, upset, shake, scare, put off, dispirit, cast down, distress, disconcert, disturb, shock, take aback, dishearten, discourage, disillusion, depress, horrify, appal, dread, worry, bother, concern, disappoint
OLD amate, heart-strike
FORMAL perturb, consternate
⬛ encourage, hearten

dismember *v*
disjoint, amputate, dissect, dislocate, mutilate, sever, divide, separate, break up, pull apart
⬛ assemble, join, unify

dismemberment *n*
dissection, mutilation, division, separation, breakup, amputation
⬛ assembly

dismiss *v*
1 *the class was dismissed*
discharge, free, let go, release, send away/off, remove, dissolve, drop, discord, banish
SLANG chassé
2 *dismiss employees*
make redundant, give notice, suspend, give someone their papers, lay off, discharge, relegate, expel, remove, cashier
COLLOQ. send packing, boot out, sack, fire, give someone their cards, give someone the sack/push/boot/elbow/bird/bum's rush/heave-ho, show someone the door
3 *dismiss it from your mind*
discount, disregard, banish, reject, repudiate, set aside, put away, put out of your mind, shelve, spurn, pour cold water on, brush aside/off
⬛ **1** retain, gather **2** appoint, hire **3** accept, think about

dismissal *n*
notice, redundancy, laying-off, discharge, removal, expulsion, marching-orders
COLLOQ. papers, sacking, firing, sack, push, boot, elbow, bird, bum's rush, heave-ho
⬛ appointment, hiring

dismissive *adj*
contemptuous, disdainful, scornful, sneering, off-hand
FORMAL dismissory
⬛ concerned, interested

dismissively *adv*
contemptuously, disdainfully, scornfully, sneeringly, off-handedly
⬛ concernedly, interestedly

dismount *v*
descend, get down, get off
FORMAL alight, disembark, light, unmount
⬛ mount

disobedience *n*
unruliness, waywardness, defiance, rebellion, wilfulness, contrariness, indiscipline, mutiny, revolt
OLD contumacity, contumacy
FORMAL infraction, insubordination, recalcitrance
⬛ obedience

disobedient *adj*
unruly, wayward, defiant, rebellious, wilful, contrary, disorderly, obstreperous, naughty, mischievous
OLD contumacious
FORMAL froward, insubordinate, intractable, refractory, recalcitrant, recusant
⬛ obedient

Synonym nuances
Unruly may be used to describe something unmanageable: *a drunk, unruly audience*, whilst **wayward** is perhaps less disapproving in tone in that it is more suggestive of being unpredictable or having lost your way: *he saw boarding school as a last chance for his wayward daughter*. **Defiant** would appropriately describe a person or actions resisting authority, while **rebellious** suggests openly flouting it, but both of these terms might be used with a hint at admiration: *a defiant sense of moral righteousness*. **Wilful**, on the other hand, may be used to suggest a less than admirable stubbornness: *her wilful refusal to go to school*, while **contrary** is similar in tone when describing something deliberately and troublesomely contradictory.
 The term **disorderly** returns to the idea of being out of control: *disorderly conduct*, whilst **obstreperous** further suggests a noisy, rowdy element, but without the same tone of disapprobation. The word **naughty** is fairly mild and generally reserved for disobedient children, while **mischievous**, which further suggests an element of playfulness, may be applied to people of all ages with a hint that it is actually endearing: *he takes mischievous delight in baiting them*.

---

disobey *v*
infringe, go against someone's wishes, overstep, step out of line, flout, disregard, defy, ignore, resist, rebel
FORMAL contravene, violate, transgress
⬛ obey, comply with

disobliging *adj*
unhelpful, unwilling, unco-operative, unaccommodating, awkward, disagreeable, discourteous, rude, uncivil, bloody-minded
⬛ obliging, helpful

disorder *n*
1 CONFUSION, chaos, muddle, disarray, mess, untidiness, clutter, disorganization, disorderliness, jumble
COLLOQ. shambles
2 DISTURBANCE, unrest, tumult, riot, breach of the peace, confusion, disruption, commotion, uproar, fracas, brawl, fight, rumpus, rout, clamour, quarrel, brouhaha, mêlée
3 ILLNESS, complaint, disease, sickness, disability, ailment, condition

FORMAL affliction, malady
See panel at **disease**.
F3 1 neatness, order **2** law and order, peace

disordered *adj*
1 UNTIDY, messy, unkempt, confused, muddled,
disorganized, jumbled, cluttered, upside-down
2 DISTURBED, deranged, confused, troubled, upset,
maladjusted, unbalanced
F3 1 organized, tidy

disorderly *adj*
1 DISORGANIZED, confused, chaotic, irregular, messy, untidy,
jumbled, cluttered, in disarray
COLLOQ. at sixes and sevens
2 UNRULY, undisciplined, unmanageable, uncontrollable,
obstreperous, rowdy, rough, boisterous, tumultuous,
turbulent, rebellious, wild, lawless, disobedient
FORMAL refractory
F3 1 neat, tidy **2** well-behaved

disorganization *n*
disarray, chaos, confusion, disorder, disruption,
dislocation, untidiness, muddle
COLLOQ. shambles
F3 order, tidiness

disorganize *v*
disorder, disrupt, disturb, disarrange, muddle, upset,
confuse, discompose, jumble, play havoc with, play hell
with, dislocate, unstring, unsettle, break up, mess up, mix
up, destroy
OLD unmechanize
F3 organize

disorganized *adj*
1 CONFUSED, disordered, haphazard, jumbled, muddled,
chaotic, unsorted, unsystematized, topsy-turvy
COLLOQ. shambolic
2 UNMETHODICAL, unorganized, unstructured,
undisciplined, unsystematic, careless, muddled
COLLOQ. untogether
F3 1 organized, tidy **2** organized, methodical

disorientate *v*
confuse, disorient, mislead, perplex, puzzle, upset, muddle
COLLOQ. faze

disorientated *adj*
disoriented, confused, bewildered, mixed up, muddled,
perplexed, puzzled, unsettled, unbalanced, lost, adrift,
astray, (all) at sea, upset

disorientation *n*
lostness, confusion, bewilderment, muddle, perplexity,
puzzlement

disown *v*
repudiate, disclaim, deny, cast off, disallow, reject, turn
your back on, abandon, unget
OLD reprobate
FORMAL renounce, forsake, disavow, abnegate,
disacknowledge
F3 accept, acknowledge

disparage *v*
belittle, criticize, defame, slander, decry, slate, run down,
degrade, detract from, disdain, discredit, dishonour,
malign, ridicule, scorn, cry down, lessen, sell short,
minimize, dismiss, underestimate, underrate, undervalue,
depreciate, mock, slur, impeach
OLD disvalue; (*Shakesp*) disable
FORMAL denigrate, deprecate, deride, cast aspersions on,
vilify, traduce, vilipend, derogate, calumniate
COLLOQ. knock, slam, rubbish
SLANG slag (off)
F3 praise

disparagement *n*
belittlement, condemnation, criticism, slander, contempt,

denunciation, discredit, disdain, ridicule, scorn,
debasement, degradation, detraction, underestimation
FORMAL derision, deprecation, aspersion, derogation,
decrial, decrying, contumely, vilification
F3 praise

disparaging *adj*
derisive, derogatory, mocking, scornful, critical, insulting,
dismissive
FORMAL deprecating, deprecatory, derisive
COLLOQ. snide, knocking
F3 flattering, praising

disparate *adj*
contrasting, different, dissimilar, unequal, unlike, contrary,
diverse, distinct
FORMAL discrepant
F3 equal, similar

disparity *n*
difference, contrast, discrepancy, gap, gulf, dissimilarity,
distinction, imbalance, inequality, inconsistency,
unevenness, unlikeness, disproportion, bias, unfairness
FORMAL dissimilitude, incongruity, inequity
F3 equality, similarity, parity

dispassionate *adj*
detached, objective, impartial, neutral, disinterested,
unbiased, unprejudiced, equitable, impersonal, fair, cool,
calm, calm and collected, composed, unemotional,
unexcited, self-possessed, self-controlled
F3 biased, emotional, involved

dispassionately *adv*
objectively, impartially, disinterestedly, fairly, equitably,
impersonally, coolly, unemotionally, unexcitedly
F3 emotionally

dispatch, despatch *v, n*
♦ *v*
1 SEND, mail, post, express, transmit, forward, consign,
expedite, convey, remit, accelerate
2 DISPOSE OF, finish, perform, discharge, conclude, settle,
perform, deal with
3 KILL, murder, execute, put to death, assassinate, slaughter
COLLOQ. bump off, knock off, do in
F3 1 receive
♦ *n*
1 SENDING, mailing, posting, consignment, transmittal,
forwarding
2 COMMUNICATION, message, report, bulletin,
communiqué, news, letter, article, account, item, piece
3 PROMPTNESS, speed, expedition, celerity, haste, rapidity,
swiftness
FORMAL alacrity, promptitude
F3 3 slowness

dispel *v*
banish, drive away, chase away, get rid of, rid, dismiss,
disperse, allay, eliminate, expel, rout, scatter, melt away
FORMAL dissipate, disseminate

dispensable *adj*
unnecessary, disposable, expendable, inessential, non-
essential, replaceable, superfluous, needless, gratuitous,
useless
F3 indispensable, essential

dispensation *n*
1 PERMISSION, exemption, exception, release, remission,
relief, reprieve, immunity, licence
2 ISSUE, distribution, allocation, allotment, provision,
handing out, sharing out
FORMAL apportionment, endowment, bestowal
3 SYSTEM, order, arrangement, plan, scheme, direction,
administration, organization, authority, discharge,
application
FORMAL economy

dispense v
1 DISTRIBUTE, pass round, give out, deal out, hand out, dole out, share out, apportion, allot, allocate, assign, share, divide out, mete out, bestow
FORMAL confer
2 ADMINISTER, carry out, apply, implement, issue, deliver, enforce, discharge, execute, operate
FORMAL effectuate
■ **dispense with**
dispose of, get rid of, abolish, do away with, do without, not need, discard, omit, disregard, give up, cancel, for(e)go, ignore, waive, relinquish
FORMAL rescind, revoke, renounce

dispersal n
scattering, breakup, breaking-up, dismissal, disbanding, separation, distribution
Ea gathering

disperse v
scatter, dispel, spread, distribute, diffuse, dissolve, break up, split up, melt away, thin out, dismiss, disband, separate, go their separate ways
FORMAL dissipate, disseminate
Ea gather

dispersion n
spreading, scattering, distribution, circulation, dispersal, diffusion, broadcast
TECHNICAL diaspora
FORMAL dissemination, dissipation

dispirit v
dishearten, discourage, deject, depress, dash, demoralize, dampen, damp, sadden, put a damper on, deter
Ea encourage, hearten

dispirited adj
disheartened, discouraged, dejected, depressed, demoralized, despondent, sad, downcast, cast down, crestfallen, gloomy, glum, morose, low
OLD (*Shakesp*) pale-hearted
COLLOQ. fed up, cheesed off, down, down in the dumps, brassed off, browned off
Ea encouraged

displace v
1 DISLODGE, move, shift, misplace, disturb, dislocate, relocate
2 DEPOSE, oust, remove, force out, dislodge, replace, dismiss, discharge, supplant, eject, expel, evict, succeed, supersede
COLLOQ. turf out, boot out

displacement n
disarrangement, dislodging, dislocation, shifting, moving, disturbance, misplacement
TECHNICAL ectopia, ectopy, heterotaxis, heterotopia
Ea order, arrangement

display v, n
♦ v
1 EXHIBIT, present, demonstrate, show, put on show, unveil, advertise, promote, publicize
2 BETRAY, disclose, reveal, show, expose
FORMAL evince, manifest
3 SHOW OFF, flourish, parade, flaunt, boast, blazon
Ea **1** conceal **2** disguise
♦ n
show, exhibition, exhibit, demonstration, presentation, parade, spectacle, pageant, array, revelation, evidence, disclosure
FORMAL manifestation, evincement

displease v
offend, annoy, irritate, anger, upset, dissatisfy, infuriate, offend, provoke, exasperate, incense, irk, vex, disturb, discompose
OLD dislike, mislike, misplease, displeasure

FORMAL perturb
COLLOQ. put out, aggravate, bug
Ea please, satisfy

displeased n
annoyed, angry, exasperated, furious, infuriated, irritated, offended, upset, disgruntled, peeved, piqued
COLLOQ. aggravated, put out
Ea pleased

displeasure n
offence, annoyance, disapproval, irritation, resentment, discontentment, disfavour, dissatisfaction, disgruntlement, distaste, disgust, anger, exasperation, indignation, chagrin, ire, pique, wrath
FORMAL disapprobation, perturbation
Ea pleasure

disport v
divert, amuse, entertain, cheer, delight, play, revel, romp, frisk, frolic, cavort, gambol, sport

disposable adj
throwaway, expendable, replaceable, non-returnable, biodegradable

disposal n
1 ARRANGEMENT, grouping, ordering, order, positioning
2 CONTROL, direction, command
3 REMOVAL, riddance, getting rid of, throwing-away, clearance, discarding, jettisoning, scrapping
■ **at someone's disposal**
available, obtainable, at/to hand, ready
COLLOQ. on tap

dispose v
1 *dispose of a problem*
deal with, decide, settle, determine, finish, attend to, see to, handle, tackle, look after, take care of, sort out, dismiss, dispatch, make short work of
COLLOQ. polish off, sew up, wrap up
2 *dispose of old books*
get rid of, discard, throw away/out, clear away/out, shed, scrap, destroy, jettison, clear out
COLLOQ. dump, get shot of, chuck out
3 *dispose troops*
arrange, align, group, place, position, plot, put, set, situate, order, organize, line up
OLD battle, dispone
4 *dispose of a person*
kill, murder, destroy, do away with, put to death
COLLOQ. do in, bump off
Ea **2** keep

disposed adj
liable, inclined, bent, prone, likely, apt, minded, subject, ready, prepared, willing, eager
FORMAL predisposed
Ea disinclined

disposition n
1 *a friendly disposition; a disposition to obey*
character, nature, temperament, inclination, make-up, bent, leaning, constitution, habit, mood, temper, spirit, humour, tendency, proneness
FORMAL predisposition, propensity, predilection, proclivity
COLLOQ. what makes someone tick
2 *the disposition of troops*
arrangement, alignment, placing, positioning, order, line-up, pattern, grouping, sequence, system
3 *the disposition of property*
distribution, giving-over, allocation, disposal, transfer, conveyance

dispossess v
deprive, take away, divest, strip, rob, eject, evict, expel, oust, dislodge
Ea give, provide

disproportion *n*
inequality, unevenness, imbalance, lopsidedness, discrepancy, inadequacy, insufficiency
FORMAL asymmetry, disparity, incommensurateness
E3 balance, equality

disproportionate *adj*
unequal, uneven, unbalanced, excessive, inordinate, unreasonable, out of proportion
FORMAL incommensurate
E3 balanced; *formal* commensurate

disproportionately *adv*
unevenly, excessively, unreasonably, inordinately
FORMAL incommensurately

disprove *v*
rebut, discredit, invalidate, contradict, prove false, deny, expose, give the lie to
OLD refel, reprove
FORMAL refute, negate, controvert, confute
COLLOQ. debunk
E3 confirm, prove

disputable *adj*
arguable, debatable, questionable, controversial, doubtful, dubious, uncertain, moot
FORMAL litigious
E3 indisputable, unquestionable

disputation *n*
debate, argument, discussion, argumentation, controversy, dispute, deliberation, polemics
TECHNICAL quodlibet
FORMAL dissension

disputatious *adj*
argumentative, contentious, polemical, quarrelsome, cantankerous, captious
FORMAL litigious, pugnacious

dispute *v, n*
◆ *v*
argue, debate, question, call into question, contend, challenge, contest, discuss, doubt, contest, contradict, deny, quarrel, clash, wrangle, bicker, squabble, wrestle, have words, moot, differ, cross swords, spar; *Scot* threap
TECHNICAL litigate, plea
OLD discept
FORMAL altercate, controvert, gainsay, traverse
E3 agree
◆ *n*
argument, debate, disagreement, controversy, conflict, contention, contest, quarrel, row, wrangle, feud, strife, squabble, variance, odds, tilt, tug-of-love; *Scot* cangle
TECHNICAL litigation
OLD controverse, disceptation
FORMAL altercation
E3 agreement, settlement

disqualification *n*
ban, bar, prohibition, veto, elimination, disentitlement, ineligibility
FORMAL preclusion

disqualified *adj*
banned, eliminated, ineligible, struck off
FORMAL debarred, precluded, disentitled
E3 accepted, eligible, qualified

disqualify *v*
1 *disqualified from the competition*
ban, bar, rule out, declare ineligible, eliminate, prohibit, suspend, strike off
FORMAL preclude, disentitle, debar
2 INCAPACITATE, disable, invalidate, immobilize, handicap, debilitate
FORMAL impair
E3 1 qualify, accept

disquiet *n, v*
◆ *n*
anxiety, worry, concern, unease, nervousness, uneasiness, restlessness, alarm, distress, agitation, fretfulness, fear, foreboding, anguish, dread, disturbance, upset, trouble
FORMAL disquietude, inquietude, perturbation
E3 calm, reassurance
◆ *v*
worry, make anxious, unsettle, make uneasy, unnerve, discompose, distress, agitate, annoy, bother, trouble, upset, concern, disturb, fret, shake, ruffle, harass, pester, plague, vex
FORMAL incommode, perturb
COLLOQ. hassle
E3 calm, reassure

disquieting *adj*
worrying, distressing, upsetting, disturbing, anxious, unsettling, unnerving, trying, troublesome
FORMAL perturbing
COLLOQ. nail-biting
E3 reassuring

disquisition *n*
explanation, dissertation, paper, essay, thesis, treatise, monograph, sermon
FORMAL discourse, exposition

disregard *v, n*
◆ *v*
1 IGNORE, overlook, discount, neglect, take no notice of, pass over, gloss over, disobey, flout, make light of, set aside, brush aside, put/rule out of court, oversee, close your eyes to, set at naught
OLD omit, waive
FORMAL dispense with
COLLOQ. turn a blind eye to, laugh off, smile at, bend
2 SLIGHT, affront, offend, snub, shun, insult, despise, disdain
FORMAL disparage, denigrate, disoblige
COLLOQ. cold-shoulder, give the go-by to, walk all over
E3 1 heed, pay attention to, listen to **2** respect
◆ *n*
neglect, negligence, carelessness, inattention, oversight, indifference, disrespect, contempt, disdain, sacrilege, desperation
OLD (*Shakesp*) non-regardance
FORMAL denigration, disesteem
COLLOQ. brush-off, cold shoulder
E3 attention, heed, notice

disrepair *n*
dilapidation, deterioration, decay, collapse, ruin, rack and ruin, shabbiness
E3 good repair

disreputable *adj*
1 DISGRACEFUL, discreditable, dubious, suspicious, dishonourable, unprincipled, unrespectable, notorious, infamous, scandalous, outrageous, shameful, unworthy, base, contemptible, corrupt, low, mean, shocking
FORMAL ignominious, opprobrious
COLLOQ. shady, shifty, dodgy
2 SCRUFFY, shabby, seedy, unkempt, slovenly, untidy, dishevelled
E3 1 honourable, respectable **2** smart

disrepute *n*
disgrace, dishonour, shame, disfavour, discredit, disreputation, infamy
FORMAL disesteem, ignominy, obloquy
E3 honour, esteem

disrespect *n*
impoliteness, disregard, discourtesy, incivility, irreverence, rudeness, dishonour, contempt, scorn, insolence, impertinence, impudence, cheek

FORMAL misesteem
E3 respect, politeness, civility, consideration

disrespectful *adj*
rude, discourteous, inconsiderate, impertinent, impolite, impudent, insolent, uncivil, unmannerly, cheeky, insulting, irreverent, contemptuous
COLLOQ. *N Am* sassy
E3 polite, respectful, civil, considerate

disrespectfully *adv*
rudely, discourteously, impertinently, impolitely, impudently, insolently, uncivilly, cheekily, insultingly, irreverently, contemptuously
E3 politely, respectfully

disrobe *v*
undress, unclothe, take off, divest, bare, uncover, strip, remove, shed, denude
FORMAL disapparel
E3 cover, dress

disrupt *v*
disturb, disorganize, confuse, cause confusion in, interfere with, interrupt, butt in, break up, unsettle, intrude, upset, throw into confusion/disorder/disarray, disarrange, dislocate, hamper, impede, sabotage
COLLOQ. throw a spanner in the works, put a spoke in someone's wheel
SLANG screw up

disruption *n*
disorder, disordering, confusion, disorganization, turmoil, disarray, disorderliness, disturbance, interference, interruption, stoppage, upheaval, upset

disruptive *adj*
troublesome, unruly, undisciplined, obstreperous, troublemaking, disorderly, boisterous, noisy, turbulent, distracting, disturbing, unsettling, upsetting
E3 well-behaved, manageable

dissatisfaction *n*
discontent, displeasure, dislike, discomfort, disappointment, disapproval, frustration, restlessness, anger, annoyance, irritation, exasperation, unhappiness, regret, resentment, vexation, chagrin
FORMAL disapprobation, disaffection, malcontentedness
COLLOQ. fed-upness
E3 satisfaction

dissatisfied *adj*
discontented, displeased, disgruntled, disappointed, disillusioned, disenchanted, frustrated, angry, annoyed, irritated, exasperated, unfulfilled, unhappy, unsatisfied
FORMAL disaffected, malcontent, malcontented
COLLOQ. fed up, cheesed off, brassed off, browned off
SLANG pissed off
E3 fulfilled, satisfied

dissatisfy *v*
displease, disappoint, let down, discontent, disgruntle, anger, annoy, irritate, exasperate, frustrate, put out, vex

dissect *v*
1 DISMEMBER, cut up, vivisect
FORMAL anatomize
2 ANALYSE, break down, investigate, scrutinize, examine, inspect, study, probe, explore, pore over

dissection *n*
1 dismemberment, cutting up, vivisection
TECHNICAL autopsy, necropsy
2 analysis, breakdown, investigation, scrutiny, examination, inspection, study, probe, exploration
Related adjective: prosectorial

dissemble *v*
feign, pretend, hide, conceal, disguise, simulate, camouflage, cloak, mask, counterfeit, fake, falsify, sham, play possum
FORMAL affect, dissimulate
COLLOQ. cover up
E3 admit

dissembler *n*
pretender, deceiver, liar, hypocrite, impostor, trickster, charlatan, fake, feigner, fraud, whited sepulchre
FORMAL dissimulator
COLLOQ. con man

disseminate *v*
circulate, distribute, spread, broadcast, scatter, sow, diffuse, disperse, publish, publicize, propagate, proclaim
FORMAL promulgate

dissemination *n*
circulation, distribution, spread, spreading, broadcasting, publishing, publication, diffusion, dispersion, propagation
FORMAL promulgation

dissension *n*
disagreement, discord, dissent, dispute, contention, argument, conflict, strife, friction, quarrel, variance, difference of opinion
E3 agreement

dissent *v, n*
♦ *v*
disagree, differ, protest, object, dispute, refuse, quibble
OLD disconsent
FORMAL demur
E3 assent
♦ *n*
disagreement, difference, dissension, discord, disharmony, friction, dispute, difference of opinion, controversy, resistance, opposition, objection, protest
E3 agreement, conformity

dissenter *n*
dissident, objector, protestant, protester, demonstrator, nonconformist, disputant, rebel, recusant, heretic, revolutionary, sectary, schismatic
FORMAL dissentient

dissentient *adj*
disagreeing, dissenting, dissident, opposing, nonconformist, protesting, conflicting, differing, rebellious, heretical, revolutionary, recusant
E3 arguing

dissertation *n*
thesis, treatise, critique, essay, monograph, paper
TECHNICAL prolegomena, propaedeutic
FORMAL discourse, disquisition, exposition

disservice *n*
disfavour, injury, wrong, bad turn, harm, hurt, unkindness, injustice, sharp practice
COLLOQ. dirty trick, con trick, kick in the teeth
E3 favour

dissidence *n*
disagreement, discordance, dispute, dissent, feud, recusancy, rupture, schism, variance
E3 agreement, peace

dissident *adj, n*
♦ *adj*
disagreeing, differing, discordant, nonconformist, opposing, protesting, conflicting, rebellious, heretical, revolutionary
FORMAL dissenting, heterodox
E3 acquiescent, orthodox
♦ *n*
dissenter, protester, objector, nonconformist, rebel, agitator, revolutionary, heretic, schismatic, recusant
E3 assenter

dissimilar *adj*
unlike, unalike, different, divergent, deviating, unrelated, contrasting, incompatible, mismatched, distinct, diverse, varying, various
TECHNICAL bifacial, hemimorphic
FORMAL disparate, heterogeneous
COLLOQ. like chalk and cheese
🠪 similar, like, alike

dissimilarity *n*
unlikeness, difference, discrepancy, divergence, distinction, unrelatedness, contrast, incomparability, diversity, variety, incompatibility
FORMAL disparity, dissimilitude, heterogeneity
🠪 compatibility, similarity

dissimulate *v*
pretend, hide, lie, fake, conceal, mask, cloak, disguise, camouflage
FORMAL feign, dissemble, affect
COLLOQ. cover up

dissipate *v*
1 *he dissipated his inheritance*
spend, waste, exhaust, squander, use up, expend, consume, lavish, drain, deplete, fritter away, burn up, run/get through
COLLOQ. blow, splurge, spend (money) like there was no tomorrow
2 *the clouds dissipated*
disperse, drive away, scatter, break up, vanish, disappear, dispel, diffuse, evaporate, dissolve, melt away
🠪 **1** accumulate **2** appear, gather

dissipated *adj*
dissolute, debauched, abandoned, self-indulgent, rakish, wasted, corrupt, wild, depraved, degenerate
FORMAL intemperate, profligate, licentious
🠪 conserved, virtuous, upright

dissipation *n*
1 *the dissipation of all fears*
dispersal, diffusion, evaporation, disappearance, squandering, expenditure, consumption, depletion
2 DEBAUCHERY, extravagance, licence, immorality, abandonment, self-indulgence, excess, prodigality, corruption, depravity
FORMAL intemperance, licentiousness
🠪 **1** conservation **2** virtue

dissociate *v*
1 *dissociate one thing from another*
separate, detach, break off/up, disunite, disassociate, disengage, disconnect, cut off, sever, disband, set apart, divorce, disrupt, isolate, segregate
2 *dissociate yourself from something*
distance, disconnect, cut off, break off, withdraw, disassociate, separate
FORMAL secede
COLLOQ. quit
🠪 associate, join

dissociation *n*
separation, detachment, break, division, divorce, disconnection, disengagement, dissevering, distancing, disassociation, segregation, isolation, setting apart, cutting-off, severance, severing, split
FORMAL disunion
🠪 association, union

dissolute *adj*
dissipated, debauched, degenerate, depraved, wanton, self-indulgent, abandoned, corrupt, immoral, lewd, rakish, unrestrained, wild
FORMAL intemperate, profligate, licentious
🠪 restrained, virtuous

dissolution *n*
1 *the dissolution of an organization/a marriage*
ending, breakup, conclusion, suspension, divorce, annulment
FORMAL termination, discontinuation
2 *the dissolution of the monarchy*
break-up, destruction, overthrow
FORMAL cessation
3 *dissolution of family life*
break-up, disintegration, collapse, decomposition, separation, division, disposal, evaporation, disappearance

dissolve *v*
1 *sugar dissolves in water*
liquefy, melt, go into solution, digest
TECHNICAL deliquesce, solvate
OLD TECHNICAL discandy
2 *the marriage/partnership dissolved*
end, bring to an end, finish, break up, divorce, unmarry, annul, disintegrate, wind up, dismiss, disband, separate, disperse, solve
FORMAL terminate, discontinue, rescind, revoke, nullify, invalidate
3 *my fears gradually dissolved*
disappear, vanish, evaporate, disperse, dwindle, melt away, crumble
FORMAL dissipate, evanesce
4 *dissolve into tears*
collapse, be overcome with, lose control, break, burst, begin, start

dissonance *n*
discord, clash, disagreement, dissension, difference, incompatibility, inconsistency, variance, disharmony, discordance, discrepancy, harshness, jangle, stridency, grating, jarring, cacophony
FORMAL inharmoniousness, disparity, incongruity
🠪 harmony, agreement

dissonant *adj*
discordant, clashing, jarring, disagreeing, jangling, grating, differing, harsh, incompatible, irregular, inconsistent, irreconcilable, raucous, strident, cacophonous, unmusical, tuneless, unmelodious
FORMAL inharmonious, anomalous, incongruous
🠪 compatible, harmonious

dissuade *v*
deter, discourage, put off, stop, discourage, persuade not to, talk out of, prevent, disincline
OLD discounsel
FORMAL dehort
COLLOQ. nobble
🠪 persuade

dissuasion *n*
discouragement, deterrence, deterring, caution
FORMAL expostulation, remonstrance, remonstration, dehortation
🠪 persuasion

distance *n, v*
♦ *n*
1 SPACE, interval, gap, separation, extent, stretch, range, reach, span, length, width, breadth, depth, height
2 REMOTENESS, farness, inaccessibility
3 ALOOFNESS, reserve, coolness, coldness, remoteness, formality, unfriendliness, detachment, stiffness
🠪 **1** closeness **2** accessibility **3** approachability, closeness, warmth
♦ *v*
separate, cut off, dissociate, disassociate, remove, withdraw, break, detach
FORMAL secede

distant *adj*
1 FAR, faraway, far-flung, far-off, out-of-the-way, remote, outlying, isolated, abroad, dispersed

COLLOQ. back of beyond
2 *a distant relative*
not close, slight, remote, indirect
3 ALOOF, cool, reserved, formal, cold, unfriendly, restrained, detached, stiff, unapproachable, uncommunicative, unresponsive, antisocial, withdrawn
COLLOQ. stand-offish
4 *a distant expression in her eyes*
detached, distracted, absent-minded, blank, preoccupied, faraway, dreamy, daydreaming
FORMAL vacant
E3 1 close, nearby **2** close **3** approachable, warm

distantly *adv*
1 FAR AWAY, a long way, great/some distance
COLLOQ. miles
2 VAGUELY, slightly, imprecisely, faintly, dimly
3 UNEMOTIONALLY, coolly, formally, coldly, stiffly, unresponsively, vacantly
4 *distantly related*
remotely, not closely
E3 1 near **2** distinctly **3** emotionally **4** closely

distaste *n*
dislike, aversion, disgust, revulsion, repugnance, horror, loathing, abhorrence, disfavour, displeasure
FORMAL antipathy
E3 liking

distasteful *adj*
disagreeable, offensive, displeasing, unpleasant, disgusting, revolting, objectionable, repellent, repulsive, repugnant, obnoxious, undesirable, uninviting, unsavoury, unpalatable, detestable, loathsome, abhorrent
E3 pleasing

distend *v*
bloat, swell, dilate, enlarge, expand, fill out, inflate, bulge, balloon, puff, stretch, widen
TECHNICAL intumesce
E3 deflate, contract, shrink

distended *adj*
bloated, swollen, dilated, enlarged, expanded, inflated, puffed-out, puffy, stretched, astrut
TECHNICAL emphysematous, tumescent, varicose
E3 deflated, shrunken

distension *n*
swelling, bloating, enlargement, expansion, extension, spread, dilation
TECHNICAL emphysema, intumescence, tumescence

distil *v*
vaporize, evaporate, condense, extract, press out, draw out, derive, express, drip, trickle, leak, flow, purify, refine, still
TECHNICAL rectify, sublimate

distillation *n*
extract, extraction, evaporation, condensation, purification, essence, spirit

distinct *adj*
1 CLEAR, plain, evident, obvious, clear-cut, apparent, manifest, marked, defined, well-defined, sharp, definite, noticeable, recognizable, unambiguous, unmistakable
FORMAL
2 SEPARATE, different, detached, individual, dissimilar, unconnected, unassociated
FORMAL discrete, disparate
E3 1 indistinct, vague

⊞ distinct or distinctive?
Distinct means 'definite', 'clearly or easily seen, heard, smelt, etc': *a distinct smell of alcohol; a distinct Scottishness in her pronunciation. Distinctive* means 'characteristic', 'distinguishing one person or thing from others': *She has a very distinctive walk; the distinctive call of a barn owl.*

distinction *n*
1 DIFFERENTIATION, discrimination, discernment, separation, difference, dissimilarity, division, contrast
FORMAL contradistinction, dissimilitude
2 EXCELLENCE, renown, fame, celebrity, prominence, eminence, importance, significance, reputation, greatness, honour, prestige, repute, superiority, worth, merit, credit, quality
FORMAL consequence
3 CHARACTERISTIC, peculiarity, individuality, feature, quality, mark
E3 2 unimportance, obscurity

distinctive *adj*
characteristic, distinguishing, individual, peculiar, different, typical, unique, particular, special, original, noteworthy, extraordinary, idiosyncratic
FORMAL singular
E3 ordinary, common

distinctiveness *n*
individuality, peculiarity, uniqueness, originality, noteworthiness, extraordinariness, idiosyncrasy
FORMAL singularity

distinctly *adv*
clearly, plainly, obviously, evidently, definitely, markedly, decidedly, noticeably, unmistak(e)ably, manifestly, unambiguously

distinguish *v*
1 DIFFERENTIATE, tell apart, tell from, set apart, discriminate, determine, tell the difference between, single out, mark off, divide, characterize, particularize, typify, mark, stamp, categorize, characterize, classify, signalize
FORMAL contradistinguish, secern
2 DISCERN, perceive, identify, ascertain, make out, recognize, see, detect, notice, pick out, discriminate, judge
FORMAL descry
3 *distinguish yourself academically*
excel, do well, acquit yourself well, bring fame to, bring honour to, bring acclaim to, glorify, dignify, ennoble

distinguishable *adj*
recognizable, discernible, clear, plain, plainly seen, evident, noticeable, conspicuous, obvious, manifest, perceptible, appreciable, observable
E3 indistinguishable

distinguished *adj*
famous, eminent, celebrated, well-known, famed, acclaimed, illustrious, prominent, notable, noted, renowned, famed, honoured, esteemed, acclaimed, outstanding, striking, marked, extraordinary, noble, aristocratic, refined, conspicuous
E3 insignificant, obscure, unimpressive

distinguishing *adj*
differentiating, different, distinctive, individual, individualistic, marked, peculiar, typical, characteristic, unique, discriminative, discriminatory
FORMAL singular, diacritical

distort *v*
1 DEFORM, contort, bend, misshape, disfigure, pull about, rack, twist, jumble, screw up, warp, buckle, hamper, torment, torture, wrench, wrest, wring; *Scot* thraw
OLD detort, writhe
2 FALSIFY, misrepresent, pervert, slant, twist, bias, colour, garble, mangle, tamper with, fudge, skew
COLLOQ. cook the books

distorted *adj*
1 DEFORMED, bent, misshapen, out of shape, disfigured, twisted, warped, awry, skew, skewed, wry; *Scot* thrawn
2 FALSE, falsified, biased, perverted, misrepresented
E3 1 straight **2** accurate

distortion *n*
1 DEFORMITY, twist, bend, buckle, contortion, crookedness, skew, slant, warp
2 MISREPRESENTATION, falsification, perversion, bias, twisting, colouring, garbling

distract *v*
1 DIVERT, sidetrack, deflect, draw away, turn aside/away, put off
2 AMUSE, occupy, divert, entertain, engross
3 CONFUSE, disconcert, bewilder, confound, disturb, perplex, puzzle, fluster, discompose

distracted *adj*
1 DISTRAUGHT, agitated, anxious, overwrought, upset, distressed, grief-stricken, beside yourself, worked up, frantic, hysterical, raving, mad, wild, crazy
2 *their attention was distracted*
abstracted, wandering, absent-minded, preoccupied, inattentive, dreaming
COLLOQ. miles away, not with it
E3 1 calm, untroubled **2** attentive

distracting *adj*
disturbing, disconcerting, confusing, bewildering, unsettling, annoying, irritating
FORMAL perturbing
COLLOQ. off-putting

distraction *n*
1 DISTURBANCE, interrupted, diversion, interference, confusion
FORMAL derangement
2 DIVERSION, amusement, entertainment, game, sport, hobby, pastime, recreation, divertissement
■ **drive to distraction**
upset, annoy, anger, madden, exasperate
COLLOQ. drive crazy, get someone's blood up, make your blood boil

distraught *adj*
agitated, anxious, overwrought, upset, worried, distressed, distracted, beside yourself, worked up, frantic, hysterical, raving, mad, wild, crazy
COLLOQ. in a state, het up
E3 calm, untroubled

distress *n, v*
♦ *n*
1 ANGUISH, grief, misery, sorrow, heartache, suffering, discomfort, torment, wretchedness, sadness, worry, anxiety, unease, desolation, pain, agony, torture
FORMAL woe, tribulation, affliction, perturbation
2 ADVERSITY, hardship, poverty, need, danger, destitution, calamity, misfortune, trouble, difficulties, trial
FORMAL peril, privation, indigence, penury
E3 1 content **2** comfort, ease
♦ *v*
upset, cause suffering to, grieve, disturb, trouble, sadden, make miserable, worry, make anxious, pain, vex, torment, harass, harrow, hurt, agonize, break someone's heart
FORMAL afflict, perturb
COLLOQ. cut up
E3 comfort

distressed *adj*
upset, hurt, troubled, worried, disturbed, dismayed, unsettled, discomposed, put out, bothered
FORMAL perturbed
COLLOQ. in a state, uptight, worked up
E3 calm

distressing *adj*
upsetting, worrying, alarming, disturbing, unsettling, off-putting, disconcerting, frightening, startling
FORMAL perturbing
E3 comforting

distribute *v*
1 DISPENSE, allocate, give out, hand out, pass out/round, dole out, dish out, ladle (out), part, serve out, share, deal (out), divide, measure out, mete out, carve, allot, issue, assort, dispose, digest; *N Am* prorate
FORMAL apportion
2 DELIVER, supply, hand out, spread, issue, circulate, pass round, transmit
TECHNICAL reticulate
3 SCATTER, diffuse, disperse, discharge
FORMAL disseminate
E3 2 collect

distribution *n*
1 DELIVERY, supply, transport, transportation, dealing, handling, conveyance
2 ALLOCATION, giving-out, handing-out, division, sharing; *N Am* proration
FORMAL apportionment
3 CIRCULATION, spreading, scattering, dispersal
FORMAL dissemination
4 ARRANGEMENT, grouping, classification, organization, placement, position
E3 1 collection

district *n*
region, area, quarter, neighbourhood, locality, sector, precinct, zone, block, parish, place, locale, community, vicinity, ward, constituency, domain, territory, shire, county, province, municipality, suburb, belt, bounds, circumscription, patch, pale, hunt, walk, *faubourg, quartier, barrio*; *N Am* section
TECHNICAL circuit

distrust *v, n*
♦ *v*
mistrust, doubt, have doubts about, disbelieve, suspect, be suspicious of, question, be sceptical about, discredit, be wary of
E3 trust
♦ *n*
mistrust, doubt, doubtfulness, disbelief, suspicion, misgiving, wariness, scepticism, question, questioning, qualm, chariness, discredit
E3 trust, confidence, faith

distrustful *adj*
mistrustful, distrusting, doubtful, doubting, dubious, disbelieving, suspicious, wary, sceptical, untrustful, untrusting, chary, uneasy, cynical
E3 trustful, unsuspecting

disturb *v*
1 DISRUPT, interrupt, put off, distract, bother, butt in on, break someone's train of thought, pester
2 AGITATE, trouble, unsettle, upset, distress, worry, make anxious, shake, fluster, annoy, bother, concern, discompose, disquiet, fret, disconcert, dismay, stir, vex, infest, racket, ruffle, touch; *Scot* mismake, sturt
OLD affray, commove, rouse, distrouble, inquiet, tumult
FORMAL discomfit, perturb, concuss
COLLOQ. beat up, turn up, hassle
3 DISARRANGE, disorder, confuse, upset, disorganize, dislocate, muddle, unsettle, throw into confusion; *Scot* jee
E3 2 reassure **3** order

disturbance *n*
1 DISRUPTION, agitation, interference, interruption, distraction, intrusion, upheaval, upset, confusion, disorder, muddle, annoyance, bother, trouble, hindrance
FORMAL inquietude
COLLOQ. hassle
2 DISORDER, uproar, commotion, tumult, turmoil, fracas, fray, brawl, riot, row, rumpus, hullabaloo, racket; *Scot* sturt
3 *emotional disturbance*

illness, sickness, disorder, complaint, neurosis
⊟ 1 peace **2** order

disturbed adj
1 *disturbed by the news*
anxious, apprehensive, bothered, concerned, troubled,
worried, upset, confused, discomposed, uneasy, flustered
OLD inquiet
2 *emotionally disturbed*
troubled, maladjusted, neurotic, unbalanced, unstable,
dysfunctional, psychotic, mentally ill, paranoid, upset
COLLOQ. screwed-up, hung-up
⊟ 1 calm

disturbing adj
alarming, distressing, troubling, unsettling, upsetting,
worrying, disconcerting, bewildering, confusing,
dismaying, disquieting, discouraging, agitating,
frightening, startling, threatening
FORMAL disturbant, disturbative, perturbing
⊟ reassuring, comforting

disunited adj
divided, split, separated, disrupted, alienated
FORMAL estranged
⊟ unify

disunity n
disagreement, conflict, discord, division, dissension,
dissent, rupture, schism, split, strife, party spirit, alienation,
breach
FORMAL estrangement, discordance
⊟ unity

disuse n
neglect, abandonment, decay
FORMAL desuetude, discontinuance
⊟ use

disused adj
unused, neglected, idle, abandoned, decayed, obsolete
FORMAL discontinued
⊟ used

ditch n, v
♦ n
trench, dyke, channel, canal, gully, gutter, furrow, moat,
drain, level, watercourse, trough
♦ v
abandon, get rid of, throw away/out, discard, dispose of,
drop, jettison, scrap
COLLOQ. dump, chuck

dither v, n
♦ v
hesitate, waver, vacillate, hang back, delay, falter, take your
time
COLLOQ. be in two minds, shilly-shally, dilly-dally, faff about
♦ n
panic, indecision, bother, flutter, fluster
COLLOQ. flap, pother, stew, tizzy
⊟ decision

divan n
couch, settee, sofa, sofa bed, chaise-longue, day bed,
lounge, lounger, ottoman, chesterfield

dive v, n
♦ v
1 *dive into water*
plunge, jump, plummet, dip, submerge, leap, nose-dive,
fall, drop, swoop, descend, go down/under, pitch, duck,
sound
2 *dive for cover*
move quickly, leap, dash, rush, hurry, fly, tear, bolt
♦ n
1 PLUNGE, lunge, header, jump, leap, plummet, nose-dive,
swoop, dash, spring, fall, drop, header, jackknife, tailspin
COLLOQ. belly-flop

2 *make a dive for the door*
leap, dash, rush, dart, bolt, spring
3 BAR, club, pub, saloon, nightclub
COLLOQ. dump, joint, hole

diverge v
1 DIVIDE, branch (off), fork, part, separate, spread (out),
split, subdivide, radiate
TECHNICAL divaricate
FORMAL bifurcate
2 DIFFER, vary, disagree, dissent, conflict, clash, contradict,
be at variance
3 DEVIATE, digress, stray, wander, depart, drift
FORMAL divagate
⊟ 1 converge **2** agree

divergence n
difference, disagreement, variation, clash, conflict,
deviation, separation, parting, deflection, departure,
digression, branching-out
TECHNICAL divarication
FORMAL disparity
⊟ agreement

divergent adj
different, differing, disagreeing, conflicting, dissimilar,
variant, varying, separate, diverging, diverse, deviating,
tangential
TECHNICAL divaricate
⊟ similar

divers adj
varying, varied, various, different, many, numerous,
several, some, miscellaneous, sundry
FORMAL manifold, multifarious

diverse adj
various, varied, varying, sundry, all means of, different,
differing, assorted, mixed, unlike, dissimilar, contrasting,
miscellaneous, separate, several, distinct
FORMAL manifold, discrete, heterogeneous
⊟ similar, identical

diversification n
modification, alteration, extension, variation, branching-
out, spreading-out
FORMAL variegation

diversify v
vary, change, expand, extend, branch out, bring variety to,
spread out, modify, alter, mix, assort
FORMAL variegate

diversion n
1 DEVIATION, detour, alternative route, redirection,
rerouteing, switching
2 AMUSEMENT, entertainment, distraction, hobby, pastime,
recreation, relaxation, play, game, sport, fun,
divertissement
3 ALTERATION, change, redirection, deviation

diversionary adj
distracting, deflecting, divertive

diversity n
variety, dissimilarity, difference, diversification, variance,
assortment, miscellany, multifariousness, embroidery,
range, mixture, medley
TECHNICAL biodiversity
FORMAL variegation, dissimilitude, pluralism, heterogeneity
⊟ similarity, likeness

divert v
1 DEFLECT, redirect, reroute, switch, sidetrack, avert,
distract, deflect, draw/turn away
2 AMUSE, entertain, occupy, distract, delight, occupy,
interest, absorb, engross, intrigue

diverting adj
enjoyable, entertaining, amusing, fun, pleasant,

pleasurable, funny, humorous, witty
⊟ irritating

divest v
deprive, strip, remove, dispossess, undress, unclothe, disrobe
OLD doff
FORMAL denude, despoil
⊟ clothe

divide v, n
♦ v
1 SPLIT, separate, sever, part, cut (up), break up/down, detach, bisect, disconnect, detach, segregate, diverge, branch, fork
OLD cleave
2 DISTRIBUTE, share (out), allocate, deal out, allot, dispense, hand out, dole out, measure out
FORMAL apportion
3 DISUNITE, separate, alienate, segregate, split (up), break up, drive apart, come between, set someone against another, polarize
FORMAL estrange
4 CLASSIFY, group, sort (out), grade, arrange, order, rank, categorize, segregate
⊟ **1** join **2** collect **3** unite
♦ n
division, gulf, gap, opening, separation, rift, split, breach, divergence
▪ **divide up**
share (out), allocate, allot, dole out, measure out, parcel out
FORMAL apportion

dividend n
1 *shareholders' dividends*
share, bonus, portion, surplus, gain, percentage
COLLOQ. cut, divvy, whack
2 BENEFIT, bonus, extra, gain, advantage, plus
FORMAL perquisite
COLLOQ. perk

divination n
clairvoyance, divining, foretelling, prophecy, prediction, fortune-telling, dukkeripen, second sight, crystal-gazing, soothsaying, augury, -mancy, presage; *Scot* taghairm
FORMAL hariolation, prognostication, rhabdomancy
Related adjective: mantic

divine adj, n, v
♦ adj
1 GODLIKE, godly, superhuman, supernatural, mystical, celestial, heavenly, angelic, seraphic, saintly, spiritual
2 HOLY, sacred, sanctified, consecrated, spiritual, transcendent, exalted, glorious, religious, supreme
3 DELIGHTFUL, beautiful, charming, lovely, wonderful, excellent, glorious, heavenly
⊟ **1** human **2** mundane
♦ n
churchman, churchwoman, clergyman, clergywoman, minister, priest, pastor, parson, reverend, cleric, ecclesiastic, prelate, theologian
♦ v
guess, deduce, suppose, infer, surmise, suspect, understand, foretell, apprehend, perceive
FORMAL conjecture, intuit, prognosticate

divinely adv
1 *divinely inspired poetry*
heavenly, supernaturally, mystically, celestially, angelically, spiritually
2 *a divinely beautiful girl*
delightfully, charmingly, wonderfully, excellently, gloriously
⊟ **1** humanly

diviner n
clairvoyant, astrologer, augur, oracle, prophet, seer,

visionary, crystal-gazer, soothsayer, haruspex, sibyl, water-finder, dowser
OLD divinator

divinity n
1 *worship a divinity; claims to divinity*
god, goddess, deity, divineness, godliness, holiness, sanctity, godhead, spirit
2 THEOLOGY, religious studies, religious education, religious knowledge, religion

division n
1 SEPARATION, dividing (up), detaching, parting, cutting (up), disunion, severance
2 BREACH, rupture, split, schism, rift, disunion, disunity, disagreement, feud, discord, conflict, alienation, difference of opinion
FORMAL estrangement
3 DISTRIBUTION, sharing (out), allotment, allocation
FORMAL apportionment
4 SECTION, group, sector, segment, part, department, category, class, subsection, compartment, branch, arm
5 BOUNDARY, divide, dividing-line, frontier, border, partition, demarcation line
⊟ **1** union **2** unity **3** collection **4** whole

divisive adj
alienating, damaging, injurious, disruptive, troublesome, troublemaking, inharmonious, schismatic
FORMAL discordant, estranging
⊟ harmonious, unifying

divorce n, v
♦ n
dissolution, annulment, break-up, split-up, split, rupture, separation, breach, division, partition, disunion, severance
TECHNICAL talaq
OLD divorcement
♦ v
separate, part, annul, break up, split up, sever, dissolve, divide, detach, dissociate, disconnect, disunite, isolate
OLD repudiate
COLLOQ. bust up, put away
⊟ marry, unite

divulge v
reveal, disclose, make known, tell, communicate, broadcast, publish, proclaim, confess, declare, let slip, betray, expose, uncover
FORMAL impart, promulgate
COLLOQ. leak, break the news, let the cat out of the bag, spill the beans, blow the gaff, put your cards on the table

dizziness n
giddiness, faintness, light-headedness
FORMAL vertiginousness
COLLOQ. wooziness

dizzy adj
1 GIDDY, faint, light-headed, wobbly, shaky, reeling, off-balance, weak at the knees, with your head swimming
FORMAL vertiginous
COLLOQ. woozy
2 CONFUSED, bewildered, dazed, muddled; *dialect* mazy
3 *a dizzy blonde*
silly, irresponsible, foolish, feather-brained, scatterbrained
COLLOQ. rattle-brained, airheaded, addle-headed; *N Am* ditsy

do v, n
♦ v
1 PERFORM, carry out, execute, accomplish, achieve, fulfil, implement, complete, discharge, undertake, work, put on, present, produce, end, finish, put into practice
FORMAL conclude, effectuate
2 BEHAVE, act, conduct yourself, acquit yourself
FORMAL comport yourself
3 *do the tea*

prepare, get ready, fix, organize, arrange, deal with, look after, take care of, manage, be in charge of, be responsible for, produce, make, create, cause, proceed

4 Will this do?
be enough, be adequate, be sufficient, be satisfactory, fit the bill, satisfy, serve
FORMAL suffice

5 What do you do?
have as a job, work as, be employed as, earn a living as

6 do something about a problem
try to solve, deal with, work out, find the answer to, sort out, resolve, figure out, work out, tackle
COLLOQ. crack, get to the bottom of; N Am dope (out)

7 do French at school
study, learn, master, read, work at/on, take, major in

8 do deliveries for you
provide, supply, furnish, offer

9 do 150 kph
travel at, go at, reach, achieve

10 do well/badly; How are you doing?
get on, get along, come on, come along, fare, progress, develop, manage, make a good/bad job of

11 do the crossword
solve, work out, figure out, resolve, puzzle out
COLLOQ. N Am dope (out)

12 do the sitting room
clean (up), decorate, tidy (up)
COLLOQ. do up, tart up

13 do your hair
arrange, style, adjust, wash, comb, brush
COLLOQ. fix

14 do Paris
visit, tour, go round, sightsee, explore, travel round
15 CHEAT, defraud, swindle, trick, deceive, dupe, fleece, hoodwink
COLLOQ. con, have
SLANG rip off, take for a ride
♦ n
function, affair, event, gathering, party, reception, celebration, soirée, occasion
COLLOQ. bash, knees-up, rave-up

■ **do away with**
1 GET RID OF, discard, dispose of, abolish, annul, remove, eliminate
FORMAL discontinue, nullify
2 KILL, murder, put to death, finish off, slaughter, slay, exterminate, assassinate
COLLOQ. do in, knock off, bump off

■ **do down**
critcize, condemn, blame, censure, belittle, find fault with
FORMAL disparage
COLLOQ. slam, rubbish, badmouth
SLANG slag (off)

■ **do in**
kill, murder, put to death, slaughter, slay, exterminate, assassinate
COLLOQ. knock off, bump off

■ **do out of**
prevent from having, deprive of, cheat out of, trick out of, swindle out of, fleece
COLLOQ. con out of, diddle out of

■ **do up**
1 FASTEN, tie (up), lace, button, zip up, pack
2 RENOVATE, redecorate, decorate, restore, modernize, repair, refurbish, recondition

■ **do without**
go without, manage without, give up, dispense with, deny yourself, refrain
FORMAL for(e)go, eschew, abstain from, relinquish

■ **dos and don'ts**
rules, regulations, code, instructions, standards, customs, etiquette

Synonym nuances
verb sense 1
Perform, **carry out** and **execute** are fairly straightforward synonyms for seeing something through; **discharge** too could be used of successfully meeting objectives, often in an official capacity: *he discharged his duties well.*
  Accomplish suggests a successful completion, with an element of satisfaction involved. **Achieve** likewise implies reaching a successful and satisfying outcome, while **fulfil**, although similar, is more suggestive of meeting all the original goals: *he fulfilled his campaign promise.* **Implement** and **put into practice**, on the other hand, have more to do with putting something into effect: *the Act is due to be implemented fully by April.* The terms **put on** and **undertake** put the focus on setting about a task rather than its completion, and **undertake** suggests a commitment to seeing it through: *we undertook to restore the cathedral.* **Work** would be used where some kind of labour is involved: *she worked in accountancy.*
  You might choose to use **present** or **produce** if what is being done involves causing or creating: *the proposals presented difficulties; we have produced the relevant data.*

docile *adj*
tractable, co-operative, manageable, submissive, obedient, compliant, amenable, willing, controllable, controlled, obliging, yielding, dutiful
🔁 truculent, unco-operative

docilely *adv*
amenably, willingly, obediently, compliantly, obligingly, co-operatively, dutifully
🔁 unco-operatively

docility *n*
amenability, tractability, manageability, submissiveness, obedience, compliance, biddableness, meekness, pliability, pliancy
FORMAL complaisance, ductility
🔁 truculence, unco-operativeness

dock¹ *n, v*
♦ n
the ship is in dock
harbour, wharf, quay, boat yard, pier, waterfront, jetty, marina
♦ v
anchor, moor, drop anchor, land, berth, put in, tie up

dock² *v*
1 dock an animal's tail
crop, clip, cut, shorten, curtail, truncate
2 dock someone's pay
deduct, reduce, lessen, withhold, decrease, subtract, remove, diminish

docket *n, v*
♦ n
certificate, ticket, label, receipt, tab, tag, bill, chit, chitty, counterfoil, coupon, voucher, tally, document, documentation, paperwork
♦ v
label, mark, tab, tag, ticket, register, record, document, catalogue, file, index

doctor *n, v*
♦ n
physician, medical officer, consultant, clinician
OLD (*Shakesp*) medicine
COLLOQ. doc, medic
SLANG bones, sawbones, quack
♦ v
1 ALTER, tamper with, interfere with, falsify, misrepresent,

pervert, adulterate, change, disguise, dilute, massage, manipulate
COLLOQ. fiddle, cook
2 CONTAMINATE, drug, weaken, lace, add drugs/poison to, adulterate
COLLOQ. spike
3 STERILIZE, castrate, spay, neuter

Types of medical doctor include:

consultant	hospital doctor	registrar
dentist	houseman	resident
family doctor	intern	veterinary
family practitioner	locum	surgeon
general	medical officer	*colloq.* vet
practitioner (GP)	(MO)	

See also **medical specialists; surgeon.**

---

doctrinaire *adj*
dogmatic, inflexible, rigid, insistent, opinionated, pedantic, biased, fanatical
E3 flexible

doctrine *n*
dogma, creed, belief, tenet, principle, teaching, precept, conviction, opinion, canon, credo

document *n, v*
♦ *n*
paper, certificate, deed, record, proof, evidence, report, form, charter
TECHNICAL affidavit
FORMAL instrument
♦ *v*
1 RECORD, put on record, keep on record, commit to film/ paper, write down, report, write up, chronicle, list, detail, register, cite, chart
2 SUPPORT, back up, prove, verify, give weight to
FORMAL corroborate, substantiate, validate

documentary *adj*
documented, recorded, chronicled, detailed, charted, written, factual

documentation *n*
paperwork, papers, record, authority, verification, evidence, qualifications

doddering *adj*
decrepit, weak, aged, feeble, frail, infirm, elderly, tottering

doddery *adj*
unsteady, shaky, weak, faltering, doddering, tottering, tottery, staggering, feeble, infirm, aged
E3 hale, youthful

dodge *v, n*
♦ *v*
1 AVOID, elude, evade, swerve, jump away, bypass, get out of, get round, side-step, shirk, shun, shift, steer clear of, fend off, veer
COLLOQ. duck
2 MOVE SUDDENLY, duck, dive, dart, dash, rush, bolt
♦ *n*
trick, ruse, ploy, wile, scheme, stratagem, manoeuvre, device, contrivance, subterfuge, deception, sharp practice
FORMAL machination
COLLOQ. *Aust & NZ* slinter
SLANG *Aust* lurk

dodger *n*
evader, avoider, shirker, trickster, slacker, layabout, dreamer
COLLOQ. lead-swinger, skiver, slyboots, lazybones
SLANG *N Am* goldbricker, goof-off

dodgy *adj*
1 SUSPECT, doubtful, dubious, unreliable, disreputable
COLLOQ. fishy, iffy; *Aust & NZ* crook
2 CHANCY, risky, dangerous, unsafe, unreliable, uncertain, fraught, problematical
COLLOQ. dicey
E3 1 honest **2** reliable

doer *n*
achiever, activist, organizer, worker, accomplisher, executor, bustler, dynamo
COLLOQ. go-getter, live wire, powerhouse, mover and shaker
E3 thinker, contemplatist

doff *v*
take off, discard, remove, shed, throw off, lift, raise, tip, touch
E3 don

dog *n, v*
♦ *n*
1 *cats and dogs*
hound, cur, mongrel; *NZ* kuri; canine, puppy, pup, bitch
COLLOQ. mutt, pooch
SLANG *Aust* tripehound
Related adjective: canine
2 VILLAIN, scoundrel, rascal, rogue, wretch
♦ *v*
pursue, follow, trail, track, tail, hound, shadow, stalk, plague, harry, haunt, trouble, worry

---

Breeds of dog include:

Afghan hound	fox terrier	poodle
Airedale	German	pug
alsatian	Shepherd	Rottweiler
Australian terrier	golden retriever	saluki
basset-hound	Great Dane	*colloq.* sausage-
beagle	greyhound	dog
Border collie	husky	schnauzer
borzoi	Irish (or red) setter	*colloq.* Scottie
boxer	Irish wolfhound	Scottish terrier
bulldog	Jack Russell	Sealyham
bull-mastiff	Kerry Blue	setter
bull terrier	(terrier)	sheltie
cairn terrier	King Charles	shih tzu
chihuahua	spaniel	springer spaniel
chow	komondor	Staffordshire
cocker spaniel	Labrador	terrier
collie	lhasa apso	St Bernard
corgi	lurcher	terrier
dachshund	Maltese	West Highland
Dalmatian	Old English	terrier
Doberman	sheepdog	*colloq.* Westie
pinscher	Pekingese	whippet
English terrier	pit bull terrier	wolfhound
foxhound	pointer	Yorkshire terrier

---

dogged *adj*
determined, resolute, persistent, persevering, intent, tenacious, firm, steadfast, staunch, single-minded, tireless, indefatigable, steady, unshak(e)able, stubborn, obstinate, relentless, unyielding, unflagging, unfaltering
FORMAL indomitable, obdurate, pertinacious
E3 irresolute, apathetic

doggedly *adv*
resolutely, persistently, tenaciously, firmly, steadfastly, staunchly, single-mindedly, tirelessly, indefatigably, unshak(e)ably, stubbornly, obstinately, relentlessly
E3 apathetically

doggedness *n*
determination, resolution, persistence, perseverance, tenaciousness, tenacity, firmness, steadfastness, steadiness, single-mindedness, stubbornness,

obstinacy, relentlessness, endurance
FORMAL indomitability, pertinacity

dogma *n*
doctrine, creed, belief, precept, principle, code (of belief),
article (of faith), credo, tenet, conviction, teaching,
opinion, maxim

dogmatic *adj*
opinionated, assertive, affirmative, authoritative,
canonical, positive, doctrinaire, domineering, dictatorial,
doctrinal, categorical, emphatic, overbearing, arbitrary,
insistent, arrogant, imperious, intolerant, opinionated,
authoritarian, ex cathedra, unquestionable,
unchallengeable, pontifical
FORMAL peremptory

dogmatically *adv*
assertively, authoritatively, domineeringly, dictatorially,
categorically, emphatically, insistently, arrogantly,
intolerantly, imperiously

dogmatism *n*
opinionatedness, assertiveness, imperiousness,
dictatorialness, bigotry, presumption, arbitrariness,
positiveness
FORMAL peremptoriness

dogsbody *n*
gofer, drudge, slave, lackey, doormat, galley-slave, menial,
factotum, maid-of-all-work, man-of-all-work
COLLOQ. skivvy

doings *n*
activities, actions, acts, exploits, feats, achievements,
enterprises, deeds, events, goings-on, happenings,
dealings, affairs, concerns, adventures, handiwork,
proceedings, transactions

doldrums *n*
depression, dejection, downheartedness, gloom,
melancholy, listlessness, low-spiritedness, apathy,
boredom, tedium, dullness, inertia, stagnation,
sluggishness, torpor
FORMAL ennui, lassitude, malaise, acedia
COLLOQ. blues, dumps

dole *n, v*
 • *n*
benefit, Job Seekers Allowance (JSA), unemployment
benefit, state benefit, social security, allowance, payment,
income, credit, support
■ **dole out**
distribute, allocate, give out, hand out, dish out, apportion,
allot, mete out, share (out), divide (up), deal (out), issue,
ration, dispense, administer, assign
FORMAL apportion

doleful *adj*
cheerless, depressing, distressing, dismal, dreary, forlorn,
gloomy, melancholy, miserable, wretched, sad, sorrowful,
mournful, sombre, rueful, painful, pathetic, pitiful,
woeful
FORMAL dolorous, lugubrious, woebegone, disconsolate
COLLOQ. blue, down in the dumps
E3 cheerful

dolefully *adv*
gloomily, mournfully, unhappily, dismally, forlornly,
miserably, wretchedly, sadly, pathetically
FORMAL disconsolately

doll *n, v*
 • *n*
figure, puppet, marionette, plaything, toy, figurine,
moppet, dolly, Barbie®, Sindy®
■ **doll up**
dress up, preen, primp, deck out, trick out, titivate
COLLOQ. tart up; *N Am* trick up

dollop *n*
lump, blob, clump, bunch, ball, glob, gob, gobbet

dolorous *adj*
anguished, distressing, melancholy, miserable, wretched,
sad, sorrowful, doleful, grievous, harrowing, heart-
rending, painful, mournful, rueful, sombre, woeful
FORMAL lugubrious, woebegone
E3 happy

dolour *n*
anguish, distress, grief, misery, sadness, sorrow, heartache,
heartbreak, mourning, suffering, lamentation

dolt *n*
fool, idiot, imbecile, simpleton
COLLOQ. ass, blockhead, nincompoop, ninny, nitwit, numskull,
twerp, dope, chump, clot, nutcase, dope, twit, dimwit
SLANG wally, dipstick, nerd, plonker, dork, geek, git

domain *n*
1 DOMINION, kingdom, realm, territory, region, empire,
estate, lands, province
2 FIELD, area, speciality, concern, section, arena,
department, region, province, realm, sphere, world,
discipline, jurisdiction

dome *n*
cupola, vault, rotunda, tholus, mound, hemisphere
TECHNICAL astrodome, brachydome, macrodome,
tope

domestic *adj, n*
 • *adj*
1 HOME, family, household, home-loving, stay-at-home,
homely, domesticated, house-trained, tame, pet, private,
personal
FORMAL domiciliary
2 INTERNAL, indigenous, native, national, home, local
3 DOMESTICATED, tame, tamed, pet, house-trained, broken
(in)
E3 2 foreign, international, export **3** wild
 • *n*
servant, maid, charwoman, char, help, daily help, domestic
help, daily, au pair

domestically *adv*
internally, locally, at/near home, nationally, in private

domestic appliances
See panel on next page

domesticate *v*
tame, house-train, break, break in, train, accustom,
familiarize, acclimatize, naturalize, assimilate
FORMAL habituate

domesticated *adj*
1 TAME, tamed, pet, house-trained, broken (in), domestic,
naturalized
2 HOME-LOVING, homely, house-proud, housewifely,
naturalized
E3 feral, wild

domestication *n*
taming, house-training, breaking-in, training,
naturalization, assimilation
FORMAL habituation

domesticity *n*
homemaking, housecraft, homecraft, housekeeping,
home economics, domestic science, domestication

domicile *n, v*
 • *n*
home, house, residence, lodging(s), residency, mansion,
quarters, settlement
FORMAL abode, dwelling, habitation
 • *v*
make your home, live, settle, establish, take up residence,
put down roots

Domestic appliances include:

FOR CLOTHES:	cylinder cleaner	electric cooker	slow cooker	juice extractor	icebox
clothes airer	floor polisher	electric grill	spit	food slicer	freezer
iron	Hoover®	fan oven	stove	food processor	*colloq.* fridge
steam iron	upright cleaner	gas stove	toaster	kettle	fridge/freezer
steam press	vacuum cleaner	griddle	waffle iron	knife sharpener	refrigerator
trouser press	wet-and-dry	grill	FOR PREPARING	liquidizer	
tumble-drier	cleaner	hob	FOOD:	mixer	MISCELLANEOUS:
washer	FOR COOKING:	hotplate	blender	percolator	dishwasher
washing machine	Aga®	kitchen range	coffee mill	tea/coffee maker	fire extinguisher
washer/drier	barbecue	microwave oven	electric knife	timer	hostess-trolley
FOR FLOORS:	cooker	oven	electric tin	water filter	humidifier
carpet sweeper	deep fryer	rotisserie	opener	FOR COOLING:	ionizer
carpet	Dutch oven	sandwich maker	ice-cream maker	deep-freeze	
shampooer			juicer		

See also **kitchen utensils**.

dominance n
supremacy, authority, power, command, pre-eminence, superiority, control, rule, domination, sway, leadership, mastery, government
FORMAL ascendancy, hegemony, paramountcy

dominant adj
1 AUTHORITATIVE, controlling, governing, ruling, presiding, powerful, all-powerful, strong, assertive, influential
2 PRINCIPAL, main, outstanding, chief, major, key, central, important, most important, predominant, overriding, primary, paramount, prime, prominent, leading, pre-eminent, supreme, prevailing, prevalent, commanding, besetting
F≡ **1** submissive **2** subordinate

Synonym nuances
sense 2
Principal and **main**, **chief** and **major** are fairly neutral terms, whilst **outstanding** and **paramount** imply superiority: *areas of outstanding beauty*. To convey the idea of something being necessary, you could use **key** and **central**: *the banks' participation was central to this bill*.
Predominant implies enjoying a high position or great number: *the predominant life forms on the planet*. Similarly, **pre-eminent** and **supreme** imply that something has high status and is the most influential: *the world's pre-eminent expert on asbestos*. **Overriding**, however, is stronger in that it suggests having power over other elements or possibilities: *the overriding sentiment was for peace*. The term **commanding** is similar in its suggestion of a dominance that lends power or requires respect: *this win gives him a commanding lead*. **Primary** and **prime** might be used to convey the idea of coming first: *the primary cause of war*; *the prime suspect*.
Prominent is a fairly restrained term to describe something that stands out in some way, but **leading** suggests being at the forefront and showing the way. To describe a dominant force whose influence may not be permanent, you might use **prevailing** or **prevalent**; the latter also suggests being widespread: *the prevailing arbiters of taste*; *nationalism is less prevalent now*.

---

dominate v
1 CONTROL, domineer, govern, preside, rule, direct, command, monopolize, predominate, master, lead, overrule, prevail, overbear, intimidate, tyrannize
FORMAL have ascendancy over
COLLOQ. have the upper/whip hand over, have under your thumb, have over a barrel, throw your weight around, wear the trousers, have on toast
SLANG rule OK
2 OVERSHADOW, eclipse, dwarf, overlook, tower over

dominating adj
commanding, powerful, strong, superior, advantageous, dominant, controlling, directing, authoritative, assertive, confident

domination n
command, control, authority, influence, power, leadership, rule, government, sway, mastery, supremacy, superiority, despotism, dictatorship, oppression, subjection, subordination, suppression, repression, tyranny, pre-eminence, predominance
FORMAL ascendancy

domineering adj
overbearing, authoritarian, imperious, autocratic, dictatorial, despotic, masterful, high-handed, iron-handed, forceful, coercive, oppressive, tyrannical, arrogant, haughty, aggressive, pushy
FORMAL peremptory
COLLOQ. bossy
F≡ meek, servile

dominion n
1 POWER, authority, domination, command, control, rule, direction, sway, jurisdiction, government, lordship, mastery, supremacy, sovereignty
FORMAL ascendancy
2 DOMAIN, country, territory, province, colony, dependency, protectorate, realm, kingdom, empire

don v, n
♦ v
put on, get into, dress in, slip into, clothe yourself in
F≡ doff
♦ n
lecturer, teacher, tutor, academic, scholar, professor, fellow, reader

Don Juan n
ladies' man, lady-killer, womanizer, lover, Casanova, philander(er), rake, romeo, gigolo

donate v
give, give away, contribute, present, make a gift, make a donation, pledge, bequeath, subscribe
FORMAL bestow, confer
COLLOQ. cough up, fork out, chip in, club together, shell out
F≡ receive

donation n
gift, present, offering, grant, gratuity, largess(e), contribution, presentation, subscription, alms, charity, bequest
FORMAL benefaction

done adj, interj
♦ adj
1 FINISHED, over, accomplished, complete, completed, ended, settled, realized, fulfilled, executed
FORMAL concluded, terminated, consummated

2 CONVENTIONAL, acceptable, proper, right, correct, suitable, appropriate, fitting
OLD seemly
FORMAL decorous
3 COOKED, well-done, tender, ready, prepared, finished, baked, boiled, browned, fried, crisp, roasted, stewed
• *interj*
settled, agreed, accepted, arranged, decided, right, absolutely
COLLOQ. OK

■ **done for**
ruined, destroyed, finished, lost, wrecked, undone, doomed, beaten, broken, dashed, defeated, foiled
FORMAL vanquished
COLLOQ. for the high jump

■ **done in**
exhausted, tired out, worn out, weary, fatigued
COLLOQ. all in, fit to drop, bushed, dead, dead beat, dog-tired, fagged out, whacked, knackered, pooped, zonked, on your last legs, bushed, flaked out, shattered, worn to a frazzle; N Am pooped (out), tuckered out

■ **have done with**
finished with, over with, thrash with, no longer involved/ associated with
COLLOQ. over and done with

Don Juan *n*
ladies' man, lady-killer, womanizer, lover, Casanova, philander(er), rake, romeo, gigolo

donkey *n*
ass, mule, burro, hinny, jackass, jenny, jennet, neddy, Jerusalem pony; *Scot* cuddy
OLD cardophagus
COLLOQ. moke
Related adjective: asinine

donnish *adj*
academic, serious, intellectual, bookish, erudite, learned, pedantic, studious, scholarly, scholastic, formalistic, pedagogic

donor *n*
giver, donator, benefactor, backer, supporter, contributor, philanthropist, provider
COLLOQ. fairy godmother, angel
F∃ beneficiary

doom *n, v*
• *n*
1 FATE, fortune, destiny, portion, lot
2 DESTRUCTION, catastrophe, downfall, disaster, ruin, ruination, death, death-knell, rack and ruin
3 CONDEMNATION, judgement, sentence, verdict, pronouncement
OLD dome
• *v*
condemn, damn, consign, judge, sentence, decree, pronounce, predestine, fate, destine; *Scot* weird
OLD devote

doomed *adj*
condemned, damned, fated, ill-fated, star-crossed, ill-omened, cursed, destined, ruined, hopeless, unlucky, luckless, ill-starred, bedevilled; *Scot* fey

door *n*
1 *the door of the house*
opening, entrance, entry, exit, doorway, portal, hatch
2 OPPORTUNITY, open door, entrance, opening, way in, access, route, way, gateway, road

doorkeeper *n*
commissionaire, doorman, gatekeeper, usher, caretaker, janitor, porter, concierge, ostiary

dope *n, v*
• *n*

1 NARCOTIC, drugs, marijuana, cannabis, heroin, opiate, hallucinogen, barbiturate, amphetamine, crack, acid, LSD, Ecstasy
COLLOQ. grass, weed, hash, pot, speed, coke
SLANG E
2 FOOL, dolt, idiot, dunce, simpleton, buffoon, halfwit, oaf, clot
COLLOQ. half-wit, dimwit, clot, blockhead, nincompoop, ninny, nitwit, twerp, twit
SLANG plonker, dork, geek, git, prat, berk, dickhead
3 INFORMATION, facts, inside information, details, specifics, particulars
COLLOQ. low-down, info, gen
• *v*
drug, sedate, anaesthetize, stupefy, medicate, narcotize, inject, knock out, doctor
COLLOQ. spike, lace

dopey *adj*
1 SLEEPY, dozy, groggy, drowsy, nodding, lethargic, confused, muddled, dozy
FORMAL somnolent, torpid
2 STUPID, foolish, silly, daft, simple
COLLOQ. dozy, addle-brained
F∃ 1 awake, alert **2** clever, bright

dormancy *n*
inactivity, inertness, sleep, rest, slumber, hibernation, latency
F∃ activity

dormant *adj*
1 INACTIVE, asleep, sleeping, inert, resting, slumbering, sluggish, hibernating, latent, fallow
TECHNICAL comatose
FORMAL torpid, quiescent
2 LATENT, unrealized, potential, undeveloped, undisclosed
F∃ 1 active, awake **2** realized, developed

dosage *n*
dose, measure, amount, portion, quantity

dose *n, v*
• *n*
measure, dosage, amount, portion, quantity, draught, potion, prescription, shot
• *v*
medicate, administer, prescribe, dispense, treat

dossier *n*
file, folder, papers, portfolio, report, case, documents, data, information, notes

dot *n, v*
• *n*
point, spot, speck, mark, fleck, dab, circle, pin-point, atom, particle, decimal point, full stop, iota, jot
• *v*
spot, speckle, mark, scatter, pepper, sprinkle, stud, dab, stipple, punctuate

■ **on the dot**
punctually, promptly, precisely, exactly, on time, sharp

dotage *n*
old age, senility, agedness, elderliness, second childhood, infirmity, weakness, feebleness, imbecility, evening/ autumn of life
FORMAL decrepitude

dote
■ **dote on**
adore, idolize, worship, treasure, admire, love, hold dear, indulge, pamper, spoil

doting *adj*
adoring, devoted, fond, loving, affectionate, tender, soft, indulgent

dotty *adj*
crazy, eccentric, feeble-minded, peculiar, touched, weird

OLD frantic-mad, lymphatic, bestraught
COLLOQ. crazy, demented, nuts, nutty, nutty as a fruitcake, wacky, mad as a hatter, barmy, bonkers, batty, cracked, crackers, dippy, daffy, dotty, loopy, potty, off your nut, off your head, wrong in the head, out of your head, off the wall, out to lunch, round the bend, round the twist, bats, having bats in the belfry, cuckoo, off the rails, screwy, up the wall, raving, not all there; *N Am* buggy, flaky, fruity; *Aust & NZ* dingbats
SLANG loony, mental, bananas, barking, wacko, doolally, off your rocker, off your chump, off your trolley, out of your tree, needing your head examined, having lost your marbles, having a screw loose, having a tile loose, having several cards short of a full deck, with one sandwich short of a picnic, meshuga, ape, apeshit; *N Am* gonzo, loco, wiggy; *Aust* out of your tree
🔁 sensible

double *adj, v, n*
♦ *adj*
1 *double doors; a double yellow line*
dual, twofold, twice, duplicate, twin, paired, doubled, duplex, two-ply, coupled
FORMAL bifarious, binal, binate
2 AMBIGUOUS, double-meaning, double-edged, two-edged, ambivalent, equivocal, paradoxical
🔁 **1** single, half **2** unambiguous
♦ *v*
1 *double your income*
duplicate, enlarge, increase, twofold, repeat, multiply by two, fold, magnify
2 *double as someone/something*
have a second job/purpose, have a dual/second role, do/function also
3 *double for someone*
substitute, stand in, fill in, understudy, be an understudy
♦ *n*
twin, duplicate, copy, clone, replica, doppelgänger, lookalike, match, image, facsimile, counterpart, impersonator
COLLOQ. spitting image, ringer
■ **double back**
return, reverse, backtrack, circle, dodge, evade, loop, go back the way you came, retrace your steps
■ **at the double**
immediately, at once, without delay, right away, straight away, quickly, at full speed, as fast as your legs can carry you

double-cross *v*
cheat, swindle, defraud, trick, hoodwink, betray, mislead
COLLOQ. con, two-time, pull a fast one on
SLANG take for a ride

double-dealing *n*
cheating, swindling, betrayal, treachery, defrauding, tricking, hoodwinking, misleading, two-facedness, two-timing
FORMAL dissembling, duplicity, perfidy, mendacity
COLLOQ. two-timing, crookedness

double entendre *n*
double meaning, innuendo, suggestiveness, ambiguity, play on words, wordplay, pun

doubly *adv*
twice, twofold, again, especially, extra
FORMAL bis

doubt *n, v*
♦ *n*
1 DISTRUST, suspicion, mistrust, scepticism, reservation, misgiving, qualm, mixed feeling, incredulity, apprehension, hesitation, uneasiness
TECHNICAL scepsis
2 UNCERTAINTY, difficulty, confusion, ambiguity, problem,

query, question, scruple, indecision, hesitation, hesitancy, wavering, perplexity, dilemma, quandary
TECHNICAL aporia
🔁 **1** trust, confidence, faith **2** certainty, belief
♦ *v*
1 DISTRUST, mistrust, query, question, call in question, suspect, be suspicious, have misgivings/qualms about, fear, wonder
OLD misdoubt, scruple, impeach
FORMAL disbelieve
COLLOQ. take with a pinch of salt
2 BE UNCERTAIN, be dubious, hesitate, vacillate, waver, be undecided
OLD dubitate, mammer
FORMAL demur
🔁 **1** believe, trust, have confidence in **2** be certain, decide
■ **in doubt**
uncertain, undecided, doubtful, unresolved, unreliable, ambiguous, in question, open to question, questionable, open to debate, debatable, moot
COLLOQ. up in the air
■ **no doubt**
doubtless, without doubt, without a shadow of a doubt, undoubtedly, definitely, unquestionably, certainly, surely, of course, no denying, probably, most likely, presumably, in anyone's book

doubter *n*
questioner, sceptic, disbeliever, unbeliever, non-believer, agnostic, doubting Thomas, cynic, scoffer
🔁 believer

doubtful *adj*
1 *it is doubtful that he will win*
unlikely, improbable, uncertain, in doubt, open to question, debatable
COLLOQ. touch and go
2 *doubtful about his future*
uncertain, unsure, undecided, suspicious, distrustful, uneasy, apprehensive, having reservations/misgivings, irresolute, wavering, hesitant, vacillating, tentative, sceptical
COLLOQ. in two minds
3 *writing of doubtful origin*
dubious, questionable, suspect, unclear, inconclusive, ambiguous, vague, obscure, debatable
COLLOQ. fishy, shady, iffy; *Aust & NZ* crook
🔁 **1** certain **2** certain, decided, confident **3** definite, settled, trustworthy

doubtfully *adv*
hesitantly, uncertainly, uneasily, apprehensively, irresolutely, sceptically

doubtless *adv*
certainly, without doubt, without a shadow of a doubt, undoubtedly, unquestionably, indisputably, no doubt, clearly, surely, of course, truly, precisely, probably, presumably, most likely, assuredly, seemingly, supposedly, in anyone's book
FORMAL indubitably
COLLOQ. bang to rights

doughty *adj*
fearless, bold, brave, confident, courageous, daring, intrepid, valiant, heroic, gallant, plucky, dauntless, unafraid, unapprehensive, unabashed, undaunted, unflinching, lion-hearted, unblenching, unblinking
FORMAL indomitable, valorous
COLLOQ. gutsy, spunky, gritty
🔁 afraid, timid

dour *adj*
1 GLOOMY, dismal, forbidding, grim, morose, unfriendly, unsmiling, dreary, austere, sour, sullen, churlish, gruff
2 HARD, harsh, inflexible, unyielding, rigid, severe,

stern, rigorous, strict, obstinate
⊟ 1 cheerful, bright **2** easy-going

douse, dowse v
1 SOAK, pour water over, saturate, flood, deluge, steep, submerge, immerse, immerge, wet, dip, souse, duck, drench, dunk, plunge, splash
2 EXTINGUISH, put out, blow out, smother, quench, snuff

dovetail v
fit together, correspond, match, coincide, conform, agree, tally, harmonize, join, interlock, link
FORMAL accord

dowdy adj
unfashionable, ill-dressed, frumpish, drab, shabby, frowsy, dingy, old-fashioned, slovenly
COLLOQ. tatty, tacky
⊟ fashionable, smart

down¹ prep, adv, adj, v
♦ prep, adv
down the road
to a lower level/position, to the ground, to the floor, to the bottom
⊟ up
♦ adj
1 SAD, depressed, unhappy, melancholy, miserable, downhearted, dejected, downcast, dispirited, wretched, low
COLLOQ. blue, down in the dumps
2 *the computer is down*
out of order, out of action, not working, crashed
FORMAL inoperative, malfunctioning
COLLOQ. bust, kaput, on the blink, wonky; *N Am* on the fritz
SLANG conked out
⊟ 1 happy **2** working, operational
♦ v
1 KNOCK DOWN, fell, floor, bring down, prostrate, throw, topple
2 SWALLOW, consume, drink, gulp (down)
COLLOQ. swig, put away, knock back, toss of, swill
■ **down with**
get rid of, away with

down² n
quilts made of down
soft feathers, fine hair, wool, pile, shag, nap, fluff, floss, fuzz, floccus, flue, bloom
TECHNICAL pappus
Related adjectives: pappose, pappous

down-and-out adj, n
♦ adj
derelict, destitute, impoverished, on your uppers, homeless, penniless, ruined
♦ n
tramp, vagrant, vagabond, piker, *clochard*, floater, straggle, stroller; *dialect* walker; *Scot* caird, gangrel, hallan-shaker, landloper, rinthereout, (*derog*) tinkler; *N Am* hobo, down-and-outer; *Aust* sundowner
OLD cursitor, rogue, scatterling, truant, vagrom
COLLOQ. loser, knight of the road, Weary Willie; *Scot* jakey
SLANG dosser, bum, toerag; (*offensive*) gook; *N Am* dingbat

down-at-heel adj
1 ILL-DRESSED, frayed, tattered, ragged, drab, frowsy, dowdy, shabby, poor, slovenly
2 *the pub looked down-at-heel*
dingy, run-down, dilapidated, ramshackle, in disrepair, neglected, tumbledown, uncared for
COLLOQ. tatty, tacky, seedy

downbeat adj
1 RELAXED, easy-going, calm, low, downcast, informal, casual, nonchalant, unhurried, unworried
FORMAL insouciant

COLLOQ. laid-back
2 GLOOMY, pessimistic, fearing the worst, negative, depressed, low, downcast, despondent, cheerless, cynical
⊟ 1 upbeat **2** happy

downcast adj
dejected, depressed, despondent, sad, unhappy, wretched, miserable, down, low, low-spirited, disheartened, downhearted, dispirited, discouraged, disappointed, crestfallen, daunted, dismayed, glum, gloomy, dull, hanging
OLD downlooked
FORMAL disconsolate
COLLOQ. blue, fed up
⊟ cheerful, happy, elated

downfall n
fall, ruin, failure, collapse, destruction, disgrace, debasement, degradation, debacle, undoing, overthrow
⊟ rise

downgrade v
1 DEGRADE, demote, lower, humble, reduce/lower in rank, relegate, depose, deflate
FORMAL disparage, denigrate
COLLOQ. take down a peg or two, take the wind out of someone's sails
2 BELITTLE, run down, decry, minimize, defame, make light of
FORMAL disparage
COLLOQ. do down, sell short
⊟ 1 upgrade, improve **2** praise

downhearted adj
depressed, dejected, despondent, sad, downcast, disappointed, discouraged, disheartened, dispirited, low-spirited, daunted, unhappy, gloomy, glum, dismayed, disappointed
FORMAL disconsolate
⊟ cheerful, enthusiastic

down-market adj
cheap, inexpensive, low-price, low-cost, affordable, bargain, reduced, cut-price, knock-down, marked-down, discounted, rock-bottom, giveaway, throwaway, budget, economy, sale, economical, no-frills, cheap-rate, bargain-basement, shoddy, cheap and cheerful, tatty, tawdry, inferior, second-rate, worthless, common, ramshackle, poor, cheapjack
COLLOQ. cheapo, tacky
⊟ up-market

downpour n
cloudburst, deluge, rainstorm, flood, inundation, torrent

downright adv, adj
♦ adv
absolutely, plainly, utterly, clearly, completely, totally, thoroughly, positively, simply, categorically
♦ adj
outright, complete, total, out-and-out, absolute, plain, utter, clear, sheer, thorough, wholesale, categorical, unqualified, unequivocal

downsize v
reduce, make smaller, contract, shrink, slim, minimize, moderate, diminish
⊟ increase

downside n
disadvantage, drawback, snag, liability, impediment, limitation, inconvenience, flaw, defect, nuisance, weakness, weak point, trouble, penalty
COLLOQ. minus, spanner in the works, fly in the ointment, weak link in the chain, chink in your armour, Achilles heel
⊟ advantage, benefit, asset

down-to-earth adj
commonsense, commonsensical, hard-headed, matter-

of-fact, mundane, no-nonsense, plain-spoken, practical, realistic, sane, sensible, unsentimental, idealistic
Ⅎ fantastic, impractical

downtrodden *adj*
oppressed, subservient, exploited, trampled on, weighed-down, burdened, overwhelmed, abused, tyrannized, bullied, victimized, helpless, powerless
FORMAL subjugated

downward *adj*
descending, declining, going/moving down, downhill, sliding, slipping
Ⅎ upward

downy *adj*
soft, feathery, fine, smooth, velvety, woolly, fluffy, fleecy, fuzzy
FORMAL pappose, pappous

dowry *n*
1 MARRIAGE SETTLEMENT, marriage portion, inheritance, legacy, portion, provision, share, wedding-dower, dot, endowment; *Scot* tocher
2 FACULTY, gift, talent

doxology *n*
hymn/song of praise, praise, hymn, psalm, song, chant, anthem, response, chorale, recessional, gloria, glorification

doze *v, n*
♦ *v*
sleep, nap, catnap, take a nap, drift off, go off, drop off
COLLOQ. snooze, kip, nod off
SLANG zizz
♦ *n*
nap, catnap, siesta
COLLOQ. snooze, forty winks, kip, shut-eye
SLANG zizz
■ **doze off**
fall asleep, drift off, catnap
COLLOQ. nod off, snooze, have forty winks

dozy *adj*
1 DROWSY, sleepy, tired, weary, nodding, dreamy, yawning, half-asleep, dopey
FORMAL somnolent, torpid
2 STUPID, foolish, silly, daft, simple
COLLOQ. dopey
Ⅎ 1 awake, alert **2** clever, bright

drab *adj*
dull, dingy, dreary, dismal, gloomy, flat, grey, colourless, lacklustre, cheerless, lifeless, sombre, shabby, featureless, tedious, boring, uninteresting
Ⅎ bright, cheerful, lively

drabness *n*
dullness, dinginess, dreariness, gloom, sombreness, greyness, shabbiness, colourlessness, cheerlessness, lifelessness
Ⅎ cheerfulness

Draconian *adj*
harsh, severe, cruel, strict, iron-handed, iron-fisted, abrasive, stern, grim, savage, brutal, unsympathetic, unfeeling, hard, inhuman, pitiless, ruthless, merciless

draft *n, v*
♦ *n*
1 OUTLINE, sketch, rough sketch, plan, abstract, rough, preliminary version, drawing, blueprint
FORMAL delineation, protocol
2 *a bank draft*
bill of exchange, cheque, money order, letter of credit, postal order
♦ *v*
draw (up), outline, sketch, plan, design, formulate, compose
FORMAL delineate

drag *v, n*
♦ *v*
1 DRAW, pull, haul, lug, tug, trail, tow, yank
2 GO SLOWLY, creep, crawl, lag, become boring/tedious, wear on, go on and on, go on for ever
♦ *n*
bore, annoyance, nuisance, bother, pest, trouble
COLLOQ. pain, pain in the neck, bind, headache
■ **drag on**
go on, run on, continue, persist, be lengthy, be long-drawn-out
■ **drag out**
spin out, prolong, draw out, extend, hang on, lengthen, persist
FORMAL protract
■ **drag up**
rake up, remind, bring up, raise, mention, introduce, revive

dragoon *v*
coerce, compel, constrain, drive, force, pressure, pressurize, harass, impel, intimidate, browbeat, bully
COLLOQ. strongarm

drain *v, n*
♦ *v*
1 EMPTY, remove, evacuate, draw off, pump off, extract, withdraw, strain, dry, milk, bleed, tap, sap, sponge, tile, ladle, leach, leech, sluice, buzz, dewater, ditch, quaff, underdrain; *dialect* sew; *Scot* pour
TECHNICAL exsanguinate, pot, unwater
OLD emulge
FORMAL void
2 *waste draining into the stream*
trickle, flow out, discharge, seep out, leak, ooze
FORMAL exude, effuse
3 EXHAUST, consume, sap, use up, drink up, suck, swallow, strain, tax, bleed, bleed dry, bleed white
FORMAL deplete
Ⅎ 1 fill
♦ *n*
1 CHANNEL, conduit, culvert, duct, outlet, trench, ditch, outlet, pipe, sink, gutter, sluice, sewer, gully, delf, fleet, grip, nulla, sough; *Scot* cundy, sheuch, stank, syver
TECHNICAL cunette, piscina
OLD common-shore
2 *a drain on resources*
exhaustion, consumption, sap, strain, tax
OLD lickpenny
FORMAL depletion

drama *n*
1 PLAY, acting, theatre, show, piece, spectacle, stagecraft, scene, comedy, melodrama, tragedy, dramatics, dramaturgy
2 EXCITEMENT, thrill, sensation, crisis, dilemma, tension, turmoil, histrionics

dramatic *adj*
1 *a dramatic change*
striking, sudden, marked, significant, substantial, considerable, abrupt, noticeable, distinct
2 EXCITING, striking, stirring, thrilling, tense, spectacular, vivid, graphic, sensational, expressive, effective, impressive, unexpected
3 HISTRIONIC, theatrical, exaggerated, melodramatic, flamboyant, artificial
4 *dramatic art*
theatrical, stage, Thespian

dramatically *adv*
1 SUDDENLY, abruptly, significantly, substantially, considerably, noticeably
2 SPECTACULARLY, vividly, impressively, expressively, strikingly

dramatist *n*
playwright, writer, scriptwriter, play-writer, screen writer, comedian, dramaturge, dramaturgist, tragedian

dramatization n
staging, adaptation, presentation, arrangement

dramatize v
1 STAGE, put on, adapt, present as a play/film, arrange for
2 EXAGGERATE, play-act, act, overdo, overstate
COLLOQ. ham (up), lay it on thick, blow up out of all proportion, make a big thing of

drape v
hang, cover, wrap, envelop, overlay, shroud, cloak, veil, arrange, decorate, adorn, fold, drop, droop, suspend

drapery n
cloth, covering(s), curtain(s), hanging(s), blind(s), arras, backdrop, tapestry, valance

drastic adj
extreme, radical, strong, serious, forceful, severe, harsh, rigorous, far-reaching, desperate, dire, Draconian
E3 moderate, cautious

drastically adv
greatly, severely, seriously, rigorously, extremely, strongly, radically, forcefully
E3 moderately

draught n
1 PUFF, breath, current, flow, rush, movement
FORMAL influx
2 DRINK, gulp, swallow, swig, quantity, cup, potion
3 PULLING, dragging, drawing, traction

draw v, n
♦ v
1 *draw a picture*
sketch, portray, trace, pencil, paint, represent, map out, depict, design, chart, scribble, doodle
FORMAL delineate
2 *the procession drew nearer*
move, go, proceed, progress, travel, walk, drive, come, approach, advance
3 PULL, drag, haul, tow, tug, lug, trail
4 *draw a knife*
take out, pull out, bring out, produce, extract, remove, withdraw
5 *draw water from a well*
extract, drain, remove, withdraw, pump, suck, siphon, tap, milk
6 *draw a breath*
breathe in
FORMAL inhale, respire, inspire
7 *draw money from a bank*
take, get, receive, obtain
FORMAL procure
8 *draw attention to something*
attract, allure, lure, entice, bring in, influence, persuade, elicit, prompt
9 *draw a conclusion*
conclude, deduce, infer, gather, come to, reason
10 *draw lots*
pick, choose, select, decide on, go for
COLLOQ. plump for
11 TIE, be equal, be even
COLLOQ. be all square
E3 3 push 8 repel
♦ n
1 ATTRACTION, enticement, lure, allure, appeal, bait, interest, magnetism
2 RAFFLE, lottery, sweepstake, sweep, tombola
3 TIE, stalemate, dead heat
■ **draw back**
recoil, wince, flinch, shrink, start back, withdraw, retract, retreat
■ **draw on**
make use of, use, put to use, call on, exploit, apply, employ, quarry, rely on, have recourse to
FORMAL utilize

■ **draw out**
1 *the train drew out of the station*
pull out, move out, set out, depart, leave, start
2 EXTEND, prolong, lengthen, spin out, drag out, elongate, stretch
FORMAL protract
3 *draw someone out*
encourage to talk, induce to talk/speak, put at ease, make feel less nervous, make
E3 2 shorten
■ **draw up**
1 DRAFT, compose, formulate, prepare, frame, write out, put in writing
2 PULL UP, stop, halt, run in

drawback n
disadvantage, snag, hitch, obstacle, hurdle, barrier, impediment, hindrance, difficulty, problem, flaw, fault, catch, stumbling-block, nuisance, trouble, defect, weak spot, handicap, deficiency, liability, limitation, imperfection, damper, discouragement
COLLOQ. fly in the ointment
E3 advantage, benefit

drawing n
sketch, picture, outline, representation, portrayal, illustration, cartoon, graphic, portrait, composition, depiction, diagram, study
FORMAL delineation

drawl v
speak/say slowly, draw out your vowels, drone, haw-haw, protract, twang

drawn adj
tired, fatigued, worn, haggard, gaunt, pinched, strained, stressed, taut, tense, fraught, harassed, sapped, washed out
COLLOQ. hassled

dread v, n, adj
♦ v
fear, shrink from, quail, cringe at, flinch, shy, shudder, tremble, be afraid of, be scared of, be terrified by, be frightened (to death) by, be anxious/worried about
COLLOQ. get cold feet about
E3 look forward to
♦ n
fear, apprehension, misgiving, dismay, alarm, horror, terror, fright, fit of terror, blind panic, cold sweat, hair standing on end, disquiet, worry, qualm
FORMAL trepidation, perturbation
COLLOQ. (blue) funk
E3 confidence, security
♦ adj
dreaded, feared, frightening, frightful, terrifying, terrible, dreadful, awful, awe-inspiring, alarming, ghastly, grisly, gruesome, horrible, dire

dreadful adj
awful, terrible, frightful, horrible, appalling, dire, shocking, outrageous, frightening, terrifying, alarming, ghastly, horrendous, horrific, grim, tragic, grievous, hideous, unpleasant, nasty
FORMAL heinous
E3 wonderful, comforting

dreadfully adv
1 *I'm dreadfully sorry*
awfully, terribly, frightfully, very, extremely, exceedingly
2 *suffer dreadfully*
appallingly, shockingly, horrendously, awfully, terribly, atrociously

dream n, v, adj
♦ n
1 VISION, illusion, reverie, trance, fantasy, daydream, nightmare, hallucination, delusion, imagination, phantasmagoria, phantom

OLD sweven; *Irish* aisling
Related adjectives: oneiric, somnial
2 ASPIRATION, ambition, wish, hope, desire, yearning, ideal, goal, design, aim, plan, speculation, expectation, castles in the air
3 DAYDREAM, fantasy, reverie, pipe dream, inattention; *Scot* dwam
4 *their new house is a dream*
ideal, beauty, perfection, joy, delight, marvel
♦ *v*
1 *dream during sleep*
imagine, envisage, fantasize, fancy, hallucinate
FORMAL somniate
2 DAYDREAM, fantasize, imagine, muse, fancy, be lost in space, not pay attention, let your thoughts wander, stare into space
COLLOQ. switch off
3 *dream of becoming a doctor*
want very much, long, desire, yearn, crave
♦ *adj*
perfect, ideal, model, supreme, superb, excellent, wonderful
▪ **dream up**
invent, devise, conceive, think up, conjure up, imagine, concoct, hatch, create, fabricate, spin, contrive
▪ **not dream of**
not think, not imagine, not consider, not conceive

Synonym nuances
noun sense 1
Vision may be used where things are envisaged in the future: *the government's vision for the inner cities*, whilst **illusion** suggests a deceptive conception or appearance, with the implication that it can never become real: *the illusion of success*. To state this idea explicitly, you might choose the term **delusion**: *to think you can beat him is a dangerous delusion*.
 The term **reverie**, however, is more appropriate for succumbing to an undirected train of thoughts, and the connotations are pleasant ones: *he drifted into a momentary reverie*. **Trance**, although similar, has more to do with absence of thought and is used of a hypnotic state that has been induced.
 The term **fantasy** could be used negatively to suggest either a misguided belief: *it is fantasy to believe this bill can be implemented*, or, more positively, of an idyllic mental projection: *we all enjoy an escapist fantasy*; whilst **daydream** likewise implies conjuring up an ideal scenario, and has pleasant connotations.
 Nightmare, conversely, can only refer to something really unpleasant, dreamed while asleep or dreaded when awake: *meeting her was his worst nightmare*. The terms **hallucination**, **delusion** and **phantom** also have unpleasant associations and again suggest something deceptive which your mind may unconsciously produce, sometimes through illness or drugs: *the ghastly phantoms of his delirious brain*, whereas **imagination** is more positive in its suggestion of conscious creativity. **Phantasmagoria** is restricted to an incredible series of unreal images or real forms: *it was a phantasmagoria of horror and mystery combined*.

---

dreamer *n*
idealist, visionary, fantasist, fantasizer, romancer, daydreamer, stargazer, theorizer, romantic, Utopian
F3 realist, pragmatist

dreamily *adv*
gently, softly, peacefully, pleasantly, romantically

dreamlike *adj*
surreal, illusory, unreal, trance-like, hallucinatory, insubstantial, unsubstantial, visionary, chimerical, fantastic, phantom, phantasmagoric, phantasmagorical, Alice-in-Wonderland
FORMAL ethereal

dreamy *adj*
1 FANTASTIC, unreal, imaginary, shadowy, unclear, indistinct, vague, misty, hazy, faint, ethereal, dim
2 DAYDREAMING, fanciful, fantasizing, romantic, idealistic, impractical, visionary, faraway, absent, musing, pensive, thoughtful, absent-minded, preoccupied, abstracted
COLLOQ. with your head in the clouds
3 *dreamy music*
relaxing, soothing, lulling, calming, gentle, soft, romantic
F3 **1** real, clear **2** practical, down-to-earth

drearily *adv*
depressingly, dismally, boringly, tediously, routinely, monstrously

dreary *adj*
gloomy, depressing, drab, dismal, bleak, sombre, cheerless, sad, mournful, overcast, dark, boring, tedious, uninteresting, uneventful, dull, humdrum, routine, monotonous, unvaried, wearisome, commonplace, colourless, lifeless, featureless, run-of-the-mill
F3 cheerful, interesting

dredge
▪ **dredge up**
dig up, discover, uncover, unearth, raise, drag up, draw up, fish up, rake up, scoop up

dregs *n*
1 SEDIMENT, deposit, residue, lees, grounds, scourings, scum, dross, trash, waste, tailings, excrement, faeces
TECHNICAL precipitate, sublimate, bottoms, draff, dunder, fecula, greaves, mother, taplash
OLD lags
FORMAL residuum, detritus
COLLOQ. ullage
2 OUTCASTS, rabble, riff-raff, scum, down-and-outs, tramps, vagrants, *faex populi*
OLD legge
SLANG dossers

drench *v*
soak, soak to the skin, saturate, steep, wet, douse, souse, immerse, inundate, duck, flood, swamp, imbue, drown, permeate

dress *n, v*
♦ *n*
1 FROCK, gown, robe
2 CLOTHES, clothing, garment(s), outfit, costume, ensemble, garb
FORMAL attire, apparel, habiliment
COLLOQ. clobber, get-up, gear, togs
Related adjective: sartorial
♦ *v*
1 CLOTHE, put on, get into, slip into, garb, rig, robe, wear, don, decorate, deck (out), garnish, trim, adorn, turn out, fit (out), drape
FORMAL attire, array, accoutre
COLLOQ. throw on
2 *dress your hair*
arrange, adjust, dispose, prepare, groom, style, straighten, tidy, comb, do, primp, preen
3 BANDAGE, bind up, put a plaster on, clean, cover, tend, treat, swathe
4 *dress meat*
clean, prepare, get ready
F3 **1** strip, undress
▪ **dress down**
1 DRESS CASUALLY, dress informally
2 REBUKE, reprimand, reprove, scold, chide
FORMAL berate, castigate, upbraid
COLLOQ. carpet, haul over the coals, tear off a strip, tell off, give someone an earful
▪ **dress up**
1 DRESS SMARTLY, dress formally

COLLOQ. doll up
2 BEAUTIFY, improve, adorn, decorate, ornament, embellish, deck, gild, disguise
COLLOQ. tart up, jazz up

Synonym nuances
verb sense 1
The phrase **slip into** suggests easy, unobtrusive movements: *he slipped into his dressing gown*. The terms **garb** and **rig** put the emphasis on the garments you are dressing in, with the suggestion they are formal or in some way untypical: *garbed in funereal black; a cavalry regiment rigged in green and gold*. **Robe** is similar, but is most appropriately used of official vestments: *the fully robed civic dignitaries*. **Drape** also puts the emphasis on the clothing, but would be used of garments which hang loosely: *draped in a loose shawl*.
To use **don** puts the emphasis back on the actual act of dressing, and suggests a very conscious act of putting on particular garments: *we donned our rain gear*. You may use **decorate** and **adorn** if you want to suggest the addition of something fancy: *a beautiful ring adorned her finger*, whilst you could use **deck** (**out**) to imply a slightly ludicrous effect: *decked out in a cowboy hat*.
Both **garnish** and **trim** return to the idea of adding something decorative but perhaps with the suggestion it is unnecessary. The term **turn out** may be used to emphasize the manner in which you present yourself and the impression it will give: *ensure that you're well turned out for the inspection*, whilst **fit out**, which also has connotations of formal or elegant dress, emphasizes the way someone organizes your attire: *he had been fitted out in a very handsome silk suit*.

---

dressing *n*
1 *a salad dressing*
sauce, condiment, relish, jus, coulis
2 BANDAGE, plaster, Elastoplast®, Band-aid®, gauze, lint, compress, poultice, tourniquet, pad, spica, ligature

dressmaker *n*
tailor, tailoress, couturier, modiste, needlewoman, garment-maker, seamstress, sewing woman, midinette

dressy *adj*
elegant, formal, smart, stylish, smart, elaborate, ornate
COLLOQ. classy, natty, ritzy, swish
F∃ dowdy, scruffy

dribble *v, n*
♦ *v*
1 TRICKLE, drip, leak, run, seep, drop, ooze
FORMAL exude
2 DROOL, slaver, slobber, drivel, foam, froth
♦ *n*
1 DRIP, trickle, droplet, leak, seepage, sprinkling
2 SALIVA, drool, spit, drivel, slaver, slobber, foam, froth

dried *adj*
arid, dehydrated, desiccated, drained, parched, wilted, withered, wizened, shrivelled, mummified
FORMAL exsiccated

drift *v, n*
♦ *v*
1 WANDER, waft, stray, float, freewheel, coast, go with the stream, be carried along, roam, rove, crab, sag, wisp
OLD hull, rack
2 GATHER, accumulate, pile up, heap up, bank, drive, amass
♦ *n*
1 ACCUMULATION, mound, pile, bank, mass, heap, wreath
2 SHIFT, movement, trend, tendency, course, direction, flow, stream, current, variation, digression, rush, sweep
3 MEANING, intention, implication, gist, vein, tenor, thrust, course, direction, trend, tendency, significance, essence,

core, substance, aim, point, design, scope
FORMAL import, purport

drifter *n*
wanderer, traveller, nomad, vagrant, itinerant, rover, tramp, vagabond, rolling stone, swagman, beachcomber; *N Am* hobo

drill *n, v*
♦ *n*
1 BORER, awl, bit, gimlet
2 INSTRUCTION, training, practice, coaching, grounding, exercise, repetition, tuition, preparation, discipline, indoctrination, procedure, routine
FORMAL inculcation
♦ *v*
1 TEACH, train, instruct, coach, practise, school, rehearse, exercise, discipline, ground, put someone through their paces
FORMAL inculcate
2 BORE, pierce, make a hole in, penetrate, puncture, perforate, prick, punch

drink *v, n*
♦ *v*
1 IMBIBE, swallow, have, sip, drain, down, gulp, sup, quaff, absorb, guzzle, swill
FORMAL partake of
COLLOQ. swig, down, knock back, throw back
2 GET DRUNK, have one too many, have (a drop) too much, overdrink, indulge, carouse, revel, be a hard drinker, be a heavy drinker, have a drink problem
COLLOQ. tipple, tank up, have one over the eight, drink like a fish; *Aust* grog on; hit the bottle, knock back a few, polish off
SLANG booze, lush, get pissed; *Aust* go on the shout
3 *drink someone's health*
drink to, toast, propose a toast to, salute, wish someone success
♦ *n*
1 BEVERAGE, liquid, brew, infusion, soft drink, cold drink, hot drink, thirst-quencher, refreshment, draught, sip, swallow, gulp
COLLOQ. swig; *Scot* swally
2 ALCOHOL, strong drink, spirits, liquor
OLD (*Shakesp*) tickle-brain
COLLOQ. tipple, the bottle, stiffener, hard stuff, hoo(t)ch, Dutch courage, firewater, the creature, jar, tipple, tiddly, tinct, sauce; *Aust & NZ* grog
SLANG booze, jungle juice, gnat's piss, rotgut; *N Am* juice; *Aust & NZ* shicker
■ **drink in**
absorb, take in, digest, realize, appreciate, grasp

Synonym nuances
verb sense 1
Imbibe is generally used to imply that alcohol has been consumed: *flushed with the Scotch he'd imbibed*.
Swallow emphasizes the act of moving food or drink down the throat, and like **down**, **gulp**, **knock back** and **throw back** it suggests drinking hastily and possibly greedily: *he downed half his wine in one gulp*. **Sip** is, by contrast, descriptive of drinking in small delicate mouthfuls, whilst **drain** suggests a more deliberate movement, trying to get the most out of your last mouthful: *she drained the last of her coffee*.
The less common **sup** and **quaff** are old-fashioned terms which are quite literary in tone, and which may also be used to describe the manner of drinking, with **sup** having connotations of relish and enjoyment, and **quaff** suggesting a faster, zealous action: *he quaffed pint after pint*. Both **guzzle** and **swill** return to the idea of greedily consuming copious amounts of drink: *champagne was guzzled like lemonade; they swilled gin in the afternoon*.

Non-alcoholic drinks include:

beef tea	Coca Cola®	sarsaparilla
julep	*colloq.* Coke®	squash
mint-julep	cordial	**MIXERS**:
tisane	cream soda	bitter lemon
MILKY DRINKS:	fizzy drink	Canada Dry®
cocoa	fruit juice	ginger ale
float	ginger beer	soda (water)
hot chocolate	Irn-Bru®	tonic (water)
Horlicks®	lemonade	**WATER**:
Ovaltine®	limeade	mineral water
milk	Lucozade®	Perrier®
milk shake	orangeade	seltzer
smoothie	Pepsi®	sparkling water
SOFT DRINKS:	*colloq.* pop	still water
Aqua Libra®	Ribena®	Vichy water
barley water	root beer	
cherryade		

See also **coffee; tea**.

Alcoholic drinks include:

BEER AND LAGER:	grog	ginger wine
ale	hot toddy	hock
beer	Irish coffee	Marsala
black-and-tan	ouzo	*colloq.* plonk
Guinness®	peach schnapps	port
lager	Pimm's®	red wine
porter	pink gin	retsina
shandy	poteen	sangria
snakebite	rum	sherry
stout	rye	*colloq.* vino
SPIRITS:	sake	vin blanc
aquavit	schnapps	vin rouge
Armagnac	Scotch	vin rosé
bourbon	Scotch and soda	white wine
brandy	sloe gin	Wincarnis®
Calvados	tequila	**MISCELLANEOUS**:
Campari	vermouth	alcopop
Cognac	vodka	cider
eggnog	whisky	*N Am*
gin	**WINE**:	malternative
gin-and-tonic	*colloq.* bubbly	mead
G&T	champagne	perry
grappa		

See also **beer; cocktails; liqueur; wine**.

---

drinkable *adj*
clean, safe, fit to drink, potable

drinker *n*
hard/serious drinker, heavy drinker, drunk, drunkard, inebriate, dipsomaniac, imbiber
COLLOQ. tippler
SLANG boozer, wino, lush, alkie, dipso, soak, piss artist, toper, tosspot, sot, sponge
E∃ abstainer, teetotaller

drip *v, n*
◆ *v*
drop, dribble, trickle, leak, ooze, plop, drizzle, splash, sprinkle, weep, filter, percolate
◆ *n*
1 DROP, trickle, dribble, leak, splash, plop, bead, tear
2 WEAKLING, bore
COLLOQ. wimp, softy, wet, weed, pansy, sissy, ninny

drive *v, n*
◆ *v*
1 STEER, ride, travel (by car), go/come (by car), motor, be behind/at the wheel, be at the controls, pilot, operate
2 TRANSPORT, take, convey, carry, move, send, run, chauffeur, give a lift to
3 PROPEL, impel, direct, power, control, manage, operate, run, handle, hurl, press, thrust

4 FORCE, compel, impel, coerce, constrain, press, move, push, urge, spur, prod, herd, round up, dragoon, goad, guide, oblige, leave someone with no choice/option
5 MOTIVATE, force, compel, pressure, pressurize, impel, lead, prompt, actuate, incite, provoke, persuade, move, spur
6 STRIKE, hammer, screw, knock, thump, dash, dig, sink, ram, thrust, plunge
7 OVERBURDEN, overwork, tax, overtax, work too hard, overdo it, exert yourself too much, burden
COLLOQ. kill yourself
◆ *n*
1 EXCURSION, outing, journey, ride, run, trip, jaunt
COLLOQ. spin, turn
2 AVENUE, driveway, road, roadway, approach
3 ENERGY, enterprise, ambition, initiative, vigour, verve, motivation, determination, will, resolve, push, spirit, effort, action
FORMAL tenacity
COLLOQ. get-up-and-go, pizazz, vim, zip
4 CAMPAIGN, crusade, appeal, effort, action, movement, fight, struggle, battle
COLLOQ. push
5 POWER, thrust, surge, pressure, propulsion, transmission, propeller shaft
6 URGE, instinct, impulse, pressure, need, desire, appetite
■ **drive at**
imply, allude to, intimate, mean, suggest, hint, have in mind, intend, refer to, signify, insinuate, indicate, aim at
COLLOQ. get at

drivel *n*
nonsense, rubbish, gibberish, gobbledygook, garbage
OLD balderdash
COLLOQ. bunkum, mumbo-jumbo, waffle, rot, baloney, blah, eyewash, hogwash, rhubarb, guff, hooey, malarkey, poppycock, tripe, hogwash, claptrap, twaddle
SLANG bull; (*vulgar*) crap, bullshit, balls, bollocks

driver *n*
motorist, motorcyclist, rider, chauffeur, cabbie, trucker

driving *adj*
compelling, forceful, vigorous, dynamic, energetic, forthright, heavy, violent, sweeping

drizzle *n, v*
◆ *n*
mist, mizzle, (light/fine) rain, spray, shower, mizzle; *dialect* skiffle; *Scot* smur
◆ *v*
1 *it's drizzling*
spit, spray, sprinkle, rain (lightly/finely), spot, shower, mizzle; *Scot* scouther, smur
2 TRICKLE, dribble, pour, sprinkle, drip, drop

droll *adj*
bizarre, odd, queer, eccentric, peculiar, comical, amusing, humorous, ridiculous, laughable, ludicrous, funny, clownish, zany, farcical, waggish, whimsical, witty, comic, diverting, entertaining, jocular
FORMAL risible

drone *v, n*
◆ *v*
1 HUM, buzz, purr, thrum, vibrate, whirr, drawl, chant, bombilate, bombinate
2 *the lecturer droned on and on*
go on and on, speak interminably, talk monotonously, intone
◆ *n*
1 HUM, buzz, purr, thrum, vibration, whirr, whirring, murmuring, chant
2 LAZY PERSON, idler, loafer, slacker, dreamer, layabout, parasite, leech, hanger-on
COLLOQ. lazybones, sponger, scrounger
SLANG *N Am* goldbricker, goof-off

drool *v*
1 DRIBBLE, slobber, salivate, drivel, salivate, slaver, water at the mouth
2 *drool over the new baby*
dote, enthuse, gloat, gush, slobber over

droop *v*
1 HANG DOWN, dangle, sag, bend, wilt, weep, stoop, bow, nod, fall down, sink, drop, slump, slouch
TECHNICAL nutate
OLD slink; (*Shakesp*) lob
2 LANGUISH, decline, flag, falter, slump, lose heart, wilt, wither, drop, faint, fall down, fade, slouch, peak
F3 1 straighten 2 flourish, rise

droopy *adj*
drooping, limp, floppy, falling, dropping, sagging, saggy, slack, loose, lax, weak, feeble

drop *v, n*
♦ *v*
1 FALL, sink, decline, plunge, plummet, tumble, dive, descend, droop
2 LET FALL, let go (of), lower
3 DRIP, trickle, leak, dribble, plop
4 LOWER, decrease, lessen, weaken, diminish, decline, dwindle, slacken off, plummet, plunge, sink
5 ABANDON, give up, desert, reject, finish (with), jilt, disown, walk out on
FORMAL forsake, relinquish, repudiate, renounce
COLLOQ. chuck, ditch, run out on, throw over
6 END, stop, cease, finish, leave out, miss out, omit, exclude
FORMAL dispense with, discontinue, terminate, for(e)go, relinquish, repudiate, renounce
COLLOQ. quit
7 *drop me at the corner*
take, bring, deliver, carry, put off, transport
8 DISMISS, discharge, make redundant
COLLOQ. sack, fire, turf out, boot out
SLANG *N Am* can
F3 1 rise
♦ *n*
1 DROPLET, bead, tear, drip, bubble, blob, globule, trickle
FORMAL goutte, globulet, spheroid, gutta
2 LITTLE, mouthful, sprinkle, bit, pinch, sip, nip, tot, trace, dab, splash; *N Am* tad
FORMAL modicum
COLLOQ. dash, spot, smidgen
3 DESCENT, fall, precipice, cliff, slope, chasm, abyss, plunge
FORMAL declivity
4 DECLINE, falling-off, fall-off, lowering, downturn, decrease, reduction, cutback, slump, plunge, depreciation, devaluation, deterioration
5 *chocolate drops*
sweet, bonbon, candy, pastille, lozenge
COLLOQ. sweetie

■ **drop back**
fall behind, lag (behind), fall back
FORMAL retreat

■ **drop in**
call (round), call by, come over, come round, visit, come by
COLLOQ. pop in

■ **drop off**
1 FALL ASLEEP, drift off, doze (off), go off, catnap
COLLOQ. nod off, snooze, have forty winks
2 DECLINE, fall off, decrease, dwindle, lessen diminish, slacken off, plummet, plunge, sink
3 DELIVER, set down, deposit, unload, hand in
F3 1 wake up 2 increase

■ **drop out**
withdraw, leave, give up, abandon
FORMAL renounce, forsake
COLLOQ. back out, cry off, quit

■ **drop out of**
back out of, withdraw from, leave, opt out, pull out, abandon
FORMAL renounce, renege
COLLOQ. cry off from, quit

dropout *n*
nonconformist, rebel, Bohemian, dissenter, hippie, beatnik, loner, deviant
FORMAL dissentient, malcontent, renegade

droppings *n*
excrement, dung, manure, ordure, spraint
TECHNICAL excreta, stools
FORMAL egesta, faeces

dross *n*
rubbish, remains, refuse, trash, waste, scum, debris, dregs, impurity, lees, slag, slack, junk
TECHNICAL scoria
FORMAL recrement

drought *n*
dryness, aridity, parchedness, dehydration, shortage, want, drouth
FORMAL desiccation

drove *n*
herd, horde, gathering, crowd, multitude, swarm, throng, flock, pack, host, company, mob, press, crush

drown *v*
1 *she drowned in the canal*
go under, suffocate in water, die, perish, go, founder, lose your life
OLD drench
COLLOQ. go to Davy Jones's locker
2 SUBMERGE, immerse, inundate, flood, sink, deluge, engulf, drench
3 *the end of her speech was drowned by applause*
drown out, silence, overwhelm, overpower, overcome, swamp, wipe out, howl out
OLD outvoice

drowsily *adv*
sleepily, wearily, lethargically, sluggishly, dopily, dozily

drowsiness *n*
sleepiness, tiredness, weariness, lethargy, sluggishness, dopiness, doziness
FORMAL oscitancy, somnolence, torpor
COLLOQ. grogginess

drowsy *adj*
sleepy, tired, weary, lethargic, nodding, dreamy, dozing, dozy, dopey, yawning, half-asleep, hardly able to keep your eyes open
FORMAL somnolent, torpid
F3 alert, awake

drubbing *n*
defeat, beating, flogging, pounding, pummelling, trouncing, walloping, whipping, hammering
COLLOQ. clobbering, licking, thrashing

drudge *n, v*
♦ *n*
toiler, menial, hack, labourer, toiler, servant, slave, factotum, worker, galley-slave, lackey
COLLOQ. dogsbody, skivvy
♦ *v*
plod, toil, work, slave, labour
COLLOQ. plug away, grind, beaver, slog away, keep your nose to the grindstone, work your fingers to the bone
F3 idle, laze

drudgery *n*
labour, menial work, hackwork, slavery, sweat, sweated labour, toil, skivvying, chore
COLLOQ. donkey-work, slog, grind

Drugs include:

slang acid	chloroquin(e)	heroin	neomycin	salbutamol
allopurinol	cocaine	hydrocortisone	opium	*slang* smack
amoxycillin	codeine	ibuprofen	paracetamol	*slang* speed
amphetamine	cortisone	insulin	penicillin	tamoxifen
amyl nitrate	*slang* crack	ipecacuanha	propranolol	temazepam
aspirin	diazepam	laudanum	Prozac®	tetracycline
cannabis	digitalis	LSD	quinine	Valium®
chlorambucil	*colloq.* dope	marijuana	ranitidine	Viagra®
chloramphenicol	*colloq.* ecstasy (or E)	methadon(e)	Ritalin®	warfarin
chloroform	heparin	morphine	Rophynol	

drug *n, v*

♦ *n*

medication, medicine, remedy, potion, cure

♦ *v*

medicate, sedate, tranquillize, anaesthetize, make unconscious, dose, stupefy, deaden, numb, shanghai
COLLOQ. dope, knock out

Types of drug include:

ace-inhibitor	bronchiodilator	opiate
anaesthetic	corticosteroid	sedative
analgesic	*slang* downer	statin
antacid	hallucinogenic	steroid
antibacterial	immuno-	stimulant
antibiotic	suppressant	sulphonamide
antidepressant	interferon	tranquillizer
antihistamine	narcotic	*slang* upper
barbiturate	NSAISD (non-	vasoconstrictor
beta-blocker	steroidal anti-	vasodilator
bronchio-	inflammatory	
constrictor	drug)	

See also **medicine**.

drug addict *n*

COLLOQ. junkie, druggie, user, dope-fiend
SLANG freak, head, coke-head, tripper, mainliner, hop-head, hype, snowbird

drugged *adj*

stupefied
TECHNICAL comatose
COLLOQ. knocked out, high, spaced out, turned on, doped, zonked, on a trip
SLANG stoned, ripped, wasted

drum *v*

beat, pulsate, tap, throb, thrum, tattoo, reverberate, rap, knock

■ **drum into**

din into, drive home, hammer, harp on, instil, reiterate, inculcate

■ **drum out**

expel, discharge, dismiss
COLLOQ. throw out

■ **drum up**

obtain, round up, collect, gather, summon, solicit, canvass, petition, attract, get

drunk *adj, n*

♦ *adj*

under the influence, drunken, inebriated, intoxicated, incapable, tipsy, mellow, merry, foxed; *dialect* fairish; *Scot* capernoity, fou; *Scot & Irish* stotious; *N Am* jagged
OLD overseen; (*Shakesp*) fap, paid
FORMAL crapulent, ebriose
COLLOQ. a sheet in the wind, three sheets in/to the wind, tight, tiddly, tiddled, well-oiled, blotto, drunk as a lord/newt, drunk as a piper, drunk as a skunk, sloshed, stewed, blind drunk, roaring drunk, the worse for drink, soused, squiffy, happy, legless, hammered, plastered, sozzled, pickled, bibulous, woozy, one over the eight, under the table, bevvied, having had a few, tired and emotional, high, footless, full, half-cut, obfuscated, pickled, pie-eyed, sow-drunk, under the weather, the worse for wear
OLD COLLOQ. corked, moppy, overshot
SLANG stoned, tanked up, loaded, lit up, canned, paralytic, smashed, pissed, bombed, wasted, wrecked, trashed, mashed, stinko, whiffled, whistled, bonkers, bottled, Brahms and Liszt, juiced (up), in liquor, liquored, maggoty, mortal, up the pole, ripped; (*vulgar*) arseholed, rat-arsed, shitfaced; *Scot* blootered; *N Am* crocked, moon-eyed; *Aust* inky, inked; *Aust & NZ* shickered
F3 sober, temperate, abstinent, teetotal

♦ *n*

drunkard, alcoholic, inebriate, drinker, hard drinker, heavy drinker, dipsomaniac
COLLOQ. tippler
SLANG boozer, wino, lush, alkie, dipso, soak, piss artist, pisshead, toper, sot, tosspot, sponge; *Aust & NZ* shicker

---

Synonym nuances

adjective

The term **under the influence** has legal connotations, but could also be used facetiously: *he claimed he was in no way 'under the influence'.* **Drunken**, however, implies a propensity to overindulge in alcohol generally: *his violent drunken father*, whereas **incapable**, although slightly euphemistic, would be used if someone is drunk to such an extent that they are rendered helpless on a particular occasion: *he was in this incapable state most afternoons.*

  Terms such as **mellow** and **merry**, on the other hand, are less judgemental, even positive, terms for someone in a relaxed or happy state induced by alcohol, though they too can often be used jocularly: *you seem particularly mellow tonight!* **Tipsy** similarly carries no tone of disapproval, and is reserved for mild drunkenness, sometimes with connotations of mischievousness: *mum is a bit tipsy and talking too much.* The term **foxed** is not often used nowadays, superseded by the abundance of colloquialisms coined, but conveys the impression of drunken confusion.

---

drunkard *n*

drunk, alcoholic, inebriate, drinker, hard drinker, heavy drinker, dipsomaniac, wine-bibber, bloater, fuddler, habitual; *N Am* souse
COLLOQ. tippler
SLANG boozer, wino, lush, alkie, dipso, soak, piss artist, pisshead, toper, sot, tosspot, sponge; *Aust & NZ* shicker

drunken *adj*

1 DRUNK
FORMAL inebriate, intoxicated, crapulent
COLLOQ. merry, tight, tipsy, tiddly, sloshed, happy
SLANG boozy, stoned, loaded, lit up, pissed, bombed
2 *a drunken party*
debauched, dissipated, riotous, intemperate, baccanalian
FORMAL crapulent
F3 1 sober

drunkenness n
intemperance, alcoholism, hard/serious drinking,
debauchery, dipsomania
TECHNICAL methysis
FORMAL inebriation, inebriety, insobriety, intoxication,
crapulence, ebriety, ebriosity, temulence
COLLOQ. bibulousness, tipsiness
Ⅰ sobriety

dry adj, v
♦ adj
1 ARID, parched, baked, scorched, thirsty, dehydrated,
barren, unwatered, waterless, rainless, moistureless, torrid,
shrivelled, withered, wilted
TECHNICAL xeric
FORMAL desiccated
COLLOQ. dry as a bone
2 THIRSTY, dehydrated
COLLOQ. parched, gasping
3 TEETOTAL, abstinent, prohibitionist, temperate, alcohol-
free, abstemious
COLLOQ. on the wagon
4 BORING, dull, dreary, tedious, monotonous, uninteresting,
unexciting, wearisome, flat
COLLOQ. dry as dust
5 *dry humour*
witty, ironic, subtle, cynical, droll, clever, deadpan,
sarcastic, cutting, low-key, laconic
Ⅰ 1 wet, damp **4** interesting, imaginative
♦ v
make/become dry, dehydrate, parch, scorch, drain, wipe,
shrivel, wither, wilt
FORMAL desiccate
Ⅰ soak, wet
■ **dry up**
1 FAIL, stop being productive, come to an end, disappear,
stop, dwindle, wane, fade, die out
2 STOP TALKING, forget your lines, shut up, someone's mind
goes blank

dryness n
aridity, aridness, drought, barrenness, dehydration, thirst,
thirstiness
Ⅰ wetness

dual adj
double, twofold, duplicate, duplex, binary, combined,
paired, coupled, twin, two-piece, matched

duality n
doubleness, duplication, duplicity, combination,
polarization, opposition, separation

dub v
name, call, entitle, confer, designate, label, nickname,
style, tag, term, christen
FORMAL bestow

dubiety n
doubt, doubtfulness, indecision, uncertainty, misgiving,
scepticism, suspicion, mistrust, qualm, hesitation
FORMAL incertitude
Ⅰ certainty

dubious adj
1 DOUBTFUL, uncertain, undecided, unsure, wavering,
vacillating, unsettled, suspicious, sceptical, hesitant,
irresolute
2 QUESTIONABLE, debatable, unreliable, untrustworthy,
ambiguous, suspect, suspicious, obscure
COLLOQ. fishy, shady, iffy, shifty; *Aust & NZ* crook
Ⅰ 1 certain **2** trustworthy

dubiously adv
1 *dubiously legal*
questionably, debatably, ambiguously, suspiciously
2 *she eyed the caller dubiously*
uncertainly, undecidedly, suspiciously, hesitantly

duck v
1 CROUCH, stoop, bob, bend, bow down, drop, squat
2 AVOID, evade, shirk, shun, sidestep, steer clear of, elude,
dodge
COLLOQ. wriggle out of, worm your way out of, skive
3 DIP, immerse, plunge, dunk, dive, submerge, douse,
souse, wet, lower

duct n
pipe, tube, channel, conduit, passage, vessel, canal,
funnel, wireway
TECHNICAL deferent, diffuser, emunctory, excretory, ureter,
vas, Venturi
FORMAL fistula

ductile adj
amenable, biddable, flexible, plastic, malleable,
manageable, pliable, pliant, tractable, manipulable,
yielding
FORMAL compliant
Ⅰ intractable; *formal* refractory

dud n, adj
♦ n
failure, flop, disappointment, let-down
COLLOQ. washout
♦ adj
broken, faulty, failed, valueless, worthless
FORMAL inoperative, nugatory
COLLOQ. bust, duff, kaput
SLANG conked out
Ⅰ working

due adj, adv, n
♦ adj
1 OWED, owing, payable, unpaid, outstanding, in arrears
2 RIGHTFUL, right, fitting, appropriate, proper, earned,
merited, deserved, justified, suitable, correct
3 ADEQUATE, enough, sufficient, ample, plenty of
FORMAL requisite
4 EXPECTED, scheduled, anticipated, awaited, long-awaited,
required
Ⅰ 1 paid **3** inadequate
♦ adv
exactly, direct(ly), precisely, straight
COLLOQ. dead
♦ n
1 *give him his due*
rights, (just) deserts, merits, prerogative, privilege,
birthright
COLLOQ. comeuppance
2 *pay dues*
charge(s), contribution, fee, membership fee, levy,
subscription
■ **due to**
owing to, as a result of, caused by, because of

duel n
affair of honour, *affaire d'honneur*, combat, contest, fight,
clash, struggle, battle, competition, rivalry, engagement,
encounter, tilt
OLD dependence, duello
FORMAL monomachy

duff adj
bad, poor-quality, poor, inferior, inadequate, weak,
mediocre, substandard, imperfect, faulty, defective,
deficient, unsatisfactory, unacceptable, second-rate,
third-rate, hopeless, incompetent, mismanaged,
ineffective
COLLOQ. awful, terrible, botched, lousy, crummy,
pathetic, ropy, useless, a load of rubbish, a load of
garbage
SLANG the pits, pants, poxy, naff, crappy

duffer n
bungler, blunderer, fool, idiot, ignoramus, oaf

COLLOQ. bonehead, clod, clot, dolt, dimwit, halfwit
SLANG plonker, dork, geek, git, prat

dulcet adj

sweet, sweet-sounding, gentle, pleasant, melodious, harmonious, mellow, soothing, soft, agreeable
FORMAL mellifluous

dull adj, v

◆ adj

1 BORING, uninteresting, unexciting, flat, dreary, monotonous, stereotyped, tedious, tiresome, wearisome, stultifying, uneventful, humdrum, unimaginative, pedestrian, dismal, lifeless, plain, bland, insipid, heavy, ponderous
COLLOQ. dull as ditchwater
2 DARK, sombre, gloomy, drab, dreary, murky, indistinct, grey, dark, cloudy, lacklustre, matt, opaque, dim, overcast
3 UNINTELLIGENT, dense, dim, stupid, slow
COLLOQ. dimwitted, thick, dumb, birdbrained, dopey, dozy, slow on the uptake
4 *dull weather*
overcast, grey, cloudy, dim, dark, leaden, dreary, sombre, gloomy
5 *feel dull*
sluggish, slow, inactive, inert, idle, heavy, lethargic, slack
FORMAL torpid
6 *a dull pain*
weak, faint, mild, troublesome, uncomfortable, distressing
7 *a dull sound/thud*
muted, indistinct, weak, soft, quiet, feeble, muffled
8 BLUNT, unsharpened, edgeless
⊟ 1 interesting, exciting, lively **2** bright **3** intelligent, clever **4** fine, sunny **5** lively, energetic **6** sharp, intense, acute **7** sharp, loud **8** sharp

◆ v

1 BLUNT, alleviate, moderate, lessen, reduce, decrease, diminish, relieve, soften, allay, assuage, tone down
FORMAL mitigate
2 DEADEN, numb, paralyse, stupefy, drug, tranquillize, desensitize
OLD (*Shakesp*) mull
3 DISCOURAGE, dampen, subdue, lower, sadden, dishearten, depress, deject
4 DIM, obscure, darken, blacken, fade, wash out

dullard n

idiot, imbecile, ignoramus, moron, oaf, simpleton, dunce
COLLOQ. blockhead, bonehead, chump, clod, clot, dumbo, dimwit, dolt, dope, dunderhead, nitwit, numskull; *N Am* bufflehead
SLANG plonker, dork, git, prat
⊟ brain

dullness n

dreariness, emptiness, flatness, dryness, plainness, monotony, slowness, tedium, sluggishness
FORMAL torpor, vacuity, vapidity
⊟ excitement, interest, sharpness, brightness, clarity

duly adv

accordingly, appropriately, correctly, fitly, fittingly, properly, rightfully, suitably, sure enough, deservedly
FORMAL befittingly, decorously

dumb adj

1 *deaf and dumb*
silent, mute, soundless, speechless, tongue-tied, inarticulate, without speech, at a loss for words, lost for words
COLLOQ. mum
SLANG shtoom
2 STUPID, unintelligent, foolish, dense
COLLOQ. dim-witted, thick, brainless, gormless, dopey, dozy, as thick as two short planks

dumbfound v

astonish, surprise, startle, amaze, astound, stun, stupefy, daze, stagger, take aback, take your breath away, shock, confound, bewilder
COLLOQ. floor, flabbergast, flummox, bowl over, gobsmack, blow your mind, knock for six, wow

dumbfounded adj

astonished, amazed, astounded, overwhelmed, speechless, taken aback, startled, stunned, overcome, confounded, lost for words, staggered, confused, baffled, bewildered, dumb, nonplussed, paralysed
COLLOQ. thrown, flabbergasted, bowled over, floored, gobsmacked, knocked for six

dumbly adv

silently, mutely, soundlessly, speechlessly, inarticulately

dumbstruck adj

speechless, dumbfounded, thunderstruck, amazed, astounded, shocked, aghast, tongue-tied, inarticulate, mute, dumb, silent, mum
FORMAL obmutescent
⊟ talkative

dummy n, adj

◆ n

1 COPY, duplicate, imitation, mock-up, counterfeit, substitute, representation, reproduction, sample
2 MODEL, lay-figure, mannequin, figure, form
3 TEAT, pacifier
4 IDIOT, imbecile, fool, oaf
COLLOQ. blockhead, chump, clot, dimwit, numskull, nitwit; *N Am* bufflehead
SLANG plonker, dork, git, prat

◆ adj

1 ARTIFICIAL, fake, imitation, false, bogus, mock, sham
FORMAL feigned
COLLOQ. phoney
2 *a dummy run*
simulated, practice, trial

dump v, n

◆ v

1 DEPOSIT, put down, set down, lay down, place, drop, offload, throw down, let fall, fling down, unload, empty out, tip out, discharge, pour out, park
COLLOQ. plonk, bung
2 GET RID OF, discard, scrap, throw away, throw out, dispose of, ditch, tip, jettison
COLLOQ. chuck away
3 *he dumped his girlfriend*
leave, abandon, walk out on, desert, jilt
FORMAL forsake
COLLOQ. ditch, chuck, give the elbow/heave-ho to

◆ n

1 RUBBISH TIP, junkyard, rubbish heap, tip, scrapyard; *Scot* midden
2 HOVEL, slum, shack, shanty, mess
COLLOQ. hole, joint, tip, pigsty; *N Am* pigpen
■ **down in the dumps**
sad, depressed, unhappy, melancholy, miserable, downhearted, dejected, downcast, dispirited, low
COLLOQ. blue

dumpy adj

short, plump, stout, chubby, chunky, podgy, pudgy, squab, squat, stubby, tubby
⊟ tall

dun adj

greyish-brown, dull, dingy, mud-coloured, mouse-coloured

dunce n

fool, idiot, imbecile, dullard, loggerhead
COLLOQ. blockhead, bonehead, nincompoop, ninny, nitwit, numskull, twerp, twit, dimwit; *N Am* bufflehead
SLANG wally, dipstick, nerd, plonker, dork, git, prat
⊟ brain, intellectual

dung *n*
excrement, animal waste, droppings, manure, ordure, spraint, dirt, muck, mulch, soil, turd, *album Graecum*, argol, chip, buffalo chips, buttons, cock, guano, scumber, spraints; *dialect* tath; *Scot* sharn
OLD fumets, fewmets; (*Shakesp*) shard, siege
FORMAL faeces
COLLOQ. cack, doo-doo
SLANG dreck

dungeon *n*
cell, prison, jail, gaol, cage, lock-up, keep, oubliette, vault

dupe *v, n*
♦ *v*
deceive, delude, fool, trick, outwit, cheat, hoax, swindle, take in, hoodwink, defraud
COLLOQ. con, bamboozle, diddle, lead up the garden path, pull the wool over someone's eyes
SLANG rip off, take to the cleaners; *N Am* goldbrick
♦ *n*
victim, fool, gull, pawn, puppet, instrument, simpleton
COLLOQ. sucker, mug, pushover, fall guy, stooge

duplicate *v, adj, n*
♦ *v*
copy, reproduce, repeat, do again, photocopy, Xerox®, Photostat®, fax, facsimile, double, clone, echo
FORMAL replicate
♦ *adj*
identical, matching, twin, twofold, corresponding, paired, matched
♦ *n*
copy, replica, reproduction, model, photocopy, Xerox®, Photostat®, carbon (copy), match, mate, facsimile, fax, double, twin, clone, imitation, forgery
COLLOQ. lookalike, (dead) ringer, spitting image

duplication *n*
repetition, copy(ing), photocopy(ing), reproduction, doubling, clone, cloning
FORMAL dittography, gemination, replication

duplicity *n*
deceit, deceitfulness, deception, dishonesty, falsehood, fraud, guile, hypocrisy, double-dealing, treachery, betrayal, artifice, chicanery
FORMAL dissimulation, mendacity, perfidy

durability *n*
permanence, imperishability, persistence, stability, strength, endurance, constancy, lastingness
FORMAL durableness, longevity
E3 fragility, impermanence, weakness

durable *adj*
lasting, enduring, long-lasting, abiding, hard-wearing, heavy-duty, reinforced, strong, solid, sturdy, tough, robust, unchanging, unfading, substantial, sound, reliable, dependable, stable, resistant, persistent, persisting, constant, permanent, firm, fixed, fast
E3 changeable, perishable, weak, fragile

duration *n*
time, time span, time scale, extent, continuation, continuance, perpetuation, prolongation, fullness, length, length of time, period, span, spell, stretch, term
E3 shortening

duress *n*
constraint, coercion, compulsion, pressure, restraint, threat, force, enforcement, exaction
COLLOQ. arm-twisting

during *conj*
at/in the time of, for the time of, in, throughout, in the course of, all the while

dusk *n*
twilight, sunset, nightfall, evening, sundown, darkness, dark, gloom, shadows, shade
OLD gloaming, owl-light
FORMAL crepuscule
E3 dawn, brightness

dusky *adj*
1 SHADOWY, dark, dim, gloomy, murky, cloudy, foggy, misty, hazy, twilit
FORMAL crepuscular, tenebrous, fuliginous, subfusc
2 DARK-SKINNED, dark-coloured, dark-complexioned, swarthy, tawny, black, brown
E3 1 bright **2** white

dust *n, v*
♦ *n*
powder, particles, dirt, earth, soil, ground, clay, grit, grime, soot, ashes, smut, smoke, smother, coom, culm, fallout, fuzz, mote, pother; *Scot* stour; *Aust* bulldust
TECHNICAL cryoconite, haemoconia, lemel, limail, bort, meteor streams, micro-meteorite, stardust, pozzolana
♦ *v*
1 CLEAN, wipe, brush, mop, burnish, polish, spray
2 SPRINKLE, powder, scatter, cover, spread, seed
OLD bedust

dust-up *n*
conflict, disagreement, quarrel, argument, disturbance, encounter, fight, fracas, brawl, brush, commotion, scuffle, skirmish, tussle
COLLOQ. argy-bargy, punch-up, bust-up, scrap, set-to, barney

dusty *adj*
1 DIRTY, grubby, grimy, filthy, dust-covered, sooty
2 POWDERY, granular, crumbly, chalky, sandy
FORMAL friable
E3 1 clean **2** solid, hard

dutiful *adj*
obedient, respectful, conscientious, devoted, filial, reverential, deferential, compliant, submissive, thoughtful, considerate

duty *n*
1 OBLIGATION, responsibility, burden, onus, assignment, calling, charge, part, role, task, job, chore, business, function, work, office, service, commission, mission, requirement
2 OBEDIENCE, respect, loyalty, allegiance, faithfulness
FORMAL fidelity
3 TAX, toll, tariff, levy, customs, excise, dues
■ **off duty**
not working, on holiday, off, off work, free, resting, inactive
■ **on duty**
at work, working, on call, engaged, busy, occupied, active
COLLOQ. tied up

Synonym nuances
sense 1
Obligation is often used of something legally or morally binding: *journalists have an obligation to protect their sources*, whilst **responsibility** and **charge** have the added implication of being accountable for something: *the manager has responsibility for the computer system; he handed the project over to their charge*. **Burden**, however, would only be appropriate of a duty that is cumbersome, as would **onus**.

For a particular, allocated duty the terms **task** or **job**, or the more specific **assignment** or **commission**, could be used: *his commission was to review teaching methods*. The term **mission** likewise suggests being assigned a specific, and highly important, purpose: *the unit's mission was to prevent any nation from mounting an attack*. **Chore** further implies a set duty that is unpleasant or tedious: *my daily household chores tire me out*.

Both **business** and **work** emphasize the aspect of labour and refer to a more continuous duty, similarly **function**, which suggests a specific purpose that is peculiar to an office or job: *the proper function of government is to manage things well*.

dwarf n, adj, v
♦ n
1 PERSON OF RESTRICTED GROWTH, midget, pygmy, Tom Thumb, Lilliputian
2 GNOME, goblin
♦ adj
miniature, little, small, tiny, pocket, diminutive, minute, petite, Lilliputian, baby, pygmy, stunted, undersized
COLLOQ. mini
₣ large
♦ v
1 STUNT, retard, check, arrest, atrophy
2 OVERSHADOW, tower over, dominate
COLLOQ. stand head and shoulders above

dwell v
live, inhabit, stay, settle, populate, people, lodge, rest
OLD (Shakesp) remain
FORMAL reside, abide, be domiciled
COLLOQ. hang out
■ **dwell on**
brood on, think about, meditate on, turn over in your mind, reflect on, mull over, harp on, linger over, elaborate, emphasize
FORMAL expatiate, ruminate on
₣ pass over

dweller n
inhabitant, occupant, occupier, resident
FORMAL denizen

dwelling n
home, house, establishment, residence, place, quarters, flat, apartment, tenement, penthouse, pied-à-terre; Scot single-end, weem; S Afr pondok; dwelling-house, lodge, lodging, cottage, hut, shanty, bothy, tent, roof, hovel, doghole, dug
TECHNICAL messuage
OLD bower, cot, won; (Spenser) grange
FORMAL abode, domicile, habitation

dwindle v
diminish, decrease, decline, reduce, become/grow less, lessen, subside, ebb, fade, weaken, taper off, tail off, shrink, fall, wane, peter out, waste away, die out, wither, shrivel, vanish, disappear
₣ increase, grow

dye n, v
♦ n
colour, colouring, agent, stain, wash, pigment, tint, shade, hue, tinge
♦ v
colour, tint, stain, shade, pigment, tinge, imbue
Related adjective: tinctorial

dyed-in-the-wool adj
entrenched, inveterate, deep-rooted, diehard, established, long-standing, settled, fixed, hard-core, hardened, inflexible, unchangeable, uncompromising, unshak(e)able, through and through, thorough, confirmed, complete, card-carrying
₣ superficial

dying adj
1 a dying woman
close/near to death, not long for this world, at death's door, on your deathbed, passing, going, mortal, perishing, failing, fading, vanishing, ebbing
FORMAL moribund
COLLOQ. with one foot in the grave, on your last legs
2 the dying moments of the match
last, final, closing, concluding, finishing
₣ 1 reviving

dynamic adj
forceful, powerful, active, strong, energetic, full of energy, vigorous, high-powered, driving, go-ahead, effective, self-starting, spirited, vital, lively, potent
COLLOQ. go-getting
₣ inactive, apathetic

dynamically adv
forcefully, powerfully, actively, strongly, energetically, vigorously, effectively, vitally
₣ inactively

dynamism n
energy, forcefulness, drive, initiative, liveliness, vigour, spirit, enterprise
COLLOQ. get-up-and-go, go, pep, pizzazz, push, vim, zap, zip
₣ apathy, inactivity, slowness

dynasty n
house, line, lineage, succession, dominion, regime, government, authority, rule, jurisdiction, empire, sovereignty

dyspepsia n
dyspepsy, heartburn, cardialgia, acidity, pyrosis, water-brash

dyspeptic adj
bad-tempered, irritable, gloomy, indigested, peevish, short-tempered, snappish, testy, touchy
COLLOQ. stroppy, in a huff, in a sulk, having got out of bed on the wrong side, having a short fuse, cross as a bear with a sore head, crotchety, crabbed, crabby, grouchy, shirty, ratty, edgy, feisty, humpy

E

each *adj, pron, adv*
- *adj*
every, every single, every individual
- *pron*
each one, each in their own way, each and every one
- *adv*
apiece, individually, per capita, per head, per person, respectively, separately, singly

eager *adj*
1 ENTHUSIASTIC, keen, fervent, intent, earnest, wholehearted, zealous, impatient, avid, ardent, diligent; *Scot* frack; *N Am* gung-ho
OLD fain, rath; (*Shakesp*) prone
SLANG up for it
2 LONGING, yearning, anxious, impatient, keen, intent, wishing, greedy, thirsty, hungry
COLLOQ. desperate, dying
E3 1 unenthusiastic, indifferent, reluctant

eagerly *adv*
keenly, enthusiastically, fervently, intently, earnestly, wholeheartedly, impatiently, ardently, avidly, zealously, greedily
E3 apathetically, listlessly

eagerness *n*
keenness, enthusiasm, fervency, fervour, intentness, earnestness, wholeheartedness, impatience, ardour, avidity, impetuosity, zeal, longing, yearning, greediness, hunger, thirst
FORMAL fervidity
COLLOQ. yen
E3 apathy, disinterest

ear *n*
1 *deaf in his right ear*
earhole; *dialect* souse
TECHNICAL auricle
COLLOQ. lug
SLANG shell-like, lughole
Related adjectives: aural, auricular, otic
2 ATTENTION, heed, notice, regard, attentiveness
3 *an ear for language*
perception, sensitivity, discrimination, appreciation, hearing, skill, ability, taste
- **play it by ear**
ad-lib, extemporize, improvise
COLLOQ. wing it, take things as they come, think on your feet

---

Parts of the ear include:

anvil (incus)	hammer	semicircular canal
auditory canal	(malleus)	stirrup (stapes)
auditory nerve	helix	tragus
auricle	labyrinth	tympanum
cochlea	lobe	vestibular nerve
concha	oval window	vestibule
eardrum	pinna	
eustachian tube	round window	

---

early *adj, adv*
- *adj*
1 *early symptoms/stages*
forward, advanced, advance, premature, untimely, undeveloped, precocious, first, initial, opening
2 *early theatre*
primitive, ancient
TECHNICAL autochthonous
FORMAL prim(a)eval, primordial
E3 1 late **2** modern, contemporary
- *adv*
1 *early in the day*
in the (early) morning, at dawn, at daybreak
2 AHEAD OF TIME, ahead of schedule, in good time, beforehand, before the usual/arranged/expected time, with time to spare, in advance, too soon, prematurely
E3 1 late

earmark *v*
set aside, put aside, lay aside, designate, allocate, keep back, reserve, label, mark out, tag

earn *v*
1 *earn a good salary*
receive, be/get paid, obtain, make, get, draw, clear, gain, realize, gross, net, collect, pocket, take home, reap
COLLOQ. bring in, pull in, rake in
2 *earn your reputation*
deserve, merit, be owed, be someone's by right, warrant, win, rate, obtain, secure, attain, achieve
E3 1 spend, lose

earnest¹ *adj*
1 SERIOUS, sincere, solemn, grave, heartfelt, intense, dedicated, committed, thoughtful, zealous, devout
OLD sad, dear
FORMAL assiduous
2 RESOLUTE, devoted, ardent, conscientious, diligent, intent, keen, fervent, firm, fixed, eager, enthusiastic, steady, persistent, urgent
OLD forward, wistful
E3 1 frivolous, flippant **2** apathetic
- **in earnest**
1 SERIOUSLY, resolutely, ardently, conscientiously, intently, steadily, wholeheartedly, passionately, purposefully, zealously
2 SINCERE, genuine, serious, not joking
E3 2 in jest, as a joke

earnest² *n*
the earnest of heavenly gifts
deposit, down payment, guarantee, pledge, token, security, assurance, determination, promise, resolution, seriousness, sincerity, truth
OLD arles, earnest-penny, press-money

earnestly *adv*
seriously, sincerely, intently, resolutely, firmly, keenly, eagerly, fervently, warmly, zealously
E3 flippantly, listlessly

earnestness *n*
seriousness, sincerity, gravity, purposefulness, resolution, intentness, determination, ardour, devotion, eagerness,

enthusiasm, fervency, fervour, zeal, keenness, passion, vehemence, warmth
F3 apathy, flippancy

earnings *n*
pay, income, salary, wages, profits, take home pay, net pay, gross pay, gain, proceeds, reward, receipts, return, revenue, fee, remuneration, honorarium, stipend
FORMAL emolument
F3 expenditure, outgoings

earth *n*
1 WORLD, planet, globe, sphere, orb
Related adjectives: terrestrial, telluric
2 LAND, ground, soil, topsoil, turf, clay, loam, sod, humus, dirt

earthenware *n*
pottery, ceramics, crockery, stoneware, pots

earthly *adj*
1 *our earthly life*
material, physical, human, worldly, mortal, mundane, fleshly, secular, sensual, materialistic, profane, temporal
FORMAL terrestrial, tellurian, telluric
2 *no earthly explanation*
possible, likely, imaginable, conceivable, slightest, feasible
F3 1 spiritual, heavenly

Synonym nuances
sense 1
Material suggests having a physical substance, and is often used as the opposite of spiritual: *our material needs*; **physical** has more to do with matters of the body: *physical pain*. **Human** is suggestive of mankind, and tends to be used in speaking of its limitations: *human nature*. **Worldly**, on the other hand, while it can be used literally of being of this world: *this is a worldly paradise*, can also be used to imply a preoccupation with material aspects: *a worldly, go-ahead, businessman*.

The term **mortal**, with its suggestion of eventual and inevitable death, is again suggestive of limitations: *no mortal man could have travelled this far*. The word **temporal** may also be used to suggest the finite nature of things: *the king rules over the Church as well as his temporal kingdom*. **Mundane** returns to the idea of being of this world: *mundane and this-worldly considerations*; however, it is more often suggestive of ordinariness: *the mundane aspects of working life*. The term **fleshly** again puts the emphasis firmly on the body and the idea of being corporeal.

You may use **secular** without any implication if you are referring to something that is not concerned with religion; **profane**, though similar in meaning, further suggests irreverence or blasphemy: *the deep gulf between sacred and profane*. **Sensual**, meanwhile, emphasizes the senses as distinct from the mind: *I take sensual pleasure in the natural world*. **Materialistic**, which is a fairly disapproving term, describes being overly concerned with material goods.

---

earthquake *n*
earth-tremor, tremor, quake, seism, shake, upheaval, convulsion, shock, aftershock
Related adjectives: seismic, seismal, terremotive

earthy *adj*
1 *an earthy smell*
soillike, earthlike, claylike, dirtlike
2 DOWN TO EARTH, natural, simple, direct, unsophisticated, unrefined, uninhibited
3 *earthy humour*
crude, coarse, rude, vulgar, bawdy, rough, ribald
FORMAL indecorous
COLLOQ. raunchy, blue
F3 2 inhibited **3** proper, modest

ease *n, v*
♦ *n*
1 EFFORTLESSNESS, facility, skilfulness, deftness, adroitness, dexterity, naturalness, cleverness
2 COMFORT, contentment, enjoyment, peace, peacefulness, affluence, prosperity, wealth, leisure, relaxation, rest, quiet, happiness, lap of luxury
FORMAL repose, opulence
COLLOQ. bed of roses, easy street, life of Riley
F3 1 difficulty **2** discomfort
♦ *v*
1 *ease the pain*
alleviate, moderate, grow/become less, lessen, reduce, diminish, lighten, relieve, relent, allay, assuage, relax, comfort, calm, soothe, facilitate, smooth, quieten, salve
FORMAL mitigate, abate, ameliorate, palliate
2 *ease it into position*
inch, steer, edge, slide, manoeuvre, guide
F3 1 aggravate, intensify, worsen

■ **ease off**
decrease, become less, die away, die down, diminish, moderate, relent, slacken, subside, wane
FORMAL abate
F3 increase

■ **at ease**
relaxed, natural, composed, calm, secure, at home, comfortable

easily *adv*
1 EFFORTLESSLY, comfortably, readily, simply, fluently, straightforwardly
2 *easily the best*
by far, undoubtedly, without doubt, indisputably, definitely, certainly, doubtlessly, clearly, far and away, undeniably, simply, surely, probably, well
F3 1 laboriously

easy *adj*
1 SIMPLE, effortless, uncomplicated, undemanding, straightforward, foolproof, manageable, painless, natural
COLLOQ. cushy, a cinch, a doddle, a piece of cake, a pushover, a cakewalk, a walk in the park, easy as ABC, easy-peasy, easy as pie, child's play, like falling off a log, not rocket science
SLANG (*vulgar*) a piece of piss
2 RELAXED, carefree, easy-going, comfortable, informal, calm, natural, leisurely, casual, unforced
COLLOQ. laid-back
F3 1 difficult, hard, demanding, exacting **2** tense, uneasy

---

Synonym nuances
sense 1
Simple a fairly positive word that can be used, as it often is in advertising, to play down potential difficulty: *a simple task; simple to use; a simple mistake*. **Effortless** makes the appealing suggestion of requiring little exertion, while **painless** also has to do with causing minimum upset: *a painless solution to council overspending*.

Natural could be used of something that is easy because it is instinctive, so implying that it requires little or no thought: *French life proceeds at its natural, inviting pace*. The terms **uncomplicated** and **straightforward** again convey the positive idea of something that may be easily followed, without any troublesome complexity: *an uncomplicated skincare routine; straightforward logic*.

The term **undemanding** can have a slightly negative aspect as it may suggest lacking a challenge: *undemanding and tedious work*. The implication of **foolproof** is that anyone could succeed with it, so it is infallible. **Manageable**, however, is not such an emphatic term, which you could use of something one is able to deal with rather than do easily: *a relatively manageable task on the computer*.

easy-going *adj*
relaxed, tolerant, lenient, amenable, undemanding, carefree, nonchalant, calm, equable, even-tempered, serene, placid
FORMAL insouciant, imperturbable
COLLOQ. laid-back, happy-go-lucky
E3 strict, intolerant, critical

eat *v*
1 CONSUME, feed, swallow, devour, chew, munch, pick, have a snack, have a bite, breakfast, lunch, dine, gulp down, bolt down, gobble, cram, chop, binge
OLD mess
FORMAL ingest, partake of, gormandize, manducate
COLLOQ. scoff, snarf, put away, wolf down, tuck in(to), polish off, graze, knock back, peck, guts; *N Am* chow down
SLANG grub, nosh, pig, pig out
2 CORRODE, erode, wear away, bite into, decay, rot, crumble, dissolve, undermine, fret
OLD begnaw

Synonym nuances
sense 1
The word **consume** is a relatively unmarked term, but can sometimes carry the added suggestion of using or taking up completely, whether literally or figuratively: *vast quantities of food were consumed*; *she was consumed with envy*. **Feed** is often used of animals, and to use the term of humans can suggest, perhaps even with a hint a disgust, an instinctive or greedy action of taking in as nourishment: *we fed hungrily on the leftovers*.
  Swallow suggests the act of moving food or drink down the throat, and like **gulp down**, **bolt down** and **gobble**, it suggests eating quickly and greedily. The term **devour** also suggests doing this with great gusto. **Gormandize** is a less common word for eating with what might seem an unappealing voraciousness. **Cram**, likewise, suggests packing in as much food as possible in the shortest time, and suggests an unpleasantly greedy action. The term **chew** is suggestive of a slower, more deliberate action, as is **munch**, which often also implies an element of enthusiasm and is used in positive contexts: *she munched on a cake and felt better*.
  The verb **pick**, on the other hand, could be used more negatively to imply a lack of interest in eating: *she seemed lifeless and picked at her meal*. The terms **breakfast**, **lunch** and **dine** tell you very little about the manner of eating, but are neutral terms which put the emphasis on the formal situation of taking a meal.

---

eatable *adj*
edible, palatable, good, wholesome, digestible
FORMAL comestible
E3 inedible, unpalatable

⚠ eatable or **edible**?
If something is *edible*, it is by nature safe or good to eat, whereas if it is *eatable*, it is in a condition that makes it possible to eat it (whether or not it is safe to do so). Poisonous mushrooms are *eatable* but they are not *edible*, while a bag of flour is perfectly *edible* but would scarcely be *eatable*.

---

eavesdrop *v*
listen in, spy, overhear, monitor
COLLOQ. snoop, tap, bug

eavesdropper *n*
listener, monitor, spy
COLLOQ. snoop, snooper

ebb *v, n*
  ♦ *v*
1 *the tide ebbed*

fall, fall back, flow back, go out, recede
FORMAL retrocede
2 *his confidence ebbed away*
decline, decrease, diminish, drop, dwindle, flag, weaken, deteriorate, decay, degenerate, fade away, shrink, sink, slacken, subside, recede, lessen, wane, peter out
FORMAL abate
E3 **1** rise **2** increase, rise
  ♦ *n*
1 *at ebb tide*
low tide, low water, ebb tide, fall, going-out, flowing-back, receding, retreat
2 *her health is at a low ebb*
decline, decrease, drop, decay, lagging, lessening, deterioration, degeneration, slackening, weakening, subsiding, subsidence, wane, waning, dwindling
FORMAL abatement
E3 **1** rise, flow **2** increase

ebony *adj*
black, dark, jet, jet-black, jetty, inky, sable, sooty

ebullience *n*
exhilaration, effusiveness, enthusiasm, excitement, exuberance, brightness, buoyancy, elation, vivacity, high spirits, breeziness, zest
COLLOQ. chirpiness, bubbliness
E3 apathy, dullness, lifelessness

ebullient *adj*
exhilarated, effusive, enthusiastic, excited, exuberant, bright, buoyant, elated, gushing, vivacious, effervescent, breezy, irrepressible, zestful
COLLOQ. chirpy, bubbly
E3 apathetic, dull, lifeless

eccentric *adj, n*
  ♦ *adj*
odd, peculiar, abnormal, unconventional, strange, quirky, weird, off, queer, outlandish, idiosyncratic, bizarre, freakish, erratic, singular, fey
FORMAL aberrant
COLLOQ. way-out, wacky, dotty, off-beat, off the wall, nutty, loopy, kinky, screwy, kooky; *N Am* flaky, ditsy
SLANG loony, spacy; *N Am* loony tunes
E3 conventional, orthodox, normal
  ♦ *n*
nonconformist, oddity, crank
COLLOQ. oddball, freak, character, case, card, nut, nutter, nutjob, nutcase, weirdo, wacko, crackpot, kook, odd fish, square peg in a round hole, fish out of water; *N Am* flake, ditz, screwball
SLANG loony, loon, geek; *N Am* dingbat, wack, cupcake; *Aust* dag

eccentricity *n*
unconventionality, strangeness, unorthodoxy, peculiarity, nonconformity, abnormality, oddity, bizarreness, weirdness, idiosyncrasy, singularity, quirk, quirkiness, freakishness, anomaly
FORMAL aberration, capriciousness
E3 conventionality, ordinariness

ecclesiastic *n*
churchman/woman, cleric, clergyman/woman, man/woman of God, man/woman of the cloth, minister, priest, reverend, father, vicar, pastor, padre, parson, rector, canon, dean, deacon, deaconess, chaplain, curate, presbyter, preacher

ecclesiastical *adj*
church, churchly, religious, clerical, priestly, holy, divine, spiritual, pastoral, ministerial
FORMAL sacerdotal
E3 secular, temporal

echelon *n*
level, rank, grade, rung, tier, degree, position, place, status

Economics terms include:

acquisition
annuity
asset
autarky
balance of trade
bear market
black economy
boom
budget
budget deficit
bull market
business cycle
buy-back
capital
capital
  expenditure
capitalism
cartel
cash flow
cash ratio
CAT standard
Central Bank
Chancellor of the
  Exchequer
(the) City
clearing-house
command
  economy
commercial bank
commodity
common market
consumer

consumer good
corporation tax
cost-benefit
  analysis
credit
credit squeeze
debt
deficit
deflation
depression
devaluation
discount
discount rate
disequilibrium
dividend
Dow-Jones
  average or index
e-economy
economic
  determinism
economic rent
economic
  sanctions
economy of scale
embargo
enterprise culture
equity finance
European
  Monetary
  Union (EMU)
excise duty or tax
financial year

fiscal drag
fiscal year
fixed capital
foreign exchange
free-market
  economy
free-trade area
FTSE
funds
futures
General
  Agreement on
  Tariffs and Trade
  (GATT)
gilt-edged
  security
gold reserve
gold standard
green fund
grey economy
gross domestic
  product (GDP)
gross national
  product (GNP)
gross profit
  margin
Group of 7 (G7)
Group of 8 (G8)
hidden economy
human capital
income tax

input-output
  analysis
interest
International
  Monetary Fund
  (IMF)
law of supply and
  demand
leverage
liability
liquid asset
liquidity
liquidization
listed company
marginal cost or
  revenue
market economy
mature
merchant bank
mixed economy
monetary
money supply
monopoly
mortgage
NASDAQ®
new economy
oligopoly
old economy
open economy
Organization for
  Economic Co-
  operation and

Development
  (OECD)
overheating
personal equity
  plan (PEP)
Phillips curve
planned
  economy
political
  economy
price control
(retail) price
  index
private enterprise
private sector
product
producer
productivity
protectionism
public sector
rationalization
recession
reflation
reserve bank
reserve currency
savings
share
siege economy
single currency
slump
socio-economic
(the) Square Mile

stagflation
stakeholder
stakeholder
  economy
stamp duty
stock
stock exchange
stock market
stop-go policy
tariff
taxation
tax evasion
tax haven
tiger economy
trade cycle
trade gap/deficit
trademark
trader
trade union
transaction
trust
unit trust
Wall Street
working capital
World Trade
  Organization
  (WTO)
yield

Economic theories or schools include:

Austrian school	Game theory	Mercantilism	Neo-Ricardian	Physiocracy
Chicago school	Keynesian	Neo-classical	New classical	Post-Keynesian
Classical school	Marxian	Neo-Keynesian	economics	

echo *n, v*
 ◆ *n*
1 REVERBERATION, ringing, resounding, reiteration, repetition, reflection
OLD (*Shakesp*) replication
2 IMITATION, copy, reproduction, reflection, mirror image, image, parallel, repeat, clone, duplicate
3 REMINDER, memory, remembrance, allusion, hint, trace, remains, vestige
FORMAL evocation
Related adjective: phonocamptic
 ◆ *v*
1 REVERBERATE, resound, repeat, reflect, reiterate, ring
2 IMITATE, copy, reproduce, mirror, reflect, resemble, mimic, repeat, parallel, parrot

éclat *n*
glory, brilliance, lustre, style, stylishness, ostentation, flamboyance, show, distinction, display, success, splendour, acclaim, renown, acclamation, applause, approval, effect, fame, celebrity
FORMAL plaudits
E3 disapproval, dullness

eclectic *adj*
diverse, wide-ranging, wide, many-sided, catholic, broad, comprehensive, diversified, general, all-embracing, liberal, varied, selective
FORMAL heterogeneous, multifarious
E3 narrow, one-sided, exclusive

eclipse *v, n*
 ◆ *v*
1 BLOT OUT, obscure, cloud, cover, block, conceal, veil, shroud, darken, dim, cast a shadow over
2 OUTDO, overshadow, outshine, surpass, exceed,

transcend, excel, dwarf, put into the shade, leave someone standing
COLLOQ. run rings around
 ◆ *n*
1 OVERSHADOWING, blotting-out, darkening, concealing, covering, veiling, shading, dimming
FORMAL obscuration
2 DECLINE, failure, fall, loss, decay, ebb, weakening

economic *adj*
1 COMMERCIAL, business, industrial, trade
2 FINANCIAL, budgetary, fiscal, monetary
FORMAL pecuniary
3 PROFITABLE, profit-making, moneymaking, productive, cost-effective, viable, rewarding, remunerative

⚠ economic or **economical**?
Economic means 'relating to economics or the economy of a country': *economic history; the country's economic future*. It also means 'giving an adequate profit or fair return', as in *We must charge an economic rent/price*. *Economical* means 'thrifty', 'not wasteful, expensive, or extravagant': *This car is very economical on petrol; the economical use of limited supplies*.

Types of economics include:

agronomics	econometrics	microeconomics
cliometrics	macroeconomics	

See also panels above

economical *adj*
1 THRIFTY, careful, prudent, saving, sparing, frugal, provident, scrimping, skimping
FORMAL parsimonious

2 CHEAP, inexpensive, low-price, low-priced, low-cost, low-budget, bargain-basement, reasonable, cost-effective, budget, modest, efficient
⊟ 1 wasteful **2** expensive, uneconomical

economics
See panels on previous page

economize *v*
save, cut back, budget, cut expenditure, use less, buy cheaply, keep down costs, live on the cheap, cut costs, be economical, scrimp and save
FORMAL retrench
COLLOQ. tighten your belt, pull/tighten the purse strings, cut corners, cut your coat according to your cloth
⊟ waste, squander

economy *n*
1 *the country's economy*
system of wealth, wealth, financial state, financial resources, financial system, financial organization, business resources
2 THRIFT, saving, restraint, carefulness, care, frugality, parsimony, providence, prudence, husbandry, scrimping, skimping
⊟ 2 extravagance

ecstasy *n*
delight, rapture, bliss, elation, joy, jubilation, euphoria, frenzy, exultation, fervour, transports of delight, pleasure
⊟ misery, torment

ecstatic *adj*
elated, blissful, joyful, jubilant, rapturous, enraptured, in raptures, overjoyed, euphoric, delirious, frenzied, fervent
FORMAL rhapsodic
COLLOQ. jumping for joy, on cloud nine, in seventh heaven, over the moon, tickled pink, high as a kite; *Aust & NZ* rapt
⊟ downcast

ecumenical *adj*
interdenominational, nondenominational, nonsectarian, broad-based, all-embracing, universal, catholic

eddy *n, v*
◆ *n*
whirlpool, swirl, swirling, vortex, twist, maelstrom
◆ *v*
swirl, whirl, spin, turn, twist, twirl, reel, roll, swish

edge *n, v*
◆ *n*
1 BORDER, rim, boundary, frontier, limit, brim, threshold, brink, fringe, margin, outline, outer limit, side, verge, line, extremity, perimeter, periphery, lip
2 ADVANTAGE, superiority, force, dominance, head, lead
FORMAL ascendancy
COLLOQ. upper hand, whip hand
3 SHARPNESS, acuteness, keenness, incisiveness, severity, zest, bite, sting
FORMAL pungency, acerbity, causticity, trenchancy
◆ *v*
creep, crawl, inch, ease, steal, sidle, elbow, worm, pick your way
■ **on edge**
nervous, tense, anxious, apprehensive, ill at ease, highly-strung, keyed-up, touchy, irritable
COLLOQ. uptight, nervy, edgy
⊟ calm, at ease

edgy *adj*
on edge, nervous, tense, anxious, highly-strung, ill at ease, keyed-up, touchy, irritable
COLLOQ. uptight, nervy
⊟ calm, at ease

edible *adj*
eatable, fit to eat, safe to eat, palatable, digestible, wholesome, good, harmless
FORMAL comestible
⊟ inedible

❗ edible or **eatable**?
See panel at **eatable**.

edict *n*
command, order, proclamation, law, decree, regulation, pronouncement, rule, ruling, act, mandate, statute, fiat, injunction, manifesto, pronunciamento, ukase

edification *n*
instruction, improvement, enlightenment, guidance, education, teaching, coaching, tuition, upbuilding, elevation, uplifting

edifice *n*
building, construction, structure, erection

edify *v*
instruct, build up, improve, enlighten, inform, guide, educate, tutor, nurture, teach, school, coach, elevate, uplift

edit *v*
1 *edit a text*
correct, revise, rewrite, rephrase, reorder, rearrange, adapt, modify, check, compile, rephrase, subedit, copy-edit, proofread, select, polish, annotate, blue-pencil
FORMAL emend, redact
2 *edit a newspaper*
be in charge of, direct, head (up), be responsible for
3 *edit an anthology*
compile, choose, select, put together, arrange, assemble, collect, gather, organize

edition *n*
copy, volume, impression, printing, publication, issue, version, number

editor *n*
1 *a newspaper editor*
publisher, director, journalist, writer, reporter, correspondent, reviewer, newspaperman/woman, newsman/woman, newscaster
2 *a freelance editor*
reviser, checker, amender, corrector, rewriter, subeditor, copy editor, proofreader

educable *adj*
instructible, teachable, trainable
⊟ ineducable

educate *v*
teach, train, instruct, tutor, coach, school, inform, cultivate, edify, enlighten, drill, improve, prepare, prime, discipline, indoctrinate, develop, bring up, nurture, nourish, take in hand
OLD institute, uptrain
FORMAL inculcate

educated *adj*
learned, taught, schooled, literate, trained, knowledgeable, enlightened, informed, instructed, lettered, well-read, cultured, civilized, cultivated, wise, tutored, refined, well-bred
FORMAL erudite, sagacious
COLLOQ. brainy, all there, clever-clever
⊟ uneducated, uncultured

education *n*
teaching, training, schooling, tuition, tutoring, coaching, guidance, instruction, informing, drilling, cultivation, culture, letters, scholarship, improvement, enlightenment, edification, knowledge, nurture, preparation, fostering, upbringing, development, indoctrination
FORMAL inculcation

educational *adj*
academic, learning, teaching, cultural, edifying, enlightening, educative, improving, informative, instructive
FORMAL didactic, scholastic, pedagogic, pedagogical
E3 uninformative

Educational establishments include:

academy	middle school
adult-education centre	non-denominational
beacon school	nursery school
boarding school	*old colloq.* poly
business school	*old* polytechnic
city technical college (CTC)	preparatory school
college	primary school
college of further education	private school
college of technology	public school
combined school	secondary school
community school	secondary modern
comprehensive school	secretarial college
convent school	seminary
finishing school	single faith school
foundation school	sixth-form college
grammar school	summer-school
grant-maintained school	Sunday school
high school	technical college
infant school	university
kindergarten	upper school
Aust kinder	voluntary school
Aust & NZ kindy	

Educational terms include:

adult education	head teacher	primary
assisted places	higher education	education
scheme	Higher Grade	proctor
A-level	Higher Still	professor
(international)	homework	pupil
baccalaureate	intake	quadrangle
board of	invigilator	qualification
governors	lecture	refresher course
break time	literacy	register
bursar	literacy hour	report
campus	matriculation	SATs (Standard
catchment area	matron	Assessment
certificate	mixed-ability	Tasks)
classroom	teaching	scholarship
coeducation	modular course	school term
common	module	secondary
entrance	national	education
course	curriculum	special education
course of studies	National Literacy	Standard Grade
curriculum	Strategy	statemented
degree	National	streaming
diploma	Numeracy	student
discipline	Strategy	student grant
double-first	newly qualified	student loan
educational	teacher	study
programme	NVQ (national	subject
eleven-plus	vocational	syllabus
enrolment	qualification)	teacher
examination	numeracy	teacher training
exercise book	Ofsted (Office for	test paper
final exam	Standards in	textbook
finals	Education)	thesis
further education	O-level	timetable
GCSE (General	opting out	top-up fees
Certificate of	parent governor	truancy
Secondary	PTA (parent-	university
Education)	teacher	entrance
governor	association)	work experience
graduation	playground	YTS (Youth
half-term	playtime	Training
head boy	prefect	Scheme)
head girl		

educative *adj*
instructive, improving, informative, edifying, educational, enlightening
FORMAL catechetic, catechismal, catechistic(al), didactic
E3 uninformative

educator *n*
instructor, teacher, tutor, schoolteacher, schoolmaster, master, schoolmistress, mistress, educationalist, lecturer, professor, academic, trainer, coach
FORMAL pedagogue

eerie *adj*
weird, strange, unnatural, unearthly, mysterious, sinister, uncanny, ghostly, frightening, scaring, scary, bloodcurdling
COLLOQ. spooky, creepy, spine-chilling

eerily *adv*
weirdly, strangely, unnaturally, mysteriously, uncannily

efface *v*
remove, destroy, delete, rub out, wipe out, cancel, eliminate, eradicate, obliterate, erase, blank out, blot out, cross out
FORMAL excise, expunge, extirpate

effect *n, v*
♦ *n*
1 OUTCOME, result, conclusion, consequence, upshot, fruit, impact, aftermath, issue
2 POWER, force, impact, action, impression, strength, influence
FORMAL efficacy
3 MEANING, significance, sense, drift, tenor, thread
FORMAL import, purport
4 *personal effects*
belongings, possessions, property, goods, mov(e)ables, paraphernalia, baggage, luggage, things, trappings
FORMAL chattels, accoutrements
COLLOQ. gear, things, stuff, clobber
♦ *v*
cause, execute, bring about, carry out, create, achieve, accomplish, perform, produce, make, initiate, give rise to, fulfil, complete
FORMAL generate, effectuate
■ **in effect**
in fact, actually, in actual fact, really, in reality, in truth, to all intents and purposes, in practice, for all practical purposes, essentially, effectively, virtually
■ **take effect**
be effective, become operative, come into force, come into operation, come into service, be implemented, become law, become valid, begin, work, take, produce results, function
COLLOQ. kick in, talk

⚠ effect or **affect**?
See panel at **affect.**

---

effective *adj*
1 EFFICIENT, productive, adequate, sufficient, capable, useful, helpful, fruitful, practical, successful, worthwhile
FORMAL efficacious
2 OPERATIVE, in force, in effect, in operation, functioning, legal, valid, current, active
FORMAL implemental
3 STRIKING, impressive, forceful, powerful, exciting, attractive, persuasive, convincing, compelling, potent, telling, prevailing
FORMAL cogent
COLLOQ. devastating
4 ACTUAL, practical, virtual, essential
E3 1 ineffective, powerless **4** theoretical

⚠ **effective** or **effectual**?
Effective has a number of meanings: 'producing, or likely to produce, the intended result': *Aspirin is effective against many types of pain*; 'impressive', 'powerful': *He's a very effective speaker*; 'in operation, in force': *The new regulations become effective at midnight*; 'in reality, even if not in theory': *Although not the king, he was the effective ruler of the country for twenty years. Effectual* puts more emphasis on the actual achievement of the desired result than *effective* does. If the police take *effective* measures to combat the rising crime rate, these measures have the desired effect, or are expected to, whereas if the police take *effectual measures*, there is no doubt that these measures are succeeding in reducing the crime rate.

effectively *adv*
1 IN EFFECT, in fact, actually, in actual fact, really, in reality, in truth, to all intents and purposes, in practice, for all practical purposes, essentially, virtually
2 SUCCESSFULLY, efficiently, productively, fruitfully

effectiveness *n*
success, strength, force, influence, productiveness, fruitfulness, usefulness, use, power, ability, capability, efficiency, validity, vigour, weight
FORMAL cogency, efficacy, potency
COLLOQ. clout
🔁 ineffectiveness, uselessness

effectual *adj*
1 *an effectual plan*
successful, effective, useful, capable, influential, serviceable, operative, sound, powerful, productive, forcible
FORMAL perficient
2 *effectual contracts*
binding, authoritative, lawful, legal, valid, authentic, proper
🔁 **1** ineffective, useless

effeminate *adj*
unmanly, womanly, womanish, feminine, delicate
OLD (*Shakesp*) meacock
COLLOQ. sissy, wimpish
🔁 manly

effervesce *v*
1 *mineral water effervescing*
sparkle, bubble, fizz, boil, foam, froth, ferment
2 *effervescing with conversation*
be lively, be vivacious, be animated, be exhilarated, sparkle
FORMAL be ebullient

effervescence *n*
1 SPARKLE, bubbles, bubbling, fizz, fizziness, gas, gassiness, foam, foaming, froth, frothing, ferment, fermentation
2 LIVELINESS, vivacity, vitality, sparkle, animation, buoyancy, enthusiasm, high spirits, excitedness, excitement, exhilaration, exuberance
FORMAL ebullience
COLLOQ. vim, zing, zip

effervescent *adj*
1 BUBBLY, bubbling, sparkling, fizzy, fizzing, gassy, aerated, frothy, carbonated, foaming, fermenting
2 LIVELY, vivacious, animated, buoyant, exhilarated, enthusiastic, exuberant, sparkling, excited, vital, irrepressible
FORMAL ebullient
🔁 **1** flat **2** dull

effete *adj*
weak, feeble, enfeebled, debilitated, exhausted, drained, fruitless, unfruitful, unproductive, played out, spent, sterile, tired out, worn out, spoiled, used up, unprolific, wasted, decayed, barren, corrupt, debased, decrepit, degenerate, decadent
FORMAL enervated, ineffectual, infecund
🔁 vigorous

efficacious *adj*
effective, productive, capable, useful, successful, competent, powerful, potent, strong, adequate, sufficient, active, effectual, operative
🔁 ineffective, useless

efficacy *n*
effectiveness, effect, usefulness, use, success, successfulness, power, energy, force, influence, potency, strength, capability, ability, competence, virtue
🔁 ineffectiveness, uselessness

efficiency *n*
effectiveness, competence, proficiency, skill, expertise, skilfulness, capability, ability, productivity, order, orderliness, organization
🔁 inefficiency, incompetence

efficient *adj*
effective, competent, proficient, skilful, capable, able, productive, organized, well-organized, well-ordered, streamlined, rationalized, methodical, systematic, businesslike, workmanlike, smart, practical, strong, powerful, well-run, well-conducted, expert
🔁 inefficient, incompetent

effigy *n*
figure, statue, carving, representation, likeness, picture, portrait, image, icon, idol, dummy, guy, Jack-straw
OLD idol, sign

effluent *n*
waste, liquid waste, discharge, sewage, emission, outflow, pollutant, pollution
FORMAL effluence, effluvium, efflux, emanation, exhalation

effort *n*
1 EXERTION, strain, application, struggle, sweat, trouble, energy, hard work, power, force, stress, toil, striving, pains, labour, muscle power
FORMAL travail
COLLOQ. elbow-grease, sweat of your brow, beef, muscles
2 ATTEMPT, try, endeavour
COLLOQ. go, shot, stab, crack, bash, whirl
3 ACHIEVEMENT, accomplishment, feat, attainment, exploit, production, creation, deed, product, result, work, opus

effortless *adj*
easy, simple, undemanding, facile, painless, uncomplicated, unexacting, straightforward, smooth
🔁 difficult, complicated, exacting, demanding

effrontery *n*
audacity, impertinence, insolence, impudence, temerity, boldness, brazenness, cheekiness, cheek, gall, nerve, presumption, disrespect, arrogance, brashness
COLLOQ. face, brass, brass neck, lip, chutzpah; *N Am* sass
🔁 respect, timidity

effulgent *adj*
brilliant, radiant, shining, glowing, splendid, glorious
FORMAL resplendent, refulgent, incandescent

effusion *n*
outpouring, outburst, outflow, gush, discharge, emission, stream, shedding
FORMAL effluence, efflux, voidance

effusive *adj*
fulsome, gushing, gushy, unrestrained, unreserved, expansive, demonstrative, profuse, overflowing, enthusiastic, exuberant, extravagant, lavish, talkative, voluble, lyrical
FORMAL ebullient, rhapsodic
COLLOQ. gabby, gassy, over the top, OTT, all mouth, big-mouthed
🔁 reserved, restrained

egalitarian *adj*
democratic, fair, just, equitable, sharing

egg *n, v*
♦ *n*
ovum, ovule
TECHNICAL oocyte, oosphere
■ **egg on**
encourage, incite, push, urge, drive, excite, stimulate, spur, prompt, coax, talk into, goad, prod, prick
FORMAL exhort
☷ discourage

egghead *n*
boffin, brain, intellect, intellectual, academic, thinker, scholar, bookworm, genius, Einstein
COLLOQ. know-all, know-it-all, brainbox

ego *n*
self, (sense of) identity, self-esteem, self-importance, self-confidence, self-image, self-worth

egocentric *adj*
self-centred, selfish, self-seeking, self-serving, self-interested, egotistic(al), narcissistic, self-absorbed, thinking only of yourself, wrapped up in yourself
☷ altruistic

egoism *n*
self-interest, self-centredness, self-importance, self-absorption, self-love, self-regard, self-seeking, selfishness, narcissism, egocentricity, egomania, egotism, amour-propre
☷ altruism

egoist *n*
self-seeker, narcissist, egotist, egomaniac

egoistic *adj*
self-absorbed, self-important, self-involved, self-centred, self-pleasing, self-seeking, narcissistic, egocentric, egoistical, egotistic, egotistical, egomaniacal
☷ altruistic

egotism *n*
egoism, egomania, self-centredness, no thought for others, self-importance, egocentricity, selfishness, superiority, conceitedness, self-regard, self-love, self-conceit, narcissism, self-admiration, pride, boastfulness, vanity, snobbery
FORMAL braggadocio
COLLOQ. bigheadedness, swank, blowing your own trumpet; *NAm* blowing your own horn
☷ humility

egotist *n*
boaster, bluffer, show-off, self-admirer, braggart, egoist, egomaniac, swaggerer, braggadocio
COLLOQ. bighead, big mouth, smart alec, clever clogs, clever dick

egotistic *adj*
egoistic, egocentric, self-centred, selfish, self-important, self-admiring, narcissistic, conceited, swollen-headed, swell-headed, superior, vain, proud, boasting, bragging
COLLOQ. bigheaded
☷ humble

egregious *adj*
grievous, outrageous, scandalous, shocking, gross, rank, infamous, notorious, insufferable, intolerable, appalling, monstrous, flagrant, glaring, arrant
FORMAL heinous
☷ slight

egress *n*
exit, way out, outlet, vent, issue, exodus, emergence, leaving, departure, escape, escape route

ejaculate *v*
1 DISCHARGE, eject, spurt, emit, release, expel

COLLOQ. come
2 EXCLAIM, call (out), blurt (out), cry (out), shout (out), yell, utter, scream

ejaculation *n*
1 *ejaculation of semen*
discharge, ejection, emission, spurt, release, expulsion, orgasm, climax
COLLOQ. coming
2 EXCLAMATION, call, cry, scream, shout, yell, utterance, interjection

eject *v*
1 EMIT, expel, discharge, release, ejaculate, spout, spew, spit, splutter, disgorge, evacuate, vomit, excrete, belch, expectorate
TECHNICAL degas
FORMAL exude, excrete
2 OUST, evict, get rid of, throw out, drive out, turn out, expel, remove, banish, deport, dismiss, discharge, exclude, exile, bounce
OLD expulse
COLLOQ. fire, sack, boot out, kick out, turf out, chuck out, give someone the boot, give someone their cards, give someone the bum's rush, show someone the door
See Synonym nuances panel at **banish**.
3 BAILOUT, propel, thrust out, throw out, get out

ejection *n*
eviction, expulsion, removal, banishment, dismissal, discharge, exile, deportation, ousting
COLLOQ. firing, sacking, the boot, the sack

eke
■ **eke out**
1 *eke out supplies*
make something stretch, stretch, spin out, fill out, husband, economize on, be economical with, add to, increase, supplement
COLLOQ. go easy with
2 *eke out a living*
scrimp and save, scrape, scratch, get by, survive
COLLOQ. live from hand to mouth, feel the pinch

elaborate *adj, v*
♦ *adj*
1 *elaborate plans*
detailed, complicated, complex, intricate, careful, thorough, exact, extensive, painstaking, precise, perfected, minute, laboured, studied
2 *elaborate designs*
intricate, complex, complicated, involved, ornamental, ornate, fancy, decorated, extravagant, ostentatious, showy, fussy, rococo, overwrought, highwrought, historiated, storiated
OLD quaint
☷ 2 simple, plain
♦ *v*
amplify, develop, enlarge on, expand on, work out, flesh out, polish, improve, refine, enhance, devise, explain
FORMAL expatiate
☷ précis, simplify

élan *n*
panache, liveliness, flair, flourish, style, stylishness, spirit, verve, vigour, vivacity, animation, confidence, zest, dash, esprit
COLLOQ. brio, oomph, pizzazz
☷ apathy, lifelessness

elapse *v*
pass, lapse, go by, go on, go past, slip away, slip by

elastic *adj*
1 PLIABLE, flexible, stretchable, stretchy, supple, resilient, yielding, springy, rubbery, pliant, elasticated, plastic, bouncy, buoyant

2 ADAPTABLE, accommodating, flexible, tolerant, adjustable, fluid, compliant
COLLOQ. easy
F3 1 rigid **2** inflexible

elasticity n
1 PLIABILITY, flexibility, resilience, stretch, stretchiness, springiness, suppleness, plasticity, bounce, buoyancy
COLLOQ. give, play
2 ADAPTABILITY, flexibility, tolerance, adjustability
F3 1 rigidity **2** inflexibility

elated adj
exhilarated, excited, delighted, euphoric, ecstatic, thrilled, rapturous, exultant, jubilant, overjoyed, joyful, happy, blissful
FORMAL joyous, rhapsodic
COLLOQ. over the moon, on cloud nine
F3 despondent, downcast

elation n
exhilaration, delight, transports of delight, euphoria, ecstasy, thrill, rapture, bliss, exultation, glee, high spirits, happiness, joy, joyfulness, jubilation
FORMAL joyousness
F3 depression, despondency

elbow v
jostle, nudge, push, force, bump, knock, crowd, shoulder
COLLOQ. shove, barge

elbow-grease n
effort, hard work, energy, strength, exertion, muscle power
COLLOQ. sweat of your brow, beef, muscles

elbow-room n
space, room, breathing space, play, scope, leeway, freedom, latitude, *Lebensraum*

elder adj, n
♦ adj
older, senior, first-born, ancient
F3 younger
♦ n
1 *no respect for their elders*
senior, older person, old person
COLLOQ. oldie
2 *a church elder*
leader, deacon, father

elderly adj, n
♦ adj
aging, aged, old, grey-haired, hoary, senile, mature, badgerly
FORMAL senescent
COLLOQ. not as young as you were, not getting any younger, over the hill, long in the tooth, past it, not long for this world
F3 young, youthful
♦ n
old people, older generation, older adults, senior citizens, retired people, pensioners, old-age pensioners, OAPs; *NAm* golden agers
COLLOQ. oldies, wrinklies, has-beens
SLANG fossils

eldest adj
first, first-born, oldest
F3 youngest

elect v, adj, n
♦ v
choose, pick, opt for, select, vote for, cast a vote, go to the polls, decide on, prefer, adopt, designate, appoint, determine, co-opt, return
OLD voice
COLLOQ. plump for
♦ adj

chosen, designate, -to-be, future, picked, prospective, selected, preferred, hand-picked
TECHNICAL nominate
♦ n
chosen, élite, select
COLLOQ. chosen few

election n
choice, selection, vote, voting, ballot, poll, hustings, referendum, appointment, determination, decision, preference, choosing, picking

electioneering n
campaigning, promotion, lobbying, canvassing, crusading, championing, fighting, struggling; *Can* mainstreeting

elector n
voter, selector, constituent, electorate

electric adj
1 *an electric light*
electric-powered, mains-operated, battery-operated, rechargeable, cordless, powered, live
2 *the atmosphere was electric*
electrifying, exciting, stimulating, thrilling, startling, charged, dynamic, stirring, tense, rousing
F3 2 unexciting, flat

electrical components

Types of electrical components and devices include:

adaptor	earthed plug	neon lamp
ammeter	electrical	socket
armature	screwdriver	test lamp
battery	electricity meter	three-core cable
bayonet fitting	extension lead	three-pin plug
cable	fluorescent tube	transducer
ceiling rose	fuse	transformer
circuit breaker	fusebox	two-pin plug
conduit	fuse carrier	universal test
continuity tester	high voltage tester	meter
copper	insulating tape	voltage doubler
conductor	lampholder	wire strippers
dimmer switch	light bulb	
dry-cell battery	multimeter	

electricity and electronics
See panel on next page

electrify v
thrill, excite, shock, charge, invigorate, animate, stimulate, stir, rouse, fire, jolt, galvanize, amaze, astonish, astound, stagger
F3 bore

elegance n
style, chic, fashionableness, stylishness, sophistication, smartness, refinement, polish, beauty, dignity, distinction, grace, gracefulness, discernment, taste, gentility, politeness, tastefulness, poise, exquisiteness, grandeur, luxury, sumptuousness
FORMAL propriety, concinnity
F3 inelegance

elegant adj
stylish, chic, fashionable, modish, smart, refined, polished, cultivated, genteel, charming, sophisticated, debonair, urbane, smooth, tasteful, lovely, fine, exquisite, beautiful, cultured, graceful, gracious, handsome, delicate, neat, artistic, bijou, humane; *Scot* jimp
OLD (*Spenser*) dainty
FORMAL concinnous
COLLOQ. ritzy, snazzy, swanky, la-di-da
F3 inelegant, unrefined, unfashionable

elegiac adj
lamenting, funereal, mournful, doleful, melancholic, sad,

Electricity and electronic terms include:

alternating current (AC)	commutator	Faraday cage	loudspeaker	siemens	truth table
alternator	condenser	Foucault current	microchip	silicon chip	turboalternator
amp	conductivity	frequency modulation	mutual induction	solenoid	tweeter
ampere	coulomb		NICAM®	solid state circuit	valve
amplifier	digital signal	galvanic	ohm	static electricity	volt
analogue signal	diode	galvanometer	optoelectronics	step-down transformer	voltaic
anode	direct current (DC)	generator	oscillator	super- conductivity	voltage amplifier
band-pass filter	Dolby® (system)	grid system	oscilloscope		watt
battery	dynamo	henry	piezoelectricity	switch	Wheatstone bridge
bioelectricity	eddy current	impedance	polarity	thermionics	woofer
capacitance	electrode	induced current	power station	thermistor	
capacitor	electrolyte	inductance	reactance	thermistor	
cathode	electromagnet	integrated circuit	resistance	thyristor	
cathode-ray tube	electron tube	isoelectric	resistor	transformer	
cell	farad	isoelectronic	rheostat	transistor	
		logic gate	semiconductor	triode	

plaintive, valedictory, keening
FORMAL threnetic, threnetical, threnodial, threnodic
E3 happy

elegy *n*
dirge, lament, requiem, funeral poem, funeral song, burial hymn, plaint
FORMAL threnody, threnode
Related adjectives: epicedial, epicedian

element *n*
1 *the elements of our discussion*
factor, component, constituent, ingredient, member, part, piece, fragment, feature, strand
2 *the elements of a subject*
basics, foundations, fundamentals, principles, first principles, rudiments, essentials
3 *an element of truth*
small amount, grain, trace, touch, hint, suspicion, soupçon
4 *the criminal element in society*
individual(s), group, faction, set, party, clique
5 *exposed to the elements*
weather, wind and rain, storms, climate, atmospheric conditions, meteorological conditions, atmospheric forces
6 *in his element*
natural environment, habitat, territory, niche, haunt
E3 1 whole

elemental *adj*
basic, fundamental, primary, principal, natural, rudimentary, primitive, radical, immense, powerful, forceful, uncontrolled

elementary *adj*
basic, fundamental, rudimentary, principal, primary, clear, easy, introductory, straightforward, uncomplicated, simple
E3 advanced, complicated

elephantine *adj*
large, vast, immense, huge, enormous, massive, great, bulky, hulking, heavy, weighty, awkward, clumsy, lumbering

elevate *v*
1 LIFT, raise, hoist, uplift, heighten, intensify, magnify, exalt
COLLOQ. hike up
2 PROMOTE, advance, exalt, aggrandize, refine, ennoble, upgrade
COLLOQ. move up the ladder, put on a pedestal, kick upstairs
3 UPLIFT, rouse, boost, buoy up, brighten, cheer, gladden, give a lift to
E3 1 lower **2** downgrade **3** depress

elevated *adj*
1 IMPORTANT, great, lofty, exalted, grand, noble, dignified
2 *elevated thoughts*

advanced, lofty, exalted, grand, high, noble, dignified, moral
FORMAL sublime
3 *elevated ground*
raised, lifted (up), rising, high, hoisted, uplifted

elevation *n*
1 RISE, promotion, advancement, preferment, upgrading, aggrandizement
COLLOQ. step up the ladder, leg-up, go-getting
2 EXALTATION, loftiness, grandeur, eminence, nobility, dignity
FORMAL sublimity
3 HEIGHT, altitude, tallness, hill, rise, mound, mount
4 *the east elevation*
face, façade, aspect, front, back, side
E3 1 demotion **3** dip

elf *n*
fairy, sprite, imp, pixie, goblin, hobgoblin, gnome, brownie, leprechaun, troll, banshee, puck, pygmy
OLD urchin
Related adjectives: elfish, elfin, elvan, elvish

elfin *adj*
small, petite, delicate, dainty, charming, elfish, elflike, frolicsome, sprightly, playful, impish, mischievous, puckish

elicit *v*
evoke, draw out, bring out, derive, extract, obtain, exact, extort, cause, wrest
FORMAL call forth, educe
COLLOQ. worm out

eligibility *n*
qualification, condition, suitability, entitlement, allowance, acceptability, desirability

eligible *adj*
qualified, fit, fitting, appropriate, suitable, acceptable, entitled, worthy, proper, desirable
E3 ineligible

eliminate *v*
1 GET RID OF, remove, cut out, take out, exclude, delete, dispense with, abolish, put an end/a stop to, rub out, omit, reject, disregard, dispose of, drop, do away with, eradicate, expel, extinguish, stamp out
2 DEFEAT, conquer, beat, overwhelm
COLLOQ. knock out, thrash, lick, hammer, annihilate
3 KILL, murder, do away with, exterminate
COLLOQ. wipe out, liquidate, rub out, bump off, do in; *N Am* whack, ice
E3 1 include, accept

elimination *n*
removal, exclusion, abolition, omission, rejection, deletion, eradication, expulsion, disposal

élite *n, adj*

• *n*

best, pick, cream, elect, aristocracy, upper classes, nobility, gentry, crème de la crème, establishment, high society
COLLOQ. pick of the bunch, jet set

• *adj*

choice, best, exclusive, selected, first-class, aristocratic, noble, upper-class

elixir *n*

cure-all, panacea, remedy, solution, mixture, concentrate, essence, extract, pith, potion, principle, quintessence, syrup, tincture, nostrum

elliptical *adj*

1 OVAL, egg-shaped, oviform, ovoid(al)
2 OBLIQUE, cryptic, obscure, ambiguous, incomprehensible, unfathomable, concise, concentrated, condensed, laconic, terse, succinct
FORMAL abstruse, recondite
F3 2 clear, direct, verbose

elocution *n*

delivery, articulation, diction, pronunciation, voice production, rhetoric, speech, utterance, phrasing
FORMAL enunciation, oratory

elongate *v*

lengthen, extend, draw out, prolong, make longer, stretch (out)
FORMAL protract

elongated *adj*

lengthened, extended, prolonged, protracted, stretched, long

elope *v*

run off, run away, decamp, bolt, make off, abscond, flee, escape, slip away, steal away, leave, disappear
COLLOQ. do a bunk, scarper, skedaddle, vamoose, do a runner, do a moonlight flit, hit the road/trail, make a bolt/break for it, hightail it

eloquence *n*

expressiveness, fluency, flow of words, expression, persuasiveness, articulateness, diction, facility, forcefulness, oratory, rhetoric
FORMAL facundity
COLLOQ. gift of the gab, blarney, gassiness
F3 inarticulateness

eloquent *adj*

articulate, fluent, well-expressed, well-spoken, glib, expressive, vocal, voluble, persuasive, moving, honey-tongued, silver-tongued, forceful, graceful, plausible, stirring, effective, vivid, Demosthenic, Mercurial
F3 inarticulate, tongue-tied

elsewhere *adv*

somewhere else, in/to another place, not here, absent, removed, abroad
F3 here, present

elucidate *v*

explain, clarify, make clear, clear up, interpret, spell out, simplify, state simply, illustrate, illuminate, unfold, throw/shed light on, fill in, exemplify, give an example
FORMAL explicate, expound
F3 confuse

elucidation *n*

explanation, clarification, comment, commentary, illumination, illustration, interpretation, footnote, gloss, annotation, marginalia
FORMAL explication, exposition

elude *v*

1 AVOID, escape, evade, shirk, shake off, flee, bilk, get away from, give someone the slip, throw someone off the scent; *Scot* jink

FORMAL circumvent
COLLOQ. dodge, duck, slip through someone's fingers
2 PUZZLE, frustrate, baffle, confound, thwart, stump, evade, foil
OLD delude

elusive *adj*

1 INDEFINABLE, difficult to describe, intangible, unanalysable, subtle, puzzling, baffling, deceptive, misleading, transient, transitory
2 EVASIVE, difficult to find, hard to catch, slippery, tricky
COLLOQ. shifty, dodgy

elusiveness *n*

indefinability, intangibility, subtlety, puzzle, evasiveness, transience, transitoriness

emaciated *adj*

thin, gaunt, lean, haggard, drawn, wasted, bony, anorexic, scrawny, skinny, skeletal, pinched, meagre
FORMAL attenuated, cadaverous
COLLOQ. thin as a rake, all skin and bone
F3 plump, well-fed

emaciation *n*

thinness, gauntness, leanness, haggardness, boniness, scrawniness, atrophy
F3 plumpness

emanate *v*

1 RADIATE, send out, emit, give out, give off, exude, discharge
FORMAL exhale
2 ORIGINATE, proceed, arise, derive, issue, spring, stem, flow, come, emerge

emanation *n*

discharge, emission, flow, effluent, effluence, radiation
FORMAL effluvium, efflux, effluxion, effusion

emancipate *v*

free, liberate, release, set free, enfranchise, deliver, discharge, loose, set loose, unchain, untie, unshackle, unfetter, unyoke
FORMAL manumit
F3 enslave

emancipation *n*

liberation, freedom, setting free, freeing, release, deliverance, liberty, discharge, enfranchisement, unbinding, unfettering, unchaining
FORMAL manumission
F3 enslavement

emasculate *v*

1 CASTRATE, geld, neuter, spay
2 WEAKEN, impoverish, cripple, debilitate, soften
FORMAL enervate
F3 2 boost, vitalize

emasculation *n*

weakening, impoverishment, debilitation, reduction, diminishment, moderation, lessening
FORMAL abatement

embalm *v*

preserve, mummify, store, lay out, enshrine, cherish, consecrate, conserve, treasure

embankment *n*

causeway, dam, rampart, mound, bank, levee, earthwork; *NZ* stopbank

embargo *n, v*

• *n*

restriction, ban, prohibition, restraint, bar, barrier, impediment, check, hindrance, obstruction, blockage, stoppage, seizure
FORMAL proscription, interdiction

• *v*

restrict, ban, bar, prohibit, restrain, block, check, impede, obstruct, seize, stop
FORMAL interdict, proscribe
F3 allow

embark *v*
board (ship), go aboard, take ship
OLD (*Shakesp*) inship
F3 disembark
▪ **embark on**
begin, start, commence, set about, launch into, undertake, venture into, enter (on), initiate, engage
F3 complete, finish

embarkation *n*
boarding, mounting, entrance, getting-on, embussing, emplaning, entrainment

embarrass *v*
make awkward/ashamed, disconcert, mortify, show up, discompose, fluster, humiliate, shame, distress, upset, confuse
FORMAL discomfit, discountenance

embarrassed *adj*
awkward, uncomfortable, ill at ease, uneasy, self-conscious, upset, confused, distressed, disconcerted, unnatural, constrained, ashamed, shamed, guilty, shown up, humiliated, mortified, abashed
FORMAL discomfited
COLLOQ. sheepish, hot under the collar
F3 unembarrassed

> **Synonym nuances**
> **Awkward** and **uncomfortable** can be used, perhaps with qualifying adverbs, of various degrees of embarrassed feelings: *there was a slightly awkward silence*. Both **ill at ease** and **uneasy** are similar, but may further imply a degree of apprehension: *she felt intimidated and uneasy*. You could use the term **self-conscious** of an embarrassed feeling characterized by a preoccupation with how you are perceived.
> The terms **upset** and **distressed** would be appropriate only where embarrassment has caused mental pain or suffering. **Disconcerted**, although similar, further suggests a loss of self-possession: *she appeared disconcerted, even flustered, at his remarks*.
> The terms **guilty** and **ashamed** suggest deep embarrassment at one's own actions or possibly, in the case of **ashamed**, those of a close associate; **humiliated** and **mortified** are even stronger terms which could refer to embarrassment at oneself, but are often reserved for deep feelings of injured self-respect. **Shamed**, on the other hand, suggests a more public embarrassment caused by exposition by others: *shamed Cabinet minister resigns*. **Shown up** also conveys the idea of being publicly humbled: *the team were shown up by their performance*. To refer to suddenly being struck by feelings of shame or embarrassment, you might use the word **abashed**: *abashed at being caught snooping*.

embarrassing *adj*
awkward, uncomfortable, disconcerting, distressing, upsetting, sensitive, mortifying, humiliating, shameful, shaming, tricky, compromising, painful
FORMAL discomfiting, indelicate, discountenancing
COLLOQ. touchy

embarrassment *n*
1 DISCOMPOSURE, self-consciousness, mortification, humiliation, shame, guilt, awkwardness, unease, uneasiness, confusion, distress, bashfulness
FORMAL chagrin, discomfiture
COLLOQ. sheepishness
2 DIFFICULTY, constraint, predicament, distress, dilemma, mess, plight

COLLOQ. fix, scrape, jam, pickle
3 *an embarrassment of riches*
abundance, surplus, excess, superabundance, overabundance
FORMAL profusion

embassy *n*
consulate, legation, ministry, delegation, deputation, mission

embed *v*
implant, plant, fix, insert, root, set, sink, hammer, drive

embellish *v*
1 *embellish a design*
adorn, ornament, decorate, deck, dress up, beautify, gild, garnish, trim, festoon
OLD bedeck, bespangle
2 *embellish a story*
elaborate, embroider, enrich, exaggerate, enhance, grace
F3 **1** simplify; *formal* denude

embellishment *n*
adornment, ornament, ornamentation, decoration, elaboration, garnish, trimming, gilding, enrichment, enhancement, embroidery

embers *n*
live coals, ashes, cinders, charcoal, residue, clinker

embezzle *v*
steal, swindle, pilfer, rob
FORMAL appropriate, misappropriate, purloin, defalcate, peculate
COLLOQ. filch, pinch, nab, nick, have your fingers/hand in the till
SLANG rip off

embezzlement *n*
pilfering, fraud, stealing, theft
FORMAL appropriation, misappropriation, defalcation
COLLOQ. filching, nabbing, nicking

embezzler *n*
cheat, fraud, thief, robber
FORMAL defalcator, peculator
COLLOQ. crook, diddler, con man

embittered *adj*
bitter, resentful, disaffected, sour, rancorous, disillusioned, disenchanted, discouraged, disheartened, angry, exasperated, piqued, rankled

emblazon *v*
1 DECORATE, adorn, ornament, blazon, embellish, depict, display, colour, illuminate, paint
2 PROCLAIM, publicize, publish, extol, praise, glorify, trumpet
FORMAL laud

emblem *n*
symbol, sign, token, representation, logo, insignia, device, crest, mark, badge, figure, image

emblematic *adj*
representative, representing, representative, symbolic, symbolical, figurative, allegorical, emblematical

embodiment *n*
personification, incarnation, exemplification, expression, epitome, example, type, model, incorporation, realization, representation, concentration
FORMAL manifestation

embody *v*
1 PERSONIFY, exemplify, represent, stand for, typify, symbolize, incorporate, express
FORMAL manifest
2 INCLUDE, contain, integrate, incorporate, assimilate, collect, combine, bring together, take in

embolden *v*
encourage, inspire, make brave/bold, give courage to,

invigorate, reassure, rouse, stimulate, stir, strengthen, vitalize, animate, fire, cheer, hearten, inflame, nerve
F3 dishearten

embrace *v, n*
♦ *v*
1 HUG, clasp, cuddle, hold, grasp, put/throw your arms around, take into your arms, squeeze, enfold, fold, enlace, inarm, lock, strain; *Scot* halse; clip
OLD coll, inclip, wrap, complect, compress
COLLOQ. neck, canoodle, smooch, tangle with
SLANG snog
2 INCLUDE, encompass, incorporate, contain, cover, involve, take in, span
OLD (*Spenser*) brace; complect
FORMAL comprise
3 ACCEPT, take up, welcome, receive eagerly, receive wholeheartedly
FORMAL espouse
COLLOQ. take on board
♦ *n*
hug, cuddle, hold, clasp, squeeze, bosom, abrazo
OLD colling, accolade, embrasure
COLLOQ. clinch, necking, slap and tickle, smooch

embrocation *n*
cream, lotion, ointment, salve
FORMAL epithem

embroider *v*
1 DECORATE, sew, stitch
2 EMBELLISH, enrich, exaggerate, colour, enhance, elaborate, dress up, garnish

embroidery *n*
fancywork, needlework, sewing, tapestry, tatting, needlepoint

---

Types of embroidery stitch include:

backstitch	half-cross	Romanian
blanket	herringbone	couching
bullion	lazy-daisy	running
chain	longstitch	satin
chevron	long-and-short	stem
cross	moss	straight
feather	Oriental	Swiss darning
fishbone	couching	tent
French knot		

---

embroil *v*
involve, implicate, entangle, enmesh, mix up, catch up in, draw into, incriminate

embryo *n*
1 UNBORN CHILD, foetus
2 *the embryo of the plan*
nucleus, germ, seed, beginning, root, rudiments, basics

embryonic *adj*
undeveloped, rudimentary, immature, beginning, emerging, fledgling, unformed, early, germinal, elementary, primary
FORMAL incipient, inchoate
F3 developed

emend *v*
correct, rectify, edit, revise, rewrite, polish, refine, improve, alter, amend, fix, repair
FORMAL redact

emend or **amend**?
See panel at **amend**.

emendation *n*
correction, editing, revision, rewriting, refinement,

improvement, alteration, amendment
FORMAL corrigendum, rectification, redaction

emerge *v*
1 *emerge from the office*
come out, come forth, come into view, emanate, issue, proceed, arise, rise, surface, appear, develop, turn up, materialize
2 *the facts emerged*
become known, come out, come to light, be revealed, become apparent, appear, transpire, turn out
COLLOQ. crop up
F3 **1** disappear

emergence *n*
appearance, rise, coming, dawn, development, arrival, coming, springing-up, unfolding, disclosure, issue
FORMAL advent
F3 disappearance

emergency *n, adj*
♦ *n*
crisis, danger, accident, catastrophe, disaster, extremity, calamity, difficulty, predicament, plight, pinch, strait, dilemma, quandary
FORMAL exigency
COLLOQ. scrape, mess, pickle, fix, hot water
♦ *adj*
1 *an emergency meeting*
urgent, crisis, immediate, top-priority, extraordinary
2 *emergency supplies*
alternative, back-up, reserve, spare, substitute, extra, fall-back

emergent *adj*
budding, coming (out), fledgling, developing, emerging, embryonic, rising, independent
FORMAL burgeoning
F3 declining, disappearing

emetic *adj, n*
♦ *adj*
emetical, vomitive, vomitory
♦ *n*
vomit, vomitary, vomitive

emigrate *v*
migrate, move abroad, relocate, move, depart, leave your home/native country, resettle

emigration *n*
moving abroad, migration, removal, departure, exodus, journey, relocation, expatriation

eminence *n*
distinction, fame, pre-eminence, prominence, renown, reputation, illustriousness, greatness, importance, esteem, celebrity, notability, note, prestige, dignity, rank

eminent *adj*
distinguished, famous, prominent, illustrious, outstanding, notable, pre-eminent, prestigious, celebrated, renowned, noted, noteworthy, conspicuous, esteemed, important, well-known, elevated, respected, great, high-ranking, high, first, superlative, grand, superior
F3 unknown, obscure, unimportant

Synonym nuances
Distinguished is a mild term for having a distinction that sets someone apart from their peers: *a distinguished philosopher*, while **prominent** would emphasize being known for this distinction: *he was among the most prominent political leaders*. You can also use **outstanding** or **pre-eminent** to appropriately describe someone who is more important or influential than most or all others.
  The terms **celebrated**, **renowned**, **respected** and **esteemed** similarly echo the idea of being widely known and having high status, as do the stronger **illustrious**,

prestigious and the particularly unequivocal **great**: *Sherlock Holmes, the world's greatest detective.* **Famous**, **well-known** and **noted**, while still positive, are perhaps less admiring in tone, in that they put the emphasis on wide recognition rather than status: *Dr Jones is a noted specialist in her field*; **conspicuous** is the least inherently approving term, given its frequent application to negative qualities. **Notable** and **noteworthy** are more approbatory, however, in their implication that something is worthy of regard.
　Elevated, along with **high-ranking**, **high** and **first** simply suggest being rated among the foremost, and do not suggest any particular attitude; **superior** and **superlative** are more marked terms to use in that they further imply supremacy: *the superlative grandeur of Verdi's music.*

eminently *adv*

highly, well, very, greatly, most, exceedingly, exceptionally, extremely, outstandingly, prominently, remarkably, notably, signally, strikingly, conspicuously, surpassingly, par excellence

emissary *n*

ambassador, agent, envoy, messenger, delegate, herald, courier, representative, diplomat, scout, deputy, intermediary, go-between, spy

emission *n*

discharge, issue, ejection, emanation, giving-out, giving-off, diffusion, transmission, exhalation, outpouring, radiation, release, production, exudation, vent

emit *v*

1 *emit fumes*
discharge, issue, eject, emanate, exude, pour out, give out, throw out, give off, send out, send forth, diffuse, radiate, release, shed, vent, ooze, leak, spew, produce, let out, express
FORMAL excrete
2 *emit a long low laugh*
produce, utter, speak, say, voice, vocalize, verbalize, express, sound
E3 1 absorb

emollient *adj, n*

◆ *adj*
1 SOOTHING, assuaging, mollifying, moisturizing, palliative, softening
FORMAL assuasive, balsamic, demulcent, lenitive, mitigative
2 CONCILIATORY, placatory, appeasing, calming
FORMAL propitiatory
◆ *n*
cream, lotion, moisturizer, oil, ointment, balm, poultice, salve
FORMAL lenitive, liniment, unguent

emolument *n*

pay, salary, wages, payment, remuneration, return, reward, allowance, benefit, earnings, fee, gain, charge, profit(s), hire, honorarium, stipend, compensation, recompense

emotion *n*

feeling, passion, sensation, sense, affection, movement, sensibility, transport, sentiment, ardour, fervour, spirit, warmth, reaction, vehemence, excitement, thrill, joy, happiness, ecstasy, sadness, sorrow, grief, reverence, sublimity, surprise, fear, despair, dread, hate, anger, pang, spasm, shock, turn, whirl, upsurge
TECHNICAL affect, anoesis
OLD motion

emotional *adj*

1 FEELING, passionate, sensitive, responsive, loving, ardent, tender, warm, roused, demonstrative, excitable, enthusiastic, fervent, fervid, glowing, radiant, swelling,

impassioned, moved, sentimental, zealous, hot-blooded, red-hot, white-hot, heated, tempestuous, overcharged, temperamental, fiery, psychological, soulful, susceptible
2 EMOTIVE, moving, poignant, thrilling, touching, stirring, heartwarming, soul-stirring, tearful, exciting, effusive, gushing, full-hearted, sentimental, pathetic
COLLOQ. tear-jerking, soppy, schmaltzy
E3 1 unemotional, cold, detached, calm

emotionally *adv*

1 *emotionally involved*
passionately, lovingly, ardently, fervently, tenderly, warmly, demonstratively, with all your heart, enthusiastically, zealously, temperamentally, poignantly, touchingly, heartwarmingly, sentimentally, psychologically
2 *emotionally charged negotiations*
awkwardly, controversially, delicately, sensitively, tensely, nervously, under pressure

emotionless *adj*

cold, cold-blooded, cool, distant, undemonstrative, unaffected, unemotional, unfeeling, unmoved, unblinking, impassive, detached, clinical, indifferent, insensible, remote, blank, toneless, frigid, glacial, cold-fish
OLD impassible
FORMAL imperturbable, phlegmatic
E3 emotional

emotive *adj*

controversial, delicate, inflammatory, sensitive, awkward, touchy

empathize *v*

share, identify with, feel for, comfort, support, understand, have a rapport, be sensitive towards
COLLOQ. be on the same wavelength, put yourself in someone's shoes

emperor *n*

ruler, sovereign, king, queen, imperial, imperator, kaiser, mikado, shogun, tsar, czar
Related adjective: imperial

emphasis *n*

1 IMPORTANCE, stress, weight, significance, priority, focus, underscoring, accent, accentuation, force, power, prominence, pre-eminence, attention, intensity, strength, urgency, positiveness, insistence, mark, moment
2 *the emphasis is on the second syllable*
stress, accent, weight, force

emphasize *v*

1 *emphasize the differences*
stress, accentuate, underline, highlight, call/draw attention to, accent, feature, dwell on, weight, point up, spotlight, play up, insist on, press home, intensify, heighten, strengthen, punctuate, bring to the fore
COLLOQ. drive the point home
2 *emphasize a syllable*
put stress on, accent, stress, accentuate
E3 1 play down, understate

emphatic *adj*

1 *an emphatic gesture*
forceful, positive, insistent, certain, definite, decided, unequivocal, absolute, categorical, earnest, marked, pronounced, significant, unmistak(e)able, distinctive, strong, striking, vigorous, distinct, energetic, forcible, vehement, firm, important, impressive, momentous, powerful, punctuated, telling, vivid, direct
2 *an emphatic win*
decisive, marked, distinctive, conclusive, momentous, unmistak(e)able
E3 1 tentative, hesitant, understated

emphatically *adv*

1 *reply emphatically*
forcefully, insistently, unequivocally, strongly, firmly,

distinctively, vigorously, vehemently
2 *this is emphatically not a lie*
certainly, definitely, absolutely, categorically
E3 1 hesitantly

empire n
1 DOMAIN, dominion, kingdom, realm, province, commonwealth, territory
Related adjective: imperial
2 SUPREMACY, sovereignty, rule, authority, dominion, command, government, jurisdiction, control, power, sway
3 *a cosmetics empire*
corporation, organization, multinational, conglomerate, consortium, business, firm, company

empirical adj
practical, pragmatic, experimental, observed
FORMAL experiential
E3 theoretical, conjectural, speculative

empirically adv
experimentally, practically, pragmatically
FORMAL experientially
E3 theoretically

employ v
1 ENGAGE, hire, appoint, take on, recruit, sign up, enlist, commission, put on the payroll, retain, fill, occupy, take up, apprentice
2 USE, utilize, make use of, put to use, apply, draw on, exploit, take advantage of, bring to bear, bring into play, ply, exercise, exert

employed adj
working, in work, in employment, with a job, earning, hired, occupied, engaged, active, preoccupied, busy
E3 unemployed, jobless

employee n
worker, working man/woman, working person, blue-collar worker, white-collar worker, member of staff, job-holder, hand, wage-earner, assistant, labourer, operative, casual, help, man, woman
OLD waterclerk
SLANG rainmaker; *N Am* gofer, munchkin

employer n
proprietor, owner, manager, head, management, director, executive, company, firm, business, establishment, organization, entrepreneur, governor, master, mistress, workmaster, workmistress, taskmaster, taskmistress
COLLOQ. boss, skipper, gaffer, guv

employment n
1 JOB, work, position, post, occupation, situation, business, calling, profession, vocation, trade, service, métier, pursuit, craft
COLLOQ. line
2 ENLISTMENT, employ, engagement, hire, hiring, taking-on, recruitment, apprenticeship, signing-up
E3 1 unemployment

emporium n
shop, store, establishment, bazaar, market, boutique, market-place, mart, fair

empower v
1 AUTHORIZE, warrant, enable, license, certify, sanction, permit, entitle, commission, delegate, qualify
FORMAL accredit
2 EQUIP, enable, set free, give power/means to

empress n
ruler, sovereign, queen, imperator, imperial, kaiserin, tsarina, czarina

emptiness n
1 VACUUM, vacantness, void, voidness, hollowness, hunger, bareness, barrenness, desolation
FORMAL hiatus

2 FUTILITY, meaninglessness, uselessness, worthlessness, aimlessness, purposelessness, senselessness, ineffectiveness, insubstantiality, hollowness, unreality
E3 1 fullness

empty adj, v
◆ adj
1 VACANT, with nothing in it, containing nothing, void, unoccupied, free, available, uninhabited, unfilled, deserted, barren, bare, hollow, desolate, blank, clear
2 *an empty gesture*
futile, aimless, meaningless, senseless, trivial, vain, idle, worthless, useless, fruitless, unreal, insubstantial, ineffective, insincere
FORMAL ineffectual
3 *an empty period of life*
aimless, meaningless, senseless, purposeless, futile, pointless, vain, hollow, worthless, useless
4 VACUOUS, inane, expressionless, blank, vacant, deadpan
E3 1 full **2** meaningful **3** interesting, eventful
◆ v
drain, exhaust, discharge, issue, clear, turn out, evacuate, vacate, leave, go out, pour out, flow out, use up, unload, unpack, void, gut
E3 fill

Synonym nuances
adjective sense 1
Vacant, **unoccupied** and **unfilled** tend to be used of an empty place or unfilled position, and **void**, although similar, has connotations of a more wasteful emptiness: *the cathedral has vast arches and void spaces*. **Free** and **available**, on the other hand, have more positive associations of potential which is yet to be fulfilled: *is this seat free?*; *there are still places available for this trip*. **Uninhabited** is specifically used to refer to a lack of resident people, while **deserted** more evocatively suggests abandonment by people: *the streets were deserted while the big match was on television*.
  Barren is more suggestive of a lack of vegetation, but again has connotations of waste. **Bare**, however, may be widely used of a lack of any form of covering, although any associations tend to be negative: *the room was bare and filthy*. You might use the word **desolate** to convey a bleak, forsaken appearance: *the dark and desolate moorlands*.
  Blank has more to do with being unmarked or, more specifically, not written on, and is not particularly connotative: *blank pages*; *a blank screen*; but **clear** has a more positive association of being free of any unwanted contents: *a clear, sunny sky*; *a clear conscience*.

---

empty-headed adj
inane, silly, stupid, foolish, unintelligent, frivolous
COLLOQ. scatter-brained, scatty, feather-brained, rattl-brained, daft, dopey, batty, dotty, dippy; *N Am* ditsy
E3 intelligent

emulate v
match, copy, mimic, follow, imitate, model yourself on, echo, reproduce, compete with, contend with, rival, vie with
COLLOQ. take a leaf out of someone's book

emulation n
copying, mimicry, following, imitation, echoing, matching, challenge, competition, contention, contest, rivalry, strife

enable v
1 AUTHORIZE, equip, qualify, entitle, empower, sanction, warrant, allow, permit, prepare, equip, fit, license, commission, endue
FORMAL accredit, validate
2 FACILITATE, make possible, make easier, let, allow, permit,

help, further, clear/pave the way for
🔁 prevent, inhibit, forbid

enact v
1 DECREE, ordain, order, authorize, command, legislate, rule, sanction, approve, ratify, pass, make law, establish
2 ACT OUT, perform, play, portray, represent, depict, appear as
🔁 **1** repeal, rescind

enactment n
1 PASSING, authorization, approval, sanction, ratification, legislation, rule, bill, act, statute, law, order, decree, edict, command, commandment, ordinance, regulation
2 PERFORMANCE, play, playing, performing, acting, portrayal, representation, staging
🔁 **1** repeal

enamoured adj
charmed, infatuated, in love with, enchanted, captivated, entranced, bewitched, enthralled, smitten, besotted, keen, wild, mad, taken, fascinated, fond

en bloc adv
en masse, all at once, all together, as a group, as a whole, as one, ensemble, in a body, wholesale

encampment n
camp, camping-ground, campsite, base, bivouac, barracks, quarters, tents

encapsulate v
sum up, summarize, typify, exemplify, epitomize, capture, include, contain, take in, represent, condense, digest, abridge, compress, précis

encapsulation n
summary, representation, digest, précis, exemplification, expression

encase v
cover, surround, enclose, bound, envelop, confine, frame, wrap

enchant v
1 CAPTIVATE, charm, fascinate, enrapture, enamour, attract, allure, appeal, delight, thrill, sirenize
OLD becharm
2 ENTRANCE, enthral, bewitch, beguile, spellbind, spell, hypnotize, mesmerize
🔁 **1** repel

enchanter n
conjurer, magician, magus, mesmerist, necromancer, reim-kennar, sorcerer, spellbinder, warlock, witch, wizard, archimage

enchanting adj
charming, delightful, attractive, fascinating, appealing, lovely, pleasant, wonderful, alluring, bewitching, captivating, endearing, entrancing, irresistible, mesmerizing, ravishing, winsome
🔁 boring, repellent

enchantment n
1 DELIGHT, fascination, charm, appeal, attractiveness, allure, allurement, glamour, bliss, rapture, ecstasy
2 SPELL, magic, witchcraft, witching, wizardry, hypnotism, sorcery, incantation, charm, mesmerism
OLD gramary, malefice
FORMAL conjuration, necromancy
🔁 **1** disenchantment

enchantress n
1 SORCERESS, magician, spellbinder, witch, conjurer, fairy, Circe, lamia
FORMAL necromancer
2 SEDUCTRESS, charmer, siren, vamp, femme fatale

encircle v
surround, encompass, compass, ring, circle, orbit, girdle,

enclose, enfold, envelop, crowd, close in, hem in
FORMAL circumscribe, gird

enclose v
1 SURROUND, encircle, encompass, ring, circle, fence, hedge, hem in, bound, encase, embrace, envelop, confine, frame, cage, cocoon, hold, shut in, close in, wrap, pen, cover, corral
OLD (*Shakesp*) inhoop, womb
FORMAL circumscribe
2 INCLUDE, insert, contain, put in, send with
FORMAL comprehend

enclosure n
1 *herded into the enclosure*
pen, pound, compound, paddock, fold, stockade, sty, run, arena, area, corral, kraal, court, yard, ring, fencing, close, cloister; *Irish* bawn; *S Afr* camp
2 INSERTION, inclusion, addition

encode v
encrypt, encipher, cipher, put into code, scramble, ravel, garble, obscure, disguise, make mysterious
🔁 decode

encompass v
1 ENCIRCLE, circle, ring, surround, envelop, close in, shut in, hem in, confine, enclose, hold
FORMAL gird, circumscribe
2 INCLUDE, cover, embrace, contain, take in, admit, incorporate, involve, embody, span
FORMAL comprise, comprehend

encore n
repeat, repetition, replay, additional/extra performance

encounter v, n
◆ v
1 *encounter difficulties*
confront, face, be faced with, experience, be/come up against, deal with, cope with, tackle
2 MEET, come across, run across, stumble across
FORMAL happen on, chance upon
COLLOQ. run into, bump into
3 FIGHT, clash with, combat, engage, grapple with, struggle, strive, contend, tussle, do battle with, come into conflict with, compete with, match
COLLOQ. cross swords with
◆ n
1 MEETING, contact, rendezvous, brush, confrontation, rencounter
2 CLASH, fight, combat, conflict, struggle, contest, battle, dispute, engagement, action, skirmish, brush, run-in, collision, joust, tilt, passage of arms
OLD ruffle; (*Shakesp*) close
COLLOQ. set-to

encourage v
1 HEARTEN, stimulate, motivate, spur, reassure, rally, give moral support to, be supportive to, animate, stir, inspire, incite, buoy up, cheer, urge, rouse, comfort, embolden, console; *Aust & NZ* barrack for
FORMAL exhort
COLLOQ. pep up, buck up
2 *encourage someone to do something*
persuade, influence, sway, win over, coax, convince, prompt, talk into
FORMAL exhort
COLLOQ. egg on
3 PROMOTE, advance, aid, boost, forward, further, foster, back, support, help, assist, advocate, favour, strengthen
🔁 **1** discourage, depress **2** discourage, dissuade **3** discourage

encouragement n
1 REASSURANCE, inspiration, motivation, cheer, cheering, heartening, incitement, urging, coaxing, persuasion, stimulation, consolation

FORMAL exhortation, succour
COLLOQ. pep talk
2 PROMOTION, help, aid, assistance, boost, incentive, support, backing, endorsement, stimulus, furtherance
COLLOQ. shot in the arm
E3 1 discouragement, disapproval

encouraging adj
heartening, promising, hopeful, reassuring, stimulating, inspiring, uplifting, cheering, comforting, supportive, bright, rosy, cheerful, satisfactory
FORMAL auspicious
E3 discouraging

encroach v
intrude, invade, impinge, trespass, infringe, usurp, overstep, overrun, infiltrate, make inroads
COLLOQ. muscle in on, tread on someone's toes

encroachment n
intrusion, invasion, trespass, trespassing, infringement, overstepping, infiltration
FORMAL incursion

encrypt v
encode, encipher, cipher, put into code, scramble, ravel, garble, obscure, disguise, make mysterious
E3 decode

encumber v
1 BURDEN, overload, load, weigh down, saddle, strain, stress, oppress, handicap, hamper, hinder, impede, restrain, slow down, obstruct, constrain, inconvenience, prevent, check, cramp
FORMAL retard
2 BLOCK, congest, jam, pack, stuff, cram

encumbrance n
burden, load, weight, cross, millstone, albatross, difficulty, restraint, constraint, handicap, impediment, obstruction, obstacle, inconvenience, strain, stress, hindrance, liability, obligation, responsibility
FORMAL cumbrance

encyclopedic adj
complete, exhaustive, comprehensive, thorough, thoroughgoing, in-depth, wide-ranging, vast, all-inclusive, broad, all-embracing, all-encompassing, universal, compendious
E3 incomplete, narrow

end n, v
♦ n
1 FINISH, conclusion, close, ending, completion, culmination, epilogue, finale, dénouement
FORMAL termination, cessation
2 EXTREMITY, boundary, border, edge, limit, margin, tip, butt, stub
3 REMAINDER, tip, butt, remnant, stub, scrap, vestige, fragment, leftovers
4 AIM, object, objective, purpose, intention, goal, target, point, reason, motive, design
FORMAL intent
5 RESULT, outcome, consequence, issue, upshot
6 DEATH, dying, destruction, extermination, downfall, doom, ruin, extinction, dissolution
FORMAL demise
7 PART, aspect, side, area, field, section, department, branch
E3 1 beginning, start **6** birth
♦ v
1 FINISH, come/bring to an end, close, stop, cease, be over, expire, complete, round off, culminate, break off, die out, fade away, run out
OLD (Shakesp) fine, period
FORMAL conclude, terminate, discontinue
COLLOQ. wind up
2 DESTROY, annihilate, exterminate, extinguish, ruin, abolish, dissolve

E3 1 begin, start; formal commence
■ **the end**
intolerable, unbearable, unendurable, too much, enough, beyond endurance, insufferable, the worst
COLLOQ. the limit, the last straw, the final blow

endanger v
hazard, risk, put at risk, jeopardize, put in jeopardy, expose, threaten, put in danger, compromise
FORMAL imperil
E3 protect

endearing adj
lov(e)able, charming, appealing, attractive, winsome, engaging, delightful, sweet, adorable, cute, captivating, enchanting

endearment n
1 AFFECTION, love, fondness, attachment
2 *whispered endearments*
sweet nothing, sweet talk, term of affection, diminutive, pet-name
FORMAL hypocorism

endeavour v, n
♦ v
attempt, try, strive, struggle, aim, aspire, undertake, venture, try your hand at, labour, take pains, do your best
FORMAL seek
♦ n
attempt, effort, try, undertaking, enterprise, aim, venture, striving
COLLOQ. go, shot, stab, bash, crack

ending n
end, close, finish, completion, conclusion, culmination, climax, resolution, dénouement, finale, epilogue
FORMAL termination, consummation, cessation
E3 beginning, start

endless adj
1 INFINITE, without end, unending, boundless, limitless, unlimited, measureless
2 EVERLASTING, perpetual, ceaseless, constant, continual, continuous, undying, eternal, interminable, boring, monotonous
OLD (Shakesp) fineless
3 UNBROKEN, continuous, constant, uninterrupted, entire, whole
E3 1 finite, limited **2** temporary

endlessly adv
infinitely, without end, without stopping, ceaselessly, unendingly, limitlessly, perpetually, constantly, continually, continuously, eternally, interminably, uninterruptedly, day in day out, day after day, through thick and thin
COLLOQ. till the cows come home

endorse v
1 APPROVE, sanction, authorize, support, back, be/get behind, favour, ratify, confirm, affirm, vouch for, advocate, uphold, warrant, recommend, subscribe to, sustain, adopt
COLLOQ. throw your weight behind
2 SIGN, countersign, sign on the back of, initial

endorsement n
1 APPROVAL, sanction, authorization, support, backing, ratification, confirmation, affirmation, advocacy, warrant, recommendation, commendation, seal of approval, testimonial, subscription
FORMAL approbation
COLLOQ. OK, green light, thumbs-up
2 SIGNATURE, countersignature, initialling

endow v
1 FINANCE, give, donate, pay for, grant, boast, present, award, fund, support, make over, leave, will
FORMAL bestow, bequeath, confer

2 HAVE, possess, give, provide, furnish, supply, present, enjoy, boast, be endued with, be blessed with

endowment n
1 FINANCE, award, grant, fund, funding, gift, present, provision, settlement, donation, dowry, legacy, income, revenue
FORMAL bequest, bestowal, benefaction
2 TALENT, attribute, faculty, gift, aptitude, capability, ability, quality, flair, power, capacity, genius, qualification, attribute, character

endurable adj
bearable, tolerable, supportable, manageable, withstandable, sustainable, sufferable
E3 intolerable, unbearable

endurance n
patience, staying power, stamina, resignation, stoicism, sufferance, tenacity, perseverance, resolution, stability, durability, backbone, persistence, strength, tolerance, toleration
FORMAL fortitude
COLLOQ. guts, spunk, bottle, stickability

endure v
1 *endure hardship*
bear, stand, put up with, tolerate, abide, weather, brave, cope with, face, go through, encounter, meet, experience, submit to, suffer, sustain, swallow, undergo, withstand, take, have, hold, stick, allow, permit, support, brook; *dialect* abear; *Scot* dree, thole
OLD bide, abrooke, outstand
COLLOQ. stomach, stick it, sweat it out, tough it out
2 *a peace that will endure for ever*
last, remain, live, survive, stay, persist, continue, hold, hold out, keep, wear, prevail
OLD aby, dure, perdure
FORMAL abide

enduring adj
lasting, long-lasting, durable, permanent, perpetual, abiding, remaining, continuing, long-standing, stable, steady, firm, steadfast, persistent, persisting, chronic, prevailing, surviving, unfaltering, unwavering, eternal, immortal, imperishable
OLD (*Spenser*) dureful
E3 changeable, fleeting

enemy n
adversary, opponent, rival, antagonist, the opposition, competitor, the competition, opposer, other side
FORMAL foe
E3 friend, ally

Synonym nuances
Adversary may be used to refer to someone who hostilely opposes you, and sounds vaguely literary: *the compelling menace of his adversary.* Other gentler terms include **opponent** which, although similar, is often used in the context of arranged competition, and does not necessarily have the same connotations of aggression. **The opposition** and **the other side** might also be used of a body of people who simply object to your views or actions.
 Rival and **competitor**, along with **the competition**, are also used specifically of people who are not necessarily enemies, but who are pursuing the same objective: *he began his campaign for the presidency with more support than his rivals.* The word **antagonist**, however, suggests someone involved in contention or a struggle, and has a more marked note of enmity: *the USA and USSR were dangerous antagonists in the Cold War.*

---

energetic adj
lively, vigorous, active, animated, dynamic, spirited,

tireless, boisterous, zestful, brisk, strong, forceful, potent, powerful, strenuous, high-powered, indefatigable; *dialect* wick
COLLOQ. bursting with energy, full of beans, go-getting, zippy, punchy
E3 lethargic, sluggish, inactive, idle

energize v
stimulate, arouse, stir, motivate, enliven, invigorate, liven, enliven, quicken, animate, vitalize, vivify, activate, electrify, galvanize
COLLOQ. pep up, fire up
E3 daunt

energy n
1 FUEL, propellant, motive power
TECHNICAL kinetic energy, potential energy
See also **fuel.**
2 LIVELINESS, vigour, activity, animation, drive, dynamism, enthusiasm, life, spirit, verve, vivacity, vitality, sparkle, effervescence, zest, zeal, ardour, fire, efficiency, force, forcefulness, effectiveness, strength, power, potency, intensity, exertion, stamina
FORMAL might
COLLOQ. get-up-and-go, zip, push, pep, brio, pizzazz
See Synonym nuances panel at **vigour.**
E3 2 lethargy, inertia, weakness, anergy

enervated adj
tired, weak, exhausted, feeble, fatigued, worn out, weakened, incapacitated, debilitated, paralysed, undermined, unmanned, unnerved, sapped, devitalized, limp, spent
FORMAL effete, enfeebled
COLLOQ. done in, run-down, washed-out; *N Am* pooped (out), tuckered out; *Aust & NZ* beaten
E3 active, energetic

enervating adj
tiring, wearying, wearisome, fatiguing, exhausting, draining, demanding, hard, tough, difficult, exacting, taxing, arduous, strenuous, laborious

enfeeble v
weaken, exhaust, fatigue, reduce, diminish, wear out, sap, geld, undermine, debilitate, unhinge, unnerve, deplete, devitalize
FORMAL enervate
E3 strengthen

enfold v
1 ENCLOSE, envelop, shroud, swathe, encircle, encompass, fold, enwrap, wrap (up)
2 EMBRACE, clasp, hug, hold, clutch

enforce v
1 IMPOSE, administer, implement, carry out, apply, execute, discharge, fulfil
2 COMPEL, insist on, oblige, urge, constrain, require, necessitate, force, pressure, pressurize, coerce, exact, prosecute, reinforce
COLLOQ. lean on, put the screws on

enforced adj
compulsory, binding, necessary, required, unavoidable, imposed, involuntary, forced, obliged, obligatory, mandatory, compelled, constrained, dictated, ordained, prescribed

enforcement n
imposition, administration, implementation, application, execution, discharge, fulfilment, insistence, coercion, obligation, compulsion, constraint, pressure, prosecution, requirement
FORMAL coaction

enfranchise v
give the right to vote to, give the vote to, free, liberate, release

FORMAL emancipate, manumit, give suffrage to
F≣ disenfranchise

enfranchisement n
giving the right to vote, voting rights, freedom, freeing,
liberating, liberation, release
FORMAL emancipation, manumission, suffrage
F≣ disenfranchisement

engage v
1 PARTICIPATE, take part, embark on, take up, practise, do,
enter into, undertake, join, involve, share, become
involved in/with
FORMAL partake of
2 ATTRACT, allure, draw, win, gain, captivate, capture,
charm, catch
3 OCCUPY, engross, absorb, employ, fill, hold, preoccupy,
busy, tie up, grip
4 EMPLOY, hire, appoint, take on, sign up/on, enlist, enrol,
commission, recruit, contract, enter into an agreement,
put on the payroll
5 INTERLOCK, mesh, enmesh, interconnect, join, fit together,
interact, attach
6 FIGHT, battle with, attack, take on, encounter,
assail, clash with, combat, join in battle with, wage war
with
F≣ 2 repel 4 dismiss, discharge 5 disengage

engaged adj
1 *engaged in his work*
occupied, busy, engrossed, immersed, absorbed,
preoccupied, involved, active, employed
COLLOQ. tied up
2 *engaged to be married*
promised, pledged, committed
FORMAL betrothed, affianced, plighted, espoused
COLLOQ. spoken for
3 *the phone is engaged*
busy, unavailable, occupied, in use, taken
COLLOQ. tied up

engagement n
1 APPOINTMENT, meeting, interview, date, arrangement,
commitment, assignation, booking, reservation, fixture,
rendezvous
COLLOQ. date, gig, snap
2 PROMISE, pledge, commitment, obligation, agreement,
contract, bond, assurance, vow
OLD plight; *Irish* hand-promise
FORMAL betrothal, betrothment, espousal, troth
3 INVOLVEMENT, participation, taking part, undertaking,
sharing
FORMAL partaking
4 FIGHT, battle, combat, conflict, attack, clash, war, assault,
strife, struggle, offensive, action, encounter, confrontation,
contest

engaging adj
charming, attractive, appealing, captivating, pleasing,
delightful, winsome, winning, lov(e)able, adorable, sweet,
lik(e)able, pleasant, fetching, fascinating, enchanting,
agreeable
F≣ repulsive, repellent

engender v
cause, produce, occasion, bring about, give rise to,
instigate, lead to, incite, induce, create, inspire, generate,
arouse, excite, encourage, nurture, kindle, breed,
propagate, provoke
OLD beget
FORMAL effect

engine n
1 *a car engine*
motor, machine, machinery, mechanism, appliance,
contraption, apparatus, device, instrument, tool,
implement, locomotive, generator, dynamo
See panels below
2 *a major engine of economic growth*
cause, instrument, vehicle, agent, medium, factor,
channel, way, means, source

engineer n, v
♦ n
1 MECHANIC, technician, operator, technician, machinist,
driver, engine driver, controller, handler
2 DESIGNER, originator, planner, builder, inventor, deviser,
mastermind, architect, civil engineer, electrical engineer,
mechanical engineer, chemical engineer, sound
engineer
♦ v
plan, contrive, devise, manoeuvre, cause, manipulate,
control, direct, bring about, mastermind, originate,
arrange, orchestrate, plot, scheme, stage-manage,
manage, create, rig
FORMAL effect

engorged adj
full, overfull, swollen, puffy, inflated, enlarged, expanded

engrave v
1 INSCRIBE, cut, carve, chisel, etch, mark, print, imprint,
impress, incise, chase
2 *engraved on her mind*
imprint, impress, fix, stamp, lodge, set, embed, engrain,
brand

engraving n
print, impression, imprint, inscription, carving, etching,
cutting, cut, woodcut, plate, block, cutting, chiselling,
mark
TECHNICAL dry-point, intaglio

engross v
absorb, occupy, engage, interest, grip, hold, preoccupy,

Types of engine include:

compression-
  ignition
	external-
	  combustion
		gas
		internal-
			jet
			oil
				reciprocating
				rocket
					turbine
					V-engine

diesel	fuel-injection	combustion	petrol	steam	water

Parts of an automotive engine and its ancillaries include:

air filter	crankshaft pulley	unit)	petrol pump	spark plug
alternator	cylinder block	fuel injector	piston	starter motor
camshaft	cylinder head	gasket	piston ring	sump
camshaft cover	drive belt	ignition coil	power-steering	tappet
carburettor	exhaust manifold	ignition distributor	pump	thermostat
choke	exhaust valve	inlet manifold	push-rod	timing belt
connecting rod	fan belt	inlet valve	radiator	timing pulley
colloq. con-rod	flywheel	oil filter	rocker arm	turbocharger
cooling fan	fuel and ignition ECU	oil pump	rocker cover	
crankshaft	(electronic control	oil seal	rotor arm	

rivet, fascinate, captivate, enthral, arrest, involve, intrigue
Ea bore

engrossed *adj*
absorbed, occupied, taken up, preoccupied, gripped,
engaged, caught up, enthralled, fascinated, captivated,
immersed, intent, intrigued, rapt, riveted, mesmerized,
wrapped, lost, fixated
Ea bored, disinterested

engrossing *adj*
absorbing, fascinating, enthralling, captivating, intriguing,
gripping, interesting, compelling, riveting, suspenseful
COLLOQ. unputdownable
Ea boring

engulf *v*
overwhelm, swamp, flood, deluge, drown, inundate,
plunge, immerse, submerge, overrun, overtake, swallow
up, devour, consume, bury, absorb, engross, envelop

enhance *v*
heighten, intensify, increase, improve, upgrade, elevate,
add to, enrich, magnify, swell, exalt, raise, lift, boost,
strengthen, emphasize, stress, reinforce, embellish
FORMAL augment
Ea reduce, minimize

enhancement *n*
heightening, increase, improvement, elevation,
enrichment, magnification, intensification, boost,
emphasis, stress, reinforcement
FORMAL augmentation

enigma *n*
mystery, riddle, puzzle, paradox, conundrum, problem,
dilemma, quandary, brain-teaser; *N Am* brain-twister
COLLOQ. poser

enigmatic *adj*
mysterious, mystifying, puzzling, cryptic, obscure,
strange, baffling, perplexing, paradoxical,
incomprehensible, inexplicable, unfathomable
FORMAL arcane, esoteric, recondite
Ea simple, straightforward

enjoin *v*
1 ORDER, command, demand, urge, direct, instruct, decree,
ordain, advise, encourage, require, charge
2 PROHIBIT, forbid, ban, bar
FORMAL disallow, interdict, proscribe

enjoy *v*
1 *enjoy dancing*
take pleasure in, delight in, appreciate, like, relish, revel in,
love, be fond of, rejoice in, savour
OLD joy, taste
COLLOQ. fancy, go for, go a bundle on, get a buzz out of, get
a kick out of
2 *enjoy an advantage*
have, have the use of, possess, be blessed with, be
endowed with, be favoured with, benefit from
OLD wield, undergo
FORMAL partake of
COLLOQ. have something going for
Ea 1 dislike, hate
■ **enjoy yourself**
have a good time, have fun, make merry, sport
COLLOQ. have a whale of a time, live it up, party, let your
hair down, paint the town red, have a ball, have a
blast, get your jollies, get your kicks, have it large, large
it
SLANG *N Am* ball; *S Afr* jol

enjoyable *adj*
pleasant, agreeable, delightful, pleasing, entertaining,
amusing, fun, pleasurable, delicious, fine, lovely, good,
nice, satisfying
FORMAL gratifying, delectable

COLLOQ. smashing, cool, ace, wizard, brilliant, brill, super,
fantastic, fab, fabulous; *N Am* neat; *S Afr* lekker
SLANG radical, wicked, bad, mega
Ea disagreeable

enjoyment *n*
1 PLEASURE, delight, amusement, entertainment, relish, joy,
fun, gladness, happiness, diversion, recreation,
indulgence, zest, satisfaction
FORMAL gratification, delectation
2 POSSESSION, use, advantage, benefit, privilege, favour,
blessing
Ea 1 displeasure

enlarge *v*
1 *enlarge the garden; glands enlarging*
make/become larger, make/become bigger, increase,
expand, extend, magnify, add to, supplement, inflate,
swell, stretch, multiply, develop, amplify, widen, broaden,
lengthen, heighten
TECHNICAL distend, dilate, intumesce
FORMAL augment, elongate
2 *enlarge a photograph*
make bigger, blow up, expand, magnify
3 *enlarge on something*
expand on, go into details, elaborate on
FORMAL expatiate on, dilate on
Ea 1 diminish, shrink

enlargement *n*
1 *enlargement of the building/a gland*
increase, expansion, growth, extension, magnification,
inflation swelling, stretching, multiplication, development,
amplification
TECHNICAL distension, dilation, intumescence, oedema
FORMAL augmentation
2 *a photographic enlargement*
blow-up, magnification
Ea 2 contraction, decrease, reduction

enlighten *v*
instruct, edify, cultivate, educate, inform, illuminate, teach,
tutor, counsel, apprise, advise, notify, make aware, open
your eyes
Ea confuse

enlightened *adj*
informed, aware, knowledgeable, educated, civilized,
cultivated, refined, cultured, sophisticated, conversant,
wise, learned, intellectual, reasonable, liberal, broad-
minded, open-minded, literate
FORMAL erudite
Ea ignorant, confused

enlightenment *n*
awareness, knowledge, teaching, understanding,
illumination, light, education, instruction, wisdom,
information, insight, comprehension, civilization,
cultivation, refinement, learning, literacy, edification,
sophistication, broad-mindedness, open-mindedness,
eye-opener, *Aufklärung*
TECHNICAL satori
FORMAL erudition, sapience
Ea confusion, ignorance

enlist *v*
1 *enlist in the army*
engage, enrol, register, sign up, recruit, conscript, hire, take
on, employ, volunteer, join (up), gather, muster
2 *enlist someone's help*
secure, obtain, enter, win, engage, get
FORMAL procure

enliven *v*
excite, exhilarate, brighten (up), cheer (up), gladden,
hearten, invigorate, rouse, wake up, liven (up), stimulate,
revitalize, inspire, animate, buoy up, fire, kindle, quicken,
spark

FORMAL vivify
COLLOQ. pep up, perk up, give a lift to
⊟ subdue

en masse adv

all at once, all together, as a group, as a whole, as one, ensemble, in a body, together, en bloc, wholesale

enmeshed adj

involved, associated, concerned, caught up, entangled, mixed up

enmity n

animosity, hostility, antagonism, discord, strife, feud, antipathy, bitterness, acrimony, malevolence, hate, hatred, aversion, ill-will, bad blood, rancour, malice, venom
⊟ friendship, reconciliation

ennoble v

dignify, uplift, elevate, raise, exalt, enhance, glorify, honour, magnify
FORMAL aggrandize, nobilitate

ennui n

boredom, tiredness, dissatisfaction, tedium, lassitude, listlessness, languor, malaise
FORMAL accidie, acedia
COLLOQ. the doldrums

enormity n

atrocity, outrage, iniquity, horror, evil, crime, abomination, violation, monstrosity, outrageousness, wickedness, vileness, depravity, evilness, atrociousness, viciousness

❗ enormity or enormousness?
Of these two nouns, only *enormousness* should be used when referring to size: *the enormousness of his ambitions*. *Enormity* means 'great wickedness, seriousness (of a crime, etc)': *the enormity of his assault on the little girl*.

enormous adj

huge, immense, vast, gigantic, massive, colossal, large-scale, gross, gargantuan, astronomic, monstrous, mammoth, considerable, tremendous, stupendous, prodigious, giant, Titanic
COLLOQ. jumbo, great big, whopping, walloping, whacking, whaling, plonking, hulking great, ginormous, humongous, monster, God-almighty
SLANG mega
⊟ small, tiny

enormously adv

very, extremely, to a vast/huge/immense extent, hugely, exceptionally, extraordinarily, exceedingly, especially, massively, tremendously, immensely
OLD jolly
COLLOQ. terribly, devilish, well, dead

enormousness n

hugeness, immensity, immenseness, vastness, massiveness, largeness, greatness, magnitude, expanse, extensiveness

enough adj, n, adv

• adj
sufficient, adequate, ample, plenty, abundant
⊟ insufficient, inadequate
• n
sufficiency, adequacy, plenty, abundance, ample supply
FORMAL amplitude
• adv
sufficiently, adequately, reasonably, tolerably, passably, moderately, fairly, satisfactorily, amply

en passant adv

in passing, by the way, while on the subject, incidentally, cursorily
FORMAL parenthetically

enquire, enquirer, enquiring, enquiringly, enquiry

see **inquire, inquirer, inquiring, inquringly, inquiry**.

enrage v

incense, infuriate, anger, make angry, annoy, madden, provoke, incite, inflame, agitate, exasperate, irritate, rile, irk, vex
COLLOQ. needle, bug, wind up, hack off, drive someone up the wall, drive someone round the bend, make someone's blood boil, make someone's hackles rise, put/get someone's back up, push too far
SLANG piss off
⊟ calm, placate

enraged adj

incensed, infuriated, angry, angered, furious, livid, raging, seething, storming, inflamed, annoyed, irritated, irate, exasperated, fuming
COLLOQ. aggravated, mad, wild
SLANG pissed off; *N Am* pissed
⊟ calm

enrapture v

enchant, fascinate, charm, thrill, delight, please greatly, captivate, bewitch, beguile, enthral, entrance, spellbind, transport, ravish

enrich v

1 ENDOW, enhance, improve, refine, develop, cultivate, add to, supplement
FORMAL augment, aggrandize, ameliorate
2 ADORN, ornament, beautify, embellish, decorate, garnish, grace, gild
⊟ 1 impoverish

enrol v

1 REGISTER, enlist, sign on, sign up, join up, recruit, go in for, enter, put your name down, engage, admit
2 RECORD, list, note, enter, put down
FORMAL inscribe

enrolment n

registration, recruitment, enlistment, enlisting, signing on/up, joining up, admission, acceptance

en route adv

in transit, on the move, on the way, on the road, on/during the journey

ensconce v

install, settle, establish, entrench, nestle, put, place, lodge, protect, shelter, shield, screen, locate

ensemble n

1 WHOLE, total, entirety, entity, unit, sum, set, group, collection, accumulation
FORMAL aggregate
COLLOQ. whole caboodle, whole (bang) shoot
2 OUTFIT, costume, suit, co-ordinates
COLLOQ. get-up, rig-out
3 GROUP, band, orchestra, company, troupe, circle, chorus, cast

enshrine v

preserve, set down, lay down, protect, guard, shield, treasure, cherish, immortalize, consecrate, dedicate, exalt, hallow, revere, sanctify, idolize, embalm
FORMAL apotheosize

enshroud v

cloak, cloud, shroud, veil, pall, wrap, conceal, hide, cover, enclose, enfold, envelop, enwrap, obscure

ensign n

banner, standard, flag, colours, pennant, jack, badge, crest, shield, coat of arms, sign, pennon, gonfalon
OLD pavilion

enslave v

subject, dominate, bind, enchain, yoke, trap
FORMAL subjugate, disenfranchise
⊟ free, emancipate

enslavement *n*
slavery, subjection, servitude, bondage, captivity, oppression, repression, serfdom, vassalage
FORMAL dulosis, enthralment, subjugation, thraldom, disenfranchisement
E3 emancipation

ensnare *v*
trap, catch, capture, net, snare, embroil, enmesh, entangle, entrap

ensue *v*
follow, issue, proceed, succeed, result, arise, happen, occur, transpire, turn out, flow, derive, develop, stem, come next
FORMAL befall
E3 precede

ensure *v*
1 MAKE CERTAIN, make sure, guarantee, warrant, secure, certify
FORMAL effect
2 PROTECT, make safe, guard, safeguard, secure

entail *v*
involve, necessitate, occasion, need, require, call for, demand, cause, produce, bring about, give rise to, lead to, result in

entangle *v*
1 *entangled in the net*
tangle, twist, knot, ravel, intertwine, enmesh, ensnare, snare, mix up
2 EMBROIL, involve, implicate, complicate, confuse, jumble, muddle
E3 1, 2 disentangle

entanglement *n*
1 TANGLE, knot, mesh, tie, trap, jumble, ensnarement, entrapment, snare
2 INVOLVEMENT, complication, embarrassment, confusion, muddle, snarl-up, difficulty, mess, mix-up, predicament, liaison, relationship, affair
E3 1, 2 disentanglement

entente *n*
agreement, arrangement, friendship, deal, pact, treaty, understanding, entente cordiale
FORMAL compact

enter *v*
1 COME IN TO, go in (to), get in (to), arrive, gain access to, cross the threshold, burst in, sneak in, break in, worm your way in, insert, introduce, board, infiltrate, penetrate, pierce, occupy
COLLOQ. pop in
2 JOIN, become a member of, enlist, set about, sign up, put your name down for, take up, participate, take part, go in for, undertake, embark upon, enrol, start, begin, engage in, get involved in
FORMAL commence
3 RECORD, log, note, list, register, put down, take down, write down, set down, inscribe, lodge, put on record, submit, go in for, input
4 *the country entered a new period of reform*
begin, start, embark on, launch into, introduce
E3 1 depart 3 delete

enterprise *n*
1 UNDERTAKING, venture, project, plan, effort, operation, campaign, programme, endeavour, task, scheme
OLD design, expedience, emprise; (*Shakesp*) designment
COLLOQ. show
2 INITIATIVE, resourcefulness, drive, adventurousness, adventure, courage, boldness, imagination, ambition, energy, enthusiasm, strong feeling, spirit, vitality, gumption
COLLOQ. get-up-and-go, push, oomph

3 BUSINESS, company, firm, establishment, operation, concern, industry
E3 2 apathy

enterprising *adj*
venturesome, adventurous, bold, daring, imaginative, resourceful, entrepreneurial, self-reliant, self-motivated, enthusiastic, energetic, keen, eager, zealous, ambitious, aspiring, pushy, go-ahead, spirited, vigorous, active, ingenious, undertaking
COLLOQ. goey
E3 unenterprising, lethargic

entertain *v*
1 AMUSE, divert, please, delight, cheer, interest, occupy, engage, engross, charm, captivate, distract
2 RECEIVE, have guests, ask over/round, have round, invite over/round, accommodate, play host to, provide hospitality, put up, treat, host, regale, junket, harbour
3 HARBOUR, contemplate, consider, think about, imagine, have, conceive, foster, nurture, cherish
FORMAL countenance
COLLOQ. flirt with
E3 1 bore 3 reject

entertainer

Entertainers include:

acrobat	fire-eater	performer
actor	game-show host	player
actress	hypnotist	pole dancer
artiste	ice-skater	presenter
busker	impressionist	singer
chat-show host	jester	song-and-dance
clown	juggler	act
comedian	lap dancer	stand-up comic
comic	magician	stripper
conjuror	mime artist	striptease artist
dancer	mimic	trapeze artist
disc jockey	mind-reader	tightrope walker
colloq. DJ	minstrel	ventriloquist
escapologist	musician	

See also **musician; singer**.

---

entertaining *adj*
amusing, diverting, fun, recreational, enjoyable, delightful, interesting, pleasant, pleasing, pleasurable, humorous, funny, comical, witty
E3 boring

entertainment *n*
1 AMUSEMENT, diversion, recreation, enjoyment, play, hobby, pastime, fun, sport, leisure, activity, distraction, pleasure

---

Forms of entertainment include:

airshow	festival	puppet show
barbecue	fête	radio
cabaret	firework party	reality television
carnival	game show	recital
cartoon show	gymkhana	revue
casino	karaoke	rodeo
chat show	makeover show	show business
cinema	laser-light show	*colloq.* show biz
circus	magic show	sitcom
computer game	musical	soap opera
concert	music hall	television
dance	nightclub	theatre
disco	opera	variety show
discothèque	pageant	video
documentary	pantomime	video game
docusoap	Punch-and-Judy	waxworks
DVD	show	zoo

See also **performance; theatrical**.

2 SHOW, spectacle, performance, play, presentation, extravaganza

enthral v
captivate, entrance, enchant, fascinate, charm, beguile, bewitch, thrill, enrapture, delight, intrigue, spellbind, hypnotize, mesmerize, engross, grip, rivet, absorb
F3 1 bore

enthralling adj
captivating, entrancing, enchanting, fascinating, intriguing, beguiling, charming, thrilling, riveting, gripping, compulsive, compelling, spellbinding, hypnotizing, mesmerizing, mesmeric
F3 boring

enthuse v
praise, rave, wax lyrical, gush, drool, excite, inspire, motivate, fire, bubble over, effervesce, go into raptures

enthusiasm n
1 ZEAL, ardour, fervour, passion, keenness, eagerness, vehemence, warmth, zest, frenzy, fire, excitement, acclamation, furore, furor, earnestness, relish, spirit, brio, wholeheartedness, commitment, devotion, fanaticism, ecstasy, delirium
OLD verve
FORMAL ebullience, schwärmerei, *entraînement*, *estro*
COLLOQ. buzz, hype, oomph
2 INTEREST, hobby, pastime, passion, preoccupation, craze, mania, rage
COLLOQ. thing
F3 1 apathy

enthusiast n
devotee, zealot, admirer, fan, supporter, follower, fanatic, lover
OLD zeal
FORMAL aficionado
COLLOQ. buff, freak, fiend

enthusiastic adj
keen, ardent, eager, fervent, vehement, intense, passionate, warm, wholehearted, zealous, vigorous, spirited, earnest, devoted, avid, committed, self-motivated, excited, fanatical, gung-ho, exuberant
FORMAL ebullient
COLLOQ. crazy, mad, wild, daft, nuts, potty, up for it; *N Am* rootin'-tootin'
F3 unenthusiastic, apathetic
See Synonym nuances panel at **intense.**

entice v
tempt, lure, allure, attract, seduce, lead on, draw, coax, persuade, induce, beguile, cajole
FORMAL inveigle
COLLOQ. sweet-talk

enticement n
inducement, lure, allure, attraction, seduction, bait, persuasion, coaxing, temptation, decoy, allurement, beguilement, cajolery
FORMAL blandishments, inveiglement
COLLOQ. come-on, sweet-talk

enticing adj
attractive, tempting, alluring, appealing, enticing, seductive, inviting, charming, captivating, irresistible

entire adj
1 *the entire factory*
complete, whole, total, full
2 *entire agreement*
absolute, utter, complete, total, whole, full, unqualified, unmitigated, outright
F3 1 incomplete, partial

entirely adv
completely, wholly, totally, fully, utterly, unreservedly, absolutely, in toto, thoroughly, altogether, perfectly, only,

solely, exclusively, in every respect, in every way, every inch
F3 partially

entirety n
totality, total, fullness, completeness, wholeness, whole, sum

entitle v
1 AUTHORIZE, give someone the right, qualify, empower, enable, make eligible, allow, permit, license, warrant, sanction
FORMAL accredit
2 NAME, call, term, title, give the title, know as, style, christen, dub, label, designate

entitlement n
right, claim, due, authority, privilege, prerogative, title, warrant, opportunity

entity n
being, existence, thing, body, creature, individual, organism, substance, object

entomb v
bury, lay to rest, shroud
FORMAL inter, tomb, sepulchre, inhume, inearth
COLLOQ. put six feet under
SLANG plant

entombment n
burial, laying to rest
FORMAL interment, inhumation, sepulture

entourage n
retinue, attendants, company, companions, followers, following, escort, staff, suite, court, train, retainers, associates, cortège, coterie
COLLOQ. hangers-on, gang, posse

entrails n
intestines, offal, viscera, bowels, internal organs, vital organs, giblets, umbles
COLLOQ. guts, innards, insides

entrance¹ n
1 OPENING, way in, entry, access, door, doorway, gate, gateway, approach, threshold, drive, driveway, passageway, lobby, porch, hall, vestibule, foyer, anteroom
2 ARRIVAL, appearance, debut, initiation, introduction, start
3 ACCESS, admission, admittance, entry, right of entry, entrée
FORMAL ingress
F3 1 exit **2** departure

entrance² v
entranced by her beauty
charm, enchant, enrapture, captivate, enthral, bewitch, beguile, spellbind, fascinate, charm, delight, ravish, transport, hypnotize, mesmerize
F3 repel

entrancing adj
enchanting, charming, delightful, attractive, fascinating, appealing, lovely, pleasant, wonderful, alluring, bewitching, captivating, endearing, irresistible, mesmerizing, ravishing, winsome
F3 boring, repellent

entrant n
1 NOVICE, beginner, starter, newcomer, new arrival, initiate, convert, probationer, apprentice, fresher, freshman, learner, student, pupil, trainee
2 COMPETITOR, candidate, contestant, contender, entry, applicant, participant, player, rival, opponent

entrap v
1 CATCH, trap, capture, snare, ensnare, entangle, enmesh, embroil, ambush, net
2 TRICK, deceive, delude, entice, seduce, tempt, implicate, beguile, allure, lure
FORMAL inveigle

entreat v
beg, implore, plead with, crave, pray, ask, petition, solicit, request, appeal to
FORMAL beseech, supplicate, invoke, importune

entrée n
1 MAIN COURSE, main dish
2 STARTER, appetizer, first course
3 ACCESS, admission, admittance, entry, right of entry
FORMAL ingress

entreaty n
appeal, plea, prayer, petition, suit, cry, solicitation, request
FORMAL supplication, invocation

entrench v
establish, fix, embed, dig in, ensconce, install, lodge, root, ingrain, settle, seat, plant, anchor, set, stop a gap, take up position
🖪 dislodge

entrenched adj
deep-rooted, deep-seated, rooted, established, well-established, firm, fixed, implanted, ingrained, inbred, set, inflexible, diehard, unshak(e)able, dyed-in-the-wool, indelible, ineradicable
FORMAL intransigent
COLLOQ. stick-in-the-mud

entrepreneur n
business executive, businessman, businesswoman, financier, industrialist, middleman, promoter, agent, dealer, broker, contractor, magnate, tycoon, speculator, moneymaker, manager, undertaker, enterpriser, impresario

entrepreneurial adj
business, commercial, industrial, trade, contractual, managerial, financial, monetary, economic, budgetary, professional

entrust v
trust, commit, make someone responsible for, put in charge, confide, consign, authorize, charge, assign, turn over, hand over, commend, depute, invest, endow, delegate, deliver

entry n
1 APPEARANCE, entrance, admittance, admission, arrival, access, entrée, introduction
2 ACCESS, admission, admittance, entry, right of entry, entrée
FORMAL ingress
3 RECORD, item, minute, note, memorandum, description, statement, account, listing
4 ENTRANT, competitor, contestant, contender, candidate, applicant, participant, player, rival, opponent
5 OPENING, entrance, door, doorway, access, threshold, way in, passage, gate, gateway, approach, lobby, porch, hall, vestibule, foyer, anteroom
🖪 5 exit

entwine v
wind, twist, intertwine, interlace, interlink, interweave, intwine, coil, braid, knit, plait, twine, weave, wreathe, knot, ravel, entangle, embroil
🖪 unravel

enumerate v
list, name, itemize, cite, detail, specify, catalogue, count, number, relate, recount, spell out, tell, mention, calculate, quote, recite, reckon, compute

enunciate v
1 ARTICULATE, pronounce, vocalize, voice, express, say, speak, utter, sound
2 STATE, declare, express, utter, proclaim, affirm, announce, put forward
FORMAL propound, promulgate

enunciation n
1 ARTICULATION, pronunciation, vocalization, expression, speech, sound, sounding, utterance
2 STATEMENT, declaration, expression, proclamation, affirmation, announcement
FORMAL promulgation

envelop v
wrap, enfold, enwrap, encase, cover, swathe, shroud, engulf, enclose, encircle, encompass, surround, cloak, veil, blanket, conceal, obscure, hide

envelope n
wrapper, wrapping, wrap, cover, case, casing, sleeve, sheath, covering, shell, skin, holder, jacket, coating

enviable adj
desirable, privileged, favoured, blessed, fortunate, lucky, attractive, advantageous, sought-after, invidious, excellent, fine
🖪 unenviable

envious adj
covetous, jealous, resentful, green (with envy), covetous, dissatisfied, grudging, begrudging, jaundiced, spiteful
COLLOQ. green-eyed

enviously adv
with envy, jealously, resentfully, grudgingly, desirously, covetously, begrudgingly

environment n
1 *a restful environment*
surroundings, conditions, climate, circumstances, milieu, atmosphere, habitat, situation, element, medium, background, ambience, scene, setting, locale, context, mood, influences, territory, domain
COLLOQ. the lie of the land, which way the wind is blowing
2 *respect the environment*
nature, creation, mother earth/nature, earth, Gaia, natural world/surroundings

---

Synonym nuances
sense 1
Surroundings may be used generally of the concrete things around you: *situated in beautiful surroundings*; whereas **conditions** has more to do with the state in which things exist: *children growing up in appalling living conditions*. **Habitat** returns to the more concrete referent of a place that is lived in.

You can use **element** to refer to the substances necessary to life, or more figuratively, the state best suited to a particular person: *the hypothetical is their element*; whilst **medium** tends to refer more narrowly to a place with the necessary attributes for supporting life: *the plant has some exacting demands as to its medium*. The term **climate** may be used of weather patterns, but can be extended to refer to the current trend in a particular area: *education has suffered in the climate of recent cuts*.

Milieu has to do with the centre of a particular place or way of thinking: *the exotic milieu of Montparnasse*; *the limitations of the milieu in which she was born*.
Atmosphere is more suggestive of pervading feeling: *an atmosphere of trust*. The terms **ambience** and **mood** similarly conjure up an idea of surrounding influences or prevailing feelings: *an ambience of unashamed luxury*.

Both **scene** and **setting** would be used to refer to where something takes place, and **locale**, likewise, may be used of a place in respect of an event: *they see the countryside as a locale for recreation*. **Context** similarly links the nature of something with its position: *literature should be read in its cultural context*.

---

environmentalist n
conservationist, ecologist, preservationist, Friends of the Earth
COLLOQ. ecofreak, econut, green; *Aust* greenie

environs n
neighbourhood, surroundings, surrounding area, vicinity, outskirts, suburbs, district, locality, precincts, purlieus
FORMAL circumjacencies, vicinage

envisage v
visualize, imagine, picture, see coming, envision, conceive of, preconceive, predict, anticipate, foresee, image, see, think of, contemplate

envision v
imagine, visualize, envisage, picture, see coming, see, think of, contemplate

envoy n
agent, representative, ambassador, diplomat, messenger, legate, consul, attaché, emissary, minister, delegate, deputy, courier, mediator, intermediary, go-between

envy n, v
◆ n
covetousness, desire, jealousy, resentfulness, resentment, dissatisfaction, grudge, ill-will, malice, spite
◆ v
covet, resent, begrudge, grudge, crave

ephemeral adj
transient, short-lived, fleeting, brief, momentary, passing, short, temporary, transitory, impermanent, flitting
FORMAL evanescent, fugacious, fungous
E∃ enduring, lasting, perpetual

epic adj, n
◆ adj
heroic, grand, majestic, elevated, exalted, lofty, imposing, impressive, vast, ambitious, long, large, large-scale, great, colossal, huge
FORMAL grandiloquent, sublime
E∃ ordinary
◆ n
long story/poem, narrative, history, legend, saga, myth, romance

epicure n
gourmet, connoisseur, *bon vivant, bon viveur,* gastronome, epicurean, gourmand, glutton, hedonist, sensualist, Sybarite, voluptuary

epicurean adj
gourmet, gastronomic, gormandizing, sensual, sensualist, voluptuous, luxurious, self-indulgent, gluttonous, luscious, lush, unrestrained, hedonistic, Sybaritic, libertine

epidemic adj, n
◆ adj
widespread, prevalent, extensive, rife, rampant, sweeping, wide-ranging, pervasive, prevailing, endemic
FORMAL pandemic
◆ n
1 PLAGUE, outbreak, scourge, pest
FORMAL pandemia
2 *the epidemic of fatherless families*
spread, rash, spate, upsurge, growth, increase, rise, wave

epigram n
witticism, quip, *bon mot,* saying, proverb, maxim, pun, play on words, aphorism, gnome
TECHNICAL apophthegm
COLLOQ. old chestnut

epigrammatic adj
concise, succinct, brief, short, terse, laconic, pithy, aphoristic, incisive, piquant, pointed, sharp, pungent, witty, ironic

epilogue n
afterword, postscript, PS, appendix, coda, conclusion, swan song
E∃ foreword, prologue, preface

episode n
1 INCIDENT, event, occurrence, happening, occasion, circumstance, experience, adventure, affair, matter, business
2 INSTALMENT, part, chapter, passage, section, scene
3 *an episode of an illness*
attack, spell, bout, period, fit, spasm
Related adjective: episodic

episodic adj
periodic, intermittent, irregular, occasional, spasmodic, sporadic, disconnected, disjointed, digressive, anecdotal
FORMAL picaresque

epistle n
letter, communication, message, missive, correspondence, bulletin, note, line, encyclical

epitaph n
commemoration, elegy, inscription, rest in peace, RIP, obituary, funeral oration
TECHNICAL lapidary expression

epithet n
description, descriptive adjective, descriptive phrase/expression, designation, name, nickname, tag, title, sobriquet, by-name, to-name
FORMAL appellation, denomination

epitome n
1 PERSONIFICATION, embodiment, representation, model, example, archetype, type, prototype, essence
FORMAL quintessence, exemplar
2 SUMMARY, abstract, abridgement, digest, synopsis, outline, précis, résumé

epitomize v
1 PERSONIFY, embody, represent, exemplify, incorporate, encapsulate, illustrate, typify, symbolize, sum up
FORMAL incarnate
2 ABRIDGE, shorten, summarize, abbreviate, abstract, précis, reduce, compress, condense, contract, curtail, cut
E∃ 2 elaborate, expand

epoch n
age, era, period, time, span, date

equable adj
1 *an equable person*
even-tempered, placid, calm, cool and collected, serene, unexcitable, tranquil, composed, level-headed, easy-going
FORMAL imperturbable
COLLOQ. unflappable, unfazed, laid-back
2 *an equable climate*
uniform, even, consistent, constant, regular, moderate, temperate, unchanging, unvarying, steady, stable, smooth
E∃ 1 excitable **2** variable, extreme

⚠ equable or equitable?
Equable means 'even-tempered': *That child would infuriate the most equable parent*; 'not extreme and without great variation': *an equable climate. Equitable* means 'fair, just': *a more equitable distribution of profits.*

equably adv
calmly, placidly, serenely, unexcitably, tranquilly, level-headedly

equal adj, n, v
◆ adj
1 IDENTICAL, the same, alike, like, equivalent, corresponding, commensurate, comparable
2 EVEN, uniform, regular, constant, level, unchanging, symmetrical, unvarying, balanced, well balanced, matched, evenly matched, on an equal footing
COLLOQ. fifty-fifty, neck and neck, even-steven(s)
3 IMPARTIAL, fair, just, unbiased, neutral, non-partisan
4 *equal to a task*

competent, able, adequate, sufficient, fit, strong, capable, suitable, suited

⊟ 1 different **2** unequal **3** biased **4** unsuitable

♦ *n*

peer, counterpart, equivalent, coequal, match, parallel, twin, fellow, mate, compeer

♦ *v*

1 *equal a number*
match, correspond to, be the same as, add up to, amount to, balance, parallel, square with, tally with, coincide with, be equivalent to, equalize, equate with, make, total

2 *equal someone's score*
match, rival, emulate, reach, be level with, be on a par with, come up to

3 *no other dancer equals her for passion*
be as good as, compare with, match, be a match for, match up to, measure up to, rival, contend, view, keep up with

equality *n*
1 UNIFORMITY, evenness, equivalence, correspondence, comparability, parallelism, balance, parity, par, symmetry, proportion, identity, sameness, likeness, similarity
2 IMPARTIALITY, fairness, justice, neutrality, partisanship, equal rights, equal opportunities, egalitarianism
⊟ 2 inequality

equalization *n*
standardization, compensation, levelling, matching, balancing, evening-out

equalize *v*
level, even up, make even, even out, match, equal, equate, draw level, keep pace, balance, redress the balance, square, standardize, regularize, compensate, smooth

equally *adv*
1 *treat people equally*
fairly, justly, evenly, uniformly, proportionally, proportionately, on equal terms
2 *equally important*
just as, similarly, as, as important, correspondingly, likewise, in the same way, in like manner, by the same token

equanimity *n*
composure, calm, calmness, tranquillity, serenity, ease, coolness, self-possession, self-control, level-headedness, confidence, assurance, self-assurance, aplomb, poise, dignity, placidity, impassivity
FORMAL imperturbability, sangfroid
COLLOQ. unflappability
⊟ alarm, anxiety, discomposure

equate *v*
1 *equate wealth with happiness*
compare (to/with), liken to, match with, identify with, connect with, link with, pair with, juxtapose with, regard as the same, bracket together
2 *costs equate to a quarter of the income*
correspond to, correspond with, balance, parallel, equalize, be equal, offset, square with, agree with, tally with

equation *n*
1 *a differential equation*
mathematical expression, mathematical statement, calculation
2 *the equation between cheap food and the plight of farmers*
equality, correspondence, equivalence, balancing, agreement, parallel, pairing, comparison, match, matching, likeness, identity, identification, similarity
FORMAL juxtaposition

equestrian *n, adj*
♦ *n*
horseman, horsewoman, rider, courier, cavalryman, knight, cavalier, hussar, trooper, cowboy, cowgirl, rancher, herder, jockey
♦ *adj*

mounted, riding, horse-riding
FORMAL equine

equilibrium *n*
1 BALANCE, poise, symmetry, evenness, stability, steadiness
TECHNICAL stasis
FORMAL equipoise, counterpoise
2 EQUANIMITY, self-possession, composure, calmness, coolness, serenity, tranquillity, self-control, level-headedness, confidence, assurance, self-assurance, aplomb, poise, dignity
FORMAL imperturbability, sangfroid
COLLOQ. unflappability
⊟ 1 imbalance, instability **2** anxiety

equip *v*
provide, fit out, supply, furnish, prepare, arm, issue, fit up, outfit, kit out, stock, endow, rig, dress, clothe, deck out
OLD equipage, accomplish, accoutre; (*Spenser*) aguise; apparel, appoint, bedight, dight

equipment *n*
apparatus, gear, supplies, tackle, kit, tools, material, furnishings, luggage, baggage, outfit, paraphernalia, accessories, appliances, articles, furniture, hardware
FORMAL accoutrements, apparelment
COLLOQ. stuff, things, rig-out

equipoise *n*
equilibrium, balance, evenness, stability, steadiness, symmetry, poise, ballast, counterbalance, counter-weight
FORMAL counterpoise, equibalance, equiponderance
⊟ imbalance

equitable *adj*
even-handed, fair, proper, reasonable, right, rightful, due, fair-and-square, square, honest, ethical, impartial, just, unbiased, unprejudiced, legitimate, disinterested, dispassionate, objective
⊟ inequitable, unfair

❗ equitable or **equable**?
See panel at **equable**.

---

equitably *adv*
fairly, justly, impartially, even-handedly, reasonably, rightfully, honestly, ethically, disinterestedly, dispassionately
⊟ unfairly, inequitably

equity *n*
even-handedness, equitableness, fairness, fair play, fair-mindedness, reasonableness, righteousness, uprightness, honesty, integrity, justice, justness, objectivity, impartiality, disinterestedness
FORMAL rectitude
⊟ inequity

equivalence *n*
identity, identicalness, correspondence, agreement, likeness, sameness, equality, interchangeability, comparability, similarity, substitutability, correlation, parallel, conformity, sameness
FORMAL parity
⊟ unlikeness, dissimilarity

equivalent *adj, n*
♦ *adj*
equal, same, similar, identical, substitutable, parallel, corresponding, alike, like, comparable, interchangeable, even, twin
TECHNICAL homologous
FORMAL tantamount, commensurate
⊟ unlike, different
♦ *n*
counterpart, opposite number, equal, parallel, match, fellow, double, twin, peer, alternative, correspondent

TECHNICAL homologue
FORMAL correlative

equivocal *adj*
ambiguous, uncertain, ambivalent, obscure, vague,
indefinite, evasive, oblique, misleading, dubious,
questionable, suspicious, confusing, indefinite
⊟ unequivocal, clear, definite

equivocate *v*
prevaricate, evade, dodge, fence, hedge, mislead, change
your mind
FORMAL tergiversate, vacillate
COLLOQ. shilly-shally, pussyfoot, waffle, chop and change,
change your tune, beat about the bush, hedge your bets,
run with the hare and hunt with the hounds

equivocation *n*
prevarication, evasion, dodging the issue, hedging, double
talk, quibbling, shifting, shuffling
FORMAL tergiversation
COLLOQ. flannel, waffle, weasel words, pussyfooting
⊟ directness

era *n*
age, epoch, period, date, day, days, time, times,
generation, aeon, season, cycle, stage, century

eradicate *v*
eliminate, annihilate, get rid of, remove, do away with, root
out, uproot, suppress, destroy, exterminate, extinguish,
weed out, stamp out, wipe out, crack down on, abolish,
erase, obliterate
FORMAL efface, expunge, extirpate

eradication *n*
elimination, annihilation, removal, riddance, obliteration,
abolition, suppression, destruction, extermination, extinction
FORMAL effacement, extirpation, deracination, expunction

erasable *adj*
removable, washable, eradicable
FORMAL effaceable
⊟ permanent, ineradicable

erase *v*
obliterate, rub out, delete, blot out, wipe out, cancel, get
rid of, remove, eradicate, put out of your mind
FORMAL expunge, efface, excise

erasure *n*
obliteration, deletion, elimination, eradication, rubbing-
out, blotting-out, wiping-out, removal, cancellation,
cleansing
FORMAL erasement, effacement, expunction

erect *v, adj*
♦ *v*
1 BUILD, construct, put up, put together, establish, set up,
elevate, assemble, raise, rear, lift, mount, pitch, create
2 erect a system
found, form, institute, set up, put up, create,
organize, establish
♦ *adj*
1 UPRIGHT, straight, vertical, upstanding, standing, raised
2 RIGID, hard, firm, stiff
TECHNICAL tumescent

erection *n*
1 BUILDING, construction, edifice, structure, assembly,
establishment, manufacture, fabrication, creation,
elevation, raising
COLLOQ. pile
2 RIGIDITY, stiffness
TECHNICAL tumescence, priapism
COLLOQ. hard
SLANG hard on, horn, stiffy, boner

ergo *adv*
therefore, consequently, accordingly, for this reason, in

consequence, so, then, this being the case
FORMAL hence, thus

erode *v*
wear away, eat away, eat into, wear down, corrode,
consume, grind down, destroy, disintegrate, deteriorate,
fragment, deplete, spoil, undermine
FORMAL abrade, excoriate

erosion *n*
wear, wearing away, corrosion, disintegration,
deterioration, destruction, undermining
FORMAL abrasion, attrition, denudation, excoriation

erotic *adj*
aphrodisiac, seductive, sensual, titillating, adult,
pornographic, lascivious, stimulating, suggestive,
erogenous, sexually arousing, amorous, venereal, carnal,
lustful, voluptuous, Lesbian, Anacreontic
FORMAL amatory
COLLOQ. sexy, blue, raunchy, steamy, hot, dirty
SLANG horny

erotically *adv*
suggestively, sensually, seductively, pornographically,
explicitly, anacreontically
COLLOQ. raunchily, steamily

err *v*
1 MAKE A MISTAKE, be wrong, be incorrect, miscalculate,
mistake, misjudge, make a slip, slip up, blunder,
misunderstand, misconstrue
COLLOQ. boob, make a booboo, mess up, duff it, bark up
the wrong tree, get hold of the wrong end of the stick, put
your foot in it, drop a clanger, come a cropper; *N Am* flub
SLANG goof (up), louse up, balls up, cock up, screw up
2 DO WRONG, sin, misbehave, go astray, offend, deviate, fall
from grace
FORMAL transgress

Synonym nuances
sense 1
Make a mistake is an unmarked term for committing a
single error: *he made a mistake when he pumped too
much money into the economy*, whilst **be wrong** and **be
incorrect** are equally unmarked but would refer to a
continuous state of being in error: *the country was wrong
in its aggressions of the 1930s.*
    The term **make a slip** returns to a single act of doing
something wrong, though the term itself is understated
and suggests something minor, whereas the term
blunder suggests a gross mistake and implies an
unfavourable judgement: *the government has blundered
in its treatment of eastern affairs.* Returning to more
neutral terms, **miscalculate** and **misjudge** are
appropriate where previously-made conclusions or
judgements are proved wrong, and **mistake** and
misunderstand could be used convey the idea of error
in comprehension: *they mistook the poisonous
toadstools for wild mushrooms.* To refer to interpreting
something wrongly, you could use **misconstrue**: *the
referee had misconstrued the rules and allowed the goal
to stand.*

---

errand *n*
task, job, duty, chore, commission, charge, mission,
undertaking, assignment, message

errant *adj*
1 WAYWARD, wrong, erring, stray, straying, deviant,
offending, criminal, lawless, disobedient, sinful, sinning,
loose
FORMAL aberrant, peccant
2 ROAMING, rambling, roving, itinerant, journeying,
wandering, nomadic
FORMAL peripatetic

erratic *adj*

changeable, variable, fitful, fluctuating, inconsistent, intermittent, sporadic, irregular, unsteady, unstable, shifting, varying, inconstant, unpredictable, volatile, unsettled, unreliable, abnormal, eccentric, wandering, meandering
FORMAL aberrant, capricious, desultory
F3 steady, consistent, stable

erratically *adv*

changeably, unpredictably, variably, fitfully, inconsistently, unreliably, intermittently, irregularly, inconstantly, sporadically
F3 steadily, consistently

erring *adj*

wayward, wrong, errant, stray, straying, deviant, offending, criminal, lawless, disobedient, guilty, sinful, sinning, loose
FORMAL culpable, peccant

erroneous *adj*

incorrect, wrong, mistaken, false, untrue, spurious, specious, inaccurate, inexact, invalid, illogical, unfounded, faulty, flawed, misguided, misplaced
FORMAL fallacious
F3 correct, right

error *n*

mistake, inaccuracy, slip, blunder, gaffe, faux pas, lapse, slip of the tongue, mix-up, miscalculation, misunderstanding, misinterpretation, misjudgement, misconception, misapprehension, misprint, literal, spelling mistake, oversight, omission, fallacy, flaw, fault, wrong
OLD (*Spenser*) mesprize
FORMAL solecism, aberration
COLLOQ. slip-up, howler, clanger, blooper, boob, booboo, foul-up, own goal, glitch, typo; *NAm* flub
SLANG goof, cock-up, balls-up

■ **in error**

mistakenly, wrongly, by mistake, erroneously, incorrectly, falsely, inaccurately, inappropriately, misguidedly, unfairly, unjustly
FORMAL fallaciously

ersatz *adj*

fake, substitute, imitation, artificial, synthetic, man-made, simulated, counterfeit, sham, bogus
COLLOQ. phoney

erstwhile *adj*

one-time, former, sometime, ex, late, old, once, past, previous, bygone

erudite *adj*

learned, scholarly, well-educated, knowledgeable, lettered, educated, well-read, literate, academic, cultured, intellectual, wise, highbrow, profound
COLLOQ. brainy
F3 illiterate, ignorant

erudition *n*

learning, scholarship, education, knowledge, facts, knowledgeableness, learnedness, scholarliness, wisdom, culture, letters
FORMAL profundity, reconditeness

erupt *v*

1 *the volcano erupted*
burst open, explode, emit lava, discharge lava, pour forth lava
2 *lava erupting from the volcano*
belch, pour forth, discharge, burst, gush, spew, spout, eject, vent, expel, emit
3 *violence erupted*
break out, flare up, explode, blow up
4 *her skin erupted in boils*
break out, flare up

eruption *n*

1 OUTBURST, discharge, ejection, emission, venting, outbreak, explosion, flare-up, blow-up
2 RASH, outbreak, inflammation

escalate *v*

increase, intensify, grow, accelerate, rise, step up, heighten, raise, spiral, magnify, mushroom, enlarge, expand, extend, develop, mount, ascend, climb, soar, shoot up, amplify
COLLOQ. rocket, go through the roof, hit the roof
F3 decrease, diminish

escalation *n*

increase, intensification, growth, acceleration, rise, heightening, magnification, expansion, extension, development, soaring, mushrooming
F3 decrease

escalator *n*

lift, elevator, moving staircase, moving walkway, travolator

escapable *adj*

avoidable, evadable, avertible, eludible
F3 inevitable

escapade *n*

adventure, exploit, fling, prank, frolic, caper, romp, spree, antic, stunt, trick
COLLOQ. lark, skylarking
SLANG *NAm* monkey shine

escape *v, n*

◆ *v*

1 GET AWAY, break free, run away, make your escape, make your getaway, bolt, abscond, flee, elope, fly, decamp, break loose, break out, flit, slip away, shake off, slip, bail out, cut and run; *dialect* overrun
COLLOQ. scoot, scram, scat, scarper, do a runner, do a bunk, run for it, do a moonlight flit, make a bolt/break for it, take to your heels, run for your life, slip through someone's fingers, have it away, take to the boats
SLANG leg it, *NAm* lam it, take it on the lam
2 AVOID, evade, elude, skip, shun, steer clear of, sidestep
FORMAL circumvent
COLLOQ. dodge, duck, ditch
3 LEAK, seep, flow, drain, spurt, gush, issue, discharge, ooze, trickle, pour out/forth, pass
4 *his name escapes me*
forget, not place, not be remembered/recalled, not know
COLLOQ. be on the tip of your tongue, not be able to put your finger on
◆ *n*

1 GETAWAY, flight, bolt, flit, breakout, absconding, decampment, jailbreak
OLD scape
COLLOQ. bunk
SLANG *NAm* lam
2 AVOIDANCE, evasion, go-by
FORMAL circumvention
COLLOQ. dodging, ducking
3 LEAK, seepage, leakage, outflow, gush, drain, hole, loophole, out, vent, discharge, issue, emission, spurt, outpour, emanation
TECHNICAL blower, efflux, extravasation
4 ESCAPISM, diversion, distraction, dreaming, fantasy, fantasizing, wishful thinking, recreation, relaxation, pastime, safety-valve

escapee *n*

absconder, escaper, jailbreaker, defector, deserter, fugitive, runaway, truant, refugee

escapism *n*

diversion, distraction, dreaming, fantasy, fantasizing, wishful thinking, recreation, relaxation, pastime, safety-valve
COLLOQ. pie in the sky, castles in the air
F3 realism

escapist *n*
dreamer, daydreamer, fantasizer, wishful thinker, non-realist, Don Quixote, Walter Mitty
COLLOQ. ostrich
F3 realist

eschew *v*
avoid, give up, abandon, keep clear of, repudiate, shun, spurn, disdain
FORMAL abjure, abstain from, refrain from, for(e)go, forswear, renounce
F3 embrace

escort *n, v*
◆ *n*
1 COMPANION, chaperon(e), partner, attendant, aide, squire, guide, bodyguard, guard, protector, defender, beau
COLLOQ. date
2 ENTOURAGE, company, retinue, suite, train, guard, convoy, cortège, attendants
◆ *v*
accompany, partner, chaperon(e), bring, come (along) with, take, take out, attend on, guide, lead, usher, conduct, guard, protect, defend, shepherd, walk

esoteric *adj*
obscure, cryptic, inscrutable, mysterious, mystic, mystical, occult, hidden, secret, confidential, private, inside
FORMAL recondite, abstruse, arcane
F3 well-known, familiar

especial *adj*
particular, special, marked, specific, striking, pre-eminent, notable, noteworthy, exceptional, outstanding, express, unique, exclusive, extraordinary, peculiar, singular, signal, uncommon, unusual, distinctive, remarkable

especially *adv*
1 PARTICULARLY, specially, markedly, notably, exceptionally, outstandingly, expressly, supremely, uniquely, exclusively, unusually, extraordinarily, uncommonly, remarkably, strikingly, very
2 CHIEFLY, mainly, principally, primarily, pre-eminently, mostly, above all, most of all

espionage *n*
counter-intelligence, infiltration, intelligence, investigation, probing, penetration, reconnaissance, spying, cloak-and-dagger operations/activities/tactics, surveillance, intercepting, secret service, industrial espionage, counter-espionage, undercover operations/work, fifth column, tradecraft
OLD scout
COLLOQ. snooping, bugging, wiretapping

espousal *n*
adoption, embracing, support, advocacy, backing, promotion, choice, defence, taking-up, championing, championship, maintenance

espouse *v*
take up, adopt, embrace, support, advocate, back, choose, stand up for, defend, champion, patronize, maintain, opt for

esprit de corps *n*
group loyalty, team spirit, public spirit, friendly relations, mutual feeling, mutal respect

espy *v*
notice, see, catch sight of, glimpse, observe, detect, discern, perceive, make out, sight, spot, spy, discover, distinguish, behold

essay *n, v*
◆ *n*
1 *an essay on 'Hamlet'*
composition, dissertation, paper, article, study, assignment, thesis, theme, piece, commentary, critique, treatise, review, leader, tract, sketch

FORMAL discourse, disquisition, causerie, prolusion
2 ATTEMPT, try, endeavour, push, go, venture
COLLOQ. bash, crack, go, stab, shot
◆ *v*
try, attempt, endeavour, test, go for, take on, strain, strive, struggle, tackle, undertake
OLD assay
COLLOQ. have a bash, have a crack, have a go, have a stab

essence *n*
1 NATURE, character, essential character, being, substance, reality, actuality, soul, spirit, core, centre, heart, meaning, point, quality, significance, life, entity, crux, kernel, marrow, pith, characteristics, attributes, principle
FORMAL quintessence
2 CONCENTRATE, extract, concentration, distillation, spirits
FORMAL distillate
■ **in essence**
basically, fundamentally, essentially, substantially, at bottom, to all intents and purposes
■ **of the essence**
crucial, indispensable, necessary, essential, vital, required, needed, important
FORMAL requisite

essential *adj, n*
◆ *adj*
1 FUNDAMENTAL, basic, intrinsic, inherent, innate, underlying, principal, main, key, central, characteristic, definitive, typical, constituent
2 CRUCIAL, indispensable, necessary, vital, required, needed, important, key
FORMAL requisite
F3 1 incidental **2** dispensable, inessential
◆ *n*
necessity, prerequisite, requisite, requirement, basic, fundamental, rudiment, necessary, principle, gist, main point(s), key point(s)
FORMAL sine qua non
COLLOQ. must

essentially *adv*
fundamentally, basically, in essence, at heart, deep down, inherently, intrinsically, primarily

establish *v*
1 SET UP, found, start, form, institute, bring into being, open, create, begin, organize, inaugurate, introduce, install, plant, settle, secure, lodge, base
2 PROVE, demonstrate, show, authenticate, ratify, verify, certify, confirm, affirm, attest
FORMAL substantiate, validate, corroborate
F3 1 uproot **2** refute

established *adj*
respected, experienced, traditional, conventional, accepted, secure, settled, entrenched, ensconced, fixed, steadfast, proved, proven, tried and tested
F3 impermanent, unreliabie

establishment *n*
1 FORMATION, setting up, founding, forming, creation, foundation, installation, institution, organization, inauguration
FORMAL inception
2 BUSINESS, company, firm, institute, organization, concern, institution, corporation, enterprise, shop, store
3 RULING CLASS, the system, the authorities, the powers that be, the government
COLLOQ. them

estate *n*
1 POSSESSIONS, effects, assets, belongings, havings, holdings, property, goods, grounds, land(s), landholding, real estate, manor, domain, park, pen, princedom, hacienda, latifundia; *Scot* udal; *N Am* realty, plantation
TECHNICAL trust, personalty, demesne, allodium, entail,

executry, conditional fee, patrimony, taluk
2 AREA, development, centre, site, land, region, tract
3 STATUS, standing, situation, position, class, place, condition, state, rank

estate agent *n*
property agent; *N Am* realtor, real-estate agent

esteem *n, v*
♦ *n*
respect, regard, good opinion, appreciation, estimation, judgement, admiration, honour, consideration, reverence, credit, reckoning, count, account, love
FORMAL veneration, approbation
♦ *v*
respect, admire, honour, regard highly, revere, reverence, value, cherish, reckon, rate, regard, think, view, consider, treasure, count, judge, hold, believe, account
FORMAL adjudge, deem, venerate

esteemed *adj*
admired, respected, well-respected, well-thought-of, worthy, highly-regarded, honoured, revered, treasured, valued, honourable, admirable, reputable, respectable, distinguished, excellent, prized
FORMAL venerated

estimable *adj*
esteemed, respected, worthy, creditable, admirable, commendable, distinguished, reputable, respectable, honourable, excellent, good, notable, noteworthy, praiseworthy, valuable, valued
FORMAL laudable, meritorious
≠ despicable, insignificant

estimate *v, n*
♦ *v*
assess, reckon, evaluate, calculate roughly, work out approximately, gauge, guess, value
FORMAL conjecture
♦ *n*
1 ROUGH CALCULATION, approximate cost/price/value/quantity, quotation, reckoning, valuation, judgement, (rough) guess, approximation, assessment, estimation, evaluation, computation
COLLOQ. guesstimate, ballpark figure
2 JUDGEMENT, consideration, opinion, belief, view, thinking, conclusion, evaluation, assessment, reckoning

estimation *n*
1 JUDGEMENT, opinion, belief, consideration, estimate, view, (way of) thinking, feeling, evaluation, assessment, reckoning, conception, calculation, computation, conclusion
2 RESPECT, regard, appreciation, esteem, credit
3 ROUGH CALCULATION, approximate cost/price/value/quantity, valuation, (rough) guess, assessment, estimate, evaluation

estrange *v*
alienate, disaffect, antagonize, disunite, divide, divorce, split up, break up, separate, sever, drive apart, part, set at variance, set against, withhold, withdraw
COLLOQ. drive a wedge between, put a barrier between
≠ attract, bind, unite

estranged *adj*
divided, separate, separated, divorced, alienated, disaffected, antagonized
≠ reconciled, united

estrangement *n*
alienation, disaffection, antagonism, disunity, division, dissociation, parting, separation, severance, split, breach, break-up, hostility, unfriendliness, antipathy, withdrawal, withholding

estuary *n*
inlet, mouth, firth, fjord, creek, cove, bay, arm, sea-loch

et cetera *adv*
and so on, and so forth, and the like, and the rest, &c, and suchlike, et al
COLLOQ. and what have you, and/or whatever

etch *v*
cut, carve, engrave, burn, furrow, dig, eat in, groove, impress, imprint, incise, ingrain, inscribe, bite, corrode, stamp

etching *n*
carving, cut, engraving, inscription, impression, imprint, print, sketch
TECHNICAL aqua fortis, aquatint

eternal *adj*
1 *eternal bliss*
unending, endless, ceaseless, everlasting, never-ending, infinite, limitless, immortal, deathless, undying, imperishable, indestructible
2 *eternal truths*
unchanging, timeless, enduring, lasting, perennial, abiding
3 *eternal quarrelling*
constant, continuous, perpetual, persistent, incessant, interminable, endless, never-ending, non-stop, relentless, remorseless
FORMAL unremitting
≠ **1** temporary; *formal* ephemeral **2** changeable

Synonym nuances
sense 1
The words **unending**, **endless** and **everlasting** can be positive or negative depending on the context: *an unending supply of money*; *his endless questions annoyed me*; *his everlasting complaints*; *everlasting glory*. **Ceaseless**, though similar, may have further implications of mundanity: *her life was a ceaseless round of hard work*; **never-ending** also tends to be used rather derogatively, again implying tediousness: *the never-ending management-union battle*.
  The terms **infinite** and **limitless**, however, can be used of something not just without end in time but also without any other fixed boundaries, and they often have positive associations: *my father had infinite patience*; *an athlete with limitless energy*.
  Immortal, meanwhile, is generally reserved for deities, whilst **undying**, and the uncommon **deathless**, are used in a positive way of more earthly notions: *undying love*. **Imperishable**, however, shifts the focus to not being subject to decay or deterioration: *the imperishable soul*, and **indestructible** emphasizes the inability to be destroyed: *CDs are not indestructible as once claimed*.

---

eternally *adv*
1 EVERLASTINGLY, endlessly, ceaselessly, indestructibly, for ever, permanently
2 INTERMINABLY, constantly, continually, lastingly, always, for ever, perpetually, incessantly
COLLOQ. 24-7
≠ briefly, temporarily

eternity *n*
1 EVERLASTINGNESS, endlessness, forever, everlasting, imperishability, infinity, timelessness, perpetuity, immutability, after-life, hereafter, immortality, deathlessness, everlasting life, heaven, paradise, next world, world to come, world without end
2 AGE, ages, long time, ages and ages
COLLOQ. donkey's years, yonks

ethereal *adj*
1 DELICATE, immaterial, dainty, exquisite, fine, light, gossamer, subtle, tenuous, insubstantial, intangible, airy-fairy, impalpable
FORMAL diaphanous
2 HEAVENLY, spiritual, celestial, refined, rarefied,

unearthly, unworldly, elemental
FORMAL empyreal, empyrean
F3 2 earthly, solid

ethical *adj*
moral, principled, just, right, proper, virtuous, honourable, fair, upright, decent, above reproach, righteous, honest, good, correct, high-minded, responsible, commendable, fitting, noble
OLD seemly
FORMAL decorous
F3 unethical

ethically *adv*
morally, rightly, justly, honestly, moralistically, virtuously, honourably, respectfully, responsibly, high-mindedly, reputably, nobly, ideologically

ethics *n*
moral values, values, morality, morals, principles, moral principles, standards, moral standards, code, moral code, moral philosophy, rules, beliefs, conscience, equity, principles of behaviour, principles of right and wrong
TECHNICAL deontology, descriptivism
FORMAL propriety

ethnic *adj*
racial, native, indigenous, traditional, tribal, folk, cultural, national, aboriginal
TECHNICAL ethnological, anthropological
FORMAL societal, autochthonous

ethnically *adv*
racially, culturally, socially, humanistically, tribally, traditionally
TECHNICAL anthropologically
FORMAL societally

ethos *n*
attitude, beliefs, standards, manners, ethics, morality, code, principles, spirit, tenor, flavour, atmosphere, rationale, character, disposition

etiquette *n*
code, code of behaviour, formalities, standards, correctness, conventions, customs, code of practice, code of conduct, rules, manners, good manners, form, good form, politeness, courtesy, ceremony, decency, unwritten law
FORMAL protocol, civility, decorum, propriety

etymology *n*
word history, word origins, word-lore, linguistics, origin, derivation, source, philology, semantics, lexicology

eulogize *v*
praise, acclaim, sing/sound the praises of, wax lyrical, applaud, approve, celebrate, exalt, extol, glorify, honour, magnify, commend, compliment, congratulate
FORMAL laud, panegyrize
COLLOQ. rave about, hype, plug
F3 condemn

eulogy *n*
praise, tribute, acclaim, acclamation, accolade, commendation, exaltation, glorification, compliment, applause, plaudit
FORMAL encomium, laud, laudation, laudatory, paean, panegyric
F3 condemnation

euphemism *n*
evasion, polite term, indirect expression, substitution, substitute, softening, genteelism, politeness, understatement, mild alternative
F3 dysphemism

euphemistic *adj*
polite, neutral, vague, indirect, substitute, evasive, soft-toned, genteel, understated, mild

euphonious *adj*
harmonious, melodious, melodic, musical, silvery, soft, sweet, dulcet, mellow, pleasant, sweet-sounding, sweet-toned, tuneful, clear
FORMAL canorous, consonant, dulcifluous, dulciloquent, euphonic, mellifluous, symphonious
F3 cacophonous

euphoria *n*
elation, ecstasy, bliss, rapture, high spirits, buoyancy, wellbeing, exhilaration, exultation, joy, intoxication, jubilation, transport, glee, exaltation, enthusiasm, happiness, cheerfulness
COLLOQ. high
F3 depression, despondency

euphoric *adj*
elated, ecstatic, blissful, rapturous, exhilarated, enraptured, enthusiastic, buoyant, intoxicated, exultant, exulted, joyful, gleeful, happy, cheerful, jubilant
FORMAL joyous
COLLOQ. high
F3 depressed, despondent

euthanasia *n*
mercy killing, assisted suicide, release, happy/merciful release, quietus

evacuate *v*
1 LEAVE, go away from, depart, withdraw, remove, move out of, retreat, retire from, abandon, desert, vacate, decamp, relinquish
FORMAL forsake
COLLOQ. quit, clear (out), pull out of
2 EMPTY, make empty, eject, void, clear, remove, expel, discharge, eliminate, purge, ease, relieve
TECHNICAL getter
OLD stool, vacuate
FORMAL defecate, excrete, stercorate
SLANG (*vulgar*) shit

evacuation *n*
1 DEPARTURE, leaving, withdrawal, retreat, exodus, flight, removal, desertion, abandonment, clearance, relinquishment, retirement, vacating
FORMAL forsaking
COLLOQ. quitting
2 EMPTYING, expulsion, ejection, discharge, clearance, removal, elimination, purging, urination
OLD vacuation
FORMAL defecation

evade *v*
1 *evade your duties*
elude, avoid, escape, shirk, steer clear of, shun, sidestep, get round, wriggle, balk, fend off, back out of, sheer
OLD blink, shift, waive
FORMAL circumvent
COLLOQ. dodge, duck, skive, chicken out, cop out, weasel out; *Aust & NZ* duckshove
SLANG skrimshank; *N Am* gold brick; *Aust & NZ* bludge
2 *evade a question*
prevaricate, equivocate, fence, fudge, avoid, parry, quibble, bypass, shuffle
COLLOQ. hedge, dodge, duck, beat about the bush
F3 1 confront, face

evaluate *v*
value, assess, estimate, reckon, calculate, gauge, measure, get/take/have the measure of, judge, determine, rate, size up, weigh, compute, rank
FORMAL appraise

evaluation *n*
valuation, assessment, estimation, estimate, appraisal, judgement, reckoning, calculation, opinion, determination, computation

evanescent *adj*
fading, fleeting, brief, short-lived, transient, transitory, impermanent, momentary, temporary, unstable, disappearing, vanishing, passing, evaporating, insubstantial, perishable
FORMAL ephemeral
EƆ permanent

evangelical *adj*
1 *evangelical Christianity*
biblical, Bible-believing, scriptural, orthodox, fundamentalist, missionary, converting, crusading
COLLOQ. Bible-bashing, Bible-thumping, Bible-punching
2 ENTHUSIASTIC, zealous, campaigning, crusading, evangelistic, missionary, propagandizing, propagandist, proselytizing

evangelist *n*
preacher, missionary, missioner, revivalist, (hot) gospeller, televangelist, proselytizer, crusader, campaigner

evangelize *v*
preach, campaign, spread the word, crusade, convert, proselytize, baptize, gospelize, missionarize, missionize, propagandize

evaporate *v*
1 DISAPPEAR, dematerialize, vanish, end, melt (away), dissolve, disperse, dispel, fade
FORMAL dissipate, evanesce
2 VAPORIZE, dry, dehydrate, boil away, distil, exhale
TECHNICAL vapour, volatilize
FORMAL desiccate

evaporation *n*
vaporization, drying, dehydration, condensation, distillation, dematerialization, dissolution, fading, melting, vanishing
FORMAL desiccation

evasion *n*
1 AVOIDANCE, equivocation, prevarication, escape, shirking, trickery, subterfuge, fencing, steering clear of, shunning
FORMAL circumvention, tergiversation
COLLOQ. hedging, ducking, cop-out, dodge, skiving
SLANG skrimshank
2 *evasions rather than straight answers*
excuse, quibble, quibbling, deception, deceit, trickery, fudging, prevarication, equivocation, shuffling
COLLOQ. ducking, hedging, dodge, dodging
EƆ **1** frankness, directness

evasive *adj*
equivocating, indirect, vague, prevaricating, devious, unforthcoming, misleading, deceitful, deceptive, fudging, quibbling, oblique, secretive, tricky, cunning
COLLOQ. shifty, slippery, cagey, waffling
EƆ direct, frank

evasiveness *n*
equivocation, indirectness, vagueness, prevarication, deceit, deceptiveness, fudging, quibbling, secrecy, cunning
COLLOQ. caginess

eve *n*
day before, time before, period before, verge, brink, edge, threshold

even *adj, adv, v*
♦ *adj*
1 LEVEL, flat, smooth, horizontal, flush, parallel, uniform, true, plane
2 STEADY, unvarying, unchanging, stable, constant, regular, uniform, consistent, unwavering
3 EQUAL, balanced, matching, same, identical, similar, like, alike, evenly matched, on an equal footing, symmetrical, level, drawn, side by side

COLLOQ. fifty-fifty, neck and neck, quits
4 EVEN-TEMPERED, calm, placid, serene, tranquil, composed, cool, equable, unruffled, unexcitable
FORMAL unperturbable
COLLOQ. unflappable
5 EVEN-HANDED, balanced, equitable, stable, fair, impartial, just, neutral, non-partisan
EƆ **1** uneven **3** unequal
♦ *adv*
1 *even worse*
all the more, still, yet, more, to a greater extent/degree
2 *even a child could do that*
surprisingly, unexpectedly, unusually, oddly, as well, also, too, still more, likewise
3 *sad, even depressed*
more exactly, more precisely, actually, indeed
4 *not even write his own name*
hardly, scarcely, at all, so much as
♦ *v*
smooth, flatten, level, plane, match, regularize, balance (out), equalize, make equal, make uniform, align, square, stabilize, steady, straighten
COLLOQ. strike a balance
■ **even so**
however, but, all the same, despite that, in spite of that, however that may be, nevertheless, nonetheless, still, yet
FORMAL notwithstanding that
■ **get even**
pay back, take/have your revenge, revenge/avenge yourself, reciprocate, requite
COLLOQ. give as good as you get, get your own back, settle a score

even-handed *adj*
fair, just, impartial, balanced, disinterested, dispassionate, equitable, neutral, unbiased, unprejudiced, reasonable, non-discriminatory, square, fair and square, without fear or favour
EƆ inequitable, discriminatory

evening *n*
night, nightfall, dusk, close of day, eve, eventide, twilight, sunset, sundown

evenly *adv*
1 STEADILY, stably, constantly, regularly, uniformly, consistently
2 EQUALLY, similarly, symmetrically, evenly matched, on an equal footing
3 *she replied evenly*
calmly, placidly, serenely, tranquilly

event *n*
1 HAPPENING, occurrence, incident, occasion, proceeding, affair, circumstance, episode, experience, matter, case, adventure, business, fact, possibility, milestone
FORMAL eventuality
2 GAME, match, fixture, competition, contest, round, race, tournament, engagement, meeting, meet, item
3 CONSEQUENCE, result, outcome, conclusion, end, aftermath, upshot, effect, issue
FORMAL termination
■ **in any event**
anyway, anyhow, in any case, no matter what, whatever happens

---

Synonym nuances
sense 1
Happening is a very general synonym, whilst occurrence implies an event that it is unplanned or unforced: *machine failure is a common occurrence.* **Incident**, while also suggestive of an unanticipated (and often unpleasant) event, would be appropriately used of a more specific one: *she reported the incident to the police.* **Circumstance** also conveys the idea of

something unplanned taking place, but as one element in a causal chain: *what to do in the circumstance of a fire*, while you might use **episode** of a distinct event taking place within a finite period of time: *the sinking of the cruiser was a highly suspicious episode.* **Case** shares this notion of a particular instance, but you would use it of an event that is being given as an example of something significant: *a case of unwitting collusion.*

  Occasion, on the other hand, tends to suggest something that has been planned, usually a grand or happy event: *on the occasion of your silver wedding*, while **affair** insinuates business that has been ongoing and is of some consequence: *extremists had set the whole affair in motion; the contemporary art show was a very significant affair.* The term **proceeding** suggests a deliberate event that involves advancement, but it is fairly formal-sounding, and has legal and political connotations. **Matter** also has connotations of seriousness, and suggests something that may cause concern or must be dealt with: *they had deeply-held views on the matter of the stolen money.* You may use **experience** to emphasize the aspect of personal engagement: *the whole experience had been a lot of fun*, while **adventure** suggests an event with an element of excitement. This is unlike **business**, which has a more pedestrian association, often further implying something complex or awkward: *the family makes rather a fuss over the whole business of baptism.*

  The term **milestone** is reserved for an event that marks an important stage: *the milestone of buying your first home.*

even-tempered *adj*
calm, level-headed, equable, placid, stable, tranquil, serene, composed, cool, cool and collected, steady, peaceful, peaceable
FORMAL imperturbable
COLLOQ. unflappable, unfazed, laid-back
E3 excitable, erratic

eventful *adj*
busy, exciting, lively, active, full, interesting, remarkable, important, significant, memorable, momentous, historic, crucial, critical, notable, noteworthy, unforgettable
COLLOQ. action-packed
SLANG ripsnorting
E3 dull, ordinary

eventual *adj*
final, ultimate, last, resulting, closing, concluding, ensuing, future, later, subsequent, prospective, projected, planned, impending

eventuality *n*
possibility, probability, likelihood, chance, contingency, event, incidence, occurrence, happening, circumstance, case, outcome, crisis, emergency, mishap
FORMAL happenstance

eventually *adv*
finally, ultimately, at last, in the end, at length, subsequently, after all, sooner or later, in the long run, in due course, in the fullness of time
COLLOQ. at the end of the day, when all is said and done, in the final analysis

ever *adv*
1 ALWAYS, evermore, for ever, perpetually, permanently, constantly, at all times, continually, incessantly, endlessly, eternally, until the end of time, till doomsday, till your dying day
COLLOQ. till the cows come home, till hell freezes over
2 AT ANY TIME, in any case, in/under any circumstances, at all, on any account, on any occasion
E3 1 never

■ **ever so**
very, very much, really, extremely, exceptionally, immensely, exceedingly
OLD jolly
COLLOQ. tremendously, frightfully, terribly, awfully

everlasting *adj*
1 ETERNAL, undying, never-ending, unending, endless, immortal, infinite, imperishable, constant, permanent, perpetual, indestructible, deathless, timeless
OLD perdurable, sempiternal
2 *everlasting noise*
constant, continual, perpetual, persistent, incessant, interminable, continuous, endless, never-ending, non-stop, relentless, remorseless
FORMAL unremitting
E3 temporary, transient

evermore *adv*
always, for ever, eternally, ever, ever after, for ever and a day, for ever and ever, unceasingly, to the end of time, till doomsday
FORMAL henceforth, hereafter, in perpetuum
COLLOQ. till the cows come home, till hell freezes over

every *adj*
1 EACH, every single, every individual
2 *make every effort*
all possible, as much as possible
3 *have every confidence*
all, complete, total, full, entire

everybody *n*
everyone, one and all, each one, each person, every person, all and sundry, the whole world
COLLOQ. all the world and his wife, every Tom Dick and Harry, every man Jack, every mother's son, Uncle Tom Cobleigh and all

everyday *adj*
ordinary, common, commonplace, day-to-day, familiar, run-of-the-mill, regular, standard, basic, plain, routine, usual, workaday, normal, average, customary, stock, accustomed, conventional, daily, habitual, monotonous, unimaginative, frequent, simple, informal
COLLOQ. common-or-garden
E3 unusual, exceptional, special

everyone *n*
everybody, one and all, each one, each person, every person, all and sundry, the whole world
COLLOQ. all the world and his wife, every Tom Dick and Harry, every man Jack, every mother's son, Uncle Tom Cobleigh and all

everything *n*
all, all things, each thing, the lot, the whole lot, the entirety, the sum, the total, lock, stock and barrel
FORMAL the aggregate
COLLOQ. the whole caboodle, the whole kit and caboodle, the whole shooting-match, the whole shebang, the whole bag of tricks, the works, everything but the kitchen sink

everywhere *adv*
all around, in/to all places, in/to each place, the world over, all over, throughout, far and near, near and far, far and wide, high and low, ubiquitous
COLLOQ. left, right and centre, here there and everywhere; N Am every place

evict *v*
expel, eject, dispossess, put out, turn out, throw out, force out, force to leave, remove, cast out, oust, dislodge
FORMAL expropriate
COLLOQ. turf out, kick out, chuck out, show someone the door, throw out on the streets, turn out of house and home

eviction *n*
expulsion, ejection, dispossession, removal, clearance, dislodgement
FORMAL defenestration, expropriation
COLLOQ. the bum's rush, the boot, the push, the elbow

evidence *n, v*
♦ *n*
1 PROOF, verification, confirmation, affirmation, grounds, support, documentation, data, test, token, credentials, warranty, guarantee, exhibit
TECHNICAL title
OLD argument, document; (*Shakesp*) avouch, instance
FORMAL substantiation, corroboration
COLLOQ. smoking gun
2 TESTIMONY, declaration, deed
TECHNICAL affidavit, adminicle, precognition, surrebut
OLD compurgation
FORMAL attestation
3 INDICATION, suggestion, sign, trace, mark, hint, demonstration, token, symptom, stamp
FORMAL manifestation
♦ *v*
show, indicate, reveal, demonstrate, display, exhibit, prove, witness, signify, confirm, affirm, establish, betray
OLD assert, bespeak
FORMAL attest, denote, evince, manifest, vouch
■ **in evidence**
clear, obvious, apparent, plain, patent, visible, conspicuous, noticeable, clear-cut, unmistakable

evident *adj*
clear, obvious, apparent, plain, patent, visible, conspicuous, noticeable, clear-cut, unmistakable, perceptible, distinct, discernible, tangible, manifest, undoubted, incontestable, indisputable, incontrovertible

evidently *adv*
1 CLEARLY, apparently, plainly, patently, obviously, manifestly, undoubtedly, doubtless(ly), indisputably
2 SEEMINGLY, apparently, outwardly, as it would seem/appear, so it seems/appears, to all appearances, on the face of it
FORMAL ostensibly

evil *adj, n*
♦ *adj*
1 WICKED, wrong, sinful, bad, immoral, vicious, vile, cruel, base, corrupt, malicious, malignant, malevolent, devilish, demonic, diabolic, depraved, mischievous, sinister, black
FORMAL iniquitous, reprehensible, nefarious, heinous
2 HARMFUL, pernicious, destructive, injurious, deadly, detrimental, hurtful, bad, poisonous
FORMAL deleterious
3 DISASTROUS, ruinous, calamitous, catastrophic, adverse, dire, unfortunate, unlucky, unfavourable
FORMAL inauspicious, unpropitious
4 OFFENSIVE, noxious, foul, nasty, vile, stinking
FORMAL noisome
F3 1 good **3** fortunate
♦ *n*
1 WICKEDNESS, wrongdoing, wrong, immorality, misconduct, badness, sin, sinfulness, vice, viciousness, vileness, depravity, baseness, corruption, devilishness, mischief
FORMAL iniquity, malignity, heinousness
2 ADVERSITY, calamity, disaster, misfortune, suffering, sorrow, ruin, catastrophe, blow, curse, distress, hurt, harm, ill, pain, injury, misery, woe
FORMAL affliction

Synonym nuances
adjective sense 1
Obviously, many of these synonyms are highly marked with disapprobation. **Wicked** is a strongly judgemental and disapproving term describing the worst extremity of badness, whilst **wrong** is comparatively tame in its suggestion of being at odds with accepted moral codes. **Sinful** and **immoral** are similar in meaning but stronger in tone, with **sinful** having strong religious associations. The word **corrupt** and the rather stronger term **depraved** also have connotations of immoral behaviour: *corrupt pleasure*.
You could use **base** or **vile** to imply that you find something loathsome or disgusting: *vile exploitation of poor workers.* **Vicious** and **cruel**, on the other hand, along with **malicious** and **malignant**, are appropriate terms for evil expressed through spite and ferocity towards others. **Devilish, demonic** and **diabolic** all convey images of the supreme spirit of evil, and so are highly judgemental: *the Nazis' demonic crimes.* The terms **sinister** and **black** have more to do with the threat of evil or potential harm: *sinister undertones, the black arts of propaganda.* Compared to all these terms, **mischievous** is fairly mild in its suggestion of a malign playfulness.

evildoer *n*
wrongdoer, bad person, criminal, delinquent, offender, miscreant, reprobate, sinner, scoundrel, rogue, villain
FORMAL transgressor

evildoing *n*
badness, wickedness, corruption, depravity, vileness, immorality, sin, sinfulness, iniquity, nastiness, cruelty

evince *v*
show, reveal, indicate, display, exhibit, make clear, express, signify, demonstrate, confess, declare, betray, establish
FORMAL attest, bespeak, betoken, evidence, manifest
F3 conceal, suppress

eviscerate *v*
disembowel, gut, draw, gralloch
FORMAL exenterate

evocation *n*
summoning-up, calling, elicitation, invocation, inducing, arousal, stirring, stimulation, suggestion, activation, excitation, kindling, recall, echo

evocative *adj*
suggestive, expressive, indicative, reminiscent, vivid, graphic, memorable
FORMAL redolent

evoke *v*
summon (up), call, elicit, invoke, induce, arouse, stir, bring/call to mind, raise, kindle, stimulate, bring about, cause, call forth, call up, conjure up, awaken, provoke, excite, recall, bring back memories of, make someone think of
F3 suppress

evolution *n*
development, growth, progression, progress, expansion, increase, ripening, derivation, descent, unrolling, unfolding, unravelling, working-out, opening-out
TECHNICAL natural selection, survival of the fittest

evolve *v*
develop, grow, increase, mature, progress, advance, unravel, unroll, unfold, work out, open out, expand, enlarge, emerge, descend, derive, result, elaborate

exacerbate *v*
aggravate, worsen, make worse, make things/matters worse, compound the problem, heighten, increase, provoke, sharpen, intensify, exaggerate, inflame, exasperate, deepen, embitter, enrage, infuriate, irritate, vex

COLLOQ. add fuel to the fire/flames, fan the flames, add insult to injury, rub salt in the wound
⊟ soothe

exacerbation n

worsening, aggravation, intensification, exaggeration, exasperation, irritation
⊟ soothing

exact adj, v

♦ adj

1 PRECISE, accurate, correct, faithful, literal, flawless, faultless, right, true, definite, explicit, detailed, specific, strict, unerring, close, just, factual, identical, express, word-perfect
FORMAL veracious
COLLOQ. blow-by-blow, on the nail, spot on, bang on, on the button
2 CAREFUL, scrupulous, particular, rigorous, precise, methodical, meticulous, orderly, exacting, painstaking, thorough
FORMAL punctilious
⊟ **1** inexact, imprecise **2** careless

♦ v

extort, extract, claim, insist on, wrest, wring, compel, demand, command, call for, force, impose, insist, require, squeeze
COLLOQ. milk, bleed

exacting adj

demanding, challenging, difficult, hard, laborious, arduous, onerous, stringent, tiring, rigorous, taxing, tough, harsh, firm, painstaking, severe, strict, stern, unsparing, unyielding
⊟ easy

exactitude n

accuracy, precision, exactness, correctness, faultlessness, carefulness, care, meticulousness, orderliness, rigorousness, rigour, scrupulousness, thoroughness, conscientiousness, painstakingness, perfectionism, strictness, detail
⊟ inaccuracy, carelessness, imprecision

exactly adv, interj

♦ adv

1 PRECISELY, accurately, literally, faithfully, correctly, specifically, rigorously, scrupulously, verbatim, carefully, faultlessly, without error, unerringly, strictly, religiously, to the letter, particularly, methodically, explicitly, expressly
OLD (Shakesp) jump
FORMAL veraciously
COLLOQ. dead
2 ABSOLUTELY, definitely, precisely, indeed, certainly, truly, quite, just, unequivocally
COLLOQ. bang on, spot on, on the dot, on the button, on the nail, to a T, smash, plumb
⊟ **1** inaccurately, roughly, vaguely

♦ interj

precisely, yes, quite, of course, just so, indeed, absolutely, agreed, certainly, right, that's right, true
COLLOQ. you got it

exactness n

accuracy, precision, exactitude, correctness, faultlessness, carefulness, care, meticulousness, orderliness, rigorousness, rigour, scrupulousness, thoroughness, strictness
⊟ inaccuracy, carelessness, imprecision

exaggerate v

overstate, overdo, magnify, overemphasize, emphasize, stress, make too much of, overdo (it/things), dramatize, overdramatize, embellish, embroider, colour, stretch (the truth), enlarge, amplify, enhance, oversell, overplay, goliathize, bounce
FORMAL aggrandize, distend

COLLOQ. lay/pile it on, lay/pile in on thick, lay/pile it on with a trowel, over-egg the pudding, make a mountain out of a molehill, blow something up out of all proportion, shoot a line, make a drama out of a crisis
⊟ understate, play down

exaggerated adj

overstated, overdone, overestimated, overcharged, excessive, extravagant, pretentious, embellished, amplified, bombastic, inflated, overblown, caricatured, burlesqued, exalted
TECHNICAL euphuistic
FORMAL hyperbolic
COLLOQ. tall, camp
⊟ understated, played down

exaggeration n

overstatement, overemphasis, emphasis, magnification, overestimation, excess, extravagance, embellishment, enlargement, pretentiousness, amplification, burlesque, caricature, parody
FORMAL hyperbole
⊟ meiosis, understatement

exalt v

1 PRAISE, extol, glorify, magnify, acclaim, applaud, bless, honour, adore, revere, worship, reverence, eulogize
FORMAL laud, venerate
2 DELIGHT, elate, overjoy, transport, uplift, enliven, excite, exhilarate
3 RAISE, advance, promote, prefer, elevate, upgrade,
FORMAL aggrandize

exaltation n

1 ELATION, ecstasy, rapture, bliss, joy, jubilation, excitement, exhilaration, high spirits
2 PRAISE, glorification, acclaim, honour, glory, reverence, worship, adoration, eulogy
FORMAL veneration
3 ELEVATION, raising, promotion, advancement
FORMAL aggrandizement

exalted adj

1 LOFTY, high, elevated, grand, regal, lordly, eminent, stately, noble, idealistic, virtuous, moral
2 ELATED, ecstatic, blissful, exultant, joyful, happy, jubilant, rapturous, in high spirits
COLLOQ. in seventh heaven

exam n

test, examination, exercises, questions, multiple-choice questions, practical, quiz, paper, viva, oral, final

examination n

1 INSPECTION, inquiry, scrutiny, study, survey, search, analysis, assessment, exploration, investigation, probe, observation, research, review, scan, perusal, check, check-up, audit, critique, post-mortem
FORMAL appraisal
COLLOQ. once-over
2 TEST, exam, quiz, questioning, cross-examination, cross-questioning, trial, inquisition, interrogation, viva, oral

---

Synonym nuances
sense 1

Inspection suggests a very close look, often in an official capacity, whilst **inquiry**, although also often official, has more to do with asking relevant questions to reach the truth. **Scrutiny**, however, implies highly detailed consideration: *parliamentary scrutiny of public sector contracts*, whilst **study**, although still suggesting attentiveness, is unlikely to delve as deeply.

Survey, on the other hand, is more appropriate a term for a general overview: *a chronological survey of art*, or sometimes, more officially, a critical look at effectiveness: *a transport survey*. **Review** is similar, but retrospective: *a review of existing legislation*. **Critique**, however, generally concentrates on the negative aspects: *a critique of society.*

If you use **search** and **research**, the implication is that you expect to uncover something, unlike **analysis**, which is suggestive of looking in detail to ascertain or resolve, whilst **assessment** has more to do with evaluation. The words **exploration**, **investigation** and **probe** suggest delving deeply into, **exploration** usually to discover something new, the other two to expose something: *a probe into the cause of the air crash.* A **post-mortem** can now refer to any thorough examination that takes place after an unfortunate event to establish what went wrong.

To refer to a more detached act of watching and noting you may choose to use the term **observation**. **Scan** suggests a quicker action, fleetingly looking over written material, while **perusal** would be the term to convey the idea of reading attentively. **Check-up** is usually used solely of a medical examination.

examine *v*
1 INSPECT, investigate, scrutinize, study, look at, look into, look over, view, observe, survey, analyse, dissect, go into, search, explore, inquire, discuss, reason, eye, consider, probe, research, review, scan, check (out), check over, ponder, pore over, sift, vet, weigh up, overhaul, assess, audit, peruse, collate, process, revise, test, try, canvass
TECHNICAL assay, cognosce
OLD quote, seek, speculate, depose; (*Spenser*) appose; overhaile
FORMAL appraise
COLLOQ. go over with a fine-tooth comb
SLANG case
2 TEST, quiz, question, cross-examine, cross-question, interrogate
OLD appose
FORMAL catechize
COLLOQ. grill, pump, give the third degree to, give someone a roasting, go to town on, put the screws on

examinee *n*
entrant, candidate, competitor, contestant, applicant, interviewee

examiner *n*
adjudicator, assessor, tester, inspector, interviewer, judge, marker, questioner, reviewer, reader, analyst, censor, critic, auditor, arbiter, scrutineer, scrutinizer
TECHNICAL assayer
FORMAL examinant, interlocutor, scrutator

example *n*
1 SAMPLE, specimen, prototype
FORMAL exemplar, archetype
2 INSTANCE, case, case in point, illustration, exemplification, representation/typical case, epitome
3 MODEL, role model, guide, lead, pattern, ideal, standard, criterion, type
FORMAL precedent, paradigm
4 LESSON, warning, caution, punishment
FORMAL admonition
■ **for example**
eg, for instance, like, such as, as an example/instance, say, to illustrate, by way of illustration, to give as an illustration

exasperate *v*
infuriate, annoy, anger, incense, irritate, madden, provoke, enrage, irk, rile, rankle, rouse, goad, vex, gall
COLLOQ. get on someone's nerves, get to, needle, bug, aggravate, wind up, drive up the wall, make someone's blood boil, put someone's back up, get someone's dander, get on someone's wick, put someone's nose out of joint
Ea appease, pacify

exasperated *adj*
infuriated, annoyed, angry, indignant, angered, incensed, irritated, maddened, provoked, riled, vexed, piqued, irked, galled, goaded
COLLOQ. aggravated, at the end of your tether, bugged, fed up, needled, nettled, peeved
Ea calm, satisfied

exasperating *adj*
infuriating, annoying, bothersome, maddening, provoking, troublesome, disagreeable, irksome, irritating, vexing, galling, pernicious, vexatious
COLLOQ. aggravating, confounded, infernal

exasperation *n*
annoyance, irritation, anger, rage, fury, chagrin, indignation, discontent, disgruntlement
COLLOQ. aggravation, stroppiness

excavate *v*
dig (out), dig up, hollow (out), burrow, tunnel, delve, unearth, mine, quarry, disinter, cut, gouge, scoop, reveal, uncover
FORMAL exhume

excavation *n*
1 HOLE, hollow, pit, quarry, mine, colliery, dugout, dig, diggings, burrow, cavity, crater, trench, trough, shaft, ditch, cutting
2 DIGGING (OUT), hollowing (out), burrowing, tunnelling, unearthing, mining
FORMAL exhumation

exceed *v*
surpass, go beyond, be greater/larger than, be more than, outnumber, outdo, outstrip, beat, better, be superior to, pass, overtake, top, outshine, eclipse, outreach, outrun, outrace, outweigh, transcend, cap, overdo, overstep, go over

exceedingly *adv*
very, very much, extremely, greatly, highly, unusually, exceptionally, especially, enormously, excessively, hugely, immensely, vastly, inordinately, unprecedentedly, superlatively, surpassingly, amazingly, astonishingly, extraordinarily

excel *v*
1 BE EXCELLENT, succeed, shine, stand out, be outstanding, be skilful, be pre-eminent, predominate
2 SURPASS, outdo, beat, be superior to, outclass, outperform, outrank, outrival, eclipse, better, be better than
OLD (*Shakesp*) outpeer

excellence *n*
superiority, pre-eminence, distinction, merit, supremacy, high quality, quality, worth, value, fineness, skill, eminence, goodness, greatness, virtue, perfection, purity, transcendence

excellent *adj*
wonderful, brilliant, marvellous, fantastic, superior, first-class, first-rate, high-quality, very good, prime, superlative, unequalled, unparalleled, matchless, rare, exceptional, outstanding, surpassing, remarkable, distinguished, great, eminent, flawless, faultless, perfect, above reproach, good, best, exemplary, select, superb, admirable, magnificent, shining, sterling, commendable, splendid, pre-eminent, praiseworthy, noteworthy, notable, noted, top-drawer, fine, A1, high, noble, worthy, inspired, Utopian, brave; *Scot* wally
OLD eximious, pure
COLLOQ. top-notch, smashing, stunning, terrific, cool, neat, ace, brill, boffo, out of this world, second to none, divine, heavenly, fabulous, sensational, not half bad, boss, bully, classic, crack, dilly, famous, jammy, knockout, the bee's knees; *N Am* hunky, jim-dandy; *Aust* bonzer, grouse;

Aust & NZ trimmer
OLD COLLOQ. capital, champion, spiffing
SLANG mega, mean, wicked, stonking, radical, rad, crucial, way-out, shit-hot, groovy, clinking, def, fab, peachy, elegant, ripping, stellar, tipping, triff, triffic; (*vulgar*) the dog's bollocks; *N Am* copacetic, dicty, righteous, socko; *Aust* beaut, castor
OLD SLANG lummy, topping
F∃ inferior, second-rate

excellently *adv*
wonderfully, brilliantly, marvellously, well, fantastically, superlatively, exceptionally, remarkably, eminently, perfectly, superbly, admirably, commendably, splendidly
COLLOQ. terrifically, divinely, sensationally
F∃ poorly

except *prep, v*
◆ *prep*
excepting, but, but for, apart from, other than, with the exception of, aside from, save, omitting, not counting, leaving out, excluding, except for, besides, bar, barring, minus, less, short of
◆ *v*
leave out, omit, bar, exclude, reject, rule out, pass over

exception *n*
oddity, deviation, departure, abnormality, irregularity, peculiarity, inconsistency, rarity, special case, freak, quirk
FORMAL anomaly
■ **take exception**
object, protest, oppose, disapprove, refuse, complain, rebut, repudiate, withstand, resist, argue, challenge, beg to differ, take issue, take a stand against
FORMAL demur, expostulate, remonstrate
■ **with the exception of**
excepting, but, apart from, other than, save, omitting, not counting, leaving out, excluding, except for, besides, bar, barring, minus, less

exceptionable *adj*
objectionable, unpleasant, disagreeable, offensive, unacceptable, disgusting, deplorable, abhorrent, repugnant
F∃ acceptable, agreeable

exceptional *adj*
1 OUTSTANDING, remarkable, marvellous, excellent, extraordinary, brilliant, phenomenal, notable, noteworthy, superior, unequalled
FORMAL prodigious
COLLOQ. one in a thousand, one in a million
2 ABNORMAL, unusual, strange, odd, irregular, extraordinary, out of the ordinary, peculiar, special, rare, atypical, uncommon
FORMAL anomalous, aberrant, singular
F∃ 1 mediocre **2** normal

exceptionally *adv*
1 EXTREMELY, extraordinarily, notably, outstandingly, especially, amazingly, remarkably, wonderfully
2 UNUSUALLY, uncommonly, irregularly, abnormally, rarely

excerpt *n*
extract, passage, portion, section, selection, quote, quotation, part, piece, cutting, clip, clipping, citation, scrap, fragment
TECHNICAL pericope

excess *n, adj*
◆ *n*
1 SURFEIT, too much, more than enough, overabundance, oversupply, glut, superabundance, surplus, backlog, overflow, overkill, remainder, rest, residue, leftovers
FORMAL plethora, superfluity
COLLOQ. bellyful; *Aust & NZ* gutful
2 OVERINDULGENCE, dissoluteness, immoderateness,

immoderation, extravagance, unrestraint, debauchery
FORMAL dissipation, intemperance, prodigality
F∃ 1 deficiency **2** restraint
◆ *adj*
extra, surplus, too much, spare, redundant, remaining, residual, left-over, additional, superfluous
FORMAL supernumerary
F∃ inadequate
■ **in excess of**
more than, over, above

excessive *adj*
immoderate, inordinate, extreme, too much, undue, uncalled-for, disproportionate, overdone, unnecessary, unneeded, needless, unwarranted, superfluous, overabundant, superabundant, unreasonable, lavish, exorbitant, extravagant
COLLOQ. steep, over the top, OTT
F∃ insufficient

excessively *adv*
immoderately, inordinately, extremely, too much, to a fault, unduly, unreasonably, overly, overmuch, disproportionately, unnecessarily, needlessly, superfluously, exorbitantly, exaggeratedly, extravagantly, intemperately
F∃ insufficiently, inadequately

exchange *v, n*
◆ *v*
barter, change, trade, swap, switch, replace, interchange, convert, commute, transpose, substitute, stand in for, reciprocate, bargain, bandy
◆ *n*
1 INTERCHANGE, swap, switch, replacement, substitution
FORMAL reciprocity
COLLOQ. give and take
2 TRADE, commerce, dealing, market, traffic, barter, bargain, trade-off
3 CONVERSATION, discussion, chat, argument, dialogue
Related adjective: catallactic

excise[1] *n*
excise duty
duty, tax, VAT, customs, levy, surcharge, tariff, toll
FORMAL impost

excise[2] *v*
excise sensitive material
cut, cut out, remove, extract, destroy, eradicate, erase, delete, exterminate
FORMAL expunge, expurgate, extirpate, rescind

excision *n*
removal, deletion, eradication, destruction, expunction
FORMAL expurgation, extermination, extirpation

excitable *adj*
temperamental, volatile, mercurial, passionate, emotional, highly-strung, fiery, hot-headed, hasty, nervous, hot-tempered, irascible, quick-tempered, sensitive, susceptible
FORMAL choleric, mercurial
COLLOQ. edgy
F∃ calm, stable

excite *v*
1 *excite a feeling*
stir up, thrill, impress, touch, move, agitate, disturb, upset, arouse, rouse, animate, awaken, evoke, stir, enliven, irritate, tickle, engender, inspire, kindle, enkindle, ferment, fire, inflame, ignite, intoxicate, flush, wake, work up, wind up, whet, waken, warm, yerk
OLD commove, upraise; (*Shakesp*) accite; (*Spenser*) emmove
COLLOQ. turn on
2 *excite an action*
provoke, motivate, stimulate, bring about, instigate, impel,

urge, incite, induce, galvanize, generate, sway, electrify, work up, suscitate
3 excite sexually
arouse, stimulate, awaken, titillate, provoke
COLLOQ. turn on
F≡ 1 calm

excited *adj*
aroused, roused, stimulated, stirred, exhilarated, thrilled, elated, in high spirits, enthusiastic, eager, moved, beside yourself, animated, worked up, wrought-up, overwrought, agitated, restless, frantic, frenzied, wild
COLLOQ. high, on the edge of your seat, on tenterhooks, thrilled to bits, turned on, uptight, hyper, fired up, hyped up
F≡ calm, apathetic

> **Synonym nuances**
> Both **aroused** and **roused** suggest a response has been elicited by something: *their secretiveness aroused considerable suspicion*, while **stimulated** could be used where interest rather than excitement has been prompted. **Stirred** and **moved** are suggestive of having the emotions activated: *stirred by thoughts of heroic deeds*, whereas **exhilarated** and **thrilled** have more to do with being thoroughly enlivened: *I was exhilarated by the run and wasn't tired*.
> Both **in high spirits** and the even more emphatic **elated** suggest excitement with a strong element of enjoyment or happiness. **Enthusiastic** focuses on an element of zealous anticipation, as does **eager**.
> To convey the sense of lively behaviour brought on by excitement you could use the term **animated**, whereas **worked up**, the fairly uncommon **wrought-up** and **overwrought** imply expending the same energy but in agitation or anxiety rather than pleasure. **Agitated**, likewise, has to do with being emotionally perturbed, whilst **restless** is similarly negative in its connotation of unease. The terms **frantic**, **frenzied** and **wild** would be appropriate only for a manic, uncontrolled excitedness: *frantic efforts to get home; a frenzied rage*.

excitement *n*
1 the excitement of winning
thrill, passion, adventure, emotion, sensation, exhilaration, pleasure, animation, elation, enthusiasm, restlessness, ferment, fever, eagerness, stimulation, agitation, discomposure, exhilaration
FORMAL perturbation
COLLOQ. kick(s)
2 UNREST, ado, action, activity, commotion, stir, fuss, tumult, flurry, furore
F≡ 1 apathy 2 calm

exciting *adj*
stimulating, stirring, intoxicating, exhilarating, thrilling, dramatic, rousing, moving, enthralling, electrifying, striking, breathtaking, sensational, provocative, inspiring, interesting
COLLOQ. nail-biting, cliff-hanging, action-packed, sexy
F≡ dull, unexciting

exclaim *v*
cry (out), declare, come out with, blurt (out), call, yell, shout, roar, shriek, bellow, proclaim, utter
FORMAL vociferate, ejaculate

exclamation *n*
cry, call, yell, shout, expletive, interjection, outcry, utterance, roar, shriek, bellow
FORMAL ejaculation

exclude *v*
1 BAN, bar, prohibit, refuse, disallow, veto, forbid, debar, blacklist
FORMAL interdict

2 OMIT, leave out, miss out, delete, keep out, refuse, reject, ignore, shut out, rule out, ostracize, eliminate, except
FORMAL preclude
COLLOQ. drop, skip, count out, include out
3 EXPEL, eject, evict, throw out, remove, excommunicate, ostracize, boycott, freeze out, ice out, lock out
COLLOQ. boot out, turf out, kick out, send to Coventry
F≡ 1 admit 2 include, consider

excluding *prep*
except, except for, with the exception of, excepting, exclusive of, not including, not counting, omitting, leaving out, ruling out, barring, debarring

exclusion *n*
1 OMISSION, rejection, elimination, ruling out, refusal, repudiation
FORMAL preclusion
2 BAN, bar, prohibition, embargo, veto, boycott
FORMAL interdict, proscription
3 EJECTION, expulsion, eviction, removal, boycott, exception
F≡ 1 inclusion 2 allowance 3 admittance

exclusive *adj, n*
◆ *adj*
1 SOLE, single, individual, unique, only, undivided, unshared, complete, whole, total, peculiar
2 RESTRICTED, limited, closed, private, narrow, restrictive, choice, select, discriminative, cliquey, chic, elegant, fashionable, up-market, high-class, upper-crust, snobbish
COLLOQ. classy, posh, snazzy, ritzy, plush, swish
◆ *n*
scoop, coup, inside story, revelation, exposé, sensation
■ **exclusive of**
except, except for, with the exception of, excepting, excluding, not including, not counting, omitting, leaving out, ruling out, barring, debarring
F≡ inclusive of

> **Synonym nuances**
> *adjective sense 2*
> **Restricted** and **limited** have a vaguely negative tone in that they describe something not available to everyone: *restricted access; limited edition; **closed** explicitly describes something that is only for a particular group: *a closed military court*. **Private** puts less emphasis on limitation and so suggests a more desirable exclusivity: *a private party for a few guests*.
> Both **narrow** and **restrictive** again have less positive connotations, by emphasizing the lack of scope: *restrictive social conventions*, unlike **choice** and **select** which suggest an element of suitability or desirability: *select schools*. **Discriminative**, on the other hand, puts the emphasis on the observance of distinctions and so can be negative in its implication, whilst **cliquey** is clearly derogatory in tone, and implicitly critical of the exclusivity of a group.
> **Chic** and **elegant** are admiring in tone and can be used to refer to the exclusivity of something stylish: *the chic cuisine of today*, while **up-market**, **high-class** and **upper-crust**, although less suggestive of admiration, have resonances with the fine living associated with the wealthier classes. **Snobbish**, however, is a markedly disapproving term, with suggestions of affectation and condescension behind the exclusivity.

excommunicate *v*
ban, banish, eject, denounce, exclude, expel, remove, bar, blacklist, debar, outlaw, repudiate, disfellowship, unchurch
FORMAL anathematize, proscribe, execrate

excommunication *n*
expulsion, exclusion, disfellowship, unchurching, banning, banishment, ejection, denunciation, barring, outlawing

excoriate *v*
condemn, carp, snipe, disapprove of, find fault with, run down, slate, denounce, attack, censure, blame
FORMAL animadvert, disparage, decry, denigrate, vituperate
COLLOQ. nag, slam, knock, come down on, give someone some stick, nit-pick

excrement *n*
waste matter, excretion, dung, ordure, droppings, turd, mess
TECHNICAL egesta, frass, scats, guano
OLD sir-reverence
FORMAL faeces, stool, rejectamenta
COLLOQ. flux, jobbie, doo-doo
SLANG poop, crud; (*vulgar*) crap, shit
Related adjective: excrementitious

excrescence *n*
1 GROWTH, swelling, bump, lump, knob, appendage, outgrowth, projection, prominence, tumour, wart, boil, cancer
FORMAL intumescence, protuberance
2 MONSTROSITY, blot, disfigurement, eyesore

excrete *v*
void, pass, eject, discharge, expel, evacuate, exude, secrete
FORMAL defecate, urinate
SLANG (*vulgar*) crap, shit

excretion *n*
discharge, excrement, droppings, dung, evacuation, ordure, perspiration
FORMAL defecation, excreta, urination, faeces, stool
SLANG (*vulgar*) crap, shit

excruciating *adj*
agonizing, painful, severe, tormenting, unbearable, insufferable, acute, intolerable, intense, sharp, piercing, extreme, atrocious, racking, harrowing, savage, burning, bitter

excruciatingly *adv*
unbearably, intolerably, painfully, severely, acutely, intensely, extremely, atrociously

exculpate *v*
clear, discharge, excuse, free, justify, let off, pardon, release, vindicate, forgive, deliver, absolve, acquit
FORMAL exonerate
E3 blame, condemn

excursion *n*
1 OUTING, trip, day trip, jaunt, expedition, journey, tour, airing, breather, ride, drive, walk, ramble
COLLOQ. junket
2 DIGRESSION, departure, straying, wandering, detour, diversion

excusable *adj*
understandable, minor, slight, allowable, permissible, defensible, explainable, forgivable, pardonable, justifiable
E3 blameworthy

excuse *v, n*
♦ *v*
1 FORGIVE, pardon, overlook, absolve, acquit, tolerate, make allowances for, ignore, indulge
FORMAL exonerate, exculpate
2 RELEASE, free, discharge, liberate, let off, relieve, spare, exempt
3 CONDONE, explain, justify, vindicate, defend, apologize for
FORMAL mitigate
E3 **1** criticize **2** punish
♦ *n*
justification, explanation, grounds, defence, plea, alibi, reason, vindication, apology, pretext, pretence, evasion, shift, substitute
FORMAL exoneration, mitigation, mitigating circumstances
COLLOQ. cop-out, front, cover-up, get-out

execrable *adj*
deplorable, abhorrent, abominable, disgusting, foul, dreadful, awful, appalling, atrocious, despicable, detestable, offensive, shocking, repulsive, revolting, horrible, loathsome, vile, nauseous, obnoxious, odious, damnable, accursed, hateful
FORMAL heinous
E3 admirable, estimable

execrate *v*
deplore, hate, abhor, loathe, abominate, condemn, denounce, denunciate, despise, detest, revile, curse, damn, imprecate
FORMAL excoriate, fulminate, inveigh against, vilify, anathematize
COLLOQ. blast
E3 commend, praise

execute *v*
1 PUT TO DEATH, kill, hang, electrocute, shoot, guillotine, behead, crucify
FORMAL decapitate
COLLOQ. liquidate
2 CARRY OUT, perform, do, accomplish, achieve, fulfil, complete, bring off, discharge, put into effect, put into practice, enact, deliver, enforce, finish, implement, administer, engineer, realize, dispatch, validate, serve, render, stage
FORMAL effect, consummate, expedite

execution *n*
1 DEATH PENALTY, death sentence, capital punishment, putting to death, killing
2 ACCOMPLISHMENT, operation, performance, completion, achievement, administration, effect, carrying-out, enactment, implementation, realization, fulfilment, discharge, dispatch, enforcement
FORMAL consummation, effecting
3 STYLE, technique, rendition, rendering, delivery, performance, staging, manner, mode, presentation

Means of execution include:

beheading	garrotting	shooting
burning	gassing	stoning
crucifixion	guillotining	*colloq.* stringing
decapitation	hanging	up
electrocution	lethal injection	
firing squad	lynching	

executioner *n*
hangman, firing squad, headsman, Jack Ketch, axeman, killer, murderer, exterminator, assassin, slayer
OLD (*Shakesp*) deathsman
COLLOQ. hit man, liquidator

executive *n, adj*
♦ *n*
1 ADMINISTRATOR, manager, organizer, leader, controller, director, governor, official, chairman, chairwoman, chairperson, superior, superintendent
2 ADMINISTRATION, management, government, leadership, hierarchy
COLLOQ. top brass, big guns, big shots
♦ *adj*
administrative, managerial, controlling, supervisory, regulating, decision-making, governing, lawmaking, organizing, directing, directorial, organizational, leading, guiding

exegesis *n*
explanation, interpretation, clarification, opening-up
FORMAL exposition, expounding, explication

exemplar n
example, standard, model, pattern, type, ideal, prototype, paragon, copy, criterion, yardstick, epitome, illustration, instance, specimen
FORMAL archetype, embodiment, exemplification, paradigm

exemplary adj
1 MODEL, ideal, perfect, admirable, excellent, faultless, flawless, correct, good, commendable, praiseworthy, worthy, honourable
FORMAL laudable, estimable, meritorious
2 CAUTIONARY, warning
FORMAL admonitory
E⁂ **1** imperfect, unworthy

exemplify v
illustrate, be an example of, demonstrate, show, instance, cite, represent, typify, characterize, embody, personify, epitomize, exhibit, depict, display
FORMAL manifest

exempt v, adj
♦ v
excuse, release, relieve, let off, free, grant immunity to, absolve, discharge, dismiss, liberate, spare, exclude, waive, make an exception
FORMAL exonerate
♦ adj
excused, not liable, not subject, immune, released, spared, absolved, discharged, excluded, free, liberated, dismissed, clear
E⁂ liable

exemption n
exception, exclusion, immunity, privilege, indulgence, release, freedom, indemnity, discharge
FORMAL absolution, dispensation, exoneration
E⁂ liability

exercise v, n
♦ v
1 USE, utilize, employ, make use of, apply, exert, practise, implement, bring to bear, bring into play, wield, try, discharge, exploit
2 TRAIN, work out, do exercises, drill, practise, keep fit, exert yourself, warm up, warm down
COLLOQ. pump iron
3 WORRY, disturb, trouble, upset, burden, distress, concern, vex, annoy, agitate, afflict, preoccupy
FORMAL perturb
♦ n
1 TRAINING, drill, movement, practice, effort, exertion, activity, keep-fit, aerobics, sports, gymnastics, PE, physical education, PT, physical training, warm-up, warm-down, jogging, running, isometrics, eurhythmics, callisthenics, Pilates, labour
COLLOQ. physical jerks, workout
2 USE, utilization, employment, application, implementation, practice, operation, discharge, assignment, fulfilment, accomplishment, exertion
3 TASK, assignment, lesson, work, discipline, problem, project, piece of work

exert v
use, utilize, employ, apply, exercise, bring to bear, bring into play, wield, spend, expend
▪ **exert yourself**
strive, struggle, try hard, strain, make every effort, take pains, do your best/utmost, toil, labour, work, endeavour, apply yourself, give your all
COLLOQ. sweat, go all out, pull out all the stops, slog away, give it your best shot, keep your nose to the grindstone, work your socks off

exertion n
1 EFFORT, industry, labour, toil, work, exercise, struggle,

diligence, assiduousness, perseverance, pains, endeavour, attempt, strain, stress, trial
FORMAL travail
COLLOQ. (hard) graft
2 USE, utilization, employment, application, exercise, operation, action
E⁂ **1** idleness, rest

exhalation n
breathing-out, respiration, evaporation, discharge, emission, expulsion
FORMAL expiration

exhale v
breathe (out), give off, blow (out), discharge, emit, expel, issue, respire, steam, evaporate
FORMAL emanate, expire
E⁂ inhale

exhaust v, n
♦ v
1 TIRE (OUT), weary, fatigue, tax, sap, drain, strain, weaken, overwork, overtax, overtire, wear out
FORMAL enervate
COLLOQ. do in, fag out, knock out, whack, knacker, take it out of, nearly/almost kill; N Am tucker out
2 CONSUME, empty, drain, sap, spend, expend, run through, waste, squander, impoverish, use up, finish, dry, bankrupt
FORMAL deplete, dissipate
E⁂ **1** refresh **2** renew
♦ n
emission, exhalation, discharge, fumes, smoke, steam, vapour
FORMAL emanation

exhausted adj
1 TIRED OUT, dead tired, worn out, fatigued, weak, washed-out, drained, jaded; Scot wabbit
FORMAL enfeebled, enervated
COLLOQ. dead-beat, all in, done (in), whacked, fagged out, knackered, bushed, burnt out, dog-tired, ready to drop, zonked, jiggered, shagged out; N Am pooped (out), tuckered out; Aust & NZ beaten
SLANG Aust & NZ euchred out
2 EMPTY, finished, consumed, spent, used up, drained, dry, worn out, void
FORMAL depleted
E⁂ **1** vigorous **2** fresh

exhausting adj
tiring, strenuous, taxing, wearying, wearing, gruelling, arduous, hard, laborious, backbreaking, draining, debilitating, severe, testing, punishing, formidable
FORMAL enervating
E⁂ refreshing, invigorating

exhaustion n
fatigue, tiredness, weariness, weakness, feebleness, lethargy, jet-lag
FORMAL enervation
E⁂ freshness, liveliness

exhaustive adj
comprehensive, all-embracing, all-inclusive, far-reaching, complete, total, extensive, encyclopedic, full-scale, thorough, full, in-depth, intensive, detailed, definitive, all-out, sweeping
E⁂ incomplete, restricted

exhaustively adv
comprehensively, all-inclusively, completely, totally, extensively, encyclopedically, thoroughly, fully, intensively, definitively
E⁂ incompletely

exhibit v, n
♦ v
display, put on display, show, present, demonstrate,

expose, unveil, parade, reveal, express, make clear, make plain, reveal, disclose, indicate, air, flaunt, offer, set out, set forth
FORMAL manifest, array
🖙 conceal, hide
♦ *n*
display, exhibition, show, showing, demonstration, illustration, model, presentation

exhibition *n*
display, show, demonstration, exhibit, presentation, diorama, pavilion, spectacle, showing, fair, performance, airing, representation, showcase, preview, retrospective, Salon, indication, expression, revelation, disclosure
TECHNICAL panopticon
FORMAL manifestation, exposition
COLLOQ. expo

exhibitionism *n*
showing-off, boastfulness, flaunting, self-display, flamboyance, histrionics, dramatics, overacting, staginess

exhibitionist *n*
show-off, extrovert, poseur, poser, self-advertiser

exhilarate *v*
thrill, excite, make excited, elate, make happy, cheer up, delight, gladden, animate, enliven, invigorate, vitalize, revitalize, raise/lift the spirits of, intoxicate, stimulate, brighten, lift
COLLOQ. perk up
🖙 bore, discourage

exhilarating *adj*
thrilling, exciting, delightful, cheerful, gladdening, cheering, enlivening, stimulating, revitalizing, invigorating, heady, breathtaking, intoxicating
COLLOQ. mind-blowing
🖙 boring, discouraging

exhilaration *n*
excitement, thrill, happiness, cheerfulness, gladness, delight, euphoria, elation, joy, joyfulness, exaltation, glee, high spirits, liveliness, vivacity, zeal, enthusiasm, animation, ardour, invigoration, revitalization, stimulation, gusto, dash, gaiety, mirth, hilarity
FORMAL élan
🖙 boredom, discouragement

exhort *v*
urge, persuade, encourage, implore, goad, incite, inflame, inspire, instigate, spur, warn, bid, call on/upon, press, advise, counsel, caution, prompt
FORMAL admonish, beseech, enjoin, entreat

exhortation *n*
urging, persuasion, encouragement, call, appeal, goading, incitement, advice, caution, warning, counsel, bidding, lecture, sermon
FORMAL admonition, beseeching, enjoinder, entreaty, paraenesis, protreptic

exhumation *n*
disinterment, disentombment, excavation, unearthing

exhume *v*
disinter, dig up, disentomb, excavate, unbury, unearth, resurrect
FORMAL disinhume
🖙 bury

exigency *n*
1 DEMAND, requirement, need, necessity
2 EMERGENCY, urgency, crisis, criticalness, difficulty, distress, imperativeness, pressure, plight, quandary, predicament, stress

exigent *adj*
urgent, demanding, insistent, necessary, pressing, stringent, exacting, critical, crucial

exiguous *adj*
meagre, insufficient, inadequate, scant, scanty, negligible, sparse, slight, slim, bare

exile *n, v*
♦ *n*
1 BANISHMENT, deportation, expatriation, expulsion, uprooting, ostracism, separating, separation, transportation, Babylon
TECHNICAL Galut
2 EXPATRIATE, refugee, émigré, expat, deportee, fugitive, displaced person, Diaspora, outcast, outlaw, pariah
OLD (*Spenser*) exul; wretch
♦ *v*
banish, expel, deport, extradite, expatriate, repatriate, drive out, cast out, uproot, separate, ostracize, oust, excommunicate, eject, outlaw, ban, bar

exist *v*
1 BE, live, have life, be alive, abide, continue, endure, have being, have existence, breathe, have breath
2 SUBSIST, survive, live, eke out a living, eke out an existence
3 BE PRESENT, occur, happen, be available, be found, remain, last, continue, prevail

existence *n*
1 BEING, life, living, reality, actuality, fact, continuance, continuation, endurance, survival, breath, subsistence
2 WAY OF LIFE, way of living, life, lifestyle
FORMAL mode of living
3 ENTITY, creature, being, thing
4 CREATION, the world
🖙 1 death, non-existence

existent *adj*
existing, in existence, actual, real, current, present, living, alive, enduring, remaining, surviving, standing, abiding, prevailing
FORMAL obtaining, extant
COLLOQ. around
🖙 non-existent

exit *n, v*
♦ *n*
1 DEPARTURE, going, leaving, retreat, withdrawal, leave-taking, retirement, farewell, exodus, flight
2 DOOR, way out, doorway, gate, vent, outlet; *Scot & dialect* outgate
FORMAL egress
🖙 1 entrance, arrival 2 entrance
♦ *v*
depart, leave, go (out), retire, withdraw, take your leave, retreat, issue
🖙 arrive, enter

exodus *n*
departure, evacuation, mass departure, mass evacuation, flight, fleeing, escape, leaving, migration, retirement, long march, retreat, withdrawal, exit, hegira

exonerate *v*
1 ABSOLVE, acquit, clear, excuse, vindicate, justify, pardon, declare innocent, discharge
FORMAL exculpate
2 EXEMPT, excuse, spare, let off, free, liberate, discharge, release, relieve
🖙 1 incriminate

exoneration *n*
1 ACQUITTAL, clearing, excusing, vindication, justification, pardon, discharge, amnesty, absolution, dismissal
FORMAL exculpation
2 EXEMPTION, excusing, discharge, liberation, freeing, release, relief, immunity, indemnity
🖙 1 incrimination

exorbitant *adj*
excessive, unreasonable, unwarranted, undue, inordinate,

immoderate, extravagant, extortionate, enormous, preposterous, monstrous
COLLOQ. daylight robbery, a rip-off
F3 reasonable, moderate, fair

exorbitantly adv
excessively, unreasonably, unduly, inordinately, immoderately, extravagantly, extortionately
F3 reasonably, moderately

exorcism n
casting out, deliverance, freeing, expulsion, purification
TECHNICAL exsufflation, insufflation
FORMAL adjuration

exorcize v
cast out, drive out, free, expel, purify
TECHNICAL exsufflate, insufflate
FORMAL adjure

exotic adj
1 FOREIGN, alien, imported, introduced, tropical, external, non-native
2 UNUSUAL, striking, different, remarkable, unfamiliar, extraordinary, bizarre, curious, strange, impressive, fascinating, colourful, glamorous, peculiar, outlandish, extravagant, outrageous, sensational
F3 1 native **2** ordinary, common

exotically adv
unusually, strikingly, remarkably, extraordinarily, curiously, strangely, impressively, sensationally, outlandishly, tropically

expand v
increase, grow, become/make larger/bigger, extend, enlarge, develop, amplify, spread, stretch, swell, widen, lengthen, thicken, intensify, escalate, magnify, multiply, inflate, amplify, broaden, blow up, open out, fill out, put out, fatten, puff out, unfold, unfurl, pad, branch out, diversify, mushroom, work up
OLD intend
FORMAL distend, dilate, dispread, intumesce
F3 contract

■ **expand on**
enlarge on, elaborate on, embroider, flesh out, go into details
FORMAL expatiate on, dilate on

expanse n
extent, space, area, breadth, range, stretch, region, sweep, field, plain, tract, vastness, extensiveness
OLD main

expansion n
growth, increase, extension, development, amplification, spread, expanse, swelling, enlargement, lengthening, thickening, broadening, magnification, multiplication, inflation, unfolding, unfurling, diversification
FORMAL augmentation, diffusion, dilation, distension, dilatation
F3 contraction

expansive adj
1 EXTENSIVE, broad, comprehensive, wide, sweeping, wide-ranging, widespread, all-embracing, thorough
2 COMMUNICATIVE, friendly, genial, outgoing, open, affable, sociable, talkative, warm, forthcoming, effusive, uninhibited
FORMAL loquacious
3 EXPANDING, growing, increasing, enlarging, developing, diversifying, magnifying, multiplying
F3 1 restricted, narrow **2** reserved, cold **3** contracting

expatiate v
expand, enlarge, amplify, elaborate, embellish, develop, expound, dwell on, hold forth on
FORMAL dilate

expatriate n, v, adj
♦ n

emigrant, émigré, exile, refugee, displaced person, outcast, expat
♦ v
banish, exile, deport, extradite, drive out, uproot, expel, oust, repatriate, ostracize
FORMAL proscribe
♦ adj
banished, exiled, deported, expelled, uprooted, emigrant, émigré

expect v
1 expect you're right
suppose, assume, believe, think, presume, imagine, reckon, trust
OLD ween
FORMAL surmise, conjecture
COLLOQ. guess
2 expect the money soon
anticipate, await, look forward to, hope for, trust, look for, watch for, bank on, bargain for, envisage, predict, forecast, contemplate, project, foresee; Scot lippen
3 expect you to comply
require, want, wish, insist on, demand, call for, ask for, look for, hope for, rely on, count on, figure on

---

Synonym nuances
sense 2
Anticipate would be appropriate for something likely, as would **look forward to**, though with the further implication of it being something pleasant: *she was looking forward to the holidays.* **Await** suggests a greater degree of certainty about something in the future: *I await your response to my complaint.*
  Hope for has a strong element of desire, while **trust** can be used as a more tentative, polite term to suggest assumption: *I trust you find everything satisfactory.* The term **look for** similarly implies confidence in the expectation at a superficial level, but might actually be used with an element of hope: *I'll be looking for your support.* **Bank on** is similar, but would be used to hint at dependency: *I am banking on you to perform well so we win the match.* **Bargain for** is different in that it would be used negatively to refer to not expecting something: *they hadn't bargained for a dramatic change in the weather.*
  For expressing what you think could happen, you might use **envisage** if it is within the realms of your imaginings: *I could envisage a long-drawn-out court case.* If you have applied what you know to your expectation for the future you might use the terms **predict**, **forecast**, **project** or **foresee**: *the fog has cleared, so I do not foresee any travel problems.*

---

expectancy n
anticipation, eagerness, expectation, hope, suspense, waiting, curiosity
FORMAL conjecture

expectant adj
1 AWAITING, anticipating, looking forward, hopeful, in suspense, ready, apprehensive, anxious, watchful, eager, excited, on tenterhooks, with bated breath, curious
2 PREGNANT, going to have a baby, carrying, big-bellied
TECHNICAL gravid
OLD with child, great, quick, in an interesting condition/state/situation
FORMAL enceinte
COLLOQ. expecting, in the family way, in the club, in a certain condition, in trouble
SLANG preggers, with a bun in the oven, in the pudding club, up the duff, up the spout

expectantly adv
in anticipation, eagerly, expectingly, hopefully, in suspense, apprehensively, optimistically

expectation *n*
hope, belief, anticipation, assumption, presumption, surmise, supposition, calculation, forecast, projection, prediction, eagerness, requirement, demand, insistence, promise, want, wish, reliance, trust, prospect, confidence, assurance, suspense, optimism, possibility, probability, outlook
FORMAL conjecture

expecting *adj*
pregnant, going to have a baby, expectant, carrying, big-bellied
TECHNICAL gravid
OLD with child, great, quick, in an interesting condition/state/situation
FORMAL enceinte
COLLOQ. in the family way, in the club, in a certain condition, in trouble
SLANG preggers, with a bun in the oven, in the pudding club, up the duff, up the spout

expedience *n*
convenience, suitability, appropriateness, fitness, aptness, advantageousness, effectiveness, desirability, helpfulness, properness, profitableness, usefulness, practicality, pragmatism, prudence, advisability, benefit, advantage, profitability, expediency, utility, utilitarianism
FORMAL judiciousness, propriety

expedient *adj, n*
 • *adj*
convenient, suitable, appropriate, fitting, opportune, politic, in your own interest, profitable, prudent, useful, beneficial, advantageous, advisable, sensible, practical, pragmatic, tactical
E3 inexpedient
 • *n*
stratagem, scheme, means, method, measure, tactic, ploy, manoeuvre, plan, trick, shift, contrivance, device, stopgap
COLLOQ. dodge

expedite *v*
speed up, accelerate, step up, quicken, hasten, hurry, further, facilitate, assist, promote, press, dispatch, discharge, hurry through
FORMAL precipitate
E3 delay

expedition *n*
1 JOURNEY, excursion, trip, voyage, tour, outing, exploration, field trip, trek, safari, hike, sail, ramble, raid, quest, pilgrimage, adventure, undertaking, enterprise, project, campaign, mission, crusade, warpath
OLD hosting
2 TEAM, group, party, crew, company
3 PROMPTNESS, speed, swiftness, haste
FORMAL alacrity, celerity

expeditious *adj*
quick, efficient, rapid, speedy, swift, fast, hasty, immediate, instant, diligent, prompt, active, alert, brisk, ready
COLLOQ. meteoric
E3 slow

expel *v*
1 DRIVE OUT, eject, evict, banish, throw out, cast out, ban, bar, oust, dismiss, sideline, reject, exile, outlaw, expatriate
FORMAL proscribe
COLLOQ. boot out, chuck out, kick out
2 DISCHARGE, let out, eject, belch, evacuate, void, cast out, spew out
E3 **1** welcome

expend *v*
1 SPEND, pay (out), buy, afford, overspend, waste, fritter, squander
FORMAL purchase, disburse, procure
COLLOQ. fork out, lay out, shell out, blow, splash out

2 CONSUME, use (up), get through, go through, exhaust, empty, drain, sap, employ, utilize
FORMAL dissipate, deplete
E3 **1** save **2** conserve

expendable *adj*
dispensable, disposable, replaceable, unimportant, unnecessary, inessential, non-essential, throwaway
E3 indispensable, necessary

expenditure *n*
1 *huge amounts of public expenditure*
spending, expense, expenses, costs, outlay, outgoings, payment, output, waste, squandering
FORMAL disbursement
2 *the expenditure of effort*
use, application, consumption, draining, sapping, employment, utilization
FORMAL dissipation
E3 income

expense *n*
1 *underestimate the expense of moving house*
spending, expenditure, outlay, payment, paying-out, loss, cost, price, charge, fee, rate
FORMAL disbursement
2 *expenses will be reimbursed*
costs, outgoings, incidentals, outlay, overheads, incidental expenses, out-of-pocket expenses, miscellaneous expenses, spending
3 *at the expense of his life*
cost, sacrifice, loss, harm, disadvantage, detriment
Related adjective: sumptuary

expensive *adj*
dear, high-priced, high-cost, costly, costing a lot, exorbitant, extortionate, overpriced, excessive, extravagant, lavish, splendid, executive
OLD chargeful
COLLOQ. steep, pricey, posh, sky-high, costing an arm and a leg, costing the earth, costing a bomb, daylight robbery; N Am big-ticket
OLD SLANG salt
E3 cheap, inexpensive

experience *n, v*
 • *n*
1 KNOWLEDGE, familiarity, contact, skill, involvement, exposure, participation, practice, training, understanding, learning, observation
COLLOQ. knowhow
2 INCIDENT, event, episode, happening, encounter, occurrence, circumstance, adventure, affair, case, ordeal
COLLOQ. *Aust & NZ* spin
E3 **1** inexperience
 • *v*
undergo, go through, live through, suffer, feel, endure, encounter, face, meet, know, try, perceive, sustain, become familiar with, participate in

experienced *adj*
1 PRACTISED, knowledgeable, familiar, capable, competent, proficient, adept, well-versed, expert, accomplished, qualified, skilful, skilled, tried, trained, professional, au fait, *au courant*
2 MATURE, seasoned, wise, veteran, sophisticated, worldly wise, suave
COLLOQ. around, streetwise
E3 **1** inexperienced, unskilled **2** inexperienced, unsophisticated

experiment *n, v*
 • *n*
trial, test, testing, investigation, experimentation, research, inquiry, demonstration, examination, observation, analysis, trial run, venture, try-out, trial and error, attempt,

procedure, proof, pilot study, piloting, dummy run, dry run
♦ *v*
try (out), test, investigate, examine, research, trial, sample,
verify, observe, explore, carry out tests, conduct an
experiment

experimental *adj*
trial, test, exploratory, tentative, provisional, investigative,
scientific, observational, speculative, pilot, preliminary,
trial-and-error, at the trial/exploratory stage
TECHNICAL empirical
FORMAL peirastic

experimentally *adv*
tentatively, provisonally, speculatively, innovatively,
scientifically, investigatively, by trial and error, by rule of
thumb
TECHNICAL empirically

experimentation *n*
investigation, exploration, research, research and
development, R & D, verification, rule of thumb,
pragmatism, inventiveness
TECHNICAL empiricism

expert *n, adj*
♦ *n*
specialist, connoisseur, authority, pundit, master, past
master, old master, old hand, practitioner, professional,
maestro, virtuoso, crack, proficient, cognoscente, nark;
Aust & NZ don
COLLOQ. pro, dab hand, ace, buff, egghead, boffin, hotshot,
whizz, wise guy; *N Am* mavin, maven; *Aust & NZ* gun; *S Afr*
fundi
♦ *adj*
proficient, adept, skilled, skilful, knowledgeable,
experienced, able, practised, professional, accomplished,
masterly, excellent, brilliant, specialist, qualified, virtuoso,
dexterous
OLD sly
COLLOQ. top-notch, up on, well up on, crack, ace; *Aust &
NZ* gun
🔁 amateurish, novice

expertise *n*
expertness, proficiency, ability, skill, skilfulness, deftness,
knowledge, understanding, professionalism, mastery,
command, dexterity, facility, cleverness, virtuosity, savoir-
faire
OLD skill
COLLOQ. knowhow, knack
🔁 inexperience, inexpertness

expertly *adv*
skilfully, proficiently, competently, ably, capably,
professionally, excellently, efficiently, masterly

expiate *v*
atone for, make amends for, purge, do penance for, make
up for, pay for, redress

expiation *n*
atonement, redemption, ransom, reparation, redress,
penance, amends, recompense, shrift

expire *v*
1 END, come to an end, cease, finish, stop, close, run out, be
no longer valid, lapse
FORMAL terminate, conclude, discontinue
2 DIE, depart, perish, pass away, pass on, depart this life,
breathe your last, lose your life
FORMAL decease
COLLOQ. peg out, bite the dust, pop off, give up the ghost,
have had it, meet your maker
SLANG snuff it, cash in your chips, kick the bucket
🔁 **1** begin, be valid **2** live, be born

expiry *n*
end, finish, close, expiration, lapse

FORMAL cessation, conclusion, termination,
discontinuation
🔁 beginning, continuation

explain *v*
1 INTERPRET, clarify, describe, define, make clear, throw/
shed light on, open up, simplify, resolve, solve, spell out,
translate, elaborate, unfold, unravel, untangle, decipher,
decode, illustrate, demonstrate, disclose, teach, set out
FORMAL elucidate, expound, delineate, explicate
2 JUSTIFY, excuse, account for, rationalize, vindicate,
defend, give a reason for, explain away, lie behind
🔁 **1** obscure, confound

Synonym nuances
sense 1

Interpret and **translate** suggest expressing something in
terms which may be understood or given due
significance: *interpreting the results of the experiment*,
whereas **clarify**, **make clear** and **simplify** would be used
of making something easier to understand. Both **resolve**
and **solve** are suggestive of finding an answer, whilst
spell out has more to do with detailing specific elements
to avoid misunderstanding: *the council's role is spelt out
in the new legislation*. **Elaborate**, although sharing the
same purpose, suggests adding to what is already there
by way of further explanation.

The term **open up** suggests making something, which
was previously difficult to penetrate, understandable: *she
longed to have the meaning of the poem opened up to
her*; or you can use **unfold** or **disclose** to similarly
suggest that something is being revealed. The term
unravel creates an image of identifying separate strands
in order to make sense of the whole: *unravelling the
philosopher's meanings is not easy*.

To refer to explanation involving practical display,
illustrate, **demonstrate** and **set out** are appropriate:
*this chapter will demonstrate ways to improve your self-
esteem.*

---

explanation *n*
1 INTERPRETATION, clarification, definition, illustration,
demonstration, simplification, account, description,
report, note, comment, commentary, gloss, footnote,
annotation, unfolding, deciphering, decoding
FORMAL elucidation, exegesis, expounding, delineation,
explication
2 JUSTIFICATION, excuse, reason, account, motive, meaning,
answer, warrant, rationalization, vindication, defence, alibi
FORMAL apologia

explanatory *adj*
descriptive, demonstrative, illustrative, justifying
FORMAL interpretative, interpretive, explicative,
expository, exegetical, elucidatory

expletive *n*
swear-word, oath, curse, blasphemy, obscenity, profanity,
bad language
FORMAL anathema, imprecation, execration
COLLOQ. four-letter word
SLANG cuss; *N Am* cussword

explicable *adj*
explainable, accountable, definable, determinable,
intelligible, justifiable, resolvable, understandable,
solvable
FORMAL interpretable, exponible

explicate *v*
explain, interpret, clarify, describe, define, make clear,
illustrate, demonstrate, spell out, set forth, unfold, unravel,
untangle, work out
FORMAL elucidate, expound
🔁 confuse, obscure

explication n
explanation, interpretation, clarification, description, illustration
FORMAL elucidation, exposition

explicit adj
1 CLEAR, distinct, clearly expressed, exact, categorical, absolute, direct, certain, positive, precise, specific, unequivocal, unambiguous, express, definite, declared, detailed, stated, straightforward
2 OPEN, direct, frank, candid, outspoken, straightforward, forthright, unreserved, unrestrained, uninhibited, plain, plain-spoken
3 *explicit sex scenes*
uncensored, offensive, shocking, obscene, pornographic, dirty, filthy, smutty, X-rated, adult
COLLOQ. near the knuckle/bone
F3 1 implicit, unspoken, vague **2** reserved, restrained, cagey

explicitly adv
clearly, overtly, directly, specifically, unequivocally, unambiguously, plainly, definitely, straightforwardly
F3 implicitly, vaguely

explode v
1 BLOW UP, burst, go off, go up, set off, detonate, discharge, blast, spring
OLD displode
FORMAL erupt
COLLOQ. go bang
2 *explode with rage*
lose your temper, blow up, erupt, flare up, burst out
FORMAL fulminate
COLLOQ. blow a fuse, blow your cool, blow your top, boil over, burst a blood vessel, do your nut, fly into a rage, fly off the handle, go off the deep end, go up the wall, hit the ceiling, hit the roof, lose your cool, lose your rag, see red
3 DISCREDIT, disprove, give the lie to, debunk, invalidate, rebut, repudiate
FORMAL refute
4 GROW RAPIDLY, increase suddenly, escalate, accelerate, boom, leap, surge, mushroom, rocket
F3 3 prove, confirm

exploit n, v
♦ n
deed, feat, adventure, achievement, accomplishment, attainment, activity, action, act, stunt
♦ v
1 USE, apply, employ, draw on, put to good use, make use of, utilize, capitalize on, use to good advantage, profit by, turn to account, take advantage of, make capital out of, tap
COLLOQ. cash in on, milk
2 MISUSE, abuse, take advantage of, take liberties, profiteer, oppress, ill-treat, impose on, fleece, manipulate
COLLOQ. milk, bleed, put something across someone, pull a fast one on, walk all over, play off against
SLANG rip off, take for a ride

exploitation n
1 *the exploitation of children*
taking (unfair) advantage, misuse, abuse, oppression, manipulation
COLLOQ. fleecing, milking, bleeding
SLANG rip-off, taking for a ride
2 *the exploitation of fossil fuels*
use, utilization, employment, application, putting to good use, making use of
COLLOQ. cashing in on, milking

exploration n
1 INVESTIGATION, examination, inquiry, research, scrutiny, study, inspection, observation, analysis, probe
2 EXPEDITION, survey, reconnaissance, search, trip, tour, voyage, travel, safari

exploratory adj
investigative, fact-finding, experimental, pilot, probing, searching, analytic, tentative, trial

explore v
1 INVESTIGATE, examine, look into, study, inspect, research, scrutinize, probe, analyse, consider, survey, inquire into, review
2 TRAVEL, tour, search, reconnoitre, prospect, scout, survey
FORMAL traverse
COLLOQ. see the world, do

explorer n
traveller, discoverer, navigator, tourer, prospector, scout, surveyor, reconnoitrer

explosion n
1 DETONATION, blast, blow-up, burst, outburst, discharge, eruption, bang, boom, outbreak, clap, crack, thunder, rumble, roll, fit; *Scot* pluff
OLD displosion
FORMAL report
2 *population explosion*
boom, surge, leap, sudden increase, dramatic growth
3 *explosion of anger*
outburst, eruption, fit, flare-up, rage, tantrum, paroxysm

explosive n, adj
♦ n
dynamite, gelignite, gunpowder, jelly, nitroglycerine, TNT, cordite, Semtex®
♦ adj
1 *an explosive device*
charged, hazardous, dangerous, unstable, volatile
FORMAL perilous
2 *an explosive situation*
tense, sensitive, fraught, charged, critical, powerful, nerve-racking, unstable, volatile, volcanic
3 FIERY, angry, unstable, volatile, overwrought, worked-up, violent, stormy, unrestrained, wild, raging, sensitive, touchy
4 *explosive growth*
sudden, dramatic, rapid, unexpected, mushrooming, rocketing, exponential, burgeoning, abrupt
COLLOQ. meteoric
F3 1, 2 stable, calm **3** composed

explosively adv
1 *explosively combustible*
dangerously, hazardously, unstably, destructively
2 *grow explosively*
suddenly, rapidly, dramatically, unexpectedly, exponentially
3 *reply explosively*
fierily, angrily, violently, wildly
4 *the play opens explosively*
tensely, critically, powerfully, volcanically, like a bolt from the blue
F3 3 calmly

exponent n
1 ADVOCATE, promoter, supporter, upholder, defender, backer, adherent, spokesman, spokeswoman, spokesperson, champion
FORMAL proponent
2 PRACTITIONER, adept, expert, master, specialist, player, performer

export v, n
♦ v
trade, deal with, sell abroad/overseas, traffic in, transport, re-export
♦ n
exported product/commodity/goods, re-export, transfer, trade, foreign trade, international trade

expose v
1 REVEAL, show, exhibit, display, disclose, uncover, bring to

light, bring out into the open, make known, present, detect, divulge, betray, unveil, unmask, unearth, lay bare, denounce
FORMAL manifest
COLLOQ. blow the whistle, take the lid off
2 ENDANGER, jeopardize, imperil, risk, hazard, put at risk, put in jeopardy, make vulnerable
3 *expose the public to art*
familiarize with, bring into contact with, acquaint with, introduce to, present with, lay open to, subject to
4 *expose yourself*
show your genitals, commit indecent exposure
COLLOQ. flash
E3 1 conceal, cover up **2** protect

exposé *n*
disclosure, divulgence, exposure, revelation, uncovering, account, article

exposed *adj*
bare, open, in the open, revealed, laid bare, unprotected, without protection, open to the elements, vulnerable, exhibited, on display, on show, on view, shown, susceptible
E3 covered, sheltered

exposition *n*
1 EXPLANATION, description, analysis, unfolding, clarification, illumination, commentary, interpretation, account, illustration, critique, presentation, paper, study, thesis, monograph
FORMAL discourse, elucidation, exegesis, explication
2 EXHIBITION, show, fair, display, demonstration
COLLOQ. expo

expository *adj*
explanatory, descriptive, illustrative, interpretative
TECHNICAL exegetic, hermeneutic
FORMAL declaratory, elucidative, explicatory, interpretive

expostulate *v*
protest, argue, plead, reason, dissuade, disagree
FORMAL remonstrate

exposure *n*
1 REVELATION, uncovering, disclosure, exposé, showing, unmasking, unveiling, display, airing, exhibition, presentation, publicity, discovery, detection, divulgence, denunciation
FORMAL manifestation
2 FAMILIARITY, experience, knowledge, contact, acquaintance, awareness
3 JEOPARDY, danger, hazard, risk, vulnerability, susceptibility
4 PUBLICITY, public attention, advertising, promotion
COLLOQ. plug, hype

expound *v*
explain, analyse, dissect, unfold, unravel, untangle, clarify, illuminate, describe, illustrate, interpret, comment on, set forth, set out, spell out, open (up), preach, sermonize
FORMAL elucidate, explicate

express *v, adj*
♦ *v*
1 ARTICULATE, verbalize, put into words, utter, voice, give voice to, say, speak, state, communicate, put/get over, pronounce, word, tell, announce, report, assert, declare, put across, formulate, point out, intimate, testify, convey, vent, ventilate, air
FORMAL enunciate
2 SHOW, demonstrate, exhibit, disclose, divulge, reveal, indicate, denote, depict, embody, couch
FORMAL manifest
3 SYMBOLIZE, stand for, represent, signify, designate
♦ *adj*
1 SPECIFIC, explicit, exact, definite, clear, categorical, precise, distinct, well-defined, clear-cut, certain, plain, particular, stated, unambiguous, unequivocal, special, sole
FORMAL manifest

2 FAST, speedy, rapid, quick, swift, high-speed, brisk, non-stop
FORMAL expeditious
E3 1 vague

expression *n*
1 LOOK, air, aspect, appearance, scowl, grimace, gesture
FORMAL countenance, mien
2 REPRESENTATION, demonstration, indication, intimation, exhibition, communication, illustration, embodiment, show, sign, symbol, style
FORMAL manifestation
3 UTTERANCE, verbalization, voicing, communication, articulation, vocalization, statement, assertion, proclamation, announcement, declaration, pronouncement, speech, wording, intimation
4 PHRASE, word, wording, term, turn of phrase, saying, maxim, adage, proverb, aphorism, axiom, set phrase, phrasing, idiom, language
5 TONE, intonation, delivery, style, idiom, diction, enunciation, modulation, phrasing
FORMAL locution
6 FEELING, emotion, passion, depth, force, power, vigour, vividness, intensity, imagination, artistry, creativity, style

expressionless *adj*
dull, blank, deadpan, impassive, emotionless, straight-faced, inscrutable, empty, vacuous, glassy, glazed
COLLOQ. poker-faced
E3 expressive

expressive *adj*
1 ELOQUENT, articulate, meaningful, forceful, telling, revealing, informative, communicative, demonstrative, emphatic, moving, evocative, poignant, lively, striking, animated, suggestive, significant, thoughtful, vivid, sympathetic
2 INDICATIVE, showing, demonstrating, revealing, suggesting

expressively *adv*
meaningfully, informatively, eloquently, demonstratively, emphatically, suggestively, evocatively, vividly
TECHNICAL espressivo

expressiveness *n*
articulateness, articulacy, demonstrativeness, meaningfulness, communicativeness, evocativeness, poignancy, vividness

expressly *adv*
specifically, explicitly, exactly, definitely, clearly, categorically, absolutely, precisely, distinctly, plainly, particularly, unambiguously, unequivocally, specially, solely, especially, decidedly, intentionally, on purpose, purposely, pointedly
FORMAL manifestly

expropriate *v*
take, take away, seize, take possession of, commandeer, confiscate, impound, usurp, assume, dispossess, annex, unhouse
TECHNICAL sequester, disseise
FORMAL appropriate, arrogate, requisition

expropriation *n*
taking-away, seizure, confiscation, impounding, dispossession
TECHNICAL sequestration
FORMAL appropriation, arrogation

expulsion *n*
1 EJECTION, eviction, exile, banishment, removal, discharge, exclusion, dismissal, throwing out, rejection
COLLOQ. sacking, the sack, the boot
2 DISCHARGE, ejection, belching, evacuation, voiding, excretion

expunge v
erase, remove, wipe out, cancel, obliterate, eradicate, destroy, exterminate, extinguish, raze, get rid of, abolish, annihilate, annul, blot out, delete, cross out, rub out
FORMAL efface, extirpate

expurgate v
censor, cut, emend, clean up, blue-pencil, bowdlerize, purge, purify, sanitize

exquisite adj
1 BEAUTIFUL, attractive, dainty, delicate, fine, charming, elegant, delightful, lovely, pretty, pleasing, fragile
2 PERFECT, flawless, fine, excellent, choice, precious, rare, outstanding
3 REFINED, discriminating, meticulous, sensitive, discerning, cultivated, cultured, impeccable
4 INTENSE, keen, sharp, acute, piercing, poignant
F3 1 ugly 2 flawed 3 unrefined

exquisitely adv
beautifully, attractively, daintily, delicately, finely, charmingly, elegantly, delightfully, pleasingly

extant adj
surviving, remaining, existent, existing, still existing, in existence, alive, living, subsistent, subsisting
F3 extinct, non-existent, dead

extempore adv, adj
◆ adv
impromptu, ad lib, on the spur of the moment, spontaneously
COLLOQ. off the cuff, off the top of your head
◆ adj
impromptu, improvised, ad-lib, unscripted, spontaneous, unplanned, unrehearsed, unprepared, extemporaneous
COLLOQ. off-the-cuff, off the top of your head
F3 planned

extemporize v
ad-lib, improvise, play it by ear, think on your feet, make up
COLLOQ. wing it, speak off the cuff, do something off the top of your head

extend v
1 SPREAD, stretch, reach, continue, carry on, run, last, come (up/down) to, go as far as, go down/up to
2 ENLARGE, increase, expand, develop, amplify, intensify, step up, lengthen, widen, broaden, draw out, stretch, prolong, spin out, drag out, unwind
FORMAL elongate, protract, augment
3 OFFER, give, grant, hold out, put out, reach out, impart, present
FORMAL bestow, confer, proffer
4 *the job extends to doing the cleaning*
include, take in, span, involve
FORMAL embrace, comprehend
F3 2 contract, shorten 3 withhold

extendable adj
enlargeable, expandable, stretchy, stretchable, elastic, magnifiable, extensive
FORMAL dilatable

extended adj
lengthy, long, lengthened, prolonged, increased, enlarged, expanded, developed, amplified

extension n
1 ENLARGEMENT, increase, stretching, broadening, widening, lengthening, expansion, development, enhancement, continuation, prolongation, proliferation
FORMAL elongation, protraction, diffusion
2 ADDITION, supplement, appendix, annexe, wing, add-on, adjunct
FORMAL addendum
3 DELAY, postponement, deferral, more/additional time

extensive adj
1 COMPREHENSIVE, far-reaching, large-scale, thorough, wide, wide-ranging, broad, widespread, universal, complete, extended, all-inclusive, unlimited, boundless, general, pervasive, prevalent
2 LARGE, huge, roomy, spacious, vast, long, lengthy, wide, substantial, fair-sized, sizeable
FORMAL capacious, commodious, voluminous
F3 1 restricted, narrow 2 small

extensively adv
1 *deal with a subject extensively*
comprehensively, thoroughly, completely, generally, boundlessly
2 *used extensively in industry*
greatly, widely, largely, generally, substantially

extent n
1 DIMENSION(S), amount, magnitude, expanse, size, area, bulk, degree, level, breadth, quantity, spread, coverage, stretch, volume, width, measure, length, duration, term, time
2 LIMIT, bounds, lengths, range, reach, scope, compass, stretch, sphere, play, sweep

extenuate v
diminish, excuse, lessen, minimize, make allowances for, modify, qualify, soften
FORMAL mitigate

extenuating adj
moderating, qualifying, justifying, palliative, diminishing, excusing, lessening, minimizing, modifying, softening
FORMAL mitigating, exculpatory, extenuative, extenuatory

exterior n, adj
◆ n
outside, surface, outer surface, covering, coating, face, façade, shell, skin, finish, externals, external surface, appearance
F3 inside, interior
◆ adj
outer, outside, outermost, surface, external, superficial, surrounding, outward, peripheral, extrinsic
F3 inside, interior

exterminate v
annihilate, kill, eradicate, destroy, eliminate, massacre, slaughter, abolish, wipe out
FORMAL extirpate
COLLOQ. do in, do away with, bump off, knock off

extermination n
annihilation, killing, eradication, elimination, destruction, massacre, genocide
FORMAL extirpation

external adj
1 OUTER, surface, outside, exterior, superficial, outward, outermost, apparent, visible, extraneous, peripheral, extrinsic
2 *external students*
extramural, independent, visiting, non-resident, outside
F3 1 internal 2 resident

externally adv
outwardly, visibly, superficially, apparently, extraneously, peripherally
F3 internally

extinct adj
1 DEFUNCT, dead, died out, non-existent, gone, obsolete, ended, exterminated, terminated, vanished, lost, wiped out, abolished
2 EXTINGUISHED, quenched, inactive, out, burnt out
3 OBSOLETE, invalid, expired, old, passé, outmoded, former, bygone, antiquated
FORMAL terminated
F3 1 living, existing, existent 2 active, erupting

extinction n
annihilation, extermination, death, dying-out, vanishing, disappearance, eradication, obliteration, destruction, abolition, excision
FORMAL termination

extinguish v
1 PUT OUT, blow out, snuff out, stifle, smother, choke, douse, quench, dampen down, stub out
2 ANNIHILATE, exterminate, eliminate, destroy, kill, eradicate, erase, abolish, remove, end, suppress
FORMAL expunge, extirpate
COLLOQ. rub out

extirpate v
destroy, annihilate, eliminate, wipe out, eradicate, cut out, remove, weed out, root out, uproot, abolish, exterminate, extinguish, erase
FORMAL deracinate, expunge

extol v
praise, acclaim, exalt, magnify, glorify, sing the praises of, applaud, celebrate, commend, wax lyrical
FORMAL laud, eulogize, rhapsodize
E3 blame; *formal* denigrate

extort v
extract, wring, exact, coerce, force, get out of, wrest, blackmail, squeeze, bully
COLLOQ. milk, bleed
SLANG screw

extortion n
force, coercion, blackmail, oppression, demand, exaction, racketeering
FORMAL malversation
COLLOQ. milking

extortionate adj
exorbitant, excessive, outrageous, grasping, exacting, immoderate, unreasonable, inordinate, preposterous, oppressive, severe, hard, harsh
FORMAL rapacious

extortionist n
extortioner, profiteer, racketeer, exploiter, blackmailer, exactor, yakuza

extra adj, n, adv
◆ adj
1 ADDITIONAL, added, auxiliary, supplementary, new, another, more, further, ancillary, fresh, other, subsidiary
2 EXCESS, excessive, spare, superfluous, surplus, unused, unneeded, unnecessary, left-over, reserve, redundant
FORMAL supernumerary
E3 1 integral 2 essential
◆ n
1 ADDITION, supplement, extension, accessory, appendage, bonus, complement, additive, adjunct, attachment
FORMAL addendum
2 *employ extras in the film*
bit player, supernumerary, spear-carrier, walk-on, walk-on part, minor role
◆ adv
1 ESPECIALLY, exceptionally, extraordinarily, particularly, unusually, remarkably, uncommonly, extremely
2 IN ADDITION, also, as well, together with, along with, besides, too, additionally, and so on, not to mention, not forgetting, let alone, above and beyond
COLLOQ. into the bargain

extract v, n
◆ v
1 REMOVE, take out, draw out, cut out, get out, pull (out), exact, uproot, prise, pluck, wrench, withdraw, suck, gut, quarry, recover, grog

TECHNICAL enucleate, decoct, render
OLD educe
FORMAL deracinate
2 DERIVE, draw, distil, boil down, obtain, get, gather, glean, wrest, wring, elicit, worm
3 CHOOSE, pick, select, cull, abstract, excerpt, copy, cite, quote, reproduce
E3 1 insert
◆ n
1 DISTILLATION, essence, concentrate, spirits, juice
TECHNICAL decoction, euonymin, logwood
FORMAL distillate
2 EXCERPT, passage, selection, clip, clipping, cutting, quotation, abstract, citation, gobbet
TECHNICAL estreat, pericope

Synonym nuances
verb sense 1
Cut out and **pull out** emphasize the manner of extracting; **draw out** is similar but suggests a slower, more deliberate movement, whereas **get out** may sometimes imply a degree of difficulty: *he finally got the device out of its wrapper.* **Exact** is also suggestive of difficulty but further suggests the use of strongly persuasive methods or even force: *the allies exacted a heavy price for their help.*

The term **uproot** would be used literally of extracting plants from the soil, but when used more figuratively, for instance of people moving from their place of origin, the implication is of a painful action, undertaken with reluctance or regret: *many were uprooted by drought or flood.* **Prise**, similarly, suggests a slow action made with effort, in this instance often physical: *he prised her fingers from the handle*; likewise **wrench**, which has further connotations of force. **Pluck**, meanwhile, would describe a much quicker, snatching movement.

Withdraw can be used of the act of extracting when it is not forceful or physical: *the bank withdrew its sponsorship.* The term **suck** is often used figuratively to suggest a slow draining, and the connotations are rarely positive: *the darkness sucked all the courage from his body*, whereas **gut** is more suggestive of violently extracting the contents from something and emphasizes the completeness of the result: *the whole house has been gutted, carpets pulled up and curtains torn down.*

---

extraction n
1 REMOVAL, taking-out, uprooting, drawing, drawing-out, pulling, withdrawal, separation, obtaining, derivation
2 ORIGIN, descent, ancestry, birth, blood, lineage, derivation, family, stock, parentage, pedigree, race
E3 1 insertion

extradite v
send back, send home, deport, repatriate, hand over, banish, expel, exile

extradition n
sending back, deportation, banishment, expulsion, handover, repatriation, exile

extraneous adj
superfluous, supplementary, redundant, irrelevant, immaterial, inapplicable, inappropriate, inessential, inapt, incidental, tangential, needless, unnecessary, unneeded, non-essential, unessential, unrelated, unconnected, extra, additional, peripheral, exterior, external, extrinsic, alien, strange, foreign
FORMAL inapposite
E3 integral, essential

extraordinarily adv
remarkably, unusually, uncommonly, exceptionally, notably, uniquely, specially, significantly, particularly, unexpectedly, strangely, oddly, bizarrely, curiously,

amazingly, astoundingly
E3 ordinarily

extraordinary *adj*
remarkable, unusual, exceptional, notable, noteworthy,
outstanding, unique, special, unexpected, strange,
peculiar, odd, bizarre, curious, unconventional, rare,
uncommon, surprising, amazing, astounding, wonderful,
unprecedented, marvellous, fantastic, significant,
particular, emergency
FORMAL singular
COLLOQ. out of this world
E3 commonplace, ordinary

extrapolate *v*
project, plan, estimate, approximate, reckon, calculate,
sample, gauge, expect

extravagance *n*
1 OVERSPENDING, squandering, waste, wastefulness,
thriftlessness, recklessness, imprudence
FORMAL profligacy, prodigality, improvidence
2 EXCESS, excessiveness, exaggeration, immoderation,
recklessness, profusion, outrageousness, folly, wildness,
ornateness, ostentation, vanity, pretentiousness,
lavishness, dissipation, splurge
OLD riotise
3 LUXURY, extra, treat
E3 1 thrift 2 moderation, restraint

extravagant *adj*
1 WASTEFUL, spendthrift, squandering, thriftless, reckless,
imprudent
FORMAL prodigal, profligate, improvident
2 IMMODERATE, exaggerated, excessive, flamboyant,
preposterous, outrageous, ostentatious, pretentious,
lavish, ornate, fanciful, fantastic, wild, unrestrained,
bizarre, outré
TECHNICAL baroque, rococo, churrigueresque
COLLOQ. flashy, over the top, OTT
3 OVERPRICED, exorbitant, expensive, excessive,
extortionate, costly, dear
COLLOQ. steep, pricey, sky-high, costing an arm and a leg,
costing the earth, costing a bomb, daylight robbery
E3 1 thrifty 2 moderate, restrained 3 reasonable

extravaganza *n*
spectacular, pageant, display, show, spectacle

extreme *adj, n*
• *adj*
1 INTENSE, great, immoderate, inordinate, utmost,
uttermost, out-and-out, maximum, acute, downright,
extraordinary, exceptional, greatest, highest, supreme,
ultimate, unreasonable, remarkable
2 FARTHEST, far-off, faraway, distant, endmost, outermost,
outlying, remotest, most remote, uttermost, final, last,
terminal, ultimate, endmost
3 RADICAL, zealous, extremist, fanatical, hardline,
immoderate, excessive, unreasonable
4 DRASTIC, dire, uncompromising, unrelenting, unyielding,
stern, strict, rigid, severe, harsh, desperate, serious,
stringent, iron-fisted, iron-handed, Draconian
E3 1 mild 3 moderate
• *n*
extremity, limit, maximum, ultimate, utmost, excess, top,
mark, line, pinnacle, peak, height, acme, apex, zenith,
end, climax, depth, edge, pole
FORMAL termination
▪ **in the extreme**
exceedingly, excessively, very, exceptionally,
extraordinarily, intensely, remarkably, utterly, greatly, highly,
immoderately, uncommonly, inordinately
COLLOQ. awfully, terribly, dreadfully, frightfully, terrifically

extremely *adv*
exceedingly, excessively, very, really, exceptionally,

extraordinarily, intensely, thoroughly, remarkably, utterly,
greatly, highly, unusually, unreasonably, immoderately,
uncommonly, inordinately, tremendously, acutely, severely,
decidedly; *N Am* mighty
OLD jolly
COLLOQ. seriously, awfully, terribly, dreadfully, frightfully,
terrifically
SLANG majorly

Synonym nuances
Very and **really** have a very general use to add emphasis.
Greatly, **highly** and the more emphatic **exceedingly**
make a stronger suggestion of great degree, whilst
excessively is negative in tone, and clearly implies too
great a degree. **Intensely**, however, is appropriate for
something that is concentrated to an extreme level: *the
most intensely populated region.* You can use the term
exceptionally to imply that something is outside of the
average, whereas **remarkably**, **unusually**, **uncommonly**
and **extraordinarily** go further by suggesting something
is beyond the norm: *an extraordinarily gifted performer.*
 More disapproving terms include **unreasonably**, which
describes levels that exceed the bounds of reason, and
immoderately, which suggests extravagance that
crosses the boundaries of taste. **Inordinately** similarly
suggests that something is unrestrained or unwarranted:
inordinately proud of her son. The tone of both **acutely**
and **severely** is not judgemental but negative in a
different way, emphasizing something felt very keenly or
deeply and connotative of difficulty: *the stuntman was
acutely aware of what could go wrong; I am severely
disappointed at your attitude.* Meanwhile **decidedly**
hints at the truth of conclusions based on the degree to
which something is happening: *nationalism is decidedly
on the wane; that shelf is decidedly crooked.*

---

extremism *n*
fanaticism, radicalism, zeal, excessiveness,
unreasonableness, terrorism
FORMAL zealotry
E3 moderation

extremist *n*
fanatic, hardliner, fundamentalist, militant, radical, zealot,
diehard, ultra, terrorist
E3 moderate

extremity *n*
1 EXTREME, limit, boundary, brink, verge, periphery, bound,
border, frontier, height, tip, top, edge, excess, end, ending,
termination, peak, pinnacle, apex, acme, zenith, apogee,
margin, terminal, terminus, ultimate, pole, maximum,
minimum, depth
2 *extremities of the body*
limb, arm, hand, finger, foot, leg, toe, tail
3 CRISIS, danger, emergency, plight, hardship, adversity,
misfortune, trouble, outrance
OLD utterance, exigent
FORMAL indigence, exigency
COLLOQ. fix, mess, jam, spot, tight spot, pickle, hole, dire
straits

extricate *v*
disentangle, extract, clear, disengage, detach, let loose,
free, deliver, liberate, release, rescue, relieve, remove, get
out, withdraw
E3 involve

extrinsic *adj*
external, extraneous, exterior, outside, alien, exotic,
foreign, imported
E3 intrinsic

extrovert *n*
mixer, socializer, mingler, outgoing person, sociable
person, conversationalist, joiner, life and soul of the party

extroverted *adj*
outgoing, friendly, sociable, amicable, amiable, exuberant, hearty, demonstrative, outward-looking
COLLOQ. hail-fellow-well-met
E3 introverted

extrude *v*
force out, squeeze out, press out, thrust out, mould

exuberance *n*
1 LIVELINESS, vitality, high spirits, zest, effervescence, enthusiasm, eagerness, excitement, animation, elation, buoyancy, exhilaration, effusiveness, cheerfulness, fulsomeness, life, vigour, energy
FORMAL ebullience, vivacity
COLLOQ. pizzazz
2 ABUNDANCE, copiousness, lushness, richness, superabundance, lavishness, luxuriance, rankness, exaggeration, excessiveness
FORMAL plenitude, prodigality, profusion
E3 1 apathy, lifelessness **2** scantiness

exuberant *adj*
1 LIVELY, vivacious, spirited, zestful, high-spirited, effervescent, enthusiastic, sparkling, excited, animated, elated, buoyant, exhilarated, effusive, cheerful, full of life, vigorous, energetic, unrestrained, fulsome, irrepressible, exaggerated
FORMAL ebullient
2 PLENTIFUL, lavish, overflowing, luxurious, lush, rich, profuse, abundant, thriving, rank
FORMAL plenteous
E3 1 apathetic **2** scarce

exude *v*
1 *exude confidence*
radiate, ooze, display, show, emanate, emit, exhibit
FORMAL manifest
2 DISCHARGE, issue, flow out, bleed, excrete, leak, secrete, give off/out, seep, perspire, sweat, trickle, weep, well

exult *v*
rejoice, revel, delight, be joyful, be delighted, glory, celebrate, relish, crow, gloat, triumph
COLLOQ. be over the moon

exultant *adj*
delighted, rejoicing, revelling, elated, thrilled, exulting, gleeful, joyful, overjoyed, jubilant, transporting, enraptured, triumphant
FORMAL joyous
COLLOQ. cock-a-hoop, over the moon, on cloud nine, in seventh heaven
E3 depressed

exultation *n*
rejoicing, joy, delight, elation, glee, revelling, glory, glorying, joyfulness, jubilation, merriness, transport, triumph, celebration, crowing, gloating
FORMAL joyousness, paean, eulogy
E3 depression

eye *n, v*
♦ *n*
1 *blind in one eye*
Scot & dialect keeker
TECHNICAL ocellus, ommateum
OLD light; *dialect* pigsney
COLLOQ. ocular, optic, water pump; *dialect & N Am* winker
SLANG peeper, peep, goggler, blinker, glim, lamp
Related adjectives: ocular, ophthalmic, optical

2 VISION, sight, eyesight, power of seeing, faculty of sight, observation
3 APPRECIATION, discrimination, discernment, perception, awareness, recognition, judgement, sensitivity, taste
4 VIEWPOINT, opinion, view, point of view, way of thinking, judgement, mind, estimation, belief
5 WATCH, observation, lookout, view, notice, watchfulness, vigilance, surveillance
♦ *v*
look at, see, watch, regard, observe, stare at, gaze at, glance at, view, scrutinize, scan, examine, peruse, study, survey, inspect, contemplate, look up and down, assess
■ **keep an eye on**
watch closely, mind, attend to, take responsibility for, look after, take care of, monitor, keep tabs on
■ **see eye to eye**
agree, be of one mind, be at one, reach an agreement
FORMAL concur
COLLOQ. go along with, go with, speak the same language, be on the same wavelength
■ **set eyes on**
see, notice, observe, come across, come upon, lay eyes on, clap eyes on, meet, encounter
FORMAL behold
■ **up to your eyes**
busy, occupied, involved, engrossed, overwhelmed, inundated
COLLOQ. snowed under, fully stretched, overstretched, having your hands full, tied up
E3 free, idle

Parts of the eye include:

anterior chamber	fovea	posterior chamber
aqueous humour	iris	
blind spot	lacrimal duct	retina
choroid	lens	rod
ciliary body	lower eyelid	sclera
cone	ocular muscle	suspension ligament
conjunctiva	optic nerve	
cornea	papilla	upper eyelid
eyelash	pupil	vitreous humour

---

eye-catching *adj*
striking, arresting, attractive, spectacular, captivating, beautiful, stunning, gorgeous, imposing, impressive, showy, conspicuous, noticeable, prominent
E3 plain, unattractive

eye-opener *n*
revelation, disclosure, surprising thing/fact, wonder, quite something, something incredible

eyesight *n*
vision, sight, perception, observation, power of seeing, faculty of sight, view
Related adjectives: optical, ocular, visual

eyesore *n*
ugliness, blemish, scar, monstrosity, blot, blot on the landscape, disfigurement, defacement, horror, blight, disgrace, atrocity, mess, carbuncle

eyewitness *n*
witness, observer, spectator, looker-on, onlooker, bystander, viewer, passer-by, watcher

F

fable *n*

Aesop's fables; fact or fable?

allegory, parable, story, tale, moral tale, yarn, myth, legend, epic, saga, fiction, fabrication, invention, lie, untruth, falsehood, yarn, *Märchen*

COLLOQ. tall story, old wives' tale

FORMAL apologue

fabled *adj*

legendary, renowned, celebrated, famous, famed, remarkable

F3 unknown

fabric *n*

1 CLOTH, material, textile, stuff, web, texture
2 STRUCTURE, framework, construction, make-up, constitution, organization, infrastructure, frame, foundations

---

Fabrics include:

alpaca	flannelette	paisley
angora	fleece	pashmina
astrakhan	gaberdine	piqué
barathea	georgette	polycotton
bouclé	gingham	polyester
brocade	Gore-Tex®	poplin
Brussels lace	gossamer	rayon
buckram	grosgrain	sateen
calico	Harris tweed®	satin
cambric	hessian	seersucker
candlewick	horsehair	serge
canvas	huckaback	shahtoosh
cashmere	jean	shantung
chambray	jersey	sharkskin
chamois	kid	sheepskin
Chantilly	lace	Shetland wool
cheesecloth	lamé	silk
chenille	lawn	suede
chiffon	leather	taffeta
chino	leather-cloth	terry towelling
chintz	linen	Terylene®
cord	lisle	ticking
corduroy	Lurex®	tulle
cotton	Lycra®	tweed
crêpe	madras	velour
crêpe de Chine	mohair	velvet
Crimplene®	moire	vicuña
crocodile skin	moleskin	Viyella®
damask	muslin	voile
denim	needlecord	webbing
drill	net	winceyette
duffel	nylon	wool
felt	organdie	worsted
flannel	organza	

---

fabricate *v*

1 FAKE, falsify, forge, counterfeit, invent, make up, trump up, concoct, hatch

COLLOQ. cook up

2 MANUFACTURE, make, construct, assemble, build, erect, put together, produce, form, shape, fashion, create, frame, devise

F3 2 demolish, destroy

fabrication *n*

1 FAKE, falsehood, forgery, invention, concoction, fable, fiction, figment, story, myth, untruth

COLLOQ. cock-and-bull story, fairy story

2 MANUFACTURE, assembly, building, construction, erection, production

FORMAL assemblage

F3 1 truth

fabulous *adj*

1 WONDERFUL, marvellous, fantastic, tremendous, remarkable, great, superb, breathtaking, spectacular, phenomenal, amazing, astounding, astonishing, unbelievable, incredible, inconceivable, unimaginable

COLLOQ. out of this world, top-notch, great, super, cool, magic, divine, heavenly, sensational, not half bad

SLANG way-out, def, fab, triff, mega, wicked, stonking, radical, rad, crucial, mean

2 *a fabulous beast*

mythological, mythical, legendary, fabled, fantastic, fictitious, fictional, invented, made-up, imaginary, unreal

F3 2 real

façade *n*

1 FRONT, exterior, frontage, face
2 SHOW, semblance, appearance, front, cover, cloak, veil, guise, mask, disguise, pretence, veneer

face *n, v*

♦ *n*

1 *she has a lovely face*

features, façade, profile

FORMAL countenance, visage, physiognomy

COLLOQ. mug, kisser, phiz, pan, clock, dial

SLANG puss

2 EXPRESSION, look, appearance, air, aspect

FORMAL mien, demeanour

3 *pull a face*

grimace, frown, scowl, pout, moue

4 EXTERIOR, outside, surface, cover, front, frontage, façade, aspect, side, flank

5 *changing the face of the city*

appearance, nature, look(s), aspect, form

6 *save/lose face*

reputation, prestige, name, standing, respect, honour, esteem, admiration

Related adjective: facial

♦ *v*

1 BE OPPOSITE, give on to, front, overlook, look onto, look towards, look out on

2 CONFRONT, face up to, deal with, come up against, cope with, tackle, defy, oppose, brave, resist, withstand, have to reckon with, encounter, meet, experience

3 COVER, line, coat, dress, clad, overlay, smooth, polish, veneer

■ **face up to**

accept, come to terms with, resign yourself to, reconcile yourself to, acknowledge, recognize, cope with, deal with, confront, meet head-on, stand up to

■ **face to face**

opposite, facing, eye to eye, confronting, in confrontation

COLLOQ. eyeball to eyeball

- **fly in the face of**

contradict, oppose, disagree, clash, conflict, contrast, go against, be at variance, be at odds, be in conflict, be inconsistent with

- **on the face of it**

apparently, seemingly, ostensibly, outwardly, to all appearances, superficially, on the surface, reputedly, plainly, clearly, obviously, manifestly, patently

- **pull a face**

frown, grimace, lour, pout, scowl, sulk, glower, knit your brows

facelift n

1 COSMETIC SURGERY, plastic surgery
TECHNICAL rhytidectomy
2 REDECORATION, renovation, restoration, refurbishment, refit, makeover, transformation

facet n

surface, plane, slant, side, face, aspect, element, angle, point, feature, characteristic, factor

facetious adj

flippant, frivolous, playful, jocular, jocose, jesting, glib, joking, tongue-in-cheek, light-hearted, funny, amusing, humorous, comic, comical, droll, witty
E3 serious

facile adj

shallow, superficial, easy, simple, simplistic, uncomplicated, ready, quick, hasty, glib, fluent, smooth, slick, plausible
E3 complicated, profound

facilitate v

ease, make easier, help, assist, encourage, further, smooth, smooth the way, lubricate, promote, advance, forward, accelerate, speed up
FORMAL expedite

facilitation n

assistance, furthering, helping, encouragement, promotion, acceleration, forwarding
FORMAL expediting

facility n

1 *a facility for learning languages*
effortlessness, ease, readiness, quickness, fluency, eloquence, articulateness, aptitude, proficiency, skill, skilfulness, talent, gift, knack, ability, dexterity
2 *sports facilities*
amenity, service, utility, convenience, resource, provision, appliance, equipment, means, feature, prerequisite, opportunity, advantage, aid
COLLOQ. mod con

facing n

coating, covering, lining, cladding, dressing, reinforcement, façade, overlay, surface, trimming, veneer, false front
TECHNICAL revetment

facsimile n

copy, imitation, reproduction, repro, replica, carbon copy, carbon, duplicate, image, fax, photocopy, Photostat®, Xerox®, mimeograph, transcript, print

fact n

1 *facts and figures*
information, datum, detail, particular, specific, point, item, feature, factor, circumstance, component, element, event, incident, occurrence, happening, act, deed, fait accompli
COLLOQ. gen, info, low-down, score, ins and outs; *NAm* poop
2 REALITY, factuality, certainty, truth
FORMAL actuality
E3 2 fiction

- **in fact**

actually, in actual fact, in point of fact, as a matter of fact, in practice, in reality, really, indeed, truly, in truth
COLLOQ. come to that

faction n

1 SPLINTER GROUP, ginger group, minority, division, section, contingent, party, band, side, group, camp, set, sector, ring, caucus, clique, coterie, cabal, junta, lobby, pressure group
2 DISAGREEMENT, conflict, argument, friction, quarrels, discord, disharmony, division, trouble, contention, infighting, strife, dissension

factious adj

conflicting, clashing, divisive, divided, split, partisan, sectarian, quarrelsome, discordant, quarrelling, at odds, at loggerheads, warring, troublemaking, turbulent, tumultuous, dissident, rival, contentious, mutinous, seditious, insurrectionary, rebellious
FORMAL disputatious, refractory
E3 calm, co-operative

factitious adj

unnatural, artificial, bogus, sham, counterfeit, imitation, pretended, false, fabricated, contrived
E3 genuine

factor n

cause, influence, circumstance, contingency, consideration, element, ingredient, component, constituent, part, point, aspect, facet, fact, item, detail, characteristic, feature
FORMAL determinant

factory n

works, plant, mill, shop floor, assembly line, assembly shop, yard, workshop, foundry, manufactory

factotum n

do-all, handyman, jack-of-all-trades, maid-of-all-work, Man (or Girl) Friday, odd-jobman

factual adj

true, historical, actual, real, genuine, authentic, true-to-life, correct, accurate, truthful, precise, exact, literal, faithful, close, strict, detailed, realistic, unbiased, unprejudiced, objective
E3 false, fictitious, imaginary, fictional

factually adv

in reality, really, actually, truly, truthfully, historically, genuinely

faculties n

wits, senses, intelligence, reason, powers, capabilities

faculty n

1 ABILITY, capability, capacity, power, facility, proficiency, knack, flair, gift, talent, skill, aptitude, bent
2 *Faculty of Medicine*
department, organization, division, section, school

fad n

craze, mania, (passing) fashion, mode, vogue, trend, enthusiasm, whim, fancy
FORMAL affectation
COLLOQ. rage

faddy adj

fussy, particular, fastidious, finicky, hard-to-please, exact
COLLOQ. pernickety, choosy, picky, nit-picking; *NAm* persnickety

fade v

1 DISCOLOUR, lose colour, bleach, blanch, blench, pale, become paler, become/grow pale, tone down, whiten, dim, dull, wash out
TECHNICAL etiolate
COLLOQ. go as white as a sheet
2 DECLINE, fall, diminish, dwindle, ebb (away), wane, fail, waste away, disappear, vanish, recede, melt (away), dissolve, pale, flag, weaken, become weaker, droop, wilt,

wither, shrivel, perish, die (away), peter out, die out
FORMAL evanesce
COLLOQ. fizzle out
▣ brighten

faeces n

waste matter, body waste, excrement, droppings, dung, ordure, turd
TECHNICAL egesta, frass, scats, guano
OLD sir-reverence
FORMAL stool, excreta, rejectamenta
COLLOQ. flux, jobbie, doo-doo
SLANG poop, crud; (*vulgar*) crap, shit
Related adjectives: stercoraceous, stercoral

fag n

1 CIGARETTE, filter-tip, king-size, high-tar, low-tar, roll-up, roll-your-own, smoke, whiff
COLLOQ. cig, ciggy, fag end, dog end, gasper, joint
SLANG cancer-stick, coffin-nail
2 NUISANCE, inconvenience, irritation, bind, bore, slog, grind, bother, chore, pest
COLLOQ. drag

fagged adj

exhausted, fatigued, weary, worn out, jaded, wasted
COLLOQ. all in, beat, knackered, on your last legs, dead-beat, done (in), whacked, bushed, burnt out, dog-tired, ready to drop, zonked, jiggered; *N Am* pooped (out), tuckered out; *Aust & NZ* beaten, euchred (out)
▣ refreshed

fail v

1 GO WRONG, be unsuccessful, break down, collapse, miscarry, abort, fall through, fall down, founder, come to grief, come to nothing, get nowhere, underachieve
COLLOQ. flop, fold, flunk, not come off, not make it, not come up to scratch, fall flat, bottle it, blow it, blow your chances, bite the dust, come a cropper, come unstuck, come unglued, come undone, not come up with the goods, fizzle out, score an own goal; *N Am* bomb; *Aust & NZ* come a gutser
2 *fail to pay the bill*
omit, neglect, forget, not do something
3 LET DOWN, disappoint, leave, desert, neglect, abandon
FORMAL forsake
4 *the engine failed*
break down, go wrong, stop, not work, cut out, not start
FORMAL malfunction
COLLOQ. pack up, crash, play up, go on the blink, go kaput, go phut; *N Am* go on the fritz; *Aust* go bung
SLANG conk out
5 *the business failed*
collapse, founder, go bankrupt, go under, become insolvent, sink
COLLOQ. fold, flop, crash, go bust, go broke, go to the wall, go into the red; *N Am* go belly-up
6 *his health failed*
weaken, fade, wane, ebb, sink, collapse, flag, decline, dwindle, diminish, decay, deteriorate, droop
▣ **1** succeed **4** work **5** prosper
■ **without fail**
without exception, unfailingly, constantly, regularly, dependably, conscientiously, reliably, faithfully, predictably, punctually, religiously
COLLOQ. like clockwork
▣ unpredictably, unreliably

Synonym nuances
sense 1
Go wrong and **be unsuccessful** can be used to describe a wide variety of things that do not go as intended: *servicemen died when an invasion exercise went wrong*, whereas **break down** suggests that something has ceased functioning: *the negotiations*

---

broke down. You could use **fall through** of plans which have come to little or no result, whilst **miscarry** has more to do with not achieving the intended end: *the plot miscarried and we were caught.*

Collapse, suggests a more dramatic or sudden failure: *war was declared when peace talks collapsed.* **Abort**, on the other hand, implies bringing to an end prematurely and usually deliberately. **Fall down**, might be used of a less deliberate failure and could be used where a cause is being identified: *where the theory fell down was in its assessment of the prospects of revolution.* The terms **founder** and **come to grief** similarly suggest failing through encountering a major setback or disaster: *many geniuses have foundered due to their lack of direction; the scheme came to grief because of entrenched opposition.*

Come to nothing and **get nowhere** are more suggestive of never actually getting underway, and hint at the frustration involved: *despite his plans, his attempts to write the novel came to nothing.*

---

failing n, prep

♦ *n*
weakness, foible, fault, defect, imperfection, flaw, blemish, drawback, deficiency, shortcoming, failure, lapse, error, weak spot
▣ strength, advantage
♦ *prep*
in the absence of, lacking, without, in default of, wanting

failure n

1 *our efforts ended in failure*
lack of success, defeat, collapse, breakdown, meltdown, downfall, miscarriage, abortion, frustration, coming to nothing
COLLOQ. flop, washout, let-down, mess
2 *the plan was a failure*
disappointment, misfortune, disaster, calamity, miss, fiasco, debacle
COLLOQ. flop, hash, botch, washout, shambles, slip-up, no go, wipeout
SLANG cock-up, balls-up, screw-up
3 *his failure to return home*
omission, neglect, negligence, disregard, oversight, forgetfulness, default
FORMAL dereliction, remissness
4 *feel that you are a failure*
loser, born loser, misfit, reject, victim
COLLOQ. dropout, non-starter, washout, write-off, no-hoper, also-ran, flop, has-been, dead loss, waste of space
5 *the failure of the machine*
breakdown, cutting-out, shutdown, stopping, stalling
FORMAL malfunction, malfunctioning
COLLOQ. crash, packing-up
SLANG conking-out
6 *the failure of the business*
collapse, bankruptcy, ruin, insolvency, foundering
COLLOQ. crash, folding, flop, going under, going to the wall
7 *the failure of his health*
weakening, fading, decline, sinking, flagging, waning, ebbing, collapse, breakdown, deterioration
▣ **1, 2** success **3** observance **4** success **6** prosperity

faint adj, v, n

♦ *adj*
1 SLIGHT, weak, feeble, soft, low, hushed, quiet, muffled, subdued, muted, faded, bleached, mild, light, pale, dull, dim, hazy, indistinct, unclear, obscure, blurred, vague
2 *I feel faint*
dizzy, giddy, unsteady, lightheaded, weak, feeble, exhausted
COLLOQ. woozy
3 *a faint smile*

slight, feeble, weak, unenthusiastic, half-hearted

E3 1 strong, clear

♦ *v*

black out, lose consciousness, pass out, collapse, drop
OLD swoon; *Scot* swelt
COLLOQ. flake out, keel over

♦ *n*

blackout, loss of consciousness, collapse, unconsciousness
TECHNICAL syncope
OLD swoon

faint-hearted *adj*

timid, timorous, weak, lily-livered, spiritless, diffident, half-hearted, irresolute, cowardly, craven, fearful, scared, white-livered, spiritless, spineless, weak-spirited, weak-kneed, soft, jittery
FORMAL pusillanimous
COLLOQ. yellow, chicken, chicken-hearted, chicken-livered, gutless, wimpish, wussy, yellow-bellied, showing the white feather
E3 courageous, confident

faintly *adv*

slightly, vaguely, a little, a bit, somewhat, weakly, feebly, softly

fair[1] *adj*

1 JUST, equitable, square, even-handed, dispassionate, impartial, objective, disinterested, unbiased, unprejudiced, detached, right, proper, above board, lawful, legitimate, honest, trustworthy, upright, honourable
COLLOQ. on the level, straight up, legit, kosher, going/done/played by the book
2 *a fair number; a fair chance of success*
reasonable, moderate, respectable, satisfactory, modest, decent, sporting
3 FAIR-HAIRED, fair-headed, blond(e), yellow, light, light-haired, golden, flaxen
4 *fair skin*
pale, cream, light, white, ivory
5 ADEQUATE, sufficient, middling, not bad, all right, satisfactory, acceptable, tolerable, reasonable, passable, mediocre
COLLOQ. OK, so-so
6 *fair weather*
fine, dry, sunny, bright, clear, warm, cloudless, unclouded
E3 1 unfair, unjust **3** dark, brunette **5** excellent, poor **6** inclement, cloudy

---

Synonym nuances
sense 1

Just is a fairly general synonym of fair, while **equitable** has more to do with natural or moral laws and the idea of treating everyone the same way: *equitable social and economic policies*. **Even-handed** and **impartial** describe a lack of favouritism: *the reports are politically impartial*, and the terms **dispassionate**, **detached**, **objective**, **disinterested**, **unbiased** and **unprejudiced** may likewise be appropriately used of being unaffected by personal feelings: *dispassionate, professional judgement; the detached scientific observer is a myth*.
 The terms **right** and **proper** return to the idea of moral correctness and imply approval of this: *it is only right that we should be sent a bill for the damage we caused*. The terms **above board**, **lawful** and **legitimate** are all suggestive of fairness with an official element of legality, whilst **honest** and **trustworthy** are more general terms which have more to do with being morally irreproachable. Similarly, **upright** and **honourable** are approving terms, which can be used to describe something or someone principled: *upright Victorians with a strong sense of family*.

---

fair[2] *n*

1 *a county fair*
market, craft fair, bazaar, exchange, fete, festival, carnival, gala
Related adjective: nundinal
2 *a trade fair*
exhibition, show, exposition, trade fair
COLLOQ. expo

fairly *adv*

1 QUITE, rather, somewhat, reasonably, tolerably, passably, moderately, adequately, pretty
2 POSITIVELY, absolutely, impartially, really, fully, veritably
3 JUSTLY, equitably, honestly, objectively, unbiasedly, impartially, neutrally, properly, legally, lawfully
E3 3 unfairly

fair-minded *adj*

fair, just, equitable, square, even-handed, dispassionate, impartial, objective, disinterested, unbiased, unprejudiced, detached, right, proper, honest, trustworthy, upright, honourable
COLLOQ. on the level, straight up

fairness *n*

justice, equitableness, equity, even-handedness, unbiasedness, impartiality, legitimacy, rightfulness, rightness, uprightness, disinterestedness, decency, legitimateness
E3 unfairness

fairy *n*

elf, pixie, imp, brownie, sandman, leprechaun, sprite, Robin Goodfellow, Puck, hob, hobgoblin, nymph, rusalka, peri, *fée*, Mab
OLD faerie, fay

fairy tale *n*

1 FAIRY STORY, folk-tale, myth, romance, fiction, fantasy
2 LIE, untruth, invention, fabrication
COLLOQ. fib, cock-and-bull story, tall story

faith *n*

1 BELIEF, trust, reliance, dependence, conviction, confidence, assurance
FORMAL credit, credence
2 RELIGION, denomination, persuasion, church, belief, creed, teaching, doctrine, dogma, sect
3 FAITHFULNESS, fidelity, loyalty, obedience, commitment, devotion, dedication, honour, sincerity, honesty, truthfulness
OLD allegiance, fealty
E3 1 mistrust, uncertainty **3** unfaithfulness, treachery, betrayal

faithful *adj, n*

♦ *adj*

1 LOYAL, devoted, committed, dedicated, staunch, steadfast, constant, trusty, trustworthy, reliable, dependable, unwavering, unflagging, unswerving, obedient, true
2 *a faithful description*
accurate, precise, exact, strict, close, true, truthful
E3 1 disloyal, treacherous **2** inaccurate, vague

♦ *n*

adherents, followers, supporters, believers, congregation, communicants, brethren

faithfully *adv*

1 LOYALLY, devotedly, staunchly, firmly, steadfastly, constantly, reliably, dependably
2 ACCURATELY, precisely, exactly, strictly, closely, truly
E3 1 disloyally **2** inaccurately

faithfulness *n*

1 LOYALTY, fidelity, devotion, dedication, commitment, allegiance, steadfastness, constancy, trustworthiness, reliability, dependability, staunchness

OLD fealty
2 ACCURACY, closeness, exactness, strictness, scrupulousness
E3 1 disloyalty, treachery **2** inaccuracy

faithless *adj*
1 DISLOYAL, unfaithful, inconstant, fickle, false, false-hearted, unreliable, untrue, untrustworthy, untruthful, traitorous, treacherous, adulterous
FORMAL perfidious
2 UNBELIEVING, doubting, disbelieving, agnostic, atheistic
FORMAL nullifidian
E3 believing, faithful

faithlessness *n*
unfaithfulness, disloyalty, deceit, infidelity, fickleness, inconstancy, treachery, betrayal, adultery, apostasy
FORMAL perfidy
E3 1 faithfulness **2** believing

fake *adj, v, n*
  • *adj*
forged, counterfeit, false, spurious, pseudo, bogus, fraudulent, assumed, sham, artificial, simulated, mock, faux, imitation, reproduction, ersatz
FORMAL affected
COLLOQ. phoney, pseud, pretend
E3 genuine
  • *v*
forge, fabricate, counterfeit, copy, pirate, imitate, simulate, feign, sham, pretend, put on, assume, fudge
FORMAL affect
COLLOQ. phoney
  • *n*
forgery, copy, reproduction, replica, imitation, mountebank, simulation, sham, counterfeit, hoax, fraud, impostor, charlatan; *Aust & NZ* bodgie
COLLOQ. phoney, quack

fall *v, n*
  • *v*
1 TUMBLE, stumble, trip, fall down, slip, topple (over), keel over, collapse, slump, crash, slide, pitch (forward)
COLLOQ. *Aust & NZ* come a gutser
2 DESCEND, go down, come down, drop, slope, incline, slant, slide, sink, dive, plunge, plummet, nose-dive, pitch
OLD (*Shakesp*) precipitate
3 DECREASE, lessen, decline, go down, diminish, dwindle, fall off, subside, recede, ebb, slump, plummet, plunge, dive, nose-dive
4 *fall ill*
become, get, grow (into), turn, come to be
5 *fall in battle*
be killed, die, perish, lose your life, be lost
FORMAL be slain
6 *the town fell in the battle*
lose control, be defeated, be conquered, be taken, surrender, yield, capitulate, submit, give in, pass into enemy hands
FORMAL be vanquished
7 *my birthday falls on a Tuesday this year*
happen, occur, take place, come about
E3 2 rise **3** increase
  • *n*
1 TUMBLE, stumble, trip, topple, keeling-over, collapse, slip, slide, crash
COLLOQ. *Aust & NZ* gutser
2 DROP, fall-off, decrease, decline, cut, reduction, lessening, dwindling, slump, descent, crash, plunge, plummeting, nose-dive
3 DEFEAT, capture, conquest, overthrow, loss of control, downfall, collapse, ruin, failure, destruction, surrender, capitulation, submission, yielding, giving-in, resignation
FORMAL demise
4 *the fall of humanity*

sin, original sin, disobedience, wrongdoing, offence
FORMAL transgression
5 WATERFALL, falls, cascade, chute, cataract, torrent
■ **fall apart**
1 *the old clothes fell apart*
break, break into pieces, fall to bits/pieces, come/go to pieces, go to bits, break up, come away, shatter, disintegrate, collapse, dissolve, crumble, decompose, decay, rot
2 CRACK UP, break down, lose control, go to pieces, have a nervous breakdown
■ **fall asleep**
pass into sleep, drift off, drop off, doze (off)
COLLOQ. nod off, flake out, go out like a light
■ **fall away**
1 SLOPE DOWN, slope away, go down, drop (away)
2 DECLINE, dwindle, drop off
■ **fall back**
retreat, withdraw, recoil, draw back, pull back, back off, disengage, depart
■ **fall back on**
resort to, make use of, have recourse to, use, employ, turn to, look to, call on, call into play
■ **fall behind**
lag (behind), trail, straggle, drop back, not keep up
E3 keep up, make progress, keep pace
■ **fall down**
fail, break down, be unsuccessful, collapse, founder, come to nothing
COLLOQ. flop, not come up to scratch, come a cropper, come unstuck, come unglued
■ **fall for**
1 FALL IN LOVE WITH, be attached to, become infatuated with, become besotted with, desire, take to
COLLOQ. fancy, be crazy about, have a crush on, fall head over heels in love with
2 ACCEPT, be taken in by, be fooled by, be deceived by
COLLOQ. swallow, buy
■ **fall in**
1 CAVE IN, come down, collapse, crash, give way, subside, sink
2 LINE UP, get in(to) formation, stand in line
FORMAL array
■ **fall in with**
1 AGREE WITH, go along with, accept, comply with, co-operate with, support
FORMAL assent to
2 BECOME FRIENDS WITH, get involved with, go around with
COLLOQ. hang with, hang about/around/out with
■ **fall off**
decrease, lessen, drop (off), slump, decline, deteriorate, worsen, slow, slacken
COLLOQ. crash
■ **fall on**
attack, descend on, set upon, lay into, pounce on, snatch, assail, assault
■ **fall out**
quarrel, argue, squabble, bicker, fight, clash, disagree, differ
E3 agree
■ **fall through**
come to nothing, go wrong, fail, miscarry, abort, founder, collapse, come to grief
E3 come off, succeed
■ **fall to**
1 *the responsibility fell to her*
be the duty of, be the responsibility of, be an opportunity for, be the task of
2 APPLY YOURSELF, begin, get stuck in, set about, set to, start
FORMAL commence

fallacious *adj*
false, wrong, untrue, incorrect, mistaken, deceptive,

erroneous, inaccurate, inexact, illogical, misleading, spurious, delusive, delusory, illusory, fictitious
FORMAL casuistical, sophistic, sophistical
Ea correct, true

fallacy *n*
misconception, misapprehension, miscalculation, misjudgement, delusion, mistake, mistaken belief, error, flaw, inconsistency, falsehood, false idea, illusion, myth
formal casuistry, sophism, sophistry
TECHNICAL equivocation, idolum, ignoratio elenchi, illicit process of the major/minor, undistributed middle
OLD idolism
Ea truth

fallen *adj*
1 *fallen in battle*
killed, murdered, died, dead, lost, perished, slaughtered
FORMAL slain
2 *fallen women*
immoral, loose, promiscuous, degenerate, shamed, disgraced
Ea 2 chaste

fallibility *n*
imperfection, failing, weakness, mortality, inaccuracy, unreliability
Ea infallibility, inerrancy

fallible *adj*
imperfect, errant, erring, frail, weak, flawed, human, mortal, ignorant, uncertain, unreliable
Ea infallible

fallow *adj*
uncultivated, unploughed, unplanted, unsown, undeveloped, unused, idle, inactive, unproductive, dormant, resting, barren, lea

false *adj*
1 WRONG, incorrect, mistaken, untrue, erroneous, inaccurate, inexact, misleading, faulty, invalid, illusory
FORMAL fallacious
2 ARTIFICIAL, synthetic, imitation, simulated, mock, fake, faux, counterfeit, fraudulent, forged, fabricated, invented, feigned, pretended, sham, bogus, assumed, fictitious
COLLOQ. phoney, pretend, trumped-up
3 *false friends*
disloyal, unfaithful, faithless, lying, unreliable, deceitful, dishonest, insincere, untrustworthy, hypocritical, two-faced, double-dealing, treacherous, traitorous
FORMAL duplicitous, perfidious
Ea 1 true, right **2** real, genuine **3** faithful, reliable, genuine

---

Synonym nuances
sense 1
The terms **incorrect**, **inaccurate** and **faulty** are suggestive of error, especially where information or conclusion is concerned: *your theory about what happened is incorrect*; *you gave me inaccurate information*. This idea is continued with **mistaken** and **erroneous**, which are further suggestive of something being misconstrued or misapprehended: *erroneous assumptions*. **Untrue**, on the other hand, could be used of something that is not genuine, but not necessarily through error: *an untrue depiction of life in that era*.
  Inexact is perhaps a less marked term to use, since it suggests a lack of precision rather than complete falseness: *an inexact calculation of the costs*. You may use **misleading** of something that prompts a wrong conclusion, giving the term an inherently negative tone: *the misleading use of figures by politicians*. **Invalid**, on the other hand, has more to do with a lack of legitimacy given accepted facts: *an invalid argument*; *the test results were invalid*, whereas **illusory** would be used to convey a deceptive element: *access to information remains an illusory right*.

---

falsehood *n*
untruth, lie, story, fairy story, fiction, fabrication, invention, untruthfulness, deceit, deception, dishonesty, insincerity, hypocrisy, two-facedness, double dealing, treachery
TECHNICAL perjury
FORMAL duplicity, perfidy
COLLOQ. fib, porky, tall story
SLANG (*vulgar*) bullshit
Ea truth, truthfulness

falsely *adv*
1 WRONGLY, wrongfully, incorrectly, mistakenly, by mistake, erroneously, in error
FORMAL fallaciously
2 INSINCERELY, hypocritically, dishonestly, deceitfully, deviously, treacherously, artificially, fraudulently
Ea 1 truly, really **2** sincerely, genuinely

falsetto *n*
high voice, high pitch, high note, shrillness

falsification *n*
alteration, tampering, distortion, perversion, misrepresentation, change, adulteration, deceit, forgery
FORMAL dissimulation

falsify *v*
alter, tamper with, doctor, distort, adulterate, twist, pervert, misrepresent, misstate, forge, counterfeit, fake, rig, fiddle, manipulate, massage
COLLOQ. cook

falter *v*
1 TOTTER, stumble, be unsteady, be shaky
2 *falter while talking*
stammer, stutter, stumble
COLLOQ. fluff your lines
3 HESITATE, waver, vacillate, delay, flinch, quail, shake, tremble, flag, fail
COLLOQ. shilly-shally, dilly-dally, be in two minds, sit on the fence, drag your feet, take your time

faltering *adj*
uncertain, hesitant, unsteady, weak, tentative, irresolute, stammering, stumbling, timid, broken, failing, flagging
Ea firm, strong

fame *n*
renown, celebrity, stardom, prominence, distinction, eminence, notability, note, illustriousness, glory, honour, greatness, importance, reputation, repute, name, kudos, esteem

famed *adj*
renowned, well-known, widely-known, famous, recognized, noted, prominent, celebrated, acclaimed, esteemed
Ea unknown

familiar *adj*
1 EVERYDAY, usual, routine, repeated, conventional, household, common, commonplace, ordinary, accustomed, customary, frequent, habitual, run-of-the-mill, well-known, known, recognized, recognizable, unmistakable
2 INTIMATE, close, near, dear, confidential, friendly, informal, free, free-and-easy, easy, relaxed, casual, comfortable, sociable, open, natural, unceremonious, unreserved
COLLOQ. pally, chummy
3 *familiar with the procedure*
aware, acquainted, abreast, knowledgeable, versed, conversant, well up, au fait, *au courant*
COLLOQ. clued up, genned up, up to speed
4 FORWARD, over-familiar, over-friendly, presumptuous, impertinent, bold, disrespectful
COLLOQ. smarmy
Ea 1 unfamiliar, strange **2** formal, reserved **3** unfamiliar, ignorant

familiarity n
1 INTIMACY, liberty, closeness, nearness, friendliness, ease, casualness, sociability, openness, naturalness, informality, casualness, unceremoniousness
COLLOQ. palliness, chumminess
2 AWARENESS, acquaintance, experience, skill, knowledge, understanding, comprehension, grasp, mastery
3 FORWARDNESS, over-familiarity, over-friendliness, presumption, liberty, liberties, impertinence, boldness, disrespect, impudence, intrusiveness
COLLOQ. pushiness

familiarize v
accustom, acclimatize, make familiar, make aware, make acquainted, acquaint, teach, school, train, coach, instruct, indoctrinate, prime, brief
FORMAL habituate
COLLOQ. clue up, gen up, get/keep up to speed

family n
1 RELATIVES, relations, household, nuclear family, extended family, one-parent family, single-parent family, next of kin, kin, kindred, kinsmen, people, parents, your own flesh and blood, you and yours, ancestors, forebears, children, offspring, issue, progeny, descendants, scions
COLLOQ. folk, little ones, kids, kiddies, patter of tiny feet
2 CLAN, tribe, race, dynasty, house, pedigree, ancestry, parentage, descent, line, lineage, extraction, blood, stock, strain, birth
3 CLASS, group, order, species, genus, type, class, subclass, kind, classification
TECHNICAL stirps

■ **family tree**
ancestry, pedigree, genealogy, line, lineage, descent, extraction, background

---

Members of a family include:

ancestor	grandchild	old man
aunt	grand-daughter	parent
brother	grandfather	sibling
cousin	grandmother	sister
colloq. dad	*colloq.* granny	son
colloq. daddy	grandparent	spouse
daughter	grandson	stepbrother
descendant	half-brother	stepchild
father	half-sister	*colloq.* stepdad
forebear	heir	stepfather
forefather	husband	stepmother
foster-child	*N Am colloq.*	*colloq.* stepmum
foster-parent	mom	step-parent
godchild	mother	stepsister
god-daughter	*colloq.* mum	twin-brother
godfather	*colloq.* mummy	twin-sister
godmother	nanny	uncle
godson	nephew	wife
colloq. gran	niece	
colloq. grandad	offspring	

---

famine n
starvation, hunger, malnutrition, lack, deprivation, scarcity, shortage of food, dearth, lack, death
FORMAL destitution, want, exiguousness
🖪 plenty

famished adj
starved, starving, famishing, ravenous, hungry, undernourished, voracious
🖪 sated

famous adj
well-known, famed, renowned, celebrated, acclaimed, world-famous, noted, great, distinguished, illustrious, eminent, honoured, respected, esteemed, glorious, legendary, legend, remarkable, notable, popular, prominent, signal, venerable, having (made) a name for yourself, your name on everyone's lips, notorious, infamous
🖪 unheard-of, unknown, obscure

Synonym nuances

Famed is an appropriate word to use when suggesting a specific cause of someone's or something's renown: *a city famed for its hospitality*. This idea continues with **acclaimed**, which carries the further notion of enthusiastic approval: *the acclaimed production of Madam Butterfly*. **Popular** also implies being much liked, if more unofficially: *the most popular singer of his day*. **Eminent** is a more formal, restrained term to use: *eminent scientists of the day*.

 Honoured is suggestive of something that has attracted plaudits, while **venerable** emphasizes that something is worthy of reverence. **Glorious**, although it again implies distinction, is more emotive and highly marked with approval: *the country's glorious history*. Both **notorious** and **infamous**, however, carry a disapproving tone, and suggest being widely known for your misdeeds rather than good works. The terms **legendary** and **legend** could be used of someone or something long-established, and have connotations of an exaggerated fame: *the legendary blues singer*. **Remarkable** has more to do with being singular in one's achievements and is fairly approbatory in tone: *a remarkable phase in the nation's history*.

 Signal is not particularly marked in tone, and returns to the idea of being singularly conspicuous and significant: *his expulsion from All Souls was the signal point of his academic career*.

---

famously adv
1 NOTABLY, eminently, prominently, conspicuously, popularly, notoriously, infamously
2 *get on famously*
well, greatly, happily, wonderfully, superbly, brilliantly, splendidly
COLLOQ. swimmingly

fan¹ n
football fans
enthusiast, admirer, supporter, backer, follower, adherent, devotee, addict, lover
FORMAL aficionado
COLLOQ. buff, fiend, freak, nut
SLANG groupie

fan² v, n
♦ v
1 COOL, ventilate, air, air-condition, air-cool, aerate, blow, freshen, refresh, winnow
2 INCREASE, provoke, intensify, stimulate, incite, instigate, rouse, arouse, excite, agitate, ignite, kindle, stir up, work up, whip up
♦ n
extractor, extractor fan, ventilator, air-conditioner, blower, cooler, air cooler, propeller, vane, wing, winnow, punka, Colmar
TECHNICAL flabellum, rhipidion

■ **fan out**
spread (out), move out, open (out), unfold, unfurl

fanatic n
zealot, devotee, enthusiast, addict, maniac, visionary, radical, bigot, extremist, militant, activist, fundamentalist
COLLOQ. fiend, freak

fanatical adj
overenthusiastic, extreme, passionate, zealous, fervent, burning, mad, wild, frenzied, rabid, obsessive, fundamentalist, activist, militant, immoderate, extremist, radical, single-minded, bigoted, narrow-minded, dogmatic
🖪 moderate, unenthusiastic

fanaticism *n*

extremism, monomania, single-mindedness, fundamentalism, activism, militancy, obsessiveness, madness, wildness, frenzy, infatuation, bigotry, narrow-mindedness, zeal, zealotry, fervour, dogmatism, enthusiasm, dedication
🞠 moderation

fancier *n*

breeder, keeper, enthusiast, fan, devotee, follower
COLLOQ. fiend, freak

fanciful *adj*

1 IMAGINARY, mythical, flighty, fabulous, fantastic, legendary, visionary, romantic, unrealistic, unreal, make-believe, illusory, fairytale, airy-fairy, vaporous, whimsical, wild
2 ELABORATE, ornate, decorated, extravagant, exotic, wild, creative, imaginative, fantastic, curious
🞠 **1** real, ordinary, realistic **2** simple, plain

fancy *v, n, adj*

♦ *v*
1 LIKE, want, feel like, wish (for), prefer, favour, desire, take a liking to, take to, go for, have in mind, not mind, not say no to, long for, yearn for
2 BE ATTRACTED TO, find attractive, desire, take to, go for, have a soft spot for, think the world of, be interested in, lust after
COLLOQ. have a crush on, have eyes for, have a soft spot for, be mad about, be wild about, be crazy about, want
SLANG have the hots for
3 THINK, conceive, imagine, dream of, picture, believe, suppose, reckon, guess
FORMAL conjecture, surmise
🞠 **1** dislike

♦ *n*
1 DESIRE, whim, caprice, raving, urge, want, wish, liking, fondness, longing, yearning, inclination, impulse, preference
FORMAL penchant, predilection
COLLOQ. itch, yen
2 NOTION, thought, idea, opinion, impression, imagination, creativity, dream, fantasy, vision, illusion, delusion
🞠 **1** dislike, aversion **2** fact, reality

♦ *adj*
elaborate, ornate, decorated, adorned, ornamented, embellished, rococo, baroque, elegant, extravagant, ostentatious, showy, lavish, fantastic, fanciful, far-fetched
🞠 plain, ordinary, simple

■ **fancy yourself**
have a high opinion of yourself, flatter yourself
COLLOQ. think that you are the cat's whiskers/pyjamas, think that you are God's gift to someone

fanfare *n*

1 *a fanfare of trumpets*
flourish, trumpet call, trump, fanfarade
OLD tucket
2 *he arrived with little fanfare*
show, display, ostentation, publicity, flamboyance, pageantry, parade, fuss

fang *n*

tooth, prong, tusk, tang, venom-tooth

fantasize *v*

imagine, daydream, dream, hallucinate, invent, romance
COLLOQ. build castles in Spain/the air, live in a dream

fantastic *adj*

1 WONDERFUL, marvellous, sensational, superb, excellent, first-rate, tremendous, impressive, terrific, great, brilliant, incredible, unbelievable, amazing, remarkable, phenomenal, overwhelming, enormous, extreme
COLLOQ. top-notch, super, cool, magic, brill, smashing, terrific, ace, out of this world, neat
SLANG mega, wicked, radical
2 STRANGE, weird, odd, eccentric, bizarre, exotic, outlandish, extravagant, wild, absurd, fanciful, fabulous, imaginary, illusory, unreal, imaginative, visionary, romantic
🞠 **1** ordinary **2** real

fantastically *adv*

extremely, tremendously, terrifically, incredibly, unbelievably, amazingly, phenomenally

fantasy *n*

1 DREAM, daydream, reverie, pipe dream, nightmare, vision, hallucination, illusion, mirage, apparition, figment of the imagination, invention, fancy, flight of fancy, myth, speculation, delusion, misconception, creativity, imagination, originality, unreality, moonshine
COLLOQ. cloud-cuckoo-land, pie in the sky
2 IMAGINATION, imaginativeness, creativity, inventiveness, fancifulness, speculation, originality, inspiration, resourcefulness
🞠 **1** reality

far *adv, adj*

♦ *adv*
a long way, a good way, great distance, some distance, distantly, nowhere near, much, very much, greatly, considerably, extremely, markedly, decidedly, significantly, incomparably, immeasurably
COLLOQ. miles
🞠 near, close

♦ *adj*
distant, far-off, faraway, far-flung, outlying, remote, inaccessible, secluded, out-of-the-way, godforsaken, removed, far-removed, further, opposite, other
COLLOQ. *N Am* in the boondocks/boonies; *Aust* (beyond) the black stump, back o' Bourke
🞠 nearby, close, accessible

■ **far and wide**
extensively, far and near, widely, everywhere, in/from all places, all about, broadly, worldwide

■ **far out**
extreme, strange, exotic, radical, bizarre, unusual, unconventional, unorthodox, weird, outlandish
COLLOQ. way out
🞠 orthodox, conventional

■ **go far**
succeed, be successful, achieve success, get on
COLLOQ. get on in the world, make your mark, make a name for yourself, arrive, go places

■ **so far**
1 UP TO NOW, up to this point, up to the present moment, till now, to date
FORMAL thus far, hitherto
2 TO A CERTAIN EXTENT, to a limited extent, to some extent, within limits

faraway *adj*

1 DISTANT, remote, outlying, far-flung, far-off, far
2 DREAMY, absent-minded, absent, abstracted, preoccupied, lost
🞠 **1** nearby **2** alert

farce *n*

1 COMEDY, slapstick, buffoonery, satire, parody, burlesque, burletta, exode, *lazzo*, mime, *opera bouffe*
OLD jig
2 TRAVESTY, sham, parody, joke, mockery, ridiculousness, absurdity, nonsense, pantomime
COLLOQ. shambles

farcical *adj*

ridiculous, absurd, ludicrous, preposterous, nonsensical, stupid, laughable, comic, silly, derisory, diverting
🞠 sensible

fare *n, v*
* *n*

1 *pay your fare*
charge, cost, price, fee, ticket, passage
2 FOOD, eatables, nourishment, nutriment, rations, meals,
diet, menu, board, table
OLD provisions
FORMAL sustenance, victuals, viands
COLLOQ. nosh, eats
* *v*

be, do, get along, get on, go, go on, happen, make out,
manage, proceed, progress, prosper, succeed, turn out

farewell *n, interj*
* *n*

goodbye, adieu, leave-taking, *au revoir*
FORMAL valediction, valedictory
* *interj*

goodbye, adieu, *au revoir, auf Wiedersehen, ciao, adios,
arrivederci*
COLLOQ. cheerio, bye, bye-bye, cheers, see you (later), see
you around, be seeing you, all the best, mind how you go,
take care, have a nice day, ta-ta, so long; *N Am* later

far-fetched *adj*
implausible, unrealistic, improbable, unlikely, dubious,
incredible, unbelievable, unconvincing, fantastic, fanciful,
preposterous, crazy
plausible

farm *n, v*
* *n*

ranch, farmstead, grange, croft, homestead, station, co-
operative, land, farmland, holding, acreage, acres
* *v*

cultivate, till, plough, work the land, plant, operate
■ **farm out**
subcontract, pass/give to others, delegate, contract out,
outsource

Types of farm include:

arable farm	free-range farm	sheep station
cattle ranch	hill farm	smallholding
croft	mixed farm	stud farm
dairy farm	organic farm	turkey farm
deer farm	ostrich farm	wind farm
estate	pig farm	
fish farm	plantation	

---

farmer *n*
agriculturist, crofter, smallholder, husbandman, rancher,
crofter, grazier, yeoman, stock-farmer, mailer, *métayer,
campesino, estanciero; Scot* store farmer; *N Am* sodbuster,
sharecropper; *Aust & NZ* cockatoo, cocky
TECHNICAL agronomist

farming *n*
agriculture, cultivation, husbandry, tilling, crofting
TECHNICAL agribusiness, agronomy, agroscience,
geoponics

far-off *adj*
faraway, far, distant, remote, outlying, far-flung
near

farrago *n*
hotchpotch, hodgepodge, jumble, medley, miscellany,
mixture, mélange, pot-pourri, hash, mishmash,
gallimaufry, salmagundi
COLLOQ. dog's breakfast

far-reaching *adj*
broad, extensive, widespread, sweeping, important, wide-
ranging, wide, comprehensive, thorough, global,
significant, momentous
limited, restricted, insignificant

far-sighted *adj*
wise, forward-looking, far-seeing, shrewd, discerning,
cautious, acute, canny, provident, prudent
FORMAL circumspect, judicious, politic, prescient
imprudent, unwise

farther *adj, adv*
* *adj*

further, more distant, remoter, more extreme
* *adv*

to a greater distance, to a more distant/remote/onward/
advanced point

farthest *adj*
furthest, most distant, remotest, most extreme

fascia *n*
1 SIGN, panel, board, front
2 CONSOLE, panel, dashboard, instrument panel

fascinate *v*
absorb, engross, intrigue, delight, charm, allure, lure, draw,
attract, entice, captivate, enchant, beguile, bewitch,
spellbind, enthral, enrapture, rivet, transfix, hypnotize,
mesmerize
bore, repel

fascinated *adj*
absorbed, engrossed, curious, intrigued, delighted,
charmed, enticed, spellbound, enthralled, entranced,
captivated, bewitched, beguiled, hypnotized,
mesmerized, infatuated, smitten
COLLOQ. hooked
bored, uninterested

fascinating *adj*
intriguing, gripping, exciting, interesting, engaging,
engrossing, irresistible, compelling, alluring, bewitching,
captivating, enchanting, riveting, enticing, seductive,
tempting, charming, absorbing, stimulating, delightful,
mesmerizing
boring, uninteresting

fascination *n*
interest, attraction, delight, appeal, lure, allure,
compulsion, magnetism, pull, draw, charm,
preoccupation, captivation, enchantment, spell, sorcery,
magic
boredom, repulsion

fascism *n*
autocracy, dictatorship, absolutism, authoritarianism,
totalitarianism, Hitlerism, Falangism, Sinarchism

fascist *adj, n*
* *adj*

autocratic, absolutist, authoritarian, totalitarian, Hitlerist,
Hitlerite, sinarchist
* *n*

autocrat, absolutist, authoritarian, totalitarian, Blackshirt,
Hitlerite, Hitlerist, Brownshirt, Falangist, sinarchist

fashion *n, v*
* *n*

1 MANNER, way, method, mode, approach, style, system,
shape, form, make, design, pattern, line, cut, look,
appearance, type, sort, kind
2 VOGUE, trend, mode, style, fad, craze, custom, tendency,
practice, convention
COLLOQ. rage, latest, in thing
3 COUTURE, clothes, clothes industry, haute couture,
fashion business, high fashion, designer label
COLLOQ. rag trade
* *v*

create, form, shape, mould, model, build, construct,
manufacture, design, fit, tailor, alter, adjust, adapt, suit
■ **after a fashion**
not very well, to some extent, to a certain extent, in a
manner of speaking

■ **in fashion**

fashionable, chic, smart, elegant, stylish, designer, modish, à la mode, in vogue, in, popular, prevailing, current, latest, up-to-the-minute, up-to-date, contemporary, modern
COLLOQ. trendy, all the rage, hot, natty, glitzy, ritzy, snazzy, swanky, funky, hip, with it, swinging, cool, dressed to the nines

■ **out of fashion**

unfashionable, outmoded, dated, out of date, out, passé, old-fashioned, démodé, antiquated, obsolete, unpopular
COLLOQ. old hat, square
E3 fashionable

Synonym nuances

noun sense 2

The term **vogue** is suggestive of what people are preferring to do or wear at a certain time: *the vogue for dressing down*, while **trend** similarly refers to an inclination at a particular time, but suggests something that is gradually increasing in popularity: *the trend towards earlier retirement*. The term **tendency** is similar, but might be used of a less significant or marked fashion: *the growing tendency towards eating out*.

Mode, however, would be more appropriate to refer to a particular way that something is done: *the dominant literary mode in New York*, while **style** could refer to the form something takes, but perhaps without the same connotations of transitoriness: *the plain façade belies the style and elegance of the interior*.

Both **fad** and **craze** strongly suggest being currently prevalent, with the further implication of being short-lived: *the latest fad in clubland*. **Custom** and **practice**, suggest an accepted and possibly long-established manner of doing things. **Convention**, likewise, is suggestive of an established method or set of rules: *she has made a virtue of flying in the face of business convention*.

---

fashionable *adj*

chic, smart, elegant, stylish, designer, modish, à la mode, in vogue, in, popular, prevailing, current, latest, up-to-the-minute, up-to-date, contemporary, modern
COLLOQ. trendy, all the rage, hot, natty, glitzy, ritzy, snazzy, swanky, funky, hip, with it, swinging, cool, dressed to the nines
E3 unfashionable

fast¹ *adj, adv*

♦ *adj*

1 QUICK, swift, rapid, brisk, accelerated, speedy, express, high-speed, hasty, hurried, flying
OLD fleet
COLLOQ. nippy
See Synonym nuances panel at **quick.**

2 *the fast life*

exciting, exhilarating, thrilling, wild, turbulent, boisterous, riotous, shameless, self-indulgent, immoral, dissipated
COLLOQ. action-packed
SLANG ripsnorting
E3 1 slow, unhurried **2** quiet, dull

♦ *adv*

quickly, swiftly, rapidly, speedily, hastily, hurriedly, in a hurry, apace, presto
COLLOQ. like a flash, like a shot, as fast as your legs will carry you, before you can say Jack Robinson, at a rate of knots, hell for leather, like lightning, like greased lightning, like the wind, like crazy, like mad, like the clappers, like a bat out of hell, lickety-spit, pdq
E3 slowly, gradually

fast² *adj, adv*

♦ *adj*

1 FASTENED, shut, closed, secure, fixed, immovable, immobile, firm, tight

2 *fast colours*

indelible, permanent, fixed
E3 1 loose **2** non-fast

♦ *adv*

1 FIRMLY, securely, tightly, immovably, fixedly, resolutely, doggedly, stubbornly

2 *fast asleep*

sound, deeply, fully

fast³ *v, n*

♦ *v*

fast for religious reasons

go hungry, diet, slim, deny yourself, starve, refrain
FORMAL abstain

♦ *n*

fasting, diet, starvation, abstinence, hunger strike
E3 gluttony, self-indulgence

fasten *v*

1 FIX, affix, attach, clamp, grip, anchor, rivet, nail, pin, clip, tack, seal, close, latch, shut, lock, bolt, secure, tie, tether, hitch, bind, chain, link, interlock, connect, join, unite, do up, button, zip up, lace, buckle

2 *fasten your attention*

focus, direct, concentrate, fix, rivet, point, aim, zero
E3 1 unfasten, untie, undo

fastener

Types of fastener include:

alligator clip	hinge	rivet
bond	holder	screw
bulldog clip	hook	shoelace
button	hook-and-eye	split pin
catch	knot	staple
clasp	lace	stitch
clip	latch	stud
collar stud	link	tie
cotter	lock	toggle
crocodile clip	loop	treasury tag
cufflink	nail	Velcro®
eyelet	padlock	zip
frog	paperclip	*N Am* zipper
hasp	press stud	

---

fastidious *adj*

fussy, particular, finicky, hard-to-please, scrupulous, faddy, discriminating, hypercritical, meticulous, precise, punctilious, overnice, squeamish, difficult, dainty
COLLOQ. choosy, pernickety, picky; *N Am* persnickety
E3 undemanding

fat *adj, n*

♦ *adj*

1 PLUMP, overweight, obese, tubby, dumpy, stout, portly, round, paunchy, well-endowed, pot-bellied, large, heavy, solid, chubby, podgy, fleshy, fleshed, buxom, tubbish, squab, pursy; *Scot* sonsy, fozy
TECHNICAL steatopygous
OLD (*Shakesp*) gor-bellied
FORMAL rotund, corpulent
COLLOQ. beefy, flabby, gross, fat as a pig, porky, well-upholstered

2 FATTY, oily, greasy, rich
TECHNICAL lipoid, pinguid
FORMAL oleaginous, adipose, sebaceous

3 *a fat book*

thick, wide, broad, big, heavy, solid, substantial

4 *fat profits*

large, handsome, considerable, generous, siz(e)able
E3 1 thin, slim **2** low-fat **3** narrow, slim, thin **4** slim, meagre, miserable, poor

♦ *n*

1 FATNESS, obesity, plumpness, stoutness, solidness, bulk, chubbiness, overweight, paunch, pot (belly), blubber

TECHNICAL lipomatosis
FORMAL corpulence
COLLOQ. flab, spare tyre
2 fats such as cream
butter, margarine, cream, cheese, lard, suet, animal
fat, vegetable fat, saturated fat, polyunsaturated fat,
tallow, blubber, grease, oil, wax, dripping, lanolin; *Scot*
creesh
TECHNICAL chylomicron, degras, deutoplasm, palmitin
OLD keech, kitchen-fee

Synonym nuances
adjective sense 1
Plump may be used to suggest roundness and softness in
appearance, and has positive connotations; the term
chubby is also suggestive of being round and soft: *she
was pretty in a chubby sort of way*. **Podgy**, although
similarly used of an endearing kind of plumpness, typical
of young children, might also be used to suggest a slightly
less appealing appearance: *the little one was podgy with
puppy fat and had a front tooth missing*.
   The term **overweight** is more technical in tone,
although it can be used in a euphemistic way, referring to
weighing more than is recommended for your age and
height. **Obese** shares this more clinical tone, but goes
further by suggesting abnormal fatness: *being obese, it
was not easy for them to climb stairs*.
   Tubby, on the other hand, conveys the idea of being
round, almost barrel-like, while **dumpy** suggests
shortness of stature as well as width. You could use **stout**
and **solid** to hint at strength behind the large size, and the
word **heavy** usually suggests solidity with weight
(although it also might be used euphemistically). **Portly**
too gives an impression of substantial but solid girth, and
is unlikely to be used of the young. The term **round**
suggests being as wide as your height, unlike **paunchy**,
which is generally used to imply a large stomach, as is
pot-bellied, although it tends to conjure up a more
concentrated mass and sounds insulting if used of
people.
   Well-endowed, however, while usually reserved to
describe a man with large genitals or a woman with large
breasts, might be used in a facetious way with regard to
fatness. **Large** may be widely used to suggest general
bigness, and again could be used as a vaguely
euphemistic, polite term: *clothes for larger ladies*. Both
fleshy and **fleshed** suggest fatness but often with a
sensual implication: *fleshy thighs*, whilst **buxom** suggests
the comeliness of women.

---

fatal *adj*
deadly, lethal, mortal, killing, incurable, malignant,
terminal, final, destructive, calamitous, catastrophic,
disastrous
F3 harmless

⚠ fatal or fateful?
Fatal means 'causing death or disaster': *a fatal accident;
She made the fatal mistake of telling him what she really
thought*. *Fateful* means 'of great importance, having important consequences, etc', as in: *At last the fateful day arrived, the day she was to be married.*

fatalism *n*
resignation, stoicism, acceptance, passivity, endurance

fatalistic *adj*
resigned, reconciled, philosophical, stoical, patient, long-
suffering, passive, submissive, yielding, defeatist
FORMAL acquiescent

fatality *n*
death, mortality, loss, casualty, dead, deadliness, lethality,
disaster, catastrophe

fate *n*
destiny, providence, God's will, kismet, karma, chance,
future, luck, fortune, horoscope, stars, lot, doom, end,
issue, outcome, ruin, disaster, destruction, catastrophe,
defeat, death
FORMAL predestiny

fated *adj*
doomed, destined, predestined, preordained,
unavoidable, inevitable, inescapable, certain, sure
FORMAL ineluctable, foreordained
F3 avoidable

fateful *adj*
crucial, critical, decisive, important, momentous,
significant, pivotal
F3 unimportant

⚠ fateful or fatal?
See panel at **fatal**.

fatefully *adv*
momentously, crucially, critically, decisively, importantly,
significantly

father *n, v*
♦ *n*
1 PARENT, birth father, patriarch, ancestor
FORMAL begetter, procreator, progenitor, sire,
paterfamilias, pater
COLLOQ. dad, daddy, da, pop, pa, papa, old man
Related adjective: paternal
2 ANCESTOR, patriarch, elder, forefather, forebear,
predecessor, progenitor
3 FOUNDER, creator, originator, inventor, initiator, maker,
architect, author, patron, leader, prime mover, guiding light
4 PRIEST, padre, pastor, parson, clergyman, minister, abbé,
curé
♦ *v*
produce, engender, give life to
OLD beget, sire
FORMAL procreate

fatherland *n*
native land, home, homeland, land of your birth, mother-
country, motherland, old country

fatherly *adj*
paternal, kind, kindly, affectionate, protective, supportive,
benevolent, benign, tender, forbearing, indulgent,
patriarchal
FORMAL avuncular
F3 cold, harsh, unkind

fathom *v*
1 MEASURE, gauge, plumb, sound, probe, estimate
2 UNDERSTAND, comprehend, grasp, see, perceive, work
out, search out, interpret, penetrate, get to the bottom of
COLLOQ. get, twig, get the hang of, latch onto, rumble, suss
out, get your head round

fathomless *adj*
deep, impenetrable, immeasurable, infinite, bottomless,
endless, mysterious, enigmatic, complex, complicated,
intricate

fatigue *n, v*
♦ *n*
tiredness, weariness, exhaustion, lethargy, listlessness,
lassitude, weakness
FORMAL debility, enervation
F3 energy
♦ *v*
tire, wear out, weary, exhaust, drain, sap, tax, weaken,
overwork
FORMAL debilitate, enervate
COLLOQ. take it out of
F3 invigorate, refresh

fatigued *adj*
exhausted, jaded, jiggered, overtired, tired, tired out, wasted, weary
COLLOQ. all in, beat, bushed, dead-beat, fagged (out), knackered, whacked, zonked, done in; *N Am* pooped (out), tuckered out; *Aust & NZ* beaten, euchred (out)
FꞋ refreshed

fatness *n*
plumpness, overweight, obesity, bulk, bulkiness, heaviness, largeness, tubbiness, stoutness, portliness, podginess, grossness, grease
TECHNICAL pinguidity, pinguitude
FORMAL corpulence, rotundity
COLLOQ. flab

fatten *v*
feed, feed up, nourish, nurture, build up, overfeed, flesh, lard, soil, cram, stuff, bloat, swell, fill out, spread, expand, widen, broaden, thicken
TECHNICAL pinguefy, saginate
OLD batten, battle, frank; (*Shakesp*) engross

fatty *adj*
fat, greasy, oily, creamy, buttery, fleshy, waxy
TECHNICAL pinguid, adipose, sebaceous, lipoid
FORMAL oleaginous, oleic, unctuous

fatuous *adj*
idiotic, foolish, silly, stupid, ludicrous, ridiculous, absurd, daft, inane, mindless, vacuous, moronic, puerile, brainless, lunatic, dense, asinine, weak-minded, witless
FꞋ sensible

fault *n, v*
• *n*
1 DEFECT, flaw, blemish, imperfection, deficiency, shortcoming, weak point, weakness, failing, foible, default, demerit, vice, beam
COLLOQ. bug, glitch, hitch
See Synonym nuances panel at **defect**.
2 ERROR, mistake, blunder, slip, lapse, negligence, omission, oversight
COLLOQ. slip-up, boob, booboo, fluff; *N Am* flub
SLANG goof
3 MISDEED, offence, wrong, wrongdoing, sin, delinquency, *culpa levis*, lapse, indiscretion, peccadillo
FORMAL misdemeanour
4 *it's your fault*
responsibility, accountability, liability, answerability, blameworthiness
FORMAL culpability
• *v*
find fault with, criticize, slate, censure, blame, call to account, judge, nag, carp, impeach, nibble, quarrel, reprehend, scold
OLD pinch
FORMAL impugn, inculpate
COLLOQ. pick holes in, knock, slam, pull to pieces
FꞋ praise, approve
■ **at fault**
(in the) wrong, blameworthy, to blame, responsible, accountable, guilty, at a loss, out
FORMAL culpable
■ **to a fault**
excessively, extremely, too much, inordinately, unduly, unnecessarily, disproportionately, in the extreme, to extremes, immoderately, out of all proportion
COLLOQ. over the top

fault-finding *n, adj*
• *n*
criticism, grumbling, complaining, complaint, carping, quibbling, cavilling, nagging, niggling, hypercriticism
FORMAL ultracrepidation
COLLOQ. finger-pointing, hair-splitting, nit-picking

FꞋ praise
• *adj*
critical, grumbling, nagging, captious, carping, cavilling, censorious, hypercritical
OLD pettifogging
FORMAL querulous, ultracrepidarian
COLLOQ. nit-picking
FꞋ complimentary

faultless *adj*
perfect, flawless, unblemished, without blemish, spotless, immaculate, unimpeachable, impeccable, unsullied, pure, blameless, exemplary, model, correct, accurate
FꞋ faulty, imperfect, flawed

faulty *adj*
1 NOT WORKING, defective, imperfect, damaged, out of order, out of action, broken
FORMAL malfunctioning, inoperative
COLLOQ. on the blink, bust, kaput, duff, wonky, playing up
SLANG conked out
2 FLAWED, defective, inaccurate, incorrect, wrong, erroneous, illogical, invalid, weak
FORMAL fallacious, casuistic
FꞋ **1** working **2** sound

faux pas *n*
blunder, gaffe, indiscretion, mistake
FORMAL impropriety, solecism
COLLOQ. boob, booboo, clanger, slip-up, howler
SLANG goof

favour *n, v*
• *n*
1 APPROVAL, esteem, support, backing, commendation, sympathy, kindness, friendliness, goodwill, patronage, assistance, aid, favouritism, preference, partiality
FORMAL approbation
2 *he did me a favour*
kindness, act of kindness, service, good turn, good deed, courtesy, benefit
FꞋ **1** disapproval
• *v*
1 PREFER, choose, select, opt for, like, pick, approve, support, back, recommend, endorse, advocate, champion, sanction, take kindly to
COLLOQ. go for, plump for
2 HELP, assist, aid, benefit, promote, encourage, pamper, spoil, indulge
FORMAL succour
FꞋ **1** dislike **2** mistreat
■ **in favour of**
for, all for, pro, supporting, on the side of, backing, behind
FꞋ against

favourable *adj*
1 *a favourable reaction*
positive, sympathetic, agreeable, well-disposed, approving, complimentary, enthusiastic, friendly, amicable, kind, understanding, encouraging, reassuring, heartening
2 *a favourable impression*
positive, good, agreeable, pleasing, effective, promising
3 *favourable conditions*
good, advantageous, beneficial, promising, fair, encouraging, convenient, suitable, appropriate, opportune
FORMAL auspicious, propitious
FꞋ **1, 2** negative **3** unhelpful

favourably *adv*
well, positively, sympathetically, agreeably, approvingly, enthusiastically, helpfully, advantageously, fortunately, conveniently, opportunely, profitably
FORMAL auspiciously, propitiously
FꞋ unfavourably

favoured adj

preferred, chosen, selected, recommended, favourite, privileged, advantaged, blessed, élite
FORMAL predilected

favourite adj, n

♦ adj

preferred, favoured, pet, best-loved, most-liked, dearest, beloved, treasured, chosen, great, esteemed, special
E₃ hated

♦ n

1 PREFERENCE, choice, first choice, number one, pick, pet, beloved, darling, idol, minion, white boy, nostrum
OLD gracioso, peat
COLLOQ. blue-eyed boy, teacher's pet, the apple of your eye, particular, best boy/girl, boyfriend, girlfriend, flavour of the week/month; N Am fair-haired boy
SLANG fave, winger
2 CERTAINTY, odds-on favourite, nap, likely winner, form horse
E₃ 1 bête noire, pet hate

favouritism n

nepotism, preferential treatment, preference, partiality, prejudice, inequality, inequity, one-sidedness, partisanship, bias, unfairness, injustice
E₃ impartiality, equality

fawn¹ adj

a fawn coat

beige, buff, yellowish-brown, pale brown, sand-coloured, sandy, khaki

fawn² v

fawning over someone famous

flatter, grovel, bow and scrape, court, curry favour, dance attendance, kowtow, pay court, ingratiate yourself, toady
FORMAL be obsequious to
COLLOQ. bootlick, crawl, creep, cringe, smarm, lick someone's boots, suck up to, butter up, soft-soap, cosy up (to); N Am cozy up (with)

fawning adj

servile, sycophantic, deferential, flattering, grovelling, ingratiating, bowing and scraping, abject, toadying, toadyish
OLD (*Shakesp*) knee-crooking
FORMAL obsequious, unctuous
COLLOQ. bootlicking, crawling, cringing
SLANG (*vulgar*) arse-licking
E₃ cold, proud

faze v

surprise, shock, startle, stun, shake, unnerve, unsettle, dumbfound, dismay, disconcert, fluster, disturb, put off/out, take aback, puzzle
FORMAL perturb
COLLOQ. rattle

fear n, v

♦ n

1 TERROR, dread, alarm, fright, panic, fearfulness, agitation, apprehension, foreboding, dismay, distress, trembling, shaking, quivering, phobia, aversion, horror, nightmare, bête noire
OLD (*Spenser*) affray
FORMAL trepidation, consternation
2 ANXIETY, worry, concern, unease, uneasiness, qualms, misgivings, disquiet, suspicion, doubt
FORMAL solicitude
3 AWE, reverence, respect, wonder, honour, fear, fear of God, terror, dread
FORMAL veneration
4 *no fear of being misunderstood*
chance, risk, likelihood, likeliness, possibility, probability, prospect, expectation, scope
E₃ 1 courage, bravery, confidence **3** contempt

♦ v

1 BE AFRAID OF, be scared of, dread, shudder at, shrink from, tremble at, lose your nerve, take fright at, have a horror of, have a phobia about, panic
COLLOQ. have your heart in your mouth, your heart melts, your stomach turns, get the wind up, be in a cold sweat, be in a blue funk, freak out, lose your bottle
2 WORRY, be anxious about, be uneasy about, be concerned about, have misgivings/qualms about, tremble for
3 *fear God*
stand in awe of, revere, hold in reverence, reverence, wonder at
FORMAL venerate
4 *I fear I can't help you*
be afraid, regret, suspect, expect, foresee, anticipate
COLLOQ. have a sneaking suspicion

Synonym nuances

noun sense 1

Terror may be used to refer to an extreme state of fear, whilst **dread** would be used of being scared of what might or will happen in future: *a dread of old age*. **Alarm**, on the other hand, is more suggestive of being alerted to danger, whereas **fright** implies a sudden reaction, and **panic** suggests a chaotic loss of control: *if there was a fire there could be panic and havoc*. **Fearfulness** may be used of a continuous state of being afraid, whilst **agitation** is more suggestive of being perturbed through fear.

Both **apprehension** and **foreboding** contain the idea of anxiety about future events, though the latter suggests a greater intensity: *a foreboding of imminent danger*. You can use **dismay** to emphasize elements of upset and concern: *I watched with dismay as the boat sank*, but **distress** has greater implications of severe mental suffering: *the threats caused me great distress*.

Phobia, which is usually reserved for a deep psychological fear of some particular thing, can also imply irrationality. **Aversion** is similar, but suggests a less obsessive feeling, and implies an overwhelming dislike, whilst **horror** goes further by suggesting an intense repugnance: *she had a horror of moths*. The terms **trembling**, **shaking**, and **quivering** all put the emphasis on the physical effects of being frightened, and so imply an intense fear.

---

fearful adj

1 FRIGHTENED, afraid, scared, alarmed, in dread, nervous, anxious, tense, uneasy, apprehensive, agitated, trembling, shaking, quivering, petrified, hesitant, nervy, panicky, faint-hearted, timid
OLD affrayed, effraide, adred, afear
FORMAL tremulous, aghast
COLLOQ. scared out of your wits, scared to death, having kittens, in a cold sweat, in a blue funk, shaking in your shoes, shaking like a leaf, with your heart in your mouth, spineless, yellow
2 TERRIBLE, dreadful, awful, frightful, atrocious, shocking, dire, harrowing, distressing, appalling, horrific, monstrous, gruesome, hideous, ghastly, horrible, grim; Scot ferly
FORMAL fearsome
E₃ 1 brave, courageous, fearless **2** wonderful, delightful

fearfully adv

1 APPREHENSIVELY, anxiously, nervously, uneasily, hesitantly, timidly, in fear and trembling
2 *fearfully insecure*
extremely, highly, intensely, unusually, exceedingly, exceptionally, very, most, incredibly, unbelievably
COLLOQ. awfully, terribly, frightfully, dreadfully, well, jolly, terrifically

fearless adj

bold, brave, confident, courageous, daring, intrepid, valiant, heroic, gallant, plucky, dauntless, aweless, unafraid, unapprehensive, unabashed, undaunted, unflinching, lion-hearted, unblenching, unblinking
OLD impavid
FORMAL doughty, indomitable, valorous
COLLOQ. game, gutsy, feisty, spunky, gritty
SLANG ballsy
F3 afraid, timid

fearsome adj

formidable, awe-inspiring, awesome, awful, daunting, terrifying, frightening, frightful, hair-raising, horrendous, horrible, horrific, horrifying, menacing, terrible, unnerving, alarming, appalling, dismaying
F3 delightful

feasibility n

practicability, achievability, workability, practicality, reasonableness, possibility, viability, expedience

feasible adj

practicable, practical, workable, doable, achievable, attainable, realizable, accomplishable, viable, expedient, reasonable, possible, likely, realistic
F3 impossible

feast n, v

♦ n

1 BANQUET, dinner, spread, junket, treat, carousal, luau; NZ kaikai
TECHNICAL love-feast, agape
FORMAL repast, epulation
OLD regale
COLLOQ. blow-out, binge, beano, slap-up meal, do
SLANG pig
2 a feast for the eyes
wealth, abundance, profusion
FORMAL cornucopia
3 FESTIVAL, holiday, gala, fete, celebration, carnival, saint's day, jour de fête, feast day, religious festival, holy day, revels, festivities, gaudy, junketing; N Am potlatch
OLD ale
Related adjective: festal
♦ v
gorge, eat your fill, wine and dine, indulge in, treat, entertain, regale, revel, banquet, junket
OLD convive
FORMAL partake of
COLLOQ. pig out

feat n

exploit, deed, act, action, accomplishment, achievement, attainment, performance, undertaking

feather n

plume, quill, down, tuft, crest
TECHNICAL penna, plumule, plumula, aigrette, egret, pinion
Related adjectives: pennaceous, plumose, plumous

feathery adj

1 feathery birds
feathered, featherlike, fleecy, fluffy, wispy, downy
TECHNICAL pennaceous, penniform, plumate, plumed, plumose, plumous, plumy
2 feathery clouds
soft, light, delicate, fluffy, wispy, flimsy

feature n, v

♦ n

1 ASPECT, facet, point, factor, attribute, quality, property, side, trait, characteristic, peculiarity, mark, hallmark, speciality, highlight, attraction, focal point
2 a person's facial features
face, looks
FORMAL countenance, lineaments, physiognomy, visage
SLANG mug, phiz, phizog, kisser, pan, clock, dial

3 a magazine feature
column, article, report, story, piece, item, comment
4 a water feature
highlight, centrepiece, focus, focus of attention, most interesting/exciting part
♦ v
1 EMPHASIZE, highlight, spotlight, play up, call/draw attention to, accentuate, promote, show, present
2 APPEAR, figure, participate, act, perform, star

featureless adj

nondescript, indeterminate, undistinctive, undistinguished, indistinguishable, unexceptional, ordinary, commonplace, plain, dull, vague, bland, anaemic, insipid, uninspiring, uninteresting, unattractive, unremarkable, unclassified
COLLOQ. run of the mill, common or garden, vanilla; N Am cookie cutter
F3 distinctive, remarkable

febrile adj

feverish, delirious, fevered, flushed, fiery, hot, inflamed, burning
FORMAL pyretic

feckless adj

incompetent, weak, feeble, useless, worthless, aimless, futile, hopeless, irresponsible
FORMAL ineffectual
COLLOQ. wimpish, no-good, wet
F3 efficient, sensible

fecund adj

fertile, productive, fruitful, prolific, teeming
FORMAL feracious, fructiferous, fructuous
F3 infertile

fecundity n

fertility, productiveness, fruitfulness
FORMAL feracity, fructiferousness
F3 infertility

fed up adj

depressed, bored, discontented, annoyed, dismal, dissatisfied, gloomy, glum, tired, weary, have had enough
COLLOQ. blue, brassed off, browned off, cheesed off, down, sick and tired, hacked off, have had it up to here, at the end of your tether
SLANG pissed off
F3 contented

federal adj

confederated, amalgamated, allied, integrated, united, unified, in league, combined, associated

federate v

confederate, amalgamate, integrate, join together, ally, league, syndicate, unify, unite, combine, associate
F3 disunite, separate

federation n

confederation, confederacy, alliance, league, amalgamation, association, coalition, combination, syndicate, union, copartnership, federacy

fee n

charge, terms, bill, account, pay, remuneration, payment, cost, price, subscription, reward, recompense, hire, rent, retainer, wage, salary, honorarium, toll, appearance money
FORMAL emolument

feeble adj

1 WEAK, faint, exhausted, frail, slight, delicate, puny, sickly, infirm, ailing, failing, powerless, helpless, decrepit, rickety, wastrel, washy, wishy-washy, debile, spiritless, dispirited, graspless, namby-pamby; dialect wearish; Scot sober, wersh, daidling, foisonless, fushionless, fizzenless
OLD impuissant, sackless, silly; (Spenser) lustless
FORMAL effete, debilitated, enervated
2 a feeble excuse

inadequate, lame, poor, weak, futile, thin, flimsy, unconvincing, tame, ineffective, unsuccessful
FORMAL ineffectual
3 *a feeble person*
ineffective, weak, incompetent, indecisive, feckless
FORMAL ineffectual
COLLOQ. pathetic, wimpish, wet
SLANG wussy
F3 1 strong, powerful

feeble-minded *adj*
slow-witted, half-witted, stupid, moronic, simple, silly, weak-minded, retarded, deficient, idiotic, imbecile, imbecilic
COLLOQ. dim-witted, dumb, slow on the uptake, soft in the head, two bricks short of a load, running on three wheels, not the sharpest knife in the box, not all there, mouth breathing; *Aust* not the full quid
F3 bright, intelligent

feebly *adv*
1 WEAKLY, faintly, slightly, powerlessly, helplessly, dispiritedly
2 *he apologized feebly*
ineffectively, weakly, indecisively, lamely
COLLOQ. pathetically

feed *v, n*
◆ *v*
1 *feed the baby*
give food to, nurture, nourish, cater for, provide for, suckle, eat, dine (on), consume, take in
FORMAL partake of
2 *animals feeding*
graze, pasture, browse, crop
FORMAL ruminate
3 *feed your sense of self-worth*
strengthen, gratify, fuel, foster, nurture, encourage, support
FORMAL fortify
4 *feed data into a computer*
put, insert, give, introduce, provide, supply, deliver, slide, slip
◆ *n*
food, fodder, foodstuff, forage, pasture, silage, provender

feedback *n*
response, answer, reply
OLD respondence
COLLOQ. comeback

feel *v, n*
◆ *v*
1 EXPERIENCE, be, go through, live through, undergo, suffer, bear, endure, be overcome by, give way to, harbour, nurse, know, enjoy
2 TOUCH, finger, handle, manipulate, hold, contact, stroke, massage, rub, caress, fondle, paw, maul, poke, fumble, grope, clutch, grasp
3 *feel soft*
seem, appear, look
4 THINK, believe, consider, reckon, judge, hold
FORMAL deem
5 SENSE, perceive, notice, observe, know, understand, realize, detect, discern, be aware of, feel in your bones
◆ *n*
1 *the feel of the material*
texture, surface, finish, touch, consistency
2 *have a feel for computer-programming*
touch, knack, ability, skill, aptitude, gift, talent, faculty, flair, bent
3 *the feel of a place*
atmosphere, impression, feeling, quality, mood, air, aura, ambience
COLLOQ. vibes
■ **feel for**
pity, sympathize (with), empathize with, commiserate

(with), be sorry for, be moved by, grieve for, weep for, pity
■ **feel like**
want, desire, wish, would like, fancy

feeler *n*
1 ANTENNA, horn, tentacle, sense organ
TECHNICAL palp, palpus
2 *put out feelers*
advance, approach, overture(s), probe, trial balloon, ballon d'essai

feeling *n*
1 EMOTION, passion, intensity, warmth, compassion, love, sympathy, understanding, pity, concern, care, affection, fondness, spirit, ardour, sentiment, sentimentality, susceptibility, sensibility, sensitivity, appreciation, fervour, intensity
FORMAL sentience
2 SENSE, perception, sensation, instinct, intuition, hunch, theory, suspicion, inkling, impression, idea, belief, thought, notion, opinion, view, point of view, way of thinking
COLLOQ. sneaking suspicion, feeling in your bones
3 *hurt someone's feelings*
emotions, passions, self-esteem, sensitivities, sensibilities, susceptibilities, ego
FORMAL affections
4 AIR, aura, atmosphere, mood, quality, feel, impression
COLLOQ. vibes
5 *have a feeling for finance*
natural ability, ability, knack, aptitude, skill, gift, talent, flair, bent

feign *v*
simulate, assume, fabricate, fake, forge, imitate, pretend, put on, put it on, sham, make a show of, make believe, invent, counterfeit, act, fable
OLD dissemble, false, falsify, fayne, gammon, misfeign; (*Shakesp*) take upon yourself
FORMAL affect, dissimulate

feint *n*
play, pretence, ruse, artifice, distraction, expedient, gambit, manoeuvre, stratagem, subterfuge, blind, bluff, deception, sham, make-believe, mock-assault, wile
OLD dissemblance
COLLOQ. dodge

feisty *adj*
tough, courageous, brave, bold, plucky, spirited, lively, determined
COLLOQ. spunky, gutsy, gritty

felicitous *adj*
1 APPOSITE, appropriate, apt, fitting, suitable, well-chosen, opportune, timely, well-timed, well-turned, fortunate
FORMAL apropos
2 DELIGHTFUL, happy, inspired, fortunate, advantageous
FORMAL propitious
F3 inappropriate

felicity *n*
1 BLISS, joy, delight, euphoria, rapture, ecstasy, happiness
FORMAL delectation
2 APPROPRIATENESS, applicability, aptness, eloquence, suitability, suitableness
FORMAL propriety
F3 1 sadness **2** inappropriateness

feline *adj, n*
◆ *adj*
catlike, graceful, sleek, slinky, smooth, stealthy, seductive, sensual, sinuous, leonine
◆ *n*
cat, kitten, tomcat, tom, tabby, queen, mouser, wildcat, alleycat, grimalkin, Tibert, eyra, jaguarundi, manul, ocelot,

ounce, quoll, rumpy, sealpoint, serval; *dialect* malkin; *Scot* baudrons
TECHNICAL felid
COLLOQ. puss, pussy, moggy

fell¹ *v*
fell trees
cut down, hew, knock down, chop down, strike down, floor, level, flatten, raze, raze to the ground, demolish, overthrow

fell²
■ **at one fell swoop**
all at once, at one time, in one go, by a single action

fellow *n, adj*
◆ *n*
1 MAN, male, boy, individual, person, character
COLLOQ. chap, bloke, guy, lad; *Aust* cove
2 PEER, compeer, equal, partner, associate, colleague, co-worker, confrère, contemporary, compatriot, companion, comrade, friend, counterpart, match, mate, twin, double
COLLOQ. crony, pal, chum, buddy
◆ *adj*
co-, associate, associated, related, like, similar

fellow feeling *n*
empathy, commiseration, compassion, care, feeling, sympathy, understanding

fellowship *n*
1 COMPANIONSHIP, camaraderie, comradeship, communion, familiarity, friendship, amiability, sociability, compatibility, affability, intimacy
COLLOQ. chumminess, matiness, palliness
2 ASSOCIATION, league, guild, society, club, union, affiliation, fraternity, brotherhood, sisterhood, order

female *adj*
feminine, she-, girlish, womanly, ladylike
🖃 male

feminine *adj*
1 FEMALE, womanly, ladylike, pretty, graceful, gentle, tender, delicate
2 EFFEMINATE, unmanly, womanish, girlish, girly, weak
COLLOQ. cissy, wimpish
🖃 **1** masculine **2** manly

Synonym nuances
sense 1
Female can be used to refer to a person's or animal's gender and has no connotations beyond specifyng sex: *most of the applicants were female.* **Womanly** has to do with the natural attributes associated with women, and is often associated with the more positive ones: *her eyes had a gentle, womanly strength.* **Ladylike**, is a rather old-fashioned sounding term to modern ears, with connotations of propriety: *she spoke with ladylike reserve.* **Pretty** implies an attractive appearance with archetypally feminine features: *his girlfriend was very pretty with a flawless complexion.*
　Other terms widely associated with femininity focus on features that are considered desirable in women; the term **graceful**, for instance, may be used to suggest an elegance of carriage or manner, **gentle** and **tender** are suggestive of being soft-hearted and **delicate** can imply a physical fragility: *her delicate white skin.*

---

femininity *n*
feminineness, womanhood, womanishness, womanliness, girlishness, effeminacy, prettiness, gracefulness, gentleness, tenderness, delicacy
COLLOQ. sissiness
🖃 masculinity

feminism *n*
women's movement, women's lib(eration), female emancipation, women's rights

femme fatale *n*
charmer, seductress, enchantress, temptress, siren, vamp, Circe, Lorelei, Mata Hari, Sirens, Delilah

fen *n*
bog, marsh, morass, moss, quag, quagmire, slough, swamp

fence *n, v*
◆ *n*
1 BARRIER, railing, rail, paling, wall, hedge, windbreak, guard, defence, barricade, stockade, enclosure, rampart, palisade
TECHNICAL sepiment
2 RECEIVER OF STOLEN GOODS/PROPERTY, trafficker
COLLOQ. pusher
◆ *v*
1 SURROUND, encircle, bound, hedge, wall, enclose, shut in, pen, coop, confine, restrict, separate, protect, secure, guard, defend
FORMAL fortify, circumscribe
2 PARRY, evade, hedge, equivocate, quibble, stonewall, prevaricate
FORMAL vacillate, tergiversate
COLLOQ. dodge, pussyfoot, shilly-shally, beat about the bush
■ **sit on the fence**
be irresolute, be uncommitted, be undecided, be unsure, be uncertain, vacillate, dither
COLLOQ. shilly-shally, blow hot and cold

fencing

Fencing terms include:

appel	foil	reprise
attack	forte	riposte
balestra	hit	counter-riposte
barrage	lunge	sabre
coquille	on guard	tac-au-tac
disengage	parry	thrust
en garde	counter-parry	touch
épée	pink	touché
feint	piste	volt
flèche	plastron	
foible	remise	

fend *v*
1 **fend for yourself**
look after, take care of, support, maintain, sustain, provide
2 **fend off an attack**
ward off, beat off, head off, parry, deflect, divert, avert, resist, repel, repulse, hold at bay, keep off, stave off, shut out, turn aside

feral *adj*
wild, ferocious, fierce, savage, vicious, brutal, brutish, bestial, undomesticated, unbroken, untamed
🖃 tame, domesticated

ferment *v, n*
◆ *v*
1 BUBBLE, effervesce, froth, foam, boil, seethe, smoulder, fester, work, brew, rise, yeast; *dialect* fret
2 ROUSE, arouse, stir up, excite, work up, agitate, foment, incite, provoke, inflame, cause, heat, yeast
◆ *n*
1 UNREST, agitation, turbulence, stir, excitement, turmoil, disruption, commotion, confusion, fuss, tumult, hubbub, stew, uproar, furore, brouhaha, frenzy, fever
2 **the action of a ferment**
leaven, zyme, enzyme, mould, bacteria
TECHNICAL ptyalin
🖃 **1** calm

ferocious *adj*
1 VICIOUS, savage, fierce, wild, untamed, barbarous, barbaric, brutal, inhuman, cruel, sadistic, murderous, bloodthirsty, violent, merciless, pitiless, bitter, ruthless
FORMAL feral
2 INTENSE, wild, vigorous, strong, extreme, severe, deep
E3 1 tame **2** gentle, mild

ferocity *n*
savagery, fierceness, violence, bloodthirstiness, ruthlessness, cruelty, inhumanity, brutality, viciousness, sadism, barbarity, wildness, intensity, severity, extremity
E3 gentleness, mildness

ferret *v*
search, rummage, hunt, go through, scour, forage, rifle
■ **ferret out**
discover, search out, find, hunt down, track down, trace, elicit, extract, unearth, dig up, nose out, root out, worm out, run to earth
COLLOQ. suss out

ferry *n, v*
♦ *n*
ferry-boat, car ferry, ship, boat, vessel, packet, packet boat, shuttle
♦ *v*
transport, ship, convey, carry, take, shuttle, taxi, drive, run, move, shift, ply

fertile *adj*
1 *fertile soil*
fruitful, productive, rich, abundant; *dialect* battle
OLD pregnant
FORMAL fecund, luxuriant
2 *a fertile imagination*
creative, resourceful, inventive, prolific, productive, ingenious, imaginative, inspired, visionary
3 *fertile animals*
generative, prolific, able to have children, potent, reproductive, virile
OLD broody
FORMAL fecund
E3 1 unfruitful, unproductive **2** barren **3** sterile, infertile, barren

fertility *n*
1 FRUITFULNESS, productiveness, abundance, richness
FORMAL luxuriance, fecundity
2 *fertility tests*
generativeness, prolificness, potency, reproductiveness, virility
E3 1 aridity **2** barrenness, sterility

fertilization *n*
impregnation, implantation, insemination, conception, pollination, propagation
FORMAL fecundation, procreation

fertilize *v*
1 IMPREGNATE, inseminate, pollinate, make pregnant, make fruitful
FORMAL procreate, fecundate, fructify
2 *fertilize land*
enrich, feed, dress, compost, manure, dung, mulch, top-dress

fertilizer *n*
dressing, compost, manure, dung, top-dressing, plant food, mulch, bone meal, humus

fervent *adj*
ardent, earnest, eager, sincere, enthusiastic, wholehearted, excited, energetic, vigorous, fiery, spirited, intense, vehement, passionate, full-blooded, zealous, devout, impassioned, heartfelt, emotional, warm
E3 cool, indifferent, apathetic

fervently *adv*
ardently, earnestly, eagerly, sincerely, enthusiastically, wholeheartedly, intensely, passionately, emotionally, excitedly, energetically, vigorously
E3 indifferently, apathetically

fervour *n*
ardour, eagerness, earnestness, sincerity, enthusiasm, excitement, animation, energy, vigour, spirit, verve, intensity, wholeheartedness, fire, vehemence, passion, emotion, zeal, warmth; *Welsh* hwyl
E3 apathy, indifference

fester *v*
1 *the wound was festering*
infect, ulcerate, gather, suppurate, discharge
TECHNICAL maturate
2 *cheese festered on the filthy counter*
rot, decay, go bad, decompose, moulder, perish
FORMAL putrefy
3 *hatred was festering*
rankle, irk, chafe, anger, annoy, gall, rankle, smoulder, brew

festival *n*
celebration, commemoration, anniversary, jubilee, holiday, feast, gala, gala day, fair, fete, carnival, fiesta, party, merrymaking, entertainment, festivities

festive *adj*
celebratory, holiday, gala, carnival, festal, happy, joyful, merry, hearty, cheerful, cheery, light-hearted, jolly, jovial, cordial, jubilant, convivial
FORMAL joyous
E3 gloomy, sombre, sober

festivity *n*
celebration, jubilation, feasting, banqueting, fun, enjoyment, pleasure, entertainment, festival, party, fun and games, carousal, junketing, sport, amusement, cheerfulness, cheeriness, merriment, merrymaking, revelry, revel, jollity, joviality, conviviality

festoon *v, n*
♦ *v*
adorn, deck, garland, wreathe, drape, hang, swathe, decorate, ornament, garnish
OLD bedeck, bedizen
FORMAL array
♦ *n*
garland, wreath, swathe, chaplet, swag

fetch *v*
1 *fetch a bucket*
get, go and get, collect, bring, carry, transport, deliver, escort, convey, conduct
2 SELL FOR, go for, bring in, yield, realize, make, earn
■ **fetch up**
end up, finish up, arrive, materialize, turn up
COLLOQ. wind up, show up

fetching *adj*
attractive, pretty, sweet, cute, charming, enchanting, appealing, fascinating, captivating, alluring, winsome, adorable
E3 repellent

fete, fête *n, v*
♦ *n*
fair, bazaar, sale of work, garden party, gala, carnival, festival
♦ *v*
entertain, treat, regale, welcome, honour, lionize

fetid, foetid *adj*
stinking, disgusting, foul, filthy, sickly, nauseating, smelly, odorous, offensive, rancid, rank, reeking
FORMAL malodorous, noisome, noxious, mephitic
COLLOQ. pongy, whiffy, humming
E3 fragrant

fetish *n*
1 FIXATION, obsession, mania, *idée fixe*
COLLOQ. thing
2 CHARM, amulet, talisman, idol, image, cult object, ju-ju, totem, obi

fetter *v*
hamper, restrain, hinder, obstruct, restrict, impede, constrain, bind, chain, confine, encumber, curb, shackle, tie (up), hamstring, manacle, truss, entrammel
F3 free

fetters *n*
1 CONSTRAINTS, obstructions, restraints, restrictions, hindrances, checks, curbs, inhibitions, captivity, bondage
2 CHAINS, bonds, bracelets, handcuffs, irons, shackles, manacles

fettle
■ **in fine fettle**
in (good) shape, fit, healthy, in good health, sound, strong, trim, in good condition, on form, in fine form, shipshape, hale and hearty
COLLOQ. in good nick

feud *n, v*
♦ *n*
vendetta, quarrel, row, argument, disagreement, dispute, bickering, conflict, strife, discord, animosity, ill will, bitterness, enmity, hostility, antagonism, rivalry, bad blood
F3 agreement, peace
♦ *v*
quarrel, argue, row, squabble, bicker, clash, contend, dispute, duel, fight, brawl, war, wrangle, be at odds
FORMAL altercate
F3 agree

fever *n*
1 FEVERISHNESS, (high) temperature, delirium, ague
TECHNICAL pyrexia
OLD calenture
Related adjective: febrile
2 EXCITEMENT, agitation, turmoil, unrest, restlessness, heat, passion, ecstasy, frenzy, ferment

fevered *adj*
1 EXCITED, impatient, restless, nervous, worked up, passionate, frenzied, frantic
2 FEVERISH, with a temperature, hot, burning, flushed, red
FORMAL febrile

feverish *adj*
1 DELIRIOUS, with a temperature, hot, burning, flushed, red
FORMAL febrile
2 EXCITED, impatient, agitated, restless, nervous, overwrought, worked up, passionate, frenzied, frantic, hectic, rushed, hasty, hurried, flustered, troubled, bothered
COLLOQ. hot and bothered, in a kerfuffle, in a tizzy, in a tizz, in a dither
F3 1 cool **2** calm

few *adj, pron*
♦ *adj*
scarce, rare, uncommon, sporadic, infrequent, sparse, thin, scant, scanty, meagre, negligible, inconsiderable, inadequate, insufficient, in short supply
COLLOQ. thin on the ground
F3 many
♦ *pron*
not many, hardly any, scarcely any, one or two, a couple, a small number of, scattering, sprinkling, handful, some, a minority
F3 many

fey *adj*
whimsical, fanciful, quirky, playful, mischievous, impulsive, childish, unpredictable, eccentric, funny, droll, curious, shy, unusual, weird, odd, peculiar, quaint
FORMAL capricious
COLLOQ. dotty

fiancé, fiancée *n*
betrothed, intended, husband-to-be, bridegroom-to-be, future/prospective husband, wife-to-be, bride-to-be, future/prospective wife

fiasco *n*
failure, catastrophe, calamity, collapse, debacle, disaster, ruin, rout, mess
COLLOQ. cropper, damp squib, flop, washout; *N Am* bomb
F3 success

fiat *n*
order, command, directive, edict, decree, injunction, mandate, sanction, warrant, authorization, ordinance, permission, dictate, precept, dictum, proclamation, diktat
COLLOQ. OK

fib *n, v*
♦ *n*
lie, untruth, white lie, falsehood, story, tale, yarn, fable, concoction, fantasy, fiction, invention, misrepresentation, evasion, prevarication
COLLOQ. whopper, porky
♦ *v*
evade, fabricate, falsify, fantasize, invent, lie, prevaricate, sidestep
FORMAL dissemble

fibre *n*
1 FILAMENT, strand, thread, tendril, fibril, nerve, sinew, pile, texture, material, cloth, substance, stuff
2 *moral fibre*
character, nature, make-up, disposition, temperament, calibre, backbone, strength, stamina, toughness, courage, resolution, resoluteness, resolve, determination, willpower, strength of character, firmness (of purpose)

fickle *adj*
inconstant, disloyal, unfaithful, faithless, treacherous, unreliable, unpredictable, variable, changeable, irresolute, vacillating, volatile, unstable, unsteady, inconsistent, flighty, wind-changing, mutable, volage; *Scot* kittle
OLD choiceful
FORMAL capricious, mercurial, labile
F3 constant, steady, stable

fickleness *n*
inconstancy, disloyalty, unfaithfulness, faithlessness, treachery, unreliability, unpredictability, changeability, changeableness, volatility, unsteadiness, instability, fitfulness, flightiness, mutability
FORMAL capriciousness
F3 constancy

fiction *n*
1 *read fiction*
novels, fantasy, romance, story, stories, tale, yarn, fable, parable, legend, myth, storytelling, creative writing
2 PRETENCE, lie, falsehood, untruth, fabrication, invention, concoction
COLLOQ. fib, tall story, cock-and-bull story
F3 1 non-fiction **2** fact, truth

fictional *adj*
literary, invented, made-up, imaginary, make-believe, legendary, mythical, mythological, fabulous, non-existent, unreal
F3 factual, real

fictitious *adj*
false, untrue, invented, made-up, fabricated, fake, apocryphal, imaginary, non-existent, bogus, counterfeit, sham, spurious, assumed, supposed, concocted, improvised
F3 true, genuine

fiddle v, n

♦ v

1 *fiddling with her necklace*
play, tinker, toy, trifle, tamper, mess around, fool around, meddle, interfere, fidget, fuss
2 CHEAT, falsify, fraud, swindle, juggle, manoeuvre, racketeer
COLLOQ. cook the books, diddle, fix, graft

♦ n

swindle, fraud, racket, sharp practice
COLLOQ. con, graft, fix
SLANG rip-off; *N Am* gold brick

fiddling adj

trifling, petty, trivial, insignificant, negligible, paltry
E3 important, significant

fidelity n

1 FAITHFULNESS, loyalty, allegiance, devotion, devotedness, constancy, reliability, dependability, trustworthiness
2 ACCURACY, exactness, precision, closeness, adherence, strictness, faithfulness, authenticity
E3 1 disloyalty, unfaithfulness, infidelity, inconstancy, treachery **2** inaccuracy

fidget v

squirm, wriggle, writhe, toss and turn, shuffle, twitch, niggle, jerk, jump, jiggle, twiddle, fret, fuss, bustle, fiddle, mess about, play around, tinker, toy, trifle, tamper; *Scot* footer, fike, hirsle, hotch

fidgety adj

restless, impatient, uneasy, nervous, agitated, excited, jumpy, twitchy, on edge
FORMAL restive
COLLOQ. jittery, uptight, afraid of your shadow, like a cat on hot bricks
E3 still

field n, v

♦ n

1 GRASSLAND, meadow, pasture, paddock, playing-field, ground, pitch, green, lawn
OLD lea, mead, sward, glebe
Related adjectives: agrestic, campestral
2 RANGE, scope, bounds, limits, confines, territory, area, province, domain, sphere, environment, department, discipline, speciality, line, forte, regime, scene
3 PARTICIPANTS, entrants, contestants, competitors, contenders, runners, candidates, applicants, opponents, opposition, competition, possibles

♦ v

1 CATCH, retrieve, stop, pick up, return
2 ANSWER, cope with, deal with, handle, parry, deflect
3 *field a team*
play, choose to play, select, put up, present, send out

fiend n

1 EVIL SPIRIT, demon, devil, monster, savage, beast, brute, ogre, ghoul; *Scot* fient
2 *a health fiend*
enthusiast, fanatic, fan, addict, devotee
FORMAL aficionado
COLLOQ. freak, nut, buff

fiendish adj

1 *a fiendish person/plot*
devilish, diabolical, infernal, wicked, malevolent, cunning, cruel, inhuman, savage, brutal, aggressive, vicious, ferocious, ruthless, bloodthirsty, barbaric, monstrous, unspeakable
2 *a fiendish problem/plan*
difficult, intricate, involved, complex, complicated, obscure, horrendous, infernal, devilish, diabolical, challenging, cunning, clever, imaginative, ingenious, resourceful

fierce adj

1 FEROCIOUS, vicious, savage, cruel, brutal, wild, merciless, ruthless, aggressive, dangerous, fell, bloodthirsty, murderous, frightening, menacing, threatening, stern, grim, terrible, relentless
OLD stout, truculent; (*Shakesp*) walleyed
2 INTENSE, strong, powerful, passionate, wild, raging, rampant, angry, violent, furious, tempestuous, severe, grave, keen, cut-throat, hot, uncontrolled, relentless
OLD felon, wood; (*Spenser*) breme
E3 1 gentle, kind **2** calm

fiercely adv

ferociously, viciously, savagely, cruelly, brutally, wildly, mercilessly, murderously, ruthlessly, aggressively, dangerously, menacingly, threateningly, sternly, terribly, intensely, implacably, fanatically, bitterly, strongly, powerfully, passionately, relentlessly, violently, furiously, tempestuously, severely, keenly
COLLOQ. tooth and nail
E3 gently, kindly

fiery adj

1 BURNING, afire, flaming, aflame, blazing, ablaze, red-hot, glowing, aglow, flushed, hot, torrid, sultry
2 PASSIONATE, inflamed, ardent, fervent, impassioned, impatient, excitable, impetuous, impulsive, hot-headed, fierce, violent, heated
3 SPICY, spiced, seasoned, hot, pungent, piquant, sharp
E3 1 cold **2** impassive

fiesta n

party, festival, celebration, jubilee, holiday, feast, gala, carnival, merrymaking

fight v, n

♦ v

1 WRESTLE, box, fence, joust, brawl, punch, hit, set about, take on, scuffle, tussle, skirmish, combat, battle, do battle, war, wage war, make war, be at war, clash, conflict, cross swords, duel, militate, spar, engage, attack, grapple, struggle, contend, come to blows; *Aust & NZ* stoush
OLD debate, camp, strike, digladiate, measure swords, snickersnee; (*Shakesp*) meddle
COLLOQ. scrap, lay into, weigh into; *N Am* duke it out
2 QUARREL, argue, have a row, row, bandy words, dispute, squabble, bicker, wrangle, feud, be at odds
OLD debate
FORMAL altercate
COLLOQ. fall out, be at each other's throats
3 OPPOSE, contest, campaign against, champion, combat, work against, resist, withstand, defy, hold out against, stand up to, dispute, object to, take issue with, strive, struggle against, do battle against
OLD repugn
4 RESIST, restrain, repress, suppress, curb, thwart, hold back, keep back, force back, stem, stifle, smother
COLLOQ. bottle up

♦ n

1 BOUT, contest, duel, combat, action, battle, war, warfare, bloodshed, hostilities, attack, brawl, scuffle, tussle, struggle, brush, skirmish, exchange, clash, engagement, encounter, confrontation, conflict, spar, fray, row, disturbance, free-for-all, fracas, rout, ruckus, ruction, riot, mêlée, ruffle, shindy, Donnybrook, fisticuffs, cockfight, dogfight, gunfight, pell-mell, monomachy; *Scot* wap, rammy; *N Am* mix-in; *Aust & NZ* stoush
OLD graplement, medley; *Scot* tuilyie
COLLOQ. aggro, bovver, scrap, set-to, scrape, punch-up, pasting, bashing
SLANG ruck, rumble, bundle
2 QUARREL, row, disagreement, difference of opinion, argument, dispute; *Aust* yike
OLD debate
FORMAL dissension, discord, altercation

COLLOQ. dust-up, ding-dong
SLANG *Aust & NZ* blue
3 *the fight for freedom*
campaign, crusade, movement, drive, struggle, battle
4 *lose all his fight*
determination, willpower, tenacity, firmness, resolve, resoluteness, drive, spirit, aggression, will to live, pluck
COLLOQ. bottle, grit, guts, spunk

■ **fight back**
1 RETALIATE, defend yourself, resist, put up a fight, counter-attack, hold out against, retort, reply
2 *fight back tears*
hold back, force back, restrain, curb, control, repress, contain, suppress, check
COLLOQ. bottle up

■ **fight off**
hold off, keep/hold at bay, ward off, stave off, resist, repel, rebuff, beat off, rout, put to flight

---

Synonym nuances
noun sense 1
Bout and **spar** are specifically used of an organized match in boxing or wrestling, but could be used figuratively, whilst **contest** is similar but not so restricted to sports: *the election will be a close contest*. **Duel**, on the other hand, has the more narrow referent of a prearranged fight between two people, although it may now be used to suggest a decisive struggle between two people: *the race soon developed into its final desperate duel*.

The terms **combat** and **action** are more suggestive of fighting in ongoing, official war, whilst **battle** has associations of one particular engagement of two opposing sides, while **attack** would be reserved for making the first aggressive move. You can use **hostilities** or **engagement** of a continuous state of antagonism, especially war, although the tone is rather formal, even euphemistic: *the commencement of hostilities is expected later this week*. **Bloodshed**, on the other hand, is an emotive and inherently disapproving term which evokes the outcome of large-scale fighting.

Encounter is a very mild term, and one which can be more widely used to imply any meeting of opposing parties: *an encounter with his rival in the semi-final*, whilst **confrontation** has more hostile implications. **Conflict** and **clash** clearly imply a more violent struggle. The terms **brawl**, **scuffle**, **tussle**, **brush** and **skirmish** are all suggestive of and appropriate for minor or limited physical disturbances: *a pub brawl*, while **struggle** implies a more protracted effort: *the struggle for human rights*.

The term **row** is usually used to suggest a verbal disagreement, whilst **disturbance** suggests a noisy outburst and smaller-scale actions: *a disturbance in the street kept me awake*. **Fracas** and **ruckus** suggest greater uproar: *she had never heard such a ruckus*, whilst **riot** implies a large-scale display which can extend into lawlessness. **Mêlée**, however, is more suggestive of confusion and disorder, as is **fray**, which is appropriate to use figuratively of bustling, active contests as well as burgeoning warfare: *other countries have been drawn into the fray over the border; key ministers have joined the election fray*.

---

fighter *n*
combatant, contestant, contender, rival, opponent, adversary, antagonist, attacker, disputant, boxer, wrestler, prizefighter, sparring partner, soldier, trouper, mercenary, warrior, man-at-arms, swordsman, gladiator
FORMAL pugilist

figment
■ **figment of your imagination**

invention, fabrication, falsehood, fancy, fiction, illusion, delusion, improvisation, fable, deception, concoction

figurative *adj*
metaphorical, symbolic, emblematic, representative, allegorical, parabolic, descriptive, pictorial, naturalistic
E3 literal

figure *n, v*
◆ *n*
1 NUMBER, numeral, digit, integer, sum, amount, total
2 *good at figures*
arithmetics, mental arithmetic, calculations, mathematics, maths, statistics
COLLOQ. sums
3 SHAPE, form, outline, silhouette
4 BODY, frame, build, physique, torso
5 *public figure*
dignitary, celebrity, leader, personality, character, person, personage, notable, worthy, authority
6 DIAGRAM, illustration, picture, drawing, sketch, image, representation, symbol, sign, emblem, design, pattern
◆ *v*
1 RECKON, guess, estimate, judge, think, suppose, believe, consider, conclude
2 FEATURE, appear, crop up, be mentioned in, be included in

■ **figure on**
bargain for, expect, plan for, be prepared for, depend on, reckon on, take into account

■ **figure out**
work out, calculate, make, compute, reckon, count, estimate, puzzle out, resolve, fathom, reason, understand, see, make out, decipher
COLLOQ. twig, tumble to, latch onto, get the picture; *N Am* dope (out)

■ **figure of speech**
figure, image, imagery, rhetorical device, turn of phrase
See panel at **rhetorical**.

figurehead *n*
1 *the president is merely a figurehead*
front man, name, mouthpiece, dummy, puppet, image, man of straw, nominal head, titular head, token
2 *a figurehead on a ship's prow*
figure, bust, carving

filament *n*
fibre, strand, thread, hair, whisker, wire, tendril, string, cord, cable, pile

filch *v*
steal, take, pilfer, thieve, rob, embezzle, palm, crib
FORMAL misappropriate, peculate, purloin
COLLOQ. lift, nab, nobble, nick, pinch, knock off, snaffle, snitch, swipe
SLANG rip off

file¹ *n, v*
◆ *n*
1 FOLDER, dossier, papers, portfolio, binder, case, box, box file, lever arch file, record, document, data, information, particulars, details
2 *a computer file*
document, text, data set, program, format
3 LINE, queue, column, row, procession, cortège, crocodile, train, string, stream, trail, rake
◆ *v*
1 *file papers*
record, register, note, enter, process, store, classify, categorize, pigeonhole, organize, catalogue, put in place
2 *file a complaint/file for divorce*
make, put in, submit, apply, ask
3 *file out of the building*
walk in line, trail, process, stream, march, parade, troop

file² v

file a rough surface
rub (down), sand, abrade, scour, scrape, grate, rasp, hone, whet, shave, plane, smooth, polish, shape; *Scot* risp

filial *adj*
dutiful, loyal, respectful, devoted, affectionate, loving, fond, daughterly
F3 disloyal, unfilial

filibuster *n, v*
• *n*
delay, delaying tactics, impediment, obstruction, postponement, hindrance
FORMAL procrastination, speechifying, peroration
• *v*
delay, obstruct, impede, put off, prevent, hinder, stall, waste time
FORMAL procrastinate, speechify, perorate
F3 expedite

filigree *n*
fretwork, lacework, lattice, latticework, interlace, lace, scrollwork, tracery, wirework

fill *v, n*
• *v*
1 fill a bucket with water
make full, stock, supply, furnish, satisfy, provide, pack, crowd, occupy, cram, stuff, congest, block, clog, plug, bung, cork, stop (up), close, seal
FORMAL replenish
2 PERVADE, imbue, permeate, soak, impregnate, saturate, charge, spread throughout, riddle
FORMAL suffuse
3 fill a post
take up, hold, occupy, fulfil, complete, perform
F3 1 empty, drain
• *n*
enough, abundance, ample, plenty, sufficiency, sufficient, all you want, more than enough, all you can take
■ **fill in**
1 fill in a form
complete, fill out, answer
2 STAND IN, deputize, understudy, substitute, replace, represent, act for
COLLOQ. *N Am* pinch-hit for
3 INFORM, brief, advise, acquaint, bring up to date
■ **fill out**
1 fill out a form
complete, fill in, answer
2 the child filled out
become/grow fatter, put on/gain weight, become plumper/chubbier

filling *n, adj*
• *n*
contents, inside, stuffing, padding, wadding, filler, substance
• *adj*
satisfying, nutritious, rich, square, solid, stodgy, substantial, heavy, large, big, generous, ample, hearty
F3 insubstantial

fillip *n*
boost, incentive, stimulus, inducement, stimulant, stimulation, encouragement, motivation, goad, impetus, spur, prod, push
COLLOQ. shove
F3 damper

film *n, v*
• *n*
1 MOTION PICTURE, picture, video, cassette, video cassette, cartridge, reel, spool, feature film, short, documentary, screenplay, footage
COLLOQ. movie, flick

Related adjective: cinematic
See panel on next page
2 LAYER, covering, cover, dusting, coat, coating, glaze, skin, membrane, tissue, sheet, veil, blanket, screen, cloud, mist, haze
• *v*
photograph, shoot, record on film, televise, video, videotape
■ **film over**
cloud over, mist over, glaze, become blurred, blur, fog, dull

filmy *adj*
cobwebby, delicate, fragile, fine, gauzy, gossamer, gossamery, light, chiffony, see-through, sheer, shimmering, thin, translucent, transparent, insubstantial, flimsy, floaty
FORMAL diaphanous
F3 opaque

filter *v, n*
• *v*
strain, sieve, sift, riddle, screen, refine, purify, clarify, percolate, ooze, seep, leak, trickle, dribble, drain, leach
FORMAL filtrate
• *n*
strainer, sieve, sifter, colander, mesh, netting, gauze, riddle, membrane

filth *n*
1 DIRT, grime, muck, dross, dung, manure, excrement, sewage, refuse, rubbish, garbage, trash, slime, sludge, soil, effluent, pollution, contamination, corruption, defilement, impurity, uncleanness, foulness, sordidness, squalor, bilge, sullage, wallow; *dialect* addle
TECHNICAL colluvies
OLD gore
FORMAL faeces, putrefaction, putrescence
COLLOQ. gunge, yuck, grot
SLANG crud, gunk, grunge, crap, dreck
2 OBSCENITY, pornography, indecency, vulgarity, coarseness, dirty books
COLLOQ. smut, sleaze, porn, hard porn, blue films, sexploitation, raunchiness
F3 1 cleanness, cleanliness, purity

filthy *adj*
1 DIRTY, soiled, unwashed, grimy, grubby, black, mucky, muddy, slimy, sooty, unclean, contaminated, polluted, decaying, rotten, impure, foul, gross, sordid, squalid, swinish, Augean
FORMAL faecal, putrid, putrefying
COLLOQ. yucky
SLANG crappy, cruddy, manky
2 OBSCENE, dirty, foul, pornographic, smutty, bawdy, adult, suggestive, indecent, explicit, offensive, foul-mouthed, vulgar, coarse, lewd, corrupt, depraved
COLLOQ. blue, raunchy, X-rated
3 DESPICABLE, contemptible, worthless, wretched, nasty, vile, low, base, mean
4 filthy weather
foul, nasty, bad, disagreeable, wet, rainy, stormy, dirty, rough, wild
5 in a filthy mood
angry, bad, bad-tempered, irritable, cross, mean
COLLOQ. stroppy, ratty, crabby, shirty
F3 1 clean, pure **2** decent **4** fine, fair **5** good

final *adj*
1 LAST, latest, closing, concluding, finishing, end, ultimate, terminal, dying, last-minute, eventual
FORMAL terminating
2 CONCLUSIVE, definitive, decisive, definite, settled, incontrovertible, indisputable, irrevocable, unalterable, irrefutable
FORMAL determinate
F3 1 first, initial **2** provisional

Kinds of film include:

action	*slang* chopsocky	expressionist	multiple-story	romantic	spaghetti western
adult	cinéma-vérité	family	murder	romantic comedy	Spielberg
adventure	classic	fantasy	murder mystery	romantic tragedy	spoof
animated	cliff-hanger	farce	musical	*colloq.* rom-com	spy
auteur	comedy	film à clef	newsreel	satirical	surrealist
avant-garde	comedy thriller	film noir	new wave	science-fiction	tear-jerker
biopic	comic-book hero	flashback	nouvelle vague	screenplay	thriller
black comedy	cowboy and	gangster	passion	screwball	tragedy
blockbuster	Indian	gay-lesbian	period epic	comedy	tragicomedy
colloq. blue	crime	historical	police	serial	travelogue
B-movie	cult	romance	police thriller	sexual fantasy	underground
Bollywood	detective	Hitchcock	political	short	Victorian
colloq.	disaster	Hollywood	pornographic	silent	adaptation
bonkbuster	Disney	horror	psychological	*slang* skin flick	vogue
buddy	documentary	James Bond	thriller	*slang* slasher	war
burlesque	Ealing comedy	kitchen sink	realist	*slang* snuff movie	war hero
Carry-on	epic	love story	remake	social comedy	western
cartoon	erotic	low-budget	rites of passage	social problem	whodunnit
chapter-play	escapist	medi(a)eval	road movie	space-age	
Charlie Chaplin	ethnographic	melodrama	robbery	space exploration	

finale *n*

climax, dénouement, culmination, crowning glory, end, ending, conclusion, close, final act, curtain, epilogue

finality *n*

conclusiveness, conviction, decidedness, decisiveness, definiteness, certitude, firmness, resolution, inevitability, inevitableness, unavoidability, incontrovertibility, irreversibility, irrevocability
FORMAL ultimacy

finalize *v*

conclude, finish, complete, round off, work out, resolve, settle, agree, decide, close
COLLOQ. clinch, sew up, wrap up, put the icing on the cake, put the finishing touches to

finally *adv*

lastly, in conclusion, to conclude, ultimately, eventually, at last, at length, in the end, conclusively, once and for all, for ever, for good, permanently, irreversibly, irrevocably, decisively, definitely, in fine
COLLOQ. when all is said and done

finance *n, v*

♦ *n*

1 *corporate finance*
economics, money management, accounting, banking, investment, stock market, business, commerce, trade, money, funding, sponsorship, subsidy
2 *the company's finances*
accounts, affairs, budget, bank account, income, revenue, liquidity, resources, funding, assets, means, capital, wealth, money, cash, funds, wherewithal, savings

♦ *v*

pay for, fund, sponsor, back, support, underwrite, guarantee, subsidize, capitalize, float, set up

financial *adj*

monetary, money, economic, fiscal, budgetary, commercial, entrepreneurial
FORMAL pecuniary

financier *n*

financialist, banker, stockbroker, moneymaker, industrialist, investor, speculator, trader

find *v, n*

♦ *v*

1 DISCOVER, locate, track down, trace, spot, retrieve, recover, regain, get back, unearth, uncover, dig out, turn up, expose, reveal, bring to light, come across, come by, stumble across/on, meet, encounter, detect, recognize, notice, observe, perceive, realize, learn
FORMAL happen upon, chance upon

2 ATTAIN, achieve, win, reach, gain, earn, acquire, secure, obtain, get
FORMAL procure
3 *find it difficult*
consider, think, judge, rate, gauge, declare, believe
FORMAL deem
4 *vitamin A is found in carrots*
be, exist, be present, occur
5 *the judge found him guilty*
judge, adjudicate, arbitrate, try, sit in judgement, deliver/pronounce a verdict, referee, umpire, decree, mediate, examine, sentence, pass sentence, give a sentence, review, rule
FORMAL adjudge
F3 **1** lose

♦ *n*

acquisition, asset, catch, coup, discovery, boon, godsend, bargain, good buy

■ **find out**

1 LEARN, ascertain, establish, identify, understand, pinpoint, discover, detect, note, observe, perceive, see, gather, realize
COLLOQ. get wind of, suss out, twig, cotton on to
2 UNMASK, expose, show up, uncover, reveal, disclose, get at, detect, bring to light, lay bare, catch
COLLOQ. tumble to
SLANG rumble

finding *n*

1 DISCOVERY, find, breakthrough, innovation
2 DECISION, conclusion, judgement, verdict, order, pronouncement, decree, recommendation, award

fine[1] *adj, adv, interj*

♦ *adj*

1 EXCELLENT, outstanding, exceptional, first-class, first-rate, great, superior, exquisite, splendid, magnificent, admirable, brilliant, beautiful, handsome, attractive, lovely, nice, good, select, choice
2 HEALTHY, in good health, well, fit, strong, flourishing, vigorous, all right, in (good) shape, sound, in good condition, on form, shipshape, hale and hearty
3 SATISFACTORY, acceptable, all right, agreeable, good
COLLOQ. OK, up to scratch; *N Am* A-OK
4 *fine weather*
bright, sunny, clear, cloudless, dry, fair, clement, temperate
5 THIN, slender, slim, slight, sheer, gauzy, diaphonous, powdery, flimsy, light, lightweight, fragile, delicate, dainty, narrow, sharp
6 POWDERY, ground, crushed, fine-grained, gossamer
7 EXPENSIVE, elegant, smart, fashionable, stylish, discerning
8 *a fine distinction*

exact, precise, accurate, nice, critical, subtle, minute
COLLOQ. hair-splitting
⊟ 1 mediocre, poor **4** cloudy, dull, inclement, stormy **5** thick, heavy, coarse
◆ *adv*
well, acceptably, all right, satisfactorily, properly, correctly, successfully
COLLOQ. OK
◆ *interj*
all right, very well, very good, good, excellent, agreed, right, yes
COLLOQ. OK

fine² *n, v*
◆ *n*
a speeding fine
penalty, punishment, forfeit, forfeiture, damages
FORMAL amercement, mulct
◆ *v*
penalize, punish
FORMAL amerce, mulct
COLLOQ. sting

finely *adv*
1 EXCELLENTLY, admirably, brilliantly, attractively, magnificently, splendidly
2 THINLY, delicately, lightly, sharply
3 SUBTLY, critically, precisely, exactly, nicely, minutely
⊟ 1 badly, poorly **2** thickly, coarsely **3** generally, widely

finery *n*
decorations, frippery, regalia, best clothes, Sunday best, jewellery, ornaments, showiness, splendour, gaudery, trappings
FORMAL bedizenment
COLLOQ. glad rags, best bib and tucker

finesse *n, v*
◆ *n*
skill, flair, expertise, deftness, adeptness, adroitness, cleverness, delicacy, diplomacy, tact, tactfulness, discretion, subtlety, savoir-faire, elegance, gracefulness, polish, neatness, refinement, sophistication, quickness
COLLOQ. knowhow
◆ *v*
bluff, evade, manipulate, manoeuvre, trick

finger *v*
touch, handle, manipulate, feel, stroke, caress, fondle, paw, fiddle with, toy with, play about with, meddle with
■ **put your finger on**
pinpoint, indicate, isolate, pin down, hit upon, identify, discover, find out, remember, place, locate, recall
COLLOQ. hit the nail on the head

finicky *adj*
1 PARTICULAR, finickety, fussy, fastidious, meticulous, scrupulous, critical, hypercritical, selective, discriminating, faddy
COLLOQ. pernickety, choosy, nit-picking, picky; *N Am* persnickety
2 FIDDLY, intricate, tricky, difficult, delicate
⊟ 1 easy-going **2** easy

finish *v, n*
◆ *v*
1 END, bring/come to an end, stop, cease, be over, complete, accomplish, attain, achieve, fulfil, carry out, get through, discharge, deal with, do, close, settle, round off, culminate, perfect
OLD absolve, outwork
FORMAL conclude, terminate, discontinue, consummate
COLLOQ. wind up, polish off, pack in, wrap up, sew up, be done with, get shot of, be through, call it a day, put paid to
2 USE UP, use, consume, devour, eat, drink, exhaust, drain, empty, run out of
FORMAL deplete, expend

COLLOQ. down, guzzle, scoff, polish off
3 DESTROY, ruin, exterminate, get rid of, do away with, annihilate, defeat, overcome, overwhelm, overpower, conquer, rout, overthrow, crush, topple, bring down, get the better of
COLLOQ. wipe out
4 VENEER, apply, lacquer, varnish, coat, polish, gloss, glaze
⊟ 1 begin, start; *formal* commence
◆ *n*
1 END, completion, conclusion, close, ending, finale, culmination, accomplishment, achievement, perfection, fulfilment, discharge, ruin, destruction
FORMAL termination, cessation
COLLOQ. winding-up, wind-up, curtains
2 SURFACE, appearance, texture, grain, polish, shine, gloss, glaze, coating, veneer, lacquer, lustre, lamination, smoothness
⊟ 1 beginning, start; *formal* commencement

finished *adj*
1 COMPLETED, complete, concluded, dealt with, over, at an end
FORMAL consummated
COLLOQ. over and done with, through, wrapped up, sewn up
2 USELESS, defeated, ruined, doomed, lost, drained, exhausted, empty, spent, undone, unwanted, unpopular
COLLOQ. done for, played out, zonked
3 **a finished performance**
accomplished, proficient, professional, expert, polished, impeccable, faultless, flawless, perfect, masterly, consummate, refined, sophisticated, urbane, virtuoso
⊟ 1 unfinished, incomplete **2** useful, productive **3** incompetent; *colloq.* hopeless

finite *adj*
limited, restricted, bounded, demarcated, terminable, definable, fixed, measurable, calculable, countable, numbered
⊟ infinite

fire *n, v*
◆ *n*
1 FLAMES, blaze, bonfire, inferno, burning, combustion, holocaust
FORMAL conflagration
Related adjective: igneous
2 GUNFIRE, attack, firing, bombing, shelling, sniping, bombardment, barrage, cannonade, fusillade, salvo, fire, flak
3 HEATER, radiator, convector, fan
4 PASSION, feeling, ardour, excitement, dynamism, eagerness, enthusiasm, spirit, energy, liveliness, life, vigour, animation, vivacity, verve, fervour, intensity, heat, radiance, inventiveness, creativity, sparkle
5 CRITICISM, condemnation, disapproval, fault-finding, censure, reproof, blame
FORMAL disparagement
COLLOQ. brickbat, flak, slating, slamming, knocking, stick
◆ *v*
1 IGNITE, light, put a match to, kindle, set fire to, set on fire, set alight, set ablaze
COLLOQ. torch
2 **fire a missile**
shoot, launch, set off, let off, detonate, discharge, explode, trigger, hurl
3 DISMISS, discharge, eject, get rid of
COLLOQ. sack, axe, boot out, kick out, show someone the door, give someone their cards, give someone the sack/ push/boot/elbow
4 EXCITE, whet, enliven, galvanize, electrify, stir (up), arouse, rouse, motivate, stimulate, inspire, animate, inflame, incite, spark off, trigger off

■ **on fire**
1 IN FLAMES, burning, alight, ignited, flaming, aflame, blazing, ablaze
2 ENTHUSIASTIC, passionate, excited, eager, ardent, fiery, energetic, creative, inventive, sparkling, inspired

firearm *n*
gun, weapon, automatic, handgun, pistol, revolver, rifle, shotgun, musket
See panel at **weapon**.

firebrand *n*
revolutionary, radical, fanatic, militant, extremist, agitator, troublemaker, rabble-rouser, incendiary, rebel, insurrectionist, insurgent

fireplace

Types of fireplace include:

backboiler	forge	open fire
boiler	furnace	oven
bonfire	gas fire	stove
brazier	grate	paraffin stove
campfire	hearth	wood burning
electric fire	incinerator	stove
firebox	kiln	

fireproof *adj*
non-flammable, incombustible, non-inflammable, flameproof, fire-resistant, flame-resistant,
F3 flammable, inflammable, combustible

fireworks *n*
1 PYROTECHNICS, explosions, illuminations, feux d'artifice
2 UPROAR, trouble, outburst, frenzy, fit, rage, rows, storm, temper, sparks, hysterics

Types of firework include:

banger	fountain	shell
cake	golden rain	sky-rocket
Catherine wheel	indoor firework	sparkler
Chinese cracker	jumping-jack	squib
cracker	mine	waterfall
firecracker	pinwheel	
firewriting	rocket	
flare	roman candle	

firm¹ *adj*
1 *firm ground*
dense, compressed, compact, close-grained, concentrated, set, solid, solidified, substantive, hard, hardened, unyielding, stiff, rigid, inflexible, inelastic
2 FIXED, embedded, established, fast, tight, secure, secured, fastened, anchored, riveted, immovable, tight, motionless, unshak(e)able, stationary, steady, stable, set, sturdy, strong
3 *a firm handshake*
strong, vigorous, forceful, solid, substantial
4 *a firm decision*
definite, settled, fixed, decided, established, unchangeable, unalterable
5 ADAMANT, unshak(e)able, resolute, resolved, decided, determined, dogged, unwavering, unfaltering, unswerving, unflinching, strict, hard, inflexible, stubborn, obstinate, constant, steadfast, staunch, tenacious
FORMAL obdurate
6 *firm friends*
close, dependable, true, sure, committed, unchanging, constant, long-standing, long-lasting, good, boon, steady, stable, steadfast, staunch
F3 1 soft, flabby **2** unsteady, shaky **3** limp, weak **4** vague, changeable **5** hesitant, non-committal

firm² *n*
a firm of accountants

company, corporation, business, enterprise, concern, house, establishment, institution, organization, association, partnership, syndicate, conglomerate

firmament *n*
sky, skies, heaven(s), atmosphere, space, expanse, the blue, ether
OLD empyrean, welkin

firmly *adv*
securely, tightly, steadily, stably, sturdily, strongly, robustly, unshakably, unwaveringly, strictly, immovably, unalterably, unchangeably, unflinchingly, resolutely, inflexibly, decisively, definitely, determinedly, doggedly, enduringly, staunchly, steadfastly
F3 loosely, vaguely, hesitantly, uncertainly

firmness *n*
1 STIFFNESS, hardness, rigidity, solidity, density, compactness, inflexibility, inelasticity, tautness, tension, fixity, immovability, tightness
2 STRENGTH, strength of will, determination, resolution, resolve, dependability, reliability, staunchness, steadfastness, steadiness, willpower, constancy, conviction, changelessness, stability, strictness, resistance, sureness, doggedness
FORMAL indomitability, obduracy
F3 1 softness **2** uncertainty

first *adj, adv, n*
♦ *adj*
1 INITIAL, opening, introductory, preliminary, beginning, inaugural, elementary, primary, basic, fundamental, rudimentary
2 ORIGINAL, earliest, earlier, prior, primitive, initial, oldest, eldest, senior
FORMAL prim(a)eval, primordial
3 CHIEF, main, key, cardinal, principal, head, leading, foremost, ruling, sovereign, highest, greatest, uppermost, paramount, best, prime, supreme, predominant, pre-eminent
F3 1 last, final
♦ *adv*
initially, to begin with, at first, first of all, firstly, in the first place, to start with, first and foremost, at the beginning, at the outset, beforehand, before anything else, originally, in preference, rather, sooner
♦ *n*
beginning, start, opening, introduction, outset, origin(s), original, prototype, unveiling, première
FORMAL commencement, inception
COLLOQ. the word go, square one

first-born *adj*
elder, eldest, older, oldest, senior
OLD eigne, primogenit
FORMAL aîné(e), primogenital, primogenitary, primogenitive

first-class *adj*
first-rate, second-to-none, matchless, peerless, top, top-flight, leading, supreme, superior, prime, excellent, outstanding, superlative, premier, exceptional, splendid, superb, fine, admirable
COLLOQ. super, cool, fabulous, top-notch, A1, ace, crack, out of this world
SLANG way-out, radical, mega, mean, wicked, crucial

firsthand *adj, adv*
direct(ly), immediate(ly), personal(ly), in service, on the job
COLLOQ. straight from the horse's mouth, hands-on
F3 indirect(ly)

firstly *adv*
in the first place, initially, to begin with, at first, first of all, to start with, first and foremost, at the outset

first name *n*
forename, Christian name, given name, baptismal name

first-rate *adj*
first-class, second-to-none, matchless, peerless, top, top-flight, leading, supreme, superior, prime, excellent, outstanding, superlative, premier, exceptional, splendid, superb, fine, admirable
COLLOQ. super, fabulous, top-notch, A1, ace, crack, out of this world
SLANG way-out, cool, radical, mega, mean, wicked, crucial
E3 inferior

fiscal *adj*
financial, tax, monetary, money, economic, budgetary, treasury, capital
FORMAL pecuniary

fiscally *adv*
financially, economically
FORMAL pecuniarily
COLLOQ. moneywise

fish *n, v*
Related adjectives: piscine, ichthyic, ichthyoid
♦ *v*
1 GO FISHING, angle, trawl
2 *she fished in her bag for a pen*
delve, hunt, search, grope
3 *fish for information*
try to get, try to obtain, angle, look, ask
FORMAL seek
■ **fish out**
produce, take out, extract, find, retrieve, haul out, pull out, come up with, dredge up

---

Types of fish, shellfish and crustaceans include:

bass	goldfish	prawn
bloater	guppy	rainbow trout
Bombay duck	haddock	roach
bream	hake	roughy
brill	halibut	salmon
brisling	herring	sardine
carp	hoki	scallop
catfish	king prawn	shark
chub	kipper	shrimp
clam	lantern fish	skate
cockle	ling	snapper
cod	lobster	sole
coley	mackerel	sprat
conger eel	marlin	squid
crab	minnow	stickleback
crayfish (or *NAm*	monkfish	stingray
crawfish)	mullet	sturgeon
cuttlefish	mussel	swordfish
dab	octopus	tench
dace	oyster	trout
dogfish	perch	tuna
dory	pike	turbot
Dover sole	pilchard	whelk
eel	piranha	whitebait
flounder	plaice	whiting
fugu	pollock	*Aust* yabbie

See also **shark**.

---

fisherman *n*
angler, fisher, rod, rodfisher, rodman, rodsman, rodster
FORMAL piscator, piscatorian

fishing *n*
catching fish, angling, trawling
Related adjectives: piscatorial, piscatory, halieutic

fishy *adj*
1 *a fishy taste*
fish-like
FORMAL piscatorial, piscatory, piscine
2 ODD, suspicious, questionable, shady, suspect, doubtful, dubious, implausible, improbable, funny, irregular, queer
E3 honest, legitimate

fission *n*
splitting, breaking, division, rupture, parting, rending, schism, severance, scission, cleavage, cleaving

fissure *n*
crack, opening, cleft, fracture, breach, break, cranny, crevasse, crevice, rent, rift, rupture, chasm, hole, gap, gape, gash, slit, split, chink, fault, vein, shake
TECHNICAL grike, foramen, sulcus, porta, zygon
OLD rime
FORMAL cleavage, interstice, scissure

fist *n*
palm, hand, clenched hand, knuckles
COLLOQ. paw
SLANG mitt, bunch of fives

fit¹ *adj, v, n*
♦ *adj*
1 HEALTHY, well, in good health, able-bodied, in good form, in good shape, in shape, in good condition, in trim, sound, sturdy, strong, hardy, robust, vigorous, flourishing, hale and hearty
2 SUITABLE, appropriate, apt, fitting, correct, right, good enough, proper, due, convenient, ready, prepared, able, capable, competent, qualified, equipped, trained, eligible, worthy
OLD seemly
FORMAL decorous, pertinent
E3 1 unfit, out of condition 2 unsuitable, unworthy
♦ *v*
1 *Do the shoes fit you?*
get into, be the right size for, be the right shape for, be a good fit
COLLOQ. fit like a glove
2 MATCH, correspond, conform, follow, agree, tally, suit, be suitable, be appropriate, harmonize, go, be right, be consistent, belong, dovetail, interlock, connect, join, put together, meet, accommodate
FORMAL concur, be consonant
3 *fit a washing machine*
install, insert, put in, position, place, put in position/place, attach, arrange, fix
4 ALTER, modify, change, adjust, adapt, regulate, tailor, shape, fashion, accommodate
5 EQUIP, qualify, train, make suitable, prepare, provide, make ready, prime, condition, arm, coach, groom, tailor
♦ *n*
correlation, relationship, correspondence, equivalence, conformity, agreement
FORMAL concurrence
■ **fit in**
match, correspond, conform, agree, square, belong, slot, squeeze
FORMAL accord, concur
■ **fit out/up**
equip, rig out, kit out, outfit, provide, supply, furnish, prepare, arm
FORMAL accoutre

fit² *n*
1 SEIZURE, convulsion, spasm, paroxysm, attack
TECHNICAL ictus
2 OUTBREAK, bout, spell, burst, surge, outburst, eruption, explosion, tantrum
■ **in fits and starts**
sporadically, fitfully, spasmodically, intermittently, occasionally, irregularly, unevenly, brokenly, erratically, off and on
E3 regularly, steadily

fitful *adj*
sporadic, intermittent, occasional, spasmodic, erratic,

irregular, disconnected, haphazard, uneven, broken, disturbed, patchy

F3 steady, regular, continuous

fitfully *adv*

in/by fits and starts, spasmodically, sporadically, intermittently, occasionally, unevenly, erratically, irregularly, haphazardly

F3 steadily, regularly, continuously

fitness *n*

1 SUITABILITY, qualifications, readiness, preparedness, eligibility, capability, appropriateness, aptness, competence, adequacy, applicability, condition
OLD opportunity, property
FORMAL pertinence

2 HEALTH, healthiness, strength, vigour, condition, shape, trim, good health, robustness, haleness

F3 1 unsuitability **2** unfitness

fitted *adj*

1 *fitted wardrobe*

built-in, permanent, integral, integrated, fixed

2 EQUIPPED, rigged out, provided, furnished, appointed, prepared, armed, tailored, shaped

3 SUITED, right, suitable, fit, qualified, cut out

fitting *adj, n*

• *adj*

apt, appropriate, suitable, fit, correct, right, proper, desirable, deserved
OLD seemly, meet
FORMAL decorous

F3 unsuitable, improper

• *n*

1 *light fittings*

attachment, accessory, connection, part, component, piece, unit, fitment, fixture, unit

2 *the price includes fittings*

equipment, furnishings, furniture, fixtures, installations, fitments, accessories, extras
FORMAL accoutrements, appointments

fix *v, n*

• *v*

1 FASTEN, secure, tie, bind, attach, join, connect, link, couple, anchor, affix, clamp, pin, nail, screw, rivet, stick, glue, cement, set, harden, solidify, stiffen, stabilize, plant, root, implant, embed, establish, install, station, lodge, locate, situate, position

2 *fix a date/price*

arrange, set, specify, define, agree on, decide, determine, name, settle, resolve, finalize, arrive at, sort
TECHNICAL valorize

3 MEND, repair, patch up, correct, rectify, adjust, restore, remedy, see to, put right

4 *fix your eyes/attention*

direct, aim, focus, concentrate, turn, point, level, hold, attract, draw

5 *fix your hair*

arrange, tidy, groom, adjust, dress, prepare, put in order, order, do, neaten, straighten, comb

6 *fix a race*

rig, set up, falsify, fake, manoeuvre, tamper with, manipulate
COLLOQ. fiddle

7 *fix some food for you*

prepare, make, get ready, put together, cook
COLLOQ. knock up, throw together

F3 1 move, shift **3** damage **5** untidy

• *n*

1 DILEMMA, quandary, predicament, plight, difficulty, corner, mess, muddle
COLLOQ. hole, (tight) spot, bind, pickle, scrape, jam, the soup

2 *there's no quick fix to the problem*

solution, answer, remedy, resolution, way out

3 INJECTION, dose, shot, hit
COLLOQ. score, slug, bang

4 RIGGING, manipulation, scam
COLLOQ. fiddle
SLANG set-up

▪ **fix up**

arrange, organize, settle, agree on, plan, lay on, provide, supply, furnish, equip, settle, sort out, produce, bring about

fixated *adj*

obsessed, preoccupied, infatuated, compulsive, pathological, dominated, gripped, phobic, neurotic
COLLOQ. hung up on

fixation *n*

preoccupation, obsession, mania, fetish, infatuation, compulsion, complex, *idée fixe*, phobia, neurosis
COLLOQ. thing, hang-up

fixed *adj*

1 *fixed times/opinions*

decided, settled, established, constant, definite, arranged, planned, set, firm, rigid, inflexible, entrenched, immobile, steady, secure, fast, rooted, permanent
COLLOQ. cast/set in stone

2 *a fixed smile*

fake, insincere, false, pretended
COLLOQ. pretend, phoney

F3 1 variable, varying, flexible, mobile

fixedly *adv*

intently, attentively, hard, watchfully, closely, steadily, searchingly, staringly

fixity *n*

permanence, persistence, constancy, stability, steadiness, fixedness
FORMAL immutability

fixture *n*

1 *fixtures and fittings*

equipment, furnishings, furniture, installations

2 *a sports fixture*

event, match, game, competition, contest, race, round, meeting

fizz *v, n*

• *v*

effervesce, sparkle, bubble, froth, foam, fizzle, hiss

• *n*

1 EFFERVESCENCE, bubbles, bubbling, fizz, fizziness, gas, gassiness, sparkle, foam, foaming, froth, frothing, ferment, fermentation

2 LIVELINESS, sparkle, vivacity, vitality, animation, buoyancy, enthusiasm, high spirits, excitedness, excitement, exhilaration, exuberance
COLLOQ. vim, zing, zip

fizzle

▪ **fizzle out**

collapse, come to nothing, die away, die down, fall through, fail, come to grief, stop, subside, disappear, evaporate, taper off, peter out
FORMAL dissipate
COLLOQ. fold, flop

fizzy *adj*

effervescent, sparkling, aerated, carbonated, gassy, bubbly, bubbling, frothy, foaming

flab *n*

fat, fatness, obesity, plumpness, stoutness, solidness, bulk, chubbiness, overweight, paunch, pot (belly), blubber
FORMAL corpulence
COLLOQ. spare tyre

flabbergasted *adj*

amazed, confounded, astonished, astounded, staggered,

dumbfounded, speechless, stunned, dazed, nonplussed, overcome, overwhelmed
COLLOQ. bowled over, blown away, knocked for six, gobsmacked

flabby adj
1 FLESHY, soft, yielding, flaccid, limp, floppy, drooping, hanging, sagging, slack, loose, lax, fat, overweight, plump
2 *flabby business corporations*
wasteful, uneconomical, disorganized, inefficient, sloppy, slack, lax
F3 1 firm, strong, lean, toned 2 lean

flaccid adj
limp, drooping, droopy, flabby, floppy, lax, loose, sagging, slack, soft, toneless, weak, nerveless, relaxed, clammy
F3 firm, hard

flag¹ n, v
♦ n
Related adjective: vexillary
♦ v
1 SIGNAL, wave, salute, motion, hail, wave down, signal to stop
2 MARK, indicate, label, tag, note

Types of flag include:

banderol	ensign	signal flag
banner	gonfalon	standard
bunting	jack	streamer
burgee	oriflamme	swallow tail
colours	pennant	vexillum
cornet	pilot flag	

Names of flags include:

Blue Ensign	Red Crescent	Star-spangled
Blue Peter	Red Cross	Banner
Crescent	Red Ensign	Tricolour
Hammer and	Rising Sun	Union Jack
Sickle	Saltire	White Ensign
Jolly Roger	Skull and	Yellow Jack
Old Glory	Crossbones	
Olympic Flag	Stars and Stripes	

---

flag² v
spirits were beginning to flag
lessen, diminish, decline, fall (off), subside, wane, ebb, sink, slump, dwindle, peter out, taper off, fade, fail, weaken, slow, falter, tire, grow tired, weary, wilt, droop, hang down, sag, flop, faint, die
FORMAL abate
F3 revive

flagellation n
beating, whipping, flogging, lashing, scourging, thrashing, flaying, whaling
OLD verberation
FORMAL castigation, chastisement, vapulation

flagging adj
lessening, diminishing, declining, subsiding, sinking, dwindling, ebbing, waning, decreasing, fading, failing, weakening, slowing, faltering, sagging, tiring, drooping, wilting
FORMAL abating
F3 returning, reviving

flagon n
bottle, decanter, carafe, jug, pitcher, flask, ewer, vessel, container

flagrant adj
scandalous, outrageous, glaring, disgraceful, dreadful, shameless, open, blatant, atrocious, enormous, infamous, notorious, bold, brazen, audacious, ostentatious,

barefaced, naked, conspicuous, unashamed, undisguised, overt, rank, gross, arrant
FORMAL egregious, heinous
F3 covert, secret

! flagrant or **blatant?**
See panel at **blatant**.

---

flail v
wave uncontrolledly, swing wildly, thresh, thrash, batter, beat, whip, strike

flair n
1 SKILL, ability, natural ability, aptitude, faculty, gift, talent, bent, facility, knack, mastery, genius, feel
2 STYLE, taste, discernment, acumen, elegance, stylishness, panache
F3 1 inability, ineptitude

flak n
criticism, blame, censure, complaints, disapproval, fault-finding, hostility, opposition, abuse, condemnation
FORMAL animadversions, aspersions, disapprobation, disparagement, invective
COLLOQ. bad press, brickbats, stick, knocking, panning

flake n, v
♦ n
scale, peeling, paring, shaving, scurf, sliver, shiver, wafer, chip, splinter, bit, particle, fragment, smut, spangle, flaught
TECHNICAL squama, flocculus, desquamation, exfoliation, furfur
OLD (*Shakesp*) flaw
♦ v
scale, peel, chip, splinter, blister
TECHNICAL desquamate, exfoliate
■ **flake out**
collapse, pass out, faint, keel over, drop, fall asleep, relax completely

flaky adj
dry, scaly, scurfy, laminar, layered
TECHNICAL squamate, squamose, squamous, flocculent, desquamative, desquamatory, exfoliative, furfuraceous, scabrous

flamboyance n
showiness, ostentation, colour, brilliance, glamour, extravagance, style, dash, élan, panache, theatricality
COLLOQ. pizzazz
F3 diffidence, restraint

flamboyant adj
showy, ostentatious, flashy, gaudy, bright, colourful, brilliant, exciting, dazzling, striking, dashing, extravagant, rich, glamorous, elaborate, ornate, florid, baroque, rococo, theatrical
F3 modest, restrained

flame v, n
♦ v
1 BURN, catch fire, flare, blaze, burst into flames
2 GLOW, glare, flash, beam, shine, sparkle, gleam, radiate, flush, go/become/turn red, redden
♦ n
1 FIRE, blaze, light, brightness, gleam, glow, heat, warmth
FORMAL conflagration
2 PASSION, ardour, fervour, warmth, fervency, excitement, enthusiasm, eagerness, keenness, zeal, intensity, radiance, fire
3 *an old flame*
lover, partner, boyfriend, girlfriend, sweetheart
■ **in flames**
on fire, burning, alight, ignited, flaming, aflame, blazing, ablaze

flameproof adj
fireproof, non-flammable, incombustible, non-

inflammable, fire-resistant, flame-resistant
F3 flammable, inflammable, combustible

flaming *adj*
1 *a flaming torch*
burning, alight, aflame, blazing, on fire, in flames, fiery, brilliant, scintillating, red-hot, glowing, raging, smouldering
2 *a flaming red*
intense, vivid, bright, brilliant, blazing
3 *a flaming row/temper*
furious, angry, enraged, raging, infuriated, incensed, mad, violent
4 CURSED, damned, wretched, detestable, abominable, hateful, loathsome, odious, vile, fiendish, annoying, unpleasant, pernicious, infamous
FORMAL execrable
COLLOQ. blasted, blooming, blinking, flipping, darned, dashed, confounded, infernal, dratting
SLANG bloody; (*vulgar*) frigging; (*taboo*) fucking

flammable *adj*
inflammable, ignitable, combustible, burnable
F3 non-flammable, incombustible, flameproof, fire-resistant, flame-resistant

flank *n, v*
♦ *n*
1 *the animal's flank*
side, quarter, wing, loin, haunch, hip, thigh
2 *the enemy's flank*
side, edge, wing
♦ *v*
edge, fringe, skirt, line, border, bound, confine, wall, screen

flannel *n*
nonsense, rubbish, flattery, blarney, smooth talk
FORMAL blandishments
COLLOQ. waffle, rot, sweet talk, soft soap, spiel

flap *v, n*
♦ *v*
flutter, vibrate, wave, agitate, shake, wag, waggle, flag, flip, slat, swing, sway, swish, thrash, thresh, beat, move up and down, move from side to side; *dialect* flacker, waff, wap; *Scot* flaff, wallop
OLD winnow
♦ *n*
1 FOLD, fly, lapel, overhang, overlap, covering, fall, tongue, tab, lug, tag, tail, skirt, apron, lap, lappet
TECHNICAL aileron, elevon, visor, epiglottis, loma, great omentum, epiploon, tuner, barn-door
OLD aventail
2 FLUTTER, fluttering, wave, shake, wag, waggle, beat, swing, sway, swish; *Scot* flaff, wap
3 PANIC, fuss, commotion, fluster, agitation, flutter, dither
COLLOQ. state, tiswas, tizwas, tizzy, stew

flare *v, n*
♦ *v*
1 FLAME, burn, blaze, glare, glow, gleam, glitter, sparkle, flash, flicker, burst, explode, erupt
2 BROADEN, widen, flare out, spread out, splay
♦ *n*
1 FLAME, blaze, glare, flash, flicker, burst, glimmer, gleam, dazzle
2 SIGNAL, distress signal, warning signal, beacon, light, rocket, beam
3 BROADENING, widening, spread, splay
■ **flare up**
erupt, break out, blaze, burst out, lose your temper, lose control
COLLOQ. explode, blow up, boil over, lose your cool, blow a fuse, blow your top, burst a blood vessel, do your nut, flip

your lid, fly into a rage, fly off the handle, foam at the mouth, freak out, go ape, go ballistic, go berserk, go mad, go off the deep end, go up the wall, hit the roof, lose your rag, throw a wobbly; *Aust* go to market; *Aust & NZ* do your block

flare-up *n*
eruption, outburst, discharge, ejection, emission, venting, outbreak, explosion, rash, inflammation

flash *v, n, adj*
♦ *v*
1 BEAM, shine, light up, lighten, flare, blaze, glare, glance, gleam, glimmer, glisten, glint, flicker, twinkle, sparkle, blink, glitter, shimmer, scintillate, dance
FORMAL coruscate, fulgurate, fulminate
2 *the train flashed past*
streak, fly, shoot, speed, dart, race, dash, tear, zoom, rush, bolt, career, bound
3 *flashed her engagement ring*
flourish, brandish, flaunt, show off, display
4 EXPOSE YOURSELF, show your genitals, commit indecent exposure
♦ *n*
1 *flash of lightning*
beam, ray, shaft, spark, blaze, flare, burst, streak, lightning, bolt, fork, glare, glimmer, glitter, gleam, glint, flicker, twinkle, sparkle, shimmer, scintillation, flaught, *bluette*
OLD fire-flag, fire-flaught; (*Spenser*) flake; *Scot* glaiks
FORMAL coruscation, fulguration
2 *a flash of inspiration*
burst, outburst, outbreak, sudden appearance, show, display, exhibition, concetto
♦ *adj*
showy, ostentatious, smart, fashionable, expensive, glamorous, gaudy, kitsch, pretentious
■ **in a flash**
in an instant, instantly, in a moment, in a split second, in a twinkling, in the twinkling of an eye, in no time (at all), in less than no time, in a trice
COLLOQ. pdq, pronto, in a jiffy, in two shakes of a lamb's tail, before you can say Jack Robinson

---

Synonym nuances
verb sense 1
Beam suggests directing a shaft of light, whilst **shine** conveys an image of constant, reflecting light: *the spotlight shone on the models.* The term **light up**, may be used to suggest infusing with light. **Flare** and **blaze** suggest a quick explosion of light or flame.
  You can use **glare** to suggest a constant, dazzling effect: *the glare of headlights.* The terms **glance** and **glint** suggest a momentary catching of the light causing a flash: *a light that glinted on the glancing raindrops.* **Gleam** and **glimmer** imply a more muted light, and **glisten** is suggestive of a wet or oily appearance: *the rain glistened on his skin.* To convey the idea of constant subtle movement of light you could use **flicker** or **scintillate**: *the waters of the river were broken and scintillating*, or **twinkle**, which is usually associated with an attractive sight such as the stars: *the stars twinkled in the black sky.*
  A sense of movement and prettiness is also conveyed in the verbs **sparkle** and **glitter**. **Blink** implies a broken ray but does not have the same appealing connotations, while **dance** implies a much more erratic but attractive movement: *the light danced on the water*, and **shimmer** conjures up images of waves of light: *a heat haze shimmered above the fields.*

---

flashy *adj*
showy, ostentatious, flamboyant, glamorous, bold, loud, garish, gaudy, jazzy, flash, pretentious, tawdry, cheap, vulgar, tasteless, kitsch, showing poor taste

COLLOQ. tacky, glitzy; *Aust* lairy
SLANG bling-bling
F3 plain, tasteful

flask *n*
bottle, carafe, flagon, decanter, vessel, container, matrass; *dialect* flacket; *Can* mick
OLD lekythos

flat *n, adj, adv*
♦ *n*
apartment, penthouse, maisonette, tenement, flatlet, rooms, suite, bedsit(ter); *Aust & NZ* home unit
COLLOQ. pad
♦ *adj*
1 LEVEL, plane, even, smooth, uniform, unbroken, levelled, horizontal, outstretched, prostrate, prone, recumbent, reclining, low, spread-eagled
TECHNICAL homaloidal
FORMAL supine
COLLOQ. flat as a pancake
2 SHALLOW, not deep, not thick, not tall
3 *a flat tyre*
punctured, burst, deflated, collapsed, ruptured
COLLOQ. blown-out
4 *a flat battery*
dead, used up, finished
COLLOQ. bust, kaput, duff
5 DULL, boring, monotonous, tedious, uninteresting, unexciting, stale, lifeless, toneless, dead, spiritless, lacklustre, vapid, insipid, bland, weak, watery, empty, pointless
6 *a flat refusal*
absolute, utter, total, unequivocal, categorical, positive, unconditional, unqualified, outright, out-and-out, downright, point-blank, direct, straight, explicit, plain, final, definite, complete
7 *feel flat*
depressed, low, discouraged, dejected, downcast, despondent, miserable, inactive, sluggish, slack, slow
COLLOQ. down
8 *charge a flat price*
set, fixed, standard, definite, stock, regular, firm, rigid, planned, arranged
9 *the market was flat*
sluggish, slow, inactive, quiet, slack, sleepy, stagnant, dull, dead, lifeless
10 STILL, dead, no longer fizzy
F3 1 bumpy, vertical, upright **2** deep, thick, tall **4** charged **5** exciting, full **6** equivocal **7** happy, cheerful, lively **8** variable, negotiable **9** active, busy **10** fizzy, effervescent, sparkling
♦ *adv*
directly, outright, categorically, absolutely, straight, point-blank, completely, totally, utterly, entirely, exactly, plainly, precisely

■ **flat out**
at top speed, at full speed, all out, as fast as possible, hard, as hard as possible, for all you are worth

flatly *adv*
categorically, point-blank, positively, absolutely, completely, uncompromisingly, unconditionally, unhesitatingly
FORMAL peremptorily

flatness *n*
1 EVENNESS, levelness, smoothness, horizontality, uniformity
2 DULLNESS, monotony, tedium, boredom, staleness, emptiness, tastelessness, insipidity, vapidity
FORMAL languor

flatten *v*
1 SMOOTH, iron, press, roll, crush, squash, compress, plane, level, make flat, make even, even out

2 KNOCK DOWN, knock to the ground, prostrate, floor, fell, demolish, raze, tear down, defeat, overwhelm, subdue

flatter *v*
1 PRAISE, compliment, adulate, fawn, cringe, sing the praises of, wheedle, toady, kowtow, humour, play up to, court, pay court to, curry favour with, palaver, sawder, soft-sawder, tickle the ear of, soap, soothe, adulate; *Scot* fleech, phrase; *Irish* soothe; *N Am* stroke
OLD claw, collogue, gloze, smooth it, bear in hand, beslobber, beslaver; (*Shakesp*) make fair weather, word
FORMAL sycophantize, eulogize, inveigle, blandish
COLLOQ. flannel, sweet-talk, butter up, creep, suck up to, make up to, soft-soap, massage someone's ego, lay it on; *N Am* cozy up (with)
2 *that dress flatters you*
show off, make someone look attractive, look good on, become, suit, enhance, embellish, grace, show to advantage, befit
F3 1 criticize

flatterer *n*
adulator, sycophant, fawner, groveller, lackey, toady, bootlicker, lickspittle
FORMAL encomiast, eulogizer
COLLOQ. back-scratcher, creep, creeper, crawler, yes-man
F3 critic, opponent

flattering *adj*
complimentary, kind, favourable, enhancing, gratifying, becoming, adulatory, ingratiating, fawning, fulsome, effusive, servile, smooth-spoken, smooth-tongued, honeyed, honey-tongued, sugared, sugary
OLD gnathonic
FORMAL laudatory, obsequious, sycophantic, unctuous
COLLOQ. sweet-talking, soft-soaping
F3 candid, uncompromising, unflattering

flattery *n*
adulation, praise, blarney, fulsomeness, compliments, cajolery, cajolement, fawning, toadyism, ingratiation, servility, butter, flapdoodle, soft sawder; *dialect* carny; *Scot* fleeching, fleechment; *N Am* taffy
OLD glozing, fair words, court holy water
FORMAL eulogy, sycophancy, blandishments, laudation
COLLOQ. sweet talk, soft soap, flannel, back scratching
SLANG sugar
OLD SLANG soap
F3 criticism

flatulence *n*
wind, windiness, gas, gassiness
FORMAL eructation, flatus, borborygmus, ventosity
COLLOQ. farting

flatulent *v*
windy, gassy
FORMAL ventose

flaunt *v*
show off, display, parade, flourish, brandish, exhibit, boast, air, sport, vaunt, wield, dangle, flash; *dialect* strout; *Scot* skyre
OLD disport, strut

⚠ flaunt or flout?
To *flaunt* something is 'to show it off or display it ostentatiously': *She was flaunting her new fur coat in front of her colleagues. Flout* means 'to treat with contempt, to refuse to obey or comply with': *He constantly flouts authority/the law.*

---

flavour *n, v*
♦ *n*
1 TASTE, tang, smack, savour, relish, piquancy, zest, aroma, odour
COLLOQ. zing
2 QUALITY, property, character, style, aspect, feeling, feel,

atmosphere, tone, spirit, essence, nature, soul
3 HINT, indication, impression, suggestion, touch, tinge, tone
♦ v
season, spice (up), ginger up, infuse, imbue, lace

flavouring n
seasoning, flavour, spice, zest, tang, relish, piquancy, essence, extract, additive
COLLOQ. zing

flaw n
defect, imperfection, fault, weakness, weak spot, Achilles' heel, foible, shortcoming, failing, fallacy, lapse, slip, error, mistake, blemish, spot, mark, speck, crack, crevice, fissure, cleft, rent, split, tear, rift, chip, break, fracture, craze
TECHNICAL brack, thief, windshake, hamartia
OLD gall
COLLOQ. fly in the ointment

flawed adj
imperfect, defective, faulty, blemished, marked, damaged, spoilt, marred, cracked, chipped, broken, unsound, fallacious, erroneous
F⊒ flawless, perfect

flawless adj
perfect, faultless, unblemished, without blemish, spotless, immaculate, impeccable, stainless, sound, intact, whole, unbroken, undamaged, unimpaired
F⊒ flawed, imperfect, blemished

flay v
1 SKIN, skin alive, upbraid, revile, scourge, flog, flench
OLD uncase
FORMAL excoriate, castigate, execrate, lambast
2 CRITICIZE, condemn, find fault with, attack, denounce, run down, slate
COLLOQ. slam, knock, pan, pull/tear apart, pull to pieces, tear a strip off

fleck v, n
♦ v
dot, spot, mark, speckle, dapple, mottle, stipple, freckle, streak, sprinkle, dust, spatter
♦ n
dot, point, spot, mark, stain, speck, speckle, freckle, streak

fledgling n, adj
♦ n
beginner, newcomer, novice, apprentice, learner, recruit, trainee, tiro, neophyte, novitiate, tenderfoot
COLLOQ. greenhorn, rookie
♦ adj
emergent, budding, coming (out), developing, emerging, embryonic, rising, independent
FORMAL burgeoning, nascent

flee v
run away, bolt, fly, take flight, take off, make off, cut and run, escape, get away, rush, decamp, abscond, leave, depart, withdraw, retreat, vanish, disappear, make yourself scarce
COLLOQ. get out, push along/off, make tracks, quit, scat, scoot, scram, take to your heels, make yourself scarce, shove off, bunk off, clear off, split, scarper, skedaddle, vamoose, skive, do a runner, do a bunk, do a moonlight flit, hit the road/trail, make a bolt/break for it, up sticks, hightail it, sling your hook
F⊒ stay

fleece n, v
♦ n
down, coat, wool
♦ v
swindle, rob, steal, cheat, defraud, overcharge, plunder, mulct, bilk
COLLOQ. do, bleed, con, diddle, squeeze, fiddle, gull, have

someone on, string along, pull a fast one, put one over on
SLANG rip off, sting, take for a ride, take to the cleaners

fleecy adj
downy, woolly, soft, velvety, shaggy, nappy, fluffy, hairy
TECHNICAL floccose, flocculate, lanuginose, pilose, eriophorous
F⊒ bald, smooth

fleet n, adj
♦ n
flotilla, armada, navy, task force, naval force, squadron
♦ adj
swift, fast, quick, rapid, nimble, flying, speedy, agile, light-footed, winged, mercurial, meteoric
FORMAL expeditious
F⊒ slow

fleeting adj
short, brief, flying, short-lived, short, quick, sudden, rushed, momentary, transient, transitory, passing, temporary
FORMAL evanescent, fugacious, ephemeral
COLLOQ. here today and gone tomorrow
F⊒ lasting, permanent

fleetingly adv
briefly, for a moment, for an instant, for a second, quickly, momentarily, casually

flesh n, v
♦ n
1 *an animal's flesh*
body, tissue, fat, muscle, brawn, skin, meat, pulp
2 SUBSTANCE, matter, physicality, pith, stuff, solidity, significance, weight
3 *pleasures of the flesh*
human nature, body, physical nature, sinful nature, carnal nature, physicality, sensuality, sexuality
FORMAL carnality, corporeality
Related adjectives: carnal, carneous, carnose
▪ **flesh out**
add/give details, elaborate on, expand on, make complete, make more substantial
▪ **flesh and blood**
family, relative, relations, kin, kindred
COLLOQ. folks
▪ **in the flesh**
in person, in real life, in actual life, before your own eyes

fleshly adj
wordly, earthy, physical, earthly, bodily, human, animal, sensual, sexual, bestial, carnal, lustful, erotic, material, brutish
FORMAL corporal, corporeal
F⊒ spiritual

fleshy adj
fat, ample, beefy, chubby, chunky, brawny, hefty, meaty, obese, plump, podgy, portly, tubby, stout, paunchy, overweight, well-padded
FORMAL corpulent, rotund
COLLOQ. flabby
F⊒ thin, slim

flex n, v
♦ n
cable, wire, lead, cord
♦ v
bend, bow, curve, angle, crook, ply, double up, stretch, tighten, contract
F⊒ straighten, extend

flexibility n
1 BENDABILITY, pliability, pliancy, elasticity, resilience, spring, springiness, suppleness, give, flexion
FORMAL tensility
2 ADAPTABILITY, agreeability, adjustability, amenability

FORMAL complaisance
F3 1, 2 inflexibility

flexible adj
1 BENDABLE, pliable, pliant, plastic, malleable, mouldable, elastic, stretchy, springy, yielding, supple, lithe, limber, double-jointed, agile, lissome, mobile, withy
COLLOQ. bendy
2 ADAPTABLE, adjustable, changeable, amenable, accommodating, variable, open, open-ended, yielding, manageable, complying, pliable, pliant, tractable
F3 1 inflexible, rigid 2 fixed, inflexible, rigid

flick v, n
♦ v
hit, strike, rap, tap, touch, dab, flip, swish, snap, click, jerk, whip, lash, fillip, flirt
♦ n
rap, tap, touch, dab, flip, jerk, click, lick, snap, swish
▪ **flick through**
flip through, browse through, thumb through, leaf through, run through, glance at, glance over, skip, skim, scan

flicker v, n
♦ v
flash, blink, wink, twinkle, sparkle, glimmer, glitter, flare, glint, shimmer, gutter, flutter, vibrate, bat, jump, lick, play, quiver, waver, flaught
♦ n
flash, gleam, glint, twinkle, glimmer, glitter, sparkle, spark, trace, drop, iota, atom, indication
FORMAL lambency

flier n
handout, leaflet, circular, bulletin, statement, press release, brochure, pamphlet, literature

flight[1] n
1 FLYING, aviation, aeronautics, air transport, air travel
2 JOURNEY, trip, voyage, shuttle, globetrotting
3 *a flight of steps*
staircase, set, stairway, stairs, steps

flight[2] n
his flight from the police
fleeing, escape, running away/off, getaway, breakaway, rush, absconding, exit, departure, exodus, retreat, withdrawal
▪ **take flight**
run, run away, bolt, flee, fly, take off, make off, cut and run, escape, get away, rush, decamp, abscond, leave, depart, withdraw, retreat, vanish, disappear
COLLOQ. push along/off, make tracks, quit, scat, scoot, scram, take to your heels, make yourself scarce, shove off, bunk off, clear off, split, scarper, skedaddle, vamoose, skive, do a runner, do a bunk, do a moonlight flit, hit the road/trail, make a bolt/break for it, up sticks, hightail it, sling your hook
SLANG leg it; N Am lam it, take it on the lam

flighty adj
inconstant, scatterbrained, impetuous, impulsive, changeable, irresponsible, silly, skittish, thoughtless, fickle, frivolous, lightheaded, rattle-brained, rattle-headed, erratic, unstable, unsteady, volatile, unbalanced, wild, mercurial, giddy, butterfly, skipping, unballasted, volage, whisky-frisky, bubble-headed; *Scot* loup-the-dyke, weather-headed, hellicat
FORMAL capricious
COLLOQ. birdbrained, hare-brained
F3 steady, responsible, sensible

flimsy adj
1 *flimsy clothing/structures*
thin, fine, light, slight, insubstantial, ethereal, lightweight, fragile, delicate, filmy, sheer, shaky, rickety, ramshackle, jerry-built, makeshift
2 *a flimsy excuse*

weak, feeble, meagre, inadequate, shallow, superficial, trivial, poor, thin, trifling, unconvincing, implausible
F3 1 sturdy, strong 2 convincing, plausible

flinch v
wince, start, cringe, cower, crouch, quail, tremble, shake, quake, shudder, shiver, shrink, shrink back, blench, recoil, falter, draw back, pull back, balk, shy away, avoid, shirk, withdraw, retreat, flee
COLLOQ. duck, dodge, funk

fling v, n
♦ v
throw, hurl, pitch, lob, toss, cast, sling, catapult, launch, propel, send, send flying, let fly, heave, jerk
COLLOQ. chuck
♦ n
1 THROW, hurl, pitch, lob, toss, cast, shot, heave
2 SPREE, venture, indulgence, good time, gamble, binge, whirl, go, trial, try, turn, attempt
COLLOQ. crack
3 AFFAIR, relationship, liaison, intrigue, love affair, romance, affaire, affaire d'amour, grande passion, amour
COLLOQ. carry-on

flinty adj
stony, hard, emotionless, blank, expressionless, deadpan, poker-faced, cold, frigid, icy, frosty, chilly, indifferent, unfeeling, heartless, adamant, steely, unresponsive, callous, merciless, pitiless, severe, stern, unforgiving, inexorable, hostile
F3 warm, soft-hearted, friendly

flip v, n
♦ v
flick, spin, twirl, twist, turn, toss, throw, cast, pitch, jerk, flap, click, snap
♦ n
flick, spin, twirl, twist, turn, toss, jerk, flap, click, snap
▪ **flip through**
flick through, browse through, thumb through, leaf through, glance at, glance over, skip, skim, scan

flippancy n
facetiousness, light-heartedness, frivolity, superficiality, shallowness, thoughtlessness, disrespect, disrespectfulness, glibness, pertness, impertinence, irreverence, levity
FORMAL persiflage
COLLOQ. cheek, cheekiness, sauciness
F3 earnestness, seriousness

flippant adj
facetious, light-hearted, frivolous, superficial, shallow, thoughtless, offhand, flip, glib, pert, impudent, impertinent, rude, disrespectful, irreverent, irresponsible
FORMAL insouciant
COLLOQ. saucy, cheeky
F3 serious, respectful

flippantly adv
facetiously, light-heartedly, frivolously, superficially, thoughtlessly, glibly, impertinently, rudely, disrespectfully, irreverently, irresponsibly
F3 seriously, respectfully

flipping adj
wretched, cursed, damned, fiendish, annoying, unpleasant
COLLOQ. blasted, blooming, blinking, darned, dashed, confounded, infernal, dratting

flirt v, n
♦ v
chat up, make eyes at, ogle, eye up, make a pass at, make up to, lead on, philander, dally
COLLOQ. carry on
OLD SLANG mash

♦ *n*
tease, vamp, trifler, heart-breaker, philanderer, wanton, hussy, coquet(te), gillet
OLD gillflirt
SLANG chippy
OLD SLANG masher
■ **flirt with**
consider, entertain, toy with, play with, trifle with, dabble in, try

flirtation *n*
affair, chatting up, dalliance, dallying, philandering, coquetry, intrigue, teasing, toying, trifling, sport
FORMAL amour
COLLOQ. come-on

flirtatious *adj*
provocative, coquettish, flirty, loose, promiscuous, teasing, sportive, amorous, wanton
OLD flirtish
COLLOQ. come-hither, come-on

flit *v*
dart, speed, dash, rush, flash, fly, wing, flutter, flitter, whisk, skim, skip, slip, pass, bob, dance

float *v*
1 GLIDE, stay afloat, sail, swim, bob, be buoyant, slide, drift, waft, hover, wander, hang, suspend
2 LAUNCH, initiate, set up, establish, promote, get going, get off the ground, be in at the beginning of, get the show on the road
3 *float an idea with you*
suggest, recommend, put forward, submit, present, propose, come up with, table
F3 1 sink

floating *adj*
1 AFLOAT, buoyant, unsinkable, sailing, swimming, bobbing, drifting, wafting, hovering
2 VARIABLE, fluctuating, movable, migratory, transitory, wandering, unsettled, unattached, free, uncommitted, indecisive
COLLOQ. sitting on the fence
F3 1 sinking, submerged **2** fixed, settled, committed

flock *v, n*
♦ *v*
herd, swarm, troop, converge, mass, bunch, cluster, huddle, mill, crowd, throng, group, assemble, come together, gather, collect, congregate
♦ *n*
herd, pack, crowd, throng, drove, fold, host, multitude, mass, bunch, cluster, group, gathering, collection, assembly, congregation; *Aust & NZ* mob

flog *v*
1 BEAT, whip, lash, scourge, birch, cane, strap, flay, drub, thrash, belt, chastise, punish, horsewhip, swish, tat, breech, knout; *S Afr* sjambok
OLD taw
FORMAL flagellate, vapulate
COLLOQ. whack, wallop, hide, larrup
2 SELL, deal in, handle, trade, peddle, hawk, offer for sale, put up for sale

flogging *n*
beating, whipping, lashing, scourging, birching, caning, flaying, strapping, belting, thrashing, horsewhipping
FORMAL flagellation, vapulation
COLLOQ. whacking, walloping, hiding

flood *v, n*
♦ *v*
1 DELUGE, inundate, soak, drench, saturate, fill, overflow, surge, swell, brim over, immerse, submerge, drown, overflow, engulf, swamp, overwhelm, drown, smother
FORMAL transgress

2 FLOW, pour, stream, rush, surge, gush, saturate, swamp, inundate
♦ *n*
1 DELUGE, inundation, downpour, torrent, flash flood, flow, tide, stream, rush, spate, outpouring, overflow, cataclysm, spate, bore, eagre, freshet
TECHNICAL debacle
OLD (*Shakesp*) rage
FORMAL alluvion, diluvium
2 EXCESS, torrent, series, succession, abundance, profusion, glut, tide, spring tide
FORMAL superfluity, plethora
F3 1 drought, trickle **2** trickle, dearth, lack

floor *n, v*
♦ *n*
1 FLOORING, ground, base, basis
2 *on the third floor*
storey, level, stage, landing, deck, tier
♦ *v*
1 BAFFLE, defeat, overwhelm, beat, frustrate, confound, perplex, nonplus, dumbfound, puzzle, bewilder, disconcert, throw
FORMAL discomfit
COLLOQ. stump, flummox
2 KNOCK DOWN, strike down, fell, level, prostrate

flop *v, n*
♦ *v*
1 COLLAPSE, slump, tumble, droop, hang, dangle, sag, drop, fall, topple, plump, whop
OLD swap
COLLOQ. flump
2 FAIL, be unsuccessful, collapse, misfire, fall flat, founder, sink
COLLOQ. fold, pack up, crash, go bust, go broke, go to the wall, come a cropper, go into the red; *N Am* bomb, lay an egg
♦ *n*
failure, fiasco, debacle, disaster
COLLOQ. washout, non-starter, shambles, slip-up, no-hoper, also-ran, has-been; *N Am* bomb

floppy *adj*
droopy, hanging, dangling, sagging, limp, loose, baggy, soft, flabby, flaccid
F3 firm

flora *n*
botany, plant life, plants, vegetable kingdom, vegetation, herbage, plantage

florid *adj*
1 FLOWERY, ornate, elaborate, fussy, overelaborate, extravagant, embellished, verbose, pompous, high-flown, high-sounding, bombastic, baroque, rococo, flamboyant
TECHNICAL melismatic
FORMAL grandiloquent
2 *a florid complexion*
ruddy, red, red-faced, reddish, blushing, flushed, purple, sanguine
FORMAL rubicund
F3 1 plain, simple **2** pale

flotsam *n*
jetsam, wreckage, floating wreckage, debris, rubbish, junk, oddments, odds and ends
FORMAL detritus
COLLOQ. dreck

flounce¹ *v*
flounce out of the room
bounce, spring, stamp, storm, toss, jerk, twist, throw, fling, bob

flounce² *n*
a flounce of flannel petticoat
frill, fringe, ruffle, trimming, valance, falbala
OLD furbelow

flounder v
wallow, thresh about, flail about, struggle, grope, fumble, blunder, stagger, stumble, falter, dither, be confused, be in difficulties, go under, be out of your depth, not know which way to turn

flourish v, n
♦ v
1 THRIVE, grow, wax, increase, flower, blossom, bloom, bear fruit, be strong, develop, progress, get on, do well, prosper, succeed, boom
FORMAL burgeon
2 BRANDISH, wave, shake, twirl, swing, swish, wag, display, wield, flaunt, show off, parade, exhibit, vaunt
⊏⊐ 1 decline, languish, fail
♦ n
1 DISPLAY, parade, show, gesture, wave, sweep, fanfare, ornament, decoration, panache, élan
COLLOQ. pizzazz
2 a *flourish on the lettering*
swirl, curlicue, serif, twist

flourishing adj
thriving, blooming, blossoming, prosperous, successful, booming
FORMAL burgeoning

flout v
defy, disobey, break, disregard, go against, spurn, treat with contempt, show contempt for, disdain, reject, scorn, jeer at, scoff at, sneer at, mock, laugh at, ridicule
FORMAL violate
⊏⊐ obey, respect, regard

⚠ flout or **flaunt**?
See panel at **flaunt**.

flow v, n
♦ v
1 CIRCULATE, move, go, run, proceed, course, ooze, seep, trickle, ripple, bubble, well, spout, spew, spurt, squirt, gush, jet, leak, drip, spill, pour, cascade, rush, stream, teem, flood, overflow, surge, sweep, drift, slip, slide, babble, gurgle, glide, roll, swirl, whirl
2 ORIGINATE, derive, arise, spring, emerge, issue, result, stem, proceed
FORMAL emanate
♦ n
course, flux, tide, current, drift, movement, passage, stream, deluge, cascade, spurt, gush, outpouring, flood, spate, abundance, plenty
OLD (Shakesp) recourse
FORMAL effusion, plethora

flower n, v
♦ n
1 BLOOM, blossom, bud, floret, floweret
TECHNICAL efflorescence, florescence, inflorescence
Related adjective: floral
See panels on next page
2 BEST, cream, pick, finest, choice, select, élite, crème de la crème
3 PRIME, height, peak, pinnacle, acme, zenith, heyday, blossom, bloom, culmination, best part, maturity, perfection
♦ v
bud, bloom, blossom, open, sprout, come out, develop, grow, mature, prosper, thrive, flourish, succeed
FORMAL burgeon

flowery adj
florid, ornate, elaborate, fancy, chintzy, bloomy, blossomy, baroque, rhetorical, high-flown, verbose, pompous, bombastic
TECHNICAL euphuistic
FORMAL grandiloquent
⊏⊐ plain, simple

flowing adj
1 *flowing rivers/traffic*
moving, oozing, seeping, bubbling, welling, gushing, pouring, rushing, cascading, streaming, surging, sweeping, overflowing
2 FLUENT, effortless, easy, natural, smooth, continuous, uninterrupted, unbroken
3 *flowing hair*
hanging, hanging loose, loose, floppy, hanging freely, falling, rolling, flaccid

fluctuate v
vary, change, alter, differ, shift, rise and fall, seesaw, go up and down, come and go, ebb and flow, alternate, swing, sway, undulate, vacillate, waver, hesitate, range, balance, trim, yo-yo
TECHNICAL float
FORMAL oscillate
COLLOQ. chop and change
⊏⊐ be steady

fluctuation n
variation, change, shift, swing, alternation, variability, range, instability, unsteadiness, wavering, irresolution, inconstancy, ambivalence, fickleness
TECHNICAL floating, nutation, seiche
FORMAL oscillation, capriciousness, vacillation

flue n
shaft, pipe, duct, vent, channel, passage, tunnel, chimney, uptake
TECHNICAL fluework
OLD tewel

fluency n
ease, eloquence, smoothness, articulateness, assurance, command, control, facility, readiness, outpouring, glibness, slickness
FORMAL facundity, volubility
⊏⊐ incoherence

fluent adj
flowing, smooth, easy, effortless, flowing, free-flowing, fluid, natural, graceful, elegant, articulate, eloquent, silver-tongued, slick, glib, ready
FORMAL voluble, mellifluous
COLLOQ. facile
⊏⊐ broken, inarticulate, tongue-tied

fluently adv
smoothly, easily, effortlessly, naturally, gracefully, elegantly, articulately, eloquently, glibly, pat

fluff n, v
♦ n
down, nap, pile, fuzz, floss, lint, dust
♦ v
botch, do badly, make a bad job of, mismanage, bungle, mess up, make a mess of, muck up, muddle, fumble, muff, spoil
COLLOQ. blot your copybook, boob, put your foot in it, foul up, mess up, blow
SLANG balls up, cock up, screw up
⊏⊐ bring off

fluffy adj
furry, fuzzy, downy, feathery, fleecy, woolly, hairy, shaggy, velvety, silky, soft

fluid n, adj
♦ n
liquid, solution, liquor, juice, gas, vapour
♦ adj
1 LIQUID, liquefied, aqueous, watery, flowing, running, runny, melted, molten
2 a *fluid situation*
variable, changeable, unstable, inconstant, shifting, mobile, adjustable, adaptable, flexible, open, unsettled, fluctuating, unsteady, unstable

Garden flowers include:

African violet	carnation	foxglove	lobelia	pink (dianthus)	stock
alyssum	chrysanthemum	(digitalis)	lupin	phlox	sunflower
anemone	coneflower	freesia	marigold	poinsettia	sweet pea
aster	cornflower	fuchsia	narcissus	polyanthus	sweet william
aubrietia	cowslip	gardenia	nasturtium	poppy	tulip
azalea	crocus	geranium	nemesia	primrose	verbena
begonia	cyclamen	gladioli	nicotiana	primula	viola
bluebell	daffodil	hollyhock	night-scented	rose	violet
busy lizzie	dahlia	hyacinth	stock	salvia	wallflower
(impatiens)	daisy	iris (flag)	orchid	snapdragon	zinnia
calendula	delphinium	lily	pansy	(antirrhinum)	
candytuft	forget-me-not	lily-of-the-valley	petunia	snowdrop	

See also **bulb; plant; shrub; wild flower.**

Parts of a flower include:

anther	corymb	nectary	petal	spadix	style
calyx	dichasium	ovary	pistil	spike	thalamus
capitulum	filament	ovule	raceme	stalk	torus
carpel	gynoecium	panicle	receptacle	stamen	umbel
corolla	monochasium	pedicel	sepal	stigma	

FORMAL protean
3 *fluid movements*
flowing, free-flowing, smooth, effortless, easy, graceful, elegant, natural
E3 1 solid, rigid **2** inflexible, fixed

fluke *n*
stroke, stroke of luck, lucky break, accident, quirk, blessing, windfall, break, chance, coincidence
FORMAL fortuity, serendipity
COLLOQ. freak

fluky *adj*
accidental, lucky, chance, fortunate, coincidental, uncertain, incalculable
FORMAL fortuitous, serendipitous
COLLOQ. jammy, freakish

flummox *v*
confuse, confound, baffle, bewilder, mystify, perplex, puzzle, nonplus, fox, defeat, stymie
COLLOQ. bamboozle, stump, floor, faze

flummoxed *adj*
baffled, confounded, bewildered, confused, perplexed, puzzled, mystified, nonplussed, foxed, stymied, at a loss, at sea
COLLOQ. bamboozled, stumped, floored, fazed

flunk *v*
be unsuccessful, founder, come to grief
COLLOQ. flop, fold, flunk, not come off, not make it, not come up to scratch, fall flat, blow it, blow your chances, bite the dust, come a cropper, come unstuck, come unglued, come undone, not come up with the goods; *N Am* bomb

flunkey *n*
lackey, assistant, servant, steward, menial, minion, slave, manservant, valet, underling, drudge, footman, hanger-on, cringer, toady, bootlicker, yes-man

flurried *adj*
upset, disturbed, flustered, unsettled, unnerved
FORMAL perturbed
COLLOQ. fazed, rattled, in a flap, in a tizzy, in a tizz, having kittens, all of a lather

flurry *n, v*
◆ *n*
1 BURST, outbreak, spell, shower, bout, spurt, gust, blast, squall, scurry, swirl, whirl
2 BUSTLE, hurry, hubbub, fluster, fuss, commotion, tumult, whirl, disturbance, agitation, excitement, stir; *Scot* swither
FORMAL perturbation

COLLOQ. to-do, flap
◆ *v*
fluster, hurry, hustle, agitate, bewilder, bother, bustle, flutter, fuss, unsettle, upset, confuse, ruffle, disconcert, disturb
FORMAL discountenance, perturb
COLLOQ. hassle, rattle

flush¹ *v, n, adj*
◆ *v*
1 BLUSH, go/turn red, redden, crimson, colour (up), burn, glow, flame
OLD gild
FORMAL suffuse
2 CLEANSE, wash, rinse, hose, swab, clear, scour, sluice, empty, eject, evacuate, expel
◆ *n*
bloom, freshness, vigour, glow, blush, reddening, colour, redness, rosiness, ruddiness, heyday
OLD rud
◆ *adj*
1 ABUNDANT, lavish, generous, full, overflowing, rich, wealthy, moneyed, prosperous, well-off, well-heeled, well-to-do
FORMAL replete
2 LEVEL, even, smooth, flat, plane, square, true

flush² *v*
flush the enemy out of the forest
force out, drive out, run to earth, discover, uncover, expel, eject, start, rouse, disturb

flushed *adj*
1 RED, rosy, ruddy, blushing, burning, crimson, scarlet, florid, aflame, ablaze, glowing, aglow, hot, embarrassed, blowzy
OLD hectic; (*Shakesp*) rosed
FORMAL rubicund
2 ELATED, thrilled, enthused, excited, exhilarated, exultant, animated, aroused, inspired, intoxicated, sanguine
E3 1 pale

fluster *v, n*
◆ *v*
bother, upset, embarrass, disturb, agitate, ruffle, flap, discompose, confuse, confound, unsettle, unnerve, make nervous, disconcert, put off, distract, pother
OLD flustrate
FORMAL perturb
COLLOQ. rattle, faze
E3 calm
◆ *n*
flurry, bustle, commotion, disturbance, confusion,

agitation, upset, turmoil, agitation, panic, embarrassment
OLD flustration
FORMAL perturbation
COLLOQ. state, flap, dither, tizzy, tizz
E3 calm

fluted *adj*
grooved, furrowed, channelled, corrugated, ribbed, ridged

flutter *v, n*
◆ *v*
flap, wave, beat, bat, flicker, vibrate, palpitate, agitate,
shake, tremble, quiver, shiver, ruffle, flitter, ripple, twitch,
pulsate, toss, waver, fluctuate, dance, hover
◆ *n*
1 FLAPPING, wave, beat, flicker, vibration, agitation,
palpitation, tremble, tremor, quiver, shiver, shudder,
twitch, ripple, ruffle
2 BET, gamble, wager, speculation, risk
COLLOQ. punt

flux *n*
fluctuation, instability, unrest, change, changeability,
alteration, modification, fluidity, flow, movement, motion,
flow, transition, development, mutation
E3 stability, rest

fly¹ *v*
1 TAKE OFF, travel/go by air, rise, ascend, mount, soar, glide,
float, hover, flit, flutter, wing
2 *fly an aeroplane*
control, operate, pilot, guide, manoeuvre, steer
3 *fly a flag*
show, wave, display, exhibit, present, reveal
4 RACE, sprint, dash, tear, rush, go/pass quickly, slip by,
hurry, speed, zoom, shoot, bolt, dart, career, jet
FORMAL hasten
5 FLEE, run away, bolt, take flight, take off, make off, cut and
run, escape, get away, rush, decamp, abscond, leave,
depart, withdraw, retreat, vanish, disappear
COLLOQ. get out, push along/off, make tracks, quit, scat,
scoot, scram, take to your heels, make yourself scarce,
shove off, clear off, split, scarper, skedaddle, vamoose,
skive, do a runner, do a bunk, do a moonlight flit, hit the
road/trail, make a bolt/break for it
E3 stay
■ **fly at**
attack, assault, go for, fall upon, hit, strike, lay into, charge,
lash out at, let someone have it, let fly
COLLOQ. bite someone's head off, have a go at, jump down
someone's throat

fly² *adj*
he's a fly fellow
alert, artful, sharp, shrewd, astute, canny, careful, prudent,
cunning, astute
FORMAL sagacious
COLLOQ. nobody's fool, on the ball, smart

fly-by-night *adj*
disreputable, discreditable, questionable, shady,
unreliable, untrustworthy, undependable, irresponsible,
dubious, short-lived, shady
FORMAL ephemeral
COLLOQ. cowboy, here today gone tomorrow
E3 reliable

flying *adj*
1 *flying insects*
gliding, floating, hovering, flapping, fluttering, airborne,
winged, winging, wind-borne, soaring, mobile
2 *a flying visit*
brief, hurried, fleeting, rapid, fast, hasty, rushed, speedy
COLLOQ. whistle-stop

foam *n, v*
◆ *n*
froth, lather, suds, head, bubbles, fizz, spume,

effervescence, mousse, surf, scum
OLD (*Shakesp*) yeast
◆ *v*
froth, lather, bubble, effervesce, fizz, boil, seethe, spume
OLD befoam; (*Spenser*) fry

foamy *adj*
frothy, lathery, bubbly, foaming, spumy, sudsy
FORMAL spumescent

fob
■ **fob off**
foist, pass off, get rid of, dump, unload, inflict, impose,
deceive, put off
COLLOQ. palm off

focus *n, v*
◆ *n*
1 *the focus of concern*
focal point, target, centre, heart, core, nucleus, kernel,
crux, hub, axis, linchpin, pivot, hinge
2 *the focus is on competition*
attention, priority, emphasis, importance, stress, weight,
significance, concentration, underscoring, accent,
accentuation, prominence, pre-eminence
◆ *v*
concentrate, aim, direct, turn, fix, spotlight, pinpoint, home
in, zoom in, converge, meet, join, centre, bring into focus
COLLOQ. zero in
■ **in focus**
clear, sharp, distinct, crisp, well-defined
■ **out of focus**
blurred, ill-defined, indistinct, hazy, fuzzy, blurry, muzzy

fodder *n*
feed, food, foodstuff, forage, eatage, nourishment, rations,
silage, soilage, provender, lucerne, browsing, provand,
proviant, pabulum; *dialect* fother
OLD stover

foe *n*
enemy, adversary, antagonist, opponent, combatant, rival,
ill-wisher
E3 friend

foetus *n*
unborn child, unborn baby, embryo
Related adjective: foetal

fog *n, v*
◆ *n*
1 MIST, haze, mistiness, haziness, cloud, gloom, murkiness,
smog, smoke, pea-souper, pease-soup, pea-soup
FORMAL brume
2 PERPLEXITY, puzzlement, confusion, bewilderment,
bafflement, disorientation, daze, trance, stupor,
vagueness, obscurity, blur, haze
◆ *v*
1 MIST, steam up, cloud, dull, dim, darken, obscure
OLD befog
2 CONFUSE, blur, muddle, bewilder, baffle, perplex
FORMAL obfuscate

foggy *adj*
1 MISTY, hazy, smoggy, cloudy, clouded, overcast, murky,
damp, dark, grey, shadowy, gloomy, dim
FORMAL brumous
2 *foggy recollections*
indistinct, vague, obscure, unclear, muddled
E3 1, 2 clear

foible *n*
quirk, weakness, weak point, idiosyncrasy, imperfection,
eccentricity, oddity, failing, fault, defect, oddness,
peculiarity, shortcoming, strangeness, habit

foil¹ *v*
foil someone's plans
defeat, outwit, frustrate, thwart, prevent, baffle, stump,

counter, nullify, stop, check, balk, obstruct, block, elude, hinder, hamper
OLD foyle
FORMAL circumvent
COLLOQ. scuttle, scupper, pip
E3 abet

foil² n
a foil to her dark hair
contrast, complement, balance, setting, set-off, background, relief, beauty spot
OLD foyle
FORMAL antithesis

foist v
force, impose, introduce, thrust, unload, saddle, pass off, get rid of, fob off, wish on
COLLOQ. palm off

fold¹ v, n
♦ v
1 BEND, ply, double, overlap, tuck, pleat, crease, gather, turn under, turn down, turn over, crumple, crimp, crinkle
2 ENFOLD, embrace, hug, clasp, squeeze, envelop, wrap (up), enclose, entwine, intertwine
3 *the business folded*
fail, shut down, close, collapse, crash, go bankrupt, go out of business
COLLOQ. flop, pack up, go to the wall, go broke, go bust
♦ n
bend, turn, layer, ply, overlap, tuck, pleat, gather, crease, knife-edge, line, wrinkle, crinkle, pucker, ruffle, furrow, corrugation

fold² n
1 ENCLOSURE, pen, pound, compound, paddock, stockade, court, yard, ring, kraal
2 CONGREGATION, church, assembly, flock, community, gathering, company, parishioners, fellowship

folder n
file, binder, folio, portfolio, envelope, holder, wallet, pocket

foliage n
leaves, greenery, leafage, vegetation, foliation
TECHNICAL frondescence, foliature, vernation
FORMAL verdure

folk n, adj
♦ n
1 PEOPLE, society, nation, persons, humans, public, population, race, tribe, clan, ethnic group
2 RELATIONS, family, parents, relatives, kin, kindred, kinsfolk
♦ adj
ethnic, national, traditional, popular, native, indigenous, tribal, ancestral

folklore n
fables, folktales, legends, myths, mythology, lore, stories, tales, customs, beliefs, tradition, superstitions

folksy adj
1 *a folksy country table*
traditional, time-honoured, rustic, plain, simple, natural, crude, basic, unsophisticated, ordinary
2 AMIABLE, affable, genial, convivial, cordial, kind, kindly, warm, neighbourly, helpful, sympathetic, fond, affectionate, familiar, intimate, inseparable, close, companionable, sociable, outgoing, approachable, receptive, hospitable, comradely, amicable, good-natured, sympathetic
COLLOQ. mat(e)y, pally, chummy, thick, tight

follow v
1 *night follows day*
come after, succeed, come next, replace, supersede, supplant, take the place of, step into the shoes of
2 CHASE, pursue, go after, run after, hunt, track, trail,

shadow, tail, stalk, dog, give chase, hound, catch, be at someone's heels
3 ACCOMPANY, go (along) with, escort, attend, trail, go behind, come behind, walk behind, tread behind, tag along
4 RESULT, ensue, develop, emanate, arise, issue, spring, flow, proceed
5 OBEY, adhere to, heed, mind, observe, note, accept, yield to, comply with, conform to, carry out, stick to, practise, take your cue from
FORMAL comply with
6 UNDERSTAND, grasp, comprehend, fathom, take in, appreciate
COLLOQ. twig, latch onto, suss (out)
7 *follow someone's example*
copy, imitate, repeat, emulate, mimic, ape
8 *she followed her father into medicine*
succeed, replace, take the place of, supplant
9 KEEP UP WITH, support, be interested in, be devoted to, be a fan of, be a supporter of, keep up to date with
E3 1 precede **3** abandon, desert **5** disobey

■ **follow through**
continue, pursue, see through, finish, complete, conclude, fulfil, implement, bring to completion

■ **follow up**
investigate, check out, look into, research, continue, pursue, reinforce, consolidate

follower n
backer, supporter, admirer, enthusiast, fan, devotee; *Irish* voteen; disciple, apostle, acolyte, pupil, imitator, emulator, adherent, hanger-on, believer, convert, attendant, retainer, helper, companion, escort
COLLOQ. sidekick, freak, buff

following adj, n
♦ adj
subsequent, next, succeeding, successive, resulting, ensuing, consequent, later
E3 previous
♦ n
followers, suite, retinue, entourage, circle, fans, admirers, adherents, supporters, support, body of support, backing, backers, patrons, patronage, clientèle, audience, public, coterie

folly n
1 FOOLISHNESS, stupidity, senselessness, rashness, recklessness, imprudence, irresponsibility, indiscretion, craziness, inanity, madness, lunacy, insanity, idiocy, imbecility, silliness, ludicrousness, ridiculousness, absurdity, nonsense, illogicality, foolhardiness, vanity, foolery, foppery, *folie*
OLD idiotcy
FORMAL fatuousness, moria
2 MONUMENT, tower, whim, belvedere, gazebo
E3 1 wisdom, prudence, sanity

foment v
incite, instigate, excite, stir up, agitate, arouse, rouse, encourage, kindle, promote, prompt, provoke, raise, activate, stimulate, spur, quicken, goad, whip up, work up, foster, brew
E3 quell

fond adj
1 *fond of someone/something*
liking, partial to, attached to, keen on, having a soft spot for, addicted to, thinking the world of
FORMAL enamoured of
COLLOQ. hooked on, crazy about, mad about, daft about, dotty about, hot, nuts about/on
2 AFFECTIONATE, warm, tender, caring, loving, adoring, devoted, doting, indulgent, amorous, amatory, spoony
3 *fond expectations*
foolish, naive, deluded, credulous, absurd, impractical, over-optimistic, vain

Kinds of food include:

SOUPS AND STEWS:
bouillabaisse
borsch
broth
chowder
cockaleekie
consommé
gazpacho
gumbo
minestrone
succotash
vichyssoise
POTATO DISHES:
boxty
bubble and
 squeak
champ
chips
colcannon
duchesse
 potatoes
French fries
gnocchi
gratin
mash
rösti
Scot stovies
SEAFOOD:
calamari
caviar
crab stick
fish and chips
fishcake
fisherman's pie
fish-finger
gefilte fish
kedgeree

kipper
pickled herring
prawn cocktail
scampi
SALAD:
coleslaw
caesar salad
Greek salad
green salad
mesclun
potato salad
Russian salad
salade niçoise
tabbouleh
Waldorf salad
winter salad
VEGETABLE DISHES:
aubergine roll
cauliflower
 cheese
macaroni cheese
nut cutlet
pease pudding
Quorn®
ratatouille
stuffed
 mushroom
tofu
MEAT AND GAME:
bacon
boeuf
bourguignon
casserole
cassoulet
cottage pie
faggot

goulash
hotpot
Irish stew
roast beef and
 Yorkshire
 pudding
salami
sausage
Scotch
 woodcock
shepherd's pie
stroganoff
toad-in-the-hole
EGG DISHES:
eggs Benedict
frittata
omelette
quiche
FAST FOOD:
Big Mac®
N Am corn dog
hamburger
hot dog
KFC®
McDonald's®
Wimpy®
**INTERNATIONAL
AND REGIONAL**:
baba ganoush
balti
bhajee (or bhaji)
biriyani
burrito
chillada
chilli con carne
chop suey
chorizo

couscous
dal (or dhal)
dolma
empanada
enchilada
fajita
feijoada
felafel
fondue
frankfurter
fritter
gado-gado
haggis
imam bayildi
kofta
laksa
latke
macédoine
moussaka
paella
pakora
peperonata
pilau
pissaladière
pizza
polenta
ragout
raita
risotto
samosa
sauerkraut
smorgasbord
sushi
taco
tortilla
Wiener schnitzel

**SNACKS AND
NIBBLES**:
canapé
panini
sandwich
vol-au-vent
welsh rarebit
wrap
BISCUITS:
amaretti
biscotto
bourbon
brandy snap
cookie
cracker
cream cracker
crispbread
digestive
flapjack
Florentine
Garibaldi
ginger nut
ginger snap
langue de chat
macaroon
oatcake
parkin
petit four
ratafia
shortbread
N Am soda
 cracker
wafer
water biscuit
zwieback
DIPS:
guacamole

hummus
salsa
tahina
taramasalata
tzatziki
**SAUCES AND
DRESSINGS**:
apple
balsamic vinegar
barbecue
bechamel
cranberry
French dressing
hollandaise
mint
olive oil
pesto
red wine sauce
salad cream
tartare
Thousand Island
 dressing
tomato ketchup
vinaigrette
white sauce
white wine sauce
Worcestershire
CONDIMENTS
chutney
horseradish
mayonnaise
mustard
Tabasco®

See also **bread; cake; cheese; cook; dessert; fish; fruit; kitchen utensils; meat; nut; pasta; pastry; sugar; sweet; vegetable**.

---

fondle *v*
   caress, stroke, pat, pet, hug, cuddle, smuggle, cosset, dandle, cocker
   COLLOQ. grope, touch up

fondly *adv*
   affectionately, warmly, tenderly, lovingly, amorously

fondness *n*
   affection, devotion, kindness, tenderness, love, liking, fancy, attachment, enthusiasm, inclination, leaning, partiality, preference, weakness, soft spot, taste, susceptibility, *tendre, tendresse*
   OLD well-liking
   FORMAL penchant, predilection
   ◘ aversion, hate

food *n*
   FOODSTUFFS, comestibles, provisions, meals, stores, rations, refreshments, sustenance, nourishment, nutrition, nutriment, subsistence, feed, fodder, diet, fare, dish, speciality, delicacy, cooking, cuisine, menu, board, table; *NZ* kai, kaikai
   OLD aliment, pabulum; (*Spenser*) pasture; (*Shakesp*) repasture
   FORMAL viands, victuals
   COLLOQ. eatables, eats, scran, tuck
   SLANG grub, nosh, chow, scoff; *Aust & NZ* tucker
   See panel above
   ▪ **food for thought**
   mental stimulation, something to be seriously considered, something to think about

fool *n, v*
   ◆ *n*
   blockhead, fat-head, dunce, dimwit, simpleton, halfwit,

idiot, cretin, imbecile, ignoramus, moron, dupe, stooge, butt, laughing-stock, clown, comic, buffoon, jester, muggins, gull, Jack-fool, jackass, lemming, mooncalf, soft, softy, Tom-noddy, tomfool, punk; *dialect* gowk, mumchance, barmpot, gump, haverel; *Scot* coof, dottle; *Scot & Irish* eejit; *Irish* omadhaun; *N Am* cluck, dumb-cluck, yap
   OLD cony, fon, fondling, want-wit, patch, sot, wigeon; (*Shakesp*) lack-brain, bauble, capocchia, snipe
   COLLOQ. nincompoop, ass, chump, ninny, neddy, clot, dope, twit, nitwit, nit, sucker, mug, twerp, birdbrain, lamebrain, knuckle-head, silly-billy, berk, (proper) Charlie, gubbins, sap, saphead, wazzock, dum-dum, coot, goat, head-banger; *Scot* bampot; *N Am* lunkhead, chowderhead, putz, doofus; *Aust* dill, boofhead
   SLANG wally, jerk, dumbo, muppet, pillock, prat, dork, geek, plonker, git, nerd, nerk, nelly, goop, josser, nig-nog, sawney, schlemiel, turkey, cloth head, dipstick, goof, kook, pillock, tosspot; *N Am* jughead, schmo, dingbat, dweeb; (*taboo*) prick, dickhead; *Aust* galah, nana; *Aust & NZ* nong
   OLD SLANG cake
   ◆ *v*
   1 DECEIVE, take in, delude, mislead, beguile, make a fool of, dupe, gull, hoodwink, put one over on, trick, hoax, cheat, swindle, bluff, tease, joke, jest, play tricks, pretend, feign, sham
   OLD fon
   COLLOQ. con, diddle, string along, have on, kid, string along, pull someone's leg, bamboozle
   2 *stop fooling about*
   lark about, play about, monkey about/around
   COLLOQ. horse around, mess about/around
   SLANG fart about/around, ponce about/around, piss about/around

3 *fooling about with my wife*
philander, flirt, play around, have an affair, womanize
COLLOQ. carry on, sleep around, mess about/around
■ **play the fool**
fool around, fool about, mess about, mess around, muck
about, muck around, clown around, monkey around, play
the giddy goat
OLD fon
COLLOQ. act the fool, horse around

foolery *n*
silliness, folly, fooling, nonsense, tomfoolery, antics,
buffoonery, drollery, waggery, zanyism, capers, carry-on,
clowning, farce, childishness, horseplay, larks, high jinks,
mischief, practical jokes, pranks, monkey tricks,
shenanigans

foolhardiness *n*
recklessness, rashness, imprudence, irresponsibility,
impulsiveness, boldness
E3 caution, prudence

foolhardy *adj*
rash, reckless, ill-advised, irresponsible, imprudent,
incautious, impulsive, bold, daring, daredevil
FORMAL temerarious
E3 cautious, prudent

foolish *adj*
stupid, senseless, silly, absurd, ridiculous, ludicrous,
imbecile, nonsensical, unwise, ill-advised, ill-considered,
vacuous, short-sighted, half-baked, crazy, mad, insane,
idiotic, moronic, hare-brained, half-witted, simple-
minded, simple, ignorant, unintelligent, inept, inane,
pointless, unreasonable, *étourdi*; *Scot* doilt, dottle, fool,
glaik; *Welsh* twp; *N Am* fool
OLD fond, gudgeon, peevish
FORMAL fatuous, risible, injudicious
COLLOQ. daft, crack-brained, rattle-brained, gormless,
dumb, dotty, mad, crazy, wacky, potty, batty, barmy, nutty,
not in your right mind, out of your mind, with a screw
missing, needing to have your head examined; *Aust* dilly
SLANG goofy
E3 wise, prudent; *formal* judicious

foolishly *adv*
stupidly, senselessly, absurdly, ridiculously, unwisely,
imprudently, ill-advisedly, idiotically, incautiously,
indiscreetly, mistakenly, ineptly, short-sightedly
OLD fonly
FORMAL fatuously, injudiciously
COLLOQ. daftly, crazily, madly, wackily
E3 wisely

foolishness *n*
folly, stupidity, silliness, senselessness, absurdity,
irresponsibility, weakness, craziness, madness, lunacy,
nonsense, rubbish, foolery, inanity, ineptitude,
indiscretion, imprudence
FORMAL incaution, unreason, unwisdom
COLLOQ. bunkum, claptrap, baloney, daftness, hogwash,
rot, piffle, poppycock, bunk, bunkum, claptrap, bilge,
cobblers
SLANG (*vulgar*) crap, balls, bullshit
E3 wisdom, prudence

foolproof *adj*
idiot-proof, infallible, unfailing, safe, fail-safe, sure, certain,
dependable, trustworthy, guaranteed
COLLOQ. sure-fire
E3 unreliable

foot *n*
1 *an animal's feet*
paw, hoof, pad, trotter, leg, toe, sole, heel
TECHNICAL pes
COLLOQ. tootsie, tootsy-wootsy
Related adjectives: pedal, pedate

2 *at the foot of the hill*
bottom, end, far end, limit, extremity, border, base,
foundation
E3 **2** head, top, summit

football
See panel on next page

footing *n*
1 BASIS, base, foundation, ground, relations, relationship,
terms, conditions, state, standing, status, grade, rank,
position
2 FOOTHOLD, balance, support, position, grip

footling *adj*
paltry, trifling, minor, trivial, insignificant, petty, irrelevant
COLLOQ. piffling
E3 major, significant

footloose *adj*
uncommitted, unattached, uninvolved, available, free,
fancy-free
E3 committed; *colloq.* tied down

footnote *n*
annotation, note, marginal note, gloss, comment,
commentary, marginalia
FORMAL scholium

footprint *n*
footmark, track, trail, trace, step, tread, spoor
FORMAL vestige

footstep *n*
footmark, track, step, tread, footfall, plod, tramp, trudge

footwear

Types of footwear include:

ballet shoe	football boot	sabot
slang beetle-	galosh	sandal
crusher	gumboot	shoe
boat shoe	hiking-boot	slingback
boot	Hush Puppies®	slip-on
bootee	jelly	slipper
bowling shoe	kitten heel	sneaker
brogue	lace-up	snowshoe
colloq. brothel	loafer	stiletto heel
creeper	moccasin	*S Afr slang* tacky
casual	mule	tennis shoe
Chelsea boot	overshoe	thong
climbing-boot	Oxford	trainer
clog	pantofle	wader
combat boot	*old* patten	walking-boot
court shoe	platform heel	wedge heel
deck shoe	plimsoll	wellington boot
Doc Martens®	pump	*colloq.* welly
espadrille	riding boot	
flip-flop	rugby boot	

---

fop *n*
dandy, coxcomb, beau, popinjay, dude, exquisite,
peacock, swell, toff, Jack-a-dandy, *petit maître*
OLD muscadin, fantastic, skipjack; (*Shakesp*) barber-
monger

foppish *adj*
dapper, dressy, spruce, overdressed, preening, vain,
dandyish, dandified, affected, dainty, finical, coxcombic,
apish
OLD fallal, fantastic; (*Shakesp*) fangled, fashionmongering
COLLOQ. la-di-da, natty, swellish
E3 unkempt

forage *n, v*
◆ *n*
fodder, pasturage, feed, food, foodstuffs, provender
◆ *v*
rummage, search, seek, cast about, scour, scratch, hunt,
scavenge, ransack, plunder, assault, ravage, loot, raid, invade

Terms used in football include:

AMERICAN FOOTBALL:
American Football Conference (AFC)
audible
backfield
blitz
block
centre
complete
cornerback
defensive end
defensive tackle
down
draw
endzone
face mask
fair catch
field goal
flag
flanker
fullback
fumble
guard
hail Mary
halfback
holding
huddle
incomplete
interception
kicker
kickoff
lateral
linebacker
lineman
National Football Conference (NFC)
National Football League (NFL)
neutral zone
nickelback
nose tackle
offensive line
offside
out of bounds
overtime
pass interference
pass rush
pocket
point after
punt
punter
quarterback
red zone
running back
rush
sack
safety
scrimmage
scrimmage line
secondary
shotgun
snap
split end
Super Bowl®
tackle
tailback
tee
tight end
touchback
touchdown
turnover
two-point conversion
wide receiver

ASSOCIATION FOOTBALL:
banana kick
bicycle kick
Bundesliga
Champions League
chip
cross
corner (kick)
defender
dugout
dummy
European Championships
extra time
FA Cup
FIFA (Fédération Internationale de Football Association)
First Division
formation
foul
fourth official
free kick
full back
goal
colloq. goalie
goalkeeper
golden goal
half-time
handball
header
injury time
kick-off
marking
midfielder
nutmeg
offside
overhead kick
own goal
pass
penalty
penalty shoot-out
Premiership
promotion
red card
referee
relegation
Serie A
silver goal
skipper
stoppage time
striker
colloq. sub
substitute
sweeper
tackle
technical area
throw-in
UEFA (Union of European Football Associations)
wing back
winger
World Cup
yellow card

AUSTRALIAN RULES:
advantage
Australian Football League (AFL)
ball-up
behind (1 point)
bouncing
boundary umpire
Brownlow Medal
bump
centre bounce
centre circle
centre square
charge
checking
drop punt
50m penalty
field umpire
flank
footpass
free kick
goal (6 points)
goal line
goal square
goal umpire
guernsey
handball
interchange
mark
Melbourne Cricket Ground (MCG)
nineteenth man
out of bounds
pockets
quarter
ruck
runner
rover
ruck-rover
shepherding
siren
colloq. torp
torpedo punt

GAELIC FOOTBALL:
All-Ireland Championships
charge
corner-back
corner-forward
Croke Park
crossbar
divot
fist
45m free kick
foul
free kick
full-forward
Gaelic Athletic Association (GAA)
goal (3 points)
handpass
kick-out
one-handed pass
overcarry
overhold
parallelogram
penalty kick
point
side-line kick
solo
square ball
Sam Maguire Cup
throw-in
tipping
toe-tap
toss
two-handed pass

---

foray *n*
raid, offensive, attack, assault, ravage, sortie, sally, swoop, invasion, inroad, incursion, reconnaissance

forbear *v*
avoid, decline, hesitate, hold, hold back, keep from, stop, cease, withhold, stay, restrain yourself, omit, pause
FORMAL refrain, abstain, desist, eschew

forbearance *n*
self-control, patience, moderation, endurance, leniency, mildness, restraint, temperance, tolerance, toleration, avoidance, self-denial, clemency, long-suffering, resignation, refraining, sufferance
FORMAL abstinence
E3 intolerance

forbearing *adj*
long-suffering, patient, moderate, lenient, self-controlled, restrained, tolerant, merciful, mild, easy, forgiving, indulgent, clement
E3 intolerant, merciless

forbid *v*
prohibit, disallow, not allow, not let, ban, veto, refuse, deny, outlaw, debar, blacklist, exclude, rule out, prevent, block, hinder, inhibit
FORMAL proscribe, interdict, preclude
COLLOQ. give the thumbs-down to; give the red light to
E3 allow, permit, let, approve

> **Synonym nuances**
> The verbs **prohibit** and **ban** are appropriate for forbidding in official contexts: *tourist coaches are to be banned from the town centre*, whilst **veto** similarly implies using official power to stop something: *the scheme was vetoed by the Treasury*, and **outlaw** is specifically used of making something illegal: *secondary picketing has been outlawed*.
>
> **Debar** and **exclude** are best used of forbidding entry: *lack of education debars half the population from employment*, whereas **blacklist** is more specific about who is forbidden in that it has to do with compiling a list of undesirables. The term **rule out** best describes forbidding something by discounting it as a possibility: *lack of funds rules out any more building work*, while **prevent** and **block** convey the idea of taking action to stop something from occurring: *MPs blocked moves to hold more talks with the French*.
>
> **Hinder** and **inhibit** would appropriately describe actions more likely to restrict or impede than to halt completely: *the conservatism that has hindered development in the past*; *his depression inhibited his writing*.

forbidden *adj*
prohibited, banned, excluded, taboo, vetoed, debarred, illicit, outlawed, out of bounds
OLD (*Shakesp*) restrained
FORMAL proscribed
COLLOQ. not on

forbidding *adj*
stern, formidable, awesome, severe, harsh, grim, hostile, unfriendly, daunting, off-putting, uninviting, menacing, threatening, ominous, sinister, foreboding, frightening
E3 approachable, friendly, congenial

force *v, n*
♦ *v*
1 COMPEL, make, oblige, urge, coerce, constrain, press,

pressure, pressurize, put pressure on, pressgang, bulldoze, bully, railroad, drive, propel, impel, push, thrust, impose, inflict

COLLOQ. lean on, put the screws on, twist someone's arm, breathe down someone's neck

2 PRISE, force open, break open, crack, blast, wrench, wrest, extort, exact, wring, extract

• *n*

1 COMPULSION, impulse, necessity, influence, coercion, constraint, pressure, duress, enforcement, violence, aggression

COLLOQ. arm-twisting, strongarm tactics, the screws, the third degree

2 POWER, might, strength, intensity, effort, energy, vigour, exertion, stamina, muscle, momentum, impetus, drive, dynamo, dynamism, vitality, passion, vehement, determination, stress, emphasis, influence, power, significance, persuasiveness, effectiveness

FORMAL cogency

3 MEANING, sense, substance, significance, gist, essence, thrust

4 ARMY, troop, body, corps, regiment, squad, platoon, squadron, battalion, division, unit, group, detachment, patrol

Ⓔ 2 weakness

■ **in force**

1 IN OPERATION, functioning, valid, binding, working, effective, current, on the statute book

FORMAL operative

2 IN STRENGTH, in crowds, in large/great numbers, in flocks, in droves

---

Synonym nuances

verb sense 1

Compel and **make** may be used to suggest that your actions are determined by certain external pressures: *he was compelled to resign because he'd been embezzling the funds*. **Oblige**, on the other hand, has more to do with feeling that something is morally binding: *I feel obliged to leave a tip even when the service is not good*.

The terms **urge** and **press** imply a powerful attempt to persuade: *he urged them to reform before it was too late*, while **coerce** suggests being made to do something against your will. Both **pressure** and **pressurize** suggest applying stronger methods to get your way, and **pressgang** has suggestions of being physically forced against your will. **Bulldoze** is a negative term echoing this use of strong tactics, or even physical strength: *the new tax was to be bulldozed through parliament*, and **bully** also suggests the use of menacing behaviour.

You can use **railroad** to further imply undue haste: *she refused to be railroaded into a decision*, whereas **drive** and **propel** have more to do with motivating factors: *driven by a need to maximize profit*. **Impel** also implies a cause for action, this time coming from within: *because he disagreed so strongly, he was impelled to speak out*. **Push** can be used to imply a determined bid to force something to be done: *they pushed the bill through parliament*, but **thrust**, although similar, can often be used to suggest a physical action: *the actor was thrust into the public eye; she thrust a leaflet in my hand*.

The forcing of unwelcome demands or measures can be conveyed in the terms **impose** and **inflict**: *the new laws were imposed without public consultation*.

---

forced *adj*

1 UNNATURAL, stiff, wooden, stilted, laboured, strained, false, artificial, contrived, feigned, insincere, overdone

FORMAL affected

2 COMPULSORY, obligatory, binding, involuntary, enforced, compelled

FORMAL mandatory

Ⓔ 1 spontaneous, natural, sincere

---

forceful *adj*

strong, mighty, powerful, potent, effective, compelling, convincing, impressive, persuasive, telling, valid, weighty, urgent, emphatic, vehement, forcible, dynamic, high-powered, assertive, energetic, vigorous

FORMAL cogent

COLLOQ. *N Am* gutty

Ⓔ weak, feeble

forcefully *adv*

strongly, powerfully, effectively, emphatically, convincingly, persuasively, vehemently, assertively, energetically, vigorously

Ⓔ weakly, feebly

forcible *adj*

1 VIOLENT, aggressive, coercive, forced, by/using force

2 POWERFUL, strong, compelling, compulsory, effective, impressive, telling, weighty, cogent, energetic, forceful, vehement, mighty, potent

Ⓔ 1, 2 feeble, weak

forcibly *adv*

violently, by force, using force, against your will, compulsorily, obligatorily, under compulsion, under duress, vigorously, vehemently, emphatically, willy-nilly

ford *n*

causeway, crossing, crossing place; *S Afr* drift

forebear *n*

ancestor, forefather, father, predecessor, forerunner, antecedent

FORMAL progenitor, primogenitor

Ⓔ descendant

foreboding *n*

misgiving, anxiety, worry, apprehension, apprehensiveness, suspicion, dread, fear, omen, sign, token, premonition, warning, prediction, intuition, feeling, sixth sense, hoodoo

OLD abodement

FORMAL presentiment, prognostication, presage

forecast *v, n*

• *v*

predict, prophesy, foretell, foresee, forewarn, anticipate, expect, tip off, estimate, calculate, extrapolate, project

FORMAL conjecture, prognosticate, portend, divine, augur, presage

COLLOQ. second-guess

• *n*

prediction, prophecy, expectation, forewarning, outlook, projection, extrapolation, calculation, permutation, guess, tip, speculation

TECHNICAL metcast

FORMAL prognosis, conjecture, prognostication, augury

COLLOQ. guesstimate

forefather *n*

ancestor, forebear, father, predecessor, forerunner, antecedent

FORMAL progenitor, primogenitor

Ⓔ descendant

forefront *n*

front, front line, firing line, van, vanguard, spearhead, lead, head, fore, leading/foremost position, avant-garde

OLD (*Shakesp*) vaward

Ⓔ rear

forego, forgo *v*

give up, yield, surrender, sacrifice, forfeit, waive, abandon, resign, pass up, do without, go without

FORMAL refrain from, relinquish, renounce, abstain from, eschew, abjure

foregoing *adj*

preceding, above, previous, earlier, former, prior

FORMAL antecedent, precedent, aforementioned, aforesaid
▣ following

foregone
■ **foregone conclusion**
inevitability, certainty, fact
COLLOQ. sure thing

foreground n
fore, forefront, front, prominence, leading/foremost position, centre, limelight
▣ background

forehead n
brow, temple(s), front
TECHNICAL metope
Related adjectives: metopic, frontal

foreign adj
1 *foreign policy*
international, overseas, external, alien, immigrant, imported, international, outside, exotic, ethnic, migrant, faraway, distant
2 *the technique was foreign to her*
unfamiliar, unknown, strange, outlandish, peculiar, odd, uncharacteristic, unconnected, extraneous, borrowed
▣ **1** home, domestic **2** familiar, known

foreigner n
alien, immigrant, incomer, stranger, outsider, newcomer, visitor, tramontane, outlander, *étranger*, *Ausländer*, *gaijin*
OLD *S Afr* uitlander; barbarian
▣ native

foreknowledge n
foresight, premonition, forewarning, clairvoyance, second sight
TECHNICAL precognition, prescience
FORMAL prevision, prognostication

foreman n
supervisor, superintendent, manager, leader, overseer, steward, ganger, overman, charge hand
COLLOQ. boss, gaffer; *N Am* honcho

foremost adj
first, leading, most important, front, chief, main, prime, principal, primary, first, top, cardinal, paramount, central, highest, advanced, uppermost, supreme, prime, premier, pre-eminent

foreordained adj
fated, destined, predestined, predetermined, appointed, preordained, prearranged
FORMAL foredoomed

forerunner n
precursor, predecessor, ancestor, antecedent, forefather, herald, envoy, sign, token
OLD (*Shakesp*) precurrer
FORMAL harbinger
▣ successor, follower

foresee v
envisage, anticipate, expect, forecast, predict, prophesy, foretell, foreknow, forebode
OLD previse
FORMAL prognosticate, divine

foreshadow v
predict, prophesy, signal, indicate, signify, mean, suggest, promise
FORMAL bode, prefigure, presage, augur, portend, prognosticate

foresight n
anticipation, planning, forward planning, forethought, far-sightedness, vision, caution, discernment, discrimination, care, prudence, readiness, preparedness, provision, precaution

FORMAL circumspection, perspicacity, judiciousness, prevision
▣ improvidence

forest n
wood, woodland, woods, trees, greenwood, monte, plantation, urman; *Aust* brush

---

Types of forest and wood include:

ancient forest	igapò	seasonal rainforest
boreal	littoral	secondary rainforest
chaparral	lowland	selva
cloud forest	maquis	taiga
coastal	mangrove	temperate broadleaf
coastal temperate	moist evergreen	temperate deciduous
coniferous	moist forest	temperate rainforest
deciduous	monsoon rainforest	tropical rainforest
equatorial	montane rainforest	vàrzea forest
evergreen rainforest	peat forest	wetland
evergreen	primary rainforest	
gallery forest	rainforest	
garrigue	savanna forest	
greenwood		
heath forest		

---

forested adj
wooded, reafforested

forestall v
pre-empt, anticipate, stop, avert, head off, ward off, stave off, parry, balk, frustrate, thwart, obstruct, hinder, prevent, impede, intercept, get ahead of
FORMAL preclude, obviate
COLLOQ. second-guess

forestry n
forestation, woodcraft, woodmanship, forest management
TECHNICAL afforestation, arboriculture, dendrology, silviculture

foretaste n
forewarning, foretoken, preview, trailer, sample, taster, appetizer, specimen, example, whiff, indication, anticipation, pre-echo, warning, premonition, *avant-goût*
OLD antepast
FORMAL pregustation, prelibation

foretell v
prophesy, forecast, predict, foresee, signify, foreshadow, indicate, forewarn
FORMAL prognosticate, augur, presage, divine

forethought n
preparation, planning, forward planning, provision, precaution, anticipation, foresight, far-sightedness, prudence, caution, discernment
FORMAL circumspection, perspicacity, judiciousness
▣ improvidence, carelessness

forever adv
1 ETERNALLY, always, ever, evermore, for all time, permanently, till the end of time
COLLOQ. till kingdom come, till the cows come home, for good, until hell freezes over
2 CONTINUALLY, constantly, always, persistently, incessantly, perpetually, endlessly
FORMAL interminably
COLLOQ. all the time

forewarn v
alert, advise, caution, tip off, give notice, warn, give advance warning to
FORMAL apprise, admonish, dissuade, previse

forewarning n
advance warning, advance notice, early warning
COLLOQ. tip-off

foreword *n*
preface, introduction, preliminary matter, prelims, frontmatter, prologue
FORMAL prolegomenon
☒ appendix, postscript, epilogue

forfeit *v, n*
◆ *v*
lose, give up, hand over, surrender, sacrifice, for(e)go, abandon
FORMAL relinquish, renounce
COLLOQ. pass up
◆ *n*
penalty, loss, surrender, confiscation, fine, damages, relinquishment, sconce; *dialect* rue-bargain
TECHNICAL sequestration, amercement
OLD cheat

forfeiture *n*
giving up, surrender, confiscation, loss, relinquishment, sacrifice, for(e)going
TECHNICAL escheat, attainder, sequestration
FORMAL *déchéance*

forge¹ *v*
1 MAKE, mould, cast, shape, form, fashion, found, beat out, hammer out, beat into shape, work, create, build, construct, invent, frame, devise, put together
2 *forge a document*
fake, counterfeit, falsify, copy, imitate, simulate, feign

forge²
▪ **forge ahead**
progress, make progress, move steadily, advance, go/move forward, make headway, push forward

forged *adj*
counterfeit, fake, faked, false, copied, pirate, fraudulent, bogus, sham, spurious, imitation, artificial, simulated, pretended, borrowed
FORMAL feigned, simular
COLLOQ. phoney, pseud, pseudo
☒ genuine, authentic, real

forger *n*
counterfeiter, contriver, faker, falsifier, framer, coiner, fabricator

forgery *n*
fake, counterfeit, copy, replica, reproduction, imitation, sham, fraud, faking, falsification, counterfeiting
COLLOQ. dud, phoney
☒ original

forget *v*
omit, fail, fail to remember, have no recollection of, neglect, let slip, overlook, disregard, ignore, lose sight of, dismiss, stop thinking about, think no more of, unlearn, not place, slip your mind, put out of your mind, put behind you, put aside; *dialect* disremember; *Scot* misremember
COLLOQ. go in one ear and out the other, have a memory like a sieve, dry up, wipe
SLANG corpse
☒ remember, recall, recollect
▪ **forget yourself**
misbehave, behave badly, be naughty, be guilty of misconduct

forgetful *adj*
absent-minded, scatterbrained, preoccupied, distracted, abstracted, dreamy, inattentive, oblivious, negligent, neglectful, remiss, lax, careless, heedless, unheeding
COLLOQ. with a head/memory like a sieve, not all there
☒ attentive, mindful, heedful

forgetfulness *n*
absent-mindedness, inattention, obliviousness, oblivion, dreaminess, heedlessness, carelessness, neglect, wool-

gathering, abstraction, amnesia, lapse, laxness
FORMAL obliviscence
☒ attentiveness, heedfulness

forgivable *adj*
excusable, pardonable, condonable, minor, petty, slight, trifling, innocent, venial
☒ unforgivable

forgive *v*
pardon, absolve, excuse, acquit, remit, let off, let it go, clear, spare, overlook, condone, forgive and forget, let bygones be bygones
FORMAL exonerate, exculpate
COLLOQ. shake hands, shake on it, think no more of, bury the hatchet
☒ punish, censure

Synonym nuances
Pardon may be used generally to suggest a willingness to put aside someone's wrongdoings, and in official contexts, specifically of allowing them to go unpunished: *the president pardoned thirty-five prisoners in an amnesty.* The term **spare** is reserved for relieving someone of their punishment.
  Absolve and **clear** go somewhat further by implying a complete discharge from blame: *the King was formally absolved from complicity in Becket's murder.* **Excuse** may be widely used to suggest making allowances for someone's behaviour, whereas **acquit** has more to do with rejecting accusations against someone and is usually reserved for legal contexts: *they were acquitted of illegally importing arms.* The term **remit**, although formerly used to suggest giving pardon, tends now to imply refraining from exacting: *parliament remitted all obligation on the king to repay.*
  Similarly, **let off** and **overlook** are suggestive of allowing someone to get away with something they have done wrong, whilst **let it go** implies a degree of reluctance about ignoring it: *I'll let it go this time, but be careful in future.* **Condone** would suggest acceptance or approval as well as forgiveness, although it is often used in the negative: *I cannot condone the behaviour of these children.*

---

forgiveness *n*
pardon, absolution, acquittal, remission, amnesty, mercy, leniency
FORMAL clemency, exoneration
☒ punishment, censure, blame

forgiving *adj*
merciful, pitying, lenient, tolerant, forbearing, indulgent, kind, humane, compassionate, soft-hearted, mild
FORMAL magnanimous, clement, placable
☒ merciless, censorious, harsh

forgo
see **forego**.

forgotten *adj*
unremembered, unrecalled, blotted out, disregarded, ignored, neglected, obliterated, overlooked, omitted, out of mind, past recollection, past recall, gone, left behind, buried, bygone, past, lost, irrecoverable, irretrievable, unretrieved, in the shade, in the wilderness
OLD oblivious
☒ remembered

fork *v, n*
◆ *v*
split, divide, part, separate, diverge, branch (off), go separate ways
TECHNICAL divaricate
FORMAL bifurcate
◆ *n*

branching, divergence, separation, split, division, junction, intersection
TECHNICAL divarication, furcation
FORMAL bifurcation

■ **fork out**
pay (up), give
COLLOQ. cough up, shell out, stump up

forked adj
branched, branching, divided, split, separated, Y-shaped, pronged
TECHNICAL divaricated, forficate, furcate, furcal, furcular
FORMAL tined, bifurcate

forlorn adj
1 a forlorn place
deserted, abandoned, forsaken, forgotten, neglected, bereft, friendless, lonely, lost, homeless, uncared-for, destitute, desolate
2 a forlorn person
unhappy, miserable, sad, desperate, despairing, hopeless, cheerless, wretched, helpless, pathetic, pitiable
FORMAL disconsolate
F∃ 1, 2 cheerful

forlornly adv
unhappily, miserably, sadly, desperately, despondently, hopelessly, pointlessly, unsuccessfully, in vain, to no avail
F∃ happily, successfully

form n, v
♦ n
1 APPEARANCE, shape, mould, cast, cut, guise, outline, silhouette, figure, build, construction, frame, framework, structure, format, formation, model, pattern, design, arrangement, planning, order, organization, system
FORMAL configuration, disposition, manifestation
2 a form of punishment
type, kind, sort, order, species, genus, variety, genre, style, manner, nature, character, description
3 CLASS, year, grade, stream, set
4 on top form
health, fitness, shape, trim, fettle, condition, spirits
5 ETIQUETTE, protocol, custom, usage, correct practice, convention, ritual, behaviour, polite behaviour, manners
COLLOQ. the done thing
6 QUESTIONNAIRE, document, application (form), paper, sheet
♦ v
1 SHAPE, mould, model, fashion, forge, make, manufacture, produce, create, found, establish, build, construct, assemble, put together, set up, devise, formulate, conceive, draw up, arrange, organize, order, line up, develop, acquire
2 COMPRISE, constitute, make (up), compose, serve as, be a part of
3 APPEAR, take shape, materialize, crystallize, come into existence, show up, grow, develop, become visible

formal adj
1 OFFICIAL, ceremonial, ritual, ritualistic, stately, solemn, conventional, customary, traditional, established, orthodox, correct, prescribed, approved, proper, fixed, set, standard, regular, ordered, organized, methodical
2 PRIM, starchy, stiff, strait-laced, strict, rigid, inflexible, unbending, precise, exact, punctilious, ceremonious, stilted, remote, reserved, aloof
3 a formal garden
symmetrical, ordered, orderly, controlled, arranged, regular, conventional
F∃ 1 informal 2 informal, casual

formality n
custom, convention, ceremony, ceremoniousness, ritual, procedure, rule, custom, form, matter of form, bureaucracy, red tape, protocol, etiquette, form, correctness, politeness

FORMAL decorum, propriety, punctilio
F∃ informality

formalization n
structuring, arrangement(s), arranging, standardization, organization, ordering, systematization, confirmation

formalize v
make formal, make official, structure, arrange, affirm, confirm, ordain, ratify, standardize, regularize, order, systematize, organize, fix, set, stylize, ritualize

formally adv
1 OFFICIALLY, conventionally, correctly, properly, methodically, ceremonially, ritually, solemnly
2 PRIMLY, rigidly, inflexibly, precisely, exactly, punctiliously
F∃ 1, 2 informally

format n
appearance, form, order, presentation, design, layout, pattern, plan, shape, structure, style, arrangement, make-up, look, type, construction, dimensions
FORMAL configuration

formation n
1 STRUCTURE, construction, composition, constitution, format, order, organization, arrangement, layout, make-up, grouping, pattern, design, figure
FORMAL configuration, disposition, phalanx
2 CREATION, generation, production, construction, building, making, shaping, manufacture, emergence, appearance, development, starting, founding, institution, establishment, inauguration

formative adj
determining, controlling, influential, dominant, shaping, growing, guiding, moulding, developmental, impressionable, teachable, malleable, mouldable, plastic, pliant, susceptible, sensitive
FORMAL determinative, creant
F∃ destructive

former adj
past, ex-, one-time, sometime, late, departed, old, old-time, ancient, bygone, historical, earlier, prior, previous, preceding, long ago, long-gone, first, first-mentioned, antecedent, foregoing, above
FORMAL erstwhile, quondam, of yore
F∃ current, present, future, following

formerly adv
once, in the past, previously, historically, earlier, at an earlier time, before, at one time, once
FORMAL heretofore, hitherto, erst, erstwhile
F∃ currently, now, later

formidable adj
daunting, challenging, redoubtable, intimidating, threatening, menacing, frightening, terrifying, horrifying, alarming, terrific, frightful, horrific, fearful, great, huge, colossal, mammoth, tremendous, impressive, powerful, awesome, dreadful, overwhelming, staggering, onerous
FORMAL prodigious
COLLOQ. scary, mind-blowing, spooky

formidably adv
menacingly, frightfully, fearfully, shockingly, horrifically, tremendously, dreadfully, awfully, overwhelmingly

formless adj
amorphous, shapeless, confused, chaotic, disorganized, indefinite, indeterminate, incoherent, nebulous, vague, unshaped, unformed
FORMAL inchoate, indigest
F∃ definite, orderly

formula n
recipe, prescription, proposal, blueprint, code, fixed/set expression, wording, rubric, rule, principle, form, precept, procedure, technique, convention, method, way

formulate v
devise, create, compose, prepare, conceive, think up, invent, originate, found, form, give form to, work out, plan, design, map out, draw up, frame, cast, propose, define, express, articulate, state, set down, put down, lay down, specify, detail, itemize, symbolize, develop, evolve
OLD formate

formulation n
1 *an experimental formulation*
production, preparation, composition, formula, product
2 *the formulation of a strategy*
devising, creating, composition, preparation, conception, framing, definition, expression, specification, development

fornication n
extramarital relations/relationship, extramarital sex, adultery, unfaithfulness, infidelity, affair, liaison, entanglement, flirtation, unchastity
OLD avoutry
COLLOQ. two-timing, cheating, a bit on the side
SLANG playing around, playing the field
E3 faithfulness, fidelity

forsake v
desert, abandon, throw over, discard, jettison, cast off, reject, repudiate, set aside, disown, leave, give up, surrender, for(e)go
OLD destitute, forlese, waive
FORMAL relinquish, renounce
COLLOQ. jilt, quit, ditch, chuck, leave in the lurch, have done with, turn your back on

forsaken adj
abandoned, deserted, neglected, godforsaken, remote, isolated, desolate, forlorn, lonely, marooned, solitary, derelict, dreary, destitute, cast off, discarded, disowned, rejected, shunned, outcast, ignored, friendless
COLLOQ. jilted, left in the lurch

forswear v
abandon, give up, for(e)go, repudiate, drop, disown, disclaim, reject, deny, do without, renege, lie, perjure yourself
FORMAL forsake, renounce, recant, disavow, abjure, retract
COLLOQ. cut out, pack in, jack in
E3 revert to

fort n
fortress, castle, tower, watchtower, citadel, keep, stronghold, fortification, turret, battlements, parapet, garrison, station, camp, donjon, redoubt

forte n
strong point, strength, skill, speciality, gift, talent, aptitude, bent, métier
E3 weak point, inadequacy

forth adv
out, away, off, outside, on, onwards, forwards, into existence, into view

forthcoming adj
1 *their forthcoming wedding*
impending, imminent, approaching, coming, future, upcoming, prospective, in the offing, projected, expected
2 AVAILABLE, accessible, obtainable, ready, at your disposal
COLLOQ. on tap, up for grabs, yours for the asking/taking
3 COMMUNICATIVE, talkative, chatty, conversational, sociable, friendly, informative, expansive, open, frank, direct
FORMAL loquacious, voluble
E3 3 reticent, reserved

forthright adj
direct, straightforward, blunt, frank, candid, plain, plain-spoken, open, honest, bold, outspoken, four-square, trenchant

COLLOQ. up-front
E3 devious, secretive

forthwith adv
immediately, as soon as possible, at once, directly, instantly, straightaway, right away, without delay, quickly
COLLOQ. pronto, asap

fortification n
defence, strengthening, reinforcement, protection, castle, citadel, fort, fortress, keep, stronghold, earthwork, rampart, bulwark, bastion, battlements, parapet, barricade, palisade, buttressing, bawn, embattlement, entrenchment, munition, outwork, redoubt, stockade
TECHNICAL contravallation

fortify v
1 STRENGTHEN, reinforce, brace, shore up, buttress, fence, fort, mound, rampart, wall, garrison, defend, guard, protect, secure, cover, embattle, entrench
OLD munite
FORMAL munify
2 INVIGORATE, sustain, support, boost, revive, energize, brace, encourage, hearten, cheer, reassure, strengthen, buoy up
E3 1 weaken

fortitude n
courage, bravery, valour, pluck, nerve, resolution, determination, tenacity, perseverance, patience, firmness, strength of mind, backbone, mettle, willpower, hardihood, endurance, stoicism
FORMAL forbearance
COLLOQ. guts, grit, spine
E3 cowardice, fear

fortress n
stronghold, castle, fort, citadel, fortification, fastness, tower, keep, garrison, battlements

fortuitous adj
accidental, chance, random, arbitrary, casual, haphazard, incidental, unforeseen, unexpected, unplanned, unintentional, lucky, fortunate, providential
COLLOQ. fluky
E3 intentional, planned, anticipated

fortuitously adv
accidentally, by chance, randomly, at random, arbitrarily, casually, haphazardly, incidentally, inadvertently, unexpectedly, unintentionally, fortunately, luckily
E3 intentionally

fortunate adj
lucky, providential, happy, prosperous, flourishing, successful, well-off, well, rich, timely, well-timed, opportune, convenient, advantageous, favourable, encouraging, promising, profitable, blessed, favoured; *Scot* canny
OLD seely
FORMAL felicitous, propitious, auspicious, providential
E3 unlucky, unfortunate, unhappy

> **Synonym nuances**
> While **lucky** is a very general synonym, **providential** is more suggestive of divine intervention having brought something about: *their progress was aided by a providential wind*. **Happy** could describe a stroke of fortune that causes something to turn out very well: *I met my wife due to a happy coincidence*. The terms **prosperous**, **well-off** and **rich** have more to do with being in a fortunate financial state, though **rich** may occasionally be used of less material possessions: *rich rewards*.
> **Flourishing**, **successful** and **profitable** could also be used of something that is thriving and generating wealth. The terms **timely**, **well-timed** and **opportune** describe something happening at the most appropriate time,

whilst **convenient** is a rather more restrained term which has wider suggestions of general suitability: *the switch of dates was convenient for my plans.* You could also use **advantageous** or **favourable** of something having a beneficial element, whereas **encouraging** and **promising** put the emphasis on offering hope of future good fortune: *there have been encouraging results in trials of the new drug.*

The terms **blessed** and **favoured** suggest being the recipient of a fortuitous gift, and again there is a divine aspect: *I considered myself blessed to be given another chance.*

fortunately *adv*
luckily, happily, thankfully, conveniently, encouragingly
FORMAL providentially
⊟ unfortunately

fortune *n*
1 WEALTH, riches, treasure, income, means, substance, assets, estate, property, possessions, affluence, prosperity, success
FORMAL opulence
COLLOQ. mint, pile, packet, bundle, bomb
SLANG megabucks, big bucks
2 LUCK, chance, coincidence, accident, providence, fate, destiny, doom, lot, portion, cup, life, history, future
FORMAL serendipity
3 *the fortunes of the company*
experience, circumstances, position, condition, situation, state of affairs

fortune-teller *n*
prophet, prophetess, visionary, soothsayer, clairvoyant, seer, augur, diviner, oracle, sibyl, psychic, telepath

forum *n*
meeting, meeting-place, arena, rostrum, stage, assembly, gathering, conference, discussion, debate, symposium

forward *adj, adv, v*
• *adj*
1 FIRST, head, front, fore, foremost, leading, advance, onward, advancing, progressing, progressive, prospective, future, forward-looking, go-ahead, enterprising
FORMAL frontal
2 CONFIDENT, over-confident, assertive, over-assertive, bold, audacious, brazen, brash, barefaced, impudent, impertinent, cheeky, cocky, familiar, overfamiliar, presumptuous, presuming, aggressive, thrusting, pushy
COLLOQ. fresh
3 EARLY, advance, precocious, premature, advanced, well-advanced, well-developed
4 *forward planning*
long-range, medium-range, long-term, medium-term, future
⊟ 1 backward, retrograde 2 shy, modest 3 late, retarded
• *adv*
forwards, ahead, on, onward, onwards, out, forth, into view, into the open
• *v*
1 ADVANCE, promote, further, foster, encourage, support, back, favour, help, assist, aid, facilitate, accelerate, speed (up), step up, hurry, hasten, dispatch
FORMAL expedite
2 SEND (ON), pass on, redirect, readdress, post, mail, transport, deliver, ship
⊟ 1 impede, obstruct, hinder, slow

forward-looking *adj*
far-sighted, enterprising, progressive, reforming, modern, innovative, dynamic, enlightened, avant-garde, liberal
COLLOQ. go-getting, goey, go-ahead
⊟ conservative, retrograde

forwardness *n*
confidence, over-confidence, boldness, audacity, brashness, brazenness, pertness, presumption, presumptuousness, impertinence, impudence, aggressiveness
OLD *N Am* forth-putting
COLLOQ. cheek, cheekiness, neck, brass neck, pushiness
⊟ reserve, retiring

forwards *adv*
forward, ahead, on, onwards, out, forth

fossil *n*
remains, remnant, petrified remains/impression, ammonite, relic, reliquiae
TECHNICAL graptolite, coprolite, trilobite

fossilized *adj*
1 HARDENED, stony
FORMAL petrified, ossified
2 OUT OF DATE, archaic, obsolete, old-fashioned, passé, outmoded, prehistoric, antediluvian, anachronistic, antiquated, extinct, dead
⊟ 2 up-to-date

foster *v*
1 *foster a child*
raise, rear, bring up, nurse, care for, take care of, look after, nurture, nourish, feed, sustain
2 *foster an activity*
help, assist, aid, back, support, uphold, promote, advance, encourage, stimulate, further, boost, cultivate, nurture, hold, cherish, make much of, entertain, harbour, nurse, foment
OLD nuzzle
⊟ 2 neglect, discourage

foul *adj, v*
• *adj*
1 DISGUSTING, offensive, repulsive, revolting, repellent, dirty, soiled, filthy, mucky, unclean, tainted, infected, impure, defiled, polluted, contaminated, rank, f(o)etid, stinking, smelly, foul-smelling, putrid, decayed, rotting, rotten, sickening, nauseating, abominable, loathsome, odious, squalid
OLD (*Shakesp*) reeky
FORMAL putrescent, putrefactive
2 *foul language*
obscene, lewd, smutty, dirty, filthy, indecent, coarse, off-colour, ribald, lewd, indelicate, vulgar, gross, low, blasphemous, profane, offensive, abusive
COLLOQ. blue
3 NASTY, disagreeable, wicked, vicious, vile, base, mean, low, loathsome, despicable, offensive, revolting, repulsive, disgusting, abhorrent, detestable, horrible, disgraceful, shameful, contemptible
FORMAL iniquitous, heinous, execrable, nefarious
4 *foul weather*
bad, nasty, unpleasant, disagreeable, rainy, wet, stormy, squally, blustery, rough, dirty, wild
FORMAL inclement
5 *in a foul temper*
bad, angry, bad, bad-tempered, irritable, cross, mean, snappy, quick-tempered, grumpy, tetchy, testy, mean, black, gnarled, peppery, prickly, fractious, narky, impatient, choleric, bilious, splenetic, dyspeptic; *dialect* stingy; *Scot* capernoity; *Scot & Irish* carnaptious
COLLOQ. stroppy, ratty, shirty, crotchety, crabbed, crabby, grouchy, edgy, feisty, humpy
⊟ 1, 2 clean 4 fine 5 good
• *v*
1 DIRTY, soil, stain, sully, muddy, blacken, defile, taint, pollute, contaminate
2 ENTANGLE, catch, snarl, twist, ensnare, tangle
3 BLOCK, obstruct, clog, choke, jam, foul up
⊟ 1 clean 2 disentangle 3 clear

■ **foul play**
criminal violence/activity, crime, unfair/dishonest behaviour, breach of the rules, deception, dirty work, double-dealing
COLLOQ. funny business, sharp practice
◩ fair play, justice

foul-mouthed *adj*
coarse, obscene, offensive, profane, abusive, blasphemous
FORMAL foul-spoken

found *v*
1 ESTABLISH, originate, create, bring into being, organize, initiate, institute, inaugurate, set up, constitute, develop, start, endow
2 BASE, ground, bottom, root, rest, set, ground, settle, fix, plant, locate, position, raise, build, erect, construct

foundation *n*
1 *the foundations of a building*
base, foot, bottom, ground, bedrock, substance, basis, footing, underpinning, understructure, substructure, substratum
2 *the foundation of a belief*
basis, support, base, groundwork, bedrock, key, keynote, reason(s), rationale, fundamental(s), fundamental point, starting-point, premise, principle, first principles, main ingredient, alpha and omega, essential(s), essence, heart, core, thrust
FORMAL quintessence, hypostasis
3 *the foundation of the college in 1900*
setting-up, establishment, founding, institution, inauguration, initiation, creation, constitution, endowment, organization, groundwork
4 *a charitable foundation*
organization, institution, charity, endowment, fund
5 *the story is without foundation*
grounds, justification, base, basis, excuse, vindication, reason, motive, inducement, cause, occasion, call, score, account, argument, principle

founder[1] *n*
the founder of the university
originator, initiator, father, mother, benefactor, creator, author, architect, designer, inventor, prime mover, maker, builder, constructor, organizer, institutor, establisher, developer, discoverer

founder[2] *v*
1 *the ship foundered*
sink, go down, go to the bottom, submerge, capsize
2 *the plan foundered*
subside, collapse, break down, fall, be unsuccessful, come to grief, fail, misfire, miscarry, abort, fall through, come to nothing, go wrong
◩ **2** succeed

foundling *n*
stray, orphan, waif, abandoned infant, outcast, urchin, *enfant trouvé*

fount *n*
source, origin, rise, well, cause, birth, beginning, mainspring, fountainhead, wellhead
FORMAL commencement, inception

fountain *n*
1 SPRAY, jet, *jet d'eau*, spout, spring, spurt, fount, well, wellspring, source, reservoir; *dialect* pant
OLD waterworks, conduit, gerbe, laver, scuttlebutt, scuttle cask
2 SOURCE, origin, fount, rise, well, cause, birth, beginning, mainspring, fountainhead, wellhead
OLD font
FORMAL commencement, inception

four-square *adv*
firmly, squarely, resolutely, solidly, frankly, honestly

fowl *n*
bird, duck, chicken, cock, hen, bantam, goose, turkey, pheasant, wildfowl, poultry
Related adjective: gallinaceous

foxy *adj*
crafty, canny, devious, cunning, artful, astute, sharp, shrewd, sly, tricky, wily, fly, knowing, guileful
◩ naive, open

foyer *n*
entrance hall, hall, hallway, reception, lobby, vestibule, antechamber, anteroom

fracas *n*
brawl, disturbance, fight, free-for-all, quarrel, riot, trouble, uproar, row, rumpus, scuffle, barney, affray, ruckus, ruction, rout, ruffle, shindy, mêlée, Donnybrook
COLLOQ. aggro, bust-up, scrap, spat, set-to

fraction *n*
proportion, amount, ratio, subdivision, part, bit

fractional *adj*
slight, small, little, minute, partial, insignificant, negligible, insubstantial, imperceptible, subtle

fractious *adj*
awkward, quarrelsome, cross, irritable, grumpy, touchy, bad-tempered, petulant, testy, unruly, choleric, captious, fretful, peevish
FORMAL querulous, recalcitrant, refractory
COLLOQ. crabby, crotchety, grouchy
◩ complaisant, placid

fracture *n, v*
♦ *n*
break, breakage, crack, fissure, cleft, rupture, split, splitting, rift, rent, schism, breach, gap, opening, aperture, slit
TECHNICAL fault
♦ *v*
break, crack, rupture, split, splinter, chip, snap
◩ join

fragile *adj*
1 BRITTLE, breakable, frail, delicate, tender, flimsy, dainty, fine, slight, insubstantial, unstable
FORMAL frangible
2 *feel fragile after an illness*
weak, feeble, delicate, infirm
◩ **1** robust, tough, durable, sturdy **2** strong

fragility *n*
brittleness, breakableness, delicacy, frailty, weakness, feebleness, infirmity
FORMAL frangibility
◩ durability, robustness, strength

fragment *n, v*
♦ *n*
piece, bit, part, portion, fraction, particle, crumb, morsel, scrap, end, remainder, remains, remnant, shred, snip, snippet, chip, splinter, shatter, shiver, sliver, chink, shard, smithereen(s), patch, morceau, mite, snatch, cantlet, flitter, potsherd; *dialect* ort; *Scot* blaud, blad
TECHNICAL sequestrum, sheave, spar, xenolith
OLD quantity, flinder, fritter, frust, rift; (*Shakesp*) flaw
♦ *v*
break, shatter, splinter, shiver, crumble, disintegrate, come to pieces, come apart, break up, divide, split (up), disunite, smash to pieces/smithereens
◩ hold together, join

fragmentary *adj*
bitty, piecemeal, scrappy, broken, disjointed, disconnected, separate, scattered, sketchy, partial, incomplete, uneven, discontinuous, incoherent
◩ whole, complete

fragmentation n
break-up, shattering, crumbling, disintegration, decomposition, division, separation, splitting, splitting-up

fragmented adj
broken, divided, separate, disintegrated, disjointed, disunited, departmentalized, compartmentalized, in pieces, in bits, incomplete
F3 complete, whole

fragrance n
perfume, scent, smell, sweet smell, odour, aroma, bouquet, balm, attar, otto
FORMAL redolence

fragrant adj
perfumed, scented, sweet-smelling, sweet-scented, sweet, balmy, aromatic, odorous
FORMAL redolent, odoriferous
F3 unscented

frail adj
delicate, brittle, breakable, easily broken, fragile, flimsy, insubstantial, slight, puny, weak, feeble, infirm, unwell, unsound, vulnerable, susceptible
FORMAL frangible
F3 robust, tough, strong

frailty n
weakness, weak point, foible, failing, deficiency, shortcoming, fault, defect, flaw, blemish, imperfection, infirmity, fallibility, susceptibility, vulnerability, brittleness, fragility, delicacy
F3 strength, robustness, toughness

frame n, v
◆ n
1 STRUCTURE, fabric, framework, skeleton, carcase, shell, casing, chassis, substructure, foundation, construction, support, bodywork, body, build, form, physique, figure, size, shape
2 MOUNT, mounting, setting, surround, border, edge
◆ v
1 COMPOSE, formulate, conceive, establish, create, devise, contrive, concoct, plan, map out, plot, sketch, draw up, draft, shape, form, model, fashion, mould, forge, assemble, put together, build, set up, erect, construct, fabricate, make, manufacture
COLLOQ. cook up
2 SURROUND, enclose, box in, case, encase, mount
3 *I've been framed*
trap, incriminate, plant
COLLOQ. set up, fit up, stitch up, pin on, cook up a charge
■ **frame of mind**
state (of mind), mood, condition, humour, temper, disposition, spirit, outlook, attitude

frame-up n
fabrication, trap, plot, conspiracy
COLLOQ. fit-up, fix, put-up job, trumped-up charge

framework n
structure, fabric, bare bones, skeleton, shell, frame, casing, outline, plan, foundation, groundwork, substructure, trestle, trestlework, lattice, rack, scheme, constraints, parameters

franchise n
concession, licence, charter, warrant, authorization, permission, consent, privilege, right, prerogative, liberty, freedom, immunity, exemption
FORMAL suffrage, enfranchisement

frank adj, v
◆ adj
honest, truthful, sincere, genuine, candid, blunt, open, free, plain, plain-spoken, direct, forthright, straight, straightforward, downright, hard-hitting, outspoken, explicit, bluff

COLLOQ. straight from the shoulder, up-front
F3 insincere, evasive
◆ v
stamp, mark, postmark, cancel

Synonym nuances
adjective
Honest is a positive term in that it implies an absence of deception in all areas of life, whilst **truthful** is more neutral and more narrow, referring only to always telling what is true. Both **sincere** and **genuine** are also approbatory terms, describing those who have belief in what they say or do. **Candid** is more neutral, having more to do with being unreservedly open: *the book's candid discussion of sexual matters.* **Blunt** is rather more disapproving, implying a lack of tact; **bluff** is similar, but also has connotations of heartiness: *he expressed himself in a macho, bluff way.*
  The terms **plain** and **straight** suggest a lack of adornment: *the plain facts*, with **plain-spoken**, **straightforward**, **direct** and **forthright** suggesting a similar absence of evasion in speech, with their use being unmarked by approval or disapproval. On the other hand, **downright**, although similar in meaning, usually suggests less admirable attributes: *downright rudeness.*
  Both **hard-hitting** and **outspoken** imply that the frankness may provoke a reaction: *an outspoken campaigner for democracy*, while **explicit** emphasizes that something is unambiguous: *art critics are not always explicit in their evaluations of works.*

---

frankly adv
to be frank, to be honest, to be blunt, in truth, to tell you the truth, honestly, candidly, bluntly, truthfully, openly, freely, plainly, directly, straight, explicitly, without reserve, straight from the shoulder, eye to eye, eyeball to eyeball
COLLOQ. straight out, laying it on the line, not beating about the bush, not mincing your words
F3 insincerely, evasively

frankness n
bluntness, candour, forthrightness, plain speaking, openness, directness, sincerity, outspokenness, truthfulness
FORMAL ingenuousness
F3 reserve

frantic adj
agitated, overwrought, fraught, desperate, beside yourself, furious, raging, mad, wild, raving, frenzied, berserk, frenetic, distressed, distracted, distraught, out of control, panic-stricken, hectic
COLLOQ. at your wits'end
F3 calm, composed

frantically adv
desperately, furiously, madly, wildly, hysterically, out of control, beside yourself
COLLOQ. at your wits'end, tearing your hair out

fraternity n
comradeship, brotherhood, kinship, camaraderie, companionship, set, society, association, circle, club, company, guild, order, league, union, fellowship, clan

fraternize v
mix, mingle, socialize, associate, keep company, move, go around, affiliate, unite, sympathize, cordialize
FORMAL consort, forgather
COLLOQ. hang about, hobnob, pal up with, gang up with, rub shoulders
F3 shun, ignore

fraud n
1 DECEIT, deception, guile, fraudulence, cheating, swindle, swindling, double-dealing, sharp practice,

embezzlement, fake, counterfeit, forgery, sham, hoax, trick, trickery, racket, roguery, humbug, imposture, supercherie
TECHNICAL stellionate, *fraus pia*
FORMAL duplicity, chicanery
COLLOQ. con, riddle, scam, fix, diddle, swiz, take-in
SLANG rip-off; *N Am* gold brick
2 CHARLATAN, impostor, pretender, sham, fake, bluffer, hoaxer, cheat, swindler, fraudster, embezzler, double-dealer, trickster, quack, mountebank
COLLOQ. phoney, con man

fraudulent *adj*
dishonest, criminal, deceitful, deceptive, false, bogus, sham, counterfeit, swindling, cheating, double-dealing, unscrupulous, exploitative, shameless, surreptitious
FORMAL duplicitous
COLLOQ. crooked, shady, phoney; *Aust* cronk
E3 honest, genuine

fraudulently *adv*
dishonestly, deceitfully, falsely, unscrupulously, shamelessly, corruptly, illegally
E3 honestly

fraught *adj*
1 FULL, filled, charged, abounding, accompanied, attended, bristling
FORMAL laden, replete
2 ANXIOUS, tense, agitated, worried, under stress, distressed, distraught, overwrought
COLLOQ. uptight, stressed out
E3 calm, untroublesome

fray *v, n*
 • *v*
1 *the rope is fraying*
become ragged, become threadbare, wear (out), frazzle, rag, unravel, wear thin
OLD fridge
2 *tempers were fraying*
irritate, vex, strain, stress, tax, overtax, make tense, make nervous, push too far, put on edge
 • *n*
brawl, scuffle, free-for-all, set-to, clash, conflict, fight, combat, battle, quarrel, row, rumpus, disturbance, riot, affray, excitement, challenge
OLD wigs on the green
COLLOQ. dust-up, aggro, bovver, scrap, scrape, punch-up, pasting, bashing

frayed *adj*
ragged, tattered, worn, threadbare, unravelled, thin, worn thin

freak *n, adj, v*
 • *n*
1 MONSTER, mutant, mutation, freak of nature, monstrosity, deformity, irregularity
TECHNICAL *lusus naturae*
FORMAL malformation
2 ANOMALY, abnormality, aberration, oddity, curiosity, quirk, whim, vagary, twist, turn
FORMAL caprice
COLLOQ. oddball, weirdo
SLANG *N Am* geek
3 ENTHUSIAST, fanatic, addict, devotee, fan
FORMAL aficionado
COLLOQ. buff, fiend, nut
 • *adj*
abnormal, atypical, unusual, exceptional, odd, queer, bizarre, erratic, unpredictable, unexpected, surprise, chance
FORMAL aberrant, capricious, fortuitous
COLLOQ. fluky
E3 normal, common

▪ **freak out**
go crazy, go wild, go berserk, go out of your mind, lose control, lose your self-control
COLLOQ. throw a wobbly, explode, go off the deep end, go bananas
SLANG *N Am* wig out

freakish *adj*
unusual, odd, abnormal, strange, peculiar, unconventional, unpredictable, weird, outlandish, freaky, whimsical, fanciful, fantastic, grotesque, monstrous, malformed, arbitrary, fitful, changeable, erratic
FORMAL aberrant, capricious
E3 ordinary, normal

free *adj, v, adv*
 • *adj*
1 *free tickets*
gratis, without charge, free of charge, for nothing, at no cost, at no extra cost, complimentary, with compliments
COLLOQ. on the house
SLANG buckshee
2 *free to move*
at liberty, at large, loose, on the loose, unattached, unrestrained, unconfined, out
COLLOQ. free as a bird
3 *a free country*
liberated, emancipated, sovereign, independent, democratic, self-governing, self-ruling, autonomous
FORMAL autarchic
4 *free of dirt*
lacking, without, unaffected by, immune to, exempt from, safe from, clear of
FORMAL devoid of
5 *free time; a free seat*
spare, available, idle, unemployed, unoccupied, off duty, with time on your hands, untaken, vacant, empty
6 CLEAR, unobstructed, unimpeded, open, unblocked, unhampered, unrestricted
7 GENEROUS, liberal, open-handed, lavish, charitable, giving, hospitable, unstinting
FORMAL munificent
8 *with his free hand*
unattached, unfastened, loose, unsecured
9 *a free translation*
loose, rough, general, broad, vague, inexact, imprecise
10 *his free manner; free movement*
easy, relaxed, easy-going, smooth, natural, uninhibited, casual, spontaneous, fluid
COLLOQ. laid-back, doing your own thing, doing as you please
E3 **2** imprisoned, bound, tied, fettered, confined, restricted **4** liable to, affected by **5** busy, occupied, at work, reserved, engaged; *colloq.* tied up **6** blocked, obstructed **7** mean, stingy **8** attached **9** literal, rigorous, exact, precise **10** inhibited, formal, tense
 • *v*
1 *free a prisoner*
release, discharge, let go, let out, loose, turn loose, set loose, set free, untie, unbind, unchain, unleash, liberate, emancipate
2 *free someone trapped*
rescue, deliver, save, ransom, disentangle, disengage, extricate
3 *free someone from debt*
clear, make available, rid, relieve, unburden, exempt, excuse, except, absolve, acquit
E3 **1** imprison, confine
 • *adv*
1 FOR NOTHING, for free, without charge, gratis, freely, for love
2 GENEROUSLY, liberally, lavishly, extravagantly, abundantly, copiously
E3 **2** meanly

■ **free and easy**
casual, informal, easy-going, relaxed, happy-go-lucky, carefree, spontaneous, tolerant
COLLOQ. laid-back
F3 inhibited, formal

■ **free hand**
authority, freedom, latitude, liberty, licence, free rein, carte blanche, permission, power, scope, discretion

freedom n
1 LIBERTY, emancipation, deliverance, release, exemption, immunity, impunity
2 INDEPENDENCE, autonomy, self-government, sovereignty, democracy, emancipation, home rule
FORMAL autarchy
3 RANGE, scope, play, leeway, flexibility, margin, latitude, licence, opportunity, privilege, right, power, prerogative, free rein, free hand; Aust & NZ open slather
F3 **1** captivity, confinement **3** restriction

free-for-all n
brawl, fight, scrap, scuffle, mêlée, fray, affray, broil, skirmish, fracas, rumpus, ruckus, disorder, row, argument, quarrel, squabble, dispute, clash, fisticuffs, Donnybrook, bagarre; dialect fratch; Aust & NZ stoush
OLD brabble, brangle; Scot tuilyie
FORMAL altercation
COLLOQ. punch-up, bust-up, dust-up

freely adv
1 READILY, willingly, voluntarily, of your own volition, of your own free will, spontaneously, easily
2 give freely
generously, liberally, lavishly, extravagantly, amply, abundantly
3 speak freely
frankly, candidly, bluntly, unreservedly, openly, plainly, spontaneously, ad-lib
4 move freely
easily, smoothly, naturally, loosely, frictionlessly, without jerking, without resistance, in all directions
F3 **2** grudgingly **3** evasively, cautiously

freethinker n
rationalist, sceptic, agnostic, doubter, nonconformist, libertine, independent, deist, unbeliever, infidel

freethinking adj
rationalist, sceptical, agnostic, nonconformist, broad-minded, open-minded, liberal, independent, unconventional

free will n
freedom, liberty, independence, self-determination, self-sufficiency, spontaneity
TECHNICAL autarky
FORMAL volition, autonomy

■ **of your own free will**
voluntarily, willingly, freely, intentionally, consciously, deliberately, purposely, spontaneously, by choice, on your own initiative, of your own accord
F3 involuntarily, unwillingly

freeze v, n
♦ v
1 ICE OVER, ice up, congeal, solidify, set, harden, stiffen
TECHNICAL glaciate
2 DEEP-FREEZE, ice, refrigerate, chill, cool, preserve, freeze-dry, enfreeze
3 GET COLD, shiver, quiver, catch a chill, turn blue with cold, your teeth be chattering
4 STOP, suspend, fix, immobilize, halt, stand still, stop dead in your tracks, become paralysed, hold
5 FIX, hold, suspend, peg
♦ n
1 FROST, freeze-up, cold snap
2 STOPPAGE, halt, standstill, shutdown, suspension,

interruption, postponement, stay, embargo, fixing, moratorium

■ **freeze out**
expel, eject, evict, throw out, remove, excommunicate, ostracize, boycott, ignore, snub, cut, ice out, lock out
COLLOQ. boot out, turf out, kick out, brush off, give the cold shoulder to, send to Coventry

freezing adj
icy, frosty, glacial, arctic, polar, Siberian, wintry, raw, bitter, bitterly cold, biting, cutting, piercing, penetrating, numbing, stinging, numb, cold, chilly
COLLOQ. baltic
SLANG brass monkeys
F3 hot, warm

freight n
1 CARGO, load, lading, payload, contents, goods, merchandise, consignment, shipment
OLD fraught
2 TRANSPORTATION, conveyance, carriage, haulage, freightage, portage

frenetic adj
frantic, wild, frenzied, hectic, overwrought, demented, distraught, excited, unbalanced, mad, insane, berserk, hysterical, manic, maniacal, obsessive, hyperactive
F3 calm, placid

frenetically adv
frantically, hectically, wildly, excitedly, intensely, madly, hysterically, manically
F3 calmly, placidly

frenzied adj
frantic, frenetic, hectic, feverish, desperate, furious, overwrought, distraught, distracted, crazed, wild, uncontrolled, mad, berserk, amok, raving, demented, hysterical, manic, panic-stricken, out of control, uncontrolled, beside yourself, obsessive, at your wits' end
F3 calm, composed

frenzy n
1 TURMOIL, agitation, wildness, distraction, madness, lunacy, insanity, mania, hysteria, delirium, fever
TECHNICAL must, musth, phrenesis
OLD derangement
COLLOQ. tailspin
2 BURST, fit, bout, spasm, paroxysm, convulsion, seizure, outburst, transport, passion, rage, fury
TECHNICAL nympholepsy, oestrus
F3 **1** calm, composure

frequency n
frequentness, incidence, prevalence, recurrence, rate of occurrence, repetition, commonness, constancy
OLD oftenness
FORMAL periodicity
F3 infrequency

frequent adj, v
♦ adj
common, commonplace, happening often, normal, everyday, familiar, usual, customary, accustomed, habitual, prevailing, prevalent, predominant, numerous, countless, incessant, constant, continual, persistent, repeated, recurring, recurrent, regular, hourly, daily, weekly, thick
OLD often
F3 infrequent
♦ v
visit, visit often, go to frequently, go to regularly, patronize, attend, haunt, associate with, lobby
OLD habituate, practise
COLLOQ. hang out at, hang about at

frequenter n
regular, regular visitor, customer, client, patron, haunter, habitué

frequently *adv*

often, commonly, many times, much, many a time, over and over, repeatedly, persistently, continually, habitually, customarily, regularly, hourly, daily, weekly, thick; *N Am* oftentimes

COLLOQ. half the time, nine times out of ten, more times than you've had hot dinners

F₃ infrequently, seldom

fresh *adj*

1 ADDITIONAL, supplementary, extra, more, further, other
2 NEW, novel, innovative, original, different, brand-new, unconventional, revolutionary, modern, up-to-date, recent, latest, exciting, unusual

COLLOQ. new-fangled

3 REFRESHING, bracing, invigorating, brisk, crisp, keen, cool, chilly, windy, fair, bright, clean, clear, pure, unfaded, unpolluted

4 *fresh fruit*
raw, natural, unprocessed, crude, firm, crisp, unpreserved, uncured, undried

5 REFRESHED, revived, restored, renewed, rested, invigorated, stimulated, energetic, vigorous, lively, vibrant, enthusiastic, alert, vital, bouncing

COLLOQ. raring to go, ready for more, yourself again, a new person, fresh as a daisy, bright-eyed and bushy-tailed

6 *a fresh complexion*
healthy, healthy-looking, glowing, bright, clear, blooming, fair, pink, rosy

7 *fresh from university*
straight, just, right, direct

8 PERT, disrespectful, impudent, insolent, impertinent, cheeky, cocky, bold, brazen, forward, familiar, overfamiliar, presumptuous

COLLOQ. saucy; *N Am* sassy

F₃ **2** old, hackneyed **3** stale **4** preserved, tinned, processed **5** tired

freshen *v*

1 AIR, ventilate, purify, clean, clear, deodorize
2 REFRESH, restore, revitalize, revive, reinvigorate, liven (up), enliven, stimulate, rouse

COLLOQ. tart up

F₃ **2** tire

■ **freshen up**
tidy yourself up, have a wash, wash yourself, get washed, spruce yourself up, get spruced up

freshly *adv*

recently, lately, of late, newly, barely, just, in the last few days, in the past few days/weeks, not long ago, a short time ago, a little while back

F₃ long ago

freshman *n*

first-year, fresher, first-year student, underclassman, newcomer

COLLOQ. *N Am* frosh

freshness *n*

brightness, cleanness, clearness, newness, originality, novelty, bloom, shine, glow, sparkle, vigour, wholesomeness

F₃ staleness, tiredness

fret *v*

1 WORRY, be anxious, be upset, agonize, anguish, be distressed, brood, pine, mope, concern yourself, make a fuss
2 VEX, irritate, nettle, bother, trouble, concern, anger, annoy, exasperate, infuriate, rile, torment

fretful *adj*

worried, anxious, unhappy, upset, distressed, disturbed, uneasy, fearful, tense, restless, troubled

COLLOQ. edgy, uptight

F₃ calm

fretfully *adv*

anxiously, worriedly, uneasily, fearfully, tensely, restlessly

COLLOQ. edgily

F₃ calmly

friable *adj*

brittle, crumbly, crisp, powdery

FORMAL pulverizable

F₃ solid

friar *n*

monk, religioner, mendicant, religious, prior, abbot, brother

friction *n*

1 DISAGREEMENT, dispute, disharmony, disunity, clashing, conflict, strife, quarrelling, arguing, antagonism, hostility, opposition, rivalry, animosity, bad/ill feeling, bad blood, resentment

FORMAL dissension, discord, disputation

2 RUBBING, chafing, irritation, scraping, grating, rasping, erosion, gnawing, wearing away, resistance, traction

FORMAL abrasion, abrading, attrition, excoriation

F₃ **1** agreement, unity

friend *n*

1 COMPANION, good friend, close friend, best friend, intimate, confidant(e), bosom friend, soul mate, comrade, ally, partner, associate, familiar, playmate, pen friend, acquaintance, well-wisher, boyfriend, girlfriend, best boy/girl, better half, schoolfriend, compadre, sparring partner, alter ego, *ami(e), belle amie, bon ami, amigo, paisano, fidus Achates*

OLD gossip, gossib, ingle, mucker, paranymph, privado; (*Shakesp*) inward, lover, cater-cousin, co-mate; (*Spenser*) belamy

COLLOQ. mate, pal, chum, buddy, buddy-buddy, crony, sidekick

2 SUPPORTER, backer, patron, well-wisher, sponsor, benefactor, subscriber, back-friend

F₃ **1** enemy **2** opponent

Synonym nuances
sense 1

Companion can be used of anyone who frequently keeps company with another, but an **intimate** is someone who is very close to another: *christened Richard, but called Dick by his intimates*. **Confidant(e)** similarly implies closeness but further involves the sharing of private secrets, whilst **soul mate** or **alter ego** would be reserved for someone with whom you feel a unique affinity.

  Comrade is more suggestive of someone with a shared, often military, experience which generates closeness: *his comrade in crime*, whereas **ally** has more to do with providing support. The term **partner** implies an equal relationship, either social or professional, but **associate** is generally reserved for varying depths of business relationships: *a close political associate and friend of Nelson Mandela*. **Compadre** also suggests an equal relationship, and might be used quite humorously of a male companion, whilst the equally light-hearted **sparring partner** suggests someone with whom you are comfortable enough to enjoy arguing.

  You can use **acquaintance** to suggest anyone of whom you have slight knowledge, while a **well-wisher** could be someone you do not necessarily know particularly well, but who, like a friend, is generally concerned for your welfare.

  The terms **boyfriend** and **girlfriend** can be used of a platonic friend of the specified sex, but usually refer to a person with whom you are having a sexual or romantic relationship. The old fashioned terms **best boy** and **best girl** are similar but would probably be used facetiously. The formal expression **fidus Achates** carries strong connotations of faithfulness and reliability.

friendless adj

alone, companionless, unpopular, unloved, unbefriended, solitary, shunned, ostracized, lonely, isolated, forlorn, abandoned, lonesome, lonely-heart, deserted, forsaken, unattached, unbeloved, by yourself, with no one to turn to
COLLOQ. cold-shouldered

friendliness n

affability, amiability, companionability, congeniality, conviviality, approachability, kindness, kindliness, warmth, neighbourliness, sociability, geniality, *Gemütlichkeit*
COLLOQ. matiness, palliness, chumminess
E3 coldness, unsociableness

friendly adj

1 AMIABLE, affable, genial, convivial, cordial, kind, kindly, warm, neighbourly, helpful, fond, affectionate, familiar, intimate, inseparable, close, companionable, sociable, outgoing, approachable, receptive, hospitable, comradely, amicable, peaceable, well-disposed, favourable, agreeable, good-natured, sympathetic
COLLOQ. mat(e)y, pally, chummy, thick, tight, folksy
2 *a friendly atmosphere*
convivial, congenial, cordial, welcoming, warm, pleasant, close, amicable, familiar
E3 1 hostile, unsociable, unfriendly **2** cold, unwelcoming, hostile

friendship n

companionship, closeness, intimacy, familiarity, amiability, affinity, rapport, attachment, affection, fondness, warmth, love, harmony, concord, understanding, goodwill, friendliness, kindliness, friendly relationship, alliance, fellowship, comradeship, camaraderie
FORMAL amity
E3 enmity, animosity

fright n

shock, scare, alarm, dismay, dread, apprehension, fear, fearfulness, terror, horror, panic, disquiet; *Scot* fleg, gliff; *S Afr* skrik
OLD affright, affrightment, tirrit
FORMAL trepidation, consternation, perturbation
COLLOQ. blind panic, cold sweat, hair standing on end, blood running cold, knocking knees, shivers, jitters, creeps, willies, heebie-jeebies, funk, blue funk, bombshell, bolt from the blue

frighten v

alarm, daunt, unnerve, unman, dismay, intimidate, terrorize, scare, startle, scare stiff, give someone a fright, terrify, petrify, horrify, appal, shock, panic; *Scot* fleg
OLD affright, affrighten; (*Spenser*) afear; (*Shakesp*) gallow, gast, ghast
COLLOQ. rattle, spook, boggle, scare out of your wits, make your blood run cold, scare the living daylights out of, scare silly, make your hair stand on end, make you jump out of your skin, put the frighteners on, put the wind up
SLANG scare the hell/shit out of
E3 reassure, calm

Synonym nuances

Alarm would describe the action of causing apprehension at the prospect of danger: *the public have been alarmed by warnings of terrorist attacks*, whilst **daunt** and **dismay** are less dramatic, suggesting discouragement: *voluntary organizations are often daunted by local bureaucracy.*

  Unnerve and **unman**, however, are more suggestive of being disconcerted and losing courage. **Intimidate** has more to do with the restriction of someone's actions through perceived or deliberate and real threats: *she was intimidated by his aggressive manner.* You might use the word **terrorize** of deliberately causing a more extreme fear: *elderly people terrorized by young thugs.* **Scare** implies a lesser degree of fear, although the extended

---

term, **scare stiff**, is stronger in its image of making someone unable to move.

  Terrify can be used of causing great fear, and **petrify** returns to the image of being rendered immobile by it: *he was sitting petrified but unhurt in the wreckage.* Both **horrify** and **appal** suggest an element of outrage or disgust in the fear caused, whilst **shock**, may be more appropriately used when someone's sensibilities are offended rather than feeling fear. **Panic** has more to do with causing a frantic, often irrational, reaction: *I was panicked into leaving town when they made their empty threats.*

---

frightened adj

afraid, dismayed, scared, terrified, unnerved, terrorized, terror-stricken, alarmed, cowed, frozen, petrified, scared stiff, startled, trembly, quivery, panicky, panic-stricken; *dialect* frit; *Scot* feart
COLLOQ. scared out of your wits, scared to death, having kittens, in a blue funk, shaking like a leaf, with your heart in your mouth
E3 calm, courageous

frightening adj

alarming, daunting, formidable, grim, fearsome, forbidding, terrifying, hair-raising, creepy, bloodcurdling, spine-chilling, petrifying, traumatic
COLLOQ. scary, hairy, spooky, white-knuckle

frightful adj

1 UNPLEASANT, disagreeable, awful, nasty, dreadful, fearful, terrible, alarming, appalling, shocking, horrendous, harrowing, unspeakable, dire, grim, ghastly, hideous, horrible, horrid, horrific, grisly, macabre, gruesome, revolting, repulsive, abhorrent, odious, loathsome, unbearable, fearsome, frightsome, *schrecklich*
OLD affrightful, ugly
COLLOQ. like nothing on earth
2 *get into a frightful mess*
awful, dreadful, very bad, terrible, appalling, horrendous
E3 1 pleasant, agreeable

frightfully adv

very, much, greatly, extremely, exceedingly, thoroughly, desperately, decidedly
COLLOQ. terribly, awfully
E3 slightly

frigid adj

1 FROZEN, bitter, freezing, icy, frosty, glacial, arctic, cold, very cold, chill, chilly, wintry, polar, Siberian
2 UNFEELING, unresponsive, unemotional, passionless, unloving, unmoved, unsympathetic, cool, chilly, icy, distant, remote, reserved, formal, clinical, impersonal, aloof, standoffish, passive, unexcitable, indifferent, stiff, dry, lifeless, stony
E3 1 hot, temperate **2** responsive, enthusiastic, approachable

---

Synonym nuances
sense 2

The terms **unfeeling** and **unemotional** appropriately describe a complete and general lack of emotion, while **unmoved**, **unsympathetic** and **unresponsive** are suggestive of an inability to identify with another's specific problems. All these terms have an inherent if not highly marked note of criticism.

  Rather more deliberately disapproving in tone are **chilly** and **icy**, which are fairly emotive terms to describe an unwelcoming manner.

  Impersonal and **clinical**, on the other hand, are not necessarily such marked terms, in that they are often more suggestive of formality and a disinterested but necessary detachment: *a clinical account of the incident.* The terms **reserved**, **distant** and **remote** all imply an inability or reluctance to relate with another: *she felt remote from her companion*; **aloof** and **standoffish** would be used of a more deliberate choice not to interact, and are therefore rather critical in tone.

Unexcitable and **indifferent** can be used fairly neutrally of a lack of any strong feeling or response, while **passionless** carries a more critical connotation of incapacity for deeply felt emotion. **Stony**, **stiff**, **dry** and **lifeless**, however, create images of a complete lack of potential for feeling, and are even more derogatory in tone: *Evelyn tried a smile, but it was met with stony indifference.*

frigidity *n*
unresponsiveness, unapproachability, frostiness, iciness, impassivity, lifelessness, passivity, stiffness, cold-heartedness, coldness, aloofness, chill, chilliness
F3 responsiveness, warmth

frill *n*
1 *a blouse with frills*
flounce, gathering, ruff, ruffle, trimming, tuck, valance, fold, fringe, furbelow, ruche, ruching, purfle, orphrey
2 *the basic model without the frills*
trimmings, addition, extra, ornamentation, decoration, embellishment, fanciness, accessory, ostentation, superfluity, finery, frilliness, fandangle, frippery

frilly *adj*
ruffled, crimped, gathered, frilled, flounced, trimmed, lacy, fancy, ornate
F3 plain

fringe *n, adj, v*
♦ *n*
1 MARGIN, periphery, outskirts, edge, perimeter, limit, rim, border, verge, borderline
2 BORDER, edging, edge, trimming, tassel, frill, valance, pelmet, fall, bullion, macramé, thrum, bangs, *frisette*
TECHNICAL fimbria, loma, peristome
♦ *adj*
unconventional, unorthodox, unofficial, alternative, avant-garde, experimental, off-beat
COLLOQ. left-field
F3 conventional, mainstream
♦ *v*
border, edge, trim, skirt, hem, surround, enclose, purl
TECHNICAL fimbria

fringed *adj*
bordered, edged, fringy, trimmed, hemmed, tasselled, tasselly
TECHNICAL fimbriated

frippery *n*
finery, adornments, decorations, ornaments, ostentation, pretentiousness, showiness, gaudiness, fanciness, flashiness, frilliness, fussiness, tawdriness, triviality, baubles, fandangles, trinkets, knickknacks, gewgaws, trifles, trivia, frills, froth, nonsense, glad rags, foppery
FORMAL meretriciousness
F3 plainness, simplicity

frisk *v*
1 JUMP, leap, skip, hop, bounce, prance, caper, dance, gambol, frolic, romp, cavort, play, sport, trip
2 BODY-SEARCH, search, inspect, check; *N Am* shake down

friskily *adv*
actively, spiritedly, exuberantly, playfully
F3 quietly

frisky *adj*
lively, active, spirited, high-spirited, in high spirits, exuberant, dashing, frolicsome, playful, romping, rollicking, bouncy

COLLOQ. high, alive and kicking, full of beans, hyper
F3 quiet, subdued

fritter *v*
waste, squander, go through, get through, idle, misuse, misspend, overspend
FORMAL dissipate
COLLOQ. spend like water
SLANG blow

frivolity *n*
fun, gaiety, flippancy, facetiousness, jest, light-heartedness, levity, triviality, superficiality, inanity, silliness, folly, foolishness, pettiness, nonsense, senselessness
COLLOQ. froth
F3 seriousness

frivolous *adj*
1 *a frivolous person*
shallow, superficial, flippant, jocular, light, light-hearted, juvenile, puerile, facetious, foolish, silly, skittish, empty-headed, featherbrained, giddy-headed, bubble-headed, airheaded
2 *frivolous activities*
futile, vain, pointless, senseless, unimportant, petty, irresponsible, trivial, trifling, shallow, superficial, inane, puerile, juvenile, foolish, silly, idle
F3 **1** serious, sensible **2** useful, sensible

frivolously *adv*
irresponsibly, foolishly, idly, vainly, pointlessly, senselessly, jocularly, light-heartedly, whimsically
F3 sensibly, seriously

frizzle[1] *v*
frizzled her hair
curl, crimp, crimple, frizz, wave, roll, crinkle, kink, bend, curve, loop, turn, twist, wind, wreathe, twirl, twine, coil, spiral, scroll, tong, purl, becurl

frizzle[2] *v*
frizzled on the fire
fry, scorch, sizzle, hiss, crackle, spit, sputter

frizzy *adj*
curled, curly, crimped, crisp, frizzed, wiry, corrugated
F3 straight

frock *n*
dress, gown, robe

frolic *v, n*
♦ *v*
gambol, caper, romp, play, lark around, rollick, make merry, frisk, prance, cavort, dance, leap, skip, hop, bounce, sport; *dialect* gammock
♦ *n*
fun, fun and games, amusement, sport, game, gaiety, jollity, merriment, mirth, revel, romp, prank, lark, caper, spree, high jinks, antics, escapade; *dialect* gammock
COLLOQ. razzle, razzle-dazzle

frolicsome *adj*
playful, ludic, frisky, lively, merry, gay, sprightly, sportive, rollicking, coltish, skittish
F3 quiet, serious, solemn

front *n, adj, v*
♦ *n*
1 *the front of the building*
face, aspect, frontage, façade, outside, exterior, facing, cover, obverse, top, head, lead, vanguard, van, forefront, front line, firing line, foreground, forepart, bow
2 PRETENCE, show, air, appearance, look, expression, manner, exterior, façade, cover, mask, disguise, pretext, cover-up, blind
FORMAL countenance
3 *fighting at the front*
front line, vanguard, firing line, battle zone
F3 **1** back, rear

◆ *adj*
leading, foremost, head, first, fore
🔁 back, rear, last

◆ *v*
face, confront, look over, look out on, meet, oppose, overlook

■ **in front**
leading, ahead, first, in advance, to the fore, before, preceding
🔁 behind

■ **in front of**
1 AHEAD OF, in advance of, before, facing
2 *in front of the children*
in the presence of, under the nose of, before

frontier *n*
border, boundary, borderline, limit, edge, perimeter, confines, marches, bounds, verge, partition

front-runner *n*
favourite, odds-on favourite, certainty, nap, likely winner, finalist, top seed, form horse
🔁 underdog, also-ran

frost *n*
freeze, freeze-up, ice, Jack Frost, hoar-frost, rime, coldness

frostily *adv*
coldly, coolly, stiffly, in an unfriendly manner
🔁 warmly, responsively, enthusiastically

frosty *adj*
1 ICY, frozen, freezing, frigid, wintry, cold, bitterly cold, chilly, rimy, glacial, arctic, Siberian, polar
COLLOQ. nippy, parky
2 UNFRIENDLY, unwelcoming, cool, cold, icy, aloof, standoffish, stiff, discouraging, hostile
🔁 **1** warm, hot **2** warm, friendly, responsive, welcoming, enthusiastic

froth *n, v*
◆ *n*
1 BUBBLES, effervescence, fizz, foam, lather, suds, head, scum, spume
2 TRIVIA, trifles, trivialities, irrelevancies
COLLOQ. pap
◆ *v*
foam, lather, ferment, fizz, effervesce, bubble, spume
Related adjectives: spumous, spumy

frothy *adj*
1 BUBBLING, bubbly, foaming, foamy, yeasty, sudsy
FORMAL spumescent, spumous, spumy
COLLOQ. fizzy
2 INSUBSTANTIAL, empty, trivial, frivolous, trifling, slight, light, lightweight, vain
🔁 **1** flat, still **2** substantial, significant

frown *v, n*
◆ *v*
scowl, glower, lour, glare, grimace, mow, pout
COLLOQ. give someone a dirty look, look daggers at
🔁 approve of, go along with
◆ *n*
scowl, glower, glare, grimace, moue, raised eyebrow
COLLOQ. dirty look

■ **frown on**
disapprove of, object to, dislike, discourage, take a dim view of, not take kindly to, think badly of, have a low opinion of, raise your eyebrows

frowsty *adj*
fusty, stuffy, airless, unventilated, fuggy, musty
🔁 airy

frowsy *adj*
untidy, dishevelled, scruffy, unwashed, unkempt, ungroomed, dirty, messy, frumpish, frumpy,

slatternly, sloppy, slovenly, sluttish
🔁 well-groomed

frozen *adj*
iced, chilled, icy, frosty, icebound, ice-covered, arctic, ice-cold, bitterly cold, raw, polar, Siberian, frigid, freezing, numb, hard, frosted, solidified, stiff, frozen-stiff, rigid, fixed
🔁 warm

frugal *adj*
thrifty, penny-wise, niggardly, penny-pinching, miserly, stingy, careful, prudent, provident, saving, scrimping and saving, economical, sparing, meagre, paltry, scanty, inadequate
FORMAL parsimonious
🔁 wasteful, extravagant

frugality *n*
thrift, economy, husbandry, saving, scrimping and saving, conservation, prudence, carefulness
FORMAL parsimony
🔁 extravagance, waste

frugally *adv*
thriftily, carefully, prudently, economically, meagrely, scantily, inadequately
FORMAL parsimoniously
🔁 wastefully, extravagantly

fruit *n*
1 CROP, harvest, produce, fruitage
2 BENEFIT, consequence, advantage, effect, outcome, reward, return, result, yield, product, profit

---

Varieties of fruit include:

APPLES:	tangerine	TROPICAL FRUIT:
Braeburn	Ugli®	date
Bramley	**BERRIES:**	fig
Cox's Orange	bilberry	guava
Pippin	blackberry	kiwi fruit
crab apple	blackcurrant	mango
Golden Delicious	blueberry	papaya (or
Granny Smith	boysenberry	pawpaw)
Pink Lady	cranberry	passion fruit
Royal Gala	elderberry	pineapple
PEARS:	gooseberry	star fruit (or
Asian pear	*colloq.* goosegog	carambola)
Conference	loganberry	**OTHER:**
William	raspberry	apricot
CITRUS FRUIT:	redcurrant	avacado
blood orange	strawberry	cherry
clementine	whitecurrant	grape
grapefruit	**PLUMS:**	kumquat
Jaffa orange	damson	lychee
lemon	greengage	olive
lime	**MELONS:**	peach
mandarin	cantaloupe	persimmon (or
mineola	casaba	sharon fruit)
nectarine	Galia	pomegranate
orange	honeydew	rhubarb
pink grapefruit	watermelon	sloe
satsuma		tomato
Seville orange		

---

fruitful *adj*
1 FERTILE, rich, teeming, plentiful, abundant, prolific, productive, fruit-bearing
OLD plenteous, pregnant; (*Shakesp*) conceptious, increaseful
FORMAL fecund, feracious, fructive
2 REWARDING, profitable, advantageous, beneficial, effective, worthwhile, well-spent, useful, successful, productive, fat
OLD increaseful
FORMAL effectual, efficacious
🔁 **1** barren, unproductive **2** fruitless, vain

fruitfully adv

successfully, profitably, advantageously, beneficially, effectively, usefully, productively
Ea fruitlessly, unsuccessfully

fruitfulness n

productiveness, profitability, fertility, usefulness
FORMAL fecundity, fecundation, feracity
Ea fruitlessness

fruition n

realization, fulfilment, attainment, achievement, completion, maturity, ripeness, perfection, success, enjoyment
FORMAL consummation, actualization

fruitless adj

unsuccessful, abortive, useless, futile, pointless, vain, idle, hopeless, worthless, unproductive, barren, sterile
OLD infructuous
FORMAL ineffectual
Ea fruitful, successful, profitable, productive

fruitlessly adv

in vain, vainly, unproductively, unsuccessfully, uselessly, pointlessly, hopelessly
Ea fruitfully, successfully

fruity adj

1 a fruity voice
rich, mellow, resonant, deep, low, full
2 INDECENT, bawdy, indelicate, juicy, suggestive, naughty, saucy, risqué, titillating, vulgar, salacious, spicy, sexy, smutty, racy
COLLOQ. blue
Ea 2 decent

frumpy adj

dowdy, dreary, drab, badly-dressed, frumpish, dingy, ill-dressed, dated, out of date
Ea chic, well-groomed

frustrate v

1 DISAPPOINT, discourage, dishearten, dissatisfy, embitter, depress, anger, annoy, irritate, exasperate, rile, infuriate
COLLOQ. aggravate, wind up, needle, get at, bug, miff, drive mad, drive crazy, get under someone's skin
SLANG nark, piss off
2 THWART, foil, balk, baffle, block, check, stop, defeat, hinder, obstruct, hamper, impede, forestall, counter, nullify, neutralize, inhibit
COLLOQ. stymie, scupper, spike, nobble
Ea 1 encourage **2** further, promote

frustrated adj

disappointed, discontented, discouraged, dissatisfied, disheartened, embittered, resentful, angry, annoyed, thwarted, blighted, repressed
COLLOQ. dished
Ea fulfilled, satisfied

frustrating adj

disappointing, discouraging, disheartening, annoying, irritating, exasperating, maddening, infuriating
Ea fulfilling

frustration n

1 DISAPPOINTMENT, discouragement, dissatisfaction, resentment, annoyance, anger, vexation, irritation, exasperation
2 THWARTING, foiling, balking, blocking, defeat, curbing, failure, non-fulfilment, obstruction, contravention
FORMAL circumvention
Ea 1 fulfilment, contentment **2** furthering, promoting

fuddled adj

hazy, confused, muddled, stupefied, muzzy, bemused, addled, drunk, groggy, woozy, inebriated, intoxicated, sozzled, tipsy
Ea clear, sober

fuddy-duddy n, adj

♦ n
conservative, traditionalist, conformist, museum piece, fossil, stick-in-the-mud
COLLOQ. old fogey, square, back number, stuffed shirt
♦ adj
old-fashioned, old-fogeyish, stick-in-the-mud, stuffy, carping, censorious, prim
COLLOQ. N Am buttoned-down
Ea up-to-date

fudge v

avoid, dodge, equivocate, evade, hedge, stall, shuffle, misrepresent, fake, falsify
COLLOQ. cook, fiddle, fix

fuel n, v

♦ n
1 COMBUSTIBLE, propellant, motive power
2 PROVOCATION, incitement, encouragement, ammunition, goading, incentive, stimulus, material
♦ v
incite, inflame, fire, encourage, fan, boost, stimulate, feed, nourish, sustain, stoke up
Ea discourage, damp down

Fuels include:

acetylene	diesel	methylated spirit
anthracite	electricity	nuclear power
biodiesel	fossil fuel	oil
butane	gas	paraffin
calor gas®	gasoline	peat
charcoal	hydroelectricity	petrol
coal	kerosine	propane
coke	logs	red diesel
derv	methane	wood

---

fug n

stuffiness, staleness, reek, stink, frowstiness, fustiness, f(o)etidness
Ea airiness

fuggy adj

stuffy, airless, close, stale, suffocating, unventilated, foul, f(o)etid, frowsty, fusty
FORMAL noisome, noxious
Ea airy

fugitive n, adj

♦ n
escapee, runaway, runner, hideaway, deserter, refugee, maroon, runagate
♦ adj
1 RUNAWAY, refugee, deserter, AWOL
2 FLEETING, transient, transitory, passing, short, short-lived, momentary, brief, flying, temporary, elusive
FORMAL ephemeral, evanescent, fugacious
Ea 2 permanent

fulfil v

complete, finish, perfect, realize, achieve, accomplish, perform, execute, discharge, implement, carry out, live out, comply with, observe, keep, obey, conform to, satisfy, fill, meet, answer, qualify, stand up to, act up to, come up to scratch; N Am fill
FORMAL conclude, consummate, effect
Ea fail, break

fulfilled adj

satisfied, gratified, pleased, happy, content
Ea dissatisfied, discontented, unhappy

fulfilling adj

satisfying, gratifying, pleasing, comforting, satisfactory
Ea unfulfilling

fulfilment n

completion, perfection, realization, achievement, accomplishment, success, performance, execution, discharge, implementation, observance, satisfaction
FORMAL consummation
✗ failure

full adj, adv

• adj

1 FILLED, loaded, laden, packed, crowded, crammed, stuffed, overflowing, bulging, well-stocked, flush, jammed, filled to capacity, full to the brim
COLLOQ. chock-a-block, chock-full, chocker, packed out, bursting at the seams, packed like sardines
2 ENTIRE, whole, intact, total, complete, unabridged, unexpurgated
3 THOROUGH, comprehensive, exhaustive, all-inclusive, broad, vast, extensive, detailed, ample, filled, generous, abundant, plentiful, copious, profuse, sufficient
4 *feel full*
satisfied, well fed, gorged, sated, stuffed
FORMAL satiated, replete
COLLOQ. bursting
5 *a full sound*
rich, resonant, loud, deep, clear, strong, distinct, fruity, sonorous
6 *at full speed*
maximum, top, highest, greatest, utmost
7 *lead a full life*
busy, active, lively, eventful, exciting, tiring, hectic, frantic
8 *a full flavour*
strong, rich, deep, intense, full-bodied, fruity, warm, vibrant
9 *a full figure*
rounded, well-rounded, plump, chubby, stout, fat, overweight, large, round, shapely, buxom, obese
FORMAL corpulent, rotund
10 *a full skirt*
wide, baggy, loose, loose-fitting
FORMAL voluminous
✗ 1 empty, bare **2** partial, incomplete **3** superficial, cursory **4** hungry, peckish **6** minimum, lowest **7** empty, boring
• adv
directly, squarely, straight, right, exactly
COLLOQ. bang, smack
▪ **in full**
fully, completely, wholly, in detail, with all the details, in its entirety, in total, uncut, with nothing missed out
▪ **to the full**
fully, to the greatest possible extent, to the utmost, fully, completely, entirely, thoroughly, utterly

full-blooded adj

committed, dedicated, devoted, enthusiastic, wholehearted, thorough, out-and-out, vigorous, hearty
✗ half-hearted

full-blown adj

full, full-scale, all-out, out-and-out, complete, intense, major, total, thorough, full-fledged

full-bodied adj

full, strong, rich, deep, intense, fruity

full-frontal adj

1 *full-frontal nudity*
complete, unexpurgated, total, absolute
2 *a full-frontal attack*
complete, out-and-out, thorough, forceful, strong, direct

full-grown adj

adult, grown-up, fully-grown, of age, mature, ripe, developed, fully-developed, fully-fledged, full-blown, full-scale
✗ young, undeveloped

fullness n

1 THOROUGHNESS, comprehensiveness, vastness, extensiveness, abundance, plenty, profusion, ampleness, completeness, totality, wholeness
2 INTENSITY, strength, depth, greatness, power, force, loudness, richness, resonance
3 SATISFACTION, glut, fill, satedness
FORMAL satiation, satiety, repletion
4 BREADTH, width, largeness, shapeliness, plumpness, curvaceousness, voluptuousness
5 SWELLING, enlargement, inflammation, growth
TECHNICAL tumescence
FORMAL dilation
✗ 1 incompleteness **3** emptiness
▪ **in the fullness of time**
eventually, in due course, in time, finally, ultimately, in the end
COLLOQ. when all is said and done, in the final analysis

full-scale adj

exhaustive, extensive, complete, sweeping, thorough, thoroughgoing, wide-ranging, comprehensive, all-out, in-depth, all-encompassing, intensive, major
✗ partial

fully adv

completely, totally, utterly, wholly, entirely, in all respects, thoroughly, altogether, quite, positively, without reserve, unreservedly, perfectly, satisfactorily, sufficiently
✗ partly

fully-fledged adj

professional, qualified, trained, senior, graduate, mature, proficient, experienced, fully-developed, full-blown
✗ inexperienced

fulminate v

criticize, condemn, curse, denounce, slate, protest, rage, rail, fume, thunder
FORMAL animadvert, inveigh, vituperate, declaim, decry
COLLOQ. slam
✗ praise

fulmination n

condemnation, criticism, denunciation, thundering, tirade, detonation
FORMAL diatribe, invective, obloquy, philippic, decrial
COLLOQ. brickbat, slating
✗ praise

fulsome adj

extravagant, excessive, immoderate, overdone, gross, inordinate, insincere, adulatory, enthusiastic, effusive, fawning, ingratiating, sycophantic, sickening, nauseating, cloying, nauseous, offensive, saccharine, fat, luscious
FORMAL obsequious, unctuous
COLLOQ. smarmy, slimy, buttery, over the top, OTT
✗ sincere

fulsomely adv

extravagantly, excessively, immoderately, inordinately, insincerely, effusively, sickeningly, nauseatingly
COLLOQ. over the top

fumble v

grope, feel (about), scrabble, blunder, bungle, botch, mishandle, mismanage, flounder, spoil, bobble
COLLOQ. faff (about)

fume v

1 SMOKE, smoulder, boil, steam
2 RAGE, be furious, storm, rant, rave, seethe, boil, be livid
COLLOQ. explode, blow up, blow your top, boil over, fly into a rage, fly off the handle, go mad, go off the deep end, lose your rag, rant and rave, blow/lose your cool, burst a blood vessel, hit the roof

fumes *n*

exhaust, smoke, gas(es), vapour(s), haze, fog, smog, pollution, stink, smell, stench, reek
FORMAL exhalation

fumigate *v*

deodorize, disinfect, sterilize, purify, cleanse, sanitize

fumigation *n*

disinfecting, sterilization, cleansing, sanitization, purifying, purification

fuming *adj*

angry, enraged, furious, livid, incensed, raging, seething, boiling
COLLOQ. ranting and raving, steamed up, uptight, mad, hopping mad, raving mad, seeing red, in a lather, disgruntled, up in arms, hot under the collar; *N Am* ticked off
F3 calm

fun *n, adj*

♦ *n*

enjoyment, pleasure, amusement, entertainment, relaxation, diversion, distraction, recreation, play, sport, game, foolery, tomfoolery, buffoonery, horseplay, skylarking, romp, merrymaking, celebration, laughter, laughs, mirth, cheerfulness, gladness, jollity, jocularity, hilarity, joy, joking, joke, jest, jesting; *dialect* gammock, gig; *Irish* crack; *N Am* music
OLD bourd

♦ *adj*

entertaining, amusing, diverting, recreational, delightful, pleasurable, enjoyable; *S Afr* lekker; lively, witty

■ **for fun**

for a laugh, for enjoyment, for no particular reason
COLLOQ. for kicks, for the hell of it

■ **in fun**

as a joke, jokingly, for a laugh, to tease, in jest, playful(ly), mischievous(ly), teasingly, tongue in cheek

■ **make fun of**

ridicule, mock, laugh at, jeer at, scoff at, sneer at, tease, taunt, humiliate, poke fun at, banter, joke, jolly
FORMAL deride
COLLOQ. rib, send up, pull someone's leg, take the mickey, get at; *Aust* have a shot at
SLANG take the piss, cod, guy; *N Am* goof; *Aust & NZ* poke borak at

function *n, v*

♦ *n*

1 ROLE, part, office, duty, charge, responsibility, concern, capacity, job, post, chore, task, occupation, situation, employment, business, activity, purpose, mission, use
2 RECEPTION, party, gathering, affair, social event, dinner, luncheon
COLLOQ. do
3 COROLLARY, concomitant, consquence, conclusion, result, upshot, deduction, induction, inference

♦ *v*

work, be in working order, operate, run, go, serve, act, perform, behave, play the part of, have the job of
F3 break down; *formal* malfunction; *slang* conk out

functional *adj*

working, operational, operative, running, practical, useful, utilitarian, utility, plain, hard-wearing, serviceable
F3 useless, decorative

functionally *adv*

operationally, practically, usefully, efficiently

functionary *n*

bureaucrat, employee, officer, official, office-bearer, office-holder, dignitary

fund *n, v*

♦ *n*

1 *contribute to the restoration fund*
pool, kitty, reserve, treasury, collection, grant, endowment, foundation, investment
2 *raise funds for the repairs*
money, finance, backing, capital, resources, savings, wealth, cash, means, assets
COLLOQ. the necessary, readies
SLANG megabucks, dough, dosh, bread, lolly, spondulicks, brass, loot, gravy, greens, shekels, moolah, gelt
OLD SLANG rhino
3 *a fund of funny stories*
reserve, repository, storehouse, store, stock, collection, accumulation, hoard, cache, stack, mine, well, source, supply, reservoir

♦ *v*

finance, provide finance for, capitalize, endow, subsidize, pay for, underwrite, sponsor, back, support, promote, float

fundamental *adj*

basic, primary, first, elementary, underlying, foundational, integral, central, principal, cardinal, prime, main, chief, key, essential, indispensable, vital, necessary, crucial, important, initial, original, profound
FORMAL rudimentary, basal, elemental

fundamentalist *adj*

rigorous, rigid, uncompromising, strict, orthodox

fundamentally *adv*

1 *fundamentally, this is a criminal, not civil, matter*
basically, essentially, in essence, at bottom, at heart, deep down, inherently, intrinsically, primarily, substantially
2 *differ fundamentally*
profoundly, deeply, inherently, intrinsically, critically, crucially, radically, acutely

fundamentals *n*

basics, essentials, first principles, laws, rules, rudiments, facts, necessaries, practicalities
COLLOQ. brass tacks, nitty-gritty, nuts and bolts

funeral *n*

burial, cremation, wake
FORMAL interment, entombment, inhumation, exequies, obsequies

funereal *adj*

solemn, serious, grave, mournful, sad, sombre, depressing, dismal, dreary, gloomy, lamenting, woeful, sepulchral, dark, deathlike
FORMAL exequial, funebral, funebrial, lugubrious
F3 happy, lively

fungus *n*

FORMAL thallophyte
Related adjective: fungous

Types of fungus include:

black spot	grey mould	saprophyte
blight	mushroom	scab
botritis	orange-peel	smut
brewer's yeast	fungus	sooty mould
brown rot	penicillium	toadstool
candida	potato blight	yeast
downy mildew	powdery mildew	
ergot	rust	

See also **mushrooms and toadstools**.

funk *v, n*

♦ *v*

balk at, flinch from, recoil from, blench, duck out of, shirk from, dodge
COLLOQ. chicken out of, cop out

♦ *n*

panic, alarm, fright, fear, terror, frenzy, fuss, commotion, fluster, agitation, dither
COLLOQ. flap, cold sweat, state, tiswas, tizwas, tizzy, stew, blue funk

funnel *v, n*
* *v*
channel, direct, convey, guide, move, transfer, pass, go, pour, siphon, filter
* *n*
chimney, smokestack, stack, vent, flue, shaft, tube, pipe, channel
TECHNICAL drogue, infundibulum, swallow hole, sink hole, windsail
OLD tun-dish

funnily *adv*
surprisingly, amazingly, astonishingly, incredibly, remarkably

funny *adj*
1 HUMOROUS, amusing, entertaining, diverting, comic, comical, hilarious, witty, facetious, droll, farcical, laughable, ridiculous, absurd, silly, hysterical, side-splitting, uproarious, riotous, rich
FORMAL risible
COLLOQ. killing, corny, rum, a scream, a hoot, knee-slapping
2 ODD, strange, peculiar, curious, queer, weird, bizarre, unusual, remarkable, puzzling, perplexing, mysterious, suspicious, dubious
COLLOQ. shady, oddball, way-out, off-beat, wacky
F3 **1** serious, solemn, sad **2** normal, ordinary, usual

Synonym nuances
sense 1
Humorous can be used of anything that causes a laugh or a smile, whilst **amusing** similarly suggests a cheery diversion. **Entertaining** implies having a wider appeal than just comedy, and **diverting** similarly suggests being engaging in a pleasurable way: *his inimitable way of telling diverting anecdotes.* Both **comic** and **comical** return to the idea of simply prompting laughter, whereas **hilarious**, **hysterical** and **side-splitting** would be reserved for something causing uncontrollable mirth.
   Witty, on the other hand, suggests a more subtle effect, and implies a sharp intelligence behind the funniness, while **facetious** goes a bit further by suggesting a degree of deprecation: *a facetious sketch on contemporary politicians*, and something **droll** would have an element of wryness about it: *his droll observations on hospital food.*
   The term **farcical** conjures up a sense of the ludicrous, whilst **laughable** and **ridiculous** also imply something unworthy of serious consideration, and all of these terms are often used of things that are not actually funny: *a laughable attempt to look cool.* Likewise, **absurd** suggests something that would prompt a degree of scorn: *trouserless men look absurd in socks*, and **silly** is similar, but with a lesser degree of scorn.
   Both **riotous** and **uproarious** suggest causing a commotion, and so appropriately describe more extreme, boisterous humour and its effects. **Rich**, on the other hand, suggests having comedic potential: *that's rich, coming from you!*

---

fur *n*
coat, hair, hide, down, fleece, pelt, fell, skin, wool, mane, pelage

furbish *v*
renovate, restore, renew, recondition, repair, overhaul, modernize, refurbish, refit, redecorate, remodel, reform, rehabilitate, revamp, improve
COLLOQ. do up, give a facelift to

furious *adj*
1 ANGRY, livid, indignant, irate, enraged, infuriated, incensed, inflamed, incandescent, raging, fuming, boiling, seething, frenzied, purple with rage
COLLOQ. mad, hopping mad, sizzling, up in arms, in a stew, in a paddy, in a lather, in a huff, gone off the deep end, hot under the collar, foaming at the mouth
2 VIOLENT, wild, fierce, intense, vigorous, frantic, boisterous, stormy, tempestuous, vehement
F3 **1** calm, pleased **2** restrained

furiously *adv*
1 ANGRILY, in anger, indignantly, irately, crossly, passionately, infuriatingly
COLLOQ. madly, seeing red, up in arms, hot under the collar, in a paddy
2 VIOLENTLY, wildly, fiercely, intensely, vigorously, vehemently, stormily, tempestuously
F3 **1, 2** calmly, gently

furnish *v*
equip, fit out, kit out, decorate, rig, appoint, stock, provide, supply, afford, grant, give, offer, present, endue, appoint
FORMAL bestow
F3 divest

furniture *n*
equipment, appliances, furnishings, fittings, appointments, fitments, household goods, movables, possessions, effects, things
See also panels on next page

furore *n*
uproar, disturbance, outcry, commotion, fuss, frenzy, fury, hullabaloo, outburst, rage, stir, to-do, tumult, storm, excitement
COLLOQ. flap
F3 calm

furrow *n, v*
* *n*
1 GROOVE, channel, trench, hollow, trough, rut, track, stria, gutter, chamfer, list; *Scot* feerin, fur
TECHNICAL sulcus, canaliculus, vallecula, rill
2 WRINKLE, line, crease, crinkle, trench, crow's foot
* *v*
crease, wrinkle, draw together, knit, seam, flute, channel, corrugate, gouge, plough, groove, engroove, rut, mill
Related adjective: sulcal

furry *adj*
hairy, woolly, fleecy, fuzzy, downy, soft, fluffy

further *adj, v, adv*
* *adj*
1 MORE, additional, supplementary, extra, fresh, new, other
2 FARTHER, more distant, remoter, more extreme
F3 **2** nearer
* *v*
advance, forward, promote, champion, encourage, foster, help, aid, assist, ease, facilitate, develop, speed (up), hasten, accelerate
FORMAL expedite
COLLOQ. push
F3 stop, frustrate
* *adv*
moreover, furthermore, besides, in addition, additionally, also, as well, too
COLLOQ. what's more

furtherance *n*
advancement, promotion, advancing, backing, boosting, encouragement, help, facilitation, carrying-out, championing, promoting, advocacy, pursuit, speeding
FORMAL preferment

Types of furniture include:

TABLES:	carver	stool	four-poster	Welsh dresser	dressing table
bedside table	chesterfield	studio couch	water bed	**FIREPLACE:**	ottoman
card table	couch	suite	**STUDY FURNITURE:**	fender	tallboy
coffee table	dining chair	swivel-chair	bookcase	firescreen	vanity unit
dining table	easy chair	**BEDS:**	bureau	overmantel	wardrobe
gateleg table	footstool	bed-settee	computer desk	**BEDROOM**	washstand
kitchen table	highchair	bunk	secretaire	**FURNITURE:**	**MISCELLANEOUS:**
lowboy	kitchen chair	camp-bed	**DINING-ROOM**	armoire	coatstand
occasional table	pouffe	chaise-longue	**FURNITURE:**	blanket box	hallstand
refectory table	recliner	cot	buffet	chest	magazine rack
side table	rocking chair	cradle	cabinet	chest of drawers	mirror
CHAIRS:	settee	daybed	china cabinet	chiffonier	umbrella stand
armchair	sofa	divan	dumb waiter	coffer	
beanbag			sideboard	commode	

See also **bed; chair; stool.**

Styles of furniture include:

Adam	boulle	Dutch Colonial	Gainsborough	Queen Anne	Vernis Martin
Anglo-Colonial	buhl	Dutch	Georgian	Regency	Victorian
Anglo-Indian	Charles II	Neoclassical	Gothic	Restoration	William and Mary
Art Deco	Chippendale	Edwardian	Hepplewhite	rococo	William IV
Art Nouveau	Colonial	Empire	Louis Philippe	Shaker	Windsor
Arts and Crafts	Continental	French Provincial	Louis-Quatorze	Sheraton	
Baroque	Empire	French Second	Louis-Quinze	Shibayama	
Biedermeier	Cromwellian	Empire	provincial	Transitional	

furthermore *adv*
moreover, in addition, further, besides, also, too, as well, additionally
COLLOQ. what's more, into the bargain

furthermost *adj*
furthest, farthest, remotest, outermost, outmost, extreme, ultimate, utmost, uttermost
F3 nearest

furthest *adj*
farthest, furthermost, remotest, outermost, outmost, extreme, ultimate, utmost, uttermost
F3 nearest

furtive *adj*
surreptitious, sly, stealthy, secretive, underhand, hidden, cloaked, veiled, covert, secret, sneaky
FORMAL clandestine
F3 open

furtively *adv*
surreptitiously, slyly, secretively, secretly, covertly
F3 openly

fury *n*
anger, rage, wrath, ire, frenzy, madness, passion, vehemence, fierceness, ferocity, violence, wildness, intensity, severity, force, turbulence, power
F3 calm, peacefulness

fuse *v*
combine, integrate, unite, join, amalgamate, blend, conflate, put together, coalesce, meld, melt, solder, weld, flux, smelt, merge, run, synthesize, intermix, mingle, interfuse
OLD colliquate
FORMAL agglutinate, commingle, intermingle

fusillade *n*
barrage, volley, discharge, burst, fire, hail, outburst, salvo, broadside

fusion *n*
melting, smelting, welding, union, synthesis, blend, blending, coalescence, amalgamation, integration, conflation, running, merger, federation
OLD colliquation

fuss *n, v*
♦ *n*
bother, trouble, palaver, furore, ado, squabble, row,

commotion, stir, fluster, confusion, upset, worry, agitation, excitement, bustle, flurry, brouhaha, chichi, hurry, racket, pother, piece of work; *Scot* fikery, paraffle, stooshie
OLD coil, do
COLLOQ. hassle, to-do, hoo-ha, flap, carry-on, kerfuffle, ballyhoo, tizzy, a song and a dance, storm in a teacup, pantomime
F3 calm
♦ *v*
complain, grumble, fret, worry, panic, take pains, bother, bustle, fidget
COLLOQ. flap, stir, make a song and dance, be in a tizzy, create, be all over, make a thing

fussiness *n*
choosiness, finicality, finicalness, pernicketiness, perfectionism, meticulousness, niceness, niggling, particularity, busyness
F3 unfastidiousness

fusspot *n*
worrier, perfectionist, hyper-critic, stickler, fidget; *NAm* fussbudget
COLLOQ. nit-picker, old maid, old woman, fantod

fussy *adj*
1 PARTICULAR, fastidious, scrupulous, finicky, finical, difficult, hard to please, grandmotherly, discriminating, faddy, fiddle-faddle, demanding, quibbling, niggling, pettifogging, pedantic, selective, prissy, chichi
OLD spoffish
COLLOQ. pernickety, choosy, picky, nit-picking, old-maidish; *NAm* persnickety
2 FANCY, elaborate, ornate, overdecorated, cluttered, busy, baroque, rococo
F3 1 casual, uncritical **2** plain, simple

fusty *adj*
1 OLD-FASHIONED, antiquated, archaic, outdated, out-of-date, passé
COLLOQ. old-fogeyish
2 STALE, damp, dank, airless, stuffy, unventilated, fuggy, ill-smelling, musty, mouldy, mouldering, frowsty, rank
FORMAL malodorous
F3 1 up-to-date **2** airy

futile *adj*
pointless, useless, worthless, vain, in vain, idle, wasted,

fruitless, meaningless, profitless, unavailing, to no avail, unsuccessful, abortive, unprofitable, unproductive, ineffective, barren, empty, hollow, forlorn, feckless, sleeveless
FORMAL ineffectual, nugatory, otiose
COLLOQ. no go
E3 fruitful, profitable

futility n

pointlessness, uselessness, fruitlessness, meaninglessness, worthlessness, ineffectiveness, waste, unproductiveness, vanity, emptiness, hollowness, barrenness, aimlessness
FORMAL nugatoriness
E3 use, purpose, success

future n, adj

◆ n
hereafter, tomorrow, time to come, coming times, outlook, prospects, expectations
E3 past
◆ adj

prospective, next, designate, to be, to come, forthcoming, in the offing, imminent, impending, coming, approaching, expected, planned, unborn, later, subsequent, eventual, fated, destined
E3 past

■ **in future**
from now on, from this time on, from this day on, after this
FORMAL henceforth, henceforward, hereafter, hereinafter, hence

fuzz n

down, floss, fluff, fug, hair, lint, nap, pile, fibre, flock

fuzzy adj

1 FRIZZY, fluffy, furry, woolly, fleecy, downy, linty, velvety, napped
2 BLURRED, unfocused, ill-defined, indefinite, unclear, indistinct, vague, faint, hazy, foggy, shadowy, woolly, muffled, distorted, fuddled, confused
COLLOQ. muzzy
E3 2 clear, distinct, focused

G

gab *v, n*
♦ *v*
chatter, talk, drivel, gossip, jaw, prattle, tattle, babble, blabber, jabber, buzz; *dialect & NAm* blather; *Scot* blether
COLLOQ. yak
♦ *v*
chat, chatter, chitchat, conversation, prattle, prattling, gossip, blab, blarney; *Scot* blethering; small talk, tittle-tattle, tongue-wagging
FORMAL loquacity
COLLOQ. yackety-yak, yak

gabble *v, n*
♦ *v*
babble, chatter, jabber, prattle, spout, splutter, cackle, sputter, gaggle, gibber, rattle, blab, blabber; *Scot* blether; rabble, patter
♦ *n*
babble, chatter, blabber, cackling, prattle, jabber, twaddle; *Scot* blethering; waffle, nonsense, drivel, gibberish, gibble-gabble, ribble-rabble

gad
■ **gad about**
gallivant, run around, travel, roam, wander, range, rove, flit about, ramble, stray, traipse, jaunt, dot about

gadabout *n*
gallivanter, rambler, rover, runabout, wanderer, pleasure-seeker; *Scot* stravaiger

gadget *n*
tool, implement, appliance, device, instrument, apparatus, mechanism, contrivance, invention, contraption, thing, novelty, gimmick, toy, widget, waldo
COLLOQ. thingamy, thingummy, thingamybob, thingummyjig, gismo, whatsit, whatnot, doodah, gubbins, jigamaree, jiggumbob, jimjam; *NAm* hickey

gaffe *n*
blunder, mistake, slip, error, indiscretion, faux pas, gaucherie
FORMAL solecism
COLLOQ. bloomer, boob, boo-boo, brick, clanger, howler, slip-up; *NAm* flub
SLANG goof

gaffer *n*
foreman, manager, overseer, superintendent, supervisor, overman, ganger
COLLOQ. boss, gov, guv, bigwig, big cheese; *NAm* honcho

gag[1] *v*
1 SILENCE, muffle, muzzle, quiet, stifle, smother, block, plug, clog, put a gag on, throttle, suppress, restrain, curb, check, still
2 RETCH, choke, heave, nearly vomit

gag[2] *n*
a comedian telling gags
joke, jest, quip, wisecrack, one-liner, pun, witticism
COLLOQ. crack, funny

gaga *adj*
crazy, insane, mad, unbalanced, disturbed, deranged, demented, unhinged, distracted

COLLOQ. dotty, batty, loopy, barmy, nuts, potty, off the rails, cuckoo, mad as a hatter, raving, wrong in the head, not all there
SLANG loony, doolally, off your rocker

gaiety *n*
happiness, glee, cheerfulness, joy, pleasure, delight, joie de vivre, jollity, merriment, mirth, gladness, blitheness, hilarity, fun, merrymaking, revelry, festivity, celebration, frolics, joviality, good humour, high spirits, light-heartedness, liveliness, exuberance, buoyancy, brightness, brilliance, sparkle, glitter, colour, colourfulness, show, showiness
FORMAL vivacity
E3 sadness, drabness, gloom

gaily *adv*
happily, joyfully, merrily, cheerfully, blithely, light-heartedly, brightly, brilliantly, colourfully, flamboyantly
E3 sadly, dully

gain *v, n*
♦ *v*
1 OBTAIN, achieve, capture, secure, get, acquire, bring in, gather, win
FORMAL procure
COLLOQ. collar, nab
2 EARN, make, produce, realize, gross, net, clear, profit, yield, bring in, reap, harvest
COLLOQ. rake in
3 REACH, arrive at, come to, get to, attain, achieve, realize
4 *gain speed*
increase, pick up, gather, collect, add, put on, advance, progress, improve
E3 1, 2, 4 lose
♦ *n*
earnings, proceeds, income, revenue, winnings, pickings, proceeds, takings, profit, return, reward, yield, interest, dividend, growth, addition, increase, increment, rise, advance, progress, headway, improvement, advantage, benefit, attainment, achievement, acquisition
FORMAL emolument, advancement, augmentation, accretion
E3 loss
■ **gain on**
close with, close in on, narrow the gap, approach, get nearer/closer to, catch up on/with, level with, overtake, outdistance
E3 leave behind
■ **gain time**
delay, stall, play for time, temporize
FORMAL procrastinate
COLLOQ. drag your feet, dilly-dally

> **Synonym nuances**
> *verb sense 1*
> **Obtain**, **get** and **acquire** refer to something coming into your possession, with no suggestion as to how it was done: *he recently acquired an honours degree.* **Achieve**, although similar, implies an element of effort was involved. The term **capture** suggests taking something, usually with effort or even by force, whilst **secure** might

be used of having taken the necessary steps to gain something desirable: *his skilful play secured a place in the finals.* **Win** is similar, but emphasizes a competitive element: *although the bidding was competitive, our company won the lucrative contract.*

The term **bring in** suggests a productive effect: *her literary work brings in the bulk of her income,* and **reap** and **harvest** similarly suggest yielding profitable returns from an initial effort or outlay, either literally or figuratively: *the prestige reaped from the royal visit was incalculable.* **Gather**, however, would be best used where bringing together or collecting is involved: *information, gathered from a variety of sources.*

gainful *adj*
profitable, beneficial, advantageous, fruitful, lucrative, remunerative, moneymaking, paying, productive, rewarding, financially rewarding, useful, worthwhile
FORMAL fructuous
F₃ useless

gainfully *adv*
profitably, productively, usefully, beneficially, advantageously, lucratively
F₃ uselessly

gainsay *v*
deny, contradict, disagree with, dispute, oppose, challenge
FORMAL contravene, controvert, disaffirm
F₃ agree

gait *n*
walk, pace, step, stride, tread, bearing, carriage, manner
OLD going
FORMAL deportment

gala *n*
festivity, celebration, party, festival, carnival, jubilee, jamboree, fete, fair, pageant, procession

galaxy *n*
1 STARS, star system, solar system, the Milky Way, constellation, cluster, nebula
Related adjective: galactic
2 ARRAY, host, collection, gathering, group assembly, mass, multitude

gale *n*
1 WIND, squall, storm, hurricane, tornado, typhoon, cyclone
2 BURST, outburst, outbreak, fit, eruption, explosion, blast

gall¹ *n*
1 IMPERTINENCE, impudence, brazenness, insolence, presumption, presumptuousness, chutzpah
FORMAL effrontery
COLLOQ. nerve, neck, cheek, sauciness, brass, brass neck
2 BITTERNESS, rancour, sourness, spite, animosity, hostility, enmity, antipathy, malice, venom, virulence, malevolence
FORMAL acrimony, animus
F₃ 1 modesty, reserve **2** friendliness

gall² *v*
it galls me to have to ask his permission
annoy, irritate, irk, exasperate, vex, bother, get to, nettle, peeve, pester, provoke, plague, rile, rankle, ruffle, harass, nag
COLLOQ. aggravate, get up your nose, get/put your back up, get on your wick
F₃ please

gallant *adj, n*
• *adj*
chivalrous, gentlemanly, courteous, polite, gracious, attentive, thoughtful, considerate, courtly, noble, honourable, dashing, manly, heroic, valiant, brave, courageous, fearless, dauntless, intrepid, audacious, bold, daring, plucky
OLD chivalric
F₃ ungentlemanly, cowardly
• *n*
cavalier, chevalier, dandy, fop, beau, *cavaliere servente*, cicisbeo
OLD chamberer, gay

gallantly *adv*
chivalrously, courteously, politely, graciously, thoughtfully, considerately, nobly, honourably, heroically, valiantly, bravely, courageously, fearlessly, dauntlessly, intrepidly, audaciously

gallantry *n*
chivalry, gentlemanliness, courtesy, courteousness, politeness, graciousness, attentiveness, thoughtfulness, consideration, courtliness, nobility, honour, manliness, heroism, valour, bravery, courage, courageousness, spirit, fearlessness, dauntlessness, boldness, intrepidity, audacity, pluck, daring
FORMAL valiance
F₃ cowardice, ungentlemanliness

gallery *n*
art gallery, exhibition area, display room, museum, arcade, passage, walk, balcony, circle, spectators
COLLOQ. gods

galling *adj*
annoying, irritating, irksome, exasperating, humiliating, infuriating, vexing, provoking, nettling, plaguing, rankling, vexatious, bitter, embittering, bothersome, harassing
COLLOQ. aggravating
F₃ pleasing

gallivant *v*
gad about, run around, travel, roam, wander, ramble, range, rove, stray, traipse, flit about, dot about; *Scot* stravaig

gallop *v*
bolt, canter, run, sprint, race, career, fly, dash, tear, speed, zoom, scurry, shoot, dart, rush, hurry
FORMAL hasten
F₃ amble

gallows *n*
scaffold, gibbet, the rope, Tyburn-tree
Related adjective: patibulary

galore *adv*
in abundance, in profusion, lots of, plenty, in numbers, to spare, everywhere
OLD aplenty
COLLOQ. heaps of, tons of, stacks of, millions of
F₃ scarce

galvanize *v*
electrify, shock, jolt, prod, spur, urge, provoke, stimulate, stir, startle, move, arouse, rouse, awaken, quicken, excite, fire, inspire, enliven, animate, invigorate, vitalize, energize

gambit *n*
device, manoeuvre, move, ploy, tactic(s), ruse, play, stratagem, trick, wile, artifice
FORMAL machination

gamble *v, n*
• *v*
bet, wager, try your luck, put money on, back, punt, play, play for money, play the horses, game, stake, chance, chance it, take a chance, risk, take a risk, hazard, venture, speculate, back
COLLOQ. have a flutter
• *n*
bet, wager, punt, lottery, chance, risk, hazard, venture, speculation, pot luck
COLLOQ. flutter, leap in the dark, toss-up

Types of indoor game include:

BOARD GAMES:				TABLE GAMES:	FLOOR GAMES:
backgammon	Pictionary®	canasta	patience	billiards	bowling
bagatelle	Scrabble®	chemin de fer	Pelmanism	craps	bowls
N Am checkers	snakes and	colloq. crib	picquet	dice	ten-pin bowling
chess	ladders	cribbage	poker	dominoes	TARGET GAMES:
Cluedo®	Trivial Pursuit®	draw poker	pontoon	Jenga®	darts
draughts	CARD GAMES:	faro	rummy	pinball	
halma	baccarat	gin rummy	snap	ping pong	
ludo	beggar-my-	happy families	solitaire	pool	
mah-jong	neighbour	nap	solo whist	roulette	
Monopoly®	bezique	napoleon	stud poker	snooker	
nine men's	blackjack	newmarket	twenty-one	shove ha'penny	
morris	brag	old maid	vingt-et-un	table tennis	
	bridge	partner whist	whist		

gambler *n*

better, punter, risk-taker, gamester, plunger, throwster; *N Am* tinhorn; tipster, bookmaker, turf accountant, desperado, daredevil

gambling *n*

betting, speculation, gaming, risk-taking, playing for money, playing the market

gambol *v*

caper, frolic, frisk, cavort, dance, skip, leap, romp, jump, bound, spring, hop, bounce, prance, kick up your heels
OLD disport

game¹ *n*

1 RECREATION, play, sport, pastime, diversion, distraction, entertainment, amusement, merriment, fun, frolic, romp, joke, practical joke, jest, prank, trick
See also panel above
2 COMPETITION, contest, match, round, tournament, event, meeting, meet, bout, round
3 GAME BIRDS, animals, wild animals, meat, flesh, wild fowl, prey, quarry, bag, spoils

Types of children's game include:

battleships	jacks	pin the tail on the
blindman's buff	jackstraws	donkey
charades	Kim's game	postman's knock
Chinese whispers	musical chairs	sardines
consequences	noughts and	Simon says
fivestones	crosses	spillikins
forfeits	pass the parcel	spin the bottle
hangman	piggy-in-the-	tiddlywinks
hide-and-seek	middle	
I-spy		

Types of game (killed for sport) include:

antelope	elephant	pheasant
badger	elk	quail
bear	fallow deer	rabbit
bison	fox	red deer
blackcock	grouse	roe deer
boar	hare	snipe
buffalo	hazel grouse	squirrel
capercailzie	lion	stag
caribou	moose	tiger
deer	mountain lion	waterfowl
duck	partridge	woodcock

game² *adj*

1 *game for anything*
willing, inclined, interested, ready, prepared, eager, enthusiastic
FORMAL desirous
COLLOQ. up for
2 BOLD, daring, intrepid, brave, courageous, fearless, resolute, spirited, unflinching, gallant, plucky, valiant, lion-hearted
F3 1 unwilling **2** cowardly, afraid, fearful

gamekeeper *n*

keeper, warden
OLD venerer

gamely *adv*

resolutely, boldly, intrepidly, bravely, courageously, fearlessly, unflinchingly, valiantly

gamut *n*

scale, series, range, sweep, scope, compass, spectrum, sequence, field, area, variety

gang *n, v*

♦ *n*
group, band, ring, pack, herd, mob, crowd, gathering, horde, circle, clique, coterie, set, lot, club, team, crew, squad, shift, party, troupe, company, core, coffle, coven; *Aust* push
OLD ging; (*Shakesp*) tribulation
COLLOQ. outfit
SLANG posse

■ **gang up on/against**
join forces against, unite against, team up against, band together against, conspire against

gangling *adj*

lanky, gawky, gangly, skinny, spindly, bony, angular, raw-boned, loose-jointed, awkward, tall, ungainly, rangy, gauche

gangster *n*

mobster, desperado, hoodlum, ruffian, rough, tough, thug, terrorist, racketeer, bandit, brigand, robber, criminal; *N Am* wise guy; yakuza
OLD tumbler
COLLOQ. crook; *N Am* goodfella
SLANG enforcer, greaser, heavy, steamer, Yardie; *N Am* gangsta, goombah, hood

gangway *n*

aisle, corridor, passage, passageway, walkway

gaol

see **jail**.

gaoler

see **jailer**.

gap *n*

1 SPACE, blank, void, hole, cavity, aperture, opening, crack, chink, crevice, cleft, cranny, breach, rift, fracture, rent, divide, gulf, divergence, difference
TECHNICAL interstice
FORMAL orifice, lacuna, vacuity, discontinuity, disparity
2 INTERRUPTION, break, recess, pause, lull, interlude, intermission, interval
FORMAL hiatus

gape *v*

1 STARE, gaze, wonder, goggle

gaping
COLLOQ. gawp, gawk
SLANG *N Am* rubberneck
2 OPEN, yawn, part, split, crack

gaping *adj*
open, yawning, broad, wide, vast, cavernous
⊟ tiny

garage *n*
lock-up, car port, petrol station, service station; *N Am* gas station

garb *n, v*
♦ *n*
1 CLOTHES, clothing, garment, costume, dress, outfit, wear, robes, uniform, vestments, habiliment
FORMAL apparel, array, attire, raiment
COLLOQ. gear, get-up, rig-out, togs
SLANG clobber
2 APPEARANCE, guise, aspect, look, form, fashion, style
♦ *v*
clothe, cover, dress, robe
FORMAL apparel, array, attire, habilitate
COLLOQ. rig out

garbage *n*
1 WASTE, rubbish, refuse, remains, leftovers, scourings, scraps, slops, swill, filth, muck, debris, dross, junk, litter, bits and pieces, odds and ends, sweepings; *N Am* trash
FORMAL detritus
2 NONSENSE, rubbish, gibberish, trash, tripe, twaddle, drivel
COLLOQ. bunk, bunkum, claptrap, piffle, bilge, cock, poppycock, hot air, cobblers, rot, tommyrot, stuff and nonsense, codswallop, baloney, blah, bosh, eyewash, hogwash, rhubarb, guff, hooey, malarkey, moonshine
SLANG bull; (*vulgar*) balls, bollocks, crap, bullshit, shit; *dialect* shite

garble *v*
confuse, muddle, jumble, scramble, mix up, twist, distort, corrupt, pervert, warp, slant, doctor, misrepresent, misinterpret, falsify, tamper with, mutilate, edit
⊟ decipher

garbled *adj*
jumbled, confused, muddled, scrambled, mixed-up, unintelligible, undecipherable

garden *n*
yard, backyard, lawn, plot; *S Afr* erf; park

Types of garden include:

allotment	hop garden	rose bed
alpine garden	indoor garden	rose garden
arboretum	Japanese garden	shrubbery
arbour	kitchen garden	sink garden
beer garden	knot garden	sunken garden
border	lawn	tea garden
botanical garden	market garden	terrarium
bottle garden	orchard	vegetable plot
cottage garden	ornamental	walled garden
fruit garden	garden	water garden
garden of rest	raised bed	window box
hanging garden	rockery	winter garden
herbaceous	rock garden	
border	roof garden	
herb garden	rose arbour	

gargantuan *adj*
colossal, huge, enormous, giant, gigantic, massive, immense, vast, tremendous, towering, mammoth, large, big, monumental, titanic, monstrous, elephantine
FORMAL leviathan, prodigious, Brobdingnagian
COLLOQ. ginormous, humongous
⊟ small, tiny, minute

garish *adj*
gaudy, lurid, loud, glaring, flashy, showy, flaunting, tawdry, vulgar, tasteless, cheap, glittering, tinselly, raffish, jazzy, criant; *Scot* roary
FORMAL meretricious
COLLOQ. glitzy, flash
⊟ quiet, tasteful

garishly *adv*
gaudily, luridly, loudly, glaringly, jazzily, tastelessly
COLLOQ. glitzily
⊟ tastefully

garland *n, v*
♦ *n*
wreath, festoon, decoration, flowers, laurels, honours, crown, coronet, coronal, headband, lei, bays, chaplet, toran
OLD crants, girlond
FORMAL stemma
♦ *v*
wreathe, festoon, decorate, deck, adorn, crown, engarland

garments *n*
clothes, clothing, wear, outfit, dress, costume, uniform
FORMAL attire, apparel
COLLOQ. gear, togs, get-up, garb

garner *v*
gather, collect, accumulate, amass, assemble, heap, pile up, stack up, hoard, lay up, put by, reserve, save, stockpile, cull, store, stow away, deposit, treasure, husband
⊟ dissipate

garnish *v, n*
♦ *v*
decorate, adorn, ornament, trim, deck (out), festoon, embellish, enhance, grace, set off, beautify
⊟ divest
♦ *n*
decoration, ornament, ornamentation, adornment, trimming, embellishment, enhancement, relish

garret *n*
attic, loft, mansard, roof space

garrison *n, v*
♦ *n*
1 ARMED FORCE, detachment, troops, unit, command
2 FORT, fortress, fortification, stronghold, station, post, base, barracks, camp, encampment, casern, zareba
Related adjective: presidiary
♦ *v*
1 PROTECT, defend, guard, engarrison
OLD stuff
2 OCCUPY, position, place, mount, station, assign, furnish, man, post

garrulous *adj*
talkative, chatty, windy, long-winded, verbose, wordy, voluble, gassy, glib; *Aust* yabbering; gossiping, gushing, chattering, babbling, effusive, prattling, prating
OLD wordish
FORMAL loquacious, prolix, voluble
COLLOQ. mouthy, gabby
⊟ taciturn, terse

garrulousness *n*
talkativeness, long-windedness, verboseness, verbosity
OLD wordishness
FORMAL loquaciousness, loquacity, prolixity, volubility
COLLOQ. mouthiness

gas *n*
Related adjective: pneumatic
See panel on next page

gash *v, n*
♦ *v*
cut, wound, slash, slit, incise, lacerate, tear, rend,

Types of gas include:

acetylene	chloroform	firedamp	laughing gas	nerve gas	tear gas
ammonia	chokedamp	helium	marsh gas	niton	town gas
black damp	CS gas	hydrogen	methane	nitrous oxide	xenon
butane	cyanogen	sulphide	mustard gas	ozone	
carbon dioxide	ether	ketene	natural gas	propane	
carbon monoxide	ethylene	krypton	neon	radon	

split, score, gouge, nick
* *n*
cut, wound, slash, slit, incision, laceration, tear, rent, split, score, gouge, nick

gasp *v, n*
* *v*
pant, puff, blow, breathe, catch your breath, wheeze, heave, choke, gulp; *dialect* chink, kink
* *n*
pant, puff, blow, breath, choke, gulp, exclamation; *dialect* chink, kink

gassy *adj*
effervescent, sparkling, aerated, carbonated, bubbly, bubbling, frothy, foaming

gastric *adj*
stomach, intestinal, abdominal, coeliac, stomachic, enteric

gate *n*
barrier, door, wicket, doorway, gateway, opening, entrance, exit, access, passage
FORMAL portal

gather *v*
1 CONGREGATE, convene, muster, rally, round up, assemble, summon, marshal, collect, come/bring together, meet, group, crowd, cluster, attract, draw, pull (in), amass, mass, accumulate, converge, hoard, stockpile, heap, pile up, hoard up, build, rake in, garner
COLLOQ. stash away
2 INFER, deduce, conclude, surmise, assume, understand, learn, hear, believe
3 *gather flowers*
pick, pluck, cull, select, reap, harvest, crop, collect, glean, collect, garner
4 *gather speed*
gain, increase, grow, pick up, build up, add, advance, progress, improve, develop
5 FOLD, pleat, tuck, pucker, ruffle, shirr
E∃ 1 scatter, dissipate

Synonym nuances
sense 1
Congregate creates an image of a group of people coming together in one place: *the beggars congregated at tube-station entrances*, while **converge** conveys the idea of people reaching the same place simultaneously. The term **convene** suggests a more formal arrangement: *a hastily convened committee meeting*. **Round up** has connotations of gathering animals together, and so is generally suggestive of getting everyone together in the same location physically, and not always voluntarily: *police have been rounding up school truants*; the word **assemble** has a more voluntary aspect to it.
  Summon would imply ordering people to gather, whilst **marshal** is more suggestive of bringing together in an orderly fashion: *she marshalled her thoughts*. The word **muster**, on the other hand, can be used specifically of military personnel or, more generally, of getting people or things to join together for a cause: *he mustered support for his scheme*; **rally** likewise suggests gathering in support of a specific cause: *the government tried to rally people behind their manifesto*.
  The terms **group** and **crowd** tend to suggest larger numbers, while **cluster** puts the emphasis on formation,

conveying an image of small tight units. The terms **amass**, **mass** and **accumulate** are appropriate for a gradual adding to what is initially present, as is **garner**, which tends to be used transitively and which you might use of gathering information or other more abstract concepts.
  Both **heap** and **pile up** again tend to be intransitive, though these suggest a more physical image and one which is often negative: *my work is piling up*. **Build** is similar in sense, although it has more constructive connotations: *I built a fine collection of miniature paintings*. **Stockpile** refers to saving up reserves for the future, and so suggests a more considered action, but without the grasping implications of **hoard** and **hoard up**. **Rake in** suggests more rapid acquisition, but also has connotations of greed: *syndicates raking in huge profits from sales of drugs*.

gathering *n*
assembly, convention, meeting, round-up, rally; *Irish* feis; get-together, jamboree, party, group, band, company, congregation, mass, crowd, flock, throng, mob, horde, turnout
FORMAL convocation, conclave, assemblage
COLLOQ. *NZ* hui

gauche *adj*
awkward, clumsy, shy, ungainly, inelegant, ungraceful, unpolished, gawky, graceless, uncultured, unsophisticated, ignorant, ill-bred, ill-mannered, insensitive, inept, farouche, tactless
FORMAL maladroit
E∃ graceful, elegant, urbane

gaudiness *n*
brightness, brilliance, garishness, loudness, harshness, showiness, tawdriness, tastelessness, raffishness
COLLOQ. flashiness
E∃ plainness, simplicity

gaudy *adj*
bright, too bright, brilliant, colourful, multicoloured, glaring, garish, loud, shrieking, harsh, stark, flashy, showy, kitsch, flaunting, ostentatious, tinselly, tawdry, vulgar, tasteless, raffish
FORMAL meretricious
COLLOQ. glitzy, flash, snazzy
E∃ drab, plain, simple

gauge *v, n*
* *v*
estimate, guess, judge, assess, evaluate, value, rate, reckon, figure, calculate, compute, count, measure, weigh, determine, check
FORMAL apprise, ascertain
COLLOQ. guesstimate
* *n*
1 SCALE, meter, measure
See panel at **measuring instruments**.
2 STANDARD, basic, guide, norm, criterion, benchmark, yardstick, touchstone, rule, guideline, indicator, measure, meter, test, sample, example, model, pattern
FORMAL exemplar
3 SIZE, magnitude, measure, capacity, bore, calibre, thickness, width, span, extent, area, scope, height, depth, degree

gaunt *adj*
1 HAGGARD, hollow-eyed, angular, bony, thin, lean, lank, skinny, skin and bones, scraggy, scrawny, spindly, skeletal, emaciated, wasted
FORMAL cadaverous
2 BLEAK, stark, bare, barren, desolate, forlorn, dismal, dreary, forbidding, grim, harsh
E3 1 plump

gauzy *adj*
filmy, flimsy, delicate, sheer, thin, transparent, light, see-through, gossamer, insubstantial, unsubstantial
FORMAL diaphanous
E3 heavy, thick

gawk *v*
gape, gawp, goggle, stare, gaze, look, ogle

gawky *adj*
awkward, clumsy, gauche, inept, loutish, oafish, ungainly, gangling, lanky, unco-ordinated, graceless, lumbering
FORMAL maladroit
E3 graceful

gawp *v*
gawk, gape, goggle, stare, gaze, look, ogle

gay *adj, n*
• *adj*
1 HOMOSEXUAL, lesbian, bisexual
FORMAL sapphic
COLLOQ. pink, camp, butch
SLANG (*offensive*) queer, bent, dykey, homo, poofy, limp-wristed
2 HAPPY, joyful, jolly, merry, cheerful, bright, blithe, sunny, carefree, debonair, fun-loving, pleasure-seeking, vivacious, lively, animated, exuberant, sprightly, playful, light-hearted, in good/high spirits
3 *gay colours*
vivid, rich, bright, brilliant, sparkling, festive, colourful, gaudy, garish, flashy, showy, flamboyant
E3 1 heterosexual; *slang* straight 2 sad, gloomy
• *n*
homosexual, lesbian
TECHNICAL invert
OLD bardash, homophile, urning
SLANG (*offensive*) queer, poof, dyke, faggot, fag, fairy, bent, pansy, queen, homo, nancy, pansy, woofter, butch, closet queen, fruit, Mary, poof, powder puff, puff, punk, quiff, shirtlifter; *Aust* tonk
E3 heterosexual; *colloq.* straight

gaze *v, n*
• *v*
stare, stare fixedly/intently, contemplate, regard, watch, view, look, look vacantly, gape, wonder, goggle, eye, muse, outstare, pore
OLD aftereye, wait upon
COLLOQ. gawk, moon around/about
• *n*
stare, look, fixed look, gape
OLD gazement

Synonym nuances
verb
Stare is a fairly general synonym of gaze, with little suggestion of motivation or manner inherent in the word, unlike **contemplate**, which suggests quiet consideration of what is being looked at: *he dropped anchor and contemplated the horizon*. **Regard** is similar, although you might wish to use an adverb to elaborate on the manner: *they regarded each other silently*, while **watch** can be used generally to suggest prolonged and deliberate observation.
 Look vacantly suggests not actually registering what your eyes see. You can use **gape** in the same way or, as **goggle**, to imply being open-mouthed in awe or

---

amazement: *he gaped at the damage to his new car*; **wonder** likewise suggests marvelling at something, but usually in a more positive fashion.
 The word **eye** returns to the idea of concentrated observation to ascertain something: *he eyed me up and down*, whilst **pore** also suggests close and steady attention, generally of written matter: *they pored over the contracts*. The term **muse** is also suggestive of deeper scrutiny, but of a more internalized nature. **Outstare** would specifically be used of keeping your eyes fixed on someone until they are forced to look away.

---

gazebo *n*
belvedere, summerhouse, shelter, pavilion, hut

gazette *n*
newspaper, journal, magazine, news-sheet, broadsheet, tabloid, periodical, paper, organ, dispatch, notice

gear *n, v*
• *n*
1 EQUIPMENT, kit, outfit, tackle, apparatus, tools, implements, instruments, appliances, accessories, supplies, utensils, contrivances
FORMAL accoutrements
COLLOQ. stuff, things
2 GEARWHEEL, cogwheel, tooth-wheel, toothed wheel, ratchet, cog, gearing, mechanism, machinery, works
FORMAL engrenage
3 BELONGINGS, possessions, personal possessions, things, baggage, luggage, paraphernalia, kit
FORMAL effects
COLLOQ. stuff
4 CLOTHES, clothing, garments, dress
FORMAL attire, apparel
COLLOQ. garb, togs, get-up
SLANG threads, clobber
• *v*
adapt, fit, design, tailor, devise, prepare, organize

gel, jell *v*
set, congeal, coagulate, crystallize, harden, thicken, solidify, stiffen, materialize, come together, finalize, form, take shape

gelatinous *adj*
jelly-like, jellied, congealed, rubbery, glutinous, gummy, gluey, sticky, viscous, viscid
FORMAL mucilaginous
COLLOQ. gooey

geld *v*
emasculate, castrate, neuter, cut, unman, unsex

gem *n*
1 GEMSTONE, precious stone, stone, jewel
2 TREASURE, prize, masterpiece, *pièce de résistance*, crème de la crème
COLLOQ. pride and joy, the bee's knees

Gems and gemstones include:

agate	fire opal	rhinestone
amber	garnet	rose quartz
amethyst	jade	ruby
aquamarine	jasper	sapphire
beryl	jet	spessartite
bloodstone	lapis lazuli	spinel ruby
chrysoprase	marcasite	tiger's eye
citrine	moonstone	topaz
coral	morganite	tourmaline
cornelian	mother-of-pearl	turquoise
cubic zirconia	onyx	uvarovite
demantoid	opal	white sapphire
diamond	pearl	zircon
emerald	peridot	

gen *n, v*

• *n*

information, facts, details, data, knowledge, background
COLLOQ. info, low-down, dope

■ **gen up on**

find out about, be well-informed about, research, read up
on, study
COLLOQ. swot up on, bone up on, brush up on

genealogy *n*

family tree, family history, pedigree, lineage, ancestry,
descent, derivation, extraction, family, dynasty, line, birth,
parentage, breeding

general *adj*

1 *a general statement*
broad, sweeping, blanket, all-inclusive, comprehensive,
universal, global, total, across-the-board, widespread,
wide-ranging, prevailing, prevalent, extensive, overall,
accepted, popular, common, panoramic
2 VAGUE, broad, ill-defined, indefinite, imprecise, inexact,
approximate, loose, rough, unspecific
3 USUAL, regular, normal, typical, ordinary, standard,
everyday, customary, conventional, common, habitual,
public
4 *a general store*
mixed, varied, assorted, diverse, miscellaneous
FORMAL heterogeneous, variegated
⊟1 particular, limited **2** specific, detailed, precise **3** rare

---

Synonym nuances
sense 1

Broad and **wide-ranging** can be used neutrally of
something covering a wide area or range: *a wide-ranging
speech*, and **blanket**, **total**, **universal** and **global** can
describe covering everything: *a blanket ban on tobacco
advertising*. **Sweeping** has further implications of being
indiscriminate: *sweeping cuts in the public sector*. The
terms **all-inclusive** and **comprehensive** can be used
where everything has been taken into account: *a
comprehensive study of classroom practice*. **Across-
the-board** is best used in narrower contexts to do with,
for instance, pay increases.
  Both **prevailing** and **prevalent** are more suggestive of
being widely practised or accepted, though they carry a
further suggestion of being current: *the prevailing
conditions of censorship*, while **accepted** and **popular**
would state these ideas more explicitly. The terms
extensive and **widespread** could be used of something
widely but more accidentally occurring, although the
latter might suggest more negative concepts: *a
widespread financial need*. The term **panoramic** is
generally reserved for a wide or complete view:
panoramic views of the coastline.

---

generality *n*

1 GENERALIZATION, generality, sweeping statement, general
statement, impreciseness, indefiniteness, inexactness,
looseness, approximateness, vagueness
2 COMMONNESS, extensiveness, popularity, prevalence,
universality, comprehensiveness, breadth, catholicity,
ecumenicity, miscellaneity
3 MAJORITY, bulk, (the) many, most, greater/larger part,
more than half, nearly all
⊟1 detail, exactness, particular **2** uncommonness **3**
minority

generalization *n*

sweeping statement, general statement, impreciseness,
indefiniteness, inexactness, looseness, approximateness,
vagueness

generalize *v*

theorize, assume, deduce, infer, conclude, deal in
generalities, make a sweeping statement, standardize

generally *adv*

usually, normally, in general, ordinarily, commonly,
habitually, customarily, as a rule, by and large, for the most
part, on the whole, more or less, mostly, in most cases,
predominantly, mainly, chiefly, broadly, largely, at large,
universally

generate *v*

produce, engender, whip up, arouse, cause, bring about,
bring into being, give rise to, create, originate, initiate,
occasion, make, form, breed, propagate
⊟ prevent

generation *n*

1 AGE GROUP, age, days, era, epoch, period, time
2 PRODUCTION, creation, origination, formation,
engendering, reproduction, propagation, breeding
FORMAL genesis, procreation

generic *adj*

1 GENERAL, common, comprehensive, inclusive, universal,
sweeping, wide, all-inclusive, all-encompassing, blanket,
collective
2 *generic drugs*
unbranded, non-trademarked, untrademarked, non-
registered, non-proprietary
⊟1 particular, specific **2** branded, trademarked,
registered, proprietary

generically *adv*

generally, commonly, comprehensively, inclusively,
universally, all-inclusively

generosity *n*

liberality, open-handedness, bounty, charity, philanthropy,
kindness, big-heartedness, benevolence, goodness,
lavishness, unselfishness, selflessness
FORMAL magnanimity, munificence
⊟ meanness, selfishness

generous *adj*

1 LIBERAL, free, bountiful, open-handed, free-handed,
unstinting, unsparing, lavish
2 CHARITABLE, philanthropic, public-spirited, unselfish,
selfless, altruistic, kind, big-hearted, benevolent, good,
high-minded, noble, lofty
FORMAL magnanimous, beneficent, munificent
COLLOQ. big
3 AMPLE, lavish, full, plentiful, abundant, rich, copious,
overflowing
⊟1 mean, miserly **2** selfish **3** meagre

generously *adv*

1 LIBERALLY, freely, bountifully, lavishly, open-handedly
2 CHARITABLY, unselfishly, selflessly, philanthropically,
nobly
FORMAL magnanimously
3 AMPLY, lavishly, fully, plentifully, richly, abundantly,
copiously
⊟1 meanly **2** selfishly **3** meagrely

genesis *n*

origin, beginning, birth, outset, root, source, start,
foundation, founding, generation, initiation, engendering,
formation, propagation, creation, dawn
FORMAL commencement, inception
⊟ end, finish

genetic *adj*

hereditary, inherited, chromosomal, biological
TECHNICAL genomic

genial *adj*

affable, amiable, friendly, amicable, convivial, cordial,
kindly, kind, sociable, warm-hearted, warm, hearty, jovial,
jolly, cheerful, happy, good-natured, good-humoured,
easy-going, agreeable, pleasant
COLLOQ. mat(e)y, pally, chummy
⊟ cold, unfriendly

geniality *n*

affability, amiability, friendliness, conviviality, congenialness, cordiality, kindliness, kindness, warm-heartedness, warmth, joviality, jollity, cheerfulness, happiness, gladness, cheeriness, good nature, agreeableness, pleasantness, bonhomie
E3 coldness, unfriendliness

genially *adv*

affably, amiably, amicably, cordially, warmly, warm-heartedly, heartily, cheerfully, pleasantly
E3 coldly

genie *n*

spirit, fairy, demon, jinni, jinnee, jann

genitals *n*

sexual organs, reproductive organs, private parts, clitoris, labia majora/minora, vagina, womb, uterus, penis, scrotum, testicles
TECHNICAL pudenda, pudendum, fourchette, vulva
FORMAL genitalia
COLLOQ. groin, privates, naughty bits, willy
SLANG (*taboo*) fanny, pussy, muff, punani, cunt, cock, prick, dick, balls

genius *n*

1 VIRTUOSO, maestro, prodigy, master, past master, expert, adept, intellectual, mastermind, brain, intellect, sage
COLLOQ. egghead, brains, boffin
2 INTELLIGENCE, brightness, brilliance, cleverness, fine mind, intellect, wisdom, ability, aptitude, gift, talent, flair, knack, bent, inclination, capacity, faculty
FORMAL propensity
COLLOQ. brains, nous, grey matter, little grey cells

genocide *n*

extermination, massacre, slaughter, ethnocide, ethnic cleansing

genre *n*

type, form, style, class, fashion, brand, group, kind, sort, variety, category, character, school, strain
TECHNICAL genus

genteel *adj*

respectable, refined, cultivated, polished, elegant, polite, stylish, fashionable, cultured, aristocratic, formal, civil, gentlemanly, graceful, mannerly, well-mannered, well-bred, courteous, courtly, ladylike, urbane
E3 crude, rough, unpolished, vulgar

gentility *n*

1 NOBILITY, aristocracy, high birth, gentle birth, good family, upper class, nobles, rank, breeding, élite, gentry, blue blood
2 COURTESY, respectability, formality, elegance, politeness, etiquette, civility, courtliness, manners, mannerliness, refinement, culture, urbanity
FORMAL decorum, propriety
COLLOQ. poshness
E3 crudeness, discourteousness, roughness

gentle *adj*

1 KIND, kindly, amiable, tender, tender-hearted, soft-hearted, compassionate, sympathetic, lenient, humane, merciful, charitable, benign, mild, placid, calm, tranquil, serene, soft, meek, sweet, maidenly, tame, milky
OLD mansuete
2 *a gentle slope*
gradual, slow, easy, smooth, moderate, slight, light, imperceptible, delicate, low-pitched
3 SOOTHING, peaceful, serene, quiet, soft, smooth
4 *gentle winds*
mild, light, moderate, calm, pleasant, balmy
FORMAL clement
E3 **1** unkind, rough, harsh, wild **2** steep, severe **4** strong, violent

gentlemanly *adj*

courteous, polite, refined, polished, urbane, well-bred, well-mannered, cultivated, civilized, civil, honourable, mannerly, gentlemanlike, noble, gallant, chivalrous, genteel, reputable, suave, obliging
OLD gent
E3 impolite, rough

gentleness *n*

kindness, warmth, tenderness, compassion, sympathy, humaneness, mildness, calmness, softness, meekness, sweetness, mercy
E3 unkindness, harshness

gently *adv*

1 *smile gently*
sympathetically, warmly, compassionately, tenderly, charitably, mildly, calmly, serenely, tranquilly
2 *gently sloping hills*
gradually, slowly, slightly, moderately
3 *blowing gently in the wind*
lightly, moderately, calmly, pleasantly
E3 **1** unkindly, harshly **2** steeply **3** strongly, violently

gentry *n*

nobility, nobles, upper class, privileged classes, aristocracy, élite, gentility
COLLOQ. top drawer, upper crust

genuflect *v*

bow, bend the knee, kneel, pay your respects, humble yourself
FORMAL prostrate yourself, make/pay obeisance

genuine *adj*

1 REAL, actual, natural, pure, original, authentic, factual, veritable, true, sound, bona fide, legitimate, legal, lawful, unadulterated, pukka
COLLOQ. real McCoy, kosher; *Aust & NZ* dinkum; *Aust* ridgy-didge
2 SINCERE, honest, frank, candid, earnest, with integrity, truthful, open, natural
E3 **1** artificial, false, fake, counterfeit **2** insincere, deceitful

---

Synonym nuances

sense 1

Real and **actual** are used of something that definitely exists. **Natural** suggests not being artificial or man-made, and has positive overtones: *made with natural ingredients*. **Pure** has further and again positive connotations of being untainted with anything else: *pure dairy butter*, whilst **unadulterated**, although it would convey this idea clearly, is more clinical in tone.

You can use **original** to imply that something has remained as it has always been; **authentic** likewise makes the positive suggestion that something has not been modified or tampered with: *authentic flamenco dancing*. **Factual** has to do with truthful details or real events: *a factual account of the war*, and while **veritable** is used of something which is undeniable, the term is often used and taken in a rather tongue-in-cheek way: *she became a veritable bag of nerves*.

Sound refers to something that is genuine in that it is well-founded: *sound arguments*. **Bona fide** would appropriately describe something which is truly what it appears: *a bona fide charity*. To emphasize that something genuine can be justified as such, you might describe it as **legitimate**: *legitimate industrial action*, while **legal** and **lawful** would be reserved for something that is actually backed by the law.

---

genuinely *adv*

sincerely, really, honestly, earnestly, actually

genus *n*

species, race, breed, genre, order, sort, set, type, division,

subdivision, kind, group, category, class
TECHNICAL taxon

geological timescale

A scale into which the Earth's geological history can be subdivided:

CENOZOIC:
Quaternary (2 million years ago to present: Holocene, Pleistocene)
Tertiary (65 million years ago to 2 million years ago: Pliocene, Miocene, Oligocene, Eocene, Palaeocene)
MESOZOIC:
Cretaceous (140 million years ago to 65 million years ago)
Jurassic (210 million years ago to 140 million years ago)
Triassic (250 million years ago to 210 million years ago)
PALAEOZOIC:
Permian (290 million years ago to 250 million years ago)

Carboniferous (360 million years ago to 290 million years ago: Pennsylvanian, Mississippian)
Devonian (410 million yeas ago to 360 million years ago)
Silurian (440 million years ago to 410 million years ago)
Ordovician (505 million years ago to 440 million years ago)
Cambrian (580 million years ago to 505 million years ago)

PRECAMBRIAN:
(before 580 million years ago)

---

germ *n*
1 MICRO-ORGANISM, microbe, bacterium, bacillus, virus
COLLOQ. bug
2 BEGINNING, start, origin, source, fountain, cause, spark, rudiment, nucleus, root, seed, embryo, bud, sprout
FORMAL commencement, inception

germane *adj*
relevant, appropriate, suitable, apt, applicable, fitting, material, proper, related, connected, akin, allied
FORMAL pertinent, apposite, apropos
F∃ irrelevant

germinal *adj*
generative, developing, embryonic, seminal, preliminary, rudimentary, undeveloped

germinate *v*
bud, sprout, shoot, develop, originate, grow, swell, spring up, take root
FORMAL burgeon

gestation *n*
development, incubation, pregnancy, conception, evolution, ripening, planning, drafting
FORMAL maturation

gesticulate *v*
wave, signal, gesture, motion, indicate, sign, make a sign

gesticulation *n*
wave, signal, gesture, motion, movement, indication, sign, body language
FORMAL chironomy

gesture *n, v*
♦ *n*
movement, motion, indication, sign, signal, wave, gesticulation, act, action
♦ *v*
indicate, sign, motion, beckon, point, signal, wave, gesticulate
OLD gest

get *v*
1 OBTAIN, acquire, come by, receive, be given, earn, gain, have, buy, bring in, clear, make, win, secure, achieve, realize
FORMAL procure, purchase
2 *it's getting dark*

become, turn, go, grow, come to be
OLD wax
3 *get him to help*
persuade, coax, induce, talk into, urge, influence, sway, win over, convince
FORMAL prevail upon
4 MOVE, go, come, travel, reach, arrive
5 FETCH, collect, go for, pick up, bring, take, catch, capture, seize, grab
6 *get a disease*
catch, pick up, develop, come/go down with, become infected with, be afflicted by
FORMAL contract, succumb to
7 *get to see the exhibition*
succeed, manage, have the opportunity, organize, arrange, find a way
COLLOQ. work it, wangle
8 *get breakfast*
prepare, get ready, cook, put together; *N Am* fix
COLLOQ. rustle up
9 *get a joke*
understand, comprehend, see, follow, take in, work out, grasp, fathom
COLLOQ. figure out, twig, get the hang of, get the point, get it, suss (out)
10 *get a thief/an animal*
catch, capture, trap, hunt down, snare, lay hold of, arrest, hit, kill
FORMAL apprehend
COLLOQ. nab, collar, nick, bust, pick up
11 *not get what she said*
hear, make out, catch, recognize, understand, follow, take in, grasp
12 *his snoring really gets me*
annoy, irritate, infuriate, exasperate, vex, provoke, rile, bother
COLLOQ. aggravate, wind up, bug, get on someone's nerves, rub someone up the wrong way, drive crazy, get on someone's wick, get up someone's nose
F∃ **1** lose **4** leave

■ **get about**
move about, move around, go/travel (widely)

■ **get across**
communicate, transmit, convey, express, impart, put across, put over, get over, make clear, bring home to

■ **get ahead**
advance, progress, get on, thrive, flourish, prosper, do well, succeed, make good, make it
COLLOQ. go places, get there, get somewhere, go great guns, make the big time, make your mark, go up in the world
F∃ fall behind, fail

■ **get along**
1 COPE, manage, get by, survive, fare, progress, develop
COLLOQ. make out
2 AGREE, be on friendly terms, harmonize, get on, relate, be on the same wavelength
COLLOQ. hit it off

■ **get at**
1 REACH, attain, gain access to, find, discover, obtain
2 BRIBE, suborn, corrupt, influence
COLLOQ. nobble
3 MEAN, intend, imply, insinuate, hint, suggest
4 CRITICIZE, find fault with, slate, pick on, attack, make fun of
COLLOQ. knock, slam, pick holes in

■ **get away**
escape, get out, break out, break away, break free, run away, flee, depart, leave
COLLOQ. scoot, scram, scat, scarper, do a runner/bunk, run for it, do a moonlight flit, make a bolt/break for it, take to your heels, run for your life
SLANG sling your hook

■ **get back**
1 RETURN, go/come back, go/come home
2 RECOVER, regain, recoup, repossess, retrieve
3 PAY BACK, retaliate, get even with, take revenge on, take vengeance on, avenge yourself on

■ **get by**
cope, get along, manage, survive, exist, fare
FORMAL subsist
COLLOQ. make ends meet, scrape through, hang on, keep your head above water, keep the wolf from the door, weather the storm, see it through

■ **get down**
1 DEPRESS, sadden, make sad, dishearten, dispirit
2 DESCEND, dismount, disembark, alight, get off
◳ 1 encourage 2 board

■ **get in**
enter, penetrate, infiltrate, arrive, come, land, embark

■ **get off**
1 *get off a train*
alight from, leave, get out (of), dismount, climb off, descend
FORMAL disembark
2 REMOVE, detach, separate, shed, get down
◳ 1 get on, board 2 put on

■ **get on**
1 BOARD, climb on, get in, get into, embark, mount, ascend
2 COPE, manage, fare, get along, prosper, succeed
COLLOQ. make out
3 CONTINUE, proceed, press on, advance, progress
4 AGREE, be on friendly terms, harmonize, relate, be on the same wavelength
COLLOQ. hit it off
◳ 1 get off

■ **get out**
1 ESCAPE, flee, break out, extricate yourself, free yourself, leave, depart, withdraw, vacate, evacuate, clear out
COLLOQ. scoot, scram, scat, scarper, do a runner/bunk, run for it, do a moonlight flit, make a bolt/break for it, take to your heels, run for your life
2 *she got out a pen*
take out, produce
3 *the news got out*
become public, become known, come out, leak out, be leaked, spread, circulate

■ **get out of**
avoid, escape, evade, shirk, dodge
COLLOQ. skive
SLANG *N Am* gold-brick, goof off

■ **get over**
1 RECOVER FROM, shake off, recuperate from, pull through, get well/better, respond to treatment, be restored, survive
2 SURMOUNT, overcome, master, get round, defeat, deal with, complete
3 COMMUNICATE, get across, convey, put over, impart, explain, make clear

■ **get ready**
prepare, arrange, fix up, ready, rehearse, set out

■ **get rid of**
do away with, dispense with, dispose of, throw away, rid yourself of, shake off, remove, unload, dump, eject, eliminate, expel, jettison
COLLOQ. get shot of, ditch
◳ accumulate, acquire

■ **get round**
1 BYPASS, evade, avoid
FORMAL circumvent
2 PERSUADE, win over, talk round, coax, cajole, induce, sway
FORMAL prevail upon

■ **get there**
advance, arrive, prosper, succeed, make good
COLLOQ. go places, make it

■ **get together**

meet, assemble, collect, gather, congregate, rally, join, unite, collaborate, organize

■ **get up**
stand (up), arise, rise, stir, get out of bed, ascend, climb, mount, scale

getaway *n*
escape, breakout, flight, start, absconding, decampment, break

get-together *n*
party, reception, meeting, reunion, function, gathering, rally, assembly, social, soirée
COLLOQ. do, bash

get-up *n*
set, outfit, clothes, clothing, garments, kit
COLLOQ. rig-out, gear, togs
SLANG clobber, threads

ghastliness *n*
awfulness, dreadfulness, frightfulness, grimness, gruesomeness, hideousness, nastiness

ghastly *adj*
1 AWFUL, dreadful, frightful, frightening, terrifying, terrible, grim, gruesome, hideous, horrible, horrid, horrendous, loathsome, nasty, repellent, shocking, appalling, lurid, macabre; *Scot* gash
OLD greisly, griesly
2 *look/feel ghastly*
ill, sick, unwell, poorly, rotten, dreadful, awful, terrible
COLLOQ. lousy, rop(e)y, off colour, under the weather
3 *a ghastly mistake*
serious, bad, grave, critical, dangerous, awful, terrible, dreadful, frightful, shocking, appalling, unrepeatable
◳ 1 delightful, attractive 2 well, healthy

Synonym nuances
sense 1
Awful, **dreadful** and **frightful** are now fairly restrained terms to describe anything thoroughly unpleasant: *a dreadful row took place between them*, while **terrible**, although still widely applied, suggests a stronger response: *I had such a terrible day at work I wanted to resign*. **Frightening** has more to do with arousing fear, as does **terrifying**, though to a greater extent, while **grim** is more suggestive of being harsh and unappealing: *a grim picture of life in the prison*. **Gruesome** suggests provoking a shudder and has overtones of disgust, as does **hideous**, although it can also be used in inoffensive contexts: *hideous injuries; a young man in a hideous jacket*. **Horrible**, although similar, again implies a strong emotional response: *I think the new building is horrible*. The term **horrid** nowadays tends to be suggestive merely of something highly disagreeable: *a horrid little boy*. By contrast, **horrendous** implies greater horror on a larger scale: *a horrendous loss of life*.
You can use **loathsome** to convey an element of contempt, while **repellent** would suggest complete aversion, and **shocking** or the even stronger **appalling** implies startling as well as offending the senses. For unsavoury descriptions or images, especially those deliberately created, you could use the term **lurid**. **Macabre** would appropriately describe something with elements of strangeness or death: *a macabre memento of a hangman's noose*.

---

ghost *n*
1 SPECTRE, phantom, apparition, visitant, spirit, wraith, soul, shadow, presence, spook, fetch, manifest, poltergeist, revenant, duppy, jumby, lemur, umbra, *duende*; *dialect* gytrash; *Scot* waff; *N Am* haunt
TECHNICAL astral body
OLD shade, larva

COLLOQ. spook

2 TRACE, suggestion, hint, shadow, impression, semblance

Synonym nuances

sense 1

Spectre can be used to suggest a being, not of this world, however it now more commonly implies any haunting fear of something unpleasant: *the spectre of war*, whilst **phantom** can be used generally of anything illusory. **Apparition** is suggestive of the unexpected appearance of something with an unreal quality: *he was startled by the apparition of a strange man with a black dog*, while **manifest** suggests the form taken by such an apparition or ghost.

   Visitant would be used of a supernatural visitor, perhaps with a specific purpose, and the more rare **revenant** could be used to refer to someone who has returned from the dead. The term **spirit** may be widely used to refer to any incorporeal body, whereas **wraith** and **fetch** would have the more narrow referent of a vision of someone living, although not present.

   Soul has less frightening connotations, suggesting merely the essence of a living creature that is believed to survive death, whilst **shadow** and **presence** are more appropriate for the influence cast by someone who has died, rather than a vision of them: *his father's shadow hung over him*. The word **spook** can be used to suggest someone otherworldly, but is now generally and relatively light-heartedly used to suggest creepiness: *his friends are real spooks*. **Poltergeist** specifically refers to a mysterious invisible force that is blamed for throwing or rearranging things.

---

ghostly *adj*

   eerie, creepy, weird, supernatural, unearthly, ghostlike, spectral, wraith-like, phantom, illusory, shadowy

   COLLOQ. spooky

ghoulish *adj*

   grisly, gruesome, macabre, morbid, unhealthy, unwholesome, revolting, sick

giant *n, adj*

   ◆ *n*

   monster, titan, colossus, behemoth, ogre, Briarean, Patagonian

   OLD eten, rounceval

   ◆ *adj*

   gigantic, colossal, titanic, mammoth, king-size, huge, enormous, massive, immense, vast, tremendous, monumental, gargantuan, cyclopean, large

   FORMAL prodigious, Brobdingnagian

   COLLOQ. jumbo, great big, whopping, ginormous, humongous

   ⊟ tiny, miniature

Famous and mythological giants include:

Albion	Fionn	Magog
Antaeus	MacCumhail	Orion
Ashuras	Fomorians	Pantagruel
Atlas	Galligantus	Paul Bunyan
Balor	Gargantua	Polyphemus
Briareus	Gog	Titans
Cyclops	Goliath	Tityus
Enceladus	Hagrid	Ymir
	Jotun	Ysbaddaden

---

gibber *v*

   babble, blab, blabber; *dialect & N Am* blather; gabble, jabber, prattle, chatter, cackle, cant

gibberish *n*

   nonsense, rubbish, drivel, jargon, twaddle,

balderdash, prattle, yammer, ravings

   OLD (*Shakesp*) linsey

   COLLOQ. gobbledygook, mumbo-jumbo, poppycock, tommyrot, cobblers, bunkum, baloney, blah, bosh, eyewash, hogwash, stuff and nonsense, codswallop, rhubarb, guff, hooey, malarkey, moonshine

   ⊟ sense

gibe, jibe *n, v*

   ◆ *n*

   jeer, sneer, mockery, ridicule, teasing, taunt, derision, scoff, poke, quip

   COLLOQ. dig, crack

   ◆ *v*

   jeer, sneer, mock, ridicule, taunt, tease, scoff, make fun of

   FORMAL deride

   SLANG *N Am* goof

giddily *adv*

1 DIZZILY, unsteadily, lightheadedly

   COLLOQ. woozily

2 EXCITEDLY, dizzily, wildly, restlessly, frantically, enthusiastically, euphorically

giddiness *n*

1 DIZZINESS, faintness, lightheadedness, wooziness, wobbliness, nausea, vertigo

2 EXCITEMENT, dizziness, frenzy, exhilaration, thrill, animation

giddy *adj*

1 DIZZY, faint, lightheaded, unsteady, reeling

   FORMAL vertiginous

   COLLOQ. woozy

2 EXCITED, wild, dizzy, exhilarated, stirred, stimulated, thrilled, elated, frenzied, silly, flighty

   COLLOQ. high

gift *n, v*

   ◆ *n*

1 PRESENT, offering, donation, contribution, bounty, largesse, gratuity, tip, bonus, inheritance, legacy, bequest, endowment

   COLLOQ. freebie

2 TALENT, genius, flair, skill, aptitude, aptness, bent, knack, facility, endowment, proficiency, power, faculty, attribute, ability, capability, capacity, turn

   ◆ *v*

   give, present, offer, contribute, donate

   FORMAL bestow, confer

gifted *adj*

   talented, endowed, adept, skilful, expert, masterly, skilled, accomplished, able, capable, proficient, clever, intelligent, bright, brilliant, sharp

   COLLOQ. smart

gigantic *adj*

   huge, enormous, immense, vast, giant, massive, colossal, king-size, monumental, titanic, mammoth, gargantuan, Herculean, Patagonian

   OLD rounceval

   FORMAL Brobdingnagian

   COLLOQ. jumbo, great big, whopping, ginormous, humongous

   SLANG mega

   ⊟ tiny, Lilliputian

giggle *v, n*

   titter, snigger, chuckle, chortle, laugh, snicker

gild *v*

   enhance, ornament, elaborate, deck, enrich, adorn, grace, beautify, embellish, embroider, festoon, garnish, brighten, dress up, paint, coat, trim

   FORMAL array, bedeck

gilded *adj*

   gilt, gold, golden, gold-plated, gold-layered

gimcrack *adj*
cheap, shoddy, jerry-built, tawdry, trashy, rubbishy, trumpery
COLLOQ. tacky
🔁 solid, well-made

gimmick *n*
attraction, publicity, novelty, ploy, stratagem, ruse, scheme, trick, stunt, dodge, device, contrivance, gadget

gimmickry *n*
novelty, modernity, innovation

gingerly *adv*
tentatively, hesitantly, warily, watchfully, cautiously, with caution, prudently, carefully, charily, attentively, delicately
FORMAL judiciously
🔁 boldly, carelessly

Gipsy
see **Gypsy**.

gird *v*
1 PREPARE, ready, get ready, brace, steel
FORMAL fortify
2 FASTEN, belt, bind, girdle, hem in, pen, surround, encircle, enclose, ring, encompass, enfold

girdle *n, v*
♦ *n*
belt, sash, band, waistband, corset
FORMAL cummerbund, ceinture, cestus, cincture, cingulum
♦ *v*
surround, encircle, circle, enclose, encompass, go round, gird, bind, bound, hem, ring

girl *n*
lass, youngster, young woman, young lady, female, madam, miss, schoolgirl, girlfriend, sweetheart, maiden, daughter, child, teenager, adolescent, au pair, tomboy, hussy, *fille*, *jeune fille*, shiksa, geisha, mousmee, gill, belle, cutie, dolly, dolly bird, baby, beauty queen, Cinderella, cub, fizgig, flirt, gamine, minx, moppet, princess, puss, nymphet, romp; *dialect* gal, mauther; *Scot* lassie, cummer, kimmer, cutty, gilpy, quean, randy, tawpie; *Irish* colleen; *N Am* bachelorette
OLD damsel, wench, gerle, jill, grisette, peat, pigeon, popsy, backfisch, blowze, blushet, gig, giglet; (*Shakesp*) maid-child
COLLOQ. kid, nipper, hen, babe, teeny-bopper; *Aust* sheila
OLD COLLOQ. filly, bobby-dazzler, bobbysoxer
SLANG chick, peach, bit, number, chit, jail-bait; (*offensive*) bit of stuff/fluff, tart, tit, tottie; *Aust* tabby
OLD SLANG Judy, dell, flapper, kinchin-mort

girlfriend *n*
young lady, girl, lady, lass, partner, date, sweetheart, lover, fiancée, woman, mistress, old flame, cohabitee, live-in lover, common-law spouse, best girl
COLLOQ. steady, babe/baby, significant other, squeeze
SLANG bird, chick, bint

girlish *adj*
youthful, childlike, adolescent, childish, immature, innocent, unmasculine

girth *n*
circumference, perimeter, measure, size, bulk, strap, band

gist *n*
pith, essence, marrow, substance, matter, meaning, significance, sense, idea, drift, direction, point, crux, nucleus, nub, core, keynote
FORMAL import, quintessence

give *v, n*
♦ *v*
1 PRESENT, award, let someone have, slip, offer, lend, donate, contribute, provide, supply, distribute, administer, furnish, grant, endow, gift, make over, hand over, turn over, deliver, entrust, bequeath, leave, will, commit, devote
FORMAL confer, bestow, accord, proffer
2 *give news*
communicate, transmit, transfer, convey, tell, utter, announce, declare, pronounce, publish, show, set forth
FORMAL impart
3 CONCEDE, allow, admit, yield, give way, give up, surrender
FORMAL cede
4 *give trouble*
cause, occasion, make, create, produce, do, perform
5 *give an impression*
show, indicate, display, present, exhibit, reveal, set forth, cause to have
FORMAL manifest
6 *give a speech*
make, perform, carry out, do
7 *give attention to something*
concentrate, direct, aim, focus, turn
8 *give someone a fright*
cause to experience/undergo, make, do, perform, occasion, create, give rise to
9 *give something a value*
allow, offer, estimate, grant
10 SINK, yield, bend, buckle, give way, break (down), collapse, fall, fall apart
11 *give a party*
organize, arrange, put on, be responsible for, have, take charge of, lay on
COLLOQ. throw
12 *be given to understand something*
lead, make, cause, move, dispose, incline, prompt, induce
🔁 **1** take, withhold **10** withstand
♦ *n*
yielding, slack, elasticity, springiness, stretch, stretchiness
COLLOQ. play

▪ **give away**
betray, inform on, expose, uncover, divulge, let slip, disclose, reveal, leak, let out, let slip, concede
🔁 keep
▪ **give in**
surrender, capitulate, submit, yield, give way, concede, admit/concede defeat, give up, succumb
COLLOQ. quit, throw in the towel/sponge, chuck it in, pack it in, jack in, call it a day, show the white flag
🔁 hold out
▪ **give off/out**
emit, discharge, release, give out, send out, throw out, pour out, exhale, vent, exude, produce
▪ **give on to**
lead to, open on to, overlook
▪ **give out**
1 DISTRIBUTE, disperse, hand out, pass around, share out, dole out, mete out, allot, deal
COLLOQ. dish out
2 ANNOUNCE, declare, broadcast, publish, make known, circulate, disseminate, communicate, transmit, impart, notify, advertise
3 STOP WORKING, break down
COLLOQ. pack up
SLANG conk out
4 RUN OUT, come to an end, be (all) mixed up, be exhausted
FORMAL be depleted
▪ **give up**
1 STOP, cease, resign, abandon, waive, leave off, sacrifice
FORMAL relinquish, discontinue, forswear, renounce
COLLOQ. quit, cut out
2 SURRENDER, capitulate, give in, admit defeat, concede, concede defeat
COLLOQ. quit, throw in the towel, turn in
SLANG *Aust* drop your bundle
🔁 **1** start **2** hold out

Synonym nuances

verb sense 1

Present can be used to suggest giving something to someone in a formal way, and **award**, while still suggesting formality, also implies that the recipient has been selected on merit. **Slip**, on the other hand, has connotations of shadiness and subterfuge: *she slipped me a fiver while his back was turned*, unlike **offer** which would only be used where someone is being given a choice.

Contribute and **donate** are more suggestive of giving to a worthy cause, although **contribute** also implies that you are not the only donor, whilst **provide** and **supply** are appropriate where something essential is being made available: *the agency provides practical care in the home*, and **distribute** suggests there are a number of recipients. The term **administer** is best used of dispensing in a professional context: *the courts administered justice; he administered first aid*, whereas **furnish** is more suggestive of equipping, and can be used of the giving of information: *the Inspector was furnished with all the documentary evidence.*

Grant, however, is often used in official contexts and implies a degree of concession in the giving: *delays in granting exit visas*, unlike **endow** or **gift** which have more voluntary implications, and suggest the giving of something valuable: *they bought the play area and gifted it to the town.* The terms **entrust** and **commit** are suggestive of passing over for safekeeping: *the courts can commit children into care*, and **devote** can be used to imply it is to the exclusion of everything else: *I've devoted my time and energy to my work.* **Bequeath**, **leave** and **will** are generally used of the transfer of your belongings after death.

---

give-and-take *n*
adaptability, compromise, negotiation, flexibility, co-operation, goodwill, willingness, compliance

given *adj, prep*
- *adj*
1 *a given number*
specified, particular, definite, specific, stated, individual, distinct
2 INCLINED, disposed, likely, liable, prone
- *prep*
considering, taking into account/consideration, bearing in mind, making allowances for, in view of, in the light of, assuming

giver *n*
benefactor, patron, sponsor, backer, supporter, promoter, donor, contributor, subscriber, provider, subsidizer, philanthropist, helper, friend, well-wisher
COLLOQ. angel, fairy godmother
F∃ opponent, persecutor

glacial *adj*
1 FREEZING, frozen, biting, bitter, chill, chilly, cold, frosty, raw, wintry, stiff, frigid, icy, piercing, polar, arctic, Siberian
FORMAL brumous, gelid
2 UNFRIENDLY, antagonistic, cold, icy, frosty, hostile
FORMAL inimical
F∃ **1** hot **2** warm

glad *adj*
1 PLEASED, delighted, gratified, contented, satisfied, happy, joyful, overjoyed, thrilled, elated, merry, cheerful, cheery, gleeful, welcome, bright
OLD gladsome, fain
COLLOQ. over the moon, chuffed, tickled pink
2 WILLING, eager, keen, ready, prepared, inclined, happy, pleased

FORMAL disposed
F∃ **1** sad, unhappy **2** unwilling, reluctant

gladden *v*
brighten, cheer, encourage, delight, please, hearten, gratify, rejoice, elate, enliven, exhilarate, raise the spirits of
COLLOQ. buck up
F∃ sadden

glade *n*
clearing, dell, space, gap, opening

gladly *adv*
happily, cheerfully, freely, willingly, readily, with good grace, with pleasure
OLD gladsomely, fain, fainly
F∃ sadly, unwillingly, reluctantly

gladness *n*
happiness, joy, cheerfulness, delight, pleasure, brightness, high spirits, jollity, glee, hilarity, mirth, gaiety
FORMAL felicity, joyousness
F∃ sadness

glamorous *adj*
smart, elegant, well-dressed, attractive, beautiful, lovely, gorgeous, enchanting, captivating, alluring, charming, appealing, fascinating, exciting, thrilling, dazzling, glittering, glossy, colourful
COLLOQ. glam, glitzy, flashy, ritzy, glammy
F∃ plain, drab, boring

glamour *n*
attraction, attractiveness, allure, appeal, fascination, excitement, thrill, captivation, enchantment, charm, magic, beauty, elegance, glitter, prestige

glance *v, n*
- *v*
peep, peek, glimpse, catch a glimpse of, view, look, look quickly/briefly at, scan, skim, leaf, flip, flick, thumb, dip, browse
- *n*
peep, peek, glimpse, look, quick/brief look
COLLOQ. butcher's, dekko, gander; *Aust & NZ* squiz
■ **glance off**
bounce off, rebound, ricochet, spring back
■ **at first glance**
apparently, at first sight, seemingly, ostensibly, outwardly, on the face of it, to all appearances, superficially, on the surface
FORMAL *prima facie*

gland *n*
Related adjectives: adenoid, glandular

Types of gland include:

adrenal	lymph	parotid
apocrine	lymph node	pineal
cortex	mammary	pituitary
eccrine	medulla	prostate
endocrine	merocrine	sebaceous
exocrine	ovary	testicle
holocrine	pancreas	thymus
lachrymal	parathyroid	thyroid

---

glare *v, n*
- *v*
1 GLOWER, look frown, scowl, stare, frown
COLLOQ. daggers, give someone a dirty look
2 DAZZLE, blaze, flame, flare, shine, beam, reflect
- *n*
1 *his fiery glare*
glower, frown, scowl, stare, look
COLLOQ. dirty look, black look

2 BRIGHTNESS, brilliance, glow, blaze, flame, flare, dazzle, spotlight

glaring adj
blatant, flagrant, open, conspicuous, patent, obvious, manifest, overt, outrageous, gross, lurid, plain as a pikestaff
F3 hidden, concealed, minor

glaringly adv
blatantly, flagrantly, obviously, manifestly, openly, conspicuously, patently, overtly

glass n
1 BEAKER, tumbler, goblet
2 CRYSTAL, glassware, vitrics
3 SPECTACLES, lens, contact lenses, lorgnette, eyeglasses, opera-glasses, pince-nez, monocle
COLLOQ. specs
Related adjectives: vitreous, hyaline
See also **spectacles**.

glassy adj
1 GLASSLIKE, smooth, polished, slippery, icy, shiny, glossy, transparent, clear, crystal clear, mirrorlike
2 *a glassy stare*
expressionless, blank, empty, vacant, dazed, unmoving, fixed, deadpan, glazed, vacuous, cold, lifeless, dull

glaze v, n
♦ v
coat, cover, enamel, gloss, varnish, lacquer, polish, burnish
♦ n
coat, coating, finish, enamel, varnish, lacquer, polish, shine, lustre, gloss

gleam n, v
♦ n
glint, flash, beam, ray, shaft, flare, flicker, glimmer, shimmer, sparkle, glitter, gloss, glow, lustre, brightness
♦ v
glint, flash, glance, flare, shine, radiate, beam, glisten, glimmer, glitter, sparkle, scintillate, shimmer, glow

glean v
gather, collect, find out, learn, pick (up), select, accumulate, amass, harvest, garner, reap, cull

glee n
delight, cheerfulness, pleasure, fun, joy, joyfulness, merriment, mirth, gladness, liveliness, exhilaration, exuberance, exultation, elation, hilarity, jocularity, jollity, joviality, gaiety, gratification, triumph, verve
FORMAL joyousness

gleeful adj
delighted, cheerful, pleased, happy, beside yourself, joyful, overjoyed, elated, exuberant, exultant, merry, mirthful, jubilant, jovial, gratified, triumphant
FORMAL joyous
COLLOQ. over the moon, cock-a-hoop
F3 sad

gleefully adv
cheerfully, happily, joyfully, exuberantly, merrily, jubilantly, triumphantly
FORMAL joyously

glib adj
fluent, easy, facile, quick, ready, talkative, plausible, insincere, smooth, slick, suave, smooth-tongued, smooth-talking, silver-tongued
FORMAL loquacious, voluble
COLLOQ. with the gift of the gab, gabby, gassy
F3 tongue-tied, implausible

glibly adv
fluently, easily, quickly, insincerely, slickly, smoothly

glide v
slide, move smoothly/effortlessly, slip, skate, skim, fly, float, drift, sail, coast, roll, run, flow, pass

glimmer v, n
♦ v
glow, shimmer, glisten, glitter, sparkle, twinkle, wink, blink, flash, flicker, gleam, shine
OLD glimpse
♦ n
1 GLOW, shimmer, shine, sparkle, twinkle, flicker, glint, gleam, ray, flash; *Scot* styme
2 TRACE, hint, suggestion, inkling, grain, flicker, ray

glimmering n
inkling, suspicion, idea, notion, clue, hint, intimation, insinuation, innuendo, suggestion, allusion, indication, sign, pointer
COLLOQ. faintest, foggiest, whisper

glimpse n, v
♦ n
peep, peek, squint, glance, look, quick/brief look, sight, sighting, view, blink, aperçu; *dialect* whiff; *Scot* gledge, gliff, glim, glisk, styme, waff
♦ v
spy, spot, catch sight of, sight, view
FORMAL espy

glint v, n
♦ v
flash, gleam, shine, reflect, glitter, sparkle, glisten, twinkle, glimmer, shimmer, scintillate
♦ n
flash, gleam, shine, reflection, glitter, sparkle, glistening, twinkle, glimmer, shimmer

glisten v
shine, gleam, glint, glitter, flash, sparkle, twinkle, flicker, glimmer, shimmer
FORMAL coruscate

glitch n
snag, delay, hold-up, trouble, problem, difficulty, mishap, setback, hiccup, drawback, catch, impediment, hindrance, obstacle, block, check, barrier, obstruction

glitter v, n
♦ v
sparkle, spangle, scintillate, twinkle, shimmer, glimmer, flicker, glisten, glint, gleam, flash, shine, dazzle, flare
OLD glister
FORMAL coruscate
♦ n
1 SPARKLE, scintillation, twinkle, shimmer, glimmer, flicker, glint, gleam, flash, shine, lustre, sheen, brightness, radiance, brilliance, splendour
FORMAL coruscation
2 SHOWINESS, glamour, tinsel, flashiness, gilt
COLLOQ. glitz, razzle-dazzle, razzmatazz

glitz n
showiness, flamboyance, pretentiousness, glitter, ostentation, razzle-dazzle, attractiveness, tastelessness, gaudiness
COLLOQ. flashiness, pizzazz, razzmatazz, swank
F3 restraint

glitzy adj
showy, flashy, flamboyant, ostentatious, gaudy, garish, glittering, brilliant, vivid, loud, tawdry, fancy, ornate, pretentious, cheap, tasteless, pompous
COLLOQ. swanky, flash, posh, ritzy
F3 quiet, restrained

gloat v
triumph, glory, exult, rejoice, revel in, delight in, relish, crow, boast, vaunt
COLLOQ. rub it in

global adj
1 WORLDWIDE, universal, international
2 GENERAL, all-encompassing, total, thorough, exhaustive,

comprehensive, all-inclusive, encyclopedic, wide-ranging, universal
F3 1 parochial **2** limited

globally *adv*

universally, throughout the world, worldwide, everywhere, in every place, in every country/land, internationally, generally, under the sun

globe *n*

world, earth, planet, sphere, ball, orb, round

globular *adj*

ball-shaped, round, globate, spherical
FORMAL orbicular, spheroid

globule *n*

bead, ball, bubble, drop, droplet, globulet, pearl, pellet, particle
TECHNICAL vesicle, vesicula

gloom *n*

1 DARK, darkness, blackness, shade, shadow, dusk, twilight, dimness, obscurity, cloud, cloudiness, dullness, murkiness
2 DEPRESSION, low spirits, despondency, dejection, sadness, unhappiness, glumness, melancholy, grief, sorrow, woe, misery, hopelessness, pessimism, desolation, despair, discouragement, damp, mood, shadow
COLLOQ. the blues
F3 1 brightness **2** cheerfulness, happiness

gloomily *adv*

despondently, downheartedly, sadly, miserably, glumly, pessimistically, depressingly, morosely, drearily, cheerlessly, dismally
F3 cheerfully, happily

gloomy *adj*

1 DARK, sombre, shadowy, dim, obscure, overcast, dull, dreary, dismal, dingy, unlit
FORMAL tenebrous, crepuscular
2 DEPRESSED, down, low, despondent, dejected, downcast, dispirited, downhearted, sad, miserable, glum, morose, dreary, drear, pessimistic, cheerless, melancholy, sorrowful, dismal, depressing, desolate, in low spirits
FORMAL disconsolate
COLLOQ. down in the dumps
F3 1 bright **2** happy, cheerful

glorification *n*

1 PRAISE, worship, adoration, honouring, thanking, gratitude, reverence, extolling
FORMAL lauding, veneration
2 *glorification of war*
celebration, praise, magnification, lionization, idolization, romanticization

glorify *v*

1 *glorify God*
praise, worship, exalt, adore, honour, thank, bless, magnify, revere, extol, sanctify
FORMAL laud, venerate
2 *glorify violence/war*
celebrate, praise, magnify, hail, lionize, idolize, elevate, enshrine, immortalize, romanticize, panegyrize
FORMAL eulogize
F3 1 denounce; *formal* vilify

glorious *adj*

1 ILLUSTRIOUS, eminent, distinguished, famous, renowned, honoured, noted, great, noble, celebrated, famed, splendid, magnificent, grand, majestic, supreme, excellent, victorious, triumphant
2 MARVELLOUS, splendid, beautiful, gorgeous, superb, perfect, splendid, excellent, wonderful, delightful, dazzling, heavenly
COLLOQ. super, terrific, great
3 *glorious weather*

fine, bright, radiant, shining, brilliant
F3 1 unknown

glory *n, v*

♦ *n*
1 FAME, renown, celebrity, illustriousness, greatness, eminence, distinction, honour, recognition, acclaim, prestige, accolade, kudos, triumph, *gloire*
2 PRAISE, homage, tribute, worship, veneration, adoration, exaltation, blessing, thanksgiving, gratitude
TECHNICAL doxology, gloria, preface
3 BRIGHTNESS, radiance, brilliance, beauty, splendour, halo, sun, resplendence, magnificence, pomp, grandeur, majesty, dignity, impressiveness, crown, diadem
TECHNICAL aureola, gloriole
OLD (*Shakesp & Spenser*) garland
♦ *v*
revel, delight, exult, pride yourself, rejoice, take great pleasure, triumph, relish, boast, crow, gloat
OLD strut, triumph

gloss¹ *n, v*

♦ *n*
1 SHEEN, polish, varnish, lustre, shine, brightness, gleam, shimmer, sparkle, brilliance
2 SHOW, appearance, semblance, surface, front, façade, veneer, camouflage, mask, disguise, veil, window-dressing
■ **gloss over**
conceal, hide, veil, draw a veil over, mask, disguise, camouflage, cover up, whitewash, explain away, evade, avoid, ignore, smooth over, deal with quickly

gloss² *n, v*

♦ *n*
glosses to the text
annotation, note, footnote, explanation, interpretation, translation, definition, comment, commentary
FORMAL elucidation, explication, scholion
♦ *v*
annotate, add glosses to, define, explain, interpret, construe, translate, comment
FORMAL elucidate

glossary *n*

word list, wordbook, index, dictionary, lexicon, concordance, thesaurus

glossy *adj*

shiny, sheeny, lustrous, sleek, silky, smooth, glassy, polished, burnished, glazed, gleaming, enamelled, bright, shining, shimmering, sparkling, brilliant
F3 matt

glove *n*

mitten, mitt, gauntlet, gage, mousquetaire glove, oven glove

glow *n, v*

♦ *n*
1 LIGHT, gleam, glimmer, radiance, glory, brightness, vividness, richness, brilliance, splendour, afterglow, sunglow, outflush
TECHNICAL phosphorescence, gegenschein
OLD leam
FORMAL luminosity, incandescence
2 ARDOUR, fervour, intensity, warmth, passion, enthusiasm, excitement, happiness, satisfaction
3 FLUSH, blush, rosiness, rose, redness, reddening, pinkness, burning, bloom
♦ *v*
1 SHINE, radiate, gleam, glimmer, burn, smoulder
2 *their faces glowed*
flush, blush, colour, redden, burn, grow/look pink

glower *v, n*

♦ *v*
glare, frown, scowl, stare, frown
COLLOQ. look daggers, give someone a dirty look

◆ *n*

glare, frown, scowl, stare, look
COLLOQ. black look, dirty look

glowing *adj*
1 BRIGHT, luminous, vivid, vibrant, rich, warm, flushed, red, ruddy, flaming, smouldering
TECHNICAL phosphorescent
FORMAL incandescent
2 *a glowing review*
complimentary, enthusiastic, favourable, ecstatic, rhapsodic
FORMAL laudatory, eulogistic, panegyrical
COLLOQ. rave
F₃ 1 dull, colourless **2** restrained

glue *n, v*
◆ *n*
adhesive, gum, paste, size, cement, fixative, mortar
◆ *v*
1 STICK, affix, gum, paste, seal, bond, cement, fix
FORMAL agglutinate
2 *glued to the radio*
grip, rivet, engross, absorb, engage, compel, hypnotize, mesmerize

gluey *adj*
adhesive, gummy, sticky, viscid, viscous
FORMAL glutinous

glum *adj*
gloomy, unhappy, forlorn, sad, miserable, depressed, despondent, moody, dejected, morose, pessimistic, doleful, crestfallen, sour, sulky, sullen, surly, grumpy, gruff, ill-humoured, churlish
COLLOQ. crabbed, down, low, down in the dumps
F₃ ecstatic, happy

glumly *adv*
gloomily, unhappily, forlornly, sadly, miserably, despondently, dejectedly, morosely, sourly, sullenly, grumpily, gruffily
F₃ ecstatically, happily

glut *n, v*
◆ *n*
surplus, excess, superfluity, surfeit, overabundance, superabundance, saturation, overflow
F₃ scarcity, lack
◆ *v*
saturate, oversupply, overload, inundate, flood, deluge, overfeed, sate, satiate, stuff, gorge, fill, cram, choke, clog

glutinous *adj*
adhesive, sticky, cohesive, gluey, gummy, mucous, viscous
FORMAL mucilaginous, viscid

glutton *n*
gourmand, gormandizer, gobbler, belly-god, free-liver, cormorant; *Aust & NZ* gutzer
OLD lurcher
COLLOQ. guzzler, greedy guts, gorger, pig
F₃ ascetic

gluttonous *adj*
greedy, gluttonish, voracious, ravenous, insatiable, gormandizing
OLD gluttonish
FORMAL edacious, esurient, omnivorous, rapacious
COLLOQ. hoggish, piggish
F₃ abstemious, ascetic

gluttony *n*
gourmandism, greed, greediness, voracity, insatiability, surfeit
OLD gulosity
FORMAL edacity, esurience
COLLOQ. piggishness
F₃ abstinence, asceticism

gnarled *adj*
gnarly, knotted, knotty, bumpy, lumpy, twisted, contorted, distorted, rough, wrinkled, rugged, weather-beaten, leathery

gnash *v*
grind, grate, grit, scrape

gnaw *v*
1 BITE, nibble, munch, chew, crunch, eat, devour, consume, erode, wear, haunt
FORMAL masticate
2 WORRY, nag, niggle, fret, trouble, plague, prey, torment, harass, harry

go *v, n*
◆ *v*
1 MOVE, pass, advance, progress, proceed, make for, head, drive, travel, journey, walk, start, begin, go away, depart, leave, take your leave, set off, set out, retreat, withdraw, disappear, vanish, melt away
FORMAL repair
COLLOQ. clear off, quit, scat, scoot, scram, make tracks, beat it; *Aust* shoot through
2 OPERATE, function, work, run, act, perform, be in working order
3 EXTEND, spread, stretch, reach, lead, span, continue, carry on, unfold
4 *time goes quickly*
pass, pass by, elapse, lapse, proceed, roll on, go by, slip away, slip by, tick away
5 *go mad*
become, turn, get, grow, come to be, be changed into
6 *the machine goes 'beep'*
emit, sound, make a sound, give off, send out, release
7 *the books go here*
belong, have as its usual place, fit in, be found, be kept, be located, be situated
8 *the interview went well*
turn out, work out, progress, proceed, manage, fare, occur, result, end up, develop
FORMAL eventuate
COLLOQ. pan out
9 *Where does all the money go?*
be used up, be spent, be finished, be exhausted, be consumed
10 *100 jobs will go*
get rid of, be discarded, be thrown away, be dismissed, be made redundant
COLLOQ. be axed, be given the sack, be sacked, be fired, be given the push, be given your cards, be shown the door, be given your marching orders; *N Am* be given the pink slip; be given your P45
11 *most of the income goes on rent*
be spent on, be given to, be allotted to, be assigned to, be awarded to
12 *the proceeds will go to charity*
be given, be donated, be presented, be pledged
13 *the hat goes well with the dress*
match, harmonize, co-ordinate, blend, go together, complement, suit, fit, correspond, go with each other
FORMAL accord
14 DIE, pass away, pass on, pass, depart, depart this life, breathe your last, draw your last breath, lose your life, perish, fail, drown, starve, close your eyes
FORMAL expire, decease
COLLOQ. peg out, bite the dust, pop off, give up the ghost, push up daisies, pop your clogs
SLANG snuff it, cash in your chips, kick the bucket, croak; *Aust* cark or kark (it)
F₃ 1 stop **2** break down, fail **13** clash
◆ *n*
1 *have a go*
attempt, try, bid, turn, endeavour, effort

COLLOQ. shot, bash, stab, crack, whirl

2 ENERGY, vitality, life, force, spirit, dynamism, vigour, animation

COLLOQ. get-up-and-go, push, pizzazz, oomph, zip, zing

■ **go about**
approach, begin, set about, embark on, address, tackle, attend to, undertake, do, engage in, perform

■ **go ahead**
begin, proceed, carry on, continue, advance, progress, make progress, move

■ **go along with**
accept, agree with, obey, follow, fall in with, support, abide by

FORMAL comply with, concur with

■ **go around/round**
circulate, be spread around, be passed round, be talked about, go about

■ **go at**
set about, tackle, attack, blame, criticize, argue

■ **go away**
depart, leave, abscond, withdraw, retreat, disappear, vanish

COLLOQ. scoot, scram, do a runner/bunk, run for it, make a bolt/break for it, take to your heels, run for your life

---

Colloquial expressions telling someone to go away include:

away!	get out!	push off!
away with you!	get lost!	run along!
be off!	go and jump in	*Aust* rack off!
beat it!	the lake!	scarper!
buzz off!	go fly a kite!	scat!
Aust choof off!	never darken my	scram!
clear off!	door again!	shove off!
clear out!	off with you!	sling your hook!
do me a favour!	off you go!	take a running
get knotted!	on your way!	jump!
get out of here!	out of my sight!	vamoose!

Slang expressions telling someone to go away include:

bugger off!	naff off!
taboo fuck off!	piss off!
get the hell out of	sod off!
here!	

■ **go back**
return, revert, backslide, retreat

■ **go back on**
renege on, default on, deny, break, break your promise

■ **go by**
1 PASS, elapse, lapse, flow
2 *go by the rules*
observe, follow, obey, heed
FORMAL comply with

■ **go down**
1 DESCEND, sink, be submerged, set, fall (down), drop, decrease, be reduced, decline, deteriorate, degenerate, fail, founder, go under, collapse
COLLOQ. fold
2 LOSE, be beaten, be defeated, suffer defeat, fail
COLLOQ. come a cropper
3 *the joke went down badly*
be received, have as a response, be reacted to, be met with, sustain
4 *go down in history*
be remembered, be recorded, be honoured, be recognized

■ **go down with**
catch, pick up, develop, come down with, become infected with, be afflicted by
FORMAL contract, succumb to

■ **go for**
1 CHOOSE, select, prefer, favour, aim for, like, admire, enjoy
2 ATTACK, assail, assault, rush at, set about, lunge at

■ **go in for**
enter, take part in, participate in, engage in, go into, take up, embrace, adopt, undertake, practise, pursue, follow
FORMAL espouse

■ **go into**
discuss, consider, review, examine, study, research, look into, scrutinize, investigate, inquire into, check out, probe, delve into, analyse, dissect

■ **go off**
1 DEPART, leave, set out, abscond, vanish, disappear
COLLOQ. quit
2 EXPLODE, blow up, blast, burst, detonate, be fired, be discharged
COLLOQ. go bang
3 *the milk has gone off*
deteriorate, turn, sour, go bad, rot, go stale

■ **go on**
1 CONTINUE, carry on, proceed, persist, stay, endure, last, remain
2 CHATTER, ramble on
COLLOQ. rabbit, witter, natter, gab, gas, talk the hind legs off a donkey
3 HAPPEN, occur, take place

■ **go out**
1 EXIT, depart, leave, withdraw
2 *the light went out*
be switched off, be turned off, be extinguished
3 *go out with a boy*
go with, go around/round, court, see each other, date, go steady

■ **go over**
examine, peruse, study, revise, scan, read, look over, inspect, discuss, think about, check, review, repeat, rehearse, list

■ **go round**
1 SPIN, turn (round), revolve, rotate, circle, twist, gyrate, twirl, swivel, pirouette, wheel, whirl, whirr, swirl, reel
2 *See* **go around**

■ **go through**
1 SUFFER, undergo, experience, bear, tolerate, endure, face, withstand, stand, be subjected to
2 INVESTIGATE, check, examine, look through, search, hunt, explore
3 USE UP, consume, exhaust, spend, squander, get through
4 *the proposal has gone through*
be approved, be passed, be authorized, be accepted, be confirmed, be adopted, be carried, be signed

■ **go together**
match, harmonize, fit, suit, blend, co-ordinate, complement
FORMAL accord

■ **go under**
1 CLOSE DOWN, collapse, default, die, fail, go out of business, founder, go bankrupt
COLLOQ. fold, flop, go to the wall, go bust
2 SINK, go down, founder, submerge, succumb, drown

■ **go with**
1 MATCH, harmonize, co-ordinate, blend, complement, suit, fit, correspond
2 ACCOMPANY, escort, take, usher
F3 1 clash

■ **go without**
abstain, deny yourself, for(e)go, do without, manage without, lack, want

goad *v*
prod, prick, spur, impel, push, drive, jolt, provoke, incite, induce, instigate, arouse, stimulate, inspire, motivate,

pressurize, prompt, urge, nag, hound, harass, taunt, annoy, irritate, vex

go-ahead n, adj

♦ n

permission, authorization, clearance, sanction, approval, assent, consent, warranty, agreement, confirmation
COLLOQ. green light, OK, thumbs-up
⊟ ban, veto, embargo

♦ adj

enterprising, pioneering, progressive, resourceful, ambitious, forward, forward-looking, opportunist, up-and-coming, dynamic, vigorous, energetic, aggressive, pushy
COLLOQ. go-getting
⊟ unenterprising, sluggish

goal n

target, mark, objective, aim, intention, object, purpose, end, design, ambition, ideal, aspiration

gobble v

bolt, guzzle, gorge, eat quickly, cram, stuff, devour, consume, swallow, gulp, slabber
COLLOQ. put away, wolf, scoff, snarf

gobbledygook n

gibberish, jargon, officialese, journalese, computerese, psychobabble, buzz words, nonsense, rubbish, drivel, twaddle, balderdash, prattle

go-between n

intermediary, mediator, liaison, contact, middleman, broker, dealer, agent, factor, messenger, medium
OLD (*Shakesp*) ring-carrier

goblet n

glass, cup, chalice, beaker, tumbler

goblin n

imp, brownie, fiend, hobgoblin, gnome, elf, sprite, spirit, gremlin, nixie, bogey, leprechaun, kelpie, kobold, demon, troll, puck, bogle, lubber fiend, barghest, *duende, esprit follet*, nis; *dialect* knocker; *Scot* bodach, redcap, red-cowl, shellycoat; *Irish* pooka
OLD gobbeline, pug

gobsmacked adj

stunned, dumbfounded, astonished, amazed, astounded, overwhelmed, speechless, taken aback, startled, overcome, confounded, lost for words, staggered, confused, baffled, bewildered, dumb, nonplussed, paralysed
COLLOQ. thrown, flabbergasted, bowled over, floored, knocked for six

God n

Deity, Supreme Being, Divine Being, Godhead, prime mover, Creator, Maker, Providence, Lord, King, Almighty, Holy One, Jehovah, Yahweh, Father, Allah, Brahma, Zeus, Holy One, Judge, Saviour, Eternal, Everlasting
Related adjective: divine

god, goddess n

deity, divine being, divinity, spirit, power, icon, idol, graven image
Related adjective: divine
See panel on next page

god-forsaken adj

remote, isolated, lonely, bleak, desolate, abandoned, deserted, forlorn, dismal, dreary, gloomy, miserable, wretched, depressing

godless adj

ungodly, atheistic, heathen, pagan, irreligious, agnostic, faithless, unholy, unrighteous, impious, sacrilegious, profane, irreverent, bad, evil, sinful, wicked
OLD atheous
FORMAL nullifidian
⊟ godly, pious

godlessness n

ungodliness, irreligion, faithlessness, unfaithfulness, impiety, irreverence, wickedness, atheism, agnosticism, paganism
⊟ godliness

godlike adj

divine, celestial, heavenly, exalted, saintly, holy, sacred, perfect, sublime, transcendent, superhuman
FORMAL deiform, theomorphic

godliness n

holiness, piety, devoutness, belief, religion, righteousness, morality, purity
⊟ godlessness

godly adj

religious, holy, pious, devout, God-fearing, believing, righteous, good, moral, virtuous, saintly, pure, innocent
⊟ godless, impious

godsend n

blessing, boon, stroke of luck, bonanza, windfall, benediction, miracle
⊟ blow, setback

goggle v

stare, gaze, wonder
COLLOQ. gawp, gawk

going-over n

1 EXAMINATION, inspection, investigation, study, survey, analysis, check, check-up, review, scrutiny
2 BEATING, attack, criticism, reprimand, scolding, rebuke, pasting, chiding, thrashing, whipping, row
FORMAL castigation, chastisement
COLLOQ. dressing-down, trouncing

goings-on n

events, activities, occurrences, happenings, affairs, scenes, business, misbehaviour, mischief
COLLOQ. funny business

gold n

bullion, nugget, bar, ingot, precious metal
Related adjectives: auric

golden adj

1 GOLD, gilded, gilt, gold-coloured, goldish, yellow, blond(e), hyacinthine, red, fair, flaxen, bright, shining, gleaming, brilliant, dazzling, lustrous
OLD gilden, inaurate
FORMAL resplendent, aureate, aurelian
2 PROSPEROUS, successful, glorious, excellent, treasured, precious, happy, joyful, delightful, rosy, favourable, promising, flourishing, bright, rewarding, millennial, Saturnian
FORMAL auspicious, propitious

golf club

Types of golf club include:

baffy	mashie	putter
brassy	mashie iron	putting-cleek
bulger	mashie niblick	sand wedge
cleek	midiron	spade mashie
driver	midmashie	spoon
driving iron	niblick	wedge
iron	pitching niblick	wood
jigger	pitching wedge	

gone adj

departed, absent, away, astray, defunct, disappeared, vanished, lost, missing, finished, done, over, elapsed, past, used, spent, dead, extinct
COLLOQ. over and done with

goo n

matter, ooze, slime, stickiness, slush, sludge, mud,

Gods and goddesses include:

GREEK GODS:
Adonis (*vegetation and rebirth*)
Aeolus (*winds*)
Apollo (*prophecy, music, youth, archery, healing*)
Ares (*war*)
Asclepius (*healing*)
Atlas (*Titan who bears Earth*)
Attis (*vegetation*)
Boreas (*north wind*)
Cronus (*father of Zeus*)
Dionysus (*wine, vegetation, ecstasy*)
Eros (*love*)
Ganymede (*rain*)
Hades (*underworld*)
Helios (*sun*)
Hephaestus (*fire*)
Hermes (*messenger of the Gods*)
Hypnos (*sleep*)
Morpheus (*dreams*)
Nereus (*sea*)
Oceanus (*river Oceanus*)
Pan (*male sexuality, woods, shepherds*)
Poseidon (*sea*)
Thanatos (*death*)
Zeus (*sky, king of the gods*)
GREEK GODDESSES:
Alphito (*barley, goddess of Argos*)
Aphrodite (*love, beauty*)
Arethusa (*springs and fountains*)
Artemis (*fertility, chastity, hunting*)
Athene (*prudence and wisdom, protectress of Athens*)
Cybele (*earth*)
Demeter (*harvest*)
the Furies (or Erinyes) (*vengeance*)
the Fates (*destiny*)
Gaia (*Earth*)
the Graces (*charm and beauty*)
Hebe (*youth*)
Hecate (*moon*)
Hera (*marriage and childbirth, queen of the gods*)
Hestia (*hearth*)
the Horae (*seasons*)
Iris (*rainbow*)
the Muses (*the liberal arts*)
Nemesis (*destiny, vengeance*)
Nike (*victory*)
Persephone (*underworld, corn*)
Rhea (*mother of Zeus*)
Selene (*moon*)
ROMAN GODS:
Apollo (*sun*)
Bacchus (*wine and ecstasy*)
Cupid (*love*)
Faunus (*crops and herbs*)
Fides (*honesty*)
Genius (*protector of individuals and the state*)

Janus (*entrances, travel, dawn*)
Jupiter (*sky, sun, moon, thunder etc*)
Lares (*house*)
Liber Pater (*human and agricultural fertility*)
Mars (*war*)
Mercury (*messenger of the gods, god of merchants*)
Mithra (*sun, regeneration*)
Neptune (*sea*)
Orcus (*death*)
the Penates (*food and drink*)
Picus (*woods*)
Pluto (*underworld*)
Portunus (*husbands*)
Saturn (*fertility, agriculture*)
Silvanus (*trees and forests*)
Vertumnus (*fertility*)
Vulcan (*fire*)
ROMAN GODDESSES:
Bellona (*war*)
Ceres (*corn, agriculture*)
Diana (*fertility, hunting*)
Egreria (*fountains, childbirth*)
Fauna (*fertility*)
Flora (*fruitfulness, flowers*)
Fortuna (*chance*)
Juno (*marriage, childbirth, light*)
Luna (*moon*)
Maia (*fertility*)
Minerva (*war, craftsmen, education, arts*)
Ops (*harvest*)
Pales (*protectress of flocks*)
Pomona (*fruits*)
Proserpina (*underworld*)
Rumina (*nursing mothers*)
Venus (*spring, gardens, love*)
Vesta (*hearth*)
Victoria (*victory*)
EGYPTIAN GODS:
Amun-Re (*universal god*)
Anubis (*funerals*)
Apis (*fertility*)
Atum (*ancestor of the human race*)
Geb (*the earth*)
Horus (*sun*)
Osiris (*vegetation, death*)
Ptah (*creation, protector of artists and artisans*)
Seth (*evil*)
Thoth (*moon, learning, scribe*)
EGYPTIAN GODDESSES:
Hathor (*love, fertility*)
Isis (*magic, fertility, mother-goddess*)
Maat (*order, law, justice*)
Nepthys (*funerals*)
Nut (*sky*)
NORSE GODS:
Aegir (*sea*)
the Aesir (*race of warlike gods*)
Balder (*son of Odin, god of light*)
Bragi (*poetry*)

Frey (*fertility, sunshine, growth*)
Heimdall (*sentinel-god of the dawn*)
Loki (*mischief*)
Njord (*ships, the sea*)
Odin (or Woden or Wotan) (*father-god, war, magic, law, poetic inspiration*)
Thor (*thunder, war*)
Tyr (*battle, sky*)
the Vanir (*race of benevolent gods*)
NORSE GODDESSES:
Freyja (*libido*)
Frigg (*fertility, wife of Odin*)
Hel (*underworld*)
Nerthus (*earth*)
the Valkyrie (*warrior-women, helpers of gods of war*)
HINDU GODS:
Agni (*fire*)
Brahma (*creator, father of gods and men*)
Krishna
Ganesh (*wisdom, success*)
Hanuman (*monkey god*)
Indra (*life, light, fertility, rain*)
Rama
Ravana
Savitri (*order*)
Shiva (*destruction, reproduction*)
Vishnu (*fertility*)
HINDU GODDESSES:
Devi
Durga
Kali (*death, destruction*)
Lakshmi (*happiness, beauty, prosperity*)
Parvati
Sarasvati (*knowledge, education*)
Uma
AZTEC GODS:
Huitzilopochtil (*war, sun*)
Quetzalcoatl (*creator, god of wind*)
Tezcatlipoca (*trickster-god of sun*)
Tlaloc (*rain, mountains, springs*)
Xiuhtecuhtli (*fire, light*)
Xochipilli (*flowers, love, song and dance*)
AZTEC GODDESSES:
Chalchiuhtlicue (*water*)
Coatlicue (*earth goddess*)
Xochiquetzal (*flowers, love, childbirth*)
MAYAN GODS:
the Bacabs (*wind gods*)
Hunab Ku (*supreme god and creator*)
Itzamna (*founder of Mayan culture, god of maize, fertility, moon*)
Kukulkan (*god of 4 elements, creator*)
MAYAN GODDESSES:
Aknah (*birth*)
Ixazaluoh (*water, inventor of weaving*)

Ixchel (*storm-goddess*)
INCA GODS:
Apu Punchau (*sun*)
Catequil (*thunder and lightning*)
Inti (*sun-god, father of Viracocha*)
Manco Capac (*sun-god, father of Incans*)
Pachacamac (*earth-god, creator*)
Viracocha (*supreme creator*)
INCA GODDESSES:
Chasca (*Venus, protectress of virgins*)
Mama Oella (*inventor of spinning*)
Mama Quilla (*moon-goddess*)
Pachamama (*earth-goddess*)
CELTIC GODS:
Aengus Mac Og (*youth, love, beauty*)
Balor (*death*)
Bran the Blessed (*prophecy, arts, war*)
Cernunnos (*fertility, underworld, animals*)
the Dagda (*earth-god, fertility, prosperity*)
Goibniu (*smithcraft*)
Gwydion (*enchantment, illusion*)
Gwynn ap Nudd (*underworld*)
Lir/Llyr (*sea, water*)
Lug (*sun-god, arts, healing, father of Cuchulainn*)
Manannan Mac Lir/Manawydan ap Llyr (*sea-god, regeneration*)
Nuada/Nuadu (*harpers, healing, learning, warfare*)
Ogma (*eloquence, physical strength*)
Pwyll
Pryderi (*underworld*)
Tuatha Dé Danann (*magical race*)
CELTIC GODDESSES:
Aine (*love, fertility*)
Badhb (*battle, enlightenment*)
Boann (*water, fertility*)
Branwen (*love, beauty*)
Brigit/Brigid (*agriculture, smithcraft, inspiration*)
Cliodhna (*beauty*)
Danu/Don (*mother of the gods, rivers, wisdom, magic*)
Epona (*horses, prosperity*)
Eriu
Macha (*warrior-goddess, death, cunning*)
Morrigan (*war-goddess, lust, revenge, magic*)
Rhiannon (*divine queen, wit*)

scum, mire, muck, grease, grime
COLLOQ. gunge, yuck, grot, gloop
SLANG crud, gunk, grunge

good *adj, n, interj*
* *adj*
1 *have a good day; do good work*
enjoyable, cheerful, pleasing, pleasurable, satisfying,
commendable, excellent, first-class, first-rate, superior,
fine, wonderful, marvellous, fantastic, terrific, superb,
exceptional, acceptable, satisfactory, pleasant, agreeable,
nice, adequate, passable, reasonable, tolerable, desirable
COLLOQ. great, super, terrific, brill, fabulous, smashing,
cracking, top
SLANG fab, mega, wicked, awesome, cushty
2 *good at her job*
competent, proficient, skilled, expert, accomplished,
professional, skilful, clever, talented, gifted, fit, brilliant,
able, capable, dependable, reliable, efficient, adept,
dexterous
3 KIND, considerate, thoughtful, gracious, friendly,
sympathetic, benevolent, charitable, altruistic,
philanthropic, kind-hearted, well-disposed
4 VIRTUOUS, exemplary, moral, upright, honest,
trustworthy, worthy, honourable, noble, admirable,
righteous, ethical
COLLOQ. salt of the earth
5 ADVANTAGEOUS, beneficial, favourable, helpful, useful,
worthwhile, profitable, convenient, appropriate, suitable,
fitting, lucky, fortunate
FORMAL auspicious, propitious
6 WELL-BEHAVED, obedient, compliant, well-mannered,
polite, respectful, under control
COLLOQ. good as gold
7 *in good health*
fine, healthy, strong, vigorous, sound, hale and hearty
COLLOQ. in the pink, the picture of health, fit as a fiddle
8 *a good reason*
sound, sensible, valid, right, genuine, persuasive,
convincing
9 *be good friends*
close, dear, intimate, best, loving, bosom, true, reliable,
faithful
10 THOROUGH, complete, whole, substantial, considerable,
siz(e)able, large
E∃ 1 bad, poor **2** incompetent **3** unkind, inconsiderate **4**
wicked, immoral **5** inconvenient, useless **6** naughty,
disobedient **7** poor **8** bad
* *n*
1 VIRTUE, morality, goodness, integrity, honesty, honour,
uprightness, righteousness, right, ethics, morals
FORMAL rectitude
2 USE, purpose, avail, advantage, profit, gain, worth, merit,
usefulness, service
3 *for your own good*
benefit, welfare, wellbeing, interest, sake, behalf,
convenience
* *interj*
fine, perfect, all right, very well, right, agreed, indeed, just
so
COLLOQ. OK
■ **for good**
for ever, always, ever, evermore, for all time, permanently,
till the end of time, eternally
COLLOQ. till kingdom come, till the cows come home, until
hell freezes over
■ **make good**
1 PUT RIGHT, make amends for, make recompense for,
compensate for, make restitution for, repair
2 SUCCEED, get ahead, go far, progress, be successful, get on
in the world
COLLOQ. arrive, make it
3 *make good a threat/promise*

fulfil, carry out, do, live up to, put into action
FORMAL effect

goodbye *interj, n*
* *interj*
farewell, adieu, *au revoir, auf Wiedersehen, ciao,
arrivederci, adiós, sayonara*
COLLOQ. cheerio, bye, bye-bye, cheers, see you (later), see
you around, be seeing you, all the best, mind how you go,
take care, have a nice day, ta-ta, so long; *N Am* later; *Aust*
hooray
* *n*
farewell, adieu, *au revoir*, leave-taking, parting, swan song
FORMAL valediction, valedictory

good-for-nothing *adj, n*
* *adj*
lazy, useless, worthless, idle, irresponsible, reprobate, no-
good
FORMAL profligate, indolent, feckless
E∃ conscientious, successful
* *n*
layabout, ne'er-do-well, reprobate, idler, waster, wastrel,
slacker
FORMAL profligate
COLLOQ. black sheep, lazybones, loafer, skiver
SLANG bum; *Aust & NZ* bludger
E∃ achiever, success, winner

good-humoured *adj*
cheerful, happy, jovial, genial, affable, amiable, friendly,
congenial, pleasant, good-tempered, approachable
E∃ ill-humoured

good-looking *adj*
attractive, handsome, beautiful, fair, pretty, lovely,
personable, presentable
OLD comely
E∃ ugly, plain

goodly *adj*
substantial, siz(e)able, considerable, ample, large, good,
significant, sufficient
COLLOQ. tidy
E∃ inadequate

good-natured *adj*
kind, kindly, kind-hearted, sympathetic, benevolent,
generous, helpful, neighbourly, gentle, good-tempered,
warm-hearted, approachable, friendly, tolerant, patient
E∃ ill-natured

goodness *n*
virtue, uprightness, integrity, righteousness, honesty,
kindness, compassion, graciousness, mercy, goodwill,
excellence, benefit, benevolence, unselfishness, generosity,
altruism, friendliness, helpfulness, wholesomeness
FORMAL rectitude, probity, beneficence
E∃ badness, wickedness, selfishness

goods *n*
1 PROPERTY, chattels, effects, possessions, belongings,
paraphernalia, things
COLLOQ. gear, stuff
FORMAL accoutrements, appurtenances
2 MERCHANDISE, wares, commodities, products, things,
lines, stock, freight

good-tempered *adj*
kind, kindly, kind-hearted, sympathetic, benevolent,
generous, helpful, neighbourly, gentle, good-natured,
warm-hearted, approachable, friendly, tolerant, patient

goodwill *n*
benevolence, kindness, compassion, generosity, favour,
friendliness, friendship, zeal, well-wishing
OLD (*Spenser*) gree
FORMAL amity
E∃ ill-will

goody-goody adj
self-righteous, sanctimonious, pious, priggish
FORMAL unctuous, ultra-virtuous

gooey adj
1 STICKY, soft, gluey, glutinous, viscous, tacky, thick, syrupy
FORMAL mucilaginous, viscid
COLLOQ. gungy
2 SENTIMENTAL, slushy, sloppy, syrupy, nauseating, maudlin, mawkish, sickly, cloying

gore v, n
• v
pierce, penetrate, stab, spear, stick, impale, wound, horn
OLD (*Spenser*) cloy, engore
• n
blood, bloodiness, bloodshed, slaughter, butchery, carnage
TECHNICAL cruor, grume

gorge n, v
• n
canyon, ravine, gully, defile, chasm, abyss, crevice, cleft, fissure, rift, gap, pass; N Am barranca
• v
feed, guzzle, gobble, devour, bolt, gulp, swallow, cram, stuff, fill, sate, surfeit, glut, overeat, stodge
COLLOQ. wolf
E3 fast

gorgeous adj
1 MAGNIFICENT, splendid, grand, glorious, superb, fine, impressive, rich, sumptuous, luxurious, brilliant, dazzling, marvellous, wonderful, delightful, pleasing, lovely, enjoyable, good, showy, glamorous
FORMAL resplendent, opulent
2 ATTRACTIVE, beautiful, pretty, fine, sweet, glamorous, handsome, good-looking, lovely
FORMAL pulchritudinous
COLLOQ. sexy, stunning, ravishing
E3 dull, plain

gorgeously adv
magnificently, splendidly, gloriously, brilliantly, impressively, superbly, richly, sumptuously, luxuriously, marvellously, wonderfully, delightfully
E3 opulently, resplendently

gory adj
bloody, bloodstained, blood-soaked, grisly, brutal, savage, violent, murderous
FORMAL sanguinary

gospel n
1 LIFE OF CHRIST, teaching of Christ, message of Christ, good news, New Testament
2 TEACHING, doctrine, creed, credo, certainty, truth, fact
TECHNICAL kerygma
FORMAL evangel, verity

gossamer adj
thin, light, delicate, flimsy, fine, cobwebby, insubstantial, sheer, shimmering, silky, airy, transparent, see-through, translucent, gauzy
FORMAL diaphanous
E3 heavy, opaque, thick

gossip n, v
• n
1 IDLE TALK, prattle, chitchat, tittle-tattle, tattle, rumour, hearsay, report, whisper, scandal, causerie, bush telegraph, reportage, *chronique scandaleuse*; Scot clatters, claver, clash, clish-clash, clishmaclaver, clash-ma-clavers; *Irish* crack
COLLOQ. mud-slinging, smear campaign, buzz, dirt
SLANG gup; N Am scuttlebutt
2 GOSSIP-MONGER, scandalmonger, whisperer, prattler, babbler, chatterbox, busybody, talebearer, tell-tale, tattler;

Scot blether, cummer, sweetie-wife; N Am yenta
OLD aunt
COLLOQ. Nosey Parker
• v
talk, chat, natter, chatter, schmooze, jabber, gabble, prattle, babble, tattle, tittle, spread gossip, tell tales, whisper, rumour, spread/circulate a rumour, chitchat; Scot blether, clash; *dialect & N Am* blather; *Scot & N Am* crack
COLLOQ. rabbit (on), gas, waffle, chinwag, jaw, chew the rag/fat

gouge v
chisel, cut, hack, incise, score, groove, scratch, claw, gash, slash, dig, scoop, hollow, extract

gourmand n
glutton, gormandizer
FORMAL omnivore
COLLOQ. gorger, guzzler, hog, pig
E3 ascetic

❗ **gourmand** or **gourmet**?
A *gourmand* is a glutton; a person who enjoys eating large quantities of food. A *gourmet* is a person who has an expert knowledge of, and a passion for, good food and wine.

gourmet n
gastronome, epicure, epicurean, connoisseur, bon vivant
COLLOQ. foodie

govern v
1 RULE, reign, be in power, hold office, direct, manage, administer, be responsible for, superintend, supervise, oversee, preside, lead, head, be in charge of, command, order, control, influence, guide, conduct, steer, pilot
2 *govern your temper*
dominate, master, control, regulate, curb, check, keep in check, hold/keep back, restrain, contain, quell, constrain, bridle, rein in, subdue, tame, discipline

governess n
teacher, guide, instructress, tutoress, tutress, mentor, companion, duenna
OLD gouvernante

governing adj
ruling, controlling, regulatory, commanding, reigning, guiding, leading, supreme, uppermost, dominant, overriding, predominant, prevailing, transcendent
FORMAL dominative

government n
1 *blame the government*
administration, executive, ministry, Establishment, authorities, state, régime, congress, parliament, council, cabinet, leadership
COLLOQ. powers that be
2 RULE, sovereignty, sway, direction, management, superintendence, supervision, surveillance, command, charge, authority, power, guidance, conduct, domination, dominion, control, regulation, restraint

Government systems include:

absolutism	empire	puppet
autocracy	federation	government
commonwealth	hierocracy	republic
communism	junta	theocracy
democracy	kingdom	triumvirate
despotism	monarchy	
dictatorship	plutocracy	

See also **parliaments and political assemblies**.

governor n
ruler, commissioner, administrator, executive, chief executive, director, manager, leader, head, chief,

president, viceroy, commander, superintendent, supervisor, master, regulator, guide, warden, overseer, controller, corrector, alderman, lieutenant-governor
OLD governess, grieve, gubernator, rector, rectrix, intendant, legate; (*Shakesp*) dominator
COLLOQ. boss
Related adjective: gubernatorial

Types of governor include:

adelantado (*of a Spanish province*)
alcaide (*of a Spanish fortress*)
eparch (*of a modern Greek province*)
castellan (*of a castle*)
ethnarch (*of an ethnic group*)
hakim (*in Pakistan*)
mudir (*in Turkey and Egypt*)
naik (*in India*)
nomarch (*of a province in modern Greece*)
pentarch (*in a government of five rulers*)
stadtholder (*of a Dutch province*)
tuchun (*Chinese military governor*)
vali (*of a Turkish province*)
HISTORICAL TERMS:
Ban (*of a district on the boundaries of the Hungarian kingdom*)
beglerbeg (*of a Turkish province*)

bey (*Turkish governor*)
burgrave (*of a German town or castle*)
catapan (*of Calabria and Apulia*)
dey (*governor of Algiers*)
exarch (*Byzantine provincial governor*)
harmost (*a Spartan governor of a subject province*)
hospodar (*of Moldavia or Wallachia*)
khan (*in Ancient Persia*)
legate (*of a Papal province*)
nomarch (*of a province in Ancient Egypt*)
podestà (*in Italy*)
proconsul (*Roman Empire*)
proveditor (*in the republic of Venice*)
satrap (*in Ancient Persia*)
subahdar (*in the Mogul empire*)
voivode (*central and eastern Europe*)

---

gown *n*
robe, dress, frock, dressing-gown, garment, habit, costume, shift
COLLOQ. garb
See panel at **clothes.**

grab *v, n*
♦ *v*
seize, snatch, take, pluck, snap up, catch/take/lay hold of, grasp, clutch, grip, catch, capture, commandeer, usurp, annex
FORMAL appropriate
COLLOQ. nab, bag, collar, nail, swipe
♦ *n*
grasp, grip, clutch, snatch, catch, capture
■ **up for grabs**
available, obtainable, at hand
COLLOQ. for the asking, to be had

grace *n, v*
♦ *n*
1 GRACEFULNESS, poise, beauty, attractiveness, loveliness, shapeliness, smoothness, elegance, ease, fluency, finesse, tastefulness, good taste, refinement, polish, breeding, cultivation, manners, etiquette, decorum, decency, consideration, courtesy, charm
OLD comeliness
FORMAL propriety
2 KINDNESS, kindliness, compassion, consideration, goodness, virtue, generosity, charity, benevolence, goodwill, favour, forgiveness, indulgence, mercy, mercifulness, leniency, pardon, reprieve, quarter
FORMAL beneficence, clemency
3 *say grace*
blessing, benediction, thanksgiving, prayer, prayer of thanks
E3 2 cruelty, harshness
♦ *v*

favour, honour, dignify, distinguish, embellish, enhance, enrich, set off, trim, garnish, decorate, ornament, adorn
E3 spoil, detract from

graceful *adj*
1 FLOWING, easy, fluid, smooth, supple, agile, deft, nimble, natural, slender, fine, tasteful, elegant, beautiful, attractive, appealing, charming, tasteful, cultured, refined, polished, cultivated, suave
2 POLITE, kind, courteous, pleasant, agreeable, cheerful, generous, respectful, gracious, tactful, diplomatic
E3 1 graceless, awkward, clumsy, ungainly **2** rude, unpleasant

gracefully *adv*
1 SMOOTHLY, deftly, nimbly, naturally, elegantly, beautifully, attractively, tastefully
2 *with good grace*
politely, courteously, pleasantly, agreeably, cheerfully, generously, respectfully, graciously, tactfully, diplomatically
E3 1 awkwardly **2** rudely, unpleasantly

graceless *adj*
clumsy, awkward, unattractive, forced, gauche, gawky, ungainly, ungraceful, inelegant, rough, rude, vulgar, coarse, crude, uncouth, unsophisticated, impolite, improper, unmannerly, ill-mannered, barbarous, shameless; *Scot* menseless
FORMAL indecorous
E3 graceful, refined

gracelessly *adv*
clumsily, awkwardly, ungracefully, inelegantly, roughly, impolitely, rudely
E3 gracefully

gracious *adj*
1 POLITE, courteous, well-mannered, refined, considerate, sweet, obliging, accommodating, kind, compassionate, kind-hearted, kindly, friendly, pleasant, benevolent, generous, charitable, hospitable, forgiving, indulgent, lenient, mild, clement, merciful, benign; *Scot* menseful
OLD hend, handsome
FORMAL beneficent, magnanimous
2 ELEGANT, luxurious, comfortable, tasteful, sumptuous
E3 1 ungracious

graciously *adv*
politely, courteously, civilly, kindly, pleasantly, respectfully, tactfully, diplomatically

gradation *n*
change, progression, degree, grading, sorting, ordering, progress, succession, arrangement, sequence, series, stage, step, level, mark, shading, rank
FORMAL array

grade *n, v*
♦ *n*
rank, status, standing, station, place, position, level, stage, degree, step, rating, rung, notch, mark, brand, quality, standard, condition, size, order, group, type, class, category, classification
FORMAL echelon
♦ *v*
sort, arrange, categorize, order, group, class, rate, size, rank, range, classify, evaluate, assess, value, mark, brand, label, pigeonhole, type
■ **make the grade**
succeed, pass, come/win through, reach the expected standard
COLLOQ. come up to scratch

gradient *n*
slope, incline, hill, bank, rise, grade
FORMAL acclivity, declivity

gradual *adj*
slow, leisurely, unhurried, easy, gentle, moderate, regular,

even, measured, steady, continuous, progressive, step-by-step
◼ sudden, steep, precipitate

gradually *adv*
little by little, bit by bit, imperceptibly, inch by inch, step by step, successively, continuously, progressively, by degrees, piecemeal, slowly, gently, cautiously, gingerly, moderately, regularly, evenly, steadily, unhurriedly

graduate *v, n*
◆ *v*
1 *graduate from medical school*
pass, qualify, complete studies
2 CALIBRATE, mark off, measure out, proportion, grade, arrange, range, order, rank, sort, group, classify, categorize
3 PROGRESS, move up, move forward, advance, be promoted, make headway, go/forge ahead
◆ *n*
qualified/skilled person, expert, specialist, consultant, professional, bachelor, doctor, master, fellow, member, graduand, alumna, alumnus, valedictorian
COLLOQ. whizz kid

graft¹ *v, n*
◆ *v*
grafted onto a tree
engraft, implant, insert, transplant, join, splice, bud, inoculate
TECHNICAL autograft
OLD graff, imp, inarch
FORMAL affix
◆ *n*
implant, implantation, transplant, growth, splice, bud, sprout, shoot, scion, take
TECHNICAL allograft, autograft, heterograft, homograft, xenograft
OLD graff, imp

graft² *n*
1 EFFORT, hard word, toil, labour, exertion
COLLOQ. sweat of your brow, slog
2 BRIBERY, corruption, dishonesty, extortion
COLLOQ. con tricks, shady business, dirty tricks/dealings, wheeling and dealing, sharp practices, sleaze
SLANG scam, rip-off, sting

grain *n*
1 BIT, piece, fragment, scrap, morsel, crumb, granule, particle, molecule, atom, jot, iota, mite, speck, modicum, trace, hint, suggestion, soupçon, scintilla
2 SEED, kernel, corn, cereals, wheat, rye, barley, oats, maize
3 TEXTURE, fabric, fibre, weave, pattern, marking, surface, nap

grammar *n*
grammatical rules, linguistic rules, correct English, good English, style, usage
TECHNICAL syntax, syntactic structure

grammatical *adj*
structural, linguistic, correct, acceptable, well-formed, well-structured, appropriate
TECHNICAL syntactic, syntactical

grand *adj*
1 MAJESTIC, regal, stately, palatial, splendid, magnificent, glorious, superb, sublime, exalting, fine, excellent, outstanding, first-rate, impressive, imposing, striking, monumental, large, luxurious, lavish, sumptuous, noble, lordly, lofty, pompous, pretentious, grandiose, showy, ostentatious, ambitious
FORMAL opulent
2 SUPREME, pre-eminent, leading, head, chief, main, principal, arch, highest, senior, great, illustrious
3 *have a grand day out*
excellent, wonderful, splendid, marvellous, fantastic,

superb, enjoyable, delightful, outstanding, first-rate
COLLOQ. great, cool, super, terrific, smashing, pretty, precious
SLANG fab, mega, wicked
4 *a grand total*
complete, final, comprehensive, inclusive, all-inclusive, in full
◼ **1** humble, plain, simple common, poor

Synonym nuances
sense 1
Majestic, **regal** and **stately** are all suggestive of a dignified manner or appearance. **Palatial** is generally used of buildings to suggest being not only luxurious, but on a grand scale, whereas **splendid** can be used of anything that merits admiration. The terms **magnificent**, **glorious** and **superb** are extremely admiring terms for something grand, whilst **sublime** would be reserved for something supreme.
　Exalting is suggestive of lifting your spirits: *this road is one of the most exalting in the Pyrenees*, while the more restrained **fine** suggests a high quality, and **excellent** goes further by suggesting it cannot be improved on. Likewise, **outstanding** and **first-rate** are highly approving terms which imply superiority. **Impressive**, **imposing** and **striking** all suggest a commanding appearance: *its striking black and white plumage.*
　While **large** is a neutral and restrained term describing size, **monumental** suggests being on a massive scale. **Luxurious**, **lavish** and **sumptuous** are all highly expressive of opulence and comfort.
　The terms **noble**, **lofty** and **lordly**, on the other hand, suggest an aristocratic demeanour, although **lofty** and **lordly** can have a rather negative connotation of aloofness. The term **pompous** is more markedly disapproving and suggests self-importance, whilst **pretentious** goes further by suggesting affectation, and **grandiose** is generally used nowadays to imply that something is overblown: *small countries dreaming of a grandiose role for themselves.* Both **showy** and **ostentatious** can also imply an excessive, even gaudy, display, whilst **ambitious** is more neutral, emphasizing an aspiration to grandeur.

---

grandeur *n*
majesty, stateliness, pomp, state, dignity, splendour, magnificence, impressiveness, luxuriousness, lavishness, nobility, greatness, illustriousness, importance, fame, renown, eminence, prominence
FORMAL opulence
◼ humbleness, lowliness, simplicity

grandfather *n*
grandparent; *Scot* luckie-dad; *dialect* granfer; *S Afr* oupa
OLD grandsire; *Scot* goodsire, gudesire, gutcher
COLLOQ. grandpa, grandpapa, papa, grand(d)ad, grand(d)addy; *N Am* gramps

grandiloquent *adj*
exaggerated, pretentious, high-flown, high-sounding, inflated, pompous, bombastic, flowery, rhetorical, fustian, euphuistic, swollen, turgid
FORMAL grandiloquous, magniloquent, orotund
◼ plain, restrained, simple

grandiose *adj*
pompous, pretentious, high-flown, high-sounding, bombastic, lofty, ambitious, extravagant, ostentatious, showy, flamboyant, grand, majestic, splendid, striking, stately, magnificent, impressive, imposing, monumental
OLD mausolean
FORMAL magniloquent
COLLOQ. over-the-top
◼ unpretentious

grandly adv
impressively, magnificently, gloriously, excellently, strikingly, majestically, regally, pompously, pretentiously

grandmother n
grandparent, babushka; *S Afr* ouma
OLD beldam, grandam, grannam; *Scot* good-dame, gude-dame
COLLOQ. grandma, granny, gran, nanny, nan, nana, grandmama, grandmamma

grant v, n
♦ *v*
1 GIVE, donate, present, award, impart, transmit, dispense, assign, allot, allocate, provide, supply, contribute
FORMAL confer, bestow, apportion, furnish
2 ADMIT, acknowledge, concede, allow, permit, consent to, accept, agree to
FORMAL accede to, vouchsafe
E3 1 withhold **2** deny
♦ *n*
allowance, subsidy, concession, award, bursary, scholarship, gift, donation, endowment, bequest, annuity, pension, honorarium, contribution

granular adj
grainy, granulated, gritty, sandy, lumpy, rough, crumbly, friable

granule n
piece, particle, grain, scrap, crumb, bead, speck, fragment, iota, jot, atom, molecule, pellet, seed, pearl
TECHNICAL microsome, bioblast, chondrule, plastid

graph n
diagram, chart, table, grid, plot, curve, bar graph, bar chart, pie chart, scatter diagram
TECHNICAL nomogram, nomograph

graphic adj
1 VIVID, descriptive, expressive, striking, telling, lively, realistic, explicit, effective, clear, lucid, specific, detailed, well-defined, blow-by-blow
FORMAL cogent
2 VISUAL, pictorial, diagrammatic, symbolic, drawn, illustrative, representational
FORMAL delineative
E3 vague, impressionistic

graphically adv
vividly, descriptively, expressively, strikingly, clearly, realistically, explicitly

grapple v
1 GRASP, seize, snatch, grab, grip, tackle, clutch, clasp, hold, lay hold of, wrestle, tussle, struggle, contend, battle, fight, combat, clash, engage, close, clinch
OLD craple
2 *grapple with a problem*
face, confront, encounter, tackle, address, deal with, cope with, get to grips with, wrestle, struggle
COLLOQ. take the bull by the horns
E3 1 release **2** avoid, evade

grasp v, n
♦ *v*
1 HOLD, clasp, clutch, grip, grapple, seize, snatch, grab, catch, lay hold of, clench
2 *grasp a concept*
understand, follow, comprehend, see, perceive, master, realize, take in, catch on, latch onto
FORMAL apprehend
COLLOQ. get
♦ *n*
1 GRIP, clasp, hold, embrace, clutches, possession, control, power, command, rule, dominion, mastery
2 UNDERSTANDING, comprehension, apprehension, mastery, familiarity, knowledge, awareness, perception

grasping adj
greedy, acquisitive, covetous, griping, mercenary, mean, selfish, miserly, close-fisted, niggardly, gripple
OLD (*Shakesp*) large-handed
FORMAL avaricious, rapacious, parsimonious
COLLOQ. money-grubbing, tight-fisted, stingy; *N Am* grabby
E3 generous

grass n, v
♦ *n*
turf, lawn, green, grassland, common, field, meadow, pasture, downs, prairie, pampas, savanna, steppe, veld, veldt
OLD lea, mead, sward
Related adjective: graminaceous
♦ *v*
inform, betray, incriminate, denounce, blab
COLLOQ. tell on, squeal, rat, blow the whistle on, sell down the river, split, snitch, stitch up
SLANG shop; *N Am* stool on; *Aust & NZ* dob in

***Types of grass include*:**

bamboo	Kentucky	rattan
barley	bluegrass	reed
beard grass	knot grass	rice
bent	maize	rye
brome	marijuana	ryegrass
buckwheat	marram grass	sorghum
cane	meadow foxtail	squirrel-tail grass
cocksfoot	meadow grass	sugar cane
corn	melick	switch grass
dog's-tail	millet	timothy grass (or
English ryegrass	moor grass	cat's-tail)
esparto	oats	twitch grass
fescue	paddy	vernal drass
Italian ryegrass	pampas grass	wheat
kangaroo grass	papyrus	wild oat
	quaking grass	

---

grate v
1 GRIND, shred, mince, pulverize, rub, rasp, scrape, scratch
OLD gride
FORMAL triturate
2 SCRATCH, squeak, screech, rasp, creak, grit, bray
3 JAR, set your teeth on edge, annoy, irritate, vex, irk, exasperate, gall, rankle
COLLOQ. aggravate, peeve, get on your nerves, get under your skin, get someone's goat

grateful adj
thankful, appreciative, pleased, indebted, obliged, obligated
FORMAL beholden
E3 ungrateful

gratefully adv
thankfully, appreciatively, with gratitude, expressing your appreciation

gratification n
pleasure, satisfaction, contentment, delight, elation, enjoyment, joy, thrill, relish, indulgence, glee
COLLOQ. kicks
E3 frustration, disappointment

gratify v
1 PLEASE, cheer, charm, gladden, delight, thrill, make happy
2 SATISFY, fulfil, indulge, pander to, humour, favour, pamper, spoil, cosset, placate
E3 1 frustrate **2** thwart

grating[1] adj
a grating noise
harsh, rasping, scraping, grinding, scratching, creaking, gritting, braying, squeaky, screeching, strident,

discordant, raucous, jarring, annoying, irritating, galling, unpleasant, disagreeable, offensive, exasperating, irksome
E3 harmonious, pleasing

grating² n
a grating over a window
grate, grille, grid, lattice, trellis, frame, fire-grate
TECHNICAL graticule, cancelli

gratis adv
free, without charge, free of charge, for nothing, at no cost, complimentary
COLLOQ. on the house
SLANG buckshee

gratitude n
gratefulness, thankfulness, thanks, appreciation, acknowledgement, recognition, indebtedness, obligation
E3 ingratitude, ungratefulness

gratuitous adj
1 WANTON, unnecessary, needless, superfluous, unwarranted, unjustified, groundless, unfounded, undeserved, unprovoked, uncalled-for, unasked-for, unmerited, unsolicited, without reason
2 VOLUNTARY, free, free of charge, gratis, for nothing, complimentary, unrewarded, unpaid
E3 1 justified, provoked

gratuitously adv
needlessly, unnecessarily, unjustifiably, undeservedly
E3 justifiably

gratuity n
tip, bonus, gift, present, donation, reward, recompense, bounty, boon, largesse, baksheesh, pourboire, donative, drink-money, lagniappe; *Scot* mags; dash, cumshaw; *S Afr* bonsella
OLD glove-money, primage; (*Shakesp*) gratillity
FORMAL perquisite
COLLOQ. perk, beer-money

grave¹ n
1 *buried in a grave*
burial place, tomb, vault, crypt, last resting-place, sepulchre, mausoleum, pit, burial mound, burial site, barrow, tumulus, cairn, dust, long home, moulds; *Scot* mouls
OLD graff
2 DEATH, loss of life, loss, departure, fatality, passing, passing away
FORMAL expiration, decease, demise
COLLOQ. last farewell, curtains

grave² adj
1 SOLEMN, dignified, sober, sedate, serious, earnest, sombre, severe, thoughtful, pensive, grim, gloomy, austere, long-faced, quiet, reserved, subdued, restrained, staid, saturnine, heavy, matronal, high
OLD sad
2 *a grave mistake*
important, significant, weighty, momentous, serious, critical, vital, crucial, urgent, pressing, acute, severe, menacing, threatening, dangerous, hazardous
FORMAL exigent, perilous
E3 1 cheerful, smiling **2** trivial, light, slight

gravel n
shingle, grit, pebbles, stones, chesil, hogging
OLD grail

gravelly adj
1 GRAINY, granular, pebbly, shingly, gritty
OLD glareous
FORMAL sabulose, sabulous
2 *a gravelly voice*
harsh, rough, thick, hoarse, guttural, throaty, grating, gruff
E3 2 clear, fine

gravely adv
1 *he shook his head gravely*
solemnly, seriously, earnestly, thoughtfully, pensively, quietly, gloomily
2 *gravely ill*
critically, importantly, significantly, seriously, crucially, dangerously, urgently, acutely, severely

gravestone n
tombstone, headstone, stone, memorial

graveyard n
cemetery, burial ground, burial place, burial site, churchyard, necropolis, charnel house, God's acre

gravitas n
seriousness, gravity, solemnity, earnestness
E3 light-heartedness

gravitate v
fall, descend, drop, head for, move, precipitate, sink, incline, lean, tend, drift, be attached to, be drawn to, settle

gravity n
1 IMPORTANCE, significance, seriousness, weightiness, momentousness, consequence, urgency, acuteness, severity, danger, hazard
OLD state
FORMAL exigency, peril
2 SOLEMNITY, dignity, seriousness, earnestness, severity, thoughtfulness, sombreness, grimness, gloominess, reserve, restraint
FORMAL sobriety
3 GRAVITATION, attraction, pull, weight, heaviness
E3 1 triviality **2** levity

graze¹ v
the cattle are grazing
crop, feed, fodder, pasture, browse
OLD gride
FORMAL ruminate

graze² v, n
♦ *v*
1 SCRATCH, scrape, skin, bruise, rub, chafe
FORMAL abrade
2 BRUSH, skim, touch, kiss, shave, glance off
♦ *n*
scratch, scrape, abrasion

grease n
oil, lubrication, fat, lard, dripping, tallow; *Scot* creesh
OLD (*Shakesp*) seam

greasy adj
oily, fatty, lardy, buttery, smeary, slimy, slippery, smooth, waxy
FORMAL oleaginous, oleic, adipose, sebaceous, unctuous

great adj
1 LARGE, big, siz(e)able, huge, enormous, massive, colossal, gigantic, mammoth, immense, vast, extensive, boundless, spacious, impressive
COLLOQ. great big, whopping, jumbo, ginormous, humongous
SLANG mega
2 *with great care*
considerable, pronounced, substantial, extreme, excessive, inordinate
3 FAMOUS, renowned, celebrated, famed, illustrious, eminent, distinguished, prominent, successful, noteworthy, notable, noted, remarkable, outstanding
FORMAL august
4 FINE, grand, glorious, impressive, imposing, magnificent, splendid
5 IMPORTANT, significant, serious, major, crucial, critical, principal, primary, main, chief, leading, powerful, essential, momentous, vital, paramount, salient
6 EXCELLENT, excellent, first-rate, superb, wonderful,

marvellous, admirable, splendid, tremendous, fantastic, fabulous
COLLOQ. super, terrific, smashing, ace, top-notch, brilliant, brill, cracking
SLANG cool, mega, wicked, awesome, cushty
7 feel great
healthy, well, fit, energetic, lively, enthusiastic, eager
8 EXPERT, proficient, adept, skilled, skilful, knowledgeable, experienced, able, practised, professional, accomplished, masterly, excellent, brilliant, specialist, qualified, virtuoso, dexterous
COLLOQ. top-notch, up on, well up on, crack, ace
F3 1 small, limited **2** slight **3** unknown **5** unimportant, insignificant **6** poor, mediocre, second-rate; *colloq.* rubbish **7** ill **8** amateurish, novice

greatly *adv*
much, very much, considerably, enormously, highly, extremely, immensely, vastly, noticeably, significantly, remarkably, impressively, notably, substantially, markedly, mightily, tremendously, hugely, powerfully, exceedingly, abundantly, sorely
SLANG majorly

greatness *n*
fame, renown, illustriousness, eminence, heroism, distinction, note, significance, importance, weight, momentousness, seriousness, power, success, successfulness, magnitude, intensity, excellence, glory, genius, grandeur
F3 insignificance, pettiness, smallness

greed *n*
1 HUNGER, ravenousness, gluttony, gourmandism, insatiability
OLD (*Spenser*) gourmandise
FORMAL voracity, edacity, esurience
COLLOQ. piggishness, hoggishness, bingeing, stuffing yourself
2 ACQUISITIVENESS, covetousness, desire, craving, longing, eagerness, impatience, selfishness, itching palm
FORMAL avidity, avarice, rapacity, cupidity, pleonexia
F3 1 abstemiousness, self-restraint

greedily *adv*
ravenously, eagerly, impatiently, selfishly
FORMAL avidly, avariciously, rapaciously, esuriently

greedy *adj*
1 HUNGRY, starving, ravenous, gluttonous, gormandizing, insatiable, open-mouthed
FORMAL voracious, edacious, esurient, omnivorous
COLLOQ. hoggish, piggish
2 ACQUISITIVE, covetous, desirous, craving, grabbing, eager, impatient, grasping, selfish, having, gripple; *Scot* gare
FORMAL avid, avaricious, rapacious, cupidinous, pleonectic
COLLOQ. on the make, money-grubbing; *N Am* grabby
F3 1 abstemious **2** generous, benevolent

green *adj, n*
◆ *adj*
1 EMERALD, jade, pine, vert, olive, avocado, sage, pea-green, apple-green, lime, chartreuse, eau de nil, aquamarine, sea-green
OLD virent
FORMAL virid, virescent, viridescent, glaucous
2 GRASSY, leafy, unripe, lush, unseasoned, tender, raw, fresh, budding, blooming, flourishing, healthy, vigorous
OLD virent
FORMAL verdant, virescent, verdurous
3 ECOLOGICAL, environmental, conservationist, eco-friendly, environmentally aware, environmentally friendly, preservationist
4 IMMATURE, naive, simple, unsophisticated, ignorant, unqualified, inexperienced, untrained, inexpert,

unversed, raw, new, recent, young
COLLOQ. wet behind the ears
5 green with envy
envious, covetous, jealous, grudging, resentful
F3 4 mature, experienced, qualified, expert
◆ *n*
common, lawn, grass, turf, field, grassland, meadow, pasture
OLD sward, lea

greenery *n*
foliage, vegetation, greenness
FORMAL verdure, verdancy, viridity, viridescence, virescence

greenhorn *n*
novice, apprentice, beginner, learner, initiate, recruit, neophyte, tenderfoot, tiro, newcomer, newbie, fledgling
COLLOQ. rookie
F3 veteran; *colloq.* old hand

greenhouse *n*
glasshouse, hothouse, conservatory, pavilion, vinery, orangery

greet *v*
salute, acknowledge, hail, address, say hello to, shake hands with, kiss, wave to, nod to, accost, meet, receive, welcome, bow, doff/tip your hat, pay your compliments, shake hands, pass the time of day, remember, bid; *dialect* pass the seel of the day; *S Afr* wish
OLD congreet, halse; (*Shakesp*) regreet
COLLOQ. give someone five
F3 ignore

greeting *n*
salutation, acknowledgement, wave, hallo, nod, handshake, the time of day, seasonal greeting, address, reception, welcome, kiss, accost, hail; *N Am* glad hand
COLLOQ. *N Am* high five

greetings *n*
regards, kind/warm regards, respects, compliments, best wishes, good wishes, congratulations, respects, love, salutations, remembrances, salaams, salve
OLD (*Shakesp*) regreet(s)

gregarious *adj*
sociable, outgoing, extrovert, friendly, affable, social, companionable, convivial, cordial, warm, hospitable
F3 unsociable

grey *adj*
1 a grey colour
neutral, colourless, pale, pallid, ashen, wan, leaden
2 a grey morning
dull, cloudy, overcast, dim, dark, dismal, dreary, bleak, cheerless, foggy, misty, murky
3 GLOOMY, dismal, cheerless, depressing, dreary, bleak, dull, uninteresting, colourless
4 a grey area
unclear, uncertain, doubtful, ambiguous, debatable, open to question

grid *n*
grating, frame, grille, grill, gridiron, lattice, trellis
TECHNICAL graticule

grief *n*
sorrow, sadness, unhappiness, depression, dejection, desolation, despondency, despair, distress, misery, woe, heartbreak, mourning, bereavement, heartache, anguish, agony, pain, suffering, dolour, trouble, regret, remorse
OLD bemoaning, dolorousness
FORMAL affliction, lamentation, tribulation
F3 happiness, delight
■ **come to grief**
go wrong, be unsuccessful, break down, collapse, fall through, fall down, founder, come to nothing

COLLOQ. flop, fold, not come off, fall flat, bite the dust, come a cropper, come unstuck, come unglued; *NAm* bomb

grief-stricken *adj*
sorrowful, sad, unhappy, sorrowing, grieving, mourning, depressed, dejected, desolate, despondent, distressed, despairing, broken, broken-hearted, heartbroken, inconsolable, overcome, overwhelmed, devastated, crushed, anguished, troubled, wretched
FORMAL disconsolate, woebegone, afflicted
F3 overjoyed, delighted

grievance *n*
complaint, resentment, objection, protest, charge, wrong, injustice, unfairness, offence, injury, damage, trouble, hardship, trial
FORMAL affliction, tribulation
COLLOQ. moan, grumble, grouse, gripe, bone to pick

grieve *v*
1 SORROW, lament, mourn, wail, cry, weep, sob, mope, brood, pine away, ache, suffer, condole; *dialect* hone
OLD rue, vex, bemoan; (*Spenser*) engrieve, wayment
2 SADDEN, upset, dismay, distress, afflict, pain, hurt, wound, crush, horrify, offend, shock, break someone's heart
F3 1 rejoice **2** please, gladden

grievous *adj*
1 SEVERE, grave, tragic, appalling, distressing, dreadful, atrocious, burdensome, calamitous, devastating, damaging, shameful, harmful, outrageous, overwhelming, shocking, deplorable, intolerable, unbearable, monstrous, flagrant, glaring
OLD doloriferous, dolorific
FORMAL sorrowful
2 WOUNDING, injurious, hurtful, painful, damaging, sore
OLD dolorous
FORMAL afflicting

grievously *adv*
severely, tragically, dreadfully, appallingly, outrageously, shockingly, unbearably, intolerably
OLD dolorously

grill *n, v*
◆ *n*
grille, gridiron, grid, grating, barbecue, lattice, frame
OLD wicket
◆ *v*
cook, heat, roast, flame-grill, toast; *NAm* broil

grim *adj*
1 STERN, severe, harsh, dour, forbidding, formidable, fierce, menacing, threatening, surly, sullen, morose, gloomy, depressing, unattractive
2 UNPLEASANT, horrible, horrid, horrendous, dire, ghastly, gruesome, grisly, sinister, dreadful, awful, frightening, fearsome, terrible, shocking, appalling, harrowing, unspeakable
3 RESOLUTE, determined, dogged, tenacious, persistent, stubborn, inexorable, unyielding, unshak(e)able
FORMAL obdurate
F3 1 attractive **2** pleasant

grimace *n, v*
◆ *n*
frown, scowl, moue, pout, smirk, sneer, face
◆ *v*
pull a face, make a face, frown, scowl, mow, pout, smirk, mouth, sneer

grime *n*
dirt, muck, filth, soot, dust, mud
COLLOQ. gunge, yuck, grot
SLANG crud, grunge

grimly *adv*
sternly, harshly, fiercely, sullenly, morosely, gloomily

grimy *adj*
dirty, mucky, grubby, soiled, stained, filthy, sooty, smutty, dusty, muddy, smudgy
FORMAL besmirched
F3 clean

grin *v, n*
smile, beam, smirk, leer, sneer, laugh, chuckle, giggle, snigger, titter

grind *v, n*
◆ *v*
1 CRUSH, pound, pulverize, crumble, powder, chew, crunch, grit, mill, granulate, grate, scrape, gnash, bray, meal, pug, slime, stamp
TECHNICAL kibble, levigate, comminute, triturate
FORMAL masticate
COLLOQ. graunch
2 SHARPEN, whet, smooth, polish, sand, file, rub, abrade
TECHNICAL chamfer
3 GRATE, scrape, rub, rasp, grit
◆ *n*
drudgery, chore, toil, labour, round, routine, exertion, task, slavery, sweat
■ **grind down**
wear down, oppress, crush, trouble, persecute, plague, torment, harass, harry, hound, tyrannize
FORMAL afflict

grip *n, v*
◆ *n*
1 HOLD, grasp, clasp, clutch, embrace, clench, hug
2 CONTROL, power, command, influence, mastery, domination, clutches
3 BAG, case, holdall, kitbag, shoulder bag, valise, suitcase, overnight bag, travelling bag
◆ *v*
1 HOLD, grasp, clasp, get/catch/grab hold of, clutch, clench, latch onto, cling, seize, grab, catch
2 FASCINATE, thrill, enthral, spellbind, mesmerize, hypnotize, entrance, rivet, engross, absorb, involve, engage, compel
■ **come/get to grips with**
deal with, tackle, cope with, take care of, look after, encounter, confront, handle, face up to, take on, grasp

gripe *v, n*
◆ *v*
complain, grumble, protest, moan, nag, groan
COLLOQ. beef, bellyache, carp, grouch, grouse, whine, whinge, have a bone to pick
SLANG bitch
◆ *n*
complaint, groan, grumble, moan, objection, protest, grievance
COLLOQ. beef, grouch, grouse, griping, whinge
SLANG bitch

gripping *adj*
fascinating, thrilling, enthralling, compelling, enchanting, compulsive, exciting, suspenseful, spellbinding, entrancing, riveting, engrossing, absorbing
COLLOQ. unputdownable

grisly *adj*
gruesome, gory, grim, macabre, horrid, horrible, horrifying, ghastly, awful, frightful, terrible, dreadful, repulsive, revolting, disgusting, hideous, loathsome, abhorrent, abominable, appalling, shocking
F3 delightful

gristly *adj*
hard, tough, rubbery, leathery, sinewy, stringy, fibrous
FORMAL cartilaginous

grit *n, v*
◆ *n*
1 GRAVEL, pebbles, shingle, sand, dust, swarf

Related adjectives: sabulous, sabulose
2 DETERMINATION, courage, bravery, strength, resolve, resolution, hardness, toughness, mettle, endurance, perseverance, doggedness, steadfastness, tenacity
COLLOQ. backbone, guts
♦ *v*
clench, gnash, grate, rasp, scrape, grind

gritty *adj*
1 GRAINY, dusty, gravelly, sandy, shingly, pebbly, powdery, granular, rough, abrasive
FORMAL sabulous, sabulose
2 DETERMINED, courageous, brave, resolute, hardy, tough, mettlesome, dogged, tenacious, steadfast, spirited, plucky
COLLOQ. spunky, feisty, gutsy
F3 **1** fine, smooth **2** cowardly; *colloq.* spineless

grizzle *v*
cry, whimper, whine, whinge, sniffle, snivel, snuffle, fret, moan, complain, grumble

grizzled *adj*
grey, grey-haired, grey-headed, greying, hoary, hoar, pepper-and-salt
TECHNICAL griseous
FORMAL canescent

groan *n, v*
♦ *n*
1 MOAN, sigh, cry, whine, whimper, wail, lament
2 COMPLAINT, grumble, objection, protest, outcry, grievance, moan
COLLOQ. beef, grouch, grouse, griping
♦ *v*
1 MOAN, sigh, cry, whine, whimper, wail, lament
2 COMPLAIN, grumble, object, protest
COLLOQ. whine, whinge, beef, bellyache, grouse

grocer *n*
dealer, storekeeper, supplier, supermarket, greengrocer
FORMAL purveyor, victualler

groggy *adj*
weak, dopey, unsteady, wobbly, shaky, staggering, stunned, dazed, confused, befuddled, bewildered, stupefied, punch-drunk, dizzy, faint, reeling
COLLOQ. muzzy, woozy
F3 healthy, strong, lucid

groin *n*
crotch, crutch, genitals; *dialect* lisk
Related adjective: inguinal

groom *v, n*
♦ *v*
1 SMARTEN, neaten, tidy (up), spruce up, prepare, put in order, arrange, adjust, fix, do, smooth
2 CLEAN, brush, curry, preen, dress
3 *groomed for her new post*
prepare, make ready, train, school, teach, educate, instruct, tutor, drill, coach, prime
♦ *n*
1 BRIDEGROOM, honeymooner, newly-wed, husband, husband-to-be, spouse, marriage partner
2 STABLEBOY, stableman, stable lad/lass, stable hand

groove *n*
furrow, rut, track, slot, channel, canal, chamfer, gutter, trough, ditch, trench, hollow, gouge, indentation, cut, score, ridge, fissure, slide, throat, chase, race, riffle, rigol; *Scot* raggle
TECHNICAL rabbet, rebate, sulcus, cannelure, croze, cullis, diglyph, flute, quirk, fossula, kerf, key-seat, mark, oche, pod, scrobe, sipe, vallecula
Related adjective: sulcal

grooved *adj*
channelled, fluted, furrowed, rutted, scored, chamfered
TECHNICAL rabbeted, scrobiculate

FORMAL sulcal, sulcate, exarate
F3 ridged

grope *v*
1 FUMBLE, feel, scrabble, flounder, pick
2 SEARCH, hunt, scrabble, fish, probe, cast about
3 FONDLE, touch, molest, abuse, abuse sexually, interfere with
COLLOQ. touch up, feel up

gross *adj, v*
♦ *adj*
1 *gross misconduct*
serious, grievous, blatant, flagrant, glaring, obvious, manifest, plain, sheer, utter, outright, shameful, shocking, outrageous
FORMAL egregious
2 OBSCENE, lewd, improper, dirty, filthy, risqué, pornographic, indecent, offensive, rude, coarse, crude, vulgar, ribald, bawdy, smutty, earthy, improper, tasteless
COLLOQ. blue
3 FAT, obese, overweight, big, large, huge, colossal, immense, massive, hulking, bulky, heavy
FORMAL corpulent
4 *gross earnings*
inclusive, all-inclusive, total, entire, complete, comprehensive, whole, before deductions, before tax
FORMAL aggregate
5 TASTELESS, vulgar, unpleasant, uncultured, unsophisticated, unrefined, insensitive, coarse, boorish
6 DISGUSTING, repulsive, revolting, repugnant, offensive, sickening, nauseating, nauseous, off-putting, odious, foul, unappetizing, unpalatable, distasteful, unpleasant, disgraceful, nasty
COLLOQ. yucky
F3 **2** polite **3** slight **4** net **5** tasteful **6** delightful
♦ *v*
earn, make, take, bring in, accumulate, total
FORMAL aggregate
COLLOQ. pull in, rake in

grossly *adv*
extremely, exceedingly, excessively, very, really, exceptionally, extraordinarily, intensely, thoroughly, remarkably, utterly, greatly, highly, unusually, unreasonably, immoderately, uncommonly, inordinately, acutely, severely, decidedly
COLLOQ. awfully, terribly, dreadfully, frightfully, terrifically

grotesque *adj*
bizarre, odd, weird, strange, peculiar, unnatural, freakish, monstrous, hideous, ugly, unsightly, misshapen, deformed, malformed, distorted, twisted, fantastic, fanciful, whimsical, extravagant, ridiculous, ludicrous, absurd, outlandish, surreal, macabre
F3 normal, graceful

grotesquely *adv*
bizarrely, strangely, unnaturally, hideously, unpleasantly, outlandishly

grotto *n*
cave, cavern, chamber, catacomb, underground chamber, subterrane

grotty *adj*
1 *a grotty little flat*
seedy, shabby, dirty, untidy, scruffy, tatty, mangy, squalid, run-down, dilapidated, decaying
COLLOQ. crummy, sleazy
2 *feel grotty*
ill, sick, poorly, unwell, ailing, off-colour
COLLOQ. groggy, rough, under the weather, out of sorts
F3 **2** well

grouch *n*
1 COMPLAINER, grumbler, moaner, fault-finder, murmurer, mutterer, grouser, kvetch, kvetcher

FORMAL malcontent
COLLOQ. grump, bellyacher, crosspatch, whiner, whinger, sourpuss, griper
2 COMPLAINT, grievance, grumble, objection, moan
COLLOQ. gripe, grouse, whinge

grouchy adj

bad-tempered, irritable, cross, dissatisfied, discontented, grumpy, sulky, surly, complaining, grumbling, testy, ill-tempered, irascible, captious, churlish, peevish, petulant
FORMAL cantankerous, querulous, truculent
COLLOQ. crotchety
F3 contented

ground n, v

♦ n

1 EARTH, soil, clay, loam, dirt, dust, dry land, terra firma, land, terrain, bottom, foundation, surface
2 *a football ground*
field, pitch, stadium, arena, park
3 *the palace grounds*
estate, property, territory, domain, gardens, lawns, park, campus, surroundings, fields, acres, land, terrain, holding, plot
4 *no grounds for such harsh treatment*
base, foundation, justification, excuse, vindication, reason, motive, inducement, cause, occasion, call, score, account, argument, principle, basis
5 *coffee grounds*
dregs, sediment, deposit, residue, lees, scourings
TECHNICAL precipitate

♦ v

1 BASE, found, establish, set, fix, settle
2 PREPARE, introduce, initiate, familiarize with, acquaint with, inform, instruct, teach, educate, train, drill, coach, tutor

groundless adj

baseless, unfounded, unsubstantiated, unsupported, empty, imaginary, false, illusory, unjustified, unwarranted, unprovoked, uncalled-for, without reason
F3 well-founded, reasonable, justified

groundwork n

basis, base, essentials, foundation, fundamentals, preparation, preliminaries, research, homework, cornerstone, footing, spadework, underpinnings

group n, v

♦ n

band, gang, pack, team, crew, troop, squad, detachment, unit, party, faction, set, circle, clique, coterie, cohort, contingent, club, society, association, guild, league, organization, company, gathering, congregation, body, assembly, crowd, flock, collection, bunch, clump, cluster, knot, batch, lot, combination, element, bracket, formation, grouping, class, category, classification, genus, species, family, school
FORMAL conglomeration

♦ v

1 GATHER, collect, assemble, congregate, unite, mass, cluster, clump, bunch, huddle
2 *group them according to size*
sort, range, arrange, marshal, line up, organize, order, rank, grade, class, classify, categorize, band, bracket, link, associate

---

Synonym nuances

noun

The terms **band**, **gang** and **pack** suggest an informal group and can have connotations of lawless intent: *a band of outlaws*. **Team** and **crew** are associated more with official or organized groups with a specific role or task: *the crew manning the ship*. **Team** in particular would be used for a competing group, and can have connotations of co-operation and camaraderie: *for this*

---

game, divide into two teams. **Squad**, **detachment** and **unit** are similar, but tend to be associated more with the armed services, and the term **contingent**, while formerly applied to armed forces, now tends to be used more loosely where a group is taken to represent something: *the British contingent at this year's Games*.

Party is appropriate to refer to a group who have gathered to take part in a particular activity: *a tour party*; *the shooting party*, and, of course, an organized political group. **Faction** would also be used in a political context, but to refer specifically to a group within a larger party, particularly a group which is potentially troublesome or divisive.

The words **set** and **circle** are appropriate to refer to a social group that is not official but widely recognized, and **set** in particular can have connotations of glamour or fashionability: *the modern art set*. **Cohort**, **clique** and **coterie** are similar in meaning, but suggest a much smaller group, and while **clique** has negative overtones of insularity, **coterie** has further, and again negative, connotations of pandering to someone: *the president had a coterie of aides and sycophants*.

Club, **society**, **association**, **guild** and **league** would refer to an organized group of individuals who have come together voluntarily to practise or promote something; **body**, **organization** and **company** are similar, but more likely to be used in a business or administrative context. On the other hand, **gathering**, **congregation**, and **assembly** suggest a group of people who have gathered for a particular purpose on a specific occasion: *she addressed a gathering of civil servants*, while **crowd** or **flock**, although suggesting large numbers, move the emphasis away from the idea of a group as individuals: *the crowd was thickening and filling the square*.

A smaller group of people or things that are so close together that the identities or natures of the individuals are unimportant or indistinguishable, could be referred to as a **bunch**, **clump**, **cluster** or **knot**: *a clump of spectators*; *there was a knot of people around the prostrate body*. The term **collection**, on the other hand, reinforces the idea of individual items making up the whole: *a motley collection of characters*.

---

grouse v, n

♦ v

complain, grumble, moan, find fault
COLLOQ. beef, bellyache, carp, grouch, gripe, whine, whinge
SLANG bitch
F3 acquiesce

♦ n

complaint, groan, grumble, moan, objection, protest, grievance
COLLOQ. bellyache, gripe, grouch, whine, whinge

grove n

wood, woodland, thicket, spinney, coppice, copse, plantation, covert, arbour, avenue
Related adjective: nemoral

grovel v

1 INGRATIATE YOURSELF, crawl, creep, toady, flatter, fawn, cringe, cower, kowtow, defer, demean yourself
COLLOQ. butter someone up, suck up, bow and scrape, lick someone's boots, kiss up to
SLANG cheese; (*vulgar*) kiss someone's arse
2 CRAWL, creep, kneel, crouch, stoop, lie low, prostrate yourself, lie down, bow down, cower, fall on your knees

grow v

1 BECOME LARGER, become/get taller, become/get bigger, increase in size/height, extend, develop, expand, enlarge, lengthen, elongate, widen, broaden, thicken, deepen, swell, fill out

2 GERMINATE, shoot, sprout, spring, bud, flower, mature, develop
FORMAL burgeon

3 INCREASE, rise, expand, enlarge, swell, spread, extend, stretch, develop, multiply, escalate, mushroom, wax
FORMAL proliferate

4 *grow cold*
become, get, go, turn, come to be, change, develop

5 PROGRESS, thrive, flourish, prosper, succeed, improve, advance, make headway

6 ORIGINATE, arise, issue, stem, spring

7 CULTIVATE, farm, produce, propagate, breed, raise, sow, plant, harvest

1 shrink **3** decrease **5** fail

growl v
snarl, snap, yap, bark, howl, yelp, grumble, rumble, roar, gnar; *Scot* gurl
OLD groin; (*Spenser*) royne

grown-up *adj, n*
• *adj*
adult, mature, of age, full-grown, fully-grown, fully-developed, fully-fledged
young, immature
• *n*
adult, man, woman
child

growth *n*
1 INCREASE, rise, extension, enlargement, expansion, spread, multiplication, magnification, amplification, deepening, development, evolution, progress, advance, improvement, success, headway, prosperity
FORMAL proliferation, augmentation, aggrandizement

2 GERMINATION, shooting, sprouting, springing, budding, flowering, development
FORMAL maturation, burgeoning

3 TUMOUR, lump, swelling, protuberance, outgrowth
TECHNICAL intumescence, excrescence
1 decrease, decline, failure

grub *v, n*
• *v*
dig, burrow, delve, excavate, probe, root, rummage, forage, ferret, hunt, search, scour, unearth, uncover, explore
• *n*
1 LAVA, maggot, worm, pupa, caterpillar, chrysalis

2 FOOD, provision, meals, refreshment(s), sustenance, nutrition
COLLOQ. eats, tuck
SLANG nosh; *Aust & NZ* tucker

grubby *adj*
dirty, soiled, unwashed, mucky, grimy, filthy, squalid, seedy, messy, scruffy, shabby
clean

grudge *n, v*
• *n*
resentment, bitterness, envy, jealousy, pique, spite, malice, enmity, antagonism, hate, hatred, venom, dislike, animosity, antipathy, aversion, ill-will, hard feelings, grievance
FORMAL malevolence, rancour, animus
favour
• *v*
begrudge, resent, envy, covet, be jealous of, dislike, take exception to, object to, mind, feel aggrieved about

grudging *adj*
reluctant, unwilling, hesitant, half-hearted, unenthusiastic, resentful, envious, jealous

gruelling *adj*
hard, difficult, taxing, demanding, tiring, exhausting, laborious, arduous, strenuous, trying, backbreaking, draining, crushing, grinding, harsh, severe, tough, punishing
easy

gruesome *adj*
horrible, disgusting, repellent, repugnant, repulsive, revolting, sickening, hideous, grisly, macabre, grim, ghastly, awful, terrible, horrific, horrid, frightful, dreadful, appalling, shocking, monstrous, abhorrent, abominable, loathsome
pleasant

gruesomely *adv*
horribly, repulsively, hideously, grimly, terribly, frightfully, dreadfully, monstrously
pleasantly

gruff *adj*
1 CURT, brusque, abrupt, blunt, rude, surly, sour, sullen, grumpy, bad-tempered, churlish, testy, tetchy, impolite, unfriendly, discourteous
COLLOQ. crotchety, crabbed

2 *a gruff voice*
rough, harsh, rasping, guttural, throaty, husky, hoarse, croaking, thick
1 friendly, courteous, polite

gruffly *adv*
1 BRUSQUELY, rudely, impolitely, curtly, abruptly, discourteously
2 ROUGHLY, harshly, hoarsely, huskily, gutturally

grumble *v, n*
• *v*
1 COMPLAIN, moan, object, protest, bleat, find fault
OLD groin
COLLOQ. bellyache, beef, grouch, gripe, whine, whinge, carp

2 RUMBLE, murmur, gurgle, growl
• *n*
1 COMPLAINT, moan, grievance, objection, protest
COLLOQ. beef, gripe, grouch, grouse, whinge, bleat
SLANG bitch

2 RUMBLE, murmur, muttering, gurgle, growl, roar

grumbler *n*
complainer, moaner, niggler, fault-finder
COLLOQ. bellyacher, grouser, fusspot, nit-picker, whiner, whinger; *N Am* fussbudget

grumpily *adv*
churlishly, crossly, sullenly, sulkily
COLLOQ. grouchily, in a huff, in a sulk, having got out of bed on the wrong side

grumpy *adj*
bad-tempered, ill-tempered, churlish, cross, irritable, surly, sullen, sulky, tetchy, snappy, petulant, discontented, grumpish
FORMAL cantankerous
COLLOQ. crotchety, crabbed, grouchy, ratty, in a huff, in a sulk, having got out of bed on the wrong side
contented

grunt *v*
snort, croak, snore, cough, grate, rasp
OLD groin

guarantee *n, v*
• *n*
warranty, warrant, guaranty, insurance, assurance, promise, word of honour, pledge, oath, bond, covenant, contract, security, collateral, surety, endorsement, testimonial, token
TECHNICAL appellation contrôlée
OLD *Scot* warrandice

FORMAL earnest

♦ v

assure, give an assurance, promise, pledge, swear, vouch for, answer for, warrant, certify, underwrite, provide security/collateral/surety for, endorse, support, back, sponsor, secure, protect, insure, ensure, make sure, make certain

OLD vouchsafe, avouch, gage, stipulate

guarantor n

underwriter, guarantee, sponsor, supporter, backer, surety, warrantor, referee, voucher, bondsman, bailsman, covenantor

COLLOQ. angel

guard v, n

♦ v

protect, safeguard, save, preserve, shield, secure, screen, shelter, cover, defend, patrol, police, escort, supervise, oversee, watch, keep, keep watch, be alert, look out, take care, mind, beware, sentinel, fence, hedge, preserve; Scot wear, weir

OLD ward, warden; (Shakesp) enguard, fortress; (Spenser) savegard

See Synonym nuances panel at **defend**.

♦ n

1 PROTECTOR, defender, custodian, warder, escort, bodyguard, keeper, captor, conductor, watch, scout, watchman, lookout, sentry, sentinel, picket, patrol, security, guardian, garda

OLD bostangi

SLANG minder

2 PROTECTION, safeguard, defence, wall, barrier, fence, screen, shield, bumper, fender, buffer, pad, cushion, rail, splasher

3 SURVEILLANCE, watch, lookout, observation, inspection, superintendence, supervision, vigilance, stewardship, guardianship, monitoring, scrutiny, check, care, charge, control, direction, regulation

■ **off your guard**
careless, unprepared, unaware(s), unready, unwary, inattentive, napping, unsuspecting, surprised, with your defences down

COLLOQ. red-handed, with your pants down

■ **on your guard**
alert, watchful, vigilant, cautious, careful, ready, prepared, attentive, on the lookout, wary, wide awake, on the alert

FORMAL circumspect, excubant

guarded adj

cautious, wary, chary, careful, watchful, discreet, non-committal, reluctant, reticent, reserved, restrained, secretive

FORMAL circumspect

COLLOQ. cagey

E3 communicative, frank

guardedly adv

cautiously, warily, carefully, charily, non-committally, reluctantly, secretively

FORMAL circumspectly

guardian n

trustee, curator, custodian, steward, caretaker, keeper, warden, protector, preserver, defender, champion, guard, warder, escort, attendant

guardianship n

trust, care, guidance, trusteeship, curatorship, custodianship, custody, tutelage, stewardship, patronage, attendance, guard, hands, keeping, wardenship, wardship, preservation, protection, safekeeping, defence

FORMAL aegis

guerrilla n

freedom fighter, terrorist, irregular, resistance fighter,

partisan, sniper, guerrillero, franc-tireur, haiduk, bushwhacker

OLD SLANG (offensive) gook

guess v, n

♦ v

speculate, make a guess, predict, estimate, judge, reckon, hypothesize, work out, put something at, suppose, assume, think, believe, judge, consider, imagine, fancy, feel, suspect

FORMAL conjecture, surmise, postulate

COLLOQ. guesstimate

♦ n

prediction, estimate, speculation, assumption, belief, judgement, reckoning, fancy, idea, notion, theory, hypothesis, guesswork, opinion, feeling, suspicion, intuition, hunch

FORMAL conjecture, supposition, surmise

COLLOQ. guesstimate, ballpark figure, shot in the dark

guesstimate n

rough calculation, approximate cost/price/value/quantity, quotation, reckoning, valuation, judgement, (rough) guess, approximation, assessment, estimation, evaluation, computation

COLLOQ. ballpark figure

guesswork n

speculation, estimation, reckoning, prediction, assumption, intuition, theory, hypothesis

FORMAL conjecture, supposition, surmise

COLLOQ. guesstimate

guest n

visitor, caller, boarder, lodger, resident, patron, regular, invitee, umbra

TECHNICAL synoecete

FORMAL visitant

guesthouse n

boarding-house, hostel, hostelry, inn, hotel, pension, rooming-house, B & B

FORMAL xenodochium

guff n

rubbish, nonsense, drivel, gibberish, trash, tripe, twaddle, stuff and nonsense

COLLOQ. bunk, bunkum, claptrap, piffle, bilge, cock, poppycock, hot air, cobblers, rot, tommyrot, codswallop, baloney, blah, bosh, eyewash, hogwash, rhubarb, hooey, malarkey, moonshine, stuff and nonsense

SLANG bull; (vulgar) balls, bollocks, crap, shit, bullshit

guffaw v, n

♦ v

laugh loudly, roar, bellow, hoot, cackle, shriek, whoop

♦ n

loud laugh, roar, bellow, hoot, cackle, shriek, whoop

guidance n

leadership, direction, management, rule, charge, control, teaching, instruction, advice, counsel, counselling, help, assistance, information, instructions, directions, guidelines, indication(s), pointer(s), hint(s), tip(s), recommendation(s), suggestion(s)

guide v, n

♦ v

1 LEAD, conduct, direct, navigate, point, steer, pilot, manoeuvre, usher, escort, show, show the way, accompany, attend

COLLOQ. hold someone's hand

2 CONTROL, govern, manage, direct, be in charge of, rule, preside over, oversee, supervise, superintend, command

3 ADVISE, counsel, give directions/recommendations to, influence, educate, teach, instruct, train

♦ n

1 MANUAL, handbook, guidebook, catalogue, directory, key, ABC
2 LEADER, courier, navigator, pilot, helmsman, steersman, conductor, director, ranger, usher, escort, chaperon(e), attendant, companion
3 ADVISER, counsellor, mentor, guru, teacher, instructor, tutor
4 GUIDELINE, example, model, pattern, norm, gauge, standard, criterion, measure, benchmark, yardstick, tombstone, indication, pointer, signpost, sign, signal, key, marker, mark, beacon
FORMAL exemplar, archetype

guidebook n
guide, handbook, manual, instruction book, book of directions, ABC, companion, prospectus, Baedeker, A to Z®

guideline n
instruction, recommendation, suggestion, direction, advice, information, indication, rule, regulation, standard, criterion, measure, benchmark, yardstick, touchstone, framework, parameter, constraint, procedure, principle, terms

guild n
organization, association, alliance, federation, society, club, union, fellowship, league, order, company, chapel, brotherhood, lodge, fraternity, sorority, corporation, incorporation

guile n
deceit, deception, cunning, treachery, double-dealing, fraud, trickery, trickiness, wiliness, cleverness, slyness, craft, craftiness, deviousness, artfulness, artifice, ruse, gamesmanship, knavery
FORMAL duplicity
E3 artlessness, guilelessness

guileless adj
artless, direct, straight, straightforward, genuine, honest, frank, sincere, trusting, truthful, innocent, naive, candid, natural, open, simple, transparent, unreserved, unsophisticated, unworldly
FORMAL ingenuous
E3 artful, cunning

guilt n
1 *he confessed his guilt*
responsibility, blame, blameworthiness, disgrace, dishonour, wrong, wrongdoing, criminality, misconduct, unlawfulness
TECHNICAL blood-guilt
FORMAL culpability
2 *a feeling of guilt*
guilty conscience, conscience, disgrace, dishonour, shame, self-condemnation, self-reproach, self-accusation, regret, remorse, contrition, repentance, penitence
FORMAL compunction
COLLOQ. guilt trip
E3 1 innocence, righteousness **2** shamelessness

guiltily adv
wrongly, illegally, unlawfully, illicitly, responsibly, unforgivably, reprehensibly, to blame, at fault, without excuse, shamefully, contritely, regretfully, penitentially, remorsefully, with sorrow, in sackcloth and ashes, caught in the act, caught red-handed

guiltless adj
blameless, innocent, clear, clean, pure, irreproachable, above reproach, sinless, spotless, faultless, stainless, immaculate, impeccable, unblamable, unimpeachable, undefiled, unspotted, unsullied, untainted, untarnished
FORMAL inculpable
E3 guilty, tainted

guilty adj
1 *guilty of a crime*
responsible, blamable, blameworthy, to blame, at fault, offending, wrong, illegal, unlawful, illicit, sinful, wicked, delinquent, criminal, convicted, evil
FORMAL culpable
2 CONSCIENCE-STRICKEN, ashamed, guilt-ridden, bad, with a bad conscience, on your conscience, shamefaced, sheepish, sorry, regretful, remorseful, contrite, penitent, repentant
FORMAL compunctious
E3 1 innocent, guiltless, blameless **2** shameless

guise n
appearance, form, shape, features, likeness, manner, disguise, mask, pretence, show, façade, front, behaviour, custom, air, aspect, face, semblance
FORMAL demeanour

gulf n
1 BAY, bight, cove, inlet, basin
2 GAP, opening, separation, division, divide, rift, split, breach, cleft, fissure, crevice, chasm, gorge, hole, ravine, abyss, void, hollow, canyon, maw
OLD vorago

gullet n
throat, craw, crop, maw
TECHNICAL oesophagus
OLD weasand
Related adjective: oesophageal

gullibility n
credulity, innocence, simplicity, naivety, trustfulness, foolishness
E3 astuteness

gullible adj
credulous, suggestible, impressionable, trusting, trustful, overtrusting, ingenuous, unsuspecting, easily deceived, foolish, naive, green, inexperienced, unsophisticated, innocent
COLLOQ. wet behind the ears
E3 astute

gully n
channel, ravine, gorge, valley, canyon, watercourse, gutter, ditch, couloir, grough; *Scot* geo; *N Am* gulch
TECHNICAL donga

gulp v, n
♦ *v*
swallow, swig, swill, quaff, bolt, gobble, guzzle, devour, stuff, gollop; *dialect* gulch
COLLOQ. knock back, wolf, tuck into
OLD SLANG swipe
E3 sip, nibble
♦ *n*
swallow, swig, draught, mouthful; *N Am* slug

gum n, v
♦ *n*
adhesive, glue, paste, cement, fixative, resin
Related adjective: mucilaginous
♦ *v*
stick, glue, paste, fix, cement, seal, clog
FORMAL affix
▪ **gum up**
obstruct, hinder, impede, choke, clog

gummy adj
sticky, adhesive, gluey, gooey, tacky, viscous
FORMAL viscid

gumption n
common sense, initiative, resourcefulness, cleverness, astuteness, nous, enterprise, shrewdness, wit, discernment, acumen, ability, acuteness
FORMAL sagacity

COLLOQ. savvy
▉ foolishness

gun *n*
firearm, weapon
COLLOQ. piece, shooter, shooting iron

gunfire *n*
shooting, firing, gunshots, bombardment, shelling, pounding, cannonade, salvo, flak

gunman *n*
assassin, terrorist, thug, killer, sniper, shootist, murderer, bandit, armed robber, gangster, mobster, bravo, desperado, gunslinger
COLLOQ. hatchet man, hit man

gurgle *v, n*
◆ *v*
BABBLE, bubble, burble, murmur, ripple, lap, splash, plash
◆ *n*
BABBLE, bubbling, murmur, ripple, crow, burble

guru *n*
expert, authority, instructor, master, teacher, tutor, leader, mentor, luminary, guiding light, pundit, maharishi, Svengali, swami, sage

gush *v, n*
◆ *v*
1 FLOW, run, pour, stream, surge, cascade, flood, rush, burst, spurt, spout, jet, well, issue, fountain, regurgitate, regorge; *dialect* boke
OLD rail
2 ENTHUSE, effervesce, bubble over, effuse, chatter, babble, fuss, jabber; *dialect & N Am* blather; drivel
COLLOQ. go on, rave
◆ *n*
flow, outflow, stream, surge, torrent, cascade, flood, tide, rush, burst, outburst, spurt, spout, outpouring, spate, jet

gushing *adj*
effusive, over-enthusiastic, excessive, cloying, emotional, saccharine, sentimental, sickly, fulsome, mawkish
COLLOQ. gushy
▉ restrained, sincere

gust *n, v*
◆ *n*
1 *a gust of wind*
blast, burst, rush, flurry, blow, puff, breeze, wind, gale, storm, squall, surge
2 *gusts of temper*
outburst, outbreak, fit, eruption, surge
◆ *v*
blast, blow, puff, squall, bluster, breeze, rush, surge, burst out, erupt

gustily *adv*
stormily, windily, breezily, tempestuously, wildly
▉ calmly

gusto *n*
zest, relish, appreciation, enjoyment, pleasure, delight, enthusiasm, exhilaration, exuberance, energy, fervour, élan, verve, zeal
▉ distaste, apathy

gusty *adj*
stormy, blowy, squally, windy, blustering, blustery, breezy, tempestuous
▉ calm

gut *n, v, adj*
◆ *n*
1 INTESTINES, belly, stomach, bowels, viscera, entrails, vital organs, insides, internal organs
COLLOQ. innards
Related adjectives: enteral, enteric, splanchnic
2 *have the guts to own up*

courage, bravery, pluck, boldness, audacity, tenacity, nerve, mettle
FORMAL fortitude
COLLOQ. grit, backbone, bottle, spunk
SLANG balls
◆ *v*
1 *gut fish*
disembowel, draw, clean (out)
FORMAL eviscerate, exenterate
2 STRIP, clear, empty, rifle, ransack, plunder, loot, sack, rob, destroy, devastate, ravage, clear out
◆ *adj*
instinctive, intuitive, emotional, unthinking, basic, deep-seated, heartfelt, innate, involuntary, natural, spontaneous, strong

gutless *adj*
weak, cowardly, feeble, irresolute, timid, faint-hearted, lily-livered, craven, abject
COLLOQ. chicken, chicken-hearted, chicken-livered, spineless
▉ courageous

gutsily *adv*
bravely, boldly, courageously, resolutely, indomitably, passionately, staunchily
COLLOQ. spunkily

gutsy *adj*
bold, brave, courageous, determined, resolute, plucky, indomitable, mettlesome, passionate, spirited, staunch, gallant, game
COLLOQ. spunky
SLANG ballsy
▉ quiet, timid

gutter *n*
drain, sluice, sewer, ditch, trench, trough, channel, gully, duct, conduit, culvert, passage, pipe, tube, grip, kennel, rigol; *Scot* strand
TECHNICAL cullis

guttersnipe *n*
urchin, waif, ragamuffin, gamin, mudlark, tatterdemalion

guttural *adj*
rasping, throaty, croaking, hoarse, harsh, gruff, rough, grating, gravelly, husky, deep, low, thick
▉ dulcet

guy *n*
fellow, man, boy, youth, lad, person, individual, character
COLLOQ. bloke, chap, fella; *Irish* bucko; *Aust* cove
SLANG sod; *N Am* dude; boyo, geezer

guzzle *v*
bolt, devour, gobble, gormandize, stuff, cram, gulp, swallow, swill, quaff, swig
COLLOQ. wolf, scoff, polish off, put away, tuck into, knock back

Gypsy, Gipsy *n*
Romany, Romani, Roma, traveller, rom, rye, wanderer, roamer, rover, rambler, hawker, huckster, nomad, tzigany, *Zigeuner, Zincalo, Zingaro,* Bohemian, tinker, diddicoy, faw, *gitano; Scot* caird, (*derog*) tinkler; *Scot & Irish* (*derog*) tinker
OLD Egyptian, gipsen
SLANG (*offensive*) gippo

gyrate *v*
turn, revolve, rotate, twirl, pirouette, spin, whirl, wheel, swirl, swivel, circle, spiral

gyration *n*
turn, revolution, rotation, twirl, pirouette, spin, spinning, whirl, whirling, swirl, swivel, wheeling, circle, spiral
FORMAL convolution

H

habit *n*
1 CUSTOM, usage, practice, routine, rule, procedure, matter of course, second nature, way(s), manner, mannerism, mode, policy, wont, inclination, tendency, leaning, bent, mannerism, quirk, ethos
FORMAL propensity, proclivity
2 ADDICTION, dependence, fixation, obsession, weakness
3 GARMENT, costume, dress, clothing, outfit, uniform, robe, vestment
COLLOQ. get-up, gear, togs

habitable *adj*
fit to live in, suitable to live in, good enough to live in, inhabitable

habitat *n*
home, domain, element, environment, natural environment, surroundings, dwelling, locality, territory, terrain, station
TECHNICAL metropolis, niche
FORMAL abode

habitation *n*
1 OCCUPANCY, occupation, quarters, residence, tenancy, housing, lodging, inhabitance, inhabitancy, inhabitation
2 HOME, house, cottage, accommodation, flat, apartment, hut, quarters, living quarters, lodging, mansion
FORMAL abode, domicile, dwelling, dwelling-place, residence, residency
COLLOQ. digs, pad, joint, roof over your head
SLANG gaff

habitual *adj*
1 CUSTOMARY, traditional, accustomed, routine, usual, ordinary, common, natural, normal, set, standard, regular, recurrent, fixed, established, systematic, familiar
FORMAL wonted
2 *habitual drinker*
confirmed, inveterate, chronic, hardened, addicted, dependent, constant, great, intemperate, pathological, persistent, obsessive
F3 **1** occasional, infrequent

habitually *adv*
usually, normally, generally, as a rule, ordinarily, typically, traditionally, regularly, routinely, commonly, by and large, on the whole, mainly, chiefly, mostly, for the most part, on average, in the main
COLLOQ. nine times out of ten
F3 exceptionally

habituate *v*
acclimatize, accustom, make used, adapt, familiarize, make familiar with, break in, condition, train, school, discipline, tame, harden, inure, season

habitué *n*
regular, regular customer, frequenter, frequent visitor, patron, denizen

hack¹ *v*
hacked them to death
cut, chop, hew, fell, saw, clear, notch, gash, slash, lacerate, mutilate, mangle
■ **hack it**

cope, manage, carry on, get on/along, get by, get through, muddle through
COLLOQ. make out

hack² *n*
write as a hack
scribbler, writer, journalist, reporter, drudge, slave

hackle
■ **make someone's hackles rise**
anger, annoy, irritate, irk, vex, rile, make angry, needle, nettle, bother, ruffle, provoke, antagonize, offend, affront, gall, madden, enrage, incense, infuriate, exasperate, outrage
COLLOQ. aggravate, get at, wind up, needle, miff, make someone's blood boil, bug, hassle, rub up the wrong way, get someone's blood up, get on someone's nerves, rattle someone's cage, ruffle someone's feathers, raise someone's dander, make sparks fly, get under someone's skin, get up someone's nose, get on someone's wick
SLANG nark, piss off

hackneyed *adj*
stale, old, overworked, overused, tired, worn-out, time-worn, threadbare, wearing thin, unoriginal, cliché-ridden, clichéd, stereotyped, stock, banal, trite, commonplace, common, pedestrian, uninspired, unimaginative
FORMAL platitudinous
COLLOQ. corny, run-of-the-mill, yawn-making
F3 original, new, fresh

haft *n*
handle, grip, handgrip, knob, stock, shaft, hilt

hag *n*
crone, witch, shrew, gorgon, termagant, vixen, virago, harridan, fury, harpy
COLLOQ. battle-axe

haggard *adj*
drawn, gaunt, careworn, thin, wasted, drained, shrunken, pinched, hollow-cheeked, pale, pallid, wan, ghastly
F3 hale

haggle *v*
bargain, negotiate, barter, beat down, chaffer, higgle, wrangle, squabble, bicker, quarrel, dispute; *N Am* dicker

hail¹ *v*
1 GREET, address, acknowledge, salute, say hello to, nod to, wave to, communicate, speak; *S Afr* hail
2 SIGNAL TO, flag down, wave down, wave to, call out to
3 ACCLAIM, applaud, honour, welcome, praise, cheer, exalt
FORMAL laud
4 *hail from Malawi*
come, originate, have your home/roots in, be born in

hail² *n, v*
♦ *n*
1 *a hail storm*
frozen rain, frozen ice, sleet, hailstones, hail-storm
TECHNICAL precipitation
2 *a hail of arrows*
barrage, bombardment, volley, torrent, shower, storm
♦ *v*
pelt, bombard, shower, rain, beat, batter, attack, assail

hail-fellow-well-met *adj*
convivial, friendly, sociable, genial, cheerful, cordial, festive, affable, hearty, jolly, jovial, lively, merry, fun-loving

hair *n*
locks, tresses, shock, mop, mane, fleece, wool, coat, fur, pelt, hide
COLLOQ. barnet

■ **let your hair down**
relax, let yourself go, have a good time, throw off your inhibitions
COLLOQ. hang loose, loosen up
SLANG let it all hang out, chill out

■ **make someone's hair stand on end**
shock, frighten, terrify, disgust, revolt, repel, appal, outrage, scandalize, horrify, startle, astound, stagger, amaze, stun, daze, stupefy, numb, paralyse, traumatize, jolt, jar, shake, agitate, unsettle, upset, distress, disquiet, unnerve, bewilder, take aback, confound, dumbfound, dismay
FORMAL perturb
E∃ delight, please, gratify, reassure

■ **not turn a hair**
remain calm, remain composed
COLLOQ. see it coming, not bat an eyelid, keep your cool, stay cool

■ **split hairs**
find fault, quibble, cavil, pettifog, argue over unimportant details
COLLOQ. nit-pick
Related adjectives: pilose, pileous, crinal, capillaceous, trichoid

hair's-breadth *n*
fraction, hair, inch, jot
COLLOQ. whisker
E∃ mile

haircut, hairdo *n*
hairstyle, coiffure, cut, style, set

hairdresser *n*
hairstylist, stylist, barber, coiffeur, coiffeuse

hairless *adj*
bald, bald-headed, shorn, tonsured, shaven, clean-shaven, beardless
E∃ hairy, hirsute

hairpiece *n*
wig, toupee, postiche, scratch-wig, spencer, bobwig, Brutus, buzz-wig, tie-wig; *Scot* gizz, jiz
OLD periwig, peruke, transformation, bagwig, caxon, major, Ramilie
OLD COLLOQ. jasey
SLANG rug

hair-raising *adj*
frightening, scary, terrifying, horrifying, shocking, bloodcurdling, spine-chilling, petrifying, eerie, alarming, startling, thrilling, exciting
COLLOQ. creepy

hairstyle *n*
style, coiffure, cut, haircut, set
COLLOQ. hairdo, barnet

hairy *adj*
1 HIRSUTE, bearded, shaggy, bushy, fuzzy, furry, woolly, fleecy, unshaven
FORMAL pilose, crinose, crinigerous, crinite
2 DANGEROUS, unsafe, insecure, risky, high-risk, fraught with danger, threatening, breakneck, hazardous, chancy, perilous, precarious, reckless, treacherous, vulnerable, menacing, ominous, exposed, susceptible, alarming, critical, severe, serious, grave, daring, nasty
COLLOQ. dicey, dodgy
E∃ 1 bald, clean-shaven **2** safe, secure

halcyon *adj*
peaceful, happy, flourishing, prosperous, carefree, calm, balmy, mild, gentle, golden, pacific, placid, quiet, serene, still, tranquil, undisturbed
E∃ stormy

hale *adj*
healthy, fit, well, youthful, strong, sound, vigorous, robust, flourishing, athletic, hearty, able-bodied, blooming
COLLOQ. in the pink, in fine fettle
E∃ ill

half *n, adj, adv*
♦ *n*
fifty per cent, equal part/share, bisection, hemisphere, semicircle, section, segment, portion, share, fraction
♦ *adj*
semi-, halved, divided, divided in two, bisected, hemispherical, fractional, part, partial, incomplete, moderate, limited, slight
E∃ whole
♦ *adv*
partly, partially, incompletely, inadequately, insufficiently, moderately, slightly, barely
E∃ completely

■ **by half**
very, considerably, excessively, too

■ **by halves**
incompletely, imperfectly, inadequately, insufficiently
E∃ thoroughly

■ **not half**
1 *not half as clever*
not at all, not nearly
2 *not half get into trouble*
very, very much, really, indeed

■ **too ... by half**
unduly, too, over, excessively, immoderately, inordinately, disproportionately, out of all proportions, unreasonably, unjustifiably, unnecessarily

half-baked *adj*
impractical, stupid, ill-conceived, unplanned, undeveloped, ill-judged, short-sighted, silly, crazy, foolish, senseless
COLLOQ. harebrained, crackpot
E∃ sensible, thought out

half-caste *n*
Creole, griff(e), mestee, mestiza, mestizo, metif, Métis, Métisse, miscegen, miscegene, miscegine, mongrel, mulatta, mulatto, mulattress, quadroon, quarteroon, quarter-blood, quintroon, sambo

---

Hairstyles include:

Afro	chignon	dreadlocks	marcel wave	ponytail	sideboards
backcombed	combover	*slang* duck's arse	mohican	pouffe	sideburns
bangs	corn rows	(or DA)	mullet	quiff	skinhead
beehive	cowlick	Eton crop	pageboy	ringlets	tonsure
bob	crewcut	French pleat	perm	shed	topknot
bouffant	crimped	fringe	pigtail	shingle	undercut
braid	crop	frizette	plait	short back and	weave
bun	curled	hair extension	pompadour	sides	

half-hearted adj
lukewarm, tepid, cool, weak, feeble, passive, apathetic, lacklustre, listless, uninterested, unenthusiastic, indifferent, unconcerned, neutral, Laodicean
F3 wholehearted, enthusiastic

half-heartedly adv
unenthusiastically, feebly, apathetically, listlessly, neutrally
F3 wholeheartedly, enthusiastically

halfway adv, adj
• adv
midway, in/to the middle, centrally
• adj
middle, central, equidistant, mid, midway, intermediate, mean, median
■ **meet someone halfway**
compromise, reach a compromise, negotiate, make concessions, come to/reach an understanding, give and take, steer a middle course, find a happy medium, make a deal
COLLOQ. go fifty-fifty with, split the difference

halfwit n
fool, blockhead, fat-head, dunce, dimwit, simpleton, idiot, cretin, imbecile, ignoramus, moron, dupe, stooge, butt, laughing-stock, clown, comic, buffoon, jester
COLLOQ. nincompoop, ass, chump, ninny, airhead, clot, dope, twit, nitwit, nit, sucker, mug, twerp, birdbrain; *Scot & Irish* eejit; *Scot* numpty; *N Am* doofus; *Aust & NZ* dill
SLANG wally, dumbo, pillock, prat, dork, geek, git, berk, nerk, plonker, prick; *Aust & NZ* nong; *Aust* galah
F3 brain

half-witted adj
simple-minded, feeble-minded, silly, foolish, idiotic, stupid, crazy, dull, moronic, simple
COLLOQ. dim-witted, crack-brained, crackpot, dumb, dotty, potty, batty, barmy, nutty, wacky, two bricks short of a load, two sandwiches short of a picnic; *Aust* not the full quid
F3 clever

hall n
1 HALLWAY, corridor, passage, passageway, entrance-hall, foyer, vestibule, lobby
2 CONCERT HALL, auditorium, chamber, assembly hall, assembly room, conference hall

hallmark n
1 *a hallmark on gold*
official mark/stamp, mark/stamp of authenticity
2 *the hallmark of her music*
typical quality, distinctive feature, stamp, mark, trademark, brand-name, sign, indication, indicator, symbol, emblem, device, badge

hallo interj
hello, hullo, good morning, good afternoon, good evening, greetings, welcome, holloa; *Can* chimo
OLD hillo
COLLOQ. hi; *Aust* g'day

hallowed adj
honoured, revered, sacred, sacrosanct, blessed, sanctified, consecrated, holy, dedicated, established, inviolable, age-old

hallucinate v
dream, imagine, imagine things, see things, see visions, daydream, fantasize
SLANG freak out, trip

hallucination n
illusion, mirage, vision, apparition, dream, daydream, fantasy, figment, figment of the imagination, delusion, delirium, phantasmagoria
TECHNICAL autoscopy
SLANG freak-out, trip

halo n
circle of light, crown, ring, corona, glory, nimbus, radiance, aura, aureole, aureola, gloria, gloriole, halation

halt v, n
• v
stop, cease, come/bring to a stop, draw up, pull up, pause, wait, rest, come to (a) rest, break off, finish, bring/draw to a close, end, put an end to, check, stem, curb, obstruct, block, arrest, crush, hold back, impede
FORMAL discontinue, desist, terminate
COLLOQ. quit, call it a day
F3 start, continue
• n
stop, stoppage, arrest, interruption, break, interval, pause, rest, respite, breathing space, standstill, end, close, deadlock, stalemate
FORMAL termination, cessation, discontinuance, discontinuation, desistance
F3 start, continuation

halting adj
hesitant, stuttering, stammering, faltering, stumbling, fumbling for words, uncertain, broken, imperfect, laboured, awkward, unsteady
F3 fluent, certain

halve v
bisect, cut in half, split in two, divide, divide equally, split, sever, share, cut down, reduce, lessen
FORMAL dichotomize

halved adj
divided, split, cut, shared, bisected
FORMAL dimidiate

ham-fisted adj
clumsy, awkward, unco-ordinated, ham, accident-prone, unhandy, heavy-handed, unskilful, inept, bungling, blundering, lumbering, cack-handed, two-fisted, thumby
FORMAL maladroit
COLLOQ. gawky, all thumbs
F3 co-ordinated, skilful

hammer v, n
• v
1 HIT, strike, beat, drum, bang, bash, hit, slap, pound, batter, knock, drive, shape, form, make, mould, fashion, forge, dolly
TECHNICAL malleate, rivet
OLD (*Spenser*) martel
2 CRITICIZE, condemn, slate, attack, blame, censure, run down
FORMAL decry, denigrate
COLLOQ. slam, knock, tear a strip off, haul over the coals
3 *hammer the opposition*
beat, trounce, defeat, overcome, overwhelm, rout, annihilate, outplay
COLLOQ. clobber, slaughter, lick, thrash, run rings round, wipe the floor with, walk all over, make mincemeat of
SLANG take to the cleaners
4 *hammer an idea into someone*
force, drum, din, drive home, instil, reiterate
5 *hammer away at his essay*
persevere, pound, persist, keep on, labour, work away, plug, grind, drudge, slog
• n
mallet, gavel, beetle, claw hammer, sledgehammer, steam hammer, stone hammer, tack hammer, tilt-hammer, trip hammer, water hammer, pick, about-sledge, madge, maul, monkey; *Scot* knapping-hammer
TECHNICAL axe, bully, percussor, plexor
OLD mall
■ **hammer out**
settle, sort out, negotiate, thrash out, achieve eventually,

produce, bring about, work out, carry through, accomplish, complete, finish, resolve

hamper v, n

♦ v

hinder, impede, obstruct, slow down, hold up, stop, inhibit, frustrate, thwart, baulk, prevent, handicap, hamstring, shackle, cramp, restrict, curb, restrain, block, check, bridle, encumber, fetter, foil

FORMAL retard

COLLOQ. stymie

 aid, facilitate

♦ n

basket, box, container, creel, pannier

hamstring v

hinder, impede, hold up, stop, frustrate, baulk, thwart, cramp, restrict, restrain, block, check, encumber, foil, cripple, disable, handicap, incapacitate, paralyse

COLLOQ. stymie

hand n, v

♦ n

1 FIST, palm

TECHNICAL manus

COLLOQ. paw

SLANG mitt, fin

Related adjective: manual

2 *give me a hand*

help, helping hand, aid, assistance, support, participation, part, influence

FORMAL succour

3 *in someone's hands*

responsibility, care, custody, possession, charge, authority, command, control, power, management, supervision, clutches

4 *give someone a hand*

applause, round of applause, clapping, handclap, cheering, acclaim, ovation

5 INDICATOR, pointer, needle, arrow, marker

6 HANDWRITING, writing, script, penmanship, calligraphy

COLLOQ. fist

7 WORKER, manual worker, employee, operative, workman, workwoman, labourer, farm-hand, hireling

♦ v

give, pass, offer, submit, present, yield, deliver, hand over, transmit, conduct, convey

■ **hand down**

bequeath, will, pass on, pass down, transfer, give, grant, leave

■ **hand on**

pass on, transfer, give, supply, let someone have, surrender

■ **hand out**

distribute, deal out, pass out, give out, share out, mete out

FORMAL dispense, disseminate

COLLOQ. dish out

■ **hand over**

yield, relinquish, surrender, turn over, deliver, consign, release, give up, give, donate, present, pass, transfer

 keep, retain

■ **at hand**

near, close, to hand, handy, accessible, available, at someone's disposal, ready, readily available, imminent, about to happen

■ **by hand**

manually, using your hands, with your hands

■ **from hand to mouth**

precariously, dangerously, insecurely, uncertainly, in poverty, from day to day

COLLOQ. on the breadline

■ **hand in glove**

very closely, in close collaboration/co-operation, in close association

COLLOQ. in cahoots

■ **hand in hand**

1 HOLDING HANDS, with hands joined/clasped/held

2 CLOSELY RELATED, closely together, in close association

■ **in hand**

1 BEING DEALT WITH, under way, considered, attended to, under control

2 SPARE, in reserve, put by, ready, available

■ **to hand**

near, close, at hand, nearby, handy, accessible, available, at someone's disposal, ready, imminent, about to happen

■ **try your hand**

attempt, try, seek, strive, see if you can do

COLLOQ. have a go, have a shot/crack/stab

■ **win hands down**

win easily/effortlessly, win without effort

handbag n

clutch bag, flight bag, grip, handgrip, holdall, vanity bag, shoulder bag; N Am purse

handbill n

circular, leaflet, pamphlet, flier, notice, announcement, advertisement, letter

handbook n

manual, instruction book, book of directions, ABC, guide, guidebook, companion, prospectus

handcuff v

fetter, shackle, manacle, fasten, secure, tie

SLANG cuff

handcuffs n

manacles, fetters, shackles, wristlets, snippers, cuffs

COLLOQ. cuffs, darbies, mittens, nippers, bracelets

OLD SLANG snitchers

handful n

1 SMALL NUMBER, few, little, small amount, sprinkling, scattering, smattering

2 NUISANCE, bother, pest

COLLOQ. pain in the neck, thorn in the flesh, pain

 1 a lot, many

handgun n

pistol, gun, revolver, sidearm, six-shooter; N Am derringer

SLANG piece, rod, iron; N Am gat

See also panel at **gun**.

handicap n, v

♦ n

obstacle, obstruction, check, block, barrier, impediment, stumbling-block, hindrance, encumbrance, constraint, drawback, disadvantage, restriction, limitation, penalty, disability, impairment, abnormality, defect, shortcoming

 assistance, advantage

♦ v

impede, hinder, disadvantage, put at a disadvantage, hold back, hamper, impair, obstruct, block, check, bridle, curb, burden, encumber, restrict, limit, disable

FORMAL retard

 help, assist

handicapped adj

disabled, differently abled, disadvantaged, incapacitated, having special needs, challenged

handicraft n

craft, art, craftwork, craftsmanship, skill, handwork, handiwork, workmanship

handily adv

1 CONVENIENTLY, practically, usefully, helpfully

2 SKILFULLY, cleverly, practically, adeptly, adroitly

3 ACCESSIBLY, within reach, readily, nearly, to hand, at hand

 1 inconveniently **2** clumsily **3** inaccessibly

handiwork n

work, doing, responsibility, achievement, action, product, result, design, invention, creation, production, skill, workmanship, craftsmanship, artisanship, handicraft, craft, art, craftwork

handkerchief n
tissue, Kleenex®, rag, romal, foulard, kerchief, blind, bandana, monteith; *Scot* napkin
OLD muckender, orarium
COLLOQ. hankie
SLANG fogle, nose-rag
OLD SLANG wipe

handle n, v
♦ *n*
grip, handgrip, knob, stock, shaft, hilt, haft
Related adjective: manubrial
♦ *v*
1 TOUCH, finger, feel, fondle, pick up, hold, grasp, grip
COLLOQ. paw
2 *handle a situation*
tackle, treat, deal with, manage, cope with, control, supervise, be in charge of, take care of
3 *handle a car*
operate, control, drive, steer, work
4 TRADE IN, do business in, deal in, market, stock, traffic, operate

---

Synonym nuances
verb sense 1
Touch refers to coming into physical contact with, but may suggest that contact is brief, whilst **hold** is suggestive of prolonged retention. The verb **finger** is indicative of movement: *she fingered the flowers to see if they were real.* Similarly, **fondle** would be used of a caressing movement, particularly an affectionate or appreciative one, but it also has sexual connotations. The terms **grasp** and **grip** imply forceful holding: *he grasped my hand fiercely.*

---

handling n
management, conduct, approach, operation, running, treatment, direction, administration, discussion, transaction, manipulation

handout n
1 CHARITY, alms, gifts, dole, largesse, share, issue, free sample
COLLOQ. freebie
2 LEAFLET, circular, bulletin, statement, press release, brochure, pamphlet, literature

handover n
transfer, change, changeover, transposition, move, shift, removal, relocation, displacement, transmission, assignment, transference
TECHNICAL conveyance

hand-picked adj
choice, select, selected, chosen, elect, élite, picked, screened, recherché

handsome adj
1 GOOD-LOOKING, attractive, fair, personable, elegant, fine, dignified, stately
OLD brave, comely, seemly, featous, featurely; (*Shakesp*) goodfaced
COLLOQ. gorgeous, dishy, hunky
2 GENEROUS, liberal, large, considerable, ample, lavish, plentiful, abundant, bountiful, siz(e)able, magnanimous, unsparing, unstinting
E3 1 ugly, unattractive **2** mean

handsomely adv
generously, lavishly, plentifully, richly, amply, abundantly, bountifully, liberally, magnanimously, unsparingly, unstintingly
FORMAL munificently
E3 stingily

handwriting n
writing, script, hand, penmanship, calligraphy, autograph
COLLOQ. fist, scrawl, scribble

handy adj
1 CONVENIENT, practical, useful, helpful, functional, practicable
2 AVAILABLE, to hand, ready, at hand, near, nearly, accessible, within reach
COLLOQ. at your fingertips
3 SKILFUL, proficient, expert, skilled, clever, practical, dexterous, adroit, adept, nimble
E3 1 inconvenient **3** clumsy

handyman n
DIYer, odd-jobman, odd-jobber, Jack-of-all-trades, factotum

hang v
1 SUSPEND, be suspended, hang down, put up, dangle, swing, drape, drop, flop, droop, sag, trail, lean, bend
2 FASTEN, attach, fix, stick, glue, paste, cement
FORMAL affix, append
3 *hang in the air*
float, drift, hover, flit, flutter, linger, remain, cling
4 *the prisoners were hanged*
execute, lynch, put to death, send to the gallows/scaffold/ gibbet, kill
COLLOQ. string up
■ **hang about**
1 LOITER, hang around, linger, dawdle, waste time
SLANG mike
2 ASSOCIATE WITH, keep company with, frequent, haunt
COLLOQ. hang out
■ **hang back**
hold back, be reluctant, hesitate, shy away, shrink back, recoil, stay behind
FORMAL demur
■ **hang fire**
hold back, hang back, delay, hold on, stall, stick, stop, wait
FORMAL procrastinate, vacillate
E3 press on
■ **hang on**
1 WAIT, hold on, remain, hold out, endure, continue, carry on, persevere, persist
2 GRIP, grasp, cling, clutch, hold fast
3 DEPEND ON, hinge on, turn on, rest on, be conditional on, be determined by
FORMAL be contingent on
E3 1 give up
■ **hang over**
impend, loom, menace, threaten, approach, be imminent
■ **get the hang of**
understand, grasp, comprehend, learn, master, fathom, get the knack of
COLLOQ. twig

hangdog adj
abject, browbeaten, defeated, guilty, shamefaced, cowed, cringing, downcast, miserable, wretched, sneaking, furtive
E3 bold

hanger-on n
follower, minion, henchman, lackey, toady, sycophant, parasite, lackey, freeloader, dependant, client, courtling, flunkey
COLLOQ. sponger, sponge

hanging adj, n
♦ *adj*
suspended, dangling, swinging, draping, drooping, flopping, floppy, flapping, loose, unattached, unsupported
FORMAL pendent, pendulous, pensile
♦ *n*

curtain, drape, drapery, drop, frontal, drop-scene, dossal, dossel

hang-out n
haunt, den, meeting-place, home, patch, local, stamping-ground
COLLOQ. dive, joint, watering-hole

hangover n
after-effects, katzenjammer, morning after, the morning after the night before
FORMAL crapulence

hang-up n
inhibition, difficulty, problem, obsession, preoccupation, fixation, phobia, *idée fixe*, block, mental block, neurosis
COLLOQ. thing

hank n
skein, coil, loop, length, roll, piece, twist; *Scot* fank

hanker
■ **hanker after/for**
crave, hunger for, thirst for, want, wish for, desire, covet, yearn for, long for, pine for, itch for, set your heart on
COLLOQ. be dying for

hankering n
craving, hunger, thirst, wish, desire, yearning, longing, pining, itch, urge

hanky-panky n
mischief, trickery, tricks, deception, dishonesty, jiggery-pokery, nonsense, chicanery, subterfuge, devilry, affair, adultery
FORMAL machinations
COLLOQ. cheating, funny business, monkey business, shenanigans, carry-on, fooling around, bit on the side, slap and tickle, fling
SLANG nookie
₤3 openness

haphazard adj
random, chance, casual, arbitrary, hit-or-miss, hitty-missy, wild, indiscriminate, irregular, aimless, orderless, unsystematic, disorganized, disorderly, careless, slapdash, slipshod, unmethodical, unplanned, promiscuous, rough-and-tumble
OLD tumultuary
₤3 methodical, orderly

haphazardly adv
randomly, by chance, arbitrarily, carelessly, wildly, indiscriminately, irregularly, unmethodically, unsystematically, willy-nilly
COLLOQ. higgledy-piggledy

hapless adj
unlucky, unhappy, unfortunate, wretched, miserable, ill-fated, ill-starred, cursed, luckless, jinxed, star-crossed
₤3 lucky

happen v
1 OCCUR, take place, fall, arise, crop up, develop, present itself, turn up, go on, come about, come true, result, ensue, follow, turn out, appear, come into being
FORMAL transpire, supervene, eventuate
COLLOQ. materialize
2 *happen to do something*
have the good/bad luck to, have the good/bad fortune to
3 *happen on something*
find, discover, hit on, light on, stumble on, come/run across, chance on
COLLOQ. bump into
4 *I wonder what happened to my schoolfriend*
become of, be the fate of
OLD befall

happening n
occurrence, phenomenon, event, incident, episode,

occasion, adventure, experience, accident, chance, proceedings, circumstance, case, affair, thing, action, scene, business
FORMAL eventuality

happily adv
1 GLADLY, joyfully, merrily, cheerfully, gleefully, heartily, delightedly, contentedly, agreeably, enthusiastically, willingly
FORMAL joyously
2 FORTUNATELY, luckily, providentially, by chance, fittingly, as luck would have it
FORMAL auspiciously, opportunely, propitiously
₤3 **1, 2** unhappily

happiness n
joy, joyfulness, gladness, cheerfulness, cheeriness, contentment, pleasure, delight, enjoyment, gaiety, glee, life, merriment, merriness, light-heartedness, exuberance, high spirits, good spirits, elation, bliss, ecstasy, euphoria
FORMAL blitheness, felicity
₤3 unhappiness, sadness

Synonym nuances
The terms **joy** and **joyfulness** would be reserved for an intense feeling of happiness, whilst **gladness** has connotations of gratitude or relief: *she was full of gladness at her deliverance*. **Cheerfulness** and **cheeriness** suggest a happy disposition that is projected to others, whereas **contentment** has more to do with a more internalized satisfaction at a current state of affairs.
 The words **pleasure** and **delight** are appropriate for the gratification to be derived from something in particular: *his delight in music*, with **enjoyment** similarly suggesting happiness while undertaking an agreeable occupation. You can use **gaiety**, **merriment** and **merriness** to refer to a bright and lively state, particularly one that has been deliberately engendered: *the day is celebrated with traditional feasting and merriment*, whilst **glee** is connotative of a degree of mischievousness, if not maliciousness: *their rivals' defeat was greeted with glee*.
 Life, like **exuberance**, could be used of vivacity and a zest for living: *she was full of life and energy*; *the sheer exuberance of youth*; and **high spirits** is also connotative of a degree of friskiness and playfulness: *the exploits were undertaken with schoolboy high spirits*. **Light-heartedness**, which has similar associations with being carefree, would be appropriate for a less boisterously expressed emotion. **Elation** is more suggestive of exhilaration, whereas **bliss** and **ecstasy** imply an unworldly, exalted state of rapture: *sexual ecstasy*. **Euphoria** is also fairly extreme, but implies a highly exaggerated sense of happiness that is usually short-lived: *a year after the revolution the euphoria has faded*.

---

happy adj
1 JOYFUL, jolly, merry, cheerful, glad, pleased, delighted, thrilled, elated, ecstatic, rapturous, overjoyed, exuberant, gleeful, euphoric, satisfied, gratified, in good/high spirits, in a good mood, content, contented, gay, carefree, light-hearted, jovial, radiant, smiling, untroubled, unconcerned, unworried
FORMAL joyous, blithe
COLLOQ. chuffed, cock-a-hoop, on top of the world, happy as Larry/a sandboy, over the moon, on cloud nine, in seventh heaven, walking/floating on air, tickled pink; *N Am* happy as a clam
2 *a happy coincidence*
lucky, fortunate, favourable, advantageous, convenient, helpful, beneficial, appropriate, apt, fitting, proper, opportune
OLD seely

FORMAL felicitous, auspicious, propitious, apposite
Ea 1 unhappy, sad, discontented **2** unfortunate, inappropriate

happy-go-lucky adj
carefree, casual, nonchalant, easy-going, cheerful, devil-may-care, light-hearted, unconcerned, untroubled, unworried, reckless, irresponsible, heedless, improvident
FORMAL blithe, insouciant
Ea anxious, wary

harangue n, v
♦ n
diatribe, tirade, lecture, speech, address
FORMAL peroration, exhortation
♦ v
lecture, preach, hold forth, spout, address
FORMAL declaim

harass v
pester, badger, harry, plague, torment, hound, afflict, bait, chivvy, distract, distress, grind, harrow, pinch, dragoon, persecute, pursue, exasperate, vex, annoy, nag, provoke, antagonize, irritate, fret, bother, disturb, trouble, worry, stress, tire, wear out, exhaust, fatigue, weary, overdo, press, trash, infest; *Scot* pingle
OLD cark, dun, trounce, turmoil
FORMAL importune
COLLOQ. hassle, have it in for, put the wind up, put the frighteners on, drive round the bend/twist, breathe down someone's neck, give someone grief

---

Synonym nuances
Pester can be used especially of one person persistently annoying another, while **badger**, although similar, is generally used to achieve a specific objective: *he badgered her into going*. **Harry**, on the other hand, is more suggestive of being troubled or beset by numerous problems: *the harried executive forgot the meeting*. **Afflict**, **plague** and **torment** would be used where something is a constant source of extreme worry or distress.
 Hound and **pursue** are suggestive of being constantly chased: *the young star was hounded by the press*. **Chivvy** also suggests chasing after someone to make them do something: *busy young mothers chivvied and scolded their children*. **Dragoon** is appropriate where someone is being forced into something: *she was dragooned into helping with the housework*. The word **bait** can be used to imply more deliberate, spiteful harassing, especially when verbal; similarly **persecute** has to do with persistent bullying, but suggests a more extreme action.
 The term **nag** tends to suggest making continual reprimands, while **vex**, **annoy** and the stronger **exasperate** put more emphasis on the victim's reaction, in this case anger or frustration. **Worry** and **stress** are appropriate for putting under mental pressure and again put emphasis on the feelings of the victim. The terms **tire**, **wear out**, **exhaust** and **fatigue** could be used if harassment has worn down the victim's energy.

---

harassed adj
distraught, pressurized, pressured, stressed, under pressure, under stress, strained, distressed, troubled, worried, careworn, hounded, pestered, plagued, tormented, harried, vexed
COLLOQ. hassled, stressed-out, uptight
Ea carefree

harassment n
annoyance, nuisance, pestering, trouble, molest, molestation, persecution, pressuring, torment, bother, distress, aggravation, badgering, bedevilment, irritation, vexation

COLLOQ. hassle, grief
Ea assistance

harbinger n
herald, forerunner, precursor, messenger, omen, portent, warning, sign, indication, *avant-courier*
FORMAL foretoken

harbour n, v
♦ n
port, dock, quay, wharf, marina, mooring, anchorage, haven, shelter, refuge, lodging
♦ v
1 HIDE, conceal, protect, shield, shelter, house, take in
OLD herd; *Scot* reset
2 harbour a feeling
hold, retain, cling to, entertain, maintain, foster, nurse, bear, nurture, cherish, receive, believe, imagine

hard adj, adv
♦ adj
1 SOLID, firm, unyielding, tough, strong, dense, condensed, compressed, compact, compacted, impenetrable, resistant, stiff, rigid, inflexible, unpliable
COLLOQ. hard as stone/iron/rock
2 a hard question/problem
complicated, difficult, complex, involved, intricate, knotty, baffling, puzzling, perplexing, bewildering
3 building a wall is hard work
strenuous, difficult, arduous, onerous, laborious, tough, tiring, toilsome, exhausting, backbreaking, tiring, heavy, exacting, rigorous
4 HARSH, severe, strict, callous, unfeeling, unsympathetic, cruel, cold-hearted, hard-hearted, stern, tyrannical, oppressive, pitiless, merciless, ruthless, implacable, unsparing, unyielding, unrelenting, distressing, painful, unpleasant, grim
FORMAL obdurate
COLLOQ. hard as flint, standing no nonsense, ruling with a rod of iron
5 hard times
tough, unpleasant, difficult, harsh, grim, severe, painful, distressing, uncomfortable, disagreeable, austere
6 a hard worker
hard-working, industrious, diligent, assiduous, conscientious, zealous, enthusiastic, keen, busy, energetic
FORMAL sedulous
7 a hard push
forceful, powerful, strong, intense, heavy, sharp, violent
8 a hard winter
cold, severe, harsh, raw, bitter, freezing
9 hard evidence
true, reliable, indisputable, undeniable, unquestionable, definite, actual, certain, real, verified
10 hard drugs
addictive, harmful, habit-forming, narcotic, heavy, strong, potent
Ea 1 soft, yielding **2** easy, simple **4** kind, pleasant, compassionate, gentle **5** easy, comfortable **6** lazy, idle **8** mild **9** uncertain, unreliable
♦ adv
1 FORCEFULLY, powerfully, energetically, intensely, strongly, heavily, sharply, forcibly, violently, vigorously
FORMAL with all your might
2 work hard
diligently, industriously, assiduously, conscientiously, energetically, intensely, busily, enthusiastically, eagerly, keenly
3 look/think hard
carefully, attentively, closely, intently, sharply, keenly
4 a hard-won victory
with difficulty, arduously, strenuously, laboriously, after a struggle, vigorously
5 the recession hit them hard

severely, acutely, critically, badly, intensely, deeply, harshly

6 snowing hard
intensely, severely, strongly, heavily, steadily
≢3 carelessly **4** effortlessly **5, 6** lightly

■ **hard and fast**
binding, fixed, definite, immutable, incontrovertible, inflexible, invariable, rigid, set, strict, stringent, unalterable, unchangeable, unchanging, uncompromising
≢ flexible

■ **hard up**
penniless, impoverished, in the red, bankrupt, short, lacking
FORMAL impecunious
COLLOQ. broke, bust, stony broke, skint, cleaned out, strapped (for cash), on your uppers, on your beam ends, not having two pennies to rub together, dirt-poor
≢ rich

hard-bitten adj
callous, case-hardened, cynical, down-to-earth, hard-boiled, hard-headed, hard-nosed, toughened, inured, matter-of-fact, practical, realistic, ruthless, shrewd, tough, unsentimental
≢ callow

hard-boiled adj
tough, cynical, hard-headed, down-to-earth, unsentimental

hard-core adj
steadfast, dedicated, blatant, obstinate, rigid, staunch, explicit, extreme, intransigent, dyed-in-the-wool, diehard
≢ moderate

harden v
solidify, set, freeze, congeal, bake, cake, stiffen, petrify, strengthen, reinforce, concrete, buttress, brace, steel, gird, nerve, toughen, temper, deaden, season, accustom, train, inure, indurate, flesh
TECHNICAL anneal, vulcanize, calcify, case-harden, work-harden, chill, sclerose
OLD bronze; (Spenser) endure
FORMAL fortify, habituate, indurate
≢ soften, weaken

hardened adj
incorrigible, inveterate, irredeemable, seasoned, set, shameless, toughened, inured, reprobate, habitual, accustomed, habituated, chronic, unfeeling, callous
FORMAL obdurate
≢ soft, callow

hard-headed adj
shrewd, astute, businesslike, sharp, level-headed, clear-thinking, cool-headed, sensible, realistic, rational, pragmatic, practical, hard-bitten, hard-boiled, tough, unsentimental, down-to-earth
COLLOQ. hard-nosed
≢ unrealistic, sentimental, idealistic, impractical

hard-hearted adj
callous, unfeeling, uncaring, unconcerned, unkind, cold, hard, stony, stony-hearted, heartless, hard, unsympathetic, cruel, inhuman, pitiless, merciless
OLD (Shakesp) flint-heart
≢ kind, merciful, compassionate, concerned

hard-hitting adj
bold, direct, blunt, forthright, frank, straight, vigorous, forceful, tough, uncompromising, condemnatory, critical, unsparing,
COLLOQ. no-holds-barred, pulling no punches
≢ mild

hardihood n
boldness, audacity, adventurousness, daring, enterprise, courage, rashness, recklessness, risk, bravery, fearlessness,

intrepidity, dauntlessness, valour, pluck
COLLOQ. bottle, guts, grit
≢ caution, reserve, timidity

hardiness n
robustness, toughness, resilience, resolution, boldness, courage, valour, ruggedness, sturdiness, intrepidity
FORMAL fortitude
≢ timidity

hardline adj
strict, tough, extreme, immoderate, inflexible, militant, uncompromising, unyielding, undeviating
FORMAL intransigent
≢ moderate, flexible

hardly adv
barely, scarcely, just, only just, not quite, not at all, almost not, by no means, none too, with difficulty; Scot jimp, jimply
OLD uneath

hardness n
toughness, severity, harshness, sternness, firmness, rigidity, difficulty, laboriousness, insensitivity, pitilessness, inhumanity, coldness
≢ ease, mildness, softness

hard-nosed adj
hard-boiled, hard-headed, hard-bitten, tough, ruthless, realistic, practical, unsentimental
COLLOQ. no-nonsense

hard-pressed adj
hard-pushed, hard put, harassed, harried, pushed, under pressure, under stress, overburdened, overtaxed
COLLOQ. up against it, in a corner, in a tight spot, between a rock and a hard place, with your back to the wall
≢ untroubled

hardship n
misfortune, adversity, trouble, difficulty, affliction, pain, distress, suffering, burdens, trial, want, need, austerity, poverty, destitution, deprivation, misery
FORMAL tribulation, privation
≢ ease, comfort, prosperity

hardware n
apparatus, equipment, gear, supplies, tackle, kit, tools, outfit, paraphernalia, accessories, appliances, articles, furniture
FORMAL accoutrements, apparelment
COLLOQ. rig-out, stuff, things

hard-wearing adj
durable, lasting, well-made, made/built to last, strong, tough, sturdy, stout, rugged, resilient
≢ delicate

hard-working adj
industrious, diligent, assiduous, conscientious, enthusiastic, keen, zealous, busy, energetic
FORMAL sedulous
COLLOQ. with your nose to the grindstone
≢ idle, lazy

hardy adj
1 STRONG, tough, sturdy, durable, heavy-duty, robust, vigorous, fit, sound, healthy, indurate, indurated, iron-sided
2 BRAVE, courageous, plucky, fearless, undaunted, bold, daring, intrepid, stalwart, stoical, stout, stout-hearted, heroic, indomitable, trusty
≢ 1 weak, tender **2** cowardly, unfaithful, fickle

hare-brained adj
foolish, stupid, silly, wild, daft, ill-conceived, careless, rash, reckless, inane, giddy
COLLOQ. half-baked, crackpot, scatty, scatterbrained
≢ sensible

hark *v*

listen, hear, give ear, mark, note, notice, pay attention, pay heed
OLD hearken

■ **hark back**

remember, recall, recollect, go back, turn back, revert
FORMAL regress

harlequin *n*

fool, jester, clown, comic, buffoon, zany, jester, joker

harlot *n*

prostitute, callgirl, whore, trollop
OLD hussy, strumpet, wagtail
COLLOQ. pro, streetwalker, tramp, hooker, working girl
OLD COLLOQ. fallen woman, loose woman
SLANG scrubber, tart, slapper, slag

harm *n, v*

◆ *n*

damage, loss, injury, hurt, pain, detriment, ill, misfortune, adversity, suffering, ruin, destruction, loss, wrong, abuse, impairment, disservice
Fз benefit, service

◆ *v*

damage, impair, work against, blemish, spoil, mar, ruin, hurt, destroy, injure, wound, ill-treat, maltreat, abuse, molest, misuse, be detrimental to
Fз benefit, improve

harmful *adj*

damaging, detrimental, bad, pernicious, unhealthy, unwholesome, injurious, wounding, dangerous, hazardous, poisonous, toxic, destructive
FORMAL noxious, deleterious
Fз harmless

harmless *adj*

safe, innocuous, non-toxic, inoffensive, gentle, mild, blameless, innocent, -friendly
Fз harmful, dangerous, destructive

harmonious *adj*

1 MELODIOUS, tuneful, musical, sweet-sounding, harmonizing, rhythmic, symphonious, euphonious, dulcet, pleasant, mellow
FORMAL mellifluous, consonous, symphonious
2 MATCHING, co-ordinated, balanced, compatible, consistent
OLD according
FORMAL congruous, consonant
COLLOQ. in sync
3 *a harmonious relationship*
agreeable, cordial, amiable, amicable, friendly, sympathetic, like-minded, peaceful, peaceable, compatible, Apollonian
FORMAL concordant, concordial, concinnous
Fз **1** discordant

harmoniously *adv*

1 *racial groups in the population that exist together harmoniously*
amicably, cordially, agreeably, sympathetically, peacefully, compatibly, in a balanced way
2 *colours that blend harmoniously*
in a balanced way, symmetrically, consistently, compatibly
FORMAL congruously

harmonization *n*

co-ordination, matching, balancing, correspondence, reconciliation, agreement, accommodation, adaptation, arrangement

harmonize *v*

match, co-ordinate, balance, mix, blend, fit in, suit, tone, correspond, go together, get on with, agree, reconcile, coincide, accommodate, adapt, arrange, compose

FORMAL be congruous, be congruent, accord
Fз clash, conflict

harmony *n*

1 TUNEFULNESS, tune, melody, melodiousness, euphony, chiming
OLD concent
FORMAL mellifluousness
2 *live in harmony*
agreement, unison, unanimity, oneness, unity, compatibility, like-mindedness, peace, goodwill, rapport, sympathy, understanding, amicability, tune, friendliness, co-operation
FORMAL accord, concord, amity, assent, concurrence
3 CO-ORDINATION, balance, blending, symmetry, correspondence, conformity, consistency, keeping
FORMAL concord, consonance, concinnity
Fз **1** discord **2** conflict

harness *n, v*

◆ *n*

tackle, gear, equipment, straps, tack
FORMAL accoutrements
See panel at **tack**.

◆ *v*

control, channel, use, utilize, exploit, make use of, employ, mobilize, apply

■ **in harness**

1 CO-OPERATING, in co-operation, collaborating, together
2 *back in harness*
at work, working, busy, active, employed

harp

■ **harp on**

go/keep on about, keep talking about, dwell on, labour, belabour the point, press, reiterate, renew, repeat, nag
COLLOQ. go on and on about, flog to death

harpoon *n*

arrow, barb, dart, spear, trident, grains

harridan *n*

virago, vixen, witch, dragon, harpy, nag, scold, shrew, tartar, fury, gorgon, termagant, Xanthippe, hell-cat
COLLOQ. battle-axe

harried *adj*

worried, anxious, agitated, troubled, bothered, distressed, harassed, hard-pressed, pressured, pressurized, plagued, tormented, ravaged, beset
COLLOQ. hassled
Fз untroubled

harrowing *adj*

distressing, upsetting, heart-rending, disturbing, alarming, daunting, tormenting, frightening, terrifying, nerve-racking, traumatic, agonizing, excruciating
FORMAL perturbing
Fз encouraging, heartening

harry *v*

badger, pester, nag, chivvy, harass, oppress, plague, hound, torment, persecute, annoy, vex, worry, trouble, bother, pressurize, disturb, molest
COLLOQ. hassle

harsh *adj*

1 SEVERE, austere, barren, stark, bitter, bleak, grim, comfortless, desolate, wild, inhospitable, spartan
2 CRUEL, strict, abrasive, severe, stern, grim, savage, brutal, unsympathetic, unfeeling, unkind, hard, inhuman, pitiless, ruthless, merciless, Draconian
FORMAL acerbic
3 *a harsh sound*
rasping, rough, coarse, croaking, guttural, hoarse, gruff, grinding, grating, jarring, jangling, discordant, strident, ear-piercing, raucous, sharp, shrill, unpleasant, dissonant, metallic

4 BRIGHT, dazzling, glaring, showy, flashy, gaudy, lurid, garish, bold
Ⅎ **1** mild, comfortable **2** compassionate, feeling, lenient **3** harmonious, soft, gentle **4** gentle

---

Synonym nuances
sense 1
Severe can be widely applied as a synonym of harsh, while **austere** and **spartan** have implications of lacking embellishments: *prisons should be austere but decent.* **Barren** goes even further by suggesting being totally bare: *a barren rolling landscape,* whilst **stark** returns to the idea of being completely unadorned. You could use **bitter** to suggest physical or mental pain: *we were buffeted by bitter winds,* or if you want to imply acrimony: *a bitter argument.*
  Bleak is more suggestive of physical emptiness or psychological pessimism: *a bleak forecast for the economy.* **Grim** strongly suggests a lack of respite or hope, while **comfortless** would more explicitly convey a lack of physical or mental ease: *a comfortless bed; comfortless days.* **Desolate** has echoes of loneliness or forlornness: *a desolate wasteland of charred tree-stumps,* whereas **wild** would be applied to a landscape or conditions that are untamed and hostile.

---

harshly *adv*
1 *harshly treated*
cruelly, brutally, unkindly, severely, sternly, grimly, ruthlessly, pitilessly, mercilessly, unsympathetically
2 *sounds that grate harshly*
roughly, hoarsely, gruffly, discordantly, stridently, sharply, unpleasantly
Ⅎ **1** compassionately, comfortably, leniently **2** harmoniously, softly, gently

harshness *n*
bitterness, acrimony, coarseness, roughness, severity, ill-temper, rigour, starkness, sternness, strictness, hardness, sourness, abrasiveness, brutality
FORMAL acerbity, asperity
Ⅎ mildness, softness, gentleness

harum-scarum *adj*
reckless, hasty, rash, impetuous, irresponsible, ill-considered, imprudent, wild, careless, haphazard, erratic
FORMAL precipitate
COLLOQ. hare-brained, scatterbrained, scatty
Ⅎ sensible

harvest *n, v*
◆ *n*
1 HARVEST-TIME, autumn, ingathering, reaping, harvesting, harvest-home, collection, store, supply, stock, accumulation, horde, rabi, *Spätlese*, vendange; *dialect* hockey; *Scot* hairst, kirn, tattie-lifting, tattie-howking
2 CROP, yield, return, produce, product, fruits, result, consequence, effect, returns
◆ *v*
reap, mow, pick, glean, pluck, garner, gather (in), ingather, in, silage, collect, accumulate, amass, horde, gain, obtain, acquire, secure

hash *n*
1 MESS, botch, muddle, bungle, mix-up, jumble, confusion, mismanagement, hotchpotch, mishmash
2 GOULASH, stew, hotpot, lobscouse, lob's course

hashish *n*
hash, hemp, marijuana, bhang, cannabis
COLLOQ. dope, ganja, grass, pot, weed

hassle *n, v*
◆ *n*
bother, inconvenience, nuisance, difficulty, trouble, problem, struggle, argument, disagreement, quarrel, squabble, trial, upset, fight, dispute, bickering, wrangle
FORMAL altercation
COLLOQ. aggro
Ⅎ agreement, peace
◆ *v*
bother, pester, trouble, annoy, badger, harass, hound, harry, chivvy
COLLOQ. bug, breathe down someone's neck, give someone grief
Ⅎ assist, calm

hassled *adj*
harassed, distraught, pressurized, pressured, stressed, under pressure, under stress, strained, distressed, troubled, worried, careworn, hounded, pestered, plagued, tormented, harried, vexed
COLLOQ. stressed-out, uptight

haste *n*
hurry, rush, hustle, bustle, speed, velocity, rapidity, swiftness, quickness, briskness, fastness, urgency, rashness, recklessness, carelessness, foolhardiness, impulsiveness, impetuosity
FORMAL alacrity, celerity, expeditiousness
▪ in haste
fast, quickly, rapidly, speedily, promptly, straightaway, apace
Ⅎ slowness

hasten *v*
hurry (up), be quick, go fast/quickly, rush, run, sprint, dash, tear, race, fly, bolt, accelerate, speed (up), quicken, dispatch, urge, assist, help, aid, boost, press, advance, forward, step up, push forward
OLD make haste
FORMAL expedite, precipitate
COLLOQ. get a move on, step on it/the gas, hotfoot it, put your foot down
Ⅎ dawdle, delay

hastily *adv*
1 RASHLY, recklessly, hurriedly, impetuously, heedlessly, impulsively
FORMAL precipitately
2 FAST, quickly, rapidly, hurriedly, speedily, promptly, straightaway, apace
COLLOQ. double-quick, chop-chop
Ⅎ **1** carefully, deliberately **2** slowly

hasty *adj*
1 *a hasty decision*
hurried, rushed, rash, reckless, heedless, thoughtless, careless, impetuous, impulsive, impatient, headlong, hotheaded
FORMAL precipitate
2 *a hasty look at the newspaper*
fast, quick, rapid, swift, speedy, rushed, hurried, brisk, prompt, short, brief, cursory, fleeting, transitory, perfunctory
FORMAL expeditious
Ⅎ **1** careful, deliberate **2** slow

hat
See panel on next page

hatch *v*
1 INCUBATE, brood, sit on, breed
2 CONCOCT, formulate, originate, think up, dream up, invent, conceive, devise, contrive, plot, scheme, design, plan, project

hatchet *n*
axe, chopper, cleaver, tomahawk, battle-axe, mattock, pickaxe, machete

hate *v, n*
◆ *v*
1 DISLIKE, despise, detest, loathe, abhor, not stand, recoil

Hats include:

Balaclava	cahperon	glengarry	mob cap	sailor hat	ten-gallon hat
balmoral	chapka	helmet	montero	school cap	top hat
baseball cap	cheesecutter	Homburg	mortarboard	shako	toque
beanie	cloche	hood	muffin-cap	skullcap	toy
bearskin	*Scot* cockernony	*Scot* hummle	*Scot* mutch	snood	trencher cap
beret	cock's-comb	bonnet	nightcap	sombrero	trilby
biggin	college cap	hunting-cap	panama	sou'wester	tuque
biretta	deerstalker	jockey cap	peaked cap	Stetson®	turban
boater	*N Am* derby	kalpak	picture hat	stovepipe hat	yarmulka
bonnet	*S Afr* doek	kepi	pileus	straw hat	
bowler	fedora	Kilmarnock	pillbox	sunhat	
Bronx hat	fez	Kilmarnock cowl	*N Am* poke-	taj	
busby	flat cap	mitre	bonnet	tammy	
bycoket	forage cap	mitre-wort	pork-pie hat	Tam o' Shanter	

from, have an aversion to, feel revulsion at, spite
FORMAL abominate, execrate
COLLOQ. hate someone's guts
2 *I hate to disturb you*
regret, apologize, be sorry, be reluctant, be unwilling, be loath
F3 **1** like, love
♦ *n*
hatred, aversion, dislike, loathing, abhorrence, animosity, ill-will, grudge, bitterness, resentment, antagonism, hostility, enmity, spite
FORMAL abomination, rancour
F3 liking, love
■ **pet hate**
bugbear, anathema, bane, bête noire, dread, fiend, horror, nightmare, bogle, bogy, poker, rawhead

> **Synonym nuances**
> *verb sense 1*
> **Dislike** is a fairly mild term for something simply being displeasing, whilst **despise** is far stronger and implies an element of contempt. Both **detest** and **loathe** would similarly refer to something deeply felt, suggesting extreme hatred, while **not stand** is also suggestive of an inability to bear: *she could not stand the sight of him, so she left the room.* **Recoil from** and **have an aversion to** put the emphasis on being more instinctively repulsed: *we recoil from the prospect of people suffering*, while **feel revulsion at** is even more strongly suggestive of complete abhorrence and disgust: *we feel some revulsion at these discriminatory policies.*

hateful *adj*
horrid, horrible, loathsome, detestable, abominable, offensive, disgusting, repellent, repugnant, obnoxious, odious, revolting, repulsive, nasty, unpleasant, disagreeable, despicable, vile, contemptible, foul, evil
FORMAL abhorrent, execrable, heinous
F3 pleasing

hatred *n*
hate, aversion, dislike, abhorrence, loathing, disgust, revulsion, animosity, ill-will, grudge, bitterness, resentment, antagonism, hostility, enmity, spite
FORMAL detestation, repugnance, abomination, execration, rancour, antipathy, animus
F3 liking, love

haughtily *adv*
arrogantly, proudly, imperiously, superciliously, disdainfully, contemptuously, scornfully, cavalierly
COLLOQ. snootily
F3 humbly

haughtiness *n*
arrogance, pride, conceit, contempt, contemptuousness, disdain, aloofness, loftiness, snobbishness,

superciliousness, airs, hauteur, insolence, pomposity
FORMAL hubris
COLLOQ. snootiness
F3 friendliness, humility

haughty *adj*
arrogant, proud, conceited, vain, swollen-headed, lofty, imperious, high, lordly, stiff-necked, supercilious, cavalier, cavalierish, contemptuous, disdainful, scornful, superior, self-important, egotistical, overbearing, condescending, patronizing, snobbish, assuming; *Scot* paughty
OLD fastuous, haught, superb, orgulous, stomachful, stomachous, stomachy; (*Shakesp*) surly
COLLOQ. snooty, stuck-up, high and mighty, hoity-toity, with your nose in the air, toploftical, on your high horse
F3 humble, modest

haul *v, n*
♦ *v*
pull, heave, tug, draw, tow, drag, trail, move, transport, convey, ship, convoy, carry, cart, lug, push
COLLOQ. hump
♦ *n*
loot, booty, plunder, spoils, takings, gain, yield, find
SLANG swag

haunches *n*
thighs, hips, buttocks, rear end, rump, nates, huckles, hucks, hunkers

haunt *v, n*
♦ *v*
1 *a ghost haunts the house*
walk, visit, appear often in, materialize, spook, possess, curse
OLD (*Shakesp*) spright
COLLOQ. show up
2 FREQUENT, patronize, spend time in, visit (regularly)
COLLOQ. hang about/around in
3 *memories haunted her*
plague, torment, trouble, disturb, worry, burden, recur, prey on, beset, harry, oppress, obsess, possess
♦ *n*
resort, stamping-ground, den, local, meeting-place, rendezvous, favourite spot; *Scot* howf
COLLOQ. hangout

haunted *adj*
1 POSSESSED, cursed, eerie, ghostly, jinxed, hag-ridden
COLLOQ. spooky
2 TROUBLED, worried, plagued, tormented, obsessed, preoccupied

haunting *adj*
memorable, unforgettable, persistent, recurrent, evocative, nostalgic, atmospheric, poignant
F3 unmemorable

hauteur *n*
arrogance, pride, conceit, contempt, contemptuousness, disdain, aloofness, loftiness, snobbishness,

superciliousness, airs, insolence, pomposity
FORMAL hubris
COLLOQ. snootiness

have v
1 OWN, possess, get, obtain, gain, be given, acquire, secure, take, receive, accept, keep, hold, use
FORMAL procure
2 FEEL, experience, enjoy, suffer, undergo, submit to, be subjected to, endure, tolerate, put up with, go through, find, meet, encounter
3 CONTAIN, include, take in, embody, incorporate, consist of
FORMAL comprise, embrace, comprehend
4 *have a party*
hold, arrange, organize, take part in, participate in
5 *have to go now*
must, be forced, be compelled, be obliged, be required, ought, should
6 *have someone do something*
cause to, make, arrange, get, oblige, require, persuade, talk into, ask, tell, request, order, command, bid, force, compel, coerce
FORMAL enjoin, prevail upon
7 *I've had measles*
suffer from, get, develop, become infected with
FORMAL contract, succumb to
8 *have an invitation to the party*
receive, get, obtain, be given, gain, acquire
9 *have pity on someone*
show, demonstrate, display, exhibit, express, feel
FORMAL manifest
10 *have food/drink*
eat, swallow, consume, take, drink, devour, down, gulp, guzzle
FORMAL partake of
COLLOQ. put away, tuck into, knock back, wolf down
11 *have a baby*
give birth to, bear, bring into the world, be delivered of
OLD beget, bring forth
12 *I won't have such behaviour*
tolerate, put up with, take, accept, allow, permit, endure, abide, brook
COLLOQ. stand
13 *you've been had*
deceive, dupe, fool, trick, cheat, swindle, take in
COLLOQ. con, diddle
F3 **1** lack

▪ **have done with**
finish with, give up, stop, cease, be through with
FORMAL desist
COLLOQ. throw over, wash your hands of

▪ **have had it**
be in trouble, have no hope, be defeated, be exhausted, be lost, have no chance of success
COLLOQ. bite the dust, come to a sticky end

▪ **have on**
1 WEAR, be dressed in, be clothed in
2 *What have you got on this week?*
have an engagement, have an appointment, have arranged, have planned
3 TEASE, trick, play a joke on
COLLOQ. kid, rag, pull someone's leg, lead up the garden path, wind someone up
SLANG take for a ride

haven n
harbour, port, dock, bay, anchorage, shelter, refuge, sanctuary, asylum, retreat, oasis

haversack n
backpack, rucksack, knapsack, kitbag

havoc n
chaos, confusion, disorder, disruption, mayhem, damage, destruction, ruin, ruination, wreck, wreckage, rack

and ruin, devastation, waste, ravaging, desolation
FORMAL despoliation
COLLOQ. shambles

hawk[1] n
hawks and other birds of prey
buzzard, kite, harrier, sparrowhawk, falcon, haggard, goshawk, tercel
Related adjective: accipitrine

hawk[2] v
hawking goods at people's houses
sell, offer for sale, peddle, market, offer, cry, tout, vend, bark

hawker n
seller, trader, dealer, pedlar, vendor, door-to-door salesman, crier, huckster, colporteur, barrow-boy, chapman, costermonger, coster

haywire adj
wrong, out of control, crazy, mad, wild, chaotic, confused, disordered, disorganized, tangled, topsy-turvy

hazard n, v
♦ n
risk, danger, jeopardy, menace, threat, deathtrap, pitfall, accident, chance, luck
OLD venture, wager, risque; (*Shakesp*) jump; (*Spenser*) hazardize
FORMAL peril, endangerment
F3 safety
♦ v
1 RISK, endanger, jeopardize, expose to danger, put at risk, put in jeopardy
OLD wage
2 CHANCE, gamble, stake, venture, suggest, put forward, submit, offer, speculate
OLD wage

hazardous adj
risky, dangerous, unsafe, precarious, menacing, threatening, insecure, chancy, uncertain, unpredictable, difficult, tricky
OLD jeopardous
FORMAL perilous
COLLOQ. hairy
F3 safe, secure

hazardously adv
dangerously, riskily, precariously, insecurely, uncertainly, unpredictably
OLD jeopardously
FORMAL perilously
F3 safely, securely

haze n
1 MIST, fog, smog, cloud, steam, vapour, film, mistiness, fogginess, cloudiness, smokiness, dimness, obscurity
2 BLUR, confusion, muddle, bewilderment, daze, uncertainty, indistinctness, vagueness

hazy adj
misty, foggy, smoky, clouded, cloudy, overcast, milky, fuzzy, blurred, muzzy, ill-defined, veiled, obscure, dim, faint, unclear, indistinct, vague, indefinite, uncertain
F3 clear, bright, definite

head n, adj, v
♦ n
1 SKULL, cranium
TECHNICAL caput
OLD (*Shakesp*) mazard, pash
COLLOQ. noddle, nut, conk, bonce
Related adjectives: capital, cephalic
2 MIND, brain, mentality, mental abilities, intellect, intelligence, wit(s), sense, understanding, wisdom, thought, reasoning, common sense

COLLOQ. brains, loaf, noddle, little grey cells, grey matter, upper storey
3 TOP, peak, summit, crown, crest, tip, apex, vertex, height, climax
4 FRONT, fore, forefront, vanguard, van, lead
5 LEADER, chief, captain, commander, director, manager, managing director, superintendent, supervisor, principal, head teacher, headmaster, headmistress, ruler, controller, administrator, president, governor, chair, chairman, chairwoman, chairperson
COLLOQ. boss, big cheese, bigwig, top banana
6 COMMAND, control(s), leadership, directorship, management, supervision, charge
7 *have a head for figures*
gift, talent, genius, flair, skill, aptitude, aptness, bent, knack, facility, endowment, proficiency, power, faculty, attribute, ability, capability, capacity
8 *come to a head*
crisis, critical point, climax, emergency, catastrophe, calamity, dilemma
COLLOQ. crunch
9 *the head of a river*
source, origin, fount, spring, rise, wellspring, wellhead
10 *no head on the beer*
froth, foam, bubbles, fizz, suds, lather
E3 1 foot, tail **3** base, foot **4** back **5** subordinate
• *adj*
leading, front, foremost, first, chief, main, prime, principal, top, topmost, highest, supreme, premier, dominant, pre-eminent
• *v*
1 *head the queue*
be at the front of, be first in, go first, lead
2 LEAD, rule, govern, command, direct, be in charge of, be in control of, manage, run, superintend, oversee, supervise, administer, control, guide, steer
■ **head for**
make for, go/move/travel towards, direct towards, go in the direction of, aim for, point to, turn for, steer for
■ **head off**
forestall, intercept, intervene, deflect, divert, turn aside, cut off, fend off, ward off, avert, prevent, stop
FORMAL interpose
■ **head over heels**
completely, utterly, uncontrollably, wholeheartedly, recklessly, thoroughly, intensely, wildly
■ **head up**
lead, direct, manage, be in charge of, take charge of, be responsible for
■ **go to your head**
1 MAKE DRUNK, intoxicate, inebriate, make dizzy, befuddle
COLLOQ. make woozy
2 *success has gone to his head*
make arrogant, make conceited, make proud, make someone full of themselves
COLLOQ. puff up
■ **keep your head**
keep calm, stay calm and collected, keep control of yourself, keep/maintain your composure
COLLOQ. keep your cool
■ **lose your head**
panic, lose control of yourself, lose your composure
COLLOQ. lose your cool, flap, freak out, go round like a headless chicken

headache *n*
1 *suffer from headaches*
migraine, neuralgia
TECHNICAL cephalalgia, hemicrania
COLLOQ. splitter
2 BOTHER, nuisance, trouble, inconvenience, problem, worry, pest, vexation, bane
COLLOQ. hassle, pain in the neck

heading *n*
title, name, headline, rubric, caption, section, division, classification, subject, category, class, head

headland *n*
promontory, cape, head, point, ness, foreland

headlong *adj, adv*
• *adj*
hasty, impetuous, impulsive, rash, reckless, careless, impulsive, dangerous, breakneck, head-first
FORMAL precipitate
• *adv*
head first, hurriedly, hastily, prematurely, rashly, recklessly, carelessly, heedlessly, impetuously, impulsively, thoughtlessly, without thinking, wildly
FORMAL precipitately

headman *n*
chief, leader, captain, ruler, chieftain, muqaddam, sachem

head-on *adj*
a head-on crash/confrontation
direct, full-frontal, straight-on, straight
COLLOQ. eyeball-to-eyeball

headquarters *n*
HQ, base (camp), head office, main office, centre of operations, nerve centre

headstone *n*
gravestone, tombstone, memorial, plaque

headstrong *adj*
stubborn, obstinate, intractable, wayward, pigheaded, wilful, self-willed, not listening to reason, perverse, contrary, unruly, ungovernable
FORMAL obdurate, refractory, recalcitrant, intransigent
E3 tractable, docile

headway *n*
advance, progress, ground, way, improvement, movement, development

heady *adj*
intoxicating, strong, stimulating, overpowering, exhilarating, invigorating, thrilling, exciting, potent, ecstatic, euphoric, rousing

heal *v*
cure, make better, make well, remedy, mend, restore, improve, treat, soothe, comfort, salve, settle, reconcile, make good, patch up, put/set right
FORMAL assuage, palliate

health *n*
fitness, constitution, form, shape, trim, fettle, condition, tone, state, healthiness, good condition, wellbeing, welfare, good shape, soundness, robustness, strength, vigour
OLD sanity
E3 illness, infirmity

healthily *adv*
well, soundly, robustly, strongly, vigorously, in condition, in good shape, in fine fettle

healthy *adj*
1 WELL, fit, good, fine, in condition, in good shape, in fine fettle, sound, sturdy, robust, strong, vigorous, hale, hale and hearty, blooming, flourishing, thriving, able-bodied, healthsome, jolly
OLD lustick, well-disposed
COLLOQ. hardy, fit as a fiddle, right as rain, in the pink, a picture of health
2 *healthy food*
wholesome, nutritious, nourishing, bracing, good, beneficial, invigorating, healthful
OLD (*Spenser*) hartie-hale
3 *healthy fresh air*
bracing, invigorating, refreshing, stimulating

FORMAL salubrious
4 _a healthy economy_
successful, strong, sound, robust, vigorous
5 _a healthy respect for authority_
wise, sensible, prudent, sound
FORMAL judicious
E3 1 ill, sick, infirm **2** _colloq._ junk **4** ailing

Synonym nuances
sense 1
Well, **good** and **fine** are suggestive of being in satisfactory rather then remarkable health, and tend to be used in answer to inquiries: _he was a bit poorly at the weekend, but now he's fine._ **Sound** has the narrower suggestion of being unimpaired, but has added implications of constant good health: _you are overweight but otherwise sound._
  The terms **robust** and **strong** could be used of someone or something with a healthy, working constitution, whilst **sturdy** is more suggestive of a strong physical build. **Fit** is generally used to suggest being in good condition and able to take on physical challenges, or you could use **vigorous** to emphasize the energy afforded by someone's good health.
  The terms **blooming**, **flourishing** and **thriving** could be applied to anyone or anything progressing in a successful manner: _the flourishing tourist industry._ You would use **able-bodied** specifically to describe a person without any disability or physical impediments.

---

heap _n, v_
♦ _n_
1 MOUND, pile, stack, mountain, lot, mass, bundle, accumulation, collection, hoard, stockpile, supply, store, bulk, cumulus, cairn, drift, rick, ruck, clamp, pit, congeries, imbroglio; _dialect_ bing, tass; _Scot_ rickle, toorie
OLD acervation, quarry, raff
FORMAL assemblage, agglomeration
2 A LOT, great deal, plenty, abundance, quantities, lots, mass, lashings; _N Am_ raft
COLLOQ. load(s), stack(s), tons, oodles, pot(s), millions, scores
♦ _v_
1 PILE, stack, mound, bank, build, amass, accumulate, cumulate, collect, gather, assemble, hoard, stockpile, store (up), load, burden, lumber, mow, ruck, congest, uphoard
TECHNICAL coacervate
2 _heap criticism/praise on someone_
shower, lavish
FORMAL confer, bestow

hear _v_
1 LISTEN, catch, pick up, make out, get, perceive, be in touch with, overhear, eavesdrop, heed, pay attention, take in
COLLOQ. latch onto
2 LEARN, find out, discover, pick up, understand, gather, be informed, be told
FORMAL ascertain
3 JUDGE, pass judgement, try, examine, investigate, consider, inquire, adjudicate

hearing _n_
1 EARSHOT, sound, range, hearing distance, reach, ear, perception
2 _gave him a fair hearing_
opportunity to speak, opportunity to express yourself, chance to speak
3 TRIAL, inquiry, investigation, examination, review, case, judgement, inquest, inquisition, adjudication, audition, interview, audience

hearsay _n_
rumour, word of mouth, talk, common talk, common

knowledge, gossip, tittle-tattle, report, say-so, _on-dit_
COLLOQ. buzz

heart _n_
1 SOUL, mind, character, disposition, nature, temperament
2 FEELING, emotion, sentiment, love, affection, passion, tenderness, kindness, compassion, concern, sympathy, pity, responsiveness, warmth
3 _lose heart_
courage, bravery, boldness, heroism, fearlessness, intrepidity, pluck, stout-heartedness, spirit, resolution, determination, enthusiasm, eagerness, keenness
FORMAL fortitude
COLLOQ. guts, bottle, spunk
4 CENTRE, middle, core, substance, kernel, nucleus, hub, nub, crux, essence, essential part, pith, marrow
FORMAL quintessence
E3 3 cowardice **4** periphery
Related adjective: cardiac
■ **at heart**
basically, really, fundamentally, essentially, in essence, at bottom
■ **by heart**
by rote, parrot-fashion, pat, off pat, from memory, word for word, verbatim
■ **change of heart**
change of mind, rethink, second thoughts
■ **from the bottom of your heart**
deeply, sincerely, passionately, fervently, earnestly, profoundly, devoutly
■ **heart and soul**
eagerly, enthusiastically, completely, unreservedly, wholeheartedly, devotedly, gladly, heartily, absolutely, entirely
■ **set your heart on**
wish for, long for, desire, yearn, crave
■ **take heart**
be encouraged, brighten up, cheer up, rally, revive
COLLOQ. buck up, perk up
■ **take to heart**
be affected by, be moved by, be upset by, be disturbed by

**Parts of the heart include**:

aortic valve	left pulmonary	right pulmonary
ascending aorta	veins	veins
bicuspid valve	left ventricle	right ventricle
carotid artery	mitral valve	superior vena
descending	myocardium	cava
thoracic aorta	papillary muscle	tricuspid valve
epicardium	pericardium	ventricular
inferior vena cava	pulmonary valve	septum
left atrium	right atrium	
left pulmonary	right pulmonary	
artery	artery	

---

heartache _n_
sorrow, anxiety, worry, grief, despair, anguish, agony, heartbreak, pain, suffering, despondency, dejection, bitterness, distress, remorse, torment, torture
FORMAL affliction

heartbreak _n_
distress, sadness, suffering, sorrow, dejection, despair, pain, grief, misery, agony, anguish, desolation
E3 elation, joy, relief

heartbreaking _adj_
distressing, sad, tragic, harsh, harrowing, heart-rending, pitiful, agonizing, painful, excruciating, grievous, bitter, cruel, disappointing, poignant
E3 heartwarming, heartening

heartbroken _adj_
broken-hearted, desolate, sad, miserable, sorrowful, in

low spirits, dejected, despondent, downcast, suffering, crestfallen, disappointed, disheartened, dispirited, grieved, desolate, crushed, anguished
E3 delighted, elated

heartburn n
indigestion, cardialgia, dyspepsia, brash
TECHNICAL peptic/reflux oesophagitis

hearten v
comfort, console, reassure, cheer (up), encourage, boost, inspire, invigorate, stimulate, energize, revitalize, animate, rouse, raise the spirits of
COLLOQ. buck up, pep up
E3 dishearten, depress, dismay

heartening adj
cheering, heartwarming, encouraging, uplifting, gladdening, touching, moving, affecting, pleasing, gratifying, rewarding, satisfying

heartfelt adj
deep, profound, sincere, honest, genuine, unfeigned, devout, earnest, ardent, fervent, wholehearted, warm, compassionate
E3 insincere, false

heartily adv
1 ENTHUSIASTICALLY, eagerly, earnestly, deeply, profoundly, warmly, warm-heartedly, gladly, cordially, feelingly, sincerely, resolutely, unfeignedly, zealously, staunchly, vigorously, genuinely
2 ABSOLUTELY, completely, very, totally, entirely, extremely, thoroughly

heartless adj
unfeeling, uncaring, cold, hard, hard-hearted, cold-hearted, cold-blooded, callous, unkind, cruel, inhuman, harsh, brutal, ruthless, pitiless, merciless, unsympathetic, unmoved, inconsiderate
E3 kind, considerate, sympathetic, merciful

heartlessly adv
coldly, cold-heartedly, hard-heartedly, unsympathetically, callously, cruelly, harshly, brutally, pitilessly, mercilessly
E3 sympathetically, kindly

heart-rending adj
harrowing, heartbreaking, agonizing, pitiful, piteous, pathetic, tragic, sad, distressing, moving, affecting, poignant

heartsick adj
sad, heavy-hearted, despondent, dejected, disappointed, depressed, downcast, melancholy, glum

heart-throb n
pin-up, star, idol
COLLOQ. hunk
OLD COLLOQ. dreamboat

heart-to-heart n
cosy chat, private conversation, tête-à-tête, friendly talk, honest talk, personal conversation

heartwarming adj
cheering, heartening, encouraging, uplifting, gladdening, touching, moving, affecting, pleasing, gratifying, rewarding, satisfying
E3 heartbreaking

hearty adj
1 ENTHUSIASTIC, eager, wholehearted, unreserved, heartfelt, sincere, genuine, unfeigned, warm, warm-hearted, affable, friendly, cordial, jovial, cheerful, ebullient, effusive, exuberant, bluff, bouncing, staunch, stalwart
COLLOQ. mat(e)y, blokeish
2 *a hearty breakfast*
large, siz(e)able, substantial, filling, solid, nourishing, nutritious, ample, abundant, generous

3 STRONG, energetic, vigorous, boisterous, robust, healthy, sound, hardy
E3 1 inhibited, reserved, cold, half-hearted 3 weak, feeble

heat n, v
♦ n
1 HOTNESS, warmth, sultriness, torridness, swelter, closeness, heaviness, high temperature, fever, feverishness
TECHNICAL calefaction
Related adjectives: calorific, thermal
2 ARDOUR, fervour, fervency, fieriness, passion, warmth, intensity, vehemence, fury, anger, excitement, impetuosity, earnestness, eagerness, enthusiasm, zeal
E3 1 cold(ness) 2 coolness
♦ v
1 WARM, boil, toast, cook, microwave, bake, roast, reheat, warm up
TECHNICAL calefy
2 INFLAME, excite, animate, stir, rouse, arouse, stimulate, enrage, annoy, flush, glow
E3 1 cool (down), chill

heated adj
angry, furious, raging, passionate, impassioned, fiery, stormy, tempestuous, bitter, fierce, intense, vehement, violent, frenzied, enraged, inflamed, excited, animated, stirred, fired, roused, stimulated
COLLOQ. worked-up
E3 calm

heatedly adv
angrily, furiously, passionately, excitedly, intensely, vehemently, violently, bitterly, fiercely
E3 calmly

heater n
fire, radiator, boiler, central heating, immersion heater, gas heater, electric heater, fan heater, convector, storage heater, solar heater

heath n
moor, moorland, fell, upland

heathen n, adj
♦ n
pagan, unbeliever, infidel, philistine, nations, idolater, idolatress, barbarian, savage
TECHNICAL Gentile
OLD paynim, proselyte of the gate
FORMAL nullifidian
E3 believer
♦ adj
pagan, unbelieving, infidel, philistine, uncivilized, unenlightened, idolatrous, godless, irreligious, savage, barbaric
FORMAL nullifidian
E3 godly, believing

heave v
1 PULL, haul, drag, tug, raise, lift, hitch, hoist, lever, rise, surge
2 THROW, fling, hurl, cast, toss, send, pitch, let fly
COLLOQ. chuck, sling
3 RETCH, vomit, be sick, spew, bring up, cough up, gag, cat, disgorge; *dialect* boke
OLD egurgitate, parbreak
COLLOQ. throw up, sick up, chuck up, puke
SLANG fetch up, honk, barf; *N Am* upchuck; *Aust* chunder
4 *heave a sigh*
give, utter, express, let out, breathe

heaven n
1 PARADISE, home of God, glory, on high, bliss, next world, hereafter, life to come, afterlife, utopia, Elysium, elysian fields, happy hunting-ground, New Jerusalem, promised land, Zion, nirvana, Valhalla, Swarga, Land o' the Leal, Asgard, Olympus
OLD firmament, empyrean, welkin

FORMAL abode of God, vault of heaven
COLLOQ. up there
2 SKY, firmament, skies, the blue, ether
3 ECSTASY, rapture, bliss, happiness, complete happiness, joy, delight, transports of delight
COLLOQ. seventh heaven
F3 1 hell

heavenly *adj*
1 CELESTIAL, unearthly, supernatural, extraterrestrial, cosmic, other-worldly, spiritual, divine, godlike, angelic, seraphic, cherubic, immortal, holy, sublime, blessed, beatific
FORMAL empyreal, empyrean
2 BLISSFUL, wonderful, glorious, marvellous, rapturous, beautiful, lovely, exquisite, perfect, enchanting, delightful, enjoyable
COLLOQ. out of this world, divine
F3 1 infernal, mundane **2** hellish

heaven-sent *adj*
unexpectedly welcome, favourable, fortunate, happy, bright, timely, opportune
FORMAL auspicious
F3 *formal* inauspicious

heavily *adv*
1 PONDEROUSLY, slowly, clumsily, awkwardly, laboriously, with difficulty, painfully, hard, sluggishly, weightily, woodenly
2 COMPACTLY, closely, densely, solidly, thick, thickly
3 COMPLETELY, utterly, decisively, thoroughly, roundly, soundly
4 EXCESSIVELY, to excess, too much, abundantly, immoderately, copiously
F3 1 lightly **2** loosely

heaviness *n*
1 WEIGHT, weightiness, ponderousness, heftiness, bulk, density, solidity, thickness
2 *a heaviness in the air*
dejection, depression, despondency, melancholy, sadness, seriousness, oppression, oppressiveness, burdensomeness, onerousness, drowsiness, sleepiness, sluggishness, deadness, gloom, gloominess
FORMAL languor, lassitude, somnolence
3 INTENSITY, seriousness, severity, depth, greatness
F3 2 lightness, liveliness

heavy *adj*
1 WEIGHTY, hefty, ponderous, burdensome, cumbersome, awkward, massive, substantial, large, bulky, hulking, solid, dense, thick
COLLOQ. weighing a ton, heavy as lead
2 *heavy work*
hard, difficult, tough, arduous, laborious, strenuous, troublesome, demanding, taxing, exacting, harsh, severe
3 SERIOUS, intense, grave, sombre, deep, profound, dull, tedious, dry, uninteresting
4 *heavy fighting; a heavy shower*
severe, intense, extreme, excessive, considerable, strong, great
5 *a heavy blow on the head*
forceful, hard, powerful, strong, intense, sharp, violent
6 *heavy responsibilities*
burdensome, onerous, unbearable, intolerable, crushing, difficult, weighty, exacting, irksome, oppressive, taxing, troublesome, trying, wearisome
7 *with a heavy heart*
sad, miserable, despondent, depressed, discouraged, downcast, gloomy, sorrowful, crushed
8 *a heavy meal*
filling, substantial, solid, big, large, stodgy, rich, hearty, indigestible, starchy
9 *tables heavy with food*
laden, loaded, full, burdened, weighed down, encumbered, groaning

10 *the weather is heavy*
sultry, humid, oppressive, muggy, close, steamy, sticky, clammy
11 *a heavy sky*
dark, cloudy, overcast, dull, grey, gloomy, leaden
12 *a heavy drinker*
excessive, immoderate, intemperate, inordinate, overindulgent
F3 1 light **2** easy **3** light **4, 5** gentle **6, 8** light **10** cool, fresh **11** bright

---

Synonym nuances
sense 1
Weighty puts the emphasis quite simply on weighing a lot, whilst **hefty** implies being of a substantial size as well as weight. **Ponderous** goes further with its implication of being massive, and this rather negative aspect is developed in **burdensome** and **cumbersome**, which suggest something is unmanageable or troublesome: *computers were meant to do away with cumbersome paper files.* **Awkward** similarly suggests being unwieldy as much as heavy.
  The terms **bulky** and **hulking** suggest something is difficult to manipulate due to size and weight: *his big hulking frame loomed over me.* To use a term such as **massive**, on the other hand, puts the emphasis firmly on enormous size, and the terms **solid**, **substantial** and **dense** can be used to suggest hardness and compactness in addition to weight and size.

---

heavy-duty *adj*
durable, lasting, enduring, long-lasting, abiding, hard-wearing, reinforced, strong, solid, sturdy, tough, robust, substantial, sound, resistant
F3 weak, perishable

heavy-handed *adj*
clumsy, awkward, blundering, bungling, unsubtle, tactless, insensitive, thoughtless, inept, oppressive, forceful, severe, harsh, stern, overbearing, domineering, autocratic, despotic
FORMAL maladroit
COLLOQ. ham-fisted, cack-handed, all fingers and thumbs, like a bull in a china shop
F3 skilful

heavy-hearted *adj*
sorrowful, sad, depressed, discouraged, disappointed, disheartened, downcast, downhearted, despondent, gloomy, miserable, morose, mournful, melancholy, glum, forlorn, crushed, heartsick
F3 light-hearted

heckle *v*
barrack, shout down, interrupt, disrupt, jeer, taunt, pester, gibe, catcall, bait, needle

hectic *adj*
busy, frantic, frenetic, chaotic, fast, feverish, excited, bustling, heated, furious, frenzied, tumultuous, turbulent, wild
F3 leisurely

hector *v*
bully, intimidate, badger, chivvy, harass, menace, threaten, nag, provoke, worry, browbeat, bluster, bullyrag, huff
COLLOQ. bulldoze

hedge *n, v*
♦ *n*
1 FENCE, hedgerow, screen, windbreak, barrier, protection, dyke, boundary, raddle, sepiment
OLD haw, hay, mound, ox-fence
2 SAFEGUARD, protection, shield, cover, guard
♦ *v*
1 SURROUND, enclose, encircle, edge, hem in, confine, restrict, limit, guard, shield, protect, safeguard, cover, insure

FORMAL fortify
2 STALL, equivocate, sidestep, evade, quibble, prevaricate, dodge
FORMAL temporize
COLLOQ. duck, sit on the fence, waffle

hedonism *n*
gratification, luxuriousness, self-indulgence, sensualism, sensuality, voluptuousness, pleasure-seeking, Epicureanism, epicurism, *dolce vita*, sybaritism
F3 asceticism

hedonist *n*
pleasure-seeker, sensualist, voluptuary, epicure, epicurean, *bon vivant, bon viveur*, sybarite
F3 ascetic

hedonistic *adj*
luxurious, pleasure-seeking, self-indulgent, voluptuous, epicurean, sybaritic
F3 ascetic, austere

heed *v, n*
♦ *v*
listen, pay attention to, mind, mark, attend to, take note/notice of, take into account, take into consideration, bear in mind, consider, note, regard, observe, follow, obey
F3 ignore, disregard
♦ *n*
attention, regard, note, notice, consideration, mind, thought, watchfulness, care, caution, heedfulness, respect, ear
OLD (*Shakesp*) observance
FORMAL animadversion
F3 inattention, indifference, unconcern

heedful *adj*
attentive, watchful, mindful, observant, careful, prudent, cautious, vigilant, chary, wary
FORMAL circumspect, regardful
F3 heedless, unthinking

heedless *adj*
oblivious, unthinking, careless, remiss, negligent, rash, reckless, irresponsible, foolhardy, inattentive, unobservant, unwary, incautious, unguarded, indiscreet, tactless, thoughtless, inconsiderate, regardless, uncaring, unconcerned, unmindful, absent-minded, forgetful
FORMAL precipitate
F3 heedful, mindful, attentive, watchful, vigilant

Synonym nuances
Many of these synonyms are inherently disapproving in tone, for example **unthinking, thoughtless** and **inattentive**: *the storyline has twists to challenge inattentive viewers.* **Inconsiderate** clearly implies selfishness on the part of the person or actions you are describing, while **uncaring** and **unconcerned** are disapproving of someone's lack of emotional involvement. To simply suggest a lack of care or regard for the consequences, you can use **incautious, regardless, heedless** or **unmindful**: *warriors, heedless of the dangers.* **Incautious** further implies a lack of care, possibly even a degree of recklessness: *the wine made her incautious.*
Both **forgetful** and **absent-minded** might be used of a slightly endearing vagueness, whereas **remiss** and **negligent** are more negative, implying the less forgivable aspect of neglect: *the Home Office has been remiss about security.* The terms **irresponsible** and **reckless** are again strongly marked by disapproval, and might be used of casualness verging on danger. **Tactless**, another critical term, has the narrower use of a tendency to hurt people's feelings. **Indiscreet** and **unguarded** both would be used more in the context of divulging secrets: *unguarded gossip.*

---

heedlessly *adv*
carelessly, unthinkingly, thoughtlessly, negligently, inattentively, rashly, recklessly
F3 attentively, watchfully, vigilantly

heel *v*
list, lean over, tilt, bank, tip, slope, slant, angle, sway
TECHNICAL seel

hefty *adj*
1 LARGE, big, huge, strapping, burly, hulking, beefy, muscular, brawny, strong, powerful, vigorous, robust, massive, stout
2 *a hefty blow*
forceful, hard, heavy, weighty, powerful, vigorous, solid, substantial, massive, immense, colossal, bulky, awkward, unwieldy
3 *a hefty sum of money*
substantial, considerable, generous, ample, siz(e)able
F3 1 small, slight **2** weak **3** small

height *n*
1 HIGHNESS, altitude, elevation, tallness, loftiness, stature
2 TOP, summit, peak, pinnacle, mountain top, hill top, apex, vertex, zenith, apogee, crest, crown, culmination, climax, perfection, extremity, maximum, limit, ultimate, uttermost, ceiling
F3 1 depth

heighten *v*
raise, elevate, lift, increase, add to, build up, magnify, intensify, strengthen, sharpen, improve, boost, amplify, enhance, exalt
FORMAL augment
F3 lower, decrease, diminish

heinous *adj*
evil, monstrous, atrocious, abominable, detestable, loathsome, abhorrent, contemptible, despicable, iniquitous, outrageous, shocking, flagrant, vicious, wicked, awful, hideous, villainous, revolting, hateful, odious, infamous, unspeakable, grave
FORMAL execrable, facinorous, nefarious

heir, heiress *n*
beneficiary, co-heir, fellow-heir, inheritor, inheritress, inheritrix, successor, next in line, scion
TECHNICAL parcener, legatee, substitute
OLD tanist

helix *n*
spiral, twist, coil, curl, whorl, loop, wreathe, screw, corkscrew
TECHNICAL curlicue, volute

hell *n*
1 *heaven and hell*
underworld, inferno, infernal regions, lower regions, abyss, fire, fire and brimstone, bottomless pit, pit, netherworld, Hades, Sheol, Acheron, Gehenna, Tophet, Abaddon, Tartarus, Malebolge, Erebus
FORMAL perdition, abode of the devil
COLLOQ. below, down there, other place
2 TORTURE, suffering, anguish, agony, torment, ordeal, nightmare, misery, wretchedness
FORMAL tribulation
3 *What the hell are you doing here?*
on earth
COLLOQ. the blazes, the heck
OLD COLLOQ. the deuce, the dickens
F3 1 heaven
■ **give someone hell**
1 TROUBLE, annoy, torment, pester, vex, harass, punish, scold, beat, flog
2 CHASTISE, criticize

COLLOQ. tell off, haul over the coals, tear off a strip, give someone an earful

■ **hell for leather**
very fast/quickly, as fast/quickly as possible, hurriedly, quickly, rapidly, swiftly, recklessly, rashly, wildly, post-haste
FORMAL precipitately
COLLOQ. like crazy, like the clappers

■ **raise hell**
1 OBJECT NOISILY, protest loudly, be very angry, be furious
COLLOQ. hit the roof
2 MAKE TROUBLE, run riot, cause a commotion

hell-bent *adj*
determined, bent, intent, fixed, resolved, set, settled, tenacious, dogged, inflexible, unhesitating, unwavering
FORMAL intransigent, obdurate

hellish *adj, adv*
♦ *adj*
infernal, devilish, satanic, diabolical, demonic, fiendish, accursed, damnable, monstrous, savage, barbaric, wicked, cruel, abominable, atrocious, dreadful, nasty, disagreeable, unpleasant
FORMAL nefarious, execrable
F3 heavenly
♦ *adv*
dreadfully, awfully, very, extremely, exceptionally, intensely, immensely, unpleasantly

hello *interj*
hallo, hullo, good morning, good afternoon, good evening, greetings, welcome, holloa, *bonjour, buon giorno*
OLD hillo
COLLOQ. hi; *Aust* g'day; *N Am* howdy, yo

helm *n*
tiller, rudder, wheel
■ **at the helm**
in control, in command, in charge, leading, directing, in the driving seat, holding the reins, in the saddle

help *v, n*
♦ *v*
1 AID, assist, be of assistance, lend a hand, do something for, do someone a good turn, serve, be of use, guide, collaborate, co-operate, stand by, rally round, support, back, encourage, oblige, contribute to, promote, nurse, give a boost to
COLLOQ. do your bit
2 IMPROVE, relieve, soothe, assuage, cure, heal, remedy, ease, facilitate, further
FORMAL ameliorate, alleviate, mitigate
F3 1 hinder **2** worsen
♦ *n*
1 AID, assistance, helping hand, collaboration, co-operation, encouragement, boost, backup, support, backing, advice, guidance, service, charity, relief, use, utility, avail, benefit, advantage
FORMAL succour
COLLOQ. shot in the arm, tower of strength
2 REMEDY, relief, cure, healing, improvement, restorative, moderator, balm, salve
FORMAL alleviation, amelioration, mitigation
COLLOQ. oil on troubled waters
3 *a daily help*
helper, home help, cleaner, worker, employee, charwoman
COLLOQ. Mrs Mop
F3 1 hindrance
■ **cannot help**
be unable to stop, be unable to control, be unable to prevent yourself
FORMAL be unable to refrain/abstain

Synonym nuances
verb sense 1
Aid can be widely used of supplying help, while **assist** suggests a more active involvement: *parent volunteers assisted in running the school library.* The phrase **lend a hand** is suggestive of contributing to the efforts of others, unlike **do something for** which implies undertaking something on someone else's behalf. **Do someone a good turn** and **oblige** have implications of a favour for which they may owe a debt. **Serve** suggests being subordinate, whereas **guide** has more to do with taking a controlling, advisory role.

The word **co-operate** has connotations of togetherness and joint effort, although it may not always refer to a willing action: *unions were asked to co-operate with management to improve production levels.* **Collaborate** would only be used where there is mutual, usually voluntary, involvement: *three prestigious galleries have collaborated in an exhibition of his works.*

You can use **support** and **stand by** to suggest remaining true to someone in troubled times when help is required, while **rally round** would be used of a number of people coming together for someone in need: *the neighbours rallied round when she became housebound.* **Support** and **aid** can also be used like **back**, of providing practical or financial help or endorsement, whilst **encourage** has more to do with providing motivation. **Promote** and **give a boost to** can also be used of helping something's progress: *the new laws promote good relations in the workplace.*

helper *n*
assistant, deputy, auxiliary, subsidiary, attendant, aid, aide, adjutant, right-hand man/woman, PA, mate, helpmate, partner, associate, colleague, collaborator, accomplice, worker, co-worker, subordinate, ally, supporter, second, second-in-command, employee, man/girl Friday, maid, servant
FORMAL paraclete

helpful *adj*
1 USEFUL, of use, practical, of service, constructive, worthwhile, valuable, beneficial, profitable, advantageous, instrumental
OLD furthersome, second
2 *a helpful person*
co-operative, obliging, accommodating, neighbourly, friendly, caring, considerate, kind, benevolent, charitable, sympathetic, supportive
F3 1 useless, futile **2** unfriendly, cruel

helpfully *adv*
kindly, obligingly, sympathetically, considerately, reassuringly, usefully, conveniently

helping *n*
serving, portion, share, ration, amount, plateful, bowlful, spoonful, piece
COLLOQ. dollop

helpless *adj*
weak, feeble, powerless, dependent, vulnerable, exposed, unprotected, defenceless, abandoned, friendless, destitute, forlorn, desolate, incapable, incompetent, infirm, disabled, impotent, paralysed
FORMAL debilitated
COLLOQ. helpless as a newborn babe
F3 strong, independent, competent

helplessly *adv*
powerlessly, defencelessly, desolately, impotently, weakly, feebly, vulnerably

helpmate *n*
partner, support, assistant, associate, companion, consort, helper, helpmeet, better half, other half, spouse, husband, wife

helter-skelter *adv, adj*

• *adv*
carelessly, confusedly, recklessly, wildly, hastily, hurriedly, pell-mell, rashly, impulsively, headlong

• *adj*
confused, disordered, disorganized, jumbled, muddled, random, unsystematic, hit-or-miss, haphazard, topsy-turvy
COLLOQ. higgledy-piggledy

hem *n, v*

• *n*
edge, edging, border, margin, fringe, trim, trimming, frill, valance, flounce
TECHNICAL fimbria

• *v*
fringe, edge, trim, bind, border, skirt, fold
TECHNICAL fimbriate

■ **hem in**
surround, enclose, box in, close in, shut in, confine, restrict, limit, hedge in, pen in, trap, constrain

hence *adv*

therefore, thus, for this reason, accordingly, consequently, as a consequence
FORMAL ergo

henceforth *adv*

from now on, from this time on, in the future, henceforward, hereafter, hereinafter, hence

henchman *n*

aide, associate, subordinate, supporter, attendant, follower, right-hand man/woman, minion, bodyguard, lackey, underling
COLLOQ. heavy, hit man, hatchet man, crony, minder, sidekick

henpecked *adj*

dominated, subjugated, browbeaten, bullied, intimidated, criticized, harassed, pestered, badgered, tormented, meek, timid
OLD (*Shakesp*) woman-tired
COLLOQ. under someone's thumb, tied to someone's apron strings, like a puppet on a string
E3 dominant

herald *n, v*

• *n*
messenger, courier, announcer, crier, forerunner, precursor, blazoner, usher, omen, token, signal, sign, indication
FORMAL harbinger, portent, augury

• *v*
1 ANNOUNCE, proclaim, broadcast, advertise, publicize, make known, make public, trumpet, fanfare
FORMAL promulgate
2 PRECEDE, usher in, show, indicate, signal, promise, foreshadow
FORMAL harbinger, augur, portend, presage
COLLOQ. pave the way

heraldry

herbs and spices

Herbs and spices include:

allspice	comfrey	nutmeg
angelica	coriander	paprika
anise	cumin	parsley
basil	curry	pepper
bay	dill	rosemary
bergamot	fennel	saffron
borage	gaillardia	sage
camomile	garlic	savory
caper	ginger	sesame
caraway seeds	hyssop	sorrel
cardamon	lavender	St John's wort (or
catmint	lemon balm	hypericum)
cayenne pepper	lovage	tarragon
chervil	mace	thyme
chilli	marjoram	turmeric
chives	mint	vanilla
cinnamon	mustard	
cloves	oregano	

herculean *adj*

arduous, laborious, onerous, toilsome, demanding, strong, tough, exacting, difficult, enormous, powerful, exhausting, strenuous, tremendous, colossal, large, gigantic, massive, great, huge, mammoth, formidable, daunting, gruelling, heavy, hard

herd *n, v*

• *n*
1 *a herd of cattle*
drove, flock, swarm, pack; *Aust & NZ* mob
2 *follow the herd*
press, crush, mass, horde, throng, multitude, crowd, mob, host, the masses, rabble
COLLOQ. riff-raff, plebs, proles

• *v*
1 FLOCK, congregate, gather, collect, get together, assemble, rally, huddle, muster
2 LEAD, guide, shepherd, look after, take care of, round up, urge, drive, goad, force

herdsman *n*

shepherd, cowherd, cowman, drover, stockman, grazier, wrangler; *N Am* vaquero

here *adv*

1 *come here*
in/to/at this place, present, around, in
2 *I must finish here*
at this point, at this time, now, at this stage
E3 1 there, away, absent, missing **2** then

here and there *adv*

in different places, in various places, hither and thither, to and fro, sporadically
COLLOQ. from pillar to post

hereabouts *adv*

here, near here, around here, in these parts, in this place

Heraldic terms include:

addorsed	centre	dormant	helmet	pall	shield
annulet	charge	eagle	impale	passant	sinister
antelope	chevron	emblazonry	insignia	phoenix	statant
arms	cinquefoil	emblem	lion	quarter	supporters
badge	coat of arms	ensign	lozenge	quatrefoil	tierced
bezant	cockatrice	escutcheon	mantling	rampant	undee
blazon	compartment	field	martlet	regalia	unicorn
bordure	couchant	fleur-de-lis	motto	roundel	urdé
caboched	crest	griffin	mullet	saltire	urinant
camelopard	dexter	gyronny	orle	semé	volant
canton	displayed	hatchment	pile	sejant	wivern

Legendary historical and fictional heroes and heroines include:

GREEK MYTH:		ARTHURIAN	CHINESE:	UNITED STATES:	
Achilles	Seven against	LEGEND:	Yu the Great	Daniel Boone	Tarzan
Agamemnon	Thebes	Galahad	SUMERIAN:	Paul Bunyan	William Tell
Ajax	Telemachus	Gawain	Gilgamesh	Davy Crockett	SUPERHEROES:
Argonauts	Theseus	Lancelot	JAPANESE:	Molly Pitcher	Batman
Atalanta	CELTIC MYTH:	Percival (Parsifal)	Raiko	Paul Revere	Spiderman
Bellerophon	Bran	HINDU:	Yamato Take	LITERATURE AND	Superman
Cadmus	Cchulainn	Rama	Yorimasa	ROMANCE:	Wonder Woman
Diomedes	Fionn	PERSIAN:	Yoshitsune	Beowulf	
Hector	MacCumhail	Rustam	SCOTTISH:	Gawain	
Hercules	Pwyll	RUSSIAN:	Rob Roy	Ivanhoe	
Jason	GERMANIC AND	Ivan Tsarevich	William Wallace	Ogier the Dane	
Odysseus	NORSE MYTH:	Mikula	BRITISH:	Robinson Crusoe	
Perseus	Brunhilde	SPANISH:	Boudicca	Roland	
	Siegfried (Sigurd)	El Cid	Robin Hood	Tam o'Shanter	

See also **god**.

hereafter *adv, n*
♦ *adv*
from now on, from this time forward/onwards, hence, henceforth, henceforward, in the future, later, eventually
♦ *n*
afterlife, heaven, paradise, life after death, life to come, next world, elysian fields, happy hunting-ground

hereditary *adj*
1 *a hereditary title*
inherited, bequeathed, handed down, family, ancestral, left, willed, transferred
2 *hereditary diseases*
inborn, inbred, innate, inherent, inherited, natural, congenital, genetic, transmissible

heredity *n*
genetics, hereditary character, gene(s), genetic make-up, DNA, chromosomes, inheritance

heresy *n*
heterodoxy, unorthodoxy, nonconformity, free-thinking, apostasy, dissidence, dissent, dissension, unbelief, atheism, agnosticism, scepticism, schism, error, sectarianism, separatism, revisionism, blasphemy
OLD recusance
E3 orthodoxy

heretic *n*
free-thinker, nonconformist, apostate, dissident, dissenter, unbeliever, atheist, agnostic, sceptic, revisionist, separatist, schismatic, sectarian, renegade, miscreant
OLD recusant, zendik
E3 conformist

heretical *adj*
heterodox, unorthodox, free-thinking, dissident, dissenting, revisionist, separatist, sectarian, renegade, unbelieving, atheistic, agnostic, sceptical, revisionist, rationalistic, schismatic, impious, irreverent, iconoclastic, blasphemous
OLD recusant
E3 orthodox, conventional, conformist

heritage *n*
1 INHERITANCE, legacy, bequest, endowment, lot, portion, share, estate, birthright, due
2 HISTORY, past, tradition, culture, cultural, traditions, background, ancestry, descent, lineage, family, extraction, dynasty

hermaphrodite *adj*
androgynous, bisexual, male and female, polygamic
TECHNICAL androdioecious, gynodioecious, heterogamous, monoclinous, monoecious, protogynous

hermetic *adj*
airtight, sealed, watertight, shut, hermetical

hermit *n*
recluse, solitary, loner, monk, ascetic, anchorite, anchoress, ancress, eremite, stylite, pillarist, pillar-saint

hermitage *n*
retreat, refuge, haven, sanctuary, cloister, shelter, asylum, hideaway, hideout, hiding-place

hero *n*
1 *the hero of a play*
protagonist, leading male role/part, leading actor, lead actor, male lead, lead
2 *heroes in battle*
conqueror, victor, champion, brave person, person of courage, cavalier, lion, celebrity
COLLOQ. good guy
See panel above
3 IDOL, star, superstar, pin-up, ideal, paragon, celebrity, god
COLLOQ. heart-throb
E3 1 villain

heroic *adj*
brave, courageous, fearless, dauntless, undaunted, lion-hearted, stout-hearted, valiant, bold, daring, intrepid, adventurous, gallant, chivalrous, noble, determined, selfless, epic, Homeric
FORMAL valorous, doughty
E3 cowardly, timid

heroically *adv*
bravely, courageously, boldly, valiantly, nobly, selflessly, fearlessly, dauntlessly
E3 timidly

heroine *n*
1 *the heroine of a play*
protagonist, leading female role/part, leading actress/lady, female lead, lead actor, lead, diva, prima donna, prima ballerina
2 *heroines in battle*
conqueror, victor, champion, brave woman, woman of courage, celebrity, Amazon
3 IDOL, star, superstar, pin-up, ideal, paragon, celebrity, goddess
E3 1 villain

heroism *n*
bravery, courage, courageousness, valour, fearlessness, dauntlessness, boldness, daring, intrepidity, gallantry, chivalry, prowess, selflessness, determination, stout-heartedness, lion-heartedness
FORMAL fortitude, doughtiness
E3 cowardice, timidity; *formal* pusillanimity

hero-worship *n*
admiration, idolization, adoration, worship, exaltation, glorification, adulation, idealization, deification
FORMAL veneration
COLLOQ. putting on a pedestal

hesitancy *n*

reluctance, misgiving, qualm, scruples, unwillingness, disinclination, doubt, doubtfulness, reservation, uncertainty, indecision, wavering
FORMAL demur, irresolution
E3 willingness, certainty

hesitant *adj*

hesitating, reluctant, unwilling, disinclined, half-hearted, uncertain, unsure, doubtful, sceptical, dubious, indecisive, irresolute, vacillating, delaying, stalling, wavering, tentative, wary, shy, timid, halting, stammering, stuttering
FORMAL demurring
E3 decisive, resolute, confident, fluent

hesitate *v*

1 PAUSE, delay, wait, think twice, doubt, hold back, hang back, hang fire, falter, stumble, halt, stammer, stutter; *Scot* swither
OLD dubitate, demur; (*Shakesp*) mammer
COLLOQ. shilly-shally, dilly-dally, hum and haw
2 BE RELUCTANT, be unwilling, be disinclined, shrink from, scruple, boggle, vacillate, waver, balance, stall, be uncertain, dither; *Scot* tarrow; *N Am* dicker
FORMAL demur
COLLOQ. shilly-shally, dilly-dally
E3 2 decide

***

Synonym nuances

sense 1

You could use the word **pause** to suggest a very short cessation: *he paused to think before answering*, whereas **delay** and the more informal **hang fire** would suggest putting off for a longer time: *he delayed his decision until he had more information*. You could use the term **think twice** specifically of stopping to reconsider one's actions: *think twice before doing anything rash.*
  Doubt would convey uncertainty about a course of action; **hold back** suggests restraint: *she started forward to hug him, then held back*; **hang back** implies reluctance to perform some action: *I hung back when volunteers were called for.* **Falter** and **stumble** are both suggestive of wavering in your intent: *their resolution failed, they faltered and then fled.* **Stammer** and **stutter** are specifically used with regard to speech, suggesting involuntary breaks or hesitation: *she started to argue, stammered, and went quiet.*

***

hesitation *n*

pause, delay, holding-back, hanging-back, waiting, reluctance, unwillingness, disinclination, hesitance, scruple(s), qualm(s), misgivings, doubt, doubtfulness, scepticism, second thoughts, vacillation, wavering, uncertainty, unsureness, indecision, stalling, faltering, stumbling, stammering, stuttering
FORMAL irresolution, demure, cunctation
COLLOQ. dilly-dallying, shilly-shallying
E3 eagerness, assurance

heterodox *adj*

unorthodox, unsound, dissident, dissenting, free-thinking, heretical, schismatic, iconoclastic, revisionist
E3 orthodox

heterogeneous *adj*

diverse, varied, miscellaneous, assorted, different, mixed, motley, diversified, divergent, catholic, opposed, unlike, unrelated, dissimilar, contrary, contrasted, discrepant, piebald
TECHNICAL polymorphic
FORMAL multiform, disparate, incongruous
E3 homogeneous

heterogeneously *adv*

diversely, differently, divergently, dissimilarly, contrarily
FORMAL disparately, incongruously
E3 homogeneously

heterosexual *adj, n*

COLLOQ. straight
SLANG hetero, breeder
E3 homosexual, gay

het up *adj*

worked up, angry, indignant, offended, resentful, upset, in a rage, beside yourself, tense, stressed, anxious, worried, agitated
COLLOQ. wound up, uptight, stressed-out
SLANG pissed off

hew *v*

1 CHOP cut, fell, saw, axe, lop, hack, sever, prune, trim, split
2 FORM, carve, sculpt, sculpture, cut, chip, whittle, chisel, hammer, fashion, model, shape, make

heyday *n*

peak, pinnacle, prime, flush, bloom, flowering, culmination, golden age, boom time

hiatus *n*

break, gap, breach, opening, rift, space, void, chasm, blank, discontinuity, pause, rest, lull, interruption, interval, lapse, suspension
FORMAL aperture, discontinuance, lacuna

hiccup *n*

snag, delay, hold-up, hitch, trouble, problem, difficulty, mishap, setback, drawback, catch, impediment, hindrance, obstacle, block, check, barrier, obstruction
COLLOQ. glitch

hidden *adj*

1 *a hidden door*
concealed, covered, shrouded, veiled, masked, disguised, camouflaged, unseen, secret, out of sight
2 OBSCURE, dark, occult, secret, covert, close, cryptic, indistinct, mysterious, abstruse, mystical, latent, ulterior
FORMAL arcane, recondite
COLLOQ. under wraps
E3 1 showing, apparent, revealed, visible, on view **2** obvious, clear, distinct

hide[1] *v*

1 CONCEAL, cover, cloak, shroud, veil, draw a veil over, put out of sight, screen, mask, disguise, camouflage, obscure, shadow, eclipse, darken, cloud, obstruct, bury, store, stow, secrete, withhold, keep dark, keep secret, suppress
FORMAL dissemble
COLLOQ. stash away, bottle up, keep under your hat, sweep under the carpet, keep under wraps
2 TAKE COVER, shelter, conceal yourself, lie low, go to ground, go into hiding, keep out of sight, cover your tracks, lurk
COLLOQ. hole up, disappear into thin air, keep a low profile, lie doggo, lay a false scent
E3 1 reveal, show, display

***

Synonym nuances

sense 1

Conceal suggests keeping something out of view, whilst **cover, cloak** and **shroud** are more specific, in the sense of placing something over an object or person: *the moon was shrouded in mist.* **Veil** is similar, but implies disguising something unpleasant or undesirable: *a thinly veiled threat*, and **draw a veil over** also implies discouraging further talk on the subject: *let's draw a veil over last night's debacle.* **Screen**, likewise, has censorial aspects: *unpleasant facts screened by fawning officials*, although it can also be used more literally: *the hedge screened the washing area.* **Mask, disguise** and **camouflage** suggest that something has being altered so as not to stand out or be recognized for what it is, so these terms might also be used of hiding unpleasant things: *nosiness disguised as* concern.

If something is coming between the viewer and their view, the terms **obscure** and **obstruct** are appropriate: *the safety notices were obscured by plants*, and both **shadow** and **eclipse** could be used where something has obstructed the light: *the square was eclipsed by tall buildings*. The term **bury** suggests putting something beneath many layers: *plants buried beneath a carpet of dead leaves*.

The terms **store**, **stow** and **secrete** can all be used of deliberately hiding something to keep for your own use: *she stowed the money in her jeans pocket when his back was turned*, whereas **withhold** and **suppress** are more appropriate for the deliberate hiding of information or facts, by preventing others from getting them: *he was withholding vital information from the public*.

hide² *n*
the hide of an animal
skin, pelt, fell, fur, coat, fleece, leather

hideaway *n*
retreat, hiding-place, hideout, refuge, sanctuary, shelter, cloister, hermitage, haven, nest, den, lair, hole

hidebound *adj*
set, rigid, fixed, entrenched, narrow, narrow-minded, intolerant, strait-laced, conventional, ultra-conservative, bigoted, uncompromising, reactionary
FORMAL intractable
F3 liberal, progressive

hideous *adj*
ugly, repulsive, repellent, grotesque, monstrous, unsightly, horrid, ghastly, awful, dreadful, frightful, terrible, grim, gruesome, macabre, abominable, terrifying, shocking, outrageous, appalling, horrifying, disgusting, revolting, horrible, horrendous; *Scot* gash
OLD deform, loathly, ugsome
F3 beautiful, attractive

hideously *adv*
repulsively, grotesquely, horridly, dreadfully, frightfully, terribly, gruesomely, abominably, terrifyingly, shockingly, outrageously, disgustingly, horribly, horrendously
F3 beautifully, attractively

hideout *n*
retreat, hiding-place, hideaway, refuge, sanctuary, shelter, cloister, hermitage, haven, nest, den, lair, hole

hiding¹ *n*
go into hiding
concealment, cover, veiling, screening, disguise, shroud, veil, mask, camouflage

hiding² *n*
give someone a good hiding
beating, flogging, whipping, caning, spanking, thrashing, drubbing, battering
COLLOQ. walloping, tanning, whacking, belting, licking

hiding-place *n*
hideaway, hideout, lair, den, hole, hide, nest, cache, cover, shelter, refuge, haven, sanctuary, retreat, cloister

hierarchy *n*
pecking order, ranking, grading, scale, series, ladder, echelons, strata, system, structure

hieroglyphics *n*
1 decipher Egyptian hieroglyphics
signs, symbols, secret symbols, picture writing, pictograms, runes, code, cipher
2 cannot understand his hieroglyphics
scribble, squiggle, bad/illegible handwriting, bad/illegible writing, scratch, scrabble
FORMAL cacography

higgledy-piggledy *adv, adj*
* *adv*
any old how, anyhow, indiscriminately, untidily, confusedly, haphazardly, pell-mell, topsy-turvy
* *adj*
confused, disorderly, disorganized, untidy, jumbled, muddled, haphazard, indiscriminate, topsy-turvy

high *adj, n*
* *adj*
1 TALL, lofty, elevated, soaring, towering
2 GREAT, strong, powerful, forceful, vigorous, violent, intense, extreme
3 IMPORTANT, influential, powerful, eminent, distinguished, notable, prominent, chief, top, principal, leading, senior, high-ranking, high-level, elevated, exalted
4 a higher form of life
advanced, complex, elaborate, progressive, ultra-modern, high-tech
5 a high standard
good, excellent, fine, outstanding, great, perfect, exemplary, commendable, noteworthy, first-class, first-rate, superior, superlative, surpassing, unequalled, unparalleled, select, choice, quality, de luxe, gilt-edged, tiptop, top-class, blue-chip
COLLOQ. classy
6 have a high opinion of someone
favourable, good, positive, well-disposed, approving, complimentary, admiring, agreeable, appreciative
7 high moral principles
noble, moral, ethical, lofty, virtuous, upright, admirable, honourable, worthy
8 a high price
expensive, dear, costly, exorbitant, excessive, inflated, unreasonable, extortionate
COLLOQ. steep
9 high winds
strong, intense, severe, extreme, forceful, violent, stormy, gusty, blustery, squally
10 HIGH-PITCHED, high-frequency, soprano, treble, falsetto, sharp, shrill, tinny, piping, piercing, penetrating, acute
11 high on drugs
intoxicated, inebriated, hallucinating
COLLOQ. turned on, having your mind blown, doped, on a trip, stoned, freaked out, spaced out, wasted, zonked; *N Am* wired
SLANG bombed, loaded, blitzed, blasted, out of it
12 meat going high
bad, off, rotting, smelling, smelly, gamy, decayed, putrid, rancid
F3 1 low, short **2** low, slight **3** unimportant, lowly **4** low **5** low, poor, inferior **6** low, poor, bad **7** low **8** cheap **9** light, gentle **10** deep, low
* *n*
1 feeling on a high
intoxication, inebriation, hallucination
COLLOQ. trip, turn-on, freak-out
2 RECORD, height, summit, peak, top, zenith
F3 1, 2 low

■ **high and dry**
abandoned, marooned, stranded, helpless, bereft, destitute
COLLOQ. ditched, dumped
■ **high and low**
everywhere, all around, in all places, in each/every place, all over, throughout, far and near
COLLOQ. left right and centre, here there and everywhere; *N Am* every place
■ **high and mighty**
arrogant, conceited, haughty, overbearing, self-important, snobbish, superior, proud, egotistic, condescending, patronizing, disdainful, cavalier, imperious, overweening

OLD hogen-mogen
COLLOQ. stuck-up, swanky, toploftical, toplofty

high-born *adj*
noble, aristocratic, blue-blooded, thoroughbred, well-born, patrician
F3 low-born

highbrow *n, adj*
• *n*
intellectual, scholar, genius, mastermind, academic
COLLOQ. egghead, brains, brainbox, know-it-all, clever clogs, boffin
• *adj*
intellectual, sophisticated, cultured, cultivated, academic, scholarly, bookish, deep, profound, serious, classical
COLLOQ. brainy
F3 lowbrow

high-class *adj*
upper-class, top-class, top-flight, high-quality, quality, de luxe, luxurious, élite, elegant, superior, excellent, first-rate, choice, select, exclusive
COLLOQ. posh, classy, super
F3 ordinary, mediocre

highfalutin, highfaluting *adj*
pretentious, pompous, supercilious, bombastic, grandiose, high-flown, high-sounding, lofty
FORMAL affected, magniloquent
COLLOQ. la-di-da, swanky

high-flown *adj*
florid, extravagant, exaggerated, elaborate, flamboyant, ornate, ostentatious, pretentious, grand-sounding, high-sounding, grandiose, pompous, bombastic, turgid, artificial, stilted, affected, lofty, highfalutin, supercilious
FORMAL grandiloquent
COLLOQ. la-di-da

high-handed *adj*
overbearing, domineering, arrogant, haughty, imperious, dictatorial, autocratic, despotic, tyrannical, oppressive, arbitrary
FORMAL peremptory
COLLOQ. bossy

high-handedness *n*
arrogance, imperiousness, arbitrariness, inflexibility
FORMAL peremptoriness
COLLOQ. bossiness

high jinks *n*
horseplay, clowning, buffoonery, foolery, fooling, fooling around, tomfoolery, skylarking, pranks, capers, antics, practical jokes, fun and games, rough-and-tumble
COLLOQ. monkey business

highland *n*
mountain, hill, upland, elevation, rise, mound, mount, height, ridge, plateau

highlight *n, v*
• *n*
high point, high spot, most interesting/exciting part, most significant feature, main feature, focus, peak, climax, best, cream
• *v*
underline, emphasize, put emphasis on, focus on, feature, call attention to, stress, accentuate, accent, play up, point up, spotlight, illuminate, show up, set off

highly *adv*
1 VERY, very much, greatly, most, thoroughly, really, considerably, decidedly, extremely, certainly, immensely, vastly, hugely, tremendously, exceptionally, extraordinarily
2 *think highly of someone*
favourably, approvingly, enthusiastically, warmly, well, appreciatively

highly-strung *adj*
sensitive, neurotic, nervous, easily upset, nervy, jumpy, on edge, temperamental, excitable, restless, overwrought, tense, stressed
COLLOQ. wound up, uptight, edgy
F3 calm

high-minded *adj*
lofty, noble, pure, moral, ethical, principled, high-principled, idealistic, elevated, virtuous, upright, righteous, honourable, fair, good, worthy
F3 immoral, unscrupulous

high-pitched *adj*
soprano, treble, falsetto, sharp, shrill, tinny, piping, piercing, penetrating, acute
F3 deep, low

high-powered *adj*
forceful, strong, mighty, powerful, potent, effective, compelling, convincing, impressive, persuasive, telling, valid, weighty, urgent, emphatic, vehement, forcible, dynamic, assertive, pushy, energetic, vigorous, go-ahead
F3 weak, feeble

high-priced *adj*
expensive, dear, costly, exorbitant, excessive, extortionate, high, pricey, unreasonable
COLLOQ. steep, stiff
F3 cheap

high-sounding *adj*
grandiose, flamboyant, ostentatious, overblown, pompous, florid, artificial, bombastic, extravagant, high-flown, ponderous, pretentious, stilted, strained
FORMAL affected, grandiloquent, magniloquent, orotund

high-speed *adj*
quick, swift, rapid, brisk, accelerated, speedy, express, hasty, hurried, flying
OLD fleet
F3 slow

high-spirited *adj*
boisterous, bouncy, exuberant, effervescent, frolicsome, ebullient, sparkling, animated, vigorous, vibrant, vivacious, lively, active, dynamic, energetic, spirited, dashing, bold, daring
COLLOQ. full of beans
F3 quiet, sedate, placid

high spirits *n*
boisterousness, exhilaration, exuberance, ebullience, animation, energy, spirit, boldness, liveliness, sparkle, good cheer, vivacity, capers, hilarity, buoyancy, joie de vivre
COLLOQ. bounce

highway *n*
road, roadway, route, thoroughfare, avenue, boulevard, broadway, grove, high street, main road, motorway, primary route, trunk road, bypass, ring road, arterial road, carriageway, clearway, dual carriageway, flyover, toll road; *N Am* expressway, freeway, turnpike

highwayman *n*
bandit, robber, land-pirate, rank-rider, knight of the road, footpad

hijack *v*
commandeer, skyjack, seize, take over
FORMAL expropriate

hike *v, n*
• *v*
1 RAMBLE, walk, trek, wander, march, tramp, trudge, plod
2 RAISE, increase, put up, lift, pull up
COLLOQ. jack up, push up

3 *hike up your clothing*
pull, tug, jerk, hoist, jack, hitch, raise, lift
COLLOQ. yank
♦ *n*
ramble, walk, trek, wander, tramp, trudge, march

hilarious *adj*
funny, amusing, comical, humorous, side-splitting,
farcical, laughable, riotous, uproarious, noisy, boisterous,
rollicking, merry, entertaining, jolly, jovial
FORMAL risible
COLLOQ. hysterical, killing, a scream
serious, grave

hilariously *adv*
comically, humorously, farcically, laughably, uproariously,
boisterously
COLLOQ. hysterically

hilarity *n*
mirth, laughter, fun, amusement, comedy, levity, frivolity,
merriment, jollity, conviviality, high spirits, boisterousness,
exuberance, exhilaration
seriousness, gravity

hill *n*
1 HILLOCK, knoll, mound, hummock, prominence,
eminence, elevation, rise, rising ground, hilltop, foothill,
down, fell, tor, mountain, mount, height, saddleback,
sugarloaf, dun, dune, pike, pimple, holt, mamelon,
monadnock, morro, jebel, tell; *dialect* how, knot, pap,
toot; *Scot* dod, kip, law; *N Am* butte, coast, cuesta, loma,
mesa; *S Afr* berg, kop, koppie
TECHNICAL cone, monticule
OLD barrow, low
2 *a steep hill*
slope, incline, gradient, ramp, rise, ascent, drop, descent,
declivity
FORMAL acclivity
■ **over the hill**
old, getting on, past your prime
COLLOQ. past it, to be no spring chicken

hillbilly *n*
bumpkin, country bumpkin, country yokel, boor, lout,
clodhopper, clodpoll, rustic, oaf, peasant, provincial,
hawbuck; *N Am & Aust* bushwhacker
COLLOQ. hick, hayseed

hillock *n*
mound, hummock, knoll, dune, barrow, knap, knob,
monticle, monticulus, tump; *Scot* knowe

hilt *n*
handle, grip, handgrip, shaft, haft, heft, helve
■ **to the hilt**
completely, fully, as fully as possible, wholly, entirely, utterly,
to the full, to the end, to the maximum extent, in every
respect
COLLOQ. all the way, from first to last, from beginning to
end

hind *adj*
rear, back, hinder, tail, after, posterior, caudal
fore

hinder *v*
hamper, obstruct, block, impede, encumber, keep off,
handicap, hamstring, hold up, delay, slow down, hold
back, check, curb, halt, stop, forestall, arrest, prevent, bar,
debar, deter, trammel, stunt, dwarf, cumber, foil, frustrate,
thwart, balk, oppose, inhibit, interfere with, interrupt,
overslaugh; *Scot* taigle
TECHNICAL estop
OLD embar, let
FORMAL retard, preclude
COLLOQ. stymie, put a spoke in someone's wheel
help, aid, assist

Synonym nuances
Hamper can be used to suggest interrupting the progress
of something, perhaps temporarily, while **obstruct** and
block suggest a more permanent situation. **Impede**
suggests getting in the way of; **inhibit**, **encumber** and
the rarer **cumber** have more to do with holding
something's progress back: *the country was
encumbered by a poorly developed industrial sector*. The
terms **check** and **curb** suggest putting restraints on
something, and **handicap** and **hamstring** are equally
suggestive of restrictions: *as a doctor, I can't be
hamstrung by sentiment*.
  Both **foil** and **frustrate** are appropriate of spoiling a
plan, while **thwart** more definitely implies putting an end
to it. The terms **arrest** and **prevent** clearly indicate that
something has been stopped. **Stunt** and **dwarf** would
be used of hindering or stopping the growth of
something.
  Forestall has more to do with taking anticipatory
action: *she tried to sidestep him but he forestalled her
movement*. You can use **bar** and **debar** where something
is hindered by exclusion or prevention, whereas **deter**
implies active discouragement, and the less common
trammel suggests an element of confinement: *the
tightness of her skirt trammelled her steps*.

---

hindmost *adj*
last, farthest behind, furthest back, rearmost, tail,
endmost, furthest, final, remotest, trailing, ultimate,
concluding, terminal
foremost

hindrance *n*
obstruction, impediment, handicap, encumbrance,
obstacle, stumbling-block, block, barrier, bar, check, curb,
restraint, restriction, thwarting, interference, interruption,
stoppage, hold-up, delay, limitation, difficulty, drag, snag,
hitch, drawback, disadvantage, inconvenience, deterrent,
foil
OLD let
help, aid, assistance

hindsight *n*
retrospect, afterthought, thinking back, reflection, re-
examination, review, survey, recollection, remembrance
prospect

hinge *v*
centre, turn, revolve, pivot, hang, depend, rest
FORMAL be contingent

hint *n, v*
♦ *n*
1 TIP, advice, suggestion, help, clue, inkling, suspicion, tip-
off, cue, reminder, indication, sign, pointer, mention,
allusion, intimation, whisper, insinuation, implication,
innuendo
COLLOQ. wrinkle
2 *a hint of garlic*
touch, trace, tinge, taste, dash, soupçon, sprinkling, speck,
whiff, suspicion, suggestion, nuance
♦ *v*
suggest, prompt, indicate, signal, imply, insinuate, intimate,
allude, mention
COLLOQ. tip off, tip someone the wink

hinterland *n*
interior, hinderland, back-country, backveld, back-blocks

hip¹ *n*
she broke her hip
haunch, loin, thigh, pelvis, hindquarters, posterior,
buttocks, rump, croup, huck, huckle

hip² *adj*
parents trying to be hip

trendy, fashionable, modish, stylish, up to the minute, voguish
COLLOQ. all the rage, cool, funky, in, happening, with it
OLD COLLOQ. groovy
E3 unfashionable

hippie n
beatnik, flower child, rebel, loner, bohemian
COLLOQ. dropout

hire v, n
• v
1 RENT, let, lease, charter, commission, book, reserve
2 EMPLOY, take on, sign up, sign on, engage, appoint, enlist, retain
E3 2 dismiss; *colloq.* fire
• n
rental, rent, lease, fee, charge, pay, cost, price, salary, wage

hire-purchase n
instalment plan, easy terms, HP, deferred payments
COLLOQ. never-never

hirsute adj
hairy, bearded, unshaven, bristly, bewhiskered, shaggy
TECHNICAL hispid
FORMAL crinal, crinate, crinigerous, crinose, crinite
E3 bald, hairless

hiss v, n
• v
1 WHISTLE, shrill, whiss, whizz, sizzle, fizzle, effervesce, siffle
TECHNICAL assibilate
FORMAL sibilate
2 JEER, mock, scoff at, scorn, ridicule, taunt, boo, hoot, shout down, catcall
OLD (*Shakesp*) hizz
FORMAL deride
COLLOQ. blow raspberries, give someone the bird, goose
• n
1 WHISTLE, hissing, buzz
FORMAL sibilance, sibilation
2 JEER, mockery, scoffing, scorn, taunting, contempt, hoot, boo, catcall
FORMAL derision
COLLOQ. raspberry, the bird

historian n
chronicler, archivist, annalist, diarist, narrator, recorder, historiographer, chronologer

historic adj
famous, famed, renowned, celebrated, momentous, important, significant, epoch-making, notable, memorable, remarkable, outstanding, extraordinary
FORMAL consequential
COLLOQ. red-letter
E3 unimportant, insignificant, unknown

⚠ historic or historical?
Historic means 'famous or important in history': *a historic battle. Historical* means 'of or about history': *books on military and historical topics*; or 'having actually happened or lived, in contrast to existing only in legend or fiction': *Is Macbeth a historical person?*

---

historical adj
1 *of historical interest*
past, old, former, prior, ancient, bygone
FORMAL of yore
2 REAL, actual, authentic, factual, documented, recorded, chronicled, confirmed, verified, verifiable
FORMAL attested
E3 2 legendary, fictional

historically adv
in the past, formerly, in former times, once, long ago, some time ago, in years gone by, originally, from past experience, yesterday, in the good old days

history n
1 THE PAST, bygone/olden days, former times, days of old, the (good) old days, antiquity, yesterday
FORMAL yesteryear, days of yore
2 CHRONICLE, record(s), annals, archives, chronology, account, study, report(s), narrative, story, tale, saga, biography, life, autobiography, memoirs
3 BACKGROUND, experience, record, credentials, qualifications, education, family, circumstances

histrionic adj
dramatic, exaggerated, theatrical, melodramatic, insincere, sensational, unnatural, forced, artificial, bogus, ham
FORMAL affected

histrionics n
overacting, theatricality, dramatics, performance, melodrama, artificiality, insincerity, unnaturalness, sensationalism, staginess, tantrums, scene
FORMAL affectation
COLLOQ. ranting and raving

hit v, n
• v
1 STRIKE, knock, tap, smack, slap, thrash, bash, bat, thump, punch, beat, pound, batter, buffet, clout, cuff, box, thrash
COLLOQ. whack, belt, wallop, biff, sock, clobber
SLANG twat
2 BUMP, collide with, bang, clip, crash into, smash into, run into, meet head-on, plough into, damage, harm
COLLOQ. prang
3 AFFECT, have an effect on, upset, disturb, trouble, devastate, overwhelm, move, touch
FORMAL perturb
COLLOQ. knock for six
4 *the thought hit me*
come to mind, come to, strike, be remembered, be thought of, occur to, dawn on, enter your mind
• n
1 STROKE, shot, blow, knock, tap, slap, smack, buffet, thrashing, beating, punch, cuff, box, clout, bash, bump, collision, impact, crash, smash
COLLOQ. whack, belt, wallop, clobbering, sock, prang
2 SUCCESS, triumph, winner, blockbuster
COLLOQ. knockout, wow
E3 2 failure

■ **hit back**
retaliate, reciprocate, counter-attack, respond, strike back, criticize in return

■ **hit it off**
get along with, get on (well) with, be/become friendly with, become friends, warm to, grow to like, relate well to each other, get on good terms with
COLLOQ. click, get on like a house on fire, become thick as thieves

■ **hit on**
realize, arrive at, guess, think of, chance on, stumble on, light on, uncover, discover, invent

■ **hit out**
lash out, assail, attack, rail, strike out, denounce, condemn, criticize
FORMAL denounce, inveigh, vilify

hitch v, n
• v
1 FASTEN, attach, tie, harness, tether, bind, yoke, couple, connect, join, unite
2 PULL, heave, tug, jerk, hoist
COLLOQ. yank, hike (up)
E3 1 unhitch, unfasten
• n
snag, delay, hold-up, trouble, problem, difficulty, mishap,

setback, drawback, catch, impediment, hindrance, obstacle, block, check, barrier, obstruction
COLLOQ. glitch, hiccup

hitherto adv
until now, up to now, till now, so far, previously, formerly, beforehand, thus far
FORMAL heretofore

hit-or-miss adj
disorganized, haphazard, indiscriminate, undirected, unplanned, careless, offhand, casual, aimless, random, trial-and-error, perfunctory, lackadaisical, apathetic, cursory, uneven
E3 directed, planned, organized

hoard n, v
♦ n
collection, accumulation, mass, heap, pile, fund, reservoir, supply, reserve, store, stockpile, cache, treasure-trove; Scot pose
FORMAL aggregation, conglomeration
COLLOQ. stash
SLANG plant
♦ v
collect, gather, amass, accumulate, heap (up), stack up, buy up, save, set aside, put by, put away, lay in, lay up, store, stock up, stockpile, coffer, salt away, squirrel away, pile up, keep, treasure, uplay, uphoard
OLD hutch, mucker, spare
COLLOQ. stash away
E3 use, spend, squander

! **hoard** or **horde**?
A *hoard* is a store or hidden stock of something: *He had a hoard of chocolate bars under the bed.* A *horde* is a crowd or large number of people, etc: *Hordes of tourists come here every year.*

---

hoarder n
collector, saver, gatherer, miser, niggard, magpie, squirrel

hoarse adj
husky, croaky, croaking, throaty, guttural, gravelly, gruff, growling, rough, harsh, rasping, raspy, grating, raucous, discordant
E3 clear, smooth

hoarsely adv
roughly, harshly, raucously, croakily, huskily, gutturally, gruffly
E3 clearly, smoothly

hoary adj
1 WHITE-HAIRED, white, grey, grey-haired, silvery, grizzled, venerable, old, aged, ancient, antique, antiquated
FORMAL canescent, senescent
2 *that hoary old joke*
old, familiar, clichéd, trite, banal, overfamiliar, predictable, ancient, archaic
COLLOQ. old-hat

hoax n, v
♦ n
trick, prank, practical joke, put-on, joke, jest, ruse, fake, fraud, deception, bluff, humbug, cheat, swindle
COLLOQ. leg-pull, con, put-up job, frame-up, fast one, scam, spoof
SLANG N Am gold brick
♦ v
trick, deceive, play a practical joke on, take in, fool, dupe, gull, delude, swindle, cheat, hoodwink, bluff
COLLOQ. con, bamboozle, have on, pull someone's leg, lead up the garden path, pull the wool over someone's eyes, pull a fast one on, double-cross, two-time
SLANG take for a ride

hoaxer n
joker, practical joker, prankster, trickster, hoodwinker, mystifier, humbug
COLLOQ. bamboozler, spoofer

hobble v
limp, walk with a limp, stumble, falter, stagger, totter, reel, dodder, shuffle, walk awkwardly, walk lamely

hobby n
pastime, interest, diversion, recreation, relaxation, pursuit, leisure activity/pursuit, sideline, game, sport, entertainment, amusement, divertissement, fad, avocation

hobgoblin n
goblin, imp, elf, dwarf, gnome, spectre, spirit, evil spirit, mischievous fairy, sprite, apparition, bugbear, bogey, bugaboo; *dialect* buggan, bull-beggar; *Scot* worricow

hobnob v
associate, fraternize, keep company, mingle, mix, go around, socialize
FORMAL consort
COLLOQ. hang about, pal around

hocus-pocus n
trickery, swindle, deception, delusion, chicanery, gibberish, humbug, imposture, nonsense, mumbo-jumbo, spell, magic words, rigmarole, sleight of hand, legerdemain, trompe-l'oeil, artifice, cant, jargon, gobbledygook, abracadabra, cheat, hoax, deceit, conjuring
FORMAL prestidigitation

hodgepodge n
hotchpotch, mishmash, medley, miscellany, collection, mix, mixture, melange, jumble, confusion, mess

hog n, v
♦ n
pig, boar, wild boar, porker, grunter, swine
♦ v
monopolize, control, dominate, corner, take over, keep to yourself

hogwash n
rubbish, nonsense, drivel, gibberish, trash, tripe, twaddle
COLLOQ. bunk, bunkum, claptrap, piffle, bilge, poppycock, hot air, cobblers, baloney, blah, bosh, guff, hooey, malarkey, moonshine, eyewash, tosh, balderdash, rot, tommyrot
SLANG (*vulgar*) balls, bollocks, crap, shit, bullshit

hoi polloi n
the common people, the ordinary people, the masses, the proletariat, the third estate, the peasants, the rabble, the herd, the great unwashed
OLD (*Shakesp*) varletry
FORMAL the populace
COLLOQ. riff-raff, the plebs, the proles
E3 aristocracy, élite, nobility

hoist v, n
♦ v
lift, elevate, raise, erect, jack up, winch up, heave, rear, uplift
♦ n
jack, winch, crane, tackle, pulley, capstan, lift, elevator

hoity-toity adj
arrogant, proud, overweening, conceited, haughty, scornful, snobbish, supercilious, lofty, disdainful, pompous
COLLOQ. stuck-up, high and mighty, toffee-nosed, snooty, uppity

hold v, n
♦ v
1 GRIP, have in your hand(s), grasp, clutch, clasp, seize, cling to, embrace, enfold, hug, have, own, possess, keep, retain

2 *hold a meeting*
run, organize, conduct, carry on, continue, call, summon, convene, assemble, preside over
3 *hold someone's attention*
keep (up), engage, occupy, maintain, catch, arrest, absorb, engross, fascinate, enthral, captivate, rivet, fill, monopolize
4 CONSIDER, regard, esteem, judge, reckon, suppose, view, treat, think, believe, maintain, assume, presume
FORMAL deem, adjudge
5 BEAR, support, hold up, keep up, sustain, carry, take, buttress, prop up, brace
6 DETAIN, imprison, confine, impound, imprison, hold in custody, lock up, stop, arrest, check, curb, restrain
FORMAL incarcerate
7 CLING, stick, adhere, stay, remain
8 *the bus holds 53 passengers*
contain, accommodate, take, have space/room for, have a capacity of
FORMAL compromise
9 *hold office as prime minister*
occupy, fill, take up, continue, fulfil, have, hold down
10 *the fine weather will hold*
continue, carry on, last, remain, stay, go on, keep up
11 *the invitation/theory still holds*
stay, apply, remain, remain in force, remain valid/true, be in force/operation, hold up
⊟ 1 drop **5** collapse, fall, break **6** release, free, liberate
♦ *n*
1 GRIP, grasp, clasp, embrace, hug
TECHNICAL purchase
2 INFLUENCE, power, sway, mastery, dominance, dominion, authority, control, grip, leverage
COLLOQ. clout
■ **hold back**
1 CONTROL, keep back, curb, check, bar, restrain, impede, stop, delay, prevent, obstruct, suppress, stifle, retain, withhold, repress, contain, inhibit
FORMAL retard
2 HESITATE, delay, pause, shrink, refuse
FORMAL desist, refrain, forbear
⊟ 1 release, disclose
■ **hold down**
1 *hold down a job*
keep, have, occupy, continue in
2 *hold someone down*
keep down, oppress, dominate, tyrannize, suppress
■ **hold forth**
speak, talk, speak/talk at length, lecture, discourse, preach, harangue
FORMAL orate, declaim
COLLOQ. spout
■ **hold off**
1 FEND OFF, fight off, ward off, stave off, keep off, keep at bay, repel, resist, rebuff
2 DELAY, postpone, put off, defer, avoid, wait
■ **hold on**
1 GRASP, grip, clutch, clasp, seize, cling to
2 CONTINUE, endure, remain, persevere, wait, carry on, keep going, survive
COLLOQ. hang on
■ **hold out**
1 OFFER, give, present, extend
FORMAL proffer
2 LAST, last out, continue, carry on, persist, endure, persevere, stand fast, stand firm, resist, withstand
COLLOQ. hang on
⊟ 2 give in, yield
■ **hold over**
defer, postpone, put off, put back, delay, adjourn, suspend, shelve
■ **hold up**
1 SHOW, display, present, exhibit, hold high

2 SUPPORT, bear, carry, hold, sustain, brace, shore up, prop up, lift, raise
3 DELAY, detain, slow, hinder, impede, obstruct, set/put back
FORMAL retard
4 ROB, steal from, burgle, knock over, break into; *N Am* burglarize
COLLOQ. mug, stick up, knock off, nobble
5 APPLY, stay, remain, remain in force, remain valid/true, be in force/operation
■ **hold water**
bear scrutiny/examination, convince, be convincing, make sense, ring true, work, stand up, pass the test
COLLOQ. wash
■ **hold with**
agree with, go along with, approve of, support, subscribe to, accept
FORMAL countenance
■ **hold your own**
resist, withstand, survive, stand fast, stand firm, stand your ground
COLLOQ. keep your head above water
⊟ be defeated, lose ground
■ **get hold of**
1 OBTAIN, get, acquire, get your hands on
2 CONTACT, reach, get in touch with, speak to, communicate with, get through to
■ **put on hold**
delay, postpone, put off, hold off, defer
COLLOQ. put on the back burner

holder *n*
1 *holders of tickets*
bearer, owner, possessor, proprietor, keeper, purchaser, custodian, occupant
FORMAL incumbent
2 CONTAINER, receptacle, case, housing, casing, cover, sheath, rest, stand

holdings *n*
investments, shares, stocks, securities, bonds, assets, resources, land, real estate, possessions, property, estate, tenure

hold-up *n*
1 DELAY, wait, hitch, setback, snag, difficulty, problem, trouble, obstruction, stoppage, (traffic) jam, bottleneck
2 ROBBERY, burglary, theft, break-in, raid
COLLOQ. mugging
SLANG heist, stick-up, stick-up job

hole *n, v*
♦ *n*
1 *dig a hole*
dent, dimple, depression, excavation, crater, mine, shaft, pothole, scoop, hollow, cavity, pit, chasm, cave, cavern, chamber, pocket, recess
2 *a hole in the roof*
aperture, opening, space, break, gap, pore, puncture, perforation, eyelet, tear, split, crack, fissure, breach, rift, vent, notch, slit, gash, rent, outlet, shaft, slot
FORMAL orifice
3 *an animal's hole*
burrow, nest, lair, den, covert, set
4 *a hole in a theory*
flaw, fault, mistake, error, defect, loophole, inconsistency, discrepancy, weakness
5 HOVEL, slum, shack
COLLOQ. dump, tip, pigsty; *N Am* pigpen
6 *in a hole*
predicament, difficulty, quandary, snag, plight
COLLOQ. fix, mess, jam, spot, corner, bind, pickle, hot/deep water, pretty pass
♦ *v*
puncture, perforate, pierce, breach, break, crack, stab, spike, slit, gash, rent

■ **hole up**
hide, conceal yourself, take cover, lie low, go to ground, go into hiding

■ **pick holes in**
criticize, find fault with, slate, run down
COLLOQ. pull to pieces, nit-pick
SLANG slag (off)

hole-and-corner *adj*
secretive, secret, underhand, clandestine, covert, furtive, stealthy, surreptitious
COLLOQ. back-door, backstairs, hush-hush, sneaky, under-the-counter
Ⅎ open, public

holiday *n*
1 *go on holiday*
vacation, trip, recess, leave, leave of absence, time off, day off, break, rest, half-term, furlough
2 *a national holiday*
public holiday, bank holiday, legal holiday, feast day, festival, celebration, anniversary, saint's day, holy day
Related adjectives: ferial, festal

holier-than-thou *adj*
self-righteous, sanctimonious, self-satisfied, complacent, self-approving, smug, priggish, pietistic, pious, religiose
FORMAL unctuous
COLLOQ. goody-goody
Ⅎ humble, modest, meek

holiness *n*
sacredness, sanctity, spirituality, divinity, piety, devoutness, godliness, consecration, dedication, saintliness, blessedness, religiousness, goodness, virtuousness, righteousness, purity, perfection, sinlessness
OLD halidom, sanctimony
Ⅎ impiety

holler *n, v*
yell, shout, bawl, bellow, roar, call, cheer, shriek, clamour, cry, howl, yelp, yowl, whoop

hollow *adj, n, v*
♦ *adj*
1 CONCAVE, indented, depressed, caved-in, sunken, deep-set, deep, cavernous, empty, vacant, void, unfilled
FORMAL incurvate
2 FALSE, artificial, deceptive, insincere, hypocritical, pretended, deceitful, sham, meaningless, empty, vain, futile, fruitless, useless, pointless, profitless, worthless, valueless, unavailing, of no avail, Pyrrhic
3 *a hollow sound*
dull, flat, low, muffled, deep, rumbling, echoing, reverberant
Ⅎ 1 solid **2** real
♦ *n*
1 HOLE, pit, well, cavity, crater, excavation, cavern, cave, depression, basin, pan, bowl, cup, dimple, dent, dip, niche, recess, nook, cranny, indentation, groove, channel, trough
FORMAL concavity
2 VALLEY, gorge, ravine, dell, glen, vale, dale, cirque
♦ *v*
dig, excavate, burrow, tunnel, scoop, gouge, channel, groove, furrow, pit, dent, indent

■ **beat someone hollow**
defeat soundly/convincingly, rout, overwhelm
COLLOQ. thrash, lick, hammer, trounce, annihilate, devastate, slaughter, clobber, wipe the floor with

holocaust *n*
conflagration, flames, inferno, destruction, disaster, cataclysm, catastrophe, devastation, annihilation, extermination, extinction, massacre, carnage, mass murder, genocide, ethnic cleansing, sacrifice, slaughter, pogrom, hecatomb
FORMAL immolation

holy *adj*
1 *holy ground*
sacred, hallowed, consecrated, sanctified, sacrosanct, dedicated, blessed, venerated, revered, religious, spiritual, divine
2 PIOUS, religious, devout, godly, God-fearing, pietistic, saintly, virtuous, good, righteous, moral, faithful, pure, perfect, sinless
Ⅎ 1 unsanctified **2** impious, irreligious

holy of holies *n*
most holy place, shrine, altar
FORMAL sanctum, inner sanctum, sanctum sanctorum

homage *n*
recognition, acknowledgement, tribute, honour, praise, adulation, admiration, regard, respect, esteem, deference, reverence, adoration, awe, worship, devotion
FORMAL veneration

home *n, adj, v*
♦ *n*
1 *invite someone to your home*
house, flat, apartment, bungalow, cottage, address
FORMAL residence, abode, domicile, dwelling, dwelling-place, habitation
COLLOQ. pad, digs, semi-, roof over your head, somewhere to live
2 BIRTHPLACE, roots, home town, native town, homeland, native country, country of origin, mother country, motherland, fatherland
3 INSTITUTION, residential home, nursing home, retirement home, old people's home, sheltered housing, children's home, Dr Barnardo's home, refuge, hostel, centre, retreat, asylum, safe place
4 *the home of jazz*
place of origin, birthplace, source, fount, cradle, habitat, natural environment, element
Related adjective: domestic
♦ *adj*
domestic, household, family, internal, local, national, native, inland, interior
Ⅎ foreign, international, overseas

■ **home in on**
pinpoint, aim, direct, focus, concentrate, zero in on, zoom in on

■ **at home**
1 COMFORTABLE, relaxed, at ease
2 FAMILIAR, knowledgeable, experienced, confident, skilled, conversant, competent
COLLOQ. well up

■ **bring home**
make someone understand, make someone aware, make someone realize, impress, emphasize, instil, inculcate

■ **nothing to write home about**
not interesting, not exciting, dull, drab, boring, ordinary, mediocre, inferior, predictable
COLLOQ. OK, not enough to set the Thames on fire, no great shakes, nothing earthshattering

homecoming *n*
return (home), arrival (at home), coming-back, return of the prodigal

homeland *n*
native land, country of origin, native country, home, fatherland, motherland, mother country

homeless *adj, n*
♦ *adj*
itinerant, travelling, nomadic, wandering, vagrant, rootless, unsettled, displaced, dispossessed, evicted, exiled, outcast, abandoned, forsaken, destitute, without a roof over your head
FORMAL of no fixed abode
COLLOQ. down-and-out, sleeping rough, on the streets

SLANG dossing

• *n*

travellers, vagabonds, vagrants, tramps, squatters
FORMAL derelicts
COLLOQ. down-and-outs
SLANG dossers

homelessness *n*

vagrancy, rootlessness, displacement, abandonment, destitution, not having a roof over your head
FORMAL no fixed abode
COLLOQ. sleeping rough
SLANG dossing

homely *adj*

1 *a homely room*
homelike, homey, comfortable, cosy, snug, relaxed, informal, friendly, welcoming, cheerful, hospitable, intimate, familiar
2 SIMPLE, plain, everyday, ordinary, domestic, natural, modest, unassuming, unpretentious, unsophisticated, folksy, homespun
3 *a homely person*
plain, unattractive, unlovely, ugly, unprepossessing
COLLOQ. not much to look at
E3 1 grand, formal 3 attractive, lovely, good-looking

homespun *adj*

plain, simple, uncomplicated, unpolished, unrefined, unsophisticated, rough, rude, crude, rustic, homely, home-made, inelegant, amateurish, coarse, artless, folksy
E3 sophisticated

homework *n*

prep, preparation, groundwork, spadework

homey *adj*

homelike, comfortable, cosy, snug, relaxed, informal, friendly, welcoming, cheerful, hospitable, intimate, familiar

homicidal *adj*

deadly, lethal, murderous, violent, bloodthirsty, mortal, death-dealing, maniacal
FORMAL sanguinary

homicide *n*

murder, manslaughter, assassination, killing, bloodshed, slaughter, slaying

homily *n*

sermon, lecture, talk, speech, address, harangue, preaching
OLD prone
FORMAL discourse, postil, oration
COLLOQ. spiel

homogeneity *n*

uniformity, consistency, identicalness, similarity, sameness, resemblance, likeness, oneness, correspondence, agreement, analogousness, comparability
FORMAL consonancy, similitude
E3 difference, disagreement

homogeneous *adj*

uniform, consistent, unvarying, unvaried, identical, similar, alike, (all) the same, of the same kind, all of a piece, akin, kindred, analogous, corresponding, comparable, harmonious, compatible
FORMAL cognate, correlative
E3 heterogeneous, different

homogeneously *adv*

uniformly, consistently, (all) the same, of the same kind, all of a piece, similarly, identically, correspondingly
E3 heterogeneously

homogenize *v*

blend, merge, combine, amalgamate, make similar/uniform, coalesce, fuse, unite

homologous *adj*

related, matching, similar, parallel, comparable, analogous, equivalent, like, correspondent, corresponding
E3 different, dissimilar

homosexual *n, adj*

• *n*

gay, lesbian, bisexual
SLANG (*offensive*) queer, poof, dyke, faggot, fag, fairy, bent, queen, homo, nancy, pansy, woofter, butch, closet queen, fruit, powder puff, puff, punk, quiff, shirtlifter; *Aust* tonk
E3 heterosexual; *colloq.* straight

• *adj*

gay, lesbian, bisexual
COLLOQ. pink; (*offensive*) camp, butch
SLANG (*offensive*) queer, bent, dykey, homo
E3 heterosexual; *colloq.* straight

hone *v*

sharpen, whet, point, edge, grind, file, polish, develop

honest *adj*

1 LAW-ABIDING, virtuous, upright, upstanding, ethical, moral, principled, high-minded, right-minded, scrupulous, honourable, dependable, reputable, respectable, reliable, trustworthy, trusty, incorruptible, true, genuine, real, round, white, yeomanly; *dialect* even-down; *Scot* aefald
OLD soothful
COLLOQ. clean; *N Am* jake; *Aust & NZ* dinkum, dinky-di
SLANG *N Am* righteous
2 TRUTHFUL, true, sincere, frank, candid, blunt, outspoken, direct, straight, outright, forthright, straightforward, plain, simple, open, plain-speaking, plain-hearted
OLD single
COLLOQ. up-front, four-square
3 FAIR, just, impartial, objective, equitable, above-board, legitimate, legal, lawful, square, bona fide
COLLOQ. on the level, fair and square, honest as the day is long, straight as a die, on the up and up
E3 1 dishonourable 2 dishonest 3 unjust

Synonym nuances

sense 1

The term **law-abiding** creates a picture of someone who is honest in an everyday sense rather than especiallyy so, and who is unlikely to cause problems: *law-abiding citizens should not have to put up with this kind of behaviour*, while **virtuous** has more to do with inherent goodness, although it can sound rather old-fashioned and hint at pomposity. **Upright**, however, is suggestive of moral rectitude, and **upstanding** suggests a basic decency.

The terms **ethical** and **moral** can be applied to someone or something that follows the accepted codes of conduct: *ethical practices in accounting*, while **principled**, although similar, would tend to be used of a more personal or voluntary quality: *a principled commitment to better housing*. **High-minded**, although suggestive of lofty principles, also has connotations of arrogance or conceit, unlike **right-minded**, which is straightforwardly descriptive of being naturally drawn to what is correct. **Scrupulous**, although guided by moral considerations, also has associations with thoroughness in these considerations: *he was scrupulous about his business affairs*, while the term **incorruptible** has more to do with unflinching rectitude even in the face of temptations.

The terms **dependable** and **reliable**, **trustworthy** and **trusty** are approving ones which would put the emphasis on the confidence merited by someone's honesty, while **reputable** and **respectable** emphasize their worthiness of esteem: *we are a reputable law firm*.

Honours and awards include:

DENMARK:	NETHERLANDS:	CBE (Commander of the British Empire)	George Cross (GC)
Order of Dannebrog	Militaire Willemsorde Orde	OBE (Officer of the British Empire)	Victoria Cross (VC)
Order of the Elephant	van Oranje Nassau	MBE (Member of the British Empire)	Victoria Medal
FRANCE:	Nederlandsche Leeuw	The Most Noble Order of the Garter (KG)	**UNITED STATES:**
Croix de Guerre	**UNITED KINGDOM:**	The Most Distinguished Order of St Michael and St George	Bronze Star
Légion d'Honneur	The Most Excellent Order of the British Empire – GBE (Knight or Dame Grand Cross)	The Distinguished Service Order	Congressional Medal of Honour
GERMANY:			Distinguished Service Cross
Iron Cross			Legion of Merit
Order of Merit	KBE/DBE (Knight or Dame Commander of the British Empire)		Purple Heart
ITALY:			Medal for Merit
Ordine al Merito della Repubblica Italiana			Silver Star

honestly *adv*

1 REALLY, truly, truthfully, sincerely, frankly, to be honest
COLLOQ. straight up, not to put too fine a point on it, no messing
2 LEGITIMATELY, legally, lawfully, morally, ethically, fairly, justly, objectively, honourably, in good faith
COLLOQ. on the level
3 TRUTHFULLY, truly, sincerely, frankly, directly, direct, straightforwardly, plainly, simply
COLLOQ. up-front
4 FAIRLY, justly, impartially, objectively, equitably, legitimately, legally, lawfully, above board
COLLOQ. fair and square
E3 2 dishonestly, dishonourably **3** dishonestly **4** unfairly

honesty *n*

1 VIRTUE, uprightness, honour, integrity, morality, morals, ethics, principles, righteousness, incorruptibility, scrupulousness, trustworthiness, genuineness, veracity
FORMAL probity, rectitude
2 TRUTHFULNESS, sincerity, frankness, candour, bluntness, outspokenness, forthrightness, straightforwardness, plain-speaking, explicitness, openness
3 FAIRNESS, legitimacy, legality, equity, justness, objectivity, impartiality, balance, even-handedness
E3 2 dishonesty **3** bias, prejudice, partiality

honeyed *adj*

sweet, pleasant, delightful, pleasing, lovely, attractive, beautiful, pretty, winning, cute, engaging, appealing, charming, agreeable, affectionate, tender, kind, precious, dear, flattering
FORMAL mellifluous, unctuous

honorarium *n*

fee, pay, payment, salary, remuneration, recompense, reward
FORMAL emolument

honorary *adj*

unpaid, unofficial, titular, nominal, in name only, honorific, ex officio, formal
E3 paid

honour *n, v*

♦ *n*
1 REPUTATION, good name, repute, renown, fame, glory, distinction, regard, respect, esteem, credit, dignity, self-respect, pride, integrity, uprightness, honesty, morals, ethics, principles, virtue, goodness, morality, decency, righteousness, trustworthiness, truthfulness
FORMAL rectitude, probity
2 AWARD, accolade, decoration, prize, reward, trophy, crown, title, distinction, laurel, commendation, acknowledgement, compliment, recognition, tribute, favour, privilege
See panel above
3 PRAISE, acclaim, acclamation, applause, homage, admiration, reverence, worship, adoration
4 CHASTITY, purity, virginity, maidenhood, modesty, abstinence, temperateness, continence, continency, celibacy, unmarried state, singleness, virtue, innocence, immaculateness
E3 1 dishonour, disgrace
♦ *v*
1 PRAISE, acclaim, applaud, commend, have a high regard for, compliment, exalt, glorify, pay homage to, pay tribute to, acknowledge, recognize, decorate, crown, celebrate, commemorate, remember, admire, respect, esteem, revere, worship, prize, value
FORMAL venerate
2 *honour a promise*
keep, observe, respect, fulfil, carry out, discharge, execute, perform, be true to
3 *honour a cheque/bill*
pay, accept, clear, take
E3 1 dishonour, disgrace

Synonym nuances
noun sense 1
Reputation may be used to suggest how you are perceived generally, without any inherent association: *I consider this a slur on my reputation*, whilst **good name** implies you are already regarded favourably. Similarly **repute** is often used alone to imply a positive opinion: *a consultant of repute*, although it may be used occasionally to suggest a less favourable view: *towns with the worst repute for infant mortality*.

The terms **regard** and **respect** are also positive in themselves, and suggest appreciation: *he has a high regard for his rival*, while **credit** is more suggestive of good character: *to his credit he made an attempt at conciliation*. Both **renown** and **fame** put more emphasis on how widely someone is known rather than the esteem in which they are held, generally in a good sense, but **distinction**, and the even more marked **glory**, suggest high esteem for something outstanding: *the victorious team returned in glory*.

The terms **dignity** and **self-respect** always suggest positive, noble attributes, whilst **pride** can imply either a positive or negative trait depending on the context: *her comments were an insult to my pride; he was full of conceit and pride*. **Integrity** and **uprightness**, on the other hand, suggest inherent rectitude.

Virtue and **goodness**, however, interpret the idea of honour as benevolence, although **virtue** suggests a more moral aspect, while the word **morality** itself would put the emphasis firmly on conforming to accepted rules of conduct. **Decency** is similar, although suggestive of a more inherent, and down-to-earth trait: *a man whose decency was unshakable*, whereas **righteousness** again has more to do with the state of moral rectitude, and is formal, even archaic, in its tone: *saints who lived lives of righteousness*.

---

honourable *adj*

great, eminent, distinguished, renowned, famous, notable,

noted, illustrious, respected, worthy, prestigious, trusty, reputable, respectable, admirable, virtuous, upright, upstanding, straight, honest, trustworthy, truthful, true, sincere, dependable, reliable, noble, high-minded, principled, high-principled, moral, ethical, fair, just, right, righteous, good, decent
F3 dishonourable, unworthy, dishonest

honourably adv
nobly, reputably, respectably, worthily, virtuously, honestly, truly, sincerely, well, decently, morally, ethically
F3 dishonourably

hood n
cowl, scarf, capuche, capeline, domino

hoodlum n
1 HOOLIGAN, ruffian, rowdy, vandal, mobster, thug, tough, lout, brute
COLLOQ. mugger
SLANG bovver boy, yob
2 CRIMINAL, lawbreaker, felon, offender, gangster, armed robber, gunman
COLLOQ. N Am mobster, hood

hoodoo n
voodoo, witchcraft, sorcery, magic, wizardry, occultism, the occult, the black art, black magic, enchantment, spell, incantation, divination, jinx
FORMAL necromancy, conjuration

hoodwink v
deceive, dupe, fool, take in, delude, mislead, outwit, hoax, trick, cheat, rook, gull, defraud, swindle, get the better of
COLLOQ. bamboozle, have on, con, lead up the garden path, pull a fast one on, pull the wool over someone's eyes
SLANG take for a ride

hoof n
foot, trotter, cloven hoof, cloot
TECHNICAL ungula

hoofed adj
cloven-footed, cloven-hoofed
TECHNICAL ungulate, unguligrade

hook n, v
♦ n
1 a hook on a door/dress
catch, peg, barb, fastener, clasp, hasp, clip, hinge, tenter, tenterhook, goose-neck; dialect snig, crome; Scot cleek
TECHNICAL becket, dog, cantdog, chape, crummock, gaff, tenaculum
OLD angle, crotchet, grappling-iron, gripple
FORMAL uncus, hamulus
2 SICKLE, scythe
3 BEND, curve, crook, angle, loop, elbow, bow, arc
4 BLOW, hit, stroke, box, thump, punch, cuff, clout, clip, knock, rap
COLLOQ. wallop
♦ v
1 BEND, crook, curve, curl
2 CATCH, capture, bag, grab, trap, entrap, snare, ensnare, enmesh, entangle, strike; Scot cleek
TECHNICAL gaff
3 FASTEN, clasp, hitch, fix, attach, secure
■ **by hook or by crook**
by any means, by some means, somehow, one way or another, come what may
COLLOQ. by fair means or foul, come hell or high water
■ **hook, line and sinker**
completely, totally, utterly, wholly, fully, in full, absolutely, perfectly, quite, thoroughly, through and through, altogether, entirely, solidly
COLLOQ. in every respect, lock stock and barrel, from first to last, root and branch, every inch, heart and soul
■ **off the hook**
cleared, acquitted, in the clear

FORMAL exonerated, vindicated
COLLOQ. scot free

hooked adj
1 CURVED, bent, curled, beaked, barbed, beaky, aquiline, sickle-shaped
FORMAL falcate, hamate, hamose, hamous, hamular, hamulate, uncate, unciform, uncinate, adunc
2 ADDICTED, dependent, devoted, obsessed, enamoured

hooligan n
ruffian, rowdy, hoodlum, mobster, thug, tough, rough, lout, vandal, delinquent
COLLOQ. mugger; Aust & NZ hoon
SLANG bovver boy, yob; Scot ned

hoop n
ring, circle, round, loop, wheel, band, girdle, circlet, stirrup, tire, basket, bail, hula-hoop, trundle; Scot gird, girr
TECHNICAL laggen-gird
OLD trochus

hoot v, n
♦ v
1 an owl hooting
call, cry, whoop, screech, tu-whit tu-whoo
FORMAL ululate
2 the car hooted
toot, beep, blare, whistle
3 the audience hooted
shout, shriek, cry, yell, whoop, howl, sneer, ridicule, taunt, mock, jeer, boo, hiss, howl down
♦ n
1 the hoot of an owl
call, cry, whoop, screech, tu-whit tu-whoo
2 the hoot of a car
toot, beep, whistle
3 the hoots of the audience
shout, shriek, cry, yell, whoop, howl, sneer, ridicule, taunt, mock, jeer, boo, hiss
3 he's a real hoot
amusing person/situation, joker, comic, wit
COLLOQ. character, scream, laugh, riot
■ **not give a hoot**
not care in the slightest, not be bothered
COLLOQ. not give a damn, not give a monkey's, not care a toss, not give a tinker's cuss/damn

hop v, n
♦ v
1 JUMP, leap, spring, bound, vault, skip, dance, prance, frisk, limp, hobble
2 hop over to Paris
pop, nip, fly quickly
♦ n
1 JUMP, leap, spring, bound, vault, bounce, step, skip, dance
2 a quick hop by plane
(quick) flight, trip, journey, excursion, jaunt
3 DANCE, disco, social, party
COLLOQ. knees-up, shindig
■ **caught on the hop**
caught unprepared/unawares, caught in the act, unready, ill-equipped
COLLOQ. caught with your trousers down

hope n, v
♦ n
hopefulness, optimism, ambition, aspiration, wish, desire, longing, yearning, craving, dream, pipe dream, expectance, expectancy, expectation, anticipation, prospect, promise, belief, confidence, assurance, conviction, assumption, faith, trust
OLD (Shakesp) esperance
F3 pessimism, despair
♦ v
aspire, wish, desire, long, yearn, crave, dream, expect, be

hopeful, await, look forward to, anticipate, aim, be ambitious, contemplate, foresee, believe, trust, have confidence, pray, rely, reckon on, assume
COLLOQ. keep your fingers crossed, pin your hopes on, hope against hope
E≥ despair

hopeful adj
1 OPTIMISTIC, confident, assured, expectant, sanguine, cheerful, buoyant, aspiring, aspirant, positive
COLLOQ. bullish
2 *a hopeful sign*
promising, encouraging, heartening, gladdening, reassuring, optimistic, pleasant, favourable, positive, rosy, bright, cheerful
FORMAL propitious, auspicious
E≥ **1** pessimistic, despairing **2** discouraging

hopefully adv
1 *hopefully the weather will improve*
I hope, if all goes well, with luck, all being well, probably, conceivably, it is to be hoped that
2 EXPECTANTLY, with hope, with anticipation, confidently, eagerly, optimistically, expectedly
FORMAL sanguinely
COLLOQ. bullishly

hopefulness n
optimism, ambition, aspiration, wish, desire, longing, yearning, craving, expectation, anticipation, prospect, belief, confidence, assurance, conviction, assumption, faith, trust

hopeless adj
1 PESSIMISTIC, defeatist, negative, despairing, desperate, gloomy, demoralized, downhearted, dejected, downcast, despondent, forlorn, wretched
2 UNATTAINABLE, unachievable, impracticable, impossible, vain, grave, foolish, futile, useless, pointless, worthless, poor, helpless, lost, past praying for, irreversible, irremediable, beyond remedy, irreparable, beyond repair, incurable
COLLOQ. all up (with), no-hope, not having a hope in hell
3 *hopeless at speaking French*
useless, incompetent, bad, weak
COLLOQ. lousy, pathetic, awful
E≥ **1** hopeful, optimistic **2** curable **3** skilled, expert

hopelessly adv
1 UNHAPPILY, pessimistically, negatively, despairingly, gloomily, desperately, despondently, dejectedly
2 INCOMPETENTLY, badly, weakly, uselessly, inefficiently
COLLOQ. pathetically, awfully

hopelessness n
despondency, pessimism, discouragement, despair, misery, gloom, gloominess, dejection, wretchedness, forlorn hope
OLD wanhope
COLLOQ. blues, dumps

horde n
band, gang, pack, troop, crew, herd, drove, flock, swarm, crowd, mob, throng, mass, multitude, host, army

❗ horde or **hoard**?
See panel at **hoard**.

horizon n
1 SKYLINE, vista, prospect, range, range of vision
2 *widen your horizons*
experience, scope, perspective, compass, outlook, perception
■ **on the horizon**
imminent, impending, forthcoming, in the offing, approaching, fast approaching, coming, on the way, near,

close, looming, menacing, threatening, brewing, in the air, at hand, about to happen, almost upon you

horizontal adj
level, flat, plane, smooth, levelled, on its side
FORMAL supine

horny adj
1 *a horny shell*
hard, corny, callous
TECHNICAL ceratoid
FORMAL corneous
2 LUSTFUL, ardent, sexy, aroused, lascivious, lecherous, ruttish
FORMAL concupiscent, libidinous
COLLOQ. randy
E≥ **2** cold, frigid

horrendous adj
horrible, horrific, shocking, appalling, horrifying, terrifying, frightening, terrible, dreadful, frightful

horrible adj
1 *horrible scenes of murder*
horrific, shocking, appalling, horrifying, terrifying, frightening, harrowing, bloodcurdling, hair-raising, terrible, black, horrendous, dreadful, frightful, repulsive, revolting, abominable, grim, hideous, gruesome, monstrous, ghastly, awful, grisly, grisy
OLD ugly
COLLOQ. scary
See Synonym nuances panel at **ghastly**.
2 *that fish smells horrible*
unpleasant, disagreeable, nasty, unkind, obnoxious, horrid, disgusting, revolting, loathsome, repulsive, detestable, abominable, offensive, ghastly, awful, terrible, dreadful, frightful, horrendous
E≥ **1** attractive **2** pleasant, agreeable, lovely

horribly adv
1 HORRIFICALLY, appallingly, terribly, dreadfully, frightfully, repulsively, grimly, hideously, gruesomely
2 UNPLEASANTLY, disagreeably, awfully, terribly, dreadfully, frightfully

horrid adj
1 HORRIFIC, shocking, appalling, horrifying, terrifying, frightening, harrowing, bloodcurdling, hair-raising, terrible, dreadful, frightful, repulsive, revolting, abominable, grim, hideous, gruesome, ghastly, awful
2 UNKIND, mean, nasty, awful, cruel, dreadful, obnoxious, hateful
COLLOQ. beastly
E≥ **1, 2** lovely, pleasant

horrific adj
horrifying, shocking, appalling, awful, terrible, frightful, dreadful, ghastly, gruesome, terrifying, frightening, harrowing, bloodcurdling
COLLOQ. scary

horrifically adv
shockingly, appallingly, terribly, dreadfully, frightfully, repulsively, disagreeably, awfully

horrify v
shock, appal, offend, outrage, scandalize, disgust, repel, revolt, sicken, nauseate, dismay, alarm, startle, scare, panic, frighten, terrify, terrorize, intimidate
OLD abhor
COLLOQ. spook, make your blood run cold, make your hair stand on end, make your flesh creep, give you the shivers, give you the heebie-jeebies, put the wind up, put the frighteners on, scare out of your wits, scare the living daylights out of, scare to death
E≥ please, delight

horror n
1 *recoil in horror*

Breeds of horse include:

Akhal-Teké	British	Frederiksborg	Karabakh	Mustang	Sardinian
Alter-Réal	Warmblood	Freiberger	Kladruber	New Kirgiz	Shagya Arab
American	Brumby	French Saddle	Knabstrup	Nonius	Shire
Quarter Horse	Budyonny	Horse	Kustanair	North Swedish	Suffolk Punch
American Saddle	Calabrese	French Trotter	Latvian Harness	Oldenburg	Swedish Halfbred
Horse	Charollais	Friesian	Horse	Orlov Trotter	Tchenaran
American Trotter	Halfbred	Furioso	Limousin	Palomino	Tennessee
Andalusian	Cleveland Bay	Gelderland	Halfbred	Paso Fino	Walking Horse
Anglo-Arab	Clydesdale	German Trotter	Lipizzaner	Percheron	Tersky
Anglo-Norman	Comtois	Groningen	Lithuanian Heavy	Peruvian Stepping	Thoroughbred
Appaloosa	Criollo	Hanoverian	Draught	Horse	Toric
Arab	Danubian	Hispano	Lokai	Pinto	Trait du Nord
Ardennias	Døle	Holstein	Lusitano	Pinzgauer	Trakehner
Auxois	Gudbrandsdal	Iomud	Mangalarga	Noriker	Vladimir Heavy
Barb	Døle Trotter	Irish Draught	Maremmana	Plateau Persian	Draught
Bavarian	Don	Irish Hunter	Masuren	Poitevin	Waler
Warmblood	Dutch Draught	Italian Heavy	Mecklenburg	Rhineland Heavy	Welsh Cob
Boulonnais	East Bulgarian	Draught	Metis Trotter	Draught	Württemberg
Brabançon	East Friesian	Jutland	Morgan	Russian Heavy	
Breton	Einsiedler	Kabardin	Muraköz	Draught	
	Finnish	Karabair	Murgese	Salerno	

The points of a horse are:

back	elbow	gaskin	loins	nostril	throat
breast	eye	haunch	lower jaw	pastern	upper lip
cannon	face	head	lower (or under)	root (or dock) of	withers
chestnut	fetlock	hind leg	lip	the tail	
crest of the neck	forearm	hip	mane	shoulder	
croup (or rump)	forefoot	hock	mouth	spur vein	
crupper	forehead	hoof	neck	stifle (joint)	
ear	forelock	knee	nose	tail	

shock, outrage, disgust, distaste, revulsion, repugnance, abhorrence, loathing, abomination, hate, dismay, alarm, fright, fear, terror, panic, dread, apprehension
FORMAL consternation, trepidation, detestation
2 GHASTLINESS, awfulness, frightfulness, hideousness, unpleasantness
E3 1 approval, delight

horror-struck *adj*
appalled, shocked, frightened, horrified, terrified, horror-stricken, aghast, stunned, petrified, scared stiff
E3 delighted, pleased

horse *n*
steed, mount, stallion, nag, mustang, mare, colt, filly, bay, sorrel, roan, hack, bronc(h)o, charger, cob, dobbin, hackney, centaur; *Welsh* keffel; *Scot* yaud; *Aust* brumby, yarraman
SLANG *Aust & NZ* moke; *Aust* neddy
Related adjectives: equine, caballine, hippic
See also panels above

Breeds of pony include:

Connemara	Hackney	Welsh Mountain
Dales	Highland	Pony
Dartmoor	New Forest	Welsh Pony
Exmoor	Przewalski's	
Falabella	Horse	
Fell	Shetland	

horseman, horsewoman *n*
equestrian, rider, jockey, cavalryman, horse soldier, hussar, dragoon, knight

horseplay *n*
clowning, buffoonery, foolery, fooling, fooling around, tomfoolery, skylarking, pranks, capers, antics, high jinks, practical jokes, fun and games, rough-and-tumble
COLLOQ. monkey business

hortatory *adj*
encouraging, edifying, heartening, inspiriting, instructive, practical, stimulating, homiletic
FORMAL didactic, exhortative, exhortatory, hortative, preceptive
COLLOQ. pep

horticulture *n*
gardening, cultivation, agriculture
TECHNICAL arboriculture, floriculture

hosanna *n*
praise, worship, alleluia, save us
FORMAL laudation

hose *n*
pipe, tube, tubing, piping, channel, conduit, duct

hosiery *n*
socks, stockings, tights, hold-ups, stay-ups, leggings, leg-coverings, hose

hospitable *adj*
friendly, sociable, welcoming, neighbourly, receptive, cordial, amicable, congenial, convivial, genial, warm, helpful, kind, kind-hearted, gracious, generous, open-handed, liberal, bountiful
E3 inhospitable, unfriendly, hostile

hospital *n*
medical centre, health centre, clinic, infirmary, institute, sanatorium, hospice
Related adjective: nosocomial

hospitality *n*
friendliness, sociability, welcome, neighbourliness, accommodation, entertainment, congeniality, conviviality, warmth, cheer, generosity, kindness, liberality, helpfulness, open-handedness, open house, entertainment
FORMAL philoxenia
COLLOQ. tea and sympathy
E3 unfriendliness, hostility
Related adjective: xenial

host[1] *n, v*

♦ *n*

1 COMPÈRE, master of ceremonies, MC, presenter, announcer, anchor, anchorman, anchorwoman, linkman, media personality, entertainer, party-giver
COLLOQ. emcee
2 PUBLICAN, innkeeper, landlord, landlady, proprietor, proprietress

♦ *v*

present, introduce, give, compère

host[2] *n*

a host of letters

multitude, myriad, array, army, horde, crowd, throng, mass, swarm, pack, troop, herd, mob, crush, band

hostage *n*

prisoner, captive, detainee, pawn, surety, security, pledge

hostel *n*

youth hostel, bed and breakfast, B & B, YMCA, YWCA, boarding-house, guesthouse, hotel, inn, motel, pension, hospice; *N Am* dormitory
OLD hospital, entry
FORMAL residence
SLANG dosshouse; *N Am* flophouse

hostelry *n*

public house, inn, tavern, bar, hotel, boarding-house, guesthouse, pension, motel; *S Afr* canteen
COLLOQ. pub

hostile *adj*

1 BELLIGERENT, antagonistic, warlike, ill-disposed, unsympathetic, unfriendly, inhospitable, inimical, opposed, malevolent
FORMAL bellicose
2 ADVERSE, unfavourable, contrary, opposite
FORMAL inauspicious
3 *hostile to trade unions*
disapproving, averse, opposed, antagonistic, unfavourable, disinclined, ill-disposed
FORMAL antipathetic
F3 **1** receptive, friendly, welcoming **2** favourable

hostilities *n*

war, warfare, battle, fighting, conflict, strife, action, bloodshed

hostility *n*

opposition, aggression, belligerence, militancy, war, enmity, antagonism, animosity, unfriendliness, cruelty, ill-will, malice, resentment, hard feelings, anger, bitterness, abhorrence, hate, hatred, malevolence, dislike, aversion, prejudice, unpleasantness, disfavour
OLD envy
FORMAL estrangement, bellicosity, antipathy, animus
F3 friendliness, friendship

hot *adj*

1 WARM, heated, fiery, burning, scalding, scorching, blistering, red hot, roasting, baking, boiling, piping, steaming, sizzling, sweltering, parching, summery, balmy, searing, sultry, torrid, tropical
2 SPICY, spiced, peppery, piquant, sharp, pungent, strong, fiery
3 FEVERISH, delirious, burning, flushed, red, with a temperature
4 *his hot temper*
fiery, furious, angry, indignant, raging, boiling, seething, fuming, livid, violent, heated, inflamed, incensed, enraged
5 *hot competition*
fierce, intense, strong, furious, keen, cut-throat
COLLOQ. dog-eat-dog
6 *not very hot on the idea*
keen, enthusiastic, eager, warm, earnest, zealous, diligent, devoted

7 *hot news*
recent, new, fresh, latest, up-to-date, exciting
8 *hot goods*
illegally obtained/imported, contraband, stolen, illicit, pilfered, ill-gotten
9 FASHIONABLE, chic, stylish, in vogue, in, popular, prevailing, current, latest, up-to-the-minute, up-to-date, contemporary, modern
COLLOQ. trendy, all the rage, glitzy, ritzy, snazzy, swanky, funky, hip, with it, cool
OLD COLLOQ. swinging
F3 **1** cold, cool, chilly **2** mild, bland **4** calm **7** old, stale

■ blow hot and cold

vacillate, waver, hesitate, fluctuate, sway, oscillate, keep changing your mind, haver, temporize
COLLOQ. dilly-dally, shilly-shally, hum and ha(w)

■ hot air

nonsense, empty talk, emptiness, mere words, bluster, bombast, vapours, foam, froth; *Scot* blethers
FORMAL verbiage
COLLOQ. balderdash, bosh, bunk, bunkum, claptrap, gas, cobblers, piffle, bilge, codswallop, baloney, eyewash, stuff and nonsense
SLANG (*vulgar*) bullshit, crap, shit
F3 wisdom

Synonym nuances
sense 1

Warm can be used of anything that is even mildly hot, whilst **heated** is similar, but more suggestive of having heat applied: *a heated swimming pool*, though, if used of conversation, it is a little more marked in its suggestion of a confrontational element: *a heated discussion*. **Fiery**, however, is often used of being hot to taste, or is more suggestive of being somewhat tempestuous: *theirs was a fiery relationship*.

The terms **burning** and **scalding**, along with **scorching** and **blistering**, suggest that damage could be sustained and thus imply dangerously high temperatures, while *red hot* offers its own warning. The terms **roasting**, **baking** and **steaming**, and **piping** and **sizzling**, make reference to how heat may have been applied or is manifesting.

Sweltering, on the other hand, is usually reserved for very hot climatic conditions, as are **sultry** and **tropical**, and while **summery** and **balmy** also suggest weather of a seasonal nature, they are associated with milder, more comfortable temperatures. **Parching**, however, puts the emphasis on the dryness effected by extreme heat: *a parching desert dust storm*, and **searing** suggests great intensity: *it was impossible to walk in the searing heat of the outback*.

---

hotbed *n*

breeding-ground, den, hive, nest, seedbed, cradle, nursery, school, forcing-house

hot-blooded *adj*

passionate, temperamental, excitable, spirited, wild, rash, impulsive, impetuous, high-spirited, heated, fervent, fiery, bold, eager, ardent, lustful, sensual, lusty
FORMAL perfervid, precipitate
F3 cool, dispassionate

hotchpotch *n*

mishmash, medley, miscellany, collection, mix, mixture, melange, jumble, confusion, mess; *N Am* hodgepodge

hotel *n*

boarding-house, guesthouse, pension, motel, inn, bed and breakfast, B & B, public house, tavern, hostel, hostelry, aparthotel

hotfoot *adv*

speedily, at top speed, quickly, rapidly, swiftly, without

Types of house include:

apartment	croft	homestead	mia-mia	semi-detached	treehouse
bedsit	detached	hut	parsonage	shack	vicarage
bungalow	*N Am* duplex	igloo	penthouse	shanty	villa
Scot but and ben	farmhouse	lodge	pied-à-terre	*Scot* single-end	*Aust* villa home
chalet	flat	log cabin	*S Afr* pondok	*NZ* state house	(or unit)
chalet bungalow	grange	maisonette	prefab	studio	*Scot* weem
condominium	granny flat	manor	ranch house	terraced	*Aust* wurley
cottage	hacienda	manse	rectory	thatched cottage	
council house	hall	mansion	*colloq.* semi	town house	

See also **building**.

---

delay, hurriedly, in haste, hastily, posthaste, helter-skelter, pell-mell
COLLOQ. at the double, at a rate of knots, flat out, hell for leather, like the clappers, like greased lightning; *N Am* lickety-split
E₃ slowly; *formal* dilatorily

■ **hotfoot it**
hurry, rush, speed, race, tear, zoom, career, bowl along, sprint, gallop, dash, accelerate, quicken
COLLOQ. belt, tear, hurtle, pelt, put your foot down, step on it
E₃ slow, delay

hothead *n*
tearaway, terror, madcap, madman, daredevil, desperado, hotspur

hotheaded *adj*
headstrong, impetuous, impulsive, hasty, rash, foolhardy, reckless, wild, fiery, excitable, volatile, explosive, volcanic, hot-tempered, quick-tempered, short-tempered, irascible
E₃ cool, calm

hothouse *n*
greenhouse, glasshouse, conservatory, orangery, vinery

hotly *adv*
1 *a hotly debated issue*
passionately, forcefully, vehemently, strongly, vigorously, keenly, fiercely, ardently, fervently, intensely
2 *hotly pursued*
closely, at close quarters, at close range, narrowly, near, nearly, tightly
FORMAL nigh

hot-tempered *adj*
fiery, choleric, explosive, quick-tempered, short-tempered, violent, volcanic, testy, hasty, irascible, irritable, petulant
COLLOQ. ratty, stroppy; *Scot & Irish* crabbit
E₃ calm, cool; *formal* imperturbable

hound *v*
chase, pursue, follow, hunt (down), track, stalk, trail, drive, force, goad, prod, urge, chivvy, nag, pester, disturb, bully, badger, harry, harass, provoke, persecute

house *n, v*
♦ *n*
1 BUILDING, home
FORMAL dwelling, residence, domicile, habitation; *NZ* whare
SLANG gaff, pad
See panel above
2 HOUSEHOLD, family, family circle, home, ménage
Related adjectives: domestic, domal
3 *a publishing/design house*
firm, company, establishment, business, enterprise, corporation, organization
4 ASSEMBLY, legislative assembly, body, chamber, legislature, parliament, congress
5 *a full house at the theatre*
audience, auditorium, gathering, assembly, turnout, crowd, spectators, onlookers, listeners, viewers
6 DYNASTY, family, clan, tribe, line, lineage, ancestry, blood, strain, race, kindred
♦ *v*
1 LODGE, quarter, billet, board, accommodate, put up, take in, have room/space for, shelter, harbour
2 HOLD, contain, protect, cover, guard, shelter, sheathe, place, keep, store

■ **on the house**
free, free of charge, without charge/cost/payment, for nothing, at no (extra) cost, gratis

household *n, adj*
♦ *n*
family, family circle, house, home, ménage, establishment, set-up
♦ *adj*
1 DOMESTIC, home, family, ordinary, plain
2 *a household name*
everyday, common, familiar, well-known, famous, established

householder *n*
resident, tenant, occupier, occupant, owner, landlady, freeholder, leaseholder, proprietor, landlord, home-owner, head of the household

housekeeping *n*
home economics, domestic science, household management, running a home, domestic work/matters, homemaking, housewifery

houseman *n*
1 DOCTOR, junior doctor, house-physician, house-surgeon, intern(e), resident
2 MANSERVANT, servant, butler, valet, retainer, gentleman's gentleman

house-trained *adj*
domesticated, tame, tamed, well-mannered, house-broken
E₃ unsocial

housing *n*
1 ACCOMMODATION, houses, homes, shelter
FORMAL dwellings, habitation
2 CASING, case, container, holder, covering, guard, cover, sheath, jacket, protection

hovel *n*
shack, shanty, cabin, hut, shed, slum
COLLOQ. dump, hole

hover *v*
1 HANG, be suspended, poise, float, drift, fly, flutter, flap
2 *he hovered by the door*
pause, linger, hang about, loiter, hesitate, waver, fluctuate, alternate, seesaw
FORMAL vacillate, oscillate

however *adv*
nevertheless, nonetheless, still, yet, even so, regardless, though, anyhow, just the same, in any case, as it comes, at the same time, actually, howsoever, leastaways; *dialect* but, howsomever, howsomdever; *N Am* leastwise
OLD howbeit
FORMAL notwithstanding

howl *v, n*

◆ *v*

wail, cry, shriek, scream, bawl, shout, yell, roar, bellow, bay, yelp, yowl, hoot, moan, groan, wow, yawl; *dialect* gowl

◆ *n*

wail, cry, shriek, scream, bawl, shout, yell, roar, bellow, bay, yelp, yowl, hoot, moan, groan, wow, yawl

howler *n*

error, mistake, blunder, gaffe, malapropism

FORMAL solecism

COLLOQ. bloomer, clanger, boob; *N Am* flub

SLANG goof

hub *n*

centre, middle, focus, focal point, axis, pivot, linchpin, nerve centre, core, heart

hubbub *n*

noise, racket, din, clamour, commotion, disturbance, riot, uproar, hullabaloo, rumpus, confusion, disorder, tumult, hurly-burly, chaos, pandemonium

F3 peace, quiet

hubris *n*

arrogance, pride, conceit, boasting, haughtiness, vanity, superciliousness, disdain, scorn, contempt, superiority, egotism, condescension, lordiness, pomposity, high-handedness, imperiousness, self-importance, snobbishness, presumption, insolence

FORMAL hauteur, contumely

COLLOQ. nerve

F3 humility, unassumingness, bashfulness

huckster *n*

hawker, dealer, trader, salesperson, barker, tinker, vendor, haggler, packman, pedlar, pitcher

huddle *v, n*

◆ *v*

cluster, gravitate, converge, meet, gather, congregate, crowd, flock, cram, pack, herd, throng, press, squeeze, cuddle, snuggle, nestle, curl up, crouch, hunch

F3 disperse

◆ *n*

1 CLUSTER, clump, knot, mass, crowd, heap, muddle, jumble

2 MEETING, conclave, conference, discussion, consultation

COLLOQ. powwow

hue *n*

colour, shade, tint, dye, tinge, nuance, tone, complexion, aspect, light

hue and cry *n*

furore, fuss, hullabaloo, outcry, commotion, rumpus, uproar, brouhaha, clamour, ado, chase

COLLOQ. ruction, to-do, hoo-ha, carry-on, kerfuffle, ballyhoo, tizzy, a song and dance

huff *n*

pique, sulks, mood, bad mood, anger, rage, passion

COLLOQ. paddy, stew

huffily *adv*

crossly, angrily, resentfully, snappily, irritably, morosely, peevishly, in a huff, in a temper

COLLOQ. hot under the collar, in a paddy, in a strop

huffy *adj*

cross, angry, resentful, snappy, disgruntled, grumpy, irritable, offended, sulky, surly, testy, touchy, moping, morose, moody, crusty, short, peevish, petulant, waspish

FORMAL querulous

COLLOQ. crabbed, crotchety, miffed, shirty, stroppy

F3 cheery, happy

hug *v, n*

◆ *v*

1 EMBRACE, cuddle, squeeze, enfold, hold, hold close, press, clasp, clutch, grip, cling to, enclose

2 *the path hugs the wall for a mile*

stay close to, follow closely, stay near, keep close to

◆ *n*

embrace, cuddle, squeeze, clasp, hold, clinch

huge *adj*

immense, vast, enormous, massive, colossal, titanic, giant, gigantic, mammoth, monumental, tremendous, stupendous, great, big, large, extensive, cavernous, monstrous, Herculean, gargantuan, titanic, bulky, heavy, unwieldy

OLD hideous, immane

FORMAL prodigious

COLLOQ. jumbo, frightful, ginormous, humongous

SLANG mega

F3 tiny, minute

hugely *adv*

enormously, immensely, vastly, massively, extremely, very, very much, really, thoroughly, greatly, highly, extraordinarily, tremendously, largely

COLLOQ. frightfully, terribly, awfully, terrifically

hugger-mugger *adj*

1 CONFUSED, muddled, jumbled, disarranged, disordered, untidy, disorderly, chaotic, disorganized, mixed-up, out of order

COLLOQ. higgledy-piggledy, at sixes and sevens

2 SECRET, clandestine, surreptitious, undercover, underhand, concealed, hidden, covert, fraudulent, sly, sneaky, stealthy, underground, closet, furtive, private

COLLOQ. backroom, behind-door, cloak-and-dagger, under-the-counter

F3 1 orderly

hulk *n*

1 WRECK, shipwreck, remains, derelict, frame, hull, shell

2 LOUT, lump, lubber, oaf

COLLOQ. clod, clodhopper

hulking *adj*

massive, heavy, weighty, unwieldy, cumbersome, bulky, big, large, awkward, clumsy, lumbering, ungainly

F3 small, delicate

hull¹ *n*

the hull of a ship

body, frame, framework, skeleton, structure, casing, covering

hull² *n, v*

◆ *n*

the hull of a fruit

husk, pod, capsule, legume, skin, rind, peel, shell; *N Am* shuck

TECHNICAL epicarp

◆ *v*

husk, pare, peel, shell, strip, skin, trim; *N Am* shuck

hullabaloo *n*

fuss, palaver, outcry, furore, hue and cry, noise, din, racket, brouhaha, uproar, pandemonium, rumpus, disturbance, commotion, hubbub, turmoil, tumult

COLLOQ. ruction, to-do, hoo-ha, carry-on, kerfuffle, ballyhoo, tizzy, a song and dance

F3 calm, peace

hum *v, n*

◆ *v*

1 BUZZ, whirr, purr, drone, thrum, throb, croon, sing

2 MURMUR, mumble

3 *humming with activity*

throb, be busy, pulse, vibrate, buzz

◆ *n*

buzz, buzzing, whirr, whirring, purring, thrum, drone, murmur, mumble, throb, throbbing, pulsation, vibration

■ **hum and haw**

be indecisive, dither, vacillate, waver, hesitate, fluctuate,

sway, oscillate, keep changing your mind
COLLOQ. dilly-dally, shilly-shally, blow hot and cold

human *adj, n*
• *adj*
1 MORTAL, physical, fleshly, fallible, flesh and blood, weak, susceptible, vulnerable, reasonable, rational
FORMAL anthropoid
2 KIND, considerate, understanding, humane, compassionate, sympathetic, tolerant
F3 2 inhuman
• *n*
human being, mortal, man, woman, child, person, individual, body, soul
TECHNICAL homo sapiens

humane *adj*
kind, compassionate, sympathetic, understanding, thoughtful, kind-hearted, good-natured, considerate, gentle, tender, loving, mild, lenient, merciful, forgiving, forbearing, kindly, generous, benevolent, charitable, humanitarian, good, benign
F3 inhumane, cruel

humanely *adv*
compassionately, sympathetically, thoughtfully, kindly, kind-heartedly, gently, lovingly, tenderly, generously, mildly, mercifully
F3 inhumanely, cruelly

humanitarian *adj, n*
• *adj*
benevolent, charitable, philanthropic, public-spirited, welfare, compassionate, humane, kind, sympathetic, understanding, considerate, generous, altruistic, unselfish
F3 selfish, self-seeking
• *n*
philanthropist, benefactor, good Samaritan, do-gooder, altruist
F3 egoist, self-seeker

humanitarianism *n*
benevolence, charitableness, charity, goodwill, philanthropy, humanism, compassionateness, generosity, loving-kindness
FORMAL beneficence
F3 egoism, self-seeking

humanities *n*
arts, liberal arts, literature, classics, classical studies, philosophy

humanity *n*
1 HUMAN RACE, humankind, mankind, womankind, mortals, mortality, people, man
TECHNICAL homo sapiens
2 HUMANENESS, kindness, compassion, fellow-feeling, brotherly love, understanding, tenderness, sympathy, gentleness, tenderness, thoughtfulness, benevolence, tolerance, generosity, goodwill, kind-heartedness, goodness, pity, mercy; *S Afr* ubuntu
F3 2 inhumanity, cruelty

humanize *v*
improve, better, polish, refine, domesticate, tame, civilize, cultivate, educate, enlighten, edify

humankind *n*
humanity, human race, mankind, womankind, mortals, mortality, people, man
TECHNICAL homo sapiens

humanness *n*
human nature, humanity, kindness, compassion, understanding, tenderness, sympathy, gentleness, tenderness, thoughtfulness, benevolence, tolerance, generosity, goodwill, kind-heartedness, goodness

humble *adj, v*
• *adj*

1 MEEK, submissive, unassertive, modest, unassuming, self-effacing, polite, respectful, deferential, servile, subservient, sycophantic, prideless, supplicatory
OLD (*Spenser*) afflicted; demiss, demissive
FORMAL obsequious
2 LOWLY, low, mean, insignificant, unimportant, common, commonplace, ordinary, poor, small, inferior, low-ranking, plain, simple, modest, unassuming, unpretentious, unostentatious, undistinguished, unrefined, yeomanly
OLD base, silly
F3 1 proud, assertive **2** important, pretentious
• *v*
bring down, lower, bring low, abase, demean, sink, discredit, belittle, disgrace, shame, put to shame, humiliate, mortify, chasten, crush, depress, deflate, subdue
OLD afflict, pluck
FORMAL disparage
COLLOQ. put someone in their place, bring/take someone down a peg or two, cut down to size
F3 exalt

humbleness *n*
humility, modesty, unassertiveness, unassumingness, self-effacement, diffidence, meekness, submissiveness, deference, self-abasement, servility, lowliness, unpretentiousness
F3 pride, arrogance, assertiveness

humbly *adv*
modestly, unassumingly, meekly, respectfully, simply, submissively, unpretentiously, deferentially, diffidently, docilely, subserviently, servilely
FORMAL obsequiously
COLLOQ. sheepishly, cap in hand
F3 confidently, defiantly

humbug *n*
1 DECEPTION, pretence, sham, fraud, swindle, trick, hoax, deceit, trickery, cheating, hypocrisy
COLLOQ. con
SLANG *N Am* gold brick
2 NONSENSE, rubbish, bluff, cant, hypocrisy
COLLOQ. bunkum, claptrap, eyewash, balderdash, poppycock, cobblers, rot
SLANG baloney; (*vulgar*) balls, shit
3 CHARLATAN, fraud, cheat, bluffer, actor, swindler, impostor, fake, sham, trickster, rogue
COLLOQ. con man, poser

humdrum *adj*
boring, tedious, monotonous, routine, dull, repetitious, tiresome, dreary, uninteresting, uneventful, unvaried, ordinary, mundane, everyday, commonplace, run-of-the-mill, banal
F3 varied, lively, unusual, exceptional

humid *adj*
damp, moist, dank, wet, clammy, sticky, close, heavy, oppressive, muggy, sultry, steamy
F3 dry

humidity *n*
humidness, damp, dampness, moisture, moistness, dankness, wetness, stickiness, closeness, heaviness, clamminess, mugginess, sultriness, steaminess, sogginess, vaporousness, dew, mist
FORMAL vaporosity
F3 dryness

humiliate *v*
mortify, embarrass, confound, crush, break, deflate, chasten, shame, bring shame on, disgrace, abash, discredit, degrade, demean, humble, bring low, abase
FORMAL discomfit
COLLOQ. put down, put someone in their place, make someone lose face, bring/take someone down a peg or

two, cut someone down to size, take the wind out of someone's sails
⊞ dignify, exalt

humiliating *adj*
humbling, mortifying, shaming, crushing, chastening, deflating, degrading, embarrassing, disgraceful, ignominious, inglorious, disgracing, snubbing
FORMAL discomfiting, humiliant, humiliative, humiliatory
⊞ gratifying, triumphant

humiliation *n*
mortification, embarrassment, shame, disgrace, chastening, crushing, confounding, dishonour, discredit, indignity, ignominy, abasement, humbling, degradation, deflation, snub, rebuff, affront
FORMAL discomfiture
COLLOQ. put-down, loss of face, humble pie
⊞ gratification, triumph

humility *n*
modesty, unassertiveness, unassumingness, self-effacement, diffidence, meekness, submissiveness, deference, self-abasement, servility, humbleness, lowliness, unpretentiousness
⊞ pride, arrogance, assertiveness

hummock *n*
hillock, hump, knoll, mound, barrow, elevation, prominence

humorist *n*
wit, satirist, caricaturist, cartoonist, comedian, comic, joker, wag, jester, clown, gagman

humorous *adj*
funny, amusing, comic, entertaining, witty, satirical, facetious, playful, waggish, droll, whimsical, comic, comical, farcical, ludicrous, absurd, ridiculous, laughable, hilarious, humoristic, side-splitting, Falstaffian, Gilbertian, Rabelaisian; *Scot* pawky
OLD (*Shakesp*) capricious
FORMAL jocular, risible
COLLOQ. zany, knee-slapping
⊞ serious, humourless

humour *n, v*
♦ *n*
1 WIT, wittiness, gags, drollery, jokes, jesting, badinage, repartee, facetiousness, absurdity, ridiculousness, hilarity, comedy, fun, amusement
FORMAL jocularity
COLLOQ. wisecracks
2 *in a bad humour*
mood, temper, frame/state of mind, spirits, disposition, temperament, vein, kidney
♦ *v*
go along with, comply with, accommodate, satisfy, gratify, indulge, pamper, spoil, cosset, favour, permit, please, mollify, flatter, pander to, tolerate, coax, jolly
OLD (*Shakesp*) observe
FORMAL acquiesce in

Types of humour include:

black	farcical	satirical
barrack-room	gallows	sick
Chaplinesque	lavatorial	slapstick
dry	Pythonesque	

---

humourless *adj*
boring, tedious, dull, dry, solemn, serious, grave, earnest, sombre, glum, morose, unsmiling, unlaughing, grim, long-faced, dour
COLLOQ. po-faced
⊞ humorous, witty

hump *n, v*
♦ *n*
hunch, lump, knob, bump, projection, protuberance, outgrowth, bulge, swelling, mound, ramp, mass, prominence, protrusion; *Scot* humph
TECHNICAL sleeping policeman
OLD bunch
FORMAL excrescence, intumescence
♦ *v*
1 ARCH, curve, crook, bend, hunch
2 CARRY, lug, haul, lift, heave, hoist, shoulder
▪ **get the hump**
sulk, mope, be annoyed, be irritated, be exasperated
COLLOQ. be rubbed up the wrong way, get the pip
▪ **give someone the hump**
annoy, irritate, rile, anger, vex, irk, madden, exasperate, tease, provoke, ruffle, gall, trouble, nag, disturb, bother, pester, plague, harass
COLLOQ. aggravate, bug, hassle, rub up the wrong way, wind up, get someone's blood up, get on someone's nerves, get up someone's nose, get under someone's skin, get someone's goat, get on someone's wick, drive up the wall, drive round the bend/twist, get someone's back up, brass off, cheese off, make someone's hackles rise, make sparks fly, get someone's dander up; *N Am* tick/hack off
▪ **over the hump**
past the crisis, past the difficulty, over the worst

hump-backed *adj*
crookbacked, hunchbacked, hunched, crooked, stooped, humped, deformed, misshapen, gibbous
TECHNICAL kyphotic
OLD (*Shakesp*) bunch-backed
⊞ straight, upright

humped *adj*
arched, bent, curved, crooked, hunched, gibbous
⊞ flat, straight

hunch *n, v*
♦ *n*
1 HUMP, lump, knob, bump, projection, protuberance, outgrowth, bulge, swelling, mound, ramp, mass, prominence, protrusion
2 SUSPICION, premonition, intuition, feeling, impression, idea, inkling, guess, sixth sense
FORMAL presentiment
♦ *v*
hump, bend, curve, arch, stoop, crouch, squat, huddle, draw in, curl up

hunger *n, v*
♦ *n*
1 HUNGRINESS, emptiness, starvation, malnutrition, famine, famishment, appetite, ravenousness, greed, greediness
TECHNICAL bulimia
FORMAL voracity, esurience, esuriency
2 *hunger for power*
desire, craving, longing, yearning, pining, hankering, want, need, yen, itch, thirst, appetite
♦ *v*
starve, want, wish, desire, need, crave, have a craving for, hanker, long, have a longing for, yearn, pine, ache, itch, thirst, raven

---

Synonym nuances
noun sense 1
The word **emptiness** places the emphasis on the physical sensations caused by needing food, but does not necessarily suggest an extreme condition.
Starvation, however, goes much further, by suggesting a debilitated physical state caused by lack of food, and **malnutrition** also suggests consequent bad health, either through a lack of food or an absence of nourishing food: *many elderly find it difficult to cook, and suffer from*

malnutrition. The term **famine** would be reserved for a widespread scarcity of food, usually with extreme results: *the famine left up to a million dead*, while the rarer **famishment** again suggests the effects of such a scarcity.

Appetite, on the other hand, suggests an everyday hunger caused by a natural desire for food: *they lost weight by taking appetite suppressors*, whereas **ravenousness** would be appropriate for immense hunger, although it can be used in a more light-hearted tone. Both **greed** and **greediness** are disapproving in that they have to do with craving much larger quantities than you actually require.

hungrily *adv*
ravenously, greedily, covetously, insatiably, eagerly, longingly, avidly

hungry *adj*
1 STARVING, underfed, undernourished, malnourished, empty, hollow, famished, ravenous, greedy, insatiable, having a wolf in the stomach, hungerful; *Scot* yaup
OLD ahungered; (*Shakesp*) hungerly, sharp
FORMAL voracious
COLLOQ. empty, peckish, could eat a horse
2 *hungry for knowledge*
desirous, craving, longing, aching, yearning, pining, hankering, itching, thirsty, eager, avid, needing, covetous
E3 1 satisfied, full

hunk *n*
1 CHUNK, lump, piece, block, slab, wedge, mass, dollop, clod, gobbet
2 STRONG MAN, macho man, he-man
COLLOQ. dish, beefcake, stud
OLD COLLOQ. dreamboat

hunt *v, n*
• *v*
1 CHASE, pursue, follow, shadow, hound, run, dog, stalk, track, trail, run to ground, persecute, prey on, tire down, chivvy, course, scare up, halloo, beagle, cub, ride to hounds, ferret, hawk, rabbit, seal, mouse, rat, slug, turtle
2 SEEK, look for, search, try to find, scour, rummage, fish, ferret, forage, investigate; *N Am* still-hunt
COLLOQ. scrounge
• *n*
chase, pursuit, search, stalking, tracking, scouring, rummaging, quest, investigation, battue
OLD chivvy, venation

hunter *n*
huntsman, chaser, chasseur, woodman, woodsman, jäger, montero, hound, beagler, hawker, rabbiter, ratter, turtler, wolfer, lion-hunter, Nimrod, seal-fisher, shikar; *N Am* still-hunter
OLD venator, venerer

hunting *n*
field sports, chase, coursing, trapping, stalking, beagling, cubbing, falconry, lamping, wolfing, wolving, ratting, turtling, birding, shikar
OLD venation, venery
Related adjectives: cynegetic, venatic, venatical

hurdle *n*
jump, fence, wall, hedge, railing, bar, barrier, barricade, obstacle, obstruction, stumbling-block, hindrance, impediment, handicap, problem, snag, difficulty, complication

hurl *v*
throw, toss, fling, sling, pitch, cast, heave, catapult, project, propel, fire, launch, send, let fly
COLLOQ. chuck

hurly-burly *n*
bustle, hustle, commotion, confusion, trouble, disorder, disruption, unrest, pandemonium, uproar, chaos, furore, upheaval, tumult, turbulence, turmoil, frenzy, distraction, agitation, hubbub, brouhaha, bedlam
COLLOQ. hassle

hurricane *n*
gale, tornado, typhoon, cyclone, whirlwind, squall, storm, tempest

hurried *adj*
rushed, hectic, hasty, speedy, fast, quick, breakneck, swift, rapid, passing, fleeting, transient, transitory, brief, short, cursory, superficial, offhand, perfunctory, shallow, careless, slapdash
FORMAL precipitate
COLLOQ. rush job
E3 leisurely, unhurried

hurriedly *adv*
speedily, at top speed, quickly, rapidly, swiftly, without delay, in haste, hastily, posthaste, helter-skelter, pell-mell, hotfoot
COLLOQ. at the double, at a rate of knots, flat out, hell for leather, like the clappers, like greased lightning; *N Am* lickety-split
E3 slowly; *formal* dilatorily

hurry *v, n*
• *v*
rush, dash, run, fly, hasten, make haste, press on, quicken, speed (up), accelerate, chase, drive, scurry, hustle, push
OLD festinate
FORMAL expedite
COLLOQ. mosey, vamoose, bettle off, run like hell, cut and run, go all out, belt, hightail it,
E3 slow down, delay
• *n*
rush, haste, quickness, swiftness, fastness, rapidity, speed, urgency, hustle, bustle, flurry, commotion, hubbub, confusion
OLD dispatch
FORMAL expedition, celerity, precipitation
E3 leisureliness, calm

Colloquial expressions telling someone to hurry up include:

buck up!	get your skates on!	out!
chop-chop!	jump to it!	put your foot
come along!	look alive/lively!	down!
come on!	look sharp!	shake a leg!
get a move on!	look slippy/ smart	show your heels!
get a wiggle on!	make it snappy!	step on it!
get cracking!	pull your finger	step on the gas!

---

hurt *v, n, adj*
• *v*
1 *my leg hurts*
ache, be painful, be sore, pain, throb, sting, smart, burn, tingle
2 INJURE, wound, maltreat, ill-treat, bruise, cut, scratch, lacerate, damage, burn, torture, maim, impair, disable
FORMAL debilitate
3 DAMAGE, impair, harm, mar, spoil, blemish, blight
4 UPSET, sadden, cause sadness, grieve, distress, wound, pain, offend, annoy
FORMAL afflict
• *n*
pain, soreness, aching, throbbing, burning, tingling, smarting, discomfort, suffering, injury, wound, cut, bruise, scratch, damage, harm, distress, sadness, upset, sorrow, grief, misery
FORMAL affliction
• *adj*

1 INJURED, wounded, bruised, grazed, cut, scarred, lacerated, maimed, painful, sore, aching, throbbing, burning, tingling, smarting
2 UPSET, sad, saddened, sorrowful, grief-stricken, miserable, in anguish, distressed, aggrieved, annoyed, offended, affronted

hurtful *adj*
1 UPSETTING, wounding, vicious, cruel, mean, unkind, nasty, malicious, spiteful, catty, derogatory, offensive, distressing, scathing, cutting
FORMAL injurious, malefactory
2 HARMFUL, damaging, detrimental, pernicious, destructive, ruinous
FORMAL injurious, deleterious
E3 1 helpful, kind, innocuous **2** advantageous

hurtle *v*
dash, tear, race, fly, shoot, speed, rush, career, charge, plunge, dive, crash, rattle
COLLOQ. belt, pelt, put your foot down, step on it/the gas/the juice

husband *n, v*
♦ *n*
spouse, partner, mate, groom, man, married man, consort, *mari complaisant; dialect* master
OLD goodman, hoddy-doddy; *N Am* gander-mooner
COLLOQ. hubby, better half, other half, old boy
Related adjective: marital
♦ *v*
conserve, economize, eke out, use sparingly, use carefully, manage, preserve, reserve, put aside, put by, budget, save, save up, store, ration, hoard
E3 squander, waste

husbandry *n*
1 FARMING, agriculture, cultivation, tillage, land management, farm management, conservation
TECHNICAL agribusiness, agronomics, agronomy
2 MANAGEMENT, saving, thrift, thriftiness, frugality, economy, good housekeeping
E3 2 wastefulness, squandering

hush *v, n, interj*
♦ *v*
quieten, silence, shush, still, settle, compose, calm, soothe, mollify, subdue
COLLOQ. pipe down, shut up, cut the cackle, dry up
E3 disturb, rouse
♦ *n*
quietness, quiet, silence, peace, peacefulness, stillness, calm, calmness, tranquillity, serenity
FORMAL repose
E3 noise, clamour
♦ *interj*
quiet, be quiet, hold your tongue, shut up, not another word
COLLOQ. belt up, button it, cut the cackle, dry up, enough said, give it a rest, give over, hold your peace, pack it in, pipe down, put a sock in it, say no more, shut your face, shut your mouth, wrap up
■ **hush up**
keep dark, keep secret, suppress, conceal, cover up, stifle, smother, gag
E3 publicize

hush-hush *adj*
secret, confidential, classified, restricted, top-secret
COLLOQ. under wraps
E3 open, public

husk *n*
covering, case, shell, pod, capsule, legume, hull, rind, peel, skin, bran, chaff; *N Am* shuck
TECHNICAL epicarp
OLD *(Shakesp)* shale

huskily *adv*
deeply, hoarsely, croakily, gutturally, gruffly, gravelly, harshly

husky *adj*
1 HOARSE, croaky, croaking, low, deep, throaty, guttural, gruff, gravelly, rasping, rough, thick, coarse, harsh
2 BRAWNY, muscular, burly, hefty, strong, strapping, well-built
COLLOQ. beefy

hussy *n*
loose woman, minx, temptress; *dialect* huzzy, limmer
COLLOQ. floozie, vamp
SLANG slut, tart, scrubber, tramp, slag

hustle *v, n*
♦ *v*
rush, hurry, dash, fly, bustle, hasten, force, pressurize, push, shove, manhandle, thrust, bundle, elbow, nudge, jostle, crowd
♦ *n*
bustle, activity, stir, commotion, tumult, agitation, fuss, hurry, rush, hurly-burly

hut *n*
cabin, shack, shanty, booth, shed, lean-to, shelter, den; *S Afr* pondok

hybrid *n, adj*
♦ *n*
cross, crossbreed, half-breed, half-blood, mongrel, composite, combination, mixture, amalgam, compound
FORMAL conglomeration
♦ *adj*
crossbred, mongrel, composite, combined, mixed, heterogeneous, compound
E3 pure-bred

hybridize *v*
crossbreed, cross, interbreed, bastardize, reproduce together

hygiene *n*
sanitariness, sanitation, sterility, disinfection, cleanliness, purity, wholesomeness
E3 insanitariness

hygienic *adj*
sanitary, sterile, sterilized, aseptic, germ-free, disinfected, clean, pure, healthy, wholesome
FORMAL salubrious
E3 unhygienic, insanitary, contaminated, polluted

hymn *n*
song of praise, song, chorus, spiritual, psalm, anthem, air, carol, chant, cantata, canticle, motet, doxology, introit, choral(e), offertory, paean, paraphrase, hymeneal, procession, recessional, dirge, mantra
TECHNICAL cathisma, sticheron, trisagion, troparion, dies irae, Stabat Mater, Tantum ergo, Te Deum, sequence

hype *n, v*
♦ *n*
publicity, advertisement, advertising, promotion, puff, puffery, ballyhoo, build-up, racket, fuss
COLLOQ. plugging, razzmatazz
♦ *v*
promote, publicize, advertise, build up
COLLOQ. plug, talk up

hyped up *adj*
excited, anxious, overwrought, stimulated, stirred, exhilarated, thrilled, elated, in high spirits, enthusiastic, eager, moved, beside yourself, animated, worked up, wrought-up, agitated, restless, frantic, frenzied, wild
COLLOQ. high, on the edge of your seat, on tenterhooks, thrilled to bits, uptight, hyper, fired up
E3 calm

hyperbole n
overstatement, exaggeration, excess, magnification, extravagance, overkill
F3 understatement; *technical* meiosis

hypercritical adj
fault-finding, over-particular, pedantic, finicky, fussy, quibbling, hair-splitting, niggling, captious, carping, strict, cavilling, censorious
FORMAL ultracrepidarian
COLLOQ. nit-picking, pernickety, choosy, picky; *NAm* persnickety
F3 tolerant, uncritical

hypnotic adj
mesmerizing, soporific, sleep-inducing, sedative, numbing, spellbinding, fascinating, compelling, irresistible, magnetic
FORMAL somniferous, stupefactive

hypnotism n
hypnosis, mesmerism, suggestion, auto-suggestion

hypnotize v
mesmerize, put into a state of unconsciousness, put to sleep, spellbind, bewitch, enchant, entrance, fascinate, captivate, beguile, magnetize

hypochondria n
neurosis, hypochondrianism, hypochondriasis
FORMAL valetudinarianism

hypochondriac n, adj
◆ n
hypochondriast
FORMAL valetudinarian
◆ adj
hypochondriacal, neurotic
FORMAL valetudinarian

hypocrisy n
insincerity, double-talk, double-dealing, two-facedness, dishonesty, falsity, deceit, deceitfulness, deception, pretence, pretended goodness, sanctimoniousness, lip service, wearing a mask, cant, pharisaism
FORMAL dissimulation, dissembling, duplicity
COLLOQ. phoneyness
F3 sincerity

hypocrite n
deceiver, fraud, impostor, pretender, mountebank, Pharisee, canter, charlatan, whited sepulchre, Holy Willie, Pecksniff, Tartuffe, Janus
FORMAL dissembler

COLLOQ. phoney, pseud, pseudo

hypocritical adj
insincere, two-faced, self-righteous, sanctimonious, double, double-dealing, false, specious, hollow, deceptive, insincere, fraudulent, spurious, deceitful, dishonest, lying, histrionic, self-pious, pharisaical, Pecksniffian, Tartuffian, Janian-faced, Janus-faced
OLD (*Shakesp*) false-faced
FORMAL dissembling, perfidious, duplicitous
COLLOQ. phoney
F3 sincere, genuine, truthful

hypothesis n
theory, thesis, theorem, axiom, proposition, notion, supposition, presumption, assumption, speculation
FORMAL premise, postulate, conjecture

hypothetical adj
theoretical, imaginary, imagined, supposed, assumed, presumed, proposed, speculative
FORMAL conjectural
F3 real, actual

hypothetically adv
in theory, theoretically, supposedly, speculatively, ideally
FORMAL conjecturally

hysteria n
agitation, frenzy, panic, hysterics, neurosis, mania, delirium, madness
COLLOQ. (screaming) habdabs
F3 calm, composure, control

hysterical adj
1 FRANTIC, frenzied, berserk, out of control, uncontrollable, mad, raving, crazed, beside yourself, delirious, demented, overwrought, neurotic, in a panic
2 HILARIOUS, extremely funny, uproarious, farcical, ridiculous, ludicrous, side-splitting
COLLOQ. priceless, rich
F3 1 calm, composed, self-possessed

hysterically adv
1 FRANTICALLY, uncontrollably, neurotically, madly, beside yourself, in a panic, out of control, out of your mind
2 HILARIOUSLY, uproariously, ridiculously, farcically, ludicrously, absurdly
COLLOQ. screamingly

hysterics n
agitation, frenzy, panic, hysteria, neurosis, mania, delirium, madness
COLLOQ. (screaming) habdabs

I

ice *n, v*

◆ *n*

1 FROZEN WATER, hail, sleet, frost, rime, icicle, glacier, floe, brash, black ice, dry ice, ground ice, anchor-ice, frazil, drift-ice, pack-ice, sea ice, shelf ice, shell ice, snow-ice, stream-ice, hummock, verglas, tickly-benders; *Scot* grue, grew; *N Am* slob ice
TECHNICAL crust, virga
2 ICINESS, frostiness, coldness, chill, coolness, unresponsiveness, distance

◆ *v*

freeze (over), refrigerate, chill, cool, frost, glaze, harden, enfreeze

▪ **put on ice**
shelve, delay, postpone, put off, defer
FORMAL hold/leave in abeyance
COLLOQ. put on the back burner

iceberg *n*
berg, calf, growler

ice-cold *adj*
frozen, iced, chilled, icy, frosty, icebound, arctic, bitterly cold, raw, polar, glacial, Siberian, frigid, freezing, numb, hard, frosted, solidified, stiff, frozen-stiff, chilled to the bone, rigid, fixed
TECHNICAL algid
FORMAL gelid
COLLOQ. baltic
F3 warm, hot

icily *adv*
coldly, coolly, stiffly, formally, rudely, morosely, forbiddingly
F3 warmly, responsively

icon *n*
idol, portrait, image, likeness, figure, representation, symbol, portrait, portrayal

iconoclast *n*
critic, denouncer, dissenter, denunciator, dissident, radical, sceptic, rebel, opponent, questioner, heretic, unbeliever, image-breaker
F3 devotee, believer

iconoclastic *adj*
critical, dissident, irreverent, innovative, questioning, radical, rebellious, sceptical, subversive, heretical, impious
FORMAL denunciatory, dissentient
F3 uncritical, unquestioning, trustful

icy *adj*
1 ICE-COLD, glacial, freezing, frozen, frosty, raw, bitter, biting, cold, chill, chilly, frigid, arctic, polar, Siberian
FORMAL gelid
2 *icy roads*
frosty, slippery, glassy, frozen, icebound, frostbound, rimy, slippy
3 HOSTILE, cold, stony, cool, frigid, frosty, indifferent, unfriendly, aloof, stiff, reserved, restrained, distant, formal, rude, morose, forbidding
F3 **1** hot **3** friendly, warm, welcoming, responsive

idea *n*
1 THOUGHT, concept, notion, theory, hypothesis, guess, belief, opinion, feeling, view, viewpoint, judgement, conception, conceptualization, vision, image, impression, perception, interpretation, understanding, inkling, suspicion, fancy, clue
FORMAL conjecture, abstraction
2 *a good idea*
brainwave, suggestion, proposal, proposition, recommendation, plan, scheme, design
3 AIM, intention, purpose, reason, point, end, goal, target, object, objective

ideal *n, adj*

◆ *n*

1 PERFECTION, epitome, acme, paragon, example, model, pattern, prototype, type, image, criterion, standard, yardstick, benchmark
FORMAL exemplar, archetype, nonpareil
2 PRINCIPLE, morals, ethics, moral standards/values, ethical standards/values

◆ *adj*

1 PERFECT, dream, utopian, best, optimum, optimal, supreme, highest, complete, absolute, model
FORMAL archetypal, quintessential, consummate
2 UNREAL, imaginary, conceptual, philosophical, theoretical, hypothetical, abstract, unattainable, impractical, visionary, romantic, fanciful, idealistic, utopian

idealism *n*
impracticality, perfectionism, romanticism, utopianism
F3 pragmatism, realism

idealist *n*
perfectionist, visionary, dreamer, optimist, romantic, romanticist
F3 realist, pragmatist

idealistic *adj*
perfectionist, utopian, visionary, romantic, quixotic, starry-eyed, optimistic, unrealistic, impractical, impracticable
F3 realistic, pragmatic, practical

idealization *n*
romanticization, romanticizing, glamorization, glorification, worship, exaltation, idolization, ennoblement
FORMAL apotheosis

idealize *v*
utopianize, romanticize, glamorize, glorify, exalt, worship, idolize
F3 caricature

ideally *adv*
perfectly, in a perfect world, in an ideal world, at best, in theory, theoretically, hypothetically

idée fixe *n*
fixation, obsession, complex, hang-up, leitmotiv, fixed idea
FORMAL monomania

identical *adj*
same, self-same, one and the same, indistinguishable, interchangeable, twin, duplicate, like, alike, similar, corresponding, matching, equal,

equivalent, consistent, right, precise
TECHNICAL cloned, congruent, identic, syngeneic
OLD self, numeric
FORMAL analogous, coincident
COLLOQ. as like as two peas in a pod, a dead ringer, spitting image
F3 different

identically *adv*
interchangeably, indistinguishably, alike, in the same way, just the same, similarly, equally, equivalently, correspondingly, consistently
FORMAL congruently, analogously
F3 differently

identifiable *adj*
recognizable, discernible, noticeable, known, perceptible, detectable, distinguishable, unmistakable
FORMAL ascertainable
F3 unidentifiable, indefinable, unfamiliar, unknown

identification *n*
1 RECOGNITION, detection, spotting, pointing-out, diagnosis, naming, labelling, classification
2 EMPATHY, association, involvement, connection, rapport, relationship, sympathy, fellow feeling
3 IDENTITY CARD, documents, ID, papers, credentials, badge, driving licence, birth certificate, passport; *S Afr* passbook
4 ASSOCIATION, bond, tie, connection, link, correlation, relation, relationship, interrelation, involvement

identify *v*
1 RECOGNIZE, know, pick out, single out, point out, distinguish, perceive, make out, discern, discover, find out, establish, notice, detect, diagnose, name, label, tag, specify, pinpoint, spot, place, catalogue, classify
FORMAL ascertain
2 ASSOCIATE, connect, relate, involve, place, think of together, couple
3 *identify with other sufferers*
empathize with, relate to, associate with, respond to, sympathize with, feel for

identity *n*
1 INDIVIDUALITY, particularity, distinctiveness, uniqueness, self, selfhood, personhood, name, ego, personality, character, existence, background, roots
FORMAL singularity
2 SAMENESS, likeness, selfsameness, closeness, similarity, resemblance, indistinguishability, oneness, unity, interchangeability, correspondence, equality, equivalence
3 *a company's corporate identity*
impression, image, profile, face, appearance, public persona, public face, public recognition

ideologist *n*
thinker, theorist, visionary, philosopher, teacher, doctrinaire, ideologue

ideology *n*
philosophy, world-view, ideas, principles, teaching, theory, tenets, doctrine(s), convictions, belief(s), opinion(s), faith, dogma, thesis
FORMAL creed, credo

idiocy *n*
folly, stupidity, silliness, senselessness, lunacy, craziness, absurdity, foolhardiness, insanity, inanity
FORMAL fatuousness
COLLOQ. daftness
F3 wisdom, sanity

idiom *n*
phrase, expression, colloquialism, language, turn of phrase, phraseology, style, usage, jargon, speech, talk, vernacular
FORMAL locution

idiomatic *adj*
colloquial, everyday, natural, vernacular, native, grammatical, correct, dialectal, dialectical, idiolectal
F3 unidiomatic

idiosyncrasy *n*
peculiarity, individuality, speciality, oddity, eccentricity, freak, quirk, habit, mannerism, trait, feature, characteristic, quality
FORMAL singularity

idiosyncratic *adj*
personal, individual, characteristic, distinctive, peculiar, odd, eccentric, quirky
FORMAL singular
F3 general, common

idiot *n*
fool, imbecile, fat-head, dunce, dimwit, simpleton, halfwit, cretin, clown, ignoramus, oaf, innocent, moron
OLD natural, nidget; (*Shakesp*) malt-horse
COLLOQ. thickhead, numskull, nincompoop, airhead, ass, chump, ninny, clot, dope, twit, nitwit, nit, sucker, mug, twerp, birdbrain, pea-brain, berk, dum-dum, knuckle-head, blockhead, airhead, lame brain, wazzock; *dialect* barmpot; *Scot* bampot, bammer, numpty; *Scot & Irish* eejit; *N Am* putz, chowderhead, bufflehead, doofus; *Aust & NZ* dill; *Aust* boofhead
SLANG jerk, nerd, wally, dumbo, divvy, pillock, prat, muppet, dork, dipstick, geek, plonker, cloth head, nana, nerk, nelly; (*taboo*) dickhead, prick, fuckwit; *N Am* flathead, jughead, klutz, schmuck, schmo, dumb-ass; *Aust & NZ* nong; *Aust* galah; *Irish* (*vulgar*) gobshite

idiotic *adj*
foolish, stupid, senseless, silly, absurd, ridiculous, ludicrous, nonsensical, unwise, ill-advised, ill-considered, short-sighted, half-baked, crazy, mad, insane, moronic, oafish, hare-brained, half-witted, simple-minded, simple, ignorant, unintelligent, inept, inane, pointless, unreasonable, gormless; *Welsh* twp
FORMAL fatuous, risible, injudicious
COLLOQ. thick-headed, daft, crack-brained, dumb, dotty, crazy, potty, batty, barmy, nutty, wacky, knuckle-headed, dozy, dim-witted
SLANG dorky, goofy; *N Am* dumb-ass
F3 sensible, sane

idle *adj, v*
♦ *adj*
1 INACTIVE, not working, inoperative, unused, dormant, dead, mothballed, unoccupied, unemployed, jobless, redundant
COLLOQ. on the dole
2 LAZY, work-shy, lethargic, sluggish, lackadaisical, do-nothing, loafish, bone-idle
FORMAL indolent, slothful
3 *idle threats*
empty, futile, vain, pointless, useless, worthless, pointless, fruitless, unsuccessful, ineffective, unproductive
FORMAL ineffectual
4 *idle gossip*
casual, trivial, petty, foolish, shallow, light, unimportant, insignificant
F3 1 active, hardworking **2** busy **4** important, deep
♦ *v*
1 DO NOTHING, laze, lounge, while, take it easy, sit back, relax, kill time, while away, potter, loiter, dawdle, dally, fritter, waste, loaf, slack, shirk, fiddle about/around, lollop, twiddle your thumbs, wanton, whip the cat; *Scot* daidle; *N Am* putter
COLLOQ. skive, horse around, fester; *N Am* lallygag
SLANG sod about, bum around, fart about, arse around, mike, lig; *Irish* doss; *N Am* gold-brick, goof off; *Aust & NZ* bludge
2 *the engine is idling*

tick over, be operational, be ready to work/run, move
F∃ 1 work, be busy

idleness n
laziness, lazing, sluggishness, torpor, inaction, inactivity,
inertia, vegetating, shiftlessness, leisure, loafing, pottering,
ease, unemployment
FORMAL indolence, sloth, slothfulness
COLLOQ. skiving
F∃ activity, employment, occupation

idler n
loafer, dawdler, slacker, lounger, malingerer, shirker, good-
for-nothing, laggard, sluggard, waster, wastrel, layabout,
do-nothing, do-naught, drone, clock-watcher, bumble,
fine gentleman/lady; *dialect* donnot
OLD Lollard, truant
FORMAL sloth
COLLOQ. dodger, lazybones, skiver, spiv, couch potato
SLANG *Irish* dosser; *N Am* gold brick, goof-off; *Aust & NZ*
bludger

idol n
1 HERO, heroine, favourite, darling, star, superstar, pet,
beloved
COLLOQ. blue-eyed boy, pin-up
2 *worship idols*
effigy, icon, image, graven image, likeness, god, deity,
fetish, mammet

idolater n
admirer, worshipper, adorer, devotee, idol-worshipper,
idolatress, idolist, iconolater, votary

idolatrous adj
adoring, worshipping, glorifying, lionizing, adulatory,
idolizing, idol-worshipping, reverential, uncritical, pagan,
heretical

idolatry n
worshipping, admiration, reverence, adoration, adulation,
deification, exaltation, glorification, hero-worship,
idolizing, idolism, iconolatry, icon worship, paganism,
heathenism, fetishism
F∃ vilification

idolize v
hero-worship, lionize, exalt, glorify, worship, deify, revere,
admire, adore, adulate, reverence, love, dote on
FORMAL venerate
COLLOQ. put on a pedestal
F∃ despise

idyllic adj
perfect, idealized, heavenly, blissful, delightful, wonderful,
charming, picturesque, pastoral, rustic, unspoiled,
peaceful, romantic, happy
F∃ unpleasant, spoiled, noisy

if conj
in the event of, in case of, on condition that, as/so long
as, provided, providing, assuming (that), supposing
(that)

iffy adj
1 *my German is a bit iffy*
unsatisfactory, substandard, disappointing, imperfect,
defective, low-grade, second-rate
COLLOQ. dodgy, not up to scratch
2 UNCERTAIN, doubtful, dubious, tentative, undecided,
unsettled

ignite v
set fire to, set alight, light, catch fire, flare up, burn, burst
into flames, conflagrate, fire, inflame, kindle, touch off, put
a match to, spark off, torch
F∃ quench

ignoble adj
low, mean, petty, base, vulgar, wretched, contemptible,

despicable, shameful, vile, infamous, disgraceful,
dishonourable
FORMAL heinous
F∃ noble, worthy, honourable

ignobly adv
meanly, pettily, wretchedly, contemptibly, despicably,
shamefully, disgracefully, dishonourably, without honour,
vilely, infamously
F∃ nobly

ignominious adj
humiliating, mortifying, degrading, undignified, shameful,
dishonourable, discreditable, sorry, disreputable,
disgraceful, despicable, infamous, abject, base,
contemptible, scandalous, embarrassing
F∃ triumphant, honourable, glorious

ignominiously adv
shamefully, disgracefully, dishonourably, disreputably,
despicably, scandalously

ignominy n
humiliation, mortification, degradation, shame, dishonour,
discredit, disgrace, disrepute, reproach, scandal,
contempt, indignity, infamy, stigma
FORMAL obloquy, odium, opprobrium
F∃ credit, honour, dignity

ignoramus n
dunce, dimwit, halfwit, imbecile, simpleton, fool, illiterate,
know-nothing, blockhead, dullard
OLD ignaro, ignorant
COLLOQ. numskull, bonehead, ass, duffer, dolt
F∃ scholar, intellectual, highbrow

ignorance n
unintelligence, illiteracy, unawareness, unconsciousness,
obliviousness, oblivion, unfamiliarity, inexperience,
innocence, naivety, stupidity
COLLOQ. greenness, thickness
F∃ knowledge, wisdom, education, intelligence

ignorant adj
uneducated, illiterate, innumerate, backward, unknowing,
unread, untaught, untrained, inexperienced, unschooled,
unlearned, stupid, uninitiated, unenlightened, in the dark,
uninformed, ill-informed, unwitting, unaware, unfamiliar,
unacquainted, unconscious, oblivious, having no idea,
know-nothing, blind, innocent, naive; *N Am* redneck
OLD benighted, ingram, inscient, lack-Latin, lewd;
(*Shakesp*) unconfirmed
FORMAL nescient
COLLOQ. clueless, dense, thick, thick as two short planks,
dumb, in the dark
SLANG not knowing one's arse from one's elbow
OLD SLANG not knowing a B from a battledore, not knowing
a B from a broomstick, not knowing a B from a bull's foot
F∃ educated, knowledgeable, learned, clever, wise; *formal*
conversant

ignore v
disregard, take no notice of, not take any notice of,
overlook, take for granted, pay no attention to, be
oblivious to, pass over, pass by, bypass, neglect, omit,
brush aside, shrug off, reject, snub, spurn, slight, cut (dead),
tune out, balk, discount, high-hat
OLD blink
COLLOQ. close/shut your eyes to, turn a blind eye to, look
the other way, turn a deaf ear to, not listen to, cold-
shoulder, turn your back on, keep in the dark, bury your
head in the sand, run away from, leave out in the cold
SLANG scrub round
F∃ notice, observe, pay attention to

ilk n
kind, sort, type, make, style, variety, brand, breed, class,
stamp, character, description

ill *adj, n, adv*
 • *adj*
1 SICK, poorly, unwell, laid up, ailing, off-colour, out of sorts, seedy, queasy, diseased, unhealthy, infirm, frail, weak, feeble, bedridden
FORMAL afflicted, indisposed, valetudinarian
COLLOQ. in a bad way, dicky, crummy, under the weather, run down, rough, groggy, like death warmed up, green about the gills; *Aust* cronk; *Aust & NZ* crook
2 *an ill omen*
bad, evil, damaging, harmful, unpleasant, injurious, destructive, ruinous, detrimental, adverse, unfavourable, unpromising, sinister, ominous, threatening, unlucky, unfortunate, difficult, harsh, severe
FORMAL inauspicious, unpropitious, infelicitous, deleterious
3 *ill feelings*
unkind, unfriendly, antagonistic, hostile, resentful, belligerent
E₃ 1 well, healthy **2** good, favourable, fortunate **3** kind, friendly
 • *n*
1 TROUBLE, problem, trial(s), pain, misfortune, suffering, disaster, unpleasantness
2 HARM, evil, hurt, cruelty, destruction, injury, sorrow
FORMAL tribulation, affliction
E₃ 1 benefit **2** good
 • *adv*
1 BADLY, unfavourably, unkindly, disapprovingly, adversely, unfortunately, unsuccessfully, unluckily, wrongfully
FORMAL inauspiciously
2 SCARCELY, hardly, barely, by no means, insufficiently, inadequately, poorly, scantily, amiss
E₃ 1 well
■ **ill at ease**
uncomfortable, awkward, fidgety, hesitant, embarrassed, self-conscious, strange, unsure, nervous, on edge, restless, tense, unrelaxed, unsettled, uneasy, worried, anxious, disquieted, disturbed
COLLOQ. edgy, like a cat on hot bricks, on tenterhooks
E₃ at ease
■ **speak ill of**
criticize, condemn, carp, disapprove of, find fault with, pass judgement on, denounce, attack, slate, censure, blame, niggle, peck at, scarify, slash, snipe at, tilt at, run down; *N Am* score
FORMAL animadvert, excoriate, decry, denigrate, disparage, vituperate, castigate, impugn, cast aspersions on
COLLOQ. nag, slam, hammer, knock, come down on, give someone some stick, go to town on, haul over the coals, pick holes in, pan, take apart, pull/tear apart, pull to pieces, tear to shreds, tear a strip off, nit-pick, do a hatchet job on, badmouth, rubbish, trash, put the boot in, wade into, cut up, roast, have a go at
SLANG slag (off)

Synonym nuances
adjective sense 1
Sick and the less common **ailing** can be widely applied as a synonym of ill, whilst **poorly** and **unwell**, while implying a fairly mild condition, suggest being in constant poor health: *she was poorly throughout most of her childhood*. The term **laid up** would be reserved for having to take to your bed, whereas **bedridden** suggests a similar, but a far more serious and permanent state.
 Off-colour is a fairly vague term which would suggest simply not feeling as well as one should, while both **seedy** and **queasy** would be appropriate for feeling mild nausea: *she felt seedy throughout the long bus journey.* **Diseased** is a more highly marked term, appropriate only for being affected by a distinctive illness: *diseased heart valves*, whereas **unhealthy** is less specific, implying continuing

poor health as much as illness: *an unhealthy pallor.*
 Infirm and **frail** suggest being in a continuous debilitated or delicate state, and are often associated with ageing: *he became very infirm in his last years.* Both **weak** and **feeble**, likewise, put the emphasis on lacking strength and vigour as a consequence of illness: *he was too feeble to get out of bed.*

---

ill-advised *adj*
unwise, foolish, ill-considered, thoughtless, careless, hasty, rash, imprudent, reckless, short-sighted, misguided, inappropriate
FORMAL injudicious
E₃ wise, sensible, well-advised, cautious; *formal* politic, circumspect

ill-assorted *adj*
incompatible, inharmonious, discordant, unsuited, mismatched, uncongenial, misallied
FORMAL incongruous
E₃ harmonious, well-matched

ill-bred *adj*
bad-mannered, ill-mannered, discourteous, impolite, rude, loutish, boorish, coarse, crude, vulgar, crass, uncouth, indelicate, uncivil, uncivilized
FORMAL unseemly
E₃ well-bred, polite, gentlemanly, ladylike

ill-considered *adj*
ill-advised, ill-judged, careless, foolish, hasty, heedless, rash, imprudent, unwise, overhasty
FORMAL improvident, injudicious, precipitate
E₃ sensible, wise

ill-defined *adj*
indistinct, unclear, vague, nebulous, imprecise, indefinite, blurred, fuzzy, hazy, woolly, blurry, dim, shadowy
E₃ clear

ill-disposed *adj*
unfriendly, unsympathetic, hostile, antagonistic, opposed, unco-operative, unwelcoming, against
FORMAL averse, inimical
COLLOQ. anti
E₃ well-disposed

illegal *adj*
unlawful, illicit, criminal, wrong, forbidden, prohibited, illegitimate, fraudulent, banned, outlawed, barred, unauthorized, under-the-counter, black-market, unconstitutional, bootleg, wrongful, criminalized
OLD wrongous
FORMAL felonious, proscribed, interdicted
COLLOQ. crooked
E₃ legal, lawful, permitted, allowed

illegality *n*
wrong, wrongfulness, wrongness, crime, criminality, illegitimacy, illicitness, lawlessness, unconstitutionality, unlawfulness
TECHNICAL felony, malfeasance
E₃ legality

illegally *adv*
unlawfully, illicitly, wrongly, against the law, contrary to the law, without authority, illegitimately, disobediently, guiltily, wrongfully, criminally
E₃ legally, lawfully

illegible *adj*
unreadable, indecipherable, hard to read, scrawled, obscure, faint, indistinct, unintelligible, hieroglyphic
E₃ legible, clear

illegitimacy *n*
illegitimateness, bastardism, bastardy, fatherlessness, birth out of wedlock
TECHNICAL baton-sinister, bend-sinister

illegitimate adj

1 *an illegitimate child*
natural, love, bastard, fatherless, misbegotten, adulterine, unfathered, spurious
OLD base, base-born; (*Shakesp*) misbegot
FORMAL born out of wedlock
COLLOQ. born on the wrong side of the blanket
2 ILLEGAL, unlawful, illicit, lawless, unauthorized, unwarranted, unlicensed, improper
3 ILLOGICAL, incorrect, inadmissible, spurious, invalid, unsound
E3 **1** legitimate **2** legal **3** well-reasoned

ill-equipped adj

unprovided (for), unsupplied, ill-supplied, exposed, unprotected, underresourced, underfinanced, underfunded, undercapitalized, understaffed, under strength, undermanned

ill-fated adj

doomed, ill-starred, ill-omened, blighted, unfortunate, unlucky, luckless, unhappy
FORMAL hapless
E3 lucky

ill-favoured adj

hideous, plain, repulsive, ugly, unattractive, unlovely, unprepossessing, unsightly; *N Am* homely
E3 beautiful, attractive

ill-feeling n

ill-will, bad blood, bitterness, grudge, hard feelings, resentment, sourness, spite, malice, hostility, enmity, animosity, antagonism, dissatisfaction, frustration, offence, anger, indignation, wrath, disgruntlement, dudgeon
FORMAL animus, odium, rancour
E3 friendship, goodwill

ill-founded adj

baseless, groundless, without foundation, unjustified, unsupported, unconfirmed
E3 substantiated, verified

ill-gotten adj

obtained dishonestly, obtained illegally, stolen, pilfered, taken, swiped
FORMAL purloined
COLLOQ. nicked, nobbled, knocked off, ripped off, dodgy
SLANG hot, bent

ill-humoured adj

bad-tempered, acrimonious, cross, impatient, irascible, quick-tempered, irritable, sharp, snappy, snappish, disagreeable, cantankerous, grumpy, sulky, sullen, petulant, huffy, moody, morose, peevish, tart, testy, waspish
COLLOQ. stroppy, shirty, ratty, crabbed, crabby, crotchety, grouchy
E3 amiable

illiberal adj

mean, narrow-minded, intolerant, petty, prejudiced, reactionary, small-minded, bigoted, hidebound, ungenerous, uncharitable, stingy, miserly, niggardly, close-fisted
FORMAL parsimonious
COLLOQ. tight-fisted, tight
E3 broad-minded, liberal

illicit adj

illegal, unlawful, criminal, wrong, illegitimate, improper, forbidden, prohibited, banned, barred, unauthorized, unlicensed, black-market, bootleg, contraband, ill-gotten, under-the-table, under-the-counter, furtive, clandestine, secretive, surreptitious, stealthy, black; *Aust* sly
SLANG *Aust* shonky
E3 legal, permissible

illicitly adv

unlawfully, illegally, wrongly, against the law, contrary to the law, without authority, illegitimately, disobediently, guiltily, wrongfully, criminally
E3 legally, lawfully

illiteracy n

inability to read, inability to read and/or write, ignorance, lack of education, lack of schooling
E3 literacy

illiterate adj

ignorant, uneducated, unschooled, unlearned, untaught, unlettered, untutored, uncultured
TECHNICAL analphabetic
OLD benighted
E3 literate

ill-judged adj

ill-advised, ill-considered, short-sighted, unwise, foolish, foolhardy, misguided, hasty, overhasty, rash, reckless, imprudent, incautious, indiscreet, wrong-headed
FORMAL impolitic, injudicious
COLLOQ. daft
E3 sensible

ill-mannered adj

rude, impolite, badly-behaved, bad-mannered, insolent, discourteous, ill-bred, ill-behaved, unmannerly, uncivil, loutish, uncouth, boorish, churlish, coarse, crude, insensitive
E3 polite, well-mannered

ill-natured adj

spiteful, vindictive, nasty, perverse, mean, surly, sulky, sullen, unfriendly, unkind, unpleasant, vicious, bad-tempered, cross, disagreeable, malicious, malevolent, malignant, churlish, petulant
COLLOQ. crabbed
E3 good-natured

illness n

disease, disorder, complaint, condition, ailment, sickness, ill/poor health, infirmity, disability, attack, bout, touch
FORMAL indisposition, malady, affliction
See panel at **disease**.

Synonym nuances

Disease would only be used of specific, and usually serious, illness characterized by a distinctive set of symptoms, while **disorder** can be used of varying degrees of illness, but particularly where some part of the body is malfunctioning: *suffering from a kidney disorder*. Similarly, **complaint** and **ailment** can be widely used of any, even minor, health problem that troubles you, while **condition** has connotations of a more permanent state, especially one that is a particular cause for concern: *an incurable heart condition*.

Sickness can be fairly widely applied to the state of being ill, although it also has associations with vomiting. **Indisposition**, on the other hand, is more suggestive of a fairly mild illness resulting in the temporary inability to perform your usual functions, unlike **infirmity**, which implies a continuous state of poor health and physical inability, often arising from age. **Disability**, however, might be used more narrowly where illness involves a particular physical or mental handicap.

Attack and **bout** are different in that they suggest a sudden and severe but temporary affliction: *an attack of gout*; *a bout of flu*, while **touch** clearly suggests a very minor case: *a touch of food poisoning*.

---

illogical adj

irrational, unreasonable, unscientific, untenable, invalid, unsound, faulty, specious, spurious, inconsistent, (*offensive*) Irish; fallible, senseless,

meaningless, absurd, incorrect, wrong
FORMAL fallacious, sophistical, casuistic
Ⓔ logical, rational, reasonable

illogicality n
irrationality, unreasonableness, unreason, unsoundness, absurdity, senselessness, speciousness, fallacy, inconsistency, invalidity
FORMAL fallaciousness
Ⓔ logicality

ill-starred adj
doomed, ill-fated, unfortunate, unhappy, unlucky, star-crossed, blighted
FORMAL inauspicious, hapless
Ⓔ fortunate

ill-tempered adj
bad-tempered, acrimonious, cross, ill-natured, ill-humoured, impatient, irritable, irascible, spiteful, vicious, curt, grumpy, cantankerous, testy, tetchy, touchy, choleric, sharp
COLLOQ. stroppy, shirty, ratty, crabbed, crabby, crotchety, grouchy
Ⓔ good-tempered

ill-timed adj
inopportune, inconvenient, inappropriate, unseasonable, untimely, wrong-timed, mistimed, unwelcome, unfortunate, awkward, tactless, inept, crass
Ⓔ well-timed

ill-treat v
mistreat, abuse, maltreat, injure, harm, damage, neglect, mishandle, misuse, wrong, oppress

ill-treatment n
abuse, mistreatment, maltreatment, damage, harm, injury, ill-use, manhandling, mishandling, misuse, neglect
Ⓔ care

illuminate v
1 LIGHT, light up, lighten, shine on, throw light on, floodlight, brighten, twilight
OLD illumine; (Shakesp) overshine
2 CLARIFY, clear up, elucidate, illustrate, explain, edify, instruct, enlighten, limelight
3 DECORATE, ornament, adorn, embellish, illustrate
OLD limn, miniate
Ⓔ 1 darken 2 mystify

illuminating adj
informative, instructive, helpful, edifying, enlightening, revealing
FORMAL explanatory, revelatory
Ⓔ unhelpful

illumination n
1 LIGHT, lights, lighting, beam, ray, irradiation, brightness, radiance, flash, candlelight
2 ENLIGHTENMENT, awareness, insight, light, understanding, instruction, perception, learning, education, revelation
3 DECORATION, ornamentation, adornment, embellishment, illustration
Ⓔ 1 darkness

illusion n
apparition, mirage, spectre, phantom, will-o'-the-wisp, hallucination, figment of the imagination, déjà vu, fantasy, fancy, delusion, misapprehension, misconception, misjudgement, error, false impression, deception, phantasm
TECHNICAL maya
OLD prestige
FORMAL chimera, fallacy
Ⓔ reality, truth

⚠ **illusion** or **allusion**?
See panel at **allusion**.

⚠ **illusion** or **delusion**?
See panel at **delusion**.

illusory adj
illusive, illusionary, deceptive, misleading, apparent, seeming, deluding, delusive, unreal, delusory, fancied, imagined, specious, unsubstantial, sham, false, untrue, mistaken, erroneous
FORMAL chimerical, fallacious
Ⓔ real, actual

illustrate v
1 DEMONSTRATE, exemplify, instance, explain, interpret, clarify, draw, sketch, depict, picture, show, exhibit
FORMAL elucidate
2 ILLUMINATE, decorate, ornament, adorn, embellish
FORMAL miniate

illustrated adj
decorated, embellished, illuminated, pictorial, with drawings/pictures
FORMAL miniated

illustration n
1 PICTURE, plate, half-tone, photograph, drawing, sketch, figure, diagram, chart, artwork, design, representation, graphic, blow-up, frontispiece, plate, vignette, decoration, ornamentation, adornment, embellishment
TECHNICAL bleed, hors texte
2 EXAMPLE, specimen, instance, case, case in point, sample, analogy, demonstration, exemplification, explanation, interpretation, clarification, quotation, quote, comment, remark, observation, note, gloss, sidelight
FORMAL exemplar, elucidation, exponent

illustrative adj
explanatory, descriptive, representative, typical, exemplifying, sample, specimen, diagrammatic, graphic, pictorial, interpretative
FORMAL explicatory, expository, delineative, illustrational, illustratory

illustrious adj
great, noble, eminent, distinguished, celebrated, acclaimed, honoured, esteemed, famous, famed, renowned, well-known, noted, prominent, outstanding, pre-eminent, remarkable, notable, brilliant, excellent, splendid, magnificent, glorious, exalted
Ⓔ ignoble, inglorious

ill-will n
hostility, antagonism, bad blood, enmity, unfriendliness, malevolence, malice, spite, animosity, ill-feeling, resentment, hard feelings, bad blood, grudge, dislike, aversion, hatred, antipathy, anger, indignation, wrath
FORMAL animus, rancour, odium
Ⓔ goodwill, friendship

image n
1 IDEA, notion, concept, conception, thought, fancy, impression, perception, vision
2 REPRESENTATION, likeness, resemblance, portrayal, depiction, picture, portrait, icon, graven image, effigy, figure, figurine, statue, statuette, bust, idol, replica, doll
3 REPRODUCTION, reflection, photograph, picture, copy, facsimile
4 *improve the company's image*
impression, identity, corporate identity, profile, face, appearance, public persona, public face, public recognition
5 *the image of his father*
likeness, representation, double, twin, duplicate, copy, clone, replica, doppelgänger, lookalike, match
COLLOQ. spitting image, (dead) ringer
6 *images in a poem*
figure of speech, figurative expression, turn of phrase, rhetorical device, imagery, simile, metaphor

imaginable adj
conceivable, thinkable, believable, credible, supposable, feasible, plausible, likely, possible, probable
F∃ unimaginable, inconceivable

imaginary adj
imagined, fanciful, fancied, illusory, hallucinatory, visionary, pretend, make-believe, dreamy, shadowy, ghostly, spectral, insubstantial, unreal, non-existent, fictional, fantastic, fabulous, legendary, mythological, mythical, made-up, invented, fictitious, assumed, supposed, hypothetical, notional
FORMAL chimerical
F∃ real

imagination n
1 CREATIVITY, imaginativeness, inventiveness, fancifulness, originality, inspiration, insight, ingenuity, ingeniousness, resourcefulness, enterprise, wit, vision
2 *see them in my imagination*
mind's eye, fancy, flight of fancy, fantasy, phantasy, mental view, contemplation, illusion, vision, dream, conceptualization, imagery, schema, dreamland
OLD wit, project
FORMAL chimera
F∃ 1 unimaginativeness **2** reality

imaginative adj
creative, inventive, innovative, full of ideas, original, inspired, visionary, ingenious, clever, resourceful, enterprising, fanciful, whimsical, fantastic, vivid
F∃ unimaginative

imagine v
1 PICTURE, form a picture of, visualize, see, see in your mind's eye, envisage, conceive, fancy, fantasize, daydream, dream, pretend, make believe, conjure up, dream up, think up, invent, devise, create, scheme, plan, project, vision
OLD image; (*Shakesp*) ween
FORMAL ideate
2 *I imagine so*
think, believe, judge, suppose, guess, reckon, assume, presume, gather, fancy, figure
OLD conceit; (*Shakesp*) propose
FORMAL conjecture, deem, surmise
COLLOQ. take it

imbalance n
unevenness, inequality, variance, disparity, disproportion, unfairness, partiality, bias
FORMAL disparity, inequity
F∃ balance, parity

imbecile n, adj
♦ *n*
idiot, halfwit, simpleton, moron, cretin, fool, blockhead, bungler, dunce, dimwit
COLLOQ. thickhead, numskull, nincompoop, ass, chump, ninny, clot, dope, twit, nitwit, nit, sucker, mug, twerp, birdbrain, berk, dum-dum, knuckle-head, lame brain, wazzock; *Scot* bampot, bammer, numpty; *Scot & Irish* eejit; *N Am* putz, chowderhead, doofus
SLANG jerk, nerd, wally, dumbo, pillock, prat, dork, geek, plonker, cloth head, nana, nerk; *N Am* flathead, jughead, klutz; *Aust & NZ* nong
♦ *adj*
stupid, silly, foolish, idiotic, inane, ludicrous, absurd, crazy, moronic, witless, asinine
FORMAL fatuous
COLLOQ. thick-headed, daft, crack-brained, dumb, dotty, crazy, potty, batty, barmy, nutty, wacky, knuckle-headed
SLANG dorky, goofy
F∃ intelligent, sensible

imbecility n
foolishness, idiocy, inanity, stupidity, incompetence, cretinism, asininity, childishness

TECHNICAL amentia
FORMAL fatuity
COLLOQ. daftness, craziness
F∃ intelligence, sense

imbibe v
1 DRINK, consume, swallow, gulp, sip, quaff
FORMAL ingest
COLLOQ. knock back, swig
2 ABSORB, take in, assimilate, drink in, receive, soak up, acquire, gain, gather
COLLOQ. lap up

imbroglio n
entanglement, tangle, involvement, confusion, difficulty, dilemma, complication, muddle, mess, quandary, embroilment
COLLOQ. scrape

imbue v
permeate, impregnate, pervade, suffuse, fill, saturate, inject, ingrain, inspire, charge, steep, inculcate, instil, tinge, tint

imitate v
1 COPY, take as a model, follow, follow suit, do likewise, ape, mimic, impersonate, do an impression of, caricature, parody, mock, act, hit, parrot, repeat, echo, mirror
FORMAL emulate
COLLOQ. take off, send up, spoof, take a leaf out of someone's book
2 REPRODUCE, duplicate, simulate, copy, fake, counterfeit, forge
FORMAL replicate

Synonym nuances
sense 1
Copy is a very general synonym, whilst **follow** implies imitating a person or adopting a style because it is believed to be better, and has vague implications of slavishness: *we would be better off following their system.* **Echo** would be used of displaying similarities to someone or something rather than copying them: *their buildings echoed those of Imperial Paris.*
  Both **ape** and **mimic** are suggestive of copying someone to rather ludicrous effect: *their lifestyle aped that of the royal household*, while **impersonate** would be reserved for pretending to be them. The terms **caricature** and **parody** are appropriate for presenting an exaggerated, often grotesque, representation, again for comic effect: *he parodied her accent*, and **mock** suggests a similarly disrespectful action. Both **parrot** and **repeat** might be used of saying something previously said by someone else, without any changes or embellishments: *he simply repeated my speech, word for word.*

---

imitation n, adj
♦ *n*
1 MIMICRY, impersonation, aping, apery, impression, caricature, parody, mocking, mockery, travesty
COLLOQ. take-off, send-up, spoof
2 COPY, duplicate, reproduction, replica, simulation, counterfeit, fake, forgery, sham, likeness, resemblance, reflection, dummy
FORMAL emulation
COLLOQ. knock-off
♦ *adj*
artificial, synthetic, man-made, ersatz, fake, mock, reproduction, simulated, sham, dummy
COLLOQ. phoney, pseudo
F∃ genuine

imitative adj
copying, mimicking, parrot-like, unoriginal, derivative, plagiarized, second-hand, simulated, mock

FORMAL emulating, mimetic
COLLOQ. me-too
F3 original

imitator n

mimic, impersonator, impressionist, parrot, ape, echo, parodist, plagiarist, copier, copyist, follower, epigone
FORMAL emulator
COLLOQ. copycat

immaculate adj

perfect, unblemished, flawless, faultless, impeccable, spotless, unsoiled, clean, spick and span, pure, unsullied, undefiled, incorrupt, untainted, stainless, blameless, guiltless, sinless, innocent
COLLOQ. squeaky clean
F3 blemished, stained, contaminated

immaculately adv

spotlessly, perfectly, to perfection, flawlessly, faultlessly, impeccably, purely, incorruptly, blamelessly, without blame, innocently, guiltlessly, without guilt, sinlessly, without sin

immanent adj

inherent, intrinsic, innate, ingrained, permeating, all-pervading
FORMAL ubiquitous, omnipresent

⚠ immanent or imminent?
Immanent means 'dwelling within', 'inherent': *divinity is immanent in many forms*. *Imminent* means 'approaching': *an imminent storm.*

---

immaterial adj

irrelevant, insignificant, unimportant, minor, trivial, petty, trifling, inconsequential, of no account
F3 relevant, important

immature adj

young, under-age, adolescent, juvenile, childish, puerile, infantile, babyish, raw, crude, callow, jejune, inexperienced, naive, unripe, undeveloped, unmellowed, incomplete, budding, fledgling, embryonic, unformed, unsiz(e)able, untimely, vealy, unready, unprepared, half-baked, unbaked
FORMAL ingenuous
COLLOQ. wet behind the ears, innocent as a newborn babe, green
F3 mature, fully-developed, grown-up

immaturity n

youth, adolescence, juvenility, childishness, puerility, babyishness, rawness, crudeness, crudity, callowness, inexperience, immatureness, unpreparedness, imperfection, unripeness, greenness
F3 maturity, mellowness

immeasurable adj

vast, immense, infinite, limitless, unlimited, illimitable, boundless, fathomless, unfathomable, unbounded, endless, never ending, interminable, bottomless, inexhaustible, incalculable, inestimable
F3 limited

immeasurably adv

infinitely, limitlessly, boundlessly, illimitably, beyond measure, endlessly, interminably, inexhaustibly, incalculably, inestimably, vastly, immensely

immediacy n

urgency, importance, criticalness, instancy, spontaneity, instantaneity, promptness, swiftness, simultaneity, directness, imminence
F3 remoteness, distance

immediate adj

1 INSTANT, instantaneous, direct, sudden, without delay, prompt, swift, speedy
2 URGENT, pressing, important, vital, crucial, critical,

current, present, existing, pressing
COLLOQ. top-priority, high-priority
3 NEAREST, closest, next, adjacent, next-door, near, close, recent
FORMAL adjoining, abutting
4 the immediate cause of death
direct, primary, basic, fundamental, chief, main, principal
F3 1 delayed **3** distant **4** indirect

immediately adv

now, then, straight away, right away, right now, at once, next, there and then, instantly, instantaneously, directly, speedily, quickly, without delay, no sooner ... than, as soon as, promptly, unhesitatingly, without hesitation, without question, this minute/instant, on the instant, on the spot, in the wake of, without further/more ado, straightforth, *statim; Scot & N Am* presently
TECHNICAL subito
OLD thereupon, straightway, therewithal, anon, incessantly, incontinent, incontinently, on the morrow
FORMAL forthwith
COLLOQ. pronto, yesterday, before you know it, before you can say Jack Robinson, in two shakes of a lamb's tail, like a shot, ASAP; *N Am* lickety-split
F3 eventually, never

immemorial adj

age-old, timeless, ancient, archaic, long-standing, fixed, time-honoured, hoary, traditional, ancestral
FORMAL of yore
F3 recent

immense adj

vast, great, extremely large, huge, enormous, massive, giant, gigantic, colossal, extensive, cosmic, limitless, myriad, tremendous, fabulous, monumental, mammoth, herculean, elephantine, titanic, Brobdingnagian, cyclopean
COLLOQ. whopping, bumper, jumbo, ginormous, humungous, mega
F3 tiny, minute, Lilliputian

immensely adv

enormously, extremely, exceedingly, excessively, very, really, exceptionally, extraordinarily, intensely, remarkably, utterly, greatly, highly, massively, unusually, unreasonably, immoderately, uncommonly, inordinately, acutely, severely, decidedly
OLD jolly
COLLOQ. awfully, terribly, dreadfully, frightfully, terrifically

immensity n

magnitude, bulk, expanse, vastness, greatness, hugeness, enormousness, massiveness, giganticness, extensiveness, limitlessness
F3 minuteness

immerse v

1 PLUNGE, submerge, submerse, sink, duck, dip, dunk, douse, souse, saturate, drench, wallow, soak, bathe, baptize
TECHNICAL blanch
OLD demerge, demerse, embathe, immerge
2 ENGROSS, preoccupy, occupy, absorb, bury, wrap up in, engage, involve, engulf

immersed adj

absorbed, engrossed, involved, occupied, preoccupied, consumed, buried, busy, deep, taken up, wrapped up, rapt, sunk

immersion n

1 SUBMERSION, plunging, sinking, ducking, dip, dipping, dunking, dousing, saturation, drenching, soaking, baptism, bathe
2 PREOCCUPATION, absorption, engrossing, engagement, involvement, concentration

immigrant n
incomer, settler, migrant, newcomer, new arrival, outsider, foreigner, alien
⊟ native

immigrate v
come in, move in, migrate, settle, resettle, remove
⊟ emigrate

imminence n
approach, nearness, closeness, immediacy, instancy, menace, threat
FORMAL propinquity
⊟ remoteness

imminent adj
impending, forthcoming, upcoming, in the offing, approaching, fast approaching, coming, on the way, near, close, looming, menacing, threatening, brewing, in the air, at hand, about to happen, almost upon you, on the horizon
COLLOQ. round the corner
⊟ remote, far-off

⚠ **imminent** or **immanent**?
See panel at immanent.

immobile adj
motionless, stationary, unmoving, immobilized, at rest, still, stock-still, static, immovable, rooted, fixed, frozen, rigid, stiff, riveted
⊟ mobile, moving

immobility n
motionlessness, immovability, steadiness, stillness, firmness, fixedness, fixity, stability, inertness, disability
⊟ mobility

immobilize v
stop, halt, inactivate, freeze, transfix, paralyse, cripple, disable, deactivate, put out of action/operation
⊟ mobilize

immoderate adj
excessive, unreasonable, unjustified, unwarranted, undue, exaggerated, fulsome, enormous, exorbitant, lavish, extravagant, extreme, wanton, inordinate, uncalled-for, uncontrolled, unrestrained, outrageous, unlimited, unrestricted, unbridled, uncurbed, intemperate, self-indulgent, distemperate, overweening
FORMAL unconscionable, profligate, hubristic, distemperate, egregious
COLLOQ. over the top, OTT, steep
⊟ moderate

immoderately adv
excessively, exorbitantly, extravagantly, extremely, inordinately, exaggeratedly, unduly, unjustifiably, unrestrainedly, without measure, unreasonably, wantonly
⊟ moderately

immoderation n
excess, excessiveness, exorbitance, extravagance, lavishness, immoderateness, intemperance, inordinacy, overindulgence, unreason, unrestraint
FORMAL prodigality, dissipation
⊟ moderation

immodest adj
improper, indecent, revealing, shameless, forward, bold, boastful, impudent, cheeky, cocky, brazen, immoral, obscene, lewd, coarse, risqué
FORMAL indecorous
COLLOQ. fresh, saucy
⊟ modest

immodesty n
audacity, boldness, forwardness, gall, impudence, shamelessness, temerity, bawdiness, coarseness, impurity, lewdness, obscenity, indelicacy

FORMAL indecorousness, indecorum
COLLOQ. brass
⊟ modesty

immolate v
sacrifice, kill, offer (up), burn

immoral adj
unethical, wrong, bad, sinful, evil, wicked, unscrupulous, unprincipled, dishonest, vile, vicious, corrupt, depraved, base, degenerate, debauched, reprobate, dissolute, loose, lewd, indecent, pornographic, obscene, licentious, impure, questionable, against nature, wanton
OLD naught, unhonest
FORMAL iniquitous, nefarious
COLLOQ. blue, raunchy, juicy
⊟ moral, right, good

Synonym nuances
Unethical is a straightforward synonym for going against the accepted code of conduct, while **unscrupulous** and **unprincipled** are more suggestive of a disregard for basic rules of morality. The words **wrong** and **bad** can be applied more widely, but imply a stronger judgement on the part of the speaker: *it was wrong of you to lie to your mother*. **Sinful** is similarly judgemental, but has added implications of offending religious tenets: *you must confess your sinful thoughts*, while **evil** and **wicked** make an extreme judgement.
  You can use **vile** to suggest that something is loathsome, while **vicious** has more to do with a penchant for inflicting hurt. Both **corrupt** and **depraved** have connotations of perversion of accepted morals, while the terms **degenerate** and **debauched** suggest a decline into a low moral state which is demonstrated by a person's behaviour: *a debauched lifestyle*. **Reprobate** similarly suggests being steeped in shame: *I have no excuse for my reprobate behaviour*. **Dissolute**, **licentious**, **loose** and **wanton** are more suggestive of a lack of discipline or restraint in one's behaviour: *gambling and other dissolute pursuits; he was accused of wanton conduct*.
  Lewd and **indecent**, and the stronger terms **pornographic** and **obscene** would only be applied to something of a sexual nature that is offensive. **Impure** suggests being tainted by immorality: *this impure world*, while **questionable** is a milder term in that it simply implies being of a morally dubious nature: *these are questionable legal practices*.

---

immorality n
wrong, wrongdoing, badness, sin, sinfulness, evil, wickedness, dishonesty, vileness, corruption, vice, depravity, dissoluteness, debauchery, impurity, lewdness, indecency, pornography, obscenity, licentiousness
OLD indiscretion
FORMAL iniquity, profligacy, turpitude
⊟ morality

immortal adj, n
♦ adj
1 UNDYING, deathless, imperishable, indestructible, unfading, eternal, everlasting, perpetual, endless, ceaseless, lasting, enduring, abiding, constant, perennial, timeless, ageless, fadeless, ambrosial
OLD amarantin; (*Shakesp*) ever-living
FORMAL sempiternal
2 *recall those immortal words*
memorable, unforgettable, well-known, celebrated, famous, honoured, distinguished
⊟ **1** mortal
♦ n
deity, god, goddess, divinity, divine being, great, hero, genius, Olympian

immortality n
1 ETERNAL LIFE, everlasting life, eternity, endlessness, deathlessness, incorruptibility, imperishability, indestructibility, timelessness, perpetuity
2 FAME, glorification, gloriousness, glory, greatness, renown, celebrity, honour, distinction
1 mortality

immortalize v
celebrate, commemorate, memorialize, perpetuate, glorify, enshrine, eternalize
FORMAL laud

immovable adj
1 FIXED, rooted, immobile, stuck, fast, secure, stable, moored, riveted, anchored, jammed, constant, firm, set
2 STEADFAST, determined, resolute, adamant, unshak(e)able, stubborn, obstinate, uncompromising, unyielding, set, firm, constant, inflexible, dogged, unwavering, unswerving
FORMAL intransigent
1 movable **2** flexible

immune adj
invulnerable, unsusceptible, resistant, proof, protected, safe, exempt, free, clear, secure, spared, excused, released, relieved, absolved
susceptible, liable, subject, exposed, open

---

*The immune system's components and responses
include*:

COMPONENTS:
antibody
antigen (or antibody
 generator)
B-lymphocytes
commensals
complement system
cytotoxic cells
helper T-cells
histamine
immunoglobulins
interferon
killer T-cells
leucocyte
lymphocyte
lysosome
lysozyme
memory T-cells
phagocyte
plasma cells
receptor (binding) site
T-cells
T-lymphocytes
RESPONSES:
acquired immunity
adaptive immune system

allergy
artificially acquired
 immunity (immunization)
autoimmune response
cell-mediated immunity
cellular response
humoral immunity/
 response
immuno-surveillance
inflammatory response
innate immune system
naturally acquired immunity
non-specific immune
 response
passive immunity
phagocyte action
 (adherence/ingestion/
 digestion)
phagocytosis
primary response
secondary response
sneeze reflex
specific immune response
tissue rejection

---

immunity n
resistance, protection, immunization, vaccination, inoculation, safety, exemption, indemnity, exception, impunity, freedom, liberty, release, licence, franchise, privilege, right, permission
TECHNICAL mithridatism
FORMAL exoneration
susceptibility

immunization n
vaccination, inoculation, injection, protection, jab

immunize v
vaccinate, inoculate, inject, protect, safeguard, shield

immure v
enclose, confine, wall in, shut up, cage, imprison, incarcerate, jail, put behind bars, cloister, enwall
free

immutability n
changelessness, immutableness, invariability, unalterableness, unchangeableness, permanence, constancy, durability, fixedness, stability
mutability

immutable adj
changeless, inflexible, invariable, unalterable, unchangeable, perpetual, permanent, abiding, constant, enduring, fixed, lasting, stable, steadfast, sacrosanct
mutable, changeable

imp n
1 SPRITE, demon, devil, goblin, hobgoblin, gnome, elf, puck
2 MISCHIEVOUS CHILD, rascal, rogue, scamp, brat, minx, troublemaker, mischief-maker, trickster, prankster, flibbertigibbet, gamin, urchin, limb

impact n, v
♦ n
1 *the impact of the reforms*
effect, consequences, results, repercussions, reverberations, impression, power, influence, significance, meaning
2 COLLISION, crash, smash, bang, bump, blow, knock, contact, clash, jolt, force, shock, brunt
♦ v
1 COLLIDE, crash, hit, clash, crush, fix, strike, press together
2 AFFECT, have an effect on, influence, act, work, apply to, impinge

impair v
damage, harm, injure, hinder, mar, spoil, cripple, disable, worsen, deteriorate, undermine, weaken, reduce, decrease, lessen, diminish, blunt
FORMAL debilitate, enervate, vitiate, enfeeble
improve, enhance

impaired adj
defective, faulty, flawed, poor, weak, disabled, handicapped, imperfect, damaged, spoilt, unsound
FORMAL vitiated
enhanced

impairment n
disability, handicap, disablement, injury, weakness, damage, deterioration, reduction, harm, hurt, fault, flaw, ruin
FORMAL dysfunction, vitiation
enhancement

impale v
pierce, puncture, perforate, run through, spear, lance, spike, skewer, spit, stick, stab, prick, transfix, disembowel

impalpable adj
imperceptible, inapprehensible, insubstantial, unsubstantial, elusive, indistinct, intangible, indefinable, shadowy, tenuous, thin, fine, delicate, airy
FORMAL incorporeal
palpable

impart v
1 CONVEY, tell, relate, communicate, make known, transmit, disclose, divulge, reveal, report, pass on
2 GIVE, grant, offer, contribute, lend, assign
FORMAL confer, bestow, accord
1, 2 withhold

impartial adj
objective, dispassionate, detached, disinterested, neutral, non-partisan, unbiased, unprejudiced, uncommitted, open-minded, fair, fair-minded, just, equitable, judicial, even-handed, equal, candid, crossbench
COLLOQ. not having an axe to grind
biased, prejudiced

impartiality n
neutrality, non-partisanship, objectivity, unbiasedness, fairness, justice, even-handedness, open-mindedness,

detachment, disinterest, disinterestedness, dispassion, equality, equity
E3 bias, prejudice, favouritism, discrimination

impassable *adj*
blocked, closed, obstructed, unnavigable, unpassable, untraversable, pathless, trackless, impenetrable, insurmountable, insuperable, unassailable, invincible
E3 passable

impasse *n*
deadlock, stalemate, checkmate, dead end, cul-de-sac, blind alley, halt, standstill, log jam

impassioned *adj*
fervent, ardent, passionate, intense, inspired, stirring, heartfelt, spirited, rousing, emotional, enthusiastic, eager, excited, fervid, vigorous, forceful, violent, furious, fiery, vehement, animated, glowing, inflamed, heated, blazing
E3 apathetic, mild

impassive *adj*
expressionless, emotionless, calm, composed, unruffled, unconcerned, apathetic, cool, unfeeling, unemotional, unmoved, unruffled, unexcitable, stoical, indifferent, dispassionate
FORMAL imperturbable, phlegmatic
COLLOQ. unflappable, laid-back
E3 responsive, moved

impassively *adv*
calmly, emotionlessly, unemotionally, unfeelingly, dispassionately, apathetically, coolly, with a straight face
FORMAL imperturbably, phlegmatically

impatience *n*
1 IRRITABILITY, intolerance, shortness, brusqueness, abruptness, curtness, tenseness, nervousness, edginess, agitation, uneasiness
OLD indignance
FORMAL dysphoria
2 EAGERNESS, keenness, excitability, restlessness, anxiety, haste, rashness, impetuosity
E3 1 contentment 2 reluctance, unwillingness

impatient *adj*
1 IRRITABLE, jittery, snappy, testy, hot-tempered, quick-tempered, angry, intolerant, brusque, abrupt, short, curt, tense, nervous, fidgety
FORMAL querulous
COLLOQ. ratty, narky, edgy
2 EAGER, keen, excitable, restless, anxious, impetuous, hasty, on tenterhooks
COLLOQ. champing at the bit, straining/panting at the leash, biting on the bridle, with ants in your pants
E3 1 pleased, happy, contented 2 reluctant, unwilling

impeach *v*
accuse, charge, denounce, criticize, revile, attack, censure, blame
TECHNICAL indict, arraign
FORMAL impugn, disparage

impeachment *n*
accusation, charge
TECHNICAL arraignment, indictment
FORMAL disparagement

impeccable *adj*
perfect, faultless, precise, exact, correct, exemplary, flawless, unblemished, stainless, immaculate, pure, upright, irreproachable, blameless, innocent
E3 faulty, flawed, corrupt

impecunious *adj*
poor, poverty-stricken, insolvent, destitute, impoverished, penniless, needy
FORMAL indigent, penurious
COLLOQ. broke, stony-broke, skint, dirt-poor, cleaned

out, strapped, on your uppers
E3 rich

impede *v*
hinder, hamper, obstruct, block, handicap, clog, slow (down), hold up, hold back, delay, check, curb, restrain, thwart, disrupt, stop, bar
FORMAL retard
E3 aid, promote, further

impediment *n*
1 HINDRANCE, obstacle, obstruction, barrier, bar, block, setback, stumbling-block, snag, difficulty, handicap, burden, encumbrance, check, curb, restraint, restriction
2 *a speech impediment*
defect, handicap, stutter, stammer
E3 1 aid

impedimenta *n*
baggage, luggage, equipment, gear, belongings, paraphernalia
FORMAL effects, accoutrements
COLLOQ. things, stuff, bits and pieces

impel *v*
urge, force, oblige, compel, constrain, drive, propel, move, get going, push, put, press, pressure, pressurize, spur, prod, goad, prompt, incite, stimulate, excite, instigate, strike, motivate, inspire
E3 deter, dissuade

impending *adj*
imminent, forthcoming, in the offing, approaching, coming, upcoming, close, near, at hand, on the way, looming, menacing, threatening, brewing, in the air, about to happen, on the horizon
E3 remote, far-off

impenetrable *adj*
1 *impenetrable jungle*
impassable, solid, thick, dense, overgrown
2 UNINTELLIGIBLE, incomprehensible, unfathomable, indiscernible, puzzling, baffling, mysterious, cryptic, enigmatic, obscure, dark, inscrutable
FORMAL abstruse, recondite
E3 1 accessible 2 understandable

impenitence *n*
impenitency, stubbornness, defiance, hard-heartedness, incorrigibility
FORMAL obduracy
E3 penitence, remorse

impenitent *adj*
unrepentant, unremorseful, uncontrite, unashamed, defiant, hardened, incorrigible, remorseless, without remorse, without regret, unabashed, unreformed, unregenerate
FORMAL obdurate
E3 penitent, contrite

imperative *adj*
vital, essential, crucial, pressing, urgent, compulsory, critical, necessary, obligatory, indispensable
E3 optional, unimportant

imperceptible *adj*
inappreciable, indiscernible, unapparent, indistinguishable, undetectable, unnoticeable, inaudible, unapparent, faint, slight, muffled, negligible, impalpable, infinitesimal, microscopic, minute, tiny, minuscule, small, fine, subtle, gradual, unclear, obscure, vague, indistinct, indefinite
E3 perceptible, noticeable, clear

imperceptibly *adv*
inappreciably, indiscernibly, unnoticeably, unobtrusively, unseen, slowly, subtly, gradually, bit by bit, little by little
FORMAL insensibly
E3 perceptibly

imperfect *adj*
faulty, flawed, defective, damaged, broken, blemished, impaired, chipped, deficient, inadequate, insufficient, incomplete, embryonic, sketchy
OLD unperfect
⊟ perfect, whole

imperfection *n*
fault, flaw, defect, blemish, deformity, crack, dent, break, tear, cut, scratch, blot, blotch, stain, taint, spot, deficiency, impairment, shortcoming, foible, weakness, failing, inadequacy, insufficiency
TECHNICAL malconformation
⊟ perfection

imperial *adj*
sovereign, supreme, absolute, royal, regal, monarchical, kingly, queenly, majestic, grand, magnificent, glorious, splendid, great, noble, lofty, stately

---
🛉 **imperial** or **imperious**?
Imperial means 'of an empire or emperor': *the imperial crown. Imperious* means 'proud and overbearing', 'behaving as if expecting to be, or in the habit of being, obeyed': *She disliked his imperious manner.*

---

imperialism *n*
empire-building, colonialism, expansionism, acquisitiveness, adventurism
COLLOQ. flag-waving, flag-wagging

imperil *v*
endanger, put in danger, jeopardize, put in jeopardy, risk, expose to risk, hazard, take a chance, expose, harm, injure, compromise, threaten

imperious *adj*
overbearing, domineering, autocratic, despotic, tyrannical, dictatorial, high-handed, lordly, masterful, commanding, assertive, arrogant, haughty
FORMAL peremptory, overweening
⊟ humble

🛉 **imperious** or **imperial**?
See panel at imperial.

---

imperishable *adj*
enduring, permanent, incorruptible, indestructible, inextinguishable, undying, unfading, unforgettable, abiding, perpetual, perennial, eternal, everlasting, immortal, deathless
⊟ perishable

impermanence *n*
transience, transiency, temporariness, inconstancy, transitoriness, briefness, elusiveness
FORMAL ephemerality
⊟ permanence

impermanent *adj*
transient, temporary, passing, short-lived, momentary, transitory, inconstant, brief, elusive, fleeting, flying, unfixed, unsettled, unstable, mortal, perishable, fugitive
FORMAL ephemeral, evanescent, fugacious
COLLOQ. fly-by-night
⊟ permanent

impermeable *adj*
impervious, impenetrable, impassable, sealed, watertight, hermetic, non-porous, damp-proof, waterproof, proof, water-resistant, resistant, water-repellent
⊟ permeable, porous

impersonal *adj*
1 COLD, cool, frigid, formal, official, aloof, remote, distant, clinical, stiff, stuffy, businesslike, detached, unemotional, unfeeling
2 OBJECTIVE, neutral, dispassionate, detached, unbiased, unprejudiced
⊟ 1 friendly, informal 2 biased

impersonally *adv*
objectively, neutrally, dispassionately, fairly, equitably, justly, without bias/prejudice, without favouritism, open-mindedly, with an open mind
COLLOQ. not having an axe to grind

impersonate *v*
imitate, mimic, parody, caricature, mock, ape, masquerade as, pose as, pass off as, act, portray
COLLOQ. take off, send up

impersonation *n*
imitation, impression, mimicry, parody, caricature, aping, apery, burlesque
COLLOQ. take-off, send-up, spoof

impertinence *n*
rudeness, impoliteness, disrespect, discourtesy, insolence, impudence, effrontery, audacity, boldness, brazenness, forwardness, presumption, shamelessness, gall, chutzpah
COLLOQ. cheek, brass, brass neck, nerve, sauce, lip, attitude, face, mouth; *Scot* snash; *N Am* sass
⊟ politeness, respect, civility

impertinent *adj*
rude, impolite, ill-mannered, unmannerly, discourteous, disrespectful, insolent, impudent, pert, bold, audacious, brash, brazen, forward, presumptuous, shameless
COLLOQ. cheeky, saucy, fresh; *N Am* sassy
SLANG smartarse
⊟ polite, respectful

imperturbability *n*
calmness, composure, coolness, complacency, self-possession, equanimity, tranquillity
⊟ jitteriness, touchiness

imperturbable *adj*
unexcitable, calm, tranquil, composed, collected, even-tempered, self-possessed, cool, impassive, unmoved, unruffled, untroubled, complacent
COLLOQ. unflappable, unfazed, laid-back, calm and collected
⊟ excitable, ruffled

impervious *adj*
1 IMPERMEABLE, waterproof, damp-proof, proof, non-porous, watertight, hermetic, closed, sealed, resistant, impenetrable
2 *impervious to criticism*
immune, invulnerable, untouched, unaffected, unmoved, closed, resistant
⊟ 1 porous, pervious 2 responsive, vulnerable

impetuosity *n*
impetuousness, impulsiveness, rashness, haste, hastiness, spontaneity, foolhardiness, recklessness, thoughtlessness, impatience, dash, élan, vehemence
FORMAL precipitateness
⊟ caution, wariness; *formal* circumspection

impetuous *adj*
impulsive, spontaneous, unplanned, unthinking, unpremeditated, spur-of-the-moment, hasty, impatient, headlong, uncontrolled, bull-headed, hot-headed, fiery, tearaway, violent, foolhardy, rash, reckless, thoughtless, unthinking, ill-conceived, unreasoned; *N Am* brash
OLD sturdy
FORMAL precipitate
⊟ cautious, wary; *formal* circumspect

impetuously *adv*
rashly, impulsively, unthinkingly, recklessly, spontaneously, passionately, vehemently
FORMAL precipitately
⊟ cautiously

impetus n
stimulus, incentive, motivation, influence, encouragement, inspiration, actuation, impulse, momentum, force, energy, power, drive, urging, boost, push, goad, spur

impiety n
irreverence, irreligion, profaneness, profanity, sinfulness, ungodliness, unholiness, unrighteousness, wickedness, godlessness, blasphemy, sacrilege, sacrilegiousness
FORMAL iniquity, hubris
F3 piety, reverence

impinge v
encroach, infringe, affect, influence, hit, touch (on), intrude, trespass, invade

impious adj
irreverent, irreligious, profane, sinful, ungodly, godless, unholy, unrighteous, wicked, blasphemous, sacrilegious
FORMAL iniquitous, hubristic
F3 pious, reverent

impish adj
mischievous, naughty, roguish, rascally, sportive, devilish, elfin, gamin, tricksome, frolicsome, tricksy, pranksome, waggish

implacability n
implacableness, inexorability, relentlessness, remorselessness, mercilessness, pitilessness, ruthlessness, rancorousness, unforgivingness, vengefulness, irreconcilability, inflexibility
FORMAL intransigence, intractability
F3 placability

implacable adj
inexorable, relentless, unrelenting, remorseless, merciless, pitiless, unappeasable, irreconcilable, vengeful, cruel, heartless, deadly, mortal, unforgiving, ruthless, rancorous, inflexible, adamant, uncompromising, unyielding
OLD impacable
FORMAL intransigent, intractable
F3 compassionate, forgiving

implant v
1 *implant ideas in someone's mind*
sow, plant, fix, root, instil, inculcate, introduce
2 *implant a new heart/new skin tissue*
insert, place, put, engraft, graft, transplant
3 EMBED, fix, sow, plant, place, root

implausible adj
improbable, unlikely, hard to believe, unbelievable, inconceivable, incredible, far-fetched, dubious, doubtful, questionable, suspect, unconvincing, weak, flimsy, thin, transparent
F3 plausible, probable, likely, reasonable

implausibly adv
improbably, unbelievably, incredibly, inconceivably, doubtfully, questionably
F3 probably, plausibly, reasonably

implement n, v
♦ n
tool, instrument, utensil, gadget, device, apparatus, appliance, contrivance
See panel at **tool**.
♦ v
enforce, bring about, carry out, perform, do, apply, execute, discharge, fulfil, complete, accomplish, realize, put into effect, put into action/operation
FORMAL effect

implementation n
carrying-out, performance, performing, fulfilling, fulfilment, application, execution, discharge, accomplishment, completion, operation, action, enforcement, realization
FORMAL effecting

implicate v
involve, embroil, entangle, incriminate, compromise, include, concern, connect, associate, be a part of, be (a) party to
FORMAL inculpate
F3 absolve; *formal* exonerate

implicated adj
involved, embroiled, entangled, incriminated, compromised, included, concerned, connected, associated, responsible, party to, suspected
FORMAL inculpated
F3 exonerated

implication n
1 INFERENCE, deduction, insinuation, suggestion, meaning, significance, overtone, undertone, ramification, repercussion, effect, consequence, conclusion
2 INVOLVEMENT, entanglement, embroilment, incrimination, connection, association
FORMAL inculpation

implicit adj
1 IMPLIED, inferred, deducible, insinuated, suggested, hinted, indirect, unsaid, unspoken, unexpressed, unstated, tacit, understood, inherent, hidden, latent
2 *implicit belief*
unquestioning, unhesitating, utter, total, full, entire, complete, absolute, perfect, sheer, positive, unqualified, unreserved, unconditional, steadfast, wholehearted
F3 1 explicit 2 half-hearted

implicitly adv
absolutely, totally, utterly, completely, unconditionally, unhesitatingly, unquestioningly, unreservedly, steadfastly, wholeheartedly, firmly
F3 explicitly

implied adj
implicit, tacit, indirect, insinuated, suggested, hinted, assumed, understood, unspoken, unexpressed, unstated, undeclared, inherent
F3 stated

implore v
beg, entreat, ask, appeal, request, press, crave, plead, pray
FORMAL importune, solicit, supplicate, beseech

imply v
suggest, insinuate, hint, intimate, infer, say indirectly, give someone to understand/believe, mean, signify, point to, indicate, signal, involve, require, entail, state
FORMAL denote

imply or **infer**?
Imply means 'to suggest or hint at (something) without actually stating it': *Are you implying that I'm a liar?* *Infer* means 'to form an opinion by reasoning from what you know': *I inferred from your silence that you were angry.*

impolite adj
rude, discourteous, bad-mannered, unmannerly, ill-mannered, ill-bred, uncivil, unrefined, ungentlemanly, unladylike, ungracious, inconsiderate, disrespectful, impertinent, insolent, rough, loutish, boorish, coarse, crude, vulgar, abrupt
FORMAL indecorous
COLLOQ. cheeky
F3 polite, courteous

impolitely adv
rudely, discourteously, uncivilly, ungraciously, inconsiderately, disrespectfully, impertinently, insolently, crudely
FORMAL indecorously
F3 politely, courteously

impoliteness n
rudeness, discourtesy, bad manners, unmannerliness,

disrespect, insolence, impertinence, incivility, inconsiderateness, boorishness, churlishness, crassness, indelicacy, roughness, coarseness, abruptness, gaucherie
FORMAL indecorousness, indecorum
F3 politeness, courtesy

impolitic adj
unwise, ill-advised, inexpedient, imprudent, ill-judged, misguided, ill-considered, short-sighted, undiplomatic, indiscreet, rash, foolish
FORMAL injudicious, maladroit
COLLOQ. daft
F3 wise, prudent; formal politic

import n, v
♦ n
1 exports and imports
imported product/commodity/goods, foreign product/commodity/goods, reimport, foreign trade
2 IMPORTANCE, consequence, significance, weight, substance, seriousness
OLD state
FORMAL moment
3 CONTENT, sense, substance, nub, meaning, implication, intention, thrust, message, drift, essence, gist
FORMAL purport
♦ v
bring in, buy in, buy from abroad, ship in, reimport, introduce

importance n
1 MOMENTOUSNESS, significance, urgency, criticalness, graveness, substance, matter, concern, interest, usefulness, value, worth, weight
OLD state
FORMAL consequence, import
2 people of importance in society
influence, power, mark, prominence, eminence, distinction, noteworthiness, prestige, status, standing, esteem
F3 1, 2 unimportance, insignificance

important adj
1 MOMENTOUS, noteworthy, significant, meaningful, relevant, material, salient, urgent, critical, paramount, crucial, vital, essential, key, central, primary, principal, major, main, chief, priority, substantial, valuable, valued, weighty, mighty, ultimate, serious, grave, far-reaching, pivotal, historic, fateful, epoch-making, world-shaking, world-shattering
FORMAL seminal
SLANG heavy
2 the most important person in the school
leading, foremost, high-level, high-ranking, top, influential, chief, main, powerful, pre-eminent, prestigious, prominent, outstanding, eminent, notable, distinguished, valued, esteemed, noted
F3 1 unimportant, insignificant, trivial **2** powerless

Synonym nuances
sense 1
Momentous can be used to suggest that something is worthy of remembrance, or you can use **historic** to suggest that something merits a place in history. **Fateful** echoes the idea of having great consequence in history: Titanic's fateful maiden voyage. **Noteworthy** is much more restrained in its suggestion that something is worthy of attention. **Significant** and **material** have implications of being of consequence: a significant proportion of the population are opposed to this tax; the merger involved material changes to the hierarchy, while **pivotal** suggests that everything else hinges on it: our pivotal problem is getting people to see the sense in this plan.
  You could use **paramount**, **primary** or **principal** to suggest something is supreme or foremost: his primary concern was the safety of his family, while **salient** would be used of something prominent among other things: we will deal with the salient points of the case first of all. **Priority**, **urgent** or **critical** can be used in cases where immediate action is essential.
  The terms **serious** and **grave**, on the other hand, suggest a cause for intense concern: the resurgence of hostage-taking has grave implications, whereas **weighty** is most appropriate for people or things that can exert power or influence: the weighty issues of the day.

---

importunate adj
insistent, persistent, troublesome, impatient, tenacious, dogged, pressing, urgent
FORMAL pertinacious

importune v
pester, badger, harass, hound, cajole, plague, appeal, beg, request, press, urge, plead with, solicit, beset
FORMAL supplicate

importunity n
insistence, persistence, pressing, pestering, harassing, hounding, urgency, urging, solicitation, harassment, cajolery, entreaties

impose v
1 ENFORCE, exact, levy, apply, charge, set, fix, put (on), place (on), lay (on), introduce, institute, establish, decree, inflict, burden, encumber, saddle, force, thrust, foist
2 FOIST, force yourself, thrust yourself, intrude, butt in, break in, encroach, trespass, obtrude, presume, exploit, put upon, abuse, mislead, take liberties, take advantage of

imposing adj
impressive, striking, grand, stately, majestic, splendid, dignified, lofty, august
F3 unimposing, modest

imposition n
1 ENFORCEMENT, introduction, infliction, exaction, levying, application, setting, fixing, establishment, decree, institution
2 CHARGE, tax, tariff, levy, toll, burden, constraint, load, encumbrance, duty, task, punishment
3 INTRUSION, encroachment, trespassing, burden, pressure
COLLOQ. hassle

impossibility n
hopelessness, impracticability, unattainableness, unobtainableness, unacceptability, untenability, unviability, inability, inconceivability, preposterousness, absurdity, ludicrousness, ridiculousness
COLLOQ. no-no, non-starter, squaring the circle
F3 possibility

impossible adj
hopeless, impracticable, unworkable, unattainable, unachievable, unobtainable, insoluble, unreasonable, unacceptable, beyond you, inconceivable, unimaginable, unthinkable, out of the question, preposterous, incredible, unbelievable, inconceivable, absurd, ludicrous, ridiculous, outlandish, intolerable, unbearable, prohibitive
COLLOQ. out, not by any stretch of the imagination, and pigs might fly, like flogging a dead horse, anybody's guess
F3 possible

impostor n
fraud, fake, quack, charlatan, sham, mountebank, impersonator, pretender, deceiver, deluder, hoodwinker, swindler, cheat, trickster, defrauder, rogue, bunyip
OLD faitor, faitour, idol, phantasm
COLLOQ. phoney, con man
SLANG N Am ringer

imposture n
deception, fraud, pretence, misrepresentation,

impersonation, quackery, swindle, trick, counterfeit, cheat, hoax, artifice
COLLOQ. con, con trick

impotence n
powerlessness, helplessness, uselessness, inability, inadequacy, incapacity, incompetence, ineffectiveness, weakness, feebleness, frailty, disability, infirmity, paralysis
FORMAL enervation, inefficacy, impuissance
E3 strength

impotent adj
powerless, helpless, useless, worthless, futile, unable, incapable, ineffective, incompetent, inadequate, weak, feeble, frail, worn out, exhausted, infirm, disabled, incapacitated, paralysed, crippled
FORMAL debilitated, enervated, impuissant
E3 potent, strong

impound v
1 CONFISCATE, seize, remove, take away, take possession of, commandeer
FORMAL appropriate, expropriate
2 CONFINE, shut up, cage, keep in, lock up, coop up, hem in, pen in
FORMAL incarcerate, immure

impoverish v
bankrupt, break, ruin, beggar, make poor, weaken, reduce, deplete, exhaust, drain, diminish, denude
FORMAL pauperize
E3 enrich

impoverished adj
1 POOR, needy, poverty-stricken, destitute, down-and-out, bankrupt, penniless, ruined
FORMAL impecunious, penurious, indigent
COLLOQ. bust, skint, broke, stony-broke, without a bean, cleaned out, on your uppers, on your beam ends, not having two pennies to rub together, dirt-poor
2 WEAKENED, drained, exhausted, desolate, empty, waste, dead, barren, bare
E3 1 rich

impracticability n
unworkability, infeasibility, unsuitableness, unviability, uselessness, impossibility, futility, hopelessness
E3 practicability

impracticable adj
unworkable, unfeasible, unattainable, unachievable, impossible, out of the question, unviable, non-viable, unrealistic, visionary, wild, useless, unserviceable, inoperable
OLD unpracticable
E3 practicable, feasible

⚠ impracticable or **impractical**?
Impracticable means 'cannot be carried out or put into practice': *The whole project has become completely impracticable*. When referring to suggestions, plans, etc, *impractical* means 'possible to carry out but not sensible or convenient': *In a modern economy barter is totally impractical*; when referring to a person, *impractical* means 'not able to do or make things in a sensible and efficient way': *He was impractical and dreamy, with a head full of foolish notions*.

---

impractical adj
unrealistic, idealistic, romantic, starry-eyed, visionary, theoretical abstract, academic, ivory-tower, impracticable, unworkable, impossible, awkward, crazy, inconvenient, unserviceable
E3 practical, realistic, sensible

impracticality n
idealism, romanticism, unworkability, unworkableness, impossibility, hopelessness, infeasibility
E3 practicality

imprecation n
curse, blasphemy, denunciation, abuse, anathema
FORMAL execration, malediction, profanity, vituperation, vilification

imprecise adj
inexact, inaccurate, approximate, estimated, rough, loose, indefinite, vague, woolly, blurred, hazy, ill-defined, sloppy, inexplicit, ambiguous, equivocal
E3 precise, exact

imprecision n
inexactitude, inexactness, inaccuracy, approximation, estimate, vagueness, ambiguity, haze, sloppiness
E3 precision, exactness

impregnable adj
impenetrable, unconquerable, invincible, unbeatable, unassailable, indestructible, inviolable, fortified, strong, solid, secure, safe, invulnerable, unquestionable, irrefutable
E3 vulnerable

impregnate v
1 SOAK, steep, saturate, drench, fill, permeate, pervade, suffuse, imbue, infuse, penetrate
2 INSEMINATE, fertilize, make pregnant
FORMAL fecundate

impregnation n
fertilization, fertilizing, insemination, saturation, imbuing
FORMAL fructification, fructifying, fecundation

impresario n
manager, organizer, director, producer, promoter, exhibitor

impress v
1 *I'm not impressed*
strike, move, touch, sway, affect, influence, stir, inspire, rouse, excite, overwhelm, possess, prepossess, bear in upon
COLLOQ. grab, bowl over, knock for six, knock out, wow, slay, go over big (with)
SLANG *NAm* gas
2 EMPHASIZE, stress, highlight, underline, bring home, hammer home, press, drum, enforce, engrave, print, indent, instil, inculcate, fix deeply
3 STAMP, imprint, print, engrave, strike, emboss, deboss, incuse, mark

impressed adj
moved, excited, affected, struck, influenced, marked, taken, touched, stamped, stirred, overawed
COLLOQ. grabbed, bowled over, knocked out, knocked for six, wowed
E3 unimpressed

impression n
1 FEELING, awareness, consciousness, sense, sensation, illusion, idea, notion, opinion, belief, thought, conviction, suspicion, fancy, hunch, memory, recollection
COLLOQ. funny feeling, gut feeling, vibes
2 *make a good impression*
effect, impact, influence, power, control, sway
3 STAMP, mark, print, dent, indentation, imprint, pressure, outline
4 IMPERSONATION, imitation, parody, mimicry, caricature, burlesque
COLLOQ. take-off, send-up, spoof

impressionability n
naivety, gullibility, susceptibility, vulnerability, sensitivity, receptiveness, receptivity, suggestibility, greenness
FORMAL ingenuousness

impressionable adj
naive, gullible, easily influenced, persuadable, susceptible, vulnerable, sensitive, pliable,

mouldable, responsive, open, receptive
FORMAL ingenuous

impressive *adj*
striking, imposing, grand, breathtaking, spectacular, superb, magnificent, commanding, dramatic, powerful, effective, dazzling, awe-inspiring, awesome, striking, scintillating, stirring, inspiring, exciting, rousing, moving, affecting, touching, emphatic, epic, monumental, noble, stately
FORMAL portentous
SLANG stonking
 unimpressive, uninspiring

impressively *adv*
strikingly, grandly, spectacularly, magnificently, powerfully, effectively, emphatically, awesomely

imprint *n, v*
  ♦ *n*
1 PRINT, mark, stamp, impression, indentation, sign, logo, emblem, badge, colophon
2 EFFECT, consequences, results, repercussions, reverberations, impression, power, influence, significance, meaning
  ♦ *v*
stamp, print, mark, brand, impress, fix, establish, engrave, emboss, etch

imprison *v*
put in prison, send to prison, jail, intern, detain, lock up, cage, pen, confine, shut in
OLD lumber
FORMAL incarcerate, immure
COLLOQ. send down, put away
SLANG bang up, lag, shop, quod
 release, free

imprisoned *adj*
jailed, locked up, behind bars, confined, caged, captive
FORMAL incarcerated, immured
COLLOQ. inside, put away, sent down, doing time
SLANG doing bird, doing porridge, banged up
 free

imprisonment *n*
internment, detention, custody, captivity, confinement
FORMAL incarceration
SLANG porridge, bird
 freedom, liberty

improbability *n*
uncertainty, doubt, doubtfulness, dubiousness, unlikelihood, unlikeliness, far-fetchedness, preposterousness, ridiculousness, implausibility
FORMAL dubiety
 probability

improbable *adj*
uncertain, questionable, doubtful, unlikely, dubious, implausible, unconvincing, far-fetched, preposterous, ridiculous, unbelievable, incredible
 probable, likely, convincing

impromptu *adj, adv*
  ♦ *adj*
improvised, extempore, ad-lib, unscripted, unrehearsed, unprepared, spontaneous
COLLOQ. off-the-cuff
 rehearsed
  ♦ *adv*
without preparation, extempore, ad lib, spontaneously
COLLOQ. on the spur of the moment, off the top of your head, off the cuff

improper *adj*
1 INDECENT, rude, vulgar, shocking, risqué, indelicate, immodest, indiscreet, immoral
FORMAL unseemly, indecorous, unbecoming

2 WRONG, incorrect, irregular, false, erroneous, unlawful
3 UNSUITABLE, inappropriate, unfitting, inopportune, inadequate, out of place
FORMAL incongruous
 1 decent 2 correct, lawful 3 suitable, appropriate

improperly *adv*
1 INDECENTLY, rudely, immodestly, indiscreetly, immorally
FORMAL indecorously
2 WRONGLY, incorrectly, irregularly, falsely, unlawfully, erroneously
3 UNSUITABLY, inappropriately, unfittingly
FORMAL incongruously
 1 decently 2 correctly, lawfully 3 suitably, appropriately

impropriety *n*
mistake, lapse, slip, blunder, faux pas, gaffe, bad taste, vulgarity, gaucherie, immodesty, indecency, unsuitability
FORMAL incongruity, indecorousness, indecorum, solecism, unseemliness
 formal propriety

improve *v*
better, make better, enhance, enrich, perfect, polish, touch up, mend, rectify, put right, set right, correct, amend, revise, reform, help, upgrade, modernize, streamline, revamp, work on/upon, increase, rise, pick up, develop, look up, advance, grow, progress, make headway, get better, recover, convalesce, recuperate, rally, rehabilitate, gain strength
FORMAL ameliorate, meliorate
COLLOQ. be on the up and up, get your act together, turn over a new leaf, mend your ways, perk up, look up, give a facelift to, do for, do up, fix up
 worsen, deteriorate, decline

Synonym nuances
Better can be used to suggest surpassing a previous state, while **enhance** would suggest adding to it: *oak furniture enhances the light feel of the room.* You might use **enrich** to suggest increasing the worth: *our lives are enriched by literature.* **Perfect** implies doing something continually until it cannot be improved upon. **Polish**, on the other hand, is more suggestive of bringing something up to a higher standard: *a slick and polished dance routine.* **Touch up** implies covering flaws.
  Both **revise** and **reform** likewise imply changes for the better, while the terms **upgrade**, **modernize** and **revamp** would be appropriate for making newer, and better, substitutions or alterations, and **streamline** has implications of doing away with anything unnecessary. You can use **pick up** to suggest that something previously disappointing has begun to get better: *trade picked up towards the end of the year*, whilst **develop** is more suggestive of steady progression.
  Look up, however, is more suggestive that things are about to improve: *Smith's fortunes in track events are looking up.* The terms **advance**, **progress** and **make headway** suggest a move forwards to a more satisfactory state or improved position: *science is making particular headway in this field.*
  The terms **get better** and **recover** are suggestive of prior failure or weakness, while **convalesce** and **recuperate** would be specifically used of getting better after a period of illness. **Rally** can also be used of getting into a better condition than previously, usually through one's own efforts: *the players rallied well but too late to save themselves from defeat.*

---

improvement *n*
betterment, enhancement, rectification, rectifying, correction, amendment, revision, reform, reformation, rehabilitation, upgrading, modernizing, increase, rise, upswing, gain, development, advance, growth, progress,

headway, furtherance, recovery, rally, upswing, pick-up
FORMAL amelioration
F3 deterioration, decline, worsening

improvident *adj*
thriftless, unthrifty, spendthrift, extravagant, shiftless,
uneconomical, wasteful, imprudent, careless, reckless,
heedless, inattentive, thoughtless, negligent, unprepared,
underprepared, Micawberish
FORMAL prodigal, profligate
F3 thrifty, economical

improvisation *n*
ad-lib, ad-libbing, extemporizing, extemporization,
impromptu, invention, spontaneity, makeshift, expedient,
vamp
FORMAL autoschediasm

improvise *v*
1 CONTRIVE, devise, concoct, invent, put together quickly,
make do
COLLOQ. throw together, cobble together, knock up, rig up,
run up
2 EXTEMPORIZE, ad-lib, compose/perform without
preparation, vamp
COLLOQ. say whatever comes into your head/mind, speak
off the cuff, speak off the top of your head, play by ear, wing
it, have a brainwave

improvised *adj*
extempore, ad-lib, spontaneous, extemporaneous,
extemporized, makeshift, unrehearsed, unprepared,
unscripted
COLLOQ. off-the-cuff
F3 rehearsed

imprudence *n*
folly, foolhardiness, short-sightedness, rashness,
recklessness, haste, irresponsibility, carelessness,
heedlessness, thoughtlessness
F3 wisdom, caution, prudence

imprudent *adj*
unwise, ill-advised, ill-considered, ill-judged, foolish,
foolhardy, short-sighted, rash, reckless, hasty,
irresponsible, unthinking, careless, heedless, thoughtless,
indiscreet
FORMAL impolitic, injudicious, improvident
F3 wise, cautious, wary, prudent

impudence *n*
impertinence, boldness, brazenness, pertness, insolence,
rudeness, presumption, chutzpah; *Scot* snash
FORMAL effrontery
COLLOQ. cheek, nerve, sauciness, attitude, lip, face, mouth,
brass neck; *N Am* sass
F3 politeness

impudent *adj*
impertinent, bold, forward, shameless, immodest, cocky,
brazen, insolent, rude, impolite, cheeky, disrespectful,
presumptuous, audacious, pert
COLLOQ. saucy, fresh; *N Am* sassy
SLANG smartarse
F3 polite

impugn *v*
challenge, attack, assail, question, call in(to) question,
criticize, oppose, resist, dispute
FORMAL berate, censure, revile, vilify, vituperate, traduce,
vilipend
F3 praise, compliment

impulse *n*
1 URGE, wish, desire, inclination, whim, notion, caprice,
instinct, feeling, passion, drive, pulse, signal, thought-wave
TECHNICAL premotion, conatus, nisus
2 IMPETUS, momentum, force, pressure, drive, impact,
thrust, motion, movement, propulsion, impulsion, surge,

push, incitement, incentive, inducement, stimulation,
stimulus, motive, motivation
■ **on impulse**
impulsively, impetuously, rashly, recklessly, impatiently,
irresponsibly, hastily, suddenly, spontaneously,
automatically, instinctively, intuitively, thoughtlessly,
without thinking

impulsive *adj*
impetuous, rash, reckless, foolhardy, thoughtless,
unthinking, impatient, madcap, headstrong, hasty, quick,
sudden, ill-judged, ill-considered, spontaneous,
automatic, instinctive, emotional, passionate, intuitive
FORMAL precipitate
F3 cautious, premeditated

impulsively *adv*
impetuously, rashly, recklessly, impatiently, irresponsibly,
hastily, suddenly, spontaneously, automatically,
instinctively, intuitively, thoughtlessly, without thinking, on
impulse
F3 cautiously

impulsiveness *n*
impetuosity, impetuousness, rashness, recklessness,
foolhardiness, thoughtlessness, impatience, haste,
hastiness, quickness, suddenness, spontaneity, instinct,
emotion, passion, intuitiveness
FORMAL precipitateness, precipitation
F3 caution

impunity *n*
exemption, freedom, immunity, liberty, licence,
dispensation, permission, security, amnesty, excusal
F3 liability
■ **with impunity**
safely, in safety, freely, without being punished, without risk

impure *adj*
1 UNREFINED, adulterated, alloyed, mixed, blended,
combined, diluted, drossy, contaminated, polluted,
tainted, infected, corrupt, defiled, debased, sullied,
unclean, dirty, foul, filthy
OLD TECHNICAL vicious
2 OBSCENE, indecent, dirty, crude, coarse, vulgar, offensive,
immoral, shameless, improper, promiscuous, depraved,
unchaste, sexy, immodest, lustful, lewd, lecherous,
licentious, risqué, suggestive, pornographic, erotic,
smutty, bawdy, ribald
F3 1 pure **2** chaste, decent

impurity *n*
1 *impurities in the petrol*
adulteration, mixture, blend, dilution, contamination,
pollution, taint, infection, corruption, debasement,
dirtiness, contaminant, pollutant, dirt, filth, grime,
foulness, dross, foreign body, mark, spot
2 OBSCENITY, indecency, crudity, coarseness, vulgarity,
offensiveness, immorality, shamelessness, impropriety,
promiscuity, unchastity, looseness, immodesty, lustfulness,
lewdness, licentiousness, pornography, eroticism, smut
F3 2 purity

impute *v*
ascribe, assign, attribute, put down to, charge, credit, refer
FORMAL accredit

in *prep, adj*
♦ *prep*
1 *in the box*
within, inside, enclosed by, surrounded by
2 *in the autumn*
during, during the time/course of, throughout, through
3 *one in ten people*
per, each, every
♦ *adj*
fashionable, in vogue, popular, current, smart, stylish,
modish

COLLOQ. all the rage, trendy, cool, hip, funky
- **in for**
due to receive, about to experience, going to suffer
- **in on**
involved in, aware of, knowledgeable about, acquainted with
COLLOQ. clued up on
- **in with**
friendly with, on good terms with, on friendly terms with, liked by

inability *n*
incapability, incapacity, powerlessness, impotence, inadequacy, incompetence, ineffectiveness, weakness, ineptitude, handicap, disability, uselessness
E3 ability

inaccessibility *n*
remoteness, isolation, distance, separation, unapproachableness, unattainability
E3 accessibility

inaccessible *adj*
isolated, remote, out of the way, god-forsaken, unfrequented, unapproachable, unreachable, out of reach, beyond reach, unattainable, impenetrable, unavailable
COLLOQ. unget-at-able
E3 accessible

inaccuracy *n*
mistake, error, miscalculation, slip, blunder, gaffe, fault, defect, imprecision, inexactness, unreliability, erroneousness, mistakenness
FORMAL corrigendum, erratum, fallaciousness
COLLOQ. boo-boo, slip-up, howler; *N Am* flub
SLANG goof
E3 accuracy, precision

inaccurate *adj*
incorrect, wrong, erroneous, mistaken, false, faulty, flawed, imperfect, defective, imprecise, inexact, out, loose, unreliable, unfaithful, untrue, unsound
FORMAL fallacious
COLLOQ. adrift
E3 accurate, correct, true, right, sound

inaccurately *adv*
incorrectly, wrongly, erroneously, falsely, imperfectly, defectively, imprecisely, inexactly, unreliably, unfaithfully, loosely, wildly, carelessly, clumsily
E3 accurately, correctly

inaction *n*
inactivity, immobility, motionlessness, inertia, rest, idleness, passivity, slowness, lifelessness, sluggishness, lethargy, stagnation
FORMAL torpor
E3 action

inactivate *v*
disable, immobilize, paralyse, stop, deactivate, cripple, mothball, stabilize
COLLOQ. knock the bottom out of, scupper
E3 activate

inactive *adj*
immobile, motionless, stationary, still, unactive, inert, idle, unused, unemployed, dormant, dead, passive, sedentary, lazy, slow, lifeless, lethargic, sluggish, vegetating, stagnant, sleepy, hibernating, shadow, slothful
FORMAL inoperative, indolent, torpid, quiescent
E3 active, working, busy, functioning, in use

Synonym nuances
Both **immobile** and **motionless** can be used where there is a total absence of movement. **Stationary** has more to do with staying in the same spot. **Still** suggests being completely at rest and has connotations of

---

calmness: *we relaxed by the still waters.* The rare **unactive** and more common **inert**, when not used in scientific contexts, have associations with disinclination and sluggishness: *she was too inert to refuse this ridiculous request.* **Idle**, likewise, would strongly suggest disinclination to do anything: *idle days in front of the television*, but may also have connotations of wasted potential: *factories lying idle.*
  Dormant returns to the idea of not currently being in action: *dormant volcano.* **Dead** would be appropriate where there is no potential for activity. **Passive** has more to do with a lack of participation: *you don't want a pantomime audience to be passive.* **Sedentary** would be specifically applied to being seated: *office work and sedentary occupations.*
  Lazy and **slothful** are disapproving terms to describe disinclination to do anything. You can use **lifeless** if you want to suggest a lack of vitality: *lifeless little villages*, whereas **lethargic** and **sluggish** have suggestions of torpor: *the sluggish global economy*, and **vegetating** goes further by implying an absence of mental activity. **Stagnant** implies not moving at all, with further connotations of being unhealthy: *stagnant and badly circulating air encourages disease to settle.*

---

inactivity *n*
immobility, inaction, inertia, inertness, idleness, unemployment, dormancy, passivity, laziness, sluggishness, lifelessness, lethargy, sloth, vegetation, stagnation, hibernation, languor, dullness, heaviness
TECHNICAL stasis
FORMAL indolence, lassitude, quiescence, dilatoriness, torpor, abeyance
E3 activeness

inadequacy *n*
1 INSUFFICIENCY, lack, shortage, deficit, dearth, deficiency, scarcity, scantiness, meagreness
FORMAL want, paucity
2 DEFECTIVENESS, ineffectiveness, inability, incapability, incompetence, ineffectiveness
FORMAL inefficacy
3 *the inadequacies of the system*
fault, defect, imperfection, weakness, foible, failing, shortcoming, flaw
E3 **1** adequacy **3** strong point

inadequate *adj*
1 INSUFFICIENT, short, wanting, deficient, too little/few, scanty, scant, scarce, skimpy, sparse, meagre, niggardly
FORMAL incommensurate
COLLOQ. thin on the ground
2 INCOMPETENT, bad, incapable, inexpert, unproficient, careless, not good enough, unequal, unqualified, ineffective, faulty, defective, imperfect, unsatisfactory, poor, unfit, substandard, disappointing, sketchy, leaving a lot to be desired
OLD unequal
FORMAL ineffectual, inefficacious
COLLOQ. pathetic, not up to scratch
E3 **1** adequate, enough **2** satisfactory

inadequately *adv*
insufficiently, poorly, meagrely, scantily, sketchily, skimpily, sparsely, thinly, imperfectly, badly, carelessly
E3 adequately

inadmissible *adj*
unacceptable, irrelevant, immaterial, inappropriate, unallowable, disallowed, prohibited, improper
FORMAL precluded, inapposite
E3 admissible, allowable

inadvertent *adj*
accidental, chance, unintentional, unintended, unplanned,

unguarded, unpremeditated, uncalculated, careless, negligent, thoughtless, unwitting, unconscious, involuntary
OLD (*Spenser*) unadvised
E3 deliberate, conscious, careful

inadvertently *adv*
accidentally, by accident, by mistake, by chance, unintentionally, unthinkingly, unwittingly, unconsciously, involuntarily, carelessly, heedlessly, negligently, mistakenly, remissly, thoughtlessly
E3 deliberately

inadvisable *adj*
unwise, foolish, silly, ill-advised, ill-judged, ill-considered, imprudent, inexpedient, misguided, indiscreet
FORMAL injudicious
E3 advisable, wise

inalienable *adj*
inherent, inviolable, unassailable, non-negotiable, non-transferable, untransferable, unremovable, permanent, sacrosanct, absolute
E3 impermanent

inane *adj*
senseless, foolish, stupid, unintelligent, silly, idiotic, absurd, ridiculous, ludicrous, frivolous, trifling, puerile, mindless, nonsensical, vapid, empty, vacuous, vain, worthless, futile
FORMAL fatuous
E3 sensible

inanely *adv*
foolishly, stupidly, idiotically, absurdly, ridiculously, ludicrously, nonsensically, vacuously, futilely
FORMAL fatuously
E3 sensibly

inanimate *adj*
lifeless, dead, defunct, extinct, unconscious, inactive, lazy, inert, dormant, immobile, stagnant, spiritless, dull, apathetic, lethargic, wooden
TECHNICAL insentient, insensate
FORMAL torpid
E3 animate, living, alive

inanity *n*
senselessness, folly, foolishness, stupidity, silliness, absurdity, ridiculousness, ludicrousness, frivolity, puerility, imbecility, vapidity, vacuity, asininity, emptiness
FORMAL fatuity
COLLOQ. daftness, waffle
E3 sense

inapplicable *adj*
irrelevant, immaterial, inapt, inappropriate, unsuitable, unsuited, unrelated, unconnected
FORMAL inapposite, inconsequent
E3 applicable; *formal* germane, pertinent

inapposite *adj*
unsuitable, inappropriate, irrelevant, immaterial, unsuitable, out of place

inappreciable *adj*
indiscernible, imperceptible, unapparent, indistinguishable, undetectable, unnoticeable, inaudible, unapparent, faint, slight, muffled, negligible, impalpable, infinitesimal, microscopic, minute, tiny, minuscule, small, fine, subtle, gradual, unclear, obscure, vague, indistinct, indefinite
E3 perceptible, noticeable, clear

inappropriate *adj*
unsuitable, unappropriate, inapt, ill-suited, ill-fitted, irrelevant, out of place, untimely, ill-timed, inopportune, tactless, improper, unbecoming, undue, unfitting, tasteless, facetious
OLD unseemly

FORMAL inapposite, incongruous, indecorous, infelicitous, malapropos
E3 appropriate, suitable

inappropriately *adv*
unsuitably, out of place, irrelevantly, without relevance, off/beside the point, inopportunely, tactlessly, tastelessly
FORMAL incongruously, infelicitously

inapt *adj*
inappropriate, unsuitable, unsuited, ill-suited, ill-fitted, irrelevant, out of place, ill-timed, inopportune, unfortunate
FORMAL inapposite, infelicitous
E3 apt

inarticulacy *n*
inarticulateness, incoherence, unintelligibility, incomprehensibility, mumbling, indistinctness, hesitancy, stumbling, stammering, stuttering, speechlessness, tongue-tiedness
E3 articulacy

inarticulate *adj*
incoherent, unintelligible, incomprehensible, unclear, indistinct, mumbled, blurred, muffled, hesitant, hesitating, stumbling, stammering, stuttering, trembling, shaking, quavery, faltering, gibbering, disjointed, halting, tongue-tied, speechless, voiceless, dumb, mute, soundless
E3 articulate

inattention *n*
carelessness, negligence, disregard, heedlessness, thoughtlessness, unmindfulness, inattentiveness, absent-mindedness, forgetfulness, daydreaming, dreaminess, preoccupation, distraction
E3 attention, care

inattentive *adj*
distracted, dreamy, daydreaming, preoccupied, absent-minded, wool-gathering, unmindful, heedless, regardless, disregarding, careless, thoughtless, negligent, forgetful, remiss
FORMAL distrait
COLLOQ. miles away, in a world of your own, somewhere else
E3 attentive

inaudible *adj*
silent, noiseless, imperceptible, faint, indistinct, muffled, stifled, muted, soft, dull, low, mumbled, muttered, murmured, whispered
E3 audible, loud

inaugural *adj*
opening, introductory, first, initial, launching, original, maiden
FORMAL exordial
E3 closing, final

inaugurate *v*
1 *inaugurate a scheme*
institute, originate, begin, start, set up, open, launch, introduce, usher in, initiate, set in motion, put into operation, get going
OLD auspicate, handsel
FORMAL commence
COLLOQ. set/start the ball rolling
2 *inaugurate the president*
induct, invest, install, ordain, instate, enthrone, admit to office, swear in
3 *inaugurate a new building*
dedicate, consecrate, open officially, commission

inauguration *n*
1 INSTITUTION, setting up, starting, opening, launch, launching, initiation
FORMAL commencement

2 INDUCTION, ordination, investiture, consecration, enthronement, installation, installing, swearing-in

inauspicious *adj*
unfavourable, bad, unlucky, unfortunate, unpromising, untimely, ill-fated, ill-starred, discouraging, threatening, ominous, black
FORMAL infelicitous, unpropitious
⊟ promising; *formal* auspicious

inborn *adj*
innate, inherent, natural, native, congenital, inbred, hereditary, inherited, in the family, ingrained, instinctive, intuitive
FORMAL connate
⊟ learned

inbred *adj*
innate, inherent, natural, native, ingrained, incrossed, constitutional
TECHNICAL sib
FORMAL connate, ingenerate
⊟ learned

inbuilt *adj*
built-in, integral, constituent, inherent, basic, fundamental, essential, elemental

incalculable *adj*
countless, innumerable, numberless, without number, untold, inestimable, immeasurable, measureless, limitless, boundless, unlimited, endless, infinite, immense, vast, enormous
⊟ limited, restricted

incandescence *n*
glow, brilliance, brightness, gleam, glimmer, radiance, glory, vividness, richness, splendour, afterglow, sunglow, outflush
TECHNICAL phosphorescence
OLD leam
FORMAL luminosity

incandescent *adj*
1 GLOWING, aglow, shining, dazzling, gleaming, brilliant, bright, white-hot
2 FURIOUS, angry, livid, indignant, irate, enraged, infuriated, incensed, inflamed, raging, fuming, boiling, seething, frenzied, purple with rage
COLLOQ. mad, hopping mad, sizzling, up in arms, in a lather, hot under the collar, foaming at the mouth

incantation *n*
chant, charm, spell, abracadabra, formula, magic formula, invocation, mantra, mantram, rune, hex
FORMAL conjuration

incapable *adj*
unable, powerless, impotent, helpless, useless, weak, feeble, unfit, unsuited, unqualified, unfitted, incompetent, inept, inadequate, ineffective
FORMAL ineffectual
COLLOQ. not up to scratch, not hacking it, out of your league
⊟ capable, experienced

incapacitate *v*
disable, cripple, paralyse, immobilize, disqualify, put out of action, lay up
FORMAL debilitate
COLLOQ. scupper

incapacitated *adj*
disabled, crippled, paralysed, immobilized, disqualified, out of action, unfit, unwell, hamstrung, prostrate, drunk
FORMAL indisposed
COLLOQ. laid up, scuppered, tipsy
⊟ operative

incapacity *n*
incapability, inability, disability, unfitness, disqualification, powerlessness, impotence, ineffectiveness, ineptitude, weakness, feebleness, inadequacy, incompetence, incompetency, uselessness
FORMAL ineffectuality
⊟ capability

incarcerate *v*
imprison, put in prison, jail, gaol, put in jail, lock up, intern, confine, impound, commit, detain, put away, restrain, restrict, cage, encage, coop up, wall in
FORMAL immure
COLLOQ. send down, put inside
SLANG bang up
⊟ free, release

incarceration *n*
imprisonment, internment, jail, custody, detention, confinement, bondage, captivity, restraint, restriction
⊟ freedom, liberation

incarnate *adj*
human, in human form, embodied, made flesh, in the flesh, fleshly, personified, typified
OLD impersonate, incardinate
FORMAL corporeal

incarnation *n*
human form, appearance in the flesh, personification, embodiment, manifestation, impersonation
TECHNICAL avatar

incautious *adj*
careless, imprudent, ill-judged, ill-advised, ill-considered, unthinking, thoughtless, inconsiderate, inattentive, unwary, unwatchful, unobservant, foolish, foolhardy, rash, reckless, hasty, impulsive
FORMAL injudicious, uncircumspect, precipitate
⊟ cautious, careful, vigilant

incendiary *adj, n*
♦ *adj*
1 *an incendiary bomb*
fire-raising, flammable, combustible, pyromaniac
2 INCITING, inflammatory, provocative, stirring, seditious, subversive, dissentious, rabble-rousing
FORMAL proceleusmatic
⊟ **2** calming
♦ *n*
1 AGITATOR, insurgent, revolutionary, demagogue, rabble-rouser, firebrand
2 FIRE-RAISER, pyromaniac, arsonist, firebug, pétroleur, pétroleuse
3 FIREBOMB, bomb, explosive, charge, grenade, mine, petrol bomb

incense¹ *n*
smell the incense
perfume, scent, aroma, balm, bouquet, fragrance, joss-stick, pastille, myrrh, frankincense, benzoin, stacte

incense² *v*
incense his teacher
anger, enrage, infuriate, madden, exasperate, inflame, agitate, irritate, irk, vex, nettle, rile, provoke, excite
COLLOQ. aggravate, hassle, get someone's blood up, make someone's blood boil, get under someone's skin, drive up the wall, get someone's dander up
⊟ calm

incensed *adj*
enraged, angry, fuming, furious, exasperated, mad, maddened, steamed up, indignant, infuriated, irate, ireful, wrathful
FORMAL furibund
COLLOQ. aggravated, cross, ratty, uptight, mad, hopping mad, raving mad, seeing red, in a lather, disgruntled, up in

arms, hot under the collar, stroppy, in a strop, choked, fit to be tied, on the warpath, in a paddy; *N Am* ticked off; *Aust* spewy, ropable; *Aust & NZ* crooked
SLANG pissed off, hairless; *N Am* burned up
F3 calm

incentive *n*
bait, lure, enticement, reward, encouragement, inducement, incitement, reason, motive, impetus, spur, stimulus, goad, lure, bait, stimulant, motivation
COLLOQ. carrot, sweetener
F3 disincentive, discouragement, deterrent

inception *n*
inauguration, initiation, opening, installation, establishment, beginning, start, birth, origin, dawn, outset, rise
FORMAL commencement
COLLOQ. kick-off
F3 end

incessant *adj*
ceaseless, unceasing, endless, never-ending, unending, continual, persistent, constant, perpetual, eternal, everlasting, continuous, unbroken, uninterrupted, recurrent, unremitting, non-stop
FORMAL interminable
F3 intermittent, sporadic, periodic, temporary

incessantly *adv*
ceaselessly, endlessly, unendingly, eternally, everlastingly, for ever, for ever and ever, uninterruptedly, continuously, unremittingly, constantly, unceasingly, interminably
COLLOQ. till the cows come home; *N Am* twenty-four seven

incidence *n*
frequency, commonness, prevalence, extent, range, amount, degree, rate, occurrence

incident *n*
1 EVENT, occurrence, happening, episode, adventure, ...ience, proceeding, affair, matter, occasion, instance, circumst... ...assage, adventure, scene, subject, period, affaire, page
2 CONFRONTATION, clash, co... ... fight, skirmish, commotion, disturbance, scene, row, fracas, ... upset, mishap

incidental *adj*
accidental, chance, by chance, random, minor, non-essential, petty, trivial, small, secondary, subordinate, background, subsidiary, ancillary, peripheral, supplementary, accompanying, attendant, related, contributory
FORMAL fortuitous, concomitant
F3 important, essential

incidentally *adv*
1 BY THE WAY, in passing, secondarily, parenthetically, as a digression, as an aside, episodically, *en passant*
FORMAL apropos
COLLOQ. by the by
2 ACCIDENTALLY, by accident, coincidentally, unexpectedly, by chance, casually, digressively
FORMAL fortuitously

incinerate *v*
burn, cremate, reduce to ashes, carbonize

incineration *n*
burning, cremation, carbonization, turning/reduction to ashes

incipient *adj*
beginning, originating, starting, inaugural, developing, rudimentary, embryonic, newborn, impending
FORMAL commencing, inceptive, inchoate, nascent
F3 developed

incise *v*
cut, cut into, carve, chisel, engrave, sculpt, sculpture, etch, gash, slit, slash, nick, notch

incision *n*
cut, opening, slit, gash, notch, slash, nick

incisive *adj*
cutting, keen, sharp, acute, piercing, penetrating, surgical, biting, stinging, pungent, caustic, acid, astute, perceptive, shrewd, sarcastic
FORMAL trenchant, mordant, perspicacious

incisively *adv*
keenly, sharply, acutely, penetratingly, piercingly, astutely, pungently, sarcastically, tartly, caustically
FORMAL trenchantly, mordantly

incisiveness *n*
keenness, sharpness, acuteness, penetration, astuteness, acidity, pungency, sarcasm, tartness
FORMAL perspicacity, astucity, trenchancy

incite *v*
prompt, instigate, rouse, arouse, inflame, foment, stir up, whip up, work up, agitate, excite, animate, provoke, stimulate, spur, goad, prod, induce, impel, drive, urge, encourage
COLLOQ. egg on
F3 restrain

incitement *n*
prompting, instigation, rousing, agitation, provocation, spur, goad, prod, impetus, stimulus, stimulation, animation, urging, drive, motivation, encouragement, inducement, incentive
F3 discouragement

inciting *adj*
incendiary, rabble-rousing, inflammatory, provocative, stirring, seditious, subversive
FORMAL proceleusmatic
F3 calming

incivility *n*
impoliteness, discourtesy, discourteousness, rudeness, disrespect, unmannerliness, bad manners, ill-breeding, inurbanity, boorishness, coarseness, roughness, vulgarity
F3 civility

inclemency *n*
harshness, bitterness, rawness, severity, storminess, tempestuousness, roughness, foulness
F3 clemency

inclement *adj*
intemperate, harsh, bitter, cold, harsh, raw, severe, wet, stormy, tempestuous, rough, foul, nasty, blustery, squally
F3 fine, clement

inclination *n*
1 LIKING, fondness, affection, attraction, affinity, taste, preference, partiality, bias, tendency, trend, disposition, leaning
FORMAL propensity, proclivity, predisposition, predilection, penchant
2 *an inclination of 45 degrees*
angle, slope, gradient, incline, ascent, steepness, bank, ramp, lift, pitch, slant, tilt, bend, bow, nod
FORMAL acclivity, declivity
F3 **1** disinclination, dislike

incline *v, n*
♦ *v*
1 DISPOSE, influence, persuade, affect, sway, bend, bias, prejudice, tend, prefer
2 LEAN, slope, slant, bank, tilt, tip, bend, curve, list, bow, nod, stoop, list, veer, deviate, swing
♦ *n*

slope, gradient, ramp, hill, rise, ascent, dip, descent
FORMAL acclivity, declivity

inclined *adj*
liable, likely, tending, given, apt, disposed, of a mind,
willing
FORMAL predisposed, wont

include *v*
comprise, incorporate, embody, contain, enclose, hold,
encompass, cover, take in, span, admit, insert, introduce,
add, enter, put in, allow for, add in, count in, take into
account, involve, let in on, reckon, contain, carry
FORMAL comprehend, comprise, embrace, subsume,
connote
COLLOQ. rope in, throw in
⊟ exclude, omit, eliminate

including *prep*
counting, inclusive of, with, together with, as well as,
included
⊟ excluding

inclusion *n*
incorporation, involvement, embodiment, encompassing,
addition, insertion
FORMAL comprehension, subsumption
⊟ exclusion

inclusive *adj*
comprehensive, full, all-in, all-inclusive, all-embracing,
across-the-board, general, catch-all, overall, sweeping
COLLOQ. blanket
⊟ exclusive, narrow

incognito *adj*
in disguise, disguised, masked, veiled, camouflaged,
unmarked, unidentified, unrecognizable, unidentifiable,
keeping your identity secret, unknown, under an
assumed/a false name, nameless
⊟ undisguised

incognizant *adj*
unaware, unconscious, unacquainted, uninformed,
unenlightened, ignorant, unknowing, unobservant,
inattentive
⊟ aware; *formal* apprised

incoherence *n*
unintelligibility, incomprehensibility, inarticulateness,
stammer, stutter, mumble, mutter, brokenness,
garbledness, muddle, mix-up, jumble, confusion,
wildness, disconnectedness, disjointedness, illogicality,
inconsistency
⊟ coherence

incoherent *adj*
unintelligible, incomprehensible, inarticulate, wandering,
rambling, stammering, stuttering, mumbled, muttered,
unconnected, disconnected, broken, garbled, scrambled,
confused, muddled, mixed-up, jumbled, disjointed,
disordered, loose, wandering, illogical, inconsistent,
unclear, rigmarole, unjointed
OLD skimble-skamble
⊟ coherent, intelligible

incombustible *adj*
fireproof, flameproof, fire-resistant, flame-resistant,
flame-retardant, non-flammable, non-inflammable,
unburnable
⊟ combustible

income *n*
revenue, returns, proceeds, gains, profits, interest, takings,
receipts, earnings, pay, salary, wages, means,
remuneration, allowance, independency, penny-rent, rent
roll, rente
OLD benefice
⊟ expenditure, expenses, outgoings

incoming *adj*
arriving, entering, approaching, coming, homeward,
returning, ensuing, succeeding, next, new
⊟ outgoing

incommensurate *adj*
disproportionate, insufficient, inadequate, unequal,
excessive, extravagant, extreme
FORMAL incommensurable, inequitable, inordinate
⊟ appropriate

incommunicable *adj*
indescribable, inexpressible, unspeakable, unutterable,
unimpartable
FORMAL ineffable
⊟ expressible, communicable

incomparable *adj*
matchless, unmatched, beyond compare, unequalled,
without equal, unparalleled, without parallel, second to
none, unrivalled, unsurpassed, peerless, inimitable,
nonpareil, paramount, supreme, superlative, superb,
brilliant
⊟ ordinary, run-of-the-mill, poor

incomparably *adv*
by far, far and away, beyond compare, immeasurably,
infinitely, easily, supremely, superbly, superlatively,
eminently, brilliantly
⊟ poorly, slightly

incompatibility *n*
irreconcilability, contradiction, clash, conflict, variance,
inconsistency, difference, disagreement, discrepancy,
antagonism, mismatch, uncongeniality
FORMAL disparateness, disparity, incongruity
⊟ compatibility

incompatible *adj*
irreconcilable, contradictory, conflicting, in conflict,
exclusive, at odds, alien, at variance, inconsistent, clashing,
antagonistic, disagreeing, discordant, ill-matched,
mismatched, ill-assorted, unsuited, uncongenial, wrong,
repugnant
TECHNICAL dissonant
OLD insociable
FORMAL incongruous, disparate
COLLOQ. like a fish out of water, like a square peg in a round
hole, like chalk and cheese
⊟ compatible, complementary, going well together

incompetence *n*
incapability, inability, unfitness, unsuitability, stupidity,
uselessness, ineptitude, ineptness, ineffectiveness,
inefficiency, inadequacy, insufficiency, bungling
FORMAL ineffectuality, ineffectualness
⊟ competence

incompetent *adj*
incapable, unable, unfit, unqualified, unsuitable,
inefficient, inexpert, amateurish, unskilful, bungling,
awkward, clumsy, fumbling, stupid, useless, botched,
ineffective, inadequate, insufficient, deficient
COLLOQ. awful, terrible, lousy, crummy, pathetic, rop(e)y, a
load of rubbish, a load of garbage
SLANG the pits, pants, poxy, naff, crappy, not able to
organize a piss-up in a brewery; (*vulgar*) a load of crap, a
load of shit
⊟ competent, able

incomplete *adj*
deficient, lacking, short, unfinished, unaccomplished,
undeveloped, embryonic, rudimentary, abridged,
shortened, partial, part, half, sketchy, fragmentary, broken,
scrappy, piecemeal, imperfect, defective
TECHNICAL catalectic
FORMAL wanting
⊟ complete, accomplished, exhaustive, total

incomprehensible *adj*
unintelligible, unreadable, impenetrable, unfathomable, unfamiliar, unaware, complex, complicated, involved, above/over your head, puzzling, perplexing, baffling, deep, profound, enigmatic, mysterious, inscrutable, obscure, opaque
FORMAL abstruse, recondite
COLLOQ. double Dutch, all Greek to you
E3 comprehensible, intelligible

incomprehension *n*
unintelligibility, lack of understanding, ignorance, unperceptiveness, incognizance, unawareness, unfamiliarity, impenetrability, complexity, mysteriousness, inscrutability, obscurity, profundity
E3 comprehension, intelligibility

inconceivable *adj*
unthinkable, unimaginable, staggering, unheard-of, impossible, unbelievable, incredible, implausible, ridiculous, ludicrous, absurd, outrageous, shocking
COLLOQ. mind-boggling
E3 conceivable, imaginable, not on

inconclusive *adj*
unsettled, undecided, indefinite, open, open to question, uncertain, indecisive, ambiguous, vague, unconvincing, unsatisfying
FORMAL indeterminate
COLLOQ. up in the air, left hanging
E3 conclusive; *colloq.* open-and-shut

incongruity *n*
inappropriateness, unsuitability, inconsistency, incompatibility, conflict, clash, irreconcilability, contradiction, discrepancy, inharmoniousness, inaptness
FORMAL disparity, dissociability, dissociableness
E3 consistency, harmoniousness

incongruous *adj*
inappropriate, unsuitable, out of place, out of keeping, inconsistent, conflicting, clashing, jarring, incompatible, irreconcilable, contradictory, contrary, at odds, odd, absurd, strange
E3 consistent, compatible

incongruously *adv*
unsuitably, inappropriately, out of place, irrelevantly, without relevance, off/beside the point, inopportunely
FORMAL infelicitously

inconsequential *adj*
minor, trivial, trifling, petty, unimportant, of no importance, insignificant, neither here nor there, negligible, immaterial, inappreciable
E3 important, significant

inconsiderable *adj*
small, slight, negligible, trivial, petty, trifling, minor, unimportant, insignificant, negligible
E3 considerable, large

inconsiderate *adj*
unkind, uncaring, unconcerned, uncharitable, selfish, self-centred, egotistic, intolerant, insensitive, tactless, rude, thoughtless, unthinking, careless, heedless, undiscerning
E3 considerate, thoughtful, gracious, kind

inconsiderateness *n*
unkindness, unconcern, selfishness, self-centredness, intolerance, insensitivity, tactlessness, rudeness, thoughtlessness, carelessness
E3 considerateness, thoughtfulness, kindness

inconsistency *n*
1 CONTRADICTION, irreconcilability, incompatibility, discrepancy, disagreement, divergence, paradox, conflict, variance, odds, gallimaufry
FORMAL contrariety, disparity, incongruity
2 CHANGEABLENESS, unpredictability, instability,

unsteadiness, unreliability, fickleness, inconstancy
E3 **1** consistency **2** consistency, constancy

inconsistent *adj*
1 CONFLICTING, at variance, at odds, out of place/keeping, in opposition, incompatible, contradictory, contrary, differing, discordant, irreconcilable, dissimilar, alien, jarring, unagreeable, repugnant, self-repugnant
TECHNICAL disconformable
FORMAL incongruous
2 CHANGEABLE, variable, irregular, erratic, unpredictable, varying, unstable, unsteady, inconstant, fickle, capricious, mercurial, playing fast and loose
COLLOQ. in and out, blowing hot and cold
E3 **1** consistent **2** consistent, constant

inconsolable *adj*
heartbroken, broken-hearted, devastated, desolate, despairing, wretched, miserable, grief-stricken
FORMAL disconsolate

inconspicuous *adj*
unobtrusive, plain, ordinary, indistinct, unremarkable, undistinguished, discreet, low-key, hidden, concealed, camouflaged, modest, unassuming, quiet, retiring, insignificant, in the background
E3 conspicuous, noticeable, obtrusive

inconspicuously *adv*
unobtrusively, unassumingly, quietly, modestly, faintly, insignificantly, in the background
E3 conspicuously, obtrusively

inconstancy *n*
variableness, unsteadiness, fluctuation, variation, change, shift, swing, alternation, variability, range, instability, wavering, irresolution, ambivalence, fickleness
FORMAL oscillation, vacillation

inconstant *adj*
changeable, variable, varying, changeful, erratic, mutable, unsteady, fluctuating, inconsistent, unsettled, unstable, volatile, wavering, uncertain, undependable, unreliable, unfaithful, irresolute, capricious, mercurial, wayward, fickle
OLD (*Shakesp*) giglet
FORMAL vacillating
E3 constant

incontestable *adj*
incontrovertible, indisputable, undeniable, indubitable, irrefutable, unquestionable, certain, obvious, clear, evident, self-evident, sure
E3 uncertain

incontinent *adj*
uncontrollable, uncontrolled, ungovernable, ungoverned, unrestrained, unbridled, unchecked, loose, promiscuous, unchaste, dissipated, dissolute, debauched, lewd, licentious, lascivious, lecherous, lustful, wanton
E3 continent

incontrovertible *adj*
indisputable, unquestionable, beyond question, undeniable, irrefutable, indubitable, beyond doubt, certain, clear, self-evident
E3 questionable, uncertain

incontrovertibly *adv*
indisputably, unquestionably, beyond question, beyond doubt, undeniably, irrefutably, indubitably, certainly, clearly

inconvenience *n, v*
♦ *n*
1 *cause inconvenience*
awkwardness, difficulty, annoyance, vexation, nuisance, bother, trouble, fuss, disruption
FORMAL incommodity, incommodiousness
COLLOQ. hassle
2 *a minor inconvenience*

difficulty, problem, annoyance, worry, nuisance, hindrance, drawback, bother, trouble, fuss, upset, disturbance, disadvantage, burden, burr
COLLOQ. drag, pain, bore, bind, headache, turn-off
EB 1, 2 convenience
♦ v
bother, disturb, disrupt, put out, trouble, upset, irk, annoy, worry, fuss, burden, impose upon
FORMAL discommode
COLLOQ. hassle
EB convenience

inconvenient adj
awkward, ill-timed, untimely, unseasonable, unsuitable, inappropriate, inexpedient, difficult, embarrassing, annoying, troublesome, bothersome, untoward, unwieldy, unmanageable, cumbersome
OLD unhandsome
FORMAL inopportune, incommodious
EB convenient, suitable, handy

incorporate v
include, embody, contain, take in, build in, absorb, assimilate, integrate, combine, amalgamate, unite, unify, merge, blend, mix, fuse, coalesce, consolidate
OLD incorpse, piece up
FORMAL subsume, embrace
EB separate

incorporation n
inclusion, absorption, embodiment, assimilation, integration, combination, amalgamation, unification, unifying, blend, fusion, coalescence, association, company, merger, society, federation
FORMAL subsuming
EB separation, splitting off

incorporeal adj
bodiless, unfleshy, spiritual, unreal, illusory, intangible, ethereal, spectral, phantasmal, phantasmic, ghostly
EB real, fleshy

incorrect adj
wrong, not right, mistaken, erroneous, inaccurate, imprecise, inexact, false, untrue, bad, ill, faulty, ungrammatical, improper, illegitimate, inappropriate, unsuitable
FORMAL fallacious
COLLOQ. (way) off beam
EB correct, accurate

incorrectly adv
wrongly, mistakenly, by mistake, in error, erroneously, falsely, inaccurately, inappropriately, misguidedly, unfairly, unjustly
FORMAL fallaciously

incorrectness n
wrongness, mistakenness, erroneousness, error, inaccuracy, imprecision, inexactitude, falseness, faultiness, impreciseness, inexactness, speciousness, unsoundness, unsuitability
FORMAL fallacy
EB correctness, accuracy

incorrigible adj
irredeemable, incurable, inveterate, hardened, hopeless, beyond hope, beyond redemption, dyed-in-the-wool
EB redeemable

incorruptibility n
honesty, honour, integrity, uprightness, virtue, morality, trustworthiness, justness, nobility
FORMAL probity
EB corruptibility

incorruptible adj
honest, straight, upright, virtuous, moral, ethical, honourable, high-principled, trustworthy, unbribable, just
EB corruptible, dishonest

increase v, n
♦ v
1 the number of tourists has increased
become greater, go up, be on the increase, climb, rise, mount, soar, maximize, improve, advance, progress, grow, develop, build up, intensify, strengthen, heighten, extend, expand, spread, swell, multiply, proliferate, escalate, mushroom, snowball, rocket, skyrocket, spiral
COLLOQ. go through the roof
2 increase the public's awareness
raise, boost, add to, improve, enhance, advance, further, step up, intensify, strengthen, heighten, develop, build up, accumulate, enlarge, magnify, broaden, widen, deepen, extend, prolong, expand, spread, breed, propagate, scale up
FORMAL augment
COLLOQ. hike up, bump up, bring to a head, bring to the boil
EB 1 decrease, reduce, decline, fall 2 decrease, reduce
♦ n
rise, growth, surge, upsurge, upturn, gain, boost, addition, increment, advance, step-up, build-up, intensification, heightening, development, enlargement, extension, expansion, spread, proliferation, escalation, mushrooming, snowballing, rocketing
FORMAL augmentation
COLLOQ. hike
EB decrease, reduction, decline

Synonym nuances
verb sense 1
Climb and **rise** are suggestive of increasing by a large amount; **mount** may be found in wider contexts suggesting a steep ascent: *mounting criticism.* **Soar** implies a huge rise, but is usually applied to figures: *crime rates have soared in the past year.* **Improve** would be used where there is a growth in price or value with a positive effect: *improved trading figures give a healthier look to the economy.*
  While **grow** suggests a natural increase, **develop** and **build up** can be used of a natural or a planned expansion: *we have built up our clientele over the years.* **Intensify** is suggestive of becoming concentrated: *yesterday's increase intensified fears for the economy.* The terms **extend, expand** and **spread** are all suggestive of horizontal growth, either physical or more figurative: *we are extending the garden by two metres; my waistline is expanding.*
  Swell suggests a more marked, inflated outcome: *the number of tourists has swelled,* and **multiply** would be used of an increase in numbers, as could **proliferate**, especially if you wish to suggest a resulting abundance. The terms **escalate, mushroom** and **snowball** use differing images to suggest the unstoppable speed with which an increase comes about. **Spiral, rocket** and **skyrocket** imply a fast and uncontrolled increase, especially where the outcome is negative: *spiralling debts have left many companies in trouble.*

---

increasingly adv
more and more, all the more, more so, to an increasing degree/extent, on the increase, progressively, cumulatively
TECHNICAL exponentially

incredible adj
1 give some incredible excuse
unbelievable, improbable, implausible, far-fetched, preposterous, absurd, impossible, inconceivable, beyond/past belief, unthinkable, unimaginable
2 walk an incredible distance
extraordinary, amazing, surprising, astonishing, astounding, fantastic, remarkable, magnificent, formidable, exceptional, marvellous, wonderful, great

COLLOQ. tremendous, terrific, smashing, out of this world, mind-boggling, jaw-dropping
Ea 1 credible, believable

⚠ incredible or incredulous?
Incredible means 'unbelievable'; *incredulous* means 'not believing, showing disbelief'. If you are told an *incredible* story, you may be *incredulous*.

---

incredibly adv
unimaginably, unbelievably, inconceivably, impossibly, very, extremely, greatly, highly, extraordinarily, inexpressibly, unspeakably, amazingly, surprisingly, fantastically, remarkably, exceptionally, wonderfully, marvellously
COLLOQ. terrifically, tremendously

incredulity n
unbelief, disbelief, scepticism, cynicism, suspicion, doubt, distrust, mistrust
Ea credulity

incredulous adj
unbelieving, disbelieving, unconvinced, sceptical, cynical, suspicious, doubting, distrusting, distrustful, dubious, doubtful, uncertain
Ea credulous

increment n
increase, gain, addition, step-up, advancement, extension, supplement, growth, enlargement, expansion, growth ring
FORMAL accretion, accrual, accrument, addendum, augmentation
Ea decrease

incriminate v
implicate, involve, accuse, charge, impeach, blame, put the blame on
TECHNICAL indict, arraign
FORMAL inculpate
COLLOQ. point the finger at
Ea exonerate

inculcate v
instil, drum into, hammer into, din into, drill into, implant, fix, imprint, engrain, impress, infuse, teach, indoctrinate

inculpate v
blame, put the blame on, censure, accuse, charge, impeach, incriminate, involve, implicate, recriminate
TECHNICAL indict, arraign
Ea exonerate

incumbent adj, n
  ♦ adj
binding, necessary, obligatory, compulsory, prescribed, up to
FORMAL mandatory
  ♦ n
office-holder, office-bearer, bearer, holder, official, officer, functionary, member

incur v
sustain, suffer, provoke, arouse, bring upon yourself, lay yourself open to, expose yourself to, risk, run, experience, arouse, meet with, run up, gain, earn, contract

incurable adj
1 *an incurable disease*
terminal, fatal, untreatable, unhealable, inoperable, hopeless
2 INCORRIGIBLE, inveterate, hardened, hopeless, beyond hope, beyond redemption, dyed-in-the-wool
Ea 1 curable

incurably adv
1 TERMINALLY, fatally, inoperably, hopelessly
2 INCORRIGIBLY, inveterately, hopelessly, beyond hope

incursion n
raid, attack, assault, invasion, onslaught, foray, sortie, sally, infiltration, inroads, penetration
FORMAL irruption

indebted adj
obliged, grateful, thankful, appreciative
FORMAL beholden

indebtedness n
obligation, debt of gratitude, gratitude, appreciation

indecency n
immodesty, impurity, indecent behaviour, obscenity, pornography, lewdness, licentiousness, vulgarity, coarseness, crudity, foulness, grossness, offensiveness
FORMAL indecorum
Ea decency, modesty

indecent adj
1 IMPURE, immodest, improper, indelicate, suggestive, offensive, free, obscene, pornographic, lewd, immoral, corrupt, perverted, depraved, degenerate, licentious, vulgar, coarse, crude, dirty, filthy, smutty, foul, gross, bawdy, ribald, risqué, outrageous, shocking, off colour
COLLOQ. blue, raunchy, sleazy, fruity, close to/near the bone, near the knuckle
2 *indecent haste*
improper, unbecoming, unsuitable, inappropriate
OLD uncomely, unseemly
FORMAL indecorous
Ea 1 decent, modest

indecipherable adj
indistinguishable, unreadable, illegible, unintelligible, indistinct, unclear, tiny, crabbed, cramped
Ea readable

indecision n
indecisiveness, irresolution, wavering, fluctuation, hesitation, hesitancy, ambivalence, uncertainty, tentativeness, doubt
FORMAL vacillation
COLLOQ. shilly-shallying
Ea decisiveness, resolution

indecisive adj
1 UNDECIDED, undecisive, irresolute, undetermined, fluctuating, wavering, ambivalent, hesitating, hesitant, faltering, tentative, uncertain, unsure, indefinite, doubtful
FORMAL vacillating
COLLOQ. in two minds, weak-willed, pussyfooting, shilly-shallying, wishy-washy, blowing hot and cold, humming and hawing, chopping and changing, sitting on the fence, giving someone the runaround
2 INCONCLUSIVE, indefinite, unclear, open, undecided, unsettled
FORMAL indeterminate
COLLOQ. up in the air, hanging in the balance
Ea 1 decisive **2** decisive; *colloq.* open-and-shut

indecorous adj
undignified, improper, immodest, indecent, rough, impolite, rude, vulgar, in bad taste, tasteless, uncouth, unsuitable, inappropriate, coarse, crude, uncivil, unmannerly, ungentlemanly, unladylike, ill-mannered, ill-bred, boorish, churlish
FORMAL unseemly, untoward
Ea decorous

indecorum n
immodesty, indecency, roughness, rudeness, impoliteness, uncivility, tastelessness, bad taste, coarseness, crudity, vulgarity
FORMAL impropriety, unseemliness

indeed adv
really, actually, in fact, in point of fact, in truth, certainly, absolutely, positively, yes, truly, undeniably, without doubt,

undoubtedly, doubtlessly, for sure, to be sure, even, definitely, for that matter, rather, in anyone's book, aye, la; *Scot* atweel, deed
OLD sooth, forsooth, insooth; (*Spenser*) soothly; yea, faith, marry, quotha, in good time
FORMAL nay
COLLOQ. just, quite

indefatigable *adj*
untiring, tireless, untireable, unflagging, unfailing, unwearied, unwearying, unweariable, unresting, relentless, unremitting, dogged, inexhaustible, diligent, patient, persevering, indomitable, undying
E3 flagging, slothful

indefatigably *adv*
tirelessly, unflaggingly, unfailingly, relentlessly, unremittingly, unrestingly, doggedly, diligently, patiently, indomitably

indefensible *adj*
1 UNJUSTIFIABLE, inexcusable, unforgivable, unpardonable, insupportable, untenable, wrong, faulty, flawed, specious
2 *an indefensible place*
vulnerable, exposed, defenceless, unshielded, unarmed, disarmed, unprotected, unguarded, undefendable, ill-equipped
FORMAL unfortified
E3 1 defensible, excusable **2** defensible, protected, guarded

indefinable *adj*
indescribable, inexpressible, indistinct, unrealized, nameless, obscure, unclear, vague, subtle, dim, hazy, impalpable
E3 definable

indefinite *adj*
unknown, uncertain, unsettled, unresolved, inconclusive, undecided, undetermined, unfixed, undefined, unspecified, unlimited, ill-defined, vague, indistinct, unclear, blurred, confused, hazy, fuzzy, obscure, ambivalent, equivocal, ambiguous, doubtful, imprecise, inexact, loose, general, nondescript
FORMAL indeterminate
COLLOQ. the jury is still out
E3 definite, limited, clear

indefinitely *adv*
for ever, eternally, endlessly, always, permanently, without limit, continually, ad infinitum
COLLOQ. till the cows come home

indelible *adj*
lasting, enduring, permanent, fast, unfading, ineffaceable, ineradicable, ingrained, imperishable, indestructible
E3 erasable

indelibly *adv*
enduringly, permanently, ineradicably, indestructibly

indelicacy *n*
immodesty, indecency, obscenity, rudeness, vulgarity, offensiveness, suggestiveness, tastelessness, bad taste, coarseness, crudity, grossness, smuttiness
FORMAL impropriety
E3 delicacy

indelicate *adj*
rude, embarrassing, suggestive, immodest, improper, indecent, offensive, tasteless, in bad taste, unbecoming, vulgar, coarse, crude, gross, low, obscene, risqué
FORMAL indecorous, unseemly, untoward
COLLOQ. blue, off-colour
E3 delicate

indemnify *v*
protect, secure, underwrite, guarantee, insure, endorse, exempt, free, reimburse, compensate, repair, repay, requite, satisfy, pay, remunerate

indemnity *n*
compensation, reimbursement, remuneration, repayment, restitution, requital, redress, reparation, insurance, assurance, guarantee, security, protection, safeguard, immunity, exemption, amnesty

indent *v*
1 CUT, mark, nick, notch, dent, dint, pink, serrate, scallop
2 ORDER, ask for, apply for, request, demand
FORMAL requisition

indentation *n*
notch, nick, cut, serration, dent, groove, furrow, depression, dip, hollow, pit, dimple

indenture *n*
contract, agreement, certificate, deed, bond, covenant, commitment, deal, settlement

independence *n*
independency, autonomy, self-government, self-determination, self-rule, home rule, sovereignty, freedom, liberty, individualism, separation, self-sufficiency, self-reliance, decolonization, nationalism
TECHNICAL autarky
E3 dependence

independent *adj*
1 AUTONOMOUS, self-governing, self-determining, self-ruling, self-legislating, sovereign, absolute, non-aligned
TECHNICAL autarkic
FORMAL autarchic
2 FREE, free-thinking, liberated, unconstrained, unrestrained, freelance, individualistic, individualist, unconventional, self-sufficient, self-supporting, self-reliant, unaided
COLLOQ. standing on your own two feet, doing your own thing, with a mind of your own, going your own way, doing something off your own bat, paddling your own canoe
3 SEPARATE, self-contained, individual, unconnected, unattacked, unrelated, free-standing, distinct
FORMAL discrete
4 FAIR, just, unprejudiced, neutral, impartial, unbiased, dispassionate, objective, disinterested
E3 1 dependent **4** biased

independently *adv*
alone, by yourself, on your own, individually, separately, solo, unaided, autonomously
COLLOQ. under your own steam, on your tod
E3 together

indescribable *adj*
inexpressible, indefinable, undefinable, unutterable, unspeakable, incredible, extraordinary, exceptional, amazing
FORMAL ineffable
E3 describable

indescribably *adv*
inexpressibly, unutterably, unspeakably, incredibly, extraordinarily, exceptionally, amazingly, extremely, very, highly, greatly

indestructible *adj*
unbreakable, durable, tough, strong, lasting, enduring, abiding, permanent, eternal, everlasting, immortal, endless, undecaying, inextinguishable, imperishable
FORMAL infrangible
E3 breakable, mortal

indeterminate *adj*
indefinite, unspecified, unstated, undefined, unknown, unfixed, imprecise, inexact, unclear, vague, hazy, ill-defined, open-ended, undecided, undetermined, unpredictable, uncertain, ambiguous, equivocal, ambivalent
E3 known, specified, fixed

index *n*

1 *an index of names*
table, key, list, catalogue, directory, guide, concordance, table
2 INDICATOR, pointer, needle, dial, hand, sign, token, mark, indication, hint, clue, symptom
TECHNICAL alidad
OLD gnomon
3 RATIO, proportion, rate, number, average, formula, scale, indicator, correspondence, difference, percentage, fraction
TECHNICAL exponent, power

indicate *v*

1 *shrugging shoulders indicates a lack of care*
show, reveal, display, mark, signify, mean, express, tell, make known, display, suggest, imply, represent, be symptomatic of
FORMAL manifest, evince, denote
2 *indicate the way to someone*
point out, show, point to, designate, specify
3 *he indicated that he would not oppose the plan*
say, declare, state, tell, announce, report, communicate, assert, affirm, specify, present, express, put, set out, make known, formulate, articulate, voice, utter, reveal, divulge, disclose
4 *the gauge indicates temperature*
show, register, record, read

indicated *adj*

needed, required, suggested, desirable, necessary, called-for, advisable, recommended

indication *n*

sign, mark, evidence, symptom, signal, record, register, warning, omen, intimation, expression, suggestion, hint, clue, note, explanation
FORMAL manifestation, augury, portent

indicative *adj*

symptomatic, suggestive, demonstrative, characteristic, typical, telltale, significant, symbolic
FORMAL denotative, exhibitive, indicatory, indicant

indicatively *adv*

symptomatically, characteristically, significantly, typically, symbolically, as a sign, as a symbol, as evidence, as an expression

indicator *n*

pointer, needle, marker, hand, index, sign, symbol, token, signal, display, dial, gauge, meter, index, guide, flasher, bezel, barometer, litmus test, mark, signpost; *N Am* turn signal
OLD gnomon

indict *v*

charge, accuse, impeach, summon, summons, prosecute, put on trial, incriminate
TECHNICAL arraign
FORMAL inculpate
☒ absolve; *formal* exonerate

indictment *n*

charge, accusation, impeachment, allegation, recrimination, summons, prosecution, incrimination
TECHNICAL arraignment
FORMAL inculpation
☒ exoneration

indifference *n*

apathy, unconcern, lack of concern, lack of interest, lack of feeling, coldness, coolness, inattention, disregard, heedlessness, negligence, impassivity, nonchalance, neutrality, disinterestedness
☒ interest, concern

indifferent *adj*

1 UNINTERESTED, unenthusiastic, unexcited, apathetic, unconcerned, unmoved, unresponsive, unfeeling, unemotional, uncaring, unsympathetic, blasé, callous, cold, cool, distant, aloof, detached, dispassionate, uninvolved, impassive, neutral, nonchalant, disinterested, careless, heedless
COLLOQ. easy, all the same to you
2 MEDIOCRE, average, middling, passable, moderate, fair, adequate, undistinguished, ordinary, medium, bad, not good
COLLOQ. OK, so-so, could be better/worse, run of the mill, nothing to write home about
☒ **1** interested, caring **2** excellent

Synonym nuances
sense 1

The word **apathetic** is fairly disapproving in tone and can be used to show that someone cannot be bothered: *young people are notoriously apathetic about voting*. **Blasé**, on the other hand, is less marked in that it suggests indifference arising from overfamiliarity. **Nonchalant** is appropriate of a very casual and perhaps studied display of indifference, while **careless** and **heedless** suggest an irresponsible lack of concern: *rushing onwards with heedless bravery*.

Other more neutral terms are **unconcerned**, **unmoved**, **unemotional**, **unsympathetic** and **uninvolved**, which are simply concerned with the absence of a particular emotion, but **unresponsive**, **unfeeling** and **uncaring** have a more disapprobatory feel, suggesting an unnatural lack of fellow feeling. **Callous** is even more strongly suggestive of a hardened attitude to the suffering of others.

Both **cold** and **cool**, however, have connotations of varying degrees of unfriendliness, and **distant** and **detached** suggest a simple lack of emotional involvement, whereas **impassive** would be appropriate for not showing it. **Aloof** has further, more disapproving implications of standoffishness. **Neutral** and **disinterested** have more to do with impartiality and not taking sides in a dispute.

---

indigence *n*

poverty, distress, destitution, deprivation, necessity, need, want
FORMAL penury, privation
☒ affluence

indigenous *adj*

native, aboriginal, original, local, home-grown
FORMAL autochthonous
☒ foreign

indigent *adj*

poverty-stricken, impoverished, poor, destitute, needy, penniless, in dire straits, in want, in need
FORMAL penurious, impecunious, necessitous
COLLOQ. down and out, bust, skint, broke, stony-broke, cleaned out, on your uppers, on your beam ends, up against it, not having two pennies to rub together, dirt-poor
☒ affluent

indigestion *n*

dyspepsia, dyspepsy, heartburn, cardialgia, acidity, pyrosis, water-brash, grass/stomach staggers
OLD apepsia

indignant *adj*

annoyed, angry, cross, irate, heated, fuming, livid, furious, incensed, infuriated, enraged, exasperated, outraged, riled, aggrieved, disgruntled, wrathful, acrimonious, bitter, resentful
COLLOQ. hot under the collar, steamed up, mad, up in arms, peeved, miffed, narked, got the hump, in a huff, in a strop
☒ pleased, delighted

indignantly *adv*

angrily, crossly, irately, furiously, reproachfully, acrimoniously, resentfully, bitterly
COLLOQ. hot under the collar, steamed up, up in arms, in a huff

indignation *n*

annoyance, anger, ire, wrath, rage, fury, exasperation, outrage, pique, scorn, contempt, resentment
E3 pleasure, delight

indignity *n*

humiliation, abuse, insult, slight, snub, affront, shame, contempt, mistreatment, offence, disgrace, outrage, reproach, dishonour, disrespect, incivility, injury
FORMAL contumely, obloquy, opprobrium
COLLOQ. slap in the face, kick in the teeth, cold shoulder, putdown
E3 honour

indirect *adj*

1 ROUNDABOUT, circuitous, divergent, devious, remote, oblique, wandering, rambling, curving, winding, meandering, zigzag, tortuous, discursive, allusive, back-handed, squint
FORMAL periphrastic, circumlocutory
2 *an indirect effect*
secondary, incidental, unintended, subordinate, subsidiary, ancillary, bye, mediate
E3 1 direct 2 primary

indirectly *adv*

roundaboutly, obliquely, second-hand, deviously, in a roundabout way, hintingly, incidentally, allusively
FORMAL periphrastically, circumlocutorily
E3 directly

indiscernible *adj*

imperceptible, minuscule, minute, microscopic, tiny, undiscernible, undetectable, unapparent, unclear, indistinct, obscure, indistinguishable, unnoticeable, invisible, hidden, impalpable
E3 clear, apparent

indiscreet *adj*

tactless, undiplomatic, insensitive, unwise, imprudent, ill-advised, ill-judged, ill-considered, foolish, foolhardy, rash, reckless, hasty, careless, heedless, unthinking, unwary, immodest, indelicate, shameless
FORMAL impolitic, injudicious
E3 discreet, cautious

indiscreetly *adv*

tactlessly, undiplomatically, unwisely, foolishly, rashly, recklessly, carelessly, heedlessly, immodestly, indelicately, insensitively, shamelessly
E3 discreetly, cautiously

indiscretion *n*

mistake, error, slip, faux pas, gaffe, blunder, lapse, tactlessness, rashness, recklessness, imprudence, foolishness, folly, carelessness, immodesty, indelicacy, shamelessness
COLLOQ. boob, slip-up; *NAm* flub
E3 caution, diplomacy, etiquette

indiscriminate *adj*

general, sweeping, wholesale, random, haphazard, hit or miss, hit and miss, aimless, careless, confused, chaotic, unsystematic, unmethodical, unselective, undifferentiating, undiscriminating, mixed, varied, diverse, motley, miscellaneous
E3 selective, specific, precise

indiscriminately *adv*

generally, wholesale, haphazardly, randomly, unselectively, aimlessly, carelessly, unsystematically, unmethodically, without fear or favour, in the mass
E3 deliberately, selectively

indispensable *adj*

vital, essential, absolutely, essential, basic, fundamental, important, key, crucial, imperative, required, needed, necessary, needful
FORMAL requisite
E3 dispensable, unnecessary

indisposed *adj*

1 ILL, sick, unwell, poorly, ailing, confined to bed, laid up
FORMAL incapacitated
COLLOQ. groggy, under the weather, out of sorts, like death warmed up
2 RELUCTANT, unwilling, not willing, not of a mind (to), disinclined, averse, loath
E3 1 well 2 inclined

indisposition *n*

1 ILLNESS, ailment, disease, complaint, disorder, sickness, ill health, bad health
FORMAL malady
2 RELUCTANCE, unwillingness, hesitancy, disinclination, aversion, dislike, distaste
E3 1 health 2 inclination

indisputable *adj*

incontrovertible, unquestionable, undeniable, indubitable, irrefutable, incontestable, absolute, undisputed, inarguable, unarguable, definite, positive, certain, sure, beyond question
SLANG *Aust* dead set
E3 doubtful, uncertain

indissoluble *adj*

indestructible, permanent, inseparable, imperishable, incorruptible, enduring, lasting, eternal, fixed, inviolable, abiding, binding, solid, unbreakable
FORMAL sempiternal
E3 impermanent, short-lived

indistinct *adj*

unclear, ill-defined, out of focus, blurred, fuzzy, misty, hazy, shadowy, obscure, dim, pale, faded, faint, low, muted, muffled, muttered, confused, unintelligible, indistinguishable, indecipherable, vague, woolly, ambiguous, indefinite, undefined
E3 distinct, clear, in focus

indistinctly *adv*

unclearly, vaguely, fuzzily, hazily, obscurely, dimly, unintelligibly, indistinguishably, out of focus
E3 clearly, distinctly

indistinguishable *adj*

identical, interchangeable, same, twin, alike, hard to make out the difference, cloned, tantamount
COLLOQ. as like as two peas in a pod
E3 distinguishable, unalike, different, dissimilar

individual *n, adj*

◆ *n*
person, being, human being, creature, party, body, soul, mortal, type, sort, character, fellow
◆ *adj*
distinctive, characteristic, typical, idiosyncratic, peculiar, unique, exclusive, original, special, personal, own, lone, solitary, isolated, proper, respective, several, separate, distinct, specific, personalized, particular, single, sole, private
FORMAL singular
E3 collective, shared, general

individualism *n*

independence, originality, self-direction, self-interest, self-reliance, freethinking, freethought, eccentricity, egocentricity, egoism, anarchism, libertarianism
E3 conventionality

individualist *n*

independent, freethinker, free spirit, egoist, egocentric,

nonconformist, original, bohemian, eccentric, maverick, loner, lone wolf, libertarian, anarchist
⊞ conventionalist

individualistic *adj*
independent, individual, nonconformist, unorthodox, eccentric, bohemian, original, self-reliant, unconventional, egocentric, egoistic, idiosyncratic, special, typical, unique, particular, libertarian, anarchistic
⊞ conventional

individuality *n*
character, personality, distinctiveness, identity, peculiarity, uniqueness, originality, separateness, distinction
OLD property; (*Shakesp*) propriety
FORMAL singularity
⊞ sameness, anonymity

individually *adv*
separately, singly, one by one, one at a time, independently, particularly, personally
FORMAL severally, in several
⊞ together

indivisible *adj*
inseparable, undividable, indissoluble, impartible
FORMAL indiscerptible
⊞ divisible

indoctrinate *v*
brainwash, propagandize, teach, instruct, school, ground, train, drill, impress, inculcate, instil

indoctrination *n*
brainwashing, instruction, schooling, training, teaching, grounding, inculcation, drilling, instilling
FORMAL catechesis, catechetics

indolence *n*
idleness, laziness, inactivity, inertia, inertness, lethargy, heaviness, listlessness, do-nothingism, apathy, slacking, sloth, sluggishness
FORMAL languidness, languor, torpidity, torpidness, torpitude, torpor
COLLOQ. shirking
⊞ activeness, enthusiasm, industriousness

indolent *adj*
idle, bone-idle, lazy, inactive, inert, lethargic, listless, do-nothing, shiftless, apathetic, slack, slow, sluggish, slothful, sluggard, lackadaisical, lumpish
FORMAL fainéant, languid, torpid
⊞ active, enthusiastic, industrious

indomitable *adj*
invincible, unconquerable, unbeatable, undefeatable, impregnable, unassailable, brave, courageous, fearless, valiant, bold, intrepid, stalwart, lion-hearted, resolute, staunch, firm, intransigent, determined, steadfast, undaunted, unflinching, unyielding
⊞ compliant, timid, submissive

indubitable *adj*
indisputable, beyond dispute, unanswerable, undeniable, beyond doubt, undoubted, undoubtable, unquestionable, unarguable, incontestable, incontrovertible, irrefutable, sure, absolute, certain, obvious, evident
FORMAL irrebuttable, irrefragable
⊞ arguable

indubitably *adv*
doubtless, certainly, without doubt, undoubtedly, unquestionably, indisputably, no doubt, clearly, surely, of course, truly, precisely, probably, presumably, most likely, assuredly

induce *v*
1 CAUSE, bring about, occasion, give rise to, lead to, bring on, get, set in motion, incite, instigate, originate, prompt, provoke, produce, generate

FORMAL effect
2 COAX, prevail upon, encourage, press, persuade, talk into, move, influence, draw, tempt, inspire, motivate, urge, actuate, impel, force, seduce
OLD entreat, procure
⊞ **2** discourage, deter

inducement *n*
lure, bait, attraction, enticement, encouragement, incentive, impetus, incitement, influence, reward, spur, goad, stimulus, motive, reason
COLLOQ. carrot, sweetener
⊞ disincentive

induct *v*
inaugurate, initiate, install, invest, ordain, introduce, consecrate, enthrone, swear in, admit

induction *n*
1 INAUGURATION, initiation, installation, institution, investiture, ordination, introduction, enthronement, consecration
2 INFERENCE, conclusion, deduction, generalization

indulge *v*
1 GRATIFY, satisfy, humour, pander to, go along with, give in to, yield to, give way to, cater to, favour, pet, cosset, mollycoddle, pamper, spoil, treat, regale
2 *indulge in something*
give way to, give free rein to, give yourself up to, revel in, wallow in, luxuriate in

indulgence *n*
1 EXTRAVAGANCE, luxury, treat, excess, gratification, self-gratification, mollycoddling, pampering, spoiling, satisfaction, fulfilment, immoderation, intemperance, dissipation, dissoluteness
2 FAVOUR, tolerance, generosity, lenience, forbearance, pardon, remission
⊞ **1** restraint

indulgent *adj*
tolerant, lenient, permissive, generous, forgiving, merciful, compassionate, sympathetic, humane, liberal, easy-going, kind, fond, tender, understanding, patient, pampering, humouring, spoiling, cosseting, mollycoddling
FORMAL forbearing
COLLOQ.
⊞ strict, harsh

indulgently *adv*
tolerantly, leniently, generously, liberally, compassionately, mercifully, sympathetically, humanely, kindly, fondly, tenderly, patiently, with compassion, with mercy, with sympathy
⊞ strictly, harshly

industrial *adj*
manufacturing, commercial, business, trade

industrialist *n*
manufacturer, producer, magnate, tycoon, baron, captain of industry, capitalist, financier

industrious *adj*
busy, productive, hard-working, hard, diligent, assiduous, conscientious, laborious, steady, dedicated, studious, workful, zealous, active, energetic, tireless, indefatigable, persistent, persevering, determined, dogged, vigorous; *dialect* deedy
OLD notable
FORMAL sedulous
COLLOQ. busy as a bee, on the go, slogging your guts out
⊞ lazy, idle

industriously *adv*
diligently, conscientiously, assiduously, steadily, hard, perseveringly, doggedly, sedulously
COLLOQ. with your nose to the grindstone
⊞ lazily

industry *n*

1 *the steel industry*

business, trade, commerce, manufacturing, production, service, enterprise, line, field

2 INDUSTRIOUSNESS, diligence, conscientiousness, assiduousness, assiduity, application, intentness, concentration, effort, labour, laboriousness, toil, persistence, hard work, zeal, energy, vigour, activity, perseverance, steadiness, determination, productiveness, tirelessness

FORMAL sedulity, sedulousness

COLLOQ. stickability

🖃 **2** laziness, indolence

inebriated *adj*

under the influence, drunk, drunken

FORMAL intoxicated, crapulent

COLLOQ. merry, tight, tipsy, tiddly, tiddled, well-oiled, blotto, drunk as a lord/newt, drunk as a piper, sloshed, stewed, blind drunk, roaring drunk, the worse for drink, soused, squiffy, happy, legless, plastered, sozzled, pickled, bibulous, woozy, one over the eight, under the table, bevvied, having had a few, tired and emotional, high, footless, full, half-cut, obfuscated, pickled, pie-eyed, sow-drunk, under the weather, the worse for wear, steaming; *Irish* jarred; *Scot & Irish* stocious

SLANG stoned, tanked up, loaded, lit up, canned, paralytic, smashed, pissed; *Scot* pished; ossified, off your face, bladdered, hammered, bombed, ripped, wasted, wrecked, stinko, whiffled, whistled, bonkers, bottled, Brahms and Liszt, juiced (up), in liquor, liquored, maggoty, mortal, up the pole; (*vulgar*) arseholed, rat-arsed; *N Am* crocked, moon-eyed; *Aust* inky, inked, rotten; *Aust & NZ* shickered

OLD SLANG corked, moppy

🖃 sober, temperate, abstinent, teetotal

inedible *adj*

uneatable, unpalatable, stale, indigestible, not fit to eat, unconsumable, rotten, off, bad, rancid, harmful, noxious, poisonous, deadly

🖃 edible, wholesome

ineducable *adj*

unteachable, incorrigible, indocile

🖃 educable

ineffable *adj*

indescribable, inexpressible, unspeakable, unutterable, beyond words, remarkable, fearful, incommunicable, unimpartible

🖃 describable

ineffably *adv*

inexpressibly, indescribably, unspeakably, unutterably, absolutely, remarkably, fearfully, beyond words

ineffective *adj*

1 *an ineffective attempt*

useless, worthless, vain, idle, futile, unavailing, to no avail, abortive, profitless, fruitless, unproductive, unsuccessful

FORMAL ineffectual

2 POWERLESS, impotent, inadequate, weak, feeble, inept, idle, lame, incompetent

🖃 **1, 2** effective

ineffectiveness *n*

uselessness, worthlessness, fruitlessness, unproductiveness, inadequacy, weakness, feebleness, futility

🖃 effectiveness

ineffectual *adj*

1 *ineffectual methods*

useless, vain, futile, worthless, fruitless, unproductive, unavailing, abortive

FORMAL inefficacious

2 *an ineffectual person*

weak, feeble, powerless, inadequate, incompetent, impotent, inept, lame

COLLOQ. wimpy

🖃 **1, 2** effectual

ineffectually *adv*

weakly, feebly, lamely, uselessly, unsuccessfully, fruitlessly, unproductively, in vain, to no purpose, to no avail

🖃 effectually

inefficacy *n*

ineffectiveness, unproductiveness, uselessness, futility, inadequacy

FORMAL ineffectuality, ineffectualness

🖃 efficacy

inefficiency *n*

waste, wastefulness, disorganization, carelessness, negligence, slackness, laxity, ineptitude, sloppiness, incompetence, muddle

🖃 efficiency

inefficient *adj*

uneconomic, wasteful, money-wasting, time-wasting, ineffective, incompetent, ineffective, inexpert, unworkmanlike, slipshod, sloppy, slack, lax, inept, careless, disorganized, unorganized, negligent

🖃 efficient

inelegant *adj*

graceless, ungraceful, clumsy, awkward, gauche, ungainly, laboured, ugly, unrefined, ill-bred, crude, vulgar, unpolished, rough, homespun, unsophisticated, uncultured, uncultivated, unfinished, uncouth

OLD unpolite

🖃 elegant

ineligible *adj*

disqualified, ruled out, unacceptable, undesirable, unworthy, unsuitable, unfit, unfitted, unqualified, unequipped

TECHNICAL incompetent

🖃 eligible

ineluctable *adj*

inescapable, inevitable, unavoidable, destined, fated, certain, sure, assured, irrevocable, unalterable, inexorable

OLD ineludible

inept *adj*

awkward, clumsy, bungling, heavy-handed, incompetent, incapable, inadequate, unskilful, inexpert, unsuccessful, foolish, stupid, useless, appalling

FORMAL maladroit

COLLOQ. pathetic, cack-handed, lousy, ham-fisted

🖃 competent, skilful

ineptitude *n*

ineptness, awkwardness, clumsiness, bungling, unhandiness, gaucheness, gaucherie, incompetence, incapability, unskilfulness, inexpertness, stupidity, unfitness, uselessness, crassness

FORMAL fatuity, incapacity

🖃 aptitude, skill

inequality *n*

unequalness, imbalance, difference, discrepancy, contrast, variation, diversity, dissimilarity, nonconformity, unevenness, roughness, irregularity, disproportion, bias, prejudice, discrimination

FORMAL disparity

🖃 equality, balance

inequitable *adj*

unfair, unjust, unequal, wrongful, one-sided, biased, prejudiced, discriminatory, bigoted, intolerant, partisan, partial, preferential

🖃 equitable

inequity *n*
unfairness, unjustness, injustice, maltreatment, mistreatment, abuse, inequality, wrongfulness, one-sidedness, prejudice, bias, discrimination, partiality
F3 equity

inert *adj*
1 IMMOBILE, motionless, unmoving, still, stock-still, inactive, static, stationary, inanimate, lifeless, dead, passive, cold, unresponsive
FORMAL comatose
2 SLUGGISH, lethargic, lazy, inactive, slack, listless, dull, apathetic, idle, dormant, stagnant, torpid, sleepy
FORMAL indolent
F3 1 moving **2** lively, animated

inertia *n*
inertness, immobility, motionlessness, stillness, stagnation, inactivity, inaction, passivity, unresponsiveness, apathy, idleness, laziness, sloth, slothfulness, lethargy, listlessness
FORMAL indolence, languor, torpor
F3 activity, liveliness

inescapable *adj*
inevitable, unavoidable, destined, fated, certain, sure, assured, irrevocable, unalterable, inexorable
OLD ineludible
FORMAL ineluctable
F3 escapable, preventable

inescapably *adv*
inevitably, unavoidably, inescapably, irrevocably, inexorably, necessarily, definitely, certainly, surely, automatically, assuredly
F3 avoidably

inessential *adj, n*
◆ *adj*
unnecessary, irrelevant, superfluous, surplus, redundant, non-essential, needless, unasked-for, uncalled-for, unimportant, secondary, spare, accidental, unessential, dispensable, expendable, extraneous, optional, extrinsic
F3 essential, necessary
◆ *n*
non-essential, extra, extravagance, luxury, superfluity, accessory, trimming, appendage
F3 essential

inestimable *adj*
incalculable, measureless, infinite, immeasurable, invaluable, precious, priceless, unlimited, uncountable, unfathomable, incomputable, immense, vast, untold
FORMAL prodigious
COLLOQ. mind-boggling, worth a fortune
F3 insignificant

inevitability *n*
certainty, absolute certainty, foregone conclusion, matter of course, truth, validity, fact, reality
COLLOQ. sure thing, safe bet, dead cert

inevitable *adj*
unavoidable, inescapable, necessary, definite, certain, sure, decreed, ordained, destined, predestined, fated, fateful, automatic, infallible, assured, fixed, settled, unalterable, irrevocable, inexorable, unpreventable, inescapable
OLD unshunned; (*Shakesp*) unavoided
FORMAL ineluctable
F3 avoidable, uncertain, alterable

inevitably *adv*
unavoidably, inescapably, irrevocably, inexorably, necessarily, infallibly, definitely, certainly, surely, automatically, assuredly, fatefully
F3 avoidably

inexact *adj*
imprecise, approximate, inaccurate, incorrect, erroneous, indefinite, indistinct, fuzzy, loose, woolly, lax, muddled
FORMAL indeterminate, fallacious
F3 exact, accurate

inexactitude *n*
inexactness, impreciseness, imprecision, inaccuracy, incorrectness, indefiniteness, approximation, miscalculation, woolliness, looseness, mistake, blunder, error
F3 exactitude, accuracy

inexcusable *adj*
indefensible, unforgivable, unpardonable, unjustifiable, intolerable, unacceptable, outrageous, shameful, blameworthy
FORMAL reprehensible
F3 excusable, justifiable

inexcusably *adv*
indefensibly, unjustifiably, unacceptably, outrageously, shamefully
FORMAL reprehensibly
F3 justfiably

inexhaustible *adj*
1 *an inexhaustible supply*
unlimited, limitless, boundless, unbounded, unrestricted, measureless, infinite, endless, never-ending, abundant, unfailing
FORMAL illimitable
2 INDEFATIGABLE, tireless, untiring, unflagging, unfailing, unwearied, unwearying, weariless
F3 1 limited

inexorable *adj*
relentless, unrelenting, remorseless, unalterable, inevitable, unpreventable, unavertable, irresistible, irrevocable, inescapable, immovable, implacable, intransigent, unyielding, unceasing, incessant, unstoppable, unfaltering, ordained, destined, fated, definite, certain, sure
FORMAL ineluctable
F3 avoidable, preventable

inexorably *adv*
relentlessly, remorselessly, inescapably, irresistibly, inevitably, irrevocably, definitely, certainly, surely, resistlessly, implacably, pitilessly, mercilessly
FORMAL ineluctably

inexpedient *adj*
unwise, unsuitable, inappropriate, disadvantageous, misguided, detrimental, unadvisable, unfavourable, indiscreet, foolish, senseless, wrong, imprudent, ill-advised, inadvisable, ill-chosen, ill-judged, inconvenient, impractical, undesirable, undiplomatic
FORMAL impolitic, injudicious
F3 expedient

inexpensive *adj*
cheap, low-priced, low-price, reasonable, modest, bargain, budget, low-cost, cut-rate, economical, reduced, discounted
COLLOQ. a snip, a steal, going for a song, dirt-cheap, dog-cheap, ten a penny, on a shoestring
F3 expensive, dear

inexperience *n*
inexpertness, ignorance, unfamiliarity, strangeness, newness, freshness, rawness, immaturity, naiveness, innocence
F3 experience

inexperienced *adj*
inexpert, untrained, unqualified, untutored, new to the job, unskilled, amateur, probationary, apprentice, unacquainted, uninformed, ignorant, unfamiliar, unaccustomed, unseasoned, new, fresh, raw, callow, young, immature, naive, unsophisticated, innocent, fledgling, unfledged

OLD unseen; (*Shakesp*) puny, unexperient
COLLOQ. rookie, green, wet behind the ears, out of your depth, wide-eyed
❌ experienced, mature

Synonym nuances
Untrained, **unqualified** and **unskilled** are straightforward synonyms, suggesting a lack of requisite knowledge. **Inexpert** and **amateur**, however, can have rather negative connotations of being unprofessional in one's practices and of the effects of this on one's work: *an enthusiastic, if amateur, cameraman*. **Unacquainted** and **uninformed**, as well as **unfamiliar** and **unaccustomed**, return to the idea of simply not having had the requisite information or introduction: *he was unacquainted with the new practices*, but **ignorant** can imply not just a lack of knowledge, but also intelligence.
 The terms **unseasoned**, **raw** and **fresh** suggest having newly come to something: *raw recruits*, while **fledgling** and **unfledged**, along with **callow**, **young** and **immature**, which also have connotations of vulnerability, continue the idea of being in the early stages: *callow undergraduates; a fledgling democracy*. **Naive**, **unsophisticated** and **innocent** put further emphasis on ingenuousness as a consequence of inexperience.

---

inexpert *adj*
unskilled, unskilful, untaught, untrained, unpractised, unworkmanlike, unprofessional, untutored, unqualified, amateur, amateurish, awkward, clumsy, unhandy, incompetent, inept, bungling, blundering
FORMAL maladroit
COLLOQ. cack-handed, ham, ham-fisted
❌ expert

inexplicable *adj*
incomprehensible, unexplainable, unintelligible, unaccountable, strange, mystifying, puzzling, perplexing, baffling, bewildering, mysterious, insoluble, enigmatic, weird, unfathomable, incredible, unbelievable, miraculous
FORMAL abstruse
❌ explicable

inexplicably *adv*
incomprehensibly, unexplainably, incredibly, unaccountably, strangely, mysteriously, mystifyingly, bafflingly, puzzlingly, miraculously
❌ explicably

inexpressible *adj*
indescribable, undescribable, unspeakable, unutterable, incommunicable, indefinable, nameless, unsayable, untellable
OLD (*Shakesp*) termless
FORMAL ineffable

inexpressibly *adv*
indescribably, unspeakably, unutterably, beyond words
FORMAL ineffably

inexpressive *adj*
unexpressive, expressionless, deadpan, poker-faced, inscrutable, blank, vacant, empty, lifeless, dead, cold, emotionless, impassive
❌ expressive

inextinguishable *adj*
unquenchable, indestructible, imperishable, irrepressible, unconquerable, unquellable, unsuppressible, deathless, enduring, lasting, eternal, everlasting, undying, immortal
❌ impermanent, perishable

inextricable *adj*
inseparable, indissoluble, indivisible, indistinguishable, intricate, irretrievable, inescapable, irreversible

inextricably *adv*
inseparably, indissolubly, indivisibly, indistinguishably, intricately, irresolubly, irretrievably, inescapably, irreversibly

infallibility *n*
accuracy, unerringness, faultlessness, inerrancy, perfection, dependability, reliability, safety, supremacy, sureness, trustworthiness, impeccability, irreproachability, inerrability
FORMAL irrefutability, omniscience
❌ fallibility

infallible *adj*
accurate, unerring, unfailing, foolproof, fail-safe, certain, sure, reliable, dependable, trustworthy, sound, perfect, flawless, faultless, impeccable, inerrable
COLLOQ. sure-fire
❌ fallible

infamous *adj*
notorious, ill-famed, disreputable, disgraceful, discreditable, dishonourable, shameful, shocking, outrageous, abominable, detestable, scandalous, evil, bad, base, vile, wicked, hateful
OLD dastardly
FORMAL iniquitous, ignominious, egregious, nefarious
❌ illustrious, glorious

infamy *n*
notoriety, disrepute, disgrace, discredit, shame, dishonour, discredit, wickedness, evil, baseness, vileness, depravity, villainy
FORMAL ignominy, turpitude
❌ glory

infancy *n*
1 BABYHOOD, childhood, youth
2 BEGINNING, start, outset, birth, dawn, cradle, seeds, roots, genesis, emergence, rise, origin(s), early stages
FORMAL commencement, inception
❌ **1** adulthood

infant *n, adj*
♦ *n*
baby, toddler, child, little one, nurseling; *Scot* bairn
FORMAL babe, babe in arms
COLLOQ. tot, sprog
❌ adult
♦ *adj*
newborn, baby, young, youthful, juvenile, immature, beginning, growing, developing, dawning, emergent, rudimentary, early, initial, new, fledgling
FORMAL nascent, burgeoning
❌ adult, mature

infantile *adj*
babyish, childish, puerile, juvenile, young, youthful, adolescent, immature
❌ adult, mature

infatuated *adj*
besotted, obsessed, enamoured, in love, spellbound, bewitched, mesmerized, captivated, fascinated, enraptured, ravished, carried away
OLD assott, assotted
FORMAL *entêté(e)*
COLLOQ. crazy/mad/daft/nuts/potty about, sweet on, wild about/for, sold on, far gone, having a crush, bowled over, swept off your feet, having a thing, smitten, head over heels in love
❌ indifferent, disenchanted

infatuation *n*
besottedness, obsession, craze, fixation, mania, passion, love, fondness, fascination
FORMAL engouement
COLLOQ. crush, thing, pash, shine, rave
OLD COLLOQ. mash
❌ indifference, disenchantment

infect v

contaminate, pollute, defile, taint, blight, mar, spoil, ulcerate, poison, corrupt, pervert, spread to, pass on, influence, affect, excite, stimulate, animate, move, touch, inspire

infection n

illness, disease, complaint, condition, virus, bacteria, germ, epidemic, contagion, pestilence, contamination, pollution, defilement, taint, tainting, spoiling, fouling, blight, poison, corruption, influence
TECHNICAL sepsis
COLLOQ. bug

infectious adj

1 an infectious disease
contagious, communicable, transmissible, transmittable, infective, catching, spreading, epidemic, virulent, deadly, toxic, contaminating, polluting, defiling, corrupting
TECHNICAL septic
FORMAL noxious

2 infectious laughter
contagious, compelling, irresistible, catching, spreading

infelicitous adj

1 INAPPROPRIATE, unfitting, unsuitable, unfortunate, inopportune, untimely, disadvantageous
FORMAL incongruous
2 UNHAPPY, unfortunate, sad, miserable, sorrowful, unlucky, despairing, wretched
F3 1 appropriate, apt **2** happy

infer v

deduce, derive, extrapolate, conclude, come to a conclusion, reason, assume, presume, surmise, gather, understand, allude
FORMAL conjecture
COLLOQ. figure out

⚠ infer or **imply**?
See panel at **imply**.

---

inference n

deduction, conclusion, consequence, assumption, presumption, construction, interpretation, reasoning, reading
FORMAL extrapolation, corollary, conjecture, surmise

inferior adj, n

♦ adj
1 LOWER, lesser, minor, secondary, junior, subordinate, ancillary, subsidiary, second-class, low, lowly, humble, menial, subservient
COLLOQ. not in the same league
2 inferior work
substandard, second-rate, low-quality, mediocre, weak, inadequate, poor, bad, awful, unsatisfactory, unacceptable, imperfect, faulty, defective, deficient, incompetent, slipshod, shoddy, cheap, useless, hopeless
COLLOQ. crummy, rop(e)y, low-rent, grotty, rubbish, pathetic
SLANG naff
F3 1 superior **2** excellent

♦ n
subordinate, junior, underling, minion, vassal, menial
F3 superior

Synonym nuances
sense 2
Poor, **weak** and **inadequate** may all be used to show that something is not up to achieving its purpose: *inadequate protection*, while **ineffective** would usually be applied to an action that has failed to make a difference: *ineffective aid schemes*. Similarly **second-rate**, **mediocre** and **substandard** all suggest that something fails to reach the accepted standard.

Imperfect, however, implies a specific fault or faults rather than overall shoddiness. Similarly **faulty** and **defective** are used of something with particular, identifiable flaws: *a faulty valve*. **Deficient**, on the other hand, is more likely to point to a lack: *deficient in imagination*.
Slipshod and **shoddy** make the critical implication that undue care has been taken with something: *he was becoming slipshod in his editing*. The terms **useless** and **hopeless** would be reserved for people or things so far below standard that they have no practical application: *hopeless public transport*, while **incompetent** is another inherently critical term used mainly of people or the results of their efforts: *incompetent scientists*.

---

inferiority n

1 SUBORDINATION, subservience, humbleness, lowliness, meanness, insignificance
2 MEDIOCRITY, imperfection, inadequacy, faultiness, defectiveness, low/poor/bad quality, unsatisfactoriness, slovenliness, shoddiness, incompetence
COLLOQ. crumminess, ropiness, grottiness
F3 1 superiority **2** excellence, perfection

infernal adj

1 HELLISH, satanic, devilish, diabolical, demonic, fiendish, accursed, damned, Hadean
2 WICKED, evil, malevolent, vile, atrocious
FORMAL execrable
3 What an infernal mess!
damned, wretched, cursed, confounded, fiendish
COLLOQ. blasted, flipping, blooming, blinking, flaming, darned, dashed
OLD COLLOQ. dashed
SLANG *Irish* fecking; (*taboo*) fucking
F3 1 heavenly

infertile adj

barren, sterile, childless, unproductive, non-productive, unfruitful, arid, parched, dried-up
FORMAL effete, unfructuous, infecund
F3 fertile, fruitful, productive, prolific

infertility n

barrenness, sterility, unfruitfulness, unproductiveness, aridity, aridness
FORMAL effeteness, infecundity
F3 fertility

infest v

swarm, teem, crawl, bristle, throng, flood, overrun, overspread, spread through, plague, take over, beset, invade, infiltrate, penetrate, permeate, pervade, ravage

infestation n

affliction, pestilence, scourge, plague, blight, pest, visitation, overrunning, infiltration, pervasion, verminousness

infested adj

swarming, teeming, crawling, bristling, beset, alive, pervaded, plagued, ravaged, ridden, overrun, overspread, infiltrated, permeated, vermined

infidel n

pagan, heathen, disbeliever, unbeliever, heretic, sceptic, atheist, freethinker, irreligionist
FORMAL nullifidian
F3 believer

infidelity n

1 ADULTERY, unfaithfulness, falseness, affair, relationship, liaison, intrigue, romance, amour
COLLOQ. fooling around, playing around, cheating
2 DISLOYALTY, faithlessness, treachery, betrayal
FORMAL duplicity, perfidy
F3 1 fidelity **2** faithfulness

infiltrate v
penetrate, enter, creep into, insinuate, intrude, invade, slip, pervade, permeate, filter, percolate, seep, soak

infiltration n
penetration, entr(y)ism, insinuation, intrusion, pervasion, invasion, permeation, percolation
FORMAL interpenetration

infiltrator n
penetrator, insinuator, intruder, spy, subversive, subverter, seditionary, entr(y)ist

infinite adj
limitless, unlimited, boundless, unbounded, endless, never-ending, interminable, inexhaustible, bottomless, fathomless, innumerable, numberless, without number, uncountable, countless, untold, incalculable, inestimable, immeasurable, unfathomable, illimitable, vast, extensive, immense, enormous, huge, absolute, total, unconditioned
FORMAL indeterminable
E3 finite, limited

⚠ infinite or **infinitesimal**?
Infinite means 'without limits', or, loosely, 'extremely large or great': *If we follow that course of action, the dangers are infinite; infinitesimal* means 'infinitely small' or, loosely, 'extremely small': *Personally, I consider the dangers infinitesimal.*

---

infinitely adv
endlessly, limitlessly, boundlessly, interminably, inexhaustibly, absolutely, inestimably, enormously, immensely, without limit, without end, *ad infinitum*

infinitesimal adj
tiny, minute, microscopic, minuscule, inconsiderable, insignificant, trifling, negligible, inappreciable, imperceptible; *Scot* wee
COLLOQ. teeny
E3 great, large, enormous

infinitesimally adv
minutely, microscopically, tinily, insignificantly, negligibly, inappreciably, imperceptibly
E3 greatly

infinity n
eternity, perpetuity, limitlessness, boundlessness, allness, endlessness, inexhaustibility, countlessness, immeasurableness, extensiveness, vastness, immensity, enormousness
E3 finiteness, limitation

infirm adj
weak, feeble, frail, ailing, ill, unwell, poorly, sickly, decrepit, failing, faltering, unsteady, shaky, wobbly, doddery, old, lame, disabled
FORMAL debilitated
E3 healthy, strong

infirmity n
weakness, feebleness, frailty, ailment, illness, ill health, disease, complaint, sickness, sickliness, disorder, failing, decrepitude, vulnerability, instability, dodderiness
FORMAL debility, malady
E3 health, strength

inflame v
anger, enrage, infuriate, incense, exasperate, madden, rile, incite, provoke, stimulate, work up, stir, excite, rouse, arouse, agitate, stir (up), whip up, foment, impassion, kindle, ignite, fire, heat, fan, fuel, increase, intensify, worsen, make worse, aggravate
FORMAL exacerbate
E3 cool, quench

inflamed adj
sore, swollen, septic, infected, festered, poisoned, red, hot, heated, fevered, angry, feverish, flushed, reddened, glowing

inflammable adj
flammable, combustible, burnable, ignitable
E3 non-flammable, incombustible, flameproof, fire-resistant, flame-resistant

inflammation n
soreness, painfulness, tenderness, swelling, abscess, festering, infection, redness, heat, hotness, rash, sore, irritation, eruption
TECHNICAL empyema, erythema, sepsis, septicity

inflammatory adj
1 PROVOCATIVE, incendiary, explosive, fiery, rabble-rousing, rabid, riotous, seditious, insurgent, intemperate, inciting, incitative, inflaming, instigative, anarchic, demagogic
2 SORE, painful, tender, swollen, allergic, festering, septic, infected
E3 1 calming, pacific

inflate v
1 *inflate a life jacket*
blow up, pump up, fill with air, bloat, expand, dilate, enlarge, aerate, swell, puff up, puff out, balloon; *dialect* blast
OLD sufflate
FORMAL distend
2 *inflate prices*
increase, raise, boost, step up, escalate, amplify, extend, intensify
FORMAL augment
COLLOQ. hike up, push up
3 *inflate the importance of something*
exaggerate, overstate, overrate, overestimate, boost, magnify
FORMAL aggrandize, bombast
E3 1 deflate 2 decrease, lower 3 understate, play down

inflated adj
1 BLOWN UP, swollen, puffed out, dilated, bloated, ballooned
FORMAL distended, tumefied, tumid
2 INCREASED, raised, escalated, extended, intensified
3 EXAGGERATED, overblown, ostentatious, pompous
FORMAL bombastic, grandiloquent, magniloquent, euphuistic
E3 deflated

inflation n
expansion, increase, rise, escalation, hyperinflation
E3 deflation

inflection n
change of tone/intonation, pitch, modulation, stress, emphasis, rhythm
TECHNICAL cadence

inflexibility n
rigidity, hardness, stiffness, fixity, immovability, immutability, immutableness, inelasticity, obstinacy, stubbornness, stringency, unsuppleness
FORMAL intractability, intransigence, obduracy
E3 flexibility

inflexible adj
1 *an inflexible mass*
stiff, firm, hard, rigid, solid, set, fixed, unelastic, unsupple, unbending, taut, iron, ramrod
FORMAL calcified
2 *inflexible rules/people*
fast, immovable, immutable, unchangeable, unvarying, uniform, standard, standardized, firm, rigorous, taut, strict, stern, stringent, unbending, unbendable, unyielding, adamant, resolute, relentless, pitiless, merciless, implacable, intolerant, uncompromising, unaccommodating, stubborn, obstinate, steely, entrenched, dyed-in-the-wool, tramlined
FORMAL intransigent, obdurate, intractable, calcified

COLLOQ. hard and fast
Ea 1 flexible, soft, elastic, supple **2** flexible, adaptable

inflict v

impose, enforce, perpetrate, wreak, administer, apply, deliver, deal (out), mete out, lay, burden, exact, levy, administer

---

⚠ inflict or afflict?
See panel at **afflict**.

---

infliction n

imposition, enforcement, perpetration, wreaking, administration, application, delivery, affliction, exaction, burden, punishment, trouble, worry, penalty
FORMAL retribution, castigation, chastisement

influence n, v

♦ n

power, sway, rule, authority, domination, dominance, supremacy, mastery, rule, hold, control, direction, guidance, bias, prejudice, pull, pressure, effect, impact, weight, importance, prestige, standing, mark, toll
COLLOQ. clout, pull
SLANG N Am drag

♦ v

dominate, control, manipulate, direct, guide, determine, manoeuvre, change, alter, modify, transform, affect, have an effect on, impress, move, mould, shape, stir, arouse, rouse, sway, persuade, impact on, induce, incite, instigate, prompt, impel, motivate, dispose, incline, colour, condition, bias, prejudice
COLLOQ. have clout, carry weight, pull strings, pull wires, have under your thumb, hold over a barrel, wheel and deal

influential adj

dominant, controlling, leading, authoritative, charismatic, persuasive, meaningful, convincing, compelling, inspiring, moving, powerful, potent, effective, telling, strong, far-reaching, prestigious, weighty, momentous, important, significant, instrumental, guiding
Ea ineffective, unimportant

influx n

inflow, inrush, invasion, arrival, intrusion, stream, flow, rush, flood, inundation
FORMAL ingress, incursion

inform v

1 TELL, advise, notify, let know, communicate, announce, relate, impart, leak, tip off, acquaint, brief, instruct, enlighten, illuminate, give notice, certify, possess
OLD advertise, resolve; (Shakesp) recommend; (Spenser) partake; N Am avail
FORMAL apprise
COLLOQ. fill in, put in the picture, clue up, clue in, put wise, wise up, keep posted, cue in
2 inform on your friends
betray, incriminate, denounce, blab
COLLOQ. tell on, squeal, rat, blow, blow the whistle on, sell down the river, split, snitch; N Am sing (like a canary); Aust put someone's pot on; Aust & NZ dob in
SLANG grass, shop, rumble, peach, fink, nark, blow the gaff; N Am stool on
3 CHARACTERIZE, typify, mark, stamp, brand, identify, distinguish, permeate

informal adj

unofficial, unceremonious, casual, everyday, relaxed, easy, easy-going, free, natural, simple, unpretentious, familiar, colloquial, vernacular
Ea formal, solemn, serious, official

informality n

unceremoniousness, casualness, congeniality, ease, freedom, familiarity, naturalness, relaxation, simplicity, unpretentiousness, approachability, homeliness, cosiness
Ea formality, ceremony

informally adj

unofficially, unceremoniously, casually, easily, familiarly, simply, colloquially, freely, confidentially, privately, on the quiet
Ea formally

information n

facts, details, particulars, data, input, intelligence, news, report, bulletin, communiqué, propaganda, message, word, advice, counsel, notice, briefing, instruction, knowledge, enlightenment, file, record, dossier, database, databank, clues, evidence
FORMAL tidings
COLLOQ. gen, info, low-down, dope, SP, score; N Am poop

informative adj

educational, instructive, edifying, enlightening, illuminating, revealing, forthcoming, communicative, chatty, gossipy, newsy, helpful, useful, constructive
Ea uninformative

informed adj

1 we'll keep you informed
familiar, conversant, acquainted, enlightened, briefed, primed, posted, up to date, abreast, au fait
COLLOQ. in the know, in the loop, clued-up, up to speed
2 an informed opinion
well-informed, authoritative, expert, versed, well-versed, well-read, well-briefed, erudite, learned, knowledgeable, well-researched
Ea 1 ignorant, unaware

informer n

informant, betrayer, traitor, Judas, tell-tale, sneak, spy, squeaker, whisperer
OLD approver, discoverer, promoter, sycophant
COLLOQ. mole, rat, finger, squealer, whistle-blower, snitch, snitcher, canary, fink, nose
SLANG grass, supergrass, stool pigeon, peacher, nark, snout; N Am stoolie; Aust fizgig
OLD SLANG stag

infraction n

breaking, breach, violation, infringement, contravention, encroachment
FORMAL transgression
Ea observance, compliance

infrequent adj

exceptional, intermittent, occasional, rare, scanty, sparse, spasmodic, sporadic, uncommon, unusual
COLLOQ. few and far between, like gold dust
Ea frequent

infringe v

1 BREAK, violate, contravene, overstep, disobey, defy, flout, ignore
FORMAL transgress
2 INTRUDE, encroach, impinge, trespass, invade

infringement n

1 infringement of the rules
breach, breaking, disobedience, violation, defiance, contravention, evasion, non-compliance, non-observance
FORMAL infraction, transgression
2 INTRUSION, encroachment, trespass, invasion

infuriate v

anger, vex, enrage, incense, exasperate, madden, inflame, provoke, rouse, annoy, irritate, rile, antagonize
COLLOQ. aggravate, wind up, get at, bug, drive mad, drive crazy, drive bananas, drive up the wall, drive round the bend/twist, miff, needle, nettle, make someone's blood boil, make someone see red, rattle someone's cage, ruffle someone's feathers, raise someone's dander, make

someone's hackles rise, make sparks fly, get under someone's skin, get up someone's nose, get on someone's wick, put someone's back up
SLANG nark, piss off
OLD SLANG get someone's shirt out
E3 calm, pacify

infuriated *adj*
angry, exasperated, enraged, agitated, provoked, roused, vexed, furious, incensed, irate, irritated, violent, wild, heated, beside yourself
COLLOQ. flaming, maddened, peeved, miffed, narked, aggravated, cross, ratty, uptight, mad, hopping mad, raving mad, seeing red, in a lather, disgruntled, up in arms, hot under the collar, stroppy, choked, fit to be tied, on the warpath, in a paddy; *Scot* radge; *N Am* ticked off; *Aust* spewy, ropable; *Aust & NZ* crooked
SLANG pissed off, hairless; *N Am* burned up
E3 calm, gratified, pleased

infuriating *adj*
annoying, exasperating, irritating, unbearable, intolerable, frustrating, galling, provoking, thwarting
FORMAL vexatious
COLLOQ. maddening, aggravating; *N Am* pesky
E3 agreeable, pleasing

infuse *v*
fill, breathe into, imbue, impart to, introduce, implant, inculcate, inspire, instil, inject, steep, soak, saturate, pervade, brew, draw

infusion *n*
implantation, inculcation, infusing, instillation, steeping, soaking, brew

ingenious *adj*
clever, shrewd, astute, adept, adroit, cunning, crafty, wily, sly, sharp, smart, skilful, masterly, bright, brilliant, neat, pretty, imaginative, creative, inventive, resourceful, talented, gifted, original, innovative
OLD artificial, quaint, witty
COLLOQ. natty, nifty, slick, patent
E3 unimaginative

! ingenious or **ingenuous**?
Ingenious means 'clever, skilful' or 'cleverly made or thought out': *an ingenious plan. Ingenuous* means 'frank, trusting, not cunning or deceitful': *It was rather ingenuous of you to believe a compulsive liar like him.*

---

ingeniously *adv*
cleverly, cunningly, skilfully, brilliantly, imaginatively, originally
COLLOQ. niftily

ingenuity *n*
ingeniousness, cleverness, shrewdness, astuteness, sharpness, skill, skilfulness, creativeness, adroitness, cunning, slyness, innovativeness, invention, inventiveness, deftness, originality, resourcefulness, genius, gift, faculty, flair, knack
COLLOQ. nattiness, niftiness, slickness
E3 clumsiness, dullness

ingenuous *adj*
artless, guileless, innocent, honest, sincere, genuine, frank, candid, open, direct, forthright, plain, simple, unsophisticated, naive, trusting, trustful
FORMAL undissembling
E3 cunning, deceitful, artful, sly

ingenuously *adv*
artlessly, guilessly, without guile, innocently, honestly, sincerely, genuinely, openly, directly, plainly, simply, naively, trustingly
E3 deceitfully, artfully

ingenuousness *n*
artlessness, guilelessness, innocence, genuineness,

honesty, openness, naivety, trustfulness, candour, frankness, forthrightness, directness, unsophisticatedness, unreserve
E3 deceit, cunning, slyness, artfulness, subterfuge

inglorious *adj*
shameful, disgraceful, discreditable, dishonourable, disreputable, humiliating, blameworthy, ignoble, infamous, mortifying, unsuccessful, unhonoured, unheroic, unknown, obscure, unsung
FORMAL ignominious
E3 glorious

ingrain *v*
fix, root, entrench, engrain, embed, establish, build in, impress, imprint, imbue, implant, infix, instil, dye

ingrained *adj*
fixed, implanted, rooted, deep-rooted, deep-seated, entrenched, embedded, established, immovable, ineradicable, permanent, inbuilt, built-in, inborn, inbred, inherent

ingratiate *v*
curry favour, flatter, creep, crawl, grovel, fawn, get in with, toady, play up to
COLLOQ. suck up to, lick someone's boots, bow and scrape, get on the right side of, get into someone's good books, soft-soap, butter someone up; *Scot & dialect* sook; *N Am* cozy up (with)
SLANG (*vulgar*) kiss/lick someone's arse, brown-nose; *N Am* (*vulgar*) kiss ass

ingratiating *adj*
flattering, servile, crawling, fawning, toadying, sycophantic, smooth-tongued, suave, time-serving
FORMAL obsequious, unctuous
COLLOQ. bootlicking

ingratitude *n*
ungratefulness, thanklessness, unappreciativeness, unthankfulness, ungraciousness
E3 gratitude, thankfulness, appreciation

ingredient *n*
constituent, element, factor, unit, component, item, feature, part

ingress *n*
access, means of approach/entry, entrance, entry, admission, admittance, right of entry, permission to enter

inhabit *v*
live in, occupy, possess, colonize, settle, make your home in, people, populate, stay in
FORMAL dwell in, reside in

inhabitable *adj*
fit to live in, suitable to live in, good enough to live in, habitable

inhabitant *n*
resident, citizen, native, settler, occupier, occupant, inmate, tenant, lodger
FORMAL dweller, habitant, denizen

inhabited *adj*
lived-in, occupied, peopled, populated, settled, possessed, colonized, held, developed, tenanted
E3 uninhabited

inhalation *n*
breathing, breath, inhaling, inspiration, suction
TECHNICAL respiration, spiration

inhale *v*
breathe in, draw in, draw, suck in, inspire, whiff
TECHNICAL respire
FORMAL inbreathe

inharmonious *adj*
1 UNMELODIOUS, unharmonious, tuneless, grating, harsh, strident, clashing, jangling, jarring, discordant, raucous,

cacophonous, untuneful, unmusical, atonal
2 INCOMPATIBLE, conflicting, out of place, contradictory, clashing, irreconcilable, unfriendly, unsympathetic, quarrelsome, perverse
FORMAL dissonant, antipathetic, inconsonant
⊟ **1, 2** harmonious

inherent adj
inborn, inbred, innate, inherited, hereditary, in the blood, native, natural, inbuilt, built-in, intrinsic, ingrained, essential, fundamental, basic

---

Synonym nuances
Inborn and **innate** can be used of something that is within from birth: *many mammals have an inborn fear of poisonous snakes*, whereas **inbred**, **inherited** and **hereditary**, although similar, would describe a characteristic that has been passed down directly by your forebears: *intelligence is an inherited characteristic*; *hereditary diseases*. **Native**, on the other hand, has more to do with being pertinent to your origins: *her native language*, whereas **natural** is positive in tone, suggesting something which has not been affected or tampered with since birth: *she has natural beauty; a natural ability*. You can use **inbuilt** and **built-in** to convey the idea of structure, and suggest that something is part of your genetic make-up, while **intrinsic** and **essential**, **fundamental** and **basic**, are appropriate to describe a crucial or prominent inherent element of that structure: *the stubbornness that is fundamental to his character*. **Ingrained**, however, is suggestive of being deeply instilled rather than inborn: *ingrained prejudices*.

---

inherently adv
intrinsically, basically, fundamentally, centrally, essentially, inwardly, constituently, integrally, constitutionally

inherit v
succeed to, assume, take over, come into, be left, be heir to, receive, be bequeathed; *dialect* heir
OLD (*Shakesp*) succeed
FORMAL accede to

inheritance n
legacy, bequest, heritage, endowment, birthright, heredity, descent, succession
TECHNICAL patrimony, primogeniture, secundogeniture
OLD fee
FORMAL accession

inheritor n
heir, heiress, inheritress, inheritrix, successor, beneficiary, recipient, reversionary, co-heir, next in line, scion, fellow-heir
TECHNICAL devisee, legatee, legatary, substitute
OLD tanist
FORMAL heritor, heritress, heritrix

inhibit v
discourage, repress, hold back, suppress, curb, rein in, check, bridle, restrain, constrain, hinder, impede, obstruct, restrict, interfere with, frustrate, thwart, hamper, balk, prevent, stop, stanch, stem, slow down
⊟ encourage, assist

inhibited adj
repressed, self-conscious, shy, embarrassed, reticent, withdrawn, introverted, self-restrained, reserved, guarded, subdued, restrained, constrained, frustrated
COLLOQ. uptight
⊟ uninhibited, open, relaxed

inhibition n
1 *lose all our inhibitions*
repression, self-consciousness, shyness, reticence, coyness, embarrassment, reserve
COLLOQ. hang-up

2 RESTRAINT, curb, check, hindrance, impediment, obstruction, restriction, interference, hampering, frustration, thwarting, bar
⊟ **1** openness **2** freedom

inhospitable adj
1 *an inhospitable place*
uninhabitable, forbidding, bare, barren, bleak, desolate, empty, lonely, uncongenial, unfavourable, uninviting, hostile
FORMAL inimical
2 *an inhospitable person*
unwelcoming, unfriendly, unreceptive, unsociable, antisocial, ungenerous, unkind, unneighbourly, uncivil, cold, cool, aloof, xenophobic
⊟ favourable, hospitable

inhuman adj
1 BARBARIC, barbarous, animal, bestial, vicious, savage, sadistic, cold-blooded, brutal, cruel, harsh, merciless, ruthless, diabolical, fiendish
2 NON-HUMAN, strange, odd, animal
⊟ **1, 2** human

⚠ **inhuman** or **inhumane**?
When referring to cruel conditions, treatment, behaviour, etc, *inhuman* is stronger than *inhumane*. *Inhumane* means 'unkind, cruel, showing lack of compassion', whereas *inhuman* means 'showing cruelty and lack of compassion to a degree almost unbelievable in a human being'.

---

inhumane adj
unkind, insensitive, inconsiderate, callous, unfeeling, uncaring, unsympathetic, heartless, cold-hearted, hard-hearted, pitiless, cruel, harsh, brutal, dehumanized
⊟ humane, kind, compassionate

inhumanity n
atrocity, barbarism, barbarity, savageness, brutality, brutishness, cruelty, cold-bloodedness, viciousness, pitilessness, ruthlessness, sadism, callousness, unkindness, cold-heartedness, hard-heartedness, heartlessness
⊟ humanity

inimical adj
hostile, adverse, antagonistic, destructive, opposed, harmful, injurious, hurtful, pernicious, intolerant, unfavourable, unfriendly, unwelcoming, inhospitable, ill-disposed, disaffected, antipathetic, contrary, repugnant
FORMAL noxious
⊟ favourable, friendly, sympathetic

inimitable adj
unique, incomparable, matchless, unmatched, unparalleled, unrivalled, unsurpassable, unsurpassed, unequalled, peerless, consummate, sublime, superlative, supreme, distinctive, exceptional, nonpareil, unexampled

iniquitous adj
evil, wicked, unrighteous, immoral, unjust, sinful, accursed, atrocious, base, vicious, awful, dreadful, criminal, abominable, infamous, reprobate
OLD facinorous
FORMAL nefarious, reprehensible, heinous, flagitious
⊟ virtuous

iniquity n
wickedness, injustice, offence, misdeed, wrong, wrongdoing, evil, evil-doing, sin, sinfulness, enormity, baseness, vice, viciousness, infamy, abomination, crime, lawlessness, unrighteousness, ungodliness
FORMAL heinousness, transgression
⊟ virtue

initial adj, v
♦ adj
first, beginning, opening, starting, introductory, inaugural, original, primary, prime, early, basic, elementary, foundational, formative

FORMAL commencing, inceptive, inchoate, incipient

F3 final, last

♦ v

write your initials on, sign, autograph, endorse, countersign

initially adv

at first, at the beginning, at the start, to begin with, to start with, originally, first, firstly, first of all, in the first instance, at the outset

COLLOQ. first off

F3 finally, in the end

initiate v, n

♦ v

1 BEGIN, start, start up, originate, pioneer, institute, set up, establish, bring about, introduce, launch, open, inaugurate, instigate, activate, trigger, prompt, stimulate, cause, induce, sow the seeds of

OLD auspicate

FORMAL commence

COLLOQ. kick off, set the ball rolling, set the wheels in motion, get off the ground, get under way, set in motion, get things moving

2 TEACH, instruct, train, drill, crash, tutor, inculcate, instil

3 *initiated into the organization*

accept, admit, let in, introduce, receive, welcome, enter, enrol, sign up, induct, install, invest, ordain

♦ n

new member, recruit, entrant, learner, newcomer, novice, beginner, convert, catechumen, novitiate, neophyte, probationer, proselyte, tenderfoot, tiro

COLLOQ. greenhorn, rookie

F3 authority, expert, connoisseur, sage

initiation n

1 BEGINNING, start, origination, setting-up, launching, opening, inauguration

FORMAL inception

2 ADMISSION, reception, entrance, entry, debut, introduction, admittance, enrolment, enlistment, induction, investiture, installation, ordination, inauguration, baptism, rite of passage

initiative n

1 ENTERPRISE, resourcefulness, inventiveness, originality, innovativeness, creativity, energy, drive, dynamism, ambition, lead, lead-off

COLLOQ. get-up-and-go, go, push

2 SUGGESTION, recommendation, scheme, proposal, plan, action, first move, opening move, first step, *démarche*

inject v

1 *inject drugs*

inoculate, immunize, vaccinate, syringe

COLLOQ. jab

SLANG shoot (up), mainline, hype (up)

2 INTRODUCE, insert, add, bring (in), infuse, instil

injection n

1 INOCULATION, immunization, vaccination, dose

COLLOQ. jab, shot

SLANG fix

2 INTRODUCTION, insertion, addition, infusion, instilling

injudicious adj

ill-advised, ill-judged, imprudent, inexpedient, ill-timed, unwise, inadvisable, incautious, inconsiderate, foolish, stupid, hasty, rash, misguided, unthinking, indiscreet, wrong-headed

FORMAL impolitic

F3 wise, cautious, prudent; *formal* judicious

injunction n

command, order, directive, ruling, mandate, direction, instruction, precept, dictum, dictate

FORMAL admonition

injure v

1 HURT, harm, damage, impair, spoil, mar, ruin, disfigure, deface, blemish, blight, weaken, undermine, mutilate, mangle, deform, wound, cut, break, fracture, maim, disable, cripple, lame

2 OFFEND, ill-treat, maltreat, abuse, wrong, upset, put out

injured adj

1 HURT, harmed, damaged, wounded, bruised, sore, tender, lame, disabled, crippled, weakened

2 OFFENDED, upset, hurt, ill-treated, maltreated, misused, pained, put out, wronged, upset, unhappy, aggrieved, maligned, abused, defamed, insulted, grieved, bruised, sore, displeased, disgruntled, vulnerable, cut to the quick

injurious adj

damaging, detrimental, harmful, hurtful, disadvantageous, destructive, prejudicial, unconducive, pernicious, adverse, corrupting, baneful, ruinous, unhealthy, unjust, bad, wrongful, insulting, libellous, slanderous

FORMAL calumnious, deleterious, iniquitous, noxious

F3 beneficial, favourable

injury n

1 WOUND, cut, bruise, sore, lesion, fracture, gash, abrasion, laceration, trauma, hurt, mischief, ill, harm, damage, impairment, ruin, disfigurement, mutilation

TECHNICAL contusion

FORMAL affliction

2 WRONG, ill-treatment, abuse, insult, grievance, offence, injustice

injustice n

unfairness, unjustness, wrong, injury, abuse, ill-treatment, offence, inequality, discrimination, oppression, bias, prejudice, one-sidedness, partisanship, partiality, favouritism

OLD unreason

FORMAL disparity, iniquity, inequity

F3 justice, fairness

inkling n

suspicion, idea, notion, glimmering, clue, hint, intimation, insinuation, innuendo, suggestion, allusion, indication, sign, pointer

COLLOQ. faintest, foggiest, whisper

inky adj

black, jet-black, coal-black, pitch-black, jet, sooty, dark-blue

inlaid adj

set, inset, enamelled, mosaic, tiled, lined, studded, enchased, damascened

FORMAL tessellated, empaestic

inland adj

interior, inner, internal, central, domestic, up-country, landward, midland, upland

OLD within land

inlay n

setting, inset, enamel, mosaic, tiling, lining, studding, damascene

FORMAL tessellation, emblema

inlet n

bay, cove, bight, creek, fiord, firth, opening, entrance, passage, sound

inmate n

patient, prisoner, convict, detainee, case, client

inmost adj

deepest, deep, central, innermost, intimate, personal, dearest, private, secret, confidential, closest, essential, hidden, buried, basic

FORMAL esoteric

inn n

public house, tavern, hostelry, hotel, bar, halfway house,

house, posthouse, roadhouse, *auberge*, imaret, khan, ryokan, *albergo*, *posada*; *Scot* change-house, howff
OLD caravanserai, watering-house
COLLOQ. pub, local

innards *n*
1 *the innards of an animal*
insides, guts, internal organs, interior, intestines, entrails, entera, organs, umbles, viscera, vitals
2 *the innards of a machine*
works, mechanism, inner workings

innate *adj*
inborn, inbred, congenital, inherited, hereditary, inherent, intrinsic, native, indigenous, natural, instinctive, intuitive
FORMAL connate
≢ acquired, learnt

innately *adv*
intrinsically, inherently, basically, fundamentally, centrally, essentially, inwardly, constituently, integrally, constitutionally

inner *adj*
internal, interior, inside, inward, innermost, central, middle, concealed, obscure, hidden, secret, private, personal, intimate, deep, profound, restricted, mental, psychological, spiritual, emotional
FORMAL esoteric
≢ outer, outward, revealed

innermost *adj*
deepest, deep, central, inmost, intimate, personal, dearest, private, secret, confidential, closest, essential, hidden, buried, basic
FORMAL esoteric

innkeeper *n*
landlord, landlady, hotel-keeper, hotelier, proprietor, manager, publican, host, hostess, mine host, barkeeper, restaurateur, innholder, padrone

innocence *n*
1 GUILTLESSNESS, blamelessness, irreproachability, unimpeachability, honesty, integrity, virtue, righteousness, sinlessness, faultlessness, impeccability, immaculateness, stainlessness, spotlessness, purity, chastity, virginity, incorruptibility
FORMAL inculpability
2 ARTLESSNESS, guilelessness, ingenuousness, naiveness, naivety, inexperience, ignorance, naturalness, simplicity, openness, frankness, unsophistication, unworldliness, childlikeness, credulity, gullibility, trustfulness
3 HARMLESSNESS, innocuousness, inoffensiveness, safety, playfulness
≢ **1** guilt **2** experience **3** harmfulness

innocent *adj, n*
• *adj*
1 *innocent of the crime*
guiltless, blameless, clear, irreproachable, above suspicion, unblameworthy, unimpeachable, honest, upright, virtuous, righteous, sinless, faultless, impeccable, stainless, spotless, immaculate, unsullied, unblemished, untainted, uncontaminated, pure, chaste, virginal, white, uncorrupted, incorrupt, crimeless
OLD offenceless, sackless
FORMAL inculpable
2 ARTLESS, guileless, ingenuous, naive, inexperienced, fresh, natural, simple, open, frank, unsophisticated, unworldly, childlike, angelic, credulous, gullible, trusting, trustful, dewy-eyed, unsuspecting, Arcadian
OLD (*Spenser*) seely
COLLOQ. green, wet behind the ears, innocent as a newborn babe
3 HARMLESS, inoffensive, innocuous, safe, playful, unsuspicious, dovelike, lamblike, gentle, bland, anodyne

≢ 1 guilty, to blame **2** experienced, sophisticated **3** harmful, offensive
• *n*
beginner, infant, novice, child, tenderfoot, babe, babe in arms, neophyte, ingénue, greenhorn
≢ connoisseur, expert

Synonym nuances
sense 1
Clear, **guiltless** and **blameless** can be used in specific cases where someone is not responsible for a wrongful action, but they can also be used to suggest not having done anything wrong generally, as can **impeccable** and **irreproachable**: *his private life was irreproachable*. The more uncommon **unblameworthy**, along with **unimpeachable**, similarly suggest being free from fault, whereas **honest** is more suggestive of being generally trustworthy.
  Likewise **upright**, **virtuous** and **righteous** all convey very positive images of integrity, while **sinless** and **faultless** would emphasize instead the lack of moral defects. **Stainless** and **spotless** imply never having been tainted by dishonest actions: *who can claim to have led a spotless life?* **Immaculate** has almost religious overtones of being free from sin, while the terms **unsullied**, **unblemished**, **untainted** and **uncontaminated** return to the idea of never having been tarnished in any way.
  You can use **pure** of being free from defilement, and **chaste**, **virginal**, and **white** share similar associations, usually of sexual innocence. Both **uncorrupted** and **incorrupt**, meanwhile, are appropriate for having resisted bad influences: *he remained incorrupt while in office, never accepting the bribes offered to him.*

---

innocently *adv*
naively, artlessly, blamelessly, harmlessly, innocuously, inoffensively, unoffendingly, trustfully, trustingly, simply, ingenuously, credulously, unsuspiciously
COLLOQ. like a lamb to the slaughter

innocuous *adj*
harmless, safe, inoffensive, unobjectionable, innocent, playful, mild, bland, unobtrusive, anodyne
≢ harmful, dangerous, toxic

innovation *n*
new product, new method, newness, novelty, neologism, introduction, modernization, progress, reform, change, alteration, variation, departure
OLD novelism, novity
FORMAL novation

innovative *adj*
new, fresh, original, creative, imaginative, inventive, resourceful, enterprising, go-ahead, progressive, reforming, bold, daring, adventurous, groundbreaking, trail-blazing, avant-garde, Promethean
≢ conservative, unimaginative

innovator *n*
originator, fresh thinker, progressive, creator, pioneer, source, deviser, developer, trailblazer, reformer, modernizer

innuendo *n*
insinuation, slur, whisper, hint, intimation, suggestion, implication, allusion, overtone
FORMAL aspersion

innumerable *adj*
countless, uncountable, numerous, numberless, unnumbered, untold, incalculable, infinite, many
COLLOQ. umpteen, oodles, tons, loads, masses, heaps, piles, stacks, dozens, hundreds, thousands, millions

inoculate v

immunize, vaccinate, inject, protect, safeguard
COLLOQ. give a jab/shot to

inoculation n

vaccination, immunization, protection, injection
COLLOQ. shot, jab

inoffensive adj

harmless, innocuous, safe, innocent, unobjectionable,
unexceptionable, peaceable, mild, bland, anodyne,
unobtrusive, unassertive, quiet, retiring
E3 offensive, harmful, provocative

inoperable adj

incurable, untreatable, unhealable, unremovable,
irremovable, terminal, fatal, deadly, hopeless
FORMAL intractable
E3 operable

inoperative adj

not working, not operative, out of order, out of action, out
of service, out of commission, defective, broken, broken-
down, non-functioning, unserviceable, unused,
unworkable, useless, invalid, idle, ineffective, inadequate,
inefficient, futile, worthless
FORMAL ineffectual, inefficacious, nugatory
COLLOQ. kaput, on the blink, bust, duff; *N Am* on the fritz
E3 working, operative

inopportune adj

untimely, inconvenient, unsuitable, inappropriate, tactless,
ill-timed, ill-chosen, mistimed, wrong-timed, unfortunate,
unseasonable, clumsy
FORMAL inauspicious, unpropitious, infelicitous
E3 opportune

inordinate adj

excessive, immoderate, extreme, exorbitant, unwarranted,
unrestricted, unrestrained, undue, unreasonable,
outrageous, preposterous, disproportionate, great
COLLOQ. over the top, OTT
E3 moderate, reasonable

inorganic adj

inanimate, lifeless, dead, mineral, non-natural, artificial
E3 organic

input v, n

◆ v

feed in, insert, key in, put in, enter, load, code, capture,
process, store
◆ n

information, data, facts, figures, statistics, material, details,
particulars, resources
E3 output

inquest n

inquiry, investigation, examination, hearing, post-mortem,
inspection

inquietude n

uneasiness, restlessness, worry, anxiety, nervousness,
agitation, unease, apprehension, discomposure, disquiet,
jumpiness
FORMAL disquietude, perturbation, solicitude
E3 composure

inquire, enquire v

ask, question, quiz, query, investigate, look into, see,
research, study, probe, examine, inspect, scrutinize, scan,
search, explore, interrogate; *Scot* speir
OLD (*Spenser*) inquere
COLLOQ. snoop

inquirer, enquirer n

questioner, student, seeker, researcher, searcher, explorer,
interrogator, investigator

inquiring, enquiring adj

inquisitive, interested, questioning, searching, curious,

analytical, eager, investigative, investigatory, interrogatory,
outward-looking, probing, prying, wondering, doubtful,
sceptical
FORMAL zetetic
COLLOQ. nos(e)y
E3 incurious, unquestioning

inquiringly, enquiringly adv

inquisitively, curiously, eagerly, keenly, wonderingly,
questioningly, analytically

inquiry, enquiry n

question, query, investigation, inquest, hearing,
inquisition, interrogation, examination, inspection,
scrutiny, study, demand, survey, poll, search, probe,
exploration, sounding, reconnaissance, quest,
interrogatory, star chamber
TECHNICAL aetiology
OLD inquire
FORMAL perquisition

inquisition n

interrogation, cross-examination, cross-questioning,
examination, investigation, questioning, quizzing, inquiry,
inquest
COLLOQ. grilling, the third degree, witch hunt

inquisitive adj

curious, inquiring, questioning, probing, searching,
scrutinizing, prying, peeping, peering, snooping, spying,
interfering, meddlesome, intrusive
COLLOQ. nos(e)y, snoopy

inquisitively adv

curiously, eagerly, keenly, inquiringly, searchingly,
questioningly, interferingly, meddlesomely

inroad n

advance, progress, encroachment, foray, impingement,
incursion, intrusion, trespassing, invasion, irruption,
onslaught, attack, assault, offensive, charge, raid, sally,
sortie, trespass

insane adj

1 MAD, lunatic, unbalanced, psychotic, disturbed,
deranged, maniacal, out of your mind, out of your senses,
of unsound mind, unhinged, crazed, unstable, *non compos
mentis*, frenzied, wild, berserk, manic, maniac, distracted,
distraught, fey, frenetic, frantic, stone-crazy, queer; *Scot*
gyte, red-mad
OLD frantic-mad, horn-mad, lymphatic, bestraught;
(*Shakesp*) wood; (*Spenser*) yond
COLLOQ. crazy, demented, nuts, nutty, nutty as a fruitcake,
wacky, mad as a hatter, barmy, bonkers, batty, cracked,
crackers, dippy, daffy, dotty, loopy, potty, off your nut, off
your head, wrong in the head, out of your head, off the
wall, out to lunch, round the bend, round the twist, bats,
having bats in the belfry, cuckoo, off the rails, screwy, up
the wall, raving, not all there; *N Am* buggy, flaky, fruity;
Aust & NZ dingbats
SLANG loony, mental, bananas, barking, wacko, doolally, off
your rocker, off your chump, off your trolley, out of your
tree, needing your head examined, having lost your
marbles, having a screw loose, having a tile loose, having
several cards short of a full deck, with one sandwich short
of a picnic, meshuga, ape, apeshit; *N Am* gonzo, loco, wiggy
2 FOOLISH, stupid, senseless, mad, crazy, impractical,
idiotic, nonsensical, absurd, ridiculous
COLLOQ. daft, potty, barmy, half-baked, hare-brained,
crackbrained, crackpot
E3 1 sane **2** sensible

insanely adv

madly, ridiculously, absurdly, ludicrously, senselessly,
foolishly, outrageously

insanitary adj

unhygienic, unsanitary, unclean, impure, unhealthy,

Insects include:

aphid	cranefly	gnat	ladybird	moth	water boatman
bee	cricket	grasshopper	*NAm* ladybug	nit	weevil
beetle	*colloq*. daddy	hornet	leatherjacket	onion fly	whitefly
blackfly	longlegs	horsefly	locust	*NAm* roach	woodlouse
bumblebee	dragonfly	flea	louse	stick insect	woodworm
butterfly	earwig	froghopper	mayfly	termite	
cicada	fly	greenfly	midge	tsetse-fly	
cockroach	glowworm	lacewing	mosquito	wasp	

See also **butterfly**; **moth**.

Arachnids include:

black widow	mite	spider
harvester (or	redback	tick
harvestman)	scorpion	

Parts of an insect:

abdomen	head	ocellus
antenna	hindwing	ovipositor
cercus	legs	segment
compound eye	mandible	spiracle
forewing	mouthpart	thorax

unsanitized, dirty, dirtied, contaminated, polluted, infected, disease-ridden, filthy, foul, infested
FORMAL unhealthful, noisome, noxious, insalubrious, feculent
F3 sanitary, clean

insanity *n*
1 *suffer from insanity*
insaneness, madness, craziness, lunacy, mental illness, neurosis, mania, dementia, delirium, frenzy, derangement, *folie*, craze
TECHNICAL psychosis, psychopathy, hebephrenia
2 FOLLY, madness, craziness, lunacy, foolishness, stupidity, senselessness, absurdity, ridiculousness, irresponsibility, *folie*
COLLOQ. daftness
F3 1 sanity 2 sensibleness

Synonym nuances
sense 1
Madness suggests a mental disorder which manifests itself in irrational behaviour, while **craziness** and **lunacy** are more informal terms suggesting any generally outlandish behaviour, not necessarily caused by a mental disorder. **Neurosis**, on the other hand, is a more clinical term which emphasizes internal effects, and has narrower implications of a specific set of disorders: *anxiety neurosis*; *obsessional neurosis*.
 The term **mania** tends to be suggestive of euphoria, and informal usage has also leant it implications of wild behaviour. The more straightforwardly medical term **dementia** is used of mental deterioration. **Delirium** suggests a fevered mental state with physical manifestations: *she thrashed and mumbled in delirium*. **Frenzy** has more to do with a state of violent excitement: *in a frenzy of wrath*. The term **derangement** is less suggestive of behaviour and returns to the general idea of mental disturbance causing disordered thought.

---

insatiable *adj*
voracious, unquenchable, unsatisfiable, unappeasable, ravenous, hungry, greedy, gluttonous, craving, avid, immoderate, inordinate
FORMAL rapacious

inscribe *v*
1 ENGRAVE, etch, carve, cut, incise, imprint, impress, stamp, brand, mark, print
2 WRITE, sign, enrol, enlist, register, record, address, autograph, dedicate

inscription *n*
engraving, etching, epitaph, caption, legend, lettering, wording, words, writing, signature, autograph, message, dedication

inscrutable *adj*
incomprehensible, unfathomable, impenetrable, deep, unintelligible, inexplicable, unexplainable, unreadable, baffling, puzzling, mysterious, enigmatic, cryptic, hidden
FORMAL arcane
F3 comprehensible, expressive

insect
See panels above

insecure *adj*
1 ANXIOUS, worried, nervous, uncertain, unsure, unassured, lacking confidence, afraid, apprehensive, fearful, hesitant, doubtful
2 UNSAFE, dangerous, hazardous, perilous, precarious, unsteady, unstable, shaky, loose, weak, frail, flimsy, unprotected, unguarded, defenceless, exposed, vulnerable, open to attack
OLD (*Shakesp & Spenser*) tickle
F3 1 confident, self-assured 2 secure, safe, protected

insecurity *n*
1 ANXIETY, worry, nervousness, uncertainty, unsureness, apprehension, fear, uneasiness, lack of confidence
2 UNSAFETY, unsafeness, danger, hazard, peril, precariousness, unsteadiness, shakiness, instability, weakness, frailness, flimsiness, defencelessness, vulnerability
F3 1 confidence, self-assurance 2 safety, security

insensate *adj*
insensible, unfeeling, unconscious, unaware, anaesthetized, numb, senseless, unresponsive, oblivious, unmindful, ignorant, blind, deaf
FORMAL insentient, comatose

insensible *adj*
1 UNCONSCIOUS, anaesthetized, numb, senseless, unresponsive
FORMAL insentient, comatose
COLLOQ. out, zonked, knocked out, out for the count, dead to the world
2 UNAWARE, unconscious, oblivious, unmindful, ignorant, blind, deaf
3 CALLOUS, insensitive, unfeeling, emotionless, detached, untouched, unmoved, unaffected, cold, hard-hearted, hard, aloof, distant
4 IMPERCEPTIBLE, indiscernible, indistinguishable, undetectable, unapparent, faint, slight
F3 1 conscious 2 aware, knowing 3 sensitive

insensitive *adj*
hardened, tough, resistant, impenetrable, impervious, immune, unsusceptible, thick-skinned, case-hardened, unfeeling, impassive, oblivious, indifferent, unaffected, unresponsive, unmoved, untouched, unsympathetic,

uncaring, unconcerned, dead, hard, hard-hearted, iron, callous, heartless, thoughtless, tactless, crass, obtuse
TECHNICAL hypalgesic, anomalous
FORMAL pachydermatous
E3 sensitive, responsive, affected

insensitivity n
hardness, toughness, resistance, impenetrability, imperviousness, immunity, unresponsiveness, hard-heartedness, hard-headedness, unconcern, bluntness, callousness, indifference, tactlessness, crassness, obtuseness
TECHNICAL hypalgesia, hypalgia
E3 sensitivity, responsiveness

inseparable adj
indivisible, indissoluble, undividable, inextricable, close, intimate, bosom, constant, devoted
E3 separable

inseparably adv
inextricably, intimately, closely, firmly, hand in hand, arm in arm, indivisibly, indissolubly, together, as one

insert v, n
♦ v
put, place, press, put in, enclose, stick in, push in, thrust in, slide in, slip in, introduce, enter, implant, embed, engraft, infix, inlay, set, inset, let in, interleave, interject
FORMAL interpose, interpolate, intercalate
♦ n
insertion, enclosure, inset, notice, advertisement, circular, supplement, addition, inlay

insertion n
addition, entry, inclusion, insert, inset, introduction, implant, supplement, intrusion
FORMAL intercalation, interpolation, intromission

inside n, adv, adj
♦ n
interior, content, contents, middle, centre, heart, core
COLLOQ. guts, belly
E3 outside
♦ adv
within, indoors, internally, inwardly, secretly, privately
E3 outside
♦ adj
1 INTERIOR, internal, inner, implicit, inherent, intrinsic, innermost, inward
2 SECRET, classified, confidential, internal, private, restricted, reserved
COLLOQ. hush-hush

insider n
member, participant, staff member, co-worker
COLLOQ. one of us, one of the in-crowd

insides n
internal organs, entrails, guts, intestines, bowels, organs, viscera, belly, stomach, abdomen
COLLOQ. innards, tummy

insidious adj
subtle, sly, crafty, cunning, wily, artful, deceptive, deceitful, dishonest, devious, stealthy, surreptitious, furtive, sneaking, sneaky, tricky, treacherous, insincere, Machiavellian
FORMAL duplicitous, perfidious
E3 direct, straightforward

insidiously adv
subtly, slyly, cunningly

insight n
awareness, knowledge, comprehension, understanding, realization, grasp, apprehension, perception, intuition, sensitivity, discernment, judgement, acumen, penetration, sharpness, shrewdness, observation,

vision, wisdom, intelligence, aperçu, epiphany
OLD sight
FORMAL perspicacity

insightful adj
perceptive, astute, sharp, shrewd, observant, penetrating, understanding, acute, discerning, seeing, intelligent, knowledgeable, wise, prudent
OLD inscient
FORMAL perspicacious, sagacious, percipient
E3 superficial

insignia n
emblem, badge, regalia, crest, sign(s), ensign, medallion, ribbon, decoration, mark, hallmark(s), symbol, trademark, brand, logo

insignificance n
unimportance, irrelevance, meaninglessness, immateriality, inconsequence, inconsequentiality, negligibility, smallness, pettiness, paltriness, tininess, insubstantiality, triviality, meanness, worthlessness
FORMAL nugatoriness
E3 significance

insignificant adj
unimportant, irrelevant, meaningless, immaterial, inconsequential, minor, trivial, trifling, petty, paltry, meagre, scanty, slight, small, tiny, insubstantial, inconsiderable, negligible, non-essential, peripheral, not worth mentioning, marginal, minimal, fractional, insect, nebbich, scrub
FORMAL nugatory
OLD petit, puisne
COLLOQ. piddling, cutting no ice, no great shakes, small-time; N Am dinky, jerkwater, no-account
SLANG Mickey Mouse, C-list
E3 significant, important

insincere adj
hypocritical, two-faced, double-dealing, lying, untruthful, dishonest, deceitful, underhand, devious, unfaithful, faithless, disloyal, untrue, treacherous, false, feigned, pretended, hollow, pretentious
FORMAL mendacious, disingenuous, dissembling, duplicitous, perfidious
COLLOQ. phoney
E3 sincere, genuine

insincerely adv
hypocritically, dishonestly, deceitfully, untruthfully, deviously, unfaithfully, disloyally, treacherously, falsely, pretentiously
FORMAL duplicitously, perfidiously

insincerity n
hypocrisy, untruthfulness, dishonesty, deceitfulness, deviousness, pretence, hollowness, pretentiousness, falseness, falsity, faithlessness, artificiality, cant, evasiveness
FORMAL disingenuousness, dissembling, dissimulation, duplicity, mendacity, perfidy
COLLOQ. phoniness, humbug, lip service
E3 sincerity

insinuate v
imply, suggest, allude, hint, mention, intimate, indicate
COLLOQ. get at, whisper
■ **insinuate yourself**
curry favour, ingratiate, sidle, work, worm, wriggle
COLLOQ. get in with

insinuation n
suggestion, implication, allusion, hint, intimation, inference, introduction, slant, slur, innuendo
FORMAL aspersion
COLLOQ. insinuendo

insipid adj

1 TASTELESS, flavourless, unsavoury, unappetizing, watery, weak, thin, bland
COLLOQ. wishy-washy
2 UNINTERESTING, dull, monotonous, boring, tedious, wearisome, tame, flat, lifeless, inanimate, spiritless, vapid, characterless, trite, banal, unimaginative, dry, anaemic, colourless, drab
COLLOQ. wishy-washy
E3 **1** tasty, spicy, piquant, appetizing **2** interesting, exciting, lively

insist v

demand, require, urge, entreat, stress, emphasize, repeat, reiterate, dwell on, harp on, assert, declare, stipulate, state firmly, ask for firmly, maintain, claim, contend, hold, press, vow, swear, persist, stand firm, stand on, stand your ground, refuse to accept an alternative, stick out for, hang out for, stick to your guns; *dialect* threap
OLD (*Shakesp*) strain
FORMAL aver
COLLOQ. put your foot down, not take no for an answer

insistence n

demand, requirement, entreaty, urging, stress, emphasis, repetition, reiteration, maintenance, assertion, declaration, claim, contention, persistence, determination, resolution, firmness, assertiveness
FORMAL exhortation

insistent adj

demanding, importunate, emphatic, resolute, determined, adamant, forceful, pressing, urgent, dogged, tenacious, persistent, persevering, assertive, constant, repeated, relentless, unrelenting, unremitting, unyielding, inexorable, incessant
FORMAL importunate, exigent

insobriety n

drunkenness, hard drinking, intemperance, inebriation, inebriety, intoxication
FORMAL crapulence
COLLOQ. tipsiness
E3 sobriety

insolence n

rudeness, abuse, insults, impudence, impertinence, gall, arrogance, audacity, boldness, forwardness, pertness, presumption, presumptuousness, disrespect, contemptuousness, defiance, insubordination, offensiveness, incivility; *Scot* snash
FORMAL hubris, effrontery, contumely
COLLOQ. cheek, cheekiness, sauce, sauciness, attitude, nerve, lip, mouth, chutzpah; *N Am* sass
E3 politeness, respect

insolent adj

rude, abusive, insulting, disrespectful, ill-mannered, impertinent, impudent, bold, audacious, brazen, brash, forward, presumptuous, arrogant, defiant, contemptuous, insubordinate
COLLOQ. cheeky, saucy, fresh, lippy, mouthy; *N Am* sassy
E3 polite, respectful

Synonym nuances
Rude can be used of someone displaying appalling manners or of a deliberate attempt to offend, while **abusive** and **insulting** specifically suggest a deliberately offensive verbal assault. **Disrespectful** has more to do with not showing a proper level of courtesy: *his intimate form of address seemed very disrespectful.*
  Ill-mannered returns to the idea of generally not conducting yourself correctly, whereas **impertinent** and **impudent** are milder terms, more suggestive of less severe insolence, or of not exhibiting the acceptable levels of restraint: *the boy gave an impertinent reply; he was greeted by impudent stares.* Both **bold** and

---

audacious also suggest insolence based on overfamiliarity; **brazen** and **brash** have implications of impetuosity and shamelessness at one's actions: *I was shocked by the brazen way she spoke to her parents.* The terms **forward** and **presumptuous** also suggest overstepping the bounds of propriety: *it was presumptuous of him to offer me advice.*
  Arrogant has more to do with an undue assumption of importance. **Defiant** could be used where conventions or demands are being flouted: *he's reached that defiant toddler stage.* You can use **contemptuous** where insolence is driven by a total lack of regard for propriety, and **insubordinate** where authority has been rejected: *you are on a training course – don't be rude or insubordinate.*

---

insoluble adj

unsolvable, unexplainable, inexplicable, incomprehensible, unfathomable, impenetrable, inscrutable, enigmatic, indecipherable, complex, intricate, involved, obscure, mysterious, mystifying, puzzling, perplexing, baffling
E3 explicable

insolvency n

bankruptcy, default, failure, liquidation, ruin, indebtedness, destitution, impoverishment, pennilessness
FORMAL impecuniosity
COLLOQ. queer street
E3 solvency

insolvent adj

bankrupt, failed, in debt, liquidated, ruined, penniless, impoverished, destitute
FORMAL impecunious
COLLOQ. bust, broke, skint, strapped (for cash), on your beam ends, gone to the wall, gone under, in the red, on the rocks, in queer street
E3 solvent

insomnia n

sleeplessness, restlessness, wakefulness
FORMAL insomnolence
E3 sleep

insouciance n

nonchalance, unconcern, carefreeness, heedlessness, indifference, light-heartedness, flippancy, airiness, breeziness, jauntiness, ease
E3 anxiety, care

insouciant adj

nonchalant, unconcerned, untroubled, unworried, indifferent, heedless, carefree, casual, free and easy, flippant, happy-go-lucky, airy, breezy, buoyant, jaunty, light-hearted, easy-going
E3 anxious, careworn

inspect v

check, vet, look into, look over, go over, pore over, examine, search, investigate, appraise, assess, audit, scrutinize, study, scan, survey, view, review, superintend, supervise, oversee, visit, reconnoitre, see over, tour
COLLOQ. check out, give something the once-over
SLANG case

inspection n

check, check-up, examination, scrutiny, scan, study, survey, review, search, investigation, vetting, analysis, appraisal, assessment, audit, supervision, visit, tour
COLLOQ. once-over, look-over, recce, dekko

inspector n

supervisor, superintendent, overseer, surveyor, controller, appraiser, assessor, auditor, scrutineer, scanner, checker, tester, examiner, investigator,

reviewer, critic, visitor, officer, searcher, viewer, conner
TECHNICAL exarch
OLD proveditor

inspiration n
1 CREATIVITY, originality, imagination, genius, inventiveness, muse, influence, encouragement, stimulation, incitement, stirring, arousing, motivation, spur, goad, stimulus, fillip, infusion, revelation, *duende, estro*; *Scot* taghairm; *Welsh* hwyl
TECHNICAL theopneusty, afflation, afflatus, Aganippe
OLD inflation, *inflatus*
2 IDEA, bright idea, stroke of genius, brainwave, brainstorm, insight, illumination, revelation, enlightenment, awakening

inspirational adj
encouraging, heartening, inspiring, motivating, suggestive, influential, emotional, spiritual, devotional, psychological, instinctive

inspire v
encourage, hearten, influence, impress, animate, breathe, enliven, quicken, energize, galvanize, fire, kindle, inflame, stir, arouse, rouse, trigger, instigate, inject, produce, bring about, spark off, touch off, prompt, spur, goad, motivate, provoke, stimulate, excite, exhilarate, thrill, enthral, enthuse, imbue, infuse, inform, infatuate, enamour, embrave

inspired adj
brilliant, impressive, superlative, wonderful, outstanding, exciting, dazzling, memorable, thrilling, enthralling, marvellous, exceptional, splendid, remarkable, creative, imaginative, talented
F3 dull, uninspired

inspiring adj
encouraging, heartening, uplifting, invigorating, stirring, rousing, interesting, enthusiastic, inspirational, stimulating, exciting, exhilarating, thrilling, enthralling, moving, affecting, memorable, impressive
F3 uninspiring, dull

inspirit v
encourage, inspire, move, stimulate, nerve, hearten, invigorate, quicken, refresh, reinvigorate, enliven, exhilarate, fire, galvanize, incite, animate, rouse, cheer, gladden, embolden

instability n
unsteadiness, shakiness, vacillation, wavering, oscillation, irresolution, uncertainty, impermanence, transience, unpredictability, changeableness, variability, fluctuation, volatility, capriciousness, flightiness, fitfulness, fickleness, inconstancy, unreliability, insecurity, precariousness, unsafeness, unsoundness, flimsiness, frailty
F3 stability

install v
1 *install a new phone system*
fix, fit, lay, put (in), plumb in, insert, place, position, locate, lodge, site, situate, station, plant, settle, establish, set up, introduce
2 *install her as president*
institute, inaugurate, invest, induct, ordain, swear in, consecrate, instate
3 ENSCONCE, settle, establish, entrench, nestle, put, place, lodge, locate

installation n
1 FITTING, insertion, positioning, location, placing, siting
2 EQUIPMENT, machinery, plant, system
3 *her installation as president*
inauguration, investiture, instatement, induction, consecration, ordination, swearing-in
4 *a military installation*
base, station, post, centre, site, settlement, establishment, headquarters, HQ, camp

instalment n
1 *pay in instalments*
payment, part payment, repayment, portion, tranche, hire purchase, HP
COLLOQ. the never-never
2 EPISODE, chapter, part, section, division, portion, segment

instance n, v
◆ n
1 *several instances of bullying*
case, example, illustration, exemplification, case in point, citation, occurrence, occasion, sample
2 *at his instance*
request, urging, incitement, demand, initiative, insistence, entreaty, instigation, pressure, prompting, solicitation
FORMAL behest, exhortation, importunity
◆ v
mention, quote, refer to, specify, give, name, cite, point to, exemplify
FORMAL adduce

instant n, adj
◆ n
flash, twinkling, trice, moment, split second, second, minute, time, occasion, juncture; *Scot* whip
COLLOQ. tick, jiffy, jiff, sec, twinkling of an eye, two shakes of a lamb's tail, mo
◆ adj
1 INSTANTANEOUS, immediate, on-the-spot, direct, prompt, urgent, unhesitating, quick, fast, rapid, swift
2 *instant food*
quickly prepared, easily prepared, pre-prepared, ready mixed, convenience, fast
F3 1 slow

instantaneous adj
immediate, instant, direct, prompt, rapid, unhesitating, sudden, on-the-spot
COLLOQ. snappy
F3 eventual

instantaneously adv
at once, directly, forthwith, immediately, right away, instantly, on the spot, promptly, speedily, quickly, rapidly, straight away, there and then, unhesitatingly, without hesitation, without delay, in the twinkling of an eye
OLD anon
COLLOQ. pronto, in a jiffy, before you can say Jack Robinson, in two shakes of a lamb's tail, ASAP
F3 eventually

instantly adv
immediately, instantaneously, at once, right away, straight away, there and then, forthwith, now, on the spot, without delay, directly
COLLOQ. pronto, in a jiffy, before you can say Jack Robinson, in two shakes of a lamb's tail, ASAP
F3 eventually

instead adv
alternatively, preferably, rather, else, by/in contrast, as an alternative, substitute, replacement
■ **instead of**
as opposed to, in contrast to, in place of, in lieu of, on behalf of, in preference to, in favour of, as an alternative to, rather than

instigate v
initiate, set on, start, begin, cause, bring about, induce, press, generate, inspire, move, influence, persuade, encourage, urge, spur, prod, goad, prompt, provoke, stimulate, kindle, incite, stir up, whip up, foment, rouse, excite

instigation n
initiation, incitement, initiative, encouragement,

prompting, urging, inducement, insistence, incentive, bidding
FORMAL behest

instigator *n*
leader, motivator, prime mover, initiator, provoker, ringleader, spur, goad, incendiary, inciter, mischief-maker, troublemaker, *agent provocateur*, agitator, fomenter, firebrand

instil *v*
infuse, imbue, insinuate, introduce, inject, implant, inculcate, impress, teach, drill
COLLOQ. din into

instinct *n*
1 NATURAL RESPONSE, inbred response, intuition, sixth sense, impulse, urge, drive, feeling, hunch, tendency
FORMAL predisposition
COLLOQ. gut feeling/reaction
2 FLAIR, knack, gift, talent, bent, feel, faculty, ability, aptitude

instinctive *adj*
natural, native, inborn, innate, inherent, intuitive, impulsive, involuntary, unintentional, automatic, mechanical, reflex, spontaneous, immediate, unlearned, untaught, unthinking, unpremeditated, visceral
COLLOQ. gut, knee-jerk
F3 conscious, voluntary, deliberate

instinctively *adv*
intuitively, naturally, spontaneously, unthinkingly, without thinking, automatically, involuntarily, mechanically
F3 consciously, deliberately, voluntarily

institute *v, n*
♦ *v*
1 START, originate, initiate, introduce, enact, begin, create, establish, develop, set up, organize, found, inaugurate, open, launch, put/set in motion
FORMAL commence
2 APPOINT, install, invest, induct, ordain, initiate
F3 1 cancel, abolish; *formal* discontinue
♦ *n*
1 *an institute for advanced research*
school, college, academy, conservatory, seminary, foundation, institution, organization
2 LAW, principle, rule, custom, regulation, decree

institution *n*
1 ORGANIZATION, association, society, guild, league, club, concern, corporation, foundation, establishment, institute, hospital, home, centre
2 CUSTOM, tradition, usage, practice, ritual, convention, rule, law, system
3 INITIATION, starting, introduction, enactment, creation, establishment, setting-up, formation, creation, founding, foundation, installation
FORMAL commencement, inception

institutional *adj*
established, organized, establishment, accepted, customary, conventional, formal, methodical, orderly, systematic, orthodox, regimented, set, routine, uniform, ritualistic, bureaucratic, clinical, impersonal, cold, unwelcoming, dreary, dull, drab, forbidding, monotonous, cheerless
F3 individualistic, unconventional

instruct *v*
1 TEACH, educate, tutor, coach, train, drill, ground, school, discipline, prime, prepare, inspire, guide, indoctrinate, lecture, show, catechize
OLD lesson; (*Shakesp*) study
2 ORDER, command, direct, demand, require, charge, mandate, tell, inform, notify, make known, tell, warn, advise, counsel, guide, enlighten, brief, call out
FORMAL enjoin, bid

instruction *n*
1 *give someone instructions*
order, direction, recommendation, advice, guidance, information, charge, command, requirement, injunction, mandate, directive, ruling, briefing
2 EDUCATION, schooling, lesson(s), classes, lecture(s), tuition, tutoring, tutelage, teaching, training, coaching, drilling, grounding, preparation, priming, guidance, enlightenment, indoctrination
3 *read the instructions carefully*
directions, orders, recommendations, rules, brief, information, advice, key, legend, guidance, guidelines, book of words, handbook, manual

instructive *adj*
informative, educational, educative, doctrinal, uplifting, edifying, enlightening, illuminating, helpful, useful
F3 unenlightening

instructor *n*
teacher, lecturer, educator, master, mistress, tutor, coach, trainer, demonstrator, exponent, adviser, mentor, guide, pedagogue, counsellor, guru, preceptor
TECHNICAL maharishi, swami
OLD institutor

instrument *n*
1 TOOL, implement, utensil, appliance, gadget, contraption, device, contrivance, apparatus, mechanism
COLLOQ. gismo
2 GAUGE, meter, measure, indicator, rule, guideline, yardstick
3 AGENT, agency, vehicle, organ, medium, factor, cause, channel, way, means
See also panels at **measuring instruments; musical instruments**.

instrumental *adj*
active, involved, contributory, conducive, influential, important, significant, useful, helpful, auxiliary, subsidiary
F3 obstructive, unhelpful

insubordinate *adj*
disobedient, rebellious, defiant, ungovernable, unruly, disorderly, undisciplined, rude, riotous, seditious, insurgent, mutinous, turbulent, impertinent, impudent
FORMAL contumacious, recalcitrant, refractory
F3 docile, obedient, compliant

insubordination *n*
disobedience, defiance, rebellion, insurrection, mutinousness, mutiny, revolt, riotousness, sedition, rudeness, ungovernability, indiscipline, impertinence, impudence
FORMAL recalcitrance
F3 docility, obedience, compliance

insubstantial *adj*
1 FLIMSY, frail, feeble, weak, tenuous, poor, slight, thin
2 UNREAL, false, illusory, fanciful, imaginary, idle, vaporous, intangible, immaterial, incorporeal, moonshine
FORMAL chimerical, ephemeral
F3 1 solid, strong **2** real

insufferable *adj*
intolerable, unbearable, unendurable, detestable, loathsome, revolting, repugnant, dreadful, shocking, outrageous, impossible, too much to bear, more than you can bear
F3 pleasant, tolerable

insufferably *adv*
unbearably, intolerably, outrageously, shockingly, impossibly, repugnantly

insufficiency *n*
inadequacy, shortage, deficiency, lack, scarcity, dearth, need, poverty, short supply
FORMAL want
F3 sufficiency, excess

insufficient *adj*
inadequate, not enough, short, deficient, lacking, wanting, meagre, sparse, scanty, scant, scarce, in short supply
🔄 sufficient, enough, excessive

insular *adj*
parochial, provincial, cut off, detached, isolated, remote, withdrawn, separate, solitary, insulated, inward-looking, short-sighted, blinkered, closed, narrow-minded, narrow, limited, restricted, petty, bigoted, biased, prejudiced, xenophobic
🔄 open-minded

insularity *n*
isolation, detachment, narrow-mindedness, short-sightedness, solitariness, pettiness, parochiality, parochialness, bigotry, bias, prejudice, xenophobia
🔄 open-mindedness, openness

insulate *v*
insulate water pipes; people insulated from outside influences
cushion, pad, lag, cocoon, protect, wrap, cover, shield, shelter, isolate, separate, cut off, exclude, detach, segregate, encase, envelop
FORMAL sequester

insulation *n*
cushioning, padding, lagging, cladding, cocooning, protection, wrapping, cover, covering, stuffing, shield, shelter, isolation, separation, exclusion, detachment, segregation

insult *v, n*
♦ *v*
abuse, call names, taunt, ridicule, bait, rebuff, libel, slander, malign, slight, slur, snub, injure, hurt, wound, offend, outrage, mortify, trample, triumph over
OLD fly in the face of
FORMAL affront, disparage, revile, impugn, calumniate, traduce
COLLOQ. kick in the teeth, slap in the face
🔄 compliment, praise

♦ *n*
abuse, rudeness, insolence, gibe, taunt, defamation, libel, slander, slight, slur, barb, snub, indignity, offence, outrage, aspersions
OLD contumely, injury, insultment; (*Spenser*) repriefe
FORMAL affront, disparagement, revilement
COLLOQ. put-down, backhanded compliment, kick in the teeth, slap in the face, verbal, mud pie
🔄 compliment, praise

Synonym nuances
verb
Abuse can be widely applied to mental maltreatment, unlike **taunt** which suggests deliberate provocation: *they taunted the beaten team with chants of 'easy'.* **Ridicule**, on the other hand, would be reserved for making someone appear absurd, while **bait** has more to do with constant harassment or goading: *on his way home he was being continually baited by a drunk.* While **malign** has to do with speaking badly of someone, it would imply it is not done in that person's presence: *he was much maligned by the critics.* Both **libel** and **slander** could be used of writing or saying injurious things about someone, but only where it is serious enough to be contested in a court of law.
 If you want to refer to disrespectfully overlooking or rejecting someone, you can use **rebuff**, **slight** or **snub**: *he felt slighted when he was passed over for promotion.* The terms **injure**, **hurt** and **wound** may all be used to put the emphasis on mental or emotional harm caused by an insult. **Offend** implies a more moral indignation, and **outrage** is suggestive of great indignation: *they were outraged at the blanket smoking ban.* **Mortify** is appropriate where severe embarrassment has resulted: *I was mortified by the things you said about me.*

---

insulting *adj*
offensive, abusive, rude, hurtful, injurious, contemptuous, degrading, slighting, outrageous, insolent, scurrilous, libellous, slanderous
OLD contumelious
FORMAL affronting, disparaging, reviling
🔄 complimentary, respectful

insuperable *adj*
insurmountable, formidable, overwhelming, invincible, unconquerable, unassailable, impassable
🔄 surmountable

insupportable *adj*
intolerable, unbearable, unendurable, insufferable, dreadful, loathsome, hateful, detestable, unacceptable, untenable, unjustifiable, indefensible
🔄 bearable

insuppressible *adj*
irrepressible, lively, unstoppable, uncontrollable, ungovernable, unruly, unsubduable, obstreperous, incorrigible, energetic
COLLOQ. go-getting
🔄 suppressible

insurance *n*
cover, protection, assurance, safeguard, security, surety, provision, assurance, indemnity, guarantee, indemnification, warranty, policy, premium

insure *v*
cover, protect, assure, underwrite, indemnify, guarantee, warrant, overinsure, reinsure
OLD ensure

insurer *n*
assurer, underwriter, protector, indemnifier, guarantor, warrantor
TECHNICAL abandonee

insurgence *n*
insurrection, rising, uprising, riot, rebellion, mutiny, revolt, revolution, sedition, coup, coup d'état, putsch

insurgent *n, adj*
♦ *n*
rebel, revolter, revolutionary, rioter, insurrectionist, seditionist, mutineer, partisan, revolutionist, resister
♦ *adj*
rebellious, revolting, revolutionary, mutinous, riotous, seditious, disobedient, insubordinate, insurrectionary, partisan

insurmountable *adj*
insuperable, unconquerable, invincible, unassailable, overwhelming, hopeless, impossible
🔄 surmountable

insurrection *n*
rising, uprising, insurgency, riot, rebellion, mutiny, revolt, revolution, sedition, coup, coup d'état, putsch

intact *adj*
unbroken, (all) in one piece, whole, complete, integral, entire, perfect, faultless, flawless, sound, undamaged, unharmed, unhurt, uninjured, unscathed
🔄 broken, incomplete, damaged

intangible *adj*
insubstantial, imponderable, elusive, fleeting, airy, unclear, shadowy, vague, subtle, obscure, indefinite, indefinable, undefinable, indescribable, abstract, unreal, invisible, immeasurable, impalpable
🔄 tangible, real

integer *n*
number, whole number, numeral, figure, digit, unit

integral *adj*
1 *an integral part*
intrinsic, constituent, component, inherent, built-in,

inbuilt, elemental, basic, fundamental, necessary, essential, indispensable
FORMAL requisite
2 COMPLETE, entire, full, whole, total, undivided, intact, integrated
⊟ 1 extra, additional, unnecessary

integrate v
assimilate, merge, join, unite, combine, amalgamate, co-ordinate, consolidate, incorporate, coalesce, fuse, knit, mesh, mix, intermix, mingle, blend, homogenize, harmonize, desegregate, mainstream
⊟ divide, separate, segregate

integrated adj
mixed, desegregated, assimilated, merged, joined, unified, unseparated, united, combined, amalgamated, consolidated, incorporated, coalesced, fused, meshed, mingled, blended, harmonized, harmonious, cohesive, connected, tight-knit, tightly-knit, interrelated, hybrid, mongrel
COLLOQ. part and parcel
⊟ unintegrated, segregated

integration n
assimilation, merger, unity, unification, combination, amalgamation, consolidation, incorporation, fusion, blend, harmony, mix, desegregation, homogenization
⊟ separation, segregation

integrity n
1 HONESTY, uprightness, incorruptibility, purity, morality, principle, sincerity, honour, decency, virtue, goodness, fairness, righteousness, justice, impartiality, truthfulness
FORMAL probity, rectitude
2 COMPLETENESS, wholeness, unity, entirety, entireness, totality, coherence, cohesion, unification
⊟ 1 dishonesty **2** incompleteness

intellect n
1 *a person of considerable intellect*
mind, brain(s), brainpower, brilliance, intelligence, genius, reason, thought, understanding, comprehension, sense, wisdom, judgement
TECHNICAL noesis, noology
COLLOQ. nous
2 THINKER, academic, highbrow, mastermind, genius, intellectual
COLLOQ. egghead, brainbox
⊟ 1 stupidity

intellectual adj, n
♦ adj
academic, scholarly, intelligent, studious, learned, thoughtful, mental, logical, highbrow, bookish, cultural, well-educated, well-read
TECHNICAL noetic, noematical
FORMAL cerebral, erudite
⊟ low-brow
♦ n
thinker, academic, highbrow, mastermind, genius, intellect, good mind, titan
COLLOQ. egghead, brainbox, rocket scientist
⊟ low-brow

intellectually adv
mentally, academically, studiously, conceptually, culturally
TECHNICAL noematically
FORMAL cerebrally

intelligence n
1 INTELLECT, reason, wit(s), brainpower, cleverness, brightness, brilliance, aptitude, quickness, alertness, sharpness, acumen, discernment, perception, thought, understanding, comprehension
COLLOQ. brain(s), grey matter, little grey cells, nous
2 INFORMATION, facts, data, knowledge, findings,

notification, news, report, notice, account, rumour, warning, advice
COLLOQ. low-down, tip-off, gen, dope
3 SURVEILLANCE, spying, espionage, observation
⊟ 1 stupidity, foolishness

intelligent adj
clever, bright, smart, brilliant, quick, alert, quick-witted, sharp, acute, discerning, perceptive, knowing, knowledgeable, well-informed, informed, thinking, educated, rational, sensible
OLD apprehensive
FORMAL perspicacious, sagacious
COLLOQ. brainy, quick on the uptake, no flies on someone, knowing a thing or two, knowing how many beans make five, using your loaf, all there
⊟ unintelligent, stupid, foolish
See Synonym nuances panel at **clever**.

intelligently adv
knowingly, rationally, sensibly, cleverly, quickly, discerningly, perceptively
FORMAL perspicaciously, sagaciously
COLLOQ. quick on the uptake, knowing a thing or two, knowing how many beans make five, using your loaf, all there
⊟ stupidly, foolishly

intelligentsia n
academics, intellectuals, cognoscenti, literati, highbrows, illuminati
COLLOQ. brains, eggheads

intelligibility n
comprehensibility, comprehensibleness, clearness, clarity, plainness, lucidity, lucidness, explicitness, distinctness, legibility, precision, simplicity
FORMAL exotericism
⊟ unintelligibility

intelligible adj
comprehensible, understandable, clear, plain, lucid, distinct, open, explicit, legible, decipherable, fathomable, penetrable
FORMAL exoteric, exoterical
⊟ unintelligible

intemperance n
excess, immoderation, self-indulgence, overindulgence, unrestraint, extravagance, drunkenness, intoxication, insobriety, licence
FORMAL crapulence, inebriation
⊟ temperance

intemperate adj
extreme, immoderate, inordinate, unrestrained, unbridled, uncontrolled, uncontrollable, irrestrainable, ungovernable, severe, violent, wild, tempestuous, passionate, excessive, unreasonable, extravagant, self-indulgent, drunken, intoxicated, dissolute, incontinent, prodigal, licentious, profligate
FORMAL inebriated
COLLOQ. over the top, OTT
⊟ temperate

intend v
aim, have a mind, have in mind, contemplate, mean, think, meditate, be going, be looking, propose, choose, plan, project, scheme, devise, plot, design, expect, purpose, determine, be determined, resolve, destine, mark out, earmark, set apart; *Scot* ettle; *N Am* calculate
OLD foremean; (*Spenser*) hight
FORMAL purport

intended adj, n
♦ adj
designated, destined, deliberate, intentional, planned, proposed, designate, future, prospective, betrothed
⊟ accidental
♦ n

fiancé, fiancée, husband-to-be, wife-to-be, future
husband, future wife, betrothed

intense *adj*
1 EXTREME, great, deep, profound, strong, powerful,
vigorous, potent, forceful, fierce, harsh, severe, acute,
sharp, keen, enthusiastic, zealous, eager, earnest, ardent,
fervent, excited, passionate, impassioned, vehement,
consuming, burning, energetic, violent, intensive,
concentrated, heightened
FORMAL fervid
2 *an intense person*
serious, thoughtful, impassioned, emotional, tense,
nervous, heavy
⊡ 1 moderate, mild, weak **2** easy-going

⚠ intense or **intensive**?
Intense means 'very great': *the intense heat from the furnace; intense bitterness. Intensive* means 'concentrated,
thorough, taking great care': *an intense search; the intensive care ward of a hospital.*

Synonym nuances
sense 1
Great can be widely applied to describe magnitude,
while **extreme** could be reserved for something of the
greatest possible degree: *extreme grief led to his suicide.*
Deep and **profound** tend to suggest being deeply rooted
psychologically or intellectually: *deep sympathy; a
profound influence.*
   Vigorous and **energetic** have associations with
liveliness and movement: *vigorous political
campaigning,* while **violent** implies furiously
unrestrained: *a violent coughing fit.* **Potent** conveys the
idea of strength, as does **forceful**, while **fierce** shares
similar implications but tends to be used in the contexts
competition or fighting.
   The terms **harsh** and **severe** imply something
unpleasant: *harsh winter; severe pain,* whereas **acute**
and **sharp** have a more penetrative effect: *sharp
criticism.* **Keen** has similar connotations, but along with
enthusiastic and **zealous** may also be suggestive of a
strong personal interest: *zealous commitment.* **Ardent,
fervent, passionate** and **impassioned** go further by
implying a heartfelt involvement.
   Vehement, on the other hand, suggests intellectual
conviction: *a vehement speech on workers' rights.*
Consuming would be appropriate for an all-engrossing
intensity: *horse-riding became her consuming passion,*
while **heightened** could be used for something that has
grown notably stronger: *heightened public awareness of
crime; heightened tension.*

---

intensely *adv*
extremely, deeply, very, strongly, greatly, profoundly,
fiercely, ardently, fervently, passionately
COLLOQ. with a vengeance
⊡ mildly

intensification *n*
increase, stepping-up, strengthening, reinforcement,
magnification, escalation, heightening, building-up, build-
up, boost, aggravation, acceleration, worsening,
deepening, concentration, emphasis, enhancement
FORMAL augmentation, exacerbescence
⊡ lessening

intensify *v*
increase, step up, build up, escalate, heighten, maximize,
fire, boost, fuel, fan, aggravate, worsen, add to, broaden,
widen, strengthen, reinforce, magnify, sharpen, whet,
quicken, deepen, concentrate, emphasize, enhance
FORMAL augment, exacerbate
COLLOQ. hot up, bump up, hike up, add fuel to

the flames, bring to a head
⊡ reduce, weaken

intensity *n*
greatness, extremity, intenseness, depth, profundity,
fullness, strength, power, vigour, potency, force,
fierceness, severity, acuteness, keenness, eagerness,
earnestness, ardour, enthusiasm, zeal, fanaticism, fervency,
fervour, fire, emotion, passion, concentration, energy,
vehemence, strain, tension

intensive *adj*
concentrated, thorough, exhaustive, comprehensive,
detailed, in-depth, rigorous, full, total, thoroughgoing, all-
out, intense
⊡ superficial

⚠ intensive or **intense**?
See panel at **intense**.

---

intensively *adv*
thoroughly, exhaustively, comprehensively, rigorously,
completely, totally, fully, closely, intensely, extensively
⊡ superficially, on the surface

intent *adj, n*
   ◆ *adj*
1 *intent on doing something*
determined, resolved, set, bent, eager, keen, committed,
firm
2 *an intent look*
attentive, alert, concentrating, fixed, close, hard, keen,
absorbed, occupied, wrapped up, focused, engrossed,
preoccupied, steady, rapt, enrapt, searching, watchful
⊡ 2 absent-minded, distracted
   ◆ *n*
intention, purpose, meaning, objective, plan, aim, goal,
target, point, idea, view, design, object, end
■ **to all intents and purposes**
almost, nearly, practically, in effect, effectively, in essence,
virtually, more or less, just about, as good as, pretty much,
pretty well

intention *n*
aim, purpose, object, end, point, target, goal, objective,
idea, plan, design, view, intent, meaning, ambition, wish,
aspiration

intentional *adj*
designed, wilful, conscious, planned, purposeful,
purposed, set, deliberate, prearranged, premeditated,
preconceived, considered, calculated, studied, systematic,
systematical, voluntary, intended, weighed-up, meant, on
purpose
TECHNICAL prepense
OLD willing
⊡ unintentional, accidental

intentionally *adv*
deliberately, on purpose, wilfully, by design, designedly,
meaningly, with malice aforethought, in cold blood
TECHNICAL prepensely
OLD willingly
⊡ accidentally

intently *adv*
attentively, watchfully, carefully, closely, steadily,
searchingly, staringly, fixedly, hard, keenly
⊡ absent-mindedly

inter *v*
bury, lay to rest, entomb, inearth, sepulchre, inhume
FORMAL inurn
⊡ exhume

interbreed *v*
cross, crossbreed, cross-fertilize, mongrelize,
hybridize, reproduce together
FORMAL miscegenate

interbreeding n
cross-breeding, crossing, hybridization
FORMAL miscegenation

intercede v
mediate, arbitrate, intervene, plead, speak, petition, negotiate, moderate
FORMAL entreat, beseech, interpose

intercept v
head off, ambush, interrupt, deflect, cut off, stop, arrest, catch, commandeer, take, seize, check, block, impede, obstruct, delay, frustrate, thwart

interception n
ambush, deflection, heading-off, cutting-off, stopping, seizure, checking, blocking, obstruction

intercession n
mediation, arbitration, negotiation, intervention, plea, pleading, advocacy, agency, solicitation, prayer, good offices
FORMAL beseeching, entreaty, supplication, interposition

intercessor n
mediator, arbitrator, negotiator, moderator, intermediary, agent, go-between, middleman, broker, prayer

interchange n, v
◆ n
1 EXCHANGE, trading, barter, swap, alternation, reciprocation, interplay, crossfire
COLLOQ. give-and-take
2 INTERSECTION, junction, crossroad(s), crossing
◆ v
exchange, swap, switch, alternate, reciprocate, replace, substitute, trade, barter, transpose, reverse

interchangeability n
comparability, similarity, transposability, exchangeability, interaction, reciprocation, exchange, barter, swap, equivalence, correspondence, synonymy, parallelism
FORMAL congruence, reciprocity

interchangeable adj
reciprocal, exchangeable, transposable, equivalent, corresponding, comparable, similar, identical, the same, synonymous, standard
E3 different

interconnect v
link, interlink, interrelate, interlock, interweave, communicate, intercommunicate

intercourse n
1 *sexual intercourse*
sex, sexual relations, intimacy, intimate relations, making love, love-making, copulation, sleeping with someone, going to bed with someone, the sex act
OLD embraces
FORMAL carnal knowledge, coition, coitus, congress
COLLOQ. it, how's your father; *Aust & NZ* naughty
SLANG nooky, bonk, bang, lay, greens, jig-a-jig, knee-trembler, pussy, rumpy-pumpy, tail, leg-over, wham bam thank you ma'am, quickie, roll in the hay, get one's oats; *N Am* jazz, poontang; (*taboo*) fuck, screw, shag, hole
2 ASSOCIATION, communication, communion, contact, connection, dealings, conversation, converse, correspondence, commerce, trade, intercommunication, congress, traffic
COLLOQ. truck

interdependent adj
interconnected, interlinked, interrelated, interlocking, reciprocal, correlated, complementary, mutual, two-way

interdict v, n
◆ v
ban, bar, debar, forbid, prohibit, prevent, embargo, rule out, veto, outlaw

FORMAL disallow, preclude, proscribe
E3 allow
◆ n
ban, injunction, prohibition, bar, embargo, taboo, veto
FORMAL disallowance, interdiction, proscription, preclusion
E3 permission

interest n, v
◆ n
1 *have an interest in dance*
curiosity, inquisitiveness, concern, care, attention, attentiveness, notice, regard, heed, charm, allure, appeal, attraction, fascination, involvement, engagement
2 IMPORTANCE, significance, consequence, concern, moment, consideration, magnitude, relevance, prominence, weight, value, note, urgency, priority, seriousness, gravity
3 *leisure interests*
activity, pursuit, pastime, hobby, diversion, recreation, amusement
4 ADVANTAGE, good, benefit, profit, gain
5 *business interests*
share, stake, concern, business, claim, involvement, participation, portion, investment, stock, equity
6 *earn interest*
dividend, return, profit, gain, receipts, revenue, proceeds, credits, bonus, premium, percentage
E3 **1** lack of interest **2** meaninglessness **4** loss
◆ v
concern, involve, touch, move, attract, appeal to, divert, amuse, occupy, engage, rivet, absorb, engross, fascinate, intrigue, captivate, grip
E3 bore
■ **in the interests of**
for the sake of, on behalf of, to the advantage of, for the benefit of

interested adj
1 ATTENTIVE, curious, absorbed, engrossed, engaged, fascinated, intent, captivated, gripped, enthralled, riveted, intrigued, enthusiastic, keen, attracted, devoted
COLLOQ. hot on, into, having the ... bug
2 CONCERNED, involved, affected, implicated
E3 **1** uninterested, indifferent, apathetic **2** disinterested, unaffected

interesting adj
attractive, appealing, entertaining, engaging, absorbing, engrossing, exciting, fascinating, captivating, intriguing, compelling, compulsive, gripping, riveting, stimulating, thought-provoking, readable, viewable, amusing, curious, unusual
COLLOQ. unputdownable
E3 uninteresting, boring, monotonous, tedious

Synonym nuances
Attractive describes anyone or anything to which you are drawn, while **appealing** may be similarly enticing but perhaps with a more emotional element: *an appealing study of a lovable eccentric*. If you describe something as **entertaining** you merely suggest it provides a diversion, while **engaging**, **absorbing** and **engrossing** are stronger terms, all suggestive of completely capturing the attention: *an absorbing book*.
  Fascinating and **captivating** have suggestions of being spellbinding and suggest interest that has less specific, worldly causes: *he was a captivating scene-stealer as Puck*. You can use **intriguing** and the more explicit **curious** to suggest that an element of puzzlement has stirred interest.
  Compelling and **compulsive** have implications of being irresistibly drawn: *a drama that makes compelling TV viewing*. With **gripping** and **riveting** we return to the idea of being enthralled, whereas **stimulating** and **thought-provoking** are more appropriate for exciting an intellectual interest: *a stimulating public debate*.

interestingly adv

curiously, intriguingly, poignantly, ingeniously

interfere v

1 INTRUDE, pry, interrupt, intervene, meddle, tamper, intermeddle, trespass
TECHNICAL intromit
OLD mar
FORMAL interpose
COLLOQ. barge in, mess about/around, poke/stick your nose in, stick/put your oar in, put in your two pennyworth, muscle in on, butt in; *N Am* put in your two cents' worth; *Aust* stick/poke/put your bib in
2 HINDER, hamper, obstruct, block, check, impede, handicap, cramp, inhibit, trammel, balk, thwart, conflict, clash, choke, jam, upset
COLLOQ. get in the way of
3 MOLEST, abuse, assault, sexually assault, attack, touch sexually, rape
COLLOQ. grope, touch up, feel up
⊟ 1 *colloq.* mind your own business **2** assist

Synonym nuances
sense 1
Intrude is critical in tone in that it suggests an uninvited or unwelcome encroachment. **Pry** is similar in tone, although it has more to do with invading someone's privacy: *her parents never pried into her affairs.* The term **interrupt** is less marked, although it also implies an element of disruption: *the speaker was interrupted by a question from the audience.* **Intervene** is more positive in that it suggests stepping in to assume a controlling role: *the government has intervened in environmental issues.* The term **meddle**, however, expresses a critical attitude and suggests unhelpful involvement, while **tamper** similarly has suggestions of causing damage: *someone had tampered with the brakes.* **Trespass** is more formal, even legal in tone, and suggests literal or figurative encroachment on someone else's territory: *trespassing on railway property; parliament must refrain from trespassing upon the province of the courts.*

---

interference n

1 INTRUSION, prying, interruption, intervention, meddling, meddlesomeness
TECHNICAL intromission
FORMAL interposition
2 OBSTRUCTION, hindrance, hampering, blocking, checking, impediment, handicap, inhibiting, trammel(s), thwarting, opposition, conflict, clashing
⊟ 2 assistance

interfering adj

meddlesome, meddling, prying, intrusive, intruding
COLLOQ. nos(e)y

interim adj, n

• *adj*
temporary, provisional, stopgap, makeshift, improvised, stand-in, acting, caretaker, pro tem
• *n*
meantime, meanwhile, interval, interregnum

interior adj, n

• *adj*
1 INTERNAL, inside, inner, innermost, central, inward, intrinsic
2 *interior thoughts*
inner, mental, personal, private, intimate, spiritual, emotional, psychological, secret, hidden, involuntary, spontaneous, impulsive, intuitive, instinctive, innate
3 HOME, domestic, central, local, inland, up-country, remote
⊟ 1 exterior, external **3** external, coastal
• *n*

inside, inside part, centre, middle, core, heart, nucleus, depths
⊟ exterior, outside

interject v

cry, shout, call, utter, introduce, interrupt, exclaim
FORMAL ejaculate, interpose, interpolate

interjection n

exclamation, cry, shout, call, utterance, interruption
FORMAL ejaculation, interpolation, interposition

interlace v

entwine, braid, twine, knit, plait, cross, enlace, interweave, interlock, intertwine, intermix, intersperse, interwreathe
FORMAL reticulate

interlink v

link, link together, interconnect, lock together, interlock, mesh, knit, intergrow, intertwine, interweave, clasp together
⊟ separate, divide

interlock v

lock together, interconnect, link, link together, mesh, engage, clasp together, intertwine, tooth, pitch
FORMAL interdigitate
⊟ disengage

interloper n

intruder, uninvited guest, trespasser, encroacher, invader
COLLOQ. gatecrasher

interlude n

interval, intermission, break, breathing space, pause, rest, recess, stop, stoppage, respite, wait, delay, halt, spell
FORMAL hiatus
COLLOQ. breather, let-up

intermediary n

mediator, go-between, negotiator, arbitrator, middleman, broker, agent

intermediate adj

midway, halfway, in-between, middle, mid, median, medial, mean, intermediary, intervening, transitional
⊟ extreme

interment n

burial, burying, funeral
FORMAL inhumation, exequies, obsequies, obsequy, sepulture
⊟ exhumation

interminable adj

endless, never-ending, perpetual, limitless, boundless, unlimited, ceaseless, without end, everlasting, eternal, long, long-winded, long-drawn-out, dragging, wearisome, tedious, boring, dull, monotonous
FORMAL prolix, loquacious
⊟ limited, brief

intermingle v

mix, mix together, merge, blend, amalgamate, combine, fuse, intermix, interlace, interweave, mix up
FORMAL commingle, commix, intermix
⊟ separate

intermission n

interval, interlude, break, recess, rest, respite, breathing space, pause, lull, remission, suspension, interruption, halt, stop, stoppage
FORMAL cessation
COLLOQ. breather, let-up

intermittent adj

occasional, periodic, sporadic, spasmodic, fitful, erratic, irregular, cyclic, broken, off and on, on and off
FORMAL discontinuous
⊟ continuous, constant

intermittently adv

occasionally, periodically, sporadically, spasmodically, erratically, irregularly, from time to time, sometimes, off and on, on and off, in/by fits and starts

Internet terms include:

access provider	dialup	host	mailing list	PNG (Portable	Internet
account	connection	host name	mail server	Network	Protocol)
address	decryption	hot spot	main menu	Graphic)	thread
ADSL	dedicated line	HTML (HyperText	message board	POP (Point of	timeout
(Asymmetric	denial of service	Markup	message-ID	Presence)	troll
Digital	digital signing	Language)	Microsoft	POP3 (Post	upload
Subscriber Line)	DNS (Domain	DHTML	Internet	Office Protocol)	uptime
alias	Name Server/	(Dynamic	Explorer®	popup	URL (Uniform or
anonymous FTP	System)	HTML)	MIME	portal	Universal
autoreply (or	domain name	HTTP or http	(Multipurpose	post	Resource
autoresponder)	dotcom	(HyperText	Internet Mail	postmaster	Locator)
applet	download	Transfer	Extensions)	PPP (Point to	Usenet
ASP (Active	e-business	Protocol)	mirror site	Point Protocol)	username
Server Page)	e-commerce	hyperlink	modem	protocol	VDSL (Very High
attachment	email (or e-mail)	hypertext	moderator	remote access	Speed Digital
authoring	emoticon	IMAP (Internet	MP3	rollover	Subscriber Line)
backbone	encryption	Message Access	MPEG (Moving	router	viral email
bandwidth	escrow	Protocol)	Picture Experts	scrollbar	virus
banner	Ethernet	intelligent agent	Group)	SDSL (Symmetric	W3C (World
baseband	extranet	Internet access	navigation bar	Digital	Wide Web
BBS (Bulletin	e-zine	provider (IAP)	netiquette	Subscriber Line)	Consortium)
Board System)	FAQ (Frequently	Internet Protocol	*colloq.* Netspeak	search engine	WAN (wide area
bookmark	Asked	(IP)	newbie	server	network)
bot	Questions)	Internet Relay	newsgroup	set-top box	WAP (Wireless
bps (bits per	favorites	Chat (IRC)	newsreader	signature file	Application
second)	firewall	Internet service	NNTP (Network	site map	Protocol)
bridge	flame	provider (ISP)	News Transfer	smiley	web bug
broadband	forum	intranet	Protocol)	snail mail	Webcam
browser	frame	ISDN (Integrated	node	spam	webcast
cable modem	FTP (File Transfer	Services Digital	offline	spider	webmaster
cache	Protocol)	Network)	online	SSI (Server Side	web page
cancelbot	gateway	Javascript	online service	Includes)	website
CGI (Common	GIF (Graphical	JPEG (Joint	packet	stylesheet	World Wide Web
Gateway	Interchange	Photographics	packet switching	cascading	(WWW or
Interface)	Format)	Experts Group)	pane	stylesheet (CSS)	www)
chatroom	helper	junk mail	Perl	surf	XML (Extensible
cookie	application	kill file	pingstorm	TCP/IP	Markup
cybercafé	hit	link	plain text	(Transmission	Language)
cyberspace	hit counter	lurk	plugin	Control	XSL (Extensible
dialer	homepage	mail bomb		Protocol/	Style Language)
	honeypot	mailbox			

FORMAL discontinuously
◨ continuously, regularly

intern *v, n*

◆ *v*
confine, detain, hold, hold in custody, jail, imprison
◨ free, release

◆ *n*
trainee, apprentice, graduate, probationer, student, pupil, learner, novice, beginner, starter, recruit, newcomer, tiro, cadet, prentice

internal *adj*
1 INSIDE, inner, interior, inward
2 HOME, domestic, civil, interior, in-house, local
3 *internal processes of the mind*
subjective, intimate, private, personal, spiritual, mental, emotional, psychological
◨ 1 external

internally *adv*
1 *known internally as 'B3'*
domestically, locally
2 SUBJECTIVELY, inwardly, inside, to yourself, within, at heart, in your heart of hearts, deep down, deep inside you, privately, secretly

international *adj*
global, worldwide, intercontinental, cosmopolitan, universal, general
◨ national, local, parochial

internecine *adj*
fierce, violent, bloody, deadly, mortal, fatal, destructive, ruinous, murderous, exterminating, family, civil, internal

Internet
See panel above

interplay *n*
exchange, interchange, interaction, reciprocation, alternation, transposition
COLLOQ. give-and-take

interpolate *v*
insert, add, put in, introduce, interject
FORMAL interpose, intercalate

interpolation *n*
insert, insertion, addition, introduction, aside, interjection
FORMAL intercalation

interpose *v*
insert, introduce, interject, add, put in, thrust in, interrupt, intrude, interfere, come between, put/place between, intervene, step in, mediate, arbitrate, intercede
FORMAL interpolate
COLLOQ. barge in, butt in, muscle in, poke your nose in, put your oar in

interpret *v*
explain, clarify, make clear, throw/shed light on, define, paraphrase, translate, render, decode, decipher, solve, make sense of, understand, read, take, construe, open up, rationalize
OLD aread, interpretate; (*Shakesp*) scan
FORMAL expound, elucidate, construe, explicate
COLLOQ. read between the lines

interpretation *n*
explanation, clarification, analysis, translation, rendering, version, paraphrase, performance, reading,

understanding, sense, meaning, opinion, decoding, deciphering
TECHNICAL anagogy
FORMAL expounding, exposition, elucidation, exegesis, explication, construe
COLLOQ. spin, take

interpretative *adj*
explanatory, clarificatory, interpretive
TECHNICAL hermeneutic
FORMAL exegetic, explicatory, expository

interpreter *n*
translator, linguist, commentator, annotator, interpretress, dragoman, dobhash, munshi, moonshee; *N Am* linguister
TECHNICAL hermeneutist, lawyer, textualist, oneirocritic, oneiroscopist
OLD Latiner, truchman
FORMAL elucidator, exegete, exponent, expositor

interrelate *v*
link, interlink, interconnect, interlock, interweave, communicate, intercommunicate

interrogate *v*
question, quiz, examine, cross-examine, cross-question, debrief
COLLOQ. grill, give a going-over, give the third degree, pump, give a roasting

interrogation *n*
questioning, quizzing, cross-questioning, examination, cross-examination, inquisition, inquiry, inquest
COLLOQ. grilling, going-over, the third degree, pumping

interrogative *adj*
questioning, quizzical, curious, inquisitive, probing, inquiring, interrogatory
FORMAL inquisitional, inquisitorial, catechetical, erotetic

interrupt *v*
1 *interrupt a conversation*
cut in, intrude, break in, disturb, punctuate, cut in, cut short, cut off, heckle, barrack, cut short, take (up) short, snap up, take up
FORMAL interpolate, interpose, interject, interjaculate
COLLOQ. barge in, butt in, chip in, chop in, put your oar in
2 *interrupt an event*
disturb, disrupt, hold up, stop, halt, end, suspend, delay, postpone, cancel, cut off, disconnect, break, block, punctuate, intercept, intervene
FORMAL interlude
3 *interrupt a view*
obstruct, block, cut off, disturb, interfere with, chequer

interruption *n*
1 *work without interruption*
intrusion, interference, disturbance, cutting-in, disruption, suspension, breaking-off, delay, disconnection
FORMAL discontinuance, cessation
COLLOQ. barging-in, butting-in
2 *no interruptions are allowed*
question, remark, interjection, obstruction, impediment, obstacle, hitch, cutting-in, blocking
OLD interpellation
FORMAL interpolation
3 PAUSE, break, halt, stop, interval, intermission, recess, interlude, cut
OLD (*Spenser*) cesure
FORMAL hiatus
COLLOQ. breather, let-up

intersect *v*
cross, criss-cross, cut across, bisect, divide, meet, converge, overlap

intersection *n*
junction, interchange, crossroads, crossing, meeting

intersperse *v*
scatter, distribute, spread, dispense, pepper, sprinkle, dot, intermix, diversify
FORMAL interpose, interlard

interstice *n*
space, gap, opening, blank, void, hole, cavity, aperture, crack, chink, crevice, cleft, cranny, breach, rift, fracture, rent, divide, gulf
FORMAL orifice, lacuna

intertwine *v*
entwine, interweave, interlace, interlink, link together, connect, interwind, twirl, twist, twine, coil, cross, weave, blend, mix

interval *n*
1 BREAK, interlude, intermission, rest, pause, space, lull, gap, delay, wait, interim, period, time, recess, meantime, meanwhile
COLLOQ. breathing space, breather
2 SPACE, gap, opening, distance, period, spell, time, season

intervene *v*
1 STEP IN, mediate, arbitrate, intercede, negotiate, involve yourself in, interfere, interrupt, intrude
2 OCCUR, happen, pass, arise, come to pass
FORMAL elapse, befall

intervening *adj*
between
FORMAL interposing, intervenient, interjacent, mediate

intervention *n*
involvement, stepping-in, mediation, arbitration, negotiation, agency, intercession, interference, interruption, intrusion

interview *n, v*
♦ *n*
discussion, audience, consultation, talk, dialogue, meeting, conference, press conference, encounter, tête-à-tête, evaluation, appraisal, assessment, oral examination, viva
♦ *v*
question, interrogate, examine, talk to, sound out, cross-examine, cross-question, evaluate, assess, vet
COLLOQ. grill, give the third degree to

interviewer *n*
examiner, questioner, investigator, reporter, correspondent, evaluator, appraiser, assessor, interrogator, inquisitor
FORMAL interlocutor, interrogant

interweave *v*
intertwine, entwine, interlace, interlink, interwind, interlock, twist, twine, coil, knit, cross, criss-cross, weave, intertangle, intertwist, interwork, interwreathe, braid, splice, blend, link together, interconnect, intermingle, connect, mix
FORMAL reticulate

intestinal *adj*
internal, abdominal, gastric, duodenal, visceral
TECHNICAL coeliac, ileac, enteric
FORMAL stomachic

intestines *n*
bowels, guts, entrails, insides, colon, offal, viscera, vitals
COLLOQ. innards

intimacy *n*
1 CLOSENESS, close relationship, friendship, familiarity, confidence, confidentiality, privacy, warmth, affection, love, understanding
2 SEXUAL INTERCOURSE, sexual relations, intimate relations, love-making, copulation, sleeping with someone, going to bed with someone
FORMAL carnal knowledge, coition, coitus

COLLOQ. it, how's your father; *Aust & NZ* naughty
SLANG nooky, bonk, bang, lay, greens, jig-a-jig, knee-trembler, pussy, rumpy-pumpy, tail, leg-over, wham bam thank you ma'am, quickie, roll in the hay, get one's oats; *N Am* jazz, poontang; (*taboo*) fuck, screw, shag, hole
🖃 distance

intimate¹ *adj, n*
• *adj*
1 *an intimate friend*
close, near, dear, bosom, cherished, friendly, informal, familiar, affectionate, boon; *Scot* chief
OLD privy, strict, gremial
COLLOQ. thick, mat(e)y, pally, chummy, tight
2 *an intimate atmosphere*
warm, welcoming, cosy, friendly, snug, *gemütlich*; *Scot* tosh; *intime*, throng
3 *an intimate conversation*
confidential, secret, private, personal, internal, innermost, heart-to-heart; *Scot* pack
4 *intimate knowledge of art*
deep, profound, in-depth, penetrating, detailed, exhaustive, thorough, special, well-acquainted
🖃 1 unfriendly, cold, distant **4** superficial
• *n*
friend, close friend, best friend, bosom friend, confidant(e), associate, boon companion, comrade, alter ego, better half, Achates, *fidus Achates*
OLD belamy, cater-cousin, inward
COLLOQ. mate, pal, chum, buddy, crony
OLD SLANG china
🖃 stranger

intimate² *v*
intimated that he'd be willing to help
hint, insinuate, imply, suggest, indicate, signal, communicate, impart, tell, state, declare, announce, make known, let it be known, give notice, allude, signal

intimately *adv*
1 CLOSELY, affectionately, personally, tenderly, warmly, familiarly, hand and/in glove
2 CONFIDENTIALLY, confidingly, privately
3 DEEPLY, fully, in detail, exhaustively, thoroughly, inside out
🖃 1 coldly, distantly **3** superficially

intimation *n*
hint, inkling, insinuation, implication, suggestion, indication, announcement, communication, signal, declaration, notice, statement, reference, warning, reminder, allusion

intimidate *v*
daunt, cow, overawe, domineer, appal, dismay, alarm, scare, frighten, terrify, subdue, threaten, extort, blackmail, menace, tyrannize, terrorize, bully, browbeat, bulldoze, coerce, compel, pressure, pressurize, warn off, bullyrag
COLLOQ. get at, lean on, twist someone's arm, put the screws on, psych out, put the frighteners on, turn the heat on

intimidation *n*
frightening, terrifying, menaces, threats, threatening, threatening behaviour, terrorization, terrorizing, domineering, tyrannization, bullying, browbeating, coercion, compulsion, pressure, fear, terror, scare tactics
COLLOQ. arm-twisting, screws, frighteners, big stick, sabre-rattling
🖃 persuasion

intolerable *adj*
unbearable, unendurable, insupportable, unacceptable, insufferable, loathsome, detestable, impossible, more than you can bear
COLLOQ. too bad, awful, dreadful, the limit, the end, the last straw, the straw that broke the camel's back
🖃 tolerable

intolerably *adv*
unbearably, insufferably, outrageously, shockingly, impossibly, repugnantly

intolerance *n*
impatience, prejudice, discrimination, narrowness, narrow-mindedness, small-mindedness, insularity, bigotry, opinionativeness, dogmatism, fanaticism, extremism, illiberality, uncharitableness, chauvinism, jingoism, racialism, racism, sexism, ageism, xenophobia, anti-Semitism
🖃 tolerance

intolerant *adj*
impatient, prejudiced, biased, discriminating, partisan, one-sided, bigoted, narrow, narrow-minded, small-minded, provincial, parochial, insular, opinionated, dogmatic, fanatical, extremist, illiberal, uncharitable, redneck, chauvinistic, jingoistic, racist, racialist, sexist, ageist, xenophobic, anti-Semitic
🖃 tolerant

intonation *n*
modulation, tone, accentuation, emphasis, stress, inflection, pitch, timbre, lilt, cadence

intone *v*
chant, croon, intonate, monotone, enunciate, pronounce, recite, sing, say, speak, voice, utter
FORMAL declaim, incant

intoxicate *n*
1 MAKE DRUNK, befuddle, fuddle, stupefy
FORMAL inebriate
2 EXCITE, elate, exhilarate, stimulate, thrill, animate, enthuse, inspire, inflame

intoxicated *adj*
1 DRUNK, drunken, under the influence
FORMAL inebriated, crapulent, ebriose
COLLOQ. merry, tight, tipsy, tiddly, tiddled, well-oiled, blotto, drunk as a lord/newt, drunk as a piper, sloshed, stewed, blind drunk, roaring drunk, the worse for drink, soused, squiffy, happy, legless, plastered, sozzled, pickled, bibulous, woozy, one over the eight, under the table, bevvied, having had a few, tired and emotional, high, footless, full, half-cut, obfuscated, pickled, pie-eyed, sow-drunk, under the weather, the worse for wear, steaming; *Irish* jarred; *Scot & Irish* stocious
SLANG stoned, tanked up, loaded, lit up, canned, paralytic, smashed, pissed, bombed, wasted, ripped, hammered, wrecked, stinko, whiffled, whistled, bonkers, bottled, Brahms and Liszt, juiced (up), in liquor, liquored, maggoty, mortal, up the pole; (*vulgar*) arseholed, rat-arsed; *N Am* crocked, moon-eyed; *Aust* inky, inked; *Aust & NZ* shickered
OLD SLANG corked, moppy
2 EXCITED, elated, exhilarated, thrilled, moved, stirred, stimulated, enthusiastic, worked up, in high spirits
COLLOQ. carried away
🖃 1 sober, abstinent

intoxicating *adj*
1 *intoxicating liquor*
alcoholic, strong, stimulant
FORMAL inebriant
COLLOQ. going to your head
2 EXCITING, stimulating, heady, exhilarating, thrilling, stirring, dramatic, rousing, moving, enthralling, inspiring
🖃 1 sobering

intoxication *n*
1 DRUNKENNESS, intemperance, alcoholism, hard/serious drinking, debauchery, dipsomania
TECHNICAL methysis
FORMAL inebriation, inebriety, insobriety, intoxication, crapulence
COLLOQ. bibulousness, tipsiness

2 EXCITEMENT, elation, exhilaration, thrill, pleasure, animation, enthusiasm, stimulation, euphoria, rapture
E3 1 sobriety

intractability n
unmanageableness, uncontrollableness, ungovernability, unco-operativeness, unamenability, waywardness, stubbornness, obstinacy, perverseness, perversity, awkwardness, pig-headedness, indiscipline, incorrigibility, cantankerousness, contrariness
FORMAL obduracy
E3 amenability

intractable adj
unmanageable, uncontrollable, unyielding, unbending, unco-operative, undisciplined, ungovernable, unamenable, wild, unruly, obstinate, perverse, self-willed, wilful, wayward, pig-headed, stubborn, disobedient, awkward, difficult, fractious, headstrong, cantankerous, contrary
FORMAL intransigent, obdurate, refractory
E3 amenable

intransigence n
stubbornness, obstinacy, relentlessness, irreconcilability, implacability, determination, toughness, tenacity, inflexibility, pig-headedness
FORMAL intractability, obduracy
COLLOQ. bloody-mindedness
E3 amenability, flexibility

intransigent adj
stubborn, obstinate, uncompromising, unamenable, unbending, unpersuadable, unyielding, unbudgeable, unrelenting, relentless, inexorable, immovable, irreconcilable, implacable, inflexible, pig-headed, hardline, determined, rigid, tenacious, tough
FORMAL intractable, obdurate
COLLOQ. uppity, bloody-minded
E3 amenable, flexible

intrepid adj
bold, daring, brave, courageous, plucky, valiant, audacious, lion-hearted, fearless, dauntless, undaunted, undismayed, unafraid, unflinching, stout-hearted, spirited, stalwart, gallant, heroic
FORMAL doughty, valorous
COLLOQ. gutsy, spunky, gritty
E3 cowardly, timid, afraid

intrepidness n
boldness, bravery, daring, intrepidity, audacity, valour, courage, heroism, dauntlessness, fearlessness, gallantry, lion-heartedness, stout-heartedness, undauntedness, pluck, prowess, spirit, nerve
FORMAL doughtiness, fortitude
COLLOQ. guts, grit
E3 cowardice, timidity

intricacy n
complexity, complexness, complexedness, complication, intricateness, elaborateness, entanglement, sophistication, involvement, knottiness, obscurity, enigma, involution
FORMAL convolution(s)
E3 simplicity, straightforwardness

intricate adj
complex, complicated, elaborate, sophisticated, involved, tortuous, tangled, entangled, ravelled, knotty, twisty, perplexing, baffling, puzzling, difficult, enigmatic, fancy, ornate, rococo
FORMAL convoluted
E3 simple, plain, straightforward

intrigue n, v
◆ n
1 PLOT, scheme, conspiracy, conniving, manoeuvre,

stratagem, artifice, ruse, wile, trickery, cabal, double-dealing, junta, web
OLD consult, courtcraft, brigue
FORMAL collusion, machination
COLLOQ. sharp practice, dodge, dirty trick
2 ROMANCE, liaison, affair, love affair, amour, intimacy, affaire, gallantry
◆ v
1 FASCINATE, arouse your curiosity, rivet, tantalize, attract, pull, draw, charm, captivate, absorb, interest, puzzle
2 PLOT, scheme, conspire, connive, manoeuvre, manipulate, work the oracle, traffic, undermine
OLD collogue, pack, brigue, practise against
FORMAL machinate
E3 1 bore

intriguer n
plotter, schemer, conspirator, collaborator, conniver, Machiavellian, intrigant(e)
FORMAL machinator
COLLOQ. wangler, wheeler-dealer, wire-puller

intriguing adj
fascinating, appealing, charming, absorbing, riveting, compelling, captivating, diverting, exciting, interesting, beguiling, attractive, tantalizing, titillating, puzzling
E3 boring, uninteresting, dull

intrinsic adj
basic, central, essential, fundamental, natural, underlying, built-in, in-built, inborn, inbred, interior, inherent, inward, native, indigenous, congenital, constitutional, elemental, genuine
E3 extrinsic

intrinsically adv
inherently, basically, fundamentally, centrally, essentially, inwardly, constituently, integrally, constitutionally

introduce v
1 INSTITUTE, begin, start, establish, found, originate, organize, develop, inaugurate, launch, usher in, open, bring in, initiate, put/set in motion, instigate
FORMAL commence
2 PUT FORWARD, advance, submit, offer, propose, suggest, float
3 PRESENT, announce, acquaint, familiarize
4 PREFACE, precede, begin, start, lead in, lead into, open
FORMAL commence
E3 1 end, conclude **2** remove, take away **4** conclude, end, finish

introduction n
1 INSTITUTION, beginning, start, establishment, origination, organization, development, inauguration, launch, presentation, debut, initiation, baptism
FORMAL commencement
2 FOREWORD, preface, preamble, prologue, preliminaries, front matter, overture, prelude, lead-in, opening
FORMAL prolegomenon, exordium, proem
COLLOQ. intro
3 PRESENTATION, announcement, familiarization, acquainting
COLLOQ. Aust knock-down
4 BASICS, fundamentals, essentials, rudiments, first principles
E3 1 removal, withdrawal, termination **2** appendix, conclusion

introductory adj
preliminary, preparatory, opening, inaugural, first, beginning, starting, initial, early, elementary, basic, fundamental, essential, rudimentary
FORMAL prefatory, initiatory, precursory, exordial, isagogic

introspection n
self-examination, contemplation, pensiveness, thoughtfulness, brooding, self-analysis, self-centredness,

self-observation, soul-searching, heart-searching, introversion
COLLOQ. navel-gazing, navel-contemplation

introspective *adj*
inward-looking, contemplative, meditative, pensive, thoughtful, brooding, musing, introverted, subjective, self-centred, self-absorbed, self-examining, self-analysing, self-observing, reserved, withdrawn
🔁 outward-looking

introverted *adj*
introspective, inward-looking, self-centred, self-absorbed, self-examining, introspective, withdrawn, shy, reserved, quiet
🔁 extroverted

intrude *v*
interrupt, meddle, interfere, violate, invade, infringe, impinge, encroach, trespass; *Scot* sorn
FORMAL interject, obtrude, interlope
COLLOQ. gatecrash, barge in, chip in, butt in
🔁 withdraw, stand back

intruder *n*
trespasser, prowler, burglar, raider, housebreaker, robber, pilferer, thief, unwelcome guest, invader, infiltrator
FORMAL interloper
COLLOQ. gatecrasher

intrusion *n*
interruption, interference, meddling, violation, infringement, encroachment, trespass, invasion
FORMAL incursion, obtrusion
COLLOQ. gatecrashing
🔁 withdrawal

intrusive *adj*
disturbing, interfering, irritating, annoying, troublesome, invasive, obtrusive, interrupting, trespassing, meddlesome, uncalled-for, unwanted, unwelcome, uninvited, forward, impertinent, officious, presumptuous, prying, pushy
FORMAL importunate
COLLOQ. nos(e)y, snooping, go-getting
🔁 unintrusive, welcome

intuition *n*
instinct, sixth sense, perception, discernment, insight, hunch, feeling, extrasensory perception, ESP, premonition, belief, anticipation, light of nature
FORMAL presentiment
COLLOQ. gut feeling, feeling in your bones
🔁 reasoning

intuitive *adj*
instinctive, intuitional, spontaneous, involuntary, automatic, innate, inborn, unlearned, untaught
🔁 reasoned

intuitively *adv*
instinctively, by instinct, spontaneously, automatically, innately, by the seat of your pants

inundate *v*
flood, deluge, swamp, engulf, submerge, soak, immerse, drown, saturate, bury, overwhelm, overburden, overrun, overflow

inundation *n*
flood, deluge, swamp, overflow, torrent, spate, tidal wave, excess, surplus, glut
🔁 trickle

inure *v*
accustom, familiarize, acclimatize, harden, temper, strengthen, desensitize, toughen, train
FORMAL habituate

invade *v*
1 *invade a country*

enter (by force), penetrate, infiltrate, burst in, descend on, attack, assault, raid, seize, storm, maraud, plunder, pillage, occupy, take over, march into, conquer, overrun, swarm over, infest, pervade
2 *invade someone's privacy*
intrude, encroach, infringe, violate, trespass, interrupt
FORMAL obtrude
🔁 withdraw, evacuate

Synonym nuances
sense 1
Penetrate can be widely used of breaking through defences, whereas **infiltrate** has more to do with gradually permeating, and has connotations of stealth or underhandedness: *microchips have infiltrated the home and the office.* **Pervade** also suggests a gradual, subtle invasion and diffusion: *a depressing atmosphere pervaded the small room.*

  The term **burst in** is suggestive of force but also of an element of surprise, whereas **descend on** is appropriate to suggest overwhelming by force of numbers: *the press descended on the town.* The terms **overrun** and **swarm over** also imply uncontrollably large numbers: *the Mediterranean is overrun with tourists*, while **infest** is an even more marked term with its connotations of harmful pests: *a mite that infests various animals.* The verb **storm** also suggests large numbers of invaders, but returns to the idea of a sudden and forced entry.

  Raid might be used of making a swift incursion, usually for the purpose of procurement, but **seize** would be appropriate for taking control: *they seized three military bases.* **Occupy** is similar in sense, but has less inherent implication of force: *the occupied territories*, while **conquer** would again imply force and an element of subjugation. The terms **maraud**, **plunder** and **pillage** would be reserved for invading in search of loot: *marauding bandits.*

---

invader *n*
aggressor, attacker, assailant, raider, plunderer, marauder, pillager, intruder, trespasser, infringer

invalid[1] *n, adj*
♦ *n*
visit an invalid in hospital
patient, sufferer, convalescent, chronic
FORMAL valetudinarian
♦ *adj*
sick, ill, unwell, poorly, ailing, sickly, weak, feeble, frail, infirm, disabled, bedridden
FORMAL debilitated, valetudinarian
🔁 healthy

invalid[2] *adj*
1 *an invalid argument*
false, unsound, ill-founded, unfounded, baseless, groundless, unjustified, unsubstantiated, untenable, unacceptable, unwarranted, illogical, irrational, unscientific, wrong, incorrect, weak, mistaken, erroneous
FORMAL fallacious
2 ILLEGAL, null, void, null and void, worthless, abolished, cancelled, quashed, overturned, expired; *Aust* informal
FORMAL inoperative, revoked, rescinded, nullified
🔁 **1** valid, sound **2** legal, binding

invalidate *v*
annul, cancel, quash, void, veto, discredit, negate, undo, overrule, overthrow, undermine, weaken
FORMAL abrogate, nullify, rescind, vitiate, revoke, terminate
🔁 validate

invalidity *n*
incorrectness, falsity, irrationality, unsoundness, sophism, speciousness, illogicality, inconsistency, voidness
FORMAL fallaciousness, fallacy

invaluable *adj*
priceless, inestimable, incalculable, indispensable, critical, crucial, precious, valuable, costly, useful
E3 worthless, cheap

invariable *adj*
fixed, set, unvarying, unchanging, unchangeable, unalterable, changeless, permanent, constant, steady, consistent, stable, unwavering, uniform, rigid, inflexible, habitual, regular
FORMAL immutable, invariant
E3 variable, changeable

invariably *adv*
always, without exception, without fail, unfailingly, consistently, regularly, repeatedly, constantly, habitually, inevitably
E3 never

invasion *n*
1 *an invasion of a country*
attack, offensive, onslaught, raid, foray, breach, occupation, storming, penetration, infiltration
FORMAL incursion
2 *invasion of privacy*
interference, interruption, intrusion, encroachment, infringement, violation
E3 1 withdrawal, evacuation

invective *n*
abuse, denunciation, reproach, scolding, reprimand, rebuke, tirade, diatribe, recrimination, sarcasm, tongue-lashing
FORMAL censure, revilement, fulmination, berating, castigation, obloquy, philippic, vilification, vituperation, contumely
E3 praise

inveigh *v*
criticize, blame, condemn, upbraid, denounce, scold, rail, recriminate, reproach, sound off, tongue-lash
FORMAL censure, fulminate, castigate, berate, lambast, expostulate, vituperate
E3 praise

inveigle *v*
cajole, persuade, beguile, coax, allure, lure, seduce, entrap, ensnare, entice, wile, decoy, manipulate, manoeuvre, lead on, wheedle
COLLOQ. bamboozle, con, sweet-talk

invent *v*
1 CONCEIVE, think up, design, discover, create, plan, originate, innovate, be the brainchild of, pioneer, formulate, frame, devise, contrive, improvise, coin, come up with, hit upon, dream up, fabricate, mint
2 *invent an excuse*
make up, concoct, cook up, trump up, imagine, dream up, manufacture, fable
TECHNICAL confabulate
FORMAL feign
SLANG swing the lead

invention *n*
1 *her latest invention*
design, creation, brainchild, innovation, discovery, development, idea, concept, construction, device, machine, system, contrivance, gadget
COLLOQ. baby
2 *the invention of the steam engine*
design, creation, discovery, development, innovation, contriving, origination, coinage, contrivance
FORMAL excogitation
3 LIE, falsehood, falsification, untruth, deceit, fabrication, concoction, fake, forgery, fiction, fantasy, myth, figment, figment of your imagination
COLLOQ. tall story, fib
4 INVENTIVENESS, imagination, creativity, innovation,

originality, ingenuity, resourcefulness, skill, artistry, talent, gift, inspiration, genius
OLD wit
E3 3 truth

inventive *adj*
imaginative, creative, innovative, original, ingenious, resourceful, fertile, skilful, inspired, artistic, talented, gifted, clever

inventiveness *n*
creativity, imaginativeness, imagination, innovation, innovativeness, originality, resourcefulness, skill, enterprise, inspiration, power, gift, talent, skill

inventor *n*
designer, discoverer, creator, originator, innovator, deviser, author, architect, developer, maker, producer, framer, scientist, engineer, father, mother

inventory *n*
list, listing, checklist, record, register, catalogue, tally, file, account, description, schedule, roll, roster, equipment, supply, stock

inverse *adj, n*
 ◆ *adj*
inverted, upside down, transposed, reversed, opposite, other, contrary, counter, reciprocal, reverse, retrograde, converse, obverse
TECHNICAL antistrophic
E3 converse
 ◆ *n*
opposite, contrary, reverse, converse, obverse
COLLOQ. the other side of the coin

inversion *n*
opposite, reversal, reverse, converse, transposal, transposition, contrary
TECHNICAL hysteron-proteron
FORMAL antithesis, contrariety, contraposition

invert *v*
upturn, turn upside down, turn back to front, turn inside out, turn around, overturn, capsize, turn turtle, upset, transpose, reverse
E3 right

invertebrate

Invertebrates include:

SPONGES:	arrow worm	fairy shrimp
calcareous	blood fluke	fiddler crab
glass	bristle worm	fish louse
horny	earthworm	goose barnacle
JELLYFISH, CORALS AND SEA ANEMONES:	eelworm	hermit crab
	flatworm	krill
box jellyfish	fluke	lobster
dead-men's fingers	hookworm	mantis shrimp
	leech	mussel shrimp
Portuguese man-of-war	liver fluke	pill bug
	lugworm	prawn
sea cucumber	peanut worm	sand hopper
sea gooseberry	pinworm	seed shrimp
sea pansy	ragworm	spider crab
sea wasp	ribbonworm	spiny lobster
Venus's girdle	roundworm	tadpole shrimp
ECHINODERMS:	sea mouse	water flea
brittle star	tapeworm	whale louse
crown-of-thorns	threadworm	woodlouse
feather star	velvet worm	**ARTHROPODS:**
sand dollar	**CRUSTACEANS:**	centipede
sea lily	acorn barnacle	millipede
sea urchin	barnacle	
starfish	brine shrimp	
WORMS:	crayfish	
annelid worm	daphnia	

See also **butterfly; insect; mollusc; moth**.

---

invest v

1 SPEND, lay out, put in, sink, subsidize, fund, tie up, lock up, sink

2 *invest time/energy in something*
spend, put in, devote, dedicate, give, place, contribute

3 PROVIDE, supply, give, endow, grant, entrust, vest, imbue, endue, empower, authorize, sanction, mandate, create, dignify, clothe, gown, robe
OLD beglamour
FORMAL confer, bestow, enrobe

4 *invest a person in authority*
induct, install, inaugurate, ordain, admit, crown, swear in, belt
OLD frock

investigate v
inquire into, look into, consider, examine, study, inspect, scrutinize, analyse, research, go into, delve into, probe, explore, search, sift, comb, trawl, pry out, spy
COLLOQ. check out, suss out, give the once-over, see how the land lies, see which way the wind is blowing, get to the bottom of, go over with a fine-tooth(ed) comb

investigation n
inquiry, inquest, hearing, consideration, examination, study, research, survey, review, inspection, scrutiny, analysis, probe, exploration, search, sifting, fact-finding mission/visit

investigative adj
fact-finding, investigating, inspecting, research, researching, analytical, exploratory
FORMAL heuristic, zetetic

investigator n
examiner, researcher, inquirer, reviewer, inspector, searcher, scrutineer, scrutinizer, analyst, analyser, explorer, prober, questioner, detective, private detective
COLLOQ. sleuth, private eye

investiture n
installation, induction, inauguration, investing, investment, ordination, coronation, enthronement, swearing-in, admission, instatement

investment n
asset, speculation, venture, stake, risk, contribution, outlay, expenditure, capital, venture capital, cash, savings, wealth, resources, money, funds, finance, principal, property, stock, reserve, transaction

inveterate adj
chronic, habitual, hardened, diehard, dyed-in-the-wool, entrenched, confirmed, established, hard-core, obstinate, incorrigible, incurable, irreformable, inured, addicted, long-standing
F3 impermanent

invidious adj
awkward, difficult, undesirable, unpleasant, objectionable, hateful, obnoxious, offensive, slighting, odious, repugnant, discriminating, discriminatory
FORMAL
F3 desirable, pleasant

invigilate v
supervise, oversee, watch (over), look after, keep an eye on, inspect, superintend, direct, be in charge of, be responsible for, be in control of, monitor

invigilation n
supervision, surveillance, care, charge, superintendence, oversight, running, direction, control, guidance, inspection

invigilator n
examiner, supervisor, overseer, inspector, superintendent, director, monitor

invigorate v
vitalize, energize, animate, enliven, liven up, quicken, strengthen, brace, motivate, stimulate, inspire, exhilarate, excite, rouse, renew, refresh, freshen, revitalize, rejuvenate
FORMAL fortify
COLLOQ. perk up, pep up, buck up, soup up, give a new lease of life to
F3 tire, weary, dishearten

invigorating adj
energizing, stimulating, refreshing, animating, exhilarating, fresh, bracing, uplifting, rejuvenating, quickening, vivifying, restorative, tonic, healthful, generous
FORMAL fortifying, inspiriting, salubrious
F3 tiring, disheartening, wearying

invincibility n
insuperability, impregnability, impenetrability, invulnerability, indestructibility, inviolability, unassailability, power, strength, force

invincible adj
unbeatable, unconquerable, insuperable, unsurmountable, undefeatable, unassailable, impregnable, impenetrable, invulnerable, indestructible, unyielding, unshak(e)able, all-powerful
FORMAL indomitable
F3 beatable, surmountable

inviolability n
inalienability, inviolableness, inviolacy, invulnerability, sacrosanctness, sanctity, sacredness, holiness
F3 violability

inviolable adj
inalienable, unalterable, untouchable, sacred, sacrosanct, holy, hallowed
FORMAL intemerate
F3 violable, alienable

inviolate adj
entire, intact, complete, whole, undisturbed, unbroken, unhurt, undamaged, unharmed, uninjured, untouched, unpolluted, unprofaned, undefiled, unstained, unsullied, unspoiled, stainless, pure, sacred, virgin
FORMAL intemerate
F3 sullied

invisible adj
unseen, unseeable, out of sight, hidden, concealed, blind, disguised, unnoticed, unobserved, inconspicuous, indiscernible, imperceptible, imperceivable, undetectable, indistinguishable, infinitesimal, microscopic, imaginary, non-existent, occulting, dematerialized, evaporated
OLD viewless; (*Shakesp*) sightless
F3 visible

invitation n
request, call, summons, bidding, petition, appeal, temptation, enticement, allurement, lure, bait, draw, attraction, encouragement, inducement, provocation, incitement, challenge, welcome, overture
FORMAL solicitation
COLLOQ. invite, come-on, come-hither, proposition

invite v

1 ASK, have round/over, entertain, call, summon, bid, press, will, petition, appeal, welcome, encourage, bring on, provoke, ask for, seek, look for
FORMAL request, solicit, request the pleasure of someone's company

2 ATTRACT, lead, draw, tempt, entice, allure, solicit, woo
COLLOQ. give the come-on to

inviting adj
welcoming, appealing, attractive, tempting, seductive, enticing, alluring, pleasing, pleasant, agreeable, delightful,

captivating, fascinating, enchanting, entrancing, intriguing, beguiling, bewitching, tantalizing, engaging, winning, irresistible
F3 uninviting, unappealing

invocation n
call, appeal, petition, prayer
TECHNICAL benediction, epiclesis
FORMAL request, supplication, solicitation, beseeching, entreaty, conjuration, imploration

invoice n
account, bill, statement of account, charges, reckoning

invoke v
1 *invoke God for help*
call upon, appeal to, petition, implore, beg, pray to
FORMAL request, supplicate, beseech, entreat, solicit, imprecate, conjure
2 *invoke a law*
turn to, resort to, have recourse to, make use of, cite, refer to

involuntary adj
1 SPONTANEOUS, unconscious, automatic, mechanical, reflex, instinctive, conditioned, impulsive, unthinking, blind, uncontrolled, unintentional
COLLOQ. knee-jerk
2 FORCED, compulsory, obligatory, compelled, coerced, reluctant, unwilling, against your wishes
FORMAL mandatory
F3 1 deliberate, intentional

involve v
1 REQUIRE, mean, assume, presuppose, imply, entail, necessitate, include, incorporate, encompass, cover, take in, affect, concern, cost
FORMAL denote, embrace, comprehend, connote
2 IMPLICATE, incriminate, draw in, let yourself in for, mix up, embroil, associate, connect, include, count in, cause to take part, compromise, embarrass, entangle, walk into; *Scot* wind someone a bonny pirn
OLD wrap
FORMAL inculpate
COLLOQ. mess with/in
3 ENGAGE, interest, occupy, absorb, engross, immerse, preoccupy, hold, grip, rivet, concern, commit
COLLOQ. dip into
F3 1 exclude

Synonym nuances
sense 1
Require suggests that the involvement of something is necessary: *a level of precision was required*, while **mean** and **entail** would be more appropriate for something resultant: *taking complete power meant silencing more liberal voices*; *the changes in housing policy entailed steep rent rises*. Both **assume** and **presuppose** are suggestive of taking certain things for granted: *this plan presupposes public support*, unlike **imply** which suggests a resultant insinuation.
  Incorporate, like **include** and **take in**, suggests being a part of, usually by design: *a demanding schedule which took in several matches and the World Cup*; *the provisions were incorporated into the act*. **Cover** and **encompass** also suggest total inclusion: *the extensive and diverse behaviour encompassed by the term 'crime'.*
  The word **affect** would be appropriate to refer to influencing or touching on: *moving house affects many areas of your life.* You might use **concern** to suggest personal involvement: *much of my work has been concerned with bereavement counselling*; *these problems do not concern you.* **Cost** is inherently negative in that it suggests loss is involved: *his addiction to work cost him his marriage.*

---

involved adj
1 CONCERNED, associated, taking part, implicated, incriminated, mixed up, participating
OLD (*Shakesp*) plighted
FORMAL inculpated
COLLOQ. in on
2 OCCUPIED, engaged, interested, absorbed, engrossed, preoccupied, immersed, caught up, held, gripped, riveted
3 *an involved explanation*
complicated, complex, intricate, difficult, elaborate, tangled, jumbled, knotty, tortuous, confusing, confused
FORMAL convoluted
F3 1 uninvolved **3** simple

involvement n
concern, interest, responsibility, association, connection, participation, contribution, action, share, part, implication, entanglement, attachment

invulnerability n
safety, security, strength, unassailability, impenetrability, invincibility, impregnability, inviolability, insusceptibility
F3 vulnerability

invulnerable adj
safe, secure, unassailable, impenetrable, impervious, invincible, indestructible
F3 vulnerable

inward adj
turned-in, incoming, entering, inside, interior, internal, inner, innermost, inmost, hidden, intrinsic, personal, private, intimate, secret, confidential, heartfelt, homefelt, infelt
TECHNICAL involute
FORMAL incurrent, introrse
F3 outward, external

inwardly adv
inside, to yourself, within, at heart, in your heart of hearts, deep down, deep inside you, privately, secretly
OLD inly
F3 externally, outwardly

inwards adv
inside, within, inward, inwardly, indoors, towards the interior

iota n
scrap, bit, mite, jot, whit, speck, trace, hint, grain, morsel, fraction, particle, atom
COLLOQ. tad

irascibility n
snappishness, bad temper, cantankerousness, irritability, irritation, petulance, impatience, ill-temper, crossness, shortness, testiness, touchiness, fieriness
COLLOQ. crabbiness, edginess
F3 placidness

irascible adj
quick-tempered, short-tempered, bad-tempered, ill-natured, ill-tempered, hot-tempered, cantankerous, petulant, irritable, prickly, testy, touchy, choleric, cross, hasty
FORMAL querulous, iracund, iracundulous
COLLOQ. crabbed, crabby, narky, ratty
F3 placid

irate adj
annoyed, irritated, indignant, up in arms, angry, enraged, furious, infuriated, incensed, worked up, fuming, raging, ranting, livid, exasperated, vexed
COLLOQ. mad, hopping mad, hot under the collar, steamed up, up in arms
SLANG pissed off
F3 calm, composed

irately adv
angrily, crossly, indignantly, furiously, reproachfully,

acrimoniously, resentfully, bitterly
COLLOQ. in a huff

ire n
anger, wrath, exasperation, annoyance, fury, rage, indignation, passion, displeasure, choler
⊟ calmness

iridescent adj
shimmering, sparkling, multicoloured, rainbow, rainbow-coloured, rainbow-like, prismatic, dazzling, glittering, shot, pearly, polychromatic
FORMAL opalescent, variegated

irk v
annoy, anger, exasperate, incense, infuriate, irritate, provoke, put out, ruffle, get, get to, vex, weary, nettle, distress, gall, disgust, rile
COLLOQ. aggravate, wind up, get at, bug, drive mad, drive crazy, drive bananas, drive up the wall, drive round the bend/twist, miff, needle, nettle, make someone's blood boil, make someone see red, rattle someone's cage, ruffle someone's feathers, raise someone's dander, make someone's hackles rise, make sparks fly, get under someone's skin, get up someone's nose, get on someone's wick
SLANG piss someone off
⊟ please

irksome adj
annoying, irritating, infuriating, exasperating, vexing, vexatious, wearisome, bothersome, burdensome, disagreeable, tiresome, troublesome, trying, tedious, boring
COLLOQ. aggravating, confounded, infernal
⊟ pleasing

iron adj, v
• adj
rigid, inflexible, adamant, determined, hard, steely, tough, strong, firm, uncompromising
⊟ pliable, weak
Related adjectives: ferrous, ferreous
• v
press, smooth, flatten
■ **iron out**
resolve, settle, sort out, straighten out, clear up, put right, reconcile, harmonize, deal with, get rid of, eradicate, eliminate

ironic, ironical adj
sarcastic, sardonic, scornful, contemptuous, derisive, sneering, scoffing, ridiculing, ridiculous, mocking, satirical, wry, paradoxical
COLLOQ. rich

irons n
chains, bonds, fetters, shackles, trammels, manacles

irony n
sarcasm, mockery, ridicule, scorn, satire, paradox, contrariness
TECHNICAL asteism, antiphrasis, enantiosis
FORMAL incongruity
COLLOQ. sting in the tail

irradiate v
brighten, enlighten, light up, lighten, illume, illuminate, illumine, expose, radiate, shine on

irrational adj
unreasonable, unreasoning, unsound, illogical, inconsistent, invalid, groundless, implausible, arbitrary, ridiculous, absurd, crazy, wild, foolish, silly, senseless, beastlike, brute, brutish, nonsensical, unwise, paranoid, phobic, beside yourself, taken leave of your senses
⊟ rational, reasonable

irrationality n
unreasonableness, unreason, unsoundness, illogicality,

groundlessness, absurdity, ridiculousness, senselessness, preposterousness, madness, lunacy, insanity
⊟ rationality

irreconcilable adj
incompatible, opposed, contrary, opposite, at odds, conflicting, clashing, contradictory, inconsistent, uncompromising, hardline, inflexible, implacable, inexorable
FORMAL incongruous, intransigent
⊟ reconcilable

irrecoverable adj
irretrievable, lost, unrecoverable, unsavable, irredeemable, irreclaimable, irremediable, irreparable, unsalvageable
⊟ recoverable

irredeemable adj
incurable, incorrigible, irreparable, irrevocable, irretrievable, beyond hope, past hope

irrefutable adj
undeniable, incontrovertible, indisputable, incontestable, unquestionable, beyond doubt/question, indubitable, unanswerable, certain, sure, definite, positive, decisive

irregular adj, n
• adj
1 ROUGH, bumpy, lumpy, uneven, pitted, crooked, ragged, jagged, asymmetric, lopsided
2 VARIABLE, fluctuating, wavering, unsteady, uneven, shaky, erratic, fitful, intermittent, sporadic, spasmodic, occasional, random, haphazard, disorganized, fragmentary, disorderly, unmethodical, unsystematic, inconsistent
3 ABNORMAL, unconventional, unorthodox, unofficial, improper, unusual, exceptional, anomalous, out of order, aberrant, extraordinary, freak, odd, strange, peculiar
4 DISHONEST, lawless, against the law/rules, deceitful, fraudulent, false, cheating, unprincipled, immoderate, indecent, improper, unscrupulous, corrupt, disreputable, dishonourable, devious
FORMAL perfidious, mendacious, duplicitous
COLLOQ. crooked, shady, bent, shifty, fishy, iffy
⊟ 1 smooth, level, uniform 2 regular 3 conventional 4 honest
• n
guerrilla, freedom fighter, terrorist, resistance fighter, partisan, sniper, guerrillero, *franc-tireur*, haiduk, bushwhacker, *maquisard*

irregularity n
1 ROUGHNESS, bumpiness, unevenness, raggedness, jaggedness, crookedness, asymmetry, lopsidedness, lumpiness
2 VARIABILITY, fluctuation, wavering, fitfulness, intermittence, spasm, occasionalness, randomness, haphazardness, disorderliness, unpunctuality, inconsistency, unsteadiness, uncertainty, inconstancy, disorganization, patchiness
3 ABNORMALITY, unconventionality, unusualness, unorthodoxy, anomaly, deviation, breach, aberration, oddity, peculiarity, eccentricity, freak
FORMAL singularity
4 DISHONESTY, lawlessness, deceit, fraudulence, fraud, cheating, malpractice, impropriety, misconduct, falsehood, falsity, criminality, insincerity, untruthfulness, treachery, double-dealing, corruption, unscrupulousness, trickery, chicanery, sharp practice
FORMAL duplicity, improbity, perfidy
COLLOQ. crookedness, shadiness, dirty trick
⊟ 1 smoothness, levelness 2 regularity 3 conventionality

irregularly adv
occasionally, now and again, off and on, unevenly, spasmodically, haphazardly, intermittently, jerkily,

unmethodically, anyhow, disconnectedly, eccentrically, erratically, fitfully, by/in fits and starts
E-I regularly

irrelevance *n*
inappropriateness, inaptness, unimportance, unrelatedness, inconsequence, irrelevancy, inapplicability, digression, tangent
FORMAL inappositeness, extraneousness, inconsequence
COLLOQ. red herring
E-I relevance, bearing

irrelevant *adj*
immaterial, beside/off the point, inapplicable, inappropriate, inapt, unimportant, out of place, inept, having no bearing, unrelated, unconnected, peripheral, tangential, beside the mark/question
FORMAL inapposite, extraneous, inconsequent, ungermane, irrelative
COLLOQ. neither here nor there, not coming into it, making no difference, not matter, going off at a tangent
E-I relevant

irreligious *adj*
atheistic, unbelieving, ungodly, unreligious, godless, undevout, unholy, unrighteous, agnostic, sceptical, heathenish, pagan, heathen, heretical, sacrilegious, iconoclastic, impious, irreverent, blasphemous, free-thinking, profane, rationalistic, sinful, wicked
FORMAL nullifidian
E-I pious, religious

Synonym nuances
Atheistic is a fairly straightforward synonym for not believing in a god, while **unbelieving** is perhaps more suggestive of not being convinced by a particular religion: *although his family was Catholic, he remained unbelieving*. **Ungodly** and **godless** are more judgemental, suggesting a lack of moral guidance and virtue: *her ungodly want of duty*; *their godless pleasures*, while the more old-fashioned **unrighteous** conveys this idea more explicitly. **Unholy** can literally suggest a lack of sanctity: *unholy ground*, but is used more generally to imply something is unconscionable: *an unholy alliance*.
  Agnostic and **sceptical** are uncritical terms relating to a tendency not to believe in unseen phenomena, while **rationalistic** can be applied to those who ascribe a practical explanation to any apparent miraculous phenomena. **Free-thinking**, on the other hand, would be used of someone who rejects religious authority, and the tone may depend on the viewpoint of the speaker.
  The terms **pagan**, **heathen** and **heathenish**, although literally meaning irreligious, can all be implicative of being primitive or uncultured: *marauding heathen tribes*. **Heretical**, which would appropriately refer to holding a belief which is at odds with an authorized religion, also tends to have negative connotations.
  Impious, **irreverent** and **blasphemous** make the inherent accusation of a lack of, or even contempt for, religious veneration: *I had no wish to indulge in such blasphemous, heretical talk*. Similarly, **sacrilegious** implies a display of extreme disrespect for anything holy. **Iconoclastic** might be used to describe an attack on established beliefs: *the book may be iconoclastic but it is not just a parody of faith*. **Profane**, although literally meaning secular: *the sacred and the profane*, can also contain the idea of being contemptuous: *profane songs*.

---

irremediable *adj*
irreparable, irretrievable, irrecoverable, irreversible, remediless, irredeemable, incurable, inoperable, incorrigible, terminal, unmedicinable, deadly, fatal, final, hopeless, mortal
E-I remediable

irremovable *adj*
durable, immovable, indestructible, ineradicable, ingrained, inoperable, fast, fixed, set, stuck, permanent, persistent, rooted, obstinate
FORMAL obdurate
E-I removable

irreparable *adj*
irreversible, irreclaimable, irrecoverable, irremediable, irretrievable, incurable, unrepairable
E-I recoverable, remediable

irreplaceable *adj*
indispensable, essential, vital, unique, priceless, precious, peerless, matchless, unmatched, special
E-I replaceable

irrepressible *adj*
lively, energetic, uninhibited, buoyant, effervescent, animated, vivacious, resilient, boisterous, uncontrollable, unrestrainable, ungovernable, unstoppable, insuppressible, uncontainable
FORMAL ebullient
COLLOQ. bubbly

irreproachable *adj*
irreprehensible, blameless, unblamable, innocent, beyond reproach, unimpeachable, faultless, guiltless, flawless, impeccable, perfect, unblemished, immaculate, stainless, spotless, sinless, pure
E-I blameworthy; *formal* culpable

irresistible *adj*
1 *irresistible desire*
overwhelming, overpowering, forceful, unavoidable, inevitable, inescapable, inexorable, unpreventable, uncontrollable, irrepressible, potent, compelling, imperative, pressing, urgent
OLD (*Shakesp*) opposeless
2 *irresistible beauty*
tempting, enticing, alluring, captivating, tantalizing, seductive, ravishing, enchanting, charming, fascinating
E-I 1 resistible, avoidable **2** unattractive, repulsive

irresolute *adj*
indecisive, hesitating, hesitant, unsure, uncertain, doubtful, dubious, ambivalent, wavering, fluctuating, shifting, dithering, variable, weak, faint-hearted, fickle, undecided, unsettled, undetermined, unstable, unsteady, half-hearted, tentative
FORMAL vacillating
COLLOQ. shilly-shallying, pussyfooting, in two minds, (sitting) on the fence
E-I resolute, decisive

irrespective
■ **irrespective of**
regardless of, disregarding, no matter, without considering, ignoring, not affecting, however, whatever, whichever, whoever, never mind
FORMAL notwithstanding

irresponsible *adj*
unreliable, untrustworthy, careless, negligent, thoughtless, unwise, heedless, ill-considered, rash, reckless, wild, carefree, flighty, fly-by-night, erratic, scatterbrained, light-hearted, immature
FORMAL injudicious
E-I responsible, dependable, cautious

irretrievable *adj*
irreparable, irrecoverable, irreversible, irredeemable, irremediable, unrecoverable, unrecallable, lost, hopeless, unsalvageable, damned
FORMAL irrevocable
E-I recoverable, reversible

irretrievably *adv*
irreparably, irrecoverably, irreversibly, irredeemably, hopelessly
FORMAL irrevocably

irreverence n
1 IMPIETY, godlessness, ungodliness, irreligion, heresy, profanity, sacrilege, blasphemy
2 DISRESPECT, disrespectfulness, discourtesy, rudeness, impoliteness, insolence, impudence, impertinence, mockery, flippancy, levity
COLLOQ. sauce, cheek, cheekiness
Ε3 1, 2 reverence

irreverent adj
1 IMPIOUS, godless, ungodly, irreligious, heretical, profane, sacrilegious, blasphemous
OLD unreverend
2 DISRESPECTFUL, discourteous, rude, impolite, impudent, impertinent, insolent, mocking, flippant
COLLOQ. cheeky, saucy
Ε3 1 reverent 2 respectful, deferential

irreversible adj
irrevocable, unalterable, final, permanent, lasting, irreparable, irremediable, irretrievable, incurable, unrectifiable, hopeless
Ε3 reversible, remediable, curable

irrevocable adj
unalterable, unchangeable, changeless, invariable, final, fixed, settled, predetermined, irreversible, irretrievable
FORMAL immutable
Ε3 alterable, flexible, reversible

irrevocably adv
irreparably, insuperably, unavoidably, inevitably, inescapably, hopelessly

irrigate v
water, flood, inundate, wet, soak, deluge, moisten, dampen, spray, sprinkle

irritability n
crossness, bad temper, ill-temper, impatience, grumpiness, prickliness, touchiness, fretfulness, edge, edginess, hypersensitivity, testiness, tetchiness, irascibility, peevishness, petulance, fractiousness
COLLOQ. rattiness, crabbiness, stroppiness
Ε3 cheerfulness, complacence, good humour, bonhomie

irritable adj
cross, bad-tempered, ill-tempered, quick-tempered, grumpy, crusty, cantankerous, testy, tetchy, short-tempered, hot-blooded, snappish, snappy, short, impatient, touchy, thin-skinned, hypersensitive, prickly, peevish, fretful, fractious, irascible, out of temper, splenetic, sore, fiery, peppery, hasty, nettlesome, spiky, on edge; *Scot* capernoity; *NAm* scratchy
OLD gustful, liverish, livery
COLLOQ. edgy, crotchety, crabby, ratty, stroppy, shirty, feisty, humpy, narky, riley; *Can* chippy
SLANG *NAm* peckish
Ε3 good-tempered, cheerful

irritant n
annoyance, nuisance, trouble, bother, menace, provocation, vexation, goad
COLLOQ. pain, thorn in the flesh
Ε3 pleasure, sweetness

irritate v
1 ANNOY, bother, harass, rouse, provoke, rile, irk, vex, goad, nettle, anger, enrage, infuriate, incense, exasperate, put out, grate, jar
COLLOQ. aggravate, wind up, get at, bug, drive mad, drive crazy, drive bananas, drive up the wall, drive round the bend/twist, miff, needle, nettle, make someone's blood boil, make someone see red, rattle someone's cage, ruffle someone's feathers, raise someone's dander, make someone's hackles rise, make sparks fly, get up someone's skin, get up someone's nose, get on someone's wick
SLANG piss someone off

2 INFLAME, chafe, rub, fret, hurt, tickle, itch
Ε3 1 please, gratify

irritated adj
annoyed, bothered, angry, cross, exasperated, irked, irritable, nettled, vexed, ruffled, roused, riled, impatient, uptight, harassed, flustered, discomposed, displeased, piqued
FORMAL exacerbated
COLLOQ. aggravated, cross, ratty, uptight, edgy, mad, hopping mad, raving mad, seeing red, in a lather, disgruntled, up in arms, hot under the collar, stroppy, in a strop, choked, fit to be tied, on the warpath, in a paddy; *N Am* ticked off; *Aust* spewy, ropable; *Aust & NZ* crooked
SLANG pissed off; *NAm* pissed
Ε3 composed, gratified, pleased

irritating adj
1 ANNOYING, infuriating, maddening, troublesome, bothersome, irksome, tiresome, grating, worrisome, vexatious, vexing, disturbing, upsetting, nagging, displeasing, galling, provoking, thorny, trying
COLLOQ. aggravating, pesky, confounded, infernal
2 ABRASIVE, rubbing, chafing, sore, ticklish, itchy
Ε3 1 pleasant, pleasing

irritation n
1 express your irritation
displeasure, dissatisfaction, annoyance, aggravation, provocation, anger, vexation, pique, indignation, fury, exasperation, irritability, crossness, testiness, snappiness, impatience
COLLOQ. aggravation
2 NUISANCE, annoyance, disturbance, bother, trouble, pest
COLLOQ. pain, pain in the neck, thorn in the flesh, drag, bind
Ε3 pleasure, satisfaction, delight

island n
isle, islet, atoll, archipelago, eyot, holm, cay, key, skerry; *Scot & Irish* inch
Related adjective: insular

The world's largest islands include:

Australia	Greenland	Sumatra
Baffin (*Canada*)	Honshu (*Japan*)	Victoria (*Canada*)
Borneo	Madagascar	
Great Britain	New Guinea	

---

isolate v
set apart, seclude, keep apart, segregate, quarantine, insulate, abstract, cut off, strand, maroon, detach, remove, disconnect, separate, divorce, alienate, shut out/away, ostracize, exclude, marginalize
FORMAL island, sequester, enisle
COLLOQ. cold-shoulder, send to Coventry
Ε3 assimilate, incorporate, integrate

isolated adj
1 REMOTE, out-of-the-way, outlying, god-forsaken, deserted, unfrequented, secluded, detached, cut off, lonely, solitary, alone, separated, segregated, apart, single
COLLOQ. off the beaten track, in the sticks
2 an isolated occurrence
unique, special, exceptional, atypical, untypical, solitary, single, unusual, uncommon, freak, abnormal, anomalous, unrelated
Ε3 1 populous, accessible 2 typical, common

isolation n
quarantine, solitude, solitariness, loneliness, aloneness, remoteness, seclusion, retirement, withdrawal, exile, segregation, insulation, separation, separateness, detachment, disconnection, dissociation,

alienation, marginalization, abstraction
FORMAL sequestration
⊟ contact

issue *n, v*

♦ *n*

1 MATTER, affair, concern, problem, point, subject, topic, question, debate, argument, dispute, controversy
2 PUBLICATION, release, distribution, supply, supplying, delivery, circulation, broadcast, announcement
FORMAL promulgation, dissemination

3 *last week's issue*

copy, number, instalment, edition, impression, version, printing

4 RESULT, consequence, upshot, outcome, conclusion, effect, finale
COLLOQ. pay-off

5 OFFSPRING, descendants, children, family, progeny, heirs, successors, seed, young
FORMAL scions

6 OUTFLOW, discharge, rush, jet, spurt, gush, emission
FORMAL effusion, effluence

♦ *v*

1 PUBLISH, announce, broadcast, proclaim, spread, put out, send out, release, deliver
FORMAL promulgate, disseminate

2 SUPPLY, provide, give out, distribute, equip, fit out/up, rig out, kit out, deal out

3 EMERGE, emanate, come, proceed, burst forth, gush, flow, exude, ooze, seep

4 RESULT, come, follow, originate, stem, spring, rise, develop, ensue

■ **at issue**

being discussed, under discussion, in question, being debated

■ **take issue**

disagree, argue, challenge, quarrel, fight, dispute, contest, protest, be at odds with, object, take exception, call into question

itch *v, n*

♦ *v*

1 TICKLE, irritate, tingle, prickle, crawl; *dialect* yuke

2 *be itching to do something*

die, long, burn, pine, crave, hanker, yearn, ache

♦ *n*

1 ITCHINESS, tickle, irritation, prickling, tingling; *dialect* yuke
TECHNICAL pruritis
OLD TECHNICAL psora
Related adjective: pruritic

2 EAGERNESS, keenness, desire, ache, hunger, thirst, longing, yearning, hankering, craving, burning, passion
FORMAL cacoethes

itching *adj*

dying, longing, burning, hankering, aching, eager, greedy, impatient, inquisitive, avid, raring

item *n*

1 OBJECT, article, thing, piece, component, ingredient, element, factor, point, detail, particular, aspect, feature, consideration, matter, circumstance, issue

2 *an item in the local paper*

article, piece, feature, report, story, account, notice, entry, paragraph, bulletin

itemize *v*

list, record, catalogue, specify, detail, document, instance, particularize, count, mention, overname, number, enumerate, tabulate, make an inventory

itinerant *adj, n*

♦ *adj*

travelling, peripatetic, running, roving, roaming, wandering, strolling, journeying, wayfaring, drifting, rambling, nomadic, migratory, vagrant, rootless, unsettled, vagabond
⊟ stationary, settled

♦ *n*

traveller, Gypsy, Romany, Romani, Roma, itinerary, peripatetic, wanderer, roamer, rover, rambler, hawker, huckster, nomad, tzigany, Zigeuner, Zincalo, Zingaro, Bohemian, tinker, diddicoy, faw, gitano, roadman, vagrant, chapman, minstrel, muffin man, preacher, evangelist, revivalist; *Scot* caird; *N Am* hobo
OLD strolling player, piepowder, Scotch draper
COLLOQ. *N Am* gandy dancer

itinerary *n*

route, course, journey, tour, way, circuit, plan, arrangements, programme, schedule, timetable

J

jab *v, n*

◆ *v*

poke, prod, dig, nudge, stab, push, elbow, lunge, punch, box, tap, thrust

◆ *n*

poke, prod, dig, nudge, stab, push, punch, box, tap, shot, injection

jabber *v*

chatter, gab, gabble, prattle, rabbit, ramble, tattle, babble, jaw, prate, rattle, mumble, witter, yap, sputter; *dialect & N Am* blather; *Scot* yatter, blether; *Aust* yabber

jack

■ **jack up**

1 LIFT, raise, hoist, elevate

2 *jack up prices*

increase, inflate, put up, push up, hike (up), raise

jacket *n*

casing, cover, covering, wrapping, wrap, wrapper, case, sheath, shell, skin, envelope, folder

See panel at **coat**.

jackpot *n*

prize, first prize, winnings, kitty, pool, pot, reward, award, bonanza, stakes

COLLOQ. big time

■ **hit the jackpot**

succeed, make it, arrive, score, get rich

COLLOQ. make a packet/bundle/pile, rake it in, hit the big time, clean up

jaded *adj*

fatigued, exhausted, dulled, played-out, tired, tired out, weary, wearied, worn out, spent, done, bored, unenthusiastic; *Scot* disjaskit

COLLOQ. fagged, done in, all in, ready to drop, shattered, knackered, whacked, jiggered, bushed, fed up, cheesed off; *N Am* pooped (out), tuckered out

F∃ fresh, refreshed

jag *n*

barb, point, projection, protrusion, snag, notch, spur, tooth

TECHNICAL denticle, dentil

jagged *adj*

uneven, irregular, notched, indented, rough, serrated, saw-edged, toothed, ragged, pointed, ridged, craggy, snagged, snaggy, barbed, spiked, nicked, broken

TECHNICAL denticulate

F∃ even, smooth

jaggedness *n*

unevenness, irregularity, roughness, brokenness, serration, raggedness

FORMAL serrature

F∃ evenness, smoothness

jail, gaol *n, v*

◆ *n*

prison, jailhouse, custody, lock-up, penitentiary, detention centre, guardhouse, house of correction

OLD kitty

COLLOQ. inside, nick; *N Am* pen, poky

SLANG porridge, clink, cooler, slammer, quod, jug, can, choky; *N Am* hoosegow, big house

◆ *v*

imprison, lock up, put away, send down, send to prison, confine, detain, intern, impound, immure

FORMAL incarcerate

jailer, gaoler *n*

prison officer, warden, warder, guard, keeper, captor

OLD turnkey, under-turnkey

SLANG screw

jam¹ *n*

bread and jam

conserve, preserve, jelly, spread, marmalade, confiture; *S Afr* konfyt

jam² *v, n*

◆ *v*

1 CRAM, pack, wedge, squash, squeeze, press, crush, crowd, congest, ram, stuff, insert, confine, force, thrust, push, press, ram

2 BLOCK, clog, obstruct, close (off), stall, stick

◆ *n*

1 CRUSH, crowd, press, congestion, pack, herd, swarm, mob, throng, horde, multitude

2 *a traffic jam*

bottleneck, congestion, gridlock, hold-up, obstruction

3 PREDICAMENT, trouble, quandary, plight, straits

COLLOQ. fix, hole, (tight) spot, bind, pickle, scrape, stew, the soup

jamb *n*

post, shaft, pole, pillar, frame, support, prop, upright, stanchion

jamboree *n*

celebration, party, rally, festivity, festival, carnival, jubilee, junket, fête, frolic, revelry, spree, carouse, merriment, field day, gathering, get-together, convention

COLLOQ. shindig

jammy *adj*

lucky, fortunate, favoured, charmed, successful, prosperous, timely, opportune, expedient, providential

FORMAL auspicious, fortuitous, propitious

F∃ unlucky

jangle *v, n*

◆ *v*

1 CLANK, clash, jar, clang, clatter, clink, jingle, chime, rattle, vibrate

2 *jangle someone's nerves*

upset, irritate, disturb, bother, trouble, make anxious

◆ *n*

clang, clash, rattle, clatter, jar, jarring, cacophony, clink, din, discord, racket, reverberation, clangour, stridor

FORMAL dissonance

F∃ euphony

janitor *n*

caretaker, doorkeeper, doorman, custodian, concierge, porter; *Scot* servitor

TECHNICAL ostiary

jar¹ *n*

a jam jar
pot, container, vessel, receptacle, crock, pitcher, urn, vase, flask, flagon, carafe, jug, mug, cruet, caddy, canister, terrine, tureen, olla, pithos, tinaja, water monkey, greybeard, amphora, dolium, stamnos

jar² *v*

1 JOLT, agitate, rattle, shake, jerk, vibrate
2 GRATE, upset, disturb, trouble, jangle, irritate, rasp, grind, annoy, offend, irk
COLLOQ. nettle
3 CLASH, conflict, be in conflict, be at odds, be at variance, quarrel, disagree, bicker, jostle

jargon *n*

1 SPECIALIST LANGUAGE, technical language, journalese, computerese, computerspeak, legalese, psychobabble, buzz words, officialese, telegraphese, parlance, slang, cant, argot, vernacular, idiom, usage
COLLOQ. Greek
2 NONSENSE, gibberish
COLLOQ. gobbledygook, mumbo-jumbo

Synonym nuances

sense 1

Both **specialist language** and **technical language** would be used without implication of language that has been tailored for its market audience, while **journalese** suggests less structured language and can imply bad or lazy journalism. **Computerese** and **computerspeak**, on the other hand, somewhat facetiously refer to language used by computer buffs, while **legalese** suggests the parallel term of the legal profession, and all hint at a deliberate arcaneness and exclusivity. **Officialese** is again fairly derogatory and conveys the idea of unnecessarily overblown bureaucratic language, whereas **telegraphese** is more straightforwardly suggestive of stark, clipped language. **Psychobabble**, while suggesting the language of psychologists, may often be used derogatively of any analytical or pseudo-psychological terms: *psychobabble portrays many criminals as the victims.*

  Parlance is a more neutral term for a manner of speaking: *in medical parlance*, while **idiom** and **usage** have to do with the everyday mode of expression: *a term in current usage.* **Buzz words** refers to the current trends in any given field, and so has positive overtones of fun and fashionability. **Slang** is also fairly unmarked, and suggests informal language that falls outside of standard language; **argot** is used of informal, but perhaps slovenly language, and **vernacular** is more suggestive of pertaining to a particular group: *a speech in the cockney vernacular.* **Cant** is more disapproving in its implication of talk that lacks sincerity or meaningful content: *the prevalent cant and humbug about political reform.*

---

jarring *adj*
clashing, discordant, jangling, harsh, grating, irritating, cacophonous, rasping, strident, upsetting, disturbing, troubling, jolting

jaundiced *adj*

1 BITTER, cynical, pessimistic, sceptical, distrustful, disbelieving, biased, prejudiced, bigoted, envious, jealous, hostile, jaded, suspicious, resentful, unenthusiastic, misanthropic
2 DISTORTED, biased, prejudiced, bigoted, preconceived

jaunt *n*
trip, outing, excursion, holiday, tour, ride, drive, spin, ramble, stroll

jauntily *adv*
cheerfully, brightly, energetically, airily, self-confidently, cheekily, smartly, perkily

jaunty *adj*

1 CHEERFUL, sprightly, lively, perky, breezy, energetic, bouncy, buoyant, high-spirited, self-confident, carefree, airy, cheeky
2 DEBONAIR, dapper, smart, trim, showy, flashy, spruce, stylish
E3 **1** depressed **2** dowdy

javelin *n*
spear, dart, harpoon, handstaff, jerid, gavelock, pilum, pile

jaw *n, v*

♦ *n*

1 *the lower jaw*
mandible, mouth, muzzle
TECHNICAL maxilla
COLLOQ. chops, trap
Related adjectives: maxillary, gnathic, gnathal
2 TALK, gossip, chat, conversation, discussion
COLLOQ. chinwag, natter, confab, rap; *N Am* visit; *Aust* wongi
SLANG schmooze
3 *the jaws of death*
clutches, grasp, control, power, claws, threshold

♦ *v*
chat, chatter, gossip, talk, gabble, jabber, babble
COLLOQ. natter, rabbit (on)

jazz *v, n*

■ **jazz up**
liven up, enliven, smarten up, brighten up, ginger up

Kinds of jazz include:

acid jazz	Dixieland	modern
Afro-Cuban	free-form	neo-classic
avant-garde	fusion	New Orleans
bebop	groove	post-bop
blues	hard bop	ragtime
boogie-woogie	hot jazz	soul jazz
bop	improvised jazz	spiel
bossa nova	jive	swing
classic	mainstream	third stream
cool	modal	West Coast

---

jazzy *adj*
lively, smart, spirited, stylish, bright, bold, wild, fancy, gaudy, vivacious, zestful
COLLOQ. flashy, snazzy, swinging
E3 conservative, square

jealous *adj*

1 ENVIOUS, covetous, desirous, grudging, begrudging, resentful, jaundiced
OLD (*Spenser*) gealous
COLLOQ. green, green-eyed
2 SUSPICIOUS, wary, doubting, distrustful, anxious, possessive, insecure
3 PROTECTIVE, watchful, mindful, careful, vigilant, wary, defensive
E3 **1** contented, satisfied

jealously *adv*
with envy, enviously, covetously, desirously, resentfully, possessively, distrustfully

jealousy *n*

1 ENVY, covetousness, grudge, grudgingness, resentment, bitterness, spite, ill-will
OLD yellowness, emulation, zelotypia; (*Spenser*) gealousy, gelosy
COLLOQ. green-eyed monster
2 SUSPICION, distrust, mistrust, doubt, possessiveness, insecurity
3 PROTECTIVENESS, watchfulness, mindfulness, carefulness, vigilance, wariness, defensiveness

jeer *v, n*

♦ *v*

mock, scoff, taunt, gibe, ridicule, sneer, make fun of, scorn, chaff, barrack, tease, twit, heckle, shout down, hiss, boo, banter, jest, laugh to scorn, flout, fleer; *dialect* gird
FORMAL deride
COLLOQ. knock; *N Am* razz; *Aust* chiack, have a shot at; *Aust & NZ* sling off at
SLANG *N Am* goof; *Aust & NZ* poke borak at

♦ *n*

mockery, ridicule, banter, taunt, gibe, sneer, scoff, teasing, abuse, catcall, hiss, boo, hoot, jest, flout, fleer
OLD frump, gird
FORMAL derision
COLLOQ. dig

jejune *adj*

1 UNSOPHISTICATED, simple, naive, immature, childish, juvenile, puerile, silly, callow
2 DULL, uninteresting, boring, unoriginal, arid, trite, banal, senseless, barren, empty, colourless, vapid, insipid, prosaic, wishy-washy, dry, spiritless
E3 1 mature **2** meaningful

jell

see **gel**.

jeopardize *v*

endanger, expose to danger, risk, put at risk, put in jeopardy, hazard, venture, gamble, chance, take a chance, threaten, menace, expose, stake
FORMAL imperil
E3 protect, safeguard

jeopardy *n*

danger, risk, hazard, endangerment, venture, vulnerability, precariousness, menace, threat, insecurity, exposure, liability
FORMAL peril
E3 safety, security

jerk *v, n*

♦ *v*

jolt, tug, twitch, jog, yank, wrench, pull, jiggle, lurch, pluck, thrust, shrug, throw, bounce

♦ *n*

1 JOLT, tug, twitch, jar, jog, yank, wrench, pull, pluck, lurch, throw, thrust, shrug
2 IDIOT, fool
COLLOQ. nincompoop, ass, chump, ninny, neddy, clot, dope, twit, nitwit, nit, sucker, mug, twerp, birdbrain, silly-billy, berk, (proper) Charlie, gubbins, sap, saphead, wazzock, dum-dum, coot, goat, headbanger
SLANG wally, dumbo, pillock, prat, dork, geek, plonker, git, nerd, dweeb, nerk, goop, josser, nig-nog, sawney, schlemiel, turkey, cloth head, dipstick, goof, kook, tosspot; (*taboo*) dickhead, prick

jerkily *adv*

fitfully, spasmodically, jumpily, bumpily, roughly, unevenly
E3 smoothly

jerky *adj*

fitful, twitchy, spasmodic, jumpy, jolting, lurching, convulsive, disconnected, bumpy, bouncy, shaky, shaking, rough, uneven, unco-ordinated, uncontrolled, incoherent
E3 smooth

jerry-built *adj*

insubstantial, ramshackle, thrown together, quickly built, built on the cheap, rickety, unstable, cheap, shoddy, defective, faulty, flimsy, unsubstantial, slipshod, cheapjack
E3 firm, stable, substantial

jersey *n*

sweater, jumper, pullover, sweatshirt, top, woolly

jest *n, v*

♦ *n*

joke, quip, witticism, banter, fooling, prank, practical joke, trick, hoax
OLD bourd
COLLOQ. wisecrack, crack, gag, kidding, leg-pull

♦ *v*

joke, tell jokes, quip, fool, tease, mock, jeer
COLLOQ. kid

■ **in jest**

in fun, as a joke, jokingly, to tease, playfully, mischievously

jester *n*

clown, fool, court-fool, comic, buffoon, comedian, humorist, joker, wag, zany, wit, prankster, quipster, gagman, juggler, joculator, pantaloon, harlequin, mummer, merry-andrew, droll
OLD patch, merryman, bourder, scop, Jack-pudding; (*Shakesp*) motley

jet¹ *n, v*

♦ *n*

a jet of water

gush, spurt, spout, spray, spring, sprinkler, sprayer, fountain, flow, stream, rush, squirt

♦ *v*

1 GUSH, spurt, spray, spring, flow, stream, rush, squirt
2 FLY, zoom, rush, shoot, career

jet² *adj*

jet black

black, pitch-black, ebony, sable, raven, sooty, inky

jetsam

See **flotsam**.

jettison *v*

discard, scrap, throw away, get rid of, abandon, offload, unload, drop, eject, expel, heave
COLLOQ. ditch, dump, chuck
E3 load, take on

jetty *n*

breakwater, pier, dock, harbour, groyne, mole, quay, wharf, landing-place, landing-stage

jewel *n*

1 GEM, precious stone, gemstone, ornament
COLLOQ. rock, sparkler
2 TREASURE, gem, find, prize, masterpiece, showpiece, rarity, paragon, pearl, jewellery, pride and joy, *crème de la crème, pièce de résistance*

jewellery *n*

jewels, gems, ornaments, trinkets, regalia, treasure, bijoux, bijouterie, finery, gemmery, gauds

---

Types of jewellery include:

amulet	cufflink	pendant
anklet	diadem	power beads
bangle	earring	ring
beads	eternity ring	rivière
bindi	friendship	signet ring
body jewel	bracelet	solitaire ring
bracelet	hatpin	stud
brooch	locket	tiara
cameo	nail jewel	tiepin
chain	navel ring	toe ring
charm bracelet	necklace	tooth jewel
choker	necklet	torque
coronet	nose ring	

Jewish calendar

See panel on next page

Jezebel *n*

seductress, temptress, *femme fatale*, hussy, scarlet woman, loose woman, Delilah, wanton, whore, harlot, jade, man-eater, witch

The Jewish calendar and its Gregorian equivalents:

Tishri (September-October)	Kislev (November-December)	Adar (February-March)	Sivan (May-June)
Hesshvan (October-November)	Tevet (December-January)	Adar Sheni (leap years only)	Tammuz (June-July)
	Shevat (January-February)	Nisan (March-April)	Av (July-August)
		Iyar (April-May)	Elul (August-September)

COLLOQ. vamp
SLANG scrubber, tart

jib *v*
balk, shrink, recoil, back off, stall, refuse, retreat, stop, stop short

jibe
see **gibe**.

jiffy *n*
instant, moment, second, sec, split second, flash, twinkling, twinkling of an eye, minute, tick, two ticks, trice, no time
COLLOQ. two shakes of a lamb's tail; *dialect* whiff
E3 age

jig *v*
jerk, prance, caper, hop, jump, leap, twitch, skip, bounce, bob, wiggle, shake, wobble

jigger *v*
wreck, destroy, break, ruin, spoil, undermine
FORMAL vitiate
COLLOQ. botch up, kibosh, louse up, make a pig's ear of, scupper
SLANG balls up, bugger up

jiggery-pokery *n*
deceit, trickery, dishonesty, fraud, deception, mischief, subterfuge, chicanery, funny business, hanky-panky
COLLOQ. monkey business

jiggle *v*
jerk, jump, bounce, twitch, fidget, shift, shake, agitate, jig, jog, joggle, waggle, wiggle, wobble

jilt *v*
abandon, reject, desert, walk out on, discard, brush off, leave, drop, spurn, betray, cast aside; *Scot* begunk
OLD throw over
COLLOQ. ditch, chuck, dump, pack in

jingle *v, n*
♦ *v*
clink, tinkle, ring, ding, chime, chink, jangle, clatter, rattle
FORMAL tintinnabulate
♦ *n*
1 CLINK, tinkle, ringing, chime, ring, ding, clang, rattle, jangle, clangour
FORMAL tintinnabulation
2 RHYME, verse, song, carol, tune, ditty, doggerel, melody, poem, chant, slogan, chorus, refrain

jingoism *n*
chauvinism, flag-waving, patriotism, nationalism, imperialism, sabre-rattling, insularity

jinx *n, v*
♦ *n*
spell, curse, bad luck, evil eye, hex, voodoo, hoodoo, Indian sign, black magic, charm, plague
FORMAL malediction, affliction
COLLOQ. gremlin
SLANG *Aust* moz, mozz
♦ *v*
curse, bewitch, bedevil, cast a spell on, doom, plague

jitters *n*
nerves, nervousness, tenseness, anxiety, fidgets, agitation, trembling, uneasiness
COLLOQ. edginess, heebie-jeebies, habdabs, the creeps, the shakes, the shivers, the willies, jimjams

jittery *adj*
nervous, anxious, agitated, uneasy, on edge, flustered, quivering, shaky, shivery, trembling, jumpy, fidgety, quaking, panicky
FORMAL perturbed
COLLOQ. edgy, nervy, twitchy, het up, keyed up, wound up, jumpy, uptight, with butterflies in your stomach, on pins and needles, shaking like a leaf/jelly, with your heart in your mouth, in a sweat, in a stew, in a tizzy
SLANG screwed-up
E3 calm, composed, confident

job *n*
1 *she has a good job*
work, employment, occupation, position, post, pursuit, situation, profession, line of work/business, career, calling, vocation, trade, métier, capacity, business, (means of) livelihood
2 *it's a difficult job*
task, piece of work, chore, duty, responsibility, charge, commission, assignment, mission, activity, affair, concern, assignment, business, proceeding, project, enterprise, office, capacity, pursuit, role, undertaking, venture, province, part, place, share, errand, function, contribution, stint, consignment, charge
▪ **have a job doing something**
find something difficult, find it a problem, have a problem with, have a hard time doing something, find something (to be) troublesome
▪ **just the job**
exactly what is needed/wanted, just the thing
COLLOQ. just the ticket, just what the doctor ordered

jobless *adj*
unemployed, out of work, without work, workless, laid off, inactive, idle, redundant
COLLOQ. on the dole
E3 employed

jockey *n, v*
♦ *n*
equestrian, horseman, horsewoman, rider, jump-jockey
COLLOQ. jockette
♦ *v*
manipulate, manoeuvre, engineer, negotiate, wheedle, cajole, coax, induce, ease, edge, manage
FORMAL inveigle

jocose *adj*
humorous, playful, funny, jesting, mischievous, pleasant, teasing, comical, droll, facetious, witty, sportive, waggish, jovial, joyous, merry, mirthful
FORMAL lepid
E3 morose

jocular *adj*
joking, jesting, funny, humorous, jovial, amusing, hilarious, comical, comic, entertaining, facetious, droll, whimsical, teasing, playful, witty, waggish, roguish
FORMAL jocose
E3 serious

jocularity *n*
jesting, funniness, humour, joviality, amusement, entertainment, laughter, hilarity, merriment, gaiety, jolliness, comicality, drollery, wit, whimsicality, waggishness, pleasantry, facetiousness, playfulness, sportiveness, sport, roguishness, fooling, teasing
FORMAL jocosity, jocoseness, desipience

jog v, n

♦ v

1 JOLT, jar, bump, jostle, jerk, joggle, nudge, poke, shake, prod, bounce, push, rock, elbow; *dialect* shog; *Scot* dunch, dunsh, hod, hotch, whig
2 PROMPT, remind, stir, arouse, activate, stimulate
3 RUN, trot, canter
COLLOQ. mosey

♦ n

1 JOLT, bump, jerk, nudge, shove, push, poke, prod, shake, jig-jog, joggle; *dialect* shog
2 RUN, trot, canter

joie de vivre n

cheerfulness, enjoyment, buoyancy, joyfulness, joy, enthusiasm, merriment, mirth, pleasure, relish, zest, gaiety, gusto
FORMAL blitheness, ebullience
COLLOQ. bounce, get-up-and-go
F3 depression

join v

1 UNITE, connect, combine, attach, link, amalgamate, ally, unify, fasten, merge, converge, marry, couple, yoke, tie, splice, knit, weld, fuse, bind, cement, glue, add, adhere, annex
OLD (*Shakesp*) injoint, interjoin
FORMAL conjoin
2 BORDER (ON), verge on, touch, meet, coincide, march with
FORMAL abut, adjoin, conjoin
3 ASSOCIATE, affiliate, become a member of, accompany, co-operate, collaborate, ally, enlist, enrol, enter, sign up, team up with
F3 1 divide, separate **3** leave

■ **join in**
take part in, participate, partake, co-operate, pitch in, lend a hand, help, contribute, chip in
COLLOQ. muck in

■ **join up**
enlist, sign up, enrol, enter

joint n, adj, v

♦ n

1 JUNCTION, connection, union, coupling, juncture, join, intersection, hinge, knot, articulation, seam
FORMAL nexus
2 CLUB, bar, nightclub, pub, haunt, place, dive
3 CIGARETTE
COLLOQ. reefer, spliff, stick, roach

♦ adj

combined, common, communal, joined, shared, united, collective, amalgamated, mutual, co-operative, co-ordinated, consolidated, concerted

♦ v

1 JOIN, connect, couple, unite, fasten, fit, articulate
2 CUT UP, carve, divide, sever, dismember, dissect

jointly adv

in agreement, in harmony, in co-operation, co-operatively, in collaboration, in partnership, together
COLLOQ. in cahoots

joke n, v

♦ n

1 JEST, quip, crack, wisecrack, witticism, funny story, pun, hoot, whimsy, yarn, banter, repartee, (old) chestnut, throwaway, jape; *Scot* bar
OLD banter, guy
COLLOQ. gag, one-liner, funny, rib-tickler, wheeze, josh
2 TRICK, jape, lark, prank, practical joke, hoax, spoof, fun, play, sport, stunt
COLLOQ. leg-pull
3 FARCE, absurdity, nonsense, ridiculousness, mockery, parody, travesty
COLLOQ. shambles

♦ v

jest, tell jokes, quip, clown, fool (about/around), pun, tease, banter, mock, laugh, frolic, gambol, crack a joke, break a jest, jape, whip the cat
COLLOQ. kid, wisecrack, pull someone's leg, have someone on, pull a fast one on
SLANG cod, josh, take for a ride

Synonym nuances
noun sense 1

Jest, although now a little old-fashioned, can be used of anything that is spoken, or done, in fun; **jape** is similar and might be used facetiously to convey the notion of something done for amusement, although often at someone else's expense: *throwing his glasses under a bus was considered a jolly jape.*

The terms **quip** and **witticism** would be used, perhaps with a hint of admiration, of a short, clever remark. The term **pun** would be reserved for a play on words that is intended to be amusing.

The word **hoot** could be applied to any person or episode that gives rise to hilarity: *your mum's a real hoot,* while **whimsy** is more suggestive of mildly quaint and fanciful behaviour: *a film characterized by Ealingesque whimsy.* **Yarn** suggests a long, rambling, but amusing, tale. **Banter** has to do with teasing and humorous chat: *he covered his shyness with a good deal of banter,* and **repartee** is appropriate for a series of sharp and witty retorts.

Chestnut, on the other hand, is rather more pejorative in its implication of a rather aged, and therefore stale, joke. **Throwaway** suggests a deliberately casual delivery of a line to increase its effect.

---

joker n

comedian, comic, wit, humorist, jester, trickster, quipster, gagman, prankster, hoaxer, practical joker, wag, clown, buffoon, kidder, droll, character, sport, farceur, funster
COLLOQ. wisecracker, card, laugh

jollity n

cheerfulness, gladness, happiness, light-heartedness, merriment, merrymaking, high spirits
F3 sadness, unhappiness

jolly adj, adv, v

♦ adj

1 a *jolly person*
jovial, merry, glad, cheerful, cheery, playful, hearty, happy, exuberant, lively, gay, joyful, gleeful, mirthful
2 ENJOYABLE, happy, delightful, pleasurable, convivial, festive
F3 1 sad, unhappy

♦ adv

extremely, very, exceptionally, intensely, greatly, highly, certainly, extraordinarily
COLLOQ. ever so, dead, well, awfully, terribly

♦ v

encourage, urge, spur, prompt, coax, persuade, influence
COLLOQ. egg on

jolt v, n

♦ v

1 JAR, jerk, jog, bump, jounce, jostle, push, knock, bounce, lurch, shake, shove, push, bang, nudge
2 UPSET, startle, shock, shake (up), surprise, stun, amaze, astound, astonish, discompose, disconcert, disturb
FORMAL perturb
COLLOQ. floor, knock for six

♦ n

1 JAR, jerk, jog, bump, blow, bang, knock, push, shove, hit, impact, lurch, shake, start
2 SHOCK, surprise, reversal, setback, start, upset, blow, fright of your life

COLLOQ. bombshell, thunderbolt, bolt from the blue, turn-up for the book

jostle v
1 PUSH, shove, jog, bump, elbow, hustle, jolt, crowd, shoulder, joggle, shake, squeeze, throng, bang, collide
2 COMPETE, vie, contend, fight, battle, struggle, jockey

jot n, v
• n
iota, glimmer, trace, fraction, scrap, atom, gleam, grain, hint, speck, trifle, whit, bit, particle, mite, morsel, scintilla, tittle, ace, detail
COLLOQ. smidgen
■ **jot down**
write down, take down, note (down), put down, list, record, scribble, register, enter

jotting n
note(s), scribble, line(s), message, reminder, comment
COLLOQ. memo

journal n
1 MAGAZINE, periodical, newspaper, paper, publication, review, weekly, monthly, fanzine, e-zine
2 DIARY, gazette, daybook, log, logbook, record, account, register, chronicle

journalism n
reporting, writing, news, news coverage, reportage, feature-writing, press, Fleet Street, fourth estate, copy-writing, correspondence, media, broadcasting, radio, television, telejournalism, photojournalism, e-journalism, web journalism, sportswriting, gutter press

journalist n
reporter, news-writer, correspondent, editor, man, newspaperman, newspaperwoman, pressman, presswoman, columnist, feature-writer, sportswriter, gossip-writer, commentator, broadcaster, contributor, reviewer, editor, subeditor, newshound, paparazzo, freelance, stringer, telejournalist, e-journalist, web journalist
OLD diurnalist, gazetteer
COLLOQ. hack, hackette, sub, journo, scribe, hatchet man, thunderer, wireman, sob sister, ink-slinger
SLANG N Am ink-jerker

journey n, v
• n
voyage, trip, travel(s), expedition, passage, trek, tour, ramble, roving, outing, excursion, jaunt, wanderings, cruise, ride, crossing, flight, drive, safari, progress, globetrotting
FORMAL odyssey, peregrination
• v
travel, voyage, go, cruise, sail, trek, hike, tour, roam, rove, proceed, wander, tramp, ramble, range, fly, gallivant
FORMAL peregrinate

journeyer n
tourist, traveller, tripper, voyager, wanderer, wayfarer, rambler, pilgrim, trekker
FORMAL peregrinator

joust v, n
• v
fight, spar, vie, compete, contest, quarrel, wrangle, skirmish, tilt
• n
fight, encounter, contest, tournament, trial, engagement, skirmish, tilt, tourney

jovial adj
jolly, happy, cheerful, glad, cheery, merry, affable, animated, cordial, genial, lively, buoyant, mirthful, gleeful, gay, in good spirits, sociable
F3 gloomy, sad, depressed

joviality n
jollity, happiness, cheerfulness, cheeriness, gladness, merriment, mirth, glee, ebullience, fun, gaiety, affability, buoyancy, hilarity
F3 moroseness, sadness

joy n
1 HAPPINESS, gladness, delight, pleasure, bliss, ecstasy, elation, joyfulness, enjoyment, exultation, cheer, jubilation, rejoicing, gratification, rapture, glee
OLD dream, list
FORMAL felicity, entrancement, transport
COLLOQ. seventh heaven, cloud nine
2 *the joys of childhood*
treasure, delight, pleasure, thrill, treat, prize, gem
COLLOQ. nuts
3 *get no joy from the inquiry desk*
satisfaction, achievement, success, successful/positive result, victory, accomplishment
F3 **1** despair, grief

joyful adj
happy, pleased, delighted, glad, elated, ecstatic, overjoyed, euphoric, thrilled, gratified, pleasing, triumphant, gleeful, merry, cheerful, jubilant
OLD gleesome
FORMAL exhilarant
COLLOQ. tickled pink, over the moon, on top of the world, on cloud nine, in seventh heaven
F3 sorrowful, mournful

joyfully adv
happily, gladly, cheerfully, ecstatically, euphorically, triumphantly, gleefully, jubilantly
F3 mournfully

joyless adj
miserable, discouraging, depressing, sad, unhappy, sombre, serious, sober, downcast, dreary, forlorn, gloomy, glum, grim, despondent, dejected, cheerless, bleak, dismal, dispirited, doleful, dour
F3 joyful

joyous adj
happy, joyful, cheerful, glad, gleeful, merry, jubilant, rapturous, ecstatic, festal, festive, gladsome
F3 sad

joyously adv
happily, joyfully, cheerfully, gladly, merrily, jubilantly, ecstatically, rapturously
F3 sadly

jubilant adj
joyful, rejoicing, overjoyed, delighted, elated, triumphant, exuberant, exultant, excited, ecstatic, euphoric, thrilled, rhapsodic
COLLOQ. tickled pink, over the moon, on top of the world, on cloud nine, in seventh heaven

jubilation n
euphoria, ecstasy, elation, triumph, excitement, exultation, jollification, joy, celebration, festivity, jamboree, jubilee
F3 depression, lamentation

jubilee n
celebration, commemoration, anniversary, festival, festivity, holiday, gala, fete, carnival, feast day

Judas n
traitor, betrayer, deceiver, renegade, quisling, turncoat
FORMAL tergiversator
COLLOQ. backstabber

judder v
shake, vibrate, shudder, tremble, quiver, quake

judge n, v
• n
1 JUSTICE, Law Lord, magistrate, sheriff, recorder, coroner,

judiciary, procurator fiscal, district attorney, seneschal, arbiter, adjudicator, arbitrator, mediator, ombudsman, moderator, referee, umpire, assessor
SLANG beak, his/her nibs
Related adjectives: judicial, judiciary
See panel at **legal terms**.
2 CONNOISSEUR, authority, expert, evaluator, assessor, critic, reviewer
◆ v
1 ADJUDICATE, arbitrate, try, sit in judgement, deliver/pronounce a verdict, referee, umpire, decree, mediate, examine, sentence, pass sentence, give a sentence, review, rule, find
FORMAL adjudge
2 ASCERTAIN, determine, decide, assess, appraise, evaluate, estimate, value, weigh (up), gauge, review, examine, distinguish, discern, reckon, believe, think, form an opinion, consider, conclude, rate
3 CONDEMN, criticize, doom, convict, damn

judgement *n*
1 VERDICT, sentence, ruling, adjudication, decree, conclusion, decision, arbitration, finding, result, mediation, order, opinion
2 DISCERNMENT, discrimination, understanding, wisdom, common sense, good sense, sense, prudence, intelligence, taste, shrewdness, perception, penetration, acumen, enlightenment
FORMAL judiciousness, sagacity, perspicacity
3 OPINION, assessment, evaluation, appraisal, estimate, view, belief, diagnosis, conviction
4 CONVICTION, damnation, punishment, doom, fate, misfortune
FORMAL retribution
Related adjective: judiciary

judgemental *adj*
critical, condemnatory, disapproving, censorious, fault-finding, scathing, carping, hypercritical, derogatory
FORMAL disparaging

judicial *adj*
legal, judiciary, magistral, forensic, official, discriminating, critical, impartial

---

⚠ judicial or **judicious**?
Judicial is a formal word meaning 'relating to judges and lawcourts'. *Judicious* means 'showing wisdom and good sense': *a judicious choice of words*.

---

judicially *adv*
legally, forensically, officially, impartially

judiciary *n*
judges, legal system, court system, magistracy, the law, justice, the bench

judicious *adj*
wise, careful, cautious, prudent, astute, discerning, informed, discriminating, shrewd, thoughtful, reasonable, sensible, clever, intelligent, smart, sound, well-judged, well-advised, considered, common-sense
FORMAL sagacious, circumspect
🔁 injudicious

judiciously *adv*
wisely, carefully, cautiously, prudently, thoughtfully, sensibly, astutely, discerningly, shrewdly
FORMAL sagaciously, circumspectly
🔁 injudiciously

jug *n*
pitcher, carafe, crock, ewer, flagon, urn, jar, decanter, vessel, Toby jug, container, receptacle

juggle *v*
alter, change, manipulate, falsify, tamper with, fake,

rearrange, balance, equalize, adjust, misrepresent, massage, rig, disguise
COLLOQ. fiddle, doctor, cook

juice *n*
liquid, fluid, extract, essence, sap, secretion, nectar, liquor, serum

juicy *adj*
1 SUCCULENT, moist, wet, lush, watery, flowing, sappy
OLD (*Shakesp*) moist
2 INTERESTING, colourful, vivid, thrilling, exciting, sensational, racy, risqué, suggestive, scandalous, lurid, spicy
COLLOQ. hot
🔁 **1** dry

jumble *v, n*
◆ v
disarrange, confuse, disorganize, mix (up), muddle, shuffle, tangle, mingle, tumble, garble; *Scot* jabble; *N Am* wuzzle
🔁 order
◆ n
1 DISORDER, disarray, confusion, mess, chaos, mix, mix-up, mixture, muddle, clutter, hotchpotch, miscellany, medley, potpourri, pastiche, huddle, mingle-mangle, praiseach, printer's pie, raffle
FORMAL conglomeration
COLLOQ. mishmash, shambles
2 *a jumble sale*
junk, clutter, oddments, bric-à-brac, rummage, cast-offs

jumbled *adj*
muddled, confused, chaotic, disorganized, disordered, disarrayed, mixed-up, tangled, unsorted, untidy, shuffled, tumbled, garbled, miscellaneous
🔁 orderly, tidy

jumbo *adj*
gigantic, colossal, giant, extra-large, mammoth, massive, huge, enormous, immense, vast, Titanic
COLLOQ. whopping, walloping, ginormous
SLANG mega

jump *v, n*
◆ v
1 LEAP, spring, bound, vault, clear, go over/across, hurdle, bounce, skip, hop, caper, cavort, frisk, romp, sport, prance, frolic, gambol
2 START, flinch, jerk, recoil, shake, quiver, twitch, jump out of your skin, wince, quail
3 OMIT, leave out, miss, skip, pass over, cut out, bypass, disregard, overlook, ignore, avoid, digress
4 RISE, increase, go up, gain, appreciate, ascend, shoot (up), leap (up), escalate, mount, advance, surge, spiral
5 POUNCE ON, attack, assault, spring on, swoop on, set upon
COLLOQ. mug, beat up, do over
◆ n
1 LEAP, spring, bound, vault, hop, skip, bounce, prance, frisk, frolic, pounce
2 START, flinch, jerk, jolt, jar, lurch, shock, spasm, quiver, shiver, shake, quiver, twitch
3 BREAK, gap, space, interruption, lapse, omission, interval, breach, switch
FORMAL hiatus, lacuna
4 RISE, increase, escalation, leap, boost, advance, increment, upsurge, elevation, upturn, mounting
COLLOQ. hike
5 HURDLE, fence, gate, hedge, barricade, barrier, obstacle, rail
Related adjective: saltatorial
■ **jump at**
accept eagerly/quickly, agree to, fall for, leap at, grab, welcome with both/open arms, seize (on), pounce on, snatch, swallow

jump on

criticize, blame, reprimand, rebuke, censure, reprove, scold, chide, fly at, tick off, reproach, upbraid
FORMAL berate, castigate, revile

jump the gun

act prematurely, act hastily, act too soon, start too early, anticipate

---

Synonym nuances
verb sense 1
Leap and **bound** can be used of jumping that takes you quickly from one point to another, and connotes great height or distance, while **spring** has further connotations of a sudden jump, made as if by elastic force: *the tiger sprang from the long grass*. **Vault**, **hurdle** and **clear** also suggest high movement, but over an obstacle: *he vaulted the gate*; *he cleared the stream*. **Bounce** is more suggestive of short, rapid and repetitive upward movements.
   You might use **skip** and **hop** to suggest carefree, casual movement. The verbs **caper**, **cavort** and **romp** are suggestive of undisciplined jumping about, while **frisk**, **frolic** and **gambol** suggest playfulness, and rather unco-ordinated jumping movements. **Prance** suggests a graceful but perhaps exaggerated action: *she pranced in little pirouettes around the kitchen*.

---

jumper *n*

sweater, jersey, pullover, sweatshirt, woolly

jumpy *adj*

1 NERVOUS, anxious, agitated, apprehensive, uneasy, nervy, jittery, tense, panicky, fidgety, shaky, on edge, keyed up, wound up
FORMAL restive
COLLOQ. twitchy, edgy, het up, uptight, with butterflies in your stomach, on pins and needles, shaking like a leaf/jelly, with your heart in your mouth, in a sweat, in a stew, in a tizzy
2 FITFUL, twitchy, spasmodic, jerky, jolting, lurching, convulsive, disconnected, bumpy, bouncy, shaky, shaking, rough, unco-ordinated, uncontrolled, incoherent
F3 1 calm, composed

junction *n*

1 *a road junction*
intersection, crossing, crossroads, T-junction, box junction, circus, interchange, meeting-point, confluence; *Scot* toll
2 JOINT, join, joining, connection, meeting, bond, seam, juncture, union, intersection, link, linking, coupling, welding, close, cornice, knitting
TECHNICAL interface, abutment, cove, graft, collar, crown, node, raphe, suture, symphysis
FORMAL infall

---

junction or **juncture**?
A *junction* is a point or place where things meet: *a road junction; a junction box for wires*. A *juncture* is a point in time: *at this/that juncture*.

---

juncture *n*

point, period, stage, time, occasion, minute, moment, crisis, emergency, crux, predicament

jungle *n*

1 *tigers in the dense jungle*
tropical forest, rainforest, equatorial rainforest, bush, growth, shola
2 *a jungle of building regulations*
mass, heap, tangle, confusion, disorder, disarray, chaos, snarl, clutter, hotchpotch, mishmash, miscellany, medley, maze, labyrinth, web

junior *adj, n*

♦ *adj*
younger, young, minor, lesser, lower, subordinate,

secondary, subsidiary, inferior, assistant, associate, chota
OLD puisne
F3 senior
♦ *n*
minor, subordinate, inferior, subsidiary, minion, servant, associate, assistant, under-boy, fils
COLLOQ. dogsbody, underling

junk *n, v*

♦ *n*
rubbish, refuse, trash, debris, garbage, waste, scrap, litter, clutter, oddments, bric-à-brac, rummage, cast-offs, leftovers, leavings, dregs, wreckage
♦ *v*
throw out, throw away, get rid of, ditch, jettison, discard, dispose of
COLLOQ. dump, chuck

junket *n*

trip, journey, visit, outing, celebration, spree
COLLOQ. do, beano, bash

junta *n*

faction, clique, gang, group, ring, set, party, cartel, coterie, council, league, conclave, confederacy, cabal, camarilla

jurisdiction *n*

1 *under the council's jurisdiction*
power, authority, control, influence, dominion, province, sovereignty, administration, leadership, mastery, command, domination, rule, right, sway
TECHNICAL competence
FORMAL prerogative, capacity
2 AREA, field, orbit, bounds, scope, range, reach, sphere, district, territory, region, province, zone

jury *n*

jurors, panel, jurymen, jurywomen, party-jury, petit jury, petty jury; *Scot* assize; *N Am* grand jury

just *adj, adv*

♦ *adj*
1 *a just ruler*
fair, equitable, impartial, unbiased, unprejudiced, fair-minded, even-handed, neutral, objective, disinterested, righteous, upright, virtuous, moral, ethical, truthful, sincere, honourable, good, honest, irreproachable, upstanding, principled
2 *a just punishment*
deserved, merited, earned, fitting, well-deserved, appropriate, suitable, apt, due, justified, valid, sound, well-grounded, well-founded, proper, reasonable, rightful, lawful, legitimate, legal
F3 1 unjust **2** undeserved
♦ *adv*
1 *he's just left*
a short time ago, a moment ago, recently, lately
2 *that's just like him*
exactly, precisely, perfectly, completely, absolutely, quite
COLLOQ. bang on, spot-on, to a T
3 *she's just a child*
only, merely, simply, purely, nothing but, barely, hardly, scarcely

just about

practically, almost, virtually, nearly, as good as, all but, well-nigh, more or less, to all intents and purposes

justice *n*

1 FAIRNESS, equity, fair play, impartiality, objectivity, neutrality, equitableness, fair-mindedness, even-handedness, justness, legitimacy, honesty, honour, uprightness, integrity, right, rightfulness, rightness, righteousness, morals, ethics, justifiableness, lawfulness, validity, soundness, reasonableness
FORMAL rectitude, propriety
2 LEGALITY, law, penalty, punishment, recompense, amends, redress, reparation, satisfaction, compensation

3 JUDGE, Justice of the Peace, JP, magistrate, sheriff
⊟ **1** injustice, unfairness, bias

justifiable adj
defensible, excusable, warranted, warrantable, reasonable, within reason, sustainable, supportable, justified, lawful, legal, legitimate, acceptable, explainable, forgivable, pardonable, understandable, plausible, valid, well-founded, sound, sensible, right, proper, fit, tenable
FORMAL explicable
⊟ unjustifiable, inexcusable

justifiably adv
rightly, properly, validly, acceptably, understandably, plausibly, defensibly, excusably, reasonably, within reason, lawfully, legally, legitimately
⊟ unjustifiably, inexcusably

justification n
defence, plea, mitigation, apology, explanation, excuse, vindication, verification, confirmation, warrant, rationalization, reason, grounds, basis

justify v
vindicate, warrant, defend, acquit, absolve, clear, excuse, forgive, explain, pardon, validate, uphold, authorize, show to be right/reasonable, sustain, support, give reasons for, give grounds for, stand up for, maintain, establish, prove, rationalize, verify, confirm, bear out, make good, deserve
TECHNICAL aver, avow
OLD darraign
FORMAL exculpate, exonerate, substantiate

justly adv
1 EQUITABLY, even-handedly, properly, fairly, honestly, impartially, lawfully, objectively, equally
2 JUSTIFIABLY, duly, rightfully, rightly, with reason, legitimately
⊟ **1, 2** unjustly

jut (out) v
project, protrude, stick out, overhang, extend, beetle, extrude
⊟ recede

juvenile n, adj
♦ n
child, youth, minor, young person, youngster, adolescent, teenager, boy, girl, infant
COLLOQ. kid
♦ adj
young, youthful, minor, junior, immature, inexperienced, childish, puerile, infantile, teenage, adolescent, babyish, unsophisticated, callow
COLLOQ. green, wet behind the ears
⊟ mature

juxtapose v
put/place together, put/place side by side, put next to each other
TECHNICAL impale

juxtaposition n
proximity, nearness, closeness, contact, vicinity, immediacy
TECHNICAL impalement
FORMAL contiguity

K

kaleidoscopic *adj*
1 MANY-COLOURED, multicoloured, many-splendoured, variegated, motley, parti-coloured
TECHNICAL poikilitic
FORMAL polychromatic, polychrome
2 EVER-CHANGING, changeable, fluctuating, manifold, fluid
FORMAL multifarious
F3 **1** dull, monochrome, monotonous

kaput *adj*
broken, finished, ruined, wrecked, smashed, undone, defunct, destroyed, extinct
COLLOQ. bust, phut, conked out

karate

Shotokan karate belts include:

JUNIOR GRADES (KYU):	
white belt (beginner)	green belt (6th Kyu)
orange belt (9th Kyu)	purple belt (5th-4th Kyu)
red belt (8th Kyu)	brown belt (3rd-1st Kyu)
yellow belt (7th Kyu)	**SENIOR GRADES (DANS):**
	black belts (1st-8th Dan)

keel *n, v*
♦ *n*
base, bottom, back, centreboard, stabilizer
TECHNICAL keelson, carina, cheesecutter, skeg
■ **keel over**
1 OVERTURN, capsize, turn upside down, turn turtle, founder, collapse, upset
2 FAINT, pass out, lose consciousness, black out, fall, drop, stagger, topple over
OLD swoon

keen¹ *adj*
1 EAGER, avid, fervent, enthusiastic, earnest, devoted, diligent, industrious, conscientious, assiduous, intent, anxious, impatient
COLLOQ. keen as mustard
2 ASTUTE, sharp, shrewd, clever, perceptive, wise, discerning, discriminating, quick, quick-witted, sharp-witted, penetrating, piercing, acute, hawkish, fine, double-eyed, quick-eyed, deep, sensitive, razor-sharp, razor-like, smart; *Scot* gleg
OLD (*Shakesp*) hawking
FORMAL perspicacious, sagacious, argute
COLLOQ. wide awake
3 SHARP, piercing, penetrating, incisive, acute, pointed, intense, pungent, acid, biting, shrill
FORMAL trenchant, mordant
4 *keen competition*
fierce, intense, strong, wild, acute, ruthless, cut-throat
COLLOQ. dog-eat-dog
5 *keen on something/someone*
fond of, devoted to, liking, attached to, enamoured, loving, caring
COLLOQ. wild, mad, crazy, potty, nuts, having a soft spot for, heavily into
6 *a keen wind*
biting, cold, sharp, severe, penetrating, piercing, nipping, stinging; *Scot* snell
F3 **1** apathetic **2** superficial **3** dull

keen² *v*
mourners keened over the body
wail, moan, cry, howl, lament, weep, sob, groan, grieve, mourn
FORMAL ululate
COLLOQ. yowl

keenly *adv*
1 INTENSELY, strongly, acutely, fiercely
2 EAGERLY, fervently, enthusiastically, earnestly, diligently, assiduously
3 ASTUTELY, sharply, acutely, shrewdly, perceptively, quickly, deeply, cleverly, sensitively, penetratingly, incisively

keenness *n*
1 ENTHUSIASM, eagerness, diligence, earnestness, industriousness, industry, sedulity
2 ASTUTENESS, sharpness, shrewdness, cleverness, discernment, penetration, sensitivity, wisdom, incisiveness
FORMAL sagacity, sapience, trenchancy
F3 **1** apathy **2** bluntness, dullness

keep *v, n*
♦ *v*
1 RETAIN, hold, preserve, hold on to, hang on to, not part with, save, store (up), stock, deal in, carry, possess, keep possession of, amass, hoard, accumulate, collect, stack, conserve, deposit, heap, pile (up), place, maintain, furnish, sustain
2 CARRY ON, keep at/on, continue, persevere, persist, remain, stay, maintain
3 LOOK AFTER, tend, care for, keep in good order, have charge of, have custody of, maintain, provide for, subsidize, support, sustain, be responsible for, foster, superintend, mind, protect, shelter, guard, defend, watch (over), shield, safeguard, feed, nurture, manage
4 DETAIN, delay, keep waiting, check, hinder, hold (up), hold back, impede, obstruct, prevent, block, curb, interfere with, restrain, limit, inhibit, deter, hamper, keep back, control, constrain, arrest, withhold, confine
FORMAL retard
5 OBSERVE, comply with, respect, obey, fulfil, adhere to, abide by, carry out, recognize, keep up, keep faith with, commemorate, celebrate, hold, maintain, perform, perpetuate, mark, honour, solemnize
FORMAL effectuate
6 *keep pets*
own, look after, take care of, support, breed, raise, rear
7 *keep a shop*
own, run, manage, be in charge of
♦ *n*
1 SUBSISTENCE, board, board and lodgings, livelihood, living, maintenance, support, upkeep, means, food, nourishment, sustenance, nurture
2 FORT, fortress, tower, castle, citadel, stronghold, dungeon, donjon
■ **keep at**
persevere, stick at, be steadfast, continue, carry on, complete, endure, finish, last, maintain, remain, stay, persist, toil, grind, drudge, labour, beaver away at
COLLOQ. slog at, plug away at
F3 abandon, neglect

■ keep back
1 RESERVE, set/lay aside, retain, save, store, hold back, stockpile, hoard, accumulate
2 HOLD BACK, restrict, suppress, restrain, check, constrain, curb, impede, limit, prohibit, stop, control, delay, withhold, conceal, censor, hide, hush up, stifle, keep secret
FORMAL retard

■ keep from
prevent, resist, stop, restrain, halt
FORMAL forbear, desist, refrain

■ keep in
1 REPRESS, keep back, inhibit, bottle up, conceal, stifle, suppress, hide, control, restrain, quell, stop up
2 CONFINE, detain, shut in, coop up
E3 1 declare **2** release

■ keep off
avoid, stay away from, stay off, keep away, avoid going near, not go near, keep at a distance from, steer clear of, keep at arm's length
COLLOQ. give a wide berth to, body-swerve

■ keep on
1 CONTINUE, carry on, go on, endure, persevere, persist, keep at it, last, remain, stay, stay the course, hold on, retain, maintain
COLLOQ. soldier on, stick at it
2 *keep an employee on*
retain, keep, continue to employ, continue to engage/hire, keep in employment, keep on the payroll, retain the services of

■ keep on at
go on at, nag, pester, plague, pursue, badger, chivvy, harass, harry
FORMAL importune

■ keep secret
hide, conceal, keep back, keep dark, suppress
FORMAL dissemble
COLLOQ. keep under your hat, keep under wraps, your lips be sealed

■ keep to
observe, comply with, respect, obey, fulfil, adhere to, stick to

■ keep track of
follow, grasp, keep up with, monitor, oversee, plot, record, trace, track, understand, watch

■ keep up
1 CONTINUE, maintain, persevere, persist, go along with, support, sustain, preserve, keep pace, equal, contend, compete, vie, rival, match, emulate
2 *keep up with the latest developments*
keep up to date with, keep abreast of, keep in touch with, stay familiar with
COLLOQ. keep tabs on, keep your finger on the pulse
E3 1 fall behind **2** lose touch

■ for keeps
for ever, for good, always, for all time

keeper *n*
guard, custodian, curator, caretaker, attendant, guardian, overseer, steward, warder, jailer, gaoler, warden, supervisor, proprietor, bodyguard, escort, inspector, defender, governor, superintendent, administrator, surveyor
FORMAL conservator
COLLOQ. minder

keeping *n*
1 CUSTODY, guardianship, supervision, care, charge, safe-keeping, retention, protection, maintenance, surveillance, trust, tutelage, ward, cure, patronage
FORMAL auspices, aegis
2 *in keeping with the architecture*
agreement, harmony, conformity, correspondence, consistency, balance, proportion
FORMAL accord, congruity

keepsake *n*
memento, souvenir, remembrance, relic, reminder, token, pledge, emblem

keg *n*
barrel, butt, cask, drum, tun, vat, firkin, hogshead

ken *n*
knowledge, understanding, perception, awareness, appreciation, comprehension, realization, field, grasp, notice, range, reach, scope, acquaintance, compass
FORMAL cognizance

kerfuffle *n*
fuss, bother, commotion, palaver, furore, ado, fluster, flurry, bustle, brouhaha
COLLOQ. to-do, hoo-ha, flap, carry-on, ballyhoo, tizzy

kernel *n*
core, crux, grain, seed, stone, nut, nucleus, centre, heart, nub, essence, germ, marrow, substance, gist
FORMAL quintessence
COLLOQ. nitty-gritty, nuts and bolts, innards

key *n, adj*
♦ *n*
1 CLUE, cue, indicator, pointer, explanation, guide, gloss, sign, answer, solution, interpretation, means, secret
FORMAL explication
2 GUIDE, glossary, translation, legend, code, table, index
3 *in a low key*
pitch, tone, style, character, mood
TECHNICAL timbre
♦ *adj*
important, essential, vital, crucial, necessary, principal, decisive, central, chief, main, major, leading, basic, fundamental

keynote *n*
core, centre, heart, substance, point, theme, gist, pith, marrow, essence, emphasis, accent, stress

keystone *n*
cornerstone, core, crux, base, basis, foundation, ground, linchpin, principle, root, mainspring, source, spring, motive

kick *v, n*
♦ *v*
1 BOOT, hit, strike, knee, jolt, foot, toe, shoot, shin, project, fling, hack, hoof, lash out, spur; *dialect* pause, punch, punce, yerk
TECHNICAL back-heel, chip, heel, punt
OLD let out, recalcitrate, spurn at/against
2 GIVE UP, quit, stop, leave off, abandon, desist from, break
COLLOQ. pack in, jack in, quit
3 RECOIL, move back, jump back, spring back, rebound, react, falter, misfire, boomerang
♦ *n*
1 BLOW, recoil, jolt, striking, boot
TECHNICAL penalty, chip, cross-kick, drop-kick, fly-kick, free kick, goal kick, place kick, point after, punt, set piece, spot kick, tap-kick, high kick, garryowen, grub kick, grubber, pile-driver
OLD spurn, wince
2 STIMULATION, thrill, excitement, fun, pleasure
COLLOQ. buzz, lift, lark, high
3 *a drink with a kick*
power, strength, potency, effect, tang, stimulus
COLLOQ. punch, pep, bite, zing, zip

■ kick against
resist, rebel, oppose, spurn, defy, withstand, protest, hold out against

■ kick around
1 DISCUSS, talk about, play with, toy with
2 TAKE ADVANTAGE OF, exploit, use, abuse, ill-treat, maltreat, push about/around, trample on, mess about/around

■ kick off

begin, start, open, get under way, open the proceedings, introduce, inaugurate, initiate
FORMAL commence
COLLOQ. set/start the ball rolling

■ kick out

eject, evict, expel, oust, remove, discharge, dismiss, get rid of, throw out, reject
COLLOQ. chuck out, sack, boot out, turf out, show someone the door, give the sack/push/boot/elbow to

kickback *n*

1 RECOIL, rebound, backlash, reaction
2 BRIBE, incentive, inducement
COLLOQ. back-hander, sweetener, pay-off

kick-off *n*

beginning, start, outset, opening, introduction
FORMAL commencement, inception
COLLOQ. word go

kid[1] *n*

she has three kids
child, young one, little one, littling, littl 'un, young 'un, toddler, youngster, young person, youth, juvenile, infant, girl, little girl, boy, little boy, adolescent, teenager, lad; *Scot* littlin, littleane, bairn, wean
COLLOQ. nipper, tot, kiddy, kiddywink, tiny tot
SLANG sprog, ankle-biter, rug rat

kid[2] *v*

1 *I was only kidding*
tease, joke, hoax, fool, pretend, trick, jest
COLLOQ. have on, rib, pull someone's leg, wind up
2 *don't kid yourself*
delude, dupe, hoodwink, deceive, humbug, gull
COLLOQ. con, bamboozle, lead up the garden path, pull the wool over someone's eyes

kidnap *v*

abduct, capture, seize, hold to ransom, snatch, hijack, take/hold as hostage, steal

kill *v, n*

♦ *v*
1 SLAUGHTER, murder, take someone's life, slay, put to death, exterminate, assassinate, stab to death, finish off, massacre, destroy, put down, put to sleep, do away with, butcher, annihilate, execute, hang, guillotine, behead, shoot, electrocute, send to the electric chair
FORMAL smite, decapitate
COLLOQ. do in, eliminate, dispatch, wipe out, decimate, polish off, take out, zap
SLANG bump off, knock off, rub out, waste, blow away, liquidate
2 *kill a project*
end, destroy, put an end to, ruin, abolish, devastate, eradicate
COLLOQ. axe, scupper, put a spanner in the works
3 *my feet are killing me*
hurt, ache, cause pain, be painful, be sore, suffer, throb, pound, twinge, sting, smart
4 *don't kill yourself with all this work*
strain, exhaust, tire out, weary, fatigue, sap, drain
COLLOQ. do in, fag out, whack, knacker, take it out of
5 *kill time*
pass, spend, occupy, fill, use (up), while away
6 *kill noise*
stifle, deaden, dull, smother, quash, quell, suppress, muffle
7 *kill pain*
alleviate, relieve, soothe, ease, deaden, moderate
♦ *n*
death, shoot-out, death-blow, end, finish, climax, conclusion, *coup de grâce*, dénouement, dispatch, mop-up

---

Synonym nuances

verb sense 1
Slaughter can refer to the large-scale killing of animals, but when applied to humans it is a more marked term which tends to suggest wanton killing of defenceless victims. The term **massacre** also conveys this idea of killing large numbers, particularly in a brutal manner. **Annihilate** would suggest totally ending the existence of someone or something: *the Native Americans were virtually annihilated.* **Exterminate** also very starkly suggests bringing about someone's or something's end: *the dissidents, unable to defend themselves, were rounded up and exterminated.*
  Slay is more poetic in tone and tends to be used in a poetic or dramatic context: *slay the dragons.* **Butcher** is an emotive term which suggests a bloody and brutal death: *they were dragged from their cars and butchered by the angry mob.*
  Destroy can be used of killing an animal, especially one that is fatally ill or injured, although it is very detached in tone, while **put down** and **put to sleep** are rather more euphemistic and gentler in tone: *we had to tell the children that the old dog had been put to sleep.*
Assassinate is reserved for the organized killing of a prominent person, while **execute** also suggests a cold, dispassionate action, and has connotations of punishment or retribution, either official or unofficial: *the terrorist was executed in a tit-for-tat killing.*
  Hang, **guillotine**, **behead**, **electrocute** and **shoot**, on the other hand, are all specific terms for the means by which someone is killed or executed.

---

killer *n*

murderer, assassin, executioner, destroyer, slayer, slaughterer, exterminator, cut-throat, gunman, homicide
COLLOQ. butcher, hatchet man, hit-man, liquidator

killing *n, adj*

♦ *n*
1 SLAUGHTER, murder, massacre, butchery, genocide, homicide, assassination, execution, slaying, manslaughter, extermination, carnage, bloodshed, elimination, destruction, fatality
FORMAL patricide, matricide, infanticide, fratricide, sororicide, uxoricide
2 GAIN, fortune, windfall, booty, profit, lucky break, coup, success, stroke of luck, hit, big hit
COLLOQ. clean-up, bonanza
♦ *adj*
1 FUNNY, hilarious, comical, amusing, uproarious, ludicrous, absurd, hysterical, rib-tickling
COLLOQ. side-splitting, a scream
2 EXHAUSTING, hard, taxing, arduous, tiring, fatiguing, wearing, draining, gruelling
FORMAL debilitating, enervating
COLLOQ. back-breaking

killjoy *n*

spoilsport, moaner, complainer, dampener, damper, misery, cynic, pessimist, sceptic, grouch, whiner, prophet of doom, Weary Willie
COLLOQ. wet blanket, buzzkill
E∃ enthusiast, optimist, sport

kilter

■ out of kilter

awry, askew, misaligned, confused, out of balance, unbalanced, lopsided
COLLOQ. skew-whiff

kin *n*

relatives, relations, family, people, flesh and blood, cousins, blood, lineage, extraction, clan, stock, tribe

OLD kindred
FORMAL consanguinity

kind *n, adj*

• *n*

sort, type, class, category, set, variety, character, genus, genre, style, brand, family, breed, race, nature, persuasion, description, species, strain, stamp, temperament, character, manner

• *adj*

benevolent, kind-hearted, kindly, good-hearted, good-natured, helpful, obliging, humane, generous, big-hearted, compassionate, merciful, forbearing, pitying, charitable, benign, philanthropic, altruistic, humanitarian, amiable, friendly, amicable, congenial, soft-hearted, thoughtful, warm, warm-hearted, genial, cordial, considerate, courteous, sympathetic, patient, tender-hearted, loving, affectionate, understanding, lenient, mild, gentle, indulgent, tolerant, unselfish, selfless, neighbourly, tactful, giving, nice, good, gracious
FORMAL magnanimous, bounteous
🔁 cruel, inconsiderate, unhelpful

■ **kind of**
rather, moderately, relatively, slightly, a bit, a little, somewhat, fairly, quite, to a limited degree/extent, to some degree/extent, pretty
COLLOQ. sort of

■ **in kind**
in like manner, in return, in exchange, similarly, tit for tat

---

Synonym nuances
adjective
Benevolent may be used of someone predisposed to doing good deeds, whereas **humane**, **compassionate** and **merciful** have more to do with showing pity or empathy: *he fought to establish humane conditions for prisoners*. You can use **benign** of someone who has a kind and sympathetic attitude: *a benign old uncle who would listen to what you had to say*, whereas **philanthropic**, **altruistic** and **humanitarian** all go somewhat further by implying actively working for the benefit of mankind. **Charitable** is similar, but can also suggest empathy and leniency: *his charitable works; be charitable, she's only young.*
  Forbearing, on the other hand, puts the emphasis on the element of patient endurance: *we are not required to be forbearing until there is a problem*. The terms **amiable**, **friendly**, **amicable** and **congenial** suggest being welcoming and outgoing, while **warm**, **genial** and **cordial** suggest an affectionate or friendly nature. You can use **lenient**, **indulgent** and **tolerant** of someone who is less severe than possible or warranted.
  The terms **unselfish**, the stronger **selfless**, and **giving**, all emphasize the quality of putting others before yourself. **Neighbourly** is milder in that it is more suggestive of a dutiful helpfulness, while **tactful** is simply being skilful in dealing with the feelings of others. **Gracious** suggests that someone's kindness lends them dignity: *our gracious queen.*

---

kind-hearted *adj*
kind, warm, warm-hearted, sympathetic, tender-hearted, kindly, generous, considerate, compassionate, amicable, good-hearted, good-natured, obliging, gracious, benign, big-hearted, helpful, philanthropic, altruistic, humanitarian, humane
🔁 ill-natured

kindle *v*
1 IGNITE, light, set alight, set on fire, set fire to
2 INFLAME, fire, stir, thrill, stimulate, rouse, arouse, awaken, excite, fan, incite, inspire, induce, provoke

kindliness *n*
kindness, benevolence, compassion, friendliness, sympathy, warmth, generosity, charity, amiability
OLD loving-kindness
FORMAL beneficence, benignity
🔁 cruelty, meanness, unkindness

kindly *adj, adv*

• *adj*

benevolent, kind, kind-hearted, compassionate, charitable, good, good-natured, helpful, considerate, thoughtful, warm, generous, big-hearted, cordial, genial, favourable, giving, indulgent, pleasant, nice, agreeable, sympathetic, understanding, tender, gentle, mild, humane, natural, patient, friendly, neighbourly, avuncular, grandfatherly, benign, fond, amicable, polite; *Scot* couthie
FORMAL magnanimous, benefic
🔁 cruel, uncharitable

• *adv*

benevolently, kind-heartedly, helpfully, humanely, compassionately, mercifully, generously, charitably, benignly, philanthropically, altruistically, thoughtfully, considerately, tolerantly, unselfishly, selflessly, tactfully, courteously, sympathetically, patiently, warmly, gently, lovingly, affectionately
OLD goodly
FORMAL magnanimously

kindness *n*
1 BENEVOLENCE, kindliness, charity, magnanimity, compassion, fellow feeling, generosity, hospitality, humanity, humaneness, courtesy, friendliness, pleasantness, goodwill, philanthropy, altruism, humanitarianism, niceness, goodness, grace, patience, indulgence, tolerance, leniency, understanding, sympathy, considerateness, consideration, warmth, warm-heartedness, love, affection, helpfulness, thoughtfulness, gentleness, mildness
OLD loving-kindness
FORMAL benignancy
2 FAVOUR, good turn, good deed, assistance, help, aid, service
🔁 1 cruelty, inhumanity 2 disservice

kindred *n, adj*

• *n*

relatives, relations, flesh and blood, family, people, folk, connections, clan, relationship, kinsfolk, lineage
OLD kin
FORMAL consanguinity

• *adj*

similar, common, related, matching, like, corresponding, affiliated, connected, allied, akin
FORMAL cognate

king *n*
1 MONARCH, ruler, head of state, sovereign, majesty, emperor, chief, chieftain, prince, lord, supremo
Related adjective: regal
2 the king of football
supremo, kingpin, star, chief, leader, master
COLLOQ. leading light, top dog, big cheese/shot/noise, bigwig, the greatest

kingdom *n*
monarchy, sovereignty, reign, realm, empire, dominion, commonwealth, nation, principality, state, country, domain, dynasty, province, sphere, territory, land, grouping, division
See panel on next page

kingly *adj*
sovereign, majestic, royal, regal, imperial, imperious, lordly, noble, stately, supreme, sublime, splendid, glorious, grand, imposing, grandiose, dignified
FORMAL august, monarchical

Historical kingdoms and empires include:

KINGDOMS:				
Akkad (*Middle East*)	Galicia (*northern Spain*)	New Kingdom (*Egypt*)	Assyria (*western Asia*)	Ottoman Empire
Alban (*Scotland*)	Lombardy (*Italy*)	Northumbria	Austro-Hungarian Empire	Persian Empire
Argolis (*Greece*)	Media (*northern Iran*)	(*northern England*)	British Empire	Roman Empire
Bohemia (*Czech Republic*)	Middle Kingdom (*Egypt*)	Old Kingdom (*Egypt*)	Byzantine Empire	
Cush or Kush (*Nile valley*)	Moab (*Jordan*)	Sardinia (*Italy*)	Chinese Empire	
Dalriada (*Scotland*)	Naples (*Italy*)	EMPIRES: Abyssinia	Holy Roman Empire	
			Mogul Empire	

kink *n, v*

♦ *n*

1 CURL, twist, twirl, bend, dent, indentation, knot, loop, crimp, coil, tangle, entanglement, crinkle, wrinkle
2 QUIRK, eccentricity, idiosyncrasy, whim, foible, peculiarity, deviation, perversion, fetish
FORMAL caprice
3 *iron out all the kinks*
defect, flaw, hitch, blemish, imperfection, deficiency, shortcoming, weak point, weakness, failing, foible
COLLOQ. bug, glitch

♦ *v*

bend, curl, twist, curve, coil, tangle, crimp, wrinkle

kinky *adj*

1 STRANGE, odd, abnormal, unusual, unconventional, freakish, eccentric, outlandish, queer, quirky, idiosyncratic, peculiar, perverted, deviant, unnatural, warped, weird, bizarre, whimsical, degenerate, depraved, licentious
FORMAL capricious
2 CURLED, coiled, twisted, crumpled, tangled, curly, wavy, wrinkled, crimped, frizzy
E3 **1** normal

kinsfolk *n*

relatives, relations, family, clan, cousins, connections
OLD kin, kindred

kinship *n*

1 KIN, family, blood, relation, relationship, ties, lineage, ancestry
FORMAL consanguinity
2 AFFINITY, similarity, association, alliance, connection, correspondence, equivalence, relationship, tie, community, likeness, kindred, conformity

kiosk *n*

booth, stall, stand, news-stand, bookstall, cabin, box, counter

kismet *n*

destiny, fate, doom, fortune, lot, portion, providence, karma
FORMAL predestiny

kiss *v, n*

♦ *v*

1 CARESS, lip, smack; *dialect* smouch; *Welsh* buss
OLD (*Shakesp*) mouth
FORMAL osculate
COLLOQ. peck, give someone a peck, smooch, neck, canoodle, bill and coo
SLANG snog; *N Am* suck face
2 TOUCH, touch gently/lightly, graze, glance off, brush, lick, scrape, fan

♦ *n*

French kiss, deep kiss, butterfly kiss; *dialect* smouch; *Welsh* buss
OLD baisemain
FORMAL osculation, pax
COLLOQ. peck, smack, smacker, plonker
SLANG snog

kit *n, v*

♦ *n*

1 EQUIPMENT, gear, apparatus, supplies, tackle, provisions, outfit, implements, set, tools, trappings, rig, instruments,
paraphernalia, utensils, effects, luggage, baggage
FORMAL accoutrements, appurtenances
COLLOQ. things, stuff
2 *football kit*
tackle, clothing, clothes, outfit, rig, colours
COLLOQ. rig-out, gear, strip, togs, things, get-up, clobber

■ **kit out**

equip, fit out, outfit, supply, provide, fix up, furnish, prepare, arm, deck out, dress, rig out

kitchen utensils

See panel on next page

kittenish *adj*

playful, sportive, ludic, frolicsome, frisky, cute, fun-loving, coquettish, flirtatious
E3 staid

knack *n*

flair, faculty, facility, bent, skill, competence, proficiency, talent, genius, gift, trick, ability, capability, adroitness, expertise, skilfulness, aptitude, forte, capacity, handiness, dexterity, quickness, turn
OLD (*Shakesp*) quirk
FORMAL propensity
COLLOQ. hang

knapsack *n*

bag, pack, haversack, rucksack, backpack, duffel bag, holdall, kitbag

knave *n*

rogue, scoundrel, villain, swindler, rascal, cheat, reprobate, scamp, scallywag, swine
OLD boy, blighter, bounder, dastard, rotter, custrel, drôle, *fripon*, varlet; (*Shakesp*) coistrel, coistril

knavery *n*

knavishness, mischief, roguery, trickery, villainy, devilry, corruption, deceit, deception, dishonesty, double-dealing, fraud, chicanery, imposture
OLD (*Shakesp*) patchery
FORMAL duplicity
COLLOQ. hanky-panky, monkey business

knavish *adj*

roguish, mischievous, rascally, fiendish, wicked, contemptible, corrupt, fraudulent, deceitful, deceptive, dishonest, dishonourable, unprincipled, unscrupulous, reprobate, scoundrelly, villainous, devilish
OLD dastardly
E3 honest, honourable, scrupulous

knead *v*

manipulate, press, massage, work, pummel, pound, ply, squeeze, shape, rub, form, mould, knuckle, conche, masticate, puddle
FORMAL malax, malaxate

kneel *v*

fall to your knees, bow (down), get down on your knees, stoop, bend, curtsy, revere, defer to, kowtow
FORMAL genuflect, make obeisance

knell *n*

toll, ringing, ring, chime, peal, sound, end
OLD knoll

Kitchen utensils include:

asparagus cooker	cruet set	kitchen scales	pie funnel	stockpot	cocktail knife
bain marie	deep-fat fryer	knife block	pie plate	stoner	cook's knife
baking sheet	dough hook	lemon reamer	potato masher	storage jar	fish knife
baster	egg coddler	lemon squeezer	potato ricer	tea caddy	grapefruit knife
biscuit press	egg poacher	liquidizer	preserving pan	tea infuser	Kitchen Devils®
blender	egg separator	loaf tin	pressure cooker	tea strainer	mezzaluna
blini pan	egg slicer	madeleine tin	pudding basin	terrine	oyster knife
blowtorch	egg-timer	mandolin	pudding mould	thermometer	palette knife
bottle opener	fish kettle	measuring jug	punch bowl	toast rack	paring knife
breadbin	fish slice	meat	quiche dish	tongs	steak knife
breadboard	fish tweezers	thermometer	ramekin	tureen	table knife
brochette	flan tin	melon baller	rice cooker	vegetable brush	tomato knife
bun tin	fondue set	milk pan	roasting pan	vegetable	vegetable knife
butter curler	flour dredger	mincer	rolling pin	steamer	**TYPES OF SPOON:**
butter dish	food processor	mixing bowl	salad spinner	waffle iron	dessert spoon
cake tin	fork	mortar and pestle	sandwich tin	whisk	draining spoon
can-opener	frying pan	mouli	saucepan	wine cooler	ladle
casserole	garlic press	muffin tin	scissors	wine rack	measuring spoon
cheese board	grater	nutcracker	sharpening steel	wok	pasta ladle
cheese slicer	gravy separator	nutmeg grater	shears	yoghurt maker	serving spoon
chestnut pan	grill pan	oil drizzler	sieve	zester	skimmer
chopping-board	ham stand	omelette pan	sifter	**TYPES OF KNIFE:**	soupspoon
cocotte	heat diffuser	paella pan	skewer	boning knife	straining spoon
colander	herb mill	pasta maker	skillet	bread knife	tablespoon
corer	ice-cream scoop	pastry board	slow cooker	butter knife	teaspoon
corkscrew	icing syringe	pastry brush	soufflé dish	canelle knife	wooden spoon
crêpe pan	jelly mould	pastry cutter	spatula	carving knife	
croquembouche	juicer	peeler	spice rack	cheese knife	
mould	karahi	pepper mill	steamer	cleaver	

See also panels at **cook**; **cutlery**; **domestic appliances**.

knickers *n*

pants, underpants, panties, briefs, underwear, lingerie, bikini briefs, g-string, camiknickers, knickerbockers, Directoire knickers, bloomers
COLLOQ. drawers, smalls, frillies, scanties

knick-knack *n*

trinket, trifle, bauble, gewgaw, gimcrack, bagatelle, ornament, bric-à-brac, plaything

knife *n, v*

◆ *n*
blade, cutter
◆ *v*
cut, rip, slash, stab, pierce, wound, lacerate, bayonet

Knives include:

Bowie knife	jackknife	scalpel
carver	Kitchen Devils®	skene-dhu
craft knife	machete	Stanley knife®
dagger	paper knife	Swiss Army knife
dirk	penknife	switchblade
flick-knife	pocket knife	

See also **dagger**; **kitchen utensils**.

knight *n*

cavalier, horseman, equestrian, cavalryman, man-at-arms, soldier, warrior, chevalier, gallant, champion, knight-errant, Bayard, carpet-knight, *preux chevalier*
OLD kemper, kempery-man, banneret, bachelor, ritter, vavasour, douzeper; (*Spenser*) doucepere, freelance, younker

knightly *adj*

chivalrous, bold, courageous, valiant, dauntless, gallant, heroic, noble, honourable, intrepid, soldierly, courtly, gracious
FORMAL valorous
F3 cowardly, ignoble, ungallant

knit *v*

1 JOIN, unite, secure, bind, ally, connect, tie, fasten, link, draw together, mend, interlace, intertwine
2 KNOT, loop, crotchet, purl, weave
3 WRINKLE, furrow, crease, gather, tighten

Types of knitting stitch include:

basketweave	fisherman's rib	plain stitch
box stitch	garter rib	purl
braided cable	garter stitch	rice stitch
cable stitch	honeycomb	roman stripe
chain cable	lattice cable	seed stitch
chain stitch	layette	stocking stitch
chevron	mistake rib	Swiss check
diagonal rib	moss panels	twin rib
double seed	moss stitch	
stitch	pavilion	

knob *n*

1 HANDLE, doorhandle, switch, button, push-button, tuner, stop
2 LUMP, ball, boss, protrusion, bump, projection, protuberance, nub, knot, knurl, gnarl, swell, knub, swelling, tumour, boll, burr, tuber, eminence, node, stud, heel, snub; *Scot* plouk
TECHNICAL umbo, tubercle
OLD knop, noop, pommel

knock *v, n*

◆ *v*
1 *knock on the door*
tap, hit, strike, rap, thump, bang, pound, slap, smack
2 *knock someone down*
hit, strike, collide with, bump into, smack, slap, punch, box, clout, cuff, clip, swipe, bang, batter
COLLOQ. wallop, whack, belt
3 *knocked her head against the wall*
bang, bump, hit, strike, collide, bash, pound, thump, stamp, dash, crash, jolt
4 CRITICIZE, condemn, run down, find fault with, slate, attack
FORMAL disparage, deprecate, censure
COLLOQ. slam, pan, rubbish, pick holes in,

pull/tear to pieces, pull apart
SLANG slag (off)
E3 4 boost, praise
◆ *n*
1 *a knock at the door*
tap, rap, hit, pounding, banging, hammering
2 BLOW, bump, bang, bash, box, rap, thump, clout, cuff, clip, pounding, hammering, slap, smack
COLLOQ. whack, belt, wallop
3 MISFORTUNE, blow, setback, failure, rejection, reversal, rebuff, defeat, bad experience/luck
COLLOQ. whammy
▪ **knock about**
1 WANDER, travel, roam, rove, saunter, traipse, ramble, gad, gallivant, range
2 ASSOCIATE, go around
FORMAL consort
COLLOQ. hang around/about
3 BEAT UP, batter, abuse, mistreat, hurt, hit, strike, punch, bash, damage, maltreat, injure, wound, manhandle, bruise, buffet
▪ **knock back**
swallow, devour, drink, gulp (down)
COLLOQ. guzzle, down, scoff, swig
▪ **knock down**
1 DEMOLISH, destroy, fell, pull down, take down, floor, level, wreck, raze, pound, batter, clout, smash, wallop
2 RUN OVER, hit, knock over, run down
3 *knocked down prices*
reduce, lower, decrease, bring down
▪ **knock off**
1 FINISH, finish/stop work, stop, cease, clock off, clock out
FORMAL terminate
COLLOQ. pack (it) in
2 STEAL, rob, pilfer, filch
COLLOQ. pinch, nick, lift, whip, snaffle, snitch, swipe
SLANG rip off
3 DEDUCT, take away
4 KILL, murder, slay, assassinate, get rid of, do away with
COLLOQ. bump off, polish off, do in
SLANG waste
▪ **knock out**
1 *knock someone out*
make unconscious, floor, strike down, fell, level, prostrate
COLLOQ. KO
2 *knocked out of a competition*
defeat, eliminate, beat, overcome, get the better of, overwhelm, rout, crush
COLLOQ. thrash, hammer, run rings round
3 STUN, astound, impress, amaze, surprise, startle, astonish, shock, overwhelm, take your breath away
COLLOQ. bowl over, knock for six
E3 1 bring round
▪ **knock up**
1 BUILD QUICKLY, jerry-build, make quickly, put together hurriedly, improvise
2 WAKE UP, waken, awake, awaken, rouse, stir, call
3 MAKE PREGNANT, impregnate
COLLOQ. put in the (pudding) club, put in the family way
E3 1 demolish

knockout *n*
success, triumph, sensation, attraction, coup, hit, winner
COLLOQ. smash, smash-hit, stunner
E3 flop, loser

knoll *n*
hill, hillock, mound, rise, barrow, elevation, hummock, koppie; *Scot* knowe

knot *v, n*
◆ *v*
tie, secure, bind, loop, tether, leash, lash, entangle, tangle, knit, entwine, ravel, weave

◆ *n*
1 TIE, bond, joint, fastening, loop, splice, twist, ligature
2 BUNCH, cluster, clump, group, circle, ring, band, gathering, crowd
3 *a knot on a tree*
knob, lump, gnarl, knurl, swelling, nodule, knub

Types of knot include:

bend	flat knot	round turn and
Blackwall hitch	Flemish eye (or	two half hitches
blood knot	double figure of	running bowline
bow	eight)	seizing
bowline	granny knot	sheepshank
carrick bend	half hitch	sheet bend (or
chain knot	highwayman's	common bend
clove hitch	hitch (or donkey	or swab hitch)
common	hitch)	simple sennit (or
whipping	hitch	plait knot)
Domhof knot	Hunter's bend	slipknot
double blood	lark's head	slippery hitch
double Cairnton	loop knot	spade-end knot
double-overhand	marling hitch	surgeon's knot
double-slipped	Matthew	thief knot
reefknot	Walker's	tie
drummer's chain	overhand knot (or	timber hitch
Englishman's tie	thumb knot)	Turk's head
(or knot)	reef knot (or	turle knot
figure of eight	square knot)	wall knot
fisherman's bend	rolling hitch	weaver's knot
fisherman's knot		Windsor knot

knotty *adj*
1 COMPLICATED, complex, intricate, difficult, hard, perplexing, thorny, tricky, troublesome, puzzling, baffling, mystifying, problematical, Byzantine
FORMAL anfractuous
2 GNARLED, knobby, knotted, rugged, rough, bumpy, nodose, nodous, nodular

know *v*
1 *know French*
understand, comprehend, apprehend, perceive, sense, notice, be aware, be conscious of, fathom, be well-versed in, be conversant with, be au fait with, experience, realize, see, undergo, go through
FORMAL be cognizant of
COLLOQ. be clued up, have at your fingertips, know like the back of your hand, have taped
2 *I know George*
be acquainted with, be familiar with, be friends with, associate with, be on good terms with, recognize, know by sight, identify
3 *know a good wine*
distinguish, discriminate, discern, differentiate, identify, make out, tell (apart)

know-all *n*
know-it-all, wiseacre
COLLOQ. clever clogs, clever dick, wise guy, smart alec, smartypants
SLANG smartass, smartarse

knowhow *n*
expertise, knowledge, experience, proficiency, competence, gumption, savoir-faire, ability, capability, skill, ingenuity, dexterity, aptitude, adroitness, adeptness, talent, faculty, bent, flair, knack
COLLOQ. savvy

knowing *adj*
meaningful, expressive, perceptive, shrewd, significant, discerning, conscious, cunning, astute, aware
COLLOQ. sussed

knowingly *adj*
intentionally, willingly, on purpose, purposely, consciously,

studiedly, wilfully, wittingly, deliberately, designedly, by design, calculatedly

knowledge n

1 LEARNING, scholarship, education, schooling, letters, instruction, wisdom, tuition, enlightenment, information, data, facts
FORMAL erudition
COLLOQ. knowhow
2 ACQUAINTANCE, familiarity, awareness, intimacy, consciousness
FORMAL cognizance
3 UNDERSTANDING, comprehension, apprehension, recognition, judgement, discernment, wisdom, intelligence, ability, grasp, skill, expertise, proficiency, conversance, savoir-faire
FORMAL cognition
COLLOQ. knowhow
E3 1 ignorance **2** unawareness

Synonym nuances
sense 1
Learning may be widely used of anything which has been retained from experience or study, while **scholarship** is more suggestive of intense academic research and expertise: *new standards of art history scholarship*. **Education** usually refers to the general instruction and culture to which a person is subject, while **schooling** suggests a more narrow training received in a formal setting: *poor standards of secondary schooling*. **Instruction** and **tuition** are also straightforward synonyms that put the emphasis on teaching, and **information**, **data** and **facts** are the basic components for building knowledge. **Letters** implies literary culture and suggests a degree of reverence: *a man of letters*. You can use **wisdom** simply of accrued knowledge: *conventional wisdom*, but it can also imply inherent good sense: *they have the wisdom to know themselves*, and it can have connotations of gravitas: a*n ancient Chinese book of wisdom*. **Enlightenment** is also very positive in tone, and implies a more internal revelation brought about by learning: *learning about history brings enlightenment*.

---

knowledgeable adj

1 EDUCATED, scholarly, learned, informed, well-informed, well-read, lettered, intelligent, enlightened
FORMAL erudite
COLLOQ. a mine of information
2 AWARE, acquainted, conscious, familiar, au fait, conversant, experienced, expert, well-versed
COLLOQ. well up in, in the know, savvy, clued-up, up to speed
E3 1 ignorant

known adj

acknowledged, recognized, well-known, noted, obvious, patent, plain, admitted, revealed, familiar, avowed, commonplace, published, proclaimed, confessed, celebrated, famous

knuckle

■ **knuckle down**
buckle down, start to work hard, begin to study
■ **knuckle under**
submit, yield, give way, give in, succumb, surrender, capitulate, defer, buckle under
FORMAL accede, acquiesce

kowtow v

defer, cringe, fawn, grovel, pander, curry favour, pay court, flatter, kneel
COLLOQ. suck up, toady, bow and scrape

kudos n

fame, glory, applause, praise, honour, laurels, prestige, renown, repute, reputation, distinction, acclaim, esteem, regard, cachet, plaudits
FORMAL laudation

L

label *n, v*

◆ *n*

1 TAG, ticket, docket, tab, mark, marker, sticker, stamp, seal, flash, trademark, number, tally, bookplate, crowner
TECHNICAL address, identifier
2 DESCRIPTION, categorization, identification, characterization, classification, designation, tag, badge, brand, name, title, nickname, epithet
3 TRADEMARK, make, logo, brand, brand name, proprietary name

◆ *v*

1 TAG, mark, stamp, attach a label to, mark, ticket
2 DESCRIBE, brand, classify, categorize, characterize, identify, class, designate, define, term, call, dub, name, designate

laboratory apparatus

Laboratory apparatus includes:

autoclave	electron	retort
beaker	microscope	separating funnel
bell jar	evaporating dish	slide
boiling tube	filter flask	spatula
Büchner funnel	filter paper	stand
Bunsen burner	flask	still
burette	fume cupboard	stirrer
centrifuge	funnel	stop clock
clamp	glove box	test tube
condenser	Kipp's apparatus	test tube rack
conical flask	Liebig condenser	thermometer
crucible	measuring	top-pan balance
cylinder	cylinder	tripod
desiccator	microscope	trough
distillation	mortar	U-tube
apparatus	pestle	volumetric flask
dropper	Petri dish	Woulfe bottle
	pipette	

laborious *adj*

1 HARD, arduous, difficult, strenuous, tough, heavy, backbreaking, wearisome, wearying, tiresome, tiring, fatiguing, uphill, onerous, tedious, heavy, toilsome, slavish, Sisyphean
OLD operose, painful; (*Shakesp*) laboursome
2 HARD-WORKING, industrious, painstaking, indefatigable, diligent, careful, assiduous
E3 **1** easy, effortless **2** lazy

laboriously *adv*

with difficulty, arduously, strenuously, wearisomely, tiresomely, toilsomely, drudgingly, slavishly
OLD operosely

labour *n, v*

◆ *n*

1 WORK, task, job, employment, chore, toil, effort, hard work, exertion, drudgery, industriousness, diligence
COLLOQ. grind, slog, sweat
2 WORKERS, employees, workforce, labourers, workmen, hands
3 CHILDBIRTH, birth, delivery, labour pains, pangs, throes, contractions
TECHNICAL parturition

E3 **1** ease, leisure **2** management

◆ *v*

1 WORK, toil, work hard, drudge, slave, strive, exert yourself, endeavour, struggle, plod
FORMAL travail
COLLOQ. grind, sweat, kill yourself
2 OVERDO, overemphasize, dwell on, elaborate, overstress, put too much emphasis on, strain
3 *labour hard to get results*
struggle, strive, endeavour, work hard, try hard
COLLOQ. do your best, give your all, go all out, give it your best shot
4 *labour under a mistaken belief*
suffer, be misled, be deceived, be blinded
5 *labour a point*
belabour, harp on about, keep talking about, dwell on, reiterate
COLLOQ. go on and on about, flog to death, do to death
6 TOSS, pitch, roll, pitch, turn
E3 **1** laze, idle, lounge

laboured *adj*

awkward, unnatural, forced, difficult, complicated, heavy, overdone, overwrought, stiff, stilted, strained, ponderous, studied, contrived
FORMAL affected
E3 easy, natural

labourer *n*

manual worker, blue-collar worker, unskilled worker, navvy, hand, worker, workman, drudge, menial, hireling, operative, boy, jack, pioneer, roustabout, hobbler, hod carrier, hodman, docker, cottager, field hand; *Aust* (*derog*) Kanaka
OLD churl
COLLOQ. *Irish* (*derog*) culchie; *N Am* gandy dancer
SLANG (*offensive*) coolie; *N Am* bohunk, grunt, (*derog*) redneck
OLD SLANG Grecian

labyrinth *n*

maze, winding, warren, complexity, intricacy, complication, network, puzzle, riddle, enigma, tangle, entanglement, jungle, confusion, web

labyrinthine *adj*

complex, intricate, complicated, perplexing, puzzling, involved, knotty, tangled, tortuous, winding, mazelike, confused, mazy, Byzantine
FORMAL convoluted
E3 simple, straightforward

lace *n, v*

◆ *n*

1 NETTING, mesh-work, open work, tatting, crochet, filigree
2 STRING, cord, twine, thong, tie, shoelace, bootlace, lacing
◆ *v*

1 TIE, do up, fasten, secure, thread, close, bind, attach, string, twine, intertwine, interweave
2 ADD TO, mix in, flavour, blend, strengthen
FORMAL fortify
COLLOQ. spike

lacerate v
tear, rip, rend, cut (open), gash, slash, wound, claw, mangle, maim, injure, mutilate, torture, torment, harrow, hurt, distress
FORMAL afflict

laceration n
tear, cut, gash, rip, rent, slash, wound, injury, mutilation, maim

lachrymose adj
tearful, crying, weeping, weepy, mournful, sad, melancholy, sobbing, teary, woeful
FORMAL dolorous, lugubrious
📧 happy, laughing

lack n, v
♦ n
need, scarcity, shortage, insufficiency, dearth, deficiency, absence, scantiness, vacancy, void, deprivation, destitution, emptiness
FORMAL want, paucity, privation
📧 abundance, profusion
♦ v
need, have need of, not have, not have enough of, miss, be deficient in, require
FORMAL want
COLLOQ. be clean/fresh out of

Synonym nuances
noun
Need can be used of a requirement: *there is a need for home care for the elderly*, while **scarcity** would be reserved for where there is a serious shortfall. The terms **shortage** and **insufficiency** simply say there is not enough, but **dearth** goes further by suggesting there are hardly any of something, and the effects are detrimental: *a dearth of written records from that time means we cannot get a clear picture.* **Deficiency**, on the other hand, suggests a missing amount that detracts from completeness: *she was suffering from an iron deficiency.* You can use **absence** if nothing is present at all, while **vacancy**, like **emptiness** and **void**, suggests an unfilled space, although **vacancy** also often applies to an unfilled job. The more emotive **deprivation** suggests inadequate supplies for physical or emotional nourishment, while **destitution** takes that to extremes by implying being entirely without such things: *the venture failed, leaving the family in destitution.*

---

lackadaisical adj
apathetic, lazy, lethargic, inert, limp, spiritless, listless, indifferent, idle, dreamy, dull, lukewarm, half-hearted, abstracted, careless
FORMAL enervated, indolent, languorous, languid
📧 active, dynamic, energetic, vigorous

lackey n
1 FAWNER, sycophant, toady, flatterer, hanger-on, parasite, minion, pawn, poodle, instrument, tool
COLLOQ. yes-man, doormat
2 ATTENDANT, steward, servant, manservant, footman, menial, valet, page, retainer, guide, equerry, vassal
OLD skip-kennel

lacking adj
1 NEEDING, without, short of, missing, absent, minus
2 DEFICIENT, inadequate, defective, flawed
FORMAL wanting

lacklustre adj
drab, dull, flat, boring, tedious, dry, leaden, lifeless, spiritless, uninteresting, unimaginative, uninspired, commonplace, dim, insipid, vapid
COLLOQ. run-of-the-mill
📧 brilliant, inspired, lively, bright

laconic adj
terse, succinct, pithy, concise, incisive, crisp, taciturn, short, curt, brief, economical, blunt, abrupt, to the point
📧 verbose, wordy

laconically adv
briefly, tersely, succinctly, pithily, concisely, incisively, bluntly, abruptly, in brief, in a word, to the point
📧 verbosely, at (great) length

lacuna n
gap, omission, space, void, break, blank, cavity
FORMAL hiatus

lad n
1 BOY, youth, youngster, stripling, juvenile, schoolboy, son; Scot callant, chield, chiel; Irish bucko, gossoon, spalpeen
OLD Scot gillie-wetfoot, gillie-white-foot
COLLOQ. kid, nipper, whippersnapper; Welsh & Irish boyo; N Am tad
2 CHAP, fellow, individual, character, sort, type
COLLOQ. guy, bloke

ladder n
1 STEPS, set of steps, stairs, rungs
Related adjective: scalar
2 RANK, ranking, level, rung, point, hierarchy, grading, scale, series, echelons, pecking order

---

Types of ladder include:

accommodation ladder	kitchen steps	scale
companion ladder	library steps	side ladder
étrier	loft ladder	stepladder
extension ladder	multipurpose ladder	stepstool
folding ladder	platform ladder	stern ladder
fruit-picking ladder	quarter ladder	stile
gangway ladder	ratline	straight ladder
hook ladder	rolling ladder	tower scaffold
	roof ladder	
	rope ladder	

---

laden adj
loaded, charged, weighed down, burdened, oppressed, packed, stuffed, weighted, full, chock-full, fraught, encumbered, hampered, taxed, jammed
📧 empty

la-di-da adj
pretentious, posh, conceited, snobbish, snooty, mannered, over-refined, foppish
FORMAL affected
COLLOQ. highfalutin, put-on, stuck-up, toffee-nosed

ladle v
shovel, spoon, lade, dish, scoop, bail, dip
■ **ladle out**
hand out, distribute, disburse, dish out, dole out

lady n
woman, young woman, female, matron, noblewoman, dame, countess, grande dame, begum, khanum, sheikha, Señora, Señorita, duenna, Signora, Signorina
OLD damsel, gentlewoman, demoiselle, miss, ladykin, lakin, burd
SLANG old dear

ladylike adj
refined, well-bred, well-mannered, polite, courteous, proper, respectable, polished, modest, cultured, elegant, courtly, queenly, genteel, matronly
FORMAL decorous

lag v
dawdle, loiter, hang back, linger, fall behind, straggle, trail, bring up the rear, saunter, delay, shuffle, idle, dally
FORMAL tarry

COLLOQ. shilly-shally, lounge, drag your feet, kick your heels
⧫ hurry, lead, keep up

laggard n
dawdler, loiterer, lingerer, straggler, sluggard, idler, saunterer, snail, loafer
COLLOQ. slowcoach, lounger
⧫ dynamo, live wire; *colloq.* go-getter

lagoon n
pool, pond, shallows, lake, marsh, bog, fen, swamp; *NAm* bayou

laid-back adj
relaxed, at ease, casual, leisurely, easy-going, unhurried, untroubled, unworried, calm, cool, free and easy
FORMAL imperturbable
COLLOQ. unflappable
⧫ tense; *colloq.* uptight

laid up adj
housebound, bedridden, confined to bed, ill, sick, incapacitated, disabled, *hors de combat*, immobilized, injured, out of action, on the sick list

lair

Lairs and homes of creatures include:

sett (*badger*)	den (*lion*)	pen (*sheep*)
den (*bear*)	fortress (*mole*)	fold (*sheep*)
lodge (*beaver*)	hole (*mouse*)	shell (*snail*)
hive (*bee*)	nest (*mouse*)	drey (*squirrel*)
nest (*bird*)	holt (*otter*)	nest (*wasp*)
byre (*cow*)	sty (*pig*)	vespiary (*wasp*)
eyrie (*eagle*)	dovecote	
coop (*fowl*)	(*pigeon*)	
earth (*fox*)	burrow (*rabbit*)	
form (*hare*)	warren (*rabbit*)	

---

laissez-faire adj
permissive, non-interfering, non-interventionist, free-enterprise, free-market, free-trade
COLLOQ. live and let live

laity n
1 THE NON-ORDAINED, unordained, parishoners, lay people
2 NON-PROFESSIONALS, amateurs, outsiders
⧫ 1 the clergy 2 experts, professionals, specialists

lake n
pond, pool, lagoon, sea, water, reservoir, dam, basin, mere, tarn, everglade, playa, salina, shott, nyanza; *Scot* loch; *Irish* lough; *NAm* bayou; *Can* saltchuck; *Aust* cowal
Related adjective: lacustrine
See panels below

lam v
beat, batter, bash, hit, knock, pound, thump,

clout, strike, thrash, leather, pelt, pummel
COLLOQ. wallop, whack, belt

lambast v
1 CRITICIZE, reprimand, rebuke, scold, upbraid
FORMAL berate, castigate, censure, reprove
COLLOQ. roast, rubbish, badmouth
SLANG slag (off)
2 BEAT, whip, flog, thrash, strike, drub, clout, thump, batter, flay, leather
COLLOQ. wallop, whack, belt, clobber, tan

lame adj
1 DISABLED, handicapped, crippled, cripple, hurt, injured, maimed, limping, hobbling, halting, game, hamstrung
TECHNICAL spavined
OLD halt, mained
FORMAL incapacitated
COLLOQ. gammy, poorly
2 WEAK, feeble, flimsy, inadequate, unsatisfactory, defective, poor, thin, unconvincing, tame
⧫ 1 able-bodied 2 convincing

lamely adv
1 *halted lamely down the path*
with a limp, hobblingly, weakly, unsteadily, shakily
2 *'It wasn't my fault,' he said lamely*
feebly, weakly, unconvincingly, tamely, inadequately, unsatisfactorily

lament v, n
♦ v
mourn, grieve, sorrow, cry, weep, sob, wail, keen, complain, groan, moan, deplore, regret; *dialect* yammer
OLD bewail, bemoan, plain, beweep, mean, mein, repine; (*Spenser*) wayment
FORMAL ululate
⧫ rejoice, celebrate
♦ n
lamentation, dirge, elegy, keen, requiem, complaint, moan, groan, wail, grieving, crying, weeping, sobbing, tears, howl
TECHNICAL dumka
FORMAL threnody

lamentable adj
1 DEPLORABLE, regrettable, mournful, distressing, sorrowful, tragic, unfortunate, terrible, wretched, grievous, woeful
2 MEAGRE, low, inadequate, insufficient, mean, unsatisfactory, pitiful, miserable, niggardly, poor, disappointing
COLLOQ. measly, lousy, grotty

lamentation n
dirge, elegy, lament, wailing, mourning, weeping, moan, sobbing, sorrow, grief, grieving, keen, keening, jeremiad
FORMAL ululation, deploration, threnody, plaint
⧫ celebration, rejoicing

Largest natural lakes are:

Caspian Sea (*Iran/ Turkmenistan/Kazakhstan/ Azerbaijan/Russia*)	Huron (*USA/Canada*)	Winnipeg (*Canada*)	Chad (*W Africa*)
	Michigan (*USA*)	Nyasa (*E Africa*)	Onega (*Russia*)
	Tanganyika (*E Africa*)	Balkhash (*Kazakhstan*)	Rudolf (*E Africa*)
Superior (*USA/Canada*)	Baikal (*Russia*)	Ontario (*Canada*)	Eyre (*Australia*)
Aral Sea (*Uzbekistan/ Kazakhstan*)	Great Bear (*Canada*)	Ladoga (*Russia*)	Titicaca (*Peru*)
	Great Slave (*Canada*)	Maracaibo (*Venezuela*)	
Victoria (*E Africa*)	Erie (*USA/Canada*)	Patos (*Brazil*)	

Other famous lakes include:

Lough Awe	Crater	Geneva	Lakes of Killarney	Peipus	Windermere
Balaton	Lough Corrib	Great Salt Lake	Loch Lomond	Tahoe	Zurich
Chiemsee	Dead Sea	Huron	Maggiore	Tiberias	
Como	Lough Derg	Loch Katrine	Lough Neagh	Turkana	
Constance	Garda	Kivu	Loch Ness	Volta	

lamentably adv

deplorably, regrettably, pitifully, miserably, disappointingly, tragically, woefully, inadequately, insufficiently

laminate v

cover, layer, overlay, plate, stratify, veneer, coat, face, flake, separate, split
TECHNICAL foliate
FORMAL exfoliate

lamp n

light, lantern, torch, bulb, light bulb
See panel at **light**.

lampoon n, v

● n

satire, skit, caricature, parody, spoof, burlesque, travesty, pasquinade
COLLOQ. send-up, take-off
● v

satirize, caricature, parody, spoof, make fun of, ridicule, mock, burlesque, pasquinade
COLLOQ. send up, take off

lampooner n

satirist, caricaturist, parodist, pasquinader, pasquilant, pasquiler

lance v, n

● v

pierce, slit, cut (open), puncture, prick, incise
● n

spear, javelin, pike, harpoon, bayonet, lancet, shaft

land n, v

● n

1 EARTH, ground, soil, loam, terrain, dry land, terra firma
Related adjective: terrestrial
2 PROPERTY, grounds, estate, real estate, country, countryside, fields, rural area, open space, farmland, agricultural land, tract, acres, acreage, manor
Related adjectives: agrarian, praedial
3 COUNTRY, nation, region, area, district, territory, province, domain, realm, state, fatherland, motherland, native country
● v

1 ALIGHT, disembark, dismount, dock, berth, anchor, moor, unload, arrive, touch down, come/bring in to land, bring/take down, go ashore, come to rest; *N Am* deplane
2 ARRIVE, deposit, reach, get, find yourself, drop, finish up, settle, turn up
COLLOQ. wind up, end up
3 OBTAIN, secure, gain, get, get hold of, acquire, net, capture, achieve, win
FORMAL procure
COLLOQ. bag, nab
4 *land you with another bill*
saddle, weigh down, burden, oppress, trouble, tax, encumber
COLLOQ. lumber
5 *land a blow on the ear*
hit, deal, give, catch, deliver, administer, direct, inflict
COLLOQ. fetch

landing n

1 TOUCHDOWN, coming in, coming in to land, coming to ground, arrival, disembarkation, putting ashore, alighting; *N Am* deplaning
2 LANDING-STAGE, landing-place, jetty, pier, dock, harbour, quay, wharf

landlady, landlord n

1 PUBLICAN, innkeeper, hotelier, hotel-keeper, host, mine host, restaurateur
2 OWNER, landowner, lessor, proprietor, proprietress, freeholder; *N Am* slumlord

landmark n

1 FEATURE, monument, signpost, milestone, milepost, boundary, beacon, cairn; *Scot* meith
2 TURNING-POINT, crisis, watershed

landscape n

scene, scenery, view, panorama, outlook, vista, prospect, perspective, countryside, aspect

landslide n, adj

● n

landslip, earthfall, rockfall, avalanche
● adj

overwhelming, decisive, emphatic, runaway

lane n

way, track, passage(way), alley(way), footpath, footway, path(way), towpath, byroad, byway, driveway, avenue, channel; *Irish* boreen

language n

1 SPEECH, tongue, vocabulary, terminology, communication, speaking, uttering, verbalizing, vocalizing
FORMAL parlance
2 TALK, conversation, utterance
FORMAL discourse, converse
3 WORDING, style, phraseology, phrasing, expression, utterance, rhetoric
FORMAL diction
Related adjective: linguistic
See also panels on next page

languid adj

listless, sluggish, lethargic, slow, inactive, lazy, feeble, heavy, uninterested, unenthusiastic, spiritless, indifferent, inert, lackadaisical, drooping, dull, weak, faint, weary, pining, limp, sickly
FORMAL debilitated, enervated, languorous, torpid
E3 alert, lively, vivacious

languidly adv

listlessly, lethargically, slowly, inactively, lazily, feebly, heavily, inertly, weakly, dully, unenthusiastically
FORMAL torpidly

languish v

1 WILT, droop, fade, fail, flag, wither, waste away, rot, deteriorate, weaken, sink, faint, decline, mope, waste, grieve, sorrow, sigh, brood, sicken
2 PINE, yearn, want, long, desire, hanker, hunger, sigh
E3 1 flourish, rise

languor n

lethargy, listlessness, laziness, faintness, fatigue, weariness, silence, inertia, drowsiness, dreaminess, sleepiness, feebleness, weakness, frailty, calm, lull, relaxation, oppressiveness, heaviness, ennui, sloth, stillness
FORMAL debility, enervation, indolence, lassitude, torpor, indolence
E3 gusto; *formal* alacrity

languorous adj

lazy, relaxed, lethargic, listless, weary, dreamy, sleepy, feeble, weak
FORMAL torpid
E3 lively, energetic

lank adj

1 *lank hair*
limp, straggling, scraggy, drooping, lifeless, lustreless
2 *lank young people*
tall, thin, long, emaciated, skinny, gaunt, lanky, lean, slender, slim, scrawny, rawboned; *N Am* slab-sided
E3 burly

lanky adj

gaunt, gangling, gangly, scrawny, tall, thin, lean, slender, slim, rangy, scraggy, weedy
E3 short, squat

lap¹ n, v

● n

Languages of the world include:

Aborigine	Chinese	Gaelic	Italian	Polish	Spanish
Afghan	Cornish	German	Japanese	Portuguese	Swahili
Afrikaans	Croat	Greek	Kurdish	Punjabi	Swedish
American Sign	Czech	Haitian	Lapp	Romany	Swiss
Language (ASL)	Danish	Hawaiian	Latin	Romanian	Tamil
Arabic	Dutch	Hebrew	Latvian	Russian	Thai
Balinese	Ebonics	Hindi	Lithuanian	Sanskrit	Tibetan
Bantu	English	Hindustani	Magyar	Scottish	Turkish
Basque	Eskimo	Hottentot	Malay	Serbian	Ukrainian
Bengali	Esperanto	Hungarian	Maltese	Shelta	Urdu
British Sign	Estonian	Icelandic	Mandarin	Siamese	Vietnamese
Language (BSL)	Ethiopian	Indonesian	Manx	Sinhalese	Volapük
Burmese	Farsi	Inuit (or Inuktitut)	Maori	Slavonic	Welsh
Belorussian	Finnish	Iranian	Mexican	Slovak	Yiddish
Catalan	Flemish	Iraqi	Norwegian	Slovenian	Zulu
Celtic	French	Irish	Persian	Somali	

Language terms include:

argot	doublespeak	*colloq.* patter	grammar	**ARTIFICIAL INTELLIGENCE**:	natural language processing (NLP)
brogue	gobbledygook	pidgin	lexicography	automatic speech recognition (ASR)	
buzz word	idiom	regionalism	linguistics		
cant	jargon	slang	orthography	language engineering	
cockney rhyming slang	journalese	tongue	phonetics		
	colloq. lingo	vernacular	semantics	machine translation	
colloquialism	lingua franca	vocabulary	sociolinguistics		
creole	localism	**LANGUAGE STUDY**:	syntax		
dialect	patois	etymology	usage		

1 *sat on her lap*
knees, thighs
Related adjective: (*old*) gremial
2 CIRCUIT, round, orbit, ambit, tour, loop, course, circle, compass, distance
3 *a lap on a journey*
stage, section, leg, stretch
♦ *v*
wrap, fold, wind, twine, envelop, enfold, swathe, encase, surround, cover, swaddle, overlap

lap² *v*
1 *animals lapping milk*
drink, sip, sup, lick, lip, scoop up
2 *the sea lapping against the boat*
splash, wash, rush, flow, roll, swish, slop, slosh, break, beat, dash
■ **lap up**
accept eagerly, take in enthusiastically, listen in, absorb, relish, delight in, savour

lapse *n, v*
♦ *n*
1 ERROR, slip, mistake, negligence, omission, oversight, fault, blunder, trip, failing, indiscretion, backsliding, relapse
FORMAL aberration, dereliction
2 FALL, descent, decline, drop, stumble, downturn, deterioration, worsening, degeneration, backslide, slipping
3 BREAK, gap, interval, lull, interruption, intermission, pause, blank, course, passage
FORMAL hiatus
♦ *v*
1 DECLINE, fall, sink, drop, deteriorate, slide, slip, sink, drift, stumble, fail, worsen, degenerate, backslide, fall from grace
COLLOQ. go downhill, go to pot, go to the dogs, go to rack and ruin, go down the tubes
2 EXPIRE, run out, end, stop, become void/invalid
TECHNICAL prescribe, resolve
FORMAL terminate, cease
3 PASS, elapse, go by, go on, slip, slip away, slip by, drift, fall
Ea **2** continue

lapsed *adj*
1 EXPIRED, ended, run out, finished, out of date, outdated, invalid, void, obsolete, unrenewed
FORMAL discontinued
2 *a lapsed Catholic*
once, former, non-practising, backslidden
Ea **1** renewed, continued

larceny *n*
stealing, theft, burglary, robbery, pilfering, piracy
FORMAL misappropriation, purloining, expropriation
SLANG heist

larder *n*
pantry, storeroom, storage room, scullery

large *adj*
1 BIG, huge, immense, massive, vast, siz(e)able, great, giant, gigantic, bulky, heavy, ample, enormous, colossal, king-sized, broad, considerable, monumental, prodigious, stupendous, mammoth, substantial, high, tall, Brobdingnagian
FORMAL commodious, voluminous
COLLOQ. jumbo, whopping, bumper, ginormous, dirty great, humungous
SLANG mega
2 FULL, extensive, generous, liberal, ample, roomy, plentiful, spacious, grand, far-reaching, wide-ranging, sweeping, broad, comprehensive, exhaustive, grandiose
Ea **1** small, tiny
■ **at large**
1 GENERALLY, in general, by and large, on the whole, chiefly, mainly, in the main
2 FREE, at liberty, on the loose, on the run, independent, unconfined
■ **by and large**
on the whole, generally, mostly, mainly, generally speaking, as a rule, for the most part, all things considered

largely *adv*
mainly, in the main, principally, chiefly, generally, primarily, predominantly, mostly, for the most part, considerably, by and large, to a large extent, widely, extensively, greatly

largeness *n*
greatness, immensity, vastness, size, heaviness, bulk, ampleness, enormousness, broadness, wideness,

expansiveness, siz(e)ableness, voluminousness, grandness, stupendousness

large-scale *adj*
extensive, far-reaching, broad, nationwide, country-wide, wide, wide-ranging, wide-reaching, expansive, wholesale, global, universal, vast, sweeping, epic
Ⅎ minor

largesse *n*
generosity, kindness, liberality, philanthropy, benefaction, open-handedness, bounty, donation, gift, present, aid, grant, handout, endowment, bequest, charity, allowance, alms
FORMAL munificence
Ⅎ meanness

lark *n, v*
• *n*
1 ESCAPADE, antic, fling, prank, romp, revel, mischief, fooling, horseplay, frolic, caper, cavorting, play, game; *dialect* gammock
OLD guy
COLLOQ. skylark
2 *this writing lark*
activity, task, job, chore
COLLOQ. business, thing
• *v*
play, play tricks, have fun, fool around/about, mess about, cavort, frolic, caper, romp, sport, rollick, gambol; *dialect* gammock
COLLOQ. skylark

lascivious *adj*
lecherous, lewd, licentious, lustful, ribald, sensual, obscene, pornographic, crude, vulgar, coarse, bawdy, wanton, dirty, indecent, offensive, suggestive, salacious, scurrilous, unchaste
FORMAL libidinous, prurient
COLLOQ. blue, horny, randy, smutty

lash *n, v*
• *n*
blow, whip, stroke, swipe, hit, stripe, thong, welt, belt
OLD wire
• *v*
1 WHIP, flog, beat, hit, thrash, strike, scourge, flail, batter, slash, switch, welt, bullwhip, horse, cat, flick
OLD swinge
COLLOQ. wallop, whack
2 ATTACK, criticize, lay into, scold, reprove, rebuke, censure
FORMAL fulminate, berate
COLLOQ. bawl out, tear a strip off, tear to shreds
3 TIE, bind, fasten, secure, make fast, join, affix, rope, tether, strap
TECHNICAL seize
4 *waves lashing the shore*
strike, smash, dash, break, beat, pound, buffet
5 *an animal lashing its tail*
flick, swish, whip, switch, wag
▪ **lash out**
1 *lash out at someone*
hit out at, thrash, yerk, attack strongly, speak out against, criticize fiercely, run down, have a go at
COLLOQ. lay into, tear a strip off, tear to pieces/shreds
2 *lash out on new clothes*
spend a lot of money, spend extravagantly
COLLOQ. splash out on, spend a fortune on, spend money like water

lashings *n*
lots, great quantity, large amount
COLLOQ. oodles, loads, masses, heaps, piles, stacks, tons

lass *n*
girl, young woman, schoolgirl, lassie, miss; *Scot* Jenny

OLD damsel, maiden, popsy
COLLOQ. hen
OLD COLLOQ. filly
SLANG bird, chick

lassitude *n*
sluggishness, tiredness, weariness, lethargy, listlessness, drowsiness, apathy, dullness, exhaustion, fatigue, heaviness
FORMAL enervation, languor, torpor
Ⅎ energy, vigour

lasso *n*
rope, lariat, noose

last¹ *adj, adv, n*
• *adj*
1 *last Sunday*
most recent, latest, previous
2 FINAL, ultimate, closing, latest, rearmost, hindmost, terminal, furthest, concluding, finishing, ending, remotest, utmost, extreme
3 *the last house on the street*
coming at the end, back, hind, hindmost, tail-end, furthest, farthest, remotest, endmost, final
4 *the last person to expect help from*
least likely, least suitable, most unlikely, most improbable, most unsuitable
Ⅎ **1** next **2** first, initial **3** first **4** most likely
• *adv*
finally, ultimately, behind, after, at the end, at the back/rear
Ⅎ first, firstly
• *n*
finish, close, end, ending, conclusion, completion
▪ **at last**
eventually, finally, in the end, in conclusion, ultimately, in due course, at length
COLLOQ. at the end of the day
▪ **last word**
1 final decision, final say, final statement, concluding remark, conclusive/definite comment, ultimatum
2 latest, best, pick, cream, ultimate, vogue, rage, perfection, crème de la crème, *dernier cri, ne plus ultra*
FORMAL quintessence

last² *v*
1 *it lasts six hours*
continue, go on, take, endure, remain, persist, carry on, keep (on), survive, hold out, hold on, exist, wear, stay, hold on, stand up
FORMAL abide, subsist
2 GET THROUGH, survive, manage to cope with, endure, keep going through
COLLOQ. stick it out
Ⅎ **1** cease, stop, fade

last-ditch *adj*
final, desperate, frenzied, wild, last-chance, straining, struggling, frantic, heroic
COLLOQ. all-out, eleventh-hour, last-gasp

last-minute *adj*
late, overdue, hasty, rushed, forced, superficial
COLLOQ. eleventh-hour

lasting *adj*
enduring, unchanging, unceasing, ceaseless, unending, abiding, surviving, continuing, persisting, permanent, durable, perpetual, external, everlasting, undying, never-ending, lifelong, long-lived, long-standing, long-term
FORMAL interminable
Ⅎ brief, fleeting, short-lived

lastly *adv*
finally, ultimately, in conclusion, in the end, to sum up
Ⅎ firstly

latch n, v

♦ n
fastening, catch, bar, bolt, lock, hook, hasp, clicket; *dialect* sneck
OLD (*Spenser*) clink

♦ v
fasten, bar, bolt, lock, hook, catch, make secure

■ **latch on to**
1 ATTACH YOURSELF TO, not want to leave, follow
2 UNDERSTAND, comprehend, grasp, learn, realize
FORMAL apprehend
COLLOQ. twig

late adj, adv

♦ *adj*
1 OVERDUE, behind, behindhand, behind schedule, behind time, slow, unpunctual, delayed, last-minute
FORMAL tardy
2 FORMER, previous, departed, dead, deceased, past, preceding, old, defunct
3 RECENT, up-to-date, current, fresh, new, up-to-the-minute, latest
F3 **1** early, punctual

♦ *adv*
1 UNPUNCTUALLY, behindhand, behind schedule, behind time, in arrears, slowly, belatedly, formerly, recently
FORMAL dilatorily, tardily
2 *work late*
after hours, overtime
F3 **1** punctually **2** early

■ **of late**
recently, lately, not long ago, newly, latterly

Synonym nuances
adjective sense 1
Overdue can be used of anything not turning up by the expected time or to suggest something has not been fulfilled by the desired time: *a change of leadership is overdue*, while **behind, behindhand, behind schedule** and **behind time** would be used of actions that should already have been carried out: *your rent payments are behind*.
Slow suggests taking a longer than average time.
Unpunctual is more disapproving, in that it suggests an inability to keep to allotted times. **Delayed** would be used of something put off until a later time: *the delayed flight will now take off at 5.30*, and **last-minute** describes something done at the latest possible moment: *last minute check-ins are common at airports*.

---

lately adv
recently, of late, not long ago, newly, latterly
OLD alate, now of late

lateness n
belatedness, delay, unpunctuality
FORMAL dilatoriness, retardation, tardiness
F3 earliness

latent adj
potential, possible, dormant, inactive, undeveloped, undiscovered, unrealized, lurking, unexpressed, unseen, unrevealed, secret, concealed, hidden, invisible, underlying, veiled, passive
FORMAL quiescent
F3 active, conspicuous, apparent

later adv, adj
♦ *adv*
next, afterwards, subsequently, eventually, after, successively, in the (near) future, at a future time/date, at a later time, later on, in due course, in a while, some other time
F3 earlier

♦ *adj*
next, subsequent, following, succeeding

lateral adj
1 SIDEWAYS, side, oblique, indirect, slanting, sideward, edgeways, marginal, flanking
2 *lateral thinking*
creative, ingenious, fresh, alternative, original, imaginative, inspired, clever, brilliant, unorthodox, unconventional, illogical
COLLOQ. outside the box

laterally adv
1 SIDEWAYS, edgeways, obliquely
2 *think laterally*
creatively, ingeniously, originally, imaginatively, unconventionally, illogically
COLLOQ. outside the box

latest adj
modern, newest, last, most recent, ultimate, up-to-date, current, now, fashionable
COLLOQ. in, with it, up-to-the-minute, hip, trendy, now
SLANG funky
F3 earliest

lather n, v
♦ *n*
1 FOAM, suds, soapsuds, froth, bubbles, soap, shampoo
2 AGITATION, fluster, anxiety, panic, fuss, dither, flutter, fever
COLLOQ. state, flap, tizzy, sweat, stew

♦ *v*
foam, froth, rub, soap, shampoo, whip up

latitude n
freedom, liberty, unrestrictedness, laxity, indulgence, carte blanche, licence, leeway, flexibility, scope, range, room, space, play, clearance, breadth, width, spread, sweep, reach, span, field, extent

latter adj
last-mentioned, last, later, closing, final, end, concluding, ensuing, succeeding, successive, second
F3 former

latter-day adj
modern, contemporary, current, present-day

latterly adv
lately, recently, most recently, of late
FORMAL hitherto
F3 formerly

lattice n
latticework, openwork, fretwork, mesh, web, grate, grating, network, espalier, grid, grille, tracery, trellis
FORMAL reticulation

laud v
praise, admire, approve, magnify, acclaim, applaud, celebrate, glorify, extol, honour, hail
F3 blame, condemn, curse, damn

laudable adj
praiseworthy, commendable, estimable, of note, excellent, exemplary, worthy, admirable, creditable, sterling
FORMAL meritorious
F3 damnable, execrable

laudation n
praise, acclaim, acclamation, reverence, adulation, blessing, accolade, celebrity, commendation, devotion, extolment, glorification, glory, kudos, homage, tribute
FORMAL encomium, encomion, eulogy, panegyric, paean, veneration
F3 condemnation, criticism

laudatory adj
complimentary, commendatory, adulatory, acclamatory, approving, congratulatory, celebratory, glorifying
FORMAL approbatory, encomiastic(al), eulogistic, panegyrical
F3 damning

laugh v, n

♦ v

chuckle, burst out laughing, dissolve into laughter, roar/ shriek with laughter, cackle, giggle, guffaw, snigger, snicker, titter, chortle, hoot, roar, peal, scream, haw-haw, ha-ha, he-he, tee-hee; *dialect* nicker; *Scot* snirtle
FORMAL cachinnate
COLLOQ. split/shake your sides, fall about, crease up, break up, howl, be rolling in the aisles, be in stitches, laugh like a drain, laugh your head off
SLANG yok, yock

♦ n

1 *have a good laugh*
giggle, chuckle, snigger, snicker, titter, guffaw, chortle, lark, roar, peal, cackle, hoot, belly-laugh, horse laugh, he-he, tee-hee, haw-haw, ha-ha; *dialect* nicker; *Scot* snirt
FORMAL cachinnation, irrision, risus
COLLOQ. scream, hoot; *N Am* boff
SLANG yok, yock
Related adjective: gelastic
2 JOKE, jest, prank, hoax, trick, sport, fun, play
3 *he's a great laugh*
joker, comedian, comic, wit, humorist, jester, trickster, quipster, prankster, hoaxer, practical joker, wag, clown, buffoon, character, sport
COLLOQ. wisecracker, card

▪ laugh at
mock, ridicule, make jokes about, jeer, make fun of, scoff at, scorn, taunt, make a fool of, poke fun at
FORMAL deride

▪ laugh off
dismiss, disregard, ignore, brush aside, belittle, shrug off, make little of, minimize
COLLOQ. pooh-pooh

Synonym nuances
verb

Burst out laughing suggests a sudden and noisy eruption of laughter, while **dissolve into laughter** implies being rendered helpless by it. **Roar/shriek with laughter** and **scream** suggest much accompanying noise, and **cackle**, with its implied squawking, is similarly raucous. **Hoot** also suggests loud hilarity, whereas **peal** is more suggestive of the emission of a series of sounds: *the laughter pealed between the two groups.*

 Chuckle can be used to suggest quiet or even suppressed laughter: *he chuckled to himself*, whereas **chortle** is connotative of gurgling and glee. **Snigger** and **snicker** have undertones of quiet derision: *many sniggered when he fell.* You can also use **titter** to suggest a degree of furtiveness: *we tittered when we heard him swear, but dared not laugh out loud.* **Giggle**, on the other hand, generally implies an element of playfulness or silliness: *the children giggled as they played their games.*

---

laughable *adj*

1 FUNNY, amusing, comical, comic, humorous, hilarious, uproarious, droll, farcical, diverting, entertaining
COLLOQ. side-splitting
2 RIDICULOUS, absurd, ludicrous, preposterous, nonsensical, derisory, derisive
EЭ 1 serious

laughably *adv*

ridiculously, ludicrously, absurdly, preposterously, farcically

laughing-stock *n*

figure of fun, butt, dupe, victim, target, object of ridicule, fair game, stooge, Aunt Sally

laughter *n*

laughing, giggling, chuckling, chortling, cackling, hooting, guffawing, sniggering, tittering, hilarity, amusement, merriment, happiness, cheerfulness, glee,

convulsions, *fou rire*, hysterics, paroxysm, haw, ha-ha
OLD mirth
FORMAL cachinnation, irrision, risibility
Related adjective: gelastic

launch *v*

1 PROPEL, dispatch, discharge, hurl, fire, send off, project, float, set afloat, set in motion, throw, fire
2 BEGIN, start, embark on, set up, establish, found, open, initiate, inaugurate, institute, introduce, organize, instigate, set in motion
FORMAL commence
COLLOQ. set/start the ball rolling

laundry *n*

1 WASHING, dirty washing, (dirty) clothes, wash
2 LAUNDERETTE, dry cleaner's; *N Am* Laundromat®

lavatory *n*

toilet, WC, bathroom, cloakroom, washroom, gents', ladies', water closet, public convenience, convenience, urinal, latrine, privy, powder room, facilities, earth-closet, Elsan®, Portaloo®, lavabo, office; *N Am* rest room, comfort station
OLD reredorter, necessary
COLLOQ. loo, lav, dunny, smallest room, throne, superloo, little boys' room, little girls' room
SLANG kazi, bog, crapper, can, cottage, rears, heads, thunderbox; *Scot* cludgie; *N Am* john; *Aust* toot
OLD SLANG dike

lavish *adj, v*

♦ adj

1 ABUNDANT, copious, lush, luxuriant, plentiful, profuse, unlimited, prolific, splendid, grand, gorgeous, rich, sumptuous
2 GENEROUS, liberal, open-handed, free, bountiful, extravagant, wasteful, thriftless, prodigal, profligate, immoderate, excessive, wild, intemperate, unsparing, unstinting
EЭ 1 scant, paltry **2** frugal, thrifty, mean

♦ v

spend, expend, heap, pour, give freely, shower, deluge, squander, waste, dissipate
FORMAL bestow

lavishly *adv*

1 *lavishly decorated*
grandly, richly, splendidly, sumptuously, luxuriously, lushly, abundantly, profusely
2 *pour cream lavishly over the pudding*
generously, liberally, freely, extravagantly, excessively, wildly, unsparingly, intemperately

law *n*

1 RULE, act, legislation, constitution, decree, edict, order, directive, statute, regulation, command, commandment, pronouncement, ordinance, charter, code, constitution, enactment
2 PRINCIPLE, axiom, maxim, criterion, standard, precept, rule, formula, tenet, code, direction, instruction, canon, guideline
3 JURISPRUDENCE, legislation, lawsuit, litigation, legal action, legal proceedings
Related adjective: legal
4 THE POLICE, the police force, police officers
COLLOQ. the force, cops, coppers, rozzers, boys in blue
SLANG the Bill, the fuzz, pigs

law-abiding *adj*

obedient, upright, orderly, lawful, complying, honest, honourable, decent, virtuous, good, righteous, upstanding, dutiful
EЭ lawless

lawbreaker *n*

offender, wrongdoer, criminal, felon, miscreant, culprit, delinquent, convict, outlaw, sinner, trespasser

FORMAL infractor, transgresser
COLLOQ. crook

lawcourt n

court, court of law, bench, bar, judiciary, tribunal, trial, session, assizes
See panel at **court.**

lawful adj

legal, legitimate, permissible, legalized, constitutional, authorized, recognized, allowable, sanctioned, warranted, valid, just, proper, rightful
FORMAL licit
COLLOQ. legit
F∃ illegal, unlawful, illicit

lawfully adv

by law, according to the law, by rights, rightfully, legally, legitimately, permissibly, validly, properly, constitutionally

lawless adj

disorderly, anarchic(al), unruly, ungoverned, riotous, mutinous, insurgent, insurrectionary, rebellious, revolutionary, seditious, unrestrained, chaotic, illegal, wrongdoing, lawbreaking, criminal, wild, reckless
F∃ law-abiding

lawlessness n

anarchy, disorder, chaos, insurgency, insurrection, rebellion, revolution, sedition, mob rule, mob law, piracy, racketeering
FORMAL ochlocracy
COLLOQ. mobocracy, rent-a-mob
F∃ order

lawsuit n

litigation, suit, action, legal action, proceedings, legal proceedings, case, prosecution, dispute, process, trial, argument, contest, cause
TECHNICAL indictment

lawyer n

solicitor, barrister, advocate, attorney, counsel, QC, legal adviser, legal representative
SLANG brief

lax adj

1 CASUAL, careless, heedless, slack, lenient, indulgent, permissive, tolerant, easy-going, negligent, neglectful, remiss, slipshod, sloppy, inattentive
COLLOQ. laid-back
2 IMPRECISE, inexact, indefinite, loose, inaccurate, vague, general, broad
F∃ 1 strict, careful 2 exact, rigorous, specific

laxative n

loosener, purgative, evacuant, lenitive, purge, salts, senna, ipecacuanha
TECHNICAL aperient, cathartic, eccoprotic

laxity n

1 CARELESSNESS, neglect, heedlessness, indulgence, negligence, slovenliness, slackness, sloppiness, tolerance, permissiveness, softness, leniency, freedom, indifference, nonchalance, latitude, latitudinarianism, laissez-faire
2 IMPRECISION, inexactness, indefiniteness, looseness
F∃ 1 severity, strictness 2 exactness, precision

lay¹ v

1 PUT, place, deposit, set down, settle, lodge, plant, set, establish, leave
FORMAL posit
COLLOQ. stick, bung, plonk
2 ARRANGE, position, set out, locate, work out, devise, make, prepare, plan, design, present, submit, offer, put forward
FORMAL dispose
3 ATTRIBUTE, ascribe, assign, charge, impute, allot
4 lay a burden on someone
impose, put, burden, inflict, apply, thrust, encumber, saddle, oppress, weigh down
5 lay a bet
place, bet, wager, gamble, risk, chance, hazard
6 lay eggs
produce, bear, deposit, give birth to, breed, engender
TECHNICAL oviposit
OLD beget
7 HAVE SEX WITH, make love with, go to bed with
SLANG make it with, have, have it off with, bonk, bang, (*taboo*) screw, shag, fuck

▪ lay aside

1 PUT ASIDE, save, keep, store
2 REJECT, set aside, put out of your mind, abandon, discard, dismiss, shelve, defer, postpone, put off, cast aside

▪ lay bare

disclose, divulge, explain, expose, reveal, show, uncover, unveil, exhibit
FORMAL manifest

▪ lay down

1 SURRENDER, yield, give up, give, discard, drop
FORMAL relinquish
2 STIPULATE, assert, postulate, affirm, state, establish, formulate, prescribe, ordain

▪ lay down the law

dictate, crack down, emphasize, dogmatize
FORMAL pontificate
COLLOQ. read the riot act, throw your weight about, rule the roost

▪ lay hands on

1 ATTACK, assault, beat up, lay into, seize, set on, grab, clasp, clutch, get, catch, lay hold of, grip
2 FIND, get hold of, locate, bring to light, obtain, acquire, discover, grasp, unearth
3 BLESS, consecrate, ordain, confirm

▪ lay in

store (up), stock up, amass, accumulate, hoard, stockpile, gather, collect, build up, glean

▪ lay into

attack, assail, pitch into, set about, tear into, let fly at, hit out at, have a go at, lash out at

▪ lay it on

exaggerate, overdo it, flatter, overpraise
COLLOQ. butter up, soft-soap, sweet-talk

▪ lay off

1 DISMISS, discharge, make redundant, pay off, let go
COLLOQ. sack
2 GIVE UP, drop, stop, leave off, leave alone, let up, refrain, cease
FORMAL desist, discontinue
COLLOQ. quit

▪ lay on

provide, supply, cater, furnish, give, set up, organize

▪ lay out

1 DISPLAY, set out, put out, spread out, exhibit, arrange, plan, design
2 KNOCK OUT, fell, floor, flatten, demolish
3 SPEND, pay, give, contribute, invest
FORMAL expend, disburse
COLLOQ. shell out, fork out

▪ lay up

store up, hoard, accumulate, amass, keep, save, put away

▪ lay waste

desolate, ravage, destroy, devastate, raze, ruin, sack, spoil, pillage, rape, vandalize
FORMAL depredate, despoil

❗ lay or **lie**?
Lay means 'to place in a flat, prone or horizontal position'. It is a transitive verb, ie, it requires an object: *If you lay the pen down there, it will roll off the table. Lie* means 'to be or move into a flat, prone or horizontal position'. It is an intransitive verb, ie, it does not have an object. The past tense is *lay*: *She went into the bedroom and lay on the bed.*

---

lay² *adj*

1 LAIC, secular
2 AMATEUR, non-professional, non-specialist, non-qualified
E **1** clergy, ordained, clerical **2** expert, professional

lay³ *n*

heavenly lays
song, poem, ballad, lyric, madrigal, ode

layabout *n*

good-for-nothing, ne'er-do-well, waster, idler, laggard, lounger; *Irish* corner-boy
COLLOQ. loafer, shirker, skiver, lazybones
SLANG *N Am* goof-off

layer *n*

1 COVER, coating, coat, covering, film, blanket, mantle, sheet, lamina
2 STRATUM, seam, vein, band, deposit, thickness, tier, bed, plate, row, ply

layman, laywoman or layperson *n*

1 PARISHIONER, unordained man/woman/person
2 AMATEUR, outsider, non-professional
E **1** clergyman, clergywoman, the clergy **2** expert, professional

lay-off *n*

redundancy, discharge, dismissal, unemployment
COLLOQ. the sack, sacking, jotters, cards, papers, firing, the push, the boot, the elbow

layout *n*

arrangement, design, outline, plan, blueprint, organization, format, sketch, draft, map, geography

laze *v*

idle, lounge, sit around, lie around, loll, relax, unwind
OLD lusk
COLLOQ. loaf, chill (out), veg (out), bum around, not pull your weight
SLANG *Aust & NZ* bludge
E work

lazily *adv*

idly, slowly, slackly, lethargically, sluggishly

laziness *n*

idleness, sloth, slothfulness, inactivity, slowness, sluggishness, lethargy, slackness, Oblomovism
FORMAL dilatoriness, fainéance, indolence, tardiness, langour
E industriousness

lazy *adj*

idle, slothful, slack, work-shy, inactive, inert, slow, slow-moving, good-for-nothing, lethargic, sluggish
OLD laesie, lither, lusk, luskish
FORMAL indolent, torpid, languid, languorous, tardy, fainéant
COLLOQ. bone-idle
E industrious, hard-working
See Synonym nuances panel at **inactive**

lazybones *n*

idler, slouch, laggard, sluggard, good-for-nothing, sleepyhead, layabout, ne'er-do-well, do-nought, do-nothing, slug, drone, lubber, lubbard
OLD bedpresser, lusk, slowback
FORMAL fainéant
COLLOQ. loafer, lounger, shirker, skiver, slob, mollusc
SLANG *N Am* goof-off

leach *v*

drain, extract, filter, strain, seep, filtrate, percolate
TECHNICAL osmose
FORMAL lixiviate

lead¹ *v, n, adj*

♦ *v*
1 GUIDE, conduct, escort, show, steer, pilot, usher
2 RULE, govern, head, be at the head of, be in charge of, preside over, direct, supervise, command, manage, regulate
COLLOQ. call the shots
3 CAUSE, result in, produce, bring about, bring on, contribute to, call forth, tend towards, prompt, induce, provoke
4 INFLUENCE, persuade, incline, sway, prompt, induce, move, dispose
5 SURPASS, outdo, excel, outstrip, outrun, outdistance, exceed, eclipse, transcend, be in the lead, be in front, come first
6 PASS, spend, live, have, undergo, experience
E **1** follow
♦ *n*
1 PRIORITY, precedence, first place, advance position, leading position, start, van, vanguard, forefront, advantage, supremacy, pre-eminence, edge, interval, gap, margin
2 LEADERSHIP, guidance, direction, example, model, pattern
3 CLUE, hint, indication, indicator, guide, pointer, tip, suggestion
COLLOQ. tip-off
4 TITLE ROLE, starring part, star role, principal, principal part, leading role, leading man/lady
5 LEASH, tether, rein, hold, cord, slip, string, line, chain
♦ *adj*
leading, first, principal, chief, main, foremost, head, premier, primary, prime, star, top

◾ lead off

begin, open, get going, start (off), inaugurate, initiate
FORMAL commence
COLLOQ. kick off, start the ball rolling

◾ lead on

entice, lure, seduce, tempt, draw on, beguile, persuade, string along, deceive, trick, mislead, dupe
COLLOQ. pull a fast one on, put one over on, lead up the garden path
SLANG take for a ride

◾ lead the way

1 GO IN FRONT, go first, show, show the way, guide
2 TAKE THE INITIATIVE, blaze a trail, pave the way, set a trend, be a pioneer, break new ground

◾ lead up to

prepare (the way) for, approach, introduce, make overtures, pave/open the way

lead² *n*

1 BULLETS, shot, ammunition, pellets, balls, slugs
2 WEIGHT, heavy weight, plumb, sinker

leaden *adj*

1 GREY, overcast, cloudy, gloomy, dingy, dismal, dreary, ashen, greyish, oppressive, sombre
2 DULL, heavy, boring, burdensome, onerous, laboured, lifeless, lacklustre, listless, spiritless, sluggish, humdrum, inert, stilted
FORMAL languid
3 CUMBERSOME, wooden, stiff, heavy, laboured, sluggish, plodding, lead

leader *n*

1 HEAD, chief, figurehead, director, ruler, principal, manager, governor, superintendent, overseer, supervisor, commander, captain, superior, chieftain, ringleader, guide, conductor, skipper, mover and shaker
COLLOQ. boss, gov, guv, top dog, bigwig, big cheese/noise/shot
2 GUIDE, courier, escort, usher
3 PIONEER, innovator, developer, expert, authority, leading light, guiding light, discoverer, inventor, founder, architect, trailblazer, pathfinder, groundbreaker, front-runner
E **1** follower

leadership *n*

direction, control, command, management, authority,

rule, guidance, supervision, superintendency, domination, pre-eminence, premiership, captaincy, administration, sway, directorship, governorship, headship

lead-in *n*
introduction, opening, foreword, preface, preamble, prologue, preliminaries, front matter, overture, prelude, beginning, start, inauguration, launch, presentation, debut
FORMAL prolegomenon, exordium, proem
COLLOQ. intro
🖃 conclusion, appendix

leading *adj*
main, principal, chief, primary, first, front, supreme, outstanding, foremost, dominant, ruling, directing, guiding, superior, greatest, highest, top, governing, paramount, top-rank, pre-eminent, number one
🖃 subordinate

leaf *n, v*
♦ *n*
1 the leaves of a tree
blade, bract, frond, pad, calyx, needle, sepal, leaflet
TECHNICAL cotyledon, foliole
Related adjectives: foliaceous, foliar, foliose
2 PAGE, sheet, folio
♦ *v*
thumb (through), browse, flip, glance, skim
■ **turn over a new leaf**
improve yourself, better yourself, mend/change your ways, pull your socks up, make a fresh start, start/begin again, start afresh, wipe the slate clean

---

Leaf parts include:

axillary bud	leaf cells	stipule
blade	margin	stomata
chloroplasts	midrib	tip
epidermis	petiole	vein
leaf axil	sheath	

Leaf shapes include:

abruptly pinnate	falcate	peltate
acerose	hastate	pinnate
ciliate	lanceolate	pinnatifid
cordate	linear	reniform
crenate	lobed	runcinate
dentate	lyrate	sagittate
digitate	obovate	spathulate
doubly dentate	orbicular	subulate
elliptic	ovate	ternate
entire	palmate	trifoliate

---

leaflet *n*
pamphlet, booklet, brochure, circular, handout, bill, handbill, flier, tract; *N Am* dodger

leafy *adj*
green, leafed, leaved, wooded, woody, shady, shaded, bosky, frondescent, frondose, bowery
TECHNICAL dasyphyllous, foliose
FORMAL verdant

league *n, v*
♦ *n*
1 ASSOCIATION, confederation, confederacy, alliance, union, federation, coalition, affiliation, group, combination, band, syndicate, conglomerate, corporation, guild, consortium, cartel, combine, partnership, co-operative, fellowship, compact, *Bund*
2 a football league
championship, tournament, division, group, band, contest, competition, cup
3 CATEGORY, class, level, group
♦ *v*

amalgamate, associate, band together, co-operate, collaborate, combine, confederate, conspire, join forces, unite, link, ally, consort
■ **in league**
allied, in co-operation, co-operating, linked, in partnership, in alliance, in collusion, in tandem, collaborating, conspiring
COLLOQ. hand in glove, in cahoots
🖃 at odds

leak *n, v*
♦ *n*
1 CRACK, hole, opening, puncture, crevice, chink, fissure, break, cut
2 LEAKAGE, leaking, seeping, seepage, spill, spillage, drip, oozing, discharge, escape, percolation
3 DISCLOSURE, divulgence, revelation, exposure, exposé, uncovering, bringing to light
♦ *v*
1 SEEP, drip, ooze, escape, overflow, run, let out, let in, make water, spill, trickle, percolate, exude, discharge, weep
2 DISCLOSE, reveal, let slip, let out, make known, make public, tell, relate, give away, pass on
FORMAL divulge, impart
COLLOQ. blab, squeal, let on, let the cat out of the bag, blow the gaffe, spill the beans

leaky *adj*
leaking, holey, perforated, punctured, dripping, split, cracked, porous, permeable

lean¹ *v*
1 SLANT, slope, incline, bend, tilt, list, bank, be at an angle
2 RECLINE, prop, rest
FORMAL repose
3 INCLINE, favour, prefer, tend, gravitate, have an inclination/preference for
FORMAL have a propensity for
■ **lean on**
1 RELY ON, depend on, trust in, have confidence in, not manage without
COLLOQ. bank on
2 FORCE, persuade, pressurize, coerce, intimidate, put pressure on
COLLOQ. twist someone's arm, put the screws on

lean² *adj*
1 THIN, skinny, bony, gaunt, lank, angular, slim, slender, scraggy, scrawny, emaciated
COLLOQ. all skin and bones
2 SCANTY, inadequate, insufficient, meagre, bare, barren, sparse, poor, arid
3 lean years
unproductive, unfruitful, unsuccessful, unprofitable, poor, hard, difficult, tough, unpleasant, uncomfortable, austere
🖃 **1** fat, flabby **2** abundant

leaning *n*
tendency, inclination, preference, partiality, liking, fondness, attraction, bent, bias, disposition, aptitude
FORMAL propensity, proclivity, penchant, predilection

leanness *n*
thinness, slimness, slenderness, boniness, gauntness, scragginess, scrawniness, lankiness, lankness
🖃 fat, flabbiness

lean-to *n*
shed, garage, lock-up, hut, outhouse, shack, penthouse; *Aust* skillion

leap *v, n*
♦ *v*
1 JUMP (OVER), bound, spring, vault, clear; *Irish* lep; skip, hop, dance, bounce, caper, gambol, romp, frisk, frolic, cavort
2 SOAR, surge, mount, increase, rocket, skyrocket, escalate, rise, spring

E₃ 2 drop, fall
* *n*
1 JUMP, bound, spring, vault, hop, skip, caper
TECHNICAL entrechat
2 INCREASE, upsurge, upswing, surge, rise, soaring, escalation
■ **leap at**
jump at, accept eagerly, agree to, fall for, grab, seize, pounce on, snatch, swallow
■ **by/in leaps and bounds**
rapidly, swiftly, quickly
COLLOQ. in no time (at all)

learn *v*
1 GRASP, comprehend, understand, master, acquire, train, study, pick up, take in, get, digest, gather, glean, read, receive, assimilate, absorb, discern, familiarize yourself in, gain knowledge of, acquire skill in, cram; *dialect* larn
OLD (*Spenser*) lear
COLLOQ. get the hang of, gen up on
2 MEMORIZE, learn by heart, commit to memory, have off pat, remember
OLD con
3 DISCOVER, find out, ascertain, understand, detect, determine, hear, see, gather, glean, realize, become aware of, become informed about
COLLOQ. get wind of, suss out

Synonym nuances
sense 1
Grasp can sometimes imply that there has been some difficulty in learning something: *they hadn't fully grasped the significance of what I said*, while **comprehend**, along with **understand** and **get**, suggests also being able to follow the meaning: *I don't get what you're saying.*
Acquire might be used of simply gaining knowledge which perhaps requires further application: *we acquired a knowledge of the tides*, whereas **master** suggests also attaining skill and proficiency: *he'd mastered the basics of sailing.*
 Glean and **gather** are more suggestive of accidental gaining of information along the way: *new ideas which he had gleaned from his trips to Europe*, while **pick up** implies a gradual improvement, perhaps again with little effort: *he picked up some French when he lived in Paris.*
Discern implies a little more mental effort in finding something out: *from the remaining evidence I tried to discern what had happened.*
 The terms **take in** and **absorb** suggest learning something and retaining it, while **assimilate** and **digest** have added suggestions of classifying and using the information learned: *I assimilated all the facts of the situation and tried to reach a decision.*

---

learned *adj*
scholarly, erudite, well-informed, well-read, well-educated, knowledgeable, cultured, academic, lettered, literary, studious, literate, widely read, intellectual, versed, pedantic
E₃ uneducated, illiterate

learner *n*
novice, beginner, student, trainee, pupil, scholar, apprentice, tiro, neophyte, intern
OLD conner
COLLOQ. rookie, greenhorn

learning *n*
scholarship, erudition, education, schooling, knowledge, information, letters, study, wisdom, tuition, culture, edification, intellect, research, pedantry; *Scot* lear
OLD conning

lease *v, n*
* *v*
1 *lease a flat from the council*

rent, hire, charter, loan
2 *lease a field to a farmer*
rent, rent out, let, let out, loan, hire, hire out, sublet
* *n*
agreement, contract, chapter, rental, tenancy

leash *n*
lead, tether, rein, hold, cord, slip, string, check, control, curb, restraint, discipline; *dialect* trash
OLD lyam
■ **strain at the leash**
be champing at the bit, be impatient, be eager, be anxious, be longing
COLLOQ. be itching, be dying

least *adj*
smallest, lowest, minimum, fewest, slightest, poorest
E₃ most
■ **at least**
1 *it'll cost at least £500*
as a minimum, at the (very) least, no less than
2 *my car may be old but at least it goes*
in any event, in any case, anyhow, however, nevertheless, at any rate, for all that, in spite of everything, whatever happens, no matter what
■ **to say the least**
 to put it mildly, at the very least, without any exaggeration, without exaggerating

leathery *adj*
hard, hardened, durable, rough, rugged, tough, wrinkled, wizened, leathern
TECHNICAL coriaceous, corious

leave¹ *v*
1 DEPART, go, go away, set out, take your leave, pull out, decamp, exit, move, retire, withdraw, retreat, emigrate, disappear
COLLOQ. push off, push along, quit, scoot, take off, clear off, shove off, make tracks, do a bunk, up sticks, take French leave, vamoose, sling your hook, hook it; *Aust* shoot through
SLANG *Aust* choof off
See Synonym nuances panel at **depart**.
2 ABANDON, cease, desert, give up, drop, pull out, surrender
FORMAL relinquish, renounce, forsake, desist
COLLOQ. quit, run out on, ditch, jilt, chuck, dump, turn your back on, leave high and dry
3 ASSIGN, commit, entrust, allot, consign, make over, hand over, deliver, transmit
4 *leave property in your will*
will, hand down, leave behind, endow, give over
TECHNICAL devise
FORMAL bequeath
5 *I must have left the tickets at home*
forget, mislay, miss, lose, drop, misplace
6 *the experience left a lasting impression on me*
cause, give rise to, lead to, result in, occasion, bring about, produce, generate, create
E₃ 1 arrive **3** receive
■ **leave off**
stop, refrain, lay off, break off, end, halt, cease
FORMAL discontinue, desist, abstain, terminate
COLLOQ. quit, give over, knock off
■ **leave out**
omit, exclude, overlook, ignore, miss out, except, disregard, pass over, count out, cut (out), eliminate, neglect, reject, cast aside, bar
E₃ include

leave² *n*
1 PERMISSION, authorization, consent, allowance, sanction, warrant, concession, indulgence, liberty, freedom
FORMAL dispensation
COLLOQ. say-so, OK, green light

2 HOLIDAY, time off, day off, break, leave of absence, vacation, sabbatical, furlough, sick leave, compassionate leave
COLLOQ. vac
F3 1 refusal, rejection

leaven *n, v*
◆ *n*
yeast, ferment, zyme, raising agent, barm
◆ *v*
1 RAISE, cause to rise, puff up, ferment, work, expand, swell
2 INSPIRE, stimulate, lighten, quicken, enliven, pervade, permeate, imbue, suffuse

leavings *n*
remains, remainder, residue, remnants, leftovers, dregs, detritus, dross, fragments, bits, pieces, oddments, sweepings, scraps, refuse, rubbish, debris, waste, spoil

lecher *n*
womanizer, adulterer, seducer, sensualist, debauchee, libertine, profligate, libidinist, rake, roué, fornicator, wanton, whoremonger, satyr, Casanova, Don Juan, Lothario, Romeo, Lovelace
COLLOQ. dirty old man, flasher, goat, wolf, lech
SLANG perv

lecherous *adj*
lewd, womanizing, carnal, promiscuous, lustful, leering, salacious, lascivious, degenerate, debauched, dissolute, dissipated, unchaste, wanton, salacious, libidinous
OLD lickerish, rammish; (*Shakesp*) codding
FORMAL concupiscent, licentious, prurient
COLLOQ. randy, raunchy, horny
SLANG pervy

lechery *n*
lewdness, womanizing, carnality, libertinism, debauchery, rakishness, lust, lustfulness, libidinousness, licentiousness, salaciousness, salacity, sensuality, wantonness, lasciviousness
OLD lickerishness
FORMAL concupiscence, prurience
COLLOQ. randiness, raunchiness

lectern *n*
desk, reading-desk, table, stand, eagle, oratory
OLD lettern

lecture *n, v*
◆ *n*
1 SPEECH, lesson, talk, instruction, sermon, address, extender, travelogue, *conférence*
OLD act
FORMAL discourse, disquisition, homily, prelection
COLLOQ. *N Am* chalk talk
2 REPRIMAND, rebuke, reproof, scolding, harangue, censure, upbraiding, chiding, reproach, curtain lecture
FORMAL berating
COLLOQ. telling-off, talking-to, dressing-down, rocket, jaw, rollicking
◆ *v*
1 TALK, give a talk, teach, hold forth, speak, make a speech, expound, address, instruct, read, give lessons in
FORMAL prelect
2 REPRIMAND, reprove, rebuke, scold, admonish, harangue, chide, censure
FORMAL berate
COLLOQ. tell off, haul over the coals, tear/pull to pieces, pick holes in, jaw

lecturer *n*
teacher, tutor, talker, speechmaker, speechifier, orator, expounder, speaker, instructor, academic, professor, reader, don, scholar, preceptor, pedagogue, sermonizer, preacher, haranguer, extensionist, *conférencier*; *N Am* docent
FORMAL declaimer, prelector

ledge *n*
shelf, shelve, sill, mantel, mantelpiece, mantelshelf, ridge, projection, overhang, step, bench, berm, offset, altar, gradin, buttery-bar; *dialect* linch, stock; *Scot* scarcement
OLD settle, fire-step, firing-step

ledger *n*
account book, books, accounts, record book, journal, register, inventory

lee *n*
shelter, refuge, protection, cover, sanctuary

leech *n*
hanger-on, parasite, sycophant, clinger, toady, bloodsucker, freeloader, extortioner, usurer
COLLOQ. sponger, scrounger

leer *v, n*
◆ *v*
eye, ogle, look lecherously at, stare, wink, squint, gloat, goggle, grin, smirk, sneer
◆ *n*
ogle, lecherous look, stare, wink, squint, grin, smirk, sneer
COLLOQ. glad eye

leery *adj*
wary, careful, cautious, guarded, uncertain, unsure, chary, suspicious, on your guard, distrustful, doubting, dubious, sceptical

lees *n*
deposit, dregs, grounds, residue, sediment, refuse, settlings, draff
FORMAL precipitate

leeway *n*
space, room, latitude, elbow-room, play, scope, freedom, slack, margin, flexibility

left *adj*
1 LEFT-HAND, port
FORMAL sinistral
2 LEFT-WING, socialist, radical, progressive, revolutionary, liberal, communist, collectivist, revisionist, Bolshevist, Leninist, Marxist, Stalinist, Trotskyist, Trotskyite, Maoist, Spartakist
COLLOQ. red
F3 1 right **2** right-wing

left-handed *adj*
1 *a left-handed person*
Scot corrie-fisted
FORMAL sinistral
COLLOQ. cack-handed, southpaw
2 AWKWARD, clumsy, gauche
3 DUBIOUS, ambiguous, equivocal, insincere, hypocritical
COLLOQ. backhanded

left-over *adj*
remaining, settled, excess, surplus, superfluous, unused, uneaten

leftovers *n*
leavings, remainder, remains, remnants, residue, surplus, scraps, sweepings, refuse, dregs, excess

left-wing *adj*
left, socialist, radical, progressive, revolutionary, liberal, communist, collectivist, revisionist, Bolshevist, Leninist, Marxist, Stalinist, Trotskyist, Trotskyite, Maoist, Spartakist

leg *n, v*
◆ *n*
1 LIMB, member, shank
TECHNICAL crus
COLLOQ. pin, stump, peg
Related adjective: crural
2 SUPPORT, prop, upright, brace, underpinning
3 STAGE, part, bit, section, portion, stretch, segment, lap

Legal terms include:

CRIMINAL LAW:	MARRIAGE AND DIVORCE:	juror	exchange of	civil law	miscarriage of
acquittal	adultery	jury	contracts	claim	justice
age of consent	alimony	justice of the	fee simple	codicil	oath
alibi	annulment	peace	foreclosure	common law	party
arrest	bigamy	JP	freehold	constitution	penalty
bail	decree absolute	juvenile	inheritance	contract	power of attorney
caution	decree nisi	Law Lord	intestacy	covenant	precedent
charge	divorce	lawyer	lease	court case	probate
confession	maintenance	Lord Advocate	leasehold	court martial	proceedings
contempt of court	settlement	Lord Chancellor	legacy	cross-examine	proof
dock	PEOPLE:	Lord Chief Justice	local search	custody	proxy
fine	accessory	liquidator	mortgage	damages	public inquiry
guilty	accomplice	magistrate	patent	defence	repeal
indictment	accused	notary public	tenancy	demand	sanction
innocent	advocate	offender	title	equity	settlement
malice	Attorney General	plaintiff	trademark	eviction	statute
aforethought	barrister	procurator fiscal	will	evidence	subpoena
pardon	*colloq.* brief	receiver	MISCELLANEOUS:	extradition	sue
parole	clerk of the court	Queen's Counsel	act of God	grant	summons
plea	client	QC	Act of Parliament	hearing	testimony
plea bargain	commissioner for	sheriff	adjournment	hung jury	trial
plead guilty	oaths	solicitor	affidavit	indemnity	tribunal
plead not guilty	convict	solicitor advocate	agreement	injunction	verdict
prisoner	coroner	witness	allegation	inquest	waiver
probation	criminal	young offender	amnesty	inquiry	ward of court
Queen's (or	defendant	PROPERTY OR	appeal	judgement	warrant
King's) evidence	Director of Public	OWNERSHIP:	arbitration	judiciary	will
remand	Prosecutions	asset	bar	lawsuit	writ
reprieve	(DPP)	conveyance	bench	legal aid	
sentence	executor	copyright	Bill of Rights	liability	
suspended	felon	deed	brief	mandate	
sentence	judge	easement	by-law	misadventure	
		endowment	charter		
		estate			

See also **court**; **crime**.

■ **leg it**
run, hurry, walk, go by foot
COLLOQ. hoof it
■ **not have a leg to stand on**
be unjustified, be unproved, lack support, lack an excuse
■ **on its last legs**
weak, failing, fading fast, ailing, nearing collapse, about to fail/collapse, near to ruin, near to death
COLLOQ. at death's door
■ **pull someone's leg**
tease, trick, joke, play a joke on, make fun of, fool, deceive
COLLOQ. kid, rib, have on, wind up, lead up the garden path
SLANG take for a ride

legacy *n*
bequest, endowment, gift, heritage, inheritance, birthright, estate, heirloom, heritance
FORMAL bequeathal, patrimony

legal *adj*
1 LAWFUL, legitimate, within the law, permissible, permitted, sanctioned, allowed, authorized, licensed, allowable, legalized, constitutional, valid, warranted, above-board, right, sound, proper, rightful, acceptable, admissible
FORMAL licit
COLLOQ. legit
2 JUDICIAL, forensic
3 JUDICIARY, statutory, constitutional
See panel above
E3 1 illegal

Synonym nuances
sense 1
Lawful would be used specifically of something that is allowed within the constraints of law, while **legitimate**, along with **valid** and **warranted**, may be used more widely of anything that is deemed acceptable or justified: *the player's claims for a penalty were legitimate.*

Permissible and **permitted**, like **allowable** and **allowed**, **acceptable** and **admissible**, similarly suggest anything that is likely to be tolerated, considered or consented to: *admissible evidence.*
  The terms **sanctioned** and **authorized** go further by implying official backing. **Licensed**, likewise, suggests the stamp of officialdom but has fairly specific contexts where licences are granted: *licensed to carry firearms.*
Legalized, on the other hand, would be reserved for something previously illegal now being encompassed by the law: *legalized abortion*, whereas **constitutional** has more to do with laws of state: *the abdication represented a constitutional crisis.*
  Above-board has more judgemental but positive connotations of a lack of deceit, as do both **right** and **sound**, which similarly suggest being trustworthy, while **proper** is also a fairly approving term for something conforming to the correct procedures. **Rightful**, on the other hand, is suggestive of legal entitlement: *the rightful heir to the throne.*

legality *n*
lawfulness, legitimacy, validity, rightness, rightfulness, soundness, admissibleness, permissibility, constitutionality
E3 illegality

legalize *v*
legitimize, make legal, license, permit, sanction, allow, decriminalize, authorize, warrant, validate, approve, ratify, accept, admit

legally *adv*
lawfully, by law, according to the law, by rights, rightfully, legitimately, permissibly, validly, properly, constitutionally

legate *n*
representative, ambassador, delegate, deputy, emissary, envoy, agent, commissioner, messenger, nuncio

legatee *n*
beneficiary, recipient, receiver, inheritor, heir, co-heir(ess), devisee, inheritrix

legation *n*
mission, diplomatic mission, commission, consulate, embassy, ministry, deputation, delegation, representation

legend *n*
1 MYTH, story, traditional story, tale, folk tale, fable, fiction, romance, narrative, saga
2 INSCRIPTION, caption, motto, key, cipher, explanation, underline
3 *he has become a legend in his own lifetime*
celebrity, star, personality, name, dignitary, famous person, superstar, living legend, household name
FORMAL personage, notable, luminary, worthy
COLLOQ. VIP, big name, bigwig, big shot, celeb

legendary *adj*
1 MYTHICAL, fabulous, fabled, storybook, fictitious, fictional, fanciful, traditional
2 FAMOUS, celebrated, renowned, well-known, illustrious, glorious, acclaimed, honoured, remembered, popular, immortal
F3 2 unknown

legerdemain *n*
trickery, sleight of hand, deception, cunning, craftiness, chicanery, artifice, artfulness, subterfuge, contrivance, manipulation, manoeuvring, feint
FORMAL prestidigitation, thaumaturgics, sophistry
COLLOQ. hocus-pocus

legibility *n*
readability, readableness, clarity, clearness, plainness, lucidity, lucidness, intelligibility, comprehensibility, comprehensibleness, explicitness, distinctness, precision, simplicity
F3 illegibility

legible *adj*
readable, easy to read, intelligible, decipherable, clear, lucid, distinct, neat, plain, comprehensible, explicit, distinct, precise, simple
F3 illegible

legibly *adv*
readably, intelligibly, clearly, lucidly, plainly, easily read, comprehensibly, explicitly, precisely, simply
F3 illegibly

legion *n, adj*
♦ *n*
1 *Roman legions*
army, battalion, brigade, company, division, regiment, unit, cohort, troop, force
2 *legions of foreign tourists*
host, number, multitude, myriad, swarm, throng, drove, mass, horde
♦ *adj*
countless, numerous, myriad, numberless, innumerable, illimitable, multitudinous

legislate *v*
enact, ordain, decree, order, pass/make laws, authorize, codify, establish, formulate
FORMAL constitutionalize, prescribe

legislation *n*
1 LAW, statute, regulation, bill, act, charter, enactment, ordinance, code, authorization, ruling, rules, measure
2 LAWMAKING, enactment, codification, formulation
FORMAL prescription

legislative *adj*
lawmaking, lawgiving, judicial, parliamentary, congressional, senatorial
TECHNICAL jurisdictive

legislator *n*
lawmaker, lawgiver, member of parliament, parliamentarian, congressman, congresswoman, senator

legislature *n*
assembly, chamber, house, parliament, congress, senate

legitimacy *n*
1 LEGALITY, lawfulness, validity, rightness, rightfulness, soundness, admissibleness, permissibility, constitutionality
2 REASONABLENESS, sensibleness, soundness, fairness, validity, rationality, admissibility, plausibility, acceptability, justifiability, credibility
F3 1 illegality **2** invalidity

legitimate *adj*
1 LEGAL, lawful, authorized, warranted, sanctioned, statutory, rightful, proper, correct, real, genuine, acknowledged
FORMAL licit
COLLOQ. legit
2 REASONABLE, sensible, rational, logical, admissible, plausible, acceptable, justifiable, justified, warranted, well-founded, sound, fair, valid, true, credible
F3 1 illegal **2** invalid

legitimize *v*
sanction, authorize, permit, allow, warrant, license, validate, charter, entitle, legalize, decriminalize
FORMAL legitimate

leisure *n*
relaxation, rest, spare time, free time, time, time off, ease, freedom, liberty, recreation, retirement, holiday, vacation, break, time out; *N Am* off-hours
OLD leasure, by-time, respite
COLLOQ. space, R and R
F3 work
■ **at your leisure**
when you want to, at your convenience, unhurriedly, in your own time, in your spare time, when it suits you, when you get round to it

leisurely *adj*
unhurried, slow, relaxed, comfortable, easy, easy-going, unhasty, tranquil, restful, gentle, carefree, lazy, slow, loose
OLD leasurable
COLLOQ. laid-back
F3 rushed, hectic

lend *v*
1 LOAN, advance, credit, put forth, allow to have, allow to use, let someone use, on-lend, overlend
OLD prest
COLLOQ. sub
2 *lend your support to something*
give, grant, provide, supply, contribute, donate, add
FORMAL bestow, furnish, confer, impart
F3 1 borrow
■ **lend an ear**
listen, pay attention, take notice, heed, give ear
FORMAL hearken
■ **lend a hand**
help, help out, assist, give assistance, aid, give a helping hand
COLLOQ. do your bit, pitch in
■ **lend itself to**
be suitable for, be appropriate for, be easily/readily used for

length *n*
1 EXTENT, distance, measure, reach, span
2 DURATION, period, term, stretch, space, span
3 PIECE, portion, section, segment
■ **at length**
1 THOROUGHLY, in great detail, fully, comprehensively, exhaustively, for a long time

2 EVENTUALLY, after a long time, finally, in due course, at last

■ **go to any lengths**
be very determined, try very hard, do anything, go to extremes

lengthen *v*
stretch, extend, draw out, grow longer, prolong, protract, spin out, eke (out), pad out, increase, expand, continue
FORMAL elongate
⊟ reduce, shorten

lengthwise *adv*
lengthways, endways, endwise, endlong, horizontally, vertically

lengthy *adj*
long, prolonged, extended, lengthened, overlong, long-drawn-out, long-winded, rambling, diffuse, wordy, verbose, drawn-out, interminable, tedious
FORMAL protracted, prolix
⊟ brief, concise

leniency *n*
lenience, tolerance, forbearance, permissiveness, indulgence, mercy, forgiveness, soft-heartedness, softness, kindness, mildness, tenderness, gentleness, compassion, humaneness, generosity, magnanimity, moderation
FORMAL clemency
⊟ severity

lenient *adj*
tolerant, forbearing, sparing, indulgent, liberal, merciful, forgiving, soft-hearted, kind, mild, tender, gentle, compassionate, humane, generous, magnanimous, moderate
⊟ strict, severe

lenitive *adj*
alleviating, calming, easing, palliative, relieving, soothing, assuaging, mollifying
FORMAL mitigating
⊟ irritant

lens
See panel at **spectacles**.

leper *n*
outcast, social outcast, undesirable, untouchable, pariah, lazar

leprechaun *n*
goblin, imp, brownie, fiend, hobgoblin, gnome, elf, sprite, spirit, gremlin, nixie, red-cap, bogey, kelpie, kobold, demon, troll, puck; *Irish* pooka

lesbian *n, adj*
♦ *n*
gay, homosexual, sapphist, tribade
COLLOQ. butch
SLANG (*offensive*) dyke, les, lez, lezzy, lesbo, queer
♦ *adj*
gay, homosexual, Sapphic, tribadic, lesbic
COLLOQ. butch
SLANG (*offensive*) dykey

lesion *n*
injury, wound, abrasion, sore, scratch, scrape, bruise, cut, gash, laceration, impairment, hurt, trauma
TECHNICAL contusion

less *n, adv, prep*
♦ *n*
fewer, smaller amount, not as/so much, not as/so many
⊟ more
♦ *adv*
to a lesser degree/extent, to a smaller extent, not as/so much
⊟ more
♦ *prep*

minus, without, short of, excluding, except, with the exception of, excepting, save, bar

lessen *v*
decrease, go/come down, reduce, diminish, decline, dip, plunge, plummet, curtail, lower, ease (off), tail off/away, peter out, contract, die down, let up, dwindle, lighten, slow down, weaken, shrink, allay, cut, abridge, de-escalate, erode, minimize, narrow, moderate, extenuate, mitigate, subside, ebb, wane, slack, slacken, flag, fail, dull, deaden, relieve, impair
OLD bate
FORMAL abate, derogate
COLLOQ. nosedive
⊟ grow, increase

lessening *n*
decrease, reduction, decline, dip, curtailment, easing, contraction, dwindling, weakening, shrinkage, cutting, de-escalation, erosion, minimization, extenuation, mitigation, moderation, ebbing, waning, slackening, flagging, failure, deadening, let-up
OLD batement, imminution
FORMAL abatement, diminution, derogation
COLLOQ. petering out
⊟ increase

lesser *adj*
lower, secondary, inferior, less important, smaller, subordinate, slighter, minor
⊟ greater

lesson *n*
1 CLASS, period, instruction, lecture, seminar, workshop, sermon, tutorial, teaching, coaching, course
2 ASSIGNMENT, exercise, homework, schoolwork, practice, task, drill
3 EXAMPLE, model, warning, deterrent, moral
4 *read the lesson at church*
Bible reading, reading, passage from the Bible, Scripture, text

lest *conj*
in case, in order to avoid, for fear that

let¹ *v*
1 PERMIT, allow, give permission, authorize, agree to, sanction, grant, enable, tolerate
FORMAL give leave, consent to, assent to
COLLOQ. OK, give the OK, give the go-ahead, give the green light to, give the nod, say the magic word
2 *let something happen*
allow, cause, enable, make
3 LEASE, hire, hire out, rent, rent out, let out
⊟ 1 prohibit, forbid

■ **let alone**
not to mention, not forgetting, never mind, apart from, also, as well as

■ **let down**
fail, disappoint, disillusion, dissatisfy, disenchant, fall short, abandon, betray, desert
COLLOQ. leave in the lurch
⊟ satisfy

■ **let fly**
fly at, attack, assault, go for, fall upon, hit, strike, lay into, charge, lash out at
COLLOQ. bite someone's head off, have a go at, jump down someone's throat, let someone have it

■ **let go**
release, give up, set free, stop holding, free, liberate, unhand
FORMAL manumit
⊟ catch, imprison

■ **let in**
admit, allow to enter, accept, receive, take in, include, incorporate, greet, welcome

▣prohibit, bar, forbid

■ **let in on**

allow to know, allow to share in, tell, inform, let know, include

■ **let off**

1 EXCUSE, absolve, pardon, exempt, discharge, reprieve, forgive, acquit, spare, ignore, liberate, release

FORMAL exonerate

2 DISCHARGE, detonate, fire, explode, emit, give off, release

▣ **1** punish

■ **let on**

disclose, reveal, let slip, make known, make public, tell, relate, give away, pass on

FORMAL divulge, impart

COLLOQ. blab, squeal, give the game away, let the cat out of the bag, spill the beans

■ **let out**

1 FREE, release, let go, discharge

COLLOQ. leak

2 REVEAL, disclose, make known, utter, betray, let slip

COLLOQ. blab, squeal, let the cat out of the bag, spill the beans

▣ **1** keep in

■ **let up**

subside, ease (off), lessen, moderate, slacken, diminish, decrease, moderate, stop, cease, end, halt, die down

FORMAL abate

▣ continue

let² *n*

without let or hindrance

check, constraint, impediment, hindrance, obstacle, obstruction, prohibition, restriction, restraint, interference

▣ assistance

let-down *n*

disappointment, anticlimax, disillusionment, setback, betrayal, desertion

COLLOQ. washout

lethal *adj*

fatal, deadly, deathly, death-dealing, mortal, dangerous, venomous, poisonous, toxic, murderous, ruinous, disastrous, destructive, devastating

FORMAL noxious

▣ harmless, safe

lethally *adv*

fatally, mortally, dangerously, toxically, disastrously, destructively, devastatingly

FORMAL noxiously

▣ harmlessly, safely

lethargic *adj*

listless, sluggish, dull, lifeless, inert, slow, lazy, inactive, idle, slothful, apathetic, drowsy, heavy, sleepy, weary

FORMAL debilitated, enervated, hebetant, languid, somnolent, torpid

▣ lively

lethargically *adv*

listlessly, sluggishly, dully, lifelessly, inertly, slowly, lazily, inactively, idly, slothfully, apathetically, drowsily, heavily, sleepily, wearily

FORMAL languidly, somnolently, torpidly

▣ energetically

lethargy *n*

listlessness, sluggishness, dullness, lifelessness, inertia, slowness, laziness, idleness, sloth, apathy, inactivity, inaction, indifference, sleepiness, drowsiness, weariness, stupor

FORMAL lassitude, torpor, langour, somnolence

▣ liveliness

let-out *n*

excuse, escape, means/way of escape, way out, cure,

remedy, safety valve, loophole, error in the law, legal flaw, technicality, escape clause

COLLOQ. get-out

letter *n*

1 NOTE, message, line, correspondence, dispatch, communication, chit, acknowledgement, reply, circular

FORMAL missive, epistle

2 CHARACTER, symbol, sign, figure

TECHNICAL grapheme

FORMAL device

3 *a woman of letters*

literature, books, culture, education, learning, humanities, writing, scholarship, academia, belles-lettres

FORMAL erudition

■ **to the letter**

exactly, strictly, strictly speaking, accurately, precisely, word for word, literally, religiously, punctiliously, in every detail, by the book

lettered *adj*

learned, scholarly, educated, informed, knowledgeable, academic, well-educated, well-read, widely read, cultivated, cultured, literary, literate, studied, versed, accomplished

FORMAL erudite

COLLOQ. highbrow

▣ ignorant

let-up *n*

break, interval, lessening, pause, recess, remission, slackening, respite, lull

FORMAL abatement, cessation

COLLOQ. breather

▣ continuation

level *adj, n, v*

◆ *adj*

1 FLAT, smooth, even, flush, plane, uniform, horizontal, aligned, abreast, plane

2 EQUAL, balanced, aligned, drawn, even, on a par, neck and neck, matching, uniform, level pegging

3 STEADY, stable, constant, unchanging, regular, uniform

4 CALM, unemotional, steady, composed, self-possessed

COLLOQ. unflappable

▣ **1** uneven **2** unequal **3** unsteady **4** emotional

◆ *n*

1 HEIGHT, elevation, altitude, highness

2 POSITION, point, rank, status, class, degree, grade, mark, standard, standing, station, plane, layer, stratum, storey, stage, zone

FORMAL echelon

3 MEASURE, degree, extent, quantity, size, magnitude, amount, quantity, volume

◆ *v*

1 DEMOLISH, destroy, devastate, flatten, knock down, raze, raze to the ground, make level, pull down, bulldoze, tear down, lay waste

2 EVEN OUT, flush, plane, smooth, equalize, even up, stabilize, make level, make flat

3 DIRECT, point, aim, train, focus, concentrate, zero in on

4 *level with someone*

admit, open up, confess, divulge, tell, tell all, speak plainly, be frank, keep nothing back

FORMAL avow

COLLOQ. come clean, put your cards on the table, be upfront, give it to someone straight, tell it like it is, bring out in the open

■ **on the level**

honest, open, candid, fair, straight

COLLOQ. fair and square, straight-up, up-front, above board

level-headed *adj*

calm, balanced, even-tempered, sensible, steady, reasonable, rational, composed, cool, cool-headed,

practical, prudent, sane, self-possessed, dependable
FORMAL circumspect, imperturbable
COLLOQ. unflappable

lever n, v

♦ n
1 HANDLE, bar, pull, switch, joystick, crank, brake, key, pedal, tiller, trigger
OLD whipstaff
2 CROWBAR, bar, jemmy, handspike, crossbar
♦ v
force, prise, pry, raise, lift, hoist, dislodge, jemmy, shift, move, heave, pinch

leverage n

1 *apply economic leverage*
force, strength, power, advantage, authority, influence, rank, weight
FORMAL ascendancy, purchase
COLLOQ. clout, pull
2 *the leverage of the straps*
grip, hold, grasp, force
FORMAL purchase

leviathan n

giant, mammoth, hulk, colossus, monster, sea monster, behemoth, whale, Titan

levitate v

float, glide, waft, drift, fly, hover, suspend, hang

levitation n

hovering, floating, hanging, gliding, wafting, drifting, flying, suspension

levity n

light-heartedness, light-mindedness, frivolity, carefreeness, facetiousness, flippancy, irreverence, hilarity, triviality, silliness, fun
E3 seriousness

levy v, n

♦ v
tax, impose, exact, demand, charge, raise, gather, collect; *Scot* stent
TECHNICAL estreat
OLD leave, tallage
♦ n
tax, toll, subscription, contribution, duty, customs, excise, duties, due, fee, tariff, collection, assessment, precept, tithe
TECHNICAL impost

lewd adj

obscene, indecent, suggestive, bawdy, pornographic, salacious, licentious, lascivious, impure, unclean, sensual, vulgar, unchaste, lustful, lecherous, carnal, promiscuous, degenerate, debauched, dissolute, wanton, harlot
OLD lubricious
FORMAL concupiscent, libidinous
COLLOQ. smutty, blue, raunchy, randy
E3 decent, chaste

lewdly adv

obscenely, indecently, pornographically, vulgarly, impurely, lustfully, lecherously, promiscuously, degenerately, dissolutely
COLLOQ. smuttily, raunchily, randily

lewdness n

obscenity, smut, smuttiness, indecency, bawdiness, pornography, salaciousness, licentiousness, lasciviousness, impurity, unchastity, lustfulness, lechery, vulgarity, wantonness, carnality, crudity, debauchery, depravity
FORMAL concupiscence
COLLOQ. randiness
E3 chasteness, politeness

lexicon n

dictionary, glossary, vocabulary, wordbook, word-list, phrase book, encyclopedia

liability n

1 ACCOUNTABILITY, duty, obligation, responsibility, answerability, blameworthiness
FORMAL culpability
2 DEBIT, arrears, obligation, dues, indebtedness
3 DRAWBACK, disadvantage, inconvenience, hindrance, impediment, burden, onus, nuisance, encumbrance
COLLOQ. drag, millstone around your neck
E3 **1** unaccountability **2** asset **3** advantage

liable adj

1 INCLINED, likely, apt, disposed, prone, tending, susceptible, vulnerable, exposed, subject, open
FORMAL predisposed
2 RESPONSIBLE, answerable, accountable, amenable, changeable, to blame, at fault
E3 **1** unlikely **2** unaccountable

liaise v

contact, communicate, intercommunicate, co-operate, work together, collaborate, exchange information, relate to, network, interface

liaison n

1 CONTACT, connection, communication, interchange, co-operation, collaboration, working together, exchange of information
2 INTERMEDIARY, link, go-between, mediator, negotiator, arbitrator, middleman, broker, agent
3 LOVE AFFAIR, affair, relationship, romance, intrigue, amour, flirtation, entanglement
COLLOQ. bit on the side, fling, carry-on, two-timing

liar n

falsifier, perjurer, deceiver, prevaricator, false witness
COLLOQ. fibber

libation n

drink offering, sacrifice
FORMAL oblation

libel n, v

♦ n
defamation, false report, untrue statement, slur, smear, slander, denigration
FORMAL disparagement, vilification, aspersion, calumny
COLLOQ. muck-raking, mudslinging
♦ v
defame, slander, malign, abuse, denigrate
FORMAL cast aspersions on, vilify, revile, disparage, calumniate, traduce
COLLOQ. slur, smear, drag someone's name through the mud, throw mud at, badmouth

> **libel** or **slander**?
> In English law, *libel* is an untrue defamatory statement made in a permanent form such as print, writing or pictures or broadcast on radio or television, whereas *slander* is one made by means of the spoken word (not broadcast) or gesture. In Scots law, both are *slander*.

libellous adj

defamatory, abusive, slanderous, derogatory, maligning, injurious, scurrilous, false, untrue, denigratory
FORMAL vilifying, disparaging, calumniatory, traducing

liberal adj

1 BROAD-MINDED, open-minded, enlightened, tolerant, lenient, unprejudiced, unbiased, impartial, flexible, broad, broad-based, wide-ranging, catholic, libertarian, latitudinarian
2 PROGRESSIVE, reformist, forward-looking, advanced, radical, moderate, left, left-wing, leftish
3 GENEROUS, giving, ample, bountiful, lavish, plentiful, abundant, copious, profuse, handsome, open-handed,

open-hearted, large-hearted, big-hearted, unsparing, philanthropic, altruistic
OLD frank, handsome
FORMAL magnanimous, munificent
E3 1 narrow-minded, exclusive 2 conservative 3 mean, miserly

liberalism *n*
progressivism, radicalism, free-thinking, leftism, humanitarianism, libertarianism, latitudinarianism
E3 conservatism, narrow-mindedness

liberality *n*
1 GENEROSITY, benevolence, free-handedness, large-heartedness, kindness, open-handedness, open-heartedness, largesse, charity, bounty, philanthropy, altruism
FORMAL magnanimity, beneficence, munificence
2 BROAD-MINDEDNESS, liberalism, impartiality, open-mindedness, permissiveness, breadth, tolerance, toleration, progressivism, flexibility, catholicity, libertarianism, latitudinarianism
E3 1 meanness 2 illiberality

liberalize *v*
relax, deregulate, lift controls on, loosen, reduce, slacken, moderate, soften, ease (off)

liberate *v*
free, emancipate, release, let loose, set loose, let go, let out, set free, deliver, unchain, unfetter, uncage, unshackle, discharge, rescue, ransom
FORMAL redeem, manumit, disimmure
E3 imprison, enslave, restrict

liberation *n*
freedom, freeing, liberating, liberty, emancipation, release, deliverance, loosing, unchaining, uncaging, unfettering, unshackling, unpenning, ransoming, enfranchisement
FORMAL manumission, redemption
COLLOQ. lib
E3 enslavement, imprisonment, restriction

liberator *n*
rescuer, deliverer, freer, saviour, ransomer, redeemer, emancipator
FORMAL manumitter
E3 enslaver, jailer

libertine *n, adj*
♦ *n*
debauchee, reprobate, seducer, sensualist, womanizer, rake, profligate, lecher, voluptary, roué, Don Juan, Casanova, Lothario, Romeo, Lovelace
♦ *adj*
debauched, degenerate, womanizing, lecherous, reprobate, dissolute, promiscuous, lustful, salacious
FORMAL licentious

liberty *n*
1 FREEDOM, emancipation, deliverance, release, liberation, independence, autonomy, self-government, self-rule, self-determination, sovereignty, discretion, leave
FORMAL manumission
2 LICENCE, permission, sanction, right, privilege, prerogative, entitlement, authorization, dispensation, franchise, indulgence
3 FAMILIARITY, disrespect, overfamiliarity, boldness, presumption, impertinence, impudence, insolence
FORMAL impropriety
E3 1 imprisonment 3 respect, politeness
■ **at liberty**
free, allowed, permitted, entitled, unconstrained, unrestricted, unhindered, without restraint, unrestrained, loose, not confined, at large
■ **take the liberty**
be so bold as to, make bold, be impertinent, be impudent,

show disrespect, act presumptuously, behave overfamiliarly

libidinous *adj*
lustful, debauched, impure, promiscuous, loose, lascivious, lecherous, carnal, lewd, salacious, unchaste, sensual, wanton, wicked
FORMAL concupiscent, cupidinous, prurient, ruttish
COLLOQ. randy, horny
E3 modest, temperate

libido *n*
sexual desire, sex drive, sexual appetite, sexual urge, erotic desire, passion, ardour, lust, eroticism
COLLOQ. randiness, the hots

libretto *n*
words, text, lines, lyrics, script, book

licence *n*
1 PERMIT, warrant, certificate, charter, document, pass, authority, grant, imprimatur
2 PERMISSION, warranty, authorization, authority, sanction, consent, certification, right, franchise, entitlement, prerogative, privilege, dispensation, carte blanche, freedom, liberty, approval, exemption, independence
FORMAL leave, accreditation
3 ABANDON, dissipation, excess, immoderation, indulgence, self-indulgence, intemperance, lawlessness, unruliness, anarchy, disorder, debauchery, decadence, dissoluteness, licentiousness, immorality, impropriety, irresponsibility
4 *poetic licence*
imaginativeness, exaggeration, fancifulness, creativity, inspiration, originality, freedom, exemption, deviation
E3 2 prohibition, restriction 3 decorum, moderation, restraint, control

license *v*
permit, give permission, consent, allow, authorize, certify, warrant, entitle, empower, sanction, commission, franchise, privilege
FORMAL accredit
E3 ban, prohibit

licentious *adj*
debauched, dissolute, dissipated, depraved, decadent, profligate, lascivious, immoral, abandoned, lewd, lecherous, promiscuous, libertine, impure, lax, lustful, disorderly, wanton, unchaste
COLLOQ. randy, raunchy
E3 modest, chaste

licentiousness *n*
debauchery, dissoluteness, immorality, abandon, lewdness, lechery, promiscuity, libertinism, impurity, lust, lustfulness, salaciousness, salacity, wantonness, dissipation
FORMAL cupidinousness, prurience
COLLOQ. randiness, raunchiness
E3 modesty, temperance

licit *adj*
legitimate, legal, lawful, authorized, warranted, sanctioned, statutory, rightful, proper, correct, real, genuine, acknowledged
COLLOQ. legit

lick *v, n*
♦ *v*
1 *lick the chocolate*
tongue, wet, moisten, lap, taste, wash, clean, fawn; *Scot* slake
2 FLICKER, dart, play over, touch, flick, ripple
3 DEFEAT, beat, conquer
FORMAL vanquish
COLLOQ. thrash, hammer, trounce, slaughter, demolish, make mincemeat (out) of, run rings round
♦ *n*

bit, dab, little, speck, spot, touch, tad, taste, stroke, sample, brush, smidgeon, hint

■ **lick your lips**
enjoy, savour, drool over, relish, anticipate

licking *n*
thrashing, whipping, flogging, hiding, smacking, spanking, tanning, beating, defeat, drubbing

lid *n*
top, cover, covering, cap, stopper

lie¹ *n, v*
♦ *n*
tell lies
falsehood, untruth, perjury, falsification, fabrication, invention, fiction, half-truth, deceit, falsity, white lie, prevarication
FORMAL dissimulation
COLLOQ. fib, whopper, porky, tall story, made-up story, cock-and-bull story
SLANG (*vulgar*) crap, bullshit
◰ truth
♦ *v*
perjure, misrepresent, tell a lie, fabricate, falsify, invent, make up a story, equivocate, prevaricate
FORMAL forswear yourself, dissemble, dissimulate
COLLOQ. fib, lie through your teeth

■ **give the lie to**
disprove, rebut, contradict, invalidate, prove false

Synonym nuances
noun
Falsehood and **untruth** can be used for untrue statements, whereas the use of **perjury** is restricted to giving dishonest evidence under oath. **Falsification** can be used to imply deliberate alteration or forgery: *the falsification of the company's accounts*, while **fabrication** suggests making something up for one's own ends. Similarly, **invention** has to do with devising something, and **fiction** suggests a tale that is a work of the imagination, but with less implication of selfish motives.
  Half-truth suggests an element of truth is involved but an important element has been hidden, whereas **deceit** suggests a deliberate attempt to mislead, while **prevarication** has more to do with deliberate deviation from and avoidance of the truth: *the minister's speech contained falsehoods and prevarications*. **White lie** is more approving in that it suggests a tactful evasion of the truth to save someone's feelings.

---

lie² *v*
1 BE, exist, be located, be placed, be positioned, be found, belong, extend, remain, stay, keep, stretch, reach, stand, continue
FORMAL dwell
2 *lie down for a rest*
rest, recline, stretch out, sprawl out, lounge, couch, laze
FORMAL repose

■ **lie in wait for**
ambush, waylay, lay a trap for, trap, attack, surprise, lurk
OLD lie at lurch
FORMAL ambuscade

■ **lie low**
go into hiding, hide, hide away, hide out, conceal yourself, go to earth, take cover, lurk, skulk
COLLOQ. hole up, lie doggo, keep a low profile

❗ lie or lay
See panel at **lay¹**.

liege *n*
lord, liege-lord, feudal lord, overlord, master, king, nobleman, superior, chief

lieutenant *n*
assistant, second-in-command, deputy, subordinate, right-hand man/woman

life *n*
1 BEING, existence, animation, breath, viability, aliveness, entity, soul
2 LIVING THINGS, human life, animal life, plant, fauna, flora, fauna and flora
3 *the loss of many lives*
person, individual, human being, man, woman, child
4 DURATION, lifetime, existence, life expectancy, course, span, lifespan, career
5 *the machine has a limited life*
duration, continuance, span, lifespan, time, course, period of usefulness, time of being active, lifetime
6 *see life*
(wide) experience, varied activities, travelling, meeting people
7 LIFE STORY, biography, autobiography, diary, diaries, memoirs, journal
8 LIVELINESS, vigour, vitality, vivacity, animation, high spirits, exuberance, enthusiasm, excitement, verve, zest, energy, élan, spirit, sparkle, effervescence, activity, cheerfulness
COLLOQ. oomph, pep, zip, zing, pizzazz
◰ **1** death
Related adjectives: vital, zoetic

■ **come to life**
become active, become interesting, become lively, become exciting, come alive, wake up

■ **give your life**
sacrifice yourself for, give up/sacrifice your life, offer up/surrender your life, die for, dedicate yourself to, devote yourself to

life-and-death *adj*
important, all-important, crucial, vital, serious, critical

lifeblood *n*
essential part/factor, life-force, spirit, soul, core, centre, heart, inspiration

lifeless *adj*
1 DEAD, deceased, defunct, cold, unconscious, gone, inanimate, insensible, stiff, stone-dead, clay-cold
OLD (*Shakesp*) key-cold
2 LETHARGIC, listless, sluggish, lacklustre, dull, apathetic, passive, insipid, uninspired, uninspiring, unemotional, bloodless, colourless, slow, flat, wooden, stiff; *Scot* cauldrife
OLD (*Shakesp*) key-cold
FORMAL exanimate
3 BARREN, bare, empty, desolate, stark, uninhabited, arid, sterile, unproductive, soulless
◰ **1** alive, exciting **2** lively

lifelike *adj*
realistic, true-to-life, real, true, vivid, natural, authentic, faithful, exact, graphic
◰ unrealistic, unnatural

lifelong *adj*
lifetime, for all your life, long-lasting, long-standing, persistent, lasting, enduring, abiding, permanent, constant
◰ impermanent, temporary

lifestyle *n*
way of life, life, way of living, manner of living, living conditions, position, situation

lifetime *n*
duration, existence, life, lifespan, span, period, time, course, day(s), career

lift *v, n*
♦ *v*
1 *she lifted the chair*
raise, pick up, elevate, hoist, uplift, upraise, hold up, hold high

2 *he lifted their spirits*
uplift, exalt, buoy up, boost, raise, elevate
3 *the ban has been lifted*
cancel, end, stop, relax, remove, withdraw, annul
FORMAL revoke, rescind, terminate
4 *lift people out of the war zone*
fly, transport, move, transfer, airlift, convey, shift
5 *the fog lifted*
clear, disperse, vanish, disappear, scatter, dissolve, thin out
6 DIG UP, dig out of the ground, pull up, pick, root out, unearth
7 *lift someone else's material*
copy, plagiarize, steal, borrow
COLLOQ. crib, nick
F∃ 1 drop, put down **2** lower, depress **3** start, apply **5** come down, gather **6** plant, sow
♦ *n*
1 ELEVATOR, escalator, hoist, paternoster
2 *give you a lift home*
drive, hitch, ride, run, transport
3 BOOST, fillip, encouragement, pick-me-up, uplift, spur, reassurance
COLLOQ. shot in the arm
F∃ 3 discouragement
■ **lift off**
take off, blast off, ascend, climb, depart
F∃ touch down

lift-off *n*
take-off, blast-off, ascent, climb, departure
F∃ touchdown

ligature *n*
band, binding, bond, link, tie, connection, cord, rope, string, tie, thong, strap, bandage, tourniquet, ligament
TECHNICAL deligation, funicle

light¹ *n, v, adj*
♦ *n*
1 ILLUMINATION, brightness, brilliance, radiance, glow, ray, beam, shaft, shine, glare, gleam, glint, lustre, flash, blaze
FORMAL luminescence, effulgence, lambency
Related adjective: photic
2 LAMP, lantern, lighter, match, torch, candle, taper, bulb, beacon
TECHNICAL luminosity, incandescence; *N Am* flashlight
3 DAY, daybreak, daylight, daytime, dawn, sunrise, first light, crack of dawn, cockcrow
4 ENLIGHTENMENT, illumination, explanation, understanding, comprehension, insight, knowledge
FORMAL elucidation
5 *presented in a different light*
aspect, way, approach, manner, style, slant, angle, side, dimension, point of view
F∃ 1 darkness **3** night
♦ *v*
1 IGNITE, fire, set alight, set fire to, set burning, kindle
COLLOQ. torch
2 ILLUMINATE, light up, lighten, floodlight, brighten, animate, cheer (up), make cheerful, switch on, turn on, put on
FORMAL irradiate
F∃ 1 extinguish **2** darken
♦ *adj*
1 ILLUMINATED, bright, brilliant, luminous, glowing, shining, well-lit, sunny
2 PALE, pastel, fair, blond, blonde, bleached, faded, whitish, faint
F∃ 1 dark **2** black
■ **bring to light**
make known, notice, reveal, expose, discover, uncover, disclose
■ **come to light**
become obvious, be made known, be noticed, be discovered, be uncovered, be exposed

■ **in the light of**
considering, taking into consideration, taking into account, because of, in view of, bearing/keeping in mind, being mindful of, remembering
■ **shed/throw/cast light on**
clarify, make clear, explain, make plain, illuminate
OLD enlight
FORMAL elucidate

Sources of light include:

NATURAL LIGHT:	headlamp	tail-light
aurora borealis	headlight	torch
daylight	indicator light	traffic light
infrared	laser	**FIRELIGHT:**
lightning	light bulb	bonfire
moonlight	light buoy	candle
starlight	lighthouse	candlelight
sunlight	navigation light	fire
ultraviolet	neon light	firework
ELECTRIC LIGHT:	night light	flare
Belisha beacon	pedestrian light	flame
brake light	range light	gaslight
chandelier	runway light	hurricane lamp
courtesy light	searchlight	lighter
fairy light	sidelight	match
flashgun	spotlight	oil lamp
N Am flashlight	standard lamp	pilot light
floodlight	streetlight	spark
fluorescent light	strip light	taper
fog lamp	strobe light	
footlight	sun-lamp	
halogen light		

light² *adj*
1 WEIGHTLESS, insubstantial, lightweight, delicate, fine, airy, buoyant, flimsy, thin, feathery, floaty, slight
2 *light rain; light winds*
slight, mild, gentle, soft, weak, faint
3 *light machinery*
small, portable, easily moved, easy to carry around
4 *light work*
easy, effortless, moderate, undemanding, unexacting, untaxing
5 *a light punishment*
mild, lenient, slight, moderate
6 *light movements*
graceful, quick, gentle, nimble, agile, deft
7 TRIVIAL, inconsiderable, trifling, superficial, unimportant, inconsequential, worthless, petty
8 CHEERFUL, cheery, carefree, light-hearted, lively, happy, merry, gay
FORMAL blithe
9 ENTERTAINING, diverting, amusing, funny, humorous, frivolous, light-hearted, witty, pleasing
10 *light food*
easy to digest, digestible, modest, delicately flavoured
11 *light soil*
easily dug, porous, loose, crumbly
FORMAL friable
F∃ 1 heavy, weighty, thick **2, 3, 4** heavy **5** severe, harsh **7** important, serious **8** solemn **9** serious **10** heavy, rich **11** solid, dense

---

Synonym nuances
sense 1
Weightless suggests being unrestrained by gravity and so is fairly technical in tone, whereas **insubstantial**, while still fairly technical, is more suggestive of a lack of solidity: *an insubstantial trail of smoke*. **Lightweight** can be used similarly, or may be applied more figuratively to imply a lack of authority: *he's a lightweight political figure*. **Delicate** and **fine** are more suggestive of physical fragility: *delicate fabrics should be washed by hand*.

Airy can be used literally or figuratively to imply a lack of tangibility or substance: *airy speculation*, whereas **buoyant** has implications of lightness with particular regard to your spirits as well as its literal meaning: *in buoyant mood*. You can use **feathery** to suggest something rather wispy: *the ferns' feathery fronds*, or **floaty** to suggest light movement: *floaty skirts*.
Flimsy, **thin** and **slight**, on the other hand, are vaguely pejorative and suggest not being solid or strong enough: *flimsy clothes that do not keep out the cold; flimsy arguments.*

light³
■ **light on/upon**
find, come across, discover, notice, hit on, spot, stumble on
FORMAL chance on, encounter, happen upon

lighten¹ v
the sky lightened
illuminate, illumine, make lighter, brighten, make brighter, light up, shine, glow
F3 darken

lighten² v
1 EASE, lessen, make lighter, unload, lift, relieve, reduce, calm
OLD levigate
FORMAL mitigate, alleviate, allay, assuage
2 BRIGHTEN, cheer (up), encourage, hearten, uplift, lift, gladden, restore, revive, elate, buoy up, inspire
FORMAL inspirit
COLLOQ. perk up
F3 **1** burden **2** depress
■ **lighten up**
relax, unwind, calm down
COLLOQ. take it easy, let yourself go, put your feet up, cool, chill (out), hang loose

light-fingered adj
dishonest, pilfering, stealing, thieving, thievish, shoplifting, crafty, furtive, shifty, sly
COLLOQ. crooked, filching
F3 honest

light-footed adj
agile, active, nimble, sprightly, spry, swift, deft, lithe, graceful
F3 clumsy, slow

light-headed adj
1 FAINT, giddy, dizzy, unsteady, airy, delirious
FORMAL vertiginous
COLLOQ. woozy
2 FLIGHTY, foolish, frivolous, silly, superficial, shallow, empty-headed, flippant, vacuous, trifling
COLLOQ. scatter-brained, feather-brained, airheaded
F3 **2** level-headed, solemn

light-hearted adj
cheerful, joyful, jolly, happy, happy-go-lucky, bright, in good spirits, in high spirits, carefree, untroubled, merry, sunny, glad, elated, gay, jovial, playful, frolicsome, amusing, entertaining
FORMAL blithe
COLLOQ. chirpy, bouncy, high
F3 sad, unhappy, serious

lighthouse n
beacon, tower, danger/warning signal, fanal, pharos

lightly adv
1 SLIGHTLY, gently, faintly, delicately, gingerly, softly, thinly, sparingly, sparsely, slightingly
2 EASILY, effortlessly, readily, airily, breezily, gaily, facilely
3 FRIVOLOUSLY, flippantly, carelessly, heedlessly, thoughtlessly, casually
4 LENIENTLY, mildly, easily
F3 **1** heavily **3** soberly

lightness n
1 *lightness of the clothes*
weightlessness, slightness, airiness, buoyancy, crumbliness, porosity, porousness, sandiness, delicacy, delicateness, flimsiness, thinness
2 *lightness of movement*
grace, gracefulness, agility, gentleness, litheness, deftness, nimbleness, mildness
3 *lightness of spirit*
cheerfulness, cheeriness, light-heartedness, liveliness, gaiety, animation
FORMAL blitheness
4 FICKLENESS, triviality, frivolity, levity
F3 **1** heaviness, solidness **2** clumsiness **3** sadness, heaviness **4** seriousness, severity, sobriety

lightning n
forked lightning, sheet lightning, ball lightning, chain lightning, zigzag lightning, summer lightning, lightning strike, thunderbolt, thunderclap, clap of thunder, thunderdart, thunderstorm, electric storm, wildfire
OLD fire, levin
FORMAL fulguration
Related adjective: fulgural
■ **like lightning**
speedily, quickly, rapidly, hastily, immediately;
COLLOQ. wildfire, a rocket

lightweight adj
1 LIGHT, insubstantial, delicate, flimsy, thin, feathery, weightless
2 UNIMPORTANT, insignificant, inconsequential, insubstantial, trivial, worthless, negligible, trifling, petty, slight, paltry
FORMAL nugatory
F3 **1** heavy, thick, strong **2** important, major, heavyweight

likable adj
lov(e)able, pleasing, appealing, nice, agreeable, charming, engaging, winsome, winning, pleasant, friendly, genial, amiable, congenial, attractive, sympathetic
F3 unpleasant, disagreeable

like¹ adj, n, prep
◆ adj
like minds
similar, resembling, alike, same, much the same, having an affinity, identical, equivalent, akin, comparable, corresponding, related, relating, parallel, allied, approximating, of a kind
FORMAL analogous
F3 unlike, dissimilar
◆ n
equal, match, counterpart, equivalent, opposite number, fellow, mate, twin, parallel, peer
◆ prep
1 *he was shaking like a leaf*
in the same way/manner as, along/on the lines of, similar to
2 *sports like running or climbing*
such as, for example, for instance, by way of example
3 *it's just like him to change his mind*
typical, characteristic, true, usual, normal

like² v
1 ENJOY, delight in, find enjoyable/interesting, find pleasant, take pleasure in, take to, appeal to, care for, admire, esteem, appreciate, be fond of, find attractive, be keen on, love, adore, hold dear, cherish, prize, relish, revel in, approve, welcome, take (kindly) to, be someone's liking
COLLOQ. have a soft spot for, dig
2 PREFER, choose, select, decide on, feel inclined, desire, want, wish, would rather, would sooner, would more willingly/readily
COLLOQ. go for, fancy, go a bundle on, take a shine to
F3 **1** dislike **2** reject

likelihood *n*
likeliness, probability, possibility, chance, prospect, liability
Ⓔ improbability, unlikeliness

likely *adj, adv*
♦ *adj*
1 PROBABLE, possible, anticipated, expected, to be expected, liable, prone, tending, inclined, predictable, inclined, foreseeable
COLLOQ. odds-on, on the cards, in the wind
2 CREDIBLE, believable, plausible, feasible, reasonable, acceptable
3 PROMISING, appropriate, acceptable, proper, fitting, fit, right, promising, hopeful, pleasing
Ⓔ **1** unlikely **3** unsuitable
♦ *adv*
probably, presumably, in all probability, no doubt, doubtlessly, (as) likely as not

like-minded *adj*
agreeing, in agreement, of one mind, of the same mind, unanimous, in harmony, in rapport, compatible, harmonious
FORMAL in accord
Ⓔ disagreeing

liken *v*
compare, equate, match, parallel, link, relate, juxtapose, associate, set beside
OLD (*Shakesp*) like
FORMAL correlate, analogize, similize

likeness *n*
1 SIMILARITY, resemblance, comparison, affinity, correspondence, parallelism
FORMAL semblance, similitude, analogy, simulacrum
2 REPRESENTATION, image, expression, copy, reproduction, replica, facsimile, statue, bust, sculpture, effigy, drawing, painting, picture, sketch, portrait, study, depiction, photograph, icon, counterpart, caricature, guise
FORMAL personation
3 SEMBLANCE, guise, appearance, form, shape
Ⓔ **1** dissimilarity, unlikeness

likewise *adv*
1 SIMILARLY, in the same way/manner, by the same token, in like manner, as also
COLLOQ. same here
2 ALSO, moreover, furthermore, in addition, further, besides, too
OLD to boot, eke

liking *n*
fondness, love, affection, preference, partiality, affinity, taste, attraction, appreciation, proneness, inclination, tendency, bias, leaning, bent, desire, weakness, fancy
FORMAL predilection, penchant, propensity, proclivity
COLLOQ. soft spot, thing
Ⓔ dislike, aversion, hatred

lilt *n*
rise and fall, rhythm, sway, swing, song, measure, beat, cadence, air

lily-white *adj*
faultless, pure, spotless, virtuous, virgin, blameless, chaste, incorrupt, innocent, irreproachable, uncorrupt, uncorrupted, unsullied, untainted, untarnished, milk-white
Ⓔ corrupt

limb *n*
1 *stretch your limbs*
arm, leg, member, appendage, extremity, quarter, flipper; *Scot* spauld
TECHNICAL pterygium
Related adjective: membral
2 BRANCH, projection, offshoot, wing, fork, extension, section, part, spur, bough

▪ **out on a limb**
exposed, isolated, in a weak position, vulnerable, in a risky/precarious situation

limber *adj, v*
♦ *adj*
flexible, supple, pliant, plastic, elastic, agile, graceful, lithe, loose-jointed, loose-limbed, pliable, lissom
Ⓔ stiff
▪ **limber up**
loosen up, warm up, work out, exercise, prepare

limbo
▪ **in limbo**
in a state of uncertainty, awaiting action, left hanging, left in the air
FORMAL in abeyance
COLLOQ. up in the air, on the back burner

limelight *n*
fame, celebrity, spotlight, stardom, recognition, renown, attention, focus of attention, notice, eminence, notability, prominence, publicity, public eye

limit *n, v*
♦ *n*
1 EXTREMITY, ultimate, utmost, extreme, maximum, terminus, greatest extent, greatest amount, lid, ceiling, maximum, cut-off point, saturation point, deadline
2 BOUNDARY, confines, parameters, bound(s), brim, border, frontier, edge, brink, threshold, verge, end, perimeter, rim, compass, demarcation, termination
3 CHECK, curb, restraint, restriction, constraint, limitation
♦ *v*
restrict, check, curb, restrain, constrain, hold/keep in check, confine, demarcate, delimit, control, contain, bound, hem in, rein, bridle, ration, reduce, specify, hinder, impede
FORMAL circumscribe
▪ **the limit**
enough, intolerable, too much, the end, the worst
COLLOQ. the final blow, the last straw

limitation *n*
1 CHECK, restriction, curb, control, constraint, restraint, delimitation, demarcation, block, hindrance, impediment
2 INADEQUACY, shortcoming, incapability, inability, imperfection, weakness, weak point, defect, disadvantage, drawback, snag, condition, qualification, reservation
Ⓔ **1** freedom, extension **2** advantage, strong point

limited *adj*
restricted, constrained, controlled, confined, checked, defined, finite, qualified, fixed, minimal, small, basic, narrow, inadequate, insufficient, scanty, incomplete, imperfect
FORMAL circumscribed
Ⓔ limitless, boundless

limitless *adj*
unlimited, unbounded, boundless, illimited, undefined, immeasurable, measureless, incalculable, infinite, countless, endless, never-ending, unending, interminable, inexhaustible, untold, vast, unspecified
Ⓔ limited

limp[1] *v, n*
♦ *v*
limp down the road
hobble, falter, stumble, hop, shuffle, shamble, stagger, totter, walk with a limp, walk unevenly, hitch; *dialect* hamble
OLD halt, dot
COLLOQ. *NAm* gimp
♦ *n*
hobble, lameness, hitch, shuffle, flop, uneven walk, hop; *Scot* hilch

TECHNICAL claudication
OLD halt

limp² adj

1 FLABBY, drooping, flaccid, floppy, loose, slack, relaxed, lax, soft, flexible, pliable, limber, flaggy, lank
2 TIRED, weary, exhausted, fatigued, spent, weak, frail, feeble, worn out, lethargic, out of energy
FORMAL debilitated, enervated
E3 1 stiff, firm **2** vigorous, energetic

limpid adj

1 CLEAR, crystal-clear, transparent, translucent, pure, glassy, bright, still, unruffled, untroubled
FORMAL pellucid
2 INTELLIGIBLE, comprehensible, clear, plain, flowing, coherent, lucid
E3 1 muddy, ripply; *formal* turbid **2** unintelligible

limply adv

loosely, slackly, flabbily, softly, flexibly, flaccidly
E3 stiffly, firmly

limpness n

flabbiness, looseness, slackness, laxity, flexibility
FORMAL flaccidness, flaccidity, claudication
E3 stiffness, firmness

line¹ n, v

♦ *n*

1 STROKE, band, bar, stripe, mark, strip, rule, dash, slash, strand, streak, seam, belt, underline, score, underscore, scratch
2 ROW, rank, queue, file, column, sequence, series, procession, parade, chain, string, trail, tier, bank
3 LIMIT, boundary, border, borderline, edge, perimeter, periphery, frontier, demarcation, margin
4 STRING, rope, cord, cable, thread, strand, filament, wire, twine
5 PROFILE, contour, outline, silhouette, figure, shape, appearance, pattern, style, formation
FORMAL configuration, delineation
6 CREASE, wrinkle, furrow, groove, crow's feet, corrugation
7 COURSE, path, direction, track, route, channel, way, trajectory, axis
8 APPROACH, avenue, course (of action), belief, ideology, attitude, policy, system, position, practice, procedure, method, way, scheme, technique, modus operandi
9 OCCUPATION, business, trade, profession, vocation, work, job, line of business/work, career, activity, interest, employment, department, calling, field, province, forte, area, activity, pursuit, specialization, specialty, specialism, speciality
10 *chat-up line*
spiel, patter, talk, sales talk, story, pitch
11 *drop you a line*
note, letter, card, postcard, message, e-mail, word, report, memo, memorandum, information
12 WORDS, part, role, text, script, book, libretto
13 *a shipping line*
company, business, firm, transport business
14 *enemy lines*
defences, position, front, front line, firing-line, battleground, battlefield, battle zone
FORMAL formation
15 *a line of products*
brand, make, kind, sort, variety, type
16 ANCESTRY, family, descent, extraction, parentage, heritage, lineage, strain, pedigree, stock, race, breed
♦ *v*

1 BORDER, skirt, verge, edge, bound, fringe, rim
2 CREASE, score, furrow, mark, draw, hatch, inscribe, rule
■ **line up**
1 ALIGN, range, straighten, marshal, order, group, regiment, queue up, form a queue, stand in line, wait in line, form ranks, fall in, assemble

FORMAL array
2 ORGANIZE, arrange, prepare, produce, secure, obtain
FORMAL procure
COLLOQ. lay on
■ **draw the line**
refuse, say no to, exclude, limit, reject, rule out, stop short of, stand firm
COLLOQ. put your foot down
■ **in line**
1 IN A ROW, in a queue, in a column, in series
2 *bring the two systems in line with each other*
in agreement, in step, in harmony
FORMAL in accord
3 *in line for promotion*
due, likely, being considered, in the running
COLLOQ. on the cards
■ **lay/put on the line**
risk, put in jeopardy, jeopardize, endanger, imperil
■ **toe the line**
conform, keep/follow the rules, be conventional

line² v

line a box with paper
encase, panel, cover, fill, inlay, pad, back, face, stuff, reinforce

lineage n

ancestry, descent, extraction, genealogy, family, line, pedigree, race, stock, birth, breed, house, heredity, ancestors, forebears, descendants, offspring, succession
OLD (*Shakesp*) descending, progeny; lignage, parage

lineaments n

features, face, lines, outline(s), appearance, aspect, profile, traits
FORMAL countenance, visage, physiognomy, configuration

lined adj

1 RULED, feint
2 WRINKLED, furrowed, creased, wizened, worn
E3 1 unlined, blank **2** smooth

linen n

bed linen, sheets, pillowcases, tablecloths, table linen, napkins, tea towels, white goods
FORMAL napery

liner n

ship, cruise ship, ocean-going vessel, steamer, boat

line-up n

array, arrangement, queue, row, line, selection, cast, team, bill, list

linger v

1 LOITER, delay, dally, wait, remain, stay, hang on, hang around, lag, dawdle, idle, stop, take your time, hover, lurk, straggle; *dialect* hanker; *Scot* taigle
OLD tarry; (*Spenser*) hove
FORMAL procrastinate
COLLOQ. stick around, dilly-dally, let the grass grow under your feet
2 CONTINUE, endure, hold out, last, persist, survive, remain
E3 1 leave, rush

lingerie n

underclothes, underwear, underclothing, undergarments, panties, knickers, camiknickers, camisole, slip, half-slip, teddy, body stocking, panty girdle, brassiere, bra, suspender belt, unmentionables, inexpressibles
COLLOQ. frillies, undies, smalls, scanties

lingering adj

persistent, remaining, surviving, persisting, slow, dragging, long-drawn-out, prolonged
FORMAL protracted
E3 quick

lingo n

language, tongue, patois, speech, talk, jargon, idiom,

vernacular, terminology, vocabulary, parlance, dialect, argot, cant, patter
COLLOQ. mumbo-jumbo

liniment n
cream, lotion, salve, ointment, embrocation, emollient, balm, balsam, wash
FORMAL unguent

lining n
inlay, interfacing, facing, padding, backing, casing, encasement, stiffening, panelling, reinforcement

link n, v
• n
1 CONNECTION, bond, tie, association, joint, relationship, tie-up, union, knot, liaison, attachment, communication, partnership
FORMAL concatenation
2 RING, loop, bond, tie, knot, joint, shackle, swivel
TECHNICAL karabiner
3 PART, piece, element, member, constituent, component, division
• v
connect, join, attach, couple, tie, fasten, unite, bind, amalgamate, merge, associate, ally, bracket, interlink, identify, relate, liaise, yoke, attach, hook up, join forces, team up, bridge, network; Scot cleek
OLD enchain
FORMAL concatenate
E3 separate, unfasten
▪ **link up**
connect, join (up), ally, amalgamate, meet up, join forces, merge, team up, unify, hook up, dock, bridge
E3 separate

linkage n
connection, bond, tie, tie-in, tie-up, association, joint, relationship, union, knot, liaison, attachment, communication, partnership, alliance, amalgamation, merger, union

link-up n
connection, alliance, amalgamation, association, relationship, partnership, merger, tie-in, union
E3 separation

lion
▪ **lion's share**
most, main part, majority, bulk, mass, greatest/largest part, preponderance, almost/nearly all

lion-hearted adj
bold, brave, courageous, heroic, daring, gallant, intrepid, stout-hearted, valiant, fearless, dauntless, resolute, stalwart, dreadless
FORMAL valorous
E3 cowardly

lionize v
glorify, hero-worship, treat as a hero, honour, idolize, magnify, fête, exalt, celebrate, praise, sing the praises of, acclaim, adulate
FORMAL aggrandize, eulogize
COLLOQ. put on a pedestal
E3 vilify

lip n
1 mouth, underlip; dialect fipple
TECHNICAL labium, labrum, flew, hare-lip, ligula, muffle, submentum
Related adjective: labial
2 EDGE, brim, border, brink, rim, margin, verge, spout
TECHNICAL helmet, corolla
3 IMPERTINENCE, impudence, insolence, rudeness, effrontery, backchat
COLLOQ. cheek, sauce, attitude
E3 politeness

lippy adj
cheeky, impertinent, impudent, insolent, disrespectful, forward, brazen, pert, audacious, overfamiliar
COLLOQ. fresh, saucy, mouthy; N Am sassy
E3 respectful, polite

liquefaction n
dissolution, dissolving, fusion, liquefying, melting, thawing
FORMAL deliquescence
E3 solidification

liquefy v
dissolve, fuse, liquidize, melt, smelt, run, thaw, flux, fluidize
FORMAL liquesce, deliquesce
E3 solidify

liqueur

Liqueurs include:

absinthe	Drambuie®	ouzo
advocaat	Frangelico®	Parfait Amour
amaretto	Galliano®	pastis
Amarula®	Glayva®	Pernod®
anisette	Goldschlager®	Ponche
Aurum®	Grand Marnier®	pousse-café
Averna	Irish Mist®	prunelle
Bailey's®	Izarra®	ratafia
Benedictine	Jägermeister	Ricard®
Chartreuse®	Kahla®	sambuca
cherry brandy	kirsch	Southern
Cherry Heering	kümmel	Comfort®
Cointreau®	limoncello	Strega®
crème de cacao	maraschino	Tia Maria®
crème de cassis	mirabelle	Triple sec
crème de menthe	Malibu®	Vana Tallinn
curaçao	Midori®	Van der Hum
Cuarenta y Tres	Nocino	
(or Licor 43)	noyau	

---

liquid n, adj
• n
liquor, fluid, juice, drink, sap, solution, lotion
• adj
1 FLUID, flowing, liquefied, watery, wet, running, runny, sloppy, thin, melted, molten, thawed, clear
FORMAL aqueous, hydrous
2 SMOOTH, flowing, steady, even, regular, unbroken, uninterrupted, pure, clear, mellow, melodious
E3 **1** solid, gas

liquidate v
1 PAY (OFF), close down, dissolve, break up, clear, discharge, wind up, sell (off), disband, cash in, convert to cash
2 ANNIHILATE, terminate, do away with, put an end to, dissolve, kill, murder, massacre, assassinate, destroy, dispatch, abolish, eliminate, exterminate, remove, finish off
COLLOQ. rub out, wipe out

liquidize v
process, blend, crush, purée, cream, mix, synthesize

liquor n
1 ALCOHOL, intoxicant, strong drink, spirits, drink
OLD (Shakesp) tickle-brain
COLLOQ. hard stuff, hoo(t)ch, juice, Dutch courage, sauce, firewater, tipple, the bottle, stiffener, the creature, tiddly, tinct; Aust & NZ grog
SLANG booze, gnat's piss, jungle juice, rotgut; Aust & NZ shicker; N Am juice
2 LIQUID, juice, gravy, essence, extract, stock, broth, infusion

lissom adj
graceful, supple, pliable, flexible, pliant, light,

nimble, agile, limber, lithe, lithesome, loose-jointed,
loose-limbed, willowy
◨ stiff, awkward

list[1] *n, v*
◆ *n*
a shopping list
catalogue, roll, inventory, register, enumeration, schedule,
programme, agenda, index, contents, listing, record, file,
directory, table, tabulation, tally, series, syllabus, calendar,
recipe, roster, rota, checklist, invoice
◆ *v*
enumerate, register, itemize, classify, catalogue,
alphabetize, index, tabulate, record, programme, file,
schedule, enrol, enter, note, bill, book, set down, write
down, compile

list[2] *v*
the ship is listing
lean (over), incline, tilt, slope, slant, heel (over), tip, cant

listen *v*
attend, pay attention, hear, heed, hang on someone's
words/lips, prick up your ears, take notice, mind, lend an
ear, eavesdrop, monitor, prick up your ears
TECHNICAL auscultate
OLD hark, hearken, give ear, intend, list, lithe
SLANG get a load of
▪ **listen in**
eavesdrop, overhear, tap, wiretap, monitor, pin back your
ears, prick up your ears
COLLOQ. bug

listless *adj*
sluggish, lethargic, spiritless, languishing, lackadaisical,
limp, lifeless, dull, passive, inert, inactive, impassive,
indifferent, uninterested, vacant, apathetic, depressed,
bored, heavy
FORMAL languid, torpid, enervated, indolent
◨ energetic, enthusiastic

listlessly *adv*
sluggishly, lethargically, spiritlessly, apathetically, lifelessly,
dully, limply, passively, inertly, inactively, impassively,
lacking energy, lacking enthusiasm
◨ energetically, enthusiastically

listlessness *n*
lethargy, sluggishness, spiritlessness, lifelessness, sloth,
inattention, indifference, ennui, apathy
FORMAL enervation, indolence, languidness, languor,
torpidity, torpor, supineness
◨ liveliness

litany *n*
1 PRAYER, petition, procession, devotion
TECHNICAL eirenicon, synapte
FORMAL supplication, invocation
2 CATALOGUE, account, enumeration, list, repetition, recital,
recitation

literacy *n*
ability to read, ability to write, proficiency, education,
culture, cultivation, intelligence, knowledge, learning,
scholarship, learnedness, articulacy, articulateness
FORMAL erudition
◨ illiteracy

literal *adj, n*
◆ *adj*
1 VERBATIM, word-for-word, verbal, strict, close, actual,
plain, clear, precise, faithful, exact, accurate, factual, true,
genuine, undistorted, unexaggerated, unembellished,
unvarnished
2 PROSAIC, unimaginative, uninspired, colourless, matter-
of-fact, down-to-earth, humdrum, boring, dull, tedious
◨ **1** imprecise, loose, deviating, free **2** imaginative
◆ *n*

misprint, mistake, error, printing error, typographical error
FORMAL corrigendum, erratum
COLLOQ. typo

literalism *n*
exact rendering, textualism, letter (of the law),
fundamentalism, biblicism, scripturalism

literally *adv*
1 *many people in Africa are literally starving*
actually, really, truly, certainly
2 *translate literally*
exactly, faithfully, to the letter, strictly, strictly speaking,
precisely, closely, plainly, word for word, verbatim
◨ **2** imprecisely, loosely

literary *adj*
1 EDUCATED, well-read, bookish, learned, scholarly, lettered,
literate, widely-read, cultured, cultivated, refined
FORMAL erudite
2 *literary phrases*
formal, poetic, written, old-fashioned
◨ **1** ignorant, illiterate **2** everyday, colloquial, informal

literate *adj*
able to read, able to write, proficient, educated, well-
educated, cultured, intelligent, learned, intellectual,
knowledgeable

literati *n*
the learned, the scholarly, the erudite, the well-informed,
men/women of letters, the studious, intelligentsia,
academics, intellectuals, cognoscenti, highbrows,
illuminati
COLLOQ. brains, eggheads

literature *n*
1 WRITINGS, printed works, published works, letters,
paper(s)
2 INFORMATION, facts, data, leaflet(s), pamphlet(s),
circular(s), brochure(s), hand-out(s), printed matter,
advertising material
COLLOQ. bumf

Types of literature include:

allegory	fiction	roman à clef
anti-novel	Gothic novel	roman novel
autobiography	historical novel	saga
formal belles-	lampoon	satire
lettres	libretto	science fiction
Bildungsroman	magnum opus	*colloq.* sex-and-
biography	non-fiction	shopping
colloq. bodice-	novel	thesis
ripper	novella	tragedy
colloq. chick lit	parody	travelogue
classic novel	pastiche	travel writing
crime fiction	*colloq.* penny	treatise
criticism	dreadful	triad
drama	picaresque novel	trilogy
epic	poetry	verse
epistle	polemic	
epistolary novel	postil	
essay	prose	
fantasy	pulp fiction	

See also **poem; story**.

---

lithe *adj*
agile, supple, flexible, pliable, pliant, lissom, limber,
lithesome, double-jointed, loose-jointed, loose-limbed
◨ stiff

litigant *n*
contender, contestant, disputant, opponent, claimant,
complainant, litigator, plaintiff, party

litigation *n*
lawsuit, law, action, legal action, dispute, suit, case, legal

proceedings, legal case, prosecution, process, contention

litigious *adj*
argumentative, quarrelsome, contentious, disputatious, disputable, belligerent
⊟ easy-going

litter *n, v*
• *n*
1 RUBBISH, debris, refuse, odds and ends, waste, mess, disorder, clutter, confusion, disarray, untidiness, muck, jumble, fragments, shreds; *N Am* trash, garbage
FORMAL detritus
COLLOQ. junk, shambles, grot
2 OFFSPRING, young, brood, family
TECHNICAL farrow
OLD kindle, team
FORMAL progeny, issue
• *v*
strew, scatter, mess up, make a mess of, disorder, clutter, make untidy
3 *litter for cattle*
bedding, straw, bed, hay, bracken, chaff
4 LIGHT COUCH, sedan, palanquin, palankeen, doolie, wagon
⊟ tidy

little *adj, adv, n*
• *adj*
1 SMALL, short, tiny, minute, diminutive, miniature, infinitesimal, mini, microscopic, petite, baby, midget, dwarf, Lilliputian, slender, slight, younger, junior
COLLOQ. wee, teeny, pint-size(d)
2 SHORT-LIVED, brief, short, fleeting, passing, momentary, transient, transitory
FORMAL ephemeral
3 INSUFFICIENT, sparse, scant, meagre, paltry, skimpy
FORMAL exiguous
4 INSIGNIFICANT, unimportant, inconsiderable, negligible, trivial, petty, minor, paltry, nominal, trifling
FORMAL nugatory
COLLOQ. peanuts
5 *a nice little house*
pleasant, attractive, nice, sweet, cute
⊟ 1 big **2** long, lengthy **3** ample **4** considerable, serious
• *adv*
barely, hardly, scarcely, slightly, faintly, rarely, seldom, infrequently, not much, next to nothing, a drop in the ocean
⊟ frequently
• *n*
bit, dash, pinch, small amount, spot, trace, drop, dab, speck, touch, taste, soupçon, smattering, particle, hint, fragment, modicum, trifle, trickle; *N Am, Aust & NZ dialect* skerrick
⊟ lot
■ **little by little**
gradually, bit by bit, progressively, slowly, step by step, by degrees, imperceptibly, piecemeal
⊟ all at one go, quickly

liturgical *adj*
ceremonial, ritual, solemn, sacramental, formal, eucharistic
FORMAL sacerdotal, hieratic
⊟ secular

liturgy *n*
service, office, form, formula, rite, usage, worship, ceremony, ritual, observance, sacrament, ordinance, celebration

live¹ *v*
1 BE, be alive, have life, exist, breathe, draw breath
2 LAST, endure, continue, remain, persist, stay,

survive, support yourself, earn your living
FORMAL abide
3 *live in Leeds*
have your home, be settled, inhabit, lodge, stay, squat
FORMAL reside, abide, dwell
4 PASS, spend, lead, experience, undergo, behave
FORMAL comport, conduct
5 *live while you're young*
enjoy life, enjoy yourself, have fun, enjoy life to the full, see life, make the most of your life
COLLOQ. live it up
⊟ 1 die **2** cease
■ **live it up**
revel, celebrate, live extravagantly, go on a spree
COLLOQ. have a ball, make merry, make whoopee, push the boat out, paint the town red
■ **live on**
live on fruit and vegetables
feed, live off, depend for nourishment, rely on, exist
FORMAL subsist on

live² *adj*
1 ALIVE, living, having life, existent, breathing, animate
2 LIVELY, vital, active, energetic, dynamic, alert, vigorous
3 BURNING, glowing, blazing, flaming, hot, red hot, ignited, alight
4 *a live appearance*
personal, in person, in the flesh, bodily, public
5 *a live TV programme*
not prerecorded, not recorded, real-time, with an audience
6 *live cables*
connected, charged, electrified, electrically charged, active
7 *a live bomb*
unexploded, explosive, unstable, volatile
8 *a live issue*
relevant, current, topical, controversial, active, important, vital, lively, urgent, pressing
FORMAL pertinent
COLLOQ. hot
⊟ 1 dead **2** apathetic **5** prerecorded **6** disconnected **7** defused **8** irrelevant
■ **live wire**
self-starter
COLLOQ. life and soul of the party; ball of fire, dynamo, go-getter, eager beaver, whizz kid
⊟ wet blanket

liveable, livable *adj*
1 INHABITABLE, habitable
2 BEARABLE, tolerable, supportable, comfortable, endurable, acceptable, adequate, satisfactory, worthwhile
⊟ 1 uninhabitable **2** unbearable
■ **liveable with**
companionable, sociable, *gemütlich*, compatible, congenial, harmonious, passable, tolerable, bearable
⊟ impossible, unbearable

livelihood *n*
occupation, employment, job, work, profession, trade, living, means of living, means, means of support, income, source of income, maintenance, daily bread, existence, support, subsistence, sustenance, upkeep, keep
OLD livelod, livelood, livelihead
COLLOQ. bread-and-butter, crust

liveliness *n*
animation, energy, quickness, spirit, life, vigour, vitality, vivacity, vivaciousness, dynamism, activity, boisterousness, briskness, smartness, sprightliness, refreshment, *esprit, entrain*
OLD livelihead
COLLOQ. brio, oomph, pizzazz
⊟ apathy, inactivity

livelong *adj*

complete, entire, full, whole, enduring, long, protracted
🔁 partial

lively *adj*

1 ANIMATED, alert, active, energetic, alive, spirited, high-spirited, enthusiastic, dynamic, vivacious, vigorous, sprightly, brisk, spry, agile, nimble, quick, keen; *dialect* wick
2 CHEERFUL, blithe, merry, frisky, perky, playful, ludic, jaunty, breezy, frolicsome, buoyant
COLLOQ. chirpy, bouncy
3 *a lively discussion*
animated, enthusiastic, heated, interesting, exciting, stimulating, vigorous
4 BUSY, bustling, quick, brisk, rapid, crowded, eventful, vibrant, exciting, buzzing, teeming, swarming, hectic
5 VIVID, bright, strong, colourful, graphic, striking, vibrant, exciting, imaginative, stimulating, stirring, invigorating, racy, refreshing, sparkling
🔁 **1** moribund, apathetic **3** dull **4** inactive **5** dull

liven *v*

enliven, vitalize, put life into, rouse, invigorate, animate, energize, brighten, stir (up), spice (up), cheer (up)
COLLOQ. buck up, pep up, perk up, hot up, jazz up
🔁 dishearten

liverish *adj*

irritable, snappy, testy, tetchy, crusty, grumpy, disagreeable, ill-humoured, quick-tempered, irascible, peevish, splenetic
COLLOQ. crabbed, crabby, crotchety
🔁 calm, easy-going

livery *n*

uniform, costume, regalia, dress, clothes, clothing, garments, vestments, suit, garb, habit
FORMAL apparel, attire, habiliments
COLLOQ. get-up, gear, clobber, togs

livid *adj*

1 ANGRY, furious, infuriated, irate, outraged, enraged, raging, seething, fuming, indignant, incensed, exasperated
COLLOQ. mad
2 LEADEN, black-and-blue, blue, bruised, discoloured, greyish, purple, purplish; *Scot* blae
3 PALE, deathly pale, pallid, ashen, blanched, white, bloodless, wan, waxy, ghastly, pasty
OLD Hippocratic
🔁 **1** calm

living *adj, n*

♦ *adj*
1 ALIVE, breathing, existing, live, animate
2 CURRENT, surviving, continuing, active, operative, in use, strong, vigorous, lively, vital, animated
FORMAL extant
COLLOQ. going strong
3 *a living likeness*
close, exact, identical, precise, faithful, true, genuine
🔁 **1** dead **2** dead, sluggish **3** inexact
♦ *n*
1 BEING, life, animation, existence
2 LIVELIHOOD, maintenance, support, means of living/support, income, source of income, subsistence, daily bread, sustenance, work, job, occupation, profession, trade, way of life, lifestyle
TECHNICAL benefice
COLLOQ. bread, bread-and-butter, crust

living room *n*

lounge, sitting room, drawing room, day room, front room, reception room, parlour

load *n, v*

♦ *n*
1 CARGO, consignment, shipment, goods, lading, freight, contents, burden, charge
2 BURDEN, onus, responsibility, duty, obligation, commitment, encumbrance, weight, pressure, charge, trouble, worry, strain, oppression, millstone, albatross
FORMAL tribulation
3 *loads of money*
a lot, lots, large amount, great deal, heaps, dozens, scores, hundreds, thousands, a million, millions, hordes, tons
COLLOQ. oodles, masses, piles, stacks, lashings, scads, miles
♦ *v*
1 PACK, pile, heap, freight, fill (up), cram, stuff, stack, lade, charge
2 *load a film into a camera*
put (in/into), insert, enter, slide, slot
3 *load a gun*
charge, prime, arm, prepare, equip, fill, plug, prepare to fire
4 BURDEN, weigh down, encumber, overburden, oppress, overwhelm, worry, trouble, weight, strain, tax, saddle with

loaded *adj*

1 BURDENED, charged, laden, full, filled, weighted, packed, piled, heaped, stacked
COLLOQ. snowed under
2 WEIGHTED, biased, to your disadvantage
COLLOQ. fixed, rigged, set up
3 RICH, wealthy, well-off, affluent
COLLOQ. well-heeled, flush, in the money, made of money, on easy street, rolling in it
4 DRUNK, under the influence, drunken, incapable, tipsy, mellow, merry, foxed; *dialect* fairish; *Scot* capernoity, fou; *Scot & Irish* stotious; *N Am* jagged
OLD overseen; (*Shakesp*) fap, paid
FORMAL inebriated, intoxicated, crapulent, ebriose
COLLOQ. a sheet in the wind, three sheets in/to the wind, tight, tiddly, tiddled, well-oiled, blotto, drunk as a lord/newt, drunk as a piper, sloshed, stewed, blind drunk, roaring drunk, the worse for drink, soused, squiffy, happy, legless, plastered, sozzled, pickled, bibulous, woozy, one over the eight, under the table, bevvied, having had a few, tired and emotional, high, footless, full, half-cut, obfuscated, pickled, pie-eyed, sow-drunk, under the weather, the worse for wear
OLD COLLOQ corked, moppy, overshot
SLANG stoned, tanked up, lit up, canned, paralytic, smashed, pissed, bombed, wasted, wrecked, trashed, stinko, whiffled, whistled, bonkers, bottled, Brahms and Liszt, juiced (up), in liquor, liquored, maggoty, mortal, up the pole, ripped; arseholed, rat-arsed, shitfaced; *Scot* blootered; *N Am* crocked, moon-eyed; *Aust* inky, inked; *Aust & NZ* shickered

loaf¹ *n*

1 *a loaf of bread*
block, slab, brick, mass, lump, cube, cake
2 *use your loaf*
common sense, sense, head, mind
COLLOQ. brains, gumption, nous, noddle

loaf² *v*

loafing about/around
stand about, idle, laze, loiter
COLLOQ. take it easy, hang around, lounge, lounge around, sit around, lie around, mooch, loll, relax, unwind, veg (out)
SLANG *Aust & NZ* bludge
🔁 toil

loafer *n*

idler, shirker, sluggard, wastrel, lounger, ne'er-do-well; *Irish* corner-boy
COLLOQ. slob, layabout, skiver, lazybones
SLANG *N Am* goof-off

loam *n*

earth, soil, clay, sand, core
TECHNICAL brickclay, malm

loan *n, v*

♦ *n*

advance, credit, mortgage, allowance, lending

OLD prest

♦ *v*

lend, advance, credit, allow, put forth, on-lend, overlend

OLD prest

COLLOQ. sub

loath *adj*

reluctant, unwilling, resisting, disinclined, opposed, grudging, hesitant, indisposed, against

FORMAL averse

Ⓔ willing

loathe *v*

hate, detest, abhor, despise, dislike, not stand, recoil from, have an aversion to, nauseate, feel revulsion at

OLD ug

FORMAL abominate, execrate

Ⓔ adore, love

loathing *n*

hatred, hate, detestation, abhorrence, repugnance, revulsion, repulsion, dislike, disgust, aversion, odium, ill-will, horror

FORMAL abomination, antipathy, execration

Ⓔ affection, love

loathsome *adj*

detestable, odious, repulsive, hateful, abhorrent, repugnant, repellent, offensive, horrible, disgusting, nauseating, vile, revolting, nasty, obnoxious, despicable, contemptible, disagreeable, abominable

OLD lothefull

FORMAL execrable

lob *v*

throw, toss, hurl, pitch, fling, heave, launch, lift, shy, loft

COLLOQ. chuck; *Irish* puck

lobby *v, n*

♦ *v*

campaign for, press for, demand, persuade, call for, urge, influence, solicit, pressure, promote

COLLOQ. push for

♦ *n*

1 VESTIBULE, foyer, porch, anteroom, hall, hallway, waiting room, entrance hall, entrance, entry, corridor, passage, passageway, box-lobby

2 PRESSURE GROUP, campaign, faction, ginger group, lobbyists

local *adj, n*

♦ *adj*

regional, provincial, community, district, neighbourhood, municipal, city, urban, town, village, parish, parochial, vernacular, small-town, limited, narrow, restricted, parish, parish-pump

Ⓔ national

♦ *n*

1 INHABITANT, citizen, resident, native

2 PUB, bar, inn, public house, tavern, bar, saloon

COLLOQ. hostelry, watering-hole

SLANG boozer

locale *n*

place, position, scene, setting, site, spot, venue, area, locality, location, neighbourhood, environment, zone

FORMAL locus

locality *n*

neighbourhood, vicinity, district, area, locale, environment, region, position, place, site, spot, scene, setting, surrounding area

localize *v*

1 IDENTIFY, specify, narrow down, pinpoint, ascribe, assign

COLLOQ. zero in on

2 RESTRAIN, limit, restrict, confine, contain, concentrate, delimit, delimitate

FORMAL circumscribe

locate *v*

1 FIND, discover, uncover, unearth, come across, track down, detect, pinpoint, identify, spot, pick out, access

COLLOQ. run to earth, lay your hands on, hit upon

2 SITUATE, settle, fix, establish, place, allocate, plant, position, put, lay, set, site, station, seat, build

location *n*

position, situation, place, whereabouts, venue, site, locale, bearings, spot, point, setting, scene

FORMAL locus

loch *n*

lake, pond, pool, sea, water, reservoir, dam, basin, mere, tarn; *Irish* lough

lock[1] *n, v*

♦ *n*

fit locks to windows

fastening, bolt, clasp, catch, padlock, mortise lock, combination lock, spring lock, Chubb® lock, Yale® lock

♦ *v*

1 FASTEN, secure, bolt, latch, bar, seal, shut, padlock

2 JOIN, unite, engage, link, mesh, entangle, entwine, clench, interlock, jam, stick

3 CLASP, hug, embrace, grasp, encircle, enclose, clutch, grapple

Ⓔ 1 unlock

■ **lock out**

shut out, refuse admittance/entrance to, keep out, exclude, bar, debar

■ **lock up**

imprison, jail, confine, shut in, shut up, put behind bars, put under lock and key, secure, cage, pen, detain, wall in, close up

FORMAL incarcerate

COLLOQ. put away

Ⓔ free

Parts of a lock include:

barrel	keyhole	rose
bolt	keyway	sash
cylinder	knob	sash bolt
cylinder hole	latch	spindle
dead bolt	latch bolt	spindle hole
escutcheon	latch follower	spring
face plate	latch lever	strike plate
hasp	mortise bolt	staple
key	pin	
key card	push button	

lock[2] *n*

locks of hair

strand, tress, tuft, plait, ringlet, curl

locker *n*

cupboard, container, cabinet, compartment

lock-up *n*

1 JAIL, gaol, prison, penitentiary, cell

SLANG can, clink, cooler, jug, slammer, quod

2 GARAGE, lock-up, storeroom, depository, warehouse

locomotion *n*

movement, motion, moving, progress, progression, travel, travelling, headway, action, walking

FORMAL ambulation, perambulation

locus *n*

place, location, position, situation, place, whereabouts, venue, site, locale, point

locution n
1 STYLE, diction, articulation, accent, intonation, inflection
2 WORDING, term, phrase, phrasing, cliché, turn of phrase, expression, idiom, collocation

lodge n, v
♦ n
1 HUT, cabin, cottage, chalet, gatehouse, house, hunting-lodge, box
2 BRANCH, chapter, section, group, club, society, association, meeting-place, habitation, campfire
3 HAUNT, retreat, shelter, nest, lair, den
♦ v
1 ACCOMMODATE, quarter, board, billet, shelter, harbour
OLD inn
COLLOQ. put up
2 LIVE, stay, have your home, be settled, lie, nest, shelter, room, barrack, keep
OLD (Spenser) bower; (Shakesp & Spenser) host
FORMAL reside, dwell, sojourn
COLLOQ. hang out, dig
3 FIX, imbed, implant, get stuck, get caught
4 DEPOSIT, place, put, put in, hand in, show up, stow, lay, submit, register, bank
5 *lodge a complaint*
register, make, submit, record, file, put forward

lodger n
boarder, paying guest, resident, tenant, roomer, inmate, guest

lodgings n
accommodation, quarters, billet, board, boarding house, rooms, place, bedsit, bedsitter, bedsitting-room
FORMAL dwelling, abode, residence
COLLOQ. digs, pad, a roof over your head, flea-bag

loftily adv
proudly, arrogantly, haughtily, disdainfully, superciliously
COLLOQ. snootily
🖃 humbly, modestly

lofty adj
1 *lofty ideals*
noble, grand, exalted, esteemed, distinguished, illustrious, majestic, sublime, stately, imposing, dignified, imperial, renowned
2 HIGH, tall, sky-high, elevated, raised, towering, soaring
OLD (Shakesp) skyish
3 ARROGANT, proud, haughty, condescending, disdainful, patronizing, supercilious, superior, lordly
COLLOQ. snooty, high and mighty, toffee-nosed
🖃 2 low 3 humble, lowly, modest

log n, v
♦ n
1 TIMBER, trunk, block, chunk, piece
2 RECORD, diary, journal, logbook, daybook, account, tally, register, chart
♦ v
record, register, write up, note, set down, book, chart, tally, file

logbook n
log, record, diary, journal, daybook, account, tally, register, chart

loggerheads
■ **at loggerheads**
disagreeing, in conflict, at odds, in opposition, quarrelling
COLLOQ. at daggers drawn, at each other's throats, like cat and dog

logic n
reasoning, reason, sense, judgement, deduction, rationale, coherence, argument, argumentation
TECHNICAL dialectics
FORMAL ratiocination

logical adj
reasonable, rational, reasoned, well-reasoned, well-founded, well-thought-out, coherent, consistent, relevant, valid, sound, clear, sensible, wise, intelligent, thinking, deducible, methodical, consecutive, well-organized
TECHNICAL Boolean, convergent, dialectic, dialectical, syllogistic
FORMAL deductive, inductive, cogent, judicious, sequacious
🖃 illogical, irrational

logically adv
rationally, coherently, consistently, relevantly, validly, clearly, sensibly, intelligently, methodically, consecutively
TECHNICAL dialectically
FORMAL deductively, inductively

logistics n
organization, co-ordination, management, masterminding, arrangement, orchestration, strategy, tactics, planning, plans, direction, engineering

logo n
symbol, sign, trademark, representation, insignia, emblem, device, mark, badge, figure, image

loiter v
dawdle, hang about/around, idle, waste time, take your time, linger, dally, delay, mooch, lag, saunter
FORMAL tarry
COLLOQ. dilly-dally, loaf, lounge

loll v
1 RELAX, slouch, slump, sprawl
FORMAL recline
COLLOQ. loaf, lounge
2 HANG, flop, droop, drop, dangle, flap, sag

lollop v
run, lope, bound, spring, stride, canter, gallop

lone adj
1 BY YOURSELF, single, sole, alone, one, only, isolated, solitary, separate
2 *a lone parent*
by yourself, on your own, single, unmarried, unattached, divorced, separated, without a partner
3 ISOLATED, uninhabited, remote, out-of-the-way, unfrequented, secluded, abandoned, deserted, forsaken, desolate, barren
🖃 1 accompanied

loneliness n
aloneness, isolation, lonesomeness, solitariness, solitude, seclusion, desolation

lonely adj
1 ALONE, friendless, lone, lonesome, solitary, abandoned, forsaken, companionless, reclusive, unaccompanied, destitute, rejected, outcast, sad, unhappy, miserable, wretched
See Synonym nuances panel at **alone**.
2 ISOLATED, uninhabited, remote, out-of-the-way, unfrequented, secluded, abandoned, deserted, forsaken, desolate, barren, god-forsaken
FORMAL solitudinous
COLLOQ. off the beaten track
🖃 1 popular, content 2 crowded, populous

loner n
individualist, recluse, solitary, hermit, introvert
FORMAL solitudinarian
COLLOQ. lone wolf

lonesome adj
1 ALONE, lonely, friendless, lone, solitary, abandoned, forsaken, companionless, reclusive, unaccompanied, destitute, rejected, outcast, sad, unhappy, miserable, wretched
2 ISOLATED, lonely, uninhabited, remote, out-of-the-way,

unfrequented, secluded, abandoned, deserted, forsaken, desolate, barren

long adj, v

♦ adj
lengthy, extensive, extended, expanded, elongated, prolonged, stretched (out), spread out, sustained, expansive, far-reaching, long-drawn-out, verbose, overlong, spun out, marathon, interminable, slow
FORMAL protracted, tardy
Ea short, brief, fleeting, abbreviated

♦ v
yearn, crave, want, wish, desire, hope, dream, hanker, pine, thirst, hunger, lust, covet, itch, ache
COLLOQ. yen

■ before long
soon, presently, shortly, in a short time, in a moment, in a minute or two, in the near future

long-drawn-out adj
lengthy, long-winded, spun out, overlong, prolonged, interminable, tedious, marathon, overextended, long-drawn
FORMAL protracted, prolix
COLLOQ. dragging on
Ea brief, curtailed

longing n, adj

♦ n
craving, desire, yearning, hunger, hungering, hankering, pining, thirst, wish, wanting, dream, hope, urge, coveting, itch, aspiration, ambition
COLLOQ. yen

♦ adj
wishful, eager, craving, pining, yearning, wistful, languishing, hungry, anxious, avid, ardent
FORMAL desirous

longingly adv
wishfully, eagerly, yearningly, wistfully, anxiously, avidly, ardently
OLD (Shakesp) wistly

long-lasting adj
permanent, imperishable, enduring, unchanging, unfading, continuing, abiding, chronic, lingering, long-standing, prolonged
FORMAL protracted
Ea short-lived, transient; formal ephemeral

long-lived adj
enduring, lasting, durable, long-lasting, long-standing
TECHNICAL macrobian, macrobiotic
FORMAL longevous
Ea brief, short-lived; formal ephemeral

long-standing adj
established, long-established, well-established, long-lived, long-lasting, enduring, abiding, time-honoured, traditional

long-suffering adj
uncomplaining, forbearing, forgiving, tolerant, indulgent, easy-going, patient, stoical, resigned
Ea complaining

long-winded adj
lengthy, overlong, prolonged, long-drawn-out, diffuse, verbose, wordy, garrulous, discursive, repetitious, rambling, tedious
FORMAL prolix, protracted, voluble
Ea brief, terse

long-windedness n
lengthiness, verbosity, wordiness, diffuseness, discursiveness, repetitiousness, tediousness, garrulity
FORMAL volubility, prolixity, longueur, macrology
Ea brevity, curtness

loo n
toilet, lavatory, WC, bathroom, cloakroom, washroom, gents', ladies', water closet, public convenience, convenience, urinal, latrine, privy, powder room, facilities, Elsan®, Portaloo®; N Am rest room, comfort station
COLLOQ. lav, dunny, smallest room, superloo, throne, little boys' room, little girls' room
SLANG bog, kazi, crapper; N Am john; Aust toot

look v, n

♦ v
1 WATCH, see, take a look, observe, view, survey, regard, gaze, eye, study, stare, examine, inspect, focus, check, take in, consider, scrutinize, glance, contemplate, scan, peep, gape
COLLOQ. gawp, run your eyes over, give the once-over, give a going-over, get a load of, get an eyeful of, take a squint at, take a dekko at, take a gander at, take a butcher's at, take a shufti at; N Am eyeball
2 SEEM, appear, give the appearance of, show, exhibit, display
3 the house looks onto the fields
face, front, front on, give on (to), overlook, be opposite, look onto

♦ n
1 VIEW, survey, inspection, examination, study, contemplation, observation, sight, review, glance, glimpse, stare, gaze, gape, peek, peep
COLLOQ. once-over, squint, eyeful, dekko, gander, butcher's, shufti
SLANG Aust & NZ squiz
2 APPEARANCE, aspect, manner, air, effect, impression, semblance, expression, face, guise, features, façade, complexion
FORMAL countenance, mien, bearing

■ look after
take care of, mind, care for, attend to, take charge of, maintain, tend, keep an eye on, watch over, nurse, protect, supervise, guard, babysit, sit, childmind
Ea neglect, disregard, ignore

■ look back
remember, recall, think back, reminisce, reflect on the past

■ look down on
despise, scorn, sneer at, hold in contempt, disdain, spurn, think of as inferior/unimportant, patronize, talk down to, act/speak condescendingly
FORMAL disparage
COLLOQ. look down your nose at, turn your nose up at, pooh-pooh
Ea esteem, approve

■ look for
try to find, search for, seek, quest, hunt for, hunt out, forage for

■ look forward to
anticipate, await, expect, hope for, long for, envisage, envision, count on, wait for, look for

■ look into
investigate, probe, research, study, go into, search into, examine, inquire about, ask about, explore, inspect, scrutinize, look over, plumb, fathom, dig, delve
COLLOQ. check out

■ look like
resemble, take after, be similar (in appearance) to, have the appearance of, remind you of

■ look on/upon
consider, regard, think, judge, count, hold
FORMAL deem

■ look out
pay attention, watch out, beware, be careful, be alert, be on your guard, guard yourself, keep your eyes open/peeled/skinned, be on the qui vive, keep an eye out, look/mind where you're going

look over

inspect, examine, check, cast an/your eye over, look through, go through, scan, read through, view, monitor
COLLOQ. check out, give a once-over

look to

1 *look to your parents for support*
turn to, reckon on, rely on, count on, resort to, fall back on
2 *look to the future*
consider, think about, give thought to, anticipate, await

look up

1 SEARCH FOR, research, seek, consult, hunt for, find, track down
2 VISIT, call on, drop in on, look in on, pay a visit to, stop by, drop by
3 IMPROVE, get better, pick up, progress, make progress, develop, advance, make headway, come on/along
FORMAL ameliorate
COLLOQ. perk up

look up to

admire, respect, regard highly, esteem, revere, honour, have a high opinion of, think highly of

---

Synonym nuances
verb sense 1
Watch, **view**, **observe**, **take in** and **regard** can be used to suggest prolonged, attentive looking. **Survey**, however, suggests a sweeping movement of the eyes to see everything: *surveying the landscape from the cliff top*, while **scan** also suggests quickly running the eyes over, but often to pick out something specific: *he scanned the rows of seats to see if she was there*. **Study**, **examine**, **scrutinize** and **inspect** share the idea of a close and lengthy look for the purpose of assessment and appraisal.

The terms **consider** and **contemplate** can be used to suggest weighing up what is seen: *I contemplated the scene of carnage before me*. **Gaze**, on the other hand, can imply an element of abstraction, or even stupefaction: *he gazed at the wall*, while **gape** suggests wide-eyed amazement: *they gaped at her as if she were an alien*. A different implication is made with **eye**, which suggests looking with a degree of suspicion: *they eyed the stranger*, while **focus** has more to do with deliberately directing your eyes: *I focused on the incident unfolding in the street below*.

The verb **check** suggests a quick movement seeking confirmation: *he checked his watch*, while **glance** is suggestive of a short but more uninterested glimpse: *he just glanced at the photos*, and **peep** suggests taking a surreptitious look: *neighbours peeping through the curtains*.

---

lookalike *n*

double, replica, twin, image, living image, exact likeness, clone, *doppelgänger*
COLLOQ. spitting image, spit, (dead) ringer

lookout *n*

1 GUARD, sentry, watch, watch-tower, watchman, sentinel, tower, post, observation post
2 CONCERN, responsibility, worry, affair, business, problem
COLLOQ. pigeon

keep a lookout

remain alert, watch, keep guard, be vigilant, be on the qui vive

loom *v*

appear, emerge, take shape, become visible, menace, threaten, impend, be imminent, hang over, dominate, tower, overhang, rise, soar, mount, overshadow, overtop

loony *adj, n*

♦ *adj*
mad, crazy, insane, lunatic, unbalanced, disturbed, deranged, demented, crazed, wild, berserk, frantic, unhinged, distracted, distraught, maniac, eccentric, strange, silly, foolish, idiotic, stupid
COLLOQ. daft, loopy, barmy, potty, bonkers, nutty
♦ *n*
madman, madwoman, lunatic, psychotic, psychopath, maniac, imbecile
COLLOQ. nutter, nut, crackpot, crank, headcase, nutcase, fruitcake, screwball, oddball, basket case; *N Am* hook
SLANG psycho

loop *n, v*

♦ *n*
hoop, ring, circle, noose, coil, eye, eyelet, loophole, spiral, curve, curl, oval, kink, twist, whorl, twirl, turn, bend, runner, sling, stitch, tab, purl, hank, knop, lug, picot
TECHNICAL becket, cannon, jubilee clip
OLD latchet
FORMAL convolution
♦ *v*
coil, encircle, surround, roll, bend, circle, curve round, turn, curl, twist, spiral, wind, connect, join, tie, knot, fasten, fold, braid

loophole *n*

let-out, escape, omission, escape clause, evasion, excuse, pretext, plea, ambiguity, pretence, mistake
COLLOQ. get-out

loose *adj, v*

♦ *adj*
1 FREE, unfastened, untied, at large, unconfined, released, undone, untethered, uncoupled, unlocked, let go, escaped, off, movable, unattached, insecure, wobbly, unsteady
2 SLACK, lax, baggy, hanging, loose-fitting, sagging, flowing, shapeless, unbound, untied
3 IMPRECISE, vague, inexact, ill-defined, indefinite, inaccurate, indistinct, general, broad, rambling
4 *loose morals*
promiscuous, dissolute, lax, unchaste, fast, debauched, disreputable, immoral, corrupt, wanton, degenerate, abandoned
E∃ 1 firm, fixed, secure **2** tight, fitting **3** exact, precise, specific, literal **4** chaste, pure
♦ *v*
1 RELEASE, set free, free, let go, liberate, loosen, unbind, unclasp, unfasten, untie, disconnect, disengage, detach, unleash, unhook, uncouple, undo, unlock, unmoor, unpen
2 RELAX, slacken, ease, moderate, lessen, loosen, weaken, diminish, reduce
E∃ 1 bind, fasten, fix, secure **2** tighten

at a loose end

with nothing to do, bored, out of action, idle, aimless, purposeless, off duty
COLLOQ. fed up, twiddling your thumbs, with time to kill

on the loose

escaped, at large, on the run, free, at liberty, unconfined

loosely *adv*

1 FREELY, insecurely, unsteadily, movably
2 SLACKLY, baggily, shapelessly
3 IMPRECISELY, inexactly, vaguely, inaccurately, generally, broadly
E∃ 1 firmly, securely **2** tightly **3** exactly, precisely, specifically

loosen *v*

1 EASE, relax, loose, slacken, moderate, weaken, diminish, undo, unbind, untie, unfasten
2 FREE, set free, release, let go, set loose, let out, deliver
E∃ 1 tighten

loosen up

1 RELAX, unwind, let up, go easy, lessen, ease up
COLLOQ. hang loose, cool it, chill out

2 LIMBER UP, warm up, warm down, work out, exercise, prepare

loot *n, v*
♦ *n*
spoils, booty, plunder, stolen money, stolen goods, pickings, riches, haul, prize
COLLOQ. swag
♦ *v*
steal, plunder, pillage, rob, steal (from), burgle, sack, rifle, raid, maraud, ransack, ravage
FORMAL despoil

lop *v*
chop, cut (off), dock, prune, sever, trim, clip, crop, hack, shorten, curtail, detach, remove, take off, reduce, truncate

lope *v*
run, lollop, bound, spring, stride, canter, gallop

lopsided *adj*
asymmetrical, unbalanced, askew, off balance, uneven, unequal, crooked, squint, tilting, sloping, slanted, one-sided
COLLOQ. skew-whiff
F3 balanced, symmetrical

loquacious *adj*
talkative, chatty, chattering, babbling, blathering, gossipy, wordy, garrulous
FORMAL voluble, multiloquent, multiloquous
COLLOQ. gabby, gassy
F3 succinct, taciturn, terse, reserved

loquacity *n*
talkativeness, chattiness, garrulity, effusiveness
FORMAL volubility, multiloquence, multiloquy
COLLOQ. gassiness
F3 succinctness, taciturnity, terseness

lord *n*
1 PEER, noble, nobleman, earl, duke, count, viscount, baron, aristocrat, patrician
2 MASTER, ruler, superior, overlord, leader, chief, captain, commander, governor, king, prince, sovereign, monarch, emperor
3 *God, the Lord*
God, Creator, Maker, King, Almighty, Holy One, Jehovah, Yahweh, Father, Eternal, Christ, Jesus Christ, Messiah, the Word, Redeemer, Saviour, Son of God, Son of Man, King of kings
▪ **lord it over**
domineer, tyrannize, be overbearing, order around, queen it over, oppress, repress, pull rank, swagger
FORMAL put on airs
OLD (*Shakesp*) overoffice
COLLOQ. act big, throw your weight around, boss around

lordliness *n*
1 NOBLENESS, magnificence, splendidness, majesty, grandness, imperiality, impressiveness
2 PRIDE, arrogance, disdain, imperiousness, haughtiness, condescension, superciliousness, high-handedness, overconfidence
COLLOQ. big-headedness
F3 1 lowliness 2 humility

lordly *adj*
1 NOBLE, dignified, aristocratic, magnificent, splendid, majestic, grand, grandiose, stately, imperial, impressive, lofty
2 PROUD, arrogant, disdainful, haughty, imperious, condescending, patronizing, supercilious, dictatorial, imperious, high-handed, domineering, overbearing, overconfident
FORMAL peremptory, hubristic
COLLOQ. big-headed, stuck-up, high and mighty, uppity, toffee-nosed, hoity-toity, too big for your boots
F3 1 lowly 2 humble

lore *n*
knowledge, wisdom, learning, scholarship, traditions, folklore, teaching, beliefs, legends, stories, sayings, superstitions, myths, mythology
FORMAL erudition

lorry *n*
truck, trailer, articulated lorry, pantechnicon, removal van, vehicle, wagon, juggernaut, pick-up, float

lose *v*
1 MISLAY, misplace, forget, miss, not find, forfeit, drop
2 FAIL, fall short, suffer defeat, be defeated, be beaten, be conquered, go down, be unsuccessful
COLLOQ. come to grief, come a cropper, throw in the towel
3 ELUDE, escape from, evade, throw off, shake off, leave behind, outrun
4 BE DEPRIVED OF, no longer have, stop having, be taken away, be bereaved of, be dispossessed of, be divested of
5 *lose an opportunity*
not take advantage of, fail to grasp, neglect, miss, disregard, ignore, waste, squander, fritter
6 *lose your way*
wander from, stray from, depart from, go astray, get lost, lose your bearings
7 WASTE, squander, spend, consume, use up, exhaust, expend, spend, drain
FORMAL dissipate, deplete
F3 1 find, keep, gain 2 win 5 grasp, take advantage of 6 find 7 make
▪ **lose out**
suffer, miss out, be unsuccessful, be beaten, be at a disadvantage, be disadvantaged
▪ **lose yourself in something**
be absorbed in, be preoccupied in, be occupied in, be taken up with, be engrossed in, be fascinated by, be enthralled by, be captivated by, be riveted by

loser *n*
failure, runner-up, the defeated
COLLOQ. also-ran, flop, no-hoper, washout, non-starter, write-off, has-been, dead loss
F3 winner

loss *n*
1 MISLAYING, misplacement, missing, forfeiture, forgetting, dropping
2 DEPRIVATION, disappearance, bereavement, dispossession, disadvantage, harm, hurt, impairment, undoing, waste
FORMAL privation
3 *losses in war*
casualty, fatality, death toll, dead, missing, wounded
4 *the business made a loss*
deficit, debt, deficiency
F3 1 finding 2 gain 4 profit
▪ **at a loss**
puzzled, perplexed, bewildered, baffled, mystified, not knowing what to do/say

lost *adj*
1 MISLAID, missing, vanished, disappeared, misplaced, stray, astray, strayed, disoriented, disorientated, off course
2 CONFUSED, disoriented, bewildered, puzzled, baffled, perplexed, nonplussed, at a loss
3 WASTED, squandered, ruined, destroyed, wrecked, demolished, neglected, missed, frittered away, unrecoverable
4 *a lost civilization*
past, dead, defunct, extinct, bygone, former, long-forgotten, vanished, untraceable
5 *lost souls*
damned, fallen, condemned, doomed, cursed, irredeemable
6 *lost in thought*
absorbed, preoccupied, occupied, taken up with,

engrossed, fascinated, enthralled, captivated, riveted, spellbound, absent-minded, dreamy
E3 1 found

■ **lost cause**
hopeless case, hopeless situation, hopeless person
COLLOQ. also-ran, flop, no-hoper, washout, non-starter, write-off, has-been, dead loss

lot *n*
1 *lots of food; a lot of people*
large amount, great number, many, a quantity, a good/ great deal
COLLOQ. oodles, tons, loads, bucketloads, shedloads, masses, heaps, piles, stacks, lashings, scads, dozens, hundreds, thousands, millions, miles; *N Am* gobs
2 COLLECTION, batch, bundle, assortment, quantity, group, set, consignment, crowd, gathering
COLLOQ. bunch, shower
3 SHARE, portion, allowance, ration, quota, percentage, part, piece, parcel
COLLOQ. cut
4 *content with your lot in life*
destiny, fate, fortune, luck, circumstances, situation
FORMAL portion
5 PLOT, allotment, parcel, piece of land, piece of ground; *S Afr* erf

■ **a lot**
much, to a great extent/degree, a great deal, often, frequently, for a long time

■ **throw in your lot with**
join forces with, align yourself with, team up with, combine with, pitch in, take part in
COLLOQ. muck in

lotion *n*
ointment, balm, balsam, cream, salve, emollient, embrocation, liniment, cleanser, wash, hairdressing, sunscreen, toner, aftershave, astringent, witch-hazel, blackwash, fomentation
TECHNICAL collyrium
OLD arquebusade, lavatory

lottery *n*
1 DRAW, raffle, sweepstake, bingo, tombola, gambling game, lotto
2 SPECULATION, venture, risk, gamble, chance, hazard, luck

loud *adj*
1 NOISY, deafening, booming, resounding, resonant, reverberating, roaring, ear-piercing, ear-splitting, piercing, penetrating, thundering, blaring, clamorous, insistent, emphatic, vehement, vociferous, strident, shrill, raucous, rowdy, aggressive, brazen, loud-mouthed, full-mouthed
FORMAL stentorian
2 GARISH, gaudy, glaring, flashy, flamboyant, brash, showy, bold, obtrusive, ostentatious, tasteless, vulgar
COLLOQ. flash
E3 1 quiet, soft **2** subdued, subtle

Synonym nuances
sense 1
Noisy is mildly disapproving in tone in that it suggests anyone or anything that is creating too much sound, while **deafening** goes further by making the negative suggestion that such a din affects your ears. **Booming**, **resounding**, **reverberating** and **resonant** have more to do with the quality of the loudness, in this instance a deep echoing sound: *a booming baritone voice*, while **roaring** and **thundering** similarly emphasize certain qualities in the sound, but again suggest great volume. **Blaring**, like deafening, implies excessive volume, with further implications of harshness: *blaring car radios*.
The terms **ear-piercing**, **ear-splitting**, **piercing** and **penetrating**, as well as **strident** and **shrill**, convey the

---

notion of exceedingly high-pitched and jarring noise, whereas **raucous** is suggestive of loud, harsh voices: *raucous cheering*. **Rowdy**, on the other hand, is more suggestive of the loudness that comes with being disorderly: *rowdy football fans*. Terms such as **clamorous**, **insistent**, **vehement** and **vociferous** also focus on the cause of loud noise, and have to do with a persistent and disturbing outcry: *clamorous criticism of capital punishment*; *a vociferous protest*.

---

loudly *adv*
noisily, strongly, deafeningly, resoundingly, clamorously, vehemently, shrilly, vigorously, uproariously, vociferously, lustily, stridently, at the top of your voice
TECHNICAL fortissimo
FORMAL streperously, strepitantly
E3 quietly, softly

loudmouth *n*
boaster, braggart, brag, blusterer, braggadocio, swaggerer
COLLOQ. windbag, gasbag, big mouth, blowhard

loud-mouthed *adj*
noisy, aggressive, bold, brazen, boasting, blustering, bragging, coarse, vulgar

lounge *v, n*
◆ *v*
relax, loll (about), idle, laze, waste time, kill time, lie about/ around, sprawl, recline, lie back, slump
FORMAL repose
COLLOQ. take it easy
◆ *n*
sitting room, living room, drawing room, day room, reception room, front room, parlour

lour, lower *v*
1 DARKEN, blacken, cloud over, threaten, menace, loom, impend, be brewing
2 SCOWL, frown, glare, glower
COLLOQ. give a dirty look, look daggers

louring, lowering *adj*
menacing, threatening, forbidding, ominous, grim, impending, foreboding, gloomy, cloudy, overcast, dark, darkening, grey, black, heavy

lousy *adj*
1 BAD, rotten, poor, second-rate, no good, inferior, unsatisfactory, inadequate, contemptible, miserable, low
COLLOQ. awful, terrible, mingy, rop(e)y, pathetic, rubbish
SLANG crap, pants
2 ILL, unwell, sick, poorly, off-colour, seedy, queasy
COLLOQ. awful, rough, rotten, out of sorts, under the weather, below par
E3 1 excellent, superb **2** well, fine

lout *n*
oaf, boor, dolt, barbarian, yahoo, gawk, lubber, calf, bull-calf, hob, lob, hallion, lumpkin, chuckle-head; *dialect* loblolly, swad; *Scot* coof, cuif; *N Am* jake
OLD (*Spenser*) loord
COLLOQ. clod, clodhopper, hick, hobbledehoy, slob, yob, yobbo, bumpkin, oik; *N Am* roughneck; *Aust* hoon

loutish *adj*
uncouth, oafish, boorish, doltish, ill-mannered, ill-bred, gawky, rude, coarse, rough, crude, vulgar, churlish, unmannerly, unrefined, uncivilized, gruff, impolite, rustic, uneducated, ignorant
COLLOQ. clodhopping, yobbish
E3 polite, refined, cultured, genteel

lovable, loveable *adj*
adorable, endearing, winsome, appealing, captivating, enchanting, bewitching, taking, dear, charming, engaging, attractive, fetching, sweet,

lovely, pleasing, delightful, lik(e)able, cute
Ⅎ detestable, hateful

love v, n

◆ v

1 *he loves his wife*
be fond of, like very much, adore, cherish, dote on, treasure, hold dear, be attracted to, feel affection for, be devoted to, care for, prize, desire, long for, be infatuated with, idolize, worship, think the world of, mean the world to someone
COLLOQ. be mad on, be sweet on, be daft/nuts on, be sold on, have a crush on
SLANG have the hots for
2 *I love macaroons*
take pleasure in, enjoy, delight in, like very much, appreciate, desire, fancy, have a liking for, be partial to, savour, relish
Ⅎ detest, hate

◆ n

1 FONDNESS, affection, adoration, attachment, care, regard, concern, compassion, liking, amorousness, ardour, intimacy, desire, devotion, adulation, passion, rapture, tenderness, warmth, inclination, infatuation, lust, delight, enjoyment, weakness, taste, friendship, brotherhood, sympathy, kindness, tendresse
COLLOQ. soft spot
2 *a love of power*
pleasure, enjoyment, delight, liking, appreciation, weakness, partiality, relish
COLLOQ. soft spot
Related adjective: amatory
3 *come here, my love*
darling, beloved, dear, dear one, dearest, favourite, sweetheart, honey, angel, pet, treasure, poppet, precious; *Irish* machree, mavourneen, acushla, asthore
COLLOQ. angel, honey, sweetie, sugar
Ⅎ 1 hate, hatred, dislike **2** detestation, loathing

■ **love affair**
affair, romance, liaison, relationship, love, intrigue, passion
OLD amour
COLLOQ. fling, carry-on

■ **fall in love with**
fall for, become infatuated with, burn with passion for, take to, lose your heart to
COLLOQ. fall head over heels in love with, have a thing for, fancy, be crazy about, have a crush on, take a shine to, have it bad

■ **in love with**
attracted to, smitten, sweet/soft on, besotted, charmed, doting, enamoured, infatuated
COLLOQ. mad/crazy/wild about, have a crush on, hooked, nuts about, potty about, stuck on

■ **make love**
have sex with
COLLOQ. sleep with, sleep together, go to bed with
SLANG have it off with, get your leg over, bang, bonk; (*taboo*) fuck, screw, shag; *N Am* make out

---

Synonym nuances
verb sense 1
Be fond of and **care for** can be used to suggest a cosy, fairly mild affection, whereas **dote on** implies an excessive, even foolish, love: *being an only child, her parents doted on her.* **Be devoted to** is also suggestive of deep attachment, often with a degree of subservience, while **adore** could refer to extreme love, with implications of reverence: *she adored her son, and admired everything he did.* **Idolize** and **worship** give emphasis to this idea of reverence and exaltation: *the doctor was worshipped by the islanders.*
You can use **treasure** and **prize** to suggest placing a high value on someone or something, while **cherish** and **hold dear** also suggest a high estimation, as well as

---

protectiveness: *she cherished her cat and looked after her well*. **Desire** and **long for**, on the other hand, suggest a yearning, unfulfilled love, while **be infatuated with** has implications of obsession, and perhaps also of being short-lived: *he was infatuated with Marilyn for a time, seeing all her films.*

---

loveless adj
cold, cold-hearted, hard, icy, insensitive, unresponsive, unloved, unloving, passionless, unfeeling, unfriendly, unappreciated, friendless, disliked, frigid, forsaken, unvalued, heartless, uncherished
Ⅎ passionate

lovelorn adj
infatuated, desiring, longing, pining, yearning, languishing, lovesick, unrequited in love

lovely adj
1 ATTRACTIVE, beautiful, charming, delightful, enchanting, pleasing, pleasant, good-looking, pretty, handsome, fair, adorable, sweet, winning, exquisite
2 MARVELLOUS, wonderful, enjoyable, pleasing, pleasant, delightful, agreeable
Ⅎ 1 ugly, hideous **2** unpleasant, disagreeable

lovemaking n
sexual intercourse, intercourse, sex, sexual relations, sexual union, copulation, intimacy, sleeping with someone, going to bed with someone, foreplay, mating
OLD embraces
FORMAL carnal knowledge, coition, coitus, congress
SLANG lay, pussy, rumpy-pumpy, tail, bonk, bang, quickie; (*taboo*) fuck, screw, shag; *N Am* making out

lover n
1 BELOVED, loved one, admirer, boyfriend, man friend, girlfriend, woman friend, lady friend, date, sweetheart, partner, live-in partner, suitor, mistress, lady love, fiancé(e), other man, other woman, significant other
COLLOQ. flame, bit on the side, bird, fella, toy boy
2 ENTHUSIAST, devotee, admirer, fan, supporter, follower, fanatic
COLLOQ. buff, freak, fiend

lovesick adj
infatuated, desiring, longing, pining, yearning, languishing, lovelorn, unrequited in love

loving adj
amorous, affectionate, devoted, doting, fond, adoring, ardent, passionate, warm, warmhearted, kind, tender, caring, friendly, sympathetic
OLD lovely; (*Shakesp*) beloving

lovingly adv
affectionately, fondly, tenderly, ardently, passionately, sympathetically, warmly

low¹ adj, n
◆ adj
1 SHORT, small, squat, stunted, little, shallow
2 INADEQUATE, insufficient, deficient, poor, sparse, scarce, inferior, unsatisfactory, meagre, paltry, trifling, scant, scanty, little, insignificant, reduced
3 *low land*
close to the ground, sea-level, ground-level, low-lying, depressed, deep, sunken, flat
4 LOWLY, humble, low-born, obscure, poor, plebeian, plain, simple, common, modest, ordinary, inferior, junior, low-ranking, peasant, meek, mild, mean, submissive, subordinate, unimportant
5 *have a low opinion of someone*
poor, unfavourable, bad, negative, adverse, hostile, opposing, antagonistic
6 *low notes*
deep, low-pitched, bass, resonant, sonorous, rich
7 *low achiever*

unintelligent, foolish, slow, dull, mediocre, inadequate, deficient, below standard
8 UNHAPPY, depressed, down, downcast, gloomy, low-spirited, miserable, despondent, sad, downhearted, disheartened, glum
FORMAL disconsolate
COLLOQ. down in the dumps, blue, fed up, cheesed off
9 BASE, coarse, vulgar, bad, evil, wicked, mean, contemptible, nasty, despicable, dishonourable, depraved, immoral, obscene, indecent, smutty
OLD dastardly
FORMAL heinous
10 CHEAP, inexpensive, reasonable, moderate, modest, reduced, slashed, sale, rock-bottom
COLLOQ. a snip, a steal, going for a song, dirt-cheap, dog-cheap, ten a penny
11 SUBDUED, muted, soft, quiet, quietened, gentle, hushed, muffled, whispered
E3 1, 2, 3 high **4** high, important **5** high, good **6** high **8** cheerful, happy **9** honourable, decent **10** high, exorbitant **11** loud, noisy
♦ *n*
all-time low, lowest point, nadir, bottom, low point, low-watermark
E3 high

low² *v*
cattle lowing
bellow, moo

low-born *adj*
humble, poor, mean-born, plebeian, unexalted, lowly, low-ranking, peasant, obscure
E3 high-born, noble

lowbrow *adj*
ignorant, uncultivated, uncultured, unrefined, uneducated, unlearned, unscholarly, unlettered, mass-market, downmarket, tabloid, crude, rude
E3 highbrow, intellectual

lowdown *n, adj*
♦ *n*
information, news, facts, data, inside information, inside story, intelligence
COLLOQ. dope, gen, info
♦ *adj*
despicable, contemptible, vile, worthless, detestable, disgusting, mean, degrading, wretched, disgraceful, disreputable, shameful, abominable, loathsome, reprobate
OLD dastardly, caitiff
FORMAL reprehensible
E3 admirable, noble

lower¹ *adj, v*
♦ *adj*
1 *the lower jaw*
under, bottom, undermost, nether
2 INFERIOR, lesser, subordinate, secondary, minor, second-class, low-level, lowly, junior
E3 1 upper **2** higher
♦ *v*
1 DROP, depress, sink, descend, let down, let fall, move down, take down
2 REDUCE, decrease, cut, lessen, diminish, curtail, slash, bring down, cheapen
FORMAL abate
3 *lower your eyes*
look down, move downwards, set down, bring low
4 *lower your voice*
speak (more) quietly, quieten, hush
5 *not lower yourself by doing something*
debase, belittle, degrade, demean, disgrace, dishonour, abase
FORMAL disparage
E3 1 raise **2** increase **3** raise

lower²
see **lour**.

lowering
see **louring**.

low-grade *adj*
bad, inferior, poor, poor-quality, substandard, below standard, second-class, second-rate, third-rate, cheap-jack
COLLOQ. not up to scratch, awful, terrible, botched, lousy, crummy, pathetic, rop(e)y, useless, a load of rubbish, a load of garbage
SLANG the pits, pants, poxy, naff, crappy; (*vulgar*) a load of crap/shit
E3 good, quality

low-key *adj*
muted, quiet, restrained, subdued, understated, easy-going, relaxed, subtle, slight, soft
E3 showy, impressive

lowliness *n*
humility, modesty, ordinariness, inferiority, meekness, mildness, submissiveness, simplicity, commonness, poverty, obscurity, unimportance, subordinateness
E3 nobility

lowly *adj*
humble, low-born, obscure, poor, plebeian, plain, simple, common, modest, ordinary, inferior, junior, low-ranking, peasant, meek, mild, mean, submissive, subordinate, unimportant
OLD base
E3 lofty, noble, pretentious

low-pitched *adj*
deep, low, bass, resonant, sonorous, rich
E3 high, high-pitched

low-spirited *adj*
depressed, gloomy, heavy-hearted, low, down, downhearted, despondent, dejected, discouraged, sad, unhappy, miserable, moody, glum
COLLOQ. fed up, cheesed off, down in the dumps
E3 high-spirited, cheerful

loyal *adj*
true, faithful, steadfast, staunch, devoted, constant, firm, unchanging, trustworthy, true-hearted, trusty, reliable, dependable, dedicated, committed, sincere, supportive, well-affected, patriotic
OLD feal, leal
E3 disloyal, treacherous

loyalty *n*
allegiance, faithfulness, fidelity, devotion, dedication, commitment, staunchness, steadfastness, constancy, trustworthiness, reliability, dependability, sincerity, patriotism
OLD fealty, lealty
E3 disloyalty, treachery

lozenge *n*
pastille, gumdrop, tablet, cough drop, jujube
TECHNICAL troche, trochiscus, trochisk

lubber *n*
oaf, boor, dolt, barbarian, yahoo, gawk, lout
COLLOQ. clod, clodhopper, hick, hobbledehoy, slob, yob, yobbo, bumpkin

lubberly *adj*
clumsy, awkward, blundering, gawky, ungainly, heavy-handed, bungling, churlish, loutish, oafish, uncouth, doltish, lumbering, clownish, lumpish, coarse, dense, crude
COLLOQ. clodhopping

lubricant *n*
oil, grease, lubrication, fat, lard
COLLOQ. *N Am & Aust* lube

lubricate *v*
1 OIL, grease, smear, wax, polish, make smooth, lard

2 FACILITATE, ease, make easier, help, assist, encourage, further, smooth, smooth the way, promote, advance, forward, accelerate, speed up
FORMAL expedite
COLLOQ. N Am & Aust lube

lucid adj
1 *lucid writing*
clear, comprehensible, plain, explicit, distinct, intelligible, obvious, evident
FORMAL perspicuous
2 CLEAR-HEADED, sane, rational, reasonable, intelligible, sensible, sober, sound, of sound mind, *compos mentis*
3 SHINING, bright, brilliant, beaming, transparent, translucent, gleaming, radiant, glassy, luminous, resplendent, crystalline, pure
FORMAL diaphanous, effulgent, limpid, pellucid
F3 1 unclear, unintelligible **2** confused, irrational **3** dark, murky

lucidity n
1 CLARITY, comprehensibility, plainness, intelligibility
2 CLEAR-HEADEDNESS, sanity, rationality, reasonableness, soundness, *compos mentis*
F3 1 unintelligibility **2** irrationality

lucidly adv
clearly, comprehensibly, plainly, explicitly, intelligibly, obviously, evidently
F3 unclearly, unintelligibly

luck n
1 CHANCE, fortune, accident, providence, fate, the stars, hazard, destiny, predestination
FORMAL fortuity
COLLOQ. fluke
2 GOOD FORTUNE, good luck, success, prosperity, godsend
FORMAL serendipity
COLLOQ. break
F3 1 design, manipulation **2** misfortune, bad luck
■ **in luck**
fortunate, happy, favoured, successful, advantaged, timely, opportune
FORMAL auspicious
COLLOQ. jammy
■ **out of luck**
unlucky, unfortunate, luckless, hapless, unsuccessful, disadvantaged
FORMAL inauspicious
COLLOQ. down on your luck

luckily adv
as luck would have it, by good luck, by chance, by accident, fortunately, happily, providentially
FORMAL fortuitously, propitiously
F3 unfortunately

luckless adj
unlucky, unfortunate, hopeless, ill-fated, ill-starred, jinxed, cursed, doomed, hapless, star-crossed, miserable, unhappy, unsuccessful, disastrous, calamitous, catastrophic
FORMAL unpropitious
F3 lucky, fortunate

lucky adj
fortunate, in luck, promising, favoured, happy, charmed, successful, prosperous, timely, opportune, expedient, providential, just as well; *Scot* canny, chancy
FORMAL auspicious, fortuitous, propitious
COLLOQ. jammy; *Aust & NZ* tinny
SLANG spawny
F3 unlucky
See Synonym nuances panel at **fortunate**.

lucrative adj
profitable, well-paid, remunerative, profit-making, moneymaking, high-paying, gainful, productive, financially rewarding, advantageous, worthwhile
F3 unprofitable

lucratively adv
profitably, gainfully, remuneratively, productively, advantageously
F3 unprofitably

lucre n
money, cash, riches, wealth, profit(s), gain(s), proceeds, winnings, pay, income, remuneration, spoils, mammon
SLANG dough, dosh, bread, lolly, spondulicks, brass, readies, ready, greenies

ludicrous adj
absurd, ridiculous, preposterous, nonsensical, laughable, farcical, silly, comical, comic, humorous, amusing, hilarious, funny, droll, burlesque, grotesque, outlandish, zany, odd, eccentric
FORMAL risible
COLLOQ. crazy
F3 serious

ludicrously adv
absurdly, ridiculously, laughably, hilariously, outlandishly, grotesquely, nonsensically, preposterously

lug v
pull, drag, haul, carry, bear, lift, tow, tote, heave, tug, hump

luggage n
baggage, belongings, paraphernalia, traps
FORMAL impedimenta
COLLOQ. gear, things, stuff, clobber

Types of luggage include:

attaché case	Gladstone bag	portfolio
backpack	grip	portmanteau
bag	hamper	rucksack
basket	hand-luggage	satchel
box	haversack	suitcase
briefcase	holdall	travel bag
case	kitbag	trunk
chest	knapsack	valise
flight bag	overnight bag	vanity-case

See also **bag**.

---

lugubrious adj
melancholy, morose, gloomy, glum, sad, woeful, woebegone, sorrowful, sombre, serious, dismal, doleful, dreary, mournful, funereal, sepulchral
F3 cheerful, jovial, merry

lukewarm adj
1 *lukewarm water*
tepid, slightly warm, warmish, coolish
2 HALF-HEARTED, cool, apathetic, tepid, indifferent, unenthusiastic, uninterested, unresponsive, unconcerned, impassive, Laodicean

lull n, v
♦ n
calm, calmness, peace, quiet, tranquillity, stillness, let-up, pause, hush, silence
F3 agitation
♦ v
soothe, subdue, calm, silence, hush, pacify, quieten down, quiet, quell, still, allay, ease, compose
FORMAL assuage, abate
F3 agitate

lullaby n
cradle song, *berceuse*, hushaby
OLD dialect & Scot baloo

lumber[1] n, v
♦ n
1 *store away lumber*
clutter, jumble, rubbish, refuse, bits and pieces, odds and ends, junk, trash

2 TIMBER, wood
* *v*
burden, encumber, saddle, land, load, hamper, impose, charge

lumber² *v*
lumber round the house
clump, shamble, plod, shuffle, stump, stamp, trundle, trudge, stumble

lumbering *adj*
awkward, clumsy, heavy-footed, ungainly, unwieldy, heavy, blundering, bumbling, lumpish, ponderous, hulking, massive, elephantine, bovine
COLLOQ. like a bull in a china shop
E3 agile, nimble

luminary *n*
expert, authority, leader, leading light, celebrity, VIP, dignitary, worthy, notable, personage, star, superstar
COLLOQ. big name, bigwig, celeb

luminescent *adj*
glowing, bright, luminous, fluorescent, radiant, shining
FORMAL effulgent, luciferous, phosphorescent

luminosity *n*
glow, brightness, light, illumination, brilliance, radiance, lustre, fluorescence

luminous *adj*
glowing, illuminated, lit, lighted, radiant, shining, dazzling, fluorescent, brilliant, lustrous, bright
FORMAL luminescent, effulgent

lump¹ *n, v*
* *n*
1 MASS, block, cluster, clump, clod, ball, dab, wad, cluster, bunch, piece, chunk, chuck, chump, cake, hunk, nugget, wedge, slug, pat, knot, node, nut, lob, gnarl, gob, knub, nub, slub; *dialect* dad, daud, hunch, lunch; *Scot* claut, nirl, slump, plouk; *N Am* rock
TECHNICAL bolus, concretion, pustule
OLD wad, loaf
COLLOQ. dollop, wodge
2 SWELLING, growth, bulge, bump, protuberance, bruise, protrusion, tumour, carbuncle, burr
TECHNICAL bunion, tuber
OLD bunch
FORMAL tumescence
* *v*
collect, mass, gather, put together, cluster, combine, pool, blend, fuse, coalesce, group, crowd, consolidate, unite, mix together, conglomerate; *Scot* slump

lump² *v*
like it or lump it
put up with, bear (with), endure, tolerate, stand, suffer, swallow, take, brook; *Scot* thole
COLLOQ. stomach

lumpish *adj*
awkward, heavy, clumsy, ungainly, hulking, gawky, bungling, lumbering, lethargic, elephantine, stupid, dull-witted, oafish, boorish, doltish, obtuse, stolid

lumpy *adj*
clotted, congealed, coagulated, curdled, bunched, bumpy, cloggy, knobbly, grainy, granular
FORMAL nodous, nodose
E3 even, smooth

lunacy *n*
madness, insanity, aberration, derangement, dementia, dementedness, mania, idiocy, imbecility, folly, foolishness, absurdity, nonsense, stupidity, preposterousness, outrageousness, irresponsibility, silliness, inanity, ridiculousness, illogicality, irrationality, senselessness
COLLOQ. craziness
E3 sanity

lunatic *n, adj*
* *n*
psychotic, psychopath, madman, madwoman, insane person, imbecile, maniac, neurotic
COLLOQ. nutcase, nutter, fruitcake, headcase, oddball
SLANG loony, psycho
* *adj*
mad, insane, deranged, unbalanced, disturbed, demented, irrational, foolish, idiotic, absurd, stupid, illogical, nonsensical, senseless, silly, inane, moonstruck
COLLOQ. crazy, bonkers, loopy, nuts, nutty, daft, barmy, potty, hare-brained, crackpot, round the bend/twist
SLANG loony, off your rocker
E3 sane

lunch *n*
midday meal, luncheon, light lunch, ploughman's lunch, packed lunch, snack, brunch, Sunday lunch, dinner

lunge *v, n*
* *v*
thrust, jab, stab, pounce, plunge, pitch into, charge, dart, dash, dive, poke, strike (at), fall upon, grab (at), hit (at), leap, spring, bound
* *n*
thrust, stab, pounce, charge, jab, poke, pass, cut, spring, plunge, leap, bound

lurch *v*
roll, rock, pitch, sway, swerve, veer, stagger, totter, stumble, reel, list
■ **leave in the lurch**
abandon, desert, disappoint, let down, fail, leave stranded, leave high and dry

lure *v, n*
* *v*
tempt, entice, draw, attract, allure, induce, decoy, seduce, ensnare, beguile, lead on, take a rise out of; *N Am* tole
TECHNICAL stool
OLD trepan
FORMAL inveigle
* *n*
temptation, enticement, attraction, draw, allurement, bait, decoy, inducement, seduction, train, honey-trap
TECHNICAL jig, spoonbait, spoonhook, trolling-bait, trolling-spoon, trout-spoon, Devon minnow
OLD stale, trepan
COLLOQ. carrot

lurid *adj*
1 SENSATIONAL, shocking, startling, explicit, graphic, exaggerated, melodramatic, macabre, gruesome, gory, ghastly, grisly, horrific, revolting
2 BRIGHTLY COLOURED, garish, glaring, loud, showy, vivid, brilliant, dazzling, intense
E3 **1** restrained, tame **2** pale, subdued

luridly *adv*
1 SHOCKINGLY, explicitly, graphically, melodramatically, gruesomely, revoltingly
2 GARISHLY, brilliantly, vividly, intensely

lurk *v*
skulk, prowl, slink, lie in wait, crouch, lie low, hide, conceal yourself, snoop, sneak

luscious *adj*
1 *luscious food*
delicious, juicy, succulent, appetizing, mouthwatering, sweet, tasty, savoury
FORMAL delectable
COLLOQ. scrumptious, yummy, mor(e)ish
2 *a luscious blonde*
attractive, beautiful, voluptuous, desirable, gorgeous, sensuous, stunning, ravishing, sexy
COLLOQ. smashing

lush *adj, n*
- *adj*
1 FLOURISHING, luxuriant, abundant, prolific, teeming, dense, overgrown, green, profuse
FORMAL verdant
2 SUMPTUOUS, opulent, ornate, plush, rich, luxurious, grand, lavish, extravagant, palatial
COLLOQ. plush, posh, glitzy, classy, swanky, ritzy
- *n*
drunk, drunkard, alcoholic, inebriate, drinker, hard drinker, heavy drinker, dipsomaniac, wine-bibber, bloater, fuddler, habitual; *N Am* souse
COLLOQ. tippler
SLANG boozer, wino, alkie, dipso, soak, piss artist, pisshead, toper, sot, tosspot, sponge; *Aust & NZ* shicker

lust *n, v*
- *n*
1 SENSUALITY, sexual desire, libido, sexual drive, lechery, licentiousness, lewdness, lasciviousness
FORMAL concupiscence, prurience
COLLOQ. randiness, raunchiness, horniness, the hots
2 CRAVING, desire, appetite, longing, passion, will, greed, greediness, covetousness, hunger, yearning, avidity
FORMAL cupidity
■ **lust after**
desire, crave, yearn for, want, need, hunger for, thirst for, covet, long for, lecher, slaver

lustful *adj*
sensual, passionate, licentious, lewd, lascivious, lecherous, carnal, unchaste, wanton, craving, hankering, salacious
OLD lickerish; (*Shakesp*) rank, ruttish
FORMAL concupiscent, libidinous, prurient, cupidinous
COLLOQ. horny, randy, raunchy

lustily *adv*
loudly, hard, heartily, robustly, strongly, vigorously, forcefully, powerfully, stoutly, with all your might
FORMAL with might and main
F∃ weakly, feebly

lustiness *n*
power, robustness, sturdiness, vigour, health, healthiness, strength, energy, haleness, hardiness, toughness, stoutness, virility

lustre *n*
1 SHINE, gloss, sheen, gleam, glow, brilliance, brightness, radiance, sparkle, shimmer, resplendence, glare, burnish, glitter, glint; *dialect* gaum
FORMAL refulgence, lambency
2 GLORY, honour, prestige, renown, distinction, fame, illustriousness, merit, credit

lustrous *adj*
bright, shiny, shining, brilliant, glossy, glowing, dazzling, gleaming, glistening, glittering, shimmering, sparkling, twinkling, burnished, luminous, radiant
FORMAL lambent
F∃ dull, lacklustre, matt

lusty *adj*
robust, strong, sturdy, vigorous, tough, hale, hearty, hale and hearty, healthy, fit, blooming, energetic, lively, strapping, rugged, forceful, powerful, virile
COLLOQ. beefy, gutsy
F∃ weak, feeble

luxuriance *n*
abundance, copiousness, lushness, denseness, rankness, fertility, lavishness, profusion, sumptuousness, richness, excess, exuberance
FORMAL fecundity

luxuriant *adj*
1 ABUNDANT, prolific, lush, superabundant, sumptuous, profuse, plentiful, plenteous, overflowing, ample, lavish,

teeming, thriving, rich, riotous, rank, copious, dense, productive, fertile
FORMAL fecund
2 ELABORATE, extravagant, fancy, ornate, flamboyant, flowery, opulent, excessive, rococo, baroque
FORMAL florid
F∃ barren, infertile

! **luxuriant** or **luxurious**?
Luxuriant means 'abundant, prolific, growing vigorously': *the luxuriant growth of the jungle plants*. *Luxurious* means 'relating to luxury and riches, expensive': *a luxurious house*.

luxuriate *v*
delight, enjoy, revel, relish, savour, thrive, bask, abound, wallow, relax in, indulge, prosper, flourish, grow, bloom, burgeon
COLLOQ. live in the lap of luxury, live off the fat of the land, live the life of Riley, live in clover, live on easy street, have a ball

luxurious *adj*
sumptuous, opulent, lavish, de luxe, magnificent, splendid, rich, expensive, costly, affluent, self-indulgent, pampered, comfortable, grand, well-appointed
COLLOQ. plush, posh, cushy, glitzy, swanky, ritzy
F∃ austere, spartan

luxuriously *adv*
sumptuously, lavishly, opulently, magnificently, affluently, comfortably
COLLOQ. poshly, plushly, swankily, glitzily

luxury *n*
1 SUMPTUOUSNESS, opulence, hedonism, splendour, affluence, richness, expensiveness, costliness, magnificence, grandness, grandeur, pleasure, indulgence, self-indulgence, gratification, comfort, milk and honey, *luxe, grand luxe*
COLLOQ. lap of luxury
2 *life's little luxuries*
extravagance, indulgence, satisfaction, extra, treat
OLD delicate
COLLOQ. pie
F∃ 1 austerity 2 essential

lying *adj, n*
- *adj*
deceitful, dishonest, false, untruthful, double-dealing
FORMAL mendacious, dissembling, dissimulating
COLLOQ. two-faced, crooked
F∃ honest, truthful
- *n*
dishonesty, untruthfulness, deceit, falsity, perjury, falsification, fabrication, invention, double-dealing
FORMAL duplicity
COLLOQ. fibbing, white lies, crookedness
F∃ honesty, truthfulness

lynch *v*
hang, hang by the neck, execute, put to death, kill
COLLOQ. string up

lyric *adj*
emotional, passionate, personal, subjective, poetic, musical, melodic

lyrical *adj*
1 POETIC, musical, romantic
2 ENTHUSIASTIC, emotional, rapturous, rhapsodic, ecstatic, effusive, passionate, carried away, expressive, impassioned, inspired

lyrically *adv*
1 POETICALLY, romantically, musically
2 ENTHUSIASTICALLY, emotionally, rapturously, passionately, expressively, effusively, ecstatically

lyrics *n*
text, words, book, libretto

M

macabre *adj*
gruesome, chilling, grisly, grim, horrible, gory, horrific, frightful, frightening, terrifying, shocking, dreadful, morbid, ghostly, eerie, hideous, ghastly, sick
COLLOQ. Gothic

mace *n*
rod, stick, staff, club, cudgel

macerate *v*
soak, steep, marinade, soften, liquefy, mash, blend, pulp, squash

Machiavellian *adj*
devious, crafty, designing, scheming, shrewd, sly, cunning, wily, artful, astute, calculating, deceitful, double-dealing, guileful, underhand, opportunist, foxy, intriguing, unscrupulous
FORMAL perfidious

machination *n*
scheme, intrigue, plot, design, manoeuvre, conspiracy, tactic, wile, ruse, ploy, stratagem, trick, device, dodge, cabal
FORMAL artifice
COLLOQ. shenanigans

machine *n*
1 INSTRUMENT, device, contrivance, tool, contraption, mechanism, engine, motor, apparatus, appliance, gadget, hardware
2 AGENCY, organization, structure, instrument, tool, organ, vehicle, influence, catalyst, system, workings
3 AUTOMATON, robot, mechanical person, tool, mechanism, zombie, android

machine-gun
See panels at **gun**; **weapon**.

machinery *n*
1 INSTRUMENTS, mechanism, tools, apparatus, equipment, tackle, gear, gadgetry
2 ORGANIZATION, channel(s), structure, system, procedure, workings, agency

---

Types of heavy machinery include:

all-terrain fork lift	excavator	road roller
bulldozer	fertilizer spreader	road-sweeping
caterpillar tractor	fire appliance	lorry
combine	fork-lift truck	Rotovator®
harvester	gantry crane	silage harvester
concrete mixer	grader	snowplough
concrete pump	grapple	straw baler
crane	gritter	threshing
crawler crane	hydraulic bale	machine
crawler tractor	loader	tower crane
digger	hydraulic shovel	tracklayer
dragline	JCB®	tractor
excavator	muck spreader	tractor-scraper
dredger	pick-up loader	truck crane
dumper	pile-driver	wheel loader
dump truck	platform hoist	
dustcart	riding mower	

---

machinist *n*
worker, operator, operative, factory hand, mechanic

machismo *n*
masculinity, maleness, manliness, virility, toughness, strength

macrocosm *n*
universe, solar system, cosmos, creation, world, planet, society, civilization, community, culture, humanity, totality, (single) entity, system, structure
F3 microcosm

mad *adj*
1 INSANE, lunatic, unbalanced, psychotic, disturbed, deranged, maniacal, out of your mind, out of your senses, of unsound mind, unhinged, crazed, unstable, *non compos mentis*, frenzied, wild, berserk, manic, maniac, distracted, distraught, fey, frenetic, frantic, stone-crazy, queer; *Scot* gyte, red-mad
OLD frantic-mad, lymphatic, bestraught
COLLOQ. crazy, demented, nuts, nutty, nutty as a fruitcake, wacky, mad as a hatter, barmy, bonkers, batty, cracked, crackers, dippy, daffy, dotty, loopy, potty, off your nut, off your head, wrong in the head, out of your head, off the wall, out to lunch, round the bend, round the twist, bats, having bats in the belfry, cuckoo, off the rails, screwy, up the wall, raving, not all there; *N Am* buggy, flaky, fruity; *Aust & NZ* dingbats
SLANG loony, mental, bananas, barking, wacko, doolally, off your rocker, off your chump, off your trolley, out of your tree, needing your head examined, having lost your marbles, having a screw loose, having a tile loose, having several cards short of a full deck, with one sandwich short of a picnic, meshuga; *N Am* gonzo, loco, wiggy
2 ANGRY, furious, enraged, raging, infuriated, incensed, irate, blazing, fuming, livid
COLLOQ. aggravated, cross, ratty, uptight, hopping mad, raving mad, seeing red, in a lather, disgruntled, up in arms, hot under the collar, stroppy, in a strop, flipped, choleric, choked, fit to be tied, on the warpath, in a paddy; *N Am* ticked off; *Aust* spewy, ropable; *Aust & NZ* crooked
SLANG pissed off, hairless, ape, apeshit; *N Am* burned up
3 IRRATIONAL, illogical, unreasonable, absurd, ludicrous, preposterous, foolish, foolhardy, idiotic, insane, stupid, silly, nonsensical, wild
COLLOQ. crazy, daft, barmy, potty, hare-brained, crackbrained, crackpot
4 FANATICAL, enthusiastic, infatuated, ardent, zealous, devoted, fond, keen, avid, passionate
COLLOQ. crazy, daft, nuts, potty, wild
5 UNCONTROLLED, wild, frantic, furious, reckless, violent, energetic, intense, rapid, hasty, hurried, unrestrained, frenzied, abandoned, excited
F3 1 sane **2** calm **3** sensible **4** apathetic **5** controlled
■ **like mad**
energetically, quickly, furiously, wildly, frantically, hurriedly, enthusiastically, fanatically, zealously, avidly

---

Synonym nuances
sense 1
You can use **insane** as a more clinical term for someone or something displaying complete mental unsoundness, while **lunatic** may be used more generally and more

offensively of hugely abnormal or irrational behaviour, and **psychotic** would be reserved for a serious mental disorder with untypical thought patterns. **Unbalanced**, however, has far less strong implications of a lack of mental equilibrium, and **unstable** is used of a variable psychological state.

Deranged again suggests more severe mental disorder, but **distracted**, on the other hand, can suggest a more temporary confusion or, more usually, lack of concentration, while **distraught** is more suggestive of being frantic with grief or worry. The term **demented** can be used of mental deterioration due to illness or age, but is often used to suggest distraction through worry, unlike **unhinged** and **crazed** which are more suggestive of wildly unpredictable behaviour, and **frenzied**, **manic**, **maniac** and **maniacal**, which are suggestive of wild and unrestrained behaviour: *a frenzied attack*; *police described the killing as maniacal.* **Frenetic** suggests hurried and chaotic activity: *the frenetic bustle of the metropolis.*

You can use **fey** if you wish to convey a slight madness or eccentricity: *she was a strange, fey woman who had become odder since her husband's death,* while **queer** simply suggests strangeness.

madcap *adj, n*
◆ *adj*
foolhardy, rash, reckless, impulsive, silly, thoughtless, wild, lively, flighty, heedless, ill-advised, imprudent, hotheaded, crazy
COLLOQ. birdbrained, hare-brained
◆ *n*
adventurer, tearaway, hothead, daredevil, firebrand, fury, desperado, eccentric
COLLOQ. crackpot

madden *v*
anger, enrage, infuriate, incense, annoy, upset, agitate, exasperate, provoke, annoy, irritate, inflame, irk, vex, distract
OLD bemad
COLLOQ. aggravate, bug, hassle, rub up the wrong way, get someone's blood up, make your blood boil, get on your nerves, get up your nose, get under your skin, get someone's goat, get on your wick, drive crazy/nuts, drive up the wall, drive round the bend/twist, get your back up, get your dander up
⊟ calm, pacify

maddening *adj*
infuriating, exasperating, annoying, troublesome, irritating, vexatious, galling, upsetting, disturbing
COLLOQ. aggravating

made-up *adj*
1 INVENTED, make-believe, unreal, untrue, false, fictional, imaginary, specious, fabricated, fairytale, mythical
COLLOQ. trumped-up
2 WEARING MAKE-UP, painted, powdered, done up
⊟ 1 real, factual, true

madhouse *n*
1 BEDLAM, chaos, disarray, disorder, uproar, turmoil, mayhem, pandemonium, Babel
2 MENTAL HOSPITAL, lunatic asylum, asylum, mental institution, psychiatric hospital
COLLOQ. funny farm, loony bin, nuthouse

madly *adv*
1 *he rolled his eyes madly*
insanely, dementedly, hysterically, frenziedly, deliriously, wildly, distractedly
COLLOQ. crazily
2 *madly cleaning up*
wildly, excitedly, frantically, furiously, recklessly, violently,

energetically, intensely, rapidly, hastily, fast, hurriedly
3 *madly in love*
intensely, wildly, fervently, devotedly, completely
4 EXTREMELY, very, wildly, exceedingly, exceptionally, utterly, unreasonably

madman, madwoman *n*
lunatic, psychotic, psychopath, maniac, imbecile, furioso
OLD bedlam, frenetic, gelt, Tom o' Bedlam
COLLOQ. nutter, nut, crackpot, crank, headcase, nutcase, fruitcake, screwball, oddball, kook; *N Am* hook
SLANG loony, psycho, basket case; *N Am* cupcake

madness *n*
1 INSANITY, insaneness, lunacy, dementia, psychosis, mental instability, mania, derangement, distraction, delusion, frenzy, deliration, *folie*, furiosity
COLLOQ. craziness, meshugaas
2 FURY, rage, raving, frenzy, hysteria, anger, agitation, exasperation, wrath, ire
3 FOLLY, craziness, irrationality, unreasonableness, insanity, stupidity, silliness, inanity, absurdity, nonsense, foolishness, foolhardiness, preposterousness, wildness
COLLOQ. daftness
4 KEENNESS, enthusiasm, ardour, craze, abandon, zeal, wildness, unrestraint, uproar, riot, passion, excitement, fanaticism, infatuation, intoxication
⊟ 1 sanity 2 calmness 3 reasonableness

maelstrom *n*
confusion, disorder, turmoil, mess, pandemonium, tumult, uproar, bedlam, chaos, turbulence, vortex, whirlpool, Charybdis

maestro *n*
expert, master, genius, prodigy, virtuoso, director, conductor
COLLOQ. wizard, ace

magazine *n*
1 JOURNAL, periodical, publication, paper, weekly, monthly, quarterly, supplement, colour supplement, fanzine, e-zine
2 ARSENAL, storehouse, ammunition dump, depot, ordnance

magic *n, adj*
◆ *n*
1 SORCERY, enchantment, supernatural, occult, occultism, black magic, black art, witchcraft, wizardry, wicca, wonder-working, voodoo, hoodoo, magical powers, spell, curse, incantation
FORMAL necromancy, thaumaturgy
2 CONJURING, illusion, sleight of hand, deception, trickery, legerdemain
FORMAL prestidigitation
3 CHARM, fascination, glamour, enticement, allure, allurement, enchantment, magnetism, pull, wonder, mystery
◆ *adj*
1 SUPERNATURAL, occult, mysterious, demonic, spellful
OLD hermetic
COLLOQ. metaphysical
2 CHARMING, enchanting, bewitching, fascinating, spellbinding, entrancing, captivating, irresistible, magnetic, romantic, stardust
3 WONDERFUL, excellent, great, tremendous, marvellous
COLLOQ. terrific, smashing, brill, ace
SLANG mega, cool, wicked

magical *adj*
1 MAGIC, mysterious, supernatural, occult, demonic
2 WONDERFUL, marvellous, charming, enchanting, fascinating, spellbinding, captivating

magician *n*
1 SORCERER, miracle-worker, enchanter, wizard, witch, warlock, spellbinder, spellworker, wonder-worker, magnus, witch doctor; *dialect* wise man; *N Am* powwow

OLD archimage
FORMAL necromancer, thaumaturge
2 CONJURER, illusionist, juggler
3 GENIUS, maestro, expert, master, virtuoso
COLLOQ. wizard, ace

magisterial *adj*
authoritative, commanding, masterful, assertive, authoritarian, domineering, imperious, high-handed, dictatorial, lordly, overbearing, arrogant, despotic
FORMAL peremptory
COLLOQ. bossy

magistrate *n*
judge, justice, justice of the peace, JP, stipendiary, bailiff, tribune
COLLOQ. beak
Related adjective: magisterial

magnanimity *n*
generosity, liberality, open-handedness, benevolence, selflessness, unselfishness, charity, charitableness, big-heartedness, bountifulness, kindness, high-mindedness, nobility, philanthropy, altruism, mercy, forgiveness, largesse
FORMAL beneficence, munificence
₣ meanness, vindictiveness

magnanimous *adj*
generous, liberal, open-handed, benevolent, selfless, charitable, big-hearted, bountiful, kind, kindly, noble, philanthropic, altruistic, unselfish, ungrudging, merciful, forgiving
FORMAL beneficent, munificent
COLLOQ. big
₣ mean

magnate *n*
tycoon, captain of industry, industrialist, mogul, entrepreneur, financier, plutocrat, baron, executive, personage, notable, leader
COLLOQ. fat cat, moneybags, bigwig, big shot, big noise, big timer, big cheese

magnet *n*
draw, bait, lure, allurement, charm, enticement, appeal, attraction, centre of attraction, focus, focal point, lodestone
TECHNICAL solenoid
₣ repellent

magnetic *adj*
attractive, alluring, fascinating, appealing, enthralling, charming, engaging, mesmerizing, hypnotic, seductive, tempting, tantalizing, irresistible, entrancing, bewitching, enchanting, captivating, gripping, absorbing, charismatic
₣ repellent, repulsive

magnetism *n*
attraction, allure, fascination, enchantment, captivation, charm, temptation, seductiveness, lure, appeal, drawing power, draw, pull, hypnotism, mesmerism, charisma, grip, magic, power, spell

magnification *n*
1 ENLARGEMENT, amplification, increase, expansion, intensification, enhancement, inflation, heightening, deepening, dilation, build-up, boost, extolment, lionization
FORMAL aggrandizement, augmentation
2 EXAGGERATION, dramatization, overemphasis, overstatement, overdoing, embellishment, embroidery, hyperbole
₣ **1** diminution, reduction

magnificence *n*
splendour, grandeur, impressiveness, glory, gorgeousness, brilliance, excellence, majesty, sumptuousness, nobility, luxuriousness, luxury, lavishness, pomp, stateliness

FORMAL resplendence, opulence, sublimity
₣ modesty, plainness, simplicity

magnificent *adj*
splendid, grand, imposing, grandiose, impressive, striking, elegant, glorious, gorgeous, brilliant, dazzling, excellent, marvellous, wonderful, majestic, superb, sumptuous, noble, exalted, elegant, fine, lavish, luxurious, rich, royal, stately
FORMAL resplendent, opulent, august, sublime
₣ modest, humble, poor

magnify *v*
1 ENLARGE, amplify, increase, expand, intensify, enhance, boost, extend, greaten, heighten, broaden, deepen, dilate, build up
2 EXAGGERATE, dramatize, overemphasize, overplay, overstate, overdo, embellish, embroider
COLLOQ. blow up, blow up out of all proportion, make a mountain out of a molehill
₣ **1** reduce, diminish **2** belittle, play down

magniloquence *n*
pomposity, pretentiousness, bombast, loftiness, rhetoric, euphuism, turgidity, fustian
FORMAL grandiloquence, orotundity
₣ simplicity, straightforwardness

magniloquent *adj*
pompous, high-sounding, lofty, overblown, elevated, exalted, bombastic, fustian, high-flown, pretentious, rhetorical, declamatory, euphuistic, sonorous, turgid, stilted
FORMAL grandiloquent, orotund
₣ simple, straightforward

magnitude *n*
1 SIZE, extent, measure, amount, expanse, dimensions, mass, proportions, quantity, weight, volume, capacity, bulk, largeness, greatness, space, strength, amplitude
2 IMPORTANCE, consequence, significance, weight, greatness, eminence, fame, distinction, moment, note, intensity
FORMAL import, moment

magnum opus *n*
masterpiece, masterwork, *chef d'oeuvre*, *pièce de résistance*

maid *n*
servant, domestic, waitress, kitchenmaid, chambermaid, housemaid, girl, au pair, maidservant, serving-maid, lady's maid, dresser, handmaiden, soubrette, abigail, maid-of-all-work, maiden, suivante, daily, charlady, charwoman
OLD bonnibell, bowerwoman, may, pucelle
COLLOQ. skivvy, slavey, Mrs Mop

maiden *n, adj*
♦ *n*
girl, young girl, young lady, young woman, virgin, lass, lassie, miss, nymph; *N Am* bachelorette
OLD damsel, popsy
♦ *adj*
1 *a maiden voyage*
first, inaugural, new, introductory, initial, initiatory
2 CHASTE, decent, demure, gentle, girlish, female, modest, proper, pure, celibate, reserved, undefiled, unsullied, unbroached, vestal, virgin, unmarried, unwed, virginal, virtuous
OLD seemly
FORMAL decorous
₣ **2** defiled, deflowered, unchaste

maidenhood *n*
purity, chastity, chasteness, virtue, honour
OLD maidenhead

maidenly *adj*
becoming, chaste, decent, demure, gentle, girlish, female,

modest, proper, pure, reserved, undefiled, immaculate, unsullied, unbroached, vestal, virgin, unmarried, unwed, virginal, virtuous
OLD seemly
FORMAL decorous
🖃 immodest

maidservant n
maid, servant, domestic, waitress, kitchenmaid, chambermaid, housemaid, girl, au pair, serving-maid, lady's maid, dresser, handmaiden, soubrette, abigail, maid-of-all-work, maiden, suivante, daily, charlady, charwoman, Mrs Mopp
OLD bonnibell, bowerwoman, may, pucelle
COLLOQ. skivvy, slavey

mail¹ n, v
◆ n
1 deliver the mail
post, general post, letters, correspondence, communications, packages, parcels, packets, delivery, registered mail, recorded mail, special delivery, direct mail, airmail, all-up service, surface mail, international mail, electronic mail, e-mail, first-class mail, second-class mail, fan mail, hate mail
COLLOQ. junk mail, snail mail, junk fax
2 POSTAL SERVICE, postal system, post, Post Office
◆ v
post, send, dispatch, forward
Related adjective: postal

mail² n
chain mail
armour, chain mail, chain armour, iron-cladding, panoply, protective covering
OLD cataphract, habergeon

maim v
mutilate, disfigure, wound, incapacitate, injure, disable, hurt, impair, mar, cripple, lame, put out of action, truncate; *dialect* main
OLD scotch

main adj, n
◆ adj
principal, chief, leading, first, foremost, major, key, predominant, dominant, pre-eminent, primary, most important, prime, premier, supreme, paramount, central, head, cardinal, outstanding, essential, critical, crucial, necessary, vital, fundamental, pivotal
See Synonym nuances panel at **dominant**.
🖃 minor, unimportant, insignificant
◆ n
pipe, duct, conduit, channel, cable, line
▪ **in the main**
chiefly, mostly, on the whole, for the most part, generally, in general, especially, as a rule, by and large, commonly, usually, largely

mainly adv
primarily, principally, chiefly, first and foremost, in the main, mostly, on the whole, for the most part, generally, in general, especially, as a rule, by and large, commonly, usually, above all, largely, overall, predominantly

mainspring n
motive, motivation, cause, reason, driving force, impulse, incentive, inspiration, origin, prime mover, generator, source, fountainhead, wellspring

mainstay n
support, buttress, bulwark, linchpin, prop, pillar, anchor, backbone, cornerstone, foundation, basis, base, key player, right-hand man/woman, tower of strength

mainstream adj
normal, average, central, general, typical, regular, standard, conventional, established, orthodox,

received, accepted, mainline
🖃 heterodox, peripheral, marginal

maintain v
1 CARRY ON, continue, keep (up), keep going, sustain, preserve, perpetuate, conserve, retain
2 CARE FOR, conserve, look after, keep (up), take care of, preserve, keep in good condition/repair
3 PROVIDE FOR, keep, support, finance, supply, feed, sustain, nourish, nurture
4 ASSERT, claim, profess, contend, declare, announce, affirm, hold, state, insist, believe, stand by, fight for, support, defend, uphold
FORMAL avow, aver, asseverate
🖃 2 neglect **4** deny

maintenance n
1 CONTINUATION, continuance, carrying-on, preservation, conservation, perpetuation
2 CARE, conservation, preservation, support, repairs, protection, upkeep, running
3 KEEP, subsistence, feeding, sustenance, nourishment, nurture, living, livelihood, financing, support, financial support, upkeep, allowance, alimony, traineeship
TECHNICAL altarage, appanage, title
OLD aliment
🖃 2 neglect

majestic adj
magnificent, grand, glorious, dignified, distinguished, noble, royal, queenly, kingly, princely, lordly, stately, splendid, imperial, marvellous, impressive, elevated, exalted, awesome, imposing, regal, superb, lofty, monumental, pompous
FORMAL resplendent, sublime, august
🖃 lowly, unimpressive, unimposing

majestically adv
magnificently, grandly, gloriously, splendidly, marvellously, impressively, superbly, pompously, nobly, royally, regally, imperially
TECHNICAL maestoso
FORMAL resplendently, sublimely

majesty n
grandeur, grandness, glory, dignity, magnificence, beauty, awesomeness, nobility, nobleness, royalty, regality, splendour, stateliness, pomp, exaltedness, impressiveness, loftiness
OLD royalty, majesticalness, majesticness
FORMAL resplendence, sublimity

major adj
greater, greatest, chief, main, larger, largest, bigger, higher, highest, best, leading, outstanding, notable, supreme, prime, paramount, uppermost, significant, crucial, important, serious, key, keynote, great, senior, older, superior, pre-eminent, vital, weighty
🖃 minor, unimportant, trivial

majority n
1 MASS, bulk, preponderance, (the) many, most, greater/larger part, greater/larger number, more than half, nearly all, plurality
COLLOQ. lion's share
2 ADULTHOOD, maturity, manhood, womanhood, legal age, coming of age, reaching full age, age of consent, years of discretion
🖃 1 minority

make v, n
◆ v
1 CREATE, manufacture, mass-produce, fabricate, construct, assemble, build, erect, produce, turn out, put together, put up, originate, compose, form, shape, fashion, mould, model
2 CAUSE, bring about, produce, accomplish, occasion, create, give rise to, engender, generate, render, perform

FORMAL effect

3 CARRY OUT, accomplish, achieve, do, perform, undertake, discharge

FORMAL effect, execute

COLLOQ. deliver (the goods), get down to, wrap up

4 COERCE, force, urge, oblige, constrain, compel, impel, prevail upon, pressure, pressurize, press, drive, require, dragoon

COLLOQ. bulldoze, strongarm, put the screws on

5 APPOINT, vote in, elect, select, designate, nominate, name, ordain, install, create, vote

6 COMPOSE, create, write, arrange, prepare, produce, devise, think up, form, formulate, frame, construct, draw up

7 EARN, gain, net, gross, obtain, acquire, get, bring in, secure, win, take home, clear

FORMAL realize

8 CONSTITUTE, compose, comprise, add up to, amount to, come to, total

9 SCORE, gain, chalk up

COLLOQ. notch up

10 PREPARE, get ready, put together, cook

COLLOQ. N Am fix

11 CALCULATE, work out, compute, reckon (up), add up (to), estimate

12 SERVE AS, have the qualifications for, become, act as, function as, play the role/part of, achieve

13 *make a decision*

reach, come to, arrive at, settle, determine

14 *make a mistake*

commit, carry out, be responsible for, be to blame for

FORMAL perpetrate

15 *make a speech*

give, communicate, convey, tell, declare, deliver, state, pronounce, set forth

FORMAL impart

E3 1 dismantle, demolish 7 spend, lose

♦ *n*

brand, sort, type, style, variety, manufacture, model, mark, kind, marque, form, structure

■ **make away with**

1 STEAL, run off with, walk off with, snatch, seize, carry off, kidnap

COLLOQ. pinch, lift, nick, nab, swipe

2 KILL, do away with, murder, slaughter, assassinate

COLLOQ. do in, knock off, bump off

■ **make believe**

pretend, play, play-act, imagine, dream, enact, fantasize, act

FORMAL feign

COLLOQ. make castles in the air

■ **make do**

cope, manage, survive, get along, get by, improvise, make out, muddle through

COLLOQ. scrape by, make the best of a bad job, keep your head above water

■ **make for**

1 HEAD FOR, aim for, go towards, move towards

2 PRODUCE, lead to, promote, contribute to, facilitate, favour, forward, further, be conducive to

■ **make it**

succeed, be successful, get on, come through, arrive, pull through, reach, survive, prosper

E3 fail

■ **make of**

assess, consider, regard, think of, evaluate, weigh up, judge, rate

■ **make off**

run off, run away, depart, bolt, leave, fly

COLLOQ. cut and run, beat a hasty retreat, clear off, make a getaway, take to your heels, skedaddle, scarper, beat it

■ **make off with**

run off with, carry off, steal, take, swipe, walk off with, pilfer, kidnap, abduct

FORMAL appropriate, purloin

COLLOQ. filch, knock off, nab, nick, pinch

■ **make out**

1 DISCERN, manage to see/hear, perceive, decipher, distinguish, recognize, see, detect, discover

FORMAL espy

2 UNDERSTAND, work out, grasp, comprehend, follow, fathom

3 DRAW UP, complete, fill in, write out

4 MAINTAIN, imply, claim, assert, affirm, declare, describe, demonstrate, prove, establish

FORMAL aver

5 MANAGE, get on, get along, get by, cope, progress, succeed

FORMAL fare

6 WRITE OUT, fill in/out, complete

7 MAKE LOVE, have sex with someone, sleep with someone, sleep together, go to bed with someone

SLANG have it off with someone, get your leg over, bang, bonk; (*taboo*) fuck, screw, shag

■ **make over**

transfer, sign over, convey, assign, bequeath, leave

■ **make up**

1 CREATE, invent, devise, fabricate, construct, originate, formulate, frame, dream up, compose, think up, concoct, hatch

2 COMPLETE, fill, supply, provide, meet, supplement, round off

3 COMPRISE, constitute, compose, form

4 BE RECONCILED, make peace, settle differences, become friends again, shake hands, repent

COLLOQ. bury the hatchet, forgive and forget, call it quits

5 PUT MAKE-UP ON, powder, rouge, perfume, paint

COLLOQ. put on your face, doll up, tart up

■ **make up for**

compensate for, make amends for, make recompense for, offset, redress

FORMAL atone for

■ **make up to**

curry favour with, toady to, court, fawn on, butter up, make overtures to

COLLOQ. chat up, suck up to; N Am cozy up (with)

■ **make up your mind**

decide, choose, determine, resolve, settle

E3 waver

■ **make way**

allow to pass, make room/space for, stand back for, not stand in the way of, clear the way, allow to succeed

make-believe *n, adj*

♦ *n*

pretence, imagination, fantasy, unreality, fabrication, play-acting, role-play, dream, dreaming, daydreaming, masquerade, charade

E3 reality

♦ *adj*

imaginary, imagined, made-up, imitated, pretended, fantasy, fantasized, dream, simulated, unreal, mock, sham

FORMAL feigned

COLLOQ. pretend

E3 real

maker *n*

creator, manufacturer, constructor, builder, producer, director, deviser, architect, author, fabricator, repairer

makeshift *adj*

temporary, improvised, rough and ready, thrown together, cobbled together, provisional, substitute, stopgap, stand-by, expedient, make-do

E3 permanent

make-up *n*
1 COSMETICS, paint, powder, greasepaint, maquillage
COLLOQ. paint, war paint
SLANG slap
See also panel at **cosmetics**.
2 CONSTITUTION, nature, composition, character, construction, form, format, formation, arrangement, organization, style, structure, assembly
FORMAL configuration
3 PERSONALITY, temperament, temper, nature, character, disposition, style

making *n*
1 PRODUCTION, producing, creation, creating, manufacture, assembly, building, composition, construction, fabrication, modelling, moulding, forging
2 POTENTIAL, qualities, potentiality, promise, capability, capacity, possibilities, beginnings, materials, ingredients
3 EARNINGS, income, profits, proceeds, revenue, returns, takings
F₃ 1 dismantling
■ **in the making**
budding, potential, promising, coming, developing, emergent, up and coming
FORMAL nascent, burgeoning, incipient

maladjusted *adj*
disturbed, unstable, confused, alienated, disordered, neurotic
FORMAL estranged
COLLOQ. dotty, round the bend, screwed-up
SLANG schizo, psycho, gaga
F₃ well-adjusted; *colloq.* together

maladministration *n*
inefficiency, incompetence, mismanagement, mishandling, misrule, blundering, bungling, misgovernment, misconduct, corruption, dishonesty, malpractice, stupidity
TECHNICAL malfeasance, misfeasance
FORMAL malversation

maladroit *adj*
clumsy, awkward, bungling, unskilful, unhandy, gauche, graceless, inelegant, inept, inexpert, tactless, insensitive, thoughtless, inconsiderate, undiplomatic, ill-timed
FORMAL untoward
COLLOQ. cack-handed, ham-fisted
F₃ skilful, adroit, tactful

maladroitness *n*
clumsiness, awkwardness, unskilfulness, ineptitude, inelegance, gracelessness, tactlessness, insensitivity, thoughtlessness
F₃ skilfulness

malady *n*
illness, disease, sickness, complaint, infirmity, ailment, disorder, breakdown
FORMAL affliction, malaise, indisposition
F₃ health

malaise *n*
uneasiness, unease, discontent, depression, discomfort, disquiet, restlessness, weariness, anxiety, unhappiness, anguish, doldrums, angst, illness, disease, sickness, weakness
FORMAL lassitude, melancholy, indisposition, enervation
F₃ happiness, wellbeing

malapropism *n*
wrong word, misuse, slip of the tongue, misapplication
FORMAL solecism, infelicity

malapropos *adj, adv*
♦ *adj*
inappropriate, unsuitable, untimely, ill-timed, inopportune, misapplied, inapt, uncalled-for, tactless

FORMAL inapposite, unseemly
F₃ appropriate, tactful
♦ *adv*
inappropriately, unsuitably, inaptly, unseasonably, tactlessly, inopportunely
FORMAL inappositely
F₃ appropriately, tactfully

malcontent *n, adj*
♦ *n*
grumbler, complainer, moaner, rebel, agitator, mischief-maker, troublemaker
COLLOQ. grouch, grouser, nit-picker, whinger
SLANG bellyacher
♦ *adj*
dissatisfied, unhappy, unsatisfied, discontented, disgruntled, ill-disposed, disaffected, morose, rebellious, fault-finding, resentful
FORMAL restive, dissentious
COLLOQ. fed up
SLANG cheesed off, bellyaching
F₃ contented

male *adj*
masculine, manly, virile, boyish, he-, manlike
COLLOQ. laddish
F₃ female

Synonym nuances
Male can be used to suggest anything living that is not female: *groin guards are mandatory for all male competitors*, whereas **manlike** suggests having the appearance of an adult human male: *I saw the shadow of a manlike creature*. **Manly**, however, may be used to refer favourably to the positive attributes associated with men: *his manly shoulders*, unlike **mannish**, which is more likely to be used, often of women, to suggest having properties normally attributed to a man: *a rather mannish woman doctor*. **Virile** has very positive implications of sexual potency: *an imposing specimen of virile manhood*.

---

malediction *n*
curse, cursing, denunciation, oath, anathema, anathematization, damnation, damning
FORMAL execration, imprecation, malison
F₃ blessing, praise

malefactor *n*
lawbreaker, criminal, offender, felon, convict, outlaw, delinquent, wrongdoer, evildoer, culprit, villain
TECHNICAL misfeasor
FORMAL miscreant, transgressor
COLLOQ. crook

malevolence *n*
malice, malignancy, malignity, maliciousness, spite, spitefulness, vindictiveness, vengefulness, ill-will, hostility, unfriendliness, hate, hatred, bitterness, venom, viciousness, fierceness, cruelty
FORMAL rancour
F₃ benevolence

malevolent *adj*
malicious, malign, spiteful, vindictive, vengeful, ill-natured, hostile, unfriendly, bitter, rancorous, resentful, vicious, fierce, cruel, venomous, pernicious, evil-minded
FORMAL baleful, maleficent
F₃ benevolent, kind

malevolently *adv*
maliciously, spitefully, vindicatively, vengefully, bitterly, resentfully, viciously, cruelly, fiercely, venomously
F₃ benevolently

malformation *n*
deformity, misshapenness, disfigurement, irregularity, distortion, warp

malformed *adj*
deformed, misshapen, irregular, disfigured, distorted, twisted, warped, crooked, bent
F3 perfect

malfunction *v, n*
♦ *v*
break down, go wrong, fail, stop working
COLLOQ. crash, go kaput, go phut, pack up
SLANG conk out
♦ *n*
fault, defect, failure, breakdown, flaw
COLLOQ. crash

malice *n*
maliciousness, enmity, hostility, animosity, ill-will, hatred, hate, bad blood, spite, vindictiveness, malevolence, venom, spleen, bitterness, resentment
OLD despite
FORMAL animus, rancour
COLLOQ. bone to pick, bloody-mindedness, bitchiness
F3 love

malicious *adj*
ill-natured, hostile, malign, malevolent, spiteful, venomous, snide, vicious, vengeful, evil, evil-minded, pernicious, bitter, rancorous, resentful
FORMAL baleful
F3 friendly, kind

maliciously *adv*
spitefully, malevolently, venomously, viciously, bitterly, resentfully, perniciously

malign *v, adj*
♦ *v*
defame, slander, libel, abuse, run down, harm, injure, insult, bait, envenom
OLD misintend
FORMAL disparage, calumniate, vilify, traduce
COLLOQ. smear, slur, badmouth, stab in the back, kick in the teeth, drag through the mud
F3 praise
♦ *adj*
harmful, malignant, malevolent, bad, evil, hurtful, injurious, destructive, hostile
F3 benign, kind

malignancy *n*
fatality, mortality, lethality, incurability, virulence, uncontrollability

malignant *adj*
1 EVIL, devilish, hostile, malicious, vicious, venomous, spiteful, destructive, harmful, hurtful, pernicious, injurious, viperous, malign, malevolent, rancorous, black, cankered, sullen, poisonous; *dialect* swart
FORMAL baleful
2 FATAL, deadly, lethal, incurable, dangerous, life-threatening, cancerous, uncontrollable, virulent
F3 1 kind **2** benign, innocent

malignity *n*
malice, maliciousness, harmfulness, malevolence, hate, hurtfulness, ill-will, hatred, bad blood, bitterness, deadliness, perniciousness, gall, destructiveness, hostility, wickedness, vengefulness, vindictiveness, spite, venom, viciousness, animosity
OLD taking
FORMAL animus, balefulness, rancour
F3 harmlessness, kindness

malinger *v*
pretend, pretend to be ill, slack, dodge, shirk
COLLOQ. loaf, skive, put it on, swing the lead
SLANG *N Am* gold-brick
F3 work

malingerer *n*
slacker, dodger, shirker
COLLOQ. loafer, skiver, lead-swinger
F3 worker

mall *n*
arcade, shopping centre, shopping complex, shopping precinct, precinct, galleria, plaza

malleability *n*
1 SUPPLENESS, flexibility, softness, plasticity, pliancy, pliability
FORMAL ductileness
2 IMPRESSIONABILITY, receptiveness, flexibility, susceptibility, pliancy, pliability, adaptability, manageability, compliance
FORMAL tractableness

malleable *adj*
1 SUPPLE, plastic, pliable, pliant, flexible, soft, yielding, workable
FORMAL ductile
2 IMPRESSIONABLE, manageable, receptive, flexible, susceptible, persuadable, pliant, pliable, adaptable, biddable, governable, compliant
FORMAL tractile, tractable
F3 1 rigid **2** *formal* intractable

malnourished *adj*
undernourished, underfed, starved, hungry, anorexic, anorectic

malnutrition *n*
starvation, undernourishment, underfeeding, hunger, unhealthy diet, anorexia (nervosa)
FORMAL inanition
F3 nourishment

malodorous *adj*
foul-smelling, evil-smelling, f(o)etid, nauseating, niffy, offensive, putrid, rank, reeking, smelly, stinking
FORMAL noisome, mephitic, miasmal, miasmatic, miasmatous, miasmic, miasmous
F3 sweet-smelling

malpractice *n*
misconduct, unethical behaviour, unprofessional conduct, mismanagement, negligence, carelessness, impropriety, wrongdoing, offence, abuse, misdeed
FORMAL dereliction of duty

maltreat *v*
mistreat, ill-treat, treat badly, mishandle, misuse, abuse, injure, harm, damage, hurt, bully, hound, victimize, torture, maul, rough-house
OLD assassinate
F3 care for

maltreatment *n*
mistreatment, ill-treatment, ill-usage, ill-use, abuse, misuse, injury, harm, damage, hurt, bullying, victimization, torture
F3 care

mammal
See panel on next page

mammoth *adj*
enormous, huge, vast, colossal, gigantic, giant, massive, immense, stupendous, monumental, mighty, prodigious, gargantuan, herculean, leviathan, Brobdingnagian
COLLOQ. whopping, jumbo, bumper, ginormous
F3 tiny, minute

man *n, v*
♦ *n*
1 MALE, gentleman
COLLOQ. guy, chap, bloke, boy, lad, fellow, geezer; *S Afr* ou
Related adjective: male
2 HUMAN BEING, person, individual, adult, human, mortal
3 HUMANITY, human race, human beings, humankind,

Mammals include:

aardvark	chimpanzee	gibbon	kangaroo	otter	sloth
African elephant	chipmunk	giraffe	koala	pig	squirrel
anteater	cow	goat	lemming	polar bear	tamarin
antelope	deer	gorilla	lemur	porcupine	tapir
armadillo	dog	grizzly bear	leopard	porpoise	tiger
baboon	dolphin	guinea pig	lion	rabbit	vole
Bactrian camel	duck-billed	hamster	manatee	raccoon	wallaby
badger	platypus	hare	marmoset	rat	walrus
bat	dugong	hedgehog	marmot	rhinoceros	weasel
bear	echidna	hippopotamus	marsupial mouse	sea cow	whale
beaver	elephant	horse	mole	sea lion	wolf
bushbaby	ferret	human being	mouse	seal	zebra
camel	fox	hyena	opossum	sheep	
cat	gerbil	Indian elephant	orang-utan	shrew	

See also **cat; cattle; dog; horse; marsupial; monkey; rodent**.

mankind, people, *Homo sapiens*, mortals
Related adjective: human
4 MANSERVANT, servant, worker, workman, labourer, employee, helper, hand, soldier, valet, houseman, houseboy, page, attendant, factotum, man-of-all-work, jack-of-all-trades, odd-jobman
5 PARTNER, husband, lover, boyfriend, fiancé, spouse, sweetheart
COLLOQ. fellow, bloke, guy, toy boy
♦ *v*
staff, crew, take charge of, be in charge of, work, operate, occupy
■ **to a man**
without exception, with no exceptions, unanimously, as one, with one voice, one and all, bar none

manacle *v*
handcuff, shackle, restrain, secure, tie, fetter, chain, put in chains, bind, curb, check, hamper, inhibit
E3 free, unshackle

manacles *n*
handcuffs, chains, fetters, cuffs, shackles, wristlets, irons, bonds
OLD gyves
COLLOQ. bracelets, darbies, mittens, nippers
OLD SLANG snitchers

manage *v*
1 ADMINISTER, direct, run, organize, command, govern, be in charge of, be responsible for, head (up), be head of, lead, guide, preside over, rule, superintend, supervise, control, oversee, conduct, negotiate, navigate
2 ACCOMPLISH, succeed, achieve, bring about, bring off, engineer
FORMAL effect
3 CONTROL, influence, deal with, master, handle, keep, operate, manipulate, work, guide, play, manoeuvre, use, wield
4 COPE, deal with, survive, get by, get along, get on, carry on, make do, shift
FORMAL fare
COLLOQ. make out
E3 1 mismanage **2** fail

manageable *adj*
1 *a manageable amount of work*
reasonable, doable, feasible, attainable, practicable, acceptable, viable, tolerable
2 CONTROLLABLE, governable, amenable, accommodating, yielding, submissive, compliant, docile, pliant, pliable, flexible
FORMAL tractable
3 *manageable blocks of ice*
handy, functional, practicable, easy-to-use, wieldy
E3 1, 2 unmanageable **3** unmanageable, unwieldy, awkward

management *n*
1 ADMINISTRATION, direction, control, government, command, leadership, organization, running, ruling, overseeing, superintendence, supervision, charge, care, handling, conduct
2 MANAGERS, directors, directorate, executive, executives, governors, board, owners, employers, proprietors, supervisors
COLLOQ. bosses
E3 1 mismanagement **2** workers

manager *n*
director, executive, employer, businessman, businesswoman, manageress, president, chairman, chairwoman, chair, chairperson, chief executive, managing director, administrator, controller, superintendent, supervisor, commissioner, overseer, governor, organizer, head, chief, head of department, comptroller, landlord, landlady, *maître d'hôtel*, hotelier, manufacturer, procurator, proctor, agent, amildar, husband, contriver, conductor, impresario, *régisseur*, intendant
COLLOQ. boss, gaffer, guv, suit; *Scot* head-bummer; *NAm* honcho

managerial *adj*
supervisory, superintendent, executive, administrative, organizational, departmental, governmental, legislative, industrial, entrepreneurial

mandate *n, v*
♦ *n*
order, command, decree, edict, injunction, dictate, charge, directive, direction, ordinance, ruling, law, statute, bidding, warrant, authorization, authority, instruction, commission, sanction
♦ *v*
authorize, legalize, make legal, validate, ratify, confirm, license, entitle, empower, give authority to, enable, commission, warrant, permit, give permission to, allow, let, consent to, sanction, approve
COLLOQ. OK, okay, give the go-ahead to, give the green light to, give the thumbs-up to

mandatory *adj*
obligatory, compulsory, binding, required, necessary, essential, imperative
FORMAL requisite
E3 optional

manful *adj*
brave, manly, gallant, courageous, heroic, intrepid, bold, lion-hearted, determined, resolute, stalwart, stout, stout-hearted, valiant, strong, powerful, indomitable, hardy, daring, unflinching, vigorous, noble, noble-minded
E3 half-hearted, timid

manfully *adv*
bravely, courageously, valiantly, heroically, intrepidly,

boldly, gallantly, pluckily, determinedly, hard, vigorously, strongly, powerfully, unflinchingly, desperately, resolutely, stalwartly, stoutly, steadfastly, nobly
☒ half-heartedly, timidly

manger n
trough, feeding trough, feeder, crib

mangle v
1 MUTILATE, disfigure, mar, maim, butcher, destroy, deform, wreck, twist, maul, distort, crush, cut, hack, tear, lacerate, rend
2 SPOIL, butcher, ruin, bungle
COLLOQ. botch, mess up, make a mess of, make a hash of
SLANG screw up

mangy adj
seedy, shabby, scruffy, scabby, shoddy, moth-eaten, worn, filthy, dirty, mean
COLLOQ. tatty

manhandle v
1 *the porters manhandled the baggage*
haul, heave, pull, push, shove, tug
COLLOQ. hump
2 *the police manhandled the demonstrators*
maul, mistreat, maltreat, misuse, abuse, handle roughly, push, shove, jostle
COLLOQ. knock about, rough up

manhood n
1 ADULTHOOD, maturity
2 MASCULINITY, virility, manliness, manfulness, maleness
COLLOQ. machismo

mania n
1 MADNESS, insanity, lunacy, dementia, psychosis, derangement, disorder, aberration, frenzy, wildness, raving, hysteria
COLLOQ. craziness
2 PASSION, craze, rage, obsession, compulsion, fetish, preoccupation, enthusiasm, infatuation, fixation, craving, urge, desire, fascination
COLLOQ. fad, thing

Manias include:

dipsomania (*alcohol*)	hippomania (*horses*)	monomania (*single idea or thing*)
bibliomania (*books*)	mythomania (*lying and exaggerating*)	kleptomania (*stealing*)
ailuromania (*cats*)		tomomania (*surgery*)
demomania (*crowds*)	ablutomania (*personal cleanliness*)	logomania (*talking*)
necromania (*dead bodies*)	hedonomania (*pleasure*)	ergomania (*work*)
thanatomania (*death*)	megalomania (*power*)	egomania (*yourself*)
cynomania (*dogs*)	theomania (*religion*)	
narcomania (*drugs*)	nymphomania (*sex*)	
pyromania (*fire-raising*)		
anthomania (*flowers*)		

See also **phobia**.

---

maniac n
1 LUNATIC, madman, madwoman, psychotic, psychopath, deranged person
COLLOQ. nutter, nut, nutcase, fruitcake, crackpot, crank, headcase, kook
SLANG loony, screwball, oddball, psycho; NAm cupcake
2 ENTHUSIAST, fan, fanatic
COLLOQ. fiend, freak, buff

manic adj
1 INSANE, mad, deranged, demented, crazed

COLLOQ. crazy, barmy, batty, dippy, daffy, loopy
2 FRENZIED, frantic, frenetic, hectic, feverish, desperate, furious, overwrought, distraught, distracted, crazed, wild, uncontrolled, mad, berserk, amok, raving, demented, hysterical, panic-stricken, uncontrolled, beside yourself, obsessive
☒ **1** sane **2** calm, composed

manically adv
frenetically, hectically, wildly, excitedly, intensely, madly, hysterically

manifest adj, v
◆ *adj*
obvious, evident, clear, apparent, plain, open, patent, distinct, noticeable, conspicuous, perceptible, glaring, blatant, unmistak(e)able, visible, unconcealed, transparent
☒ unclear
◆ *v*
show, exhibit, display, demonstrate, reveal, appear, set forth, present, express, declare, indicate, expose, make clear/plain, prove, illustrate, establish, be evidence of, extrovert
OLD confess
FORMAL evince, attest
☒ conceal, hide

manifestation n
display, exhibition, demonstration, show, presentation, declaration, revelation, exposure, disclosure, appearance, expression, representation, reflex, illustration, exemplification, evidence, mode, sign, indication, token, mark
TECHNICAL incarnation
FORMAL exposition

manifesto n
statement, declaration, announcement, proclamation, publication, policies, programme, platform

manifold adj
many, several, numerous, varied, various, diverse, multiple, kaleidoscopic, abundant, copious
FORMAL multifarious, multitudinous

manipulate v
1 MANOEUVRE, influence, control, exploit, work, milk, engineer, guide, direct, steer, use/turn to your advantage, negotiate, capitalize on, finesse
COLLOQ. wangle, cash in on, pull strings, have in the palm of your hand, twist round your little finger, have over a barrel, wheel and deal, frame, fit up
2 FALSIFY, rig, juggle with, massage, tamper with, gerrymander, shuffle, thimblerig, cog
COLLOQ. doctor, cook, fiddle
3 HANDLE, control, manage, wield, operate, work, knead, massage, use, utilize, employ, process, ply, nurse; NAm tong
OLD hand

manipulation n
1 MANOEUVRING, influence, exploitation, control, working, guidance, directing, steering, negotiation, milking
COLLOQ. wheeling and dealing, wangling, pulling strings
2 FALSIFICATION, rigging, juggling, massaging
COLLOQ. doctoring, fiddling, cooking the books
3 HANDLING, control, wielding, operation, kneading, using, utilization

manipulative adj
scheming, crafty, cunning, deceitful, sly, underhand, unscrupulous, wily, devious, artful, calculating, conniving, designing, insidious, tricky, slippery, foxy, Machiavellian
FORMAL duplicitous
☒ artless, honest, open, transparent

manipulator n
1 EXPLOITER, controller, manoeuvrer, influencer, schemer,

engineer, director, negotiator
COLLOQ. wheeler-dealer, smoothy, smart guy
2 HANDLER, operator, user, worker, controller, wielder

mankind *n*
human race, humanity, human beings, humankind, man,
Homo sapiens, people, mortals

manliness *n*
masculinity, maleness, virility, manfulness, bravery,
boldness, courage, valour, fearlessness, heroism,
intrepidity, resoluteness, resolution, stout-heartedness,
stalwartness, hardihood, independence, manhood,
strength, vigour, mettle, firmness
FORMAL fortitude
COLLOQ. machismo
Ⅎ timidity, unmanliness

manly *adj*
masculine, male, virile, manful, brave, courageous, bold,
intrepid, fearless, heroic, determined, strong, powerful,
firm, tough, rugged, vigorous, sturdy, robust
COLLOQ. macho

man-made *adj*
synthetic, manufactured, simulated, imitation, artificial,
mock, faux
COLLOQ. ersatz
Ⅎ natural

manner *n*
1 WAY, method, means, fashion, style, variety, procedure,
technique, approach, practice, process, routine, form
FORMAL mode
2 BEHAVIOUR, conduct, appearance, look, character,
attitude, posture, stance
FORMAL bearing, demeanour, air, mien, aspect,
deportment
3 *good manners*
behaviour, conduct, way of behaving, etiquette,
politeness, courtesy, protocol, good form, formalities,
social graces
FORMAL decorum, propriety, demeanour, bearing
COLLOQ. p's and q's, the done thing

mannered *adj*
artificial, posed, pretentious, stilted, precious
FORMAL affected, euphuistic
COLLOQ. pseudo, put-on
Ⅎ natural

mannerism *n*
idiosyncrasy, peculiarity, characteristic, quirk, trait, feature,
foible, habit

mannerly *adj*
polite, courteous, refined, well-behaved, well-bred, well-
mannered, gentlemanly, ladylike, respectful, civil, civilized,
deferential, gracious, formal, genteel, polished
FORMAL decorous
Ⅎ unmannerly

mannish *adj*
masculine, unfeminine, unladylike, unwomanly,
tomboyish, viraginian, viraginous, viragoish, Amazonian
OLD (*Shakesp*) mankind
FORMAL virilescent
COLLOQ. butch, laddish
Ⅎ womanish

mannishness *n*
masculinity, unfemininity, unladylikeness, unwomanliness,
virilism
FORMAL virilescence
COLLOQ. butchness
Ⅎ womanishness

manoeuvre *v, n*
• *v*
1 MOVE, manipulate, handle, guide, pilot, steer, navigate,

dock, berth, negotiate, jockey, direct, drive, turn, cut in,
ease, exercise
TECHNICAL chandelle
2 CONTRIVE, engineer, plot, scheme, intrigue, manipulate,
manage, plan, devise, negotiate
COLLOQ. wangle, pull strings, jockey for position
• *n*
1 EXERCISE, move, movement, turn, roll, operation,
deployment, action
OLD decursion
2 MANIPULATION, skilful plan, ploy, plot, ruse, stratagem,
device, gambit, tactic, trick, scheme, subterfuge, stall
FORMAL machination, artifice
COLLOQ. dodge, wangle

manor *n*
house, country house, seat, hall, villa, barony, château,
Schloss, Hof
Related adjective: manorial

manpower *n*
workers, skilled workers, workforce, staff, employees,
human resources, personnel

manse *n*
vicarage, rectory, parsonage, deanery, glebe-house

manservant *n*
butler, gentleman's gentleman, valet, attendant, retainer

mansion *n*
home, hall, house, manor, manor-house, castle, château,
Schloss, villa, seat, place, *casa*
FORMAL abode, dwelling, habitation, residence

manslaughter *n*
killing, slaughter, murder, massacre, butchery, genocide,
homicide, assassination, execution, slaying,
extermination, carnage, bloodshed, elimination,
destruction, fatality
FORMAL patricide, matricide, infanticide, fratricide,
sororicide, uxoricide
COLLOQ. liquidation

mantle *n, v*
• *n*
1 CLOAK, cape, hood, shawl, veil, wrap, shroud, screen
2 COVER, covering, veil, shroud, blanket, layer, cloak, mask,
cloud, envelope
• *v*
cover, cloak, veil, mask, wrap, blanket, shroud, cloud,
envelop, hide, disguise, conceal

manual *n, adj*
• *n*
handbook, guide, guidebook, instruction book,
instructions, ABC, companion, bible, prospectus, vade-
mecum, directions
COLLOQ. book of words
• *adj*
hand-operated, by hand, (done) with your hands, physical,
human
Ⅎ mental, automatic

manually *adv*
by hand, with your hands, done/operated with your hands,
physically

manufacture *v, n*
• *v*
1 MAKE, produce, construct, build, fabricate, create,
assemble, mass-produce, put together, turn out, fashion,
process, forge, model, form
2 INVENT, make up, devise, construct, frame, concoct,
fabricate, think up, dream up
• *n*
production, making, construction, building, fabrication,
mass-production, assembly, processing, creation,
formation, fashioning, modelling, forming

manufacturer *n*
maker, producer, industrialist, constructor, factory-owner,
builder, creator
OLD fabricant

manure *n*
fertilizer, compost, muck, dung, animal excrement,
droppings, guano, ordure, top-dressing; *dialect* vraic; *Scot*
hen-pen, police-manure
FORMAL animal faeces

manuscript *n*
document, text, typescript, paper, parchment, scroll,
vellum

many *adj, n*
• *adj*
a lot of, a large number of, several, numerous, innumerable,
countless, various, multiple, copious, varied, sundry,
diverse
FORMAL manifold, multitudinous
COLLOQ. umpteen
🖙 few
• *n*
a lot, a large number, a mass, a multitude, plenty, scores
COLLOQ. lots, loads, hundreds, thousands, millions,
billions, zillions, masses, piles, heaps, stacks, oodles,
scads, wads, tons

map *n, v*
• *n*
chart, plan, projection, town plan, street plan, street guide,
road-map, atlas, gazetteer, graph, plot, inset, cartogram,
card, *carte du pays*, horoscope
TECHNICAL hypsography, planisphere
OLD mappemond
• *v*
chart, plot, plan, mark, sketch
FORMAL delineate
■ **map out**
sketch, draw (up), draft, outline, work out

mar *v*
spoil, impair, harm, hurt, damage, blemish, deface,
deform, disfigure, mutilate, injure, maim, scar, detract
from, mangle, ruin, wreck, taint, tarnish, contaminate, stain
🖙 enhance

maraud *v*
plunder, raid, ravage, ransack, loot, pillage, harry, forage,
foray, sack
FORMAL despoil, spoliate, depredate

marauder *n*
bandit, brigand, robber, raider, plunderer, looter, pillager,
pirate, buccaneer, freebooter, outlaw, highwayman,
ravager, predator, rustler, rover
COLLOQ. mugger

march *v, n*
• *v*
walk, file, parade, pace, step, tread, stride, tramp, hike,
footslog, stalk, strut, swagger, forward, advance, progress,
make headway, countermarch, debouch, defile
• *n*
1 STEP, pace, stride, walk, gait
2 WALK, route-march, trek, hike, tramp, footslog, *étape*
COLLOQ. yomp
3 PROCESSION, parade, demonstration
TECHNICAL walk-around
COLLOQ. demo
4 ADVANCE, development, progress, evolution, passage,
headway, evolution

marches *n*
boundary, border, border district, borderland, frontier

margin *n*
1 BORDER, edge, boundary, bound, periphery, perimeter,
frontier, demarcation line, rim, brim, brink, limit(s),
confine(s), verge, side, skirt
2 ALLOWANCE, play, leeway, latitude, scope, room, room for
manoeuvre, difference, differential, space, surplus, extra

marginal *adj*
borderline, doubtful, peripheral, on the edge, negligible,
minute, minimal, insignificant, minor, slight, tiny, low, small
🖙 central, core, mainstream

marginalization *n*
isolation, separation, separateness, detachment,
disconnection, dissociation, alienation, abstraction,
solitude, solitariness, loneliness, aloneness, remoteness,
seclusion, retirement, withdrawal, exile, segregation
FORMAL sequestration
🖙 assimilation, integration

marginalize *v*
isolate, set apart, seclude, keep apart, segregate, abstract,
cut off, detach, remove, disconnect, separate, divorce,
alienate, shut out/away, ostracize, exclude, strand, maroon
FORMAL sequester
COLLOQ. cold-shoulder
🖙 assimilate, integrate

marijuana *n*
cannabis, hemp, hashish, ganja, bhang, kef, kaif, kif,
sinsemilla
COLLOQ. joint, dope, pot, gage, puff, wacky baccy
SLANG hash, blow, weed, grass, reefer, spliff, roach, toke,
blunt, bomber, skunk, leaf, greens, shit; *N Am* locoweed,
Mary Jane, splay
OLD SLANG *N Am* tea

marina *n*
dock, harbour, mooring, port, yacht station

marinade *v*
steep, soak, immerse, marinate, souse, saturate, imbue,
permeate, infuse

marine *adj*
sea, maritime, naval, nautical, seafaring, seagoing, ocean-
going, oceanic, saltwater, seawater, aquatic
FORMAL pelagic, thalassian, thalassic

mariner *n*
sailor, seaman, seafarer, deckhand, navigator
COLLOQ. tar, Jack Tar, matlo, matlow, matelot, sea dog, salt,
limey

marital *adj*
married, marriage, wedding, wedded
FORMAL matrimonial, conjugal, nuptial, connubial, spousal

maritally *adv*
in/by marriage
OLD in/by wedlock
FORMAL matrimonially, conjugally, nuptially, connubially

maritime *adj*
marine, nautical, naval, seafaring, sea, seaside, sea-trade,
sea-coast, seagoing, oceanic, coastal
FORMAL littoral, pelagic

mark *n, v*
• *n*
1 SPOT, stain, blemish, patch, pimple, freckle, birthmark,
blot, blotch, smudge, smear, dent, impression, trace,
fingerprint(s), track(s), imprint, speck, notch, chip, cut,
scar, scratch, bruise, score, line, nick
FORMAL stigma
COLLOQ. zit
2 SIGN, indication, character, symbol, stamp, token,
characteristic, feature, quality, attribute, symptom, clue,
proof, hint, evidence, impression, print, imprint
3 SYMBOL, emblem, brand, stamp, seal, badge, device, logo,
trademark, motto, monogram
4 SCORE, grade, percentage, tick, assessment, evaluation

5 *inflation reaching the 5% mark*
point, level, stage, norm, standard, criterion, gauge, scale, measure, yardstick
6 TARGET, goal, aim, objective, object, purpose, end, intention, bull's-eye
♦ *v*
1 STAIN, blemish, blot, smudge, discolour, dent, scar, scratch, bruise, dent, chip, cut, score, nick
2 BRAND, label, stamp, tag, flag, characterize, indicate, put your name on, identify, distinguish
3 EVALUATE, assess, correct, grade
FORMAL appraise
4 WRITE DOWN, note (down), indicate, name, label, specify, designate, jot down
5 CHARACTERIZE, identify, stamp, brand, typify, distinguish
6 *mark an event/occasion*
observe, remember, celebrate, commemorate, keep, honour, recognize, acknowledge, pay tribute to
7 *the war marked a turning point in the city's history*
represent, indicate, signify, denote, designate
8 *mark my words*
listen, mind, note, spot, observe, regard, see, notice, take note of, discern, pay attention to, bear in mind, take to heart
FORMAL heed, take heed of
▪ **mark down**
reduce, lower, decrease, cut
COLLOQ. slash
◲ mark up
▪ **mark out**
1 *mark out a football pitch*
draw lines, demarcate, show the boundaries of, fix, delimit
FORMAL delineate
2 DISTINGUISH, differentiate, tell apart, set apart, discriminate, single out, tell the difference between
▪ **mark up**
increase, raise, put up
COLLOQ. hike up, jack up
▪ **make your mark**
succeed, be successful, prosper, get on
COLLOQ. make it, make the grade, hit/make the big time
▪ **up to the mark**
good enough, satisfactory, acceptable
COLLOQ. up to scratch, OK
▪ **wide of the mark**
incorrect, inaccurate, imprecise, irrelevant, beside the point, off target

marked *adj*
1 SPOTTED, spotty, stained, blemished, blotched, blotchy, scarred, pimply, freckled, bruised, scratched
2 NOTICEABLE, obvious, conspicuous, prominent, signal, evident, clear, pronounced, distinct, noted, decided, emphatic, considerable, remarkable, apparent, glaring, striking, blatant, unmistakable
3 SUSPECTED, watched, doomed, condemned
◲ **1** unnoticeable, slight

markedly *adv*
noticeably, obviously, conspicuously, prominently, signally, evidently, clearly, distinctly, decidedly, emphatically, considerably, remarkably, glaringly, strikingly, blatantly, unmistakably

market *n, v*
♦ *n*
1 *buy goods at the market*
mart, market-place, shopping centre, mall, bazaar, fair, exchange, outlet, souk
OLD agora
2 *no market for these goods*
demand, call, requirement, need, occasion, want, desire
3 BUSINESS, trade, trading, buying, selling, industry, dealings
Related adjective: nundinal
♦ *v*

sell, retail, hawk, peddle, offer for sale
◲ buy
▪ **on the market**
for sale, on sale, up for sale, available

marketable *adj*
in demand, sought after, wanted, saleable, sellable, merchantable
FORMAL vendible
◲ unsaleable

marketing *n*
sales, promotion, publicity, advertising, merchandizing, distribution
COLLOQ. hype, pushing, plugging
See panel on next page

marksman, markswoman *n*
crack shot, dead shot, sharpshooter, sniper

mark-up *n*
increase, price increase, rise, escalation, leap, upsurge
COLLOQ. hike

maroon *v*
abandon, strand, cast away, desert, put ashore, strand, leave (behind), isolate, turn your back on
FORMAL forsake
COLLOQ. leave in the lurch, leave high and dry

marriage *n*
1 *the marriage ceremony*
union, married relationship, married state, wedding
OLD wedlock
FORMAL matrimony, nuptials, spousage, espousals
2 UNION, alliance, partnership, merger, coupling, fusion, amalgamation, unification, combination, link, connection, association, confederation, affiliation
◲ **1** divorce **2** separation
Related adjectives: marital, matrimonial, conjugal, connubial

married *adj*
marital, wedded, united, wed, joined, husbandly, wifely, wived, yoked
FORMAL conjugal, connubial, matrimonial, nuptial, spousal
COLLOQ. hitched, spliced
◲ divorced, single, widowed

marrow *n*
essence, heart, nub, kernel, core, nucleus, centre, pith, soul, spirit, substance, quick, stuff, gist
FORMAL quintessence
COLLOQ. nitty-gritty, nuts and bolts
Related adjective: myeloid

marry *v*
1 WED, get married, become husband and wife, intermarry, unite, elope; *Scot* cleek
OLD spouse, take to wife, wive; (*Shakesp*) go to the world
FORMAL join in matrimony, become espoused
COLLOQ. tie the knot, get hitched, hitch up, get spliced, take the plunge, lead to the altar, lead up the aisle, make an honest woman of
2 UNITE, ally, join (together), merge, combine, amalgamate, couple, affiliate, match, link, connect, associate, weld, fuse, knit
◲ **1** divorce **2** separate

marsh *n*
marshland, bog, swamp, fen, morass, mire, quagmire, slough; *N Am* bayou
Related adjective: paludal

marshal *v*
1 ARRANGE, dispose, order, line up, align, array, rank, organize, put in order, assemble, gather (together), muster, group, collect, draw up, deploy
2 GUIDE, lead, take, escort, conduct, usher, shepherd

Terms used in marketing include:

PEOPLE IN MARKETING:
account executive
commando salesman
media buyer
media planner
SELLING METHODS:
cold call
door-to-door
face-to-face
field selling
hard sell
high-pressure selling
house-to-house
inertia selling
low-pressure selling
mailshot
missionary selling
party selling
personal selling
pyramid selling
telephone selling
**ADVERTISING AND
PROMOTION TECHNIQUES:**
above-the-line advertising
below-the-line advertising
blanket coverage
blind advertisement
BOGO(F)F (buy one get
  one (for) free)
classified advertising
commercial
comparative advertising
co-operative advertising
flash pack
free gift (or sample)
gimmick
giveaway
industrial advertising
institutional advertising
island display
jingle
loyalty card
outdoor advertising
personality promotion
piggyback promotion
predatory pricing
sales campaign
sales drive
slogan
subliminal advertising
BRANDING:
brand awareness
brand image
brand loyalty

corporate identity
corporate image
dealer brand
family brand
market leader
multi-brand strategy
own-brand
own-label
recognition
MARKET RESEARCH:
aided (or prompted)
  recall
area sampling
attitude research
audience research
buying motives
canvass
cluster sampling
concept testing
consumer panel
consumer research
filter question
focus group survey
Gallup poll
group discussion
leading question
motivation research
random sampling
reference group
unaided recall
unprompted response
BUYERS:
adopter
captive audience
early adopter
heavy user
late adopter
target audience
PRODUCTS:
articles of ostentation
cash cow
dog
FMCGs (fast-moving
  consumer goods)
heterogenous products
homogenous products
loss-leader
low-involvement
  products
problem children (or
  wildcats)
star

MISCELLANEOUS:
ACORN (a classification of
  residential neighbour-
  hoods)
after-sales service
AIDA (Attention Interest
  Desire Action)
ASA (Advertising Standards
  Authority)
buyers' market
call rate
campaign
cannibalism
captive market
churn
competitive market
concentrated marketing
consumer sovereignty
corner a market
coverage
credibility gap
customer orientation
customer profile
DAGMAR (defining
  advertising goals for
  measured advertising
  results)
demarketing
demographic
elasticity of demand
family life cycle
footfall
four p's (Product,
  Price, Promotion and Place)
frequency
gap analysis
generic
geographical concentration
Giffen good
growth-share matrix
halo effect
harvesting strategy
hierarchy of effects
hierarchy of needs
high-involvement products
hit rate
horizontal marketing
impulse buying
incentive marketing
international marketing
journey planning
key prospects
launch

macro marketing
market demand
marketing audit
marketing board
marketing concept
marketing intelligence
marketing mix
market orientation
market penetration
market potential
market profile
market segmentation
market share
matched sample
media independent
merchandizing
micro marketing
mock-up
necessity good
Nielsen index
normal good
observation
opportunity to see
opinion leaders
paired comparisons
perceptual map
perfect competition
product differentiation
product orientation
product positioning
psychographic
  measurement
response rate
retail audit
rolling launch
sales aid
saturation point
skimming pricing
social marketing
socio-economic groups
solus position
static market
tachistoscope
Target Group Index
test marketing
undifferentiated marketing
up-market
USP (unique selling
  proposition)
vertical marketing
viral marketing
visualizer

---

marshy *adj*
  boggy, fenny, fennish, swampy, quaggy, waterlogged, wet,
  muddy, squelchy, miry, slumpy, spongy
  FORMAL paludal, paludinal, paludine, paludinous
  E3 solid, firm, dry

marsupial

Marsupials include:

bandicoot	marsupial mole	Tasmanian Devil
cuscus	marsupial rat	Tasmanian wolf
kangaroo	opossum	tree kangaroo
koala	pademelon	wallaby
marsupial	phalanger	wallaroo
anteater	rat kangaroo	wombat
marsupial mouse	rock wallaby	

mart *n*
  market, market-place, shopping centre, bazaar, mall, fair,
  exchange, outlet, souk

martial *adj*
  warlike, military, army, soldierly, militant, heroic, brave,
  belligerent, combative, aggressive, hawkish
  FORMAL pugnacious, bellicose

martial arts

Martial arts include:

UNARMED:	kickboxing	bojutsu
aikido	kung fu	jojutsu
capoeira	tae kwon do	kendo
judo	t'ai chi	kenjutsu
jujitsu	wushu	kumdo
karate	**WITH WEAPONS:**	kyodo
kempo	bandesh	

martinet *n*
  dsciplinarian, stickler, tyrant, taskmaster, taskmistress,
  formalist
  COLLOQ. slave-driver

martyr v

put to death, make a martyr of, crucify, stone, persecute, torture, torment, burn at the stake, throw to the lions, put on the rack
COLLOQ. give the works, give the third degree

martyrdom n

death, suffering, torture, torment, persecution, excruciation, ordeal, agony, anguish, witness

marvel v, n

• v

wonder, gape, gaze, stare, goggle, not expect, be amazed, be astonished, stand in amazement
COLLOQ. gawp, be flabbergasted, not believe your eyes, not know what to say

• n

wonder, miracle, surprise, something amazing/incredible, phenomenon, prodigy, spectacle, sensation, genius
COLLOQ. eye-opener, quite something

marvellous adj

1 WONDERFUL, excellent, splendid, superb, great, magnificent, terrific, super, fantastic
COLLOQ. ace, neat, brill, sensational, magic
SLANG awesome, wicked, bad, def, phat, mean, crucial, rad, radical, cool, mega
2 EXTRAORDINARY, amazing, surprising, astonishing, astounding, sensational, spectacular, miraculous, remarkable, awesome, unbelievable, incredible, stupendous, glorious
E3 1 terrible, awful **2** ordinary, run-of-the-mill

marvellously adv

extremely, exceedingly, excessively, very, really, exceptionally, extraordinarily, intensely, thoroughly, remarkably, utterly, greatly, highly, unusually, uncommonly, inordinately, acutely, severely, decidedly
COLLOQ. awfully, terribly, dreadfully, frightfully, terrifically

masculine adj

1 MALE, manlike, manly, mannish, virile
COLLOQ. macho, butch
2 VIGOROUS, strong, strapping, robust, powerful, muscular, rugged, red-blooded, virile, bold, brave, gallant, fearless, heroic, determined, confident, resolute, stout-hearted
E3 1 feminine

masculinity n

manliness, maleness, virility, manfulness, bravery, boldness, courage, valour, fearlessness, heroism, intrepidity, resolution, stout-heartedness, stalwartness, hardihood, independence, manhood, strength, vigour, mettle, firmness
FORMAL fortitude
COLLOQ. machismo
E3 femininity

mash v, n

• v

crush, pulp, beat, pound, purée, pulverize, pummel, grind, smash, squash

• n

mush, pulp, crush, purée, squash, pap, paste

mask n, v

• n

disguise, camouflage, façade, front, concealment, cover-up, cover, guise, pretence, semblance, cloak, veil, blind, screen, show, veneer, visor, goggles, vizard, false face, domino
TECHNICAL matte, persona
OLD masque

• v

disguise, camouflage, cover (up), conceal, cloak, veil, hide, obscure, screen, shield
OLD vizard; (*Shakesp*) immask
FORMAL dissemble
E3 expose, uncover

masquerade n, v

• n

1 MASQUE, masked ball, costume ball, fancy dress ball/party
2 DISGUISE, counterfeit, cover-up, cover, deception, front, pose, pretence, guise, cloak

• v

disguise, impersonate, pose, pass yourself off, mask, play, pretend, profess
FORMAL dissimulate

mass¹ n, adj, v

• n

1 HEAP, pile, load, accumulation, collection, combination, entirety, whole, total, totality, sum, lot, group, batch, stack, bunch
FORMAL aggregate, conglomeration, assemblage
2 QUANTITY, abundance, multitude, large number, throng, troop, crowd, band, horde, mob
COLLOQ. loads, heaps, bags, piles, lots, tons, scores, oodles
3 MAJORITY, body, bulk, greater part, most, preponderance
4 SIZE, dimension, magnitude, immensity, bulk, weight, capacity
5 LUMP, piece, chunk, block, hunk
COLLOQ. wodge
6 *the masses*
crowd, herd, mob, lower classes, working class(es), common people, proletariat, rabble, hoi polloi, the rank and file
COLLOQ. plebs, riff-raff

• adj

widespread, large-scale, extensive, comprehensive, general, universal, indiscriminate, popular, across-the-board, sweeping, wholesale, blanket
FORMAL pandemic
E3 limited, small-scale

• v

collect, gather, assemble, congregate, amass, accumulate, draw together, come/bring together, crowd, rally, cluster, muster, swarm, throng
E3 separate

mass² n

go to mass
Eucharist, Communion, Holy Communion, Lord's Supper, Lord's Table

massacre n, v

• n

slaughter, murder, homicide, extermination, carnage, butchery, wholesale slaughter, indiscriminate killing, holocaust, bloodbath, annihilation, killing, genocide, ethnic cleansing, pogrom, liquidation, decimation, purge

• v

slaughter, butcher, murder, mow down, exterminate, annihilate, kill (off), slay, decimate, liquidate
COLLOQ. wipe out

massage n, v

• n

manipulation, kneading, rub, rubbing, rub-down, pummelling, reflexology, aromatherapy, acupressure, shiatsu, Jacuzzi®, tripsis, osteopathy, physiotherapy, Reichian therapy, reiki

• v

1 *massaged her thigh*
manipulate, knead, rub (down), pummel, shampoo
2 *massage statistics*
alter, tamper with, interfere with, falsify, misrepresent, manipulate
COLLOQ. doctor, fiddle, cook

massive adj

huge, immense, enormous, vast, colossal, mammoth, gigantic, big, bulky, monumental, solid, hulking, hefty, weighty, substantial, heavy, large,

large-scale, great, extensive, mighty
COLLOQ. whopping, jumbo, ginormous
E3 tiny, small

massively *adv*
immensely, greatly, very much, substantially, heavily,
extensively, enormously, vastly, monumentally

mast *n*
pole, shaft, rod, bar, spar, boom, yard, heel, post, staff,
stick, upright, support

master *n, adj, v*
• *n*
1 RULER, chief, governor, head, lord, captain, employer,
commander, controller, director, manager,
superintendent, overseer, principal, overlord, owner; *S Afr*
baas
COLLOQ. boss, gaffer, skipper, guv; *N Am* honcho
2 EXPERT, genius, professional, pundit, virtuoso, past master,
grand master, maestro, adept
COLLOQ. dab hand, ace, pro, buff, egghead, wise guy;
N Am mavin
3 TEACHER, tutor, mentor, instructor, schoolteacher,
schoolmaster, schoolmistress, guide, guru
FORMAL pedagogue, preceptor
E3 **1** servant, underling **2** amateur, beginner **3** learner, pupil
• *adj*
1 CHIEF, principal, main, leading, foremost, most important,
prime, predominant, controlling, great, grand
2 EXPERT, masterly, skilled, skilful, experienced, proficient,
practised, adept, dexterous
E3 **1** subordinate **2** inept
• *v*
1 CONQUER, defeat, subdue, triumph over, overcome,
overpower, quell, suppress, rule, control, govern, tame,
bridle, check, curb
FORMAL subjugate, vanquish
2 LEARN, grasp, acquire, manage, pick up
COLLOQ. get the hang of

masterful *adj*
arrogant, authoritative, domineering, overbearing,
controlling, high-handed, despotic, dictatorial, autocratic,
tyrannical, powerful, dominating, imperious
FORMAL peremptory
COLLOQ. bossy
E3 humble, downtrodden; *colloq.* hen-pecked

⚠ masterful or **masterly**?
Masterful means 'showing power, authority or determination': *The directors show a masterful approach to their employees. Masterly* means 'showing the skill of a master': *a
masterly display of swordsmanship.*

---

masterly *adj*
expert, professional, accomplished, polished, skilled,
skilful, dexterous, adept, adroit, first-rate, excellent,
superb, superior, supreme
FORMAL consummate
COLLOQ. ace, crack, top-notch
E3 inept, clumsy

mastermind *v, n*
• *v*
devise, think up, contrive, engineer, direct, control,
organize, manage, originate, plan, conceive, design,
dream up, frame, hatch, forge, inspire, be behind
• *n*
organizer, initiator, manager, planner, creator, director,
originator, authority, genius, intellect, mind, engineer,
architect, prime mover, virtuoso
COLLOQ. brains

masterpiece *n*
masterwork, *pièce de résistance, chef d'oeuvre*, magnum
opus, work of art, creation, jewel

masterstroke *n*
superior performance, triumph, victory, success,
achievement, accomplishment, attainment, feat, coup

mastery *n*
1 PROFICIENCY, skill, ability, capability, command, expertise,
virtuosity, knowledge, understanding, comprehension,
knowhow, dexterity, familiarity, grasp
FORMAL prowess
2 CONTROL, command, domination, supremacy,
superiority, victory, triumph, dominion, authority,
sovereignty, rule, direction
FORMAL ascendancy
COLLOQ. upper hand
E3 **1** incompetence **2** subjugation

masticate *v*
champ, chew, munch, chomp, crunch, eat, ruminate,
knead
FORMAL manducate

mastication *n*
chewing, champing, munching, eating, rumination
FORMAL manduction

masturbate *v*
stimulate yourself, gratify yourself
COLLOQ. jerk off, jack off, toss (it) off, play with yourself,
enjoy yourself
SLANG wank, frig

masturbation *n*
self-gratification, self-stimulation, autoeroticism, onanism,
self-abuse, tribadism, tribady
COLLOQ. playing with yourself, enjoying yourself, hand
relief
SLANG wank, wanking, frig, frigging, frottage

mat *n*
1 CARPET, doormat, felt, rug, underfelt, underlay, drugget,
table mat, place mat, coaster
2 TANGLE, knot, twist, cluster, mass

match¹ *n, v*
• *n*
1 CONTEST, competition, bout, game, test, trial, event,
meet, tournament
2 EQUAL, equivalent, peer, counterpart, fellow, mate, rival,
competitor, one of a pair, copy, double, companion,
complement, replica, lookalike, twin, duplicate
COLLOQ. dead ringer
3 MARRIAGE, alliance, union, combination, partnership,
affiliation, pairing, merger, coupling
• *v*
1 EQUAL, compare, measure up to, rival, parallel, compete,
oppose, contend, vie, keep up with, pit against
OLD (*Spenser*) amate
2 FIT, go with, agree, suit, harmonize, tally, co-ordinate,
blend, complement, adapt, go together, correspond, be in
agreement, relate, tone with, accompany, connect
OLD (*Shakesp*) besort, pattern
FORMAL accord
3 JOIN, marry, unite, mate, link, couple, combine, ally, pair
(up), yoke, team
COLLOQ. hitch up
E3 **2** clash, conflict **3** separate, divorce
▪ **match up to**
come up to, reach, meet, measure up to, live up to, make
the grade, compare with, approach, bear comparison with

match² *n*
light the fire with matches
light, safety match, spill, taper, fuse, vesta

matching *adj*
corresponding, comparable, complementing, equivalent,
parallel, like, identical, co-ordinating, blending,
harmonizing, complementary, correlative, similar,

duplicate, same, twin, paired, double, coupled
FORMAL analogous
▣ clashing, conflicting

matchless adj
unequalled, without equal, peerless, incomparable,
beyond compare, unmatched, unparalleled, unsurpassed,
unexcelled, unrivalled, inimitable, perfect, unique
▣ ordinary

mate n, v
♦ n
1 FRIEND, companion, comrade, colleague, partner, fellow
worker, co-worker, workmate, associate, mucker; *dialect*
marrow, wack; *Welsh* wus
OLD (*Shakesp*) co-mate; (*Spenser*) paragon
FORMAL compeer
COLLOQ. chum, crony, buddy, pal; *Aust & NZ* cobber
SLANG china, fere
OLD SLANG cully
2 PARTNER, husband, wife, spouse, boyfriend, girlfriend,
companion; *Scot* maik
OLD make, fere, paragon
COLLOQ. better half, other half, hubbie, missis, missus, Mr
Right, opposite number
3 ASSISTANT, helper, subordinate, apprentice, accomplice,
partner
COLLOQ. sidekick
4 MATCH, fellow, twin, equivalent, counterpart
♦ v
1 COUPLE, pair, breed, copulate, line, leap, nick
OLD gender
2 JOIN, match, marry, wed

material n, adj
♦ n
1 STUFF, substance, body, matter, medium
2 FABRIC, textile, cloth, stuff
3 INFORMATION, facts, facts and figures, numbers, data,
details, particulars, ideas, evidence, constituents, work,
notes
COLLOQ. low-down, gen, info
♦ adj
1 PHYSICAL, bodily, concrete, tangible, palpable, substantial,
earthly, worldly
FORMAL corporeal
2 RELEVANT, significant, important, momentous,
consequential, meaningful, essential, vital, key,
indispensable, serious, weighty
FORMAL pertinent, germane, apposite
▣ **1** spiritual, abstract **2** irrelevant, insignificant

materialism n
1 CORPOREALISM, hylicism, hylism, somatism
2 CONSUMERISM, worldliness, greed, acquisitiveness
▣ **1** spiritualism

materialistic adj
consumerist, worldly, acquisitive, mercenary, money-
grabbing, mammonist, mammonistic

materialize v
appear, arise, become visible, show/reveal yourself, take
shape, turn up, happen, occur, take place, come into being
▣ disappear

materially adv
significantly, essentially, fundamentally, substantially,
basically, considerably, seriously, gravely, greatly, much
▣ insignificantly

maternal adj
motherly, motherlike, nurturing, nourishing, loving,
caring, affectionate, warm, tender, gentle, fond, kind,
protective, comforting, understanding, vigilant, doting

matey
see **maty**.

mathematics
See panel on next page

mating n
breeding, copulating, sexual intercourse, copulation,
coupling, fusing, uniting, pairing, joining, matching,
twinning
FORMAL coition

matrimonial adj
marital, marriage, wedding, married, wedded
FORMAL nuptial, conjugal, spousal

matrimony n
marriage, married relationship/state, union
OLD wedlock
FORMAL espousals, nuptials, spousage

matrix n
1 TABLE, arrangement, analysis, context, frame, framework
TECHNICAL array
2 MOULD, cast, form, template, frame, framework
OLD plasm

matted adj
knotted, tangled, entangled, tangly, tousled, dishevelled,
uncombed
▣ tidy, untangled

matter n, v
♦ n
1 SUBJECT, issue, topic, question, affair, business, case,
point, concern, event, occurrence, happening, situation,
proceeding, circumstance, episode, incident, thing
2 IMPORTANCE, significance, consequence,
momentousness, interest, value, note, weight
FORMAL import
3 *What's the matter?*
trouble, problem, difficulty, distress, upset, worry, bother,
nuisance, inconvenience, shortcoming, weakness
4 SUBSTANCE, stuff, material, medium, physical elements,
body, content
5 DISCHARGE, pus, secretion
FORMAL purulence, suppuration
♦ v
count, be important, be of importance, be relevant, have
influence, carry weight, make a difference, mean
something
COLLOQ. make a stir, make waves, cut a lot of ice
■ **as a matter of fact**
in fact, actually, as it happens, really, truly, in actual fact
■ **no matter**
never mind, it does not matter, it is unimportant

matter-of-fact adj
unemotional, prosaic, down-to-earth, emotionless,
unsentimental, straightforward, practical, sober,
pedestrian, unimaginative, lifeless, dry, dull, flat
COLLOQ. deadpan
▣ emotional

mattress n
bed, feather bed, Lilo®, airbed, futon, water bed, crash-
mat, pallet, palliasse
SLANG biscuit

maturation n
ripening, seasoning, development, growth

mature adj, v
♦ adj
1 ADULT, grown-up, grown, full-grown, of age, sensible,
responsible, balanced, experienced, wise, fully fledged,
complete, finished, finalized, perfect, perfected, well-
developed, precocious, well-thought-out
2 RIPE, ripened, seasoned, mellow, ready
▣ **1** childish **2** immature
♦ v
grow up, become adult, become sensible, come of age,

Mathematical terms include:

acute angle
addition
algebra
algorithm
analysis
angle
apex
approximate
arc
area
argument
arithmetic
arithmetic
 progression
asymmetrical
average
axis
axis of symmetry
bar chart
bar graph
base
bearing
binary
binomial
breadth
calculus
capacity
cardinal number
Cartesian
 coordinates
chance
chord
circumference
coefficient
combination
common fraction
commutative
 operation
complement

complementary
 angle
complex number
concave
concentric circles
congruent
conjugate angles
constant
continuous
 distribution
converse
convex
coordinate
correlation
cosine
covariance
cross section
cube
cube root
curve
decimal
degree
denominator
depth
derivative
determinant
diagonal
diameter
differentiation
directed number
distribution
dividend
division
divisor
edge
enlargement
equal
equation
equidistant
even number

exponent
exponential
face
factor
factorial
Fibonacci
 sequence
formula
fraction
function
geometric
 progression
geometry
gradient
graph
greater than
group
harmonic
 progression
height
helix
histogram
horizontal
hyperbola
hypotenuse
identity
infinity
integer
integration
irrational number
latitude
length
less than
linear
line
locus
logarithm
longitude
magic square
mapping

matrix
maximum
mean
measure
median
minimum
minus
mirror image
mirror symmetry
mixed fraction
Möbius strip
mode
modulus
multiple
multiplication
natural logarithm
natural number
negative number
number
numerator
oblique
obtuse angle
odd number
operation
ordinal number
origin
parabola
parallel lines
parallel planes
parameter
percentage
percentile
perimeter
permutation
perpendicular
pi
pie chart
place value
plane figure
plus

point
positive number
prime number
probability
product
proportion
protractor
Pythagoras's
 theorem
quadrant
quadratic
 equation
quadrilateral
quartile
quotient
radian
radius
random sample
ratio
rational number
real number
reciprocal
recurring decimal
reflection
reflex angle
regression
remainder
right-angle
right-angled
 triangle
root
rotation
rotational
 symmetry
sample
scalar segment
secant
sector
set
side

simultaneous
 equation
sine
speed
spiral
square
square root
standard
 deviation
statistics
straight line
subset
subtractor
supplementary
 angles
symmetry
tangent
three-
 dimensional
total
transcendental
 number
transformation
triangulation
trigonometry
unit
universal set
variable
variance
vector
velocity
Venn diagram
vertex
vertical
volume
vulgar fraction
whole number
width
zero

See also **shape**.

---

develop, be fully developed, become ripe, become mellow, mellow, ripen, perfect, age, bloom, prepare, concoct, draw to a head, season, evolve, fall due
OLD maturate

maturity *n*
1 ADULTHOOD, full growth, majority, age, coming of age, womanhood, manhood, wisdom, experience, responsibility, sensibleness, age/years of discretion
2 RIPENESS, readiness, mellowness, perfection
E3 1 childishness **2** immaturity

maty, matey *adj*
friendly, affable, genial, convivial, cordial, kind, warm, neighbourly, helpful, sympathetic, affectionate, familiar, intimate, inseparable, close, companionable, sociable, outgoing, approachable, receptive, comradely, amicable, peaceable, well-disposed, favourable, agreeable, good-natured
COLLOQ. pally, chummy, thick, tight, folksy

maudlin *adj*
sentimental, mawkish, emotional, tearful, half-drunk, drunk, fuddled, tipsy
FORMAL lachrymose
COLLOQ. gushy, schmaltzy, mushy, sickly, slushy, soppy, weepy
E3 pleasant

maul *v*
attack, abuse, ill-treat, mutilate, mangle, manhandle, maltreat, assault, molest, paw, beat (up), claw, lacerate, thrash
COLLOQ. batter, wallop, belt, do over, mug, knock about, rough up, knock someone's block off

maunder *v*
1 MUTTER, ramble, babble, blather, chatter, jabber, gabble
COLLOQ. prattle, witter, natter, waffle, rabbit (on)
2 WANDER, meander, stray, amble, ramble, stroll, roam, rove, ease, shuffle, inch
COLLOQ. laze, mosey, mooch

mausoleum *n*
tomb, crypt, vault, burial chamber, catacomb, sepulchre, undercroft

maverick *n*
outsider, rebel, agitator, nonconformist, individualist
COLLOQ. fish out of water

maw *n*
mouth, jaws, throat, stomach, gullet, gulf, abyss, chasm

mawkish *adj*
sentimental, maudlin, emotional, offensive, nauseous, nauseating, feeble, flat, disgusting, foul, loathsome
COLLOQ. soppy, gushy, schmaltzy, mushy, sickly, slushy
E3 matter-of-fact, pleasant

mawkishly *adv*
sentimentally, emotionally, nauseatingly, loathsomely, feebly
COLLOQ. soppily, mushily

maxim *n*
saying, proverb, adage, axiom, aphorism, saw, epigram, motto, byword, precept, rule
TECHNICAL apothegm, apophthegm
FORMAL gnome

maximize *v*
increase, raise, boost, add to, enhance, advance, further, step up, intensify, strengthen, heighten, develop, build up, accumulate, enlarge, magnify, broaden, widen, deepen, extend, prolong, expand, spread, breed, propagate, scale up
FORMAL augment
COLLOQ. hike up, bump up
E3 decrease, reduce

maximum *adj, n*
◆ *adj*
greatest, highest, largest, biggest, most, utmost, supreme, top, topmost
E3 minimum
◆ *n*
most, top (point), utmost, uttermost, upper limit, peak, pinnacle, summit, zenith, apogee, acme, height, ceiling, extremity
E3 minimum

maybe *adv*
perhaps, possibly, conceivably, for all you know
FORMAL perchance, peradventure
E3 definitely

mayhem *n*
chaos, disorder, confusion, disorganization, tumult, disruption, uproar, riot, bedlam, madhouse, mess, anarchy, lawlessness

maze *n*
labyrinth, network, tangle, jungle, web, mesh, complex, confusion, puzzle, intricacy

meadow *n*
field, grassland, grass, pasture, pastureland, paddock, green, lea, saeter; *dialect* leasow; *Scot* haugh; *Scot & Irish* inch
OLD mead

meagre *adj*
1 SCANTY, sparse, inadequate, insufficient, deficient, skimpy, paltry, negligible, small, poor, slight, stingy, niggardly
FORMAL exiguous
COLLOQ. measly
2 THIN, puny, insubstantial, bony, emaciated, skinny, scraggy, gaunt, scrawny, slight
E3 1 ample, generous **2** fat, plump

meagreness *n*
scantiness, sparseness, inadequacy, insufficiency, deficiency, smallness, slightness, stinginess, puniness
COLLOQ. measliness

meal *n*
NZ kai
FORMAL repast

Meals include:

afternoon tea	*colloq.* elevenses	snack
banquet	evening meal	spread
barbecue	feast	supper
colloq. barbie	fork supper	takeaway
colloq. bite	harvest supper	tea
colloq. blow-out	high tea	tea break
breakfast	lunch	tea party
brunch	luncheon	tiffin
buffet	midday meal	TV dinner
cold table	*slang* nosh-up	wedding
cream tea	picnic	breakfast
dinner	*colloq.* slap-up	
dinner party	meal	

---

mealy-mouthed *adj*
hesitant, indirect, mincing, over-squeamish, overdelicate, reticent, plausible, equivocal, flattering, smooth-tongued, euphemistic, prim, glib

mean¹ *v*
1 SIGNIFY, represent, stand for, symbolize, show, designate, convey, express, suggest, indicate, imply, intimate
FORMAL denote, betoken, purport, connote
2 INTEND, aim, propose, design, purpose, plan, aspire, wish, wont, have in mind, think of
3 CAUSE, give rise to, lead to, bring about, produce, involve, entail, result in, necessitate
FORMAL effect
4 *it was meant to happen*
destine, predestine, fate, design, intend, appoint, ordain
5 *your approval means a lot to me*
matter, be important, have influence, carry weight, make a difference

mean² *adj*
1 MISERLY, niggardly, selfish, grasping, close-fisted/handed
FORMAL parsimonious
COLLOQ. tight, tight-fisted, stingy, penny-pinching, mingy
2 UNKIND, unpleasant, nasty, bad-tempered, cruel, disagreeable, unfriendly, cross, spiteful
COLLOQ. beastly, crotchety, crabby, grouchy
3 LOWLY, base, poor, humble, ordinary, common, obscure, wretched, shabby, dirty, miserable, dismal, squalid
4 *she makes a mean rice salad*
excellent, wonderful, brilliant, marvellous, fantastic, first-class/rate, high-quality, very good, prime, superlative, unequalled, unparalleled, matchless, rare, exceptional, outstanding, surpassing, remarkable, perfect, superb, admirable, magnificent, splendid, fine
COLLOQ. top-notch, smashing, stunning, terrific, neat, ace, brill, boffo, out of this world, second to none, divine, heavenly, fabulous, sensational, crack, not half bad
SLANG mega, cool, radical, rad, crucial, way-out
E3 1 generous, liberal **2** kind **3** noble, splendid **4** inferior, second-rate

> **Synonym nuances**
> *sense 1*
> Naturally, the synonyms tend to be disapproving in tone. **Miserly** can be used disapprovingly of someone with an antipathy to spending money, whereas **niggardly** has more to do with undertaking expenditure grudgingly: *niggardly payouts*. **Selfish**, on the other hand, emphasizes self-interest, and therefore a reluctance to give to others, while **grasping** has the negative implication of greed: *the grasping acquisitiveness of an affluent society*. Both **tight-fisted** and the less common **close-fisted** can be used more informally, and sometimes more jocularly, to suggest an unwillingness to spend money: *being tight-fisted, we bypassed the museums with entrance fees.*

mean³ *adj, n*
◆ *adj*
the mean score
average, intermediate, middle, medium, middling, halfway, median, normal
E3 extreme
◆ *n*
average, middle, mid-point, norm, median, mode, compromise, middle course, middle way, medium, happy medium, golden mean
E3 extreme

meander *v*
1 WIND, zigzag, turn, twist, snake, bend, curve; *Scot* wimple
2 WANDER, stray, amble, ramble, stroll, roam, rove, ease, shuffle, inch
COLLOQ. laze, mosey, mooch

meandering *adj*
wandering, winding, twisting, turning, rambling, tortuous, circuitous, snaking, serpentine, sinuous, indirect, roundabout, meandrous
FORMAL convoluted
E3 straight, direct

meaning *n*
1 SIGNIFICANCE, sense, implication, message, expression, gist, drift, substance, essence, thrust, trend, definition, explanation, interpretation
FORMAL import, signification, connotation, explication, elucidation
2 AIM, intention, purpose, plan, goal, object, objective, aspiration, wish, idea
3 VALUE, worth, point, significance, purpose, usefulness
Related adjective: semantic

meaningful *adj*
1 IMPORTANT, significant, relevant, valid, useful, worthwhile, material, purposeful, effective, serious
2 EXPRESSIVE, speaking, suggestive, eloquent, pregnant, warning, pointed, telling
E3 1 unimportant, worthless

meaningfully *adv*
1 SIGNIFICANTLY, effectively, importantly, relevantly, usefully, purposefully
2 EXPRESSIVELY, suggestively, eloquently, pointedly

meaningless *adj*
1 SENSELESS, pointless, purposeless, useless, insignificant, incomprehensible, unintelligible, aimless, motiveless, irrational, futile, insubstantial, trifling, trivial
2 EMPTY, hollow, vacuous, vain, worthless, nonsensical, absurd
E3 1 important, meaningful **2** worthwhile, productive

meaninglessly *adv*
pointlessly, purposelessly, aimlessly, senselessly, uselessly, incomprehensibly, unintelligibly, irrationally, futilely, vainly, in vain, without rhyme or reason

meanly *adv*
1 SELFISHLY, niggardly, graspingly, ungenerously
2 UNKINDLY, unpleasantly, nastily, cruelly, spitefully, contemptibly
3 *a meanly furnished flat*
poorly, commonly, beggarly, shabbily, miserably, scurvily
E3 1 generously **2** kindly **3** splendidly

meanness *n*
mean-spiritedness, miserliness, narrow-mindedness, niggardliness, close-fistedness/handedness, illiberality
FORMAL parsimony, penuriousness
COLLOQ. stinginess, tight-fistedness
E3 generosity, kindness

means *n*
1 METHOD, way, manner, medium, course, agency, process, instrument, avenue, channel, vehicle
FORMAL mode
2 RESOURCES, funds, money, income, wealth, capital, riches, substance, wherewithal, fortune, affluence, assets, property
■ **by all means**
of course, naturally, certainly, surely, with pleasure
■ **by means of**
using, with, through, via, with the help of, with the aid of, as a result of
FORMAL by dint of
■ **by no means**
certainly not, not at all, never, in no way
COLLOQ. no way

meantime, meanwhile *adv*
at the same time, for the time being, for now, for the moment, in the meantime, in the meanwhile, in the interim, in the interval, simultaneously
FORMAL concurrently

measly *adj*
mean, miserable, paltry, meagre, pitiful, scanty, skimpy, petty, poor, puny, trivial, ungenerous, miserly, niggardly, beggarly, contemptible
COLLOQ. stingy, piddling, pathetic, mingy
E3 generous

measurable *adj*
perceptible, significant, quantifiable, noticeable, appreciable, determinable, assessable, computable, gaugeable, fathomable, material, quantitative
FORMAL mensurable
E3 measureless

measure *n, v*
♦ *n*
1 SIZE, quantity, magnitude, amount, degree, extent, range, scope, proportion(s), dimension(s), area, expanse, capacity, height, depth, length, width, weight, volume, mass, bulk
2 RULE, gauge, ruler, scale, level, standard, system, unit(s), criterion, norm, touchstone, yardstick, benchmark, test, meter, barometer, litmus test, acid test
3 STEP, course, action, act, deed, expedient, procedure, proceeding, means, method, act, bill, statute, resolution
4 PORTION, ration, share, piece, part, allocation, quota, division, lot, allotment
COLLOQ. rake-off, cut
♦ *v*
quantify, evaluate, assess, weigh, value, gauge, judge, sound, fathom, read, record, meter, time, determine, calculate, estimate, size (up), be, rate, plumb, survey, compute, measure out, measure off
FORMAL appraise
■ **measure off**
mark out, measure (out), determine, fix, lay down, limit, pace out, delimit, demarcate
FORMAL circumscribe
■ **measure out**
share out, divide, distribute, proportion, dispense, deal out, dole out, allot, apportion, hand out, mete out, parcel out, pour out, issue, assign
■ **measure up**
do, come up to standard, make the grade, pass muster, fit/fill the bill
FORMAL suffice
COLLOQ. come up to scratch, shape up
■ **measure up to**
equal, meet, live up to, come up to, match, match up to, compare with, touch, rival, satisfy, make the grade
Related adjective: mensural
■ **beyond measure**
beyond belief, immensely, infinitely, endlessly, limitlessly, incalculably, inestimably
■ **for good measure**
as well, besides, in addition, furthermore, over and above, as a bonus
■ **get/take the measure of**
get a handle on, evaluate, value, assess, estimate, reckon, calculate, gauge, judge, determine, rate, size up, handle
FORMAL appraise
COLLOQ. get a handle on

measured *adj*
deliberate, planned, reasoned, slow, unhurried, steady, regular, studied, well-thought-out, calculated, careful, considered, premeditated, precise

measureless *adj*
endless, immeasurable, inestimable, incalculable, innumerable, limitless, unbounded, infinite,

boundless, bottomless, immense, vast
▣ measurable

measurement *n*

1 DIMENSION, size, extent, amount, proportion(s), amplitude, unit, magnitude, area, range, expanse, capacity, height, depth, length, width, weight, volume, mass, bulk, quantity
2 ASSESSMENT, evaluation, estimation, computation, calculation, calibration, quantification, sizing, weighing, reading, gauging, judgement, appraisal, appreciation, survey

Units of measurement include:

acre	foot-pound	month
ampere	furlong	nautical mile
angstrom	gallon	newton
atmosphere	gill	ohm
bar	gram (or	ounce
barrel	gramme)	pascal
becquerel	hand	peak
bushel	hectare	pint
cable	hertz	pound
calorie	horsepower	pound per square
candela	hour	inch
centigram (or	hundredweight	radian
centigramme)	inch	rod
centilitre	joule	second
centimetre	kelvin	siemens
century	kilogram (or	span
chain	kilogramme)	square
coulomb	kilolitre	centimetre
cubic centimetre	kilometre	square foot
cubic foot	knot	square inch
cubic inch	league	square kilometre
cubic metre	litre	square metre
cubic yard	lumen	square mile
day	metre	square yard
decade	micrometre	steradian
decibel	mile	stone
degree	millennium	therm
dyne	millibar	ton
erg	milligram (or	tonne
farad	milligramme)	volt
fathom	millilitre	watt
fluid ounce	millimetre	week
fresnel	minute	yard
foot	mole	year

measuring instruments

Measuring instruments include:

altimeter	hygrometer	rule
ammeter	hypsometer	saccharometer
anemometer	manometer	salinometer
audiometer	measuring	seismograph
balance	cylinder	sextant
barometer	meter	speedometer
bathometer	micrometer	spherometer
Breathalyser®	multimeter	sphygmomano-
burette	octant	meter
callipers	optometer	steelyard
calorimeter	pedometer	stopwatch
chronometer	photometer	tachometer
clinometer	pipette	tachymeter
colorimeter	planimeter	tape measure
cyclometer	plumb line	tensiometer
densitometer	protractor	theodolite
galvanometer	psychrometer	thermometer
gauge	pyranometer	vinometer
Geiger counter	pyrometer	voltmeter
gravimeter	quadrant	weighbridge
hourglass	radiosonde	Wheatstone
hydrometer	rheometer	bridge

Gauges include:

cutting gauge	mortise gauge	steam gauge
drill gauge	paper gauge	strain gauge
feeler gauge	pressure gauge	taper gauge
gauge glass	radius gauge	tide gauge
gauge rod	rain gauge	vacuum gauge
gauge wheel	ring gauge	water gauge
marking gauge	snap gauge	

meat *n*

1 FLESH
2 FOOD, rations, provisions, nourishment, sustenance, subsistence, fare, comestibles
FORMAL viands, victuals
COLLOQ. eats, eatables, tuck, scran
SLANG grub, nosh; *Aust & NZ* tucker
3 ESSENCE, substance, fundamentals, heart, kernel, marrow, core, crux, nub, nucleus, pith, point, gist

Meats and meat products include:

bacon	hamburger	pigeon
beef	hare	pig's knuckle
beefburger	heart	pork
black pudding	kidney	quail
brains	lamb	rabbit
brawn	liver	rissole
chicken	mince	sausage
duck	minced beef	steak
faggot	mutton	sweetbread
gammon	offal	tongue
goose	oxtail	tripe
grouse	partridge	trotters
haggis	pâté	turkey
ham	pheasant	venison

Cuts of meat include:

breast	hand	scrag
brisket	hock	shin
chine	knuckle	shoulder
chop	leg	silverside
collar	loin	sirloin
cutlet	neck	spare-rib
escalope	rib	topside
fillet	rump	
flank	saddle	

meaty *adj*

1 FLESHY, hearty, solid, heavy, brawny, beefy, burly, muscular, strapping, sturdy
COLLOQ. hunky
2 SUBSTANTIAL, interesting, significant, meaningful, profound, rich, pithy

mechanic *n*

engineer, repairman, operative, operator, technician, machinist, mechanician, artificer

mechanical *adj*

1 *a mechanical device*
automatic, automated, mechanized, machine-powered, power-driven, electric
2 AUTOMATIC, involuntary, instinctive, routine, machine-like, unthinking, habitual, impersonal, emotionless, unemotional, unconscious, cold, matter-of-fact, unfeeling, perfunctory, lifeless, dead, dull
▣ **2** conscious

mechanically *adv*

1 *mechanically sorted letters*
as/by a machine, automatically, electronically
2 *waved his arm mechanically*
involuntarily, automatically, instinctively, intuitively,

habitually, unconsciously, unthinkingly, routinely, as a matter of routine, on autopilot

E3 2 consciously

mechanism n

1 MACHINE, machinery, engine, appliance, instrument, tool, contraption, motor, works, workings, action, movement, system, gadget, device, apparatus, contrivance, gears, components

COLLOQ. guts

2 MEANS, method, agency, process, procedure, system, technique, medium, channel, structure, workings, operation, functioning, performance

mechanize v

automate, computerize, program

medal n

award, medallion, prize, trophy, decoration, honour, ribbon, reward, gold medal, silver medal, bronze medal, cross, contorno, vernicle

OLD model

SLANG gong

See panel at **honour**.

meddle v

interfere, intervene, pry, intrude, butt in, tamper

COLLOQ. fiddle, poke/stick your nose in, stick/put your oar in, snoop

meddlesome adj

interfering, meddling, prying, snooping, intrusive, intruding, mischievous

COLLOQ. nos(e)y

mediaeval

See **medieval**.

mediate v

arbitrate, conciliate, intervene, referee, umpire, intercede, intermediate, moderate, reconcile, act as mediator/intermediary/peacemaker, negotiate, resolve, settle, step in

OLD stickle

FORMAL interpose

mediation n

arbitration, reconciliation, negotiation, conciliation, intercession, peacemaking, good offices, intervention

FORMAL interposition

mediator n

arbitrator, referee, umpire, intermediary, negotiator, go-between, interceder, judge, arbiter, reconciler, middleman, intervener, moderator, intercessor, conciliator, peacemaker, Ombudsman

medical equipment

See panel on next page

medical specialists

Medical specialists include:

anaesthetist	geriatrician	orthoptist
audiologist	gerontologist	paediatrician
bacteriologist	gynaecologist	pathologist
cardiologist	haematologist	pharmacist
chiropodist	hom(o)eopath	pharmacologist
chiropractor	immunologist	physiotherapist
dentist	microbiologist	psychiatrist
dermatologist	neurologist	psychologist
dietician	obstetrician	radiologist
embryologist	oncologist	rheumatologist
endocrinologist	ophthalmologist	toxicologist
forensic	optician (or	vaccinologist
pathologist	optometrist)	
gastro-	orthodontist	
enterologist	orthopaedist	

See also **doctor**; **nurse**; **surgeon**.

medical terms

See panel on next page

medicinal adj

therapeutic, healing, remedial, health-giving, curative, restorative, medical

medicinally adv

therapeutically, remedially, curatively, restoratively, medically

medicine n

medication, drug, cure, remedy, medicament, prescription, pharmaceutical, panacea

TECHNICAL analeptic

Types of medicine include:

analgesic	eye drops	pessary
antacid	gargle	pill
antibiotic	gripe-water	pastille
anti-histamine	inhaler	sedative
anti-	laxative	steroid
inflammatory	linctus	suppository
antiseptic	lozenge	tablet
arnica	nasal spray	tonic
capsule	ointment	tranquillizer
cough medicine	painkiller	Ventolin®
ear drops	paregoric	
emetic	penicillin	

Forms of alternative medicine include:

acupressure	craniosacral	osteopathy
acupuncture	therapy	reflexology
aromatherapy	herbal medicine	reiki
Ayurveda	hom(o)eopathy	rolfing
Chinese	hypnotherapy	shiatsu
medicine	iridology	
chiropractic	naturopathy	

---

medieval, mediaeval adj

1 *medieval history*

of the Middle Ages, of the Dark Ages, historic, old, archaic

2 OLD-FASHIONED, obsolete, primitive, antiquated, archaic, antique, antediluvian, old-world, outmoded, unenlightened

mediocre adj

ordinary, average, middling, medium, indifferent, unexceptional, undistinguished, commonplace, pedestrian, insignificant, second-rate, passable, adequate, inferior, uninspired, tolerable

COLLOQ. so-so, run-of-the-mill, bog standard, fair to middling, not up to much, not all that it is cracked up to be, nothing much to write home about, no great shakes, not much cop

E3 exceptional, extraordinary, distinctive

mediocrity n

1 ORDINARINESS, unimportance, averageness, unexceptionableness, adequacy, passableness, insignificance, poorness, inferiority, indifference

2 NONENTITY, nobody, nothing

COLLOQ. non-starter, no-hoper, dead loss

E3 1 distinction, exceptionableness

meditate v

reflect, ponder, ruminate, chew, contemplate, muse, brood, think (over), consider, deliberate, mull over, study, concentrate, speculate, scheme, plan, design, intend, have in mind, study

OLD devise

FORMAL cogitate

COLLOQ. put on your thinking cap, chew the cud

meditation n

contemplation, reflection, pondering, musing, thought,

Medical and surgical equipment includes:

aspirator	ECG (electro-cardiograph)	MRI (magnetic resonance imaging) scanner	speculum
audiometer	electro-encephalograph	nebulizer	sphygmomanometer
aural speculum	endoscope	obstetrical forceps	sterile donor-pack
auriscope	first aid kit	oesophagoscope	sterilizer
autoclave	forceps	operating table	stethoscope
body scanner	haemodialysis unit	ophthalmoscope	stomach pump
bronchoscope	hypodermic needle	oxygen cylinder	surgical mask
ca(n)nula	hypodermic syringe	oxygen mask	surgical suture materials
catheter	incubator	rectoscope	swabs
CAT scanner	inhalator	respirator	syringe
clamp	inhaler	resuscitator	thermometer
CT (computed tomography) scanner	instrument table	retractor	tracheostomy tube
curette	iron lung	rhinoscope	traction apparatus
defibrillator	isolator tent	scales	tweezers
dilator	kidney dish	scalpel	ultrasound
disposable enema pack	laparoscope	sliding-weight scales	urethroscope
ear syringe	laryngoscope	specimen glass	vaginal speculum
	microscope		X-ray unit

Medical terms include:

abortion	case history	dissection	inflammation	prosthesis	syndrome
allergy	casualty	doctor	injection	psychosomatic	therapy
amniocentesis	cauterization	donor	injury	quarantine	tourniquet
amputation	cervical smear	dressings	inoculation	radiotherapy	transfusion
assisted conception	check-up	enema	intensive care	recovery	transplant
bandage	chemotherapy	examination	in-vitro fertilization (IVF)	rehabilitation	trauma
barium meal	childbirth	gene	keyhole surgery	relapse	treatment
biopsy	circulation	genetic	labour	remission	tumour
blood bank	circumcision	counselling	laser treatment	respiration	ultrasound scanning
blood count	clinic	health screening	microsurgery	resuscitation	vaccination
blood donor	complication	home visit	miscarriage	scan	vaccine
blood group	compress	hormone replacement therapy (HRT)	mouth-to-mouth	side effect	virus
blood pressure	consultant		nurse	sling	X-ray
blood test	consultation	hospice	operation	smear test	
Caesarean (section)	contraception	hospital	paraplegia	specimen	
cardiopulmonary resuscitation (CPR)	convulsion	immunization	post-mortem	splint	
	cure	implantation	pregnancy	sterilization	
	diagnosis	incubation	prescription	surgery	
	dialysis	infection	prognosis	suture	
	dislocate			symptom	

See also **therapy**.

---

ruminating, rumination, deliberation, brooding, mulling over, speculation, study, reverie, concentration, brown study
FORMAL cerebration, cogitation, excogitation

meditative *adj*
contemplative, deliberative, reflective, thoughtful, studious, museful, pensive, ruminant, ruminative, prayerful
FORMAL cogitative

medium *adj, n*
♦ *adj*
average, middle, median, mean, medial, intermediate, middling, midway, midpoint, standard, fair
♦ *n*
1 AVERAGE, middle, median, mean, mode, intermediate point, midpoint, norm, compromise, centre, middle ground/way, happy medium, golden mean
2 MEANS, means of expression, means of communication, way of expressing, agency, channel, vehicle, instrument, way, form, substance, material, stuff, avenue, organ
FORMAL instrumentality, mode
3 ENVIRONMENT, element, setting, surroundings, atmosphere, conditions, habitat, circumstances, influences, ambience, milieu
4 PSYCHIC, spiritualist, spiritist, clairvoyant, fortune-teller, necromancer

medley *n*
assortment, mixture, mix, miscellany, variety, melange, potpourri, hotchpotch, hodgepodge, helter-skelter, confusion, farrago, salmagundi, smorgasbord, collection, pastiche, patchwork, gallimaufry, jumble, mess, mingle, olio, macaroni, *macédoine*
FORMAL conglomeration
COLLOQ. mixed bag, mishmash, omnium-gatherum

meek *adj*
modest, long-suffering, forbearing, humble, docile, patient, unassuming, quiet, lowly, mild, unpretentious, resigned, gentle, peaceful, tame, timid, submissive, yielding, compliant, deferential, weak, spiritless
COLLOQ. spineless
₣₃ arrogant, assertive, rebellious

meekly *adv*
humbly, mildly, gently, modestly, patiently, quietly, submissively, deferentially, like a lamb to the slaughter
₣₃ arrogantly, assertively, rebelliously

meekness *n*
modesty, long-suffering, forbearance, humility, docility, patience, unpretentiousness, lowliness, mildness, gentleness, humbleness, peacefulness, submission, submissiveness, compliance, deference, tameness, softness, self-abasement, self-disparagement, self-effacement, timidity, spiritlessness, resignation, weakness
FORMAL acquiescence
COLLOQ. spinelessness, wimpishness
₣₃ arrogance, assertiveness, rebelliousness

meet *v, n*
♦ *v*
1 ENCOUNTER, come across, run across, run into, make contact with, join up with, chance on

FORMAL happen upon
COLLOQ. bump into
2 GATHER, get together, collect, come together, muster, assemble, congregate, rally, rendezvous
FORMAL convene, convoke, for(e)gather
3 FULFIL, fill, satisfy, match, answer, come up to, measure up to, equal, comply with, discharge, perform, execute
4 EXPERIENCE, encounter, face, come across, go through, undergo, bear, endure, suffer
5 *meet a challenge*
deal with, manage, handle, tackle, look after, cope with, get to grips with
6 *meet the cost*
pay (for), settle, discharge, honour
7 JOIN, converge, come together, connect, link (up), cross, intersect, touch, unite
FORMAL abut, adjoin
8 *the reports were met with disbelief*
receive, give, greet, get, take, react to, respond to, hear, listen to
E3 2 scatter, disperse **7** diverge, separate
◆ *n*
event, game, match, fixture, competition, contest, round, race, tournament, engagement, meeting

meeting *n*

1 ENCOUNTER, confrontation, rendezvous, appointment, date, engagement, contact, assignation, introduction
FORMAL tryst
2 ASSEMBLY, gathering, session
3 CONVERGENCE, confluence, junction, intersection, union, venue, (point of) contact, interface, watersmeet
FORMAL concourse, abutment, conjunction

Types of meeting include:

AGM (annual general meeting	*formal* convocation	interview
assignation	council	meet
audience	debate	panel
audition	discussion	party
board	EGM	rally
brainstorming	(extraordinary general meeting)	rendezvous
briefing	*Welsh* eisteddfod	reunion
cabinet	*Irish* feis	seminar
committee	forum	service
formal conclave	general meeting	social
conference	*colloq.* get-together	soirée
congregation		summit
congress	*Welsh* gorsedd	symposium
consultation	*NZ* hui	talk-in
convention	inaugural meeting	teleconference
		workshop

See also **committee**.

---

megalomania *n*

overestimation, self-importance, exaggerated sense of power, delusions of grandeur, *folie de grandeur*, conceitedness

melancholy *adj, n*

◆ *adj*
melancholic, depressed, dejected, down, downhearted, downcast, gloomy, glum, low, low-spirited, heavy-hearted, sad, unhappy, despondent, dispirited, miserable, mournful, dismal, sombre, sorrowful, doleful, rueful, moody, hypochondriac, *pensieroso*
OLD adust, allicholy, hipped
FORMAL disconsolate, lugubrious, woeful, woebegone
COLLOQ. blue, down in the dumps, in the doldrums
E3 cheerful, elated, joyful
◆ *n*
depression, dejection, gloom, despondency, low spirits,

sadness, unhappiness, sorrow, misery, pessimism, the black dog
OLD tristesse
COLLOQ. blues, doldrums, dumps
E3 cheerfulness, elation, joy

melange *n*

assortment, mixture, mix, miscellany, variety, potpourri, hotchpotch, hodgepodge, confusion, farrago, salmagundi, smorgasbord, collection, pastiche, patchwork, gallimaufry, jumble
FORMAL conglomeration
COLLOQ. mixed bag, mishmash, omnium-gatherum

mêlée *n*

1 BRAWL, rumpus, scuffle, set-to, fight, tussle, ruckus, ruction, broil, affray, fracas, fray, free-for-all, scrum; *Scot* stramash
2 MUDDLE, confusion, chaos, disorganization, disorder, mess, mix-up, jumble, clutter, tangle

mellifluous *adj*

smooth, sweet-sounding, sweet, soothing, soft, tuneful, harmonious, dulcet, mellow, honeyed, silvery
FORMAL canorous, euphonious
E3 discordant, grating, harsh

mellow *adj, v*

◆ *adj*
1 MATURE, ripe, juicy, soft, tender, full-flavoured, sweet, luscious, mild
2 GENIAL, cordial, affable, pleasant, relaxed, easy-going, good-natured, amiable, amicable, placid, gentle, serene, tranquil, cheerful, happy, jolly, jovial, kind, kind-hearted
3 SMOOTH, melodious, tuneful, harmonious, smooth, rich, rounded, full, soft, sweet, fruity, resonant, pear-shaped, dulcet
FORMAL euphonious
E3 1 unripe **2** cold **3** harsh
◆ *v*
mature, ripen, improve, sweeten, soften, temper, make/become less extreme, season, perfect

melodic *adj*

melodious, tuneful, musical, harmonious, dulcet, sweet, sweet-sounding, silvery
FORMAL euphonious
E3 discordant, grating, harsh

melodically *adv*

melodiously, tunefully, musically, harmoniously, sweetly
E3 discordantly, harshly

melodious *adj*

tuneful, musical, melodic, harmonious, dulcet, sweet, sweet-sounding, silvery
FORMAL euphonious
E3 discordant, grating, harsh

melodrama *n*

histrionics, overacting, theatricality, staginess, dramatics, performance, tragedy, tragicomedy, high drama

melodramatic *adj*

histrionic, theatrical, overdramatic, exaggerated, extravagant, overemotional, sensational, overdone, stag(e)y
COLLOQ. hammy, over-the-top, OTT

melody *n*

1 TUNE, music, song, refrain, harmony, rhythm, theme, air, strain, chant, part, carillon
TECHNICAL counterpoint, canto, cantus, plainsong, aria, augmentation, cabaletta, cantilena, cavatina, melisma, musette
OLD ayre
2 TUNEFULNESS, musicality, musicalness, harmony, harmoniousness, sweetness
FORMAL euphony

melt *v*
1 LIQUEFY, dissolve, thaw, defrost, unfreeze, fuse
FORMAL deliquesce
2 *melt someone's heart*
soften, move, affect, touch, make/become tender,
moderate, calm
F3 1 freeze, solidify **2** harden, inure
■ **melt away**
disappear, vanish, fade (away), evaporate, dissolve,
disperse
FORMAL evanesce
COLLOQ. disappear into thin air

meltdown *n*
failure, defeat, collapse, breakdown, downfall,
miscarriage, disaster, calamity, fiasco, debacle, abortion,
frustration, coming to nothing

member *n*
1 *members of a club*
adherent, associate, subscriber, representative, comrade,
fellow
2 PART, limb, arm, leg, appendage, extremity, organ,
element

membership *n*
1 *membership of a club*
affiliation, adherence, allegiance, participation,
enrolment, fellowship
2 MEMBERS, associates, body, adherents, subscribers,
representatives, comrades, fellows, fellowship

membrane *n*
sheet, film, skin, tissue, layer, veil, partition, diaphragm
TECHNICAL integument, septum, velum, hymen

memento *n*
souvenir, keepsake, remembrance, reminder, token,
memorial, trophy, record, vestige, relic

memo *n*
memorandum, message, note, reminder, aide-mémoire,
e-mail, fax, letter
COLLOQ. memory-jogger

memoir *n*
account, biography, autobiography, essay, journal, life,
monograph, narrative, chronicle, record, register, report

memoirs *n*
reminiscences, recollections, memories, autobiography,
life story, diary, diaries, chronicles, annals, journals,
records, confessions, experiences

memorable *adj*
unforgettable, remarkable, significant, impressive, striking,
notable, noteworthy, historic, extraordinary, important,
consequential, distinguished, distinctive, special,
outstanding, momentous, unique
F3 forgettable, trivial, unimportant

memorandum *n*
message, note, reminder, aide-mémoire, e-mail, fax, letter
COLLOQ. memo, memory-jogger

memorial *n, adj*
♦ *n*
remembrance, monument, statue, stone, plaque,
shrine, cenotaph, mausoleum, record, souvenir,
memento
♦ *adj*
commemorative, celebratory, monumental

memorize *v*
learn, learn by heart, learn by rote, commit to memory,
remember
F3 forget

memory *n*
1 RECALL, powers of recall, retention, recollection,
remembrance, reminiscence

2 COMMEMORATION, remembrance, tribute, honour,
observance, recognition
F3 1 forgetfulness

menace *n, v*
♦ *n*
1 THREAT, intimidation, terrorism, ominousness, threatening
behaviour, terrorizing, tyrannization, bullying,
browbeating, coercion, pressure, warning; *Scot* shore
COLLOQ. screws, frighteners, big stick
2 DANGER, peril, hazard, jeopardy, risk, threat
3 NUISANCE, annoyance, pest, bother, public enemy,
troublemaker
COLLOQ. pain, thorn in your side/flesh
♦ *v*
threaten, frighten, alarm, daunt, dismay, appal, intimidate,
scare, terrorize, terrify, browbeat, coerce, press, pressure,
pressurize, bully, loom, lour; *Scot* shore

menacing *adj*
threatening, intimidating, intimidatory, warning, ominous,
alarming, frightening, dangerous, looming, sinister, grim,
louring, Damoclean
FORMAL impending, portentous, minacious, minatory

mend *v*
1 REPAIR, fix, renovate, restore, renew, refit, patch (up), put
back together, run up, solder, cobble, darn, toe, stick, sew,
cure, heal, make whole, clout, plash, solution; *N Am*
bushel
OLD beet
2 RECOVER, get better, improve, recuperate
3 REMEDY, correct, rectify, reform, revise, amend, improve,
put right, put in order, mend your fences
FORMAL ameliorate, emend
F3 1 break **2** deteriorate **3** destroy
■ **mend your ways**
reform, improve yourself, make a fresh start, turn over a
new leaf, come/get back onto the straight and narrow, see
the error of your ways, wipe the slate clean
■ **on the mend**
convalescing, convalescent, recovering, improving,
recuperating, reviving, healing

mendacious *adj*
untruthful, untrue, false, fictitious, insincere, deceitful,
deceptive, dishonest, lying, perjured, fraudulent
FORMAL fallacious, perfidious, duplicitous
F3 honest, truthful; *formal* veracious

mendacity *n*
untruthfulness, untruth, lie, lying, misrepresentation,
distortion, falsehood, falsification, insincerity, deceit,
deceitfulness, dishonesty, fraudulence, perjury
FORMAL inveracity, duplicity, perfidy
F3 honesty, truthfulness; *formal* veracity

mendicant *adj, n*
♦ *adj*
begging, scrounging
FORMAL petitionary, supplicant
COLLOQ. cadging
♦ *n*
beggar, supplicant, pauper, down-and-out, tramp,
vagabond, vagrant, beachcomber, craver, canter,
besognio; *N Am* hobo, panhandler
OLD whipjack
COLLOQ. bum, cadger, scrounger, sponger, freeloader;
N Am moocher
SLANG blighter, toerag; *Aust & NZ* bludger
OLD SLANG jarkman

menial *adj, n*
♦ *adj*
low, lowly, humble, base, dull, humdrum, routine, boring,
degrading, demeaning, ignominious, unskilled,
subservient, servile, slavish

◆ *n*

servant, domestic, labourer, minion, attendant, drudge, slave, underling
COLLOQ. skivvy, dogsbody

menstruation *n*

period, time of the month, menstrual cycle, monthly flow, courses, flow, menses
TECHNICAL menorrhoea
COLLOQ. monthlies, the usual, the curse
Related adjective: menstrual

mensuration *n*

measurement, measuring, calibration, computation, estimation, calculation, assessment, evaluation, survey, surveying, valuation
TECHNICAL metage

mental *adj*

1 INTELLECTUAL, abstract, unconscious, conceptual, theoretical, rational
FORMAL cognitive, cerebral
2 MAD, insane, lunatic, unbalanced, psychotic, disturbed, deranged, maniacal, out of your mind/senses, of unsound mind, unhinged, crazed, unstable, *non compos mentis*, frenzied, wild, berserk, manic, maniac, distracted, distraught, fey, frenetic, frantic, stone-crazy, queer; *Scot* gyte, red-mad
OLD frantic-mad, lymphatic, bestraught
COLLOQ. crazy, demented, nuts, nutty, nutty as a fruitcake, wacky, mad as a hatter, barmy, bonkers, batty, cracked, crackers, dippy, daffy, dotty, loopy, potty, off your nut/head, wrong in the head, out of your head, off the wall, out to lunch, round the bend/twist, bats, having bats in the belfry, cuckoo, off the rails, screwy, up the wall, raving, not all there; *N Am* buggy, flaky, fruity; *Aust & NZ* dingbats
SLANG loony, bananas, barking, wacko, doolally, off your rocker, off your chump, off your trolley, out of your tree, needing your head examined, having lost your marbles, having a screw loose, having a tile loose, having several cards short of a full deck, with one sandwich short of a picnic, meshuga, ape, apeshit; *N Am* gonzo, loco, wiggy
See Synonym nuances panel at **mad**.
F3 1 physical **2** sane

mentality *n*

1 FRAME OF MIND, mind, way of thinking, (mental) attitude, make-up, character, disposition, personality, psychology, outlook, mindset
2 INTELLECT, intelligence, understanding, mind, comprehension, faculty, rationality
COLLOQ. brains, little grey cells, grey matter

mentally *adv*

intellectually, in the mind, inwardly, psychologically, rationally, temperamentally, subjectively, emotionally

mention *v, n*

◆ *v*

1 SPEAK OF, refer to, say, name, acknowledge, report, make known, impart, introduce, declare, note, notice, communicate, divulge, disclose, broach, cite, reveal, state, quote, specify, instance, particular
OLD bename, remember, hight
FORMAL nominate, condescend upon
2 TOUCH ON, allude to, cite, refer to, speak about briefly, bring up, hint at, intimate, point out, exhume, drag up, cast up

◆ *n*

reference, allusion, hint, citation, observation, recognition, remark, speech, talk, statement, acknowledgement, announcement, notification, notice, tribute, indication
OLD mind

■ **don't mention it**

not at all, don't worry, forget it, it was nothing, it's a pleasure, think nothing of it, *bitte*

■ **not to mention**

not including, to say nothing of, besides, as well as, let alone, not forgetting, much less

mentioned *adj*

quoted, reported, stated, cited
FORMAL above-mentioned, aforementioned, forementioned, forenamed, fore-quoted, foresaid, aforesaid, fore-cited

mentor *n*

teacher, tutor, adviser, counsellor, guru, swami, guide, confidant(e), coach, instructor, pedagogue, therapist

menu *n*

bill of fare, tariff, list, card, *carte du jour*

mercantile *adj*

trade, trading, commercial, merchantable, marketable, sal(e)able

mercenary *adj, n*

◆ *adj*

1 GREEDY, covetous, grasping, acquisitive, money-orientated, materialistic, mammonistic, sordid
FORMAL avaricious
COLLOQ. money-grubbing, on the make
2 HIRED, paid, professional, venal
◆ *n*

soldier of fortune, hired soldier, freelance, free companion, hireling, *condottiere*, galloglass, *landsknecht*, lansquenet
COLLOQ. merc

merchandise *n*

goods, commodities, stock, produce, products, wares, cargo, freight, shipment
FORMAL vendibles

merchandize *v*

1 TRADE, deal in, market, retail, sell, buy and sell, carry, distribute, supply, traffic in, peddle
FORMAL vend
2 PROMOTE, publicize, advertise, market, sell
COLLOQ. push, plug, hype

merchant *n*

trader, dealer, broker, agent, trafficker, wholesaler, distributor, retailer, seller, salesperson, salesman, saleswoman, sales executive, shopkeeper, vendor, factor, jobber, bourgeois, *négociant, bunnia*
OLD (*Shakesp*) marcantant
Related adjective: mercantile

merciful *adj*

compassionate, forgiving, forbearing, humane, lenient, sparing, tender-hearted, soft-hearted, pitying, gracious, humanitarian, kind, liberal, tolerant, sympathetic, generous, mild
F3 hard-hearted, merciless

mercifully *adv*

1 COMPASSIONATELY, graciously, kindly, generously, tender-heartedly, sympathetically, tolerantly
2 THANKFULLY, fortunately, luckily
F3 1 hard-heartedly, mercilessly

merciless *adj*

pitiless, relentless, unmerciful, ruthless, barbarous, hard-hearted, hard, heartless, implacable, inexorable, intolerant, inhumane, unforgiving, remorseless, unpitying, unsympathetic, unfeeling, unsparing, severe, rigid, stern, cruel, callous, harsh, inhuman
F3 compassionate, merciful

mercilessly *adv*

ruthlessly, hard-heartedly, cruelly, severely, sternly, callously, harshly, heartlessly, pitilessly, relentlessly, implacably, inexorably, remorselessly
F3 compassionately, mercifully

mercurial *adj*
volatile, temperamental, unpredictable, unstable, variable, changeable, inconstant, erratic, fickle, impetuous, impulsive, irrepressible, flighty, light-hearted, lively, spirited, sprightly, active, mobile
FORMAL capricious
E3 saturnine

mercy *n*
1 COMPASSION, grace, forgiveness, forbearance, leniency, pity, humaneness, humanitarianism, kindness, tender-heartedness, tenderness, mildness, sympathy, generosity, quarter
OLD loving-kindness, misericord
FORMAL clemency
2 BLESSING, godsend, boon, favour, good luck, stroke of good luck, relief
E3 1 cruelty, harshness
■ **at the mercy of**
in the control of, in the power of, in someone's clutches, defenceless against, unarmed against, exposed to, vulnerable to, unprotected against, at the whim of, prostrate

> **Synonym nuances**
> *sense 1*
> **Compassion** is a fairly strong term for having mercy towards others, whereas **grace** suggests a divine reprieve: *there but for the grace of God go I.*
> **Forbearance** has more to do with patience: *it requires the forbearance of a saint to keep making allowances for others.* **Leniency**, however, is more suggestive of displaying perhaps too much tolerance, while **sympathy** and **pity** would be appopriate synonyms for mercy springing from feeling sorry for someone.
> The term **humaneness** suggests the essential nature of mankind, and so fellow feeling, whereas **humanitarianism** is less abstract in its reference to benevolence to your fellow man: *his humanitarianism led him to work for children's charities abroad.* **Tender-heartedness** and **tenderness** too suggest a condition whereby you are sensitive and easily moved: *an unexpected tenderness towards the misfortunes of others.* **Mildness** is less marked in that it simply suggests gentleness. **Quarter** has narrower implications of clemency granted to an antagonist, and is usually used in the negative: *expect no quarter to be given when the sides meet again.*

mere *adj*
sheer, plain, simple, pure and simple, no more than, bare, utter, pure, absolute, complete, stark, unadulterated, common, paltry, petty

merely *adv*
simply, just, only, purely, nothing but, barely, hardly, scarcely

meretricious *adj*
flashy, flash, showy, ostentatious, flamboyant, glamorous, bold, loud, garish, gaudy, jazzy, pretentious, tawdry, cheap, vulgar, tasteless, kitsch, showing poor taste
COLLOQ. tacky, glitzy
E3 plain, tasteful

merge *v*
join, unite, combine, come/bring together, join forces, team up, converge, amalgamate, blend, coalesce, mix, intermix, mingle, melt into, run into, fuse, meet, meld, be swallowed up in, be assimilated in, become lost in, be engulfed, incorporate, consolidate

merger *n*
amalgamation, union, fusion, combination, coalition, alliance, consolidation, confederation, incorporation, convergence, blend, assimilation

merit *n, v*
♦ *n*
1 GOODNESS, worth, excellence, value, quality, high quality, good, virtue, worthiness
2 STRONG POINT, virtue, asset, credit, advantage, talent, justification, reward, recompense, due, deserts, claim
COLLOQ. plus
E3 1 fault, drawback; *colloq.* minus
♦ *v*
deserve, be worthy of, be worth, earn, justify, have a right to, be entitled to, warrant

merited *adj*
deserved, earned, justified, entitled, fitting, appropriate, warranted, worthy, due, just, rightful
FORMAL condign
E3 inappropriate, unjustified

meritorious *adj*
commendable, deserving, right, righteous, virtuous, excellent, good, honourable, praiseworthy, worthy, estimable, admirable, creditable, exemplary
FORMAL laudable
E3 unworthy

mermaid *n*
sea nymph, water-spirit, water sprite, undine, siren
OLD seamaid

merrily *adv*
happily, jovially, cheerfully, gladly, pleasantly
FORMAL blithely
COLLOQ. chirpily

merriment *n*
fun, jollity, hilarity, laughter, conviviality, high spirits, joyfulness, cheerfulness, gaiety, festivity, amusement, revelry, frolic, liveliness, joviality, buoyancy, carefreeness
FORMAL mirthfulness, mirth, jocundity, blitheness
E3 gloom, seriousness

merry *adj*
1 JOLLY, light-hearted, jovial, joyful, happy, high-spirited, in good spirits, convivial, festive, cheerful, cheery, amusing, carefree, glad
FORMAL mirthful, blithe
COLLOQ. chirpy
2 TIPSY, slightly drunk, happy, tiddly
COLLOQ. squiffy
E3 1 gloomy, melancholy **2** sober
■ **make merry**
have fun, enjoy yourself, celebrate, have a party, sing, dance, drink, carouse

merry-go-round *n*
roundabout, carousel, joy-wheel, whirligig

merrymaking *n*
merriment, celebration, fun, gaiety, jollification, rejoicings, conviviality, festivity, party, carousal, carousing, revel, revelry

mesh *n, v*
♦ *n*
net, network, netting, lattice, latticework, tracery, gauze, trellis, web, tangle, entanglement, snare, trap
♦ *v*
engage, interlock, dovetail, fit together (closely), connect, harmonize, match, co-ordinate, combine, go/come together, entangle, enmesh, inmesh

mesmerize *v*
transfix, hypnotize, magnetize, spellbind, hold spellbound, captivate, enthral, fascinate, grip, entrance, stupefy, benumb

mess *n, v*
♦ *n*
1 CHAOS, untidiness, disorder, disarray, confusion, muddle, jumble, clutter, litter, turmoil, disorganization, mix-up, dirt,

dirtiness, filth, filthiness, squalor
COLLOQ. shambles, hole, dump, tip, dog's breakfast, pig's breakfast, dog's dinner
2 DIFFICULTY, trouble, predicament, plight, dilemma, quandary
COLLOQ. fix, (tight) spot, jam, pickle, hiccup, hole, stew, hot/deep water, pretty pass
3 BOTCH, bungle, muddle, failure
COLLOQ. farce, shambles, hash
SLANG cock-up, balls-up, screw-up
⊟ **1** order, tidiness

▪ **mess about/around**
fool around, play, play around, play about, potter about, fiddle around; *N Am* putter
COLLOQ. muck about, faff about/around
SLANG frig about/around, piss about/around; *N Am* goof about/around; (*taboo*) fuck about/around

▪ **mess about/around with**
interfere with, treat badly, upset, bother, trouble, inconvenience, meddle with, play (about/around) with, fool about/around with, tamper with

▪ **mess up**
1 DISARRANGE, jumble, untidy, clutter up, throw into disorder, disrupt, confuse, muddle, tangle, dishevel, dirty, foul
2 BOTCH, bungle, spoil, ruin, make a mess of
COLLOQ. muck up, bodge, fluff, muff, foul up, make a hash of
SLANG louse up, cock up, screw up
⊟ **1** order, tidy

message *n*
1 COMMUNICATION, bulletin, dispatch, communiqué, report, news, piece of information, word, intimation, errand, task, letter, memorandum, note, notice, fax, cable
FORMAL missive, tidings, epistle
COLLOQ. memo
2 MEANING, idea, sense, significance, point, theme, implication, gist, drift, essence, thrust, moral
FORMAL purport, import

▪ **get the message**
understand, comprehend, take in, follow, see, grasp
COLLOQ. get it, get the point, get the picture, get the idea, get the hang, catch the drift, catch on, latch on, cotton on (to), tumble to, twig

messenger *n*
courier, envoy, go-between, herald, runner, errand-boy, errand-girl, express, carrier, bearer, dispatch, forerunner, agent, ambassador, angel, nuncio, page, commissionaire, footpost, pursuivant, *valet de place*, Mercury, Hermes, chaprassi, internuncio, peon; *Scot* send, corbie messenger, shellycoat
OLD post, beadle; (*Shakesp*) missive; *Scot* caddie, gillie-wetfoot
FORMAL emissary, harbinger

messy *adj*
1 DIRTY, sloppy, slovenly, grubby, filthy
2 DISORGANIZED, untidy, unkempt, dishevelled, disordered, in disarray, chaotic, confused, muddled, cluttered, littered
COLLOQ. shambolic, slobbish
⊟ **1** clean **2** neat, ordered, tidy

metallic *adj*
1 *metallic elements*
copper, iron, tin, lead, nickel, steel, gold, silver, shiny, polished, gleaming
2 *metallic sounds*
harsh, grating, jarring, unpleasant, rough, dissonant, jangling, tinny

metamorphose *v*
change, alter, transform, remake, remodel, reshape, convert, modify, translate

TECHNICAL mutate, transubstantiate
FORMAL transmute, transfigure
COLLOQ. transmogrify

metamorphosis *n*
change, alteration, rebirth, regeneration, transfiguration, conversion, modification, changeover
TECHNICAL mutation
FORMAL transformation, transmutation
COLLOQ. transmogrification

metaphor *n*
figure of speech, allegory, analogy, symbol, emblem, emblematic, visual, picture, image, representation
FORMAL trope

metaphorical *adj*
figurative, allegorical, symbolic, analogical, emblematic, visual, representational
⊟ literal

metaphysical *adj*
philosophical, theoretical, abstract, unreal, essential, fundamental, basic, subjective, spiritual, supernatural, transcendental, unsubstantial, insubstantial, general, immaterial, speculative, intellectual, ideal, high-flown, intangible, deep, profound, universal, eternal
FORMAL abstruse, esoteric, impalpable, incorporeal, recondite

mete *v*
▪ **mete out**
allot, apportion, deal out, dole out, hand out, measure out, share out, ration out, portion, distribute, dispense, divide out, assign, administer

meteor *n*
falling star, meteorite, meteoroid, comet, shooting star, fireball, aerolite, aerolith, bolide

meteoric *adj*
rapid, speedy, swift, quick, fast, sudden, lightning, overnight, instantaneous, momentary, brief, transient, spectacular, brilliant, dazzling, flashing

meteorologist *n*
weather forecaster, climatologist, weatherman, weathergirl, weatherlady, met man, weather prophet

method *n*
1 WAY, approach, means, course, manner, fashion, form, process, procedure, system, practice, route, technique, style, plan, arrangement, scheme, rule, programme, modus operandi
FORMAL mode
2 ORGANIZATION, order, structure, system, pattern, arrangement, form, design, plan, planning, regularity, orderliness, routine

methodical *adj*
systematic, structured, organized, ordered, orderly, well-ordered, logical, tidy, regular, planned, efficient, formal, disciplined, businesslike, deliberate, neat, scrupulous, precise, meticulous, painstaking
⊟ chaotic, irregular, confused

methodically *adv*
systematically, logically, tidily, uniformly, regularly, efficiently, formally, as planned, tidily, in place, neatly, scrupulously, precisely, meticulously, painstakingly, by the book, according to the rules, to the rule
⊟ chaotically, irregularly

meticulous *adj*
precise, scrupulous, careful, conscientious, rigorous, exact, punctilious, fussy, particular, detailed, accurate, thorough, fastidious, painstaking, strict
⊟ careless, slapdash

meticulously *adv*
accurately, thoroughly, precisely, exactly, carefully,

scrupulously, painstakingly, conscientiously, rigorously,
punctiliously, strictly
☒ chaotically

métier *n*
calling, vocation, line, line of business, business, job,
occupation, profession, sphere, field, forte, trade, pursuit,
speciality, craft; *N Am* specialty

metropolis *n*
capital city, main city, large city, municipality, megalopolis,
cosmopolis, industrial/cultural centre

mettle *n*
1 CHARACTER, temperament, disposition, nature, calibre,
personality, personal qualities, make-up
2 SPIRIT, courage, bravery, vigour, nerve, boldness, daring,
intrepidity, indomitability, fearlessness, pluck, nerve, resolve,
determination, endurance, valour, gallantry, fortitude
COLLOQ. guts, backbone, spunk

mettlesome *adj*
high-spirited, spirited, bold, daring, intrepid, brave,
courageous, fearless, resolute, unflinching, gallant, plucky,
valiant, lion-hearted, stout-hearted
COLLOQ. spunky
☒ cowardly, afraid, fearful

mew *v*
miaow, meow, mewl, caterwaul, whine

mewl *v*
whine, whimper, whinge, cry, blubber, grizzle, snivel

miasma *n*
odour, smell, stench, stink, pollution, reek
FORMAL fetor, effluvium, mephitis

miasmal *adj*
foul, foul-smelling, noxious, putrid, reeking, smelly,
stinking, polluted, unwholesome
FORMAL f(o)etid, malodorous, noisome, mephitic,
miasm(at)ic, miasm(at)ous

miaow *v*
mew, meow, mewl, caterwaul, whine

microbe *n*
micro-organism, bacterium, bacillus, germ, virus,
pathogen
COLLOQ. bug

microscopic *adj*
minute, tiny, extremely small, minuscule, infinitesimal,
indiscernible, imperceptible, negligible
☒ huge, enormous

microscopically *adv*
minutely, extremely, infinitesimally, imperceptibly
☒ hugely, gigantically

midday *n*
noon, twelve, twelve o'clock, twelve noon, lunchtime
FORMAL noonday, noontide
Related adjective: meridian

middle *adj, n*
  ♦ *adj*
central, mid, midway, halfway, mean, medium, medial,
median, equidistant, intermediate, inner, inside,
intervening
  ♦ *n*
1 CENTRE, halfway point, midpoint, mean, median, heart,
core, midst, inside
COLLOQ. bull's eye
2 MIDRIFF, waist, stomach, belly, paunch
COLLOQ. tummy
SLANG bread basket
☒ extreme, end, edge, beginning, border
▪ **in the middle of**
busy with, during, engaged in, in the process of, occupied
with, surrounded by, while, in the midst of, among

middle-class *adj*
conventional, suburban, professional, white-collar,
gentrified, bourgeois

middleman *n*
intermediary, go-between, negotiator, entrepreneur,
distributor, retailer, broker, fixer

middling *adj*
mediocre, medium, ordinary, moderate, average, fair,
unexceptional, unremarkable, run-of-the-mill, indifferent,
modest, adequate, passable, tolerable
COLLOQ. so-so, OK, fair to middling, not up to much, no
great shakes, not much cop, nothing much to write home
about

midpoint *n*
middle point, central point, halfway point

midget *n, adj*
  ♦ *n*
person of restricted growth, small person, pygmy, dwarf,
Lilliputian, Tom Thumb, gnome, man(n)ikin, homunculus
☒ giant
  ♦ *adj*
tiny, small, minute, diminutive, dwarf, miniature, little, baby,
pocket, pocket-sized, toy, pygmy, Lilliputian
COLLOQ. teeny, itsy-bitsy, teeny-weeny
☒ giant

midst *n*
middle, centre, midpoint, heart, core, bosom, nucleus,
hub, depths, thick, interior
▪ **in the midst**
during, in the middle/thick of, among, surrounded by

midway *adv*
halfway, in the middle, at the midpoint, in the centre,
equidistant between, betwixt and between

mien *n*
appearance, look, manner, aspect, expression, air,
complexion, presence, semblance, aura
FORMAL bearing, carriage, countenance, demeanour,
deportment

miffed *adj*
annoyed, irritated, displeased, aggrieved, nettled, hurt,
offended, put out, resentful, upset, vexed, irked,
disgruntled, chagrined, piqued
COLLOQ. in a huff, peeved
SLANG cheesed off, narked
☒ delighted, pleased; *colloq.* chuffed

might *n*
power, strength, force, forcefulness, energy, powerfulness,
ability, capability, capacity, sway, vigour, stamina, heftiness,
muscularity, potency, valour, prowess
FORMAL efficacy, puissance
COLLOQ. clout, muscle

mightily *adv*
exceedingly, very, very much, much, extremely, greatly,
highly, hugely, decidedly, intensely, powerfully, strongly,
vigorously, energetically, forcefully, lustily, manfully,
strenuously

mighty *adj, adv*
  ♦ *adj*
1 STRONG, powerful, almighty, potent, forceful, vigorous,
hefty, robust, tough, stalwart, stout, strapping, muscular,
dominant, influential, doughty, grand, hardy, indomitable,
lusty, manful
OLD puissant; (*Shakesp*) mightful
2 LARGE, enormous, colossal, huge, immense, vast,
massive, gigantic, great, tremendous, towering, titanic,
stupendous, monumental, bulky, prodigious; *Scot* fell
OLD *Scot* felon
☒ **1** frail, weak **2** small
  ♦ *adv*

extremely, very, really, exceedingly, excessively,
exceptionally, extraordinarily, intensely, thoroughly,
remarkably, utterly, greatly, highly, unusually, unreasonably
COLLOQ. awfully, terribly, dreadfully, frightfully, terrifically

migrant n, adj
+ n
traveller, wanderer, itinerant, emigrant, immigrant,
Gastarbeiter, transmigrant, rover, nomad, transient,
globetrotter, drifter, Gypsy, tinker, vagrant
+ adj
travelling, wandering, peripatetic, itinerant, immigrant,
roving, nomadic, shifting, transient, globetrotting, drifting,
Gypsy, migratory, vagrant

migrate v
move, resettle, relocate, wander, roam, rove, journey,
emigrate, travel, voyage, hike, trek, drift

migration n
movement, travel, journey, voyage, wandering, roving,
emigration, shift, trek
TECHNICAL diaspora
FORMAL transhumance

migratory adj
travelling, wandering, peripatetic, itinerant, immigrant,
roving, nomadic, shifting, transient, globetrotting, drifting,
Gypsy, migrant, vagrant

mild adj
1 *a mild form of the disease*
slight, faint, feeble, weak, gentle, modest, subtle, vague,
imperceptible
2 *mild manners*
gentle, calm, peaceable, placid, tender, tender-hearted,
sensitive, soft, soft-hearted, good-natured, easy-going,
kind, sympathetic, warm, warm-hearted, meek, amiable,
lenient, humane, compassionate, merciful, forbearing
3 *mild weather*
calm, temperate, warm, balmy, clement, fair, moderate,
pleasant
4 *mild food*
bland, mellow, smooth, subtle, soothing, tasteless,
flavourless, insipid
Ⓔ **1** strong, severe, extreme **2** harsh, aggressive, fierce **3**
cold, stormy **4** strong, sharp, spicy

mildewy adj
rotten, fusty, musty
FORMAL f(o)etid, mucedinous, mucid

mildly adv
1 SLIGHTLY, faintly, weakly, vaguely, gently, subtly,
imperceptibly
2 GENTLY, calmly, tenderly, sensitively, softly, warmly,
meekly, compassionately, mercifully
Ⓔ **1** strongly, severely, extremely **2** harshly, aggressively,
fiercely

mildness n
1 GENTLENESS, calmness, placidity, tenderness, softness,
docility, kindness, sympathy, warmth, meekness,
indulgence, leniency, lenity, compassion, mercy,
forbearance, tranquillity, passivity
2 TEMPERATENESS, calmness, warmth, clemency,
moderation
3 BLANDNESS, mellowness, smoothness, tastelessness,
insipidness
Ⓔ **1** harshness, aggressiveness, violence **2** storminess,
chilliness **3** sharpness, spiciness

milieu n
environment, location, scene, setting, surroundings,
background, locale, medium, arena, element, sphere

militancy n
aggressiveness, belligerence, extremism, assertiveness,
activism, vigorousness

militant adj, n
+ adj
aggressive, belligerent, vigorous, fighting, combative,
embattled, warring, assertive, activist
FORMAL pugnacious
Ⓔ pacifist, peaceful
+ n
activist, combatant, fighter, struggler, soldier, warrior,
aggressor, belligerent, partisan

militantly adv
aggressively, belligerently, vigorously, assertively

military adj, n
+ adj
martial, armed, army, soldierly, warlike, service,
disciplined
+ n
army, armed forces, soldiers, forces, services, militia, air
force, navy
See panel on next page

militate v
▪ **militate against**
oppose, discourage, counter, counteract, go/count
against, act/tell against, work against, weigh against, be
detrimental/harmful/disadvantageous to, damage, hurt,
prejudice, be a decisive factor against, contend, resist
▪ **militate for**
help, promote, speak for, back, further, advance, aid

militia n
reserve, reservists, Territorial Army, yeomanry, National
Guard, home guard, minutemen
OLD fencibles, trainband

milk v
1 DRAIN, bleed, tap, extract, draw (off), exploit, use,
express, press, pump, siphon, squeeze, wring
2 EXPLOIT, use, squeeze, wring, pump, take advantage of,
oppress, impose on, manipulate
COLLOQ. bleed
SLANG screw, rip off

milksop n
coward, weakling, namby-pamby, pansy, cissy
COLLOQ. wimp, mummy's boy; *Scot* jessie
SLANG wuss

milky adj
white, milk-white, snow-white, chalky, opaque, clouded,
cloudy

mill n, v
+ n
1 FACTORY, plant, processing plant, works, workshop, shop,
foundry
2 GRINDER, crusher, quern, roller
+ v
grind, pulverize, powder, pound, crush, crunch, roll, press,
grate
FORMAL comminute
▪ **mill around**
move about, crowd around, throng, swarm, stream, press
around

millstone n
1 GRINDSTONE, quernstone
2 BURDEN, load, encumbrance, weight, dead-weight,
obligation, duty, onus, trouble, affliction
COLLOQ. cross to bear

mime n, v
+ n
dumb show, pantomime, gesture, mimicry, mummery,
charade
+ v
gesture, signal, indicate, act out, represent, simulate,
impersonate, mimic, imitate

Military terms include:

about turn
absent without
leave (AWOL)
action
action stations
adjutant
aide-de-camp
(ADC)
Airborne
Warning and
Control System
(AWACS)
air cover
air-drop
air force
allies
ambush
arm
armed forces
armistice
army
arsenal
artillery
assault course
atomic warfare
attack
attention
barracks
base
battle
battle fatigue
beachhead
billet
biological
warfare
bivouac
blockade
bomb

bombardment
brevet
bridgehead
briefing
brigade
bugle call
call up
camouflage
camp
campaign
canteen
ceasefire
charge
chemical warfare
citation
close ranks
collateral damage
colours
combat
command
commission
company
conquest
conscript
conscription
corps
counter-attack
court-martial
crossfire
debriefing
decamp
decoration
defeat
defence
demilitarize
colloq. demob
demobilize
demotion

depot
desertion
detachment
detail
disarmament
discharge
dispatches
division
draft
drill
duty
encampment
enemy
enlist
ensign
epaulette
evacuation
excursion
expedition
fall out
fatigues
firing line
first post
flank
fleet
flight
flotilla
foe
foray
forced march
friendly fire
front line
fusillade
garrison
guard
incursion
infantry
insignia

inspection
installation
insubordination
intelligence
invasion
kit bag
landing
last post
latrine
leave
left wheel
liaison
lines
logistics
manoeuvres
march
marching orders
march past
married quarters
martinet
mess
minefield
mission
mission creep
mobilize
munitions
muster
mutiny
national service
navy
Navy, Army and
Air Force
Institutes
(NAAFI)
nuclear warfare
observation post
offensive

operational
command
operational fleet
operations
orders
ordnance
outpost
padre
parade
parade ground
parley
parole
patrol
pincer movement
platoon
posting
prisoner of war
(POW)
quartermaster
quarters
quick march
radar
range
rank
ration
rearguard
colloq. recce
reconnaissance
recruit
regiment
reinforcements
requisition
retreat
reveille
rifle range
roll-call
rout
route march

salute
sentry
shell
shell-shock
signal
skirmish
slow march
sniper
sortie
squad
squadron
slang square-
bashing
standard
stores
strategy
supplies
surrender
tactics
tank
target
task force
tattoo
the front
training
trench
trench warfare
troop
truce
unit
van
vanguard
victory
white flag
wing

See also **armed services; rank; sailor; soldier.**

---

mimic *v, n*

♦ *v*

imitate, parody, caricature, copy, ape, monkey, parrot, impersonate, echo, mirror, resemble, simulate, mime, mock, play, look like
FORMAL emulate, personate
COLLOQ. take off, send up

♦ *n*

imitator, impersonator, impressionist, mimicker, caricaturist, parrot, ape, mime, starling, copy, copyist
COLLOQ. copycat

mimicry *n*

imitation, imitating, impersonation, copying, parody, mockery, simulation, impression, caricature, aping, burlesque
TECHNICAL mimesis
COLLOQ. take-off

minatory *adj*

threatening, menacing, intimidatory, warning, cautionary, ominous, foreboding, sinister, grim, looming
FORMAL inauspicious, impending, minacious

mince *v*

1 CHOP, cut, cut into very small pieces, hash, dice, grind, crumble
2 WALK AFFECTEDLY, attitudinize, pose, strike a pose, posture, ponce, simper, walk in an effeminate/a dainty way, prance

■ **not mince your words**
talk plainly, speak directly, not hold anything back
COLLOQ. call a spade a spade, not beat about the bush, not pull any punches

mincing *adj*

dainty, effeminate, nice, precious, foppish, pretentious,

minikin, niminy-piminy, coxcombic(al)
FORMAL affected
COLLOQ. la-di-da, poncy, cissy

mind *n, v*

♦ *n*

1 INTELLIGENCE, intellect, reason, powers of reasoning, judgement, sense, understanding, comprehension, wits, mentality, thinking, thoughts, subconscious, head, genius, concentration, application, attention, spirit, psyche
FORMAL ratiocination
COLLOQ. brains, brainbox, grey matter, little grey cells
Related adjective: mental
2 MEMORY, remembrance, recollection, recall, retention
3 OPINION, view, viewpoint, point of view, way of thinking, belief, attitude, judgement, outlook, feeling, sentiment
4 INCLINATION, disposition, tendency, will, wish, intention, desire, fancy, urge, notion
5 THINKER, intellect, intellectual, genius, academic, mastermind, scholar, expert
COLLOQ. egghead, brain, brainbox

■ **be in two minds**
be uncertain, hesitate, be hesitant, be unsure, be undecided, waver, vacillate, dither
COLLOQ. shilly-shally, dilly-dally, sit on the fence

■ **bear/keep in mind**
consider, remember, note, take note of, make a mental note of, take into account/consideration, give thought to

■ **cross your mind**
think of, remember, occur to, come to, strike, hit

■ **have in mind**
plan, design, aim, think of, contemplate, want, intend

■ **make up your mind**

decide, come to/arrive at a decision, reach/make a decision, choose, determine, settle, resolve

■ **mind's eye**

imagination, mind, head, contemplation, memory, recollection, remembrance

■ **out of your mind**

mad, insane, lunatic, unbalanced, psychotic, deranged, maniacal, demented, out of your senses, of unsound mind, unhinged, crazed, unstable, *non compos mentis*, frenzied, manic, maniac, distracted, distraught

COLLOQ. crazy, nuts, nutty, nutty as a fruitcake, barmy, bonkers, batty, crackers, dippy, daffy, loopy, off your head, wrong in the head, off the wall, round the bend, round the twist, having bats in the belfry, mad as a hatter, barking mad, cuckoo, flipped, off the rails, screwy, up the wall, potty, raving, not all there

SLANG bananas, loony, off your rocker, off your chump, off your trolley, needing your head examined, having lost your marbles, having a screw loose, having a tile loose, mental, doolally

See Synonym nuances panel at **mad**.

■ **put you in mind of**

remind, prompt, bring to mind, call to mind, make you think of

■ **put your mind to**

concentrate on, persevere, exert yourself, rise to the occasion, take pains, buckle down

■ **speak your mind**

talk plainly, not mince your words, give it to someone straight

COLLOQ. tell it like it is, call a spade a spade

■ **to my mind**

in my opinion, in my view, personally, personally speaking, according to what I think, I think/believe, as I see it

♦ *v*

1 OBJECT (TO), take offence (at), be offended by, be bothered by, be annoyed by, be troubled by, care about, resent, disapprove, dislike

2 *mind the traffic*

watch, watch out, be careful, heed, pay attention, pay heed to, regard, note, obey, respect, listen to, concentrate on, comply with, follow, mark, observe, watch

3 MAKE SURE, ensure, make certain, take care, remember, not forget, note

4 LOOK AFTER, take care of, watch over, keep an eye on, guard, have charge of, attend to

■ **mind out**

be careful, take care, look out, watch out, watch, pay attention, beware, be on your guard, keep your eyes open

■ **never mind**

1 TAKE NO NOTICE OF, not bother about, don't worry, forget it

2 LET ALONE, not to mention, not forgetting, apart from, also, as well as, too

---

Synonym nuances

noun sense 1

Intelligence may be used straightforwardly of mental skill or knowledge: *I didn't have the intelligence to become a doctor*, while **intellect** implies a person's capacity for developed thought: *his was a heavyweight intellect with a lightweight judgement*. **Reason**, although similar, is more appropriate for processing thought to draw conclusions, whereas **judgement** has more to do with assessment and discernment. **Wits**, however, is suggestive of alertness and ingenuity: *you need your wits about you in this place.*

  Subconscious puts the emphasis on innate mental influences rather than formulated thought, while **head** suggests the overall concept of the brain: *for goodness' sake, use your head*; *a good head for figures*. **Genius** is a highly approbatory term reserved for a unique inborn ability. **Concentration** and **attention** would be

---

appropriate where the mind is focused on something, while **application** implies a level of diligence.

  To suggest the essential nature of a person, you can use **spirit**, whereas **mentality** or **psyche** might be used of their mental make-up or a particular, set way of thinking: *this country is entrenched in a litigation mentality*; *staking a claim to a piece of land is deeply rooted in the American psyche.*

---

mind-boggling *adj*

incredible, unbelievable, impossible, inconceivable, unthinkable, unimaginable, extraordinary, amazing, surprising, astonishing, astounding, formidable, exceptional

mindful *adj*

aware, conscious, alive (to), alert, attentive, paying attention to, careful, watchful, wary, chary, heedful

FORMAL cognizant, sensible

E3 heedless, inattentive

mindless *adj*

1 THOUGHTLESS, senseless, illogical, irrational, stupid, foolish, witless, dull, unintelligent, gratuitous, negligent

COLLOQ. dumb, dopey, thick, birdbrained

2 MECHANICAL, automatic, robotic, tedious, routine, involuntary, instinctive

COLLOQ. knee-jerk

E3 **1** thoughtful, intelligent

mindlessly *adv*

1 THOUGHTLESSLY, senselessly, foolishly, stupidly, irrationally, illogically

2 MECHANICALLY, automatically, routinely, involuntarily, instinctively

E3 **1** thoughtfully

mine *n, v*

♦ *n*

1 PIT, colliery, coalfield, excavation, quarry, well, vein, lode, seam, shaft, trench, deposit

2 SUPPLY, source, stock, store, storehouse, reserve, reservoir, quarry, fund, repository, hoard, treasury, wealth

3 LANDMINE, explosive, depth charge, bomb

♦ *v*

excavate, dig for, dig up, delve, quarry, extract, search, unearth, tunnel, remove, undermine

---

Parts of a mine include:

air lock	hydraulic pit prop	shaft
bord-and-pillar	jib coal-cutter	shearer loader
bunker	lateral	skip winding
cage	long-wall	system
cage-winding	long-wall face	spoil
system	main shaft	staple shaft
capping	overburden	sump/sink
charging	pan	tunnelling
conveyor	pithead frame	machine
coal-bearing rock	pithead gear	ventilation shaft
coal-cutter	pit prop	winding engine
coal seam	plough coal-	
fan drift	cutter	
fault line	powered support	
gallery	retreat long-wall	
goaf/gob/waste	scraper chain	

---

miner *n*

coalminer, mineworker, collier, pitman, digger, faceman, faceworker, tributer; *Aust* hatter

mineral

See panel on next page

mingle *v*

1 MIX, intermingle, intermix, combine, blend, merge, unite,

Minerals include:

alabaster	calamine	fluorite	idocrase	microcline	silica
albite	calcite	fluorspar	jacinth	montmorillonite	smithsonite
anhydrite	calcspar	fool's gold	jargoon	olivine	sodalite
asbestos	cassiterite	French chalk	jet	orthoclase	spar
aventurine	chalcedony	galena	kandite	peridot	sphalerite
azurite	chlorite	graphite	kaolinite	plumbago	spinel
bentonite	chrysoberyl	gypsum	lapis lazuli	pyrites	talc
blacklead	cinnabar	haematite	lazurite	quartz	uralite
bloodstone	corundum	halite	magnetite	rock salt	uranite
blue john	dolomite	haüyne	malachite	rutile	vesuvianite
borax	emery	hornblende	meerschaum	saltpetre	wurtzite
cairngorm	feldspar	hyacinth	mica	sanidine	zircon

alloy, fuse, amalgamate, coalesce, join, compound
2 ASSOCIATE, socialize, circulate
FORMAL commingle
COLLOQ. hobnob, rub shoulders

mingy *adj*
1 NIGGARDLY, mean, miserly, close, ungenerous, ungiving, sparing, grudging, hard-fisted, close-fisted/handed
FORMAL parsimonious
COLLOQ. stingy, tight-fisted, cheese-paring
2 *a mingy amount*
paltry, meagre, pitiful, miserable, scanty, skimpy, poor, puny, trivial
COLLOQ. measly, piddling, pathetic
E3 1 generous, liberal **2** great, large

miniature *adj*
tiny, small, small-scale, scaled-down, minute, reduced, diminutive, midget, toy, dwarf, baby, pocket-sized, little, cameo, microcosmic; *Scot* wee
COLLOQ. pint-size(d), mini, young
E3 giant

minimal *adj*
least, smallest, minimum, slightest, littlest, negligible, minute, token, nominal

minimize *v*
1 REDUCE, decrease, diminish, cut, curtail, shrink
COLLOQ. slash
2 BELITTLE, make light of, make little of, deprecate, discount, play down, underestimate, underrate, trivialize, laugh off
FORMAL disparage, decry
COLLOQ. soft-pedal
E3 1 maximize **2** emphasize, play up

minimum *n, adj*
♦ *n*
least, lowest, lowest point, nadir, lowest number, smallest quantity, slightest, bottom
E3 maximum
♦ *adj*
minimal, least, lowest, slightest, smallest, littlest, tiniest
E3 maximum

minion *n*
1 ATTENDANT, follower, underling, lackey, flunkey, henchman/woman/person, hireling, servant, menial, drudge
2 DEPENDANT, hanger-on, favourite, darling, sycophant, fawner, parasite, leech
COLLOQ. yes-man, bootlicker

minister *n, v*
♦ *n*
1 OFFICIAL, office-holder, politician, dignitary, diplomat, ambassador, delegate, legate, envoy, emissary, representative, consul, leader, cabinet minister, chancellor, agent, aide, administrator, executive, department secretary
2 CLERGYMAN/woman, churchman, cleric, parson, priest, dean, pastor, vicar, rector, verger, curate, deacon, elder, chaplain, preacher, divine, padre

FORMAL ecclesiastic
♦ *v*
attend, serve, tend, take care of, look after, administer, wait on, cater to, accommodate, nurse
Related adjective: ministerial

ministration *n*
help, aid, assistance, care, service, relief, supervision, backing, support, favour, patronage
FORMAL succour

ministry *n*
1 GOVERNMENT, cabinet, department, office, bureau, administration
2 THE CHURCH, holy orders, the priesthood, the clergy, the cloth
Related adjective: ministerial

minor *adj, n*
♦ *adj*
lesser, secondary, small, smaller, inferior, subordinate, subsidiary, junior, younger, unimportant, insignificant, inconsiderable, unknown, little known, negligible, petty, trivial, trifling, second-class, unclassified, slight, light
E3 major, significant, important
♦ *n*
child, boy, girl, son, daughter, youngster, young person, juvenile, infant, junior, little one, young one, baby, toddler
COLLOQ. tot, tiny tot, kid, nipper

minstrel *n*
singer, musician, troubadour, bard, rhymer, joculator, jongleur

mint *v, adj, n*
♦ *v*
1 COIN, stamp, strike, cast, forge, punch, make, manufacture, produce, construct, devise, fashion
2 INVENT, make up, coin, fabricate, forge, falsify, fake, trump up, concoct, hatch
♦ *adj*
perfect, brand-new, new, as new, mint-new, fresh, immaculate, undamaged, unblemished, unused, excellent, first-class
♦ *n*
fortune, wealth, riches
COLLOQ. pile, packet, bomb, bundle, heap, stack, million(s), billion(s), king's ransom
SLANG megabucks, loadsamoney

minus *prep*
less, without, short of, excluding, except, with the exception of, excepting, save, bar

minuscule *adj*
tiny, fine, little, very small, minute, miniature, microscopic, infinitesimal, diminutive, Lilliputian
COLLOQ. teeny, teeny-weeny, itsy-bitsy
E3 gigantic, huge

minute[1] *n*
1 *ten minutes*
moment, second, instant, short (length of) time, flash

COLLOQ. jiffy, tick, sec, mo

2 the minute something happens
the moment, immediately, the instant, the point, directly, no sooner, as soon as

■ **in a minute**
soon, very soon, shortly, in a moment, in a flash, before long, in the near future
COLLOQ. pronto, in a jiffy/tick, in two shakes of a lamb's tail, before you can say Jack Robinson

■ **this minute**
this instant, immediately, now, then, straight away, right away, right now, at once, next, there and then, instantly, instantaneously, directly, speedily, quickly, without delay, no sooner… than, as soon as, promptly, unhesitatingly, without hesitation, without question, without further/ more ado
FORMAL forthwith
COLLOQ. pronto, yesterday, before you know it, before you can say Jack Robinson, in two shakes of a lamb's tail, like a shot

■ **up to the minute**
latest, most modern, newest, most recent, fashionable
COLLOQ. with it, in, all the rage, now

minute² adj
1 TINY, very small, infinitesimal, minuscule, microscopic, diminutive, miniature, inconsiderable, insignificant, infinitesimal, negligible, slight, trifling, trivial, Lilliputian
2 DETAILED, precise, accurate, exact, meticulous, painstaking, close, strict, critical, exhaustive, punctilious
E3 1 gigantic, huge **2** cursory, superficial

minutely adv
closely, in detail, meticulously, painstakingly, scrupulously, systematically, precisely, exactly, exhaustively, critically
COLLOQ. with a fine-tooth comb

minutes n
proceedings, record(s), notes, memorandum, transcript, transactions, details, tapes

minutiae n
details, fine details, finer points, intricacies, complexities, particulars, niceties, subtleties, trifles, trivialities
COLLOQ. small print

miracle n
wonder, marvel, sign, prodigy, phenomenon
Related adjective: miraculous

miraculous adj
1 WONDERFUL, marvellous, phenomenal, extraordinary, remarkable, incredible, amazing, surprising, astounding, astonishing, unbelievable, unexpected
2 SUPERNATURAL, inexplicable, unaccountable, phenomenal, unnatural, extraordinary, remarkable, unbelievable, superhuman, monstrous
E3 2 natural, normal

miraculously adv
1 WONDERFULLY, remarkably, incredibly, amazingly, surprisingly, unbelievably, unexpectedly
2 SUPERNATURALLY, extraordinarily, remarkably, superhumanly, inexplicably, unaccountably
E3 2 naturally, normally

mirage n
illusion, optical illusion, hallucination, loom, fantasy, phantasm, phantasmagoria
TECHNICAL fata Morgana

mire n, v
♦ n
1 QUAGMIRE, quag, marsh, marshland, morass, bog, fen, swamp, slough; Scot glaur
2 MUCK, mud, dirt, slime, ooze
3 DIFFICULTIES, trouble, mess
COLLOQ. spot, jam, pickle, fix, hole, stew

♦ v
sink, bog down, overwhelm, deluge

mirror n, v
♦ n
1 GLASS, looking-glass, reflector, driving-mirror, rear-view mirror, wing mirror, hand-glass, pier-glass, cheval-glass; dialect keeking-glass
TECHNICAL condenser, laryngoscope, siderostat, Claude Lorraine glass
OLD (Shakesp) stone
FORMAL speculum
2 REFLECTION, likeness, exact likeness, image, double, twin, copy, clone
COLLOQ. dead ringer, spitting image
♦ v
reflect, echo, imitate, copy, follow, represent, show, depict, mimic, parrot, ape, image
FORMAL emulate
Related adjective: specular

mirth n
merriment, hilarity, gaiety, fun, laughter, enjoyment, pleasure, jollity, jocularity, amusement, frolics, revelry, glee, cheerfulness, light-heartedness, high spirits, buoyancy
FORMAL blitheness
E3 gloom, melancholy

mirthful adj
merry, hilarious, laughing, laughable, uproarious, pleasurable, jolly, jovial, amusing, funny, amused, happy, gay, cheerful, cheery, glad, gladsome, light-hearted, light-spirited, vivacious, buoyant, playful, ludic, sportive, frolicsome, festive
FORMAL blithe, jocund
E3 gloomy, glum, melancholy, mirthless

mirthless adj
glum, gloomy, unhappy, humourless, unamused, sad, miserable, depressed, despondent, moody, dejected, morose, pessimistic, doleful, crestfallen, sour, sulky, sullen, surly, grumpy, gruff, ill-humoured, churlish
E3 happy, cheerful

miry adj
marshy, swampy, boggy, fenny, muddy, mucky, dirty, oozy, slimy; Scot glaury

misadventure n
bad luck, hard luck, accident, ill fortune, ill luck, misfortune, mischance, calamity, catastrophe, tragedy, mishap, disaster, failure, problem, debacle, cataclysm, reverse, setback

misanthrope n
solitary, loner, recluse, hermit, unsocial person, cynic, miser
COLLOQ. meanie

misanthropic adj
antisocial, unfriendly, surly, unsociable, unsympathetic, malevolent, egoistic, inhumane
E3 philanthropic

misanthropy n
antisociality, unsociableness, malevolence, egoism, inhumanity
E3 philanthropy

misapply v
misuse, use unwisely/unsuitably, pervert, misappropriate, misemploy, abuse, exploit

misapprehend v
misunderstand, misinterpret, miscomprehend, misconceive, misconstrue, mistake, misread, get the wrong idea, get a false impression
COLLOQ. get hold of the wrong end of the stick
E3 apprehend

misapprehension *n*
misunderstanding, misconception, misinterpretation, misreading, error, mistake, wrong idea, false impression, fallacy, delusion, mix-up

misappropriate *v*
steal, embezzle, pocket, thieve, pilfer, rob, swindle, misspend, misuse, misapply, abuse, pervert
FORMAL peculate, defalcate
COLLOQ. filch, pinch, nab, nick, have your fingers/hand in the till

misappropriation *n*
embezzlement, stealing, theft, pilfering, robbing, pocketing, misapplication, misuse
FORMAL defalcation, peculation

misbegotten *adj*
1 DISHONEST, disreputable, contemptible, stolen, unlawful, illicit, ill-gotten, shady
FORMAL purloined
2 ILL-CONCEIVED, ill-advised, unadvised, imprudent, ill-judged, poorly thought-out, abortive
COLLOQ. hare-brained
3 ILLEGITIMATE, natural, bastard, born out of wedlock

misbehave *v*
behave unacceptably/badly, behave improperly, be naughty, be rude, mess about, fool about/around, be beyond the pale, get up to mischief, offend, disobey, lapse, trespass
FORMAL transgress, misdemean
COLLOQ. muck about, play up, act up, carry on

misbehaviour *n*
unacceptable/bad behaviour, misconduct, bad manners, disobedience, naughtiness, mischief, insubordination
FORMAL misdemeanour, impropriety
COLLOQ. mucking about, carrying-on

misbelief *n*
wrong belief, delusion, illusion, error, mistake, misapprehension, misunderstanding, misconception, fallacy, heresy, unorthodoxy, heterodoxy

miscalculate *v*
misjudge, get wrong, go wrong, make a mistake, slip up, blunder, err, miscount, overestimate, underestimate
COLLOQ. boob

miscalculation *n*
misjudgement, mistake, blunder, overestimate, underestimate, error, inaccuracy, slip, oversight, aberration, lapse, slip, gaffe, fault, misunderstanding, misapprehension
COLLOQ. slip-up, boob, booboo, bloomer, howler, clanger

miscarriage *n*
1 *have a miscarriage*
spontaneous abortion
2 FAILURE, breakdown, abortion, aborting, mishap, mismanagement, error, perversion, ruination, disappointment
F3 **2** success, fulfilment

miscarry *v*
1 *she miscarried*
abort, lose the baby, have a spontaneous abortion
2 FAIL, abort, come to nothing, fall through, go wrong, go amiss, misfire, founder, come to grief
COLLOQ. flop, fold, not come off, come a cropper, bite the dust
F3 **2** succeed

miscellaneous *adj*
mixed, varied, various, assorted, diverse, diversified, eclectic, sundry, motley, mingled, jumbled, chow, farraginous
FORMAL heterogeneous, multifarious, variegated

miscellany *n*
assortment, mixture, mix, variety, collection, anthology, medley, potpourri, hotchpotch, jumble, diversity, pastiche, patchwork, olio, olla, gallimaufry, farrago, salmagundi, smorgasbord
FORMAL conglomeration, collectanea, miscellanea
COLLOQ. mixed bag, mishmash, omnium-gatherum

mischance *n*
accident, misfortune, bad break, ill-chance, ill fortune, ill luck, misadventure, disaster, tragedy, calamity, mishap, blow, contretemps
FORMAL infelicity

mischief *n*
1 TROUBLE, harm, hurt, evil, damage, injury, disruption
2 MISBEHAVIOUR, bad behaviour, naughtiness, impishness, roguishness, devilment, pranks, tricks, escapade, wrongdoing; *Scot* pliskie
COLLOQ. monkey business, shenanigans, carry-on, lark, hanky-panky, jiggery-pokery, funny business; *Scot* barnsbreaking; *N Am* dido
SLANG *N Am* monkey shine
3 IMP, elf, puck, monkey, wag, rascal, rogue, stirrer, scallywag, scamp, nuisance, terror, pest, tyke, urchin, villain, devil, limb (of Satan), flibbertigibbet, gamin(e), varmint, *esprit follet*; *Scot* cutty, nickum; *Irish* spalpeen
OLD makebate
COLLOQ. cockatrice; *N Am* hellion

mischievous *adj*
1 MALICIOUS, evil, spiteful, vicious, wicked, malignant, pernicious, destructive, harmful, hurtful, injurious, detrimental, pestilent
OLD litherly, shrewd; *Scot* ill-deedly
2 NAUGHTY, badly-behaved, bad, disobedient, misbehaving, up to no good, impish, rascally, roguish, playful, teasing, waggish, frolicsome, troublesome, tricksy, arch, elfish, elfin; *dialect* gallows
OLD unhappy
F3 **1** kind **2** well-behaved, good

mischievously *adv*
1 MALICIOUSLY, spitefully, wickedly, viciously, harmfully, injuriously, destructively
2 NAUGHTILY, disobediently, roguishly, playfully, impishly, teasingly, waggishly

misconceive *v*
misunderstand, misapprehend, misinterpret, misread, misjudge, misconstrue, mistake
COLLOQ. get hold of the wrong end of the stick

misconception *n*
misapprehension, misunderstanding, misreading, misinterpretation, error, mistake, fallacy, delusion, wrong idea, false impression
COLLOQ. the wrong end of the stick

misconduct *n*
misbehaviour, bad/unacceptable behaviour, malpractice, unethical/unprofessional behaviour, mismanagement, wrongdoing
FORMAL impropriety, misdemeanour

misconstrue *v*
misinterpret, misjudge, misread, misunderstand, misconceive, misapprehend, mistranslate, misreckon, mistake, take the wrong way
COLLOQ. get hold of the wrong end of the stick

miscreant *n*
wrongdoer, criminal, evildoer, sinner, rogue, rascal, scoundrel, scamp, scallywag, villain, vagabond, wretch, reprobate, profligate, mischief-maker, knave, dastard, troublemaker
FORMAL malefactor
F3 worthy

misdeed n
wrong, wrongdoing, crime, felony, offence, peccadillo, delinquency, error, fault, misconduct, villainy, sin, trespass
FORMAL misdemeanour, transgression

misdemeanour n
wrongdoing, wrong, misdeed, offence, infringement, lapse, fault, error, indiscretion, misbehaviour, misconduct, trespass, peccadillo
FORMAL malfeasance, transgression

misdirect v
divert, avert, misuse, misapply, misguide, mislead, misaddress, misinform, misappropriate
COLLOQ. throw off the scent
SLANG give a bum steer

miser n
niggard, skinflint, cheeseparer, Scrooge, save-all, curmudgeon, muckworm, hunks; *Scot* carl
OLD scrapegood
COLLOQ. penny-pincher, cheapskate, meanie, tightwad, money-grubber
SLANG tight arse
E∃ spendthrift

miserable adj
1 UNHAPPY, sad, sorrowful, sorry, dejected, despondent, depressed, down, downcast, downhearted, heartbroken, low-spirited, wretched, distressed, crushed, desolate, forlorn, gloomy, glum
FORMAL disconsolate, melancholic
COLLOQ. down in the dumps, blue
2 *miserable weather*
cheerless, depressing, dreary, gloomy, dismal, disagreeable, unpleasant, forlorn, joyless
COLLOQ. lousy
3 *miserable living conditions*
impoverished, shabby, squalid, poor, wretched, rotten, punk
4 CONTEMPTIBLE, despicable, ignominious, detestable, vile, base, mean, disgraceful, deplorable, low, shameful, pitiable
5 MEAGRE, paltry, niggardly, scanty, poor, worthless, pathetic, pitiful
COLLOQ. measly
6 GRUMPY, bad-tempered, ill-tempered, irritable, surly, sullen
COLLOQ. grouchy, crotchety
E∃ 1 cheerful, happy **2** pleasant, fair **3** comfortable **5** generous, liberal

miserably adv
1 UNHAPPILY, sadly, sorrowfully, despondently, desolately, gloomily, glumly
FORMAL disconsolately
2 NIGGARDLY, poorly, scantily, paltrily, pathetically, pitifully
COLLOQ. stingily
3 *fail miserably*
greatly, very much, desperately, dangerously, markedly

miserliness n
meanness, niggardliness, tightness, close-fistedness, frugality, parsimony, penny-pinching, cheeseparing, covetousness, avarice
FORMAL penuriousness
COLLOQ. tight-fistedness, minginess, stinginess
E∃ generosity, lavishness; *formal* prodigality

miserly adj
mean, niggardly, close, close-fisted/handed, sparing, parsimonious, cheeseparing, beggarly, chintzy, candle-paring; *Scot* gare
FORMAL penurious
COLLOQ. tight, tight-fisted, stingy, penny-pinching, mingy, money-grubbing
E∃ generous, spendthrift

misery n
1 UNHAPPINESS, sadness, suffering, sorrow, distress, desolation, depression, melancholy, melancholia, discomfort, despair, anguish, agony, gloom, grief, wretchedness, adversity, misfortune, living death, hell, perdition
OLD bale
FORMAL woe, affliction
2 DEPRIVATION, hardship, poverty, want, oppression, destitution
FORMAL privation, penury, indigence
3 SPOILSPORT, pessimist, killjoy, moaner, complainer, prophet of doom, Jeremiah
COLLOQ. wet blanket, grouch, whiner, whinger, sourpuss, dog in the manger, buzzkill
E∃ 1 contentment **2** comfort

misfire v
miscarry, go wrong, go amiss, go awry, abort, fail, fall through, founder, fizzle out, come to grief
COLLOQ. flop, not come off, come a cropper, bite the dust
E∃ succeed

misfit n
individualist, nonconformist, eccentric, maverick, dropout, loner, lone wolf
COLLOQ. oddball, weirdo, freak, odd one out, fish out of water, square peg in a round hole
E∃ conformist

misfortune n
bad luck, mischance, mishap, ill luck, hard luck, misadventure, setback, reverse, failure, calamity, catastrophe, disaster, blow, accident, tragedy, trouble, adversity, evil, sorrow, hardship, trial
FORMAL tribulation, affliction, woe
E∃ luck, success

Synonym nuances
The less common synonym **mischance** suggests any unfortunate happening, and the term **mishap**, although similar, is more appropriate for an unhappy accident: *his death was a million-to-one mishap*. **Ill-luck** again suggests the general concept of chance conspiring against you, and **hard luck** echoes this suggestion, with a hint of sympathy: *you've had your share of hard luck*. **Adversity** and **evil** imply particular circumstances working against you to a more serious degree: *we all need support in times of adversity*; similarly both **hardship** and **trial** are suggestive of a period of suffering. **Misadventure**, on the other hand, is now most commonly applied to an accidental cause of death, unlike **setback** which is appropriate where there is an element of disappointing delay, while **reverse** could be used of a complete regression of fortune: *a reverse in the profits of the company*.
To refer to a sudden and dreadful occurrence, you might choose **calamity**, **catastrophe** or **disaster**, while **tragedy** is liable to suggest more dire human consequences: *neighbours were shocked by the tragedy*. **Blow**, although similar, would be a less serious impediment: *losing the match was a bit of a blow*. **Sorrow** can be used to put more emphasis on the grief caused.

---

misgiving n
doubt, uncertainty, unease, hesitation, qualm, reservation, apprehension, scruple, suspicion, distrust, second thoughts, niggle, anxiety, worry, fear
E∃ confidence

misguided adj
misled, misconceived, ill-considered, ill-advised, ill-judged, imprudent, rash, misdirected, misinformed, misplaced, deluded, foolish, erroneous, wrong, mistaken

FORMAL fallacious, injudicious
F3 sensible, wise

mishandle v
mismanage, make a mess of, bungle, misjudge, mess up
COLLOQ. botch, make a hash of, make a pig's ear of, fluff, muff
SLANG balls up, make a balls(-up) of, screw up
F3 cope, manage

mishap n
misfortune, ill fortune, stroke of bad luck, misadventure, accident, reverse, setback, calamity, catastrophe, disaster, adversity, blow, incident, trouble, trial
FORMAL tribulation

mishmash n
hotchpotch, hodgepodge, jumble, medley, potpourri, pastiche, mess, muddle, salad, hash, farrago, gallimaufry, salmagundi, olla, olio
FORMAL conglomeration

misinform v
mislead, misdirect, misguide, deceive, bluff, hoodwink
COLLOQ. lead up the garden path
SLANG give a bum steer, take for a ride

misinformation n
disinformation, misleading, deception, misdirection, nonsense, bluff, lies, baloney
COLLOQ. dope, eyewash, guff, hype
SLANG bum steer

misinterpret v
misconstrue, misread, misunderstand, mistake, misjudge, misconceive, misapprehend, distort, garble, take the wrong way
COLLOQ. get hold of the wrong end of the stick

misinterpretation n
misunderstanding, misconception, misjudgement, misapprehension, misreading, misconstruction, false impression

misjudge v
miscalculate, mistake, misinterpret, misconstrue, misunderstand, overestimate, underestimate, get the wrong idea about, have a wrong opinion about

misjudgement n
miscalculation, misinterpretation, misunderstanding, mistake, wrong opinion/idea/conclusion
COLLOQ. the wrong end of the stick

mislay v
lose, misplace, miss, forget where you have put, lose sight of, lose track of, be unable to find, misfile

mislead v
misinform, misdirect, misguide, misrepresent, deceive, fool into, delude, lead astray, blindfold, lead into error, put on, impose on/upon, fool, hoodwink
COLLOQ. send on a wild-goose chase, lead up the garden path, pull a fast one on, pull the wool over someone's eyes, put/throw off the scent
SLANG give a bum steer, take for a ride; N Am snow

misleading adj
deceptive, deceiving, confusing, unreliable, equivocal, ambiguous, biased, loaded, evasive, delusive, illusory
FORMAL fallacious
COLLOQ. tricky
F3 unequivocal, authoritative, informative

mismanage v
mishandle, botch, bungle, make a mess of, mess up, misrule, misspend, misjudge, foul up, mar, waste
COLLOQ. botch, make a hash of, make a pig's ear of, muff
SLANG balls up, make a balls(-up) of, screw up

mismanagement n
mishandling, misjudgement, failure, muddle, bungling, mess
COLLOQ. hash, pig's ear, pig's breakfast, shambles, farce
SLANG balls-up, cock-up

mismatched adj
clashing, discordant, ill-assorted, incompatible, unmatching, misallied, mismated, unsuited, unreconcilable, irregular
FORMAL incongruous, disparate, antipathetic
F3 compatible, matching

misogynist n
woman-hater, anti-feminist, male chauvinist, male supremacist, sexist
COLLOQ. male chauvinist pig (MCP)
F3 feminist

misogyny n
anti-feminism, male chauvinism, male supremacy, sexism, sexual discrimination

misplace v
lose, mislay, miss, misapply, misassign, misfile, forget where you have put, lose sight of, lose track of, be unable to find

misprint n
mistake, error, literal (error), printing error, typographical error
FORMAL corrigendum, erratum
COLLOQ. typo

misquote v
misrepresent, misreport, muddle, misstate, twist, distort, pervert, falsify, garble, misremember

misread v
misinterpret, misconstrue, misunderstand, mistake, misjudge, misconceive, misapprehend, distort, garble, take the wrong way
COLLOQ. get hold of the wrong end of the stick

misrepresent v
distort, falsify, slant, pervert, manipulate, twist, garble, misquote, exaggerate, minimize, misconstrue, misinterpret, misreport, misstate, give a false/wrong account of

misrepresentation n
distortion, perversion, falsification, twisting, manipulation, exaggeration, misreporting, misconstruction, misinterpretation

misrule n
disorder, disorganization, maladministration, misgovernment, mismanagement, chaos, confusion, indiscipline, lawlessness, anarchy, riot, tumult, turmoil, turbulence, unreason

miss¹ v, n
♦ v
1 *miss a target*
fail, lose, let slip, let go, omit, fail, fail to hit/get/catch, miscarry, overlook, pass over, slip, leave out, mistake, trip, misunderstand, err
COLLOQ. blow, muff
2 *miss a meeting*
be absent from, be away from, fail to attend, not take part in, not go to, not go to see, not see, not be part of, be too late for
3 *miss an opportunity*
let go, let slip, fail to seize, not take advantage of, neglect, disregard, overlook, pass up
4 NOT NOTICE, not spot, fail to notice, fail to notice the absence of, overlook, disregard, pass over
5 AVOID, escape, evade, beat, dodge, for(e)go, skip, bypass, sidestep
FORMAL circumvent

6 PINE FOR, long for, yearn for, regret, feel the loss of, grieve for, mourn, sorrow for, ache for, want, wish, need, lament
1 hit, get, catch **2** take part in, attend **3** seize, grab **4** notice, spot
♦ *n*
failure, error, blunder, mistake, omission, oversight, fault, slip, fiasco
COLLOQ. flop; *N Am* flub
■ **miss out**
bypass, dispense with, disregard, ignore, jump, leave out, exclude, omit, pass over, skip

miss² *n*
Miss Bancroft
girl, schoolgirl, young lady, young woman, teenager, Ms, mademoiselle, damsel, lass, maid, maiden

missal *n*
breviary, formulary, mass-book, office-book, prayerbook, servicebook, euchologion, Triodion

misshapen *adj*
deformed, distorted, twisted, malformed, warped, contorted, crooked, crippled, bent, misproportioned, grotesque, ugly, monstrous
◼ regular, shapely

missile *n*
projectile, shot, guided missile, ballistic missile, arrow, shaft, dart, rocket, bomb, shell, flying bomb, grenade, torpedo, weapon

missing *adj*
absent, lost, lacking, gone, mislaid, unaccounted-for, wanting, disappeared, astray, gone astray, strayed, misplaced, nowhere to be found
◼ found, present

mission *n*
1 TASK, undertaking, assignment, operation, commission, campaign, crusade, business, errand, work, duty, chore
2 CALLING, duty, purpose, vocation, *raison d'être*, aim, goal, quest, pursuit, charge, office, job, work
3 DEPUTATION, ministry, delegation, commission, task force, legation, embassy
4 *a bombing mission*
operation, raid, sortie, campaign, exercise, manoeuvre, action

missionary *n*
evangelist, campaigner, preacher, converter, proselytizer, apostle, minister, crusader, propagandist, champion, promoter, emissary, envoy, ambassador

missive *n*
communication, dispatch, letter, line, message, report, note, bulletin, communiqué, memorandum
FORMAL epistle
COLLOQ. memo

misspent *adj*
wasted, frittered away, squandered, thrown away, idle, idled away, misused, profitless, misapplied, dissipated, unprofitable
FORMAL prodigal
◼ profitable

misstate *v*
misreport, misrepresent, misquote, misrelate, pervert, twist, distort, falsify, garble, misremember

mist *n, v*
♦ *n*
haze, fog, vapour, smog, cloud, murk, condensation, film, spray, drizzle, mizzle, dew, steam, veil, dimness
■ **mist over/up**
cloud over, become cloudy, become hazy, fog (up), dim, blur, become blurred, steam up, obscure, veil, glaze
◼ clear

mistake *n, v*
♦ *n*
error, inaccuracy, omission, oversight, aberration, lapse, slip, slip of the tongue, mix-up, blunder, gaffe, fault, flaw, fallacy, faux pas, indiscretion, misjudgement, miscalculation, misunderstanding, misapprehension, misprint, misspelling, misreading, mispronunciation, miscommunication, misstep, boss, miscue, misprise, misprision
TECHNICAL domino
OLD misprize; (*Spenser*) mesprize
FORMAL solecism, erratum, corrigendum
COLLOQ. bloomer, howler, clanger, slip-up, muff, fluff, botch-up, boob, booboo, bad move, blooper, bish, foul-up, own goal; *Scot* stumer
SLANG goof
♦ *v*
1 MISUNDERSTAND, misapprehend, misconstrue, misjudge, misread, miscalculate, misconceive, get wrong, go wrong, slip up, make a slip, blunder, err, misstep, miscue
OLD misprise; (*Spenser*) mesprize
COLLOQ. muff, boob, duff it, mess up, make a booboo, foul up, put your foot in it, get your wires crossed, bark up the wrong tree, get hold of the wrong end of the stick, drop a clanger, come a cropper; *N Am* flub
SLANG louse up, balls up, cock up, screw up, goof (up)
2 *mistake a person for another*
confuse, mix up, confound, muddle (up), take for

> **Synonym nuances**
> *noun*
> **Error** can be widely applied to anything that has been done wrong, while **fault** suggests a flaw: *a simple technical fault*. **Inaccuracy** has more to do with a lack of precision, but suggests a less obvious mistake; **slip** is also suggestive of a smaller mistake but one made through a degree of carelessness. The word **oversight**, similarly, suggests an inadvertent omission: *an administrative oversight*, whereas **aberration** and **lapse** are appropriate for a deviation from normal practices or expectations: *Vichy was an aberration in French history*. **Blunder** and **gaffe** are more suggestive of stupidity and more contemptuous in tone.
> **Indiscretion** is a gentler term which has more to do with a misdeed through lack of judgement: *a youthful indiscretion*. This more tolerant tone is continued by **misjudgement** and **miscalculation** which both simply imply an incorrect assessment, while **misunderstanding** and **misapprehension** suggest taking the wrong meaning.

mistaken *adj*
wrong, incorrect, in error, erroneous, inaccurate, inexact, untrue, unfounded, inappropriate, ill-judged, inauthentic, false, deceived, deluded, misguided, misinformed, misled, faulty, at fault, misprised
FORMAL fallacious
COLLOQ. having got hold of the wrong end of the stick, got the wrong idea, wide of the mark
◼ correct, right

mistakenly *adv*
wrongly, by mistake, erroneously, in error, incorrectly, falsely, inaccurately, inappropriately, misguidedly, unfairly, unjustly
FORMAL fallaciously
◼ appropriately, correctly, fairly, justly

mistimed *adj*
inconvenient, unfortunate, untimely, ill-timed, inopportune, unseasonable, unsynchronized, tactless
FORMAL infelicitous, malapropos
◼ opportune

mistreat v
abuse, misuse, ill-treat, ill-use, maltreat, treat badly, mishandle, harm, hurt, bully, batter, injure, molest, maul
COLLOQ. knock about, beat up, walk (all) over
☒ cosset, pamper

mistreatment n
maltreatment, abuse, ill-treatment, ill-use, harm, hurt, battering, injury, molestation, bullying, cruelty, unkindness, manhandling, mauling, mishandling, misuse, ill-usage, brutalization
☒ cosseting, pampering

mistress n
1 LOVER, live-in lover, partner, girlfriend, woman, lady, kept woman, concubine, courtesan, paramour, woman, lady-love, inamorata, hetaera, *amie, belle amie*, canary-bird
OLD miss, wench; (*Shakesp*) doxy
COLLOQ. bit on the side, fancy woman
OLD SLANG stepney
2 TEACHER, schoolteacher, governess, tutor

mistrust n, v
♦ n
distrust, doubt, suspicion, wariness, misgiving, reservations, qualm, hesitancy, chariness, caution, uncertainty, scepticism, apprehension
☒ trust
♦ v
distrust, doubt, have doubts about, have no faith in, suspect, be suspicious of, be wary of, beware, have reservations, have misgivings, fear
☒ trust

mistrustful adj
distrustful, doubtful, dubious, hesitant, sceptical, suspicious, uncertain, wary, cautious, apprehensive, fearful, shy, chary, cynical
COLLOQ. leery
☒ trustful

misty adj
hazy, foggy, cloudy, blurred, fuzzy, murky, smoky, unclear, dim, indistinct, obscure, opaque, vague, nebulous, veiled
☒ clear, distinct

misunderstand v
misapprehend, misconstrue, misinterpret, misread, misjudge, mistake, get wrong, get the wrong idea, get a false impression, miss the point, mishear
COLLOQ. get hold of the wrong end of the stick, not make head or tail of, get your wires crossed
☒ understand

misunderstanding n
1 MISTAKE, error, misapprehension, misconception, misjudgement, misinterpretation, wrong idea, false impression, misreading, mix-up
COLLOQ. the wrong end of the stick, crossed wires
2 DISAGREEMENT, argument, dispute, conflict, clash, difference, difference of opinion, breach, quarrel, rift, row, squabble
FORMAL discord
COLLOQ. falling-out, tiff
☒ **1** understanding, right idea **2** agreement, accord

misunderstood adj
misappreciated, misconstrued, misjudged, misread, misrepresented, mistaken, unappreciated, unrecognized, misheard, misinterpreted, ill-judged

misuse n, v
♦ n
mistreatment, maltreatment, mishandling, injury, abuse, wrong use, harm, ill-treatment, misapplication, misemployment, misappropriation, waste, squandering, perversion, corruption, exploitation
♦ v

abuse, misapply, misemploy, ill-use, ill-treat, treat badly, harm, mistreat, wrong, distort, injure, hurt, corrupt, pervert, waste, squander, misappropriate, exploit, dissipate

⚠ **misuse** or **abuse**?
See panel at **abuse**.

mite n
bit, trace, spark, whit, touch, atom, morsel, scrap, grain, jot, iota, modicum, ounce
COLLOQ. smidgen, tad

mitigate v
moderate, temper, alleviate, relieve, reduce, lessen, calm, pacify, soften, soothe, still, subdue, tone down, weaken, placate, quiet, decrease, diminish, dull, check, ease, mollify, lighten, sweeten, modify, qualify, help, blunt; *Scot* mease
OLD aslake, slake
FORMAL abate, allay, appease, assuage, extenuate, palliate, remit, lenify
☒ increase, exacerbate, aggravate

mitigating adj
extenuating, justifying, vindicating, tempering, modifying, lenitive, qualifying, vindicatory, mitigant
FORMAL palliative, assuasive

mitigation n
moderation, lessening, tempering, reduction, relief, easement, alleviation, decrease, diminution, qualification, mollification
FORMAL abatement, allaying, appeasement, assuagement, extenuation, palliation, remission
☒ increase, exacerbation, aggravation

mix v, n
♦ v
1 COMBINE, blend, mingle, put together, intermingle, intermix, amalgamate, compound, homogenize, synthesize, merge, join, unite, coalesce, fuse, alloy, incorporate, stir, whisk, mash, emulsify, infiltrate, introduce, fold in
FORMAL interpolate
2 ASSOCIATE, consort, fraternize, socialize, meet others, mingle, join
COLLOQ. hobnob
3 BE COMPATIBLE, harmonize, get along/on, agree, complement, go well with, suit
COLLOQ. be on the same wavelength
☒ **1** divide, separate
♦ n
mixture, blend, amalgam, amalgamation, assortment, combination, union, compound, merger, coalition, alloy, fusion, synthesis, medley, hotchpotch, hodgepodge, composite, jumble, potpourri, pastiche, hash, farrago, gallimaufry, salmagundi, olla-podrida, olio
FORMAL conglomerate
COLLOQ. mishmash
■ **mix in**
add in, blend, merge, introduce, incorporate, infiltrate
FORMAL interpolate
☒ extract, isolate
■ **mix up**
confuse, bewilder, muddle (up), mistake, perplex, puzzle, confound, mix, jumble, get jumbled up, complicate, garble, involve, implicate, disturb, upset, snarl up

mixed adj
1 *of mixed race*
combined, hybrid, mingled, crossbred; (*offensive*) half-caste; mongrel, interbred, blended, composite, compound, incorporated, united, alloyed, amalgamated, fused
2 *mixed biscuits*

assorted, varied, miscellaneous, diverse, diversified, motley

3 *mixed feelings*
ambivalent, equivocal, conflicting, contradicting, uncertain, unsure

■ **mixed up**
1 *a mixed-up person*
maladjusted, disturbed, disordered, disoriented, distracted, distraught, confused, bewildered, muddled, perplexed, puzzled, upset, chaotic, complicated, *désorienté*
COLLOQ. messed up, hung up
SLANG screwed up
2 *mixed up in a crime*
INVOLVED, embroiled, incriminated, caught up, entangled, implicated
FORMAL inculpated
COLLOQ. in on

mixer *n*
1 *a food mixer*
blender, food processor, liquidizer, beater, whisk
2 EXTROVERT, joiner, socializer, everybody's friend
COLLOQ. life and soul of the party
3 INTERFERER, busybody, disrupter, meddler, mischief-maker, subversive, troublemaker
OLD makebate
COLLOQ. stirrer
E3 2 introvert, loner, recluse **3** peacemaker

mixing *n*
1 AMALGAMATION, combination, synthesis, intermingling, coalescence, blending, union, fusion, hybridization, interbreeding, interflow
FORMAL minglement
2 ASSOCIATION, fraternization, socializing, mingling
E3 1 separation

mixture *n*
mix, blend, combination, amalgamation, amalgam, compound, composite, coalescence, alloy, brew, synthesis, union, fusion, concoction, cross, hybrid, assortment, variety, miscellany, medley, melange, farrago, smorgasbord, pastiche, patchwork, potpourri, jumble, hotchpotch, hodgepodge, olio, olla-podrida
FORMAL conglomeration
COLLOQ. mixed bag, mishmash

mix-up *n*
mess, mistake, misunderstanding, muddle, nonsense, chaos, confusion, jumble, disorder, complication, snarl-up, tangle
COLLOQ. foul-up
SLANG balls-up; *N Am* snafu

moan *n, v*
♦ *n*
1 GROAN, lament, lamentation, sob, wail, howl, whimper, whine
2 COMPLAINT, grumble, grievance, groan, dissatisfaction, annoyance, fault-finding, criticism, carping, censure, accusation, charge, representation
COLLOQ. beefing, beef, grouse, gripe, bleating, whingeing, whinge
SLANG bellyaching
♦ *v*
1 GROAN, wail, sob, weep, howl, whimper, mourn, lament, sigh, grieve; *dialect* hone; *Scot* mean
2 COMPLAIN, grumble, whine, carp; *Scot* mean
COLLOQ. whinge, gripe, grouse, bleat, beef, kick up a fuss
SLANG bellyache
E3 1 rejoice

moaner *n*
complainer, grumbler, niggler, fault-finder

COLLOQ. whinger, grouser, fusspot, nit-picker, whiner; *N Am* fussbudget
SLANG bellyacher

mob *n, v*
♦ *n*
1 CROWD, mass, throng, multitude, horde, rabble, host, swarm, gathering, group, collection, body, flock, herd, drove, brood, pack, press, set, tribe, troop, company, crew, gang, ribble-rabble
FORMAL assemblage
2 POPULACE, rabble, masses, proletariat, hoi polloi, rank and file, common people, common herd, great unwashed, ribble-rabble, king mob, many-headed beast/monster, *canaille, faex populi*
OLD mobile, rabble rout
COLLOQ. plebs, riff-raff, proles
SLANG mobility
♦ *v*
crowd, crowd round, surround, swarm round, gather round, jostle, overrun, set upon, fall upon, besiege, descend on, throng, pack, fill, pester, attack, charge

mobile *adj*
1 MOVING, movable, able to move, portable, transportable, travelling, roaming, roving, itinerant, wandering, migrant
FORMAL peripatetic, motile, locomotive, ambulatory
2 FLEXIBLE, adjustable, adaptable, supple, agile, active, energetic, nimble
3 CHANGING, changeable, ever-changing, expressive, suggesting, revealing, lively
E3 1 immobile

mobility *n*
movability, movableness, portability, flexibility, motion, expressiveness, vivacity, agility, animation, suppleness
FORMAL locomobility, locomotion, locomotivity, motility, motivity
E3 immobility, inflexibility, rigidity

mobilization *n*
activation, organization, preparation, summoning, assembly, marshalling, mustering

mobilize *v*
assemble, marshal, rally, conscript, muster, call up, enlist, call into action, activate, cause to take action, galvanize, organize, prepare, get ready, make ready, ready, summon, animate

mob rule *n*
mob law, lynch law, kangaroo court, Reign of Terror
FORMAL ochlocracy
COLLOQ. mobocracy

mobster *n*
gangster, desperado, hoodlum, ruffian, rough, tough, thug, terrorist, racketeer, bandit, brigand, robber, criminal, bovver boy, hooligan, skinhead
COLLOQ. crook
SLANG heavy

mock *v, adj*
♦ *v*
1 RIDICULE, jeer, make fun of, poke fun at, laugh at, scoff, sneer, taunt, gibe, scorn, insult, tease, chaff, laugh in someone's face, flout, fleer; *dialect* geck; *Scot* murgeon; *Aust* poke mullock at
OLD bemock, dor, jape, scout
FORMAL disparage, deride
COLLOQ. kid, rib, rag, knock, take the mickey out of
SLANG slag (off), take the piss out of; *N Am* goof; *Aust & NZ* poke borak at
2 IMITATE, simulate, mimic, ape, caricature, parody, burlesque, lampoon, satirize
FORMAL emulate
COLLOQ. send up, take off
♦ *adj*

imitation, imitative, counterfeit, artificial, sham, mimic, simulated, synthetic, substitute, ersatz, false, fake, forged, fraudulent, bogus, pseudo, spurious, feigned, faked, pretended, dummy
COLLOQ. phoney, pretend
SLANG cod

mocker *n*
jeerer, ridiculer, scoffer, scorner, sneerer, satirist, tease, tormentor, flouter, lampooner, lampoonist, critic, detractor, pasquinader
FORMAL derider, reviler, vilifier, iconoclast
SLANG piss-taker
Ⅎ flatterer, supporter

mockery *n*
1 RIDICULE, jeering, scoffing, scorn, sneer, sneering, taunting, teasing, contempt, disdain, disrespect, sarcasm, sport, fleer, banter, raillery, quiz
OLD dor, gab
FORMAL derision, disparagement, contumely
COLLOQ. kidding, ribbing, ragging, mickey-taking
SLANG piss-taking; *Aust* serve
2 PARODY, satire, sham, travesty, caricature, farce, burlesque, lampoon, apology, charivari, horning
FORMAL emulation
COLLOQ. send-up, take-off, spoof

mocking *adj*
scornful, derisive, derisory, contemptuous, sarcastic, satirical, taunting, scoffing, sardonic, sneering, insulting, irreverent, impudent, disrespectful, disdainful, cynical
COLLOQ. snide

mock-up *n*
model, copy, replica, representation, facsimile, image, imitation, dummy

mode *n*
1 WAY, style, manner, approach, condition, method, form, plan, practice, procedure, process, technique, system, convention
2 FASHION, style, custom, trend, vogue, fad, look
COLLOQ. craze, latest thing, rage, *dernier cri*

model *n, adj, v*
♦ *n*
1 COPY, replica, representation, facsimile, image, imitation, mock-up, dummy
2 EXAMPLE, pattern, design, standard, ideal, epitome, paragon, perfect example, embodiment, byword, mould, original, type, prototype, sample, template, version
TECHNICAL stereotype
FORMAL exemplar, archetype, paradigm
3 DESIGN, style, form, sort, kind, variety, type, version, mark
FORMAL mode
4 MANNEQUIN, fashion model, artist's model, photographer's model, dummy, sitter, subject, poser
♦ *adj*
1 EXEMPLARY, perfect, typical, ideal
FORMAL archetypal, prototypical
2 *a model railway*
miniature, small-scale, reduced, replica, reproduction, toy
♦ *v*
1 MAKE, form, fashion, mould, sculpt, carve, cast, shape, work, create, design, plan, base
2 DISPLAY, wear, sport, pose, show off

moderate *adj, v, n*
♦ *adj*
1 MEDIOCRE, medium, modest, ordinary, fair, fairish, indifferent, average, middling, adequate, tolerable, passable, middle-of-the-road
COLLOQ. so-so, fair to middling, not up to much, no great shakes, not much cop, nothing much to write home about
2 REASONABLE, restrained, fair, just, modest, sensible, calm, steady, sober, controlled, temperate, cool, mild, well-regulated

Ⅎ **1** exceptional, extreme **2** immoderate, excessive
♦ *v*
1 CONTROL, regulate, decrease, lessen, slacken, die down, soften, restrain, tone down, play down, diminish, ease, curb, calm, check, keep in check, keep under control, modulate, repress, subdue, assuage, tame, subside, pacify, dwindle
FORMAL attenuate, mitigate, allay, alleviate, abate, appease, palliate
COLLOQ. soft-pedal
2 *moderate a debate*
chair, act as chair/chairperson/chairman/chairwoman at, preside over, direct, supervise
♦ *n*
nonextremist, centrist, liberal, neutral person, don't know
Ⅎ extremist, hardliner

moderately *adv*
reasonably, somewhat, quite, rather, fairly, slightly, passably, within reason, to some extent, to a certain degree, conservatively, within measure
Ⅎ extremely

moderation *n*
1 RESTRAINT, self-control, self-restraint, caution, control, composure, sobriety, abstemiousness, temperance, temperateness, reasonableness
2 DECREASE, reduction, lessening, regulation, curbing, subsidence, relaxation
FORMAL attenuation, mitigation, alleviation, abatement
Ⅎ **1** (over-)indulgence, self-indulgence
▪ in moderation
within limits, within bounds, within reason, moderately, with self-control
Ⅎ to excess

modern *adj*
current, contemporary, up-to-date, existing, new, fresh, latest, late, novel, present, present-day, recent, up-to-the-minute, advanced, avant-garde, progressive, modernistic, innovative, inventive, state-of-the-art, go-ahead, forward-looking, futuristic, fashionable, in fashion, stylish, in vogue, in style, voguish, modish
COLLOQ. newfangled, in, now, trendy, with it, spanking new, faddish, all the rage, the latest, hot off the press(es), hip, cool
Ⅎ old-fashioned, old, out-of-date, antiquated, traditional

Synonym nuances
Current, **contemporary**, **up-to-date** and **up-to-the-minute** can be used with overtones of fashionability: *pubs of the 1950s adopted a contemporary 'Festival of Britain' look*, while **existing**, **present** and **present-day** straightforwardly refer to what is presently available or happening: *present-day standards; customer needs are being met by existing products*, whereas **fresh** has positive implications of not being stale: *we need a fresh outlook*. **Novel** too has suggestions of newness as well as originality.

The terms **advanced** and **avant-garde** would actually suggest something is ahead of its time, the latter often in a shocking way, and **progressive**, **go-ahead** and **forward-looking** too echo the idea of pushing old boundaries: *progressive thinking leads to scientific advance*. **Innovative** and **inventive** are also more positively suggestive of being imaginatively creative. The term **modernistic**, however, can be used to imply a stylized representation and is not necessarily approving: *the car was given a modernistic design, intended to look like a space ship*; **futuristic** is similar but indicates looking to the imagined future for inspiration: *futuristic houses with labour-saving gadgets*. **State-of-the-art**, on the other hand, is more approbatory in its suggestion of being unsurpassed at a given time: *state-of-the-art technology*.

The various terms **in vogue**, **voguish** and **modish** all return to the idea of the present and its prevailing trends, while **fashionable** and **stylish** express approval of them.

modernity n

innovation, innovativeness, newness, novelty, originality, contemporaneity, fashionableness, freshness, recentness
F3 antiquatedness, antiquity

modernization n

renovation, refurbishment, regeneration, renewal, revamping, updating, redesign, remodelling, transformation, modification, improvement

modernize v

renovate, refurbish, rejuvenate, regenerate, streamline, revamp, renew, make modern, update, bring up-to-date, improve, do up, redesign, reform, remake, remodel, refresh, transform, modify, progress
COLLOQ. do over, do up, fix up, move with the times, get with it
F3 regress

modest adj

1 UNASSUMING, humble, self-effacing, self-deprecating, quiet, reserved, retiring, lowly, unpretentious, unpretending, discreet, bashful, shy, self-conscious, coy, timid, diffident, shamefaced
FORMAL verecund
2 MODERATE, ordinary, unexceptional, fair, satisfactory, reasonable, tolerable, passable, decent, adequate, limited, small
3 *a modest house*
unassuming, unpretentious, simple, ordinary, plain, small, inexpensive
4 *modest behaviour*
proper, prudent, discreet, pure, chaste, virtuous, demure, maidenly
OLD seemly
FORMAL decorous
F3 1 immodest, conceited, arrogant **2** exceptional, excessive **3** pretentious, expensive, extravagant **4** immoral, indecent

modestly adv

1 HUMBLY, unassumingly, quietly, bashfully, shyly, self-consciously, coyly, timidly, diffidently, unpretentiously
2 MODERATELY, reasonably, satisfactorily, adequately, decently
3 *behave modestly*
discreetly, purely, chastely, virtuously, demurely
F3 1 arrogantly **2** excessively **3** immorally

modesty n

1 HUMILITY, humbleness, self-effacement, self-deprecation, reticence, reserve, quietness, shyness, bashfulness, coyness, self-consciousness, timidity
2 *modesty of behaviour*
decency, propriety, demureness, chasteness
OLD seemliness
FORMAL decorum
3 UNPRETENTIOUSNESS, simplicity, plainness, inexpensiveness
F3 1 immodesty, vanity, conceit **3** extravagance

modicum n

little, bit, small amount, little bit, particle, molecule, fragment, grain, scrap, shred, speck, touch, degree, trace, tinge, atom, crumb, dash, drop, pinch, ounce, hint, suggestion, inch, iota, mite
COLLOQ. tad

modification n

adaptation, adjustment, alteration, change, revision, tweak, variation, improvement, transformation, mutation, refinement, reformation, reorganization, remoulding, reworking, recasting, limitation, moderation, qualification, restriction, tempering
FORMAL modulation

modify v

1 CHANGE, alter, redesign, revise, vary, adapt, adjust,

transform, reform, convert, improve, reorganize, reshape, remould, rework, recast, sculpt, retrofit, diversify, temper, touch, tweak, invert, overrule, explain away, trim your sails
TECHNICAL assimilate, dash, vowel, vowelize, umlaut
2 MODERATE, reduce, lessen, decrease, diminish, temper, tone down, limit, soften, dull, qualify
OLD attemper
FORMAL abate, mitigate

modish adj

fashionable, stylish, smart, vogue, voguish, contemporary, current, modern, modernistic, avant-garde, chic, *à la mode*
COLLOQ. cool, all the rage, hip, in, jazzy, latest, mod, trendy, up-to-the-minute, with it, now
F3 dowdy, old-fashioned

modulate v

modify, adjust, balance, alter, soften, temper, moderate, lower, regulate, change, vary, harmonize, inflect, tune

modulation n

modification, adjustment, balance, alteration, softening, lowering, moderation, regulation, change, variation, harmonization, tuning, tone, shift, inflection, inflexion, intonation, accent, shade

module n

component, unit, part, section, element, factor, item, piece

modus operandi n

method, way, operation, plan, practice, procedure, process, manner, technique, system, rule, rule of thumb
FORMAL praxis

mogul n

magnate, tycoon, baron, potentate, notable, personage, supremo
COLLOQ. big cheese, big gun, big noise, big pot, big shot, big wheel, bigwig, Mr Big, top dog, VIP
F3 nobody

moist adj

damp, clammy, dank, humid, wet, wettish, liquid, dewy, rainy, muggy, marshy, drizzly, drizzling, watery, washy, soggy, dripping
FORMAL humectant, hydric, hygrophil, hygrophilous
F3 dry, arid

moisten v

moisturize, dampen, damp, wet, make wet, soak, water, humidify, humify, lick, irrigate, slake; *Scot* sparge, spairge
FORMAL humect, humectate
F3 dry

moisture n

water, liquid, wetness, wet, wateriness, damp, dampness, dankness, humidity, vapour, rain, drizzle, dew, mugginess, condensation, soaking, steam, spray, perspiration, sweat
TECHNICAL precipitate, precipitation
OLD humour
FORMAL humectation
F3 dryness

mole¹ n

a mole on the skin
spot, blemish, blotch, mark, speckle, freckle

mole² n

a mole in the organization
agent, infiltrator, secret agent, spy, double agent

mole³ n

a mole stretching out to sea
barrier, breakwater, pier, causeway, dyke, groyne, jetty, embankment

molest v

1 ANNOY, disturb, bother, harass, irritate, agitate, vex, exasperate, persecute, pester, nag, chivvy, harry, plague,

tease, torment, hound, upset, fluster, worry, trouble, provoke, badger
COLLOQ. aggravate, needle, hassle, bug
2 ATTACK, accost, assail, hurt, ill-treat, maltreat, mistreat, abuse, interfere with, (sexually) assault, rape, harm, injure
FORMAL ravish

molestation n
abuse, interference, harm, injury, attack, assault, rape

molester n
abuser, attacker, assaulter, rapist
FORMAL ravisher

mollify v
placate, appease, calm, pacify, compose, conciliate, cushion, ease, relax, relieve, lessen, moderate, temper, modify, quell, soften, soothe, lull, quieten, quiet, blunt, sweeten, mellow
FORMAL abate, allay, mitigate, assuage, propitiate
E3 aggravate, anger

mollusc

Molluscs include:

abalone	limpet	scallop
conch	marine snail	sea slug
cowrie	mussel	slug
cuttlefish	nautilus	squid
clam	nudibranch	tusk shell
cockle	octopus	whelk
freshwater snail	oyster	
land snail	periwinkle	

mollycoddle v
pamper, coddle, indulge, spoil, overprotect, pander to, cosset, spoon-feed, mother, pet, baby, ruin
E3 ill-treat, neglect

molten adj
melted, liquefied, flowing, fusil
TECHNICAL magmatic

moment n
1 *stop for a moment*
second, instant, (very) short time, little while, less than no time, point in time, minute, split second, flash, twinkling of an eye, trice
COLLOQ. mo, sec, jiffy, tick, two ticks, two shakes of a lamb's tail
2 *the moment something happens*
the minute, immediately, the instant, the point, directly, no sooner..., as soon as
3 IMPORTANCE, significance, substance, note, interest, value, worth, concern, consequence, gravity, seriousness, weight, weightiness
FORMAL import
E3 3 insignificance

momentarily adv
briefly, for a moment, for a short time, for a second, for an instant, instantaneously, fleetingly, temporarily

momentary adj
brief, short, short-lived, temporary, transient, transitory, fleeting, hasty, quick, passing, spasmodic, instantaneous, momentaneous
OLD (*Shakesp*) momentany
FORMAL ephemeral, evanescent
E3 lasting, permanent

momentous adj
significant, important, of importance, of great consequence, of significance, critical, crucial, decisive, weighty, grave, serious, vital, consequential, fateful, historic, pivotal, earth-shaking, earth-shattering, world-shattering, epoch-making, eventful, major, pregnant
E3 insignificant, unimportant, trivial

momentum n
impetus, force, energy, impulse, drive, power, driving-power, thrust, propulsion, speed, velocity, impact, incentive, stimulus, urge, strength, push

monarch n
sovereign, the Crown, crowned head, ruler, king, queen, emperor, empress, prince, princess, Caesar, tsar, potentate, autocrat

monarchy n
1 KINGDOM, empire, principality, realm, sovereign state, domain, dominion
2 ROYALISM, sovereignty, kingship, autocracy, absolutism, despotism, tyranny
FORMAL monocracy

monastery n
friary, priory, nunnery, convent, abbey, cloister, charterhouse, religious community
FORMAL coenobium

monastic adj
reclusive, withdrawn, secluded, cloistered, anchoritic, canonical, austere, ascetic, celibate, meditative, contemplative
FORMAL sequestered, eremitic, coenobitic
E3 secular, worldly
See panel **religious orders** *at* **religious**.

monasticism n
asceticism, austerity, recluseness, reclusion, seclusion, monkhood
FORMAL monachism, eremitism, coenobitism

monetary adj
financial, money, fiscal, budgetary, economic, capital, cash
FORMAL pecuniary

money n
currency, cash, legal tender, banknotes, coin, funds, finances, assets, means, savings, resources, capital, riches, wealth, prosperity, affluence
COLLOQ. the necessary
SLANG loot, readies, bucks, ready, megabucks, dough, dosh, bread, lolly, spondulicks, brass, loot, gravy, greens, shekels, moolah, greenies, scratch, smash, stumpy, chink; *Aust & NZ* Oscar
OLD SLANG blunt, rhino
Related adjectives: monetary, pecuniary
■ **in the money**
rich, wealthy, affluent, prosperous, well-off, well-to-do
COLLOQ. rolling in it, well-heeled, stinking rich, flush
SLANG loaded
E3 poor

Synonym nuances
Currency refers to money in circulation, with an exchangeable value: *foreign currency*. **Legal tender**, likewise, is a more formal term for a country's legitimate units of payment. **Cash** can be used to put the emphasis on the physical nature of money: *you can pay by cash or cheque*.

Funds and **finances**, on the other hand, have more to do with the money available for a particular project, or to a particular person or group: *the party has started raising funds for its campaign; the company's finances are strong*. **Capital** is also appropriate for available money, but more suggestive of that provided by an initial investment. **Assets**, **means** and **resources** are similar, but can also refer to anything owned that is of monetary value and which you can use to support yourself: *she tried to make the most of her limited resources*.

While **riches** and **wealth** have more to do with an abundance of money and valuable possessions, **prosperity** and **affluence** suggest potential for increase in monetary wealth.

money-box *n*
cash box, chest, safe, coffer, piggy-bank

moneyed *adj*
wealthy, rich, affluent, comfortable, well-off, prosperous, well-to-do
FORMAL opulent
COLLOQ. flush, well-heeled, rolling in it
SLANG loaded
▣ poor, impoverished

money-grubbing *adj*
acquisitive, grasping, miserly, mercenary, mammonish, mammonistic
FORMAL quaestuary

moneymaking *adj*
profitable, profit-making, lucrative, commercial, remunerative, paying, successful

mongrel *n, adj*
♦ *n*
cross, crossbreed, hybrid, half-breed, mixed breed, cur; *NZ* kuri
♦ *adj*
crossbred, hybrid, half-bred, bastard, mixed, of mixed breed, ill-defined
▣ pure-bred, pedigree

monicker *n*
name, alias, nickname, pseudonym, assumed/false name, so(u)briquet, pen name, stage name

monitor *v, n*
♦ *v*
check, watch, keep track of, keep under surveillance, keep an eye on, follow, track, supervise, oversee, observe, note, survey, trace, scan, record, plot, detect
♦ *n*
1 SCREEN, display, VDU, recorder, scanner, detector, security camera, CCTV
2 SUPERVISOR, watchdog, observer, overseer, invigilator, adviser, prefect, head boy/girl

monk *n*
brother, religious, friar, frater, prior, abbot, hermit, monastic, mendicant, contemplative, cloisterer, beguin, conventual, *religieux*, religionary, religioner, anchorite, possessionate, *talapoin*, abbey-lubber
OLD gyrovague
FORMAL coenbite
Related adjectives: monastic, monasterial

monkey *n, v*
♦ *n*
1 PRIMATE, simian
Related adjective: simian

Monkeys include:

ape	macaque	spider monkey
baboon	mandrill	squirrel monkey
capuchin monkey	mangabey	tamarin
colobus	marmoset	titi
drill	night monkey (or	toque
guenon	douroucouli)	uakari (or
guereza	proboscis	cacajou)
howler	monkey	woolly monkey
langur	rhesus monkey	
leaf monkey	saki	

---

2 SCAMP, imp, urchin, brat, rogue, rascal, mischief-maker, scallywag, tyke
♦ *v*
play, fool, tinker, tamper, trifle, fiddle, fidget, interfere, meddle, mess, potter
COLLOQ. muck, clown, footle

▪ **monkey business**
mischief, tomfoolery, trickery, chicanery, clowning, pranks, dishonesty, skulduggery, legerdemain, sleight-of-hand, foolery
COLLOQ. carry-on, hanky-panky, jiggery-pokery, monkey tricks, shenanigans, funny business

monochrome *adj*
black-and-white, monotone, sepia, monochromatic, monotonous
FORMAL monochroic, unicolor, unicolorate, unicolorous, unicolour, unicoloured
▣ kaleidoscopic, multicoloured

monocle *n*
eyeglass, glass

monogamous *adj*
having only one marriage partner
FORMAL monandrous, monogamic, monogynous
▣ bigamous, polygamous

monogamy *n*
FORMAL monandry, monogyny
▣ bigamy, polygamy

monolingual *adj*
FORMAL monoglot, unilingual
▣ polyglot

monolith *n*
megalith, standing stone, shaft, menhir, sarsen

monolithic *adj*
massive, vast, colossal, gigantic, huge, monumental, giant, immovable, immobile, rigid, solid, unmoving, unchanging, inflexible, faceless, undifferentiated, fossilized, hidebound, intractable, unvaried

monologue *n*
speech, soliloquy, lecture, sermon, address, oration, homily
COLLOQ. spiel
▣ conversation, dialogue, discussion

monomania *n*
obsession, fixation, ruling passion, fanaticism, *idée fixe*, mania, neurosis, fetish
COLLOQ. bee in your bonnet, hobby-horse, thing

monopolize *v*
dominate, take over, keep to yourself, have (all) to yourself, corner, control, not share with others, have exclusive/sole rights, engross, occupy, preoccupy, take up, tie up
FORMAL appropriate
COLLOQ. hog
▣ share

monopoly *n*
domination, control, corner, exclusive right(s), sole right(s), privilege, franchise, *appalto, régie*
TECHNICAL monopsony
FORMAL ascendancy

monotonous *adj*
boring, dull, tedious, uninteresting, unexciting, tiresome, wearisome, unchanging, uneventful, unvarying, unvaried, all the same, uniform, toneless, flat, colourless, repetitive, repetitious, routine, mechanical, plodding, humdrum, soul-destroying
COLLOQ. run-of-the-mill, samey, deadly, ho-hum
▣ lively, varied, colourful

monotony *n*
tedium, dullness, boredom, sameness, tiresomeness, uneventfulness, flatness, wearisomeness, uniformity, routine, routineness, repetitiveness, repetition
▣ liveliness, colour, variety, excitement, interest

monster *n, adj*
♦ *n*
1 *sea monsters*

frightening creature, imaginary creature, mythical creature, mythological creature, Frankenstein, chimera, prodigy, bandersnatch, jabberwock
TECHNICAL wivern, satyral, teratism
OLD mooncalf, wasserman, whirlpool
See panel at **mythical**.
2 BEAST, fiend, brute, barbarian, savage, villain, Frankenstein, giant, ogre, ogress, devil, troll
3 FREAK, freak of nature, monstrosity, mutant, malformation, miscreation
TECHNICAL teratism
4 MAMMOTH, jumbo, giant, colossus, leviathan, behemoth, cyclops, Brobdingnagian
♦ *adj*
huge, gigantic, giant, colossal, enormous, immense, massive, monstrous, jumbo, mammoth, vast, tremendous
COLLOQ. whopping, ginormous, mega
F3 tiny, minute

monstrosity *n*
1 EYESORE, blot on the landscape, atrocity, abnormality, enormity, freak, monster, mutant, miscreation, obscenity
TECHNICAL teras
2 DREADFULNESS, frightfulness, hideousness, loathsomeness, horror, hellishness, evil
FORMAL heinousness

monstrous *adj*
1 WICKED, evil, vicious, savage, cruel, criminal, outrageous, scandalous, shocking, disgraceful, abominable, atrocious, abhorrent, dreadful, frightful, horrible, horrifying, grisly, terrible, vile, foul, nasty, inhuman
FORMAL heinous
2 UNNATURAL, inhuman, freakish, abnormal, grotesque, hideous, gruesome, deformed, malformed, misshapen
TECHNICAL teratoid
3 HUGE, enormous, colossal, gigantic, vast, immense, tremendous, massive, mammoth

monstrously *adv*
1 OUTRAGEOUSLY, shockingly, atrociously, scandalously, dreadfully, frightfully, terribly
2 IMMENSELY, hugely, enormously, colossally, gigantically, vastly, massively, tremendously

monument *n*
memorial, cenotaph, headstone, gravestone, tombstone, shrine, mausoleum, cairn, barrow, cross, marker, obelisk, pillar, column, statue, relic, remembrance, commemoration, witness, testament, reminder, record, memento, evidence, token

monumental *adj*
1 IMPRESSIVE, imposing, striking, awe-inspiring, awesome, overwhelming, significant, important, epoch-making, historic, magnificent, remarkable, majestic, memorable, unforgettable, notable, outstanding, abiding, permanent, enduring, immortal, lasting, classic
2 HUGE, immense, enormous, colossal, vast, tremendous, extraordinary, massive, great, exceptional
3 COMMEMORATIVE, celebratory, memorial
F3 1 insignificant, unimportant

monumentally *adv*
immensely, hugely, enormously, colossally, gigantically, vastly, massively, tremendously

mood *n*
1 DISPOSITION, frame of mind, state of mind, temper, humour, vein, spirit, tenor, whim
2 BAD TEMPER, bad mood, sulk, the sulks, pique, melancholy, low spirits, depression, doldrums
COLLOQ. blues, dumps
3 ATMOSPHERE, feeling, feel, spirit, tenor, tone, climate, ambience
■ **in the mood for**
wanting to do/have, feeling like, willing to, eager to, keen

on/to, inclined to, ready for, in the right frame of mind to
FORMAL disposed to

moody *adj*
changeable, temperamental, unpredictable, volatile, unstable, irritable, short-tempered, bad-tempered, crotchety, testy, touchy, morose, angry, broody, irritable, irascible, cantankerous, petulant, mop(e)y, sulky, sullen, gloomy, melancholy, miserable, downcast, in a huff, in a (bad) mood, doleful, glum, impulsive, fickle, flighty
FORMAL capricious
COLLOQ. crabby, crusty
F3 equable, cheerful

moon *v*
idle, loaf, languish, pine, mope, brood, daydream, dream, fantasize
COLLOQ. mooch
■ **once in a blue moon**
very rarely, seldom, not often, hardly ever, almost never
■ **over the moon**
ecstatic, elated, blissful, joyful, jubilant, rapturous, enraptured, overjoyed, euphoric, delirious, frenzied, fervent
FORMAL rhapsodic
COLLOQ. jumping for joy, on top of the world, on cloud nine, in seventh heaven, tickled pink, high as a kite

moonlike *adj*
lunar, moon-shaped, crescent, crescentic, moony
TECHNICAL lunate
FORMAL lunular, meniscoid, selenic

moonshine *n*
1 NONSENSE, rubbish, fantasy, stuff; *dialect & N Am* blathers; *Scot* blethers
COLLOQ. hot air, guff, hogwash, baloney, bosh, bunk, bunkum, claptrap, eyewash, tommyrot, tosh, tripe, twaddle, piffle, rot
SLANG (*vulgar*) shit, bullshit, crap
2 SPIRITS, liquor, bootleg, hoo(t)ch, pot(h)een
F3 1 sense

moor¹ *v*
to moor a boat
fasten, secure, tie up, drop anchor, anchor, berth, dock, make fast, fix, fix firmly, hitch, lash, bind
F3 loose

moor² *n*
the Yorkshire moors
moorland, heath, fell, upland

moot *v, adj*
♦ *v*
put forward, propose, suggest, submit, advance, bring up, raise, broach, introduce, pose, discuss, argue, debate
FORMAL propound
♦ *adj*
controversial, problematic, difficult, questionable, vexed, unsettled, unresolved, unresolvable, undecided, undetermined, disputed, disputable, arguable, doubtful, insoluble, knotty, open, open to debate, debatable, crucial, contestable, academic

mop *n, v*
♦ *n*
1 *a floor mop*
sponge, wiper, swab, squeegee
2 *a mop of hair*
head of hair, shock, mane, tangle, thatch, mat, mass
♦ *v*
swab, sponge, wipe, clean, wash, absorb, soak
■ **mop up**
1 WIPE UP, wash, absorb, soak up, sponge, swab, clean up, tidy up
2 FINISH OFF, deal with, wipe up, dispose of, account for, round up, neutralize, eliminate, secure, take care of

mope v, n

♦ v

brood, fret, sulk, pine, languish, droop, despair, be miserable, grieve

♦ n

melancholic, misery, depressive, pessimist, killjoy, melancholiac, moaner, introvert

COLLOQ. grouch, grump, moper

■ **mope about**

idle, wander, moon, languish

COLLOQ. mooch, lounge, loll

moral adj, n

♦ adj

1 ETHICAL, virtuous, good, right, principled, honourable, decent, upright, upstanding, straight, righteous, high-minded, honest, incorruptible, proper, blameless, chaste, clean-living, pure, just, noble

2 *give moral support*

encouraging, emotional, psychological

E3 1 immoral

♦ n

lesson, message, significance, teaching, point, dictum, meaning, maxim, adage, precept, saying, proverb, aphorism, epigram

---

Synonym nuances

adjective sense 1

Ethical can be used to suggest anything that conforms to acceptable forms of human conduct: *the ethical dilemma of cloning*, while **virtuous** and **good** are more judgemental, suggesting an inherent goodness. **Decent**, **principled** and **upstanding** similarly suggest adherence to conventions of social morality: *fine, upstanding young men*, but **honourable** is stronger in that it further implies integrity, while **upright** implies strong moral rectitude. **Righteous** and **high-minded** are similar, but can on occasion imply a degree of self-satisfaction or arrogance: *a school with high-minded staff and prissy pupils.*

Proper, although it is rather prim in tone, might be used in a variety of contexts to suggest behaving appropriately: *I didn't feel her forwardness was quite proper.* **Chaste**, **pure** and **clean-living**, however, more specifically suggest an avoidance of wrong-doing and debauchery. **Straight** tends to suggest an adherence to the law, whereas **just** is more suggestive of fairness or sometimes simply validity: *a just cause*, and **noble** suggests morality with an element of dignity: *enlightened, noble thoughts.*

---

morale n

confidence, spirit(s), *esprit de corps*, self-esteem, self-confidence, state of mind, heart, mood, optimism, hopefulness

moralistic adj

self-righteous, smug, complacent, superior, priggish, pious, sanctimonious, holier-than-thou, pietistic, hypocritical, pharisaical

COLLOQ. goody-goody

E3 humble

morality n

ethics, morals, moral values, moralism, ideals, principles, principles of behaviour, principles of right and wrong, standards, virtue, righteousness, decency, purity, chastity, goodness, honesty, integrity, justice, uprightness, conduct, manners, *Sittlichkeit*

OLD morale

FORMAL rectitude, propriety

E3 immorality

moralize v

preach, lecture, pontificate, edify, sermonize

FORMAL discourse, ethicize

morally adv

ethically, honourably, properly, justly, nobly, socially, behaviourally

morals n

morality, moral values, moral code, ethics, principles, principles of behaviour, right and wrong, standards, ideals, integrity, scruples, behaviour, conduct, habits, manners

morass n

1 QUAGMIRE, bog, moss, marsh, marshland, swamp, slough, mire, fen, quag, quicksand

2 CONFUSION, clutter, chaos, mess, jam, jumble, muddle, mix-up, tangle

COLLOQ. can of worms

moratorium n

delay, postponement, halt, freeze, suspension, stay, standstill, stoppage, respite, ban, embargo

E3 *colloq.* go-ahead, green light

morbid adj

1 GHOULISH, obsessed with death, ghastly, gruesome, grisly, macabre, hideous, horrible, horrid, dreadful, grim

2 GLOOMY, pessimistic, melancholy, dejected, down, morose, sombre

FORMAL lugubrious

COLLOQ. down in the dumps

3 SICK, ailing, diseased, unhealthy, unwholesome

FORMAL insalubrious

morbidly adv

ghoulishly, gruesomely, horribly, horridly, grimly, dreadfully, hideously

mordant adj

biting, acid, caustic, bitter, acrimonious, astringent, critical, scathing, sharp, harsh, incisive, waspish, stinging, wounding, vicious, venomous, cutting, sarcastic, pungent, edged

FORMAL acerbic, trenchant

E3 gentle, mild, sparing

more adj, adv, pron

♦ adj

further, extra, additional, added, new, fresh, increased, other, another, supplementary, repeated, alternative, spare

E3 less

♦ adv

further, longer, to a greater extent/degree, again, better

E3 less

♦ pron

greater number/quantity, additional people/things, extra

■ **more or less**

generally, in general, by and large, for the most part, on the whole, mostly, in most cases, predominantly, mainly, broadly

moreover adv

furthermore, further, besides, in addition, as well, also, additionally, what is more

mores n

custom, traditions, habits, procedures, practices, ways, manners, ways of life, ways of behaving, conventions, usages, etiquette

morgue n

mortuary, funeral parlour, deadhouse, charnel house

moribund adj

1 DYING, failing, fading, expiring, declining, wasting away, senile, in extremis

TECHNICAL comatose

COLLOQ. on your last legs, on the way out, with one foot in the grave, not long for this world

2 WEAK, feeble, lifeless, declining, wasting away, waning, ebbing, stagnating, stagnant, obsolescent, doomed, dwindling, collapsing, crumbling

E3 1 alive, lively; *formal* nascent **2** flourishing

morning *n*
before noon, a.m., dawn, sunrise, first light, daybreak, break of day, cock-crow, crack of dawn, daylight, forenoon
OLD morn; (*Shakesp*) matin
Related adjectives: matutinal, antemeridian

moron *n*
fool, blockhead, fat-head, dolt, dunce, dimwit, simpleton, halfwit, idiot, cretin, imbecile, ignoramus, dupe, stooge, butt, laughing-stock, clown, comic, buffoon, jester
COLLOQ. nincompoop, ass, chump, ninny, neddy, clot, dope, twit, nitwit, nit, sucker, mug, twerp, birdbrain, silly-billy, berk, (proper) Charlie
SLANG wally, jerk, dumbo, muppet, pillock, prat, dork, geek, plonker, git, nerd, dweeb, nerk, cloth head, dipstick, goof, kook, pillock, tosspot; (*taboo*) dickhead, prick

moronic *adj*
foolish, stupid, senseless, silly, absurd, ridiculous, ludicrous, nonsensical, unwise, ill-advised, ill-considered, shortsighted, half-baked, crazy, mad, insane, idiotic, hare-brained, half-witted, simple-minded, simple, ignorant, unintelligent, inept, inane, pointless, unreasonable
COLLOQ. daft, crack-brained, gormless, dumb, dotty, mad, crazy, wacky, potty, batty, barmy, nutty, not in your right mind, out of your mind
SLANG with a screw/tile loose, needing your head examined

morose *adj*
ill-tempered, bad-tempered, moody, sombre, sullen, sulky, surly, gloomy, grim, gruff, sour, taciturn, glum, saturnine, depressed, mournful, melancholic, pessimistic
FORMAL lugubrious
COLLOQ. grouchy, crabby
E3 cheerful, communicative

morosely *adv*
sullenly, gloomily, moodily, gruffly, sourly, mournfully
FORMAL lugubriously
E3 cheerfully

morsel *n*
bit, scrap, piece, fragment, crumb, bite, mouthful, nibble, taste, soupçon, titbit, slice, segment, fraction, modicum, grain, atom, part, particle

mortal *adj, n*
◆ *adj*
1 WORLDLY, earthly, bodily, fleshly, human, perishable, transient, temporal
FORMAL corporeal, ephemeral
2 FATAL, lethal, dying, deadly, killing, murderous, deathful
3 EXTREME, great, severe, intense, grave, awful, dire, terrible, unbearable
4 *mortal enemies*
implacable, relentless, unrelenting, deadly, cruel, bitter, vengeful
5 *a mortal sin*
unforgivable, unpardonable, irremissible
E3 1 immortal **5** venial
◆ *n*
human being, human, individual, person, man, woman, being, body, creature, earthling
OLD worldling
E3 immortal, god

mortality *n*
1 HUMANITY, impermanence, worldliness, earthliness, perishability, transience
FORMAL ephemerality
2 FATALITY, death, death rate, killing, slaughter, carnage, casualty, loss of life
E3 1 immortality

mortally *adv*
1 *mortally wounded*
fatally, lethally, finally, terminally destructively, disastrously

2 EXTREMELY, greatly, severely, intensely, gravely, awfully, terribly

mortgage *n*
loan, pledge, security, bond, debenture; *Scot* wadset
FORMAL lien

mortification *n*
1 EMBARRASSMENT, humiliation, confounding, shame, disgrace, dishonour, loss of face, abasement, annoyance, chastening, vexation
FORMAL chagrin, discomfiture, ignominy
2 DISCIPLINE, punishment, asceticism, control, self-control, denial, self-denial, conquering
FORMAL subjugation

mortified *adj*
humiliated, horrified, shamed, ashamed, disgraced, dishonoured, humbled, embarrassed, crushed, confounded, defeated, sick

mortify *v*
1 HUMILIATE, horrify, shame, put to shame, embarrass, offend, disgrace, dishonour, chastise, chasten, abash, confound, humble, bring low, crush, deflate, affront, annoy, disappoint, wither
FORMAL discomfit, chagrin
COLLOQ. take down a peg or two
2 DISCIPLINE, restrain, suppress, deny, die, control, conquer, subdue

mortifying *adj*
embarrassing, humbling, humiliating, salutary, shaming, ignominious, overwhelming, crushing, chastening, punishing, thwarting
FORMAL discomfiting

mortuary *n*
morgue, funeral parlour, deadhouse, charnel house

most *n*
bulk, mass, majority, overwhelming majority, preponderance, greatest/largest part, almost all, nearly all
COLLOQ. lion's share
■ **for the most part**
mostly, mainly, on the whole, principally, especially, chiefly, generally, in general, usually, largely, predominantly, overall, in the main, as a rule, above all

mostly *adv*
mainly, on the whole, principally, especially, chiefly, generally, in general, usually, largely, predominantly, overall, for the most part, in the main, as a rule, above all

moth

Types of moth include:

brown-tail	gypsy	peppered
buff-tip	hawk moth	privet hawk moth
burnet	Kentish glory	puss
six-spot	lackey	red underwing
carpet	lappet	silkworm
cinnabar	leopard	silver-Y
clothes	lobster	swallowtail
death's-head	magpie	turnip
moth	oak hook-tip	wax
emperor	pale tussock	winter
garden tiger	peach blossom	

See also **butterfly**.

moth-eaten *adj*
old, worn, worn-out, old-fashioned, obsolete, outdated, outworn, ragged, tattered, threadbare, dated, ancient, antiquated, archaic, decrepit, dilapidated, decayed, musty, shabby, stale, mouldy, mangy, moribund, seedy
E3 fresh, new

mother *n, v*

◆ *n*

1 PARENT, birth mother, dam, matriarch, ancestor, matron
FORMAL procreator, progenitress, materfamilias, mater
COLLOQ. mum, mummy, ma, mam, mumsy, ma(m)ma, old
woman, old lady; *N Am* mom, mommy
Related adjective: maternal

2 ORIGIN, source, spring, fount, foundation, base, cause,
derivation, roots, wellspring

◆ *v*

1 BEAR, give birth to, produce, bring forth, nurture, raise,
rear, tend, nurse, care for, take care of, look after, cherish
2 PAMPER, spoil, baby, indulge, overprotect, fuss over,
nanny

motherly *adj*

motherlike, maternal, caring, comforting, affectionate,
kind, loving, protective, nurturing, warm, tender, gentle,
fond
F3 neglectful, uncaring

motif *n*

theme, idea, topic, concept, pattern, design, figure, form,
logo, shape, device, emblem, ornament, decoration

motion *n, v*

◆ *n*

1 MOVEMENT, action, mobility, moving, activity,
locomotion, travelling, travel, transit, going, changing
place(s), passage, passing, progress, change, flow,
inclination
FORMAL motility
Related adjective: kinetic

2 GESTURE, gesticulation, movement, act, action,
indication, signal, sign, wave, nod

3 PROPOSAL, suggestion, recommendation, proposition,
plan, scheme, project, manifesto, presentation, bid, offer

◆ *v*

signal, gesture, gesticulate, sign, wave, nod, beckon, direct,
usher

■ **in motion**

under way, moving, on the move, going, on the go,
travelling, in progress, functioning, running, operational
F3 stationary, at rest

■ **set in motion**

begin to happen, begin, start, set about, embark on, get
going, launch into, activate, actuate, set off, initiate,
introduce, found, institute, open, instigate
FORMAL commence
COLLOQ. kick off, get cracking, set the ball rolling, take the
plunge, set the wheels turning

motionless *adj*

unmoving, still, stationary, static, immobile, immovable,
unmovable, moveless, at a standstill, stock-still, fixed, set,
halted, at rest, resting, sleeping, standing, paralysed,
inanimate, inert, lifeless, frozen, transfixed, rigid, stagnant
OLD becalmed
F3 active, moving

motivate *v*

prompt, incite, impel, spur, provoke, stimulate, drive, lead,
stir, urge, goad, push, propel, persuade, move, inspire,
encourage, cause, trigger, actuate, activate, induce, kindle,
draw, excite, arouse, bring, initiate
COLLOQ. kick-start
F3 deter, discourage, prevent, inhibit

motivation *n*

reason, incitement, inducement, prompting, spur,
stimulus, provocation, drive, push, hunger, desire, wish,
urge, impulse, incentive, ambition, inspiration, instigation,
momentum, motive, persuasion, interest
F3 discouragement, prevention

motive *n*

ground(s), cause, reason, basis, purpose, motivation, aim,
occasion, object, intention, influence, rationale, thinking,
incentive, impulse, stimulus, inspiration, incitement,
inducement, urge, goad, spur, encouragement,
inspiration, design, desire, attraction, lure, consideration,
persuasion, pretext, mainspring, propellant
TECHNICAL sanction
OLD instance, moment
F3 deterrent, disincentive

Synonym nuances

Grounds and **basis** can be used to suggest sufficient
foundation or justification: *an appeal for clemency on the
grounds of ill health; he was elected on the basis of his
local reputation*, whereas **purpose** and **motivation**,
object and **intention** put the emphasis on a desired
outcome. **Occasion**, on the other hand, has more to do
with a specific set of circumstances: *the family gathering
afforded the occasion to reveal a few home truths*, unlike
influence which suggests an external force: *the
influence of religion on lifestyle is on the decline*.

The words **rationale**, **thinking** and **consideration**
imply the application of constructive thought to a
motive: *what is the rationale behind this seemingly
impetuous move?*. **Design** is similar but also implies a
degree of contrivance. The word **pretext** would be
reserved for a false objective: *I went uninvited to the
party, on the pretext of helping with the food*. The terms
impulse and **urge**, conversely, imply a sudden
inclination. **Incentive** and **inducement** suggest an
encouraging or rewarding element: *what is my incentive
to do this for you?*, while **attraction** and **lure** imply an
element of temptation.

Stimulus, **inspiration** and **spur** have suggestions of a
response that has been provoked: *hunger was the main
spur for our hunting*, as does **incitement**, though
perhaps with less desirable consequences: *the
incitement of racial hatred*. The terms **encouragement**
and **inspiration** suggest a very positive infusion with
spirit or enthusiasm. The less common **propellant** and
mainspring might be used of a powerful, driving
motive: *being a supreme athlete was the mainspring of
his life*.

---

motley *adj*

1 ASSORTED, varied, mixed, miscellaneous, diverse,
diversified, multifarious
FORMAL heterogeneous
2 MULTICOLOURED, variegated, particoloured, colourful,
many-hued, pied, piebald, tabby, dappled, brindled,
mottled, spotted, striped, streaked
F3 1 uniform, homogeneous **2** monochrome

motor vehicle

See **car.**
See also panel on next page

mottled *adj*

speckled, dappled, blotchy, blotched, flecked, piebald,
stippled, streaked, marbled, splotchy, tabby, spotted,
freckled, brinded, brindled, brindle, variegated
TECHNICAL poikilitic
F3 monochrome, uniform

motto *n*

saying, slogan, maxim, watchword, cry, catchword,
byword, precept, proverb, aphorism, saw, axiom, adage,
formula, rule, golden rule, dictum, truism
FORMAL epigram, gnome

mould[1] *n, v*

◆ *n*

1 CAST, form, shape, die, template, pattern, matrix, frame,
framework, blister pack
2 SHAPE, form, format, pattern, structure, style, type, build,
construction, formation, cast, cut, figure, design, kind,

Parts of a motor vehicle include:

ABS (anti-lock braking system)
accelerator
airbag
air brake
air-conditioner
air inlet
antidazzle mirror
antiglare switch
anti-roll bar
antitheft device
ashtray
axle
N Am backup light
battery
bench seat
bezel
bodywork
bonnet
boot
brake drum
brake light
brake pad
brake shoe
bumper
car radio

car phone
catalytic converter
central locking
centre console
chassis
child-safety seat
cigarette-lighter
clock
clutch
courtesy light
crankcase
cruise control
dashboard
differential gear
dimmer
disc brake
door
door-lock
drive shaft
drum brake
electric window
emergency light
engine
exhaust pipe
N Am fender
filler cap

flasher switch
fog light (or lamp)
folding seat
four-wheel drive
fuel gauge
N Am gas tank
gear
gearbox
gear-lever (or gear-stick)
N Am gearshift
glove compartment
grill
handbrake
hazard warning light
headlight
headrest
heated rear window
heater
N Am hood
horn
hub-cap
hydraulic brake

hydraulic suspension
ignition
ignition key
indicator
instrument panel
jack
jump lead
kingpin
N Am license plate
lift gate
monocoque
number plate
oil gauge
overrider
parcel shelf
parking-light
petrol tank
pneumatic tyre
power brake
prop shaft
quarterlight
rack and pinion
radial-ply tyre
rear light
rear-view mirror

reclining seat
reflector
Aust & NZ registration plate
colloq. rev counter
reversing light
roof rack
screen-washer bottle
seat belt
shaft
shock absorber
sidelight
side-impact bar
side mirror
silencer
sill
solenoid
spare tyre
speedometer
spoiler
steering-column
steering-wheel
N Am stick shift
stoplight
sunroof

sun visor
suspension
temperature gauge
towbar
track rod
transmission
N Am trunk
tyre
vent
wheel
wheel arch
windscreen
windscreen-washer
windscreen-wiper
N Am windshield
wing
wing mirror

See also **engine**.

---

model, sort, stamp, arrangement, brand, frame, framework, character, nature, quality, calibre, line, outline, make
FORMAL configuration
♦ *v*
1 FORGE, cast, shape, stamp, make, form, fashion, create, design, construct, sculpt, carve, model, work, frame
2 INFLUENCE, affect, form, shape, direct, control

mould² *n*
a smell of mould
mildew, must, fungus, mouldiness, mustiness, fust, blight, rot

moulder *v*
decay, decompose, perish, rot, waste, corrupt, crumble, disintegrate, turn to dust, humify

mouldy *adj*
mildewed, blighted, musty, muggy, decaying, corrupt, rotten, fusty, putrid, bad, spoiled, stale, vinewed; *dialect* foughty; *Scot* fousty, mochie
OLD hoar
FORMAL mucedinous, mucid
E3 fresh, wholesome

mound *n*
1 HILL, hillock, hummock, mount, rise, knoll, bank, dike, dune, dun, elevation, ridge, embankment, whaleback, earthwork, rampart, tumulus, barrow, cairn, kurgan, tell; *dialect* tump; *Scot* barp
TECHNICAL butt
OLD agger, motte, tuffet
FORMAL monticule
2 HEAP, pile, stack, accumulation, collection, supply, store, hoard, abundance, mountain, lot, stack, bundle, stockpile; *dialect* hog
TECHNICAL mogul, pingo, termitarium

mount *v, n*
♦ *v*
1 ORGANIZE, produce, put on, set up, prepare, stage, exhibit, display, launch, arrange, install
2 INCREASE, grow, build (up), accumulate, pile up, tot up, multiply, rise, intensify, escalate, soar, swell, accrue

3 CLIMB (UP), ascend, get up, go up, get on, clamber up, scale, step up, climb on (to), jump on (to), get astride, ride, horse, escalade; *S Afr* saddle up
OLD back, sty
E3 2 decrease, descend **3** descend, dismount, go down
♦ *n*
1 HORSE, steed
2 SUPPORT, mounting, backing, base, fixture, stand, frame

mountain *n*
1 HEIGHT, elevation, mount, peak, pinnacle, hill, fell, mound, alp, tor, massif; *S Afr* berg
2 HEAP, pile, mound, stack, mass, abundance, accumulation, lot, stack, backlog

---

The highest mountains of the world include:

ASIA:
Everest (*Himalaya-Nepal/ Tibet*)
K2 (*Pakistan/India*)
Kanchenjunga (*Himalaya-Nepal/India*)
Makalu (*Himalaya-Nepal/ Tibet*)
Dhaulagiri (*Himalaya-Nepal*)
Nanga Parbat (*Himalaya-India*)
Annapurna (*Himalaya-Nepal*)

SOUTH AMERICA:
Aconcagua (*Andes-Argentina*)
NORTH AMERICA:
McKinley (*Alaska Range*)
AFRICA:
Kilimanjaro (*Tanzania*)
EUROPE:
Elbruz (*Caucasus*)
Mont Blanc (*Alps-France*)
ANTARCTICA:
Vinson Massif
AUSTRALASIA:
Jaja (*New Guinea*)

---

mountaineering
See panel on next page

mountainous *adj*
1 CRAGGY, rocky, hilly, high, highland, upland, alpine, soaring, lofty, towering, steep
2 HUGE, towering, enormous, immense, vast, colossal, massive, gigantic, giant, mammoth
COLLOQ. jumbo, ginormous, humongous
SLANG mega
E3 1 flat **2** tiny

Mountaineering and climbing terms include:

abseiling	cam	debolting	ice ridge	rock	snow goggles
abseil piton	carabiner (or	descender	ice screw	rock face	solo ascent
abseil sling	karabiner)	descent	ice slope	rock spike	spike
abseil station	chalk bag	drive-in ice piton	ice step	rock wall	sport climbing
N Am adz	chalk cliff	Dülfer seat	kernmantel rope	rope	spur
adze	climbing	dynamic rope	Munro	rope sling	stack
Alpinism	chimney	étrier	non-belayer	saddle	standing rope
arête	chock	fissure	nut	scree	summit
ascender	chockstone	glacier	on the rope	sea stack	top out
ascent	cleft	gully	overhang	self-belaying	trad route
avalanche	climbing harness	hammer axe	pick	*sérac*	traverse
N Am ax	climbing wall	harness	piolet	Sherpa	tying in
axe	col	hand hold	pitch	shunt	unrope
base camp	corkscrew piton	helmet	piton	sit harness	wallnut
belay	cornice	helmet lamp	prusik knot	sling	wrist sling
belayer	corrie	hut	prusik loop	sling seat	
bivouac	crag	ice axe	rapelling	snow bridge	
bolting	crampon	ice climbing	ridge	snow cornice	
bouldering	crevasse	ice piton	ringed piton	snow gaiters	

mountebank *n*

charlatan, swindler, cheat, fake, fraud, impostor, pretender, rogue, trickster

COLLOQ. con man, phoney, pseud, quack

mourn *v*

grieve, lament, sorrow, miss, regret, deplore, weep, wail, keen

OLD bemoan, bewail

F3 rejoice

mourner *n*

griever, bereaved, sorrower, mute, keener

mournful *adj*

sorrowful, sad, unhappy, desolate, doleful, rueful, grief-stricken, heavy-hearted, heartbroken, broken-hearted, cast-down, downcast, miserable, tragic, melancholy, melancholic, plaintive, funereal, sombre, depressed, dejected, gloomy, dismal, *funèbre*

OLD dernful

FORMAL woeful, lugubrious, disconsolate, elegiac

F3 happy, joyful, cheerful

mournfully *adv*

sadly, unhappily, sorrowfully, desolately, dolefully, ruefully, plaintively, broken-heartedly, miserably, sombrely, gloomily, dismally

F3 happily, joyfully, cheerfully

mourning *n*

grief, grieving, bereavement, lamentation, sadness, sorrow, sorrowing, desolation, weeping, wailing, keening

F3 rejoicing

moustache *n*

whiskers, mustachio, handlebar moustache, toothbrush moustache, zapata moustache, walrus, Charlie

OLD excrement

COLLOQ. tache, tash, face fungus

mousey, mousy *adj*

1 BROWNISH, greyish, colourless, drab, dull, plain, uninteresting, diffident

2 SHY, quiet, timid, withdrawn, unassertive, unforthcoming, shrinking, self-effacing, meek, timorous

F3 2 assertive, bright, extrovert, irrepressible

mouth *n, v*

♦ *n*

1 LIPS, jaws, embouchure

COLLOQ. chops, kisser

SLANG trap, gob, traphole, cakehole; *N Am* bazoo

Related adjectives: oral, stomatic

2 OPENING, aperture, cavity, vent, entrance, door, doorway, gateway, hatch, portal, inlet, estuary, outlet, delta

TECHNICAL stoma

FORMAL orifice

3 BOASTING, bragging, bragging, blustering, babble, empty/idle talk

COLLOQ. hot air, gas

4 CHEEK, nerve, gall, impudence, impertinence, insolence, disrespect, rudeness, backchat

FORMAL effrontery

COLLOQ. sauce, lip, brass neck

♦ *v*

enunciate, articulate, utter, say, pronounce, whisper, form

■ **keep your mouth shut**

keep quiet, shut up, say nothing, not breathe a word, hold your tongue, cover up

COLLOQ. pipe down, clam up, keep mum

SLANG keep your trap shut

Parts of the mouth include:

alveolar ridge	lower lip	tongue
gum	palatoglossal arch	tonsil
hard palate	palato-	upper lip
inferior dental	pharyngeal arch	uvula
arch	soft palate	
isthmus of fauces	superior dental	
labial commissure	arch	

See also **tooth**.

mouthful *n*

sample, morsel, spoonful, swallow, taste, bite, nibble, bit, gulp, sip, titbit, drop, forkful, slug, sup, bonne-bouche

mouthpiece *n*

spokesperson, spokesman, spokeswoman, representative, agent, delegate, propagandist, journal, periodical, publication, voice, organ

movable *adj*

mobile, portable, transportable, changeable, alterable, adjustable, flexible, transferable

FORMAL portative

F3 fixed, immovable

movables *n*

belongings, possessions, goods, furniture, property

FORMAL chattels, effects, impedimenta, plenishings

COLLOQ. gear, stuff, things, clobber

move *v, n*

♦ *v*

1 GO, advance, travel, walk, shift, stir, change, pass, act, take action, proceed, progress, develop, make strides

COLLOQ. budge
2 TRANSPORT, carry, bring, take, fetch, relocate, transfer, shift, switch, shunt, swing
FORMAL transpose
3 DEPART, go away, leave, transfer, decamp, migrate, remove, move house, move away, relocate
4 STIMULATE, prompt, incline, urge, impel, drive, cause, lead, propel, actuate, motivate, incite, excite, rouse, arouse, push, persuade, induce, inspire, influence, provoke
5 AFFECT, touch, agitate, stir, impress, strike, excite, disturb, upset, agitate
6 PROPOSE, put forward, request, suggest, advocate, recommend, submit
7 FRATERNIZE, circulate, mix, mingle, socialize, associate, keep company, go around
FORMAL consort
COLLOQ. hang about, hang out, hobnob, pal up, gang up, rub shoulders
♦ *n*
1 MOVEMENT, motion, manoeuvre, gesture, gesticulation, activity
2 REMOVAL, relocation, migration, transfer, repositioning, change of address
3 MEASURE, initiative, step, act, manoeuvre, action, activity, action, device, stratagem, tack
■ **get a move on**
hurry up, speed up, make haste
COLLOQ. get cracking, shake a leg, put your foot down, step on it/the gas
■ **make a move**
1 GO, depart, leave, get going, take your leave
COLLOQ. make tracks, push/clear off, split
2 TAKE A COURSE OF ACTION, do something, take the initiative
COLLOQ. get cracking, take the plunge, get the show on the road
■ **on the move**
moving, travelling, journeying, progressing, advancing, moving forward, making progress, active, on the go, astir, under way

movement *n*
1 REPOSITIONING, move, moving, gesture, gesticulation, relocation, activity, act, action, agitation, stirring, shifting, transfer, transportation, passage
2 CHANGE, development, variation, advance, improvement, breakthrough, evolution, passage, current, drift, flow, current, fall, rise, swing, shift, progress, progression, trend, tendency
3 CAMPAIGN, crusade, drive, group, organization, party, coalition, faction, wing
4 MECHANISM, works, workings, machinery, system, action
COLLOQ. guts
5 *a movement in a symphony*
section, part, division, piece, bit, portion, passage

movie *n*
1 FILM, motion picture, picture, feature film, video, silent film, talkie
OLD flick
2 *What's on at the movies?*
cinema, film theatre, movie theatre, entertainment centre, multiplex, picture-house, picture-palace
COLLOQ. fleapit

moving *adj*
1 MOBILE, active, dynamic, in motion, astir, manoeuvrable
TECHNICAL kinetic
FORMAL motile
2 TOUCHING, affecting, poignant, impressive, emotive, arousing, stirring, emotional, inspiring, inspirational, exciting, thrilling, persuasive, stimulating, disturbing, upsetting, worrying, pathetic
3 *the moving force/spirit*
driving, motivating, leading, influential, dynamic,

stimulating, inspiring, urging
E∃ 1 immobile, fixed **2** unemotional

movingly *adv*
touchingly, with feeling/emotion, poignantly, inspirationally, expressively, pathetically

mow *v*
cut, trim, crop, clip, shear, scythe
■ **mow down**
butcher, slaughter, massacre, kill, shoot down, decimate, gun down, cut down, cut to pieces

much *adv, adj, n*
♦ *adv*
greatly, to a great extent, to a great degree, a great deal, considerably, a lot, frequently, often
♦ *adj*
copious, plentiful, ample, considerable, a lot, abundant, great, substantial, a great number of, extensive, widespread
COLLOQ. lots, masses, piles, stacks, scads, lashings, oodles
♦ *n*
plenty, a great deal, a lot
COLLOQ. lots, loads, heaps, lashings
E∃ little

muck *n, v*
♦ *n*
1 DIRT, mire, filth, mud, slime, grime, scum, sludge; *Aust & NZ* scunge
COLLOQ. gunge, yuck; *N Am* guck
SLANG grunge, crud
2 EXCREMENT, dung, manure, ordure, sewage
TECHNICAL guano
FORMAL faeces
■ **muck about/around**
1 FOOL ABOUT/AROUND, play around, play about
COLLOQ. mess about/around, lark about/around
SLANG *N Am* goof about/around
2 INCONVENIENCE, upset, bother, trouble
COLLOQ. lead a merry dance, lead up the garden path, send on a wild goose chase, make life hell for
3 INTERFERE, tamper, meddle, untidy, disorder, disarrange, dishevel, mess up
■ **muck up**
ruin, wreck, spoil, mess up, make a mess of, botch, bungle
SLANG cock up, screw up, louse up

mucky *adj*
begrimed, bespattered, dirty, filthy, grimy, messy, miry, mud-caked, muddy, oozy, slimy, soiled, sticky; *Aust & NZ* scungy
COLLOQ. *N Am* gucky
E∃ clean

mucous *adj*
gelatinous, glutinous, gummy, viscous, viscid, slimy, snotty
FORMAL mucilaginous

mud *n*
clay, mire, ooze, dirt, soil, sludge, silt, slab; *Scot & Irish* clabber

muddle *n, v*
♦ *n*
chaos, confusion, disorganization, disorder, disarray, mess, mix-up, jumble, clutter, tangle
♦ *v*
1 DISORGANIZE, disorder, throw into disorder, mix up, mess up, jumble (up), scramble, tangle
2 CONFUSE, bewilder, bemuse, perplex, daze, puzzle, confound, befuddle
■ **muddle through**
get by, get along, cope, manage, make do

muddled *adj*
confused, chaotic, disorganized, disordered, jumbled,

mixed-up, tangled, scrambled, disarrayed, messy, loose, higgledy-piggledy, disorient(at)ed, bewildered, perplexed, unclear, vague, woolly, befuddled, stupefied, dazed, incoherent
COLLOQ. at sea, addle-headed

muddy adj, v

♦ adj

1 DIRTY, filthy, foul, miry, mucky, grimy, grubby, slimy, slushy, oozy, marshy, boggy, swampy, quaggy, grimy, sludgy, sloppy, splashy, dreggy, slabby, waterlogged; *dialect* grouty; *Scot* drumly
OLD limous
2 CLOUDY, indistinct, obscure, opaque, murky, turbid, hazy, smoky, blurred, fuzzy, dull, dingy; *Scot* drumly
F3 1 clean **2** clear

♦ v

1 DIRTY, soil, make muddy, puddle, smear, smirch, cloud
FORMAL begrime, bespatter, bedash, bedaub
2 CONFUSE, cloud, make unclear, muddle, mix up, jumble (up), disorganize, scramble, tangle, trouble
F3 1 clean **2** clarify

muff v

botch, bungle, mess up, mismanage, mishandle, miss, spoil, mishit
COLLOQ. fluff

muffle v

1 WRAP, wrap up, envelop, cloak, swathe, swaddle, cover (up)
2 DEADEN, dull, quieten, soften, mute, hush, silence, stifle, dampen, muzzle, suppress, smother, gag
F3 2 amplify

mug¹ n

drink coffee from a mug
cup, beaker, pot, tankard, stein, noggin, sconce, *bock*
COLLOQ. tinny

mug² v

mugged on his way home
set upon, attack, assault, waylay, steal from, rob, beat up, bash, jump (on), knock about
COLLOQ. do over, rough up, batter, knock someone's block off, knock into the middle of next week

mug³ n

like a mug, I agreed
fool, simpleton, gull, dupe
COLLOQ. sucker, chump, muggins, soft touch

mug⁴ n, v

♦ n

his ugly mug
face, features
FORMAL countenance, visage, physiognomy
COLLOQ. kisser, mush, clock, phiz

■ **mug up**
bone up, con, cram, get up, study, swot

muggy adj

humid, sticky, stuffy, sultry, close, clammy, oppressive, airless, sweltering, moist, damp; *Scot* mochie
F3 dry

mulish adj

obstinate, stubborn, defiant, difficult, headstrong, inflexible, self-willed, stiff-necked, unreasonable, wilful, perverse, rigid, wrong-headed
FORMAL intractable, intransigent, recalcitrant, refractory
COLLOQ. pig-headed

mull

■ **mull over**
reflect on, ponder, contemplate, think over, think about, consider, weigh up, muse on, chew over, meditate, study, examine, deliberate
FORMAL ruminate

multicoloured adj

variegated, particoloured, colourful, kaleidoscopic, motley, pied, piebald, dappled, brindled, spotted, striped
COLLOQ. psychedelic

multifarious adj

diverse, diversified, different, miscellaneous, varied, sundry, variegated, numerous, many, multiple, multitudinous, legion
FORMAL manifold, multiform

multiple adj

many, numerous, various, several, sundry, collective
FORMAL manifold

multiplicity n

abundance, array, number, numerousness, profusion, variety, diversity, mass, host, lot, myriad
FORMAL manifoldness
COLLOQ. heaps, loads, lots, oodles, piles, scores, stacks, tons

multiply v

increase, proliferate, expand, grow, spread, reproduce, propagate, breed, accumulate, intensify, extend, build up, boost
FORMAL augment, manifold
F3 decrease, lessen

multipurpose adj

versatile, adaptable, flexible, all-round, all-purpose, multifaceted, adjustable, many-sided, general-purpose, functional, resourceful, handy, variable
F3 inflexible

multitude n

1 CROWD, throng, horde, swarm, mob, mass, herd, congregation, assembly, host, lot, legion
COLLOQ. lots
2 PUBLIC, people, populace, crowd, mob, common people, rank and file, rabble, hoi polloi, herd, common herd, great unwashed, *canaille*
COLLOQ. plebs, riff-raff
F3 1 few, scattering

multitudinous adj

numerous, many, profuse, swarming, copious, considerable, abundant, abounding, teeming, innumerable, countless, great, infinite, legion, myriad
FORMAL manifold
COLLOQ. umpteen

mum adj

quiet, mute, dumb, silent, reticent, secretive, tight-lipped, close-lipped, close-mouthed, uncommunicative, unforthcoming

mumble v

murmur, rumble, talk to yourself, talk under your breath, mutter, stutter, splutter, speak unclearly, speak softly, speak in a low voice, slur

mumbo-jumbo n

nonsense, claptrap, gibberish, incantation, jargon, magic, superstition, spell, chant, cant, charm, ritual, rite, mummery, rigmarole, abracadabra
FORMAL conjuration
COLLOQ. double talk, gobbledygook, hocus-pocus, humbug

munch v

eat, chew, crunch, champ, chomp
FORMAL masticate

mundane adj

1 ORDINARY, banal, hackneyed, boring, dull, stale, trite, everyday, common, commonplace, usual, normal, typical, regular, customary, prosaic, humdrum, workaday, routine
2 WORLDLY, secular, earthly, terrestrial, fleshly, temporal
FORMAL terrene
F3 1 extraordinary **2** spiritual

municipal *adj*
civic, city, civil, town, metropolitan, urban, borough, community, public

municipality *n*
city, town, township, borough, department, district, precinct, council, local government, burgh, *département*

munificence *n*
generosity, generousness, liberality, magnanimousness, open-handedness, bounty, benevolence, philanthropy, charitableness, altruism, hospitality
FORMAL largesse, beneficence, bounteousness
E3 meanness

munificent *adj*
generous, open-handed, big-hearted, bountiful, free-handed, magnanimous, lavish, liberal, hospitable, benevolent, philanthropical, charitable, altruistic, rich, unstinting, princely
FORMAL beneficent, bounteous
E3 mean

munitions *n*
equipment, supplies, apparatus, gear, tackle, kit, tools, materials, provisions, bombs, shells, guns

murder *n, v*
◆ *n*
1 KILLING, homicide, manslaughter, slaying, slaughter, assassination, execution, massacre, butchery, bloodshed, blood, foul play, dispatch
OLD murther, petty treason
FORMAL patricide, matricide, infanticide, fillicide, fratricide, sororicide, uxoricide, parricide
COLLOQ. liquidation, removal, rubout
2 *driving in town is murder*
hell, torment, torture, agony, ordeal, nightmare, misery, wretchedness, suffering, anguish
◆ *v*
1 KILL, slaughter, slay, put to death, execute, assassinate, butcher, massacre, rid, burke
COLLOQ. do in, wipe out
SLANG bump off, eliminate, liquidate, knock off, hit, rub out, take out, waste, blow away, fill in, stiff, whack
2 RUIN, spoil, destroy, botch, mess up, wreck, make a mess of
3 DEFEAT EASILY, beat, overwhelm, rout, annihilate, outplay, outwit, outsmart, trounce
COLLOQ. slaughter, hammer, clobber, lick, thrash, wipe the floor with

murderer *n*
killer, homicide, slayer, slaughterer, assassin, butcher, cut-throat
OLD murtherer

murderous *adj*
1 HOMICIDAL, brutal, barbarous, bloodthirsty, bloody, cut-throat, killing, lethal, fatal, mortal, cruel, savage, ferocious, deadly
2 DIFFICULT, exhausting, strenuous, arduous, punishing, gruelling, unpleasant, dangerous
COLLOQ. killing

murderously *adv*
dangerously, alarmingly, menacingly, threateningly, ominously, sinisterly, fatally, homicidally, unpleasantly, grimly, bloodthirstily
FORMAL portentously

murk *n*
murkiness, dark, darkness, dimness, blackness, gloom, gloominess, night, dusk, twilight, half-light, shadows, shade, shadiness, sunlessness, cloudiness
FORMAL tenebrity, tenebrosity

murky *adj*

1 DARK, dismal, gloomy, dreary, cheerless, dull, overcast, misty, foggy, dim, cloudy, obscure, veiled, grey
FORMAL tenebrose, tenebrious, tenebrous
2 *murky water*
dirty, dark, dingy, cloudy, turbid
3 MYSTERIOUS, shady, dark, secret, suspicious, questionable
COLLOQ. fishy, shady
SLANG sus
E3 1 bright, clear, fine **2** clear

murmur *n, v*
◆ *n*
1 MUMBLE, muttering, whisper, undertone, humming, rumble, drone, grumble
2 *the murmur of voices*
hum, buzz, drone, purring, thrum, rumbling
3 GRUMBLE, complaint, moan, grievance, protest, objection, dissatisfaction, annoyance, fault-finding, criticism, carping, censure
COLLOQ. grouse, gripe, beefing, whingeing
SLANG bellyaching
◆ *v*
1 MUTTER, mumble, whisper, intone, buzz, drone, hum, rustle, rumble, purr, purl, burble, babble
2 COMPLAIN, criticize, find fault, object, protest, grumble, carp, fuss, whine
COLLOQ. beef, grouse, gripe, whinge
SLANG bellyache

murmuring *adj, n*
◆ *adj*
mumbling, murmurous, muttering, rumbling, whispering, humming, buzzing, droning, purring
◆ *n*
drone, mumble, mumbling, muttering, rumble, rumbling, whisper(ing), buzz(ing), purr(ing)
FORMAL murmuration, susurrus

muscle *n, v*
◆ *n*
1 *strong muscles*
sinew, tendon, ligament
Related adjective: muscular
2 FORCE, brawn, beef, power, forcefulness, strength, stamina, potency, sturdiness, weight
FORMAL might
COLLOQ. beef, clout
▪ **muscle in**
butt in, push in, shove, strongarm, impose yourself, force your way in, interfere with, elbow your way in, jostle

---

Muscles include:

abdominal	latissimus dorsi	rectus
biceps	(or lat)	rhomboideus
buccinator	masseter	risorius
cardiac	omohyid	sartorius
ciliary body	pectoralis major	scalenus
complexus	pectoralis minor	soleus
deltoid	perforans	splenius
detrusor	peroneal muscles	stapedius
eye-string	platysma	supinator
gastrocnemius	pronator	trapezius
gluteus	psoas	triceps
iliacus	quadriceps	xiphihumeralis

---

muscular *adj*
brawny, sinewy, fibrous, athletic, strong, powerfully built, strapping, hefty, burly, powerful, husky, robust, stalwart, rugged, sturdy, vigorous, potent
COLLOQ. beefy
E3 puny, flabby, weak

muse *v*

ponder, think, think over, meditate, mull over, weigh, contemplate, consider, brood, reflect, review, study, chew over, dream, deliberate, speculate

FORMAL cogitate, ruminate

mush *n*

1 PASTE, pulp, pap, dough, corn, slush, swill, mash, cream, purée

2 SENTIMENTALITY, mawkishness

COLLOQ. schmaltz

mushroom *v*

proliferate, shoot up, grow, increase, expand, flourish, boom, spread, spring up, sprout, luxuriate

FORMAL burgeon

mushrooms and toadstools

Types of mushroom and toadstool include:

EDIBLE:	man on	INEDIBLE/
beefsteak fungus	horseback	POISONOUS:
blewit	march mushroom	amanita
boletus	meadow	common ink cap
button mushroom	mushroom	copper trumpet
cep	oyster mushroom	death cap
champignon	parasol	destroying angel
chanterelle	mushroom	devil's boletus
chestnut boletus	penny bun	earth ball
clouded agaric	porcini	false morel
common morel	saffron milk cap	fly agaric
cramp ball	shaggy parasol	mower's
cultivated	shiitake	mushroom
mushroom	slippery jack	panther cap
dingy agaric	sweetbread	purple boletus
elf cup	mushroom	satan's mushroom
fairy ring	truffle	shaggy milk cap
gypsy mushroom	trumpet agaric	stinking parasol
honey fungus	velvet shank	sulphur tuft
horn of plenty	winter mushroom	verdigris agaric
horse mushroom	wood hedgehog	woolly milk cap
lawyer's wig		yellow-staining
		mushroom

mushy *adj*

1 PULPY, pappy, pulpous, squashy, squelchy, squidgy, soft, doughy, wet

2 SENTIMENTAL, maudlin, mawkish, saccharine, sugary, syrupy, weepy

COLLOQ. schmaltzy, soppy, sloppy, slushy

music *n*

tune, melody, harmony
See panel below

musical *adj*

tuneful, melodious, melodic, harmonious, mellow, dulcet, sweet-sounding, lyrical

FORMAL euphonious, mellifluous

◼◼ discordant, unmusical

musical composition

Musical compositions include:

arabesque	fugue	prelude
aubade	gavotte	requiem
bagatelle	humoresque	rhapsody
berceuse	impromptu	rondo
bourrée	intermezzo	round
canon	lied	scherzo
capriccio	march	serenade
cavatina	minuet	sinfonietta
chaconne	nocturne	sonata
concerto	opus	sonatina
concerto grosso	overture	suite
divertimento	partita	symphony
étude	pastorale	toccata
extravaganza	pavane	voluntary
fanfare	polka	waltz
fantasia	polonaise	

See also **song**.

musical instruments

See panel on next page

musical terms

See panel on next page

musician

Musicians include:

GENERAL:	oboist	chamber
accompanist	organist	orchestra
busker	percussionist	choir
instrumentalist	pianist	duo
minstrel	piper	duet
performer	soloist	ensemble
player	trombonist	nonet
virtuoso	trumpeter	octet
PARTICULAR	violinist	orchestra
INSTRUMENTS:	SINGERS:	quartet
bugler	balladeer	quintet
cellist	bard	sextet
clarinettist	diva	trio
clarsair	minstrel	OTHER:
drummer	prima donna	composer
flautist	vocalist	conductor
fiddler	GROUPS:	maestro
guitarist	backing group	
harpist	band	
lutenist		

musing *n*

thinking, meditation, introspection, dreaming, daydreaming, wool-gathering, abstraction, absent-mindedness, contemplation, study,

Types of music include:

acid house	calypso	folk	honky-tonk	middle-of-the-	rock and roll
acid jazz	chamber	folk rock	house	road (MOR)	sacred
adult-orientated	choral	*colloq.* funk	incidental	muzak	salsa
rock (AOR)	classical	fusion	indie	nu-metal	samba
ambient	country-and-	gamelan	instrumental	operatic	ska
ballet	western	gangsta	jazz	orchestral	skiffle
ballroom	country rock	garage	jazz-funk	pop	soft rock
bebop	dance	glam rock	jazz-pop	punk rock	soul
bhangra	disco	gospel	jazz-rock	ragtime	swing
Big Beat	Dixieland	grunge	jive	rap	techno
bluegrass	doo-wop	hardcore	jungle	reggae	*slang* thrash metal
blues	drum and bass	hard rock	karaoke	rhythm and blues	trance
boogie-woogie	easy listening	heavy metal	lounge	(R & B)	trip-hop
cajun	electronic	hip-hop		rock	world

See also **jazz**.

Musical instruments include:

STRINGED INSTRUMENTS:
balalaika
bandore
banjo
bazouki
cello
clarsach
crwth
double-bass
erhu
colloq. fiddle
guitar
gusla
harp
hurdy-gurdy
lute
lyre
mandolin

oud
sarangi
saz
sitar
spinet
surbahar
tambura
ukulele
viola
violin
zither
KEYBOARD INSTRUMENTS:
accordion
concertina
clavichord
grand piano
harmonium

harpsichord
mbira
Mellotron®
melodeon
organ
piano
Pianola®
player-piano
colloq. squeeze-box
synthesizer
virginals
Wurlitzer®
WIND INSTRUMENTS:
bagpipes
bassoon
bugle

clarinet
cor anglais
cornet
didgeridoo
euphonium
fife
flugelhorn
flute
French horn
gaita harmonica
horn
kazoo
mouth-organ
oboe
Pan-pipes
piccolo
recorder
saxophone

sousaphone
Swanee whistle
tin whistle
trombone
trumpet
tuba
uillean pipes
PERCUSSION INSTRUMENTS:
bass-drum
bodhran
bongo
castanets
cymbal
gamelan
glockenspiel
kettle drum
maracas

marimba
rainstick
snare drum
steel pan
tabla
tambourine
tenor drum
timpani
tom-tom
triangle
tubular bells
xylophone

Musical terms include:

accelerando
acciaccatura
accidental
accompaniment
acoustic
adagio
ad lib
a due
affettuoso
agitato
al fine
alla breve
alla cappella
allargando
allegretto
allegro
al segno
alto
alto clef
amoroso
andante
animato
appoggiatura
arco
arpeggio
arrangement
a tempo
attacca
augmented interval
bar
bar line
baritone
bass
bass clef
beat
bis
breve
buffo
cadence

cantabile
cantilena
chord
chromatic
clef
coda
col canto
compound time
con brio
concert
con fuoco
con moto
consonance
contralto
counterpoint
crescendo
crotchet
cross-fingering
cue
da capo
decrescendo
demisemiquaver
descant
diatonic
diminished
interval
diminuendo
dissonance
dolce
doloroso
dominant
dotted note
dotted rest
double bar line
downbeat
drone
duplet
double trill
double sharp
encore

ensemble
expression
fifth interval
finale
fine
fingerboard
flat
double flat
forte
fortissimo
four-four time
fourth interval
fret
glissando
grave
harmonics
harmony
hemidemi-semiquaver
hold
imitation
improvisation
interval
intonation
key
key signature
langsam
larghetto
largo
leading note
ledger line
legato
lento
lyric
maestoso
major
major interval
manual
marcato
mediant

medley
melody
metre
mezza voce
mezzo forte
microtone
middle C
minim
minor
minor interval
mode
moderato
modulation
molto
mordent
movement
mute
natural
non troppo
note
obbligato
octave
orchestra
orchestration
ostinato
part
pause
pedal point
pentatonic
perdendo
perfect interval
phrase
pianissimo
piano
piece
pitch
pizzicato
presto
quadruplet
quarter tone

quaver
quintuplet
rallentando
recital
refrain
resolution
rest
rhythm
rinforzando
ritenuto
root
scale
score
second interval
semibreve
semiquaver
semitone
semplice
sempre
senza
sequence
seventh interval
sextuplet
sforzando
shake
sharp
simple time
six-eight time
sixth interval
slur
smorzando
solo
soprano
sostenuto
sotto voce
spiritoso
staccato
staff
stave
subdominant

subito
submediant
sul ponticello
supertonic
swell
syncopation
tablature
tacet
tanto
tempo
tenor
tenor clef
tenuto
theme
third interval
three-four time
tie
timbre
time signature
tone
tonic sol-fa
transposition
treble
treble clef
tremolo
triad
trill
triplet
tune
tuning
turn
tutti
two-two time
upbeat
unison
vibrato
vigoroso
virtuoso
vivace

---

studying, reflection, reverie, brown study
FORMAL cerebration, cogitation, ponderment, rumination

muss *v*
ruffle, make untidy, dishevel, tousle, disarrange, make a mess of

must *n*
necessity, prerequisite, obligation, requirement, stipulation, essential, fundamental, imperative, duty, basic, provision
FORMAL requisite, sine qua non

muster *v, n*
♦ *v*

assemble, convene, gather (together), call together, mobilize, round up, marshal, bring/come together, congregate, collect, group, meet, rally, mass, throng, call up, summon (up), enrol
FORMAL convoke
♦ *n*
gathering, assembly, collection, congregation, convention, mass, mobilization, rally, round-up, turnout, meeting, parade, review, march past, throng, concourse
OLD hosting
FORMAL assemblage, convocation
■ **pass muster**
be acceptable, be accepted, come up to standard, be good

enough, measure up, fit/fill the bill, make the grade, muster
COLLOQ. come up to scratch, shape up

musty *adj*
mouldy, mildewy, mildewed, stale, stuffy, fusty, damp, dank, airless, decayed, decaying, smelly, vinewed; *dialect* foughty; *Scot* fousty, mochie; *N Am* funky
OLD frowy
FORMAL mucid

mutability *n*
changeableness, interchangeability, alterability, variability, permutability, variation

mutable *adj*
changing, interchangeable, changeable, adaptable, alterable, vacillating, variable, volatile, wavering, inconsistent, uncertain, undependable, unreliable, unsettled, inconstant, fickle, flexible, irresolute, unstable, unsteady, permutable
E3 constant, invariable, permanent

mutate *v*
metamorphose, change, alter, transform, remake, remodel, reshape, convert, modify, evolve, translate
TECHNICAL transubstantiate
FORMAL transmute, transfigure
COLLOQ. transmogrify, morph

mutation *n*
change, alteration, variation, modification, adaptation, transformation, deviation, anomaly, evolution
FORMAL metamorphosis
COLLOQ. transmogrification

mute *adj, v*
• *adj*
silent, dumb, voiceless, uncommunicative, taciturn, wordless, speechless, unspoken, noiseless, unexpressed, unpronounced
TECHNICAL aphasic
COLLOQ. mum, shtoom
E3 vocal, talkative
• *v*
tone down, subdue, muffle, lower, moderate, dampen, deaden, dull, smother, quieten, stifle, suppress, soften, silence
COLLOQ. soft-pedal
E3 intensify

muted *adj*
quiet, soft, softened, low-key, subtle, discreet, subdued, restrained, faint, dull, muffled, suppressed, dampened, stifled

mutely *adv*
silently, in silence, dumbly, voicelessly, speechlessly, noiselessly, taciturnly

mutilate *v*
1 MAIM, injure, dismember, disable, disfigure, lame, cripple, mangle, lacerate, cut to pieces, cut up, butcher, hack (up)
2 SPOIL, mar, damage, impair, ruin, distort, mangle, cut, censor
FORMAL bowdlerize
COLLOQ. hack, butcher

mutilation *n*
amputation, maiming, disfigurement, dismembering, damage
FORMAL detruncation

mutinous *adj*
rebellious, insurgent, insubordinate, disobedient, disorderly, uncontrollable, ungovernable, seditious, revolutionary, riotous, anarchistic, subversive, unruly
FORMAL refractory, contumacious

COLLOQ. bolshie
E3 obedient, compliant

mutiny *n, v*
• *n*
rebellion, insurrection, revolt, revolution, rising, uprising, insurgence, insubordination, disobedience, defiance, resistance, riot, strike, protest
• *v*
rebel, revolt, rise up, resist, protest, disobey, defy, strike

mutt *n*
1 MONGREL, dog, cur, hound, bitch
COLLOQ. pooch
2 FOOL, idiot, imbecile, ignoramus, moron, dolt
COLLOQ. dunderhead, thickhead

mutter *v*
1 MUMBLE, murmur, talk to yourself, talk under your breath, stutter, splutter, rumble, witter; *dialect* mump; *Scot* whittie-whattie
OLD mussitate; (*Spenser*) royne
COLLOQ. chunter
2 COMPLAIN, grumble, criticize, find fault, object, protest, carp, fuss, whine
OLD maunder
COLLOQ. grouse, beef, gripe, whinge, chunter
SLANG bellyache

mutual *adj*
reciprocal, shared, common, joint, collective, interchangeable, interchanged, exchanged, complementary

muzzle *v*
restrain, inhibit, check, stifle, suppress, gag, fetter, mute, silence, censor, choke

muzzy *adj*
1 GROGGY, tipsy, confused, dazed, befuddled, addled, muddled, bewildered
2 FUZZY, blurred, unfocused, unclear, indistinct, faint, hazy
E3 2 clear

myopic *adj*
1 *myopic vision*
short-sighted, near-sighted, purblind, half-blind
2 *myopic attitudes*
short-sighted, unwise, ill-considered, imprudent, thoughtless, narrow, narrow-minded, localized, parochial, unimaginative, unadventurous, short-term
FORMAL uncircumspect
E3 2 far-sighted

myriad *adj, n*
• *adj*
countless, innumerable, limitless, immeasurable, incalculable, untold, boundless
FORMAL multitudinous
• *n*
multitude, throng, horde, army, flood, host, swarm, sea
COLLOQ. scores, thousands, millions, zillions, mountain

mysterious *adj*
1 ENIGMATIC, cryptic, mystifying, inexplicable, incomprehensible, puzzling, perplexing, obscure, shadowy, sinister, shady, strange, unfathomable, unsearchable, inscrutable, mystical, baffling, curious, hidden, insoluble
FORMAL abstruse, arcane, recondite, esoteric
2 SECRET, as if by magic, occult, weird, secretive, veiled, dark, furtive, obscure, strange, creepy, mystic, mystical, baffling, curious, hidden, surreptitious, reticent
E3 1 straightforward, comprehensible

Mythical creatures and spirits include:

abominable snowman (or yeti)	dragon	gnome	lamia	orc	taniwha
	dryad	goblin	leprechaun	oread	troll
afrit	dwarf	golem	Lilith	Pegasus	Typhoeus
basilisk	Echidna	Gorgon	lindworm	phoenix	unicorn
Bigfoot	elf	Grendel	Loch Ness monster	pixie	vampire
brownie	Erinyes (or Furies)	griffin		roc	werewolf
bunyip	Fafnir	hamadryad	Medusa	salamander	windigo
Cecrops	fairy	Harpies	mermaid	sasquatch	wivern
centaur	faun	hippocampus (or seahorse)	merman	satyr	yaksha
Cerberus	Frankenstein's monster	hippogriff	Minotaur	Scylla	yowie
Charybdis	genie	hobgoblin	naiad	sea serpent	
Chimera	Geryon	imp	nereid	selkie	
cockatrice	giant	kelpie	nymph	Siren	
Cyclops	Gigantes	kraken	ogre	Sphinx	
			ogress	sylph	

Synonym nuances
sense 1
Enigmatic can be used of people or things that are complex and therefore not readily understood by other people, and can have a vaguely romantic tone: *an enigmatic stranger*, while **cryptic** can be used with implications of secret meanings: *cryptic crossword clues; a cryptic code*. **Mystifying** and **baffling**, on the other hand, are more suggestive of creating confusion in the mind, and both **puzzling** and **perplexing** suggest someone or something that elicits many unanswered questions in the mind: *the perplexing phenomenon of racism in Europe.*

Obscure could be used straightforwardly to suggest a lack of clarity, especially of something that can never be known or deciphered: *obscure ancient languages*. To use **shadowy**, however, would suggest an element of furtiveness: *shadowy figures hiding in doorways*, and **sinister** and **shady** go further with their implication of being underhand: *shady dealings not declared to the taxman*. **Inscrutable** and the rarer **unsearchable** have implications of foiling attempts at analysis: *the inscrutable workings of providence.*

To suggest an element of sacred mystery, the term **mystical** is appropriate, whereas **curious** is more suitable for something that deviates a little from what is expected, and so elicits interest: *that was a curious thing for him to say, don't you think?*

mysteriously *adv*
1 ENIGMATICALLY, cryptically, puzzlingly, inexplicably, incomprehensibly, curiously, strangely, inscrutably
FORMAL abstrusely, arcanely, esoterically
2 SECRETLY, in secret, magically, obscurely, strangely, mystically, surreptitiously

mystery *n*
1 ENIGMA, puzzle, secret, riddle, problem, conundrum, closed book, question, question mark
OLD concealment
FORMAL arcanum
2 OBSCURITY, mystique, secrecy, ambiguity, curiosity, strangeness, weirdness, incomprehensibility, inexplicability, inscrutability, unfathomability, furtiveness, surreptitiousness, reticence

mystic *n*
esotericist, psychic, supernaturalist, metaphysicist, spiritist, spiritualist, transcendentalist, swami, Sufi, occultist

mystical *adj*
occult, mystic, esoteric, spiritual, supernatural, paranormal, other-worldly, transcendental, metaphysical, hidden, mysterious, obscure, incomprehensible, inexplicable, unfathomable, strange, weird, baffling
FORMAL preternatural, abstruse, arcane, recondite
E3 rational, logical

mysticism *n*
spirituality, deism, theism, spiritism, supernaturalism, transcendentalism, esotericism, occultism, mystery, mysteriousness, incomprehensibility, inexplicability
FORMAL arcaneness

mystification *n*
bewilderment, perplexity, confusion, uncertainty, daze, disconcertion, disorientation, puzzlement, stupefaction, surprise, awe, muddle, fog

mystify *v*
puzzle, bewilder, baffle, perplex, confound, confuse
COLLOQ. bamboozle

mystique *n*
mystery, secrecy, fascination, glamour, magic, spell, charm, appeal, adventure, romance, charisma, awe

myth *n*
1 LEGEND, fable, fairy tale, fairy story, allegory, parable, saga, story, tale, folk tale, bestiary
2 FICTION, fancy, fallacy, delusion, fantasy, invention, fabrication, lie, untruth, pretence, misconception
COLLOQ. fib, tall story

mythical *adj*
1 MYTHOLOGICAL, legendary, fabled, fairytale, fictitious
FORMAL chimerical, fabulous, fantastic
See panel above
2 FICTITIOUS, imaginary, made-up, invented, non-existent, unreal, untrue, fantasy, fabricated, pretended, make-believe, fanciful
COLLOQ. pretend, put-on, phoney
E3 **1** historical **2** actual, real, true

mythological *adj*
legendary, mythical, traditional, mythic, fabled, fairytale, fictitious
FORMAL fabulous, folkloric

mythology *n*
legend, myths, lore, tradition(s), stories, folklore, folk tales, tales

N

nab *v*

catch, arrest, capture, grab, seize, snatch
FORMAL apprehend
COLLOQ. collar, pull in, run in, nail, nick, nobble

nabob *n*

celebrity, magnate, personage, tycoon, VIP, millionaire,
multimillionaire, billionaire, financier
FORMAL luminary
COLLOQ. bigwig, celeb

nadir *n*

low point, lowest point, minimum, zero, bottom, depths,
all-time low, low-watermark
COLLOQ. rock bottom
E3 zenith, peak, acme, apex

nag¹ *v*

1 SCOLD, pester, badger, plague, torment, harass, harry, vex,
upbraid, pick on, keep on at, moan, complain
FORMAL berate
COLLOQ. henpeck, hassle, grouse, earbash
2 NIGGLE, tease, worry, bother, trouble, annoy, irritate
COLLOQ. bug, aggravate, get someone's back up

nag² *n*

ride a nag
horse, hack, jade, rip, Rosinante; *Welsh* keffel
COLLOQ. plug
SLANG *Aust & NZ* moke

nagging *adj*

1 *a nagging pain*
continuous, critical, distressing, upsetting, worrying,
irritating, niggling, painful, aching, persistent
2 SCOLDING, shrewish, critical, tormenting, moaning
COLLOQ. nit-picking

nail *v, n*

♦ *v*
1 FASTEN, attach, secure, pin, tack, fix, join, hammer
2 CATCH, arrest, capture, grab, seize, trap, snatch, corner,
pin down
FORMAL apprehend
COLLOQ. collar, nick, nab, nobble
3 EXPOSE, detect, identify, reveal, uncover, unearth, unmask
♦ *n*
1 FASTENER, pin, tack, rivet, brad, sprig, clout, sparable,
spike, skewer, screw
2 FINGERNAIL, toenail, nipper, pincer, claw, talon
■ *hit the nail on the head*
be accurate, be exactly/precisely right, score a bull's eye

naive *adj*

unsophisticated, ingenuous, innocent, naif, artless,
guileless, simple, simplistic, unrealistic, natural, frank,
childlike, inexperienced, immature, primitive, open,
candid, trusting, born yesterday, having no idea,
unsuspecting, unsuspicious, unaffected, unworldly,
gullible, unpretentious, bread-and-butter, credulous,
wide-eyed, pollyannaish
FORMAL jejune
COLLOQ. green, wet behind the ears
E3 experienced, sophisticated

Synonym nuances
Unsophisticated may be widely applied to anything
displaying a lack of artifice, and **ingenuous** to someone
or something without wiles. **Innocent**, on the other
hand, suggests an endearing vulnerability brought about
by lack of exposure to the ways of the world, and while
unaffected and **unpretentious** have more to do with a
lack of pretension, they also suggest positive qualities.
Both **artless** and **guileless** would suggest a complete
lack of ability to deceive, but can occasionally hint at lack
of intelligence: *artless prattle*.
  The term **simple** can be used in many contexts to
describe a lack of complexity, unlike **simplistic** which,
like **unrealistic**, more negatively implies a shallow
reduction of complexities: *she rejected the simplistic
connection between unemployment and rioting*.
  The term **childlike** again suggests a more endearing
outlook comparable to that of a child, whereas
immature is a rather more disapproving term, suggestive
of retarded development, and **primitive** can have
additional, negative connotations of a lack of
advancement: *the primitive mores of the rustics*.
  Like **innocent**, **unworldly** suggests a vulnerability
arising from lack of experience: *a schoolgirl who was
unworldly in the extreme*, whereas both **gullible** and
credulous further imply a tendency to be duped and are
rather more contemptuous in tone: *he treated her as a
credulous imbecile*.

---

naively *adv*

artlessly, guilelessly, simply, simplistically, naturally,
ingenuously, without affectation, innocently,
unsuspiciously, gullibly, immaturely

naivety *n*

ingenuousness, innocence, inexperience, immaturity,
naturalness, artlessness, guilelessness, childlikeness,
simplicity, openness, frankness, candidness, gullibility,
credulity
E3 experience, sophistication

naked *adj*

1 NUDE, bare, with nothing on, undressed, unclothed,
uncovered, exposed, stripped, stark-naked, disrobed,
denuded, raw, mother-naked, Adamic, skyclad,
undraped, *in puris naturalibus*; *dialect* start-naked; *Scot* in
the scud
COLLOQ. in the altogether, starkers, in your birthday suit, in
the raw, in the buff, not a stitch on, naked as the day you
were born
SLANG bollock-naked
2 OPEN, unadorned, undisguised, unqualified,
unvarnished, plain, stark, bald, simple, evident, overt,
patent, blatant, flagrant, glaring, exposed
3 DEFENCELESS, exposed, unprotected, unguarded,
uncovered, weak, vulnerable, helpless, powerless
4 *a naked landscape*
denuded, stripped, grassless, treeless, exposed, barren,
bare, stark
E3 **1** clothed, covered **2** concealed, veiled

nakedness *n*
1 NUDITY, bareness, undress, starkness
COLLOQ. the altogether, the buff
2 PLAINNESS, openness, simplicity, baldness, barrenness, bareness, starkness

namby-pamby *adj*
sentimental, feeble, spineless, weak, weedy, wet, wishy-washy, mawkish, vapid, maudlin, insipid, colourless, anaemic, pretty-pretty, prim, prissy
COLLOQ. soppy, cissy, wimpish
SLANG wussy

name *n, v*
♦ *n*
1 TITLE, designation, label, tag, style, term, epithet, nickname
FORMAL appellation, denomination, cognomen
COLLOQ. handle
SLANG monicker
Related adjective: nominal
2 REPUTATION, character, repute, renown, eminence, prominence, fame, honour, prestige, distinction, note, esteem, standing, popularity, celebrity
3 STAR, expert, authority, leading light, celebrity, dignitary, VIP, luminary, hero
COLLOQ. big noise, big name, celeb, bigwig, somebody
♦ *v*
1 CALL, christen, baptize, give name to, term, title, entitle, dub, label, tag, style, identify
FORMAL denominate
2 DESIGNATE, nominate, mention, cite, choose, pick, select, specify, classify, commission, appoint

---

Synonym nuances
noun sense 1
The term **title** tends to be reserved for a form of address conferred on a person, whereas **designation** more widely encompasses any term indicating who or what someone or something is: *his designation as a 'comic' novelist*; *the area's designation as an enterprise zone.*
  Label, likewise, suggests a descriptive name, but a more informal one given for purposes of classification, and **tag** has further implications of this being an unwelcome summary: *he had to live up to the tag of anti-hero that the media gave him.* **Term** is a more neutral, widely applicable word for a way of referring to something: *the technical term is 'codification'.*
  Epithet, however, is a more formal-sounding word which returns to the idea of description through a name: *the epithet 'Clyde-built' was a badge of quality,* but **nickname**, while perhaps similarly descriptive, is an informal name which usually suggests affection: *Martinique deserves its nickname 'island of flowers',* but could be a taunt: *his nickname is Mouse because he is small and weedy.*

Kinds of name include:

agnomen	first name	place name
alias	full name	proper name
assumed name	given name	pseudonym
baptismal name	last name	second name
brand name	maiden name	so(u)briquet
Christian name	middle name	stage-name
code name	nickname	surname
diminutive	nom-de-plume	term of
false name	pen-name	endearment
family name	pet name	trademark

---

named *adj*
called, known as, by the name of, labelled, termed, titled, entitled, dubbed, styled, baptized, christened, identified, designated, mentioned, chosen, picked, selected, singled out, specified, classified, commissioned, cited, nominated, appointed, *dit*
FORMAL denominated
⊟ nameless

nameless *adj*
1 UNNAMED, anonymous, unidentified, untitled, unlabelled, unspecified, undesignated, unknown, obscure
OLD (*Shakesp*) titleless
FORMAL innominate
2 INEXPRESSIBLE, indescribable, unutterable, unspeakable, unmentionable, unheard-of
⊟ 1 named

namely *adv*
that is, ie, specifically, viz, that is to say, specifically, in other words
FORMAL to wit

nanny *n, v*
♦ *n*
nurse, nursemaid, governess, nursery-governess, childminder, au pair, amah, ayah
♦ *v*
mollycoddle, pamper, coddle, indulge, spoil, overprotect, pander to, cosset, spoon-feed, mother, pet, baby

nap¹ *n, v*
♦ *n*
have a nap
rest, lie-down, doze, sleep, light sleep, siesta, catnap
COLLOQ. snooze, forty winks, kip
♦ *v*
doze (off), sleep, sleep lightly, drop off, catnap, lie down, rest
COLLOQ. nod off, snooze, kip, have forty winks, get some shut-eye

nap² *n*
the nap of the carpet
down, pile, weave, shag, surface, texture, fibre, grain, fuzz, downiness

nappy *n*
diaper, napkin, towel, serviette

narcissism *n*
self-love, egotism, egomania, egocentricity, self-centredness, self-obsession, self-regard, self-conceit, conceit, vanity

narcissistic *adj*
self-loving, egotistic, egomaniacal, egocentric, self-centred, self-obsessed, self-absorbed, conceited, vain

narcotic *n, adj*
♦ *n*
drug, opiate, sedative, tranquillizer, sleeping pill, painkiller, analgesic, anodyne, anaesthetic, palliative, soporific
SLANG upper, downer
♦ *adj*
soporific, sleep-inducing, hypnotic, sedative, analgesic, anaesthetic, tranquillizing, opiate, painkilling, numbing, dulling, pain-dulling, calming, stupefying
FORMAL somnolent, stupefacient

narked *adj*
annoyed, bothered, irritated, piqued, irked, exasperated, provoked, riled, vexed, galled
COLLOQ. bugged, miffed, nettled, peeved, cheesed off, brassed off, got the hump, in a huff, in a paddy, hot under the collar
SLANG pissed off

narrate *v*
tell, read, report, describe, portray, unfold, recite, state, explain, set out, detail, chronicle, record
FORMAL relate, recount, rehearse, set forth

narration n

account, story, tale, description, explanation, telling,
report, statement, history, chronicle, detail, sketch,
portrayal, reading, recital, storytelling, voice-over
FORMAL rehearsal, recountal

narrative n

story, tale, chronicle, account, history, report, description,
sketch, portrayal, reading, detail, statement, relation, saga,
novel, allegory, fable, anecdote
OLD prose; (*Shakesp*) process
FORMAL récit

narrator n

storyteller, chronicler, reporter, raconteur, tale-teller,
anecdotist, commentator, writer, author, describer, relater,
relator, annalist
TECHNICAL mythographer, sagaman
FORMAL recounter

narrow adj, v

◆ *adj*
1 TIGHT, confined, constricted, cramped, small, slim,
slender, thin, fine, spare, tapering, close
FORMAL attenuated
2 LIMITED, restricted, cramped, squeezed, tight, close,
meagre, scant
FORMAL circumscribed, incommodious, exiguous
3 NARROW-MINDED, biased, bigoted, prejudiced, dogmatic,
intolerant, illiberal, reactionary, hidebound, strait-laced,
dyed-in-the-wool, close-minded, set, rigid, conservative,
small-minded, insular, petty
4 *in the narrow sense of the word*
strict, literal, exact, precise, true, original
Ea **1** wide **2** broad **3** broad-minded, tolerant **4** broad
◆ *v*
constrict, limit, tighten, confine, restrict, cramp, reduce,
diminish, taper, simplify
FORMAL attenuate, circumscribe
Ea broaden, widen, increase

narrowing n

compression, constriction, curtailment, contraction,
reduction, tapering, thinning, emaciation, constipation
TECHNICAL stenosis
FORMAL attenuation
Ea broadening, widening

narrowly adv

1 BARELY, scarcely, just, only just
COLLOQ. by a hair's breadth, by a whisker
2 CAREFULLY, closely, strictly, scrutinizingly, attentively,
precisely, exactly, painstakingly

narrow-minded adj

illiberal, biased, bigoted, prejudiced, reactionary,
hidebound, strait-laced, dyed in the wool, opinionated,
diehard, small-minded, close-minded, set, rigid, inflexible,
entrenched, conservative, ultra-conservative, blimpish,
intolerant, insular, provincial, parochial, twisted, warped,
jaundiced, petty, petty-minded, exclusive, unreasonable
Ea broad-minded, liberal, tolerant

narrow-mindedness n

bigotry, bias, prejudice, small-mindedness, close-
mindedness, petty-mindedness, conservativeness,
parochialism, exclusiveness, inflexibility, rigidity
Ea broadmindedness, tolerance

narrowness n

1 THINNESS, tightness, slenderness, limitation,
restrictedness, nearness, constriction, closeness,
meagreness
FORMAL attenuation
2 NARROW-MINDEDNESS, insularity, parochialism,
exclusiveness, bias, bigotry, prejudice, intolerance,
pettiness, small-mindedness, rigidity, conservatism
Ea **1** breadth, width **2** broad-mindedness, tolerance

narrows n

straits, sound, channel, passage, waterway

nascent adj

budding, developing, growing, rising, young, embryonic,
beginning, evolving, advancing
FORMAL burgeoning, incipient, naissant
Ea dying

nastily adv

unpleasantly, disagreeably, offensively, obnoxiously,
objectionably, repulsively, disgustingly
Ea kindly, pleasantly

nastiness n

1 UNPLEASANTNESS, repulsiveness, horribleness,
disagreeableness, offensiveness, filth, dirtiness,
defilement, filthiness, foulness, impurity, pollution,
squalor, uncleanliness, unsavouriness
2 OBSCENITY, indecency, filth, pornography
COLLOQ. porn, smuttiness
3 MALICE, spitefulness, spite, malevolence, viciousness,
meanness

nasty adj

1 UNPLEASANT, awful, repulsive, hateful, loathsome,
objectionable, disagreeable, offensive, distasteful,
disgusting, obnoxious, repellent, repugnant, revolting,
sickening, horrible, horrid, dirty, filthy, squalid, foul, mucky,
vile, odious, polluted, rank
FORMAL noisome, malodorous
COLLOQ. grotty, yucky, rough; *Aust & NZ* crook
SLANG ribby
2 OBSCENE, offensive, indecent, dirty, filthy, pornographic,
ribald
COLLOQ. blue, smutty
3 MALICIOUS, mean, malevolent, spiteful, vicious, cruel,
unkind, bad-tempered, disagreeable, unpleasant
4 SERIOUS, grave, critical, dangerous, worrying, alarming,
disquieting, unpleasant, difficult, tricky
5 *a nasty situation*
difficult, tricky, awkward, annoying, exasperating,
delicate, ticklish
COLLOQ. dodgy
6 *nasty weather*
stormy, wet, rainy, foggy, foul, disagreeable, unpleasant,
vile, wild, rough, dirty, filthy, awful
Ea **1** agreeable, nice, pleasant **2** decent **3** benevolent, kind
6 fine

nation n

country, people, race, tribe, state, kingdom, land, realm,
republic, population, community, society, folk, vassal; *S Afr*
volk
OLD public

national adj, n

◆ *adj*
countrywide, civil, civic, domestic, nationwide, state,
internal, domestic, native, general, governmental, federal,
public, widespread, comprehensive, social
◆ *n*
citizen, native, subject, inhabitant, resident

nationalism n

patriotism, allegiance, loyalty, chauvinism, xenophobia,
jingoism

nationalist n

patriot, loyalist, chauvinist, jingoist, flag-waver,
xenophobe

nationalistic adj

patriotic, loyal, chauvinistic, jingoistic, xenophobic
FORMAL ethnocentrist

nationality n

race, nation, ethnic group, birth, citizenship, tribe,
clan

nationally adv

generally, comprehensively, countrywide, nationwide, throughout all the country, across the whole country

nationwide adj

national, countrywide, general, overall, extensive, widespread, comprehensive, state, coast-to-coast

native adj, n

* adj

1 INDIGENOUS, local, domestic, vernacular, home, home-grown, aboriginal, mother, original
FORMAL autochthonous
2 INHERENT, inborn, innate, inbred, ingrained, hereditary, inherited, congenital, instinctive, intuitive, natural, built-in, intrinsic
FORMAL natal, connate

* n

inhabitant, resident, national, citizen, dweller, aborigine
FORMAL autochthon
E3 foreigner, outsider, stranger, alien

Synonym nuances
adj sense 1
Indigenous is a straightforward, fairly technical term to refer to something originating from the place indicated: *gibbons are indigenous to Burma*, whereas **local** has to do with being a more immediate vicinity: *local customs in this part of Spain*. **Vernacular** tends to be reserved for language to suggest being particular to an area.
  Domestic is also a fairly technical term for pertaining to one's native place, and can be used in political contexts: *domestic and foreign policy*, while **home** is perhaps more affectionate in tone, and **home-grown** has overtones of pride at something being created in one's native land: *home-grown talent*.
  Original is widely used to suggest being there at the start: *the original settlements found by discoverers*, while **aboriginal** would be appropriate for an original inhabitant of a country, though the term is now strongly associated with Australia. **Mother**, with its connotations of nurture, is a more affectionate-sounding term for something belonging to your land: *mother tongue*.

---

nativity n

birth, childbirth, delivery
FORMAL parturition

natter v, n

* v

chat, chatter, gabble, jabber, gossip, talk, confabulate; *dialect & N Am* blather; *Scot* blether
COLLOQ. confab, gab, jaw, prattle, rabbit (on), chinwag, witter, chew the fat, shoot the breeze

* n

chat, conversation, talk, gossip, prattle, chit-chat; *dialect & N Am* blather; *Scot* blether
COLLOQ. chinwag, confab, gab, jaw

nattily adv

smartly, neatly, elegantly, fashionably, stylishly

natty adj

smart, neat, dapper, chic, elegant, well-dressed, fashionable, spruce, stylish, trim
COLLOQ. ritzy, snazzy, swanky

natural adj

1 ORDINARY, normal, common, regular, standard, everyday, routine, run-of-the-mill, usual, typical
2 INNATE, inborn, inbred, ingrained, built-in, normal, instinctive, intuitive, inherent, inherited, congenital, native, indigenous
FORMAL connate
3 *natural fibres*
genuine, pure, authentic, additive-free, chemical-free, organic, raw, virgin, unrefined, unprocessed, unmixed, plain, real, whole
4 SINCERE, unaffected, genuine, artless, ingenuous, guileless, simple, unpretentious, unsophisticated, frank, open, candid, spontaneous, relaxed
E3 1 unnatural **2** acquired **3** artificial, man-made, synthetic **4** affected, disingenuous, contrived

naturalist n

life scientist, plant scientist, botanist, biologist, zoologist, ecologist, evolutionist, Darwinist, creationist

naturalistic adj

natural, realistic, true-to-life, representational, lifelike, graphic, real-life, photographic, factual
E3 idealistic, unrealistic

naturalize v

introduce, adopt, incorporate, familiarize, acclimatize, accept, assimilate, accustom, adapt, enfranchise, give citizenship to, domesticate
FORMAL acclimate, acculturate, endenizen, habituate

naturally adj

1 OF COURSE, obviously, clearly, as a matter of course, simply, logically, typically, certainly, absolutely, as you would expect, as might be expected
SLANG natch
2 NORMALLY, genuinely, sincerely, instinctively, spontaneously, artlessly, ingenuously, candidly, frankly

naturalness n

sincerity, genuineness, artlessness, ingenuousness, simpleness, simplicity, plainness, pureness, purity, wholeness, candidness, frankness, openness, realism, unpretentiousness, unaffectedness, unselfconsciousness, spontaneousness, spontaneity, informality

nature n

1 ESSENCE, quality, character, essential quality/character, identity, features, disposition, attributes, personality, stamp, make-up, characteristic(s), complexion, constitution, temperament, mood, outlook, humour, temper
COLLOQ. chemistry
2 KIND, sort, type, description, category, variety, style, species, class, category
3 UNIVERSE, world, creation, cosmos, earth, mother earth/nature, Gaia, environment
4 COUNTRYSIDE, country, landscape, scenery, natural history

naught n

nothing, nothingness, zero, nought, nil; *dialect* nowt
COLLOQ. zilch, sweet Fanny Adams, sweet FA

naughtily adv

1 BADLY BEHAVED, mischievously, disobediently, waywardly, defiantly, perversely, playfully
2 INDECENTLY, obscenely, bawdily, vulgarly, coarsely, lewdly

naughtiness n

1 BAD BEHAVIOUR, misbehaviour, mischief, disobedience, waywardness, defiance, lack of discipline, playfulness
2 INDECENCY, obscenity, bawdiness, vulgarity, coarseness, lewdness
COLLOQ. smuttiness

naughty adj

1 BAD, badly behaved, misbehaving, mischievous, disobedient, wayward, defiant, undisciplined, unruly, exasperating, playful, roguish, perverse, incorrigible
FORMAL refractory
2 INDECENT, obscene, bawdy, risqué, vulgar, off-colour, coarse, ribald, lewd
COLLOQ. blue, smutty
E3 1 good, well-behaved **2** decent

nausea n

1 VOMITING, sickness, retching, gagging, queasiness,

biliousness, morning sickness, travel sickness, motion sickness, seasickness, carsickness, airsickness, sick headache; *dialect* wamble
COLLOQ. throwing up, puking
2 DISGUST, revulsion, loathing, aversion, distaste, hatred
FORMAL repugnance, detestation

nauseate *v*
sicken, make sick, disgust, revolt, repel, offend, make your gorge rise, turn your stomach
COLLOQ. turn off; *N Am* gross out

nauseating *adj*
sickening, disgusting, stomach-churning, stomach-turning, repulsive, offensive, distasteful, repellent, repugnant, odious, loathsome, abhorrent, nauseous, revolting
FORMAL detestable
SLANG *Aust* chunderous

nauseous *adj*
queasy, nauseated, sick, ill, travel sick, seasick, carsick, airsick
COLLOQ. under the weather, about to throw up

nautical *adj*
naval, maritime, seagoing, seafaring, sailing, oceanic, boating, yachting

Nautical terms include:

afloat	harbour	reef
aft	harbour-bar	refit
air-sea rescue	harbour dues	ride out
amidships	harbour-master	riptide
ballast	haven	roll
beam	head to wind	row
bear away	heave to	run
beat	heavy swell	run aground
becalmed	heel	run before the
bow-wave	helm	wind
breeches-buoy	high tide	salvage
broach	inflatable life-raft	seafaring
capsize	jetsam	sea lane
cargo	jetty	sea legs
cast off	knot	seamanship
chandler	launch	seasick
circumnavigate	lay a course	seaworthy
coastguard	lay up	set sail
compass bearing	lee	sheet in
convoy	lee shore	shipping
course	leeward	shipping lane
cruise	life buoy	ship's company
current	life-jacket	ship water
Davy Jones's	life-rocket	shipwreck
locker	list	shipyard
dead reckoning	low tide	shore leave
deadweight	make fast	sink
disembark	marina	slip anchor
dock	marine	slipway
dockyard	maroon	stevedore
dry dock	mayday	stowaway
ebb tide	moor	tack
embark	mooring	tide
ferry	mutiny	trim
fleet	navigation	voyage
float	neap tide	wake
flotilla	on board	wash
flotsam	pitch and toss	watch
foghorn	plane	wave
fore	put in	weather
foreshore	put to sea	weigh anchor
go about	quay	wharf
gybe	reach	wreck

See also **navigational aids; sail; sailing; ship.**

naval *adj*
marine, maritime, nautical, sea, seagoing, seafaring

navel *n*
umbilicus, centre, middle, hub
FORMAL omphalos
COLLOQ. belly-button, tummy-button
Related adjective: umbilical

navigable *adj*
passable, crossable, negotiable, open, clear, unblocked, unobstructed, surmountable
FORMAL traversable

navigate *v*
steer, drive, direct, pilot, guide, plan a course, handle, manoeuvre, negotiate, cruise, sail, voyage, journey, cross, helm, plot, plan
COLLOQ. skipper

navigation *n*
sailing, steering, piloting, pilotage, directing, direction, guiding, guidance, cruising, voyaging, seamanship, helmsmanship, manoeuvring
Related adjective: nautical

Navigational aids include:

astronavigation	flux-gate	magnetic
bell buoy	compass	compass
channel-marker	Global	marker buoy
buoy	Positioning	nautical table
chart	System (GPS)	parallel ruler
chronometer	gyrocompass	pilot
conical buoy	lighthouse	radar
Decca®	lightship	sectored leading-
navigator system	log	light
depth gauge	loran (long-range	sextant
dividers	radio navigation)	VHF radio
echo-sounder		

navigator *n*
pilot, seaman, helmsman, steersman, mariner

navvy *n*
labourer, common labourer, worker, manual worker, workman, digger, ganger

navy *n*
fleet, naval fleet, naval force, ships, flotilla, armada, warships, merchant navy, merchant service, mercantile marine

nay *adv*
1 NO, not at all, not really, of course not, absolutely not, certainly not, most certainly not, under no circumstances; *Scot* nae
2 INDEED, actually, in fact, in truth, in point of fact, or rather

near *adj, adv, prep, v*
♦ *adj*
1 NEARBY, close, close-range, close by, within reach, within range, at hand, accessible, convenient, bordering, adjacent, alongside, local, neighbouring, surrounding; *Scot* ewest
FORMAL adjoining, contiguous
COLLOQ. a stone's throw from; *Aust & NZ* within cooee
2 IMMINENT, close, impending, forthcoming, coming, looming, immediate, approaching, in the offing
FORMAL proximate
3 DEAR, familiar, close, related, closely related, intimate, akin
4 SIMILAR, close, like, alike, comparable, corresponding
E3 1 far, far off, far-away **2** distant **3** remote
♦ *adv*
nearby, close, close by, not far away, at close quarters, alongside, within reach, at hand, within close range; *Scot* ewest
OLD forby
COLLOQ. a stone's throw away; *Aust & NZ* within cooee

See Synonym nuances panel at **close**.
• *prep*
nearby, close to, next to, bordering on, adjacent to, alongside, in the neighbourhood of, within reach of
OLD forby
FORMAL adjoining, contiguous to
• *v*
approach, get closer to, come nearer/closer, advance towards, come/move towards, draw near to, draw nearer to, close in on, cling to
F∃ withdraw, keep your distance
▪ **near thing**
near miss, narrow escape, nasty moment, close call
COLLOQ. close shave, narrow squeak

nearby *adj, adv*
• *adj*
near, close, neighbouring, adjoining, adjacent, accessible, convenient, handy, within reach
F∃ faraway
• *adv*
near, within reach, at close quarters, close by, close at hand, not far away, a short distance away, in the vicinity
COLLOQ. on your doorstep, in your own backyard

nearly *adv*
almost, practically, virtually, as good as, closely, close to, approximately, more or less, all but, just about, roughly, verging on, well-nigh

nearness *n*
1 CLOSENESS, vicinity, handiness, accessibility, availability, immediacy, imminence
FORMAL proximity, contiguity, propinquity
2 INTIMACY, dearness, familiarity, closeness, chumminess

near-sighted *adj*
short-sighted, myopic, half-blind, purblind

neat *adj*
1 TIDY, orderly, ordered, well-ordered, organized, well-organized, well-groomed, straight, tight, smart, smug, spruce, dapper, trim, dainty, clean, clean-cut, shipshape; *dialect* jemmy; *Scot* dink, jimpy, snod, tosh, trig, genty; *N Am* band-box
OLD net, featous; *Scot* donsie
COLLOQ. dinky, natty, spick-and-span, in apple-pie order, shipshape and Bristol fashion
2 DEFT, clever, adroit, nimble, skilful, practised, dexterous, expert
OLD (*Shakesp*) feat
COLLOQ. nifty
3 COMPACT, handy, dainty, convenient, efficient, well-designed, well-made, user-friendly
4 *a neat solution*
clever, convenient, nice, simple, apt, sensible, ingenious, elegant, slick, clean, crisp
COLLOQ. nifty
5 GREAT, excellent, wonderful, marvellous, superb, admirable, tremendous, fantastic, fabulous
COLLOQ. super, terrific, smashing
SLANG cool, mega, wicked
6 UNDILUTED, unmixed, unadulterated, straight, pure
COLLOQ. short
F∃ 1 untidy, scruffy, shabby, slovenly **2** clumsy **6** diluted

neaten *v*
tidy (up), straighten, smarten (up), spruce up, clean (up), arrange, trim, edge, round off, groom, put to rights; *N Am* square away

neatly *adv*
1 TIDILY, smartly, stylishly, sprucely, methodically, systematically, efficiently
2 CLEVERLY, conveniently, handily, aptly, nicely, daintily, elegantly
3 DEFTLY, skilfully, adeptly, adroitly, agilely, nimbly,

dexterously, effortlessly, expertly, precisely, accurately, gracefully
OLD (*Shakesp*) featly; (*Spenser*) feateously
F∃ 1 untidily **2** inelegantly **3** unskilfully, inexpertly

neatness *n*
1 TIDINESS, smartness, trimness, spruceness, stylishness, style, orderliness, straightness, efficiency, methodicalness
2 CLEVERNESS, aptness, handiness, elegance, daintiness, niceness, nicety
3 SKILFULNESS, skill, adeptness, deftness, adroitness, agility, dexterity, gracefulness, grace, nimbleness, expertness, preciseness, precision, accuracy
F∃ 1 untidiness, disorderliness **2** inelegance

nebulous *adj*
vague, hazy, imprecise, indefinite, indistinct, cloudy, misty, shadowy, obscure, uncertain, unclear, dim, ambiguous, confused, fuzzy, abstract, shapeless, unformed
FORMAL amorphous, indeterminate
F∃ clear

necessarily *adv*
inevitably, unavoidably, incontrovertibly, certainly, compulsorily, by definition, inescapably, of necessity, indispensably, inexorably, of course, naturally, consequently, automatically, therefore, thus, accordingly, axiomatically, willy-nilly, *nolens volens*
TECHNICAL obligate
OLD no remedy
FORMAL ineluctably, perforce

necessary *adj*
needed, required, essential, compulsory, indispensable, vital, crucial, de rigueur, obligatory, needful, unavoidable, sure, inevitable, inescapable, inexorable, certain
OLD needful; (*Shakesp*) needy
FORMAL mandatory, imperative, requisite, ineluctable
F∃ unnecessary, inessential, unimportant

necessitate *v*
require, involve, entail, make necessary, need, take, mean, call for, demand, oblige, exact, force, constrain, compel

necessity *n*
1 REQUIREMENT, obligation, prerequisite, essential, fundamental, indispensable, need, want, compulsion, demand
OLD extremes
FORMAL exigency, requisite, desideratum, sine qua non
COLLOQ. must
2 INDISPENSABILITY, inevitability, certainty, inescapability, inexorability, destiny, fate, obligation, need, needfulness; *Scot* mister
3 POVERTY, destitution, hardship, want, need, deprivation
FORMAL penury, privation, indigence
F∃ luxury
▪ **of necessity**
inevitably, unavoidably, incontrovertibly, certainly, compulsorily, indispensably, by definition, inescapably, inexorably, automatically
OLD no remedy

neck *n, v*
• *n*
nape, scruff, scrag, halse
TECHNICAL cervix
Related adjective: cervical
• *v*
kiss, pet, caress
COLLOQ. smooch, canoodle
SLANG snog
▪ **neck and neck**
level, equal, balanced, aligned, drawn, even, on a par, matching, uniform, level pegging

necklace *n*
chain, string, band, pearls, beads, jewels, choker, locket,

pendant, *lavallière*, negligee, torque, torc, gorget, carcanet, *rivière*

necromancer n
magician, conjurer, diviner, sorcerer, sorceress, witch, wizard, warlock, spiritist, spiritualist
FORMAL thaumaturge, thaumaturgist

necromancy n
divination, enchantment, wonder-working, magic, magical powers, black magic, black art, sorcery, witchcraft, witchery, spiritism, spiritualism, wizardry, demonology, voodoo, hoodoo
FORMAL conjuration, thaumaturgy

necropolis n
cemetery, graveyard, burial ground, burial place, burial site, churchyard, God's acre, charnel house

need v, n
• v
miss, lack, want, require, demand, call for, have need of, necessitate, be necessary to have, have occasion for, have to, must, be compelled/obliged to, desire, crave, pine for, yearn for, be desperate for, cry out for, be dependent on, depend on, be reliant on, rely on
OLD mister
• n
1 *a need for caution*
call, demand, obligation, necessity, want, wish, justification, requirement; *Scot* mister
FORMAL exigency
2 *the country's needs*
essential, necessity, prerequisite
FORMAL requisite, desideratum
3 *a need for equipment*
want, lack, insufficiency, inadequacy, neediness, demand, shortage
■ **in need**
poor, impoverished, needy, penniless, disadvantaged, deprived, poverty-stricken, underprivileged
FORMAL destitute, penurious, indigent, impecunious
COLLOQ. on the breadline, hard up, dirt-poor, unable to keep the wolf from the door

needed adj
called for, desired, required, wanted, lacking, compulsory, necessary, obligatory, essential
FORMAL requisite
E3 unnecessary, unneeded

needful adj
required, needed, necessary, essential, indispensable, vital, stipulated, needy
FORMAL requisite
E3 excess, needless, superfluous

needle n, v
• n
1 *needle and thread*
knitting needle, pin, sharp, stylus, nib, bodkin, darner, darning-needle, packing-needle, hypodermic needle, syringe, stylus
TECHNICAL spud, dry-point, microneedle
SLANG hype, hypo
2 POINTER, indicator, arrow, marker, hand
3 THORN, prickle, spike, splinter, barb, spine, quill, briar, bristle, bramble
FORMAL spicule
• v
annoy, irritate, harass, pester, goad, spur, provoke, ruffle, prick, rile, bait, prod, nag, irk, taunt, torment, sting
COLLOQ. aggravate, wind up, get at, bug, drive mad, drive crazy, drive bananas, drive up the wall, drive round the bend/twist, miff, make someone's blood boil, make someone see red, rattle someone's cage, ruffle someone's feathers, raise someone's dander, make someone's

hackles rise, make sparks fly, get under someone's skin, get up someone's nose, get on someone's wick
SLANG nark, piss off
OLD SLANG get someone's shirt out

needless adj
unnecessary, gratuitous, uncalled-for, unwanted, undesired, redundant, dispensable, superfluous, expendable, useless, pointless, purposeless, luxury
E3 necessary, essential, indispensable
■ **needless to say**
of course, naturally, certainly, surely, by all means, definitely, without a doubt, no doubt, undoubtedly, doubtlessly, indubitably

needlessly adv
unnecessarily, superfluously, redundantly, pointlessly, uselessly, dispensably
E3 necessarily, indispensably

needlework n
embroidery, fancywork, stitching, sewing, crocheting, tapestry, tatting, needlepoint

needy adj
poor, impoverished, in need, needful, penniless, disadvantaged, deprived, poverty-stricken, underprivileged
OLD strait, wanting
FORMAL destitute, penurious, indigent, impecunious
COLLOQ. on the breadline, hard up, dirt-poor, unable to keep the wolf from the door
E3 affluent, wealthy, well-off

ne'er-do-well n
good-for-nothing, idler, layabout, loafer, slacker, lounger, shirker, wastrel, waster, do-nothing
COLLOQ. black sheep, skiver, dodger, spiv
SLANG *Irish* dosser; *N Am* goof-off; *Aust & NZ* bludger

nefarious adj
wicked, detestable, dreadful, evil, foul, loathsome, vile, vicious, shameful, outrageous, horrendous, terrible, odious, monstrous, villainous, abominable, atrocious, base, sinful, unholy, criminal, depraved, infamous, horrible, satanic, infernal
FORMAL execrable, heinous, iniquitous, opprobrious
E3 exemplary

negate v
1 CANCEL, annul, invalidate, undo, neutralize, quash, reverse, wipe out, void, repeal
FORMAL nullify, countermand, abrogate, retract, revoke, rescind
2 DENY, contradict, oppose, disprove, repudiate, reject, discredit
FORMAL renounce, refute, gainsay
COLLOQ. explode, squash
E3 **2** affirm

negation n
1 CANCELLATION, repeal, neutralization, veto
FORMAL disavowal, nullification, abrogation, countermanding
2 DENIAL, contradiction, rejection, renunciation, disclaimer
3 OPPOSITE, reverse, contrary
FORMAL inverse, antithesis, converse
E3 **2** affirmation

negative adj, n
• adj
1 *a negative impact*
adverse, bad, unfavourable, disadvantageous, hostile, antagonistic, opposing, opposite, counter, contrary, conflicting, counter-productive, negative, unfortunate, unlucky, detrimental, harmful, injurious, hurtful, unfriendly, uncongenial
FORMAL inauspicious, unpropitious

2 a negative attitude
pessimistic, defeatist, gloomy, unenthusiastic, uninterested, unwilling, unco-operative, unhelpful, cynical, critical, weak, spineless
3 a negative reply
contrary, denying, saying no, refusing, opposing, opposed, invalidating, neutralizing, annulling
FORMAL nullifying, dissenting, gainsaying
E3 1 positive **2** constructive, positive **3** affirmative
♦ *n*
contradiction, denial, opposite, refusal, rejection
FORMAL dissension

negativity *n*
pessimism, defeatism, gloominess, lack of interest/enthusiasm, unco-operativeness, cynicism, unwillingness, unhelpfulness, criticalness

neglect *v, n*
♦ *v*
1 DISREGARD, ignore, overlook, leave alone, leave out, abandon, pass by, pass up, rebuff, scorn, disobey, infringe, disdain, slight, spurn, pigeon; *dialect* mislippen
FORMAL forsake
2 FORGET, fail (in), omit, overlook, let slide, shirk, skimp, be lax about
E3 1 cherish, appreciate **2** remember, pay attention to, attend to
♦ *n*
negligence, disregard, carelessness, shortcoming, failure, abuse, non-performance, inattention, disuse, disrepair, rack and ruin, indifference, slackness, laxity, forgetfulness, ignoring, rebuff, scorn, disdain, slight, spurning, oversight, disrespect
TECHNICAL incivism, misprision
FORMAL remissness, default, dereliction of duty, heedlessness, desuetude
E3 care, attention, concern

neglected *adj*
1 they feel neglected
uncared-for, disregarded, unheeded, abandoned, undervalued, unappreciated, deserted, stranded, forsaken
2 a neglected garden
derelict, overgrown, uncultivated, unmaintained, untended, untilled, unweeded, unhusbanded, dilapidated
COLLOQ. run-down
E3 1 cherished, treasured **2** tended, cared for

neglectful *adj*
uncaring, careless, sloppy, inattentive, disregardful, forgetful, thoughtless, unmindful, indifferent, lax, negligent, oblivious
FORMAL heedless, remiss
E3 attentive, careful

negligence *n*
inattentiveness, inattention, carelessness, sloppiness, laxity, neglect, slackness, thoughtlessness, forgetfulness, indifference, omission, oversight, disregard, shortcoming, failure
FORMAL default, remissness, dereliction of duty, heedlessness
E3 attentiveness, care, regard

negligent *adj*
neglectful, inattentive, thoughtless, casual, lax, cursory, careless, indifferent, offhand, nonchalant, slack, uncaring, unmindful, forgetful
FORMAL remiss, heedless, dilatory
COLLOQ. sloppy
E3 attentive, careful, scrupulous

negligible *adj*
unimportant, insignificant, small, imperceptible, inappreciable, minimal, trifling, trivial, petty, paltry, minor,
minute, tiny, not worth bothering about, off the map
OLD neglectable
E3 significant

negotiable *adj*
1 DEBATABLE, arguable, questionable, contestable, open to discussion/question, undecided, unsettled
2 NAVIGABLE, passable, crossable, open, clear, unblocked, unobstructed, surmountable
FORMAL traversable
E3 1 non-negotiable, fixed, definite

negotiate *v*
1 negotiate an agreement
deal, mediate, arbitrate, intervene, intercede, debate, haggle, bargain, arrange, agree, come to an agreement, resolve, hammer out, thrash out, pull off, transact, work out, manage, complete, settle, fulfil, consult, contract, talk, discuss, broker, treat, reach a compromise
FORMAL confer, execute, conclude
COLLOQ. parley, wheel and deal
2 GET ROUND, cross, clear, surmount, pass (over/through)
FORMAL traverse

negotiation *n*
mediation, arbitration, debate, conference, discussion, diplomacy, bargaining, haggling, parleying, transaction, reaching an agreement, thrashing-out, hammering-out, pulling-off, talks
COLLOQ. parley, wheeling and dealing

negotiator *n*
arbitrator, go-between, mediator, intermediary, bargainer, haggler, moderator, intercessor, adjudicator, broker, ambassador, diplomat
COLLOQ. parleyer, wheeler-dealer

neigh *v*
whinny, hinny, bray, nicker

neighbourhood *n*
district, locality, vicinity, community, locale, quarter, part, precinct, environs, confines, surroundings, area, region, presence
OLD convicinity, voisinage
FORMAL proximity, purlieus, vicinage
COLLOQ. *N Am* hood
■ in the neighbourhood of
near, close to, about, roughly, almost, approximately, nearby, next to, round, around, up to

neighbouring *adj*
adjacent, bordering, near, nearby, nearest, near at hand, close at hand, local, connecting, next, surrounding
FORMAL adjoining, abutting, contiguous
E3 distant, remote, far away

neighbourly *adj*
sociable, friendly, amiable, kind, generous, helpful, genial, warm, cordial, easy to get on/along with, affable, hospitable, obliging, considerate, companionable

nemesis *n*
retribution, vengeance, punishment, just punishment, destruction, ruin, downfall, destiny, fate

neologism *n*
new word/term, new expression, new phrase, innovation, coinage, novelty, vogue word

neophyte *n*
beginner, learner, novice, newcomer, apprentice, probationer, trainee, recruit, raw recruit, new member, tiro, rookie
FORMAL noviciate, novitiate
COLLOQ. greenhorn, newbie

nepotism *n*
favouritism, bias, partiality, preferential treatment, keeping it in the family, looking after your own

COLLOQ. jobs for the boys, Old Boy network, old school tie

nerve *n, v*

◆ *n*

1 COURAGE, bravery, mettle, pluck, spirit, vigour, intrepidity, valour, daring, fearlessness, cool-headedness, hardihood, firmness, self-confidence, resolution, steadfastness, will, determination, endurance, force
FORMAL fortitude
COLLOQ. guts, spunk, grit, bottle
2 AUDACITY, impudence, effrontery, brazenness, gall, boldness, impertinence, insolence, presumption, temerity
COLLOQ. cheek, chutzpah, face, neck, brass neck, sauce, mouth, lip
1 weakness **2** timidity

◆ *v*

steel, strengthen, invigorate, encourage, bolster, prepare, brace, hearten, embolden
FORMAL fortify
unnerve

nerveless *adj*

feeble, weak, flabby, inert, slack, nervous, spineless, timid, unnerved, afraid, cowardly
FORMAL debilitated, enervated
bold, brave, strong

nerve-racking *adj*

harrowing, distressing, trying, stressful, tense, maddening, worrying, anxious, disquieting, difficult, frightening
COLLOQ. nail-biting

nerves *n*

nervousness, tension, nervous tension, stress, anxiety, worry, shock, strain, fretfulness, apprehensiveness, twitter, *crise de nerfs*
COLLOQ. jitters, butterflies (in your stomach), collywobbles, wobbly, willies, heebie-jeebies
Related adjective: neural

■ **get on someone's nerves**

annoy, irritate, rile, displease, anger, vex, irk, madden, exasperate, tease, provoke, ruffle, gall, trouble, nag, disturb, bother, pester, plague, harass, molest; *Scot* fash
COLLOQ. aggravate, bug, wind up, hassle, rub up the wrong way, get someone's blood up, make someone's blood boil, get up someone's nose, get under someone's skin, get someone's goat, get on someone's wick, drive crazy/nuts, drive bananas, drive up the wall, drive round the bend/twist, get someone's back up, brass off, cheese off, make someone's hackles rise, make sparks fly, give someone the hump, get your dander up; *N Am* tick/hack off

nervous *adj*

highly-strung, excitable, anxious, agitated, on edge, tense, strained, fidgety, apprehensive, neurotic, overwrought, shaky, uneasy, worried, flustered, disquieted, fretful, quaking, on tenterhooks, fearful, timid, timorous
FORMAL perturbed
COLLOQ. edgy, nervy, twitchy, het up, keyed up, wound up, jumpy, jittery, uptight, with/having butterflies in your stomach, on pins and needles, having kittens, shaking like a leaf/jelly, with your heart in your mouth, in a sweat, in a stew, in a tizzy
SLANG screwed-up
calm, relaxed

nervous breakdown *n*

mental breakdown, nervous disorder, nervous exhaustion, neurosis, crisis, depression, clinical depression, melancholia
COLLOQ. cracking-up

nervously *adv*

anxiously, apprehensively, uneasily, on edge, fretfully, fearfully, timidly
COLLOQ. twitchily, edgily, with/having butterflies in your

stomach, having kittens, shaking like a leaf/jelly, with your heart in your mouth, in a sweat, in a stew, in a tizzy
calmly

nervousness *n*

anxiety, tension, strain, stress, edginess, worry, uneasiness, disquiet, apprehensiveness, agitation, restlessness, fluster, excitability, timidity, timorousness, tremulousness
FORMAL perturbation
COLLOQ. habdabs, heebie-jeebies, touchiness, willies
calmness, coolness

nervy *adj*

highly-strung, excitable, anxious, agitated, on edge, tense, strained, fidgety, apprehensive, neurotic, shaky, uneasy, worried, flustered, fearful
COLLOQ. edgy, twitchy, het up, keyed up, wound up, jumpy, jittery, uptight, with/having butterflies in your stomach, on pins and needles, having kittens, shaking like a leaf/jelly, with your heart in your mouth
calm, relaxed

nescient *adj*

ignorant, uneducated, illiterate, innumerate, backward, unread, untaught, untrained, inexperienced, unschooled, unlearned, stupid, uninitiated, unenlightened, uninformed, ill-informed, unwitting, unaware, unfamiliar, unacquainted
COLLOQ. clueless, dense, thick, thick as two short planks
educated, knowledgeable, learned, clever; *formal* conversant

nest *n*

1 *a bird's nest*
breeding-ground, den, roost, perch, lair, cote, nesting-box, hive-nest; *N Am* bird-house
OLD (*Shakesp*) cabinet
FORMAL nidus, nidification
2 RETREAT, refuge, shelter, haunt, hideaway, hideout, hiding-place, den, mew
Related adjective: nidal

Nests of creatures include:

formicarium (or formicary) (*ants*)	*dialect* cage (*squirrel*)	*Scot* bike (*wasps, wild bees*)
hive (*bees*)	drey (*squirrel*)	
eyrie (*eagle*)	termitarium (*termites*)	*Scot* bink (*wasps, wild bees*)
nid (*pheasant*)		
Aust wurley (*rat*)	vespiary (*wasps*)	

See also **lair**.

---

nest egg *n*

fund(s), reserve(s), savings, store, cache, deposit, bottom drawer
COLLOQ. money saved for a rainy day

nestle *v*

snuggle (up), huddle (together), cuddle (up), nuzzle, curl up

nestling *n*

fledgling, chick, suckling, weanling, baby

net¹ *n, v*

◆ *n*
a fishing net
mesh, meshwork, web, webbing, network, netting, open work, tracery, lattice, latticework, filigree, lace, fishnet, drag, dragnet, drift, drift-net, drop-net, seine, seine net, snare, trap
FORMAL reticulum
Related adjectives: retiary, reticular
◆ *v*
catch, trap, capture, take captive, bag, ensnare,

snare, enmesh, entangle
COLLOQ. nab, collar, nick

net² adj, v
♦ adj
1 *net salary*
nett, clear, after tax(es), after deductions, take-home, final, lowest
2 OVERALL, general, broad, total, inclusive, final, end, ultimate
E3 1 gross
♦ v
bring in, clear, earn, take, take home, raise, get, make, receive, gain, pocket, obtain, accumulate
FORMAL realize
COLLOQ. pull in, rake in

nether adj
1 LOWER, under, lower-level, bottom, below, beneath, underground, low
FORMAL basal, inferior
2 INFERNAL, hellish, underworld, Plutonian, Stygian

netherworld n
hell, underworld, inferno, infernal regions, lower regions, abyss, fire, fire and brimstone, bottomless pit, pit, Hades, Sheol, Acheron, Gehenna, Tophet, Abaddon, Tartarus, Malebolge, Erebus
FORMAL perdition, abode of the devil
COLLOQ. below, down there, other place

nettle v
annoy, chafe, discountenance, exasperate, fret, goad, harass, incense, irritate, rile, pique, provoke, ruffle, sting, tease, torment, vex, upset
COLLOQ. aggravate, wind up, get at, bug, needle, drive mad, drive crazy, drive bananas, drive up the wall, drive round the bend/twist, miff, make someone's blood boil, make someone see red, rattle someone's cage, ruffle someone's feathers, make sparks fly, get under someone's skin, get up someone's nose, get on someone's wick, make someone's hackles rise
SLANG nark, piss off

nettled adj
annoyed, offended, irritated, angry, aggrieved, incensed, exasperated, cross, harassed, provoked, piqued, riled, ruffled, stung, vexed, galled, goaded, huffy, irritable
COLLOQ. aggravated, wound up, got at, bugged, driven mad, driven crazy, driven bananas, driven up the wall, driven round the bend/twist, miffed, needled, rattled
SLANG narked, pissed off

network n
1 NET, maze, mesh, labyrinth, circuitry, grill, meshwork, web, webbing, network, netting, open work, tracery, lattice, latticework, filigree, lace
FORMAL convolution
2 SYSTEM, organization, arrangement, structure, interconnections, complex, grid, matrix, web, channels, tracks
FORMAL nexus
COLLOQ. grapevine, bush telegraph, Old Boy network, old school tie

neurosis n
(mental) disorder, psychological disorder, affliction, abnormality, disturbance, instability, maladjustment, derangement, deviation, fixation, obsession, mania, phobia

neurotic adj
paranoid, irrational, disturbed, maladjusted, deranged, anxious, overanxious, nervous, overwrought, hysterical, unstable, unhealthy, deviant, abnormal, compulsive, obsessive, manic, phobic

neuter adj, v
♦ adj

sexless, asexual, agamic, agamous
TECHNICAL clonal, conidial, monogenetic
♦ v
castrate, emasculate, doctor, geld, spay, dress, caponize, sterilize
COLLOQ. fix

neutral adj
1 IMPARTIAL, uncommitted, unbiased, unprejudiced, non-aligned, disinterested, undecided, non-partisan, non-combatant, non-committal, objective, detached, indifferent, dispassionate, uninvolved, even-handed, open-minded
2 DULL, bland, inoffensive, unexceptionable, unremarkable, unassertive, ordinary, uninteresting, nondescript, colourless, grey, insipid, drab, expressionless, indistinct, anodyne, anaemic, anonymous
3 *a neutral colour*
pale, pastel, indefinite, indistinct, grey, fawn, beige, white, colourless
E3 1 biased, prejudiced, partisan **2** remarkable, exciting **3** colourful

neutrality n
unbiasedness, impartiality, impartialness, detachment, disinterest, disinterestedness, non-alignment, non-intervention, non-involvement
COLLOQ. sitting on the fence
E3 bias, partiality

neutralize v
counteract, counterbalance, offset, balance, compensate for, make up for, negate, cancel (out), invalidate, annul, undo, frustrate, incapacitate
FORMAL nullify

never adv
at no time, not ever, not for a moment, under no circumstances, not at all, on no account
COLLOQ. not on your life, not on your nellie, when pigs fly, no way, not in a month of Sundays, not in a million years
E3 always

never-ending adj
everlasting, eternal, non-stop, endless, unending, without end, perpetual, unceasing, uninterrupted, continuous, unbroken, unremitting, interminable, incessant, unbroken, permanent, persistent, constant, unchanging, relentless, infinite, boundless, limitless
E3 fleeting, transitory

nevertheless adv
nonetheless, still, anyway, even so, yet, however, in spite of everything, though, after all, by any means, in any case/event, by some means, anyhow, but, regardless, for all that, all/just the same, at the same time, *tout de même, quand même, malgré tout*
OLD algate, none but what, withal
FORMAL notwithstanding
COLLOQ. at that

new adj
1 MODERN, contemporary, current, latest, recent, state-of-the-art, present-day, up-to-date, up-to-the-minute, topical, modish, ultra-modern, futuristic, advanced, avant-garde
COLLOQ. trendy, newfangled, way out
See Synonym nuances panel at **modern**.
2 NOVEL, original, fresh, different, creative, resourceful, imaginative, innovative, pioneering, revolutionary, ground-breaking, experimental, ingenious, unfamiliar, strange, unconventional, unusual, brand-new, mint, unknown, unused, newly discovered, virgin, newborn
3 CHANGED, altered, modernized, improved, renewed, refreshed, reinvigorated, restored, remodelled, redesigned
COLLOQ. born-again
4 *new or used cars*

fresh, unused, brand-new, spanking-new
5 ADDED, additional, another, further, extra, more, supplementary
6 *new to the work*
unfamiliar, unacquainted, unknown, inexperienced, unversed, unaccustomed, ignorant, a stranger, alien
E3 1 out-of-date, old-fashioned, outdated **2** usual, ordinary, just another **3** old **4** used **6** familiar

---

Synonym nuances
sense 2
Novel and **original** have positive connotations and can be used of something, perhaps a bit quirky, that has not been previously encountered: *an entirely novel perspective*; *original thoughts*. **Fresh**, however, implies replacing something or someone jaded: *fresh ideas; a fresh investigation*.

The similarly positive **creative**, **imaginative** and **resourceful** emphasize the initiative behind something new, as does **ingenious**, which would appropriately describe something that cleverly meets its requirements: *ingenious booby-traps*.

The terms **innovative**, **pioneering** and *ground-breaking* are appropriate for something that initiates further developments: *pioneering medical work*, but **revolutionary** would be reserved for some radical change: *revolutionary farming methods that hugely increase crop yields*. **Experimental**, although similar, is more suggestive of varying degrees of success and less inherently positive.

Less complimentary terms for something that deviates from the usual are **unfamiliar** and **strange**, while **unconventional** and **unusual** would be more neutral terms to use.

If you want to refer to a more physical newness, the term **mint** can be used to suggest that something is in a perfect condition, while **virgin** is appropriate for something so far untainted by use or experience: *virgin green grass*.

---

newcomer *n*
1 IMMIGRANT, alien, foreigner, incomer, colonist, settler, (new) arrival, outsider, intruder, stranger
2 NOVICE, beginner, learner, pupil, trainee, recruit, probationer, apprentice, tiro
FORMAL neophyte
COLLOQ. greenhorn, rookie, newbie

newfangled *adj*
modern, new, recent, state-of-the-art, contemporary, ultra-modern, futuristic, fashionable, modernistic, novel, gimmicky
COLLOQ. trendy
E3 old-fashioned

newly *adv*
recently, lately, latterly, just, freshly, of late, afresh, anew

newness *n*
freshness, innovation, novelty, originality, oddity, uniqueness, unusualness, strangeness, unfamiliarity
FORMAL recency
E3 oldness, ordinariness

news *n*
report, account, information, data, facts, intelligence, dispatch, message, communication, announcement, press release, communiqué, bulletin, news item, newsflash, newscast, gossip, hearsay, rumour, statement, story, word, latest, developments, scandal, revelation, exposé, disclosure, advice
FORMAL tidings
COLLOQ. lowdown, gen, info, dope

newspaper *n*
daily, paper, publication, broadsheet, tabloid, sheet, journal, periodical, magazine, weekly, local paper, local,

regional paper, regional, provincial paper, provincial, national paper, national, morning paper, evening paper, press, gazette, organ
COLLOQ. rag

newsreader *n*
newscaster, journalist, newsman/woman, reporter, correspondent, announcer, commentator, presenter, anchor, anchorman/woman

newsworthy *adj*
reportable, hitting/making the headlines, important, significant, interesting, remarkable, stimulating, notable, noteworthy, topical, arresting, unusual

next *adj, adv*
♦ *adj*
1 ADJACENT, neighbouring, bordering, along, alongside, beside, nearest, closest
FORMAL adjoining, contiguous, tangential
2 FOLLOWING, succeeding, successive, ensuing, later
FORMAL subsequent
E3 2 previous, preceding
♦ *adv*
afterwards, after that time, later, then
FORMAL subsequently, thereafter

nibble *n, v*
♦ *n*
bite, peck, gnaw, munch, morsel, taste, titbit, bit, crumb, snack, piece
♦ *v*
bite, eat, peck, pick at, munch, gnaw; *dialect* chumble
COLLOQ. snack
SLANG nosh

nice *adj*
1 *have a nice time*
pleasant, agreeable, enjoyable, lovely, good, delightful, satisfying, acceptable, pleasurable, fine, appealing, amusing, entertaining, welcome
FORMAL delectable
COLLOQ. decent
2 *he seems a nice man*
pleasant, agreeable, delightful, charming, lik(e)able, attractive, good, good-natured, good-humoured, kind, kindly, friendly, genial, sweet, amiable, sympathetic, understanding, endearing, well-mannered, polite, respectable, civil, courteous; *dialect* canny
3 SUBTLE, delicate, fine, minute, fastidious, refined, particular, discriminating, scrupulous, meticulous, precise, exact, accurate, careful, strict, close, ticklish
OLD tickle
E3 1 unpleasant, horrible **2** nasty, disagreeable, unpleasant **3** careless

nicely *adv*
1 SATISFACTORILY, well, agreeably, delightfully, pleasurably, pleasantly, pleasingly, attractively, respectably, properly
2 POLITELY, respectably, civilly, courteously
E3 1 unpleasantly, disagreeably, nastily **2** rudely, impolitely, disrespectfully

niceness *n*
pleasantness, kindness, agreeableness, friendliness, delightfulness, lik(e)ableness, attractiveness, charm, amiability, politeness, respectability
E3 unpleasantness, disagreeableness, nastiness

nicety *n*
1 SUBTLETY, refinement, delicacy, distinction, nuance, fine point
2 PRECISION, accuracy, meticulousness, exactness, scrupulousness, minuteness, finesse

niche *n*
1 POSITION, place, vocation, calling, métier, slot, specialized/specialist area

2 RECESS, alcove, hollow, nook, cranny, cubbyhole, corner, opening

nick n, v

◆ n

1 NOTCH, indentation, chip, cut, groove, dent, scar, scratch, mark
2 PRISON, jail, jailhouse, police station
COLLOQ. inside
SLANG porridge, clink, cooler, slammer, quod, jug, can, choky
3 *in good nick*
condition, shape, form, state, health, fettle

◆ v

1 NOTCH, cut, dent, indent, chip, score, scratch, scar, mark, damage, snick
2 STEAL, pilfer, take, pocket
COLLOQ. knock off, pinch, swipe, lag, snitch
3 ARREST, catch, capture, pick up
FORMAL apprehend
COLLOQ. bust, nab, collar, run in, pull in, pick up, do, nail

nickname n

pet name, familiar name, so(u)briquet, epithet, diminutive, byname, to-name
FORMAL cognomen
SLANG monicker

nifty adj

slick, neat, clever, pleasing, enjoyable, excellent, quick, skilful, deft, chic, smart, stylish, spruce, sharp, adroit, agile, nippy, apt

niggardliness n

1 MEANNESS, miserliness, closeness, grudgingness, ungenerousness
FORMAL parsimony
COLLOQ. stinginess, tight-fistedness, cheeseparing
2 MEAGRENESS, paltriness, smallness, scantiness, skimpiness, inadequacy, insufficiency
F3 **1** generosity **2** bountifulness

niggardly adj

1 MEAN, miserly, close, ungenerous, ungiving, sparing, grudging, illiberal, hard, hard-fisted, penny-wise, nippy; *Scot* near-begaun, near-gaun, nirly
OLD nithing
FORMAL parsimonious, penurious
COLLOQ. mingy, stingy, tight-fisted, cheeseparing
2 MEAGRE, small, miserable, scanty, skimpy, paltry, inadequate, insufficient
COLLOQ. measly, mingy
F3 **1** generous, liberal **2** bountiful, abundant

niggle v, n

◆ v

1 BOTHER, worry, trouble, annoy, irritate, upset
COLLOQ. bug
2 NAG, criticize, keep on at, pick on, complain, moan, carp, quibble
COLLOQ. nit-pick, hassle, henpeck

◆ n

quibble, complaint, objection, criticism, query, protest, cavil, equivocation, prevarication
OLD pettifogging
COLLOQ. nit-picking

night n

night-time, darkness, hours of darkness, dark, dead of night
F3 day, daytime
Related adjective: nocturnal

nightclub n

club, disco, discotheque, cabaret, nightspot
COLLOQ. niterie, nitery

nightfall n

sunset, dusk, twilight, dark, evening, sundown
FORMAL gloaming, crepuscule
F3 dawn, sunrise

nightly adv

every night, each night, night after night, at night, after dark, nocturnally

nightmare n

1 BAD DREAM, hallucination, *cauchemar*
OLD ephialtes; (*Shakesp*) cacodemon
FORMAL incubus, oneirodynia
2 ORDEAL, horror, torment, torture, trial, calamity, agony, anguish, awful experience

nightmarish adj

terrifying, alarming, dreadful, frightening, ghostly, harrowing, horrible, horrific, agonizing, disturbing, scaring, unreal
COLLOQ. creepy

night-time n

night, darkness, hours of darkness, dark, dead of night
F3 day, daytime

nihilism n

rejection, repudiation, negation, denial, pessimism, scepticism, nothingness, oblivion, emptiness, non-existence, lawlessness, anarchy, terrorism, disorder, agnosticism, atheism, cynicism, disbelief, negativism
FORMAL abnegation, nullity, renunciation

nihilist n

pessimist, revolutionary, extremist, agitator, anarchist, terrorist, negationist, negativist, agnostic, atheist, disbeliever, cynic, sceptic, antinomian

nil n

nothing, zero, none, nought, naught, love, cipher
COLLOQ. duck, zilch

nimble adj

1 AGILE, active, lively, sprightly, spry, smart, graceful, lithe, quick, quick-moving, brisk, deft, light-footed, light, lissome, prompt, ready, swift, sure-footed; *dialect* wandle; *Scot* swack, yauld
OLD fleet, flippant, wight, deliver; (*Shakesp*) fleet-foot, quiver; (*Spenser*) wimble
FORMAL volant
COLLOQ. nippy
2 ALERT, quick-witted, quick, quick-thinking, clever, smart, sharp-witted, sharp-eyed
F3 **1** clumsy, slow **2** slow

nimbleness n

agility, adroitness, dexterity, grace, lightness, deftness, finesse, sprightliness, spryness, smartness, skill, alertness
FORMAL alacrity
COLLOQ. niftiness, nippiness

nimbly adv

smartly, agilely, fast, sharply, snappily, speedily, swiftly, spryly, quickly, readily, promptly, actively, lightly, proficiently, dexterously, deftly, briskly, easily, alertly, quick-wittedly
F3 awkwardly, clumsily

nincompoop n

fool, idiot, dunce, dimwit, simpleton, ignoramus, dolt
COLLOQ. blockhead, nitwit, numskull, chump, clot, twit, twerp
SLANG nerd, plonker, wally

nip¹ v

1 BITE, pinch, squeeze, snip, clip, dock, lop, tweak, catch, grip, nibble
2 DASH, go, hurry, rush, fly, tear, dart, run
COLLOQ. pop
■ **nip in the bud**

Members of the nobility include:

baron	dowager	governor	liege lord	nawab	thane
baroness	duchess	jarl	life peer	patrician	toiseach
baronet	duke	Junker	lord	peer	vavasour
count	earl	knight	magnifico	peeress	*vicomte*
countess	grand duchess	lady	marchioness	seigneur	*vidame*
daimio	grand duke	laird	marquess	squire	viscount
dame	grand seigneur	liege	marquis	starosta	viscountess

halt, arrest, stop, stem, check, curb, block, frustrate, obstruct, impede

**nip² ** *n*

a nip of brandy
dram, draught, shot, swallow, mouthful, drop, sip, taste, portion

nipple *n*
teat, udder, breast, dug
TECHNICAL mamilla, papilla
COLLOQ. *dialect* diddy, pap
SLANG tit

nippy *adj*
1 CHILLY, cold, biting, sharp, raw, nipping, piercing, icy, stinging
2 FAST, quick, speedy, nimble, brisk, active, agile, sprightly, spry
E3 1 warm **2** slow

nirvana *n*
enlightenment, paradise, heaven, tranquillity, bliss, joy, peace, ecstasy, exaltation, serenity

nit-picking *adj*
quibbling, carping, finicky, fussy, hair-splitting, hypercritical, pedantic, captious, pettifogging, cavilling

nitty-gritty *n*
basics, essentials, fundamentals, main points, key points
COLLOQ. bottom line, nuts and bolts, brass tacks

nitwit *n*
fool, idiot, dimwit, simpleton
COLLOQ. nincompoop, ass, chump, ninny, neddy, clot, dope, twit, birdbrain, silly-billy
SLANG wally, jerk, dumbo, pillock, prat, plonker

no *adv, interj*
not at all, not really, of course not, absolutely not, certainly not, most certainly not, no thanks, under no circumstances; *Scot* nae
COLLOQ. no way, nope, not on your life, over my dead body

nob *n*
VIP, aristocrat, personage
COLLOQ. big shot, bigwig, fat cat, toff

nobble *v*
1 BRIBE, buy (off), influence, warn off, threaten, intimidate
2 DOPE, drug, interfere with, disable, incapacitate, hamstring
COLLOQ. get at
3 CATCH, arrest, grab, seize
COLLOQ. nab, collar, nick, bust, run in, pull in, pick up, do, nail
4 STEAL, grab, take, pilfer, pinch
COLLOQ. nick, knock off, snitch, swipe
5 THWART, frustrate, foil, check, defeat, hinder

nobility *n*
1 NOBLENESS, dignity, grandeur, grandness, illustriousness, stateliness, majesty, magnificence, splendour, impressiveness, illustriousness, glory, eminence, excellence, superiority, uprightness, integrity, honour, virtue, worthiness, generosity
FORMAL magnanimity
2 ARISTOCRACY, peerage, peers, nobles, gentry, élite, lords, high society, family, rank
COLLOQ. nobs, toffs

Related adjective: nobiliary
See panel above
E3 1 baseness **2** proletariat

noble *n, adj*
♦ *n*
aristocrat, peer, lord, lady, nobleman, noblewoman, magnate
OLD grandee, atheling; (*Spenser*) douzeper
E3 commoner
♦ *adj*
1 ARISTOCRATIC, high-born, titled, landed, high, high-ranking, patrician
OLD (*Spenser*) gent
COLLOQ. blue-blooded, born with a silver spoon in your mouth
2 MAGNIFICENT, glorious, splendid, stately, generous, dignified, distinguished, fine, eminent, grand, great, exalted, lofty, honoured, honourable, venerated, imposing, impressive, majestic, illustrious
FORMAL magnanimous
3 VIRTUOUS, unselfish, honourable, worthy, excellent, elevated, fine, gentle, generous, great-hearted, self-sacrificing, noble-minded, brave, gallant, manful
OLD handsome
FORMAL magnanimous
E3 1 low-born, common **3** ignoble, base, contemptible

nobly *adv*
worthily, unselfishly, honourably, virtuously, gallantly, manfully, bravely, generously
E3 contemptibly

nobody *pron, n*
no one, nothing, nonentity, menial, cipher, mediocrity; *Scot* naebody
COLLOQ. lightweight
E3 somebody

nocturnal *adj*
night, night-time, occurring at night, active at night

nod *v, n*
♦ *v*
1 GESTURE, indicate, sign, signal, salute, acknowledge, beckon, beck, incline, dip, bow, nid-nod, noddle
FORMAL nutate
2 AGREE, approve, support, accept, say yes to
FORMAL assent
♦ *n*
gesture, indication, sign, signal, salute, greeting, beck, acknowledgement
■ **nod off**
sleep, fall asleep, doze (off), drop off, drowse, nap
FORMAL slumber
■ **give the nod to**
approve, agree to, assent to, consent to, allow, permit, pass, sanction, authorize, mandate, ratify, validate, endorse, support, hold with, uphold, second, back, accept, adopt, carry, confirm
COLLOQ. give the go-ahead to, give the green light to, OK, rubber-stamp, give the thumbs-up to, buy

node *n*
swelling, protuberance, lump, knob, knot, growth, bud, bump, nodule, carbuncle, junction, convergence

noise n, v

◆ n

sound, din, racket, row, clamour, clash, clatter, commotion, outcry, hubbub, uproar, cry, blare, talk, pandemonium, tumult, babble

F∃ quiet, silence

◆ v

report, rumour, publicize, announce, circulate

noiseless adj

silent, inaudible, soundless, quiet, mute, still, soft, hushed

F∃ loud, noisy

noiselessly adv

silently, inaudibly, soundlessly, quietly, softly

F∃ noisily

noisily adv

loudly, deafeningly, resoundingly, tumultuously, boisterously, rowdily, at the top of your voice

TECHNICAL fortissimo

FORMAL vociferously

COLLOQ. so loud you can't hear yourself think

F∃ quietly, softly

noisome adj

disgusting, offensive, repulsive, disagreeable, obnoxious, nauseating, harmful, hurtful, injurious, pernicious, bad, unhealthy, unwholesome, smelly, stinking, foul, putrid, reeking, poisonous

FORMAL deleterious, f(o)etid, malodorous, mephitic, noxious, pestiferous, pestilential

F∃ balmy, pleasant, wholesome

noisy adj

booming, roaring, thundering, loud, deafening, blasting, blaring, ear-splitting, clamorous, piercing, vocal, tumultuous, rowdy, rackety, rumbustious, boisterous, obstreperous, turbulent

FORMAL vociferous

COLLOQ. so loud you can't hear yourself think

F∃ quiet, silent, peaceful

nomad n

traveller, wanderer, itinerant, transient, rambler, roamer, rover, migrant, vagabond, vagrant

nomadic adj

travelling, itinerant, wandering, roaming, migrant, migratory, drifting, roving, roaming, Gypsy, unsettled, vagrant

FORMAL peregrinating, peripatetic

nom-de-plume n

pseudonym, pen-name, assumed name, alias

nomenclature n

naming, classification, vocabulary, terminology, phraseology

TECHNICAL taxonomy

FORMAL codification, locution

nominal adj

1 TITULAR, in name only, supposed, professed, ostensible, so-called, theoretical, formal, self-styled, puppet, symbolic

FORMAL purported

2 TOKEN, minimal, trifling, trivial, insignificant, small, tiny, peppercorn, symbolic

F∃ 1 actual, genuine, real

nominally adv

in name only, ostensibly, theoretically, symbolically, formally

nominate v

1 PROPOSE, designate, submit, suggest, recommend, present

COLLOQ. put up

2 APPOINT, choose, select, name, elect, assign, commission, elevate, term

TECHNICAL postulate, present

OLD voice

nomination n

1 PROPOSAL, submission, suggestion, recommendation

2 APPOINTMENT, choice, selection, designation, election

nominee n

candidate, entrant, contestant, appointee, runner, assignee

non-aligned adj

neutral, independent, impartial, non-partisan, uncommitted, undecided, uninvolved, disinterested

nonchalance n

calm, calmness, cool, composure, aplomb, equanimity, indifference, detachment, unconcern, self-possession

FORMAL imperturbability, insouciance, sang-froid, pococurant(e)ism

F∃ anxiousness, worriedness

nonchalant adj

unconcerned, detached, dispassionate, offhand, blasé, indifferent, casual, easy-going, cool, calm, collected, apathetic, careless

FORMAL insouciant, imperturbable

COLLOQ. laid-back, cool and collected, cool as a cucumber

F∃ concerned, careful

non-combatant adj, n

◆ adj

non-fighting, non-violent, non-belligerent, unaggressive, civilian, neutral, non-aligned, pacifist, conciliatory, peacemaking, dovish

◆ n

pacifist, passive resister, conscientious objector

COLLOQ. conchie

non-committal adj

guarded, unrevealing, cautious, wary, reserved, ambiguous, discreet, equivocal, evasive, careful, prudent, neutral, indefinite, tactful, diplomatic, tentative, vague

FORMAL circumspect, politic

COLLOQ. sitting on the fence, playing your cards close to your chest

non compos mentis adj

insane, mad, lunatic, unbalanced, psychotic, disturbed, deranged, maniacal, out of your mind, out of your senses, of unsound mind, unhinged, crazed, unstable, frenzied, wild, berserk, manic, maniac, distracted, distraught, fey, frenetic, frantic, stone-crazy, queer; Scot gyte, red-mad

OLD frantic-mad, lymphatic, bestraught

COLLOQ. crazy, demented, nuts, nutty, nutty as a fruitcake, wacky, mad as a hatter, barmy, bonkers, batty, cracked, crackers, dippy, daffy, dotty, loopy, potty, off your nut, off your head, wrong in the head, out of your head, off the wall, out to lunch, round the bend, round the twist, bats, having bats in the belfry, cuckoo, off the rails, screwy, up the wall, raving, not all there; N Am buggy, flaky, fruity; Aust & NZ dingbats

SLANG loony, mental, bananas, barking, wacko, doolally, off your rocker, off your chump, off your trolley, out of your tree, needing your head examined, having lost your marbles, having a screw loose, having a tile loose, having several cards short of a full deck, with one sandwich short of a picnic, meshuga, ape, apeshit; N Am gonzo, loco, wiggy

See Synonym nuances panel at **mad**.

nonconformist n, adj

◆ n

dissenter, rebel, individualist, dissident, radical, protester, heretic, iconoclast, eccentric, maverick, seceder, secessionist

FORMAL dissentient
COLLOQ. fish out of water, square peg in a round hole
🔁 conformist
• *adj*
rebel, dissident, unco-operative, radical, heretical, eccentric, individualist
FORMAL dissentient

nonconformity *n*
unconventionality, originality, eccentricity, dissent, deviation, heterodoxy, heresy, secession
🔁 conformity, conventionality

nondescript *adj*
featureless, indeterminate, undistinctive, undistinguished, indistinguishable, unexceptional, ordinary, commonplace, plain, dull, vague, bland, anaemic, insipid, uninspiring, uninteresting, unattractive, unremarkable, unclassified
COLLOQ. run of the mill, common or garden, vanilla, nothing much to write home about, no great shakes, not going to set the Thames on fire; *N Am* cookie-cutter
🔁 distinctive, remarkable

none *pron*
no one, not any, not one, not even one, not a single one, nothing, nobody, not a soul, nil, zero

■ **none the ...**
no, not at all, to no extent, not a bit

nonentity *n*
nobody, nothing, menial, cipher, mediocrity
COLLOQ. lightweight
🔁 somebody

non-essential *adj*
unnecessary, unimportant, superfluous, redundant, unneeded, inessential, peripheral, dispensable, excessive, extraneous, expendable, supplementary
🔁 essential, necessary

nonetheless *adv*
nevertheless, still, anyway, even so, yet, however, in spite of everything, though, after all, by any means, in any case/event, by some means, anyhow, but, regardless, for all that, all/just the same, at the same time
FORMAL notwithstanding

non-event *n*
anticlimax, comedown, let-down, disappointment, fiasco
COLLOQ. damp squib, not all that it was cracked up to be

non-existence *n*
unreality, fancy, illusion, illusiveness, insubstantiality, unbeing
FORMAL chimera
🔁 existence, reality

non-existent *adj*
missing, unreal, null, legendary, mythical, fictitious, fictional, fancied, fanciful, hallucinatory, illusory, hypothetical, imaginary, imagined, fantasy, immaterial, insubstantial
FORMAL chimerical, incorporeal, suppositional
🔁 actual, existing, real

non-flammable *adj*
not flammable, fireproof, fire-resistant, flame-resistant, incombustible, uninflammable
🔁 flammable, inflammable

non-intervention *n*
non-involvement, non-participation, non-alignment, non-interference, laissez-faire, inaction, inertia, passivity, apathy
COLLOQ. hands-off policy

nonpareil *adj*
unparalleled, incomparable, beyond compare, without equal, unequalled, matchless, unrivalled, unique, inimitable

non-partisan *adj*
unbiased, unprejudiced, impartial, independent, neutral, objective, even-handed, detached, dispassionate
🔁 partisan, biased, prejudiced

nonplus *v*
puzzle, perplex, take aback, stagger, baffle, bewilder, confound, confuse, dumbfound, stun, astonish, astound, dismay, embarrass, disconcert, mystify
FORMAL discomfit, discountenance
COLLOQ. stump, flabbergast, flummox, faze, sew up

nonplussed *adj*
disconcerted, confounded, taken aback, at a loss, stunned, bewildered, astonished, astounded, dumbfounded, perplexed, puzzled, baffled, dismayed, embarrassed, blank
COLLOQ. stumped, flabbergasted, flummoxed, fazed, floored, out of your depth

nonsense *n*
rubbish, trash, drivel, balderdash, gibberish, gobbledygook, senselessness, stupidity, silliness, foolishness, folly, twaddle, ridiculousness, blague, doggerel; *dialect* faddle, havers; *dialect & N Am* blathers; *Scot* blethers, clamjamphrie
OLD galimatias
COLLOQ. stuff and nonsense, double Dutch, mumbo-jumbo, bunk, bunkum, claptrap, cobblers, poppycock, piffle, waffle, flannel, rot, tripe, tosh, bosh, tommyrot, codswallop, baloney, humbug, hooey, bilge, bull, blah, eyewash, hogwash, rhubarb, guff, malarkey, moonshine
SLANG (*vulgar*) crap, cack, shit, balls, bollocks, bullshit; *N Am* jazz; *Aust & NZ* borak
🔁 sense, wisdom

nonsensical *adj*
ridiculous, meaningless, senseless, foolish, stupid, inane, irrational, silly, incomprehensible, unintelligible, gibberish, ludicrous, preposterous, absurd, fatuous
COLLOQ. crazy, crackpot, potty, nutty, dotty, barmy, hare-brained, wacky
🔁 reasonable, sensible, logical

non-stop *adj, adv*
• *adj*
never-ending, uninterrupted, continuous, unceasing, ceaseless, incessant, constant, endless, interminable, persistent, relentless, unending, unbroken, without interruption, unfaltering, round-the-clock, ongoing
🔁 intermittent, occasional
• *adv*
uninterruptedly, continuously, constantly, incessantly, unceasingly, ceaselessly, endlessly, interminably, unendingly, unbrokenly, round-the-clock, unfalteringly, steadily, relentlessly, unrelentingly, unremittingly
🔁 intermittently, occasionally

non-violent *adj*
peaceable, peaceful, pacifist, passive, dovish
FORMAL irenic
🔁 violent

nook *n*
1 RECESS, alcove, corner, cranny, niche, cubbyhole
2 SHELTER, retreat, hideout, hideaway, den, refuge, cavity, opening

noon *n*
midday, twelve o'clock, twelve p.m., twelve noon, lunchtime

norm *n*
average, mean, standard, rule, usual rule, pattern, type, criterion, gauge, model, yardstick, benchmark, touchstone, measure, scale, reference

normal *adj*
usual, standard, general, commonplace, common,

ordinary, conventional, popular, average, regular, routine, everyday, accepted, typical, mainstream, natural, habitual, accustomed, well-adjusted, straight, rational, reasonable
COLLOQ. run of the mill, bog standard
☒ abnormal, irregular, peculiar, deviant

normality n
usualness, commonness, ordinariness, regularity, routine, conventionality, balance, adjustment, averageness, typicality, naturalness, reason, reasonableness, rationality
FORMAL normalcy
☒ abnormality, irregularity, peculiarity

normally adv
ordinarily, usually, as usual, as a rule, generally, typically, commonly, conventionally, characteristically, naturally, regularly, routinely
☒ abnormally, exceptionally

northern adj
north, northerly, polar, Arctic
OLD septentrional
FORMAL boreal, hyperborean
☒ southern

nose n, v
♦ n
1 the animal's nose
beak, bill, neb
FORMAL proboscis
COLLOQ. boko, hooter, snitch, snout, snoot
SLANG conk, schnozzle, schnoz
Related adjectives: nasal, rhinal
2 a nose for a good story
sense, flair, feel, perception, instinct
♦ v
nudge, inch, edge, ease, move slowly, push
▪ **nose around**
poke around, search, pry
COLLOQ. snoop, rubberneck, poke your nose in
▪ **nose out**
discover, detect, find out, uncover, reveal, inquire
COLLOQ. sniff out
▪ **get up your nose**
irritate, rile, displease, anger, vex, irk, madden, exasperate, tease, provoke, ruffle, gall, trouble, nag, disturb, bother, pester, plague, harass, molest; Scot fash
COLLOQ. aggravate, bug, wind up, hassle, rub up the wrong way, get your blood up, make your blood boil, get on your nerves, get under your skin, get your goat, get on your wick, drive crazy/nuts, drive bananas, drive up the wall, drive round the bend/twist, get your back up, brass off, cheese off, make your hackles rise, make sparks fly, give you the hump, get your dander up; N Am tick/hack off
☒ please, gratify, comfort
▪ **poke your nose into**
interfere, intervene, pry, intrude, butt in, tamper
COLLOQ. fiddle, stick your nose into, stick/put your oar in, snoop
▪ **under your nose**
in front of you, right in front of you, plainly, obviously, clearly, staring you right in the face, plain to see, plain as a pikestaff, for all to see

nosedive v, n
♦ v
plummet, dive, drop, plunge, decline, get worse, go down, submerge, swoop
♦ n
plummet, dive, drop, plunge, swoop, header, purler

nosegay n
bouquet, posy, spray, bunch

nosey, nosy adj
inquisitive, meddlesome, prying, interfering,

curious, eavesdropping, probing
COLLOQ. snooping

nosh n
food, foodstuffs, comestibles, provisions, meals, stores, rations, refreshments, sustenance, nourishment, nutrition, nutriment, subsistence, feed, fodder, diet, fare, dish, speciality, delicacy, cooking, cuisine, menu, board, table
FORMAL viands, victuals
COLLOQ. eatables, eats, tuck, scran
SLANG grub

nosiness n
inquisitiveness, curiousness, meddlesomeness, interference, intrusiveness, prying
COLLOQ. snooping

nostalgia n
yearning, longing, wistfulness, regretfulness, regret(s), remembrance, recollection(s), reminiscence(s), homesickness, pining, mal du pays

nostalgic adj
yearning, longing, pining, wistful, emotional, regretful, sentimental, homesick, reminiscent

nostrum n
medicine, pill, drug, potion, cure, remedy, elixir, panacea, cure-all, cure for all ills, universal cure/remedy

notability n
1 NOTEWORTHINESS, impressiveness, importance, significance, distinction, fame, eminence, esteem, renown, observableness
2 CELEBRITY, dignitary, magnate, worthy, luminary
FORMAL notable, personage
COLLOQ. somebody, VIP, bigwig, big shot, big noise, big cheese, heavyweight, top brass, someone, celeb
☒ nonentity

notable adj, n
♦ adj
noteworthy, remarkable, noticeable, observable, particular, striking, extraordinary, signal, impressive, outstanding, special, important, significant, marked, unusual, uncommon, celebrated, distinguished, famous, great, illustrious, eminent, pre-eminent, well-known, momentous, notorious, memorable, renowned, unforgettable, rare
☒ ordinary, commonplace, usual
♦ n
celebrity, notability, personage, dignitary, luminary, star, worthy
COLLOQ. somebody, VIP, bigwig, big shot, big noise, big cheese, heavyweight, top brass, someone, celeb
☒ nobody, nonentity

notably adv
markedly, noticeably, particularly, in particular, significantly, remarkably, strikingly, signally, conspicuously, distinctly, especially, impressively, outstandingly, extraordinarily, eminently, uncommonly

notation n
symbols, characters, code, cipher, signs, alphabet, system, script, hieroglyphics, noting, record, shorthand

notch n, v
♦ n
1 CUT, nick, indentation, incision, dent, indent, score, groove, gouge, cleft, gash, scratch, mark, snip, nail-hole, nock, hack, jag, kerf
TECHNICAL joggle, sinus, swan-mark
FORMAL crena, insection
2 DEGREE, grade, step, level, stage
♦ v
cut, nick, score, dent, gouge, groove, indent, mark, gash, scratch, serrate, tally, vandyke, nock, raffle; dialect gap, gimp; Scot lip, mush

■ **notch up**
achieve, gain, attain, make, score, record, register
COLLOQ. chalk up

notched *adj*
jagged, jaggy, pinked, serrate(d), serrulate(d), eroded
TECHNICAL emarginate
FORMAL crenellate(d), erose

note *n, v*
◆ *n*
1 MESSAGE, letter, communication, memorandum, reminder, line, jotting, account, record, entry, comment, e-mail
FORMAL epistle, missive
COLLOQ. memo
2 ANNOTATION, comment, commentary, explanation, gloss, footnote, remark
FORMAL explication, marginalia
3 INDICATION, signal, element, tone, inflection, token, mark, symbol
4 EMINENCE, distinction, importance, significance, consequence, fame, renown, greatness, illustriousness, reputation, pre-eminence, prestige
5 HEED, attention, attentiveness, care, mindfulness, regard, notice, observation, consideration
◆ *v*
1 NOTICE, observe, perceive, become aware of, heed, detect, mark, remark, mention, allude to, refer to, touch on, see, witness
2 RECORD, register, log, write down, mark, enter, put in writing, put down, jot down

notebook *n*
notepad, pocket-book, exercise book, jotter, logbook, log, record, diary, journal, daybook, address book, table-book, field book, *cahier, index rerum*

noted *adj*
famous, well-known, renowned, notable, celebrated, eminent, pre-eminent, prominent, great, of note, acclaimed, illustrious, distinguished, respected, recognized
E3 obscure, unknown

notes *n*
jottings, record, impressions, report, commentary, sketch, impressions, outline, synopsis, transcript, minutes, draft

noteworthy *adj*
remarkable, significant, important, notable, memorable, striking, exceptional, impressive, extraordinary, unusual, outstanding, marked
E3 commonplace, unexceptional, ordinary

nothing *n*
1 NOUGHT, zero, not a thing, naught, nothingness; *dialect* nowt; *Scot* naething; *S Afr* nix-nie
COLLOQ. zilch, sweet Fanny Adams, sweet FA; *N Am* diddly-squat, squat
SLANG bugger all, sod all; (*taboo*) fuck all
2 NON-EXISTENCE, emptiness, void, vacuum, oblivion
FORMAL nullity
3 NOBODY, nonentity, menial, cipher, mediocrity
COLLOQ. lightweight
E3 something
■ **nothing but**
only, simply, just, merely, solely, exclusively
■ **for nothing**
1 FREE, gratis, without charge, free of charge, at no cost, complimentary
COLLOQ. on the house
2 IN VAIN, unsuccessfully, futilely, needlessly, with no result, to no avail

nothingness *n*
non-existence, oblivion, vacuum, void, emptiness
FORMAL nihilism, nihility, nullity
E3 life, existence

notice *v, n*
◆ *v*
note, remark, perceive, observe, mind, see, discern, distinguish, make out, mark, detect, spot, become aware of, take note of, pay attention to
FORMAL heed, take heed of, behold, espy
E3 ignore, overlook, miss
◆ *n*
1 ANNOUNCEMENT, notification, information, declaration, communication, intimation, intelligence, news, warning, instruction, advice, order
FORMAL apprisal
2 ADVERTISEMENT, poster, sign, bill, handbill, bulletin, leaflet, pamphlet, circular, information sheet
3 REVIEW, comment, criticism, critique, write-up
COLLOQ. crit
4 ATTENTION, observation, awareness, note, regard, thought, interest, watchfulness, consideration
FORMAL heed, cognizance
■ **give/hand in your notice**
quit, leave, resign, stand down, step down, walk out
COLLOQ. chuck/pack in your job
■ **give someone notice**
fire, dismiss, discharge, eject, get rid of
COLLOQ. sack, axe, boot out, kick out, show someone the door, give someone their cards/jotters, give someone the sack/push/boot/elbow

noticeable *adj*
perceptible, observable, appreciable, unmistakable, conspicuous, visible, discernible, evident, clear, distinct, significant, striking, plain, patent, obvious, manifest, marked, pronounced, bold, notable, detectable, distinguishable, measurable, impressive, powerful
COLLOQ. sticking out like a sore thumb
E3 inconspicuous, unnoticeable

noticeably *adv*
perceptibly, unmistakably, evidently, clearly, distinctly, significantly, strikingly, plainly, patently, obviously, notably, conspicuously, visibly, discernibly

notification *n*
announcement, information, notice, declaration, advice, warning, telling, informing, intelligence, message, publication, statement, communication, divulgence, disclosure

notify *v*
inform, tell, make known, advise, announce, declare, communicate, broadcast, warn, acquaint, caution, alert, publish, disclose, reveal, divulge
FORMAL apprise

notion *n*
1 IDEA, thought, concept, conception, belief, impression, view, opinion, conviction, theory, hypothesis, assumption, understanding, apprehension
FORMAL conceptualization
2 INCLINATION, desire, wish, impulse, whim, fancy, caprice

notional *adj*
theoretical, abstract, imaginary, hypothetical, illusory, conceptual, speculative, fanciful, fancied, unfounded, unreal, visionary, thematic, classificatory
FORMAL ideational
E3 real

notionally *adv*
theoretically, in theory, hypothetically, conceptually
FORMAL conjecturally, putatively

notoriety *n*
infamy, disrepute, dishonour, disgrace, scandal
FORMAL ignominy, obloquy, opprobrium

notorious *adj*
infamous, disreputable, scandalous, dishonourable, ill-

famed, of ill repute, disgraceful, flagrant, blatant, noted, glaring, well-known, proverbial, arrant
TECHNICAL Scot notous
FORMAL ignominious, egregious, opprobrious

notoriously adv
infamously, disreputably, scandalously, dishonourably, disgracefully, flagrantly, blatantly, glaringly, overtly, notably, obviously, openly, particularly, patently, arrantly, spectacularly
FORMAL egregiously, opprobriously, ignominiously

notwithstanding adv, prep
nevertheless, nonetheless, although, though, even so, however, yet, despite, in spite of, regardless of

nought n
zero, nil, naught, nothing, nothingness
COLLOQ. zilch

nourish v
1 NURTURE, feed, foster, care for, provide for, take care of, sustain, support, attend to, tend, nurse, bring up, rear, maintain, have, cherish
2 STRENGTHEN, encourage, promote, cultivate, stimulate, foster, further, forward, advance, boost, help, aid, assist

nourishing adj
nutritious, wholesome, healthful, health-giving, good, beneficial, substantial, strengthening, invigorating
TECHNICAL alimentative
FORMAL nutritive

nourishment n
nutrition, food, sustenance, diet, nutriment, subsistence
TECHNICAL ingesta
OLD aliment, nouriture, pabulum
COLLOQ. eats, tuck, scran
SLANG grub, nosh

nouveaux riches n
the new rich, upstarts, parvenus, arrivistes

novel adj, n
◆ adj
new, original, fresh, innovative, unfamiliar, unique, rare, unusual, uncommon, different, creative, imaginative, resourceful, ingenious, inventive, unconventional, unorthodox, modern, unprecedented, pioneering, ground-breaking, strange
E3 hackneyed, familiar, ordinary
See Synonym nuances panel at **new**.
◆ n
story, tale, narrative, romance, book, paperback, hardback, fiction

novelist n
writer, author, storyteller, man/woman of letters, creative writer, fabler, fiction writer

novelty n
1 NEWNESS, originality, freshness, innovation, unfamiliarity, unusualness, uniqueness, rareness, difference, creativity, imaginativeness, unconventionality, strangeness
2 GIMMICK, gadget, trifle, memento, knick-knack, curiosity, souvenir, trinket, bauble, gimcrack

novice n
beginner, tiro, learner, student, pupil, trainee, probationer, recruit, raw recruit, apprentice, amateur, newcomer
FORMAL neophyte, noviciate
COLLOQ. greenhorn, rookie, newbie
E3 expert

noviciate n
novitiate, apprenticeship, trainee period, training, initiation, probationary period, trial period

now adv
1 AT PRESENT, right now, just now, at the moment, for the time being, at the present time, at the moment, at this

moment in time, at this time, currently, nowadays, today, these days; N Am presently
2 IMMEDIATELY, at once, directly, instantly, straight away, right away, promptly, without delay, next

■ **now and then**
at times, sometimes, from time to time, now and again, occasionally, on and off, on occasion, once in a while, periodically, infrequently, intermittently, spasmodically, sporadically
FORMAL desultorily

nowadays adv
at present, today, at the present time, at the moment, at this moment in time, at this time, currently, these days, in this day and age; N Am presently

noxious adj
harmful, poisonous, pernicious, toxic, injurious, unhealthy, deadly, destructive, ruinous, damaging, detrimental, malignant, foul, disgusting, threatening, menacing
FORMAL noisome, deleterious
E3 innocuous, wholesome

nozzle n
sprinkler, sprinkler head, rose, sprayer, jet, nose, sparger, adjutage, twyer; Scot stroup

nuance n
subtlety, suggestion, shade, shading, hint, suspicion, gradation, (fine) distinction, overtone, refinement, touch, trace, tinge, degree, nicety

nub n
centre, central point, heart, core, nucleus, kernel, crux, gist, pith, marrow, meat, pivot, focus, point, essence

nubile adj
mature, adult, marriageable, attractive, desirable, voluptuous
COLLOQ. sexy

nucleus n
centre, heart, nub, core, kernel, basis, marrow, meat, pivot, focus, crux

nude adj
naked, bare, with nothing on, undressed, unclothed, uncovered, exposed, stripped, disrobed, denuded, raw, mother-naked, Adamic, skyclad, undraped, in puris naturalibus; dialect start-naked; Scot in the scud
COLLOQ. in the altogether, starkers, in your birthday suit, in the raw, in the buff, not a stitch on, naked as the day you were born
SLANG bollock-naked
E3 clothed, dressed

nudge v, n
poke, prod, jab, shove, dig, jog, prompt, push, elbow, bump; Scot dunch, dunsh

nudity n
nakedness, bareness, undress, state of undress, nudism, dishabille, déshabillé
COLLOQ. in the altogether

nugatory adj
worthless, futile, useless, vain, valueless, unavailing, null and void, invalid, inoperative, insignificant, negligible, inconsequential, trifling, trivial, inadequate
FORMAL ineffectual
E3 important, significant

nugget n
lump, mass, piece, chunk, clump, hunk, wad, wodge

nuisance n
annoyance, inconvenience, bother, irritation, irritant, vexation, pest, bore, difficulty, problem, trial, trouble, weight, burden, plague, inconvenience, drawback
FORMAL affliction, tribulation

COLLOQ. pain, drag, thorn in your side/flesh
SLANG chizz; *N Am* hoop

null *adj*

void, invalid, invalidated, annulled, revoked, cancelled, useless, vain, worthless, powerless, inoperative
FORMAL ineffectual, nullified, abrogated
F∃ valid

nullify *v*

annul, revoke, cancel, invalidate, declare null and void, abolish, rescind, quash, repeal, void, set aside, bring to an end, reverse, offset, counteract
FORMAL abrogate, negate, countermand, renounce, discontinue
F∃ validate

nullity *n*

non-existence, voidness, characterlessness, immateriality, invalidity, powerlessness, uselessness, worthlessness
FORMAL incorporeality, ineffectualness
F∃ validity

numb *adj, v*

• *adj*
benumbed, insensible, unfeeling, dead, deadened, insensitive, without feeling, sleeping, drugged, anaesthetized, stunned, dazed, frozen, paralysed, immobilized, in shock
FORMAL insensible, insensate, torpid
F∃ sensitive
• *v*
deaden, benumb, anaesthetize, drug, freeze, immobilize, paralyse, dull, daze, stupefy, stun
FORMAL torpefy
F∃ sensitize

number *n, v*

• *n*
1 FIGURE, numeral, digit, integer, unit, character, cipher, fraction, decimal, statistics, data
2 TOTAL, sum, aggregate, tally, score, count, collection, amount, quantity, several, many, company, crowd, group, multitude, throng, horde
3 COPY, issue, edition, impression, imprint, volume, printing
4 PIECE OF MUSIC, song, dance, item, track, turn, act, sketch, routine, performance
• *v*
1 COUNT, calculate, enumerate, reckon, total, add (up to), compute, estimate, include
2 *your days are numbered*
limit, restrict, restrain, delimit, specify

numberless *adj*

innumerable, countless, endless, uncounted, without number, many, unnumbered, unsummed, infinite, untold, myriad, immeasurable
FORMAL multitudinous

numbness *n*

deadness, paralysis, anaesthetization, unfeelingness, dullness, insensitivity, stupefaction, stupor, torpor
FORMAL insensateness, insensibility
F∃ sensitivity

numeral *n*

number, figure, digit, integer, unit, character, cipher

numerical *adj*

integral, digital, whole, figural, computational, statistical, in numerical order, ranked, graded, hierarchical

numerically *adv*

arithmetically, algebraically, digitally, mathematically, in numerical order, in ascending order, in order, measurably, quantifiably, exponentially

numerous *adj*

many, innumerable, countless, endless, abundant, several, great (in number), strong, quite a few, a lot of, legion, plentiful, copious, profuse, various, sundry
OLD (*Shakesp*) populous
FORMAL manifold, multitudinous
COLLOQ. a good few
F∃ few, scarce, rare

numerousness *n*

plentifulness, abundance, copiousness, countlessness, plurality, profusion
FORMAL manifoldness, multiplicity, multitudinousness, multeity
F∃ scantiness, scarcity

numinous *adj*

spiritual, mystical, supernatural, religious, holy, sacred, divine, transcendent, mysterious

numskull *n*

fool, dimwit, dunce, simpleton
COLLOQ. nincompoop, ass, chump, ninny, neddy, clot, dope, twit, nitwit, nit, sucker, mug, twerp, birdbrain, silly-billy, berk, (proper) Charlie, gubbins, sap, saphead, wazzock, dum-dum, coot, goat, headbanger; *Scot* bampot; *N Am* lunkhead, chowderhead, putz, doofus; *Aust* dill, boofhead
SLANG wally, jerk, dumbo, pillock, prat, dork, geek, plonker, git, nerd, dweeb, nerk, goop, josser, nig-nog, sawney, schlemiel, turkey, yo-yo, cloth head, dipstick, muppet, goof, kook, pillock, tosspot; (*taboo*) prick, dickhead; *N Am* jughead, schmo, dingbat; *Aust* galah, nana; *Aust & NZ* nong

nun *n*

sister, abbess, prioress, mother superior, anchoress, ancress, canoness, vestal, deaconess, religieuse, conventual, zelatrix
OLD vowess; (*Shakesp*) cloistress

nuncio *n*

representative, envoy, ambassador, legate

nunnery *n*

convent, priory, cloister, abbey

nuptial *adj*

wedding, wedded, marital, bridal
FORMAL matrimonial, conjugal, connubial, hymeneal, epithalamial, epithalamic

nuptials *n*

wedding celebrations, wedding, marriage, bridal
FORMAL matrimony, spousals, espousal

nurse *v*

1 TEND, care for, look after, treat, attend to, take care of, cradle
2 BREAST-FEED, feed, suckle, wet-nurse, nurture, nourish
3 PRESERVE, sustain, support, nourish, cherish, harbour, entertain, encourage, keep, foster, boost, promote, advance, further, nurture, help, aid, assist

---

Nurses include:

auxiliary nurse	matron	General Nurse
charge nurse	midwife	(RGN)
children's nurse	nanny	school nurse
community nurse	night nurse	sicknurse
dental nurse	night sister	sister
district nurse	nurse consultant	staff nurse
dry-nurse	nursemaid	State Enrolled
healthcare	nurse practitioner	Nurse (SEN)
assistant	nursery nurse	State Registered
health visitor	nurse tutor	Nurse (SRN)
home nurse	occupational	theatre sister
Iain Rennie nurse	health nurse	ward sister
locality manager	psychiatric nurse	wet nurse
Macmillan nurse	Registered	

nurture *n, v*

◆ *n*

1 FOOD, nourishment, nutrition, sustenance, diet, subsistence, nouriture
COLLOQ. eats, tuck, scran
SLANG grub, nosh
2 REARING, upbringing, training, care, cultivation, stimulation, encouragement, fostering, promotion, help, aid, assistance, furtherance, advance, boosting, development, education, tending, feeding, schooling, discipline
FORMAL nouriture

◆ *v*

1 FEED, nourish, nurse, tend, care for, foster, support, sustain, cherish
2 BRING UP, rear, cultivate, develop, stimulate, promote, foster, help, aid, assist, further, advance, boost, educate, instruct, train, school, coach, tutor, discipline

nut *n*

1 *a bag of mixed nuts*
kernel, pip, seed, stone
2 MANIAC, insane person, lunatic, psychopath, madman, madwoman
COLLOQ. oddball, nutcase, nutter, fruitcake, crackpot, crank, headcase, basket-case
SLANG loony, psycho, screwball
3 ENTHUSIAST, fan, fanatic, follower, supporter, devotee, zealot, admirer
FORMAL aficionado
COLLOQ. buff, freak, fiend

■ **do your nut**
explode, blow up, blow a fuse, blow your top/cool, boil over, burst a blood vessel, flip your lid, fly into a rage, fly off the handle, foam at the mouth, freak out, go ballistic, go berserk, go mad, go off the deep end, go up the wall, have kittens, hit the ceiling, lose your cool, lose your rag, raise hell, see red, throw a tantrum/wobbly

---

Varieties of nut include:

almond	coconut	peanut (or
beech nut	filbert	groundnut)
brazil nut	hazelnut	pecan
cashew	macadamia	pine nut
chestnut	monkey nut	pistachio
cobnut		walnut

---

nutriment *n*
food, nourishment, nutrition, sustenance, diet, subsistence
COLLOQ. eats, tuck, scran

SLANG grub, nosh

nutrition *n*
food, nourishment, sustenance, diet, nutriment, subsistence
TECHNICAL eutrophy
COLLOQ. eats, tuck, scran
SLANG grub, nosh
Related adjective: trophic

nutritious *adj*
nourishing, wholesome, healthful, health-giving, good, beneficial, strengthening, body-building, substantial, sustaining, invigorating
FORMAL nutritive
E₃ bad, unwholesome

nuts *adj*
1 MAD, crazy, insane, lunatic, unbalanced, disturbed, deranged, demented, crazed, wild, berserk, unhinged, out of your mind
COLLOQ. loopy, bonkers, barmy, batty, dippy, daffy, potty, nutty, nutty as a fruitcake, out to lunch, round the bend, round the twist
SLANG loony, doolally, with one sandwich short of a picnic, off your rocker, off your trolley
2 *nuts about computers*
crazy, enthusiastic, fanatical, zealous, devoted, fond, keen, avid, ardent, passionate, infatuated, enamoured, smitten, mad, wild
COLLOQ. daft, potty
E₃ 1 sane 2 indifferent

nuts and bolts *n*
basics, essentials, fundamentals, details, components, bits and pieces, practicalities
COLLOQ. nitty-gritty

nutty *adj*
mad, crazy, insane, lunatic, unbalanced, disturbed, deranged, demented, crazed, wild, berserk, unhinged, out of your mind
COLLOQ. loopy, bonkers, barmy, batty, dippy, daffy, potty, nuts, nutty as a fruitcake, out to lunch, round the bend, round the twist
SLANG loony, doolally, with one sandwich short of a picnic, off your rocker, off your trolley

nuzzle *v*
snuggle, cuddle, pet, nestle, fondle, nudge, burrow

nymph *n*
sprite, sylph, dryad, hamadryad, naiad, oread, maelid, mermaid, oceanid, undine, girl, damsel, lass, maid, maiden, houri, Tethys

O

oaf *n*
lout, boor, dolt, yahoo, barbarian, gawk, lubber
COLLOQ. clod, clodhopper, hick, hobbledehoy, slob,
yobbo, bumpkin, oik; *N Am* roughneck; *Aust* hoon

oafish *adj*
boorish, churlish, doltish, lumpish, lubberly, stolid, swinish,
uncouth, unmannerly, bungling, rough, coarse, gross, ill-
bred, ill-mannered, gawky, lumpen
COLLOQ. clodhopping, yobbish

oar *n*
paddle, scull, blade, spoon, sweep, bow-oar, stroke oar,
stroke

oasis *n*
1 SPRING, watering-hole
2 REFUGE, haven, island, sanctuary, retreat, hideaway,
hideout
FORMAL sanctum

oath *n*
1 VOW, pledge, promise, bond, word, assurance,
affirmation, word of honour
FORMAL avowal, attestation
2 CURSE, swear-word, obscenity, profanity, expletive, bad
language, blasphemy; *N Am* curse-word
FORMAL imprecation
COLLOQ. four-letter word
SLANG cuss; *N Am* cussword

obduracy *n*
obstinacy, stubbornness, inflexibility, hard-heartedness,
persistence, perseverance, resoluteness, tenacity,
wilfulness, wrongheadedness, perversity, firmness,
doggedness, relentlessness, mulishness
FORMAL frowardness, intransigence, pertinacity
COLLOQ. pigheadedness
■ co-operativeness, flexibility, submissiveness

obdurate *adj*
obstinate, stubborn, inflexible, hard-hearted, implacable,
iron, stiff-necked, stony, unfeeling, immovable, unyielding,
unbending, unrelenting, persistent, dogged, headstrong,
strong-minded, self-willed, steadfast, firm, determined,
adamant, wilful
FORMAL intractable, intransigent
COLLOQ. pigheaded, bloody-minded
■ submissive, tender

obedience *n*
submissiveness, submission, respect, reverence,
amenableness, amenability, malleability, allegiance,
conformability, compliance, accordance, agreement,
deference, duty, dutifulness, passivity, subservience,
observance, docility
FORMAL acquiescence, tractability
■ disobedience, rebellion

obedient *adj*
submissive, docile, yielding, conforming, pliable,
compliant, malleable, amenable, dutiful, duteous,
biddable, law-abiding, deferential, respectful, well-
trained, disciplined, subservient, observant; *N Am* bridle-
wise

OLD (*Spenser*) bent
FORMAL acquiescent, tractable, obsequious
■ disobedient, rebellious, wilful

Synonym nuances
Submissive and **yielding** can be used of someone who
habitually gives in to others, and have negative
suggestions of weakness, whereas **docile** implies a
willingness to comply, and is more connotative of
gentleness. **Conforming**, which has more to do with
falling in with the plans of others, is not so marked by
approval or disapproval.
  The terms **pliable**, **malleable** and **biddable** again have
implications of weakness making someone suggestible
to whatever is proposed, while **amenable** is suggestive
of not being obstructive, and is more positive in tone: *he
was quite amenable to her suggestion.*
  Both **dutiful** and the less common **duteous** are
suggestive of strict obligations of responsibility and also
tend to convey approval, as does **law-abiding**.
Deferential, on the other hand, has more to do with
humbly resigning yourself to the wishes of others and has
overtones of criticism: *the prince's fawning and
deferential friends*, and **subservient** echoes this idea of
ingratiating humility.
  While **respectful** is similar, it suggests a less extreme
aspect and perhaps a more admirable quality.
Observant is more suggestive of careful adherence to
ritual, especially with regard to religion: *I married a
traditional, observant Jew.*

---

obeisance *n*
respect, reverence, submission, deference, homage, bow,
curtsy, kowtow, salaam, salute
FORMAL genuflection, salutation, veneration

obelisk *n*
pillar, column, monument, memorial, needle

obese *adj*
fat, overweight, tubby, stout, big, large, portly, fleshy,
round, well-endowed, paunchy, ponderous, plump,
podgy, chubby, roly-poly, heavy, bulky, outsize, Falstaffian
FORMAL corpulent, rotund
COLLOQ. gross, flabby, beefy, porky, well-upholstered
■ skinny, slender, thin

obesity *n*
fatness, overweight, stoutness, plumpness, portliness,
chubbiness, podginess, tubbiness, bulk
FORMAL corpulence, rotundness
COLLOQ. grossness, flabbiness
■ thinness, slenderness, skinniness

obey *v*
1 *obey an order*
follow, observe, abide by, adhere to, conform, comply,
consent to, heed, keep (to), mind, respond, submit,
surrender, yield, be ruled by, bow to, take orders from, do
as you are told, defer (to), respect, give way
FORMAL acquiesce in
COLLOQ. stick to the rules, go by the book, toe the line

2 CARRY OUT, discharge, execute, act upon, fulfil, perform
🖃 **1** disobey

obfuscate v
obscure, cover, blur, confuse, muddle, complicate, conceal, cloud, hide, disguise, mask, overshadow, shadow, shade, cloak, veil, shroud
🖃 clarify

obfuscation n
confusion, muddle, obscurity, concealment, complication, disguise
🖃 clarification

obituary n
death notice, eulogy
OLD necrology
COLLOQ. obit

object[1] n
1 THING, article, item, entity, body, something, device, gadget, artefact, phenomenon
2 AIM, objective, purpose, goal, target, intention, point, idea, motive, end, reason, ambition, design
FORMAL intent
3 TARGET, focus, recipient, butt, victim

object[2] v
object to something
protest, oppose, take exception, disapprove, refuse, complain, rebut, repudiate, withstand, resist, argue, challenge, beg to differ, take issue, take a stand against, cavil, jib
OLD recuse
FORMAL demur, expostulate, remonstrate, recalcitrate
🖃 agree, approve; *formal* acquiesce, accede, assent

objection n
protest, dissent, disapproval, opposition, complaint, dissatisfaction, argument, challenge, grievance, scruple, difficulty, question, exception, but, boggle, cavil
TECHNICAL recusation
OLD quarrel
FORMAL demur, expostulation, remonstration, recalcitrance
🖃 agreement, approval, assent

objectionable adj
unacceptable, unpleasant, offensive, obnoxious, disagreeable, hateful, detestable, deplorable, despicable, contemptible, intolerable, loathsome, abhorrent, revolting, repugnant, repellent, repulsive, nauseating, sickening
FORMAL reprehensible
🖃 acceptable, pleasant, delightful

objective adj, n
• adj
1 IMPARTIAL, unbiased, detached, unprejudiced, open-minded, equitable, dispassionate, even-handed, neutral, disinterested, uninvolved, just, fair
2 ***objective information***
factual, real, true, actual, authentic, genuine
🖃 **1** subjective
• n
object, aim, goal, end, purpose, ambition, mark, target, intention, point, idea, design
FORMAL intent

objectively adv
impartially, equitably, dispassionately, disinterestedly, even-handedly, neutrally, justly, fairly, with an open mind

objectivity n
impartiality, detachment, disinterest, disinterestedness, equitableness, even-handedness, justness, justice, fairness, open-mindedness, open mind
🖃 subjectivity, bias, prejudice

objector n
protester, demonstrator, opposer, opponent, complainer, agitator, striker, rebel, dissident, dissenter

obligate v
oblige, compel, constrain, coerce, require, make, necessitate, force, impel, pressurize, pressure, press, bind

obligation n
duty, responsibility, onus, charge, task, function, assignment, job, commitment, liability, accountability, requirement, agreement, bond, deed, covenant, contract, debt, indebtedness, burden, trust, compulsion, demand, command, pressure, duress

obligatory adj
1 COMPULSORY, statutory, required, binding, essential, necessary, unavoidable, enforced
FORMAL mandatory, imperative, requisite
2 CUSTOMARY, traditional, conventional, accepted, established, set, habitual, routine, regular, usual, normal, ordinary, familiar, fashionable
🖃 **1** optional

oblige v
1 COMPEL, constrain, coerce, require, make, necessitate, force, impel, pressurize, pressure, press, bind, tie, leave/be given no option
OLD astringe
FORMAL obligate
2 HELP, assist, accommodate, do someone a favour, serve, do someone a service, put yourself out for, gratify, please

obliged adj
under an obligation, indebted, in debt (to), grateful, thankful, gratified, appreciative, bound, forced, compelled, constrained, duty-bound, honour-bound, required, having (got) to, under compulsion
OLD debted
FORMAL obligated, beholden

obliging adj
accommodating, co-operative, helpful, considerate, willing, generous, pleasant, agreeable, friendly, kind, good-natured, polite, courteous, civil, indulgent
OLD officious
FORMAL complaisant
🖃 unhelpful, unkind, rude

obligingly adv
helpfully, considerately, willingly, generously, agreeably, politely, courteously, civilly
🖃 unhelpfully, rudely

oblique adj, n
• adj
1 SLANTING, sloping, inclined, angled, skew, cross, sidelong, sideways, squint, traverse, tilted
TECHNICAL bevelled
OLD awkward
COLLOQ. skew-whiff
2 INDIRECT, roundabout, circuitous, divergent, devious, rambling, winding, meandering, zigzag, tortuous, discursive
FORMAL periphrastic, circumlocutory
🖃 **2** direct
• n
diagonal, slant, slash, forward slash, stroke, solidus
FORMAL virgule

obliquely adv
1 DIAGONALLY, at an angle, aslant, aslope, askance, askant, slantwise, askew
2 INDIRECTLY, in a roundabout way, circuitously, evasively, not in so many words
🖃 **2** directly

obliterate v
eradicate, destroy, eliminate, annihilate, strike out,

delete, blot out, wipe out, rub out, erase
FORMAL efface, expunge, extirpate

obliteration n

eradication, destruction, elimination, annihilation, blotting out, deletion, erasure
FORMAL effacement, expunction, extirpation

oblivion n

1 UNCONSCIOUSNESS, blankness, darkness, stupor, void, limbo, inattentiveness, unmindfulness, absent-mindedness, carelessness, blindness, deafness, ignorance
FORMAL insensibility, Lethe
2 OBSCURITY, nothingness, non-existence, disuse
E3 1 awareness
Related adjective: lethean

oblivious adj

unaware, unconscious, inattentive, unmindful, preoccupied, absent-minded, careless, forgetful, heedless, unheeding, blind, deaf, ignorant, negligent, unconcerned
FORMAL insensible
E3 aware, conscious

obliviousness n

ignorance, unintelligence, illiteracy, unawareness, unconsciousness, unfamiliarity, inexperience, innocence, naivety, stupidity
COLLOQ. greenness, thickness

obloquy n

disgrace, dishonour, discredit, disfavour, shame, reproach, humiliation, criticism, attack, abuse, blame, censure, defamation, slander, detraction, bad press
FORMAL animadversion, aspersion, calumny, contumely, ignominy, invective, odium, opprobrium, stigma, vilification

obnoxious adj

unpleasant, disagreeable, disgusting, offensive, objectionable, unacceptable, loathsome, nasty, horrid, horrible, odious, vile, repulsive, repugnant, repellent, revolting, sickening, nauseating, hateful, detestable, abhorrent, contemptible, deplorable, intolerable
E3 pleasant

obscene adj

1 INDECENT, rude, improper, immoral, immodest, shameless, unchaste, impure, coarse, vulgar, filthy, dirty, foul, gross, vile, bawdy, fruity, lewd, licentious, X-rated, pornographic, hard-core, scurrilous, suggestive, sexy, risqué, smutty, disgusting, nasty, greasy
OLD paw, pawpaw
FORMAL carnal, lubricious, prurient
COLLOQ. blue, near the knuckle/bone, raunchy, sleazy, off-colour
2 SHOCKING, shameless, offensive, outrageous, disgraceful, immoral, scandalous
E3 1 decent, wholesome

obscenity n

1 INDECENCY, immodesty, immorality, impurity, impropriety, unchasteness, lewdness, licentiousness, bawdiness, suggestiveness, eroticism, pornography, dirt, dirtiness, filth, filthiness, foulness, coarseness, grossness, indelicacy, vulgarity, shamelessness, scurrilousness, salaciousness, lasciviousness, ribaldry, scatology; *dialect* balderdash
FORMAL carnality, prurience, lubricity
COLLOQ. raunchiness, sleaze, smut
2 ATROCITY, evil, outrage, offence, wickedness, vileness
FORMAL heinousness
3 SWEAR-WORD, curse, profanity, expletive, bad language
FORMAL imprecation
COLLOQ. four-letter word
SLANG cuss; *N Am* cussword

obscure adj, v

◆ *adj*
1 UNKNOWN, unimportant, insignificant, little-known, unheard-of, remote, out-of-the-way, god-forsaken, undistinguished, nameless, unsung, unrecognized, inconspicuous, humble, minor
COLLOQ. off the beaten track
2 INCOMPREHENSIBLE, unclear, complex, involved, enigmatic, cryptic, opaque, mysterious, unexplained, inexplicable, unfathomable, impenetrable, deep, hidden, concealed, confusing, puzzling, perplexing
FORMAL recondite, esoteric, arcane, abstruse
3 INDISTINCT, unclear, indefinite, uncertain, doubtful, shadowy, blurred, cloudy, faint, hazy, fuzzy, dim, misty, shady, vague, murky, dark, gloomy, dusky
E3 1 famous, renowned **2** intelligible, straightforward **3** clear, definite

◆ *v*
conceal, cloud, hide, cover, blur, confuse, muddle, complicate, disguise, mask, overshadow, shadow, shade, cloak, veil, shroud, darken, dim, eclipse, screen, block out
FORMAL obfuscate
E3 clarify, illuminate

obscurity n

1 UNIMPORTANCE, insignificance, lowliness, namelessness, inconspicuousness, lack of fame/recognition
2 INCOMPREHENSIBILITY, impenetrability, unclearness, complexity, intricacy, ambiguity, mystery, depth, night, fog, murkiness, shade, confusion, mysticism
FORMAL abstruseness, reconditeness
E3 1 fame, renown **2** intelligibility, clarity, lucidity

obsequies n

funeral, burial, cremation, wake
FORMAL interment, entombment, inhumation, exequies

obsequious adj

servile, ingratiating, grovelling, fawning, menial, sycophantic, cringing, toadying, toadyish, deferential, flattering, oily, fulsome, submissive, subservient, slavish, abject, knee-crooking
FORMAL unctuous
COLLOQ. smarmy, bootlicking, crawling, creepy
SLANG (*vulgar*) arse-licking; *N Am* kiss-ass

observable adj

noticeable, perceptible, discernible, appreciable, detectable, recognizable, measurable, significant, visible, apparent, clear, obvious, evident, open, patent

observance n

1 ADHERENCE, performance, execution, discharge, obedience, compliance, keeping, following, fulfilment, honouring, notice, attention
FORMAL heeding
2 RITUAL, custom, ceremony, rite, practice, tradition, formality, service, celebration, festival

observant adj

1 ATTENTIVE, alert, vigilant, on guard, seeing, watchful, mindful, perceptive, sharp, sharp-eyed, hawk-eyed, eagle-eyed, wide-awake, on the lookout, on the qui vive
FORMAL heedful, percipient, observative
COLLOQ. with your eyes skinned/peeled, with eyes like a hawk
2 DUTIFUL, committed, devoted, obedient, practising, orthodox
COLLOQ. card-carrying
E3 1 unobservant

observation n

1 ATTENTION, notice, noticing, seeing, viewing, examination, inspection, scrutiny, monitoring, study, review, watching, consideration, discernment, perception
2 REMARK, comment, utterance, thought, statement, pronouncement, declaration, reflection, opinion, finding,

result, description, note, information, data
FORMAL annotation

observatory n
planetarium, planisphere, orrery

observe v
1 WATCH, see, view, spot, study, notice, note, contemplate, inspect, examine, monitor, keep an eye on, discern, perceive, detect, catch sight of, keep watch on, keep under surveillance
FORMAL behold, espy
COLLOQ. keep tabs on, miss nothing, keep an eye on, keep your eyes skinned/peeled, watch like a hawk
2 REMARK, comment, say, mention, utter, state, declare
3 *observe a law/custom*
abide by, honour, keep, follow, obey, adhere to, fulfil, celebrate, mark, commemorate, remember, recognize, perform, conform to, respect, execute, discharge
FORMAL comply with
ᇤ **1** miss, ignore **3** break, violate

> **Synonym nuances**
> *sense 3*
> **Abide by** can be used of being governed by: *they abided by the umpire's decision*, whereas **honour** and **respect** additionally imply showing due deference.
>   **Keep**, however, is suggestive of maintaining something, usually a ritual or a faith, while **follow** and **adhere to** can be used more widely: *he faithfully followed the cabinet's line*. The terms **obey** and **conform to** suggest compliance but not necessarily willingness, while **fulfil**, along with **perform** and **execute**, has more to do with carrying something out: *they fulfilled the conditions of the pact; the will had been duly executed*.
>   **Celebrate** is more suggestive of performing with appropriate ceremony: *celebrating the seasonal festivals*, and **mark** similarly implies making distinct in some way, although not necessarily as a cause for celebration: *we must mark the occasion*. **Commemorate**, however, is appropriate for remembrance of something that has happened in the past: *commemorating the deeds of our war heroes*, while you could use **recognize** to simply suggest acknowledgement: *we must recognize the multicultural nature of our society*.

observer n
watcher, spectator, viewer, witness, reporter, looker-on, onlooker, sightseer, eyewitness, commentator, bystander
FORMAL beholder

obsess v
preoccupy, dominate, rule, control, monopolize, haunt, hound, torment, bedevil, grip, have a grip/hold on, plague, prey on, possess, engross, consume, be uppermost in your mind
COLLOQ. eat up

obsessed adj
preoccupied, dominated, gripped, in the grip of, immersed in, haunted, hounded, plagued, infatuated, bedevilled, beset
COLLOQ. hung up on, having ... on the brain
ᇤ detached, indifferent, unconcerned

obsession n
preoccupation, fixation, *idée fixe*, ruling passion, compulsion, fetish, infatuation, mania, complex, phobia, enthusiasm, fascination, hobby-horse, neurosis
COLLOQ. hang-up, thing, bug, bee in your bonnet, one-track mind

obsessive adj
consuming, all-consuming, compulsive, gripping, fixed, haunting, tormenting, maddening

obsolescence n
redundancy, obsoleteness, disuse, rejection, scrapping, disappearance, failure

obsolescent adj
out of date, old-fashioned, outdated, dated, dying out, disappearing, declining, fading, waning, ag(e)ing, redundant, on the way out, past its prime, on the decline, on the wane
FORMAL moribund
COLLOQ. past its sell-by date, old hat, on the shelf, out of the ark, antediluvian

obsolete adj
outmoded, disused, in disuse, discarded, out of date, old-fashioned, out of fashion, passé, dated, outworn, old, ancient, antiquated, antique, superannuated, dead, extinct, bygone, behind the times, on the way out, past its prime
FORMAL discontinued
COLLOQ. past its sell-by date, old hat, on the shelf, out of the ark, antediluvian
ᇤ modern, current, up-to-date, in use

obstacle n
barrier, bar, obstruction, blockade, barricade, impediment, hurdle, jump, hindrance, check, snag, stumbling-block, blockage, drawback, handicap, difficulty, hitch, catch, stoppage, stop, curb, interference, interruption, deterrent, drag, entanglement, rock, boyg, remora
OLD stay
COLLOQ. hiccup, fly in the ointment, spanner in the works
ᇤ advantage, help

obstinacy n
stubbornness, inflexibility, hard-heartedness, persistence, perseverance, resoluteness, tenacity, wilfulness, wrongheadedness, perversity, firmness, doggedness, relentlessness, mulishness
FORMAL frowardness, intransigence, obduracy, pertinacity
COLLOQ. pigheadedness
ᇤ co-operativeness, flexibility, submissiveness

obstinate adj
stubborn, inflexible, hard-hearted, immovable, unyielding, unbending, unrelenting, persistent, dogged, headstrong, strong-minded, self-willed, steadfast, firm, persevering, determined, adamant, wilful, diehard, hidebound, dour, hard-set, restive, wrongheaded, stiff-necked, mulish, bullish, camelish, rusty, sturdy; *Scot* kittle, thrawart, thrawn
OLD stomachful, pervicacious, stiff-hearted, stoor; (*Shakesp*) high-stomached
FORMAL intractable, intransigent, refractory, recalcitrant, contumacious, pertinacious
COLLOQ. pigheaded, bloody-minded, obstinate as a mule, cussed
ᇤ flexible, tractable

obstreperous adj
disorderly, unruly, tumultuous, unmanageable, undisciplined, wild, uncontrolled, out of hand, noisy, loud, boisterous, clamorous, raucous, riotous, rip-roaring, tempestuous, rowdy, rough, turbulent, uproarious, vociferous
FORMAL refractory, restive, intractable
COLLOQ. stroppy, bolshie, bloody-minded
ᇤ calm, disciplined, quiet

obstruct v
block, impede, hinder, prevent, check, frustrate, hamper, clog, choke, bar, barricade, stop, halt, bridle, stall, restrict, limit, thwart, encumber, hamstring, inhibit, hold up, brake, curb, arrest, slow down, delay, interrupt, interfere with, shut off, cut off, obscure, cross, hedge, blanket, stuff, sandbag, crab, foul, portcullis
OLD stap, waylay
FORMAL retard, arrest
COLLOQ. stymie
ᇤ assist, further

obstruction n
barrier, blockage, bar, barricade, hindrance, impediment,

obstacle, stumbling-block, check, stop, stoppage, restriction, embargo, sanction, difficulty, deterrent
ᴇ϶ help

obstructive *adj*

hindering, delaying, blocking, stalling, unhelpful, unco-operative, awkward, difficult, restrictive, inhibiting, interrupting
ᴇ϶ co-operative, helpful

obtain *v*

1 ACQUIRE, get, gain, gain possession of, come by, attain, secure, seize, earn, achieve
FORMAL procure
COLLOQ. get your hands on
2 PREVAIL, exist, hold, be in force, be the case, be effective, be in use, hold sway, stand, reign, rule, be prevalent

obtainable *adj*

available, at hand, ready, to be had, accessible, achievable, attainable, realizable, on call
FORMAL procurable
COLLOQ. on tap
ᴇ϶ unobtainable, unavailable

obtrude *v*

impose, intrude, foist, force yourself, thrust yourself, butt in, break in, encroach, presume, exploit, put upon, abuse, mislead, take advantage of

obtrusive *adj*

1 PROMINENT, protruding, projecting, noticeable, obvious, conspicuous, blatant, flagrant, bold, forward
2 INTRUSIVE, interfering, forward, pushy, prying, meddling
COLLOQ. nos(e)y
ᴇ϶ 1 unobtrusive

obtuse *adj*

slow, slow-witted, stupid, unintelligent, dull, dense, crass, stolid, dull-witted, thick-skinned
COLLOQ. thick, dumb, dim, dim-witted, dopey, dozy, slow on the uptake
ᴇ϶ bright, sharp

obverse *n*

reverse, opposite, inverse, contrary, converse
FORMAL antithesis

obviate *v*

avert, prevent, divert, forestall, remove, counter, counteract, anticipate
FORMAL preclude

obvious *adj*

evident, self-evident, manifest, patent, clear, crystal clear, plain, visible, distinct, transparent, undeniable, unmistakable, conspicuous, glaring, apparent, open, unconcealed, visible, noticeable, detectable, perceptible, pronounced, recognizable, self-explanatory, straightforward, clear-cut, prominent
COLLOQ. as plain as a pikestaff, as plain as the nose on your face, as clear as daylight, staring you in the face, sticking out a mile, right under your nose, shouting from the rooftops
ᴇ϶ unclear, indistinct, obscure

obviously *adv*

plainly, clearly, evidently, noticeably, patently, manifestly, undeniably, unmistakably, without doubt, undoubtedly, certainly, distinctly, of course

occasion *n, v*

◆ *n*

1 EVENT, occurrence, incident, episode, experience, situation, circumstance, happening, affair, time, instance, point, chance, case, opportunity, juncture
2 REASON, cause, excuse, justification, call, ground(s)
3 CELEBRATION, function, affair, party, (social) event
COLLOQ. do, get-together, bash

◆ *v*

cause, bring about, bring on, make, produce, create, give rise to, generate, induce, lead to, provoke, prompt, evoke, elicit, influence, inspire, persuade, originate, engender
FORMAL effect

occasional *adj*

periodic, intermittent, irregular, sporadic, infrequent, uncommon, incidental, odd, rare, casual, off and on, on and off, incidental, fugitive; *Scot* daimen, orra
ᴇ϶ frequent, regular, constant

occasionally *adv*

sometimes, on occasion, from time to time, at times, at intervals, now and then, now and again, irregularly, periodically, every so often, once in a while, off and on, on and off, infrequently, intermittently, sporadically
OLD once in a way
ᴇ϶ frequently, often, always

occlude *v*

block, stop (up), choke, clog (up), plug, dam up, close, seal, bar, obstruct, impede, hinder, fill, check, arrest, halt, thwart
COLLOQ. bung up

occlusion *n*

blockage, obstruction, blocking, stoppage, block, clot, jam, log jam, congestion, hindrance, impediment

occult *adj, n*

◆ *adj*

mystical, supernatural, magical, magic, mysterious, concealed, obscure, secret, hidden, veiled
FORMAL esoteric, arcane, recondite, abstruse, transcendental, preternatural, metaphysical

◆ *n*

the supernatural, black arts, mysticism, supernaturalism, art(s)

Terms associated with the occult include:

amulet	hoodoo	satanic
astral projection	horoscope	Satanism
astrologer	horseshoe	Satanist
astrology	hydromancer	séance
bewitch	hydromancy	second sight
black cat	illusion	shaman
black magic	incantation	shamrock
black mass	influence	sixth sense
cabbala	jinx	sorcerer
charm	juju	sorcery
chiromancer	magic	spell
chiromancy	magician	spirit
clairvoyance	mascot	spiritualism
clairvoyant	medium	spiritualist
conjure	necromancer	supernatural
coven	necromancy	superstition
crystal ball	obi	talisman
curse	omen	tarot card
déjà vu	oneiromancer	tarot reading
divination	oneiromancy	telepathist
diviner	Ouija board®	telepathy
divining-rod	palmist	totem
dream	palmistry	trance
ectoplasm	paranormal	vision
evil eye	pentagram	voodoo
evil spirit	planchette	Walpurgis Night
exorcism	poltergeist	warlock
exorcist	possession	white magic
extrasensory	prediction	witch
perception (ESP)	premonition	witchcraft
familiar	psychic	witch doctor
fetish	psychometer	witch's
fortune-teller	psychometry	broomstick
garlic	rabbit's foot	witch's sabbath
Hallowe'en	relic	
hallucination	rune	

Occupations include:

accountant	claims assessor	farmer	landscape	pharmacist	security guard
account	cleaner	fashion designer	architect	pharmacologist	set designer
executive	coach	financial advisor	landscape	philosopher	shop assistant
actor/actress	commercial artist	financial analyst	gardener	photographer	shopkeeper
actuary	composer	financial	lawyer	physicist	signalman
administrator	computer analyst	controller	lecturer	physiotherapist	singer
advertising	computer	firefighter	librarian	pilot	social worker
executive	engineer	fisherman	lighting	plasterer	sociologist
air traffic	computer	fitness instructor	technician	plumber	sound engineer
controller	programmer	fitter	linguist	podiatrist	speech therapist
animator	computer	flight attendant	machinist	poet	spokesperson
anthropologist	support	florist	management	police officer	stage manager
archaeologist	specialist	food scientist	consultant	political scientist	statistician
architect	conductor	forensic scientist	marketing	postal worker	stenographer
archivist	conservationist	forester	manager	potter	stockbroker
art director	construction	fund manager	marine biologist	printing-press	stock controller
artist	manager	fundraiser	massage therapist	operator	stonemason
arts administrator	construction	funeral director	mathematician	prison officer	streetcleaner
astronomer	worker	game warden	mechanic	private	subeditor
athlete	consultant	gardener	media planner	investigator	surgeon
author	costume designer	general	meteorologist	producer	surveyor
baker	counsellor	practitioner	microbiologist	proofreader	systems analyst
banker	crane operator	(GP)	military member	property	tailor
bank teller	criminologist	geneticist	(or officer)	developer	taxi driver
barista	critic	geologist	midwife	psychologist	teacher
barperson	curator	glazier	minister	publicist	tourism
barrister	customer	graphic designer	model	public relations	development
blacksmith	services	groundskeeper	MP	(PR) consultant	officer
biologist	representative	historian	musician	publishing	toxicologist
biotechnologist	dancer	home economist	music therapist	manager	traffic warden
bodyguard	data entry	horticulturalist	nurse	purchasing	trainer
bookbinder	operator	hotel manager	nutritionist	manager	translator
bookkeeper	dental hygienist	human resource	oceanographer	radiographer	travel agent
botanist	dentist	manager	occupational	railwayman	truck driver
bricklayer	dietician	illustrator	therapist	receptionist	upholsterer
broadcaster	director	industrial	office	recruitment	urban planner
bus driver	DJ	designer	administrator	consultant	van driver
business analyst	doctor	insurance	operations	refuse collector	veterinarian
butcher	draughtsperson	underwriter	research analyst	restaurant	waiter/waitress
buyer	ecologist	interior designer	optician	manager	weaver
camera operator	economist	interpreter	optometrist	retail manager	web designer
carpenter	editor	IT consultant	orthodontist	roofer	welder
cashier	electrician	janitor	osteopath	sales and	writer
chauffeur	engineer	joiner	painter/decorator	marketing	youth worker
chef	environmental	journalist	panel beater	manager	zookeeper
chemist	health officer	judge	paralegal	sales	zoologist
chiropractor	environmental	keyboarder	paramedic	representative	
choreographer	scientist	laboratory	personal assistant	scriptwriter	
civil engineer	estate agent	technician	(PA)	sculptor	
civil servant	event manager		personal trainer	secretary	

See also **medical specialists**.

---

occupancy n
  tenancy, residence, tenure, term, occupation, owner-occupancy, ownership, possession, holding, use
  FORMAL domiciliation, habitation, inhabitancy

occupant n
  occupier, owner, owner-occupier, homeowner, holder, inhabitant, resident, householder, tenant, user, renter, leaseholder, lessee, squatter, inmate
  FORMAL incumbent

occupation n
  1 JOB, profession, work, career, vocation, employment, employ, trade, post, calling, business, field, line, province, pursuit, craft, walk of life, activity, interest, métier
  See panel above
  2 INVASION, seizure, conquest, control, possession, capture, overthrow, foreign rule, foreign domination, takeover
  FORMAL subjugation
  3 OCCUPANCY, possession, holding, tenancy, tenure, residence, residency, use
  FORMAL habitation

> **Synonym nuances**
> *sense 1*
> **Job** can be used widely to suggest any task, or used more particularly to suggest a task undertaken on a daily basis for payment, whereas **profession** tends to be used more generally of a skilled occupation: *the medical profession*. **Post** has the narrower referent of a particular appointment: *he was appointed to the post of Managing Director*.
>
>   **Work** and **employment**, again, can be used to imply a specific task or more generally that done regularly for money: *he's been out of work for a year now*, and **employ** usually implies the state of being employed: *in the employ of local government*.
>
>   **Career**, on the other hand, suggests the progress charted throughout your working life and implies an impressive or skilled occupation: *a career in law*, while the terms **vocation** and **calling** particularly suggest an occupation one feels drawn to by principles or religion: *a vocation to the priesthood*.
>
>   To refer more generally to a form of skilled livelihood you could use **trade**: *the building trade*, while **business**

has more commercial implications: *the freight business.* The terms **field**, **line** and **province** are appropriate for a wider referent of a particular area of expertise: *his line of research*, and **métier** further implies a particular aptitude. **Craft** conveys the involvement of highly specialized, even artistic skills.

More personal occupations can be referred to with the terms **interest**, **activity** or **pursuit**: *horticultural work supplanted his pursuit of agriculture.*

occupational *adj*
job-related, professional, vocational, career, work, employment, trade, business

occupied *adj*
1 UNAVAILABLE, in use, taken, busy, full, engaged, tenanted
2 ABSORBED, engrossed, taken up, employed, engaged, preoccupied, immersed, busy, working, tied up
COLLOQ. hard at it
E3 1 unoccupied, vacant

occupier *n*
occupant, owner-occupier, homeowner, holder, inhabitant, resident, householder, tenant, user, renter, leaseholder, lessee, squatter, inmate
FORMAL incumbent

occupy *v*
1 INHABIT, live in, possess, reside in, stay in, make your home in, settle, people, tenant, take possession of, move in, own, rent, nest
OLD occupate, possess, manure; *N Am* improve
FORMAL dwell in
2 ABSORB, take up, engross, employ, engage, hold, involve, possess, fill in, take up, preoccupy, immerse, amuse, entertain, busy, overbusy, interest, stimulate, divert, obsess
OLD tire, trade; (*Spenser*) entreat, embusy
3 INVADE, seize, capture, overrun, take over, take possession of
OLD beset
4 FILL, take up, use (up), hold, have
OLD obtain

occur *v*
1 HAPPEN, come about, take place, chance, come to pass, turn out, materialize, develop, crop up, turn up, result
FORMAL transpire, befall, eventuate
2 EXIST, be present, be found, have its being, arise, appear
FORMAL obtain, manifest itself
3 *the idea occurred to me*
come to you, dawn on, strike, hit, suggest itself, come to mind, cross your mind, enter your head, present itself, spring to mind, sink in

occurrence *n*
1 INCIDENT, event, happening, affair, proceedings, circumstance, episode, instance, case, development, action
2 INCIDENCE, existence, appearance, arising, springing-up, development
FORMAL manifestation

ocean *n*
main, profound, sea, the deep
COLLOQ. briny, the drink
Related adjective: pelagic

The world's oceans and largest seas include:

Antarctic Ocean	Caribbean Sea	Pacific Ocean
Arctic Ocean	Gulf of Mexico	Sea of Okhotsk
Atlantic Ocean	Indian Ocean	South China Sea
Bering Sea	Mediterranean	

---

ocean-going *n*
seafaring, seagoing, sailing, marine, maritime, nautical, naval

odd *adj*
1 UNUSUAL, strange, uncommon, peculiar, funny, exceptional, curious, quaint, atypical, abnormal, different, queer, bizarre, eccentric, deviant, singular, idiosyncratic, remarkable, original, unconventional, uncanny, droll, drôle, freakish, weird, irregular, wild, extraordinary, outlandish, quirky, whimsical, whimsy, rare; *Scot* orra, odd-like
OLD rum
COLLOQ. out of the ordinary, freaky, kinky, wacky, oddball, zany, barmy, crackers, off the wall
SLANG rum, far-out, way-out
2 OCCASIONAL, incidental, haphazard, irregular, periodic, seasonal, random, casual, part-time, temporary
FORMAL fortuitous
3 UNMATCHED, unpaired, single, spare, surplus, superfluous, left-over, remaining, mismatched, sundry, various, miscellaneous
E3 1 normal, usual **2** regular

■ **odd one out**
nonconformist, eccentric, odd man/woman out
COLLOQ. freak, oddball, weirdo, case, odd bod, odd/queer fish, fish out of water, square peg in a round hole
SLANG cure

oddball *n*
eccentric, nonconformist, oddity, crank
OLD rum
COLLOQ. freak, character, case, card, nut, nutter, weirdo, crackpot, loon, kook, odd/queer fish, square peg in a round hole, fish out of water; *N Am* flake
SLANG geek; *N Am* dingbat, wack, cupcake; *Aust* dag

oddity *n*
1 ABNORMALITY, strangeness, peculiarity, queerness, rarity, eccentricity, idiosyncrasy, phenomenon, twist, quirk
2 CURIOSITY, anomaly, rarity, phenomenon, misfit
OLD rum
COLLOQ. oddball, freak, character, case, card, nut, nutter, weirdo, crackpot, loon, kook, odd/queer fish, square peg in a round hole, fish out of water; *N Am* flake
SLANG geek; *N Am* dingbat, wack, cupcake; *Aust* dag

oddly *adv*
strangely, curiously, unusually, abnormally, remarkably, unconventionally, irregularly, weirdly
E3 normally, usually, regularly

oddment *n*
bit, scrap, piece, leftover, fragment, offcut, end, remnant, shred, snippet, patch; *dialect* fent

odds *n*
1 LIKELIHOOD, probability, chances, the line, price
2 ADVANTAGE, edge, lead, superiority, supremacy
FORMAL ascendancy

■ **odds and ends**
bits and pieces, bits, oddments, junk, remnants, bric-à-brac, job-lot, rubbish, litter, scraps, cuttings, snippets, tatt, debris, flotsam and jetsam, leavings
OLD odd-come-shorts
COLLOQ. odds and sods, this and that

■ **at odds**
disagreeing, in disagreement, in conflict, at variance, differing, clashing, quarrelling, arguing, at loggerheads, out of step; *N Am* at outs

odious *adj*
offensive, loathsome, unpleasant, disagreeable, obnoxious, disgusting, hateful, objectionable, repulsive, repugnant, revolting, foul, detestable, abhorrent, horrible, horrid, abominable, vile, contemptible, despicable
FORMAL execrable, heinous
E3 pleasant

odium n

dislike, hatred, abhorrence, disapproval, disrepute, dishonour, shame, disgrace, disfavour, discredit, censure, condemnation, contempt
FORMAL detestation, disapprobation, animosity, antipathy, obloquy, opprobrium, infamy, reprobation, execration

odorous adj

scented, sweet-smelling, balmy, aromatic, fragrant, perfumed, pungent
FORMAL odoriferous, redolent
F3 odourless

odour n

smell, scent, aroma, fragrance, bouquet, perfume, stench
FORMAL redolence
COLLOQ. stink, pong, niff, whiff

odourless adj

having no smell, without smell, unscented, deodorized
FORMAL inodorous

odyssey n

journey, voyage, trek, travels, wandering, adventure
FORMAL peregrination

off adv, adj

• adv
1 AWAY, elsewhere, out, at a distance, apart, aside
2 ILL, out of sorts, unwell, sick, seedy, queasy, off form, off-colour, poorly
FORMAL indisposed
COLLOQ. rough, under the weather
• adj
1 AWAY, absent, gone, unavailable, unobtainable
2 CANCELLED, postponed, called off, abandoned, dropped
COLLOQ. shelved, scrapped
3 ROTTEN, bad, sour, turned, high, spoilt, rancid, mouldy, decomposed
4 SUBSTANDARD, below par, disappointing, unsatisfactory, slack, wrong, incorrect

offbeat adj

unorthodox, weird, unconventional, untraditional, abnormal, strange, unusual, bizarre, out of the ordinary
COLLOQ. oddball, freaky, kooky, wacky
SLANG far-out, way-out

off-colour adj

1 ILL, out of sorts, unwell, sick, seedy, queasy, off form, poorly
FORMAL indisposed
COLLOQ. under the weather, run down, rough, crummy
2 RUDE, indecent, improper, immoral, immodest, indelicate, coarse, crude, foul, gross, vulgar, impure, filthy, dirty, obscene, pornographic, lewd, perverted, depraved, degenerate, licentious, offensive, suggestive, sexy, risqué, smutty
COLLOQ. blue, sleazy

off-duty adj

off, off work, not at work, on holiday, free, at leisure
F3 on-duty

offence n

1 a criminal offence
infringement, crime, trespass, wrong, wrongdoing, illegal act, breach of the law, sin
FORMAL misdemeanour, transgression, violation, misdeed, infraction
2 AFFRONT, insult, injury, hurt, outrage, snub, slight, indignity, atrocity, ire
3 RESENTMENT, indignation, anger, annoyance, exasperation, disapproval, pique, umbrage, outrage, hurt, hard feelings
FORMAL antipathy

■ **take offence**
resent, be indignant, be angry, be annoyed, be exasperated, be hurt, be offended, be insulted, be upset, be/feel put out, take exception, take personally, take umbrage
COLLOQ. be miffed, get huffy, go into a huff, get the hump, get/have your nose put out of joint

offend v

1 HURT, insult, injure, affront, wrong, wound, displease, snub, upset, annoy, anger, outrage, exasperate, incense, provoke; *Scot* kittle
OLD distaste, umbrage, hip
FORMAL disoblige
COLLOQ. miff, needle, put out, put someone's back up, rub someone up the wrong way, put someone's nose out of joint, raise someone's hackles, rattle someone's cage, ruffle someone's feathers, tread on someone's toes, give someone the pip
2 DISGUST, repel, sicken, revolt, nauseate, put off
3 BREAK THE LAW, do wrong, sin, err, go astray
FORMAL transgress, violate
F3 1 please

offended adj

upset, hurt, resentful, disgruntled, affronted, displeased, angered, annoyed, exasperated, incensed, outraged, wounded, smarting, stung, piqued, pained, disgusted
COLLOQ. huffy, in a huff, miffed, put out
F3 pleased, happy

offender n

wrongdoer, culprit, criminal, miscreant, guilty party, lawbreaker, delinquent
FORMAL malefactor, transgressor

offensive adj, n

• adj
1 DISAGREEABLE, unpleasant, objectionable, displeasing, disgusting, odious, obnoxious, revolting, repellent, repugnant, abhorrent, loathsome, vile, sickening, nauseating, nasty, foul, detestable, abominable
2 INSOLENT, abusive, rude, insulting, affronting, upsetting, hurtful, wounding, annoying, exasperating, impolite, disrespectful, discourteous, impertinent
3 ATTACKING, hostile, antagonistic, aggressive, invading, belligerent
F3 1 pleasant 2 polite
• n
attack, assault, onslaught, invasion, raid, drive, thrust, push, sortie, charge
FORMAL incursion

offensively adv

unpleasantly, disagreeably, objectionably, disgustingly, detestably, nauseatingly
F3 pleasantly

offer v, n

• v
1 PRESENT, make available, advance, extend, put forward, submit, suggest, propose, recommend, hold out
FORMAL propound, proffer
2 PROVIDE, give, supply, sell, put on the market
FORMAL afford
3 offer £100
propose, bid, put in a bid, tender
4 VOLUNTEER, come forward, make yourself available, be at someone's service
COLLOQ. show willing
5 offer prayers/a sacrifice
offer up, sacrifice, dedicate, present, worship, give, consecrate, celebrate
6 offer resistance
show, express, give, present, try, attempt
• n
proposal, bid, submission, tender, suggestion, proposition, overture, approach, attempt, presentation

offering n

1 GIFT, present, donation, handout, contribution, subscription

2 SACRIFICE, dedication, consecration, tithe, celebration
FORMAL oblation

offhand adj, adv

• adj

casual, unconcerned, uninterested, indifferent, unceremonious, discourteous, rude, brusque, abrupt, curt, snap, terse, airy, perfunctory, cursory, informal, cavalier, careless, blasé, nonchalant
COLLOQ. take-it-or-leave-it, happy-go-lucky, free-and-easy, laid-back, couldn't-care-less

• adv

impromptu, immediately, ad lib, without thinking about it, without preparation, without checking, at the first blush
FORMAL extempore
COLLOQ. off the cuff, off the top of your head
F3 calculated, planned

office n

1 RESPONSIBILITY, duty, obligation, charge, commission, occupation, tenure, situation, post, position, employment, function, work, appointment, business, role, place, service

2 WORKPLACE, workroom, place of business, base, bureau

3 *our Edinburgh office*
branch, department, local/regional office, agency, bureau, part, section, division, subsidiary, subsection, subdivision, affiliate, wing

4 *through the offices of someone*
support, advocacy, help, aid, assistance, favour, recommendation, word, back-up, backing, patronage, mediation, intervention, referral
FORMAL auspices, aegis, intercession

office equipment and furniture

Office equipment includes:

acoustic hood	information	reference book
adhesive binder	board	rotary filing-
answering	inkpad	system
machine	intercom	scanner
calculator	keyboard	screen
cash box	laminator	screen filter
collating machine	laptop computer	share certificate
comb binder	letter-folding	book
comb binding	machine	shredder
computer	letter opener	slide projector
copy holder	letter scales	stapler
data cartridge	letter tray	staple-remover
date-stamp	message board	switchboard
desk organizer	microcassette	tacker
desk-top display	microcassette	telephone
calculator	recorder	telephone
Dictaphone®	microfiche reader	directory
dictation machine	monitor	telephone index
disk storage-	monitor arm	telex machine
system	mouse	terminal trolley
diskette mailer	mouse mat	textphone
duplicator	noticeboard	thermal binder
dust cover	overhead	time clock
electric	projector (OHP)	trimmer
typewriter	paper-folding	typewriter
electronic	machine	visitors' book
organizer	paper punch	visual display unit
electronic	parcel scales	(VDU)
typewriter	photocopier	wages book
facsimile machine	plan file	waste-paper bin
(or fax)	planner	wire-binding
flip-chart easel	planning board	machine
guillotine	printer	wire bindings
hole puncher	printwheel	word processor
	projection screen	

Office furniture includes:

boardroom table	filing cabinet	safe
computer desk	filing cupboard	secretarial desk
conference table	filing trolley	stationery
desk	fire cupboard	cupboard
desk lamp	fire-extinguisher	stepstool
display cabinet	fire safe	storage unit
draughtsman's	lectern	swivel chair
chair	partition	typist's chair
drawing-board	plan chest	workstation
executive chair	printer stand	work table
executive desk	reception chair	

See also **computer; stationery.**

officer n

official, office-holder, office-bearer, public servant, functionary, dignitary, bureaucrat, committee member, administrator, representative, executive, board member, agent, appointee, envoy, messenger, deputy

official adj, n

• adj

1 AUTHORIZED, authoritative, legal, lawful, legitimate, formal, accepted, recognized, licensed, certified, validated, endorsed, sanctioned, approved, authenticated, authentic, bona fide, proper
FORMAL accredited
COLLOQ. kosher

2 *official activities*
formal, ceremonial, stately, dignified, solemn, ritual
F3 1 unofficial

• n

office-bearer, office-holder, officer, functionary

❗ official or **officious?**
Official means 'done by someone in authority; relating to authority': *We think she has won, but we're still waiting for the official result of the race. Officious* means 'too eager to meddle, offering unwanted advice or assistance' or, more often, 'holding too rigidly to rules and regulations': *An officious little man told us that we would have to move our bicycles.*

Officials include:

administrator	diplomat	member of
agent	director	parliament (MP)
ambassador	elder	minister
bailiff	envoy	monitor
bureaucrat	equerry	notary
captain	Eurocrat	ombudsman
chairman (or	Euro-MP	overseer
chairwoman or	executive	prefect
chairperson)	executor	president
chancellor	Gauleiter	principal
chief	governor	proctor
civil servant	hakim	proprietor
clerk	inspector	public prosecutor
commander	justice of the	registrar
commissar	peace (JP)	representative
commissioner	magistrate	*N Am* senator
congressman	manager	sheriff
congresswoman	mandarin	steward
consul	marshal	superintendent
coroner	mayor	supervisor
councillor	mayoress	usher
delegate		

officialdom n

officials, bureaucracy, administration, administrator, government, central/national/regional/local government, ministry, civil service, civil servants, the authorities, the system, the establishment, mandarins
COLLOQ. them

officialese n
gobbledygook, gibberish, jargon, journalese, computerese, psychobabble, buzz words, nonsense, rubbish

officially adv
authoritatively, formally, authentically, properly, correctly, on the record, procedurally, bureaucratically, administratively, managerially
E3 unofficially, off the record

officiate v
preside, superintend, conduct, chair, take the chair, manage, oversee, run, be in charge, take charge

officious adj
obtrusive, domineering, dictatorial, intrusive, interfering, prying, meddlesome, meddling, inquisitive, over-zealous, overbusy, self-important, forward, pushy, opinionated, superserviceable, bustling
OLD spoffish, pragmatical
FORMAL importunate
COLLOQ. bossy

! officious or official?
See panel at **official**.

---

officiously adv
dictatorially, over-zealously, self-importantly
FORMAL with importunity
COLLOQ. bossily, pushily

offing
= in the offing
imminent, near, coming/happening soon, coming up, (close) at hand, just round the corner, in sight, on the way, on the horizon
COLLOQ. on the cards
E3 far off

offish adj
standoffish, aloof, cool, haughty, unsociable
COLLOQ. stuck-up
E3 friendly, sociable

off-key adj
out of tune, discordant, unsuitable, inappropriate, out of keeping, inharmonious, jarring
FORMAL dissonant
E3 in tune

offload v
unburden, unload, jettison, dump, drop, deposit, get rid of, shift, discharge
FORMAL disburden
COLLOQ. dump, chuck

off-putting adj
intimidating, daunting, frightening, unpleasant, disconcerting, discouraging, disheartening, dispiriting, formidable, unnerving, unsettling, unappealing, demoralizing, disturbing, upsetting
FORMAL discomfiting

offset v
counterbalance, compensate for, cancel out, counteract, make up for, balance (out), neutralize
FORMAL counterpoise, countervail

offshoot n
1 BRANCH, outgrowth, limb, arm
2 SPIN-OFF, by-product, product, result, consequence, outcome, development, branch, appendage

offspring n
child, children, son(s), daughter(s), infant(s), young, young one(s), youngster(s), family, brood, baby, babies, little one(s), heirs, successors, descendants
FORMAL issue, progeny, fruit of your loins
COLLOQ. kid(s), nipper(s)
E3 parent(s), ancestor(s)

often adv
frequently, repeatedly, regularly, generally, again and again, over and over again, time after time, time and (time) again, day in day out, week in week out, month in month out, many times, many a time, much
E3 rarely, seldom, never

ogle v
eye, eye up, leer, make eyes at, look, stare
COLLOQ. give someone the glad eye

ogre n
1 GIANT, monster, devil, demon, troll, fiend, bogey, bogeyman, boyg
2 his father is a bit of an ogre
monster, beast, brute, villain, savage, barbarian, fiend

oil v, n
♦ v
lubricate, grease, make smooth, anoint
♦ n
lubricant, grease, ointment, lotion, liniment, cream, balm, salve
FORMAL unguent

Types of oil include:

INDUSTRIAL:	peppermint	croton
benzaldehyde	rapeseed	eucalyptus
diesel	safflower	evening primrose
kerosene	sesame	jojoba
mineral	soybean	lavender
neat's foot	sunflower	lemon grass
palm	vegetable	macassar
paraffin	walnut	neroli
rapeseed	**AROMATIC,**	nim (or neem)
rosin	**COSMETIC AND**	orange
sperm	**MEDICINAL:**	patchouli
tung	attar (rose)	peppermint
EDIBLE:	avocado	rose
canola	baby oil	sandalwood
coconut	bergamot	sassafras
corn	cajeput	savin
grapeseed	camphor	tea tree
lemon grass	castor	vetiver
maize	chaulmoogra	wheatgerm
nut	cinnamon	wintergreen
olive	citronella	ylang ylang
palm	clove	
peanut (or	coconut	
groundnut)	cod-liver	

---

oily adj
1 GREASY, fatty, buttery, slippery
FORMAL oleaginous
2 SMOOTH-TALKING, smooth, ingratiating, glib, slippery, suave, urbane, flattering, servile, subservient
FORMAL unctuous, obsequious
COLLOQ. smarmy, slimy

ointment n
salve, balm, cream, gel, lotion, liniment, preparation, Vaseline®, basilicon
TECHNICAL emollient, cerate, collyrium, pomade, pomatum
FORMAL embrocation, unction, unguent

OK adj, adv, n, v, interj
♦ adj
acceptable, all right, fine, permitted, in order, fair, satisfactory, reasonable, tolerable, passable, good, adequate, convenient, correct, accurate
COLLOQ. not bad, so-so, up to par, up to scratch; N Am A-OK; N Am & Aust jake
♦ adv
fine, all right, in order, well, satisfactorily, reasonably,

tolerably, passably
 ◆ *n*
authorization, approval, endorsement, permission, agreement, consent, sanction
FORMAL approbation
COLLOQ. go-ahead, green light, thumbs-up
 ◆ *v*
approve, authorize, pass, rubber-stamp, consent to, agree to, say yes to
COLLOQ. give the go-ahead to, give the green light to, give the thumbs-up to
 ◆ *interj*
all right, fine, very well, very good, agreed, right, yes

old *adj*
1 AGED, ag(e)ing, elderly, advanced in years, mature, sensible, wise, past your prime, grey, senile
FORMAL senescent
COLLOQ. getting on, past it, no spring chicken, not as young as you were, not getting any younger, over the hill, (a bit) long in the tooth, not long for this world, gaga
2 ANCIENT, age-old, bygone, antique, classic, vintage, veteran, original, primitive, early, earlier, earliest, antiquated, prehistoric, primal
FORMAL pristine, prim(a)eval, primordial
3 LONG-STANDING, long-established, long-lived, enduring, lasting, time-honoured, traditional, age-old
COLLOQ. old as the hills
4 OBSOLETE, old-fashioned, unfashionable, out of date, behind the times, oudated, passé, archaic
COLLOQ. on the way out, past it, past its sell-by date, Dickensian, out of the ark, antediluvian
5 WORN OUT, cast-off, torn, shabby, decayed, decaying, decrepit, broken down, crumbling, ramshackle, tumbledown
COLLOQ. have seen better days
6 HACKNEYED, stale, overworked, overused, tired, worn-out, time-worn, threadbare, wearing thin, unoriginal, cliché-ridden, clichéd, stereotyped, stock, banal, trite, commonplace, common, pedestrian, uninspired, unimaginative
FORMAL platitudinous
COLLOQ. corny, run-of-the-mill, yawn-making
7 TRADITIONAL, conventional, customary, habitual, usual, routine, accustomed, ceremonial, established, fixed, set, long-established, time-honoured, age-old, historic, folk, oral, unwritten
8 FORMER, previous, earlier, one-time, sometime, ex-
FORMAL erstwhile, quondam
E3 **1** young, youthful **2** new, recent **4** modern, contemporary, state-of-the-art, up-to-date, fashionable, new **5** new **6** original, new, fresh **7** innovative, new, modern, contemporary **8** current, present

■ **old age**
age, agedness, oldness, elderliness, advancing years, declining years, second childhood, senility, dotage, twilight of your life
FORMAL senescence
E3 youth
Related adjective: geriatric

■ **old man**
father, grandfather, husband, elder, old-age pensioner, OAP, pensioner, senior citizen, employer, greybeard, white-beard, patriarch, elder statesman
COLLOQ. old codger, old stager, old-timer, oldster, boss, gaffer, geezer, fuddy-duddy; *N Am* golden ager
SLANG (*offensive*) coffin-dodger

■ **old woman**
mother, grandmother, granny, wife, old-age pensioner, OAP, pensioner, senior citizen, old dear, complainer, grumbler
COLLOQ. bag, fusspot, grouch, hag; *N Am* golden ager
SLANG (*offensive*) coffin-dodger

Synonym nuances
sense 1
Aged can refer to someone or something of advanced years: *his aged parents*, unlike **ag(e)ing** which is more appropriate for the process of getting older: *an ageing population*. **Elderly**, on the other hand, is reserved for people who have passed their middle age.
 The term **mature** has more to do with development, and when used of humans, and particularly of the emotions, it has positive associations: *mature judgement*. **Sensible**, too, is suggestive of good reasoning brought about by experience, and **wise** goes further by emphasizing inherent prudence.
 The term **past your prime**, however, disrespectfully suggests physical and mental decline, and **grey**, while literally reflecting hair colour, can also have connotations of the dullness of old age. **Senile**, while used technically of a medical condition, can also be used rather offensively to suggest that someone's mental faculties are diminished through age.

old-fashioned *adj*
outmoded, out of date, outdated, dated, old, unfashionable, out of fashion, obsolete, past, bygone, ancient, old-time, dead, moth-eaten, written off, behind the times, antiquated, antique, archaic, passé, obsolescent, primitive, quaint, schmaltzy, fusty, *arriéré, vieux jeu*
OLD auld-farrant, auld-farand, rococo
COLLOQ. antediluvian, out of the ark, fuddy-duddy, old hat, past it, square, past its sell-by date, on the way out, Neanderthal, steam, oldfangled, uncool, mumsy; *N Am* rinky-dink
E3 modern, up-to-date

old-time *adj*
old-fashioned, outmoded, out of date, outdated, dated, old, unfashionable, out of fashion, obsolete, past, bygone, behind the times, antiquated, archaic, passé

old-world *adj*
old-fashioned, quaint, traditional, picturesque, antiquated, past, archaic, bygone
COLLOQ. olde-worlde

omen *n*
sign, warning, token, premonition, foreboding, indication, forecast, prediction, harbinger, forerunner, prognosis, presage, boding, bodement; *Scot* freit
OLD abodement, presagement, soothsay
FORMAL portent, augury, auspice, presentiment, prodrome, prodromus
Related adjective: ominous

ominous *adj*
menacing, foreboding, sinister, fateful, unpromising, unlucky, unfavourable, threatening, sinister, bodeful
FORMAL portentous, inauspicious, unpropitious, minatory
E3 favourable; *formal* auspicious

ominously *adv*
alarmingly, dangerously, frighteningly, grimly
E3 favourably

omission *n*
exclusion, gap, exception, leaving-out, erasure, oversight, failure, lack, neglect, negligence, disregard, default, deletion, avoidance
FORMAL lacuna, expunction, dereliction
E3 inclusion

omit *v*
leave out, exclude, miss (out), pass (over), except, overlook, drop, skip, eliminate, forget, neglect, leave undone, fail, fail to mention, disregard, skip, overskip, edit out, erase, delete, cross out, rub out, white out

OLD let, pretermit
FORMAL expunge
⊟ include, mention

omnibus *adj, n*
♦ *adj*
comprehensive, inclusive, wide-ranging, all-embracing, compendious, encyclopedic
⊟ selective
♦ *n*
anthology, collection, compilation, compendium, encyclopedia

omnipotence *n*
absolute/total power, complete authority, all-powerfulness, almightiness, divine right, invincibility, mastery, sovereignty, supremacy
FORMAL plenipotence
⊟ impotence

omnipotent *adj*
all-powerful, almighty, invincible, supreme
FORMAL plenipotent
⊟ impotent

omnipresent *adj*
universal, all-present, present everywhere, pervasive, all-pervasive, limitless, infinite, ubiquitous
FORMAL ubiquitary

omniscient *adj*
all-knowing, all-seeing, all-wise
FORMAL pansophic

omnivorous *adj*
all-devouring, eating anything, gluttonous, indiscriminate, undiscriminating

on *prep, adv*
♦ *prep*
1 *on the shelf*
touching, resting on, in contact with, attached to, stuck to, being supported by
2 *a book on China*
on the subject of, about, concerning, relating to, connected with, concerned with, regarding, as regards, referring to, with regard to, with respect to, with reference to, in the matter of, re, dealing with
FORMAL apropos of
■ **on and off**
now and then, occasionally, on occasion, off and on, periodically, sometimes, from time to time, now and again, every so often, irregularly, at intervals, intermittently, spasmodically, sporadically, fitfully
FORMAL discontinuously
■ **on and on**
continually, constantly, perpetually, incessantly, ceaselessly, interminably, ever, forever, eternally, everlastingly, always, endlessly, non-stop, regularly, frequently, recurrently, repeatedly, persistently, habitually, all the time
⊟ occasionally, intermittently

once *adv, prep*
♦ *adv*
1 FORMERLY, previously, in the past, at one time, long ago, in times past, in times gone by, once upon a time, in the old days
2 ON ONE OCCASION, at one point, one time
♦ *conj*
after, immediately after, as soon as, when
■ **once and for all**
permanently, decisively, definitively, conclusively, positively, finally, for good, for the last time
■ **once in a while**
now and again/then, at times, sometimes, from time to time, occasionally, on and off, on occasion, periodically, infrequently, intermittently, sporadically, off and on

■ **at once**
1 IMMEDIATELY, instantly, directly, right away, straightaway, without delay, now, right now, promptly, on the spot
FORMAL forthwith
COLLOQ. pronto, before you know it, before you can say Jack Robinson, in two shakes of a lamb's tail, like a shot, yesterday
2 SIMULTANEOUSLY, together, at the same time, at the same moment

once-over *n*
checkup, check, look, examination, inspection, scrutiny, investigation, inquiry, audit, test, research, monitoring, analysis, probe, confirmation, verification, glance, glimpse, stare, gaze, gape, peek, peep
COLLOQ. squint, eyeful, dekko, gander, butcher's, shufti

oncoming *adj*
approaching, advancing, upcoming, looming, nearing, onrushing, gathering

one *adj*
1 SINGLE, solitary, lone, individual, only, sole, ace
2 UNITED, joined, fused, bound, married, wedded, harmonious, like-minded, whole, entire, complete, equal, identical, alike

oneness *n*
singleness, unity, completeness, wholeness, identity, individuality, identicalness, sameness, consistency

onerous *adj*
oppressive, burdensome, demanding, tiring, wearying, laborious, arduous, strenuous, back-breaking, crushing, hard, taxing, difficult, troublesome, exacting, fatiguing, exhausting, heavy, weighty
FORMAL exigent

oneself
■ **by oneself**
1 ALONE, by yourself, on your own, lonely, lonesome, deserted, isolated, abandoned, forsaken, forlorn, desolate, unaccompanied, unescorted, unattended, solo
2 ON YOUR OWN, independently, unaided, unassisted, without help, without assistance, singly, single-handed, unaccompanied

one-sided *adj*
1 UNBALANCED, unequal, uneven, lopsided
2 UNFAIR, unjust, prejudiced, biased, bigoted, partial, partisan, narrow-minded, discriminatory, inequitable
3 UNILATERAL, independent, one-way, separate, separated, disconnected
⊟ **1** balanced **2** impartial **3** bilateral, multilateral

one-time *adj*
former, previous, old, ex-, late, sometime
FORMAL erstwhile, quondam

ongoing *adj*
1 CONTINUING, continuous, unending, unbroken, uninterrupted, non-stop, constant, incessant
2 DEVELOPING, evolving, progressing, advancing, growing, in progress, current, unfinished, unfolding

onlooker *n*
bystander, observer, spectator, looker-on, eyewitness, witness, sightseer, watcher, viewer
COLLOQ. rubberneck, gawper

only *adv, adj*
♦ *adv*
just, at most, merely, simply, purely, barely, not more than, no more than, nothing but, exclusively, solely
FORMAL but
♦ *adj*
sole, single, one and only, solitary, lone, unique, exclusive, individual

onrush *n*
surge, rush, push, stream, flood, flow, charge, cascade, career, onset, onslaught, stampede

onset *n*
1 BEGINNING, start, outset, outbreak
FORMAL commencement, inception
COLLOQ. kick-off
2 ASSAULT, attack, onslaught, onrush, charge
E3 1 end, finish

onslaught *n*
attack, assault, offensive, charge, onrush, storming, raid, drive, push, thrust, foray, bombardment, blitz

onus *n*
burden, responsibility, weight, load, obligation, duty, charge, encumbrance, liability, task
COLLOQ. millstone, albatross

onwards *adv*
forward(s), on, ahead, in front, beyond
FORMAL forth
E3 backward(s)

oodles *n*
lots, masses, abundance
COLLOQ. bags, heaps, lashings, loads, tons
E3 scarcity

oomph *n*
vitality, sparkle, vigour, energy, vivacity, enthusiasm, exuberance, animation
COLLOQ. bounce, get-up-and-go, pep, pizzazz, zing, sexiness

ooze *v, n*
• *v*
seep, exude, leak, percolate, escape, dribble, drip, trickle, drop, discharge, bleed, secrete, emit, flow, overflow with, pour forth, filter, drain
FORMAL filtrate, excrete
• *n*
sludge, silt, slime, muck, mire, mud, sediment, deposit, seepage
FORMAL alluvium

oozy *adj*
sludgy, muddy, slimy, mucky, miry, dripping, dewy, moist, weeping, sweaty, sloppy
FORMAL uliginous

opacity *n*
1 CLOUDINESS, opaqueness, dullness, unclearness, impermeability, milkiness, murkiness, filminess, density
2 OBSCURITY, impenetrability, incomprehensibility, unintelligibility
FORMAL obfuscation
E3 1 transparency **2** clarity

opalescence *n*
multicolour, shimmering, sparkling, dazzling, glitter, glittering, rainbow, rainbow colours, prism
FORMAL iridescence

opalescent *adj*
shimmering, sparkling, multicoloured, rainbow, rainbow-coloured, rainbow-like, prismatic, dazzling, glittering, shot, pearly, polychromatic
FORMAL iridescent, variegated

opaque *adj*
1 CLOUDY, clouded, murky, unclear, dull, dim, hazy, misty, muddied, muddy, dingy, blurred, dense, thick, turbid
2 OBSCURE, unclear, impenetrable, unfathomable, incomprehensible, unintelligible, enigmatic, cryptic, difficult, dense, confusing, baffling, puzzling
FORMAL abstruse, recondite, esoteric
COLLOQ. as clear as mud
E3 1 transparent, see-through **2** clear, obvious

open *adj, v*
• *adj*
1 UNCLOSED, ajar, gaping, wide open, uncovered, unfastened, unbolted, unlocked, unsealed, unbarred, unlatched, unfolded, spread out, yawning, lidless, topless, coverless
2 UNRESTRICTED, free, unobstructed, unblocked, passable, navigable, unenclosed, unfenced, clear, accessible, exposed, unprotected, unsheltered, vacant, wide, obtainable, available, unoccupied
3 OVERT, obvious, manifest, plain, clear, visible, patent, evident, noticeable, apparent, flagrant, blatant, conspicuous, unhidden, unconcealed, undisguised
4 UNDECIDED, unresolved, unsettled, debatable, arguable, problematic, moot
COLLOQ. up in the air
5 FRANK, candid, honest, guileless, natural, simple, ingenuous, unreserved, forthright, blunt, direct
6 LOOSELY WOVEN, airy, holey, openwork, porous, honeycombed, cellular, spongelike
7 *an open secret*
widely known, well known, public, general, accessible, unrestricted
8 *open to misinterpretation*
liable, vulnerable, susceptible, subject, open to the risk of, receptive, exposed, disposed, accessible
E3 1 shut, closed **2** restricted, exclusive **3** hidden, concealed **4** decided, resolved **5** reserved **6** close, dense, compact **7** private, closed, exclusive
• *v*
1 UNFASTEN, undo, unlock, unlatch, uncover, unseal, untie, unbolt, unblock, uncork, crack, broach, break open, burst open, slide open, push open, force open, prise open, clear, expose
2 EXPLAIN, divulge, expose, disclose, bare, lay bare, uncover, reveal
3 EXTEND, spread (out), unroll, unfold, unfurl, flower, come apart, separate, split
4 BEGIN, start, commence, inaugurate, initiate, set in motion, launch
COLLOQ. set the ball rolling, kick off, get cracking, take the plunge
E3 1 close, shut **2** hide, cover up **4** end, finish
■ **open onto**
give onto, overlook, lead to, command a view of, face

open-air *adj*
outdoor, out-of-doors, outside, afield, alfresco
E3 indoor

open-and-shut *adj*
straightforward, obvious, simple, clear, easily decided, easily solved

open-handed *adj*
generous, free, liberal, large-hearted, lavish, bountiful, unstinting
FORMAL bounteous, eleemosynary, magnanimous, munificent
E3 *colloq.* tight-fisted

opening *n, adj*
• *n*
1 APERTURE, breach, gap, space, break, chink, crack, fissure, cleft, crevice, chasm, hole, cave, slot, split, inlet, outlet, vent, rupture
FORMAL orifice, interstice
2 START, onset, beginning, outset, inauguration, birth, dawn, launch
FORMAL inception
COLLOQ. the word go, square one, kick-off, first base
3 OPPORTUNITY, chance, occasion, place, possibility, vacancy, job, position
COLLOQ. break
E3 2 close, end

♦ *adj*

first, beginning, starting, introductory, initial, early, primary

FORMAL commencing, inaugural

E3 closing

openly *adv*

overtly, frankly, candidly, directly, forthrightly, bluntly, honestly, blatantly, flagrantly, plainly, unashamedly, brazenly, unreservedly, glaringly, publicly, in public, in full view, immodestly, shamelessly

COLLOQ. with no holds barred

E3 secretly, slyly

open-minded *adj*

unprejudiced, unbiased, broad-minded, broad, impartial, tolerant, liberal, receptive, reasonable, objective, free, catholic, dispassionate, enlightened

FORMAL latitudinarian

E3 bigoted, intolerant, prejudiced, narrow-minded

open-mindedness *n*

impartiality, neutrality, non-partisanship, objectivity, unbiasedness, fairness, justice, even-handedness, detachment, disinterest, disinterestedness, dispassion, equality, equity

E3 bias, prejudice, favouritism, discrimination

open-mouthed *adj*

amazed, astounded, astonished, spellbound, dumbfounded, shocked, clamorous, thunderstruck, expectant, wide-eyed

COLLOQ. flabbergasted

operate *v*

1 *it operates on batteries*

function, act, perform, run, work, go, make go, serve, set, trip, actuate

OLD play

2 *she can operate that machine*

control, handle, manage, direct, work, run, be in charge of, drive, pilot, fly, use, utilize, employ, manoeuvre

operation *n*

1 FUNCTIONING, action, running, motion, movement, performance, working

2 INFLUENCE, manipulation, handling, control, working, running, management, use, using, utilization

3 UNDERTAKING, enterprise, affair, procedure, proceeding, process, exercise, action, activity, business, deal, job, task, transaction, effort

4 CAMPAIGN, action, task, manoeuvre, exercise, attack, assault, charge, raid

5 SURGERY, surgical operation, surgical intervention

COLLOQ. op

■ in operation

operational, in force, functioning, active, effective, efficient, in action, in effect, taking effect, working, workable, viable, serviceable, functional, valid

operational *adj*

working, in working order, in use, usable, functioning, functional, in action, going, running, up and running, viable, workable, ready, prepared, in service

E3 out of order

operative *adj, n*

♦ *adj*

1 OPERATIONAL, in operation, in force, functioning, active, effective, efficient, in action, working, workable, viable, serviceable, functional, valid

2 KEY, crucial, important, relevant, significant, vital

E3 1 inoperative, out of service

♦ *n*

1 WORKER, workman, employee, labourer, hand, mechanic, machinist, operator, artisan

2 DETECTIVE, private detective, (private) investigator

COLLOQ. private eye, sleuth, gumshoe, shamus, dick

3 SECRET AGENT, agent, spy, double agent

COLLOQ. mole

operator *n*

1 OPERATIVE, worker, mechanic, machinist, technician, mover, driver, practitioner

2 TRADER, contractor, dealer, manager, director, administrator, handler

3 MANIPULATOR, machinator, punter, manoeuvrer, speculator

COLLOQ. wheeler-dealer, shyster

opiate *n*

drug, narcotic, sedative, pacifier, anodyne, tranquillizer, soporific, stupefacient, depressant, bromide

FORMAL nepenthe

COLLOQ. downer

opine *v*

think, believe, suppose, suggest, guess, say, volunteer, presume, declare, judge, conceive, conclude, suspect, venture

FORMAL conjecture, surmise

opinion *n*

belief, judgement, view, point of view, viewpoint, idea, perception, stance, standpoint, theory, impression, feeling(s), sentiment, assumption, assessment, conception, mind, notion, way of thinking, thought(s), school of thought, conviction, persuasion, attitude

FORMAL estimation

■ in my opinion

I think, I believe, in my view, from my point of view, from my standpoint, as I see it, (according) to my way of thinking, personally (speaking)

COLLOQ. in my book, if you ask me, for my money

Synonym nuances

Belief can be used of something that you are sure is true, while **conviction** further implies an unshakable confidence in it. **Judgement** has more to do with your evaluation, a suggestion made even more explicit with the term **assessment**. **Idea**, however, suggests something less well formulated: *his own ideas of democracy*, while **theory** suggests a hypothetical explanation: *I have no theory as to how this happened.*

Perception, conception and **impression** have more to do with a personal interpretation of events: *I had the impression he was frightened of me; one's conception of the world.* **Feeling(s)** likewise has suggestions of personal sensitivities, whereas **sentiment** hints at an emotional reaction: *public sentiment turned against the war.*

You can use **mind** to suggest your current opinion: *he was of a mind to sack them*, whereas **notion** is more suggestive of a passing whim. **Persuasion** is again suggestive of assured opinion, often relating to a creed: *voters of every political persuasion.* **Attitude** could be used of the particular position someone has adopted on an issue, and both **stance** and **standpoint** imply a view that is firmly held: *I have urged him to reconsider his stance on the issue.*

---

opinionated *adj*

dogmatic, doctrinaire, dictatorial, arrogant, inflexible, obstinate, stubborn, pigheaded, uncompromising, with preconceived ideas, single-minded, adamant, prejudiced, biased, bigoted, self-important, pompous, cocksure, pontifical

E3 open-minded

opponent *n*

adversary, enemy, antagonist, foe, competitor, contestant, challenger, opposer, opposition, rival, contender, objector, dissenter, dissident

FORMAL dissentient

E3 ally, friend, supporter

opportune adj

suitable, proper, convenient, appropriate, advantageous, apt, fit, seasonable, timely, well-timed, favourable, providential, fitting, fortunate, good, lucky, happy
FORMAL auspicious, felicitous, pertinent, propitious
E3 unsuitable; *formal* inopportune

opportunism n

exploitation, expediency, pragmatism, realism, taking advantage, unscrupulousness, Machiavellianism
COLLOQ. making hay while the sun shines

opportunity n

chance, opening, occasion, possibility, hour, moment, room, scope, power, privilege, pick, overture, turn
OLD (*Shakesp*) vantage
COLLOQ. break, look-in, space, a bite of the cherry, crack of the whip

oppose v

1 RESIST, withstand, counter, attack, combat, contest, challenge, contradict, disapprove of, argue against, disagree with, stand up to, take a stand against, be against, take issue with, confront, defy, face, fight, hinder, obstruct, bar, check, prevent, thwart
COLLOQ. fly in the face of
2 COMPARE, contrast, match, offset, balance, counterbalance, set against, play off
FORMAL juxtapose
E3 1 defend, support

Synonym nuances

sense 1

Resist and **withstand** are suggestive of opposition while under pressure: *the party is resisting calls for modernization*. **Counter**, on the other hand, implies a positive retaliation, unlike **attack**, which suggests the initial incursion. The term **combat** has implications of an organized struggle against something: *combating drug abuse*, while **contest** and **challenge** are appropriate for disputing something verbally: *many anthropologists challenged his conclusions*. **Take issue with** a bit more forceful: *local scientists took issue with some of his evidence*.

  The term **disapprove of** likewise suggests a lack of accord, though not a vociferous one and without necessarily involving any active steps, whereas **stand up to**, **confront** and **face** are more suggestive of bravely encountering your opponents. **Defy** also suggests a degree of boldness in actively resisting: *I defied my father's wishes*, and the term **fight** is appropriate if you want to suggest a more fierce struggle against adversity.

---

opposed adj

in opposition, against, hostile, conflicting, disagreeing, opposing, opposite, antagonistic, clashing, contrary, incompatible
FORMAL averse, inimical
COLLOQ. anti
E3 in favour

■ **as opposed to**
rather than, instead of, in contrast to, as against, versus

opposing adj

opposite, contrary, differing, at odds, at variance, rival, clashing, conflicting, irreconcilable, incompatible, opposed, contentious, enemy, hostile, antagonistic, fighting, contending, warring, combatant
FORMAL antipathetic, disputatious, oppugnant

opposite adj, n

◆ *adj*
1 FACING, face to face, fronting, corresponding
2 OPPOSED, antagonistic, conflicting, contrary, hostile, contradictory, clashing, irreconcilable, unlike, reverse, inconsistent, different, contrasted,

differing, at odds, at variance, opposing
FORMAL adverse, antithetical, dissident
COLLOQ. poles apart
E3 2 same

◆ *n*
reverse, converse, contrary, contradiction, inverse
FORMAL antithesis
COLLOQ. flip side, the other side of the coin, the other side of the fence
E3 same

opposition n

1 ANTAGONISM, hostility, resistance, confrontation, obstructiveness, unfriendliness, dislike, disapproval
2 OPPONENT, adversary, enemy, antagonist, rival, foe, opposing side, other side, competition
E3 1 co-operation, support **2** ally, supporter

oppress v

1 OVERWHELM, subjugate, suppress, subdue, overpower, crush, trample, tyrannize, repress, enslave, quell, quash, persecute, maltreat, abuse, ride, grind, gripe, tread on the neck of
COLLOQ. bully, bring someone to their knees, treat like dirt, use as a doormat, walk all over
SLANG (*vulgar*) treat like shit
2 BURDEN, afflict, lie heavy on, bear hard upon, bear heavily upon, weigh down, weight, hang on/over, crush, harass, depress, press, sadden, discourage, dishearten, deject, dispirit, torment, vex, tread
FORMAL desolate

oppressed adj

tyrannized, burdened, persecuted, downtrodden, enslaved, subject, crushed, repressed, harassed, abused, maltreated, misused, troubled, disadvantaged, underprivileged
FORMAL subjugated
E3 free

oppression n

tyranny, overwhelming, overpowering, subjection, repression, despotism, suppression, injustice, cruelty, brutality, ruthlessness, abuse, persecution, maltreatment, harshness, hardship
FORMAL subjugation

oppressive adj

1 TYRANNICAL, tyrannous, despotic, overbearing, overwhelming, repressive, iron-fisted, domineering, crushing, harsh, unjust, inhuman, extortionate, cruel, brutal, ruthless, pitiless, merciless, burdensome, onerous, intolerable, Draconian
2 AIRLESS, stuffy, close, stifling, suffocating, sultry, muggy, heavy, sweltry, leaden
OLD faint
E3 1 just, gentle **2** airy

oppressor n

tyrant, bully, (hard) taskmaster, slave-driver, despot, dictator, persecutor, tormentor, torturer, intimidator, autocrat
FORMAL subjugator

opprobrious adj

contemptuous, insulting, offensive, scandalous, abusive, damaging, defamatory, derogatory, insolent, scurrilous, vitriolic, venomous
FORMAL calumniatory, calumnious, contumelious, invective, vituperative

opprobrium n

censure, disgrace, dishonour, reproach, disrepute, disfavour, discredit, degradation, debasement, shame, infamy, scurrility, stigma
FORMAL calumny, contumely, ignominy, obloquy, odium
COLLOQ. slur

opt *v*

choose, pick, decide (on), elect, prefer, select, settle on, single out
COLLOQ. go for, plump for

optical instrument

Optical instruments and devices include:

astronomical telescope	magnifying glass	simple microscope
binoculars	opera-glass	slide projector
camera	periscope	spyglass
compound microscope	photo-microscope	stereocamera
endoscope	reflecting telescope	telescope
field-glasses	refracting telescope	telescopic sight
film projector		theodolite
laser	sextant	

See also **spectacles**.

optimism *n*

cheerfulness, cheer, confidence, hopefulness, brightness, morale, buoyancy, idealism, expectancy, sanguineness
COLLOQ. feel-good factor
✑ pessimism

optimistic *adj*

confident, assured, sanguine, hopeful, positive, cheerful, buoyant, bright, idealistic, expectant, bullish, pollyann(a)ish, Panglossian, Panglossic
COLLOQ. upbeat, happy-go-lucky, looking on the bright side, through rose-coloured spectacles
✑ pessimistic

optimum *adj*

best, ideal, model, perfect, optimal, flawless, supreme, highest, superlative, top, choice, most favourable, utopian
✑ worst

option *n*

choice, alternative, preference, possibility, selection

optional *adj*

voluntary, discretionary, elective, free, unforced
✑ compulsory, required; *formal* mandatory

opulence *n*

1 RICHES, fortune, wealth, prosperity, affluence
COLLOQ. easy street
2 SUMPTUOUSNESS, lavishness, richness, luxury, plenty
3 ABUNDANCE, fullness, copiousness, profusion, superabundance, luxuriance
FORMAL cornucopia
✑ 1 poverty; *formal* penury

opulent *adj*

1 RICH, wealthy, prosperous, affluent, well-to-do, well-off, moneyed
COLLOQ. well-heeled, rolling in it
2 SUMPTUOUS, lavish, luxurious
COLLOQ. plush, posh
3 ABUNDANT, copious, prolific, plentiful, profuse, superabundant, luxuriant
✑ 1 poor; *formal* penurious

opus *n*

work, piece, production, composition, creation, oeuvre, brainchild

or *conj*

as an alternative, alternatively, conversely, in preference to, on the other hand

oracle *n*

1 SEER, prophet, prophetess, sage, soothsayer, wizard, sibyl, high priest, augur, fortune teller, forecaster
2 AUTHORITY, adviser, mentor, expert, specialist
COLLOQ. guru, mastermind, pundit

3 PROPHECY, vision, divination, prediction, forecast, revelation, answer, augury
FORMAL prognostication

oracular *adj*

prophetic, wise, significant, positive, authoritative, dogmatic, dictatorial, grave, predictive, obscure, mysterious, cryptic, Delphic, venerable, ominous, portentous, ambiguous, equivocal, two-edged
FORMAL arcane, abstruse, auspicious, haruspical, prescient, sage

oral *adj*

verbal, spoken, said, uttered, unwritten, vocal
✑ written

orally *adv*

verbally, vocally, in spoken language, by mouth, *viva voce*
✑ in written language

orate *v*

speak, talk, hold forth, lecuture, sermonize, pontificate, discourse, harangue, speechify
FORMAL declaim

oration *n*

address, speech, lecture, sermon, discourse, harangue, homily
FORMAL declamation
COLLOQ. spiel

orator *n*

public speaker, speaker, lecturer, rhetorician, demagogue, declaimer, spellbinder, phrasemonger
COLLOQ. spieler

oratorical *adj*

rhetorical, eloquent, sonorous, high-flown, elocutionary, silver-tongued, smooth-tongued, Ciceronian, Demosthenic
FORMAL bombastic, declamatory, grandiloquent, magniloquent

oratory *n*

rhetoric, eloquence, public speaking, speech, speechifying, speechmaking, diction, elocution, declamation
FORMAL grandiloquence

orb *n*

ball, sphere, globe, circle, ring, mound, round, globule, spherule

orbit *n, v*

♦ *n*
1 CIRCUIT, cycle, circle, course, path, trajectory, track, revolution, rotation, orb
FORMAL circumgyration
2 RANGE, scope, reach, domain, influence, sphere of influence, sweep, ambit, compass
♦ *v*
revolve, circle, encircle, circumnavigate

orchestrate *v*

arrange, co-ordinate, organize, stage-manage, put together, prepare, present, mastermind, fix, integrate, score, compose

orchestration *n*

1 *orchestration of the event*
organization, arrangement, management, running, planning, preparation, co-ordination, stage-managing, masterminding, engineering
2 *orchestration of the music*
arrangement, adaptation, interpretation, setting, score, instrumentation, harmonization, version

ordain *v*

1 CONSECRATE, invest, appoint, call, elect, anoint, frock, lay hands on
OLD ordinate

OLD SLANG japan
2 DECREE, order, require, instruct, rule, set, lay down, fix, dictate, establish, pronounce, will, fate, destine, predestine, preordain, predetermine
OLD ordinate, foresay
FORMAL dispose, foreordain, prescribe

ordeal *n*
trial, test, trouble(s), suffering, anguish, distress, agony, pain, torment, persecution, torture, nightmare, gruelling, baptism of fire
FORMAL tribulation(s), affliction

order *n, v*
♦ *n*
1 COMMAND, directive, decree, injunction, summons, writ, warrant, instruction, direction, edict, dictate, ordinance, stipulation, mandate, regulation, rule, precept, law
2 REQUISITION, request, requirement, booking, commission, reservation, application, demand, call, notification
3 ARRANGEMENT, organization, grouping, sequence, cycle, categorization, classification, codification, method, form, pattern, plan, system, rota, regularity, uniformity, symmetry, array, layout, line-up, set-up, structure
FORMAL disposition
4 ORDERLINESS, neatness, tidiness, method, system
5 PEACE, quiet, calm, tranquillity, harmony, law and order, lawfulness, discipline, control
6 ASSOCIATION, society, club, community, fellowship, fraternity, brotherhood, sisterhood, sorority, lodge, guild, league, company, organization, denomination, sect, union, secret society
7 CONDITION, state, shape, form, order, working order, fettle, kilter
COLLOQ. nick
8 CLASS, kind, sort, type, group, variety, species, genus, rank, position, level, grade, degree, station, hierarchy, family, caste
COLLOQ. pecking order
E3 3 disorder **4** confusion, chaos **5** anarchy
Related adjective: ordinal
♦ *v*
1 COMMAND, instruct, direct, bid, decree, rule, legislate, require, authorize
FORMAL prescribe, enjoin
2 REQUEST, reserve, book, apply for, call for, send away for, write off for
FORMAL requisition
3 ARRANGE, organize, systematize, dispose, classify, group, marshal, tidy up, sort out, lay out, manage, control, regulate, catalogue, codify
■ **order around**
order about, domineer, dominate, tyrannize, bully, bulldoze, browbeat, boss around
COLLOQ. push about/around, throw your weight about/around, lay down the law
■ **in order**
1 WORKING, functioning, operative, mended
2 ORDERED, orderly, organized, tidy, neat, shipshape, arranged, well-organized, systematic, regular, methodical, categorized, classified, in sequence, in alphabetical order
3 ACCEPTABLE, proper, correct, right, lawful, allowed, permitted, suitable, appropriate, fitting, all right, done
COLLOQ. OK
■ **in order to**
with the purpose, with the intention of, intending to, to, with a view to, so that, with the result
■ **out of order**
1 BROKEN, broken down, not working, not functioning, inoperative, out of commission
COLLOQ. gone phut, haywire, on the blink, bust, kaput
SLANG conked out
2 DISORDERED, disorganized, untidy, messy,

confused, muddled, out of sequence
3 UNACCEPTABLE, improper, un-called-for, incorrect, wrong, irregular, inappropriate, unsuitable, unlawful
OLD unseemly

orderliness *n*
neatness, tidiness, smartness, organization, straightness, methodicalness, regularity, trimness, spruceness
E3 untidiness, disorderliness

orderly *adj*
1 ORDERED, systematic, neat, tidy, regular, methodical, efficient, businesslike, in order, well-organized, well-regulated, trim
COLLOQ. in apple-pie order
2 WELL-BEHAVED, controlled, disciplined, restrained, law-abiding, ruly
E3 1 chaotic **2** disorderly, unruly

ordinance *n*
1 REGULATION, law, rule, ruling, command, decree, dictum, directive, injunction, canon, statute, edict, enactment, fiat
2 SACRAMENT, ceremony, order, practice, observance, rite, ritual, institution

ordinarily *adv*
as a rule, usually, commonly, normally, in general, generally, familiarly, customarily, habitually, conventionally

ordinary *adj*
normal, usual, customary, common, commonplace, regular, routine, standard, mainstream, average, everyday, workaday, quotidian, unexceptional, unremarkable, fair, typical, plain, familiar, habitual, simple, conventional, modest, mediocre, indifferent, uninteresting, dull, mundane, banal, bland, nondescript, pedestrian, prosaic, undistinguished, unpretentious, unmemorable
COLLOQ. run-of-the-mill, common-or-garden, bog standard
E3 extraordinary, unusual
■ **out of the ordinary**
unusual, exceptional, remarkable, memorable, noteworthy, extraordinary, different, unique, rare, outstanding, surprising, unexpected

ordnance *n*
munitions, weapons, military supplies, arms, artillery, cannon, guns
COLLOQ. big guns

ordure *n*
dirt, dung, excrement, excretion, waste matter, droppings, filth
TECHNICAL egesta, frass, scats, guano
FORMAL faeces, stool
SLANG poo, poop; (*vulgar*) crap, shit

organ *n*
1 DEVICE, instrument, implement, tool, element, constituent, part, component, process, structure, unit, member
2 MEDIUM, agency, forum, vehicle, voice, mouthpiece, publication, newspaper, paper, magazine, periodical, journal
See also panel on next page

organic *adj*
1 *organic matter*
biological, living, animate, natural
TECHNICAL biotic
2 *organic vegetables*
natural, not artificial, non-chemical, chemical-free, pesticide-free, additive-free, GM-free
3 *an organic whole*
structured, organized, ordered, harmonious, coherent

organism *n*
1 LIVING THING, being, creature, entity, body, structure, cell, animal, plant, bacterium

Major organs of the body include:

DIGESTIVE SYSTEM:	ENDOCRINE SYSTEM:	LYMPHATIC/ IMMUNE SYSTEM:	REPRODUCTIVE SYSTEM:		SENSORY:
bowel	adrenal glands	adenoids	cervix	uterus	ear
colon	hypothalamus	appendix	clitoris	vagina	eye
gall bladder	ovaries	lymph	ejaculatory duct	vas deferens	nose
intestines	pancreas	lymph nodes and	epididymis	vulva	skin
large intestine	parathyroid	vessels	fallopian tubes	RESPIRATORY SYSTEM:	taste buds
liver	glands	spleen	ovaries	bronchus	URINARY SYSTEM:
oesophagus	pituitary	thymus	oviduct	diaphragm	bladder
pancreas	testes	tonsils	penis	lungs	kidneys
rectum	thymus glands	NERVOUS SYSTEM:	prostate	nose	ureter
small intestine	thyroid gland	brain	scrotum	throat (or	urethra
stomach		peripheral nerves	seminal vesicles	pharynx)	
		spinal cord	testes	windpipe (or	
				trachea)	

2 SYSTEM, structure, entity, whole, unity, organization, set-up

organization *n*
1 ASSOCIATION, institution, institute, society, company, firm, corporation, concern, operation, federation, group, body, union, league, club, confederation, consortium, conglomeration, syndicate, authority, council, outfit
2 ARRANGEMENT, management, running, co-ordination, administration, development, planning, regulation, establishment
3 SYSTEM, classification, methodology, order, formation, grouping, method, plan, structure, arrangement, unity, whole, set-up, pattern, composition, design
FORMAL configuration

organize *v*
1 ARRANGE, co-ordinate, structure, manage, run, see to, administer, be in charge of, be responsible for, order, standardize, group, marshal, dispose, orchestrate, rationalize, put in order, sort out, classify, systematize, regiment, tabulate, catalogue
OLD embody
TECHNICAL lemmatize
2 ESTABLISH, found, set up, create, originate, start, begin, institute, prepare, develop, form, mould, frame, construct, assemble, put together, shape
E₃ 1 disorganize

organized *adj*
arranged, neat, tidy, orderly, planned, ordered, well-ordered, structured, systematic, efficient, regular, methodical, businesslike, in order, well-organized, well-regulated
E₃ disorganized

orgiastic *adj*
bacchanalian, orgic, Dionysiac, Bacchic, debauched, wild

orgy *n*
1 PARTY, wild party, debauch, carousal, revelry, revel(s), bout, bacchanalia, Saturnalia, Dionysia
COLLOQ. binge, splurge
2 INDULGENCE, excess, spree, frenzy, bout
COLLOQ. binge, splurge

orient *v*
accustom, accommodate, familiarize, acclimatize, adapt, adjust, orientate, attune, align, get your bearings, find your bearings
FORMAL habituate

oriental *adj*
Eastern, Far Eastern, Asian, Asiatic

orientation *n*
1 SITUATION, bearings, location, direction, position, positioning, alignment, placement, attitude, inclination
2 INDUCTION, initiation, training, guiding, leading, acclimatization, familiarization, adaptation, adjustment, getting your bearings, finding your bearings, settling-in

orifice *n*
opening, hole, gap, space, aperture, breach, break, inlet, pore, rent, slit, slot, vent, mouth, cleft, crack, rift, crevice, fissure, perforation
FORMAL aperture

origin *n*
1 SOURCE, spring, fount, foundation, basis, base, cause, derivation, root(s), fountain, fountainhead, well-spring
TECHNICAL etymology
FORMAL provenance
2 BEGINNING, start, inauguration, foundation, launch, birth, dawn, dawning, creation, conception, emergence
FORMAL commencement, inception, genesis
3 ANCESTRY, descent, line of descent, line, extraction, heritage, family, lineage, parentage, pedigree, birth, paternity, stock
E₃ 2 end, termination
Related adjective: genetic

original *adj, n*
♦ *adj*
1 FIRST, early, earliest, initial, primary, archetypal, rudimentary, embryonic, starting, opening, commencing, first-hand, primitive, primal
FORMAL indigenous, autochthonous, prim(a)eval, primordial
2 CREATIVE, innovative, new, novel, fresh, imaginative, ingenious, inventive, resourceful, unconventional, unorthodox, unusual, unique, pioneering, ground-breaking
3 GENUINE, real, authentic, true, actual
E₃ 1 latest **2** hackneyed, unoriginal **3** copied
♦ *n*
prototype, master, paradigm, model, pattern, archetype, standard, type
E₃ copy

originality *n*
inventiveness, creativeness, creativity, imaginativeness, imagination, freshness, boldness, cleverness, creative spirit, daring, innovativeness, innovation, ingenuity, individuality, resourcefulness, newness, novelty, unconventionality, unorthodoxy, singularity, eccentricity

originally *adv*
initially, at first, at the start, at the outset, in the beginning, first, to begin with, in origin, by derivation, by birth

originate *v*
1 RISE, arise, spring, stem, issue, flow, emanate, proceed, derive, result, come, evolve, emerge, be born
2 CREATE, invent, inaugurate, introduce, give birth to, develop, discover, establish, begin, start, set up, set in motion, launch, pioneer, conceive, form, produce, generate, be the father/mother of, seed, plant
FORMAL commence
E₃ 1 end, terminate

origination _n_
creation, development, forming, production, conception, generation, invention

originator _n_
architect, author, creator, designer, father, mother, founder, generator, developer, establisher, innovator, discoverer, inventor, initiator, pioneer, prime mover
COLLOQ. the brains

ornament _n, v_
♦ _n_
1 ADORNMENT, decoration, embellishment, garnish, trimming, accessory, frill, pattern
2 TRINKET, decoration, bauble, jewel, knick-knack, accessory, gewgaw, furbelow, fallal
♦ _v_
decorate, adorn, embellish, garnish, trim, beautify, brighten, dress up, deck, gild

ornamental _adj_
decorative, embellishing, adorning, embroidering, attractive, showy, fancy

ornamentation _n_
decoration, adornment, embellishment, embroidery, ornateness, elaboration, garniture, frills, fallalery

ornate _adj_
elaborate, ornamented, decorated, elegant, fine, fancy, decorated, embellished, showy, ostentatious, baroque, rococo, florid, flowery, flamboyant, fussy, busy, grandiose, sumptuous
OLD adorn
COLLOQ. flash
E3 plain, simple

orotund _adj_
1 _orotund voices_
full, loud, round, powerful, strong, deep, rich, sonorous, booming, resonating
2 _orotund speaking_
dignified, imposing, ornate, pompous, strained, pretentious
FORMAL magniloquent

orthodox _adj_
1 CONFORMIST, conventional, accepted, correct, official, traditional, usual, regular, well-established, established, received, customary, conservative, recognized, authoritative, _bien pensant_
COLLOQ. square
2 _orthodox religious views_
sound, conservative, correct, true, faithful, devout, traditional, strict, canonic, canonical, fundamentalist, hardshell
E3 1 nonconformist, unorthodox

orthodoxy _n_
1 CONVENTIONALITY, conformity, conformism, correctness, properness, authoritativeness, received wisdom
2 TRADITIONALISM, soundness, conservatism, devoutness, devotion, trueness, faithfulness, inflexibility, strictness, fundamentalism
3 DOCTRINE, dogma, creed, belief, tenet, principle, teaching, precept, conviction, canon, credo

oscillate _v_
fluctuate, vary, waver, sway, swing, vacillate, move backwards and forwards, move to and fro, vibrate, wigwag, go from one extreme to the other
COLLOQ. seesaw, yo-yo

oscillation _n_
fluctuation, wavering, variation, vacillation, swinging, swing, instability
COLLOQ. shilly-shallying, seesawing

ossify _v_
fossilize, harden, solidify, make/become fixed,
make/become hard
FORMAL indurate, petrify, rigidify

ostensible _adj_
alleged, apparent, presumed, seeming, supposed, so-called, professed, claimed, outward, pretended, superficial, specious
FORMAL feigned, purported, ostensive
E3 real, genuine

ostensibly _adv_
allegedly, apparently, professedly, supposedly, seemingly, reputedly, outwardly, superficially, on the surface, to all intents and purposes
FORMAL purportedly

ostentation _n_
showiness, showing-off, flamboyance, pretension, pretentiousness, show, flaunting, vaunting, pomp, dash, pride, puff, exhibitionism, boasting, display, flourish, pageantry, parade, trappings, pretence, vanity, window-dressing, splash, fuss, fanfaronade, peacockery
TECHNICAL phylactery
OLD ostent
FORMAL affectation
COLLOQ. flash, flashiness, swank, tinsel, dog
E3 unpretentiousness

ostentatious _adj_
showy, pretentious, vulgar, loud, obtrusive, flaunting, demonstrative, garish, gaudy, flamboyant, conspicuous, extravagant, splashy, barbarous
OLD fastuous
FORMAL affected
COLLOQ. flashy, flash, kitsch, glitzy, over the top, OTT
E3 restrained, modest

ostentatiously _adv_
showily, flamboyantly, pretentiously, loudly, obtrusively, demonstratively, garishly, extravagantly, conspicuously
COLLOQ. flashily, over the top, OTT
E3 modestly

ostracism _n_
exclusion, isolation, rejection, barring, avoidance, banishment, boycott, exile, expulsion, excommunication
FORMAL disfellowship, proscription
COLLOQ. cold-shoulder
E3 acceptance, reinstatement, welcome

ostracize _v_
exclude, banish, exile, expel, excommunicate, reject, segregate, isolate, send to Coventry, shun, snub, boycott, bar, outlaw, avoid
COLLOQ. cold-shoulder, cut
E3 accept, welcome

other _adj_
1 DIFFERENT, dissimilar, unlike, variant, separate, distinct, contrasting
FORMAL disparate
2 MORE, further, extra, additional, supplementary, spare, alternative

otherwise _adv_
1 UNLESS, if not, or, or else, failing that
2 DIFFERENTLY, in a different way, in another way, along different lines, in other respects

otherworldly _adj_
dreamy, absent-minded, ethereal, preoccupied, rapt, bemused, fey
E3 worldly, mundane, solid, substantial

otiose _adj_
redundant, superfluous, extra, spare, excess, surplus, remaining, to spare, unnecessary, unneeded, needless, gratuitous, unwanted, unwarranted, uncalled-for, excessive

FORMAL supernumerary
🖅 necessary, needed, required, wanted

ounce n
particle, scrap, speck, spot, trace, touch, tad, iota, jot, shred, whit, atom, crumb, drop, grain, modicum, morsel
Related adjective: uncial

oust v
expel, eject, depose, displace, supplant, turn out, throw out, overthrow, evict, drive out, thrust out, force out, put out, get rid of, dismiss, unseat, dislodge, dispossess, disinherit, replace, topple
COLLOQ. sack, fire, kick out, boot out, show the door to, give someone the boot/elbow
🖅 install, settle

out adj
1 AWAY, absent, elsewhere, not at home, gone, outside, abroad
2 UNCONSCIOUS, knocked out, out cold
TECHNICAL comatose
FORMAL insensible
COLLOQ. KO'd
3 *the book is out*
published, available, obtainable, ready, in print
4 REVEALED, exposed, known, disclosed, divulged, public, evident, manifest, in the open
5 FORBIDDEN, unacceptable, impossible, excluded, inadmissible, unwelcome, undesirable, inappropriate, unsuitable
FORMAL disallowed
6 OUT-OF-DATE, unfashionable, old-fashioned, dated, passé, antiquated, *démodé*
COLLOQ. old hat
7 EXTINGUISHED, finished, expired, dead, not burning, doused, not shining, used up
8 *the flowers are out*
in bloom, in full bloom, blooming, blossoming, in flower
9 *out to make money*
determined, bent, insistent, intent, set
🖅 **1** in, here, at home **2** conscious **3** out of print, unavailable **4** hidden, concealed **5** allowed, permitted **6** in fashion, up-to-date; *colloq.* in **7** burning

out-and-out adj
absolute, thorough, total, complete, utter, outright, perfect, downright, inveterate, thoroughgoing, unmitigated, unqualified, uncompromising
FORMAL arrant, consummate
COLLOQ. dyed-in-the-wool

outbreak n
eruption, outburst, explosion, flare-up, clash, upsurge, sudden start, flash, rash, burst, epidemic, storm, upbreak
FORMAL recrudescence, ebullition, excrescence

outburst n
outbreak, eruption, explosion, flare-up, outpouring, outcry, burst, fit, gush, surge, storm, spasm, seizure, gale, attack, fit of temper, paroxysm

outcast n
castaway, exile, pariah, outsider, untouchable, leper, refugee, evacuee, reject, *persona non grata*

outclass v
surpass, outshine, beat, excel over, be much better than, outrival, transcend, top, eclipse, outdo, outdistance, outrank, outstrip, overshadow, leave standing, put in the shade

outcome n
result, consequence, upshot, conclusion, effect, after-effect, product, issue, sequel, end result, answer, proceeds, dénouement, pay-off, outspring, upcome
OLD proof
SLANG *Aust* wash-up

outcry n
protest, complaint, protestation, objection, dissent, indignation, uproar, cry, exclamation, clamour, row, fuss, commotion, noise, tumult, hue and cry, outburst
COLLOQ. hullaballoo, racket

outdated adj
out of date, old-fashioned, out of fashion, dated, unfashionable, outmoded, behind the times, obsolete, obsolescent, superseded, antediluvian, antiquated, antique, archaic, passé, *démodé*
COLLOQ. out of the ark, fuddy-duddy, old-fogeyish, old hat, past it, square, past its sell-by date, on the way out, steam, oldfangled, uncool, mumsy
🖅 modern, up-to-date, fashionable

outdistance v
outstrip, outpace, outrun, pass, overtake, pull ahead of, shake off, overhaul, surpass, leave behind, leave standing

outdo v
surpass, exceed, beat, excel, outstrip, outshine, get the better of, have the advantage over, come first, overcome, defeat, outclass, outdistance, eclipse, transcend
COLLOQ. cap, gain the upper/whip hand over, stand/be head and shoulders above, run rings/circles round

outdoors adv
out, outside, in the open air, out-of-doors, alfresco, *en plein air*
🖅 indoors

outer adj
1 EXTERNAL, exterior, outside, outermost, outward, surface, superficial, peripheral
2 OUTLYING, distant, remote, further, fringe, peripheral, faraway
🖅 **1** internal **2** inner

outface v
brave, confront, defy, stand up to, outstare, stare down, brazen out, beard
🖅 capitulate; *formal* succumb

outfit n, v
♦ n
1 CLOTHES, dress, suit, costume, ensemble, separates, turnout, setout
OLD weed
FORMAL accoutrements
COLLOQ. get-up, togs, garb, gear
2 EQUIPMENT, kit, tools, apparatus, rig, trappings, paraphernalia, layout
OLD fit-out
COLLOQ. gear, bag of tricks
3 ORGANIZATION, firm, business, company, corporation, group, team, unit, set, set-up, clique, coterie, crew, gang, squad
♦ v
fit out, furnish, provide, supply, equip, stock, turn out, fit up, kit out, appoint, provision
FORMAL accoutre, apparel, attire

outfitter n
tailor, clothier, costumer, costumier, dressmaker, sartor, modiste, haberdasher, couturier, *couturière*

outflow n
discharge, rush, spout, gush, jet, emergence, effusion, emanation, outrush, outpouring, drainage, ebb, outfall
FORMAL debouchment, disemboguement, effluence, effluent, effluvium, efflux, effluxion
🖅 inflow

outflowing adj
discharging, gushing, leaking, rushing, spurting, effluent, emanant
FORMAL debouching

outfox *v*
outsmart, outwit, outperform, outmanoeuvre, best, out-think, beat, get the better of, deceive, trick, dupe
COLLOQ. kid, con, have on, pull a fast one on
SLANG take for a ride

outgoing *adj*
1 SOCIABLE, friendly, unreserved, uninhibited, affable, amiable, warm, affectionate, approachable, expansive, open, talkative, extrovert, gregarious, cordial, genial, easy-going, communicative, demonstrative, sympathetic
2 DEPARTING, retiring, leaving, former, last, past, ex-, emissary
F3 1 reserved **2** incoming

outgoings *n*
costs, expenditure, outlay, overheads, spending, expenses
FORMAL disbursal, disbursement
F3 income

outgrowth *n*
1 CONSEQUENCE, effect, product, offshoot, by-product, spin-off, emanation
2 SWELLING, shoot, sprout
FORMAL protuberance, excrescence

outing *n*
excursion, expedition, jaunt, trip, pleasure trip, tour, mystery tour, spin, picnic, hike, sally, junket; *dialect* out
COLLOQ. jolly

outlandish *adj*
unconventional, unfamiliar, unheard-of, unknown, bizarre, strange, odd, unusual, peculiar, weird, eccentric, alien, exotic, curious, quaint, barbarous, grotesque, foreign, extraordinary, preposterous, unreasonable
COLLOQ. freaky, oddball, wacky
SLANG way-out, far-out
F3 familiar, ordinary

outlandishness *n*
bizarreness, oddness, unusualness, strangeness, weirdness, queerness, eccentricity, exoticness, quaintness, grotesqueness
F3 commonplaceness, familiarity

outlast *v*
survive, come through, outlive, outstay, ride, weather

outlaw *n, v*
♦ *n*
fugitive, bandit, brigand, robber, desperado, highwayman, criminal, marauder, pirate, outcast, exile, Robin Hood; *N Am* badman
♦ *v*
ban, disallow, forbid, prohibit, exclude, embargo, bar, debar, banish, excommunicate, condemn
OLD TECHNICAL *Scot* horn
FORMAL proscribe, interdict
F3 allow, legalize

outlay *n*
expenditure, expenses, outgoings, payment, charge, cost, price, spending
FORMAL disbursement
F3 income

outlet *n*
1 RETAILER, retail outlet, shop, store, market, supplier
2 EXIT, way out, vent, duct, escape, issue, let-off, outfall, opening, port, sea gate, release, valve, safety valve, sluice, nozzle, channel, culvert, conduit, *débouché*, emissary
TECHNICAL femerall
OLD going forth
FORMAL egress
3 *an outlet for your feelings*
channel, means of release, means of expression, safety valve
F3 2 entry, inlet

outline *n, v*
♦ *n*
1 SUMMARY, sketch, synopsis, précis, résumé, main points, prospectus, programme, scenario, rough idea, bare facts, bare bones, framework, skeleton, thumbnail sketch, abstract, aperçu, *croquis, esquisse*
2 PROFILE, sketch, tracing, form, shape, design, figure, layout, plan, contour, silhouette, keyline, skyline, waterline, chart, diagram, map, schema, ground plan, underdrawing, balloon
TECHNICAL trick
FORMAL configuration, delineation, lineament, contorno
♦ *v*
1 SKETCH (OUT), summarize, draft, trace, rough out, give a rough idea of, chalk out
FORMAL delineate, adumbrate
2 EDGE, trim, fringe, dress, braid

outlive *v*
survive, outlast, come through, live through, weather
F3 predecease

outlook *n*
1 VIEW, viewpoint, point of view, attitude, mindset, perspective, frame of mind, interpretation, angle, slant, standpoint, opinion, world-view, *Weltanschauung*
2 EXPECTATIONS, future, forecast, prospect(s), prognosis
3 *a house with a pleasant outlook*
view, prospect, aspect, panorama

outlying *adj*
distant, remote, isolated, far-off, far-away, far-flung, outer, out-of-the-way, inaccessible, provincial
COLLOQ. off the beaten track
F3 inner

outmanoeuvre *v*
outdo, outthink, outwit, outsmart, outfox, beat, outflank, outgeneral, get the better of
FORMAL circumvent

outmoded *adj*
out of date, old-fashioned, out of fashion, dated, unfashionable, behind the times, obsolete, obsolescent, superseded, antediluvian, antiquated, archaic, passé, démodé
COLLOQ. out of the ark, fuddy-duddy, old-fogeyish, old hat, past it, square, past its sell-by date, on the way out, steam, oldfangled, uncool
F3 modern, new, fashionable, fresh

out of date *adj*
old-fashioned, outdated, outmoded, out of fashion, dated, unfashionable, behind the times, obsolete, obsolescent, superseded, antediluvian, antiquated, archaic, passé, démodé
COLLOQ. out of the ark, fuddy-duddy, old-fogeyish, old hat, past it, square, past its sell-by date, on the way out, steam, oldfangled, uncool
F3 modern, new, fashionable, fresh

out-of-the-way *adj*
remote, isolated, far-flung, far-off, far-away, distant, outlying, outer, inaccessible, lonely, little-known, obscure, unfrequented, peripheral, god-forsaken
COLLOQ. off the beaten track

out of work *adj*
unemployed, redundant, out of a job, jobless, idle, laid off, workless
COLLOQ. on the dole, resting, between jobs
F3 employed, occupied, busy

outpace *v*
outstrip, outrun, outdistance, outdo, beat, pass, overtake, surpass, overhaul

outpouring *n*
flood, deluge, torrent, stream, spate, spurt, flow, outflow,

flux, cascade, effusion, emanation
FORMAL debouchment, disemboguement, effluence, efflux

output *n*
production, productivity, product, manufacture, achievement, performance, accomplishment, gain, yield, fruits, harvest, return, outturn, turnout, throughput

outrage *n, v*
• *n*
1 ANGER, fury, rage, indignation, shock, affront, horror, wrath
2 ATROCITY, offence, injury, enormity, barbarism, brutality, crime, violation, evil, scandal, horror, affront
• *v*
1 APPAL, anger, infuriate, affront, incense, enrage, madden, disgust, injure, offend, shock, horrify, scandalize
2 ASSAULT, violate, abuse, desecrate, defile, ravish, ravage

outrageous *adj*
1 ATROCIOUS, abominable, shocking, scandalous, offensive, disgraceful, dreadful, terrible, monstrous, unspeakable, flagrant, diabolical, horrible, ghastly, gruesome, vile, foul, unacceptable, intolerable, unbearable, insufferable
OLD enormous
FORMAL heinous, egregious
COLLOQ. unchristian, ungodly, unholy, infernal
2 EXCESSIVE, exorbitant, immoderate, unreasonable, extortionate, scandalous, obscene, inordinate, preposterous
E3 **2** acceptable, reasonable

outrageously *adv*
scandalously, disgracefully, obscenely, unspeakably, unacceptably, intolerably, unbearably, terribly, dreadfully, horribly

outré *adj*
unconventional, unusual, strange, odd, extraordinary, eccentric, weird, bizarre, shocking, outrageous
COLLOQ. oddball, freaky
SLANG way-out, far-out

outrider *n*
advance guard, escort, attendant, guard, bodyguard, vanguard, herald, precursor

outright *adj, adv*
• *adj*
1 TOTAL, utter, absolute, complete, downright, out-and-out, unqualified, unconditional, unmitigated, perfect, pure, thorough, direct
2 CLEAR, definite, categorical, unequivocal, unmistakable, undeniable, straightforward
E3 ambiguous, indefinite
• *adv*
1 TOTALLY, absolutely, completely, wholly, entirely, categorically, utterly, thoroughly, openly, without restraint, straightforwardly, positively, directly, explicitly
2 *killed outright*
instantaneously, at once, there and then, instantly, immediately, straight away

outrun *v*
outstrip, outpace, outdistance, overtake, outdo, shake off, pass, overhaul, surpass, exceed, excel, beat, lose, run faster than, leave behind

outset *n*
start, beginning, opening, inauguration
FORMAL inception, commencement
COLLOQ. kick-off
E3 end, conclusion

outshine *v*
outclass, outstrip, outdo, overshadow, transcend, eclipse,

surpass, beat, best, upstage, excel, dwarf, outrank, top, put in the shade, put to shame

outside *adj, n*
• *adj*
1 EXTERNAL, exterior, outer, surface, superficial, outward, extraneous, outdoor, outermost, extreme
2 *an outside chance*
remote, marginal, distant, small, faint, slight, slim, slender, vague, negligible, improbable, unlikely
3 *outside examiners*
external, independent, consulting, non-resident, casual, temporary, visiting, self-employed, extramural, peripatetic, subcontracted, neutral, objective, impartial, unbiased
E3 **1** inside, internal **2** likely, real, substantial **3** resident, internal
• *n*
exterior, façade, front, surface, outer surface, face, appearance, cover
E3 inside

outsider *n*
stranger, intruder, alien, non-member, non-resident, foreigner, newcomer, visitor, emigrant, émigré, immigrant, outlander, interloper, misfit, gatecrasher, outlier
COLLOQ. odd one out
SLANG *N Am* ringer

outsize *adj*
huge, immense, vast, enormous, massive, colossal, titanic, giant, gigantic, mammoth, tremendous, stupendous, great, very big, very large, extensive, monstrous, gargantuan
FORMAL prodigious
COLLOQ. jumbo, frightful, ginormous, humongous
SLANG mega
E3 tiny, minute

outskirts *n*
suburbs, suburbia, vicinity, neighbourhood, environs, periphery, edges, fringes, borders, boundary, limit, frontier, edge, margin, perimeter
E3 centre

outsmart *v*
outwit, outperform, outmanoeuvre, best, out-think, beat, get the better of, deceive, trick, dupe, outfox
COLLOQ. kid, con, have on, pull a fast one on
SLANG take for a ride

outsource *v*
contract out, farm out, delegate, pass/give to others

outspoken *adj*
candid, frank, forthright, free, unreserved, unequivocal, unceremonious, plain-spoken, plain, direct, straightforward, bluff, broad, straight, vocal, explicit, blunt, brusque, rude, Rabelaisian
E3 diplomatic, reserved

outspokenness *n*
candidness, frankness, plainness, directness, forthrightness, straightforwardness, bluntness, bluffness, brusqueness, rudeness

outspread *adj*
spread out, outstretched, open, opened, wide, wide-open, unfolded, unfurled, stretched, extended, fanned out, flared, expanded

outstanding *adj*
1 EXCELLENT, distinguished, eminent, pre-eminent, famous, famed, well-known, renowned, celebrated, exceptional, superior, remarkable, prominent, superb, great, notable, impressive, striking, salient, superlative, important, noteworthy, memorable, special, extraordinary, arresting, golden, chief
FORMAL prosilient

COLLOQ. ace, top-notch, smashing, brill, out of this world; *NAm* some
SLANG cool, wicked, radical
2 OWING, unpaid, due, unsettled, unresolved, uncollected, pending, payable, remaining, unfinished, to be done, ongoing, left-over
E3 1 ordinary, unexceptional **2** paid, settled

outstandingly *adv*
exceptionally, remarkably, greatly, notably, extremely, especially, extraordinarily, impressively, strikingly, amazingly

outstrip *v*
surpass, exceed, better, outdo, beat, top, transcend, outshine, pass, gain on, go/travel faster than, leave behind, leave standing, outrun, outdistance, overtake, eclipse

outward *adj*
external, exterior, outer, outside, outermost, surface, superficial, visible, apparent, perceptible, noticeable, discernible, observable, evident, supposed, professed, public, obvious, ostensible
E3 inner, private

outwardly *adv*
apparently, externally, to all appearances, visibly, superficially, supposedly, seemingly, on the surface, on the outside, at first sight, as far as you can see, on the face of it

outweigh *v*
exceed, surpass, be greater than, be more than, be superior to, override, prevail over, overcome, take precedence over, cancel out, make up for, compensate for, predominate
FORMAL preponderate

outwit *v*
outsmart, outthink, outmanoeuvre, get the better of, be cleverer than, trick, better, beat, dupe, cheat, deceive, defraud, swindle
COLLOQ. kid, con, have on, pull a fast one on
SLANG take for a ride

outworn *adj*
outdated, out of date, outmoded, ancient, antiquated, archaic, stale, discredited, defunct, old-fashioned, behind the times, hackneyed, rejected, obsolete, obsolescent, disused, rejected, exhausted, abandoned
COLLOQ. old hat, moth-eaten, past it, past its sell-by date
E3 fresh, new

oval *adj*
egg-shaped, elliptical, ovoid, ovate, ellipsoidal
TECHNICAL obovate, oviform
FORMAL vulviform

ovation *n*
applause, acclaim, acclamation, praise(s), tribute, clapping, handclapping, cheering, cheers, accolade, bravos
FORMAL plaudits, laudation
COLLOQ. bouquet
E3 abuse, catcalls

oven *n*
cooker, stove, microwave (oven), kiln

over *adj, adv, prep*
   ◆ *adj*
finished, ended, at an end, done with, past, gone, no more, completed, closed, in the past, settled, up, forgotten, accomplished
FORMAL concluded, terminated
COLLOQ. over and done with, ancient history
   ◆ *adv*
1 ABOVE, beyond, overhead, on high
FORMAL aloft
2 EXTRA, remaining, surplus, superfluous, left, left over, unclaimed, unused, unwanted, in excess, in addition

   ◆ *prep*
1 ABOVE, on, on top of, upon, in charge of, in command of, higher than, superior to
2 EXCEEDING, more than, in excess of
3 ON THE SUBJECT OF, about, on, concerning, relating to, connected with, concerned with, regarding, as regards, referring to, with regard to, with respect to, with reference to, on the subject of, in the matter of, re, dealing with
FORMAL apropos of
■ **over and above**
in addition to, on top of, together with, plus, along with, as well as, besides, added to, let alone, not to mention
■ **over and over (again)**
again and again, repeatedly, frequently, often, continually, endlessly, time and (time) again, ad infinitum, ad nauseam

overabundance *n*
surplus, surfeit, excess, glut, profusion, oversupply, *embarras de choix, embarras de richesses*
FORMAL superfluity, superabundance, plethora
COLLOQ. too much of a good thing
E3 lack, dearth

overact *v*
overplay, exaggerate, overdo
COLLOQ. ham, lay/pile it on, lay/pile it on thick, lay/pile it on with a trowel
E3 underact, underplay

overall *adj, adv*
   ◆ *adj*
total, all-inclusive, all-embracing, comprehensive, inclusive, complete, sweeping, general, universal, global, broad, all-over, out to out
COLLOQ. blanket, umbrella
E3 narrow, specific
   ◆ *adv*
in general, on the whole, by and large, broadly, broadly/generally speaking, altogether

overalls *n*
dungarees, coverall, boiler suit, workwear, dust-coat, pinafore, crawler, tablier; *dialect* save-all
OLD jumper
COLLOQ. pinnie

overawe *v*
intimidate, daunt, dismay, disconcert, abash, frighten, scare, terrify, petrify, alarm, awe, unnerve, browbeat, cow
E3 reassure, comfort

overbalance *v*
lose your balance, fall over, tip over, topple over, trip, slip, tumble, upset, somersault, lose your footing, capsize, keel over, overturn, turn turtle

overbearing *adj*
imperious, domineering, arrogant, officious, dictatorial, despotic, lordly, tyrannical, high-handed, haughty, proud, cavalier, autocratic, dogmatic, oppressive, presumptuous, contemptuous, disdainful
COLLOQ. bossy, la-di-da, snobby, snooty, snotty, stuck-up, toffee-nosed, too big for your boots
SLANG smartarse, smartass
E3 meek, unassertive

overblown *adj*
overstated, overdone, overestimated, overcharge, excessive, extravagant, pretentious, embellished, amplified, bombastic, inflated, caricatured, burlesqued, exalted, self-important
COLLOQ. over the top, OTT

overcast *adj*
cloudy, clouded (over), grey, dull, dark, darkened, sombre, gloomy, dreary, dismal, sunless, hazy, misty, foggy, leaden, louring
E3 bright, clear

overcharge v
surcharge, short-change, cheat, extort, fleece, swindle
COLLOQ. do, diddle, rook
SLANG rip off, sting
🖃 undercharge

overcoat n
See panel at **coat**.

overcome v, adj
♦ v
conquer, defeat, beat, surmount, prevail, triumph over, get the better of, be victorious over, rise above, master, overpower, overwhelm, overthrow, subdue, trounce, best, worst, rout, break, knock out, outdo, outplay, outwit, outsmart, be more than a match for, have the edge on, master, wear down, put on the foil
OLD convince, evince, fordo, superate; (*Spenser*) underfong
FORMAL vanquish, subjugate, expugn
COLLOQ. hammer, slaughter, clobber, lick, thrash, wipe the floor with, hit/knock for six
♦ adj
overwhelmed, overpowered, exhausted, broken, moved, speechless, choked up
COLLOQ. dead-beat, bowled over, swept off your feet, lost for words
FORMAL affected

over-confident adj
arrogant, brash, cocksure, self-assured, blustering, swaggering, presumptuous, overweening, foolhardy, rash, incautious, over-optimistic, sanguine
FORMAL hubristic, temerarious
COLLOQ. cocky, uppity, uppish
🖃 cautious, diffident

overcritical adj
overparticular, fault-finding, hypercritical, hard to please, pedantic, over-nice, purist, captious, carping, cavilling, Zoilean
FORMAL ultra-crepidarian
COLLOQ. nit-picking, pernickety, hair-splitting; *NAm* persnickety
🖃 easy-going, tolerant, uncritical

overcrowded adj
congested, packed (out), crammed full, chock-full, chock-a-block, overpopulated, overloaded, swarming, teeming, overrun, full to overflowing
COLLOQ. jam-packed, packed like sardines
SLANG chocker
🖃 deserted, empty

overdo v
exaggerate, go too far, carry to excess, overindulge, overstate, overact, overplay
COLLOQ. ham it up, go overboard, camp it up, lay/pile it on, lay/pile it on thick, lay/pile it on with a trowel, stretch a point
■ **overdo it**
overwork, work too hard, do too much, overstretch yourself, strain yourself, overreach yourself, overexert yourself
COLLOQ. sweat blood, burn yourself out, bite off more than you can chew, run yourself into the ground, burn the candle at both ends, work your fingers to the bone, crack up

overdone adj
1 OVERCOOKED, burnt, spoiled, dried up, overbaked, charred
COLLOQ. burnt to a cinder, burnt to a frazzle
2 EXAGGERATED, overstated, overelaborate, undue, unnecessary, overplayed, excessive, immoderate, fulsome, effusive, gushing, inordinate, histrionic
COLLOQ. over the top, OTT
🖃 **1** underdone, raw **2** underplayed, understated

overdraft n
overdrawn account, debt, arrears, liabilities, borrowings, unpaid amounts, deficit, insufficient funds

overdue adj
late, behindhand, behind schedule, delayed, owing, unpaid, due, unsettled, pending, payable, unpunctual, slow
FORMAL tardy, belated
🖃 early

overeat v
gorge, overindulge, guzzle, eat too much, go on a binge, stuff yourself, gormandize
COLLOQ. binge, make a pig of yourself, pig out, have eyes bigger than your stomach
🖃 abstain, starve

overeating n
guzzling, overindulgence, gluttony, bulimia, hyperphagia, gourmandism, gormandism, gourmandise, gormandise
COLLOQ. bingeing
🖃 abstemiousness, abstention

overemphasize v
exaggerate, overstress, lay/put too much emphasis on, attach too much importance to, make too much of, labour, belabour, overdramatize
COLLOQ. make a mountain out of a molehill, blow up out of all proportion
🖃 minimize, play down, underplay, understate, belittle

overexert
■ **overexert yourself**
overdo it, overstrain yourself, overtax yourself, overtire yourself, overwork, strain yourself, wear yourself out, drive yourself too hard, work too hard, run yourself into the ground, fatigue, work yourself to death, push yourself too hard
COLLOQ. burn the candle at both ends, knock yourself out
🖃 idle, laze

overflow v, n
♦ v
spill (over), overrun, run over, pour over, well over, flow over, brim over, bubble over, surge, discharge, flood, cover, inundate, deluge, shower, submerge, soak, swamp, teem
♦ n
overspill, spill, inundation, flood, spillage, overabundance, surplus

overflowing adj
crowded, filled, full, swarming, teeming, thronged, bountiful, abounding, superabundant, brimful, plentiful, copious, profuse, rife
FORMAL inundant, plenteous
🖃 lacking, scarce

overgrowth n
escalation, overabundance, overdevelopment, superabundance
TECHNICAL hypertrophy
🖃 decline, failure, shrinkage, wasting

overhang v
jut (out), project, bulge (out), protrude, stick out, poke (out), stand out, extend, beetle

overhanging adj
projecting, protruding, jutting (out), bulging (out), sticking out, standing out, beetling, prominent
FORMAL pensile

overhaul v, n
♦ v
1 RENOVATE, repair, service, recondition, revamp, mend, examine, inspect, investigate, check, check over/up, survey, go over, re-examine, fix
OLD rummage
2 OVERTAKE, pull ahead of, outpace, outstrip,

outdistance, gain on, pass, get ahead of
* *n*
reconditioning, repair, renovation, check, check-up,
service, examination, inspection
COLLOQ. going-over

overhead *adv, adj*
* *adv*
above, up above, on high, upward
OLD aloft
Ea below, underfoot
* *adj*
elevated, aerial, overhanging, raised, air

overheads *n*
running costs, outgoings, operating costs, regular costs,
fixed costs, expenses, expenditure, burden, oncost(s)
FORMAL disbursement
Ea income, profit

overheated *adj*
angry, agitated, inflamed, fiery, flaming, overwrought,
passionate, roused, impassioned, excited, overexcited
Ea calm, cool, impassive, dispassionate

overindulge *v*
1 GORGE, gormandize, gluttonize, guzzle, debauch, eat/
drink too much, satiate, sate
COLLOQ. binge, pig out, make a pig of yourself
SLANG booze, get pissed, lush
2 PAMPER, mollycoddle, spoil, cosset, pander, pet
COLLOQ. spoon-feed
Ea 1 abstain

overindulgence *n*
excess, immoderation, overeating, intemperance, surfeit,
debauch
COLLOQ. binge
Ea abstemiousness, abstention

overjoyed *adj*
delighted, elated, euphoric, ecstatic, in raptures, joyful,
enraptured, rapturous, thrilled, jubilant, in transports of
delight
COLLOQ. over the moon, tickled pink, on cloud nine, in
seventh heaven, on top of the world, like a child with a new
toy, pleased as Punch, high as a kite
Ea sad, disappointed

overlap *v*
coincide, cover, overlay, overlie, flap over
TECHNICAL imbricate, shingle

overlay *v*
cover, wrap, envelop, blanket, inlay, face, surface, line,
decorate, ornament, adorn, veneer, varnish, laminate

overload *v, n*
* *v*
burden, overburden, oppress, strain, tax, overtax, weigh
down, overcharge, encumber, saddle, lumber
* *n*
overabundance, surplus, surfeit, excess, glut, oversupply
FORMAL superfluity, superabundance, plethora
Ea lack, dearth

overlook *v*
1 FRONT ONTO, face, look onto, open onto, look over,
command/have a view of
2 MISS, disregard, ignore, omit, neglect, pass over, pass by,
leave, forget, take no notice of, let pass, let ride, slight, take
no account of; *dialect* mislippen
3 EXCUSE, forgive, pardon, condone, wink at, turn a blind
eye to, pass over
Ea 2 notice, observe **3** penalize, condemn

overlooked *adj*
unhonoured, unvalued, unregarded, unnoted,
unremarked, unprized, unconsidered, unheeded
Ea appreciated, prized, sought-after, valued

overly *adv*
too, over, unduly, excessively, exceedingly, immoderately,
unreasonably, inordinately, unnecessarily
Ea inadequately, insufficiently

overmuch *adv*
too much, unduly, excessively, unreasonably,
immoderately, inordinately, unnecessarily

overnice *adj*
overfastidious, over-meticulous, overparticular,
overprecise, oversensitive, overscrupulous, oversubtle,
finical
COLLOQ. nit-picking, pernickety; *N Am* persnickety
Ea casual, uncritical

overplay *v*
exaggerate, overstate, overdo, magnify, overemphasize,
emphasize, stress, make too much of, dramatize,
overdramatize, embellish, embroider, colour, stretch the
truth, enlarge, amplify, enhance, oversell
FORMAL aggrandize
COLLOQ. lay/pile it on, lay/pile it on thick, lay/pile it on with
a trowel, make a mountain out of a molehill, blow
something up out of all proportion, shoot a line
Ea understate, play down

overpopulated *adj*
overcrowded, congested, packed (out), crammed full,
chock-full, overloaded, swarming, teeming, overrun, full to
overflowing
COLLOQ. jam-packed, packed like sardines
Ea deserted, empty

overpower *v*
1 OVERWHELM, overcome, conquer, defeat, beat, trounce,
rout, subdue, overthrow, quash, quell, crush, immobilize,
overbear, master, gain mastery over, gain the upper hand
over
OLD evince, whelm, swelt
FORMAL vanquish, subjugate
2 *overpowered by a feeling*
move, affect deeply/strongly, touch, confuse, perplex,
daze, stagger, dumbfound, leave speechless, hypnotize,
take aback, dazzle
OLD bedazzle
COLLOQ. bowl over, floor, flabbergast, hit/knock for
six

overpowering *adj*
overwhelming, powerful, strong, forceful, irresistible,
undeniable, irrefutable, uncontrollable, compelling,
extreme, oppressive, suffocating, stifling, unbearable,
nauseating, sickening

overrate *v*
overestimate, overvalue, overpraise, magnify, overprize,
make too much of, attach too much importance to
COLLOQ. blow up
Ea underrate

overreach
▪ **overreach yourself**
overstretch yourself, try to do too much, overdo it, go too
far, strain yourself
COLLOQ. bite off more than you can chew, spread yourself
too thinly, burn yourself out

overreact *v*
get upset over nothing, make a lot of fuss about nothing,
lose your sense of proportion
COLLOQ. blow something up out of all proportion, make a
mountain out of a molehill

override *v*
1 OUTWEIGH, be more important than, exceed, surpass, be
greater than, be superior to, prevail over, overcome
2 OVERRULE, cancel, annul, set aside, supersede, quash,
reverse, disregard, ignore, trample over

FORMAL abrogate, countermand, nullify, rescind, vanquish
COLLOQ. ride roughshod over

overriding adj

most important, most significant, principal, first, major, predominant, primary, prime, supreme, compelling, dominant, essential, final, ultimate, overruling, prior, prevailing, ruling, paramount, pivotal, cardinal, determining, number one
E∃ insignificant, unimportant

overrule v

overturn, override, revoke, set aside, disallow, reject, reverse, invalidate, cancel, annul, vote down
FORMAL countermand, abrogate, rescind, nullify

overrun v

1 INVADE, occupy, besiege, attack, storm, infest, overwhelm, inundate, permeate, penetrate, spread over, swamp, swarm over, surge over, ravage, overgrow
OLD depopulate
COLLOQ. run riot, spread like wildfire
2 EXCEED, go over, overshoot, overstep, overreach
TECHNICAL bleed, lip

overseas adj, adv

◆ adj
foreign, international, external, exotic, faraway, distant, remote, ultramarine
E∃ domestic, home
◆ adv
abroad, in/to a foreign country, out of the country, in/to foreign parts, in/to foreign climes, far and wide, widely

oversee v

supervise, watch (over), look after, keep an eye on, inspect, superintend, run, manage, administer, direct, guide, conduct, preside over, be in charge of, be responsible for, be in control of, control

overseer n

supervisor, chief, foreman, forewoman, manager, manageress, superintendent, steward, captain, surveyor, workmaster, workmistress, overman; *Scot* grieve; *S Afr* baas, induna
OLD decurion
COLLOQ. boss, gaffer, guv, guv'nor

overshadow v

1 OBSCURE, cloud, darken, dim, mar, spoil, blight, veil, take the edge off, put a damper on
2 OUTSHINE, eclipse, excel, surpass, be superior to, dominate, dwarf, put in the shade, rise above, tower above

oversight n

1 LAPSE, omission, fault, error, slip-up, mistake, blunder, carelessness, neglect
FORMAL dereliction
COLLOQ. slip-up, howler, boob; *N Am* flub
2 SUPERVISION, responsibility, care, charge, control, custody, superintendence, handling, keeping, administration, management, surveillance, direction

oversize adj

huge, immense, vast, enormous, massive, colossal, giant, gigantic, mammoth, monumental, tremendous, stupendous, great, very big, very large, extensive, titanic, monstrous, gargantuan
FORMAL prodigious
COLLOQ. jumbo, frightful, ginormous, humongous
SLANG mega
E∃ tiny, minute

overstate v

exaggerate, overdo, magnify, overemphasize, emphasize, stress, make too much of, dramatize, overdramatize, embellish, embroider, colour, stretch the truth, enlarge, amplify, enhance, oversell
FORMAL aggrandize

COLLOQ. lay/pile it on, lay/pile it on thick, lay/pile it on with a trowel, make a mountain out of a molehill, blow something up out of all proportion, shoot a line
E∃ understate, play down

overstatement n

exaggeration, overemphasis, emphasis, magnification, overestimation, excess, extravagance, embellishment, enlargement, pretentiousness, amplification, burlesque, caricature, parody
FORMAL hyperbole
E∃ meiosis, understatement

overt adj

open, plain, evident, patent, observable, obvious, manifest, noticeable, visible, conspicuous, apparent, public, professed, unconcealed, undisguised
E∃ covert, secret

overtake v

1 PASS, go past, drive/run past, catch up with, outdistance, leave behind, outstrip, draw level with, gain on, come up with, pull ahead of, ride down, overhaul
OLD overcatch
2 COME UPON, happen to, happen suddenly/unexpectedly to, take by surprise, catch unawares, strike, overwhelm, engulf
FORMAL befall

overthrow v, n

◆ v
1 DEPOSE, oust, bring down, put down, bear down, down, topple, unseat, displace, dethrone, conquer, beat, defeat, crush, confound, overcome, overpower, overwhelm, overcast, subvert, quash, quell, trounce, best, worst, subdue, master, abolish, upset, lay low
FORMAL vanquish
OLD smite, supplant
SLANG stonker
2 OVERTURN, upset, upturn, tip over, topple, tumble, overbalance, keel over, knock over, spill, turn over, invert, prostrate, run over/down, ride down, trip up someone's heels; *dialect* whemmle
E∃ 1 install, protect, reinstate, restore
◆ n
ousting, unseating, defeat, deposition, dethronement, fall, rout, undoing, suppression, downfall, end, humiliation, upsetting, destruction, ruin, subversion, confusion; *dialect* whemmle
FORMAL vanquishing, bouleversement, labefactation, labefaction

overtly adv

plainly, clearly, obviously, manifestly, openly, noticeably, conspicuously, in full view, for all to see, patently
E∃ covertly, secretly

overtone n

suggestion, intimation, nuance, hint, undercurrent, insinuation, innuendo, connotation, hidden meaning, indirect reference, association, feeling, implication, sense, flavour

overture n

1 APPROACH, advance(s), feeler(s), offer, invitation, proposal, proposition, suggestion, signal, move(s), motion
2 PRELUDE, opening, introduction, opening move, (opening) gambit

overturn v

1 CAPSIZE, upset, upturn, tip over, topple, overbalance, keel over, knock over, spill, turn over, invert, skittle
2 OVERRULE, repeal, override, reverse, cancel, annul, abolish, destroy, quash, set aside, veto
FORMAL abrogate, nullify, rescind, revoke
3 OVERTHROW, depose, oust, bring down, topple, unseat, displace, dethrone, confound, subvert, conquer, beat,

defeat, crush, overcome, overpower, overwhelm
FORMAL vanquish

overused adj
overworked, hackneyed, trite, stereotyped, worn, tired, unoriginal, stale, played out, commonplace, bromidic, cliché(e)d, threadbare
FORMAL platitudinous
E3 fresh, original, new

overview n
survey, review, examination, inspection, consideration, study, appraisal, scrutiny, assessment, measurement, valuation

overweening adj
arrogant, conceited, haughty, proud, self-confident, over-confident, supercilious, vain, presumptuous, overblown, high-handed, cocksure, excessive, immoderate, inflated, extravagant, swollen, opinionated, lordly, egotistical, cavalier, pompous, insolent
FORMAL hubristic, vainglorious
COLLOQ. cocky
E3 unassuming, modest, diffident

overweight adj
fat, plump, stout, massive, huge, chunky, obese, ample, hefty, bulky, outsize, podgy, portly, pot-bellied, fleshy, heavy, tubby, chubby, buxom, voluptuous
FORMAL corpulent
COLLOQ. flabby, gross, well-padded, well-upholstered
E3 underweight, thin, skinny, emaciated

overwhelm v
1 OVERCOME, overpower, overthrow, destroy, defeat, beat, trounce, worst, best, subdue, oppress, overbear, quash, quell, prevail, get the better of, be victorious over, outplay, outwit, outsmart, be more than a match for, have the edge on, crush, rout, devastate
FORMAL vanquish, subjugate
COLLOQ. hammer, slaughter, clobber, lick, thrash, wipe the floor with
2 OVERRUN, deluge, inundate, bury, submerge, overburden, swamp, engulf
COLLOQ. snow under
3 CONFUSE, stagger, move, affect deeply/strongly, amaze, daze, touch
COLLOQ. bowl over, floor, kill, knock out, knock sideways, knock/hit for six

overwhelming adj
1 OVERPOWERING, powerful, strong, forceful, irresistible, undeniable, irrefutable, uncontrollable, compelling, extreme, oppressive, suffocating, stifling, unbearable, nauseating, sickening
2 an overwhelming majority
great, large, enormous, massive, vast, immense, huge, formidable
E3 1 resistible **2** insignificant, negligible

overwork v
overstrain, overload, exploit, exhaust, overuse, overtax, strain, wear out, oppress, burden, weary, work too hard, overdo it, do too much, overstretch yourself, strain yourself, overreach yourself, overexert yourself

COLLOQ. sweat blood, burn yourself out, bite off more than you can chew, run yourself into the ground, burn the candle at both ends, work your fingers to the bone, crack up

overworked adj
1 overworked employees
overstrained, exhausted, worn out, overtaxed
COLLOQ. stressed out
2 an overworked expression
hackneyed, trite, stereotyped, worn, tired, unoriginal, stale, played out, commonplace, bromidic, cliché(e)d, threadbare
FORMAL platitudinous
E3 fresh, original, new

overwrought adj
tense, on edge, distraught, agitated, worked up, wound up, nervous, highly, strung, frantic, overcharged, overexcited, excited, beside yourself
COLLOQ. edgy, uptight, nervy, keyed up
E3 calm

owe v
be in debt to, be overdrawn, get into debt, run up debts, be indebted to, be in arrears to, be under an obligation to
COLLOQ. be in the red, be up to your ears in debt

owing adj
unpaid, due, owed, in arrears, outstanding, payable, unsettled, overdue
■ **owing to**
because of, as a result of, on account of, thanks to, in consequence of, due to

own adj, v
♦ adj
personal, individual, private, particular, idiosyncratic
♦ v
possess, be the owner of, have, have got, have as your belongings/property, have in your possession, have (all) to yourself, monopolize, hold, retain, keep, enjoy, use, occupy
■ **own up**
admit, confess, tell the truth, acknowledge, plead guilty
COLLOQ. come clean, make a clean breast of it
■ **on your own**
alone, isolated, by yourself, singly, unaccompanied, unaided, unassisted, independently
COLLOQ. off your own bat, on your tod

owner n
possessor, holder, keeper, householder, homeowner, landlord, landlady, proprietor, proprietress, master, mistress, freeholder

ownership n
possession, proprietary rights, right of possession, proprietorship, rights, freehold, dominion
TECHNICAL title

ox n
bull, bullock, steer, buffalo, bison, yak
Related adjective: bovine

P

pace *n, v*

◆ *n*

1 STEP, stride, walk, gait, tread
2 SPEED, movement, motion, progress, rate, rate of progress, velocity, quickness, rapidity, swiftness, tempo, measure
FORMAL celerity

◆ *v*

step, stride, walk, walk up and down, march, tramp, pound, patrol, mark out, measure

pacific *adj*

peaceable, peaceful, peace-loving, mild, peacemaking, pacifist, appeasing, friendly, gentle, equable, placid, still, unruffled, quiet, serene, tranquil, smooth, calm, conciliatory, nonbelligerent, non-violent, diplomatic, dovelike, dovish
FORMAL irenic, complaisant, pacificatory, placatory, propitiatory, halcyon
Ⅎ belligerent, aggressive, contentious; *formal* pugnacious

pacification *n*

conciliation, soothing, calming, moderation, moderating, quietening (down), silencing
FORMAL appeasement, placating, propitiation

pacifism *n*

non-violence, pacificism, peacemaking, passive resistance, satyagraha

pacifist *n*

peacemaker, pacificist, peace-lover, conscientious objector, peace-monger, dove
COLLOQ. conchy
Ⅎ warmonger, hawk

pacify *v*

conciliate, mollify, calm, calm down, compose, soothe, assuage, allay, defuse, moderate, soften, lull, still, quiet, quieten, silence, quell, crush, put down, tame, subdue
FORMAL appease, placate, propitiate
Ⅎ anger

pack *n, v*

◆ *n*

1 PACKET, box, carton, container, parcel, package, blister card, bundle, truss, bale, burden, load
OLD fardel
2 BAG, backpack, rucksack, haversack, knapsack, kitbag
3 GROUP, company, set, troop, crew, herd, flock, drove, band, bunch, crowd, gang, mob, rout

◆ *v*

1 WRAP, wrap up, tie up, parcel, package, bundle, put in, cover, crate, stow, store, prepack
2 FILL, load, charge, cram, stuff, crowd, throng, mob, jam, press, squeeze, ram, wedge, compact, compress, crate, stow, tin, canister, canisterize
TECHNICAL steeve

■ **pack in**

1 CRAM IN, fill, load, charge, stuff, crowd, throng, mob, jam, press, squeeze, ram, wedge
2 STOP, end, give up, leave, resign
COLLOQ. throw in, jack in, chuck

■ **pack off**

send, dismiss, dispatch, bundle off

■ **pack up**

1 TIDY UP, tidy away, clear up, put things away, bundle, break camp
OLD empacket, truss
2 STOP, finish, end, give up
COLLOQ. throw in, jack in, wrap up, call it a day
3 BREAK DOWN, stop working, fail
FORMAL malfunction
COLLOQ. seize up, go phut, go kaput, crash; *N Am* go on the fritz
SLANG conk out

package *n, v*

◆ *n*

1 PARCEL, pack, packet, box, container, carton, bale, consignment
2 WHOLE, unit, group, collection, set, entity, lot, bundle, package deal

◆ *v*

parcel (up), wrap (up), pack (up), gift-wrap, box, batch

packaging *n*

container, box, packet, packing, wrapping(s), wrapper(s), presentation

packed *adj*

filled, full, crammed, jammed, crowded, congested, brimful, overflowing, overloaded
COLLOQ. jam-packed, chock-a-block, chocker, chockfull, packed like sardines
Ⅎ empty, deserted

packet *n*

1 PACK, carton, box, bag, package, parcel, case, container, sachet, wrapper, wrapping, envelope, packing, padded bag, padded envelope, Jiffy bag®
2 *cost a packet*
a lot, lots, fortune, small fortune, king's ransom
COLLOQ. mint, pile, pots, pretty penny, a bob or two, bomb, bundle, tidy sum
SLANG loadsamoney, megabucks

pact *n*

treaty, convention, covenant, bond, alliance, cartel, contract, deal, bargain, settlement, agreement, arrangement, entente, understanding
FORMAL compact, concordat
Ⅎ disagreement, quarrel

pad[1] *n, v*

◆ *n*

1 CUSHION, pillow, bolster, squab, wad, wadding, buffer, padding, pack, stuffing, compress, dressing, protection
2 WRITING PAD, notepad, jotter, notebook, block
COLLOQ. memo pad
3 *an animal's pad*
foot, paw, sole, print, footprint
4 HOME, place, room, rooms, quarters, penthouse, flat, apartment
COLLOQ. hang-out

◆ *v*

fill, stuff, wad, pack, wrap, line, cushion, protect

■ **pad out**

expand, inflate, fill out, amplify, elaborate, increase, flesh

out, lengthen, stretch, spin out
FORMAL augment, protract

pad² *v*
to pad softly
walk, move, step, run, tread, trudge, tramp, tiptoe, lope

padding *n*
1 FILLING, stuffing, wadding, packing, cushioning, lining, protection
2 VERBOSITY, verboseness, wordiness, bombast, hot air
FORMAL verbiage, prolixity
COLLOQ. waffle

paddle¹ *n, v*
♦ *n*
the paddles of a canoe
oar, scull, sweep
♦ *v*
row, oar, scull, propel, pull, punt, steer, canoe

paddle² *v*
children paddling in the water
wade, splash, slop, dabble, plunge

paddock *n*
enclosure, field, pen, fold, yard, pound, compound, stockade, corral

paddy *n*
rage, tiff, temper, tantrum, fit of temper, fury, passion, taking, pet, bate
COLLOQ. strop

padlock *n, v*
♦ *n*
lock, mortise lock, spring lock, fastening, bolt, clasp, catch
♦ *v*
lock, fasten, secure, bolt, latch, bar, seal, shut

padre *n*
chaplain, minister, priest, pastor, vicar, cleric, curate, reverend, father, parson, rector, deacon, deaconess, clergyman, churchman

paean *n*
eulogy, song of praise, ode to joy, hymn, doxology, anthem, psalm, ovation
FORMAL dithyramb, encomium, panegyric
Ea denunciation, satire

pagan *n, adj*
♦ *n*
heathen, atheist, unbeliever, nonbeliever, infidel, idolater
TECHNICAL Gentile
OLD paynim
FORMAL nullifidian
Ea believer
♦ *adj*
heathen, irreligious, atheistic, godless, ungodly, infidel, idolatrous, pantheistic
FORMAL nullifidian

page¹ *n*
1 ***write on a new page***
leaf, sheet, folio, side, recto, verso
2 ***start a new page of your life***
episode, incident, event, period, stage, chapter, phase, era, epoch

page² *n, v*
♦ *n*
a page at a wedding
pageboy, attendant, servant, messenger, bellboy, footman; *N Am* bellhop
♦ *v*
call, ask for, send for, summon, bid, announce

pageant *n*
procession, parade, show, display, tableau, scene, play,

representation, cavalcade, spectacle, extravaganza, triumph
OLD antic

pageantry *n*
pomp, ceremony, grandeur, magnificence, splendour, glamour, glitter, flourish, spectacle, parade, display, show, showiness, extravagance, theatricality, drama, melodrama

pageboy *n*
page, attendant, servant, messenger, bellboy, footman; *N Am* bellhop

paid-up *adj*
committed, active, dedicated, devoted, loyal, involved, enthusiastic, zealous, fervent, red-hot, evangelical
COLLOQ. card-carrying
Ea apathetic, uncommitted

pail *n*
bucket, can, tub, bail, scuttle, pitcher, vessel, churn, piggin

pain *n, v*
♦ *n*
1 HURT, ache, throb, cramp, stitch, spasm, twinge, pang, stab, sting, smart, smarting, soreness, irritation, aching, throbbing, tenderness, discomfort, distress, suffering, trouble, anguish, agony, torment, torture
OLD teen
FORMAL affliction
2 ANGUISH, grief, sorrow, agony, anxiety, desolation, distress, suffering, torment, torture, heartache, heartbreak, broken-heartedness, misery, pang, rack, woe, wretchedness
FORMAL tribulation
3 NUISANCE, bother, pest, annoyance, vexation, burden
COLLOQ. bore, drag, headache, pain in the neck/backside
SLANG pain in the arse, bummer
♦ *v*
1 HURT, ache, be sore, sting, smart, irritate, be tender
2 AFFLICT, torment, torture, agonize, distress, worry, trouble, upset, make miserable, make anxious, sadden, grieve
Ea **2** please, delight, gratify

Synonym nuances
noun sense 1
Hurt can be used to suggest any painful feeling, but more usually an emotional one, while **ache** is likely to imply one that is continuous. **Throb** is also suggestive of the form pain takes, in this instance occurring in waves, whereas **cramp** suggests muscular contractions.
 Spasm implies a sudden convulsive movement, unlike **twinge** which is a shorter, shooting pain. **Pang** and **stab** on the other hand, though similarly short and sharp, suggest a more violent pain. The terms **sting**, **smart** and **smarting** would be used of a tingling or nipping pain. **Irritation** suggests a reaction, and **tenderness** suggests something painful to the touch, but neither suggest an extreme pain.
 While you could also use **discomfort** to suggest minor degrees of pain, **distress**, **suffering** and **anguish** would suggest a more extreme experience. **Agony** is similar, but tends to be used of more concentrated pain. Both **torment** and **torture** are best reserved to refer to enduring extreme physical or mental pain.

---

pained *adj*
hurt, injured, wounded, stung, offended, aggrieved, reproachful, distressed, upset, worried, unhappy, sad, saddened, grieved, piqued, vexed
Ea pleased, gratified

painful *adj*
1 SORE, tender, hurting, irritating, inflamed, aching, throbbing, smarting, stabbing, agonizing, excruciating

OLD baleful, poignant, pungent; (*Shakesp*) panging
2 *a painful experience*
unpleasant, disagreeable, distressing, upsetting, bad, bitter, saddening, wretched, miserable, agonizing, disturbing, harrowing, traumatic, grievous
OLD baleful, poignant, pungent
FORMAL disquieting
COLLOQ. tortured
3 EMBARRASSING, awkward, touchy, uncomfortable, disconcerting, distressing, upsetting, sensitive, mortifying, humiliating, shameful, shaming, guilty
FORMAL discomfiting
4 HARD, difficult, tough, trying, exacting, laborious, tedious, arduous, rigorous, strenuous
E3 1 painless, soothing **2** pleasant, agreeable **4** easy, simple

painfully *adv*
distressingly, dreadfully, terribly, excessively, clearly, markedly, alarmingly, pitiably, pitifully, sadly, unfortunately, wretchedly, agonizingly, excruciatingly, woefully, deplorably

painkiller *n*
analgesic, anodyne, anaesthetic, palliative, sedative, drug, remedy, lenitive

painless *adj*
pain-free, trouble-free, comfortable, effortless, easy, simple, undemanding
COLLOQ. cushy, a piece of cake, child's play, like falling off a log, plain sailing
E3 painful, difficult

painlessly *adv*
effortlessly, simply, easily, undemandingly, comfortably
E3 painfully

pains *n*
trouble, bother, effort, labour, care, diligence, assiduousness
▪ **be at pains**
be anxious, be concerned, make every effort, try hard, put yourself out, take care, bother, go to great lengths

painstaking *adj*
careful, meticulous, scrupulous, thorough, conscientious, attentive, diligent, assiduous, industrious, hardworking, dedicated, devoted, persevering, searching
FORMAL punctilious, sedulous
E3 careless, negligent

paint *n, v*
◆ *n*
colour, colouring, pigment, colorant, vinyl wash, dye, tint, stain
◆ *v*
1 COLOUR, dye, tint, stain, lacquer, varnish, glaze, apply, daub, wash, whitewash, coat, plaster, smear, cover, spray, respray, decorate, redecorate
2 PORTRAY, depict, tell, describe, narrate, draw, sketch, picture, evoke, represent
FORMAL recount, delineate
▪ **paint the town red**
celebrate, have/throw a party, rejoice, enjoy yourself, have fun, go out
COLLOQ. rave, binge, have a ball, live it up, whoop it up, go out on the town, go on the razzle, have a night on the tiles, push the boat out, kill the fatted calf, put the flags out

---

Paints include:

acrylic paint	gloss paint	poster paint
colourwash	gouache	primer
distemper	lacquer	stencil paint
eggshell	masonry paint	undercoat
emulsion	matt paint	varnish
enamel	oil paint	watercolour
fabric paint	oils	whitewash
glaze	pastel	

painter *n*
artist, colourist, oil painter, watercolourist, miniaturist, dauber, limner, depicter
FORMAL delineator

painting *n*
oil painting, oil, watercolour, picture, portrait, landscape, portrayal, representation, likeness, still life, miniature, illustration, fresco, mural
FORMAL delineation
Related adjective: pictorial

Painting terms include:

abstract	frottage	pigment
alla prima	gallery	pochade box
aquarelle	genre painting	pointillism
aquatint	gesso	portrait
art gallery	gouache	primer
bleeding	grisaille	round brush
bloom	grotesque	sable brush
brush	hair-pencil	scumble
brush strokes	hard edge	seascape
canvas	icon	secco
canvas board	illustration	sfumato
capriccio	impasto	sgraffito
cartoon	landscape	silhouette
charcoal	maulstick (or	sketch
chiaroscuro	mahlstick)	skyscape
collage	miniature	still life
composition	monochrome	stipple
craquelure	montage	tempera
diptych	mural	thinners
drawing	oil painting	tint
easel	paint	tondo
encaustic	palette	tone
facture	palette knife	triptych
fête champêtre	pastels	trompe l'oeil
fête galante	pastoral	turpentine
figurative	paysage	underpainting
filbert brush	pencil sketch	vignette
flat brush	pentimento	wash
foreshortening	perspective	watercolour
fresco	picture	
frieze	pieta	

See also **art**; **paint**; **picture**.

---

pair *n, v*
◆ *n*
couple, couplet, brace, two, twosome, duo, twins, two of a kind, set
◆ *v*
match (up), twin, team (up), mate, marry, wed, unite, splice, join (up), couple, link (up), bracket, put together, arrange in pairs
E3 separate, part

paired *adj*
coupled, joined, linked, matched, double, twinned, in twos, yoked, mated, associated, bracketed
E3 single

pal *n, v*
◆ *n*
friend, comrade, companion, partner, confidant(e), intimate, soul mate
COLLOQ. buddy, chum, crony, mate, sidekick; *Aust & NZ* cobber
E3 enemy, opponent
▪ **pal up**
get together, become friends, make friends, join up
COLLOQ. gang up, chum up

palace *n*
castle, château, *schloss*, mansion, stately home, basilica, dome, court, Savoy, *hôtel*, *alcázar*, Alhambra, *palazzo*, seraglio
Related adjectives: palatial, palatine

palatable _adj_

1 TASTY, appetizing, eatable, edible, flavoursome, flavorous, succulent, mouthwatering, delicious, savoury
FORMAL delectable
COLLOQ. yummy, mor(e)ish, scrumptious, scrummy, delish, done to a turn
2 ACCEPTABLE, satisfactory, pleasant, pleasing, nice, agreeable, enjoyable, attractive
F3 1 unpalatable **2** unacceptable, unpleasant, disagreeable

palate _n_

taste, sense of taste, taste buds, appreciation, liking, relish, gout, enjoyment, enthusiasm, appetite, stomach, heart

palatial _adj_

grand, magnificent, splendid, majestic, regal, stately, grandiose, imposing, luxurious, de luxe, sumptuous, opulent, spacious
COLLOQ. plush, posh, ritzy

palaver _n_

fuss, bother, fuss about nothing, rigmarole, procedure, carry-on, activity, business, bustle, commotion, fluster
COLLOQ. song and dance, kerfuffle, hoo-ha, to-do, flap

pale[1] _adj, v_

◆ _adj_
1 PALLID, livid, ashen, ashy, white, whitish, colourless, chalky, pasty, pasty-faced, waxen, waxy, wan, peaky, sallow, anaemic, drained, lurid, complexionless, whey-faced, bloodless; _Scot_ peelie-wally
OLD pallescent; (_Shakesp_) maid-pale
COLLOQ. washed out
2 _pale blue_
light, pastel, lily, faded, bleached, colourless, insipid, vapid, weak, muted, feeble, thin, faint, dim, restrained, low-key, delicate
TECHNICAL etiolated, high-key
COLLOQ. washed-out
F3 1 ruddy, florid **2** dark, strong, intense
◆ _v_
1 WHITEN, blanch, bleach, fade, dim, grow white, grow pale, change colour
TECHNICAL etiolate
OLD appal, blank, pall
2 _pale into insignificance_
fade, dim, lessen, diminish, melt, dwindle
OLD stain
F3 1 colour, blush

Synonym nuances

adjective sense 1
Pallid can be used to suggest weakness of colour or, sometimes, a lack of vigour: _his pallid cheeks; their pallid apathy._ **Livid** occasionally refers to an extreme lack of colour: _his scar became a livid white;_ **lurid** is similar, though this usage is not common.

Ashen and **ashy** are more suggestive of being tinged with grey, and have overtones of unhealthiness. **Whey-faced** is a similar, if more poetic, way of conveying paleness. **Chalky** suggests not only paleness but also a powdery texture; **pasty** and **pasty-faced** suggest an unhealthy sheen, but with a more derogatory tone: _the pasty complexion of a kid raised in institutions._ Similarly, **waxen** and **waxy** connote an unnatural, deathly lustre. **Wan** returns to the idea of a lack of colour, while **peaky** suggests an aura of sickliness: _he looked a bit peaky and green around the gills._

The term **sallow** is often used to suggest a yellowy complexion, while **anaemic, bloodless**, the uncommon **complexionless** and **drained** more straightforwardly refer to lack of blood: _thin bloodless lips._

---

pale[2] _n_

the pales of the fence
post, pole, stake, fence, column, shaft, upright

■ **beyond the pale**
unacceptable, intolerable, unreasonable, improper, unsuitable, inappropriate, inadmissible
FORMAL unseemly

paleness _n_

pallor, pale, whiteness, colourlessness, pastiness, wanness, sallowness, anaemia
OLD pallescence
F3 ruddiness

palisade _n_

fence, paling, defence, enclosure, barricade, bulwark, fortification, stockade

pall[1] _n_

a pall over a coffin; a pall of smoke
shroud, veil, mantle, cloak, cloud, shadow, gloom, damper
■ **cast a pall over**
spoil, mar, upset, impair, harm, ruin, destroy, wreck

pall[2] _v_

interest began to pall
wear off, tire, weary, become tired, become bored, lose its attraction, jade, sate, satiate, cloy, sicken

palliate _v_

ease, diminish, moderate, mollify, relieve, soften, soothe, temper, lessen, lighten, allay, alleviate, excuse, minimize, mitigate, cover, conceal, cloak
FORMAL abate, assuage, extenuate, lenify

palliative _adj, n_

◆ _adj_
sedative, soothing, mollifying, alleviative, calming, lenitive, calmative, anodyne
TECHNICAL demulcent, paregoric
FORMAL mitigative, mitigatory, assuasive
F3 irritant
◆ _n_
analgesic, anodyne, painkiller, sedative, tranquillizer, calmative, lenitive
TECHNICAL demulcent, paregoric

pallid _adj_

1 PALE, pasty, whitish, sallow, colourless, pasty-faced, ashen, ashy, bloodless, anaemic, wan, waxen, waxy, whey-faced, lurid, complexionless, bloodless; _Scot_ peelie-wally
TECHNICAL etiolated
OLD pallescent
2 UNEXCITING, weak, dull, boring, uninteresting, bland, uninspired, tame, sterile, tired, lifeless, insipid, spiritless, vapid
F3 1 vigorous, ruddy, high-complexioned **2** lively, exciting

pallor _n_

paleness, whiteness, pallidness, wanness, sallowness, bloodlessness, anaemia, chalkiness
TECHNICAL etiolation
OLD pallescence
F3 ruddiness

pally _adj_

friendly, close, affectionate, familiar, intimate, warm
COLLOQ. chummy, thick, tight, folksy
F3 unfriendly

palm _n, v_

◆ _n_
hand
TECHNICAL thenar
COLLOQ. paw
SLANG mitt
Related adjectives: palmar, volar
◆ _v_
take, grab, snatch, appropriate
■ **palm off**
foist, impose, fob off, thrust, offload, unload, pass off, get rid of

■ **have someone in the palm of your hand**
have power/control/authority over, have someone at your mercy
COLLOQ. have someone in your clutches, have someone eating out of your hand, be able to twist someone round your little finger

palmist *n*
fortune-teller, clairvoyant, palm reader

palmistry *n*
fortune-telling, clairvoyancy, palm reading, chirognomy, chiromancy

palmy *adj*
carefree, thriving, prosperous, flourishing, successful, fortunate, happy, glorious, triumphant, joyous, luxurious, golden
FORMAL halcyon

palpable *adj*
1 SOLID, substantial, material, concrete, real, touchable, tangible
2 OBVIOUS, visible, apparent, clear, plain, evident, patent, manifest, conspicuous, glaring, blatant, unmistak(e)able, staring you in the face
COLLOQ. plain as a pikestaff
E3 1 intangible, insubstantial **2** impalpable, imperceptible, elusive

palpably *adv*
obviously, clearly, apparently, visibly, plainly, evidently, patently, manifestly, conspicuously, blatantly, glaringly, unmistak(e)ably
E3 imperceptibly

palpitate *v*
flutter, quiver, tremble, shiver, vibrate, quake, shake, beat, pulse, pulsate, pound, thump, thud, throb

palpitation *n*
pounding, vibration, trembling, shaking, shake(s), flutter(ing), quiver(ing), throbbing, throb

paltry *adj*
meagre, miserly, derisory, contemptible, mean, low, miserable, wretched, poor, sorry, small, slight, trifling, inconsiderable, negligible, trivial, minor, contemptible, petty, unimportant, insignificant, puny, worthless
COLLOQ. measly, piddling
E3 substantial, significant, valuable

pamper *v*
spoil, cosset, coddle, mollycoddle, baby, featherbed, humour, gratify, indulge, overindulge, pander, pet, fondle, cocker; *dialect* cosher; *Scot* cuiter
OLD pompey
COLLOQ. spoon-feed, wait on someone hand and foot
E3 neglect, ill-treat

pampered *adj*
spoilt, cosseted, coddled, mollycoddled, indulged, overfed, high-fed, petted
COLLOQ. spoon-fed
E3 abused, neglected

pamphlet *n*
leaflet, brochure, booklet, folder, circular, handout, flyer, notice

pan¹ *n, v*
♦ *n*
1 *pots and pans*
saucepan, frying-pan, fryer, pot, skillet, casserole, wok, container, vessel, pancheon
2 *a salt pan*
hollow, basin, bowl, hole, pit, well, cavity, crater, excavation, cavern, cave, depression, channel
FORMAL concavity
♦ *v*

criticize, censure, flay, slate, find fault with, hammer
COLLOQ. knock, pull to pieces, roast, rubbish, slam
SLANG slag (off)
E3 praise
■ **pan out**
work out, turn out, result, happen, yield, culminate, come to an end, be exhausted
FORMAL eventuate

pan² *v*
pan the camera
sweep, scan, move, turn, follow, track, swing, circle
FORMAL traverse

panacea *n*
cure-all, universal remedy, elixir, nostrum
FORMAL catholicon, diacatholicon, panpharmacon

panache *n*
flourish, flamboyance, ostentation, style, flair, élan, dash, spirit, enthusiasm, zest, brio, energy, vigour, verve

pancake *n*
crêpe, waffle, wafer, blini, griddle-cake, tortilla, taco, crumpet, omelette, spring roll, blintz, latke, drop scone, froise, fraise; *Scot* bannock; *N Am* battercake, flapjack
OLD flawn, flaune, flam

pandemic *adj*
widespread, extensive, general, common, prevalent, far-reaching, rife, pervasive, universal, global

pandemonium *n*
chaos, disorder, confusion, commotion, rumpus, turmoil, turbulence, tumult, uproar, din, bedlam, hubbub, hullaballoo, hue and cry
COLLOQ. to-do, shemozzle, all hell breaking loose
E3 order, calm, peace

pander *v*
■ **pander to**
humour, indulge, pamper, please, gratify, satisfy, fulfil, provide, cater to

pane *n*
window, windowpane, glass

panegyric *n, adj*
♦ *n*
eulogy, praise, speech of praise, tribute, commendation, homage, accolade, citation
FORMAL paean, encomium, eulogium
E3 censure, criticism
♦ *adj*
eulogistic, favourable, flattering, glowing, praiseful, praising, complimentary, commendatory
FORMAL encomiastic, laudatory, panegyrical
E3 censorious, critical, damning

panel *n*
1 *a wooden panel*
board, sheet, table, tablet, sign, slab, plank, beam, timber, cartouche, pane, plate, faceplate, headboard, valance
2 *a panel of judges*
board, committee, council, jury, team, commission, directorate, trustees, advisory group, focus group
3 *a control panel*
board, console, unit, dashboard, instrument panel, instruments, controls, switches, knobs, dials, buttons, levers, patchboard

panelling *n*
panelwork, wainscot, wainscot(t)ing, dado, coffer, lacunar

pang *n*
pain, ache, twinge, stab, sting, prick, stitch, gripe, spasm, throe, misgiving, scruple, qualm, agony, anguish, uneasiness, discomfort, distress

panic *n, v*
♦ *n*

agitation, alarm, dismay, fright, fear, scare, horror, terror, frenzy, hysteria, *sauve qui peut*
OLD amaze, amazedness
FORMAL consternation, disquiet, trepidation, perturbation
COLLOQ. flap, funk, flat spin, tailspin
E3 calmness, confidence
♦ *v*
lose your nerve, lose your head, overreact, unnerve
COLLOQ. flap, go to pieces, lose your cool, have kittens, get the jitters, get the shakes, get the willies, got into a flat spin, lose your bottle, feel your hair stand on end, run round like a headless chicken
E3 relax

panic-stricken *adj*
alarmed, frightened, horrified, terrified, terror-stricken, petrified, scared, scared stiff, aghast, in a cold sweat, panicky, frantic, frenzied, hysterical
FORMAL perturbed
COLLOQ. in a tizzy, in a blue funk, in a flat spin
E3 relaxed, confident

panoply *n*
array, range, equipment, show, regalia, insignia, armour, dress, raiment, trappings
FORMAL attire
COLLOQ. garb, gear, get-up, turn-out

panorama *n*
view, wide-broad view, bird's-eye view, vista, prospect, scenery, landscape, scene, spectacle, perspective, overview, survey, cyclorama

panoramic *adj*
scenic, wide, broad, sweeping, extensive, far-reaching, wide-ranging, widespread, overall, comprehensive, general, universal
E3 narrow, restricted, limited

pant *v, n*
♦ *v*
1 PUFF, blow, gasp, wheeze, breathe, sigh, heave, throb, palpitate
COLLOQ. huff and puff
2 LONG, pine, desire, want, yearn, covet, crave, hanker, sigh, ache, thirst
COLLOQ. yen
♦ *n*
gasp, puff, huff, throb, wheeze

panting *adj*
1 PUFFED OUT, breathless, out of breath, gasping, short-winded, winded, puffing, puffed
2 ANXIOUS, eager, impatient, longing, craving, hankering

pantomime *n*
show, charade, farce, commedia dell'arte, harlequinade, masque
COLLOQ. panto

pantry *n*
larder, storeroom, scullery

pants *n*
1 UNDERPANTS, drawers, panties, briefs, knickers, camiknickers, teddy, panty girdle, Y-fronts, boxer shorts, trunks, shorts
COLLOQ. undies, smalls, frillies
2 TROUSERS, slacks, jeans

pap *n*
1 MUSH, pulp, purée, soft food, semi-liquid food
COLLOQ. goo
2 RUBBISH, drivel, trash, nonsense, drivel, twaddle, gibberish
COLLOQ. poppycock, hot air, rot, claptrap
SLANG crap

paper *n, v*
♦ *n*

1 NEWSPAPER, daily, broadsheet, tabloid, magazine, periodical, weekly, journal, organ
COLLOQ. rag
2 *a paper on alternative medicine*
essay, composition, dissertation, thesis, treatise, article, study, report, work, examination, analysis
FORMAL monograph
▪ **paper over**
hide, conceal, cover up, obscure, put out of sight, disguise, camouflage
▪ **on paper**
1 IN WRITING, written down, officially, on the record, recorded, in black and white
2 IN THEORY, hypothetically, ideally, theoretically, supposedly, seemingly, in your mind's eye
Related adjective: papyraceous

Types of paper include:

acid-free paper	greaseproof	silver paper
art paper	paper	sugar paper
bank	handmade paper	tissue paper
blotting paper	manila	toilet paper
bond	notepaper	tracing paper
carbon paper	papyrus	vellum
card	parchment	wallpaper
cardboard	pasteboard	wrapping paper
cartridge paper	rag paper	writing-paper
crêpe paper	recycled paper	
graph paper	rice paper	

Paper sizes include:

A3	atlas	*N Am* legal
A4	crown	letter
A5	foolscap	quarto

papers *n*
documentation, document, records, certificates, evidence, qualifications, driving licence, birth certificate, marriage certificate, deeds, credentials, authorization, identification, identity card, ID, passport; *S Afr* passbook

papery *adj*
thin, paper-thin, light, lightweight, delicate, insubstantial, flimsy, fragile, frail, translucent

par *n*
level, standard, norm, usual, correspondence, similarity, equivalence, equal footing, equality, balance, equilibrium, accordance, average, mean
TECHNICAL median
FORMAL parity
▪ **below par**
1 UNSATISFACTORY, inadequate, inferior, below average, not up to par
COLLOQ. not up to scratch
2 UNWELL, under par, tired, rough, out of sorts
COLLOQ. lousy, under the weather
▪ **on a par with**
equal to, equivalent to, as good as, the same standard as
▪ **par for the course**
typical, normal, standard, usual, predictable, only to be expected
▪ **up to par**
satisfactory, adequate, acceptable, fine
COLLOQ. OK, up to scratch

parable *n*
fable, allegory, lesson, moral tale, story, story with a moral

parade *n, v*
♦ *n*
1 PROCESSION, cavalcade, motorcade, march, column, file, train, line-up, progression, review, ceremony, stand-to
OLD decursion

2 SPECTACLE, pageant, show, display, demonstration, exhibition
FORMAL array
• *v*
1 MARCH, process, file past
2 SHOW, display, exhibit, show off, vaunt, flaunt, brandish, prance

paradigm *n*
pattern, model, example, original, ideal, framework, prototype
FORMAL archetype, exemplar

paradise *n*
1 HEAVEN, home of God, bliss, next world, hereafter, life to come, afterlife, utopia, Elysium, Elysian Fields, happy hunting ground, Shangri-La, Eden, Garden of Eden, Swarga
2 ECSTASY, rapture, bliss, happiness, complete happiness, joy, delight, transports of delight
FORMAL felicity
COLLOQ. seventh heaven, cloud nine
E3 1 hell, Hades

paradox *n*
contradiction, inconsistency, absurdity, oddity, mystery, enigma, riddle, puzzle
FORMAL incongruity, anomaly

paradoxical *adj*
self-contradictory, contradictory, conflicting, inconsistent, absurd, illogical, improbable, impossible, mysterious, enigmatic, puzzling, baffling
FORMAL incongruous, anomalous

paragon *n*
ideal, epitome, model, pattern, perfect example, crème de la crème, masterpiece, prototype, standard, criterion
FORMAL exemplar, quintessence, archetype, nonpareil
COLLOQ. the bee's knees

paragraph *n*
passage, section, part, portion, segment, subsection, subdivision, article, piece, clause, item

parallel *adj, n, v*
• *adj*
1 ALIGNED, equidistant, alongside, side by side, coextensive, collateral
2 SIMILAR, like, matching, resembling, equivalent, comparable, uniform, corresponding, co-existing
FORMAL analogous, homologous
E3 2 divergent, different
• *n*
1 MATCH, equal, twin, duplicate, equivalent, counterpart
FORMAL analogue
2 SIMILARITY, resemblance, likeness, correspondence, equivalence, analogy, comparison
FORMAL correlation
• *v*
match, echo, be similar to, resemble, be like, be equivalent, equal, conform, agree, correspond, compare, liken
FORMAL be analogous, correlate
E3 diverge, differ

paralyse *v*
1 *paralysed his leg*
cripple, lame, disable, incapacitate, debilitate, immobilize, palsy, anaesthetize, numb, dull, deaden, freeze, shock, terrify, transfix, torpefy; *dialect* scram
OLD benumb
2 *paralyse the transport system*
bring to a standstill, immobilize, cripple, halt, stop, disable, deactivate

paralysed *adj*
paralytic, paraplegic, quadriplegic, crippled, lame,

disabled, incapacitated, immobilized, numb
E3 able-bodied

paralysis *n*
1 *paralysis in the legs*
paraplegia, quadriplegia, palsy, numbness, deadness, immobility, powerlessness, debilitation
TECHNICAL paresis
2 *paralysis of the transport system*
standstill, halt, stoppage, shutdown, breakdown, immobility

paralytic *adj*
1 CRIPPLED, disabled, paralysed, incapacitated, lame, immobilized, immobile, numb, palsied, quadriplegic, monoplegic, hemiplegic
2 DRUNK, inebriated, intoxicated, incapable
COLLOQ. a sheet in the wind, three sheets in/to the wind, legless, plastered, pie-eyed, blotto, sloshed, soused, sozzled, stewed
SLANG wasted, wrecked, stoned, pissed, canned, smashed; (*vulgar*) arseholed, rat-arsed, shitfaced
E3 2 (stone-cold) sober

parameter *n*
variable, guideline, indication, criterion, specification, factor, limiting factor, limitation, restriction, framework, limit, boundary

paramount *adj*
supreme, highest, topmost, predominant, pre-eminent, prime, principal, main, chief, outstanding, cardinal, primary, first, foremost, first and foremost, most important, of greatest importance
E3 lowest, last

paramour *n*
lover, beloved, beau, courtesan, mistress, woman, kept woman, inamorato, inamorata, concubine, hetaera
COLLOQ. fancy man, fancy woman, bit on the side, bit of fluff

paranoia *n*
obsession, delusions, psychosis, megalomania, monomania, persecution complex

paranoid *adj*
suspicious, distrustful, bewildered, confused, afraid, fearful, fazed

paranormal *adj*
supernatural, unnatural, abnormal, otherworldly, metaphysical, spiritual, psychic, mystic, mystical, occult, hidden, mysterious, miraculous, magical, magic, phantom, ghostly, eerie, weird
FORMAL preternatural
E3 natural, normal

parapet *n*
1 WALL, railing, fence, rail, paling, balustrade, barrier
2 EMBANKMENT, defence, guard, battlement, bulwark, fortification, rampart, barricade, barbican, bastion

paraphernalia *n*
equipment, gear, tackle, apparatus, tools, implements, materials, accessories, trappings, belongings, possessions, stuff, things, baggage
FORMAL effects, accoutrements
COLLOQ. gear, bits and pieces, odds and ends

paraphrase *v, n*
• *v*
reword, rephrase, restate, put in other words, express differently, interpret, render, translate, gloss
COLLOQ. rehash
• *n*
rewording, rephrasing, restatement, different expression, other form of words, version, interpretation, rendering, translation, gloss

parasite *n*

1 LEECH, bloodsucker
TECHNICAL endophyte, entozoon, endozoon, epiphyte, epizoon, epizoan
2 *parasites in society*
hanger-on, passenger, leech, drone, bloodsucker
COLLOQ. sponger, scrounger, cadger, freeloader, ligger, bum, moocher

parasitic *adj*

1 *parasitic animals*
parasitical, biogenous, leechlike
TECHNICAL epizoan, epizoic
2 *a parasitic person*
bloodsucking, freeloading
COLLOQ. cadging, scrounging, sponging

parasol *n*

sunshade, shade, umbrella, shelter, protection, shield, veil

parcel *n, v*

♦ *n*
1 PACKAGE, packet, pack, box, carton, bundle, *dak*
2 *a parcel of land*
plot, patch, area, piece, portion, lot, allotment, tract
3 GROUP, company, troop, herd, flock, band, crowd, gang, mob, crew, bunch, collection
OLD sort
4 LOT, deal, transaction, package, pack, collection
♦ *v*
package, pack (up), wrap (up), gift-wrap, bundle (up), make up, put up, tie up

■ **parcel out**
divide (out), carve up, apportion, allocate, allot, share out, distribute, hand out, dispense, dole out, deal out, mete out
COLLOQ. whack

parch *v*

dry (up), dehydrate, bake, burn, scorch, sear, blister, wither, shrivel
FORMAL desiccate

parched *adj*

1 ARID, waterless, dry, dried up, dehydrated, baked, burned, seared, blistered, scorched, withered, shrivelled
FORMAL desiccated, sear, sere
COLLOQ. dry as a bone
2 THIRSTY, dry, dehydrated
COLLOQ. gasping

parchment *n*

scroll, vellum, document, certificate, charter, diploma, palimpsest
Related adjective: pergameneous

pardon *v, n, interj*

♦ *v*
forgive, condone, overlook, excuse, absolve, let off, reprieve, free, liberate, release
FORMAL vindicate, acquit, remit, exonerate, exculpate
COLLOQ. let off the hook
E3 punish, discipline
♦ *n*
forgiveness, mercy, clemency, indulgence, forbearance, lenience, amnesty, excuse, absolution, reprieve, release, discharge, act of grace
OLD grace, oblivion
FORMAL acquittal, condonation, exoneration, exculpation, remission
E3 punishment, condemnation
♦ *interj*
sorry, I beg your pardon, what did you say?, excuse me, *bitte*
OLD cry you mercy
COLLOQ. come again?, say again?, you what?, what?, eh?

Synonym nuances

verb

Forgive can be used to suggest a charitable readiness to forget about someone's misdeeds, while **condone** implies an element of acceptance: *society by its silence is condoning racism*. **Overlook** is appropriate for letting someone's misdemeanours go unpunished, and **excuse** further suggests making allowances for them. **Absolve** goes further with its suggestion of completely discharging from blame, whereas **let off** has more to do with allowing someone to get away with something, for which they were responsible. **Reprieve**, on the other hand, is more suggestive of overturning the proposed punishment or fate: *many rail projects facing the axe have been reprieved.*

   Free and **liberate** suggest the removal of restraints or confinement, literally or figuratively: *Paris has been liberated by the Allies; his new direction liberated his art*. **Release** has narrower associations of setting someone free from imprisonment.

pardonable *adj*

forgivable, excusable, justifiable, warrantable, understandable, allowable, permissible, slight, minor, venial, condonable
E3 inexcusable

pare *v*

peel, skin, shear, clip, trim, crop, cut, dock, lop, prune, cut back, whittle, reduce, decrease

parent *n, v*

♦ *n*
1 *a single parent*
father, mother, biological/birth parent, bioparent, single parent, guardian, step-parent, adoptive parent, foster parent, custodial parent, dam, sire; *Aust & NZ* solo parent
OLD begetter, generant, genitor
FORMAL progenitor, procreator
COLLOQ. folks, dad, daddy, pop, pa, papa, old man, mum, mummy, ma, mam, mumsy, mamma, old woman, empty-nester; *N Am* mom, mommy
2 SOURCE, origin, root, cause, creator, originator, author, architect, prototype, forerunner
OLD begetter
♦ *v*
be the father/mother of, bring into the world, create, look after, take care of, nurture, bring up, raise, foster, educate, teach, train
OLD beget
FORMAL rear, procreate
Related adjective: parental

parentage *n*

family, birth, origin(s), source, stock, extraction, filiation, affiliation, ancestry, lineage, derivation, descent, line, race, pedigree, paternity
FORMAL stirps

parenthetical *adj*

in parenthesis, incidental, as an aside, qualifying, explanatory, bracketed, inserted, extraneous
FORMAL elucidative, interposed, intervening
E3 basic, original

parenthetically *adv*

incidentally, by the way, secondarily, as a digression, as an aside
COLLOQ. btw

par excellence *adj*

first-class, first-rate, excellent, wonderful, brilliant, marvellous, fantastic, superior, high-quality, very good, prime, superlative, unequalled, unparalleled, matchless, rare, exceptional, outstanding, surpassing, remarkable, distinguished, great, eminent, flawless, faultless, perfect,

best, exemplary, select, superb, magnificent, shining, commendable, splendid, pre-eminent, praiseworthy, noteworthy, notable, noted, fine, A1
COLLOQ. top-notch, smashing, stunning, terrific, neat, ace, brill, out of this world, second to none, divine, heavenly, fabulous, sensational
SLANG wicked, cool, mean
F3 inferior, second-rate

pariah *n*
outcast, outlaw, exile, castaway, leper, undesirable, unperson, untouchable, *persona non grata*, Ishmael
COLLOQ. black sheep

paring *n*
peel, peeling, skin, shaving, shred, clipping, trimming, fragment, cutting, flake, rind, slice, sliver, snippet, flaught

parish *n*
1 DISTRICT, community, village, town
2 PARISHIONERS, church, churchgoers, congregation, community, flock, fold
Related adjective: parochial

parity *n*
equality, equivalence, parallelism, consistency, conformity, analogy, agreement, correspondence, similarity, resemblance, likeness, sameness, uniformity, unity, semblance, affinity, par
FORMAL congruence, congruity, consonance, similitude

park *n, v*
♦ *n*
grounds, woodland, grassland
♦ *v*
1 *park your car*
stop, pull up, draw up, leave
2 *park your bag down*
put, position, place, deposit, set, leave
COLLOQ. bung, plonk

Types of park include:

amusement park	municipal park	reserve
arboretum	national park	safari park
botanical garden	parkland	sanctuary
business park	play area	science park
caravan site/park	playground	theme park
estate	pleasance	wildlife park
fun park	pleasure garden	zoological
game reserve	pleasure ground	garden/park
industrial park	recreation ground	

---

parlance *n*
phraseology, language, talk, speech, tongue, idiom, jargon, diction, argot, cant
COLLOQ. lingo

parley *n, v*
♦ *n*
talk(s), negotiation, meeting, conference, council, deliberation, discussion, get-together, dialogue, tête-à-tête
FORMAL colloquy
COLLOQ. confab, powwow
♦ *v*
talk, speak, discuss, get together, negotiate, consult, deliberate
FORMAL confer
COLLOQ. powwow

parliament *n*
legislature, senate, congress, house, lower house, upper house, assembly, chamber, convocation, council, diet
See panel below

parliamentary *adj*
governmental, senatorial, congressional, legislative, lawmaking, lawgiving, elected, democratic, popular, representative, official, republican
FORMAL legislatorial

parlour *n*
sitting room, lounge, living room, front room, drawing room, morning room

parlous *adj*
dire, disastrous, dreadful, terrible, frightful, awful, appalling, calamitous, catastrophic, horrible, atrocious, shocking, alarming, distressing, desperate, grave

parochial *adj*
insular, provincial, parish-pump, small-town, petty, small-minded, narrow-minded, narrow, inward-looking, blinkered, limited, restricted, confined
COLLOQ. hick
F3 national, international

parochialism *n*
insularity, provincialism, small-mindedness, pettiness, narrow-mindedness, narrowness

parody *n, v*
♦ *n*
caricature, lampoon, burlesque, satire, pasquinade, skit, mimicry, imitation, travesty, distortion, corruption, misrepresentation, perversion
COLLOQ. send-up, spoof, take-off
♦ *v*
caricature, lampoon, burlesque, satirize, mimic, imitate, ape
COLLOQ. send up, spoof, take off

paroxysm *n*
fit, seizure, spasm, convulsion, attack, eruption, flare-up, outbreak, outburst, explosion

parrot *v, n*
♦ *v*
repeat, copy, imitate, mimic, echo, rehearse, reiterate, ape

Names of parliaments and political assemblies include:

House of Representatives & Senate (*Australia*)	National Assembly & Senate (*France*)	Staten-Generaal (*Netherlands*)	House of Assembly (*South Africa*)
Nationalrat & Bundesrat (*Austria*)	Bundesrat & Bundestag & Landtag (*Germany*)	House of Representatives (*New Zealand*)	Cortes (*Spain*)
Narodno Sobraniye (*Bulgaria*)	Althing (*Iceland*)	Northern Irish Assembly (*Northern Ireland*)	Riksdag (*Sweden*)
House of Commons & Senate (*Canada*)	Lok Sabha & Rajya Sabha (*India*)	Storting (*Norway*)	Nationalrat & Ständerat & Bundesrat (*Switzerland*)
National People's Congress (*China*)	Majlis (*Iran*)	Sejm (*Poland*)	Porte (*Turkey*)
Folketing (*Denmark*)	Dáil & Seanad (*Ireland*)	Cortes (*Portugal*)	House of Commons & House of Lords (*UK*)
People's Assembly (*Egypt*)	Knesset (*Israel*)	Congress of People's Deputies & Supreme Soviet (*Russia*)	House of Representatives & Senate (*USA*)
Eduskunta (*Finland*)	Camera del Deputati & Senato (*Italy*)	Scottish Parliament (*Scotland*)	National Assembly (*Vietnam*)
	Diet (*Japan*)		Welsh Assembly (*Wales*)

♦ *n*

mimic, repeater, imitator, copycat, phraser, ape
Related adjective: psittacine

parrot-fashion *adv*

by rote, mechanically, mindlessly, unthinkingly,
automatically

parry *v*

ward off, fend off, repel, repulse, rebuff, field, deflect, stave
off, block, avert, turn aside, avoid, evade, keep/hold at bay,
sidestep, steer clear of, shun
FORMAL circumvent
COLLOQ. duck, dodge, bodyswerve

parsimonious *adj*

mean, niggardly, miserly, stinting, sparing, scrimpy, saving,
close, cheeseparing, close-fisted, close-handed, frugal,
grasping
FORMAL penurious
COLLOQ. mingy, penny-pinching, stingy, tight, tight-
fisted
◼ generous, liberal, open-handed

parsimony *n*

meanness, miserliness, frugality, niggardliness
COLLOQ. minginess, penny-pinching, stinginess, tightness,
tight-fistedness
◼ generosity, liberality

parson *n*

vicar, rector, priest, minister, pastor, deacon, preacher,
clergyman, reverend, curate, cleric, churchman

part *n, v, adj*

♦ *n*

1 COMPONENT, constituent, module, element, factor,
ingredient, side, dimension, aspect, facet, piece, bit,
particle, fragment, slice, scrap, segment, fraction,
proportion, percentage, portion, extract, excerpt,
share, section, division, department, branch, sector,
wing
2 ROLE, character, portrayal, representation, persona
3 INVOLVEMENT, duty, job, work, charge, task, responsibility,
chore, office, function, capacity, participation
4 SECTION, chapter, volume, book, passage, scene,
episode, instalment
5 AREA, district, sector, region, neighbourhood, territory,
locality, quarter
6 *a person of many parts*
skill, gift, talent, ability, capability, attribute,
accomplishment, faculty, endowment, expertise, genius,
intellect, intelligence, calibre
◼ **1** whole, totality
♦ *v*

1 SEPARATE, detach, disconnect, sever, split, tear, break,
break up, take apart, dismantle, come apart, split up,
divide
FORMAL disjoin, cleave
2 PART COMPANY WITH, split up from, separate from, divorce
from, get divorced from, leave, withdraw from, go away
from, go your separate ways, depart from, take your leave,
say goodbye, get going
COLLOQ. push along/off, split, scarper, clear off, take off, hit
the road/trail, make tracks
3 DISPERSE, separate, diverge, disband, scatter, split up,
break up
◼ **1, 2** join
♦ *adj*

partial, half, not complete, limited, restricted, imperfect,
fragmentary, unfinished

◼ **part with**

relinquish, let go of, give up, yield, surrender, for(e)go,
abandon, discard, jettison
FORMAL renounce
◼ hold onto

◼ **for the most part**

by and large, on the whole, generally, usually, mostly,
mainly, in the main, chiefly, largely, commonly

◼ **in part**

to some degree, partly, somewhat, to some extent, to
a certain extent, to a certain degree, up to a point,
slightly

◼ **on the part of**

by, caused by, carried out by, on behalf of, from the side
of

◼ **take part in**

join in, opt in, be involved in, participate in, share in,
engage in, help with, assist in, play a part in, play a role in,
contribute to
FORMAL partake

Synonym nuances
verb sense 2
The phrase **part company with** can be used where
someone has opted to take a different direction from
their previous associates, while **split up from** is generally
used of a marital or familial rift: *she split up from her
husband*. **Separate from** can refer to any type of
severance, as can **divorce from**, but **get divorced from**
is generally appropriate only for marital break-ups.
Withdraw from is appropriate for ending an association
with someone or something: *he withdrew from politics*,
while **go away from** suggests removing yourself from a
person or place: *they went away from the conference,
convinced by his argument*.
  The phrase **go your separate ways** implies two or
more parties have mutually decided to follow their
individual choices, unlike **depart from**, which again
implies only one party is diverging. **Take your leave**,
along with **say goodbye**, suggests a definite ending of
contact on a specific occasion: *we said goodbye at the
station*, whereas **get going**, although similarly
suggesting parting, also implies embarking on a fresh
activity.

---

partake *v*

take part, share, participate, be involved, engage, enter
◼ **partake of**
1 *partake of food*
consume, eat, drink
2 *partake of the divine nature*
receive, share, have, show, demonstrate, take, suggest, evoke
FORMAL evince, manifest

partial *adj*

1 *a partial victory*
incomplete, in part, part, limited, restricted, imperfect,
fragmentary, unfinished
2 BIASED, prejudiced, partisan, one-sided, discriminatory,
preferential, unfair, unjust, inequitable, coloured, affected
FORMAL predisposed
◼ **1** complete, total **2** impartial, disinterested, unbiased,
fair
◼ **partial to**
fond of, liking, loving, keen on, taken with, with a weakness
for
FORMAL with a penchant for
COLLOQ. crazy about, mad about, with a soft spot for

partiality *n*

1 BIAS, prejudice, discrimination, unfairness, injustice,
inequity, inequitableness, partisanship, favour,
respect
2 LIKING, fondness, love, inclination, preference
FORMAL predilection, predisposition, proclivity

partially *adv*

incompletely, not fully, to a limited degree/extent,
fractionally, somewhat, in part, partly

participant *n*

entrant, competitor, contestant, contributor, participator, member, party, co-operator, helper, associate, partner, worker, sharer, shareholder

participate *v*

take part, join in, contribute, engage, be involved, be associated, enter, opt in, share, play a part, play a role, co-operate, help, assist
FORMAL partake
COLLOQ. muck in, be in

participation *n*

involvement, sharing, partnership, co-operation, contribution, assistance, association
FORMAL partaking
COLLOQ. mucking in

particle *n*

bit, piece, fragment, scrap, trace, touch, shred, sliver, speck, morsel, mite, crumb, iota, whit, jot, tittle, atom, molecule, grain, drop, spot
COLLOQ. smidgen, tad

parti-coloured *adj*

motley, variegated, piebald
FORMAL polychromatic, polychromic, versicoloured
E3 monochromatic, plain

particular *adj, n*

◆ *adj*
1 *on that particular day*
specific, precise, exact, distinct, certain, individual, special, peculiar
2 EXCEPTIONAL, remarkable, notable, marked, special, outstanding, thorough, unusual, uncommon, peculiar, notable, noteworthy
FORMAL especial
3 FUSSY, discriminating, finicky, fastidious, selective, meticulous, painstaking, exacting
COLLOQ. choosy, pernickety, picky, faddy; *N Am* persnickety
4 EXACT, detailed, thorough, precise, faithful, accurate
E3 **1** general
◆ *n*
detail, specific, point, feature, item, fact, circumstance
■ **in particular**
particularly, especially, specifically, exactly, precisely, to be specific, in detail

particularity *n*

feature, trait, detail, instance, fact, item, circumstance, characteristic, idiosyncrasy, individuality, point, property, distinctiveness, uniqueness, peculiarity, quirk, singularity

particularize *v*

detail, specify, itemize, stipulate, individualize, enumerate
FORMAL individuate

particularly *adv*

especially, exceptionally, remarkably, notably, markedly, extraordinarily, unusually, uncommonly, surprisingly, in particular, specifically, explicitly, distinctly, expressly

parting *n, adj*

◆ *n*
1 DEPARTURE, going, leaving, leave-taking, farewell, goodbye, adieu
FORMAL valediction
2 DIVERGENCE, separation, divorce, division, partition, rift, split, rupture, breaking, breaking-up
E3 **1** meeting **2** convergence
◆ *adj*
departing, leaving, farewell, goodbye, last, dying, final, closing, concluding
FORMAL valedictory
E3 first, arriving, opening

partisan *n, adj*

◆ *n*
1 SUPPORTER, devotee, adherent, follower, party man, disciple, backer, upholder, champion, fan, votary, stalwart
2 GUERRILLA, irregular, freedom fighter, resistance fighter
◆ *adj*
biased, prejudiced, unfair, unjust, inequitable, partial, predisposed, discriminatory, one-sided, factional, sectarian
E3 impartial

partisanship *n*

bias, prejudice, partiality, partyism, sectarianism, factionalism
E3 impartiality

partition *n, v*

◆ *n*
1 DIVIDER, barrier, wall, dividing wall, panel, screen, room-divider, dividing screen, separator
TECHNICAL diaphragm
2 DIVISION, break-up, splitting, separation, segregation, parting, severance, subdivision
Related adjectives: septiform, septiferous
◆ *v*
1 SEPARATE, separate off, divide, subdivide, bar, wall off, fence off, screen (off)
2 SHARE, divide (up), split up, break up, segregate, sever, parcel out

partly *adv*

somewhat, to some extent, to some degree, a little, to a certain extent, to a certain degree, (up) to a point, slightly, fractionally, in some measure, moderately, relatively, in part, partially, incompletely, half
E3 completely, totally, fully, wholly

partner *n*

1 ASSOCIATE, ally, confederate, colleague, co-worker, teammate, opposite number, collaborator, co-operator, accomplice, helper, mate, companion, comrade, consort, pair, yoke-fellow; *dialect* butty
OLD copesmate, copemate; (*Shakesp*) rival
COLLOQ. sidekick, oppo, pal
SLANG *N Am* pard, pardner
2 *bring your partner to the party*
spouse, husband, man, wife, woman, lady, boyfriend, girlfriend, fiancé, fiancée, friend, common-law wife/husband, cohabitee, live-in lover, significant other, SOP (significant other person), companion, consort, cavalier, catch
COLLOQ. other half, better half, bit on the side, kept man/woman

---

Synonym nuances

sense 1

The term **associate** is appropriate for someone you are involved with in a business sense, while **confederate** suggests someone you are in league with. **Ally** suggests a slightly closer relationship and someone who will stand up for you.

    Colleague, **co-worker** and **teammate** are more suggestive of a person whom you work alongside, whereas **opposite number** would be reserved for someone with equivalent status in a different organization: *the Foreign Minister met his Chinese opposite number*.

    Collaborator is more suggestive of someone who works in association with you: *his musical collaborator*, and may be used in a narrower sense, and with connotations of underhandedness, of people who assist the enemy: *a Nazi collaborator*. The less common **co-operator** similarly suggests mutual support.

Accomplice has strong connotations of illegality: *an accomplice to murder*. A person you are closer to could be described as a **mate**, which could also be used of either a friend or a fellow worker, or **companion**, if they are someone who often accompanies you. **Comrade** is more suggestive of someone you have shared experiences with and so have forged a bond with: *old war comrades*. **Consort** is a more formal term which tends to be reserved for a spouse: *the queen's consort*.

partnership *n*

1 *the partnership between teachers and parents*
association, alliance, co-operation, collaboration, participation, sharing, confederation, affiliation, combination, union, fellowship, fraternity, brotherhood
OLD consort
2 *a business partnership*
company, firm, corporation, syndicate, co-operative, association, society, conglomerate

party *n, v*

♦ *n*
1 CELEBRATION, festivity, social, get-together, gathering, reunion, function, reception, at-home
COLLOQ. do, bash, thrash, beanfeast, beano, blow-out, bunfight, knees-up, rave, rave-up, shindig; *Irish* hooley; *Aust* shivoo; *S Afr* jol
2 *a search party*
team, squad, crew, gang, band, group, body, company, unit, contingent, detachment
SLANG posse
3 *a political party*
faction, side, league, cabal, alliance, association, affiliation, grouping, camp, combination
4 *the parties in a contract*
person, individual, litigant, plaintiff, defendant
♦ *v*
celebrate, have/throw a party, enjoy yourself, have fun, go out
COLLOQ. rave, binge, have a ball, live it up, whoop it up, go out on the town, go on the razzle, have a night on the tiles, paint the town red, kill the fatted calf, put the flags out, push the boat out
COLLOQ. large it, have it large
■ **be a party to**
be involved in, be associated with, know about, share in the responsibility for

---

Kinds of party include:

acid-house party	fancy dress party	orgy
N Am baby	farewell party	picnic
shower	flatwarming	*N Am* potluck
barbecue	garden party	party
colloq. beanfeast	*colloq.* gathering	pyjama party
birthday party	of the clan	slumber party
N Am bridal	*Aust colloq.* grog-	social
shower	on	soirée
ceilidh	Hallowe'en party	stag night
cheese and wine	*NZ* hangi	stag party
party	hen party	supper party
Christmas party	*N Am colloq.*	tea party
cocktail party	hootenanny	toga party
dinner party	housewarming	welcoming party
disco	leaving party	wrap party
discotheque	new year party	

---

parvenu *n*
upstart, pretender, climber, social climber, arriviste, *nouveau riche*, new rich, vulgarian

pass¹ *v, n*
♦ *v*

1 GO, move, proceed, travel, progress, flow, run, drive, make your way
2 OVERTAKE, go past, drive/run past, outdistance, outstrip, beat, lose, lap, leave behind, draw level with, pull ahead of, overhaul
3 GO THROUGH, go across, go over, get across, get over, run, move, traverse
4 *pass the salt*
hand, give, reach, let someone have, transfer, transmit
5 *time passes quickly*
go by, go past, elapse, proceed, advance, slip by, slip away, drag
6 *pass time wisely*
spend, fill, occupy, employ, use up, take up, devote, while away
7 EXCEED, surpass, go beyond, go over, outdo, outstrip
8 *pass an exam*
succeed, be successful in, get through, qualify, graduate, pass with flying colours, sail/breeze through, scrape through
9 *the examiner passed him*
declare successful, approve, accept, declare satisfactory
10 *pass a new law*
enact, ratify, validate, adopt, authorize, sanction, approve, vote for, agree to, accept
11 *pass from one state to another*
change, go, move, turn, become, develop, transfer, evolve
12 HAPPEN, take place, occur, come about
FORMAL transpire, befall
13 *the estate passed to her daughter*
be left, be willed, be bequeathed, be inherited, be made over, be given, be handed down, be transferred, be endowed, be granted, be consigned, transfer
14 *pass the ball*
throw, kick, hit, move, swing, lunge
15 *pass comment*
make, say, speak, voice, utter, express, declare
16 *pass judgement*
pronounce, deliver, issue, announce, proclaim, decree, assert
17 *we let her attempt at humour pass*
go unnoticed, stand, go without comment
18 *pass urine*
discharge, expel, emit, let out, release
FORMAL excrete
E3 2 fall behind, trail 7 fail to reach, miss 8, 9 fail
♦ *n*
1 THROW, kick, move, hit, lunge, swing
2 PERMIT, passport, visa, identification, ticket, licence, authorization, warrant, permission
3 *make a pass at someone*
advances, approach, overture, suggestion, proposition, play
■ **pass as/for**
appear to be, be taken for, be mistaken for, be regarded as
■ **pass away**
die, pass on, go, depart this life, breathe your last
FORMAL expire, decease
COLLOQ. give up the ghost, go the way of all flesh, peg out, pop off, kick the bucket
■ **pass off**
1 HAPPEN, occur, take place, go off
2 *the effects passed off quickly*
wear off, fade away, die down, disappear, vanish
3 FEIGN, misrepresent, counterfeit, fake, palm off
■ **pass out**
1 FAINT, lose consciousness, black out, collapse, drop
OLD swoon
COLLOQ. flake out, keel over
2 GIVE OUT, hand out, distribute, deal out, allocate, allot, share out, dole out

- **pass over**
  disregard, ignore, overlook, miss, omit, leave, neglect, forget, take no notice of, not take into consideration, turn a blind eye to, turn a deaf ear to
- **pass up**
  not take advantage of, ignore, miss, refuse, neglect, reject, let slip

pass² *n*

a pass through the mountains
way, route, path, col, defile, gorge, ravine, canyon, gap, passage

passable *adj*

1 SATISFACTORY, acceptable, allowable, tolerable, average, ordinary, unexceptional, moderate, fair, adequate, all right, mediocre
COLLOQ. OK, run of the mill, so-so, nothing to write home about, not much cop, no great shakes
2 CLEAR, unobstructed, unblocked, open, navigable, traversable
E3 1 unacceptable, excellent **2** obstructed, blocked, impassable

passably *adv*

fairly, rather, quite, somewhat, tolerably, relatively, reasonably, moderately, after a fashion

passage *n*

1 PASSAGEWAY, aisle, corridor, hall, hallway, lobby, vestibule, doorway, opening, entrance, exit
2 THOROUGHFARE, way, route, road, avenue, path, track, lane, alley
3 CHANNEL, duct, conduit, main, groove, furrow, trough, gutter, gully, canal, flume, watercourse, waterway, strait, neck, sound
TECHNICAL orifice
4 MOVEMENT, passing, flow, running, course, advance
5 TRANSITION, progress, advance, change, transfer, turning, development
TECHNICAL mutation, metamorphosis
6 *the passage of a bill*
acceptance, approval, passing, adoption, authorization, validation, sanction, enactment, ratification
7 *grant passage through a country*
access, entry, admission, permission to travel through, safe conduct
8 EXTRACT, excerpt, quotation, text, paragraph, section, piece, clause, verse
FORMAL citation
9 JOURNEY, voyage, trip, crossing, tour, trek

passageway *n*

passage, corridor, hall, hallway, lobby, entrance, exit, aisle, lane, path, way, track, alley, gangway, arcade, runway

passé *adj*

outdated, old-fashioned, out-of-date, dated, obsolete, outmoded, unfashionable, outworn, *démodé*, antiquated, past its best
COLLOQ. old hat, out, on the way out, past it, past its sell-by date
E3 fashionable, in

passenger *n*

1 TRAVELLER, voyager, commuter, rider, fare, fare-payer, strap-hanger, hitchhiker
2 *get rid of passengers who don't work*
hanger-on, drone, shirker
COLLOQ. freeloader

passer-by *n*

bystander, looker-on, onlooker, observer, spectator, witness, eyewitness
COLLOQ. rubberneck, gawper

passing *adj, n*

 ♦ *adj*

1 SHORT-LIVED, temporary, momentary, transitional, fleeting, brief, short
FORMAL ephemeral, transient
2 CASUAL, incidental, cursory, hasty, quick, rapid, slight, superficial, shallow
E3 1 lasting, permanent
 ♦ *n*
1 *the passing of time*
passage, flow, march, course, advance, movement
2 DEATH, departure, passing away, perishing, end, finish, loss
FORMAL decease, demise, expiration, quietus, termination

- **in passing**
  incidentally, by the way, parenthetically, *en passant*
  COLLOQ. by the by(e)

passion *n*

1 FEELING, emotion, ardour, zeal, fervour, warmth, heat, spirit, intensity, fire, vehemence
2 OUTBURST, explosion, anger, indignation, wrath, rage, fit, temper, fury, tantrum
3 LOVE, desire, sexual desire, ardour, lust, adoration, infatuation, fondness, affection, craving
4 *a passion for football*
enthusiasm, obsession, mania, craze, fascination, eagerness, keenness, avidity, zest, fanaticism, zeal
E3 1 coolness, indifference

passionate *adj*

1 ARDENT, fervent, eager, keen, avid, enthusiastic, fanatical, zealous, warm, hot, fiery, inflamed, aroused, excited, impassioned, intense, strong, fierce, vehement, violent, stormy, tempestuous, wild, frenzied
COLLOQ. crazy, mad, nuts, potty
2 EMOTIONAL, excitable, hotheaded, intense, warm, impetuous, impulsive, frenzied, quick-tempered, irritable, stormy, headstrong, wilful, self-willed, obstinate, choleric, Latin, torrid
OLD affectionate; (*Shakesp*) waspish-headed
3 LOVING, affectionate, ardent, aroused, lustful, erotic, sexy, sensual, sultry
COLLOQ. turned on, randy, horny, gutsy
E3 1 phlegmatic; *colloq.* laid-back **3** frigid, cold

passionately *adv*

1 ENTHUSIASTICALLY, ardently, fervently, keenly, fanatically, zealously, intensely, strongly, hotly, violently, fiercely
2 LOVINGLY, affectionately, ardently, lustfully, sensually, erotically
E3 1 apathetically **2** coldly

passionless *adj*

emotionless, unfeeling, unemotional, unloving, impassive, calm, cold, cold-hearted, frigid, callous, frosty, icy, cold-blooded, apathetic, restrained, unresponsive, uncaring, indifferent, insensible, uninvolved, detached, dispassionate, impartial, neutral, withdrawn
E3 passionate, caring, sensitive, sympathetic

passive *adj*

1 DOCILE, receptive, unassertive, yielding, submissive, unresisting, non-violent, patient, resigned, compliant, long-suffering
2 UNEMOTIONAL, apathetic, lifeless, emotionless, unmoved, indifferent, detached, distant, uninvolved, unenterprising, non-participating, remote, aloof, dispassionate, inert, inactive
E3 1 involved, lively, active **2** responsive

passively *adv*

submissively, unassertively, patiently, emotionlessly, lifelessly
E3 actively

passport *n*

1 *show your passport at the border*

travel documents, papers, identity card, ID, visa, permit, pass, authorization, laissez-passer
2 *the passport to success*
key, entry, door, doorway, avenue, path, way, route, admission, means of access

password *n*
watchword, signal, key, word, open sesame, parole, shibboleth, countersign

past *adj, n, prep*
♦ *adj*
1 OVER, ended, finished, completed, done, over and done with
2 FORMER, previous, preceding, foregoing, foregone, late, sometime, last, latter, recent
FORMAL erstwhile
3 ANCIENT, bygone, olden, early, gone, gone by, elapsed, long ago, no more, extinct, defunct, forgotten
F3 2 future, next
♦ *n*
1 *in the past*
history, former times, olden days, olden times, days gone by, bygone times/days, good old days, antiquity
FORMAL days of yore
2 LIFE, background, experience, record, track record
F3 1 future
♦ *prep*
1 *walking past the trees*
by, near, beside, beyond
OLD forby
2 *past childish jokes*
after, over, beyond, too old for, too mature for

pasta

Forms and shapes of pasta include:

agnolotti	fettuccine	pappardelle
anelli	fiochetti	penne
angel's hair	fusilli	pennine
bombolotti	gnocchi	ravioli
bucatini	lasagne	rigatoni
cannelloni	lasagne verde	ruoti
capelletti	linguini	spaghetti
casarecci	lumache	stelline
conchiglie	macaroni	strangozzi
crescioni	mafalde	tagliatelle
ditali	manicotti	taglierini
elbow macaroni	maruzze	tortellini
farfalla	mezzani	trofie
farfalline	noodle	vermicelli
fedelini	noodle farfel	ziti

paste *n, v*
♦ *n*
1 ADHESIVE, glue, gum, mastic, putty, cement
2 *fish paste*
pap, pulp, mush, blend, pâté, purée, spread, mixture
♦ *v*
stick, glue, gum, cement, fix, fasten

pastel *adj, n*
♦ *adj*
soft, soft-hued, light, light-coloured, pale, delicate, subtle, discreet, muted, low-key, subdued, faint
♦ *n*
1 CHALK, crayon, pastille
2 DRAWING, sketch, vignette

pastiche *n*
assortment, mixture, mix, miscellany, variety, melange, potpourri, hotchpotch, hodgepodge, olio, olla-podrida, confusion, farrago, salmagundi, smorgasbord, collection, medley, patchwork, gallimaufry, jumble
FORMAL conglomeration
COLLOQ. mixed bag, mishmash, omnium-gatherum

pastille *n*
lozenge, pastel, sweet, tablet, cough sweet, cough drop, confection, jujube, troche

pastime *n*
hobby, activity, leisure activity, leisure pursuit, game, sport, recreation, play, fun, amusement, entertainment, diversion, distraction, relaxation, avocation, *Zeitvertreib*
OLD pastance; (*Shakesp*) abridgement, suppliance
F3 work, employment

past master *n*
expert, proficient, virtuoso, adept, artist
COLLOQ. ace, old hand, dab hand, wizard
F3 incompetent

pastor *n*
minister, clergyman, priest, rector, vicar, parson, deacon, cleric, churchman, canon, prebendary, divine, ecclesiastic
Related adjective: pastoral

pastoral *adj*
1 RURAL, country, rustic, agricultural, agrarian, simple, idyllic
FORMAL bucolic
2 ECCLESIASTICAL, clerical, priestly, ministerial
F3 1 urban

pastry

Types of pastry include:

American crust	one-stage	rich shortcrust
biscuit-crumb	pâte à savarin	rough-puff
cheese	pâte brisée	short
choux	pâte frolle	shortcrust
Danish	pâte sablée	suetcrust
filo	pâte sucrée	sweet
flaky	plain pastry	wholewheat
flan	pork-pie	
hot-water crust	puff	

pasture *n*
grass, grassland, meadow, field, paddock, pasturage, grazing, grazing land; *N Am* range
Related adjective: pastoral

pasty *adj*
sallow, pale, pallid, wan, anaemic, pasty-faced, sickly, unhealthy
F3 ruddy, healthy

pat *v, n, adj, adv*
♦ *v*
tap, dab, slap, touch, stroke, caress, fondle, pet, patter, burp; *Scot* clap
OLD bepat, tick
♦ *n*
1 *gave the dog a pat*
tap, dab, slap, touch, stroke, caress; *Scot* clap
OLD tick
2 *a pat of butter*
dab, lump, mass, chunk, ball, coquille, print
♦ *adj*
glib, fluent, smooth, slick, ready, easy, facile, simple, simplistic
♦ *adv*
precisely, exactly, perfectly, flawlessly, faultlessly, fluently, word-for-word
F3 imprecisely, inaccurately, wrongly
■ **pat someone on the back**
congratulate, praise, compliment, say well done to
COLLOQ. take your hat off to

patch *n, v*
♦ *n*
1 *a patch of land*
bed, plot, lot, parcel, tract, area, piece, spot

2 COVER, material, cloth, covering, shield, protection
3 *go through a bad patch*
phase, period, stretch, time, term, spell
◆ *v*
mend, repair, sew, stitch, fix, cover, reinforce

patchwork *n*
medley, jumble, mixture, assortment, farrago, gallimaufry, hash, hotchpotch, pastiche
COLLOQ. mishmash

patchy *adj*
uneven, irregular, inconsistent, varying, variable, random, fitful, erratic, sketchy, bitty, spotty, blotchy
Ⓔ even, uniform, regular, consistent

patent *adj, n*
◆ *adj*
obvious, manifest, evident, self-evident, conspicuous, clear, crystal clear, plain, transparent, apparent, visible, undeniable, unmistak(e)able, palpable, unequivocal, open, overt, blatant, flagrant, glaring
COLLOQ. plain as a pikestaff, plain as the nose on your face, clear as daylight, staring you in the face
Ⓔ hidden, opaque
◆ *n*
privilege, right, certificate, licence, invention, copyright, registered trademark

patently *adv*
clearly, manifestly, plainly, visibly, conspicuously, unmistak(e)ably, unequivocally, palpably, blatantly, glaringly

paternal *adj*
fatherly, fatherlike, protective, benevolent, concerned, vigilant

path *n*
1 FOOTPATH, pathway, bridleway, trail, towpath, track, walk
2 ROUTE, course, direction, approach, way, circuit, passage, road, avenue, lane

pathetic *adj*
1 PITIABLE, poor, sorry, lamentable, miserable, wretched, sad, dismal, distressing, moving, affecting, touching, pitiful, poignant, plaintive, heart-rending, heartbreaking, woeful
2 FEEBLE, poor, sorry, miserable, useless, worthless, inadequate, unsatisfactory, meagre, contemptible, derisory, deplorable, woeful
Ⓔ **1** cheerful **2** admirable, excellent, valuable

pathetically *adv*
1 PITIABLY, lamentably, wretchedly, sadly, dismally, pitifully, woefully
2 INADEQUATELY, unsatisfactorily, miserably, deplorably, contemptibly, woefully
Ⓔ **1** happily **2** admirably

pathological *adj*
compulsive, habitual, inveterate, obsessive, confirmed, chronic, hardened, addicted, dependent, persistent

pathos *n*
poignancy, misery, sadness, tragedy, pitiableness, pitifulness, plaintiveness, inadequacy

patience *n*
calmness, composure, self-control, equanimity, even-temperedness, restraint, tolerance, forbearance, endurance, fortitude, long-suffering, submission, resignation, stoicism, tranquillity, serenity, inexcitability, persistence, perseverance, diligence, doggedness, tenacity
OLD sufferance
FORMAL imperturbability
COLLOQ. unflappability, cool, stickability
Ⓔ impatience, intolerance, exasperation

patient *adj, n*
◆ *adj*
calm, composed, serene, self-possessed, self-controlled, restrained, even-tempered, mild, unhurried, leisurely, easy-going, lenient, indulgent, kind, tender, understanding, forgiving, tolerant, accommodating, forbearing, long-suffering, uncomplaining, submissive, resigned, philosophical, stoical, persistent, persevering, resolute
OLD forbearant
FORMAL imperturbable
COLLOQ. patient as Job, unflappable, cool, laid-back, hanging in there
Ⓔ impatient, restless, intolerant, exasperated
◆ *n*
invalid, sufferer, case, client, subject, out-patient
OLD ambulant

Synonym nuances
adjective
Calm and **serene** can be used to suggest being in a fairly constant tranquil state. **Composed**, **self-possessed** and **self-controlled** are more suggestive of having your emotions under control, while **restrained** implies a greater difficulty in achieving this: *restrained enthusiasm*. You can use **lenient** to suggest being influenced by mercy, but **indulgent** goes further by implying an excessive tolerance: *a rather indulgent parent who was never put out by anything*. **Understanding** has added associations of empathy, whereas **forgiving** implies compassion in the face of trying behaviour, and both **tolerant** and **forbearing** suggest an element of permissiveness. **Accommodating**, however, suggests being more actively obliging: *he is a most accommodating interviewee, talking freely about his projects*.
  Uncomplaining, **submissive** and **resigned** have more to do with yielding to the wishes of others, while **long-suffering** is suggestive of martyred endurance: *a long-suffering mother of four*. Both **philosophical** and **stoical** have implications of acceptance: *he was philosophical about their defeat*, while **resolute** is less connotative of gentleness, and suggests intractability.

---

patiently *adv*
calmly, unhurriedly, leisurely, mildly, considerately, tenderly, kindly, tolerantly, enduringly, resolutely, persistently, perseveringly
COLLOQ. unflappably, through thick and thin

patois *n*
dialect, vernacular, local parlance, local speech, argot, cant, lingo, lingua franca, patter, slang, jargon

patriarch *n*
elder, father, grandfather, paterfamilias, greybeard, founder, sire
COLLOQ. grand old man

patrician *n, adj*
◆ *n*
aristocrat, noble, nobleman, gentleman, grandee, peer
COLLOQ. nob
Ⓔ commoner, plebeian
◆ *adj*
aristocratic, noble, lordly, high-class, high-born, blue-blooded, gentle, thoroughbred, well-born
COLLOQ. upper-crust
Ⓔ common, humble

patrimony *n*
inheritance, legacy, bequest, heritage, estate, property, possessions, birthright, revenue, share, portion

patriot *n*
nationalist, loyalist, chauvinist, flag-waver, jingoist, jingo

patriotic *adj*
nationalistic, nationalist, chauvinistic, jingoistic, loyal, loyalist, flag-waving

patriotism *n*
chauvinism, flag-waving, jingoism, loyalty, nationalism

patrol *v, n*
♦ *v*
police, guard, keep guard on, protect, defend, keep watch on/over, monitor, go the rounds, make your/do the rounds, be on the beat, tour, inspect
♦ *n*
1 GUARD, patrolman, patrolwoman, sentry, sentinel, police officer, security guard, defender, night-watchman, watchman
2 *on patrol*
watch, guard, vigil, surveillance, policing, patrolling, protection, defence, round, beat

patron *n*
1 BENEFACTOR, philanthropist, sponsor, backer, supporter, friend, promoter, sympathizer, advocate, upholder, champion, defender, protector, guardian, guardian angel, helper, Maecenas; *Scot* stoop, stoup
OLD fautor
COLLOQ. angel, fairy godmother
2 CUSTOMER, client, frequenter, shopper, buyer, purchaser, subscriber
COLLOQ. regular

patronage *n*
1 SPONSORSHIP, funding, backing, support, promotion, financial help/aid/assistance, encouragement, protection, aegis, auspices
2 CUSTOM, business, trade, commerce, buying, purchasing, shopping, subscription

patronize *v*
1 LOOK DOWN ON, talk down to, despise, scorn, act/speak condescendingly towards
FORMAL disparage
COLLOQ. look down your nose at, turn your nose up at
2 SPONSOR, fund, finance, back, support, maintain, protect, help, assist, aid, promote, champion, foster, encourage
OLD (*Shakesp*) empatron
3 FREQUENT, shop at, buy from, deal with
COLLOQ. be a regular at

patronizing *adj*
condescending, stooping, overbearing, high-handed, haughty, lofty, superior, snobbish, supercilious, scornful, contemptuous, disdainful
COLLOQ. snooty, toffee-nosed, stuck up, high-and-mighty, on your high horse
E3 humble, lowly

patter[1] *v, n*
♦ *v*
rain pattering on the window
tap, pat, pitter-patter, drum, pound, beat, pelt, trip, scuttle, scurry
♦ *n*
pattering, tapping, pitter-patter, beating

patter[2] *n*
a salesman's patter
chatter, gabble, jabber, line, pitch, jargon, monologue
COLLOQ. spiel, lingo, yak

pattern *n, v*
♦ *n*
1 SYSTEM, method, order, plan, arrangement
2 DECORATION, ornamentation, ornament, figure, motif, device, design, style, markings
3 MODEL, template, stencil, guide, plan, design, instruction, original, prototype, blueprint, standard, criterion, norm, ideal, example

4 *a book of fabric patterns*
sample, swatch
♦ *v*
model, style, order, form, follow, imitate, match, stencil, emulate, copy, decorate, design, shape, mould, influence, trim

patterned *adj*
decorated, ornamented, figured, printed, watered, moiré
E3 plain

paucity *n*
lack, shortage, insufficiency, scarcity, scantiness, poverty, rarity, fewness, sparseness, sparsity, want, dearth, deficiency, smallness, slightness, slenderness, meagreness, paltriness
FORMAL exiguousness
E3 abundance

paunch *n*
fat stomach, abdomen, belly, pot-belly, beer belly, beer gut
COLLOQ. corporation

paunchy *adj*
pot-bellied, fat, podgy, pudgy, portly, tubby
TECHNICAL adipose
FORMAL corpulent, rotund

pauper *n*
insolvent, down-and-out, have-not, bankrupt, beggar, mendicant, church mouse
FORMAL indigent

pause *v, n*
♦ *v*
halt, stop, cease, break (off), interrupt, adjourn, take a break, rest, sit down, stay, wait, delay, hold back, hesitate, breathe
FORMAL discontinue, desist
COLLOQ. let up, take a breather, take a rest, take five
♦ *n*
halt, stoppage, stop, close, interruption, break, rest, lull, stay, respite, gap, interval, interlude, intermission, wait, delay, hesitation, hold
TECHNICAL caesura, diaeresis, limma, fermata, dwell
OLD demur
FORMAL cessation
COLLOQ. breather, breathing space, let-up, time out

pave *v*
flag, tile, floor, surface, cover, asphalt, tar, macadamize, tarmac, concrete

■ **pave the way for**
get/make ready for, prepare for, lead up to, introduce, take steps/measures, clear the ground, lay/do the groundwork for, do the spadework for

pavement *n*
footpath, footway, walkway, path, way, floor, bed, causeway; *N Am* sidewalk

paw *n, v*
♦ *n*
foot, pad, forefoot, hand
♦ *v*
maul, touch, stroke, manhandle, mishandle, poke, molest
COLLOQ. touch up

pawn[1] *n*
mere pawns in the power struggle
dupe, puppet, tool, instrument, toy, plaything
COLLOQ. cat's paw, stooge

pawn[2] *v*
pawn your watch
deposit, pledge, stake, mortgage, dip; *Scot* wadset
OLD impawn, lumber, pignorate, oppignorate; (*Shakesp*) fine
FORMAL impignorate
COLLOQ. hock, pop, lay in lavender
OLD SLANG spout

pawnbroker n

pawnshop, lender, money-lender, usurer, gombeen-man, *mont-de-piété, monte di pietà*
OLD lumberer; (*offensive*) sheeny
COLLOQ. pop-shop
SLANG uncle

pay v, n

◆ v

1 *pay money to someone*

spend, pay out, meet the cost of, lay out, outlay, hand over, recompense, invest, reimburse, repay, refund, settle, settle up, discharge, reward
FORMAL remunerate, remit, expend, disburse, indemnify
COLLOQ. dip (your hand) into your pocket, foot the bill, pick up the tab, fork out, shell out, cough up, stump up; *N Am* ante up

2 BENEFIT, profit, pay off, bring in, produce, yield, return, be beneficial to, be advantageous to, be worthwhile to
COLLOQ. rake in

3 *pay attention/a compliment/a visit*

give, make, do, let someone have, offer, extend, grant, supply
FORMAL afford, proffer, bestow

4 ATONE, make amends, compensate, avenge yourself on, pay back, answer, suffer, be punished

◆ n

wages, salary, earnings, income, gross/net pay, take-home pay, commission, fee, stipend, honorarium, payment, reward, recompense, compensation, reimbursement
FORMAL remuneration, emoluments

■ **pay back**

1 REPAY, refund, return, reimburse, recompense, settle, pay off, give back, square

2 RETALIATE, get your own back, take revenge, get your revenge on, avenge yourself on, get even with, punish, repay, reciprocate, counter-attack, give someone a taste of their own medicine

■ **pay for**

answer for, atone, be punished for, compensate, make amends, suffer, pay a penalty for, pay the price for, count the cost (of), cost dearly
COLLOQ. face the music, get your deserts

■ **pay off**

1 DISCHARGE, settle, square, clear, meet, honour, repay, pay in full

2 DISMISS, discharge, make redundant, lay off
COLLOQ. fire, sack

3 *the preparations paid off*

succeed, be successful, work, get results

4 BRIBE, buy off, suborn, take care of
COLLOQ. fix, grease, grease someone's palm

■ **pay out**

spend, hand over, part with, lay out
FORMAL disburse, remit, expend
COLLOQ. fork out, shell out, cough up; *N Am* ante up

Synonym nuances
verb sense 1
Pay out generally suggests a financial payment made from duty or necessity, whereas **meet the cost** implies taking on the responsibility of payment: *it was the government, rather than the UN, which met the cost*. Both **settle** and **settle up** suggest the final payment of accumulated costs, while **discharge** would be appropriate for meeting a debt. You can use **hand over** to suggest the actual transference of money, but it has connotations of unwillingness: *forced to hand over the money at gunpoint*.
  Invest implies devoting money or time to a project in the hope of an augmented return: *they had invested heavily in new technology; she invested a great deal of time in the project*. **Lay out**, on the other hand, implies

---

an element of extravagance, whilst **outlay** is again more suggestive of necessary costs incurred, though is less common in its verbal form.
  Recompense and **repay** have suggestions of an equable return for something proffered: *he was adequately recompensed for his loyalty*, whereas **reimburse** and **refund** are more specifically to do with compensating someone for their expenses. **Reward** would suggest giving something in recognition of merit.

---

payable adj

owed, owing, unpaid, to be paid, outstanding, in arrears, due, mature

payload n

cargo, freight, load, haul, lading, tonnage, shipment, consignment, contents, goods, merchandise, baggage

payment n

settlement, discharge, clearance, premium, outlay, advance, deposit, instalment, amount, contribution, donation, allowance, reward, pay, fee, hire, fare, toll
FORMAL remittance, remuneration

pay-off n

1 RESULT, outcome, benefit, advantage, reward, settlement, consequence, upshot
COLLOQ. crunch, moment of truth, punchline

2 BRIBE, inducement, allurement, enticement
COLLOQ. back-hander, sweetener, hush money, slush fund, protection money

3 PAYMENT, pay, wages, salary, earnings, income, gross/net pay, take-home pay, commission, fee, stipend, honorarium, reward, recompense, compensation, reimbursement
FORMAL remuneration, emoluments

peace n

1 CALM, quiet, quietness, peacefulness, hush, silence, still, stillness, rest, restfulness, relaxation, tranquillity, calmness, serenity, composure, contentment, placidity
FORMAL repose

2 ARMISTICE, truce, ceasefire, peace treaty, non-violence, non-aggression, law and order, conciliation, harmony, pax, friendship, amicableness, goodwill, agreement, pact, treaty
FORMAL concord, amity, accord
E3 1 noise, disturbance **2** war, disagreement, discord
Related adjective: irenic

peaceable adj

pacific, peace-loving, unwarlike, dovish, non-violent, non-aggressive, conciliatory, friendly, cordial, easy-going, even-tempered, good-natured, amicable, harmonious, inoffensive, gentle, placid, mild
FORMAL irenic
E3 aggressive, violent, quarrelsome, belligerent

peaceably adv

amicably, harmoniously, pacifically, inoffensively, gently, placidly, mildly, cordially
E3 aggressively, violently

peaceful adj

quiet, still, restful, relaxing, tranquil, serene, calm, placid, sleepy, unruffled, undisturbed, untroubled, friendly, harmonious, amicable, peaceable, pacific, gentle
FORMAL halcyon, irenic, reposeful, in repose
E3 noisy, disturbed, troubled, violent

peacefully adv

quietly, calmly, serenely, gently, sleepily, restfully, harmoniously, amicably, placidly
E3 noisily

peacemaker n

appeaser, conciliator, mediator, arbitrator, intercessor, broker, peace-monger, pacifier, pacifist, dove
OLD (*Shakesp*) make-peace

peacemaking adj

appeasing, conciliatory, pacific, mediating, mediative, mediatorial, mediatory
FORMAL irenic

peak n, v

• n

top, summit, pinnacle, crest, crown, zenith, apogee, height, high point, elevation, mountain, mount, hill, pinnacle, maximum, climax, culmination, apex, tip, point, rise, spire, pin, summer, aiguille, nib, crise; *Scot & Irish* ben
OLD (*Spenser*) prick
E≡ trough, nadir

• v

climax, culminate, come to a head, reach the highest point, spike

peaky adj

pale, pallid, wan, ill, sick, unwell, off-colour, sickly, poorly, out of sorts, seedy, queasy
COLLOQ. under the weather, washed-out, dicky, crummy, green about the gills
E≡ healthy; *colloq.* in the pink

peal n, v

• n

chime, carillon, toll, knell, ring, clang, ringing, reverberation, resounding, triple, rumble, boom, roar, crash, clap, firing
FORMAL tintinnabulation

• v

chime, toll, ring (out), clang, resonate, reverberate, resound, rumble, boom, roll, roar, crash

peasant n

rustic, provincial, country person, yokel, bumpkin, oaf, lout, churl, campesino, contadino, Cossack, kulak, muzhik, fellah, jungli, kisan, ryot; *Scot* cottar, blue-bonnet
OLD boor, carlot, kern, swain
COLLOQ. country bumpkin, clodhopper, hick

pebble n

stone, agate, chip, gallet

peccadillo n

error, fault, indiscretion, lapse, slip, minor offence, misdeed, misdemeanour, delinquency
FORMAL infraction
COLLOQ. boob, slip-up

peck v

nip, jab, tap, rap, hit, strike, bite, prick, kiss

peculiar adj

1 *a peculiar sound*
strange, odd, curious, funny, queer, weird, bizarre, quaint, extraordinary, unusual, abnormal, exceptional, unconventional, offbeat, droll, eccentric, outlandish, freakish, grotesque, exotic
SLANG way-out
2 CHARACTERISTIC, distinctive, distinguishing, specific, particular, special, distinct, remarkable, individual, individualistic, personal, idiosyncratic, unique
FORMAL singular
3 *feel peculiar*
unwell, ill, sick, poorly, out of sorts, dizzy, queasy
COLLOQ. under the weather
E≡ **1** ordinary, normal **2** general

■ **peculiar to**
unique to, characteristic of, like, belonging to, in keeping with, typical of, representative of
FORMAL indicative of

peculiarity n

oddity, bizarreness, weirdness, abnormality, exception, eccentricity, quirk, foible, mannerism, feature, trait, mark, hallmark, quality, attribute, property, characteristic, distinctiveness, particularity, idiosyncrasy
FORMAL singularity
COLLOQ. jimjam

peculiarly adv

1 STRANGELY, oddly, bizarrely, quaintly, curiously, extraordinarily, unusually, exceptionally, unconventionally
2 CHARACTERISTICALLY, distinctively, uniquely, particularly, remarkably, distinctly
FORMAL singularly
E≡ **1** ordinarily, normally **2** generally

pecuniary adj

monetary, financial, fiscal, commercial
FORMAL nummary, nummulary

pedagogic adj

educational, teaching, instructional, tuitional, academic, scholastic, didactic

pedagogue n

teacher, instructor, educator, master, mistress, educationalist, educationist, schoolteacher, schoolmaster, schoolmistress, don, pedant, dogmatist, preceptor, dominie

pedagogy n

teaching, instruction, training, tuition, tutelage, didactics, pedagogics

pedant n

purist, formalist, literalist, perfectionist, precisionist, precisian, dogmatist, quibbler, casuist, doctrinaire, academic, intellectual, pettifogger, Dryasdust, scholastic
FORMAL academe
COLLOQ. hair-splitter, nit-picker, egghead, highbrow, schoolmarm

pedantic adj

stilted, fussy, purist, perfectionist, literalist, formalist, particular, precise, exact, meticulous, punctilious, scrupulous, quibbling, finical, pompous, pretentious, academic, scholastic, intellectual, bookish, heavy, inkhorn, stuffy, erudite
TECHNICAL sesquipedalian, sesquipedal
OLD blue
COLLOQ. hair-splitting, nit-picking, schoolmarmish
E≡ imprecise, informal, casual

pedantry n

punctiliousness, exactness, meticulousness, dogmatism, cavilling, finicality, quibbling, pomposity, pretentiousness, academicness, intellectualism, bookishness, stuffiness, pedagogism, pedagoguishness, pedantism
COLLOQ. hair-splitting, nit-picking

peddle v

sell, sell from house to house, sell from door to door, sell from place to place, vend, hawk, tout, push, trade, traffic, market, offer/present for sale, huckster; *S Afr* smouch
COLLOQ. flog

pedestal n

plinth, pillar, column, stand, support, mounting, foot, base, foundation, platform, podium

■ **put on a pedestal**
idolize, hero-worship, exalt, revere, admire, look up to, adulate

pedestrian n, adj

• n

walker, foot-traveller, hiker; *S Afr* voetganger

• adj

dull, boring, flat, uninspired, unexciting, unimaginative, banal, mundane, commonplace, humdrum, ordinary, mediocre, indifferent, prosaic, stodgy, plodding, turgid
COLLOQ. run-of-the-mill, not up to much, no great shakes, nothing much to write home about
E≡ exciting, imaginative

pedigree n, adj
* n

genealogy, family tree, lineage, ancestry, descent, line, line of descent, family, parentage, derivation, extraction, race, breed, stock, strain, blood
FORMAL stirps
* adj

pure-bred, pedigree, full-blooded, thoroughbred, aristocratic

pedlar n

seller, house-to-house salesman, door-to-door salesman, hawker, huckster, vendor, walker, street-trader, colporteur, chapman, gutter-man, gutter-merchant, boxwallah, cheap-jack, camelot; dialect bodger, jagger; Scot yagger, pedder, pether; S Afr smouch, smouser
OLD cadger

peek v, n
* v

peep, glance, peer, spy, look
COLLOQ. have a gander, have a look-see
* n

peep, glance, glimpse, look, blink
COLLOQ. dekko, look-see, shufti
SLANG gander; Aust & NZ squiz

peel v, n
* v

pare, skin, strip, scale, shell, flake (off), take off, remove; dialect pill; N Am shuck
FORMAL decorticate, desquamate
* n

skin, rind, zest, peeling
TECHNICAL epicarp, exocarp, integument
■ **keep your eyes peeled**
watch closely, observe, monitor, keep a lookout for, be alert, keep your eyes skinned

peep¹ v, n
* v

peep through the keyhole
look, peek, glimpse, spy, squint, peer, blink, pink, pry, emerge, issue, appear; Scot cook, kook, keek
OLD (Spenser) toot
* n

look, quick look, peek, glimpse, glance, squint; Scot keek
COLLOQ. dekko, look-see, shufti, gander

peep² v, n
* v

birds peeping
chirp, cheep, chirrup, pipe, tweet, chatter, twitter, warble, squeak
* n

chirp, cheep, chirrup, pipe, tweet, chatter, twitter, warble, squeak, cry, utterance, sound, noise, word

peephole n

spyhole, keyhole, pinhole, hole, opening, aperture, slit, chink, slink, crack, fissure, cleft, crevice, Judas hole, Judas window
FORMAL interstice

peer¹ v

peer through the window
look, gaze, scan, scrutinize, examine, inspect, spy, pry, snoop, peep, squint, pink; Scot styme
OLD squinny; (Shakesp) twire; (Spenser) toot
SLANG dick

peer² n

1 ARISTOCRAT, peeress, noble, nobleman, lady, lord, Law Lord, duke, marquess, marquis, earl, count, viscount, baron, patrician, trier, backwoodsman
2 EQUAL, counterpart, equivalent, like, match, fellow, confrère, compeer

peerage n

aristocracy, nobility, lords and ladies
COLLOQ. upper crust, top drawer

peeress n

aristocrat, noble, noblewoman, lady, dame, duchess, marchioness, countess, viscountess, baroness

peerless adj

matchless, without equal, unequalled, unexcelled, unmatched, incomparable, beyond compare, unparalleled, unrivalled, unsurpassed, unbeatable, unique, supreme, excellent, paramount, outstanding, superlative
FORMAL nonpareil
COLLOQ. second to none

peeve v

annoy, exasperate, irritate, vex, irk, exasperate, gall, rile
COLLOQ. aggravate, bug, wind up, hassle, rub up the wrong way, get someone's blood up, make someone's blood boil, get on someone's nerves, get up someone's nose, get under someone's skin, get someone's goat, get on someone's wick, drive crazy/nuts, drive up the wall, drive round the bend/twist, get someone's back up, brass off, cheese off, make someone's hackles rise, make sparks fly, give someone the hump, get someone's dander up; N Am tick/hack off
SLANG drive bananas

peeved adj

annoyed, irritated, exasperated, put out, upset, vexed, irked, galled, riled, sore, piqued, nettled
COLLOQ. miffed, narked, bugged, stroppy, shirty, hassled, driven crazy, driven nuts, cheesed off, brassed off, got the hump, in a huff, in a paddy, hot under the collar; N Am ticked off

peevish adj

petulant, querulous, fractious, fretful, touchy, complaining, irritable, cross, grumpy, ill-tempered, in a bad mood, cantankerous, crusty, snappy, short-tempered, moody, testy, tetchy, churlish, surly, sullen, sulky
COLLOQ. crotchety, crabbed, ratty, grouchy
F3 good-tempered

peevishly adv

irritably, crossly, grumpily, churlishly, sullenly, fractiously, fretfully, petulantly, in a bad mood

peevishness n

ill-temper, irritability, perversity, petulance, querulousness, testiness, pique, pet, captiousness, acrimony
FORMAL protervity

peg n, v
* n

pin, nail, screw, spike, brad, dowel, hook, knob, marker, post, stake, picket, plug, tap, hatpeg, knag, nog, thole, key
TECHNICAL cheville, piton, spigot, soft spile
OLD perch
* v

1 FASTEN, secure, fix, attach, join, mark
2 *peg prices*
control, stabilize, hold down, limit, freeze, fix, set
■ **peg away**
apply yourself, work away, work hard, persevere, persist, plug away, plod along
COLLOQ. beaver away, hang in, keep at it, stick at it
■ **take/bring down a peg or two**
humiliate, humble, bring/cut down to size, put someone in their place, take the wind out of someone's sails

pejorative adj

derogatory, disparaging, belittling, slighting, unflattering, uncomplimentary, unpleasant, bad, negative
FORMAL deprecatory
F3 complimentary

pellet *n*
ball, shot, bullet, pill, drop, capsule, lozenge
COLLOQ. slug

pell-mell *adv*
hurriedly, hastily, feverishly, precipitously, posthaste, recklessly, rashly, heedlessly, impetuously, at full tilt
COLLOQ. helter-skelter, hurry-scurry

pellucid *adj*
clear, limpid, transparent, translucent, pure, glassy, bright

pelt¹ *v*
1 THROW, hurl, bombard, shower, attack, assail, batter, beat, hit, strike
2 POUR, teem
COLLOQ. bucket (down), rain cats and dogs
3 RUSH, hurry, charge, tear, race, dash, run, speed, sprint, career
COLLOQ. belt, scoot, zip

pelt² *n*
a beaver pelt
skin, coat, fur, fleece, hide, fell

pen¹ *n, v*
• *n*
write with a pen
fountain pen, ballpoint, ballpoint pen, Biro®, felt-tip pen, felt-tip, felt pen, self-filler, highlighter, marker pen, Rollerball®, stylograph, Magic Marker®, J-pen, quill
• *v*
write (down), note (down), take down, compose, draft, scribble, jot down, dash off

pen² *n, v*
• *n*
a sheep pen
enclosure, fold, pound, compound, stall, sty, coop, cage, hutch, mew, corral, crawl, kraal, cruive
• *v*
enclose, fence, hedge, hem in, confine, cage, coop, shut (up), corral, kraal

penal *adj*
punitive, disciplinary, corrective, retaliatory, retributive, vindictive

penalize *v*
punish, discipline, correct, fine, disadvantage, handicap
FORMAL castigate, chastise
⊟ reward

penal servitude *n*
hard labour, stretch, time
SLANG bird, lag, porridge

penalty *n*
1 PUNISHMENT, retribution, sentence, fine, forfeit, chastisement
FORMAL mulct, castigation
2 DISADVANTAGE, handicap, drawback, snag, weak point
COLLOQ. downside, minus
⊟ **1** reward **2** advantage, benefit

penance *n*
atonement, reparation, punishment, penalty, self-punishment, self-abasement, mortification, penitence, sackcloth and ashes
Related adjective: penitentiary

penchant *n*
fondness, liking, tendency, taste, preference, affinity, bent, inclination, leaning, bias, partiality, weakness, soft spot, proneness
FORMAL disposition, predilection, predisposition, proclivity, propensity
⊟ dislike

pendant *n*
medallion, locket, necklace

pendent *adj*
hanging, suspended, dangling, drooping, swinging
FORMAL pendulous, pensile, nutant

pending *adj, prep*
• *adj*
imminent, impending, in the offing, forthcoming, coming, approaching, nearing, near, undecided, unresolved, unsettled, awaiting settlement, uncertain
COLLOQ. in the balance, up in the air
⊟ finished, settled
• *prep*
until, till, to, before, so long as, while, whilst, throughout

pendulous *adj*
sagging, hanging, suspended, dangling, drooping, droopy, swaying, swinging
FORMAL pendent

penetrable *adj*
clear, open, passable, permeable, pervious, porous, fathomable, understandable, intelligible, accessible, comprehensible, explicable
⊟ impenetrable

penetrate *v*
1 PIERCE, stab, prick, perforate, puncture, spike, probe, sink, bore
2 GET INTO, enter, infiltrate, make your way, permeate, fill, seep, saturate, pervade, suffuse, imbue
3 GRASP, understand, fathom, comprehend, make out, work out, see, register, sink in
COLLOQ. crack, cotton on, suss out, twig, get to the bottom of

penetrating *adj*
1 PIERCING, stinging, biting, incisive, sharp, keen, cutting
2 *a penetrating sound*
loud, clear, strident, shrill, piercing, carrying
3 *a penetrating mind*
keen, acute, shrewd, discerning, discriminating, wise, perceptive, observant, profound, deep, searching, insightful, probing
⊟ **1** blunt

penetration *n*
1 PIERCING, puncturing, perforation, stabbing, pricking, incision
2 ENTRANCE, entry, inroad, infiltration, permeation, pervasion, invasion
FORMAL interpenetration
3 DISCERNMENT, perception, insight, acumen, astuteness, sharpness, keenness, acuteness, shrewdness, wit
FORMAL perspicacity

peninsula *n*
cape, point, mull, tongue, chersonese, doab

penis *n*
male organ of copulation/urination, pizzle; *dialect* jock
OLD pillicock, pintle, yard
FORMAL phallus, *membrum virile*
COLLOQ. willy; *N Am* putz
SLANG pecker, chopper, JohnThomas, schmuck, tail, todger, winkle, joystick; *N Am* dork; *Aust* tonk
TABOO dick, cock, prick, knob, tool, rod, cory, dong, plonker, roger, shaft, whang, wang
Related adjective: penile

penitence *n*
repentance, contrition, sorrow, shame, remorse, regret, self-reproach
FORMAL compunction, ruefulness

penitent *adj*
repentant, contrite, sorry, sorrowful, apologetic, remorseful, ashamed, regretful, conscience-stricken, shamefaced, humble
FORMAL rueful
⊟ unrepentant, hard-hearted, callous

pen-name n

assumed name, pseudonym, stage-name, *nom de plume*, false name
FORMAL allonym

pennant n

flag, banner, ensign, standard, streamer, colours, banderol, gonfalon, jack

penniless adj

poor, poverty-stricken, impoverished, destitute, bankrupt, ruined
FORMAL indigent
COLLOQ. dirt-poor, broke, stony-broke, down and out, on the breadline, cleaned out, strapped for cash, on your beam-ends, on your uppers, bust
SLANG skint
E3 rich, wealthy, affluent

penny-pincher n

miser, niggard, skinflint, cheeseparer, Scrooge
COLLOQ. meanie, cheapskate, money-grubber

penny-pinching adj

miserly, mean, close, niggardly, scrimping, cheeseparing, ungenerous, frugal
FORMAL parsimonious
COLLOQ. tight, tight-fisted, mingy, stingy
E3 generous, open-handed

pension n

old-age pension, retirement pension, state pension, personal pension, company pension, index-linked pension, stakeholder pension, annuity, superannuation, support, welfare, social assistance, income, allowance, benefit, corrody

pensioner n

retired person, old-age pensioner, OAP, senior citizen, out-pensioner

pensive adj

thoughtful, reflective, contemplative, meditative, thinking, pondering, musing, ruminative, absorbed, preoccupied, absent-minded, dreamy, wistful, solemn, serious, sober
FORMAL cogitative
E3 carefree

pensively adv

thoughtfully, contemplatively, meditatively, absent-mindedly, wistfully, dreamily, seriously

pent-up adj

repressed, inhibited, restrained, bridled, curbed, suppressed, stifled, held in
COLLOQ. bottled-up

penurious adj

1 POOR, impoverished, destitute, poverty-stricken, beggarly, penniless, hard up, in straitened circumstances, inadequate
FORMAL impecunious, indigent
COLLOQ. bust, flat broke, on your beam-ends, on your uppers
2 MISERLY, mean, niggardly, close, close-fisted, grudging, ungenerous
FORMAL parsimonious
COLLOQ. cheeseparing, tight-fisted, tight, mingy, stingy
E3 1 wealthy, generous

penury n

poverty, destitution, pauperism, impoverishment, insolvency, straitened circumstances, straits, deficiency, need, want, dearth, beggary
FORMAL indigence, mendicity
E3 prosperity

people n, v

♦ *n*
1 PERSONS, individuals, humans, human beings, the human race, mankind, humankind, humanity, mortals, folk(s)
2 CITIZENS, ordinary citizens, public, general public, populace, rank and file, hoi polloi, population, men women and children, inhabitants, community, society, electorate, masses, mob, rabble, great unwashed, riff-raff
COLLOQ. punters, plebs, proles
3 NATION, race, tribe, clan, ethnic group
OLD *Irish* tuath
4 *his people are from Wales*
parents, relations, relatives, folks, family, kith and kin
♦ *v*
populate, inhabit, occupy, settle, colonize

pep n, v

♦ *n*
energy, vigour, verve, spirit, sparkle, vitality, life, liveliness, dynamism, exuberance, effervescence, high spirits
FORMAL ebullience
COLLOQ. get-up-and-go, oomph, pizzazz, zing, zip
■ **pep up**
invigorate, vitalize, liven up, quicken, improve, stimulate, animate, excite, exhilarate, inspire, energize
E3 tone down

pepper v

1 BOMBARD, attack, assail, pelt, blitz, bomb
2 SPRINKLE, shower, scatter, spatter, bespatter, strew, dot, stud

peppery adj

1 SPICY, hot, pungent, seasoned, piquant
2 QUICK-TEMPERED, hot-tempered, irritable, irascible, choleric, testy, touchy, fiery, grumpy, snappish
3 INCISIVE, sharp, sarcastic, biting, stinging, astringent, caustic, waspish
FORMAL trenchant

peppy adj

lively, energetic, alive, spirited, high-spirited, animated, alert, active, enthusiastic, dynamic, vivacious, vigorous, sprightly, brisk, spry, agile, nimble, quick
E3 inactive, apathetic

perceive v

1 SEE, discern, make out, detect, discover, spot, catch sight of, glimpse, notice, observe, view, remark, note, distinguish, recognize
FORMAL espy, behold
2 SENSE, feel, apprehend, learn, realize, appreciate, be aware of, discern, recognize, see, know, grasp, understand, gather, deduce, conclude, comprehend
FORMAL be cognizant of
COLLOQ. get wind of

perceptible adj

perceivable, discernible, detectable, appreciable, distinguishable, observable, noticeable, obvious, evident, manifest, conspicuous, clear, plain, distinct, patent, apparent, tangible, visible
E3 imperceptible, inconspicuous

perception n

1 VIEW, interpretation, understanding, sense, feeling, impression, idea, conception, knowledge, apprehension
2 DISCERNMENT, awareness, consciousness, observation, recognition, insight, understanding, grasp, discrimination, sensitivity, responsiveness
FORMAL cognizance

perceptive adj

discerning, observant, sensitive, responsive, aware, alert, quick, quick-witted, keen, sharp, acute, sharp-eyed, astute, penetrating, discriminating, shrewd, understanding, deep, insightful
FORMAL perspicacious, percipient
E3 unobservant

perceptively *adv*
astutely, observantly, sensitively, keely, sharply, discriminatingly, insightfully
FORMAL perspicaciously

perch *n, v*
♦ *n*
rod, pole, bar, roost
♦ *v*
land, alight, settle, sit, roost, balance, rest, overperch; *dialect* perk

perchance *adv*
perhaps, maybe, possibly, conceivably, feasibly

percipience *n*
perception, discernment, astuteness, awareness, insight, intuition, understanding, sensitivity, penetration, judgement, alertness, acuteness
FORMAL perspicacity, sagacity

percipient *adj*
perceptive, observant, discerning, discriminating, sharp, aware, alive, astute, alert, penetrating, quick-witted, knowing, intelligent, wide-awake
FORMAL judicious, perspicacious
E3 unaware, obtuse

percolate *v*
filter, strain, seep, ooze, leach, leak, drip, drain, sift, sieve, penetrate, pass through, spread (slowly) through, trickle through, permeate, pervade

perdition *n*
damnation, hell, everlasting punishment, condemnation, hellfire, destruction, doom, downfall, ruin, ruination, annihilation

peregrination *n*
travel, travelling, voyage, wandering, roaming, roving, journey, tour, expedition, exploration, trek, trekking, trip, excursion, globetrotting, wayfaring, odyssey

peremptory *adj*
imperious, commanding, dictatorial, autocratic, tyrannical, lordly, authoritative, assertive, high-handed, overbearing, domineering, dogmatic, absolute, irrefutable, abrupt, curt, summary, arbitrary
COLLOQ. bossy

perennial *adj*
lasting, enduring, abiding, everlasting, eternal, immortal, undying, imperishable, unceasing, ceaseless, endless, unending, incessant, never-ending, constant, continual, unchanging, uninterrupted, unfailing, perpetual, persistent, permanent

perfect *adj, v*
♦ *adj*
1 FAULTLESS, impeccable, flawless, immaculate, sinless, unmarred, unblemished, spotless, blameless, pure, superb, wonderful, excellent, matchless, peerless, incomparable, superlative
2 IDEAL, model, textbook, exemplary, ultimate, expert, accomplished, finished, completed, experienced, skilful
FORMAL consummate
COLLOQ. just the job
3 EXACT, precise, accurate, right, correct, true, faithful
4 *perfect strangers*
utter, absolute, sheer, complete, entire, total, thorough, downright, out-and-out
E3 1 imperfect, flawed, blemished **2** inexperienced, unskilled **3** inaccurate, wrong
♦ *v*
fulfil, complete, finish, better, improve, polish, refine, mature, elaborate
FORMAL consummate
E3 spoil, mar

perfection *n*
1 EXCELLENCE, faultlessness, flawlessness, superiority, immaculateness, impeccability
2 IMPROVEMENT, betterment, polishing, refinement, completion, realization, maturity, ripeness, roundedness
FORMAL consummation
3 IDEAL, model, paragon, crown, pinnacle, peak of perfection, prime, best, flower, bloom, ultimate, *ne plus ultra*, acme
COLLOQ. one in a million

perfectionism *n*
1 PEDANTRY, formalism
2 IDEALISM, purism, Utopianism

perfectionist *n*
1 PEDANT, formalist, stickler, precisionist
2 IDEALIST, purist

perfectly *adv*
1 UTTERLY, absolutely, quite, thoroughly, very, completely, entirely, wholly, totally, fully, altogether
2 FAULTLESSLY, flawlessly, immaculately, without blemish, impeccably, ideally, wonderfully, superbly, exactly, correctly, to perfection
COLLOQ. *N Am* down pat
E3 1 partially **2** imperfectly, badly

perfidious *adj*
treacherous, untrustworthy, deceitful, dishonest, disloyal, double-dealing, double-faced, false, traitorous, two-faced, unfaithful, faithless, corrupt, Machiavellian, treasonous, Punic
FORMAL duplicitous
E3 faithful, honest, loyal

perfidy *n*
treachery, betrayal, deceit, falsity, faithlessness, infidelity, disloyalty, double-dealing, traitorousness, treason
FORMAL duplicity, perfidiousness
E3 faithfulness, honesty, loyalty

perforate *v*
hole, make holes in, punch, drill, bore, pierce, prick, puncture, spike, stab, gore, burst, rupture, tear, split, penetrate
TECHNICAL trephine

perforated *adj*
pierced, holed, bored, drilled, punctured, punched, porous
TECHNICAL ethmoid, fenestrate(d), fenestrial, foraminous

perforation *n*
hole, bore, prick, pierce, puncture, dotted line
TECHNICAL fenestra, fenestration, foramen

perforce *adv*
unavoidably, inevitably, necessarily, of necessity, willy-nilly

perform *v*
1 DO, carry out, discharge, fulfil, satisfy, complete, achieve, accomplish, conduct, bring off, pull off, bring about
FORMAL execute, effect
2 *perform a play*
stage, put on, present, enact, represent, act, do, play, appear as, portray, recite
3 FUNCTION, work, operate, go, run, behave, produce

performance *n*
1 SHOW, appearance, presentation, production, interpretation, rendering, rendition, representation, portrayal, acting, recital
See panel on next page
2 ACTION, deed, doing, carrying-out, implementation, discharge, fulfilment, conducting, completion, achievement, accomplishment
FORMAL execution, effecting
3 FUNCTIONING, operation, working, running, going, behaviour, conduct

Types of performance include:

act	concert	farewell	last night	production	sell-out
audition	debut	performance	last night of the	read-through	short run
benefit	dress rehearsal	first house	Proms	recital	show
N Am colloq.	dry run	first night	matinée	rehearsal	sketch
bomb	encore	*colloq.* flop	one-night stand	rendition	*colloq.* smash hit
cabaret	entertainment	full house	opening night	review	sneak preview
charity concert	exhibition	gala night	play	revue	song and dance
command	extended run	*colloq.* gig	première	run-through	theatre
performance		*colloq.* hit	preview	second house	turn

See also **theatrical**.

performer *n*
1 *circus performer*
actor, actress, player, musician, singer, dancer, comic, comedian, clown, artiste, entertainer, trouper, Thespian
See panels at **entertainer; musician; singers**.
2 ACHIEVER, doer, operator, author
FORMAL executor

perfume *n*
scent, fragrance, smell, odour, aroma, bouquet, sweetness, balm, essence, cologne, eau-de-cologne, eau-de-toilette, toilet water, incense
FORMAL redolence

perfunctorily *adv*
quickly, carelessly, superficially, cursorily, hurriedly, inattentively
E3 carefully

perfunctory *adj*
quick, careless, superficial, cursory, negligent, offhand, slipshod, slovenly, inattentive, hurried, heedless, automatic, mechanical, routine, indifferent, brief, wooden
FORMAL desultory
E3 careful, enthusiastic

perhaps *adv*
maybe, possibly, conceivably, feasibly
FORMAL perchance

peril *n*
danger, hazard, risk, jeopardy, uncertainty, insecurity, threat, menace
E3 safety, security

perilous *adj*
dangerous, unsafe, hazardous, risky, high-risk, chancy, precarious, insecure, unsure, vulnerable, fraught with danger, exposed, menacing, threatening, dire
COLLOQ. dicey, hairy, dodgy
E3 safe, secure

perimeter *n*
circumference, edge, border, boundary, frontier, limit(s), outer limits, bounds, confines, circuit, fringe, margin, periphery
E3 middle, centre, heart

period *n*
1 TIME, season, stretch, duration, space, span, spell, stint, shift, term, while, turn, session, interval, cycle
COLLOQ. *Aust & NZ* spin
2 STAGE, phase, era, epoch, age, eon, generation, date, years
3 CLASS, lesson, lecture, session, seminar, tutorial, instruction
4 *a woman's monthly period*
menstruation, menstrual flow, menstrual cycle, time of the month, monthlies
FORMAL menses
COLLOQ. the curse
5 *a period at the end of the sentence*
full stop, stop, full point, point
6 *you may not go, period*
full stop, stop, end, end of story, finish, conclusion

periodic *adj*
occasional, infrequent, sporadic, intermittent, once in a while, recurrent, recurring, repeated, regular, periodical, seasonal, cyclical, cyclic

periodical *n*
magazine, journal, publication, weekly, monthly, quarterly, review, organ

periodically *adv*
occasionally, sometimes, on occasion, from time to time, at times, at intervals, now and then, now and again, irregularly, every so often, once in a while, off and on, on and off, infrequently, intermittently, sporadically
E3 frequently, often, always

peripatetic *adj*
travelling, itinerant, journeying, mobile, roaming, roving, migrant, migratory, nomadic, wandering, vagabond, vagrant
FORMAL ambulant, ambulatory
E3 fixed

peripheral *adj*
1 MINOR, secondary, lesser, incidental, unimportant, irrelevant, subsidiary, ancillary, unnecessary, marginal, sidelined, tangential, borderline, surface, superficial
COLLOQ. beside the point, neither here nor there
2 OUTLYING, outer, outermost, surrounding
3 *peripheral devices*
additional, add-on, auxiliary, computer, input, output, storage
E3 1 major, crucial **2** central, inner

periphery *n*
edge, boundary, border, circumference, fringe, perimeter, brim, brink, rim, skirt, outskirts, outer regions, margin, verge, hem, circuit, ambit
E3 centre, nub, middle

periphrastic *adj*
roundabout, indirect, circuitous, wandering, oblique, discursive, tortuous, rambling, long-drawn-out
FORMAL circumlocutory
E3 direct

perish *v*
1 DIE, pass away, pass on, pass, depart, depart this life, breathe your last, draw your last breath, lose your life, fail, go, drown, starve, go west, succumb, close your eyes, go over to the majority
OLD exit, famish, be gathered to your fathers, give up the ghost, go the way of all flesh, go the way of the earth, pip out, sterve, swelt; (*Shakesp*) go off; (*Spenser*) quell, tine, vade
FORMAL expire, decease
COLLOQ. peg out, bite the dust, pop off, have had it, meet your maker, push up daisies, shuffle off this mortal coil; *Aust* go bung; slip the cable, turn up your toes
SLANG snuff it, cash in your chips, cash/pass in your checks, kick the bucket, kick off, kiss off, spark out, choke, croak, flatline, hop the twig, pop your clogs; *N Am* go belly up; *Aust* cark
2 COLLAPSE, disintegrate, crumble, fail, fall, come to an end, disappear, vanish, die away, rot, decay, decompose, go off

perishable *adj*
destructible, biodegradable, decomposable, short-lived
Ⓔ imperishable, durable

perjure *v*
■ **perjure yourself**
lie, lie under oath, commit perjury, bear false witness/testimony, make false statements, give false evidence
FORMAL forswear yourself

perjury *n*
false evidence, false testimony, false witness, false swearing, false oath, false statement, lying under oath, falsification, hard swearing
TECHNICAL *crimen falsi*
OLD (*Shakesp*) oath-breaking
FORMAL forswearing, mendacity

perk *n, v*
♦ *n*
fringe benefit, benefit, bonus, advantage, dividend, gratuity, tip, extra, baksheesh
FORMAL perquisite
COLLOQ. plus, freebie, golden handshake
■ **perk up**
brighten (up), cheer up, take heart, revive, rally, liven up, make/become lively, rally, recover, revitalize, improve, look up
COLLOQ. buck up, pep up

perky *adj*
lively, jaunty, spirited, vivacious, sprightly, cheerful, cheery, gay, bright, animated, bouncy, buoyant, bubbly, effervescent, sunny
FORMAL ebullient
COLLOQ. bouncy, peppy
Ⓔ cheerless, dull, gloomy

permanence *n*
fixedness, stability, imperishability, indestructibility, perpetuity, constancy, endurance, steadfastness, persistence, durability
Ⓔ impermanence, transience

permanent *adj*
1 LASTING, enduring, durable, imperishable, indestructible, unfading, eternal, everlasting, lifelong, perpetual, constant, steadfast, immutable, invariable, unchangeable, indelible, perennial, long-lasting
2 FIXED, stable, unchanging, constant, solid, firm, established
Ⓔ **1** temporary, fleeting; *formal* ephemeral

permanently *adv*
always, continually, constantly, ceaselessly, endlessly, eternally, perpetually, in perpetuity, incessantly, unceasingly, unremittingly, unendingly, once and for all, indelibly, everlastingly, ever more, for ever, for ever and ever, for all time
COLLOQ. for keeps, till doomsday, till kingdom come, till the cows come home, till hell freezes over
Ⓔ temporarily

permeable *adj*
porous, absorbent, absorptive, penetrable, pervious, passable, spongy
Ⓔ impermeable, watertight

permeate *v*
pass through, soak through, filter through, seep through, spread through, penetrate, infiltrate, percolate, pervade, imbue, saturate, impregnate, fill, diffuse

permissible *adj*
permitted, allowable, allowed, admissible, all right, tolerable, acceptable, proper, authorized, sanctioned, lawful, legal, legitimate
COLLOQ. OK, kosher, legit
Ⓔ prohibited, banned, forbidden

permission *n*
consent, assent, agreement, approval, allowance, clearance, authorization, sanction, leave, warrant, permit, licence, dispensation, freedom, liberty
FORMAL approbation
COLLOQ. green light, thumbs-up, go-ahead
Ⓔ prohibition

permissive *adj*
liberal, broad-minded, tolerant, forbearing, easy-going, lenient, indulgent, overindulgent, lax, free
FORMAL latitudinarian
Ⓔ strict, rigid, narrow-minded

permit *v, n*
♦ *v*
allow, let, consent, agree, admit, grant, authorize, give, enable, empower, sanction, warrant, license, indulge, tolerate
OLD suffer
COLLOQ. give the go-ahead to, give the green light to, give the thumbs up to, give the nod to
Ⓔ prohibit, forbid
♦ *n*
pass, passport, visa, licence, warrant, authorization, sanction, permission, safe-conduct, docket, *carnet*, green card, laissez-passer, *permis de séjour*
OLD placard
Ⓔ prohibition

permutation *n*
alteration, change, shift, transformation, variation
FORMAL transposition, configuration, transmutation, commutation

pernicious *adj*
harmful, damaging, dangerous, destructive, ruinous, detrimental, bad, hurtful, injurious, offensive, malicious, poisonous, venomous, pestilent, toxic, wicked, evil, malevolent, malignant, fatal, deadly, unhealthy, unwholesome
FORMAL deleterious, maleficent, noisome, noxious
Ⓔ innocuous

pernickety *adj*
fussy, particular, over-particular, over-precise, carping, nice, punctilious, fastidious, difficult to please, fiddly, finical, finicky, exacting, detailed, careful, painstaking, fine, tricky
COLLOQ. choosy, picky, hair-splitting, nit-picking; *NAm* persnickety

peroration *n*
1 SUMMING-UP, summary, conclusion, closing remarks, reiteration, recapitulation
COLLOQ. recapping
2 SPEECH, lecture, talk, address
FORMAL oration, diatribe, declamation

perpendicular *adj, n*
♦ *adj*
vertical, upright, erect, straight, right, at right angles, sheer, steep, abrupt, precipitous, plumb
TECHNICAL anticlinal, normal
OLD downright
Ⓔ horizontal
♦ *n*
TECHNICAL apothem, cathetus, offset, sine

perpetrate *v*
commit, carry out, execute, do, accomplish, be responsible for, be to blame for, perform, inflict, wreak
FORMAL effect, effectuate

perpetration *n*
carrying-out, implementation, execution, doing, performance, achievement, accomplishment, commitment, committal

perpetrator *n*
doer, committer, offender, agent
FORMAL executor, executant
COLLOQ. *N Am* perp

perpetual *adj*
eternal, everlasting, infinite, endless, unending, never-ending, interminable, ceaseless, unceasing, incessant, continuous, unbroken, uninterrupted, unremitting, constant, persistent, continual, repeated, recurrent, perennial, permanent, lasting, enduring, abiding, persisting, unchanging, unfailing, undying, unvarying, intermittent
temporary; *formal* ephemeral, transient

perpetually *adv*
eternally, endlessly, interminably, ceaselessly, unceasingly, incessantly, unremittingly, constantly, persistently, continually, permanently

perpetuate *v*
continue, keep up, maintain, sustain, preserve, keep alive, keep going, immortalize, commemorate, eternalize, memorialize

perpetuation *n*
continuation, prolongation, maintenance, preservation, commemoration, sustaining, keeping alive, lengthening, extension
FORMAL protraction
formal cessation, termination

perpetuity
■ **in perpetuity**
for ever, for ever and ever, for all time, always, endlessly, eternally, perpetually, ever more
COLLOQ. till the cows come home

perplex *v*
puzzle, baffle, mystify, stump, confuse, confound, muddle, bewilder, dumbfound, tickle, bother, pother, embarrass, entangle, gravel, hobble, beset; *Scot* bumbaze, fickle
OLD distrouble, embrangle, feague, pose
COLLOQ. throw, bamboozle, flummox, nonplus

perplexed *adj*
puzzled, baffled, bewildered, mystified, stumped, confused, muddled, confounded, disconcerted, fuddled, worried, at a loss
COLLOQ. bamboozled, flummoxed, nonplussed

perplexing *adj*
puzzling, baffling, bewildering, confusing, mystifying, amazing, complex, complicated, intricate, inexplicable, hard, strange, weird, paradoxical, difficult, taxing, involved, knotty, thorny, enigmatic, mysterious
FORMAL labyrinthine
easy, simple

perplexity *n*
1 PUZZLEMENT, bafflement, bewilderment, confusion, incomprehension, mystification, nonplus; *Scot* fickleness
2 COMPLEXITY, complication, difficulty, intricacy, involvement, dilemma, enigma, mystery, puzzle, paradox, obscurity, labyrinth
FORMAL obfuscation

perquisite *n*
perk, fringe benefit, benefit, bonus, advantage, dividend, gratuity, tip, extra, baksheesh, plus
COLLOQ. freebie

persecute *v*
1 ILL-TREAT, abuse, mistreat, maltreat, oppress, tyrannize, victimize, martyr, distress, afflict, torment, torture, crucify
2 HARASS, hound, pursue, hunt (down), bother, worry, annoy, pester, badger, bait, molest
COLLOQ. hassle
1 pamper, spoil

persecution *n*
ill-treatment, mistreatment, abuse, maltreatment, discrimination, oppression, harassment, molestation, suppression, tyranny, victimization, punishment, torture, martyrdom, crucifixion
FORMAL subjugation

perseverance *n*
persistence, determination, resolution, resolve, doggedness, tenacity, diligence, application, assiduity, dedication, commitment, purpose, purposefulness, constancy, steadfastness, stamina, endurance, indefatigability
FORMAL pertinacity, intransigence
COLLOQ. stickability; *N Am* stick-to-it-iveness

persevere *v*
continue, carry on, go on, keep going, struggle on, soldier on, persist, remain, be persistent, be determined, be resolute, stand firm, stand fast, hold on, hang on
OLD prosecute
COLLOQ. stick at it, plug away, hang in there, hammer away, bash on, truck, go the whole distance, stick to your guns, leave no stone unturned, mean business; *Scot* stick in
give up, stop; *formal* discontinue

persist *v*
1 CONTINUE, carry on, go on, keep on, keep going, soldier on, keep at it, persevere, stand firm, stand fast, hold on, hang on, be persistent, be determined, be resolute, insist
COLLOQ. stick at it, hang in, plug away
2 REMAIN, keep on, hold, linger, last, endure, continue
FORMAL abide
1 stop, give up; *formal* desist

persistence *n*
perseverance, determination, endurance, doggedness, diligence, assiduousness, assiduity, constancy, resolution, tenacity, steadfastness, tirelessness, stamina, indefatigableness
FORMAL pertinacity, sedulity
COLLOQ. grit, stickability; *N Am* stick-to-it-iveness

persistent *adj*
1 INCESSANT, endless, never-ending, interminable, continual, unceasing, ceaseless, lasting, unrelenting, relentless, unremitting, constant, steady, repeated, perpetual, lasting, enduring, continuous
2 *persistent effort*
persevering, determined, resolute, purposeful, diligent, assiduous, dogged, tenacious, stubborn, obstinate, steadfast, zealous, tireless, unflagging, indefatigable
FORMAL intractable, obdurate, pertinacious
COLLOQ. *N Am* stick-to-it-ive

persistently *adv*
1 CONTINUALLY, incessantly, interminably, unceasingly, ceaselessly, relentlessly, constantly, continuously
2 RESOLUTELY, diligently, assiduously, obstinately, stubbornly, tenaciously, tirelessly

person *n*
individual, human being, human, being, man, woman, mortal, body, soul, character, type, someone, somebody
■ **in person**
personally, face to face, actually, bodily
COLLOQ. in the flesh, as large as life

persona *n*
image, face, public face, role, part, character, personality, front, façade, mask

personable *adj*
pleasant, pleasing, likeable, presentable, nice, agreeable, amiable, affable, attractive, good-looking, handsome, charming, warm, winning, outgoing
unpleasant, disagreeable, unattractive

personage *n*
celebrity, name, notable, worthy, public figure,

personality, luminary, dignitary, headliner
COLLOQ. VIP, celeb, big shot, somebody, big noise, big cheese, bigwig

personal *adj*
1 *give you my personal attention*
individual, special, particular, exclusive
2 *a personal appearance*
live, in person, in the flesh, bodily
3 *your personal style*
individual, idiosyncratic, peculiar, characteristic, distinctive, unique, own, subjective
4 PRIVATE, confidential, intimate, secret
5 *personal remarks*
offensive, insulting, critical, rude, abusive, hurtful, wounding, disrespectful, derogatory, upsetting
E3 **3** general, universal **4** public, official

personality *n*
1 CHARACTER, nature, disposition, temperament, temper, identity, individuality, mind, self, selfhood, psyche, traits, make-up, charm, charisma, magnetism
COLLOQ. the real you
2 CELEBRITY, notable, personage, (public) figure, person, dignitary, worthy, star
COLLOQ. VIP

personalize *v*
customize, adapt, convert, modify, tailor, alter, adjust, suit, fit, transform

personally *adv*
1 *personally, I don't approve*
from my point of view, in my opinion, I think, I believe, in my view, from my standpoint, the way I see it, as I see it, (according) to my way of thinking
COLLOQ. if you ask me, in my book, for my money
2 INDIVIDUALLY, in person, specially, particularly, exclusively, solely, alone, independently, subjectively, idiosyncratically, distinctively, characteristically, uniquely, privately, confidentially
3 *take something personally*
directed against you, as personal criticism, as hurtful comments, as a slight, insultingly, offensively

personification *n*
essence, embodiment, incarnation, likeness, image, representation, recreation, portrayal, semblance
FORMAL delineation, manifestation, quintessence

personify *v*
embody, epitomize, typify, exemplify, symbolize, represent, mirror, incarnate, be the incarnation of, personize, personalize
OLD impersonate
FORMAL hypostatize

personnel *n*
staff, workforce, workers, employees, crew, human resources, labour force, manpower, people, members
COLLOQ. liveware

perspective *n*
1 VIEW, point of view, viewpoint, aspect, angle, slant, attitude, frame of mind, vantage point, standpoint, vista, scene, prospect, outlook
COLLOQ. take
2 *get things into perspective*
proportion, relation, balance, equilibrium

perspicacious *adj*
discerning, observant, sensitive, responsive, aware, alert, quick, quick-witted, keen, sharp, sharp-eyed, astute, penetrating, discriminating, shrewd, understanding
FORMAL sagacious, percipient, judicious
E3 unobservant, obtuse

perspicacity *n*
discernment, astuteness, perceptiveness, discrimination, insight, acuteness, cleverness, sharpness, keenness, acumen, shrewdness, penetration, wit
FORMAL percipience, perspicaciousness, perspicuity, sagaciousness, sagacity
COLLOQ. brains

perspicuity *n*
clarity, clearness, plainness, precision, lucidity, straightforwardness, distinctness, explicitness, intelligibility, comprehensibility, comprehensibleness, penetrability, transparency
FORMAL limpidity, limpidness

perspicuous *adj*
clear, crystal-clear, unambiguous, plain, obvious, manifest, self-evident, transparent, understandable, lucid, straightforward, apparent, explicit, distinct, intelligible, comprehensible
FORMAL limpid

perspiration *n*
sweat, secretion, moisture, wetness, foam
TECHNICAL sudor, diaphoresis, hidrosis
FORMAL exudation

perspire *v*
sweat, secrete, swelter, drip
TECHNICAL sudate
FORMAL exude

persuadable *adj*
amenable, agreeable, compliant, flexible, persuasible, malleable, pliable, receptive, susceptive, impressionable
FORMAL acquiescent
E3 firm, inflexible, stubborn

persuade *v*
coax, prevail upon, cajole, wheedle, talk into, argue (into), induce, bring round, win over, convince, satisfy, convert, lobby, sway, influence, tempt, lure, lead on, incite, prompt, urge, coerce, move, get round, bring yourself
OLD perswade
FORMAL inveigle
COLLOQ. lean on, sweet-talk, fast-talk, soft-soap, swing it, pull strings, twist someone's arm, put the screws on, con, nobble, moody; *N Am* snow
E3 dissuade, deter, discourage, talk out of, put off

Synonym nuances
Coax or **induce** would be appropriate to refer to enticing someone with an element of flattery or encouragement, while **prevail upon** is more suggestive of successfully convincing someone: *he was prevailed upon to become chairman.* **Cajole** and **wheedle**, however, both have slight implications of deception or trickery, whereas **get round**, **talk into**, **bring round** and **win over** suggest convincing someone to do something they were originally opposed to. **Convince** and **satisfy** have similar connotations but with suggestions of supplying evidence rather than just encouragement to effect the change, while the term **convert** further implies getting someone to turn from one viewpoint to another.
    Lobby is generally used in the context of persuading public officials, while **sway** and **influence** are suggestive of the use of power in persuasion: *the Home Secretary denied influencing the Prime Minister in his decision.* Both **tempt** and **lure** imply a degree of enticement with promises of a favourable result, whereas **lead on** implies delusion: *you led me on into taking part - now we shall both go to prison.*
    Incite suggests rousing into action, often with undesirable or dramatic results: *opposition incited him to drastic methods.* You could use **prompt** to suggest a causal effect, although a less dramatic one: *what happened recently has prompted me to write to you.* Meanwhile **urge** has more to do with persuasion through persistence, and **coerce** implies a degree of compulsion.

persuasion n
1 COAXING, prevailing, cajolery, wheedling, talking into, winning over, inducement, enticement, pull, power, influence, sway, conviction, conversion, incitement, prompting, urging, coercion
COLLOQ. clout, sweet-talking, arm-twisting
2 OPINION, school (of thought), party, faction, side, camp, affiliation, philosophy, conviction, faith, belief, view, point of view, viewpoint, denomination, sect

persuasive adj
convincing, plausible, sound, valid, influential, forceful, pushy, weighty, effective, slick, telling, potent, compelling, moving, touching
FORMAL cogent, effectual
COLLOQ. smooth-talking
E3 unconvincing

persuasively adv
convincingly, plausibly, influentially, powerfully, forcefully, effectively, compellingly
FORMAL cogently, effectually
E3 unconvincingly

pert adj
impudent, cheeky, presumptuous, impertinent, insolent, bold, cocky, brash, gay, forward, fresh, flippant, lively, spirited, brisk, daring, sprightly, jaunty, tossy
COLLOQ. perky, saucy; N Am sassy
E3 coy, shy

pertain v
relate, apply, be appropriate, be part of, be relevant, bear on, have a bearing on, befit, belong, come under, concern, refer, regard
FORMAL appertain ·

pertinacious adj
persistent, persevering, determined, dogged, purposeful, tenacious, relentless, resolute, uncompromising, unyielding, wilful, headstrong, inflexible, obstinate, stubborn, self-willed, strong-willed, perverse, mulish
FORMAL intractable, obdurate

pertinent adj
relevant, suitable, appropriate, fitting, apt, apposite, to the point, material, applicable
FORMAL germane, apropos, ad rem
E3 inappropriate, unsuitable, irrelevant

pertness n
impudence, cheek, cheekiness, impertinence, insolence, presumption, rudeness, effrontery, forwardness, freshness, boldness, brashness, audacity, brazenness
COLLOQ. sauciness, brass, cockiness, face, chutzpah; N Am sass, sassiness

perturb v
worry, alarm, disturb, bother, trouble, upset, make anxious, disconcert, unsettle, discompose, disquiet, ruffle, fluster, confuse, agitate, vex
COLLOQ. put the wind up, rattle
E3 reassure, compose

perturbation n
worry, fright, scare, alarm, fear, terror, panic, horror, shock, consternation, dismay, distress, anxiety, nervousness, apprehension, trepidation, uneasiness
COLLOQ. flap

perturbed adj
worried, anxious, alarmed, upset, fearful, shaken, troubled, nervous, restless, disturbed, unsettled, discomposed, disconcerted, flustered, agitated, uncomfortable, uneasy, harassed, flurried
E3 calm, composed

perusal n
read, reading, look, scrutiny, study, examination, inspection, check, browse, glance, skim, run-through

peruse v
study, pore over, read, scan, scrutinize, examine, inspect, check, browse, look through, run through, leaf through, glance through, skim

pervade v
affect, penetrate, permeate, percolate, charge, fill, pass through, spread through, be disseminated through, imbue, infuse, suffuse, diffuse, infiltrate, saturate, impregnate

pervasive adj
prevalent, common, extensive, widespread, general, universal, inescapable, rife, diffuse, ubiquitous
FORMAL omnipresent, immanent

perverse adj
contrary, wayward, wrong-headed, wilful, headstrong, stubborn, obstinate, unyielding, disobedient, awkward, unruly, difficult, rebellious, troublesome, worrying, alarming, obstructive, unhelpful, unco-operative, uncontrollable, unmanageable, pig-headed, ill-tempered, cantankerous, unreasonable, senseless, incorrect, improper, deviant, cross-grained, thwart, balky; Scot thrawn, camstairy
OLD overthwart, cussed, froward, wry; (Shakesp) peevish; Scot donsie
FORMAL intransigent, obdurate, refractory, intractable
COLLOQ. crabbed, stroppy, bolshie, bloody-minded
E3 obliging, co-operative, reasonable

perversely adv
waywardly, stubbornly, obstinately, worryingly, alarmingly, obstructively, unhelpfully, unco-operatively
E3 obligingly, reasonably

perversion n
1 CORRUPTION, depravity, debauchery, immorality, vice, wickedness, deviance, abnormality, irregularity
COLLOQ. kinkiness
2 TWISTING, distortion, misrepresentation, travesty, misinterpretation, deviation, misuse, misapplication, falsification
FORMAL aberration

perversity n
contrariness, waywardness, wrong-headedness, wilfulness, stubbornness, obstinacy, disobedience, awkwardness, unruliness, rebelliousness, troublesomeness, uncontrollability, unreasonableness, senselessness, contradictoriness, frowardness, gee
OLD cussedness
FORMAL contumacy, intransigence, obduracy, refractoriness

pervert v, n
♦ v
1 *pervert the truth*
twist, warp, distort, misrepresent, falsify, garble, misinterpret, misdirect, turn aside, deflect, avert, wrest
OLD prevaricate, wry
2 CORRUPT, lead astray, deprave, debauch, debase, degrade, subvert, warp, abuse, misuse, misapply
OLD wry
FORMAL vitiate
♦ n
deviate, deviant, debauchee, degenerate
COLLOQ. weirdo, oddball; N Am sicko
SLANG perv

perverted adj
corrupt, depraved, debauched, debased, immoral, evil, wicked, corrupted, deviant, unnatural, abnormal, unhealthy, twisted, warped, distorted
FORMAL vitiated
COLLOQ. kinky
SLANG pervy
E3 natural, normal

pesky adj
irritating, annoying, infuriating, maddening, troublesome, bothersome, irksome, tiresome, grating, worrisome, vexatious, vexing, disturbing, upsetting, nagging, displeasing, galling, provoking, thorny, trying
COLLOQ. aggravating, confounded, infernal

pessimism n
defeatism, fatalism, hopelessness, cynicism, depression, dejection, despair, gloom, gloominess, glumness, despondency, doomwatch, melancholy, negative thinking, distrust, *Weltschmerz*
COLLOQ. looking on the black side
F3 optimism, hopefulness

pessimist n
defeatist, fatalist, alarmist, doubter, cynic, melancholic, worrier, prophet of doom, gloom-monger, doomster, doomwatcher, doubting Thomas
OLD saturnist
COLLOQ. dismal Jimmy, gloom and doom merchant, doom merchant, killjoy, wet blanket, no-hoper, crapehanger
F3 optimist, hopeful

pessimistic adj
negative, cynical, fatalistic, defeatist, resigned, distrustful, suspicious, doubting, hopeless, alarmist, discouraging, depressing, off-putting, despairing, despondent, dejected, downhearted, glum, morose, melancholy, depressed, dismal, gloomy, bleak
COLLOQ. looking on the black side, doomy
F3 optimistic

pest n
nuisance, bother, annoyance, irritation, irritant, vexation, trial, curse, scourge, bane, blight, bug
COLLOQ. pain, pain in the neck, thorn in the flesh

pester v
nag, badger, hound, harass, plague, torment, provoke, worry, irk, fret, bother, disturb, annoy, irritate, pick on
COLLOQ. hassle, get at, get on someone's nerves, drive round the bend, drive up the wall

pestilence n
plague, epidemic, disease, sickness, infection, contagion, infestation, cholera
OLD lues
FORMAL pandemic
Related adjective: luetic

pestilent adj
1 HARMFUL, destructive, ruinous, diseased, disease-ridden, plague-ridden, poisonous, contaminated, contagious, infectious, infected, communicable, catching, corrupting, detrimental, pernicious
FORMAL deleterious
2 INFURIATING, troublesome, annoying, bothersome, irritating, tiresome, vexing, irksome

pestilential adj
1 HARMFUL, destructive, ruinous, diseased, disease-ridden, plague-ridden, poisonous, contaminated, contagious, infectious, infected
2 INFURIATING, annoying, troublesome, bothersome, irritating, tiresome, vexing, irksome, pernicious

pet¹ n, adj, v
♦ *n*
teacher's pet
favourite, darling, idol, treasure, jewel
COLLOQ. teacher's pet, apple of your eye, blue-eyed boy/girl
♦ *adj*
1 *my pet rabbit*
tame, domesticated, trained, house-trained, manageable, subdued
See also panel at **animal**.

2 *her pet project*
favourite, favoured, preferred, dear, dearest, cherished, prized, preferred, chosen, special, particular, personal
♦ *v*
stroke, caress, fondle, cuddle, embrace, kiss
COLLOQ. neck, canoodle, smooch
SLANG snog

pet² n
in a pet
bad mood, bad temper, temper, sulk(s), tantrum
COLLOQ. paddy, hump, huff, stew, strop, grumps, the pits

peter v
■ **peter out**
dwindle, taper off, fade, wane, evaporate, ebb, diminish, fail, cease, stop, die away, come to an end, come to nothing
COLLOQ. fizzle out

petite adj
dainty, small, slight, little, delicate, bijou, dinky
F3 big, large

petition n, v
♦ *n*
appeal, round robin, protest, application, request, representation, solicitation, plea, entreaty, prayer, supplication
TECHNICAL supplicat
OLD boon, suit
FORMAL invocation
♦ *v*
appeal, call upon, ask, crave, solicit, bid, urge, press, implore, beg, plead, entreat, beseech, pray, request, memorialize
OLD sue
FORMAL supplicate, adjure

pet name n
diminutive, endearment, term of endearment, nickname
FORMAL hypocorisma

petrified adj
terrified, terror-stricken, aghast, horrified, horror-stricken, appalled, stunned, dumbfounded, shocked, speechless, stupefied, transfixed, numb, benumbed, dazed, frozen
COLLOQ. scared stiff, scared out of your wits, scared to death, having kittens, in a blue funk, shaking like a leaf, with your heart in your mouth

petrify v
1 TERRIFY, horrify, frighten, alarm, panic, appal, paralyse, numb, stupefy, stun, dumbfound
COLLOQ. rattle, spook, boggle, scare someone out of their wits, make someone's blood run cold, scare the living daylights out of, make someone's hair stand on end, make someone jump out of their skin, put the frighteners on, put the wind up
SLANG scare the shit out of
2 TURN TO STONE, ossify, fossilize

petticoat n
slip, underskirt, jupon, kirtle

pettifogging adj
mean, petty, quibbling, paltry, captious, niggling, over-refined, subtle, sophistical, cavilling, casuistic, equivocating
COLLOQ. hair-splitting, nit-picking

pettiness n
small-mindedness, narrow-mindedness, meanness, quibbling, spitefulness
COLLOQ. nit-picking

pettish adj
peevish, sulky, irritable, petulant, thin-skinned, tetchy, touchy, grumpy, bad-tempered, ill-humoured, fractious, cross, fretful, querulous, snappish, waspish, splenetic
COLLOQ. huffy

petty *adj*

1 MINOR, unimportant, insignificant, inconsequential, inessential, trivial, secondary, lesser, small, in a small way, little, slight, trifling, paltry, inconsiderable, negligible, pimping, poking, twopenny-halfpenny; *N Am* shoestring
OLD puisne, scantle
COLLOQ. measly, grotty, piffling, piddling, potty; *N Am* picayune
2 SMALL-MINDED, small, narrow-minded, mean, ungenerous, grudging, niggling, quibbling, parochial, spiteful
COLLOQ. nit-picking, parish-pump
F∃ 1 important, significant **2** generous, open-minded

petulance *n*

bad temper, irritability, ill-temper, ill-humour, sulkiness, sullenness, waspishness, peevishness, pique
FORMAL procacity, querulousness, spleen
COLLOQ. crabbedness, crabbiness

petulant *adj*

fretful, peevish, touchy, cross, irritable, snappish, bad-tempered, ill-humoured, complaining, impatient, moody, sullen, sulky, sour, ungracious
FORMAL querulous
COLLOQ. crotchety, crabby, crabbed, ratty, browned off, in a paddy, in a stew

phantasmagorical *adj*

phantasmagoric, dreamlike, surreal, illusory, unreal, trance-like, hallucinatory, insubstantial, unsubstantial, visionary, chimerical, fantastic, Alice-in-Wonderland
FORMAL ethereal

phantom *n*

ghost, spectre, spirit, apparition, wraith, vision, hallucination, illusion, figment
FORMAL revenant
COLLOQ. spook

pharisaical *adj*

sanctimonious, self-righteous, holier-than-thou, formal, hypocritical, insincere, pietistic, preachy, moralizing
COLLOQ. goody-goody

Pharisee *n*

hypocrite, fraud, pietist, whited sepulchre
FORMAL dissembler, dissimulator
COLLOQ. phoney, humbug

phase *n, v*

♦ *n*
stage, step, time, juncture, period, spell, season, chapter, position, part, point, aspect, form, shape, state, condition, development
▪ **phase in**
introduce, ease in, bring in, start, start using, initiate
▪ **phase out**
wind down, run down, ease off, taper off, wind up, eliminate, dispose of, get rid of, remove, withdraw, close, stop, stop using
FORMAL terminate

phenomenal *adj*

unbelievable, incredible, wonderful, fantastic, sensational, stupendous, amazing, astounding, astonishing, marvellous, breathtaking, remarkable, extraordinary, exceptional, unprecedented, unparalleled, unique, singular, unheard of, unusual
COLLOQ. mind-blowing, mind-boggling, too good to be true

phenomenally *adv*

incredibly, unbelievably, remarkably, extraordinarily, exceptionally, amazingly, astoundingly, astonishingly, wonderfully, marvellously, sensationally

phenomenon *n*

1 OCCURRENCE, happening, event, incident, episode, circumstance, fact, experience, appearance, sight
2 WONDER, marvel, miracle, prodigy, rarity, curiosity, spectacle, sensation
SLANG phenom

philander *v*

womanize, flirt, dally, play/fool around, have an affair
COLLOQ. sleep around, play the field

philanderer *n*

womanizer, ladies' man, lady-killer, flirt, dallier, libertine, rake, playboy, Casanova, Don Juan
COLLOQ. stud, wolf

philanthropic *adj*

humanitarian, public-spirited, altruistic, unselfish, selfless, benevolent, kind, kind-hearted, humane, charitable, alms-giving, generous, liberal, open-handed
FORMAL munificent, bounteous, bountiful
F∃ misanthropic

philanthropist *n*

humanitarian, benefactor, patron, sponsor, giver, donor, helper, backer, contributor, alms-giver, altruist
F∃ misanthrope

philanthropy *n*

humanitarianism, public-spiritedness, altruism, unselfishness, selflessness, social concern/awareness, social conscience, benevolence, kind-heartedness, kindness, charity, alms-giving, giving, patronage, sponsorship, help, backing, generosity, liberality, open-handedness
FORMAL beneficence, munificence, bounteousness, bountifulness
F∃ misanthropy

philippic *n*

diatribe, tirade, abuse, harangue, attack, onslaught, denunciation, criticism, insult, reviling, upbraiding, reproof, reprimand, rebuke
FORMAL invective, vituperation

philistine *n, adj*

♦ *n*
lowbrow, ignoramus, barbarian, bourgeois, vulgarian, yahoo
COLLOQ. boor, lout
♦ *adj*
uncultivated, uncultured, uneducated, unrefined, unread, unlettered, ignorant, lowbrow, tasteless, boorish, bourgeois, crass

philosopher *n*

philosophizer, thinker, theorist, theorizer, analyser, scholar, expert, guru, metaphysicist, sage, logician
TECHNICAL epistemologist, dialectician
FORMAL deipnosophist

philosophical *adj*

1 *a philosophical discussion*
metaphysical, abstract, theoretical, analytical, rational, logical, erudite, learned, wise, thoughtful, pensive, reflective, contemplative, meditative
COLLOQ. unflappable
2 RESIGNED, patient, stoic, stoical, self-possessed, dispassionate, serene, unruffled, calm, composed, unemotional, impassive, collected, cool, placid, rational, logical, realistic
FORMAL phlegmatic, imperturbable

philosophically *adv*

1 METAPHYSICALLY, theoretically, abstractly, analytically, logically
2 *they accepted their fate philosophically*
stoically, calmly, patiently, resignedly, unemotionally, impassively, placidly
COLLOQ. unflappably

Philosophical schools, doctrines and theories include:

absolutism	critical	existentialism	intuitionalism	phenomenalism	scepticism
agnosticism	rationalism	experimentalism	Kantianism	Platonism	scholasticism
altruism	cynicism	fatalism	libertarianism	pluralism	sensationalism
analytic	deism	feminism	logical positivism	positivism	solipsism
philosophy	descriptivism	fideism	Marxism	post-	Stoicism
antinomianism	determinism	Frankfurt School	materialism	structuralism	structuralism
Aristotelianism	dialectical	gnosticism	monism	pragmatism	subjectivism
ascetism	materialism	hedonism	naturalism	prescriptivism	Taoism
atheism	dogmatism	Hegelianism	neo-Kantianism	Pyrrhonism	theism
atomism	dualism	historicism	Neoplatonism	Pythagoreanism	Thomism
behaviourism	egoism	humanism	nihilism	rationalism	transcendenta-
Cartesianism	Eleaticism	idealism	nominalism	realism	lism
conceptualism	empiricism	immaterialism	Nyaya-Vaisesika	reductionism	utilitarianism
Confucianism	Epicureanism	instrumentalism	objectivism	relativism	Vedanta-
consequentialism	essentialism	interactionism	pantheism	Sankhya-Yoga	Mimamsa

Philosophical terms include:

a posteriori	deontology	identity	jurisprudence	sense data	teleology
a priori	entailment	induction	ontology	substance	
deduction	falsafa	intuition	phenomenology	syllogism	

Branches of philosophy include:

aesthetics	ethics	philosophy of biology	philosophy of informatics	philosophy of mathematics	philosophy of psychology
AI and cognitive science	history of philosophy	philosophy of economics	philosophy of language	philosophy of medicine	philosophy of religion
applied ethics	logic	philosophy of education	philosophy of law (jurisprudence)	philosophy of mind	philosophy of science
axiology	metaphysics				
bioethics	moral philosophy	philosophy of history	philosophy of literature	philosophy of politics	semiotics
eastern philosophy	ontology				
epistemology	phenomenology				

philosophy *n*

1 *study philosophy*
reason, thought, thinking, wisdom, knowledge
See panels above
2 IDEOLOGY, world-view, doctrine, beliefs, convictions, tenets, values, principles, attitude, viewpoint, point of view, view

phlegmatic *adj*
placid, stolid, impassive, calm, tranquil, cool, unemotional, unconcerned, indifferent, matter-of-fact, self-controlled, stoical, dispassionate, saturnine
FORMAL imperturbable
COLLOQ. unflappable, cool and collected
Ⅎ emotional, passionate, nervous

phobia *n*
fear, irrational fear, terror, dread, anxiety, neurosis, obsession, aversion, dislike, hatred, horror, loathing, revulsion, repulsion
FORMAL antipathy, detestation
COLLOQ. hang-up, thing
Ⅎ love, liking

Phobias (by name of fear) include:

zoophobia (*animals*)	hippophobia (*horses*)
bacteriophobia (*bacteria*)	entomophobia (*insects*)
apiphobia (*bees*)	astraphobia (*lightning*)
ailurophobia (*cats*)	autophobia (*loneliness*)
cyberphobia (*computers*)	bacillophobia (*microbes*)
necrophobia (*corpses*)	belonephobia (*needles*)
scotophobia (or achluophobia) (*darkness*)	agoraphobia (*open spaces*)
cynophobia (*dogs*)	toxiphobia (*poison*)
claustrophobia (*enclosed places*)	herpetophobia (*reptiles*)
	ophiophobia (*snakes*)
panphobia (*everything*)	tachophobia (*speed*)
pyrophobia (*fire*)	arachnophobia (*spiders*)
xenophobia (*foreigners*)	triskaidekaphobia (*thirteen*)
phasmophobia (*ghosts*)	brontophobia (*thunder*)
acrophobia (*high places*)	hydrophobia (*water*)

phone *n, v*

♦ *n*

1 TELEPHONE, receiver, handset, mobile phone, cordless phone, car phone, cell phone
COLLOQ. blower
2 *give me a quick phone*
ring, call, phone call
COLLOQ. buzz, tinkle, bell

♦ *v*

telephone, ring (up), call (up), dial, contact, get in touch, give someone a call, make a call
COLLOQ. buzz, give a buzz, give a tinkle, give a bell

phonetic alphabet

The NATO phonetic alphabet code words for letters are:

Alpha	Juliet	Sierra
Bravo	Kilo	Tango
Charlie	Lima	Uniform
Delta	Mike	Victor
Echo	November	Whisky
Foxtrot	Oscar	X-ray
Golf	Papa	Yankee
Hotel	Quebec	Zulu
India	Romeo	

phoney *adj, n*

♦ *adj*
fake, counterfeit, forged, fraudulent, bogus, trick, false, mock, spurious, assumed, feigned, simulated, affected, put-on, contrived, sham, imitation, ersatz
COLLOQ. pseudo
Ⅎ real, genuine

♦ *n*
impostor, pretender, fraud, sham, fake, faker, forgery, counterfeit, mountebank
COLLOQ. humbug, pseud, quack

phosphorescent *adj*
glowing, bright, luminescent, luminous, radiant
TECHNICAL noctilucent, noctilucous
FORMAL refulgent

photocopy *v, n*
• *v*
copy, duplicate, Photostat®, Xerox®, print, run off
• *n*
copy, duplicate, facsimile, Photostat®, Xerox®

photograph *n, v*
• *n*
photo, snap, snapshot, print, shot, still, slide, transparency, picture, image, likeness, visual aid, retake, close-up, enlargement, blow-up, exposure, abstract, composition, montage, landscape, portrait, seascape, centrefold, panel, pin, sepia, hologram, headshot, heliochrome, microdot, microgram, micrograph, microphotograph, nephogram, pyrophotograph, skiagram, wirephoto
TECHNICAL angiogram, cathodograph, encephalogram, karyotype, mammogram, radiogram, radiograph, X-ray, röntgenogram, chlorobromide, chromatype, daguerreotype, ferro-print, rotograph, spectrogram, spectroheliogram
OLD ferrotype, photogene, platinotype, sun picture, sun print
COLLOQ. pic, piccy, mug shot
• *v*
snap, take, take a picture of, take a photograph of, take a snapshot of, film, shoot, video, record, capture on film/ videotape, blow up, enlarge
TECHNICAL X-ray, daguerreotype, rotograph
OLD Kodak®

Photographic equipment includes:

boom arm	film-drying	safelight
camcorder	cabinet	screen
camera	film projector	slide projector
contact printer	fixing bath	slide viewer
developer bath	flash umbrella	stand
developing tank	focus magnifier	stop bath
dry mounting	light-box	tripod
press	negative carrier	Vertoscope®
easel	print-drying rack	viewer
enlarger	print washer	
enlarger timer	paper drier	

Photographic accessories include:

afocal lens	film	parabolic
air-shutter release	film pack	reflector
auxiliary lens	filter	polarizing filter
barn doors	fish-eye lens	remote control
battery	flashbulb	right-angle finder
cable release	flash card	sepia filter
camcorder	flashcube	skylight filter
battery charger/	flashgun	slide mount
discharger/	flash unit	snoot
tester	heat filter	spot meter
camera bag	honeycomb	supplementary
cartridge film	diffuser	lens
cassette adaptor	hot shoe	tele-cine
cassette film	light meter	converter
close-up lens	lens	teleconverter
colour filter	lens cap	telephoto lens
diffuser	lens hood	video editor
disc film	lens shield	video light
exposure meter	macro lens	video mixer
eye-cup	memory card	viewfinder
eyepiece	memory reader	wide-angle lens
magnifier		zoom lens

See also **camera**.

---

photographer *n*
camera operator, cameraman, camerawoman, paparazzo

photographic *adj*
1 *photographic equipment*
filmic, graphic, cinematic, pictorial
2 *photographic memory*
accurate, exact, detailed, faithful, precise, realistic, retentive, vivid, minute, visual, lifelike, natural, naturalistic, representational

Photostat® *n, v*
• *n*
copy, duplicate, facsimile, photocopy, Xerox®
• *v*
copy, duplicate, photocopy, Xerox®, print, run off

phrase *n, v*
• *n*
construction, clause, idiom, expression, group of words, saying, utterance, remark, comment, language, phraseology, usage, way/style of speaking
• *v*
word, formulate, frame, couch, present, put, put into words, express, say, utter, pronounce

phraseology *n*
terminology, phrase, phrasing, wording, expression, idiom, language, parlance, speech, writing, style, syntax, diction, argot, cant, patois

phrasing *n*
wording, words, choice of words, language, expression, idiom, phraseology, terminology, style, diction, wordage, verbiage

physical *adj*
1 BODILY, corporeal, fleshy, fleshly, carnal, incarnate, mortal, earthly, unspiritual
FORMAL somatic
2 MATERIAL, concrete, solid, substantial, tangible, palpable, visible, real, actual, spatial
E3 **1** mental, spiritual **2** abstract, theoretical

physically *adv*
1 *physically fit*
in your body, bodily, physiologically
2 *the school is physically unable to expand*
materially, substantially, concretely, tangibly, actually, really, visibly
E3 **1** mentally, spiritually

physician *n*
doctor, medical practitioner, general practitioner, GP, houseman, intern, internist, registrar, consultant, specialist, healer, external, hakim, Paean
OLD leech, mediciner, physicianer; (*Shakesp*) medicine
COLLOQ. medic, doc, quack, medico

physics *n*
natural philosophy
See panel on next page

physiognomy *n*
face, features, look
OLD visnomy; (*Shakesp*) fisnomie
FORMAL countenance, visage
COLLOQ. clock, dial, mug, phiz, phizog, kisser

physique *n*
body, figure, shape, form, build, frame, structure, constitution, make-up

pick *v, n*
• *v*
1 SELECT, choose, go for, opt for, decide on, settle on, fix on, single out, prefer, favour, make up your mind
COLLOQ. plump for
2 GATHER, collect, pluck, pull, harvest, cull, take in
3 *pick a lock/safe*
open, crack, break open, prise open, force open
4 *pick a quarrel*

Terms used in physics include:

absolute zero	electricity	incandescence	mass	quantum
acceleration	electrodynamics	indeterminacy	mechanics	chromo-
acoustics	electromagnetic	principle	microwaves	dynamics
alpha particle	spectrum	inertia	mirror	(QCD)
analogue signal	electromagnetic	infrared	Mohs scale	quantum electro-
applied physics	waves	interference	molecule	dynamics (QED)
Archimedes	electron	ion	moment	quantum
principle	energy	Kelvin effect	momentum	mechanics
area	engine	kinetic energy	motion	quantum theory
atom	entropy	kinetic theory	neutrino	quark
beta particle	equation	laser (light	neutron	radiation
Big Bang theory	equilibrium	amplification by	nuclear	radioactive
boiling point	evaporation	stimulated	nuclear fission	element
bubble-chamber	field	emission of	nuclear fusion	radioactivity
capillary action	flash point	radiation)	nuclear physics	radioisotope
centre of gravity	force	latent heat	nucleus	radio wave
centre of mass	formula	law	optical centre	ratio
centrifugal force	freezing point	laws of motion	optics	reflection
chain reaction	frequency	laws of reflection	oscillation	refraction
charge	friction	laws of refraction	parallel motion	relativity
charged particle	fundamental	laws of thermo-	particle	resistance
circuit	constant	dynamics	periodic law	resonance
circuit-breaker	gamma ray	lens	perpetual motion	rule
couple	gas	lever	phonon	semiconductor
critical mass	gate	light	photon	sensitivity
cryogenics	Grand Unified	light emission	photosensitivity	separation
density	Theory (GUT)	light intensity	polarity	SI unit
diffraction	gravity	light source	potential energy	sound
digital	half-life	liquid	power	sound wave
dynamics	heat	longitudinal wave	pressure	specific gravity
efficiency	heavy water	luminescence	principle	specific heat
elasticity	hydraulics	Mach number	process	capacity
electric current	hydrodynamics	magnetic field	proton	spectroscopy
electric discharge	hydrostatics	magnetism		spectrum

speed
states of matter
statics
substance
superstring
theory
supersymmetry
surface tension
temperature
tension
theory
theory of relativity
thermodynamics
Thomson effect
transverse wave
ultrasound
ultraviolet
uncertainty
principle
velocity
viscosity
visible spectrum
volume
wave
wave property
weight
white heat
work
X-ray

See also **atom; electricity**.

---

cause, start, begin, provoke, produce, lead to, prompt, give rise to

♦ *n*

1 CHOICE, selection, option, decision, preference, favour

2 BEST, cream, choicest, prize, flower, élite, elect, crème de la crème

■ **pick at**

nibble, peck, play with, toy with, eat small amounts of

■ **pick off**

1 SHOOT, hit, kill, remove, strike, fire at, gun down, take out

2 REMOVE, detach, take away, pull off

■ **pick on**

bully, torment, victimize, persecute, criticize, blame, find fault with, nag, bait

COLLOQ. get at, needle

■ **pick out**

1 CHOOSE, select, go for, opt for, decide on, settle on, fix on, single out, prefer, favour, make up your mind

2 DISCERN, make out, spot, notice, perceive, recognize, distinguish, tell apart, discriminate, separate, single out, hand-pick

■ **pick up**

1 LIFT, raise, hoist, take up

2 *I'll pick you up at eight*

call for, fetch, collect, give a lift/ride

3 LEARN, master, grasp, acquire, get to know, gather

4 IMPROVE, get better, rally, recover, make progress, make headway

COLLOQ. perk up

5 ARREST, take into custody, apprehend

COLLOQ. nick, nab, collar, pinch, bust, run in, take in

6 RESUME, begin again, start again, continue, go on, carry on

7 OBTAIN, acquire, gain, learn, hear, find, discover, come across, buy, purchase

FORMAL chance upon

8 *pick up an infection*

catch, contract, get, become ill with, become infected with, go down with

9 *pick up a girl at a party*

COLLOQ. get off with, pull, cop off with

10 *pick up a radio signal*

receive, detect, get, hear

picket *n, v*

♦ *n*

1 PICKETER, protester, objector, rebel, dissident, demonstrator, striker

2 GUARD, sentry, watch, patrol, lookout, outpost, blockade

3 STAKE, post, spike, upright, peg, pike, stanchion, pale, paling

♦ *v*

protest, demonstrate, boycott, blockade, go on a picket line, enclose, surround

pickings *n*

proceeds, profits, returns, rewards, earnings, yield, take, spoils, booty, loot, plunder

SLANG gravy

pickle *n, v*

♦ *n*

1 *cheese and pickle*

chutney, relish, vinegar, sauce, flavouring, seasoning, condiment, piccalilli

2 MESS, difficulty, dilemma, predicament, plight, crisis, quandary, straits

FORMAL exigency

COLLOQ. bind, fix, hot water, jam, pinch, scrape, spot, tight spot

♦ *v*

preserve, conserve, souse, marinade, steep, cure, salt; *dialect* put down

pick-me-up *n*

tonic, boost, refreshment, restorative, fillip, stimulant, stimulus, cordial

TECHNICAL roborant
COLLOQ. shot in the arm

pickpocket *n*
thief, snatcher, pick-purse, bagsnatcher
OLD file, cutpurse; (*Shakesp*) bung
COLLOQ. dip, diver, wire, nipper, whizzer
OLD SLANG cly-faker

pick-up *n*
1 IMPROVEMENT, betterment, enhancement, rectification, rectifying, correction, amendment, revision, reform, reformation, rehabilitation, upgrading, modernizing, increase, rise, upswing, gain, development, advance, growth, progress, headway, furtherance, recovery, rally, upswing
FORMAL amelioration
2 *load boxes into a pick-up*
truck, lorry, van, wagon, float
F3 1 deterioration, decline, worsening

picky *adj*
fussy, choosy, selective, discriminating, particular, finicky, fastidious, exacting, faddy
COLLOQ. pernickety; *N Am* persnickety

picnic *n*
1 *a picnic lunch*
outing, excursion, outdoor meal, *fête champêtre*, junket
OLD a kettle of fish, wayzgoose
2 *minding young children is no picnic*
COLLOQ. child's play, cinch, doddle, piece of cake, pushover, walkover, a fine/pretty kettle of fish

pictorial *adj*
graphic, diagrammatic, schematic, representational, vivid, striking, expressive, illustrated, picturesque, scenic, in pictures, in photographs

picture *n, v*
♦ *n*
1 DESCRIPTION, portrayal, depiction, account, report, story, narrative, tale, semblance, impression
FORMAL delineation, similitude
Related adjective: pictorial
2 *the picture of health*
embodiment, personification, epitome, essence
FORMAL archetype, exemplar, quintessence
3 FILM, motion picture
COLLOQ. movie
OLD COLLOQ. flick
4 *go to the pictures*
cinema, movies, picture-house, film theatre, entertainment centre, multiplex, picture-palace
OLD COLLOQ. flicks
♦ *v*
1 IMAGINE, envisage, envision, conceive, visualize, call to mind, see, see in your mind's eye
2 DEPICT, describe, represent, reproduce, show, portray, draw, sketch, paint, photograph, illustrate, appear
FORMAL delineate
▪ **get the picture**
understand, comprehend, grasp, take in, follow, see

COLLOQ. get the message, get it, get the idea, get the point, catch on, cotton on, latch on, tumble to
▪ **put someone in the picture**
inform, tell, notify, communicate, explain, update
COLLOQ. fill in, clue up, keep posted

picturesque *adj*
1 ATTRACTIVE, beautiful, pretty, lovely, delightful, charming, pleasant, pleasing, quaint, idyllic, romantic, scenic
2 DESCRIPTIVE, depictive, graphic, vivid, colourful, striking, impressive
F3 1 unattractive **2** dull, boring

piddling *adj*
paltry, meagre, derisory, contemptible, mean, low, miserable, wretched, poor, sorry, small, slight, trifling, inconsiderate, negligible, trivial, minor, contemptible, petty, unimportant, insignificant, puny, worthless
COLLOQ. measly, piffling
F3 substantial, significant, valuable

pie *n*
pastry, flan, tart
See also **food**.
▪ **pie in the sky**
daydream, dream, delusion, fantasy, reverie, romance, mirage, notion
COLLOQ. jam tomorrow, hot air, castle in Spain, castle in the air

piebald *adj*
black and white, dappled, flecked, mottled, pied, spotted, speckled, variegated, brindled, skewbald

piece *n, v*
♦ *n*
1 FRAGMENT, bit, scrap, crumb, morsel, flake, speck, fleck, titbit, mouthful, bite, lump, chunk, wedge, hunk, dollop, block, slab, bar, slice, sliver, snippet, chip, splinter, shred, offcut, length, sample, component, constituent, element, part, segment, section, unit, division, fraction, share, allocation, allotment, percentage, quota, portion, quantity; *N Am* tidbit
COLLOQ. smithereen, cut, slice
2 ARTICLE, item, study, work, opus, story, review, composition, report, illustration, creation, specimen, example, instance
▪ **piece together**
assemble, join, put together, unite, attach, compose, fit, mend, fix, repair, patch, restore
▪ **all in one piece**
intact, unbroken, whole, complete, integral, entire, undamaged, unharmed, unhurt, uninjured
F3 broken, incomplete, damaged
▪ **go to pieces**
lose control, break down, have a breakdown, be overcome, collapse
COLLOQ. crack up
▪ **in pieces**
in bits, broken, damaged, disintegrated, ruined, shattered, smashed
COLLOQ. kaput, in smithereens

Kinds of picture include:

abstract	effigy	landscape	passport photo	silhouette	transfer
bitmap	engraving	likeness	Photofit®	sketch	transparency
bricolage	etching	miniature	photograph	slide	triptych
cameo	fresco	montage	photogravure	snap	trompe l'oeil
canvas	graffiti	mosaic	pin-up	snapshot	vignette
caricature	graphics	*colloq.* mugshot	plate	still	watercolour
cartoon	icon	mural	portrait	still life	
collage	identikit	negative	print	study	
design	illustration	oil painting	representation	tableau	
doodle	image	old master	reproduction	tapestry	
drawing	kakemono	painting	self-portrait	tracing	

■ **pull/tear to pieces**
criticize, condemn, disapprove of, find fault with, denounce, attack, censure, slate, snipe, run down, come down on, pick holes in, blame
COLLOQ. nag, slam, knock, give someone some stick, go to town on, haul over the coals, pan, tear to shreds, tear a strip off, do a hatchet job on, badmouth, rubbish, put the boot in
SLANG slag (off)

pièce de résistance n
masterpiece, masterwork, prize, showpiece, magnum opus, *chef-d'oeuvre*, jewel

piecemeal *adv, adj*
• *adv*
little by little, intermittently, parcel-wise, partially, at intervals, slowly, bit by bit, by degrees, fitfully
COLLOQ. in dribs and drabs
E∃ completely, entirely, wholly
• *adj*
fragmentary, intermittent, interrupted, partial, unsystematic, scattered, patchy, sporadic
FORMAL discrete
E∃ complete, entire, whole, wholesale

pied *adj*
flecked, irregular, motley, mottled, multicoloured, parti-coloured, piebald, dappled, brindle(d), spotted, streaked, skewbald, varicoloured, variegated

pier n
1 JETTY, breakwater, landing-stage, dock, quay, wharf
2 SUPPORT, upright, pile, pillar, post, column

pierce v
1 PENETRATE, enter, pass through, stick into, puncture, drill, bore, probe, perforate, punch, prick, stab, lance, bayonet, pike, stake, run through, spear, skewer, spike, barb, pink, impale, transfix, transpierce, punch, needle, probe, thrust, gore, pith, broach, tap, jag, peg, gimlet, spile, drift; *dialect* thirl; *Scot* slap, steek
OLD pearce, perse, perce, cleave, engore, gride, launch, nail, prog, rive, thrill (through); (*Spenser*) empierce
FORMAL lancinate
2 *pierce someone's spirit*
stab, sting, pain, hurt, move, prick, cut to the quick
3 *pierce the darkness*
burst through, penetrate, fill, enter, light up

pierced *adj*
perforated, perforate, impaled, punctured, pinked, stung
TECHNICAL foraminated, foraminous
OLD pearst, pierst
FORMAL pertusate, pertuse(d), fenestrate

piercing *adj*
1 *a piercing cry*
shrill, high-pitched, loud, ear-splitting, ear-piercing, penetrating, sharp, acute, keen
OLD perceant
2 PENETRATING, probing, searching, discerning, perceptive, shrewd, alert, astute, sharp, sharp-witted
OLD perceant; (*Spenser*) thrillant
3 COLD, bitter, raw, biting, numbing, keen, fierce, severe, wintry, frosty, freezing, Arctic
4 PAINFUL, agonizing, excruciating, extreme, severe, intense, stabbing, lacerating, shooting

piercingly *adv*
1 *shriek piercingly*
shrilly, loudly, sharply, keenly
2 *look piercingly*
penetratingly, discerningly, sharply, alertly, astutely
3 *piercingly cold*
bitterly, numbingly, fiercely, keenly, severely
4 *piercingly poignant*
intensely, extremely, severely, painfully, agonizingly, excruciatingly, bitterly

piety n
piousness, devoutness, godliness, saintliness, holiness, sanctity, spirituality, religiousness, religion, faith, devotion, reverence, respect, fear of God, deference
E∃ impiety, irreligion

piffle n
nonsense, rubbish, trash, tripe, drivel, balderdash, rot, tarradiddle
COLLOQ. bunk, bunkum, codswallop, guff, hooey, poppycock, cock, tommyrot, tosh, twaddle, baloney, blah, bosh, eyewash, hogwash, rhubarb, malarkey, moonshine
SLANG bull; (*vulgar*) balls, shit, bullshit

piffling *adj*
trifling, small, paltry, slight, negligible, inadequate, insufficient, inconsiderable, unimportant, insignificant, minor, trivial, superficial, petty, silly, foolish, frivolous, idle, empty, shallow, worthless
FORMAL inconsequential
E∃ important, significant, serious

pig *n, v*
• *n*
1 SWINE, hog, sow, boar, grunter, piglet
COLLOQ. piggy
2 ANIMAL, beast, brute, monster, boor
3 GLUTTON, gormandizer, gourmand
COLLOQ. greedy guts, guzzler
• *v*
gorge, feast, gobble, guzzle, cram, stuff
COLLOQ. wolf, scoff, snarf
Related adjective: porcine

pigeonhole *n, v*
• *n*
1 COMPARTMENT, niche, slot, cubby-hole, cubicle, locker, box, place, section
2 CATEGORY, class, classification, compartment
• *v*
1 LABEL, compartmentalize, categorize, classify, sort, file, tag, slot, catalogue, alphabetize
2 SHELVE, defer, postpone, put off
COLLOQ. put on the back burner

pig-headed *adj*
stubborn, obstinate, perverse, self-willed, stiff-necked, inflexible, contrary, mulish, stupid, unyielding, wilful, wrong-headed, headstrong, bull-headed
OLD froward
FORMAL intractable, intransigent
E∃ flexible, tractable

pigment n
colour, hue, tint, dye, stain, paint, colouring, tincture

pile¹ *n, v*
• *n*
1 STACK, heap, bundle, mound, mountain, mass, accumulation, collection, assortment, hoard, stockpile, store
FORMAL assemblage
2 LARGE QUANTITY, a great deal, a lot, quantities
COLLOQ. loads, lots, lashings, stacks, heaps, masses, oodles, millions, thousands, hundreds, tons
3 *make a pile*
fortune, wealth, riches
COLLOQ. mint, packet, bundle, bomb
SLANG megabucks, big bucks, loadsamoney
4 *a pile in the country*
large building, imposing/impressive building, edifice, mansion
• *v*
1 STACK (UP), heap (up), mass, amass, accumulate, build up, gather, assemble, collect, hoard, stockpile, store, load
2 PACK, jam, crush, squeeze, crowd, flock, flood, stream, rush, charge

■ **pile it on**

exaggerate, overstate, overdo, magnify, overemphasize, emphasize, stress, make too much of, overplay, dramatize, overdramatize

COLLOQ. lay it on, lay/pile it on thick, lay/pile it on with a trowel, make a mountain out of a molehill, blow something up out of all proportion

Ⅎ understate, play down

■ **pile up**

mount up, increase, grow, accumulate, multiply, escalate, soar

pile² n

houses built on piles

post, piling, column, upright, support, bar, beam, foundation

pile³ n

the pile of a carpet

nap, shag, plush, fur, hair, fluff, fuzz, down, wool, fibres, threads, (soft) surface, texture

Related adjectives: villose, villous

pile-up n

crash, accident, collision, bump, wreck

COLLOQ. smash, smash-up, prang

pilfer v

steal, filch, shoplift, rob, thieve, make away with, run off with; *dialect* mag; *N Am* boost

FORMAL purloin, peculate

COLLOQ. pinch, nick, knock off, lift, snaffle, nobble, have sticky fingers, snitch, swipe, whip, bag

SLANG heist, hoist, pull, lag, blag, mill, smug, sneak

pilgrim n

crusader, traveller, wanderer, wayfarer, worshipper, devotee, palmer, hadji

OLD peregrine

pilgrimage n

crusade, mission, expedition, journey, trip, tour, hadj

FORMAL peregrination

pill n

tablet, capsule, lozenge, pellet, ball, bolus, caplet

pillage v, n

◆ v

plunder, raid, sack, vandalize, maraud, loot, spoil, ransack, ravage, raze, freeboot, rifle, rob, strip

FORMAL depredate, despoil, spoliate

◆ n

plunder, sack, devastation, marauding, harrying, seizure, spoils, robbery, loot, booty

FORMAL depredation, rapine, spoliation

pillar n

1 COLUMN, shaft, pole, post, mast, pier, upright, pile, support, prop, stanchion, obelisk, baluster, pilaster, stack, lat, man, monolith, trumeau, lamppost, standard, lamp-standard; *dialect* stoop

TECHNICAL cippus, telamon

OLD goal

2 *a pillar of society*

mainstay, bastion, support, rock, stalwart, tower of strength

pillory v

ridicule, mock, pour scorn on, laugh at, denounce, attack, criticize, lash, hold up to shame, show up, brand, cast a slur on, stigmatize

pillow n

cushion, bolster, rest, headrest, bed

pilot n, v, adj

◆ n

1 FLYER, aviator, airman, airwoman, captain, commander, first officer, flight engineer, crew, aircrew

2 NAVIGATOR, steersman, helmsman, coxswain, captain, leader, director, guide

◆ v

fly, drive, steer, direct, control, handle, manoeuvre, manage, operate, run, conduct, lead, guide, navigate

◆ adj

experimental, trial, test, model, sample

pimp n

pander, panderer, procurer, fancy man, fleshmonger, whoremonger, solicitor

OLD bawd, broker, mackerel

SLANG hustler, ponce, mack; *Aust* hoon

pimple n

spot, blackhead, boil, swelling, papula, papule, pustule, whitehead, carbuncle, whelk, button, milium, rum-blossom, rum-bud; *dialect* quat; *Scot* plouk

OLD botch, bubukle

COLLOQ. zit

Related adjectives: papulose, papulous

pin v, n

◆ v

1 TACK, nail, fix, stick, affix, attach, join, staple, clip, fasten, secure

2 HOLD DOWN, hold, hold fast, restrain, constrain, press, immobilize

3 *pin the blame on someone*

attach, put, place, lay, attribute, ascribe

FORMAL impute

◆ n

tack, nail, screw, spike, rivet, bolt, peg, dowel, fastener, clip, staple, skewer, brooch

■ **pin down**

1 PINPOINT, identify, define, determine, specify

COLLOQ. nail down, put your finger on

2 FORCE, make, compel, press, pressurize, hold down, hold fast, restrain, constrain

COLLOQ. nail down

pincers n

forceps, tweezers, forfex

pinch v, n

◆ v

1 SQUEEZE, compress, crush, press, tweak, nip, hurt, confine, cramp, grip, gripe, grasp, twinge, twitch, shut, pincer, sneap, check, lace; *Scot* chack, pook

OLD wring

2 STEAL, pilfer, filch, snatch

FORMAL appropriate, purloin, peculate

COLLOQ. nick, walk off with, knock off, lift, swipe, whip, bag; *Aust & NZ* souvenir

3 ECONOMIZE, save, cut back, budget, keep costs down, live on the cheap, scrimp and save, eke out

COLLOQ. tighten your belt, cut your coat according to your cloth, scrape a living

4 ARREST, capture, catch, seize, detain

COLLOQ. bust, nick, collar, nab, book, run in, pull in, pick up, nail

◆ n

1 SQUEEZE, tweak, nip, twinge; *Scot* chack

2 DASH, soupçon, trace, taste, bit, touch, speck, spot, jot, mite, pugil, snuff; *Scot* tate, sneesh

COLLOQ. smidgen, tad

3 EMERGENCY, crisis, predicament, difficulty, hardship, pressure, stress

■ **at a pinch**

if necessary, if absolutely necessary, in an emergency, with great difficulty

■ **feel the pinch**

have a hard time, hit/strike a bad patch, not have enough money, be short of money, be poor, scratch a living, tighten your belt

pinched *adj*
pale, thin, drawn, strained, haggard, gaunt, peaky, careworn, worn, narrowed, straightened, starved

pine *v*
1 YEARN, long, ache, sigh, wish, desire, crave, hanker, hunger, thirst
2 *pine away from grief*
grieve, mourn, fret, weaken, fade, languish, waste away

pinion *v*
pin down, tie, fasten, confine, bind, chain, fetter, manacle, shackle, hobble, immobilize, truss

pink¹ *adj, n*
♦ *adj*
pink flowers
reddish, flushed, rose, rosy, salmon, roseate
♦ *n*
perfection, height, peak, acme, extreme, best, flower, prime, summit, top, tiptop
■ **in the pink**
fit, healthy, well, very well, in good shape, trim, in fine fettle, in good/perfect health, in the best of health
COLLOQ. right as rain, in good nick, on good form

pink² *v*
to pink cloth
cut, notch, serrate, perforate, score, incise, prick, punch, scallop
FORMAL crenellate

pinnacle *n*
1 PEAK, summit, top, cap, crown, crest, apex, vertex, acme, zenith, apogee, height, eminence, culmination
2 SPIRE, steeple, turret, minaret, pyramid, cone, obelisk, needle

pinpoint *v, adj*
♦ *v*
identify, spot, distinguish, locate, place, home in on, pin down, discover, determine, specify, define
COLLOQ. zero in on, nail down, put your finger on
♦ *adj*
precise, exact, accurate, right, scrupulous, punctilious, meticulous, rigorous

pint-size *adj*
pint-sized, little, small, pocket, pocket-sized, tiny, diminutive, miniature, dwarf, midget, pygmy; *Scot* wee
COLLOQ. mini, teeny, teeny-weeny, dinky
F3 giant, huge, enormous

pioneer *n, v*
♦ *n*
1 SETTLER, colonist, frontiersman, frontierswoman, explorer
2 *a pioneer in science*
developer, pathfinder, trailblazer, groundbreaker, leader, innovator, inventor, discoverer, founder, founding father
♦ *v*
invent, discover, originate, create, initiate, instigate, begin, start, launch, institute, introduce, found, establish, set up, develop, open up, prepare the way for, lead the way, spearhead, break new ground, blaze a trail, make the first move
COLLOQ. set/start the ball rolling, pave the way

pious *adj*
1 DEVOUT, godly, saintly, holy, spiritual, religious, reverent, sanctified, faithful, dedicated, devoted, good, virtuous, righteous, moral, wise, *pia*
2 SANCTIMONIOUS, self-righteous, hypocritical, insincere, priggish
FORMAL unctuous
COLLOQ. holier-than-thou, goody-goody, pi
F3 1 impious, irreligious, irreverent

piously *adv*
1 DEVOUTLY, religiously, spiritually, reverently, faithfully,

morally, righteously, virtuously
2 SELF-RIGHTEOUSLY, sanctimoniously, insincerely, hypocritically, priggishly

pipe *n, v*
♦ *n*
1 TUBE, hose, piping, tubing, pipeline, line, main, flue, duct, conduit, drainpipe, channel, passage, cylinder, conveyor, overflow, tap, faucet, jet, manifold, blast-pipe, blow pipe, feed-pipe, stopcock, standpipe, service pipe, gas-bracket, goose-neck, dip-pipe, exhaust pipe, tailpipe, stovepipe, throttle-pipe, uptake, chimney pot, dry riser, riser, wastepipe, crane, worm, dead-end, soil pipe, aqueduct, ventiduct
TECHNICAL kill/injection string, kelly
OLD clyster-pipe
2 *pipe and tobacco*
tabacco-pipe, clay, claypipe, hookah, hubble-bubble, kalian, water pipe, brier, dudeen, meerschaum, narghile, calumet, peace-pipe, calumet, chibouk, churchwarden, cob-pipe; *Scot* cutty
3 *play music on a pipe*
recorder, flute, fife, whistle, penny whistle, bagpipes, reed, quill, aulos, chanter, cornpipe, drone, pitch-pipe, tibia
OLD oat
♦ *v*
1 CHANNEL, funnel, siphon, carry, bring, take, convey, conduct, duct, transmit, supply, deliver
2 WHISTLE, chirp, tweet, cheep, chirrup, peep, twitter, sing, warble, trill, shrill, tweedle, play, sound, pule
OLD shrike
■ **pipe down**
be quiet, stop talking
COLLOQ. shut up

pipe dream *n*
daydream, dream, delusion, fantasy, reverie, romance, false hope, mirage, notion
FORMAL chimera, vagary
COLLOQ. castle in Spain, castle in the air, pie in the sky

pipeline *n*
passage, pipe, tube, line, conduit, channel, duct, conveyor
■ **in the pipeline**
in preparation, planned, already started, on the way, under way

pipsqueak *n*
nobody, nonentity, nothing
COLLOQ. upstart, squirt, twerp, whippersnapper, creep, hobbledehoy
F3 somebody

piquancy *n*
1 SPICINESS, pungency, tang, pepperiness, spice, relish, flavour, strong flavour, sharpness, ginger, bite
2 LIVELINESS, excitement, interest, vigour, vitality, spirit, zest, colour, raciness, punch
COLLOQ. edge, kick, oomph, pep, pizzazz, zip

piquant *adj*
1 *piquant sauce*
spicy, tangy, savoury, salty, peppery, seasoned, highly seasoned, pungent, zesty, sharp, biting, tart, stinging
2 LIVELY, spirited, stimulating, provocative, interesting, sparkling, intriguing, fascinating, sharp, racy, colourful
COLLOQ. juicy
F3 1 bland, insipid 2 dull, banal

pique *n, v*
♦ *n*
annoyance, anger, irritation, gall, vexation, displeasure, offence, resentment, grudge, umbrage
COLLOQ. huff
♦ *v*
1 AROUSE, stimulate, excite, goad, rouse, provoke, stir, spur, whet, kindle, galvanize

2 ANNOY, anger, irritate, affront, displease, gall, irk, get, put out, rile, incense, offend, mortify, vex, wound, sting
COLLOQ. aggravate, wind up, get at, bug, drive mad, drive crazy, drive up the wall, drive round the bend/twist, miff, needle, peeve, nettle, make someone's blood boil, make someone see red, rattle someone's cage, ruffle someone's feathers, make sparks fly, get under someone's skin, get up someone's nose, get on someone's wick, make someone's hackles rise
SLANG drive bananas, nark, piss off
OLD SLANG get someone's shirt out

piqued adj
annoyed, irritated, vexed, riled, angry, cross, displeased, offended, put out, resentful
COLLOQ. miffed, peeved, aggravated, ratty, uptight, mad, hopping mad, raving mad, seeing red, in a lather, disgruntled, up in arms, hot under the collar, stroppy, choked, fit to be tied, on the warpath, in a paddy
SLANG narked, pissed off

piracy n
buccaneering, freebooting, bootlegging, robbery, stealing, theft, hijacking, infringement, plagiarism
FORMAL rapine

pirate n, v
♦ n
1 BUCCANEER, brigand, freebooter, filibuster, corsair, marauder, raider, picaroon, sea robber, sea rover, sea dog, sea wolf, sea rat, water rat, marque, viking, arch-pirate
OLD sallee-man, rover, algerine; (*Shakesp*) water-thief
2 INFRINGER, plagiarist, plagiarizer
♦ v
copy, reproduce illegally, steal, pinch, plagiarize, poach
FORMAL appropriate
COLLOQ. borrow, crib, lift, nick, knock off

pirouette n, v
♦ n
gyration, spin, turn, twirl, whirl, pivot
♦ v
gyrate, spin, turn, twirl, whirl, pivot

pistol n
gun, handgun, revolver, sidearm, six-shooter, Luger®, Colt®, puffer; *N Am* derringer
OLD dag, pistole
COLLOQ. gat, iron, piece
SLANG pop, barking iron
OLD SLANG barker; *N Am* heater, rod

pit n, v
♦ n
1 *dig a pit*
hole, cavity, crater, pothole, gulf, chasm, abyss, mine, coalmine, quarry, diggings, trench, ditch, excavations, workings
2 HOLLOW, depression, dent, indentation, pockmark
♦ v
pockmark, blemish, scar, mark, dent, notch, depress, indent, dimple, pothole
■ **pit against**
compete, match, oppose, set against
■ **the pits**
awful, very poor, abysmal, inferior, dreadful, unsatisfactory, inadequate, second-rate, third-rate
COLLOQ. terrible, lousy, pathetic, crummy, a load of rubbish
SLANG pants, naff, cruddy; (*vulgar*) crap, shit; *Aust* spewy

pitch¹ v, n
♦ v
1 THROW, fling, toss, cast, lob, bowl, hurl, heave, sling, fire, launch, aim, direct
COLLOQ. chuck
2 PLUNGE, dive, plummet, drop, fall, fall headlong, topple, tumble

3 *pitch camp*
erect, put up, set up, place, station, settle, plant, fix
4 MOVE UP AND DOWN, lurch, sway, roll, toss, reel, keel, list, flounder, wallow
♦ n
1 *a cricket pitch*
ground, field, sports field, playing-field, park, arena, stadium
2 SOUND, tone, timbre, tonality, modulation, frequency, level
3 GRADIENT, incline, slope, slant, tilt, angle, degree, inclination, steepness, cant
4 *reach a high pitch*
level, degree, extent, height, point, position, intensity, grade, mark
5 THROW, fling, toss, lob, cast, hurl
COLLOQ. chuck
6 TALK, patter, line, gabble, chatter, jargon
COLLOQ. spiel, yak
■ **pitch in**
join in, co-operate, be involved, participate, help (out), lend a hand
COLLOQ. muck in, do your bit
■ **make a pitch for**
bid for, try to sell, put in for, try to get/obtain, offer, tender, submit, put up, put forward, advance, propose
FORMAL proffer

pitch² n
to coat a surface with pitch
tar, bitumen, asphalt
Related adjective: piceous

pitch-black adj
pitch-dark, black, dark, jet-black, inky, coal-black, unilluminated, unlit

pitcher n
jug, ewer, jar, vessel, crock, bottle, can, container, urn

piteous adj
poignant, moving, touching, distressing, heartbreaking, heart-rending, plaintive, mournful, sad, sorrowful, woeful, wretched, lamentable, pitiful, pitiable, pathetic

---

🛈 **piteous**, **pitiable** or **pitiful**?
Pitiful means 'very sad, arousing or deserving pity': *She was a pitiful sight*; and also 'arousing or deserving contempt, very bad, very poor': *a pitiful attempt at catching the ball. Pitiable* means the same as *pitiful* but is less common: *He was in a pitiable condition; That was a pitiable attempt you made. Piteous* is a rather formal word meaning 'arousing or deserving pity': *She gave a piteous cry.*

---

pitfall n
danger, peril, hazard, risk, trap, snare, stumbling-block, catch, snag, drawback, difficulty

pith n
gist, essence, essential part, salient point, point, crux, nub, heart, core, meat, kernel, importance, significance, moment, weight, value, consequence, substance, forcefulness, vigour, matter
TECHNICAL medulla
OLD marrow, papyrus
FORMAL import, quintessence

pithily adv
concisely, succinctly, compactly, tersely, in brief, in a few words, in a word, to the point, meaningfully
COLLOQ. in a nutshell
🔁 wordily, verbosely

pithy adj
succinct, concise, compact, terse, short, brief, condensed, summary, pointed, expressive, meaningful, forceful, incisive, telling
FORMAL trenchant, cogent
🔁 wordy, verbose

pitiable adj

contemptible, distressed, distressful, distressing, doleful, grievous, lamentable, miserable, mournful, piteous, poor, sad, sorry, woeful, woesome, wretched
COLLOQ. pathetic

🚹 **pitiable**, **piteous** or **pitiful**?
See panel at **piteous**.

pitiful adj

1 PITEOUS, doleful, mournful, distressing, heartbreaking, heart-rending, affecting, moving, pathetic, pitiable, sad, miserable, wretched, lamentable, poor, sorry; *Scot* waeful
OLD ruthful, seely
2 CONTEMPTIBLE, meagre, despicable, low, base, mean, poor, vile, shabby, miserable, deplorable, lamentable, woeful, inadequate, hopeless, insignificant, paltry, worthless
COLLOQ. pathetic, lousy, terrible, crummy
SLANG the pits

🚹 **pitiful**, **piteous** or **pitiable**?
See panel at **piteous**.

pitifully adv

1 *pitifully thin*
piteously, distressingly, sadly, miserably, lamentably, pathetically
2 *pitifully inadequate*
deplorably, lamentably, woefully, contemptibly, despicably, hopelessly
COLLOQ. terribly, pathetically

pitiless adj

merciless, cold-hearted, unsympathetic, unfeeling, uncaring, heartless, hard-hearted, callous, cruel, inhuman, inhumane, brutal, cold-blooded, ruthless, relentless, unremitting, inexorable, harsh, severe
F3 merciful, compassionate, kind, gentle

pitilessly adv

mercilessly, cruelly, callously, harshly, brutally, ruthlessly, hard-heartedly, cold-heartedly, cold-bloodedly
F3 mercifully, compassionately

pittance n

modicum, crumb, drop (in the ocean), trifle
COLLOQ. chickenfeed
SLANG peanuts

pitted adj

dented, holey, potholed, pockmarked, blemished, scarred, marked, notched, depressed, indented, rough

pity n, v

♦ *n*
1 SYMPATHY, commiseration, regret, sorrow, sadness, distress, understanding, fellow-feeling, feeling, emotion, condolence, compassion, kindness, tenderness, mercy, forgiveness, grace
OLD piety, bowels, misericord, rue, ruth; (*Spenser*) remorse
FORMAL forbearance
2 *What a pity!*
shame, disappointment, misfortune, unfortunate thing, bad luck
COLLOQ. crying shame
OLD COLLOQ sin
F3 **1** cruelty, anger, scorn
♦ *v*
feel sorry for, feel for, sympathize with, be sympathetic towards, empathize with, show understanding towards, feel/have compassion for, commiserate with, grieve for, weep for, have a heart, bleed
OLD bemoan, bepity, compassion; (*Spenser*) mercify
■ **take pity on**
feel sorry for, feel for, sympathize with, be sympathetic

towards, empathize with, show understanding towards, feel/have compassion for, commiserate with, show mercy, have mercy on, pardon, spare, rue

---

Synonym nuances

noun sense 1
Sympathy can be used to suggest having concern for another's predicament, while **commiseration** would be used more appropriately of expressing that concern to them: *I offered my commiserations on her loss.*
Condolence, is similar, but is more narrowly used in cases of bereavement: *he gave his condolences to the widow.*
Regret, **sorrow** and **sadness**, on the other hand, imply a heartfelt upset and unhappiness at the suffering of another, while **distress** goes further by suggesting extreme feeling.
Understanding and **fellow-feeling** have more to do with empathy and an ability to appreciate how others are feeling. Both **kindness** and **tenderness** also suggest a condition in which you are sensitive and easily moved, as well as displays of thoughtful attention: *an unexpected tenderness towards the misfortunes of others*, while **compassion** is a fairly strong term for caring about the suffering of others, combined with a desire to alleviate it.
Mercy is more suggestive of pity and consequent leniency when one is in a superior position.
Forgiveness, although similar, would be appropriate where pity prompts forgetting or overlooking a misdemeanour; likewise **grace**, although its usage is less common, and tends to connote divine mercy.

---

pivot n, v

♦ *n*
the wheel turns on a pivot; the pivot of her life
axis, hinge, axle, spindle, fulcrum, kingpin, linchpin, swivel, hub, central point, focal point, focus, centre, heart
♦ *v*
1 SWIVEL, turn, spin, revolve, rotate, swing
2 DEPEND, rely, revolve, hinge, hang, lie
FORMAL turn, be contingent

pivotal adj

vital, important, focal, central, critical, crucial, decisive, determining, climactic, axial

pixie n

elf, brownie, goblin, leprechaun, fairy, imp, sprite

pizzazz n

liveliness, animation, energy, quickness, spirit, life, vigour, vitality, vivacity, vivaciousness, dynamism, activity, boisterousness, briskness, smartness, sprightliness, refreshment, *esprit*, *entrain*
COLLOQ. brio, oomph
F3 apathy, inactivity

placard n

poster, bill, notice, sticker, sign, advertisement
COLLOQ. ad, advert

placate v

appease, pacify, conciliate, win over, mollify, calm (down), assuage, soothe, lull, quiet
FORMAL propitiate
F3 anger, enrage, incense, infuriate

placatory adj

appeasing, calming, soothing, mollifying, conciliatory, peace-making
FORMAL pacificatory, propitiatory, propitiative

place n, v

♦ *n*
1 SITE, venue, location, locus, scene, setting, situation, station, spot, point, position, locale, part, whereabouts, seat, space, room

2 *a place name*
city, town, village, hamlet, locality, neighbourhood, whereabouts, district, area, region, state, country
3 BUILDING, establishment, hotel, restaurant, institution, property, accommodation, house, flat, apartment, home
FORMAL dwelling, residence, abode, domicile
COLLOQ. pad, digs
4 JOB, position, appointment, situation, role, part, niche, status, standing, grade, rank, footing
5 *not your place to comment*
role, function, task, duty, responsibility, right, concern, business

♦ *v*

1 PUT, put down, set, set down, plant, fix, position, locate, situate, station, rest, settle, install, establish, lay, lay down, stand, deposit, lodge, leave
2 ARRANGE, put, class, sort, classify, categorize, order, group, rank, grade
3 *I can't quite place her*
recognize, know, remember, identify, establish, pinpoint
4 *place graduates in companies*
find a job for, find employment for, find accommodation for, allocate, assign
■ **in place**
arranged, in order, in position, in the correct position, set up, working
■ **in place of**
instead of, in lieu of, as a replacement for, as an alternative to, in exchange for, as a substitute for, taking the place of
■ **out of place**
inappropriate, unsuitable, unfitting, improper, tactless, unbecoming
FORMAL unseemly, inapposite
■ **put someone in their place**
humble, humiliate, shame, crush, deflate, bring low, bring/take someone down a peg or two, take the wind out of someone's sail
■ **take place**
happen, occur, come about, be held, come off, fall
OLD befall, betide
FORMAL transpire, come to pass
■ **take the place of**
replace, substitute for, supersede, stand in for, take over from, act for

placement *n*
locating, location, installation, ordering, arrangement, deployment, appointment, positioning, ranking, stationing, distribution, classification, job, assignment, disposition, engagement, employment
FORMAL emplacement

placid *adj*
1 *a placid person*
calm, composed, unmoved, undisturbed, unruffled, untroubled, unexcitable, cool, self-possessed, level-headed, imperturbable, easy-going, mild, gentle, equable, serene, unemotional, even-tempered, peaceable, tranquil
COLLOQ. unflappable
2 *live in placid surroundings*
tranquil, still, quiet, calm, peaceful, restful
FORMAL pacific
E3 **1** excitable, agitated, disturbed

placidly *adv*
calmly, gently, mildly, imperturbably, peacefully, restfully, serenely
COLLOQ. unflappably
E3 excitably

plagiarism *n*
infringement, copying, reproduction, counterfeiting, piracy, theft
FORMAL appropriation
COLLOQ. borrowing, cribbing, lifting

plagiarist *n*
copier, robber, thief, pirate, imitator

plagiarize *v*
crib, copy, reproduce, imitate, counterfeit, pirate, infringe copyright, poach, steal, borrow
FORMAL appropriate
COLLOQ. crib, lift, nick

plague *n, v*
♦ *n*
1 PESTILENCE, epidemic, disease, sickness, infection, contagion, infestation, cholera, bubonic plague, pneumonic plague, Black Death
FORMAL pandemic
2 *a plague of rats*
infestation, influx, swarm, invasion, huge number, epidemic
3 NUISANCE, annoyance, curse, scourge, trial, affliction, torment, calamity, bane
COLLOQ. thorn in the flesh, pain in the neck
♦ *v*
annoy, vex, bother, disturb, trouble, distress, upset, irritate, worry, cause problems for, pester, harass, hound, dog, hamper, hinder, haunt, bedevil, afflict, torment, torture, persecute
COLLOQ. bug, hassle, aggravate, cause headaches to

The ten Biblical plagues are:

Nile Waters Turn to Blood	Disease of Livestock	Darkness Death of the Firstborn
Frogs	Boils	
Lice	Hailstorm	
Flies	Locusts	

---

plain *adj, adv, n*
♦ *adj*
1 *plain cookery*
ordinary, basic, simple, unpretentious, unsophisticated, modest, unadorned, unelaborate, restrained, stark, austere, spartan
2 *plain fabric*
undecorated, unadorned, unembellished, unpatterned, unvariegated, uncoloured, self-coloured, restrained, muted
3 OBVIOUS, evident, patent, manifest, clear, understandable, apparent, noticeable, perceptible, discernible, visible, overt, unmistakable, transparent
COLLOQ. plain as a pikestaff, plain as the nose on your face, clear as daylight
4 UNATTRACTIVE, ordinary, ugly, unprepossessing, unlovely; *NAm* homely
5 *plain language*
clear, intelligible, understandable, lucid, unambiguous, uncomplicated, simple, direct, straightforward, accessible
6 FRANK, candid, blunt, outspoken, direct, forthright, straightforward, unambiguous, plain-spoken, open, honest, sincere, truthful, simple, unassuming
E3 **1** fancy, elaborate **2** patterned, ornate **3** unclear, obscure **4** attractive, beautiful, good-looking **5** complicated, obscure **6** devious, deceitful
♦ *adv*
completely, utterly, totally, thoroughly, undeniably, simply, quite, downright
♦ *n*
grassland, prairie, steppe, lowland, pampas, flat, flatland, plateau, tableland, savannah, tundra

plain-spoken *adj*
candid, frank, open, honest, blunt, outspoken, straightforward, direct, truthful, unequivocal, outright, explicit, forthright, downright, round

plaintive *adj*
doleful, mournful, melancholy, wretched, woeful, wistful, sad, unhappy, sorrowful, grief-stricken, heartbroken, piteous, pitiful, heart-rending, high-pitched
FORMAL disconsolate

plaintively *adv*
mournfully, sadly, unhappily, pitifully, wistfully, dolefully, wretchedly, woefully
FORMAL disconsolately

plan *n, v*
• *n*
1 IDEA, suggestion, intention, aim, arrangement, proposal, proposition, project, scheme, plot, system, method, means, way, policy, procedure, strategy, formula, programme, schedule, scenario
COLLOQ. *Aust* dart
2 BLUEPRINT, layout, diagram, chart, map, drawing, scale drawing, sketch, representation, illustration, design
FORMAL delineation
• *v*
1 PLOT, scheme, design, invent, think of, devise, contrive, develop, formulate, frame, shape, draft, outline, sketch, map out, work out, prepare, organize, arrange, schedule, programme, mastermind
2 AIM, intend, want, wish, propose, purpose, mean, resolve, seek, contemplate, envisage, foresee

plane¹ *n, adj*
• *n*
1 FLAT SURFACE, level surface, flat, level
2 LEVEL, stage, position, class, condition, degree, rank, footing, rung, stratum, echelon
• *adj*
level, smooth, uniform, regular, plain, flat, flush, even, horizontal
TECHNICAL homaloidal
FORMAL planar

plane² *n, v*
• *n*
travel by plane
aeroplane, aircraft, jet, jumbo jet, jumbo, airliner, glider, bomber, fighter, seaplane, swing-wing, VTOL; *N Am* airplane
See also panel at **aircraft**.
• *v*
skim, skate, fly, glide, sail, volplane, wing

planet *n*
Related adjective: planetary

Planets within the Earth's solar system (nearest the sun shown first) are:

Mercury	Mars	Uranus
Venus	Jupiter	Neptune
Earth	Saturn	Pluto

plank *n*
board, sheet, panel, slab, beam, timber, slat

planner *n*
designer, deviser, originator, maker, stylist, inventor, creator, contriver, producer, fashioner, architect, author, arranger, developer, organizer, mastermind

planning *n*
organization, arrangement, management, preparation, design, running, co-ordination, administration, development, regulation, establishment, control

plant *n, v*
• *n*
1 *garden plants*
flower, tree, shrub, herb, bush, vegetable
Related adjective: botanical

2 FACTORY, works, foundry, mill, shop, yard, workshop, machinery, apparatus, equipment, gear
• *v*
1 SOW, seed, scatter, implant, put into the ground, bury, transplant
2 INSERT, put, place, set, position, situate, fix, lodge, imbed, root, settle, found, establish
3 HIDE, put secretly, conceal, bury, disguise, put out of sight
FORMAL secrete

Types of plant include:

air-plant	fern	sapling
algae	flower	seedling
annual	fungus	shrub
biennial	grass	succulent
bulb	herb	tree
bush	herbaceous plant	vegetable
cactus	house plant	vine
cereal	hybrid	water plant
climber	lichen	weed
corm	moss	wild flower
cultivar	perennial	
evergreen	pot plant	

See also **algae and lichen; bulb; flower; grass; leaf; poisonous; shrub; weed; wild flower**.

plaque *n*
plate, slab, tablet, panel, sign, plaquette, brass, shield, plateau, medal, medallion, badge, brooch
TECHNICAL cartouche

plaster *n, v*
• *n*
1 *apply plaster to walls*
stucco, mortar, plasterwork, gypsum, plaster of Paris, gesso, plasterboard, grout, Polyfilla®, laying, rendering, scratchcoat, screed, roughcast, pugging
2 *put a plaster on a wound*
sticking-plaster, patch, dressing, adhesive dressing, bandage, Band-aid®, Elastoplast®, butterfly clip/plaster
TECHNICAL cataplasm, peloid
FORMAL emplastron, emplastrum
OLD plaister, emplaster
• *v*
daub, smear, coat, cover, cover thickly, overlay, spread, mortar, render, mud, parget, parge, leep; *dialect* smarm; *Scot* clatch
TECHNICAL teer
OLD bedaub, beplaster, emplaster

plastic *adj*
1 *plastic toys*
soft, pliable, flexible, supple, malleable, mouldable, ductile, shapeable
2 EASILY INFLUENCED, receptive, compliant, malleable, pliable, pliant, impressionable, manageable, mouldable
FORMAL tractable
3 ARTIFICIAL, unnatural, false, synthetic, man-made
COLLOQ. phoney
E3 1 rigid, inflexible **2** inflexible; *formal* intractable **3** natural

Types of plastic include:

Bakelite®	polymethyl	PVC (polyvinyl
Biopol®	methacrylate	chloride)
celluloid®	polynorbornene	uPVC
epoxy resin	polypropylene	silicone
Perspex®	polystyrene	Teflon®
phenolic resin	polythene	trans-
plexiglass	polyurethane	polyisoprene
polyester	PTFE (polytetra-	urea
polyethylene	fluoroethylene)	formaldehyde
		vinyl

plasticity *n*
flexibility, softness, suppleness, pliancy, pliableness, pliability, malleability
FORMAL tractability
Ea inflexibility, rigidity

plate *n, v*
• *n*
1 DISH, bowl, platter, salver, helping, serving, portion, ashet
2 SHEET, layer, slab, pane, panel, sign, plaque, tablet
FORMAL lamina
3 ILLUSTRATION, photograph, picture, print, lithograph
• *v*
coat, cover, overlay, veneer, laminate, electroplate, anodize, galvanize, platinize, gild, silver, tin

plateau *n*
1 *a grassy plateau*
plane, highland, tableland, table, upland, mesa
2 STABILITY, level, grade, stage

platform *n*
1 STAGE, podium, dais, rostrum, stand
COLLOQ. soapbox
2 POLICY, party line, principles, tenets, manifesto, programme, objectives, aims, ideas, intentions, strategy

platitude *n*
banality, generality, commonplace, truism, cliché, bromide, inanity, stereotype, hackneyed statement, trite expression, overworked phrase; *NAm* glittering generality
COLLOQ. chestnut

platitudinous *adj*
banal, commonplace, truistic, trite, clichéd, hackneyed, overworked, stale, stereotyped, set, stock, inane, tired, dull, flat, well-worn, vapid
COLLOQ. corny

platonic *adj*
non-physical, spiritual, non-romantic, non-sexual, intellectual, ideal, idealistic, transcendent
FORMAL incorporeal
Ea sexual

platoon *n*
company, group, patrol, troop, unit, battery, team, squad, squadron, outfit

platter *n*
plate, dish, salver, tray, charger, trencher

plaudits *n*
commendation, approval, praise, acclaim, acclamation, applause, congratulations, hurrahs, accolade, ovation, standing ovation, clapping
FORMAL approbation
COLLOQ. hand, bouquet, pat on the back, rave review, good press
Ea criticism

plausible *adj*
credible, believable, reasonable, logical, likely, fair, possible, probable, imaginable, conceivable, convincing, persuasive, smooth-talking, glib, soft-spoken, silver-tongued, colourable
FORMAL cogent, specious
Ea implausible, unlikely, improbable

plausibly *adv*
reasonably, logically, probably, possibly, conceivably, convincingly, persuasively, imaginably
Ea implausibly, improbably

play *v, n*
• *v*
1 AMUSE YOURSELF, have fun, enjoy yourself, play games, occupy yourself, divert yourself, revel, sport, romp, frolic, caper, gambol, frisk, cavort

2 PARTICIPATE IN, take part in, join in, be involved in, do, compete
3 *France played Italy*
oppose, compete against, vie with, rival, challenge, take on
4 ACT, perform, play the part of, portray, represent, impersonate
5 *light playing on the water*
dance, move lightly, flicker, twinkle, flash, gleam, glance
Ea **1** work
• *n*
1 FUN, amusement, enjoyment, entertainment, diversion, leisure, recreation, sport, game, hobby, pastime, merrymaking
2 DRAMA, tragedy, comedy, farce, show, melodrama, plot, performance, work
3 MOVEMENT, action, flexibility, give, freedom of movement, slack, looseness, leeway, latitude, freedom, liberty, free rein, margin, scope, range, licence, room, space
COLLOQ. give
4 ACTION, operation, exercise, interaction, interplay, transaction
5 JEST, fun, joking, teasing, laugh
COLLOQ. kicks
Ea **1** work

■ **play around with**
1 FIDDLE WITH, toy with, fidget with, meddle with, tamper with, interfere with
2 DALLY WITH, mess around with, flirt with, fool with, trifle with, womanize with, philander with

■ **play at**
pretend (to be), put on an act, make out
FORMAL affect
COLLOQ. go through the motions

■ **play down**
minimize, make light of, gloss over, underplay, downplay, understate, undervalue, underestimate
Ea exaggerate, emphasize, play up

■ **play on**
exploit, take advantage of, turn to account, profit by, trade on, capitalize on

■ **play out**
continue, go on, carry on, unfold, be revealed, act, enact

■ **play up**
1 EXAGGERATE, highlight, spotlight, accentuate, emphasize, stress, underline, point up, call attention to
2 MISBEHAVE, be mischievous, be naughty, give trouble, be difficult to control, trouble, bother, annoy, hurt
3 MALFUNCTION, not work, go wrong
COLLOQ. go/be on the blink
Ea **1** play down, underplay **3** work properly

■ **play up to**
flatter, ingratiate yourself, suck up to, curry favour with, blandish, fawn, toady
COLLOQ. bootlick, butter up, soft-soap; *NAm* cozy up

play-act *v*
pretend, put on, assume, feign, sham, counterfeit, fake, fabricate, simulate, bluff, impersonate, pass yourself off, act, put on an act, mime, go through the motions
FORMAL affect, dissemble
COLLOQ. keep up appearances

playboy *n*
philanderer, womanizer, ladies' man, lady-killer, rake, libertine, roué, debauchee
COLLOQ. man about town, socialite

player *n*
1 CONTESTANT, competitor, participant, sportsman, sportswoman
2 PERFORMER, entertainer, artiste, actor, actress, artist,

comedian, trouper, player, musician, instrumentalist, accompanist

playful *adj*
1 *as playful as a kitten*
frisky, sportive, frolicsome, ludic, lively, fun-loving, spirited, mischievous, roguish, impish, puckish, kittenish
2 *a playful remark*
humorous, funny, friendly, light-hearted, tongue-in-cheek, jesting, joking, facetious, waggish, teasing
F3 2 serious

playfully *adv*
light-heartedly, jokingly, humorously, facetiously, in jest
F3 seriously

playground *n*
park, playing-field, play area, adventure playground, amusement park, pleasure ground, recreation ground

playmate *n*
friend, companion, comrade, neighbour, playfellow
COLLOQ. buddy, chum, pal, mate

plaything *n*
toy, trifle, amusement, game, puppet, trinket, pastime, bauble, gewgaw, gimcrack

playwright *n*
dramatist, writer, scriptwriter, screen writer, dramaturge, dramaturgist, tragedian

plea *n*
1 APPEAL, petition, request, entreaty, supplication, prayer
FORMAL invocation, imploration
2 DEFENCE, justification, excuse, explanation, claim, pretext, alibi
TECHNICAL declinature, demurrer, *nolo contendere*
FORMAL vindication, placitum

plead *v*
1 BEG, implore, entreat, appeal, petition, ask, request, urge, intercede (for), moot
OLD persuade
FORMAL beseech, solicit, make supplication
2 *plead ignorance*
assert, state, argue, maintain, claim, allege, put forward
FORMAL adduce

pleasant *adj*
1 *a pleasant chat*
enjoyable, agreeable, nice, fine, lovely, delightful, charming, amusing, pleasing, gratifying, satisfying, acceptable, welcome, entertaining, refreshing; *S Afr* lekker
2 *a pleasant person*
friendly, amiable, affable, likeable, cheerful, congenial, good-humoured, charming, nice, lovely, winsome
F3 1, 2 unpleasant, nasty **2** unfriendly

pleasantly *adv*
enjoyably, delightfully, pleasingly, entertainingly, refreshingly

pleasantry *n*
1 *exchange pleasantries about the weather*
friendly remark, polite comment, casual remark
2 JOKE, jest, banter, badinage, quip, sally, witticism, *bon mot*

please *v, interj*
♦ *v*
1 DELIGHT, make happy, give pleasure to, charm, attract, appeal to, captivate, entertain, amuse, divert, cheer (up), gladden, humour, flatter, indulge, gratify, satisfy, fulfil, content, suit
OLD aggrate, agree, arride; (*Spenser*) queme
COLLOQ. tickle
2 WANT, will, wish, desire, like, prefer, choose, think fit, see fit
OLD list

F3 1 displease, annoy, anger, sadden
♦ *interj*
if you please, *bitte, je vous en prie*
OLD prithee, I'll trouble you to

pleased *adj*
contented, satisfied, gratified, glad, happy, cheerful, delighted, thrilled, euphoric, elated
COLLOQ. chuffed, over the moon, tickled pink; *Aust & NZ* rapt
F3 displeased, annoyed

pleasing *adj*
gratifying, satisfying, acceptable, good, pleasant, pleasurable, agreeable, nice, fine, delightful, enjoyable, amusing, entertaining, charming, attractive, engaging, winning, taking
F3 unpleasant, disagreeable

pleasurable *adj*
enjoyable, delightful, fun, good, lovely, nice, pleasant, gratifying, welcome, entertaining, amusing, diverting, agreeable, congenial
OLD COLLOQ. groovy
F3 bad, disagreeable

pleasure *n*
1 HAPPINESS, contentment, joy, delight, gladness, enjoyment, satisfaction, gratification
FORMAL solace
2 *the pleasure of playing a sport*
joy, delight, enjoyment, thrill, glory, treasure, prize, gem
3 *combine business with pleasure*
recreation, amusement, entertainment, leisure, fun
4 PREFERENCE, wish, will, desire, choice, inclination
F3 1 sorrow, pain, trouble, displeasure **2** disappointment, sadness
■ **it's a pleasure**
my pleasure, you're welcome, not at all, it's no trouble, any time, don't mention it, forget it, it was nothing, it's all right, that's all right, think nothing of it, no problem
■ **with pleasure**
gladly, willingly, of course, happily, readily
OLD fain

pleat *n*
tuck, fold, crease, flute, crimp, gather, pucker
FORMAL plication

plebeian *adj, n*
♦ *adj*
1 LOWER-CLASS, working-class, proletarian, low-born, peasant, mean
2 COMMON, uncultured, unrefined, uncultivated, coarse, base, ignoble, low
COLLOQ. non-U
F3 1 aristocratic, noble, patrician **2** refined, sophisticated
♦ *n*
common person, commoner, person in the street, proletarian, worker, peasant
COLLOQ. pleb, prole
F3 aristocrat, noble, patrician

plebiscite *n*
vote, referendum, ballot, poll, straw poll

pledge *n, v*
♦ *n*
1 PROMISE, vow, word of honour, word, oath, bond, hand, covenant, guarantee, warrant, commitment, committal, assurance, undertaking
OLD plight, band, sacrament, wager
2 DEPOSIT, security, surety, bail, guarantee, pawn
OLD gage, earnest, borrow, wed; *Scot* wad
FORMAL collateral
♦ *v*
1 PROMISE, vow, give your word, swear, take an oath, commit, contract, engage, undertake, give an

undertaking, vouch, guarantee, secure, pass
OLD plight, betroth, engage, propine
FORMAL impignorate
2 GUARANTEE, mortgage, secure
OLD impawn, pignorate, wage; (*Shakesp*) fine
FORMAL put up as collateral, impledge

plenary *adj*
full, complete, entire, open, absolute, unrestricted, whole,
general, integral, unconditional, unlimited, unqualified,
thorough, sweeping

plenipotentiary *n*
ambassador, envoy, minister, dignitary, diplomat, emissary,
legate, nuncio

plenitude *n*
abundance, plenty, plentifulness, profusion, fullness,
completeness, copiousness, bounty, excess, wealth,
entireness
FORMAL amplitude, plenteousness, plethora, cornucopia,
repletion
F3 scarcity

plenteous *adj*
abundant, plentiful, bountiful, copious, fruitful, lavish,
abounding, ample, generous, liberal, productive, fertile,
profuse, prolific, overflowing, inexhaustible, infinite
FORMAL bounteous, luxuriant
COLLOQ. bumper
F3 scarce, paltry

plentiful *adj*
ample, abundant, profuse, copious, overflowing, lavish,
generous, liberal, bountiful, fruitful, productive,
inexhaustible, infinite
FORMAL bounteous
COLLOQ. bumper
F3 scarce, scanty, rare

plentifully *adv*
abundantly, amply, profusely, copiously, generously,
lavishly, liberally, bountifully, fruitfully
F3 scarcely

plenty *n*
1 ABUNDANCE, profusion, copiousness, enough, fullness,
sufficiency, quantity, mass, volume, fund, mine, store, milk
and honey; *Scot* scouth, scowth
OLD foison; *Scot* stouth and routh
FORMAL plethora, plenteousness, cornucopia
2 AFFLUENCE, wealth, wealthiness, riches, fortune,
substance, prosperity
F3 **1** scarcity, lack, want **2** need
■ **plenty of**
many, large amount, large number, enough, more than
enough, more than is needed
COLLOQ. bags, lots, loads, masses, heaps, piles, stacks,
shedloads

plethora *n*
surfeit, surplus, excess, glut, abundance, overabundance,
profusion, overfullness, superabundance
FORMAL superfluity

pliability *n*
1 BENDABILITY, elasticity, flexibility, plasticity, ductility
2 ADAPTABILITY, amenability, susceptibility, malleability,
suggestibility, impressionableness, compliance, docility
FORMAL tractableness
F3 **1, 2** inflexibilty, rigidity

pliable *adj*
1 *pliable pieces of wood*
pliant, flexible, bendable, supple, lithe, malleable, elastic,
plastic, superplastic, cheverel
COLLOQ. bendy
2 *a pliable person*
yielding, adaptable, flexible, accommodating,

manageable, docile, biddable, compliant, persuadable,
responsive, receptive, impressionable, susceptible
FORMAL tractable
F3 **1** rigid, inflexible **2** headstrong, stubborn

pliant *adj*
1 *pliant pieces of wood*
pliable, flexible, bendable, supple, lithe, malleable, elastic,
plastic
COLLOQ. bendy
2 *a pliant person*
yielding, adaptable, flexible, accommodating,
manageable, docile, biddable, compliant, persuadable,
responsive, receptive, impressionable, susceptible
FORMAL tractable
F3 **1** rigid, inflexible **2** headstrong, stubborn

plight¹ *n*
the plight of starving children
predicament, quandary, dilemma, extremity, trouble,
difficulty, difficult/distressing situation, straits, dire straits,
state, condition, situation, circumstances, case; *Scot*
pliskie
OLD liking, point; (*Spenser*) taking
COLLOQ. jam, hole, tight spot, scrape, fix, pickle

plight² *v*
plight your troth
promise, pledge, vow, swear, contract, covenant, engage,
guarantee, propose, vouch, secure
OLD affiance

plod *v*
1 TRUDGE, tramp, stump, clump, stomp, lumber, walk
heavily, plough through
2 DRUDGE, labour, toil, grind, slog, persevere, peg away,
plug away, soldier on

plodder *n*
drudge, dullard, toiler, slogger, mug, sap
F3 high-flier

plot *n, v*
♦ *n*
1 CONSPIRACY, intrigue, scheme, plan, ruse, stratagem, cabal
FORMAL machination
2 STORY, narrative, action, subject, theme, storyline, thread,
outline, scenario
3 *plot of land*
patch, piece, tract, area, allotment, lot, parcel; *S Afr* erf
♦ *v*
1 CONSPIRE, intrigue, collude, connive, scheme, hatch, lay,
devise, contrive, plan, project, design, draft, concoct,
frame
FORMAL machinate
COLLOQ. cook up
2 CHART, map (out), mark, locate, draw, sketch, plan,
calculate

plotter *n*
conspirator, intriguer, schemer, planner
FORMAL machinator

plough *n, v*
♦ *n*
tractor, drill-plough, ridger, beam, sill, subsoiler, swing-
plough, wheel plough; *N Am* plow, lister, scooter
OLD ard
♦ *v*
cultivate, dig, till, work, ridge, spade, break (up), turn up,
furrow, fallow, rafter, rib, thwart; *Scot* rive; *N Am* plow, list
OLD ear
■ **plough into**
crash into, drive into, smash into, run/go into, hit, collide,
bump into
■ **plough through**
plod through, move through laboriously, trudge through,
wade through

ploy *n*

manoeuvre, stratagem, tactic, move, device, contrivance, scheme, game, trick, artifice, dodge, wile, ruse, subterfuge
See Synonym nuances panel at **trick¹**.

pluck *v, n*

◆ *v*

1 PULL, draw, tug, snatch, pull (off), remove, extract, pick, collect, gather, take in, harvest
COLLOQ. yank
2 *pluck a guitar*
pick, twang, strum, finger, thrum

◆ *n*

courage, bravery, daring, boldness, spirit, intrepidity, audacity, fearlessness, mettle, backbone, resolution, determination
FORMAL fortitude, valour
COLLOQ. nerve, guts, grit
🖃 cowardice

pluckily *adv*

bravely, daringly, courageously, confidently, boldly, fearlessly, audaciously, valiantly, intrepidly, heroically, adventurously
🖃 cowardly, cautiously, timidly

plucky *adj*

brave, courageous, bold, daring, audacious, fearless, intrepid, heroic, valiant, spirited, determined
COLLOQ. gutsy, spunky, gritty, feisty
🖃 cowardly, weak, feeble

plug *n, v*

◆ *n*

1 STOPPER, bung, cork, seal, spigot, spile, dossil; *Scot* dook
TECHNICAL access eye, neck, fipple, tampion
OLD stopple
2 ADVERTISEMENT, publicity, commercial, promotion, recommendation, blurb, mention, puff, good word
COLLOQ. hype, ad, push, promo
3 *a plug of tobacco*
chew, wad, twist, cake, dottle

◆ *v*

1 STOP (UP), stopper, bung, cork, block, choke, close, seal, fill, pack, stuff
TECHNICAL tampon, stem
OLD stopple
2 ADVERTISE, publicize, promote, market, tout, mention
COLLOQ. hype, push

▪ **plug away**
keep trying, persevere, plod on, slog away, peg away, toil (away), soldier on

plum *adj*

first-class, best, choice, prize, especially valued, excellent
COLLOQ. cushy

plumb *adv, v*

◆ *adv*

1 VERTICALLY, perpendicularly, sheer, straight up, straight down, up and down
2 PRECISELY, right, exactly, dead
COLLOQ. slap, bang, spot-on

◆ *v*

sound (out), fathom, measure, gauge, penetrate, delve into, probe, search (out), examine, investigate, explore
▪ **plumb in** install, fix, fit, put (in), place, position, set up
▪ **plumb the depths of**
experience the worst extremes of, experience fully, hit the lowest point/level, reach the nadir, reach rock bottom

plumbing
See panel below

plume *n*

feather, crest, pinion, quill, tuft, aigrette, streamer, marabou, osprey, plumule
TECHNICAL pappus
OLD panache
▪ **plume yourself on**
congratulate yourself, boast about, pride yourself, preen yourself, exult in
COLLOQ. pat yourself on the back

plummet *v*

plunge, dive, nose-dive, descend, drop, fall, drop/fall rapidly, decrease quickly, tumble, hurtle
🖃 soar

plummy *adj*

high-class, aristocratic, upper-class, affected, refined
COLLOQ. posh, U

plump¹ *adj*

a plump person
fat, obese, dumpy, tubby, stout, round, well-rounded, portly, chubby, podgy, fleshy, full, ample, buxom
FORMAL rotund, corpulent
COLLOQ. well-upholstered, beefy, flabby, gross
🖃 thin, skinny

plump² *v*

plump the sacks on the floor
put down, set down, deposit, drop, flop, sink, slump, collapse, descend, fall
COLLOQ. dump
▪ **plump for**
choose, select, prefer, opt for, back, side with, support, favour

plumpness *n*

fatness, fat, fleshiness, chubbiness, stoutness, portliness, tubbiness, podginess, obesity, pudginess

---

Plumbing fittings and equipment include:

auger	copper pipe	gate valve	nipple key	shower	toilet
back boiler	copper tube	geyser	overflow bend	attachment	trap
ballcock	coupler	hopper	pan	shower head	tube (or pipe)
ball valve	cylinder	hose	pedestal	sink	cutter
basin	deburring tool	immersion heater	pipe	siphon washer	tube flaring tool
basin spanner	draincock	joint	pipe bender	soil vent	U-bend
bath	drain rod	jointing	pipe clip	solder	union
bend	elbow joint	compound	pipe coupling	Stillson® wrench	urinal
bidet	electric water	lavatory	pipe wrench	stopcock	valve
blowtorch	heater	lavatory chain	plug	stop end	valve key
boiler	expansion (or	lever tap	plunger	sump pump	washer
bottle trap	header) tank	lockshield valve	programmer	tank	waste disposal
bowl	*N Am* faucet	mains pipe	P-trap	tap	unit
ceiling joint	flare joint	mixer tap	pump	tee	waste pipe
check valve	float	monkey wrench	radiator	Teflon® tape	water closet
cistern	flux	motorized zone	reducer	thermostat	WC
compression	gasket	valve	septic tank	thermostatic	Y-branch
fitting	gas water heater	nipple	shower	valve	

FORMAL corpulence, rotundity
▰ thinness, skinniness

plunder v, n
◆ v
loot, pillage, ravage, lay waste, devastate, sack, raid, ransack, maraud, rifle, steal, rob, strip, fleece
FORMAL despoil, depredate
◆ n
loot, pillage, booty, spoils, pickings, ill-gotten gains, prize
SLANG swag
Related adjective: predatory

plunge v, n
◆ v
1 DIVE, jump, nose-dive, swoop, dive-bomb, plummet, crash, descend, go down, sink, drop, fall, drop/fall rapidly, decrease quickly, throw, pitch, tumble, hurtle, career, launch, charge, dash, rush, tear, bull (into), enew yourself
COLLOQ. go in at the deep end
2 THRUST, push, drive, stick, stab, shove, ram, jab, pitch, lunge
3 IMMERSE, submerge, dip, sink, douse, mire, plump, souse
TECHNICAL enew
OLD beduck, merge, demerge, demerse, immerge, implunge, whelm; (*Shakesp*) emplonge
◆ n
dive, nose-dive, dip, duck, jump, swoop, descent, drop, fall, tumble, charge, rush, hurtle, immersion, submersion
■ **take the plunge**
decide to do something, commit yourself
COLLOQ. bite the bullet, go for it

plurality n
diversity, variety, number, numerousness, profusion, mass, bulk, majority, most
FORMAL multiplicity, multitudinousness, preponderance
COLLOQ. galaxy

plus n, prep
◆ n
advantage, benefit, bonus, good point, asset, credit, gain, extra, surplus
COLLOQ. perk
▰ disadvantage, drawback; *colloq*. minus
◆ prep
and, with, together with, as well as, in addition to, added to, over and above
COLLOQ. not to mention
▰ minus

plush adj
luxurious, luxury, lavish, de luxe, palatial, stylish, affluent, sumptuous, costly, rich
FORMAL opulent
COLLOQ. ritzy, glitzy, posh, swanky

plutocrat n
rich man, capitalist, millionaire, tycoon, magnate, billionaire, multimillionaire, Dives, Croesus
COLLOQ. fat cat, moneybags

ply[1] v
1 KEEP SUPPLYING, provide, supply, furnish, feed, lavish, assail, beset, bombard, harass, importune
2 TRAVEL, go, ferry, make regular journeys between/along
3 *ply a trade*
practise, carry on, follow, pursue, engage in, exercise, work at
4 *ply a tool*
use, employ, utilize, wield, handle, manipulate

ply[2] n
three-ply wool
thickness, strand, leaf, layer, sheet, fold

poach v
1 STEAL, pilfer, copy, take

FORMAL appropriate
COLLOQ. lift, borrow, nick
2 TRESPASS, encroach, infringe, intrude, catch/hunt illegally

pocket n, adj, v
◆ n
1 *a pocket on the back of the seat*
pouch, bag, envelope, receptacle, compartment, hollow, cavity; *Scot* plaid-neuk
OLD placket, bin, poke
2 *the fees are a drain on my pocket*
resources, funds, means, money, finances, budget, assets, capital, wherewithal
3 *pocket of resistance/unemployment*
patch, small area, isolated area, small group
◆ adj
small, little, concise, abridged, potted, compact, portable, miniature
COLLOQ. mini, pint-size
◆ v
take, gain, win unfairly, help yourself to, pilfer, filch, steal
OLD fob
FORMAL appropriate, purloin
COLLOQ. lift, nick, pinch, trouser, whip; *Aust & NZ* souvenir

pockmark n
blemish, pock, pit, scar, pockpit

pod n
shell, husk, case, hull
TECHNICAL legume

podgy adj
fat, chubby, paunchy, plump, fleshy, roly-poly, squat, chunky, dumpy, stout, tubby, stubby, stumpy
FORMAL corpulent, rotund
▰ thin, skinny

podium n
dais, platform, stage, stand, rostrum

poem

Types of poem include:

ballad	haiku	rondeau
bucolic	idyll	roundelay
cinquain	lay	sestina
clerihew	limerick	shape poem
concrete poem	lipogram	song
couplet	lyric	sonnet
ditty	madrigal	tanka
eclogue	monody	thin poem
elegy	nursery rhyme	triolet
epic	ode	verse
epigram	palinode	verselet
epithalmium	pantoum	versicle
epode	pastoral	villanelle
epopee	prothalamion	virelay
georgic	rhyme	

See also **prosody; song; verse.**

poet n
versifier, verse-maker, rhymer, rhymester, rhymist, lyricist, idyllist, sonneteer, balladeer, elegist, bard, minstrel, beat poet, performance poet, poetaster, poeticule

poetic adj
poetical, lyrical, moving, artistic, graceful, flowing, expressive, sensitive, beautiful, creative, imaginative, metrical, rhythmical, rhyming, prosaic, figurative, symbolic

poetry n
verse, lyrics, rhyme, rhyming, versing, poems, poesy, free verse, versification, vers libre, pennill, iambics, muse, Parnassus

pogrom *n*

slaughter, murder, homicide, extermination, carnage, massacre, butchery, wholesale slaughter, indiscriminate killing, holocaust, bloodbath, annihilation, killing, genocide, ethnic cleansing, liquidation, decimation

poignancy *n*

pathos, feeling, sentiment, emotion, evocativeness, intensity, keenness, painfulness, piquancy, tenderness, piteousness, sharpness, pungency, sadness, pain, distress, tragedy, misery, wretchedness, bitterness

poignant *adj*

moving, touching, affecting, emotional, tender, distressing, tragic, upsetting, heartbreaking, heart-rending, heartfelt, piteous, pathetic, sorrowful, sad, tearful, painful, agonizing, miserable, wretched
OLD poynant

poignantly *adv*

movingly, emotionally, tenderly, sadly, sorrowfully, pathetically, tearfully, painfully, miserably, wretchedly, tragically

point *n, v*

◆ *n*

1 *the main points of the argument*
issue, matter, subject, topic, question, item
2 FEATURE, attribute, quality, aspect, characteristic, trait, property, facet, detail, particular, item, subject, topic
3 *What's the point?*
use, sense, purpose, motive, reason, object, objective, intention, aim, end, goal, objective
4 ESSENCE, main point, crux, core, central point, heart, heart of the matter, pith, gist, nub, meat, marrow, thrust, meaning, significance, importance, theme, vein, tenor, drift, burden, keynote
5 PLACE, position, situation, location, locality, area, site, spot
6 MOMENT, instant, juncture, stage, time, period, position
7 DOT, spot, mark, speck, full stop, stop, full point, period, decimal point
8 *the point of a needle*
sharp end, end, extremity, tip, top, taper, spike, tine, nib
9 HEADLAND, head, foreland, promontory, cape, ness
10 MARK, score, goal, run, hit, total

◆ *v*

1 *point a gun*
aim, direct, train, level
2 INDICATE, signal, gesture at/towards, show, signify, designate, suggest
FORMAL denote, evidence
■ **point out**
show, indicate, draw/call attention to, point to, reveal, identify, specify, mention, bring up, allude to, remind
■ **point up**
emphasize, stress, underline, highlight, call attention to
■ **beside the point**
irrelevant, immaterial, unrelated, unconnected, out of place
COLLOQ. neither here nor there
■ **in point of fact**
actually, in fact, as a matter of fact, in reality, really
■ **on the point of**
on the verge of, (just) about to, going to, ready to, preparing to
■ **point of view**
1 OPINION, view, belief, judgement, attitude, feeling, sentiment, position, standpoint, viewpoint
2 PERSPECTIVE, outlook, approach, angle, slant, aspect
■ **to the point**
relevant, related, connected, germane, applicable, appropriate
FORMAL apposite, pertinent
■ **up to a point**
partly, somewhat, to some extent/degree, slightly

point-blank *adv, adj*

◆ *adv*
outright, directly, forthrightly, straightforwardly, straight, plainly, explicitly, openly, bluntly, frankly, candidly, rudely, abruptly, unequivocally

◆ *adj*
1 OUTRIGHT, direct, forthright, straightforward, plain, explicit, open, unreserved, blunt, frank, candid
2 AT CLOSE RANGE, closely, close to, near, touching

pointed *adj*

1 SHARP, keen, edged, tapering, barbed
TECHNICAL acicular, cuspidate(d)
FORMAL aculeate(d), fastigiate, lanceolate(d), mucronate(d)
2 *a pointed comment*
cutting, incisive, biting, forceful, penetrating, telling, striking, clear, obvious
FORMAL mordant, trenchant

pointedly *adv*

intentionally, on purpose, plainly, provocatively, defiantly, explicitly, bluntly

pointer *n*

1 ARROW, indicator, needle, hand
2 TIP, recommendation, suggestion, sign, hint, guide, guideline, clue, indication, indicator, advice, piece of advice, warning, caution
3 STICK, rod, cane, pole

pointless *adj*

useless, futile, vain, fruitless, unproductive, unprofitable, worthless, senseless, valueless, absurd, ridiculous, nonsensical, foolish, inane, meaningless, insignificant, a waste of time/effort, aimless, to no avail, unavailing
COLLOQ. a mug's game
F∃ useful, profitable, meaningful

pointlessly *adv*

senselessly, in vain, meaninglessly, aimlessly, unproductively, unprofitably
F∃ usefully, profitably, meaningfully

poise *n, v*

◆ *n*
calmness, composure, self-control, self-possession, presence of mind, assurance, self-assurance, dignity, elegance, grace, serenity, balance, equanimity, equilibrium, aplomb
COLLOQ. cool, coolness

◆ *v*
balance, position, steady, hover, hang, suspend, support

poised *adj*

1 DIGNIFIED, graceful, calm, composed, collected, self-possessed, self-controlled, self-confident, assured, serene, suave, urbane
COLLOQ. cool, cool calm and collected, unruffled, unflappable
2 *poised for action*
prepared, ready, set, all set, waiting, expectant

poison *n, v*

◆ *n*
1 *poison such as arsenic*
toxin, venom
2 *a poison spreading through society*
bane, blight, cancer, malignancy, contagion, pollution, contamination, corruption, canker

◆ *v*
kill by poison, envenomate, infect, contaminate, pollute, taint, adulterate, corrupt, deprave, defile, pervert, warp, spoil, blight
OLD (*Shakesp*) bane

poisonous *adj*

1 TOXIC, venomous, lethal, deadly, fatal, mortal
2 HARMFUL, noxious, pernicious, malicious, vicious,

Poisonous plants include:

aconite	common	dwale	jimson weed	naked lady	wild arum
amanita	nightshade	foxglove	laburnum	oleander	windflower
anemone	cowbane	giant hockweed	lantana	poison ivy	wolfsbane
banewort	cuckoo pint	helmet flower	lords-and-ladies	stinkweed	
belladonna	deadly	hemlock	meadow saffron	stramonium	
black nightshade	nightshade	hemlock water	monkshood	thorn apple	
castor oil plant	digitalis	dropwort	naked boys	wake-robin	

See also **mushrooms and toadstools**.

---

spiteful, virulent, malignant, contaminating, corrupting, cancerous, cankerous

poke *v, n*
* *v*

prod, stab, jab, stick, thrust, push, shove, nudge, nuzzle, pick, elbow, dig, butt, hit, punch; *dialect* poach, pote, proke, snuzzle; *Scot* powter; *N Am* scuffle
OLD prick, prog
* *n*

prod, jab, thrust, shove, nudge, dig, butt, punch; *dialect* peg
■ **poke around**
grope around, search for, look (all over) for, rummage around, rake through, root, rout
■ **poke fun at**
ridicule, mock, jeer, make fun of, tease, parody, joke, quiz; *Aust* poke mullock at
COLLOQ. rag, rib, send up, spoof, take the mickey; *Aust & NZ* poke borak at
■ **poke out**
stick out, jut out, protrude, project, overhang, extend, beetle, extrude
■ **poke your nose into**
meddle in, interfere in, tamper with, pry in
COLLOQ. put/stick your oar in, stick/thrust your nose into, butt in

poker-faced *adj*
blank, expressionless, deadpan, impassive, emotionless, without feeling, lifeless, apathetic, uninterested, indifferent, glazed, empty, vacant, vacuous, inscrutable, uncomprehending

poky *adj*
confined, restricted, cramped, small, tight, tiny, narrow, crowded
FORMAL incommodious
EЭ spacious, roomy

polar *adj*
1 COLD, freezing, frozen, icy, glacial, arctic, Siberian, Antarctic
2 OPPOSITE, completely/utterly different, diametrically opposed, conflicting, ambivalent, contradictory
FORMAL antithetical, dichotomous

polarity *n*
opposition, oppositeness, contradiction, ambivalence, separation, difference, contrariety, duality, paradox
FORMAL antithesis, dichotomy

polarize *v*
divide, disunite, separate, alienate, split (up), segregate, break up, drive apart, come between, set someone against another
FORMAL estrange
EЭ unite

pole[1] *n*
a telegraph pole
bar, rod, stick, shaft, spar, upright, pillar, support, post, stake, mast, staff, stanchion

pole[2] *n*
views that represent opposite poles
extremity, extreme, limit

■ **poles apart**
completely different, extremely different, incompatible, irreconcilable, worlds apart
COLLOQ. like chalk and cheese

polemic *n, adj*
* *n*

argument, controversy, debate, dispute
FORMAL diatribe, invective
* *adj*

argumentative, contentious, controversial, polemical
FORMAL disputatious, eristic(al)

polemicist *n*
debater, controversialist, arguer, contender, disputer, disputant, polemist
FORMAL logomachist

polemics *n*
debate, dispute, argument, controversy, contention, argumentation
FORMAL disputation, logomachy

police *n, v*
* *n*

police force, police officers, constabulary; *Scot & Irish* polis
COLLOQ. the law, the force, cops, coppers, boys in blue
SLANG the Bill, bizzies, the fuzz, rozzers, pigs
* *v*

1 PATROL, guard, protect, defend, keep watch, keep the peace
2 CHECK, control, keep under control, regulate, monitor, watch, observe, supervise, oversee

police officer *n*
officer, policeman, policewoman, constable, PC, WPC; *Scot & Irish* polis
COLLOQ. cop, copper, bobby
SLANG pig, nark, rozzer, flat-foot, bluebottle; *Aust & NZ* John Hop
OLD SLANG *N Am* bull

policy *n*
1 CODE OF PRACTICE, rules, guidelines, procedure, method, system, practice, custom, protocol
2 COURSE OF ACTION, line, course, plan, programme, scheme, schedule, stance, position, guideline(s), approach, strategy

polish *v, n*
* *v*

1 SHINE, brighten, smooth, rub (up), buff, burnish, clean, wax, brilliant, slick, beeswax, furbish, sand, scour, supercalender, glaciate, rottenstone
OLD glass, lap
FORMAL planish
COLLOQ. posh up
SLANG bull
2 IMPROVE, enhance, brush up, touch up, finish, perfect, refine, cultivate, file
EЭ 1 tarnish, dull
* *n*

1 *a tin of polish*
wax, varnish
2 SHINE, gloss, sheen, lustre, brightness, brilliance, sparkle,

smoothness, finish, glaze, veneer, burnish
3 REFINEMENT, cultivation, class, breeding, sophistication, finesse, style, elegance, grace, poise
E3 2 dullness **3** clumsiness

■ **polish off**
1 EAT UP, consume, devour, put away, bolt, gobble, finish, complete, dispose of, down, stuff
COLLOQ. wolf
2 MURDER, kill, destroy
COLLOQ. do in, eliminate, dispatch, wipe out, take out, zap
SLANG bump off, knock off, rub out, waste, blow away, liquidate

polished *adj*
1 SHINING, shiny, waxed, burnished, glossy, lustrous, gleaming, smooth, glassy, slippery
2 FAULTLESS, flawless, impeccable, perfect, outstanding, superlative, remarkable, excellent, masterly, expert, professional, skilful, accomplished, proficient, adept, perfected
FORMAL consummate
3 REFINED, cultivated, genteel, well-bred, well-mannered, polite, sophisticated, civilized, urbane, suave, elegant, graceful
E3 1 tarnished, dull **2** inexpert, unskilful **3** gauche, awkward

polite *adj*
1 COURTEOUS, well-mannered, respectful, civil, well-bred, well-behaved, deferential, refined, cultured, gentlemanly, ladylike, gallant, chivalrous, gracious, obliging, thoughtful, considerate, tactful, diplomatic, suave, courtlike, delicate, humane, bland, Grandisonian
2 *in polite society*
refined, cultured, genteel, well-bred, well-mannered, polite, sophisticated, civilized, urbane, suave, elegant
E3 1 impolite, rude, discourteous

Synonym nuances
sense 1
Courteous may be used to describe paying someone due regard and attention, although it suggests a rather formal manner, and while **well-mannered** describes similarly formal behaviour, it is more suggestive of adhering to social conventions.
  You can use **respectful** to imply displaying an attentive regard for someone; **deferential** goes further by implying an element of submissiveness: *the media are deferential to Prime Ministers.* **Civil**, however, generally implies showing the minimum courtesy required to avoid rudeness: *it was an effort to remain civil to her.*
  Well-bred puts the emphasis on someone's upbringing, while **refined** and **cultured** further imply tastefulness and a complete lack of vulgarity. **Gallant** and **chivalrous** would be reserved for a man's attentive conduct towards women, while **suave** also tends to be used of men, but conveys an ease of manner.
  Gracious has implications of dignity: *she accepted his gift with a gracious smile.* The terms **tactful** and **diplomatic** put the emphasis on skill in dealing with people's feelings: *I showed a diplomatic interest in his inane ramblings.* **Delicate** has more negative suggestions of tentativeness. More critical is the term **bland**, which quite pointedly suggests an absence of personality.

---

politely *adv*
courteously, respectfully, thoughtfully, considerately, diplomatically, tactfully, graciously, obligingly, chivalrously, gallantly
E3 impolitely, rudely, discourteously

politeness *n*
courtesy, manners, good manners, deference, cordiality, gentility, mannerliness, polish, refinement, elegance, courtliness, culture, thoughtfulness, cultivation, civility, considerateness, graciousness, grace, gentlemanliness,

good breeding, respect, respectfulness, diplomacy, tact, discretion, attention, savoir-vivre
FORMAL complaisance
E3 impoliteness, rudeness, discourtesy

politic *adj*
wise, prudent, shrewd, sensible, tactful, diplomatic, advisable, advantageous, opportune, expedient
FORMAL judicious, sagacious, sage
E3 impolitic

⚠ politic or **political**?
Politic is a rather formal word meaning 'wise, sensible': *He considered it politic to leave before there was any further trouble.* *Political* means 'relating to politics': *the political system of the USA; party political broadcasts.*

political *adj*
governmental, parliamentary, constitutional, ministerial, administrative, executive, bureaucratic, civil, public, judicial, party political

⚠ political or **politic**?
See panel at **politic**.

political ideology

Political ideologies include:

absolutism	federalism	pluralism
anarchism	holism	republicanism
authoritarianism	imperialism	social democracy
Bolshevism	individualism	socialism
Christian	liberalism	syndicalism
democracy	Maoism	Thatcherism
collectivism	Marxism	theocracy
communism	nationalism	third way
conservatism	Nazism	totalitarianism
democracy	neocolonialism	Trotskyism
egalitarianism	neo-fascism	unilateralism
fascism	neo-nazism	Whiggism

---

political party
See panel on next page

politics *n*
1 *go into politics*
public affairs, civics, affairs of state, statecraft, government, national government, regional government, local government, diplomacy, statesmanship, political science, party politics, political views/beliefs
2 *office politics*
power struggle, power game, power politics, manipulation, manoeuvring, jockeying for position/power
FORMAL machination(s)
COLLOQ. wheeler-dealing
See also panels on page 770

poll *n, v*
♦ *n*
ballot, ballot-box, vote, voting, plebiscite, referendum, straw poll, straw vote, head count, show of hands, sampling, canvass, opinion poll, market research, Gallup poll, survey, returns, census, count, tally
♦ *v*
1 WIN, net, get, receive, return, gain, obtain
2 BALLOT, survey, canvass, sample, question, interview, solicit, electioneer, campaign
3 CLIP, cut, trim, shear, pollard, dod, dishorn

pollute *v*
contaminate, infect, poison, taint, adulterate, debase, corrupt, dirty, make dirty, foul, befoul, soil, defile, deprave, warp, sully, stain, tarnish, blacken, mar, spoil; *Scot* file
FORMAL vitiate

Political parties include:

AUSTRALIA:
Australian Democrats
Australian Greens
Australian Labor Party (ALP)
Liberal Party of Australia
National Party of Australia
One Nation

AUSTRIA:
Freiheitliche Partei Österreichs (FPÖ) [Freedom Party]
Liberales Forum (LF) [Liberal Forum]
Österreichische Volkspartei (ÖVP) [Austrian People's Party]
Sozialdemokratische Partei Österreichs (SPÖ) [Social Democratic Party of Austria]

BELGIUM:
Anders gaan Leven (AGALEV) [Flemish Greens]
Christen-Democratisch en Vlaams (CD&V) [Christian-Democratic and Flemish Party]
Ecologistes Confédérés pour l'Organisation de Luttes Originales (ECOLO) [French Greens]
Parti Réformateur Libéral (PRL) [Liberal Reform Party]
Parti Social Chrétien (PSC) [Christian Social Party]
Parti Socialiste (PS) [Socialist Party]
Social Progressive Alternative (SPA) [Flemish Socialist Party]
Vlaams Blok (VB) [Flemish Bloc]
Vlaamse Liberalen en Democraten (VLD) [Flemish Liberal Democrats]

CANADA:
Bloc Québécois
Canadian Alliance/Alliance Canadienne
Liberal Party of Canada/Parti Libéral du Canada
New Democratic Party of Canada (NDP)/Nouveau Parti Démocratique du Canada (NPD)
Progressive Conservative Party of Canada/Parti Progressiste-Conservateur du Canada

DENMARK:
Dansk Folkeparti (DF) [Danish People's Party]
Enhedslisten – De Rød-Grønne [Unity List – The Danish Red-Green Alliance]
Kristeligt Folkeparti [Christian People's Party]
Konservative Folkeparti [Conservative People's Party]
Det Radikale Venstre ['The Radical Left' – Danish Social Liberal Party]
Social-demokratiet [Social Democrats]
Socialistisk Folkeparti (SF) [Socialist People's Party]
Venstre [Left – Danish Liberal Party]

FRANCE:
Front National (FN) [National Front]
Parti Communiste Français (PCF) [French Communist Party]

Parti Socialiste (PS) [Socialist Party]
Rassemblement pour la République (RPR) [Movement for the Republic]
Union pour la Démocratie Française (UDF) [Union for the French Democracy]

GERMANY:
Bündnis 90/Die Grünen [Alliance 90/The Greens]
Christlich Demokratische Union Deutschlands (CDU) [Christian Democratic Union of Germany]
Christlich-Soziale Union in Bayern (CSU) [Christian Social Union in Bavaria]
Freie Demokratische Partei (FDP) – Die Liberalen [Free Democratic Party – The Liberals]
Partei des Demokratischen Sozialismus (PDS) [Party of the Democratic Socialism]
Sozial-demokratische Partei Deutschlands (SPD) [Social-democratic Party of Germany]

GREECE:
Dimokratiko Kinoniko Kinima (DIKKI) [Democratic Social Movement]
Kommounistiko Komma Elladas (KKE) [Communist Party of Greece]
Nea Dimokratia (ND) [New Democracy]
Panellinio Socialistiko Kinima (PASOK) [Panhellenic Socialist Movement]
Politiki Anixi [Political Spring]
Synaspismos tis Aristeras kai tis Proodou (SYN) [Coalition of the Left and Progress]

ITALY:
Alleanza Nazionale (AN) [National Alliance]
Democratici di Sinistra (DS) [Democratic Left]
Forza Italia (FI) [Italian Force]
Lega Nord [Northern League]
Margherita [Daisy]
Partito dei Comunisti Italiani (PDCI) [Party of Italian Communists]
Unione Democratico Cristiana e di Centro (UDC) [Christian Democratic and Centrist Union]
I Verdi [Greens]

THE NETHERLANDS:
Christen Democratisch Appèl (CDA) [Christian Democratic Party]
Democraten 66 (D66)
GroenLinks [GreenLeft]
Lijst Pim Fortuyn (LPF) [List Pim Fortuyn]
Partij van de Arbeid (PvdA) [Labour Party]
Socialistische Partij (SP) [Socialist Party]
Volkspartij voor Vrijheid en Democratie (VVD) [People's Party for Freedom and Democracy]

PORTUGAL:
Partido Comunista Português (PCP) [Portuguese Communist Party]
Partido Social Democrata (PSD) [Social Democratic Party]
Partido Socialista (PS) [Socialist Party]
Partido Popular (CDS-PP) [People's Party]

SPAIN:
Batasuna
Convergència i Unió (CiU) [Convergence and Union]
Euzko Alderdi Jeltzalea (EAJ)/Partido Nacionalista Vasco (PNV) [Basque Nationalist Party]
Izquierda Unida (IU) [United Left]
Partido Popular (PP) [People's Party]
Partido Socialista Obrero Español (PSOE) [Spanish Socialist Workers' Party]

REPUBLIC OF IRELAND:
Fianna Fáil
Fine Gael
Green
Labour
People of Ireland Party/Muintir na hEireann
Progressive Democrats
Sinn Féin
Socialist
Workers' Party

UK:
Alliance
British National (BNP)
Communist
Conservative and Unionist
Co-operative
Democratic
Democratic Unionist (DUP)
Green
Labour
Liberal
Liberal Democratic
Militant Labour
National Front
Parliamentary
Parliamentary Labour
Plaid Cymru
Progressive Unionist (PUP)
Republican
Scottish Conservative and Unionist
Scottish Liberal Democratic
Scottish National (SNP)
Scottish Socialist
Sinn Féin
Social and Liberal Democratic
Social Democratic and Labour (SDLP)
Socialist Workers
UK Independence
UK Unionist
Ulster Democratic Unionist
Ulster Popular Unionist
Ulster Unionist
Welsh Liberal Democratic

See also **government systems; parliaments and assemblies; political ideology**.

---

pollution *n*
impurity, contamination, infection, taint, adulteration, corruption, dirtiness, filthiness, foulness, fouling, defilement, debasement, depravity, sullying, staining, tarnishing, blackening
OLD soilure
COLLOQ. muckiness
F3 purification, purity, cleanness

polychromatic *adj*
multicoloured, many-coloured, kaleidoscopic, many-hued, mottled, motley, rainbow, variegated, varicoloured, polychrome, parti-coloured
F3 monochromatic, monochrome, black and white

polyglot *adj, n*
♦ *adj*
multilingual, cosmopolitan, international, multiracial

People in politics include:

activist	Democrat	lawmaker	moderate	presiding officer	statesman
AM (Assembly Member)	Deputy Speaker	left-winger	MP (Member of Parliament)	prime minister	stateswoman
ambassador	dictator	*colloq.* lefty		radical	Tánaiste
backbencher	dissident	legislator	MSP (Member of the Scottish Parliament)	*colloq.* red	Taoiseach
Black Rod	*colloq.* dry	Liberal		Republican	TD (Member of the Dáil)
capitalist	Eurosceptic	Liberal Democrat	party chairman	revolutionary	
Communist	extremist	loyalist	party member	right-winger	Tory
colloq. commie	first minister	Marxist	party worker	secretary of state	Trotskyite
comrade	frontbencher	Marxist-Leninist	*colloq.* pinko	senator	true-blue
congressman	Green	MEP (Member of the European Parliament)	politician	Social Democrat	*colloq.* wet
congresswoman	high commissioner		premier	Socialist	Whig
Conservative	independent	minister	president	speaker	
				spin doctor	

Terms used in politics include:

alliance	coup d'état	government	nationalization	referendum	trade union
apartheid	détente	green paper	parliament	right wing	veto
ballot	devolution	Hansard	party	sanction	vote
bill	election	hung parliament	party line	shadow cabinet	welfare state
blockade	electoral register	judiciary	prime minister's question time	sovereignty	whip
cabinet	first-past-the-post	left wing		state	white paper
campaign		lobby	privatization	summit	
civil service	focus group	local government	propaganda	summit conference	
coalition	general election	majority	proportional representation	term of office	
constitution	ginger group	mandate		three-line whip	
council	go to the country	manifesto	rainbow coalition		

FORMAL polyglottal, polyglottic
Ⅎ monoglot
♦ *n*
linguist, multilinguist

polymath *n*
all-rounder, oracle, mine of information
FORMAL pansophist, polyhistor
COLLOQ. know-all, walking encyclopaedia
Ⅎ ignoramus

pomp *n*
ceremony, ceremonial, ritual, solemnity, formality, ceremoniousness, state, grandeur, splendour, magnificence, pageantry, show, display, parade, spectacle, ostentation, flourish, brilliance, glory, majesty
OLD triumph
COLLOQ. glitter
Ⅎ austerity, simplicity

pomposity *n*
1 SELF-IMPORTANCE, arrogance, vanity, pride, haughtiness, loftiness, presumption, pretension, pretentiousness, imperiousness, superciliousness, condescension, airs
FORMAL affectation
2 *his annoying pomposities*
turgidity, rhetoric, stuffiness, preachiness
FORMAL bombast, euphuism, fustian, grandiloquence, magniloquence
Ⅎ 1 modesty **2** simplicity, economy

pompous *adj*
1 SELF-IMPORTANT, arrogant, proud, haughty, lofty, conceited, vain, presumptuous, grandiose, supercilious, patronizing, condescending, overbearing, imperious, solemn, magisterial, aldermanlike, aldermanly, pretentious, ostentatious, magnificent, portentous, budge
OLD magnific
FORMAL affected
COLLOQ. snooty, big
2 *pompous language/occasions*
elaborate, grant, high-flown, overblown, windy, stilted, flowery, ostentatious, turgid, stuffy, state, inflated, fustian
FORMAL euphuistic, magniloquent, bombastic, orotund
COLLOQ. heavy, preachy, la-di-da

Ⅎ 1 unassuming, modest, unaffected **2** simple, unpretentious

pond *n*
pool, puddle, lake, mere, tarn, watering-hole, waterhole, rink, stew, oceanarium, seaquarium; *Scot* pound; *Irish* turlough; *N Am* tank
OLD flash
FORMAL piscary

ponder *v*
deliberate, give thought to, reflect, reason, think, contemplate, meditate, consider, brood, examine, analyse, study, ruminate over, turn over, weigh, muse (on), puzzle over, mull over, pore (over), revolve, incubate
OLD poise, volve
FORMAL cerebrate, cogitate, excogitate, ratiocinate, ponderate

ponderous *adj*
1 *ponderous writing*
dull, serious, dreary, tedious, stilted, long-winded, plodding, verbose, laborious, pedantic, pedestrian, stodgy, stolid, humourless, laboured, lifeless
FORMAL prolix
2 CLUMSY, unwieldy, awkward, cumbersome, graceless, heavy, bulky, weighty, heavy-handed, heavy-footed, huge, massive, hefty, slow-moving, lumbering, elephantine
Ⅎ 1 light, simple **2** delicate, nimble

ponderously *adv*
1 TEDIOUSLY, seriously, laboriously, verbosely, pedantically, stodgily
2 CLUMSILY, awkwardly, cumbersomely, heavily, slowly, gracelessly
Ⅎ 1 simply **2** delicately

ponderousness *n*
seriousness, tedium, heaviness, laboriousness, stodginess, stolidity, weightiness, humourlessness, gravitas
Ⅎ delicacy, lightness, subtlety

pontifical *adj*
1 PAPAL, apostolic, ecclesiastical, prelatic
2 SELF-IMPORTANT, pompous, overbearing, condescending, imperious, pretentious, magisterial, dogmatic, didactic, portentous, sermonizing
COLLOQ. snooty, preachy
Ⅎ 2 reticent, unassuming

pontificate *v*
preach, hold forth, lecture, expound, pronounce, sermonize, sound off, harangue, dogmatize, moralize
FORMAL declaim, perorate
COLLOQ. lay down the law, spiel

pony *n*
See panel at **horse**.

pooh-pooh *v*
dismiss, scorn, make little of, belittle, brush aside, ridicule, disdain, disregard, slight, sneer, sniff at, scoff, spurn, reject, play down, minimize
FORMAL deride, disparage
COLLOQ. turn up your nose at
F3 exaggerate, magnify

pool¹ *n*
a pool of water
puddle, pond, lake, mere, tarn, watering-hole, waterhole, paddling-pool, swimming-pool, swimming-bath(s)
OLD flash; (*Spenser*) plesh

pool² *n, v*
♦ *n*
1 FUND, reserve, supply, accumulation, bank, kitty, purse, pot, jackpot, ante
2 SYNDICATE, cartel, ring, combine, consortium, collective, group, team
♦ *v*
share, merge, put together, combine, amalgamate, contribute
COLLOQ. chip in, muck in

poor *adj*
1 IMPOVERISHED, poverty-stricken, badly off, in need, hard-up, bankrupt, penniless, as poor as a church mouse, without means, without the wherewithal, destitute, deprived, underprivileged, disadvantaged, reduced, humble, lowly, mean, miserable, wretched, distressed, straitened, beggared, needy
FORMAL penurious, impecunious, exiguous, obolary, indigent
COLLOQ. dirt-poor, broke, stony, stony-broke, flat broke, skint, strapped (for cash), cleaned-out, on your uppers, on your beam ends, not having two pennies to rub together, not having a penny to your name, on the breadline, in Queer Street
2 BAD, substandard, unsatisfactory, inferior, mediocre, below standard, below par, low, low-quality, low-grade, low-rent, second-rate, third-rate, shoddy, imperfect, defective, faulty, jerry, weak, feeble, sorry, worthless, fruitless, unproductive, barren
COLLOQ. pathetic, rubbish, rop(e)y, rotten, duff, measly, crumm; *Aust* cronk; *Aust & NZ* crook
SLANG cruddy, naff, pants
3 LACKING, deficient, inadequate, insufficient, scanty, skimpy, meagre, sparse, paltry, depleted, exhausted
4 UNFORTUNATE, unlucky, luckless, ill-fated, ill-starred, unhappy, miserable, wretched, sorry, sad, spiritless, pathetic, pitiable, pitiful
FORMAL hapless
F3 **1** rich, wealthy, affluent **2** good, superior, impressive **3** sufficient, ample **4** fortunate, lucky

---

Synonym nuances
sense 1
While both **bankrupt** and **penniless** emphasize the idea of having absolutely no money, **impoverished**, **poverty-stricken** and **distressed** suggest a complete lack of any resources, and suffering as a result. Likewise **destitute** suggests being entirely bereft of money or possessions.
  The terms **badly off** and **hard-up** suggest having very little rather than nothing, while **in need** and **needy** put the emphasis on what you do not have but require: *cash grants for those in need*. **Deprived**, likewise, implies

---

being without, while **underprivileged** and **disadvantaged** suggest financial misfortunes arising from a lack of opportunity: *the unemployed and other disadvantaged groups*. Similarly, **straitened** can be used to suggest limitations through reduced resources.
  You can use **reduced** and **impoverished** where there has been a deterioration in circumstances, whereas **humble** and **lowly** are more suggestive of being modest or basic: *lowly accommodation in run-down areas*. The terms **mean**, **miserable** and **wretched** could be used to suggest an element of pitiable shabbiness: *the mean little houses; poor immigrants in their wretched clothes*.
  You can use **without means** or **without the wherewithal** to refer to a lack of pecuniary resources for something in particular: *we were without the wherewithal for private health care*.

poorly *adj, adv*
♦ *adj*
ill, sick, unwell, ailing, sickly, off colour, below par, seedy, groggy
FORMAL indisposed
COLLOQ. out of sorts, under the weather, rotten
F3 well, healthy
♦ *adv*
badly, inadequately, unsatisfactorily, unsuccessfully, faultily, incompetently, inexpertly, insufficiently, inferiorly, rottenly, shabbily, shoddily, meanly, feebly
F3 well

pop *v, n*
♦ *v*
1 BURST, explode, go off, bang, crack, snap
2 RUSH, dash, hurry, go quickly, leave quickly, go for a short time
COLLOQ. nip
3 PUT, push, insert, slide, slip, thrust, drop, shove
♦ *n*
1 BANG, crack, snap, burst, explosion, boom
FORMAL report
2 FIZZY DRINK, fizzy lemonade, cola, soda
■ **pop off**
die, pass away, pass on
COLLOQ. peg out, have had it
SLANG snuff it, kick the bucket, flatline
■ **pop up**
appear, occur, materialize, crop up, turn up, show up, come along

pope *n*
pontiff, sovereign pontiff, Bishop of Rome, Holy Father, Vicar of Christ, His Holiness, *Il Papa*
Related adjectives: papal, pontifical

popinjay *n*
dandy, fop, beau, coxcomb, peacock, pansy, swell, dude
COLLOQ. toff
F3 he-man, macho

poppycock *n*
nonsense, rubbish, trash, drivel, balderdash, gibberish, gobbledygook, stupidity, silliness, foolishness, folly, twaddle; *Scot* blether; *dialect & N Am* blathers
COLLOQ. stuff and nonsense, bunk, rot, claptrap, cobblers, piffle, waffle, flannel, tripe, tosh, bosh, tommyrot, codswallop, baloney, humbug, hooey, bilge, hogwash, blah, guff, rhubarb
SLANG bull; (*vulgar*) crap, shit, balls, bollocks, bullshit
F3 sense

populace *n*
inhabitants, natives, residents, citizens, occupants, community, society, people, folk, general public, crowd, masses, proletariat, public, common people, mob, multitude(s), canaille, hoi polloi, third estate, rabble, rank

and file, herd, common herd, great unwashed, riff-raff
COLLOQ. punters, plebs, proles
■ aristocracy, élite, nobility

popular adj
1 WELL-LIKED, favourite, liked, favoured, in favour, admired, wanted, desired, approved, in demand, sought-after, fashionable, modish
COLLOQ. trendy, in, now, hip, cool, big, all the rage
2 FAMOUS, well-known, celebrated, renowned, acclaimed, noted, idolized
3 PREVAILING, current, accepted, usual, customary, conventional, standard, stock, common, prevalent, widespread, universal, general, generally recognized, household
4 *a popular history of science*
general, non-specialist, non-technical, amateur, understandable, accessible, simple, simplified, ordinary, mass-market, lay
■ 1 unpopular, disliked, out of favour 2 unheard of, obscure, unknown 3 rare, unusual 4 specialist, technical, expert, professional

popularity n
approval, acceptance, recognition, reputation, favour, vogue, kudos, mass appeal, regard, fame, renown, esteem, currency, repute, acclaim, adoration, adulation, glory, worship, idolization, lionization
FORMAL approbation
■ unpopularity

popularize v
spread, propagate, familiarize, universalize, democratize, generalize, give currency to, simplify, make understandable, make accessible

popularly adv
commonly, widely, universally, generally, usually, customarily, non-technically, ordinarily, regularly, conventionally, traditionally

populate v
people, occupy, settle, colonize, inhabit, live in, overrun
FORMAL dwell

population n
inhabitants, natives, residents, citizens, occupants, community, society, people, folk
FORMAL populace

populous adj
crowded, packed, swarming, teeming, crawling, densely populated, overpopulated, overpeopled
■ deserted, empty

porcelain

Types of porcelain include:

biscuit	copper red	Kakiemon
bisque	eggshell	Kraak
blue and white	faience	nankeen
bone china	famille-rose	Parian
Canton	famille-verte	saltglazed
Capodimonte	First Period	soapstone paste
chinoiserie	Worcester	soft paste
Compagnie des	hard paste	Yingqing
Indes	Imari	

Famous makers of porcelain include:

Arita	Copeland	Rockingham
Belleek	Derby	Royal Doulton
Bow	Dresden	Royal Worcester
Bristol	Limoges	Satsuma
Caughley	Meissen	Sèvres
Chantilly	Ming	Vienna
Chelsea	Minton	Wedgwood®
Coalport	Nanking	Worcester

porch n
vestibule, hall, hallway, entrance-hall, lobby, foyer; N Am stoop; S Afr stoep
TECHNICAL galilee

pore¹ v
■ **pore over**
study, study intensely, examine, examine closely, scrutinize, go over, read, scan, contemplate, ponder, dwell on, brood
OLD con
FORMAL peruse

pore² n
sweating from every pore
hole, opening, perforation, aperture, outlet, vent
TECHNICAL foramen, micropore, stoma, stigma, lenticel
FORMAL orifice

pornographic adj
obscene, indecent, dirty, filthy, X-rated, pink, adult, risqué, bawdy, coarse, gross, lewd, salacious, erotic, titillating
FORMAL prurient
COLLOQ. blue, off-colour, porn

pornography n
indecency, obscenity, filth, dirt, smut, erotica, grossness, bawdiness, facetiae, curiosa, peep-show, snuff film/movie/video
COLLOQ. porn, porno, sexploitation, girlie magazines, (video) nasty, skinflick

porous adj
permeable, pervious, penetrable, absorbent, spongy, spongelike, honeycombed, cellular, holey, open, airy
TECHNICAL foraminous, foveate
■ impermeable, impervious

port n
seaport, harbour, jetty, dock, anchorage, harbourage, haven, roads, roadstead, hithe

portability n
movability, transportability, manageability, handiness, convenience, compactness

portable adj
movable, transportable, compact, lightweight, manageable, conveyable, handy, convenient
■ fixed, immovable

portal n
gateway, opening, entrance, access, way in, door, doorway

portend v
indicate, point to, be a sign of, be an indication of, warn of, announce, forecast, predict, foretell, promise, signify, threaten, herald
FORMAL augur, bode, forebode, foreshadow, foreshow, forewarn, harbinger, foretoken, prognosticate, adumbrate, presage, purport, betoken, bespeak

portent n
sign, indication, warning, threat, omen, precursor, forecast, foreboding, forerunner, prefiguration, premonition
FORMAL augury, signification, prognostication, foreshadowing, forewarning, prognostic, presage, presentiment, prodrome, harbinger

portentous adj
1 FOREBODING, ominous, sinister, menacing, threatening, momentous, fateful
2 REMARKABLE, significant, important, amazing, astounding, extraordinary, awe-inspiring, earth-shaking, epoch-making, miraculous, crucial
3 POMPOUS, self-important, arrogant, proud, haughty, conceited, vain, presumptuous, grandiose, supercilious, patronizing, condescending, overbearing, imperious,

magisterial, pretentious, ostentatious
FORMAL affected
COLLOQ. snooty
◨2 insignificant, unimportant, unimpressive

portentously adv

pompously, self-importantly, arrogantly, haughtily, conceitedly, superciliously, condescendingly, patronizingly
COLLOQ. snootily

porter¹ n

a porter at a hotel
bearer, carrier, baggage-attendant, baggage-handler, baggage-carrier, out-porter, ticket-porter, bellhop, page, bummaree, hammal; NAm redcap
OLD caddie
COLLOQ. humper

porter² n

a porter at a college
doorman, commissionaire, door-keeper, gatekeeper, door attendant, janitor, caretaker, concierge, night-porter, dvornik
OLD doorsman

portion n, v

◆ n
1 SHARE, allocation, tranche, allotment, parcel, quantity, allowance, ration, quota, measure, part, section, division, fraction, percentage, bit, fragment, morsel, piece, segment, slice, wedge, serving, helping
COLLOQ. cut, whack, rake-off
2 DESTINY, fate, lot, kismet, fortune, luck, chance
◆ v
distribute, divide, deal, share out, allocate, allot, apportion, assign, slice up, parcel, partition
COLLOQ. carve up, dole out

portliness n

ampleness, stoutness, roundness, plumpness, fatness, paunchiness, obesity, heaviness, fullness, dumpiness, tubbiness, chubbiness, fleshiness
FORMAL corpulence, rotundity
COLLOQ. beefiness

portly adj

stout, round, fat, plump, obese, overweight, stocky, ample, heavy, large
FORMAL corpulent, rotund
◨slim, thin, slight

portrait n

picture, painting, drawing, sketch, caricature, miniature, carte-de-viste, icon, photograph, likeness, image, representation, self-portrait, pin-up, full-length, whole-length, half-length, profile, Kit-Cat, vignette, profile, study, thumbnail sketch, characterization, description, depiction, portrayal, story, account; NAm composite
OLD pourtray; (Spenser) retrate, retraitt
◨landscape

portray v

1 DRAW, sketch, paint, illustrate, picture, represent
OLD pourtray, portrait
2 DESCRIBE, depict, picture, represent, present, take, characterize, illustrate, evoke
OLD pourtray, portrait
3 PLAY, act, play/act the part of, perform, impersonate, characterize, image, personify
OLD pourtray, portrait

portrayal n

representation, characterization, depiction, description, picture, painting, drawing, sketch, study, evocation, presentation, acting, performance, interpretation, rendering
FORMAL delineation

pose v, n

◆ v
1 MODEL, sit, position, arrange
2 PRETEND, feign, act, put on an act, put on airs, masquerade, pass yourself off, impersonate, attitudinize
FORMAL affect
3 pose a question
put forward, ask, submit, suggest, propose, put, set, advance
FORMAL posit, postulate, propound
4 pose a problem/threat
create, present, cause, produce, give rise to, lead to, result in
FORMAL constitute
◆ n
1 POSITION, stance, air, posture, attitude
FORMAL bearing, carriage, deportment
2 PRETENCE, sham, façade, front, masquerade, airs, role, act, pretence
FORMAL affectation

poser¹ n

he's a poser
poseur, poseuse, posturer, attitudinizer, exhibitionist, show-off, play-actor, charlatan, sham, impostor
COLLOQ. pseud, phoney

poser² n

this is a poser
puzzle, riddle, conundrum, mystery, enigma, problem, dilemma, vexed question, brainteaser, mind-bender; NAm brain-twister

poseur n

poser, poseuse, posturer, attitudinizer, exhibitionist, show-off, play-actor, charlatan, sham, impostor
COLLOQ. pseud, phoney

posh adj

smart, stylish, fancy, fashionable, elegant, high-class, upper-class, grand, luxurious, lavish, sumptuous, luxury, de-luxe, rich, up-market, exclusive, select
FORMAL opulent
COLLOQ. la-di-da, swanky, classy, swish, plush, snazzy
◨inferior, cheap

posit v

put forward, pose, advance, state, submit, assert, assume, presume
FORMAL postulate, predicate, propound

position n, v

◆ n
1 PLACE, situation, location, site, spot, scene, setting, area, locality, whereabouts, point
2 POSTURE, stance, pose, attitude, arrangement, disposition
FORMAL bearing
3 JOB, post, occupation, employment, situation, appointment, office, duty, function, role, capacity
4 RANK, grade, level, place, status, standing, ranking, influence, prestige
5 SITUATION, state, condition, state of affairs, circumstances, case, factor(s), background, plight, predicament
6 OPINION, point of view, belief, view, outlook, viewpoint, attitude, stance, standpoint, stand
◆ v
put, place, set, settle, fix, stand, arrange, dispose, lay out, deploy, station, locate, situate, site, install, establish
FORMAL array

positive adj

1 SURE, certain, convinced, confident, assured
2 OPTIMISTIC, hopeful, confident, encouraged, good, favourable, cheerful, promising, encouraging
COLLOQ. upbeat
3 positive criticism
helpful, constructive, practical, useful, productive, affirmative

4 DEFINITE, decisive, conclusive, real, actual, concrete, clear, clear-cut, unmistakable, explicit, precise, unequivocal, express, direct, firm, emphatic, categorical, undeniable, indisputable, incontestable, incontrovertible
FORMAL irrefutable
5 ABSOLUTE, utter, sheer, complete, rank, perfect, unmitigated, outright, out-and-out, thorough, veritable
FORMAL consummate
E3 **1** uncertain, doubtful **2** negative, pessimistic **3** negative, unhelpful **4** indefinite, vague

positively *adv*
absolutely, definitely, categorically, firmly, finally, decisively, emphatically, expressly, conclusively, certainly, assuredly, surely, unmistakably, unquestionably, incontestably, incontrovertibly, indisputably, unequivocally, undeniably, uncompromisingly

possess *v*
1 OWN, have, hold, be in possession of, acquire, gain, get, enjoy, be endowed with, be gifted with, be blessed with, boast
OLD wield
2 SEIZE, take, obtain, acquire, take over, take possession of, take control of, get, occupy; *dialect* overget
3 INFLUENCE, control, dominate, bewitch, haunt, enchant, infatuate, obsess, demonize

possessed *adj*
dominated, controlled, mesmerized, enchanted, berserk, bedevilled, demonized, bewitched, haunted, cursed, hag-ridden, frenzied, demented, crazed, mad, maddened, raving, consumed, infatuated, obsessed, besotted

possession *n*
1 OWNERSHIP, title, tenure, occupation, holding, tenancy, custody, proprietorship, control, hold, grip
2 OBSESSION, infatuation, domination, control, haunting, craze

possessions *n*
lose your possessions
belongings, property, baggage, luggage, paraphernalia, effects, goods, chattels, personal effects, goods and chattels, movables, assets, estate, wealth, riches, temporalities, temporalties, ana
OLD aver, worth
FORMAL accoutrements
COLLOQ. things, stuff, gear, clobber, (all your) worldly wealth

possessive *adj*
selfish, clinging, overprotective, domineering, dominating, controlling, jealous, covetous, acquisitive, grasping, greedy
E3 unselfish, sharing

possessiveness *n*
selfishness, jealousy, exclusiveness, greed, covetousness, acquisitiveness

possibility *n*
1 LIKELIHOOD, probability, odds, chance, risk, danger, hazard, hope, prospect, potentiality, conceivability, practicability, feasibility, attainability
2 *a place with possibilities*
promise, potential, prospects, advantages, capabilities, expectations, talent
FORMAL potentiality
3 OPTION, alternative, choice, preference, recourse
E3 **1** impossibility, impracticability **2** disadvantages, liabilities

possible *adj*
likely, probable, promising, potential, imaginable, conceivable, practicable, feasible, that can be done,

viable, tenable, credible, workable, achievable, attainable, doable, accomplishable, realizable
COLLOQ. on the cards, odds-on
E3 impossible, unthinkable, impracticable, unattainable

possibly *adv*
perhaps, maybe, conceivably, by any means, at all, by any chance
FORMAL peradventure
COLLOQ. hopefully

post¹ *n, v*
♦ *n*
a fence post
pole, stake, picket, pale, pillar, column, shaft, standard, support, prop, baluster, banister, palisade, upright, newel, stanchion, jamb, strut, leg
♦ *v*
1 DISPLAY, stick up, pin (up), put up, attach, affix
2 ANNOUNCE, advertise, publicize, make known, circulate, report, publish, broadcast

post² *n, v*
♦ *n*
a teaching post
office, job, employment, position, situation, place, vacancy, appointment, assignment, station, beat
♦ *v*
station, locate, situate, position, place, put, put on duty, appoint, assign, second, transfer, move, send

post³ *n, v*
♦ *n*
1 *deliver the post*
mail, letters, correspondence, communications, packages, parcels, packets, delivery, registered mail, recorded mail, special delivery, direct mail, airmail, all-up service, first-class mail, second-class mail, surface mail, international mail, electronic mail, e-mail
COLLOQ. junk mail, snail mail
2 POSTAL SERVICE, postal system, mail, Post Office
♦ *v*
mail, send, dispatch, transmit, forward
■ **keep someone posted**
inform, keep up to date, keep informed, give the latest information
COLLOQ. fill in, keep in the picture, keep in the loop

poster *n*
notice, bill, sign, placard, sticker, advertisement, bulletin, announcement, show bill
COLLOQ. ad, advert

posterior *adj, n*
♦ *adj*
rear, rearward, behind, back, hind, hinder, after, ensuing, following, subsequent, succeeding, later, latter
TECHNICAL dorsal, posticous
E3 anterior, front, previous
♦ *n*
bottom, rear, behind, buttocks, rump, seat, haunches, hinder end, hindquarters
COLLOQ. backside, bum, tail; *NAm* butt
SLANG (*vulgar*) arse; *NAm* ass
Related adjective: pygal

posterity *n*
descendants, successors, future generations, succeeding generations, heirs, offspring, seed, children
FORMAL progeny, issue

posthaste *adv*
quickly, speedily, straightaway, immediately, at once, as quickly as possible, directly, promptly, hastily, swiftly, with all speed
COLLOQ. double-quick, full tilt, pronto
E3 eventually, gradually, slowly

postman, postwoman *n*
delivery officer, letter-carrier, mail-carrier, mail handler, postal worker; *N Am* mailman
COLLOQ. postie

post-mortem *n*
autopsy, dissection, necropsy, analysis, examination, review

postpone *v*
put off, defer, put back, do later, hold over, carry over, delay, adjourn, suspend, reschedule, shelve, pigeonhole, freeze, mothball, waive, stand over; *N Am* table
OLD frist, protract, refer, rejourn, retard, withhold; (*Shakesp & Spenser*) prolong
FORMAL prorogue, procrastinate
COLLOQ. put on ice, put/place on the back burner, sleep on it, wait, take a raincheck on
☒ advance, forward, bring forward

postponed *adj*
put off, adjourned, deferred, carried over, held over, shelved, suspended, pigeonholed, frozen
FORMAL in abeyance
COLLOQ. on ice, on the back burner
☒ advanced

postponement *n*
adjournment, put-off, deferment, delay, deferral, moratorium, freeze, suspension, stay, respite
FORMAL prorogation

postscript *n*
addition, supplement, afterthought, addendum, appendix, afterword, epilogue
TECHNICAL codicil
COLLOQ. PS
☒ introduction, prologue

postulate *v*
theorize, suppose, assume, presume, presuppose, hypothesize, propose, advance, put forward, lay down, stipulate
FORMAL posit

posture *n, v*
♦ *n*
1 POSITION, stance, pose, attitude, disposition, set, motion, counter-view, defensive, guard, offensive, sprawl
TECHNICAL decubitus, mudra, pike
OLD gesture, site
FORMAL bearing, carriage, deportment
2 ATTITUDE, opinion, point of view, belief, view, outlook, viewpoint, stance, standpoint, stand
♦ *v*
pose, put on airs, show off, strike attitudes, attitudinize, strut
FORMAL affect

posy *n*
bouquet, spray, buttonhole, nosegay, corsage

pot *n*
1 RECEPTACLE, vessel, teapot, coffee pot, urn, jar, vase, bowl, basin, pan, cauldron, crucible, cruse, can, box, caster, crock, casserole, *pot-au-feu*, marmite, pipkin, flowerpot, planter, lota, tajine, chamberpot; *Scot* pat
TECHNICAL aludel, test, gallipot
OLD boughpot, bowpot, crewe, pottle; (*Shakesp & Spenser*) stew
2 KITTY, purse, pool, bank, fund, reserve

potable *adj*
drinkable, clean, safe, fit to drink

pot-bellied *adj*
bloated, distended, fat, gor-bellied, obese, overweight, paunchy, portly, tubby
FORMAL corpulent

pot-belly *n*
belly, beer belly, paunch, gut, pot
COLLOQ. corporation, spare tyre

potency *n*
power, strength, force, influence, potential, vigour, powerfulness, control, authority, effectiveness, persuasiveness, energy, sway, capacity
FORMAL cogency, efficaciousness, efficacy, might, puissance
COLLOQ. headiness, kick, muscle, punch
☒ weakness, impotence

potent *adj*
effective, powerful, mighty, strong, intoxicating, pungent, impressive, convincing, persuasive, eloquent, compelling, forceful, dynamic, energetic, active, vigorous, authoritative, commanding, dominant, influential, overpowering, virile
OLD puissant
FORMAL cogent, efficacious
COLLOQ. still having a shot in your locker
☒ impotent, weak

potentate *n*
ruler, monarch, sovereign, autocrat, head of state, king, queen, despot, dictator, tyrant, emperor, empress, prince, chief, chieftain, mogul, leader, dynast, overlord

potential *adj, n*
♦ *adj*
possible, likely, probable, prospective, future, aspiring, would-be, promising, budding, developing, embryonic, inherent, implicit, undeveloped, dormant, latent, hidden, concealed, unrealized, virtual
♦ *n*
possibility, ability, capability, capacity, aptitude, gift, flair, talent, promise, powers, resources

potentiality *n*
likelihood, possibilities, potential, promise, prospect, virtuality, ability, capability, aptitude, capacity

potentially *adv*
possibly, probably, in all likelihood, virtually, inherently, implicitly, dormantly, latently
FORMAL in potentia

potion *n*
mixture, concoction, brew, beverage, drink, draught, dose, medicine, tonic, elixir, philtre, potation

potpourri *n*
medley, mixture, assortment, jumble, hotchpotch, miscellany, collection, melange, confusion, smorgasbord, pastiche, patchwork, gallimaufry, hodgepodge, hotchpotch, olla-podrida, olio
COLLOQ. mishmash

potter *v*
dawdle, amble, loiter; *N Am* putter
COLLOQ. mess about, toddle, dilly-dally, pootle
■ **potter about**
tinker about/around, fiddle about/around, fool about/around, play about/around, do nothing much
COLLOQ. mess about/around, muck about/around
SLANG fart about/around

pottery *n*
ceramics, crockery, china
See panel on next page

potty *adj*
1 MAD, insane, lunatic, unbalanced, psychotic, disturbed, deranged, maniacal, out of your mind, out of your senses, of unsound mind, unhinged, crazed, unstable, *non compos mentis*, frenzied, wild, berserk, manic, maniac, distracted, distraught, fey, frenetic, frantic, stone-crazy, queer; *Scot* gyte, red-mad
OLD frantic-mad, lymphatic, bestraught

Terms used in pottery include:

armorial	crackleware	firing	lustre	raku	terracotta
art pottery	crazing	flambé	majolica (or	sagger	tin-glazed
basalt	creamware	flatback	maiolica)	scratch blue	earthenware
blanc-de-chine	delft	glaze	maker's mark	sgraffito	transfer printing
bronzing	earthenware	grotesque	mandarin palette	slip	underglaze
celadon	enamel	ground	model	slip-cast	Willow pattern
ceramic	faience	ironstone	monogram	spongeware	
china clay	fairing	jasper	overglaze	Staffordshire	
cloisonné	figure	kiln	porcelain	stoneware	

See also **porcelain**.

COLLOQ. crazy, demented, nuts, nutty, nutty as a fruitcake, wacky, mad as a hatter, barmy, bonkers, batty, cracked, crackers, dippy, daffy, dotty, loopy, off your nut, off your head, wrong in the head, out of your head, off the wall, out to lunch, round the bend, round the twist, bats, having bats in the belfry, cuckoo, off the rails, screwy, up the wall, raving, not all there; *N Am* buggy, flaky, fruity; *Aust & NZ* dingbats
SLANG loony, mental, bananas, barking, wacko, doolally, off your rocker, off your chump, off your trolley, out of your tree, needing your head examined, having lost your marbles, having a screw loose, having a tile loose, having several cards short of a full deck, with one sandwich short of a picnic, meshuga, ape, apeshit; *N Am* gonzo, loco, wiggy
2 FANATICAL, enthusiastic, infatuated, ardent, zealous, devoted, fond, keen, avid, passionate, mad, wild
COLLOQ. crazy, daft, nuts
E3 1 sane **2** apathetic

pouch *n*
bag, purse, pocket, container, receptacle, sack, wallet, sporran, poke; *Scot* gaberlunzie; *Scot & Irish* spleuchan
TECHNICAL marsupium, sac, bursa, diverticulum, spur
OLD scrip, codpiece
FORMAL reticule
Related adjectives: marsupial, saccate

pounce *v, n*
♦ *v*
fall (on), dive (on), swoop (on), drop, descend (on), attack, strike, ambush, spring, jump (on), leap, bound, lunge, snatch, grab, take by surprise, catch/take unawares, catch off guard
♦ *n*
attack, assault, bound, dive, grab, jump, leap, swoop, lunge, spring

pound¹ *n*
it cost 100 pounds
pound coin, £, pound sterling
OLD *Irish* punt
COLLOQ. quid
SLANG nicker, smacker, smackeroo, oncer, sov, squid
OLD SLANG bar, jimmy-o'goblin; *Aust* iron man

pound² *n*
keep animals in a pound
enclosure, compound, corral, yard, pen, fold, penfold, pinfold

pound³ *v*
1 STRIKE, thump, beat, drum, pelt, hammer, batter, bang, bash, smash, pummel, bruise; *Scot* nevel
TECHNICAL contuse
OLD contund, pun
2 PULVERIZE, powder, grind, mash, bray, pestle, crush, beat, smash, granulate, stamp
OLD pun
FORMAL levigate, comminute, triturate
3 *his heart was pounding*

throb, pulsate, palpitate, thump, thud, hammer
OLD pownd
4 *pound the streets*
tread, tramp, walk, pace, trudge, plod, stomp

pour *v*
1 *pour a drink*
make flow, let flow, serve, pour out, decant, tip, spill, sprinkle
2 SPILL, issue, come out, discharge, flow, emit, leak, ooze, stream, run, rush, spout, spew, jet, spurt, gush, course, cascade, flood, crowd, throng, swarm
FORMAL disgorge, disembogue
3 RAIN, teem down, pelt down
COLLOQ. rain cats and dogs, bucket down, come down in buckets/stair rods/torrents
SLANG piss down

pout *v, n*
♦ *v*
scowl, glower, lour, grimace, pull a face, make a moue, sulk, mope, boody; *Scot* tout
OLD (*Shakesp*) make a lip
E3 grin, smile
♦ *n*
scowl, glower, grimace, long face, moue
E3 grin, smile

poverty *n*
poorness, impoverishment, insolvency, bankruptcy, pennilessness, destitution, deprivation, beggary, distress, hardship, need, necessity, want, lack, deficiency, shortage, inadequacy, insufficiency, depletion, scarcity, meagreness, paucity, dearth, narrow circumstances, shabbiness, locust-years; *Scot* poortith
FORMAL penury, impecuniosity, indigence, privation
E3 wealth, richness, affluence, plenty

Synonym nuances
Impoverishment suggests having lost what you once owned: *the north is an area of progressive impoverishment*. **Insolvency** means being unable to meet one's debts, and **bankruptcy** also suggests being at the mercy of your creditors. Similarly, **pennilessness** suggests a total absence of funds, while **destitution** would further refer to a lack of possessions, and **beggary** has clear connotations of being reduced to asking for handouts.
   Both **distress** and **hardship** again have implications of a lack of money and its potential effects: *they are in dire distress financially*. **Deprivation** too implies a state of being without, while **need** and **necessity** emphasize a condition requiring aid. The terms **want**, **lack**, **deficiency** and **shortage** are less forceful, and concentrate on what is absent: *the want of funding*; *a shortage of science teachers*. **Inadequacy** and **insufficiency**, **meagreness** and **paucity** do suggest a presence, but have implications of being somewhat insubstantial: *a paucity of research*. **Scarcity** and **dearth**, on the other hand, suggest a more serious lack: *a dearth of skilled applicants is damaging industry*.

poverty-stricken *adj*
poor, penniless, impoverished, needy, destitute, distressed, bankrupt, beggared
FORMAL impecunious, obolary, indigent, penurious
COLLOQ. dirt-poor, broke, skint, stony, stony-broke, cleaned-out, flat broke, strapped, on your beam-ends, on your uppers, in Queer Street
F3 rich, affluent

powder *n, v*
♦ *n*
dust, grains, pounce, bran, talc
TECHNICAL triturate, pulvil, pulville, pulvil(l)io
FORMAL efflorescence
See panel on next page
♦ *v*
1 PULVERIZE, grind, mash, bray, pestle, crush, beat, smash, granulate
FORMAL levigate, comminute, triturate
2 SPRINKLE, scatter, cover, dust, strew

powdery *adj*
dusty, sandy, grainy, granular, granulated, powdered, pulverized, ground, fine, loose, dry, floury, crumbly, chalky, mealy
FORMAL friable, pulverulent, pulverous, efflorescent, levigate

power *n*
1 COMMAND, authority, sovereignty, rule, dominion, domination, control, say, influence, mastery, supremacy, sway
FORMAL ascendancy
COLLOQ. clout, pull, muscle, teeth, clutches
2 RIGHT, authority, privilege, prerogative, authorization, licence, warrant
3 POWERFULNESS, strength, intensity, energy, force, forcefulness, effectiveness, vigour, potency
FORMAL might
COLLOQ. juice, oomph
4 ABILITY, capability, capacity, potential, faculty, competence
FORMAL potentiality
5 *the western powers*
nation, state, country, people, superpower
F3 1 subjection, servitude **3** weakness, impotence **4** inability, incapacity
■ **the powers that be**
the establishment, the authorities, the system
COLLOQ. them

powerful *adj*
1 INFLUENTIAL, dominant, prevailing, leading, high-powered, authoritative, commanding, potent, effective, energetic, forceful, telling, impressive, convincing, persuasive, compelling, winning, overwhelming, all-powerful
FORMAL cogent
2 STRONG, mighty, robust, tough, muscular, brawny, strapping, burly, hardy
OLD puissant; (*Shakesp*) mightful
F3 1 powerless, ineffective, impotent **2** weak, puny

powerfully *adv*
strongly, strong, vigorously, hard, high, highly, forcefully, forcibly, potently, convincingly, persuasively, impressively, tellingly
FORMAL cogently, mightily, with might and main

powerless *adj*
helpless, unfit, unable, impotent, incapable, ineffective, weak-handed, weak, having a say, feeble, toothless, frail, infirm, incapacitated, debilitated, disabled, paralysed, vulnerable, defenceless, unarmed, hamstrung, numb, castrated
OLD benumbed, impuissant

FORMAL ineffectual
COLLOQ. with your hands tied, had by the short and curlies
F3 powerful, influential, able, potent

practicability *n*
possibility, feasibility, practicality, viability, workability, workableness, handiness, operability, use, usefulness, value, utility
F3 impracticability

practicable *adj*
possible, feasible, performable, achievable, doable, attainable, viable, workable, practical, realistic
F3 impracticable

❗ practicable or **practical**?
Practicable means 'able to be done, used, carried out, etc': *a practicable plan. Practical*, when applied to things, suggestions, etc also means 'able to be done, used, or carried out' but has the further connotation of 'efficient, sensible, useful': *Both these suggested courses of action are practicable, but John's is certainly the more practical of the two; High heels aren't very practical for hill-walking.* Applied to people, *practical* means 'able to do, make, or deal with things well or efficiently': *He's not a very practical person: he has lots of ideas for redesigning the bathroom but he doesn't have a clue how to put up a shelf.*

---

practical *adj*
1 *put knowledge to practical use*
applied, hands on, real, actual
2 *a practical person*
down-to-earth, matter-of-fact, sensible, realistic, pragmatic, hard-headed, businesslike, efficient, experienced, trained, qualified, skilled, accomplished, proficient
COLLOQ. hard-nosed, having both feet on the ground
3 *practical ideas*
realistic, workable, feasible, sensible, commonsense, applied, workaday, practicable
4 *wear practical shoes*
sensible, strong, suitable, utilitarian, functional, working, everyday, ordinary, serviceable, useful, handy
5 *a practical walkover*
virtual, effective, in effect, essential
F3 1 theoretical **2** impractical, unskilled **3, 4** impractical
■ **practical joke**
trick, hoax, joke, prank, antic, caper, frolic, gag, jape, feat, stunt
COLLOQ. leg-pull, frame-up, fast one, scam

❗ practical or **practicable**?
See panel at **practicable**.

---

practicality *n*
sense, common sense, realism, basics, experience, practicability, pragmatism, practicalness, serviceability, soundness, usefulness, utility, workability, feasibility, practice
COLLOQ. nitty-gritty, nuts and bolts

practically *adv*
1 ALMOST, nearly, well-nigh, virtually, all but, just about, in principle, in effect, essentially, fundamentally, to all intents and purposes
COLLOQ. pretty much, pretty well
2 REALISTICALLY, sensibly, reasonably, rationally, pragmatically, matter-of-factly

practice *n*
1 CUSTOM, tradition, convention, usage, habit, routine, way, method, system, procedure, policy
FORMAL wont
2 REHEARSAL, run-through, dry run, dummy run, try-out, training, drill, exercise, work-out, study, preparation, warm-up, experience
3 *in practice*

Kinds of powder include:

baking powder	custard powder	fly powder	itching powder	polishing-	soap powder
black powder	diamond-powder	giant powder	pearl-powder	powder	talcum powder
bleaching	Dover's powder	Goa powder	pebble-powder	priming-powder	tea powder
powder	dusting powder	Gregory's	percussion-	projecting-	tooth powder
calamine powder	egg powder	powder	powder	powder	washing powder
coffee powder	emery powder	gunpowder	Persian powder	putty-powder	worm powder
chilli powder	face powder	hair-powder	plate-powder	Rochelle-powder	yeast powder
curry powder	flea powder	insect powder		Seidlitz powder	

effect, reality, actuality, action, operation, performance, use, exercise, application

4 the practice of medicine
business, work, profession, career, occupation, employment, job, following, pursuit

5 a lawyer's practice
business, partnership, establishment, company, firm
E3 3 theory, principle

■ **out of practice**
unpractised, disused, out of (the) habit, rusty
FORMAL disaccustomed

■ **put into practice**
apply, put into effect/operation, put into action, use, make use of, put to use, exercise, perform

practise v
1 DO, perform, implement, carry out, apply, put into practice, observe, follow, pursue, engage in, undertake
FORMAL execute
2 REHEARSE, run through, go through, go over, repeat, drill, exercise, train, study, work on, work at, prepare, perfect, refine, polish

practised adj
experienced, seasoned, veteran, trained, qualified, accomplished, skilled, skilful, versed, knowing, knowledgeable, able, adept, proficient, expert, masterly, finished, old
OLD experimented; (Shakesp) traded
FORMAL consummate
E3 unpractised, inexperienced, inexpert

practitioner n
expert, specialist, authority, professional, pundit, master, maestro, virtuoso, crack, proficient, doer
COLLOQ. pro, dab hand, old hand, ace, buff

pragmatic adj
practical, realistic, sensible, matter-of-fact, businesslike, efficient, utilitarian, hard-headed, unsentimental
COLLOQ. hard-nosed
E3 unrealistic, idealistic, romantic

pragmatism n
practicality, realism, utilitarianism, hard-headedness, humanism, practicalism, opportunism, unidealism
E3 idealism, romanticism

pragmatist n
realist, utilitarian, opportunist, practicalist
E3 idealist, romantic

praise v, n
♦ v
commend, congratulate, express approval of, speak highly of, speak well of, admire, compliment, flatter, sing the praises of, wax lyrical, extol, promote, applaud, cheer, acclaim, hail, recognize, acknowledge, pay tribute to, honour, glorify, magnify, exalt, worship, adore, bless
FORMAL eulogize, laud
COLLOQ. talk up, rave over
E3 criticize, revile
♦ n
approval, admiration, commendation, congratulation, compliment, flattery, adulation, applause, plaudits, ovation, cheering, acclaim, recognition, testimonial,
tribute, accolade, homage, honour, glory, worship, adoration, devotion, thanks, thanksgiving, hallelujah, hosanna
FORMAL approbation, eulogy, encomium, laudation, panegyric
COLLOQ. bouquets, puff
E3 criticism, revilement

Synonym nuances
verb
Commend can be used of singling someone out for an honourable mention: *I commend you for arriving early*, while **congratulate** conveys more enthusiasm in extending recognition for something well done. **Admire**, on the other hand, suggests holding someone in high regard, and **compliment** might be used of expressing that regard. **Flatter**, although similar, has more negative implications of insincerity.

While you can use **promote** to suggest praise bringing to the attention of others, the term **extol** would be appropriate for paying a more lavish tribute: *the poem extolled his achievements.*

Acclaim, often used in the passive, suggests enthusiastic public recommendation: *the acclaimed violinist.* **Recognize** and **acknowledge**, on the other hand, are less effusive, much less so than the term **honour**, which again suggests paying tribute; the terms **glorify, magnify, exalt** and **worship** go much further by attributing with the highest status: *life in Britain may be glorified by ex-pats.*

Adore similarly suggests having feelings of reverence, whereas **bless** has more to do with giving thanks, and has strong religious connotations.

---

praiseworthy adj
commendable, fine, excellent, admirable, exemplary, worthy, deserving, honourable, reputable, estimable, sterling
FORMAL laudable
E3 blameworthy, dishonourable, ignoble

praising adj
approving, complimentary, congratulatory, favourable, flattering, commendatory, adulatory, recommendatory, promotional, worshipful
FORMAL approbatory, eulogistic, encomiastic, laudative, laudatory, panegyric, plauditory
E3 condemnatory, critical

pram n
buggy, Baby Buggy®, pushchair; N Am baby carriage, stroller
FORMAL perambulator

prance v
1 LEAP, jump, spring, skip, dance, frisk, frolic, gambol, cavort, caper, bound, romp, vault
OLD (Shakesp) jaunce
2 SHOW OFF, strut, swagger, stalk, parade, curvet
COLLOQ. swank

prank n
trick, practical joke, joke, stunt, caper, frolic, lark, antic, escapade
SLANG N Am monkey shine

prankster *n*
joker, jester, trickster, quipster, hoaxer, practical joker

prat *n*
idiot, fool, imbecile, fat-head, dunce, dimwit, simpleton, halfwit, cretin, clown, ignoramus, oaf, innocent
COLLOQ. thickhead, numskull, nincompoop, ass, chump, ninny, clot, dope, twit, nitwit, nit, sucker, mug, twerp, birdbrain, berk, dum-dum, knuckle-head, lamebrain
SLANG jerk, nerd, wally, muppet, dumbo, pillock, dork, geek, plonker; (*taboo*) prick, dickhead

prattle *v, n*
◆ *v*
chat, chatter, gabble, babble, jabber, rattle, twitter, twaddle, twattle, patter, drivel, gossip; *Scot* blether; *dialect & N Am* blather
COLLOQ. blabber, witter
◆ *n*
chat, chatter, gossip, talk, babble, jaw, gab, tattle, nonsense, prating, gibberish, foolishness, drivel; *Scot* blether; *dialect & N Am* blather
COLLOQ. hot air

prattler *n*
chatterer, talker, gossip, gabbler, babbler, tatler, tattler, magpie; *Scot* blether
COLLOQ. blabbermouth, chatterbox, loudmouth, windbag
F3 clam

pray *v*
1 *pray to God*
invoke, call on, commune with, talk to, speak to, say a prayer, be at prayer, say your prayers, praise, worship, adore, confess, thank
TECHNICAL daven
OLD beseech, bid, wrestle with God
FORMAL imprecate, supplicate
2 ENTREAT, implore, plead, beg, petition, ask, request, crave, solicit
OLD beseech
FORMAL supplicate

prayer *n*
1 *prayer to God*
collect, litany, devotion, doxology, communion, invocation, fellowship, intercession, praise, worship, adoration, confession, thanksgiving, mantra, novena
FORMAL imprecation, supplication, orison
2 ENTREAT, plea, appeal, petition, request
FORMAL supplication

Prayers include:

Act of Contrition	Habdalah (or	Om
adhan	Havdalah)	Our Father
Agnus Dei	Hail Mary	Paternoster
Amidah	Kaddhish	requiescat
Angelus	khutbah (or	Rosary
Ardas	khotbah)	salat
Ave Maria	Kol Nidre	shahadah
Benedictus	Kyrie eleison	Shema
Confiteor	Lord's Prayer	Sursum Corda
Divine Office	Lychnapsia	Yizkor
Gloria	Magnificat	
grace	Nunc Dimittis	

---

prayer-book *n*
ordinal, service-book, Book of Common Prayer, Alternative Service Book, liturgy, missal, breviary, mahzor, euchologion, euchology, formulary, Triodion

preach *v*
address, lecture, teach, proclaim, harangue, pontificate, sermonize, evangelize, give a sermon, spread the gospel, moralize, exhort, advise, admonish, urge, advocate

OLD prophesy, sermon, predicate
COLLOQ. preachify

preacher *n*
minister, clergyman, parson, evangelist, televangelist, missionary, apostle, revivalist, lay preacher, local preacher, sermonizer, moralizer, licentiate, predicant, predikant, ranter, homilist, pontificater, gospeller, prophet, itinerant, open-air preacher, field preacher, tent preacher, spintext, mullah, Boanerges; *Scot* probationer
OLD circuit rider, pulpit(e)er, martext
COLLOQ. Bible-pounder, Bible-thumper, Bible-basher, tub-thumper, holy Joe, Holy Roller
SLANG devil-dodger

preaching *n*
teaching, instruction, doctrine, precepts, message, homiletics, homilies, dogma, gospel, sermons, sermonizing, pulpit, open-air/tent preaching, evangelism, pontificating
TECHNICAL evangel, kerygma
OLD prophecy
FORMAL exhortation
COLLOQ. Bible-bashing, tub-thumping
Related adjective: homiletic

preachy *adj*
moralizing, moralistic, pontificating, sermonizing, religiose, pietistic, pharisaic, pontifical, sanctimonious, self-righteous, pious, dogmatic, didactic, edifying, homiletic
FORMAL exhortatory, hortatory
COLLOQ. holier-than-thou, pi

preamble *n*
introduction, lead-in, preliminaries, preparation, prelude, foreword, preface, prologue, overture
FORMAL exordium, proem, prolegomenon
F3 postscript, epilogue

prearrange *v*
arrange in advance, arrange beforehand, plan ahead, pre-plan, prepare, prepare beforehand, prepare in advance, organize, schedule, diarize
FORMAL predetermine

precarious *adj*
unsafe, dangerous, treacherous, risky, hazardous, chancy, uncertain, unsure, unsettled, dubious, doubtful, unpredictable, unreliable, undependable, unsteady, unstable, shaky, wobbly, insecure, vulnerable
COLLOQ. chancy, dicey, dodgy, hairy, iffy, dicky
F3 safe, certain, stable, secure

precariously *adv*
dangerously, riskily, unsafely, hazardously, insecurely, unsteadily, unstably, shakily, unpredictably, unreliably
F3 safely, securely

precaution *n*
safeguard, security, preventive/preventative measure, protection, insurance, providence, forethought, care, caution, prudence, attentiveness, foresight, farsightedness, anticipation, preparation, provision
FORMAL circumspection

precautionary *adj*
safety, protective, preventive, preventative, provident, prudent, cautious, far-sighted, preparatory, preliminary
FORMAL judicious

precede *v*
come before, lead, come first, go before, go ahead of, take precedence, introduce, herald, usher in, head, forego, preface, prelude
OLD anticipate, prevent, prevene
FORMAL antecede, antedate
F3 follow, succeed

precedence n

priority, preference, pride of place, superiority, supremacy, eminence, pre-eminence, lead, first place, seniority, rank, right of way
FORMAL ascendancy

■ **take precedence over**

take priority over, come before, be more important than

precedent n

example, instance, case, parallel, pattern, model, standard, criterion, yardstick
FORMAL paradigm, exemplar

preceding adj

above, earlier, former, past, previous, prior, precedent, foregoing, antecedent
FORMAL aforementioned, aforesaid, supra, precursive, anterior
E3 following, later

precept n

principle, axiom, command, commandment, charge, direction, directive, ordinance, regulation, guideline, order, injunction, institute, law, instruction, decree, dictum, mandate, rule, statute, convention, canon, maxim, motto, saying, sentence, rubric

precinct n

1 ZONE, area, district, quarter, sector, division, section, shopping centre, mall, galleria, food court
2 BOUNDARY, limit, bound, confine, enclosure, close, court, neighbourhood, surrounds, locality, vicinity, environs, milieu, verge, purlieus
3 *the precinct of a cathedral*
close, enclosure, land(s), building(s)
TECHNICAL temenos, vihara

preciosity n

artificiality, pretentiousness, floweriness, over-refinement, affectation, tweeness, chichi

precious adj

1 VALUED, treasured, prized, cherished, beloved, dear, dearest, darling, favourite, loved, revered, adored, idolized
2 VALUABLE, expensive, costly, high-priced, dear, priceless, inestimable, rare, choice, fine
3 AFFECTED, overrefined, simulated, contrived, artificial, mannered, pretentious, flowery, twee, chichi

precipice n

cliff, cliff face, bluff, brink, steep, escarpment, crag, drop, sheer drop, height, escarp, scarp, krantz

precipitate v, adj

♦ v

1 HASTEN, hurry, speed (up), accelerate, quicken, expedite, advance, further, bring about, bring on, induce, trigger, cause, occasion
2 THROW, plunge, hurl, shoot, heave, thrust, fling
♦ adj
sudden, unexpected, abrupt, quick, swift, speedy, rapid, brief, hasty, hurried, headlong, breakneck, frantic, violent, impatient, hot-headed, impetuous, impulsive, rash, reckless, heedless, indiscreet
OLD precipitant, precipitous
E3 cautious, careful

! **precipitate** or **precipitous**?
Precipitate means 'hasty or too hasty': *precipitate decision. Precipitous* means 'very steep, like a precipice': *The path through the mountains is narrow and precipitous.*

---

precipitately adv

suddenly, unexpectedly, abruptly, quickly, rapidly, hastily, frantically, violently, recklessly, rashly, impulsively, impetuously
E3 carefully, cautiously

precipitation

Types of precipitation include:

dew	mist	sleet
downpour	rain	snow
drizzle	rainfall	snowfall
fog	rainstorm	snowflake
hail	shower	

---

precipitous adj

steep, sheer, perpendicular, vertical, abrupt, sharp, high, sudden
E3 gradual

! **precipitous** or **precipitate**?
See panel at **precipitate**.

---

précis n, v

♦ n

summary, abridgement, contraction, abbreviation, condensation, synopsis, abstract, digest, epitome, outline, résumé, sketch, compendium, run-down, table
FORMAL conspectus, encapsulation
♦ v
summarize, shorten, sum up, outline, abstract, abridge, condense, synopsize, digest, abbreviate, encapsulate, epitomize, contract, compress
E3 amplify, expand

precise adj

exact, accurate, right, punctilious, correct, factual, faithful, authentic, literal, word-for-word, actual, express, definite, explicit, very, specific, particular, unequivocal, unambiguous, clear-cut, distinct, detailed, blow-by-blow, minute, nice, particular, specific, fixed, rigid, strict, tight, careful, scrupulous, punctilious, meticulous, conscientious, rigorous, fastidious, finical, formal, starchy, narrow, prim, priggish, ceremonious, dry, razor, surgical, buckram; *Scot* preceese
OLD punctual
E3 imprecise, inexact, indefinite, ambiguous, careless

precisely adv

1 *one o'clock precisely; speak precisely*
exactly, absolutely, just so, accurately, on the dot, dead on, correctly, literally, verbatim, word for word, strictly, minutely, clearly, distinctly; *N Am* on the button
COLLOQ. dead on, bang on, spot-on, plumb, slap, smack, to a T
2 YES, exactly, quite, of course, just so, indeed, absolutely, agreed, certainly, right, that's right, true
COLLOQ. you got it

precision n

preciseness, exactness, exactitude, accuracy, correctness, faithfulness, explicitness, distinctness, detail, particularity, rigour, care, reliability, meticulousness, scrupulousness, punctiliousness, conscientiousness, neatness, fastidiousness
E3 imprecision, inaccuracy

preclude v

prevent, exclude, eliminate, rule out, hinder, inhibit, prohibit, restrain, stop, avoid, check, debar, forestall
FORMAL obviate
E3 incur, involve

precocious adj

forward, ahead, far ahead, advanced, advanced/old for your age, early, premature, mature, developed, gifted, talented, clever, bright, brilliant, smart, quick, fast
E3 backward, slow, stupid

preconceive v

presuppose, presume, assume, anticipate, project,

imagine, conceive, envisage, expect, visualize, picture
FORMAL predetermine, ideate

preconception *n*
presupposition, presumption, assumption, notion, idea,
anticipation, expectation, prejudgement, bias, prejudice
FORMAL conjecture, predisposition

precondition *n*
condition, stipulation, requirement, prerequisite, essential,
necessity
FORMAL sine qua non
COLLOQ. must

precursor *n*
forerunner, antecedent, sign, indication, prelude, herald,
messenger, usher, morning star, pioneer, trailblazer, way-
maker, curtain-raiser, ancestor, forebear
FORMAL progenitor, harbinger
⊟ follower, successor

precursory *adj*
preceding, warning, introductory, antecedent,
preliminary, preparatory, previous, prior, prefatory, anterior
FORMAL preambulatory, precursive, preludial, prelusive,
prevenient, prodromal
⊟ following, resulting, subsequent

predatory *adj*
hunting, preying, voracious, carnivorous, greedy,
acquisitive, avaricious, covetous, despoiling, thieving,
ravaging, plundering, marauding, pillaging, wolfish,
lupine, vulturine, vulturous
FORMAL predacious, predative, rapacious, raptatorial,
raptorial

predecessor *n*
ancestor, forefather, forebear, antecedent, forerunner,
precursor
FORMAL progenitor
⊟ successor, descendant

predestination *n*
destiny, fate, lot, doom, foreordination
FORMAL predetermination

predestine *v*
intend, mean, destine, fate, preordain, predetermine, pre-
elect, doom, foredoom
FORMAL foreordain, predestinate

predetermined *adj*
1 PREDESTINED, destined, fated, doomed, ordained
FORMAL foreordained
2 PREARRANGED, arranged, agreed, fixed, set, settled

predicament *n*
situation, plight, trouble, mess, pass, quandary, dilemma,
impasse, crisis, emergency, box
OLD taking
COLLOQ. spot, tight spot, scrape, pickle, jam, fix, hiccup,
hole, stew, hot/deep water, kettle of fish, how-d'ye-do,
cart, chancery, praemunire

predicate *v*
1 ASSERT, affirm, state, declare, proclaim, contend
FORMAL aver, avouch, avow, posit, postulate, premise
2 BE DEPENDENT, rest, base, build, found, establish, maintain,
ground

predict *v*
forecast, foretell, prophesy, foresee, bet, project
TECHNICAL cast
OLD warrant
FORMAL prognosticate, vaticinate, augur, portend, presage,
divine, auspicate
COLLOQ. second-guess

predictable *adj*
foreseeable, expected, anticipated, likely, probable,
imaginable, foreseen, foregone, certain, sure, reliable,

dependable, unsurprising, usual, customary
COLLOQ. on the cards, odds-on
⊟ unpredictable, unforeseeable, uncertain

prediction *n*
prophecy, forecast, prognosis, fortune-telling,
soothsaying
FORMAL augury, divination, prognostication, auspication

predictive *adj*
prophetic, foretelling, diagnostic
FORMAL augural, divinatory, prognostic

predilection *n*
fondness, preference, inclination, leaning, liking, affection,
love, partiality, tendency, bent, bias, enthusiasm, fancy,
taste, affinity, soft spot, weakness
FORMAL penchant, predisposition, proclivity, propensity
⊟ dislike, disinclination; *formal* antipathy

predispose *v*
dispose, incline, prompt, induce, make, make liable, sway,
move, influence, persuade, affect, bias, prejudice

predisposed *adj*
inclined, liable, prepared, ready, susceptible, willing,
disposed, well-disposed, minded, not unwilling, subject,
agreeable, amenable, favourable, prone, biased,
prejudiced
⊟ unwilling, reluctant, loath

predisposition *n*
likelihood, inclination, leaning, tendency, preference,
disposition, bent, proneness, willingness, liability,
susceptibility, vulnerability, bias, prejudice
FORMAL penchant, potentiality, predilection, proclivity,
propensity

predominance *n*
dominance, dominion, power, control, leadership,
mastery, prevalence, superiority, supremacy, influence,
sway, weight, hold, numbers
FORMAL hegemony, ascendancy, paramountcy,
preponderance, prepotence, prepotency, prepollence,
prepollency
COLLOQ. edge, upper hand
⊟ ineffectiveness, weakness

predominant *adj*
dominant, prevailing, chief, main, principal, primary,
capital, paramount, supreme, sovereign, ruling,
controlling, in control, leading, powerful, potent, prime,
important, most important, influential, forceful, strong,
most noticeable, most obvious
FORMAL preponderant, ascendant, in the ascendancy
⊟ minor, lesser, weak

predominantly *adv*
mainly, primarily, principally, chiefly, in the main, mostly, on
the whole, for the most part, generally, in general,
especially, as a rule, by and large, commonly, usually, above
all, largely, overall

predominate *v*
prevail, dominate, outnumber, be in the majority,
outweigh, override, overrule, overshadow, transcend, tell,
reign, rule
FORMAL obtain, preponderate

pre-eminence *n*
supremacy, distinction, excellence, fame, prestige,
renown, repute, predominance, prominence, superiority,
incomparability, peerlessness, matchlessness,
paramountcy, transcendence

pre-eminent *adj*
supreme, unsurpassed, unrivalled, unequalled,
unmatched, matchless, incomparable, inimitable, chief,
first, most important, foremost, leading, eminent,
distinguished, renowned, famous, prominent,

outstanding, exceptional, excellent, superlative, transcendent, superior
F3 inferior, unknown

pre-eminently *adv*
especially, notably, particularly, exceptionally, eminently, signally, superlatively, singularly, strikingly, surpassingly, par excellence, exclusively, supremely, primarily, principally, emphatically, conspicuously, incomparably, inimitably, matchlessly, peerlessly

pre-empt *v*
prevent, forestall, anticipate, assume, acquire, secure, seize, usurp
FORMAL appropriate, arrogate

preen *v*
1 CLEAN, smooth, groom, plume, trim, spruce up, dress up, trick out, slick, prettify, adorn, beautify, deck, primp, prink; *N Am* trick up
FORMAL array
COLLOQ. do up, doll up, tart up
2 CONGRATULATE, pride, exult, bask, plume, gloat, pique
COLLOQ. pat yourself on the back

preface *n, v*
♦ *n*
foreword, introduction, preamble, prologue, prelude, frontmatter, preliminaries
FORMAL proem, prolegomenon, exordium
COLLOQ. prelims
F3 epilogue, postscript
Related adjective: prefatory
♦ *v*
precede, prefix, lead up to, introduce, launch, open, begin, start
F3 end, finish, complete

prefatory *adj*
introductory, opening, preparatory, preliminary, explanatory, antecedent
FORMAL exordial, preambulatory, precursory, prefatorial, preludial, prelusive, prelusory, proemial, prolegomenal
F3 closing, final

prefect *n*
monitor, administrator, supervisor, praeposter, prepositor, praefect

prefer *v*
1 *I prefer tea to coffee*
favour, like better, would rather, would sooner, be partial to, want, wish, desire, choose, select, pick (out), opt (for), go for, single out, advocate, recommend, back, support, elect, adopt
FORMAL elect
COLLOQ. plump for, fancy
2 PROMOTE, favour, advance, move up, raise, elevate, exalt, honour
FORMAL aggrandize
3 *prefer charges*
bring, file, lodge, press, present, place
F3 **1** reject **2** demote

preferable *adj*
better, superior, nicer, preferred, favoured, more desired, chosen, desirable, advantageous, advisable, recommended
F3 inferior, undesirable

preferably *adv*
rather, much rather, if possible, ideally, sooner, much sooner, from choice, for choice, by/for preference, first

preference *n*
1 FAVOURITE, first choice, choice, pick, selection, option, wish, desire
COLLOQ. cup of tea; *N Am* druthers

2 LIKING, fancy, inclination, will, bent, leaning, bias, discrimination, partiality, favouritism, priority, precedence, preferential treatment, fad, forehand
OLD pre-election
FORMAL predilection
COLLOQ. kink
OLD SLANG mark
■ **in preference to**
rather than, instead of, in place of, before, by/for/from choice

preferential *adj*
better, superior, favoured, privileged, special, favourable, advantageous, partial, partisan, biased
F3 equal

preferment *n*
promotion, advancement, furtherance, improvement, rise, step up, betterment, dignity, elevation, exaltation, upgrading
FORMAL aggrandizement
F3 demotion

preferred *adj*
favoured, selected, approved, choice, chosen, desired, recommended, authorized, sanctioned
FORMAL predilect
F3 rejected, undesirable

prefigure *v*
foreshadow, signal, indicate, signify, mean, suggest, promise, predict, prophesy
FORMAL bode, presage, augur, portend, prognosticate

pregnancy *n*
child-bearing, conception, fertilization, impregnation, gestation
TECHNICAL parturition
OLD being with child
FORMAL gravidity
COLLOQ. family way

pregnant *adj*
1 *a pregnant woman*
expectant, expecting, big-bellied
TECHNICAL parturient, gravid
OLD with child, great, quick, in an interesting condition/ state/situation; (*Shakesp*) great-bellied
FORMAL enceinte
COLLOQ. in the family way, in the club, in a certain condition, in trouble
SLANG preggers, with a bun in the oven, up the spout, in the pudding club, up the duff
2 *a pregnant pause*
meaningful, significant, eloquent, rich, expressive, suggestive, telling, pointed, charged, loaded, heavy, full, filled, fraught
FORMAL replete

prehistoric *adj*
primitive, earliest, early, ancient, archaic, antiquated, antediluvian, old, obsolete, out-of-date, outmoded
FORMAL prim(a)eval, primordial
COLLOQ. out of the ark, before the flood
F3 modern

prejudge *v*
judge prematurely, anticipate, presume, assume, presuppose, forejudge
FORMAL predetermine, prejudicate

prejudice *n, v*
♦ *n*
1 BIAS, partiality, partisanship, discrimination, preference, one-sidedness, unfairness, injustice, intolerance, narrow-mindedness, bigotry, chauvinism, racism, sexism, misogyny, ageism, xenophobia, misanthropy, anti-Semitism

2 HARM, damage, impairment, hurt, injury, detriment, disadvantage, loss, ruin
⊟ 1 fairness, tolerance **2** benefit, advantage
♦ v
1 BIAS, incline, sway, influence, condition, colour, jaundice, slant, distort, load, weight
FORMAL predispose
2 HARM, damage, impair, be detrimental to, be disadvantageous to, hinder, undermine, hurt, injure, mar, spoil, ruin, wreck
⊟ 2 benefit, help, advance

prejudiced adj
biased, partial, subjective, partisan, one-sided, slanted, discriminatory, unfair, unjust, loaded, weighted, intolerant, narrow-minded, bigoted, blinkered, chauvinist, chauvinistic, xenophobic, anti-Semitic, racist, sexist, ageist, jaundiced, distorted, warped, influenced, conditioned, insular, parochial, illiberal, prepossessed
TECHNICAL *ex parte*
OLD prejudicial
FORMAL predisposed
⊟ impartial, fair, tolerant

prejudicial adj
harmful, damaging, hurtful, injurious, detrimental, disadvantageous, counter-productive, unfavourable, inimical
FORMAL deleterious, noxious
⊟ beneficial, advantageous

preliminary adj, n
♦ adj
preparatory, prior, advance, exploratory, experimental, trial, test, pilot, early, earliest, first, initial, beginning, primary, qualifying, inaugural, introductory, opening, prefatory
FORMAL precursory, exordial
⊟ final, closing
♦ n
preparation, groundwork, foundations, basics, rudiments, formalities, introduction, preface, foreword, prelude, preamble, opening, beginning, start
FORMAL proem, exordium, prolegomenon, prodrome

prelude n
overture, introduction, preface, foreword, preamble, prologue, opening, opener, preliminary, preparation, beginning, start, forerunner, herald, precursor, curtain-raiser
FORMAL proem, exordium, prolegomenon, prodrome, commencement, harbinger
⊟ finale, epilogue
Related adjectives: preludial, preludious, proemial

premature adj
1 *a premature baby*
COLLOQ. prem; *N Am* preemie
2 *her premature death*
early, soon, too early, too soon, untimely
3 *it is premature to dismiss the suggestion*
hasty, ill-considered, rash, impetuous, impulsive, precipitate, inopportune, untimely, ill-timed
COLLOQ. jumping the gun
⊟ 1 overdue, late **2** timely, overdue **3** well-timed, timely

prematurely adv
1 *born prematurely*
early, too early, too soon
2 *a decision taken prematurely*
early, too early, too soon, incompletely, hastily, impulsively, rashly, impetuously

premeditated adj
planned, intended, intentional, deliberate, wilful, conscious, cold-blooded, calculated, considered, contrived, preplanned, prearranged, predetermined
⊟ unpremeditated, spontaneous

premeditation n
planning, prearrangement, purpose, intention, deliberation, deliberateness, determination, forethought, design, scheming, plotting
TECHNICAL malice aforethought
OLD aforethought
FORMAL predetermination
⊟ impulse, spontaneity

premier n, adj
♦ n
head of government, prime minister, chief minister, first minister, chancellor, secretary of state
♦ adj
principal, leading, highest, top, head, foremost, chief, primary, prime, main, supreme, paramount, pre-eminent, first, cardinal, earliest, original, initial

première n
first performance, first showing, opening, opening night, first night, debut

premise n, v
♦ n
proposition, statement, assertion, postulate, thesis, argument, basis, supposition, hypothesis, assumption
FORMAL presupposition, postulate
♦ v
lay down, state, assert, assume, stipulate, take as true, presuppose, hypothesize
FORMAL posit, postulate, predicate

premises n
building, property, establishment, office, grounds, estate, site, place

premium n
1 *pay an insurance premium*
regular payment, instalment
2 SURCHARGE, extra sum/charge, overcharging, bonus
COLLOQ. an arm and a leg, daylight robbery
▪ **at a premium**
scarce, rare, hard to come by, in short supply, in great demand, few and far between
COLLOQ. like gold dust
▪ **put a premium on**
value greatly, treasure, appreciate, favour, hold dear, attach great/special importance to, regard highly, set great store by

premonition n
feeling, intuition, sixth sense, hunch, idea, suspicion, sneaking suspicion, foreboding, misgiving, fear, apprehension, anxiety, worry, warning, omen, sign
OLD prevention
FORMAL presentiment, presage, portent
COLLOQ. feeling in your bones, funny feeling, gut feeling

preoccupation n
1 OBSESSION, fixation, concern, interest, enthusiasm, hobby-horse
COLLOQ. hang-up, thing, bee in your bonnet, one-track mind
2 DISTRACTION, absent-mindedness, daydreaming, reverie, abstraction, heedlessness, obliviousness, oblivion, inattentiveness, wool-gathering, pensiveness, absorption, engrossment

preoccupied adj
1 OBSESSED, intent, immersed, engrossed, absorbed, engaged, fixated, taken up, wrapped up, involved, pensive, deep in thought
2 DISTRACTED, abstracted, absent-minded, daydreaming, absorbed, faraway, heedless, oblivious
FORMAL distrait

preoccupy v
occupy, absorb, engage, take up, involve, obsess, fixate, prepossess, occupy the attention of
COLLOQ. eat (up)

preordain v
destine, prearrange, foreordain, doom, fate
FORMAL predestine, predetermine

preparation n
1 *preparations for the wedding; in preparation for the event*
planning, plan, arrangement, organization, development, basics, rudiments, preliminaries, readiness, provision, supply, equipping, assembly, composition, construction, production, homework, foundation, groundwork, spadework
2 TRAINING, coaching, study, revision, practice
3 MIXTURE, compound, composition, concoction, potion, medicine, lotion, application, cosmetic

preparatory adj
preliminary, introductory, opening, initial, primary, basic, fundamental, rudimentary, elementary
FORMAL precursory, prefatory

■ **preparatory to**
before, in advance of, in anticipation of, in expectation of, previous to, prior to, in preparation for, as a preparation for

prepare v
1 GET READY, make ready, make preparations for, set up, plan, organize, arrange, adjust, provide, supply, equip, fit out, rig out, prime, put together, construct, assemble, concoct, contrive, devise, draft, fashion, draw up, compose, pave the way, do your homework for, lay the foundations for, lay the groundwork for, do the spadework for, take the necessary steps for, set the scene for
COLLOQ. gear up, psych up, tee up
2 TRAIN, teach, instruct, exercise, coach, study, practise, prime, warm up, get into shape, make ready
3 *prepare a meal*
make, produce, concoct, put together, throw together, get ready; *N Am* fix

■ **prepare yourself**
brace yourself, steel yourself, gird yourself
FORMAL fortify yourself, gird up your loins

prepared adj
ready, willing, disposed, waiting, set, fit, inclined, arranged, planned, organized, in order, fixed
FORMAL predisposed
E3 unprepared, unready

preparedness n
readiness, preparation, order, fitness, alertness, anticipation, expectancy
E3 unreadiness

preponderance n
dominance, supremacy, greater number, superiority, majority, bulk, mass, extensiveness, prevalence, predominance, domination, dominion, power, force, sway, weight
FORMAL ascendancy
COLLOQ. lion's share

preponderant adj
greater, larger, superior, predominant, dominant, prevailing, overriding, overruling, controlling, foremost, important, significant

preponderate v
dominate, predominate, prevail, be in the majority, outnumber, override, overrule, rule, tell, weigh with, turn the balance, turn the scales

prepossessing adj
attractive, charming, good-looking, winning, winsome, appealing, beautiful, likeable, lov(e)able, amiable, delightful, fair, handsome, pleasing, striking, captivating, bewitching, enchanting, engaging, inviting, alluring, magnetic, fascinating, fetching, taking
E3 unattractive, unprepossessing

preposterous adj
incredible, unbelievable, absurd, ridiculous, ludicrous, foolish, farcical, crazy, nonsensical, irrational, unreasonable, senseless, monstrous, shocking, outrageous, asinine, intolerable, unthinkable, impossible
E3 sensible, reasonable, acceptable

preposterously adv
absurdly, ludicrously, ridiculously, incredibly, unbelievably, unreasonably, shockingly, outrageously, intolerably

prerequisite n, adj
♦ *n*
condition, proviso, qualification, requirement, imperative, necessity, essential
FORMAL precondition, requisite, sine qua non
COLLOQ. must
E3 extra
♦ *adj*
indispensable, necessary, obligatory, required, needed, needful, essential, basic, fundamental, vital, imperative
FORMAL mandatory, requisite
E3 unnecessary, superfluous

prerogative n
privilege, right, authority, advantage, choice, sanction, exemption, immunity, liberty, due, claim, entitlement, licence, carte blanche, birthright, royalty
TECHNICAL droit
OLD purvey

presage v, n
♦ *v*
indicate, point to, be a sign of, be an indication of, warn of, announce, forecast, predict, foretell, promise, signify, threaten, herald, foretoken
FORMAL augur, portend, bode, forebode, foreshadow, forewarn, harbinger, bespeak, betoken, adumbrate, prognosticate
♦ *n*
sign, indication, warning, threat, omen, precursor, forecast, foreboding, forerunner, prefiguration, premonition
FORMAL augury, portent, signification, prognostication, foreshadowing, forewarning, prognostic, presentiment, harbinger

prescience n
foreknowledge, foresight, far-sightedness, second sight, prophecy, clairvoyance, propheticness
FORMAL precognition, prevision

prescient adj
foreknowing, far-sighted, far-seeing, prophetic, foresighted, perceptive, discerning, clairvoyant, divinatory, divining, psychic
FORMAL previsional
E3 imperceptive

prescribe v
1 *prescribe medicine*
advise, act, specify, stipulate
2 *prescribe a duty*
ordain, decree, dictate, rule, command, order, require, direct, specify, stipulate, lay down, set, appoint, impose, fix, define, limit

⚠ prescribe or **proscribe**?
To *prescribe* is to advise or order: *The doctor prescribed a course of antibiotics; The law prescribes severe penalties for such offences.* To *proscribe* is to ban, outlaw or forbid: *This book was formerly proscribed by the church; Such actions are proscribed by law.*

prescribed adj
laid down, specified, stipulated, set, ordained, assigned, decreed
FORMAL formulary

prescription *n*
1 INSTRUCTION, direction, formula, recipe, advice, recommendation, guideline(s)
2 MEDICINE, drug, preparation, mixture, remedy, treatment, concoction
TECHNICAL optometry
OLD leechdom

prescriptive *adj*
dictatorial, legislating, prescribing, didactic, dogmatic, rigid, authoritarian, customary
FORMAL preceptive

presence *n*
1 ATTENDANCE, company, companionship, occupancy, residence, existence, being
2 AURA, air, appearance, dignity, poise, self-confidence, self-assurance, attraction, personality, charisma, appeal, magnetism
FORMAL demeanour, bearing, carriage
3 NEARNESS, closeness, proximity, neighbourhood, vicinity
FORMAL propinquity
4 SPIRIT, ghost, phantom, spectre, apparition, visitant, shadow
Ⅎ **1** absence **3** remoteness, distance
■ **presence of mind**
calmness, self-possession, composure, coolness, self-assurance, self-command, level-headedness, alertness, aplomb, equanimity, poise
FORMAL imperturbability, sang-froid
COLLOQ. cool, unflappability
Ⅎ agitation, confusion

present¹ *adj*
1 ATTENDING, in attendance, here, there, near, nearby, at hand, close at hand, to hand, available, ready, existing
2 *at the present time*
current, contemporary, present-day, immediate, instant, existent, existing
Ⅎ **1** absent, far away **2** past, out-of-date
■ **the present day**
today, now, nowadays, at this time, currently, here and now
■ **at present**
at the moment, now, just now, at this time, today, currently
■ **for the present**
for the time being, for the moment, for now, in the meantime, pro tem

present² *v*
1 AWARD, grant, give, donate, hand over, entrust, extend, hold out
FORMAL confer, bestow
2 OFFER, tender, submit, put forward
FORMAL proffer
3 SHOW, display, put on display, exhibit, demonstrate, organize, mount, stage, perform, put on, introduce, host, make known
5 *present a television show*
introduce, compère, host, announce
6 *the story presents her sympathetically*
describe, depict, represent, portray, characterize, picture
FORMAL delineate
■ **present yourself**
1 *present yourself somewhere*
appear, arrive, attend, show up, turn up
COLLOQ. pop up
2 *an idea presents itself*
occur, arise, crop up, emerge, materialize, come to light, happen

present³ *n*
Christmas presents
gift, offering, donation, contribution, handout, award, grant, endowment, bounty, largesse, gratuity, tip, favour
FORMAL benefaction
COLLOQ. prezzie, freebie, perk, sweetener

presentable *adj*
1 NEAT, tidy, clean, smart, smartly dressed, spruce, respectable, decent
2 QUITE GOOD, satisfactory, tolerable, passable, acceptable
Ⅎ **1** untidy, shabby

presentation *n*
1 APPEARANCE, arrangement, organization, structure, system, layout, form, format, packaging
2 AWARD, awarding, presenting, granting, donating, investiture
FORMAL conferral, bestowal
3 TALK, address, lecture, speech, seminar, demonstration
FORMAL disquisition
4 SHOW, performance, production, staging, showing, mounting, representation, rendition, recital, display, exhibition, demonstration, introduction, making known, launch

present-day *adj*
current, present, existing, living, contemporary, modern, up-to-date, fashionable, latest
Ⅎ past, future

presenter *n*
host, announcer, compère, anchor, anchorman, anchorwoman, frontman, master of ceremonies, MC
COLLOQ. emcee

presentiment *n*
premonition, intuition, apprehension, fear, feeling, misgiving, hunch, anticipation, foreboding, expectation, forecast, forethought
OLD bodement
FORMAL forebodement, presage, presension
COLLOQ. bad vibes

presently *adv*
1 SOON, shortly, in a short time, in a short while, in a minute, in a moment, in a second, before long, by and by
COLLOQ. in a jiffy, pronto, in a mo, in a tick, in two shakes of a lamb's tail, before you can say Jack Robinson
2 CURRENTLY, at present, now, at the moment, at the present time, these days, at this moment in time

preservation *n*
protection, defence, maintenance, keeping, guarding, safeguarding, safekeeping, safety, security, conservation, storage, upkeep, support, retention, upholding, continuation, perpetuation, reservation
Ⅎ destruction, ruin

preserve *v, n*
♦ *v*
1 PROTECT, safeguard, guard, defend, shield, shelter, care for, look after, take care of, maintain, uphold, secure, sustain, continue, perpetuate, commemorate, keep, retain, conserve, reserve, save, store, lay up, cocoon, embalm; *Scot* hain
OLD salve
2 *preserve food*
bottle, tin, can, chill, freeze, freeze-dry, quick-freeze, pickle, salt, cure, dry, desiccate, smoke, kipper, candy, corn; *dialect* put down
OLD confect
3 *preserve timber*
season, creosote, kyanize, powellize
Ⅎ **1** destroy, ruin
♦ *n*
1 *home made preserves*
conserve, jam, marmalade, jelly, pickle, chow-chow; *S Afr* konfyt
2 DOMAIN, realm, sphere, area, field, speciality
3 RESERVATION, sanctuary, reserve, game reserve, nature reserve, safari park, chase, forest

preside *v*
chair, be in the chair, be the chairman/chairwoman/

chairperson of, officiate, conduct, direct, manage, administer, control, run, head, lead, govern, rule, be responsible for, be in charge of
COLLOQ. head up, call the shots

president n
head of state, ruler, leader, controller, governor, head, director, manager, principal, chief
COLLOQ. boss
Related adjective: presidial

press v, n
♦ v
1 CRUSH, squash, squeeze, mash, pinch, knead, compress, stuff, jam, cram, crowd, push (down), depress, surge, swarm, throng, trample
2 *press clothes*
iron, smooth (out), flatten, roll
3 HUG, embrace, clasp, enfold, hold close, grasp, squeeze, caress, cuddle, crush
4 URGE, plead, petition, campaign, demand, call for, insist on, exhort, entreat, implore, push for, push forward, compel, constrain, force, coerce, pressure, pressurize, put pressure on, harass, besiege, afflict, vex, worry, trouble
FORMAL supplicate
COLLOQ. sweet-talk, fast-talk, soft-soap, twist someone's arm, lean on, put/turn/tighten the screws on, swing it, pull strings
♦ n
1 CROWD, throng, multitude, mob, horde, troop, swarm, pack, crush, flock, push
2 JOURNALISTS, reporters, correspondents, photographers, paparazzi, newspapermen, newspaperwomen, pressmen, presswomen, the media, news media, newspapers, papers, Fleet Street, journalism, fourth estate
COLLOQ. hacks
3 PRINTING PRESS, printing-machine, rotary press
4 *get a good/bad press*
coverage, treatment, articles, reports, reviews, praise, criticism
■ **press on**
press ahead, continue, carry on, go on, keep going, persevere, go ahead, proceed, keep trying, plod on, slog away, peg away, toil (away)
COLLOQ. plug away, soldier on, stick at it

pressed adj
1 FORCED, pressured, pressurized, coerced, bullied, browbeaten, constrained, hurried, pushed, rushed, harassed
COLLOQ. bludgeoned, railroaded
2 *be pressed for time*
short of, having too little, not having enough, lacking, deficient in
Ｅ **1** unhurried **2** well-off

pressing adj
urgent, needing to be dealt with immediately, high-priority, burning, crucial, demanding, vital, essential, imperative, serious, important, critical, key
FORMAL exigent
Ｅ unimportant, trivial

pressure n, v
♦ n
1 FORCE, power, load, burden, weight, heaviness, compression, crushing, squeezing, stress, strain
2 COMPULSION, force, constraints, coercion, duress, bullying, harassment
3 STRESS, tension, strain, difficulty, problem, demand, adversity, burden, trouble, constraint, obligation
COLLOQ. hassle, aggro
♦ v
force, compel, constrain, oblige, drive, bulldoze, dragoon, coerce, press, pressurize, put pressure on, browbeat, bully
COLLOQ. lean on, put the screws on, sweet-talk, fast-talk,

soft-soap, swing it, pull strings, twist someone's arm, railroad, bludgeon

pressurize v
force, compel, constrain, oblige, drive, bulldoze, dragoon, coerce, press, pressure, put pressure on, browbeat, bully
COLLOQ. lean on, put the screws on, sweet-talk, fast-talk, soft-soap, swing it, pull strings, twist someone's arm, railroad, bludgeon; *Aust & NZ* put the acid on

prestige n
status, reputation, standing, stature, eminence, distinction, regard, importance, authority, influence, fame, renown, esteem, kudos, credit, honour, izzat
Ｅ humbleness, unimportance

prestigious adj
respected, reputable, important, influential, distinguished, high-ranking, great, eminent, prominent, illustrious, esteemed, renowned, celebrated, famous, well-known, exalted, imposing, impressive, up-market
COLLOQ. blue-chip
Ｅ humble, modest, down-market

presumably adv
most likely, very likely, in all likelihood, in all probability, I presume, I guess, doubtless, doubtlessly, no doubt, probably, apparently, seemingly

presume v
1 ASSUME, take it, think, believe, imagine, suppose, surmise, infer, presuppose, hypothesize, deduce, take for granted, take as read
2 *presume to criticize*
dare, make so bold, have the audacity, take the liberty, go so far, venture, undertake, take upon yourself
■ **presume on**
count on, rely on, depend on, bank on, trust, take (unfair) advantage of, exploit

presumption n
1 ASSUMPTION, belief, opinion, surmise, deduction, inference, hypothesis, presupposition, supposition, conjecture, guess, likelihood, probability
2 PRESUMPTUOUSNESS, boldness, arrogance, effrontery, temerity, audacity, cheek, impertinence, impudence, insolence, forwardness, assurance
COLLOQ. nerve, sauce, gall, lip, mouth, neck, brass neck, chutzpah
Ｅ **2** humility

presumptive adj
expected, assumed, believed, designate, prospective, likely, possible, probable, reasonable, supposed, understood, believable, conceivable, hypothetical, credible, inferred, plausible
FORMAL conjectural
Ｅ known, unlikely

presumptuous adj
bold, audacious, impertinent, impudent, insolent, over-familiar, forward, arrogant, pushy, over-confident, conceited, cocky, cocksure
COLLOQ. cheeky, fresh, saucy, lippy, mouthy, bigheaded, too big for your boots
Ｅ humble, modest

presuppose v
assume, presume, necessitate, suppose, accept, consider, imply, take for granted
FORMAL posit, postulate, premise

presupposition n
assumption, presumption, belief, supposition, hypothesis, theory, preconception
FORMAL premise, premiss

pretence n
show, display, appearance, cover, front, charade, façade, veneer, cloak, veil, mask, masquerade, guise, sham,

feigning, faking, false show, false colours, semblance, hypocrisy, simulation, deception, trickery, wile, ruse, excuse, pretext, bluff, falsehood, deceit, lie, fabrication, invention, acting, play-acting, make-believe, posturing, posing, showiness, ostentation, pretentiousness, profession, humbug, feint, daubery
FORMAL affectation, dissimulation, dissembling, pretension
E3 honesty, openness

Synonym nuances
Show and **display** can be used to suggest a false image, especially one projected for public consumption. **Charade** has an element of the absurd about it: *they have finally ended their charade of a marriage;* **masquerade** is similar, although more suggestive of an elaborate deception. **Façade** suggests a carefully contrived image and **veneer** an outward gloss which may be more easily seen through: *underneath her veneer of kindness there lay a devious imp.*

Both **cover** and **front** have stronger implications of keeping something undesirable hidden, as do **cloak, veil** and **mask**, which make this more explicit, while **guise** also implies presenting something in another form: *promoting his ambitions under the guise of revenge.* **Semblance** is a straightforward term for appearing to be like, while **sham** implies a hollow display: *the country's democracy is a sham.* **Humbug** shares this idea of hollowness: *the humbug of suburban life.*

Simulation is a fairly neutral term for a recreation of something. **Feigning** and **faking** are far more disapproving in tone, like **deception, trickery, wile** and **ruse**, which all imply deliberate misleading. While you might use **invention** for something devised, **bluff** and **falsehood** would convey the same idea with more disapprobation.

The terms **acting, posturing** and **posing** return to the idea of presenting a false image, and again suggest mild disapproval, while the more negative terms **showiness, ostentation** and **pretentiousness** all make suggestions of vulgar affectation.

Hypocrisy is a strongly critical term, particularly relevant where someone's real views or actions belie the beliefs they profess.

---

pretend v
1 *pretend to be asleep*
put on, assume, feign, sham, counterfeit, fake, fabricate, simulate, bluff, impersonate, pass yourself off, act, play-act, put on an act, mime, go through the motions
OLD pass the bottle of smoke
FORMAL affect, dissemble
COLLOQ. keep up appearances
2 CLAIM, allege, profess
FORMAL purport
3 IMAGINE, make believe, suppose

pretended adj
artificial, put on, alleged, ostensible, professed, supposed, spurious, bogus, fake, false, feigned, sham, fictitious, counterfeit, so-called, imaginary, specious
FORMAL affected, avowed, purported, supposititious
COLLOQ. phoney, pretend, pseudo
E3 real

pretender n
claimant, aspirant, claimer, candidate

pretension n
1 PRETENTIOUSNESS, pomposity, self-importance, airs, conceit, vanity, snobbishness, hypocrisy, pretence, show, showiness, floweriness, ostentation
FORMAL affectation, magniloquence
2 CLAIM, profession, demand, aspiration, ambition

FORMAL purporting
E3 **1** modesty, humility, simplicity

pretentious adj
pompous, self-important, conceited, immodest, snobbish, mannered, flaunting, showy, ostentatious, extravagant, flamboyant, elaborate, exaggerated, high-sounding, uppish, chichi, twee, artificial, inflated, grandiose, ambitious, overambitious, kitschy; *Scot* fantoosh
OLD fine
FORMAL affected, magniloquent, vainglorious, bombastic
COLLOQ. over-the-top, OTT, pseud, pseudo, big
E3 modest, humble, simple, straightforward

pretentiously adv
pompously, self-importantly, snobbishly, ostentatiously, uppishly, showily, artificially, flamboyantly
E3 modestly, humbly

pretentiousness n
ostentation, posing, pretension, show, theatricality, floweriness, floridness, flamboyance, attitudinizing, ambitiousness, overambitiousness, uppishness, chichi, kitsch; *Scot* paraffle
FORMAL posturing
COLLOQ. pseudery, side
E3 humbleness, modesty, simplicity, straightforwardness

preternatural adj
extraordinary, unusual, exceptional, abnormal

pretext n
excuse, alleged/ostensible reason, ploy, ruse, cover, cloak, mask, veil, guise, sham, semblance, appearance, pretence, show
COLLOQ. red herring

prettify v
decorate, smarten up, ornament, adorn, beautify, bedeck, deck, deck out, embellish, gild, garnish, trick out, trim; *N Am* trick up
COLLOQ. do up, doll up, tart up
E3 mar, uglify

prettily adv
attractively, charmingly, beautifully, nicely, delightfully, pleasantly, engagingly, winsomely, gracefully, daintily, elegantly
E3 plainly, unattractively

pretty adj, adv
• adj
attractive, good-looking, beautiful, fair, lovely, delightful, nice, cute, pleasant, pleasing, engaging, personable, prepossessing, winsome, appealing, charming, handsome, dainty, graceful, elegant, fine, delicate, chocolate-box, twee; *dialect* purty; *Scot* bonny
OLD comely; (*Shakesp*) incony
E3 plain, unattractive, ugly
• adv
fairly, somewhat, rather, quite, reasonably, moderately, tolerably
COLLOQ. not half

prevail v
1 WIN, triumph, be victorious, succeed, overcome, overrule, override, conquer, reign, rule, gain mastery, have it
FORMAL gain ascendancy
COLLOQ. carry the day
2 PREDOMINATE, abound, hold sway, occur, be common, be customary, be present, be normal, be accepted, be current
FORMAL preponderate; obtain
E3 **1** lose

■ **prevail upon**
persuade, talk into, prompt, induce, incline, sway, influence, convince, urge, win over, bring round, pressure, pressurize

COLLOQ. sweet-talk, lean on, soft-soap, pull strings, twist someone's arm

prevailing adj
predominant, preponderant, main, principal, chief, supreme, dominant, controlling, powerful, compelling, influential, reigning, ruling, current, fashionable, in fashion, in style, in vogue, popular, mainstream, accepted, established, set, usual, most usual, customary, general, common, most common, average, prevalent, widespread
FORMAL prepotent, ascendant
minor, subordinate

prevalence n
commonness, currency, frequency, order of the day, pervasiveness, acceptance, popularity, predominance, universality, regularity, rule, hold, mastery, sway, profusion
FORMAL ascendancy, omnipresence, preponderance, primacy, ubiquity
uncommonness

prevalent adj
widespread, extensive, rampant, rife, pervasive, epidemic, frequent, general, customary, usual, universal, established, accepted, set, ubiquitous, common, vulgar, everyday, popular, current, prevailing, dominant
TECHNICAL enzootic
FORMAL endemic, regnant
uncommon, rare

prevaricate v
equivocate, quibble, evade, be evasive, shift, shuffle, lie, deceive, stonewall
FORMAL cavil, tergiversate
COLLOQ. hedge, dodge, shilly-shally, waffle, pussyfoot, beat about the bush, sit on the fence

⚠ prevaricate or procrastinate?
To *prevaricate* is 'to talk evasively in order to avoid telling the truth, coming to the point, or answering a question': *When faced with difficult questions, politicians usually prevaricate.* To *procrastinate* is to put off until later things that should be done immediately.

prevarication n
evasion, equivocation, pretence, quibbling, lie, falsehood, untruth, falsification, fibbing, fib(s), half-truth, misrepresentation, deception, deceit
FORMAL cavilling, tergiversation
COLLOQ. shilly-shallying, pussyfooting, beating about the bush, sitting on the fence

prevaricator n
evader, equivocator, quibbler, liar, hypocrite, deceiver
OLD pettifogger
FORMAL casuist, caviller, dissembler, sophist
COLLOQ. dodger, fibber

prevent v
stop, avert, avoid, keep from, halt, arrest, hold back, inhibit, head off, ward off, fend off, stave off, intercept, forestall, anticipate, frustrate, thwart, restrain, hinder, hamper, impede, obstruct, block, check, hold in check, foil, balk, deter, bar
FORMAL preclude, obviate
cause, help, foster, encourage, allow

Synonym nuances
Both **avert** and **avoid** might be used of taking action to escape something unwanted: *full-scale civil war was averted.* The term **keep from** is also a fairly restrained one, which usually implies the intervention of another party: *her youthful outlook kept him from becoming staid.*
  Head off and **ward off** are more appropriate for keeping something at bay, as are **fend off** and **stave off**, which have further implications of deflecting an onslaught: *he fended off all challenges to his leadership.* **Intercept**, on the other hand, suggests a less defensive action, interrupting something before it can continue: *she was about to strike him but he intercepted her, taking the stick from her hand.* **Forestall** and **anticipate** are more appropriate for pre-emptive action: *he anticipated her punch and ducked.*
  The terms **hinder** and **hamper** can be used of interfering with the progress of something, but **impede**, **block**, **balk** and **obstruct** suggest more effectively, and perhaps more deliberately, handicapping: *his refusal to talk obstructed the police inquiry.* **Frustrate, foil** and **thwart** imply putting paid to the plans of others in a definite fashion: *bad weather frustrated the attack.*
  Deter, on the other hand, is more relevant to providing discouragement: *alarms help deter burglars.*

prevention n
avoidance, halting, arresting, heading off, warding off, fending off, staving off, frustration, check, hindrance, impediment, obstruction, obstacle, bar, elimination, exclusion, precaution, safeguard, deterrence, hampering, foiling, balking
TECHNICAL contraception, prophylaxis
OLD impeach
FORMAL preclusion, obviation
cause, help

preventive adj, n
♦ adj
preventative, anticipatory, pre-emptive, inhibitory, obstructive, precautionary, protective, counteractive, deterrent
TECHNICAL prophylactic
OLD prevenient
causative, fostering
♦ n
prevention, protection, precautionary measure, protective, impediment, hindrance, deterrent, block, obstruction, obstacle, safeguard, remedy, shield, neutralizer
TECHNICAL prophylactic
cause, encouragement, incitement

previous adj
preceding, foregoing, earlier, prior, past, former, ex-, one-time, sometime, antecedent
FORMAL erstwhile, quondam
following, subsequent, later

previously adv
formerly, once, earlier, earlier on, until now, before, beforehand, already, at one time, in the past
OLD afore, fore
FORMAL heretofore, hitherto, erst, erstwhile
later

prey n, v
♦ n
quarry, game, kill, victim, target, spreagh
OLD (*Spenser*) soyle, ravin
FORMAL rapine
COLLOQ. mug, fall guy
■ **prey on**
1 HUNT, kill, seize, catch, pounce on, prowl, devour, eat, feed on, moth-eat, raven on, vampire, live off, exploit, fleece, take advantage of
FORMAL depredate, predate
COLLOQ. con, bleed
2 *prey on your mind*
haunt, trouble, distress, worry, burden, weigh down, hang over, oppress, plague, torment

price n, v
♦ n
1 *the price of the car*

value, worth, cost, expense(s), outlay, expenditure, fee, charge, levy, toll, rate, bill, assessment, valuation, estimate, quotation, figure, amount, sum, payment, reward

2 *publicity is the price of fame*
penalty, forfeit, sacrifice, consequence(s), result

♦ *v*
value, rate, cost, evaluate, assess, estimate, set/fix the price at
FORMAL appraise, valorize

■ **at a price**
expensive, at a high price, at a high cost

■ **at any price**
at any cost, whatever it takes, whatever the cost, no matter what it costs

priceless *adj*
1 INVALUABLE, inestimable, incalculable, expensive, costly, dear, precious, valuable, prized, treasured, cherished, irreplaceable, incomparable, rare
COLLOQ. worth its weight in gold
2 FUNNY, amusing, comic, hilarious, riotous, side-splitting
COLLOQ. killing, rich, a scream
E3 1 cheap, run-of-the-mill

pricey *adj*
costly, dear, excessive, exorbitant, expensive, extortionate, high-priced
COLLOQ. steep, over the odds, sky-high, costing an arm and a leg, costing the earth, costing a bomb, daylight robbery
E3 cheap

prick *v, n*
♦ *v*
1 PIERCE, puncture, perforate, point, punch, jab, jag, nick, slit, gash, wound, spike, prod, thorn, rowel, bore, stab, sting, bite, prickle, itch, tingle, smart; *Scot* brog
OLD prog, accloy, cloy
2 *prick your conscience*
trouble, distress, worry, torment, plague, harass, harry, gnaw at, prey on
♦ *n*
puncture, perforation, pinhole, hole, stab, pierce, prickle, jab, jag, nick, wound, pang, twinge, sting, pain, smarting, tingle, bite; *dialect* brod

■ **prick up your ears**
listen eagerly, listen expectantly, listen carefully, attend, lend an ear, pay attention, pin back your ears, take note/notice of

prickle *n, v*
♦ *n*
1 THORN, spine, barb, spur, point, spike, needle, prong, tine
TECHNICAL aculeus
FORMAL spicula, acantha
2 *feel a prickle of fear*
sensation, sting, stinging, itching, smarting, twinge, pang, tingle
TECHNICAL paraesthesia
FORMAL formication
COLLOQ. pins and needles
♦ *v*
tingle, itch, smart, sting, prick, nip

prickly *adj*
1 THORNY, brambly, spiny, barbed, spiky, spiked, armed, pronged, bristly, bearded, rough, scratchy; *Scot* jaggy
TECHNICAL acanaceous, acanthaceous, aculeate, echinate
2 IRRITABLE, on edge, touchy, grumpy, short-tempered, bad-tempered
COLLOQ. stroppy, ratty, crabby, crotchety, edgy, shirty, grouchy
3 *a prickly subject*
complicated, difficult, hard, thorny, problematic(al), tough, troublesome, tricky, delicate, sensitive
E3 1 smooth **2** relaxed, easy-going

pride *n, v*
♦ *n*
1 SATISFACTION, gratification, sense of achievement, pleasure, delight, joy, elation, triumphalism
2 DIGNITY, self-respect, self-esteem, self-image, self-worth, ego, honour
3 CONCEIT, vanity, egotism, boastfulness, smugness, disdain, arrogance, self-importance, self-conceit, presumption, haughtiness, superciliousness, snobbery, pretentiousness
COLLOQ. bigheadedness
E3 1 shame, embarrassment **3** humility, modesty

■ **pride and joy**
glory, joy, delight, apple of your eye, beloved/treasured possession, darling, best, pick, élite, flower, choice/select part, finest, pick of the bunch, *crème de la crème*

■ **pride yourself on**
take satisfaction in, congratulate yourself, flatter yourself, take pride in, revel in, glory in, exult in, vaunt, crow about, boast about, brag about, plume yourself, preen yourself
COLLOQ. pat yourself on the back for
E3 belittle, humble

priest *n*
minister, vicar, parson, pastor, padre, father, man/woman of God, man/woman of the cloth, clergyman, clergywoman, churchman, churchwoman, deacon, deaconess, cleric, clerk, neophyte, orator, concelebrant, high priest, pontiff, prelate, presbyter, secular, seminarian, seminarist, hierarch, hierophant, ecclesiastic, arch-priest, redemptorist; (*derog*) hedge-parson, hedge-priest
OLD masspriest; (*derog*) lack-Latin, Sir John Lack-Latin
Related adjective: sacerdotal

Priests include:

arch-flamen & flamen (*Ancient Rome*)	lucumo (*Etruscan*)
bacchant & bacchanal (*Bacchus*)	magus (*Ancient Persia*)
	mambo (*voodoo*)
bonze & lama (*Buddhism*)	papa & pope (*Greek Orthodox*)
Brahman (*Hindu*)	presbyter (*Episcopal churches*)
corybant & Pythian (*Ancient Greece*)	tohunga (*Maori*)
druid (*Celtic*)	
Levite & rabbi (*Judaism*)	

---

priestess *n*
clergywoman, canoness, deaconess, nun, prioress, sister, abbess, religious, vestal, beguine, mambo

priesthood *n*
holy orders, the church, the ministry, the pastorate, the cloth, full orders, priestship, hierocracy, sacerdotalism

priestly *adj*
clerical, ecclesiastical, canonical, pastoral, priestlike, sacerdotal, Aaronic(al)
FORMAL hieratic

prig *n*
prude, puritan, killjoy, precisian, old maid, Mrs Grundy
COLLOQ. goody-goody, holy Joe, holy Willie

priggish *adj*
smug, self-righteous, sanctimonious, puritanical, prim, prudish, narrow-minded, starchy, stuffy, strait-laced
COLLOQ. goody-goody, holier-than-thou
E3 broad-minded

prim *adj*
prudish, strait-laced, formal, demure, proper, smug, priggish, prissy, fussy, particular, stuffy, starchy, puritanical, precise, fastidious, old-maidish, governessy; *dialect* mimsy; *Scot* mim, perjink, primsie
OLD (*Spenser*) quaint

COLLOQ. fuddy-duddy, schoolmarmish
🔄 relaxed, easy-going

primacy n
supremacy, greatest importance, dominance,
paramouncy, pre-eminence, sovereignty, superiority,
command, seniority, dominion, leadership
FORMAL ascendancy
🔄 inferiority

prima donna n
1 LEADING LADY, female lead, leading female singer, leading
soprano, diva
2 TEMPERAMENTAL PERSON, over-sensitive person, moody
person, unpredictable person

primal adj
original, basic, earliest, fundamental, primitive, first,
primary, initial, major, greatest, highest, main, central,
chief, paramount, principal, prime
FORMAL prim(a)eval, primordial
🔄 later, minor

primarily adv
chiefly, principally, mainly, mostly, basically, first, firstly, first
and foremost, fundamentally, especially, particularly,
predominantly, essentially, in essence, in the main, in the
first place

primary adj
1 CHIEF, principal, main, dominant, leading, foremost,
supreme, prime, predominant, cardinal, capital,
paramount, greatest, highest, ultimate
2 FIRST, basic, fundamental, essential, radical, rudimentary,
elementary, simple, earliest, original, initial, introductory,
beginning, opening
FORMAL elemental, prim(a)eval, primordial
🔄 **1** secondary, subsidiary, minor

prime¹ adj, n
♦ adj
1 BEST, choice, select, quality, first-class, first-rate,
excellent, top, top-grade, supreme, highest, pre-eminent
2 CHIEF, principal, main, leading, foremost, supreme,
predominant
3 CLASSIC, typical, standard, characteristic
FORMAL paradigmatic, quintessential, prototypical
🔄 second-rate, secondary
♦ n
height, peak, pinnacle, acme, zenith, heyday, flower,
blossom, bloom, culmination, best part, maturity,
perfection

prime² v
1 PREPARE, equip, get ready, make ready, gear up, coach,
train
2 BRIEF, inform, notify, prepare, fill, fill in
COLLOQ. clue up, gen up

prime minister n
premier, head of government, chief minister, first minister,
chancellor, secretary of state

primer n
introduction, manual, textbook
OLD (Shakesp) absey-book
FORMAL prodrome, prodromus

primeval, primaeval adj
1 EARLIEST, first, original, early, old, ancient, prehistoric,
primitive
FORMAL primordial, autochthonal
2 INSTINCTIVE, basic, intuitive, natural, innate, inherent,
inborn, primal
🔄 **1** modern

primitive adj
1 CRUDE, rough, unsophisticated, uncivilized, simple,
natural, uncultured, undeveloped, barbarian, wild,
savage

2 EARLY, elementary, rudimentary, primary, first, original,
earliest, ancient
FORMAL prim(a)eval, primordial
🔄 **1** advanced, sophisticated, civilized

primly adv
prudishly, prissily, fussily, stuffily

primordial adj
earliest, first, original, early, old, ancient, prehistoric,
primitive, instinctive
FORMAL prim(a)eval, autochthonal
🔄 modern

primp v
groom, smarten, tidy, dress up, spruce up, brush up,
beautify, preen
COLLOQ. titivate, doll up, tart up, put on your best bib and
tucker, put on your glad rags

prince n
lord, ruler, monarch, potentate, sovereign, duke, prince
consort, princekin, princelet, princeling, khan, ras, sherif,
Tunku
OLD archduke, atheling, infante, hospodar, raja(h),
maharaja(h), nizam, rana, Upper Roger, nawab,
porphyrogenite, tetrarch, lucumo; (Shakesp)
potent

princely adj
1 SOVEREIGN, imperial, royal, regal, majestic, stately, grand,
imposing, magnificent, splendid, glorious, impressive,
superb, noble, en prince
2 princely sum
handsome, generous, liberal, lavish, sumptuous,
magnificent, enormous, huge, immense, vast, massive,
colossal, large-scale, mammoth, considerable,
tremendous, stupendous
FORMAL bounteous, magnanimous

princess n
lady, ruler, monarch, potentate, sovereign, crown princess,
begum
OLD archduchess, infanta

principal adj, n
♦ adj
main, chief, key, major, essential, cardinal, primary, first,
foremost, leading, controlling, dominant, in charge, prime,
paramount, pre-eminent, most important, supreme,
highest, arch
🔄 minor, subsidiary, lesser, least
♦ n
1 HEAD, head teacher, headmaster, headmistress, rector,
chief, leader, director, manager, superintendent,
controller, ruler
COLLOQ. boss
2 MONEY, capital, capital sum, capital funds, assets

🔲 **principal** or **principle**?
As an adjective, *principal* means 'most important': *Ship-
building and coal-mining were two of Britain's principal
industries.* As a noun, *principal* means 'the head of a
school, college or university'. *Principle* can only be used as
a noun. It means 'a general rule' or 'the theory underlying a
method or way of working': *the principles of economic
theory.*

principality n
princedom, principate, duchy, dukedom, grand duchy,
archduchy, archdukedom, earldom, palatinate, sultanate,
protectorate, kingdom, realm, dominion, empire,
dependency, federation, confederation

principally adv
mainly, mostly, chiefly, primarily, predominantly, above all,
particularly, especially, in the main, for the most part, first
and foremost, capitally

principle *n*

1 RULE, formula, law, canon, axiom, dictum, precept, maxim, truth, tenet, doctrine, creed, dogma, code, theory, idea, standard, criterion, proposition, basis, fundamental, essential
FORMAL postulate

2 *a man of principle*
honour, integrity, uprightness, virtue, decency, morality, morals, ethics, standards, scruples, conscience
FORMAL rectitude, probity

■ **in principle**
theoretically, in theory, ideally, in essence, *en principe*

🔃 **principle** or **principal**?
See panel at **principal**.

principled *adj*
upright, virtuous, moral, ethical, high-minded, upright, honourable, conscientious, decent, respectable, righteous, just, right-minded, scrupulous
🖃 unprincipled

print *v, n*
◆ *v*
mark, stamp, imprint, impress, engrave, etch, record, register, copy, reproduce, run off, publish, issue
COLLOQ. put to bed
See panels on next page
◆ *n*
1 LETTERS, characters, lettering, type, typescript, typeface, fount, font
2 MARK, impression, fingerprint, footprint
3 COPY, reproduction, replica, facsimile, design, picture, engraving, lithograph, photograph, photo, snapshot
COLLOQ. snap

■ **in print**
published, available, obtainable, in stock, in circulation
🖃 out of print

■ **out of print**
no longer available, unavailable, unobtainable, out of stock, sold out, off the market, out of/withdrawn from circulation
🖃 in print

prior *adj*
earlier, preceding, foregoing, previous, former
🖃 later

■ **prior to**
before, preceding, earlier than, up to, until, till, in advance of
🖃 after, following

priority *n*
1 *a top priority*
most important thing, most urgent matter, matter of highest/greatest importance, main thing, supreme matter, first concern, primary issue, essential, requirement, pole position
COLLOQ. top of the tree
2 PRECEDENCE, right of way, seniority, rank, superiority, pre-eminence, supremacy, paramouncy, the lead, greater/greatest importance, first/highest place
🖃 **2** inferiority

priory *n*
monastery, abbey, cloister, friary, priorate, convent, nunnery, religious community, religious house, béguinage

prise *v*
lever, force, jemmy, pry, raise, lift, hoist, dislodge, shift, move, winkle

prison *n*
jail, jailhouse, guardhouse, penitentiary, cell, lock-up, cage, dungeon, imprisonment, confinement, detention centre, custody
OLD kitty; (*Shakesp*) confine

COLLOQ. nick, inside
SLANG porridge, clink, cooler, slammer, jug, can, choky, quod; *N Am* big house, hoosegow

prisoner *n*
captive, hostage, convict, prisoner of war, POW, inmate, internee, detainee, recidivist, prisoner of conscience, political prisoner, Rule 43, state prisoner, trust, *détenu(e)*
TECHNICAL culprit
COLLOQ. jailbird, con, lifer, (old) lag, yardbird
OLD SLANG passman

prissily *adv*
prudishly, primly, fussily, stuffily

prissy *adj*
prim, squeamish, prudish, strait-laced, formal, demure, proper, priggish, fussy, particular, stuffy, starchy, puritanical, precise, fastidious, old-maidish
COLLOQ. finicky, po-faced, schoolmarmish

pristine *adj*
1 IMMACULATE, undefiled, uncorrupted, untouched, virgin, unspoiled, unsullied
2 ORIGINAL, earliest, first, initial, former, primary, primitive, primal
FORMAL prim(a)eval, primordial, primigenial
🖃 **1** spoiled, defiled **2** developed, later

privacy *n*
secrecy, confidentiality, independence, solitude, quietness, isolation, seclusion, privateness, concealment, retirement, retreat
FORMAL sequestration
🖃 publicness, interruption, interference

private *adj, n*
◆ *adj*
1 *private discussions*
confidential, classified, secret, top secret, privileged, unofficial, off the record
COLLOQ. hush-hush
2 *your private life/feelings*
personal, confidential, intimate, innermost, secret, hidden, individual
3 *a private bathroom*
exclusive, particular, own, special, individual, personal
4 *a private person*
quiet, reserved, withdrawn, independent, solitary, retiring, separate, self-contained, introverted
5 *a private place*
secluded, isolated, hidden, concealed, closed, secret, remote, undisturbed, quiet, out-of-the-way
FORMAL sequestered
6 *private industries*
independent, commercial, free-enterprise, free-market, privatized, non-governmental, denationalized, self-governing, self-determining
🖃 **1** official, public **5** public, open **6** public, state-controlled, state-run, nationalized
◆ *n*
enlisted man, private soldier, Tommy, squaddy, swad, swaddy, gunner
COLLOQ. Tommy Atkins

■ **in private**
privately, in confidence, confidentially, secretly, in secret, with no one else present, behind closed doors, in camera, *sub rosa*
🖃 publicly, openly

■ **private detective**
private eye, private investigator, pinkerton
COLLOQ. sleuth, shamus, dick

■ **private parts**
genitals, sexual organs, reproductive organs, vagina, womb, uterus, penis, scrotum, testicles
TECHNICAL pudenda, vulva

Printing methods include:

bubble-jet printing	die-stamping	ink-jet printing	offset lithography	thermography
collotype	duplicating	intaglio	offset printing	twin-etching
colour-process printing	electrostatic printing	laser printing	photoengraving	xerography
computer-to-plate (CTP)	engraving	letterpress	rotary press	
	etching	lino blocking	screen printing	
	flexography	litho	silk-screen printing	
copper engraving	gravure	lithography	stencilling	

Printing terms include:

anodized plate	collograph	flong	Linotype®	perfecting	strike-on
author's proof	colour control bar	font	literal	phototypesetting	strip in
backing-up	colour separation	forme	logotype	planographic	take in
back margin	column inch/	galley	lower-case	printing press	take over
bad break	centimetre	gutter	machine	progressive	text
base alignment	compose	hard hyphen	composition	proofs	thermal printer
batter	composing room	hot-metal	machine proof	proof	tint
bi-directional	composition size	typesetting	mackle	quoin	trim marks
printing	compositor	image printing	makeready	ragged right/left	type
black printer	condensed	imposition	manuscript	registration	typeface
blanket-to-	copy	impression	margin	relief printing	type scale
blanket press	cylinder press	indent	matrix	reprint	typescript
bold face	dampers	initial caps	misprint	roman	typesetting
bromide	dot-etching	inking roller	moiré	run-around	type spec
camera-ready	dot gain	Intertype®	Monophoto®	running head	typo
copy	drum printer	italic	Monotype®	running text	typographer
carding	electrotype	justification	mottling	sans serif	upper-case
caret	em	keep standing	newsprint	see-through	web-fed
cast-off	en	kern	non-image area	signature	web offset
catchword	end even	kiss impression	non-impact	small capitals	widow
centre	expanded type	large print	printing	soft hyphen	woodcut
character set	feathering	leaders	offprint	specimen page	wood engraving
chase	finishing	leading	orphan	spoilage	zinco
cliché	first proof	letterset	overprint	stereotype	
cold composition	flat-bed press	line printer	Ozalid®	stet	

FORMAL genitalia
COLLOQ. privates
SLANG (*taboo*) fanny, pussy, muff, cunt, cock, prick, dick, balls

privateer *n*
buccaneer, pirate, brigand, filibuster, freebooter, corsair, marque, sea robber, sea wolf

privately *adv*
1 *we need to talk privately*
in private, in confidence, confidentially, secretly, in secret, with no one else present, behind closed doors, in camera, *sub rosa*
2 *privately, I'm worried about him*
personally, inwardly, inside, to yourself, within, at heart, in your heart of hearts, deep down, deep inside you, secretly

privation *n*
hardship, destitution, deprivation, affliction, neediness, poverty, suffering, lack, need, austerity, loss, misery, distress
FORMAL indigence, penury, want
🔁 affluence, wealth

privilege *n*
advantage, benefit, concession, birthright, title, due, right, prerogative, entitlement, honour, freedom, liberty, franchise, licence, sanction, dispensation, authority, immunity, exemption, priority, status symbol, patent, faculty
TECHNICAL octroi
OLD commodity; (*Shakesp*) prise
🔁 disadvantage

privileged *adj*
1 FAVOURED, advantaged, special, indulgent, sanctioned, authorized, immune, excepted, exempt, élite, honoured, ruling, powerful, rich, wealthy
2 CONFIDENTIAL, private, classified, secret, top secret,

unofficial, off the record
COLLOQ. hush-hush
🔁 **1** disadvantaged, under-privileged **2** public, common

privy *n*
toilet, lavatory, water closet, WC, public convenience, washroom, cloakroom, latrine, gents', ladies', urinal, powder room; *N Am* rest room, comfort station
COLLOQ. bog, loo, lav, dunny, smallest room
SLANG kazi, crapper, can, cottage, heads, thunderbox
■ **privy to**
aware of, cognizant of, informed about, wise to
FORMAL apprised of
COLLOQ. genned up on, clued up on, in on, in the know about
🔁 unaware of

prize *n, adj, v*
♦ *n*
1 REWARD, trophy, medal, award, winnings, jackpot, purse, premium, stake(s), honour, accolade, laurels, pennant
2 AIM, goal, gain, hope, desire, honour
3 BOOTY, loot, spoils, plunder, pickings, capture, pillage, trophy
♦ *adj*
best, top, first-rate, excellent, outstanding, champion, winning, prize-winning, award-winning
COLLOQ. top-notch, terrific, smashing, out of this world
🔁 second-rate
♦ *v*
treasure, value, appreciate, revere, cherish, love, hold dear, think highly of, hold in high regard, set great store by, esteem
🔁 despise, undervalue

prize-winner *n*
winner, champion, cup-winner, medallist, prizeman, prizewoman, dux
COLLOQ. champ

pro[1] n

a tennis pro
professional, expert, authority, specialist, consultant, practitioner, master, past master, old hand, virtuoso
COLLOQ. dab hand, wizard, ace
Ⓔ amateur

pro[2] prep

• prep
pro democracy
in favour of, for, supporting, backing
Ⓔ against

■ pros and cons
advantages and disadvantages, reasons for and reasons against, arguments for and arguments against, strengths and weaknesses, pluses and minuses

probability n

likelihood, likeliness, odds, chance(s), expectation, prospect, possibility
Ⓔ improbability

probable adj

likely, expected, to be expected, anticipated, credible, believable, plausible, feasible, forseeable, predictable, possible, apparent, seeming
COLLOQ. odds-on, on the cards, a fair bet
Ⓔ improbable, unlikely

probably adv

in all likelihood, in all probability, likely, it looks like, the chances are, most likely, as likely as not, doubtless, presumably, arguably, possibly, perhaps, maybe
COLLOQ. (as) like as not, a fair bet
Ⓔ improbably

probation n

trial period, experimental period, trial, test, test period, apprenticeship, supervision

probationer n

trainee, apprentice, novice, beginner, learner, student, pupil, recruit, raw recruit, amateur, newcomer, tiro
FORMAL neophyte, noviciate
COLLOQ. greenhorn, rookie

probe v, n

• v
1 INVESTIGATE, scrutinize, examine, study, inquire, analyse, research, go into, look into, search, sift, test
2 PROD, poke, pierce, penetrate, sound, plumb, check, explore, examine, feel
• n
1 INQUIRY, inquest, investigation, exploration, examination, test, scrutiny, scrutinization, study, analysis, research
2 *examine with a probe*
instrument, bore, drill, device
OLD tent

probity n

uprightness, righteousness, integrity, honour, honourableness, virtue, morality, worth, honesty, goodness, equity, fairness, justice, truthfulness, trustworthiness, sincerity
FORMAL fidelity, rectitude
Ⓔ *formal* improbity

problem n, adj

• n
1 TROUBLE, worry, predicament, quandary, plight, dilemma, difficulty, complication, snag; *S Afr* indaba
COLLOQ. hassle, hole, pickle, fix, mess, tight spot, dire straits, no-win situation, catch-22
2 QUESTION, issue, matter, poser, puzzle, conundrum, riddle, enigma, brainteaser, mind-bender; *N Am* braintwister
3 NUISANCE, annoyance, inconvenience, bother, irritation, irritant, vexation, pest, bore

COLLOQ. pain, pain in the neck, drag, thorn in your side/ flesh
• adj
difficult, unmanageable, uncontrollable, unruly, troublesome, disobedient, delinquent
FORMAL recalcitrant, intransigent
Ⓔ well-behaved, manageable

Synonym nuances
noun sense 1
Trouble and **difficulty** can be widely used to refer to anything that is hard to deal with, while **worry** has a narrower suggestion of causing mental anguish.
Predicament can be used of physical problems: *he was in a bit of a predicament when he missed his plane*, as can **plight**, but this is far more suggestive of a position of danger.
  Both **predicament** and **quandary** can appropriately refer to being in an awkward situation, especially one requiring action: *the government is in a quandary trying to reconcile the conflicting demands*; **dilemma** would specifically suggest being faced with two equally undesirable choices.
  The term **complication** can be used to suggest something that increases the complexity of a situation, and **snag**, although similar, often implies something that is not initially evident: *another unexpected snag*.

---

problematic adj

1 DIFFICULT, fraught with difficulties, troublesome, awkward, hard, puzzling, perplexing, intricate, involved, tricky, thorny, problematical, enigmatic, moot
COLLOQ. a can of worms, a minefield
2 UNCERTAIN, questionable, debatable, doubtful, dubious
Ⓔ 1 easy, straightforward 2 certain

procedure n

routine, process, method, methodology, system, technique, custom, practice, means, measure, policy, formula, way, course, course of action, scheme, strategy, plan of action, move, step, action, conduct, operation, modus operandi, performance

proceed v

1 *the permission to proceed*
advance, go ahead, move on, go on, go forward, progress, continue, carry on, press on, make your way
2 START, begin, make a start, take steps, get under way, set in motion
3 ORIGINATE, derive, flow, start, stem, spring, arise, issue, emanate, result, ensue, follow, come
Ⓔ 1 stop, retreat

proceedings n

1 MATTERS, affairs, business, dealings, transactions, report(s), account, minutes, records, archives, annals
2 EVENTS, activities, happenings, deeds, doings, moves, steps, measures, action, course of action, operations, procedures, manoeuvres
3 *legal proceedings*
lawsuit, case, trial, action, process, litigation

proceeds n

revenue, income, returns, receipts, takings, earnings, gain, profit(s), yield, produce
Ⓔ expenditure, outlay

process n, v

• n
1 PROCEDURE, operation, practice, action, method, system, technique, means, manner, way, stage, step
FORMAL mode
2 COURSE, progression, advance, progress, development, change(s), evolution, formation, growth, movement, action, proceeding
• v

deal with, sort, attend to, handle, treat, prepare, refine, transform, convert, change, alter

■ **in the process of**
in the course of, in the middle of, being, in the making, in preparation

procession n
march, parade, cavalcade, motorcade, pageant, cortège, file, column, walk, funeral, train, succession, stream, series, sequence, course, run, progress, pomp, corso, demonstration, manifestation
TECHNICAL Moharram
OLD triumph
FORMAL exequy

proclaim v
announce, declare, pronounce, affirm, give out, publish, advertise, circulate, broadcast, make known, notify, profess, testify, blaze abroad, blazon, trumpet, show, indicate, bid, cry, herald, preach, show forth, summon, knell, ring, sing, sound, apostolize; *dialect* out-ask
TECHNICAL preconize
OLD ask, annuntiate, denounce; (*Shakesp*) protest
FORMAL promulgate, enounce

proclamation n
announcement, declaration, affirmation, pronouncement, publication, circulation, advertisement, notice, notification, preaching, broadcast, manifesto, order, order of the day, rule, command, decree, edict, banns
TECHNICAL kerygma
OLD proclaim, annunciation, indiction, hue and cry, placard; (*Shakesp*) oyez
FORMAL promulgation, pronunciamento

proclivity n
tendency, leaning, inclination, weakness, disposition, bent, bias, liability, proneness, liableness
FORMAL penchant, predilection, predisposition, propensity
Ea disinclination

procrastinate v
defer, put off, postpone, delay, stall, play for time, dally, drag your feet, prolong, protract
FORMAL retard, temporize
COLLOQ. dilly-dally
Ea advance, proceed

🛈 **procrastinate** or **prevaricate**?
See panel at **prevaricate**.

---

procrastination n
delaying, deferral, stalling, delaying tactics
FORMAL temporizing, cunctation
COLLOQ. dilly-dallying

procreate v
reproduce, produce, father, mother, breed, conceive, generate, propagate, multiply, engender, sire, spawn
OLD beget

procure v
1 ACQUIRE, buy, purchase, get, obtain, find, come by, pick up, lay hands on, earn, gain, win, secure, get hold of
FORMAL appropriate, requisition
2 *procure a prostitute*
pimp, pander, ponce, solicit, importune
COLLOQ. hook, hustle
Ea **1** lose

procurer n
procuress, pimp, pander, panderer, madam, fancy man, whoremonger, fleshmonger, solicitor
OLD bawd, broker, mackerel
SLANG hustler, ponce, mack; *Aust* hoon

prod v, n
♦ v

1 POKE, jab, dig, elbow, nudge, push, butt, thrust
COLLOQ. shove
2 URGE, goad, spur, prompt, stimulate, motivate, stir, move, encourage, incite
COLLOQ. egg on
♦ n
1 POKE, jab, dig, elbow, nudge, push
COLLOQ. shove
2 PROMPT, prompting, reminder, push, stimulus, spur, goad, motivation, encouragement

prodigal adj, n
♦ adj
wasteful, extravagant, squandering, excessive, improvident, intemperate, unsparing, unthrifty, unthrift, wanton, reckless, spendthrift, immoderate, lavish, profuse, sumptuous, exuberant, bountiful, copious
FORMAL bounteous, luxuriant, profligate
Ea modest, thrifty, parsimonious
♦ n
squanderer, waster, spendthrift, spendall, wastrel
FORMAL profligate
COLLOQ. big spender

prodigality n
wastefulness, extravagance, recklessness, squandering, waste, wantonness, unthriftiness, immoderation, intemperance, dissipation, excess, abandon, exuberance, richness, profusion, lavishness, sumptuousness, plenty, abundance
FORMAL luxuriance, plenteousness, profligacy, bounteousness, amplitude, copiousness
Ea modesty, thrift, parsimony

prodigious adj
1 ENORMOUS, gigantic, huge, massive, vast, immense, colossal, giant, mammoth, immeasurable
2 EXTRAORDINARY, marvellous, startling, amazing, astounding, staggering, fabulous, fantastic, flabbergasting, striking, impressive, miraculous, wonderful, monumental, inordinate, spectacular, remarkable, stupendous, tremendous, phenomenal, unusual, exceptional, abnormal
Ea **1** small **2** commonplace, unremarkable

prodigiously adv
vastly, massively, immensely, astoundingly, amazingly, wonderfully, staggeringly, fantastically, impressively, unusually, remarkably, phenomenally, exceptionally, spectacularly
Ea commonly, usually, unremarkably

prodigy n
genius, virtuoso, child genius, wonder child, wunderkind, gifted child, mastermind, wonder, marvel, miracle, phenomenon, sensation, freak, curiosity, rarity
OLD monster; (*Shakesp*) monument
FORMAL portent
COLLOQ. whizz kid
SLANG phenom

produce v, n
♦ v
1 CAUSE, occasion, give rise to, provoke, bring about, result in, create, evoke, originate, invent, develop, prepare, make, manufacture, fashion, fabricate, build, construct, put together, assemble, compose, generate, yield, bear, breed, grow, deliver
FORMAL effect
2 ADVANCE, put forward, present, offer, give, supply, provide, furnish, bring out, bring forward, bring forth, show, exhibit, demonstrate, come up with
FORMAL proffer
3 *produce a play*

direct, stage, present, perform, manage,
organize, arrange, mount, put on
• *n*
crop, harvest, yield, output, product(s), food, foodstuffs,
fruit, vegetables, dairy products, eggs

producer *n*
1 *the producer of a play*
director, presenter, impresario, manager, régisseur
2 *a producer of wine*
manufacturer, maker, farmer, grower

product *n*
1 COMMODITY, merchandise, goods, wares, end-product,
artefact, work, article, item, creation, invention,
production, output, yield, produce, fruit, return
2 RESULT, consequence, effect, outcome, issue, upshot,
fruit, offshoot, spin-off, by-product, legacy
Ea 2 cause

production *n*
1 MAKING, manufacture, manufacturing, producing,
building, fabrication, construction, assembly, creation,
origination, preparation, formation, composition,
development
2 OUTPUT, yield, harvest, fruit(s), return(s), productivity,
manufacture, achievement, performance
3 *the production of a play*
staging, mounting, performance, presentation, direction,
management, organization
4 SHOW, play, drama, concert, musical, opera, film, revue,
presentation, performance
Ea 1 consumption

productive *adj*
fruitful, profitable, rewarding, valuable, beneficial,
worthwhile, useful, constructive, gainful, creative,
inventive, fertile, prolific, rich, high-yielding, teeming,
busy, energetic, vigorous, efficient, effective
FORMAL fecund, fructiferous
Ea unproductive, fruitless, useless

productivity *n*
productiveness, fruitfulness, yield, output, production,
capacity, work rate, efficiency

profanation *n*
desecration, violation, abuse, misuse, defilement,
debasement, dishonouring, sacrilege, blasphemy,
perversion

profane *adj, v*
• *adj*
1 SACRILEGIOUS, irreligious, blasphemous, idolatrous,
godless, ungodly, irreverent, disrespectful, abusive, crude,
vulgar, coarse, foul, foul-mouthed, foul-spoken, filthy,
unclean
2 SECULAR, temporal, lay, worldly, unconsecrated,
unhallowed, unsanctified, unholy, impious
Ea 1 religious, respectful **2** sacred, holy
• *v*
desecrate, pollute, contaminate, defile, debase, pervert,
violate, abuse, misuse, misemploy
Ea revere, honour

profanity *n*
1 SACRILEGE, irreverence, profaneness, impiety, blasphemy,
abuse
FORMAL execration, imprecation, malediction
2 OBSCENITY, swear-word, swearing, oath, expletive, curse,
cursing
COLLOQ. four-letter word
Ea politeness, reverence

profess *v*
1 CLAIM, maintain, allege, lay claim to, make out,
pretend
FORMAL dissemble, purport

2 DECLARE, admit, confess, acknowledge, own, confirm,
certify, announce, proclaim, state, assert, affirm
FORMAL aver, avow

professed *adj*
1 SELF-ACKNOWLEDGED, self-confessed, self-styled, so-
called, soi-disant, confirmed, declared, certified,
acknowledged, proclaimed
FORMAL avowed
2 PRETENDED, supposed, ostensible, alleged, apparent,
would-be
FORMAL purported

profession *n*
1 CAREER, job, occupation, employment, business, line (of
work), walk of life, craft, trade, vocation, calling, métier,
craft, office, appointment, post, position, situation
2 ADMISSION, confession, acknowledgement, declaration,
announcement, statement, testimony, assertion,
affirmation, claim
FORMAL averment, avowal

professional *adj, n*
• *adj*
qualified, licensed, trained, experienced, practised,
dexterous, skilful, skilled, educated, knowledgeable,
specialist, expert, masterly, adept, able, accomplished,
proficient, competent, businesslike, efficient
Ea amateur, unprofessional
• *n*
expert, authority, specialist, consultant, practitioner,
master, past master, maestro, old hand, virtuoso
COLLOQ. pro, dab hand, wizard, whizz, ace; *N Am* mavin,
maven
Ea amateur

professor *n*
head of department, chair, head of faculty, vice chancellor,
dean, principal, provost, don, fellow, reader, academic,
lecturer, intellectual

proffer *v*
offer, tender, advance, extend, hold out, hand, suggest,
present, propose, submit, volunteer

proficiency *n*
skill, skilfulness, expertise, experience, mastery, talent,
knack, dexterity, finesse, aptitude, accomplishment,
capability, ability, competence, aptness, adeptness
Ea incompetence

proficient *adj*
able, capable, skilled, qualified, trained, experienced,
accomplished, expert, masterly, gifted, talented, clever,
skilful, competent, efficient, effective, apt, adept, keeping
your eye in
OLD wise
Ea unskilled, incompetent

profile *n*
1 SIDE VIEW, outline, contour, silhouette, cameo,
description, shape, form, line(s), figure, sketch, drawing,
diagram, chart, graph, template
TECHNICAL thalweg
OLD half-cheek, purfle
2 BIOGRAPHY, curriculum vitae, CV, thumbnail sketch,
vignette, portrait, sketch, study, analysis, examination,
survey, review
COLLOQ. biog
■ **high profile**
exposure, prominence, public attention, visibility,
conspicuous position, noticeable position, the limelight,
the spotlight
■ **keep a low profile**
blend/merge into the background, be/keep/stay in the
background, lie low, escape notice, hide yourself, avoid
publicity, escape the limelight

profit *n, v*
* *n*

1 *the company's profits*
revenue, return, yield, proceeds, receipts, takings, earnings, winnings, dividend, interest, bonus, gain, surplus, excess, bottom line
COLLOQ. fast buck, gravy, killing, rake-off
2 ADVANTAGE, benefit, gain, use, usefulness, avail, value, worth
1, 2 loss
* *v*

gain, make money, pay, serve, avail, benefit
COLLOQ. line your pockets
SLANG make megabucks, make loadsamoney
lose
■ **profit by/from**
exploit, take advantage of, use, utilize, turn to advantage, put to good use, gain a benefit from, gain an advantage from, capitalize on, reap the benefit of
COLLOQ. cash in on, milk

profitable *adj*
1 *a profitable business*
cost-effective, economic, commercial, moneymaking, lucrative, remunerative, fat, paying, rewarding, successful, juicy, plummy, expedient
FORMAL gainful
COLLOQ. in the black
2 *a profitable discussion*
helpful, useful, valuable, worthwhile, fruitful, productive, advantageous, beneficial
OLD advantageable, available, behovely, utile
1 unprofitable, loss-making, non-profit-making **2** unhelpful, useless

profitably *adv*
1 *a business operating profitably*
economically, commercially, successfully
2 *spend your leisure time profitably*
usefully, productively, beneficially, valuably, fruitfully
1 unprofitably **2** uselessly

profiteer *n, v*
* *n*

racketeer, exploiter, extortioner, extortionist
* *v*

exploit, extort, racketeer, fleece, overcharge
COLLOQ. make a fast/quick buck, make a quick killing

profiteering *n*
exploitation, extortion, racketeering, Rachmanism

profitless *adj*
useless, worthless, fruitless, futile, vain, pointless, thankless, ineffective, idle, unavailing, unproductive, unprofitable, unremunerative, gainless, to no purpose, to no avail
FORMAL ineffectual
profitable

profligacy *n*
1 WASTE, wastefulness, extravagance, excess, unrestraint, lavishness, unthriftiness, recklessness, squandering, improvidence, prodigality
2 IMMORALITY, promiscuity, corruption, debauchery, degeneracy, depravity, libertinism, licentiousness, wantonness, dissipation, dissoluteness
morality, parsimony, thrift, uprightness

profligate *adj, n*
* *adj*

1 WASTEFUL, extravagant, squandering, immoderate, excessive, improvident, reckless, spendthrift, prodigal
2 IMMORAL, corrupt, dissolute, unprincipled, wicked, loose, dissipated, depraved, degenerate, debauched, iniquitous, promiscuous, licentious, wanton, libertine
1 thrifty; *formal* parsimonious **2** upright, moral

* *n*

1 WASTER, wastrel, squanderer, spendthrift, prodigal
2 REPROBATE, debauchee, libertine, degenerate, wanton, rake, roué

profound *adj*
1 DEEP, great, intense, extreme, heartfelt, sincere, marked, thorough, complete, absolute, thoroughgoing, far-reaching, radical, extensive, exhaustive
2 *a profound remark*
serious, weighty, deep, penetrating, discerning, thoughtful, philosophical, wise, learned, impenetrable
FORMAL sagacious, erudite, esoteric, abstruse, recondite
1 shallow, slight, mild **2** shallow, superficial

profoundly *adv*
deeply, intensely, extremely, seriously, acutely, greatly, heartily, thoroughly, keenly, sincerely
slightly

profundity *n*
depth, profoundness, extremity, intensity, severity, strength, seriousness, penetration, learning, insight, intelligence, wisdom, perceptiveness, acumen
FORMAL abstruseness, erudition, perspecuity, perspicacity, sagacity
shallowness

profuse *adj*
ample, abundant, plentiful, copious, generous, liberal, lavish, rich, excessive, immoderate, extravagant, large-handed, fulsome, unsparing, unstinting, overabundant, superabundant, overflowing
TECHNICAL colliquative
FORMAL luxuriant, inordinate
COLLOQ. over the top
inadequate, sparse

profusely *adv*
abundantly, copiously, liberally, lavishly, immoderately, extravagantly, unstintingly, unsparingly
inadequately, sparsely

profusion *n*
abundance, copiousness, plenty, wealth, multitude, glut, riot, excess, surplus, superfluity, superabundance, extravagance, unsparingness
FORMAL plethora, plenitude
COLLOQ. loads, lots, heaps, tons
inadequacy, scarcity

progenitor *n*
1 ANCESTOR, forebear, forefather, father, mother, parent
OLD begetter
FORMAL procreator, primogenitor
2 ORIGINATOR, forerunner, founder, instigator, precursor, predecessor, antecedent, source

progeny *n*
offspring, children, young, descendants, family, issue, lineage, race, breed, seed, stock, quiverful
FORMAL posterity, scions

prognosis *n*
diagnosis, expectation, forecast, prediction, outlook, projection, assessment, evaluation, prospect, speculation, surmise
FORMAL prognostication

prognosticate *v*
forecast, foreshadow, foretell, predict, prophesy, herald, indicate, soothsay, divine
FORMAL augur, betoken, harbinger, portend, presage

prognostication *n*
prediction, projection, forecast, expectation, speculation, surmise, horoscope, prophecy
FORMAL prognosis

programme *n, v*
• *n*
1 SCHEDULE, timetable, agenda, calendar, order of events, listing, list, line-up, plan, plan of action, scheme, project, syllabus, course, prospectus, curriculum
2 *radio programme*
broadcast, transmission, show, performance, production, presentation, episode, simulcast
• *v*
arrange, plan, schedule, work out, formulate, itemize, lay on, line up, design, list, map out, book, prearrange

progress *n, v*
• *n*
movement, progression, passage, going, journey, way, advance, headway, step(s) forward, forward movement, breakthrough, development, evolution, growth, increase, improvement, upgrading, betterment, promotion
FORMAL advancement
🖪 recession, deterioration, decline
• *v*
proceed, advance, go forward, move forward, forge ahead, make progress, make headway, make your way, make strides, continue, go on, come on, develop, grow, mature, blossom, bloom, flourish, thrive, improve, better, recover, prosper, increase
COLLOQ. be getting there, shape up
🖪 deteriorate, decline
▪ **in progress**
under way, proceeding, going on, happening, occurring, continuing, in preparation, not finished, not completed
COLLOQ. in the pipeline, on the stocks

progression *n*
cycle, chain, string, succession, series, sequence, process, stream, train, order, course, advance, headway, passage, progress, development, forward movement
TECHNICAL movement, motion, direct motion, resolution, paraphonia
OLD precession
FORMAL advancement

progressive *adj, n*
• *adj*
1 MODERN, avant-garde, advanced, forward-looking, forward-thinking, enlightened, liberal, radical, revolutionary, reformist, innovative, dynamic, enterprising, go-ahead, up-and-coming
2 ADVANCING, continuing, developing, growing, increasing, escalating, intensifying, accelerating, gradual
🖪 **1** conservative **2** regressive
• *n*
reformer, modernizer, innovator, originator, fresh thinker, creator, pioneer, deviser, developer, trailblazer

progressively *adv*
gradually, increasingly, step by step, by degrees, by/in stages, little by little, piecemeal, bit by bit

prohibit *v*
forbid, ban, bar, veto, outlaw, rule out, prevent, exclude, stop, hinder, hamper, impede, obstruct, restrict
OLD defend, injunct
FORMAL proscribe, preclude, interdict, enjoin
🖪 permit, allow, authorize

prohibited *adj*
forbidden, banned, barred, taboo, vetoed, embargoed, *verboten*
FORMAL disallowed, interdicted, proscribed
🖪 permitted, allowed

prohibition *n*
forbidding, forbiddance, ban, bar, constraint, veto, restriction, obstruction, exclusion, prevention, negation, embargo
TECHNICAL injunction

FORMAL disallowance, forbiddal, interdict, interdiction, proscription
🖪 permission

prohibitionist *n*
teetotaller, abolitionist, dry, pussyfoot

prohibitive *adj*
forbidding, preposterous, excessive, exorbitant, extortionate, impossible, restrictive, restraining, suppressive, repressive, prohibiting, prohibitory
FORMAL proscriptive
COLLOQ. sky-high, steep
🖪 encouraging, reasonable

project *n, v*
• *n*
scheme, campaign, plan, venture, programme, design, proposal, assignment, contract, task, job, work, occupation, activity, enterprise, undertaking, idea, conception
• *v*
1 PREDICT, forecast, plan, propose, intend, extrapolate, estimate, reckon, calculate, gauge, expect, design, map out
FORMAL predetermine
2 THROW, fling, hurl, cast, launch, propel, discharge
COLLOQ. chuck
3 PROTRUDE, stick out, stand out, extend, bulge, jut out, overhang
FORMAL obtrude

projectile *n*
missile, rocket, shell, shot, grenade, bullet, ball, bomb, mortar

projecting *adj*
overhanging, protruding, sticking out, protrusive, beetling
FORMAL exsertile, extrusive, extrusory, protrudent

projection *n*
1 PREDICTION, forecast, expectation, extrapolation, estimate, estimation, reckoning, calculation, computation, plan, design
2 PROTUBERANCE, bulge, jutting, overhang, ledge, sill, shelf, ridge

proletarian *adj*
working-class, ordinary, common, plebeian

proletariat *n*
working class, common people, masses, mob, lower classes, rabble, herd, hoi polloi, rank and file, canaille, commoners, commonalty, third estate, great unwashed, riff-raff
COLLOQ. plebs, proles

proliferate *v*
multiply, reproduce, grow quickly, breed, increase, increase rapidly, build up, intensify, extend, escalate, mushroom, snowball, rocket, spread, expand, flourish, thrive
FORMAL burgeon
🖪 dwindle

proliferation *n*
multiplication, increase, rapid increase, intensification, escalation, expansion, spread, extension, build-up, concentration, duplication, mushrooming, snowballing, rocketing
TECHNICAL ecblastesis
🖪 decrease

prolific *adj*
productive, fruitful, fertile, profuse, copious, plentiful, abundant, rank
OLD broody
FORMAL fecund, luxuriant
🖪 unproductive

prolix adj
long-winded, verbose, lengthy, prolonged, prosy, discursive, digressive, long, diffuse, rambling, tedious, tiresome, wordy
TECHNICAL pleonastic
FORMAL protracted
E3 succinct

prolixity n
long-windedness, verboseness, verbiage, wordiness, prosiness, rambling, discursiveness, diffuseness, wandering, verbosity, boringness, tediousness
TECHNICAL pleonasm
E3 succinctness

prologue n
introduction, foreword, preface, preamble, preliminary, prelude
FORMAL exordium, proem, prolegomena, prooemion, prooemium

prolong v
lengthen, extend, elongate, stretch (out), draw out, spin out, drag out, delay, continue, perpetuate, sustain
OLD prorogue; (Shakesp) linger, respite
FORMAL protract
E3 shorten

prolongation n
extension, lengthening, stretching, continuation, perpetuation
FORMAL protraction
E3 shortening

promenade n, v
♦ n
1 SEAFRONT, walkway, front, parade, esplanade, prom, boulevard, terrace
2 WALK, stroll, breather, airing, saunter, turn, walkabout
FORMAL constitutional
♦ v
walk, stroll, saunter, strut, swagger, sally forth, parade
FORMAL perambulate
COLLOQ. mosey

prominence n
1 FAME, celebrity, renown, eminence, pre-eminence, illustriousness, distinction, greatness, note, importance, conspicuousness, reputation, name, standing, stature, rank, prestige, weight, emphasis, top billing, pride of place
OLD prominency
2 BULGE, protuberance, swelling, jutting, protruding, bump, hump, lump, mound, rise, rising, elevation, projection, rib, boss, embossment, process, headland, promontory, pinnacle, crest, height, cliff, crag
TECHNICAL antitragus, tragus, mastoid, cusp, colliculus, torus
OLD prominency
E3 **1** unimportance, insignificance

prominent adj
1 a prominent writer
famous, well-known, celebrated, renowned, noted, notable, eminent, pre-eminent, distinguished, respected, illustrious, leading, foremost, chief, main, important, popular, outstanding, top, acclaimed
COLLOQ. A-list
2 NOTICEABLE, conspicuous, obvious, unmistak(e)able, striking, eye-catching
3 BULGING, protuberant, projecting, jutting (out), standing out, sticking out, protruding, obtrusive, protrusive
E3 **1** unknown, unimportant, insignificant **2** inconspicuous

promiscuity n
looseness, laxity, permissiveness, wantonness, immorality, dissoluteness, dissipation, licentiousness, debauchery, depravity
FORMAL profligacy, protervity

COLLOQ. sleeping around
E3 chastity, morality

promiscuous adj
loose, immoral, licentious, dissolute, debauched, dissipated, abandoned, wanton, fast, of easy virtue, sluttish, casual, random, haphazard, indiscriminate, mixed
FORMAL profligate
COLLOQ. swinging, slack, sleeping around
E3 chaste, moral

promise v, n
♦ v
1 VOW, pledge, swear, take an oath, contract, give an undertaking, undertake, give your word, vouch, warrant, guarantee, assure, give an assurance
OLD plight, betroth
2 clouds that promise rain
indicate, suggest, hint at, signify, denote, be a sign of
FORMAL augur, presage, betoken
♦ n
1 VOW, pledge, oath, word, word of honour, bond, hand, guarantee, assurance, contract, undertaking, engagement, commitment, committal
FORMAL compact, covenant
2 POTENTIAL, ability, capability, aptitude, talent, flair
3 a promise of autumn sunshine
sign, hint, suggestion, indication, evidence
■ promised land
paradise, heaven, land of milk and honey, Zion, Elysium, Elysian fields, Shangri-la, El Dorado, Utopia

---

Synonym nuances
verb sense 1
Vow can be used to suggest a firm resolve, particularly one binding you to a person or a cause, and **pledge** or **take an oath** are similar, though often given more formally or ritually. **Swear** suggests an assertion made in earnest: she swore she would behave. You might choose to use **contract** of a more legally binding commitment. **Give an undertaking** and **undertake** suggest a less officially binding but serious expression of intent. **Vouch**, **warrant** and **guarantee** are generally used for affirming something is true or will happen: her colleagues vouched for her good character. **Assure** and **give an assurance** are perhaps least suggestive of strongly expressed promise, but have added implications of instilling, or attempting to instil, confidence: the tutor assured me that my exam results would be fine.

---

promising adj
favourable, rosy, bright, encouraging, optimistic, hopeful, talented, able, gifted, budding
FORMAL auspicious, propitious
COLLOQ. up-and-coming
E3 unpromising, inauspicious, discouraging

promontory n
cliff, headland, head, foreland, bluff, precipice, point, projection, prominence, ridge, spur, cape, naze, ness, peninsula

promote v
1 UPGRADE, advance, move up, raise, elevate, exalt, honour
FORMAL aggrandize, prefer
2 ENCOURAGE, recommend, advocate, champion, endorse, sponsor, support, back, help, aid, assist, advance, foster, nurture, further, forward, boost, stimulate, urge, contribute to
FORMAL espouse
3 ADVERTISE, publicize, popularize, market, merchandise, sell
COLLOQ. plug, hype, push, puff up
E3 **1** demote, relegate **2** discourage, hinder; formal disparage

promoter n
supporter, upholder, champion, advocate, campaigner, pleader, vindicator, proponent, exponent, evanglist, speaker, spokesman, spokeswoman, spokesperson

promotion n
1 ADVANCEMENT, upgrading, rise, elevation, exaltation, move-up
TECHNICAL remove
FORMAL preferment, aggrandizement, prelation
2 ENCOURAGEMENT, support, recommendation, advocacy, urging, fostering, contribution, backing, furtherance, development, speeding, boosting
FORMAL espousal
3 ADVERTISING, publicity, campaign, propaganda, marketing, payola, puff, puffery
COLLOQ. plugging, hype, pushing, promo
E3 1 demotion 2 discouragement, obstruction; *formal* disparagement

prompt adj, adv, v, n
• adj
punctual, on time, immediate, instantaneous, instant, sudden, direct, quick, swift, rapid, speedy, unhesitating, willing, ready, alert, eager, responsive, timely, early; *Scot* frack
OLD expedite, pernicious
FORMAL expeditious
E3 slow, hesitant, late
• adv
promptly, punctually, exactly, on time, on the dot, to the minute, sharp
COLLOQ. dead on, bang on, spot-on
• v
cause, give rise to, result in, lead, occasion, produce, make, instigate, call forth, elicit, provoke, induce, incite, urge, encourage, inspire, move, stimulate, motivate, spur, impel, prod, remind
OLD premove
FORMAL expedite
E3 deter, dissuade
• n
reminder, cue, refresher, encouragement, hint, help, jolt, prod, spur, stimulus

prompting n
encouragement, reminder, reminding, advice, assistance, hint, influence, jogging, prodding, pushing, suggestion, urging, persuasion, incitement, pressing, pressure
FORMAL admonition, protreptic
E3 dissuasion

promptly adv
1 IMMEDIATELY, instantly, directly, unhesitatingly, quickly, speedily, swiftly, without further ado, smartly
FORMAL forthwith
COLLOQ. pronto, yesterday, before you know it, before you can say Jack Robinson, in two shakes of a lamb's tail, like a shot
2 PUNCTUALLY, on time, on target, exactly, on the dot, to the minute, sharp, as soon as possible, posthaste
COLLOQ. bang on, spot-on, dead on, pronto, asap, pdq, pretty damn quick

promptness n
punctuality, quickness, readiness, speed, swiftness, willingness, briskness, dispatch, eagerness, alertness, haste
FORMAL alacrity, expedition, promptitude
E3 *formal* tardiness

promulgate v
announce, proclaim, declare, decree, promote, circulate, notify, communicate, make known, make public, publish, spread, publicize, broadcast, advertise, issue
FORMAL disseminate

promulgation n
announcement, communication, declaration, proclamation, publication, publicizing, issuance, promulgating
FORMAL dissemination

prone adj
1 LIKELY, given, inclined, disposed, bent, apt, liable, subject, tending, susceptible, vulnerable
OLD proclive
FORMAL predisposed
2 *she lay prone*
face down, prostrate, flat, horizontal, full-length, stretched
OLD proclive
FORMAL recumbent, procumbent
E3 1 unlikely, immune 2 upright, supine

proneness n
inclination, leaning, tendency, susceptibility, aptness, bent, bias, disposition, liability, weakness
FORMAL penchant, proclivity, propensity
E3 dislike

prong n
point, spike, projection, spur, tine, tip, fork, grain

pronounce v
1 SAY, utter, speak, express, voice, vocalize, sound, enunciate, articulate, stress
2 DECLARE, announce, proclaim, decree, judge, affirm, assert

pronounceable adj
speakable, utterable, sayable, vocable, articulable, enunciable, expressible
E3 unpronounceable

pronounced adj
clear, distinct, definite, positive, decided, marked, noticeable, conspicuous, evident, obvious, striking, unmistak(e)able, strong, broad, thick
E3 faint, vague

pronouncement n
declaration, statement, announcement, judgement, notification, proclamation, assertion, decree, edict, manifesto, dictum
FORMAL pronunciamento, *ipse dixit*, promulgation

pronunciation n
speech, diction, elocution, enunciation, articulation, saying, uttering, voicing, vocalization, delivery, accent, stress, inflection, intonation, modulation

proof n, adj
• n
evidence, documentation, demonstration, verification, confirmation, corroboration, certification, validation, substantiation, authentication
FORMAL attestation
COLLOQ. smoking gun
• adj
impenetrable, impervious, proofed, repellent, resistant, strong, tight, treated, fireproof, weatherproof, waterproof, rainproof, leakproof, windproof, bombproof, bulletproof, childproof, foolproof, tamperproof, soundproof
E3 permeable, untreated

prop v, n
• v
1 SUPPORT, sustain, uphold, hold up, maintain, shore (up), stay, brace, buttress, bolster (up), underpin, set, underwrite
2 *propped against the wall*
lean, rest, stand, balance, steady
• n
1 *a clothes prop*
support, stick, post, column, shaft, stay, mainstay, strut, buttress, upright, bolster, brace, truss, stanchion

2 *drink is the prop in his life*
mainstay, support, pillar, column, supporter, anchor

propaganda *n*
advertising, publicity, promotion, information,
indoctrination, brainwashing, disinformation, Agitprop
COLLOQ. hype, ballyhoo

propagandist *n*
promoter, advocate, canvasser, publicist, pamphleteer,
evangelist, proselytizer, indoctrinator
FORMAL proponent
COLLOQ. plugger

propagandize *v*
1 *propagandize communism*
champion, advocate, promote, uphold, campaign for,
argue for, press for, preach
2 BRAINWASH, indoctrinate, pressurize, re-educate,
persuade, talk into, win over

propagate *v*
1 SPREAD, transmit, broadcast, communicate, distribute,
proclaim, diffuse, circulate, publish, publicize, promote
FORMAL disseminate, promulgate
2 INCREASE, multiply, proliferate, grow, generate, produce,
breed, spawn, reproduce
OLD beget
FORMAL procreate

propagation *n*
1 COMMUNICATION, spread, spreading, transmission,
promotion, distribution, circulation, diffusion
FORMAL dissemination, promulgation
2 INCREASE, generation, breeding, multiplication,
proliferation, spawning, reproduction
OLD procreation

propel *v*
move, drive, impel, force, thrust, push (forward), project,
launch, shoot, send, wheel, leg, row, oar, paddle, scull,
punt, pole, pump, sail, swim, waft, frogmarch, loft;
Scot ca'
COLLOQ. power, shove
EJ stop

propeller *n*
screw, airscrew, rotor, vane, prop

propensity *n*
tendency, liability, susceptibility, inclination, leaning,
disposition, aptness, proneness, bent, bias, readiness,
foible, weakness
FORMAL penchant, predisposition, proclivity
EJ disinclination

proper *adj*
1 RIGHT, correct, accurate, exact, precise, true, genuine,
real, actual
2 ACCEPTED, correct, suitable, appropriate, fitting,
acceptable, conventional, orthodox, established, decent,
respectable, polite, refined, genteel, strict, gentlemanly,
ladylike, prim, prudish, formal, respectable
EJ 1 wrong, incorrect **2** improper, indecent

properly *adv*
1 ACCEPTABLY, appropriately, suitably, fittingly,
conventionally, correctly, respectably
2 CORRECTLY, accurately, rightly, right, exactly, precisely,
actually, faultlessly, flawlessly, unerringly
EJ 1 unacceptably, rudely **2** incorrectly, wrongly,
inaccurately

property *n*
1 ESTATE, land, real estate, acres, premises, buildings,
house(s), wealth, riches, resources, means, capital, assets,
holding(s), belongings, possessions, goods, chattels,
paraphernalia
FORMAL effects
COLLOQ. gear, things, clobber

2 FEATURE, trait, quality, attribute, characteristic,
idiosyncrasy, quirk, peculiarity, mark

prophecy *n*
prediction, forecast, prognosis, second sight, fortune-
telling, divination, soothsaying, message
FORMAL augury, prognostication, vaticination
Related adjective: vatic

prophesy *v*
predict, foresee, augur, foretell, forewarn, forecast
FORMAL prognosticate, augur, vaticinate

prophet, prophetess *n*
seer, soothsayer, foreteller, forecaster, oracle, clairvoyant,
fortune-teller
FORMAL prognosticator, vaticinator
■ **prophet of doom**
pessimist, doomwatcher, Jeremiah, Cassandra
COLLOQ. doom merchant, doomster

prophetic *adj*
forecasting, predictive, prognostic, foreshadowing,
oracular, fey
FORMAL sibylline, presaging, prescient, augural, divinatory,
fatidical, mantic, vatic, vaticidal
EJ unprophetic

prophylactic *adj, n*
◆ *adj*
preventive, preventative, anticipatory, pre-emptive,
inhibitory, obstructive, precautionary, protective,
counteractive, deterrent
EJ causative, fostering
◆ *n*
1 PREVENTIVE, preventative, preservative, precaution,
immunization
2 CONDOM, sheath, contraceptive, female condom,
Femidom®; *N Am* protective
SLANG French letter, johnnie, rubber; *N Am* scumbag, safe

propinquity *n*
nearness, closeness, connection, tie, vicinity,
neighbourhood, proximity, adjacency, relation,
relationship, blood, kinship, affiliation, affinity
FORMAL consanguinity, contiguity, kindredness,
kindredship
EJ remoteness

propitiate *v*
reconcile, pacify, placate, satisfy, appease, conciliate,
mollify, soothe
EJ anger, provoke

propitiation *n*
reconciliation, peacemaking, appeasement, conciliation,
mollification, pacification, placation, pacifying
EJ angering, provocation

propitiatory *adj*
reconciliatory, peacemaking, soothing, pacifying,
pacificatory, appeasing, conciliatory, mollifying, assuaging
FORMAL placative, placatory, propitiative
EJ provocative

propitious *adj*
favourable, fortunate, advantageous, happy, friendly,
gracious, opportune, timely, promising, prosperous,
encouraging, reassuring, well-disposed, bright, lucky,
kindly, rosy, benign, beneficial, benevolent
FORMAL auspicious
EJ inauspicious

proponent *n*
advocate, supporter, backer, proposer, subscriber,
apologist, partisan, defender, enthusiast, exponent,
upholder, vindicator, champion, friend, patron
FORMAL propounder
EJ opponent, enemy

proportion n

1 PERCENTAGE, fraction, part, segment, portion, measure, division, share, quota, amount
COLLOQ. cut, split, whack, slice of the cake, piece of the action
2 RATIO, relationship, correspondence, symmetry, balance, distribution, quotient
3 *a task/building of huge proportions*
dimensions, measurements, size, magnitude, extent, volume, capacity, bulk, mass, height, length, depth, breadth, width, scale
F3 2 disproportion, imbalance

proportional adj

proportionate, relative, equivalent, commensurate, consistent, corresponding, analogous, comparable, equitable, even
F3 disproportionate

proportionally adv

proportionately, relatively, correspondingly, comparably, commensurately, evenly, pro rata
F3 disproportionately

proposal n

plan, scheme, project, design, programme, manifesto, presentation, proposition, suggestion, recommendation, motion, bid, offer, tender, terms

propose v

1 SUGGEST, recommend, move, advance, put forward, introduce, bring up, advocate, plan, table, place, submit, present, offer, tender, slate; *Scot* propone
FORMAL move, proffer, propound, moot, motion, put forth
COLLOQ. vote
2 INTEND, mean, aim, purpose, plan, design, have in mind
OLD bethink
3 NOMINATE, put up, name, recommend, suggest
4 *propose marriage*
ask to marry, ask for someone's hand in marriage
OLD plight your troth
COLLOQ. pop the question, go down on bended knee
F3 1 withdraw

proposition n, v

◆ *n*
1 PROPOSAL, suggestion, theory, plan, project, programme, recommendation, scheme, manifesto, motion, tender
FORMAL hypothesis, theorem
2 TASK, activity, undertaking, venture, job
3 *a sexual proposition*
advance, overture, approach, indirect proposal/suggestion, pass
COLLOQ. come-on
◆ *v*
accost, solicit, make sexual advances/overtures to, make an indecent proposal to, make a pass at

propound v

put forward, suggest, propose, advance, set forth, advocate, contend, lay down, present, submit
FORMAL move, postulate
F3 oppose

proprietor, proprietress n

landlord, landlady, title-holder, freeholder, leaseholder, landholder, landowner, owner, possessor, deed holder, entrepreneur, patron
OLD proprietrix

propriety n

1 MODESTY, decorum, decency, civility, etiquette, protocol, delicacy, respectability, refinement, rightness, correctness, manners, good manners, politeness, courtesy, breeding, appropriateness, aptness, becomingness, suitableness, fitness, gentlemanliness, ladylikeness
OLD seemliness

FORMAL punctilio, rectitude
2 *observe proprieties*
civility, standard, etiquette, convention, decency, social graces, social niceties
COLLOQ. the done thing, p's and q's
F3 1, 2 impropriety

propulsion n

drive, driving force, power, pressure, push, thrust, motive force, momentum, impetus, impulse, impulsion

pro rata adv

proportionally, proportionately, relatively, correspondingly, comparably, commensurately, evenly
F3 disproportionately

prosaic adj

mundane, ordinary, routine, dull, stale, boring, commonplace, humdrum, matter-of-fact, unimaginative, uninspired, uninspiring, monotonous, bland, tame, trite, banal, vacuous, vapid, pedestrian, workaday, flat, dry, hackneyed, everyday
F3 imaginative, interesting

prosaically adv

mundanely, ordinarily, unimaginatively, uninspiringly, monotonously, blandly, dully
F3 imaginatively, interestingly

proscribe v

forbid, prohibit, ban, outlaw, bar, banish, condemn, embargo, reject, exclude, boycott, censure, damn, doom, black, blackball, denounce, deport, expel, exile, excommunicate, expatriate, ostracize
FORMAL interdict, disallow
F3 allow, permit

---

proscribe or **prescribe**?
See panel at **prescribe**.

---

proscription n

prohibition, ban, bar, barring, embargo, outlawry, censure, condemnation, damning, denunciation, ostracism, rejection, banishment, boycott, deportation, expulsion, ejection, eviction, exclusion, exile, excommunication, expatriation
FORMAL interdict
F3 admission, allowing

prosecute v

accuse, sue, charge, bring charges, bring an action against, prefer charges, take to court, litigate, summon, put on trial, try, proceed, process; *Scot* pursue
FORMAL arraign, indict
F3 defend

prosecution n

accusation, bringing charges, charging, trial, taking to court, litigation, indictment, impeachment

proselyte n

convert, neophyte, new believer, changed person, new person, recruit, catechumen

proselytize v

convert, evangelize, make converts, persuade, win over, propagandize, spread the gospel, bring into the fold, bring to God

prosody

See panel on next page

prospect n, v

◆ *n*
1 *the prospect of rain*
chance(s), odds, probability, likelihood, likeness, possibility, hope, expectation, anticipation, outlook, future, promise
2 *a prospect of the bay*
outlook, vista, view, scene, panorama, aspect, spectacle, perspective, landscape, opening

Terms used in prosody include:

abstract verse	bouts rimés	enjambment	iamb	Petrarchan sonnet	Spenserian stanza
Alcaic verse	broken rhyme	envoy	ictus	Pherecratean	spondee
alexandrine	caesura	epitrite	Ionic	Pindaric	sprung rhythm
alliteration	canto	epode	internal rhyme	poulters' measure	strophe
amphibrach	catalexis	eye rhyme	kyrielle	pyrrhic	substitution
amphimacer	choliamb	false quantity	laisse	Pythian verse	synaphea
Anacreontic	choree	feminine caesura	Leonine rhyme	quatorzain	tetrameter
verse	choriamb	feminine ending	linked verse	quatrain	tetrapody
anacrusis	cinquain	feminine rhyme	long-measure	reported verses	tetrastich
analysed rhyme	consonance	foot	macaronic	rhopalic	tribrach
anapaest	couplet	free verse	masculine ending	rhyme royal	trimeter
antibacchius	dactyl	galliambic	masculine rhyme	rime riche	triolet
antispast	decastich	glyconic	metre	rime suffisante	tripody
Archilochian	dipody	half-rhyme	miurus	rondeau	triseme
verse	dispondee	heptameter	monometer	rondel	trochee
asclepiad	distich	heptapody	monorhyme	rove-over	villanelle
assonance	ditrochee	heroic couplet	paeon	Sapphic	virelay
asynartete	dizain	hexameter	pantoum	senarius	
ballade	dochmius	hexastich	pentameter	septenarius	
blank verse	elision	hypermetrical	pentastich	sonnet	

⊟ 1 unlikelihood

♦ *v*

explore, search, look for, seek, survey, examine, inspect, quest, fossick

COLLOQ. nose

prospective *adj*

future, -to-be, would-be, intended, designate, destined, forthcoming, approaching, coming, imminent, awaited, expected, anticipated, hoped-for, likely, possible, probable, potential, aspiring

prospectus *n*

syllabus, manifesto, outline, synopsis, pamphlet, leaflet, brochure, catalogue, list, literature, announcement, description, plan, scheme, programme

FORMAL conspectus

prosper *v*

boom, thrive, flourish, flower, bloom, succeed, be successful, get on, get on well, do well, turn out well, advance, progress, make progress, grow rich

FORMAL burgeon

COLLOQ. get ahead, get on in the world, go up in the world, make your pile, hit the big time, hit the jackpot, live on easy street

⊟ fail

prosperity *n*

boom, plenty, affluence, wealth, riches, fortune, wellbeing, luxury, success, good fortune

COLLOQ. the good life, the life of Riley, easy street, bed of roses, land of milk and honey, clover, lap of luxury

⊟ adversity, poverty

prosperous *adj*

booming, thriving, flourishing, blooming, successful, fortunate, lucky, rich, wealthy, affluent, well-off, well-to-do

FORMAL burgeoning, opulent

COLLOQ. well-heeled, rolling in it

⊟ unfortunate, poor

prostitute *n, v*

♦ *n*

harlot, call-girl, rent-boy, woman of the streets, woman of the town, woman of ill repute, loose woman, fallen woman, scarlet woman, whore, trollop, street-walker, cocotte, courtesan, bawd, *fille de joie, fille des rues*, drab, grande cocotte, lorette, lady of the night, geisha, hetaera, hierodule, loose fish, magdalen, night-walker, vizard-mask

OLD bulker, convertite, trull, moll, strumpet, cockatrice, public woman, wench, pug, punk, stew, stale; (*Shakesp*)quail, bona-roba, callet, polecat, road, venture

COLLOQ. hooker, hustler, pro, hostess, fancy woman; *N Am* working girl

SLANG *poule de luxe*, quiff, rough trade, tart, tom, tramp, brass, floozie; *N Am* broad

OLD SLANG dell, mutton, dolly-mop, plover; (*Shakesp*) laced mutton

♦ *v*

cheapen, degrade, debase, demean, devalue, pervert, betray, sacrifice, misapply, misuse, profane

prostitution *n*

harlotry, whoredom, whoring, street-walking, vice, meretriciousness

OLD social evil

COLLOQ. the game, the oldest profession

Related adjective: meretricious

prostrate *adj, v*

♦ *adj*

1 FLAT, horizontal, prone, lying down, lying flat, fallen
2 OVERCOME, overwhelmed, devastated, crushed, paralysed, powerless, helpless, defenceless, laid low, brought to your knees, exhausted, worn out, tired out

COLLOQ. devastated, bushed, whacked, all-in, dead beat; *N Am* pooped (out), tuckered out

⊟ 1 erect **2** triumphant

♦ *v*

lay low, flatten, level, knock down, overcome, overwhelm, crush, overthrow, bring to your knees, tire, wear out, fatigue, exhaust, sap, drain, ruin

⊟ strengthen

■ **prostrate yourself**

bow down, kneel, kowtow, submit, grovel, cringe, abase yourself

prostration *n*

collapse, abasement, kneeling, kowtow, submission, depression, desolation, despair, despondency, dejection, grief, helplessness, weakness, weariness, exhaustion, paralysis, bow

FORMAL slough of despond, obeisance, genuflection

⊟ elation, exaltation, happiness, triumph

protagonist *n*

hero, heroine, lead, principal, leader, main/chief/leading character, leading figure/player, title role, prime mover, champion, advocate, supporter, banker, adherent, mainstay, standard-bearer, exponent, moving spirit

FORMAL proponent

⊟ critic, opponent

protean *adj*

ever-changing, changeable, versatile, inconstant, many-sided, variable, volatile, mercurial, multiform, mutable

TECHNICAL polymorphic, polymorphous, amoebic

⊟ stable, unchanging

protect v

safeguard, defend, guard, escort, cover, screen, shield, secure, watch over, look after, care for, take care of, support, shelter, harbour, keep, keep safe, conserve, preserve, save, ring-fence
E3 attack, neglect
See Synonym nuances panel at **defend**.

protection n

1 *protection of the environment*
care, custody, charge, guardianship, safekeeping, conservation, preservation, safety, security, safeguard, defence
2 BARRIER, buffer, bulwark, defence, guard, shield, armour, screen, cover, shelter, safeguard, refuge, security, insurance
E3 1 neglect, attack

protective adj

1 *protective clothing*
waterproof, fireproof, windproof, insulating, covering, shielding, defensive
2 POSSESSIVE, defensive, motherly, maternal, fatherly, paternal, watchful, vigilant, careful, wary, over-protective
E3 2 aggressive, threatening

protector n

1 DEFENDER, benefactor, advocate, guardian, patron, champion, counsel, bodyguard, minder, keeper, father-figure
OLD (*Shakesp*) guardant
FORMAL protectress, protectrix
2 GUARD, safeguard, shield, cushion, bolster, pad, buffer, buckler, screen
E3 1 attacker, threat

protégé, protégée n

pupil, student, ward, charge, dependant, disciple, follower, discovery
COLLOQ. blue-eyed boy
E3 guardian

protest v, n

♦ *v*
1 OBJECT, make/raise an objection to, speak out, take exception, complain, appeal, demonstrate, march, go on strike, down tools, sit in, work to rule, picket, oppose, disapprove, disagree, argue, reject, take issue
OLD abhor, obtest, reclaim
FORMAL remonstrate, demur
COLLOQ. gripe, whinge, kick up a fuss
2 *protest your innocence*
assert, maintain, contend, insist (on), profess, proclaim, announce, declare, affirm, testify
FORMAL attest, avow
E3 1 accept
♦ *n*
1 OBJECTION, disapproval, disagreement, opposition, outcry, scruple, dissent, complaint, exception, protestation, outcry, fuss, appeal, demonstration, mass meeting, march, boycott, strike, hunger strike, sit-in, work-in, industrial action, work-to-rule, riot, civil disobedience
FORMAL demurral, remonstration, remonstrance
COLLOQ. demo, squawk
2 ASSERTION, contention, declaration, affirmation, proclamation, announcement
FORMAL attestation, avowal
E3 1 acceptance

protestation n

1 STATEMENT, declaration, profession, affirmation, pledge, vow, assurance, oath
FORMAL asseveration, avowal, expostulation
2 OBJECTION, complaint, outcry, disagreement, protest, dissent
FORMAL remonstrance, remonstration

protester n

demonstrator, opposer, opponent, objector, complainer, agitator, striker, picket, rebel, mutineer, dissident, dissenter

protocol n

procedure, formalities, convention, custom, etiquette, manners, code of behaviour, civilities, good form
FORMAL propriety, decorum
COLLOQ. p's and q's

prototype n

original, model, mock-up, example, standard, type, pattern, precedent
FORMAL archetype, exemplar, paradigm

protract v

continue, draw out, extend, keep going, lengthen, prolong, make longer, spin out, stretch out, sustain
COLLOQ. drag out
E3 shorten

protracted adj

long, lengthy, prolonged, extended, drawn-out, long-drawn-out, stretched out, spun out, overlong, endless, interminable
E3 brief, shortened

protrude v

stick out, poke out, come through, bulge, jut out, project, extend, stand out, goggle, poke, pout, pop, beetle; *dialect* strout
OLD peer, strut
FORMAL protract, obtrude, extrude, exsert

protruding adj

jutting (out), prominent, protuberant, sticking out, proud
FORMAL exsertive, extrusive, extrusory, protrudent, protrusive
E3 flat, flush

protrusion n

lump, bulge, knob, bump, outgrowth, projection, protuberance, swelling, jut
FORMAL obtrusion, process

protuberance n

lump, bump, bulge, bulging-out, bulb, knob, outgrowth, swelling, prominence, protrusion, projection, tumour, wart, welt, tuber, tubercle, paunch, beer belly, ball; *dialect* wame
TECHNICAL apophysis
OLD wallet
FORMAL excrescence, process
COLLOQ. pot-belly

protuberant adj

swelling, swollen, jutting, prominent, popping, full, bulging, bulbous, protruding, proud, beetling, bunched, gibbous, bunched
OLD astrut
FORMAL protrusive, exsertive, extrusive, extrusory, protrudent, rotund
E3 flat

proud adj

1 CONCEITED, vain, egotistical, boastful, smug, complacent, arrogant, self-important, self-satisfied, cocky, presumptuous, haughty, full of yourself, scornful, high-handed, imperious, lordly, pompous, overweening, puffed up, overbearing, supercilious, snobbish; *dialect* proudful
OLD cockhorse, misproud, stout, sublime, superb, top-proud; (*Spenser*) brag
FORMAL hubristic
COLLOQ. high and mighty, snooty, toffee-nosed, stuck-up, jumped-up, too big for your boots, bigheaded
SLANG *N Am* dicty
2 SATISFIED, contented, gratified, pleased, delighted, happy, glad, content, thrilled, honoured

3 DIGNIFIED, noble, honourable, worthy, self-respecting, walking tall
4 *a proud moment*
satisfying, gratifying, pleasing, memorable, notable, splendid, marvellous, wonderful
COLLOQ. red-letter
5 *a proud sight*
splendid, grand, imposing, glorious, magnificent, outstanding, notable, honourable, worthy
6 *the surface stands proud*
projecting, jutting, prominent, protuberant, sticking out, jutting out
🗉 **1** humble, modest, unassuming **2** ashamed, abashed **3** deferential, ignoble

---

Synonym nuances
sense 1
Many of the synonyms, for example **conceited**, **bigheaded** and **vain**, are very disapproving in tone. **Egotistical** suggests a selfish concern for your own interests as well as a high opinion of yourself. **Boastful** is appropriate for bragging about your own perceived accomplishments, while both **smug** and **complacent** suggest a more internalized feeling of being very pleased with yourself, with the latter having further implications of blinkeredness: *a complacent belief in his own abilities lost him the match.*

  Arrogant and **cocky** can be used to suggest a visibly over-confident attitude, while **presumptuous**, although similar, further implies taking things for granted: *the way I have been treated by people has been patronizing and presumptuous.*

  Haughty and **supercilious** suggest someone has belief in their own superiority and acts with disdain, whereas **scornful** goes further and would describe someone who openly displays their contempt for others. Meanwhile **high-handed**, **lordly**, **imperious** and **overweening** are appropriate terms for someone who adopts a dominant role. **Pompous** and **puffed up**, although similar, have further implications of affectation, while **snobbish** tends to be reserved for someone's awareness of their own and others' social standing.

---

proudly *adv*
1 *she smiled proudly at her son*
with satisfaction, with delight, contentedly, delightedly, appreciatively
2 ARROGANTLY, vainly, boastfully, smugly, conceitedly, haughtily
COLLOQ. bigheadedly, snootily

provable *adj*
demonstrable, establishable, confirmable, verifiable, testable
FORMAL attestable, corroborable, evincible
🗉 unprovable

prove *v*
1 SHOW, demonstrate, verify, confirm, bear out, bear witness to, document, certify, authenticate, validate, justify, establish, determine, ascertain, try (out), test, check, examine, analyse
FORMAL attest, corroborate, substantiate
2 TURN OUT, come about, be the case
FORMAL transpire, eventuate
COLLOQ. pan out
🗉 **1** disprove, discredit, falsify

proven *adj*
proved, confirmed, certified, checked, established, accepted, dependable, reliable, tested, tried, definite, authentic, trustworthy, valid, verified, undoubted
FORMAL attested, corroborated
🗉 unproven

provenance *n*
source, origin, derivation, birthplace, spring
FORMAL provenience

provender *n*
food, provisions, foodstuffs, eats, supplies, stores, rations, sustenance, groceries, edibles, comestibles, fare, feed, fodder, forage
OLD aliment, pabulum; (*Spenser*) pasture; (*Shakesp*) repasture
FORMAL viands, victuals
COLLOQ. eatables, eats, tuck
SLANG grub, nosh, chow, scoff; *Aust & NZ* tucker

proverb *n*
saying, adage, aphorism, maxim, byword, motto, dictum, axiom, precept, saw, gnome
FORMAL apophthegm, paroemia

proverbial *adj*
axiomatic, accepted, conventional, traditional, customary, time-honoured, famous, famed, well-known, renowned, acknowledged, legendary, notorious, infamous, typical, archetypal

provide *v*
1 SUPPLY, furnish, stock, equip, outfit, kit out, prepare for, cater, serve, present, give, offer, contribute, yield, lend, add, bring, lay on, put on
FORMAL afford, impart
2 PLAN FOR, make plans for, allow, make provision, accommodate, arrange for, anticipate, take precautions, take measures/steps
3 STATE, specify, stipulate, lay down, require
🗉 **1** take, remove
▪ **provide for**
support, maintain, sustain, look after, take care of, keep, endow, fend
🗉 ignore, neglect

provided *conj*
given, as/so long as, on condition, on the understanding, presuming, assuming, in the event, with the proviso

providence *n*
1 FATE, destiny, divine intervention, God's will, fortune, luck
2 PRUDENCE, far-sightedness, foresight, forethought, judgement, wisdom, caution, care, thrift, economy
FORMAL sagacity, circumspection, judiciousness
🗉 **2** improvidence

provident *adj*
prudent, far-sighted, cautious, careful, thrifty, economical, frugal
FORMAL sagacious, circumspect, judicious
🗉 improvident

providential *adj*
fortunate, lucky, opportune, timely, happy, convenient, welcome, heaven-sent
FORMAL fortuitous
🗉 unfortunate, untimely

providentially *adv*
fortunately, luckily, coveniently, happily, opportunely
FORMAL fortuitously
🗉 unfortunately

provider *n*
supplier, supporter, sponsor, patron, benefactor, wage-earner, breadwinner, earner, giver, donor, funder, source, mainstay
COLLOQ. angel

providing *conj*
provided, given, as long as, on condition, on the understanding, presuming, assuming, in the event, with the proviso

province *n*
1 REGION, area, district, zone, county, shire, department,

territory, state, colony, dependency
2 *live out in the provinces*
backwater, backwoods
COLLOQ. middle of nowhere, the sticks, dorp; *N Am* the boondocks, the boonies
3 RESPONSIBILITY, concern, duty, office, business, role, function, charge, field, sphere, area, domain, department, line
COLLOQ. pigeon

provincial *adj, n*
⬩ *adj*
1 *a provincial theatre*
regional, local, rural, rustic, country, mofussil
OLD presidial
2 *provincial attitudes*
parochial, insular, inward-looking, limited, intolerant, narrow, narrow-minded, small-minded, naive, suburban, unsophisticated, home-grown, small-town, outlying, parish-pump
COLLOQ. hick
E₃ 1 national, metropolitan, capital, cosmopolitan, urban **2** sophisticated, urbane
⬩ *n*
country bumpkin, yokel, rustic, peasant
COLLOQ. hillbilly, hick, hayseed

provincialism *n*
parochialism, provinciality, regionalism, sectionalism, insularity, localism, narrow-mindedness
E₃ sophistication

provision *n*
1 SUPPLY, giving, equipping, furnishing, preparation, service, contribution, outfitting
2 FACILITIES, amenities, services, resourses
3 PLAN, arrangement, preparation, measure, step, allowance, contingency, concession, precaution
4 STIPULATION, specification, proviso, condition, term, requirement, clause, qualification, rider
5 FOOD, foodstuff, groceries, sustenance, rations, supplies, stocks, stores
OLD victuals, viands
COLLOQ. eatables

provisional *adj*
temporary, interim, transitional, stopgap, makeshift, conditional, tentative, pencilled in, subject to confirmation
COLLOQ. pro tem
E₃ permanent, fixed, definite, confirmed

provisionally *adv*
temporarily, tentatively, for the time being, interim, meanwhile
COLLOQ. pro tem

proviso *n*
condition, term, requirement, stipulation, qualification, reservation, restriction, limitation, provision, clause, rider
COLLOQ. strings

provocation *n*
1 ANNOYANCE, enraging, angering, irritation, exasperation, vexation, grievance, offence, insult, affront, injury, taunt, challenge, dare
COLLOQ. aggravation
2 CAUSE, grounds, justification, reason, motive, stimulus, stimulation, motivation, incitement, inducement, inspiration, eliciting, production, generation, instigation

provocative *adj*
1 ANNOYING, irritating, infuriating, exasperating, galling, outrageous, offensive, insulting, abusive
COLLOQ. aggravating
2 STIMULATING, exciting, challenging
3 EROTIC, titillating, arousing, sexy, sexually arousing, seductive, alluring, tempting, inviting, tantalizing, teasing, suggestive
E₃ 1 conciliatory

provocatively *adv*
1 ANNOYINGLY, infuriatingly, exasperatingly, offensively, outrageously
2 EROTICALLY, sexily, sexually, seductively, suggestively, temptingly, alluringly, invitingly

provoke *v*
1 ANNOY, irritate, rile, offend, insult, anger, enrage, infuriate, incense, madden, exasperate, tease, taunt, pique, vex, nettle, harass
FORMAL exacerbate
COLLOQ. aggravate, get at, bug, needle, hassle, miff, wind up, make someone's blood boil, get someone's back up, rattle someone's cage, ruffle someone's feathers, drive mad, drive crazy, drive up the wall, drive round the bend/ twist, make someone see red, make sparks fly, get under someone's skin, get under someone's nose, get on someone's wick, make someone's hackles rise
SLANG drive bananas, nark, piss off
OLD SLANG get someone's shirt out
2 GOAD, stir, spur, prod, move, prompt, stimulate, motivate, incite, rouse, inflame, kindle, instigate, entice
COLLOQ. egg on
SLANG *N Am* sound
3 CAUSE, occasion, give rise to, produce, generate, induce, elicit, evoke, call forth, engender, promote, excite, inspire, move
E₃ 1 please, pacify **3** result

provoking *adj*
annoying, exasperating, infuriating, irritating, offensive, maddening, obstructive, tiresome, vexatious, vexing, irking, irksome, galling
COLLOQ. aggravating
E₃ pleasing

prow *n*
bow(s), fore, stem, front, head, nose, forepart, cut-water
E₃ stern

prowess *n*
1 ACCOMPLISHMENT, attainment, ability, capability, aptitude, skill, skilfulness, expertise, facility, mastery, command, proficiency, talent, genius, dexterity, adeptness, adroitness, vassalage
2 BRAVERY, courage, dauntlessness, fearlessness, daring, heroism, gallantry, pluck, valour, audacity, intrepidity
COLLOQ. grit, nerve, guts, bottle, spunk

prowl *v*
creep, hunt, rove, roam, move stealthily, slink, sneak, stalk, lurk, skulk, steal, range, search, scavenge, cruise, patrol, nose, snoop, mouse; *dialect* ratch
OLD prole, proll, proul, lurch

prowler *n*
stalker, scavenger, patrol, roamer, nighthawk, tenebrio
OLD proler, proller, prouler

proximity *n*
closeness, nearness, vicinity, neighbourhood, adjacency, juxtaposition
FORMAL contiguity, propinquity
E₃ remoteness

proxy *n*
agent, deputy, stand-in, substitute, surrogate, representative, delegate, attorney, factor

prude *n*
prig, old maid, puritan, Mrs Grundy
COLLOQ. goody-goody, schoolmarm

prudence *n*
wisdom, judgement, good sense, common sense, care, foresight, forethought, far-sightedness, economy, heedfulness, preparedness, discretion, caution, cautiousness, vigilance, wariness, planning, providence,

precaution, policy, happy medium, canniness, frugality, saving, thrift, husbandry
FORMAL circumspectness, circumspection, judiciousness, sagacity, advisedness
⊟ imprudence, rashness, improvidence

> **Synonym nuances**
> Many of these synonyms are approving in tone; both **good sense** and **common sense** share suggestions of everyday practicality, while **care**, **heedfulness** and the more active **vigilance** have more to do with being aware of possible eventualities. Similarly, **foresight**, **forethought** and **far-sightedness** imply consideration of future possibilities, and **preparedness** and **precaution** further suggest being ready for them.
>   **Economy**, on the other hand, is more appropriate for careful management of resources: *she attempted to combine good living with economy*, and the less common **husbandry** would describe careful financial management. The terms **canniness**, **frugality** and **thrift** could also all be used of shrewdness in handling financial resources, although they may have slight but unpleasant connotations of meanness.
>   **Discretion** is more approving and implies due reserve in someone's conduct, while both **caution** and **cautiousness**, along with **wariness**, return to the general idea of exercising restraint, and do not suggest approval or disapproval.
>   **Providence** and **policy** are positive terms to convey the notion of skilful management or timely organization: *a scheme of forward planning and providence.*

prudent adj
wise, sensible, politic, shrewd, discerning, careful, well-advised, cautious, wary, vigilant, discreet, provident, far-sighted, frugal, economical, thrifty
OLD considerate, ware and wise
FORMAL judicious, circumspect, sagacious
⊟ imprudent, unwise, careless, rash, improvident

prudently adv
sensibly, wisely, carefully, shrewdly, discreetly, far-sightedly, warily, vigilantly, economically, providently
⊟ imprudently, rashly, unwisely, carelessly

prudery n
overmodesty, primness, squeamishness, starchiness, strictness, stuffiness, priggishness, prissiness, old-maidishness, puritanism, Grundyism
⊟ laxness

prudish adj
overmodest, overnice, proper, prim, narrow-minded, squeamish, demure, starchy, strait-laced, stuffy, puritanical, old-maidish, prissy, priggish, po-faced, ultra-virtuous, Victorian, mimsy
FORMAL pudibund
COLLOQ. goody-goody, schoolmarmish
⊟ lax, easy-going

prune v
clip, trim, snip, cut, cut back, cut off, dock, lop, pare, shape, reduce, shorten

prurient adj
salacious, lewd, dirty, obscene, indecent, lustful, desirous, itching, erotic, pornographic, lascivious, lecherous, voyeuristic
FORMAL concupiscent, cupidinous, libidinous
COLLOQ. smutty, blue
⊟ decent

pry v
meddle, interfere, intrude, peep, peer, nose, ferret, dig, delve
OLD prodnose; (*Spenser*) toot

COLLOQ. snoop, poke/stick your nose in, put your oar in
SLANG *N Am* gumshoe
⊟ mind your own business

prying adj
meddlesome, meddling, interfering, intrusive, nos(e)y, curious, inquisitive, spying, peering, peery
COLLOQ. snooping, snoopy
⊟ uninquisitive

psalm n
hymn, song, poem, prayer, chant, canticle, paean, paraphrase

pseud n
poser, poseur, trendy, fraud, humbug
COLLOQ. phoney

pseudo adj
false, sham, mock, pretended, imitation, fake, counterfeit, bogus, artificial, spurious, ersatz, quasi-, ungenuine
COLLOQ. phoney, pseud
⊟ genuine, real, authentic

pseudonym n
false name, assumed name, alias, incognito, pen-name, *nom de plume*, stage name
FORMAL allonym

psych v
■ **psych out**
intimidate, daunt, cow, overawe, domineer, appal, dismay, upset, unsettle, put off balance, alarm, scare, frighten, terrify, menace, tyrannize, terrorize, bully, browbeat, bulldoze, coerce, compel, pressure, pressurize, warn off
COLLOQ. throw, rattle, get to, lean on, twist someone's arm, put the screws on, put the frighteners on, turn the heat on

■ **psych yourself up**
prepare yourself mentally, get yourself prepared, work yourself up, gear yourself up, nerve yourself, steel yourself, brace yourself, pluck up courage

psyche n
spirit, soul, anima, mind, self, inner self, inmost self, innermost self, deepest feelings, heart of hearts, consciousness, personality, awareness, individuality, subconscious, intellect, intelligence, understanding
TECHNICAL pneuma

psychiatrist n
analyst, psychoanalyst, therapist, psychotherapist, psychologist, psychoanalyser
COLLOQ. headshrinker, shrink, trick cyclist, head doctor, man in a white coat

psychic adj, n
♦ adj
1 *psychic power*
spiritual, supernatural, occult, mystic(al), clairvoyant, extrasensory, telepathic, telekinetic
2 MENTAL, psychological, intellectual, emotional, cognitive, spiritual
♦ n
clairvoyant, fortune-teller, prophet, prophetess, visionary, seer, soothsayer, augur, oracle, diviner, telepath

psychological adj
mental, intellectual, cognitive, emotional, subjective, subconscious, unconscious, psychosomatic, irrational, unreal, imaginary, theoretical, conceptual
FORMAL cerebral
COLLOQ. all in the mind
⊟ physical, real

psychologically adv
mentally, emotionally, intellectually, cognitively, unconsciously, subjectively, theoretically, conceptually

Psychological conditions and disorders include:

abreaction	antisocial	bulimia	Munchausen	sociopathy
acatamathesia	personality	dementia	neurosis	Tourette's
addiction	disorder	depression	paranoia	syndrome
affective	Asperger's	dysmorphia	personality	
disorders	syndrome	Huntington's	disorder	
agnosia	autism	disease	phobias	
Alzheimer's	battle fatigue	hypochondria	postpartum	
anhedonia	bipolar disorder	kleptomania	depression	
anorexia nervosa	blindsight	manias		

and more... (antisocial personality disorder; post traumatic stress disorder; psychopathy; psychosexual dysfunctions; psychosis; schizophrenia; separation anxiety)

Forms of psychological therapy include:

art therapy	colour therapy	Gestalt therapy	psychodynamic therapy
aversion therapy	counselling	group therapy	psychotherapy
behavioural therapy	drama therapy	hypnotherapy	regression therapy
cognitive behaviour therapy	electroconvulsive (or	interpersonal therapy	
cognitive therapy	electroshock) therapy	person-centred therapy	

psychology n

1 *study psychology*
science of the mind, study of the mind, study of mental processes, science of human/animal behaviour
TECHNICAL metapsychology
See also panels on next page

2 *the psychology of crowds*
mind, mental characteristics, behavioural characteristics, mental chemistry, make-up, attitudes, habits, motives, mindset
TECHNICAL conation
COLLOQ. what makes someone tick

psychopath n
lunatic, mad person, madman, madwoman, maniac, sociopath, psychotic
COLLOQ. psycho

psychopathic adj
lunatic, mad, insane, maniacal, psychotic, deranged, unbalanced, mentally disturbed, demented

psychosomatic adj
psychological, irrational, subjective, unreal, imaginary
COLLOQ. all in the mind

psychotic adj
insane, lunatic, unbalanced, disturbed, deranged, maniacal, out of your mind, out of your senses, of unsound mind, unhinged, crazed, unstable, *non compos mentis*, frenzied, wild, berserk, manic, maniac, distracted, distraught, fey, frenetic, frantic, stone-crazy, queer; *Scot* gyte, red-mad
OLD frantic-mad, lymphatic, bestraught
COLLOQ. crazy, demented, nuts, nutty, nutty as a fruitcake, wacky, mad as a hatter, barmy, bonkers, batty, cracked, crackers, dippy, daffy, dotty, loopy, potty, off your nut, off your head, wrong in the head, out of your head, off the wall, out to lunch, round the bend, round the twist, bats, having bats in the belfry, cuckoo, off the rails, screwy, up the wall, raving, not all there; *N Am* buggy, flaky, fruity; *Aust & NZ* dingbats
SLANG loony, mental, bananas, barking, wacko, doolally, off your rocker, off your chump, off your trolley, out of your tree, needing your head examined, having lost your marbles, having a screw loose, having a tile loose, having several cards short of a full deck, with one sandwich short of a picnic, meshuga; *N Am* gonzo, loco, wiggy

pub n
public house, inn, tavern, wine bar, free house, bar, saloon, taproom, lounge, lounge bar, grill, brasserie, counter, table, brewpub, jerry-shop; *Scot* howf; *S Afr* canteen
COLLOQ. local, hostelry, watering-hole
SLANG boozer

puberty n
pubescence, adolescence, teens, teenage years, youth, young adulthood, growing up, maturity
F3 childhood, immaturity, old age

public adj, n
◆ adj
1 *public buildings*
state, government, national, nationalized, federal, official, civil, community, social, civic, collective, communal, common, general, popular, universal, open, available, accessible, unrestricted
2 KNOWN, well-known, famous, important, influential, respected, eminent, prominent, illustrious, celebrated, popular, widespread, recognized, acknowledged, plain, overt, obvious, open, exposed, published
F3 **1** private, privatized, personal **2** secret, exclusive
◆ n
people, nation, country, population, populace, masses, citizens, society, everyone, community, voters, electorate, multitude, crowd, followers, supporters, fans, audience, spectators, patrons, clientèle, customers, buyers, consumers
■ **in public**
publicly, openly, in the open, in full view, for all to see
F3 in secret
■ **public house**
bar, saloon, inn, tavern, taproom, lounge, lounge bar, grill, brasserie, counter, table; *Scot* howf
COLLOQ. pub, local, hostelry, watering-hole
SLANG boozer

publican n
landlord, landlady, barman, barmaid, barperson, hotelier, hotel-keeper, innkeeper, taverner, licensed victualler, tapster, host, mine host; *N Am* saloon-keeper

publication n
1 *the publication of a book*
publishing, production, printing, distribution, circulation, release, issue
2 BOOK, volume, title, paperback, hardback, newspaper, magazine, fanzine, journal, periodical, newsletter, weekly, monthly, daily, quarterly, booklet, leaflet, pamphlet, brochure, handbill
3 ANNOUNCEMENT, declaration, notification, reporting, proclamation, disclosure, broadcasting

publicity n
advertising, promotion, marketing, puff, propaganda, build-up, boost, attention, limelight, splash, air, notoriety, réclame
COLLOQ. plug, hype

publicize v
advertise, promote, market, spotlight, broadcast, make

Branches of psychology include:

abnormal psychology	criminal psychology	evolutionary psychology	industrial and organizational psychology	psychobiology psychogeriatrics psycholinguistics psychometrics psychopathology psychopharmacology psychophysiology social psychology	sport psychology structural psychology transpersonal psychology
behaviour analysis	depth psychology	experimental psychology	narrative psychology		
biospsychology	developmental psychology	forensic psychology	neuropsychology		
child psychology	educational psychology	health psychology	occupational psychology		
clinical psychology	environmental psychology	hedonics	parapsychology		
cognitive psychology			psychoanalysis		

Terms used in psychology include:

affect	conditioning	externalization	mechanism	projection	superego
anal stage	configuration	extrovert	metacognition	psychosexual	superiority complex
anima/animus	consciousness	fixation	Oedipus complex	psychosomatic	symbol
anxiety	cue	horme	over-compensation	puerilism	transference
body image	death wish	id	paragnosis	reality principle	unconscious
bonding	delusion	identification	passive-aggressive	regression	wish fulfilment
catharsis	denial	illusion	penis envy	repression	word salad
cathexis	displacement	image	perception	role reversal	Zener cards
chunking	dissociation	imago	Phaedra complex	Rorschach test	
co-dependency	ego	inferiority complex	phallic	schema	
cognitive map	ego ideal	introvert	preconscious	self	
collective unconscious	Electra complex	libido	primal therapy	Stockholm syndrome	
complex	escape mechanism	limen		subconscious	

Theories of psychology include:

Adlerian	connectionism	humanistic theory	psychoanalytic theory
associationism	environmentalism	Jamesian	Skinnerian
atomism	Freudian	Jungian	structural theory (or structuralism)
attachment theory	functional theory (or functionalism)	Lacanian	
behavioural theory	Gestalt theory	Pavlovian	
cognitive theory		personality theory	

known, announce, make public, bring to the public's attention, blaze
FORMAL disseminate, promulgate
COLLOQ. plug, hype, push

public-spirited *adj*
community-minded, humanitarian, philanthropic, altruistic, charitable, unselfish, generous, conscientious
E3 selfish

publish *v*
1 *publish a book*
produce, print, issue, bring out, release, distribute, circulate, gazette, paperback, paragraph, spread, diffuse
FORMAL disseminate, promulgate
COLLOQ. pirate
2 ANNOUNCE, declare, communicate, broadcast, report, notify, make known, carry, run, serialize, syndicate, put about, make public, proclaim, celebrate, diffuse, import, divulge, disclose, reveal, sound, release, publicize, advertise, notice, poster, placard
OLD evulgate, delate, vent
FORMAL give forth, set forth, fulminate

pucker *v, n*
♦ *v*
gather, ruffle, wrinkle, pleat, ruckle, ruck, shrivel, crinkle, crumple, crease, furrow, purse, screw up, contract, compress
♦ *n*
crinkle, crumple, fold, crease, ruck, wrinkle, ruckle, shirr

puckered *adj*
creased, gathered, rucked, ruckled, wrinkled, pursy
E3 smooth

puckish *adj*
impish, mischievous, naughty, playful, roguish, sly,

waggish, whimsical, teasing, frolicsome, sportive
E3 serious, solemn

pudding *n*
dessert, sweet, tart, pie, pastry
COLLOQ. afters, pud
See panel at **dessert**.

puddle *n*
pool, sop, plash, slop, plashet; *dialect* dub, pant, soss, sump
OLD flush; (*Spenser*) plesh

puerile *adj*
childish, babyish, infantile, juvenile, immature, adolescent, irresponsible, silly, foolish, inane, trivial
E3 mature

puff *n, v*
♦ *n*
1 BREATH, waft, whiff, draught, flurry, gust, blast, waff, waif; *Scot* fuff, pluff
OLD huff, whift
FORMAL flatus
2 *a puff on a cigarette*
pull, drag
SLANG *N Am* toke
3 ADVERTISEMENT, publicity, promotion, marketing, commendation
COLLOQ. plug, push
♦ *v*
1 BREATHE, pant, gasp, gulp, wheeze, blow, waft, whiff, inflate, expand, swell; *Scot* flaff, fuff, pluff, skiff
OLD huff
2 *puff a cigarette*
smoke, pull, drag, draw, suck
3 ADVERTISE, praise, publicize, promote, market, commend
COLLOQ. plug, push

■ **puff out**
bulge, balloon, swell, hump, expand, enlarge, bulb, project, protrude, bag, belly, billow, bloat, blouse, heave
OLD bepuff
FORMAL dilate, distend
COLLOQ. sag

puffed *adj*
out of breath, breathless, panting, winded, exhausted, gasping
COLLOQ. done in

■ **puffed up**
arrogant, proud, swollen-headed, self-important, full of yourself, prideful
COLLOQ. bigheaded, high and mighty, too big for your boots
E∃ modest

puffy *adj*
puffed up, inflated, swollen, bloated, enlarged
TECHNICAL oedematous
FORMAL distended, dilated

pugilism *n*
boxing, fighting, prize-fighting, the noble art, the noble science, the ring, the prize-ring
COLLOQ. the fancy, fistiana

pugilist *n*
boxer, fighter, prize-fighter
COLLOQ. bruiser

pugnacious *adj*
hostile, aggressive, belligerent, contentious, combative, antagonistic, argumentative, quarrelsome, bad-tempered, hot-tempered
FORMAL disputatious, bellicose
E∃ peaceable

puke *v, n*
◆ *v*
vomit, retch, regurgitate, bring up, disgorge, heave, cat; *dialect* boke
OLD egurgitate, parbreak
COLLOQ. spew, throw up, sick up, chuck up, fetch up
SLANG honk; *N Am* barf, upchuck; *Aust* chunder
◆ *n*
vomit, sick, spew, retch(ing); *dialect* boke
TECHNICAL emesis
OLD parbreak
COLLOQ. spew
SLANG technicolour yawn

pull *v, n*
◆ *v*
1 TOW, drag, haul, trail, heave, draw, tug, jerk
COLLOQ. yank
2 REMOVE, take out, draw out, extract, root out, pull out, pluck, uproot, pull up, rip, tear, wrench
3 ATTRACT, draw, bring in, pull in, lure, allure, charm, entice, tempt, magnetize
4 DISLOCATE, sprain, wrench, strain, turn, damage, tear
E∃ 1 push, press 3 repel, deter, discourage
◆ *n*
1 TOW, drag, tug, haul, jerk, power, forcefulness, exertion
COLLOQ. yank
2 ATTRACTION, lure, allurement, draw, drawing power, magnetism, influence, weight, sway
COLLOQ. clout, muscle

■ **pull apart**
1 SEPARATE, part, dismember, demolish, dismantle, take to pieces, tear apart
2 CRITICIZE, take apart, run down, slate, attack
COLLOQ. slam, pan, tear to shreds, pick holes in, pull to pieces, do a hatchet job on
E∃ 1 join

■ **pull back**
draw back, withdraw, retreat, fall back, retire, disengage, back out

■ **pull down**
destroy, demolish, knock down, dismantle, bulldoze, raze to the ground
E∃ build, erect, put up

■ **pull in**
1 STOP, arrive, draw in, pull up, halt, park
2 ATTRACT, draw, bring in, lure, allure, entice
3 ARREST, capture, seize, apprehend, detain, take into custody
COLLOQ. bust, nick, collar, nab, book, run in
4 EARN, receive, be paid, make, clear, collect, bring in, take home
COLLOQ. rake in
E∃ 1 pull away 2 repel 3 lose

■ **pull off**
1 ACCOMPLISH, achieve, bring off, succeed, manage, fulfil, carry off, carry out
2 DETACH, remove, separate, take off, tear off, rip off
E∃ 1 fail 2 attach

■ **pull out**
retreat, withdraw, leave, depart, quit, move out, back out, evacuate, desert, abandon
E∃ join, arrive

■ **pull through**
recover, come through, improve, get better, get well again, rally, recuperate, survive, weather

■ **pull together**
co-operate, work together, collaborate, team up
E∃ fight

■ **pull up**
1 STOP, halt, come to a halt, park, draw up, pull in, pull over, brake
2 REPRIMAND, take to task, rebuke, scold, criticize, reprove, chide, lecture, censure, blame
FORMAL admonish, berate, castigate
COLLOQ. tell off, tick off, carpet, give someone a ticking-off, give someone a dressing-down, haul over the coals, read the riot act, rap over the knuckles, give someone a rap over the knuckles, give someone a flea in their ear

■ **pull yourself together**
control yourself, regain your self-control, get a grip on yourself
COLLOQ. get your act together, get yourself together, snap out of it, buck up your ideas

---

Synonym nuances
verb sense 1
Tow is usually reserved for an act of assistance, often aided by the attachment of a rope, while **drag** may suggest reluctance or resistance from the object: *she dragged him round the shops.* **Haul** and **heave** suggest exertion on the part of the subject: *I hauled my luggage to the nearest hotel,* whereas **trail** has connotations of weariness or inertia: *he stumbled along, trailing his bag behind him.*
   If you want to suggest short and sudden movements, the terms **tug** and **jerk** would be appropriate: *she tugged at the zip,* while **draw** suggests a more gradual, deliberate action: *he pushed the notebook aside and drew the typewriter to him.*

---

pullover *n*
jersey, sweater, jumper, sweatshirt, top, woolly

pulp *n, v*
◆ *n*
1 *crushed to a pulp*
paste, purée, cream, mash, mush, pap, flesh, pith, must, pomace
TECHNICAL chyme, furnish

OLD marrow
FORMAL triturate
2 SENTIMENTALITY, tenderness, sentimentalism, emotionalism, romanticism, mawkishness, nostalgia
FORMAL bathos
COLLOQ. corniness, gush, mush, schmaltz, sloppiness, slush, gloop
• v
crush, squash, pulverize, mash, purée, liquidize, shred, beat, pound

pulpit *n*
platform, rostrum, stand, lectern, dais, podium
COLLOQ. soapbox

pulpy *adj*
soft, sloppy, pappy, mushy, crushed, squashy, fleshy, succulent
Ea hard

pulsate *v*
pulse, beat, throb, pound, hammer, drum, thud, thump, vibrate, oscillate, quiver, palpitate

pulsating *adj*
vibrating, oscillating, pulsing, palpitating
FORMAL pulsatile, pulsative, pulsatory, vibrative, vibratile

pulsation *n*
vibration, oscillation, palpitation, vibratiuncle
TECHNICAL ictus

pulse¹ *n, v*
• *n*
felt his pulse
beat, stroke, rhythm, throb, pulsation, beating, throbbing, thud, thudding, thump, thumping, pounding, drumming, vibration, oscillation, flutter
TECHNICAL sphygmus
• *v*
beat, drum, pulsate, vibrate, pound, thud, throb, tick, flutter

pulse² *n*
beans and pulses
bean, legume, gram, dal
TECHNICAL calavance, caravance
Related adjective: leguminous
See panel at **bean**.

pulverize *v*
1 CRUSH, pound, grind, mill, powder, crumble, pulp, squash
FORMAL triturate
2 DEFEAT, destroy, demolish, annihilate, smash
FORMAL vanquish
COLLOQ. thrash, hammer, wipe the floor with

pummel *v*
hit, knock, hammer, beat, batter, pound, punch, strike, thump, bang

pump *v*
1 PUSH, drive, force, send, inject, siphon, draw, drain, jet, surge, spurt, spout, gush
2 CROSS-EXAMINE, cross-question, interrogate, quiz
COLLOQ. grill, give someone the third degree, put the screws on
■ **pump out**
bail out, drain, draw off, empty, force out, siphon
■ **pump up**
blow up, inflate, puff up, fill

pun *n*
play on words, *double entendre*, double meaning, witticism, quip
TECHNICAL paronomasia

punch¹ *v, n*
• *v*
hit, strike, pummel, jab, bash, knock, clout, cuff, box, slug, thump, thwack, wind, black, fib, counter-punch
COLLOQ. sock, wallop, bop, biff, plug; *N Am* boff, bust, sucker-punch; *Aust* job
• *n*
1 BLOW, jab, bash, knock, hit, clout, thump, thwack, plug, bolo punch, roundhouse, *coup de poing*; *dialect* pounce
COLLOQ. sock, wallop, bop, biff, whammy; *N Am* boff, bust, sucker-punch
OLD SLANG fourpenny one
2 FORCE, strength, power, energy, impact, effectiveness, drive, vigour, forcefulness, verve, panache, zap
COLLOQ. bite, pizzazz, stingo

punch² *v*
punch a hole
perforate, pierce, puncture, make a hole in, prick, bore, drill, hole, stamp, cut, clip, check, keypunch

punch-drunk *adj*
dazed, confused, befuddled, stupefied, unsteady, reeling, staggering, dizzy, groggy, woozy

punch-up *n*
stand-up fight, brawl, fight, row, scuffle, fracas, free-for-all, argument, ruckus
COLLOQ. scrap, set-to, ding-dong, dust-up, shindy

punchy *adj*
incisive, effective, forceful, aggressive, dynamic, lively, powerful, strong, spirited, vigorous
COLLOQ. zappy
Ea feeble, weak

punctilio *n*
1 SCRUPULOUSNESS, strictness, exactness, ceremony, finickiness, formality, convention, punctiliousness, precision, meticulousness, refinement, preciseness
2 FINE POINT, detail, nicety, particular, exactitude, delicacy, distinction, particularity
Ea **1** informality

punctilious *adj*
scrupulous, conscientious, meticulous, careful, exact, precise, strict, formal, proper, particular, finicky, fussy
COLLOQ. pernickety, choosy, picky, nit-picking; *N Am* persnickety
Ea lax, informal

punctiliously *adv*
conscientiously, meticulously, scrupulously, carefully, exactly, precisely

punctual *adj*
prompt, on time, exact, precise, well-timed, early, in good time
COLLOQ. on the dot, dead on time, bang on time, on cue
Ea unpunctual, late

punctuality *n*
promptness, promptitude, regularity, readiness, strictness
Ea unpunctuality

punctually *adv*
on time, prompt, promptly, precisely, exactly, sharp, to the minute
COLLOQ. dead on, bang on, spot-on, on the dot, on the button, on the stroke (of), up to time
Ea unpunctually, late

punctuate *v*
interrupt, sprinkle, break (up), intersperse, pepper, emphasize, point, accentuate
FORMAL interject

punctuation

Punctuation marks include:

apostrophe	exclamation mark	quotation marks
asterisk	full stop	*colloq.* quotes
backslash	hyphen	semicolon
brackets	inverted commas	solidus
colon	oblique stroke	speech marks
comma	parentheses	square brackets
dash	period	star
ellipsis	question mark	

---

puncture *n, v*

♦ *n*

1 FLAT TYRE, blow-out

COLLOQ. flat

2 LEAK, hole, holing, piercing, perforation, cut, rupture, prick, nick, slit

♦ *v*

1 PRICK, pierce, penetrate, perforate, hole, make a hole in, bore, spike, cut, nick, burst, rupture

2 DEFLATE, flatten, let down, humiliate

COLLOQ. put down

pundit *n*

authority, expert, master, teacher, adviser, maestro, guru, sage, savant

COLLOQ. buff

pungency *n*

1 *the pungency of the herbs*

spiciness, strong flavour, tang, pepperiness, sharpness, bite

2 *writing that lacks pungency*

incisiveness, sharpness, power, strength, bite, causticity, sarcasm

FORMAL trenchancy, mordancy

COLLOQ. oomph, kick, pizzazz

F₃ 1 mildness, blandness, tastelessness **2** blandness

pungent *adj*

1 *a pungent taste/smell*

strong, powerful, hot, peppery, fiery, spicy, aromatic, tangy, tart, piquant, sharp, keen, acute, sour, bitter, acid, acrid, caustic, stinging, burning, biting

2 *pungent comments*

cutting, incisive, pointed, piercing, penetrating, sarcastic, scathing, caustic, stinging, burning, biting

FORMAL trenchant, mordant

F₃ 1 mild, bland, tasteless **2** bland

punish *v*

1 PENALIZE, discipline, correct, scold, beat, make someone pay, smack, slap, flog, whip, scourge, lash, cane, spank, knee-cap, crucify, hang, fine, imprison, strafe, make an example of, fine, log, gate, bring to justice, pay out, serve out, scour, trounce; *Scot* give it laldie

OLD justify, shend, visit, wreak

FORMAL chastise, chasten, castigate, amerce

COLLOQ. teach someone a lesson, make an example of, bring to book, throw the book at, come down (heavily) on, give someone stick, ground, sort, give someone hell

2 BEAT, defeat, trounce, batter

COLLOQ. hammer, thrash, rough up

3 MISUSE, maltreat, harm, damage, abuse

F₃ 1 reward

Synonym nuances

sense 1

Penalize suggests imposing a penalty on someone for their misdeeds or mistakes: *councils spending too much are penalized by a reduction in grants*, unlike **discipline**, which is more suggestive of training for the prevention of undesirable behaviour: *it's up to the parents to discipline their children*. **Correct** suggests showing someone the

---

error of their ways as well as punishing them: *can criminals be corrected by prison sentences?*

 Crucify used literally refers to a form of capital punishment, but used figuratively it is an emotive term for subjecting someone to extremely humiliating or severe treatment: *his infidelities crucified his wife*. The rarely used **pay out** and **serve out** suggest retaliation and revenge, and while **scour** and **trounce** also suggest punishing severely, they do not have such strong implications of avenging a previous misdeed.

---

punishable *adj*

criminal, convictable, chargeable, unlawful, illegal, blameworthy

FORMAL culpable, indictable

punishing *adj*

arduous, strenuous, crippling, crushing, burdensome, taxing, grinding, demanding, hard, harsh, severe, cruel, gruelling, fatiguing, tiring, wearying, exhausting, backbreaking

F₃ easy

punishment *n*

1 *corporal punishment*

discipline, correction, chastisement, penalty, sentence, deserts, retribution, revenge

COLLOQ. short sharp shock

Related adjective: penal

2 *punishment from the wind*

damage, harm, injury, ill-use, maltreatment, rough handling, force, turbulence, storminess, ferocity

F₃ 1 reward

See panel on next page

punitive *adj*

1 PENAL, disciplinary, retributive, retaliatory, vindictive

FORMAL chastising, castigatory

2 CRIPPLING, crushing, burdensome, demanding, hard, harsh, severe, cruel, gruelling, stiff, punishing, corrective

punter *n*

1 GAMBLER, better, backer, wagerer

2 CUSTOMER, client, consumer, person, individual, fellow, chap

COLLOQ. guy, bloke

puny *adj*

weak, feeble, frail, sickly, undeveloped, underdeveloped, stunted, small, undersized, diminutive, little, tiny, insignificant, minor, inconsequential, trifling, petty, trivial

COLLOQ. measly, piddling

F₃ strong, sturdy, large, important

pupil *n*

student, scholar, schoolboy, schoolgirl, learner, apprentice, beginner, novice, disciple, protégé(e), class-fellow, classmate, monitor, prefect, boarder, day-boarder, parlour-boarder, gymnasiast, bluecoat, grey-coat, alumnus, old boy/girl, pupil teacher, abiturient; *Scot* academical; *Scot & NZ* bursar; *N Am* kindergartener

TECHNICAL ashrama

COLLOQ. prep; *N Am* preppy; *Aust* schoolie; St Trinian

Related adjective: pupillary

F₃ teacher

puppet *n*

1 MARIONETTE, finger puppet, glove puppet, hand puppet, doll, rod puppet, Guignol, *fantoccino, fantoccio; dialect* puppy

OLD poppet, Jack of Lent; (*Shakesp*) mammet, motion, motion generative

2 *a mere puppet of a government*

pawn, tool, instrument, dupe, cat's-paw, pawn, quisling, stooge, gull, figurehead, mouthpiece, creature, dependant

Forms of punishment include:

banishment	confiscation	exile	incarceration	probation	spanking
beating	corporal	expulsion	internment	the rack	the stocks
belting	punishment	fine	jail	rap across the	strappado
the birch	decimation	flaying	jankers	knuckles	suspension
borstal	defrocking	flogging	keelhauling	scourging	tarring and
breaking upon the	demotion	gaol	knee-capping	sending to	feathering
wheel	deportation	gating	*colloq*. larruping	Coventry	thrashing
the cane	detention	grounding	lashing	sequestration	torturing
capital	dressing-down	hiding	leathering	slapping	transportation
punishment	exclusion	hitting	lines	the slipper	unfrocking
cashiering	excommunica-	horsewhipping	masteheading	smacking	walking the plank
chain gang	tion	house arrest	penal colony	solitary	whipping
confinement	execution	imprisonment	prison	confinement	

See also **execution**.

---

puppy *n*
pup, young dog, whelp

purchase *v, n*
♦ *v*
buy, pay for, invest in, acquire, obtain, get, pick up, shop for, go shopping, secure, gain, earn, win
FORMAL procure
COLLOQ. snap up, splash out on
E₃ sell
♦ *n*
1 ACQUISITION, gain, buy, bargain, deal, investment, asset(s), possession(s), property, goods, holdings
FORMAL emption
2 GRASP, foothold, grip, hold, advantage, leverage
E₃ 1 sale

purchaser *n*
buyer, consumer, shopper, customer, client, hirer, patron
FORMAL vendee, emptor
E₃ seller; *formal* vendor

pure *adj*
1 *pure gold*
unadulterated, unalloyed, unmixed, undiluted, 100%, flawless, perfect, neat, straight, solid, simple, natural, real, authentic, genuine, true
2 STERILE, uncontaminated, unpolluted, uninfected, germ-free, aseptic, antiseptic, disinfected, sterilized, hygienic, sanitary, clean, immaculate, spotless, clear, fresh, natural
3 SHEER, utter, complete, total, thorough, absolute, perfect, unqualified, unmitigated, downright
4 CHASTE, virgin, virginal, virtuous, undefiled, unsullied, moral, unblemished, upright, virtuous, honourable, honest, good, righteous, decent, noble, worthy, blameless, innocent
5 *pure mathematics*
theoretical, abstract, conjectural, speculative, academic
E₃ 1 impure, adulterated **2** contaminated, polluted **4** immoral, corrupt, defiled **5** applied, practical

pure-bred *adj*
pedigree, pedigreed, pure-blood, pure-blooded, thoroughbred, full-blooded, blooded
E₃ cross-bred, hybrid, mixed, mongrel

purely *adv*
1 UTTERLY, completely, totally, entirely, wholly, thoroughly, absolutely
2 ONLY, simply, merely, just, solely, exclusively

purgative *n, adj*
♦ *n*
laxative, enema, evacuant, purge
TECHNICAL emetic, aperient, cathartic, eccoprotic
FORMAL depurative
♦ *adj*
cleansing, laxative, purging, evacuant
TECHNICAL aperient, cathartic, cathartical, eccoprotic
FORMAL abstersive, depurative

purgatory *n*
torment, torture, hell, agony, ordeal, anguish, misery, wretchedness, hopelessness

purge *v, n*
♦ *v*
1 PURIFY, cleanse, clean out, scour, clear (out), expurgate, absolve; *dialect* work
TECHNICAL absterge, soil
FORMAL catharize
2 OUST, remove, get rid of, rid, eject, expel, depose, root out, clear (out), dismiss, eradicate, exterminate, wipe out, kill
♦ *n*
removal, ejection, expulsion, witch hunt, eradication, rooting-out, extermination, cleansing, disposal, ousting

purification *n*
1 DECONTAMINATION, refinement, cleaning, cleansing, disinfection, filtration, sanitization, fumigation, deodorization, desalination
TECHNICAL sublimation, elution, reverse osmosis
FORMAL depuration, epuration
2 SANCTIFICATION, redemption, absolution, purge, cleansing
FORMAL lustration, purgation, catharsis
E₃ 1 contamination, defilement, pollution

purify *v*
1 DECONTAMINATE, refine, filter, distil, clarify, clean, cleanse, sanitize, freshen, disinfect, sterilize, fumigate, deodorize, filtrate, fine, expurgate
TECHNICAL clay, defecate, rectify, retort, scrub, sublime
OLD chastise, chasten, mundify, try
FORMAL depurate, epurate, furbish
2 SANCTIFY, redeem, absolve, purge, cleanse, shrive
FORMAL catharsize, lustrate
E₃ 1 contaminate, pollute, defile

purifying *adj*
cleansing, purificatory, refining, purging, purgative
TECHNICAL cathartic
FORMAL depurative, lustral, mundificative
E₃ contaminating, defiling, polluting

purism *n*
fastidiousness, formalism, fussiness, over-precision, pedantry, restraint, strictness, orthodoxy, austerity, classicism, Atticism
E₃ liberality, open-mindedness, tolerance

purist *n, adj*
♦ *n*
pedant, literalist, formalist, precisionist, dogmatist, stickler, quibbler
COLLOQ. nit-picker
♦ *adj*
fastidious, over-exact, over-fastidious, over-meticulous, over-particular, over-precise, pedantic, quibbling,

uncompromising, strict, captious, finicky, fussy, hypercritical, puristic
COLLOQ. nit-picking
F∃ liberal, open-minded, tolerant

puritan n
pietist, rigorist, disciplinarian, zealot, fanatic, moralist, killjoy, spoilsport, prude
COLLOQ. goody-goody
F∃ hedonist, libertarian

puritanical adj
puritan, moralistic, disciplinarian, ascetic, abstemious, austere, severe, stern, strict, strait-laced, prim, proper, prudish, disapproving, stuffy, stiff, rigid, narrow-minded, bigoted, fanatical, zealous
COLLOQ. goody-goody
F∃ hedonistic, liberal, indulgent, broad-minded

puritanism n
rigorousness, self-discipline, self-denial, strictness, uncompromisingness, austerity, propriety, sternness, severity, stiffness, rigidity, zealotry, fanaticism, bigotry, narrow-mindedness, narrowness, priggishness, primness, prudishness, abstemiousness, abstinence, asceticism
F∃ broad-mindedness, hedonism, indulgence, liberality

purity n
1 CLEARNESS, clarity, cleanness, cleanliness, pureness, freshness, untaintedness, flawlessness, wholesomeness
TECHNICAL chiarezza, orient
OLD pure
2 SIMPLICITY, authenticity, genuineness, truth, perfection
3 CHASTITY, virginity, decency, morality, integrity, rectitude, uprightness, goodness, virtue, virtuousness, honour, honesty, decency, nobility, worthiness, innocence, blamelessness, sanctity
OLD candour
F∃ 1 impurity, pollution, contamination **3** immorality

purlieus n
neighbourhood, surroundings, vicinity, suburbs, environs, precincts, periphery, borders, bounds, confines, limits, fringes, perimeter, outskirts

purloin v
steal, rob, remove, take, pilfer, make away with, run off with
FORMAL appropriate
COLLOQ. swipe, nick, pinch, filch, finger, lift, nobble, pocket, snaffle, snitch, thieve, bag, whip; *Aust & NZ* souvenir
SLANG rip off

purport v, n
♦ v
claim, allege, profess, seem, pose as, pretend, imply, proclaim, show, mean, intend, indicate, denote, signify, suggest, express, convey, declare, assert, maintain
FORMAL import, portend, betoken
♦ n
meaning, significance, point, gist, drift, idea, spirit, substance, theme, tendency, tenor, thrust, bearing, direction, implication
FORMAL import

purportedly adv
allegedly, supposedly, apparently, reportedly, by all accounts, doubtfully, dubiously
FORMAL ostensibly, putatively

purpose n, v
♦ n
1 INTENTION, aim, objective, end, goal, target, plan, design, vision, idea, ambition, hope, wish, desire, aspiration, point, object, function, reason, motive, motivation, rationale, justification, principle, result, outcome, basis
2 DETERMINATION, resolve, resolution, drive, single-

mindedness, firmness, dedication, devotion, constancy, backbone, steadfastness, perseverance, persistence, doggedness, tenacity, zeal
3 USE, function, application, good, advantage, benefit, gain, effect, value, usefulness
♦ v
intend, mean, plan, propose, resolve, decide, determine, settle, design, aspire, aim, desire, contemplate, meditate
■ **on purpose**
deliberately, intentionally, consciously, knowingly, wittingly, wilfully, purposely, by design, premeditatedly
F∃ accidentally, impulsively, spontaneously

purposeful adj
determined, decided, purposed, resolved, resolute, single-minded, constant, steadfast, persistent, persevering, unwavering, unfaltering, tenacious, dogged, strong-willed, positive, firm, deliberate
F∃ purposeless, aimless

purposefully adv
resolutely, steadfastly, single-mindedly, persistently, perseveringly, unwaveringly, unfalteringly, tenaciously

🛈 purposefully or **purposely**?
Purposefully means 'obviously, or apparently, having some purpose': *She stole purposefully towards him, clearly intent on settling things once and for all.* Purposely means 'intentionally, on purpose': *She didn't want to go to college so she purposely failed her exams.*

purposeless adj
pointless, senseless, aimless, objectless, empty, unmeaning, goalless, thoughtless, gratuitous, unasked-for, uncalled-for, unnecessary, useless, needless, motiveless, nonsensical, vain, wanton, vacuous
OLD (*Shakesp*) shapeless
F∃ purposeful

purposely adv
on purpose, intentionally, deliberately, consciously, calculatedly, by design, specifically, wilfully, knowingly, premeditatedly, designedly, expressly, with malice aforethought
F∃ unintentionally, by accident, impulsively, spontaneously

🛈 purposely or **purposefully**?
See panel at **purposefully**.

purse n, v
♦ n
1 MONEY-BAG, wallet, pouch, burse, *porte-monnaie*; *Scot & Irish* spleuchan; *N Am* pocketbook
OLD (*Spenser*) crumenal
OLD SLANG bung
2 MONEY, means, resources, finances, funds, coffers, treasury, exchequer
OLD fisc
3 REWARD, award, prize, present, gift
♦ v
pucker, wrinkle, draw together, press together, close, tighten, contract, compress, prim

pursuance n
discharge, pursuit, pursuing, performance, fulfilment, following, accomplishment, achievement, completion
FORMAL effecting, effectuation, execution, prosecution

pursue v
1 CHASE, go after, run after, follow, give chase, make after, run after, track, stalk, trail, shadow, tail, dog, harass, harry, hound, hunt, seek, search for, investigate, inquire into
OLD persue, poursew, pursew, prosecute, sue
2 *pursue an activity*

perform, engage in, practise, conduct, follow, carry on, continue, keep on, keep up, maintain, persevere in, persist in, apply yourself to, hold to, whore after
3 STRIVE FOR, aspire to, aim for, seek, search for, try for, work towards, have your goal

pursuit *n*
1 CHASE, hue and cry, tracking, pursuing, stalking, trail, tailing, shadowing, hunt
OLD poursuit
2 SEARCH, quest, aim, aspiration, goal, investigation, following, continuance, persistence, perseverance
3 ACTIVITY, interest, hobby, pastime, occupation, trade, craft, line, speciality, vocation

purvey *v*
1 SUPPLY, cater, deal in, provide, furnish, stock, sell, retail, trade in
FORMAL provision, victual
2 TRANSMIT, spread, communicate, publicize, publish, put about, pass on
FORMAL propagate, disseminate

purveyor *n*
1 SUPPLIER, stockist, trader, dealer, seller, provider, provisor, retailer
FORMAL victualler, vendor
2 TRANSMITTER, communicator
FORMAL disseminator, propagator

pus *n*
discharge
TECHNICAL matter, diapyesis, seropus
OLD quitter
FORMAL suppuration
Related adjective: purulent

push *v, n*
♦ *v*
1 PROPEL, thrust, ram, shove, jostle, hustle, manhandle, butt, jolt, elbow, prod, nudge, poke, press, depress, squeeze, plunge, squash, cram, drive, force, constrain
2 PRESS (FOR), encourage, urge, incite, impel, spur, prod, goad, force, influence, persuade, press, pressurize, coerce, bully
COLLOQ. egg on, twist someone's arm, put the screws on
3 PROMOTE, advertise, market, publicize, boost
COLLOQ. hype, plug
F3 **1** pull **2** discourage, dissuade
♦ *n*
1 KNOCK, shove, nudge, jolt, prod, poke, thrust, ram, jostle, butt
2 OFFENSIVE, assault, advance, charge, drive, invasion, incursion, raid, onslaught, foray
3 ENERGY, vigour, vitality, drive, effort, force, forcefulness, dynamism, enterprise, initiative, ambition, determination
COLLOQ. go, get-up-and-go
4 *get/be given the push*
dismissal, discharge, your cards, notice, marching orders
COLLOQ. the boot, the elbow, the axe, the chop, papers, sacking, firing
■ **push around**
bully, torment, terrorize, intimidate, victimize, pick on
■ **push off**
go away, depart, leave, run along, move
COLLOQ. push along, shove off, beat it, buzz off, scarper, scat, scram, clear off/out, make a move, make tracks
■ **push on**
press on, advance, continue, go on, carry on, keep going, persevere, go ahead, proceed, keep trying, plod on, slog away, peg away, toil (away)
COLLOQ. plug away, soldier on, stick at it

> **Synonym nuances**
> *verb sense 1*
> **Propel** can be used of causing something to move forward, usually briskly: *I propelled myself through the doorway and rushed down the corridor*, while **thrust** and **drive** have implications of greater force: *he thrust his way through the crowds; he was driven by his commitment*. **Ram** also suggests the use of great force, resulting in a collision, while **shove** is more suggestive of a rough physical push by another person. **Manhandle** and **jostle** also have suggestions of treating roughly, although they tend to suggest more continual pushing.
> The word **jolt** is appropriate for a short, sudden action: *the crowd suddenly jolted forwards and he fell over*. **Nudge** too suggests a sudden action, although a more gentle one, whereas **prod** and **poke** have more painful connotations of a stab with, for example, a finger. **Press** and **squeeze** are appropriate for pushing with continuous force, while **depress**, although similar, generally implies a downward movement. Likewise, **plunge** suggests a downwards action, but a more sudden and dramatic one: *he missed his footing and plunged to the ground*.

pushed *adj*
short of, stretched, under pressure, harassed, rushed, hard-pressed, hard-up, hurried, in difficulties, strapped, pinched, pressed, harried

pushover *n*
1 *he's a pushover*
sucker, dupe, mug, weakling, stooge, gull
COLLOQ. fall guy, sitting duck, sitting target, soft touch, easy touch
2 *the job's a pushover*
COLLOQ. child's play, cinch, doddle, picnic, piece of cake, walkover
SLANG (*vulgar*) piece of piss
F3 **2** challenge, labour

pushy *adj*
assertive, self-assertive, ambitious, forceful, aggressive, over-confident, forward, bold, brash, arrogant, presumptuous, impertinent, assuming
COLLOQ. bossy
F3 unassertive, unassuming

pusillanimity *n*
cowardliness, faint-heartedness, fearfulness, feebleness, timidity, timorousness, weakness, spinelessness, cravenness
FORMAL poltroonery
COLLOQ. gutlessness

pusillanimous *adj*
cowardly, faint-hearted, craven, fearful, timorous, scared, weak, weak-kneed, chicken-hearted, spineless, lily-livered, feeble, timid
COLLOQ. chicken, gutless, yellow, wimpish
F3 brave, courageous, strong

pussyfoot *v*
1 PREVARICATE, equivocate, hedge
FORMAL tergiversate
COLLOQ. mess about, beat about the bush
2 CREEP, slink, tiptoe, prowl, pad, steal

pustule *n*
boil, pimple, abscess, carbuncle, eruption, fester, whitehead, blotch, ulcer, pock, whitlow, blister, papule
TECHNICAL uredosorus

put *v*
1 PLACE, lay (down), deposit, set (down), fix, settle, rest, establish, stand, position, dispose, situate, locate, station, post

COLLOQ. plonk, dump

2 ARRANGE, place, class, sort, classify, categorize, group, rank, grade

3 APPLY, impose, inflict, levy, assign, subject, exact, demand, require

4 *put the blame on someone*

place, attribute, attach, fix, ascribe, assign, lay, pin, charge, impute

5 EXPRESS, word, phrase, formulate, frame, couch, say, speak, voice, pronounce, utter, state

6 *put a suggestion*

submit, present, offer, suggest, propose, tender, set/lay before, set forth, bring forward

FORMAL proffer

7 *put money/energy into a project*

invest, spend, sink, devote, dedicate, give, contribute

8 TRANSLATE, transcribe, turn, render, convert

9 *put money on a horse*

bet, gamble, place, lay, risk, chance

10 *put the number of casualties at 50*

estimate, reckon, calculate roughly, work out, gauge, guess

COLLOQ. guesstimate

■ **put about**

tell, spread, make known, circulate, announce

FORMAL disseminate

■ **put across**

put over, get across/over, communicate, convey, express, explain, clarify, make clear, make understood, spell out, bring home to, get through to

■ **put aside**

put by, set aside, lay aside/by, keep, retain, save, reserve, keep in reserve, store, stow, stockpile, hoard, salt away, put to one side

COLLOQ. stash

■ **put away**

1 CONSUME, devour, eat (up), drink, swallow, down

COLLOQ. wolf, tuck in, guzzle, scoff, snarf, polish off

2 IMPRISON, jail, lock up, confine, commit, certify

FORMAL incarcerate

COLLOQ. send down

SLANG bang up

3 SAVE, put aside/by, set aside, lay aside/by, keep, retain, reserve, keep in reserve, store, stow, stockpile

■ **put back**

1 DELAY, defer, postpone, reschedule, adjourn, suspend, shelve, freeze

FORMAL procrastinate

COLLOQ. put on ice

2 REPLACE, return, restore, reinstate, return to its place, clear away/up, tidy away/up

E3 1 bring forward

■ **put down**

1 WRITE DOWN, note down, jot down, transcribe, enter, log, register, list, record

2 CRUSH, quash, suppress, defeat, quell, stop, stamp out, silence

3 *put down a sick dog*

kill, destroy, put to sleep, put out of its misery

4 ASCRIBE, attribute, blame, charge, set down, fix, attach, lay

5 HUMILIATE, snub, slight, squash, belittle, deflate, humble, crush, shame, mortify

FORMAL disparage, deprecate

COLLOQ. take down a peg

■ **put forward**

advance, suggest, recommend, nominate, propose, move, table, introduce, present, submit, offer, tender

FORMAL proffer

■ **put in**

insert, enter, input, submit, present, install, fit

■ **put in for**

apply for, request, ask for, fill in a form for, write off for, order

FORMAL requisition

■ **put off**

1 DELAY, defer, postpone, reschedule, adjourn, suspend, shelve

FORMAL procrastinate

COLLOQ. put on ice, put on the back burner

2 DETER, dissuade, talk out of, discourage, dishearten, demoralize, daunt, dismay, intimidate, disconcert, confuse, distract, sicken, nauseate

3 DISTRACT, divert, sidetrack, deflect, turn away/aside

E3 2 encourage

■ **put on**

1 *put on new clothes*

get dressed in, dress in, change into, get into, slip into, wear, don, try on

COLLOQ. throw on, get dolled up in

2 SWITCH ON, turn on, start up, activate, plug in, connect

3 ATTACH, affix, apply, place, add, impose

4 *put on a service*

lay on, provide, supply, give, add

5 PRETEND, feign, sham, fake, simulate, make believe, affect, assume

6 STAGE, mount, organize, produce, present, do, perform

E3 1 take off

■ **put out**

1 PUBLISH, announce, broadcast, circulate, issue, disclose, make known, bring out

2 EXTINGUISH, quench, douse, smother, stamp out

3 INCONVENIENCE, cause inconvenience to, impose on, bother, disturb, trouble, disconcert, upset, hurt, offend, annoy, irritate, irk, anger, exasperate, provoke, infuriate, unsettle

FORMAL perturb, discommode

COLLOQ. faze

E3 2 light

■ **put through**

accomplish, achieve, complete, conclude, finalize, execute, manage, bring off

■ **put together**

assemble, join, build, construct, fit/piece together

E3 take apart

■ **put up**

1 ERECT, build, construct, assemble, raise

2 ACCOMMODATE, give accommodation to, house, lodge, shelter, give a room to, provide with board and lodging

3 *put up prices*

raise, increase, escalate

COLLOQ. jack up, hike up, bump up

4 PAY, invest, give, advance, float, provide, supply, pledge, offer

5 *put up a candidate*

nominate, put forward, propose, suggest, recommend, choose

E3 1 take down, pull down **3** bring down

■ **put up to**

prompt, incite, encourage, urge, persuade, goad

COLLOQ. egg on

E3 discourage, dissuade

■ **put up with**

stand, bear, abide, stomach, endure, suffer, tolerate, allow, accept, stand for, take, brook

COLLOQ. swallow, wear, take lying down

E3 object to, reject

■ **put upon**

impose on, exploit, take advantage of, take for granted, take liberties, inconvenience

putative *adj*

supposed, assumed, presumed, alleged, reported, reputed, hypothetical, theoretical, suppositional, reputative

FORMAL conjectural, suppositious

Types of puzzle include:

acrostic	crossword	jigsaw puzzle	quiz	sorites	wordsearch
alphametic	cryptogram	magic pyramid	rebus	tangram	
anagram	hangman	maze	Rubik's Cube®	wordgame	

---

put-down *n*
affront, humiliation, insult, slight, sneer, snub, rebuff, sarcasm, gibe
FORMAL disparagement
COLLOQ. slap in the face, dig

put-off *n*
deterrent, discouragement, disincentive, hindrance, constraint, curb, damper, obstacle, restraint
F3 encouragement, incentive

putrefaction *n*
decay, decomposition, rot, rotting, going bad, perishing, mould, fungus, mildew
FORMAL putrescence, putridity

putrefy *v*
rot, perish, go bad, decay, corrupt, mould, spoil, stink, taint, gangrene, decompose, deteriorate, fester, addle

putrescent *adj*
rotting, perishing, decaying, decomposing, putrefying, stinking, festering
FORMAL mephitic

putrid *adj*
rotten, decayed, decaying, decomposed, decomposing, mouldy, off, bad, rancid, addled, addle, turned, corrupt, contaminated, tainted, polluted, foul, rank, f(o)etid, stinking
F3 fresh, wholesome

put-upon *adj*
imposed on, taken advantage of, exploited, used, inconvenienced, abused, maltreated, persecuted

puzzle *v, n*
   ◆ *v*
1 BAFFLE, mystify, perplex, confound, confuse, stagger, bewilder, intrigue, fascinate, riddle, gravel, metagrobolize; *Scot* bumbaze, fickle, kittle
OLD bemuse, pose
COLLOQ. stump, floor, flummox, beat, nonplus, bamboozle
2 THINK, ponder, meditate, consider, brood, mull over, muse over, deliberate, think hard about, figure, rack your brains, beat your brains (out)
   ◆ *n*
question, poser, anagram, riddle, conundrum, mystery, enigma, dilemma, paradox, tickler, crux, brainteaser, mind-bender; *N Am* brain-twister
See panel above

■ **puzzle out**
solve, work out, figure out, think out, decipher, decode, unravel, untangle, find the answer to, piece together, sort out, resolve, clear up
COLLOQ. crack, get, suss (out)

puzzled *adj*
baffled, mystified, perplexed, confounded, at a loss, beaten, confused, bewildered, lost, in a haze
COLLOQ. stumped, nonplussed, at sea, flummoxed, floored, bamboozled
F3 clear

puzzlement *n*
bafflement, perplexity, bewilderment, confusion, disorientation, astonishment, mystification, surprise, wonder, uncertainty, doubt, doubtfulness
FORMAL incertitude
COLLOQ. bamboozlement
F3 certainty, clarity, lucidity

puzzling *adj*
baffling, bewildering, confusing, perplexing, unclear, hard to understand, difficult to understand, queer, peculiar, strange, bizarre, mystifying, mysterious, arcane, mystical, misleading, unaccountable, unfathomable, impenetrable, inexplicable, intricate, involved, ambiguous, equivocal, mind-bending, mind-boggling, curious, enigmatic, cryptic, tortuous, knotty, Sphynx-like
FORMAL abstruse, labyrinthine

pygmy *n, adj*
   ◆ *n*
person of restricted growth, dwarf, midget, Tom Thumb, Lilliputian, manikin, thumbling, fingerling, hop-o'-my-thumb, Negrito
OLD (*Shakesp*) atomy
FORMAL homunculus
F3 giant
   ◆ *adj*
miniature, small, tiny, baby, diminutive, half-pint, undersized, minuscule, minute, pint-sized, pocket, elfin, stunted, dwarf, midget, dwarfish, toy, Lilliputian; *Scot* wee
F3 gigantic

pyromaniac *n*
arsonist, incendiary, fire-raiser
COLLOQ. firebug

Q

quack *n, adj*

♦ *n*

charlatan, impostor, fraud, mountebank, pretender, masquerader, humbug, sham, fake, cowboy, swindler, trickster

OLD quacksalver

COLLOQ. phoney, pseud

♦ *adj*

false, bogus, counterfeit, fake, pretended, fraudulent, spurious, supposed, sham, so-called, unqualified

COLLOQ. phoney

F3 genuine, real

quackery *n*

charlatanism, mountebankery, mountebankism, fraud, fraudulence, sham, imposture

COLLOQ. humbug, phoniness

quadrangle *n*

courtyard, court, square, cloister, enclosure, plaza, esplanade, piazza

COLLOQ. quad

quaff *v*

down, drink, gulp, knock back, swallow, swig, toss off, swill, carouse, drain

FORMAL imbibe

COLLOQ. booze, guzzle, tipple

quagmire *n*

1 BOG, marsh, quag, fen, swamp, morass, mire, slough, quicksand

OLD (*Spenser*) wagmoire

2 MESS, problem, dilemma, quandary, perplexity

COLLOQ. fix, hole, pickle, tight spot, hot/deep water

quail *v*

recoil, back away, shy away, shrink, flinch, pull back, draw back, cringe, cower, tremble, quake, shake, shiver, blench, shudder, falter

quaint *adj*

picturesque, charming, attractive, sweet, old-fashioned, antiquated, old-world, unusual, strange, odd, queer, curious, droll, bizarre, fanciful, whimsical, whimsy; *Scot* auld-farand

OLD queint

COLLOQ. twee, olde-worlde, funky

F3 modern

quaintly *adv*

charmingly, attractively, strangely, oddly, curiously, unusually, picturesquely, whimsically

quaintness *n*

charm, attractiveness, picturesqueness, old-fashionedness, unusualness, whimsicalness

quake *v*

shake, tremble, shudder, quiver, shiver, quail, vibrate, throb, pulsate, wobble, rock, sway, move, convulse, heave, dither; *dialect* wamble

qualification *n*

1 CERTIFICATE, diploma, degree, training, certification, skill, competence, proficiency, ability, capability, capacity,

aptitude, suitability, fitness, accomplishment, eligibility

2 RESTRICTION, limitation, reservation, exception, allowance, exemption, condition, caveat, rider, provision, proviso, stipulation, modification, adjustment, adaptation

qualified *adj*

1 CERTIFIED, chartered, licensed, professional, trained, experienced, practised, skilled, accomplished, expert, knowledgeable, skilful, talented, proficient, competent, efficient, able, capable, adept, fit, fitted, equipped, prepared, eligible

2 *qualified praise*

reserved, guarded, cautious, restricted, limited, bounded, modified, conditional, provisional, equivocal

FORMAL contingent, circumscribed

F3 1 unqualified, untrained **2** unconditional, wholehearted

qualify *v*

1 TRAIN, prepare, make ready, teach, instruct, equip, fit, coach, ground, pass, graduate, certify, empower, entitle, authorize, license, sanction, permit, allow, warrant, capacitate, be allowed, be eligible, fit/meet the requirements

TECHNICAL habilitate

2 MODERATE, reduce, lessen, diminish, temper, soften, weaken, ease, adjust, modify, restrain, restrict, limit, delimit, make conditional, define, classify, alloy

TECHNICAL contemper

FORMAL mitigate, alleviate

F3 1 disqualify

quality *n*

1 *of poor quality*

standard, grade, class, kind, sort, type, make, variety, calibre, status, rank, level, value, worth, merit, condition

2 EXCELLENCE, superiority, eminence, pre-eminence, distinction, merit, value, worth, refinement

3 CHARACTERISTIC, property, attribute, aspect, feature, trait, peculiarity, mark, nature, character, make-up

qualm *n*

misgiving, apprehension, fear, anxiety, worry, apprehension, concern, disquiet, uneasiness, scruple, hesitation, hesitancy, disinclination, reluctance, uncertainty, doubt

FORMAL compunction

quandary *n*

dilemma, predicament, impasse, perplexity, confusion, bewilderment, muddle, mess, problem, difficulty

COLLOQ. fix, hole, pickle, jam, tight spot

quantify *v*

measure, calculate, number, count, weigh, enumerate, calibrate, evaluate, determine, specify

quantity *n*

1 AMOUNT, number, sum, total, aggregate, mass, lot, share, portion, quota, allotment, measure, dose, proportion, part, content, capacity, volume, weight, bulk, size, magnitude, expanse, extent, area, length, breadth

2 *quantities of food*

much, many, lots

COLLOQ. loads, heaps, stacks, oodles, tons, masses

quarantine *n*
detention, isolation, segregation, lazaretto

quarrel *n, v*
♦ *n*
row, argument, wrangle, squabble, tiff, misunderstanding, disagreement, dispute, dissension, controversy, difference, difference of opinion, conflict, clash, contention, strife, fight, brawl, fracas, feud, vendetta, schism
FORMAL altercation, disputation
COLLOQ. barney, broil, spat, miff, bust-up, punch-up, slanging match, scrap, set-to, dust-up
E3 agreement, harmony
♦ *v*
1 ROW, argue, bicker, squabble, wrangle, be at loggerheads, fall out, disagree, dispute, dissent, differ, be at variance, clash, contend, fight, feud, spat, have words; *Scot* cast out, flyte
OLD jangle
COLLOQ. scrap
SLANG part brass rags
2 FIND FAULT WITH, fault, slate, criticize, dispute, censure
COLLOQ. pick holes in, knock, slam, pull to pieces
E3 **1** agree

quarrelling *n, adj*
♦ *n*
bickering, contention, dissension, feuding, rowing, variance, strife, wrangling, disharmony, argumentation
FORMAL altercation, discord, disputation, vitilitigation
COLLOQ. argy-bargying
E3 concord, harmony
♦ *adj*
bickering, contending, fighting, squabbling, wrangling, warring, feuding, rowing, at odds, at variance, at loggerheads
FORMAL discordant, dissentient
COLLOQ. scrapping
E3 amicable, friendly

quarrelsome *adj*
argumentative, disputatious, contentious, irascible, belligerent, ill-tempered, hot-tempered, irritable, ready for a fight
FORMAL bellicose, pugnacious
E3 peaceable, placid

quarry *n*
prey, victim, object, goal, target, game, kill, prize

quarter *n, v*
♦ *n*
1 DISTRICT, sector, zone, neighbourhood, locality, vicinity, area, region, province, territory, division, section, part, place, spot, point, direction, side
COLLOQ. digs
2 MERCY, leniency, favour, pardon, pity, compassion, grace, indulgence, forgiveness, clemency
3 *living quarters*
accommodation, lodgings, billet, residence, rooms, barracks, station, post
FORMAL dwelling, habitation, domicile
COLLOQ. digs, pad
♦ *v*
station, post, billet, accommodate, put up, lodge, board, house, shelter

quash *v*
1 ANNUL, revoke, rescind, cancel, repeal, void, invalidate, reverse, set aside, overturn, overrule, override
FORMAL nullify, abrogate, countermand
2 CRUSH, squash, quell, suppress, scotch, put an end to, subdue, defeat, overthrow
E3 **1** confirm, vindicate, reinstate

quaver *v, n*
♦ *v*
shake, tremble, quake, waver, shudder, quiver, wobble,

vibrate, pulsate, oscillate, flutter, flicker, trill, warble
♦ *n*
tremble, trembling, tremor, trill, break, quiver, shake, throb, sob, quaveriness, vibration, vibrato, warble, tremolo

quay *n*
wharf, pier, jetty, dock, harbour

queasiness *n*
nausea, vomiting, sickness, retching, gagging, biliousness, morning sickness, travel sickness, motion sickness, seasickness, carsickness, airsickness, sick headache

queasy *adj*
sick, ill, unwell, queer, groggy, green, nauseous, nauseated, sickened, bilious, squeamish, faint, dizzy, giddy
COLLOQ. rough, under the weather, out of sorts

queen *n*
1 MONARCH, sovereign, ruler, head of state, majesty, princess, empress, consort
OLD prince
FORMAL regina
Related adjectives: royal, regal, reginal
2 BEAUTY, belle, idol, charm, Venus

queenly *adj*
sovereign, majestic, regal, royal, imperial, imperious, noble, stately, splendid, dignified, gracious, grand
FORMAL reginal, august, monarchical, sublime
E3 undignified

queer *adj, v*
♦ *adj*
1 ODD, mysterious, strange, unusual, uncommon, weird, unnatural, extraordinary, bizarre, eccentric, outlandish, peculiar, funny, puzzling, curious, unconventional, unorthodox, abnormal, deviant, remarkable; *dialect* quare
OLD rum
FORMAL singular
2 *I feel queer*
unwell, ill, sick, queasy, light-headed, faint, giddy, dizzy
COLLOQ. rough, under the weather, out of sorts
3 SUSPICIOUS, suspect, shifty, dubious, doubtful, irregular, peculiar, strange
COLLOQ. shady, fishy, iffy
4 HOMOSEXUAL, gay, lesbian, bisexual
COLLOQ. camp, butch
E3 **1** ordinary, usual, common **2** well, fine **4** heterosexual; *colloq.* straight
♦ *v*
spoil, harm, ruin, upset, wreck, mar, botch, thwart, impair, foil, frustrate, endanger, jeopardize, stymie

queerness *n*
oddity, peculiarity, strangeness, unusualness, uncommonness, unconventionality, unnaturalness, bizarreness, anomalousness, curiousness, abnormality, irregularity, eccentricity, unorthodoxy
FORMAL singularity

quell *v*
subdue, quash, crush, squash, suppress, rout, put down, put an end to, overcome, conquer, defeat, overpower, moderate, allay, soothe, calm, pacify, appease, hush, quiet, silence, stifle, extinguish
FORMAL mitigate, alleviate, vanquish

quench *v*
1 *quench your thirst*
slake, satisfy, sate, cool; *Scot* slocken
OLD stanch
FORMAL satiate
2 EXTINGUISH, stifle, smother, douse, put out, snuff out, stamp out; *Scot* slocken

querulous *adj*
peevish, fretful, fractious, cross, irritable, complaining, grumbling, sour, testy, petulant, discontented, dissatisfied,

critical, carping, captious, fault-finding, fussy, irascible
FORMAL cantankerous
COLLOQ. grouchy, shirty, ratty
E3 placid, uncomplaining, contented

query *v, n*
♦ *v*
ask, inquire, question, challenge, dispute, quarrel with, doubt, throw doubts on, suspect, be sceptical of, have suspicions about, distrust, mistrust, disbelieve
E3 accept
♦ *n*
question, inquiry, problem, uncertainty, doubt, suspicion, scepticism, reservation, hesitation, uneasiness, qualm(s), quibble

quest *n*
search, seeking, hunt, pursuit, investigation, inquiry, purpose, aim, goal, mission, crusade, enterprise, undertaking, venture, journey, voyage, expedition, exploration, pilgrimage, adventure

■ **in quest of**
searching for, seeking after, trying to find, trying to obtain, in pursuit of, for, out for, hunting for, harking after, questing

question *n, v*
♦ *n*
1 QUERY, inquiry, poser, problem, difficulty
2 ISSUE, matter, problem, subject, theme, topic, point, point at issue, proposal, proposition, motion, debate, dispute, controversy
3 DOUBT, query, debate, dispute, argument, controversy, uncertainty
♦ *v*
1 INTERROGATE, quiz, grill, pump, interview, examine, cross-examine, cross-question, debrief, ask, inquire, investigate, probe, catechize
COLLOQ. give the third degree to
2 QUERY, challenge, dispute, have doubts about, have reservations/qualms about, doubt, disbelieve

■ **in question**
at issue, being discussed, under discussion, concerned

■ **out of the question**
impossible, unthinkable, unbelievable, absurd, ridiculous, unacceptable, not worth considering
COLLOQ. not by any stretch of the imagination

■ **without question**
without arguing, immediately, unhesitatingly, unquestionably, without a shadow of doubt

---

Synonym nuances
verb sense 1
Interrogate can be used to suggest a thorough questioning, often in official circumstances, and **quiz** likewise implies a detailed investigation. **Grill**, too, has connotations of pressure, or even harassment: *he was grilled by detectives for two hours*, while **pump** is more suggestive of persistently trying to extract particular information: *she pumped me about his movements*.
  The word **interview**, while suggesting a formal situation, suggests a less intense questioning, but both **cross-examine** and **cross-question** return to the idea of close questioning in minute detail, and are usually associated with court cases. The term **debrief** has the specific use of questioning someone on their return from business or a mission: *the aircrews had yet to be debriefed as to the operations*.
  Inquire is not a particularly marked term, and can be generally used of seeking information, but the terms **investigate** and **examine** return to the idea of looking more carefully into a matter. To suggest an even deeper scrutiny, you could use **probe**: *police probed allegations of assault and arrests were made*.
  The uncommon **catechize** is reserved for a systematic questioning, usually regarding religious tenets.

---

questionable *adj*
debatable, disputable, unsettled, undetermined, unproven, uncertain, arguable, controversial, vexed, doubtful, dubious, suspicious, suspect, at question, problematic(al), equivocal
COLLOQ. shady, fishy, iffy
E3 unquestionable, indisputable, certain

questioner *n*
1 INTERVIEWER, examiner, inquirer, question-master, quizmaster, inquisitor, interrogator, investigator, catechizer, catechist
2 DISBELIEVER, doubter, sceptic, agnostic
FORMAL interlocutor

questionnaire *n*
quiz, test, form, survey, opinion poll, market research

queue *n, v*
♦ *n*
line, tailback, tail, file, row, column, crocodile, procession, train, string, chain, succession, series, sequence, order, breadline
FORMAL concatenation
♦ *v*
line up, form a queue, form a line, stand in line, wait in line, fall in, tail back; *N Am* back up

quibble *v, n*
♦ *v*
carp, cavil, split hairs, find fault with, equivocate, avoid the issue, prevaricate, dodge, haggle, peck at
OLD pettifog
COLLOQ. nit-pick, split hairs
♦ *n*
complaint, objection, criticism, query, protest, cavil, niggle, equivocation, prevarication, dodge, quip, quirk
OLD quiblin, pettifogging, brabble, carriwitchet; (*Shakesp*) snatch
FORMAL quiddity, equivoke, quillet
COLLOQ. nit-picking

quibbler *n*
caviller, niggler, sophist, equivocator, casuist
OLD pettifogger
COLLOQ. hair-splitter, nit-picker

quibbling *adj*
niggling, critical, overnice, carping, captious, ambiguous, cavilling, evasive, casuistic, equivocating, logic-chopping
OLD pettifogging
COLLOQ. hair-splitting, nit-picking

quick *adj*
1 FAST, swift, rapid, speedy, express, hurried, hasty, cursory, fleeting, brief, perfunctory, prompt, ready, immediate, without delay, instant, instantaneous, sudden, brisk, nimble, sprightly, agile
FORMAL expeditious
COLLOQ. like greased lightning, nifty, nippy, zippy, pdq, pretty damn quick
2 CLEVER, intelligent, quick-witted, smart, sharp, sharp-witted, keen, shrewd, astute, discerning, perceptive, responsive, alive, receptive, quick off the mark, quick on the uptake
E3 1 slow, sluggish, lethargic **2** unintelligent, dull

Synonym nuances
sense 1
Swift can imply not lasting long: *the swift burst of curiosity flickered out*, while **rapid** is appropriate for something accomplished within a short time: *the patient has made rapid progress*. Both **speedy** and **nippy** can be used to suggest agility and mobility: *a nippy little car*. Similarly **nimble**, **sprightly** and **agile** can suggest both speed and lightness or suppleness of movement.

Express, however, implies the fastest of various set options: *express delivery*, unlike the more critical **hurried**, **hasty** and **cursory**, which suggest not being apportioned enough time or attention: *a cursory examination of an important issue*. You can use **brief** or **fleeting** fairly neutrally of something transitory, whereas **perfunctory** returns to the idea of merely going through the motions and is more disapproving.

Prompt and **ready** have connotations of efficiency, when referring to something quickly achieved or available: *prompt payment of bills will help you to budget*. **Brisk** can have similar connotations of efficiency but can also suggest brusqueness in manner: *a brisk retort*, or purposeful movement: *a brisk walk*.

quicken v

1 ACCELERATE, speed (up), hurry (up), hasten, dispatch, advance
FORMAL precipitate, expedite
2 ANIMATE, enliven, invigorate, energize, galvanize, activate, incite, instigate, rouse, arouse, stimulate, stir (up), excite, kindle, inspire, whet, revive, refresh, reinvigorate, strengthen, revitalize, reactivate
FORMAL revivify
F3 **1** slow, retard **2** dull, enervate

quickly adv

rapidly, quick, fast, speedily, swiftly, express, briskly, apace, hurriedly, hastily, immediately, instantaneously, readily, smartly, soon, abruptly, instantly, promptly, unhesitatingly, cursorily, posthaste
TECHNICAL presto, prestissimo
FORMAL expeditiously, perfunctorily
COLLOQ. pronto, lickety-split, at a rate of knots, at the double, before you can say Jack Robinson, by leaps and bounds, hell for leather, like a bat out of hell, like the clappers, like greased lightning, a mile a minute
F3 slowly; *formal* tardily

quickness n

1 SPEED, speediness, rapidity, swiftness, hastiness, immediacy, briskness, promptness, readiness, suddenness, instantaneousness, agility, nimbleness
OLD nimblesse
FORMAL expedition, precipitation, promptitude, celerity
2 INTELLIGENCE, shrewdness, sharpness, penetration, acuteness, astuteness, keenness, quick-wittedness, alertness
FORMAL acumen
F3 **1** slowness; *formal* tardiness **2** dullness; *colloq.* dim-wittedness

quick-tempered adj

fiery, impatient, impulsive, hot-tempered, irascible, testy, touchy, irritable, explosive, volcanic, waspish, choleric, excitable, quarrelsome, shrewish, snappy, temperamental, splenetic, petulant
F3 cool, dispassionate

quick-witted adj

intelligent, clever, resourceful, keen, bright, sharp, shrewd, penetrating, acute, perceptive, smart, wide-awake, alert, astute, crafty, ingenious, witty, ready-witted, nimble-witted, quick off the mark, quick on the uptake
F3 dull, slow, stupid

quid pro quo n

exchange, swap, trade-off, give-and-take, equivalent, equivalence, co-operation, compensation, remuneration, damages
FORMAL reciprocity, reciprocation, mutuality
COLLOQ. tit for tat

quiescent adj

quiet, at rest, resting, calm, peaceful, serene, placid, tranquil, undisturbed, untroubled, still, passive, silent, motionless, inactive, inert, sleeping, asleep, latent, dormant
FORMAL in abeyance, reposeful
F3 active

quiet adj, n

♦ adj
1 SILENT, soundless, without a sound, noiseless, inaudible, hushed, soft, faint, indistinct, muffled, low
COLLOQ. you could hear a pin drop
2 PEACEFUL, still, tranquil, serene, calm, mild, gentle, restrained, composed, undisturbed, untroubled, placid
3 SHY, reserved, reticent, uncommunicative, taciturn, placid, unforthcoming, undemonstrative, retiring, withdrawn, introvert, unexcitable, stoic, thoughtful, discreet, subdued, meek
FORMAL imperturbable, phlegmatic
COLLOQ. unflappable
4 *have a quiet word with you*
secret, private, confidential, discreet, off-the-record, personal, man-to-man, woman-to-woman
5 *a quiet spot*
isolated, unfrequented, lonely, secluded, undisturbed, private, sleepy, peaceful
FORMAL sequestered
COLLOQ. off the beaten track
6 *quiet colours*
muted, subdued, soft, subtle, faint, pale, restrained, low-key
F3 **1** noisy, loud **2** excitable, animated **3** extrovert, talkative **4** public **5** noisy, busy **6** loud, ostentatious
♦ n
quietness, silence, hush, peace, lull, stillness, peacefulness, soundlessness, noiselessness, tranquillity, serenity, calm, rest
FORMAL repose
F3 noise, loudness, disturbance, bustle

quieten v

1 SILENCE, hush, shush, mute, soften, lower, diminish, reduce, stifle, muffle, deaden, dull
COLLOQ. shut up
2 SUBDUE, pacify, quell, quiet, still, smooth, calm (down), tranquillize, soothe, compose, sober
F3 **2** disturb, agitate

quietly adv

calmly, noiselessly, inaudibly, mutely, silently, softly, soundlessly, surreptitiously, placidly, tranquilly, peacefully, gently, mildly, meekly, unobtrusively, unostentatiously, undemonstratively, modestly, secretly, privately
F3 noisily, obtrusively

quietness n

calm, quiet, silence, serenity, tranquillity, calmness, hush, peace, peacefulness, placidity, lull, still, stillness, composure, inactivity, inertia, uneventfulness, dullness
FORMAL quiescence, quietude, repose
F3 activity, bustle, commotion, disturbance, noise, racket

quietude n

tranquillity, calm, peace, peacefulness, serenity, calmness, composure, quiet, quietness, rest, restfulness, stillness, hush, silence, imperturbability, coolness, equanimity, sedateness, placidity
TECHNICAL ataraxia, ataraxy
FORMAL repose
F3 disturbance, agitation, noise

quietus n

release, end, silencing, discharge, dispatch, acquittance, death, death-blow, death-stroke, finishing stroke, *coup de grâce*, extinction
FORMAL decease, demise

quilt n

bedcover, coverlet, bedspread, counterpane, eiderdown,

duvet, continental quilt, patchwork quilt, kantha; *N Am* comforter; *Aust* doona
OLD counterpoint
COLLOQ. *N Am* comfort

quintessence *n*
embodiment, personification, essence, core, distillation, marrow, pith, soul, spirit, extract, gist, heart, kernel, pattern, sum and substance
FORMAL exemplar, quiddity

quintessential *adj*
typical, essential, ideal, perfect, ultimate, complete, definitive, entire
FORMAL archetypical, consummate, prototypical

quip *n, v*
♦ *n*
joke, jest, crack, wisecrack, witticism, riposte, retort, gibe, epigram, pleasantry
COLLOQ. gag, one-liner
♦ *v*
jest, joke, retort, riposte, gibe, quirk, gag, wisecrack

quirk *n*
freak, eccentricity, curiosity, oddity, peculiarity, idiosyncrasy, mannerism, habit, trait, characteristic, feature, foible, whim, vagary, caprice, obsession, turn, twist, kink
COLLOQ. thing, hang-up, fluke

quirkiness *n*
eccentricity, unconventionality, strangeness, unorthodoxy, peculiarity, nonconformity, abnormality, oddity, bizarreness, weirdness, idiosyncrasy, singularity, freakishness, anomaly
FORMAL aberration, capriciousness
COLLOQ. freakiness, wackiness, zaniness
E3 conventionality, ordinariness

quirky *adj*
odd, unusual, strange, eccentric, idiosyncratic, uncommon, peculiar, funny, abnormal, exceptional, curious, atypical, different, queer, bizarre, deviant, singular, remarkable, original, unconventional, uncanny, droll, drôle, freakish, weird, irregular, wild, extraordinary, outlandish, whimsical, whimsy
FORMAL aberrant, capricious
COLLOQ. out of the ordinary, freaky, kinky, wacky, oddball, zany, barmy, crackers, off the wall
SLANG far-out, way-out, funky

quisling *n*
betrayer, traitor, turncoat, collaborator, renegade, fifth columnist, puppet, Judas
FORMAL collaborationist

quit *v*
1 *quit smoking*
give up, stop, end, cease, abandon, drop, leave off
FORMAL discontinue, desist, abstain
COLLOQ. pack in
2 LEAVE, depart, go (away), exit, decamp, desert, abandon, relinquish, surrender, give up, resign, retire, withdraw
FORMAL renounce, forsake

quite *adv*
1 MODERATELY, rather, somewhat, reasonably, fairly, relatively, comparatively, to some extent/degree
2 UTTERLY, absolutely, totally, completely, entirely, wholly, fully, perfectly, exactly, precisely

quits *adj*
equal, even, level, square

■ **call it quits**
stop, cease, break off, make peace, stop fighting
FORMAL discontinue
COLLOQ. call it a day, bury the hatchet, lay down your arms

quitter *n*
defector, delinquent, renegade, shirker, deserter, apostate
OLD recreant
COLLOQ. rat, skiver

quiver *v, n*
♦ *v*
shake, tremble, shudder, shiver, quake, quaver, vibrate, pulsate, tingle, thrill, palpitate, flutter, flicker, oscillate, wobble, tremor, bicker; *Scot* flichter
♦ *n*
shake, tremble, shudder, shiver, tremor, throb, vibration, palpitation, quaver, pulsation, flutter, flicker, oscillation, wobble, twinkle

quixotic *adj*
unrealistic, unworldly, idealistic, impracticable, visionary, extravagant, fanciful, Utopian, fantastical, romantic, starry-eyed, impetuous, impulsive, chivalrous
E3 hard-headed, practical, realistic

quiz *n, v*
♦ *n*
questionnaire, test, examination, competition, questioning, cross-examination, cross-questioning
♦ *v*
question, interrogate, examine, cross-examine, cross-question
OLD smoke
COLLOQ. grill, pump, give the third degree to, trail

quizzical *adj*
questioning, inquiring, curious, amused, humorous, teasing, mocking, satirical, sardonic, sceptical, mystified, perplexed, puzzled, baffled

quizzically *adv*
questioningly, inquiringly, curiously, mockingly, sceptically

quota *n*
ration, allowance, allocation, assignment, share, portion, part, slice, percentage, proportion, contingent
TECHNICAL numerus clausus
FORMAL quotum
COLLOQ. cut, whack, slice of cake

quotation *n*
1 CITATION, extract, excerpt, line, passage, selection, piece, cutting, reference, allusion
COLLOQ. quote
2 ESTIMATE, tender, figure, price, cost, charge, rate, bid
COLLOQ. quote

quote *v*
cite, refer to, mention, name, reproduce, echo, repeat, recite, recall, recollect, allude to

quoted *adj*
cited, referred to, reported, reproduced, stated, above-mentioned
FORMAL forementioned, instanced

quotidian *adj*
everyday, normal, ordinary, routine, workaday, regular, daily, day-to-day, repeated, common, commonplace, customary, recurrent, habitual
FORMAL diurnal
COLLOQ. run-of-the-mill, bog-standard

R

rabbit *n, v*

♦ *n*

bunny, cony, bunny rabbit, daman, hyrax, dassie, buck, doe; *N Am* cottontail

COLLOQ. bun

Related adjective: oryctolagine, lagomorphic

■ **rabbit on**

chatter, babble, go on (and on), maunder (on); *Scot* blether; *dialect & N Am* blather

COLLOQ. natter, witter (on), waffle, gab

Breeds of rabbit and hare include:

Alaska	Harlequin	sable
Angora	Havana	sage rabbit
Arctic hare	Himalayan	satin
Argente	hotot	silver
Belgian hare	jack rabbit	snowshoe hare
black silver	lop	(or rabbit)
brown hare	New Zealand	swamp (or water)
chinchilla	oar-lap	rabbit
cottontail	pika	tan
Dutch	Polish	tapeti
English spot	Rex	Van Beveren
European	Rhinelander	Vienna
Flemish	riverine rabbit	
fox	rock rabbit	

rabble *n*

1 CROWD, throng, horde, herd, mob

2 MASSES, populace, crowd, herd, mob, common people, proletariat, hoi polloi, rank and file, riff-raff, great unwashed

COLLOQ. plebs, proles

rabble-rouser *n*

agitator, troublemaker, incendiary, firebrand, demagogue, ringleader

COLLOQ. tub-thumper

rabble-rousing *n*

stirring up, troublemaking

COLLOQ. tub-thumping

Rabelaisian *adj*

satirical, exuberant, extravagant, coarse, bawdy, earthy, gross, vulgar, uninhibited, unrestrained, indecent, lewd, racy, ribald, risqué

rabid *adj*

1 FANATICAL, ferocious, extreme, burning, ardent, raging, fervent, frantic, unreasoning, intolerant, irrational, furious, obsessive, zealous, overzealous, bigoted, narrow-minded

2 MAD, hydrophobic, maniacal, wild, berserk, frenzied, crazed, violent, hysterical

rabies *n*

hydrophobia, rabidity, rabidness

race¹ *n, v*

♦ *n*

a horse race

competition, contest, contention, rivalry, chase, pursuit, quest

♦ *v*

run, sprint, dash, tear, fly, gallop, speed, career, dart, bolt, zoom, rush, hurry, hasten, accelerate, take part in a race

COLLOQ. get a move on, go all out, get cracking, scoot, zip, zap, run like hell

Types of race include:

CYCLING:	stock car race	**FUN RACES:**
cyclo-cross	**SAILING:**	egg-and-spoon
keirin race	regatta	race
road race	yacht race	pancake race
time trial	**RUNNING:**	sack race
HORSE RACING:	cross-country	three-legged race
N Am harness	dash	wheelbarrow
race	hurdles	race
steeplechase	marathon	**OTHER:**
trotting race	relay	greyhound race
MOTORCYCLING:	sprint	swimming race
motocross	steeplechase	walkathon
scramble	track event	walking race
speedway	**SKIING:**	
MOTOR-RACING:	downhill	
Formula One	slalom	
scramble		

Famous races include:

CYCLING:	One Thousand	Melbourne
Giro d'Italia	Guineas	Grand Prix
Tour de France	Prix de l'Arc de	Monte Carlo rally
GREYHOUND RACING:	Triomphe	RAC Rally
	St. Leger	**ROWING:**
Greyhound	Two Thousand	Boat Race
Derby	Guineas	Diamond Sculls
HORSE RACING:	**MOTORCYCLE RACING:**	**RUNNING:**
Breeder's Cup		London
Cheltenham Gold	Isle of Man Tourist	Marathon
Cup	Trophy (TT)	New York
Derby	**MOTOR-RACING:**	Marathon
Grand National	Grand Prix	**YACHTING:**
Kentucky Derby	Indianapolis 500	Admiral's Cup
Melbourne Cup	Le Mans	America's Cup
Oaks		

race² *n*

a race of people

nation, people, ethnic group, racial group, colour, tribe, clan, house, dynasty, family, kindred, ancestry, line, lineage, blood, ancestry, extraction, stock, parentage, strain, stirps, genus, species, breed

Related adjective: ethnic

racecourse *n*

racetrack, course, track, circuit, lap, turf, speedway

racial *adj*

national, tribal, ethnic, folk, ethnological, genealogical, ancestral, inherited, genetic

raciness *n*

1 RIBALDRY, indecency, indelicacy, bawdiness, naughtiness, lewdness, smuttiness, suggestiveness, vulgarity, crudeness, coarseness

2 LIVELINESS, animation, zest, zestfulness, energy, exhilaration, freshness, dynamism
FORMAL ebullience
COLLOQ. pep, pizzazz

racism *n*
racialism, xenophobia, chauvinism, jingoism, discrimination, racial discrimination, prejudice, racial prejudice, apartheid, bias

racist *n, adj*
• *n*
racialist, discriminator, bigot, chauvinist
• *adj*
racialist, discriminatory, bigoted, intolerant

rack *n, v*
• *n*
1 HOLDER, shelf, stand, support, structure, frame, framework, trestle, flake, hack; *dialect* heck
OLD portmanteau
2 SUFFERING, pain, misery, affliction, agony, anguish, distress, pangs, torment, torture, persecution
• *v*
afflict, oppress, distress, agonize, pain, harass, convulse, shake, strain, stress, tear, stretch, wrench, wrest, wring, excruciate, harrow, lacerate, torment, torture, crucify
OLD touse
▪ **rack your brains**
think hard, think deeply, concentrate, study, put your mind to
▪ **on the rack**
suffering, in distress, under pressure/stress, in difficulties, in trouble, in agony, in pain

racket *n*
1 NOISE, din, uproar, row, fuss, outcry, clamour, shouting, yelling, tumult, commotion, disturbance, hullabaloo, pandemonium, hurly-burly, hubbub
2 SWINDLE, fraud, fiddle, deception, trick, dodge, scheme, business
COLLOQ. scam, con, game
SLANG *N Am* gold brick

racketeering *n*
cheating, swindling, fraud, defrauding, extortion, stealing, overcharging, fleecing, fiddling
COLLOQ. cooking the books
SLANG ripping off, stinging, chiselling, taking for a ride, taking to the cleaners

raconteur *n*
narrator, storyteller, chronicler, reporter, anecdotist, commentator, describer, relater

racy *adj*
1 RIBALD, bawdy, risqué, vulgar, crude, rude, coarse, dirty, naughty, indecent, indelicate, suggestive, off-colour, smutty
COLLOQ. blue
2 LIVELY, animated, spirited, vigorous, vivacious, fast-moving, energetic, dynamic, buoyant, enthusiastic, boisterous, sparkling, piquant, witty, spicy
FORMAL ebullient
COLLOQ. peppy, zippy

raddled *adj*
haggard, drawn, gaunt, wasted, worn out, unkempt, dishevelled, in a mess, the worse for wear

radiance *n*
1 LIGHT, luminosity, radiation, brightness, brilliance, shine, lustre, gleam, glow, glitter, resplendence, splendour
TECHNICAL incandescence
FORMAL effulgence, refulgence
2 JOY, happiness, pleasure, delight, elation, ecstasy, bliss, rapture

radiant *adj*
1 BRIGHT, luminous, shining, illuminated, gleaming, glowing, beaming, glittering, sparkling, brilliant, splendid, magnificent, glorious, beamish, beamy
TECHNICAL incandescent
FORMAL resplendent, effulgent, refulgent, lambent, profulgent
2 JOYFUL, happy, delighted, elated, pleased, blissful, ecstatic, in raptures
COLLOQ. in seventh heaven, on top of the world, on cloud nine, over the moon
E3 1 dull **2** miserable

radiate *v*
1 *radiate light/an emotion*
shine, gleam, glow, beam, shed, pour, send out/forth, give off, emit, emanate, diffuse, issue
2 SPREAD (OUT), scatter, disperse, diverge, branch
FORMAL disseminate, divaricate

radiation *n*
emanation, emission, rays, waves, transmission
TECHNICAL insolation

Types of radiation include:

alpha radiation	electromagnetic	radio waves
background	radiation	soft radiation
radiation	gamma radiation	synchroton
beta radiation	hard radiation	radiation
black body	Hawking	ultraviolet
radiation	radiation	radiation
bremsstrahlung	infrared radiation	visible radiation
Cerenkov	insolation	X-rays
radiation	ionizing	
cosmic radiation	microwaves	

---

radical *adj, n*
• *adj*
1 BASIC, fundamental, rudimentary, primary, elementary, elemental, essential, natural, native, innate, intrinsic, deep-seated, profound
2 *radical changes*
drastic, comprehensive, thorough, sweeping, far-reaching, exhaustive, thoroughgoing, profound, complete, absolute, total, entire, utter
3 FANATICAL, militant, extreme, extremist, rebellious, revolutionary
E3 1 superficial **3** conservative, moderate
• *n*
fanatic, militant, extremist, revolutionary, rebel, reformer, reformist, fundamentalist

raffish *adj*
disreputable, dissipated, dissolute, cheap, tawdry, vulgar, uncouth, trashy, bohemian, rakish, showy, sporty, jaunty, casual, careless, devil-may-care, improper, gross, flamboyant, flashy, garish, gaudy, tasteless, loud, coarse
OLD dashing
FORMAL meretricious
E3 proper, sedate, staid; *formal* decorous

raffle *n*
draw, lottery, sweepstake, sweep, tombola

rag¹ *n*
1 *an old clothes rag*
cloth, flannel, floorcloth, duster, towel; *S Afr* lap, l appie
OLD slut
2 *dressed in rags*
remnant, shred, raggedness, tatter, tat, clout, tagrag; *Scot* wallop
COLLOQ. duddery, duds, schmutter

rag² v

rag the new boy
tease, badger, jeer, mock, ridicule, taunt, torment, bait, haze
OLD row
COLLOQ. rib, kid, take the mickey out of
SLANG *N Am* goof

ragamuffin n

urchin, guttersnipe, waif, street arab, gamin

ragbag n

confusion, miscellany, assortment, mixture, mix, jumble, medley, pastiche, hotchpotch, hodgepodge, salad, potpourri, olio, olla-podrida
FORMAL assemblage
COLLOQ. omnium-gatherum, mishmash

rage n, v

◆ *n*
anger, wrath, fury, frenzy, raving, madness, tumult, tantrum, temper, paroxysm
◆ *v*
fume, seethe, rant, rave, storm, thunder, explode, rampage
COLLOQ. blow a fuse, blow a gasket, blow your cool, blow your top, boil over, burst a blood vessel, do your nut, explode, flip your lid, fly off the handle, go mad, foam at the mouth, go off the deep end, go up the wall, hit the roof, lose your cool, lose your rag, raise hell, see red
■ **all the rage**
fashionable, popular, the craze, in vogue, stylish
COLLOQ. cool, in, the in thing, trendy, now

ragged adj

1 ragged clothes
frayed, torn, ripped, tattered, in tatters, worn-out, in holes, holey, threadbare, falling to pieces, tatty, shabby
OLD rent
2 ragged children
scruffy, untidy, unkempt, poor, destitute, down and out, down-at-heel
FORMAL indigent
3 JAGGED, serrated, indented, notched, rugged, rough, uneven, irregular
4 a ragged group of people
fragmented, erratic, disorganized, straggling

raging adj

1 VIOLENT, wild, stormy, turbulent, tumultuous
2 ANGRY, furious, enraged, infuriated, ireful, irate, fuming, incensed, raving, seething, wrathful, frenzied, mad
FORMAL fulminating, furibund

raid n, v

◆ *n*
attack, onset, assault, charge, onslaught, inroad, invasion, descent, excursion, incursion, foray, sortie, sally, strike, blitz, air raid, Baedeker raid, swoop, robbery, break-in, hold-up, smash-and-grab raid, dawn raid, ram-raid, sneak-raid, spreagh
OLD (*Shakesp & Spenser*) road; (*Spenser*) bodrag
SLANG bust
◆ *v*
loot, pillage, plunder, sack, ransack, forage, rifle, maraud, break into, attack, assail, rush, set upon, descend on, invade, storm, foray, ram-raid
SLANG bust, do, pull

raider n

attacker, invader, looter, plunderer, pillager, ransacker, marauder, robber, thief, criminal, brigand, villain, pirate
COLLOQ. crook, shark

rail v

censure, criticize, attack, abuse, protest, decry, upbraid, vociferate, mock, jeer, revile, ridicule, scoff
FORMAL arraign, castigate, denounce, fulminate, inveigh, vituperate

railing n

fence, fencing, paling, barrier, parapet, rail(s), balustrade

raillery n

mockery, teasing, jeering, jesting, banter, chaff, badinage, repartee, irony, joke, joking, ridicule, satire, sport, pleasantry, persiflage
OLD dicacity
FORMAL diatribe, invective
COLLOQ. kidding, ragging, ribbing; *Aust* chiacking

railway n

track, line, rail(s); *N Am* railroad

Types of railway include:

branch line	high-speed line	rack-and-pinion
broad gauge	InterCity®	railway
cable railway	light railway	rack railway
cutting	main line	rapid transit
electric railway	marshalling yard	system
elevated railway	metro	siding
express	model railway	standard gauge
feeder line	monorail	subway
freight	mountain railway	tramway
funicular railway	narrow gauge	trunk line
garden railway	passenger line	*colloq.* tube
goods line		underground

---

rain n, v

◆ *n*
1 RAINFALL, precipitation, raindrops, drizzle, mizzle, shower, cloudburst, downpour, deluge, torrent, storm, rainstorm, thunderstorm, squall
2 a rain of stones
torrent, volley, shower, deluge
◆ *v*
spit, drizzle, mizzle, sprinkle, shower, pour (down), tipple down, teem, pelt, deluge
COLLOQ. bucket (down), rain cats and dogs, come down in buckets/sheets/stair rods/torrents, the floodgates/clouds open
SLANG piss down
Related adjectives: pluvial, hyetal

rainbow n, adj

◆ *n*
arc, arch, bow, spectrum, prism, iris, fog-bow, moon-bow, weather gall, *arc-en-ciel*; *Scot* weather gaw
OLD water gall
◆ *adj*
rainbow-like, kaleidoscopic, prismatic, variegated, spectral, opalescent
FORMAL iridescent, irisated, irised
E3 monochrome

The colours of the rainbow are:

red	yellow	blue	violet
orange	green	indigo	

---

rainy adj

wet, damp, moist, watery, showery, drizzly; *dialect* soft
FORMAL inclement, pluvial, pluviose, pluvious, hyetal
E3 dry

raise v

1 LIFT, lift up, elevate, hoist, uplift, heave up, jack up, put up, set up, erect, build, construct, weigh
2 INCREASE, escalate, put up, magnify, heighten, strengthen, step up, push up, intensify, amplify, boost, enhance, upgrade
FORMAL augment
COLLOQ. jack up, bump up, hike up

3 raise funds
get, obtain, collect, gather, get together, amass, accumulate, assemble, rally, muster, recruit
4 BRING UP, rear, breed, propagate, grow, cultivate, educate, produce, develop, nurture
5 raise a subject
bring up, broach, introduce, present, put forward, moot, suggest
6 PROVOKE, cause, create, arouse, rouse, activate, give rise to, evoke, excite, stir
F3 1 lower, drop **2** decrease, reduce **5** suppress

raised adj
embossed, relief, applied, appliqué, cameo, relievo
F3 engraved, incised, intaglio

rake¹ v, n
• v
1 rake the grass
scratch, hoe, scrape, graze, comb, level, smooth
2 SEARCH, scour, hunt, ransack, rifle, rummage, comb
3 GATHER, collect, amass, accumulate
• n
harrow, muck-rake, buckrake, stubble rake, horse rake

rake² n, v
• n
DEGENERATE, debauchee, playboy, roué, wanton, dissolute, libertine, hedonist, lecher, sensualist, pleasure-seeker, spendthrift, swinger, rakehell, Lothario, gay dog
FORMAL profligate, prodigal
F3 ascetic, puritan
■ **rake in**
earn, receive, get paid, make, fetch, haul in, net, gross, reap
COLLOQ. bring in, pull in
■ **rake up**
remind, bring up, raise, mention, revive, introduce, drag up, dredge up, dig up

rake-off n
cut, share, slice, cut, part, portion, proportion, percentage

rakish adj
1 STYLISH, sporty, smart, dapper, sharp, flamboyant, flashy, jaunty, debonair, nonchalant, adventurous, casual, breezy, devil-may-care
OLD dashing
COLLOQ. natty, snazzy
2 DEBAUCHED, dissolute, dissipated, abandoned, libertine, loose, lecherous, raffish, sinful, depraved, degenerate, immoral, licentious
FORMAL prodigal, profligate

rally n, v
• n
1 GATHERING, assembly, convention, convocation, conference, meeting, mass meeting, jamboree, reunion, march, demonstration
FORMAL assemblage
2 RECOVERY, recuperation, revival, comeback, improvement, resurgence, renewal
• v
1 GATHER, collect, come/bring together, get together, assemble, congregate, group, band together, muster, summon, round up, unite, marshal, organize, mobilize, reassemble, regroup, reorganize, reform
OLD really, rely; (Shakesp) re-enforce
FORMAL convene
2 RECOVER, recuperate, revive, improve, pick up, get well, get better, gain strength, pull through
COLLOQ. perk up, bounce back, get back on your feet, be on the mend

ram v
1 HIT, strike, beat, butt, hammer, pound, drive, drum, bump, crash, smash, dash, slam, stem
OLD pun

2 FORCE, drive, thrust, cram, stuff, pack, crowd, jam, squeeze, compress, wedge
TECHNICAL tamp

ramble v, n
• v
1 WALK, hike, trek, tramp, traipse, stroll, amble, saunter, stray, straggle, wander, roam, range, jaunt, rove, diverge, meander, wind, zigzag
2 CHATTER, babble, digress, wander, drift; Scot blether; dialect & N Am blather
FORMAL expatiate
COLLOQ. rabbit (on), witter (on), gas, jaw, natter, waffle, go off at a tangent
• n
walk, hike, trek, tramp, stroll, saunter, wander, roam, amble, jaunt, tour, trip, excursion

rambler n
hiker, walker, traveller, stroller, rover, roamer, saunterer, wanderer, drifter, wayfarer

rambling adj
1 SPREADING, sprawling, straggling, trailing
2 ROUNDABOUT, digressive, wandering, wordy, verbose, long-winded, long-drawn-out, disjointed, disconnected, incoherent
FORMAL circuitous, periphrastic, errant
F3 2 direct

ramification n
1 RESULT, consequence, effect, upshot, outcome, sequel
2 BRANCH, offshoot, limb, outgrowth, development, implication, complication
FORMAL divarication

ramp n
slope, incline, gradient, rise, grade
FORMAL acclivity, declivity

rampage v, n
• v
run wild, run amok, run riot, go berserk, rush, rush violently/wildly, charge, tear, storm, rage, rant, rave
• n
rage, fury, frenzy, turmoil, mayhem, storm, uproar, violence, destruction, furore
■ **on the rampage**
wild, amok, berserk, frenzied, in a frenzy, violent(ly), wild(ly), out of control

rampant adj
unrestrained, uncontrolled, out of control, out of hand, unbridled, unchecked, wanton, excessive, fierce, violent, raging, wild, riotous, rank, profuse, rife, widespread, prevalent, epidemic, pandemic
COLLOQ. spreading like wildfire

rampart n
earthwork, embankment, bank, fence, barricade, bastion, bulwark, defence, stronghold, guard, wall, security, parapet, fort, fortification, breastwork, vallum

ramshackle adj
dilapidated, tumbledown, broken-down, run-down, crumbling, ruined, neglected, derelict, jerry-built, unsafe, rickety, shaky, flimsy, unsteady, tottering, decrepit, gone to rack and ruin
F3 solid, stable

ranch n
farm, estate, plantation, fazenda, hacienda, estancia, dude ranch; N Am range, spread; Aust & NZ station

rancid adj
sour, off, bad, turned, high, overripe, unpleasant, musty, stale, rank, foul, f(o)etid, putrid, rotten
FORMAL noxious, noisome, malodorous
F3 sweet

rancorous *adj*
resentful, bitter, acrimonious, acerbic, hostile, spiteful, malevolent, malignant, vindictive, venomous, vengeful, implacable, virulent, splenetic

rancour *n*
resentfulness, resentment, spite, hate, hatred, animosity, malevolence, malice, malignity, ill-feeling, ill-will, hostility, bitterness, acrimony, enmity, grudge, venom, vindictiveness, spleen
FORMAL animus, antipathy

random *adj*
arbitrary, chance, casual, incidental, haphazard, irregular, sporadic, unsystematic, unarranged, unplanned, unmethodical, accidental, aimless, purposeless, indiscriminate, stray
FORMAL fortuitous, serendipitous
COLLOQ. hit-or-miss
E3 systematic, deliberate
■ **at random**
randomly, haphazardly, incidentally, fortuitously, arbitrarily, sporadically, irregularly, unsystematically, unmethodically, aimlessly, purposelessly, indiscriminately
E3 systematically, deliberately

randomly *adv*
at random, haphazardly, incidentally, arbitrarily, sporadically, irregularly, unsystematically, unmethodically, aimlessly, purposelessly, indiscriminately
E3 systematically, deliberately

randy *adj*
horny, sexy, raunchy, amorous, aroused, hot, lustful, goatish, lascivious, lecherous, satyric
FORMAL concupiscent
COLLOQ. turned-on

range *n, v*
♦ *n*
1 *a range of fittings*
variety, diversity, assortment, selection, array, sort, kind, type, class, order, species, genus, series, string, chain, line, row, file
2 SCOPE, compass, scale, gamut, spectrum, radius, sweep, spread, extent, distance, reach, span, confines, limits, bounds, parameters, area, field, domain, province, sphere, orbit
3 *a mountain range*
line, row, chain, string, sierra, cordillera
4 PASTURE, grass, grassland, meadow, field, paddock, pasturage, grazing, grazing land
5 *a cooking range*
stove, cooker, oven
♦ *v*
1 EXTEND, stretch, reach, go, run, cover, spread, vary, fluctuate
2 ALIGN, arrange, draw up, line up, order, rank, class, classify, catalogue, group, categorize, grade, pigeonhole, compartmentalize
FORMAL dispose
3 ROAM, wander, stroll, stray, drift, amble, ramble, rove

rangy *adj*
long-legged, leggy, lanky, gangling, long-limbed, skinny, weedy, rawboned
E3 compact, dumpy

rank¹ *n, v*
♦ *n*
1 GRADE, degree, class, caste, status, standing, position, station, condition, estate, mark, echelon, level, stratum, tier, classification, sort, type, group, division
COLLOQ. place in the pecking order
See panel on next page
2 ARISTOCRACY, nobility, peerage, peers, nobles, gentry, élite, lords, high society, family

COLLOQ. nobs, toffs
3 ROW, line, range, column, file, string, series, order, formation
♦ *v*
1 GRADE, class, rate, place, position, range, sort, classify, categorize, order, arrange, organize, marshal
2 ALIGN, arrange, order, draw up, line up
FORMAL dispose
■ **rank and file**
1 ORDINARY SOLDIERS, ordinary men, soldiers, private soldiers
2 RABBLE, masses, populace, crowd, herd, mob, common people, proletariat, hoi polloi, riff-raff
COLLOQ. proles, plebs

rank² *adj*
1 UTTER, total, complete, absolute, unmitigated, unqualified, thorough, sheer, downright, out-and-out, arrant, gross, flagrant, glaring, blatant, outrageous
2 FOUL, repulsive, disgusting, unpleasant, offensive, disagreeable, revolting, stinking, evil-smelling, acrid, pungent, putrid, f(o)etid, rancid, stale
FORMAL malodorous, mephitic, graveolent
3 *rank disobedience*
gross, coarse, shocking, outrageous, vile
4 OVERGROWN, lush, abundant, dense, profuse, vigorous
FORMAL luxuriant

rankle *v*
annoy, irritate, rile, nettle, gall, irk, vex, peeve, fester, cause bitterness/resentment in/to, embitter, anger
COLLOQ. bug, get your blood up, get your back up, make your blood boil, get on your nerves, get up your nose, get under your skin, get your goat, get on your wick

ransack *v*
1 PLUNDER, rifle, raid, sack, strip, ravage, devastate, maraud, harry, loot, pillage
FORMAL depredate
2 SEARCH, scour, comb, rake, hunt, fish, rummage through, go through, turn inside out, turn upside down; *Scot* ripe
OLD ranshackle
FORMAL despoil

ransom *n, v*
♦ *n*
1 PAYMENT, price, money, pay-off
2 REDEMPTION, deliverance, rescue, freedom, setting free, liberation, restoration, release
♦ *v*
buy off, buy/purchase the freedom of, redeem, deliver, rescue, liberate, free, set free, release

rant *v, n*
♦ *v*
shout, cry, yell, roar, bellow, bluster, rave, harangue, rant and rave
FORMAL declaim, vociferate, hold forth
COLLOQ. tub-thump
♦ *n*
storm, shouting, crying, yelling, roaring, bluster, tirade, oration, harangue, rhetoric, bombast
FORMAL declamation, diatribe, philippic, vociferation

rap *v, n*
♦ *v*
1 KNOCK, hit, strike, tap, clout, clip, cuff, hammer, thump, bang, batter, flick, flirt, knap
COLLOQ. whack
2 REPROVE, reprimand, criticize, pick holes in, pull/tear to pieces, slate, run down, come down on, censure, punish, blame, scold
FORMAL castigate
COLLOQ. rail, slam, knock, pan, haul over the coals, tear to shreds

Ranks in the armed services include:

UK AIR FORCE:
aircraftsman/aircraftswoman
corporal
sergeant
master aircrew
warrant officer
pilot officer
flying officer
flight lieutenant
squadron leader
wing commander
group captain
air-commodore
air vice-marshal
air-marshal
air-chief-marshal
marshal of the Royal Air Force

US AIR FORCE:
airman
airman first class
senior airman
staff sergeant
chief master sergeant
second-lieutenant
first-lieutenant
captain
major
lieutenant-colonel
colonel
brigadier-general
major-general
lieutenant-general
general
general of the air force

UK ARMY:
private
lance-corporal
corporal
sergeant
warrant officer
lieutenant
captain
major
lieutenant-colonel
colonel
brigadier
major general
lieutenant-general
general
field marshal

US ARMY:
private
private first class
corporal
sergeant
staff sergeant
sergeant first class
first sergeant
master sergeant
sergeant major
command sergeant major
second lieutenant
first lieutenant
captain
major
lieutenant colonel
colonel
brigadier general
major general
lieutenant general
general
general of the army

UK NAVY:
able seaman
rating
petty officer
chief petty officer
sublieutenant
lieutenant
lieutenant-commander
commander
captain
commodore
rear admiral
vice-admiral
admiral
admiral of the fleet

US NAVY:
seaman recruit/apprentice
seaman
petty officer third class
petty officer second class
petty officer first class
chief petty officer
senior chief petty officer
master chief petty officer
lieutenant junior grade
lieutenant
lieutenant commander
commander
captain
rear admiral (lower half)
rear admiral (upper half)
vice-admiral
admiral
fleet admiral

UK POLICE:
constable/detective constable
sergeant/detective sergeant
inspector/detective inspector
chief inspector/detective chief inspector
superintendent/detective superintendent
chief superintendent/detective chief superintendent
commander
deputy assistant commissioner
assistant commissioner
deputy commissioner
commissioner

US STATE POLICE:
Trooper (or Trooper Second Class)
Trooper First Class
Corporal
Sergeant
Lieutenant
Captain
Major
Lieutenant Colonel
Colonel

See also **soldier**.

• *n*
1 KNOCK, hit, blow, tap, clout, clip, cuff, hammer, thump, bang, batter; *Scot* yanker
COLLOQ. whack
2 REBUKE, reprimand, censure, blame, punishment
FORMAL castigation
COLLOQ. flak, slating, slamming, knocking, stick

■ **take the rap**
take the blame, be punished, suffer the consequences, pay for it, face the music, get it in the neck, lay your head on the block

rapacious *adj*
uncaring, greedy, grasping, extortionate, preying, ravening, ravenous, voracious, plundering, predatory, marauding, insatiable, wolfish, wolvish, vulturish, vulturous, usurious
FORMAL avaricious, esurient

rapacity *n*
greed, greediness, graspingness, avarice, insatiableness, predatoriness, rapaciousness, ravenousness, voraciousness, voracity, wolfishness, usury
FORMAL avidity, esurience, esuriency
COLLOQ. shark's manners

rape *v, n*
• *v*
1 ***rape a woman***
violate, ravish, assault, assault sexually, abuse, maltreat, defile, deflower, gang-rape
OLD vitiate
2 ***rape the land***
ravage, sack, ransack, strip, raid, loot, rob, pillage, plunder, devastate, violate, defile
FORMAL despoil, depredate, spoliate
• *n*
1 ***the rape of a young girl***
violation, assault, sexual assault, violence, ravishment, abuse, outrage, maltreatment, date rape, gang rape; *N Am* statutory rape
2 ***rape of the countryside***
ravaging, sacking, ransacking, stripping, raid, looting, plundering, devastation, violation, defilement
FORMAL rapine, despoliation, depredation, spoliation

rapid *adj*
swift, speedy, quick, fast, express, prompt, lively, brisk, hurried, hasty, headlong
FORMAL precipitate, expeditious
COLLOQ. like lightning, like greased lightning, nifty, zippy, pdq, pretty damn quick
≠ slow, leisurely, sluggish; *formal* tardy

rapidity *n*
quickness, hurry, speed, speediness, rush, haste, briskness, swiftness, velocity, fleetness, promptness, dispatch
FORMAL alacrity, celerity, expedition, expeditiousness, precipitateness, promptitude
≠ slowness

rapidly *adv*
fast, quickly, speedily, swiftly, hastily, hurriedly, briskly, promptly
FORMAL expeditiously, precipitately
COLLOQ. pronto, lickety-split, at a rate of knots, at the double, before you can say Jack Robinson, by leaps and bounds, hell for leather, like a bat out of hell, like the clappers, like greased lightning, a mile a minute
≠ slowly

rapine *n*
ravaging, sacking, ransacking, rage, stripping, raid, looting, plundering, devastation, violation, defilement
FORMAL despoliation, depredation, spoliation

rapport *n*
bond, link, affinity, relationship, empathy, sympathy, understanding, good understanding, harmony

rapprochement *n*
increased friendliness, agreement, reconciliation, reunion, détente, softening, harmonization, reconcilement

rapt *adj*
engrossed, absorbed, preoccupied, intent, gripped, spellbound, enthralled, bewitched, captivated, concentrated, fascinated, entranced, charmed,

enchanted, ecstatic, delighted, thrilled, ravished, enraptured, transported

rapture *n*
delight, happiness, joy, bliss, ecstasy, elation, exhilaration, enchantment, euphoria, exaltation, transport
OLD (*Spenser*) enragement
FORMAL delectation, felicity
COLLOQ. seventh heaven, cloud nine, top of the world

■ **go into raptures**
enthuse, praise, rave, wax lyrical, gush, drool, excite, inspire, motivate, fire, bubble over, effervesce

rapturous *adj*
joyful, joyous, overjoyed, happy, delighted, enthusiastic, blissful, ecstatic, entranced, euphoric, exalted, ravished, transported, rhapsodic
COLLOQ. over the moon, on cloud nine, in seventh heaven, tickled pink, on top of the world

rare *adj*
1 UNCOMMON, unusual, exceptional, scarce, sparse, sporadic, infrequent
COLLOQ. thin on the ground, few and far between, like gold dust
2 EXQUISITE, superb, excellent, superlative, superior, outstanding, unparalleled, incomparable, matchless, exceptional, remarkable, precious, choice
COLLOQ. one in a million
E3 1 common, abundant, frequent, ordinary, typical

rarefied *adj*
exclusive, select, private, esoteric, refined, high, noble, sublime, special

rarely *adv*
seldom, hardly ever, scarcely ever, infrequently, occasionally, little, scarcely, hardly, intermittently, sporadically, spasmodically
COLLOQ. once in a blue moon
E3 often, frequently

raring *adj*
eager, keen, enthusiastic, ready, willing, impatient, longing, itching, desperate

rarity *n*
1 CURIOSITY, curio, gem, pearl, treasure, find, collector's item, marvel, wonder, nonpareil
2 UNCOMMONNESS, unusualness, strangeness, scarcity, shortage, sparseness, infrequency
E3 2 commonness, frequency

rascal *n*
rogue, scoundrel, scamp, scallywag, imp, devil, villain, good-for-nothing, ne'er-do-well, mischief-maker, wastrel, vagabond, loon, rascallion, rapscallion, hallion, scapegrace; *dialect* skellum; *Scot* smaik; *Irish* spalpeen; *N Am* skeesicks; *S Afr* skelm
OLD rascaille, cullion, varlet
COLLOQ. tinker, toerag
SLANG son of a gun, a bad hat

rascally *adj*
dishonest, wicked, mischievous, scoundrelly, unscrupulous, villainous, good-for-nothing, evil, vicious, disreputable, base, crooked, bad, knavish, low, mean, reprobate
COLLOQ. furciferous

rash[1] *adj*
a rash action
impulsive, impetuous, hasty, over-hasty, fast, reckless, ill-considered, inconsiderate, foolhardy, ill-advised, madcap, hare-brained, hot-headed, headstrong, headlong, unguarded, unwary, indiscreet, imprudent, adventurous, audacious, careless, premature, heedless, unthinking, dare-devil, harum-scarum

OLD furthersome, hasty-witted, temerarious; (*Shakesp*) madbrain(ed)
FORMAL precipitate, temerous
E3 cautious, wary, careful

rash[2] *n*
1 *a rash on the skin*
eruption, outbreak, hives, nettlerash, heat rash, epidemic, plague, itch, irritation
TECHNICAL pompholyx, urticaria, rosacea
2 *a rash of burglaries*
spate, flood, deluge, torrent, run, series, rush, wave

rashly *adv*
impulsively, on impulse, impetuously, hastily, over-hastily, recklessly, heedlessly, carelessly, without thinking, unwarily, indiscreetly, imprudently, audaciously
E3 cautiously, carefully

rashness *n*
impulsiveness, incaution, hastiness, foolhardiness, carelessness, incautiousness, imprudence, recklessness, thoughtlessness, adventurousness, audacity, heedlessness, brashness, indiscretion
FORMAL precipitance, precipitation, precipitancy, temerity
E3 carefulness, cautiousness, wariness

rasp *n, v*
♦ *n*
grating, scrape, grinding, scratch, harshness, hoarseness, croak
♦ *v*
1 GRATE, scrape, grind, file, sand, scour, scratch, abrade, rub; *Scot* risp
FORMAL excoriate
2 IRRITATE, grate, jar
COLLOQ. peeve, bug, get on your nerves
3 CROAK, screech, squawk, cackle; *Scot* risp

rasping *adj*
harsh, hoarse, creaking, croaking, grating, jarring, raspy, gravelly, gruff, husky, croaky, scratchy, rough, raucous
FORMAL stridulant

rat *n, v*
♦ *n*
informer, informant, betrayer, traitor, Judas, tell-tale, sneak, spy, squeaker, whisperer
OLD approver, discoverer, promoter, sycophant
COLLOQ. mole, finger, squealer, whistle-blower, snitch, snitcher, canary, fink, nose
SLANG grass, supergrass, stool pigeon, nark, peacher, snout; *N Am* stoolie; *Aust* fizgig
OLD SLANG stag
♦ *v*
inform, betray, incriminate, denounce, blab
COLLOQ. tell on, squeal, blow, blow the whistle on, sell down the river, split, snitch; *N Am* sing; *Aust* put someone's pot on, dob on
SLANG peach, grass, shop, rumble

rate *n, v*
♦ *n*
1 SPEED, velocity, tempo, time, ratio, proportion, percentage, relation, degree, grade, rank, rating, standard, basis, measure, scale
2 CHARGE, fee, hire, toll, tariff, price, cost, value, evaluate, assess, worth, pay, payment, tax, duty, amount, figure, percentage
♦ *v*
1 JUDGE, regard, consider, deem, esteem, count, reckon, figure, estimate, evaluate, value, assess, weigh (up), sum (up), measure, grade, rank, categorize, class, classify
FORMAL appraise, adjudge
2 ADMIRE, respect, value, prize, have a high opinion of, esteem
3 DESERVE, merit, be worthy of, have a right to, warrant, justify, be entitled to

■ at any rate
in any case, anyway, anyhow, in any event, nevertheless, regardless, at all

rather *adv*
1 MODERATELY, relatively, slightly, a bit, a little, somewhat, fairly, quite, to some degree/extent, pretty, noticeably, significantly, very
2 PREFERABLY, sooner, much rather, much sooner, instead, by/for preference, by/for/from choice

ratification *n*
approval, endorsement, corroboration, authorization, affirmation, confirmation, certification, validation, authentication, seal/stamp of approval
E3 rejection

ratify *v*
approve, uphold, endorse, corroborate, sign, countersign, legalize, sanction, authorize, warrant, establish, affirm, agree to, confirm, certify, validate, authenticate, seal, strike, amen
TECHNICAL preconize
FORMAL homologate
E3 repudiate, reject

rating *n*
assessment, classification, category, score, mark, evaluation, class, rank, degree, status, standing, position, placing, order, grade, grading
FORMAL appraisal, adjudging

ratio *n*
proportion, percentage, fraction, index, relation, relationship, correspondence, correlation, symmetry, balance

ration *n, v*
♦ *n*
1 QUOTA, allowance, allocation, allotment, share, proportion, percentage, portion, helping, part, measure, lot, amount
2 *rations in times of shortage*
food, foodstuffs, provisions, supplies, stores, iron ration
TECHNICAL compo ration
FORMAL viands, victuals
♦ *v*
allot, allocate, apportion, budget, share, deal out, distribute, hand out, divide out, measure out, mete out, dole out, dispense, supply, issue, control, restrict, limit, conserve, save, point
FORMAL apportion

rational *adj*
logical, reasonable, sound, well-founded, realistic, sensible, prudent, clear-headed, wise, sane, normal, balanced, in your right mind/senses, lucid, reasoning, thinking, intelligent, intellectual, enlightened, Apollonian; *Scot* wice
TECHNICAL discursive
OLD sober
FORMAL judicious, sagacious, circumspect, philosophical, cognitive, cerebral, ratiocinative
E3 irrational, unreasonable, illogical, insane, crazy

rationale *n*
logic, reasoning, philosophy, thesis, principle, basis, grounds, explanation, reason(s), purpose, *raison d'être*, motive, motivation, hypothesis, theory

rationalization *n*
1 JUSTIFICATION, excuse, excusing, vindication, explanation
2 REORGANIZATION, modernization, streamlining, updating

rationalize *v*
1 JUSTIFY, excuse, vindicate, explain, account for, make allowances for, explain away
2 REORGANIZE, streamline, trim, modernize, update, make more efficient, cut back on, cut out waste

rationally *adv*
logically, reasonably, sensibly, prudently, sanely, lucidly, thinkingly, intelligently, without bias/prejudice
FORMAL judiciously, sagaciously, philosophically
E3 irrationally, illogically, insanely

rattle *v, n*
♦ *v*
1 CLATTER, jingle, jangle, clang, clank, clink, shake, vibrate, jolt, jar, bounce, bang, rap, bump, knock
2 UNNERVE, disconcert, unsettle, disturb, confuse, upset, put off/out, shake, alarm, throw off balance
COLLOQ. faze, put someone's nose out of joint
♦ *n*
clatter, jingle, jangle, clank, clanking, clink, clinking, shaking, vibration, jolting, jarring

■ rattle off
reel off, list, list quickly, run through, recite, repeat

■ rattle on
chatter, gabble, jabber, prate, prattle, blether, cackle
COLLOQ. gab, rabbit on, witter, yack, chunter

ratty *adj*
irritable, annoyed, angry, cross, impatient, testy, touchy, short, snappy, short-tempered
COLLOQ. crabbed, peeved, grouchy
E3 calm, patient

raucous *adj*
harsh, rough, hoarse, husky, scratching, rasping, grating, jarring, screeching, piercing, ear-piercing, discordant, strident, shrill, sharp, noisy, loud

raunchy *adj*
sexy, alluring, desirable, attractive, sensual, voluptuous, nubile, seductive, inviting, flirtatious, arousing, stimulating, slinky, provoking, provocative, titillating, pornographic, erotic, salacious, suggestive

ravage *v, n*
♦ *v*
destroy, devastate, lay waste, demolish, level, raze, wreck, ruin, leave in ruins, spoil, damage, loot, harry, maraud, pillage, plunder, sack, depredate
FORMAL despoil
♦ *n*
destruction, devastation, havoc, damage, ruin, ruination, looting, ransacking, desolation, wreckage, pillage, plunder
FORMAL despoliation, depredation, spoliation

ravaged *adj*
devastated, destroyed, desolate, wrecked, ransacked, spoilt, shattered, war-worn, war-torn, battle-torn, war-wasted
E3 unspoilt

rave *v, adj, n*
♦ *v*
1 TALK WILDLY, rant and rave, shout, cry, yell, roar, bellow, babble, jabber, ramble
2 RAGE, storm, thunder, roar, rant, rant and rave, fume, seethe, explode, lose your temper
COLLOQ. lose your cool, boil over, flip your lid, hit the roof, blow up, blow a fuse, blow a gasket, blow your cool, blow your top, burst a blood vessel, do your nut, explode, fly into a rage, fly off the handle, foam at the mouth, freak out, go berserk, go mad, go off the deep end, go up the wall, have kittens, lose your rag, raise hell, see red, sizzle, throw a tantrum, throw a wobbly, get all steamed up
SLANG go bananas, go ape, go apeshit
3 ENTHUSE, sing the praises of, wax lyrical, go into raptures, extol, acclaim, hail
COLLOQ. be mad about
♦ *adj*
enthusiastic, praising, rapturous, favourable, excellent, ecstatic, wonderful
FORMAL laudatory

♦ *n*
party, disco, celebration, carousal, orgy, acid-house party
COLLOQ. do, knees-up, rave-up, bash, blow-out

raven *adj*
black, jet-black, coal-black, jet, ebony, sable, inky, dusky

ravenous *adj*
hungry, very hungry, starving, starved, famished, greedy, voracious, insatiable, wolfish

rave-up *n*
party, celebration, carousal, debauch, orgy
COLLOQ. bash, blow-out, do, shindig, thrash

ravine *n*
canyon, gorge, deep narrow valley, gully, abyss, gap, pass, chine, gill, khor, linn, nulla, flume; *dialect* clough, grike, gullet; *Scot* heuch; *N Am* arroyo, coulée, gulch, purgatory; *S Afr* kloof

raving *adj*
mad, insane, hysterical, delirious, deranged, demented, unbalanced, wild, frenzied, furious, berserk, irrational, out of your mind
COLLOQ. crazy, barmy, batty, loopy, round the bend/twist
SLANG loony, mental
E3 rational, sane, balanced

ravings *n*
gibberish, nonsense, rubbish, drivel, twaddle, balderdash, prattle, yammer
COLLOQ. gobbledygook, mumbo-jumbo
E3 sense

ravish *v*
1 DELIGHT, enrapture, overjoy, enchant, charm, captivate, enthral, entrance, fascinate, spellbind, bewitch
OLD rape
2 RAPE, violate, assault, assault sexually, abuse, maltreat, defile, force yourself on, outrage
OLD stuprate, constuprate, oppress; (*Spenser*) suppress

ravishing *adj*
delightful, enchanting, bewitching, enthralling, charming, lovely, beautiful, gorgeous, stunning, radiant, dazzling, alluring, seductive

raw *adj*
1 *raw vegetables*
uncooked, fresh
2 UNPROCESSED, unrefined, untreated, unprepared, unfinished, rough, crude, natural
3 PLAIN, bare, naked, basic, harsh, brutal, strong, intense, realistic, true-to-life, candid, blunt, outspoken, frank, forthright
4 SCRATCHED, grazed, scraped, abraded, chafed, open, bloody, red, sore, exposed, tender, sensitive
FORMAL excoriated
5 COLD, chilly, chill, bitter, biting, nippy, piercing, freezing, bleak, wet, damp
6 *a raw recruit*
inexperienced, new, green, immature, callow, ignorant, naive, untrained, untutored, unpractised, unskilled
COLLOQ. wet behind the ears
E3 1 cooked, done 2 processed, refined, treated 5 warm, mild 6 experienced, skilled

ray *n*
beam, shaft, flash, streak, stream, gleam, flicker, glimmer, twinkle, glint, spark, trace, hint, suggestion, indication

raze *v*
demolish, pull down, tear down, knock down, bulldoze, flatten, level, wreck, ruin, destroy, fell

razor

Types of razor include:

battery shaver	electric razor	safety razor
cut-throat	Ladyshave®	shaver
disposable razor	razor blade	wet-and-dry
double-edged	rechargeable	shaver
razor	razor	wet razor

re *prep*
about, concerning, regarding, with regard to, with reference to, on the subject of

reach *v, n*
♦ *v*
1 ARRIVE AT, get to, attain, achieve, make, make it to, amount to, come to, touch
COLLOQ. hit
2 *reach for a pen*
stretch (out), extend, spread, touch, contact, grasp, hold, hit, strike
3 EXTEND, stretch, spread, project, continue, come to, go as far as, go down/up to, come down/up to
4 CONTACT, get in touch with, get hold of, communicate with, get through to, write to, speak to, get onto, telephone, phone, ring, call, fax
♦ *n*
range, scope, compass, distance, span, spread, extent, extension, stretch, ambit, latitude, grasp, command, power, influence, authority, control, jurisdiction

react *v*
1 RESPOND, retaliate, reciprocate, reply, answer, acknowledge, act, behave
2 *react against something*
rebel, rise up, oppose, defy, resist
FORMAL dissent

reaction *n*
response, reply, answer, acknowledgement, repercussion, counteraction, reflex, recoil, reciprocation, counterbalance, reversal, reversion, retaliation
COLLOQ. feedback, backlash, kickback

reactionary *adj, n*
♦ *adj*
conservative, ultraconservative, right-wing, rightist, diehard, counter-revolutionary, traditional
E3 progressive, revolutionary
♦ *n*
conservative, ultraconservative, right-winger, rightist, diehard, counter-revolutionary, traditionalist
E3 progressive, revolutionary

read *v, n*
♦ *v*
1 STUDY, look at, pore over, scan, examine, scrutinize, skim, glance
FORMAL peruse
COLLOQ. dip into, browse through, leaf through, thumb through, flick through
2 INTERPRET, understand, comprehend, decipher, decode
FORMAL construe
3 RECITE, deliver, speak, utter
FORMAL declaim
4 *the gauge read zero*
indicate, show, display, register, record, measure
♦ *n*
study, look, perusal, scan, scanning, skimming, scrutiny, browsing
■ **read into**
interpret, deduce, infer, reason, misinterpret, take out of context
FORMAL construe

COLLOQ. read between the lines, get hold of the wrong end of the stick

readable *adj*
1 LEGIBLE, decipherable, intelligible, clear, easy to read, understandable, comprehensible
2 INTERESTING, enjoyable, worth reading, entertaining, stimulating, captivating, enthralling, gripping
COLLOQ. unputdownable
F3 1 illegible 2 unreadable

reader *n*
addressee, listener, hearer, audience

readership *n*
audience, following, regulars, subscribers

readily *adv*
willingly, unhesitatingly, happily, gladly, eagerly, enthusiastically, promptly, quickly, swiftly, rapidly, speedily, freely, smoothly, with ease, easily, effortlessly
F3 unwillingly, reluctantly, with difficulty

readiness *n*
willingness, preparedness, skill, preparation, aptitude, fitness, eagerness, keenness, inclination, quickness, rapidity, ease, promptness, facility, availability, handiness
COLLOQ. gameness
■ **in readiness**
in preparation, available, prepared, ready, on standby, standing by, on call, on full alert

reading *n*
1 STUDY, perusal, scrutiny, scan, browsing, examination, inspection
2 INTERPRETATION, understanding, decoding, deciphering, rendering, version, edition, rendition, recital
3 *the reading on a meter*
indication, display, register, record, measurement, figure
4 *a reading from the Bible*
passage, lesson, text, recitation, piece, section

ready *adj, v*
♦ *adj*
1 *ready to go*
prepared, waiting, set, all set, fit, fitted out, equipped, rigged out, arranged, organized, completed, finished
COLLOQ. geared up
2 WILLING, inclined, disposed, happy, pleased, eager, enthusiastic, keen
FORMAL predisposed
COLLOQ. game, psyched up
3 AVAILABLE, to hand, on hand, present, near, close, accessible, convenient, handy, within reach
COLLOQ. at your fingertips
4 ABOUT TO, on the point of, likely to, liable to, on the verge of
5 PROMPT, immediate, quick, swift, rapid, speedy, easy, sharp, astute, perceptive, clever, discerning, alert, resourceful
F3 1 unprepared 2 unwilling, reluctant, disinclined 3 unavailable, inaccessible 5 slow
♦ *v*
prepare, organize, arrange, equip, order, prime, set, alert
■ **at the ready**
prepared, ready, set, all set, mobilized, poised

real *adj*
1 *in the real world*
actual, existing, physical, material, substantial, tangible, concrete
2 *real leather*
genuine, authentic, bona fide, official, rightful, legitimate, valid, true, factual, occurring, certain, sure, positive, veritable
3 SINCERE, honest, truthful, genuine, true, from the heart, fervent, heartfelt, unfeigned, unaffected

4 *this is a real mess*
right, complete, absolute, utter, thorough
F3 1 unreal, imaginary 2 false, imitation 3 insincere, feigned

Synonym nuances
sense 2
Genuine can be widely used to suggest a lack of artificiality, while **authentic** is more suggestive of being an original rather than a modification or derivative: *an authentic Spanish galleon*. The phrase **bona fide** may be used to imply being absolutely as presented: *a bona fide charity*, while **official** could be used where there is an element of authorization.
 Rightful, on the other hand, has implications of entitlement: *the rightful Scottish queen*. Similarly, both **legitimate** and **valid** echo the idea of being justified: *he has a legitimate claim to the throne*. The word **factual** is appropriate for real events that can be verified: *a factual account of the war*.
 Certain could be used to suggest there is a lack of any doubt, or in some instances suggests an inevitability, and both **sure** and **positive** share similar connotations of dependability: *this job requires a positive commitment*. **Veritable** implies being undeniably as described, and can be used in a rather tongue-in-cheek way: *a veritable explosion of laughter*.

realism *n*
1 ACTUALITY, practicality, pragmatism, sanity, saneness, sensibleness, rationality
2 LIFELIKENESS, faithfulness, truthfulness, authenticity, naturalness, genuineness

realistic *adj*
1 PRACTICAL, down-to-earth, commonsense, sensible, matter-of-fact, level-headed, clear-sighted, businesslike, hard-headed, pragmatic, rational, logical, objective, detached, unsentimental, unromantic
COLLOQ. hard-boiled, hard-nosed
2 LIFELIKE, faithful, truthful, true, true-to-life, vivid, genuine, authentic, natural, close, real, real-life, graphic, representational, figurative
F3 1 unrealistic, impractical, irrational, idealistic 2 fake, imitation, unrealistic, unfaithful, abstract

Synonym nuances
sense 1
Practical can be used to suggest looking at things in the most straightforward way: *we need some practical thinking on what to do next*, while **down-to-earth** implies an absence of fanciful ideas. Both **commonsense** and **sensible** are more suggestive of exhibiting sound judgement: *he has tackled these issues with a commonsense approach*, whereas **matter-of-fact** is best used to suggest an absence of personal input or bias: *a matter-of-fact analysis*.
 The term **level-headed** suggests an ability to keep calm in a crisis: *any hiccups in the relationship are best addressed in level-headed discussion*, while **clear-sighted** has more to do with discerning the reality of a situation. **Businesslike** implies a brisk effectiveness coupled with emotional detachment, but **hard-headed**, although similar, has further connotations of shrewdness: *hard-headed investigators examined the data*.
 Pragmatic suggests accepting the actual rather than theory: *pragmatic compromises*, while **rational** implies the use of reason, and **logical** similarly suggests deduction and analysis.
 You might use **objective** to suggest a lack of emotional involvement, and **detached** implies a similar absence of subjectivity, whereas both **unsentimental** and **unromantic** put the emphasis more firmly on a lack of emotion.

realistically *adv*
1 PRACTICALLY, sensibly, pragmatically, rationally, logically, objectively, unsentimentally, unromantically
2 *the film follows the book's storyline realistically*
faithfully, truly, truthfully, vividly, genuinely, authentically, graphically, representationally, figuratively
E3 1 impractically, idealistically **2** unfaithfully

reality *n*
truth, fact, certainty, realism, actuality, real world, real life, existence, materiality, tangibility, substantiality, genuineness, authenticity, validity
FORMAL corporeality
E3 fiction, fantasy
■ **in reality**
in fact, actually, in actual fact, in point of fact, as a matter of fact, in practice, really, indeed, truly, in truth

realization *n*
1 UNDERSTANDING, comprehension, grasp, recognition, discernment, perception, acceptance, appreciation, awareness, consciousness
FORMAL cognizance, apprehension
2 ACHIEVEMENT, accomplishment, fulfilment, completion, implementation, performance
FORMAL actualization, consummation
3 EARNING, selling, fetching, making, gain, clearing

realize *v*
1 UNDERSTAND, grasp, comprehend, discover, learn, ascertain, catch on, take in, become aware/conscious of, recognize, perceive, discern, accept, register, appreciate, glean
FORMAL apprehend
COLLOQ. cotton on, twig, tumble to, get
2 ACHIEVE, accomplish, fulfil, complete, implement, perform, bring about
FORMAL effect, effectuate, consummate
3 SELL FOR, fetch, make, earn, gain, produce, get, obtain, net, clear, bring in, encash

really *adv*
1 ACTUALLY, in fact, truly, honestly, sincerely, genuinely, positively, surely, certainly, undoubtedly, absolutely, categorically
2 VERY, extremely, exceptionally, intensely, thoroughly, remarkably, highly, severely, indeed

realm *n*
1 *defence of the realm*
kingdom, queendom, monarchy, royalty, principality, empire, country, state, land, territory, area, region, province, domain
OLD reame, reign
2 *the realm of politics*
sphere, area, region, province, domain, world, orbit, field, department

reap *v*
1 HARVEST, cut, crop, gather, mow; *dialect* swap; *Scot* shear
FORMAL garner
2 GAIN, obtain, secure, acquire, get, derive, collect, receive, realize, win

rear *n, adj, v*
♦ *n*
back, stern, end, hind, tail, rump, buttocks, posterior, behind, bottom
COLLOQ. backside
E3 front
♦ *adj*
back, hind, hindmost, rearmost, last, tail-end
E3 front
♦ *v*
1 *rear a child*
bring up, care for, look after, raise, breed, grow, cultivate, foster, nurse, nurture, instruct, train, educate, parent

2 RISE, rise up, loom, tower, soar, raise, elevate, lift (up), hoist

rearrange *v*
change, adjust, alter, shift, vary, reorder, reschedule, reposition, rejig

reason *n, v*
♦ *n*
1 CAUSE, motive, motivation, incentive, impetus, inducement, explanation, excuse, justification, defence, warrant, ground(s), basis, case, argument, aim, intention, purpose, object, end, goal
FORMAL rationale, *raison d'être*
See Synonym nuances panel at **motive**.
2 SENSE, logic, reasoning, rationality, sanity, mind, thought, wit, brain, intellect, intellectuality, intelligence, understanding, comprehension, wisdom, judgement, common sense, gumption
FORMAL ratiocination
COLLOQ. nous
♦ *v*
work out, solve, reckon, resolve, conclude, deduce, infer, think, use your brain
FORMAL cerebrate, ratiocinate, cogitate, syllogize
■ **reason with**
urge, persuade, coax, move, argue with, debate with, discuss with, plead with
FORMAL remonstrate with
■ **within reason**
within limits, in moderation, moderately, within bounds, with self-control
E3 to excess

reasonable *adj*
1 SENSIBLE, wise, well-advised, sane, intelligent, rational, logical, practical, sound, fair, reasoned, understandable, well-thought-out, plausible, credible, possible, viable, justifiable, sane
OLD (*Shakesp*) wholesome
FORMAL sagacious, judicious
2 *a reasonable price*
acceptable, satisfactory, moderate, average, fair, just, modest, competitive, inexpensive, low
3 *a reasonable standard of work*
tolerable, acceptable, satisfactory, moderate, average, fair
COLLOQ. OK, not a lot to write home about, no great shakes, not to be sneezed at
E3 1 unreasonable, irrational **2** exorbitant, expensive **3** poor, bad

reasonably *adv*
1 SENSIBLY, wisely, rationally, intelligently, fairly, plausibly
2 *a reasonably large crowd*
fairly, quite, rather, somewhat, tolerably, passably, moderately, adequately
E3 1 unreasonably, irrationally

reasoned *adj*
clear, logical, methodical, organized, rational, sensible, sound, systematic, well-thought-out
FORMAL judicious
E3 illogical, unsystematic

reasoning *n*
logic, thinking, thought, analysis, interpretation, deduction, supposition, hypothesis, rationalization, argument, case, proof
FORMAL rationale, ratiocination, cerebration
Related adjective: logistical

reassurance *n*
comfort, encouragement, inspiration, motivation, cheer, cheering, heartening, incitement, urging, coaxing, persuasion, stimulation, consolation
FORMAL exhortation, succour

reassure *v*
comfort, cheer (up), encourage, hearten, inspire, brace, bolster, buoy up, nerve, rally
FORMAL inspirit
▄▄ alarm, unnerve

rebate *n*
refund, repayment, reduction, decrease, discount, deduction, allowance

rebel *n, v, adj*
• *n*
1 REVOLUTIONARY, agitator, insurgent, insurrectionary, guerrilla, freedom fighter, mutineer, revolter, paramilitary
OLD (*Shakesp*) mutine, revolt
2 DISSENTER, nonconformist, schismatic, apostate, heretic
OLD recusant
COLLOQ. aginner
• *v*
revolt, mutiny, rise up, riot, run riot, dissent, disobey, oppose, turn against, defy, resist, recoil, shy away, pull back, shrink, flinch
OLD mutine
▄▄ conform, obey
• *adj*
revolutionary, insurgent, insurrectionary, mutinous, rebellious, defiant, disobedient, malcontent(ed)
FORMAL insubordinate

rebellion *n*
revolt, revolution, rising, uprising, insurrection, insurgence, insurgency, mutiny, riot, military takeover, coup, coup d'état, resistance, opposition, defiance, disobedience, civil disobedience, dissent, heresy
OLD mutine
FORMAL insubordination

rebellious *adj*
rebelling, resistant, defiant, disobedient, unruly, disorderly, ungovernable, unmanageable, obstinate, revolutionary, insurrectionary, insurgent, seditious, mutinous, rioting
FORMAL contumacious, insubordinate, intractable, recalcitrant
▄▄ obedient, submissive

rebirth *n*
restoration, revival, renewal, regeneration, renaissance, revitalization, reawakening, rejuvenation, resurrection, reincarnation

rebound *v, n*
• *v*
recoil, backfire, return, bounce (back), spring (back), ricochet, boomerang, fail, defeat itself, be self-defeating
COLLOQ. come home to roost, score an own goal
• *n*
recoil, backfiring, return, bounce, spring, ricochet, repercussion, reverberation, reflection

---

⊞ rebound or **redound**?
To *rebound* is 'to bounce back', in either a neutral, a good, or a bad sense: *She was throwing the ball against the wall and catching it as it rebounded; His overweening ambition rebounded on him, as, having displaced his father from the throne, he was in turn ousted by those who would not accept him as the legitimate ruler.* To *redound* (now a rather old-fashioned or formal word) is 'to have advantageous or disadvantageous consequences': *His actions redounded to the credit of the regiment; A child's bad behaviour in public inevitably redounds on the parents.*

---

rebuff *v, n*
• *v*
spurn, reject, refuse, decline, repudiate, turn down, repulse, discourage, snub, slight, cut, counterbuff, put someone's nose out of joint

COLLOQ. cold-shoulder, give the cold shoulder to, put down, knock back
• *n*
rejection, refusal, repulse, check, discouragement, spurning, repudiation, snub, slight, counterbuff, noser, rubber, set-down, squelch
COLLOQ. brush-off, put-down, cold shoulder, slap in the face, kick in the teeth, one in the eye, a flea in your ear

rebuild *v*
restore, remake, remodel, renovate, reassemble, reconstruct, refashion, re-edify
▄▄ demolish, destroy

rebuke *v, n*
• *v*
reprove, chide, scold, reprimand, upbraid, rate, censure, blame, reproach, snub, speak to, talk to, take someone to task, trim, trounce, slap, keelhaul, countercheck; *dialect* threap; *N Am* score
OLD lesson, objurgate; (*Shakesp*) sauce
FORMAL castigate, admonish, remonstrate
COLLOQ. tell off, tick off, dress down, carpet, read the riot act to, throw the book at, give an earful, tear off a strip, give someone some stick, go to town on, haul over the coals, come down on like a ton of bricks, give someone hell, rollick, pin back someone's ears, talk like a Dutch uncle; *N Am* call down; *Aust & NZ* go crook on/at
▄▄ praise, compliment
• *n*
reproach, reproof, reprimand, scolding, lecture, censure, blame, countercheck
FORMAL admonition, castigation, remonstration
COLLOQ. dressing-down, telling-off, ticking-off, carpeting, earful, rollicking, stick, comeuppance
▄▄ praise, commendation

rebut *v*
refute, quash, defeat, discredit, disprove, invalidate, negate, overturn, give the lie to
FORMAL confute
COLLOQ. explode

rebuttal *n*
refutation, negation, defeat, disproof, invalidation, overthrow
FORMAL confutation

recalcitrance *n*
disobedience, defiance, waywardness, wilfulness, stubbornness, obstinacy, unwillingness
FORMAL insubordination
▄▄ amenability

recalcitrant *adj*
disobedient, defiant, uncontrollable, ungovernable, unmanageable, unruly, wayward, wilful, contrary, obstinate, stubborn, unsubmissive, unwilling, unco-operative
OLD renitent
FORMAL contumacious, insubordinate, intractable, refractory
▄▄ amenable, tractable

recall *v, n*
• *v*
1 REMEMBER, think of, call to mind, recollect, reminisce, think back to, cast your mind back, evoke, call up, summon up, bring back
2 ORDER BACK, summon (back), call back, order to return
3 CANCEL, revoke, withdraw, repeal, annul
FORMAL rescind, retract, countermand, abrogate, nullify
• *n*
1 REMEMBRANCE, memory, recollection
2 CANCELLATION, annulment, repeal, withdrawal
FORMAL abrogation, nullification, countermanding, retraction, revocation, recision

recant v

deny, disown, repudiate, rescind, apostatize, retract, revoke, withdraw, recall, unsay, renounce
FORMAL abjure, abrogate, disavow, disclaim, forswear

recantation n

denial, renunciation, repudiation, apostasy, withdrawal, revocation, revoke, disownment
FORMAL abjuration, disavowal, disclaimer, retractation

recapitulate v

recap, summarize, sum up, review, repeat, reiterate, restate, recount, run over, go over

recapitulation n

summarizing, summary, review, repetition, reiteration, restatement

recce v, n

• v

reconnoitre, explore, survey, scan, spy out, inspect, examine, scrutinize, investigate, patrol, observe, probe
COLLOQ. check out, see how the land lies, see the lie of the land

• n

reconnaissance, exploration, reconnoitring, scouting, survey, expedition, examination, inspection, probe, observation, scrutiny, scan, investigation, search, patrol

recede v

1 GO BACK, return, retire, withdraw, move away, retreat
2 DIMINISH, decline, fade, dwindle, decrease, lessen, fall off, drop, shrink, slacken, subside, ebb, wane, sink
FORMAL abate
E3 1 advance, approach **2** grow, increase

receipt n

1 VOUCHER, ticket, slip, proof of purchase, counterfoil, stub, acknowledgement, paper, chit, deposit-receipt
TECHNICAL warrant, dock-warrant
OLD note, quittance
FORMAL acquittance
2 RECEIVING, reception, acceptance, getting, obtaining, deriving, gaining, delivery
3 MONEY RECEIVED, takings, income, earnings, pay, proceeds, profits, gains, return(s), turnover

receive v

1 TAKE, take up, accept, get, be given, obtain, derive, gain, acquire, come by, pick up, collect, gather, inherit
2 *receive guests*
admit, let in, greet, welcome, entertain, take, contain, hold, accommodate
3 EXPERIENCE, undergo, go through, suffer, bear, sustain, meet with, encounter
4 REACT TO, respond to, hear, find out about, be informed of, learn about, perceive
FORMAL apprehend
E3 1 give, donate

receiver n

1 RECIPIENT, beneficiary, donee, assignee, grantee, legatee
2 RADIO, tuner, wireless, apparatus, handset
E3 1 donor

recent adj

late, latest, current, present-day, contemporary, modern, up-to-date, up-to-the-minute, new, novel, fresh, young
E3 old, out-of-date

recently adv

lately, of late, newly, freshly, in the last few days/weeks/ months, in the past few days/weeks/months, not long ago, a short time ago, a little while back
E3 long ago

receptacle n

container, vessel, holder
FORMAL repository, reservatory
See panel at **container**.

reception n

1 ACCEPTANCE, admission, greeting, recognition, welcome, entertaining, treatment, response, reaction, acknowledgement, receipt
2 PARTY, function, social, get-together, gathering, reunion, at-home, occasion, entertainment
COLLOQ. do, bash, beano, shindig, rave-up

receptive adj

open-minded, open to reason, amenable, accommodating, suggestible, susceptible, flexible, willing, quick, sensitive, responsive, open, accessible, approachable, friendly, hospitable, welcoming, sympathetic, favourable, interested
E3 narrow-minded, resistant, unresponsive

recess n

1 BREAK, breaktime, playtime, interval, intermission, rest, respite, time off, holiday, vacation
COLLOQ. time out
2 ALCOVE, niche, nook, corner, bay, cavity, hollow, depression, indentation, indent, cupboard, closet, press, bay, cove, bower, bunk, bunker; *Scot* bole, ingo, outshot
TECHNICAL apse, confessional, ambry, sepulchre, columbarium, embrasure, oriel, exedra, loculus, corrie, hitch, mortise
3 *in the recesses of your mind*
innards, heart, depths, interior, reaches, bowels
FORMAL penetralia

recession n

slump, depression, downturn, decline, economic decline, slide, trough, collapse, crash, failure
E3 boom, upturn

recherché adj

refined, select, choice, rare, far-fetched, obscure, exotic
FORMAL esoteric, abstruse, arcane
E3 commonplace

recipe n

formula, prescription, ingredients, instructions, directions, method, system, way, means, procedure, guide, process, technique
OLD receipt

recipient n

receiver, beneficiary, assignee, donee, grantee, legatee
E3 donor, giver

reciprocal adj

mutual, joint, exchanged, shared, give-and-take, returned, requited, complementary, alternating, corresponding, equivalent, interchangeable, interdependent, reflex
FORMAL correlative, commutual
E3 irreciprocal

reciprocate v

respond, reply, return, give in return, exchange, swap, repay, trade, match, equal, correspond, interchange, alternate
FORMAL requite
COLLOQ. do the same, give as good as you get, give an eye for an eye

reciprocity n

exchange, mutuality, give-and-take, alternation, correspondence, equivalence, interchangeability, interdependence
E3 irreciprocity

recital n

1 *a music recital*
performance, show, concert
2 RECITATION, reading, narration, report, telling, account, description, rendition, rendering, interpretation, repetition, enumeration
FORMAL declamation

recitation *n*

passage, reading, piece, party piece, poem, verse, monologue, narration, story, tale, recital, rendering, telling, performance

recite *v*

repeat, repeat from memory, tell, narrate, relate, recount, speak, say aloud, deliver, articulate, perform, reel off, rattle off, itemize, enumerate, improvise, chant, chime, rhapsodize
TECHNICAL daven, scan
FORMAL declaim

reckless *adj*

heedless, thoughtless, mindless, careless, negligent, inattentive, irresponsible, imprudent, incautious, ill-advised, indiscreet, rash, hasty, foolhardy, desperate, daredevil, devil-may-care, wild, madcap, tearaway
FORMAL precipitate
🖭 cautious, wary, careful, prudent

> **Synonym nuances**
>
> Many of these synonyms are inherently disapproving in tone.
>   **Heedless** can be used to suggest a disregard for consequences: *warriors, heedless of the dangers*, while **thoughtless** suggests a more general lack of concern. **Mindless** has implications of stupidity: *a brutal and mindless sport*, while **careless** is more appropriately used to imply either a lack of concern or an element of clumsiness: *careless disposal of toxic waste.*
>   **Negligent** is more suggestive of a deliberate dereliction of duty, and is very negative in tone. Similarly, **irresponsible** implies casualness, often verging on the dangerous, while **incautious** more straightforwardly suggests a failure to consider risks: *the wine made her incautious*, and **indiscreet** has more to do with divulging confidences. **Ill-advised**, meanwhile, appropriately describes an erroneous choice: *you would be ill-advised to go out on your own.*
>   Both **rash** and **hasty** could be used to suggest something done quickly without proper consideration, while the term **foolhardy** can be used to more explicitly express unwise recklessness. **Desperate** would suggest actions that have to do with a loss of hope, whereas **daredevil** implies those motivated by absence of fear and even a sense of adventure. While **madcap** is more suggestive of exuberant eccentricity, **tearaway** implies a lack of restraint, usually a characteristic of youth: *his tearaway son.*

recklessly *adv*

carelessly, negligently, irresponsibly, rashly, mindlessly, thoughtlessly, hastily, desperately
🖭 carefully, cautiously

recklessness *n*

carelessness, heedlessness, inattention, irresponsibility, irresponsibleness, negligence, rashness, thoughtlessness, incaution, imprudence, foolhardiness, mindlessness, madness
🖭 carefulness, caution, prudence

reckon *v*

1 THINK, believe, imagine, fancy, suppose, assume, guess
FORMAL surmise, conjecture
2 CONSIDER, regard, esteem, think of, look upon, value, rate, judge, make, put down, count, evaluate, assess, estimate, gauge, designate, call
OLD vogue
FORMAL deem, appraise, impute
3 CALCULATE, compute, figure out, work out, add up, total, tally, count, sum (up), number, enumerate, account

■ **reckon on**
rely on, depend on, bank on, count on, take for granted,

trust in, hope for, expect, anticipate, foresee, plan for, bargain for, figure on, trade on, take into account, face

■ **reckon with**
anticipate, bargain for, consider, take into account, plan for, expect, foresee, handle, cope, deal, face, treat

■ **reckon without**
not expect, fail to think of, ignore, disregard, overlook, not notice, not take into consideration/account

■ **to be reckoned with**
strong, powerful, influential, forceful, great, important, significant, considerable, formidable, weighty
FORMAL mighty

reckoning *n*

1 *by my reckoning*
calculation, computation, addition, working-out, total, tally, score, number, enumeration, estimate
2 BILL, account, charge, due, score, paying, payment, settlement
3 JUDGEMENT, opinion, estimation, evaluation, assessment
FORMAL appraisal
4 *the day of reckoning*
judgement, punishment, retribution, doom, damnation

reclaim *v*

recover, regain, get back, claim back, take back, recapture, retrieve, salvage, rescue, redeem, restore, reinstate, regenerate

reclamation *n*

salvage, recovery, regaining, retrieval, rescue, restoration, reinstatement, regeneration

recline *v*

rest, lean back, lie (down), lounge, loll, sprawl, stretch out
FORMAL repose

recluse *n*

ascetic, hermit, solitary, loner, monk, eremite, stylite, solitarian, solitaire, anchorite, anchoret, anchoress

reclusive *adj*

isolated, solitary, withdrawn, secluded, retiring, recluse, cloistered, monastic, ascetic, eremitic, hermitical, anchoritic
FORMAL sequestered

recognition *n*

1 IDENTIFICATION, detection, discovery, recollection, recall, remembrance, awareness, knowing, knowledge, consciousness, perception, realization, admission, confession, understanding, placing, spotting
FORMAL cognizance
2 ACCEPTANCE, allowing, admittance, endorsement, grating, approval, acknowledgement, validation, sanction
3 *receive recognition for your work*
appreciation, honour, reward, respect, salute, gratitude, thankfulness, thanks

recognize *v*

1 IDENTIFY, know, remember, recollect, recall, call to mind, pick out, tell, place, see, notice, spot, perceive, not miss, not mistake
2 *recognize your faults*
accept, acknowledge, admit, grant, concede, allow, endorse, appreciate, discern, perceive, understand, realize, confess, own, be aware of, be conscious of
FORMAL apprehend
3 *recognize a qualification*
accept, allow, admit, endorse, grant, approve, acknowledge, adopt, validate, sanction
4 APPRECIATE, be thankful for, honour, respect, salute, show your gratitude/thankfulness
COLLOQ. take your hat off to

recoil *v, n*

◆ *v*

move back, draw back, jump back, spring back, shy away, withdraw, flinch, shrink, quail, rebound, react, redound, reverberate, falter, kick, backfire, boomerang, misfire, come home to roost
TECHNICAL resile
OLD requoyle; (*Spenser*) recuile, rebut
✦ *n*
rebound, reaction, resilience, spring, kick, backlash, repercussion
TECHNICAL undertow
OLD requoyle

recollect *v*
recall, remember, call to mind, cast your mind back, reminisce

recollection *n*
memory, recall, remembrance, souvenir, reminiscence, (mental) impression

recommend *v*
commend, approve, endorse, praise, vouch for, advocate, urge, advise, counsel, preach, guide, suggest, propose, put forward, advance, move, tout, put in a good word for
OLD wish
FORMAL exhort, set forth
COLLOQ. plug
E3 disapprove

recommendation *n*
commendation, endorsement, approval, advice, counsel, guidance, suggestion, urging, proposal, advocacy, sanction, blessing, praise, tip, good word, special mention, reference, testimonial
TECHNICAL coupon
FORMAL exhortations
COLLOQ. plug
E3 disapproval

recompense *n, v*
✦ *n*
compensation, indemnification, damages, reparation, restitution, amends, requital, satisfaction, repayment, reward, payment, remuneration, pay, wages
FORMAL guerdon
✦ *v*
compensate, indemnify, remunerate, pay, reward, repay, redress, reimburse, make up for, requite, satisfy
FORMAL guerdon

reconcile *v*
1 *be reconciled with someone*
reunite, conciliate, pacify, appease, placate, mollify, bring together, make (your) peace, put on friendly terms
OLD agree, atone
FORMAL propitiate
COLLOQ. make up, bury the hatchet, become friends again, shake hands, forgive and forget
2 *reconcile different aims*
harmonize, accommodate, adjust, resolve, settle, mend, remedy, put right, rectify, square, accord
OLD (*Spenser*) upknit
COLLOQ. patch up
3 *reconcile yourself to an unpleasant situation*
resign yourself to, face up to, accept, come to accept, submit, wean
E3 **1** estrange, alienate

reconciliation *n*
reunion, conciliation, pacification, peace, mollification, appeasement, rapprochement, détente, settlement, agreement, harmony, harmonizing, accommodation, resolution, squaring, adjustment, compromise
FORMAL propitiation, accord
E3 estrangement, separation

recondite *adj*
obscure, difficult, involved, complicated, intricate, mysterious, mystical, deep, profound, dark, concealed, hidden, secret
FORMAL abstruse, arcane, esoteric
E3 simple, straightforward

recondition *v*
renovate, repair, restore, renew, refurbish, overhaul, fix, remodel, revamp

reconnaissance *n*
exploration, reconnoitring, scouting, survey, expedition, examination, inspection, probe, observation, scrutiny, scan, investigation, search, patrol
COLLOQ. recce

reconnoitre *v*
explore, survey, scan, spy out, inspect, examine, scrutinize, investigate, patrol, observe, probe
COLLOQ. recce, check out, see how the land lies, see the lie of the land

reconsider *v*
think over, rethink, review, revise, re-examine, think twice, modify, reassess, think better of, have second thoughts

reconsideration *n*
review, rethink, re-examination, reassessment, review, further reflection, fresh look, second thoughts

reconstruct *v*
remake, rebuild, reassemble, re-establish, refashion, remodel, recondition, revamp, reform, reorganize, redo, recreate, restore, renovate, regenerate

record *n, v, adj*
✦ *n*
1 REGISTER, log, chart, report, account, minutes, memorandum, note(s), entry, document(s), file, dossier, diary, logbook, journal, chronicle, memoir, memorial, history, annals, archives, documentation, data, evidence, photography, testimony, reminder, trace
2 RECORDING, disc, single, CD, compact disc, DVD, MiniDisc®, album, release, LP, single, 45, 78, cassette, microcassette, tape, audio tape, DAT, digital audio tape
COLLOQ. vinyl
3 *break the record*
fastest time, best performance, furthest distance, personal best, world record
4 BACKGROUND, history, previous performance, track record, curriculum vitae, career
✦ *v*
1 NOTE, enter, inscribe, write down, transcribe, register, log, chart, put down, take down, put on record, enrol, report, list, catalogue, minute, chronicle, document, keep, preserve
2 TAPE-RECORD, make a recording of, tape, videotape, video, burn, cut, edit, make, produce
3 *the gauge records electrical activity*
show, register, indicate, display, read, express
4 ACHIEVE, accomplish, obtain, manage, complete, produce
COLLOQ. notch up, chalk up
✦ *adj*
best, best ever, fastest, record-breaking, world-beating, unsurpassed, unequalled, unparalleled, without equal, supreme, superlative, top-ranking
■ **off the record**
unofficial, unofficially, confidential, confidentially, private, privately
FORMAL sub rosa
E3 officially
■ **on record**
1 *the wettest April on record*
noted, documented, written down

2 *to go on record as saying*
officially recorded, publicly known, documented

recorder *n*
1 REGISTRAR, archivist, annalist, chronicler, diarist, historian, chronologer, secretary, clerk, stenographer, scribe, scorer, score-keeper
2 TAPE RECORDER, cassette recorder, cassette-player, CD burner, video recorder, VCR, video cassette recorder, Walkman®
COLLOQ. video

recording

Types of recording include:

album	45	tape-recording
audiotape	gramophone	tele-recording
cassette	record	video
CD (compact	LP (long-playing)	video cassette
disc)	magnetic tape	video disc
DAT (digital audio	MiniDisc®	videotape
tape)	mono recording	*colloq.* vinyl
digital recording	MP3	
disc	record	
DVD (digital	78	
versatile disk)	single	
EP (extended	stereo recording	
play)	tape	

recount *v*
tell, relate, impart, communicate, report, narrate, describe, depict, portray, unfold, detail, repeat, rehearse, recite

recoup *v*
recover, retrieve, regain, get back, win back, claw back, make good, repossess, repay, refund, indemnify, reimburse, recompense, compensate
OLD recruit

recourse *n*
appeal, resort, access, turning to, choice, option, alternative, possibility, remedy, refuge, way out
■ **have recourse to**
resort to, turn to, use, utilize, make use of, avail yourself of, fall back on, employ, exercise

recover *v*
1 *recover from illness*
get better, feel better, get well, improve, pick up, rally, mend, heal, respond to treatment, get over, recuperate, feel yourself again, revive, convalesce, gain strength, get stronger, come round
FORMAL ameliorate
COLLOQ. pull through, bounce back, turn the corner, get back on your feet, be on the mend
2 REGAIN, get back, win back, recoup, retrieve, retake, recapture, repossess, reclaim, recycle, restore
OLD (*Spenser*) recure
Ⓔ **1** worsen, fail **2** lose, forfeit

recovery *n*
1 RECUPERATION, convalescence, rehabilitation, mending, healing, improvement, upturn, rally, rallying, revival, restoration
OLD convalescency, reconvalescence, recure, recover
FORMAL amelioration
2 *recovery in a country's economy*
improvement, rally, comeback, upturn, upswing, pick-up, *Wirtschaftswunder*
TECHNICAL amelioration
SLANG dead-cat bounce
3 RETRIEVAL, salvage, rescue, reclamation, recouping, regaining, repossession, recapture, recycling, revival
TECHNICAL regeneration
Ⓔ **1, 2** worsening **3** loss, forfeit

recreation *n*
fun, enjoyment, pleasure, amusement, diversion, distraction, entertainment, hobby, pastime, game, sport, play, leisure pursuit, leisure activity, leisure, relaxation, refreshment
COLLOQ. R & R

recrimination *n*
accusation, countercharge, counter-attack, reprisal, retaliation, retort, bickering, quarrel

recruit *v, n*
♦ *v*
enlist, draft, conscript, enrol, sign up, levy, engage, take on, mobilize, raise, muster, gather, assemble, put together, obtain, acquire, unionize, talent-spot, headhunt
FORMAL procure
♦ *n*
beginner, newcomer, novice, new entrant, initiate, learner, trainee, apprentice, tiro, conscript, draftee, convert
COLLOQ. greenhorn, rookie
SLANG nozzer, sprog, yob, nig-nog; *NAm* swabby, yardbird

recruitment *n*
enrolment, enlisting, drafting, conscription, signing-up, engaging, engagement, mobilization

rectification *n*
correction, improvement, amendment, putting/setting right, making good, adjustment, reformation

rectify *v*
correct, put right, right, set right, make good, remedy, cure, repair, fix, mend, reform, improve, better, amend, adjust, reform
FORMAL emend, ameliorate, redress

rectitude *n*
integrity, uprightness, virtue, honesty, honour, goodness, justice, morality, incorruptibility, irreproachability, exactness, decency, correctness, righteousness, scrupulousness
FORMAL probity

recumbent *adj*
lying down, lying, flat, horizontal, resting, reclining, leaning, lounging, prostrate, prone, sprawling
FORMAL supine
Ⓔ erect, upright

recuperate *v*
recover, get better, get well, get stronger, regain your strength, improve, pick up, rally, revive, mend, convalesce
COLLOQ. pull through, bounce back, turn the corner, get back on your feet, be on the mend
Ⓔ worsen, weaken

recuperation *n*
recovery, convalescence, rehabilitation, mending, healing, improvement, upturn, rally, rallying, revival, restoration
OLD convalescency, reconvalescence, recure
FORMAL amelioration

recur *v*
repeat itself, happen again, persist, return, reappear, run, come round (again), revert
TECHNICAL perseverate

recurrence *n*
repetition, return, appearance, reversion, regularity, persistence, continuation

recurrent *adj*
recurring, chronic, persistent, repeated, repetitive, continual, habitual, regular, periodic, cyclical, frequent, intermittent

recycle *v*
re-use, reprocess, reclaim, recover, salvage, save

red *adj*
1 SCARLET, vermilion, cherry, ruby, crimson, rose, maroon,

russet, pink, reddish, bloodshot, inflamed
2 RUDDY, florid, glowing, rosy, flushed, blushing, embarrassed, shamefaced
TECHNICAL rufescent
FORMAL rubicund
3 *red hair*
flaming red, ginger, carroty, auburn, chestnut, Titian
4 COMMUNIST, socialist, leftist, Bolshevik, revolutionary
■ **in the red**
overdrawn, insolvent, bankrupt, in debt, in arrears, owing money, penniless, impoverished
COLLOQ. on the rocks, broke, bust, gone to the wall, on your beam ends, on your uppers
Ⓔ₃ in the black
■ **see red**
become angry, lose your temper
COLLOQ explode, blow your cool, blow your top, boil over, burst a blood vessel, hit the roof, do your nut, fly into a rage, fly off the handle, go mad, lose your cool, lose your rag

red-blooded *adj*
virile, strong, vigorous, manly, masculine, robust, hearty, lively, lusty

redden *v*
blush, flush, colour, go red, crimson, suffuse

reddish *adj*
red, bloodshot, rosy, ruddy, russet, ginger, sandy, pink
TECHNICAL rufescent
FORMAL rubicund, rufous

redeem *v*
1 BUY BACK, repurchase, cash (in), convert, trade in, exchange, give in exchange, change, trade, ransom, reclaim, regain, get back, repossess, recoup, recover, recuperate, retrieve, salvage
2 COMPENSATE FOR, make up for, offset, outweigh
3 *a saviour who redeems sinners*
atone for, absolve, acquit, remove guilt from, discharge, release, liberate, emancipate, free, set free, deliver, rescue, save, reprieve; *Scot* lowse
TECHNICAL buy
FORMAL ransom, expiate

redemption *n*
1 REPURCHASE, repossession, reclamation, recovery, reparation, retrieval, exchange, reinstatement, trade-in, fulfilment, compensation
2 ATONEMENT, deliverance, expiation, emancipation, freedom, rescue, salvation, ransom, liberation, release

red-handed *adv*
in the act, in the very act, by surprise, unawares, off-guard, napping
FORMAL in flagrante delicto
COLLOQ. on the hop, with your trousers down

redolent *adj*
1 EVOCATIVE, reminiscent, suggestive, remindful
2 AROMATIC, fragrant, perfumed, scented, sweet-smelling
FORMAL odorous

redoubtable *adj*
formidable, fearsome, strong, terrible, powerful, resolute, mighty, awful, dreadful, fearful

redound *v*
contribute, ensue, reflect, result, tend
FORMAL conduce, effect

❗ **redound** or **rebound**?
See panel at **rebound**.

---

redress *v, n*
♦ *v*
1 RIGHT, put right, rectify, remedy, avenge, requite, recompense, make compensation for, compensate
2 ADJUST, amend, correct, balance, regulate

♦ *n*
compensation, recompense, indemnification, remedy, relief, assistance, help, aid, correction, requital, restitution, satisfaction, reparation, payment, justice, atonement

reduce *v*
1 LESSEN, make less, make smaller, decrease, contract, shrink, slim, shorten, abbreviate, curtail, trim, minimize, downsize, lower, moderate, weaken, diminish, impair, deplete, beat down, clip, bring/come down, condense, cut back/down, deduct, minimize, restrict, step down, take down, trim, wind down, dock, de-escalate, scant, take the edge off, water down, dilute
OLD slake
FORMAL mitigate
COLLOQ. axe
2 DRIVE, force, degrade, bring down, lower, downgrade, demote, humble, humiliate, impoverish, subdue, overcome, overpower, conquer, master
FORMAL vanquish
3 *reduce prices*
lower, decrease, cut, slash, knock down, discount, rebate, halve, deduct, deflate, devalue
COLLOQ. axe
4 SLIM, diet, go on a diet, lose weight
COLLOQ. weight-watch
Ⓔ₃ 1 increase, raise **2** boost

reduction *n*
decrease, drop, fall, decline, lessening, moderation, weakening, contraction, abbreviation, compression, shrinkage, downsizing, narrowing, shortening, minimization, curtailment, restriction, limitation, cutback, cut, discount, discounting, rebate, concession, allowance, devaluation, depreciation, deduction, subtraction, loss, clipping, condensation
FORMAL diminution
Ⓔ₃ increase, rise, enlargement

redundancy *n*
1 DISMISSAL, notice, laying-off, discharge, removal, expulsion, marching-orders, downsizing, outplacement
COLLOQ. papers, cards, jotters, sacking, firing, sack, push, boot, elbow
2 SUPERFLUITY, surplus, uselessness, wordiness, excess, repetition, tautology
TECHNICAL pleonasm, cheville
FORMAL prolixity, verbosity, exuberance
Ⓔ₃ 1 appointment, hiring

redundant *adj*
1 UNEMPLOYED, out of work, jobless, laid off, dismissed
COLLOQ. sacked, fired
2 SUPERFLUOUS, surplus, excess, extra, unneeded, unnecessary, unwanted, inessential
FORMAL supernumerary, otiose
3 WORDY, verbose, padded, repetitious, tautological
TECHNICAL pleonastic
FORMAL periphrastic
Ⓔ₃ 2 necessary, essential, required **3** concise, pithy

reef *n*
sandbank, sandbar, ridge, shoal, cay, key, motu, scar, skerry; *Aust* bombora

reek *v, n*
♦ *v*
smell, stink, fume, whiff
FORMAL exhale
COLLOQ. hum, pong; *Scot* ming
SLANG honk, niff
♦ *n*
smell, odour, whiff, stink, stench, vapour, fume(s)
FORMAL exhalation, effluvium, malodour, mephitis, fetor
COLLOQ. pong; *Scot* ming

reel v

stagger, totter, wobble, rock, sway, waver, falter, stumble, fling, lurch, pitch, swim, roll, revolve, gyrate, spin, wheel, twirl, whirl, swirl

■ **reel off**

rattle off, list, list quickly, run through, recite, repeat

refer v

1 MENTION, allude, touch on, speak of, bring up, recommend, cite, quote, hint at

2 *refer to a catalogue*

consult, look up, turn to, look at, resort to

3 SEND, direct, point, guide, pass on, hand on, transfer, commit, deliver

FORMAL remit

4 APPLY, concern, be relevant, relate, belong, mean, describe, indicate

FORMAL pertain

referee n, v

◆ n

umpire, judge, adjudicator, arbitrator, mediator

COLLOQ. ref

SLANG *N Am* zebra

◆ v

umpire, judge, adjudicate, mediate, intercede, arbitrate

reference n

1 MENTION, remark, allusion, hint, citation, quotation, illustration, source, authority, instance, note, footnote

2 TESTIMONIAL, recommendation, endorsement, credentials, character

3 RELATION, applicability, regard, respect, connection, bearing

FORMAL pertinence

■ **with reference to**

referring to, concerning, about, regarding, with regard to, as regards, respecting, with respect to, relating to, relevant to, in the matter of, on the subject of, re

FORMAL apropos

referendum n

poll, vote, voting, plebiscite, survey

referral n

transfer, sending, direction, pointing, passing/handing on, handover

refine v

1 PURIFY, process, treat, clarify, filter, sift, strain, distil, clear, cleanse

2 IMPROVE, polish, hone, perfect, elaborate, civilize, elevate, exalt

refined adj

1 CIVILIZED, cultured, cultivated, polished, sophisticated, stylish, urbane, genteel, gentlemanly, ladylike, well-bred, well-mannered, polite, civil, elegant, gracious, courtly, fine, delicate, subtle, precise, exact, sensitive, discriminating

2 PURIFIED, processed, treated, distilled, filtered, clear

1 coarse, vulgar, rude

refinement n

1 MODIFICATION, alteration, amendment, addition, improvement

FORMAL amelioration

2 CULTIVATION, sophistication, culture, urbanity, gentility, breeding, style, elegance, grace, civility, good manners, polish, taste, discrimination, subtlety, finesse

1 deterioration, degeneration **2** coarseness, vulgarity

reflect v

1 MIRROR, echo, glass, imitate, reproduce, image, send back, throw back, bounce off, shine, glint, reverberate

TECHNICAL scatter

OLD repercuss

2 SHOW, portray, depict, reveal, display, exhibit, demonstrate, indicate, express, communicate

FORMAL manifest, bespeak

3 THINK, ponder, consider, mull (over), dwell, brood, deliberate, contemplate, meditate, muse, speculate, study, chew

OLD advise

FORMAL ruminate, cogitate, cerebrate

COLLOQ. chew the cud

4 *his behaviour reflects badly on the school*

discredit, disgrace, tarnish, put in a bad light, give a bad name to

OLD redound

reflection n

1 IMAGE, likeness, echo, mirror image

2 INDICATION, impression, expression, display, demonstration, portrayal, observation, view

FORMAL manifestation

3 THINKING, thought, study, consideration, deliberation, contemplation, meditation, musing, view, opinion, impression, belief, viewpoint, idea, feeling(s)

FORMAL rumination, cogitation, cerebration

4 DISCREDIT, slur, disgrace, shame, criticism, disrepute, blame, reproach

FORMAL aspersion

reflective adj

thoughtful, contemplative, pondering, deliberative, meditative, pensive, reasoning, absorbed, dreamy

FORMAL cogitating, ruminative

reflex adj

automatic, spontaneous, without thinking, unwilled, uncontrollable, involuntary, natural, instinctive, mechanical

TECHNICAL re-entrant, re-entering

COLLOQ. knee-jerk

reform v, n

◆ v

change, amend, improve, better, rectify, correct, mend, repair, revise, refashion, rehabilitate, rebuild, reconstruct, remodel, revamp, renovate, restore, regenerate, reconstitute, reorganize, revolutionize, purge

FORMAL ameliorate

COLLOQ. shake up, turn over a new leaf

◆ n

change, amendment, improvement, betterment, rectification, correction, rehabilitation, renovation, reorganization, revision, rebuilding, reconstruction, remodelling, restoration, purge

COLLOQ. shake-up

reformation n

improvement, amendment, revision, rehabilitation, progress, renovation, restoration, rectification

FORMAL amelioration

reformer n

revolutionary, progressive, liberal; (*derog*) do-gooder, bleeding heart

COLLOQ. whistle-blower

refractory adj

stubborn, obstinate, headstrong, unmanageable, uncontrollable, naughty, unruly, wilful, unco-operative, perverse, mulish, difficult, disobedient, resistant, defiant, cantankerous, contentious

FORMAL intractable, contumacious, recalcitrant, disputatious, restive

1 co-operative, malleable, obedient

refrain[1] v

refrain from smoking

stop, cease, give up, do without, leave off, hold off, avoid, keep

FORMAL desist, abstain, forbear, for(e)go, renounce, eschew

OLD withhold, spare, supersede, surcease, restrain

COLLOQ. quit

refrain² n
sing the refrain twice
chorus, response, burden, strain, melody, song, tune, tag, falderal, overture
TECHNICAL epistrophe, faburden, hemistich, ritornello
OLD undersong, bob, wheel, fading, tirra-lirra, turnagain
FORMAL repetend

refresh v
1 COOL, freshen, energize, stimulate, enliven, invigorate, revive, brace, restore, renew, rejuvenate, reanimate, revitalize, reinvigorate
FORMAL fortify, revivify
COLLOQ. breathe new life into
2 *refresh your memory*
jog, stimulate, stir, prompt, prod, arouse, activate, remind
E3 1 tire, exhaust

refreshing adj
1 *a refreshing bath/drink*
invigorating, energizing, stimulating, exhilarating, reviving, cool, thirst-quenching, bracing
2 *a refreshing change from routine*
different, fresh, freshening, stimulating, inspiring, new, novel, original, welcome, unexpected
COLLOQ. not another

refreshment n
sustenance, food, food and drink, drink(s), snack, freshening, stimulation, revival, restoration, renewal, reanimation, invigoration, reinvigoration, revitalization

refreshments n
aliment, drinks, food, food and drink, provisions, snacks, elevenses, sustenance, titbits
COLLOQ. eats, eatables
SLANG nosh, grub; *Aust* tucker

refrigerate v
chill, cool, keep cold, freeze
E3 heat, warm

refuge n
sanctuary, asylum, shelter, protection, security, retreat, place of safety, hideout, hideaway, resort, harbour, haven, bolthole, island

refugee n
exile, émigré, displaced person, stateless person, asylum seeker, fugitive, runaway, escapee
OLD contraband
SLANG *Aust* reffo

refulgent adj
brilliant, shining, beaming, bright, radiant, gleaming, glistening, glittering
FORMAL irradiant, lambent, lustrous, resplendent

refund v, n
• v
repay, pay back, reimburse, rebate, return, give back, restore
• n
repayment, reimbursement, rebate, return

refurbish v
renovate, redecorate, re-equip, refit, remodel, revamp, repair, mend, overhaul, restore, recondition
COLLOQ. do up

refurbishment n
renovation, redecoration, restoration, recondition, revamping, refitting, repairing
COLLOQ. doing-up

refusal n
rejection, turning-down, no, rebuff, spurning, repudiation, repulse, denial, negation, withholding
OLD nay-say
FORMAL incompliance
E3 acceptance, agreement

■ **first refusal**
option, choice, consideration, opportunity, right of purchase

refuse¹ v
refuse to go; refuse permission
reject, turn down, say no, spurn, repudiate, rebuff, repel, deny, withhold
FORMAL decline
COLLOQ. pass up, knock back, shake your head, draw the line at, dig your heels in
E3 accept, agree, allow, permit, grant

refuse² n
piles of refuse
rubbish, waste, garbage, junk, litter, debris, dregs, dross, scum, offscum; *N Am* trash
TECHNICAL scoria, draff

refutation n
disproof, negation, rebuttal, overthrow
TECHNICAL elenchus
FORMAL confutation

refute v
disprove, rebut, give the lie to, discredit, counter, negate, overthrow, silence, deny (strongly)
FORMAL confute

regain v
recover, get back, win back, recoup, reclaim, repossess, retake, take back, recapture, retrieve, return to

---

Synonym nuances
Recover and **get back** can be widely used to suggest taking or finding something previously yours: *she's got back her figure.* **Win back**, however, suggests that a contest or at least some kind of effort has been involved. **Recoup**, is more suggestive of compensation or making up for losses: *basic costs must be recouped for the retailer to stay in business.*
  Reclaim is appropriate for reasserting ownership of something that is rightfully yours, while **repossess** tends to be used of items taken back as a debt: *failure to meet mortgage payments will result in your house being repossessed.* The term **recapture** has implications of effort or even force: *trying to recapture the magic of those days; government forces recaptured the towns.* **Retrieve**, meanwhile, is appropriate for successfully bringing something back that may have been lost: *we finally retrieved our lost luggage.*

---

regal adj
majestic, kingly, queenly, princely, imperial, royal, sovereign, stately, magnificent, noble, lordly

regale v
amuse, entertain, delight, divert, captivate, fascinate, feast, ply, gratify, serve, refresh

regard v, n
• v
1 CONSIDER, judge, rate, value, gauge, estimate, think, believe, suppose, imagine, contemplate, weigh up
FORMAL deem, appraise
2 LOOK AT, look upon, see, view, observe, watch, gaze at, scrutinize, eye
FORMAL behold
COLLOQ. give the once-over
3 HEED, listen to, observe, follow, note, bear in mind, take notice of, pay attention to, take into account/consideration
• n
1 CARE, concern, consideration, attention, notice, heed, respect, deference, esteem, honour, admiration, affection, love, sympathy, approval
FORMAL approbation
2 *in this regard*

matter, subject, aspect, respect, point, detail, particular
3 send her my regards
best wishes, good wishes, greetings, respects,
compliments, love
FORMAL salutations
E3 1 disregard, contempt
■ **with/in regard to**
as regards, concerning, with reference to, with respect to,
in relation to, in connection with, re, about, as to, on the
subject of
FORMAL apropos

Synonym nuances
noun sense 1
Care and **concern** can widely be used to suggest feeling
for the situation of others. **Consideration**, however,
conveys a less intense feeling, more suggestive of
modifying your behaviour to take account of others,
whereas **attention** implies a more focused
concentration: *children need a great deal of attention*.
Both **notice** and **heed** have similar implications, though
to a less intense degree.
 Respect has further connotations of looking up to
someone, while **deference** goes further by implying
submission: *in deference to his elders*. **Honour**, on the
other hand, has more to do with veneration, whereas
admiration implies high esteem. You could use
affection to suggest fond feelings, and **love**, although
similar, suggests something much stronger.

---

regardful *adj*
attentive, mindful, thoughtful, noticing, observant,
aware, careful, considerate, watchful, respectful, dutiful,
heedful
FORMAL circumspect
E3 heedless, inattentive, regardless, unobservant

regarding *prep*
with regard to, in regard to, as regards, concerning, with
reference to, with respect to, in relation to, in connection
with, re, about, as to, on the subject of, vis-à-vis
FORMAL apropos

regardless *adj, adv*
• *adj*
disregarding, heedless, unmindful, neglectful, negligent,
inattentive, careless, unconcerned, indifferent
E3 heedful, mindful, attentive
• *adv*
anyway, nevertheless, nonetheless, no matter what,
despite everything, come what may, anyhow
COLLOQ. at any price/cost, irregardless

regenerate *v*
revive, reinvigorate, revitalize, reawaken, rekindle, renew,
restore, reconstitute, reconstruct, re-establish, renovate,
refresh, uplift, change, invigorate, rejuvenate, reproduce
FORMAL inspirit, revivify

regeneration *n*
renewal, renovation, restoration, re-establishment,
reinvigoration, reconstruction, reconstitution,
rejuvenation, reproduction
FORMAL homomorphosis

regime *n*
1 GOVERNMENT, rule, administration, management,
leadership, command, control, direction, reign,
establishment, system
2 a daily regime of training
routine, system, procedure, way, method, order, pattern,
schedule, programme, formula, practice
3 REGIMEN, diet, fast, abstinence

regiment *n*
army, brigade, cohort, battery, band, company, platoon,
squadron, group, crew, gang, body, pultun
OLD tercio
See panel on next page

regimented *adj*
strict, disciplined, controlled, regulated, standardized,
ordered, methodical, systematic, organized, systematized
E3 free, lax, disorganized

region *n*
1 LAND, terrain, expanse, tract, place, area, territory,
reservation, country, continent, subcontinent,
hemisphere, time zone
2 DISTRICT, neighbourhood, estate, area, quarter, zone,
belt, borough, burgh, county, shire, state, bailiwick, postal
district, catchment area, diocese, parish, mission,
municipality, territory, domain, dominion, duchy, manor,
emirate, empire, kingdom, realm, principality, province,
riding, heartland, interior, inner city, ghetto, red-light
district, outskirts, suburbs
OLD hundred; (*Shakesp*) climate, climature
3 SECTOR, division, section, part
4 a region of influence
range, scope, expanse, sphere, world, field, ambit, orbit,
domain
■ **in the region of**
approximately, roughly, around, about, some, something
like, odd, circa, more or less, loosely, round about, or
thereabouts, approaching, close to, nearly, just about, not
far off, in the neighbourhood/vicinity of, in round
numbers, rounded up/down
COLLOQ. give or take
E3 exactly

Types of geographical region include:

Antarctic	lowlands	seaside
Arctic	marshland	steppe
basin	midlands	Third World
coast	occident	tropics
countryside	orient	tundra
desert	outback	urban district
developed world	pampas	veld
developing world	plain	wasteland
forest	prairie	wilderness
grassland	riviera	woodland
green belt	rural district	
heath	savannah	
jungle	scrubland	

See also **park**.

---

regional *adj*
district, local, localized, provincial, sectional, zonal,
parochial
E3 national, international, worldwide

register *n, v*
• *n*
1 a doctor's register
roll, roster, list, listing, index, catalogue, directory, log,
diary, journal, record, chronicle, annals, archives, file(s),
ledger, schedule, diary, almanac, enrolment, muster, poll
TECHNICAL obituary, patent-rolls, transfer book, cadastre,
cartulary, diptych, menology, docket, matricula
OLD album, regest, terrier
FORMAL notitia
Related adjective: matricular
2 a musical register
range, voice, tone, note(s)
• *v*
1 RECORD, note, log, enter, put in writing, put down, set
down, take down, inscribe, mark, list, catalogue, chronicle,
enrol, enlist, sign on, check in, book in, turn in, cast, clock
TECHNICAL matriculate, tax

Regiments include:

Argyll and Sutherland Highlanders	Highlanders (Seaforth Gordons and Camerons)	Prince of Wales's Own Regiment of Yorkshire	Royal Horse Artillery
Army Air Corps	Household Cavalry	Princess of Wales's Royal Regiment	Royal Irish Regiment
The Black Watch (Royal Highland Regiment)	The Inns of Court and City Yeomanry	Queen's Dragoon Guards	Royal Lancers – 9th/12th
Blues and Royals (formerly Royal Horse Guards and Royal Dragoons)	Irish Guards	Queen's Lancashire Regiment	Royal Military Police
Brigade of Gurkhas	King's Own Royal Border Regiment	Queen's Royal Hussars	Royal Regiment of Artillery
Cheshire Regiment	King's Own Scottish Borderers	Queen's Royal Lancers	Royal Regiment of Fusiliers
Coldstream Guards	King's Regiment	Royal Anglian Regiment	Royal Regiment of Wales
Devonshire & Dorset Regiment	King's Royal Hussars	Royal Armoured Corps	Royal Scots
Duke of Wellington's Regiment	King's Troop Royal Horse Artillery	Royal Corps of Signals	Royal Scots Dragoon Guards
Green Howards (Alexandra Princess of Wales's Own Yorkshire Regiment)	Life Guards	Royal Dragoon Guards	Royal Tank Regiment
General Support Regiment	Light Dragoons	Royal Engineers	Royal Welch Fusiliers
Grenadier Guards	Light Infantry	Royal Gloucestershire Berkshire and Wiltshire Regiment	Scots Guards
	Lowland Regiment (TA)	Royal Green Jackets	Special Air Service (SAS)
	Parachute Regiment	Royal Gurkha Rifles	Staffordshire Regiment
		Royal Highland Fusiliers	Welsh Guards
			Worcestershire & Sherwood Foresters Regiment

FORMAL enregister
2 SHOW, reveal, betray, display, exhibit, indicate, demonstrate, express, say
FORMAL manifest
3 *the gauge registers a measurement*
read, indicate, record, show, display

registrar *n*
official, recorder, secretary, clerk, administrator, cataloguer, annalist, archivist, chronicler, protocolist

registration *n*
enrolment, record, recording, inscription, list, noting, logging, entering, signing-on, checking-in

regress *v*
deteriorate, recede, relapse, retreat, return, revert, wane, backslide, degenerate, lapse, ebb
FORMAL retrocede, retrogress
⊟ progress

regret *v, n*
♦ *v*
feel/be sorry, wish that you had not done, be disappointed, be distressed, rue, repent, lament, bemoan, weep, mourn, grieve, deplore
♦ *n*
remorse, contrition, repentance, penitence, self-reproach, shame, sorrow, grief, disappointment, bitterness
OLD rue, had-I-wist
FORMAL compunction

> ### Synonym nuances
> *noun*
> **Remorse** can refer to a strong feeling of being extremely upset by your actions, while **contrition** goes further by implying more deeply felt pain for your deeds. **Repentance**, although similar, has further implications of seeking to change: *he was released as he had shown repentance*, whereas **penitence** is more appropriate where there is atonement. **Self-reproach** is a more restrained term for blaming yourself, while **shame** is stronger, with the implication of humiliation.
>   **Sorrow** can be used to cover a wide range of sad feelings, not just where one blames oneself, while **grief** is generally associated with loss or bereavement: *the grief of a child's death*. You can use **disappointment** of feelings of being let down either by oneself or by others, but **bitterness** would further imply resentment: *he spoke of his loss without bitterness or self-pity*.

regretful *adj*
remorseful, rueful, repentant, contrite, penitent,

conscience-stricken, ashamed, sorry, apologetic, sad, sorrowful, disappointed
⊟ impenitent, unashamed

> **⚠ regretful** or **regrettable**?
> *Regretful* means 'full of regret, sad, sorry'; *regrettable* means 'causing regret, to be regretted': *It is regrettable that you have behaved so foolishly, and I feel regretful that I must now ask you to leave.*

---

regrettable *adj*
unfortunate, unlucky, unhappy, sad, disappointing, upsetting, distressing, lamentable, deplorable, disgraceful, shameful, sorry, wrong, ill-advised
FORMAL reprehensible
⊟ fortunate, happy

> **⚠ regrettable** or **regretful**?
> *See panel at* **regretful**.

---

regrettably *adv*
unfortunately, unhappily, unluckily, sadly, alas, sad to say, sad to relate
COLLOQ. worse luck
⊟ fortunately

regular *adj*
1 ROUTINE, habitual, typical, usual, customary, time-honoured, classic, conventional, established, orthodox, correct, official, approved, proper, standard, normal, average, ordinary, common, commonplace, daily, everyday
2 PERIODIC, rhythmic, frequent, recurring, hourly, daily, weekly, monthly, yearly, steady, constant, fixed, set, unchanging, unvarying, uniform, consistent, even, level, flat, evenly spread, smooth, balanced, symmetrical, orderly, systematic, methodical, well-organized
COLLOQ. regular as clockwork
⊟ 1 unusual, unconventional **2** irregular, intermittent

regulate *v*
1 CONTROL, direct, guide, govern, rule, administer, oversee, superintend, supervise, manage, handle, conduct, run, organize, order, arrange, settle, square, monitor
2 ADJUST, set, synchronize, control, tune, moderate, balance

regulation *n, adj*
♦ *n*
1 RULE, statute, law, act, ordinance, by-law, edict, decree, order, ruling, directive, command, supervision, commandment, principle, precept, dictate, dictum, pronouncement, requirement, procedure, curfew
2 CONTROL, direction, guidance, rule, administration, superintendence, supervision, management

FORMAL dispensation
* *adj*
standard, official, statutory, obligatory, required, fixed, set, orthodox, accepted, customary, usual, normal
FORMAL prescribed, mandatory
SLANG pusser

regurgitate *v*
1 VOMIT, bring up, spew, retch, heave
FORMAL disgorge
COLLOQ. puke, throw up, sick up, fetch up
2 REPEAT, say/tell again, restate, recapitulate
FORMAL reiterate

rehabilitate *v*
reintegrate, restore, renew, reinvigorate, normalize, reform, reinstate, reconstitute, re-establish, renovate, recondition, rebuild, convert, adjust, clear, mend, reconstruct, save, redeem
COLLOQ. rehab

rehash *n, v*
* *n*
reworking, rearrangement, rejig, rejigging, restatement, reshuffle, rewrite
* *v*
rework, change, alter, rearrange, rejig, rejigger, restate, reshuffle, refashion, rewrite

rehearsal *n*
practice, drill, exercise, trial run, run-through, walk-through, preparation, reading, recital
COLLOQ. dry run, dummy run

rehearse *v*
1 PRACTISE, drill, train, go over, run through, prepare, try out, block (out)
2 REPEAT, recite, recount, relate, narrate, go over, enumerate, pour forth/out

reign *v, n*
* *v*
1 RULE, be king/queen, sit on the throne, be in power, be in charge, be in control, govern, be in government, command, be in command
2 *silence reigns*
prevail, predominate, occur, hold sway, be present, exist, influence
FORMAL obtain
* *n*
rule, sway, monarchy, empire, sovereignty, supremacy, government, power, command, dominion, control, influence
FORMAL ascendancy

reigning *adj*
1 *the reigning king*
ruling, governing, in power, in command, in control, current
FORMAL regnant
2 *the reigning champion*
present, current, presiding, victorious, world
FORMAL incumbent

reimburse *v*
refund, repay, pay back, give back, return, restore, recompense, compensate, indemnify, remunerate

reimbursement *n*
refund, repayment, recompense, compensation, idemnity

rein *n, v*
* *n*
check, control, curb, restraint, hold, overcheck, restriction, brake, bridle, harness
* *v*
check, control, curb, restrain, restrict, limit, hold back, stop, hold, halt, arrest, bridle
■ **free rein**
carte blanche, blank cheque, free hand, free-for-all, liberty, freedom, laissez-faire; *Aust & NZ* open slather

reincarnation *n*
rebirth
TECHNICAL samsara
FORMAL palingenesis, metempsychosis

reinforce *v*
1 STRENGTHEN, toughen, harden, stiffen, steel, brace, support, buttress, shore, prop, stay, supplement, increase
FORMAL fortify, augment
2 EMPHASIZE, stress, underline, consolidate
⊟1 weaken, undermine

reinforcement *n*
1 STRENGTHENING, supplement, support, addition, increase, enlargement, prop, shore, stay, brace, buttress, emphasis, hardening, amplification
OLD re-enforcement
FORMAL fortification, augmentation
2 *send reinforcements*
auxiliaries, reserves, additional soldiers/troops/police officers, supplementaries, back-up, support, help
OLD recruit

reinstate *v*
restore, return, give back, replace, recall, reappoint, reinstall, re-establish

reinstatement *n*
restoration, return, giving-back, replacement, recall, re-establishment

reiterate *v*
repeat, recapitulate, resay, restate, retell, emphasize, stress
FORMAL iterate, rehearse
COLLOQ. recap

reject *v, n*
* *v*
1 *reject a proposal*
refuse, deny, decline, turn down, say no to, veto, disallow, condemn, despise, spurn, rebuff, jilt, exclude, repudiate, repel
TECHNICAL athetize
FORMAL renounce
COLLOQ. have nothing to do with, take a raincheck on, wash your hands of, turn your back on, turn your nose up at, not touch with a bargepole, kick into touch
2 DISCARD, scrap, jettison, eliminate, cast off, throw away, set aside
FORMAL forsake
COLLOQ. give the brush-off to, give the cold shoulder to
⊟1 accept, agree **2** choose, select
* *n*
failure, second, discard, outcast, cast-off

Synonym nuances
verb sense 1
The term **refuse** gives a impression of a strong or definite rejection, while **deny** is more suggestive of refuting: *the anger of those who were denied passports*. **Decline** and **turn down**, however, would be appropriate for a rejection of an offer or proposal.

Veto, on the other hand, suggests forbidding, often with official overtones: *the government vetoed the proposal*, whereas **disallow** implies a failure to grant legitimacy: *his confession was disallowed*. You can use **condemn** to suggest censure, while **despise** is more implicative of contempt, and **spurn** is similarly disdainful, but further implies an element of discarding. Likewise, **rebuff** suggests a snub, often unexpectedly: *his suggestions were constantly rebuffed by the Prime Minister*. **Jilt** too shares connotations of abruptness or unexpectedness: *on his wedding day, he was afraid of being jilted at the altar*.

Repudiate implies disowning or rejecting completely: *previous theories have been thoroughly repudiated by latest research*.

rejection *n*
refusal, turning-down, denial, declining, veto, dismissal, rebuff, exclusion, discarding, jettisoning, repudiation, elimination
TECHNICAL athetesis
FORMAL renunciation, reprobation
COLLOQ. brush-off, cold shoulder, Dear John letter, push, heave-ho
Ӗ acceptance, choice, selection

rejig *v*
reorganize, restructure, rearrange, shake up, modernize, streamline, rationalize

rejoice *v*
celebrate, revel, delight, be delighted/pleased, be joyful/happy, take pleasure, glory, exult, triumph
OLD make merry
COLLOQ. jump for joy, whoop it up

rejoicing *n*
celebration, revelry, festivity, happiness, gladness, joy, delight, pleasure, euphoria, elation, jubilation, glory, exultation, triumph
OLD merrymaking

rejoin *v*
retort, answer, reply, respond, quip, repartee, riposte

rejoinder *n*
retort, answer, reply, response, quip, repartee, riposte

rejuvenate *v*
revitalize, reinvigorate, reanimate, revive, renew, freshen up, refresh, restore, rekindle, recharge, regenerate
FORMAL revivify

rejuvenation *n*
reinvigoration, revival, renewal, restoration, regeneration, revitalization

relapse *v, n*
◆ *v*
worsen, deteriorate, degenerate, weaken, sink, fail, lapse, revert, regress, fall away, backslide
FORMAL retrogress
◆ *n*
worsening, deterioration, setback, recurrence, weakening, lapse, decline, reversion, regression, backsliding
FORMAL retrogression

relate *v*
1 LINK, connect, join, couple, ally, associate, compare
FORMAL correlate
2 REFER, apply, concern, have a bearing on, be relevant
OLD respect
FORMAL pertain, appertain
3 *relate an anecdote*
tell, recount, narrate, report, describe, recite, present, communicate, detail, make known, impart, fable
OLD story
FORMAL delineate
4 IDENTIFY, sympathize, empathize, understand, have a rapport, feel for, get on (well) with
COLLOQ. hit it off, speak the same language, be on the same wavelength

related *adj*
kindred, of the same family, akin, affiliated, allied, associated, connected, linked, interrelated, interconnected, accompanying, joint, mutual, relevant
FORMAL concomitant, correlated, cognate, consanguineous, agnate
Ӗ unrelated, unconnected

relation *n*
1 LINK, linking, connection, bond, relationship, comparison, similarity, affiliation, alliance, interrelation, interconnection, interdependence

FORMAL correlation
2 REGARD, reference, relevance, bearing, application
FORMAL pertinence
3 RELATIVE, family, kin, kinsman, kinswoman, kinsfolk, kindred

relations *n*
1 RELATIVES, family, kin, kinsman, kinswoman, kinsfolk, kindred
COLLOQ. folks
2 RELATIONSHIP, terms, rapport, liaison, interaction, affairs, dealings, connections, communications, contact(s), associations
FORMAL intercourse
3 *sexual relations*
intercourse, sex, union, intimacy, intimate relations, sleeping with someone, going to bed with someone, love-making, copulation
FORMAL coition, coitus, carnal knowledge, consummation

relationship *n*
1 CONNECTION, bond, link, tie(s), tie-up, association, alliance, liaison, rapport, friendship, affinity, closeness, similarity, parallel, ratio, proportion
FORMAL correlation
COLLOQ. chemistry
2 AFFAIR, love affair, romance, intimacy, liaison, friendship, flirtation
COLLOQ. fling, thing

relative *adj, n*
◆ *adj*
1 COMPARATIVE, proportional, proportionate, moderate, comparable, corresponding, respective, parallel, reciprocal
FORMAL commensurate, correlative
2 APPROPRIATE, relevant, applicable, related, connected, interrelated, dependent
FORMAL apposite, germane, pertinent
◆ *n*
relation, family, kin, kinsman, kinswoman, kinsfolk, kindred

relatively *adv*
comparatively, in/by comparison, fairly, quite, rather, somewhat

relax *v*
1 *relax on holiday*
calm (down), rest, unwind, wind down, loosen up, tranquillize, sedate, unbend, slump, unknit, unpurse
COLLOQ. take it/things easy, let yourself go, make yourself at home, let your hair down, put your feet up, hang loose, cool it, chill (out), veg (out), lighten up
2 *relax the rules*
moderate, soften, ease (off), liberalize, lessen, reduce, diminish, weaken, lower, slacken, loosen, loose, unrein, mollify
OLD relent
FORMAL abate, remit, resolve
Ӗ2 tighten

relaxation *n*
1 REST, unwinding, loosening up, refreshment, leisure, recreation, fun, amusement, entertainment, enjoyment, pleasure
FORMAL repose
COLLOQ. R & R
2 SLACKENING, loosening, weakening, lessening, abatement, reduction, softening, easing, moderation, détente, easing
FORMAL abatement
COLLOQ. let-up
Ӗ2 tension, intensification

relaxed adj
1 feel relaxed
at ease, comfortable, uninhibited, carefree, happy-go-lucky, cool, calm, composed, restful, collected, unhurried, leisurely, easy-going
2 a relaxed situation
informal, casual, restful
COLLOQ. laid-back
F3 1 tense, nervous, worried 2 formal, tense

relay n, v
• n
1 BROADCAST, transmission, programme, communication, message, dispatch
2 work in relays
shift, turn, stint, time, spell, period
• v
broadcast, transmit, communicate, pass on, hand on, send, circulate, spread, carry, supply

release v, n
• v
1 SET FREE, free, liberate, deliver, emancipate
2 LOOSEN, loose, unloose, let go, untie, undo, unlock, unfasten, unchain, unbind, unshackle, unleash
3 EXCUSE, exempt, discharge, let go, let off, acquit, absolve
FORMAL exonerate
4 ISSUE, publish, make available, make known, make public, announce, disclose, reveal, circulate, distribute, present, launch, divulge, unveil
F3 1 imprison 3 detain
• n
1 FREEDOM, liberty, liberation, deliverance, emancipation
FORMAL manumission
2 ACQUITTAL, absolution, exoneration, exemption, discharge
COLLOQ. let-off
3 ISSUE, publication, publishing, disclosure, revelation, declaration, bulletin, announcement, proclamation
F3 1 imprisonment, detention

relegate v
demote, downgrade, degrade, sideline, reduce, consign, entrust, assign, refer, dispatch, delegate, transfer, banish, expatriate, deport, eject, exile, expel
F3 promote

relent v
1 GIVE IN, give way, come round, yield, allow, change your mind, capitulate
2 the storm relented
ease (off), let up, die down, slacken, soften, weaken, unbend, relax
FORMAL abate

relentless adj
unrelenting, unremitting, incessant, persistent, unflagging, unceasing, ruthless, remorseless, implacable, merciless, pitiless, cold-hearted, hard-hearted, unforgiving, cruel, harsh, fierce, grim, hard, punishing, uncompromising, inflexible, unyielding, inexorable
F3 merciful, yielding

relevance n
suitability, aptness, appropriateness, appositeness, significance, applicability
FORMAL pertinence
F3 irrelevance

relevant adj
material, significant, related, to the point, applicable, live, apposite, apt, appropriate, suitable, fitting, proper, admissible, relative, to the purpose
OLD german

FORMAL pertinent, germane, congruous, apropos
F3 irrelevant, inapplicable, inappropriate, unsuitable

reliability n
dependability, trustworthiness, constancy, steadiness, responsibility, faithfulness, honesty, integrity, conscientiousness, certainty
F3 unreliability, fickleness

reliable adj
unfailing, certain, sure, dependable, responsible, trusty, trustworthy, dutiful, honest, true, devoted, conscientious, faithful, constant, staunch, solid, safe, sound, well-grounded, well-founded, stable, tested, predictable, regular
F3 unreliable, doubtful, untrustworthy

reliance n
dependence, trust, faith, belief, conviction, credit, confidence, assurance

relic n
memento, souvenir, keepsake, token, reminder, monument, remembrance, survival, remains, artefact, heirloom, antique, remnant, scrap, fragment, vestige, trace; N Am holdover
TECHNICAL fossil
OLD relique, relict
Related adjective: reliquary

relief n
1 relief from pain
respite, alleviation, easing, lessening, reduction, soothing, release, cure, remedy, deliverance, remission
FORMAL mitigation, abatement, allaying, assuaging, palliation
2 COMFORT, reassurance, happiness, relaxation, calmness, consolation
3 REST, refreshment, diversion, relaxation, respite, break, interruption
FORMAL repose
COLLOQ. breather, let-up
4 famine relief
aid, help, assistance, rescue, saving, support, back-up, sustenance
FORMAL succour
5 SUBSTITUTE, replacement, reserve, stand-by, stand-in, supply, locum, understudy, proxy, surrogate

relieve v
1 relieve the pain
alleviate, soothe, lessen, soften, slacken, reduce, cure, heal, comfort, console, reassure
FORMAL mitigate, abate, allay, assuage, palliate
2 DELIVER, set free, free, liberate, release, unburden, discharge
3 SUBSTITUTE, replace, stand in for, take the place of, take over from
4 HELP, aid, assist, rescue, save, support, sustain
FORMAL succour
5 DISCHARGE, exempt, excuse, dismiss, expel, remove, free, release
6 relieve the tedium
break (up), interrupt, pause, stop, bring to an end, punctuate
FORMAL discontinue
F3 1 aggravate, intensify

relieved adj
happy, glad, pleased, thankful, cheered, encouraged, refreshed, eased

religion n
faith, belief system, beliefs, creed, code, doctrine, dogma
See panels on next page

Religions include:

CHRISTIANITY:		ISLAM:	Reform	Hinduism	Taoism
Anglicanism	evangelicalism	Ismaili	OTHER:	Jainism	voodoo
Baptists	Jehovah's	Shi'ah	Amish	New Age	Zen
Calvinism	Witnesses	Sufi	Bahaism	paganism	Zoroastrianism
Catholicism	Methodism	Sunni	Buddhism	Santeria	
Church of England	Mormonism	Wahabi	Confucianism	Scientology	
(C of E)	Presbyterianism	JUDAISM:	druidism	Shintoism	
Congrega-	Protestantism	Conservative	Hare Krishna	Sikhism	
tionalism	Quakerism	Orthodox			

See also **scripture**; **worship**.

Religious festivals include:

BUDDHIST:	Pentecost	Id-ul-Zuha	Sukkoth (Feast of	SHINTO:	Martyrdom of
Buddha Purnima	HINDU:	(Bakrid)	Tabernacles)	Ohinamatsuri	Guru Arjan Dev
Dhamma	Baisakhi	Milad-un-Nabi	Yom Kippur	Oshogatsu	Martyrdom of
Sangha	Basant	Muharram	PAGAN:	Tanabata Matsuri	GuruTeg
Vesak	Diwali	JEWISH:	Beltane	Tango no Sekku	Bahadur
CHRISTIAN:	Dusserah	Hanukkah	Imbolc	SIKH:	ANCIENT ROMAN:
All Saints' Day	Holi	Pesach (Passover)	Lammas	Baisakhi	Bacchanalia
Ascension	Oram	Purim	(Lughnasadh)	Birthday of Guru	Saturnalia
Christmas	ISLAMIC:	Rosh Hashanah	Litha	Gobind Singh	Vulcanalia
Corpus Christi	Id-al-Adha	Shavuot	Samhain	Birthday of Guru	
Easter	Id-al-Fitr	Simchat Torah	Yule	Nanak (Prakash	
Epiphany				Utsav)	
Good Friday					

See also **celebration**.

Religious officers include:

abbess	chancellor	dean	monk	parson	rector
abbot	chaplain	elder	Monsignor	pastor	vicar
archbishop	clergyman	father	mother superior	pope	
archdeacon	clergywoman	friar	muezzin	prelate	
ayatollah	curate	guru	mullah	priest	
bishop	Dalai Lama	imam	nun	prior	
canon	deacon	kohen	Pachen Lama	proctor	
cardinal	deaconess	minister	padre	rabbi	

See also **priest**.

Religious orders include:

Augustinians	Cistercians	Marists (Society of Mary)	Sisters of Mercy
Benedictines	Dominicans	Missionary Sisters of Charity	Trappists
Capuchins	Franciscans	Oratorians (Congregation of	Ursulines
Carmelites	Jesuits	the Oratory)	
Carthusians	Loreto (The Institute of the	Poor Clares	
Celestines	Blessed Virgin Mary)	Salesians	

---

religious *adj*
  1 SACRED, holy, divine, spiritual, devotional, scriptural, theological, doctrinal
  2 *a religious person*
  believing, having a living faith, devout, godly, pious, God-fearing, church-going, practising, committed, reverent, righteous
  3 CONSCIENTIOUS, scrupulous, rigorous, meticulous, strict
  Ea 1 secular **2** irreligious, ungodly

religiously *adv*
  1 CONSCIENTIOUSLY, strictly, rigorously, scrupulously, meticulously
  2 *he converted religiously*
  spiritually, theologically, doctrinally

relinquish *v*
  let go, release, hand over, surrender, yield, cede, give up, resign, repudiate, waive, for(e)go, part with, retreat, abandon, desert, drop, discard; *Scot* demit
  OLD (*Shakesp*) give out, cease
  FORMAL renounce, forsake, discontinue, desist, abstain, abdicate
  COLLOQ. quit
  Ea keep, retain

Synonym nuances
Let go is a synonym which can be generally applied, while **release** has added implications of setting free, or relinquishing something firmly held: *he agreed to release his claims on the estate for a one-off payment*. **Hand over** implies placing in someone else's care, whereas **surrender** has the added suggestion of defeat: *the trade unions retained influence in negotiations, but surrendered control*. The terms **give up**, **yield** and **cede** are also suggestive of a degree of reluctance, with **cede** generally used of political situations: *a region ceded to Russia*.
  The terms **renounce** and **repudiate**, on the other hand, imply a more heartfelt disowning, and waive and **for(e)go** describe a conscious refraining from exercising your rights or claims: *some celebrities waive their appearance fees for charity*. **Retreat** has a more military tone and implies moving back, thereby giving ground to the enemy, while **abandon** and **desert** suggest leaving behind something that is no longer profitable or productive: *the artist abandoned her old palette in favour of bolder colours*. **Drop** is more suggestive of a loss of interest or willingness: *he dropped friends at the bat of an eye*, and **discard** is similarly dismissive.

relish v, n

♦ v

like, enjoy, savour, appreciate, taste, adore, love, revel in, delight in

OLD degust; (*Shakesp*) palate

♦ n

1 SEASONING, flavouring, condiment, sauce, pickle, chutney, garnish, spice, flavour, piquancy, tang, palate, savour, gout, goût; *Scot* kitchen

OLD gust, lust

FORMAL opsonium

2 ENJOYMENT, pleasure, delight, appreciation, satisfaction, taste, appetite, stomach, tooth, gusto, zest, liveliness, vivacity, vigour, charm

relocate v

move, move house, move away, remove, transfer, go (away), leave, change address

COLLOQ. up sticks

reluctance n

unwillingness, hesitancy, hesitation, disinclination, indisposition, dislike, distaste, repugnance, loathing, aversion, backwardness

OLD renitency

FORMAL recalcitrance

E∃ eagerness, enthusiasm, willingness

reluctant adj

unwilling, indisposed, hesitant, slow, backward, loath, averse, disinclined, unenthusiastic, grudging, shy, squeamish, loathful

OLD renitent

E∃ willing, ready, eager, enthusiastic

rely v

depend, lean, be sure, count, bank, reckon, trust, swear by

remain v

stay, rest, stand, last, endure, survive, stay behind, be left over, prevail, persist, continue, linger, wait

OLD bide; (*Shakesp*) climate

FORMAL dwell, abide, tarry

E∃ go, leave, depart

remainder n

rest, balance, surplus, excess, residue, leftovers, carry-over, remnant, remains, vestiges; *Scot* lave

OLD remanent, remanet

FORMAL superfluity, residuum

remaining adj

left, left over, spare, unused, unspent, unfinished, residual, last, outstanding, surviving, persisting, lingering, lasting, abiding

remains n

1 REST, remainder, residue, dregs, leavings, leftovers, scraps, crumbs, fragments, remnants, oddments, traces, vestiges, relics

FORMAL detritus, reliquiae

COLLOQ. odds and ends

2 CORPSE, body, dead body, cadaver, carcase, ashes, debris

remark v, n

♦ v

comment, observe, note, notice, mention, say, state, assert, pronounce, declare

♦ n

comment, observation, opinion, reflection, mention, reference, utterance, statement, assertion, pronouncement, acknowledgement, declaration, notice

remarkable adj

striking, impressive, noteworthy, surprising, amazing, strange, odd, unusual, uncommon, rare, extraordinary, phenomenal, exceptional, memorable, momentous, outstanding, notable, considerable, conspicuous,

prominent, important, significant, pre-eminent, signal, surpassing, distinguished

FORMAL singular

E∃ average, ordinary, commonplace, usual

remarkably adv

surprisingly, unusually, uncommonly, significantly, signally, extraordinarily, exceptionally, outstandingly, considerably

remedy n, v

♦ n

cure, antidote, countermeasure, corrective, restorative, medicine, medication, treatment, therapy, relief, solution, answer, panacea

FORMAL medicament, physic, nostrum

♦ v

correct, put right, redress, control, counteract, cure, heal, restore, treat, help, relieve, soothe, ease, mend, repair, sort (out), fix, solve

FORMAL rectify, mitigate

Synonym nuances

noun

The word **antidote** and the less clinical-sounding **countermeasure** are suggestive of counteraction: *rules are the only antidote to chaos*, whereas **corrective** is appropriate for putting right: *the book provides a much-needed corrective to the film's lack of atmosphere.* **Restorative** has stronger implications of returning to a previous state or full strength: *restorative sleep.* While **medicine** and **medication** tend to be reserved for chemical preparations, **treatment** can be used more generally of a medical remedy, and **therapy** can be used for any non-surgical practice. To emphasize the alleviation of suffering you can use **relief**, whereas the terms **solution** and **answer** could be used of anything that satisfactorily addresses a problem: *the solution to most problems is anticipation.* **Panacea** would be reserved for an almost hypothetical remedy, effective against all ills: *there is no panacea for economic problems.*

---

remember v

1 RECALL, recollect, summon up, think back, think of, look back, hark back, cast your mind back, call to mind, reminisce, recognize, place

2 MEMORIZE, learn, learn by heart, commit to memory, make a mental note of, retain

3 COMMEMORATE, honour, mark, keep, recognize, celebrate, pay tribute to

4 *remember me to your parents*

send good/best wishes, send greetings, send your regards/respects

E∃ 1 forget

remembrance n

1 MEMORY, recollection, mind, reminder, recall, reminiscence, thought, testimonial, retrospect, nostalgia

2 COMMEMORATION, memorial, monument, souvenir, memento, token, keepsake, relic, recognition

remind v

prompt, nudge, hint, jog your memory, refresh your memory, bring to mind, call to mind, put you in mind of, make you think of, call up, evoke, take back

reminder n

prompt, nudge, hint, suggestion, note, memorandum, aide-mémoire, souvenir, memento, token, remembrance, keepsake, phylactery

TECHNICAL prompt-note

COLLOQ. memo

reminisce v

remember, recall, recollect, think back, look back, hark back, review, retrospect

reminiscence *n*
memory, remembrance, memoir, anecdote, recollection, recall, retrospection, review, reflection

reminiscent *adj*
suggestive, evocative, nostalgic
FORMAL redolent

remiss *adj*
careless, negligent, neglectful, forgetful, unmindful, heedless, lackadaisical, inattentive, indifferent, lax, slack, slipshod, sloppy, slow, thoughtless, casual, wayward
FORMAL culpable, tardy, dilatory
F3 careful, scrupulous

remission *n*
1 LESSENING, moderation, slackening, relaxation, release, weakening, decrease, reduction, respite, reprieve, ebb, lull
FORMAL abatement, alleviation, diminution
COLLOQ. let-up
2 CANCELLATION, repeal, annulment, suspension
TECHNICAL acceptilation
FORMAL rescinding, abrogation, revocation
3 PARDON, forgiveness, acquittal, excuse, absolution, exemption, discharge, indulgence, amnesty
TECHNICAL baptismal regeneration, plenary indulgence
OLD remitment
FORMAL exoneration, absolution, remittal

⚠ remission or **remittance**?
Remission means 'a lessening in force or effect': *Remissions in that form of cancer are not unknown*, 'the shortening of a prison sentence', 'the cancelling of a debt or punishment', and, in Christian theology, 'the forgiveness (of sins)'. *Remittance* is a formal word for the sending of money in payment for something, or for the money itself: *We are grateful for your remittance of the correct sum of money*.

---

remit *v, n*
♦ *v*
1 SEND, transmit, dispatch, post, mail, forward, pay, settle
2 REFER, transfer, direct, pass on
3 CANCEL, set aside, hold over, suspend, repeal
FORMAL rescind, abrogate, revoke
♦ *n*
brief, orders, instructions, guidelines, terms of reference, scope, authorization, (area of) responsibility

remittance *n*
sending, dispatch, payment, fee, allowance, consideration

⚠ remittance or **remission**?
See panel at **remission**.

---

remnant *n*
scrap, piece, bit, fragment, end, offcut, leftover, remainder, oddment, balance, residue, remains, shred, trace, vestige, butt, rump; *dialect* fent
TECHNICAL outlier, witness
OLD odd-come-short, wrack
FORMAL remanent

remonstrance *n*
grievance, complaint, objection, opposition, protest, protestation, reprimand, reproof, exception, petition
FORMAL expostulation

remonstrate *v*
protest, argue, challenge, oppose, take exception to, take issue with, complain, object, dispute
FORMAL dissent, expostulate
COLLOQ. gripe

remorse *n*
regret, ruefulness, repentance, penitence, contrition, contriteness, self-reproach, shame, guilt, bad conscience, sorrow, grief, worm
OLD rue, ruth, ayenbite, had-I-wist

FORMAL compunction
See Synonym nuances panel at **regret**.

remorseful *adj*
guilty, regretful, repentant, ashamed, penitent, conscience-stricken, guilt-ridden, sorrowful, sorry, sad, apologetic, rueful, contrite
FORMAL chastened, compunctious
COLLOQ. on a guilt trip
F3 impenitent, remorseless

remorseless *adj*
relentless, unrelenting, unremitting, unstoppable, undeviating, inexorable, implacable, pitiless, unforgiving, merciless, hard, hard-hearted, harsh, ruthless, savage, unmerciful, unremorseful, callous, cruel, stern, inhumane
F3 sorry, remorseful

remorselessly *adv*
relentlessly, unremittingly, inexorably, implacably, callously, cruelly, mercilessly, harshly, ruthlessly, savagely

remote *adj*
1 DISTANT, far, faraway, far-off, outlying, out-of-the-way, inaccessible, god-forsaken, isolated, secluded, lonely
COLLOQ. off the beaten track
2 DETACHED, aloof, distant, standoffish, unapproachable, uncommunicative, unconcerned, uninvolved, reserved, withdrawn
3 *a remote possibility*
slight, small, slim, poor, meagre, slender, faint, inconsiderable, negligible, doubtful, dubious, unlikely, improbable, insignificant, outside
4 *official policies remote from everyday experience*
irrelevant, immaterial, beside/off the point, inapplicable, inappropriate, inapt, unimportant, out of place, having no bearing, unrelated, unconnected, peripheral, tangential, beside the mark/question
FORMAL inapposite, extraneous, inconsequent, ungermane, irrelative
COLLOQ. neither here nor there, not coming into it, making no difference, not matter, going off at a tangent
F3 **1** close, nearby, accessible **2** friendly, warm, approachable **3** strong, distinct **4** relevant, pertinent

removable *adj*
detachable, movable, separable, eradicable, transferable

removal *n*
1 MOVE, transferral, departure, relocation, uprooting, shift, shifting, transporting, conveyance
2 WITHDRAWAL, taking away, detachment, extraction, deletion, obliteration, abolition, purging
3 DISMISSAL, discharge, departure, riddance, ejection, ousting, eviction, expulsion, relegation, disposal
FORMAL dislodgement
COLLOQ. firing, sacking, sack, push, boot, elbow

remove *v*
1 MOVE, transfer, relocate, take away, shift, dislodge, transport, carry, convey
2 TAKE AWAY, withdraw, take off, detach, tear off, pull off, amputate, destroy, cut off, lop off, take out, cut out, extract, excise, pull out, get out, strip, shed, doff
TECHNICAL deaccession
3 ELIMINATE, get rid of, erase, rub out, delete, strike out, cross out, obliterate, abolish, purge, blue-pencil
FORMAL expurge, efface
4 DISMISS, discharge, eject, throw out, get rid of, oust, evict, expel, dislodge, unseat, depose, cast out, cashier, relegate
COLLOQ. fire, sack, boot out

remunerate *v*
pay, reimburse, recompense, compensate, reward, indemnify, redress, repay

remuneration *n*
pay, payment, wages, salary, emolument, stipend, fee,

honorarium, retainer, earnings, income, profit, reward, recompense, remittance, repayment, reimbursement, compensation, indemnity
OLD (*Spenser*) sold

remunerative *adj*
profitable, lucrative, moneymaking, paying, rewarding, rich, (financially) worthwhile, gainful, fruitful

renaissance *n*
revival, renewal, rebirth, reawakening, awakening, resurrection, rejuvenation, regeneration, re-emergence, restoration, new birth, new dawn, reappearance, resurgence
FORMAL recrudescence, renascence

renascent *adj*
revived, resurgent, renewed, re-emergent, reborn, resurrected, reawakened, reanimated
FORMAL redivivus
COLLOQ. born again

rend *v*
tear (apart), split, break, burst, divide, separate, rupture, sever, rip, fracture, pierce, shatter, smash, splinter, stab, lacerate, wring
OLD dilacerate, cleave, rent, rive, to-rend

render *v*
1 *they rendered it harmless*
make, cause to be, leave, change, turn
2 GIVE, provide, supply, tender, present, contribute, furnish, submit, hand over, deliver
FORMAL proffer
3 TRANSLATE, transcribe, interpret, explain, clarify, represent, perform, play, sing
4 SHOW, describe, represent, display, exhibit, depict
FORMAL manifest

rendering *n*
1 PERFORMANCE, rendition, show, appearance, presentation, production, interpretation, representation, portrayal, acting
2 TRANSLATION, version, rendition, explanation, interpretation, gloss, crib, rewording, rephrasing, paraphrase, simplification, transliteration, transcription
FORMAL metaphrasis

rendezvous *n, v*
♦ *n*
1 MEETING, appointment, engagement, assignation, date
OLD tryst
2 MEETING-PLACE, venue, haunt, resort
OLD trysting-place
♦ *v*
meet, come together, gather, collect, assemble, rally, muster, converge
FORMAL convene

rendition *n*
1 PERFORMANCE, presentation, version, rendering, portrayal, reading, translation, arrangement, construction, delivery
FORMAL execution
2 TRANSLATION, version, interpretation, explanation, transcription, gloss, rewording, rephrasing, paraphrase, simplification, transliteration, depiction

renegade *n, adj*
♦ *n*
deserter, defector, traitor, turncoat, dissident, mutineer, outlaw, rebel, betrayer, apostate, backslider, runaway, runagate
OLD recreant
FORMAL tergiversator
COLLOQ. rat
⊟ adherent, disciple, follower

♦ *adj*
disloyal, rebel, rebellious, traitorous, treacherous, unfaithful, apostate, backsliding, dissident, mutinous, outlaw, runaway
OLD recreant
FORMAL perfidious
⊟ loyal, faithful

renege *v*
default, repudiate, go back on your promise, backslide, apostatize, welsh, cross the floor

renew *v*
1 RENOVATE, modernize, refurbish, refit, recondition, innovate, mend, repair, overhaul, remodel, reform, transform, recreate, reconstitute, re-establish, regenerate, revive, resuscitate, refresh, rejuvenate, reinvigorate, boost, brush up, revitalize, restore, replace, replenish, restock
OLD new, renforce
2 RESUME, repeat, restate, reaffirm, extend, prolong, continue, recommence, restart
FORMAL reiterate, reprise

renewal *n*
1 RENOVATION, reconditioning, re-creation, repair, refurbishment, reconstitution, reconstruction, reinvigoration, rejuvenation, revitalization, replenishment, resurrection, resuscitation
OLD recruit, recruital
FORMAL revivification
COLLOQ. kiss of life
2 RESUMPTION, repetition, restatement, reaffirmation, continuance, recommencement
FORMAL reiteration

renounce *v*
abandon, give up, resign, relinquish, surrender, waive, sign away, discard, reject, spurn, shun, disown, for(e)go, disinherit, repudiate, deny, refuse, revolt, cut, declare off, swear off, pass up, put away, recede
TECHNICAL disgown, forisfamiliate
OLD renay; (*Spenser*) forsay
FORMAL forsake, disclaim, desist, abstain, eschew, abnegate, recant, abjure, abdicate, renege, disprofess, forswear
COLLOQ. wash your hands of

renovate *v*
restore, renew, recondition, repair, overhaul, modernize, refurbish, refit, redecorate, remodel, reform, rehabilitate, revamp, improve
COLLOQ. do up, give a facelift

renovation *n*
refurbishment, improvement, modernization, repair, restoration, renewal, reconditioning, refit
COLLOQ. facelift

renown *n*
fame, celebrity, stardom, acclaim, glory, eminence, pre-eminence, illustriousness, distinction, prestige, esteem, prominence, note, mark, reputation, repute, honour
⊟ obscurity, anonymity

renowned *adj*
famous, well-known, celebrated, acclaimed, famed, noted, eminent, pre-eminent, distinguished, prestigious, prominent, illustrious, notable, of repute
⊟ unknown, obscure

rent¹ *n, v*
♦ *n*
pay the rent
rental, lease, hire, payment, cost, rate, fee
♦ *v*
1 *rent a television*
hire, lease
2 LET (OUT), rent out, sublet, lease, hire (out), charter

**rent² **n

a world rent by conflict
torn apart, split, ripped apart, ruptured, divided, severed
OLD riven

renunciation n
abandonment, giving up, relinquishment, surrender,
waiving, discarding, rejection, spurning, shunning,
disowning, disinheriting, repudiation, denial
FORMAL forsaking, disclaiming, desistance, abstinence,
abnegation, abdication

reorganize v
restructure, rearrange, shake up, modernize, streamline,
rationalize, rejig

repair¹ v, n
 • v

repair a faulty machine
mend, fix, patch up, sew, darn, overhaul, refit, service,
maintain, put right, rectify, adjust, redress, restore, make
good, heal, renovate, renew
 • n
1 MEND, patch, darn, overhaul, service, refit, maintenance,
restoration, adjustment, improvement
2 *in good/bad repair*
condition, shape, state, form, (working) order, fettle, kilter
COLLOQ. nick

repair² v
repair to a place
go, move, turn, withdraw, retire, resort, remove, wend your
way

reparable adj
recoverable, rectifiable, remediable, restorable,
retrievable, salvageable, savable, corrigible, curable
⊟ irreparable

reparation n
amends, redress, requital, restitution, satisfaction, renewal,
compensation, recompense, damages, indemnity,
atonement
TECHNICAL solatium
FORMAL propitiation

repartee n
banter, bantering, badinage, jesting, wit, witticism, riposte,
retort

repast n
meal, snack, food, nourishment, spread, board, table, feed
FORMAL refection, collation, victuals

repatriate v
deport, expel, banish, exile, extradite, transport, oust,
ostracize

repay v
1 REFUND, reimburse, pay back, compensate, recompense,
reward, remunerate, pay, settle, settle up with, square
OLD yield
2 GET EVEN WITH, get back at, retaliate, return, reciprocate,
revenge, avenge
OLD apay, quit
COLLOQ. get your own back on, settle the score, give as
good as you get, not take it lying down

repayment n
1 REFUND, reimbursement, compensation, recompense,
reward, remuneration, payment, reparation, redress,
restitution, amends, requital, rebate
2 VENGEANCE, revenge, retribution, reciprocation,
retaliation
COLLOQ. tit for tat, eye for an eye

repeal v, n
 • v
quash, annul, void, invalidate, cancel, set aside, lift, recall,
withdraw, reverse, abolish

FORMAL revoke, rescind, abrogate, nullify, abjure, retract,
countermand, recant
⊟ enact
 • n
cancellation, invalidation, quashing, reversal, withdrawal,
abolition, annulment
FORMAL abrogation, nullification, rescinding, rescindment,
rescission, revocation
⊟ enactment, establishment

repeat v, n
 • v
restate, say again, go over, recapitulate, reiterate, echo,
parrot, quote, recite, relate, retell, reproduce, duplicate,
renew, rebroadcast, reshow, replay, rerun, redo
FORMAL iterate, rehearse
COLLOQ. recap
 • n
repetition, restatement, recapitulation, echo,
reproduction, copy, duplicate, duplication, rebroadcast,
reshowing, replay, rerun, ditto

repeated adj
frequent, constant, continual, regular, recurrent, periodic,
rhythmical, persistent, recurring

repeatedly adv
time after time, time and (time) again, again and again,
over and over (again), frequently, often

repel v
1 DRIVE BACK, repulse, check, hold off, ward off, parry, resist,
keep at bay, oppose, fight (off), beat off, force back, beat
back, push back, refuse, decline, reject, spurn, rebuff,
rebut
2 DISGUST, revolt, nauseate, sicken, make you sick, offend
FORMAL be repugnant to
COLLOQ. turn off, turn your stomach
⊟ **1** attract **2** delight

repellent adj
repulsive, revolting, disgusting, nauseating, sickening,
offensive, shocking, distasteful, objectionable, off-putting,
obnoxious, foul, vile, nasty, repugnant, loathsome,
abominable, abhorrent, contemptible, despicable,
hateful, horrid, unpleasant, disagreeable
⊟ attractive, pleasant, delightful

repent v
regret, rue, feel remorse, sorrow, be sorry, be ashamed, be
contrite, confess, lament, deplore, reproach yourself, turn,
be converted
OLD (*Spenser*) relent
FORMAL recant
COLLOQ. go down on your knees, beat your breasts, see
the error of your ways, see the light, do a U-turn, wipe the
slate clean

repentance n
penitence, confession, penance, contrition, remorse,
regret, sorrow, grief, guilt, shame, conversion
FORMAL compunction, recantation
COLLOQ. U-turn

repentant adj
penitent, contrite, sorry, sorrowful, apologetic,
remorseful, regretful, guilty, rueful, chastened, ashamed,
conscience-stricken
⊟ unrepentant, impenitent

repercussion n
result, consequence, effect, side-effect, spin-off,
reverberation, echo, rebound, recoil, backwash
COLLOQ. backlash, ripple, shock wave

repertoire n
collection, list, range, repertory, reserve, reservoir, stock,
store, supply
FORMAL repository

repetition _n_

restatement, reiteration, recapitulation, quoting, copying, echo, echoing, return, reappearance, recurrence, duplication, redundancy, superfluity, tautology
TECHNICAL echolalia
FORMAL iterance, iteration, rehearsal, reprise

repetitious _adj_

tedious, monotonous, boring, dull, unchanging, unvaried, redundant, tautological, long-winded, verbose, wordy, windy
TECHNICAL pleonastic(al)
FORMAL prolix

repetitive _adj_

recurrent, monotonous, tedious, boring, dull, mechanical, automatic, unchanging, unvaried
COLLOQ. samey, soul-destroying

rephrase _v_

paraphrase, reword, put in other/different words, put another way, ask/express/say differently, rewrite, recast

repine _v_

grumble, complain, murmur, fret, lament, grieve, languish, moan, brood, sulk, mope
COLLOQ. beef, grouse, grouch

replace _v_

1 _replace the lid_
put back, return, restore, make good, reinstate, re-establish, hang up
2 SUPERSEDE, take the place of, succeed, come after, follow, supplant, relieve, oust, deputize, substitute, stand in for, act for, fill in for, displace, exchange, change, pre-empt, refund
TECHNICAL replant

Synonym nuances

sense 2

While the terms **succeed**, **come after** and **follow** are suggestive of a time sequence, and natural or expected progression: _Reagan succeeded Carter as president_, **supersede** generally suggests replacing something due to its obsolescence: _sheep netting has been superseded by electric fencing._

Supplant and **displace** imply a more marked removal by a rival person or cause: _a sense of Britishness has been supplanted by Scottish and Welsh nationalism; he displaced the long-time title holder_, while **oust** would more clearly convey a forcible ejection: _Allende was ousted in a military coup._

Relieve is appropriate where replacement gives respite: _they were relieved by the morning shift._ **Substitute** suggests a straightforward replacing of a person or thing for practical reasons: _substitute skimmed milk for full fat milk if you are on a diet_; you could use **deputize**, **act for**, **stand in for** or **fill in for** if you want to suggest a more temporary arrangement: _Mr Smith will deputize for the manager while he is in hospital._

Where a replacement is made in advance you may use the term **pre-empt**: _the latest episode of the soap will be pre-empted for the prime ministerial address._

---

replaceable _adj_

1 DISPOSABLE, throwaway, expendable, non-returnable, biodegradable
2 _he thinks he's not replaceable_
substitutable, exchangeable, interchangeable
F3 1 returnable **2** irreplaceable

replacement _n_

substitute, stand-in, reserve, understudy, fill-in, supply, proxy, surrogate, successor, spare part

replenish _v_

refill, restock, reload, recharge, replace, restore, renew, supply, provide, furnish, stock, fill, fill up, top up, make up

replenishment _n_

restocking, recharging, replacement, restoration, renewal, provision, supply, filling, refilling

replete _adj_

1 FILLED, full, full up, charged, abounding, brimful, brimming, teeming, well-provided, well-stocked, jammed, stuffed, crammed
COLLOQ. chock-a-block, chock-full, chocker, jam-packed
2 WELL-FED, gorged, sated, glutted
FORMAL satiated
COLLOQ. full, full up, stuffed

repletion _n_

fullness, overfullness, glut, completeness, superabundance, superfluity
FORMAL plethora, satiation, satiety

replica _n_

model, imitation, reproduction, facsimile, copy, duplicate, dummy, clone

replicate _v_

repeat, duplicate, copy, mimic, follow, reduplicate, reproduce, recreate, clone, ape

reply _v, n_

◆ _v_
answer, respond, retort, rejoin, react, acknowledge, return, come back, write back, echo, reciprocate, counter, retaliate, riposte
◆ _n_
answer, response, retort, rejoinder, riposte, repartee, reaction, comeback, acknowledgement, return, echo, retaliation
COLLOQ. comeback

Synonym nuances

verb

The term **respond** implies that something has been directly prompted: _she responded to the cheering with a curtsy._ **Return**, **come back**, **retort** and **rejoin** are similar but suggest swift verbal retaliation for a perceived taunt, and **riposte** too suggests speed and wit.

React, however, can be used of a more instinctive reply brought about by a stimulus: _he reacted angrily to their proposal_, whereas **acknowledge** is more suggestive of replying through courtesy, and **reciprocate** could be used of any verbal interchange.

While **echo** would suggest a remark made in agreement, **counter** suggests a contradictory or retaliatory reply. **Retaliate** more explicitly returns to the idea of requital of a perceived insult.

---

report _n, v_

◆ _n_
1 ACCOUNT, article, piece, item, write-up, record, relation, narrative, description, story, tale, statement, communiqué, press release, bulletin, register, chronicle, minutes, write-up, declaration, announcement, communication, information, news, word, message, note, brief, file, dossier
FORMAL delineation
2 _a school report_
evaluation, assessment, inspection, appraisal, examination, judgement
3 GOSSIP, hearsay, rumour, talk, whisper
4 REPUTATION, honour, character, standing, stature, opinion, credit, esteem, repute, fame, renown, celebrity, distinction, name
5 EXPLOSION, shot, bang, crack, boom, crash, blast, reverberation, noise
◆ _v_
1 STATE, announce, declare, proclaim, air, broadcast, relay, publish, circulate, pass on, communicate, notify, tell, recount, relate, narrate, describe, detail, set forth, disclose, divulge, cover, document, chronicle, record, note

FORMAL delineate
2 COMPLAIN, inform on
COLLOQ. tell on, squeal, rat, split, blow the whistle on
SLANG shop, grass; *N Am* stool on

reportedly *adv*
allegedly, supposedly, apparently, by all accounts
FORMAL ostensibly, putatively

reporter *n*
journalist, correspondent, columnist, newspaperman,
newspaperwoman, newscaster, commentator, announcer
COLLOQ. hack

repose¹ *n, v*
◆ *n*
moments of repose
rest, calm, peace, restfulness, ease, relaxation, respite,
stillness, tranquillity, serenity, calmness, composure,
inactivity, quietness, quiet, poise, equanimity, dignity, self-
possession, sleep, night-rest, kef
FORMAL slumber, aplomb, quietude
⊟ activity, strain, stress
◆ *v*
lie, lay, lean, rest, recline, relax, sleep
FORMAL slumber
COLLOQ. laze

repose² *v*
repose confidence in someone
place, put, set, rest, store, lodge, deposit, confide, entrust,
invest
OLD affy

repository *n*
store, storehouse, depository, depot, warehouse, safe, bank,
treasury, vault, archive, container, receptacle, magazine

reprehensible *adj*
disgraceful, deplorable, discreditable, objectionable,
shameful, unworthy, blamable, blameworthy, bad, ill,
remiss, censurable, condemnable, delinquent, erring,
errant, ignoble, base
FORMAL culpable, opprobrious
⊟ creditable, good, praiseworthy

represent *v*
1 STAND FOR, symbolize, designate, denote, mean, mark,
be, amount to, constitute, correspond to, be equivalent to
2 ACT FOR, stand for, speak for, act/speak on behalf of, act
as representative of, act as spokesperson for, act/speak in
the name of, appear for/on behalf of, deputize for
3 EXEMPLIFY, typify, stand for, epitomize, embody, personify,
show
4 DEPICT, portray, describe, picture, display, exhibit, draw,
sketch, illustrate, evoke, characterize
OLD refer
5 ACT AS, enact, perform, appear as

representation *n*
1 LIKENESS, image, icon, picture, portrait, drawing,
illustration, sketch, model, statue, bust, depiction,
portrayal, description, account, explanation
FORMAL delineation
2 REPRESENTATIVE, delegate, delegation, deputy, deputation,
proxy, stand-in, spokesperson, spokesman,
spokeswoman, envoy, ambassador, mouthpiece, MP,
member of parliament, Congressman, Congresswoman,
councillor
3 PERFORMANCE, production, presentation, play, show,
spectacle
4 *make representations*
request, report, account, statement, allegation, protest,
complaint

representative *n, adj*
◆ *n*
1 DELEGATE, delegation, deputy, deputation, proxy, stand-in,

spokesperson, spokesman, spokeswoman, envoy,
ambassador, mouthpiece, MP, member of parliament,
councillor
2 *a sales representative*
salesman, saleswoman, salesperson, traveller, commercial
traveller, travelling salesman, commissioner, agent; *N Am*
drummer
OLD bagman, rider
COLLOQ. rep, knight of the road
◆ *adj*
1 TYPICAL, illustrative, exemplary, characteristic, usual,
normal, symbolic, indicative
FORMAL archetypal
2 DELEGATED, chosen, elected, elective, nominated,
appointed, commissioned, authorized, decentralized,
devolved
⊟ unrepresentative, atypical

repress *v*
1 INHIBIT, check, control, curb, restrain, suppress, bottle up,
hold back, stifle, smother, muffle, silence, keep back,
swallow, cork (up)
COLLOQ. sit on, bite your lip
2 *repress a revolt*
quell, put down, crush, quash, subdue, overpower,
overcome, master, dominate, domineer, oppress, stifle,
sneap
OLD reprime; (*Spenser*) repeal
FORMAL subjugate, vanquish

repressed *adj*
frustrated, inhibited, withdrawn, introverted, self-
restrained
COLLOQ. hung-up, uptight
⊟ uninhibited, relaxed

repression *n*
1 OPPRESSION, suppression, quashing, quelling, crushing,
suffocation, gagging, censorship, authoritarianism,
dictatorship, despotism, tyranny, domination, control,
constraint, coercion
FORMAL subjugation
2 *repression of your feelings*
suppression, inhibition, restraint, control, holding-back,
stifling, smothering, muffling

repressive *adj*
oppressive, authoritarian, despotic, tyrannical, dictatorial,
dominating, autocratic, totalitarian, absolute, harsh, cruel,
severe, strict, tough, coercive

reprieve *v, n*
◆ *v*
pardon, forgive, acquit, show mercy/pity, spare, rescue,
redeem, relieve, respite
OLD repreeve, reprive
COLLOQ. let off, let off the hook, forgive and forget
◆ *n*
pardon, amnesty, suspension, postponement, deferment,
stay of execution, remission, respite, relief
OLD (*Shakesp*) repreeve; (*Spenser*) reprive
FORMAL abatement, abeyance
COLLOQ. let-up

reprimand *v, n*
◆ *v*
rebuke, reprove, reproach, scold, chide, lecture, criticize,
censure, slate, blame, lambast, bring/call to account, lace
into, jobe; *Scot* targe; *Aust* rouse on
FORMAL admonish, berate, castigate
COLLOQ. tell off, tick off, take/pull apart, bawl out, bounce,
carpet, catch it, chew out, see off, give someone a ticking-
off, dress down, give someone a dressing-down, haul over
the coals, read the riot act to, rap over the knuckles, give
someone a rap over the knuckles, give someone a flea in
their ear, give someone an earful, give someone a piece of

your mind, shoot down in flames, tear a strip off someone;
Scot give someone their kale through the reek
SLANG bollock; *Aust* go off at
♦ *n*
rebuke, reproof, reproach, lecture, censure, blame,
schooling, tongue-lashing
FORMAL upbraiding, admonition, castigation
OLD check
COLLOQ. telling-off, ticking-off, talking-to, dressing-down,
slap/smack on the wrist, rap over the knuckles, a flea in
someone's ear, rocket, wigging, carpeting, earful

reprisal *n*
retaliation, counter-attack, retribution, requital, revenge,
vengeance, recrimination, redress
OLD ultion
COLLOQ. tit for tat, eye for an eye, a taste of someone's own
medicine

reprise *n, v*
♦ *n*
repetition, restatement, recapitulation, quoting, copying,
echoing
FORMAL reiteration, iterance, iteration, rehearsal
♦ *v*
play, sing, put on, perform, act, relate, narrate

reproach *v, n*
♦ *v*
rebuke, reprove, reprimand, upbraid, scold, chide,
reprehend, blame, censure, condemn, slate, criticize, find
fault with, defame
FORMAL disparage, admonish
COLLOQ. tell off, tick off, take/pull apart, bawl out, bounce,
carpet, catch it, chew out, see off, give someone a ticking-
off, dress down, give someone a dressing-down, haul over
the coals, read the riot act to, rap over the knuckles, give
someone a rap over the knuckles, give someone a flea in
their ear, give someone an earful, give someone a piece of
your mind, shoot down in flames, tear a strip off someone
♦ *n*
1 REBUKE, reproof, reprimand, scolding, blame, censure,
condemnation, criticism, disapproval, scorn, contempt
FORMAL admonition
COLLOQ. telling-off, ticking-off, talking-to, dressing-down,
slap/smack on the wrist, rap over the knuckles, a flea in
someone's ear, rocket, wigging, carpeting, earful
2 DISGRACE, shame, disrepute, disrespect, discredit,
stigma, dishonour, degradation, blemish, blot, smear, stain,
slur
FORMAL ignominy, opprobrium, obloquy

reproachful *adj*
reproving, upbraiding, scolding, censorious, critical, fault-
finding, disapproving, disappointed, scornful
FORMAL castigating, disparaging, opprobrious
F3 complimentary

reprobate *adj, n*
♦ *adj*
immoral, corrupt, depraved, sinful, unprincipled, vile,
wicked, bad, shameless, incorrigible, dissolute,
degenerate, base, abandoned, hardened, damned
FORMAL profligate, reprobative, reprobatory
F3 upright, virtuous
♦ *n*
degenerate, miscreant, rake, *roué*, wrongdoer, criminal,
evildoer, sinner, rogue, rascal, scoundrel, scamp,
scallywag, villain, vagabond, wretch, mischief-maker,
ne'er-do-well, knave, dastard, troublemaker
FORMAL profligate

reproduce *v*
1 COPY, transcribe, print, duplicate, photocopy, Xerox®,
Photostat®, mirror, echo, repeat, imitate, emulate, match,
follow, cline, ape, mimic, simulate, recreate, remake, redo,

reconstruct, repeat, enlarge, facsimile, express, reflect,
render, pirate
TECHNICAL autotype, phototype, hectograph
OLD (*Shakesp*) refigure
FORMAL replicate
2 BREED, spawn, bear young, give birth, generate,
propagate, multiply, proliferate, clone, regenerate
TECHNICAL gemmate
FORMAL procreate, replicate

reproduction *n*
1 COPY, print, picture, duplicate, photocopy, Xerox®,
Photostat®, facsimile, replica, clone, imitation
2 BREEDING, generation, propagation, multiplication
FORMAL procreation
F3 1 original
Related adjective: genital

reproductive *adj*
generative, sexual, sex, genital, propagative
FORMAL procreative, progenitive

reproof *n*
rebuke, reproach, reprimand, scolding, censure,
condemnation, criticism
FORMAL upbraiding, admonition, castigation,
disapprobation, berating
COLLOQ. telling-off, ticking-off, talking-to, dressing-down,
slap/smack on the wrist, rap over the knuckles, a flea in
someone's ear, rocket, wigging, carpeting, earful
F3 praise

reprove *v*
rebuke, reproach, reprimand, scold, chide, reprehend,
censure, slate, condemn, criticize; *Aust* rouse on
FORMAL upbraid, admonish, berate, castigate
COLLOQ. tell off, tick off, take/pull apart, bawl out, bounce,
carpet, catch it, chew out, see off, give someone a ticking-
off, dress down, give someone a dressing-down, haul over
the coals, read the riot act to, rap over the knuckles, give
someone a rap over the knuckles, give someone a flea in
their ear, give someone an earful, give someone a piece of
your mind, shoot down in flames, tear a strip off someone
F3 praise

reptile

Reptiles include:

alligator	hawksbill turtle	snake
chameleon	iguana	terrapin
crocodile	lizard	tortoise
frilled lizard	skink	turtle
gecko	slowworm (or	
giant tortoise	blindworm)	
green turtle		

See also **dinosaurs; snake**.

repudiate *v*
reject, denounce, deny, disown, discard, retract, reverse,
revoke, cast off, desert, abandon, repel, divorce
TECHNICAL notchel
FORMAL abjure, disaffirm, disavow, disclaim, disprofess,
forsake, rescind, renounce
COLLOQ. not touch with a barge pole, have nothing to do
with, turn your back on
F3 admit, own

repudiation *n*
rejection, denial, disclaimer, disowning
FORMAL renunciation, abjuration, disaffirmance,
disaffirmation, disavowal, recantation, retraction
F3 acceptance

repugnance *n*
reluctance, distaste, dislike, aversion, hatred, loathing,
abhorrence, horror, repulsion, revulsion, nausea, disgust

OLD reluctation, repugnancy
FORMAL odium, antipathy
COLLOQ. allergy
F3 liking, pleasure, delight

repugnant adj
repellent, objectionable, obnoxious, offensive,
unacceptable, antagonistic, antipathetic, hostile, alien,
averse, opposed, distasteful, inconsistent, incompatible,
contradictory, adverse, disgusting, foul, vile, hateful,
horrid, abhorrent, abominable, revolting, sickening,
nauseating, loathsome, odious
FORMAL inimical
F3 acceptable, consistent, pleasant

repulse v, n
◆ v
repel, drive back, defeat, beat off, check, rebuff, reject,
refuse, disregard, disdain, snub, spurn
◆ n
check, defeat, disappointment, failure, rebuff, refusal,
rejection, repudiation, reverse, snub, spurning
F3 acceptance, success

repulsion n
revulsion, disgust, distaste, hatred, aversion, repugnance,
abhorrence, loathing
FORMAL detestation, disrelish, repellence, repellency
F3 liking

repulsive adj
repellent, revolting, disgusting, nauseating, sickening,
offensive, shocking, distasteful, objectionable, off-putting,
obnoxious, foul, vile, nasty, loathsome, abominable,
abhorrent, contemptible, odious, repugnant, despicable,
hateful, horrid, unpleasant, disagreeable, ugly, hideous,
unattractive, forbidding
OLD evil-favoured, loth
FORMAL reprehensible, heinous
COLLOQ. gross, icky
F3 attractive, pleasant, delightful

repulsively adv
unpleasantly, disagreeably, disgustingly, shockingly,
abominably, objectionably, despicably, obnoxiously,
nauseatingly
F3 attractively, delightfully

reputable adj
respectable, respected, reliable, dependable, trustworthy,
upright, honourable, honest, creditable, admirable, of
high/good repute, well-thought-of, esteemed, worthy,
good, virtuous, excellent, irreproachable
FORMAL estimable
F3 disreputable, infamous

reputation n
1 NAME, good name, opinion, credit, repute, character,
standing, stature, status, rank, position, infamy, notoriety
FORMAL estimation
2 FAME, renown, celebrity, distinction, prestige, esteem,
image, character, good name, good standing, honour,
respect, respectability

repute n
reputation, name, standing, stature, renown, fame, good
name, celebrity, distinction, esteem, estimation
F3 infamy

reputed adj
alleged, supposed, said, rumoured, believed, thought,
considered, regarded, reckoned, estimated, held, judged,
seeming, assumed, presumed, apparent
FORMAL ostensible
F3 actual, true

reputedly adv
allegedly, apparently, seemingly, supposedly, by all
accounts, reputatively

FORMAL ostensibly
F3 actually

request v, n
◆ v
ask for, demand, require, seek, desire, beg, petition, apply
for, call for, appeal, invite, order, send for, wish, write in/off for
OLD bespeak, require
FORMAL solicit, entreat, requisition, supplicate, beseech,
adjure, impetrate
COLLOQ. put in for; N Am hit
◆ n
appeal, call, demand, desire, application, suit, petition,
petitioning, plea, pleading, prayer, invitation
OLD boon, behest
FORMAL requisition, solicitation, entreaty, supplication,
imploration

require v
1 NEED, want, wish, desire, crave, lack, miss, be short of, be
deficient in
2 **you are required to attend**
oblige, force, compel, necessitate, make, ask, request, call
on, instruct, direct, command, order, demand, entail, insist
on, take, involve
FORMAL constrain, enjoin

required adj
compulsory, essential, obligatory, recommended, advised,
demanded, necessary, stipulated, set, needed,
unavoidable, vital
FORMAL mandatory, prescribed, requisite
F3 optional, inessential

requirement n
need, necessity, essential, sine qua non, demand, lack,
want, stipulation, condition, term, specification, proviso,
prerequisite, qualification, provision, obligation, occasion
FORMAL requisite, precondition, desideratum
COLLOQ. must

requisite adj, n
◆ adj
required, needed, needful, necessary, essential,
indispensable, obligatory, compulsory, set, prerequisite,
vital
FORMAL prescribed, mandatory
◆ n
requirement, essential, due, necessity, need, condition,
prerequisite, stipulation, specification, qualification, sine
qua non
FORMAL desideratum, precondition, desiderative
COLLOQ. must
F3 inessential

requisition v, n
◆ v
commandeer, take, take over, take possession of, use,
confiscate, seize, occupy, request, put in for, demand,
summons
FORMAL appropriate
◆ n
commandeering, confiscation, seizure, takeover,
occupation, order, use, application, summons, request,
call, demand
FORMAL appropriation

requital n
amends, redress, restitution, satisfaction, recompense,
compensation, indemnification, indemnity, repayment,
payment, pay-off, reparation
FORMAL quittance

requite v
repay, reciprocate, respond, retaliate, return, pay, pay off,
recompense, reimburse, remunerate, reward, satisfy,
redress, even up on, compensate, avenge
OLD requight, apay, quit

rescind v

cancel, set aside, overturn, quash, reverse, recall, repeal, annul, invalidate, void, negate
FORMAL revoke, abrogate, countermand, nullify, retract
E3 enforce

rescission n

cancellation, negation, reversal, invalidation, annulment, recall, repeal
FORMAL abrogation, nullification, rescindment, retraction, revocation, voidance
E3 enforcement

rescue v, n

♦ v

save, recover, salvage, deliver, free, set free, liberate, emancipate, extricate, release, relieve, bring off, pluck, redeem, ransom, reprieve, retrieve, come/go to someone's rescue
OLD reskew
COLLOQ. throw a lifeline to, pull the chestnuts out of the fire
E3 capture, imprison

♦ n

saving, recovery, salvage, deliverance, liberation, freeing, release, emancipation, relief, redemption, salvation
E3 capture

research n, v

♦ n

investigation, inquiry, fact-finding, groundwork, examination, analysis, assessment, scrutiny, inspection, testing, test(s), study, review, search, probe, exploration, experiment, experimentation

♦ v

investigate, examine, look into, analyse, scrutinize, study, inspect, search, probe, test, assess, review, explore, experiment

researcher n

investigator, student, analyst, inspector, inquirer, field worker, boffin

resemblance n

likeness, similarity, sameness, conformity, nearness, closeness, affinity, uniformity, parallel, parallelism, comparison, comparability, agreement, analogy, correspondence, image, facsimile
FORMAL parity, similitude, congruity
E3 dissimilarity

resemble v

be like, look like, be similar to, bear resemblance to, take after, favour, mirror, echo, duplicate, parallel, approach
E3 differ from

resent v

grudge, begrudge, envy, feel bitter about, feel aggrieved at, be angry at, take offence at, take umbrage at, take amiss, object to, grumble at, take exception to, dislike
SLANG Aust & NZ have a derry on
E3 accept, like

resentful adj

grudging, envious, jealous, bitter, embittered, hurt, wounded, offended, aggrieved, put out, piqued, incensed, in high dudgeon, indignant, angry, irritated, irked, vindictive, malicious, spiteful
COLLOQ. miffed, peeved
E3 satisfied, contented

resentment n

grudge, envy, jealousy, bitterness, spite, malice, ill-will, ill-feeling, bad feeling, hard feelings, (high) dudgeon, bad blood, ill blood, animosity, hostility, hurt, umbrage, pique, offence, displeasure, irritation, indignation, annoyance, ire, vexation, anger, vindictiveness, snuff
COLLOQ. miff

SLANG Aust derry
E3 contentment, happiness

reservation n

1 DOUBT(S), scepticism, misgiving(s), qualm(s), scruple(s), hesitancy, hesitation, second thoughts, arrière-pensée
FORMAL demur
2 BOOKING, advance booking, engagement, appointment, arrangement, order, prearrangement
3 RESERVE, preserve, park, sanctuary, homeland, enclave, tract
COLLOQ. N Am res
4 PROVISO, stipulation, qualification, condition, limitation
TECHNICAL salvo
5 PRESERVATION, keeping, storage, protection, defence, maintenance, guarding, safeguarding, safekeeping, safety, security, conservation, upkeep, support, retention, upholding, continuation, perpetuation
E3 destruction, ruin

■ **without reservation**

unreservedly, completely, entirely, utterly, wholeheartedly, outright, unhesitatingly, without hesitation, without qualification
COLLOQ. gloves-off; Aust & NZ boots and all

reserve v, n, adj

♦ v

1 SET ASIDE, earmark, keep, retain, hold back, keep back, save, store, lay aside, put on one side, put to one side, set apart, stockpile, hoard, accumulate, ring-fence
2 reserve a seat
book, engage, order, arrange for, secure, prearrange
3 DELAY, postpone, defer, put off, suspend, shelve, hold over, adjourn
E3 1 use up

♦ n

1 STORE, stock, supply, fund, stockpile, pool, reservoir, bank, cache, hoard, accumulation, savings
2 SUBSTITUTE, replacement, stand-in, understudy, fill-in, supply, proxy, surrogate, successor
3 RESERVATION, preserve, park, area, sanctuary, tract, enclave
4 SHYNESS, reticence, unresponsiveness, secretiveness, coldness, coolness, aloofness, detachment, modesty, restraint, self-restraint, distance, remoteness, unapproachability
5 military reserves
backup, auxiliaries, support, help, reinforcements, additional soldiers/troops/police officers, supplementaries
E3 4 friendliness, openness, approachability

♦ adj

spare, substitute, additional, auxiliary, alternative, extra, stand-in, secondary

■ **in reserve**

for use when needed, available, to hand, in hand, unused, stored, spare, set aside

reserved adj

1 BOOKED, engaged, ordered, arranged, prearranged, taken, spoken for, set aside, earmarked, meant, intended, designated, destined, saved, held, kept, retained
2 SHY, retiring, backward, reticent, unresponsive, unforthcoming, uncommunicative, secretive, silent, taciturn, introverted, unsociable, cool, cold, aloof, standoffish, unapproachable, modest, diffident, restrained, cautious, distant, remote
E3 1 unreserved, free, available 2 friendly, open

reservoir n

1 LAKE, pond, pool, cistern; Scot loch; Aust gilgai
OLD reservatory
2 TANK, cistern, vat, basin, container, receptacle, holder, header, header tank
TECHNICAL sump, hot well, steam chest, wind chest

OLD TECHNICAL urinary

3 STORE, stockpile, stock, supply, source, reserves, accumulation, fund, holder, bank, well, fountain
FORMAL repository, reservatory

reshuffle *n, v*
♦ *n*
reorganization, upheaval, redistribution, regrouping, rearrangement, realignment, restructuring, revision, change, interchange
COLLOQ. shake-up
♦ *v*
reorganize, restructure, shake up, change, interchange, shift, shuffle, revise, rearrange, regroup, realign, redistribute

reside *v*
1 LIVE, inhabit, lodge, stay, board, occupy, settle, remain
FORMAL dwell, sojourn
2 BE PRESENT, exist, lie, rest, be inherent, be contained
FORMAL dwell, abide

residence *n*
home, house, flat, apartment, seat, place, lodgings, quarters, hall, manor, mansion, mansionary, palace, villa, country house, country seat, stay, lodging
FORMAL dwelling, habitation, domicile, abode, sojourn
COLLOQ. pad, digs

resident *n, adj*
♦ *n*
inhabitant, citizen, local, householder, occupant, occupier, tenant, lodger, guest, patient, inmate, client, transient
OLD ledger, resiant
FORMAL resider, dweller, sojourner
Ⓔ non-resident
♦ *adj*
live-in, living-in, dwelling, local, permanent, inhabiting, inhabitant, neighbourhood, settled, stationary, ledger
TECHNICAL commorant
OLD gremial, resiant
FORMAL *en poste*
Ⓔ non-resident

residential *adj*
commuter, suburban, dormitory
FORMAL exurban

residual *adj*
remaining, left-over, unused, unconsumed, net, excess, surplus

residue *n*
remainder, remains, remnant, rest, surplus, excess, extra, overflow, balance, difference, lees, dregs, leftovers, carry-over
FORMAL residuum
Ⓔ core

resign *v*
stand down, retire, step down, leave, abdicate, vacate, give up, throw up, hand in your notice, give in your notice, for(e)go, waive, surrender, yield, abandon, submit; *Scot* demit
OLD waive, forelend
FORMAL renounce, relinquish, forsake
COLLOQ. quit
Ⓔ join

▪ **resign yourself**
reconcile yourself, accept, comply, bow, submit, yield, come to terms, put something behind you, turn your face to the wall
FORMAL acquiesce
Ⓔ resist

resignation *n*
1 STANDING-DOWN, stepping-down, abdication,

retirement, departure, notice, letter of resignation, surrender, giving-up, waiving
FORMAL renunciation, relinquishment
2 ACCEPTANCE, reconciliation, submission, non-resistance, passivity, patience, stoicism, yielding, compliance, defeatism
FORMAL acquiescence
Ⓔ **2** resistance

resigned *adj*
reconciled, philosophical, stoical, patient, long-suffering, unprotesting, uncomplaining, unresisting, passive, submissive, yielding, defeatist
FORMAL acquiescent
Ⓔ resistant, protesting

resignedly *adv*
stoically, philosophically, submissively, uncomplainingly, patiently

resilience *n*
1 FLEXIBILITY, elasticity, springiness, spring, pliability, plasticity, suppleness, give, bounciness, bounce, recoil
2 STRENGTH, toughness, hardiness, adaptability, buoyancy, irrepressibility, unshockability
Ⓔ inflexibility, rigidity

resilient *adj*
1 *resilient material*
flexible, pliable, supple, plastic, elastic, springy, bouncy, rubbery
2 STRONG, tough, hardy, adaptable, buoyant, springing, irrepressible, unshockable
Ⓔ **1** rigid, brittle **2** weak

resist *v*
oppose, defy, confront, face, fight (off), struggle, contend, battle, combat, weather, withstand, defend, buck, stand up to, stand against, stick out, hold out against, obstruct, repel, counter, counteract, check, stop, halt, avoid, refuse, prevent, hinder, obstruct, thwart, impede, restrain, curb, stem, wear
TECHNICAL deforce
OLD gainstrive
SLANG *Aust* jack up
Ⓔ submit, accept

resistance *n*
opposition, defiance, confrontation, fight, fighting, struggle, combat, contention, counteraction, battle, withstanding, repulsion, avoidance, refusal, prevention, thwarting, hindrance, obstruction, impedance, impediment, restraint
FORMAL intransigence
Ⓔ acceptance, submission

resistant *adj*
1 OPPOSED, antagonistic, defiant, unyielding, unwilling
OLD renitent
FORMAL intransigent
2 PROOF, impervious, waterproof, immune, unaffected, invulnerable, unsusceptible, tough, strong, windproof, shellproof, shockproof
Ⓔ **1** compliant, yielding

resolute *adj*
determined, resolved, intent, decided, dedicated, constant, serious, earnest, adamant, stalwart, set, strong, fixed, unwavering, unyielding, unswerving, inflexible, staunch, firm, steadfast, steady, relentless, single-minded, persevering, dogged, tenacious, stubborn, obstinate, strong-willed, undaunted, dauntless, unflinching, bold, diehard, granite, hardy; *N Am* flat-footed
FORMAL obdurate
Ⓔ irresolute, weak-willed, half-hearted

resolutely *adv*
firmly, steadily, strongly, with determination, unwaveringly,

unswervingly, steadfastly, relentlessly, single-mindedly, unflinchingly, adamantly, inflexibly, seriously, earnestly, staunchly, obstinately, stubbornly, dauntlessly
⊟ irresolutely, half-heartedly

resolution *n*

1 DECISION, judgement, finding, declaration, proposition, motion, decree, verdict, declaration
2 DETERMINATION, resolve, willpower, commitment, dedication, devotion, constancy, firmness, intentness, seriousness, earnestness, steadfastness, persistence, perseverance, doggedness, inflexibility, tenacity, zeal, courage, boldness
3 SOLVING, answer, solution, unravelling, disentangling, working out, sorting out
⊟ 2 half-heartedness, uncertainty, indecision

resolve *v, n*

♦ *v*
1 DECIDE, make up your mind, determine, fix, settle (on), conclude, talk out, patch
2 SOLVE, answer, unravel, untie, disentangle, sort out, straighten out, work out
OLD dissolve
3 BREAK UP, break down, analyse, reduce, divide, separate, dissolve, disintegrate, detail, convert, anatomize, itemize
TECHNICAL decompose, factorize, sublate
♦ *n*
determination, willpower, commitment, dedication, devotion, constancy, firmness, intentness, seriousness, earnestness, steadfastness, persistence, perseverance, doggedness, inflexibility, tenacity, zeal, courage, boldness, sense of purpose, vow
COLLOQ. bottle, pecker
⊟ indecision

resonance *n*

depth, strength, richness, vibrancy, fullness, reverberation
FORMAL canorousness, plangency

resonant *adj*

deep, strong, sonorous, ringing, booming, rich, fruity, vibrant, full, plummy, resounding, reverberant, reverberating, echoing, pear-shaped
FORMAL canorous, plangent
⊟ weak, faint, tinny

resonate *v*

resound, reverberate, echo, re-echo, ring, sound, boom, thunder

resort *v, n*

♦ *v*
go, visit, frequent, patronize, haunt
FORMAL repair
♦ *n*
1 HOLIDAY CENTRE, centre, holiday destination, spot, health resort, spa
2 RECOURSE, refuge, course (of action), measure, step, alternative, option, chance, possibility
■ **resort to**
turn to, use, utilize, make use of, avail yourself of, fall back on, have recourse to, employ, exercise
■ **in the last resort**
ultimately, finally, eventually, at last, in the end, after all, sooner or later, fundamentally
COLLOQ. at the end of the day

resound *v*

resonate, reverberate, echo, re-echo, ring, sound, boom, thunder

resounding *adj*

1 RESONANT, reverberating, echoing, ringing, loud, sonorous, booming, resonating, thunderous, full, rich, vibrant
2 *a resounding victory*
decisive, conclusive, impressive, striking, outstanding,

roaring, great, memorable, remarkable, notable, emphatic, thorough
⊟ 1 faint

resource *n*

1 *a shortage of resources*
materials, supplies, reserves, holdings, funds, money, wealth, riches, capital, assets, property, means, power, wherewithal
2 SUPPLY, reserve, pool, accumulation, stockpile, store, fund, source, contrivance, device, course, resort, expedient
3 RESOURCEFULNESS, initiative, enterprise, ingenuity, inventiveness, wit, imagination, talent, ability, capability
OLD artifice, chevisance

resourceful *adj*

ingenious, imaginative, creative, inventive, enterprising, innovative, original, versatile, clever, bright, sharp, quick-witted, witty, with your wits about you, able, capable, talented, adroit; *Scot* fendy

resourceless *adj*

inadequate, useless, hopeless, helpless, feeble, feckless, shiftless
⊟ unimaginative

respect *v, n*

♦ *v*
1 ADMIRE, regard, have a good opinion of, think highly of, hold in high regard, set great store by, appreciate, value, praise, honour, approve of, revere, esteem
FORMAL venerate
2 OBEY, observe, heed, comply with, follow, adhere to, honour, fulfil
3 CONSIDER, show consideration for, pay attention to, take into account, show regard for
FORMAL take cognizance of
⊟ 1 despise, scorn **2** ignore, disobey
♦ *n*
1 ADMIRATION, appreciation, recognition, honour, deference, reverence, high opinion, esteem, regard, high regard, homage
FORMAL veneration, approbation, obeisance
2 CONSIDERATION, attention, attentiveness, notice, regard, heed, thoughtfulness, politeness, courtesy
FORMAL cognizance
3 GREETINGS, compliments, regards, salutations, best wishes, good wishes
FORMAL devoirs
4 *in every respect*
point, aspect, facet, feature, characteristic, particular, detail, sense, matter, way, regard, reference, bearing, relation, connection
⊟ 1 disrespect
■ **with respect to**
with regard to, in regard to, as regards, concerning, with reference to, in relation to, in connection with, re, about, as to, on the subject of
FORMAL apropos

respectability *n*

worthiness, trustworthiness, integrity, honesty, uprightness, decency, gentility

respectable *adj*

1 REPUTABLE, honourable, worthy, respected, dignified, upright, honest, above-board, trustworthy, decent, superior, good, presentable, neat, tidy, clean, clean-living, clean-cut; *dialect* sponsible; *Scot* menseful
FORMAL decorous, salubrious
2 ACCEPTABLE, tolerable, passable, adequate, fair, fairly good, nice, reasonable, all right, appreciable, considerable
COLLOQ. not bad, OK
⊟ 1 dishonourable, disreputable **2** inadequate, paltry

respected *adj*
admired, valued, esteemed, highly esteemed, highly regarded, highly valued, held in high regard, thought highly of

respectful *adj*
deferential, reverent, reverential, humble, polite, well-mannered, courtly, dutiful, courteous, civil, subservient
≠ disrespectful

respectfully *adv*
courteously, civilly, politely, deferentially, reverently, reverentially
≠ disrespectfully

respecting *prep*
about, concerning, considering, in respect of, with regard to, regarding, with respect to, vis-à-vis

respective *adj*
corresponding, relevant, various, several, separate, individual, personal, own, specific, particular, special

respectively *adv*
correspondingly, in the order stated/given/listed, in turn, one by one, individually, specifically, particularly, specially

respite *n*
1 PAUSE, rest, relief, break, adjournment, intermission, recess, relaxation, interval, interruption, halt, gap, lull, reprieve, truce
FORMAL cessation, hiatus
COLLOQ. breather, let-up
2 DELAY, reprieve, postponement, deferment, remission, stay, suspension, moratorium
OLD frist
FORMAL abatement

resplendent *adj*
glorious, magnificent, splendid, dazzling, shining, radiant, brilliant, bright, irradiant, luminous, beaming, gleaming, glittering
FORMAL effulgent, fulgent, lustrous, refulgent
COLLOQ. splendiferous
≠ dull

respond *v*
answer, reply, acknowledge, retort, rejoin, answer back, react, return, counter, reciprocate

response *n*
answer, reply, acknowledgement, retort, rejoinder, riposte, return, reaction, feedback
OLD (*Spenser*) respondence
COLLOQ. comeback
≠ query

responsibility *n*
1 DUTY, obligation, burden, onus, charge, care, role, task, authority, power, trust, business, affair, concern
COLLOQ. baby, pidgin
2 FAULT, blame, guilt, answerability, accountability
FORMAL culpability
3 DEPENDABILITY, reliability, conscientiousness, trustworthiness, honesty, soundness, maturity, adulthood, stability

responsible *adj*
1 IN CHARGE OF, in control of, controlling, managing, leading, accountable, answerable
2 TO BLAME, guilty, at fault, blameworthy, liable, answerable, accountable
FORMAL culpable
3 DEPENDABLE, reliable, conscientious, trustworthy, honest, sound, steady, sober, mature, adult, stable, reasonable, sensible, rational, sane, level-headed
4 IMPORTANT, authoritative, powerful, executive, decision-making
COLLOQ. high-level
≠ **3** irresponsible, unreliable, untrustworthy

> **Synonym nuances**
> *sense 3*
> Most of these synonyms are, naturally, approbatory in tone.
> Both **dependable** and **reliable** suggest someone who can be counted on, while **trustworthy** and **honest** clearly suggest someone morally deserving of peoples' confidence. **Conscientious** is suggestive of a high degree of diligence; the terms **sound**, **steady** and **stable** are more appropriate if you want to suggest firmness of character, and **mature** and **adult** have suggestions of emotional responsibility: *women show a more adult approach to driving, and tend not to show off.*
> The terms **reasonable**, **rational** and **sane** put more emphasis on intellectual responsibility and judiciousness: *he had a sane approach to the controversy, seeing both sides*, while **sensible** and **level-headed** emphasize the use of common sense: *he is sensible enough to become a nurse: as it was raining, he drove at a sensible speed.*

responsibly *adv*
sensibly, reasonably, steadily, dependably, reliably, honestly, conscientiously, rationally
≠ irresponsibly

responsive *adj*
alert, aware, sensitive, awake, open, sharp, quick, reactive, amenable, receptive, susceptible, sympathetic, perceptive, forthcoming, impressionable, alive, respondent, teachable, stimulable
TECHNICAL excitable
FORMAL responsorial, sentient
COLLOQ. on the ball, with it, swinging, switched on
≠ unresponsive

responsiveness *n*
alertness, awareness, openness, receptiveness, susceptibility, sensitivity

rest¹ *n, v*
♦ *n*
1 LEISURE, relaxation, lie-down, sleep, snooze, nap, siesta, idleness, inactivity, ease, motionlessness, standstill, stillness, tranquillity, calm
FORMAL repose, quietude, slumber
COLLOQ. R & R
2 BREAK, pause, breathing space, intermission, interlude, interval, recess, holiday, vacation, time off, halt, lull, respite
FORMAL cessation
COLLOQ. breather
3 SUPPORT, prop, stand, base, holder
≠ **1** action, activity, work
♦ *v*
1 PAUSE, halt, stop, cease
2 RELAX, sit (down), recline, lounge, laze, lie down, sleep, snooze, doze
FORMAL repose
COLLOQ. put your feet up, take it easy, recharge your batteries, veg (out)
3 DEPEND, rely, hinge, hang, lie, be based
4 LEAN, prop, support, stand, steady
≠ **1** continue **2** work

rest² *n, v*
♦ *n*
the rest of us stayed behind
remainder, others, balance, surplus, excess, residue, remains, leftovers, remnant(s)
FORMAL residuum
♦ *v*
continue, remain, stay, last, endure, persist

restaurant
See panel on next page

Types of restaurant include:

bistro	creperie	ice-cream parlour	pull-in	tea room
brasserie	*N Am* diner	Internet café	refectory	tea shop
buffet	dining-car	*N Am* luncheonette	rotisserie	transport café
burger bar	dining room	McDonald's®	sandwich bar	trattoria
café	drivethrough	mess room	self-service restaurant	
cafeteria	eating-house	milk bar	snack-bar	
canteen	fish-and-chip shop	motorway café	steakhouse	
carvery	*slang* greasy spoon	NAAFI (Navy Army	sushi bar	
Irish colloq. chipper	grill	and Air Force	taqueria	
colloq. chippy	grill room	Institutes)	taverna	
coffee bar	health food restaurant	pizzeria	teahouse	

restful *adj*
relaxing, soothing, calming, calm, tranquil, serene, peaceful, quiet, still, placid, undisturbed, relaxed, comfortable, leisurely, unhurried
FORMAL languid
E3 tiring, restless

restitution *n*
amends, reparation, requital, restoration, restoring, return, satisfaction, redress, repayment, damages, compensation, recompense, remuneration, refund, reimbursement, indemnification, indemnity

restive *adj*
1 UNRULY, impatient, wayward, wilful, turbulent, uncontrollable, undisciplined, unmanageable
FORMAL recalcitrant, refractory
2 RESTLESS, agitated, fidgety, fidgeting, unsettled, nervous, uneasy, anxious, fretful, tense, on edge
COLLOQ. edgy, jumpy, uptight
E3 2 calm, relaxed

restiveness *n*
unruliness, waywardness, wilfulness, uncontrollableness, unmanageableness, restlessness, turbulence
E3 calmness

restless *adj*
1 FIDGETY, fidgeting, unruly, turbulent, impatient, changeable; *Scot* wanrestful
FORMAL restive
COLLOQ. having ants in your pants
2 AGITATED, nervous, anxious, worried, uneasy, fretful, troubled, unsettled, on edge, unquiet
TECHNICAL agitato
OLD disquiet
COLLOQ. edgy, jittery, jumpy, uptight
SLANG *Aust* toey
3 SLEEPLESS, uncomfortable, broken, disturbed, tossing and turning
E3 1 still, motionless **2** calm, relaxed **3** restful, comfortable

restlessly *adv*
nervously, anxiously, fretfully, impatiently, turbulently
E3 calmly

restlessness *n*
agitation, disturbance, unsettledness, uneasiness, unrest, turbulence, turmoil, worriedness, anxiety, nervousness, fermentation, fitfulness, insomnia, fretfulness, bustle, disquiet, hurry, activity, dynamism, instability, movement, inconstancy, transience
TECHNICAL jactitation
FORMAL inquietude, restiveness
COLLOQ. edginess, jitters, jumpiness, heebie-jeebies
SLANG gate fever
E3 calmness, relaxation

restoration *n*
1 RENOVATION, repair, refurbishing, rebuilding, reconstruction, renewal, rehabilitation
OLD instauration
2 REVIVAL, refreshment, rejuvenation, revitalization, recovery

OLD recruit, recruital
COLLOQ. kiss of life
3 RETURN, replacement, reinstallation, restitution, reinstatement, re-establishment, reconstitution
TECHNICAL restitutio in integram
E3 1 damage **2** weakening **3** removal

restore *v*
1 *restore a building*
renovate, renew, rebuild, reconstruct, redecorate, refurbish, retouch, recondition, rehabilitate, revamp, repair, mend, fix
COLLOQ. do up
2 REVIVE, refresh, recover, rejuvenate, revitalize, reinvigorate, strengthen, build up
FORMAL revivify
3 REPLACE, return, give back, hand back, reinstate, re-establish, reintroduce, re-impose, re-enforce
E3 1 damage **2** weaken **3** remove

restrain *v*
restrain your feelings; restrain a prisoner
hold back, keep back, suppress, subdue, repress, inhibit, check, hold in check, curb, bridle, stop, arrest, prevent, hinder, obstruct, impede, bind, tie, chain, fetter, manacle, imprison, detain, jail, confine, hold captive, restrict, regulate, control, keep under control, govern
COLLOQ. bottle up
E3 encourage, liberate

Synonym nuances
Hold back, **keep back** and **detain** are fairly unmarked terms which suggest preventing progress. **Control** and **keep under control** have connotations of dominance, and **subdue** is similar but implies something has been overcome, while **suppress** is more suggestive of forcibly quashing. **Repress** would also suggest preventing using a more forcible control: *she repressed a shudder.*
The idea of curtailing something can be conveyed in a fairly neutral way by **inhibit**, **check** and **hold in check**, but **restrict**, **curb** and **bridle** imply subjecting to rigid limitations: *the government must curb spending.* **Arrest** and **prevent** could be used of bringing completely to a standstill. **Hinder** implies interfering with progress in a way that is unwelcome: *there is a difference between not helping and actually hindering our plans*; both **obstruct** and **impede** suggest even more effective handicaps: *the doctor did not make it on time, as he was impeded by the weather conditions.*
The terms **bind**, **tie**, **chain**, **fetter** and **manacle** all suggest physical restraints, though they may also be used figuratively to imply powerful and perhaps frustrating restrictions: *she is not fettered by preconceptions.*
The term **regulate** would be appropriate where restraining involves the application of rules, whereas **govern**, although similar, has perhaps a more democratic and less strict element: *a contract which regulates the rights of the parties; our upbringing can govern how we think.*

restrained *adj*

1 CALM, controlled, steady, self-controlled, self-restrained, unemotional, formal, cold, aloof, uncommunicative, sober, measured, ordered, reserved, abstemious, chaste, relaxed, cool
TECHNICAL ritenuto

2 *restrained decorations*
tasteful, moderate, temperate, mild, subdued, subtle, muted, quiet, soft, low-key, unobtrusive, discreet, refined, modest, dry, severe
F3 **1** emotional, demonstrative **2** garish, ostentatious; *colloq.* loud

restraint *n*

behave with restraint; no restraints in modern life
moderation, prudence, inhibition, self-control, self-discipline, hold, grip, check, curb, rein, bridle, suppression, bondage, captivity, confinement, imprisonment, bonds, chains, fetters, straitjacket, restriction, control, constraint, limit(s), restriction(s), duress, block, barrier, stint, limitation, tie, hindrance, prevention
FORMAL judiciousness
F3 liberty

restrict *v*

limit, bound, demarcate, control, keep under control, keep within limits, regulate, tighten, confine, contain, localize, cramp, constrict, strangle, constrain, hold, impede, hinder, hamper, handicap, tie, restrain, curtail, curb, inhibit, pinch, bind, condition, peg down, go slow, fast, ration, scant
TECHNICAL astrict
OLD stint, straiten, thirl; (*Shakesp*) combine
COLLOQ. hem in, cramp someone's style, draw/pull in your horns
F3 broaden, free

restricted *adj*

1 SMALL, narrow, cramped, confined, constricted, tight
2 SECRET, private, limited, exclusive, closed, controlled, regulated

restriction *n*

limit, bound, confine, limitation, constraint, handicap, check, curb, restraint, ban, stint, embargo, control, regulation, rule, stipulation, qualification, condition, proviso
F3 freedom

restructure *v*

reorganize, rearrange, shake up, modernize, streamline, rationalize, rejig

result *n, v*

◆ *n*
effect, consequence, sequel, repercussion, reaction, implication, outcome, upshot, end, issue, end-product, by-product, side effect, fruit(s), score, grade, mark, answer, verdict, judgement, decision, conclusion
COLLOQ. pay-off, spin-off
F3 cause

◆ *v*
follow, ensue, happen, occur, issue, emerge, arise, spring, derive, stem, flow, evolve, emanate, proceed, come out of, develop, end, finish, terminate, culminate
FORMAL eventuate
F3 cause

resultant *adj*

ensuing, consequent, resulting, subsequent, following

resume *v*

restart, start again, begin again, recommence, reopen, reconvene, re-occupy, continue, carry on, go on, proceed, take up (again)
TECHNICAL rejuvenesce
F3 cease

résumé *n*

summary, précis, synopsis, outline, sketch, breakdown, abstract, digest, recapitulation, review, overview, run-down, epitome; *N Am* wrap-up
COLLOQ. recap

resumption *n*

restart, recommencement, reopening, re-establishment, renewal, resurgence, continuation, proceeding
F3 cessation

resurgence *n*

re-appearance, re-emergence, resumption, return, rebirth, resurrection, revival, renaissance
FORMAL renascence, recrudescence, revivification, risorgimento
F3 decrease

resurrect *v*

1 *Jesus Christ was resurrected*
bring back to life, raise from the dead, restore, restore to life, revive

2 *resurrect an old idea*
restore, revive, resuscitate, reactivate, bring back, reintroduce, re-establish, re-install, renew, revitalize
F3 **1** kill, bury

resurrection *n*

1 *the resurrection of Jesus Christ*
bringing back to life, raising/rising from the dead, restoration to life, return from the dead
TECHNICAL anastasis

2 *resurrection of former procedures*
restoration, revival, resuscitation, renaissance, rebirth, renewal, revitalization, re-establishment, resurgence, reappearance, return, comeback

resuscitate *v*

revive, bring round, resurrect, save, rescue, reanimate, quicken, reinvigorate, breathe new life into, revitalize, restore, renew
FORMAL revivify
COLLOQ. give the kiss of life to

resuscitated *adj*

restored, revived, resurrected
FORMAL redivivus, redintegrate(d)

resuscitation *n*

revival, restoration, renewal, reinvigoration, revitalizing, quickening
FORMAL revivification

retain *v*

1 KEEP, hold, keep hold of, grasp, grip, reserve, hold back, hold fast to, save, continue, maintain, preserve
COLLOQ. hang on to

2 *retain information*
remember, recall, recollect, memorize, bear in mind, keep in mind, call to mind

3 EMPLOY, engage, hire, pay, contract, commission
F3 **1** release **2** forget **3** dismiss

retainer *n*

1 FEE, retaining fee, deposit, advance
2 SERVANT, lackey, footman, domestic, attendant, supporter, follower, valet, dependant, vassal, menial, jackman
OLD galloglass, samurai

retaliate *v*

reciprocate, counter-attack, get back at, pay someone back, hit back, strike back, fight back, avenge, take revenge
COLLOQ. get your own back, get even with, give as good as you get, return like for like, give someone a taste of their own medicine

retaliation *n*

reprisal, counter-attack, revenge, vengeance,

retribution, reciprocation, retort
OLD talion
FORMAL ultion, quid pro quo, *lex talionis*
COLLOQ. tit for tat, like for like, an eye for an eye (and a tooth for a tooth), a taste of your own medicine

retard *v*
slow down, delay, hold up, decelerate, brake, put a/the brake on, handicap, incapacitate, obstruct, hinder, impede, check, curb, restrict
E3 speed up, accelerate

retardation *n*
slowness, slowing, incapability, mental handicap, deficiency, incapacity, impeding, hindering, hindrance, delay, lag, obstruction, dullness
FORMAL retardment
E3 advancement

retch *v*
vomit, spew, heave, disgorge, regurgitate, gag, disgorge; *dialect* reach
COLLOQ. puke, throw up, chuck up, fetch up, sick up
SLANG *NAm* barf

retching *n*
vomiting, nausea, reaching, gagging
FORMAL vomiturition
COLLOQ. puking, spewing

retention *n*
keeping, holding, keeping hold, holding (on), saving, continuance, maintenance, preservation
COLLOQ. hanging-on

rethink *v*
reconsider, think over, review, revise, re-examine, think twice, modify, reassess, think better of, have second thoughts

reticence *n*
reserve, restraint, quietness, uncommunicativeness, unforthcomingness, secretiveness, silence, taciturnity, muteness, diffidence
E3 communicativeness, forwardness, frankness

reticent *adj*
reserved, shy, restrained, uncommunicative, unforthcoming, tight-lipped, close-lipped, close-mouthed, secretive, taciturn, silent, quiet, diffident, boutonné
E3 communicative, forward, frank

retinue *n*
entourage, following, followers, personnel, staff, suite, train, attendants, escort, cortège, aides, servants, tail, sowarry
TECHNICAL comitatus
OLD attendancy, equipage, port; (*Shakesp*) meinie; (*Spenser*) many

retire *v*
1 STOP WORK, stop working, leave work, give up work, resign
COLLOQ. bow out, be put out to pasture
2 LEAVE, depart, go away, withdraw, retreat, recede, move, go, decamp, go aside, step, scratch, den, lick your wounds
E3 **1** join **2** enter, advance

retired *adj*
former, ex-, emeritus, past

retirement *n*
withdrawal, retreat, exit, departure, resignation, solitude, loneliness, seclusion, privacy, obscurity

retiring *adj*
shy, bashful, timid, shrinking, quiet, reticent, reserved, self-effacing, unassertive, diffident, coy, modest, unassuming, humble
E3 bold, forward, assertive

retort *v, n*
♦ *v*
answer, reply, respond, rejoin, return, counter, retaliate, return, repartee, throw back, turn upon
COLLOQ. give as good as you get
♦ *n*
answer, reply, response, rejoinder, riposte, repartee, quip, wisecrack, comeback, backword, clinch, outfling, sally, squelch
COLLOQ. floorer; *NAm* zinger

retract *v*
1 *retract criticism*
take back, withdraw, recant, reverse, cancel, repeal, repudiate, disown, disclaim, deny, renege
OLD (*Shakesp*) unspeak
FORMAL renounce, revoke, rescind, disavow, abjure, abrogate
2 *retract like cat's claws*
pull back, move back, move in, draw in, withdraw
E3 **1** assert, maintain

retreat *v, n*
♦ *v*
draw back, pull back, fall back, turn back, shrink, withdraw, decamp, give ground, climb down, give way, retire, leave, depart, flee, beat a retreat
OLD disadvance, recoil, retrate
COLLOQ. turn tail, quit, back-pedal; *NAm* bug out, crawfish
E3 advance
♦ *n*
1 WITHDRAWAL, drawing-back, pulling-back, pull-back, falling-back, climb-down, departure, evacuation, flight, katabasis
OLD recoil, retraict, retrate
2 SECLUSION, privacy, solitude, retirement, hideaway, hideout, den, refuge, asylum, sanctuary, shelter, harbour, haven, tower, lair, lodge, mew, nest, nook, hermitage, ivory tower, arbour, ashram
TECHNICAL redoubt, hibernaculum, reduit, interglacial, interstadial
OLD privacy, alcove, growlery
COLLOQ. sanctum sanctorum
SLANG funkhole
E3 **1** advance, charge

retrench *v*
cut back, economize, cut, slim down, live more economically, save, reduce, lessen, limit, decrease, diminish, curtail, trim, pare, prune, husband
COLLOQ. tighten your belt
E3 increase

retrenchment *n*
cutback, cutting back, cut, economy, reduction, pruning, curtailment, cost-cutting, run-down, contraction, shrinkage
COLLOQ. tightening your belt, tightening/pulling the purse strings
E3 increase

retribution *n*
punishment, reckoning, justice, satisfaction, retaliation, requital, reward, reprisal, redress, repayment, payment, compensation, recompense, revenge, vengeance, Nemesis, utu
TECHNICAL karma
OLD talion, vengement
COLLOQ. just deserts

retrieve *v*
recover, get back, fetch, bring back, regain, recapture, repossess, recoup, reclaim, put to rights, make good, salvage, save, rescue, redeem, restore, remedy, return, mend, repair
E3 lose

retro *adj*
old, old-time, old-fashioned, antique, olde-worlde, former, past, bygone, passé, period, in period style

retrograde *adj*
backward, reverse, retrogressive, negative, downward, worsening, declining, deteriorating
F3 progressive

retrogress *v*
regress, retrograde, return, revert, relapse, withdraw, recede, drop, ebb, fall, sink, wane, retire, retreat, backslide, decline, deteriorate, worsen, degenerate
F3 progress, advance

retrogression *n*
regression, regress, return, relapse, decline, worsening, deterioration, drop, ebb, fall
FORMAL recidivism, retrogradation
F3 increase, progress

retrospect *n*
hindsight, afterthought, thinking back, reflection, re-examination, review, survey, recollection, remembrance
F3 prospect
■ **in retrospect**
retrospectively, with hindsight, looking back, thinking back, on reflection, with the wisdom of hindsight
FORMAL retroactively

retrospective *adj*
backward-looking, retro-active, retro-operative

retrospectively *adv*
in retrospect, with hindsight, looking back, thinking back, on reflection, with the wisdom of hindsight
FORMAL retroactively

return *v, n*
♦ *v*
1 COME BACK, reappear, recur, go back, get back, come home, come again, happen again, backtrack, regress, revert
2 GIVE BACK, hand back, pay back, send back, take back, deliver, put back, replace, reinstate, restore
FORMAL remit
3 *return a favour*
reciprocate, repay, refund, reimburse, recompense, exchange, match, equal, correspond
FORMAL requite
COLLOQ. do the same
4 ANSWER, reply, respond, rejoin, retort, riposte, counter
5 *return a verdict*
announce, pronounce, declare, deliver, bring in, hand down
F3 1 leave, depart **2** take, keep
♦ *n*
1 REAPPEARANCE, recurrence, home-coming
COLLOQ. comeback
2 REPAYMENT, recompense, replacement, restoration, reinstatement, reciprocation
3 REVENUE, income, proceeds, takings, yield, gain, profit, interest, reward, advantage, benefit
4 *the return of the books*
giving-back, handing-back, taking-back, reinstatement, restoration, delivery, replacement
5 *a tax return*
form, statement, document, account, report, record, data
F3 1 departure, disappearance **2** removal **3** payment, expense, loss
■ **in return for**
in exchange for, in response to, in consideration of, equivalently, mutually, reciprocally

re-use *v*
recycle, reconstitute

revamp *v*
renovate, recondition, rebuild, reconstruct, repair, restore, revise, refit, refurbish, modernize, rehabilitate, overhaul, recast
COLLOQ. do up

reveal *v*
expose, bring to light, make aware, uncover, unveil, unmask, unearth, unfold, unshadow, expose to view, show, display, exhibit, lay bare, manifest, disclose, divulge, give away, betray, leak, tell, let out, let slip, impart, communicate, express, publicize, broadcast, publish, make public, make known, announce, proclaim, confess, undeceive, unbosom, disbosom, throw up
OLD discover, bewray, decipher, descry; (*Spenser*) presage
COLLOQ. take the wraps off, let on, blow someone's cover, take/lift/blow the lid on, tell tales out of school
F3 hide, conceal, mask

Synonym nuances
Expose and **bring to light** can be used of bringing something into view or making others aware of it, particularly something underhand or unwelcome: *a drugs ring exposed by investigative journalists*. Both **uncover** and **unveil** are similar, and have implications of prior secrecy, while **unmask** is more appropriate for making known someone's true identity: *the trial unmasked him as a charlatan*.
   The archaeological image of **unearth** suggests an element of perseverance, and has connotations of finding something valuable or useful: *the club unearthed a prodigious talent in this young player*, whereas **throw up** implies something produced incidentally: *the medical detective work threw up new uncertainties*. **Unfold** suggests gradually opening out, without any element of effort involved: *the Watergate drama unfolded*. **Manifest**, likewise, can be used of something becoming apparent: *the crisis manifested itself in a variety of ways*, while **display** and **exhibit** could be used to suggest a more deliberate element of presentation.
   A lack of intention is conveyed by **give away**, and **betray** has further implications of an unwanted revelation: *his expression betrayed how he really felt*, while both **let out** and **let slip** could be used of accidentally passing on information. **Leak** can convey being deliberately indiscreet, while both **disclose** and **divulge** suggest revelations of an intimate nature, without the same connotations of stealth or secrecy.
   Express is appropriate for deliberately revealing your feelings: *he expressed his concern*, while **confess** has more to do with admission. **Announce** and **proclaim** would be appropriate for a strong verbal gesture bringing something to public attention, while **publicize**, **broadcast** and **publish** could be used where such a gesture is aimed at a wider audience, often through the media.

---

revealing *adj*
1 *a revealing interview*
indicative, significant, revelatory, giveaway
2 *a revealing dress*
low-cut, daring, see-through, diaphanous, sheer

revel *v, n*
♦ *v*
1 *revel in an experience*
enjoy, delight, take delight, take pleasure, relish, glory, joy, indulge, thrive, wallow, savour, bask, rejoice, lap up, gloat, crow, luxuriate
2 *revelling through the night*
celebrate, carouse, have a party, make merry, riot, roist, roister
OLD wake

COLLOQ. live it up, whoop it up, paint the town red, push the boat out, raise the roof, large it, have it large

E3 1 dislike

♦ *n*

celebration, party, carousal, carouse, festivity, spree, gala, merrymaking, jollification, bacchanal, orgy, debauch, saturnalia, comus

OLD night-rule

COLLOQ. rave, rave-up, do, knees-up

revelation *n*

1 UNCOVERING, unveiling, unearthing, exposure, unmasking, show, display, exhibition, disclosure, divulgence, expression, vision, confession, admission, betrayal, giveaway, broadcasting

OLD revealment

FORMAL manifestation, apocalypse, epiphany

2 NEWS, fact, detail, information, secreted/confidential information, communication, giveaway, publication, announcement, proclamation, leak

COLLOQ. eye-opener

reveller *n*

celebrator, party-goer, raver, pleasure-seeker, merrymaker, carouser, roisterer, wassailer, bacchanal

revelry *n*

celebration(s), festivity, festivities, party, merrymaking, fun, carousal, jollity, jollification, debauchery

E3 sobriety

revenge *n, v*

♦ *n*

vengeance, satisfaction, reprisal, retaliation, requital, retribution, redress, vendetta, revanche

OLD avenge, avengement, ultion

COLLOQ. tit for tat, eye for an eye (and a tooth for a tooth), a dose/taste of your own medicine

♦ *v*

avenge, take vengeance on, repay, pay off, retaliate, settle a score/an old score, pay someone back, put someone back in their own court, get back at, hit back, fight back, settle accounts with, square an account with, serve out

OLD wreak of

COLLOQ. get, get your own back, get even with, give as good as you get

---

Synonym nuances

noun

Vengeance is an emotive word which suggests a deeply felt need for revenge, while **satisfaction** puts more emphasis on reparation: *he demanded satisfaction for his losses*. **Reprisal** conveys the more clinical idea of a deliberate action striking back at the actions of another: *the hostages were executed in reprisal for the bombing raid*. **Retaliation** likewise suggests a fairly immediate return in kind, but one made more instinctively.

Both **requital** and **retribution** imply an element of punishment, with **retribution** in particular suggesting a large-scale or dramatic action, unlike **redress**, which implies restoration as an important element: *the farmers' best hope of redress lay in court action*. **Vendetta** is appropriate for a continued state of hostility and acts of revenge between two parties, while the uncommon **revanche** more narrowly refers to recovery of territory.

---

revengeful *adj*

bitter, resentful, implacable, vengeful, vindictive, malignant, malevolent, spiteful, malicious, merciless, unmerciful, pitiless, unforgiving

E3 forgiving, merciful

revenue *n*

income, return, yield, interest, profit(s), gain, proceeds, receipts, rewards, takings

E3 expenditure

reverberate *v*

echo, re-echo, resound, resonate, ring, boom, vibrate

COLLOQ. repercuss

reverberation *n*

1 ECHO, re-echoing, resounding, resonance, ringing, vibration, wave, rebound, recoil, reflection

2 *reverberations following the resignation*

repercussion, effect, consequence, result

COLLOQ. shock wave, ripple

revere *v*

respect, admire, esteem, honour, look up to, think highly of, pay homage to, worship, reverence, adore, exalt

FORMAL venerate

E3 despise, scorn

reverence *n, v*

♦ *n*

respect, deference, honour, (high) esteem, homage, admiration, awe, worship, exaltation, adoration, devotion, idolism

OLD obeisance

FORMAL veneration

E3 irreverence, contempt, scorn

♦ *v*

admire, respect, honour, acknowledge, revere, adore, worship, hallow, fear, dread, overawe, prostrate yourself

FORMAL venerate

E3 despise, scorn

reverent *adj*

reverential, respectful, admiring, deferential, humble, dutiful, devoted, awed, solemn, pious, devout, adoring, worshipping, loving

OLD obeisant

E3 irreverent, disrespectful

reverie *n*

daydream, daydreaming, musing, trance, abstraction, absent-mindedness, inattention, preoccupation, brown study, woolgathering

reversal *n*

1 NEGATION, cancellation, annulment, nullification, countermanding, repeal, reverse, turnabout, turnaround, exchange, swap, volte-face, upset

FORMAL revocation, rescinding

COLLOQ. U-turn

2 MISFORTUNE, mishap, misadventure, adversity, affliction, hardship, trial, blow, disappointment, upset, setback, check, delay, problem, difficulty, failure, defeat

E3 1 advancement, progress

reverse *v, n, adj*

♦ *v*

1 *reverse a car*

back, move backwards, drive backwards, retreat, backtrack, withdraw

FORMAL regress

2 *reverse a decision*

undo, negate, set aside, cancel, annul, invalidate, overrule, repeal, quash, overthrow

FORMAL countermand, revoke, rescind, retract

3 TRANSPOSE, turn round, invert, up-end, overturn, turn upside-down, put back to front, upset, change, change round, exchange, swap, alter

E3 1 go forwards, progress **2** advance, enforce

♦ *n*

1 UNDERSIDE, other side, back, rear, inverse, verso, counter, converse, contrary, opposite

FORMAL antithesis

2 MISFORTUNE, mishap, misadventure, adversity, affliction, hardship, trial, blow, disappointment, upset, setback, check, delay, problem, difficulty, failure, defeat, reversal

FORMAL vicissitude

• *adj*
opposite, contrary, converse, inverse, inverted, backward, back, rear, verso

reversion *n*
return, restoration, reinstatement, handing-back, giving-back, taking-back, throwback

revert *v*
return, go back, resume, lapse, relapse, regress

review *n, v*
• *n*
1 ASSESSMENT, criticism, critique, evaluation, appraisal, judgement, report, commentary, examination, scrutiny, analysis, study, survey, rating, recapitulation, reassessment, re-evaluation, re-examination, revision, notice, reviewal, revise, summing-up, write-up, *tour d'horizon*
FORMAL recension
COLLOQ. rethink
2 MAGAZINE, periodical, journal
• *v*
1 ASSESS, criticize, evaluate, judge, weigh (up), discuss, examine, view, inspect, scrutinize, analyse, study, survey, recapitulate, write up, comment on
FORMAL appraise
2 *review the situation*
reassess, re-evaluate, re-examine, reconsider, rethink, revise, take stock of, go over; *N Am* appeal
COLLOQ. size up

reviewer *n*
commentator, critic, judge, observer, connoisseur, arbiter, essayist

revile *v*
despise, hate, scorn, slander, libel, defame, abuse, smear, reproach, malign, blackguard, rail; *dialect* miscall
FORMAL calumniate, denigrate, traduce, vituperate, vilify, inveigh
OLD missay
✖ praise

revise *v*
1 *revise your opinion*
change, alter, modify, amend, correct, update, edit, rewrite, reword, redraft, recast, rework, revamp, reconsider, re-examine, review, go over, peruse, think better of, have second thoughts about, expurgate
FORMAL emend, recense
2 STUDY, learn, memorize
COLLOQ. swot up, cram, bone up on, mug up

revision *n*
1 CHANGE, amendment, editing, modification, alteration, correction, recast, recasting, reworking, re-examination, reconstruction, review, rewriting, rereading
FORMAL emendation
2 STUDYING, memorizing, homework, learning, updating
COLLOQ. swotting

revitalize *v*
revive, renew, restore, refresh, reactivate, reanimate, rejuvenate, resurrect, reinvigorate
FORMAL revivify
✖ dampen, suppress

revival *n*
resuscitation, revitalization, restoration, re-establishment, reintroduction, renewal, renaissance, rebirth, resurrection, reawakening, resurgence, upsurge, upturn
COLLOQ. the kiss of life, comeback

revive *v*
resuscitate, bring round, reanimate, revitalize, restore, renew, refresh, animate, invigorate, reinvigorate, quicken, rouse, awaken, recover, rally, comfort, cheer up, reawaken, breathe new life into, rekindle, reactivate, re-establish, reintroduce, wake, resurrect

OLD relive
FORMAL revivify
COLLOQ. give the kiss of life to, rake up
✖ weary

revivify *v*
revive, revitalize, invigorate, restore, resuscitate, refresh, renew, reactivate, reanimate
FORMAL inspirit
✖ dampen, depress

reviving *adj*
refreshening, invigorating, reinvigorating, exhilarating, bracing, stimulating, tonic, reanimating, enheartening, regenerating
FORMAL revivescent, revivifying, reviviscent
✖ disheartening, exhausting

revocation *n*
revoking, repeal, repealing, quashing, reversal, withdrawal, annulment, nullification, invalidation, negation, cancellation, abolition, repudiation
FORMAL countermanding, rescinding, rescission, retractation, retraction
✖ enforcement

revoke *v*
repeal, quash, annul, nullify, invalidate, negate, cancel, abolish, reverse, withdraw, recall, recant, lift, unpray, unshout
FORMAL rescind, abrogate, countermand, retract, renege
✖ enforce

revolt *n, v*
• *n*
revolution, rebellion, mutiny, rising, uprising, insurrection, putsch, coup (d'état), secession, defection
TECHNICAL apostasy, expressionism
• *v*
1 REBEL, mutiny, rise, rise up, riot, resist, defect, take up arms, take to the streets, fall away
FORMAL dissent
2 DISGUST, sicken, nauseate, repel, turn your stomach, offend, shock, outrage, scandalize
✖ **1** submit **2** please, delight

revolting *adj*
disgusting, sickening, nauseating, repulsive, repellent, obnoxious, nasty, horrible, vile, hateful, foul, loathsome, abhorrent, repugnant, abominable, distasteful, off-putting, offensive, shocking, appalling
FORMAL reprehensible, heinous
✖ pleasant, delightful, attractive, palatable

revolution *n*
1 REVOLT, rebellion, mutiny, rising, uprising, insurrection, insurgence, putsch, coup (d'état)
2 CHANGE, reformation, transformation, innovation, upheaval, cataclysm
TECHNICAL metamorphosis
COLLOQ. sex change
3 ROTATION, turn, spin, wheel, whirl, cycle, circuit, round, circle, orbit, gyration

revolutionary *n, adj*
• *n*
rebel, mutineer, insurgent, insurrectionist, anarchist, revolutionist, Leninist, Bolshevik, Sandinista, filibuster, sansculotte
OLD Menshevik
COLLOQ. red
• *adj*
1 REBEL, rebellious, mutinous, insurgent, insurrectionary, subversive, seditious, extremist, anarchistic, extremist, Leninist, Bolshevik
OLD Menshevik
COLLOQ. red

2 *revolutionary ideas*
new, innovative, novel, progressive, ground-breaking, experimental, avant-garde, different, drastic, radical, thoroughgoing, complete
F3 1 conservative

revolutionize *v*
transform, reform, restructure, cause radical changes in, reorganize, transfigure, turn upside-down

revolve *v*
1 ROTATE, turn, go, move, pivot, swivel, spin, wheel, whirl, gyrate, circle, orbit, run, twist, rev
TECHNICAL circumduct
FORMAL circumvolve
2 *his life revolves around sport*
centre on, focus on, concentrate on, be preoccupied with, turn on, hinge on, hang on

revolver *n*
gun, handgun, firearm, pistol, rifle, shotgun, airgun, six-shooter, bulldog, Colt®
OLD peacemaker
COLLOQ. shooter
SLANG iron, shooting iron; *N Am* gat, rod

revolving *adj*
rotating, turning, spinning, whirling, gyrating, gyratory
F3 stationary

revulsion *n*
disgust, distaste, dislike, repulsion, repugnance, aversion, hatred, hate, loathing, nausea, abhorrence, recoil, abomination
FORMAL detestation
F3 delight, pleasure, approval

reward *n, v*
◆ *n*
1 *a reward for long service*
present, prize, honour, medal, decoration, bounty, pay-off, bonus, premium, payment, remuneration, recompense, repayment, compensation, gain, profit, return, benefit, merit, desert
2 REQUITAL, punishment, retribution
COLLOQ. just deserts
◆ *v*
pay, remunerate, recompense, repay, requite, compensate, honour, decorate
OLD yield; (*Shakesp*) reguerdon
F3 punish

rewarding *adj*
worthwhile, satisfying, gratifying, pleasing, fulfilling, enriching, profitable, remunerative, lucrative, productive, fruitful, valuable, advantageous, beneficial, edifying
F3 unrewarding

rewording *n*
rephrasing, rewriting, paraphrase, revision
TECHNICAL metaphrase, metaphrasis

rework *v*
revise, rewrite, reword, redraft, recast, revamp, reconsider, re-examine, review, change, alter, modify, amend, correct, update, edit, go over, peruse, think better of, have second thoughts about, expurgate
FORMAL emend, recense

rewrite *v*
revise, rework, reword, redraft, recast, correct, edit
FORMAL emend

rhetoric *n*
eloquence, oratory, bombast, pomposity, hyperbole, verbosity, wordiness, long-windedness, fustian
FORMAL grandiloquence, magniloquence, prolixity

rhetorical *adj*
oratorical, bombastic, pompous, high-sounding, long-winded, verbose, wordy, stylistic, grand, high-flown, flowery, florid, flamboyant, showy, pretentious, artificial, insincere
FORMAL grandiloquent, magniloquent, declamatory, prolix
F3 simple
See panel on next page

rhyme *n*
poetry, verse, poem, ode, limerick, jingle, song, ditty, couplet, chime, tink, crambo
OLD rhime, rhythm
See panel below

rhythm *n*
beat, pulse, time, throb, tempo, metre, measure, movement, harmony, flow, lilt, swing, accent, cadence, pattern

rhythmic *adj*
rhythmical, metric, metrical, pulsating, pulsing, throbbing, flowing, lilting, periodic, regular, repeated, steady

rib *n*
bone, band, bar, support, vein, moulding, ribbing, ridge, shaft, welt, wale
FORMAL costa
Related adjective: costal

ribald *adj*
rude, obscene, risqué, racy, off-colour, bawdy, earthy, coarse, smutty, vulgar, filthy, foul-mouthed, gross, base, scurrilous, low, mean, lewd, disrespectful, licentious, indecent, irreverent, satirical, jeering, mocking, derisive, Rabelaisian
COLLOQ. blue, naughty
F3 polite

ribaldry *n*
rudeness, obscenity, bawdiness, raciness, vulgarity, smut, smuttiness, earthiness, coarseness, filth, grossness, lowness, baseness, licentiousness, indecency, scurrility, jeering, derision, mockery
COLLOQ. naughtiness

ribbing *n*
teasing, mocking, taunting, ridicule, banter, provocation, baiting, goading, annoying, badgering
COLLOQ. ragging, kidding

ribbon *n*
band, cord, cloth, line, sash, strip, braid, shred, tatter, jag, hair-band, headband, fillet, taenia
Related adjectives: taeniate, taenioid

rich *adj*
1 WEALTHY, affluent, moneyed, prosperous, well-to-do, well-off
COLLOQ. flush, well-heeled, made of money, in the money, rolling in it, with money to burn
OLD COLLOQ. oofy

Forms of rhyme include:

apocopated rhyme	end rhyme	half-rhyme (or near-rhyme)	male (or masculine) rhyme	rich rhyme (or rime riche)	tail(ed) rhyme
assonance (or vowel-rhyme)	eye-rhyme	head-rhyme	pararhyme	riding-rhyme	
cynghanedd	female (or feminine) rhyme	identical rhyme internal rhyme	rhyme royal	rime suffisant slant rhyme	

See also **prosody**.

Rhetorical devices include:

abscission	asyndeton	enumeration	hypallage	onomatopoeia	synchoresis
alliteration	auxesis	epanadiplosis	hyperbole	oxymoron	synchrysis
amplification	bathos	epanalepsis	hypostrophe	parabole	synecdoche
anacoluthon	catachresis	epanaphora	hypotyposis	paradox	synoeciosis
anadiplosis	cataphora	epanodos	hysteron-	paraleipsis	tautology
anaphora	chiasmus	epanorthosis	proteron	parenthesis	transferred
anastrophe	climax	epigram	increment	pathetic fallacy	epithet
anticlimax	diallage	epiphonema	innuendo	personification	trope
antimetabole	diegesis	epistrophe	irony	prolepsis	vicious circle
antimetathesis	dissimile	epizeuxis	litotes	pun	zeugma
antiphrasis	double entendre	erotema	meiosis	rhetorical	
antithesis	dramatic irony	erotetic	metalepsis	question	
antonomasia	dysphemism	euphemism	metaphor	simile	
aporia	ellipsis	figure of speech	metonymy	syllepsis	
apostrophe	enantiosis	hendiadys	mixed metaphor	symploce	

SLANG loaded, filthy rich, stinking rich
2 EXPENSIVE, precious, valuable, priceless, costly, lavish, magnificent, sumptuous, luxurious, lush, splendid, grand, gorgeous, palatial, fine, elaborate, ornate
FORMAL opulent
3 PLENTIFUL, abundant, abounding, copious, profuse, prolific, ample, full, high, packed, steeped, overflowing, well-provided, well-supplied
FORMAL replete, plenteous
4 FERTILE, fruitful, productive, lush
FORMAL fecund
5 *rich food*
creamy, fatty, oily, full-bodied, heavy, full-flavoured, strong, spicy, savoury, tasty, delicious, luscious, juicy, sweet
6 *rich colours*
deep, intense, vivid, strong, bright, brilliant, vibrant, warm
7 IRONIC, laughable, ridiculous, outrageous, unreasonable, preposterous, absurd
8 *a rich voice*
deep, mellow, full, sonorous, resonant
FORMAL mellifluous
9 *a rich life*
full, eventful, active, busy, lively, exciting
E3 1 poor, impoverished **2** plain, basic **4** barren, infertile **5** plain, bland **6** dull, soft **9** dull, empty

---

Synonym nuances
sense 1
Wealthy and **affluent** can be used to suggest having an abundance of money and possessions, whereas **well-to-do** and **well-off** suggest a more moderate degree of wealth. **Moneyed** puts the focus solely on pecuniary riches. **Prosperous** is suggestive of being continually financially successful: *the prosperous southern half of Britain.*

---

riches *n*
wealth, affluence, prosperity, money, gold, treasure, fortune, assets, property, substance, resources, means
OLD (filthy) lucre
FORMAL opulence
COLLOQ. the necessary
SLANG loot, readies, ready, megabucks, dough, dosh, bread, lolly, spondulicks, brass, loot, gravy, greens, shekels, moolah, greenies, scratch, smash, stumpy
E3 poverty

richly *adv*
1 LAVISHLY, splendidly, gorgeously, sumptuously, elegantly, elaborately, expensively, exquisitely, luxuriously, palatially
FORMAL opulently, floridly
2 FULLY, thoroughly, completely, well, strongly, suitably, appropriately, properly
E3 1 poorly, scantily

richness *n*
1 *the richness of mineral deposits*
plentifulness, abundance, fullness, provision
2 *the richness of the pudding*
fattiness, creaminess, oiliness, heaviness, taste, juiciness
3 *the richness of the furnishings*
lavishness, magnificence, splendour, luxuriousness, luxuriance, sumptuousness, elegance, exquisiteness
4 *Japan's cultural richness*
depth, fullness, eventfulness, business, liveliness, excitement
5 RESONANCE, mellowness, fullness, intensity, loudness

rickety *adj*
unsteady, wobbly, shaky, unstable, insecure, flimsy, jerry-built, decrepit, ramshackle, broken-down, dilapidated, derelict
E3 stable, strong

ricochet *v, n*
♦ *v*
bounce (back), rebound, spring back, bob, recoil, throw, dap; *Scot* stoit, stot
♦ *n*
bounce, rebound, bound, spring, jump, leap; *Scot* stot

rid *v*
free, deliver, relieve, unburden, clear, purge, cleanse, purify
▪ **get rid of**
throw away, throw out, dispose of, discard, dump, scrap, jettison, abolish, put an end to, eliminate, do away with
COLLOQ. chuck (out), get shot of, ditch, junk

riddance *n*
deliverance, release, relief, removal, freedom, elimination, clearance, disposal, ejection, expulsion, extermination, purgation
E3 burdening

riddle¹ *n*
tell me a riddle
enigma, mystery, conundrum, puzzle, poser, problem, teaser, charade, brainteaser, mind-bender; *Scot* guess; *N Am* brain-twister
TECHNICAL koan, logograph
OLD (*Shakesp*) conclusion

riddle² *v*
1 PERFORATE, pierce, puncture, pepper, fill, permeate, pervade, infest
2 SIFT, sieve, strain, filter, mar, winnow
OLD cribble

ride *v, n*
♦ *v*
sit, move, go, progress, travel, journey, gallop, trot, pedal, drive, steer, control, dominate, handle, manage
FORMAL bestride

◆ *n*
journey, trip, outing, jaunt, spin, drive, lift

rider *n*
horseman, horsewoman, equestrian, jockey, cavalryman, horse soldier, hussar, dragoon, knight

ridge *n*
band, escarpment, hill, hummock, lump, arête, drum, drumlin, hog's back, reef, ripple, saddle, knurl, wale, welt, crinkle
TECHNICAL esker, yardang, sastruga
FORMAL costa

ridicule *n, v*
◆ *n*
mockery, jeering, laughter, scorn, derision, taunting, teasing, chaff, banter, badinage, satire, irony, sarcasm, jest, depreciation
⊟ praise
◆ *v*
laugh at, mock, make fun of, poke fun at, jeer, scorn, gibe, scoff, deride, sneer, tease, humiliate, taunt, satirize, send up, caricature, lampoon, burlesque, parody, jest, mimic, have a game with, make a game of, pillory, crucify; *Aust* poke mullock at
OLD smoke
COLLOQ. rib, kid, rag, pull someone's leg, pooh-pooh, take the mickey out of, guy, josh, queer
SLANG *N Am* goof
⊟ praise

Synonym nuances
verb
You can use **laugh at** as a fairly general synonym, while **mock** and **deride** have greater implications of disparagement and contempt: *intellectuals who deride romance novels.* **Jeer** is more suggestive of expressing this contempt: *the team's performance was jeered by fans.* You could use **scoff** or **sneer** to imply a degree of superciliousness in the expression, while **scorn** also implies rejection: *he scorned my attempts to humour him.*
  Tease is a fairly mild term, which can even suggest affection, whereas **gibe** and **taunt** are more suggestive of hurtful provocation: *Bremner was taunted mercilessly by rival fans.* **Humiliate** is a strong term to use, appropriately describing belittling someone to their extreme embarrassment. **Crucify** is similarly extreme, especially referring to holding up to public derision: *the press crucified him for the affair.*
  Other synonyms relate to ridicule as a source of humour, for example **satirize**, which suggests the use of witty invective, and **lampoon**, which might be used of a more concentrated assault on an individual. **Mimic**, **parody**, and the less common verb **burlesque** can be used to suggest impersonating in a ridiculous way: *every movement was ridiculed and parodied*, while **caricature** is appropriate for the use of gross exaggeration: *scientists caricatured as absent-minded professors.* **Send up** suggests similar activity, but perhaps to a less sophisticated degree.

---

ridiculous *adj*
ludicrous, absurd, nonsensical, silly, foolish, stupid, contemptible, derisory, laughable, facetious, farcical, comical, funny, humorous, droll, hilarious, outrageous, shocking, preposterous, incredible, unbelievable
FORMAL risible
⊟ sensible

ridiculously *adv*
absurdly, ludicrously, laughably, shockingly, unreasonably, unbelievably, incredibly, outrageously, surprisingly, preposterously
⊟ sensibly

rife *adj*
abundant, abounding, rampant, teeming, swarming, overflowing, raging, epidemic, prevalent, widespread, predominant, extensive, general, common, frequent, ubiquitous
⊟ scarce

riff-raff *n*
mob, rabble, hoi polloi, scum, dregs, undesirables, *canaille*
COLLOQ. rent-a-mob

rifle¹ *n*
shoot with a rifle
gun, firearm, shotgun, weapon
SLANG bundook
See also **gun**.

rifle² *v*
rifle through some files
search, rummage, sack, pillage, plunder, ransack, rob, maraud, loot, strip, burgle, gut
FORMAL despoil

rift *n*
1 SPLIT, breach, break, fracture, crack, fault, chink, cleft, fissure, slit, cavity, cranny, crevice, gap, space, opening, hole
2 DISAGREEMENT, difference, fight, split, row, feud, argument, conflict, breach, separation, division, schism, alienation
FORMAL estrangement, altercation
⊟ 2 unity

rig *n, v*
◆ *n*
equipment, kit, outfit, gear, tackle, apparatus, structure, machinery, fittings, fixtures
FORMAL accoutrements
◆ *v*
falsify, tamper with, doctor, fiddle, distort, twist, pervert, manipulate, massage, misrepresent, forge, fake
COLLOQ. cook
▪ rig out
1 EQUIP, kit out, outfit, fit (out), supply, provide, furnish, make ready
2 CLOTHE, dress (up), wear, put on, get into, garb, robe, trim, turn out; *N Am* trick up
FORMAL array, accoutre, attire
COLLOQ. get up, trick out
▪ rig up
arrange, build, assemble, construct, erect, fit up, fix up, put together, improvise
COLLOQ. knock up, throw together, cobble together
⊟ dismantle

right *adj, adv, n, v*
◆ *adj*
1 *the right answer*
correct, accurate, exact, precise, true, factual, actual, real, genuine, authentic, valid
COLLOQ. spot on, bang-on
2 PROPER, fitting, correct, accepted, approved, becoming, appropriate, suitable, fit, fitting, admissible, acceptable, satisfactory, reasonable, desirable, favourable, preferable, advantageous, convenient, opportune
OLD seemly
FORMAL propitious, auspicious
COLLOQ. the done thing
3 FAIR, just, equitable, lawful, legal, honest, upright, good, virtuous, righteous, moral, ethical, proper, principled, honourable, impartial
4 RIGHT-WING, conservative, Tory, reactionary, true-blue
5 *he's a right fool*
complete, absolute, utter, real, thorough
⊟ 1 wrong, incorrect, erroneous **2** improper, unsuitable **3** unfair, wrong **4** left-wing, liberal

♦ *adv*
1 CORRECTLY, accurately, exactly, precisely, factually, properly, satisfactorily, well, favourably, fairly
COLLOQ. by the book
2 *right to the bottom*
straight, in a straight line, directly, as the crow flies, completely, utterly, entirely, absolutely, exactly, wholly, totally, all the way
COLLOQ. slap bang
3 *I'll be right back*
straight, immediately, without delay
COLLOQ. pronto, yesterday, before you know it, before you can say Jack Robinson, in two shakes of a lamb's tail, like a shot
E∃ 1 wrongly, incorrectly, unfairly
♦ *n*
1 JUSTICE, legality, lawfulness, good, goodness, virtue, righteousness, morality, ethics, honour, honesty, integrity, uprightness, truthfulness, impartiality, fairness
FORMAL rectitude, propriety
2 PRIVILEGE, prerogative, due, claim, entitlement, birthright, business, authority, power, permission, warrant, freedom, opportunity, licence, charter, sanction, title deed
TECHNICAL droit
FORMAL lien
E∃ 1 wrong
♦ *v*
rectify, correct, put right, put in order, fix, repair, redress, vindicate, avenge, settle, straighten (out), stand up

▪ **right away**
straight away, immediately, at once, now, instantly, directly, forthwith, without delay, promptly
COLLOQ. from the word go, pronto, yesterday, before you know it, before you can say Jack Robinson, in two shakes of a lamb's tail, in a jiffy, like a shot
E∃ later, eventually

▪ **right-hand man/woman**
assistant, PA, personal assistant, executive assistant, secretary, helper, helping hand, aide, deputy, lieutenant, second-in-command, number two, subordinate, understudy, man/girl Friday, backroom boy/girl

▪ **right of way**
precedence, priority, preference, superiority, supremacy, eminence, pre-eminence, lead, first place, seniority, rank

▪ **by rights**
rightfully, correctly, properly, rightly, in fairness, justifiably, justly, lawfully, legally, legitimately;
TECHNICAL de jure

▪ **in the right**
justified, right, warranted, vindicated
E∃ in the wrong, at fault

▪ **put/set to rights**
rectify, correct, put in order, fix, remedy, settle, straighten (out)

▪ **within your rights**
justified, entitled, permitted, allowed, reasonable, right

Synonym nuances
adjective sense 1
Correct may be widely used to suggest an absence of error, while **accurate**, **exact** and **precise** suggest a complete lack of deviation: *the precise measurements*. **True** has implications of depth, and can be used to suggest an absolute: *the true meaning of the word*, whereas **factual** more narrowly refers to correctness based on actual events and proof: *factual news stories*. **Actual** and **real**, although similar, go further by suggesting the validity of the existence of something: *the actual words that were said*. The terms **genuine** and **authentic** are more suggestive of being right, in the sense of being as perceived and therefore not fraudulent, while **valid** appropriately describes something that can be ratified: *a valid marriage*, or is justifiable: *valid suggestions*.

---

righteous *adj*
1 *a righteous person/action*
just, good, virtuous, moral, worthy, honourable, upright, fair, ethical, equitable, honest, law-abiding, blameless, irreproachable, incorrupt, guiltless, God-fearing, saintly, pure, sinless
2 *righteous anger*
justifiable, defensible, excusable, warranted, reasonable, supportable, justified, lawful, legal, legitimate, acceptable, explainable, valid, well-founded, proper
E∃ 1 unrighteous **2** unjustifiable

righteousness *n*
goodness, honesty, honour, virtue, uprightness, morality, integrity, justice, blamelessness, faithfulness, equity, ethicalness, purity, holiness, sanctification
TECHNICAL dharma
FORMAL probity, rectitude
E∃ unrighteousness

rightful *adj*
legitimate, lawful, legal, just, bona fide, true, real, genuine, valid, authorized, correct, proper, suitable, due
E∃ wrongful, unlawful

rightfully *adv*
correctly, properly, rightly, by rights, justifiably, justly, lawfully, legally, legitimately
TECHNICAL de jure
E∃ incorrectly, unjustifiably

rightly *adv*
1 CORRECTLY, properly, rightly, by rights, justifiably, justly, lawfully, legally, legitimately, fairly, equitably, morally
2 PROPERLY, fittingly, correctly, appropriately, reasonably
E∃ 1 wrongly, unfairly, incorrectly **2** improperly, unsuitably

rigid *adj*
1 STIFF, inflexible, inelastic, unbending, cast-iron, hard, firm, set, fixed, unyielding, unalterable, invariable
2 *a rigid political system*
austere, harsh, severe, inflexible, unrelenting, strict, rigorous, stringent, stern, uncompromising, unyielding, spartan
FORMAL intransigent
E∃ 1 flexible, elastic, bending, malleable **2** variable, weak

rigidity *n*
inflexibility, hardness, stiffness, fixity, immovability, immutability, immutableness, inelasticity, obstinacy, stubbornness, stringency, unsuppleness
FORMAL intractability, intransigence, obduracy
E∃ flexibility

rigmarole *n*
process, bother, performance, fuss, palaver, nonsense, jargon, gibberish, twaddle, riddle-me-ree
OLD *Scot* ragman
COLLOQ. carry-on, hassle, to-do

rigorous *adj*
1 EXACT, precise, accurate, meticulous, painstaking, scrupulous, conscientious, punctilious, laborious, thorough
2 STRICT, stringent, rigid, firm, tough, harsh, hard, severe, stern, austere, exacting, uncompromising, spartan
FORMAL intransigent
E∃ 1 lax, superficial

rigorously *adv*
meticulously, painstakingly, scrupulously, thoroughly, accurately, exactly, precisely, punctiliously
E∃ carelessly, superficially

rigour *n*
1 *the rigours of war*
trial, hardship, severity, suffering, ordeal
FORMAL privation
2 THOROUGHNESS, exactness, meticulousness, accuracy,

preciseness, precision, conscientiousness,
punctiliousness, inflexibility
3 STRICTNESS, stringency, rigidity, firmness, toughness,
harshness, hardship, hardness, severity, sternness, austerity
FORMAL intransigence
F3 leniency, mildness

rig-out *n*
clothing, clothes, garments, outfit, kit, uniform, dress,
costume, habit, livery
FORMAL apparel, raiment
COLLOQ. clobber, garb, gear, get-up, togs, things

rile *v*
annoy, irritate, nettle, pique, put out, upset, irk, vex, anger,
exasperate
COLLOQ. peeve, aggravate, bug, wind up, hassle, rub up the
wrong way, get your blood up, make your blood boil, get
on your nerves, get up your nose, get under your skin, get
your goat, get on your wick, drive crazy/nuts, drive
bananas, drive up the wall, drive round the bend/twist, get
your back up, brass off, cheese off, make your hackles rise,
make sparks fly, give you the hump, get your dander up; *N
Am* tick/hack off
F3 calm, soothe

rim *n*
lip, edge, brim, brink, verge, margin, border,
circumference, ring, skirt, apron, shoe, strake
TECHNICAL felloe, helix, velum, bezel, wood, chime, fiddle,
girdle
OLD rymme
F3 centre, middle

rind *n*
peel, zest, skin, husk, crust, shell, bark, gourd, crackling
OLD rine
FORMAL epicarp, integument

ring¹ *n, v*
◆ *n*
1 CIRCLE, round, loop, hoop, disc, halo, band, circlet, belt,
girdle, collar, circuit, area, arena, enclosure, atoll
2 GROUP, cartel, syndicate, association, organization,
league, alliance, combine, society, club, fraternity, sorority,
gathering, circle, gang, crew, mob, band, cell, clique,
coterie
◆ *v*
surround, encircle, gird, loop, encompass, enclose, cage
in, hem in
FORMAL circumscribe

ring² *v, n*
◆ *v*
1 CHIME, peal, toll, knell, ding, ding-dong, tinkle, clink,
jingle, clang, sound, resound, resonate, echo, reverberate,
buzz
2 TELEPHONE, phone, call (up), ring up, reach, dial
COLLOQ. buzz, give a buzz, give a tinkle, give a bell
◆ *n*
1 CHIME, peal, toll, knell, tinkle, clink, jingle, clang, ding-
dong
2 PHONE CALL, call
COLLOQ. buzz, tinkle, bell

ringleader *n*
leader, spokesman, spokeswoman, spokesperson,
mouthpiece, chief, fugleman, bell-wether
COLLOQ. brains

rinse *v*
swill, bathe, wash (out), wash clean, clean, cleanse, flush
(away), wet, dip

riot *n, v*
◆ *n*
1 *a riot in the streets*
insurrection, rising, uprising, revolt, rebellion, insurgence,

anarchy, lawlessness, fight, brawl, fray, fracas, mêlée, affray,
disturbance, race riot, turbulence, disorder, confusion,
commotion, tumult, turmoil, uproar, row, quarrel, strife,
breach of the peace, rout, hubbub
2 REVELRY, feasting, partying, indulgence, debauchery, orgy
OLD merrymaking
COLLOQ. rave, rave-up
3 *a riot of colour*
display, show, flourish, exhibition, extravaganza
4 LAUGH
COLLOQ. scream, hoot
F3 1 order, calm
◆ *v*
revolt, rebel, mutiny, rise up, run riot, run wild, run amok,
go berserk, rush wildly, charge, tear, storm, rage, rant, rave,
rampage, go on the rampage
▪ **run riot**
rampage, go on the rampage, run wild, run amok, go
berserk, rush wildly, charge, tear, storm, rage, rant, rave

riotous *adj*
1 WILD, violent, uncontrollable, unrestrained, unruly,
rebellious, lawless, insurrectionary, insubordinate,
disorderly, mutinous, ungovernable, wanton
2 NOISY, loud, rowdy, tumultuous, boisterous, uproarious
F3 1 orderly, restrained

riotously *adv*
wildly, uncontrollably, noisily, loudly, tumultuously, ariot

rip *v, n*
◆ *v*
tear, rend, split, separate, rupture, burst, cut, shred, slit,
slash, gash, lacerate, hack
◆ *n*
tear, rent, split, cleavage, rupture, cut, ladder, slit, slash,
gash, hole
▪ **rip off**
overcharge, swindle, defraud, fleece, cheat, diddle, trick,
dupe, exploit
COLLOQ. do, con
SLANG sting; *N Am* gold-brick

ripe *adj*
1 RIPENED, mature, mellow, seasoned, grown, fully-grown,
developed, fully-developed, complete, finished, perfect,
in season, forward, rare-ripe, drop-ripe, premature, under-
ripe
OLD ratheripe
2 READY, suitable, fit, right, advantageous, favourable,
timely, opportune
FORMAL auspicious, propitious
COLLOQ. spoiling (for)
F3 2 untimely, inopportune; *formal* inauspicious

ripen *v*
develop, mature, bring/come to maturity, mellow, season,
age

rip-off *n*
robbery, exploitation, cheat, swindle, theft, fraud, diddle
COLLOQ. scam, con, con trick, daylight robbery
SLANG sting, swiz; *N Am* gold brick

riposte *n, v*
◆ *n*
retort, rejoinder, repartee, quip, answer, reply, response,
return, sally, comeback
◆ *v*
retort, rejoin, quip, reciprocate, answer, reply, respond,
return

ripple *n, v*
◆ *n*
1 WAVE, disturbance, eddy, gurgle, lapping, ripplet,
wavelet, undulation, burble, babble, purl, wimple
2 REPERCUSSION, effect, result, consequence, reverberation
COLLOQ. shock wave

  ♦ *v*

ruffle, wrinkle, flow, undulate, purl, wimple, crease, pucker, crumple

rise *v, n*

  ♦ *v*

1 GO UP, move upwards, ascend, climb (up), mount, slope (up), soar, tower, loom, grow, get higher, increase, escalate, swell, intensify, rocket
2 STAND UP, get up, arise, jump up, leap up, spring up, get to your feet, get out of bed
3 ADVANCE, progress, make progress, approach, improve, prosper, be promoted
4 ORIGINATE, spring, flow, issue, emanate, emerge, appear, start, begin
FORMAL commence
5 REBEL, revolt, mutiny, riot, resist, defect, take up arms, take to the streets
FORMAL dissent
6 *rise to the challenge*
attempt, try, do your best, respond, react to, exert yourself
Ѳ **1** fall, descend **2** sit down, lie down **3** decline, fall back
  ♦ *n*
1 ASCENT, climb, slope, upward slope, soaring, towering, incline, hill, elevation
FORMAL acclivity
2 INCREASE, growth, escalation, leap, increment, upsurge, upturn, advance, progress, improvement, advancement, promotion; *N Am* raise
FORMAL amelioration, aggrandizement
Ѳ **1** descent, valley **2** fall, descent
▪ **give rise to**
cause, bring about, bring on, make, produce, create, generate, induce, lead to, provoke, prompt, evoke, elicit, influence, inspire, persuade, originate, engender
FORMAL effect

Synonym nuances
verb sense 1
Go up can be widely applied as a synonym of rise: *house prices went up*; *the curtain went up*. **Ascend** generally describes the action of making your way up something, while both **climb (up)** and **mount** have suggestions of overcoming a slope or height with a degree of difficulty. **Slope (up)** would be reserved for simply increasing in gradient. **Tower** suggests a superiority of height: *horse and rider towered above her*, while **loom** has perhaps more menacing implications.
  To refer to a rise in size or amount, **grow**, **get higher** and **increase** can be widely used, while **escalate** implies a rapid rise and possibly a loss of control, and **rocket** implies rising at an incredible rate: *exports rocketed*. You can use **swell** to suggest inflating or a more lateral growth: *holiday-makers swelled the local population*, and **intensify** to imply building in strength: *the new, extreme policy intensified opposition*.

---

risible *adj*
ridiculous, ludicrous, funny, hilarious, humorous, laughable, absurd, amusing, comic, comical, droll, farcical
COLLOQ. rib-tickling, side-splitting
Ѳ serious, unfunny

rising *n, adj*
  ♦ *n*
riot, revolution, revolt, uprising, insurrection
  ♦ *adj*
ascending, growing, increasing, intensifying, mounting, soaring, swelling, advancing, emerging, approaching
Ѳ decreasing

risk *n, v*
  ♦ *n*
danger, peril, jeopardy, hazard, threat, chance, possibility,

uncertainty, gamble, speculation, venture, adventure
COLLOQ. throw, flier
Ѳ safety, certainty
  ♦ *v*
endanger, imperil, jeopardize, put in jeopardy, hazard, chance, take a chance, gamble, venture, dare
COLLOQ. chance it, put on the line, go for broke, stick your neck out, play with fire

risky *adj*
dangerous, unsafe, perilous, hazardous, chancy, uncertain, touch-and-go, touchy, high-risk, tricky, precarious, venturesome
COLLOQ. dicey, dodgy, iffy, hairy
Ѳ safe

risqué *adj*
indecent, improper, rude, immodest, indelicate, suggestive, coarse, crude, earthy, dirty, bawdy, racy, smutty, naughty, adult, ribald, off-colour
COLLOQ. blue, saucy, fruity, near the knuckle
Ѳ decent, proper

rite *n*
ceremony, custom, act, usage, office, form, formality, ceremonial, ordinance, practice, procedure, ritual, service, worship, liturgy, sacrament, observance

ritual *n, adj*
  ♦ *n*
custom, tradition, convention, usage, practice, habit, wont, routine, procedure, ordinance, prescription, form, formality, ceremony, ceremonial, solemnity, rite, sacrament, service, liturgy, celebration, observance, act, mumbo-jumbo, trumpery
TECHNICAL cultus
OLD sacring
FORMAL consuetude
  ♦ *adj*
ceremonial, prescribed, set, formal, customary, traditional, conventional, habitual, routine, procedural
FORMAL formulary

ritualistic *adj*
ritual, ceremonial, formulaic, traditional, formal, official, solemn, dignified, stately, customary, festive
FORMAL formulary

ritzy *adj*
sumptuous, luxurious, opulent, lavish, de luxe, magnificent, splendid, rich, expensive, costly, affluent, self-indulgent, pampered, comfortable, grand, well-appointed
COLLOQ. plush, posh, cushy, glitzy, swanky
Ѳ austere, spartan

rival *n, adj, v*
  ♦ *n*
competitor, contestant, contender, challenger, opponent, opposition, adversary, antagonist, vier, fellow, match, equal, peer, collateral, nemesis
OLD corrival, paragon
Ѳ colleague, associate
  ♦ *adj*
competitive, competing, in competition, in conflict, conflicting, opposed, opposing, in opposition
OLD corrival
Ѳ associate
  ♦ *v*
compete with, contend with, vie with, oppose, compare with, measure up to, emulate, match, equal, parallel, touch
OLD mate
Ѳ co-operate

rivalry *n*
competitiveness, competition, contest, contention, conflict, struggle, strife, vying, opposition, antagonism
OLD corrivalry, corrivalship; (*Shakesp*) rivality
Ѳ co-operation

Forms of river or watercourse include:

beck	burn	cut	inlet	rivulet	wadi
billabong	canal	delta	mountain stream	runnel	waterway
bourn	channel	estuary	mouth	source	
broads	confluence	firth	rill	stream	
brook	creek	frith	rillet	tributary	

The world's longest rivers include:

Nile (*Africa*)	Mississippi-Missouri (*North America*)	Amur-Argun-Kerulen (*Asia*)	Yellow (*Asia*)
Amazon (*South America*)		Ob-Irtysh (*Asia*)	Congo (or Zaire) (*Africa*)
Yangtze (*Asia*)	Yenisey-Angara-Selenga (*Asia*)	Plata-Parena-Grande (*South America*)	

riven *adj*

torn apart, split, ripped apart, ruptured, divided, severed
OLD rent

river *n*

waterway, watercourse
Related adjectives: fluvial, potamic
See panels above

rivet *v*

fascinate, absorb, intrigue, interest very much, excite, grip,
captivate, engross, enthral, arrest
E3 bore

riveting *adj*

fascinating, absorbing, interesting, exciting, gripping,
arresting, captivating, engrossing, enthralling,
spellbinding, magnetic, hypnotic
E3 boring

road *n*

route, way, roadway

Types of road include:

A-road	course	path
alley	crescent	pathway
arterial road	cul-de-sac	primary route
autobahn	dead end	ring road
avenue	dirt road	service road
B-road	dirt track	side road
boulevard	drive	side street
bridle path	driveway	single-track road
bridle way	dual carriageway	slip road
broadway	*N Am* expressway	square
bypass	flyover	street
byroad	freeway	terrace
byway	grove	thoroughfare
carriageway	high street	toll road
cartroad	highway	towpath
cart-track	lane	track
cartway	main road	trail
causeway	motorway	trunk road
circle	one-way street	turnpike
circus	overpass	unadopted road
clearway	parade	underpass
close	passage	walk

roam *v*

wander, rove, range, travel, traverse, walk, tramp, trek,
ramble, meander, stroll, amble, prowl, raven, drift, stray;
dialect rake, stroam
OLD squander; (*Shakesp*) wheel
FORMAL ambulate, perambulate, peregrinate
E3 stay

roar *v, n*

♦ *v*

1 BELLOW, yell, shout, cry, scream, shriek, bawl, howl, hoot,
guffaw, thunder, crash, blare, rumble, boom, bell; *dialect*
rout
OLD (*Spenser*) royne

2 LAUGH, shriek with laughter, guffaw, hoot
COLLOQ. split your sides, fall about, break up, crease up,
laugh like a drain
E3 1 whisper
♦ *n*
bellow, yell, shout, cry, scream, shriek, bawl, howl, hoot,
guffaw, thunder, crash, blare, boom, rumble

roaring *adj*

1 RESONANT, reverberating, echoing, ringing, loud,
sonorous, booming, resounding, resonating, thunderous,
full, rich, vibrant
2 CONCLUSIVE, resounding, decisive, impressive, striking,
outstanding, roaring, great, memorable, remarkable,
notable, emphatic, thorough

rob *v*

steal from, hold up, raid, burgle, loot, pillage, plunder, sack,
rifle, ransack, swindle, cheat, defraud, deprive, bereave,
despoil, pluck, ramp, fake, hijack, pirate, steal someone's
thunder; *Scot* rub; *N Am* bunko
OLD pad, reave; (*Spenser*) berob
FORMAL deprecate
COLLOQ. do, mug, knock off, nick
SLANG rip off, sting, heist, screw, stiff, turn over, blag, flimp,
mill; *N Am & NZ* roll

robber *n*

thief, burglar, stealer, bandit, swindler, embezzler, fraud,
cheat, plunderer, raider, pirate, highwayman, looter, brigand
COLLOQ. con man, mugger

robbery *n*

theft, stealing, larceny, break-in, housebreaking, hold-up,
pilferage, raid, burglary, pillage, plunder, fraud,
embezzlement, swindle
COLLOQ. mugging
SLANG rip-off, stick-up, heist

robe *n, v*

♦ *n*
costume, gown, vestment, habit, bathrobe, dressing-
gown, nightgown, housecoat, peignoir, wrap, wrapper,
talar, cassock, dolman, kimono
TECHNICAL chimer, purple, chrisom, killut
OLD palliament, vest, parament, peplos; (*Spenser*) camis
♦ *v*
clothe, dress, drape, garb, vest
FORMAL apparel, attire

robot *n*

automaton, machine, android, zombie

robust *adj*

1 STRONG, sturdy, tough, hardy, energetic, vigorous,
powerful, muscular, well-built, strapping, stalwart,
athletic, fit, healthy, well
2 *robust opinions*
strong, forceful, vigorous, straightforward, direct, down-
to-earth, no-nonsense
3 COARSE, earthy, rude, crude, ribald, risqué, raw
E3 2 weak, feeble, unhealthy

rock[1] n
rocks rolling down the hill
boulder, stone, pebble, crag, outcrop
■ **on the rocks**
in a bad way, failing, in difficulty, in difficulties, unstable, hopeless, slipping, doomed, in a mess, in pieces, in shreds, at an impasse
COLLOQ. in a fix/scrape/hole/jam

Rocks include:

basalt	granite	porphyry
breccia	gravel	pumice stone
chalk	lava	sandstone
coal	limestone	schist
conglomerate	marble	serpentine
flint	marl	shale
gabbro	obsidian	slate
gneiss	ore	

---

rock[2] v
1 SWAY, swing, tilt, tip, shake, wobble, roll, undulate, pitch, toss, lurch, reel, stagger, totter, oscillate, move to and fro
2 *news that rocked the nation*
shock, stun, stagger, bewilder, daze, dumbfound, astound, astonish, surprise, startle, take back

rocket n, v
♦ n
projectile, missile, guided missile, ballistic missile, flying bomb
♦ v
soar, tower, increase quickly/suddenly, escalate, shoot up

rocky[1] adj
rocky moorland
stony, pebbly, craggy, rugged, rough, hard, flinty
Ｆ₃ smooth, soft

rocky[2] adj
a rocky marriage
unsteady, shaky, wobbly, wobbling, staggering, tottering, unstable, unreliable, uncertain, weak
Ｆ₃ steady, stable, dependable, strong

rococo adj
flamboyant, baroque, florid, extravagant, elaborate, ornate, flowery, embellished, exuberant, vigorous, bold, convoluted, decorated, overelaborate, overdecorated, overwrought, showy, fanciful, fantastic, whimsical, grotesque
TECHNICAL churrigueresque
Ｆ₃ plain, simple, unadorned, austere

rod n
bar, shaft, strut, pole, stick, baton, wand, cane, switch, staff, mace, sceptre
Related adjective: rhabdoid

rodent

Kinds of rodent include:

agouti	gerbil	muskrat
bandicoot	gopher	musquash
beaver	grey squirrel	pika
black rat	groundhog	porcupine
brown rat	guinea pig	prairie dog
cane rat	hamster	rabbit
capybara	hare	rat
cavy	harvest mouse	red squirrel
chinchilla	hedgehog	sewer rat
chipmunk	jerboa	squirrel
cony	kangaroo rat	vole
coypu	lemming	water rat
dormouse	marmot	water vole
ferret	meerkat	woodchuck
fieldmouse	mouse	

---

rogue n
scoundrel, rascal, scamp, villain, miscreant, deceiver, swindler, fraud, fraudster, cheat, reprobate, good-for-nothing, wastrel, ne'er-do-well, rascallion, scallywag, drôle, hedge-creeper; *dialect* skellum; *Scot* hempy, limmer
OLD knave, palliard, slip-string, varlet, Greek, gypsy
COLLOQ. terror, wrong 'un, crook, con man, nasty piece of work
SLANG son of a gun, bugger; *S Afr* donder
OLD SLANG dummerer

roguish adj
mischievous, playful, cheeky, impish, knavish, rascally, waggish, frolicsome, coquettish, swindling, villainous, deceiving, deceitful, dishonest, criminal, crooked, fraudulent, shady, unprincipled, unscrupulous, rascal-like, hempy
OLD slip-string
Ｆ₃ honest, serious

roister v
revel, rollick, celebrate, carouse, frolic, romp, strut, swagger, brag, bluster, boast
OLD make merry
COLLOQ. paint the town red, whoop it up, have it large, large it

roisterer n
reveller, carouser, ranter, roister, swaggerer, boaster, braggart, blusterer

roisterous adj
loud, noisy, wild, rowdy, uproarious, disorderly, exuberant, boisterous, clamorous, obstreperous
Ｆ₃ orderly, restrained

role n
part, character, representation, portrayal, impersonation, function, capacity, task, duty, job, post, position, situation, place

roll v, n
♦ v
1 ROTATE, revolve, turn (round), go round, spin, wheel, twirl, whirl, gyrate, move, go, run, pass, elapse
2 WIND, coil, furl, twist, curl, wrap, envelop, fold, enfold, bind
3 *the ship rolled*
rock, sway, swing, pitch, toss, lurch, reel, billow, tumble, stagger, wallow, undulate
4 PRESS, press down, flatten, crush, smooth, level
5 RUMBLE, grumble, roar, thunder, boom, resound, reverberate, echo
♦ n
1 *a bread roll*
bap, bun, bagel, bridge roll, finger roll, petit pain, brioche, burger bun, burger, hamburger, hot dog, submarine sandwich, crescent, croissant, twist; *dialect* barm cake; *N Am* hoagie
2 ROLLER, cylinder, drum, reel, spool, bobbin, scroll
3 REGISTER, roster, census, list, inventory, index, catalogue, directory, schedule, record, file, chronicle, annals
4 ROTATION, revolution, cycle, turn, spin, wheel, twirl, whirl, gyration, undulation
5 RUMBLE, roar, thunder, boom, resonance, reverberation
6 SWELL, pitching, tossing, rocking, reeling, billowing, undulation
■ **roll in**
1 *money is rolling in*
be received, pour in, come in, flow in, rush in, flood in
2 *he rolled in an hour late*
turn up, appear, come, arrive, put in an appearance, be present
COLLOQ. show up, blow in
■ **roll up**
arrive, assemble, gather, congregate, convene
Ｆ₃ leave

■ **rolling in it**
rich, wealthy, affluent, moneyed, prosperous, well-to-do, well-off
COLLOQ. flush, well-heeled, made of money, in the money, with money to burn
SLANG loaded, filthy rich, stinking rich

rollicking[1] adj
a rollicking story
lively, noisy, light-hearted, hearty, romping, sprightly, exuberant, frolicsome, jovial, carefree, boisterous, joyous, merry, spirited, sportive, jaunty, cavorting, devil-may-care, roisterous, roisting, frisky, playful, rip-roaring, swashbuckling
F∃ restrained, serious

rollicking[2] n
given a rollicking by the boss
reprimand, rebuke, reproof, scolding, harangue, censure, upbraiding, chiding, reproach, lecture
FORMAL berating
COLLOQ. telling-off, talking-to, dressing-down, rocket

rolling adj
heaving, surging, waving, rippling, undulating, undulant
F∃ flat

roly-poly adj
fat, plump, chubby, overweight, rounded, tubby, buxom, podgy, pudgy
FORMAL rotund
F∃ slim

romance n, v
♦ n
1 LOVE AFFAIR, affair, relationship, liaison, attachment, intrigue, amour, passion
COLLOQ. fling, thing
2 LOVE STORY, romantic fiction, novel, story, tale, fairy story, fairytale, legend, idyll, fiction, fantasy, whimsy, bodice-ripper
3 ADVENTURE, excitement, melodrama, mystery, charm, fascination, glamour, colour, sentiment, crusade
♦ v
1 LIE, fantasize, exaggerate, overstate
2 GO OUT WITH, court, woo, chase, see, date, go steady with

romantic adj, n
♦ adj
1 IMAGINARY, fictitious, fanciful, fantastic, legendary, fairytale, idyllic, utopian, optimistic, idealistic, quixotic, visionary, starry-eyed, dreamy, unrealistic, impractical, improbable, unlikely, wild, extravagant, exciting, fascinating, mysterious, stardust
2 SENTIMENTAL, loving, amorous, passionate, tender, fond
COLLOQ. soppy, sloppy, lovey-dovey
F∃ 1 real, practical 2 unromantic, unsentimental
♦ n
sentimentalist, dreamer, visionary, idealist, utopian
F∃ realist

romantically adv
1 *dance romantically*
lovingly, tenderly, fondly, sentimentally, amorously, passionately
2 *as they romantically call it*
fancifully, optimistically, idealistically, unrealistically, impractically, extravagantly, excitingly, mysteriously

Romeo n
lover, ladies' man, Don Juan, Casanova, Lothario, lady-killer, gigolo

romp v, n
♦ v

gambol, frolic, skip, play, sport, frisk, caper, cavort, revel, rollick, roister
♦ n
caper, frolic, lark, rig, spree

roof n
covering, canopy, vault; *dialect & Scot* rigging
Related adjective: tectiform
■ **hit the roof**
COLLOQ. explode, fly off the handle, blow up, blow your cool/top, boil over, burst a blood vessel, do your nut, flip your lid, freak out, go mad, go off the deep end, go up the wall, lose your cool/rag, see red

Types of roof include:

bell roof	gambrel roof	onion dome
conical broach	geodesic dome	pavilion roof
roof	helm roof	pendentive dome
cupola	hip roof	pitched roof
dome	imbricated roof	saddle roof
flat roof	imperial roof	saucer dome
French roof	lean-to roof	sawtooth roof
gable roof	mansard roof	sloped turret
gable-and-valley	monitor roof	span roof
roof	ogee roof	thatched roof

rook v
cheat, swindle, defraud, fleece, overcharge
COLLOQ. do, diddle, con, bilk
SLANG rip off, sting, take for a ride, take to the cleaners; *N Am* gold-brick

room n
space, volume, capacity, area, headroom, legroom, elbow-room, *Lebensraum*, scope, range, extent, expanse, volume, leeway, latitude, margin, allowance, chance, opportunity

Types of room include:

anteroom	family room	parlour
assembly room	fitting-room	playroom
attic	foyer	porch
basement	front room	reading-room
bathroom	games room	reception room
bedroom	greenroom	recreation room
boardroom	guardroom	*N Am* restroom
boudoir	guest room	rumpus room
box-room	hall	saddleroom
breakfast room	kitchen	salon
buttery	kitchen-diner	scullery
cabin	kitchenette	seminar room
cell	laboratory	sick-room
cellar	landing	sitting room
chamber	larder	smoking room
chambers	laundry	spare room
changing room	lavatory	staffroom
classroom	lecture room	stateroom
cloakroom	library	stockroom
common room	living room	storeroom
conservatory	lobby	strongroom
consulting room	locker room	studio
control room	loft	study
courtroom	*colloq.* loo	sun lounge
cubicle	lounge	tack room
darkroom	lounge-diner	toilet
day room	lumber room	utility room
colloq. den	meeting room	waiting-room
dining-room	mezzanine	washroom
dormitory	morning room	WC
drawing room	music-room	workroom
dressing-room	nursery	workshop
engine-room	office	
en suite bathroom	pantry	

roomy *adj*

spacious, large, sizeable, broad, wide, extensive, ample, generous

FORMAL capacious, voluminous, commodious

E3 cramped, small, tiny

root¹ *n, v*

◆ *n*

1 TUBER, rhizome, stem, radical, radicle, radix

Related adjective: radical

2 ORIGIN, source, derivation, reason, cause, starting point, fount, fountainhead, seed, germ, kernel, nucleus, heart, core, nub, essence, seat, base, bottom, basis, foundation, fundamental

3 *tracing your family roots*

beginning(s), origins, family, heritage, background, birthplace, home

◆ *v*

anchor, moor, fasten, fix, set, stick, implant, embed, entrench, establish, ground, base

■ **root out**

unearth, dig out, uncover, discover, uproot, eradicate, eliminate, put an end to, exterminate, destroy, abolish, clear away, remove, get rid of

FORMAL extirpate

■ **put down roots**

settle down, establish yourself, make your home, set up home

■ **root and branch**

completely, entirely, wholly, totally, utterly, thoroughly, radically, finally

E3 not at all, slightly

■ **take root**

become established, become fixed, become entrenched, take hold, establish itself, become acceptable

root²

■ **root around**

rummage, ferret, poke, pry, nose, dig, delve, burrow, forage, hunt

root³ *v*

root for your team

support, shout, cheer (on), encourage, applaud, hail; *N Am* pull

rooted *adj*

entrenched, established, felt, firm, fixed, deep, deeply, deep-seated, ingrained, confirmed, rigid, radical

E3 superficial, temporary

rootless *adj*

unsettled, homeless, free, carefree, transient, of no fixed abode, moving, wandering, drifting, floating, nomadic, itinerant

E3 settled, established

rope *v, n*

◆ *v*

tie, bind, lash, fasten, hitch, moor, tether

■ **rope in**

enlist, engage, involve, persuade, talk into

FORMAL inveigle

Related adjective: funicular

■ **know the ropes**

understand what should be done, learn, master, get the hang of what to do, know what's what

COLLOQ. know the score, know the drill

See panel on next page

ropy, ropey *adj*

poor, substandard, deficient, inadequate, inferior, unsatisfactory, rough, unwell, off colour

COLLOQ. duff, not up to scratch, below par

E3 good, well

roster *n*

rota, schedule, register, roll, list, listing, index, directory

rostrum *n*

platform, stage, dais, podium

rosy *adj*

1 PINK, reddish, red, rose, rose-coloured, rose-hued, roselike, rose-pink, rose-red, rose-scented, roseate, glowing, fresh, sunny, healthy-looking, blooming, blushing, ruddy, flushed, florid, inflamed, bloodshot

FORMAL rubicund

2 PROMISING, cheerful, bright, encouraging, optimistic, hopeful, reassuring, favourable

FORMAL auspicious

E3 2 depressing, sad, unhappy

rot *v, n*

◆ *v*

decay, decompose, fester, perish, corrode, spoil, go bad, go off, degenerate, go sour, deteriorate, crumble, disintegrate, taint, corrupt, ret

FORMAL putrefy

◆ *n*

1 DECAY, decomposition, deterioration, corruption, disintegration, corrosion, rust, mould

FORMAL putrefaction

2 NONSENSE, rubbish, drivel, claptrap

COLLOQ. poppycock, bunk, bunkum, baloney, humbug, piffle, tosh, bosh, codswallop, cobblers, kibosh, blah, hogwash, rhubarb, hooey, malarkey, moonshine

rota *n*

roster, schedule, register, roll, list, listing, index, directory

rotary *adj*

rotating, revolving, turning, spinning, whirling, gyrating, gyratory

E3 fixed

rotate *v*

1 REVOLVE, turn (round), spin (round), go round, move round, reel, whirl, gyrate, pivot, swivel, roll

2 ALTERNATE, take (it) in turns, interchange, reciprocate

rotation *n*

revolution, turn, turning, spin, spinning, swivel, swivelling, whirl, whirling, gyration, orbit, cycle, alternation, sequence, succession

rote

■ **learn by rote**

memorize, commit to memory, learn from memory, learn off by heart, learn off pat, learn word for word, learn parrot-fashion

rotten *adj*

1 DECAYED, decomposed, putrid, addled, bad, off, gone off, sour, spoilt, tainted, mouldy, f(o)etid, stinking, rank, foul, rotting, decaying, disintegrating, mouldering

OLD putid

FORMAL putrescent

2 INFERIOR, bad, poor, inadequate, low-grade, terrible, dreadful, mean

COLLOQ. lousy, crummy, rop(e)y

SLANG manky, poxy, punk, putrid

3 NASTY, evil, wicked, horrible, beastly, dirty, despicable, contemptible, dishonourable, dishonest, immoral, corrupt, unprincipled

4 ILL, sick, unwell, poorly, awful, off colour, guilty

COLLOQ. grotty, rough, rop(e)y

5 *I'm fed up with your rotten questions*

damned, confounded, wretched, horrible, unpleasant

COLLOQ. blasted, blooming, blinking, flipping, flaming, darned, dashed, confounded, infernal, dratting

SLANG bloody; (*taboo*) fucking, frigging

E3 1 fresh **2, 3** good **4** well

rotter *n*

scoundrel, rogue, cad, blackguard, dastard, cur

Kinds of rope include:

bobstay	cordage	guy-rope	lariat	painter	tether
bowline	cringle	hackamore	lashing	ratline	towrope
brace	dockline	halter	lasso	runner	vang
bridle	downhaul	halyard	line	stay	warp
buntline	dragline	hawser	marline	strand	widdy
cable	dragrope	head rope	mooring rope	string	
clew-line	gantline	hobble	noose	tack	
cord	guy	lanyard	outhaul	tackle	

COLLOQ. bounder, blighter, stinker, swine, beast, pig, rat, fink, louse

rotund *adj*
1 FAT, round, stout, tubby, full, fleshy, plump, podgy, portly, chubby, roly-poly, heavy, obese, spherical, globular, spheric, spheral, spherular, bulbous
FORMAL corpulent, rotundate, orbicular
2 RESONANT, rich, sonorous, full, rounded
FORMAL grandiloquent, magniloquent, orotund
E3 1 flat, slim, gaunt

roué *n*
rake, lecher, libertine, profligate, wanton, debauchee, sensualist, rakehell

rough *adj, n, v*
♦ *adj*
1 UNEVEN, bumpy, lumpy, stony, rugged, craggy, jagged, irregular, gnarled, coarse, bristly, hairy, shaggy, scaly, prickly, scratchy
2 BOISTEROUS, forceful, energetic, lively, disorderly, violent, aggressive, belligerent, wild, noisy, rowdy, raucous, discordant
3 HARSH, severe, stern, tough, hard, difficult, insensitive, unfeeling, merciless, cruel, unkind, brutal, drastic, extreme, vulgar, impolite, coarse, brutish, brusque, curt, sharp
4 *in a rough voice*
husky, throaty, gruff, harsh, hoarse, rasping, croaking, guttural, raucous, discordant, strident
5 APPROXIMATE, estimated, imprecise, inexact, hazy, vague, general, quick, cursory, hasty, sketchy, incomplete, unfinished, unpolished, unrefined, crude, plain, basic, rudimentary
6 *rough sea*
choppy, agitated, turbulent, stormy, tempestuous, violent, wild
7 ILL, sick, unhealthy, unwell, poorly, off colour
COLLOQ. below par, rotten, grotty, lousy, under the weather
E3 1 smooth, level 2 gentle, sensitive 3 kind, mild 5 accurate, exact 6 calm, smooth 7 well
♦ *n*
1 SKETCH, mock-up, outline, draft, model
2 THUG, hooligan, bully, rowdy, ruffian, bruiser, roughneck, tough
SLANG yob, yobbo
■ **rough out**
sketch, draft, draw in rough, outline, mock up, give a summary of
■ **rough up**
beat up, maltreat, manhandle, mistreat
COLLOQ. do in, knock about, bash, mug

Synonym nuances
adjective sense 1
Uneven and **irregular** are very general terms to describe a surface that is not flat, while **bumpy, lumpy** and **stony** are more descriptive of the physical appearance. The terms **rugged** and **craggy** are suggestive of broken rock and have connotations of rough beauty: *the craggy coastline*, but **jagged** suggests a more dangerous

outline. **Gnarled** is suggestive of a twisted and knotted appearance.
  Coarse suggests being in need of refining and is mildly pejorative: *a coarse woollen coat*, while both **bristly** and **hairy** again describe the finish in more detail and have similar connotations of discomfort, connotations which are made more explicit with **prickly** and **scratchy**. **Shaggy** is usually associated with hair, and has implications of being unkempt.

rough-and-ready *adj*
approximate, crude, sketchy, simple, basic, plain, makeshift, make-do, provisional, stop-gap, hurried, unpolished, unrefined
E3 exact, refined

rough-and-tumble *n*
scuffle, struggle, fight, fracas, rumpus, affray, brawl, mêlée
COLLOQ. dust-up, punch-up, scrap

roughen *v*
abrade, asperate, coarsen, granulate, graze, harshen, rough, chafe, chap, rasp, ruffle, scuff
E3 smooth

roughly *adv*
1 *speak to someone roughly*
harshly, toughly, cruelly, unkindly, brutally, insensitively, mercilessly
2 *hustled roughly*
forcefully, energetically, violently, wildly, noisily, rowdily, boisterously
3 *roughly £5million*
approximately, around, about, something like, circa, more or less, loosely, round about, or thereabouts, approaching, close to, nearly, just about, not far off, in the region/ neighbourhood/vicinity of, somewhere in the region of, in round numbers, rounded up/down
COLLOQ. give or take
E3 1, 2 gently 3 exactly

roughneck *n*
tough, thug, rough, rowdy, ruffian, hooligan, lout, bully boy, bruiser; *Scot* keelie

round *prep, adv, adj, n, v*
♦ *prep, adv*
1 SURROUNDING, around, encircling, encompassing, enclosing, on all sides (of), on every side (of), about, framed by
2 EVERYWHERE (IN), to all parts (of), all over, in all directions, on all sides (of), throughout, about, around, here and there, to and fro
♦ *adj*
1 SPHERICAL, globular, ball-shaped, circular, ring-shaped, disc-shaped, disclike, globelike, hooplike, cylindrical, rounded, curved
FORMAL spheroid, discoid, discoidal, orbicular, globate
2 CHUBBY, fat, plump, stout, portly, ample
FORMAL corpulent, rotund
3 APPROXIMATE, rough, imprecise, estimated
♦ *n*
1 CIRCLE, ring, band, hoop, circlet, disc, sphere, cylinder, globe, ball, orb

2 CYCLE, series, sequence, succession, period, bout, session, heat, game, level, stage
3 BEAT, circuit, route, path, lap, course, routine
◆ *v*
go round, move past, circle, skirt, travel round, flank, bypass

■ **round off**
finish (off), complete, end, close, conclude, cap, crown, top off
⊟ begin

■ **round on**
turn on, set upon, attack, lay into, abuse

■ **round up**
bring together, herd, marshal, assemble, gather, rally, muster, collect, group
⊟ disperse, scatter

■ **round about**
approximately, roughly, around, about, something like, circa, more or less, loosely, or thereabouts, approaching, close to, nearly, just about, not far off, in the region/neighbourhood/vicinity of, somewhere in the region of, in round numbers, rounded up/down
COLLOQ. give or take

roundabout *adj*
indirect, circuitous, tortuous, twisting, winding, meandering, oblique, devious, evasive
FORMAL periphrastic, circumlocutory
⊟ straight, direct

roundly *adv*
completely, thoroughly, forcefully, violently, vehemently, fiercely, intensely, rigorously, severely, sharply, bluntly, openly, frankly, outspokenly
⊟ mildly

round-up *n*
1 SUMMARY, survey, overview, précis, collation, collection, assembly
2 GATHERING, herding, marshalling, muster, rally
⊟ **2** dispersal

rouse *v*
1 WAKE (UP), waken, awake, awaken, arouse, call, stir, get up, raise, look alive, unbed; *dialect* rear
TECHNICAL flush
OLD abraid
2 EXCITE, arouse, awake, awaken, waken, move, start, disturb, agitate, anger, provoke, stimulate, instigate, incite, fire, inflame, impel, induce, kindle, enkindle, evoke, call up, galvanize, whip up, work up, stir, raise, summon, send, yerk, roust, irritate, put someone on their mettle
OLD firk; (*Spenser*) amove
FORMAL suscitate
COLLOQ. turn on, shake
⊟ **2** calm

rousing *adj*
stirring, exciting, inspiring, lively, moving, stimulating, spirited, vigorous, exhilarating, brisk, electrifying
⊟ dull, boring, calming

rout *n, v*
◆ *n*
defeat, conquest, overthrow, beating, trouncing, drubbing, flight, retreat, stampede
OLD hurricane
FORMAL subjugation
COLLOQ. thrashing
⊟ win
◆ *v*
defeat, conquer, overthrow, crush, beat, trounce, put to flight, chase, dispel, scatter, shoot down
FORMAL vanquish, subjugate, discomfit
COLLOQ. hammer, thrash, lick, slaughter, clobber, walk all over, wipe the floor with

route *n, v*
◆ *n*
course, run, path, road, avenue, way, flight path, direction, itinerary, journey, passage, circuit, round, beat
◆ *v*
direct, send, forward, convey, dispatch

routine *n, adj*
◆ *n*
1 PROCEDURE, way, method, system, order, pattern, schedule, programme, formula, practice, usage, custom, wont, habit, regime, rut, groove, rota, round, mechanics, treadmill, jogtrot, journey-work, heigh; *Scot* heich-how
TECHNICAL chain, run
COLLOQ. drill; *N Am* milk run
2 *comedy routine*
act, piece, programme, performance, lines
COLLOQ. patter, spiel, yak
SLANG shtick
◆ *adj*
customary, habitual, usual, typical, ordinary, run-of-the-mill, normal, standard, common, wonted, workaday, conventional, unoriginal, predictable, familiar, everyday, banal, humdrum, dull, boring, monotonous, tedious, tiresome, hackneyed, institutional, bread-and-butter, day-to-day, perfunctory
COLLOQ. ho-hum
⊟ unusual, different, exciting, inspiring

routinely *adv*
regularly, usually, normally, commonly, conventionally, typically, customarily, habitually
⊟ surprisingly, irregularly, unusually

rove *v*
roam, wander, ramble, range, meander, drift, cruise, stroll, stray, gallivant, traipse; *Scot* stravaig
⊟ stay

rover *n*
rambler, wanderer, transient, vagrant, traveller, drifter, itinerant, ranger, nomad, Gypsy, gadabout; *Scot* stravaiger
⊟ stay-at-home

row[1] *n*
a row of seats
line, tier, bank, rank, range, column, file, queue, string, chain, series, sequence, arrangement

■ **in a row**
consecutively, successively, sequentially, continuously, uninterruptedly, one after the other, in turn
COLLOQ. on the trot, back to back

row[2] *n, v*
◆ *n*
1 ARGUMENT, quarrel, disagreement, dispute, controversy, squabble, tiff, fight, conflict, fracas, brawl
FORMAL altercation
COLLOQ. slanging match, falling-out, set-to, scrap, dust-up
2 NOISE, racket, din, uproar, commotion, clamour, disturbance, rumpus, hubbub, tumult
⊟ **2** calm
◆ *v*
argue, quarrel, wrangle, bicker, squabble, fight
COLLOQ. scrap, be at each other's throats

rowdy *adj, n*
◆ *adj*
noisy, loud, rough, boisterous, disorderly, unruly, unrestrained, riotous, wild, obstreperous, blowzy
COLLOQ. stroppy; *Aust* rorty
⊟ quiet, peaceful, restrained
◆ *n*
rough, ruffian, tough, tearaway, hooligan, lout, brawler, apache; *Scot* keelie; *Aust* larrikin
COLLOQ. hoodlum
SLANG yahoo, yob, yobbo, brat packer, bovver boy

royal *adj*
regal, majestic, kingly, kinglike, queenly, queenlike, princely, imperial, monarchical, sovereign, august, grand, impressive, imposing, stately, magnificent, splendid, superb

royally *adv*
impressively, grandly, greatly, wonderfully, tremendously, magnificently, splendidly, superbly

rub *v, n*
  ♦ *v*
1 STROKE, caress, fondle, pat, massage, scratch, knead
FORMAL embrocate
2 CLEAN, smooth, polish, buff (up), burnish, shine
3 SCOUR, scratch, scrape, scrub, wipe, clean, abrade
4 PUT ON, apply, work in, spread, smear
5 CHAFE, grate, scrape, pinch
  ♦ *n*
1 MASSAGE, stroke, caress, kneading, rub-down
2 POLISH, shine, wipe, clean
3 DIFFICULTY, drawback, hindrance, trouble, impediment, problem, obstacle, hitch, catch
COLLOQ. snag
▪ **rub along**
get along/on, cope, manage, get by
▪ **rub down**
clean, smooth, wash (down), sponge, dry, massage
▪ **rub in**
emphasize, stress, underline, highlight, make much of, insist on, keep going on about, harp on
▪ **rub off on**
influence, affect, have an effect on, change, alter, transform
▪ **rub out**
1 ERASE, obliterate, delete, cancel
FORMAL efface
2 KILL, assassinate, murder, put to death, finish off, do away with
SLANG do in, bump off, eliminate, liquidate
▪ **rub up the wrong way**
annoy, anger, irk, irritate, get, vex, niggle, get to
COLLOQ. bug, wind up, get your goat, get under your skin, needle, peeve
🖃 calm

rubberneck *v*
gape, stare, look at, watch, view, goggle
COLLOQ. gawp, gawk

rubbish *n*
1 REFUSE, junk, litter, scrap, waste, dross, debris, rubble, flotsam and jetsam; *N Am* garbage, trash
FORMAL detritus
2 NONSENSE, drivel, twaddle, gibberish, gobblydegook, balderdash
COLLOQ. stuff and nonsense, claptrap, poppycock, rot, cobblers, bunk, bunkum, piffle, rot, tripe, tosh, bosh, baloney, blah, eyewash, hogwash, rhubarb, guff, hooey, malarkey, moonshine; *Aust & NZ* bulldust; *Aust* bull's wool
SLANG bull; (*vulgar*) crap, cack, shit, bullshit, balls, bollocks
🖃 **2** sense

rubbishy *adj*
worthless, valueless, trashy, cheap, tawdry, low-quality, inferior, unsatisfactory, second-rate, third-rate, grotty, paltry, petty, shoddy, throw-away, gimcrack, tatty, twopenny-halfpenny
COLLOQ. crummy
SLANG cruddy
🖃 high-quality, classy

rubble *n*
debris, remains, ruins, waste, wreck, wreckage, fragments

ruction *n*
protest, quarrel, trouble, fracas, fuss, row, rout, rumpus,

disturbance, noise, din, hue and cry, dispute, commotion, racket, uproar, storm, brawl, rookery, ruffle
FORMAL altercation
COLLOQ. scrap, to-do, carry-on, kerfuffle
🖃 calm

ruddy *adj*
1 *a ruddy complexion*
red, reddish, scarlet, crimson, blushing, flushed, rosy, glowing, healthy, blooming, florid, fresh, sunburnt, apple-cheeked
FORMAL rubicund
2 *the ruddy machine has broken down again*
annoying, infernal, confounded
COLLOQ. blasted, blooming, flipping, darned, dashed
🖃 **1** pale, unhealthy

rude *adj*
1 IMPOLITE, discourteous, disrespectful, bad-tempered, bad-mannered, impertinent, impudent, cheeky, insolent, offensive, insulting, abusive, ill-mannered, ill-bred, unpleasant, uncouth, uncivilized, unrefined, unpolished, uneducated, untutored, uncivil, curt, brusque, abrupt, sharp, short; *Scot* goustrous
OLD giant rude
2 *a rude joke*
obscene, vulgar, coarse, smutty, crude, offensive, improper, indecent, indelicate, dirty, filthy, risqué, ribald, lewd, bawdy, salacious, naughty, gross
COLLOQ. blue, near the bone, near the knuckle
3 *get a rude shock*
unpleasant, harsh, disagreeable, nasty, unexpected, sudden, startling
4 SIMPLE, rough, crude, primitive, rudimentary, basic, makeshift, rough-and-ready
5 IGNORANT, illiterate, uncivilized, unrefined, uneducated, untutored, unpolished, uncouth, rough, coarse, peasant, barbaric, bestial, boorish, churlish, heathenish
🖃 **1** polite, courteous, civil **2** clean, decent **3** pleasant, welcome **4** advanced, well-developed **5** educated, sophisticated

rudely *adv*
1 IMPOLITELY, discourteously, disrespectfully, impudently, insolently, abusively, curtly, brusquely, abruptly
2 *be made rudely aware*
harshly, unexpectedly, suddenly, unpleasantly, disagreeably
🖃 **1** politely, courteously, civilly, respectfully **2** pleasantly, agreeably

rudeness *n*
discourtesy, disrespect, impoliteness, bad manners, impertinence, impudence, insolence, abuse, ill manners, incivility, unpleasantness, uncouthness
🖃 politeness, courtesy, civility, respect

rudimentary *adj*
1 BASIC, primary, initial, introductory, elementary, fundamental, essential
2 PRIMITIVE, undeveloped, embryonic, crude, unsophisticated, rough and ready, simple, rough
3 VESTIGIAL, remaining, surviving, undeveloped, imperfect, incomplete, reduced, functionless
🖃 **1** advanced **2** developed

rudiments *n*
basics, fundamentals, essentials, principles, first principles, elements, ABC, beginnings, foundations

rue *v*
regret, be regretful, be sorry, mourn, grieve, lament, deplore, feel remorse for, reproach yourself, repent
OLD bemoan, bewail
🖃 rejoice

rueful *adj*
regretful, remorseful, penitent, sad, melancholy,

repentant, sorrowful, sorry, mournful, dismal, apologetic, grievous, conscience-stricken, doleful, pitiable, pitiful, plaintive, self-reproachful
FORMAL contrite, lugubrious, woebegone, woeful
F3 glad, joyful

ruffian *n*

villain, scoundrel, bully, bully-boy, brute, thug, lout, rowdy, rogue, cut-throat, rascal, roughneck, hooligan, bruiser, desperado, Apache; *N Am* highbinder, plug-ugly
OLD sweater, trailbastion
FORMAL miscreant
COLLOQ. hoodlum, rough, tough, toerag, yobbo
SLANG yob, bovver boy, lager lout; *Scot* ned

ruffle *v, n*

♦ *v*
1 RUMPLE, dishevel, tangle, tousle, wrinkle, crease, pucker, crumple, ripple
FORMAL disarrange
2 ANNOY, upset, irritate, anger, put out, vex, irk, exasperate, fluster, rile, nettle, discompose, confuse, trouble
FORMAL perturb
COLLOQ. aggravate, bug, hassle, rattle, wind up, rub up the wrong way, get someone's blood up, make someone's blood boil, get on someone's nerves, get up someone's nose, get under someone's skin, get someone's goat, get on someone's wick, drive crazy/nuts, drive bananas, drive up the wall, drive round the bend/twist, get someone's back up, brass off, cheese off, make someone's hackles rise, make sparks fly, give someone the hump, get someone's dander up
F3 1 smooth **2** pacify
♦ *n*
fold, tuck, pleat, gather, crease, flounce, frill, fringe, trimming, valance, falbala, line, wrinkle, crinkle, pucker, furrow

rug *n*

mat, carpet, floor-covering, covering, matting, kali, kilim, Persian carpet, doormat, felt, underfelt, underlay

rugged *adj*

1 ROUGH, bumpy, uneven, irregular, jagged, rocky, stony, craggy, stark
2 STRONG, robust, hardy, tough, sturdy, stalwart, vigorous, burly, well-built, muscular, sinewy, weather-beaten, furrowed
3 DETERMINED, strong, robust, tough, resolute, firm, tenacious, unflinching, unwavering
F3 1 smooth

ruggedly *adv*

1 ROUGHLY, unevenly, irregularly, rockily, starkly
2 STRONGLY, toughly, vigorously, muscularly

ruin *n, v*

♦ *n*
1 DESTRUCTION, devastation, wreckage, havoc, damage, disrepair, decay, disintegration, breakdown, collapse, fall, downfall, failure, defeat, overthrow, ruination, undoing
2 *financial ruin*
insolvency, bankruptcy, loss, failure, crash, disaster
FORMAL indigence, penury
3 *the ruins of the castle*
remains, debris, rubble, fragments, traces, vestiges, relics, remnants, chaos, devastation, havoc, shambles
FORMAL detritus
F3 1 development, reconstruction
♦ *v*
1 DAMAGE, harm, spoil, mar, botch, break, smash, shatter, injure, wreck, wreak havoc, destroy, demolish, raze, devastate, lay waste, overwhelm, overthrow, defeat, cripple, crush
COLLOQ. mess up
SLANG screw up

See Synonym nuances panel at **destroy**.
2 IMPOVERISH, bankrupt, make bankrupt, make insolvent, cripple
F3 1 develop, restore
■ **in ruins**
ruined, damaged, dilapidated, broken-down, ramshackle, decrepit, destroyed, devastated, wrecked, falling apart, tumbledown

ruination *n*

destruction, devastation, wreckage, havoc, damage, disrepair, decay, disintegration, breakdown, collapse, fall, downfall, failure, defeat, overthrow, undoing

ruinous *adj*

1 *ruinous costs*
exorbitant, extortionate, excessive, unreasonable, immoderate, crippling
2 RUINED, in ruins, damaged, dilapidated, broken-down, ramshackle, decrepit, destroyed, devastated, wrecked, shattered, catastrophic, calamitous, disastrous, devastating, cataclysmic
OLD tottered, waste
F3 1 low **2** beneficial

ruinously *adv*

exorbitantly, extortionately, unreasonably, immoderately, excessively

rule *n, v*

♦ *n*
1 REGULATION, law, statute, ordinance, decree, ruling, order, command, commandment, guide, corrective, restriction, precept, tenet, canon, maxim, axiom, truth, truism, principle, formula, guideline, direction, instruction, standard, criterion
2 REIGN, sovereignty, supremacy, kingship, queenship, dominion, mastery, influence, sway, power, authority, command, direction, control, influence, regime, administration, government, leadership, jurisdiction
3 CUSTOM, convention, practice, standard, routine, procedure, protocol, form, habit, wont
♦ *v*
1 *rule a country*
reign, govern, command, lead, preside over, officiate, administer, manage, direct, guide, control, be in control, administer, regulate, prevail, dominate
COLLOQ. call the shots, sit in the driving seat
2 JUDGE, adjudicate, decide, find, settle, determine, resolve, establish, decree, direct, order, lay down, pronounce
■ **rule out**
exclude, eliminate, reject, dismiss, prevent, ban, prohibit, forbid, disallow
FORMAL preclude
■ **as a rule**
usually, normally, mainly, in the main, ordinarily, generally, in general, on the whole, by and large, for the most part

---

Synonym nuances
noun sense 1
You can use **regulation** of a strict rule controlling various organizations or procedures, whereas **law** and **statute** are appropriate for a legal constitution devised by a corporation or body. **Ordinance**, likewise, implies the legal guidelines of an authority: *the German Drinking Water Ordinance*, while **decree** and **ruling**, although similar, suggest a judicial decision.
 Order or **command** can be used of a direction issued by anyone in a superior position, whereas **commandment** tends to suggest a divine or religious element.
Instruction suggests a dictatorial element; the term **direction** suggests a less strict rule advising on how to proceed, and **guide** is even more suggestive of a helping hand. **Corrective** would be appropriate to refer to a rule

that has been issued to put something right: *this policy could prove a strong corrective to inefficient practices*, whereas a **restriction** would refer to one which applies limitations.

   Principle, **precept** and **tenet** suggest a rule that is part of a moral code or belief system, while **canon** has ecclesiastical connotations. Both **maxim** and **axiom** would be appropriate to refer to a generally accepted adage, and **truism** used for something that is self-evident: *the truism that you get what you pay for*. The terms **principle**, **formula** and **guideline**, along with **standard** and **criterion**, can be used of fundamental truths, laws or norms that can be used as rules in doing something: *we will work on the principle of first come, first served*.

ruler

Titles of rulers include:

Aga	kaiser	princess
begum	khan	queen
caesar	king	rajah
caliph	leader	rani
commander	lord	regent
consul	maharajah	shah
controller	maharani	sheikh
duce	mikado	shogun
emir	monarch	sovereign
emperor	nawab	sultan
empress	nizam	sultana
Führer	overlord	suzerain
governor	pharaoh	tsar (or czar)
governor-general	potentate	tsarina (or
head	president	czarina)
head of state	prince	viceroy

ruling *n, adj*

 ◆ *n*
judgement, adjudication, verdict, decision, finding, resolution, decree, pronouncement
 ◆ *adj*
1 REIGNING, sovereign, on the throne, supreme, governing, controlling, in control, in charge, commanding, leading
2 MAIN, chief, leading, principal, dominant, predominant, most influential

rum *adj*

strange, unusual, odd, peculiar, abnormal, bizarre, curious, weird, funny, freakish, queer, suspect, suspicious
FORMAL singular
COLLOQ. funny-peculiar

rumble *v, n*

 ◆ *v*
roar, thunder, boom, roll, reverberate
 ◆ *n*
roar, thunder, boom, roll, reverberation

rumbustious *adj*

boisterous, loud, noisy, rowdy, disorderly, clamorous, exuberant, unmanageable, unruly, uproarious, wild, rough, wayward, wilful, robust, roisterous, roisting
FORMAL obstreperous, refractory
F3 quiet, restrained, sensible

ruminate *v*

ponder, think, reflect, meditate, mull over, muse, brood, consider, contemplate, deliberate, chew over
FORMAL cogitate

rummage *v, n*

 ◆ *v*
root (around), search (through), turn over, poke around, hunt, explore, examine, delve, ransack, forage, rifle
 ◆ *n*
jumble, junk, tat, bric-à-brac, odds and ends

rumour *n, v*

 ◆ *n*
hearsay, gossip, talk, speculation, whisper, scandal, word, information, news, report, story, the word on the street, say-so, underbreath, cry, kite, canard, on-dit, sough; *dialect* tittle-tattle; *Scot* fama clamosa; *Aust* furphy
OLD noise, speech, voice, fame, bruit; (*Shakesp*) murmur
FORMAL tidings
COLLOQ. grapevine, bush telegraph, buzz, breeze; *N Am* scuttlebutt
 ◆ *v*
say, tell, hint, put about, noise abroad, report, publish, gossip, circulate, whisper, bruit (about/abroad)

rump *n*

1 BUTTOCKS, bottom, behind, rear, seat, dock, hindquarters, breech, haunches, nache, croup, *derrière*
COLLOQ. backside, bum, posterior, fundament, tail; *N Am* butt, heinie, booty
SLANG duff, prat; (*vulgar*) arse; *N Am* ass, can, fanny, keister, tush; *Aust* coit, quoit
2 LEFTOVERS, remains, remainder, residue, trace, vestige

rumple *v*

wrinkle, crease, pucker, crumple, ruffle, dishevel, disorder, tousle, crinkle, crush, derange, scrunch
F3 smooth

rumpus *n*

disturbance, noise, uproar, confusion, commotion, disruption, furore, rout, row, tumult, fuss, fracas, brawl, brouhaha, ruction, bagarre, ruckus
COLLOQ. kerfuffle, shindy, rhubarb, shemozzle
F3 calm

run *v, n*

 ◆ *v*
1 SPRINT, jog, race, charge, career, tear, dash, hurry, rush, speed, run away, flee, bolt, dart, gallop, trot, scuttle, scamper, scurry
COLLOQ. step on it, scoot, scarper
2 GO, pass, move, travel, proceed, issue, flow
3 FUNCTION, work, go, operate, be in operation, perform, progress
4 CARRY OUT, do, perform, execute, fulfil, implement, undertake
5 *run a company*
head, lead, administer, direct, operate, own, carry on, carry out, conduct, manage, superintend, supervise, organize, co-ordinate, oversee, control, be in control of, regulate, be in charge of
6 COMPETE, contend, stand, enter, take part in, put yourself forward, challenge
7 LAST, continue, go, go on, extend, reach, stretch, proceed, spread, range
8 FLOW, stream, glide, roll, course, pour, gush, issue, jet, spurt, cascade, drip, trickle
9 *run your hand over something*
move, pass, spread, slide, cross
10 *run you to the station*
drive, take, convey, transport, give a lift; *N Am* give a ride
11 *run a car*
own, possess, have, drive, use, keep, maintain
12 *run for president*
stand, be a candidate in the election of, offer yourself as a candidate for
13 *that train doesn't run on a Sunday*
travel regularly, go, ply, shuttle
14 *the contract runs for three years*
be valid, be in effect, last, continue, operate, be in operation
15 *the play ran for four years*
be performed, be presented, be produced, be staged, be mounted, be played, last, go on
16 *the newspaper ran a story*

publish, print, carry, feature, include, communicate, broadcast

♦ *n*

1 JOG, gallop, race, sprint, spurt, dash, rush, hurry
2 DRIVE, ride, jaunt, excursion, outing, trip, journey
COLLOQ. spin
3 SERIES, sequence, string, cycle, chain, course, round, succession, spell, stretch, period
4 COURSE, route, way, line, track, road, flight path
5 ENCLOSURE, coop, pen, pound, fold, sty, paddock, yard
6 *a run on a currency*
demand, need, call, rush, clamour, pressure
7 POINT, goal, hit, mark, score
8 *gave us the run of their apartment*
free use of, permission to go anywhere in, permission to use anythig in, unrestricted access to
9 *different from the average run of things*
sort, kind, type, class, set, variety, category
10 *a run in a stocking*
ladder, rip, tear, cut, hole, split, slit, slash, snag, gash

■ **run across**
meet, encounter, come across, meet by chance, meet unexpectedly, run into
FORMAL chance upon
COLLOQ. bump into

■ **run after**
chase, pursue, follow, tail
◪ flee

■ **run along**
go away, away with you, off with you, off you go, be off, on your way
COLLOQ. buzz off, clear off, scarper, scat

■ **run away**
1 ESCAPE, flee, abscond, decamp, bolt, run off, make off
COLLOQ. scarper, beat it, clear off, make a run for it, vamoose
2 *run away from problems*
avoid, ignore, disregard, evade, neglect, overlook, take no notice of, brush aside, dodge
COLLOQ. shut your eyes to, turn your back on
3 *run away with your neighbour's wife*
run off, elope, make off, leave
4 *run away with the money*
make off with, walk off with, steal, filch, pocket
FORMAL appropriate, purloin
COLLOQ. pinch, nick, lift
5 *run away with a competition*
win easily, win hands down, coast home
◪ **1** stay **2** deal with

■ **run down**
1 CRITICIZE, slate, denounce, attack, pull/tear to pieces, belittle, defame
FORMAL disparage, denigrate
COLLOQ. slam, knock, pan, rubbish
SLANG slag (off)
2 RUN OVER, knock down, knock over, knock to the ground, hit, strike
3 TIRE, weary, exhaust, weaken
4 *run down production*
reduce, decrease, drop, cut, cut back on, trim, curtail
◪ **1** praise **4** increase

■ **run for it**
escape, flee, fly, make off, retreat, bolt
COLLOQ. scarper, scram, do a bunk, skedaddle
◪ stay

■ **run in**
arrest, jail
FORMAL apprehend
COLLOQ. nick, pick up, nab, lift, pinch, bust, nail, collar

■ **run into**
1 MEET, encounter, run across, meet by chance, meet unexpectedly
FORMAL chance upon

COLLOQ. bump into
2 HIT, strike, collide with, bump into, crash, ram
3 *run into difficulties*
encounter, meet, face, experience, come up against
4 *debts running into thousands of pounds*
amount to, come to, equal, add up to
◪ **2** miss

■ **run off**
1 RUN AWAY, escape, make off, abscond, bolt, decamp, elope
COLLOQ. scarper, skedaddle
2 DUPLICATE, print, produce, copy, photocopy, Xerox®, Photostat®
◪ **1** stay

■ **run off with**
1 *run off with your neighbour's wife*
run away with, make off with, elope with
2 *run off with the money*
run away with, make off with, walk off with, steal, filch, pocket
FORMAL appropriate, purloin
COLLOQ. pinch, nick, lift

■ **run on**
continue, go on, carry on, last, extend, reach

■ **run out**
expire, terminate, cease, end, close, finish, be used up, be finished, exhaust, be exhausted, dry up, give out, fail

■ **run out on**
abandon, leave, strand, desert, maroon
FORMAL forsake
COLLOQ. walk out on, jilt, ditch, chuck, dump, leave in the lurch

■ **run over**
1 HIT, knock down, run down, strike
2 REPEAT, go over, run through, practise, rehearse, review, recapitulate, reiterate, survey
COLLOQ. recap

■ **run through**
1 REHEARSE, go through, run over, practise, read, read through, review, survey, examine
2 SPEND, waste, squander, exhaust, fritter away
FORMAL dissipate

■ **run to**
amount to, add up to, total, come to, equal, afford, have enough of

■ **run together**
join, mix, unite, blend, combine, fuse, merge, mingle, amalgamate, coalesce
FORMAL commingle
◪ separate

■ **in the long run**
eventually, ultimately, at last, in the end
COLLOQ. when all is said and done, at the end of the day

■ **on the run**
trying to escape, running away, on the loose, escaped, at large, free, at liberty, unconfined
SLANG *N Am* on the lam

Synonym nuances
verb sense 1
While **jog** suggests a comparatively slow, regular pace, **sprint** and **race** can be used of covering a short distance at speed. The term **charge** usually implies a fixed purpose: *she charged off in search of her mother*, while **career** implies a degree of wildness and lack of direction. The terms **tear**, **dash** and **speed** have suggestions of a rather sudden, fleeting action: *she grabbed her mobile phone and dashed out into the street*; *something sped past me*. **Rush** is similar, but with overtones of impetuosity: *Why are you rushing from room to room?* **Dart** also suggests quick and sudden movement, although perhaps more brief in duration: *he darted across the road*.

The terms **run away** and **flee** are appropriate words for running to escape, and **bolt** likewise implies a hurried departure made to escape: *the gate was left open and the animals bolted*. **Gallop** returns to the idea of moving at a fast rhythmic pace, while **trot** is more suggestive of a quickened walk. While the association of these terms with horses lend suggestions of almost exaggerated movements, the terms **scuttle**, **scurry** and **scamper** are connotative of the short rapid steps of small animals, especially those taken nervously or playfully: *the blast sent people scurrying for cover; the boy scampered away, pleased with himself.*

runaway *n, adj*

◆ *n*

escaper, escapee, fugitive, absconder, truant, deserter, refugee

◆ *adj*

escaped, fugitive, loose, out of control, uncontrolled, wild

run-down *n, adj*

◆ *n*

1 REDUCTION, decrease, curtailment, decline, drop, cut, cutback
2 SUMMARY, résumé, synopsis, analysis, outline, sketch, briefing, review, run-through
COLLOQ. recap

◆ *adj*

1 WEAK, ill, unwell, tired, weary, drained, exhausted, fatigued, debilitated, worn-out, unhealthy, seedy, peaky
FORMAL enervated
2 NEGLECTED, uncared-for, dilapidated, tumble-down, ramshackle, broken-down, decrepit, dingy, shabby
COLLOQ. grotty
F3 1 healthy **2** well-kept

run-in *n*

fight, quarrel, argument, dispute, wrangle, skirmish, tussle, confrontation, difference of opinion, brush, contretemps
FORMAL altercation
COLLOQ. dust-up, set-to

runner *n*

1 JOGGER, sprinter, athlete, competitor, participant
2 COURIER, messenger, racer, dispatch rider, bearer
3 STEM, shoot, offshoot, sprout, tendril, sprig, sarmentum, stolon
TECHNICAL flagellum

■ **do a runner**

depart, go, go away, set out, take your leave, pull out, decamp, exit, disappear
COLLOQ. push off, push along, quit, scoot, take off, clear off, shove off, make tracks, do a bunk, up sticks, take French leave, vamoose, sling your hook, hook it

running *n, adj*

◆ *n*

1 SPRINTING, jogging, racing, rushing
2 ADMINISTRATION, direction, management, organization, co-ordination, superintendency, supervision, leadership, charge, control, controlling, regulation
3 FUNCTIONING, working, operation, performance, conduct
4 *out of the running*
contention, contest, competition, shortlist, candidacy

◆ *adj*

1 UNBROKEN, uninterrupted, continuous, ongoing, constant, perpetual, ceaseless, incessant, moving, flowing
FORMAL unceasing
2 IN SUCCESSION, successive, consecutive, in a row
COLLOQ. on the trot
F3 1 broken, occasional

runny *adj*

flowing, fluid, liquid, liquefied, melted, molten, watery, diluted
F3 solid

run-of-the-mill *adj*

ordinary, common, normal, everyday, average, unexceptional, mediocre, middling, tolerable, fair, unremarkable, undistinguished, unimpressive
COLLOQ. OK, so-so, bog standard, common-or-garden, not up to much, no great shakes
F3 exceptional, remarkable

rupture *n, v*

◆ *n*

1 SPLIT, tear, burst, puncture, break, breaking, breach, fracture, crack
TECHNICAL hernia, scissure, rhexis, amniotomy, cerebral haemorrhage
2 DIVISION, separation, split, schism, rift, disagreement, quarrel, falling-out, scissure
OLD rent
FORMAL estrangement
COLLOQ. bust-up

◆ *v*

split, tear, burst, puncture, break, fracture, crack, sever, separate, divide, cut off
OLD rend

rural *adj*

country, rustic, countryside, pastoral, agricultural, agrarian, bucolic, sylvan
F3 urban

Synonym nuances

Country can be used to suggest anything that is not urbanized, and **countryside**, less usual in its adjectival form, suggests the general area: *the Countryside Commission*. **Rustic** can be used to describe something characteristic of a rural way of life, usually with connotations of old-fashionedness or simplicity: *a rustic kitchen with wooden floors*. Both **agricultural** and **agrarian**, on the other hand, are appropriate for a more practical view of farming life, unlike **bucolic** and **pastoral**, which are literary in tone and often imply an idealized image: *a romantic, pastoral scene*. **Sylvan** is similar, but is suggestive of a wooded area: *beautiful trees, and vistas of sylvan charm*.

---

ruse *n*

plan, trick, deception, dodge, hoax, imposture, stratagem, tactic, manoeuvre, ploy, plot, scheme, wile, subterfuge, artifice, device, blind, sham, stall

rush *v, n*

◆ *v*

1 HURRY, dash, hasten, quicken, accelerate, speed (up), press, push, dispatch, bolt, dart, shoot, fly, tear, career, race, run, sprint, scramble, gallop, stampede, charge
OLD make haste
COLLOQ. belt, bomb, pelt, get a move on, run like hell
2 ATTACK, charge, assault, storm, raid, strike, run at

◆ *n*

1 HURRY, haste, urgency, speed, rapidity, swiftness, dash, race, scramble, stampede, charge, flow, flood, surge, stream, gush
2 BUSTLE, activity, hustle and bustle, stir, commotion, excitement, flurry, hurry, hurly-burly
COLLOQ. hive of activity, comings and goings
3 ATTACK, charge, onslaught, assault, storm, raid, strike
4 DEMAND, call, need, run, clamour, pressure

rushed *adj*

busy, hurried, emergency, careless, cursory, superficial, quick, fast, rapid, swift, brisk, hasty, prompt, urgent
FORMAL expeditious

rust *n, v*
* *n*

corrosion, oxidation, verdigris, stain, decay, dross
TECHNICAL uredo, ferrugo
* *v*

corrode, oxidize, tarnish, deteriorate, decline, decay, rot

rust-coloured *adj*
rusty, reddish-brown, brown, red, reddish, coppery,
copper, auburn, chestnut, russet, ginger, gingery, sandy,
tawny, titian
FORMAL ferruginous, ferrugineous, rubiginous,
rubiginose

rustic *adj, n*
* *adj*

1 PASTORAL, sylvan, bucolic, countrified, country,
countryside, rural
2 PLAIN, simple, rough, crude, coarse, rude, clumsy,
awkward, artless, homespun, ingenuous, unsophisticated,
unrefined, uncultured, provincial, uncouth, graceless,
indelicate, boorish, clodhopping, oafish
FORMAL maladroit
1 urban **2** urbane, sophisticated, cultivated,
polished
* *n*

bumpkin, countryman, countrywoman, oaf, peasant,
provincial, yokel, boor, churl, clodhopper, clod, country
cousin
COLLOQ. hayseed, hick, hillbilly
sophisticate , dandy

rustle *v, n*
* *v*

crackle, whoosh, swish, whisper, sigh; *Scot* fissle
FORMAL susurrate
* *n*

crackle, crinkling, rustling, swish, whoosh, whisper,
whispering
FORMAL crepitation, crepitus, susurration, susurrus
■ **rustle up**

prepare quickly, get/provide quickly, make, get/put
together
COLLOQ. scare up

rusty *adj*
1 CORRODED, rusted, rust-covered, oxidized, tarnished,
discoloured, dull
TECHNICAL aeruginous
2 RUST-COLOURED, reddish-brown, brown, red, reddish,
coppery, copper, auburn, chestnut, russet, ginger, gingery,
sandy, tawny, titian
FORMAL ferruginous, ferrugineous, rubiginous, rubiginose
3 *my German is a bit rusty*
unpractised, out of practice, weak, poor, impaired,
deficient, dated, old-fashioned, outmoded, antiquated,
stale, stiff, creaking

rut *n*
1 DITCH, channel, furrow, groove, gutter, indentation,
trough, track, gouge, pothole, wheelmark, wheel track
2 ROUTINE, habit, pattern, system, humdrum, grind, daily
grind, treadmill, same old round/place, no change of
scenery

ruthless *adj*
merciless, pitiless, hard-hearted, hard, heartless,
unforgiving, unmerciful, unfeeling, unsparing, callous,
cruel, inhuman, grim, stern, vicious, brutal, savage,
barbarous, fierce, ferocious, relentless, remorseless,
unrelenting, inexorable, implacable, harsh, severe,
Draconian, stopping/sticking at nothing, hard-bitten,
third-degree
OLD fell; (*Spenser*) felonous
COLLOQ. cut-throat, dog-eat-dog
merciful, compassionate

ruthlessly *adv*
hard-heartedly, unmercifully, mercilessly, pitilessly,
callously, unfeelingly, fiercely, cruelly, brutally, savagely,
harshly, grimly, severely, inexorably, remorselessly
compassionately

S

sable *adj*
dark, black, coal-black, pitch-black, pitch-dark, pitchy, ebony, inky, jet, raven, dusky, sombre, midnight

sabotage *v, n*
◆ *v*
damage, spoil, mar, disrupt, vandalize, wreck, destroy, thwart, ruin, scupper, cripple, incapacitate, disable, undermine, impair, weaken
OLD ratten
◆ *n*
vandalism, damage, impairment, disruption, wrecking, destruction, ruin, spoiling, crippling, disabling, weakening
OLD rattening

sac *n*
bag, pocket, pouch, pod, bladder, capsule, follicle, cyst, saccule, vesicle
TECHNICAL bursa, theca, vesica, vesicula
Related adjective: thecal

saccharine *adj*
sickly, sweet, sentimental, honeyed, cloying, maudlin, mawkish, nauseating, oversweet, sugary, syrupy, sickly-sweet
COLLOQ. soppy, sloppy, mushy, gushy, schmaltzy
F3 bitter, tart

sachet *n*
packet, pack, bag, package, container, wrapping, envelope

sack¹ *v, n*
◆ *v*
sack 100 workers
dismiss, fire, discharge, lay off, make redundant, give notice, give someone their papers, remove
COLLOQ. axe, send packing, boot out, fire, give someone their cards, give someone their jotters, give someone the sack/push/boot/elbow/heave-ho, show someone the door
COLLOQ. *N Am* can, select out
◆ *n*
1 BAG, pocket, pouch, pack, satchel, mat
OLD budget
2 DISMISSAL, discharge, notice, marching orders
COLLOQ. the boot, the push, the elbow, the axe, the chop, the heave-ho, papers, cards, jotters, sacking, firing

sack² *v, n*
◆ *v*
the army sacked the town
destroy, raid, plunder, ravage, raze, lay waste, waste, level, devastate, desecrate, demolish, maraud, pillage, rifle, rob, loot, ruin, rape, spoil, strip
FORMAL depredate, despoil
◆ *n*
destruction, devastation, ravage, razing, ruin, waste, levelling, looting, plunder, plundering, marauding, desecration, rape, pillage
FORMAL depredation, despoliation, rapine

sacrament *n*
ordinance, ceremony, order, practice, observance, rite, ritual, institution

sacred *adj*
1 HOLY, divine, heavenly, blessed, hallowed, sanctified, consecrated, dedicated
2 RELIGIOUS, spiritual, devotional, ecclesiastical, priestly, saintly, godly
3 REVERED, venerable, respected, sacrosanct, inviolable, defended, protected, hallowed, untouchable, impregnable, secure
F3 **1** profane, secular **2** temporal

sacredness *n*
holiness, divinity, godliness, sanctity, solemnity, saintliness, sacrosanctity, invulnerability, inviolability
F3 profaneness, worldliness

sacred writings
See **scripture**.

Sacred writings of religions include:

BAHAI:	Shu Ching	**JAINISM:**
Most Holy Book	Ch'un Ch'iu	Svetambara
The Seven	I Ching	canon
Valleys	Lun Yu	Digambara texts
The Hidden	Chung Yung	**JUDAISM:**
Words	Ta Hsueh	Hebrew Bible
The Bayan	Meng Tzu	Talmud
BUDDHISM:	**HINDUISM:**	Zohar
Tipitaka	Bhagavad-Gita	**MORMONISM:**
Mahayana Sutras	Mahabharata	Book of Mormon
Milindapandha	Puranas	**SHINTOISM:**
Bardo Thodol	Ramayana	Kojiki
CHRISTIANITY:	the Vedas (Rig,	Nihon Shoki
Old Testament	Yajur, Sama,	**SIKHISM:**
Pentateuch	Atharva)	Adi Granth
Gospel	Upanishads	**TAOISM:**
Apocrypha	**ISLAM:**	Chuang Tzu
Epistles	Koran	Lao Tzu (Tao Te
CONFUCIANISM:	Hadith	Ching)
Shih Ching		**ZOROASTRIANISM:**
Li Ching		Avesta

sacrifice *v, n*
◆ *v*
1 *sacrifice an animal in a religious ceremony*
offer, offer up, slaughter, martyrize
TECHNICAL molochize
OLD sacrify; (*Spenser*) sacrifide
FORMAL immolate, lustrate
2 GIVE UP, surrender, forfeit, relinquish, let go, abandon, for(e)go
TECHNICAL gambit
FORMAL renounce
◆ *n*
1 OFFERING, slaughter, victim, blood-sacrifice
TECHNICAL burnt-offering, heave-offering, heave-shoulder, sin-offering, propitiation, acceptilation, hecatomb
OLD suovetaurilia, taurobolium
FORMAL oblation, immolation, lustration, holocaust, juggernaut
2 GIVING-UP, destruction, surrender, abandonment, loss
TECHNICAL gambit
FORMAL renunciation

sacrificial *adj*
atoning, votive
TECHNICAL propitiatory, expiatory, piacular
FORMAL oblatory, reparative

sacrilege *n*
blasphemy, profanity, heresy, desecration, profanation, violation, outrage, irreligion, impiety, irreverence, disrespect, mockery
F3 piety, reverence, respect

sacrilegious *adj*
blasphemous, profane, heretical, desecrating, disrespectful, irreverent, impious, irreligious, godless, ungodly, unholy
FORMAL profanatory
F3 pious, reverent, respectful

sacrosanct *adj*
sacred, hallowed, untouchable, inviolable, impregnable, respected, protected, secure

sad *adj*
1 UNHAPPY, sorrowful, tearful, grief-stricken, heavy-hearted, upset, distressed, miserable, low-spirited, in low spirits, downcast, glum, long-faced, crestfallen, dejected, downhearted, despondent, melancholy, depressed, mournful, doleful, wistful, joyless, gloomy, dismal, wretched
FORMAL woebegone, disconsolate
COLLOQ. fed up, blue, low, down, down in the dumps, (at) rock bottom
2 *sad news*
upsetting, distressing, painful, depressing, touching, poignant, heart-rending, heartbreaking, tragic, grievous, lamentable, regrettable, miserable, sorry, sorrowful, unfortunate, unhappy, serious, grave, calamitous, disastrous
3 *in a sad state*
grievous, lamentable, regrettable, deplorable, disgraceful, shameful, sorry, unfortunate, wretched, pitiful, pitiable
COLLOQ. pathetic
F3 **1** happy, cheerful **2** fortunate, lucky **3** good, healthy

---

Synonym nuances
sense 1
Unhappy can be widely used as a synonym for sad, while **sorrowful** implies a more intense feeling, often with further implications of regret: *a homesick and sorrowful refugee*, and **grief-stricken** has suggestions of a crushing loss. **Upset** can suggest various depths of emotional disturbance, while **distressed** suggests acute mental anguish.
  Miserable and the stronger **wretched** have connotations of a pitiful state, whilst **downcast** and **glum** often suggest a sad appearance. Similarly, **crestfallen** suggests a facial expression, implying disappointment as the cause: *her crestfallen countenance revealed her feelings at the news*. Both **dejected** and **downhearted** are appropriate to convey a slump in spirits, and **despondent** suggests a lack of hope: *many people who have lost their jobs become despondent, fearing they will never work again*.
  Melancholy implies a lingering condition, often tinged with self-indulgence: *a melancholy reverie*, while **wistful** suggests sadness tinged with yearning. The term **depressed** may be used to describe a persistent, clinical state. **Mournful** suggests bereavement or loss, while **doleful** is more suggestive of a heavy heart. **Gloomy** and **dismal** suggest a more pervasive feeling of darkness or lack of hope: *don't look so gloomy, I am sure there are good times coming.*

---

sadden *v*
upset, distress, grieve, depress, deject, dismay, discourage,

dishearten, cast down, dispirit, break your heart, drive to despair
OLD attrist, contrist
COLLOQ. get someone down
F3 cheer, please, gratify, delight

saddle *n, v*
♦ *n*
See panel at **tack**.
♦ *v*
burden, encumber, lumber, land, impose, tax, charge, load

sadism *n*
cruelty, inhumanity, brutality, savagery, viciousness, heartlessness, ruthlessness, unnaturalness, sado-masochism, spite, malevolence, callousness, barbarity, bestiality
FORMAL *schadenfreude*

sadist *n*
torturer, abuser, molester, monster, brute, savage, barbarian
COLLOQ. terror

sadistic *adj*
cruel, inhuman, brutal, savage, vicious, merciless, pitiless, barbarous, bestial, unnatural, perverted

sadly *adv*
1 UNHAPPILY, sorrowfully, gloomily, dismally, tearfully, weepingly, heavy-heartedly, dejectedly, despondently, miserably
2 UNFORTUNATELY, regrettably, unhappily, unluckily, alas, sad to say, sad to relate
COLLOQ. worse luck
F3 **1** happily, cheerfully **2** fortunately, luckily

sadness *n*
unhappiness, sorrow, sorrowfulness, grief, misery, misfortune, despondency, desolation, depression, dejection, cheerlessness, bleakness, joylessness, dolefulness, dismalness, poignancy, sombreness, mournfulness, distress, low spirits, glumness, gloominess, tearfulness, wretchedness, tragedy, pain, regret, pathos
OLD contristation
FORMAL disconsolateness, lugubriousness, melancholy, woe
COLLOQ. heartache
F3 happiness, cheerfulness, delight

safe *adj, n*
♦ *adj*
1 HARMLESS, innocuous, non-toxic, non-poisonous, uncontaminated
2 UNHARMED, undamaged, unscathed, uninjured, out of danger, unhurt, intact, secure, sound, protected, sheltered, defended, guarded, impregnable, invulnerable, unassailable, immune
COLLOQ. out of harm's way, safe and sound, safe as houses, in good hands
3 DEPENDABLE, reliable, trustworthy, responsible, honest, honourable, sure, proven, tried, tested, sound, upright
4 UNADVENTUROUS, unenterprising, cautious, prudent, timid, conservative
FORMAL circumspect
F3 **1** dangerous, harmful **2** vulnerable, at risk, exposed **3** risky, uncertain **4** adventurous, reckless
♦ *n*
cash box, deposit box, safety-deposit box, strongbox, chest, coffer, vault, depository, repository

safe-conduct *n*
authorization, pass, passport, permit, safeguard, warrant, licence, convoy, *laissez-passer*
OLD SLANG jark

safeguard *v, n*
♦ *v*
protect, preserve, defend, look after, take care of, guard,

shield, screen, shelter, secure
Ea endanger, jeopardize
* *n*
protection, defence, shield, security, surety, guarantee,
assurance, insurance, cover, precaution, preventive,
preventative

safekeeping *n*
protection, care, custody, keeping, charge, trust,
guardianship, surveillance, supervision, ward, wardship

safely *adv*
securely, out of danger, without injury, without risk,
without harm, impregnably
COLLOQ. out of harm's way

safety *n, adj*
* *n*
1 PROTECTION, security, safeguard, immunity, welfare,
sanctuary, impregnability, safeness, harmlessness,
soundness, reliability, dependability, trustworthiness
2 SANCTUARY, refuge, shelter, cover
Ea 1 danger, jeopardy, risk
* *adj*
precautionary, preventive, preventative, protective, fail-
safe

sag *v, n*
* *v*
1 HANG LOOSELY, bend, give, bag, droop, hang, swag
2 *prices/her spirits started to sag*
fall, drop, sink, dip, decline, slump, subside, flop, fail, flag,
falter, weaken, wilt
Ea 1 bulge **2** rise
* *n*
drop, fall, low, low point, reduction, slump, slip, slide, dip,
decline, depression, downturn, dwindling
Ea peak, rise

saga *n*
chronicle, epic, history, narrative, adventure, story, tale,
yarn, romance, soap opera, *roman fleuve*
FORMAL epopee, epopeia, epos

sagacious *adj*
wise, discerning, insightful, penetrating, perceptive, far-
sighted, able, intelligent, knowing, acute, sharp, astute,
canny, quick, shrewd, prudent, smart, wary, wide-awake,
wily, fly
FORMAL judicious, percipient, perspicacious, sage,
sapient
Ea foolish, obtuse

sagacity *n*
wisdom, discernment, understanding, judgement, insight,
foresight, penetration, sense, sharpness, shrewdness,
prudence, acumen, knowingness, astuteness, acuteness,
canniness, wariness, wiliness
FORMAL judiciousness, percipience, perspicacity,
sapience
Ea folly, foolishness, obtuseness

sage *n, adj*
* *n*
wise person, wise man, wise woman, teacher, master,
expert, authority, pundit, savant, guru, maharishi, oracle,
elder, philosopher, wiseacre, Solomon, mahatma,
maharishi, hakam, rishi, Solon
Ea ignoramus
* *adj*
wise, intelligent, discerning, knowing, learned,
knowledgeable, astute, canny, politic, prudent,
sensible
FORMAL judicious, perspicacious, sagacious, sapient
Ea foolish

sagely *adv*
wisely, perceptively, discerningly, ably, intelligently,

knowingly, sharply, quickly, acutely, astutely, prudently,
shrewdly
FORMAL judiciously, perspicaciously

saggy *adj*
sagging, droopy, drooping, limp, floppy, falling, dropping,
slack, loose, lax, weak, feeble

sail *v*
1 *sail for France*
embark, set sail, leave port, weigh anchor, put to sea, put
off, go/travel by sea, cruise, yacht, boat, ship, voyage
2 CAPTAIN, skipper, pilot, navigate, steer
3 GLIDE, plane, sweep, float, drift, coast, skim, scud, fly,
wing, soar
■ **sail into**
attack, let fly, set about, turn on, assault
COLLOQ. lay into, tear into
■ **sail through**
deal with successfully, succeed in/pass easily, romp
through
Ea scrape through
See panel on next page

sailing *n*
boating, yachting

Terms used in sailing include:

abaft	going about	sailing by the lee
across the wind	gybe	sail trimming
alongside	handing (a sail)	sheeting in a sail
astern	hard on the wind	spilling wind
backing	heeling (to the	standing on
beam reach	wind)	starboard
bearing	in irons/in stays	stepping/
beat	knockdown (by	unstepping (the
beating	the wind)	mast)
bending (on a	laying off (a	tacking
sail)	course)	starboard tack
blanketing effect	lay up	steerage way
breaking out (the	lee helm	taking soundings
anchor)	lee-oh!	unbending (a sail)
broad reach	leeway	under way
casting off/letting	lift	upwind
go	points of sailing	veer (the anchor)
close-hauled	port	weather helm
close reach	port tack	weathering
coming about	reaching	windward
downwind	ready about!	yawing
fetch	running	
fitting-out	running goose-	
fixing a position	winged	

---

sailor *n*
seafarer, mariner, seaman
OLD (*Shakesp*) canvas-climber
COLLOQ. hearty, tar, Jack, Jack tar, sea dog, water rat; *Scot*
tarry-breeks
SLANG limey, matlo, matelot, salt

Types of sailor include:

AB	crewman	oarsman
able seaman	deck hand	pilot
bargee	fisherman	pirate
bluejacket	galiongee	purser
boatman	*N Am slang* gob	rating
boatswain (or	helmsman	rower
bosun)	lascar	sculler
buccaneer	leatherneck	skipper
cabin boy	*N Am* marine	Wren
captain	master	yachtsman
cox	mate	yachtswoman
coxswain	navigator	

Types of sail include:

Bermuda rig	foretop	jib	mainsail	spanker	topsail
canvas	fore-topgallant	jigger	maintopsail	spinnaker	trysail
course	fore-topsail	jury rig	mizzen	spritsail	
fore-and-aft rig	gaff sail	kite	moonraker	square sail	
foreroyal	gaff-topsail	lateen sail	rig	staysail	
foresail	genoa	lugsail	royal	studdingsail	
forestaysail	headsail	main course	skysail	topgallant	

saint *n*

sant, santon, patron saint, guardian saint, tutelar; *Scot* saunt
OLD hallow
See panel below

saintliness *n*

godliness, piety, devoutness, holiness, spirituality, blessedness, purity, spotlessness, faith, innocence, blamelessness, sinlessness, virtue, selflessness, morality, goodness, righteousness, sanctity, chastity, self-denial, self-sacrifice, asceticism, uprightness, unselfishness
E3 godlessness, unholiness, wickedness

saintly *adj*

saintlike, godly, pious, devout, God-fearing, holy, religious, spiritual, believing, blessed, angelic, pure, spotless, innocent, blameless, sinless, virtuous, moral, ethical, good, upright, worthy, righteous
E3 godless, unholy, wicked

sake *n*

benefit, advantage, good, welfare, wellbeing, gain, profit, behalf, interest, account, regard, respect, purpose, aim, goal, object, objective, cause, reason, consideration

salacious *adj*

prurient, bawdy, indecent, improper, obscene, scurrilous, pornographic, lecherous, lewd, carnal, coarse, erotic, horny, ribald, wanton, randy, lustful, raunchy, fruity, ruttish
OLD salt
FORMAL concupiscent, lascivious, libidinous, lubricious

COLLOQ. blue, smutty, steamy
E3 clean, decent, proper

salaciousness *n*

prurience, lewdness, obscenity, bawdiness, lustfulness, indecency, pornography, lecherousness
FORMAL concupiscence, lasciviousness
COLLOQ. smuttiness, steaminess

salaried *adj*

paid, remunerated, waged, stipendiary
FORMAL emolumental, emolumentary
E3 unpaid, voluntary, honorary

salary *n*

pay, remuneration, stipend, honorarium, wages, earnings, income, fee, allowance, weighting allowance
FORMAL emolument
SLANG screw

sale *n*

selling, marketing, vending, bargaining, disposal, trade, market, traffic, transaction, deal
See panel on next page
▪ **for sale**
on sale, up for sale, available, obtainable, on the market, for purchase, in the shops
COLLOQ. up for grabs

saleable *adj*

marketable, merchantable, sought-after, desirable
FORMAL vendible
E3 unmarketable, unsaleable

Groups of people with a patron saint include:

Accountants (Matthew)
Actors (Genesius; Vitus)
Advertisers (Bernardino of Siena)
Architects (Thomas Apostle)
Artists (Luke; Angelico)
Astronauts (Joseph of Cupertino)
Astronomers (Dominic)
Athletes (Sebastian)
Authors (Francis de Sales)
Aviators (Our Lady of Loreto)
Bakers (Honoratus)
Bankers (Bernardino (Feltre))
Barbers (Cosmas and Damian)
Blacksmiths (Eligius)
Bookkeepers (Matthew)
Book trade (John of God)
Brewers (Amand; Wenceslas)
Builders (Barbara; Thomas Apostle)
Butchers (Luke)
Carpenters (Joseph)
Chemists (Cosmas and Damian)
Comedians (Vitus)
Cooks (Lawrence; Martha)
Dancers (Vitus)
Dentists (Apollonia)
Doctors (Cosmas and Damian; Luke)
Editors (Francis de Sales)
Farmers (Isidore)
Firemen (Florian)

Fishermen (Andrew; Peter)
Florists (Dorothy; Thérèse of Lisieux)
Gardeners (Adam; Fiacre)
Glassworkers (Luke; Lucy)
Gravediggers (Joseph of Arimathea)
Grocers (Michael)
Hotelkeepers (Amand; Julian the Hospitaler)
Housewives (Martha)
Jewellers (Eligius)
Journalists (Francis de Sales)
Labourers (James; John Bosco)
Lawyers (Ivo; Thomas More)
Librarians (Jerome; Catherine of Alexandria)
Merchants (Francis of Assisi)
Messengers (Gabriel)
Metalworkers (Eligius)
Midwives (Raymond Nonnatus)
Miners (Anne; Barbara)
Motorists (Christopher)
Musicians (Cecilia; Gregory the Great)
Nurses (Camillus de Lellis; John of God)
Philosophers (Thomas Aquinas; Catherine of Alexandria)
Poets (Cecilia; David)
Police (Michael)
Postal workers (Gabriel)
Pregnant women (Margaret of Antioch)
Priests (Jean-Baptiste Vianney)

Printers (John of God)
Prisoners (Leonard)
Radio workers (Gabriel)
Sailors (Christopher; Erasmus; Francis of Paola)
Scholars (Thomas Aquinas)
Scientists (Albert the Great)
Sculptors (Luke; Louis)
Secretaries (Genesius)
Servants (Martha; Zita)
Shoemakers (Crispin; Crispinian)
Singers (Cecilia; Gregory)
Soldiers (George; Joan of Arc; Martin of Tours; Sebastian)
Students (Thomas Aquinas)
Surgeons (Luke; Cosmas and Damian)
Tailors (Homobonus)
Tax collectors (Matthew)
Taxi drivers (Fiacre)
Teachers (Gregory the Great; John Baptist de la Salle)
Television workers (Gabriel)
Theologians (Augustine; Alphonsus Liguori; Thomas Aquinas)
Undertakers (Dismas; Joseph of Arimathea)
Waiters (Martha)
Widows (Monica; Paula)
Workers (Joseph)
Writers (Lucy)

Types of sale include:

auction	*Aust* clearing sale	fleamarket	online auction	sale of bankrupt	telesales
autumn sale	closing-down	forced sale	online sale	stock	trade show
bargain offer	sale	garage sale	on-promotion	sale of the	trash and treasure
bazaar	cold call	grand opening	open market	century	sale
bazumble	e-auction	sale	pre-season sale	sale of work	warrant sale
boot-sale	end-of-line sale	introductory offer	private sale	second-hand sale	winter sale
bring-and-buy	end-of-season	January sale	public sale	special offer	
car-boot sale	sale	jumble sale	pyramid selling	spring sale	
charity sale	exhibition	mail order	remainder sale	stocktaking sale	
church bazaar	exposition	market	rummage sale	summer sale	
clearance sale	fair	mid-season sale		tabletop sale	

salesperson *n*
salesman, saleswoman, saleslady, sales assistant, shop
assistant, shop-boy, shop-girl, salesgirl, shopkeeper,
representative; *N Am* clerk, salesclerk
COLLOQ. rep

salient *adj*
important, significant, chief, main, principal, striking,
arresting, conspicuous, noticeable, obvious, prominent,
pronounced, outstanding, signal, remarkable
TECHNICAL saltant

saliva *n*
spit, spittle, slaver, drool, dribble, sputum, phlegm
FORMAL expectoration

sallow *adj*
yellowish, pale, pallid, wan, waxen, pasty, sickly, jaundiced,
unhealthy, anaemic, colourless, ashen
E3 rosy, healthy

sally[1] *v, n*
♦ *v*
1 RUSH, surge, attack, sortie, charge, breeze, venture, erupt,
foray, issue
2 SAUNTER, stroll, wander, promenade, amble
COLLOQ. mosey
E3 1 retire, retreat
♦ *n*
1 RUSH, raid, assault, attack, foray, incursion, offensive,
surge, sortie, thrust, venture, dash
2 EXCURSION, jaunt, wander, trip, drive, frolic, escapade

sally[2] *n*
RETORT, riposte, witticism, wisecrack, joke, jest, crack, quip,
bon mot, jeu d'esprit

salt *n, adj, v*
♦ *n*
1 *add a pinch of salt*
seasoning, taste, flavour, savour, relish, piquancy,
pungency, smack, punch, rock-salt, sea-salt
TECHNICAL sodium chloride
Related adjective: saline
2 LIVELINESS, zest, interest, wit, vigour, zip
FORMAL trenchancy, mordancy
3 SAILOR, seafarer, mariner, seaman, marine, rating
♦ *adj*
salted, saltish, salty, saline, brackish, briny
E3 fresh
■ **salt away**
store up, hoard, save, stash, stockpile, collect, cache, bank,
accumulate, amass, put/set aside, put away, hide
E3 spend, squander
■ **take with a pinch/grain of salt**
have reservations, have hesitations, have misgivings,
disbelieve, not fully believe, hesitate, question

salty *adj*
1 SALT, salted, saline, briny, brackish, savoury, spicy, piquant,
tangy
2 LIVELY, vigorous, witty, exciting, stimulating,
animated

FORMAL trenchant, mordant
E3 fresh, sweet

salubrious *adj*
sanitary, hygienic, health-giving, healthy, healthful,
wholesome, pleasant, beneficial, salutary, refreshing,
invigorating

salutary *adj*
1 GOOD, beneficial, advantageous, profitable, valuable,
helpful, useful, practical, timely
2 HEALTHY, sanitary, hygienic, health-giving, refreshing,
invigorating

salutation *n*
greeting, address, welcome, salute, reverence, respects,
homage
FORMAL obeisance

salute *v, n*
♦ *v*
1 GREET, acknowledge, recognize, wave, hail, address, nod,
bow, cap, honour, present arms
OLD halse, move, make your manners, salue
2 HONOUR, acknowledge, recognize, mark, celebrate, pay
tribute to
♦ *n*
1 GREETING, acknowledgement, recognition, welcome,
wave, gesture, hail, address, handshake, nod, bow,
reverence, banzai
TECHNICAL coupé
OLD half-cap
2 HONOUR, celebration, recognition, acknowledgement,
tribute, homage, salvo

salvage *v, n*
♦ *v*
save, preserve, conserve, rescue, recover, recuperate, retrieve,
get back, reclaim, redeem, repair, restore, retain, salve
E3 waste, abandon
♦ *n*
rescue, saving, recovery, retrieval, reclamation, raising,
restoration, reinstatement, regeneration, rescue, regaining

salvation *n*
deliverance, liberation, rescue, saving, preservation,
lifeline, redemption, reclamation
TECHNICAL soteriology
Related adjective: soterial
E3 loss, damnation

salve *n, v*
♦ *n*
ointment, lotion, cream, balm, liniment, medication,
preparation, application
FORMAL embrocation
♦ *v*
ease, lighten, relieve, calm, comfort, soothe

salver *n*
plate, dish, platter, tray, charger, trencher

same *adj, n*
♦ *adj*
1 IDENTICAL, twin, indistinguishable, equal, selfsame, the

very same, one and the same, very, alike, like, similar, duplicate, carbon copy, comparable, equivalent, matching, corresponding, mutual, reciprocal, interchangeable, unchanging, substitutable, synonymous
COLLOQ. samey
2 UNCHANGING, consistent, uniform, unvarying, unvariable, changeless, unchanged
COLLOQ. samey
E3 1 different **2** inconsistent, variable, changeable
◆ *n*
the above-mentioned, the above-named, ditto
FORMAL the aforementioned, the aforesaid
■ **all the same**
nevertheless, nonetheless, still, anyway, even so, yet, however, by any means, in any case/event, by some means, anyhow, but, regardless, for all that, in spite of everything
FORMAL notwithstanding

sameness *n*
changelessness, invariability, consistency, monotony, predictability, repetition, tedium, uniformity, standardization, resemblance, similarity, indistinguishability, likeness, identicalness, identity, oneness, duplication, déjà vu
E3 variety, difference

samey *adj*
same, similar, identical, uniform, indistinguishable, unchanging, monotonous, tedious, predictable
COLLOQ. *N Am* cookie-cutter

sample *n, v, adj*
◆ *n*
specimen, example, cross-section, representative, model, pattern, type, test, sampling, swatch, piece, demonstration, illustration, instance, sign, indication, foretaste
◆ *v*
try (out), test, taste, sip, inspect, examine, experience
◆ *adj*
representative, specimen, demonstrative, illustrative, typical, dummy, trial, test, pilot

sanatorium *n*
clinic, medical centre, health centre, hospital, infirmary

sanctification *n*
holiness, sacredness, piety, godliness, purity, righteousness, blessedness, devotion, spirituality

sanctify *v*
1 HALLOW, consecrate, make holy, make sacred, bless, anoint, dedicate, set apart, cleanse, purify, wash, absolve, exalt, canonize
2 SANCTION, authorize, allow, permit, approve, ratify, confirm, support, back, endorse, underwrite, accredit, license, warrant, legitimize
E3 1 desecrate, defile **2** veto, forbid, disapprove

sanctimonious *adj*
self-righteous, holier-than-thou, holy, pious, pietistic, moralizing, smug, superior, hypocritical, priggish, pharisaical
FORMAL unctuous
COLLOQ. goody-goody, pi
E3 humble

sanctimoniousness *n*
self-righteousness, moralizing, righteousness, hypocrisy, self-satisfaction, priggishness, pietism, preachiness, complacency, cant, smugness, humbug, pharisaism
FORMAL unctuousness
E3 humility

sanction *n, v*
◆ *n*
1 AUTHORIZATION, permission, agreement, approval,

ratification, confirmation, support, backing, endorsement, licence, authority, suffrage
OLD approof
FORMAL approbation, accreditation, subscription, countenance
COLLOQ. OK, go-ahead, green light, thumbs-up
2 *impose sanctions on a country*
restriction, boycott, embargo, ban, prohibition, penalty, deterrent, punishment, sentence
◆ *v*
authorize, allow, permit, approve, ratify, confirm, support, back, endorse, underwrite, accredit, license, warrant, legitimize, ratify, sustain
TECHNICAL royalize
OLD sanctify
FORMAL accredit, fiat
COLLOQ. OK, give the go-ahead to, give the green light to, give the thumbs-up to
E3 veto, forbid, disapprove

sanctity *n*
holiness, sacredness, inviolability, piety, godliness, saintliness, blessedness, religiousness, devotion, grace, spirituality, purity, goodness, virtue, righteousness, sanctification
FORMAL sacrosanctity
E3 unholiness, secularity, worldliness, godlessness, impurity

sanctuary *n*
1 CHURCH, temple, tabernacle, shrine, altar, place of worship, holy place, holy of holies
TECHNICAL oracle, nymphaeum
FORMAL sacrarium, sanctum, sanctum sanctorum, delubrum
2 ASYLUM, refuge, protection, shelter, haven, retreat, hideout, hideaway
OLD grith
3 SAFETY, protection, security, safeguard, immunity
OLD privilege, frith
4 RESERVE, reservation, park, area, enclave, tract, preserve

sanctum *n*
1 HOLY PLACE, holy of holies, shrine, sanctuary
FORMAL sanctum sanctorum
2 REFUGE, retreat, den, hideaway, hideout, study, cubbyhole

sand *n*
beach, shore, strand, sands, seashore, desert, wilderness, grit, rock
Related adjectives: arenaceous, sabulous

sandbank *n*
dune, reef, sand bar, sandhill, bar, hurst, key, yardang

sandy *adj*
gritty, ginger, rusty, tawny, reddish, reddish-yellow, yellow, yellowish, yellowy, gingerous, gingery, auburn, coppery, red, Titian
TECHNICAL arenaceous, psammitic

sane *adj*
normal, rational, right-minded, balanced, well-balanced, lucid, in your right mind, of sound mind, stable, sound, sober, level-headed, yourself, herself, himself, sensible, responsible, wise, reasonable, moderate, *compos mentis*; *Scot* wice
OLD (*Shakesp*) formal
FORMAL judicious, *mens sana in corpore sano*
COLLOQ. all there
E3 insane, mad, crazy, foolish

sang-froid *n*
composure, aplomb, self-control, poise, self-possession, indifference, equanimity, assurance, calmness, dispassion, cool-headedness, nonchalance, coolness, imperturbability
FORMAL phlegm

COLLOQ. nerve, cool, unflappability
E3 discomposure, excitability, hysteria, panic

sanguinary *adj*
bloody, bloodied, gory, grim, bloodthirsty, brutal, cruel, merciless, murderous, savage, pitiless, ruthless

sanguine *adj*
1 CHEERFUL, confident, hopeful, lively, expectant, optimistic, over-confident, over-optimistic, assured, animated, ardent, buoyant, spirited, roseate, unabashed, unbowed
2 RUDDY, rosy, florid, red, pink, fresh-complexioned, fresh, flushed, roseate
FORMAL rubicund
E3 1 cynical, depressive, gloomy, melancholy, pessimistic
2 pale, sallow

sanitary *adj*
clean, pure, uncontaminated, unpolluted, aseptic, antiseptic, germ-free, disinfected, sterile, hygienic, healthy, wholesome
FORMAL salubrious
E3 insanitary, unwholesome

sanitize *v*
1 PURIFY, sterilize, decontaminate, refine, filter, clean, cleanse, freshen, disinfect, fumigate, deodorize
2 MAKE ACCEPTABLE, make presentable, expurgate, make palatable

sanity *n*
normality, rationality, reason, sense, common sense, good sense, balance of mind, soundness of mind, lucidity, right-mindedness, stability, soundness, level-headedness, prudence, wisdom, responsibility
FORMAL judiciousness
E3 insanity, madness

sap *v, n*
♦ *v*
bleed, drain, exhaust, weaken, wear down/away, erode, enfeeble, debilitate, undermine, deplete, reduce, diminish, impair
FORMAL enervate
E3 strengthen, build up, increase
♦ *n*
1 *sap in a plant*
lifeblood, vital fluid, plant fluid, juice, essence, vigour, energy
2 FOOL, idiot, imbecile, moron
COLLOQ. clot, twit, nit, nitwit
SLANG jerk, prat, git, fink

sarcasm *n*
irony, satire, mockery, sneering, ridicule, scoffing, derision, scorn, contempt, gibing, cynicism, resentment, acidity, acrimony, spitefulness, bitterness
OLD wipe
FORMAL invective, trenchancy, mordancy

sarcastic *adj*
ironical, satirical, satiric, mocking, snide, taunting, sneering, derisive, derisory, scornful, sardonic, jeering, scoffing, scathing, cynical, incisive, cutting, sharp, witty, biting, caustic, acid, pungent, back-handed, Juvenalian, Voltairian
FORMAL disparaging, acerbic, mordant, invective
COLLOQ. sarky

sarcastically *adv*
ironically, satirically, scornfully, cynically, jeeringly, tauntingly, scathingly

sardonic *adj*
mocking, jeering, sneering, derisive, scornful, contemptuous, sarcastic, dry, biting, cruel, heartless, malicious, cynical, acrimonious, bitter
FORMAL acerbic, mordant

sash *n*
belt, girdle, scarf, waistband, cummerbund, cincture, lungi, obi, baldric
OLD shash, burdash

sassy *adj*
cheeky, impertinent, impudent, insolent, disrespectful, forward, brazen, pert, audacious, overfamiliar
COLLOQ. fresh, saucy, lippy, mouthy
E3 respectful, polite

Satan *n*
the Devil, the Enemy, the Adversary, the Evil One, the Tempter, the serpent, Beelzebub, Lucifer, Old Nick, Prince of Darkness, prince of this world, Mephistopheles, Belial, Apollyon, Abaddon, arch-enemy, Shaitan
OLD leviathan

satanic *adj*
satanical, diabolical, diabolic, devilish, demonic, fiendish, hellish, infernal, damned, accursed, inhuman, wicked, malevolent, sulphurous, evil, sinful, abominable, black, dark
FORMAL iniquitous
E3 holy, divine, godly, saintly, benevolent

sate *v*
satisfy, overfill, saturate, surfeit, fill, glut, gorge, gratify, cloy, sicken, slake
FORMAL satiate
E3 deprive, dissatisfy, starve

satellite *n*
1 ORBITING BODY, natural/artificial satellite, spacecraft, moon, planet, spaceship, space station, sputnik
2 *the USSR and its former satellites*
dependency, colony, province, protectorate, dominion
3 DEPENDANT, hanger-on, parasite, sycophant, subordinate, follower, attendant, aide, adherent, disciple, minion, lackey, sidekick, retainer, vassal
COLLOQ. puppet

satiate *v*
sate, overfill, fill, overfeed, satisfy, gorge, slake, glut, cloy, engorge, stuff, surfeit, jade, nauseate
E3 deprive, dissatisfy, underfeed

satiety *n*
satiation, saturation, satisfaction, gratification, fullness, over-fullness, overindulgence, surfeit
OLD (*Shakesp*) cloyment
FORMAL repleteness, repletion

satire *n*
ridicule, irony, sarcasm, wit, burlesque, lampoon, skit, parody, caricature, travesty, jeer, comedy of manners
OLD glance
FORMAL invective
COLLOQ. send-up, spoof, take-off, mickey-taking
SLANG piss-taking

satirical *adj*
ironical, sarcastic, mocking, ridiculing, irreverent, taunting, derisive, sardonic, incisive, cutting, biting, caustic, cynical, bitter, Swiftian, Archilochian
FORMAL trenchant, acerbic, mordant, invective

satirist *n*
cartoonist, mocker, parodist, ridiculer, caricaturist, lampooner, lampoonist, pasquilant, pasquiler, pasquinader

satirize *v*
ridicule, mock, make fun of, poke fun at, burlesque, lampoon, parody, caricature, criticize
FORMAL deride
COLLOQ. send up, take off, take the mickey out of
SLANG take the piss out of
E3 acclaim, honour

satisfaction *n*
1 GRATIFICATION, contentment, happiness, pleasure, enjoyment, delight, comfort, ease, wellbeing, fulfilment, self-satisfaction, pride, sense of achievement
2 SETTLEMENT, compensation, reimbursement, indemnification, indemnity, damages, reparation, amends, redress, recompense, requital, vindication, restitution
1 dissatisfaction, displeasure

satisfactorily *adv*
acceptably, passably, adequately, competently, sufficiently, favourably, nicely
unsatisfactorily, unacceptably, inadequately

satisfactory *adj*
acceptable, passable, up to the mark, all right, fair, average, competent, adequate, fine, sufficient, suitable, proper, well, favourable, nice
COLLOQ. OK, up to scratch, tickety-boo; *N Am* copacetic, A-OK; *Aust* sweet
unsatisfactory, unacceptable, inadequate

satisfied *adj*
1 HAPPY, contented, pleased, self-satisfied, content, smug
2 CONVINCED, reassured, persuaded, sure, certain, positive, pacified
3 FULL, sated, satiated
FORMAL replete
1 dissatisfied; *colloq.* disgruntled **2** unconvinced, unsure **3** hungry

satisfy *v*
1 GRATIFY, indulge, content, please, delight, appease, quench, slake, sate, satiate, surfeit
OLD agree, pay, apay
FORMAL assuage
2 *satisfy requirements*
meet, fulfil, discharge, settle, answer, fill, be sufficient for, be adequate for, comply with, supply, serve, qualify
FORMAL suffice
3 ASSURE, reassure, convince, persuade
4 COMPENSATE FOR, indemnify, make reparation for, stay
FORMAL appease, placate, requite
OLD defray
1 dissatisfy **2** fail

satisfying *adj*
pleasing, fulfilling, gratifying, cheering, pleasurable, satisfactory, convincing, persuasive, filling, cool, refreshing, harmonious, enough, square
dissatisfying, frustrating, unsatisfactory

saturate *v*
1 SOAK, make wet through, wet, steep, flood, souse, drench, waterlog
2 IMPREGNATE, permeate, imbue, pervade, suffuse, fill, overfill, sate, glut, surfeit

saturated *adj*
1 SOAKED, soaking, sopping, dripping, soused, steeped, drenched, flooded, wringing, waterlogged, sodden
2 IMBUED, impregnated, permeated, suffused

saturation *n*
filling, flooding, soaking, pervading, permeation, suffusion, glutting, sating, satiation

saturnine *adj*
morose, gloomy, unfriendly, sombre, severe, austere, dismal, dour, dull, grave, melancholy, moody, glum, stern, heavy, withdrawn, taciturn, uncommunicative, phlegmatic
cheerful, jovial

sauce *n*
1 DRESSING, relish, condiment, flavouring, dip, mayonnaise
2 CHEEKINESS, cheek, impudence, impertinence, presumption, presumptuousness, audacity, freshness, flippancy, pertness, backchat, brazenness, insolence, disrespectfulness, disrespect, irreverence, rudeness, sass

FORMAL malapertness
COLLOQ. brass, lip, nerve, sauciness, mouth
2 politeness, respectfulness

saucepan *n*
pan, pot, skillet, casserole, wok, container, vessel, frying-pan, fryer, pancheon

saucy *adj*
impertinent, impudent, insolent, brazen, presumptuous, disrespectful, irreverent, rude, cheeky, pert, forward, presumptuous, flippant
COLLOQ. fresh, lippy; *N Am* sassy
polite, respectful

saunter *v, n*
♦ *v*
stroll, amble, wander, ramble, meander; *dialect* dander, shool; *Scot* dacker
OLD promenade
COLLOQ. mosey, mooch, knock about/around, toddle
♦ *n*
stroll, amble, walk, constitutional, ramble
OLD promenade
COLLOQ. mosey, mooch

savage *adj, n, v*
♦ *adj*
wild, untamed, undomesticated, uncivilized, primitive, barbaric, barbarous, fierce, ferocious, vicious, beastly, cruel, terrible, inhuman, grim, brutal, sadistic, bloodthirsty, bloody, murderous, pitiless, merciless, ruthless, harsh, catamountain, warrigal
OLD salvage, fell, immane
FORMAL feral
COLLOQ. cut-throat, dog-eat-dog
tame, civilized, humane, mild
♦ *n*
brute, boor, churl, beast, monster, barbarian, wild person, wild man, wild woman
OLD salvage
♦ *v*
1 *savaged by a dog*
attack, bite, claw, tear, tear to pieces, lacerate, maul, mangle
2 *savaged by the critics*
attack, slate, run down, denounce
COLLOQ. slam, rubbish, pull/tear to pieces, pull/tear to shreds, go to town on, pick holes in, do a hatchet job on

savagely *adv*
viciously, brutally, cruelly, ruthlessly, harshly, mercilessly, pitilessly, fiercely, ferociously, barbarically, barborously

savagery *n*
cruelty, fierceness, ferocity, viciousness, wildness, roughness, barbarity, bestiality, brutality, inhumanity, ruthlessness, mercilessness, pitilessness, murderousness, bloodthirstiness, brutishness, sadism, primitiveness
FORMAL ferity
civilization, civility, humanity

savant *n*
authority, scholar, intellectual, pundit, guru, mastermind, man/woman of letters, master, philosopher
FORMAL sage
amateur, ignoramus

save *v, prep*
♦ *v*
1 RESCUE, come to the rescue of, deliver, liberate, free, set free, release, get someone out of, redeem, salvage, recover, reclaim
COLLOQ. bail out
2 *save food*
conserve, preserve, keep, retain, hold, reserve, store, lay up, set aside, put by, put aside, hoard, stockpile, collect, gather

COLLOQ. stash

3 ECONOMIZE, cut back, cut costs, use less, budget, buy cheaply, live on the cheap, be thrifty, scrimp and save
COLLOQ. tighten your belt, cut your coat according to your cloth
4 PROTECT, guard, screen, keep, shield, safeguard, keep safe, preserve, spare, prevent, hinder
FORMAL obviate
E3 2 waste, discard **3** spend, squander

♦ *prep*
apart from, except (for), not counting, excepted, aside from, excluding, with the exception of, but for

---

Synonym nuances
verb sense 1
You can use **rescue** to suggest removal from a dangerous or disagreeable situation, while **deliver** likewise has connotations of removing from potential harm or evil: *people delivered from fear, oppression and famine.* **Liberate**, on the other hand, suggests restoring freedom, and the terms **free**, **set free** and **release** all echo this suggestion of getting someone out of captivity.
  Redeem, however, might be used with a more figurative sense of undoing damage: *her performance redeemed the show,* though it may also be used more literally to imply getting back in return for money: *redeem a debt.* It can also have religious connotations of being saved from sin. **Salvage** and **recover** can be used for retrieving whatever you can from being lost: *stained glass windows salvaged from ruined churches.*

---

saving *adj, n*
♦ *adj*
1 ECONOMICAL, careful, sparing, thrifty, frugal
2 *a saving grace*
redeeming, compensating, qualifying, compensatory, extenuating, mitigating
♦ *n*
1 ECONOMY, thrift, discount, reduction, bargain, cut, conservation, preservation
2 *put your savings in the bank*
capital, investments, nest egg, fund, store, reserves, resources
E3 1 expense, loss, waste **2** expenditure, outgoings

saviour *n*
1 RESCUER, deliverer, redeemer, liberator, emancipator, guardian, protector, defender, champion, messiah
2 *Jesus Christ, the Saviour*
Redeemer, Deliverer, Lamb of God, Mediator, Emmanuel, Christ, Messiah
E3 1 destroyer

savoir-faire *n*
capability, ability, accomplishment, confidence, assurance, discretion, expertise, finesse, poise, diplomacy, tact, urbanity, social grace(s)
COLLOQ. knowhow
E3 awkwardness, clumsiness, incompetence, inexperience

savour *n, v*
♦ *n*
1 TASTE, flavour, smack, tang, piquancy, salt, spice, relish, zest; *Scot* sair
2 SMELL, aroma, bouquet, fragrance, perfume, scent, odour
3 TRACE, hint, suggestion, touch, smattering
♦ *v*
1 RELISH, taste to the full, enjoy, enjoy to the full, delight in, take pleasure in, revel in, like, appreciate; *Scot* sar, sair
2 SMACK, suggest, speak, smell, seem like, have all the signs of, have the hallmarks of
OLD resent
E3 1 shrink from

savoury *adj, n*
♦ *adj*
1 TASTY, flavoursome, appetizing, delicious, mouthwatering, luscious, palatable, sapid; *Scot* gustie
OLD gustful
COLLOQ. yummy, scrumptious, scrummy
2 *savoury pancakes*
salty, spicy, aromatic, piquant, tangy
E3 1 unappetizing, unsavoury, tasteless, insipid **2** sweet, sugary
♦ *n*
appetizer, snack, *hors d'œuvre*, bonne-bouche, canapé, tapas

savvy *adj*
shrewd, astute, well-advised, calculated, far-sighted, smart, clever, intelligent, sharp, keen, acute, alert, perceptive, observant, discerning, discriminating, knowing, calculating, cunning, crafty, wily, canny, artful, sly
FORMAL callid, judicious, sagacious, perspicacious
E3 unwise, obtuse, naive, unsophisticated

saw¹

Kinds of saw include:

band-saw	fretsaw	pruning saw
bench saw	hacksaw	rabbet saw
chainsaw	handsaw	radial-arm saw
circular saw	jigsaw	ripsaw
compass saw	panel saw	scroll saw
coping-saw	power-driven	tenon saw
crosscut saw	saw	

---

saw² *n*
SAYING, byword, proverb, maxim, aphorism, adage, axiom, dictum, epigram, commonplace, gnome, mot
FORMAL apophthegm

say *v, n*
♦ *v*
1 EXPRESS, phrase, put, put into words, mention, render, utter, voice, articulate, enunciate, pronounce, deliver, speak, rehearse, recite, repeat, perform, read, indicate
FORMAL orate
2 ANSWER, reply, respond, rejoin, retort, exclaim, comment, remark, observe, mention, add, drawl, mutter, grunt
FORMAL ejaculate
3 TELL, instruct, order, communicate, convey, intimate, report, announce, declare, state, assert, affirm, maintain, claim, allege, rumour, suggest, imply, signify, reveal, disclose, divulge
4 GUESS, estimate, reckon, judge, imagine, suppose, assume, presume, surmise
♦ *n*
1 *have a say in something*
voice, word, opinion, vote, right to express yourself, opportunity to speak, turn/chance to speak
2 *have no say in the matter*
influence, power, authority, sway, weight
COLLOQ. clout
■ **that is to say**
ie, that is, in other words, to put it another way

saying *n*
adage, proverb, dictum, precept, axiom, aphorism, maxim, motto, slogan, phrase, catch phrase, cliché, platitude, expression, quotation, epigram, statement, remark, word/pearl of wisdom
FORMAL apophthegm

say-so *n*
authorization, permission, agreement, approval, consent, affirmation, authority, backing, assertion, assurance, word, guarantee, ratification, sanction

FORMAL asseveration, dictum
COLLOQ. OK, go-ahead, green light, thumbs-up

scaffold n
1 PLATFORM, framework, scaffolding, gantry, stage, tower
2 GALLOWS, gibbet, the rope
OLD catasta

scald v
burn, sear, brand, scorch, blister
FORMAL cauterize

scalding adj
extremely hot, burning, boiling, blistering, piping hot,
steaming

scale¹ n, v
♦ n
1 *the Richter scale*
graduation, calibration, system of measurement,
measuring system, calibrated system, register
2 EXTENT, level, degree, measure, spread, reach, range,
scope, compass, spectrum, gamut
3 *What is the scale of the map?*
ratio, proportion, relative size
4 SEQUENCE, series, gamut, progression, hierarchy, ranking,
order, ladder
COLLOQ. pecking order
♦ v
climb, go up, ascend, mount, clamber, scramble, shin up,
conquer, surmount
■ **scale down**
decrease, make less, lessen, reduce, cut back/down, drop,
contract, shrink
■ **scale up**
increase, expand, raise, boost, improve, enhance, further,
step up, intensify, strengthen, develop, build up,
accumulate, expand
FORMAL augment
COLLOQ. hike up, bump up

scale² n
scale in a kettle; scales on a fish
encrustation, deposit, crust, layer, coat, coating, limescale,
tartar, plaque, film, lamina, plate, flake, scurf, furfur
FORMAL squama
Related adjective: squamose

scaliness n
dandruff, flakiness, furfur, scurfiness, scabrousness
FORMAL squamosity

scaly adj
flaky, scurfy, scabby, scabrous, rough, branny
FORMAL lepidote, furfuraceous, furfurous, squamose,
squamous, squamulose, desquamative, desquamatory

scam n
racket, swindle, fraud, fiddle, deception, trick, dodge,
scheme, business
COLLOQ. con, game
SLANG rip-off; *N Am* gold brick

scamp n
rogue, rascal, scallywag, monkey, mischief-maker,
troublemaker, imp, devil, wretch, good-for-nothing,
reprobate, vagabond, losel, *fripon*; *dialect* skellum; *Irish*
spalpeen
COLLOQ. whippersnapper, blighter, bugger

scamper v
scuttle, scurry, dart, dash, run, sprint, rush, hurry, race,
scramble, fly, romp, frolic, gambol
FORMAL hasten
COLLOQ. scoot

scan v, n
♦ v
1 EXAMINE, scrutinize, inspect, study, search, survey, sweep,
investigate, check, spell

OLD con
2 SKIM, have a quick look at, browse through, run through,
run over, go over, glance at, flick through, flip through,
thumb through, leaf through, run your eye over
♦ n
screening, examination, scrutiny, inspection, search,
probe, check, study, investigation, test, survey, review
TECHNICAL scintilliscan, sector scan, CAT scan

scandal n
1 OUTRAGE, offence, outcry, uproar, furore, discredit,
dishonour, disgrace, shame, embarrassment, ignominy,
-gate
FORMAL obloquy, opprobrium
2 GOSSIP, rumours, libel, slander, smear, dirt, *chronique
scandaleuse*
FORMAL defamation, calumny
COLLOQ. dirty linen/washing/laundry, skeleton in the
cupboard
3 DISGRACE, shame, pity, reproach, blot, slur, smear, stain,
black mark
COLLOQ. crying shame

scandalize v
shock, horrify, appal, dismay, disgust, repel, revolt, offend,
insult, affront, outrage

scandalmonger n
gossip, gossip-monger, tattler, tattle, talebearer, busybody,
quidnunc
FORMAL calumniator, defamer, traducer
COLLOQ. muck-raker, Nosey Parker

scandalous adj
shocking, appalling, atrocious, abominable, monstrous,
unspeakable, outrageous, blatant, flagrant, disgraceful,
shameful, disreputable, dishonourable, infamous,
improper, malicious, scurrilous, sensational, gamey,
slanderous, libellous, untrue
FORMAL unseemly, defamatory, opprobrious
COLLOQ. juicy

scant adj
little, sparse, limited, little or no, bare, deficient, minimal,
hardly any, inadequate, insufficient
FORMAL exiguous
COLLOQ. measly
F∃ adequate, ample, sufficient

scantily adv
poorly, meagerly, inadequately, insufficiently, deficiently,
skimpily, barely, sparsely
F∃ adequately, sufficiently

scanty adj
deficient, short, inadequate, insufficient, scant, little,
limited, restricted, narrow, poor, meagre, insubstantial,
thin, skimpy, sparse, bare
F∃ adequate, sufficient, ample, plentiful, substantial

scapegoat n
victim, whipping-boy, sucker
COLLOQ. fall guy; ; *Aust* bunny
SLANG *N Am* patsy

scar n, v
♦ n
mark, lesion, wound, injury, shock, trauma, defacement,
disfigurement, discolouration, blemish, blotch, stigma,
trauma, pockmark, pockpit, sword-cut, cicatrice
TECHNICAL desmoid, hilum, leaf-cushion, keloid, ulosis
OLD (*Shakesp*) wipe
FORMAL cicatricula
♦ v
mark, deface, disfigure, discolour, spoil, damage, injure,
shock, traumatize, brand, stigmatize

scarce adj
few, rare, infrequent, uncommon, unusual, sparse, scanty,

scant, meagre, in short supply, too little, not enough, insufficient, inadequate, deficient, lacking, dear
COLLOQ. few and far between, like gold dust
E3 plentiful, common
■ **make yourself scarce**
leave quickly, go fast, dash off, rush away, take to your heels
COLLOQ. scoot, make tracks, run for it

scarcely adv
1 *I can scarcely hear you*
hardly, barely, only just
2 *that is scarcely a reason to hit him*
hardly, not, not at all, certainly not, definitely not
3 *scarcely had I put the phone down when it rang again*
hardly, barely, only just, no sooner

scarcity n
lack, shortage, dearth, deficiency, insufficiency, rareness, rarity, infrequency, uncommonness, sparseness, scantness, scantiness
FORMAL paucity, want, exiguity
E3 glut, plenty, abundance, sufficiency, enough

scare v, n
♦ v
frighten, startle, alarm, make afraid, make frightened, dismay, daunt, intimidate, unnerve, threaten, menace, terrorize, shock, appal, panic, terrify, petrify
FORMAL perturb
COLLOQ. rattle, scare someone out of their wits, make someone's blood run cold, scare silly, scare the living daylights out of, make someone's hair stand on end, make someone's flesh creep, make someone jump out of their skin, put the frighteners on, put the wind up
SLANG scare the shit out of
E3 reassure, calm
♦ n
fright, start, shock, alarm, panic, hysteria, horror, terror, fearfulness
E3 reassurance, comfort

scared adj
afraid, frightened, fearful, nervous, anxious, worried, startled, alarmed, cowed, shaken, panic-stricken, panicky, quivery, terrified, petrified, terrorized, terror-stricken, unnerved, jittery, nervous
COLLOQ. scared out of your wits, scared to death, with your heart in your mouth, shaking like a leaf, having kittens, in a blue funk
E3 confident, reassured

scaremonger n
alarmist, pessimist, prophet of doom, doom and gloom merchant, doomwatcher, jitterbug, Cassandra

scarf n
headscarf, headsquare, kerchief, neckerchief, muffler, necktie, shawl, stole, cravat, babushka, sash, comforter, pagri, vexillum
TECHNICAL orarium, tippet
OLD screen, nightingale

scarper v
leave, depart, go, run away, vanish, disappear, abscond, bolt, escape, flee, decamp, flit
COLLOQ. clear off, beat it, bunk off, run for it, make a run for it, scram, skedaddle, vamoose, hightail it, do a bunk

scary adj
frightening, alarming, daunting, formidable, fearsome, forbidding, intimidating, disturbing, shocking, horrifying, terrifying, petrifying, hair-raising, bloodcurdling, spine-chilling, chilling, creepy, eerie
COLLOQ. spooky, hairy, white-knuckle

scathing adj
withering, sarcastic, scornful, critical, cutting, biting, stinging, caustic, acid, vitriolic, ferocious, fierce, severe,

bitter, harsh, brutal, savage, unsparing, devastating
FORMAL trenchant, mordant
E3 complimentary

scatter v
disperse, dispel, dissipate, disband, disunite, separate, divide, break up, disintegrate, diffuse, broadcast, spread, sprinkle, sow, strew, fling, shower, spatter, splutter, shake, dissipate, dot, intersperse, litter, blind, cast/fling/throw to the winds; *dialect* scamble; *Scot* skail
TECHNICAL backscatter
OLD bescatter, flurr, shatter, squander
FORMAL disseminate, disject
E3 gather, collect

scatterbrained adj
forgetful, absent-minded, empty-headed, feather-brained, hare-brained, careless, inattentive, thoughtless, unreliable, impulsive, irresponsible, wool-gathering, frivolous, slaphappy, carefree
COLLOQ. scatty, dizzy, having your head in the clouds, airheaded; *N Am* ditsy
E3 sensible, sober, efficient, careful

scattering n
sprinkling, few, handful, smattering, break-up
E3 mass, abundance

scavenge v
forage, rummage, rake, search, look for, hunt, scrounge

scavenger n
rummager, scavager, forager, scrounger, raker

scenario n
1 SITUATION, scene, circumstances, state, state of affairs, sequence of events, plan, programme
2 OUTLINE, synopsis, summary, résumé, storyline, script, screenplay, plot, scheme, plan, programme, projection, sequence

scene n
1 PLACE, area, spot, location, locale, site, situation, position, whereabouts, locality, environment, milieu, setting, context, background, backdrop, arena, set, stage
2 LANDSCAPE, scenery, panorama, view, vista, outlook, prospect, sight, spectacle, picture, tableau, pageant
3 EPISODE, incident, proceeding, part, division, act, clip
4 *don't make a scene*
fuss, commotion, outburst, tantrum, furore, performance, drama, exhibition, display, show
COLLOQ. to-do, kerfuffle
5 *not my scene*
area of interest, area of activity, field, area, speciality
■ **behind the scenes**
secretly, not in public, out of the public eye, privately, in private, behind closed doors, surreptitiously, on the quiet, out of sight, backstage

scenery n
landscape, terrain, panorama, view, vista, outlook, prospect, scene, background, setting, surroundings, backdrop, set, *mise-en-scène*

scenic adj
panoramic, picturesque, attractive, pretty, beautiful, grand, striking, impressive, spectacular, breathtaking, awe-inspiring
E3 dull, dreary

scent n, v
♦ n
1 FRAGRANCE, aroma, perfume, bouquet, smell, odour
FORMAL redolence
2 PERFUME, essence, cologne, eau-de-cologne, eau-de-toilette, toilet water
3 *follow the scent*
track, trail, trace, spoor
E3 **1** stink

• v

1 SMELL, sniff (out), nose (out), track, trail, trace
2 SENSE, become aware of, become conscious of, perceive, detect, discern, recognize

scented adj
perfumed, fragrant, sweet-smelling, aromatic
Ea malodorous, stinking

sceptic n
doubter, unbeliever, disbeliever, agnostic, atheist, rationalist, questioner, scoffer, cynic, doubting Thomas
Ea believer

sceptical adj
doubting, doubtful, unconvinced, unbelieving, disbelieving, incredulous, questioning, distrustful, mistrustful, hesitating, hesitant, dubious, suspicious, scoffing, cynical, academic, pessimistic, infidel, Voltairian
Ea convinced, confident, trusting

scepticism n
doubt, unbelief, disbelief, hesitancy, agnosticism, atheism, rationalism, distrust, doubtfulness, dubiety, suspicion, incredulity, cynicism, pessimism
Ea belief, faith

schedule n, v
• n
timetable, programme, agenda, diary, calendar, itinerary, plan, scheme, list, syllabus, inventory, catalogue, table, form
• v
timetable, time, table, programme, plan, organize, arrange, appoint, assign, book, list; N Am slate
OLD (Shakesp) enschedule
■ **behind schedule**
behind time, behindhand, late, running late, overdue
■ **on schedule**
on time, on target, according to plan, on course, on track

schema n
outline, profile, sketch, tracing, form, shape, design, figure, layout, plan, chart, diagram, map
FORMAL configuration, delineation, lineament

schematic adj
diagrammatic, representational, symbolic, simplified, illustrative, graphic

scheme n, v
• n
1 PROGRAMME, schedule, plan, project, strategy, tactics, system, method, procedure, course of action, idea, proposal, proposition, suggestion, draft, outline, blueprint, schema, diagram, chart, map, layout, sketch, pattern, design, shape, arrangement
OLD practice
FORMAL configuration, disposition, delineation
COLLOQ. Aust & NZ dart
2 INTRIGUE, plot, conspiracy, device, stratagem, ruse, ploy, shift, manoeuvre, tactic(s), strategy
FORMAL machinations
• v
plot, conspire, connive, collude, intrigue, manoeuvre, manipulate, pull strings, mastermind, plan, project, contrive, devise, frame, work out
FORMAL machinate

schemer n
plotter, intriguer, politician, conniver, deceiver, mastermind, intrig(u)ant(e), Machiavelli, Machiavellian, éminence grise, fox, contriver
FORMAL machinator
COLLOQ. wangler, wheeler-dealer, wire-puller

scheming adj
crafty, cunning, deceitful, sly, underhand, unscrupulous, wily, devious, artful, manipulative, calculating, conniving,

designing, insidious, tricky, slippery, foxy, Machiavellian
FORMAL duplicitous
Ea artless, honest, open, transparent

schism n
1 DIVISION, split, rift, rupture, break, breach, disunion, separation, severance, discord
FORMAL estrangement, scission
2 SPLINTER, group, faction, sect, detachment

schismatic adj
breakaway, rebel, dissenting, separatist, renegade, heretical
FORMAL apostate, seceding, secessionist

schmaltz n
sentimentality, emotionalism, romanticism, mawkishness
COLLOQ. slush, mush, gush, pulp, soppiness, sloppiness

scholar n
1 STUDENT, pupil, learner, schoolchild, schoolboy, schoolgirl, day-scholar, day-boy, day-girl
COLLOQ. schoolie
2 ACADEMIC, intellectual, authority, expert, philosopher, mastermind, pundit, bookman, man/woman/person of letters, savant, scholastic, schoolman
OLD artsman, clerk
COLLOQ. egghead, bookworm

scholarly adj
learned, erudite, lettered, academic, scholastic, school, intellectual, highbrow, bookish, studious, knowledgeable, well-read, conscientious, analytical, scientific
Ea uneducated, illiterate

scholarship n
1 LEARNING, learnedness, knowledge, wisdom, education, schooling, academic achievements/attainments
FORMAL erudition
2 *a scholarship to a public school*
grant, award, bursary, endowment, fellowship, exhibition

scholastic adj
academic, scholarly, educational, pedagogic, learned, lettered, literary, bookish, analytical, pedantic, precise

school n, v
• n
1 *go to school*
college, academy, institute, institution, university, seminary, faculty, department, division, discipline, class, group, pupils, students, yeshiva(h)
See also **educational establishments.**
2 *a school of artists*
group, set, circle, clique, coterie, faction, association, club, society, guild, league, company
• v
educate, teach, instruct, tutor, coach, train, discipline, drill, verse, prime, prepare, indoctrinate

schooling n
education, learning, book-learning, teaching, instruction, tuition, coaching, training, drill, preparation, grounding, guidance, indoctrination

schoolteacher n
teacher, instructor, educator, schoolmaster, master, schoolmistress, mistress, schoolmarm, pedagogue; Scot dominie
COLLOQ. Aust schoolie

science n
technology, discipline, specialization, knowledge, skill, proficiency, expertise, technique, dexterity, art
See panel on next page

scientific adj
methodical, systematic, controlled, regulated, orderly, analytical, mathematical, exact, precise, accurate, scholarly, thorough

Sciences include:

acoustics	biophysics	electronics	information	microbiology	sociology
aerodynamics	botany	engineering	technology	mineralogy	space technology
aeronautics	chemistry	entomology	inorganic	morphology	telecom-
agricultural	chemurgy	environmental	chemistry	natural science	munications
science (or	climatology	science	life science	nuclear physics	thermodynamics
agriscience)	computer science	food science	linguistics	organic chemistry	toxicology
anatomy	cybernetics	genetics	macrobiotics	ornithology	ultrasonics
anthropology	diagnostics	geoarchaeology	materials science	pathology	veterinary science
archaeology	dietetics	geochemistry	mathematics	pharmacology	zoology
astronomy	domestic science	geographical	mechanical	physics	
astrophysics	dynamics	science	engineering	physiology	
behavioural	earth science	geology	mechanics	political science	
science	ecology	geophysics	medical science	psychology	
biochemistry	economics	graphology	metallurgy	radiochemistry	
biology	electrodynamics	hydraulics	meteorology	robotics	

scientific instruments
See panel below

scientist *n*
experimenter, researcher, investigator, research worker, technologist, doctor, analyst, expert, engineer, designer, planner, inventor, mastermind, genius, brain, intellect, intellectual, thinker
COLLOQ. boffin, backroom-boy

scintilla *n*
shred, scrap, snippet, bit, piece, fragment, remnant, particle, modicum, speck, spot, jot, iota, atom, grain, mite, whit, trace; *N Am, Aust & NZ* skerrick

scintillate *v*
sparkle, spark, shine, flash, gleam, glint, glisten, glitter, twinkle, blaze, wink
FORMAL coruscate

scintillating *adj*
sparkling, glittering, flashing, bright, shining, brilliant, dazzling, exciting, stimulating, lively, animated, vivacious, witty, exhilarating, invigorating
FORMAL ebullient
E3 dull

scion *n*
1 CHILD, descendant, offspring, heir, successor
2 OFFSHOOT, shoot, branch, sprout, graft, twig

scoff[1] *v*
scoff at something
mock, ridicule, laugh at, poke fun, taunt, tease, jeer, sneer, gibe, scorn, despise, revile, belittle, rail; *dialect* geck at
OLD dor; (*Shakesp*) gall at
FORMAL deride, disparage
COLLOQ. rib, pooh-pooh, knock
E3 praise, compliment, flatter

scoff[2] *v, n*
♦ *v*
scoff food
eat, consume, devour, finish off, gobble, guzzle, bolt, gulp, binge

COLLOQ. put away, wolf, snarf
♦ *n*
food, foodstuffs, comestibles, provisions, meal, refreshments, sustenance, nourishment, nutrition, nutriment, subsistence; *Scot* scaff
COLLOQ. eatables, eats, tuck, scran
SLANG grub, nosh, nosh-up; *N Am* chow

scoffing *adj*
mocking, taunting, sneering, derisive, scathing, cynical, sarcastic, fiendish, Mephistophelian
FORMAL disparaging

scold *v, n*
♦ *v*
reprimand, reprove, rebuke, chide, take to task, reproach, blame, censure, lecture, nag, rant, row, speak to, rate; *Scot* flyte, rage, yaff; *Aust* rouse on
OLD clapperclaw, rattle
FORMAL admonish, upbraid, castigate, berate, lambast, objurgate
COLLOQ. tell off, tick off, start on, take apart, tear into, yap, blow up, give it to someone, give someone a piece of your mind, give a dressing-down, read the riot act to, haul over the coals, rap over the knuckles, jaw, slang, wig; *Aust & NZ* go crook at
SLANG *Aust* go off at
E3 praise, commend
♦ *n*
shrew, dragon, nag, termagant, virago, vixen, harridan, henpecker, spitfire, Fury, Xantippe; *Scot* yankie
OLD brimstone, callet, trimmer

scolding *n*
telling-off, reprimand, reproof, rebuke, lecture, talking-to
FORMAL castigation, upbraiding
COLLOQ. a piece of your mind, ticking-off, dressing-down, carpeting, wigging, earful, earbashing
E3 praise, commendation

scoop *n, v*
♦ *n*
1 LADLE, spoon, dipper, bailer, bucket, shovel

Types of scientific instrument include:

absorptiometer	dipleidoscope	hydrophone	optical character	rheostat	telethermoscope
barostat	electromyograph	hydroscope	reader	slide rule	tesla coil
cathode ray	electrosonde	hydrostat	oscillograph	spectroscope	thermostat
oscilloscope	eudiometer	hygrograph	oscilloscope	stactometer	thyratron
centrifuge	fluoroscope	hygrostat	pantograph	stauroscope	torsion balance
chronograph	Fresnel lens	iconoscope	parametric	strobe	transformer
coherer	Geissler tube	image converter	amplifier	stroboscope	transponder
collimator	heliograph	image tube	phonendoscope	tachistoscope	tunnel diode
cryostat	heliostat	interferometer	radarscope	tachograph	vernier
decoherer	hodoscope	microtome	radiosonde	teinoscope	zymoscope
dephlegmator	humidistat	nephograph	rheocord	telemeter	

See also **laboratory apparatus; measuring instruments; medical equipment**.

2 PORTION, helping, ladleful, spoonful
3 EXCLUSIVE, coup, inside story, revelation, exposé, sensation
COLLOQ. latest
♦ *v*
gouge, scrape, hollow, empty, excavate, dig, shovel, remove, ladle, spoon, dip, bail

scoot *v*
rush, hurry, dash, dart, career, bolt, shoot, run, sprint, zip, scurry, scud, scuttle, tootle
COLLOQ. belt, tear, vamoose, skedaddle, beat it, scarper

scope *n*
1 RANGE, compass, field, area, sphere, ambit, terms of reference, realm, confines, limits, reach, orbit, extent, span, sweep, breadth, coverage
2 *scope for improvement*
room, space, capacity, elbow-room, latitude, leeway, freedom, liberty, opportunity

scorch *v*
burn, singe, char, blacken, discolour, scald, roast, sear, parch, shrivel, wither, dry up, fry, frizzle, sizzle, blast, sear, scathe; *dialect* plot, sweal; *Scot* birsle, scouther
OLD adust
FORMAL torrefy

scorching *adj*
burning, roasting, sizzling, blistering, sweltering, torrid, tropical, searing, extremely hot, red-hot
COLLOQ. boiling, baking

score *n, v*
♦ *n*
1 RESULT, goals, runs, hits, total, sum, tally, points, marks, record, outcome
2 SCRATCH, line, groove, mark, cut, gouge, incision, nick, notch, gash, slit, scrape
3 *scores of people*
crowds, lots, masses, multitudes, hundreds, thousands, millions, myriads, swarms, shoals, droves, hosts, legions
4 REASON, grounds, basis, motives, explanation, case, argument
5 *no worries on that score*
matter, subject, question, issue, concern, aspect
6 *know the score*
state of affairs, situation, facts, truth
COLLOQ. what's what, the (whole) picture, the gen
7 *settle old scores*
grievance, grudge, complaint, dispute, quarrel, argument, bone of contention
♦ *v*
1 RECORD, register, get, count, total, keep a tally, make, earn, gain, achieve, attain, win, be successful, have the advantage, have the edge, be one up
COLLOQ. chalk up, notch up, hit the jackpot
2 SCRATCH, scrape, graze, mark, groove, gouge, cut, incise, engrave, indent, nick, slit, gash, slash, notch
3 *score a piece of music*
set, arrange, adapt, write, orchestrate, instrument
■ **score off**
gain an advantage over, make a clever reply to, humiliate, have the edge
COLLOQ. get one over on
■ **score out**
cross out, cancel, remove, strike out, erase, delete
FORMAL efface, expunge, obliterate
▉ reinstate, restore

scorn *n, v*
♦ *n*
contempt, scornfulness, disdain, sneering, derision, mockery, haughtiness, ridicule, sarcasm, disgust; *dialect* geck
OLD misprise
FORMAL disparagement, contumely

▉ admiration, respect
♦ *v*
despise, look down on, disdain, sneer at, sniff at, scoff at, mock, laugh at, slight, rebuff, spurn, refuse, shun, reject, dismiss, crucify, scorch, spit
OLD blurt, misprise
FORMAL deride, disparage
SLANG *N Am* zing
▉ admire, respect

❗ scorn or **spurn**?
In *scorn*, the main focus is on contempt for someone or something: *Courbet had little formal art training and scorned the rigid classical outlook of the time.* In *spurn*, the emphasis is on the rejection rather than the contempt: *Spurned by her family, she moved to London; He spurned their offer of help.*

scornful *adj*
contemptuous, disdainful, supercilious, haughty, arrogant, sneering, scoffing, derisive, mocking, jeering, sarcastic, scathing, insulting, slighting, dismissive
FORMAL disparaging
▉ admiring, respectful

scornfully *adv*
contemptuously, disdainfully, superciliously, haughtily, arrogantly, scathingly, slightingly, sneeringly, derisively, dismissively, witheringly
FORMAL disparagingly
▉ admiringly, respectfully

scotch *v*
put an end to, put a stop to, bring to an end, stop, halt, ruin, wreck, scupper, scuttle
COLLOQ. pull the plug on, put the lid on

scot-free *adj*
clear, unpunished, unrebuked, unreprimanded, unreproached, unharmed, unhurt, unscathed, undamaged, safe, uninjured, without a scratch

scoundrel *n*
rogue, rascal, villain, vagabond, ruffian, ne'er-do-well, good-for-nothing, miscreant, scamp, scallywag, cheat, reprobate, dog, cur, hound; *Irish* spalpeen
OLD blighter, bounder, dastard, rotter, stinker, blackguard
COLLOQ. rat, swine; *Irish* louser
SLANG louse, scab; *S Afr* donder

scour[1] *v*
scour pots and pans
scrub, scrape, clean, wash, cleanse, purge, flush, rub, polish, wipe, burnish
TECHNICAL full
FORMAL abrade

scour[2] *v*
scour the hillside
search, hunt, comb, drag, ransack, rummage, turn upside-down, forage, rake, skirt, *battre la campagne*; *Scot* skirr

scourge *n, v*
♦ *n*
1 AFFLICTION, misfortune, torment, terror, torture, bane, evil, curse, menace, plague, trial, penalty, nuisance, punishment, thorn in your side
2 WHIP, lash, strap, flail, birch, cat-o'-nine-tails, switch, disciplinarium, scorpion
OLD flagellum
▉ **1** blessing, godsend, boon
♦ *v*
1 AFFLICT, torment, torture, burden, curse, plague, devastate, punish, chastise, discipline
2 WHIP, flog, beat, lash, strap, birch, cane, flail, thrash

scout *v, n*
♦ *v*
spy out, reconnoitre, explore, investigate, check out,

survey, inspect, spy, snoop, search, seek, hunt, probe, look (for), watch, observe
COLLOQ. recce
SLANG case
♦ *n*
spy, reconnoitre, vanguard, advance guard, outrider, escort, lookout, recruiter, spotter, talent spotter, A & R person

scowl *v, n*
♦ *v*
frown, glower, glare, grimace, pout, lour, look daggers at
OLD gloom, overgloom
E∃ smile, grin, beam
♦ *n*
frown, glower, glare, grimace, lour, pout; *Scot* gloom
COLLOQ. dirty/black look
E∃ smile, grin, beam

scrabble *v*
clamber, scramble, scrape, scratch, claw, grope, grub, paw, dig, root

scraggy *adj*
scrawny, skinny, thin, lean, lanky, bony, raw-boned, angular, gaunt, undernourished, emaciated, wasted
E∃ plump, sleek

scram *v*
go away, leave, depart, disappear, flee
COLLOQ. take to your heels, get out, clear out, clear off, quit, beat it, shove off, skedaddle, vamoose, do a bunk, scarper, scoot, bolt, buzz off, scat

scramble *v, n*
♦ *v*
1 CLIMB, scale, clamber, crawl, shuffle, scrabble, grope, grabble
OLD scamble
2 RUSH, hurry, run, push, jostle, jockey, struggle, tussle, strive, vie, contend, compete, battle; *Scot* sprattle
FORMAL hasten
3 MIX, jumble, mix up, infuse, disturb, disorganize, shuffle
♦ *n*
1 CLAMBER, climb, scrabble, shuffle, scaling
2 RUSH, hurry, race, dash, hustle, bustle, scurry, commotion, confusion, muddle, struggle, tussle, vying, competition, free-for-all, mêlée, stampede
OLD (*Shakesp*) muss
COLLOQ. rat race

scrap¹ *n, v*
♦ *n*
1 *a scrap of paper*
bit, piece, fragment, part, fraction, crumb, morsel, bite, mouthful, sliver, shred, shard, snippet, tatter, patch, atom, iota, grain, particle, mite, trace, vestige, remnant, leftover, waste, junk, snap, stitch, rag, scrip; *Scot* glim; *N Am, Aust & NZ* skerrick
OLD quantity
2 *scraps of meat*
leftovers, bits, scrapings, leavings, remains, residue
COLLOQ. bits and pieces, odds and ends
SLANG odds and sods
♦ *v*
discard, throw away, get rid of, jettison, shed, abandon, drop, dump, cancel, axe, demolish, break up, write off
COLLOQ. chuck out, ditch, junk
E∃ recover, restore
■ **on the scrap heap**
discarded, forgotten, jettisoned, redundant, rejected, written off
COLLOQ. ditched, dumped

scrap² *n, v*
♦ *n*
a scrap in the school playground

fight, scuffle, brawl, quarrel, row, argument, squabble, wrangle, dispute, disagreement, tiff, fracas; *Scot* splore
COLLOQ. dust-up, set-to, punch-up
SLANG bundle
E∃ peace, agreement
♦ *v*
fight, brawl, quarrel, argue, fall out, squabble, bicker, row, wrangle, disagree
E∃ agree

scrape *v, n*
♦ *v*
1 GRATE, grind, rasp, file, scour, rub, clean, remove, erase, scrabble, claw, shave, descale, flesh, hoe, shred
TECHNICAL curette
OLD scalp
FORMAL abrade
2 SCRATCH, graze, skin, cut, bark, scuff, rake, raze, paw; *Scot* claut, scart
OLD scrab
♦ *n*
1 GRAZE, scratch, rub, abrasion, scuff, shave
TECHNICAL curettage
2 DIFFICULTY, dilemma, predicament, trouble, plight, distress; *Scot* snapper
OLD hobble
COLLOQ. fix, hole, mess, pickle, tight spot, pretty kettle of fish, wrong box, shemozzle, praemunire
■ **scrape by**
just manage to live, get by, scrimp, skimp, scarcely have enough to live on, muddle through, eke out
COLLOQ. keep the wolf from the door, keep your head above water
■ **scrape through**
just pass, only just/barely win, just succeed in
COLLOQ. get through by a whisker
■ **scrape together**
get together, round up, pool together, get with difficulty, collect with difficulty, obtain with difficulty, just manage to get, scuffle

scrappy *adj*
bitty, disjointed, piecemeal, fragmentary, incomplete, untidy, disorganized, sketchy, superficial, slapdash, slipshod
E∃ complete, finished

scratch *v, n, adj*
♦ *v*
claw, gouge, score, mark, cut, nick, incise, etch, engrave, scrape, rub, scuff, graze, gash, skin, tear, lacerate, curry, race; *dialect* scram, scrawm; *Scot* claut, rit, scart
TECHNICAL tease
OLD clapperclaw, scrab, scrat
FORMAL abrade
♦ *n*
mark, line, scrape, scuff, abrasion, graze, gash, wound, laceration, score, streak, race; *Scot* claut, rit, scart
♦ *adj*
improvised, impromptu, unrehearsed, rough-and-ready, rough, haphazard
E∃ polished
■ **up to scratch**
good enough, satisfactory, adequate, acceptable, up to the mark, reasonable, tolerable, competent
COLLOQ. OK, up to snuff
E∃ unsatisfactory

scrawl *v, n*
♦ *v*
scribble, write quickly, pen, jot (down), dash off, doodle
♦ *n*
scribble, squiggle, writing, handwriting, bad/illegible handwriting, scratch, scrabble
FORMAL cacography

scrawny *adj*
scraggy, skinny, thin, lean, lanky, angular, bony, raw-boned, underfed, undernourished, emaciated
F3 fat, plump

scream *v, n*
* *v*

shriek, screech, cry, shout, yell, bawl, roar, howl, wail, squeal, yelp, squawk
COLLOQ. holler, shout/cry blue murder; *NAm* yawp
F3 whisper
* *n*

1 SHRIEK, screech, cry, shout, yell, bawl, roar, howl, wail, squeal, yelp, squawk
COLLOQ. holler; *NAm* yawp
2 *he's a scream*
joker, comic, comedian, wit
COLLOQ. character, hoot, laugh, riot
OLD SLANG yell
F3 1 whisper **2** bore

screech *v, n*
* *v*

squeal, cry, scream, shriek, howl, yell, squawk, yelp
F3 whisper
* *n*

squeal, cry, scream, shriek, howl, yell, squawk, yelp
F3 whisper

screen *n, v*
* *n*

1 PARTITION, divider
2 SHIELD, guard, protection, cover, mask, veil, cloak, shroud, concealment, front, façade, disguise, camouflage, shelter, shade, curtain, blind, awning, canopy, net, netting, mesh
* *v*

1 *screen a film*
show, present, broadcast
2 SHIELD, protect, safeguard, defend, guard, cover, mask, veil, cloak, shroud, hide, conceal, disguise, camouflage, shelter, shade
3 SORT, grade, sift, sieve, riddle, filter, process, evaluate, test, check, investigate, gauge, examine, scan, vet
F3 2 uncover, expose

■ screen off
partition (off), separate (off), divide (off), fence off, hide, conceal

screw *n, v*
* *n*

fastener, pin, tack, nail, rivet, brad, bolt
* *v*

1 FASTEN, adjust, tighten, clamp, fix, contract, compress, squeeze, turn, wind, twist, wring, distort, wrinkle
2 *screw money out of him*
extract, extort, force, constrain, pressurize
COLLOQ. bleed, milk
F3 1 unscrew

■ screw up
1 *screw up your face*
wrinkle, distort, tighten, knot, crumple, contract, pucker, contort; *Can* squinch
2 MESS UP, spoil, botch, bungle, mishandle, mismanage
COLLOQ. make a hash of
SLANG louse up, cock up
F3 2 manage

■ screwed up
mixed up, disturbed, disordered, disoriented, distracted, distraught, confused, bewildered, muddled, perplexed, puzzled, upset, maladjusted
COLLOQ. messed up, hung up

■ put the screws on
pressurize, force, strongarm, compel, constrain, dragoon, coerce
COLLOQ. lean on

screwy *adj*
crazy, eccentric, mad, odd, weird, queer
COLLOQ. daft, dotty, nutty, batty, crackers, round the twist, round the bend
F3 sane

scribble *v, n*
* *v*

write, pen, jot (down), dash off, scrawl, doodle
OLD bescrawl, bescribble
* *n*

squiggle, writing, handwriting, bad/illegible handwriting, scratch, scrabble
FORMAL cacography

scribbler *n*
writer
COLLOQ. hack, pen-pusher, pot-boiler

scribe *n*
writer, author, reporter, copyist, transcriber, amanuensis, secretary, clerk, recorder, mallam
TECHNICAL hierographer
OLD scrivener
COLLOQ. hack, pen-pusher

scrimmage *n*
brawl, fight, riot, row, struggle, scuffle, skirmish, squabble, disturbance, fray, free-for-all, affray, shindy, mêlée
COLLOQ. bovver, dust-up, scrap, set-to

scrimp *v*
skimp, save, economize, cut back on, limit, reduce, restrict, scrape, curtail, shorten, stint, pinch
COLLOQ. tighten your belt, cut your coat according to your cloth
F3 spend

script *n*
1 a *film script*
text, lines, words, manuscript, dialogue, screenplay, shooting script, libretto, book
2 WRITING, handwriting, hand, longhand, running-hand, calligraphy, letters, manuscript, copy

scripture

scroll *n*
paper, parchment, roll, volume, list, inventory

Scrooge *n*
miser, skinflint, niggard
COLLOQ. cheapskate, meanie, money-grubber, penny-pincher, tightwad
F3 spendthrift

scrounge *v*
cadge, beg, borrow
COLLOQ. sponge, bum
SLANG *Aust & NZ* bludge

scrounger *n*
cadger, parasite, beggar, borrower; *dialect* scunge
COLLOQ. sponger, bum, freeloader, moocher
SLANG *Aust & NZ* bludger

scrub¹ *v*
1 *scrub the floor*
rub, brush, clean, wash, cleanse, wipe, scour
2 ABOLISH, cancel, delete, abandon, give up, drop, forget
FORMAL discontinue
COLLOQ. axe, wipe

scrub² *n*
an area of scrub
scrubland, bush, backwoods, brush, undergrowth, thicket

scruffy *adj*
untidy, messy, unkempt, dishevelled, bedraggled,

ungroomed, run-down, tattered, shabby, down-at-heel, disreputable, slatternly, worn-out, ragged, seedy, squalid, slovenly, sloppy
COLLOQ. grotty; *Aust & NZ* daggy
SLANG sluttish
F3 tidy, well-dressed

scrumptious *adj*
delicious, appetising, tasty, mouthwatering, succulent, luscious, delightful, gorgeous, exquisite, magnificent
FORMAL delectable
COLLOQ. mor(e)ish, yummy, scrummy
F3 unappetizing; *colloq.* yucky

scrunch *v*
crunch, crumple (up), twist, crush, grate, grind, screw (up), mash, squash, chew, champ

scruple *n, v*
• *n*
1 RELUCTANCE, hesitation, doubt, qualm, reservation, misgiving, second thoughts, uneasiness, difficulty, perplexity, objection, boggle, point of honour
FORMAL vacillation, compunction
2 *has no scruples*
standards, principles, morals, ethics
• *v*
hesitate, be reluctant, think twice, hold back, shrink, balk, doubt
OLD stick, stickle
FORMAL vacillate

scrupulous *adj*
1 PAINSTAKING, meticulous, conscientious, careful, rigorous, thorough, strict, exact, precise, minute, fastidious, nice
FORMAL punctilious
2 PRINCIPLED, high-principled, moral, ethical, honourable, honest, upright
F3 1 superficial, careless, reckless 2 unscrupulous, unprincipled

scrutinize *v*
examine, inspect, study, scan, go over, go through, look over, look through, run over, run through, analyse, sift, investigate, probe, search, explore
FORMAL peruse

scrutiny *n*
examination, inspection, study, analysis, investigation, inquiry, search, exploration, probe
FORMAL perusal

scud *v*
sail, skim, race, blow, fly, speed, shoot, dart

scuff *v*
scrape, scratch, graze, rub, brush, drag
FORMAL abrade

scuffle *v, n*
• *v*
fight, quarrel, tussle, brawl, come to blows, grapple, struggle, contend, clash
OLD cuffle, pull caps
COLLOQ. scrap
• *n*
fight, tussle, brawl, fray, rumpus, commotion, disturbance, affray, row, quarrel, rough-and-tumble, *bagarre*
COLLOQ. scrap, punch-up, set-to, dust-up

sculpt *v*
sculpture, carve, chisel, hew, cut, model, mould, cast, form, shape, fashion, represent

sculptor *n*
sculptress, carver, stone-carver, chiseller, hewer, mason, modeller, caster, moulder, figurist, artist, craftsman, craftswoman

sculpture

Types of sculpture include:

bas-relief	figurine	moulding
bronze	group	plaster cast
bust	head	relief
carving	herm	statue
caryatid	high-relief	statuette
cast	kinetic	telamon
effigy	maquette	waxwork
figure	marble	

scum *n*
1 *scum floating on a liquid*
froth, foam, film, layer, covering, impurities, dross, dregs
2 *they're the scum of the earth*
rabble, dregs of society, dirt, undesirables, lowest of the low, rubbish, trash, great unwashed, riff-raff
COLLOQ. plebs

scupper *v*
1 *scupper a plan*
foil, wreck, ruin, mess up, scuttle, disable, demolish, defeat, destroy, overthrow, overwhelm
COLLOQ. axe, kill, put a spanner in the works
SLANG louse up, cock up, screw up
2 *scupper a ship*
sink, destroy, submerge, torpedo
F3 1 advance, promote

scurf *n*
scale, scaliness, dandruff, flakiness, furfur, scruff, scabrousness
OLD scald
Related adjective: furfuraceous

scurfy *adj*
scaly, flaky, scabby, scabrous
OLD scaberulous, scabrid, scald
FORMAL furfuraceous, furfurous, lepidote

scurrility *n*
scurrilousness, rudeness, offensiveness, vulgarity, nastiness, obscenity, coarseness, foulness, indecency, grossness, abuse, abusiveness
FORMAL invective, obloquy, vituperation
F3 politeness

scurrilous *adj*
rude, vulgar, coarse, foul, obscene, indecent, salacious, offensive, abusive, insulting, slanderous, libellous, scandalous, Fescennine, Sotadic, Sotadean
FORMAL disparaging, defamatory, vituperative
F3 polite, courteous, complimentary

scurry *v, n*
• *v*
dash, rush, hurry, bustle, scramble, scuttle, scamper, dart, run, sprint, trot, race, fly, skim, scud
FORMAL hasten
COLLOQ. scoot
• *n*
rush, bustling, hurry, flurry, scampering, whirl
COLLOQ. hustle and bustle
F3 calm

scurvy *adj*
contemptible, vile, dirty, shabby, worthless, dishonourable, sorry, ignoble, despicable, rotten, pitiful, mean, low, bad, base
FORMAL abject
COLLOQ. low-down
F3 good, honourable

scuttle *v*
scurry, hurry, rush, scutter, bustle, scamper, scramble, scud, run
FORMAL hasten

sea *n, adj*
+ *n*
1 OCEAN, waves, main, deep
COLLOQ. briny
See also **ocean**.
Related adjectives: marine, maritime, thalassic, pelagic
2 *a sea of faces*
large number, multitude, abundance, profusion, host,
mass, expanse
+ *adj*
marine, maritime, ocean, oceanic, salt, saltwater, aquatic,
seafaring, afloat
F3 land, air
■ **at sea**
adrift, lost, confused, bewildered, baffled, puzzled,
perplexed, mystified, disoriented, disorientated

seafaring *adj*
sea-going, ocean-going, oceanic, sailing, nautical, naval,
marine, maritime

seal *v, n*
+ *v*
1 *seal a jar*
close (up), shut, stop (up), plug, cork, stopper, waterproof,
fasten, secure, tighten, make airtight/watertight
TECHNICAL plumb, tar-seal
2 SETTLE, conclude, finalize, confirm, ratify, stamp, shake
hands
OLD consign, counterseal, enseal, obsign, obsignate
COLLOQ. clinch
F3 1 unseal
+ *n*
stamp, signet, insignia, imprimatur, authentication,
assurance, confirmation, ratification
TECHNICAL cachet, bulla
FORMAL attestation, sigil
OLD SLANG jark
Related adjectives: sigillary, sphragistic
■ **seal off**
block up, cordon off, close off, shut off, fasten, fence off, cut
off, segregate, isolate, quarantine, cap
F3 open up

sealed *adj*
closed, shut, corked, plugged, hermetic
F3 unsealed

seam *n*
1 JOIN, joint, junction, weld, closure, line, stitching
2 *a coal seam*
layer, stratum, vein, lode

seaman *n*
sailor, rating, seafarer, steersman, AB, tar, deck hand, Jack
tar, sea dog
SLANG matelot

seamy *adj*
disreputable, sordid, squalid, unsavoury, rough, dark, low,
nasty, unpleasant
COLLOQ. sleazy
F3 respectable, wholesome, pleasant

sear *v*
burn, scorch, char, singe, brown, fry, sizzle, seal, brand,
parch, shrivel, wither, wilt, dry up
OLD sere
FORMAL cauterize

search *v, n*
+ *v*
1 SEEK, look for, look through, go through, hunt, rummage,
rifle, ransack, forage, scour, comb, sift
COLLOQ. go through with a fine-tooth comb, turn upside-
down/inside-out
2 EXAMINE, probe, explore, examine, scrutinize, inspect,
check, investigate, inquire, pry

COLLOQ. frisk
+ *n*
1 HUNT, quest, pursuit, rummage, rifling, forage, ransacking
2 EXAMINATION, exploration, probe, scrutiny, inspection,
investigation, inquiry, research, survey
■ **search me**
I don't know
COLLOQ. I've no idea, I haven't got a clue, it beats me, I
haven't got the faintest/foggiest, you've got me there,
dunno, ask me another
■ **in search of**
searching for, looking for, seeking, in pursuit of, in quest of,
on the lookout for

Synonym nuances
verb sense 1
The terms **seek** and **look for** can be employed widely for
attempting to find someone or something. **Look
through**, however, suggests cursorily riffling through
papers or such like, whereas **go through** implies a
greater degree of systematic attention. **Hunt**, on the
other hand, implies an element of desperation, while
rummage and **rifle** convey the idea of a haphazard
execution: *she rifled through her wardrobe in an attempt
to find a decent dress*. **Ransack** goes further by
suggesting resultant disarray.
  You can use **forage** of scrabbling about to retrieve
anything useful, whereas **scour** could be used for a
wide-ranging quest: *she scoured all the antique shops for
authentic pieces*. The terms **comb** and **sift** are both
suggestive of a close and thorough examination: *he
methodically sifted through the files, papers and
notebooks*.

---

searching *adj*
penetrating, piercing, alert, discerning, observant, keen,
sharp, close, intent, probing, thorough, minute,
inquisitional, trying, home
F3 vague, superficial

searing *adj*
1 *searing pain/heat*
extreme, severe, intense, fierce, unbearable, insufferable,
blazing, burning, scorching
2 *a searing personal attack on the politician*
savage, fierce, ferocious, cruel, brutal, devastating,
scathing, vitriolic
FORMAL trenchant, mordant

seaside *n*
coast, shore, seashore, beach, sands, strand
Related adjective: littoral

season *n, v*
+ *n*
period, spell, phase, term, time, span, interval
+ *v*
1 *season food*
flavour, spice, salt, add flavouring, add pepper to, add
herbs to, add relish/sauce to
COLLOQ. pep up
2 AGE, mature, ripen, mellow, harden, toughen, train,
prime, prepare, condition, treat
3 TEMPER, moderate, tone down
■ **in season**
available, obtainable, growing plentifully, growing, on the
market

seasonable *adj*
timely, well-timed, welcome, opportune, providential,
convenient, suitable, appropriate, fitting
F3 unseasonable, inopportune

seasoned *adj*
mature, experienced, practised, established, well-versed,
veteran, long-serving, battle-scarred, old, hardened,

toughened, conditioned, acclimatized, weathered
FORMAL habituated
F3 inexperienced, novice

seasoning n

flavouring, spice, condiment, salt, pepper, herbs, relish,
sauce, dressing

seat n, v

• n
1 CHAIR, bench, pew, stool, throne, stall, form, settle
2 *country seat*
residence, house, mansion, stately home
FORMAL abode
3 PLACE, site, situation, location, headquarters, centre,
heart, hub, axis, source, cause, origin, reason, bottom,
base, foundation, footing, ground
• v
1 SIT, place, put, position, deposit, set, locate, install, fit, fix,
settle
2 *the theatre seats 1000*
accommodate, hold, contain, take, have room for

seating n

seats, chairs, places, room, accommodation

seaweed n

alga, seaware, kelp, varec(h), vraic
Related adjective: fucoid

Seaweed species include:

bladderwrack	gulfweed	sargasso
carrageen	Irish moss	sea moss
channelled wrack	laver	tangle
coral weed	oarweed	thongweed
dulse	peacock's tail	wrack

---

secede v

separate, split off, withdraw, break away, break, resign,
retire, leave, disaffiliate, turn your back on
FORMAL apostatize
COLLOQ. quit
F3 join, unite with

secession n

seceding, split, withdrawal, defection, break, breakaway,
disaffiliation, schism
FORMAL apostasy
F3 amalgamation, unification

secluded adj

private, secret, withdrawn, cloistered, shut away, cut off,
isolated, lonely, unfrequented, solitary, remote, out-of-
the-way, sheltered, hidden, concealed, close, recluse,
retired, shadowy, shy, in purdah, purdahed
FORMAL sequestered, claustral, cloistral, umbratic
F3 public, accessible

seclusion n

privacy, retirement, withdrawal, retreat, isolation, solitude,
remoteness, shelter, secrecy, hiding, concealment,
hermitage, nook, recess, byplace, bypath, bolt hole
FORMAL sequestration

second¹ adj, n, v

• adj
1 NEXT, following, subsequent, succeeding
2 ADDITIONAL, further, extra, supplementary, alternative,
other, alternate, back-up, spare
3 DUPLICATE, twin, double, repeated, another
4 SECONDARY, subordinate, lower, inferior, lesser,
supporting
• n
helper, assistant, backer, supporter, attendant, second-in-
command, right-hand man/woman, deputy
• v

approve, agree with, endorse, back, back up, support,
help, assist, aid, further, advance, forward, promote,
encourage
■ **second to none**
incomparable, matchless, beyond compare, without
equal, without parallel, unrivalled, unsurpassed, peerless,
inimitable, nonpareil, paramount, supreme, superlative,
superb, brilliant
F3 ordinary, run-of-the-mill, poor

second² n

in ten seconds
minute, moment, instant, flash, split second, twinkling,
twinkling of an eye, trice
COLLOQ. tick, mo, jiff, jiffy, two shakes of a lamb's tail

second³ v

seconded to Australia for a year
transfer, relocate, change, move, shift, assign, send

secondary adj

subsidiary, subordinate, lower, inferior, lesser, minor,
unimportant, non-essential, ancillary, auxiliary,
supporting, relief, back-up, reserve, spare, extra, second,
alternative, indirect, derived, derivative, resulting
F3 primary, main, major, essential

second-class adj

second-best, second-rate, mediocre, inferior,
unimportant, indifferent, uninspiring, undistinguished,
uninspired
F3 valuable

second-hand adj, adv

• adj
used, old, formerly owned, pre-owned, nearly-new, worn,
hand-me-down, borrowed, derivative, secondary,
indirect, vicarious
F3 brand-new
• adv
indirectly, in a roundabout way, obliquely, incidentally
COLLOQ. on the grapevine
F3 directly

second-in-command n

deputy, helper, assistant, backer, supporter, attendant,
right-hand man/woman

secondly adv

furthermore, moreover, in addition, further, next, besides,
also, too, as well, additionally
COLLOQ. what's more, into the bargain

second-rate adj

inferior, substandard, lesser, unimportant, second-class,
second-best, poor, low-grade, shoddy, cheap, tawdry,
mediocre, undistinguished, uninspired, uninspiring
COLLOQ. rop(e)y, tacky, lousy, tinpot, grotty; *Aust & NZ*
crook
F3 first-rate

secrecy n

privacy, seclusion, confidentiality, confidence, disguise,
covertness, concealment, camouflage, furtiveness,
surreptitiousness, stealthiness, stealth, mystery
F3 openness

secret adj, n

• adj
1 PRIVATE, discreet, covert, hidden, concealed, unseen,
shrouded, covered, disguised, camouflaged, undercover,
furtive, surreptitious, stealthy, sly, underhand, under-the-
counter, underground, backstairs, back-door
FORMAL clandestine
COLLOQ. cloak-and-dagger, hole-and-corner, closet
2 CLASSIFIED, restricted, confidential, sensitive,
unpublished, undisclosed, unrevealed, unknown
COLLOQ. hush-hush, top secret, between you and me,
between you me and the gatepost

3 CRYPTIC, mysterious, occult, deep
FORMAL arcane, recondite, abstruse
4 CONCEALED, private, cloistered, shut away, cut off,
isolated, lonely, unfrequented, solitary, remote, close,
sheltered, hidden, retired, secluded, out-of-the-
way
FORMAL sequestered
⊟ **1** public, open **2** well-known, widely-known **4** public,
accessible

◆ *n*
1 CONFIDENTIAL MATTER, confidence, private matter,
mystery, enigma
COLLOQ. inside story
2 *the secret of eternal youth*
code, key, answer, solution, formula, recipe

■ **in secret**
confidentially, in confidence, in private, secretly, under
cover, privately, quietly, surreptitiously, stealthily,
unobserved, covertly, furtively, on the quiet
FORMAL clandestinely, in camera, privily
COLLOQ. on the q.t., on the sly, behind closed doors,
hugger-mugger
⊟ openly

■ **secret agent**
spy, undercover agent, foreign agent, enemy agent, double
agent, fifth columnist, scout, snooper
COLLOQ. mole

Synonym nuances
adjective sense 1
Private can be used to suggest something of a personal,
intimate nature, while **discreet** implies being rather low-
key: *the discreet intervention of the bank*. **Covert**, on the
other hand, would be used of something being kept from
the knowledge of others: *covert payments to amateur
players*. **Unseen** has suggestions of protecting identity:
an unseen associate, while **shrouded** and **covered** both
have connotations of mystery: *the writer's sensitive and
shrouded lyrics*.

The term **undercover** conveys the idea of false
representation, often to undertake sensitive work, and
underground also has connotations of confidential
activity which, if not illegal, is outside of the mainstream:
*she worked for an underground movement, forging
passports and papers*. The more negative term **furtive**
suggests an element of shiftiness, and **surreptitious** and
stealthy share the idea of being deliberately
unobtrusive, although again with connotations of being
up to no good. The term **sly** clearly implies an element of
craftiness, and you might use **underhand** to imply a
degree of deception.

---

secretary *n*
personal assistant, PA, assistant, office administrator,
executive assistant, administrative assistant, typist,
stenographer, clerk, scribe, man/girl/person Friday,
amanuensis
OLD chancellor, famulus, prothonotary

secrete[1] *v*
secrete a weapon
hide, conceal, bury, cover, cover up, cache, screen, shroud,
veil, disguise, take, appropriate
FORMAL sequester
COLLOQ. stash away
⊟ uncover, reveal, disclose

secrete[2] *v*
secrete a liquid
exude, discharge, release, excrete, give off, emit, send out,
emanate, produce, leach, leak, ooze
TECHNICAL water, lactate, salivate
OLD secern

secretion *n*
exudation, discharge, release, production, emission,
emanation, leakage, oozing
TECHNICAL osmosis, lactation
OLD secernment

secretive *adj*
tight-lipped, close, uncommunicative, unforthcoming,
reticent, taciturn, reserved, withdrawn, intent, quiet, deep,
cryptic, enigmatic
COLLOQ. cagey, playing your cards close to your chest
⊟ open, communicative, forthcoming

secretively *adv*
quietly, silently, enigmatically, uncommunicatively,
reticently, taciturnly
⊟ openly, communicatively

secretly *adv*
confidentially, in confidence, in private, in secret, under
cover, privately, quietly, surreptitiously, stealthily,
unobserved, covertly, furtively, on the quiet
FORMAL clandestinely, in camera, privily
COLLOQ. on the q.t., on the sly, behind closed doors,
between you me and the gatepost
⊟ openly

sect *n*
denomination, cult, division, subdivision, group, splinter
group, order, faction, camp, wing, party, school, tradition

sectarian *adj, n*
◆ *adj*
factional, partisan, cliquish, exclusive, narrow, hidebound,
limited, parochial, insular, narrow-minded, bigoted,
prejudiced, fanatical, extreme, doctrinaire, dogmatic, rigid
⊟ non-sectarian, broad-minded
◆ *n*
bigot, fanatic, partisan, zealot, dogmatist, extremist,
separatist, fractionalist

section *n*
division, subdivision, chapter, paragraph, passage,
instalment, part, component, fraction, fragment, bit,
piece, slice, portion, segment, sector, zone, district, area,
region, department, branch, wing
⊟ whole

sectional *adj*
separate, divided, exclusive, factional, separatist,
individual, regional, local, localized, partial, class, racial,
sectarian
⊟ general, universal

sector *n*
zone, district, quarter, area, precinct, region, branch, field,
category, section, division, subdivision, part
⊟ whole

secular *adj*
lay, temporal, worldly, earthly, civil, state, non-religious,
non-spiritual, profane
⊟ religious, spiritual

secure *adj, v*
◆ *adj*
1 SAFE, unharmed, undamaged, protected, sheltered,
shielded, immune, impregnable, fast, tight, closed, sealed,
fastened, locked
FORMAL fortified
COLLOQ. out of harm's way
2 CONFIDENT, self-confident, assured, self-assured,
reassured, certain, safe, comfortable, relaxed, happy,
contented
3 FIXED, immovable, stable, steady, sturdy, solid, firm
4 CERTAIN, sure, well-founded, reliable, dependable,
steadfast, conclusive, definite, established, settled
⊟ **1** insecure, vulnerable **2** uneasy, ill at ease, embarrassed,
uncomfortable

◆ v
1 OBTAIN, acquire, gain, get, get hold of
FORMAL procure
COLLOQ. come by, land
2 FASTEN, attach, fix, make fast, tie (up), moor, lash, anchor, chain, lock (up), shut, close, padlock, bolt, batten down, nail, rivet
3 PROTECT, make safe, strengthen, guard, safeguard, defend, cover, shield, screen
4 GUARANTEE, assure, ensure, establish, confirm, sponsor, underwrite, endorse
Ea 1 lose **2** unfasten

securely adv
firmly, tightly, steadily, stably, sturdily, strongly, robustly, safely, impregnably, out of danger, immovably, steadfastly
Ea uncertainly, unsoundly

security n
1 SAFETY, immunity, asylum, sanctuary, refuge, cover, protection, defence, invulnerability, surveillance, safe-keeping, preservation, care, custody
2 *security for a loan*
collateral, surety, pledge, guarantee, warranty, assurance, insurance, precaution(s), safeguard(s), protection, defence
OLD gage
3 CONFIDENCE, assurance, ease, peace of mind, conviction, certainty, positiveness
Ea 1 insecurity, danger **3** anxiety, worry, embarrassment

sedate adj, v
◆ adj
staid, dignified, solemn, grave, stiff, serious, earnest, sober, proper, noble, worthy, demure, composed, unruffled, serene, tranquil, calm, quiet, unexciting, dull, cool, collected, deliberate, slow-moving
OLD seemly
FORMAL decorous, imperturbable
COLLOQ. unflappable
Ea undignified, lively, agitated
◆ v
tranquillize, calm, calm down, quieten down, soothe, relax, pacify

sedately adv
calmly, quietly, serenely, deliberately, seriously, earnestly, soberly, with dignity, nobly, worthily, demurely
FORMAL decorously, imperturbably

sedative adj, n
◆ adj
calming, soothing, anodyne, lenitive, quietive, tranquillizing, relaxing, soporific, depressant
Ea rousing
◆ n
tranquillizer, sleeping-pill, narcotic, barbiturate, opiate, calmative, depressant, quietive
COLLOQ. downer

Sedatives and tranquillizers include:

amobarbital	diazepam	pentobarbitone
Amytal®	dichloral-	phenobarbitone
Ativan®	phenazone	promethazine
barbitone	laurel-water	Rohypnol®
chloral hydrate	Librium®	scopalamine
clonazepam	lorazepam	Temazepam
clozapine	lupulin	tetronal
codeine	meprobramate	thalidomide
cyclobarbitone	methaqualone	thridace
deserpidine	Nembutal®	Valium®

---

sedentary adj
sitting, seated, desk-bound, inactive, still, stationary, immobile, unmoving
Ea active

sediment n
deposit, residue, grounds, lees, dregs, silt
FORMAL precipitate, residuum

sedition n
agitation, rabble-rousing, subversion, disloyalty, treachery, treason, mutiny, rebellion, revolt
FORMAL insubordination, fomentation, incitement to riot
Ea calm, loyalty

seditious adj
agitating, inciting, rabble-rousing, subversive, disloyal, traitorous, mutinous, rebellious, revolutionary
FORMAL insubordinate, dissident, insurrectionist, fomenting, refractory
Ea calm, loyal

seduce v
entice, lure, allure, attract, tempt, charm, beguile, ensnare, lead astray, mislead, deceive, corrupt, dishonour, deprave, ruin, betray, debauch
OLD jape, undo, wrong
FORMAL inveigle
COLLOQ. get into bed, chat up, vamp, make a play for
SLANG pull
Ea repel

seducer n
charmer, philanderer, rake, womanizer, flirt, deceiver, libertine, Romeo, Don Juan, Casanova, Lothario
COLLOQ. wolf, goat

seduction n
enticement, lure, allure, allurement, attraction, appeal, temptation, charm, beguilement, corruption, deception, misleading, ruin
COLLOQ. come-on

seductive adj
enticing, alluring, luring, attractive, appealing, tempting, tantalizing, inviting, flirtatious, sexy, provocative, arousing, beguiling, charming, captivating, bewitching, deceiving, misleading, irresistible, sultry
COLLOQ. come-hither
Ea unattractive, repulsive

seductress n
femme fatale, temptress, siren, Delilah, Lorelei, Circe
COLLOQ. vamp

sedulous adj
diligent, industrious, conscientious, painstaking, persevering, persistent, laborious, busy, constant, assiduous, tireless, untiring, unflagging, unremitting, resolved, determined
Ea half-hearted

see v
1 PERCEIVE, catch sight of, set eyes on, glimpse, discern, spot, make out, recognize, distinguish, identify, sight, notice, observe, watch, view, look at, get a look at, witness, mark, note
FORMAL espy, behold
2 *I see your point*
understand, grasp, comprehend, fathom, follow, know, take in, make out, realize, recognize, appreciate, think, regard, consider, reflect, deem
COLLOQ. get, get it, latch onto, cotton onto
3 IMAGINE, picture, visualize, envisage, forecast, foresee, predict, anticipate
4 DISCOVER, find out, ask, learn, ascertain, investigate, inquire, determine, decide
5 ACCOMPANY, usher, lead, show, take, escort
6 VISIT, consult, speak to, interview, meet, encounter
FORMAL chance upon, confer with
COLLOQ. bump into, run into, come across
7 GO OUT WITH, court, date, take out, keep company with, go with

■ **see about**
arrange, attend to, deal with, take care of, look after, organize, manage, be responsible for, do, fix, repair, sort out

■ **see through**
1 *see through a trick*
realize, understand, fathom, penetrate, not be deceived by, not be taken in by
COLLOQ. rumble, get wise to
2 *see a task through*
stick out, continue, persist, persevere, not give up
COLLOQ. hang in
3 *she saw me through the difficult times*
sustain, get through, encourage, support, keep going

■ **see to**
attend to, deal with, take care of, look after, arrange, organize, manage, be responsible for, do, fix, repair, sort out, mind, ensure, make sure, make certain

---

Synonym nuances
sense 1
You can use **perceive** to suggest becoming visually aware, while **catch sight of** or **glimpse** suggests a brief and unexpected look. The phrase **set eyes on** tends to be used for emphasis: *I tell you, I've never set eyes on him before*. **Discern** and **make out** imply an ability to make visual sense of something despite possible obstacles: *she could no longer make out the hills through the mist*. **Spot** and **notice** are more suggestive of suddenly detecting, or you can use **sight** to suggest seeing a rare occurrence: *he sighted a herd of whales*.
  Recognize suggests previous familiarity, whereas **distinguish** suggests differentiation from surrounding items, and **identify** takes this further by suggesting an ability to name what is seen. Both **observe** and **watch** suggest prolonged attentiveness. **View** and **look at**, on the other hand, are more appropriate for focusing on a particular image. **Get a look at** implies managing to overcome some difficulty: *did you manage to get a look at the new museum?*
  Witness has implications of being able to testify to what has been seen, especially something significant: *he had witnessed the actual event*. The terms **mark** and **note**, meanwhile, both have suggestions of carefully heeding what is seen: *I noted her flushed countenance*.

---

seed *n*
1 *the seeds of a plant*
pip, stone, kernel, nut, pit, nucleus, grain, germ, sperm, ovum, egg, ovule, spawn, embryo, semen, spermatozoon
Related adjective: seminal
2 *the seeds of rebellion*
source, start, beginning, root, origin, cause, reason(s)
FORMAL genesis
3 OFFSPRING, child, children, young, young one(s), family, heirs, successors, descendants

■ **go/run to seed**
deteriorate, decay, decline, degenerate, get worse
COLLOQ. go downhill, got to pot, go to the dogs, go down the tubes, go to hell

seediness *n*
shabbiness, dirtiness, untidiness, squalidness, dilapidation, decay

seedy *adj*
1 SHABBY, dirty, untidy, scruffy, tatty, mangy, squalid, run-down, dilapidated, decaying
COLLOQ. grotty, crummy, sleazy, ribby
2 UNWELL, ill, sick, poorly, ailing, off-colour, chippy
COLLOQ. groggy, rough, under the weather, out of sorts
Ｅ**2** well

seek *v*
look for, search for, try to find, hunt for, pursue, follow, inquire, ask, invite, request, beg, petition, want, desire, aim, try, attempt, endeavour, strive
FORMAL solicit, entreat, aspire

seeker *n*
inquirer, searcher, student, disciple, novice
FORMAL chela, zetetic

seem *v*
appear, look, have/give the appearance of being, look like, come across as, have the look of, show signs of, give the impression of being, strike you as, feel, sound, pretend to be

seeming *adj*
apparent, outward, external, superficial, surface, supposed, pretended, quasi-, pseudo, specious
FORMAL ostensible, assumed
Ｅ real

seemingly *adv*
apparently, superficially, on the surface, on the face of it, as far as you can see, outwardly, allegedly
FORMAL ostensibly
Ｅ really

seemly *adj*
appropriate, proper, suitable, suited, befitting, fit, fitting, decent, nice, attractive, handsome, maidenly, becoming, *comme il faut*
OLD comely, meet
FORMAL decorous
Ｅ unseemly

seep *v*
ooze, leak, exude, well, trickle, drip, dribble, percolate, drain, permeate, soak; *dialect* sipe

seepage *n*
leak, leakage, dripping, oozing, exudation, percolation
TECHNICAL osmosis

seer *n*
seeress, augur, prophet, prophetess, soothsayer, sibyl, wise man, spaeman, spaewife

seesaw *v*
alternate, swing, go from one extreme to the other, fluctuate, oscillate, teeter, pitch
COLLOQ. yo-yo

seethe *v*
1 BOIL, simmer, bubble, effervesce, fizz, foam, froth, ferment, rise, swell, surge, teem, swarm; *Scot* buller
2 RAGE, be angry, fume, smoulder, storm, be furious, be outraged, be livid, be incensed
COLLOQ. explode, boil over, see red, foam at the mouth, blow up, blow a fuse, blow a gasket, blow your cool, burst a blood vessel, fly off the handle, go off the deep end, lose your cool
SLANG go ape, go ballistic

see-through *adj*
transparent, translucent, sheer, filmy, gauzy, gossamer(y), flimsy
Ｅ opaque

segment *n, v*
♦ *n*
section, division, compartment, part, bit, piece, joint, link, slice, portion, wedge; *Scot* scliff
TECHNICAL ring, urite, somite, arthromere, metamere, uromere
OLD article, lith
SLANG pig
Ｅ whole
♦ *v*
cut up, separate, divide, split, slice, halve, anatomize

segregate v
separate, keep apart, cut off, isolate, dissociate, ostracize, quarantine, set apart, exclude
FORMAL sequester
F3 unite, join

segregation n
separation, setting apart, isolation, quarantine, dissociation, apartheid, discrimination, separate development
FORMAL sequestration
F3 unification, desegregation

seize v
1 GRAB, snatch, grasp, clutch, grip, hold, get/take hold of, grab hold of
2 *seize property/a plane*
take, confiscate, impound, usurp, appropriate, commandeer, hijack, annex, kidnap, abduct
FORMAL sequestrate
3 *seize a criminal*
catch, capture, arrest, apprehend
COLLOQ. nab, collar, nail, nobble
F3 1, 2 let go, release, hand back
▪ **seize on**
grab, grasp eagerly, grasp with both hands, exploit
▪ **seize up**
stop, break down, stop working
FORMAL malfunction
COLLOQ. pack up, go phut, conk out

seizure n
1 FIT, attack, convulsion, paroxysm, spasm
2 TAKING, confiscation, commandeering, hijack, annexation, abduction, snatching, capture, arrest, apprehension
FORMAL appropriation, sequestration
F3 2 release, liberation

seldom adv
rarely, infrequently, occasionally, hardly ever, scarcely ever
COLLOQ. once in a blue moon
F3 often, usually

select v, adj
♦ v
choose, pick, single out, decide on, settle on, appoint, elect, favour, prefer, opt for, invite
COLLOQ. cherry-pick
♦ adj
selected, choice, top, prime, first-class, first-rate, best, finest, supreme, high-quality, hand-picked, élite, exclusive, limited, privileged, special, excellent, superior
COLLOQ. posh
F3 second-rate, ordinary, general

selection n
1 CHOICE, pick, option, preference
2 ASSORTMENT, variety, choice, range, line-up, miscellany, medley, potpourri, collection, anthology

selective adj
particular, careful, fussy, finicky, fastidious, discerning, discriminating
COLLOQ. choosy, picky, pernickety; N Am persnickety
F3 indiscriminate

selectively adv
carefully, particularly, discerningly, by choice, preferentially, discriminatingly, differentially

self n
ego, personality, identity, I, person, inner being, soul
COLLOQ. the real me, heart of hearts

self-assembly adj
DIY, flat-pack, kit-form, prefabricated

self-assertive adj
forceful, pushing, pushy, aggressive, authoritarian,

commanding, dictatorial, overbearing, heavy-handed, high-handed, overweening, domineering
FORMAL peremptory
COLLOQ. bossy, not backward in coming forward
F3 compliant

self-assurance n
confidence, overconfidence, belief in yourself, self-confidence, assurance, self-possession, positiveness, aplomb, cocksureness
COLLOQ. cockiness
F3 humility, unsureness

self-assured adj
self-confident, confident, assured, sure of yourself, self-collected, self-possessed, overconfident, cocksure, cocky
F3 humble, unsure

self-centred adj
selfish, self-seeking, self-serving, self-interested, egotistic(al), narcissistic, self-absorbed, egocentric, thinking only of yourself, wrapped up in yourself
F3 altruistic

self-confidence n
assurance, self-assurance, confidence, belief in yourself, self-reliance, positiveness, composure, aplomb
F3 insecurity, self-consciousness

self-confident adj
confident, self-reliant, self-assured, assured, self-possessed, composed, cool, bold, fearless, positive, unabashed
F3 unsure, insecure, self-conscious

self-conscious adj
uncomfortable, ill at ease, awkward, embarrassed, blushing, shamefaced, sheepish, shy, diffident, bashful, coy, retiring, timid, timorous, shrinking, self-effacing, nervous, insecure
F3 natural, unaffected, confident

self-contained adj
1 *a self-contained person*
independent, self-reliant, self-sufficient, private, quiet, secretive
2 *a self-contained flat*
separate, independent, free-standing
FORMAL discrete

self-control n
calmness, composure, patience, self-restraint, restraint, self-denial, temperance, self-discipline, self-mastery, willpower
COLLOQ. cool

self-denial n
moderation, temperance, abstemiousness, asceticism, self-sacrifice, unselfishness, selflessness
FORMAL self-abnegation, self-renunciation
F3 self-indulgence

self-discipline n
willpower, self-control, self-mastery, persistence, resolve, determination, single-mindedness

self-employed adj
independent, freelance, out-of-house, consultant, casual, temporary, part-time

self-esteem n
ego, self-respect, self-regard, self-assurance, self-image, self-confidence, pride, self-pride, dignity, *amour-propre*
F3 inferiority complex

self-evident adj
obvious, clear, plain, manifest, undeniable, axiomatic, unquestionable, incontrovertible, inescapable

self-explanatory adj
easy-to-understand, easy-to-read, easy-to-follow, self-

evident, obvious, clear, plain, understandable, intelligible, approachable, accessible, comprehensible

self-glorification *n*
self-exaltation, self-aggrandizement, self-admiration, self-advertisement, egotism, egotheism
E3 humility

self-governing *adj*
independent, autonomous, free, sovereign, self-determining

self-government *n*
autonomy, independence, home rule, democracy, self-sovereignty, self-determination
FORMAL autarchy
E3 subjection

self-importance *n*
arrogance, cockiness, pushiness, pompousness, conceit, conceitedness, vanity, pomposity, self-opinion, donnism, self-consequence
COLLOQ. bigheadedness, bumptiousness
E3 humility

self-important *adj*
arrogant, pompous, conceited, egoistic, vain, proud, overbearing, swaggering, strutting, cocky, pushy, self-consequent, swollen-headed, swell-headed
COLLOQ. bigheaded, bumptious
E3 humble

self-indulgence *n*
extravagance, excess, self-gratification, sensualism, dissoluteness, intemperance, high living, hedonism
FORMAL dissipation, profligacy
E3 self-denial

self-indulgent *adj*
hedonistic, pleasure-seeking, dissolute, extravagant, intemperate, immoderate
FORMAL dissipated, profligate
E3 abstemious

self-interest *n*
selfishness, self-love, self-regard, self-serving, self
E3 selflessness

selfish *adj*
self-interested, self-seeking, self-serving, mean, miserly, mercenary, greedy, covetous, self-centred, inconsiderate, egocentric, egotistic(al)
COLLOQ. thinking of nobody except yourself, looking after number one
E3 unselfish, selfless, generous, considerate

selfishly *adv*
thinking only of yourself, only for yourself, from personal motives, inconsiderately, ungenerously, greedily, egotistically, egocentrically
E3 unselfishly, generously

selfishness *n*
self-centredness, self-seeking, self-serving, self-love, self-interest, self-regard, greed, meanness, egotism
E3 selflessness

selfless *adj*
unselfish, altruistic, self-denying, self-sacrificing, generous, philanthropic
FORMAL magnanimous
E3 selfish, self-centred

selflessness *n*
unselfishness, generosity, consideration of others, thinking of others first, altruism, philanthropy, self-denial, self-sacrifice
FORMAL magnanimity
E3 selfishness, self-centredness

self-possessed *adj*
self-assured, assured, self-collected, calm, collected,

composed, confident, unruffled, poised
COLLOQ. cool, unflappable, together
E3 worried

self-possession *n*
self-assurance, assurance, calmness, confidence, composure, aplomb, self-confidence, coolness, self-command, poise
FORMAL sang-froid
COLLOQ. cool, unflappability

self-reliance *n*
independence, self-support, self-sufficiency, self-sustenance, self-sustainment
TECHNICAL autarky
FORMAL self-sustentation
E3 dependence

self-reliant *adj*
independent, self-supporting, self-sufficient, self-sustaining
TECHNICAL autarkic(al)
E3 dependent

self-respect *n*
pride, dignity, self-esteem, self-assurance, self-confidence, self-regard, *amour-propre*
E3 inferiority complex

self-restraint *n*
self-discipline, self-denial, self-control, patience, forbearance, moderation, abstemiousness, self-government, temperance, self-command, willpower
FORMAL encraty
E3 licence

self-righteous *adj*
smug, complacent, superior, priggish, pious, sanctimonious, holier-than-thou, pietistic, hypocritical, pharisaical, moralistic
COLLOQ. goody-goody, pi
E3 humble

self-righteousness *n*
priggishness, piousness, goodiness, sanctimoniousness, pharisaicalness, pharisaism
COLLOQ. goody-goodiness
E3 humility

self-sacrifice *n*
self-denial, selflessness, altruism, unselfishness, generosity
FORMAL self-abnegation, self-renunciation
E3 selfishness

self-satisfaction *n*
smugness, complacency, contentment, pride, self-appreciation, self-approval
FORMAL self-approbation
E3 humility

self-satisfied *adj*
smug, complacent, self-congratulatory, self-righteous, proud
COLLOQ. puffed up
E3 humble

self-seeking *adj*
mercenary, self-interested, selfish, self-loving, self-serving, self-endeared, opportunistic, acquisitive, calculating, careerist, fortune-hunting, gold-digging
COLLOQ. on the make
E3 altruistic

self-styled *adj*
self-appointed, self-titled, professed, so-called, *soi-disant*, would-be, pretended

self-sufficient *adj*
independent, self-contained, self-supporting, self-reliant, self-sustaining
E3 dependent

self-supporting *adj*
self-sufficient, self-financing, independent, self-reliant, self-sustaining
F3 dependent

self-willed *adj*
stubborn, obstinate, stiff-necked, opinionated, self-opinionative, self-opinionated, headstrong, pig-headed, ungovernable, wilful, bloody-minded, perverse
FORMAL intractable, refractory
COLLOQ. cussed
F3 complaisant

sell *v*
1 *sell cars*
exchange, trade, barter, auction, dispose of, vend, retail, hawk, peddle, tout; *S Afr* smouch
COLLOQ. flog
2 *it sold for £10,000*
be priced at, go for, retail at
3 STOCK, handle, deal in, carry, market, trade in, traffic in, merchandize, import, export
4 PROMOTE, advertise, market, get support/approval for, persuade, win over, bring round
COLLOQ. push, hype
F3 1 buy
■ **sell out**
1 *sell out of fruit*
run out of, have none left, be out of stock, be exhausted
2 BETRAY, fail, double-cross
COLLOQ. rat on, sell down the river, stab in the back
SLANG fink on; *N Am* stool on

seller *n*
vendor, merchant, trader, supplier, stockist
F3 buyer, purchaser

Types of seller include:

agent	huckster	saleswoman
auctioneer	jobber	shop assistant
bagman	knight of the road	shopkeeper
barrow-boy	market trader	*S Afr* smouch
broker	merchandizer	*S Afr* smouser
cold caller	milklady	store clerk
colporteur	milkman	storekeeper
commercial	*N Am* peddler	street trader
traveller	pedlar	tallyman
costermonger	*colloq.* rep	telephone sales-
dealer	representative	person
demonstrator	retailer	ticket agent
door-to-door	sales assistant	tout
salesman/	sales clerk	tradesman
saleswoman	sales executive	tradeswoman
estate agent	saleslady	traveller
factor	salesman	wholesaler
hawker	salesperson	

See also **shops**.

---

selling *n*
dealing, marketing, trading, transactions, traffic, trafficking, merchandizing, salesmanship, promotion
FORMAL vending, vendition
F3 buying

semblance *n*
appearance, air, show, pretence, guise, mask, front, façade, veneer, look, aspect, image, resemblance, likeness, similarity
FORMAL apparition

semen *n*
seminal fluid, sperm, ejaculate
OLD seed
SLANG come, cum; *Aust* spoof; (*taboo*) jism, spunk

seminal *adj*
influential, major, important, original, innovative, productive, creative, formative, imaginative, seminary
F3 derivative

seminar *n*
1 *a business seminar*
meeting, discussion, workshop, conference, convention, forum, symposium, colloquy
2 *a seminar at a university*
tutorial, lecture, class, session, workshop, study group

seminary *n*
college, institute, institution, training college, academy, school, theological college

send *v*
1 POST, mail, get off, address, put in the post/mail, dispatch, consign, forward, redirect, convey, deliver
FORMAL remit
2 TRANSMIT, broadcast, beam, relay, communicate, convey, radio, televise
3 PROPEL, drive, move, throw, cast, fling, hurl, launch, fire, shoot, discharge, project, emit, direct
4 *the heat sent him to sleep*
make, cause to be, drive
5 THRILL, stimulate, excite, arouse, give pleasure to
COLLOQ. turn on, give a buzz/kick
■ **send for**
summon, call for, request, order, command
F3 dismiss
■ **send off**
order to leave, order off, tell to leave the field
■ **send up**
satirize, mock, ridicule, parody, mimic, imitate
COLLOQ. take off, take the mickey out of
SLANG take the piss out of

send-off *n*
goodbye, farewell, leave-taking, departure, start
F3 arrival

send-up *n*
mockery, parody, skit, satire, imitation, burlesque
COLLOQ. mickey-take, spoof, take-off

senile *adj*
old, aged, doddering, decrepit, failing, confused; *Scot* doited
FORMAL senescent
COLLOQ. gaga

senility *n*
old age, infirmity, dotage, second childhood, senile dementia, decrepitude, anility
FORMAL paracme, caducity, senescence

senior *adj*
older, elder, higher, superior, high-ranking, first, major, chief
FORMAL doyen(ne), âiné(e)
F3 junior
■ **senior citizen**
pensioner, retired person, old-age pensioner, OAP
COLLOQ. *N Am* golden ager
SLANG (*offensive*) coffin-dodger

seniority *n*
priority, precedence, rank, standing, status, age, superiority, importance

sensation *n*
1 FEELING, sense, impression, perception, awareness, consciousness, emotion
COLLOQ. vibes
2 *the report caused a sensation*
commotion, stir, agitation, excitement, thrill, furore, outrage, scandal
3 SUCCESS, hit, triumph
COLLOQ. winner, wow

sensational *adj*
1 EXCITING, thrilling, electrifying, galvanic, breathtaking, startling, stirring, amazing, astounding, staggering, incredible, dramatic, spectacular, impressive, exceptional, excellent, wonderful, superb, marvellous, fantastic, gorgeous
COLLOQ. smashing, terrific, fabulous, drop-dead, shock
2 SCANDALOUS, shocking, horrifying, revealing, melodramatic, lurid, gamy
COLLOQ. juicy, sensational, pulp
F₃ 1 ordinary, run-of-the-mill

sense *n, v*
• *n*
1 FEELING, sensation, impression, perception, awareness, consciousness, appreciation, faculty, ability
FORMAL sensibility
2 REASON, logic, mind, brain(s), wit(s), wisdom, common sense, intelligence, cleverness, understanding, comprehension, apprehension, discernment, prudence, judgement, appreciation, intuition
FORMAL judiciousness
COLLOQ. gumption, nous, savvy
3 MEANING, significance, definition, interpretation, implication, drift, tenor, nuance, point, purpose, substance
FORMAL denotation, import, purport
F₃ 2 foolishness **3** nonsense
• *v*
feel, suspect, be aware of, be conscious of, discern, perceive, detect, experience, notice, observe, recognize, realize, appreciate, understand, comprehend, grasp
FORMAL intuit, divine
COLLOQ. pick up
■ **make sense of**
understand, grasp, comprehend, make out
COLLOQ. figure out, fathom, make head or tail of

senseless *adj*
1 FOOLISH, stupid, unwise, silly, idiotic, mad, crazy, moronic, ridiculous, ludicrous, absurd, meaningless, nonsensical, fatuous, irrational, illogical, unreasonable, mindless, pointless, purposeless, futile, inane
OLD surd
COLLOQ. daft, dotty, batty, load of nonsense/rubbish
2 UNCONSCIOUS, stunned, anaesthetized, deadened, numb, unfeeling
FORMAL insensible, insensate
COLLOQ. out, out cold
F₃ 1 sensible, meaningful, intelligent **2** conscious, aware

sensibility *n*
1 *show sensibility*
sensitiveness, sensitivity, susceptibility, discernment, perceptiveness, appreciation, awareness, responsiveness, insight, intuition, delicacy, taste
2 *offend someone's sensibilities*
feelings, emotions, sentiments, susceptibilities, sensitivities
F₃ 1 insensibility

sensible *adj*
1 WISE, well-advised, prudent, shrewd, sharp, far-sighted, intelligent, clever, mature, level-headed, clear-headed, down-to-earth, commonsense, commonsensical, sober, sane, rational, logical, reasonable, realistic, practical, functional, sound
FORMAL judicious, sagacious
COLLOQ. with both feet on the ground, with your head screwed on (the right way)
See Synonym nuances panel at **realistic**.
2 SENSITIVE, responsive, aware, perceptive, discerning, susceptible, vulnerable
3 *wear sensible shoes*
practical, ordinary, everyday, working, serviceable, hard-wearing, strong, tough, functional

F₃ 1 senseless, foolish, unwise **2** insensitive, unresponsive **3** impractical, fashionable, decorative
■ **sensible of**
sensitive to, understanding, conscious of, aware of, acquainted with, mindful of, observant of, alive to, convinced of
FORMAL cognizant of
F₃ unaware of

sensibly *adv*
1 WISELY, prudently, shrewdly, cleverly, rationally, logically, reasonably, realistically, practically
FORMAL judiciously, sagaciously
2 *sensibly dressed*
practically, strongly, suitably, usefully, handily, functionally, serviceably
F₃ 1 foolishly, unwisely **2** impractically, fashionably

sensitive *adj*
1 SUSCEPTIBLE, vulnerable, impressionable, tender, emotional, thin-skinned, temperamental, touchy, irritable, sensitized, responsive, reactive, aware, perceptive, discerning, appreciative
FORMAL sentient
2 DELICATE, fine, fragile, soft, exact, precise
3 *a sensitive issue*
delicate, tricky, controversial, difficult, problematic, awkward, touchy
4 *needs sensitive handling*
tactful, delicate, diplomatic, careful, considerate, sympathetic, discerning, discreet, well-thought-out
F₃ 1 insensitive, thick-skinned **2** imprecise, approximate

sensitivity *n*
1 SUSCEPTIBILITY, vulnerability, responsiveness, awareness, perceptiveness, receptiveness, reactiveness, discernment, appreciation, sympathy
2 DELICACY, fineness, fragility, softness
F₃ 1 insensitivity

sensual *adj*
self-indulgent, voluptuous, voluptuary, sultry, worldly, physical, animal, carnal, fleshly, bodily, embodied, animal, brute, gross, sexual, erotic, sexy, lustful, lecherous, lewd, licentious
OLD swinish
FORMAL encarnalized, pandemian
COLLOQ. randy, horny
F₃ ascetic

❗ sensual or sensuous?
Sensual means 'of or concerning the physical senses and the body rather than the mind', and is used especially with a connotation of sexuality or sexual arousal: *a full, sensual mouth; a strong desire for sensual pleasure*. *Sensuous* means 'perceived by or affecting the senses, especially in a pleasant way', as in *I find his music very sensuous; Her sculptures have a certain sensuous quality to them*.

sensuality *n*
pleasure, voluptuousness, lewdness, lustfulness, salaciousness, sexiness, licentiousness, libertinism, eroticism, carnality, animalism, lasciviousness, debauchery, lecherousness, gourmandise
FORMAL profligacy, prurience
F₃ asceticism, Puritanism

sensuous *adj*
pleasurable, gratifying, pleasing, pleasant, voluptuous, rich, lush, luxurious, sumptuous, aesthetic
F₃ ascetic, plain, simple

❗ sensuous or sensual?
See panel at **sensual**.

sensuously *adv*
pleasurably, gratifyingly, voluptuously, richly, lushly,

sumptuously, luxuriously
F3 plainly

sentence *n, v*
♦ *n*
judgement, decision, verdict, condemnation, pronouncement, ruling, decree, order, punishment
♦ *v*
judge, pass judgement on, impose a sentence on, condemn, doom, punish, penalize

sententious *adj*
1 MORALIZING, moralistic, judgemental, sanctimonious, canting, pompous
2 BRIEF, concise, compact, pithy, short, terse, succinct, pointed, epigrammatic, aphoristic, laconic, axiomatic, gnomic
COLLOQ. preachy
F3 1 humble **2** verbose

sentient *adj*
conscious, aware, sensitive, responsive, feeling, live, living, reactive
F3 *formal* insentient

sentiment *n*
1 THOUGHT, idea, feeling, opinion, view, point of view, judgement, belief, persuasion, attitude
2 EMOTION, sensibility, tenderness, soft-heartedness, softness, romance, romanticism, sentimentality, mawkishness

sentimental *adj*
tender, soft-hearted, emotional, loving, gushing, sugary, touching, pathetic, tear-jerking, maudlin, mawkish, nostalgic, romantic, affectionate
COLLOQ. soppy, weepy, lovey-dovey, slushy, mushy, schmaltzy, corny, sickly, gushy, sloppy, gooey, gloopy, yucky
F3 unsentimental, realistic, cynical

> **Synonym nuances**
> You can use **tender** to suggest having a sensitive nature, while **soft-hearted** implies generosity, although perhaps to a fault: *James cursed himself for being a soft-hearted fool.* **Emotional** can be widely used to suggest exaggerated sensibilities, while **gushing** is disapproving in tone, implying over-effusiveness, often tinged with insincerity: *the gushing praise of the critics.* **Sugary** is similarly critical in its implication that something is cloyingly sweet: *sugary heroines in old movies.*
> If you want to express approval of sentimentality, you might use **touching** to suggest that something is positively affecting. **Pathetic**, however, would imply a degree of being pitiable, and while **tear-jerking** literally suggests prompting crying, it is often used facetiously. You can use **maudlin** to imply being foolishly lachrymose, while **mawkish**, although similar, implies a more nauseating or embarrassing aspect: *he wrote a mawkish poem when his father died, an attempt to suggest feelings that had never existed.*
> Whereas **nostalgic** straightforwardly suggests a hankering for the past, **romantic** has connotations, mostly positive, of idealized love. The terms **sloppy** and **soppy**, by contrast, share negative implications of causing embarrassment: *soppy love songs that make us cringe.*

sentimentality *n*
tenderness, sentimentalism, sentiment, emotionalism, feeling, sensibility, romanticism, mawkishness, nostalgia, treacle
FORMAL bathos
COLLOQ. corniness, gush, mush, pulp, schmaltz, sloppiness, slush, goo, gloop, yuck

sentry *n*
sentinel, guard, picket, watchman, watch, lookout, out-sentry, vedette
OLD centry

separable *adj*
divisible, detachable, removable, distinguishable, distinct, independent, different, particular
OLD (*Shakesp*) dividant
FORMAL partible
F3 inseparable

separate *v, adj*
♦ *v*
divide, sever, take/come apart, keep apart, break off, break up, part, split (up), divorce, part company, diverge, dismantle, disconnect, uncouple, disunite, disaffiliate, disentangle, single out, segregate, isolate, cut off, partition, abstract, remove, detach, withdraw, secede
OLD sunder
FORMAL disjoin, become estranged
F3 join, unite, combine
♦ *adj*
different, distinct, unattached, unconnected, unrelated, single, individual, particular, independent, alone, solitary, segregated, isolated, apart, divorced, divided, disunited, disconnected, disjointed, detached, sundry
FORMAL disparate, discrete, several, autonomous
F3 together, attached

separated *adj*
separate, split up, divided, disconnected, parted, isolated, disunited, disassociated, apart, segregated
OLD sundered
F3 attached, together

separately *adv*
independently, individually, singly, one by one, apart, discriminately, discretely, alone, personally
FORMAL severally
F3 together

separating *adj*
divisive, isolating, dividing, intervening, partitioning, segregating
F3 unifying

separation *n*
division, parting, parting of the ways, leave-taking, farewell, split-up, break-up, divorce, split, rift, schism, gap, divergence, disconnection, uncoupling, disengagement, dissociation, segregation, isolation, apartheid, detachment
FORMAL severance, estrangement, disseverment
F3 unification

separatist *adj*
breakaway, rebel, dissenting, renegade, heretical
FORMAL apostate, schismatic, seceding, secessionist

septic *adj*
infected, poisoned, festering, putrefying, putrid
FORMAL putrefactive, suppurating

sepulchral *adj*
gloomy, grave, melancholy, sombre, cheerless, mournful, sad, solemn, dismal, funereal, morbid, deep, hollow
FORMAL lugubrious, sepulchrous, woeful
F3 happy, cheerful

sepulchre *n*
tomb, grave, burial place, vault, mausoleum

sequel *n*
follow-up, continuation, development, result, consequence, outcome, issue, upshot, pay-off, end, conclusion

sequence *n*
succession, series, run, progression, chain, string, train,

line, procession, order, arrangement, consequence, course, track, cycle, set

sequester v
1 ISOLATE, set apart, seclude, insulate, detach, remove, alienate, shut away, shut off
2 CONFISCATE, seize, impound, take, commandeer
FORMAL sequestrate, appropriate

sequestered adj
isolated, secluded, lonely, outback, out-of-the-way, private, remote, quiet, retired, unfrequented, cloistered
🔁 public, busy, frequented

sequestrate v
seize, confiscate, impound, take, commandeer, sequester
FORMAL appropriate

seraphic adj
seraphical, angelic, heavenly, celestial, holy, divine, pure, saintly, innocent, blissful
FORMAL beatific, sublime
🔁 demonic

serendipitous adj
chance, lucky, happy, accidental, unexpected, fortunate
FORMAL fortuitous

serendipity n
chance, coincidence, happy coincidence, accident, luck, fortune, good fortune
FORMAL fortuity

serene adj
calm, tranquil, cool, composed, placid, untroubled, undisturbed, unclouded, unruffled, still, quiet, peaceful, seraphic
FORMAL halcyon, imperturbable
COLLOQ. unflappable
🔁 troubled, disturbed

serenely adv
calmly, placidly, quietly, peacefully, tranquilly
FORMAL imperturbably

serenity n
calm, calmness, stillness, tranquillity, cool, composure, placidity, peace, peacefulness, quietness
FORMAL quietude
COLLOQ. unflappability
🔁 anxiety, disruption

serf n
slave, servant, thrall, villein, bondservant, bond-slave, bond(s)man, bond(s)woman, bondmaid, helot, thirl, thete, adscript
🔁 master

series n
set, cycle, succession, sequence, run, progression, row, chain, string, line, train, stream, order, arrangement, course
FORMAL concatenation

serious adj
1 IMPORTANT, significant, weighty, momentous, crucial, critical, urgent, pressing, acute, grave, worrying, difficult, life-and-death, grim, severe, deep, far-reaching
FORMAL of consequence, consequential
COLLOQ. no joke, no laughing matter
2 UNSMILING, long-faced, humourless, unlaughing, grim, dour, solemn, sober, sombre, grave, stern, thoughtful, quiet, pensive, preoccupied, earnest, genuine, honest, sincere
COLLOQ. heavy
3 *serious injuries*
severe, acute, critical, grave, bad, dangerous, precarious, life-and-death, grievous
FORMAL perilous
4 *serious money*

considerable, great, large, big, siz(e)able, substantial, ample, plentiful, abundant, lavish, generous, significant
COLLOQ. tidy
🔁 1 trivial, unimportant, insignificant 2 smiling, laughing, joking, light-hearted, facetious, frivolous 3 slight, mild 4 small, slight, insignificant

> **Synonym nuances**
> *sense 2*
> **Unsmiling** and **unlaughing** can be used to suggest facial expressions that show you will brook no nonsense, but **long-faced** can have further implications of deeper sadness. **Humourless**, on the other hand, has more to do with temperament, implying an inability to enjoy levity, while the equally negative **grim** suggests a forbidding manner or countenance: *a grim look on his face*; *grim resolve*. **Dour** is similar, but further implies a degree of moroseness.
>   **Sober** implies a restrained and quiet persona, and the term **solemn** too has connotations of quiet dignity: *a solemn funeral ceremony*. **Sombre** can be more suggestive of gloominess: *a sombre death-haunted melancholic*, while **grave** suggests significance.
>   **Stern** carries suggestions of being slightly fearsome, while **quiet**, **thoughtful** and **pensive** suggest an introspective nature. **Preoccupied** suggests a somewhat abstracted air, while **earnest** implies being rather focused in intent: *earnest conviction*. To suggest an absence of affectation or pretence, you could use **genuine**, **honest** and **sincere**, which are all approving in tone.

seriously adv
1 SOLEMNLY, thoughtfully, earnestly, sincerely, joking apart, *au sérieux*
COLLOQ. for real
2 ACUTELY, gravely, badly, severely, critically, dangerously, sorely, distressingly, grievously
3 EXTREMELY, exceedingly, excessively, very, really, exceptionally, extraordinarily, intensely, thoroughly, remarkably, utterly, greatly, highly, unusually, unreasonably, immoderately, uncommonly, inordinately, acutely, severely, decidedly
OLD jolly
COLLOQ. awfully, terribly, dreadfully, frightfully, terrifically
🔁 1 casually, in fun 3 slightly

seriousness n
1 IMPORTANCE, significance, urgency, weight, gravity
FORMAL moment
2 SOLEMNITY, earnestness, humourlessness, sternness, staidness, sedateness
FORMAL sobriety, gravitas
🔁 1 triviality, slightness 2 casualness

sermon n
address, discourse, lecture, talk, message, harangue, homily, khutbah
FORMAL oration, exhortation, declamation
COLLOQ. talking-to, preach

serpentine adj
winding, twisting, tortuous, meandering, coiling, crooked, sinuous, snakelike, snaking, snaky
FORMAL serpentiform
🔁 straight

serrated adj
toothed, notched, indented, jagged, sawlike, saw-toothed, saw-edged
FORMAL serratulate, serrulated
🔁 smooth

serried adj
dense, close, close together, close-set, crowded, compact, massed
🔁 scattered

servant n

attendant, retainer, hireling, help, helper, assistant, ancillary
Related adjectives: menial, servile
Ea master, mistress

Kinds of servant include:

au pair	domestic help	maid
barmaid	drudge	manservant
barman	equerry	menial
batman	errand boy	nanny
bellboy	factotum	ostler
NAm bellhop	fag	page
body servant	flunkey	pageboy
boot-catcher	footman	parlour-maid
boots	garçon	retainer
butler	*Irish* gossoon	scullery maid
care assistant	governess	scullion
carer	groom	seneschal
chambermaid	haiduk	*old* servitor
colloq. char	*old* handmaid(en)	*colloq.* skivvy
charlady	henchman	slave
chauffeur	henchperson	steward
chauffeuse	henchwoman	stewardess
chef	home help	tapsman
chokra	house boy	*colloq.* tweeny
cleaner	housekeeper	valet
coachman	housemaid	waiter
commissionaire	kitchen-maid	waitress
cook	lackey	wench
colloq. daily	lady-in-waiting	wet nurse
dogsbody	lady's maid	
domestic	livery-servant	

---

serve v

1 WAIT ON, attend, minister to, be employed by, work for, help, aid, assist, be of assistance to, benefit, be of benefit to, be of service to, further, support, be of use to
FORMAL succour
COLLOQ. do a good turn to
2 *serve a purpose*
fulfil, complete, answer, satisfy, perform, carry out, go through, act, function, do the work of
FORMAL discharge, suffice
3 DISTRIBUTE, give out, dish up, dish out, wait, dole out, present, deliver, take care of, provide, supply

service n, v

♦ *n*
1 EMPLOYMENT, work, labour, business, duty, duties, job, function, performance, activity, assistance
2 USE, usefulness, usage, utility, advantage, benefit, help, assistance
COLLOQ. turn
3 SERVICING, maintenance, repair(s), overhaul, check
4 *church service*
worship, observance, ceremony, rite, ritual, sacrament, ordinance
5 *armed services*
forces, military, air force, navy, army
See also panel at **armed services**.
6 *railway/postal services*
facility, amenity, resource, utility
♦ *v*
maintain, overhaul, check, repair, go over, recondition, tune
= in service
in use, in regular use, in working order, working, in operation, functional, operative
= of service
useful, helpful, profitable, advantageous, beneficial, of benefit
= out of service
out of use, no longer in service, out of order, not

working, not in working order, defective, faulty
COLLOQ. on the blink, packed up, conked out, kaput, phut; *NAm* on the fritz

serviceable adj

usable, useful, helpful, profitable, advantageous, beneficial, utilitarian, simple, plain, unadorned, strong, tough, durable, hard-wearing, dependable, efficient, functional, practical, sensible, convenient
Ea unserviceable, unusable

servile adj

sycophantic, toadying, cringing, fawning, grovelling, bootlicking, slavish, subservient, subject, submissive, humble, abject, low, lowly, mean, base, menial, slavish, vassal
FORMAL obsequious, unctuous
COLLOQ. slimy
Ea assertive, aggressive

servility n

sycophancy, toadyism, grovelling, fawning, bootlicking, self-abasement, slavishness, submissiveness, subservience, meanness, abjection, abjectness, baseness
FORMAL obsequiousness, unctuousness
Ea aggressiveness, boldness

serving n

helping, portion, share, amount, plateful, bowlful, spoonful, ration

servitude n

slavery, enslavement, bondage, obedience, bonds, chains, serfdom, thrall, thraldom, vassalage, villeinage
FORMAL subjugation
Ea freedom, liberty

session n

1 MEETING, sitting, hearing, assembly, conference, discussion; *Scot* down-sitting
TECHNICAL séance
COLLOQ. talkathon
2 PERIOD, stretch, spell, time, term, semester, year, drill, clinic, scrimmage, shoot
TECHNICAL church court
COLLOQ. bevvy, sesh; *Aust* grog-on, grog-up

set v, n, adj

♦ *v*
1 PUT, place, lay (down), locate, situate, position, station, arrange, prepare, make ready, install, lodge, insert, fix, stick, park, deposit, rest
COLLOQ. plonk, dump
2 SCHEDULE, appoint, arrange, organize, designate, specify, name, prescribe, ordain, assign, allocate, impose, fix, establish, determine, stipulate, decide, conclude, confirm, settle, agree on, resolve
3 ADJUST, regulate, synchronize, co-ordinate, harmonize, put right
4 *set the table*
lay, prepare, get ready, make ready, arrange, set out
5 *set something in motion*
cause, start, begin, occasion, bring about, produce, prompt, set off, give rise to, lead to, result in, trigger (off)
6 *set someone a task*
assign, allocate, give, grant, delegate, choose, select, consign
7 *set a record/precedent*
establish, provide, inaugurate, start, begin, create, bring into being
8 *set a trap*
prepare, arrange, organize, lay, set up, plan, devise
9 *set words to music*
arrange, score, adapt, write, orchestrate, harmonize
10 *the sun sets*
go down, go below the horizon, sink, dip, decline, subside, disappear, vanish

11 CONGEAL, thicken, gel, stiffen, become firm/hard, solidify, harden, cake, coagulate, crystallize

F3 10 rise

♦ *n*

1 COLLECTION, batch, series, sequence, kit, outfit, compendium, assortment, class, category

FORMAL array, assemblage

2 *a set of people*
group, band, gang, crowd, circle, clique, faction

3 *the set of a film*
setting, background, scene, scenery, stage, backdrop, wings, *mise-en-scène*

4 *the set of someone's face/body*
expression, turn, look, position, posture

FORMAL bearing

♦ *adj*

1 FIXED, established, scheduled, appointed, arranged, prearranged, ordained, specified, decided, agreed, settled, firm, strict, rigid, inflexible, ingrained, entrenched

FORMAL predetermined, prescribed

2 REGULAR, routine, usual, customary, everyday, traditional, habitual, standard, stock, stereotyped, conventional

3 READY, prepared, equipped, arranged, organized, completed, finished, all set

F3 1 undecided, movable **2** spontaneous **3** unprepared

■ **set about**
begin, start, get down to, embark on, undertake, tackle, attack

FORMAL commence

COLLOQ. set the ball rolling

■ **set against**

1 BALANCE, compare, contrast, weigh

FORMAL juxtapose

2 OPPOSE, divide, disunite, alienate

FORMAL estrange

■ **set apart**
distinguish, make different, differentiate, mark off, put aside, separate

■ **set aside**

1 PUT ASIDE, lay aside, lay by, keep (back), put away, save, give over to, keep in reserve, reserve, set apart, separate, select, earmark, mothball

COLLOQ. stash away

2 ANNUL, cancel, reverse, overturn, overrule, reject, ignore, discount, discard

FORMAL abrogate, revoke

■ **set back**
delay, hold up, slow, thwart, check, hinder, impede

FORMAL retard

■ **set down**

1 LAY DOWN, record, stipulate, assert, affirm, state, establish, formulate, prescribe

2 WRITE DOWN, note (down), record, put in writing

■ **set forth**

1 EXPLAIN, expound, describe, present, set out, clarify

FORMAL delineate, elucidate, explicate

2 *set forth on a journey*
depart, set out, set off, leave, start out

■ **set in**
begin, start, come, arrive

FORMAL commence

■ **set off**

1 LEAVE, depart, set out, start (out), set forth, begin

2 DETONATE, blow up, light, ignite, touch off, trigger off, explode

3 ACTIVATE, trigger (off), touch off, prompt, encourage, initiate, set in motion

4 DISPLAY, show off, enhance, contrast, throw into relief, heighten, intensify

■ **set on**

1 set upon, attack, assault, turn on, go for, fall upon, lay into, mug

COLLOQ. beat up

2 determined, resolved, fixed, bent, decided, resolute, firm, purposeful, strong-willed, single-minded, persevering, persistent, strong, strong-minded, steadfast, tenacious, dogged, insistent, intent, unflinching, unwavering, uncompromising, stubborn

COLLOQ. hell-bent, dead set, out

■ **set out**

1 LEAVE, depart, set off, start (out), begin

2 ARRANGE, lay out, display, exhibit, present, describe, explain

■ **set up**

1 BUILD, raise, elevate, erect, construct, assemble, compose

FORMAL dispose, array

2 START, form, create, establish, institute, found, inaugurate, initiate, begin, introduce, bring into being, organize, arrange, prepare

3 FRAME, trap, incriminate, accuse falsely

COLLOQ. fit up

setback *n*
delay, problem, difficulty, hitch, hiccup, reverse, reversal, stumbling-block, impediment, hindrance, obstruction, misfortune, upset, disappointment, defeat, rebuff, throwback, blight

COLLOQ. hold-up, snag, blow, body blow, whammy, knock

F3 boost, advance, help, advantage

settee *n*
sofa, couch, chesterfield, davenport, lounge, canapé, day-bed, bed-settee, sofa bed, futon, dos-à-dos, squab, tête-à-tête, bergère

setting *n*
mounting, frame, surroundings, milieu, environment, background, context, perspective, period, position, location, locale, site, scene, scenery, *mise-en-scène*

setting-up *n*
start, establishment, institution, initiation, inauguration, foundation, founding, introduction, creation

FORMAL inception

F3 abolition, termination

settle *v*

1 AGREE (ON), decide (on), resolve, reconcile, solve, compromise, fix, establish, determine, accept, choose, confirm, appoint, arrange

COLLOQ. patch up, clinch

2 ARRANGE, order, put in order, organize, adjust, complete, conclude

3 *the dust settled*
sink, subside, drop, go down, fall, come down, descend, land, alight, light upon

FORMAL repose

4 COLONIZE, occupy, populate, people, inhabit, live, make your home, put down roots

FORMAL reside

5 *settle a bill*
pay, clear, discharge, settle up, square (up)

COLLOQ. fork out, cough up, foot; *N Am* ante up

■ **settle down**

1 CALM DOWN, make comfortable, quieten, still, soothe, compose

2 CONCENTRATE ON, apply yourself to, get down to, knuckle/buckle down to

3 *time to settle down*
put down roots, get married, buy a house, start a family

settlement *n*

1 RESOLUTION, agreement, arrangement, contract, decision, conclusion, reconciliation, satisfaction

FORMAL termination

COLLOQ. patching up

2 ARRANGEMENT, ordering, organization, completion, conclusion

3 PAYMENT, clearance, clearing, liquidation, discharge
FORMAL defrayal
4 COLONY, outpost, community, kibbutz, camp, encampment, hamlet, village, plantation, establishment, colonization, occupation, population

settler *n*
colonist, colonizer, pioneer, frontiersman, frontierswoman, planter, immigrant, incomer, newcomer, squatter, pilgrim, beachcomber; *Aust & NZ* bushman
OLD inhabiter, Cromwellian, Varangian; *NZ* shagroon
F∃ native

set-to *n*
argument, quarrel, conflict, fight, row, squabble, wrangle, disagreement, exchange, fracas, brush, contest, slanging-match
FORMAL altercation
COLLOQ. argy-bargy, barney, bust-up, dust-up, scrap, spat

set-up *n*
system, structure, organization, composition, arrangement, format, framework, business, conditions, circumstances
FORMAL disposition

sever *v*
1 CUT, split, part, separate, divide, break off, tear off, lop off, chop (off), hack, cut off, amputate, detach, disconnect, disjoin, disunite, divorce, dissever, disbranch, hew, nip off
TECHNICAL pith
OLD rend, cleave
2 *sever a relationship*
dissociate, alienate, break (off), make a clean break with, divorce, dissolve, cease, end
TECHNICAL cut the painter
FORMAL terminate, estrange
F∃ 1 join, combine, attach, unite

several *adj*
some, many, a number of, (quite) a few, various, assorted, sundry, diverse, different, distinct, separate, particular, individual
FORMAL disparate

severally *adv*
separately, individually, singly, discretely, particularly, respectively, specifically, seriatim, apiece
F∃ simultaneously, together

severe *adj*
1 EXTREME, acute, intense, fierce, violent, strong, forceful, powerful, cruel, pitiless, merciless, relentless, inexorable, harsh, tough, hard, difficult, grim, forbidding, rigorous, stringent, drastic, Draconian, tyrannical, iron-handed, iron-fisted
2 STRICT, rigid, unbending, stern, grim, dour, cold, unsympathetic, disapproving, sober, serious, unsmiling, strait-laced
3 AUSTERE, ascetic, plain, simple, modest, stark, spartan, undecorated, unembellished, unadorned, functional
4 *a severe illness*
serious, grave, critical, acute, dangerous, intense, unbearable, agonizing, excruciating, perilous
5 HARD, difficult, demanding, rigorous, arduous, burdensome, taxing, exacting, punishing
F∃ 1 mild, kind, compassionate, sympathetic **2** lenient **3** decorated, ornate **4** minor **5** easy, simple

severely *adv*
1 EXTREMELY, acutely, intensely, badly, critically, dangerously, gravely
2 STRICTLY, rigorously, disapprovingly, sternly, hard, harshly, sharply, sorely, grimly, bitterly, coldly, unsympathetically, dourly

severity *n*
1 EXTREMITY, acuteness, severeness, intensity, strength,

forcefulness, fierceness
2 HARSHNESS, hardness, toughness, sharpness, ungentleness, ruthlessness, pitilessness, mercilessness, grimness, wrath, stringency, coldness, sternness, strictness, seriousness, gravity
3 AUSTERITY, plainness, rigour, asceticism, simplicity, bareness, plainness, spartanism
F∃ 1 mildness **2** compassion, kindness, leniency

sew *v*
stitch, tack, baste, hem, darn, mend, seam, embroider
Related adjectives: sutorial, sutorian

sex *n*
1 GENDER, sexuality, sex appeal, sexual desire, libido, sexual attraction, sensuality, desirability, allure, seductiveness, glamour, sexiness, magnetism, voluptuousness
FORMAL nubility
COLLOQ. it
2 SEXUAL INTERCOURSE, intercourse, sexual relations, copulation, lovemaking, fornication, reproduction, union, intimacy, intimate relations, sleeping with someone, going to bed with someone
OLD congress, commixtion, embraces
FORMAL carnal knowledge, consummation, coitus, coition
COLLOQ. how's your father, it; *Aust & NZ* naughty
SLANG lay, bang, greens, jig-a-jig, knee-trembler, nooky, bonk, leg-over, wham bam thank you ma'am, pussy, rumpy-pumpy, tail; *N Am* jazz, poontang; (*taboo*) fuck, fucking, screw, screwing, shag, shagging
Related adjective: sexual
■ **have sex with**
make love to, sleep with, go to bed with
OLD know, lie with
FORMAL copulate with
COLLOQ. do it, go all the way
SLANG lay, get your leg over, have it off with, bonk, bang; (*taboo*) fuck, screw, shag; *Aust & NZ* root

sexless *adj*
asexual, unsexual, unsexed, unfeminine, unmasculine, undersexed, neuter
TECHNICAL parthenogenetic

sexton *n*
caretaker, verger, grave-digger, fossor, sacristan
OLD (*Shakesp*) grave-maker

sexual *adj*
sex, reproductive, procreative, genital, coital, venereal, carnal, sensual, erotic

---

Sexual orientations include:

bisexual	homosexual	transsexual
heterosexual	lesbian	unisexual

---

sexuality *n*
sexual instincts, sexual urge, sexual orientation, sexual desire, sexiness, sensuality, desire, carnality, eroticism, virility, lust, voluptuousness

sexy *adj*
alluring, desirable, attractive, sensual, voluptuous, nubile, seductive, inviting, flirtatious, arousing, stimulating, slinky, provoking, provocative, titillating, pornographic, erotic, salacious, suggestive
COLLOQ. raunchy, beddable
F∃ sexless

shabbily *adv*
1 *dressed shabbily*
unfashionably, inelegantly, scruffily, disreputably
2 *he's been treated shabbily*
unfairly, unacceptably, dishonourably, shamefully,

despicably, contemptibly, rottenly
E3 1 smartly **2** fairly, honourably

shabby *adj*
1 RAGGED, tattered, frayed, threadbare, worn, worn-out, mangy, moth-eaten, faded, scruffy, tatty, dowdy, disreputable
2 DILAPIDATED, run-down, broken-down, tumbledown, ramshackle, seedy, dirty, squalid, dingy, poky, in disrepair
COLLOQ. tacky
3 *a shabby trick*
unfair, unacceptable, contemptible, despicable, rotten, mean, low, cheap, shoddy, unworthy, shameful, dishonourable
E3 1, 2 smart **3** honourable, fair

shack *n*
hut, cabin, shanty, hovel, shed, hutch, lean-to
COLLOQ. dump, hole

shackle *v, n*
♦ *v*
1 HAMPER, inhibit, impede, encumber, limit, restrict, restrain, secure, thwart, bind, tie, constrain, obstruct, handicap, hamstring
2 CHAIN, handcuff, bind, restrain, manacle, fetter, trammel, tether
TECHNICAL hamshackle
OLD gyve
E3 1 free **2** unshackle
♦ *n*
1 BOND, tether, chain, fetter, iron, handcuff, rope, manacle, trammel, hamper
TECHNICAL fetterlock
OLD gyve
COLLOQ. bracelets, darbies
2 *throw off the shackles of tyranny*
restriction, restraint, constraint, tie, encumbrance, obstruction, trammel

shade *n, v*
♦ *n*
1 SHADINESS, shadow(s), darkness, obscurity, semi-darkness, dimness, gloom, gloominess, murkiness, twilight, dusk, gloaming
2 AWNING, canopy, cover, covering, shelter, protection, screen, blind, curtain, veil, shield, visor, umbrella, parasol, sunshade
3 COLOUR, hue, tint, tone, tinge
4 TRACE, dash, hint, suggestion, suspicion, touch, memory, reminder, nuance, gradation, degree, difference, amount, variety
COLLOQ. tad
5 GHOST, spectre, phantom, spirit, apparition, semblance
♦ *v*
shield, screen, protect, cover, shroud, veil, hide, conceal, obscure, block light from, cloud, dim, darken, shadow, overshadow
■ **a shade**
a little, a bit, rather, slightly, a touch, a trace, a trifle
■ **put in the shade**
outshine, outclass, surpass, beat, excel, eclipse, outrank, top, dwarf

shadow *n, v*
♦ *n*
1 SHADE, darkness, obscurity, inconspicuousness, semi-darkness, dimness, gloom, twilight, dusk, gloaming, cloud, cover, protection
FORMAL tenebrosity
2 SILHOUETTE, shape, outline, image, representation
3 *cast a shadow over the proceedings*
cloud, gloom, sadness, blight, pall, foreboding
4 FOLLOWER, companion, inseparable companion, pal, detective, sleuth

COLLOQ. sidekick
5 TRACE, hint, suggestion, suspicion, vestige, remnant, remainder
♦ *v*
1 OVERSHADOW, overhang, shade, shield, screen, obscure, darken
2 FOLLOW, tail, dog, stalk, trail, watch
■ **a shadow of your former self**
vestige, remnant, apology, weaker version, poor imitation
■ **without a shadow of a doubt**
doubtless, certainly, without doubt, undoubtedly, unquestionably, indisputably, no doubt, clearly, surely, of course, truly, most likely, assuredly, indubitably

shadowy *adj*
1 DARK, gloomy, murky, obscure, dim
FORMAL crepuscular, tenebrous, tenebrose, tenebrious
2 VAGUE, faint, indistinct, ill-defined, indistinguishable, indeterminate, unclear, hazy, nebulous, intangible, unsubstantial, ethereal, ghostly, spectral, phantom, illusory, dreamlike, imaginary, unreal, mysterious

shady *adj*
1 SHADED, shadowy, shielded, screened, protected, covered, shrouded, veiled, dim, dark, obscure, clouded, cool, leafy, bowery, opaque, bosky
OLD caliginous
FORMAL umbrageous, umbratile, umbratilous, umbriferous, umbrose, umbrous, tenebrous, tenebrose, tenebrious
2 DUBIOUS, questionable, suspect, suspicious, dishonest, crooked, unreliable, untrustworthy, disreputable, unscrupulous, unethical, underhand, shifty, louche
COLLOQ. fishy, slippery, iffy
E3 1 sunny, sunlit, bright **2** honest, trustworthy, honourable

shaft *n*
1 PASSAGE, duct, tunnel, well, flue
2 HANDLE, shank, stem, hilt, butt, stock, upright, pillar, pole, rod, bar, stick, arrow
3 *a shaft of light*
ray, dart, pencil, beam, duct, passage
TECHNICAL winze

shaggy *adj*
hairy, long-haired, hirsute, bushy, woolly, unshorn, dishevelled, unkempt
FORMAL crinose
E3 bald, shorn, close-cropped

shake *v, n*
♦ *v*
1 *the windows are shaking in the wind*
rattle, jolt, jerk, bump, roll, bounce, judder, wag, agitate, twitch, convulse, heave, throb, vibrate, oscillate
2 TREMBLE, quiver, quake, wobble, totter, sway, rock, shiver, shudder, judder, convulse
3 WAVE, swing, flourish, brandish, wield
4 *the news shook her*
upset, distress, alarm, shock, shake up, frighten, unnerve, intimidate, disturb, discompose, unsettle, agitate, stir, rouse
FORMAL perturb
COLLOQ. rattle, faze
5 *shake someone's confidence*
weaken, undermine, reduce, diminish, lower, lessen
♦ *n*
1 JOLT, rattle, roll, bounce, rocking, jerk, judder, jiggle, twitch, throbbing, vibration, oscillation
2 TREMBLING, convulsion, quiver, quake, quaking, shiver, shivering, shudder, shuddering
3 SHOCK, upset, alarm, disturbance, jolt, unsettling
■ **shake a leg**
hurry, get a move on
COLLOQ. get cracking, step on it, look lively, get your skates on

■ shake off
1 *shake someone off*
get rid of, dislodge, lose, elude, escape, give the slip, get away from, leave behind, outdistance, outstrip
2 *shake off an illness*
recover from, get better, feel better, get well, improve, pick up, rally, mend, heal, respond to treatment, get over, recuperate, revive, convalesce, gain strength
COLLOQ. pull through, bounce back, turn the corner, get back on your feet, be on the mend

■ shake up
1 *the accident shook me up*
upset, distress, alarm, shock, unnerve, unsettle
COLLOQ. rattle
2 *shake up an organization*
reorganize, rearrange, restructure
COLLOQ. reshuffle

shake-up *n*
reorganization, rearrangement, restructuring, disturbance, upheaval
COLLOQ. reshuffle

shaky *adj*
1 TREMBLING, quivering, quavery, faltering, unsteady, wobbly, tottering, tottery, staggering, doddering, tentative, uncertain
FORMAL tremulous
2 UNSTABLE, unsteady, insecure, precarious, wobbly, rocky, tottery, rickety, weak
3 DUBIOUS, questionable, suspect, weak, flimsy, unreliable, unsound, unfounded, ungrounded, unsupported, untrustworthy
Ⓔ **2** firm, strong

shallow *adj*
1 *shallow water/containers*
superficial, surface, skin-deep
2 *a shallow person*
superficial, slight, flimsy, trivial, frivolous, foolish, idle, empty, petty, trifling, meaningless, unscholarly, ignorant, simple, insincere, one-dimensional
COLLOQ. rattle-brained
Ⓔ **1** deep, profound **2** deep, profound, serious, careful

sham *n, adj, v*
◆ *n*
1 PRETENCE, fraud, counterfeit, imposture, forgery, fake, copy, imitation, simulation, feigning, hoax
COLLOQ. humbug
SLANG *N Am* gold brick
2 IMPOSTOR, fraud, fake, charlatan, impersonator, pretender, deceiver, cheat, swindler
COLLOQ. phoney, con man
◆ *adj*
false, fake, counterfeit, spurious, bogus, pretended, feigned, make-believe, put-on, simulated, artificial, mock, imitation, synthetic
COLLOQ. phoney
Ⓔ genuine, authentic, real
◆ *v*
pretend, feign, put on, make believe, simulate, imitate, fake, counterfeit
FORMAL affect, dissemble

shaman *n*
magician, sorcerer, witch doctor, medicine man, medicine woman, healer, powwow, pawaw, angekok

shamble *v*
shuffle, scrape, drag, falter, limp, toddle, doddle, hobble

shambles *n*
mess, chaos, muddle, confusion, disorganization, disorder, havoc, anarchy, bedlam, wreck
FORMAL disarray
COLLOQ. madhouse, pigsty

shambling *adj*
awkward, clumsy, unsteady, ungainly, lumbering, lurching, shuffling, unco-ordinated, disjointed, loose
Ⓔ agile, neat, nimble, spry

shambolic *adj*
chaotic, messy, muddled, in disarray, disorganized, confused
COLLOQ. at sixes and sevens, all over the shop

shame *n, v*
◆ *n*
1 HUMILIATION, degradation, shamefacedness, remorse, guilt, embarrassment, mortification, modesty, confusion, *aidos*
OLD pudor; (*Spenser*) repriefe
FORMAL compunction
2 DISGRACE, dishonour, discredit, stain, stigma, disrepute, infamy, scandal, reproof, reproach
FORMAL ignominy, opprobrium
3 *it's a shame*
pity, disappointment, misfortune, unfortunate thing, bad luck
COLLOQ. too bad
OLD COLLOQ. sin
Ⓔ **1** pride **2** honour, credit, distinction
◆ *v*
embarrass, mortify, abash, confound, humiliate, ridicule, humble, put to shame, show up, disgrace, dishonour, discredit, debase, degrade, sully, taint, stain
OLD ashame, beshame, rebuke, shend

■ put to shame
show up, humiliate, humble, embarrass, mortify, disgrace, upstage, outshine, outclass, outstrip, surpass, eclipse
COLLOQ. show up

shamefaced *adj*
ashamed, conscience-stricken, guilty, regretful, penitent, remorseful, contrite, apologetic, sorry, red-faced, blushing, embarrassed, mortified, abashed, humiliated, uncomfortable
COLLOQ. sheepish
Ⓔ unashamed, proud

shameful *adj*
1 *a shameful waste of money*
disgraceful, outrageous, shocking, scandalous, indecent, abominable, atrocious, wicked, mean, base, foul, poor, low, vile, reprehensible, dishonourable, discreditable, inglorious, contemptible, unworthy, ignoble
OLD pudendous
FORMAL heinous
2 EMBARRASSING, mortifying, shaming, humiliating
FORMAL ignominious
Ⓔ **1** honourable, creditable, worthy

shamefully *adv*
shockingly, scandalously, atrociously, embarrassingly, disgracefully, outrageously, reprehensibly
FORMAL ignominiously

shameless *adj*
1 UNASHAMED, unabashed, unshamed, unrepentant, unregretful, impenitent, barefaced, bald-faced, flagrant, blatant, brazen, brash, audacious, unblushing, insolent, impudent, defiant, hardened, incorrigible
OLD browless, frontless; (*Shakesp*) unbashful
2 IMMODEST, indecent, improper, unprincipled, wanton, dissolute, corrupt, depraved
FORMAL unbecoming, indecorous, unseemly
Ⓔ **1** ashamed, shamefaced, contrite **2** modest

shamelessly *adv*
unashamedly, blatantly, defiantly, incorrigibly, immodestly, indecently, improperly

shanty *n*
hut, cabin, shed, shack, lean-to, hovel, bothy, hutch

shape *n, v*

+ *n*

1 FORM, outline, outward appearance, silhouette, profile, model, mould, pattern, cut, lines, contours, figure, physique, build, structure, frame, design, format
FORMAL configuration
2 APPEARANCE, guise, likeness, form, look, aspect, image, air, guise, semblance
3 *in good shape*
condition, state, form, health, trim, fettle, kilter
4 PATTERN, mould, model, format, structure, character
FORMAL configuration

+ *v*

form, fashion, model, mould, cast, forge, sculpt, sculpture, carve, whittle, make, guide, influence, develop, produce, construct, create, design, define, determine, devise, frame, block, plan, prepare, organize, develop, adapt, adjust, regulate, accommodate, alter, modify, remodel

■ **shape up**
develop, come on, take shape, progress, make progress, move forward, make headway, improve, flourish

■ **take shape**
become clear, become recognizable, become definite, gel, come together, form

---

Geometrical shapes include:

circle	isosceles triangle	quadrant
cone	kite	quadrilateral
crescent	nonagon	rectangle
cube	oblong	rhombus
cuboid	octagon	right-angled
cylinder	octahedron	triangle
decagon	oval	scalene triangle
diamond	parallelogram	semicircle
ellipse	pentagon	sphere
equilateral	pentahedron	square
triangle	polygon	tetrahedron
hemisphere	polyhedron	trapezium
heptagon	prism	triangle
hexagon	pyramid	

---

shapeless *adj*

formless, amorphous, unformed, unfashioned, undeveloped, unframed, nebulous, unstructured, chaotic, irregular, misshapen, badly proportioned, ill-proportioned, deformed, dumpy
OLD unfashionable
FORMAL indigest

shapely *adj*

elegant, pretty, attractive, well-formed, well-proportioned, well-turned, trim, neat, graceful, gainly, curvaceous, voluptuous, clean-limbed; *dialect* tidy, gainly; *Scot* trig
TECHNICAL forehanded
OLD comely, featous

shard *n*

fragment, piece, bit, part, chip, particle, splinter, shiver, sherd

share *v, n*

+ *v*

divide, split, go halves, partake, participate, have a share in, share out, distribute, dole out, give out, hand out, deal out, allot, allocate, assign
OLD (*Shakesp*) common
FORMAL apportion
COLLOQ. go fifty-fifty, go Dutch, go halvesies, carve up

+ *n*

portion, ration, quota, allowance, allocation, allotment, lot, part, division, proportion, percentage, dividend, due, contribution
OLD (*Shakesp*) allottery

COLLOQ. cut, whack, rake-off, slice of the cake, piece/slice of the action

■ **share out**
give out, distribute, hand out, mete out, divide up, parcel out, allot, apportion, assign
Ⅎ monopolize

shark *n*

CROOK, extortioner, swindler, parasite, slicker
COLLOQ. fleecer, sponger, wheeler-dealer

Types of shark include:

angelfish	great white	sand tiger
basking	Greenland	saw
beagle	grey reef	school
blacktip	hammerhead	sea cat
blind	lemon	sevengill
blue	leopard	sharpnose
bramble	mackerel	shovelhead
bull	mako	sleeper
carpet	man-eating	smooth-hound
cat	night	soupfin
Colclough's	nurse	swell
dogfish	porbeagle	thresher
dusky	Portuguese	tiger
epaulette	ragged-tooth	whale
fox	requiem	whitetip
ghost	sagre	wobbegong
goblin	salmon	zebra

---

sharp *adj, adv*

+ *adj*

1 *a sharp needle*
pointed, keen, edged, knife-edged, razor-edged, razor-sharp, needle-like, cutting, serrated, jagged, barbed, spiky
2 QUICK-WITTED, quick, clever, bright, intelligent, alert, shrewd, astute, perceptive, observant, discerning, penetrating
COLLOQ. on the ball, all there
3 HARSH, brusque, curt, incisive, cutting, biting, bitter, cruel, hurtful, malicious, acrimonious, caustic, sarcastic, sardonic, scathing, vitriolic, venomous
FORMAL trenchant
4 CLEAR, clear-cut, well-defined, definite, distinct, crisp, stark, marked
5 SUDDEN, abrupt, unexpected, violent, fierce, rapid, tight, intense, extreme, severe, keen, acute, piercing, stinging, shooting, stabbing
6 PUNGENT, strong, piquant, tangy, sour, tart, vinegary, bitter, biting, acerbic, acid, acidic, burning, acrid
7 *a sharp bend*
tight, sudden, hairpin, abrupt
8 *a sharp wind*
biting, cold, freezing, bitter, harsh, severe, penetrating, piercing, nipping, stinging
9 CRAFTY, clever, shrewd, deceptive, dishonest, cunning, artful, wily, sly
10 *a sharp dresser*
neat, tidy, smart, elegant, stylish, fashionable
COLLOQ. snappy, natty
Ⅎ **1** blunt **2** slow, stupid **3** mild **4** blurred **5** gentle **6** bland **7** gentle **8** gentle, mild **10** shabby

+ *adv*

1 *six o'clock sharp*
punctually, promptly, on the dot, exactly, precisely
2 *pull up sharp*
abruptly, suddenly, unexpectedly
Ⅎ **1** approximately, roughly

sharpen *v*

edge, whet, hone, grind, file, keen, strop
FORMAL acuminate
Ⅎ blunt, blur

sharp-eyed *adj*
observant, perceptive, noticing, eagle-eyed, hawk-eyed, keen-sighted
F3 short-sighted, unobservant

sharply *adv*
1 *prices rose sharply*
suddenly, abruptly, unexpectedly, rapidly, quickly, acutely
2 *speak to someone sharply*
harshly, brusquely, curtly, bitterly, acrimoniously, fiercely, sarcastically, vitriolically, venomously
3 *the road turns sharply*
abruptly, tightly, suddenly
4 *opinions are sharply divided*
clearly, distinctly, starkly, definitely, markedly
F3 1 slowly **2** gently

sharpness *n*
1 DISCERNMENT, penetration, acuteness, keenness, astuteness, shrewdness, observation, perceptiveness, incisiveness, eagerness
2 INTENSITY, fierceness, severity
3 HARSHNESS, brusqueness, cruelty, incisiveness, sarcasm, vitriol, venom
4 CLARITY, definition, precision, crispness

shatter *v*
1 BREAK, smash, splinter, shiver, crack, split, burst, explode, blast, crush, demolish, smash/blow to smithereens, star
OLD craze, smithereen
FORMAL pulverize
COLLOQ. bust
2 *shatter your hopes*
destroy, devastate, dash, crush, wreck, ruin, disappoint, overturn
3 *shattered by her death*
upset, devastate, crush, overwhelm, break your heart

shattered *adj*
1 OVERWHELMED, devastated, crushed, broken
2 WORN OUT, exhausted, weary, tired out
COLLOQ. all in, dead beat, dog-tired, done in, fagged out, ready to drop, knackered, zonked; *N Am* pooped (out), tuckered out

shattering *adj*
devastating, damaging, crushing, overwhelming, paralysing, severe

shave *v, n*
♦ *v*
cut, trim, barber, shear, crop, fleece, graze, brush, touch, pare, cut, plane, scrape
OLD barb
♦ *n*
■ **close shave**
narrow miss, narrow escape, lucky escape, close thing, close call, near touch

shawl *n*
wrap, scarf, stole, blanket, afghan, zephyr, tonnag, dopatta, tallith, prayer shawl, Kashmir shawl, India shawl, Paisley shawl, pashmina, shahtoosh; *dialect* whittle
OLD turnover, tozie

sheaf *n*
bundle, bunch, armful, truss

shear *v*
shave, fleece, trim, cut, crop, barber

sheath *n*
1 SCABBARD, case, sleeve, envelope, shell, wrapping, casing, covering
2 CONDOM, protective contraceptive; *N Am* prophylactic
SLANG rubber, French letter, johnnie
Related adjective: thecal

shed[1] *v*
1 DROP, let fall, remove, cast (off), moult, discard, get rid of, slough, spill
2 SEND OUT, pour, spill, scatter, diffuse, emit, shower, throw, radiate, shine
■ **shed tears**
weep, sob, be in tears, blubber, wail, howl, bawl, whimper, whine, snivel
COLLOQ. burst into tears, cry your eyes out, turn on the waterworks

shed[2] *n*
a garden shed
hut, outhouse, lean-to, building, shack; *Aust* skillion

sheen *n*
lustre, gloss, shine, gleam, sparkle, shimmer, brightness, brilliance, shininess, polish, varnish, burnish
OLD shine
FORMAL patina
F3 dullness, tarnish, lacklustre

sheep *n*
ram, ewe, lamb, wether, tup, bell-wether
COLLOQ. *Aust* jumbuck
Related adjective: ovine
See panel on next page

sheepish *adj*
ashamed, shamefaced, embarrassed, mortified, chastened, abashed, uncomfortable, self-conscious, silly, foolish
F3 unabashed, brazen, bold

sheer[1] *adj*
1 UTTER, complete, total, absolute, thorough, full, pure, mere, simple, perfect, unadulterated, downright, out-and-out, flat, stark, rank, veritable, thoroughgoing, unconditional, unqualified, blank, plumb
FORMAL unmitigated
2 *a sheer drop*
vertical, perpendicular, precipitous, abrupt, steep, sharp
3 THIN, fine, light, delicate, flimsy, gauzy, gossamer, translucent, transparent, see-through
FORMAL diaphanous
F3 2 gentle, gradual **3** thick, heavy

sheer[2] *v*
sheer away to the right
swerve, turn, bend, veer, swing, shift, drift, deviate, diverge, deflect

sheet *n*
1 *cotton sheets*
cover, blanket, bed linen
2 COVERING, coating, coat, film, layer, stratum, skin, membrane, veneer, overlay, plate, piece, panel, slab, plate, pane
FORMAL lamina
3 *a sheet of paper*
leaf, page, folio
4 *a sheet of ice*
expanse, stretch, reach, sweep, surface

shelf *n*
1 *put books on the shelf*
ledge, mantelpiece, mantelshelf, sill, step, bench, bracket, counter, bar, shelve, shelving, stage, rack, chimney piece; *Scot* bink
TECHNICAL credence, retable, shrine
2 *the shelf on the seabed*
bank, sandbank, reef, ledge, terrace, continental shelf, sand bar, bar, step, shoal
■ **on the shelf**
unmarried, unattached, single, on your own, without a partner, spouseless

Breeds of sheep include:

Arcott	Charollais	Galway	Meatlinc	Scottish Blackface	White Face
Awassi	Cheviot	German	Merino	Scottish Greyface	Dartmoor
Badger Face	Clun Forest	Blackheaded	Montadale	Shetland	White Faced
Welsh Mountain	Colbred	Mutton	Morada Nova	Shetland-Cheviot	Marsh
Balwen	Columbia	Gotland	Navajo-Churro	Shropshire	White Faced
Barbados	Coopworth	Greenland	Norfolk Horn	Soay	Woodland
Blackbelly	Corriedale	Greyface	North Country	Southdown	Wicklow Cheviot
Beltex	Cotentin	Dartmoor	Cheviot	South Wales	Wiltshire Horn
Berrichon du Cher	Cotswold	Gute	North of England	Mountain	Zwartbles
Beulah Speckled	Dalesbred	Hampshire Down	Mule	St Croix	**WILD SHEEP:**
Face	Derbyshire	Hebridean	North Ronaldsay	Steigar	argali
Blackface	Gritstone	Herdwick	Ouessant	Suffolk	barbary (or
Blackfaced	Devon Closewool	Hill Radnor	Oxford Down	Swaledale	aodad)
Mountain	Devon and	Icelandic	Peliquey	Swiss Black-	bighorn
Blackheaded	Cornwall	Ile de France	Perendale	Brown Mountain	blue sheep
Persian	Longwool	Jacob	Poll Dorset	Swiss White	Dall Sheep
Black Welsh	Dala	Karakul	Polwarth	Alpine	Desert Bighorn
Mountain	Danish Landrace	Karaman	Portland	Teeswater	mouflon
Bleu du Marine	Dorper	Katahdin	Rambouillet	Texel	Rocky Mountain
Bluefaced	Dorset Down	Kerry Hill	Romanov	Tibetan	Bighorn
Leicester	Dorset Horn	Leicester	Romney	Troender	snow sheep
Borderdale	East Friesian	Longwool	Rouge de l'Ouest	Tunis	stone sheep
Border Leicester	English Leicester	Lincoln	Rough Fell	Tyrol Mountain	thinhorn
Brecknock Hill	Est A Laine	Llanwenog	Roussin	Vendeen	urial
Cheviot	Merino	Lleyn	Rya	Welsh Halfbred	
British Milksheep	Exmoor Horn	Lonck	Ryeland	Welsh Hill	
Cambridge	Faroe Islands	Manx Loghtan	Rygja	Speckled Face	
Castlemilk Moorit	Finn Sheep	Masai	Scotch Halfbred	Welsh Mule	
Charmoise	Fuglestad	Masham	Scotch Mule	Wensleydale	

shell *n, v*

• *n*

1 COVERING, hull, husk, pod, rind, crust, case, carapace, casing, body, chassis, frame, framework, structure, skeleton; *N Am* shuck

TECHNICAL integument

Related adjective: conchoidal

2 EXPLOSIVE, bullet, shot, pellet, bomb, projectile, missile, grenade

• *v*

1 *shell nuts*

hull, husk, pod; *N Am* shuck

2 BOMB, bombard, fire on, barrage, blitz, attack

■ **shell out**

pay out, spend, lay out, give, contribute, donate, expend

FORMAL disburse

COLLOQ. cough up, fork out; *N Am* ante up

shelter *n, v*

• *n*

cover, roof, shade, shadow, protection, shield, screen, defence, guard, security, safety, sanctuary, asylum, haven, refuge, harbour, retreat, accommodation, lodging

F3 exposure

• *v*

cover, shroud, screen, shade, shadow, protect, defend, guard, safeguard, shield, harbour, hide, conceal, accommodate, put up

F3 expose

sheltered *adj*

covered, shaded, shady, shielded, protected, screened, cosy, snug, warm, quiet, secluded, isolated, retired, withdrawn, reclusive, cloistered, unworldly

F3 exposed

shelve *v*

postpone, defer, put off, suspend, halt, put aside, lay aside, pigeonhole, mothball

COLLOQ. put on ice, put on the back burner

F3 expedite, implement

shepherd *n, v*

• *n*

shepherdess, herdess, shepherdling, herdsman, pastor, protector, shepherd boy, herdboy, guardian, flockmaster, tar-box

OLD feeder, herd-groom

Related adjective: pastoral

• *v*

guide, lead, conduct, convoy, escort, usher, steer, pastor, marshal, herd

shield *n, v*

• *n*

buckler, defence, bulwark, rampart, support, screen, guard, cover, shelter, protection, protector, safeguard, targe

TECHNICAL escutcheon

• *v*

defend, guard, protect, safeguard, keep safe, screen, shade, shadow, cover, shelter

OLD (*Shakesp*) buckle

F3 expose

shift *v, n*

• *v*

1 CHANGE, vary, fluctuate, alter, adjust, modify, move, budge, relocate, reposition, rearrange, transfer, carry, switch, swerve, veer

FORMAL transpose

2 REMOVE, dislodge, displace, get rid of

• *n*

1 CHANGE, variation, fluctuation, alteration, modification, move, movement, removal, switch, displacement, relocation, rearrangement, transfer

FORMAL transposition

COLLOQ. U-turn

2 *work shifts*

period, spell, time, stretch, span, stint

shiftless *adj*

lazy, idle, unambitious, unenterprising, resourceless, aimless, directionless, goalless, incompetent, inefficient, irresponsible, inept, feckless

FORMAL indolent, ineffectual, slothful
COLLOQ. good-for-nothing, lackadaisical
🠔 enterprising, ambitious, aspiring, eager

shifty *adj*
untrustworthy, dishonest, deceitful, scheming, contriving, tricky, wily, crafty, cunning, devious, evasive, furtive, underhand, dubious
FORMAL duplicitous
COLLOQ. shady, slippery, iffy
🠔 dependable, honest, open

shilly-shally *v*
dither, hesitate, vacillate, be indecisive, waver, fluctuate, falter, teeter, seesaw
FORMAL prevaricate
COLLOQ. dilly-dally, hem and haw, sit on the fence, mess about

shimmer *v, n*
• *v*
glisten, gleam, sparkle, glimmer, glint, glitter, scintillate, glow, play, flicker, twinkle
• *n*
lustre, gleam, sparkle, glint, glimmer, glitter, glistening, glow, haze, flicker, twinkle
FORMAL iridescence

shimmering *adj*
glittering, glowing, glistening, gleaming, shining, shiny, lustrous, luminous
TECHNICAL aventurine
FORMAL incandescent, iridescent
🠔 dull, matt

shin *v*
climb, mount, soar, scramble, scrabble, ascend, clamber, scale, shoot, swarm

shine *v, n*
• *v*
1 BEAM, radiate, glow, flash, glare, dazzle, gleam, glint, glitter, flicker, sparkle, twinkle, shimmer, glisten, glimmer, give off, emit
FORMAL incandesce
See Synonym nuances panel at **flash**.
2 POLISH, burnish, gloss, buff, brush, rub (up), wax
3 *shine at athletics*
excel, stand out, be brilliant, be excellent, be outstanding, be pre-eminent
• *n*
1 LIGHT, radiance, glow, brightness, glare, dazzle, flash, gleam, sparkle, shimmer, glitter, glint, flicker, twinkle
FORMAL effulgence, luminescence, incandescence, lambency
2 GLOSS, polish, burnish, gleam, sheen, lustre, glaze
FORMAL patina

shininess *n*
brightness, gleam, glitter, shine, sheen, polish, lustre, glossiness, burnish
FORMAL effulgence
🠔 dullness

shining *adj*
1 BRIGHT, radiant, glowing, beaming, flashing, gleaming, glittering, glinting, glistening, shimmering, twinkling, sparkling, flickering, luminous, brilliant, splendid, glorious
FORMAL phosphorescent, resplendent, effulgent, incandescent
2 *a shining example*
conspicuous, outstanding, splendid, magnificent, glorious, brilliant, leading, eminent, pre-eminent, perfect, celebrated, distinguished, illustrious
🠔 1 dark

shiny *adj*
polished, burnished, shining, sheeny, lustrous, glossy, silky,

sleek, bright, gleaming, glistening, shimmering
🠔 dull, matt

ship *n*
vessel, craft, liner, steamer, tanker, trawler, ferry, boat, yacht

---

Parts of a ship include:

afterdeck	flight deck	port
anchor	forecastle	porthole
berth	(fo'c'sle)	promenade deck
bilge	funnel	prow
boat deck	galley	quarter
boiler room	gangplank	quarter deck
bollard	gangway	radio room
bridge	gun deck	rigger
brig	gunwale (gunnel)	rowlock
bulkhead	hammock	rudder
bulwarks	hatch	sail
bunk	hatchway	stabilizer
cabin	hawser	stanchion
capstan	head	starboard
chain locker	hold	stateroom
chart room	keel	stern
cleat	landing	superstructure
companion	lower deck	tiller
ladder	main deck	top deck
companionway	mast	transom
crow's nest	oar	wardroom
davit	paddle wheel	waterline
deck	pilot house	wheel
engine room	Plimsoll line	winch
figurehead	poop deck	

See also **boat**; **sail**.

---

shipshape *adj*
tidy, neat, orderly, spruce, trim, well-organized, well-planned, businesslike, well-regulated, spick and span; *Scot* trig
🠔 disorderly, untidy

shirk *v*
dodge, get out of, evade, avoid, shun, shrink from, play truant, wriggle out of, balk, slack, soldier
COLLOQ. duck, skive, funk; *Aust & NZ* duckshove
SLANG *N Am* gold-brick, goof off; *Aust & NZ* bludge

shirker *n*
dodger, slacker, idler, layabout, loafer, absentee, truant, malingerer, shirk
COLLOQ. quitter, skiver; *Aust & NZ* duckshover
SLANG *N Am* gold brick, goof-off; *Aust & NZ* bludger

shiver[1] *v, n*
• *v*
shivering with cold
shudder, tremble, quiver, quake, shake, vibrate, palpitate, flutter, dither; *dialect* chitter
OLD shrug
• *n*
shudder, quiver, shake, tremor, twitch, start, vibration, flutter, frisson; *Scot* grue

shiver[2] *n, v*
• *n*
shivers of light
splinter, piece, bit, fragment, shred, sliver, shaving, chip, shard
COLLOQ. smithereen(s)
• *v*
shatter, break, smash, splinter, crack, split
OLD disshiver

shivery *adj*
cold, chilly, trembly, trembling, shuddery, shaking, quivery, quaking, chilled, nervous, fluttery; *Scot* ourie

shoal n

group, mass, multitude, mob, throng, swarm, horde, flock
FORMAL assemblage

shock¹ v, n

• v

his attitude shocked her

disgust, revolt, repel, sicken, offend, nauseate, appal,
outrage, scandalize, outrage, horrify, startle, astound,
stagger, amaze, stun, daze, stupefy, numb, paralyse,
traumatize, jolt, jar, shake, agitate, unsettle, upset, distress,
disquiet, unnerve, bewilder, take aback, confound,
dumbfound, dismay
FORMAL perturb
COLLOQ. bowl over
F3 delight, please, gratify, reassure

• n

1 FRIGHT, start, jolt, surprise, blow, trauma, upset, distress,
dismay, disgust, outrage, horror
FORMAL consternation, perturbation
COLLOQ. bombshell, thunderbolt, bolt from the blue,
whammy, rude awakening
2 IMPACT, crash, collision, blow, shake, jolt, jarring, jerk
F3 **1** delight, pleasure, reassurance

shock² n

a shock of hair

mop, head, mane, tangle, thatch, mat, mass

shocking adj

appalling, outrageous, scandalous, offensive, horrifying,
disgraceful, deplorable, intolerable, unbearable, atrocious,
abominable, monstrous, vile, foul, unspeakable,
detestable, abhorrent, dreadful, loathsome, awful, terrible,
frightful, ghastly, hideous, horrible, horrific, disgusting,
revolting, repulsive, repugnant, sickening, nauseating,
unsettling, disquieting, distressing
FORMAL perturbing
F3 acceptable, satisfactory, pleasant, delightful

shockingly adv

outrageously, appallingly, scandalously, disgracefully,
deplorably, unbearably, abominably, disgustingly,
revoltingly, repulsively, sickeningly, atrociously, dreadfully,
terribly, frightfully

shoddy adj

inferior, second-rate, cheap, tawdry, tatty, trashy, rubbishy,
poor, poor-quality, careless, slipshod, slapdash,
cheapjack, second-rate, third-rate
COLLOQ. rop(e)y, tacky, rubbish; *Aust & NZ* crook
F3 superior, well-made

shoe n

See **footwear.**

shoemaker n

cobbler, bootmaker, snob, snab

shoemaking n

bootmaking, cobblery, cobbling

shoot v, n

• v

1 FIRE, discharge, launch, propel, kick, hit, throw, hurl, fling,
lob, project, let off, aim, direct
2 HIT, kill, injure, wound, open fire, blast, bombard, gun
down, mow down, shell, snipe at, pick off
COLLOQ. zap
3 DART, bolt, dash, tear, rush, race, sprint, speed, hurry,
charge, fly, hurtle, streak, whisk, whiz
COLLOQ. scoot, zip, zap, belt, get a move on, go all out
4 *shoot a film*
film, photograph, take photographs of, video
COLLOQ. snap
5 GROW, germinate, shoot up, sprout, burgeon, bolt, bud,
stretch

• n

sprout, bud, offshoot, branch, twig, sprig, cutting, slip,
scion, graft, tendron

shop n, v

• n

store, retail outlet
FORMAL emporium

• v

1 *shop for clothes*
go shopping, buy, buy things, do the shopping, stock up
on, get, pick up, purchase
2 INFORM ON, betray
COLLOQ. tell on, tell tales on, split, squeal, rat, blow the
whistle on
SLANG grass; *N Am* stool on

Types of shop include:

baker	e-shop	*Aust & NZ*
barber	farmers' market	opportunity
bazaar	farm shop	shop (or op-
betting shop	fish and chip shop	shop)
bookmaker	fishmonger	outfitter
colloq. bookie	*N Am* five-and-	pawnbroker
bookshop	dime	pharmacy
Aust & NZ bottle	florist	phone shop
shop (or store)	general store	post office
boutique	greengrocer	radio and TV shop
butcher	grocer	record shop
candy store	*Aust & NZ* grog-	saddler
cash-and-carry	shop	second-hand
chain store	haberdasher	shop
charity shop	hairdresser	shoe shop
chemist	hardware shop	stall
Irish colloq.	health-food shop	stationer
chipper	hypermarket	*Aust & N Am*
colloq. chippy	indoor market	superette
clothes shop	ironmonger	supermarket
computer store	jeweller	superstore
confectioner	launderette	sweet shop
corner shop	market	tailor
dairy	milliner	takeaway
delicatessen	mini-market	tobacconist
department store	newsagent	toy shop
draper	off-licence	tuck shop
dress shop	*colloq.* offie	video shop
N Am drugstore	online shop (or	
electrical shop	store)	

---

shopkeeper n

dealer, salesman, saleswoman, retailer, stockist, trader,
tradesman, manager, owner, proprietor, storekeeper,
merchant

shopper n

buyer, purchaser, client, customer, consumer

shore¹ n

walk along the shore

seashore, beach, sand(s), shingle, strand, waterfront,
waterside, front, promenade, coast, seaside, seaboard,
foreshore, lakeside, bank
OLD strand, rivage
FORMAL littoral
Related adjective: littoral

shore² v

shore up a building

support, hold (up), prop (up), stay, underpin, buttress,
brace, strengthen, reinforce

shorn adj

cut, cropped, shaved, shaven, stripped, polled, bald,
beardless, crew-cut, deprived

short adj, adv

• adj

1 *a short visit*

brief, short-lived, cursory, hasty, quick, swift, fleeting, passing, momentary, transitory, transient, temporary, limited
FORMAL ephemeral, evanescent, fugacious
2 CONCISE, brief, succinct, terse, crisp, pithy, to the point, compact, compressed, shortened, condensed, truncated, curtailed, abbreviated, abridged, summarized, summary
FORMAL aphoristic
3 SMALL, little, low, petite, slight, minuscule, diminutive, squat, dumpy, stubby, Lilliputian; *Scot* wee
COLLOQ. teeny, teensy, pint-size(d)
4 INADEQUATE, insufficient, deficient, lacking, wanting, low, poor, meagre, scarce, scanty, scant, sparse
COLLOQ. tight
5 BRUSQUE, curt, gruff, snappy, sharp, abrupt, terse, blunt, direct, rude, impolite, discourteous, uncivil
Ea 1 long, lasting **3** tall, big **4** adequate, ample **5** polite, civil
♦ *adv*
unexpectedly, suddenly, abruptly
■ **short of**
1 DEFICIENT IN, lacking, missing, short on, less than, low on, other than
FORMAL wanting
COLLOQ. pushed for
2 EXCEPT FOR, apart from, excepting, but, but for, other than, with the exception of, aside from, save, omitting, not counting, leaving out, excluding, besides, bar, barring
■ **fall short**
be less than required, be lacking, be insufficient, be inadequate
■ **in short**
in brief, briefly, in a word, in a few words, in conclusion, summarizing, concisely, to sum up, in fine
COLLOQ. in a nutshell, to cut a long story short

Synonym nuances
adjective sense 1
You can use **short-lived** of something lasting only for a little time, with an intimation of regret at this: *my joy was short-lived*. **Temporary** and **limited**, however, may be used to show that something, in addition to lasting a short time, is also known from the outset to be impermanent: *a temporary repair; the seasonal positions they seek to fill are of limited duration*. **Momentary** suggests something of exceedingly limited duration, likewise **ephemeral**, which also carries the added suggestion that its brevity is expected: *statistics, ephemeral though they may be*. Similarly **fleeting**, **transient**, **passing** and **transitory** all describe restricted existence, though the first emphasizes great speed: *a fleeting glimpse of the star*.
  Quick and **swift** are not particularly marked terms, although the second may be used to hint that the speed is desirable. **Cursory** presents a more negative aspect, often implying superficiality: *the book is similarly cursory in its treatment of style*, and **hasty** might appropriately be used of a brief act not thought to be well done: *a hasty transition from one system to another*.

---

shortage *n*
inadequacy, insufficiency, deficiency, shortfall, deficit, lack, want, need, scarcity, poverty, absence, dearth; *N Am* wantage
TECHNICAL skills gap
FORMAL paucity
Ea sufficiency, abundance, surplus

shortcoming *n*
defect, imperfection, fault, flaw, drawback, failing, weak point, weakness, frailty, foible

shorten *v*
cut (down), trim, prune, crop, dock, pare (down), make/

become shorter, curtail, truncate, abbreviate, abridge, condense, compress, contract, sum up, reduce, lessen, decrease, diminish, take up
Ea lengthen, enlarge, amplify

shortened *adj*
abridged, condensed, summarized, abbreviated, abstracted
FORMAL abbreviatory
Ea amplified

shortfall *n*
deficit, shortage, deficiency, loss, arrears, lack, default
Ea excess

short-lived *adj*
brief, momentary, passing, short, temporary, transient, transitory, fleeting, impermanent
TECHNICAL caducous
FORMAL ephemeral, evanescent, fugacious
Ea abiding, enduring, lasting, long-lived

shortly *adv*
1 SOON, in a little while, in a while, before long, presently, by and by
2 BRUSQUELY, curtly, gruffly, sharply, abruptly, tersely, bluntly, directly, rudely, impolitely, discourteously, uncivilly

short-sighted *adj*
1 MYOPIC, near-sighted
2 IMPROVIDENT, imprudent, unwise, unthinking, impolitic, ill-advised, thoughtless, careless, rash, heedless, hasty, ill-considered
FORMAL injudicious, uncircumspect
Ea 1 long-sighted, far-sighted

short-staffed *adj*
shorthanded, understaffed, with insufficient staff, below strength

short-tempered *adj*
bad-tempered, impatient, irritable, hot-tempered, quick-tempered, fiery, irascible, choleric, crusty, touchy
COLLOQ. ratty, testy, grouchy
Ea calm, patient, placid

short-winded *adj*
breathless, gasping, panting, puffing

shot[1] *n*
1 GUNFIRE, discharge, blast, bang, crack, explosion
2 BULLET, ammunition, missile, projectile, ball, pellet
COLLOQ. slug
3 *he's a good shot*
shooter, marksman, markswoman, gunner, sniper, hunter
4 *have a shot at goal*
kick, hit, throw, stroke, fling, lob
5 PHOTOGRAPH, photo, snap, snapshot, print, picture, image, slide, transparency
6 ATTEMPT, try, effort, endeavour, guess, turn
COLLOQ. go, bash, whack, crack, stab; *Aust & NZ* burl
7 INJECTION, inoculation, immunization, vaccination, dose
COLLOQ. jab
SLANG fix
■ **shot in the arm**
encouragement, stimulus, boost, fillip, lift, uplift, impetus, fresh talent
■ **shot in the dark**
guess, guesswork, wild guess, blind guess, conjecture, speculation
■ **call the shots**
be in charge, lead, give a lead, head (up), manage, direct, supervise, command
COLLOQ. be in the driving seat, wear the trousers
■ **like a shot**
without delay, without hesitation, unhesitatingly, immediately, instantly, at once, eagerly, enthusiastically, willingly

shot

■ **not by a long shot**
by no means, never, certainly not, not at all, not in the least, in no way
COLLOQ. no way

shot² adj
shot fabric
variegated, mottled, watered, moiré, iridescent

shoulder v
1 ACCEPT, assume, take on, take upon yourself, bear, carry, sustain, support
2 PUSH, shove, jostle, thrust, press, force, elbow

■ **shoulder to shoulder**
side by side, hand in hand, united, together, co-operatively, working together, closely, in alliance

■ **give someone the cold shoulder**
snub, rebuff, shun, spurn, insult, disregard, ignore, brush off, cut, slight, rebuke, put down, squash, humble, shame, humiliate, mortify
COLLOQ. slap in the face, kick in the teeth, blank

■ **rub shoulders with**
meet with, associate with, socialize with, mix with, fraternize with
COLLOQ. hang/knock about/around with, hobnob with

shout v, n
♦ *v*
call (out), cry (out), scream, shriek, yell, raise your voice, rant and rave, squawk, roar, bellow, bawl, howl, bay, cheer
COLLOQ. holler; *N Am* yawp
♦ *n*
call, cry, scream, shriek, yell, squawk, roar, bellow, bawl, howl, bay, cheer
COLLOQ. holler; *N Am* yawp

Synonym nuances
verb
You can use **call** (**out**) of deliberately projecting your voice so your words may be heard, whereas **cry** (**out**) is more suggestive of instinctively emitted sounds: *he cried out in pain*. **Scream** suggests a loud, high-pitched emission, with connotations of negative emotions such as pain, fear or anger, while **shriek** suggests an even more piercing sound: *children shrieking in the playground*. **Yell**, too, implies sounding loud and sharp, as well as implying a degree of effort, and is often used in the context of anger: *he yelled at them to keep quiet*, whereas **rant and rave** is more suggestive of an inarticulate tirade.

More instinctive, animal-like sounds are suggested by **squawk**: *she squawked in surprise*, and **roar** and **bellow**, which could be used to describe a deeper and hoarser sound. The term **bay** may be used to suggest vengeful jeers like the prolonged wailing of hounds in pursuit of quarry: *the crowd bayed for the referee's blood*. **Bawl** returns to the idea of loudness, often with an element of anger, whereas **howl** is more connotative of being in distress.

In comparison, **raise your voice** suggests a far more restrained increase in volume.

---

shove v, n
♦ *v*
push, thrust, drive, propel, force, barge, jolt, jostle, elbow, shoulder, press, crowd
♦ *n*
push, thrust, jolt, jostle, elbow, shoulder

■ **shove off**
leave, depart
COLLOQ. beat it, clear off, push off, get lost, scram, scarper, clear out, skedaddle, vamoose, do a bunk, scoot, run for it, buzz off, scat
SLANG *Aust* choof off

shovel n, v
♦ *n*
spade, scoop, bucket, backhoe, backhoe loader, excavator, dust-pan, peel; *dialect* shool
TECHNICAL van
OLD main
♦ *v*
dig, excavate, scoop, dredge, clear, move, shift, spade, heap; *dialect* shool

show v, n
♦ *v*
1 REVEAL, expose, uncover, disclose, divulge, make visible, make clear, make plain, make known
FORMAL manifest
2 EXPRESS, mean, indicate, signify, register, record, portray, depict, make it clear, prove, demonstrate, be evidence, bear witness to, suggest
FORMAL manifest
3 TEACH, instruct, clarify, make clear, elucidate, point out, explain, demonstrate, prove, illustrate, exemplify
FORMAL expound
4 DISPLAY, exhibit, demonstrate, set out, present, produce, offer
5 *show him out*
lead, guide, direct, conduct, steer, take, usher, escort, accompany, attend
6 *he didn't show*
appear, arrive, come, turn up
E3 1 hide, cover (up)
♦ *n*
1 ENTERTAINMENT, performance, programme, production, staging, showing, spectacle, extravaganza
2 EXHIBITION, fair, parade, presentation, demonstration, display, spectacle
FORMAL exposition
COLLOQ. expo
3 DISPLAY, representation, demonstration, presentation, sign, indication, arrangement
FORMAL manifestation, array
4 PRETENCE, semblance, façade, front, illusion, ostentation, parade, flamboyance, panache, showiness, exhibitionism, pose
FORMAL affectation
COLLOQ. window dressing, play-acting, pizzazz
5 APPEARANCE, air, impression, guise, display, profession
6 *Who's running the show?*
affair, proceedings, organization, undertaking, operation

■ **show off**
1 BOAST, parade, strut, swagger, brag, flaunt, brandish
COLLOQ. swank; *S Afr* pronk
2 DISPLAY, exhibit, demonstrate, show to advantage, advertise, set off, enhance

■ **show up**
1 REVEAL, show, make visible, expose, unmask, lay bare, highlight, pinpoint
2 HUMILIATE, embarrass, mortify, shame, put to shame, disgrace, let down
3 ARRIVE, come, turn up, appear
COLLOQ. materialize

showdown n
confrontation, clash, crisis, climax, moment of truth, culmination, dénouement, face-off

shower n, v
♦ *n*
rain, drizzling, stream, torrent, sprinkling, deluge, hail, volley, barrage, drift, scud, thunder-shower; *dialect* scat, skit; *Scot* scouther
TECHNICAL avalanche, pelter
OLD (*Shakesp*) aspersion

• *v*
spray, sprinkle, rain, pour, fall, deluge, inundate, overwhelm, load, heap, lavish, pelt, pepper, play, hail
OLD (*Spenser*) pound

showiness *n*
flamboyance, pretentiousness, glitter, ostentation, razzle-dazzle
COLLOQ. flashiness, pizzazz, razzmatazz, glitz, swank, ritziness
E- restraint

showing *n, adj*
• *n*
display, evidence, impression, representation, record, presentation, performance, exhibition, show, staging, account, statement, appearance, past performance
COLLOQ. track record
• *adj*
explanatory, demonstrative, descriptive, illustrative, indicative, representative, significant, symbolic
FORMAL explicatory, elucidative, revelatory

showing-off *n*
boasting, self-advertisement, bragging, exhibitionism, braggadocio, swagger, egotism, peacockery
FORMAL vainglory
COLLOQ. swank
E- modesty

showman *n*
performer, entertainer, impresario, publicist, ring-master, self-advertiser
COLLOQ. show-off

show-off *n*
swaggerer, braggart, boaster, exhibitionist, peacock, poser, poseur, egotist
COLLOQ. swanker, know-all

showy *adj*
flashy, flamboyant, ostentatious, gaudy, garish, glittering, loud, conspicuous, tawdry, fancy, ornate, pretentious, pompous
COLLOQ. swanky, flash, ritzy, glitzy
SLANG bling-bling
E- quiet, restrained

shred *n, v*
• *n*
1 SCRAP, ribbon, tatter, rag, snippet, sliver, bit, piece, fragment, remnant, particle, modicum, speck, vestige, peeling, clipping, snip, tag, wisp, frazzle, screed, hangnail, agnail; *dialect* mammock, mummock; *Scot* taver
2 JOT, iota, atom, spot, grain, mite, whit, trace, wisp
• *v*
cut (up), tear (up), rip (up), chop, slice, julienne
OLD mammock

shrew *n*
dragon, nag, scold, termagant, virago, vixen, Xanthippe, harridan, henpecker, spitfire, Fury
OLD shrow
SLANG bitch

shrewd *adj*
astute, prudent, well-advised, calculated, far-sighted, smart, clever, intelligent, sharp, keen, acute, alert, perceptive, observant, discerning, discriminating, knowing, calculating, cunning, crafty, wily, canny, artful, sly, wise, hard-headed, long-headed, sharp-sighted, arch, cut-and-thrust, argute, gnostic
OLD callid
FORMAL judicious, sagacious, perspicacious
COLLOQ. smart, savvy, knowing a thing or two
E- unwise, obtuse, naive, unsophisticated

Synonym nuances
Astute can be used to suggest having an insightful ability to understand: *an astute awareness of the way events are unfolding*. **Sharp, keen, perceptive** and **acute** echo this idea of being able to deftly assess a situation: *with her sharp pen and keen observation*. **Alert**, on the other hand, is more suggestive of being attentive, while **observant** implies being deliberately watchful.
 Discerning, again, has implications of insight but further suggests an element of good taste; **discriminating**, likewise, implies an ability to distinguish between options: *make a discriminating selection from your range of reference materials*. **Calculated** is more suggestive of having weighed up the pros and cons: *a calculated bid for media coverage*.
 You can use **knowing** to imply having the advantage of privileged information: *with a knowing look*, whereas **calculating** has rather more negative implications of scheming. Similarly, **cunning, crafty, wily** and **sly** are more disapproving, and suggest an underhand element, but **canny** is merely suggestive of being prudent: *canny investors*, like the approbatory **wise**, which implies innate knowledge and judgement. **Artful** suggests a degree of mental dexterity, again with overtones of deception. **Arch** would be reserved for someone with expertise, but again in deception and cunning: *an arch manipulator*.

---

shrewdly *adv*
astutely, cleverly, far-sightedly, wisely, knowingly, perceptively, craftily, cannily, artfully, slyly, argutely
FORMAL judiciously, sagaciously, perspicaciously

shrewdness *n*
discernment, intelligence, perceptiveness, sharpness, acuteness, astuteness, grasp, judgement, penetration, wisdom, acumen, canniness, prudence
FORMAL perspicacity, astucity, sagacity
OLD callidity
COLLOQ. smartness
E- foolishness, naivety, obtuseness

shrewish *adj*
scolding, bad-tempered, ill-tempered, ill-humoured, ill-natured, nagging, peevish, quarrelsome, complaining, discontented, fault-finding, henpecking, petulant, captious, sharp-tongued, vixenish
FORMAL querulous
E- affectionate, peaceable, placid, supportive

shriek *v, n*
• *v*
scream, screech, squawk, squeal, cry (out), shout, yell, wail, howl, yelp
• *n*
scream, screech, squawk, squeal, cry, shout, yell, wail, howl, yelp

shrill *adj*
high, high-pitched, treble, sharp, acute, piercing, penetrating, screaming, screeching, strident, ear-splitting
E- deep, low, soft, gentle

shrine *n*
holy place, sacred place, chapel, sanctuary, church, tabernacle, temple, martyry, fane, dome, delubrum, dagoba, stupa, tope, darga, vimana

shrink *v*
1 CONTRACT, shorten, grow/become smaller, narrow, decrease, lessen, reduce, diminish, drop off, fall off, dwindle, shrivel, wrinkle, wither, atrophy
2 RECOIL, draw back, back away, shy away, withdraw, retire, balk, quail, cower, cringe, wince, flinch, start back, shun, have scruples/qualms about
E- **1** expand, stretch **2** accept, embrace

shrivel v

wrinkle, pucker (up), wither, wilt, shrink, dwindle, parch, dry (up), dehydrate, desiccate, scorch, sear, burn, frizzle; *Scot* gizzen

shrivelled adj

wrinkled, puckered, shrunken, withered, emaciated, wizened, dried up, dry, desiccated; *Scot* gizzen
OLD writhled
FORMAL sere

shroud v, n

♦ v

wrap, envelop, swathe, cloak, veil, screen, cloud, hide, conceal, enshroud, blanket, cover, fog
ᴇᴈ uncover, expose

♦ n

winding-sheet, cloth, graveclothes, cerecloth, cerement, pall, mantle, cloak, veil, screen, cloud, blanket, covering
OLD sindon

shrouded adj

wrapped, enveloped, swathed, cloaked, enshrouded, hidden, concealed, covered, clouded, blanketed, veiled
ᴇᴈ exposed, uncovered

shrub

Shrubs include:

azalea	fuchsia	mallow
berberis	heather	mimosa
broom	hebe	mock orange
buddleia	holly	musk rose
camellia	honeysuckle	peony
clematis	hydrangea	phlomis
cotoneaster	ivy	privet
daphne	japonica	rhododendron
dogwood	jasmine	rose
eucryphia	laburnum	spiraea
euonymus	laurel	viburnum
firethorn	lavender	weigela
flowering currant	lilac	wistaria
forsythia	magnolia	witch hazel

See also **flower**; **plant**.

shrug v

■ **shrug off**

brush off, ignore, disregard, dismiss, neglect, take no notice of

shrunken adj

reduced, shrunk, shrivelled, contracted, emaciated, gaunt
FORMAL cadaverous
ᴇᴈ full, generous, rounded, sleek

shudder v, n

♦ v

shiver, shake, tremble, quiver, quake, heave, convulse, judder

♦ n

shiver, quiver, tremble, quake, heave, tremor, spasm, convulsion, judder

shuffle v

1 MIX (UP), intermix, jumble (up), confuse, disorder, rearrange, reorganize, move around, shift around, switch, reshuffle
OLD pack
2 *shuffle across the room*
shamble, scuffle, scrape, drag, falter, limp, toddle, doddle, hobble, dodge, hedge

shun v

avoid, evade, elude, steer clear of, shy away from, keep away from, spurn, ignore, snub, ostracize

OLD evite
FORMAL eschew
COLLOQ. give a wide berth to, cold-shoulder, avoid like the plague
ᴇᴈ accept, embrace

shunt v

move, transport, carry, bring, take, fetch, relocate, transfer, shift, switch, swing
FORMAL transpose
COLLOQ. budge

shut v

close, slam, seal, fasten, secure, put the lid on, lock, latch, bolt, bar
ᴇᴈ open
2 CONFINE, lock up, cage in, coop up, imprison, jail, intern
FORMAL incarcerate, immure

■ **shut down**

close (down), stop, cease, halt, suspend, switch off, inactivate
FORMAL terminate, discontinue

■ **shut in**

enclose, box in, hem in, fence in, confine, imprison, cage (in), keep in, restrain
FORMAL immure

■ **shut off**

seclude, isolate, cut off, separate, segregate

■ **shut out**

1 EXCLUDE, bar, debar, lock out, ostracize, banish, outlaw, exile
2 HIDE, conceal, cover (up), block out, mask, screen, veil

■ **shut up**

SILENCE, gag, quiet, quieten, hush (up), hold your tongue
COLLOQ. pipe down, clam up, keep mum

Colloquial ways of telling someone to shut up include:

belt up!	hold your peace!	say no more!
button it!	keep shtoom!	shut it!
can it!	mum!	shut up!
cut the cackle!	not another	shut your face!
drop dead!	word!	shut your gob!
dry up!	one more word	shut your mouth!
enough said!	out of....!	wrap up!
get knotted!	pack it in!	
give it a rest!	pipe down!	
give over!	put a sock in it!	

shutter n

screen, shade, blind, louvre, jalousie

shuttle v

go to and fro, travel, ply, run, alternate, commute, shunt, shuttlecock, seesaw

shy adj, v

♦ adj

timid, timorous, bashful, reticent, reserved, demure, diffident, introverted, retiring, coy, self-conscious, embarrassed, inhibited, modest, self-effacing, shrinking, withdrawn, hesitant, cautious, chary, suspicious, nervous, backward, squab, farouche; *Scot* skeigh, willyard
COLLOQ. mous(e)y, backward in coming forward
ᴇᴈ bold, assertive, confident

■ **shy away**

avoid, balk, shrink, recoil, wince, back away, flinch, swerve, start, quail, rear, buck, jib, startle, spook

■ **fight shy of**

avoid, steer clear of, shun, spurn
FORMAL eschew
COLLOQ. give a wide berth to, keep at arm's length

Synonym nuances
adjective

You might use **timid** to suggest a slightly fearful aspect to someone's shyness, while **diffident** would suggest an deeper lack of confidence. **Bashful** is more suggestive of a restraining modesty rather than fear, while **demure** suggests primness, and hints at a more affected modesty. **Coy** also implies a degree of affectedness: *a coy smile of invitation*, but can also be used to suggest evasion: *the company is coy about revealing its profits.*

 Reticent is more straightforwardly suggestive of a disinclination to talk: *he was reticent about the perks of his job*, while **reserved**, too, implies an uncommunicative element more explicitly expressed by **withdrawn**. The term **introverted** may be used to suggest an inward-looking nature, and while **retiring** is more suggestive of being deliberately unobtrusive, the term **inhibited** implies being more subconsciously restrained: *Charles felt inhibited in mixed company, and found it difficult to talk*. The term **self-effacing** is suggestive of someone who prefers to keep their presence or achievements hidden, and **backward** and **shrinking** similarly suggest keeping a low profile.

 Both **hesitant** and **cautious** put more focus on the cause of shyness and suggest a degree of apprehension, whereas **chary** and **suspicious** put more emphasis on mistrust. **Self-conscious** would be used specifically of shyness brought about by being overly concerned about how you are perceived.

shyly *adv*
timidly, bashfully, reticently, diffidently, coyly, self-consciously, hesitantly, cautiously, cagily, charily
E∃ boldly, assertively, confidently

shyness *n*
timidity, timidness, timorousness, hesitancy, diffidence, bashfulness, reticence, self-consciousness, inhibition, embarrassment, modesty, constraint, nervousness, coyness, caginess, chariness
COLLOQ. mousiness
E∃ boldness, assertiveness, confidence

sibling *n*
brother, sister, twin
OLD german

sibyl *n*
wise woman, oracle, prophetess, seer, seeress, sorceress, Pythia, pythoness

sick *adj*
1 ILL, unwell, laid up, poorly, ailing, sickly, weak, feeble
FORMAL indisposed
COLLOQ. under the weather, rough, groggy, seedy, off colour, out of sorts
See Synonym nuances panel at **ill**.
2 VOMITING, retching, heaving, nauseous, queasy, bilious, travel-sick, carsick, seasick, airsick
COLLOQ. throwing up, spewing up, puking
3 *sick of waiting*
bored, tired, weary, disgusted, nauseated
COLLOQ. fed up
4 DISGUSTED, annoyed, disappointed, angry, enraged, disgruntled
COLLOQ. fed up, sick and tired, cheesed off, browned off, hacked off
SLANG pissed off
5 *a sick joke*
cruel, black, tasteless, vulgar, gross, macabre, in bad taste
E∃ 1 well, healthy
■ **be sick**
vomit, retch, heave, gag, feel nauseous, feel queasy

COLLOQ. throw up, spew, puke, fetch up
SLANG *N Am* barf

sicken *v*
1 NAUSEATE, revolt, disgust, repel, appal, put off
COLLOQ. turn off, turn your stomach
2 BECOME ILL, catch, develop, pick up, get, go down with, come down with, become infected with, become ill with
FORMAL contract, succumb to
E∃ 1 delight, attract

sickening *adj*
nauseating, revolting, disgusting, offensive, appalling, shocking, distasteful, off-putting, foul, vile, loathsome, nauseous, repulsive, repellent, stomach-turning
SLANG *Aust* chunderous
E∃ delightful, pleasing, attractive

sickly *adj*
1 UNHEALTHY, infirm, delicate, weak, feeble, frail, wan, pale, pallid, insipid, ailing, sick, bilious, faint, languid
FORMAL indisposed
COLLOQ. washed out
2 NAUSEATING, revolting, sweet, syrupy, cloying, mawkish
COLLOQ. soppy, schmaltzy, gushy, mushy, slushy
E∃ 1 healthy, robust, sturdy, strong

sickness *n*
1 ILLNESS, disease, ailment, complaint, ill-health, disorder, infirmity
FORMAL malady, affliction, indisposition
COLLOQ. bug, virus
2 VOMITING, retching, heaving, nausea, queasiness, biliousness, travel sickness, motion sickness, morning sickness, carsickness, seasickness, airsickness
COLLOQ. throwing up, spewing up, puking
E∃ 1 health

side *n, adj, v*
♦ *n*
1 *the side of an object*
face, facet, surface, end, profile
2 EDGE, margin, fringe, periphery, border, boundary, limit, end, verge, rim, brink, bank, shore, flank, hand
TECHNICAL jamb
Related adjective: lateral
3 *the other side of the city*
district, quarter, area, region, sector, neighbourhood, section, zone
4 *draw the figure from all sides*
aspect, angle, slant, facet, standpoint, view, viewpoint, point of view, profile
5 *hear one side of the story*
standpoint, viewpoint, point of view, view, aspect, angle, slant
6 TEAM, party, faction, wing, camp, sect, splinter group, cause, interest
♦ *adj*
1 LATERAL, flanking, wing
2 MINOR, marginal, secondary, subsidiary, subordinate, lesser, incidental
3 OBLIQUE, sideward, sideways, sidelong
■ **side-effect**
spin-off, repercussion, result, consequence, effect, outcome, reverberation, echo, rebound, recoil, backwash, aftermath
COLLOQ. ripple
■ **side with**
agree with, team up with, take someone's side, be on the side of, support, give your support to, back, give your backing to, join with, vote for, favour, prefer
■ **side by side**
next to each other, close to each other, alongside each other, shoulder to shoulder
■ **take someone's side**
be on the side of, support, give your support to, back, give

your backing to, join with, vote for, favour, prefer, encourage, help, motivate, sympathize with

sideline n, v
* n

second job, subsidiary activity, hobby, pastime, interest, diversion, recreation, relaxation, pursuit, leisure activity/pursuit, game, sport, entertainment, amusement, divertissement
* v

exclude, demote, downgrade, degrade, relegate, transfer, banish, expatriate, deport, eject, exile, expel

sidelong adj
indirect, oblique, sideward, sideways, secret, covert, surreptitious
⧉ direct, overt

side-splitting adj
hilarious, funny, amusing, comical, humorous, farcical, laughable, riotous, uproarious
COLLOQ. hysterical, killing, a scream
⧉ serious, grave

sidestep v
avoid, find a way around, dodge, evade, elude, skirt, bypass
FORMAL circumvent
COLLOQ. duck, shirk, give a miss
⧉ tackle, deal with

sidetrack v
deflect, head off, lead away from, divert, distract

sideways adv, adj
* adv

from side to side, sidewards, to the side, edgeways, edgewise, crabwise, laterally, obliquely, askance, athwart
* adj

sideward, side, lateral, slanted, oblique, indirect, sidelong

sidle v
slink, edge, inch, creep, sneak

siege n
blockade, encirclement, besiegement, beleaguerment
Related adjective: obsidional

siesta n
rest, sleep, relaxation, nap, afternoon nap, doze
FORMAL repose
COLLOQ. catnap, forty winks, snooze

sieve v, n
* v

sift, strain, filter, screen, riddle, separate, remove, sort, winnow; dialect sye, temse
OLD cribble, searce
* n

colander, strainer, filter, sifter, riddle, screen, boulter, cribble, trommel; dialect sye, temse
OLD searce
Related adjectives: cribrate, cribrose, coliform, cribriform, ethmoid

sift v
1 SIEVE, strain, filter, riddle, screen, winnow, separate, sort
OLD cribble, garble, searce
2 EXAMINE, scrutinize, investigate, analyse, study, pore over, probe, review, search

sigh v
1 BREATHE, moan, complain, lament, grieve
OLD suspire, besigh, sithe
FORMAL exhale
2 the wind sighing through the valley
rustle, whisper, crackle, swish, sough
FORMAL susurrate
■ **sigh for**
grieve, lament, languish, long, mourn, pine, weep, yearn, cry, cry for the moon

sight n, v
* n

1 VISION, eyesight, seeing, ability to see, faculty/sense of sight, observation, perception
2 VIEW, look, glance, glimpse, range, field of vision, range of vision, visibility
3 APPEARANCE, spectacle, show, display, exhibition, scene, monstrosity
COLLOQ. eyesore, fright
4 see the sights of London
place of interest, landmark, amenity, beauty, feature, curiosity, wonder, splendour, marvel
* v

see, observe, spot, glimpse, perceive, discern, distinguish, make out
FORMAL espy, behold
Related adjective: visual
■ **catch sight of**
see, perceive, notice, note, watch, view, look at, mark, glimpse, discern, make out, recognize, spot, identify
■ **lose sight of**
forget, omit, fail to remember, neglect, overlook, disregard, ignore, put aside, slip your mind
■ **set your sights on**
aim at, plan for, seek to, intend to, strive for, aspire towards, work towards

sightless adj
blind, visually impaired, unsighted, unseeing, visionless, eyeless
⧉ sighted

sightseer n
tourist, visitor, holidaymaker, tripper, excursionist; N Am rubberneck

sign n, v
* n

1 SYMBOL, token, character, figure, code, cipher, representation, emblem, badge, insignia, logo
2 INDICATION, mark, signal, gesture, evidence, proof, clue, pointer, token, hint, suggestion, trace, symptom
FORMAL manifestation
3 GESTURE, signal, movement, motion, wave, indication, act, action, gesticulation
4 NOTICE, poster, board, placard, signpost, marker, indicator
5 PORTENT, omen, forewarning, foreboding
FORMAL augury, prognostication, harbinger, presage
* v

1 sign your name
autograph, countersign, initial, endorse, write
FORMAL inscribe, attest, ratify, witness
2 SIGNAL, wave, gesticulate, gesture, beckon, wink, motion, nod, indicate, express, show, mark, communicate
3 RECRUIT, enlist, draft, conscript, enrol, sign up, levy, engage, take on, mobilize, raise, muster, gather, assemble, put together, obtain, acquire, talent-spot, headhunt
■ **sign over**
make over, transfer, turn over, surrender, entrust, deliver, convey, consign
■ **sign up**
enlist, enrol, join (up), join the services, volunteer, register, sign on, put your name down for, recruit, take on, hire, engage, employ

signal n, v, adj
* n

sign, indication, mark, gesture, evidence, clue, message, symptom, pointer, token, hint, light, alert, warning, tip-off
COLLOQ. shot across the bows
* v

wave, gesticulate, gesture, beckon, wink, motion, nod, sign, indicate, express, show, mark, communicate
FORMAL signify

♦ *adj*

significant, important, exceptional, notable, noteworthy, outstanding, extraordinary, impressive, memorable, momentous, remarkable, striking, eminent, distinguished, conspicuous, glorious, famous

---

Kinds of signal and warning include:

alarm	hand signal	a shot across the
alarm-bell	heliograph	bows
alarm clock	honk	shout
amber light	hooter	signal box
beacon	horn	signal letters
Belisha beacon	hurricane	siren
bell	warning	smoke alarm
bicycle bell	indicator	smoke signal
bleeper	klaxon	SOS
bugle	knell	starter's gun
buoy	larum	storm cone
burglar alarm	larum-bell	storm signal
buzzer	lighthouse	storm warning
car alarm	beacon	tattoo
car horn	Lutine bell	time signal (pips)
cue	mayday	tocsin
curfew bell	Morse code	toot
distress signal	pager	trafficator
drumbeat	password	traffic lights
final warning	personal alarm	Very light
fire	police whistle	vigia
fire alarm	red alert	warning light
flag	red card	whistle
flare	red flag	winker
flashing light	red light	written warning
foghorn	reveille	yellow card
gale warning	rocket	yellow flag
go-ahead	security alarm	
gong	semaphore signal	
green light		

---

signature *n*

autograph, name, initials, mark, endorsement, inscription, subscription, hand, countersignature, frank, sheet, tag
COLLOQ. *N Am* John Hancock

significance *n*

importance, relevance, consequence, seriousness, solemnity, magnitude, matter, interest, consideration, weight, force, meaning, implication(s), sense, essence, gist, point, message
FORMAL significance, import, purport
E3 insignificance, unimportance, pettiness

significant *adj*

1 IMPORTANT, relevant, consequential, momentous, memorable, weighty, serious, noteworthy, material, critical, vital, crucial, key, fateful, marked, considerable, appreciable
2 MEANINGFUL, symbolic, expressive, suggestive, indicative, symptomatic, eloquent, pregnant, ominous
E3 1 insignificant, unimportant, trivial **2** meaningless

significantly *adv*

1 VITALLY, crucially, considerably, appreciably, remarkably, notably, noticeably, perceptibly, critically, materially
2 MEANINGFULLY, eloquently, meaningly, expressively, knowingly, suggestively

signify *v*

1 MEAN, symbolize, be a sign of, represent, stand for, indicate, mark, show, exhibit, signal, express, convey, transmit, communicate, declare, proclaim, intimate, imply, suggest
FORMAL denote, betoken, portend
2 MATTER, count, be of importance, be important, be relevant, have influence, carry weight
FORMAL be of consequence
COLLOQ. make waves

signpost *n*

sign, pointer, marker, indicator, placard, guidepost, fingerpost, handpost, waypost, clue

silence *n, v*

♦ *n*

quiet, quietness, hush, peace, peacefulness, stillness, still, calm, calmness, tranquillity, lull, noiselessness, soundlessness, muteness, dumbness, speechlessness, wordlessness, voicelessness, taciturnity, uncommunicativeness, reticence, reserve, secretiveness
TECHNICAL quiescence
COLLOQ. mum
E3 noise, sound, din, uproar

♦ *v*

quiet, quieten, hush, mute, strike dumb, deaden, muffle, stifle, gag, muzzle, suppress, subdue, quell, still, dumbfound
FORMAL abate

silent *adj*

inaudible, noiseless, soundless, quiet, peaceful, still, calm, hushed, muted, mute, dumb, speechless, tongue-tied, tight-lipped, taciturn, reticent, reserved, secretive, tacit, unspoken, implicit, implied, unexpressed, understood, unvoiced, voiceless, wordless, dummy, sulking, sullen
TECHNICAL quiescent
OLD hush, conticent, creepmouse, tuneless, whisht, whist; (*Shakesp*) languageless
FORMAL obmutescent
COLLOQ. mum, shtoom
E3 noisy, loud, talkative

silently *adv*

noiselessly, quietly, calmly, inaudibly, soundlessly, speechlessly, wordlessly, without a word, unheard, dumbly, mutely, tacitly
TECHNICAL quiescently

silhouette *n, v*

♦ *n*

outline, contour, shape, form, profile, shadow, shadow figure, skyline
FORMAL delineation, configuration

♦ *v*

outline, shadow, shape, profile, stand out
FORMAL delineate, configurate, configure

silky *adj*

silken, fine, sleek, lustrous, glossy, satiny, smooth, soft, velvety
FORMAL diaphanous

silliness *n*

foolishness, folly, stupidity, absurdity, ridiculousness, ludicrousness, preposterousness, idiocy, frivolousness, frivolity, childishness, inaneness, fatuousness, immaturity, irresponsibility, senselessness, pointlessness, meaninglessness, irrationality, foolhardiness, recklessness, rashness
COLLOQ. daftness, looniness, loopiness, barminess, pottiness
E3 sense, sensibleness, wisdom, maturity

silly *adj, n*

♦ *adj*

foolish, stupid, unintelligent, unwise, senseless, pointless, thoughtless, idiotic, ridiculous, ludicrous, preposterous, absurd, meaningless, unreasonable, irrational, illogical, frivolous, childish, puerile, inane, fatuous, immature, irresponsible, imprudent, foolhardy, rash, reckless, scatterbrained, feather-brained
FORMAL injudicious
COLLOQ. airheaded, daft, dizzy, soft, dotty, loopy, barmy, potty, nutty
E3 wise, sensible, sane, mature, clever, intelligent

♦ *n*
fool, idiot, ignoramus, simpleton, ninny, halfwit
COLLOQ. dumbo, silly-billy, nincompoop, clot, dope,
duffer, berk, nit, twit, wally, goose; *Aust* bunny

silt *n, v*
♦ *n*
sediment, deposit, residue, sludge, mud, ooze, sullage
FORMAL alluvium, illuvium

■ **silt up**
block (up), clog (up), dam, choke, congest

silvan *adj*
leafy, tree-covered, wooded, woodland
FORMAL arboreous, forestal, forested, forestine
F3 treeless

silver *adj*
greyish-white, whitish-grey, pale grey, snowy
OLD argent
Related adjective: argentine

similar *adj*
like, alike, close, much the same, related, akin,
corresponding, equivalent, coincident, comparable,
uniform, cut from the same cloth
TECHNICAL homologous
FORMAL analogous, homogeneous
COLLOQ. samey
F3 dissimilar, different

similarity *n*
likeness, resemblance, sameness, closeness, relation,
kinship, correspondence, parallelism, equivalence,
comparability, compatibility, agreement, affinity,
uniformity
FORMAL similitude, congruence, analogy, homogeneity,
concordance
F3 dissimilarity, difference, clash

similarly *adv*
in the same way, likewise, correspondingly, uniformly, by
the same token, by analogy
F3 differently

similitude *n*
similarity, likeness, resemblance, sameness, closeness,
relation, correspondence, parallelism, equivalence,
comparability, compatibility, agreement, affinity,
uniformity
FORMAL congruence, analogy

simmer *v*
1 BOIL GENTLY, bubble, cook gently, seethe, stew
2 *simmer with anger*
fume, rage, boil, seethe, burn, smoulder
■ **simmer down**
calm down, cool down, subside, lessen, become less
angry, control yourself, collect yourself

simpering *adj*
self-conscious, silly, coy, giggling, smirky, missish,
schoolgirlish
FORMAL affected

simple *adj*
1 *a simple question; in simple language*
easy, elementary, straightforward, uncomplicated,
uninvolved, effortless, clear, lucid, plain, understandable,
comprehensible
COLLOQ. cushy, easy-peasy, easy as pie, rough and ready,
a cinch, a doddle, a piece of cake, a pushover, a walkover,
a cakewalk, as easy as falling off a log, not rocket
science
2 BASIC, plain, crude, primitive, natural, undecorated,
unadorned, unembellished, unsophisticated, ordinary,
mere, unpretentious, unfussy, classic, rudimentary, stark,
austere, spartan
COLLOQ. low-tech, no-frills

3 *the simple fact is ...*
plain, basic, straightforward, bald, stark, direct,
unambiguous, open, honest, sincere, candid, blunt
4 UNSOPHISTICATED, unpretentious, natural, innocent,
artless, guileless, ingenuous, naive, green
5 FOOLISH, stupid, silly, idiotic, half-witted, simple-minded,
feeble-minded, slow, backward, retarded
F3 1 difficult, hard, complicated, intricate **2** elaborate,
fancy, luxurious **4** sophisticated, worldly, artful **5** clever,
sharp, intelligent

simple-minded *adj*
unsophisticated, simple, natural, artless, stupid, foolish,
idiot, idiotic, imbecile, moronic, cretinous, brainless,
backward, retarded, feeble-minded, addle-brained; *Welsh*
twp
COLLOQ. dim-witted, dopey, goofy
F3 bright, clever

simpleton *n*
idiot, fool, moron, ninny, imbecile, dolt, dullard, dunce,
dupe, jackass, flathead, softhead, noddy, spoon, wiseacre,
Johnny, Gothamite, Abderite; *dialect* gaby, zany; *Scot*
gomeril, sumph
OLD simple, rook, cokes, daw, dawcock, woodcock,
hoddy-doddy, shot-clog, Gothamist
COLLOQ. mug, dope, nincompoop, numskull, nitwit,
stupid, twerp, clot, twit, greenhorn, goose, gander,
blockhead, booby, noodle, flat, mafflin; *Aust* bunny
SLANG juggins, patsy
OLD SLANG green goose, tony
F3 brain

simplicity *n*
simpleness, ease, easiness, facility, straightforwardness,
uncomplicatedness, elementariness, clarity, purity,
plainness, lucidity, intelligibility, restraint, starkness,
naturalness, clean lines, innocence, guilelessness,
naivety, artlessness, unpretentiousness, directness,
frankness, candour, openness, sincerity, honesty,
directness
F3 difficulty, complexity, intricacy, sophistication,
elaborateness

simplification *n*
explanation, clarification, paraphrase, abridgement,
reduction, interpretation, popularization
F3 complication, elaboration

simplify *v*
disentangle, untangle, unravel, decipher, make easy/
easier, make easier to understand, make (more)
comprehensible, make (more) accessible, popularize,
remove complexities in, explain, interpret, clarify,
paraphrase, abridge, reduce, sort out, streamline
F3 complicate, elaborate

simplistic *adj*
oversimplified, superficial, shallow, sweeping, facile,
simple, oversimple, naive, pat
F3 analytical, detailed

simplistically *adv*
superficially, shallowly, simply, facilely, naively

simply *adv*
1 MERELY, just, only, solely, purely, utterly, completely, totally,
wholly, altogether, absolutely, positively, quite, really,
undeniably, unquestionably, without doubt, unreservedly,
unconditionally, clearly, plainly, obviously
2 EASILY, straightforwardly, directly, intelligibly, plainly,
clearly, lucidly, naturally

simulate *v*
pretend, make believe, assume, put on, act, feign, sham,
fake, mock, counterfeit, reproduce, duplicate, copy,
imitate, mimic, parrot, echo, reflect, parallel
FORMAL affect

simulated *adj*

pretended, feigned, artificial, assumed, imitation, put-on, sham, fake, faux, mock, make-believe, bogus, spurious, substitute, synthetic, man-made, inauthentic, insincere
COLLOQ. phoney, pseudo
F3 real, genuine

simultaneous *adj*

happening at the same time, existing at the same time, done at the same time, synchronous, synchronic, coexistent, coinciding, parallel
FORMAL concurrent, contemporaneous, concomitant
F3 asynchronous

simultaneously *adv*

at the same time, at once, all at once, together, all together, in parallel, in unison, synchronically, synchronously

sin *n, v*

♦ *n*
wrong, offence, misdeed, lapse, fault, error, trespass, crime, wrongdoing, sinfulness, wickedness, badness, evil, impiety, immorality, ungodliness, unrighteousness, irreligiousness, guilt
FORMAL transgression, misdemeanour, iniquity
♦ *v*
offend, commit a sin, lapse, err, trespass, misbehave, go wrong, do wrong, stray, go astray, fall, fall from grace
FORMAL transgress

The seven deadly sins are:

pride	sloth	greed/avarice
envy	lust	
anger/wrath	gluttony	

---

since *adv, prep, conj*

♦ *adv, prep, conj*
from that time, from the time (that/of), until (now), after, following, subsequent to, ago
♦ *conj*
as, because, seeing that, considering that, inasmuch as, being, the reason is..., through, on account of, as a result of, owing to, in view of the fact that

sincere *adj*

genuine, true, real, honest, truthful, bona fide, trustworthy, candid, frank, open, direct, straightforward, no-nonsense, plain-spoken, plain-hearted, serious, fervent, earnest, heartfelt, wholehearted, hearty, pure, unadulterated, unmixed, undesigning, unfeigned, natural, artless, ingenuous, guileless, simple, cordial; *Scot* aefald
OLD simple-hearted, single
FORMAL unaffected
COLLOQ. above board, up front
F3 insincere, hypocritical, affected

Synonym nuances

Many of these synonyms are marked by a note of approval.
  Genuine and **real** can be used to suggest being exactly as you seem, while **true** implies being correct in all aspects. **Honest** and **truthful** have more to do with virtue, whilst **trustworthy** suggests someone honourable. The term **bona fide** suggests authenticity or a lack of intention to deceive: *a bona fide money-back guarantee*.
  The less marked terms **candid** and **frank** describe someone who is simply forthright, and **direct**, **straightforward** and **plain-spoken** are similarly uncompromising. **Open** has further suggestions of being unrestrained: *an open exchange of views*.

  Serious and **earnest** suggest commitment: *a serious foray into acting*, and both **fervent** and **heartfelt**, although similar, perhaps suggest an even greater degree of passion. **Wholehearted**, too, remains with the idea of unreserved involvement, while **hearty** and **cordial** convey extra enthusiasm and an element of affability: *hearty congratulations were sent to the trophy winners*.
  Both **pure** and **unadulterated** put the emphasis on a lack of defilement or distraction, and **natural** and **simple**, likewise, imply an absence of artificiality or complexity. The terms **artless**, **ingenuous** and **guileless** suggest sincerity that stems from basic innocence: *the artless writing style of a child*.

---

sincerely *adv*

genuinely, honestly, earnestly, in earnest, seriously, really, simply, truly, truthfully, wholeheartedly, unfeignedly
FORMAL unaffectedly

sincerity *n*

genuineness, honour, integrity, probity, uprightness, honesty, truth, truthfulness, candour, frankness, openness, directness, straightforwardness, seriousness, earnestness, wholeheartedness, trustworthiness, artlessness, ingenuousness, guilelessness
F3 insincerity

sinecure *n*

soft option
COLLOQ. plum job, picnic, doddle, cinch, cushy job, money for jam, money for old rope, gravy train

sinewy *adj*

muscular, burly, brawny, strapping, stalwart, strong, sturdy, robust, vigorous, athletic, wiry, stringy

sinful *adj*

wrong, wrongful, criminal, evil, bad, wicked, erring, fallen, immoral, corrupt, depraved, impious, ungodly, unholy, unrighteous, irreligious, guilty
FORMAL iniquitous
F3 sinless, righteous, godly

sinfulness *n*

immorality, wickedness, sin, ungodliness, unrighteousness, impiety, corruption, guilt
FORMAL iniquity, depravity, peccability, peccancy, transgression
F3 righteousness

sing *v*

chant, intone, vocalize, burst into song, chorus, croon, serenade, yodel, trill, warble, chirp, quaver, pipe, whistle, hum

■ **sing out**
shout, yell, cry (out), call, bawl, bellow, cooee
COLLOQ. holler

singe *v*

scorch, char, blacken, burn, sear

singer

Singers include:

		REGISTERS:
balladeer	pop singer	alto
carol-singer	pop star	baritone
chanteuse	precentor	bass
choirboy	prima donna	castrato
choirgirl	soloist	coloratura
chorister (or	songster	soprano
chorist)	songstress	contralto
crooner	torch singer	soprano
diva	troubadour	tenor
folk-singer	vocalist	treble
minstrel	warbler	
opera singer		

single *adj, v*

+ *adj*
1 ONE, unique, singular, individual, particular, exclusive, sole, only, one and only, by yourself/itself, lone, solitary, isolated, separate, distinct, unshared, undivided, unbroken, simple, one-to-one, person-to-person, man-to-man, woman-to-woman
2 UNMARRIED, unwed, free, unattached, celibate, on your own, by yourself, available
E3 1 multiple **2** married

■ **single out**
choose, select, pick, hand-pick, distinguish, identify, separate (out), set apart, decide on, isolate, highlight, pinpoint

single-handed *adj, adv*

by yourself, on your own, alone, solo, independent(ly), without help, unaided, unassisted, unaccompanied

single-minded *adj*

determined, resolute, dogged, persevering, tireless, unwavering, fixed, set, unswerving, undeviating, steadfast, dedicated, committed, devoted, obsessive, onefold, monomaniacal; *Scot* aefald

singly *adv*

one by one, on their own, one at a time, individually, separately, distinctly, solely, independently

singular *adj*

1 REMARKABLE, exceptional, unusual, extraordinary, noteworthy, unique, unparalleled, pre-eminent, outstanding, eminent, conspicuous
2 PECULIAR, odd, queer, unusual, strange, uncommon, curious, eccentric, atypical
E3 1 usual **2** normal

singularity *n*

peculiarity, strangeness, queerness, quirk, particularity, oddness, oddity, abnormality, curiousness, eccentricity, idiosyncrasy, irregularity, extraordinariness, uniqueness, oneness, twist
E3 normality

singularly *adv*

remarkably, exceptionally, extraordinarily, notably, outstandingly, particularly, uncommonly, unusually, especially, surprisingly, signally, conspicuously, prodigiously, bizarrely

sinister *adj*

ominous, menacing, threatening, disturbing, disquieting, terrifying, frightening, unlucky, evil, dark, forbidding, Gothic, louche, harmful, cruel, malevolent, wicked, vicious
FORMAL inauspicious, portentous
COLLOQ. shady
E3 harmless, innocent; *formal* auspicious

sink *v*

1 DESCEND, slip, fall, drop, go down, slump, lower, go lower, plummet, plunge, stoop, succumb, lapse, droop, sag, dip, set, disappear, vanish
2 DECREASE, lessen, subside, abate, dwindle, diminish, ebb, fade, flag, weaken, fail, decline, worsen, degenerate, degrade, decay, collapse, fall (in)
FORMAL abate
COLLOQ. go downhill, go to pot
3 FOUNDER, dive, plunge, plummet, go under, capsize, submerge, immerse, engulf, drown
4 *sink a well*
bore, drill, penetrate, dig, excavate, drive, put down, embed, lay, conceal
5 *sink money into a project*
invest, put in, lay out, fund, risk, venture, plough
6 RUIN, destroy, wreck, devastate, demolish, foil, scupper, scuttle
COLLOQ. put a spanner in the works
E3 1 rise **2** increase, improve **3** float

sinless *adj*

innocent, virtuous, faultless, guiltless, immaculate, pure, unblemished, uncorrupted, undefiled, unsullied, unspotted, impeccable
E3 sinful

sinner *n*

wrongdoer, offender, trespasser, criminal, backslider, reprobate, evil-doer
FORMAL malefactor, miscreant, transgressor

sinuous *adj*

lithe, slinky, curved, curving, wavy, undulating, weaving, tortuous, twisting, winding, bending, turning, meandering, serpentine, coiling, curling, wriggly, ogee
FORMAL sinuate
E3 straight

sip *v, n*

+ *v*
taste, sample, drink, drink slowly, sup
+ *n*
taste, drop, drink, spoonful, mouthful

siren *n*

1 ALARM, tocsin, burglar alarm, car alarm, fire alarm, personal alarm, security alarm
2 SEDUCTRESS, *femme fatale*, temptress, vamp, charmer, Lorelei, Circe, Delilah

sissy, cissy *n, adj*

+ *n*
baby, coward, weakling, pansy, softy, mummy's boy, milksop
COLLOQ. wimp, namby-pamby, wet
SLANG wuss; *Aust & NZ* tonk
+ *adj*
unmanly, weak, soft, cowardly, effeminate, feeble, pansy
COLLOQ. wimpish, namby-pamby, wet

sister *n*

1 *brothers and sisters*
sibling, blood-sister, full sister, twin-sister, half-sister, relation, relative, sib
OLD german
COLLOQ. sis
2 *sisters in the struggle against injustice*
comrade, friend, partner, colleague, associate, fellow, companion
3 *sisters in a convent*
nun, abbess, prioress, vowess
Related adjective: sororal

sit *v*

1 SETTLE, sit down, take your seat, be seated, lie, hang, rest, squat (down), place, put, deposit, position, situate, locate, stand, perch, roost, brood, pose
2 SEAT, accommodate, hold, contain, have room/space for
3 MEET, assemble, gather, convene, consult, deliberate, be in session
4 *sit an exam*
take, do, study for
5 *sit for an artist*
pose, model
6 *sit on a committee*
be a member (of), serve, take part (in)

■ **sit back**
relax, do nothing, not be involved in/with

■ **sit in on**
be present at, attend, observe, watch

site *n, v*

+ *n*
1 LOCATION, place, spot, position, situation, locality, station, setting, scene
2 PLOT, lot, ground, area
+ *v*
locate, place, position, situate, station, put, set, install

sitting n

session, period, spell, meeting, assembly, hearing, consultation

sitting room n

living room, lounge, drawing room, day room, front room, reception room, parlour

situate v

locate, place, position, site, station, put, set, install

situation n

1 SITE, location, position, place, spot, seat, locality, locale, setting, environment, milieu, scenario

2 STATE OF AFFAIRS, case, circumstances, predicament, affairs, environment, climate, set-up, state, state of play, condition(s), status, rank, station

COLLOQ. scenario, lie of the land, picture, what's going on, score

3 JOB, post, office, position, appointment, place, employment

sizable, sizeable adj

substantial, fairly large, considerable, respectable, goodly, largish, biggish, decent, generous

F3 small, tiny

size n, v

♦ n

magnitude, measurement(s), dimensions, proportions, volume, bulk, mass, expanse, height, length, area, extent, range, scale, amount, greatness, largeness, bigness, vastness, immensity

■ **size up**

gauge, assess, evaluate, judge, weigh up, estimate, rate, measure

FORMAL appraise

COLLOQ. suss out

sizzle v

hiss, crackle, spit, sputter, fry, frizzle

skeletal adj

skin-and-bone, wasted, drawn, emaciated, gaunt, haggard, hollow-cheeked, shrunken, fleshless, unfleshed

FORMAL cadaverous

skeleton n, adj

♦ n

bones, frame, structure, framework, support, bare bones, outline, blueprint, plan, draft, sketch

TECHNICAL endoskeleton, coenosteum, corallum

OLD anatomy; (Shakesp) atomy

♦ adj

smallest, lowest, minimum, reduced, basic

sketch v, n

♦ v

draw, depict, portray, represent, pencil, paint, outline, delineate, draft, rough out, block out, line, platform

♦ n

1 DRAWING, vignette, design, plan, diagram, outline, skeleton, plan, abstract, draft, representation, description, rough, visual, memoir, cartoon, pencilling, thumbnail; Scot skiff

TECHNICAL bozzetto, modello, trick

FORMAL delineation, prosopography

2 SUMMARY, synopsis, précis, résumé, main points, prospectus, programme, scenario, rough idea, bare facts, bare bones, framework, skeleton, thumbnail sketch, abstract, aperçu, croquis, ébauche, esquisse

3 SKIT, satire, parody, caricature, burlesque, scene, act, turn

COLLOQ. spoof, take-off, send-up, mickey-taking

SLANG piss-taking

sketchily adv

roughly, vaguely, incompletely, inadequately, imperfectly, patchily, cursorily, perfunctorily, hastily

F3 fully

sketchy adj

rough, vague, incomplete, unpolished, unfinished, scrappy, crude, provisional, patchy, bitty, imperfect, inadequate, insufficient, defective, deficient, slight, superficial, cursory, meagre, perfunctory, hasty

F3 full, complete

skew v

distort, slant, twist, bias, weigh, falsify, misrepresent, colour

skilful adj

able, capable, adept, competent, proficient, efficient, good, dexterous, deft, adroit, handy, expert, (well-)versed, masterly, clever, smart, accomplished, skilled, gifted, talented, practised, experienced, trained, professional, tactical, cunning

F3 inept, clumsy, awkward

skilfully adv

ably, capably, competently, proficiently, deftly, cleverly, handily, expertly

F3 ineptly, awkwardly

skill n

skilfulness, ability, aptitude, facility, handiness, adeptness, deftness, adroitness, talent, knack, art, technique, training, experience, expertise, expertness, professionalism, finesse, mastery, proficiency, competence, efficiency, accomplishment, cleverness, smartness, intelligence

skilled adj

trained, schooled, qualified, professional, experienced, practised, accomplished, gifted, talented, expert, masterly, proficient, competent, efficient, able, capable, good, adept, skilful

F3 unskilled, inexperienced

skim v

1 BRUSH, touch, skate, plane, hydroplane, float, sail, glide, graze, fly, skip, bounce, skiff, skitter

2 SCAN, look through, glance at, skip, read (through) quickly, run through/over, have a quick look at, browse through, flick through, flip through, thumb through, leaf through

COLLOQ. graze

3 CREAM, separate, take off; Scot ream

FORMAL despumate

skimp v

economize, be economical, cut back on, scrimp, pinch, stint, be mean with, withhold

COLLOQ. cut corners, tighten your belt, cut your coat according to your cloth

F3 squander, waste

skimpy adj

small, scanty, short, sparse, thin, tight, sketchy, meagre, miserly, niggardly, inadequate, insufficient, insubstantial, beggarly

FORMAL exiguous

COLLOQ. measly

F3 generous

skin n, v

♦ n

hide, fleece, fell, pelt, membrane, film, coating, layer, surface, covering, cover, complexion, outside, peel, rind, husk, hull, pod, casing, crust

TECHNICAL corium, derma, dermis, cutis, integument, tegument, epidermis

FORMAL cuticle

Related adjectives: dermatoid, cutaneous

♦ v

flay, fleece, strip, peel, scrape, graze

■ **by the skin of your teeth**

narrowly, barely, only just

COLLOQ. by a whisker, a near/close thing

skin-deep *adj*
shallow, superficial, surface, external, outward, artificial, empty, meaningless

skinflint *n*
miser, niggard, cheeseparer, Scrooge
COLLOQ. meanie, penny-pincher, tightwad
⊟ spendthrift

skinny *adj*
thin, lean, scrawny, scraggy, skin-and-bone, skeletal, emaciated, underfed, undernourished
⊟ fat, plump

skip *v*
1 HOP, jump, leap, dance, spring, bounce, bob, bound, cavort, gambol, frisk, caper, prance, scamper, ricochet, tittup; *dialect* trounce; *Scot* flisk
See Synonym nuances panel at **jump.**
2 *skip a page*
miss (out), omit, leave out, overskip
COLLOQ. dodge, cut
3 *skip from one thing to another*
move quickly, jump, rush, pass, dart, tear, race

skirmish *n, v*
• *n*
fight, combat, battle, engagement, encounter, confrontation, conflict, clash, brush, affray, fracas, mêlée, tussle, argument, dispute, difference of opinion
FORMAL altercation
COLLOQ. scrap, set-to, dust-up, punch-up
• *v*
clash, fight, tussle, brawl, scuffle, combat, battle, contend, argue, quarrel, wrangle
COLLOQ. scrap, fall out, be at each other's throats

skirt *v*
1 CIRCLE, move/go round, border, edge, flank
FORMAL circumnavigate
2 AVOID, evade, bypass, find a way round
FORMAL circumvent

skit *n*
satire, parody, caricature, burlesque, sketch, scene, act, turn
COLLOQ. spoof, take-off, send-up, mickey-taking
SLANG piss-taking

skittish *adj*
nervous, excitable, fidgety, lively, playful, jumpy, highly-strung, frivolous, fickle
FORMAL restive

skittles *n*
ninepins, pins, tenpin bowling, tenpins, skittle-pins, kettle-pins

skive *v*
dodge, laze, idle, shirk, avoid work, malinger, skulk, slack
COLLOQ. bunk off, swing the lead
SLANG *N Am* goof off

skiver *n*
dodger, idler, do-nothing, shirker, slacker, loafer, malingerer
SLANG *N Am* goof-off

skulduggery *n*
trickery, swindling, fraudulence, double-dealing, underhandedness, unscrupulousness, chicanery
FORMAL duplicity, machinations
COLLOQ. jiggery-pokery, shenanigans, hanky-panky

skulk *v*
lurk, hide, prowl, sneak, creep, slink, lie in wait, steal, slide, pad, pussyfoot, loiter

sky *n*
space, atmosphere, air, heavens, the blue
OLD firmament, empyrean, welkin

FORMAL vault of heaven
Related adjectives: celestial, supernal, empyreal

skyscraper *n*
high-rise building, tower block, splinter building, sliver building

slab *n*
piece, block, lump, chunk, hunk, brick, briquette, wedge, slice, portion
COLLOQ. wodge

slack *adj, n, v*
• *adj*
1 LOOSE, relaxed, flexible, limp, hanging, sagging, flapping, flabby, nerveless, baggy
OLD lash
FORMAL flaccid
2 *a slack period*
sluggish, slow, quiet, idle, lazy, inactive, languid
3 NEGLECTFUL, negligent, careless, sloppy, slapdash, inattentive, permissive, lax, remiss, relaxed, easy-going
OLD lash
FORMAL tardy
⊟ 1 tight, taut, stiff, rigid **2** busy **3** diligent
• *n*
looseness, give, play, room, leeway, excess, spare capacity
• *v*
1 IDLE, shirk, dodge, malinger, neglect
COLLOQ. skive
2 SLACKEN, ease, moderate, reduce, lessen, get less, decrease, diminish, slow (down), become slower, become less intense/active

slacken
■ **slacken off**
loosen, release, relax, ease, moderate, reduce, lessen, get less, decrease, diminish, abate, slow (down), become slower, become less intense/active
OLD forslack
FORMAL abate
COLLOQ. take it easy
⊟ tighten, increase, intensify, quicken

slacker *n*
idler, shirker, dawdler, loafer, malingerer, clock-watcher, good-for-nothing, layabout
COLLOQ. skiver

slag *v*
■ **slag off**
criticize, slate, abuse, mock, malign, berate, run down, lambast, insult
FORMAL deride
COLLOQ. slam, knock

slake *v*
satisfy, satiate, quench, moisten, sate, gratify, allay, reduce, extinguish, moderate
FORMAL abate, assuage, mitigate

slam *v*
1 BANG, crash, dash, smash, thump, slap, throw, hurl, fling
2 CRITICIZE, attack, slate, denounce, run down, find fault with
COLLOQ. pan, rubbish, pull/tear to pieces, tear to shreds, do a hatchet job on
SLANG slag (off)

slander *n, v*
• *n*
defamation, misrepresentation, libel, scandal, smear, smear campaign, slur, denigration, backbiting, character assassination, mudslinging, evil-speaking, detraction
OLD sclaunder
FORMAL aspersion, disparagement, calumny, vilification, traducement, obloquy
COLLOQ. muck-raking, mudslinging

◆ *v*

defame, malign, libel, smear, blacken the name of, slur, backbite, speak evil of
OLD missay
FORMAL vilify, cast aspersions on, asperse, disparage, denigrate, vilipend, calumniate, traduce
COLLOQ. sling/throw mud at, drag someone's name through the mud; *N Am* badmouth
Ⓔ praise, compliment

⚠ slander or **libel**?
See panel at **libel**.

---

slanderous *adj*

defamatory, false, untrue, libellous, damaging, malicious, abusive, insulting, backbiting
OLD venom'd-mouth'd
FORMAL aspersory, aspersive, calumniatory, calumnious

slang *n*

cant, jargon, argot, patois, patter, cockney, cockney rhyming slang, vulgarism, doublespeak, gobbledygook, colloquialism, informal expressions
COLLOQ. lingo, mumbo-jumbo

slanging match *n*

argument, row, quarrel, dispute, shouting match
FORMAL altercation
COLLOQ. argy-bargy, barney, set-to, spat

slant *v, n*

◆ *v*

1 TILT, slope, incline, lean, list, oblique, dip, skew, bevel, be askew, angle, shelve; *Scot* sklent
TECHNICAL splay
2 DISTORT, twist, warp, bend, weight, bias, skew, colour; *Scot* sklent

◆ *n*

1 SLOPE, incline, inclination, bevel, leaning, gradient, ramp, camber, pitch, tilt, dip, angle, diagonal, oblique, slash, forward slash; *Scot* sklent
TECHNICAL embrasure, splay
2 BIAS, prejudice, distortion, twist, one-sidedness, emphasis, attitude, angle, opinion, view, viewpoint, point of view

slanting *adj*

sloping, tilting, tilted, inclining, leaning, listing, dipping, on an incline, at a slant, aslant, askew, oblique, diagonal; *Scot* asklent

slap *n, v, adv*

◆ *n*

smack, spank, cuff, blow, buffet, hit, bang, clap, clout, thump, punch; *dialect* skelp, twank; *Scot* scud, yank, clatch, sclaff
OLD spat
COLLOQ. whack, wallop, biff, sock, clobber
SLANG paddy-whack

◆ *v*

1 SMACK, spank, hit, strike, thump, punch, clout, cuff, bang, clap, strike hands; *dialect* skelp; *Scot* scud
OLD spat
COLLOQ. whack, wallop, biff, sock, clobber, pandy
2 PUT DOWN, set (down), plump, plonk, slam, stick; *dialect* swap
3 DAUB, plaster, spread, apply

◆ *adv*

right, directly, straight, exactly, precisely, dead, plumb
COLLOQ. bang, slap-bang, smack

■ **slap in the face**
insult, humiliation, blow, affront, rejection, repulse, snub, rebuke, rebuff, indignity
COLLOQ. put-down

■ **slap on the wrist**
rebuke, reprimand, punishment, censure, blame

FORMAL castigation
COLLOQ. flak, slating, slamming, knocking, stick, dressing-down, telling-off, ticking-off, carpeting, earful, rollicking, comeuppance

slapdash *adj*

careless, thoughtless, haphazard, slovenly, sloppy, disorderly, clumsy, offhand, negligent, messy, slipshod, thrown-together, untidy, hurried, last-minute, hasty, rash, perfunctory
Ⓔ careful, orderly

slap-happy *adj*

casual, irresponsible, boisterous, haphazard, reeling, happy-go-lucky, nonchalant, reckless, slapdash, hit-or-miss, dazed, giddy, punch-drunk, woozy

slapstick *n*

comedy, farce, buffoonery, tomfoolery, knockabout, horseplay

slap-up *adj*

excellent, splendid, lavish, elaborate, first-class, first-rate, magnificent, superb, sumptuous, luxurious, princely, superlative

slash *v, n*

◆ *v*

1 *slash your wrists*
cut, slit, gash, lacerate, knife, rip, tear, hack, score, rend
2 *slash costs*
cut, reduce, decrease, curb, curtail, prune
COLLOQ. axe

◆ *n*

1 CUT, incision, slit, gash, laceration, score, rip, tear, rent
2 OBLIQUE, diagonal, forward slash, solidus, stroke
FORMAL virgule

slate *v*

scold, rebuke, reprimand, berate, censure, blame, criticize, run down, pull apart, pull/tear to pieces
COLLOQ. slam, pan, knock, rubbish, tear to shreds, do a hatchet job on
SLANG slag (off)
Ⓔ praise

slatternly *adj*

slovenly, sloppy, dirty, slipshod, untidy, unkempt, unclean, dowdy, bedraggled, frowzy, frumpish, frumpy, sluttish

slaughter *v, n*

◆ *v*

1 KILL, put to death, slay, butcher, murder, massacre, exterminate, liquidate, annihilate
2 DEFEAT, beat, trounce, best, worst, conquer, overcome, overwhelm, overpower, subdue, rout, annihilate, outplay, outwit, outsmart, be more than a match for, get the better of, have the edge on, drub
FORMAL vanquish, subjugate
COLLOQ. hammer, clobber, lick, thrash, wipe the floor with

◆ *n*

killing, putting to death, murder, massacre, extermination, liquidation, annihilation, butchery, carnage, bloodbath, bloodshed

slaughterhouse *n*

abattoir, butchery, shambles

slave *n, v*

◆ *n*

servant, drudge, menial, lackey, vassal, serf, villein, captive, thrall, bondservant, bond-slave, bond(s)man, bond(s)woman, bondmaid, abject, galley slave, maroon, praedial
TECHNICAL odalisque
OLD sclave, boy, contraband, esne, theow, Mameluke, Gibeonite
COLLOQ. skivvy
Related adjective: servile

◆ *v*
toil, labour, drudge, sweat, grind, slog, work your fingers to the bone, work your guts out

slave-driver *n*
taskmaster, tyrant, dictator, despot, autocrat, bully, oppressor, martinet

slaver *v*
dribble, drivel, slobber, drool
FORMAL salivate

slavery *n*
servitude, bondage, yoke, captivity, enslavement, serfdom, vassalage, thrall, thraldom
FORMAL subjugation
Ⅎ freedom, liberty

slavish *adj*
1 UNORIGINAL, imitative, unimaginative, uninspired, literal, strict
2 SERVILE, abject, submissive, meek, sycophantic, deferential, grovelling, cringing, fawning, menial, low, mean
FORMAL obsequious
Ⅎ **1** original, imaginative **2** independent, assertive

slavishly *adv*
unimaginatively, unoriginally, strictly, submissively, meekly, unresistingly
Ⅎ imaginatively

slay *v*
kill, butcher, massacre, murder, dispatch, destroy, eliminate, execute, slaughter, annihilate, assassinate, exterminate
COLLOQ. rub out

slaying *n*
murder, killing, butchery, slaughter, assassination, massacre, destruction, dispatch, elimination, annihilation, extermination
FORMAL mactation

sleazy *adj*
disreputable, low, seedy, sordid, corrupt, squalid
COLLOQ. crummy, tacky

sledge *n*
sleigh, toboggan, slide, luge, bobsled, bobsleigh, skeleton bob, Ski-doo®, dray, kibitka, pulka; *Scot* hurly-hacket; *N Am* dogsled, travois; *Can* train
TECHNICAL slipe

sleek *adj*
shiny, glossy, lustrous, smooth, silky, silken, soft, well-groomed, stylish, thriving, prosperous, slick, smug
Ⅎ rough, unkempt

sleep *v, n*
◆ *v*
be asleep, get some sleep, fall asleep, doze, drowse, hibernate, drop off, go off, drift off, nap, rest
OLD slumber
FORMAL repose
COLLOQ. snooze, have a snooze, have forty winks, nod off, be in the land of Nod, sleep like a log, flake out, go out like a light
SLANG kip, doss (down), crash out
◆ *n*
doze, nap, catnap, hibernation, rest, siesta
OLD slumber
FORMAL repose
COLLOQ. snooze, forty winks, shut-eye
SLANG kip
Related adjectives: hypnic, hypnoid, hypnoidal
■ **go to sleep**
fall asleep, drift off, drop off, doze (off), go off, catnap
COLLOQ. crash out, nod off, snooze, have forty winks
SLANG kip

■ **put to sleep**
put down, destroy, put out of its misery

sleepily *adv*
drowsily, wearily, heavily, inactively, lethargically, quietly, slowly, sluggishly
FORMAL languidly, torpidly

sleepiness *n*
drowsiness, doziness, heaviness, lethargy, torpor
FORMAL languor, oscitancy, oscitation, somnolence
Ⅎ alertness, wakefulness

sleeping *adj*
asleep, daydreaming, idle, inactive, unaware, becalmed, passive, off guard, inattentive, dormant, hibernating
FORMAL slumbering
Ⅎ alert, awake

sleepless *adj*
unsleeping, awake, wide-awake, alert, vigilant, watchful, wakeful, restless, disturbed, insomniac

sleeplessness *n*
insomnia, wakefulness
FORMAL insomnolence

sleepwalker *n*
somnambulist, noctambulist

sleepwalking *n*
somnambulism, somnambulation, noctambulism, noctambulation

sleepy *adj*
1 DROWSY, tired, weary, heavy, slow, sluggish, lethargic, inactive, quiet, dull, soporific, hypnotic; *Scot* sleepery
TECHNICAL comatose, soporose
OLD slumberous
FORMAL somnolent, languid, languorous, torpid
2 *a sleepy little village*
quiet, dull, peaceful, still, tranquil, isolated, lonely, unfrequented, undisturbed
FORMAL sequestered
COLLOQ. off the beaten track
Ⅎ **1** awake, alert, wakeful, restless **2** bustling, lively

sleigh *n*
sledge, toboggan, slide, luge, bobsled, bobsleigh, skeleton bob, Ski-doo®, dray, kibitka, pulka; *Scot* hurly-hacket; *N Am* dogsled, travois; *Can* train
TECHNICAL slipe

sleight of hand *n*
trickery, skill, artifice, dexterity, legerdemain, deception, magic, adroitness, manipulation
FORMAL prestidigitation

slender *adj*
1 SLIM, thin, lean, slight, svelte, graceful, trim, sylphlike, willowy, willowish
2 *a slender chance*
faint, remote, small, little, slim, slight, inconsiderable, tenuous, flimsy, feeble, deficient, inadequate, insufficient, meagre, scant, scanty
Ⅎ **1** fat, plump, overweight **2** appreciable, considerable, ample

sleuth *n*
detective, private investigator, shadow, tail, tracker, Pinkerton
COLLOQ. private eye, bloodhound, dick, gumshoe

slice *n, v*
◆ *n*
piece, sliver, wafer, rasher, tranche, slab, wedge, segment, section, hunk, chunk, part, share, portion, allocation, allotment, helping
COLLOQ. cut, whack, slice of the cake
◆ *v*
carve, cut (up), chop, sever, divide, separate, segment

slick *adj*
1 GLIB, plausible, easy, simplistic, deft, adroit, sharp, dexterous
2 SMOOTH, sleek, glossy, shiny, polished, quick, streamlined, well-oiled, well-organized, skilful, smooth, professional, efficient, masterly
3 INSINCERE, glib, smarmy, smooth-speaking, smooth-talking, persuasive, polished, sophisticated, urbane, suave
FORMAL unctuous

slide *v, n*
♦ *v*
1 MOVE SMOOTHLY, go smoothly, slip, slither, skid, skate, ski, toboggan, glide, plane, coast, skim
2 DETERIORATE, lessen, decrease, decline, fall, descend, drop, plummet, plunge, lapse, worsen, get worse, depreciate
♦ *n*
decrease, decline, fall, drop, descent, plunge, depreciation

slight *adj, v, n*
♦ *adj*
1 MINOR, unimportant, insignificant, inconsequential, negligible, inappreciable, imperceptible, trivial, petty, scant, paltry, subtle, modest, small, little, minute, inconsiderable, insubstantial
2 SLENDER, slim, small, dainty, diminutive, petite, frail, fragile, delicate, elfin
E3 1 major, significant, noticeable, considerable 2 large, muscular, burly
♦ *v*
scorn, despise, disdain, insult, affront, offend, snub, rebuff, spurn, slur, cut, ignore, disregard, neglect
FORMAL disparage
COLLOQ. give the cold shoulder to, cold-shoulder, give someone the brush-off
E3 respect, praise, compliment, flatter
♦ *n*
insult, affront, scorn, slur, snub, rebuff, rudeness, discourtesy, disrespect, contempt, disdain, indifference, disregard, neglect
COLLOQ. cold shoulder, slap in the face, kick in the teeth, brush-off

slighting *adj*
disdainful, disrespectful, belittling, insulting, scornful, offensive, defamatory, derogatory, slanderous, abusive, supercilious, uncomplimentary
FORMAL disparaging
E3 complimentary

slightly *adv*
rather, quite, a little, a bit, somewhat, to some degree, to some extent, to a certain extent

slim *adj, v*
♦ *adj*
1 SLENDER, thin, slight, lean, svelte, trim, graceful, sylphlike, willowy, willowish, leggy
2 SLIGHT, remote, faint, poor, small, little, scant, scanty, meagre, inconsiderable, tenuous, flimsy, insufficient, inadequate
E3 1 fat, chubby 2 strong, considerable
♦ *v*
1 LOSE WEIGHT, diet, go on a diet, reduce
2 *slim down the workforce*
lessen, make less, make smaller, reduce, decrease, contract, shrink, curtail, trim, minimize, downsize, lower, moderate, weaken, bring down, cut back/down, restrict, trim, wind down
COLLOQ. axe

slime *n*
mud, ooze, muck, sludge, mess; *dialect* slake
COLLOQ. goo, gunk, yuck

slimy *adj*
1 MUDDY, miry, sludgy, oozy, sticky, mucous, viscous, oily, greasy, slippery
2 SERVILE, sycophantic, toadying, ingratiating, grovelling, creeping, oily
FORMAL obsequious, unctuous
COLLOQ. smarmy

sling *v, n*
♦ *v*
1 THROW, hurl, fling, catapult, heave, pitch, lob, toss, shy
COLLOQ. chuck
2 HANG, suspend, dangle, swing
♦ *n*
bandage, loop, strap, support, band, catapult
TECHNICAL parbuckle, prusik
OLD scarf

slink *v*
sneak, steal, creep, sidle, slip, lurk, prowl, skulk

slinky *adj*
tight-fitting, close-fitting, figure-hugging, clinging, tight, skin-tight, sleek, sinuous

slip^1 *v, n*
♦ *v*
1 SLIDE, glide, skate, skid, stumble, lose your balance, trip, lose your footing, fall, slither, slink, sneak, steal, creep
2 *slip into/out of clothes*
put on, get dressed in, change into, get into, take off, change out of, pull on, wear, don
3 *standards are slipping*
fall, drop, sink, decrease, decline, plummet, plunge, slump, deteriorate, worsen, lapse, get worse
COLLOQ. go to the dogs, go to pot, go down the tubes
♦ *n*
1 MISTAKE, error, blunder, fault, indiscretion, omission, oversight, failure
COLLOQ. slip-up, bloomer, boob, booboo, howler, clanger; *N Am* flub
SLANG cock-up, goof
2 PETTICOAT, underskirt, jupon, kirtle
■ **slip up**
make a mistake, go wrong, get wrong, miscalculate, bungle, blunder, err, stumble
COLLOQ. boob, botch, fluff
SLANG cock up, screw up, goof (up)
■ **give someone the slip**
escape from, run away from, get away from, flee from, break loose from, shake off
COLLOQ. slip through someone's fingers, dodge, duck
■ **let slip**
let out, reveal, divulge, disclose, give away, betray, leak, tell
COLLOQ. blab, squeal, give the game away, let the cat out of the bag, spill the beans

slip^2 *n*
a slip of paper
piece, strip, scrap, paper, note, voucher, chit, coupon, certificate
■ **a slip of a**
small, thin, slender, slim, slight, delicate, fragile, young

slipper *n*
houseshoe, moccasin, mule, flip-flop, sandal, pump, loafer, pabouche, pantof(f)le, pantoufle, pantable, carpet-slipper, babouche; *Scot* panton
OLD slip-shoe

slippery *adj*
1 SLIPPY, icy, wet, greasy, oily, slimy, slithery, glassy, smooth, dangerous, treacherous, perilous
COLLOQ. skiddy
2 *a slippery character*
dishonest, untrustworthy, unreliable, false, two-faced, crafty, cunning, devious, clever, shifty, deceitful, foxy,

evasive, smooth, smarmy
FORMAL duplicitous, perfidious
2 trustworthy, reliable

slipshod adj
careless, slapdash, sloppy, slovenly, untidy, disorganized, negligent, lax, casual
> careful, fastidious, neat, tidy, methodical, organized

slip-up n
slip, mistake, error, blunder, fault, indiscretion, omission, oversight, failure
COLLOQ. bloomer, boob, booboo, howler, clanger; NAm flub
SLANG cock-up, goof

slit v, n
◆ v
cut, gash, slash, slice, split, pierce, lance, knife, rip, tear; Scot rit, speld
OLD rend
◆ n
opening, aperture, fissure, vent, cut, incision, gash, slash, split, rip, tear, slot, snip, peep, rent, fent, loop, race, buttonhole; Scot rit, spare
TECHNICAL sipe
FORMAL pertusion

slither v
slide, skid, slip, glide, slink, creep, snake, worm

sliver n
flake, shaving, paring, slice, wafer, shred, fragment, piece, bit, scrap, chip, splinter, shiver, shard

slob n
lout, oaf, layabout, good-for-nothing, sloven, churl, boor, philistine
COLLOQ. yob

slobber v
drool, dribble, drivel, slaver, foam at the mouth
FORMAL salivate

slog v, n
◆ v
1 HIT, strike, thump, belt, clout
FORMAL smite
COLLOQ. bash, slosh, slug, sock, wallop
2 PERSEVERE, labour, slave, work, work hard, plough through, toil, plod, trudge, trek, tramp
COLLOQ. plug away at, peg away at, sweat blood, work your fingers to the bone, work till you drop
◆ n
struggle, effort, exertion, grind, labour, hike, trek, trudge, tramp
COLLOQ. sweat, graft

slogan n
jingle, motto, catch phrase, catchword, watchword, cry, battle-cry, rallying cry, war cry, chant, logo, splash; NAm tag line
OLD slughorn
FORMAL shibboleth

slop v
spill, overflow, slosh, splash, splatter, spatter; dialect slattern; NAm slather

slope v
slant, lean, tilt, tip, dip, pitch, incline, rise, fall (away), drop
■ **slope off**
slip away, sneak off, steal away, go away, leave quietly
See panel on next page

sloping adj
inclined, inclining, at a slant, slanting, leaning, oblique, tilting, askew, angled, canting, bevelled
FORMAL acclivitous, acclivous, declivitous, declivous
> level

sloppily adv
carelessly, hurriedly, hastily, untidily, messily, lackadaisically, haphazardly
> carefully, precisely, methodically

sloppy adj
1 WATERY, wet, liquid, runny, soggy, splashy, mushy, slushy
2 sloppy work
careless, hit-or-miss, slapdash, slipshod, hurried, hasty, slovenly, slack, lackadaisical, haphazard, untidy, disorganized, messy, clumsy, amateurish
3 SENTIMENTAL, romantic, gushing, mawkish, maudlin
COLLOQ. mushy, soppy, schmaltzy, gushy, gooey, slushy, sickly, corny
> **1** solid **2** careful, exact, precise, organized, methodical

slosh v
1 SPLASH, wade, slop, slog, pour, shower, flounder, spray, swash
2 HIT, strike, thump, clout, thwack, slap, swipe, punch
COLLOQ. bash, biff, slug, sock, wallop

slot n, v
◆ n
1 HOLE, opening, aperture, crack, slit, vent, notch, groove, channel
2 a slot in your schedule
gap, space, time, vacancy, place, opening, spot, position, niche
COLLOQ. window
◆ v
insert, fit, put, install, place, position, assign, pigeonhole

sloth n
laziness, idleness, inactivity, slackness, listlessness, slothfulness, sluggishness, torpor, inertia
FORMAL indolence, acedia, accidie, fainéance
> diligence, industriousness; formal sedulity

slothful adj
lazy, idle, inactive, inert, slack, listless, sluggish, workshy, torpid, do-nothing
FORMAL indolent, fainéant
COLLOQ. skiving
> diligent, industrious; formal sedulous

slouch v
stoop, hunch, bend, droop, slump, lounge, mooch, loll, shuffle, shamble

slovenly adj
sloppy, careless, slipshod, untidy, messy, disorganized, scruffy, unclean, dirty, unkempt, slatternly, sluttish
> careful, tidy, neat, smart

slow adj, v
◆ adj
1 LEISURELY, unhurried, lingering, loitering, lagging, dawdling, lazy, sluggish, slow-moving, slow-motion, ponderous, creeping, gradual, deliberate, measured, plodding, at a snail's pace, delayed, late
FORMAL tardy, dilatory
2 STUPID, unintelligent, slow-witted, dim, dull, dull-witted, dense, retarded, daft; Welsh twp
FORMAL obtuse
COLLOQ. thick, dumb, dopey, slow off the mark, slow on the uptake
3 PROLONGED, time-consuming, protracted, long-drawn-out, tedious, boring, dull, tiresome, wearisome, uninteresting, uneventful
4 QUIET, sleepy, dull, slack, sluggish, stagnant, dead
5 slow to anger
unwilling, reluctant, hesitant, averse, disinclined, loath, indisposed
> **1** fast, quick, swift, rapid, speedy **2** bright, clever, intelligent **3** brief, exciting **4** brisk, lively, exciting

Words used for slopes include:

UP:	DOWN:			
acclivity	decline	drop	escarp	slant
ascent	declivity	fall	glacis	staircase
climb	descent	**UP AND DOWN:**	gradient	stairs
incline	dip	bajada	inclination	stairway
rise	downgrade	brae	pitch	steps
uphill	downhill	cant	ramp	tilt
upward	downward	escalator	scarp	versant

■ **slow down**
1 BRAKE, decelerate, ease up, reduce speed, put the brakes on, delay, hold up, handicap, check, curb, detain, keep/hold back, restrict
FORMAL retard
2 BECOME LESS ACTIVE, relax, do less, take it easy, ease up, calm down
COLLOQ. chill out, hang loose
F3 1 speed, accelerate

> **Synonym nuances**
> *adjective sense 1*
> The term **leisurely** suggests taking your time in a relaxed way, and **unhurried** could describe similarly dilatory action. **Loitering** and **dawdling**, however, are more negative in that they are suggestive of wasting time, and **lagging** also suggests falling behind: *conversation was lagging and everyone wanted to go home.* **Lazy**, on the other hand, although it implies a reluctance to exert oneself, is not necessarily disapproving in tone: *happy, lazy summer days.* **Sluggish** could be used to describe more undesirable inactivity: *the sluggish economy.* **Ponderous** and **plodding** also have more unpleasant implications of a lumbering slowness.
> The terms **creeping** and **gradual** would appropriately describe a slow but stealthy progress: *creeping privatization of the health service*, whereas **deliberate** and **measured** have vaguely positive connotations of a more careful consideration: *she slowed her words to a more measured pace so we could understand her.*

slowly *adv*
leisurely, at a leisurely pace, slowly but surely, unhurriedly, gradually, little by little, by degrees, steadily, lazily, ploddingly, ponderously, sluggishly, at a snail's pace
TECHNICAL lento, adagio, largo, larghetto
F3 fast, quickly

sludge *n*
mud, ooze, mire, muck, residue, sediment, silt, slime, slush, swill, slop, slob, slag, dregs
COLLOQ. gunge, gunk, mudge

sluggish *adj*
lethargic, listless, torpid, heavy, dull, slow, slow-moving, slothful, languid, lazy, idle, inactive, apathetic, lifeless, unresponsive, phlegmatic
FORMAL languorous, indolent, somnolent
F3 brisk, vigorous, lively, dynamic

sluggishness *n*
lethargy, listlessness, torpor, phlegm, heaviness, inertia, dullness, slowness, slothfulness, apathy, drowsiness, stagnation, lassitude
FORMAL indolence, languor, somnolence, fainéance
F3 dynamism, eagerness, quickness

sluice *n, v*
◆ *n*
1 DRAIN, channel, passage, conduit, outlet, inlet
TECHNICAL penstock
OLD sasse
2 FLOODGATE, lock gate, water gate

◆ *v*
wash, cleanse, drain, flush, swill, drench, irrigate, slosh, slush

slum *n*
ghetto, shanty town, hovel, favela; *Can* cabbagetown
OLD rookery
COLLOQ. the wrong side of the tracks

slumber *n, v*
◆ *n*
sleep, rest, doze, nap
FORMAL repose
COLLOQ. snooze, forty winks, shut-eye
SLANG kip
◆ *v*
doze, drowse, nap, rest, sleep
FORMAL repose
COLLOQ. snooze

slummy *adj*
run-down, squalid, dirty, decayed, seedy, sordid, ramshackle, overcrowded, wretched
COLLOQ. sleazy

slump *v, n*
◆ *v*
1 COLLAPSE, fall, go down, decrease, drop, plunge, plummet, sink, subside, nosedive, decline, deteriorate, worsen, crash, fail
COLLOQ. go downhill
2 DROOP, sag, bend, stoop, slouch, loll, lounge, flop
COLLOQ. flump
◆ *n*
recession, depression, stagnation, devaluation, downturn, slide, low, lowering, trough, downswing, decline, deterioration, worsening, fall, drop, decrease, plunge, collapse, crash, failure
F3 boom, upturn

slur *n, v*
◆ *n*
smear, slight, insult, disgrace, discredit, reproach, slander, libel, affront, stain, blot, innuendo, insinuation, stigma
FORMAL aspersion, calumny
◆ *v*
mumble, speak unclearly, splutter, stumble

slush *n*
1 SNOW, melting snow, wet snow
2 SENTIMENTALITY, emotionalism, romanticism, mawkishness, soppiness, sloppiness
COLLOQ. mush, gush, pulp, schmaltz

slut *n*
1 LOOSE WOMAN, hussy, drab, prostitute
OLD pucelle; (*Shakesp*) pussel
COLLOQ. hooker
SLANG tart, floozie, scrubber, slag
OLD SLANG dolly-mop
2 SLATTERN, sloven, trollop, draggle-tail; *dialect* dratchell, drazel, slummock; *Scot* clatch

sly *adj*
wily, foxy, crafty, cunning, artful, guileful, clever, canny, shrewd, smart, astute, knowing, subtle, devious, shifty,

tricky, furtive, stealthy, surreptitious, insidious, underhand, covert, secret, secretive, scheming, conniving, mischievous, impish, roguish, peery, sleeky, weaselly; *dialect* carny; *Scot* slee, sleekit
FORMAL clandestine
COLLOQ. sneaky
SLANG fly
E3 honest, frank, candid, open
■ **on the sly**
in secret, secretly, in private, under cover, privately, stealthily, surreptitiously, underhandedly, furtively, covertly
FORMAL clandestinely
COLLOQ. on the q.t.
E3 openly

slyly *adv*
cunningly, artfully, cannily, shrewdly, deviously, stealthily, surreptitiously, underhandedly, furtively, covertly
E3 openly

smack¹ *v, n, adv*
◆ *v*
Do you ever smack your children?
hit, strike, slap, spank, clap, box, thump, punch, bang, crash, thud, clout, cuff, pat, tap
COLLOQ. whack, thwack, belt, wallop, biff, sock, clobber, put over your knee, give a hiding to
◆ *n*
1 BLOW, slap, spank, box, thump, punch, bang, crash, thud, clout, cuff, pat, tap
COLLOQ. whack, thwack, belt, wallop, biff, sock, clobber
SLANG paddy-whack
2 KISS, smacker; *dialect* smouch
◆ *adv*
bang, slap-bang, right, plumb, straight, directly, exactly, precisely
■ **smack your lips**
enjoy, relish, savour, drool over, delight in, anticipate

smack² *v, n*
◆ *v*
1 *his attitude smacks of hypocrisy*
suggest, savour of, hint at, give the impression of, intimate, evoke, bring to mind, remind you of
2 SAVOUR, relish, taste, enjoy, delight in, take pleasure in, revel in, like, appreciate
OLD smatch
◆ *n*
1 TASTE, flavour, savour, tang, spice, relish, piquancy, zest; *dialect* tack
OLD smatch
2 SUGGESTION, hint, trace, impression, intimation, tinge, touch, dash, speck, smell, whiff, nuance; *dialect* twang

small *adj*
1 LITTLE, tiny, minute, minuscule, short, slight, puny, petite, diminutive, compact, pocket, cramped, poky, miniature, microscopic, infinitesimal, mini, pocket-sized, young, peewee; *Scot* wee
COLLOQ. pint-size(d), knee-high to a grasshopper, teeny, teensy, teensy-weensy
2 PETTY, trifling, trivial, unimportant, insignificant, minor, inconsiderable, inappreciable, negligible
3 INADEQUATE, insufficient, scanty, meagre, paltry, mean, limited
4 *make you feel small*
humiliated, ashamed, embarrassed, foolish, crushed, broken, deflated, degraded, disgraced, stupid, unimportant, insignificant
E3 1 big, large, tall, huge **2** great, major, considerable **3** ample, generous, liberal

---

Synonym nuances
sense 1
Little can be widely applied as a synonym of small, although it can have overtones of cuteness: *a little boy; a little kitten.* **Tiny** and **minute** would be reserved for something extremely small, with **minute** having the more scientific tone: *minute quantities of uranium.* **Minute** also tends to be used when implying something is not enough: *she poured a minute amount of milk on my cereal.* **Teeny** can be used with a suggestion of amused affection: *she has such teeny hands.*
  Minuscule goes further by suggesting another step down in size, suggesting something hardly visible: *a minuscule particle,* while **microscopic** would be the more scientific term. Likewise, **infinitesimal** is reserved for something immeasurable: *an infinitesimal speck.* **Miniature** and **mini**, while still suggesting something very small, are usually applied to a scaled-down version of something: *a miniature railway; a mini disc; a mini riot.*
  Short, on the other hand, is more often associated with a lack of height, whereas **slight** suggests a lightness of build. However, this is more flattering than **puny**, which further implies weakness. **Petite** is more complimentary in tone, and suggests a neat, dainty frame.
  Compact suggests convenience and manageability, whereas **cramped** and **poky** obviously have more claustrophobic implications when applied to spaces.

---

small-minded *adj*
petty, mean, ungenerous, illiberal, intolerant, bigoted, narrow-minded, prejudiced, biased, parochial, insular, rigid, hidebound
E3 liberal, generous, tolerant, broad-minded, open-minded

smallness *n*
small size, littleness, tininess, slightness, compactness, diminutiveness, minuteness
E3 largeness, bigness

small-time *adj*
unimportant, minor, insignificant, small-scale, petty, piddling, inconsequential, no-account
E3 important, major, big-time

smarminess *n*
oiliness, servility, sycophancy, toadying, suavity
FORMAL obsequiousness, unctuousness, unctuosity

smarmy *adj*
smooth, oily, servile, sycophantic, bootlicking, suave, toadying, ingratiating, crawling, fawning
FORMAL obsequious, unctuous

smart *adj, v*
◆ *adj*
1 *smart clothes*
elegant, stylish, snappy, chic, fashionable, modish, neat, tidy, spruce, trim, presentable, dapper, well-dressed, well-groomed, well-turned-out
COLLOQ. natty, cool, snazzy
2 CLEVER, intelligent, bright, sharp, acute, shrewd, astute
COLLOQ. on the ball, all there
3 *a smart hotel*
fashionable, elegant, expensive, stylish, chic, modish
COLLOQ. posh, glitzy, ritzy
E3 1 dowdy, unfashionable, untidy, scruffy **2** stupid, slow **3** cheap, shabby, down-at-heel
◆ *v*
sting, hurt, prick, burn, nip, ache, tingle, twinge, throb
■ **smart alec**
know-all, wise guy, wiseacre
COLLOQ. clever clogs, clever dick, smartypants, smartyboots
SLANG smartarse

smarten *v*
neaten, make neat, tidy (up), make tidy, spruce up, groom, clean, polish, beautify

smartly *adv*
1 *dress smartly*
stylishly, elegantly, fashionably, neatly, tidily, presentably
COLLOQ. snazzily, nattily
2 *move away smartly*
quickly, promptly, immediately, instantly, directly, unhesitatingly, speedily, swiftly, rapidly, briskly, hurriedly, hastily, instantaneously, readily, abruptly, without further ado
◼ **1** unfashionably, untidily **2** slowly, later

smash *v, n*
♦ *v*
1 *smash a window*
break, shatter, crack, splinter, disintegrate, shiver, ruin, wreck, demolish, destroy, dash, defeat, crush; *Scot* stramash
FORMAL pulverize
2 CRASH, collide, wreck, strike, bang, bump, drive, go, run, knock, hit, plough, bash, thump
COLLOQ. prang
♦ *n*
1 ACCIDENT, crash, collision, pile-up, bump, wreck
COLLOQ. smash-up, prang
SLANG *Aust* bingle
2 SUCCESS, smash hit, sensation, triumph, winner
COLLOQ. knockout, wow

smashing *adj*
excellent, wonderful, marvellous, superb, tremendous, great, fantastic, magnificent, sensational, superlative, stupendous, super, exhilarating, first-class, first-rate
COLLOQ. fabulous, fantastic, terrific

smattering *n*
bit, modicum, dash, sprinkling, basics, rudiments, elements
OLD smatch

smear *v, n*
♦ *v*
1 DAUB, plaster, spread, cover, slap, coat, rub, smudge, streak
2 SULLY, blacken, stain, tarnish, slur, taint
FORMAL defame, malign, vilify, calumniate
COLLOQ. drag someone's name through the mud; *N Am* badmouth
♦ *n*
1 STREAK, smudge, blot, spot, patch, blotch, splodge, splotch, daub
2 *a smear campaign against a politician*
taint, slur, stain, false report, slander, libel
FORMAL defamation, aspersion, vilification, obloquy
COLLOQ. mudslinging, muck-raking

smell
Related adjective: olfactory

Words used for types of smell include:

PLEASANT:	UNPLEASANT:	reek
aroma	b.o. (body odour)	sniff
bouquet	fetor	stench
fragrance	*N Am* funk	stink
incense	hum	whiff
nose	malodour	
odour	mephitis	
pot pourri	miasma	
perfume	niff	
redolence	pong	
scent	pungency	

---

smelly *adj*
stinking, reeking, foul, foul-smelling, bad, off, putrid, high, strong-smelling
FORMAL malodorous, f(o)etid, mephitic, noisome
COLLOQ. pongy, humming; *Scot* mingin
SLANG honking

smile *v, n*
♦ *v*
grin, beam, simper, smirk, leer, sneer, laugh, chuckle, giggle, snigger, titter
♦ *n*
grin, beam, simper, smirk, leer, sneer, laugh, chuckle, giggle, snigger, titter
COLLOQ. someone's face lights up, be all smiles

> **Synonym nuances**
> *verb*
> You can use **grin** to suggest the wideness of a smile, while **beam** suggests brightness and underlying enthusiasm. **Simper**, on the other hand, is a pejorative term, and implies affectation or weakness, whereas **smirk** carries a negative suggestion of smugness: *he smirked in triumph*, and **sneer** is strongly associated with contempt: *he sneered at her bookish tastes*. **Leer**, however, would be reserved for smiling lecherously.

smirk *v, n*
grin, sneer, snigger, leer, simper

smitten *adj*
obsessed, bewitched, beguiled, charmed, attracted, enthusiastic, captivated, infatuated, enamoured, afflicted, plagued, struck, troubled, burdened, beset
COLLOQ. bowled over

smog *n*
fog, pea-souper, smoke, pollution, exhaust, fumes, haze, mist, vapour

smoke *n, v*
♦ *n*
fumes, exhaust, gas, vapour, mist, fog, smog
♦ *v*
fume, draw (on), puff (on), light up, smoulder, preserve, cure, dry

smoky *adj*
sooty, black, grey, dark, grimy, murky, cloudy, hazy, foggy, smoggy, smudgy, reechy, reeky, fuggy, peaty

smooch *v*
cuddle, hug, embrace, clasp, hold, enfold, nurse, nestle, snuggle, pet, fondle, caress
COLLOQ. snog, canoodle, neck

smooth *adj, v*
♦ *adj*
1 LEVEL, plane, even, flat, horizontal, flush
2 *a smooth sauce*
even, creamy, velvety, rich, thick
3 *a smooth wine*
full-flavoured, mellow, sweet, mature, soft, mild
4 STEADY, even, unbroken, uninterrupted, continuous, flowing, regular, uniform, rhythmic, easy, simple, straightforward, effortless, problem-free, trouble-free
COLLOQ. plain sailing
5 SHINY, polished, burnished, glossy, silky, silken, velvety, sleek, like a mirror, glassy
6 CALM, still, undisturbed, serene, tranquil, peaceful
7 SUAVE, agreeable, smooth-talking, urbane, sophisticated, over-confident, glib, plausible, persuasive, slick, ingratiating, crawling, fawning
FORMAL unctuous
COLLOQ. smarmy
◼ **1** rough, coarse **2** lumpy **3** sharp, bitter **4** troublesome, irregular, erratic, unsteady **6** bumpy, rough, choppy

♦ *v*

1 IRON, press (down), roll, flatten, plaster (down), slick, rub down, level, plane, even (out), file, sand, grind, polish

2 EASE, alleviate, pacify, soothe, allay, calm (down), palliate, mollify

FORMAL assuage, mitigate, appease

3 *smooth the way*

make easier, facilitate, ease, help, assist, aid, encourage, clear the way for

⊟ 1 roughen, wrinkle, crease

smoothly *adv*

evenly, calmly, steadily, soothingly, peacefully, tranquilly, serenely, pleasantly, mildly, easily, effortlessly, equably, fluently

smoothness *n*

1 LEVELNESS, evenness, flatness

2 STEADINESS, evenness, flow, regularity, rhythm, unbrokenness, ease, efficiency, effortlessness, facility, fluency, finish

3 SHINE, polish, silkiness, velvetiness, sleekness, glassiness, serenity, calmness, stillness, softness

⊟ 1 roughness, coarseness

smooth-talking *adj*

persuasive, plausible, slick, suave, silver-tongued, facile, glib, bland

COLLOQ. smooth

smother *v*

suffocate, asphyxiate, strangle, throttle, choke, stifle, put out, extinguish, snuff, smoulder, damp (down), dampen, muffle, inundate, overwhelm, overlie, suppress, repress, keep back, hide, conceal, cover, shroud, cocoon, envelop, surround, wrap; *Scot* smore

OLD oppress

smoulder *v*

burn, smoke, fume, rage, foam, boil, seethe, fester, simmer

smudge *n, v*

♦ *n*

(dirty) mark, blot, blotch, stain, spot, blemish, blur, smear, streak, smutch

♦ *v*

blur, smear, streak, daub, mark, spot, stain, dirty, make dirty, soil, blacken, besmirch

smug *adj*

complacent, self-satisfied, superior, smirking, holier-than-thou, self-righteous, pleased with yourself, priggish, conceited

FORMAL unctuous

⊟ humble, modest

smuggler *n*

runner, contrabandist, moonshiner, free-trader, courier

OLD owler

COLLOQ. bootlegger, mule

smutty *adj*

dirty, crude, coarse, rude, filthy, indecent, improper, indelicate, obscene, pornographic, risqué, racy, bawdy, suggestive, vulgar, gross, lewd, salacious, ribald

FORMAL prurient

COLLOQ. blue, off colour, raunchy, sleazy

⊟ clean, decent

snack *n*

refreshment(s), light meal, sandwich, bite, nibble(s), titbit, buffet, bar lunch/meal, snap, snatch, nacket, supper, *hors d'œuvre*, appetizer, tapas, meze, zakuska; *dialect* bever, butty; *Scot* chack; *N Am* gorp

OLD lunch

COLLOQ. elevenses, fours, bite to eat, pick-me-up

snaffle *v*

grab, seize, steal, make off with, take, take/get hold of,

pluck, pull, wrench, wrest, gain, win, clutch, pounce on, grasp, grip, secure

COLLOQ. nab, swipe, bag, collar, nail

snag *n, v*

♦ *n*

disadvantage, inconvenience, drawback, catch, problem, difficulty, complication, setback, hitch, obstacle, stumbling-block

♦ *v*

catch, rip, tear, hole, ladder

snake *n, v*

♦ *n*

serpent, naga

OLD worm

TECHNICAL ophidian

SLANG *Aust* Joe Blake

Related adjective: anguine, ophidian, serpentine

See panel on next page

♦ *v*

wind, curve, bend, loop, spiral, zigzag, twine, deviate, meander, ramble

snap *v, n, adj*

♦ *v*

1 *the twig snapped*

break, crack, split, splinter, fracture, separate, crackle, chop, give way, collapse, knap

FORMAL crepitate

2 CLICK, clink, snip, snick, tick, gnash

3 BITE, nip, bark, growl, snarl, retort, crackle; *dialect* snack; *Scot* hanch

4 SNATCH, seize, catch, grasp, grip

OLD snip

5 SPEAK ANGRILY TO, growl at, snarl at, lash out at, bark at, speak sharply/brusquely to

COLLOQ. jump down someone's throat

6 PHOTOGRAPH, take, film, shoot, record

♦ *n*

1 BREAK, crack, bite, nip, flick, fillip, crackle; *Scot* snack

2 CLICK, clink, snip, snick, tick, crackle, gnash

3 *a cold snap*

spell, period, time, stretch, span, stint

4 PHOTOGRAPH, photo, snapshot, print, shot, still, picture

♦ *adj*

sudden, immediate, instant, on-the-spot, abrupt

■ **snap up**

grab, grasp, seize, snatch, pounce on, buy quickly, pick up, pluck

COLLOQ. nab

snappy *adj*

1 SMART, stylish, chic, elegant, fashionable, up-to-date, up-to-the-minute, modish

COLLOQ. trendy, snazzy, natty

2 QUICK, hasty, brisk, lively, energetic

3 CROSS, irritable, brusque, bad-tempered, quick-tempered, short-tempered, ill-tempered, ill-natured, irascible, testy

COLLOQ. ratty, grouchy, stroppy, edgy, crabby, crabbed, touchy, crotchety

⊟ 1 dowdy **2** slow

■ **make it snappy**

hurry up

COLLOQ. get cracking, step on it, go all out, pull your finger out, shake a leg, buck up, come along, jump to it, look lively, look sharp, get your skates on

snare *v, n*

♦ *v*

trap, ensnare, entrap, catch, capture, seize, net

♦ *n*

trap, wire, net, noose, gin, springe, catch, pitfall

Types of snake include:

adder	coachwhip	diamond python	hoop-snake	puff adder	smooth snake
anaconda	cobra	dipsas	indigo snake	python	taipan
asp	colubrid	dugite	jararaca	racer	tiger snake
bandy-bandy	constrictor	file snake	king snake	rat snake	tree snake
black snake	copperhead	flying snake	krait	rattlesnake	viper
blind snake	coral snake	gaboon snake	langaha	ribbon snake	water moccasin
boa	corn snake	garter-snake	mamba	ringhals	water snake
boomslang	cottonmouth	gopher snake	massasauga	ring snake	whip snake
brown snake	cylinder snake	grass snake	milk snake	rock snake	worm snake
bull snake	death adder	green snake	pine snake	sand snake	
bushmaster	dendrophis	hamadyrad	pipe snake	sea snake	
carpet snake	diamondback	hognose	pit viper	sidewinder	

snarl¹ *v*

the dog snarled

growl, show your teeth, snap, bark, howl, yelp, lash out at, grumble, complain

snarl² *v*

the rope was snarled in the bushes

tangle, knot, ravel, twist, entangle, enmesh, entwine, embroil, confuse, muddle, jumble, complicate

snarl-up *n*

muddle, tangle, mess, mix-up, jumble, confusion, entanglement, traffic jam, gridlock

snatch *v, n*

♦ *v*

grab, seize, steal, kidnap, abduct, take as hostage, make off with, take, take/get hold of, pluck, pull, wrench, wrest, gain, win, clutch, pounce on, grasp, grip, secure
COLLOQ. nab, swipe, bag, collar, nail

♦ *n*

part, piece, bit, section, segment, fraction, fragment, smattering, snippet, spell

snazzy *adj*

stylish, showy, fashionable, smart, attractive, flamboyant, raffish, sporty, dashing, sophisticated
COLLOQ. flashy, jazzy, ritzy, snappy, swinging, with it
E₃ drab, unfashionable

sneak *v, n, adj*

♦ *v*

1 CREEP, steal, slip, slink, sidle, slide, skulk, pad, lurk, prowl, snook, smuggle, spirit
OLD (*Shakesp*) peak
2 TELL TALES, inform on
COLLOQ. split, squeal, snitch, blow the whistle on, rat
SLANG shop, grass on; *N Am* stool on

♦ *n*

tell-tale, informer, stool pigeon
COLLOQ. squealer, mole, rat, whistle-blower
SLANG grass; *N Am* stoolie

♦ *adj*

secret, surprise, quick, covert, furtive, stealthy, surreptitious
FORMAL clandestine

sneaking *adj*

private, secret, furtive, surreptitious, hidden, lurking, suppressed, unvoiced, unexpressed, grudging, nagging, niggling, persistent, worrying, uncomfortable, intuitive

sneaky *adj*

shady, shifty, furtive, dishonest, devious, guileful, deceitful, unethical, unreliable, unscrupulous, untrustworthy, sly, snide, double-dealing, base, contemptible, cowardly, nasty, mean, low, low-down, malicious
FORMAL disingenuous
COLLOQ. slippery
E₃ honest, open; *colloq.* up front

sneer *v, n*

♦ *v*

scorn, disdain, look down on, scoff, jeer, mock, ridicule, deride, insult, taunt, slight, gibe, laugh, snigger, snicker, smirk, twitch, curl your lips

♦ *n*

scorn, disdain, derision, jeer, mockery, ridicule, insult, taunt, slight, gibe, snigger, snicker, smirk

snicker *v, n*

snigger, laugh, giggle, titter, chuckle, chortle, sneer

snide *adj*

derogatory, sarcastic, cynical, scornful, sneering, hurtful, mocking, taunting, jeering, scoffing, derisive, scathing, biting, caustic, unkind, nasty, mean, spiteful, malicious, ill-natured
FORMAL disparaging
E₃ complimentary

sniff *v, n*

♦ *v*

1 BREATHE, inhale, snuff, snuffle, snivel, snift, vent
2 SMELL, nose, scent, whiff, get a whiff of

♦ *n*

1 SNIFFLE, snivel, snuff, snuffle
2 SMELL, scent, whiff, aroma
3 HINT, whiff, suggestion, trace, impression, intimation

■ **sniff at**

look down on, disdain, sneer at, scoff at, scorn, mock, laugh at, slight, spurn, refuse, shun, reject, dismiss, disregard, overlook
FORMAL deride, disparage
E₃ admire, respect

sniffy *adj*

snobbish, snobby, contemptuous, scoffing, sneering, scornful, condescending, superior, supercilious, disdainful, haughty

snigger *v, n*

snicker, laugh, giggle, titter, chuckle, chortle, sneer, smirk

snip *v, n*

♦ *v*

cut, clip, trim, crop, dock, prune, slit, nick, snick, notch, incise

♦ *n*

1 CUT, clip, trim, crop, prune, slit, clipping
2 BIT, fragment, piece, scrap, shred, snippet
3 BARGAIN, giveaway, special offer, good buy, discount, reduction, value for money
COLLOQ. steal

sniper *n*

guerrilla, freedom fighter, terrorist, irregular, resistance fighter, partisan, bushwhacker, *franc-tireur*, guerrillero, haiduk

snippet *n*

piece, scrap, bit, cutting, clipping, fragment, particle, shred, snatch, part, portion, segment, section

snivel *v*

cry, weep, bawl, sniff, sniffle, snuffle, sob, blub, blubber, whimper, grizzle, moan, whinge, whine

snivelling *adj*
crying, weeping, sniffling, snuffling, blubbering, whimpering, grizzling, moaning, whingeing, whining

snob *n*
élitist, social climber, swank, parvenu
COLLOQ. bighead, high-hat

snobbery *n*
snobbishness, superciliousness, airs, loftiness, arrogance, haughtiness, pride, pretension, pretentiousness, condescension, superiority, disdain, airs and graces
COLLOQ. snootiness, uppishness, side

snobbish *adj*
supercilious, disdainful, proud, haughty, snobby, superior, lofty, arrogant, pretentious, affected, condescending, patronizing
COLLOQ. snooty, stuck-up, toffee-nosed, uppity, jumped-up, hoity-toity, too big for your boots, high and mighty

snog *v*
cuddle, hug, embrace, clasp, hold, enfold, nurse, nestle, snuggle, pet, fondle, caress
COLLOQ. smooch, canoodle, neck

snoop *v, n*
• *v*
spy, sneak, pry, nose, interfere, meddle
COLLOQ. poke/stick your nose in, stick/put your oar in
• *n*
1 *have a snoop around*
sneak, pry, nose, interference, meddling
2 SNOOPER, spy, busybody, pry, meddler
COLLOQ. Nosey Parker, Paul Pry

snooper *n*
snoop, spy, busybody, pry, meddler, eavesdropper
COLLOQ. Nosey Parker, Paul Pry

snooty *adj*
supercilious, disdainful, proud, haughty, snobbish, snobby, superior, lofty, arrogant, pretentious, affected, condescending, patronizing
COLLOQ. stuck-up, toffee-nosed, uppity, jumped-up, hoity-toity, too big for your boots, high and mighty

snooze *v, n*
• *v*
nap, drop off, catnap, doze, sleep
OLD slumber
COLLOQ. have forty winks, nod off
SLANG kip
• *n*
nap, catnap, doze, siesta, sleep
OLD slumber
FORMAL repose
COLLOQ. forty winks, shut-eye
SLANG kip

snout *n*
nose, muzzle, neb, trunk
FORMAL proboscis
COLLOQ. schnozzle, snitch

snow *n*
snowfall, snowstorm, snowflakes, snowdrift, blizzard, snow flurries, sleet, slush, ice
Related adjective: niveous

snub *v, n*
• *v*
rebuff, shun, spurn, insult, disregard, ignore, brush off, cut, slight, rebuke, put down, squash, humble, shame, humiliate, mortify, squelch, sneap; *Scot* snool
OLD frump, sneb, snib
FORMAL affront
COLLOQ. cold-shoulder, give the cold shoulder to, slap in the face, kick in the teeth, blank, give the heave-ho

• *n*
rebuff, brush-off, slight, affront, insult, rebuke, put-down, humiliation, slap, set-down, down-setting, sneap; *Scot* sloan
OLD frump, snib
COLLOQ. slap in the face, kick in the teeth, cold shoulder, heave-ho

snuff
▪ **snuff out**
1 *snuff out a candle*
put out, blow out, stifle, smother, choke, douse, quench, dampen down
2 CRUSH, eliminate, destroy, eradicate, erase, abolish, remove, end, suppress

snug *adj*
cosy, warm, comfortable, homely, friendly, intimate, sheltered, secure, tight, skintight, close-fitting, figure-hugging; *Scot* snod
COLLOQ. comfy, snug as a bug in a rug

snuggle *v*
nestle, nuzzle, curl up, cuddle, embrace, hug
COLLOQ. *N Am* cozy up

snugly *adv*
warmly, cosily, comfortably, securely, tightly

soak *v*
wet, drench, saturate, penetrate, permeate, infuse, bathe, marinate, souse, steep, submerge, immerse, mop, sop, sog, sponge, macerate, seethe, imbue, ret; *dialect* sipe
TECHNICAL *dialect* buck

soaking *adj*
soaked, soaked to the skin, wet through, drenched, sodden, waterlogged, saturated, sopping, sopping wet, wringing, dripping, streaming
🔁 dry

soar *v*
1 *the bird soared up into the air*
fly (up), wing, glide, plane, tower, rise, take off, ascend
2 *temperatures soared*
climb, mount, increase quickly, escalate, spiral, rocket, skyrocket
🔁 **1** fall, descend **2** decrease, plummet

sob *v*
cry, weep, shed tears, bawl, howl, blubber, snivel
COLLOQ. boohoo, turn on the waterworks

sober *adj, v*
• *adj*
1 TEETOTAL, temperate, moderate, abstinent, abstemious, clear-headed
COLLOQ. sober as a judge, dry, drying out, stone-cold sober, on the wagon, off the bottle, having taken/signed the pledge
2 SOLEMN, dignified, serious, earnest, grave, thoughtful, staid, steady, sedate, quiet, serene, calm, composed, unruffled, unexcited, cool, dispassionate, level-headed, practical, realistic, reasonable, rational, clear-headed, self-controlled
3 *sober dress*
sombre, staid, drab, dull, dark, plain, severe, austere, subdued, restrained
🔁 **1** drunk, intemperate **2** frivolous, excited, unrealistic, irrational **3** flashy, garish
▪ **sober up**
clear your head
COLLOQ. dry out, sleep it off

sobriety *n*
1 ABSTEMIOUSNESS, soberness, abstinence, moderation, temperance, teetotalism
2 SOLEMNITY, seriousness, staidness, steadiness, calmness, composure, level-headedness, coolness, sedateness,

restraint, self-restraint, gravity
E3 1 drunkenness 2 excitement, frivolity

sobriquet, soubriquet n
name, title, designation, label, tag, style, term, epithet, nickname
FORMAL appellation, denomination, cognomen
COLLOQ. handle
SLANG monicker

so-called adj
alleged, supposed, ostensible, nominal, self-styled, professed, would-be, pretended, soi-disant
FORMAL purported

sociability n
friendliness, companionability, congeniality, conviviality, cordiality, affability, neighbourliness, gregariousness
COLLOQ. chumminess

sociable adj
friendly, outgoing, gregarious, affable, companionable, genial, convivial, cordial, warm, hospitable, neighbourly, approachable, accessible, familiar, clubbable, extrovert, conversable; N Am folksy
COLLOQ. chummy, mat(e)y
E3 unsociable, withdrawn, unfriendly, hostile

! **sociable** or **social**?
Sociable is usually applied to people and means 'friendly, fond of the company of others': *Our new neighbours aren't very sociable; He's a cheerful, sociable sort of bloke. Social* means 'of or concerning society': *Problems such as this are social rather than medical in origin; social class. Social* also means 'concerning the gathering together or meeting of people for recreation and amusement': *a social club; His reasons for calling round were purely social.*

---

social adj, n
• adj
1 *social policies*
communal, public, community, civic, common, general, collective, group, organized
2 *social activities*
leisure, recreational, entertainment, amusement
• n
party, get-together, gathering, function, dance, at-home
COLLOQ. do, bash, blow-out, knees-up, rave-up, thrash

! **social** or **sociable**?
See panel at **sociable**.

---

socialism n
leftism, communism, welfarism, Leninism, Marxism, Stalinism, Trotskyism

socialist adj, n
• adj
left-wing, leftist, hard-left, communist, Trotskyist, Trotskyite
COLLOQ. commie, leftie, red, Trot
• n
left-winger, leftist, communist, welfarist, Trotskyist, Trotskyite
COLLOQ. commie, leftie, red, pink, pinko, Trot

socialize v
mix, mingle, be sociable, meet people, meet socially, fraternize, converse, get together, go out, entertain
COLLOQ. hobnob

society n
1 COMMUNITY, population, culture, civilization, nation, public, people, mankind, humanity, human race, humankind
2 CLUB, circle, group, band, body, association, organization, company, corporation, federation, alliance, league, union, guild, fellowship, fraternity, brotherhood, sisterhood, sorority

3 FRIENDSHIP, companionship, camaraderie, fellowship, company
4 UPPER CLASSES, high society, polite society, aristocracy, gentry, nobility, élite
COLLOQ. nobs, toffs, swells, top drawer, the smart set, the upper crust, Sloane Rangers

sodden adj
wet, soaking, soaked, drenched, saturated, sopping, waterlogged, soggy, marshy, boggy, miry; *Scot* drookit
E3 dry

sofa n
settee, couch, chesterfield, davenport, lounge, canapé, day-bed, bed-settee, futon, dos-à-dos, squab, tête-à-tête, bergère

soft adj
1 YIELDING, pliable, flexible, pliant, elastic, springy, plastic, supple, malleable, tender, spongy, squashy, mushy, squelchy, pulpy
FORMAL ductile
COLLOQ. squishy
2 *soft colours; speak in a soft voice*
pale, light, pastel, delicate, subdued, shaded, muted, restrained, quiet, low, low-key, whispered, hushed, dim, faint, diffuse, mild, bland, gentle, flowing, soothing, sweet, mellow, melodious, dulcet, pleasant
FORMAL mellifluous
3 FURRY, downy, fleecy, velvety, silky, silken, smooth
4 LENIENT, lax, easy-going, liberal, permissive, indulgent, tolerant, forgiving, forbearing, weak
COLLOQ. spineless
5 TENDER, kind, generous, sympathetic, affectionate, gentle, mild, merciful, soft-hearted, sensitive
6 *a soft life*
easy, comfortable, easy-going, luxurious, successful, prosperous
COLLOQ. cushy, a bed of roses, all beer and skittles
E3 1 hard, firm 2 harsh, hard, sharp, bright, loud 3 rough, abrasive 4 hard, strict, severe 5 unsympathetic, cruel 6 hard

■ **soft in the head**
foolish, stupid, unintelligent, unwise, senseless, childish, puerile, immature, irresponsible
COLLOQ. daft, dotty, loopy, barmy, potty, nutty

■ **soft spot**
fondness, liking, partiality, weakness
FORMAL penchant, proclivity

soften v
1 MODERATE, temper, lessen, diminish, alleviate, ease, cushion, soothe, palliate, quell, subdue, mollify, appease, calm (down), still, relax
FORMAL abate, mitigate, assuage
2 MELT, liquefy, dissolve, reduce
3 CUSHION, pad, muffle, quicken, lower, lighten

■ **soften up**
persuade, conciliate, disarm, win over, weaken, melt
COLLOQ. butter up, soft-soap

soft-hearted adj
sympathetic, compassionate, gentle, kind, benevolent, charitable, generous, warm-hearted, tender, tender-hearted, affectionate, sentimental
E3 hard-hearted, callous

softly-softly adj
cautious, restrained, low-key, diplomatic, patient, tentative, indirect
FORMAL circumspect
E3 aggressive, direct, assertive

soft-pedal v
moderate, minimize, go easy, play down, subdue, tone down
E3 highlight, emphasize

soggy *adj*
wet, damp, moist, soaked, soaking, drenched, sodden, waterlogged, marshy, swampy, saturated, sopping, sopping wet, dripping, heavy, boggy, spongy, pulpy

soil[1] *n*
1 EARTH, clay, loam, humus, dirt, dust, ground
Related adjective: edaphic
2 LAND, region, country, territory
FORMAL terra firma

soil[2] *v*
1 DIRTY, begrime, stain, spot, smudge, smear, foul, muddy, pollute, defile
2 *soil your reputation*
stain, smear, sully, tarnish, damage, defile
OLD besmirch

soiled *adj*
dirty, grimy, stained, spotted, sullied, polluted, tarnished
FORMAL maculate
COLLOQ. manky
E3 clean, immaculate

sojourn *n, v*
◆ *n*
stay, rest, visit, stop, stopover
FORMAL peregrination
◆ *v*
lodge, rest, stay, stop
FORMAL dwell, reside, abide, tarry, tabernacle

solace *n, v*
◆ *n*
comfort, consolation, relief, alleviation, support, condolence, cheer
FORMAL succour
◆ *v*
comfort, console, support, allay, alleviate, soften, soothe
FORMAL mitigate, succour

soldier
Related adjective: military
■ **soldier on**
continue, persevere, keep on, keep going, remain, hold on, hang on
COLLOQ. keep at it, stick at it, hang in there, plug away

Types of soldier include:

cadet	gunner	private
cavalryman	hussar	recruit
centurion	infantryman	regular
commando	lancer	rifleman
conscript	legionnaire	sapper
dragoon	marine	sentry
ensign	mercenary	serviceman
fighter	NCO	Territorial
fusilier	officer	*colloq.* terrier
N Am GI	orderly	tommy
guardsman	paratrooper	trooper
guerrilla	partisan	warrior

See also **rank**[1].

---

sole *adj*
only, unique, exclusive, individual, single, singular, one, lone, solitary, alone
E3 shared, multiple

solecism *n*
error, mistake, blunder, lapse, gaucherie, impropriety, absurdity, faux pas
TECHNICAL anacoluthon
FORMAL cacology, incongruity, indecorum
COLLOQ. boob, booboo, howler, gaffe

solely *adv*
exclusively, only, singly, uniquely, merely, simply, just, completely, entirely, alone, single-handedly

solemn *adj*
1 *a solemn expression*
serious, grave, sober, sedate, sombre, glum, thoughtful, earnest, formal, awed, reverential, devout, pious
COLLOQ. po-faced
2 GRAND, stately, majestic, ceremonial, ritual, formal, ceremonious, pompous, dignified, august, venerable, awe-inspiring, impressive, imposing, momentous
3 *a solemn promise*
sincere, formal, earnest, genuine, wholehearted, committed, honest
E3 1 light-hearted **2** frivolous

solemnity *n*
1 SERIOUSNESS, earnestness, gravity, sacredness, sanctity, momentousness, dignity, impressiveness, grandeur, stateliness
FORMAL portentousness
2 CEREMONY, celebration, observance, rite, ritual, ceremonial, proceedings, formality
E3 1 frivolity

solemnize *v*
keep, honour, observe, commemorate, celebrate, perform, dignify

solemnly *adv*
seriously, gravely, soberly, earnestly, formally, in a dignified manner
E3 frivolously, light-heartedly

solicit *v*
1 *solicit advice*
ask (for), request, crave, beg, implore, plead, pray, apply (for), petition, canvass, woo, court; *N Am* drum
OLD beseech
FORMAL seek, entreat, supplicate, sue, importune
COLLOQ. tout
2 *solicit as a prostitute*
accost, importune, proposition
SLANG hustle, bash

solicitor *n*
lawyer, advocate, attorney, barrister, QC, commissioner of oaths, recorder, barrister; *Scot* crown agent, law agent

solicitous *adj*
caring, attentive, considerate, concerned, anxious, worried, apprehensive, uneasy, troubled, eager, earnest, zealous

solicitude *n*
care, concern, attentiveness, considerateness, consideration, regard, worry, anxiety, uneasiness, disquiet, trouble

solid *adj*
1 HARD, firm, dense, thick, compact, compressed, strong, concrete, sturdy, substantial, stable, sound, well-built, durable, long-lasting, unshak(e)able
2 RELIABLE, dependable, trusty, trustworthy, worthy, decent, upstanding, upright, sensible, level-headed, steadfast, stable, serious, sober, respectable
3 *solid evidence*
reliable, sound, valid, strong, firm, authoritative, weighty, well-grounded, well-founded
FORMAL cogent
4 REAL, genuine, pure, concrete, tangible, unadulterated, unmixed, unalloyed
5 *a solid white line*
unbroken, continuous, undivided, uninterrupted
E3 1 liquid, gaseous, hollow **2** unreliable, unstable **3** unsound, unreliable **4** unreal **5** broken, dotted

solidarity *n*
unity, agreement, accord, unanimity, consensus, harmony, concord, cohesion, like-mindedness, single-mindedness, camaraderie, team spirit, *esprit de corps*, soundness, stability
⊟ discord, division, schism

solidify *v*
harden, go/become hard, set, gel, jell, congeal, coagulate, clot, cake, crystallize
⊟ soften, liquefy, dissolve

soliloquy *n*
monologue, speech, lecture, sermon, address, oration, homily
⊟ conversation, dialogue, discussion

solitary *adj, n*
♦ *adj*
1 LONELY, sole, single, lone, alone, lonesome, by yourself, friendless, companionless, unsociable, introverted, recluse, reclusive, hermitical, withdrawn, retired, monasterial
OLD dernful
2 REMOTE, lonely, separate, isolated, desolate, out-of-the-way, inaccessible, cloistered, secluded, unfrequented, unvisited, untrodden
FORMAL sequestered
COLLOQ. off the beaten track
⊟ 1 accompanied, gregarious, busy **2** accessible
♦ *n*
loner, individualist, hermit, recluse, ascetic, monk, anchorite, anchoress, ancress, eremite, stylite
COLLOQ. lone wolf; *Aust & NZ* Jimmy Woodser

solitude *n*
aloneness, loneliness, singleness, friendlessness, lonesomeness, introversion, unsociability, reclusiveness, retirement, privacy, seclusion, isolation, remoteness, desolation
⊟ companionship

solo *adj*
unaccompanied, alone, unescorted, unattended, by yourself, on your own, lone, single, single-handed
⊟ accompanied

solution *n*
1 ANSWER, result, explanation, resolution, key, remedy, way out, panacea, cure-all, clarification, decipherment, disentanglement, unfolding, unravelling
FORMAL elucidation
COLLOQ. (quick) fix
2 MIXTURE, blend, mix, compound, suspension, emulsion, liquid, solvent

solve *v*
work out, figure out, puzzle out, decipher, read, resolve, crack, disentangle, unravel, unfold, answer, put right, remedy, settle, clear up, clarify, explain, interpret, think out, riddle, unriddle, undo, untie, guess, get to the bottom of; *N Am* work, solution
OLD assoil; (*Spenser*) loose
FORMAL rectify, expound
COLLOQ. fathom

solvent *adj*
sound, financially sound, able to pay, creditworthy, out of debt, unindebted
COLLOQ. in the black
⊟ insolvent

sombre *adj*
1 SAD, serious, solemn, grave, melancholy, mournful, depressed, doleful, morose, joyless, sober
FORMAL lugubrious
2 *sombre colours*
dark, dull, gloomy, funereal, drab, dim, obscure,

shady, shadowy, dismal, dingy
⊟ 1 happy, cheerful **2** bright, cheerful

somebody *n*
someone, celebrity, dignitary, name, personage, star, superstar, VIP, notable, luminary, magnate, mogul, heavyweight, nabob, panjandrum
COLLOQ. household name, bigwig, big noise, big shot, big wheel
⊟ nobody

someday *adv*
sometime, at some time in the future, one day, one of these (fine) days, sooner or later, later, later on, in due course, by and by, eventually, ultimately
⊟ never

somehow *adv*
by some means, one way or another, come what may
COLLOQ. by fair means or foul, by hook or by crook, come hell or high water

sometime *adv, adj*
♦ *adv*
someday, one day, at some time in the future, at some time in the past, another time, in the past, then, previously, earlier
♦ *adj*
former, previous, one-time, late, retired, emeritus
FORMAL erstwhile, quondam
COLLOQ. ex

sometimes *adv*
occasionally, on occasion(s), now and again, now and then, on and off, off and on, every so often, once in a while, at times, from time to time
⊟ always, never

somewhat *adv*
rather, moderately, relatively, slightly, a bit, a little, fairly, quite, to a limited degree/extent, to some degree/extent, pretty
COLLOQ. kind of, sort of

somnolent *adj*
sleepy, drowsy, dozy, half-awake, heavy-eyed, soporific, torpid
TECHNICAL comatose
FORMAL oscitant

son *n*
boy, child, lad(die), offspring, descendant, inhabitant, disciple
Related adjective: filial

song *n*
■ **song and dance**
commotion, stir, fuss, bother, ado, to-do, tumult, furore, performance
COLLOQ. flap, hoo-ha, kerfuffle, pother, tizzy
See panel on next page

songster *n*
singer, vocalist, chorister, balladeer, chanteuse, soloist, minstrel, troubadour, crooner, warbler

sonorous *adj*
resonant, resounding, ringing, rich, rounded, orotund, ororotund, full, full-mouthed, full-voiced, full-throated, loud, sounding, high-flown, high-sounding
FORMAL grandiloquent, plangent

soon *adv*
shortly, presently, in a little while, in no time (at all), in a short time, in a minute, in a moment (or two), any minute (now), just now, early, without delay, in a hurry, before long, in the near future
OLD anon, betimes, ere long, timely
COLLOQ. quick, pronto, in a jiffy, in a tick, in two shakes of a lamb's tail, before you can say Jack Robinson, (just) round the corner

Types of song include:

air	calypso	descant	lay	ode	rock song
amoret	cantata	dirge	lied	penillion-singing	roundelay
anthem	canticle	dithyramb	lilt	plainchant	serenade
aria	cantilena	ditty	love-song	plainsong	shanty
art-song	canzone	elegy	lullaby	pop song	spiritual
ballad	canzonet	epinikion	lyric(s)	psalm	threnody
barcarole	carol	epithalamium	madrigal	pub song	torch song
birdcall	chanson	folk song	melody	recitative	tune
birdsong	chansonette	gospel song	Negro spiritual	refrain	war song
blues	chant	hymn	number	requiem	wassail
bothy ballad	chorus	jingle	nursery rhyme	rock and roll	yodel

See also **poem**.

■ **as soon as**
directly after, immediately after, once, when, no sooner ... than, right after, in the wake of
OLD eftsoons

sooner *adv*
1 EARLIER, before, in advance, beforehand
2 RATHER, preferably, much rather, instead, by/for preference, by/for/from choice

■ **sooner or later**
eventually, finally, ultimately, at last, in the end, at length, subsequently, after all, in the long run, in due course, in the fullness of time
COLLOQ. at the end of the day, when all is said and done, in the final analysis

■ **no sooner than**
scarcely, hardly, barely, only just

soothe *v*
alleviate, relieve, ease, salve, comfort, allay, calm (down), compose, tranquillize, settle (down), still, quiet, quieten (down), hush, lull, pacify, mollify, soften, palliate, temper
FORMAL appease, assuage, mitigate
Ɛ∃ aggravate, irritate, annoy, vex

soothing *adj*
relaxing, restful, calming, easeful, emollient, lenitive, balmy, palliative, balsamic
TECHNICAL anetic
FORMAL assuasive, demulcent
Ɛ∃ annoying, irritating, vexing

soothsayer *n*
prophet, prophetess, diviner, foreteller, seer, sibyl, augur
OLD Chaldaic
FORMAL haruspex

sophisticated *adj*
1 URBANE, cosmopolitan, worldly, worldly-wise, experienced, seasoned, cultured, cultivated, civilized, stylish, elegant, refined, polished, suave, couth, slick
OLD (*Shakesp*) inland
COLLOQ. having been around, cool
2 *sophisticated technology*
advanced, highly-developed, high-tech, hi-tech, space-age, state-of-the-art, complicated, complex, intricate, elaborate, delicate, subtle, gold, expensive, executive
Ɛ∃ **1** unsophisticated, naive **2** primitive, simple

sophistication *n*
urbanity, worldliness, culture, experience, elegance, finesse, poise, savoir-faire, savoir-vivre
Ɛ∃ naivety, simplicity

sophistry *n*
false reasoning, casuistry, sophism, quibble, fallacy
TECHNICAL paralogism, elenchus

soporific *adj, n*
♦ *adj*
sleep-inducing, hypnotic, sedative, opiate, narcotic, tranquillizing, sleepy
FORMAL somnolent

Ɛ∃ stimulating, invigorating
♦ *n*
tranquillizer, sleeping pill, sleeping tablet, sedative, opiate, narcotic, hypnotic, anaesthetic, hypnic
Ɛ∃ stimulant

soppy *adj*
sentimental, overemotional, mawkish, maudlin, cloying, soft, crazy, wild, silly
COLLOQ. slushy, mushy, sloppy, lovey-dovey, weepy, schmaltzy, gooey, cheesy, corny, wet, wimpish, daft

sorcerer *n*
sorceress, wizard, warlock, witch, magician, enchanter, magus, mage, magian, reim-kennar, necromancer, voodoo, angek(k)ok
FORMAL thaumaturgist
Related adjective: magian

sorcery *n*
magic, black magic, witchcraft, wizardry, necromancy, wicca, voodoo, spell, incantation, charm, enchantment, pishogue
FORMAL thaumaturgy

sordid *adj*
1 DIRTY, filthy, unclean, foul, vile, squalid, grimy, stained, soiled, mucky, seamy, seedy, disreputable, shabby, tawdry; *Aust & NZ* scungy
COLLOQ. sleazy
2 CORRUPT, degraded, degenerate, immoral, debased, dishonest, dishonourable, disreputable, debauched, low, base, vile, foul, despicable, shameful, abhorrent, wretched, mean, miserly, niggardly, grasping, mercenary, self-seeking
FORMAL ignominious
Ɛ∃ **1** clean, pure **2** honourable, upright

sore *adj, n*
♦ *adj*
1 PAINFUL, hurting, aching, smarting, stinging, burning, chafed, tender, sensitive, inflamed, red, reddened, bruised, injured, raw, wounded, nasty; *Scot* sair
2 ANNOYED, irritated, vexed, angry, upset, hurt, wounded, afflicted, aggrieved, offended, bitter, resentful, distressed; *Scot* sair
COLLOQ. peeved, miffed, cheesed off
Ɛ∃ **2** pleased, happy
♦ *n*
wound, cut, graze, laceration, lesion, scrape, abrasion, chafe, swelling, inflammation, boil, abscess, ulcer, the raw, bite, felon, fester, gall, nerve; *Scot* sair
TECHNICAL anthrax, quittor
OLD botch

sorely *adv*
greatly, much, very much, highly, extremely, noticeably, significantly, remarkably, notably, substantially, markedly, powerfully, exceedingly

sorrow *n, v*
♦ *n*
1 SADNESS, unhappiness, grief, mourning, misery, woe,

distress, suffering, pain, dejection, anguish, heartache, heartbreak, misfortune, wretchedness
FORMAL affliction, disconsolateness, dolour
2 TROUBLE, misfortune, hardship, worry, trial, regret, remorse
FORMAL tribulation, affliction
F3 1 happiness, joy **2** joy, delight
♦ v
grieve, lament, bewail, bemoan, be/feel sad, be/feel miserable, weep, agonize, moan, mourn, pine
F3 rejoice

sorrowful *adj*
miserable, mournful, sad, unhappy, tearful, sorry, distressing, depressed, dejected, wretched, painful, lamentable, woeful, melancholy, grievous, doleful, heartbroken, heart-rending, heavy-hearted, piteous, rueful; *Scot* wae
OLD woe
FORMAL afflicted, disconsolate, lugubrious, woebegone
F3 happy, joyful

sorry *adj*
1 APOLOGETIC, regretful, ashamed, remorseful, contrite, penitent, repentant, rueful, conscience-stricken, guilt-ridden, shamefaced
COLLOQ. bad
2 *sorry to hear the news*
sad, unhappy, upset, distressed
3 SYMPATHETIC, compassionate, understanding, pitying, concerned, moved
4 *in a sorry state*
pathetic, pitiful, poor, mean, simple, wretched, miserable, sad, unfortunate, unhappy, dismal, grievous, heart-rending, shameful
F3 1 impenitent, unashamed **2** happy, pleased **3** uncaring **4** happy, cheerful

sort *n, v*
♦ n
kind, type, ilk, family, race, breed, species, variety, order, class, set, category, group, denomination, style, make, brand, stamp, quality, nature, character, description
TECHNICAL genus
FORMAL genre
♦ v
class, group, categorize, distribute, divide, separate, segregate, sift, screen, grade, rank, order, classify, catalogue, arrange, put in order, organize, systematize
■ **sort out**
1 ARRANGE, order, put in order, organize, work out
2 CLASSIFY, class, group, categorize, rank, order, grade, separate, divide, segregate, choose, select
3 RESOLVE, clear up, work out, put right, solve
■ **sort of**
rather, moderately, relatively, slightly, a bit, a little, somewhat, fairly, quite, to a limited degree/extent, to some degree/extent, pretty
COLLOQ. kind of
■ **out of sorts**
1 UNWELL, ill, sick, poorly, laid up, ailing, off-colour, seedy, queasy, diseased, unhealthy, infirm, frail, weak, feeble, bedridden
COLLOQ. in a bad way, dicky, below par, down in the dumps, down in the mouth, under the weather, run-down, rough, groggy
2 BAD-TEMPERED, irritable, cross, snappy, quick-tempered, grumpy, fractious, in a (bad) mood, narky, impatient, choleric
COLLOQ. crotchety, crabbed, crabby, grouchy, stroppy, shirty, ratty, in a huff, in a sulk

sortie *n*
foray, raid, offensive, attack, charge, assault, sally, swoop, invasion, rush

so-so *adj*
average, middling, moderate, mediocre, indifferent, fair, adequate, ordinary, respectable, neutral, tolerable, unexceptional, undistinguished, passable, *comme ci comme ça*
COLLOQ. fair to middling, not bad, OK, no great shakes, run-of-the-mill

sought-after *adj*
in great demand, popular, well-liked, favourite, liked, favoured, in favour, admired, wanted, desired, approved, in demand, fashionable, modish
COLLOQ. trendy, now, in, hip, cool, big, all the rage
F3 unpopular, disliked, out of favour

soul *n*
1 SPIRIT, psyche, mind, reason, intellect, character, inner being, inner self, essence, life, life-giving principle, vital force
FORMAL anima
COLLOQ. heart of hearts
2 INDIVIDUAL, person, human being, man, woman, creature
COLLOQ. character
3 *a singer with no soul*
sensitivity, sympathy, compassion, feeling, humanity, understanding, appreciation, tenderness, inspiration, passion
4 *he's the soul of discretion*
epitome, personification, embodiment, essence, model, example
F3 1 body

soulful *adj*
sensitive, emotional, expressive, heartfelt, moving, profound, mournful, meaningful, eloquent
F3 soulless

soulless *adj*
unfeeling, spiritless, unsympathetic, inhuman, lifeless, cold, callous, cruel, unkind, dead, uninteresting, characterless, ignoble, mean, mean-spirited, soul-destroying, mechanical
F3 soulful

sound¹ *n, v*
♦ n
1 *hear a tapping sound*
noise, din, report, resonance, reverberation, tone, timbre, tenor, description
Related adjectives: acoustic, audial, sonic
See panels on next page
2 *I don't like the sound of that idea*
impression, sense, notion, feeling, implication
COLLOQ. vibe
♦ v
1 RING, toll, chime, peal, resound, resonate, reverberate, echo, go off
2 ARTICULATE, enunciate, pronounce, voice, express, utter, say, declare, announce
3 *that sounds like an excellent idea*
seem, appear, look, give the impression

sound² *adj, adv*
♦ adj
1 FIT, well, healthy, in good health, in good condition/ shape, vigorous, robust, sturdy, firm, solid, whole, sane, complete, intact, perfect, disease-free, unbroken, undamaged, unimpaired, unhurt, uninjured
COLLOQ. in fine fettle, sound as a bell
2 VALID, well-founded, well-grounded, reasonable, rational, logical, orthodox, authoritative, weighty, right, true, proven, reliable, dependable, trustworthy, secure, substantial, solid, sturdy, thorough, good, complete
FORMAL judicious, cogent
3 *a sound sleep*
deep, intense, serious, very great, extreme, severe, strong, vigorous, profound

Sounds include:

bang	clatter	gurgle	pop	smack	thunder
beep	click	hiccup	rattle	snap	tick
blare	clink	hiss	report	sniff	ting
blast	crack	honk	reverberate	snore	tinkle
bleep	crackle	hoot	ring	snort	toot
boom	crash	hum	roar	sob	twang
bubble	creak	jangle	rumble	splash	wail
buzz	crunch	jingle	rustle	splutter	whimper
chime	cry	knock	scrape	squeak	whine
chink	drone	moan	scream	squeal	whirr
chug	echo	murmur	screech	squelch	whistle
clack	explode	patter	sigh	swish	whoop
clang	fizz	peal	sizzle	tap	yell
clank	grate	ping	skirl	throb	
clap	grizzle	pip	slam	thud	
clash	groan	plop	slurp	thump	

Animal sounds include:

bark	chirp	growl	miaow	snarl	woof
bay	chirrup	grunt	moo	squawk	yap
bellow	cluck	hiss	neigh	squeak	yelp
bleat	coo	hoot	purr	tweet	yowl
bray	croak	howl	quack	twitter	
cackle	crow	low	roar	warble	
caw	gobble	mew	screech	whinny	

⨥ 1 unfit, ill, shaky **2** unsound, unreliable, poor **3** light, shallow
* *adv*
deeply, intensely, extremely, completely, thoroughly, very much, greatly, severely, vigorously, seriously, profoundly

sound³ *v*
to sound the depths
measure, plumb, fathom, probe, gauge, examine, test, inspect, investigate
■ **sound out**
ask, canvass, examine, investigate, research, survey, probe, pump, question
COLLOQ. suss out

sound⁴ *n*
the Sound of Jura
channel, estuary, inlet, passage, strait, firth, fjord, voe

soundly *adv*
1 *soundly asleep*
deeply, intensely, extremely, completely, thoroughly, very much, greatly, severely, vigorously, seriously, profoundly
2 *soundly beaten in the finals*
fully, perfectly, completely, absolutely, downright, entirely, quite, totally, utterly
3 *a soundly based decision*
validly, reasonably, logically, dependably, securely, solidly, authoritatively
⨥ 1 lightly **2** partially

soup *n*
broth, potage, consommé, stock, chowder, bisque, cockieleekie, borsch, gazpacho, mulligatawny, julienne

sour *adj, v*
* *adj*
1 TART, sharp, acid, tangy, acidy, acidulous, acetic, pungent, vinegary, bitter, rancid, curdled, turned, verjuice, acerbic, acerb, subacid; *Scot* wersh
OLD eager; (*Shakesp*) aygre
FORMAL acetous
COLLOQ. off, bad
2 EMBITTERED, bad-tempered, surly, churlish, ill-tempered, peevish, crusty, resentful, unpleasant, acrimonious, nasty, disagreeable, austere, subacid, vinegary

COLLOQ. crabbed, grouchy, shirty, ratty
⨥ 1 sweet, sugary **2** good-natured, generous
* *v*
disenchant, embitter, make bitter, exacerbate, exasperate, alienate, spoil, envenom, canker

source *n*
origin, derivation, beginning, start, cause, root, rise, spring, wellspring, fountainhead, wellhead, supply, mine, originator, author, authority, informant
TECHNICAL ylem
FORMAL commencement, provenance, primordium, *fons et origo*

sourpuss *n*
misery, grumbler, killjoy, shrew, whiner, kvetch
COLLOQ. crosspatch, grouse, grump, whinger, dog in the manger, buzzkill

souse *v*
douse, drench, dunk, sink, immerse, marinate, marinade, pickle, plunge, soak, saturate, steep, dip, submerge

souvenir *n*
memento, reminder, remembrance, keepsake, relic, token, trophy

sovereign *n, adj*
* *n*
ruler, monarch, king, queen, emperor, empress, tsar, chief
FORMAL potentate
* *adj*
1 RULING, royal, kingly, queenly, princely, imperial, majestic, absolute, unlimited, supreme, paramount, predominant, principal, chief, dominant, independent, autonomous, self-governing, self-ruling
2 UNRIVALLED, outstanding, utmost, extreme, unequalled

sovereignty *n*
autonomy, independence, supremacy, domination, sway, dominion, kingship, queenship, regality, primacy, raj
FORMAL ascendancy, imperium, suzerainty

SOW *v*
plant, seed, scatter, strew, bestrew, spread, distribute, disperse, broadcast, lodge, implant
FORMAL disseminate

space *n, v*

♦ *n*

1 ROOM, place, seat, accommodation, capacity, area, volume, extent, expanse, sweep, stretch, expansion, latitude, scope, range, play, clearance, elbow-room, *Lebensraum*, leeway, margin
FORMAL amplitude
Related adjective: spatial
2 BLANK, omission, gap, break, empty space, opening, interval, intermission, chasm
FORMAL lacuna, interstice
Related adjective: lacunary
3 *in a short space of time*
period, stretch, span, spell, time, shift, stint
4 OUTER SPACE, the Milky Way, galaxy, universe, cosmos, solar system, deep space
Related adjective: cosmic

♦ *v*

arrange, order, put in order, range, be apart, set apart, space out, stretch out, string out, place at intervals
FORMAL array, dispose

spaceman, spacewoman *n*

astronaut, space traveller, cosmonaut

spacious *adj*

roomy, ample, big, large, siz(e)able, broad, wide, huge, vast, immense, extensive, expansive, open, uncrowded, palatial
FORMAL capacious, commodious
F3 small, narrow, cramped, confined, poky

spadework *n*

foundation, groundwork, homework, preparation, preliminary work, labour, drudgery
COLLOQ. donkey-work

span *n, v*

♦ *n*

spread, stretch, reach, range, scope, compass, piece, extent, length, distance, duration, time, interval, term, period, spell

♦ *v*

arch, vault, bridge, link, cross, traverse, range, extend, stretch, last, cover, include
OLD overlay
FORMAL bestride

spank *v*

smack, slap, thrash, slipper, cane
COLLOQ. wallop, whack, thwack, tan, put over your knee

spanking *adj, adv*

♦ *adj*

brisk, fast, quick, lively, smart, speedy, swift, vigorous, energetic, snappy, invigorating, fine, gleaming
F3 slow

♦ *adv*

absolutely, completely, utterly, totally, exactly, strikingly, positively, brand

spar *v*

argue, dispute, contest, fall out, contend, quarrel, wrangle, squabble, bicker, wrestle, box, skirmish
COLLOQ. scrap, spat, tiff

spare *adj, v*

♦ *adj*

1 RESERVE, emergency, extra, additional, supplementary, subsidiary, leftover, remaining, unused, over, surplus, surplus to requirements, superfluous, supernumerary, auxiliary, unwanted
OLD subsecive
SLANG buckshee, gash
2 *spare time*
free, unoccupied, leisure
3 LEAN, thin, skinny, bony, gaunt, lank, slim, slender, scraggy, scrawny

COLLOQ. all skin and bones
4 FRUGAL, scanty, scant, meagre, modest, sparing, skimpy
F3 **1** necessary, vital, used **3** fat, plump

♦ *v*

1 PARDON, let off, reprieve, show mercy to, forgive, release, free, forbear, withhold
2 GRANT, allow, provide, give, afford, part with, do without, manage without
FORMAL dispense with
3 NOT HARM, protect, save, guard, safeguard, secure, take care of, defend, reserve, stint; *Scot* hain

■ **to spare**
left over, remaining, extra, in reserve, unused, surplus

sparing *adj*

economical, thrifty, careful, prudent, frugal, meagre, miserly
FORMAL penurious
COLLOQ. stingy, mingy, tight-fisted, close-fisted
F3 unsparing, liberal, lavish

sparingly *adv*

economically, carefully, prudently, meagrely, frugally
COLLOQ. stingily
F3 unsparingly, lavishly

spark *n, v*

♦ *n*

1 FLASH, flare, gleam, glint, glimmer, flicker, sparkle, flame, flake, flaught, funk, *bluette*
2 *not a spark of intelligence*
flicker, hint, trace, vestige, scrap, bit, touch, suggestion, iota, atom, jot, scintilla; *dialect* spunk; *N Am, Aust & NZ* skerrick

■ **spark off**
kindle, set off, trigger (off), start (off), cause, touch off, occasion, prompt, give rise to, provoke, stimulate, stir, incite, excite, inspire
FORMAL precipitate

sparkle *v, n*

♦ *v*

1 TWINKLE, glitter, scintillate, flash, flicker, gleam, glint, glisten, glow, glimmer, shimmer, shine, beam
OLD glister
FORMAL coruscate, emicate
2 EFFERVESCE, fizz, bubble
3 BE LIVELY, be animated, be spirited, be enthusiastic, be witty, be vivacious, be effervescent
FORMAL be ebullient
COLLOQ. be bubbly

♦ *n*

1 TWINKLE, glitter, flash, shimmer, gleam, glow, shine, glint, flicker, spark, fire, radiance, brilliance, dazzle
FORMAL coruscation, emication
2 SPIRIT, vitality, life, animation, vivacity, liveliness, energy, dash, brio, zest, enthusiasm
FORMAL ebullience
COLLOQ. get-up-and-go, vim, pizzazz

sparkling *adj*

1 EFFERVESCENT, fizzy, carbonated, bubbly
2 TWINKLING, flashing, glittering, glistening, gleaming, scintillating, scintillant
FORMAL coruscating
3 LIVELY, animated, scintillating, witty
F3 **1** flat **3** dull

sparse *adj*

scarce, scanty, meagre, slight, scattered, infrequent, sporadic
F3 plentiful, thick, dense

sparsely *adv*

scarcely, scantily, meagrely, slightly, sporadically, few and far between
F3 plentifully

spartan *adj*
austere, harsh, severe, rigorous, strict, disciplined, self-denying, ascetic, abstemious, stringent, temperate, frugal, plain, simple, bleak, joyless
Ⅎ luxurious, self-indulgent

spasm *n*
burst, eruption, outburst, frenzy, fit, bout, convulsion, seizure, attack, paroxysm, contraction, cramp, crick, jerk, twitch, tic, start, grip, throe
TECHNICAL clonic spasm, clonus, tonic spasm, tonus
FORMAL access
Related adjective: spastic

spasmodic *adj*
sporadic, occasional, intermittent, erratic, periodic, irregular, fitful, jerky
Ⅎ continuous, uninterrupted

spasmodically *adv*
sporadically, occasionally, intermittently, periodically, intermittently, now and again, off and on, on and off
Ⅎ continuously, uninterruptedly

spate *n*
flood, deluge, torrent, rush, series, outpouring, flow

spatter *v*
splatter, splash, splodge, spray, sprinkle, shower, speckle, scatter, daub, bedaub, bestrew, besprinkle, bespatter, dirty, soil

spawn *v*
give rise to, cause, bring about, bring on, make, produce, create, generate, lead to, originate, engender

spay *n*
neuter, sterilize, castrate, emasculate, doctor, geld

speak *v*
talk, say, state, declare, express, utter, voice, articulate, enunciate, pronounce, tell, chat, communicate, address, lecture, harangue, hold forth, argue, discuss
FORMAL converse, declaim
COLLOQ. have a word with, chatter, gab, witter, yak

■ **speak for**
speak on behalf of, represent, act for, stand for, act as spokesperson for

■ **speak of**
refer to, make reference to, mention, make mention of, discuss

■ **speak out/up**
say publicly, speak openly, defend, support, protest
COLLOQ. stand up and be counted

■ **speak to**
rebuke, reprimand, scold, warn, lecture, accost, address; *Aust* rouse on
FORMAL admonish, upbraid
COLLOQ. bring to book, tell off, tick off, take/pull apart, bawl out, bounce, carpet, give someone a ticking-off, dress down, give someone a dressing-down, haul over the coals, read the riot act to, throw the book at, rap over the knuckles, give someone a rap over the knuckles, give someone a flea in their ear, give someone an earful, give someone a piece of your mind, shoot down in flames, tear a strip off someone, give someone some stick, go to town on, come down on like a ton of bricks, give someone hell; *Aust & NZ* go crook at

■ **speak up**
talk (more) loudly, raise your voice, make yourself heard

Synonym nuances
State has added implications of emphasis and clarity: *everything I have stated in my report is accurate*, and **declare** also suggests an announcement. While **utter** is merely to vocalize, **express** implies conveying meaning or feeling: *a speech expressing grave misgivings*, and **voice** could also be used of making your feelings known: *he voiced his support for the proposal.*

Articulate, similarly, suggests the verbal conveying of a precise meaning, whereas **enunciate** puts the emphasis on the physical formation of words: *he enunciated his words with clarity and force.* **Pronounce** can be used similarly, but is also appropriate for making a formal declaration: *a death sentence was pronounced.*
Address would be used of directing words to an audience, while **harangue** has suggestions of forcefulness and aggression. **Lecture** can be used of delivering a more specific talk, but can also describe delivering a perhaps rather overbearing reproof: *he lectured them on their appalling manners.* The term **hold forth** suggests engaging an audience: *Asimov could hold forth on almost any subject with lucidity.* However, it may have overtones of pompousness: *a bulky woman was holding forth in stentorian tones.*

speaker *n*
talker, lecturer, orator, spokesperson, spokesman, spokeswoman, mouthpiece
FORMAL prolocutor

spear *n*
javelin, dart, harpoon, pike, trident, handstaff, assegai, boar-spear, fish-spear, gig, leister, truncheon; *dialect* gleave; *Scot* waster
OLD ash, demi-lance, gad, glaive, lancegay, gavelock, pilum, pile

spearhead *v, n*
◆ *v*
lead, head, initiate, launch, front, pioneer
◆ *n*
vanguard, front line, leading position, pioneer, trailblazer, leader, guide, overseer
COLLOQ. van, cutting edge

special *adj*
1 *a special occasion*
important, significant, momentous, major, noteworthy, notable, distinguished, distinctive, memorable, remarkable, extraordinary, outstanding, exceptional, unusual
COLLOQ. out of the ordinary, red-letter
2 DIFFERENT, distinctive, characteristic, peculiar, individual, unique, exclusive, select, choice, particular, exact, specific, precise, detailed
FORMAL singular
Ⅎ 1 normal, ordinary, usual; *colloq.* run-of-the-mill **2** general, common

specialist *n*
consultant, authority, expert, master, professional, connoisseur
COLLOQ. brains

speciality *n*
strength, feature, forte, talent, gift, field/area of study, field, *pièce de résistance*; *N Am* specialty

specialization *n*
special interest, special subject, specialist subject, special study, concentration, focus, particularization

specialize *v*
concentrate on, focus on, study, follow, have as your specialist subject; *N Am* major in

specially *adv*
for a special purpose, for a particular purpose, particularly, exclusively, uniquely, in particular, specifically, explicitly, distinctly, expressly

species *n*
class, kind, breed, sort, type, category, variety, group, collection, description
TECHNICAL genus

specific *adj*
particular, precise, exact, fixed, set, limited, determined,

special, definite, well-defined, unequivocal, clear-cut, detailed, explicit, express, unambiguous
E vague, approximate, unspecific

specifically *adv*
1 *designed specifically for the elderly*
particularly, specially, exclusively, in particular, for a special purpose, for a particular purpose
2 *I specifically told you not to go there*
distinctly, exactly, clearly, plainly, unambiguously, expressly, definitely

specification *n*
requirement, condition, qualification, stipulation, instruction, description, listing, naming, statement, designation, item, particular, detail
FORMAL delineation

specify *v*
stipulate, spell out, set out, define, particularize, detail, itemize, enumerate, list, mention, state, cite, name, designate, indicate, describe
FORMAL delineate

specimen *n*
sample, example, instance, illustration, model, pattern, type, representative, copy, exhibit
FORMAL paradigm, exemplar

specious *adj*
false, misleading, unsound, untrue, deceptive, plausible
FORMAL fallacious, casuistic, sophistic, sophistical
E valid, true

speck *n*
mark, fleck, dot, speckle, shred, grain, particle, bit, blot, defect, blemish, fault, flaw, stain, spot, atom, mite, iota, jot, trace, whit, tittle, mote, peep, pip, spangle
TECHNICAL floater, sheave

speckled *adj*
spotted, spotty, flecked, dotted, dappled, mottled, sprinkled, stippled, brinded, brindle(d), fleckered, freckled
TECHNICAL lentiginous

spectacle *n*
show, performance, display, exhibition, parade, pageant, extravaganza, scene, sight, picture, curiosity, wonder, marvel, phenomenon

spectacles

Types of spectacles include:

bifocals	monocle	shooting glasses
diving mask	pince-nez	sports spex
eyeglass	Polaroid® glasses	sunglasses
goggles	quizzing glass	trifocals
half-glasses	reading glasses	varifocals
lorgnette	safety glasses	

---

spectacular *adj, n*
♦ *adj*
grand, splendid, magnificent, sensational, impressive, glorious, striking, stunning, staggering, amazing, astonishing, extraordinary, outstanding, remarkable, dramatic, daring, breathtaking, dazzling, eye-catching, colourful, ostentatious, flamboyant
FORMAL resplendent, opulent
E unimpressive, ordinary
♦ *n*
extravaganza, show, display, exhibition, pageant, spectacle

spectacularly *adv*
amazingly, astonishingly, strikingly, stunningly, staggeringly, extraordinarily, outstandingly, remarkably, magnificently, sensationally, impressively, gloriously
E ordinarily

spectator *n*
watcher, viewer, onlooker, looker-on, bystander, passer-by, witness, eyewitness, observer, ringsider
OLD groundling; (*Shakesp*) supervisor
FORMAL beholder
COLLOQ. wallflower
SLANG *N Am* rubberneck
E player, participant

spectral *adj*
ghostly, incorporeal, insubstantial, disembodied, supernatural, unearthly, weird, uncanny, phantom, shadowy, eerie; *Scot* eldritch
COLLOQ. spooky

spectre *n*
1 GHOST, phantom, phantasm, spirit, wraith, apparition, vision, presence, shade, shadow, revenant, visitant, bogle, Empusa; *Scot* bodach
OLD larva, phantosme
COLLOQ. spook
2 THREAT, menace, fear, dread

spectrum *n*
See **rainbow**.

speculate *v*
1 GUESS, wonder, imagine, contemplate, meditate, muse, reflect, consider, deliberate, theorize, hypothesize, suppose
FORMAL conjecture, surmise, cogitate
2 GAMBLE, risk, hazard, venture

speculation *n*
1 GUESS, guesswork, consideration, supposition, theory, contemplation, deliberation, imagination, flight of fancy
FORMAL conjecture, surmise, hypothesis
2 GAMBLE, gambling, hazard, risk

speculative *adj*
hypothetical, theoretical, notional, indefinite, vague, abstract, academic, tentative, risky, hazardous, uncertain, unpredictable, unproven
FORMAL conjectural, suppositional
COLLOQ. iffy, chancy, dicey

speech *n*
1 COMMUNICATION, spoken communication, language, dialogue, conversation, talk, articulation, pronunciation, diction, enunciation, elocution, accent, delivery, utterance, voice, tongue, parlance, dialect, jargon
COLLOQ. lingo
2 *make a speech*
oration, address, discourse, talk, lecture, homily, sermon, message, harangue, patter, conversation, dialogue, monologue, soliloquy, tirade
FORMAL diatribe, philippic
COLLOQ. spiel

speechless *adj*
dumbfounded, dumbstruck, lost for words, thunderstruck, amazed, astounded, shocked, aghast, tongue-tied, inarticulate, mute, dumb, struck dumb, silent, mum
FORMAL obmutescent
E talkative

speed *n, v*
♦ *n*
velocity, rate, pace, tempo, momentum, quickness, swiftness, promptness, rapidity, haste, hurry, dispatch, rush, acceleration
FORMAL alacrity, celerity, expeditiousness
E slowness, delay
♦ *v*
race, tear, zoom, career, bowl along, sprint, cruise, whisk, gallop, hurry, rush, dash, accelerate, quicken
FORMAL hasten

COLLOQ. belt, hurtle, pelt, put your foot down, step on it/the gas/the juice
E3 slow, delay

■ **speed up**
1 ACCELERATE, quicken, speed, drive faster, go faster, pick up/gather speed, gain momentum
COLLOQ. open up, put your foot down, step on it/the gas/the juice, put on a spurt
2 *speed up a process*
accelerate, hurry, step up, stimulate, facilitate, advance, further, promote, spur on, forward
FORMAL hasten, expedite, precipitate

speedily *adv*
fast, quickly, rapidly, swiftly, hastily, hurriedly, promptly, posthaste
FORMAL expeditiously
COLLOQ. pronto, lickety-split, at a rate of knots, at the double, before you can say Jack Robinson, by leaps and bounds, hell for leather, like a bat out of hell, like the clappers, like greased lightning, a mile a minute
E3 slowly

speedy *adj*
fast, quick, swift, rapid, nimble, express, prompt, immediate, hurried, hasty, cursory, summary, posthaste
FORMAL precipitate, expeditious
COLLOQ. nippy, zippy, zappy, like greased lightning, pdq, pretty damn quick
E3 slow, leisurely

spell[1] *v*
his expression spelt trouble
signal, suggest, mean, indicate, imply, promise, amount to, lead to, signify, herald
FORMAL augur, portend, presage

■ **spell out**
explain, clarify, make clear, elucidate, emphasize, detail, stipulate, specify

spell[2] *n*
a spell of sunny weather
period, time, bout, session, term, season, interval, extent, course, stretch, span, patch, turn, shift, stint

spell[3] *n*
1 CHARM, incantation, abracadabra, magic, sorcery, witchery, bewitchment, enchantment, trance
2 FASCINATION, charm, glamour, pull, attraction, influence, drawing power, allure, magnetism

■ **cast a spell on**
fascinate, charm, attract, bewitch, enchant, enthral, captivate, mesmerize

spellbinding *adj*
gripping, fascinating, riveting, enthralling, captivating, enchanting, bewitching, entrancing, mesmerizing

spellbound *adj*
transfixed, hypnotized, mesmerized, fascinated, enthralled, gripped, entranced, riveted, captivated, bewitched, transported, enraptured, enchanted, charmed, rapt

spend *v*
1 *spend money*
pay out, invest, lay out, waste, squander, fritter, expend, consume, use up, exhaust, finish
FORMAL disburse
COLLOQ. fork out, shell out, splash out, stump up, cough up, spend like water, dip/dig into your pocket
SLANG blow
2 *spend time*
pass, fill, occupy, use (up), take up, while away, put in, employ, apply, devote
COLLOQ. do, kill
E3 1 save, hoard

Synonym nuances
sense 1
Pay out can be used to suggest spending a substantial amount of money from duty or necessity, while **invest** implies an expectation of increased returns, and has positive suggestions of prudent action. The term **lay out** has implications of more extravagant expenditure, while **waste**, **fritter** and **squander** more specifically and negatively suggest misuse.
    Expend is a term which might be used in more formal contexts: *resources expended on community programmes*. The terms **consume**, **use up** and **exhaust**, however, are more suggestive of depletion and carry the negative implication of lost resources: *the museum's funds were exhausted by its purchases*.

spendthrift *n, adj*
♦ *n*
squanderer, prodigal, wastrel
FORMAL profligate
E3 miser, hoarder, saver
♦ *adj*
improvident, extravagant, prodigal, wasteful, squandering
FORMAL profligate

spent *adj*
1 USED (UP), finished, expended, exhausted, consumed, gone
2 TIRED OUT, exhausted, weary, wearied, drained, weakened, debilitated
FORMAL effete
COLLOQ. worn out, fagged (out), burnt out, all in, bushed, dead beat, dog-tired, done in, jiggered, knackered, shattered, whacked, zonked; *N Am* pooped (out), tuckered out

sperm *n*
germ cell, sex cell, semen, seminal fluid
TECHNICAL spermatozoon, gamete

spew *v*
vomit, bring up, spit out, spurt, gush, issue, emit, retch, regurgitate, disgorge, belch
COLLOQ. puke, throw up, sick up, chuck up, fetch up
SLANG barf; *Aust* chunder

sphere *n*
1 BALL, globe, orb, round, globule
2 DOMAIN, realm, province, department, territory, discipline, speciality, field, area, range, scope, compass, extent, rank, function, capacity
3 *a sphere of people*
circle, class, group, set, band, crowd, clique

spherical *adj*
round, ball-shaped, globe-shaped, globular
FORMAL rotund, globoid, globate, globose, orbicular

spice *n, v*
♦ *n*
1 FLAVOURING, seasoning, piquancy, relish, savour, tang
See also **herbs**.
2 EXCITEMENT, life, colour, zest, gusto
COLLOQ. kick, pep, zap, zip
♦ *v*
liven (up), enliven, vitalize, put life into, rouse, invigorate, animate, energize, brighten, ginger up, stir (up)
COLLOQ. buck up, jazz up, pep up, perk up, hot up

spick and span *adj*
tidy, clean, polished, scrubbed, trim, well-kept, neat, immaculate, spotless, spruce, shipshape, uncluttered
E3 dirty, untidy

spicy *adj*
1 PIQUANT, hot, peppery, pungent, sharp, tangy, tart, seasoned, well-seasoned, flavoured, strongly flavoured,

flavoursome, aromatic, fragrant
2 RACY, risqué, adult, ribald, suggestive, indelicate, indecent, improper, scandalous, sensational
FORMAL indecorous, unseemly
COLLOQ. raunchy, juicy, blue, near the bone/knuckle
F3 1 bland, insipid **2** clean, decent

spiel *n*
patter, pitch, sales patter, line, speech, recital
FORMAL oration

spike *n, v*
♦ *n*
point, prong, projection, tine, spine, barb, nail, stake, rowel, spick, tang, chape, nib, pricket, beard, catkin, spire; *dialect* brod
TECHNICAL spadix, strobilus
OLD gad
Related adjectives: spicate, spicated
♦ *v*
1 IMPALE, stick, prick, spear, skewer, spit
2 *spike a drink*
lace, drug, add, mix in, contaminate

spill *v, n*
♦ *v*
overturn, upset, slop, flow, overflow, disgorge, run (out/over), pour, tip, discharge, slop, well, shed, scatter; *dialect* slatter, swatter; *Scot* skail
♦ *n*
1 LEAK, spillage, leakage, leaking, seeping, seepage, drip, oozing, discharge, escape, percolation
2 FALL, accident, tumble, overturn, upset
COLLOQ. cropper
■ **spill the beans**
inform, tell (on), tell all
COLLOQ. blab, rat, split, squeal, blow the gaff, give the game away, let the cat out of the bag
SLANG grass

spin *v, n*
♦ *v*
1 TURN (ROUND), go round, revolve, rotate, circle, twist, gyrate, twirl, swivel, pirouette, wheel, whirl, whirr, swirl, reel
2 *spin a story/yarn*
tell, narrate, relate, make up, invent, fabricate, dream up
♦ *n*
1 TURN, revolution, rotation, circle, twist, gyration, twirl, swivel, pirouette, wheel, whirl, swirl, reel
2 COMMOTION, agitation, panic
COLLOQ. flap, state, dither, fluster, tizzy, tizz
3 DRIVE, ride, run, trip, journey, outing, jaunt
■ **spin out**
prolong, extend, lengthen, keep going, amplify, pad out
FORMAL protract

spindle *n*
axis, pivot, pin, rod, axle, staff, verge, spit
TECHNICAL arbor, fusee
Related adjective: fusiform

spindly *adj*
long, thin, lanky, gangly, gangling, skinny, spidery, skeletal, spindle-shanked
FORMAL attenuate(d), fusiform
COLLOQ. weedy
F3 stocky, thickset

spine *n*
1 BACKBONE, spinal column, vertebral column, vertebrae, dorsum, rachis
Related adjective: vertebral
2 THORN, barb, prickle, bristle, spike, needle, quill, rachis
3 STRENGTH OF CHARACTER, courage, bravery, determination, spirit, resolution, mettle, pluck
FORMAL fortitude
COLLOQ. guts, bottle, grit, spunk

spine-chilling *adj*
frightening, hair-raising, horrifying, scary, terrifying, bloodcurdling, eerie
COLLOQ. spooky

spineless *adj*
weak, feeble, irresolute, indecisive, ineffective, cowardly, faint-hearted, spiritless, lily-livered, soft, submissive, weak-kneed, timid, timorous
COLLOQ. chicken, cissy, yellow, wet, wimpish
SLANG wussy
F3 strong, brave, courageous

spin-off *n*
repercussion, result, consequence, effect, side effect, reverberation

spiny *adj*
thorny, thistly, prickly, briery, spiky
FORMAL spinose, spinous, acanthaceous, acanthous, spinigerous, spiniferous, spicular, spiculate

spiral *adj, n, v*
♦ *adj*
winding, twisting, coiled, corkscrew, helical, whorled, scrolled, circular
TECHNICAL cochlear
FORMAL cochleate(d)
♦ *n*
coil, helix, corkscrew, screw, twist, whorl, convolution, wreath, curlicue
TECHNICAL cochlea
FORMAL gyre, volute, volution, volute(d)
Related adjective: helical
♦ *v*
1 WIND, twist, coil, circle, screw, whorl, wreathe, gyrate, gyre
2 *costs spiralling*
rise, increase, go up, soar, climb, escalate, rocket, skyrocket
3 *prices spiralling downwards*
fall/drop rapidly, decrease quickly, plunge, dive, plummet, nosedive, dive-bomb

spire *n*
steeple, belfry, tower, turret, pinnacle, peak, summit, crown, crest, top, tip, point, spike, broach, spear, flèche
OLD spyre

spirit *n, v*
♦ *n*
1 SOUL, psyche, inner being, inner self, mind, breath, life, life-giving principle, vital force, *élan vital*
FORMAL anima
2 GHOST, spectre, phantom, apparition, supernatural being, presence, wraith, shade, shadow, revenant, visitant, angel, demon, fiend, devil, fairy, sprite
COLLOQ. spook
3 MOOD, atmosphere, air, humour, temper, disposition, temperament, character, feeling(s), morale, make-up, quality, state/frame of mind, attitude, outlook, mindset
OLD complexion
4 DETERMINATION, strength of character, resolution, willpower, courage, bravery, backbone, mettle, pluck, dauntlessness, stout-heartedness
COLLOQ. guts, bottle, grit, spunk
5 TENDENCY, characteristic, principle, essence, essential quality, force
6 LIVELINESS, vivacity, animation, sparkle, vigour, energy, zest, fire, ardour, motivation, enthusiasm, zeal, enterprise
COLLOQ. pizzazz, zip, kick
7 *the spirit of the law*
meaning, sense, substance, essence, drift, gist, tenor, implication, character, quality
FORMAL purport

■ **spirit away**
remove, capture, carry, convey, abstract, seize, kidnap, abduct, steal, whisk
FORMAL purloin
COLLOQ. snaffle

spirited *adj*
lively, vivacious, animated, sparkling, high-spirited, vigorous, energetic, fiery, passionate, active, ardent, zealous, bold, determined, resolute, courageous, valiant, mettlesome, plucky, confident
FORMAL valorous
COLLOQ. feisty
ⅎ spiritless, lethargic, cowardly

spiritless *adj*
apathetic, weak, lifeless, listless, dull, unenthusiastic, unmoved, lacklustre, anaemic, despondent, depressed, dejected, dispirited, low, melancholy, torpid, droopy
FORMAL languid
COLLOQ. wishy-washy
ⅎ spirited

spirits *n*
1 LIQUOR, alcohol, strong drink, strong liquor, moonshine
COLLOQ. firewater, hooch, the hard stuff
2 FEELINGS, emotions, mood, temperament, temper, attitude, humour

---

Spirits include:

añejo tequila	gold tequila	rum
apple-jack	grappa	rye
armagnac	kir	sambucca
Bacardi®	kirsch	schnapps
bitters	framboise	Scotch
bourbon	malt whisky	silver tequila
brandy	mezcal	slivovitz
calvados	mirabelle	sloe gin
cognac	ouzo	spiced rum
dark rum	pastis	tequila
eau de vie	Pernod®	vodka
genever	poteen	whiskey
gin	raki	whisky
golden rum	reposado tequila	white rum

See also **drink; liqueur.**

---

spiritual *adj*
1 UNWORLDLY, transcendent, incorporeal, immaterial, ethereal, otherworldly, intangible
FORMAL metaphysical
2 RELIGIOUS, devotional, heavenly, divine, holy, sacred, ecclesiastical
ⅎ **1** physical, material, temporal **2** secular

spit¹ *v, n*
♦ *v*
he spat at me
eject, discharge, issue, rasp, hawk, splutter, hiss, sputter; *Scot* fuff, yex
OLD bespit, spawl, spet
FORMAL expectorate
SLANG gob; *Aust* slag
♦ *n*
spittle, saliva, slaver, drool, dribble, sputum, phlegm; *Scot* yex
TECHNICAL emptysis
OLD spawl
FORMAL expectoration
SLANG *Aust* slag
■ **spitting image**
likeness, exact likeness, double, lookalike, picture, replica, twin, clone
COLLOQ. spit, dead spit, dead ringer, ringer

spit² *n*
to roast meat on a spit
skewer, rotisserie, brochette, turnspit, broach, jack
OLD smoke-jack

spite *n, v*
♦ *n*
spitefulness, malice, maliciousness, malevolence, venom, gall, bitterness, resentment, rancour, animosity, ill-feeling, ill-will, grudge, vengeance, vindictiveness, ill nature, hostility, evil, hate, hatred
OLD spight, maugre
FORMAL malignity
COLLOQ. hard feelings
ⅎ goodwill, compassion, affection
♦ *v*
annoy, irritate, irk, vex, provoke, gall, hurt, upset, injure, wound, offend, put out; *Scot* maugre
■ **in spite of**
despite, regardless of, undeterred by, against, defying, in the face of, for, with, after all, be that as it may, nevertheless, *malgré*
OLD malgrado, maugre
FORMAL notwithstanding

spiteful *adj*
malicious, venomous, snide, barbed, resentful, bitter, cruel, hostile, rancorous, vindictive, vengeful, ill-natured, ill-disposed, nasty, malevolent
FORMAL malignant
COLLOQ. catty, bitchy
ⅎ charitable, affectionate

spitefully *adv*
maliciously, bitterly, resentfully, cruelly, vindictively, venomously, malevolently
COLLOQ. bitchily

splash *v, n*
♦ *v*
1 BATHE, wallow, paddle, wade, lap, dabble, plunge, wet, wash, shower, spray, squirt, sprinkle, spatter, splatter, splodge, splotch, scatter, spread, daub, plaster, slop, slosh, slush, plop, surge, break, dash, beat, strike, batter, buffet, smack, swash, plash, squatter; *dialect* flouse, slatter, swatter, sozzle; *Scot* jabble, jaup
OLD bedash
COLLOQ. splosh, splish
2 PUBLICIZE, show, display, exhibit, flaunt, blazon, trumpet, plaster
♦ *n*
1 SPOT, patch, splatter, splodge, splotch, splurge, stain, burst, touch, streak, dash, beating, spat; *Scot* blash, jaup; *Scot & N Am* splatch
COLLOQ. splosh, splish
2 PUBLICITY, display, ostentation, blaze, effect, impression, impact, stir, excitement, sensation
COLLOQ. splurge
■ **splash out**
invest in, lash out, spend, splurge, be extravagant
COLLOQ. push the boat out

spleen *n*
anger, bad temper, bitterness, resentment, hatred, hostility, ill-will, ill-humour, spite, spitefulness, malice, vindictiveness, peevishness, venom, malevolence, wrath, pique, rancour, bile, biliousness, gall, acrimony, animosity
FORMAL animus, malignity

splendid *adj*
1 *splendid Georgian buildings*
impressive, great, fine, grand, stately, imposing, brilliant, dazzling, glittering, lustrous, bright, radiant, glowing, glorious, magnificent, gorgeous, sumptuous, luxurious, lavish, rich, distinguished, illustrious, renowned, celebrated

FORMAL resplendent, opulent, refulgent
2 have a splendid time
marvellous, wonderful, superb, excellent, first-class, outstanding, remarkable, exceptional, sublime, supreme, admirable
COLLOQ. fabulous, terrific, super
F3 **1** drab, ordinary, run-of-the-mill **2** poor, bad

splendidly adv
1 IMPRESSIVELY, brilliantly, magnificently, grandly
2 MARVELLOUSLY, wonderfully, remarkably, exceptionally, superbly, admirably, outstandingly

splendour n
brightness, radiance, brilliance, dazzle, glow, gleam, lustre, glory, luxury, sumptuousness, magnificence, richness, grandeur, majesty, illustriousness, solemnity, pomp, ceremony, display, show, spectacle
FORMAL resplendence, opulence
F3 drabness, squalor

splenetic adj
angry, cross, bad-tempered, irritable, irascible, rancorous, sullen, spiteful, choleric, morose, peevish, petulant, churlish, fretful, bilious, envenomed, acid, sour, testy
OLD atrabilious
COLLOQ. bitchy, crabbed, crabby, touchy, ratty

splice v
join, fasten, connect, marry, bind, tie, plait, braid, interweave, interlace, intertwine, entwine, mesh, knit, graft
■ **get spliced**
get married, wed, become husband and wife
OLD plight your troth
COLLOQ. get hitched, tie the knot, take the plunge

splinter n, v
♦ n
sliver, shiver, chip, shard, fragment, bit, piece, shred, flake, shaving, paring, splint, spall, spicula, spicule; dialect skelf, speel, spelk, spell; Scot spale
OLD flinders; (Shakesp) flaw
COLLOQ. smithereens
♦ v
split, break, break into pieces, fracture, smash, shatter, shiver, crumble, fragment, disintegrate, spall, spalt
FORMAL cleave

split v, n, adj
♦ v
1 split the logs; the cloth split
break, cut, splinter, shiver, crack, burst, rupture, tear, rip, chop, slit, slash, open
OLD rend
FORMAL cleave
2 split in two
divide, separate, partition, halve, bisect, share
3 split the profits
share, separate, divide, halve, allocate, allot, apportion, distribute, hand out, dole out, parcel out
COLLOQ. carve up
4 PART COMPANY, part, disunite, disband, break up, set apart, dissociate from, divide, separate, divorce, become estranged, become alienated
5 INFORM ON, betray, incriminate
COLLOQ. tell on, squeal, rat, blow the whistle on, stitch
SLANG shop, peach, grass, rumble; N Am stool on
♦ n
1 DIVISION, separation, partition, break, cut, breach, gap, cleft, crevice, crack, fissure, rupture, tear, rip, rift, slit, slash
OLD rent
2 SCHISM, disunion, dissension, discord, difference, division, separation, rupture, estrangement, alienation, divergence, break-up
♦ adj

divided, cleft, bisected, dual, twofold, broken, fractured, cracked, ruptured
FORMAL cloven
■ **split hairs**
find fault, quibble, pettifog, over-refine, cavil
COLLOQ. nit-pick
■ **split up**
part, part company, disband, break up, separate, divorce, get divorced

split-up n
break-up, separation, divorce, estrangement, alienation, parting, parting of the ways

spoil v
1 MAR, upset, wreck, ruin, destroy, damage, botch, bodge, butcher, impair, harm, hurt, injure, distort, mutilate, deface, disfigure, blemish, taint, contaminate, pollute, corrupt, foul, tarnish, cook, mangle, deform, obliterate, poison, ret; Scot bauchle, blunk; N Am mux
OLD wrong, distaste, prejudicate
FORMAL vitiate
COLLOQ. mess up, throw a spanner in the works, queer, pour cold water on, put a damper on, cast a shadow over, foul up, wash up, kill, murder
SLANG louse up, screw up, gum up, bitch up, bugger up
2 spoil a child
indulge, overindulge, pamper, cosset, coddle, mollycoddle, baby, spoon-feed
COLLOQ. wait on hand and foot
3 DETERIORATE, go bad, go off, go sour, sour, turn, curdle, decay, decompose, rot, go/become rotten
■ **spoil for**
be eager for, be keen on, be intent on, long for, yearn for

spoils n
plunder, loot, booty, haul, gain, benefit, profit, acquisitions, prizes, winnings, the game, boodle; Scot spulzie
OLD bribe
FORMAL spoliation, despoliation
COLLOQ. pickings
SLANG swag

spoilsport n
misery, killjoy, meddler, damper
COLLOQ. dog in the manger, party-pooper, wet blanket, buzzkill
SLANG Aust & NZ wowser, nark

spoken adj
verbal, oral, voiced, said, stated, told, uttered, phonetic, expressed, declared, unwritten, viva voce
F3 unspoken, unexpressed, written

spokesman, spokeswoman n
spokesperson, representative, delegate, agent, voice, negotiator, arbitrator, intermediary, mediator, go-between, broker, mouthpiece, propagandist

sponge v
1 WIPE, mop, clean, wash, swab
2 sponge off/on other people
cadge, beg, borrow, scrounge
COLLOQ. bum, freeload
SLANG Aust & NZ bludge

sponger n
cadger, scrounger, parasite, hanger-on, beggar, borrower
COLLOQ. freeloader, bum, moocher
SLANG Aust & NZ bludger

spongy adj
soft, cushioned, cushiony, yielding, elastic, resilient, springy, squashy, porous, absorbent, light

sponsor n, v
♦ n
patron, supporter, backer, friend, promoter, subsidizer,

underwriter, guarantor, surety, godfather
OLD gossip, susceptor, undertaker
COLLOQ. angel
♦ v
finance, fund, bankroll, subsidize, patronize, be a patron of, back, support, promote, underwrite, guarantee, put up the money for, stand for
OLD promise, vouch

sponsorship n
(financial) backing, (financial) support, (financial) aid, (financial) assistance, endorsement, patronage, finance, funds, grant, subsidy, promotion

spontaneity n
naturalness, instinctiveness, instinct, impulse, improvisation, extemporization

spontaneous adj
1 UNPLANNED, voluntary, unprompted, uncompelled, impromptu, extempore, unrehearsed, unpremeditated, free, willing, unhesitating, reflex, automatic
COLLOQ. spur of the moment, knee-jerk
2 NATURAL, unforced, untaught, instinctive, impulsive
E3 1 planned, deliberate 2 forced, studied

spontaneously adv
voluntarily, willingly, freely, impromptu, extempore, impulsively, on impulse, unplanned, unprompted, instinctively, of your own accord, without being asked, on the spur of the moment
COLLOQ. off the cuff, off the top of your head

spoof n
joke, hoax, game, travesty, trick, prank, fake, deception, caricature, bluff, burlesque, parody, mockery, satire, lampoon
COLLOQ. send-up, take-off, con, leg-pull

spooky adj
creepy, chilling, eerie, frightening, hair-raising, ghostly, scary, mysterious, spine-chilling, supernatural, weird, unearthly, uncanny

spoon n
See panel at **kitchen utensils**.

spoon-feed v
indulge, overindulge, cosset, pamper, spoil, mollycoddle, baby, featherbed
COLLOQ. wait on hand and foot

sporadic adj
occasional, intermittent, infrequent, isolated, spasmodic, erratic, irregular, uneven, random, scattered
E3 frequent, regular

sporadically adv
spasmodically, occasionally, intermittently, periodically, intermittently, now and again, off and on, on and off
E3 continuously, uninterruptedly

sport n, v
♦ n
1 GAME, exercise, activity, physical activity, pastime, amusement, entertainment, diversion, recreation, pleasure, fun, play
See panel on next page
2 FUN, mirth, humour, joking, joke, jesting, jest, banter, teasing, mockery, ridicule, sneering
COLLOQ. kidding
♦ v
wear, display, exhibit, show off

sporting adj
sportsmanlike, decent, modest, considerate, fair, reasonable, respectable, just, honourable, gentlemanly, ladylike
E3 unsporting, ungentlemanly, unfair

sportive adj
playful, lively, frisky, frolicsome, gamesome, gay, jaunty, merry, skittish, sprightly, prankish, rollicking, coltish, kittenish, ludic

sports equipment
See panel on next page

sporty adj
1 ATHLETIC, fit, energetic, outdoor
2 STYLISH, jaunty, showy, loud, flashy, casual, informal
COLLOQ. trendy, natty, snazzy

spot n, v
♦ n
1 DOT, speckle, fleck, mark, speck, blotch, blot, splodge, splotch, smudge, daub, splash, stain, discoloration, blemish, flaw
2 PIMPLE, blackhead, boil, pock, papula, papule, pustule
3 PLACE, point, position, situation, location, site, scene, setting, locality, locale, area
4 *have a spot of lunch*
bit, little, some, small amount, bite, morsel
5 *have a spot on television*
slot, niche, opening, position, place, time, airtime, show, programme
6 PLIGHT, predicament, quandary, difficulty, trouble, mess
COLLOQ. fix, hole, jam, scrape, pickle, fine/pretty kettle of fish
♦ v
1 NOTICE, see, observe, detect, discern, identify, recognize, make out, catch sight of
FORMAL descry, espy
2 MARK, dot, speckle, fleck, soil, blemish, taint, stain
■ **spot-on**
exact, precise, accurate, correct, flawless, faultless, right, true, definite, explicit, detailed, specific, strict, unerring, close, factual
COLLOQ. on the nail, bang on, on the button
■ **on the spot**
immediately, straight away, right away, right now, at once, next, there and then, instantly, instantaneously, directly, speedily, quickly, without delay, promptly, unhesitatingly, without hesitation, without question, this minute/instant, without further/more ado, straightforth
FORMAL forthwith
COLLOQ. pronto, before you know it, before you can say Jack Robinson, in two shakes of a lamb's tail, in a jiffy, like a shot

spotless adj
immaculate, clean, white, gleaming, shining, spick and span, unmarked, unstained, unblemished, unsullied, untainted, pure, chaste, virgin, virginal, untouched, innocent, blameless, faultless, irreproachable
E3 dirty, impure

spotlight v, n
♦ v
emphasize, stress, accentuate, focus on, highlight, underline, illuminate, feature, point up, draw attention to, give prominence to, throw into relief
E3 tone down, play down
♦ n
attention, public attention, public eye, fame, emphasis, notoriety, interest
COLLOQ. limelight

spotted adj
dotted, speckled, flecked, mottled, dappled, brindle(d), pied, piebald, polka-dot, spotty
FORMAL macular, guttate(d)

spotty adj
1 PIMPLY, pimpled, acned, blotchy, spotted, dotted, speckled, flecked, mottled, dappled, pied, piebald
2 PATCHY, uneven, inconsistent, varying, erratic, bitty

Sports include:

RACKET SPORTS:
badminton
fives
lacrosse
colloq. ping-pong
squash
table-tennis
tennis
BALL GAMES:
American football
Australian Rules
 football
baseball
basketball
billiards
boules
bowls
camogie
Canadian football
cricket
croquet
football
futsal
Gaelic football
golf

handball
hockey
hurling
netball
pelota
pétanque
pitch and putt
polo
pool
putting
rounders
rugby
shinty
snooker
soccer
tenpin bowling
volleyball
ATHLETICS:
cross-country
decathlon
discus
high-jump
hurdling
javelin

long-jump
marathon
pentathlon
pole vault
running
shot put
triple-jump
WATER SPORTS:
aqua aerobics
angling
canoeing
diving
fishing
rowing
sailing
skin-diving
surfing
swimming
synchronized
 swimming
water polo
water-skiing
windsurfing
yachting

WINTER SPORTS:
bobsleigh
cross-country
 skiing
curling
downhill skiing
ice-hockey
ice-skating
skeleton bob
skiing
slalom
snowboarding
speed skating
tobogganing
 (luging)
TARGET GAMES:
archery
clay-pigeon
 shooting
darts
quoits
shooting
COMBAT SPORTS:
boxing
fencing

judo
jujitsu
karate
kung fu
tae kwon do
wrestling
**OUTDOOR
PURSUITS:**
climbing
jogging
mountaineering
orienteering
pot-holing
rock-climbing
walking
RACING:
cycle racing
drag-racing
go-karting
greyhound-
 racing
horse racing
motor racing
Nascar®
speedway racing

stock-car racing
ON HORSEBACK:
horse-racing
hunting
show-jumping
trotting
IN THE AIR:
gliding
hang-gliding
paragliding
sky-diving
MISCELLANEOUS:
aerobics
gymnastics
keep-fit
roller-skating
trampolining
weightlifting

Sports equipment includes:

ANGLING:
bait
disgorger
fishing-line
fishing-rod
float
fly
fly reel
fly rod
gaff
gang-hook
hook
jig
keep-net
lure
net
paternoster
priest
reel
spinning rod
trace
ARCHERY:
arrow
bolt
bow

crossbow
ATHLETICS:
discus
hammer
javelin
shot
BADMINTON:
badminton racket
net
shuttlecock
BASEBALL:
baseball
baseball bat
catcher's glove
mitt
BOWLING:
boule
bowl
jack
wood
BOXING:
boxing glove
gum shield
punch-bag

punch-ball
CRICKET:
bail
cricket ball
cricket bat
nets
stump
wicket
CURLING:
brush
curling stone
DEEP-SEA DIVING:
aqualung
snorkel
FENCING:
épée
face-guard
foil
mask
sabre
GOLF:
golfball
golf club
golfing glove

tee
GYMNASTICS:
asymmetrical
 bars
balance beam
beam
horizontal bar
isometric bar
mat
parallel-bars
pommel horse
rings
rope
springboard
trampoline
vaulting horse
HOCKEY:
hockey ball
hockey stick
ICE-HOCKEY:
hockey skate
ice-hockey stick
puck

SKATING:
ice-skate
in-line skate
rollerblade
roller boot
roller-skate
speed skate
SKIING:
ski
ski stick
**SNOOKER AND
BILLIARDS:**
billiard ball
bridge
chalk
cue
cue ball
rack
rest
snooker ball
spider
table
TENNIS:
net

racket press
tennis ball
tennis racket
TENPIN BOWLING:
bowling ball
pins
OTHER:
basketball
caman
football
hurley
netball
oar
rugby ball
sailboard
skateboard
snow board
surfboard
toboggan
volleyball
water-ski

See also **golf club**.

---

spouse n
husband, wife, partner, companion, consort, mate
OLD fere
COLLOQ. better half, other half, hubby, missus

spout v, n
  ◆ v
1 SPURT, jet, squirt, spray, shoot, gush, flow, stream, pour,
surge, erupt, emit, discharge, disgorge, spew, blow
OLD bespout
2 *spouting poetry*
pontificate, go on, rant, hold forth, spout off/forth, mouth
OLD bespout
FORMAL expatiate, sermonize, orate
COLLOQ. spiel, rabbit on, waffle, witter (on)
  ◆ n
stream, jet, fountain, geyser, gargoyle, outlet, nozzle, rose,
spray, waterspout; *Scot* stroup

sprain v
twist, wrench, turn, injure, dislocate, pull, rick, crick

sprawl v
1 *sprawl on the couch*
flop, slump, stretch, slouch, recline
FORMAL repose
COLLOQ. loll, lounge
2 STRAGGLE, spread, stretch, trail, ramble

spray[1] n, v
  ◆ n
1 MOISTURE, drizzle, mist, foam, froth, spume, shower, jet,
spindrift, spoondrift, swish, waterspout, scud
OLD (*Shakesp*) aspersion
2 AEROSOL, atomizer, sprinkler, vaporizer, mister, sprayer,
nebulizer, propellant, spray gun; *N Am* squirt gun
  ◆ v
shower, spatter, spout, sprinkle, scatter, diffuse, disperse,
gush, jet, wet, drench, squirt, vaporize, mothball
FORMAL disseminate

spray[2] n
a spray of flowers/leaves

sprig, branch, corsage, posy, nosegay, bouquet, garland, wreath, aigrette

spread *v, n*

♦ *v*

1 STRETCH, extend, sprawl, broaden, widen, dilate, enlarge, develop, grow, increase, advance, expand, grow/become bigger, swell, mushroom, proliferate, escalate, spill over, open (out), unroll, unfurl, unfold, fan out, cover, lay (out), order, set, arrange

2 SCATTER, strew, diffuse, radiate, fan out, broadcast, transmit, communicate, propagate, make public, make known, publicize, advertise, publish, circulate, go/get round, distribute

FORMAL disseminate, promulgate

3 COAT, cover, put on, apply, smear, layer

F3 1 close, fold **2** suppress

♦ *n*

1 STRETCH, reach, span, extent, expanse, sweep, compass

2 *the spread of disease*

advance, development, expansion, increase, proliferation, escalation, swelling, mushrooming, diffusion, dispersion, distribution, transmission, broadcasting, communication, propagation

FORMAL dissemination

3 LARGE MEAL, banquet, feast, party, dinner, dinner party, treat

FORMAL repast

COLLOQ. blow-out

spree *n*

bout, fling, orgy, revel, carouse, debauch

COLLOQ. binge, splurge, razzle, razzle-dazzle, bender

sprig *n*

twig, stem, spray, shoot, branch, bough

sprightly *adj*

agile, nimble, spry, active, energetic, lively, animated, spirited, vivacious, hearty, brisk, jaunty, playful, frolicsome, cheerful, light-hearted, blithe, airy

COLLOQ. perky

F3 doddering, inactive, lifeless

spring *v, n*

♦ *v*

1 JUMP, leap, vault, bound, hop, bounce, rebound, recoil

2 ORIGINATE, derive, come, stem, arise, start, proceed, issue, descend, emerge, emanate, appear, sprout, grow, develop

3 *spring the news on someone*

tell/announce unexpectedly, reveal suddenly, present without warning

♦ *n*

1 JUMP, leap, vault, bound, hop, bounce, rebound, recoil

2 SPRINGINESS, resilience, give, flexibility, elasticity, bounciness, buoyancy

3 LIVELINESS, energy, spirit, briskness, cheerfulness, light-heartedness, animation

4 SOURCE, origin, beginning, basis, cause, root, fountainhead, wellhead, wellspring, well, geyser, spa

■ **spring up**

appear suddenly, come into existence, come into being, develop, grow, shoot up, sprout up, proliferate, mushroom

springy *adj*

bouncy, resilient, flexible, elastic, stretchy, rubbery, spongy, buoyant, tensible, tensile

F3 hard, stiff, rigid

sprinkle *v*

shower, spray, spatter, splash, trickle, scatter, strew, dot, pepper, dust, powder

sprinkling *n*

few, handful, dash, scattering, scatter, smattering, sprinkle, trickle, touch, trace, dusting

FORMAL admixture

sprint *v*

run, race, dash, tear, fly, dart, career, shoot

COLLOQ. belt, scoot, zip

sprite *n*

gnome, spirit, elf, fairy, goblin, imp, kelpie, nymph, naiad, puck, pouke, pixie, sylph, brownie, leprechaun, dryad, apparition, bogy, bogle, spright

TECHNICAL apsaras

OLD pug

sprout *v*

shoot, bud, germinate, grow, develop, come up, put forth, spring up

spruce *adj, v*

♦ *adj*

smart, elegant, neat, trim, dapper, well-dressed, chic, well-turned-out, well-groomed, sleek

COLLOQ. natty, cool, snazzy

F3 scruffy, untidy

■ **spruce up**

neaten, tidy (up), smarten up, groom, preen, primp, titivate

COLLOQ. tart up

spry *adj*

sprightly, quick, alert, agile, energetic, brisk, ready, nimble, active, supple

COLLOQ. nippy, peppy

F3 doddering, inactive, lethargic

spume *n*

foam, froth, lather, suds, head, bubbles, fizz, effervescence

spunk *n*

courage, nerve, spirit, pluck, resolution, toughness, backbone, gameness, heart, mettle, chutzpah

COLLOQ. guts, grit, bottle

F3 *colloq.* funk

spur *v, n*

♦ *v*

stimulate, prompt, incite, drive, propel, impel, urge, induce, encourage, motivate, goad, prod, poke, prick

OLD (*Spenser*) spurne

F3 curb, discourage

♦ *n*

1 INCENTIVE, encouragement, inducement, motive, motivation, stimulus, stimulant, urge, incitement, impetus, prompt, fillip

2 SPIKE, prong, rowel, stud, projection, protuberance, protrusion, heel

TECHNICAL calcar, spica, star wheel

3 *a mountain spur*

limb, branch, offset, embranchment

F3 1 curb, disincentive, discouragement

■ **on the spur of the moment**

on impulse, impulsively, impetuously, spontaneously, impromptu, extempore, unexpectedly, suddenly, thoughtlessly, unpremeditatedly, without planning

OLD (*Shakesp*) upon the gad

COLLOQ. on the spot

spurious *adj*

false, fake, counterfeit, forged, fraudulent, deceitful, contrived, bogus, mock, sham, feigned, pretended, simulated, imitation, artificial, make-believe

COLLOQ. pseudo, phoney, trumped-up; *Aust* cronk

F3 genuine, authentic, real

spurn *v*

reject, turn down, turn away, say no to, scorn, condemn, despise, disdain, rebuff, repulse, repudiate, slight, snub, ignore, disregard

COLLOQ. cold-shoulder, look down on, turn up your nose at

F3 accept, embrace

⚠ spurn or **scorn**?

See panel at **scorn.**

spurt *v, n*

♦ *v*

gush, spray, squirt, jet, shoot, pour, stream, well, burst, erupt, issue, surge

♦ *n*

1 JET, gush, stream, spray, squirt, outpouring, welling, eruption

2 *a spurt of activity*

burst, rush, surge, rush, increase, spate, fit, access

spy *n, v*

♦ *n*

secret agent, agent, undercover agent, foreign agent, enemy agent, double agent, fifth columnist, scout, snooper, shadow, emissary, setter, sleeper, *mouchard*
OLD spie, intelligencer, beagle, spial, under-espial, wait; (*Spenser*) spyal
COLLOQ. mole
SLANG plant, nark, spook

♦ *v*

spot, glimpse, notice, see, observe, discern, discover, make out, catch sight of, tout
OLD spie, survey
FORMAL descry, espy
SLANG nark

▪ **spy on**

watch, observe (closely), keep an eye on, keep tabs on, keep under surveillance

squabble *v, n*

♦ *v*

bicker, wrangle, fight, quarrel, row, argue, dispute, have words, clash, brawl
COLLOQ. scrap, set to

♦ *n*

row, clash, dispute, fight, argument, quarrel, disagreement, spat
COLLOQ. barney, scrap, set-to, tiff

squad *n*

crew, team, gang, band, group, company, unit, brigade, platoon, troop, force, outfit

squalid *adj*

1 DIRTY, filthy, unclean, grimy, grubby, mucky, foul, disgusting, repulsive, sordid, seedy, dingy, untidy, slovenly, unkempt, broken-down, run-down, ramshackle, dilapidated, neglected, uncared-for, Dickensian
COLLOQ. sleazy, grotty, slummy
SLANG ribby
2 REPULSIVE, low, mean, nasty, sordid, unpleasant, wretched, vile, shameful, obscene, offensive, improper, disgraceful
E₃ 1 clean, attractive **2** pleasant

squall *n, v*

♦ *n*

wind, storm, gale, gust, hurricane, blow, flurry, tempest, windstorm

♦ *v*

wail, yell, cry, howl, yowl, moan, groan

squally *adj*

windy, stormy, rough, wild, gusty, blowy, blustery, tempestuous, turbulent

squalor *n*

squalidness, dirtiness, dirt, filthiness, filth, uncleanness, grime, griminess, grubbiness, muckiness, foulness, dinginess, decay, neglect, meanness, wretchedness, slum, dung-heap, dung-hill; *N Am* skid row/road
COLLOQ. sleaziness

squander *v*

waste, misspend, misuse, lavish, fritter away, throw away, dissipate, scatter, spend, expend, consume, blue, fool away, muck, muddle away, gamble, plunge; *dialect* scamble; *N Am* slather

OLD bezzle, lash, sport away
COLLOQ. splash out on, splurge, throw/pour down the drain, spend money like water, spend money as if it grows on trees, spend money as if it's going out of style/fashion, spend money like there's no tomorrow, make/play ducks and drakes of/with
SLANG blow

square *n, v, adj*

♦ *n*

1 QUADRANGLE, market square, town square, marketplace, plaza
COLLOQ. quad
2 TRADITIONALIST, conservative, conventionalist, conformer, conformist, diehard
COLLOQ. fuddy-duddy, (old) fogey, stick-in-the-mud

♦ *v*

settle (up), reconcile, tally, agree, harmonize, conform, accord, correspond, match, be compatible with, balance, straighten, level, align, even, make equal, adjust, regulate, set/put right, adapt, tailor, fit, suit, resolve
FORMAL be congruous with

♦ *adj*

1 QUADRILATERAL, rectangular, right-angled, perpendicular, straight, true, even, level
2 FAIR, equitable, just, ethical, upright, straight, honourable, honest, genuine, above-board
COLLOQ. on the level; *Aust & NZ* dinkum
3 TRADITIONALIST, conservative, conventionalist, conformist, diehard, old-fashioned, strait-laced
COLLOQ. fuddy-duddy; *N Am* buttoned-down

squarely *adv*

directly, straight, unswervingly, right, dead, just, exactly, precisely
COLLOQ. bang, smack, plumb

squash *v*

1 CRUSH, flatten, press, squeeze, compress, crowd, pack, jam, trample, stamp, pound, grind, pulp, mash, smash, distort, squidge
FORMAL macerate, pulverize
2 SUPPRESS, silence, quell, quash, crush, annihilate, put down, squelch, snub, humiliate
E₃ 1 stretch, expand

squashy *adj*

soft, spongy, springy, squelchy, mushy, pappy, pulpy, squishy, yielding
E₃ firm

squat *v, adj*

♦ *v*

crouch, stoop, bend, kneel, hunch, sit on your haunches, sit, hunker (down), ruck; *dialect* croup
COLLOQ. *N Am* absquatulate

♦ *adj*

short, stocky, thickset, dumpy, chunky, stubby, podgy, pudgy, squabby, Humpty-dumpty; *dialect* fubby
TECHNICAL pyknic
E₃ slim, lanky, slender

squawk *v, n*

♦ *v*

1 SCREECH, shriek, cry, scream, yelp, croak, cackle, crow, hoot
2 COMPLAIN, criticize, find fault, kick up a fuss, object, protest, air your grievances, grumble, carp, fuss, moan, nag, whine, carry on, groan, growl
COLLOQ. beef, bellyache, grouse, grouch, gripe, grump, bleat, whinge, squeal, raise a stink, have a bone to pick
SLANG bitch

♦ *n*

screech, shriek, cry, scream, yelp, croak, cackle, crow, hoot

squeak v, n
squeal, whine, creak, peep, cheep, pipe

squeal v, n
◆ v
1 CRY, shout, yell, howl, yelp, wail, scream, screech, shriek, squawk
2 INFORM, tell tales, sneak, betray
COLLOQ. tell, sell out, sell down the river, snitch, split, rat
SLANG grass, shop; N Am stool
◆ n
cry, shout, yell, howl, yelp, wail, scream, screech, shriek, squawk

squeamish adj
queasy, nauseated, nauseous, sick, delicate, fastidious, finicky, particular, punctilious, prudish, strait-laced, scrupulous

squeeze v, n
◆ v
1 PRESS, squash, crush, pulp, mash, pinch, nip, tighten, compress, gripe, strain, twist, wring, extract, grip, clasp, clutch, hold tight, hug, embrace, enfold, cuddle, suck, chirt, squidge; *dialect* scruze, thrutch
2 *squeeze into a corner*
cram, stuff, pack, crowd, crush, squash, wedge, jam, force, ram, push, thrust, shove, jostle, shoe, sandwich; *dialect* scrouge, scrowdge
3 WRING, wrest, extort, milk, force, pressurize, pressure, extract, juice, mangle, sweat
COLLOQ. bleed, lean on, put the screws on
◆ n
1 PRESS, squash, crush, crowd, congestion, jam, chirt; *dialect* thrutch
2 HUG, embrace, cuddle, hold, grasp, grip, clutch, clasp

squint n, v, adj
◆ n
glance, side-glance, glimpse, sideways look, cast, cross-eye; *Scot* gley
TECHNICAL strabism
Related adjective: strabismal
◆ v
peer, look askance, blink, gaze, scan, peep, pink; *Scot* gledge, gley, skelly
OLD twire, squinny
◆ adj
crooked, indirect, oblique, off-centre, aslant, askew, awry, cockeyed, walleyed; *Scot* gleyed
TECHNICAL strabismic
COLLOQ. skew-whiff
✑ straight

squirm v
wriggle, twist, writhe, squiggle, move, shift, wiggle, fidget, agonize, flounder

squirrel
■ **squirrel away**
hoard, stash away, store, hide, conceal, lay up, save (up), set aside, put by, put away, lay in, stock up, stockpile, salt away
COLLOQ. stash away

squirt v, n
◆ v
spray, spurt, jet, shoot, spout, gush, stream, spew (out), ejaculate, discharge, issue, pour, well, surge, emit, eject, expel; *Scot* scoosh
◆ n
spray, spurt, jet, stream, gush, surge; *Scot* scoosh

stab v, n
◆ v
pierce, puncture, cut, wound, injure, gore, knife, spear, skewer, slash, bayonet, transfix, stick, push, jab, thrust, pink, fork, prong, kris, poniard, stilleto
OLD dirk

◆ n
1 ACHE, pang, pain, spasm, throb, twinge, prick
2 CUT, puncture, incision, slash, gash, injury, wound, jab, pierce, prick, pink, thrust
3 TRY, attempt, go, endeavour, venture
FORMAL essay
COLLOQ. bash, crack, shot, whirl
■ **stab in the back**
betray, deceive, let down, slander, double-cross, inform on, sell out
COLLOQ. sell down the river

stabbing adj
shooting, stinging, piercing, throbbing, painful, sharp, acute

stability n
steadiness, firmness, secureness, soundness, sturdiness, solidity, reliability, durability, uniformity, constancy, regularity, unchangeability
✑ instability, unsteadiness, insecurity, weakness

stabilize v
make stable, keep steady, steady, fix, secure, support, establish, firm up, balance, equalize, make uniform
TECHNICAL valorize

stable adj
1 *a stable structure*
balanced, fixed, static, steady, firm, secure, fast, sound, strong, sturdy, solid, sure, reliable
2 *a stable government/relationship*
established, well-founded, deep-rooted, lasting, long-lasting, durable, enduring, abiding, permanent, dependable, reliable, unchangeable, invariable, unwavering, unswerving
3 *the patient's condition is stable*
regular, uniform, steady, constant, unchanging, static
✑ **1** wobbly, shaky, weak, unstable **2** unstable, changeable **3** irregular, erratic, unstable

stack n, v
◆ n
1 HEAP, pile, mound, mass, load, collection, accumulation, store, hoard, stock, stockpile, rick, ruck
COLLOQ. stash
2 *stacks of money*
a large amount, lot, great numbers, many, a good/great deal
COLLOQ. oodles, tons, loads, masses, heaps, piles
3 *a chimney stack*
chimney, clamp, funnel, shaft, vent, flue
TECHNICAL blow-out preventer
◆ v
heap, pile, load, amass, accumulate, assemble, gather, save, hoard, stockpile, rick
COLLOQ. stash

stadium n
sports ground, sports field, field, arena, bowl, ring, track, pitch

staff n, v
◆ n
1 *member of staff*
personnel, workforce, employees, workers, human resources, manpower, crew, team, teachers, officers
2 STICK, pole, cane, crook, rod, baton, crutch, wand, truncheon, prop, crosier
◆ v
man, work, operate, occupy, provide, supply, equip

stage n, v
◆ n
1 PHASE, point, juncture, step, time, period, division, lap, leg, length, level, floor
2 PLATFORM, podium, dais, rostrum, stand, apron
COLLOQ. soapbox

3 ARENA, setting, scene, sphere, field, realm, background, backdrop
♦ *v*
mount, put on, lay on, put together, present, produce, give, do, perform, direct, arrange, organize, stage-manage, orchestrate, engineer

■ **the stage**
theatre, drama, the play, dramatics, theatrics, show business
FORMAL Thespian art
COLLOQ. the boards, the footlights, rep

stagger *v*
1 LURCH, totter, teeter, wobble, bumble, blunder, sway, rock, roll, pitch, reel, recoil, falter, hesitate, waver, keel over, titubate; *Scot* daidle, stoit, stoiter, stot, wintle
OLD *N Am* step
2 SURPRISE, amaze, astound, astonish, stun, stupefy, dumbfound, shake, shock, confound, overwhelm
COLLOQ. flabbergast, nonplus, bowl over

staggered *adj*
astonished, surprised, startled, amazed, astounded, stunned, dazed, dumbfounded, taken aback, shocked, confounded, bewildered, open-eyed
COLLOQ. lost for words, knocked for six, bowled over, flabbergasted, gobsmacked

staggering *adj*
amazing, astounding, astonishing, surprising, dramatic, shocking, stunning, stupefying, unexpected, unforeseen
COLLOQ. mind-boggling

stagnant *adj*
1 *stagnant water*
still, motionless, unflowing, standing, brackish, stale, foul, dirty, filthy, smelly, unhealthy
2 *a stagnant economy*
inactive, slow, quiet, dull, sluggish, torpid, lethargic, dying, moribund
F3 1 fresh, moving **2** busy, brisk, booming

stagnate *v*
vegetate, become stagnant, idle, languish, do nothing, decline, deteriorate, degenerate, decay, rot, putrefy, fester, rust

staid *adj*
sedate, calm, composed, sober, demure, solemn, serious-minded, serious, proper, formal, grave, sombre, quiet, steady, stiff, starchy, prim
FORMAL decorous
COLLOQ. *N Am* buttoned-down
F3 jaunty, debonair, frivolous, adventurous

stain *v, n*
♦ *v*
1 MARK, spot, blemish, blot, blotch, smear, smudge, discolour, dirty, soil, taint, contaminate, corrupt, sully, tarnish, blacken, disgrace, damage, injure
FORMAL besmirch
2 DYE, tint, tinge, colour, paint, varnish
♦ *n*
mark, spot, blemish, blot, blotch, smear, splodge, smudge, discoloration, smear, slur, taint, disgrace, shame, dishonour, damage, injury
OLD mote

stake¹ *n, v*
♦ *n*
a stake supporting a young tree
post, pole, standard, picket, pale, paling, spike, stick, rod
♦ *v*
1 SUPPORT, fasten, brace, tie, tie up, prop (up), secure, hold (up), tether, pierce
2 *stake a claim*
establish, lay claim to, state, declare, demand, assert, put in
FORMAL requisition

■ **stake out**
demarcate, define, delimit, stake off, mark off/out, outline, reserve, survey, watch, keep an eye on

stake² *n, v*
♦ *n*
1 INVESTMENT, share, claim, involvement, concern, (financial) interest, bet, wager, pledge
COLLOQ. ante
2 *the leadership stakes*
contest, competition, race, prize, winnings
♦ *v*
risk, gamble, bet, wager, pledge, chance, hazard, venture
COLLOQ. ante

stale *adj*
1 *stale bread*
dry, hard, hardened, old, musty, mouldy, fusty, flat, insipid, tasteless, sour
COLLOQ. (gone) off
2 OVERUSED, hackneyed, corny, clichéed, cliché-ridden, stock, stereotyped, tired, jaded, worn-out, worthless, blown, overfamiliar, unoriginal, uninspired, flat, trite, insipid, banal, commonplace
FORMAL platitudinous
COLLOQ. run-of-the-mill
F3 1 crisp, fresh **2** new, original, imaginative

stalemate *n*
draw, tie, deadlock, impasse, standstill, halt, blockade, stand-off
TECHNICAL *zugzwang*
F3 progress

stalk¹ *n*
the stalk of a flower
stem, shoot, twig, branch, trunk
TECHNICAL peduncle, petiole
Related adjective: peduncular

stalk² *v*
stalk a person/an animal
1 TRAIL, track, hunt, chase, give chase, follow, pursue, shadow, track down, tail, creep up on, haunt
2 STRIDE, walk, step, pace, march

stall¹ *v*
stall them to give you more time
temporize, play for time, delay, hold up, put off, slow (down), defer, postpone, hedge, equivocate, obstruct, stonewall
COLLOQ. beat about the bush, drag your feet, put on ice, put on the back burner

stall² *n*
1 STAND, table, booth, kiosk, counter, surface, place, platform
2 CUBICLE, compartment, enclosure, coop, pen, corral

stalwart *adj*
1 STAUNCH, loyal, faithful, devoted, committed, steady, trusty, steadfast, reliable, dependable, vigorous, valiant, daring, intrepid, indomitable, determined, resolute
2 STRONG, sturdy, robust, rugged, stout, hardy, strapping, muscular, athletic, brawny, burly
F3 1 disloyal, unfaithful **2** weak, feeble, timid

stamina *n*
energy, vigour, strength, power, power to stay the course, force, grit, resilience, resistance, endurance, indefatigability, staying power, fibre, bottom
FORMAL fortitude
COLLOQ. grit, guts
F3 weakness

stammer *v, n*
♦ *v*
stutter, stumble, falter, hesitate, splutter, lisp, mumble, gibber, babble, hum

◆ *n*

stutter, speech impediment, speech defect

stamp *v, n*

◆ *v*

1 TRAMPLE, tread, crush, beat, pound, pulp, mash, squash
2 IMPRINT, impress, print, inscribe, engrave, emboss, mark, brand, fix, label, categorize, designate, identify, characterize

◆ *n*

print, imprint, impression, seal, signature, authorization, mark, hallmark, tag, label, brand, cast, mould, cut, form, fashion, sort, kind, type, quality, variety, breed, character, description
FORMAL attestation

■ **stamp out**

eradicate, suppress, crush, quell, quash, curb, put down, scotch, destroy, eliminate, end, put an end to, extinguish, quench, kill
FORMAL extirpate

stampede *n, v*

◆ *n*

charge, rush, onrush, dash, sprint, flight, rout, scattering, debacle, *sauve qui peut*; *Aust* breakaway

◆ *v*

charge, rush, dash, tear, run, race, sprint, gallop, shoot, fly, flee, scatter

stance *n*

position, posture, deportment, carriage, bearing, stand, standpoint, viewpoint, policy, angle, slant, line, point of view, opinion, attitude

stanch *v*

stem, stop, check, block, arrest, stay, halt, plug, dam
E3 increase, promote

⚠ stanch or staunch?
In the sense of 'to stop the flow of', either form is correct, but *staunch* is the commoner: *staunched the flow of blood from the wound; staunch the decline of royal authority; This helped to staunch the Danish invasion*. As an adjective, the form to use is *staunch*, meaning 'loyal, trusty, steadfast': *a staunch ally/Catholic/opponent*.

---

stand *v, n*

◆ *v*

1 RISE, rise to your feet, get on/to your feet, get up, stand up, be on your feet, straighten up, be erect, be upright
2 PUT, place, set, erect, up-end, place, position, station, locate
3 *I can't stand it*
bear, tolerate, put up with, cope with, endure, allow, brook, suffer, experience, live with, undergo, withstand, weather
FORMAL abide
COLLOQ. stomach, swallow
4 *the offer still stands*
exist, be, remain, hold, be valid, be in effect, be in force
FORMAL prevail, obtain

◆ *n*

1 BASE, pedestal, support, shelf, case, frame, rack
2 STALL, booth, counter, table, stage, dais, platform, place
3 STANCE, position, standpoint, viewpoint, policy, angle, slant, line, point of view, opinion, attitude

■ **stand by**

support, back, champion, defend, stand up for, stick up for, uphold, side with, adhere to, hold to, stick by
E3 let down

■ **stand down**

step down, resign, abdicate, quit, give up, retire, withdraw
E3 join

■ **stand for**

1 REPRESENT, symbolize, mean, signify, denote, indicate
FORMAL betoken

2 *not stand for such nonsense*
put up with, tolerate, bear, endure, allow, brook
COLLOQ. stomach

■ **stand in for**

deputize for, cover for, understudy, replace, take the place of, substitute for
COLLOQ. hold the fort for

■ **stand out**

show, be noticeable, be obvious, be conspicuous, stick out, jut out, extend, project, poke out
COLLOQ. catch the eye, stick out a mile, jump out

■ **stand up**

1 RISE, rise to your feet, get up, get to your feet, straighten up, stand
2 REMAIN VALID, cohere, hold up, hold water, stand
COLLOQ. wash
3 *she stood me up*
fail to meet, not keep a date with, let down, jilt

■ **stand up for**

defend, stick up for, side with, fight for, stand by, support, remain loyal to, protect, champion, uphold, adhere
E3 attack

■ **stand up to**

defy, oppose, resist, withstand, challenge, endure, face, face up to, confront, brave
E3 give in to

standard *n, adj*

◆ *n*

1 NORM, average, type, model, pattern, example, sample, guide, guideline, benchmark, touchstone, yardstick, principle, rule, measure, gauge, criterion, requirement, specification, grade, level, quality
FORMAL archetype, paradigm, exemplar
2 PRINCIPLE, scruple, ethic, moral, code, ideal
3 FLAG, ensign, pennant, pennon, streamer, colours, banner, gonfalon
TECHNICAL vexillum

◆ *adj*

normal, average, typical, stock, classic, basic, staple, usual, ordinary, customary, habitual, popular, prevailing, regular, approved, accepted, recognized, official, authoritative, orthodox, conventional, set, fixed, established, definitive
E3 abnormal, unusual, irregular

standard-bearer *n*

ensign, standard, gonfalonier, cornet, vexillary

standardize *v*

normalize, equalize, systematize, regiment, regularize, homogenize, stereotype, mass-produce
E3 differentiate

stand-in *n*

deputy, representative, delegate, proxy, substitute, surrogate, second, second-in-command, understudy, locum
COLLOQ. *N Am* pinch-hitter

standing *n, adj*

◆ *n*

1 REPUTATION, status, rank, position, seniority, eminence, station, repute, experience, footing
2 DURATION, existence, continuance

◆ *adj*

1 UPRIGHT, erect, perpendicular, vertical, up-ended, on your feet
2 PERMANENT, perpetual, lasting, fixed, regular, repeated
3 *standing water*
stagnant, still, motionless, unflowing, brackish, stale, foul, dirty, filthy, smelly, unhealthy
E3 **1** horizontal, lying **2** temporary

stand-off *n*

deadlock, impasse, standstill, halt, blockade

standoffish adj
aloof, remote, distant, unapproachable, unsociable, unfriendly, uncommunicative, withdrawn, detached, reserved, cold, cool
E3 friendly, approachable

standpoint n
viewpoint, angle, slant, point of view, perspective, position, station, vantage point, stance

standstill n
stop, halt, pause, lull, rest, stoppage, jam, log jam, hold-up, tie-up, gridlock, stand, dead stop, impasse, deadlock, stalemate, dead-finish, stall, jib
OLD (Shakesp) still-stand
FORMAL cessation
E3 advance, progress

staple adj
basic, fundamental, primary, key, main, chief, major, important, foremost, principal, essential, indispensable, vital, necessary, standard
E3 minor, dispensable

star n, adj
* n
1 the stars in the sky
asteroid, planet, sun, moon, heavenly/celestial body, sphere, orb, satellite
Related adjectives: stellar, astral, sidereal
2 CELEBRITY, personage, luminary, idol, lead, leading man, leading lady, superstar, principal
COLLOQ. household name, big name, bigwig, big shot, leading light, celeb
* adj
brilliant, well-known, famous, leading, illustrious, celebrated, prominent, talented, principal, major, pre-eminent, paramount
E3 minor

Types of star include:

brown dwarf	North Star	red dwarf
comet	nova	red giant
falling star	Polaris	shooting star
Halley's comet	Pole Star	supergiant
meteor	pulsar	supernova
neutron star	quasar	white dwarf

See also **constellation**.

---

starchy adj
formal, stiff, prim, punctilious, ceremonious, conventional, stuffy, staid, strait-laced
E3 informal

stare v, n
* v
gaze, look, watch, gape, gawp, gawk, goggle, glare, glower, ogle, outface
OLD dare
SLANG rubberneck
* n
gaze, look, glare, gawp, glower, goggle
SLANG fisheye
■ **be staring you in the face**
be very obvious, be glaringly obvious, be blatant, be conspicuous
COLLOQ. stick out a mile

stark adj, adv
* adj
1 faced with the stark reality
bald, bare, plain, simple, blunt, harsh, grim, severe, undecorated, unembellished, unadorned
2 a stark contrast
sharp, clear, clear-cut, distinct, obvious

3 a stark landscape
bare, barren, desolate, bleak, austere, forsaken, empty, harsh, severe, grim, dreary, gloomy, depressing
4 UTTER, complete, unmitigated, unqualified, total, absolute, sheer, pure, downright, thorough, out-and-out, flagrant, arrant
FORMAL consummate
* adv
completely, entirely, wholly, totally, absolutely, altogether, quite, utterly, clean
E3 mildly, slightly

stark-naked adj
naked, nude, in the nude, stripped, undressed, stark, in puris naturalibus, en cueros
FORMAL unclad
COLLOQ. in the altogether, in the buff, in your birthday suit, in the raw, starkers
E3 clothed, dressed

start v, n
* v
1 BEGIN, originate, initiate, introduce, pioneer, create, embark on/upon, bring/come into being, bring/come into existence, get under way, found, establish, set up, institute, inaugurate, launch, pioneer, open, instigate, activate, turn on, trigger (off), set off, get going, set out, leave, depart, appear, arise, issue
FORMAL commence
COLLOQ. kick in, kick off, set the ball rolling, get things moving, get cracking, fire away
See Synonym nuances panel at **begin**.
2 JUMP, jerk, leap, twitch, flinch, shrink, wince, recoil
E3 1 stop, finish, end
* n
1 BEGINNING, outset, dawn, birth, break, outburst, onset, origin, origination, initiation, introduction, foundation, institution, inauguration, launch, opening, emergence
FORMAL commencement, inception
COLLOQ. kick-off; N Am get-go
2 JUMP, jerk, leap, twitch, flinch, wince, spasm, convulsion, fit
E3 1 stop, finish, end

starter n
appetizer, first course, canapé, hors d'œuvre, meze, apéritif, cocktail, tapas, bhajee, whet, relish
OLD antepast

startle v
surprise, amaze, astonish, astound, shock, make you jump, scare, frighten, alarm, agitate, upset, unsettle, disturb, alarm
OLD start, affray
FORMAL perturb
COLLOQ. rock, spook
E3 calm

startling adj
surprising, astonishing, astounding, extraordinary, shocking, staggering, unexpected, sudden, dramatic, alarming, unforeseen, electrifying, galvanic
E3 boring, calming, ordinary

starvation n
hunger, extreme hunger, undernourishment, malnutrition, famine, fasting, death, famishment
E3 plenty, excess

starve v
hunger, fast, diet, deprive, deny, die, perish, faint, famish, atrophy, pine, clem
OLD (Spenser) sterve
E3 feed, gorge

starving adj
(very) hungry, underfed, undernourished, ravenous, famished, faint, dying

stash v, n
* v
store, hide, conceal, hoard, squirrel away, closet, lay up, save up, stockpile, stow, cache
FORMAL secrete
COLLOQ. salt away
☞ bring out, uncover
* n
hoard, store, collection, accumulation, mass, heap, pile, fund, reservoir, reserve, stockpile, cache

state n, v, adj
* n
1 CONDITION, shape, situation, position, circumstances, case, predicament
2 NATION, country, land, territory, kingdom, republic, realm, government, federation
3 PANIC, bother, plight, predicament
COLLOQ. fluster, flap, tizzy, dither, tizwas
4 GOVERNMENT, administration, authorities, parliament, council, Establishment
5 POMP, ceremony, dignity, majesty, grandeur, glory, splendour, display
* v
say, declare, tell, announce, report, communicate, assert, affirm, specify, present, express, put, set out, make known, proclaim, formulate, articulate, voice, utter, reveal, divulge, disclose
FORMAL aver, promulgate
* adj
national, governmental, parliamentary, public, official, formal, ceremonial, pompous, stately
☞ private, commercial
■ **state of affairs**
case, situation, position, circumstances, condition, plight, predicament, crisis, juncture
COLLOQ. kettle of fish, lie of the land
■ **in a state**
agitated, anxious, worried, distressed, troubled, upset, worked up, panic-stricken, ruffled
COLLOQ. flustered, hassled, het up, in a stew, in a tizzy
☞ calm

stately adj
grand, imposing, impressive, splendid, glorious, magnificent, elegant, majestic, regal, royal, imperial, noble, lofty, pompous, dignified, measured, deliberate, solemn, ceremonial, ceremonious, graceful
FORMAL august
☞ informal, unimpressive

statement n
account, report, bulletin, communiqué, announcement, declaration, assertion, proclamation, communication, presentation, utterance, revelation, divulgence, disclosure, testimony, affirmation
FORMAL averment, promulgation

statesman, stateswoman n
politician, leader, elder statesman, diplomat
COLLOQ. grand old man, GOM

state-of-the-art adj
modern, up-to-the-minute, advanced, highly-developed, high-tech, hi-tech, space-age, complicated, complex, progressive, modernistic, innovative, inventive, go-ahead, forward-looking, futuristic, contemporary, up-to-date, new, fresh, latest, novel, present, present-day, recent, in vogue, modish
COLLOQ. newfangled, in, trendy, with it, the latest, hip, cool
☞ old, old-fashioned, out-of-date, antiquated

static adj
stationary, motionless, immobile, unmoving, still, at a standstill, inert, resting, fixed, constant, steady, changeless,
unchanging, undeviating, unvarying, stable
☞ dynamic, mobile, varying

station n, v
* n
1 a bus/railway station
stop, stopping-place, halt, fare-stage, terminus, exchange, park-and-ride
2 OFFICE, base, depot, headquarters
3 a pumping station
establishment, base, centre, office, post
4 a television station
channel, wavelength, broadcasting company
5 your station in life
status, standing, position, rank, level, grade, class
6 PLACE OF DUTY, post, place, site, location, position
* v
locate, set, establish, install, garrison, post, send, appoint, assign

stationary adj
motionless, immobile, unmoving, still, at a standstill, static, constant, inert, standing, resting, parked, moored, fixed
☞ mobile, moving, active

stationery
See panel on next page

statue n
figure, head, bust, effigy, image, idol, statuette, figurine, carving, sculpture, bronze, representation, monument, torso, acrolith, polychrome, xoanon; *Scot* stookie
OLD colossus, ka, kore, kouros

statuesque adj
dignified, imposing, impressive, majestic, stately, regal, handsome, tall
☞ small

stature n
1 HEIGHT, tallness, elevation, attitude, loftiness, size, inches
2 IMPORTANCE, reputation, standing, prominence, prestige, fame, renown, eminence, rank, consequence, weight
☞ **2** unimportance

status n
1 POSITION, rank, grade, degree, level, class, station, standing, state, condition
2 IMPORTANCE, prestige, eminence, standing, distinction, reputation, consequence, weight
☞ **2** unimportance, insignificance

statute n
law, rule, regulation, act, decree, ordinance, edict, enactment, act of parliament, written law, ukase
TECHNICAL capitular, *lex scripta*
OLD assize
FORMAL interlocution
Related adjective: statutory

staunch[1] adj
a staunch supporter
steadfast, loyal, faithful, devoted, hearty, strong, stout, firm, resolute, sound, sure, constant, true, trusty, trustworthy, committed, reliable, dependable, zealous, yeomanly
☞ unfaithful, weak, unreliable

🛈 **staunch** or **stanch**?
See panel at **stanch**.

staunch[2] v
staunch the flow of blood
stanch, stem, stop, check, block, arrest, stay, halt, plug
☞ increase, promote

🛈 **staunch** or **stanch**?
See panel at **stanch**.

Items of stationery include:

account book	correction fluid	file tab	marker	printer label	shorthand
address book	correction ribbon	filing tray	memo pad	printer paper	notebook
adhesive tape	desk diary	Filofax®	notepaper	printer ribbon	spiral notebook
blotter	diary	flip chart	paper clip	reinforcement	stamp pad
Blu-Tack®	divider	floppy disk	paper fastener	ring	staple
bulldog clip	document folder	folder	paper knife	reply-paid	suspension file
calendar	document wallet	graph paper	pen	envelope	tape dispenser
carbon paper	drawing pin	headed	pencil	ring binder	Tipp-Ex®
card index	dry-transfer	notepaper	pencil-sharpener	rubber	toner
cartridge ribbon	lettering	index card	personal	rubber band	treasury tag
cash book	elastic band	ink	organizer	rubber stamp	typewriter ribbon
clipboard	envelope	Jiffy bag®	pin	ruler	wall chart
computer disk	eraser	label	pocket calculator	scissors	window envelope
copying paper	expanding file	lever arch file	pocket folder	self-seal envelope	writing paper
correcting paper	file	manila envelope	Post-it note®	Sellotape®	

See also **paper**.

---

staunchly *adv*
steadfastly, firmly, resolutely, unswervingly, unfalteringly, implacably, unflinchingly
Ɛɪ unfaithfully, unreliably

stave
■ **stave off**
fend off, ward off, avoid, avert, deflect, repel, repulse, turn aside, prevent, parry, foil, keep back, keep at bay
Ɛɪ cause, encourage

stay[1] *v, n*
♦ *v*
1 REMAIN, last, continue, endure, linger, persist, keep, stay put
FORMAL abide, tarry
2 *stay in a hotel*
live, settle, stop, board, lodge, put up, rest, halt, pause, wait, visit, be accommodated at, take a room at
FORMAL reside, dwell, sojourn
3 *stay judgement*
suspend, halt, postpone, put off, delay, defer, adjourn, reprieve
FORMAL prorogue
COLLOQ. put on ice
4 *stay your anger*
control, restrain, arrest, check, curb, stop, halt, prevent, hinder, block, obstruct
♦ *n*
1 VISIT, holiday, vacation, stopover
FORMAL sojourn
2 *a stay of execution*
suspension, postponement, deferment, delay, reprieve
FORMAL remission

stay[2] *n*
a stay supporting a mast
prop, brace, buttress, reinforcement, stanchion, support, wire, strut, shoring

staying power *n*
stamina, energy, vigour, strength, power, power to stay the course, force, grit, resilience, resistance, endurance, indefatigability, fibre, bottom
FORMAL fortitude
COLLOQ. grit, guts

steadfast *adj*
firm, fixed, resolute, stable, steady, intent, single-minded, loyal, faithful, stout-hearted, sturdy, strong, dedicated, constant, dependable, staunch, reliable, fast, established, persevering, unswerving, unwavering, immovable, unfaltering, implacable, unflinching, perseverant
OLD sad
Ɛɪ unreliable, wavering, weak

steadily *adv*
1 *work away steadily*
constantly, uninterruptedly, regularly, evenly, on an even keel, round the clock, all year round
2 CALMLY, sensibly, rationally, seriously, soberly
Ɛɪ 1 sporadically, intermittently **2** excitably, impulsively

steady *adj, v*
♦ *adj*
1 *hold the camera steady*
stable, balanced, well-balanced, poised, fixed, secure, immovable, unmoving, motionless, firm
2 *make steady progress*
regular, even, uniform, on an even keel, consistent, unvarying, unvariable, unchanging, ceaseless, perpetual, constant, persistent, uninterrupted, unbroken, unfaltering, unwavering
FORMAL incessant, unremitting
3 CALM, stable, settled, controlled, self-controlled, well-balanced, still, imperturbable, unexcitable, unexcited
COLLOQ. unflappable
4 RELIABLE, dependable, balanced, well-balanced, serious, sober, sensible, steadfast
5 *a steady boyfriend*
regular, constant, usual, customary, established, habitual
Ɛɪ 1 unsteady, shaky, wobbly **2** uneven, irregular, variable, wavering **3** excitable, worried **4** unreliable
♦ *v*
1 STABILIZE, balance, fix, secure, brace, support
2 COMPOSE, control, soothe, relax, tranquillize, still, subdue, check, restrain

steal *v, n*
♦ *v*
1 *steal a car*
make off/away with, run off with, go/walk off with, thieve, pilfer, take, misappropriate, snatch, break in, pocket, shoplift, poach, embezzle, kidnap, abduct, plagiarize, rob, burgle, hijack, crib, knap, nap, twitch; *dialect* mag; *N Am* boost
OLD bribe, condiddle, purse
FORMAL appropriate, purloin, peculate
COLLOQ. pinch, nick, filch, lift, snaffle, knock up, nobble, knock off, swipe, whip, bag, nip, liberate, relieve of, help yourself to, have your fingers in the till; *Aust & NZ* duckshove, souvenir
SLANG rip off, heist, hoist, pull, lag, blag, mill, smug, sneak; *N Am* glom
OLD SLANG cabbage, cly, nim
2 CREEP, tiptoe, slip, slink, slide, slither, sneak
Ɛɪ 1 return, give back
♦ *n*
bargain, giveaway, special offer, good buy, value for money, discount, reduction
COLLOQ. snip

Synonym nuances
verb sense 1
The phrases **make off with**, **run off with** and **go off with** widely refer to taking something without the knowledge of the owner, whereas **thieve** more directly refers to illegal procurement and is more accusatory in tone.
  Pilfer, although similar, suggests taking small quantities: *she regularly pilfered the office stationery.*
Misappropriate refers to wrongly taking something for your own use, and may be used rather euphemistically: *the branch secretary had misappropriated funds,* whereas **embezzle** more directly refers to fraudulently acquiring large sums of money.
  Pocket is appropriate for furtively taking possession of something small: *she pocketed his keys,* while **snatch** suggests elements of speed and surprise.

---

stealing *n*
theft, robbery, thieving, shoplifting, pilfering, pilferage, burglary, break-in, embezzlement, larceny, misappropriation, plagiarism, poaching, piracy, thievery, snatch
FORMAL peculation, appropriation, purloining
COLLOQ. filching, pinching, nicking, stick-up, mugging, swipe, smash-and-grab

stealth *n*
stealthiness, furtiveness, surreptitiousness, covertness, secrecy, slyness, sneakiness, unobtrusiveness
F3 openness

stealthily *adv*
by stealth, surreptitiously, covertly, secretly, furtively, slyly, cunningly, à la dérobée; *Scot* stownlins
OLD stolenwise

stealthy *adj*
surreptitious, covert, secret, unobtrusive, secretive, quiet, furtive, sly, cunning, sneaky, underhand
FORMAL clandestine
F3 open

steam *n, v*
♦ *n*
1 VAPOUR, water vapour, mist, haze, exhalation, condensation, moisture, dampness
2 *run out of steam*
energy, activity, enthusiasm, eagerness, liveliness, vigour, stamina, momentum
▪ **steam up**
mist up, fog up, become covered with steam, become covered with mist
▪ **let off steam**
let yourself go, release surplus energy, air your feelings, sound off
▪ **under your own steam**
by your own efforts, independently, by yourself, alone, unaided, without (others') help
▪ **get steamed up**
get annoyed, get angry, get flustered, get excited
COLLOQ. get het up, boil over, fly into a rage, blow a fuse, blow your cool, do your nut, explode, fly off the handle, have kittens, hit the roof, lose your cool, lose your rag

steamboat *n*
steamer, steamship, steam-packet, steam vessel, packet-boat, packet-ship, packet, paddle-boat, paddle steamer, vaporetto

steamy *adj*
1 HUMID, hot, steaming, sweltering, hazy, muggy, sticky, misty, sweaty, close, damp, sultry, stewy, vaporous, vapourish, vapoury, gaseous
FORMAL vaporiform
2 EROTIC, passionate, sensual, lustful, amorous, seductive
COLLOQ. sexy, raunchy, blue

steed *n*
horse, charger, hack, mount, nag, jade, Rosinante

steel *v*
brace, harden, toughen, nerve, prepare
FORMAL fortify
COLLOQ. psych
F3 weaken

steely *adj*
1 GREY, steel-coloured, steel-blue, blue-grey
2 DETERMINED, firm, resolute, strong, hard, harsh, inflexible, pitiless, merciless, unyielding

steep[1] *adj*
1 *a steep slope*
sheer, precipitous, headlong, abrupt, sudden, sharp, vertical, perpendicular, precipiced, bluff, bold, cragged, high-pitched, arduous, exponential; *dialect* stickle; *Scot* brent, stey
OLD steepy
FORMAL acclivitous, declivitous
2 EXCESSIVE, extreme, stiff, unreasonable, uncalled-for, high, exorbitant, extortionate, inordinate, expensive, costly, dear, overpriced
COLLOQ. over the top
F3 **1** gentle, gradual **2** moderate, low

steep[2] *v*
steep something in liquid
saturate, seethe, soak, moisten, damp, souse, submerge, suffuse, drench, fill, bathe, imbue, immerse, infuse, permeate, pervade, marinate, pickle, brine, macerate, imbrue, sop; *dialect* plot; *Scot* mask
OLD buck; (*Shakesp*) ensteep; (*Spenser*) embay

steeple *n*
spire, belfry, tower, turret, spire-steeple, rood-steeple

steeply *adv*
sharply, abruptly, rapidly, suddenly
F3 gradually

steer *v*
pilot, guide, direct, control, drive, govern, conduct, navigate, cox, lead, usher, helm, tack
OLD steare
▪ **steer clear of**
avoid, keep away from, shun, evade, bypass, escape, skirt, dodge
FORMAL circumvent, eschew
COLLOQ. give a wide berth to
F3 seek

stem[1] *n, v*
♦ *n*
the stem of a plant
stalk, shoot, stock, branch, trunk
TECHNICAL peduncle
Related adjective: cauline
♦ *v*
come, develop, flow, originate, have its origins, derive, emanate, spring, issue, arise
F3 give rise to, cause

stem[2] *v*
stem the flow of blood
stop, halt, arrest, stanch, staunch, block, dam, check, curb, restrain, contain, resist, oppose
F3 encourage

stench *n*
stink, reek, smell, odour, whiff
FORMAL mephitis, miasma
COLLOQ. pong
SLANG niff

stentorian *adj*
loud, strong, booming, thunderous, thundering, resonant, sonorous, ringing, full, vibrant, reverberating, strident

step *n, v*

◆ *n*

1 PACE, stride, footstep, walk, gait, tread, tramp, footprint, print, impression, trace, track
2 MOVE, act, action, course of action, deed, measure, procedure, process, proceeding, progression, advance, development, movement, manoeuvre, expedient, effort, stage, rank, grade, level, phase, degree
3 RUNG, stair, tread, stage, level, rank, point

◆ *v*

pace, stride, tread, stamp, walk, move, advance, progress

■ **step down**
stand down, resign, abdicate, quit, leave, retire, withdraw, give up your post

■ **step in**
intervene, mediate, arbitrate, intercede, interfere, interrupt, intrude, involve yourself in

■ **step up**
increase, raise, boost, build up, intensify, escalate, accelerate, speed up
FORMAL augment
F3 decrease

■ **step by step**
gradually, slowly, progressively, one step at a time, bit by bit, gradatim

■ **in step**
together, in agreement, in harmony, in unison, in accord

■ **out of step**
in disagreement, not in step, having different opinions, at odds, at loggerheads

■ **watch your step**
be careful, look out, watch out, take care, be attentive, have your wits about you
COLLOQ. mind how you go

stereotype *n, v*

◆ *n*

formula, convention, mould, pattern, model, cliché, hackneyed expression, conventional/standardized image, fixed set of ideas

◆ *v*

typecast, cast, pigeonhole, standardize, formalize, tag, label, conventionalize, mass-produce, categorize
F3 differentiate

stereotyped *adj*

conventional, stereotypical, standardized, standard, unoriginal, stock, overused, mass-produced, hackneyed, clichéed, cliché-ridden, banal, stale, trite, tired, threadbare, corny
FORMAL platitudinous
F3 different, unconventional

sterile *adj*

1 GERM-FREE, germless, clean, pure, aseptic, sterilized, disinfected, antiseptic, uncontaminated, uninfected
2 INFERTILE, barren, arid, bare, unproductive, unprofitable, fruitless, unfruitful, moorish
TECHNICAL acarpous
FORMAL infecund
3 *a sterile argument*
dry, unimaginative, uninspired, lifeless, stale, unproductive, unfruitful, pointless, futile, vain, useless, unyielding, abortive
FORMAL ineffectual
F3 1 septic **2** fertile **3** fruitful

sterility *n*

1 CLEANNESS, purity, disinfection
TECHNICAL asepsis
2 INFERTILITY, barrenness, unfruitfulness, unproductiveness, impotence
TECHNICAL atocia
FORMAL unfecundity
3 UNPRODUCTIVENESS, fruitlessness, futility, pointlessness,

uselessness, ineffectiveness, unfruitfulness, unimaginativeness
FORMAL inefficacy
F3 1 infection, contamination **2** fertility **3** fruitfulness

sterilize *v*

1 DISINFECT, fumigate, purify, clean, cleanse; *N Am* retort
TECHNICAL autoclave
2 MAKE INFERTILE, castrate, neuter, doctor, geld, spay
F3 1 contaminate, infect

sterling *adj*

excellent, great, superlative, first-class, genuine, real, sound, standard, authentic, true, pure, worthy
COLLOQ. top-notch, smashing, terrific, neat, ace, brill, out of this world, second to none, mean
F3 false, poor

stern¹ *adj*

a stern look/person
strict, severe, authoritarian, rigid, inflexible, unyielding, hard, tough, rigorous, demanding, exacting, stringent, harsh, cruel, tyrannical, Draconian, unsparing, relentless, unrelenting, unsmiling, grim, sombre, forbidding, stark, austere
F3 kind, gentle, mild, lenient

stern² *n*

the stern of the ship
rear, back, tail, tail end, poop
F3 bow

sternly *adv*

harshly, cruelly, grimly, forbiddingly, sombrely, strictly, severely, inflexibly, relentlessly
F3 gently, kindly

stew *v, n*

◆ *v*

1 *stew the meat*
boil, simmer, braise, cook, casserole, ragout, jug; *Scot* stove
2 *let him stew in his own juice*
worry, sweat, fret, fuss, agonize

◆ *n*

1 *beef stew*
casserole, goulash, pot-au-feu, *daube*, ragout, hash, chowder, lobscouse, bouillabaisse, Irish stew, paella, zarzuela, ratatouille, haricot, matelote, carbonado, cassoulet, cholent, tzimmes, maconochie, navarin, potpourri, olla-podrida, succotash, tajine; *Scot* stovies; *N Am* burgoo
COLLOQ. scouse; *N Am* mulligan
2 FLUSTER, worry, fuss, bother, agitation, pother, fret
COLLOQ. tizzy, tizwas

steward *n*

stewardess, attendant, flight attendant, air hostess, waiter, waitress, official, butler, supervisor, overseer, custodian, caretaker, marshal, factor, chamberlain, manciple, major-domo, *homme d'affaires*, *maître d'hôtel*, commis, manciple, sommelier
OLD mormaor, reeve, seneschal

stick¹ *v*

1 THRUST, poke, stab, jab, push, pierce, prick, penetrate, insert, puncture, spear, impale, transfix
2 GLUE, gum, paste, cement, bond, fuse, weld, solder, tape, adhere, grip, cling, hold, attach, affix, fasten, secure, fix, pin, tack, join, bind
3 PUT, place, lay, position, site, locate, set (down), install, deposit, drop
4 *the car got stuck in the mud*
fix, jam, clog (up), get bogged down, trap, stop, come to a halt, come to a standstill
5 REMAIN, stay, linger, persist, continue, carry on, rest, last, endure
FORMAL dwell, abide

6 TOLERATE, bear, stand, endure, put up with
FORMAL abide
COLLOQ. stomach, swallow

■ **stick at**
1 PERSEVERE, persist, continue, keep at
COLLOQ. plug away
2 HESITATE, recoil, shrink from, stop at, doubt, pause, balk, scruple
FORMAL demur
COLLOQ. draw the line at
F3 1 give up

■ **stick by**
stand by, support, back, champion, defend, stand up for, stick up for, uphold, side with, adhere to, hold to
F3 let down

■ **stick it out**
persevere, persist, continue
COLLOQ. plug away, see things through to the end, keep at it, grin and bear it, hang in there

■ **stick out**
protrude, jut out, poke out, bulge, project, extend, be noticeable, be obvious, be conspicuous

■ **stick to**
obey, observe, follow, go along with, carry out, stand by, abide by, hold to, keep to, agree to, accept, respect, uphold, fulfil, comply with, adhere to, conform to, submit to, discharge
COLLOQ. go by the book, toe the line
F3 ignore, reject; *colloq.* flout

■ **stick up for**
stand up for, speak up for, fight for, stand by, defend, protect, champion, support, uphold, take the side/part of
F3 attack

Types of stick include:

alpeen	hockey stick	stake
alpenstock	kierie	tripod stick
baton	knobkerrie	truncheon
billy	lathi	waddy
birch	lug	walking stick
bludgeon	pike	wand
cane	pole	whip
club	post	woomera
cosh	rod	
crook	sceptre	
crutch	shillelagh	
cudgel	staff	

**stick² ** *n*
gather dry sticks
1 BRANCH, branch, twig, switch
2 CRITICISM, hostility, punishment, reproof, blame, abuse
COLLOQ. flak, rocket, dressing-down
F3 praise

■ **the sticks**
remote areas, backwoods, bush, outback; *Aust & NZ* back-blocks; *S Afr* backveld
COLLOQ. middle of nowhere, end of the earth, hickdom, yokeldom; *N Am* boondocks, boonies; *Aust & NZ* scrub, beyond the black stump

stickiness *n*
adhesiveness, gumminess, glueyness, tackiness, syrupiness
FORMAL glutinousness, viscidity
COLLOQ. goo, gooeyness

stick-in-the-mud *adj, n*
♦ *adj*
fuddy-duddy, unadventurous, conservative, fossilized, fogeyish, outmoded, antiquated, antediluvian, Victorian
COLLOQ. square; *N Am* buttoned-down
F3 adventurous, modern

♦ *n*
fuddy-duddy, conservative
COLLOQ. (old) fogey, back number, fossil

stickler *n*
fanatic, maniac, perfectionist, pedant, purist, precisianist, fusspot; *N Am* fussbudget
COLLOQ. nut

sticky *adj*
1 ADHESIVE, gummed, tacky, gluey, gummy, viscous
FORMAL glutinous, viscoid
COLLOQ. gooey
2 *a sticky situation*
difficult, tricky, thorny, unpleasant, awkward, embarrassing, delicate, sensitive, ticklish
3 HUMID, clammy, muggy, close, oppressive, sweltering, sultry, sweaty
F3 1 dry **2** easy **3** fresh, cool

stiff *adj*
1 RIGID, unbending, unyielding, inflexible, hard, solid, hardened, solidified, firm, tight, taut, inelastic, tense
2 *stiff muscles/joints*
aching, arthritic, rheumatic, tight, tense, rheumaticky
3 DIFFICULT, hard, tough, tiring, harsh, arduous, laborious, awkward, demanding, exacting, challenging, rigorous
4 FORMAL, ceremonial, ceremonious, reserved, pompous, standoffish, cold, chilly, awkward, prim, priggish
FORMAL decorous
5 SEVERE, extreme, rigorous, hard, harsh, tough, demanding, austere, strict, drastic, stringent, Draconian
6 *a stiff breeze*
strong, fresh, brisk, windy, forceful, vigorous
7 *a stiff drink*
large, alcoholic, strong, intoxicating, potent
F3 1 flexible, supple **3** easy **4** informal, relaxed, friendly **5** lenient, easy-going **6** light, gentle **7** weak

stiffen *v*
1 HARDEN, solidify, tighten, tense (up), starch, thicken, congeal, coagulate, gel, jell, set
2 STRENGTHEN, steel, brace, harden, reinforce
FORMAL fortify

stiff-necked *adj*
proud, stubborn, obstinate, arrogant, haughty, uncompromising, pig-headed, opinionated
FORMAL contumacious
F3 humble, flexible

stifle *v*
1 *stifle opposition*
repress, silence, hush (up), suppress, quell, quash, check, curb, restrain, constrain, keep in, hold back, gulp back/down, smother, crush, subdue, extinguish, muffle, dampen, deaden
2 SMOTHER, suffocate, asphyxiate, strangle, choke, funk; *Scot* scomfish
F3 1 encourage

stigma *n*
brand, mark, stain, blot, spot, note, blemish, slur, taint, disgrace, shame, dishonour
F3 credit, honour

stigmatize *v*
stain, mark, blemish, disgrace, shame, condemn, denounce, discredit, brand, label, mark
OLD note
FORMAL vilify, vilipend
F3 praise

still *adj, v, adv, n*
♦ *adj*
1 STATIONARY, motionless, immobile, unmoving, unstirring, static, stock-still, lifeless, stagnant, inert, inactive, sedentary

2 QUIET, undisturbed, unruffled, calm, smooth, tranquil, serene, mild, restful, peaceful, hushed, silent, noiseless
≡ 1 moving, active **2** disturbed, agitated, noisy
♦ *v*
calm, soothe, allay, tranquillize, subdue, restrain, hush, quieten, silence, pacify, settle, moderate, smooth
FORMAL abate, assuage, appease
≡ agitate, stir up
♦ *adv*
1 UNTIL NOW, up to the present time, up to this time, yet
2 YET, but, even so, though, although, nevertheless, nonetheless, however, in spite of this/that, for all that
FORMAL notwithstanding
♦ *n*
stillness, quiet, quietness, hush, peace, peacefulness, silence, noiselessness, serenity, tranquillity
≡ agitation, disturbance, noise

stillness *n*
tranquillity, calm, peace, peacefulness, serenity, calmness, composure, quiet, quietness, rest, restfulness, hush, silence, imperturbability, coolness, equanimity, sedateness, placidity
FORMAL quietude, repose
≡ disturbance, agitation, noise

stilted *adj*
artificial, unnatural, laboured, stiff, wooden, forced, constrained
≡ natural, relaxed, fluent, flowing

stimulant *n*
tonic, restorative, whetstone
TECHNICAL analeptic
COLLOQ. pick-me-up, pep pill
SLANG reviver

⚠ stimulant or **stimulus**?
Stimulant is normally used only of a drug or medicine which makes a person more alert or part of their body more active: *Tea and coffee contain stimulants; a powerful heart stimulant. Stimulus* is used to mean 'something which causes or encourages a person to make greater efforts': *Many people think that children need the stimulus of competition to make them work well at school.*

---

stimulate *v*
rouse, arouse, animate, quicken, kindle, fan, fire, inflame, excite, inspire, motivate, encourage, induce, fillip, urge, impel, spur, prompt, goad, provoke, incite, instigate, trigger (off)
COLLOQ. whip up, hype (up)
≡ discourage, hinder, prevent

stimulating *adj*
stimulant, inspiring, rousing, stirring, interesting, exciting, exhilarating, intriguing, provoking, provocative, thought-provoking, piquant, suggestive, galvanic, excitant
≡ uninspiring, boring, depressing, bland

stimulation *n*
animation, quickening, kindling, excitement, arousal, inspiration, motivation, encouragement, prompting, provocation, incitement, instigation
≡ discouragement, prevention, hindrance

stimulus *n*
incentive, encouragement, impetus, inducement, spur, goad, prod, provocation, incitement, fillip, drive, push, jolt, jog
COLLOQ. shot in the arm
≡ discouragement

⚠ stimulus or **stimulant**?
See panel at **stimulant**.

---

sting *v, n*
♦ *v*
1 *bees sting*
bite, prick, hurt, injure, wound; *Scot* stang

2 SMART, tingle, burn, pain, irritate
3 HURT, distress, wound, upset, offend, annoy, grieve, torment, provoke, exasperate, incense, needle, nettle
4 CHEAT, swindle, defraud, deceive, trick, fiddle, fleece
COLLOQ. do, con
SLANG rip off, take for a ride, take to the cleaners; *N Am* gold-brick
♦ *n*
1 PRICK, point, bite, nip, wound, injury, hurt, pain, smart, tingle, irritation, tang, piercer; *Scot* stang
TECHNICAL aculeus
OLD TECHNICAL stimulus
2 *the memory lost its sting*
sharpness, viciousness, spite, malice, pungency, incisiveness, sarcasm, causticness, causticity, edge, bite, heartache, barb
3 SWINDLE, fraud, fiddle, diddle, racket, sharp practice, double-dealing, trickery, deception
COLLOQ. con, scam
SLANG rip-off; *N Am* gold brick; *Aust* lurk

stinging *adj*
burning, smarting, tingling, irritating, hurtful, injurious, wounding, offensive, distressing
FORMAL urent, urticant, aculeate(d)
≡ mild, soothing, comforting

stingy *adj*
mean, miserly, niggardly, cheeseparing
FORMAL parsimonious, penurious
COLLOQ. tight-fisted, tight, penny-pinching, mingy
≡ generous, liberal

stink *v, n*
♦ *v*
1 SMELL, reek
COLLOQ. pong, hum; *Scot* ming
SLANG honk
2 *the whole set-up stinks*
be bad, be awful, be nasty, be unpleasant, be despicable
COLLOQ. suck
♦ *n*
1 SMELL, bad/foul smell, odour, stench
FORMAL malodour, mephitis
COLLOQ. pong; *Scot* ming, guff
SLANG niff
2 FUSS, trouble, bother, furore, row, commotion, stir, fluster
COLLOQ. hassle, hoo-ha, flap, song and dance

stinker *n*
1 PROBLEM, difficulty, predicament, plight, impediment, horror, shocker
2 SCOUNDREL, rogue, rascal, good-for-nothing, villain, vagabond, ruffian, ne'er-do-well, miscreant, scamp, scallywag, cheat, reprobate, dog, cur, hound
OLD blighter, bounder, dastard, rotter, blackguard
COLLOQ. rat, swine; *Irish* louser
SLANG louse, scab

stinking *adj*
bad, unpleasant, vile, awful, f(o)etid, stenchy, nasty, contemptible, awful, disgusting, terrible, foul, rotten
COLLOQ. pongy, humming; *Scot* mingin
SLANG niffy
≡ good, pleasant

stint *n, v*
♦ *n*
spell, stretch, period, time, shift, turn, bit, share, quota
♦ *v*
economize, save, withhold, pinch, begrudge, scrimp
COLLOQ. skimp on

stipend *n*
allowance, payment, grant, income, maintenance, subsistence allowance, expenses, expense allowance,

contribution, benefit, pension, annuity, assistance, alimony

stipulate v

specify, lay down, set down, require, demand, insist on

stipulation n

specification, requirement, point, clause, rider, demand, condition, proviso, prerequisite
FORMAL precondition

stir v, n

♦ v

1 MOVE, budge, shift, rouse, disturb, agitate, shake, tremble, twitch, quiver, flutter, rustle, turn, riffle, jog, torment; *Scot* jee
OLD steer, stire, tempest, wag; (*Spenser*) quich, quinche
2 MIX, blend, whip, beat, agitate, churn, puddle; *N Am* muddle
3 AFFECT, touch, inspire, excite, thrill, provoke, pique
OLD tempest

♦ n

activity, movement, bustle, flurry, commotion, ado, fuss, uproar, tumult, disturbance, disorder, agitation, excitement, ferment; *dialect* clutter
OLD steer, stire
COLLOQ. to-do, hoo-ha, flap, kerfuffle, tizzy, song and dance
E3 calm

■ stir up

encourage, rouse, arouse, awaken, waken, wake, awake, inspire, animate, quicken, kindle, fire, inflame, excite, stimulate, spur, motivate, drive, impel, prompt, provoke, incite, instigate, agitate, electrify, galvanize, raise, rummage, rustle, poke, disturb, racket, rattle someone's cage, put the cat among the pigeons; *dialect* poach, rear
OLD amove
E3 calm, discourage

stirring adj

rousing, exciting, spirited, inspiring, stimulating, moving, animating, thrilling, exhilarating, heady, emotive, dramatic, lively, impassioned, intoxicating
E3 calming, uninspiring

stitch v

sew, stitch, tack, darn, mend, repair, seam, embroider, hem
See panel at **embroidery**.

■ stitch up

trap, incriminate, plant, double-cross
COLLOQ. set up, con, stab in the back, fit up, sell down the river
SLANG shop, grass, rumble

stock n, adj, v

♦ n

1 GOODS, merchandise, wares, commodities, inventory, repertoire, quantity, collection, range, selection, variety, assortment, source, supply, quantity, fund, reservoir, store, reserve, cache, stockpile, hoard, heap, pile, amassment, accumulation
2 *stocks and shares*
investment, holding, shares, bonds, securities, equities, portfolio, money, capital, funds, assets
3 PARENTAGE, ancestry, genealogy, background, descent, extraction, family, relatives, line, lineage, pedigree, race, breed, strain, species, blood
4 REPUTATION, name, good name, opinion, credit, repute, standing
FORMAL estimation
5 LIVESTOCK, animals, farm animals, cattle, cows, pigs, horses, sheep, herds, flocks

♦ adj

standard, basic, regular, routine, ordinary, average, run-of-the-mill, usual, common, customary, essential, basic, traditional, conventional, set, stereotyped, tired, worn-

out, hackneyed, clichéed, overused, banal, trite
E3 original, unusual

♦ v

keep, carry, sell, market, trade in, traffic in, merchandize, deal in, handle, carry, supply, provide, furnish, equip
FORMAL accoutre
COLLOQ. kit out

■ stock up

gather, accumulate, amass, lay in, fill (up), load, store (up), buy (up), put aside, put away, save, hoard, stockpile, stack up, pile up, heap (up)
FORMAL provision, replenish
COLLOQ. salt away, stash away

■ in stock

available, for sale, on sale, on the market, on the shelves

■ take stock

assess, reassess, estimate, review, survey, evaluate, re-evaluate, re-examine, size up, weigh up
FORMAL appraise

stockpile v, n

♦ v

hoard, stock, store (up), save, gather, accumulate, amass, pile up, heap (up), keep, put aside, put away

♦ n

store, stock, hoard, fund, reservoir, reserve, cache, pile, heap, amassment, accumulation

stock-still adj

motionless, unmoving, unstirring, static, still, immobile, inactive, inert, stationary

stocky adj

sturdy, solid, thickset, chunky, broad, short, squat, dumpy, stubby, stumpy
FORMAL mesomorphic
E3 tall, skinny

stodgy adj

1 *stodgy food*
solid, heavy, indigestible, filling, starchy, substantial
2 STUFFY, unimaginative, uninspired, unexciting, unenterprising, solemn, heavy, boring, dull, tedious, staid, formal, leaden, laboured, turgid, spiritless
COLLOQ. fuddy-duddy
E3 exciting, informal, light

stoical adj

patient, long-suffering, uncomplaining, accepting, resigned, philosophical, indifferent, impassive, unexcitable, unemotional, dispassionate, self-disciplined, self-controlled, forbearing, cool, calm, imperturbable
FORMAL phlegmatic
E3 excitable, anxious

stoicism n

patience, long-suffering, resignation, indifference, dispassion, unexcitability, impassivity, calmness, acceptance, forbearance, imperturbability, stolidity, fatalism, philosophy
FORMAL fortitude, ataraxia, ataraxy
E3 anxiety, depression, fury

stoke v

add fuel to, feed with fuel, add wood to, add coal to, keep burning, tend

stolen adj

ill-gotten, obtained dishonestly, obtained illegally, pilfered, taken
FORMAL purloined
COLLOQ. punched, swiped, nicked, nobbled, knocked off, ripped off
SLANG hot

stolid adj

slow, heavy, dull, bovine, wooden, blockish, l
umpish, impassive, unemotional, uninspiring,

unimaginative, solemn, indifferent, apathetic
FORMAL phlegmatic
🔁 lively, interested

stomach n, v
♦ n
1 GUT, inside(s), belly, abdomen, paunch, pot-belly
COLLOQ. tummy, tum, corporation; *Aust* bingy
SLANG bread basket
Related adjective: gastric
2 *have the stomach for food*
desire, relish, hunger, appetite, taste, zest
3 *not have the stomach for a fight*
courage, determination, desire, inclination, liking, passion,
appetite
COLLOQ. guts
♦ v
tolerate, bear, stand, endure, suffer, approve of, submit to,
take, brook, put up with
FORMAL abide

stomachache n
colic, gripes, grass/stomach staggers
TECHNICAL dyspepsia
OLD hypochondria
COLLOQ. tummy ache, bellyache

stone n
1 ROCK, boulder, cobble, pebble
FORMAL concretion
Related adjectives: lapidarian, lithic
2 *precious stones*
jewel, gemstone, gem, lapis
3 GRAVESTONE, tombstone, headstone, slab, flagstone,
set(t)
4 PIP, kernel, pit, seed
TECHNICAL endocarp

stonewall v
prevaricate, equivocate, quibble, evade, be evasive, shift,
shuffle, lie, deceive
COLLOQ. hedge, dodge, shilly-shally, waffle, pussy-foot,
beat about the bush, sit on the fence

stony adj
1 *stony beach*
pebbly, shingly, rocky, gravelly, gritty
2 BLANK, expressionless, deadpan, poker-faced, hard, cold,
frigid, icy, frosty, chilly, indifferent, unfeeling, heartless,
adamant, steely, unresponsive, callous, merciless, pitiless,
severe, stern, unforgiving, inexorable, unfriendly, hostile
🔁 **2** warm, soft-hearted, friendly

stooge n
puppet, pawn, lackey, henchman, dupe, foil, butt
COLLOQ. cat's paw, fall guy

stool

Types of stool include:

bar stool	*technical* cutty-	music stool
dialect buffet	stool	piano stool
camp-stool	*old* ducking-stool	stillage
close-stool	faldstool	*Scot* sunk
dialect coppy	fender-stool	tabouret
creepie	footstool	*technical* tripod
dialect cricket	*old* joint-stool	
old cucking stool	milking-stool	

---

stoop v, n
♦ v
1 HUNCH, bow, bend, lower, incline, lean, poke, duck,
squat, crouch, kneel
OLD courb, lout
2 *stoop to blackmail*
descend, sink, lower yourself, resort, go so far as,

condescend, go so low as, deign, decline, cringe; *dialect*
steep
FORMAL vouchsafe
♦ n
droop, hunch, hunching, round-shoulderedness, sag,
slouch, slump, bending, inclination, lowering, ducking

stop v, n
♦ v
1 HALT, end, finish, conclude, cease, discontinue, abandon,
bring/come to an end, bring/come to a rest, suspend,
interrupt, pause, quit
FORMAL terminate, arrest, refrain, desist
COLLOQ. quit, wind up, pack in, kick, knock off, leave off,
give over
2 PREVENT, bar, frustrate, thwart, intercept, hinder, impede,
obstruct, block, check, restrain, stall
3 SEAL, close, plug, block, bung, stop up, cover, obstruct,
arrest, stem, stanch, staunch
4 STAY, live, settle, lodge, board, visit, put up, rest, pause,
break your journey
FORMAL reside, dwell, sojourn
🔁 **1** begin, start, continue
♦ n
1 HALT, standstill, stoppage, end, finish, close, conclusion
FORMAL cessation, termination, discontinuance,
discontinuation
2 STATION, halt, bus stop, fare stage, stopping-place,
terminus, destination
3 REST, break, stay, pause, stage, stopover, visit
FORMAL sojourn
🔁 **1** start, beginning, continuation

Synonym nuances
verb sense 1
You can use **halt** to suggest coming to a complete
standstill, whereas **end**, **finish** and **conclude** imply a
more permanent but less sudden cessation. **Discontinue**
suggests putting a stop to an ongoing process: *the patient
asked for his treatment to be discontinued*. **Abandon**
suggests a degree of disenchantment, or loss of interest:
the party has now abandoned monetarism.
 Suspend carries implications of being a temporary
measure. Similarly, **interrupt** implies a short-term
intervention, while **pause** implies a brief break.
However, **quit** has implications of a permanent
departure from something, with overtones of resolve: *he
quit smoking years ago.*

---

stopgap n, adj
♦ n
improvisation, makeshift, substitute, temporary substitute,
expedient, resort, shift
♦ adj
improvised, makeshift, provisional, temporary, emergency,
impromptu
FORMAL expediential
COLLOQ. rough-and-ready
🔁 finished, permanent

stopover n
stop-off, stop, visit, rest, break, overnight stay; *NAm* layover
FORMAL sojourn

stoppage n
1 STOP, halt, standstill, arrest, blockage, obstacle,
obstruction, check, hindrance, interruption
FORMAL cessation, termination, discontinuance,
discontinuation, occlusion
2 STRIKE, shutdown, closure, walk-out, sit-in, industrial
action; *S Afr* stayaway
3 DEDUCTION, subtraction, reduction, decrease, taking
away/off, withdrawal, removal, discount, allowance
🔁 **1** start, continuation

stopper *n*
cork, bung, plug, seal, spigot
OLD stopple

store *v, n*
♦ *v*
save, keep, put aside, lay by, reserve, stock, stock up with, lay in, deposit, put down, lay down, lay up, squirrel away, bank, gather, collect, accumulate, hoard, stockpile
COLLOQ. salt away, stash, save for a rainy day
Ǝ⅃ use
♦ *n*
1 STOCK, supply, provision, fund, reserve, mine, reservoir, hoard, cache, stockpile, heap, load, accumulation, amassment, deposit, quantity, abundance, plenty, lot
2 SHOP, retail outlet, supermarket, hypermarket, chain store, department store, corner shop.
See panel at **shop**.
3 STOREROOM, storehouse, warehouse, repository, depository, larder, buttery
Ǝ⅃ **1** scarcity
■ **set/lay store by**
value, think highly of, consider highly, admire, hold in high regard, esteem

storehouse *n*
repository, warehouse, treasury, wealth, vault, depository, depot, garner, granary, hold, cellar, armoury, arsenal, fund, entrepot, repertory, barn, buttery, larder, pantry, silo

storey *n*
floor, level, stage, tier, flight, deck
FORMAL stratum

storm *n, v*
♦ *n*
outburst, uproar, furore, outcry, row, rumpus, commotion, disturbance, clamour, tumult, brouhaha, turmoil, stir, agitation, rage, roar, outbreak, offensive, attack, assault, onslaught
COLLOQ. to-do, kerfuffle
Ǝ⅃ calm
♦ *v*
1 *storm a citadel*
charge, rush, attack, assault, assail
2 RAGE, roar, rant, rave, shout, fume, thunder, explode, seethe
COLLOQ. hit the roof, lose your cool, foam at the mouth
3 *storm out of the room*
charge, rush, stamp, tear, flounce

Kinds of storm include:

blizzard	gale	snow storm
buran	haboob	squall
cloudburst	hailstorm	tempest
cyclone	hurricane	thunderstorm
downpour	ice storm	tornado
dust devil	monsoon	typhoon
dust storm	rainstorm	whirlwind
electrical storm	sand storm	

See also **wind**.

---

stormy *adj*
tempestuous, squally, rough, choppy, turbulent, rainy, wild, raging, windy, gusty, blustery, foul, dirty, boisterous, unruly, gustful, stormful, wintry; *N Am* rugged
OLD oragious, wroth
FORMAL inclement
Ǝ⅃ calm, peaceful

story *n*
1 TALE, fiction, anecdote, episode, plot, storyline, narrative, history, chronicle, record, account, relation, recital, report, item, article, feature

2 LIE, falsehood, untruth
COLLOQ. rib

Types of story include:

adventure story	fantasy	saga
Aga saga	folk tale	science fiction
anecdote	ghost story	*colloq.* sci-fi
bedtime story	historical novel	shaggy-dog story
black comedy	horror story	short story
colloq.	interactive story	spiel
blockbuster	legend	spine-chiller
colloq.	love story	spy story
bonkbuster	Mills & Boon®	supernatural tale
children's story	mystery	tall story
comedy	myth	thriller
crime story	novel	western
detective story	novelization	*colloq.*
fable	novella	whodunnit
fairy story	parable	yarn
fairy tale	romance	

---

storyteller *n*
narrator, writer, author, novelist, raconteur, raconteuse, anecdotist, chronicler, bard, romancer, tell-tale

stout *adj*
1 FAT, stocky, plump, fleshy, portly, obese, overweight, heavy, tubby, bulky, big, brawny, beefy, hulking, thickset, burly, muscular, athletic, lusty, chopping, embonpoint; *dialect* stuggy
FORMAL corpulent
2 *stout packaging*
strong, tough, durable, thick, solid, heavy, sturdy, substantial, robust, hardy, vigorous
3 BRAVE, courageous, valiant, plucky, tough, fearless, bold, gallant, heroic, intrepid, dauntless, resolute, stalwart, determined, strong, forceful, fierce, staunch, manful; *dialect* cobby; *Scot* stuffy
OLD tall
FORMAL valorous
COLLOQ. gutsy, spunky, gritty
Ǝ⅃ **1** thin, lean, slim **2** weak **3** cowardly, timid, afraid

stoutly *adv*
strongly, fiercely, toughly, fearlessly, boldly, resolutely, staunchly
Ǝ⅃ weakly, timidly, fearfully

stove *n*
cooker, oven, range, furnace, kiln, grill, heater

stow *v*
put away, store, place, deposit, load, pack, cram, bundle, stuff
COLLOQ. stash
Ǝ⅃ unload
■ **stow away**
hide, travel secretly, conceal yourself

straggle *v*
stray, wander, drift, lag, amble, loiter, ramble, roam, rove, trail, range, scatter, spread, string out
COLLOQ. dilly-dally

straggly *adj*
untidy, rambling, drifting, straying, straggling, aimless, disorganized, irregular, random, spreading, loose, strung out
Ǝ⅃ tidy, organized, grouped

straight *adj, adv*
♦ *adj*
1 *a straight line*
direct, undeviating, unswerving, unbending, unbent, uncurving
2 LEVEL, even, flat, horizontal, upright, vertical, aligned, true, right

3 FRANK, honest, candid, blunt, forthright, direct, outspoken, straightforward
4 CONSECUTIVE, successive, continuous, unbroken, uninterrupted, one after the other
5 TIDY, neat, in order, orderly, shipshape, arranged, organized
6 HONOURABLE, honest, law-abiding, respectable, upright, trustworthy, reliable, upstanding, decent, straightforward, fair, just, faithful, sincere, conventional
7 *straight whisky*
undiluted, neat, pure, unadulterated, unmixed
E3 1 bent, crooked, curved, wavy, curly **2** sloping **3** evasive **5** untidy **6** dishonest **7** diluted
◆ *adv*
1 DIRECTLY, with no changes of direction, without deviating, as the crow flies
2 IMMEDIATELY, directly, instantly, promptly, right away, without delay, at once, as soon as possible
COLLOQ. pronto
3 *tell someone straight*
frankly, honestly, candidly, bluntly, directly, plainly, clearly, forthrightly, straightforwardly, point-blank
COLLOQ. not pulling any punches, straight from the shoulder
4 CONSECUTIVELY, successively, continuously, uninterruptedly, one after the other
COLLOQ. on the trot
■ **straight away**
at once, immediately, instantly, right away, directly, without delay, now, there and then
COLLOQ. pronto
E3 later, eventually

straighten *v*
unbend, make/become straight, align, tidy (up), neaten, order, arrange, adjust, put in order, put right
E3 bend, twist
■ **straighten out**
clear up, sort out, settle, resolve, correct, realign, disentangle, regularize, tidy up, put in order, put right
FORMAL rectify
E3 confuse, muddle
■ **straighten up**
stand up, stand, stand erect, stand upright, straighten your back/body

straightforward *adj*
1 EASY, simple, uncomplicated, clear, elementary, unexacting, undemanding, plain, penny-plain, point-blank, pukka
COLLOQ. child's play, a piece of cake, like falling off a log, no frills
2 HONEST, truthful, sincere, genuine, open, frank, candid, direct, forthright, outspoken, plain-speaking, undesigning, on the level; *dialect* jannock
COLLOQ. up-front
E3 1 difficult, complicated, complex, tricky **2** evasive, devious, underhand

strain¹ *v, n*
◆ *v*
1 PULL, heave, tug, wrench, twist, sprain, hurt, injure, wrick, tear, stretch, extend, elongate, tighten, tauten
FORMAL distend
2 SIEVE, sift, screen, separate, filter, percolate, riddle, purify, drain, wring, squeeze, compress, express
3 WEAKEN, tire, fatigue, tax, overtax, overwork, pressure, labour, try, endeavour, struggle, strive, exert, force, drive, push to/beyond the limit, make every effort, do your utmost
COLLOQ. go all out, put your heart and soul into, pull out all the stops
◆ *n*
1 SPRAIN, pull, wrench, twist, injury, wrick

2 PRESSURE, tension, stress, anxiety, worry, duress, effort, struggle, exertion, pressure, force, burden, demand, tiredness, weariness, fatigue, exhaustion, overwork
E3 2 relaxation

strain² *n*
1 STOCK, ancestry, descent, extraction, breed, family, lineage, pedigree, blood, variety, type, sort, kind
2 TRAIT, streak, quality, characteristic, vein, tendency, way, trace, element, suggestion, suspicion
FORMAL disposition, proclivity
3 *the strains of music*
theme, tune, melody, music, sound, song, air

strained *adj*
forced, constrained, laboured, false, artificial, unnatural, stiff, wooden, tense, unrelaxed, uneasy, uncomfortable, awkward, embarrassed, self-conscious
E3 natural, relaxed

strainer *n*
sieve, colander, sifter, filter, screen, riddle

strait *n*
1 *the Straits of Gibraltar*
sound, narrows, inlet, channel, kyle
2 *in desperate straits*
crisis, difficulty, emergency, hardship, predicament, plight, perplexity, distress, dilemma, embarrassment, extremity, poverty
COLLOQ. hole, mess, fix, pickle, jam, pretty/fine kettle of fish

straitened *adj*
poor, reduced, difficult, distressed, limited, restricted, impoverished, embarrassed
E3 easy, well-off

strait-laced *adj*
prudish, stuffy, starchy, prim, prim and proper, priggish, proper, strict, narrow, narrow-minded, puritanical, moralistic
E3 broad-minded

strand¹ *n*
1 FIBRE, filament, wire, thread, string, piece, length
2 *the strands of a theory*
element, feature, component, factor, ingredient

strand² *n*
walk along the strand
shore, beach, seashore, foreshore, sand(s), waterfront, front

stranded *adj*
marooned, high and dry, abandoned, forsaken, helpless, penniless, aground, grounded, beached, shipwrecked, wrecked
COLLOQ. (left) in the lurch

strange *adj*
1 ODD, peculiar, curious, queer, weird, bizarre, eccentric, offbeat, abnormal, irregular, uncommon, unusual, unexpected, exceptional, remarkable, fantastic, extraordinary, unreal, surreal, mystifying, perplexing, unexplained, inexplicable, uncanny; *dialect* unked; *Scot* unco
OLD rum, selcouth
FORMAL singular
COLLOQ. funny, freaky, wacky, oddball, kinky, off the wall
2 NEW, novel, untried, unknown, unheard-of, unfamiliar, unaccustomed, unacquainted, foreign, alien, exotic; *Scot* fremd
OLD straunge
E3 1 ordinary, common **2** well-known, familiar

Synonym nuances
sense 1
You can use **odd** and **peculiar** to suggest an element of quirkiness: *a distinctly odd appearance*; *a peculiar brand of humour*, and **curious** also suggests raising questions in the mind: *a curious tale*. **Queer** and **weird** continue the idea of singularity, but with a more negative or slightly sinister tone: *I had a queer feeling we were being watched*, while **bizarre** would be reserved for something very outlandish. **Eccentric** suggests being somewhat unconventional in a more endearing way: *eccentric old ladies*.

Abnormal more alarmingly and negatively implies deviation from what is considered the norm: *abnormal behaviour*; *abnormal cells*. **Irregular**, although negative in its connotations, is more suggestive of being unpredictable: *irregular behaviour*. The terms **uncommon** and **unusual**, however, have different connotations, and imply a degree of rarity, and this is conveyed more positively by **exceptional** and **remarkable**, which suggest outstanding qualities.

Both **fantastic** and **extraordinary** suggest something beyond reality, in the realms of the imagination, and the connotations tend to be positive. **Unreal** and **surreal**, although more neutral in tone, echo these suggestions, the first suggesting something unbelievable, and the latter something akin to dreaming: *a surreal nightmare of fire engines and police cars.*

strangely *adv*
peculiarly, oddly, curiously, weirdly, bizarrely, abnormally, unusually, uncommonly, unexpectedly, exceptionally, remarkably, inexplicably
F3 commonly, familiarly

strangeness *n*
oddity, oddness, peculiarity, bizarreness, extraordinariness, irregularity, abnormality, queerness, eccentricity, uncanniness, eeriness, exoticness
FORMAL singularity
F3 ordinariness

stranger *n*
newcomer, new arrival, visitor, guest, non-member, outsider, incomer, foreigner, alien, pilgrim; *Scot* fremd, unco
F3 local, native

■ a stranger to
unfamiliar with, inexperienced in, unversed in, unacquainted with, unaccustomed to

strangle *v*
1 THROTTLE, choke, asphyxiate, suffocate, stifle, smother, strangulate, bowstring, thropple
2 SUPPRESS, gag, repress, inhibit, restrain, check, keep in, hold back, stifle, smother

strap *n, v*
♦ *n*
thong, tie, band, belt, cord, leash
♦ *v*
1 BEAT, lash, whip, flog, belt, scourge
2 FASTEN, secure, tie, bind, truss, lash, bandage

strapping *adj*
brawny, strong, sturdy, well-built, beefy, big, burly, hefty, robust, hulking, husky
COLLOQ. hunky
F3 puny

stratagem *n*
plan, scheme, plot, intrigue, ruse, ploy, trick, deception, dodge, manoeuvre, device, tactic, artifice, wile, subterfuge
FORMAL machination

⚠ stratagem or strategy?
A *stratagem* is a plan or trick, intended to deceive someone or gain an advantage over them: *He was a master of the cunning stratagem and the bare-faced lie*. *Strategy* is used to describe tactics, especially in a long-term plan of campaign: *adopt a strategy of civil disobedience*; *guerrilla tactics were replaced by a strategy of conventional warfare.*

strategic *adj*
strategical, important, key, critical, decisive, crucial, vital, essential, tactical, planned, calculated, deliberate, politic, diplomatic, commanding
F3 unimportant

strategy *n*
tactics, planning, policy, approach, procedure, plan, plan of action, programme, schedule, design, scheme
TECHNICAL geostrategy, maximin, minimax
COLLOQ. blueprint, game plan

⚠ strategy or stratagem?
See panel at **stratagem**.

stratification *n*
division, classification, categorization, ranking, layering, hierarchy, graduation, sorting, gradation

stratum *n*
1 LEVEL, grade, class, rank, table, tier, category, bracket, caste, station, group, region
2 LAYER, seam, vein, lode, bed, stratification

stray *v, adj, n*
♦ *v*
wander (off), get lost, err, go astray, ramble, saunter, amble, roam, rove, range, meander, straggle, drift, diverge, deviate, digress, go wrong, go off the subject; *Scot* stravaig, traik
OLD estray, exorbitate, wilder; (*Spenser*) forwander
COLLOQ. go off at a tangent
♦ *adj*
1 LOST, abandoned, homeless, wandering, roaming, drifting; *Scot* waff
2 RANDOM, chance, occasional, accidental, freak, odd, erratic, scattered, isolated
♦ *n*
straggle, straggler, waif, tag, maverick, stray cat, alleycat, stray dog

streak *n, v*
♦ *n*
1 LINE, stroke, smear, band, stripe, strip, layer, vein, mark, stria, wave, wake, weal, waif
TECHNICAL vibex
OLD freak, strake
2 TRACE, dash, touch, element, strain
3 *on a lucky streak*
spell, time, period, stint, stretch, roll
♦ *v*
1 BAND, stripe, mark, fleck, smear, smudge, daub, fleck, ribbon, lace
OLD freak
FORMAL striate
2 SPEED, tear, rush, hurtle, sprint, race, gallop, fly, dart, dash, flash, whistle, zoom, whizz, sweep, scurry
COLLOQ. belt, tear, vamoose, skedaddle, beat it, scarper

streaked *adj*
flecked, fleckered, streaky, lined, banded, barred, brinded, brindle(d)
FORMAL striate

stream *n, v*
♦ *n*
1 RIVER, creek, brook, beck, burn, rill, rillet, rivulet, tributary

2 *a stream of traffic*
course, drift, flow, surge, current, outpouring, succession, jet, run, gush, rush, tide, flood, deluge, cascade, torrent, volley, burst
FORMAL efflux
♦ *v*
1 ISSUE, well, surge, run, flow, course, pour, spout, gush, flood, cascade, crowd, spill, shed; *Irish* streel
2 *streaming in the wind*
float, trail, flap, fly, flutter

streamer *n*
ribbon, banner, pennant, pennon, flag, ensign, standard, gonfalon
FORMAL vexillum

streamlined *adj*
1 AERODYNAMIC, smooth, sleek, graceful
2 EFFICIENT, well-run, smooth-running, rationalized, time-saving, organized, modernized, slick
COLLOQ. up-to-the-minute
E₃ 2 clumsy, inefficient

street *n*
road, way, thoroughfare, avenue, lane
■ **man/woman in the street**
ordinary person, ordinary citizen, average person, Mr/Mrs Average, average punter
COLLOQ. Joe Bloggs, person/man/woman on the Clapham omnibus

strength *n*
1 POWER, force, energy, vigour, brawn, muscle, sinew, stoutness, toughness, stamina, fitness, health, vigour
COLLOQ. clout
2 TOUGHNESS, resilience, robustness, sturdiness, impregnability, durability, solidity, solidness, resistance, firmness, soundness, hardiness
3 DETERMINATION, resolution, forcefulness, firmness, assertiveness, persistence, spirit, bravery, courage
FORMAL fortitude
COLLOQ. guts, grit
4 INTENSITY, depth, vividness, graphicness, sharpness, keenness, pungency, passion, fervency, ardour, vehemence
5 FORCEFULNESS, effectiveness, power, force, potency, persuasiveness, influence, weight, validity, soundness, urgency
FORMAL cogency
6 STRONG POINT, talent, gift, aptitude, advantage, asset, bent, forte, specialty, speciality, métier
COLLOQ. thing
E₃ 1 weakness, frailty **2** weakness **3** weakness, feebleness **4** mildness, blandness, faintness **5** weakness, ineffectiveness **6** weakness
■ **on the strength of**
because of, because of the influence of, on account of, based on, on the basis of
FORMAL by virtue of

strengthen *v*
reinforce, brace, steel, buttress, build up, prop up, shore up, bolster, support, back up, protect, toughen, man, harden, stiffen, consolidate, substantiate, corroborate, reinforce, confirm, encourage, hearten, refresh, restore, rally, invigorate, nourish, edify, increase, turn up, heighten, intensify, arm, stay, picket
TECHNICAL work-harden, anneal, cleat, fish, line, afforce
OLD munite, sinew, wharf; (*Shakesp*) force
FORMAL fortify
COLLOQ. beef up
E₃ weaken, undermine

strenuous *adj*
1 *strenuous work*
hard, tough, demanding, gruelling, taxing, difficult, laborious, heavy, uphill, arduous, tiring, exhausting, warm, weighty
2 ACTIVE, energetic, vigorous, eager, keen, earnest, tenacious, determined, forceful, resolute, spirited, bold, tireless, indefatigable, blistering
E₃ 1 easy, effortless

strenuously *adv*
vigorously, boldly, actively, resolutely, tirelessly, tenaciously, forcefully

stress *n, v*
♦ *n*
1 PRESSURE, strain, tension, worry, uneasiness, apprehension, anxiety, distress, difficulty, trouble, weight, burden, trauma
COLLOQ. hassle
2 EMPHASIS, accent, accentuation, beat, force, weight, value, priority, importance, significance
TECHNICAL ictus
E₃ 1 relaxation
♦ *v*
emphasize, accentuate, highlight, underline, underscore, point up, spotlight, repeat, exaggerate
E₃ understate, play down, moderate, downplay, tone down

stressed *adj*
tense, nervous, anxious, worried, strained, distraught, under pressure, jittery, uneasy, apprehensive, fidgety, restless, jumpy, overwrought, on edge
COLLOQ. edgy, uptight, keyed up, stressed out
SLANG screwed up
E₃ relaxed, calm

stressful *adj*
tense, worrying, uneasy, strained, charged, fraught, nerve-racking, nail-biting
E₃ easy, light, relaxing, calm

stretch *v, n, adj*
♦ *v*
1 LENGTHEN, extend, make/become longer, broaden, widen, make/become wider, expand, spread, elongate, prolong, draw out
FORMAL protract
2 *stretch from one point to another*
reach, extend, spread, unfold, unroll, continue, project, go as far as, go/come down/up to, last, range
3 TIGHTEN, pull, tauten, strain
4 REACH OUT, straighten, extend, hold out, present, offer
FORMAL proffer
5 *the job will stretch you*
challenge, extend, push, test, tax, try, stimulate, put demands on
E₃ 1 shorten, condense, compress
♦ *n*
1 EXPANSE, spread, sweep, reach, extent, distance, space, area, tract
2 PERIOD, time, term, spell, stint, run
♦ *adj*
elastic, pliable, flexible, stretchable, stretchy, supple, resilient, yielding, springy, rubbery, pliant, elasticated, plastic, bouncy, buoyant
■ **stretch out**
extend, relax, hold out, put out, lie down, sprawl, reach
FORMAL recline
E₃ draw back
■ **stretch your legs**
exercise, go for a walk, move about, stroll, take a walk, take the air
FORMAL promenade
COLLOQ. take a breather

strew *v*
scatter, spread, disperse, bestrew, litter, sprinkle, toss

OLD bespread, besprinkle
☙ gather

stricken *adj*
affected, afflicted, hit, struck, injured, wounded, smitten
☙ unaffected

strict *adj*
1 *a strict teacher*
stern, authoritarian, no-nonsense, hard, firm, rigid, inflexible, uncompromising, stringent, rigorous, disciplinarian, iron-handed, iron-fisted, harsh, tough, severe, austere, narrow
2 EXACT, precise, accurate, clear, clear-cut, literal, faithful, close, true, absolute, utter, total, complete, thoroughgoing, meticulous, scrupulous, conscientious, particular, orthodox, religious
☙ **1** liberal, soft, flexible, easy-going **2** loose

> **Synonym nuances**
> *sense 1*
> You can use **stern** to suggest a rather fearsome attitude or manner, while **authoritarian** implies a dictatorial element: *the premier's authoritarian leadership.*
> **No-nonsense**, however, is slightly more positive in its implication of being sensible, while **hard**, **firm** and **tough** have more to do with resolve.
> The words **rigid** and **inflexible** imply an unyielding determination and are rather more negative in their connotations. **Uncompromising** also suggests complete resistance to concession, but tends to suggest that this is a strength: *a staunch defence of France's uncompromising stand on trade.*
> **Stringent** implies being rigidly applied: *stringent airport checks.* **Rigorous**, too, has more positive overtones and suggests being scrupulous, but **harsh** and **severe** imply a degree of injustice. The synonym **austere** could be used of an absence of any ameliorating traits: *life was austere in the war years*, while **narrow** might be used critically to imply something rather limiting: *companies fail because of their narrow view of how profits are made.*

strictly *adv*
1 *he was brought up very strictly*
sternly, firmly, inflexibly, uncompromisingly, rigorously, severely, narrowly
2 *strictly forbidden*
absolutely, completely, totally, wholly, categorically, definitely, positively, in every way/respect, unequivocally, unambiguously, unquestionably
3 *strictly for the use of members*
only, purely, exclusively, uniquely
☙ **1** liberally
■ **strictly speaking**
literally, strictly, exactly, precisely, to the letter

strictness *n*
1 STERNNESS, authoritarianism, firmness, harshness, rigidity, rigidness, severity, stringency, stringentness, austerity
2 EXACTNESS, precision, accuracy, meticulousness, rigorousness, rigour, scrupulousness
☙ **1** flexibility, mildness

stricture *n*
1 CRITICISM, rebuke, reproof, blame, censure
FORMAL animadversion
COLLOQ. flak
2 RESTRICTION, limit, bound, confine, constraint, restraint, control, tightness
☙ **1** praise

stride *v, n*
♦ *v*
walk, step, pace, tread, advance, progress, lope, overstride, stalk, galumph; *dialect* stroam; *Scot* lamp, stend

OLD bestride
♦ *n*
step, pace, walk, tread, movement, advance, progression; *Scot* stend
■ **take something in your stride**
deal with easily, cope with easily, make light of, do with both eyes shut, do blindfold, do with one hand tied behind your back, do standing on your head, think nothing of

strident *adj*
loud, thundering, roaring, booming, clamorous, vociferous, harsh, rough, raucous, grating, rasping, shrill, screeching, unmusical, discordant, clashing, jarring, jangling
FORMAL stentorian, stridulant
☙ quiet, soft

strife *n*
conflict, disagreement, discord, dissension, controversy, animosity, hostility, friction, rivalry, contention, ill-feeling, ill-will, quarrel, quarrelling, row, argument, dispute, bickering, wrangling, struggle, fighting, combat, battle, warfare, trouble, contest, contestation, feud, mutiny, brigue; *Scot* sturt
OLD bargain, barrat, colluctation, conteck, debate; (*Spenser*) bate
☙ peace

strike *n, v*
♦ *n*
1 INDUSTRIAL ACTION, work-to-rule, go-slow, stoppage, sit-in, walk-out, mutiny, revolt
2 HIT, blow, stroke, slap, smack, thump
COLLOQ. wallop, clobber, whack, thwack, belt, biff
3 ATTACK, charge, raid, storming, assault, rush, ambush, trap
♦ *v*
1 STOP WORK, down tools, take industrial action, work to rule, walk out, protest, mutiny, revolt
2 HIT, knock, collide with, crash, slap, smack, cuff, clout, thump, thrash, rap, beat, bang, pound, punch, box, hammer, buffet, batter
COLLOQ. wallop, sock, clobber, swipe, whack, thwack, belt, biff
SLANG twat; *N Am* lam
3 ATTACK, charge, storm, assail, assault, raid, rush, set about, pounce on, ambush, trap
4 FIND, discover, come upon, unearth, uncover, encounter, reach
FORMAL chance upon, happen upon
5 *the idea suddenly struck me*
occur to, hit, come to, come to mind, dawn on, register
6 *it strikes me as odd*
seem, appear, look, look like, feel, sound, give the impression, impress, affect, touch, have the look of
7 *strike a particular pose*
adopt, take on, assume, embrace, affect
8 *strike a bargain*
reach, come to, agree on, come to an agreement on, settle on, arrive at, achieve
COLLOQ. clinch
■ **strike back**
retaliate, hit back, fight back, reciprocate, get back at, pay someone back
COLLOQ. get your own back, get even with
■ **strike down**
afflict, ruin, destroy, kill, murder, assassinate
FORMAL slay, smite
■ **strike out**
cross out, delete, rub out, erase, strike through, cancel, strike off, remove, obliterate
☙ add

■ **strike up**
begin, start, initiate, instigate, introduce, establish
FORMAL commence
COLLOQ. kick off

striking *adj*
1 NOTICEABLE, conspicuous, obvious, evident, salient, outstanding, remarkable, extraordinary, memorable, distinct, visible, impressive, dazzling, arresting, astonishing, stunning
2 ATTRACTIVE, stunning, beautiful, good-looking, gorgeous, pretty, glamorous
SLANG drop-dead gorgeous
⊟ 1 unimpressive 2 ugly

string *n, v*
♦ *n*
1 *a piece of string*
twine, cord, rope, yarn, cable, line, strand, fibre
2 SERIES, succession, sequence, chain, line, row, column, file, queue, procession, stream, train
♦ *v*
thread, link, connect, fasten, tie up, sling, hang, suspend, festoon, loop

■ **string along**
deceive, mislead, fool, bluff, dupe, play (someone) false, hoax, humbug
COLLOQ. play fast and loose with, put one over on
SLANG take for a ride

■ **string out**
space out, spread out, stretch out, straggle, fan out, disperse, extend, lengthen, wander
FORMAL protract
⊟ gather, shorten

■ **string up**
hang, kill, lynch, send to the gallows/scaffold/gibbet
COLLOQ. top

with no strings attached
unconditional, without qualifications, without limitations, without stipulations, with no obligation

stringency *n*
strictness, rigour, rigorousness, toughness, firmness, inflexibility, exactness, demands
⊟ flexibility

stringent *adj*
binding, strict, severe, rigorous, tough, firm, rigid, inflexible, uncompromising, exacting, demanding, tight, hard, harsh
⊟ lax, flexible

stringy *adj*
tough, gristly, chewy, fibrous, sinewy, leathery, wiry, rop(e)y
⊟ tender

strip *v, n*
♦ *v*
1 UNDRESS, take your clothes off, unclothe, disrobe, remove your clothes, uncover, expose, lay bare
FORMAL denude
2 CLEAN OUT, clear, empty, divest, deprive, dispossess, gut, ransack, pillage, plunder, loot
OLD disfurnish
3 PEEL, skin, flay, flake off
FORMAL excoriate
4 DISMANTLE, take apart, disassemble, separate, pull apart, take to pieces
⊟ 1 clothe, dress, get dressed 2 cover, fill 4 assemble, put together
♦ *n*
1 *a strip of wood*
ribbon, thong, strap, belt, sash, band, bar, stripe, lath, slat, piece, bit, slip, shred

2 *a strip of land*
stretch, belt, expanse, extent, area, tract, swathe, zone
3 *a football strip*
outfit, clothing, clothes, outfit, rig, colours
COLLOQ. rig-out, gear, togs, things, get-up, clobber

stripe *n*
band, line, bar, chevron, flash, streak, fleck, strip, belt, ribbon, slash, snip, list, pin-stripe, streak, zone, whelk
TECHNICAL vitta, pale, endorse
OLD strake, laticlave

striped *adj*
banded, barred, streaky, stripy, variegated, striated, vittate
TECHNICAL endorsed
OLD bausond

stripling *n*
boy, fledgling, lad, teenager, adolescent, youth, youngster
COLLOQ. young 'un

strive *v*
1 TRY, attempt, endeavour, struggle, strain, work, toil, labour, try hard, campaign, exert yourself, give your all, do your best, do your utmost
2 FIGHT, battle, contend, engage, contest, combat, do battle, vie, compete

stroke *n, v*
♦ *n*
1 CARESS, pat, rub
2 BLOW, hit, knock, swipe, slap, thump, smack
COLLOQ. wallop, clobber, whack, thwack, belt, biff
3 SWEEP, flourish, movement, action, move, motion, line
4 ACCOMPLISHMENT, achievement, coup
5 COLLAPSE, shock, spasm, attack, seizure, thrombosis, cerebral haemorrhage
♦ *v*
caress, fondle, pet, touch, pat, rub, massage

stroll *v, n*
♦ *v*
saunter, amble, dawdle, ramble, wander, meander, go for a walk
COLLOQ. stretch your legs
♦ *n*
walk, saunter, amble, constitutional, turn, ramble

stroller *n*
saunterer, rambler, walker, wanderer, dawdler

strong *adj*
1 POWERFUL, mighty, potent, lusty, strapping, sturdy, stout, burly, well-built, beefy, brawny, muscular, sinewy, athletic, fit, well, healthy
2 TOUGH, resilient, durable, hard-wearing, heavy-duty, industrial-strength, solid, long-lasting, well-built, well-protected, reinforced, secure, robust, hardy, sturdy, vigorous, stalwart, rugged
3 DETERMINED, forceful, firm, confident, resolute, assertive, aggressive, formidable, strong-willed, strong-minded, single-minded, persistent, brave, courageous
COLLOQ. gutsy
4 *a strong colour*
intense, deep, vivid, graphic, fierce, violent, powerful, sharp, heady, keen, pungent, piquant, biting, highly-flavoured, highly-seasoned, hot, spicy
5 *a strong impression*
marked, clear, clear-cut, obvious, evident, remarkable, pronounced
6 *take strong action*
decisive, firm, definite, positive, active, severe, resolute, forceful
7 *a strong interest in railways*
keen, enthusiastic, eager, devoted, committed, deep, passionate
8 *a strong case/argument*
convincing, persuasive, powerful, potent, plausible, valid,

sound, effective, telling, forceful, weighty, compelling, urgent
FORMAL cogent, efficacious
9 *strong feelings*
intense, passionate, fervent, great, powerful, deep, profound, ardent, vehement
10 UNDILUTED, concentrated, potent
F3 1 weak, frail, sickly, unhealthy **2** weak, insubstantial **3** feeble, weak **4** weak, faint, mild, bland **6** weak, indecisive **8** weak, unconvincing **9** weak, feeble **10** diluted
■ **strong point**
strength, talent, gift, aptitude, advantage, asset, bent, forte, speciality, specialty, métier
COLLOQ. thing

Synonym nuances
sense 1
Most of the synonyms are positive in tone.
  You can use **powerful** or **mighty** to suggest having great strength, while **potent** has further implications of effectiveness: *the most potent political force in the country.* **Lusty**, meanwhile, suggests vigour, while **strapping** conveys a picture of a tall, robust build.
  Other synonyms make suggestions about appearance; **sturdy** and **stout** imply a firm, stocky body, while **burly** additionally suggests height: *burly bouncers on the door.* The term **beefy** has suggestions of fleshiness: *his great wide beefy back*, while **brawny** implies muscularity, and **sinewy** echoes this toned form: *his long sinewy body.* **Athletic** and **fit**, although similar, are more suggestive of concomitant physical prowess.

---

strongarm *adj*
forceful, physical, violent, oppressive, terror, aggressive, bullying, coercive, threatening, intimidatory, thuggish
COLLOQ. bully-boy
F3 gentle

strongbox *n*
safe, cash box, deposit box, safety-deposit box, chest, coffer, vault, depository, repository

stronghold *n*
citadel, bastion, fort, fortress, castle, tower, keep, hold, centre, refuge, fastness, outpost, eyrie, hill-fort
OLD holt

strongly *adv*
1 *a strongly built man*
powerfully, muscularly, athletically
2 *strongly-constructed apparatus*
durably, solidly, toughly, resiliently, substantially
3 *strongly opposed to the idea*
firmly, positively, resolutely, deeply, intensely, definitely, forcefully
4 *his breath smells strongly of garlic*
intensely, powerfully, markedly
F3 1 insubstantially **2** weakly **3** mildly **4** faintly

strong-minded *adj*
resolute, steadfast, strong-willed, tenacious, firm, determined, independent, iron-willed, uncompromising, unbending, unwavering
F3 weak-willed

strong-willed *adj*
stubborn, obstinate, intractable, wayward, inflexible, wilful, self-willed
FORMAL obdurate, refractory, recalcitrant, intransigent

stroppy *adj*
bad-tempered, difficult, unhelpful, unco-operative, perverse, awkward, bloody-minded, quarrelsome, rowdy, cantankerous, obstreperous

FORMAL refractory
COLLOQ. bolshie, ratty, shirty
F3 co-operative, sweet-tempered

structural *adj*
design, constructional, organizational
TECHNICAL tectonic
FORMAL configurational, formational, edificial

structure *n, v*
♦ *n*
1 *the structure of society*
framework, frame, construction, fabric, form, shape, design, make-up, formation, arrangement, organization, composition, constitution, system, set-up, chassis
FORMAL configuration, conformation
2 BUILDING, construction, edifice, erection
♦ *v*
construct, assemble, build, form, shape, design, arrange, organize

struggle *v, n*
♦ *v*
1 STRIVE, work, toil, labour, strain, try hard, exert yourself, give your all, do your best, do your utmost, agonize
2 FIGHT, battle, wrestle, grapple, engage, contest, combat, contend, compete, vie
F3 2 yield, give in
♦ *n*
clash, conflict, strife, fight, battle, skirmish, encounter, combat, scuffle, brawl, hostilities, contest, competition, difficulty, problem, effort, exertion, trouble, pains, agony, work, labour, toil
F3 ease, submission, co-operation

strut *v*
parade, prance, stalk, swagger, peacock; *S Afr* pronk
COLLOQ. swank

stub *n*
end, stump, remnant, butt, counterfoil
COLLOQ. fag end, dog-end

stubborn *adj*
obstinate, stiff-necked, mulish, pig-headed, rigid, uncompromising, inflexible, unbending, unyielding, dogged, persistent, tenacious, headstrong, self-willed, strong-willed, adamant, hidebound, wilful, difficult, unmanageable, stubborn as a mule, not listening/open to reason, opinionated, overdetermined, stiff, inveterate, perverse, cantankerous; *Scot* rigwiddie, thrawn
OLD stoor, stout; (*Shakesp*) obstacle
FORMAL obdurate, intransigent, refractory, intractable, recalcitrant, contumacious
COLLOQ. *N Am* ornery
F3 compliant, flexible, yielding

Synonym nuances
You can use **obstinate** to suggest unreasonable determination, and **rigid**, **inflexible**, **stiff**, **unbending** and **unyielding** are also rather negative in their implication of being fixed in your ideas and not open to suggestion. **Uncompromising** suggests a refusal to allow any concessions, but can be more suggestive that this is a strength.
  The terms **dogged** and **tenacious** suggest a refusal to give up, which can be interpreted as admirable: *a thorough and tenacious businesswoman.* **Persistent**, although similar, has implications of repetition and being a nuisance: *persistent demands.* The terms **headstrong** and **self-willed** suggest acting on your own wishes, regardless of others, and are rather disapproving; however, **strong-willed**, which also suggests single-mindedness, is far more approbatory: *he is strong-willed, and a great competitor.* **Wilful** suggests an untamed

element, and the terms **difficult** and **unmanageable** make more explicit these problems of control.

Hidebound is a fairly critical term which implies habitual behaviour and attitudes: *a liberator from hidebound convention*, while **inveterate** has slightly less criticism inherent in its tone: *an inveterate rebel who would not be shifted*. **Opinionated** is also negative in its implication of undue adherence to your own assertions: *entrenched, opinionated and bombastic idiots*. You might use the disapproving term **perverse** of being deliberately provocative by championing the opposite viewpoint, and **cantankerous**, too, has suggestions of being deliberately contrary: *he can be a cantankerous old fossil at times*.

stubbornly *adv*
obstinately, pig-headedly, inflexibly, uncompromisingly, doggedly, persistently, tenaciously, perversely, wilfully
FORMAL intransigently
ᴇ⅃ compliantly

stubby *adj*
stumpy, dumpy, chunky, short, squat, thickset
ᴇ⅃ long, tall, thin

stuck *adj*
1 FAST, jammed, firm, fixed, embedded, rooted, fastened, unmovable, immobile, joined, glued, cemented
COLLOQ. bogged down
2 BEATEN, perplexed, baffled
COLLOQ. stumped, at a loss, at your wits' end, nonplussed
ᴇ⅃ **1** loose

■ **stuck on**
fond of, enthusiastic about, keen on, obsessed with, infatuated with, wild about, crazy about
COLLOQ. dotty about, mad on, nuts on, sweet on

■ **get stuck into**
set about, tackle, get down to, start, begin, embark on
ᴇ⅃ indifferent to

stuck-up *adj*
snobbish, supercilious, haughty, patronizing, condescending, proud, arrogant, conceited
COLLOQ. snooty, bigheaded, toffee-nosed, high and mighty, hoity-toity, uppish, toploftical
ᴇ⅃ humble, modest

stud *n*
knob, boss, tack, rivet, doornail, press fastener, seg; *Aust* stop

studded *adj*
dotted, flecked, set, spotted, speckled, sprinkled, ornamented, spangled, scattered
OLD bejewelled, bespangled

student *n*
undergraduate, postgraduate, scholar, schoolboy, schoolgirl, pupil, disciple, learner, probationer, trainee, apprentice

studied *adj*
deliberate, conscious, wilful, intentional, premeditated, planned, purposeful, calculated, contrived, forced, affected, unnatural, artificial, over-elaborate
ᴇ⅃ unplanned, impulsive, natural

studio *n*
workshop, workroom, gallery, school, atelier, bottega

studious *adj*
scholarly, academic, intellectual, bookish, serious, thoughtful, reflective, diligent, hard-working, industrious, meticulous, thorough, assiduous, careful, attentive, earnest, eager
FORMAL sedulous
ᴇ⅃ lazy, idle, negligent

study *v, n*
♦ *v*
read, learn, train, revise, cram, read up, research, work, major in, investigate, analyse, survey, scan, examine, scrutinize, peruse, pore over, contemplate, meditate, ponder, consider, deliberate
COLLOQ. swot, mug up, bone up
♦ *n*
1 READING, homework, preparation, learning, scholarship, revision, cramming, research, investigation, inquiry, analysis, examination, scrutiny, inspection, contemplation, thought, consideration, attention
COLLOQ. swotting
See panel on next page
2 REPORT, essay, thesis, paper, monograph, article, work, survey, review, critique
3 OFFICE, studio, library, workplace, workroom
COLLOQ. den

stuff *v, n*
♦ *v*
1 PACK, stow, load, fill, pad, press, cram, crowd, force, push, ram, thrust, wedge, jam, squeeze, stow, compress, block, obstruct, bung up
COLLOQ. shove
2 GORGE, gormandize, overindulge, guzzle, gobble, sate, satiate
COLLOQ. pig out, gross out, make a pig of yourself, binge
ᴇ⅃ **1** unload, empty **2** nibble
♦ *n*
1 MATERIAL, fabric, matter, substance, essence
2 BELONGINGS, possessions, things, objects, articles, items, goods, luggage, paraphernalia, kit, tackle, equipment, materials
COLLOQ. gear, clobber

stuffing *n*
padding, wadding, quilting, packing, kapok, filling, forcemeat, farce

stuffy *adj*
1 *a stuffy room*
musty, stale, airless, unventilated, suffocating, stifling, oppressive, heavy, close, muggy, sultry, fuggy, fusty
2 STAID, strait-laced, prim, conventional, old-fashioned, pompous, dull, dreary, uninteresting, fusty, stodgy, stiff, starchy
COLLOQ. fuddy-duddy; *N Am* buttoned-down
ᴇ⅃ **1** airy, well-ventilated **2** informal, modern, lively

stultify *v*
blunt, dull, stupefy, numb, smother, stifle, suppress, thwart, invalidate, negate, nullify
FORMAL hebetate
ᴇ⅃ prove, sharpen, electrify

stumble *v*
1 TRIP, slip, fall, falter, lurch, reel, stagger, flounder, founder, blunder, lose your balance, peck, titubate; *dialect* hamble; *Scot* snapper, stoit
2 STAMMER, stutter, hesitate, falter

■ **stumble across/on**
come across, find, discover, encounter
FORMAL chance upon, happen upon

stumbling-block *n*
obstacle, hurdle, barrier, bar, obstruction, hindrance, impediment, difficulty, snag

stump *n, v*
♦ *n*
end, remnant, trunk, stub, butt, remains
COLLOQ. fag end, dog-end
♦ *v*
defeat, outwit, confound, perplex, puzzle, baffle, mystify, confuse, bewilder, dumbfound, foil

Subjects of study include:

accountancy	craft	fitness	languages	natural history	religious studies
agriculture	creative writing	food technology	law	oceanography	science
anatomy	dance	forensics	leisure studies	ornithology	shorthand
anthropology	design	gender studies	lexicography	pathology	social sciences
archaeology	design and	genetics	librarianship	penology	sociology
architecture	technology	geography	linguistics	personal and	sport
art	(D & T)	geology	literature	social education	statistics
astrology	drama	heraldry	logistics	(PSE)	surveying
astronomy	dressmaking	history	management	personal health	technology
biology	driving	home economics	studies	and social	theology
botany	ecology	horticulture	marine studies	education	tourism and
building studies	economics	hotel	marketing	(PHSE)	hospitality
business studies	education	management	mathematics	pharmacology	translation and
calligraphy	electronics	humanities	mechanics	philosophy	interpretation
chemistry	engineering	information and	media studies	photography	typewriting
citizenship	environmenal	communication	medicine	physics	visual arts
civil engineering	studies	technology	metallurgy	physiology	web design
the Classics	erotology	(ICT)	metaphysics	politics	women's studies
commerce	ethnology	information	meteorology	pottery	word processing
computer studies	eugenics	technology (IT)	music	psychology	zoology
cosmology	fashion	journalism	mythology	publishing	

COLLOQ. flummox, bamboozle, nonplus

E≡ assist

■ **stump up**
pay, pay out/up, hand over, donate, contribute

COLLOQ. fork out, shell out, chip in, cough up; *N Am* ante up

E≡ receive

stumped *adj*
perplexed, stuck, baffled

COLLOQ. floored, bamboozled, flummoxed, nonplussed, stymied

stumpy *adj*
chunky, heavy, short, squat, stocky, stubby, thickset, thick, dumpy

E≡ long, tall, thin

stun *v*
amaze, astonish, astound, stagger, shock, daze, deafen, stupefy, dumbfound, overcome, overpower, confound, confuse, bewilder, stupefy, settle; *Scot* devvel, dover; *N Am* Taser®

OLD stonn, bedeafen; (*Spenser*) stoun, stound

COLLOQ. flabbergast, knock out, knock for six, bowl over, take your breath away

stunned *adj*
amazed, astounded, devastated, dumbfounded, dazed, numb, shocked, staggered, stupefied

COLLOQ. flabbergasted, floored, gobsmacked

E≡ indifferent

stunner *n*
beauty, charmer, good-looker, sensation, dazzler, heart-throb, looker, *femme fatale*, lovely, siren

COLLOQ. smasher, cracker, knock-out, peach, wow, eye-catcher

stunning *adj*
beautiful, lovely, gorgeous, ravishing, dazzling, brilliant, striking, impressive, spectacular, remarkable, extraordinary, amazing, wonderful, marvellous, great, sensational, incredible, staggering

COLLOQ. smashing, fabulous

E≡ ugly, awful

stunningly *adv*
brilliantly, strikingly, impressively, remarkably, spectacularly, amazingly, extraordinarily, staggeringly, marvellously, wonderfully, beautifully, gorgeously

COLLOQ. fabulously

stunt¹ *n*
a publicity stunt

feat, exploit, act, deed, action, enterprise, trick, turn, performance, ramp

COLLOQ. wheeze, hype

stunt² *v*
stunt someone's growth
stop, arrest, check, restrict, curb, slow, hinder, hamper, inhibit, impede, dwarf; *dialect* stock; *Scot* nirl

FORMAL retard

E≡ promote, encourage

stunted *adj*
small, little, tiny, undersized, diminutive, dwarfed, dwarfish

OLD (*Shakesp*) scrubbed

E≡ large, sturdy

stupefaction *n*
daze, numbness, state of shock, blackout, senselessness, bewilderment, wonder, bafflement, amazement, astonishment

stupefy *v*
daze, stun, numb, dumbfound, shock, devastate, stagger, dull, amaze, astound, fuddle, drowse, drug, etherize, hocus; *dialect* moider; *Scot* dozen

OLD bemuse, benumb, somniate; (*Shakesp*) mull

COLLOQ. knock out, knock for six, bowl over

stupendous *adj*
huge, enormous, immense, gigantic, colossal, vast, phenomenal, tremendous, breathtaking, wonderful, extraordinary, overwhelming, staggering, stunning, amazing, astounding, superb, marvellous, fantastic

FORMAL prodigious

COLLOQ. fabulous

E≡ ordinary, unimpressive

stupid *adj*
1 SILLY, foolish, irresponsible, ill-advised, indiscreet, foolhardy, rash, senseless, mad, lunatic, brainless, mindless, half-witted, idiotic, imbecilic, moronic, feeble-minded, simple-minded, slow, dim, dull, dull-witted, dense, crass, inane, fatuous, puerile, futile, pointless, meaningless, nonsensical, absurd, ludicrous, laughable; *Welsh* twp

OLD (*Shakesp*) clay-brained, fatbrained, sodden-witted

FORMAL injudicious

COLLOQ. gormless, thick, dumb, dopey, not all there, loopy, barmy, potty, slow on the uptake, thick as a plank/two short planks

SLANG loony

2 DAZED, groggy, stupefied, stunned, sluggish, semiconscious, unconscious

E≡ **1** sensible, wise, clever, intelligent **2** alert, sharp

Synonym nuances

sense 1

Many of the synonyms are disapproving in tone.

Silly and **foolish** are fairly restrained terms to suggest a lack of good sense or wisdom. **Irresponsible**, on the other hand, makes the accusation of recklessness, and **foolhardy** also suggests an absence of caution: *an example of foolhardy daring*, while **rash** is appropriate to suggest a degree of impulsiveness in an action: *take your time rather than make rash decisions based on wishful thinking*. **Ill-advised** is more restrained, and has more to do with lack of judgement: *his ill-advised return to television failed miserably*.

To emphasize the purposelessness of an action you might use **senseless**, **pointless**, **meaningless** or **futile**: *futile departmental infighting*. However, to convey the idea of a lack of mental sharpness or ability **slow**, **dim**, **dull** and **dense** are more useful. More strongly critical terms are **idiotic**, **imbecilic** and **moronic**, which suggest total intellectual incapacity.

Crass suggests not just stupidity but also insensitivity or lack of taste: *crass comments made to try to cheer me up*, while **inane** is suggestive of being vacuous. **Fatuous** further implies cheerful complacency: *their fatuous optimism*, while **puerile** could be used to suggest that something is childish. **Absurd**, **ludicrous** and **laughable** all suggest an element of the ridiculous and so convey contempt: *the idea that these weapons deter anyone is laughable*.

stupidity *n*

silliness, folly, foolishness, foolhardiness, irresponsibility, indiscretion, rashness, senselessness, madness, lunacy, denseness, crassness, absurdity, dimness, asininity, feeble-mindedness, dullness, puerility, fatuousness, fatuity, futility, impracticality, brainlessness, idiocy, imbecility, inanity, ineptitude, naivety, obtuseness, pointlessness, ludicrousness, slowness
COLLOQ. dopiness, doziness, dumbness, thickness
E3 intelligence, alertness, cleverness

stupidly *adv*

foolishly, irresponsibly, unthinkingly, sillily, inanely, fatuously, absurdly, mindlessly
E3 sensibly

stupor *n*

daze, state of shock, stupefaction, lethargy, inertia, trance, blackout, coma, numbness, oblivion, insensibility, unconsciousness
FORMAL torpor
E3 alertness, consciousness

sturdy *adj*

strong, robust, durable, well-made, stout, substantial, solid, well-built, powerful, muscular, lubberly, burly, stocky, athletic, hardy, rugged, vigorous, flourishing, hearty, staunch, stalwart, steadfast, firm, resolute, determined, tenacious; *dialect* turnsick; *Scot* stuffy, steeve
FORMAL mighty
E3 weak, flimsy, puny

stutter *v, n*

◆ *v*
stammer, hesitate, splutter, falter, stumble, mumble, lisp
◆ *n*
stammer, speech impediment, speech defect

style *n, v*

◆ *n*
1 *style of working*
technique, approach, method, methodology, manner, fashion, way, custom
FORMAL mode

2 APPEARANCE, cut, design, pattern, shape, form, sort, type, kind, variety, category
FORMAL genre
3 ELEGANCE, smartness, chic, flair, panache, stylishness, dash, taste, polish, refinement, sophistication, urbanity, suaveness, fashion, vogue, trend, mode, dressiness, flamboyance, wealth, affluence, comfort, luxury, grandeur
4 WORDING, phrasing, expression, language, tone, tenor
E3 3 inelegance, tastelessness
◆ *v*
1 DESIGN, cut, tailor, fashion, make, shape, produce, adapt
2 DESIGNATE, term, name, call, address, title, dub, tag, label
FORMAL denominate

stylish *adj*

chic, fashionable, *à la mode*, modish, in vogue, voguish, snappy, dressy, smart, elegant, polished, refined, sophisticated, urbane
COLLOQ. trendy, natty, snazzy, classy, ritzy
E3 old-fashioned, shabby

stylus *n*

needle, pointer, pen, index, hand, style, probe
FORMAL graphium

stymie *v*

foil, frustrate, hinder, stump, thwart, hamper, impede, interfere, defeat, confound, baffle, balk, mystify, puzzle
COLLOQ. bamboozle, flummox, nonplus, snooker
E3 help, assist

suave *adj*

debonair, refined, polite, courteous, charming, civil, civilized, agreeable, affable, soft-spoken, smooth, polished, bland, glib, sophisticated, urbane, worldly
FORMAL unctuous
E3 rude, unsophisticated

suavity *n*

refinement, politeness, courtesy, sophistication, urbanity, charm, civility, agreeability, blandness, smoothness, worldliness
FORMAL unctuousness
E3 coarseness

sub *n*

1 SUBSTITUTE, reserve, stand-by, supply, locum, understudy, stand-in, replacement, relief, surrogate, proxy, agent, deputy, makeshift, stopgap
FORMAL *locum tenens*
COLLOQ. temp, fill-in; *N Am* pinch-hitter
2 SUBSCRIPTION, membership fee, dues, payment, donation, contribution, offering, gift

subaquatic *adj*

underwater, undersea, submersed, submarine
FORMAL subaqua, subaqueous, demersal

subconscious *adj, n*

◆ *adj*
subliminal, unconscious, intuitive, instinctive, inner, innermost, deep, hidden, latent, underlying, repressed, suppressed
E3 conscious
◆ *n*
psyche, mind, unconscious, unconscious self, inner self, inner being, ego, super-ego, id

subcontract *v*

contract out, pass/give to others, delegate, farm out, outsource

subdue *v*

overcome, quell, suppress, repress, overpower, crush, quash, defeat, conquer, overrun, subject, gain mastery over, get the better of, humble, bring under, cow, crucify, take in, break, tame, master, discipline, chasten, chastise, control, check, stifle, restrain, moderate, reduce, soften, quieten, damp, mellow, soft-pedal, quell, step on, charm,

daunt, mortify, starve; *Scot* daunton
OLD subdew, do down, quail, mate; (*Spenser*) accoy, adaw
FORMAL vanquish, subjugate, subact
SLANG settle someone's hash
F3 arouse, awaken

subdued *adj*
1 SAD, downcast, dejected, crestfallen, depressed, quiet,
unexcited, lifeless, serious, grave, solemn
COLLOQ. down in the dumps
2 QUIET, muted, hushed, silent, noiseless, still, soft,
softened, pastel, dim, shaded, sombre, sober, restrained,
delicate, unobtrusive, low-key, subtle, toned-down
F3 1 lively, excited **2** bright, loud, striking, obtrusive

subject *n, adj, v*
◆ *n*
1 TOPIC, theme, matter, issue, question, aspect, point,
substance, case, affair, business, discipline, area of study,
field, field of study, motif
2 NATIONAL, citizen, native, inhabitant, resident
3 PARTICIPANT, client, patient, case, victim
COLLOQ. guinea pig
4 SUBORDINATE, vassal, liegeman, inferior, dependant,
captive
COLLOQ. underling
F3 4 monarch, ruler, master
◆ *adj*
1 LIABLE, disposed, prone, susceptible, vulnerable, likely,
apt, open, exposed
2 *subject to a law*
captive, bound, constrained, obedient, answerable,
accountable, subordinate, inferior, subservient, submissive
FORMAL subjugated
3 DEPENDENT, depending, conditional, resting, hanging
FORMAL contingent
F3 1 invulnerable, immune **2** free, superior **3** unconditional
◆ *v*
expose, lay open, submit, subdue, submit
FORMAL subjugate

subjection *n*
captivity, bondage, slavery, oppression, domination,
mastery, defeat, enslavement, chains, shackles
FORMAL subjugation

subjective *adj*
biased, prejudiced, bigoted, personal, individual,
personal, idiosyncratic, emotional, intuitive, instinctive
F3 objective, unbiased, impartial

subjugate *v*
conquer, overpower, overcome, master, overthrow, gain
mastery over, get the better of, crush, defeat, subdue,
suppress, oppress, quell, reduce, enslave, tame, thrall
FORMAL vanquish
F3 free, liberate

sublimate *v*
channel, divert, transfer, redirect, turn, exalt, heighten,
elevate, purify, refine
FORMAL transmute
F3 let out

sublime *adj*
1 GLORIOUS, exalted, elevated, high, lofty, noble, winged,
august, majestic, great, grand, imposing, magnificent,
transcendent, spiritual, heavenly, celestial, Dantean
FORMAL empyreal
2 SUPREME, great, intense, extreme, complete, utter
F3 1 lowly, base

subliminal *adj*
subconscious, hidden, concealed, unconscious

submerge *v*
submerse, immerse, plunge, plummet, duck, dip, dive,
dunk, sink, go down, go/put under water, drown, engulf,

overwhelm, swamp, overflow, flood, inundate, deluge,
submerse, bury; *Scot* take
OLD whelm, implunge, indrench
F3 surface

submerged *adj*
submersed, immersed, underwater, sunk, sunken,
drowned, swamped, inundated, hidden, concealed,
cloaked, veiled, unseen

submission *n*
1 SURRENDER, giving in, capitulation, resignation,
agreement, acquiescence, compliance, obedience,
deference, submissiveness, meekness, passivity
FORMAL assent
2 PRESENTATION, offering, contribution, entry, introduction,
tendering, tabling, tender, suggestion, proposal,
statement, assertion
FORMAL averment
F3 1 resistance, opposition, intransigence, intractability **2**
withdrawal, retraction

submissive *adj*
yielding, passive, unresisting, resigned, patient,
uncomplaining, accommodating, malleable, biddable,
compliant, acquiescent, obedient, deferential, ingratiating,
subservient, resisting, servile, humble, meek, self-effacing,
docile, weak, weak-willed, downtrodden, subdued
FORMAL supine
F3 intractable, assertive; *formal* intransigent

submissively *adv*
passively, patiently, uncomplainingly, obediently,
deferentially, humbly, meekly, subserviently, weakly
F3 assertively, intractably

submit *v*
1 YIELD, give in, give way, surrender, lay down your arms,
capitulate, knuckle under, bow, bend, bend/bow the
knee, stoop, succumb, agree, comply, defer, acquiesce,
subject, resign, come to terms, bow, expose, violate, bite
the bullet, come to heel, kiss the rod
TECHNICAL passage
OLD permit; (*Shakesp*) subscribe
FORMAL accede
2 PRESENT, tender, offer, put forward, suggest, propose,
introduce, table, move, state, claim, assert, lay before, put,
refer, render, argue, send in
TECHNICAL prefer
FORMAL proffer, propound, aver
F3 1 resist, oppose **2** withdraw

subnormal *adj*
below normal, below average, low, backward, inferior,
slow, retarded, feeble-minded
F3 gifted

subordinate *adj, n*
◆ *adj*
secondary, auxiliary, ancillary, subsidiary, dependent,
inferior, lower, lower in rank, lower-ranking, junior, minor,
lesser, subservient, lowly
F3 superior, senior
◆ *n*
inferior, junior, assistant, attendant, second, deputy, aide,
dependant, menial, vassal
COLLOQ. underling, sidekick, skivvy, dogsbody, second
fiddle
F3 superior, boss

subordination *n*
inferiority, subjection, submission, dependence, servitude,
subservience
F3 superiority

subscribe *v*
1 *subscribe to a magazine*
pay for regularly, buy regularly, receive/take regularly,

take, sign up to
2 DONATE, give, contribute, pledge
COLLOQ. chip in, shell out, fork out
3 *subscribe to a theory*
support, endorse, back, approve, agree
FORMAL advocate

subscriber n
regular reader, member, customer

subscription n
membership fee, dues, payment, donation, contribution, offering, gift

subsequent adj
following, later, future, next, succeeding, consequent, resulting, ensuing
☞ previous, earlier, prior

subsequently adv
later, after, afterwards, consequently
☞ previously

subservience n
servility, servitude, deference, submissiveness, obedience, acquiescence, dutifulness, humility, subjection, subordination

subservient adj
1 SERVILE, deferential, submissive, fawning, ingratiating, toadying, sycophantic
FORMAL obsequious, unctuous
COLLOQ. bootlicking
2 SUBORDINATE, less important, secondary, ancillary, auxiliary, subsidiary, dependent, inferior, lower, junior, minor, lesser
☞ **1** domineering, rebellious **2** superior, senior, more important

subside v
1 DECREASE, lower, get lower, lessen, diminish, dwindle, decline, wane, peter out, ebb, recede, moderate, die down, quieten, let up, fall, slacken, ease, lull, slake
OLD adaw, assuage, quell, quench
FORMAL abate
COLLOQ. pipe down
2 SINK, collapse, cave in, settle, descend, lower, fall, drop, founder, dissolve
OLD swoon
☞ **1** rise, increase

subsidence n
collapse, decline, decrease, descent, settlement, sinking, slackening, lessening, ebb, de-escalation, settling
FORMAL abatement, detumescence, diminution
☞ increase

subsidiary adj, n
◆ adj
auxiliary, supplementary, additional, ancillary, assistant, supporting, contributory, secondary, subordinate, subservient, lesser, minor
☞ primary, chief, major
◆ n
branch, offshoot, division, section, part, wing

subsidize v
support, back, endorse, underwrite, sponsor, finance, fund, invest in, give a subsidy to, pay part of the cost of, contribute to, aid, promote

subsidy n
grant, allowance, assistance, help, aid, contribution, sponsorship, finance, funding, investment, support, backing, endorsement, underwriting
FORMAL subvention

subsist v
exist, continue, endure, hold out, live, survive, remain, last, eke out an existence

subsistence n
living, survival, existence, continuance, livelihood, maintenance, support, keep, sustenance, nourishment, food, provisions, rations, aliment

substance n
1 MATTER, material, stuff, fabric, essence, mass, medium, entity, body, solidity, materiality, tangibility, concreteness, reality, actuality, ground, foundation
FORMAL corporeality
2 SUBJECT, subject matter, matter, topic, theme, text, burden, pith, gist, meaning, meaningfulness, significance, validity, truth, foundation, ground, basis, force, power, weight
FORMAL import
3 *a person of substance*
wealth, money, prosperity, riches, fortune, assets, means, resources, affluence, power, influence

substandard adj
second-rate, inferior, imperfect, damaged, shoddy, poor, inadequate, unacceptable
COLLOQ. below par, not up to scratch; *Aust & NZ* crook
☞ first-rate, superior, perfect

substantial adj
1 LARGE, big, siz(e)able, ample, measurable, generous, great, considerable, significant, important, meaningful, notable, remarkable, weighty, worthwhile, valuable
COLLOQ. tidy, pretty
2 WELL-BUILT, solid, stout, sturdy, strong, tough, hard, durable, sound, cast-iron
3 TANGIBLE, material, existing, concrete, real, actual, true
FORMAL corporeal
4 BASIC, essential, central, primary, main, principal, fundamental, inherent, intrinsic
5 WEALTHY, prosperous, rich, successful, affluent, powerful, influential
☞ **1** small, insignificant **2** flimsy **3** insubstantial, imaginary **5** poor

substantially adv
1 SIGNIFICANTLY, largely, considerably, to a great extent
2 ESSENTIALLY, fundamentally, mainly, in the main, materially, to all intents and purposes, in effect, at heart
☞ **1** slightly

substantiate v
prove, verify, confirm, uphold, support, back up, bear out, authenticate, validate
FORMAL corroborate
☞ disprove, refute

substantive adj
real, substantial, material, factual, valid, concrete, solid, fundamental, intrinsic

substitute v, n, adj
◆ v
1 CHANGE, exchange, swap, switch, interchange, replace, use instead
2 STAND IN, cover, deputize, understudy, relieve, take over, take the place of, double, act instead of
COLLOQ. fill in, sub
◆ n
reserve, stand-by, supply, locum, understudy, stand-in, replacement, relief, surrogate, proxy, agent, deputy, makeshift, stopgap
FORMAL *locum tenens*
COLLOQ. temp, sub, fill-in; *N Am* pinch-hitter
◆ adj
reserve, temporary, relief, acting, deputy, surrogate, proxy, replacement, alternative, stand-by, stand-in

substitution n
change, exchange, replacement, interchange, swap, swapping, switch, switching

subsume v
include, incorporate, embody, contain, enclose, hold,
encompass, cover, take in, admit, insert, introduce, add,
enter, put in, add in, count in, contain
FORMAL comprehend, comprise, embrace
ᙖ exclude, omit

subterfuge n
trick, stratagem, scheme, ploy, ruse, wile, intrigue,
expedient, manoeuvre, deviousness, evasion, deception,
artifice, pretence, excuse, pretext
FORMAL machination, duplicity
COLLOQ. dodge
ᙖ openness, honesty

subtle adj
1 DELICATE, understated, implied, indirect, low-key, slight,
minute, tenuous, elusive, faint, indistinct, indefinite, mild,
toned-down, fine, nice, refined, sophisticated, deep,
profound, scholastic
OLD subtil, suttle
2 ARTFUL, cunning, crafty, sly, devious, wily, indirect,
shrewd, astute, discreet, discriminating, tactful, clever,
strategic, intricate, complex
OLD subtil, suttle
ᙖ 1 blatant, obvious 2 artless, open, indiscreet, tactless

subtlety n
1 DELICACY, nicety, nuance, refinement, finesse, faintness,
indistinctness, indefiniteness, mutedness, sophistication
OLD suttletie
2 ARTFULNESS, cunning, wiliness, guile, deviousness,
craftiness, cleverness, discernment, astuteness, skill,
discrimination, intricacy, slyness, acuteness, acumen
OLD suttletie
FORMAL sagacity

subtly adv
1 *subtly different*
indirectly, tenuously, mildly, faintly, indistinctly, indefinitely
OLD suttly
2 *subtly manipulate an audience*
deceitfully, deviously, artfully, cunningly, slyly, cleverly,
astutely
OLD suttly
ᙖ 1 obviously 2 openly

subtract v
deduct, take away, remove, dock, withdraw, debit, detract,
diminish
ᙖ add

suburb n
suburbia, outskirts, commuter belt, residential area,
dormitory (town), *banlieue, faubourg*; N Am bedroom
suburb
FORMAL purlieus
ᙖ centre, heart

suburban adj
1 *a suburban railway*
commuter, residential
2 *suburban attitudes*
conventional, dull, unimaginative, narrow, narrow-
minded, parochial, provincial, insular, bourgeois, middle-
class
COLLOQ. common-or-garden

subversive adj, n
♦ adj
seditious, treasonous, treacherous, traitorous,
revolutionary, inflammatory, incendiary, disruptive,
troublemaking, riotous, weakening, undermining,
discrediting, destructive
ᙖ loyal
♦ n
seditionist, terrorist, dissident, traitor, quisling, troublemaker
COLLOQ. freedom fighter, fifth columnist

subvert v
undermine, destroy, ruin, pervert, corrupt, confound,
overthrow, deprave, demoralize, contaminate, poison,
overturn, upset, disrupt, invalidate, wreck, demolish,
debase, raze, sabotage
FORMAL vitiate
ᙖ boost, uphold

subway n
1 UNDERGROUND RAILWAY, underground, metro
COLLOQ. tube
2 UNDERPASS, tunnel, pedestrian tunnel, underground
passage

succeed v
1 TRIUMPH, do well, be successful, thrive, flourish, prosper,
make good, manage, carry out, complete, achieve,
accomplish, reach, realize, attain, fulfil, prevail, work, work
out, get results
COLLOQ. make it, get on, bring off, pull off, turn up trumps,
take over, steal the show, go places, win the day, land/fall
on your feet, bring home the bacon, strike gold, hit the
jackpot
2 *winter succeeds autumn*
follow, come after, replace, take the place of, result, ensue
ᙖ 1 fail; *colloq.* flop 2 precede, come before
▪ **succeed to**
come into, enter upon, inherit, replace, take over,
supersede
FORMAL accede, assume
ᙖ abdicate, precede

succeeding adj
following, next, subsequent, ensuing, coming, to come,
later, successive
TECHNICAL hereditary
ᙖ previous, earlier, prior

success n
1 TRIUMPH, victory, positive result, luck, fortune, prosperity,
happiness, fame, eminence, completion, achievement,
accomplishment, realization, attainment, fulfilment
2 CELEBRITY, star, winner, bestseller, hit, sensation
COLLOQ. somebody, VIP, celeb, big name, bigwig, big shot,
wow, sell-out, box-office hit, smash hit, smash
ᙖ 1 failure, disaster 2 failure, loser; *colloq.* write-off, flop,
dead loss

successful adj
1 VICTORIOUS, triumphant, winning, lucky, fortunate,
prosperous, wealthy, affluent, thriving, flourishing,
booming, moneymaking, lucrative, profitable, rewarding,
satisfying, fruitful, productive
2 *a successful writer*
famous, well-known, popular, leading, bestselling, top,
unbeaten
ᙖ 1 unsuccessful, unprofitable, fruitless 2 unknown, little-
known

successfully adv
great, fine, well, victoriously, beautifully, famously
COLLOQ. swimmingly
ᙖ unsuccessfully

succession n
1 SERIES, sequence, order, progression, run, chain, string,
cycle, continuation, flow, course, line, train, procession
2 *the succession to the throne*
accession, attaining, elevation, inheritance
FORMAL assumption
▪ **in succession**
successively, consecutively, sequentially, uninterruptedly,
running, in a row, one after the other
COLLOQ. on the trot

successive adj
consecutive, sequential, following, succeeding, running,
serial

successively *adv*
consecutively, in succession, sequentially, uninterruptedly, running, one after the other
COLLOQ. on the trot

successor *n*
replacement, substitute, relief, descendant, beneficiary, heir, co-heir, inheritor, next in line

succinct *adj*
concise, short, brief, terse, crisp, pithy, compact, condensed, summary, to the point, in a word, Laconian
long, lengthy, wordy, verbose

succinctly *adv*
concisely, briefly, in brief, tersely, crisply, pithily, compactly, to the point, in a word
wordily, verbosely

succour *n, v*
♦ *n*
help, aid, assistance, support, comfort, relief
FORMAL ministrations
COLLOQ. helping hand
♦ *v*
help, help out, aid, assist, comfort, encourage, support, relieve, foster, minister to, nurse, befriend
undermine

succulent *adj*
fleshy, juicy, moist, luscious, mouthwatering, lush, rich, mellow
dry

succumb *v*
1 GIVE IN, give way, yield, submit, knuckle under, surrender, capitulate, collapse, fall
2 *succumb to an illness*
catch, go down with, pick up, die of/from
FORMAL contract
1 overcome, overwhelm, master

suck *v*
draw (in), imbibe, absorb, blot up, soak up, extract, drain, absorb, pull, sponge, suckle, hoover
■ **suck up to**
fawn, flatter, ingratiate, toady, creep, grovel, curry favour, truckle
COLLOQ. lick someone's boots

sucker *n*
fool, victim, dupe, stooge, sap, leech
COLLOQ. pushover, mug, butt, cat's-paw

suckle *v*
breastfeed, feed, nurse

suction *n*
sucking, drawing-in, absorbing, extraction, draining

sudden *adj*
unexpected, unforeseen, unanticipated, surprising, startling, dramatic, abrupt, sharp, quick, fast, swift, rapid, speedy, meteoric, immediate, instantaneous, prompt, hurried, hasty, rash, impetuous, impulsive
COLLOQ. snap, spur-of-the-moment
expected, predictable, gradual, slow

suddenly *adv*
unexpectedly, all of a sudden, quickly, abruptly, sharply, immediately, instantaneously, without warning, all at once
COLLOQ. out of the blue, from out of nowhere

suddenness *n*
unexpectedness, abruptness, hurriedness, haste, hastiness, impulsiveness
slowness

suds *n*
bubbles, soapiness, lather, froth, foam

sue *v*
1 PROSECUTE, charge, bring charges against, take (legal)
action against, indict, take to court, bring to trial
2 SUMMON, solicit, appeal, beg, petition, plead
FORMAL beseech

suffer *v*
1 HURT, ache, be in pain, be afflicted, agonize, grieve, sorrow
COLLOQ. go through the mill
2 UNDERGO, experience, go through, feel, meet with, endure, sustain
3 BEAR, support, stand, put up with, allow, permit, tolerate, endure
FORMAL abide

suffering *n*
pain, discomfort, hurt, hurting, agony, anguish, affliction, distress, misery, hardship, wretchedness, plight, adversity, ordeal, torment, torture
ease, comfort

suffice *v*
do, satisfy, be sufficient, be enough, be adequate, answer, measure up, serve, content
COLLOQ. fit/fill the bill

sufficiency *n*
adequateness, adequacy, enough, plenty, satiety, competence
FORMAL sufficience
insufficiency, inadequacy

sufficient *adj*
enough, adequate, ample, plenty, satisfactory, effective
COLLOQ. decent
insufficient, inadequate

suffocate *v*
asphyxiate, smother, stifle, choke, strangle, throttle, be/make breathless, smoke; *dialect* stive; *Scot* smore

suffrage *n*
franchise, right to vote, right of representation
FORMAL enfranchisement

suffuse *v*
spread, imbue, infuse, permeate, pervade, steep, transfuse, cover, flood, mantle, bathe, colour, redden

sugar

Kinds of sugar include:

beet sugar	golden syrup	powdered sugar
brown sugar	granulated sugar	refined sugar
cane sugar	icing sugar	sucrose
caster sugar	invert sugar	sugar loaf
crystallized sugar	jaggery	sugar lump
demerara	lactose	syrup
dextrose	maltose	treacle
fructose	maple syrup	unrefined sugar
glucose	molasses	

sugary *adj*
1 *sugary drinks*
sweet, syrupy, sweetened, saccharine, sickly
2 SENTIMENTAL, emotional, gushing, touching, maudlin, mawkish
COLLOQ. soppy, lovey-dovey, slushy, mushy, schmaltzy, corny, sickly, gushy, sloppy

suggest *v*
1 PROPOSE, put forward, advocate, recommend, submit, advise, counsel, move, table, nominate, bring forward, come up with, envisage, present
COLLOQ. float, vote
2 IMPLY, insinuate, hint (at), intimate, evoke, bring to mind, indicate, give the impression, allude, connote, prompt, savour, smack (of), smell (of)

suggestion *n*

1 PROPOSAL, proposition, motion, recommendation, submission, idea, plan, hint, piece of advice, pointer
COLLOQ. wrinkle, kite
2 IMPLICATION, insinuation, intimation, innuendo, allusion, prompting
OLD (*Shakesp*) prompture
3 HINT, intimation, suspicion, trace, touch, indication, note, pointer, smack, wind, whiff; *dialect* twang

suggestive *adj*

1 EVOCATIVE, reminiscent, expressive, meaning, indicative
FORMAL redolent
2 *a suggestive remark*
indecent, immodest, improper, indelicate, titillating, off-colour, sexual, risqué, bawdy, dirty, smutty, ribald, lewd, provocative
COLLOQ. blue
F3 1 inexpressive **2** decent, clean

suicide *n*

killing yourself, self-destruction, self-murder, taking of your (own) life, self-slaughter, parasuicide, hara-kiri, suttee
FORMAL *felo de se*, self-immolation
COLLOQ. topping yourself, doing away with yourself, cutting your (own) throat, ending it all, hari-kari
■ **commit suicide**
kill yourself, take your (own) life
COLLOQ. top yourself, do yourself in, do away with yourself, end it all, commit hari-kari

suit *n, v*

♦ *n*
1 *wear a suit*
outfit, costume, dress, clothing, set of clothes, ensemble
OLD suite
2 LAWSUIT, action, case, cause, dispute, argument, contest, prosecution, litigation, proceedings, process, trial
OLD suite
♦ *v*
1 GO WELL WITH, complement, match, tally with, agree with, harmonize with, fit, befit, become, look good/attractive on, flatter
2 PLEASE, satisfy, answer, gratify
3 BE CONVENIENT FOR, be suitable for, be appropriate for, be applicable to, be acceptable to, be satisfactory to, qualify for
FORMAL suffice
COLLOQ. fit/fill the bill
F3 1 clash, jar **2** displease, dissatisfy **3** be unsuitable for, be inconvenient for

suitability *n*

appropriateness, aptness, fitness, fittingness, opportuneness, timeliness, convenience, rightness
FORMAL appositeness
F3 unsuitability, inappropriateness

suitable *adj*

appropriate, fitting, convenient, opportune, suited, in keeping, right, compatible, well-suited, well-matched, due, apt, relevant, applicable, fit, adequate, satisfactory, acceptable, befitting, becoming, proper, right
OLD seemly; (*Shakesp*) liable
FORMAL apposite, pertinent
COLLOQ. (right/just) up someone's street
F3 unsuitable, inappropriate

suitably *adv*

appropriately, fittingly, properly, fitly, acceptably, as well, accordingly, quite
F3 unsuitably

suitcase *n*

case, vanity-case, bag, holdall, portmanteau, valise, overnight-bag, flight bag, hand-luggage, travel bag, attaché case, portfolio, trunk

suite *n*

1 APARTMENT, rooms, set of rooms, chambers, flat, household
2 SET, series, collection, sequence, train, furniture
TECHNICAL partita
3 ATTENDANTS, retinue, entourage, court, train, tail, escort, followers, retainers, servants

suitor *n*

admirer, boyfriend, lover, young man, wooer, beau, follower, pretendant
OLD swain

sulk *v, n*

♦ *v*
mope, brood, pout, grouse, grump, pull a long face
COLLOQ. be miffed, be in a huff
♦ *n*
mood, temper, bad mood, bad temper, pique
COLLOQ. huff, miff

sulkily *adv*

morosely, moodily, resentfully, grudgingly, sullenly, crossly
F3 cheerfully

sulky *adj*

brooding, moody, morose, resentful, grudging, disgruntled, put out, cross, moping, grumpy, out of sorts, bad-tempered, sullen, aloof, unsociable
COLLOQ. miffed, ratty, huffy
F3 cheerful, good-tempered, sociable

sullen *adj*

1 SULKY, moody, morose, glum, gloomy, silent, uncommunicative, surly, sour, cross, churlish, perverse, obstinate, stubborn, resentful
2 DARK, gloomy, sombre, dismal, cheerless, dull, leaden, heavy
F3 1 cheerful, happy **2** fine, clear

sullenly *adv*

glumly, morosely, moodily, sulkily, gloomily, crossly, sourly, churlishly, stubbornly, resentfully, obstinately

sullenness *n*

moroseness, sulkiness, surliness, moodiness, brooding, glowering, sourness, glumness, heaviness
F3 cheerfulness

sully *v*

dirty, soil, defile, pollute, contaminate, taint, spoil, mar, spot, blemish, besmirch, stain, tarnish, damage, disgrace, dishonour
OLD befoul
F3 cleanse, honour

sultry *adj*

1 *sultry weather*
hot, sweltering, sweltry, stifling, stuffy, oppressive, suffocating, close, airless, humid, muggy, soggy, sticky
2 SENSUAL, voluptuous, passionate, attractive, sexy, provocative, seductive, tempting, alluring
F3 1 cool, cold

sum *n, v*

♦ *n*
total, sum total, aggregate, whole, entirety, number, quantity, amount, tally, reckoning, score, result, answer, summary, culmination
■ **sum up**
1 SUMMARIZE, review, recapitulate, conclude, close
COLLOQ. put in a nutshell, recap
2 EPITOMIZE, embody, encapsulate, exemplify
3 ASSESS, evaluate, gauge, review, consider, size up

summarily *adv*

immediately, promptly, speedily, swiftly, without delay, hastily, abruptly, arbitrarily
FORMAL expeditiously, peremptorily, forthwith

summarize v

outline, précis, condense, abridge, abbreviate, shorten, sum up, epitomize, encapsulate, review, sketch, outline, synopsize, minute, abstract, resume, docket
COLLOQ. recap
◨ expand (on)

summary n, adj

◆ n

synopsis, résumé, outline, main points, abstract, précis, condensation, digest, compendium, abridgement, summing-up, review, recapitulation, overview, plan, summation, short, tabloid, argument, minutes, epitome, docket, aide-mémoire, aperçu, curriculum vitae; N Am wrap-up
TECHNICAL brief, memorandum, balance-sheet, bank statement, creed
FORMAL conspectus, summa
COLLOQ. rundown, recap

◆ adj

short, succinct, brief, curt, cursory, swift, speedy, hasty, prompt, without delay, immediate, instant, instantaneous, direct, unceremonious, offhand, without formality, arbitrary; Scot summar
FORMAL peremptory
◨ lengthy, careful

summerhouse n

belvedere, gazebo, pavilion

summit n

1 TOP, peak, pinnacle, point, crest, crown, head, vertex, acme, apex, zenith, apogee, climax, culmination, height
2 a NATO summit
meeting, conference, negotiation, talks, discussion, consultation
◨ 1 bottom, foot, nadir

summon v

call, send for, order, demand, invite, bid, beckon, gather, assemble, convene, rally, muster (up), mobilize, rouse, arouse, challenge, warn, drum up, work up, pluck up, screw up, hail, recollect, cite, page, ring, buzz, gong, knell, toll, trumpet, whistle, whoop, throw the handkerchief
TECHNICAL conjure; Scot sist
OLD provoke, accite, history; (Shakesp & Spenser) convent
FORMAL convoke, preconize
COLLOQ. shake
◨ dismiss

■ **summon up**

gather, assemble, convene, rally, muster, mobilize, rouse, arouse, evoke, revive, call to mind

summons n

writ, subpoena, citation, order, call, injunction

sumptuous adj

luxurious, plush, lavish, extravagant, rich, costly, expensive, dear, splendid, magnificent, gorgeous, superb, grand, de luxe
FORMAL opulent
◨ plain, poor

sun n, v

◆ n

star, daystar, sunlight, light, daylight, sunshine
Related adjective: solar

◆ v

sunbathe, tan, brown, bake, bask
FORMAL insolate

sunbathe v

sun, bask, tan, brown, bake, sunbake
FORMAL insolate

sunburnt adj

burnt, red, weather-beaten, blistered, blistering, peeling, inflamed
◨ pale

sunder v

split, separate, divide, part, cut, chop, sever
FORMAL cleave, dissever, dissunder
◨ join

sundry adj

various, diverse, miscellaneous, assorted, varied, different, several, some, a few

sunk adj

failed, lost, ruined, finished, doomed
COLLOQ. done for, up the creek, up the spout, in a fix/jam

sunken adj

1 SUBMERGED, buried, recessed, lower, lowered, below ground level
2 sunken eyes
depressed, concave, hollow, hollowed, haggard, drawn

sunless adj

bleak, overcast, dark, cloudy, grey, hazy, gloomy, depressing, dismal, dreary, sombre, cheerless
◨ sunny, bright

sunlight n

light, daylight, sun, sun's rays, natural light

sunny adj

1 FINE, cloudless, unclouded, clear, summery, sunshiny, sunlit, bright, brilliant
2 CHEERFUL, happy, joyful, smiling, cheery, glad, bright, merry, beaming, radiant, light-hearted, bubbly, bouncy, buoyant, optimistic, hopeful, pleasant
FORMAL blithe
◨ 1 sunless, cloudy, dull 2 gloomy, pessimistic, glum

sunrise n

dawn, crack of dawn, break of day, daybreak, daylight, first light, sun-up, cock-crow, aurora

sunset n

sundown, dusk, twilight, gloaming, evening, close of day, nightfall

super adj

great, excellent, superb, wonderful, outstanding, marvellous, magnificent, glorious, incomparable, peerless, matchless, sensational
COLLOQ. smashing, terrific, top-notch, neat, ace, brill
SLANG mega, cool, wicked
◨ poor; colloq. lousy

superannuated adj

antiquated, old, elderly, pensioned off, obsolete, senile, retired, aged, decrepit
FORMAL moribund
COLLOQ. past it, put out to grass
◨ young

superb adj

excellent, first-rate, first-class, superior, superlative, choice, fine, exquisite, brilliant, gorgeous, magnificent, splendid, lavish, grand, wonderful, great, outstanding, remarkable, unrivalled, unsurpassed, marvellous, admirable, impressive, breathtaking, dazzling
COLLOQ. fabulous, smashing, terrific, neat, ace, brill
◨ bad, poor, inferior

supercilious adj

arrogant, condescending, patronizing, overbearing, scornful, lofty, lordly, imperious, insolent, proud, disdainful, haughty, contemptuous
FORMAL vainglorious
COLLOQ. snooty, snotty, stuck-up, toffee-nosed, uppish, uppity, hoity-toity, jumped-up, too big for your boots
◨ humble, self-effacing

superficial adj

surface, external, exterior, peripheral, outward, outer, apparent, alleged, seeming, cosmetic, skin-deep, shallow, one-dimensional, slight, trivial, facile, lightweight,

insignificant, frivolous, casual, cursory, sketchy, careless, slapdash, perfunctory, hasty, hurried, passing
FORMAL ostensible
◪ internal, deep, thorough

superficiality n

shallowness, slightness, triviality, lightness, worthlessness, frivolousness, simplicity
◪ depth, seriousness

superficially adv

externally, on the surface, outwardly, apparently, seemingly, casually, carelessly, hurriedly
FORMAL ostensibly
◪ in depth

superfluity n

redundancy, excess, surfeit, surplus, extra, exuberance, glut, superabundance, excessiveness
TECHNICAL pleonasm
FORMAL plethora
◪ lack

superfluous adj

extra, spare, excess, surplus, remaining, redundant, waste, to spare, unnecessary, unneeded, needless, gratuitous, unwanted, unwarranted, uncalled-for, excessive, frilly, at a discount, fifth-wheel
OLD (*Shakesp*) prolixious
FORMAL supernumerary, otiose, *de trop*, excrescent
◪ necessary, needed, required, wanted, essential

superhuman adj

great, immense, supernatural, herculean, heroic, extraordinary, stupendous, divine, paranormal, phenomenal
FORMAL preternatural, prodigious
◪ average, ordinary

superimpose v

put on, add, overlay, lay over, lay on, transfer

superintend v

supervise, oversee, overlook, inspect, run, manage, administer, direct, be in charge of, be responsible for, control, be in control of, handle, steer

superintendence n

supervision, oversight, inspection, direction, control, government, charge, care, management, administration, running, guidance, surveillance

superintendent n

supervisor, overseer, director, governor, controller, conductor, administrator, manager, inspector, chief, curator, warden, intendant, viewer
TECHNICAL provincial
COLLOQ. gaffer, boss, super

superior adj, n

♦ adj
1 EXCELLENT, first-class, first-rate, high-class, high-quality, good-quality, exclusive, prime, premium, quality, prize, choice, select, fine, de luxe, admirable, distinguished, exceptional, unrivalled, par excellence
COLLOQ. top-notch, top-flight, top-drawer
2 BETTER, preferred, greater, higher, higher in rank, senior
3 HAUGHTY, lordly, lofty, pretentious, snobbish, supercilious, disdainful, condescending, patronizing
COLLOQ. snooty, stuck-up, toffee-nosed, uppish, uppity, jumped-up, too big for your boots
◪ **1** inferior, average **2** inferior, worse, lower **3** humble, self-effacing
♦ n
senior, elder, better, chief, principal, director, manager, foreman, supervisor
COLLOQ. boss
◪ subordinate, inferior, junior, assistant

superiority n

advantage, lead, edge, supremacy, pre-eminence, eminence, dominance, predominance
FORMAL ascendancy
◪ inferiority

superlative adj

best, greatest, highest, first-class, first-rate, supreme, unbeatable, unrivalled, unparalleled, matchless, peerless, unsurpassed, unbeaten, excellent, brilliant, magnificent, outstanding
FORMAL transcendent, consummate
COLLOQ. ace, brill
◪ poor, average, mediocre

supermarket n

superstore, hypermarket, cash-and-carry

supernatural adj

paranormal, unnatural, abnormal, otherworldly, spiritual, miraculous, psychic, mystic, mystical, occult, daemonic, witchlike, hidden, mysterious, magical, magic, phantom, fey, ghostly, eerie, weird, uncanny; *Scot* eldritch
FORMAL metaphysical, transcendental, preternatural, hyperphysical
◪ natural, normal

supernumerary adj

superfluous, surplus, redundant, spare, excess, excessive, extra, extraordinary
◪ necessary

supersede v

succeed, replace, supplant, usurp, oust, displace, take the place of, take over from, remove
SLANG Stellenbosch

superstition n

myth, old wives' tale, fallacy, delusion, illusion, magic

superstitious adj

mythical, false, fallacious, irrational, groundless, delusive, illusory
◪ rational, logical, factual

supervise v

oversee, watch (over), look after, keep an eye on, inspect, superintend, run, manage, administer, direct, guide, conduct, preside over, be in charge of, be responsible for, be in control of, control, handle, administer, monitor, invigilate, umpire, edit, nanny, bear-lead; *Scot* targe

supervision n

surveillance, care, charge, superintendence, oversight, running, management, administration, direction, control, guidance, inspection, instruction

supervisor n

overseer, inspector, superintendent, chief, director, administrator, manager, steward, foreman, forewoman, monitor, invigilator, umpire, governor, warden
COLLOQ. boss

supervisory adj

administrative, managerial, executive, overseeing, superintendent
FORMAL directorial

supine adj

1 PROSTRATE, flat, horizontal
FORMAL recumbent
2 LAZY, idle, inactive, lethargic, careless, heedless, resigned, bored, uninterested, apathetic, indifferent, weak, sluggish, slothful, inert, languid, negligent, passive, listless, spiritless, unresisting
FORMAL indolent, torpid
COLLOQ. spineless
◪ **1** upright **2** alert

supper *n*
dinner, evening meal, tea, snack
OLD rere-supper; (*Shakesp*) aftersupper

supplant *v*
replace, supersede, usurp, oust, displace, take the place of, take over from, remove, overthrow, topple, unseat

supple *adj*
flexible, bending, stretching, elastic, pliant, pliable, plastic, lithe, limber, graceful, loose-limbed, loose-jointed, double-jointed, willowish, agile, sinuous, whippy, lofty; *dialect* souple, wandle; *Scot* leish
🖪 stiff, rigid, inflexible

supplement *n, v*
♦ *n*
addition, additive, extra, insert, pull-out, add-on, addendum, appendix, rider, postscript, sequel, annex, schedule, relay
TECHNICAL codicil
OLD sooterkin
♦ *v*
add to, boost, reinforce, increase, fill up, top up, complement, extend, eke out
FORMAL augment
🖪 deplete, use up

🛈 **supplement, complement** or **compliment**?
See panel at **complement**.

supplementary *adj*
additional, extra, added, auxiliary, second, secondary, attached, complementary, accompanying, ancillary, bolt-on
TECHNICAL ripieno
OLD (*Shakesp*) suppliant
FORMAL expletory

🛈 **supplementary, complementary** or **complimentary**?
See panel at **complementary**.

suppliant *adj*
begging, entreating, imploring, supplicating, craving
FORMAL beseeching, importunate

supplicant *n*
petitioner, pleader, suitor, applicant, suppliant
FORMAL postulant

supplicate *v*
request, entreat, appeal, petition, plead, pray, solicit
FORMAL invoke, beseech

supplication *n*
request, appeal, entreaty, petition, plea, pleading, prayer, orison, suit
FORMAL invocation, imploration, solicitation, rogation

supplicatory *adj*
begging, petitioning, supplicating, imploring
FORMAL beseeching, imprecatory, precative, precatory

supplier *n*
dealer, seller, vendor, wholesaler, retailer, outfitter, provider, contributor, donor

supply *v, n*
♦ *v*
provide, furnish, equip, outfit, fit out, stock, fill, replenish, give, donate, grant, endow, contribute, yield, produce, sell
FORMAL endue, proffer
🖪 take, receive
♦ *n*
1 STOCK, source, amount, quantity, fund, reservoir, store, reserve, heap, mass, pile, stockpile, hoard, cache
2 PROVISIONS, stores, food, rations, equipment, materials, necessities
🖪 1 lack

support *v, n*
♦ *v*
1 BACK, second, defend, champion, advocate, further, be in favour of, be in sympathy with, be behind/with, promote, foster, help, aid, assist, rally round
FORMAL espouse, give countenance to
COLLOQ. run with, throw your weight behind
2 HELP, encourage, comfort, motivate, befriend, care for, sympathize with, be kind to, give strength to, give moral support to, be supportive to
3 HOLD UP, bear, carry, take the weight of, sustain, brace, reinforce, strengthen, prop (up), shore up, buttress, underpin, bolster (up)
4 MAINTAIN, keep, look after, take care of, provide for, sustain, feed, nourish
5 *support a statement*
endorse, confirm, back up, bear out, verify, authenticate, substantiate, validate, ratify, document
FORMAL corroborate
6 FINANCE, fund, subsidize, underwrite, back, sponsor, contribute to, give a donation to
🖪 1 oppose 4 live off 5 contradict
♦ *n*
1 BACKING, allegiance, loyalty, defence, protection, patronage, approval, encouragement, comfort, relief, help, aid, assistance
FORMAL espousal
2 PROP, stay, post, pillar, brace, buttress, bolster, trestle, crutch, foundation(s), underpinning, substructure, skeleton, base
3 HELP, encouragement, comfort, care, sympathy, motivation, strength, friendship, moral support
COLLOQ. tower of strength
4 MAINTENANCE, keep, provision, sustenance, food, subsistence
5 FINANCE, funding, assistance, capital, sponsorship, grant, donation, subsidy, contribution, patronage
6 EVIDENCE, confirmation, backing, verification, authentication, substantiation, validation, ratification
🖪 1 opposition, hostility

Synonym nuances
verb sense 2
Help can be widely used to suggest giving assistance, while **encourage** has more to do with inspiring with confidence, and **motivate** suggests providing the necessary incentive to achieve something.
Comfort, however, would be specifically used of cheering or consoling someone: *he was comforted by her reassurances*, while **sympathize with** is more suggestive of identifying with another's problems. **Care for** also implies emotional concern and involvement: *he cared for his elderly parents at home*, and **befriend** could be used of a specific support born of compassion and given at a time of need: *numerous Czechoslovaks befriended the refugees*.

---

supporter *n*
fan, follower, adherent, advocate, champion, defender, upholder, promoter, sympathizer, seconder, second, apostle, patron, sponsor, donor, contributor, partner, co-worker, helper, ally, friend, voter, well-wisher, apologist, henchman, militant, prop, bottle-holder, ideologist, janizary; *N Am* booster; *Scot* stoop
OLD understander
COLLOQ. angel
🖪 opponent

supportive *adj*
helpful, caring, attentive, sympathetic, understanding, comforting, reassuring, encouraging, affirmative, positive, sensitive, in someone's corner, on someone's side
🖪 discouraging

suppose v

1 THINK, guess, believe, consider, imagine, reckon, fancy, judge, expect, infer, conclude, take for granted, perceive; *N Am* calculate
OLD (*Shakesp*) propose; (*Spenser*) devise
FORMAL conjecture, surmise, opine
COLLOQ. dare say
2 ASSUME, presume, imply, require, take, say, put (the) case, hypothesize, uphold, warrant, sepad
FORMAL postulate, posit, presuppose

supposed *adj*

alleged, reported, rumoured, assumed, presumed, reputed, so-called, believed, imagined, hypothetical
FORMAL putative

■ **supposed to**

meant to, intended to, expected to, required to, obliged to

supposedly *adv*

allegedly, apparently, reportedly, by all accounts
FORMAL ostensibly, putatively

supposition *n*

assumption, presumption, guess, speculation, theory, hypothesis, idea, notion
FORMAL conjecture, surmise, postulation, presupposition
E3 knowledge

suppress v

crush, stamp out, put an end to, quash, squash, quell, subdue, stop, silence, hush up, censor, stifle, smother, strangle, strangulate, throttle, choke, squelch, block out, blank out, conceal, withhold, hold back, control, keep under control, contain, restrain, check, keep in check, repress, inhibit, cancel, cushion, elide, black out, gulp back/down, mince, sink, submerge, vote down, burke
OLD stay
FORMAL vanquish
COLLOQ. crack/clamp down on, kill, knock on the head, put the tin lid/hat on
E3 encourage, incite

suppression *n*

crushing, quashing, quelling, elimination, prohibition, censorship, check, inhibition, dissolution, smothering, cover-up, termination, extinction
COLLOQ. clampdown, crackdown
E3 encouragement, incitement

suppurate v

gather, discharge, fester, ooze, weep
TECHNICAL maturate

suppuration *n*

festering, pus, mattering
TECHNICAL diapyesis

supremacy *n*

dominance, domination, dominion, mastery, lordship, rule, power, control, predominance, primacy, sovereignty, sway, pre-eminence
FORMAL ascendancy, hegemony, paramountcy

supreme *adj*

1 GREATEST, best, highest, excellent, top, crowning, culminating, first, first-rate, first-class, leading, foremost, chief, principal, head, sovereign, pre-eminent, predominant, prevailing, world-beating, unsurpassed, second-to-none, incomparable, peerless, matchless, consummate, transcendent, superlative, prime
2 *the supreme sacrifice*
utmost, extreme, ultimate, final, last, greatest, highest
E3 1 lowly, poor

supremely *adv*

extremely, exceedingly, excessively, very, really, exceptionally, extraordinarily, intensely, thoroughly, remarkably, utterly, greatly, highly, unusually, uncommonly, inordinately, acutely, severely, decidedly
COLLOQ. terrifically

sure *adj, interj*

♦ *adj*
1 CERTAIN, convinced, assured, confident, decided, positive, definite, unmistakable, unfaltering, unwavering, clear, accurate, precise, unquestionable, indisputable, undoubted, undeniable, irrevocable, inevitable, guaranteed, bound
COLLOQ. pukka, as sure as eggs is eggs
2 SAFE, secure, fast, solid, firm, steady, stable, guaranteed, reliable, dependable, tested, loyal, faithful, trustworthy, steadfast, unwavering, unerring, unfailing, never-failing, infallible, effective, foolproof
FORMAL efficacious
COLLOQ. home and dry, sure-fire, sure-footed, safe as houses
E3 1 unsure, uncertain, hesitating, doubtful **2** unsafe, insecure
♦ *interj*
all right, fine, of course, right, indeed, agreed, very well
COLLOQ. OK, okay

■ **for sure**

definitely, for certain, positively, unquestionably, without question, absolutely, certainly, categorically, undeniably, clearly, undoubtedly, without doubt, unmistakably, plainly, obviously, indeed, indubitably

■ **make sure**

make certain, check, ensure, guarantee, confirm, verify

surely *adv*

certainly, without doubt, doubtlessly, undoubtedly, unquestionably, indubitably, definitely, assuredly, firmly, confidently, inevitably, inexorably

surety *n*

guarantee, indemnity, pledge, security, safety, warrant, warranty, certainty, bail, insurance, mortgagor, sponsor, bond, deposit, guarantor, hostage, bondsman

surface *n, v, adj*

♦ *n*
outside, outward appearance, exterior, façade, veneer, covering, skin, top, side, face, plane
E3 inside, interior
♦ *v*
rise, arise, come up, come to the surface, emerge, appear, reappear, materialize, come to light
E3 sink, disappear, vanish
♦ *adj*
superficial, outer, outside, outward, exterior, external, apparent
E3 interior

■ **on the surface**

superficially, externally, at first glance, apparently, seemingly
FORMAL ostensibly

surfeit *n, v*

♦ *n*
surplus, superfluity, excess, glut, satiation, satiety, superabundance, overindulgence, repleteness, repletion, stall; *Scot* staw
OLD (*Shakesp*) cloyment
FORMAL plethora
COLLOQ. bellyful; *Aust & NZ* gutful
E3 lack
♦ *v*
fill, overfill, overfeed, stuff, cram, glut, gorge, satiate, overcloy

surge *n, v*

♦ *n*
1 RUSH, gush, stream, sweep, pouring, flow, wave(s), billow, breaker, roller, swell, eddy; *Scot* jaw

OLD whelm

FORMAL efflux

2 INCREASE, upswing, upsurge, rise, escalation, intensification

♦ *v*

1 RUSH, gush, stream, sweep, pour, flow, break, swell, swirl, eddy, heave, roll, seethe, wallow

OLD welter; (*Spenser*) redound

2 INCREASE, rise, escalate, upsurge

surgeon *n*

COLLOQ. sawbones

Types of surgeon include:

brain surgeon	heart surgeon	tree surgeon
cosmetic surgeon	house surgeon	veterinary
dental surgeon	neurosurgeon	surgeon
eye surgeon	oral surgeon	
general surgeon	plastic surgeon	

---

surly *adj*

gruff, brusque, churlish, ungracious, uncivil, ill-natured, bad-tempered, cross, crusty, grumpy, testy, cantankerous, irascible, sullen, sulky, morose

COLLOQ. crabbed, grouchy, crotchety

Ea friendly, polite

surmise *v, n*

♦ *v*

infer, suppose, presume, assume, conclude, deduce, imagine, fancy, guess, consider, speculate, suspect

FORMAL conjecture, opine

Ea know

♦ *n*

inference, conclusion, deduction, supposition, hypothesis, assumption, presumption, speculation, guess, idea, suspicion, thought, opinion, notion, possibility

FORMAL conjecture

Ea certainty

surmount *v*

overcome, get over, conquer, master, triumph over, prevail over, surpass, exceed

FORMAL vanquish

surpass *v*

beat, outdo, exceed, outstrip, outclass, better, excel, transcend, tower above, outshine, overshadow, eclipse, surmount, go beyond, put down, cap, top, outbrag; *dialect* overgo; *Scot* ding

OLD outrival, pass; (*Shakesp*) outpeer, paragon; (*Spenser*) underlay

COLLOQ. whop, leave for dead, knock (the) spots off, knock the socks off, beat to sticks, bang

surpassing *adj*

exceptional, incomparable, outstanding, matchless, unrivalled, unsurpassed, rare, inimitable, extraordinary, supreme, phenomenal, transcendent

Ea poor

surplus *n, adj*

♦ *n*

excess, residue, remainder, balance, carry-over, superfluity, glut, surfeit, leftovers

Ea lack, shortage

♦ *adj*

excess, superfluous, redundant, extra, spare, remaining, unused, left over

surprise *v, n*

♦ *v*

1 AMAZE, startle, astonish, astound, stagger, take aback, stun, bewilder, confuse, disconcert, dismay

COLLOQ. flabbergast, nonplus, bowl over, wow, blow away, knock for six, knock someone down with a feather, take someone's breath away

2 CATCH RED-HANDED, catch in the act, catch unawares, expose, unmask, startle, burst in on, find (out)

COLLOQ. catch someone with their pants/trousers down

♦ *n*

amazement, astonishment, incredulity, wonder, bewilderment, dismay, shock, start, revelation

FORMAL surprisal

COLLOQ. bombshell, thunderbolt, bolt from the blue, curveball

Ea composure

See panel below

Synonym nuances

verb sense 1

You can use **amaze** to suggest filling with wonder as well as great surprise. The terms **astonish** and **astound** are even stronger, while **stagger** and **stun** suggest being overwhelmed, possibly even stupefied: *they were staggered by the distance he'd covered.*

  Startle can be used where there is a degree of fright: *startled by a sudden noise*, but **take aback** has more to do with the unexpected causing dismay: *he was taken aback by their outburst.*

  To use **bewilder** or **confuse** would put the emphasis on perplexity caused by the unexpected. Likewise, **disconcert** conveys a degree of disturbance at surprising events: *he was disconcerted by her sudden departure*, and **dismay** an element of alarm.

---

surprised *adj*

startled, amazed, astonished, astounded, staggered, thunderstruck, dumbfounded, speechless, lost for words, open-mouthed, shocked, stunned, jiggered, with raised eyebrows

COLLOQ. flabbergasted, nonplussed, gobsmacked

Ea unsurprised, composed

surprising *adj*

amazing, astonishing, astounding, staggering, stunning, incredible, extraordinary, remarkable, wonderful, startling, funny, strange, unexpected, unforeseen, unlooked-for

COLLOQ. shock, jaw-dropping

Ea unsurprising, expected

Expressions of surprise include:

bless my soul!	good grief!	*N Am* jeepers	my eye!	*Aust* strewth!	you could have
blimey!	good heavens!	I ask you!	my foot!	that's news to me!	knocked me
blow me down!	good lord!	I don't know!	my goodness!	the (very) idea!	down with a
by Jove!	Gordon Bennett!	I'll be blessed!	my word!	to think!	feather!
come off it!	gosh!	I'll be blowed!	no kidding!	well I never!	you don't say!
did you ever!	great Scott!	I'll be damned!	of all the ...!	wonders will	you're joking!
fancy that!	heavens above!	imagine that!	oh mother!	never cease!	you're kidding!
for goodness	holy smoke!	in heaven's name!	oh my!	would you	
sake!	how about that	Mama Mia!	stone me!	believe!	
for heaven's sake!	then!	*Irish* musha!	stone the crows!		

surprisingly *adv*
amazingly, astonishingly, incredibly, extraordinarily, remarkably, wonderfully, staggeringly, stunningly, funnily, strangely, unexpectedly
🔁 unsurprisingly, as expected

surrender *v, n*
♦ *v*
capitulate, submit, resign, concede, yield, give in, lay down your arms, strike/lower the flag, render, strike, kamerad, sacrifice, cede, give up, leave behind, let go of, relinquish, abandon, abdicate, for(e)go, waive, release, turn in; *Aust* bail up
TECHNICAL remise
OLD enfeoff
FORMAL succumb, renounce
COLLOQ. quit, throw in the towel/sponge, throw in your hand
♦ *n*
capitulation, resignation, submission, yielding, relinquishment, renunciation, abandonment, abdication, waiving, sacrifice, rendition
TECHNICAL remise
OLD surrendry
FORMAL cession

surreptitious *adj*
furtive, stealthy, sly, covert, veiled, hidden, secret, underhand, unauthorized
FORMAL clandestine
COLLOQ. sneaky
🔁 open, obvious

surrogate *n*
substitute, replacement, representative, stand-in, deputy, proxy

surround *v, n*
♦ *v*
encircle, ring, go round, gird, girdle, encompass, confine, envelop, encase, enclose, fence in, hem in, besiege, beset
OLD (*Shakesp*) enround
FORMAL environ
♦ *n*
border, edging, setting, edge, rim, brim, verge, margin, fringe, periphery, perimeter, circumference, bound, bounds, confine, confines, limit, brink

surrounding *adj*
encircling, bordering, adjacent, adjoining, neighbouring, nearby

surroundings *n*
neighbourhood, vicinity, locality, scene, setting, environment, habitat, environs, background, milieu, element, ambience

surveillance *n*
watch, observation, inspection, superintendence, supervision, vigilance, stewardship, guardianship, monitoring, spying, scrutiny, check, care, charge, control, direction, regulation

survey *v, n*
♦ *v*
1 VIEW, contemplate, observe, look at, look over, supervise, scan, scrutinize, examine, inspect, study, research, poll, review, consider, reconnoitre, prospect
TECHNICAL traverse, triangulate, plane-table
OLD overeye
FORMAL surview
COLLOQ. recce
2 ASSESS, estimate, evaluate, measure, plot, plan, map, chart
FORMAL appraise
COLLOQ. size up
♦ *n*
1 REVIEW, overview, view, scrutiny, examination, inspection, consideration, study, poll, appraisal, assessment,

measurement, valuation, prospect, reconnaissance, *tour d'horizon*
TECHNICAL traverse, triangulation, level
OLD perambulation
FORMAL conspectus
COLLOQ. once-over
2 QUESTIONNAIRE, quiz, test, form, study, probe, opinion poll, market research

surveyor *n*
inspector, examiner, assessor
TECHNICAL geodesist

survival *n*
continuance, endurance, persistence, perseverance, existence, withholding, coping, managing, will to live, staying power

survive *v*
outlive, outlast, endure, last, continue, persist, stay, remain, live (on), exist, withstand, get/come through, live through, hold out, cope, manage, weather, die hard, recover, rally
FORMAL be extant
COLLOQ. pull through, make it, keep your head above water
🔁 succumb, die

susceptibility *n*
liability, openness, vulnerability, defencelessness, weakness, proneness, responsiveness, sensitivity, suggestibility, gullibility, tendency
FORMAL predisposition, proclivity, propensity
🔁 impregnability, resistance

susceptible *adj*
liable, prone, inclined, disposed, predisposed, given, capable, subject, receptive, responsive, impressionable, impressible, easily led, credulous, gullible, suggestible, weak, vulnerable, at risk, defenceless, open, sensitive, tender
🔁 resistant, immune

suspect *v, adj*
♦ *v*
1 DOUBT, have doubts about, distrust, mistrust, fear, be wary of, have misgivings/qualms about, be uneasy about, call into question; *dialect* mislippen; *Scot* jalouse; *N Am* suspicion
OLD misdoubt
COLLOQ. smell a rat
2 *I suspect you're right*
believe, fancy, feel, guess, suppose, speculate, consider, conclude, infer, sniff, snuff; *Scot* jalouse; *N Am* suspicion
OLD misconceive, misdeem, smoke
FORMAL conjecture, surmise
COLLOQ. have a hunch, get it into your head, suss
♦ *adj*
suspicious, doubtful, dubious, questionable, debatable, unreliable, inadequate, insufficient
COLLOQ. iffy, dodgy, fishy
🔁 acceptable, reliable

suspend *v*
1 HANG, dangle, swing
TECHNICAL disperse, entrain
2 ADJOURN, interrupt, delay, defer, postpone, put off, arrest, shelve, pigeonhole, side, cease; *N Am* hold
FORMAL discontinue, put in abeyance, prorogue, stay
COLLOQ. put on ice, put on the back burner, take a raincheck on
3 EXPEL, dismiss, exclude, remove, debar, keep out, shut out, unfrock
COLLOQ. ground, stand off
🔁 **2** continue, carry on **3** restore, reinstate

suspended *adj*
1 HANGING, dangling
FORMAL pendent, pensile

2 POSTPONED, delayed, deferred, put off, shelved, pending
COLLOQ. put on ice

suspense n
uncertainty, insecurity, doubt, doubtfulness, anxiety, tension, nervousness, apprehension, anticipation, expectation, expectancy, excitement
Fa certainty, knowledge
■ **in suspense**
expectantly, eagerly, anxiously, with bated breath, on edge, on tenterhooks
COLLOQ. keyed up

suspension n
1 ADJOURNMENT, interruption, break, intermission, respite, remission, stay, moratorium, delay, deferral, deferment, postponement
OLD inhibition
FORMAL cessation, abeyance
2 EXPULSION, dismissal, exclusion, removal, debarment, unfrocking
COLLOQ. grounding, standing-off
Fa 1 continuation

suspicion n
1 DOUBT, scepticism, distrust, mistrust, chariness, wariness, qualm(s), caution, misgiving(s), apprehension, paranoia
OLD suspect, misdeeming, misdoubt, surmise
COLLOQ. suss
2 TRACE, hint, suggestion, soupçon, touch, tinge, shade, glimmer, shadow, scintilla, dash
OLD surmise
3 IDEA, notion, intuition, feeling, belief, opinion, inkling, intimation, sniff
FORMAL conjecture
COLLOQ. hunch, sixth sense, funny feeling
Fa 1 trust

suspicious adj
1 DOUBTFUL, sceptical, unbelieving, disbelieving, suspecting, unsure, distrustful, mistrustful, wary, chary, apprehensive, uneasy
OLD misdeeming, suspectful
2 DUBIOUS, questionable, suspect, irregular, equivocal, strange, queer, odd, funny, peculiar, dishonest, guilty, shifty
OLD smoky
COLLOQ. shady, dodgy, fishy, iffy
Fa 1 trustful, confident **2** trustworthy, innocent

suspiciously adv
1 DOUBTFULLY, sceptically, unbelievingly, disbelievingly, distrustfully, mistrustfully, warily, apprehensively
2 DUBIOUSLY, questionably, strangely, oddly, dishonestly
COLLOQ. shadily
Fa 1 confidently **2** trustworthily

sustain v
1 NOURISH, feed, provide for, nurture, foster, help, aid, assist, comfort, encourage, relieve, support, uphold, give strength to, endorse, bear, carry
OLD aliment, upbear
2 MAINTAIN, keep going, keep up, carry on, continue, prolong, hold, uphold, buoy (up), prop (up), ride out, stand, scaffold, upstay
FORMAL protract
3 SUFFER, go through, experience, undergo, endure, receive, happen to, face
OLD underbear
FORMAL abide

sustained adj
prolonged, long-drawn-out, steady, continuous, continuing, constant, ongoing, perpetual
FORMAL protracted, unremitting
Fa broken, interrupted, intermittent, spasmodic

sustenance n
nourishment, food, provisions, fare, maintenance,

subsistence, support, livelihood
FORMAL refection, aliment, comestibles, provender, viands, victuals
COLLOQ. grub, nosh, scoff

svelte adj
slender, slim, lithe, elegant, graceful, lissom, willowy, sylphlike, shapely, sophisticated, urbane, polished
Fa bulky, ungainly

swagger v, n
♦ v
bluster, boast, crow, brag, prance, parade, strut; *S Afr* pronk
COLLOQ. swank, show off, play to the gallery, make an exhibition of yourself, go over the top
♦ n
bluster, show, ostentation, arrogance, prancing, parading

swallow v
1 CONSUME, devour, eat, gobble up, drink, quaff, gulp (down)
FORMAL ingest
COLLOQ. guzzle, knock back, down, scoff, swig, polish off
2 ACCEPT, believe, trust, be certain of
COLLOQ. buy, fall for, swallow hook line and sinker
3 STIFLE, smother, repress, hold back, contain, suppress
4 TOLERATE, put up with, accept, endure, stand, take, bear; *Scot* thole
FORMAL abide
COLLOQ. stomach
■ **swallow up**
overwhelm, overrun, engulf, enfold, envelop, absorb, assimilate, take over

swamp n, v
♦ n
bog, marsh, fen, slough, quagmire, quag, quicksand, mire, morass, mud, swampland; *N Am* loblolly, purgatory; *Can* muskeg; *Aust* cowal; *S Afr* vlei
OLD Lerna; *N Am* Dismals
♦ v
flood, inundate, deluge, engulf, submerge, bog down, mire, sink, drench, saturate, waterlog, wash out, weigh down, overload, overwhelm, besiege, beset

swampy adj
boggy, marshy, wet, miry, fenny, soggy, quaggy, squelchy, waterlogged
FORMAL paludal, uliginous
Fa arid, dehydrated, dry

swank v, n
♦ v
brag, boast, show off, strut, swagger, parade, posture, preen yourself, attitudinize; *S Afr* pronk
♦ n
bragging, boastfulness, pretentiousness, showing-off, show, display, ostentation, conceit, conceitedness, swagger, self-advertisement
FORMAL vainglory
Fa modesty, restraint

swanky adj
glamorous, ostentatious, fashionable, expensive, luxurious, rich, lavish, smart, grand, stylish, showy, exclusive, de luxe, sumptuous, fancy, pretentious
COLLOQ. flash, flashy, plush, plushy, posh, ritzy, swish
Fa discreet, unobtrusive

swap, swop v, n
♦ v
exchange, transpose, switch, interchange, substitute, barter, trade, bandy, traffic
♦ n
exchange, switch, substitution, interchange, trade, trade-off, transposition

swarm *n, v*

♦ *n*

crowd, throng, mob, mass, stream, body, multitude, myriad, host, army, horde, pack, herd, flock, drove, shoal

♦ *v*

flock, flood, surge, stream, mass, congregate, crowd, throng

■ be swarming with

be crowded with, be teeming with, be overrun with, be crawling with, be bristling with, be thronged with, abound in; *Scot* be hotching with

swarthy *adj*

dark, dark-complexioned, dark-skinned, tanned, dusky, brown, black

Ⅎ fair, pale

swashbuckling *adj*

daring, courageous, adventurous, bold, spirited, swaggering, exciting, gallant, flamboyant, dare-devil, dashing, robust

Ⅎ tame, unadventurous, unexciting

swat *v, n*

♦ *v*

swipe, hit, strike, lash out, lunge
COLLOQ. whack, wallop, biff

♦ *n*

swipe, hit, strike, lunge
COLLOQ. whack, wallop, biff

swathe *v*

wrap, bandage, bind, wind, cloak, envelop, drape, enshroud, enwrap, fold, shroud, swaddle, lap, sheathe, furl

Ⅎ unwind, unwrap

sway *v, n*

♦ *v*

1 ROCK, roll, reel, lurch, stagger, swing, wave, shake, wobble, oscillate, vacillate, fluctuate, bend, incline, lean, divert, veer, swerve, sally, swag, teeter, thraw, swale, titter, totter, waddle; *dialect* shog; *Scot* shoogie, shoogle, swee
2 INFLUENCE, affect, persuade, win over, bring round, induce, convince, convert, overrule, rule, direct, dominate, govern
OLD swinge
FORMAL prevail upon

♦ *n*

1 ROCKING, swing, roll, reeling, lurch, stagger, wave, shake, wobble, oscillation, fluctuation, swerve; *Scot* shoogie, shoogle, swee
2 CONTROL, command, authority, power, influence, leadership, government, rule, sovereignty, dominion, predominance, jurisdiction
TECHNICAL hegemony
OLD swinge
FORMAL ascendancy, preponderance
COLLOQ. clout

■ hold sway

have power, exercise/wield power, have influence, have authority, reign, rule, prevail, lay down the law

swear *v*

1 VOW, promise, promise solemnly, pledge, pledge yourself, take an oath, be on/under oath, take the oath, testify, affirm, assert, declare, insist, rap
OLD adjure, abjure, depose, objure
FORMAL avow, attest, asseverate, aver, forswear, overswear
2 CURSE, blaspheme, utter profanities, abuse, damn, use bad language, take the Lord's name in vain, turn the air blue
FORMAL imprecate, maledict
COLLOQ. damn and blast, eff, eff and blind, blind
SLANG cuss

■ swear by

believe in, trust in, depend on, rely on, have confidence in, have faith in, put your faith in

swearing *n*

bad language, foul language, cursing, profanity, expletives, blasphemy
TECHNICAL coprolalia
FORMAL imprecations, maledictions
COLLOQ. effing and blinding
SLANG cussing

swear-word *n*

expletive, four-letter word, curse, oath, obscenity, profanity, blasphemy, swearing, bad language, foul language
FORMAL imprecation
SLANG cuss; *N Am* cussword

sweat *n, v*

♦ *n*

1 PERSPIRATION, moisture, stickiness, lather, bloody-sweat, mucksweat, death-damp
TECHNICAL sudor, diaphoresis, hidrosis, osmidrosis
OLD sudation
Related adjective: sudatory
2 ANXIETY, worry, agitation, panic, fuss, dither, cold sweat
COLLOQ. fluster, flap, tizzy, tizwas
3 TOIL, labour, drudgery, chore, effort

♦ *v*

perspire, secrete, swelter, drip, break out in a sweat, swelter
OLD sudate, perspirate
FORMAL exude
COLLOQ. sweat like a pig, sweat buckets

sweaty *adj*

damp, moist, clammy, sticky, sweating, perspiring
OLD forswatt
Ⅎ dry, cool

sweep *v, n*

♦ *v*

1 *sweep the floor*
brush, dust, clean (up), clear (up), remove, vacuum, broom, besom (away/out), overrake; *Scot* soop
OLD ensweep
2 PUSH, thrust, drive, move quickly, spread quickly, force, shove, drag, jostle, elbow, poke
3 PASS, sail, fly, glide, scud, skim, glance, whisk, race, swing, whip, tear, hurtle, roll, wash
OLD swoop

♦ *n*

1 *give the room a good sweep*
brush, dust, clean, clear, wipe, vacuum
2 ARC, curve, bend, swing, stroke, move, movement, action, gesture, stroke, sling, lash, scoop, swipe, sway
FORMAL curvature
3 SCOPE, compass, range, extent, span, stretch, vastness, immensity, expanse, vista

■ sweep under the carpet

hide, conceal, cover up, hush up, suppress, paper over, gloss over

sweeping *adj*

general, global, universal, all-inclusive, all-embracing, broad, wide, wide-ranging, extensive, far-reaching, comprehensive, thorough, thoroughgoing, radical, wholesale, indiscriminate, oversimplified, simplistic
COLLOQ. blanket, across-the-board
Ⅎ specific, narrow

sweepstake *n*

draw, lottery, gambling, sweep, sweepstakes

sweet *adj, n*

♦ *adj*

1 SUGARY, syrupy, sickly, sickly sweet, sweetened, honeyed, candied, glacé, saccharine, luscious, delicious, ripe
OLD soot
2 AROMATIC, fragrant, perfumed, balmy, sweet-scented

OLD soot
FORMAL ambrosial, odoriferous, odorous, redolent
3 *sweet music*
melodious, tuneful, harmonious, sweet-sounding, euphonious, musical, dulcet, soft, mellow
OLD soot
FORMAL mellifluous
4 PLEASANT, delightful, pleasing, lovely, attractive, beautiful, pretty, winsome, winning, cute, engaging, appealing, likeable, lov(e)able, adorable, charming, agreeable, amiable, affectionate, tender, kind, kindly, treasured, precious, cherished, dear, darling
OLD soot
5 FRESH, clean, wholesome, pure, clear
E3 1 savoury, salty, sour, bitter **2** foul, off **3** discordant, cacophonous **4** unpleasant, nasty, ugly **5** foul
♦ *n*
1 DESSERT, pudding
COLLOQ. afters, pud
2 BONBON, candy, sweetmeat, confectionery
FORMAL confection
COLLOQ. sweetie
▪ **sweet on**
fond of, liking, keen on, having a soft spot for, infatuated with, ravished with
COLLOQ. crazy about, mad about, far gone on

Sweets include:

alcorza	halva	nougat
aniseed ball	humbug	pear drop
barley sugar	jelly	peppermint
bonbon	jelly baby	pineapple chunk
bull's eye	jelly bean	pomfret
butterscotch	*Aust* jujube (or	praline
caramel	jube)	rock
chewing-gum	lemon drop	*Scot* tablet
chocolate	liquorice	toffee
dolly mixture	liquorice allsort	toffee apple
Edinburgh rock	lollipop	truffle
fondant	lozenge	Turkish delight
fruit pastille	Mars®	wine gum
fudge	marshmallow	
gobstopper	marzipan	
gumdrop	noisette	

---

sweeten *v*
1 SUGAR, add sugar to, honey
2 MELLOW, soften, soothe, mollify, appease
3 TEMPER, cushion, alleviate, ease, relieve
FORMAL mitigate
E3 2 sour, embitter

Artificial sweeteners include:

acesulfame K	cyclamate	saccharin
aspartame	Hermesetas®	sorbitol
Canderel®	NutraSweet®	Sweetex®

See also **sweet**.

---

sweetheart *n*
darling, dear, boyfriend, beau, girlfriend, love, lover, truelove, suitor, valentine, admirer, beloved, betrothed, follower, inamorata, inamorato, Romeo
OLD swain
COLLOQ. flame, steady, sweetie

sweetly *adv*
1 *smile sweetly*
pleasantly, delightfully, kindly, affectionately, lovingly, winsomely, tenderly, charmingly
2 *sing sweetly*
tunefully, in tune, melodiously, harmoniously,

euphoniously, softly, mellowly
3 *a machine working sweetly*
smoothly, easily, effortlessly, evenly, steadily

sweetness *n*
1 SUGARINESS, syrup, succulence, lusciousness, mellowness, freshness
2 FRAGRANCE, balminess, aroma
3 KINDNESS, amiability, winsomeness, tenderness, sweet temper, love, loveliness, charm
4 HARMONY, euphony
FORMAL dulcitude
E3 1 saltness, sourness, bitterness, acidity **2** foulness **3** nastiness **4** cacophony

sweet-smelling *adj*
aromatic, fragrant, perfumed, balmy, sweet-scented
FORMAL ambrosial, odoriferous, odorous, redolent
E3 f(o)etid, malodorous

swell *v, n, adj*
♦ *v*
1 EXPAND, inflate, blow up, puff up, bloat, fatten, bulge, balloon, billow, raise, bag, belly (out), berry, boll, bulb, bulk, plump, bunch, hove; *dialect* blast, plim, strout
OLD blab, outswell, huff; (*Shakesp*) farce
FORMAL dilate, distend, intumesce, tumesce, tumefy
2 RISE, surge, mount, increase, enlarge, grow larger, escalate, extend, grow, step up, accelerate, mushroom, proliferate, snowball, skyrocket, heighten, intensify, heave
OLD hove, volume
FORMAL augment
E3 1 shrink, contract **2** decrease, dwindle
♦ *n*
1 BILLOW, wave, undulation, sea, roughness, surge, rise, increase, enlargement, backwater
OLD wallow
2 DANDY, fop, beau, dude, cockscomb
COLLOQ. bigwig, toff, don
E3 2 down-and-out, scarecrow, tramp
♦ *adj*
wonderful, excellent, great, grand, smart, stylish, exclusive, fashionable, de luxe
COLLOQ. flashy, posh, ritzy, swanky
E3 seedy, shabby

swelling *n*
lump, tumour, bump, bruise, blister, boil, inflammation, bulge, protuberance, puffiness, enlargement
FORMAL distension, tumescence, intumescence, tumefaction

sweltering *adj*
hot, tropical, baking, boiling, roasting, scorching, torrid, stifling, suffocating, airless, oppressive, sultry, clammy, muggy, steamy, sticky, humid
COLLOQ. baking, roasting, sizzling
E3 cold, cool, fresh, breezy, airy

swerve *v*
change direction suddenly, turn, bend, incline, veer, swing, twist, shift, deviate, stray, wander, diverge, deflect, skew, sheer

swift *adj*
fast, quick, rapid, brisk, speedy, express, flying, hurried, hasty, short, brief, sudden, abrupt, immediate, prompt, ready, agile, lively, nimble
OLD fleet; (*Shakesp*) flighty
FORMAL expeditious
COLLOQ. nippy
E3 slow, sluggish, unhurried

swiftly *adv*
quickly, posthaste, fast, rapidly, speedily, express, hurriedly, instantly, promptly, at full tilt
FORMAL expeditiously
COLLOQ. double-quick, hotfoot
E3 slowly; *formal* tardily

swiftness n

quickness, rapidity, speed, speediness, suddenness, velocity, immediacy, immediateness, instantaneity, readiness, promptness, dispatch
OLD fleetness
FORMAL alacrity, celerity, expedition
E∃ delay, slowness; *formal* tardiness

swill v, n

♦ v

drink, swallow, swig, quaff, gulp, guzzle, drain, consume
FORMAL imbibe
COLLOQ. knock back, toss off

♦ n

1 DRINK, gulp, swallow, swig
2 WASTE, slops, hogwash, pigswill, scourings, refuse

■ **swill out**

wash out, wash down, rinse, clean, cleanse, drench, flush, sluice

swim v

bathe, take a dip, tread water, float, bob, snorkel, paddle, run, strike out; *Scot* soom
COLLOQ. swan
Related adjectives: natatorial, natant

The main swimming strokes include:

backstroke	butterfly	doggy-paddle
breaststroke	crawl	sidestroke

---

swimmingly adv

very well, smoothly, easily, without a hitch
COLLOQ. like clockwork, like a house on fire

swimming-pool n

swimming-bath(s), baths, leisure pool, lido, swimming-pond

swimsuit n

swimming costume, bathing costume, bathing suit, bikini, trunks

swindle v, n

♦ v

cheat, defraud, fiddle, diddle, overcharge, exploit, trick, deceive, dupe, nobble, fleece, skin, ramp, skelder, financier, mulct, chouse; *NAm* beat, bunko
OLD bucket, let in
COLLOQ. do, con, take, bamboozle, rook, stitch up, shaft, put one over on, pull the wool over someone's eyes, sell smoke
SLANG rip off, sting, gyp, pluck, tweedle, hand someone a lemon, sell a pup, take for a ride, take to the cleaners; *NAm* grift, gold-brick

♦ n

fraud, fiddle, diddle, racket, sharp practice, double-dealing, trickery, deception, clean-out, fake, chouse
COLLOQ. con, scam, do, rig
SLANG chizz, rip-off, gyp; *NAm* gold brick; *Aust* lurk

swindler n

cheat, fraud, fraudster, fiddler, impostor, trickster, rogue, rascal, charlatan, mountebank
COLLOQ. con man/woman, con artist, shark, rook, hustler, hood, hoodlum; *NAm* bunko-steerer
SLANG *NAm* grifter

swine n

1 PIG, beast, boar, hog
2 SCOUNDREL, rogue, rascal, good-for-nothing, brute, boor

swing v, n

♦ v

1 HANG, dangle, wave, spin, rotate, pivot, sway, rock
2 SWERVE, veer, turn, twist, wind, curve, bend, incline, lean, oscillate, fluctuate, change, vary

FORMAL pendulate
3 ARRANGE, achieve, get, set up, make, organize
COLLOQ. fix (up)

♦ n

sway, rock, oscillation, waving, vibration, fluctuation, variation, change, shift, move, movement, motion, stroke, rhythm

swingeing adj

harsh, severe, stringent, drastic, serious, extreme, punishing, devastating, excessive, extortionate, exorbitant, oppressive, heavy, Draconian
COLLOQ. thumping
E∃ mild

swinging adj

lively, exciting, dynamic, fashionable, contemporary, modern, up-to-date, up-to-the-minute, stylish
COLLOQ. jet-setting, trendy, with it
SLANG hip
E∃ old-fashioned, fuddy-duddy

swipe v, n

♦ v

1 HIT, strike, clout, lunge, lash out, slap, swat
COLLOQ. whack, wallop, sock, biff
2 STEAL, pilfer, lift
COLLOQ. pinch, whip, nick, filch

♦ n

stroke, strike, blow, clout, slap, smack, swat
COLLOQ. whack, wallop, biff

swirl v

churn, agitate, spin, revolve, circulate, twirl, whirl, wheel, eddy, twist, curl

swish¹ v

the horses swished their tails
flourish, whisk, swing, swirl, thrash, flog, lash, birch, whip, rustle, twirl, whizz, swoosh, wave, brandish, whirl, whistle, whoosh

swish² adj

a swish hotel
smart, grand, fashionable, exclusive, plush, stylish, elegant, sumptuous, de luxe
COLLOQ. flash, posh, ritzy, swanky, swell
E∃ seedy, shabby

switch v, n

♦ v

change, exchange, swap, trade, barter, interchange, substitute, replace, shift, rearrange, turn, put, veer, deviate, divert, deflect, beat, scutch, twig, convert
FORMAL transpose
COLLOQ. chop and change

♦ n

1 BUTTON, control, on-off device, lever, circuit-breaker, relay, shunt, toggle
TECHNICAL cryotron
2 CHANGE, alteration, shift, exchange, swap, interchange, substitution, replacement, reversal, about-turn
3 TWIG, shoot, branch, cane, rod, birch, lash, twitch, whisk, whip, thong

■ **switch off**

turn off, close down, shut off, flick off, stop working, cut

■ **switch on**

turn on, put on, flick on, operate, activate, set off, trigger off

swivel v

pivot, spin, rotate, revolve, turn, twirl, pirouette, gyrate, wheel

swollen adj

bloated, inflated, tumid, puffed up, puffy, bulbous, bulging, inflamed, enlarged, expanded, engorged
FORMAL distended, dilated, tumescent
E∃ shrunken, shrivelled

swoop v, n

◆ v

dive, plunge, drop, fall, descend, stoop, pounce, lunge, rush, souse

◆ n

dive, plunge, drop, descent, pounce, stoop, lunge, rush, attack, onslaught

■ **at/in/with one fell swoop**
by a single action, by one complete action, by one decisive action, on one occasion, suddenly, by one blow, with one deadly blow

swop

see **swap**.

sword n

blade, foil, rapier, sabre, scimitar, steel, épée, katana

■ **cross swords**
disagree, argue, quarrel, fight, contend, dispute, contest, wrangle, bicker, be at odds, be at loggerheads

sworn adj

devoted, confirmed, eternal, implacable, inveterate, relentless
FORMAL attested

swot v

study, work, learn, memorize, revise, cram
COLLOQ. mug up, bone up, burn the midnight oil

sybarite n

parasite, pleasurer, pleasure-seeker, sensualist, bon vivant, epicure, epicurean, hedonist, playboy, voluptuary
 ascetic, toiler

sybaritic adj

easy, pleasure-loving, pleasure-seeking, self-indulgent, sensual, voluptuous, hedonistic, epicurean, luxurious, parasitic
 ascetic

sycophancy n

cringing, fawning, flattery, toadyism, toad-eating, grovelling, servility, slavishness, kowtowing, backscratching, adulation, truckling, oleaginousness
FORMAL obsequiousness
COLLOQ. bootlicking
SLANG (vulgar) arse-licking

sycophant n

cringer, fawner, flatterer, groveller, backscratcher, slave, parasite, hanger-on, toady, truckler, claqueur
OLD placebo, toad-eater
COLLOQ. crawler, bootlicker, sponger, yes-man
SLANG (vulgar) arse-licker; NAm cookie-pusher

sycophantic adj

cringing, fawning, flattering, grovelling, servile, slavish, ingratiating, parasitical, backscratching, slimy, toad-eating, toadying, time-serving, truckling, oleaginous
OLD sycophantical
FORMAL obsequious, unctuous
COLLOQ. bootlicking, smarmy
SLANG (vulgar) arse-licking

syllabus n

curriculum, course, programme, schedule, plan, outline

syllogism n

deduction, argument, proposition
TECHNICAL epicheirema

sylph-like adj

slim, slight, slender, elegant, graceful, lithe, willowy, streamlined, svelte
 bulky, plump

symbiotic adj

co-operative, interactive, interdependent
TECHNICAL endophytic, epizoan, epizoic, epizootic
FORMAL commensal, synergetic

symbol n

sign, token, representation, mark, emblem, badge, logo, character, ideograph, figure, image
FORMAL type

Symbols include:

badge	logogram	**TEXT SYMBOLS:**
brand	monogram	ampersand
cipher	motif	asterisk
coat of arms	pictograph	at sign
crest	swastika	caret
emblem	token	dagger
hieroglyph	totem	double-dagger
icon	trademark	emoticon
ideogram	watermark	hash
insignia		obelus
logo		smiley

---

symbolic adj

symbolical, representative, typical, illustrative, emblematic, token, figurative, metaphorical, allegorical, meaningful, significant

symbolically adv

representationally, figuratively, representatively, characteristically, emblematically, as a symbol, as a sign, as an emblem, by this token

symbolize v

represent, stand for, denote, mean, signify, express, symbol, typify, exemplify, epitomize, personify, personate
TECHNICAL type
OLD betoken, emblem, figure, present

symmetrical adj

balanced, even, regular, well-proportioned, parallel, uniform, consistent, harmonious, corresponding, proportional
 asymmetrical, irregular

symmetry n

balance, evenness, regularity, parallelism, correspondence, proportion(s), harmony, uniformity, consistency, agreement
FORMAL congruity
 asymmetry, irregularity

sympathetic adj

understanding, appreciative, supportive, comforting, encouraging, consoling, commiserating, pitying, interested, concerned, caring, compassionate, tolerant, tender, kind, kindly, warm, warm-hearted, kind-hearted, well-disposed, affectionate, agreeable, favourable, considerate, solicitous, friendly, pleasant, likeable, companionable, congenial, sociable, neighbourly, like-minded, compatible, feeling, genial, soft, tender, commiserative
OLD sympathetical, social
FORMAL solicitous
COLLOQ. simpatico
 unsympathetic, indifferent, callous, antipathetic

sympathetically adv

appreciatively, supportively, understandingly, compassionately, comfortingly, consolingly, responsively, sensitively, warmly, warm-heartedly, feelingly, kindly, pityingly

sympathize v

understand, comfort, console, encourage, be supportive, appreciate, show concern/interest, care for, offer condolences, commiserate, pity, feel sorry for, feel for, your heart goes out, empathize, identify with, respond to, condole
 ignore, disregard

sympathizer *n*
supporter, condoler, admirer, backer, adherent, well-wisher, fan, fellow-traveller, partisan
E3 enemy, opponent, adversary

sympathy *n*
1 UNDERSTANDING, comfort, encouragement, support, appreciation, consolation, condolences, commiseration, pity, compassion, tenderness, kindness, warmth, warm-heartedness, thoughtfulness, empathy, fellow-feeling, closeness, consideration, affinity, rapport, commiseration, *Weltschmerz*
FORMAL solace
2 AGREEMENT, approval, correspondence, accord, harmony
FORMAL approbation
E3 **1** indifference, insensitivity, callousness **2** disagreement

symptom *n*
sign, indication, signal, evidence, expression, display, demonstration, note, feature, characteristic, mark, token, warning, diagnostic
TECHNICAL prodrome, prodromus
FORMAL manifestation

symptomatic *adj*
indicative, typical, characteristic, associated, suggesting, suggestive

syndicate *n*
association, alliance, combination, group, bloc, cartel, ring, combine

synonymous *adj*
interchangeable, substitutable, the same, identical, similar, comparable, tantamount, equivalent, corresponding
E3 antonymous, opposite

synopsis *n*
outline, abstract, summary, sketch, résumé, précis, condensation, digest, abridgement, review, recapitulation, compendium, tabulation, schema
FORMAL summation, conspectus
COLLOQ. run-down, recap

synthesis *n*
amalgamation, combination, compound, fusion, integration, union, welding, blend, alloy, amalgam, coalescence, composite, pastiche
FORMAL unification

synthesize *v*
unite, combine, amalgamate, integrate, merge, blend, compound, alloy, fuse, weld, coalesce, unify
E3 separate, analyse, resolve

synthetic *adj*
manufactured, man-made, simulated, artificial, ersatz, imitation, fake, faux, bogus, mock, sham, pseudo
E3 genuine, real, natural

syrupy *adj*
1 SWEET, sugary, sickly sweet, oversweet, sweetened, honeyed, saccharine
2 SENTIMENTAL, emotional, loving, gushing, sugary, pathetic, tear-jerking, maudlin, mawkish, romantic, affectionate
COLLOQ. soppy, weepy, lovey-dovey, slushy, mushy, schmaltzy, sloppy, corny, sickly, gushy

system *n*
1 METHOD, technique, procedure, process, routine, practice, approach, way, means, usage, rule, modus operandi
FORMAL mode
2 ORGANIZATION, structure, set-up, systematization, co-ordination, orderliness, methodology, logic, classification, arrangement, network, framework, order, plan, scheme, apparatus, mechanism
3 THE ESTABLISHMENT, the government, the authorities, the powers that be
COLLOQ. them

systematic *adj*
methodical, methodic, logical, ordered, well-ordered, planned, well-planned, organized, well-organized, structured, systematized, standardized, scientific, orderly, businesslike, efficient
E3 unsystematic, unstructured, arbitrary, disorderly, inefficient

systematize *v*
arrange, order, structure, plan, organize, rationalize, methodize, standardize, schematize, regulate, regiment, classify, tabulate, make uniform
FORMAL dispose

T

tab *n*

flap, tag, marker, label, sticker, ticket, fob, strap, trimmer

■ **keep tabs on**

watch closely, keep an eye on, observe, keep a close watch on, keep a close check on

tabby *adj*

stripy, striped, streaked, wavy, mottled, variegated, banded, brindle(d)

table *n, v*

◆ *n*

1 BOARD, slab, counter, bar, worktop, desk, bench, stand
2 DIAGRAM, chart, figure, graph, timetable, schedule, programme, plan, list, inventory, catalogue, tabulation, index, register, record
3 FOOD, board, diet, fare, dish, speciality, menu
COLLOQ. tuck
SLANG grub, nosh; *N Am* chow

◆ *v*

propose, suggest, submit, put forward, move

tableau *n*

representation, picture, portrayal, scene, spectacle, vignette, diorama, *tableau vivant*

tablet *n*

1 PILL, capsule, lozenge, pellet, ball, bolus, caplet, purple heart
FORMAL troche
COLLOQ. sleeper
SLANG benny
2 SLAB, surface, plate, plaque, pad, medallion, monument, stele; *N Am* marker
TECHNICAL abacus, triglyph
OLD tablature

taboo *adj, n*

◆ *adj*

forbidden, prohibited, banned, ruled out, vetoed, sacrosanct, unacceptable, unmentionable, unthinkable
FORMAL proscribed
E₃ permitted, acceptable

◆ *n*

ban, prohibition, veto, restriction, anathema, curse
FORMAL interdiction, proscription
E₃ permission, acceptance

tabulate *v*

order, arrange, arrange in columns, chart, classify, list, sort, systematize, table, catalogue, categorize, range, index, codify, tabularize

tabulation *n*

arrangement, ordering, sorting, classification, listing, cataloguing, categorization, indexing

tacit *adj*

unspoken, unexpressed, unstated, unvoiced, silent, wordless, understood, implicit, implied, inferred
E₃ express, explicit

taciturn *adj*

silent, quiet, uncommunicative, unforthcoming, untalkative, close-mouthed, tight-lipped, reticent, reserved, withdrawn, aloof, detached, distant, cold, dumb, mute
E₃ talkative, communicative, forthcoming

tack *n, v*

◆ *n*

1 NAIL, pin, drawing-pin, staple, tintack, tingle; *N Am* thumbtack
2 COURSE, path, bearing, heading, direction, line, line of action, course of action, approach, method, way, technique, procedure, process, policy, strategy, plan, tactic, attack

◆ *v*

1 ADD, append, attach, annex
2 FIX, fasten, affix, nail, pin, staple, tag, stitch, sew, baste
3 CHANGE COURSE, turn, change direction, go/come about, swerve
TECHNICAL club-haul

Parts of a horse's tack include:

alforja	girth	saddlebow
old arson	hackamore	saddlecloth
backband	halter	saddle-girth
bearing rein	hames	saddlepad
bellyband	*N Am* headstall	saddletree
bit	housing	*old* shabrack (or
N Am blinders	martingale	shabracque)
blinkers	noseband	stirrup
breeching	numnah	surcingle
bridle	pommel	throatlatch (or
cantle	reins	throatlash)
N Am cinch	saddle	traces
collar	saddlebag	
crupper	saddle blanket	

---

tackle *n, v*

◆ *n*

1 *a rugby tackle*
attack, challenge, interception, intervention, block
2 EQUIPMENT, tools, implements, apparatus, rig, outfit, gear, things, trappings, paraphernalia, harness
FORMAL accoutrements
COLLOQ. stuff, clobber, things

◆ *v*

1 BEGIN, embark on, set about, go about, try, attempt, undertake, take on, challenge, confront, encounter, face up to, grapple with, get to grips with, apply yourself to, address, deal with, attend to, handle, grab, seize, grasp, take hold of
2 INTERCEPT, block, take, halt, stop, deflect, catch, grapple with, challenge, obstruct
E₃ 1 avoid, sidestep

tacky¹ *adj*

tacky paint
sticky, wet, adhesive, gluey, gummy
COLLOQ. gooey

tacky² *adj*

1 SHABBY, scruffy, tatty, threadbare, shoddy, dingy, tattered, ragged, untidy, messy, sloppy

COLLOQ. grotty
2 TASTELESS, vulgar, tawdry, flashy, gaudy, kitschy
SLANG naff

tact *n*

tactfulness, diplomacy, discretion, prudence, delicacy,
subtlety, sensitivity, perception, discernment, judgement,
understanding, thoughtfulness, consideration, skill,
dexterity, adroitness, finesse, savoir-faire
FORMAL judiciousness
⊟ tactlessness, indiscretion

tactful *adj*

diplomatic, discreet, politic, prudent, careful, delicate,
tender, subtle, sensitive, perceptive, discerning,
thoughtful, understanding, considerate, polite, skilful,
adroit, kid-glove
FORMAL judicious
⊟ tactless, indiscreet, thoughtless, rude

tactfully *adv*

diplomatically, discreetly, carefully, sensitively, delicately,
tenderly, thoughtfully, skilfully, politely, prudently
FORMAL judiciously
⊟ tactlessly, thoughtlessly

tactic *n*

1 APPROACH, course, course of action, way, means, method,
procedure, plan, stratagem, scheme, ruse, ploy,
subterfuge, trick, device, shift, expedient, move,
manoeuvre
2 *military tactics*
strategy, campaign, plan, policy, approach, line of attack,
moves, manoeuvres
COLLOQ. game plan, hardball, soft sell

tactical *adj*

strategic, planned, calculated, artful, cunning, shrewd,
adroit, skilful, clever, smart, prudent, politic
FORMAL judicious

tactician *n*

strategist, orchestrator, planner, politician, diplomat,
director, campaigner, co-ordinator, mastermind
COLLOQ. brain

tactless *adj*

undiplomatic, indiscreet, indelicate, unsubtle,
inappropriate, impolitic, imprudent, careless, clumsy,
awkward, blundering, gauche, insensitive, unfeeling,
hurtful, unkind, thoughtless, inconsiderate, rude, rough,
impolite, discourteous
FORMAL injudicious, maladroit
⊟ tactful, diplomatic, discreet

tactlessness *n*

insensitivity, impoliteness, indelicacy, indiscretion,
thoughtlessness, discourtesy, rudeness, ineptitude, bad
timing, clumsiness, gaucherie, boorishness
FORMAL maladroitness
⊟ tact, tactfulness, diplomacy

tag *n, v*

♦ *n*
1 LABEL, sticker, tab, ticket, mark, identification, note, slip,
docket, bracelet, anklet, strap, flap, tally, treasury tag,
aglet, Kimball tag
OLD dag
2 IDENTIFICATION, label, description, name, title, nickname,
epithet, identity disc, badge
3 QUOTATION, saying, expression, phrase, maxim, moral,
motto, proverb, dictum, epithet, allusion, stock phrase,
cliché, remnant
COLLOQ. quote
♦ *v*
1 LABEL, mark, identify, designate, term, title, entitle, call,
name, christen, nickname, style, dub
2 ADD, attach, append, annex, adjoin, affix, fasten, tack

■ **tag along**
follow, shadow, tail, trail, accompany

tail *n, v*

♦ *n*
1 END, extremity, rear, rear end, bottom, back, rump,
appendage, conclusion
FORMAL termination
COLLOQ. behind, posterior, backside
Related adjective: caudal, cercal
2 DETECTIVE, (private) investigator, shadow
COLLOQ. private eye, sleuth, gumshoe, shamus
♦ *v*
follow, pursue, shadow, dog, stalk, track, trail
■ **tail back**
queue, jam, line; *N Am* back up
■ **tail off**
decrease, decline, drop (off), fall away, fade, wane,
dwindle, taper off, peter out, die (out)
⊟ increase, grow
■ **turn tail**
run away, escape, flee, abscond, decamp, bolt
COLLOQ. skedaddle, scarper, beat it

tailback *n*

queue, line, tail, file, row, column, crocodile, procession,
train; *N Am* backup

tailor *n, v*

♦ *n*
outfitter, dressmaker, costumer, costumier, couturier,
seamster, seamstress, modiste, clothier, cutter, knight of
the shears, whipcat, darzi; *dialect* teller; *Scot* prick-louse
COLLOQ. sartor
SLANG snip
OLD SLANG dung, flint
Related adjective: sartorial
♦ *v*
fit, suit, cut, trim, style, fashion, shape, mould, alter, modify,
convert, adapt, adjust, accommodate, customize,
personalize

tailor-made *adj*

made-to-measure, custom-built, bespoke, ideal, perfect,
right, suited, tailored, fitted
⊟ off-the-peg, ready-made

taint *v, n*

♦ *v*
contaminate, infect, pollute, adulterate, corrupt, deprave,
stain, blemish, blot, smear, tarnish, blacken, dirty, soil,
muddy, defile, sully, harm, damage, injure, blight, spoil,
ruin, shame, disgrace, dishonour, envenom, mildew,
smoke, poison
OLD attainder
FORMAL befoul
♦ *n*
contamination, infection, contagion, adulteration,
pollution, corruption, stain, blemish, fault, flaw, defect,
spot, blot, smear, stigma, shame, disgrace, dishonour

take *v, n*

♦ *v*
1 SEIZE, grab, snatch, clutch, grasp, hold, get/lay hold of,
grip, catch, capture, get, obtain, acquire, secure, gain,
receive, win, derive, adopt, assume, pick, choose, select,
decide, settle on, accept, receive
FORMAL procure
2 REMOVE, draw, eliminate, take away, subtract, deduct,
extract, steal, seize, kidnap, abduct, carry off, confiscate
FORMAL purloin, appropriate
COLLOQ. filch, nick, pinch, lift, have your fingers in the till
3 *take me home*
convey, carry, bring, fetch, deliver, drive, transport, ferry,
accompany, escort, show, lead, guide, conduct, help,
usher, shepherd

FORMAL bear
COLLOQ. whisk
4 BEAR, tolerate, put up with, stand, endure, suffer, undergo, experience, withstand
FORMAL abide
COLLOQ. stomach
5 *the journey takes 6 hours*
need, necessitate, require, demand, call for, use (up), last
6 CAPTURE, win, seize, catch, conquer, occupy
FORMAL vanquish
7 *take pleasure in something*
derive, obtain, draw, gain, receive, attain, secure, achieve, be given, come by, get
FORMAL procure
8 *take the blame/responsibility*
accept, bear, be responsible for, admit, acknowledge, undertake
9 CONSIDER, believe, assume, presume, suppose, note, remember, examine, bear in mind
10 UNDERSTAND, comprehend, grasp, gather, apprehend, follow, fathom (out)
COLLOQ. cotton on, twig
11 *take the news badly*
react to, accept, respond to, cope with, deal with, handle
12 *take him for a fool*
believe, think, consider, regard, look upon, view, reckon, suppose, hold
FORMAL deem
13 *the hall takes 400 people*
hold, contain, accommodate, seat, have a capacity of, have room for, have space for
14 *take a measurement*
find out, discover, measure, establish, determine, ascertain
15 BUY, purchase, rent, hire, lease, pay for, book, receive, subscribe to
16 *take a subject at university*
study, learn, pursue, be taught, research, read, major in
17 *take the new road*
use, travel along, drive along, go along, follow
18 *take food/drink*
consume, swallow, eat, drink, devour
FORMAL imbibe, ingest
COLLOQ. tuck in, guzzle, scoff
19 *will the drug take?*
succeed, work, produce results, take effect, be effective
FORMAL be efficacious
E3 1 leave, refuse **2** replace, put back **6** lose **15** sell **19** fail
♦ *n*
1 CATCH, gate, haul, bag, yield
2 INCOME, revenue, takings, proceeds, profit(s), receipts, return(s), yield, gate, gate-money
3 PERSPECTIVE, view, point of view, viewpoint, aspect, angle, slant, attitude, frame of mind, vantage point, standpoint, interpretation

■ **take after**
resemble, look like, be like, be similar to, favour, mirror, echo

■ **take against**
dislike, object to, disapprove of, despise, regard with distaste
E3 take to

■ **take apart**
1 *take apart a machine*
pull/take to pieces, separate, dismantle, disassemble, analyse
2 CRITICIZE, condemn, carp, disapprove of, find fault with, snipe, pass judgement on, denounce, slate, attack, run down, censure, blame
FORMAL disparage
COLLOQ. nag, slam, knock, come down on, give someone some stick, go to town on, haul over the coals, pick holes in, pan, pull/take to pieces, tear to shreds, tear a strip off,

nit-pick, do a hatchet job on, badmouth, rubbish, put the boot in
SLANG slag (off)

■ **take back**
1 WITHDRAW, retract, recant, repudiate, disclaim, deny
FORMAL renounce
COLLOQ. eat your words
2 REPOSSESS, reclaim, regain, get back
3 RETURN, replace, restore, give back, hand back, send back
4 REMIND, put you in mind of, make you think of, call up, evoke

■ **take down**
1 DISMANTLE, disassemble, remove, demolish, raze, level, lower
2 NOTE, make a note of, record, write down, put down, set down, get down, transcribe, put on paper
E3 1 put up

■ **take in**
1 ABSORB, assimilate, digest, realize, appreciate, understand, comprehend, grasp
2 ACCOMMODATE, admit, receive, shelter, welcome
3 INCLUDE, contain, comprise, incorporate, embrace, encompass, cover
4 DECEIVE, fool, dupe, mislead, trick, hoodwink, cheat, swindle
COLLOQ. con, bamboozle, pull the wool over someone's eyes, lead up the garden path

■ **take off**
1 *watch the plane take off*
depart, fly, lift off, ascend, climb, rise, soar, mount, become airborne
2 REMOVE, undress, get undressed, strip, divest, shed, discard, detach, pull off, throw off, tear off, drop, doff
3 SUBTRACT, take away, remove, deduct, discount
4 LEAVE, depart, go, run away, decamp, disappear, flee, abscond
COLLOQ. skedaddle, scarper, bunk off, do a runner
5 IMITATE, impersonate, mimic, parody, caricature, satirize, mock
COLLOQ. send up
6 *the project has really taken off*
succeed, work, do well, become fashionable, become popular, catch on, prosper, flourish
COLLOQ. make it, become all the rage, go places, hit the jackpot, strike gold

■ **take on**
1 ACCEPT, assume, acquire, undertake, tackle, face
2 COMPETE WITH, contend with, fight, oppose, vie with, tackle
3 *take on staff*
employ, hire, enlist, recruit, engage, enrol, retain
4 GET UPSET, get angry, make a fuss

■ **take out**
1 REMOVE, extract, get out, detach, excise, cut out, pull out
2 *take someone out to a restaurant*
go with, go out with, accompany, escort, see
3 *take out a loan*
arrange, organize, set up, settle on, work out
COLLOQ. fix
4 *take out a book from the library*
borrow, use temporarily, have a loan, be lent
5 KILL, murder, put to death, exterminate, assassinate, finish off, massacre, execute, destroy, do away with, butcher, execute, shoot
COLLOQ. do in, bump off, eliminate, dispatch, liquidate, knock off, rub out, wipe out, polish off, waste, blow away, zap

■ **take over**
gain control of, take charge of, become responsible for, assume control/responsibility for, buy out

■ **take to**
1 LIKE, find pleasant, find attractive, become friendly with, become keen on, appreciate
2 BEGIN, start, launch into, undertake, set about
FORMAL commence

■ **take up**
1 OCCUPY, fill, engage, engross, absorb, become interested in, become involved in, monopolize, use (up), fill, consume
2 RAISE, lift, pick up
3 *take up a hobby*
start, begin, embark on, pursue
FORMAL commence
4 RESUME, carry on, continue, pick up
COLLOQ. pick up the threads
5 ACCEPT, adopt, assume, agree to
6 *what made you take up with him?*
become friends with, become friendly with, hang/knock about with, get involved with
F3 5 refuse

take-off *n*
1 DEPARTURE, flight, flying, lift-off, ascent, climbing
2 IMITATION, mimicry, impersonation, parody, caricature, travesty
COLLOQ. spoof, send-up

takeover *n*
gaining of control, merger, amalgamation, combination, incorporation, buyout, coalition, coup

taking *adj, n*
♦ *adj*
catching, attractive, charming, pleasing, delightful, winning, winsome, appealing, fascinating, fetching, engaging, enchanting, compelling, alluring, beguiling, captivating, intriguing, prepossessing
F3 repellent, repulsive, unattractive
♦ *n*
receipts, proceeds, profits, gain, returns, income, revenue, yield, earnings, winnings, pickings, gate, gate-money

tale *n*
1 STORY, yarn, anecdote, narrative, account, report, rumour, tall story, old wives' tale, superstition, fable, myth, legend, epic, saga, parable, allegory, fairy story, fairytale, novel, romance, roman, tradition, mystery, jeremiad, hair-raiser, traveller's tale, odyssey, sob story, toy, weird
TECHNICAL fabliau
OLD rede, gest
COLLOQ. spiel
2 LIE, falsehood, untruth, fabrication, hoax
COLLOQ. fib, whopper, porky, tall story, cock-and-bull story, fairy story, fairytale, bam

talent *n*
gift, endowment, genius, flair, feel, knack, bent, aptitude, faculty, facility, skill, ability, capacity, aptness, power, strength, strong point, forte, showmanship, long suit
OLD ingenium
COLLOQ. nous, shot in the arm
F3 inability, weakness, limitation

talented *adj*
gifted, brilliant, well-endowed, versatile, accomplished, able, capable, proficient, adept, adroit, deft, artistic, clever, skilful
F3 inept

talisman *n*
amulet, charm, fetish, mascot, totem, symbol, idol, ju-ju, phylactery, periapt, abraxas

talk *v, n*
♦ *v*
1 SPEAK, say, utter, articulate, voice, communicate, express, chat, chatter, babble; *Scot* blether
FORMAL converse, confer, orate
COLLOQ. natter, jabber, babble, prattle, chinwag, jaw

2 NEGOTIATE, discuss, bargain, haggle, work out an agreement
3 GOSSIP, spread rumours, chat, chatter, natter
4 *talk to the police*
tell, confess, give (secret) information to, inform on
COLLOQ. tell tales, squeal, blab, spill the beans, let the cat out of the bag, give the game away
SLANG grass
♦ *n*
1 CONVERSATION, dialogue, discussion, chat, chatter, tête-à-tête; *Scot* blether; *NZ* korero
COLLOQ. natter, confab, jaw, jaw-jaw, chinwag
2 *give a talk*
lecture, seminar, symposium, speech, address, discourse, sermon
FORMAL disquisition, oration
COLLOQ. spiel
3 GOSSIP, hearsay, rumour, tittle-tattle
4 *the two sides are holding talks*
negotiation, discussion, interview, meeting, consultation, debate, conference, summit conference, dialogue, seminar, symposium, bargaining, haggling
FORMAL conclave
5 LANGUAGE, dialect, slang, cant, jargon, speech, utterance, words
TECHNICAL idiolect
COLLOQ. lingo

■ **talk back**
answer back, answer rudely, be cheeky to, retort, riposte, retaliate

■ **talk big**
bluster, boast, brag, show off, crow, exaggerate, vaunt
COLLOQ. swank

■ **talk down to**
patronize, speak condescendingly towards, look down on, despise

■ **talk into**
persuade, encourage, coax, sway, convince, bring round, win over
F3 dissuade, talk out of

■ **talk out of**
dissuade, discourage, deter, put off, prevent, stop
F3 persuade, convince, talk into

talkative *adj*
garrulous, vocal, communicative, forthcoming, unreserved, expansive, chatty, gossipy, verbose, wordy, long-winded
FORMAL voluble, loquacious
COLLOQ. gabby, gassy, mouthy, can talk the hind legs off a donkey
F3 taciturn, quiet, reserved

Synonym nuances
You can use **garrulous** of someone who talks excessively, but with the negative suggestion that what they say has little meaningful content, while **vocal** is more appropriate for someone who likes to make their opinions known, and is not particularly disapproving: *his most vocal critics.*
  More positive-sounding synonyms include **communicative**, which is suggestive of an ability to impart meaning, and **forthcoming**, which further implies sociability. **Unreserved** suggests an element of wholeheartedness: *unreserved enthusiasm*, while **expansive** appropriately describes being able to talk extensively on a subject: *he was expansive on both himself and his future plans.*
  The term **chatty**, again, returns to the idea of being friendly, but a more disapproving tone is discernible in **gossipy**, with its implications of idle speculation. The terms **verbose** and **wordy** suggest a propensity for using more words than are necessary and are also critical: *much academic language is obtuse and verbose*, and **long-winded** suggests a similarly tedious quality.

talker *n*
speaker, conversationalist, communicator, lecturer, orator, speechmaker
COLLOQ. chatterbox

talking-to *n*
lecture, scolding, reprimand, rebuke, reproof, reproach, criticism
COLLOQ. dressing-down, telling-off, carpeting, wigging, ticking-off, rocket
F3 praise, commendation

tall *adj*
1 HIGH, lofty, elevated, soaring, towering, sky-high, lanky, big, great, giant, gigantic
2 *a tall story*
unlikely, unbelievable, incredible, improbable, remarkable, implausible, absurd, far-fetched, exaggerated, dubious, preposterous, overblown
3 *a tall order*
difficult, demanding, exacting, taxing, hard, challenging, trying
F3 1 short, low, small **2** reasonable **3** easy

tallness *n*
altitude, height, loftiness, stature

tally *n, v*
  ♦ *n*
1 RECORD, count, total, sum, score, enumeration, reckoning, account, register, list, roll, stick
OLD stock, nickstick
2 COUNTERFOIL, counterpart, duplicate, ticket, tag, tab, stub; *N Am* tab
  ♦ *v*
1 AGREE, concur, tie in, square, harmonize, coincide, correspond, match, conform, suit, fit
OLD nick
FORMAL accord, concur
2 ADD (UP), total, count, reckon, figure
F3 1 disagree, differ

tame *adj, v*
  ♦ *adj*
1 *a tame rabbit*
pet, domesticated, domestic, broken in, trained, disciplined, manageable, tractable, amenable, gentle, docile, meek, subdued, submissive, unresisting, obedient, biddable
OLD mansuete
2 DULL, boring, tedious, uninteresting, unexciting, humdrum, flat, bland, insipid, weak, feeble, lame, uninspired, unadventurous, unenterprising, wearisome, lifeless, spiritless, vapid
COLLOQ. kids' stuff
F3 1 wild, unmanageable, rebellious **2** exciting, adventurous
  ♦ *v*
domesticate, house-train, break (in), train, discipline, master, overcome, conquer, bring to heel, bridle, curb, repress, suppress, quell, subdue, temper, soften, mellow, calm, pacify, humble
OLD (*Shakesp*) entame; (*Spenser*) amenage
FORMAL subjugate

tamper *v*
interfere, meddle, tinker, fiddle, manipulate, juggle, alter, damage
COLLOQ. mess about, muck about, monkey, fix, rig, poke/stick your nose in, stick/put your oar in

tan *adj, v*
  ♦ *adj*
brown, light brown, yellowish brown
  ♦ *v*
1 BROWN, go/turn brown, make/become darker, bronze

2 BEAT, flog, lash, thrash, whip, flay, cane, birch, strap, spank, clout
COLLOQ. wallop, whack, belt

tang *n*
1 SHARPNESS, piquancy, spice, pungency, taste, flavour, savour, smack, smell, aroma, scent, whiff
COLLOQ. bite, edge, kick, pep, punch
2 TINGE, touch, trace, hint, suggestion, overtone

tangible *adj*
touchable, palpable, solid, concrete, material, substantial, physical, real, actual, hard, perceptible, discernible, visible, evident, definite, well-defined, unmistakable, positive
FORMAL tactile, manifest
F3 intangible, abstract, unreal

tangle *n, v*
  ♦ *n*
1 KNOT, snarl-up, snarl, twist, coil, mesh, mat, web, maze, ravel, skein, wilderness; *Scot* fank
FORMAL convolution
2 MESS, muddle, jumble, mix-up, confusion, entanglement, embroilment, complication, labyrinth, imbroglio, raffle, skein, perplexity; *Scot* burble, fankle
  ♦ *v*
1 ENTANGLE, knot, snarl, ravel, twist, coil, interweave, interlace, intertwine, intertwist, intertangle, catch, ensnare, entrap, enmesh, mat; *Scot* fankle, taut
FORMAL convolve
2 INVOLVE, embroil, ensnare, entrap, enmesh, implicate, muddle, confuse, perplex, come into conflict
COLLOQ. mess with
F3 1, 2 disentangle

tangled *adj*
1 *tangled hair*
knotty, knotted, twisted, snarled, matted, tousled, dishevelled, messy, entangled
2 CONFUSED, muddled, jumbled, twisted, tortuous, involved, mixed up, complicated, complex, intricate
FORMAL convoluted

tangy *adj*
sharp, biting, acid, tart, spicy, piquant, pungent, strong, fresh
F3 tasteless, insipid

tank *n*
1 *a hot-water tank*
container, reservoir, header, receptacle, cistern, flush-box, aquarium, stew, vat, basin, gasometer, septic tank
TECHNICAL sponson, shield pond
2 *anti-tank missiles*
armoured car, armoured vehicle, panzer, whippet, Valentine

tantalize *v*
tease, taunt, torment, torture, provoke, lead on, titillate, tempt, allure, entice, beguile, bait, balk, frustrate, thwart, disappoint
F3 gratify, satisfy, fulfil

tantamount *adj*
as good as, equivalent, equal, synonymous, the same as
FORMAL commensurate

tantrum *n*
temper, rage, fury, storm, outburst, fit, fit of temper, flare-up, blow-up, pet, scene, paroxysm
COLLOQ. paddy, hissy fit

tap¹ *v, n*
  ♦ *v*
tap someone on the shoulder
hit, strike, knock, rap, beat, drum, pat, touch, blip, bob, chuck, broach, percuss, pitapat, tat
OLD tick
  ♦ *n*

knock, rap, beat, pat, touch, light blow, blip, chuck, tack, tip, tat; *dialect* tit, tuck
OLD tick

tap² *n, v*
♦ *n*
1 STOPCOCK, valve, faucet, spigot, spout, cock, bibcock, petcock; *Scot* stroup
2 STOPPER, plug, bung
3 BUG, listening device, hidden microphone, receiver
♦ *v*
1 *tap a supply*
use, make use of, utilize, exploit, draw on, take advantage of, mine, quarry, siphon, bleed, milk, drain
2 *tap someone's telephone*
monitor, listen in on, listen to, eavesdrop on, bug, wiretap
■ **on tap**
available, ready, on/at hand, handy, accessible

tape *n, v*
♦ *n*
1 BAND, strip, string, binding, ribbon
2 VIDEO, videotape, cassette, video cassette, recording, tape-recording, video recording, audio cassette, audiotape, magnetic tape
3 *with tape over their mouths*
adhesive tape, Sellotape®, Scotch tape®, masking tape, gaffer tape, sticky tape
♦ *v*
1 BIND, secure, tie, fasten, stick, seal, Sellotape®
2 RECORD, tape-record, video, video-record

taper *v, n*
♦ *v*
narrow, make/become narrow, thin, thin out, make/become thin, slim, decrease, reduce, lessen, diminish, dwindle, fade, wane, peter out, tail off, die away/off
FORMAL attenuate
E3 widen, flare, swell, increase
♦ *n*
spill, candle, wick

tardily *adv*
late, slowly, unpunctually, sluggishly, late in the day, at the last minute
FORMAL belatedly
COLLOQ. at the eleventh hour
E3 promptly, punctually

tardiness *n*
lateness, delay, slowness, unpunctuality, sluggishness, dawdling
FORMAL procrastination, dilatoriness, belatedness
E3 promptness, punctuality

tardy *adj*
slow, slack, sluggish, late, unpunctual, overdue, delayed, dawdling, loitering, behindhand, backward, last-minute, eleventh-hour
FORMAL belated, dilatory, procrastinating, retarded
E3 prompt, punctual

target *n, v*
♦ *n*
1 MARK, aim, goal, bull's eye, victim, butt, game, prey, quarry
2 AIM, object, objective, end, purpose, intention, ambition, goal, destination
♦ *v*
aim for, try for, seek, have as your goal
■ **on target**
1 ACCURATE, precise, exact
COLLOQ. spot-on, bang on
2 ON SCHEDULE, on time, on course, according to plan

tariff *n*
1 TOLL, tax, levy, customs, excise, duty, *zabeta*
2 PRICE LIST, schedule, (list of) charges, menu, bill of fare, rate

tarnish *v, n*
♦ *v*
discolour, corrode, rust, dull, dim, darken, blacken, sully, taint, stain, blemish, spot, blot, mar, spoil
FORMAL befoul, besmirch
E3 polish, brighten
♦ *n*
blemish, spot, stain, taint, blot, discoloration, blackening, film, rust, patina
E3 brightness, polish

tarry *v*
linger, remain, stay, stop, rest, wait, pause, delay, lag, dally, dawdle, loiter
FORMAL abide, bide, sojourn

tart¹ *n, v*
♦ *n*
1 *cherry tart*
pie, flan, pastry, tartlet, patty, quiche, strudel
2 PROSTITUTE, call girl, loose woman, fallen woman, slut, street-walker, whore, harlot, scarlet woman, trollop, drab, *fille de joie*, woman of the streets, rent-boy, woman of the town, woman of ill repute, cocotte, courtesan, bawd, *fille des rues*, grande cocotte, lorette, lady of the night, geisha, hetaera, hierodule, loose fish, magdalen, night-walker, vizard-mask
OLD strumpet, wench
COLLOQ. hooker, hustler, moll, pro, hostess, fancy woman; *N Am* working girl
SLANG floozie, scrubber, tramp, *poule de luxe*, quiff, rough trade, tom, brass; *N Am* broad
■ **tart up**
smarten (up), dress up, renovate, decorate, redecorate, embellish
COLLOQ. doll up

tart² *adj*
1 *the food tastes tart*
sharp, acid, sour, bitter, vinegary, tangy, acidulous, piquant, pungent
2 *tart remarks*
biting, sharp, cutting, sarcastic, incisive, caustic, acid, acerbic, scathing, sardonic
FORMAL trenchant, astringent
E3 1 bland, sweet **2** kind

task *n*
job, chore, duty, charge, imposition, assignment, commission, exercise, mission, engagement, errand, undertaking, enterprise, business, occupation, activity, employment, work, piece of work, labour, toil, burden
■ **take to task**
reprimand, rebuke, criticize, blame, scold, reproach, reprove, censure, lecture
FORMAL upbraid
COLLOQ. tell off, tick off, give someone a dressing-down, slate, slam, knock, give someone stick
E3 commend, praise

taste *n, v*
♦ *n*
1 FLAVOUR, savour, relish, smack, tang
Related adjective: gustative, gustatory
2 SAMPLE, bit, piece, morsel, titbit, bite, nibble, mouthful, sip, drop, dash, soupçon
3 *a taste for adventure*
liking, fondness, partiality, preference, inclination, bent, leaning, hankering, desire, hunger, thirst, appetite
FORMAL penchant, predilection
4 DISCRIMINATION, discernment, judgement, perception, appreciation, sensitivity, refinement, polish, culture, cultivation, breeding, decorum, stylishness, etiquette, finesse, style, grace, elegance, tastefulness, propriety

⊟ 1 blandness **3** distaste **4** tastelessness
◆ v
1 SAMPLE, nibble, sip, try, test
2 SAVOUR, smack, relish
3 EXPERIENCE, undergo, feel, encounter, meet, know
4 DIFFERENTIATE, distinguish, discern, make out, perceive

Synonym nuances
noun sense 1
While **taste** can be used to refer to both pleasant and unpleasant sensations, the associations of **flavour** tend to be positive: *a delicious flavour.* While still positive, **savour** is more suggestive of a distinctive quality: *the salt has lost its savour.* **Relish** could be used of an appetizing element that enhances, whereas **smack** suggests an identifiable trace of something: *a beer with a modest smack of hops,* but **tang** is more suggestive of a strong, sharp ingredient: *the tang of fresh lemons.*

Ways of describing taste include:

acid(ic)	meaty	sharp
acrid	*colloq.* mor(e)ish	sour
appetizing	mouthwatering	spicy
bitter	peppery	sugary
bittersweet	piquant	sweet
citrus	pungent	tangy
creamy	salty	tart
delicious	sapid	tasty
flavoursome	savoury	vinegary
fruity	*colloq.*	*colloq.* yummy
hot	scrumptious	

---

tasteful *adj*
refined, polished, cultured, cultivated, elegant, pleasing, charming, smart, stylish, aesthetic, artistic, harmonious, beautiful, pretty, exquisite, delicate, dainty, gracious, graceful, restrained, well-judged, correct, fastidious, discriminating
FORMAL judicious
COLLOQ. tasty
⊟ tasteless, garish, tawdry

tastefully *adv*
elegantly, graciously, smartly, stylishly, artistically, harmoniously, beautifully, charmingly, exquisitely, delicately
FORMAL judiciously
⊟ tastelessly

tasteless *adj*
1 FLAVOURLESS, insipid, bland, mild, weak, thin, watery, watered-down, flat, plain, stale, dull, boring, uninteresting, vapid
2 INELEGANT, graceless, unseemly, improper, unfitting, indiscreet, crass, rude, tactless, crude, vulgar, kitsch, cheap, tawdry, flashy, showy, gaudy, garish, loud, uncouth
COLLOQ. tacky
SLANG naff
⊟ **1** tasty **2** tasteful, elegant

tasting *n*
testing, sampling, trial, assay, assessment
FORMAL gustation

tasty *adj*
luscious, palatable, appetizing, mouthwatering, delicious, flavoursome, toothsome, succulent, tangy, spicy, piquant, savoury, sweet
FORMAL flavorous, delectable
COLLOQ. mor(e)ish, scrumptious, yummy
⊟ tasteless, insipid

tatter
■ **in tatters**
1 IN RAGS, ragged, in shreds, in ribbons, in pieces, in bits
2 DESTROYED, ruined, in ruins, wrecked, broken, shattered, devastated

tattered *adj*
ragged, frayed, threadbare, ripped, torn, tatty, shabby, scruffy
⊟ smart, neat

tattler *n*
gossip, busybody, tell-tale, scandalmonger, tale-teller, newsmonger, rumour-monger, talebearer

taunt *v, n*
◆ v
tease, torment, provoke, bait, goad, jeer, mock, ridicule, make fun of, poke fun at, gibe, deride, sneer, insult, revile, reproach, dig, twit, cast/throw/fling in someone's teeth
OLD gird
COLLOQ. rib
◆ n
jeer, catcall, gibe, dig, barb, fling, jest, sneer, insult, reproach, taunting, teasing, provocation, mockery, ridicule, sarcasm, derision, censure
OLD gird
COLLOQ. brickbat

taut *adj*
tight, stretched, tightened, contracted, strained, tense, tensed, unrelaxed, worried, anxious, fraught, stiff, rigid
⊟ slack, loose, relaxed

tautological *adj*
repetitive, superfluous, redundant, wordy
TECHNICAL pleonastic
FORMAL verbose
⊟ succinct, economical

tautology *n*
repetition, repetitiveness, duplication, superfluity, redundancy
TECHNICAL pleonasm, perissology
FORMAL iteration, verbosity

tavern *n*
public house, local, inn, bar, alehouse, tap-house, roadhouse, trust-house, *Kneipe, fonda*
OLD public, bush, night-cellar
COLLOQ. dive, hostelry, joint, pub
SLANG boozer

tawdry *adj*
cheap, vulgar, tasteless, fancy, showy, flashy, gaudy, garish, tinselly, glittering, chintzy, tatty, gingerbread
COLLOQ. tacky, cheapo
⊟ fine, tasteful

tawny *adj*
golden, golden brown, khaki, sandy, yellow, tan, fawn
FORMAL fulvous, fulvid, xanthous

tax *n, v*
◆ n
1 LEVY, charge, rate, duty, tariff, customs, contribution
FORMAL imposte
Related adjective: fiscal
2 BURDEN, load, strain, stress, pressure, imposition, weight
◆ v
1 LEVY, charge, demand, exact, assess, impose
2 BURDEN, weigh (down), load, overload, strain, stretch, encumber, impose, exact, try, test, tire, wear out, weary, exhaust, drain, sap, weaken, make demands on
FORMAL enervate
See panel on next page

Taxes include:

airport tax	estate duty	property tax
capital gains tax	excise	rates
capital transfer	*Can & Aust* goods	surtax
tax	and services tax	tithe
capitation	(GST)	toll
community	income tax	value added tax
charge	inheritance tax	(VAT)
corporation tax	insurance tax	
council tax	PAYE (pay as you	
customs	earn)	
death duty	poll tax	

taxi *n*

cab, minicab, taxicab, hansom-cab, hackney carriage, fiacre, samlor
OLD hackney cab, hackney coach

taxing *adj*

burdensome, exacting, demanding, exhausting, punishing, stressful, heavy, tough, hard, tiring, trying, onerous, draining, wearing, wearying, wearisome
FORMAL enervating
E3 easy, gentle, mild

tea *n*

infusion, tisane, cha
SLANG char

Types of tea include:

Assam	herbal tea	orange pekoe
black tea	iced tea	Broken Orange
camomile tea	instant tea	Pekoe (BOP)
Ceylon	Irish Breakfast	Flowery Orange
China tea	Jasmine	Pekoe (FOP)
CTC (crush, tear,	Keemun	Golden Flowery
curl)	Lapsang	Orange Pekoe
Darjeeling	Souchong	(GFOP)
decaffeinated tea	lemon tea	rosehip tea
Dragon Well	Macha	Russian Caravan
Earl Grey	mint tea	Scottish Breakfast
English Breakfast	Nilgiri	Sencha
fruit tea	oolong	Yunnanchai
green tea	pekoe	

teach *v*

instruct, train, coach, tutor, lecture, drill, give lessons, ground, verse, discipline, school, educate, enlighten, edify, inform, impart, indoctrinate, condition, brainwash, advise, counsel, guide, direct, show, demonstrate, read, perfect, preach, take, cram, parrot; *dialect* larn
OLD disciple, foreteach, lear
FORMAL inculcate, pedagogue
COLLOQ. hammer in/into, din in/into
E3 learn

Synonym nuances

Instruct is a synonym with fairly general application, while **train** would suggest a more structured process, to pass on a skill. **Coach**, however, might also be used of preparing someone for a specific test: *coaching for my French exam.* **Tutor** similarly suggests individual attention.

  Drill, on the other hand, suggests physical training, while **ground** and **verse** suggest instilling a rudimentary but thorough knowledge: *in his day, students were grounded in spelling.* **Discipline**, meanwhile, implies a more rigid application: *disciplined in dance from a young age,* whereas **school** and **educate** both suggest a lengthy and structured formal programme.

While these synonyms are fairly neutral in tone, **enlighten** has very positive overtones of enhanced awareness or comprehension, and **edify**, likewise, suggests a beneficial outcome: *an edifying lesson in self-sufficiency.* Negative ideas are conveyed by **indoctrinate**, which suggests a forceful and narrow practice of imbuing with your own opinions. Similarly, **condition** and **brainwash** have unhealthy suggestions of controlling another's mind.

  The terms **advise** and **counsel** convey the more positive suggestion of supplying help. The terms **guide** and **direct** echo this, while **show** and **demonstrate** suggest the provision of a practical example. The more disapproving **preach**, however, suggests overbearing proclamations, usually with a religious or moralistic tone: *we ignored his pompous preaching on his favourite topics.*

teacher *n*

schoolteacher, educator, guide; *Scot* dominie
COLLOQ. *Aust* schoolie
E3 pupil

Kinds of teacher include:

adviser	housemaster	professor
coach	housemistress	pundit
college lecturer	instructor	reader
counsellor	lecturer	reception teacher
crammer	maharishi	*N Am*
dean	master	schoolmarm
demonstrator	mentor	schoolmaster
deputy head	middle school	schoolmistress
doctor	teacher	schoolteacher
don	mistress	secondary school
duenna	nursery school	teacher
fellow	teacher	senior lecturer
form teacher	pastoral head	student teacher
governess	pedagogue	subject co-
guru	pedant	ordinator
headmaster	preceptor	supply teacher
headmistress	preceptress	trainer
head of	primary school	tutor
department	teacher	university lecturer
head of year	principal	upper school
headteacher	private tutor	teacher

teaching *n*

1 INSTRUCTION, tuition, education, pedagogy, didactics
2 DOGMA, doctrine, tenet, precept, principle
Related adjective: doctrinal

Methods of teaching include:

apprenticeship	home-learning	rote learning
briefing	indoctrination	schooling
coaching	induction training	seminar
computer-aided	in-service training	shadowing
learning	instruction	special tuition
correspondence	job training	theory
course	lecturing	training
counselling	lesson	tuition
demonstration	master-class	tutelage
distance learning	on-the-job	tutorial
drilling	training	vocational
familiarization	practical	training
grounding	preaching	work experience
guidance	private tuition	
hands-on training	role-play	

---

team *n, v*

  ♦ *n*

side, line-up, squad, shift, crew, gang, band, group,

set, troupe, bunch, company, stable

■ **team up**

join, join forces, unite, couple, combine, come together, band together, co-operate, collaborate, work together, match, yoke

teamwork *n*

collaboration, co-operation, co-ordination, joint effort, team spirit, fellowship, *esprit de corps*

E3 disharmony, disunity

tear[1] *v, n*

♦ *v*

1 RIP, rend, divide, pull apart, break apart, split, ladder, rupture, sever, shred, scratch, claw, gash, wound, injure, lacerate, slash, mutilate, mangle

OLD sunder

2 PULL, snatch, grab, seize, pluck, wrest

COLLOQ. yank

3 *tear down the street*

dash, rush, hurry, speed, race, run, sprint, fly, shoot, dart, bolt, career, gallop, charge

COLLOQ. belt, nip, rip, bomb, scoot, whizz, vroom, zap, zing, zip, zoom, step on it

♦ *n*

rip, rent, slit, hole, split, run, rupture, scratch, gash, wound, injury, laceration, slash, mutilation

■ **tear down**

destroy, demolish, pull down, knock down, dismantle

tear[2]

■ **in tears**

crying, weeping, tearful, sobbing, wailing, whimpering, blubbering, sad, sorrowful, upset, distressed, emotional

COLLOQ. weepy

Related adjective: lachrymal

tearaway *n*

rough, tough, rowdy, ruffian, rascal, daredevil, delinquent, hooligan, hoodlum, hothead, madcap, roughneck

COLLOQ. good-for-nothing

tearful *adj*

crying, in tears, weeping, sobbing, whimpering, blubbering, sad, sorrowful, upset, distressed, emotional, upsetting, distressing, mournful, doleful

FORMAL lachrymose

COLLOQ. weepy

E3 happy, smiling, laughing

tease *v*

taunt, provoke, bait, make fun of, poke fun at, goad, annoy, vex, irritate, badger, bother, worry, pester, plague, torment, tantalize, mock, ridicule, gibe, banter, chaff, perplex, grig; *dialect* mag

OLD teaze

COLLOQ. aggravate, needle, wind up, rag, kid, rib, have a go at, take the mickey out of, pull someone's leg, chip; *Aust* chiack

SLANG nark, josh, take the piss out of; *NAm* sound, goof

technical *adj*

mechanical, scientific, technological, electronic, computerized, specialist, specialized, practical, applied, expert, professional

technically *adv*

technologically, mechanically, scientifically, electronically, practically, professionally

technician *n*

operator, operative, mechanic, engineer, fitter, mechanical engineer, machinist, mechanician

technique *n*

1 METHOD, system, procedure, manner, fashion, style, way, means, approach, course, performance, execution, modus operandi

FORMAL mode

2 SKILL, skilfulness, ability, capability, delivery, artistry, mastery, craftsmanship, dexterity, facility, proficiency, expertise, art, craft, knack, touch

COLLOQ. knowhow

tedious *adj*

boring, monotonous, uninteresting, unexciting, dull, dreary, uninspired, unvaried, lifeless, flat, drab, banal, routine, humdrum, tiresome, wearisome, wearying, weary, tiring, laborious, long, long-winded, long-drawn-out, irksome

OLD operose

FORMAL prosaic

COLLOQ. run-of-the-mill, samey, a drag

SLANG balls-aching, dragsville

E3 lively, interesting, exciting

tedium *n*

boredom, tediousness, monotony, monotonousness, dullness, dreariness, lifelessness, drabness, irksomeness, banality, sameness, routine, prosiness, ennui, vapidity

COLLOQ. rut

E3 excitement, interest

teem[1] *v*

streets teeming with tourists

swarm, bristle, crawl, burst, proliferate, abound, be full, increase, multiply, overflow, produce, bear, brim

FORMAL pullulate

E3 lack, want

teem[2] *v*

it was teeming with rain

pour, rain, pelt down

COLLOQ. rain cats and dogs, bucket down, come down in buckets/stair rods/torrents

SLANG piss down, chuck it down

teeming *adj*

swarming, crawling, alive, bristling, seething, full, packed, brimming, overflowing, bursting, numerous, abundant, fruitful, thick

FORMAL replete, pullulating

COLLOQ. chock-a-block, chock-full

E3 lacking, sparse, rare

teenage *adj*

teenaged, adolescent, young, youthful, juvenile, immature

teenager *n*

young person, young adult, adolescent, youth, boy, girl, minor, juvenile, emerging adult

COLLOQ. teen, teeny-bopper, bobbysoxer

teeny *adj*

tiny, minute, minuscule, miniature, diminutive, microscopic; *Scot* wee

COLLOQ. titchy, teeny-weeny, teensy-weensy

teeter *v*

sway, rock, roll, reel, stagger, totter, shake, tremble, waver, wobble, balance, lurch, pitch, pivot, seesaw

teetotal *adj*

temperate, abstinent, abstemious, sober

COLLOQ. on the wagon, TT, tee-tee

teetotaller *n*

non-drinker, abstainer, nephalist, Rechabite, water-drinker

COLLOQ. tee-tee

telegram *n*

Telemessage®, cable, telex, fax, telegraph

COLLOQ. wire

telegraph *n, v*

♦ *n*

cable, teleprinter, telex, telegram, radiotelegraph

COLLOQ. wire

♦ *v*

send, transmit, signal, cable, telex
COLLOQ. wire

telepathy n
mind-reading, thought transference, sixth sense, ESP,
extrasensory perception, second sight, clairvoyance

telephone n, v
♦ n
phone, handset, receiver
COLLOQ. blower, hot line
♦ v
phone, ring (up), call (up), dial, contact, get in touch, give
someone a call, make a call
COLLOQ. buzz, give a buzz, give a tinkle, give a bell

Types of telephone include:

Ansaphone®	fax	3G phone
answering	fax-phone	tone-dialling
machine	hands-free phone	phone
caller display	hazardous area	Touchtone®
phone	phone	Uniphone®
camera phone	Minicom®	videophone
cardphone	mobile phone	WAP (Wireless
carphone	pager	Application
cashphone	payphone	Protocol) phone
cellphone	picture mobile	weather-resistant
cellular phone	push-button	phone
corded phone	telephone	
cordless phone	system phone	
dual-band phone	textphone	

---

telescope v
contract, shrink, compress, condense, abridge, squash,
squeeze, crush, shorten, compact, curtail, truncate,
abbreviate, reduce, cut, trim, concertina

televise v
broadcast, screen, show, put on, transmit, air, beam, relay,
cable

television n
TV, receiver, set, small screen
COLLOQ. telly, the box, goggle-box, idiot box, the tube,
tele; N Am boob tube

tell v
1 INFORM, notify, let know, brief, mention, acquaint, impart,
communicate, make known, report, speak, utter, say, state,
confess, divulge, show, disclose, reveal, announce,
broadcast, declare, proclaim
FORMAL apprise
COLLOQ. give the low-down
2 *tell a story*
narrate, recount, relate, recite, report, announce, describe,
sketch, portray, mention
FORMAL delineate
3 ORDER, command, direct, instruct, require, charge, bid,
dictate, advise, authorize, decree
4 DIFFERENTIATE, distinguish, discriminate, tell apart,
discern, recognize, identify, discover, see, perceive, make
out, understand, comprehend
5 AFFECT, have an effect on, take its toll of, exhaust, drain,
change, transform, alter
6 INFORM ON, talk, betray, denounce
COLLOQ. rat, squeal, tell tales, blab, blow the whistle on,
spill the beans, let the cat out of the bag, give the game
away, blow the gaff
SLANG grass, shop
■ **tell off**
scold, chide, reprimand, rebuke, reprove, lecture,
reproach, censure
FORMAL upbraid, berate
COLLOQ. tick off, dress down, slate, slam, knock, bawl out,
bounce, carpet, catch it, chew out, see off, take/pull apart,

give a talking-to, give someone a ticking-off/a dressing-
down, haul over the coals, read the riot act to, (give
someone a) rap over the knuckles, give someone a flea in
their ear/an earful/a piece of your mind, shoot down in
flames, tear a strip off someone

teller n
cashier, clerk, bank clerk, banker, treasurer

telling adj
revealing, significant, impressive, marked, effective,
powerful, convincing, persuasive, impressive
FORMAL cogent

telling-off n
scolding, chiding, rebuke, reprimand, reproach, reproof,
lecture, row
FORMAL castigation, upbraiding
COLLOQ. dressing-down, ticking-off, bawling-out, talking-
to, slap/smack on the wrist, rap over the knuckles, flea in
someone's ear, rocket, wigging, carpeting, earful

tell-tale adj, n
♦ adj
revealing, suggestive, meaningful, revelatory, noticeable,
perceptible, unmistakable
COLLOQ. give-away
♦ n
informer, secret agent, sneak, spy, tale-teller; *Scot* clype; *N
Am* tattle-tale
OLD (*Shakesp*) buzzer
COLLOQ. squealer, snake in the grass, snitch, snitcher
SLANG grass; *N Am* stoolie

temerity n
presumption, impudence, impertinence, effrontery, gall,
audacity, boldness, daring, rashness, recklessness,
impulsiveness
COLLOQ. cheek, nerve
F∃ caution, prudence

temper n, v
♦ n
1 MOOD, humour, nature, temperament, character,
attitude, disposition, constitution, frame/state of mind
2 ANGER, bad mood, rage, fury, passion, tantrum, fit of
temper, flare-up, scene, storm, annoyance, resentment,
irritability, petulance, ill-humour
COLLOQ. paddy, wax
3 CALM, calmness, composure, self-control, tranquillity
SLANG cool
F∃ **2** calmness, self-control **3** anger, rage
♦ v
1 MODERATE, lessen, weaken, reduce, calm, soothe, allay,
alleviate, palliate, modify, soften
FORMAL mitigate, assuage
COLLOQ. tone down
2 HARDEN, roughen, toughen, strengthen
TECHNICAL anneal
FORMAL fortify
■ **lose your temper**
lose your patience, get aggravated, get angry
COLLOQ. boil over, get all steamed up, foam at the mouth,
fly off the handle, go mad, see red, get up in arms, get
aggravated, blow a fuse, blow a gasket, blow your cool,
blow your top, burst a blood vessel, do your nut, explode,
flip your lid, fly into a rage, go off the deep end, go up the
wall, hit the ceiling, hit the roof, lose your cool, lose your
rag, raise hell, freak out, throw a tantrum, throw a wobbly

temperament n
1 CHARACTER, temper, nature, personality, disposition,
tendency, bent, constitution, make-up, complexion, soul,
spirit, mood, humour, temper, frame/state of mind,
attitude, outlook, mettle, idiosyncrasy, kidney
OLD composure, complexion
2 MOODINESS, excitability, sensitivity, touchiness, irritability,

impatience, fieriness, explosiveness, hot-headedness, red-headedness, volatility

temperamental adj
1 MOODY, emotional, over-emotional, neurotic, highly-strung, sensitive, over-sensitive, hypersensitive, touchy, irritable, impatient, passionate, fiery, excitable, explosive, hot-blooded, hot-headed, petulant, volatile, mercurial, capricious, artistic, unpredictable, unreliable
2 NATURAL, inborn, innate, inherent, constitutional, ingrained, congenital
F3 1 calm, level-headed, steady

temperamentally adv
naturally, constitutionally, innately, inherently, basically, fundamentally

temperance n
1 TEETOTALISM, prohibition, abstinence, abstemiousness, sobriety
2 MODERATION, restraint, self-restraint, self-control, self-discipline, self-denial, austerity, continence
F3 2 intemperance, excess

temperate adj
1 *temperate climate*
mild, clement, balmy, fair, equable, balanced, stable, moderate, gentle, pleasant, agreeable
2 TEETOTAL, abstinent, abstemious, self-denying, sober, continent, moderate, restrained, self-restrained, controlled, self-controlled, even-tempered, calm, composed, continent, reasonable, sensible
F3 2 intemperate, extreme, excessive

tempest n
1 STORM, gale, squall, tornado, typhoon, hurricane, cyclone
2 FURORE, upheaval, uproar, ferment, disturbance, commotion, turmoil, tumult

tempestuous adj
stormy, windy, gusty, blustery, squally, turbulent, tumultuous, rough, wild, uncontrolled, violent, furious, raging, heated, boisterous, impassioned, fierce, feverish, passionate, intense
F3 calm, peaceful, quiet

template n
prototype, model, pattern, form, frame, mould, matrix, blueprint, profile, jig, master
TECHNICAL strickle

temple n
place of worship, shrine, sanctuary, church, tabernacle, mosque, pagoda
See also **worship**.

tempo n
time, rhythm, metre, measure, beat, cadence, pulse, throb, speed, velocity, rate, pace

temporal adj
secular, profane, worldly, earthly, terrestrial, material, carnal, fleshly, mortal
F3 spiritual

temporarily adv
for the time being, momentarily, for now, in the interim, pro tem, transiently, transitorily, briefly, fleetingly
F3 permanently

temporary adj
impermanent, provisional, interim, short-term, fill-in, makeshift, stopgap, pro tem, temporal, transient, transitory, passing, fleeting, brief, short-lived, momentary
FORMAL ephemeral, evanescent, fugacious
F3 permanent, everlasting

temporize v
delay, hang back, pause, stall, equivocate, play for time
FORMAL procrastinate, tergiversate
COLLOQ. hum and haw

tempt v
1 ENTICE, coax, cajole, persuade, woo, bait, lure, induce, educe, provoke, incite, egg on
OLD assay, attempt; (*Shakesp*) suggest
FORMAL inveigle
2 ALLURE, attract, draw, invite, tantalize
COLLOQ. make someone's mouth water
F3 1 discourage, dissuade **2** repel

temptation n
enticement, inducement, incitement, coaxing, cajolery, persuasion, urging, bait, snare, lure, allure, allurement, appeal, attraction, influence, draw, pull, trial, seduction, invitation, suggestion
OLD tentation, attempt, invitement, cloven hoof

tempting adj
attractive, inviting, alluring, tantalizing, enticing, appetizing, mouthwatering, seductive
F3 unattractive, uninviting

temptress n
enchantress, seductress, siren, vamp, flirt, sorceress, *femme fatale*, coquette, Delilah, Lorelei, Circe

tenable adj
credible, defensible, justifiable, reasonable, rational, sound, arguable, believable, defendable, plausible, maintainable, supportable, viable, feasible
F3 untenable, indefensible, unjustifiable

tenacious adj
1 DETERMINED, persistent, dogged, firm, single-minded, adamant, resolute, purposeful, steadfast, relentless, persevering, unyielding, unshak(e)able, unswerving, obstinate, stubborn
FORMAL intransigent, obdurate
2 ADHESIVE, cohesive, sticky, clinging, secure, firm, tight, fast
F3 1 loose, slack, weak

tenacity n
determination, persistence, single-mindedness, firmness, fastness, perseverance, doggedness, resoluteness, resolution, resolve, steadfastness, staunchness, toughness, diligence, power, solidity, solidness, strength, force, forcefulness, inflexibility, indomitability, application, stubbornness, obstinacy
FORMAL intransigence, obduracy, pertinacity
F3 looseness, slackness, weakness

tenancy n
occupancy, possession, renting, residence, tenure, holding, lease, leasehold, occupation, incumbency

tenant n
renter, lessee, leaseholder, occupier, occupant, resident, inhabitant, landholder
FORMAL incumbent

tend[1] v
tends to arrive late
incline, be inclined, lean, show a tendency, be liable, bend, bear, head, aim, point, lead, go, move, gravitate

tend[2] v
tend someone who is ill
look after, take care of, care for, cultivate, keep, maintain, see to, manage, handle, guard, protect, watch (over), keep an eye on, mind, nurture, nurse, minister to, serve, attend (to), wait on
F3 neglect, ignore

tendency n
trend, drift, movement, course, direction, bearing, heading, bias, partiality, readiness, liability, susceptibility, proneness, inclination, leaning, bent, aptness, disposition
FORMAL predisposition, propensity, proclivity, conatus

tendentious *adj*
controversial, contentious, polemical, disputed, doubtful, questionable, debatable, disputable, at issue
E3 uncontroversial

tender¹ *adj*
1 KIND, gentle, caring, humane, generous, benevolent, considerate, compassionate, merciful, sympathetic, warm, kindly, fond, affectionate, loving, amorous, romantic, sentimental, emotional, evocative, sensitive, vulnerable, tender-hearted, soft-hearted
TECHNICAL affetuoso, amoroso
OLD (*Spenser*) frail
2 YOUNG, youthful, immature, green, raw, new, early, callow, inexperienced, impressionable, vulnerable
3 SOFT, easy to chew/cut, succulent, fleshy, juicy, dainty, delicate, fragile, frail, sensitive, weak, feeble; *dialect* nesh
4 SORE, painful, aching, smarting, bruised, throbbing, inflamed, red, raw, sensitive, footsore
E3 1 hard-hearted, callous **2** mature **3** tough, hard

tender² *v, n*
♦ *v*
tender an apology
offer, extend, give, present, submit, propose, suggest, advance, volunteer, bid, render
FORMAL proffer
♦ *n*
1 *legal tender*
currency, money, coins, banknotes
2 OFFER, bid, estimate, quotation, price, proposal, proposition, suggestion, submission

tender-hearted *adj*
caring, gentle, kind, kind-hearted, kindly, mild, warm, warm-hearted, sympathetic, soft-hearted, feeling, considerate, compassionate, benevolent, loving, fond, affectionate, responsive, sensitive, humane, merciful, pitying, sentimental, benign
E3 callous, cruel, hard-hearted, unfeeling

tenderly *adv*
gently, warmly, generously, benevolently, considerately, compassionately, sympathetically, sensitively, lovingly, affectionately, fondly, romantically, sentimentally, emotionally
E3 cruelly, hard-heartedly, unfeelingly

tenderness *n*
1 KINDNESS, gentleness, warmth, warm-heartedness, tender-heartedness, sympathy, sweetness, sensitivity, loving-kindness, humaneness, benevolence, attachment, devotion, affection, fondness, amorousness, love, liking, mercy, pity, care, compassion, consideration, humanity, sentimentality, soft-heartedness, vulnerability
2 YOUTH, youthfulness, immaturity, callowness, greenness, inexperience
3 SOFTNESS, succulence, juiciness, weakness, delicateness, frailness, fragility, feebleness
4 SORENESS, rawness, bruising, sensitiveness, ache, aching, inflammation, irritation, pain, painfulness
E3 1 cruelty, hardness, harshness **2** maturity **3** toughness, hardness

tenet *n*
principle, belief, precept, presumption, conviction, opinion, teaching, rule, thesis, view, doctrine, dogma, maxim, creed, credo, canon, article of faith

tennis
See panel on next page

tenor *n*
meaning, tendency, theme, trend, essence, substance, gist, aim, point, direction, drift, purpose, sense, spirit, intent, course, path, way, burden
FORMAL purport

tense *adj, v*
♦ *adj*
1 TIGHT, taut, stretched, strained, stiff, rigid
2 NERVOUS, anxious, worried, strained, distraught, under pressure, jittery, uneasy, apprehensive, on edge, fidgety, restless, jumpy, overwrought, keyed up
COLLOQ. edgy, uptight, stressed out
SLANG screwed up
3 STRESSFUL, exciting, worrying, uneasy, strained, charged, fraught, nerve-racking, nail-biting
E3 1 loose, slack **2** calm, relaxed
♦ *v*
tighten, contract, brace, stretch, strain, stiffen, work
E3 loosen, relax

tensely *adv*
worriedly, anxiously, nervously, apprehensively, uneasily, restlessly
COLLOQ. stressed out, in a state, with butterflies in your stomach
E3 calmly, in a relaxed manner

tension *n*
1 TIGHTNESS, tautness, stiffness, rigidity, strain, straining, stretching, stress, pressure
2 NERVOUSNESS, anxiety, worry, strain, stress, pressure, uneasiness, apprehension, edginess, restlessness, agitation, disquiet, distress, suspense, hypertension
COLLOQ. nerves, jitters, butterflies, butterflies in your stomach, collywobbles, wobbly, willies, heebie-jeebies
3 CONFLICT, disagreement, friction, quarrel, dissension, dispute, opposition, antagonism, hostility, strife, unrest, confrontation, feud, discord, contention, ill-will, difference of opinion, variance, clash
FORMAL antipathy
E3 1 looseness **2** calm(ness), relaxation **3** harmony

tent

Types of tent include:

barrel-vaulted tent	dome tent	sloping wedge tent
bell tent	double-A pole mountain tent	tabernacle
big top	frame tent	tepee
bivvy	hooped bivvy	touring tent
black tent	kata	trailer tent
box tent	lodge	tunnel tent
canopy	marquee	tupik
canvas	mat tent	wigwam
conical tent	ridge tent	yaranga
crossover pole tent	single hoop tent	yurt
	sloping ridge tent	

tentative *adj*
1 PROVISIONAL, experimental, exploratory, speculative, test, trial, pilot, indefinite, unconfirmed, to be confirmed, unproven
FORMAL conjectural, peirastic
2 HESITANT, wavering, faltering, cautious, unsure, uncertain, timid, doubtful, undecided
E3 1 definite, conclusive, final, firm **2** decisive, confident

tentatively *adv*
1 PROVISIONALLY, experimentally, indefinitely, speculatively, on spec
FORMAL peirastically
2 HESITANTLY, cautiously, doubtfully, timidly, gingerly
E3 1 definitely, firmly **2** decisively, confidently

tenterhooks
▪ **on tenterhooks**
anxious, in suspense, impatient, nervous, excited, waiting, watchful, expectant, eager, with bated breath
COLLOQ. keyed up

Terms used in tennis include:

ace	break point	Flushing	let	return	topspin
advantage	bye	Meadows	line judge	Roland Garros	tournament
advantage court	call	follow-through	linesman	royal tennis	tramlines
All England Lawn	Centre Court	foot fault	lob	runback	umpire
Tennis and	centre mark	forecourt	love	second serve	unforced error
Croquet Club	change of ends	forehand	love game	seeding	US Open
N Am alley	clay court	French Open	match	serve	volley
approach shot	continental grip	game	match point	serve and volley	western grip
Association of	court	game point	Melbourne Park	service court	whites
Tennis	cross-court	Grand Slam	mini-break	service line	wild card
Professionals	cut	grass court	mixed doubles	set	Wimbledon
(ATP)	Davis Cup	grip	moon-ball	set point	Women's Tennis
Australian Open	deuce	ground stroke	net	shot	Association
backcourt	deuce court	half volley	net cord	singles	(WTA)
backhand	double fault	hard court	not up	slice	
backspin	doubles	hit	overhead	smash	
ball	down the line	kick serve	overrule	sphairistike	
ball-boy	drive	kill	passing shot	spin	
ball-girl	drop-shot	knock-up	racket (or	straight sets	
baseline	eastern grip	lawn tennis	racquet)	stringing	
baseliner	En-Tout-Cas®	Lawn Tennis	rally	stroke	
baseline rally	exhibition match	Association	real tennis	sweet spot	
break (of service)	fault	(LTA)	retrieve	tie-break	

tenuous *adj*

thin, slim, slender, fine, slight, insubstantial, flimsy, fragile, delicate, weak, vague, hazy, shaky, indefinite, subtle, recherché, doubtful, dubious, questionable
E3 strong, substantial

tenure *n*

possession, proprietorship, residence, tenancy, term, time, holding, occupancy, occupation
FORMAL habitation, incumbency

tepid *adj*

lukewarm, cool, lew, warmish, half-hearted, indifferent, unenthusiastic, apathetic
E3 cold, hot, passionate

term *n, v*

◆ *n*
1 WORD, name, title, epithet, phrase, expression
FORMAL designation, denomination, appellation, locution
2 TIME, period, course, duration, spell, span, stretch, interval, space, semester, session, season
3 on good terms
relations, relationship, footing, standing, position
4 the terms of the contract
condition, point, detail, specification, stipulation, clause, proviso, provision, qualification, restriction, particular
5 CHARGES, rates, fees, prices, costs, tariff
6 END, interval, conclusion, limit, finish, duration, period, culmination, close, bound, boundary, fruition, terminus
◆ *v*
call, name, dub, style, designate, label, tag, title, entitle
FORMAL denominate

terminal *adj, n*

◆ *adj*
1 LAST, final, concluding, ultimate, extreme, utmost, ending, confining, limiting
2 terminal illness
fatal, deadly, lethal, mortal, incurable, untreatable, dying, killing
E3 1 initial, first
◆ *n*
1 END, extremity, limit, termination, boundary, station, last stop, end of the line, garage, depot, terminus
2 a computer terminal
VDU, computer workstation, input-output device, keyboard, console, monitor

terminally *adv*

incurably, fatally, mortally, malignantly, lethally

terminate *v*

finish, bring/come to an end, cease, complete, conclude, end, stop, close, cut off, result, put an end to, leave off, dismiss, abort, lapse, run out, expire, dissolve, issue
FORMAL discontinue
COLLOQ. wind up
E3 begin, start, initiate

termination *n*

end, ending, finish, conclusion, close, abortion, completion, boundary, issue, result, consequence, effect, dénouement, expiry, finale, success, finis
FORMAL demise, cessation, discontinuation
E3 beginning, initiation, start

terminology *n*

language, jargon, phraseology, vocabulary, words, expressions, terms, nomenclature

terminus *n*

end, close, termination, extremity, limit, boundary, destination, goal, target, depot, station, garage, end of the line, terminal

terrain *n*

land, ground, territory, country, countryside, landscape, topography

terrestrial *adj*

earthly, worldly, global, mundane
E3 cosmic, heavenly

terrible *adj*

1 BAD, awful, frightful, dreadful, shocking, appalling, outrageous, disgusting, revolting, repulsive, nasty, offensive, abhorrent, hateful, horrid, horrible, unpleasant, obnoxious, foul, vile, monstrous, hideous, gruesome, horrific, harrowing, grim, distressing, unspeakable, fearful, pokerish
COLLOQ. abortional
2 EXTREME, serious, severe, great, intense, exceptional, big, large
COLLOQ. frightful, awful
3 my arithmetic is terrible
poor, bad, inferior, inadequate, weak, mediocre, substandard, imperfect, faulty, defective, deficient, unsatisfactory, unacceptable, second-rate, third-rate, useless, hopeless, incompetent, ineffective
COLLOQ. awful, lousy, crummy, pathetic, rop(e)y, useless, a load of rubbish, a load of garbage; *N Am* hellacious
SLANG the pits, pants, poxy, naff, crappy; (*vulgar*) a load of crap/shit

4 GUILTY, bad, sorry, ashamed, shamefaced, apologetic, conscience-stricken, remorseful, contrite
5 ILL, unwell, sick, poorly, diseased, painful, in pain, aching, unhappy, despondent, gloomy
FORMAL indisposed
COLLOQ. under the weather
E3 **1** excellent, wonderful, superb **3** good **5** well, happy

terribly adv
very, much, greatly, extremely, exceedingly, thoroughly, desperately, decidedly, seriously
COLLOQ. frightfully, awfully

terrific adj
1 EXCELLENT, wonderful, great, marvellous, fantastic, super, remarkable, outstanding, brilliant, magnificent, superb, sensational, amazing, stupendous, breathtaking
COLLOQ. smashing, fabulous, neat, ace, brill, crack, out of this world, hell of a, wild
SLANG mega, cool, wicked, awesome, crucial, triff
2 HUGE, enormous, gigantic, tremendous, great, intense, extreme, excessive, extraordinary
E3 **1** awful, terrible, appalling

terrifically adv
extremely, exceedingly, excessively, very, really, exceptionally, extraordinarily, intensely, thoroughly, remarkably, utterly, greatly, highly, unusually, unreasonably, immoderately, uncommonly, inordinately, acutely, severely, decidedly
OLD jolly
COLLOQ. awfully, terribly, dreadfully, frightfully

terrified adj
frightened, petrified, scared, scared stiff, panic-stricken, intimidated, horrified, horror-struck, dismayed, appalled, alarmed, awed, aghast
COLLOQ. scared out of your wits, scared to death, having kittens, in a blue funk

terrify v
petrify, horrify, appal, shock, terrorize, intimidate, frighten, scare, scare stiff, panic, alarm, dismay, paralyse, numb
OLD fear, grise, affright; (Shakesp & Spenser) gast, ghast; (Spenser) agrise
COLLOQ. rattle, scare someone out of their wits, make someone's blood run cold, scare the living daylights out of, make someone's hair stand on end, make someone jump out of their skin, put the frighteners on, put the wind up
SLANG scare the shit out of

territorial adj
geographical, area, district, zonal, regional, sectional, topographic, localized
FORMAL domainal

territory n
country, land, state, dependency, province, domain, preserve, jurisdiction, sector, region, area, district, county, zone, tract, terrain, field

terror n
1 FEAR, panic, dread, trepidation, horror, shock, fright, alarm, dismay, terrorism, intimidation
OLD affright, amazedness
FORMAL consternation
COLLOQ. blue funk, cold sweat
2 that child's a terror
rascal, rogue, horror, tearaway
3 FIEND, monster, devil, demon, bogy, scarecrow, bugbear, bogle, poker
OLD bug

terrorist n
revolutionary, gunman, guerrilla, urban guerrilla, militant, anarchist, butcher, seditionist, freedom fighter, bomber, attacker, aggressor, agitator, assailant, assassin, fundamentalist

terrorize v
threaten, menace, intimidate, oppress, coerce, bully, browbeat, frighten, scare, alarm, terrify, petrify, horrify, shock
COLLOQ. strongarm, put the frighteners on, put the wind up

terse adj
short, brief, succinct, concise, to the point, compact, crisp, condensed, pithy, incisive, snappy, curt, blunt, brusque, abrupt, laconic
FORMAL epigrammatic, elliptical, gnomic
E3 long-winded, verbose

test v, n
♦ v
1 test them on spelling
try (out), experiment, examine, assess, evaluate, check, scrutinize, inspect, investigate, study, analyse, screen, sample, prove, verify
FORMAL appraise, assay
COLLOQ. probe
2 test someone's patience
strain, burden, load, overload, stretch, encumber, impose, exact, try, test, tire, wear out, weary, exhaust, drain, sap, weaken, make demands on
FORMAL enervate
♦ n
trial, try-out, experiment, examination, audition, pilot study, assessment, evaluation, questions, questionnaire, quiz, check, check-up, scrutinization, investigation, inspection, analysis, exploration, proof, probation, ordeal

testament n
testimony, witness, demonstration, proof, evidence, exemplification, tribute, will, earnest
FORMAL attestation

testicles n
SLANG goolies, nuts; (vulgar) balls, bollocks, rocks
Related adjective: testicular

testify v
give evidence, state, declare, assert, swear, vouch, affirm, certify, confirm, verify, establish, demonstrate, substantiate, show, bear witness, back up, support, endorse, speak to, rap
TECHNICAL Scot depone
FORMAL avow, attest, corroborate

testimonial n
reference, character, credential, certificate, (letter of) recommendation, endorsement, commendation, tribute

> **⚠ testimonial** or **testimony**?
> A testimonial is a letter describing a person's character and abilities. A testimony is a statement of evidence, for example that of a witness at a trial: he was convicted mainly by the testimony of his former partner; her book is a remarkable testimony to her vision for the future of her country.

testimony n
evidence, statement, submission, declaration, profession, assertion, support, proof, verification, confirmation, affirmation, witness, demonstration, indication
TECHNICAL affidavit, deposition
OLD (Shakesp) attest
FORMAL attestation, corroboration, manifestation

> **⚠ testimony** or **testimonial**?
> See panel at **testimonial**.

testy adj
bad-tempered, cross, quarrelsome, crusty, quick-tempered, short-tempered, irritable, impatient, touchy, grumpy, irascible, snappish, snappy, waspish, sullen, fretful, peevish, splenetic, petulant, captious
FORMAL cantankerous

COLLOQ. crabbed, tetchy, crotchety, stroppy, shirty, ratty
E3 even-tempered, good-humoured

tetchy *adj*
irritable, irascible, peevish, bad-tempered, crusty, grumpy, touchy, short-tempered, snappish
COLLOQ. grouchy, crotchety, shirty, ratty

tête-à-tête *n*
conversation, chat, talk, heart-to-heart, dialogue
COLLOQ. jaw, chitchat, confab, natter

tether *n, v*
• *n*
chain, rope, cord, line, lead, leash, bond, fetter, shackle, restraint, fastening
• *v*
tie, fasten, secure, restrain, chain, rope, leash, bind, lash, fetter, shackle, manacle

text *n*
1 WORDS, wording, content, matter, main matter, body
2 SUBJECT, subject matter, topic, theme, issue, point
3 READING, passage, verse, chapter, paragraph, sentence
4 BOOK, set book, textbook, source

texture *n*
consistency, feel, touch, surface, finish, grain, appearance, weave, tissue, fabric, structure, composition, constitution, character, quality

thank *v*
say thank you to, be grateful, show/express your gratitude, express your thanks, appreciate, show your appreciation, acknowledge, recognize, credit, owe
OLD aggrate; (*Spenser*) remercy

thankful *adj*
grateful, appreciative, obliged, indebted, pleased, contented, relieved
FORMAL beholden
E3 ungrateful, unappreciative

thankfulness *n*
gratitude, appreciation, obligation, indebtedness

thankless *adj*
unrecognized, unappreciated, ungrateful, unacknowledged, unrequited, unrewarded, unrewarding, unprofitable, useless, fruitless
E3 rewarding, worthwhile

thanks *n, interj*
• *n*
gratitude, gratefulness, appreciation, acknowledgement, recognition, credit, thanksgiving, thank-offering
• *interj*
thank you, many thanks, bless you, much obliged, that's very kind of you, that's very good of you, you shouldn't have
COLLOQ. cheers, ta
■ **thanks to**
because of, owing to, due to, on account of, as a result of, through

thaw *v*
1 MELT, defrost, defreeze, unfreeze, de-ice, soften, liquefy, dissolve, warm, heat up
2 BECOME FRIENDLIER, become more relaxed, relax, loosen up
E3 1 freeze

theatre *n*
1 *go to the theatre*
auditorium, hall, playhouse, amphitheatre, lyceum, odeon, opera house
2 DRAMA, the stage, dramatics, theatrics, show business
FORMAL Thespian art
COLLOQ. the boards, the footlights, rep
See panel on next page

theatrical *adj*
1 DRAMATIC, thespian
2 MELODRAMATIC, histrionic, dramatic, mannered, affected, unreal, artificial, forced, pompous, ostentatious, showy, extravagant, emotional, exaggerated, overdone
COLLOQ. over the top, OTT

***Theatrical forms include*:**

ballet	Grand Guignol	operetta
burlesque	kabuki	pageant
cabaret	kitchen-sink	pantomime
circus	legitimate drama	play
comedy	masque	Punch and Judy
black comedy	melodrama	puppet theatre
comedy of	mime	revue
humours	miracle play	street theatre
comedy of	monologue	tableau
manners	morality play	theatre-in-the-
comedy of	mummery	round
menace	musical	Theatre of Cruelty
commedia	musical comedy	Theatre of the
dell'arte	music hall	Absurd
duologue	mystery play	tragedy
farce	Noh	
fringe theatre	opera	

See also **performance**.

---

theft *n*
robbery, thieving, burglary, stealing, pilfering, larceny, shoplifting, kleptomania, fraud, swindling, embezzlement, walk-in, autocrime
OLD mainor, pilferage, plagiary; *Scot* stouth, stouthrie, stouthrief
FORMAL purloining
COLLOQ. pinching, nicking, swiping, lifting, nobbling, filching, mugging, steal, job, stick-up, swipe, smash-and-grab
SLANG heist, touch, blag, sting, rip-off

thematic *adj*
conceptual, notional, classificatory
FORMAL taxonomic

theme *n*
1 SUBJECT, topic, subject matter, thread, motif, keynote, idea, gist, essence, burden, argument, text, story, talk
TECHNICAL subtext, topos
FORMAL leitmotif, lemma, mythus
COLLOQ. the name of the game, peg
2 THESIS, paper, dissertation, composition, essay, text, matter
3 MELODY, tune, motif, song
TECHNICAL leitmotiv

then *adv*
1 AT THAT TIME, at that point, at that moment, in those days, by that time
FORMAL whereupon
2 AFTERWARDS, after, next, soon, subsequently, at a later date
3 IN ADDITION, additionally, also, as well, moreover, besides, too, further, furthermore
4 THEREFORE, and so, accordingly, consequently, as a result
FORMAL thus

theological *adj*
religious, divine, doctrinal, ecclesiastical, scriptural
TECHNICAL hierological

theorem *n*
formula, principle, rule, statement, deduction, proposition
FORMAL dictum, postulate, hypothesis

theoretical *adj*
hypothetical, speculative, abstract, conceptual, notional, academic, doctrinaire, pure, ideal
TECHNICAL a priori

Parts of a theatre include:

apron	coulisse	footlights	loge	pit	spots
auditorium	cut drop	forestage	loggia	prompt side	stage
backstage	cyclorama	fourth wall	logum	proscenium	stalls
balcony	decor	gallery	mezzanine	proscenium arch	tormentor
border	downstage	*colloq.* the gods	open stage	revolving stage	trapdoor
box	flat	green room	opposite prompt	rostrum	upper circle
bridge	flies	grid	orchestra pit	safety curtain	upstage
catwalk	floats	leg drop	picture-frame	scruto	wings
circle	floods	lights	stage	set	

FORMAL conjectural, suppositional
COLLOQ. on paper, armchair
E3 practical, applied, concrete, hands-on

theoretically *adv*
in theory, in principle, hypothetically, notionally,
conceptually, ideally, seemingly
TECHNICAL a priori
COLLOQ. on paper
E3 in practice

theorize *v*
suppose, guess, speculate, formulate, hypothesize
FORMAL conjecture, postulate, propound

theory *n*
hypothesis, supposition, assumption, presumption, guess,
speculation, idea, view, opinion, notion, abstraction,
rationale, philosophy, thesis, plan, proposal, scheme,
system, principle, law
FORMAL conjecture, surmise, postulation
E3 certainty, practice; *formal* praxis
■ **in theory**
theoretically, in principle, hypothetically, notionally,
conceptually, ideally, seemingly
TECHNICAL a priori
COLLOQ. on paper
E3 in practice

therapeutic *adj*
remedial, curative, healing, curing, restorative, tonic,
medicinal, corrective, good, advantageous, beneficial,
salutary, health-giving
FORMAL ameliorative, sanative
E3 harmful, detrimental

therapy *n*
treatment, remedy, cure, healing, tonic

Types of therapy include:

acupressure	electrotherapy	phototherapy
acupuncture	faith healing	physiotherapy
Alexander	family therapy	play therapy
technique	Gestalt therapy	primal therapy
aromatherapy	group therapy	psychotherapy
art therapy	heat treatment	radiotherapy
aversion therapy	herbalism	reflexology
beauty therapy	homeopathy	regression
behaviour	hormone-	therapy
therapy	replacement	reiki
biofeedback	therapy (HRT)	reminiscence
chemotherapy	horticulture	therapy
chiropractic	therapy	*colloq.* retail
cognitive therapy	hydrotherapy	therapy
confrontation	hypnotherapy	Rolfing
therapy	irradiation	sex therapy
craniosacral	lymphatic	shiatsu
therapy (CST)	drainage therapy	speech therapy
drama therapy	(LDT)	ultrasound
dream analysis	moxibustion	zone therapy
drug therapy	music therapy	
electroconvulsive	naturopathy	
(or	occupational	
electroshock)	therapy	
therapy	osteopathy	

thereabouts *adv*
about, approximately, roughly, near that number, near that
date

thereafter *adv*
subsequently, afterwards, after that, after that time, next

therefore *adv*
and so, then, accordingly, consequently, as a result, for that
reason
FORMAL thus, ergo

thesaurus *n*
dictionary, lexicon, wordbook, wordfinder, vocabulary,
synonymy, encyclopedia, storehouse, repository, treasury

thesis *n*
1 *a doctoral thesis*
dissertation, essay, composition, treatise, paper, monograph
FORMAL disquisition
2 SUBJECT, topic, theme, idea, opinion, view, theory,
hypothesis, proposal, proposition, premise, statement,
argument, contention, position
E3 **2** antithesis

thick *adj, n*
♦ *adj*
1 WIDE, broad, fat, stout, chunky, heavy, bulky, deep, big,
substantial, stiff, solid, dense, impenetrable, close,
compact
2 FULL, packed, crowded, filled, overflowing, swarming,
teeming, bristling, brimming, crawling, bursting,
numerous, abounding, abundant
COLLOQ. chock-a-block, chocker
3 *a thick soup*
semi-solid, heavy, concentrated, condensed, viscous,
coagulated, creamy, lumpy, clotted
4 *thick clothes*
heavy, warm, woollen, chunky, bulky
5 *thick fog*
impenetrable, dense, heavy, murky, smoggy, soupy,
opaque, concentrated
6 *a thick voice*
husky, rough, unclear, indistinct, throaty, guttural, hoarse,
croaky, croaking, gruff, gravelly, rasping
7 *a thick accent*
strong, pronounced, broad, marked, definite, obvious,
noticeable, striking
8 STUPID, foolish, slow, unintelligent, dense, dull, brainless,
simple
COLLOQ. dim-witted, dumb, gormless, dopey, daft, dippy,
thick as a plank/two short planks
E3 **1** thin, slim, slender, slight **2** sparse **3** clear, watery **4** thin,
light, lightweight **6** clear, distinct **7** faint, vague **8** clever,
intelligent; *colloq.* brainy
♦ *n*
middle, centre, focus, midst, hub, heart

thicken *v*
1 *thicken a soup*
make/become more solid, solidify, stiffen, condense,
congeal, coagulate, curdle, clot, cake, gel, jell, set, reduce;
Scot meal
TECHNICAL upset

OLD incrassate, inspissate
2 the plot thickens
become more mysterious/complicated/involved/intricate
F3 1 thin

thicket *n*
wood, copse, coppice, grove, spinney, maquis

thickhead *n*
fool, idiot, dunce, imbecile
COLLOQ. nitwit, twit, numskull, fathead, blockhead,
dimwit, dope, clot, dummy, pinhead, chump, moron,
nincompoop, ninny, twerp, oaf, halfwit, buffoon
SLANG prat, dork, geek, git, berk; (*taboo*) dickhead

thick-headed *adj*
stupid, foolish, dense, slow, brainless, obtuse, dull-witted,
idiotic, imbecilic, moronic, asinine, doltish, slow-witted
COLLOQ. dim-witted, blockheaded, dopey, thick,
gormless, dumb, not all there, loopy, barmy, potty, slow on
the uptake, thick as a plank/two short planks
SLANG loony
F3 clever, intelligent, sharp; *colloq.* brainy

thickness *n*
1 WIDTH, breadth, diameter, extent, density, viscosity,
consistency, bulk, bulkiness, body, solidness, closeness
2 LAYER, stratum, seam, vein, band, deposit, bed, ply, sheet,
coat, film, lamina
F3 1 thinness

thickset *adj*
stocky, heavy, heavily built, well-built, sturdy, powerful,
strong, muscular, burly, beefy, brawny, solid, bulky,
squabby, squat, dense
F3 lanky

thick-skinned *adj*
insensitive, unfeeling, callous, tough, invulnerable,
hardened, case-hardened, inured, impervious
COLLOQ. hard-boiled, hard-nosed, tough as old boots
F3 thin-skinned, sensitive, vulnerable

thief *n*
robber, bandit, pickpocket, shoplifter, burglar,
housebreaker, crook, highwayman, plunderer, poacher,
stealer, pilferer, kleptomaniac, fraud, fraudster, swindler,
embezzler, brigand, larcener, snatch-purse, sneak, coon,
knight of industry, land-rat, river-rat, area-sneak,
Autolycus, nut-hook; *dialect* limmer
OLD abactor, footpad, water thief, bulker; (*Shakesp*) lifter
COLLOQ. mugger, filcher, nicker, nobbler, hotter
SLANG tea leaf, chummy, kiddy; *N Am* ice man
OLD SLANG snow-dropper, snow-gatherer; (*Shakesp*) prig

thieve *v*
steal, rob, pinch, cheat, swindle, make/run off with,
misappropriate, burgle, embezzle, pilfer, plunder, poach,
abstract
FORMAL peculate, purloin
COLLOQ. nobble, snaffle, filch, knock off, lift, nick, swipe,
whip, bag
SLANG rip off, heist, hoist, pull, blag, lag

thieving *n, adj*
• *n*
stealing, theft, robbery, burglary, pilferage, pilfering,
shoplifting, plundering, embezzlement, larceny, thievery,
banditry, crookedness, piracy
FORMAL peculation
COLLOQ. mugging, knocking off, ripping off, lifting, nicking,
filching
• *adj*
dishonest, fraudulent, crooked, light-fingered, larcenous,
predatory
OLD furacious; (*Shakesp*) pugging
FORMAL rapacious
COLLOQ. sticky-fingered

thievish *adj*
dishonest, fraudulent, crooked, light-fingered, thieving,
larcenous, predatory
OLD furacious
FORMAL rapacious
COLLOQ. sticky-fingered

thin *adj, v*
• *adj*
1 LEAN, slim, slender, fine, light, svelte, narrow, paper-thin,
wafer-thin, attenuated, slight, skinny, bony, skeletal,
scraggy, scrawny, spindly, lanky, gaunt, spare, anorexic,
wasted, shrunken, underweight, undernourished,
emaciated
COLLOQ. thin as a rake
2 thin fabric
fine, delicate, light, lightweight, flimsy, filmy, gauzy,
gossamer, sheer, see-through, transparent, translucent
FORMAL diaphanous
3 SPARSE, scarce, scattered, scant, paltry, meagre, poor,
inadequate, deficient, scanty, skimpy, straggly, wispy
4 WEAK, feeble, runny, watery, diluted, dilute
COLLOQ. wishy-washy
5 the evidence is thin
weak, flimsy, unconvincing, implausible, insubstantial,
feeble, lame, inadequate, inconclusive, untenable,
defective, deficient
6 a thin voice/sound
high-pitched, soft, quiet, weak, faint
F3 1 fat, broad **2** substantial, thick, dense, solid **3** thick,
plentiful, abundant **4** strong, thick **5** strong, convincing,
substantial
• *v*
1 DIMINISH, reduce, dwindle, decrease, lessen, make/
become less in number, trim, narrow, weed out
FORMAL attenuate
2 WEAKEN, dilute, make more watery, water down, rarefy,
refine
■ **on thin ice**
precarious, unsafe, at risk, vulnerable, insecure, in
jeopardy, open to attack

Synonym nuances
adjective sense 1
Lean can be used positively to suggest an athletic
thinness. Also complimentary-sounding, but usually
used of women, are **slim** and **slender**, which suggest an
attractively shaped figure, and **svelte**, which suggests
sleekness. **Narrow**, on the other hand, is more
straightforwardly descriptive of width: *a narrow waist*,
while **attenuated** is more appropriate to suggest being
elongated: *an attenuated El Greco face.*
  Slight returns to the idea of a dainty build, and is not
particularly suggestive of any point of view, but **skinny**,
bony and **skeletal** all suggest an extreme and
unattractive lack of flesh, and are uncomplimentary in
tone: *his skeletal fingers.* **Scraggy** and **scrawny** are
similar, but more suggestive of resultant stretched skin:
her scrawny neck. You can use **spindly** and **lanky** to
suggest an awkward ungainliness, whereas **gaunt**
creates an unattractive image of a pinched face.
  Spare returns to the idea of having no excess flesh and is
not judgemental: *a spare man, in middle age*, unlike
underweight and **undernourished**, which are more
technical in tone and suggest an unhealthy look. This is
more explicit in the rather more emotive terms **anorexic**,
wasted and **emaciated**, implying seriously debilitating
conditions. **Shrunken** has more to do with having
contracted, and again is associated with ill health: *his
grey and shrunken face dwarfed by the pillow.*

---

thing *n*
1 ARTICLE, item, object, entity, creature, body, substance

2 DEVICE, contrivance, gadget, tool, implement, instrument, apparatus, machine, mechanism, waldo
COLLOQ. gismo, doodah, thingy, thingummy, thingamy, thingummyjig, thingummybob, what-d'you-call-it, whatsit, what's-its-name; *S Afr* dinges
3 *take your things with you*
clothes, clothing, garments, belongings, possessions, paraphernalia, goods, luggage, baggage, equipment, tools, apparatus, tackle, oddments, odds and ends, bits and pieces
FORMAL apparel, attire, effects
COLLOQ. stuff, gear, togs, bits and bobs, clobber
4 ASPECT, detail, particular, characteristic, trait, feature, quality, property, factor, element, attribute, point, fact, concept, notion, thought, idea
5 ACT, deed, feat, exploit, action, activity, undertaking, job, chore, task, responsibility, problem
6 CIRCUMSTANCE, situation, eventuality, happening, occurrence, event, episode, matter, incident, phenomenon, affair, proceeding, arrangement, condition
7 OBSESSION, preoccupation, fixation, *idée fixe*, fetish, mania, phobia, dislike, fear, horror, aversion
COLLOQ. hang-up, one-track mind
8 LIKING, fondness, love, affection, preference, partiality, affinity, taste, attraction, appreciation, proneness, inclination, tendency, bias, leaning, bent, desire, weakness, fancy
FORMAL predilection, penchant, propensity, proclivity
COLLOQ. soft spot
9 *computers are his thing*
speciality, what you like, what interests you
COLLOQ. cup of tea, baby, bag, what turns you on, what floats your boat, what lights your candle
- **the thing**
fashionable, popular, in fashion, in vogue, current, latest, modish
COLLOQ. the latest, all the rage, hip, cool

think *v, n*
- *v*
1 BELIEVE, hold, consider, regard, judge, esteem, estimate, reckon, calculate, determine, conclude, reason
FORMAL deem, opine
COLLOQ. figure, reckon
2 CONCEIVE, imagine, suppose, guess, presume, expect, foresee, envisage, visualize, anticipate
OLD conceit
FORMAL surmise, conjecture
3 *think it over*
ponder, mull over, chew over, brood, ruminate, meditate, contemplate, muse, reflect, concentrate, deliberate, weigh up, recall, review, take stock, recollect, remember
FORMAL cogitate, cerebrate
COLLOQ. sleep on it
- *n*
consideration, contemplation, deliberation, muse, ponder, reflection, meditation, assessment, evaluation
FORMAL cogitation
- **think better of**
change your mind about, think again, think twice, reconsider, rethink, revise, have second thoughts about, decide not to do
COLLOQ. get cold feet
- **think much of**
think highly of, admire, esteem, prize, respect, value, set store by, rate
E3 abominate
- **think nothing of**
consider normal, consider usual, take in your stride, have no qualms about
- **think over**
reflect upon, consider, weigh up, contemplate, meditate, ponder, chew over, ruminate, mull over

- **think up**
devise, contrive, dream up, imagine, conceive, visualize, invent, design, create, concoct

---

Synonym nuances
verb sense 3
You can use **ponder**, **mull over** and **chew over** to suggest turning a matter over in your mind, while **brood** implies less focused thought, and a degree of moroseness. **Ruminate**, **meditate** and **contemplate**, on the other hand, suggest intense thought and consideration, while **muse** and **reflect** would be appropriate of a mental aside: *what a daft world this is, he mused*.
  Concentrate, however, suggests focusing strongly on a particular matter, whereas **deliberate** has implications of lengthy and careful thought with the purpose of arriving at an answer: *the jury deliberated for five days*. Similarly, **weigh up** suggests looking at the benefits and disadvantages of a situation, and **take stock** and **review** also suggest careful judgement, but after looking back over past events.

---

thinkable *adj*
likely, imaginable, possible, feasible, reasonable, supposable, conceivable
FORMAL cogitable
E3 unthinkable

thinker *n*
philosopher, scholar, theorist, ideologist, intellect, sage, mastermind
FORMAL theoretician
COLLOQ. brain

thinking *n, adj*
- *n*
reasoning, philosophy, thought(s), conclusion(s), theory, idea, opinion, view, outlook, position, judgement, assessment, evaluation, appraisal
- *adj*
reasoning, rational, sensible, intellectual, intelligent, cultured, sophisticated, philosophical, analytical, logical, reflective, contemplative, meditative, thoughtful

thin-skinned *adj*
sensitive, easily upset, snappish, soft, susceptible, tender, vulnerable, hypersensitive, irritable, touchy
E3 thick-skinned, unfeeling, callous

third-rate *adj*
low-grade, low-quality, poor, poor-quality, bad, awful, inferior, substandard, unsatisfactory, mediocre, indifferent, slipshod, shoddy, cheap and nasty
COLLOQ. not up to scratch, awful, terrible, botched, lousy, crummy, pathetic, rop(e)y, useless, a load of rubbish/garbage
SLANG the pits, pants, poxy, naff, crappy; (*vulgar*) a load of crap/shit
E3 first-rate

thirst *n, v*
- *n*
1 THIRSTINESS, dryness, drought, parchedness, aridity, drouth, drouthiness
OLD thrist
2 DESIRE, longing, yearning, hankering, craving, hunger, appetite, lust, passion, eagerness, keenness
COLLOQ. yen
- *v*
hunger, desire, want, long, yearn, hanker, crave, lust
COLLOQ. have a yen for

thirsty *adj*
1 DRY, dehydrated, arid, droughty, drouthy
OLD athirst, hydropic
COLLOQ. parched, gasping

2 *thirsty for knowledge*
desirous, longing, yearning, hankering, craving, hungry, thirsting, burning, itching, dying, eager, keen, avid, greedy, athirst

thong *n*
band, strip, belt, cord, lash, strap

thorn *n*
spike, point, barb, prickle, spine, bristle, needle, acantha; *S Afr* doorn
TECHNICAL aculeus
OLD prick
Related adjective: spiniform

thorny *adj*
1 SPIKY, pointed, sharp, barbed, prickly, spiny, bristly, armed, briery
FORMAL acanthous, spinous, spinose
2 *a thorny problem*
difficult, troublesome, irksome, vexed, worrying, trying, upsetting, problematic, knotty, complex, intricate, tough, awkward, delicate, tricky, ticklish
FORMAL convoluted
COLLOQ. dicey, sticky

thorough *adj*
1 *a thorough person*
painstaking, scrupulous, meticulous, careful, conscientious, efficient, methodical
2 *thorough research*
sweeping, all-embracing, comprehensive, rigorous, in-depth, all-inclusive, exhaustive, scrupulous, meticulous, extensive, deep, thoroughgoing, intensive, widespread
3 *a thorough waste of time*
full, complete, total, entire, utter, absolute, perfect, pure, sheer, unqualified, unmitigated, out-and-out, downright
F∃ 1 superficial, careless **2** partial

thoroughbred *adj*
pedigree, pedigreed, pure-blood, pure-blooded, full-blooded, blooded
F∃ cross-bred, hybrid, mixed, mongrel

thoroughfare *n*
road, street, roadway, way, highway, avenue, motorway, passage, passageway, access, turnpike, boulevard, concourse

thoroughgoing *adj*
1 *a thoroughgoing Socialist*
full, complete, total, entire, utter, absolute, perfect, pure, sheer, unqualified, unmitigated, out-and-out, downright, uncompromising
2 *thoroughgoing reform/research*
sweeping, all-embracing, comprehensive, rigorous, in-depth, all-inclusive, exhaustive, scrupulous, extensive, deep, thoroughgoing, intensive, widespread, meticulous, painstaking, scrupulous, careful, methodical

thoroughly *adv*
1 CAREFULLY, painstakingly, meticulously, scrupulously, intensively, conscientiously, assiduously, efficiently, comprehensively, sweepingly, exhaustively, root and branch, inside out
2 FULLY, perfectly, completely, absolutely, downright, entirely, quite, totally, utterly, soundly
OLD throughly
COLLOQ. every inch, with a fine-tooth comb
F∃ 1 carelessly, haphazardly **2** partially

though *conj, adv*
♦ *conj*
although, even if, while, allowing, granted
FORMAL notwithstanding
♦ *adv*
however, but, nevertheless, nonetheless, yet, still, even so, for all that
COLLOQ. all the same

thought *n*
1 THINKING, attention, care, heed, regard, consideration, reasoning, study, scrutiny, introspection, meditation, pondering, contemplation, musing, rumination, reflection, deliberation
OLD conceit
FORMAL cogitation, cerebration
2 IDEA, notion, concept, conception, belief, conviction, opinion, view, point of view, feeling, judgement, theory, assessment, estimation, appraisal, conclusion, plan, design, intention, purpose, reason, aim, hope, dream, prospect, expectation, anticipation, aspiration
OLD conceit
3 THOUGHTFULNESS, consideration, kindness, care, concern, regard, compassion, sympathy, tenderness, gesture, touch
FORMAL solicitude

thoughtful *adj*
1 PENSIVE, wistful, dreamy, abstracted, reflective, contemplative, introspective, thinking, absorbed, studious, serious, solemn, quiet, lost in thought, deep, profound, sobering, *pensieroso*
OLD (*Spenser*) conceitful
FORMAL cogitative
COLLOQ. in a brown study
2 CONSIDERATE, kind, unselfish, helpful, caring, compassionate, sympathetic, tender, attentive, mindful, careful, methodical, prudent, cautious, wary
FORMAL heedful, solicitous
F∃ 2 thoughtless, insensitive, selfish

thoughtfully *adv*
1 PENSIVELY, wistfully, dreamily, reflectively, contemplatively, introspectively, seriously, quietly, deeply, profoundly
2 CONSIDERATELY, unselfishly, helpfully, compassionately, sympathetically, carefully, methodically, mindfully, cautiously
F∃ 2 inconsiderately, thoughtlessly

thoughtless *adj*
1 INCONSIDERATE, unthinking, insensitive, unfeeling, tactless, undiplomatic, indiscreet, unkind, rude, impolite, selfish, uncaring
OLD (*Shakesp*) unweighing
FORMAL incogitant
2 ABSENT-MINDED, inattentive, heedless, mindless, foolish, stupid, silly, rash, hasty, reckless, ill-considered, ill-advised, unwise, imprudent, careless, negligent, remiss, vain, improvident, frivolous, giddy-headed, light-headed, blindfold, *étourdi(e)*
FORMAL precipitate
F∃ 1 thoughtful, considerate **2** careful

thoughtlessly *adv*
inconsiderately, insensitively, unfeelingly, tactlessly, undiplomatically, indiscreetly, impolitely, rudely, inattentively, foolishly, stupidly, carelessly, recklessly, rashly
F∃ thoughtfully, carefully

thrall *n*
thraldom, power, control, bondage, enslavement, servitude, slavery, subjection, serfdom, vassalage, hands, grip, clutches
FORMAL subjugation
F∃ freedom

thrash *v*
1 PUNISH, beat, whip, lash, flog, scourge, cane, spank, clobber, lay into
COLLOQ. wallop, tan, whack, belt
SLANG *N Am* lam; *S Afr* donder
2 DEFEAT, beat, trounce, drub, be more than a match for, have the edge on, crush, overwhelm, rout
FORMAL vanquish
COLLOQ. hammer, slaughter, clobber, lick, pound,

demolish, wipe the floor with, walk all over
SLANG take to the cleaners
3 THRESH, flail, hit, flog, toss, jerk, swish, writhe
■ **thrash out**
discuss, debate, negotiate, hammer out, settle, resolve, clear the air

thrashing *n*
1 PUNISHMENT, flogging, lashing, caning, hiding, beating, tanning, whipping, leathering, pasting
FORMAL chastisement
COLLOQ. belting
2 DEFEAT, drubbing, beating, rout, crushing, trouncing, lamming
COLLOQ. hammering, clobbering, licking

thread *n, v*
♦ *n*
1 YARN, strand, fibre, filament, string, line, strip, streak
Related adjective: fibrillary, fibrillous
2 COURSE, direction, drift, tenor, theme, subject, motif, plot, storyline, train of thought
♦ *v*
pass, ease, move, push, inch, meander, wind, string, weave

Types of thread and wool include:

THREAD:		chunky wool
button thread	mercerized cotton	crewel wool
coton à broder	metallic thread	double-knitting wool
cotton	pearl cotton	embroidery wool
embroidery silk	polyester	knitting wool
embroidery thread	purl	Persian wool
floss	quick-match	tapestry wool
machine embroidery thread	silk	2-ply
machine embroidery thread	stranded cotton	2-ply
machine twist	WOOL:	3-ply
	Arran wool	4-ply
	baby wool	

---

threadbare *adj*
1 *threadbare clothes*
worn, frayed, ragged, moth-eaten, scruffy, tatty, tattered, shabby
2 HACKNEYED, overused, old, stale, tired, trite, worn-out, well-worn, cliché-ridden, commonplace, stock, stereotyped
COLLOQ. corny
E3 **1** new **2** fresh

threat *n*
menace, warning, ultimatum, omen, foreboding, danger, risk, hazard, peril, blackmail, denunciation, enemy at the door, gunboat diplomacy, war drum, *brutum fulmen*
FORMAL portent, presage, commination
COLLOQ. stick, big stick

threaten *v*
1 MENACE, intimidate, browbeat, cow, pressurize, bully, extort, blackmail, terrorize, warn (off), endanger, jeopardize, imperil, flank, lift a/your hand to; *Scot* shore
OLD comminate
COLLOQ. push around, lean on, put the frighteners on, put the screws on
2 BE IMMINENT, be in the offing, approach, loom (up), forebode, foreshadow, impend, hang over, look like
FORMAL portend, presage, augur, comminate

threatening *adj*
menacing, intimidatory, warning, cautionary, ominous, foreboding, sinister, grim, looming
FORMAL inauspicious, impending, minacious, minatory, comminative

threesome *n*
trio, trilogy, triple, triplet, triumvirate, triad, triune, troika, trinity, triptych

thresh *v*
thrash, flail, hit, flog, toss, jerk, swish, writhe

threshold *n*
doorstep, sill, doorway, door, entrance, entry, brink, verge, starting-point, dawn, beginning, start, commencement, outset, opening
FORMAL inception

thrift *n*
economy, husbandry, prudence, saving, conservation, frugality, carefulness
FORMAL parsimony
COLLOQ. scrimping and saving
E3 extravagance, waste

thriftless *adj*
extravagant, lavish, spendthrift, unthrifty, imprudent, wasteful, prodigal
FORMAL improvident, dissipative, profligate
E3 thrifty

thrifty *adj*
economical, saving, frugal, sparing, prudent, careful, conserving, provident, husbandly; *Scot* fendy
OLD wary
FORMAL parsimonious
E3 extravagant, profligate, prodigal, wasteful, thriftless, unthrifty

thrill *n, v*
♦ *n*
excitement, adventure, pleasure, delight, joy, stimulation, charge, sensation, feeling, glow, tingle, throb, frisson, shudder, flutter, vibration, quiver, tremor, bang, pulse; *Scot* dinnle
COLLOQ. kick, buzz, the shivers
SLANG charge; *N Am* gas
♦ *v*
excite, exhilarate, rouse, arouse, move, stir, stimulate, electrify, galvanize, flush, glow, tingle, throb, shudder, flutter, vibrate, tremble, shiver, quiver, shake, pulsate; *dialect* thirl; *Scot* dirl
COLLOQ. give a buzz/kick to
E3 bore

thrilling *adj*
exciting, stimulating, stirring, rousing, riveting, sensational, exhilarating, gripping, electrifying, rip-roaring, heart-stirring, soul-stirring, shaking, shuddering, shivering, trembling, vibrating, quaking, tinglish
COLLOQ. hair-raising, action-packed

thrive *v*
flourish, prosper, boom, grow, increase, advance, develop, bloom, blossom, gain, profit, succeed, do well, make progress, make headway
FORMAL burgeon
E3 languish, stagnate, fail, die

thriving *adj*
prosperous, successful, blossoming, booming, developing, flourishing, growing, healthy, wealthy, affluent, well, comfortable, blooming
FORMAL burgeoning
E3 ailing, failing, languishing, stagnating, dying

throat *n*
throttle, windpipe, gullet, gorge, oesophagus, craw, thropple, fauces, halse; *Scot* thrapple
TECHNICAL trachea, pharynx
OLD weasand
COLLOQ. the Red Lane
Related adjectives: guttural, pharyngeal, jugular

throaty *adj*
guttural, hoarse, rasping, raucous, low, husky, deep, gruff, thick

throb *v, n*
• *v*
pulse, pulsate, beat, palpitate, vibrate, pound, thump, drum, jump, tingle, stound
OLD quop
• *n*
pulse, pulsation, beat, heartbeat, palpitation, vibration, pant, pounding, thumping, drumming

throe *n*
convulsion, fit, pain, pang, paroxysm, seizure, spasm, stab, suffering, distress, agony, anguish, torture
FORMAL travail
■ **in the throes of**
struggling with, wrestling with, deeply involved in, busy with, preoccupied with, in the process of, in the middle of, in the midst of

thrombosis *n*
heart attack, coronary, coronary thrombosis, blood clot, apoplexy

throng *n, v*
• *n*
crowd, mass, mob, multitude, pack, press, crush, jam, swarm, flock, congregation, herd, bevy, horde, host; *Scot* thrang
FORMAL assemblage, *grex venalium*
• *v*
flock, fill, crowd, cram, converge, herd, press, swarm, pack, bunch, congregate, jam, besiege; *Scot* thrang
OLD press
COLLOQ. mill around

throttle *v*
1 STRANGLE, strangulate, choke, asphyxiate, suffocate, smother, stifle, scrag, thropple
2 SUPPRESS, gag, silence, inhibit, restrain, check, keep in, hold back, strangle, stifle, smother

through *prep, adv, adj*
• *prep*
1 ACROSS, all the way across, from one side of to the other, from one end of to the other
2 BETWEEN, by, with the help of, via, by way of, by means of, using, through the agency of
FORMAL through the good offices of, by virtue of
3 *all through the night*
throughout, during, in, to/until the end of, from the beginning to the end of, without a break/interruption in
4 BECAUSE OF, as a result of, owing to, due to, thanks to, on account of, by virtue of
• *adv*
1 ALL THE WAY ACROSS, from one side to the other, from one end to the other
OLD throughly
2 FROM BEGINNING TO END, from start to finish, during the whole time, continuously, uninterruptedly
OLD throughly
3 *warmed/soaked through*
thoroughly, completely, fully, entirely, totally
• *adj*
1 FINISHED, ended, completed, done, no longer having anything to do with, no longer involved with
FORMAL terminated
2 *through train*
direct, express, non-stop
■ **through and through**
completely, totally, thoroughly, utterly, wholly, entirely, fully, unreservedly, in every respect, altogether, to the core, from top to bottom

throughout *adv, prep*
• *adv*
everywhere, in every part, extensively, widely, completely, from beginning to end
FORMAL ubiquitously
• *prep*
1 DURING, during/in the whole of, all through, in the course of, for the duration of
2 IN ALL PARTS, in every part of, all over, all round, everywhere

throughput *n*
output, production, productivity, product, manufacture, yield, fruits, harvest, return, outturn, turnout

throw *v, n*
• *v*
1 HURL, heave, lob, pitch, sling, cast, fling, flip, toss, shy, launch, project, propel, catapult, send
COLLOQ. chuck; *Irish* puck
2 MOVE QUICKLY, fling, turn, force, put, cast
3 *throw light*
shed, cast, project, send, direct, cause to fall, emit, radiate, give off
4 BRING DOWN, floor, fell, prostrate, upset, overturn, dislodge, unseat, unsaddle, unhorse
5 *throw a switch*
put on, switch on, operate, work
6 PERPLEX, baffle, confound, disturb, put out, confuse, disconcert, surprise, astonish, dumbfound
FORMAL discomfit
COLLOQ. floor, faze, rattle
7 *throw a party*
arrange, organize, give, put on, lay on, host
• *n*
heave, lob, pitch, sling, fling, flip, toss, cast
COLLOQ. chuck
■ **throw away**
1 DISCARD, jettison, get rid of, reject, scrap, dispose of, throw out
FORMAL dispense with
COLLOQ. dump, ditch, chuck away/out
2 WASTE, lose, squander, fritter away
SLANG blow
F3 1 keep, preserve, salvage, rescue 2 exploit, make use of, capitalize on
■ **throw off**
shed, cast off, drop, abandon, shake off, free yourself from, get rid of, discard, divest, jettison, elude, escape from
■ **throw out**
1 EVICT, turn out, expel, eject
COLLOQ. turf out
2 REJECT, discard, dismiss, turn down, jettison, throw away, scrap
FORMAL dispense with
COLLOQ. dump, ditch
3 EMIT, radiate, give off, emanate, exude, send out, diffuse, produce
4 MENTION, speak about, refer to, bring up, point out, introduce
■ **throw over**
abandon, desert, discard, drop, finish with, jilt, leave, reject
FORMAL forsake
COLLOQ. chuck, quit
■ **throw up**
1 VOMIT, bring up, spew, regurgitate, disgorge, retch, heave, gag
COLLOQ. puke, sick up, chuck up, fetch up
SLANG barf, upchuck; *Aust* chunder
2 ABANDON, resign, quit, leave
FORMAL relinquish, renounce
COLLOQ. chuck in, pack in, jack in

Synonym nuances

verb sense 1

You can use **hurl** to suggest a violent movement, while **heave** suggests the movement of something heavy and implies a degree of effort involved. **Lob**, on the other hand, implies a slow but effective underhand motion, whereas **pitch** often suggests a specific target. **Sling**, however, implies a much more casual aspect, and **fling** is equally haphazard: *she flung the cutlery on the table.* **Cast** has overtones of a decisive or powerful action: *the die is cast; Adam and Eve were cast from Eden.*

The term **flip** is appropriate where a throw sends something spinning, while **toss** implies an upward movement, and again a casual one: *let's toss a coin.* You can use **launch** to suggest the provision of an initial force, and **project**, **propel** and **catapult** likewise suggest strongly driving something forward: *he propelled me off the terrace.*

---

throwaway *adj*

1 *throwaway comments*
careless, casual, offhand, passing, unemphatic, undramatic
2 *a throwaway product*
disposable, cheap, expendable, non-returnable, biodegradable

throwback *n*
reversion, return, retrogression, restoration, reinstatement, taking back

thrust *v, n*
* *v*
1 PUSH, shove, butt, ram, jam, wedge, stick, poke, prod, jab, lunge, pierce, stab, plunge, drive, press, force, impel, drive, propel
2 IMPOSE, press, urge, force, inflict, burden, saddle, encumber, foist
* *n*
1 PUSH, shove, poke, prod, lunge, jab, ram, stab
2 DRIVE, motive, power, force, pressure, impetus, momentum
3 *the thrust of an argument*
gist, essence, drift, tenor, theme, message, point, force, substance

thud *n, v*
thump, clump, knock, clunk, clonk, smack, bash, crash, bang, thunder, bounce, dump, plod
COLLOQ. wallop, wham, flump

thug *n*
ruffian, tough, rough, roughneck, robber, bandit, killer, murderer, cut-throat, assassin, hoodlum, gangster, hooligan, villain, goonda; *N Am* plug-ugly; *S Afr* tsotsi
OLD phansigar
COLLOQ. mugger, yobbo
SLANG gorilla, cosh boy; *N Am* goon

thuggery *n*
violence, hooliganism, vandalism, brutality, abuse, viciousness, inhumanity, atrocity, foul play, murder, killing, butchery

thumb
▪ **thumb through**
glance at, scan, skim, peruse, browse through, flick through, flip through, leaf through

thumbnail *adj*
short, brief, concise, pithy, quick, small, compact, succinct, miniature

thumbs-down *n*
refusal, rejection, disapproval, negation, rebuff, no, turn down
🖙 thumbs-up

thumbs-up *n*
approval, affirmation, encouragement, acceptance, yes, sanction
COLLOQ. go-ahead, green light, OK
🖙 thumbs-down

thump *v, n*
* *v*
1 HIT, strike, knock, punch, box, cuff, clout, smack, thrash, slap, rap, crash, bang, thud, batter, pound, cob, dump, pummel; *dialect* dad; *Scot* daud, dunt, paik
OLD bethump, ding, tund
COLLOQ. whack, thwack, wallop, bonk, whop
2 THROB, pound, hammer, beat, pulsate, palpitate
* *n*
knock, blow, punch, box, cuff, clout, smack, rap, crash, bang, thud, beat, throb, bump, clunk, souse; *dialect* dad, dunt; *Scot* paik
COLLOQ. whack, thwack, wallop, bonk

thumping *adj, adv*
* *adj*
big, enormous, great, intense, extreme, severe, immense, massive, huge, colossal, monumental, terrific, thundering, tremendous, impressive, mammoth, excessive, exorbitant, gigantic, towering, gargantuan, titanic
COLLOQ. whopping
🖙 insignificant, petty, trivial; *colloq.* piddling
* *adv*
extremely, very, intensely, really, greatly, severely, unusually, remarkably, tremendously, highly
COLLOQ. seriously
SLANG mega

thunder *n, v*
* *n*
boom, reverberation, crash, crashing, bang, crack, clap, peal, rumble, roll, roar, outburst, blast, explosion
* *v*
1 BOOM, resound, reverberate, crash, bang, crack, clap, peal, rumble, roll, roar, blast
OLD intonate, upthunder; (*Spenser*) foulder
FORMAL fulminate
2 BELLOW, roar, yell, shout, bawl, cry, scream, shriek, howl, clamour, raise your voice
COLLOQ. holler

thundering *adj, adv*
* *adj*
great, enormous, excessive, remarkable, monumental, tremendous, unmitigated
FORMAL tonant, altitonant
* *adv*
extremely, very, intensely, really, greatly, severely, unusually

thunderous *adj*
booming, resounding, reverberating, roaring, rumbling, loud, noisy, deafening, tumultuous, ear-splitting

thunderstruck *adj*
stunned, shocked, staggered, amazed, astonished, astounded, dazed, dumbfounded, open-mouthed, paralysed, aghast, agape, petrified
COLLOQ. flabbergasted, floored, flummoxed, nonplussed, bowled over, knocked for six

thus *adv*
1 THEREFORE, so, consequently, then, accordingly
FORMAL hence, ergo
2 LIKE THIS, in this way, so, as follows
▪ **thus far**
up to/till now, until now, so far, up to the present, up to this point

thwack *v, n*
* *v*
beat, strike, bash, hit, flog, smack, thump, slap, buffet, clout, cuff

COLLOQ. wallop, whack

♦ *n*

blow, bash, slap, thump, smack, cuff, buffet

COLLOQ. wallop, whack

thwart *v*

frustrate, foil, defeat, hinder, hamper, impede, obstruct, block, balk, check, baffle, stop, prevent, oppose, cross, nobble, forestall, pre-empt, snooker, spite, transverse, traverse, hogtie, thraw, clip someone's wings, put a spoke in someone's wheel, put the skids on/under; *N Am* crimp

COLLOQ. stymie

SLANG pip, stonker

ᗓ help, assist, aid

tic *n*

jerk, spasm, twitch, tic douloureux

tick *n, v*

♦ *n*

1 CLICK, tap, stroke, beat, tock, tick-tock

OLD (*Shakesp*) jar

2 *wait a tick*

moment, instant, flash, second, minute, twinkling

COLLOQ. jiffy, mo, sec, trice

3 MARK, line, stroke; *N Am* check

♦ *v*

1 MARK, indicate, choose, select; *N Am* check

2 CLICK, tap, beat

OLD jar

▪ **tick off**

1 *tick off items on a list*

put a tick against, mark, indicate, select, pick; *N Am* check (off)

2 SCOLD, chide, reprimand, rebuke, reproach, reprove

FORMAL upbraid

COLLOQ. tell off, take/pull apart, bawl out, bounce, carpet, catch it, chew out, see off, give someone a ticking-off, dress down, give someone a dressing-down, haul over the coals, read the riot act to, give someone a rap over the knuckles, give someone a flea in their ear, give someone an earful, give someone a piece of your mind, shoot down in flames, tear a strip off someone, throw the book at, give someone some stick, go to town on, come down on like a ton of bricks, give someone hell, rollick, pin back someone's ears, talk like a Dutch uncle; *N Am* call down; *Aust & NZ* go crook on/at

ᗓ **2** praise, compliment

ticket *n*

pass, card, certificate, authorization, warrant, permit, token, voucher, coupon, docket, stub, counterfoil, slip, label, tag, sticker

tickle *v*

touch, stroke, excite, thrill, delight, please, gratify, amuse, entertain, divert, interest, stimulate

ticklish *adj*

sensitive, touchy, delicate, thorny, awkward, problematic, difficult, tricky, knotty, critical, risky, hazardous, precarious

COLLOQ. dodgy

ᗓ easy, simple, straightforward

tide *n, v*

♦ *n*

1 CURRENT, ebb, flow, stream, flux, movement, sea, water, flood

2 COURSE, movement, run, direction, drift, trend, tendency, tenor, rising tide

▪ **tide over**

help (through), assist, aid, see through, keep going, sustain, help out

tidily *adv*

neatly, orderly, just so, systematically, methodically, smartly, immaculately, in order, in place

ᗓ untidily, in a muddle, in a mess

tidings *n*

news, communication, report, bulletin, message, advice, word, information, intelligence, greetings

COLLOQ. dope, gen

tidy *adj, v*

♦ *adj*

1 NEAT, orderly, methodical, efficient, businesslike, systematic, organized, in order, well-ordered, ordered, uncluttered, clean, spick, spick-and-span, immaculate, shipshape, smart, spruce, trim, well-groomed, well-kept, kempt; *N Am* band-box

COLLOW. tiddley

2 *a tidy sum*

large, substantial, siz(e)able, considerable, fair, respectable, good, generous, ample

ᗓ **1** untidy, messy, disorganized **2** small, insignificant

♦ *v*

neaten, straighten (out), clear out, clear the decks, declutter, do, straighten up, order, arrange, clean (up), clear up, smarten, spruce up, groom, trim, brush up, primp, slick; *dialect* fettle; *Scot* redd (up); *N Am* square away

tie *v, n*

♦ *v*

1 FASTEN, knot, fix, secure, moor, tether, attach, join, connect, link, couple, unite, rope, lash, strap, lace, chain, bind

2 RESTRAIN, restrict, confine, limit, curb, constrain, hamper, impede, hinder, cramp, shackle

3 DRAW, be equal, be even, be neck and neck

COLLOQ. be all square

♦ *n*

1 KNOT, fastening, link, band, bond, ribbon, lace, tape, clip

2 CONNECTION, link, liaison, relationship, bond, friendship, affiliation, allegiance, kinship

3 OBLIGATION, commitment, duty, restraint, constraint, restriction, limit, limitation, hindrance

4 DRAW, dead heat, stalemate, deadlock

▪ **tie down**

restrain, constrain, restrict, confine, limit, hamper, hinder

▪ **tie in with**

be consistent with, be connected with, fit in with, relate to, be associated with, agree with, correlate with

▪ **tie up**

1 MOOR, tether, attach, fasten, secure, rope, lash, chain, bind, connect, truss, wrap up, restrain

COLLOQ. do up

2 CONCLUDE, settle, finalize

FORMAL terminate

COLLOQ. wind up, wrap up

3 OCCUPY, engage, engross, keep busy

4 *tie up your money*

reserve, make unavailable, commit

tie-in *n*

connection, relationship, link, relation, co-ordination, association, liaison, tie-up, affiliation

COLLOQ. hook-up

tier *n*

floor, storey, level, stage, layer, stratum, belt, zone, band, echelon, rank, row, line, bank, deck, gradin; *N Am* bleachers

tie-up *n*

connection, link, tie-in, association, bond, alliance, relation, relationship, interrelation, parallel, correlation, analogy, correspondence, reference

tiff *n*

disagreement, squabble, row, difference, difference of opinion, quarrel, words, dispute, temper, ill-humour, sulk, tantrum

COLLOQ. falling-out, huff, scrap, set-to, dust-up, pet, barney, spat

tight *adj*

1 TAUT, stretched, tense, strained, rigid, stiff, firm, fixed, fast, secure, close, cramped, clenched, constricted, compressed, limited, restricted, narrow, compact, snug, close-fitting, skin-tight, figure-hugging

2 SEALED, hermetic, soundproof, impervious, impenetrable, airtight, watertight

3 *tight security*
strict, tough, firm, severe, stringent, rigorous, hard, harsh, rigid, inflexible

4 *money is tight; a tight budget*
scarce, limited, insufficient, inadequate, scanty, too little, not enough, in short supply

5 *a tight contest*
close, evenly matched, well-matched, even, hard-fought
COLLOQ. neck and neck

6 *in a tight corner/spot*
difficult, awkward, problematic, tricky, delicate
COLLOQ. dodgy

7 MEAN, stingy, miserly, niggardly, penny-pinching
FORMAL parsimonious
COLLOQ. tight-fisted

8 DRUNK, intoxicated, tipsy, under the influence
COLLOQ. sloshed, sozzled, plastered, tiddly, merry, well-oiled, legless
SLANG pissed, stoned, tanked up, smashed
E3 **1** loose, slack **2** open **3** lax **4** plentiful **6** easy **7** generous **8** sober

tighten *v*

1 *tighten a rope/hold*
tauten, stretch, pull tight, tense, stiffen, fix, fasten, make fast, secure, narrow, close, cramp, constrict, crush, squeeze, take in, wind up, pull up, screw, brace; *N Am* cinch
TECHNICAL swift, swig
OLD strait, straiten; (*Shakesp*) restrain
FORMAL rigidify, constringe

2 *tighten up the security/rules*
make stricter, make more rigorous, increase, heighten, toughen up, firm up, strengthen
COLLOQ. beef up
E3 **1** loosen **2** relax

tight-fisted *adj*

mean, stingy, miserly, niggardly, penny-pinching, sparing, grasping
FORMAL parsimonious
COLLOQ. mingy, tight
E3 generous, charitable

tight-lipped *adj*

silent, uncommunicative, unforthcoming, close-lipped, close-mouthed, quiet, reticent, taciturn, reserved, secretive, mum, mute
E3 talkative, forthcoming, garrulous

till¹ *prep*

till the end of June
until, up to, to, up to the time of, all through; *N Am* through

till² *n*

take money from the till
cash register, cash box, cash drawer, checkout

till³ *v*

till the land
cultivate, work, plough, dig, farm

tilt *v, n*

• *v*
1 SLOPE, incline, slant, pitch, list, tip, lean, cant, bank, careen, cock, heel, rock, toss, trip
TECHNICAL peak
2 ATTACK, charge, rush, fight, contend, encounter, clash, duel, spar, joust
OLD jostle

• *n*
1 SLOPE, incline, angle, inclination, slant, pitch, list, bank
TECHNICAL attitude
2 ATTACK, charge, fight, contest, encounter, combat, clash, duel, spar, joust, tournament, *pas d'armes*

■ **at full tilt**
very quickly, very fast, at full speed, at top speed, at full blast, at full pelt, with full force
COLLOQ. all out, flat out

timber *n*

1 WOOD, trees, forest; *N Am* lumber
2 BEAM, lath, plank, pole, spar, board, log

timbre *n*

quality, voice quality, tone, tonality, sound, resonance, ring, colour
TECHNICAL klang

time *n, v*

• *n*
1 SPELL, stretch, period, term, season, session, span, duration, interval, space, while
2 TEMPO, beat, rhythm, metre, measure
3 MOMENT, point, juncture, stage, instance, instant, occasion, date
4 AGE, era, epoch, life, lifetime, lifespan, generation, heyday, peak
Related adjective: temporal

• *v*
1 ARRANGE, set, schedule, programme, timetable, fix
2 MEASURE, clock, calculate, count, meter, regulate, control, adjust

■ **time after time**
repeatedly, frequently, often, recurrently, many times, on many occasions, time and (time) again, again and again, over and over again

■ **ahead of time**
in advance, early, beforehand, previously, earlier, sooner, ahead, in front
COLLOQ. up front
E3 later, behind

■ **ahead of your time**
new, innovative, novel, progressive, experimental, revolutionary, avant-garde, radical

■ **all the time**
continually, constantly, perpetually, incessantly, interminably, always, forever, all along
E3 never

■ **at one time**
once, formerly, previously, at one point, long ago, in times past

■ **at the same time**
1 SIMULTANEOUSLY, all together, in parallel
FORMAL concurrently
2 NEVERTHELESS, nonetheless, still, but, however, anyway, even so, for all that

■ **at times**
sometimes, on occasions, occasionally, from time to time, now and again, now and then, off and on, every so often

■ **behind time**
late, overdue, unpunctual, delayed, behind, behind schedule
FORMAL tardy
E3 early

■ **behind the times**
old-fashioned, oldfangled, out of date, dated, old, unfashionable, out of fashion, obsolete, past
COLLOQ. fuddy-duddy, old hat, past its sell-by date
E3 up to date

■ **for the time being**
at present, for now, right now, just now, at the moment, for the moment, for the present, at the present time, temporarily, (in the) meantime, meanwhile, pro tem

■ **from time to time**
now and again, now and then, at times, sometimes, occasionally, on occasion, once in a while, periodically, intermittently, spasmodically, sporadically, every now and then, every so often
⊟ constantly, always

■ **in good time**
early, with time to spare, ahead of time, ahead of schedule, punctually, on time
⊟ late

■ **in time**
not too late, early enough, punctually, on time

■ **on time**
punctually, promptly, exactly, precisely, sharp, on the dot
COLLOQ. dead on, bang on, spot-on
⊟ late

■ **play for time**
delay, hesitate, stall, temporize, stonewall, hang fire, filibuster
FORMAL procrastinate
COLLOQ. drag your feet

Times and periods of time include:

afternoon	hour	p.m.
age	instant	quarter
a.m.	lifetime	quinquennium
autumn	light-year	season
bedtime	long-weekend	second
century	microsecond	spring
chiliad	midday	summer
dawn	midsummer	sunrise
day	midweek	sunset
daytime	millennium	sun-up
decade	millisecond	teatime
decennium	minute	today
dusk	moment	tomorrow
the early hours	month	tonight
eon	morn	twilight
epoch	morning	week
era	morrow	weekday
eternity	nanosecond	weekend
evening	night	*colloq.* wee small
N Am fall	nightfall	hours
fortnight	night-time	winter
generation	noon	year
high noon	period	yesteryear

---

time-honoured *adj*
age-old, traditional, long-established, usual, accustomed, conventional, customary, established, fixed, old, ancient, historic, venerable

timeless *adj*
ageless, immortal, deathless, everlasting, eternal, endless, permanent, lasting, enduring, changeless, unchanging, unending, indestructible, imperishable
FORMAL immutable, abiding

timely *adj*
well-timed, at the right time, seasonable, suitable, appropriate, convenient, opportune, prompt, punctual
FORMAL propitious, felicitous
⊟ ill-timed, unsuitable, inappropriate

timetable *n, v*
◆ *n*
schedule, programme, agenda, calendar, diary, rota, roster, list, listing, curriculum
◆ *v*
schedule, programme, diarize, set (up), fix, arrange, list

time-worn *adj*
worn, old, aged, dog-eared, out of date, passé, outworn, worn out, ruined, well-worn, tired, trite, stock, stale, threadbare, bromidic, cliché(e)d, hackneyed, weathered, dated, decrepit, ancient, broken-down, run-down,

shabby, ragged, hoary, wrinkled, lined
⊟ fresh, new

timid *adj*
shy, bashful, modest, shrinking, retiring, nervous, apprehensive, timorous, afraid, scared, frightened, fearful, cowardly, faint-hearted, spineless, irresolute, mousey, lily-livered, chicken-hearted, chicken-livered, pigeon-hearted, hen-hearted, pavid
OLD meticulous
FORMAL pusillanimous
COLLOQ. chicken, yellow, gutless, wimpish, wimpy, cissy, afraid of your own shadow
⊟ brave, bold, confident

timidity *n*
shyness, bashfulness, apprehensiveness, fear, fearfulness, cowardice
FORMAL pusillanimity
⊟ braveness, boldness, confidence

timorous *adj*
shy, timid, bashful, afraid, fearful, scared, frightened, apprehensive, shrinking, retiring, faint-hearted, nervous, diffident, coy, tentative, irresolute, modest, unadventurous, cowardly, trembling
OLD aspen
FORMAL pusillanimous
COLLOQ. mous(e)y
⊟ assertive, assured, bold

tincture *n, v*
◆ *n*
trace, flavour, touch, tinge, tint, colour, hint, hue, dash, suggestion, shade, stain, seasoning, smack, aroma
◆ *v*
flavour, scent, season, stain, tinge, tint, colour, dye, infuse, permeate, imbue, suffuse

tinge *n, v*
◆ *n*
1 TRACE, touch, suggestion, hint, smack, flavour, pinch, drop, dash, bit, sprinkling, smattering, tang
2 TINT, dye, colour, shade, wash, tincture, cast, tinct
OLD taint; (*Shakesp*) eye
◆ *v*
tint, dye, stain, colour, flavour, shade, suffuse, imbue, touch, encolour, tincture
OLD taint, tinct

tingle *v, n*
◆ *v*
sting, prickle, tickle, itch, prick, thrill, throb, tremble, quiver, vibrate
◆ *n*
stinging, prickling, tickle, tickling, itch, itching, thrill, tremor, throb, quiver, shiver, gooseflesh, goosepimples
COLLOQ. pins and needles

tinker *v, n*
◆ *v*
fiddle, play, toy, trifle, potter, dabble, meddle, fool about/around, tamper, tink
COLLOQ. mess about/around
◆ *n*
itinerant, Gypsy, fixer, mender, botcher, bungler, diddicoy, pedlar, hawker; *Scot* caird, (*derog*) tinkler, tink
OLD SLANG prig

tinkle *v, n*
◆ *v*
ring, ding, jingle, jangle, clink, chink, peal, chime
◆ *n*
1 *the tinkle of the bell*
ring, ding, jingle, jangle, clink, chink, peal, chime
2 *give you a tinkle*
ring, phone call, call
COLLOQ. buzz, bell

tinny *adj*
1 *tinny sounds*
metallic, jangling, jingly, harsh, jarring, high-pitched
2 *his tinny old car*
flimsy, insubstantial, thin, cheap, poor-quality, cheapjack

tinpot *adj*
inferior, substandard, second-rate, low-quality, mediocre, bad, poor, awful, unsatisfactory, insignificant, imperfect, defective, incompetent, slipshod, shoddy
COLLOQ. crummy, rop(e)y, useless, pathetic
Ⓕ excellent

tinsel *adj, n*
♦ *adj*
showy, ostentatious, cheap, gaudy, tawdry, trashy, superficial, specious, gimcrack, sham
FORMAL meretricious
COLLOQ. flashy
♦ *n*
glitter, spangle, frippery, show, triviality, display, ostentation, flamboyance, garishness, gaudiness, sham, worthlessness, artificiality, meaninglessness, insignificance, pretension

tint *n, v*
♦ *n*
dye, stain, rinse, wash, colour, hue, shade, tincture, tinge, tone, cast, streak, trace, touch
♦ *v*
dye, colour, tinge, streak, stain, taint, affect

tiny *adj*
minute, microscopic, infinitesimal, minuscule, small, little, slight, trifling, negligible, insignificant, diminutive, petite, dwarfish, midget, pocket, miniature, Lilliputian; *Scot* wee
COLLOQ. pint-sized, mini, teensy, teeny, teeny-weeny, itsy-bitsy
Ⓕ huge, enormous, immense

tip¹ *n, v*
♦ *n*
the tip of a finger
end, extremity, point, nib, apex, peak, pinnacle, summit, acme, top, cap, crown, head
♦ *v*
cap, crown, top, surmount

tip² *v, n*
♦ *v*
tip your head
lean, incline, slant, list, tilt, cant, topple (over), capsize, upset, overturn, spill, pour (out), empty, unload, dump
♦ *n*
dump, rubbish-heap, refuse-heap, slag heap, midden

tip³ *n, v*
♦ *n*
1 HINT, pointer, clue, suggestion, advice, recommendation, warning, tip-off, information, inside information, forecast
2 GRATUITY, gift, bonus, reward, present, baksheesh, *pourboire*
FORMAL perquisite
COLLOQ. perk
♦ *v*
1 ADVISE, suggest, warn, caution, forewarn, tip off, inform, tell
2 *tip the driver*
reward, remunerate

tip-off *n*
hint, pointer, clue, suggestion, warning, information, inside information

tipple *v, n*
♦ *v*
drink, imbibe, indulge, quaff, bib
COLLOQ. swig, booze, down, knock back

♦ *n*
drink, regular drink, favourite drink, alcohol, liquor
COLLOQ. booze, poison, usual

tippler *n*
drinker, hard drinker, drunk, drunkard, dipso(maniac), bibber, inebriate, winebag
COLLOQ. boozer, sponge
SLANG lush, soak, sot, toper, wino, alkie, dipso, piss artist, tosspot

tipsy *adj*
drunk, under the influence, mellow, merry, totty, muzzy, nappy, rocky, top-heavy, a peg too low, a pip out
COLLOQ. happy, squiffy, tiddly, tight, tiddled, woozy, the worse for wear, oiled, well-oiled, bosky, cockeyed, sprung, pleasant
OLD COLLOQ. glorious
SLANG lushy, moony, wet, screwed, slewed
Ⓕ sober

tirade *n*
harangue, diatribe, denunciation, abuse, lecture, admonishment, outburst, rant
FORMAL fulmination, invective, philippic

tire *v*
weary, fatigue, wear out, tire out, exhaust, tax, strain, drain, drop, flag, bore
FORMAL enervate
Ⓕ enliven, invigorate, refresh

tired *adj*
1 WEARY, drowsy, sleepy, flagging, fatigued, wearied, worn out, exhausted, dog-tired, drained, jaded, blown, outspent; *Scot* forjeskit, wabbit
OLD wappend; (*Shakesp*) fatigate
FORMAL enervated
COLLOQ. fagged out, bushed, whacked, shattered, beat, dead-beat, all in, knackered, clapped-out, rough, ready to drop, washed-out, hardly able to keep your eyes open, zonked; *N Am* pooped (out), tuckered out
SLANG (*taboo*) shagged out
2 *tired of waiting*
bored, sick; *Aust* jack
COLLOQ. fed up, sick and tired
3 HACKNEYED, old, stale, worn-out, trite, cliché(e)d
COLLOQ. corny, past its sell-by date
Ⓕ **1** lively, energetic, rested, refreshed **3** new, original

---

Synonym nuances
sense 1
You can use **weary** to suggest having depleted reserves of vigour, while **drowsy** and **sleepy** are more appropriate for having an inclination to sleep. **Flagging**, on the other hand, suggests being unable to maintain your levels of energy: *even in old age he showed no signs of flagging*, whereas **fatigued** suggests that your physical or mental resources are almost expended.
  Similarly, both **worn out** and **exhausted** imply having used up your strength, but perhaps more completely, while **drained** has also to do with being physically or emotionally spent: *she felt quite drained by the whole experience*. **Jaded**, however, has implications of suffering from over-indulgence or over-exposure to something: *after three years in the job she felt jaded*.

---

tireless *adj*
untiring, unwearied, unflagging, indefatigable, energetic, vigorous, diligent, industrious, resolute, determined
Ⓕ tired, lazy, unenthusiastic

tirelessly *adv*
untiringly, indefatigably, energetically, vigorously, diligently, resolutely
Ⓕ lazily, idly, unenthusiastically

tiresome *adj*
troublesome, trying, annoying, irritating, exasperating, irksome, vexatious, wearisome, dull, boring, routine, humdrum, tedious, monotonous, uninteresting, unexciting, tiring, fatiguing, laborious
Ε∃ interesting, stimulating, easy

tiring *adj*
wearying, wearisome, fatiguing, exhausting, draining, demanding, hard, tough, difficult, exacting, taxing, arduous, strenuous, laborious
FORMAL enervating

tiro, tyro *n*
beginner, novice, apprentice, freshman, learner, pupil, starter, student, trainee, tenderfoot, greenhorn, initiate, neophyte, novitiate, catechumen
Ε∃ veteran; *colloq.* old hand

tissue *n*
1 MATTER, substance, material
2 *a box of tissues*
paper handkerchief, disposable handkerchief, Kleenex®, facial tissue, toilet paper, toilet tissue
3 *tissue paper*
fabric, stuff, gauze, gossamer
4 *a tissue of lies*
web, mesh, network, structure, texture

tit for tat *n*
blow for blow, retaliation, revenge, requital, reprisal, measure for measure, counterblow, counterbuff, countercharge
FORMAL quid pro quo, *lex talionis*
COLLOQ. like for like, an eye for an eye (and a tooth for a tooth), a taste of your own medicine

titan *n*
colossus, giant, superman, Hercules, Atlas, leviathan

titanic *adj*
colossal, huge, enormous, massive, vast, immense, giant, gigantic, jumbo, mammoth, monumental, prodigious, stupendous, towering, mountainous, monstrous, herculean, cyclopean
FORMAL mighty
Ε∃ insignificant, small

titbit *n*
morsel, scrap, appetizer, snack, delicacy, dainty, treat, bonne-bouche

tithe *n, v*
◆ *n*
tenth, tax, levy, duty, tariff, toll, tribute, rent, assessment, impost
◆ *v*
give, hand over, pay, take in, tax, assess, charge, levy, rate

titillate *v*
stimulate, arouse, excite, thrill, tickle, provoke, tease, tantalize, intrigue, interest
COLLOQ. turn on

titillating *adj*
stimulating, arousing, exciting, sexy, erotic, seductive, lewd, lurid, thrilling, provocative, sensational, suggestive, intriguing, interesting, teasing, captivating

titivate *v*
smarten up, touch up, refurbish, preen, make up, groom, primp, prink
COLLOQ. doll up, tart up

title *n, v*
◆ *n*
1 NAME, term, designation, form of address, label, epithet, nickname, so(u)briquet, pseudonym, *nom-de-plume*, rank, status, office, position
FORMAL appellation, denomination

COLLOQ. handle
SLANG monicker
Related adjective: titular
2 PUBLICATION, book, work
3 HEADING, headline, caption, legend, inscription, credit(s)
4 RIGHT, prerogative, privilege, claim, entitlement, ownership, proprietorship, deeds
5 CHAMPIONSHIP, match, contest, competition, game, prize, trophy, stakes, laurels, crown
◆ *v*
entitle, name, call, dub, style, term, designate, tag, label

titter *v, n*
◆ *v*
giggle, snigger, snicker, chuckle, cackle, laugh, chortle, mock
◆ *n*
giggle, snigger, snicker, chuckle, cackle, laugh, chortle

tittle-tattle *n, v*
◆ *n*
gossip, rumour, hearsay, chatter, babble, cackle, prattle; *Scot* blether; *dialect & N Am* blather
COLLOQ. chitchat, jaw, natter, twaddle, ya(c)k, yackety-yak
◆ *v*
gossip, chat, chatter, babble, cackle, prattle; *Scot* blether; *dialect & N Am* blather
COLLOQ. chitchat, tell tales, witter, jaw, rabbit on, natter, ya(c)k, yack-yack, yackety-yak

titular *adj*
nominal, in name only, token, so-called, self-styled, honorary, formal, official
FORMAL putative
COLLOQ. puppet

toadstool
See panel at **mushrooms and toadstools**.

toady *n, v*
◆ *n*
fawner, flatterer, sycophant, groveller, lackey, minion, parasite, flunkey, jackal
COLLOQ. yes-man, sucker, bootlicker, crawler, creep, hanger-on, truckler
SLANG (*vulgar*) arse-licker; *Aust* suck-hole
◆ *v*
curry favour, crawl, flatter, grovel, fawn, creep, cringe, kowtow
COLLOQ. bootlick, bow and scrape, butter up, kiss the feet, suck up, truckle

toast *v, n*
◆ *v*
1 *toast bread*
grill, brown, roast, crisp, bake, heat (up), warm (up), barbecue, scorch; *Scot* birsle, scouther
2 *toast the bride and groom*
drink to, drink the health of, honour, salute, pledge
◆ *n*
drink, pledge, tribute, salute, salutation, compliment(s), best wishes, health, sentiment, *brindisi*

Toasts include:

all the best!	good luck!	prosit!
auf Ihre	happy landings!	skoal!
Gesundheit!	here's how!	slàinte!
à votre santé!	here's looking at	to absent friends!
bottoms up!	you!	your health!
cheers!	here's mud in your	
chin-chin!	eye!	
down the hatch!	here's to ...!	
good health!	here's to you!	

tobacco *n*

COLLOQ. baccy, the weed

Forms of tobacco include:

chewing tobacco	**CIGARS:**	filter-tip
flake tobacco	cheroot	high-tar
pipe tobacco	cigarillo	king-size
plug	corona	low-tar
shag tobacco	Havana cigar	menthol
snuff	panatella	roll-up
Turkish tobacco	**CIGARETTES:**	Russian
Virginia tobacco	cork-tipped	

Tobacco accessories include:

ashtray	cigar holder	pipe-cleaner
box of matches	clay pipe	pipe-light
chibouk	gas lighter	pipe rack
church-warden	hookah	pipe rest
cigar box	humidor	smoker's
cigar case	match	companion
cigar cutter	matchbook	snuffbox
cigarette box	match striker	tobacco pipe
cigarette case	meerschaum	tobacco pouch
cigarette holder	narghile	vesta
cigarette lighter	peace pipe (pipe	
cigarette machine	of peace)	
cigarette paper	petrol lighter	
cigarette roller	pipe	

---

toboggan *n*

sledge, sleigh, slide, luge, bobsled, bobsleigh, skeleton bob, Ski-doo®, dray, kibitka, pulka; *Scot* hurly-hacket; *N Am* dogsled, train, travois
TECHNICAL slipe

today *n, adv*

♦ *n*
THIS DAY, the present day, this very day, the present time, this morning, this afternoon, this evening
♦ *adv*
AT THIS MOMENT, at this moment in time, now, right now, just now, at the present time, these days, nowadays

toddle *v*

walk/move unsteadily, totter, wobble, stagger, waddle, reel, lurch, stumble, falter, waver, teeter, sway, rock, shake

to-do *n*

commotion, fuss, furore, bother, disturbance, flurry, stir, tumult, turmoil, uproar, unrest, excitement, bustle, agitation, rumpus, ruction, quarrel
COLLOQ. performance, brouhaha, flap, hullabaloo, hoo-ha, stew

together *adv, adj*

♦ *adv*
1 UNITED, collectively, jointly, mutually, in concert, in unison, in company, working together, in collaboration, in conjunction, as one, as a partnership, as a team
2 *travel together*
side by side, shoulder to shoulder, hand in hand, in a row
3 SIMULTANEOUSLY, at the same time, at one time, all at once
FORMAL concurrently
4 CONTINUOUSLY, consecutively, successively, in succession, without a break, without interruption, on end
COLLOQ. on the trot, back to back
F3 1 separately, individually **2** alone
♦ *adj*
well-balanced, well-adjusted, stable, well-organized, organized, level-headed, sensible, down-to-earth, composed, calm, commonsensical
COLLOQ. cool, unflappable

toil *n, v*

♦ *n*
labour, hard work, slog, drudgery, sweat, slaving, industry, application, effort, exertion
COLLOQ. donkey-work, graft, elbow grease
♦ *v*
labour, work, slave, drudge, sweat, grind, push yourself, slog, persevere, strive, struggle
COLLOQ. graft, plug away, work like a Trojan, work your fingers to the bone

toiler *n*

worker, workaholic, drudge, grafter, slogger, struggler, slave, workhorse, labourer, menial, navvy
F3 idler, loafer, shirker

toilet *n*

lavatory, WC, bathroom, cloakroom, washroom, water closet, public convenience, convenience, urinal, latrine, powder room, the ladies', the gents', facilities, earth-closet, Elsan®, Portaloo®, lavabo; *N Am* rest room, comfort station
OLD reredorter, necessary
COLLOQ. loo, lav, dunny, smallest room, superloo, throne, little boys' room, little girls' room
SLANG bog, kazi, crapper, can, cottage, heads, thunderbox; *Scot* cludgie; *N Am* john; *Aust* toot
OLD SLANG dike

toilsome *adj*

difficult, hard, laborious, arduous, burdensome, backbreaking, fatiguing, painful, tough, wearisome, severe, strenuous, taxing, tedious, tiresome, uphill, herculean

token *n, adj*

♦ *n*
1 SYMBOL, emblem, representation, mark, sign, indication, demonstration, expression, evidence, proof, recognition, clue, warning, signal, index, reminder, remembrance, memorial, memento, souvenir, keepsake
FORMAL manifestation
2 *gift token*
voucher, coupon, counter, disc
♦ *adj*
symbolic, emblematic, nominal, slight, minimal, perfunctory, superficial, cosmetic, hollow, insincere

tolerable *adj*

1 BEARABLE, endurable, sufferable, acceptable
2 ACCEPTABLE, satisfactory, passable, adequate, reasonable, fair, fairly good, average, all right, mediocre, indifferent, unexceptional, ordinary, middling
COLLOQ. OK, so-so, run-of-the-mill, not bad, nothing (much) to write home about, no great shakes, not much cop
F3 1 intolerable, unbearable, insufferable

tolerably *adv*

reasonably, fairly, ordinarily, adequately, sufficiently, bearably, acceptably

tolerance *n*

1 TOLERATION, patience, forbearance, open-mindedness, broad-mindedness, liberalism, sympathy, good-humour, understanding, leniency, lenity, laxness, indulgence, permissiveness
FORMAL magnanimity
2 VARIATION, fluctuation, allowance, clearance
COLLOQ. play, give, swing
3 RESISTANCE, resilience, toughness, endurance, stamina
FORMAL fortitude
F3 1 intolerance, prejudice, bias, bigotry, narrow-mindedness

tolerant *adj*

patient, forbearing, long-suffering, open-minded, fair, unprejudiced, broad-minded, catholic, liberal, charitable,

kind-hearted, sympathetic, understanding, forgiving, lenient, compliant, indulgent, permissive, easy-going, lax, soft, mellowed
FORMAL magnanimous
COLLOQ. decent
⊟ intolerant, biased, prejudiced, bigoted, unsympathetic

tolerate v
endure, suffer, put up with, bear, stand, take, have, receive, accept, admit, allow, permit, warrant, sanction, condone, indulge, pardon; *dialect* abear; *Scot* thole
FORMAL abide, countenance
COLLOQ. stomach, swallow, wear

toleration n
1 PATIENCE, forbearance, open-mindedness, broad-mindedness, liberalism, sympathy, understanding, leniency, lenity, laxness, indulgence, permissiveness
FORMAL magnanimity
2 RESISTANCE, resilience, toughness, endurance, stamina
FORMAL fortitude
3 ACCEPTANCE, allowance, endurance, sufferance, sanction, indulgence

toll¹ v
the bell tolls
ring, peal, chime, knell, sound, strike, clang, announce, call, signal, warn, herald; *dialect* jowl; *Scot* jow

toll² n
1 *motorway tolls*
charge, fee, payment, levy, tax, duty, tariff, rate, cost, penalty, demand, tollage, due, pike; *N Am* streetage
TECHNICAL pontage, pierage, octroi
OLD scavage, tallage
2 *the casualty toll*
cost, loss, damage, injury, death
3 *take its toll*
adverse effect, cost, price, harm, damage, suffering, hardship

tomb n
grave, burial-place, vault, crypt, sepulchre, catacomb, mausoleum, cenotaph, shrine, marble, monument, sarcophagus, speos, tholus, heroon, hypogeum, mastaba, sacellum
TECHNICAL cist
OLD burial, reposit; (*Spenser*) funeral
Related adjective: sepulchral

tombstone n
gravestone, headstone, stone, memorial, memorial stone, monument, marble; *Scot* through-stone

tome n
book, volume, work, opus

tomfoolery n
mischief, horseplay, silliness, stupidity, messing about, carrying on, foolishness, childishness, idiocy, inanity, skylarking, clowning, buffoonery, hooey
COLLOQ. larking about, larks, shenanigans

tone n, v
♦ n
1 *tone of voice*
note, timbre, pitch, sound, quality, volume, expression, intonation, modulation, inflection, accent, accentuation, stress, emphasis, force, strength
2 TINT, tinge, colour, hue, shade, cast, tonality, tincture
3 AIR, manner, attitude, mood, spirit, humour, temper, character, quality, feel, style, effect, vein, tenor, drift
Related adjective: tonal
♦ v
match, co-ordinate, suit, blend, harmonize, go (well) with
■ **tone down**
moderate, temper, subdue, restrain, soften, lighten, dim, dampen, play down, reduce, alleviate

FORMAL assuage, mitigate
COLLOQ. soft-pedal
■ **tone up**
shape up, touch up, trim, tune up, sharpen up, limber up, freshen, invigorate, brighten

toneless adj
tuneless, unmelodious, unmusical, dull, colourless, neutral, grey, faded, dim, unexpressive, listless
⊟ tuneful, melodious, musical, bright

tongue n
language, speech, discourse, talk, utterance, articulation, vernacular, idiom, dialect, patois, jargon, slang, argot, cant
FORMAL parlance
COLLOQ. lingo
Related adjective: lingual, glottic

tongue-tied adj
speechless, dumbstruck, inarticulate, silent, mute, dumb, wordless, voiceless, lost for words
⊟ talkative, garrulous, voluble

tonic n
1 *a herbal tonic*
cordial, pick-me-up, restorative, refresher, bracer, stimulant, analeptic, boost, fillip, roborant
OLD saloop
COLLOQ. shot in the arm
2 *a tonic of a musical scale*
keynote, fundamental note, final, home key

too adv
1 ALSO, as well, in addition, furthermore, besides, moreover, likewise
2 EXCESSIVELY, inordinately, unduly, over, overly, unreasonably, ridiculously, extremely, very

tool n, v
♦ n
1 IMPLEMENT, instrument, utensil, gadget, device, contrivance, contraption, apparatus, artefact; *Irish* yoke; appliance, machine, means, vehicle, medium, agency, agent, intermediary
COLLOQ. gismo
See Synonym nuances panel at **device.**
2 PUPPET, pawn, dupe, stooge, flunkey, minion, hireling, cat's-paw
♦ v
work, machine, cut, shape, decorate, fashion, ornament, chase
See panel on next page

tooth n
cog, denticle, denticulation, dentil, fang, incisor, jag, masticator, molar, prong, tush, tusk

---

Types of tooth include:

baby tooth	gold tooth	second premolar
back tooth	grinder	snaggletooth
bicuspid	incisor	tush
bucktooth	central incisor	tusk
canine	lateral incisor	wisdom tooth
carnassial	milk tooth	**FALSE TEETH**:
denture	molar	bridge
dog-tooth	first molar	cap
eye tooth	second molar	crown
false tooth	third molar	plate
fang	premolar	
first tooth	first premolar	

---

toothsome adj
appetizing, delicious, tasty, tempting, mouthwatering, palatable, nice, agreeable, flavoursome, sweet, luscious, savoury, dainty
FORMAL delectable

Types of tool include:

auger	crochet hook	hod	pestle	rasp	socket-wrench
awl	crowbar	hoe	pick	rule	soldering-iron
axe	dibber	jack	pick-axe	sander	spade
bevel	dividers	jackhammer	pincers	saw	spirit level
billhook	dolly	jack-plane	pinking-shears	scalpel	spraygun
bodkin	drill	jig-saw	pitchfork	scissors	stapler
bolster	file	jointer	plane	screwdriver	steel
brace and bit	forceps	level	pliers	scriber	tenon-saw
bradawl	fork	mace	plough	scythe	thresher
caulking-iron	fretsaw	mallet	plumb-line	secateurs	tommy bar
chainsaw	gimlet	mattock	pocket-knife	set-square	tongs
chaser	grass-rake	mortar	protractor	shears	trowel
chisel	hacksaw	needle	pruning-knife	shovel	T-square
chopper	hammer	paper-cutter	pruning-shears	sickle	tweezers
clamp	handsaw	paper-knife	punch	sledgehammer	vice
cleaver	hay fork	penknife	rake	snips	wrench

COLLOQ. scrumptious, yummy, scrummy, mor(e)ish
⊟ disagreeable, unpleasant

top n, adj, v

◆ *n*

1 HEAD, tip, highest point, apex, crest, crown, peak, pinnacle, summit, vertex, acme, zenith, apogee, climax, culmination, height
2 LID, cap, cover, cork, stopper
3 *a sleeveless top*
blouse, shirt, sweatshirt, T-shirt, tee shirt, jumper, jersey, sweater, pullover, tank top, smock
⊟ 1 bottom, base, nadir **3** bottoms

◆ *adj*

highest, topmost, upmost, uppermost, upper, superior, head, chief, leading, main, first, foremost, premier, principal, sovereign, ruling, pre-eminent, dominant, prime, paramount, utmost, greatest, maximum, best, finest, premium, supreme, crowning, culminating
⊟ bottom, lowest, inferior

◆ *v*

1 TIP, cap, crown, cover, finish (off), decorate, garnish
2 BEAT, exceed, outstrip, better, excel, best, surpass, eclipse, outshine, outdo, surmount, transcend
3 HEAD, lead, be first in, rule, command

■ **top up**
refill, recharge, reload, add to, supplement, increase, boost
FORMAL replenish, augment

■ **on top of the world**
thrilled, happy, overjoyed, ecstatic, elated, exhilarated, exultant
COLLOQ. on cloud nine, over the moon

■ **over the top**
excessive, immoderate, inordinate, extreme, too much, undue, uncalled-for, disproportionate, unreasonable, lavish, exorbitant, extravagant
COLLOQ. OTT, a bit much

Synonym nuances
noun sense 1
You can use **head** to refer to the uppermost part of anything, while **tip** suggests something that tapers up to a point. **Apex**, likewise, implies the high point, literally or figuratively: *the apex of the pyramid; the apex of military command.* **Crown** can also be used of the highest extremity: *the crown of the hill; the crown of his head,* but **crest** tends to be reserved for the top edge of something: *the crest of a wave.*
Other synonyms lend themselves more to figurative uses. **Peak** can either suggest a pointed end or, like **pinnacle** and **summit**, suggest the highest position: *the pinnacle of his career.* You can use the terms **climax** and **culmination** if you want to refer to the highest that is achievable, or the defining point: *the culmination of a lifetime's dream.*

---

topic n

subject, subject matter, theme, issue, question, argument, matter, point, talking point, thesis, text, hobby-horse, *cheval de bataille*, touch-me-not; *N Am* hot button
TECHNICAL topos
OLD commonplace, place
COLLOQ. hardy annual, old chestnut

topical adj

current, contemporary, up-to-date, up-to-the-minute, recent, newsworthy, relevant, popular, familiar

topmost adj

uppermost, highest, loftiest, top, upper, supreme, first, leading, foremost, principal, maximum, paramount, dominant
TECHNICAL apical
⊟ bottom, bottommost, lowest

top-notch adj

first-rate, first-class, second-to-none, matchless, peerless, top, top-flight, leading, supreme, superior, prime, excellent, outstanding, superlative, premier, exceptional, splendid, superb, fine, admirable
COLLOQ. super, A1, ace, crack, out of this world
SLANG wicked, way-out, cool, radical, mega

topple v

1 OVERBALANCE, totter, tumble, fall (over), collapse, upset, tip over, knock over/down, keel over, overturn, capsize
2 OVERTHROW, oust, bring down, unseat, displace, dethrone

top-secret adj

confidential, highly confidential, secret, classified, restricted, off-the-record, private, personal, intimate, sensitive
COLLOQ. hush-hush

topsy-turvy adj

confused, in confusion, jumbled, chaotic, inside out, upside down, disorganized, disarranged, disorderly, in disorder, untidy, mixed-up, messy
⊟ ordered, tidy

torch n, v

◆ *n*

light, firebrand, brand, flambeau; *N Am* flashlight
OLD cresset

◆ *v*

ignite, set fire to, set on fire, set alight, burn, put a match to

torment n, v

◆ *n*

1 ANGUISH, distress, misery, affliction, suffering, pain, agony, ordeal, worry, torture, persecution, martyrdom, furnace, Gehenna
2 ANNOYANCE, provocation, irritation, vexation, bane, scourge, curse, pest, trouble, bother, nuisance, harassment, worry

COLLOQ. thorn in the flesh, pain in the neck

♦ *v*

1 AFFLICT, plague, distress, trouble, distress, harrow, pain, torture, persecute, crucify, grill, wrack
OLD pine

2 ANNOY, tease, provoke, irritate, vex, trouble, worry, harass, hound, pester, bother, plague, badger, bedevil, tantalize

torn *adj*

1 CUT, ragged, ripped, slit, split, rent, lacerated
2 DIVIDED, uncertain, undecided, unsure, in two minds, irresolute, vacillating, wavering, dithering

tornado *n*

storm, cyclone, gale, hurricane, whirlwind, typhoon, monsoon, tempest, squall
COLLOQ. twister

torpid *adj*

sluggish, lethargic, slow, dull, lifeless, inert, inactive, apathetic, lazy, passive, listless, drowsy, sleepy, dead, deadened, numb, nerveless, insensible
FORMAL languorous, somnolent, supine, indolent
F3 active, lively, vigorous

torpor *n*

torpidity, sluggishness, lethargy, listlessness, slowness, dullness, lifelessness, inactivity, inertia, inertness, drowsiness, sleepiness, numbness, apathy, laziness, passivity, sloth
FORMAL indolence, languor, somnolence, hebetude
F3 activity, vigour, enthusiasm

torrent *n*

1 *torrent of water*
stream, gush, rush, flood, storm, outburst, volley, barrage, inundation, spate, deluge, cascade, downpour
2 *a torrent of abuse*
outburst, volley, barrage, stream, gush, rush, flood, storm, inundation, spate, deluge; *Scot* blatter
F3 1 trickle

torrential *adj*

heavy, persistent, pouring down, pelting, driving, teeming, inundating
COLLOQ. raining cats and dogs, bucketing down, coming down in stair rods
SLANG pissing

torrid *adj*

1 HOT, blazing, sweltering, blistering, boiling, sizzling, scorching, tropical, stifling, arid, parched, scorched, waterless, desert
2 PASSIONATE, erotic, red-hot, sexy, amorous
COLLOQ. steamy

tortuous *adj*

1 *a tortuous road*
twisting, winding, meandering, curving, serpentine, zigzag, circuitous, roundabout, indirect
FORMAL sinuous
2 COMPLICATED, involved, serpentine, zigzag, circuitous, roundabout, indirect
FORMAL convoluted
F3 1 straight **2** straightforward

torture *v, n*

♦ *v*

pain, agonize, excruciate, crucify, rack, martyr, persecute, abuse, ill-treat, mistreat, torment, harrow, plague, punish, afflict, worry, distress, trouble

♦ *n*

pain, agony, suffering, affliction, distress, punishment, misery, anguish, torment, abuse, ill-treatment, mistreatment, martyrdom, persecution
See panel on next page

toss *v, n*

♦ *v*

1 FLIP, cast, fling, throw, pitch, heave, sling, hurl, lob, shy, loft, tip, cant; *Scot* birl, bum
COLLOQ. chuck; *Irish* puck
2 ROLL, heave, sway, pitch, lurch, jolt, shake, jerk, agitate, rock, thrash, squirm, writhe, wriggle, tumble, welter, bandy, dandle

♦ *n*

flip, cast, fling, throw, pitch, cant
COLLOQ. chuck

tot¹ *n*

1 TODDLER, child, infant, mite, baby; *Scot* bairn
2 *a tot of whisky*
dram, measure, nip, shot, slug, swallow, swig, finger

tot²

▪ **tot up**
add (up), calculate, compute, count (up), reckon, mount (up), sum, tally, total

total *n, adj, v*

♦ *n*

sum, whole, entirety, grand total, subtotal, totality, all, lot, mass, amount
FORMAL aggregate

♦ *adj*

full, complete, entire, whole, comprehensive, integral, all-out, utter, absolute, unconditional, unqualified, outright, undisputed, perfect, thoroughgoing, rank, sheer, downright, out-and-out, thorough
FORMAL consummate, unmitigated
F3 partial, limited, restricted

♦ *v*

add (up), sum (up), tot (up), count (up), reckon, amount to, come to, reach, make

totalitarian *adj*

authoritarian, one-party, despotic, dictatorial, oppressive, tyrannous, monolithic, undemocratic
FORMAL omnipotent, monocratic
F3 democratic

totality *n*

total, sum, whole, wholeness, entirety, entireness, everything, fullness, completeness, all, cosmos, universe
FORMAL aggregate, pleroma

totally *adv*

completely, fully, wholly, entirely, perfectly, utterly, quite, thoroughly, wholeheartedly, absolutely, unconditionally, comprehensively, undividedly, undisputedly
FORMAL consummately, unmitigatedly
COLLOQ. *Aust & NZ* boots and all
F3 partially

totter *v*

1 STAGGER, waddle, move unsteadily, reel, lurch, stumble, falter, waver, teeter, sway, roll, rock, shake, wobble, quiver, tremble, dodder, titter, topple; *dialect* daddle; *Scot* hotter
2 *the economy is tottering*
be unstable, be unsteady, be insecure, be shaky, teeter, be precarious, be about to collapse
COLLOQ. wobble

touch *v, n*

♦ *v*

1 FEEL, handle, hold, finger, run your finger over, brush, skim, graze, stroke, caress, fondle, pet, tickle, pat, tap, hit, strike, contact
2 ADJOIN, bring/come into contact, meet, abut, border, impinge
FORMAL be contiguous to
3 MOVE, stir, upset, sadden, disturb, impress, inspire, influence, affect, have an effect on, have an influence/impact on, involve, concern, regard
4 EQUAL, match, rival, better, come near, approach

Forms and instruments of torture include:

Austrian ladder	cave of roses	German chair	knee-capping	saw	squassation
ball and chain	confession chair	gridirons	knotting	scarpines	starvation
bastinado	devil-on-the-	harrow	pear	scavenger's	stocks
bilboes	neck	head crusher	peine forte et	daughter	stoning
boiling	disembowelment	heretic's forks	dure	scold's bridle	strappado
boot (or bootikin)	drunkard's cloak	hooding	pendulum	scourge	suspension
branding	(or Spanish	impalement	picana	shabeh	thumbscrews
brank	mantle)	iron collar	picketing (or	shin vice	treadmill (or
brazen bull	ducking-stool	iron maiden	picquet)	shrew's fiddle	treadwheel)
cage	electric shock	irons	pilliwinks	skull crusher	turcas
carcan	flesh tearers	jougs	pillory	sleep deprivation	water torture
cat-o'-nine-tails	forciption	Judas cradle (or	pincers	Spanish chair	wheel
cat's paw	garrotte	scale)	pressing	spider	wooden horse
cattle prod	gauntlets	keelhauling	rack	spiked hare	

COLLOQ. hold a candle to
5 REACH, attain, make, come to
COLLOQ. hit
6 *not touch alcohol*
consume, use, eat, drink, take, devour
7 MENTION, broach, speak of, remark on, refer to, allude to, cover, deal with
♦ *n*
1 FEEL, brush, stroke, caress, pat, tap, blow, hit, contact, tactility
Related adjective: tactile, haptic
2 TEXTURE, feel, surface, finish, grain, weave
3 SKILL, art, knack, flair, craftsmanship, dexterity, style, method, manner, technique, approach, way, direction, influence
4 *finishing touches*
detail, feature, point, addition, aspect, nicety, minutia
5 *keep/lose touch*
contact, communication, correspondence, connection, association
6 *a touch of garlic*
trace, spot, dash, pinch, taste, soupçon, suspicion, hint, suggestion, bit, speck, jot, tinge, smack
COLLOQ. whiff
■ **touch down**
land, come in, come in to land, come to earth
■ **touch off**
spark off, trigger (off), detonate, begin, cause, set off, initiate, provoke, foment, fire, ignite, inflame, light, arouse
FORMAL actuate
■ **touch up**
renovate, improve, brush up, retouch, revamp, enhance, finish off, round off, patch up, perfect, polish up

touch-and-go *adj*
close, critical, dangerous, uncertain, hazardous, near, nerve-racking, offhand, perilous, dire, precarious, risky, sticky, tricky
FORMAL parlous
COLLOQ. dodgy, hairy

touchdown *n*
landing, coming in, coming in to land, arrival
E3 take-off

touched *adj*
1 MOVED, stirred, inspired, influenced, affected, impressed, disturbed, upset
2 MAD, crazy, insane, deranged, disturbed, eccentric, unbalanced
COLLOQ. dotty, daft, barmy, nutty, bonkers, batty, loopy

touchiness *n*
bad temper, irritability, grumpiness, irascibility, peevishness, pettishness, surliness, testiness, tetchiness, petulance, captiousness
COLLOQ. crabbedness, grouchiness

touching *adj*
moving, stirring, impressive, affecting, upsetting, disturbing, poignant, pitiable, pitiful, heartbreaking, heart-rending, pathetic, sad, emotional, tender
FORMAL piteous

touchstone *n*
criterion, standard, test, norm, proof, measure, gauge, guide, model, pattern, template, benchmark, yardstick

touchy *adj*
1 IRRITABLE, bad-tempered, quick-tempered, grumpy, cross, prickly, over-sensitive, thin-skinned, peevish, captious, irascible
COLLOQ. grouchy, crabbed, edgy; *Can* chippy
2 *a touchy subject*
delicate, sensitive, tricky, difficult, problematic, awkward, controversial
E3 1 calm, imperturbable

tough *adj, n*
♦ *adj*
1 STRONG, durable, resilient, resistant, firm, hardy, sturdy, solid, rigid, stiff, inflexible, hard, leathery
2 *tough criminal*
rough, violent, disorderly, rowdy, vicious, callous, hardened, obstinate
3 HARSH, severe, strict, stern, firm, resolute, adamant, determined, tenacious, unyielding, uncompromising
4 ARDUOUS, strenuous, laborious, exacting, hard, taxing, grim, difficult, puzzling, perplexing, baffling, knotty, thorny, troublesome
COLLOQ. uphill
5 FIT, muscular, hardy, burly, well-built, robust, sturdy, rugged, vigorous, stalwart
6 *the meat is tough*
rubbery, chewy, fibrous, gristly
COLLOQ. tough as leather
7 *tough luck*
hard, unpleasant, unfortunate, unlucky, uncomfortable, distressing
E3 1 fragile, delicate, weak, tender **2** gentle, soft **3** gentle, easy-going **4** easy, simple **5** weak, frail **6** tender **7** good, fortunate
♦ *n*
brute, thug, bully, ruffian, hooligan, lout, rowdy, roughneck
COLLOQ. rough, yobbo
SLANG yob, bovver boy, lager lout

toughen *v*
strengthen, harden, reinforce, brace, stiffen, considerate, substantiate, make stricter
TECHNICAL anneal
FORMAL fortify

toughness *n*
strength, resilience, resistance, firmness, hardiness, sturdiness, tenacity, determination, inflexibility, ruggedness, obduracy
COLLOQ. grit
E3 weakness, vulnerability, softness, liberality

toupee *n*
hairpiece, wig, postiche, scratch-wig, spencer, bobwig, Brutus, buzz-wig, tie-wig; *Scot* gizz, jiz
OLD periwig, peruke, transformation, bagwig, caxon, major, Ramilie
OLD COLLOQ. jasey

tour *n, v*
* *n*
circuit, round, visit, expedition, journey, trip, outing, excursion, inspection, drive, ride, jaunt, course, hike
FORMAL peregrination
COLLOQ. walkabout, road
* *v*
visit, go round, sightsee, explore, travel round, journey through, drive through, ride, tramp, barnstorm
COLLOQ. do

tourist *n*
holidaymaker, visitor, sightseer, tripper, day-tripper, tourer, excursionist, traveller, voyager, globetrotter
OLD emmet
FORMAL sojourner
COLLOQ. *dialect* (*derog*) grockle
SLANG *N Am* rubberneck

tournament *n*
championship, series, competition, contest, match, event, meeting, meet, joust, round robin
OLD tourney

tousled *adj*
dishevelled, ruffled, unkempt, untidy, messed up, disordered, in disarray, disarranged, tangled, rumpled, tumbled

tout *v*
1 SELL, hawk, peddle, trade
2 ADVERTISE, promote, market, endorse, commend, solicit, petition, ask, appeal, seek
COLLOQ. plug, hype, push

tow *v, n*
* *v*
pull, tug, draw, trail, drag, lug, haul, transport
* *n*
pull, tug, haul, trail, lug
■ **in tow**
following closely, accompanying, by your side, in convoy

towards *prep*
1 TO, in the direction of, on the way to, approaching, nearing, close to, nearly, almost, -wards
2 *his feelings towards her*
regarding, with regard to, with respect to, concerning, about, for
3 *£500 towards the cost of the project*
to help pay for, as a contribution to, for

tower *v*
rise, rear, ascend, mount, soar, loom, overlook, dominate, surpass, transcend, overshadow, eclipse, exceed, excel, top, cap
■ **tower of strength**
supporter, support, pillar, pillar of the community, prop, mainstay, friend in need

towering *adj*
1 HIGH, soaring, tall, lofty, elevated, monumental, colossal, gigantic, great
2 MAGNIFICENT, imposing, impressive, outstanding, sublime, supreme, incomparable, unrivalled, surpassing, overpowering, extraordinary, extreme, inordinate
F3 1 low, small, tiny 2 minor, trivial

town *n*
borough, village, municipality, burgh, market town, county town, new town, city, suburbs, outskirts, conurbation, metropolis, urban district, urban area, settlement, township, pueblo; *Scot* burgh
Related adjective: urban
F3 country

town-dweller *n*
citizen, townsman, townswoman, burgher, urbanite
FORMAL oppidan
COLLOQ. towny
F3 country-dweller, rustic

toxic *adj*
poisonous, harmful, noxious, unhealthy, dangerous, deadly, lethal, baneful
F3 harmless, safe

toy *n, v, adj*
* *n*
plaything, knick-knack, trinket, trifle, bauble
See panel on next page
* *v*
play, tinker, fiddle, sport, trifle, dally, flirt
COLLOQ. mess about/around
* *adj*
model, miniature, small-scale, reduced, replica, reproduction

trace *n, v*
* *n*
1 *leave traces of blood*
hint, suggestion, suspicion, soupçon, dash, pinch, drop, spot, bit, jot, touch, tinge, shadow, smack, thought, scintilla, whiff, dreg
2 MARK, token, sign, indication, impression, scar, evidence, record, relic, remains, monument, remnant, vestige, trail, track, spoor, footprint, footmark, scent, fossil
TECHNICAL engram
OLD (*Shakesp & Spenser*) tract
COLLOQ. hide nor/or hair
* *v*
1 FIND, discover, detect, unearth, track (down), uncover, dig up, trail, track, stalk, hunt, seek, follow, pursue, dog, shadow, analyse, derive
OLD (*Shakesp & Spenser*) tract
COLLOQ. run down
2 COPY, draw, draft, sketch, outline, show, depict, mark (out), record, map, chart, describe, chalk out, counterdraw
TECHNICAL generate
FORMAL delineate

track *n, v*
* *n*
1 WAY, rail, path, route, orbit, line, trail, trajectory, slot,

---

Types of tower include:

barbican	castle	fort	Leaning Tower of	pagoda	stronghold
bastille	church tower	fortification	Pisa	peel-tower	tower block
bastion	citadel	fortress	lookout tower	scaffold tower	tower mill
belfry	column	gate-tower	Martello tower	skyscraper	Tower of London
bell tower	demi-bastion	high-rise building	minar	smock mill	turret
belvedere	donjon	hill-fort	minaret	spire	watchtower
campanile	Eiffel Tower	keep	mirador	steeple	water tower

Kinds of toy include:

action figure	crayons	golliwog	ocarina	Scalextric®	Tiny-Tears doll®
Action Man®	Digimon®	guitar	paddling-pool	scooter	toy soldier
activity centre	doll	gun	paints	seesaw	train set
aeroplane	doll's buggy	gyroscope	pantograph	Sega®	trampoline
baby-bouncer	doll's cot	hobby-horse	peashooter	sewing machine	tricycle
baby-walker	doll's house	hula-hoop	pedal-car	shape-sorter	trike
ball	doll's pram	jack-in-the-box	Plasticene®	Sindy doll®	Turtles®
balloon	dreidel	jigsaw puzzle	Play-Doh®	skateboard	typewriter
Barbie doll®	drum set	kaleidoscope	playhouse	skipping-rope	video game
bicycle	electronic game	kewpie doll	PlayStation®	slide	walkie-talkie
colloq. bike	executive toy	kite	pogo stick	soft-toy	water pistol
blackboard and	farm	Lego®	Pokémon®	Sonic the	Wendy house
easel	fivestones	marbles	pop-gun	Hedgehog®	XBox®
Bob the Builder®	football	Matchbox®	Powerpuff Girls®	spacehopper	yo-yo
boxing-gloves	fort	Meccano®	Power Rangers®	Space Invaders®	
box-kite	Frisbee®	model car	puzzle	spinning top	
building-blocks	game	model kit	rag doll	Subbuteo®	
building-bricks	Game Boy®	modelling clay	rattle	Super Mario®	
cap-gun	GameCube®	model railway	rocker	swing	
catapult	garage	mountain bike	rocking-horse	swingball	
climbing-frame	glove puppet	musical box	Rubik's Cube®	tea set	
computer game	go-kart	Nintendo®	sandpit	teddy-bear	

See also **game**.

---

groove, course, drift, sequence, argument
OLD sleuth; (*Shakesp & Spenser*) tract
2 FOOTPRINT, footstep, footmark, scent, spoor, trail, wake, mark, trace

♦ *v*
stalk, trail, hunt, trace, follow, pursue, chase, dog, tail, shadow

■ **track down**
find, discover, trace, detect, hunt down, run to earth, nose out, sniff out, ferret out, turn up, dig up, uncover, unearth, expose, catch, capture
COLLOQ. run down

■ **keep track of**
monitor, check, watch, follow, observe, record, keep an eye on
E3 lose track of

■ **lose track of**
forget, misplace, miss, lose touch/contact with

■ **make tracks**
leave, go, depart, make off, dash (off), disappear
COLLOQ. scram, beat it, hit the road

■ **on track**
on course, on schedule, on target, on time

tract *n*
1 *a tract of land*
stretch, extent, expanse, plot, lot, territory, area, region, zone, district, quarter
2 *a religious tract*
booklet, leaflet, brochure, pamphlet, treatise, sermon, essay, dissertation, homily, discourse, monograph
FORMAL disquisition

tractable *adj*
pliant, pliable, manageable, obedient, persuadable, willing, submissive, docile, controllable, amenable, biddable, governable, malleable, compliant, yielding, workable, tame, tractile
FORMAL complaisant
E3 headstrong, intractable, obstinate, refractory, stubborn, unruly, wilful

traction *n*
drawing, pull, pulling, haulage, propulsion, drag, draught, grip, friction, adhesion

trade *n, v*
♦ *n*
1 COMMERCE, traffic, trafficking, business, dealing, buying, selling, buying and selling, marketing,

shopkeeping, barter, exchange, switch, swap, transactions, custom
Related adjective: mercantile
2 OCCUPATION, employment, job, work, business, line (of work), profession, career, calling, vocation, métier, craft, skill

♦ *v*
do business, deal, transact, buy, sell, run, traffic, peddle, market, merchandize, barter, exchange, swap, switch, bargain

trademark *n*
1 *a registered trademark*
brand, brand name, brand label, tradename, proprietary name, proprietary brand, label, name, sign, symbol, logo, insignia, crest, emblem, badge
2 HALLMARK, stamp, mark, speciality, typical quality, (distinctive) feature, attribute, characteristic, idiosyncrasy, peculiarity, quirk

trader *n*
merchant, tradesman, tradeswoman, broker, dealer, buyer, seller, marketeer, marketer, vendor, supplier, wholesaler, retailer, shopkeeper, trafficker, peddler
OLD plier

tradesman, tradeswoman *n*
1 SHOPKEEPER, retailer, buyer, seller, merchant, dealer, trader, vendor
2 ARTISAN, craftsman, craftswoman, worker, mechanic, journeyman

tradition *n*
convention, custom, belief, ceremony, usage, way, habit, routine, practice, observance, ritual, rite, institution, folklore, legend
FORMAL praxis

traditional *adj*
conventional, customary, habitual, usual, routine, accustomed, conservative, ceremonial, established, fixed, set, long-established, time-honoured, old, age-old, historic, folk, oral, unwritten; *N Am* old-line
E3 unconventional, innovative, new, modern, contemporary

traditionalist *n*
conventionalist, conservative, formalist, reactionary, diehard, old guard, one of the old school; *N Am* old-liner
COLLOQ. old fogey, stick-in-the-mud

traduce *v*
misrepresent, slander, run down, revile, decry, defame, blacken, abuse, insult, malign, smear
FORMAL disparage, detract, asperse, denigrate, deprecate, depreciate, calumniate, vilify
COLLOQ. knock
SLANG slag (off)

traducer *n*
defamer, slanderer, abuser, smearer
FORMAL disparager, asperser, calumniator, denigrator, deprecator, detractor, vilifier
COLLOQ. knocker, mud-slinger

traffic *n, v*
♦ *n*
1 VEHICLES, cars, shipping, transport, transportation, freight, passengers
2 CONGESTION, traffic jam, queue, tailback, gridlock, hold-up
3 TRADE, commerce, business, dealing, trading, trafficking, buying and selling, peddling, barter, exchange
4 COMMUNICATION, dealings, relations, contact
FORMAL intercourse
♦ *v*
peddle, buy, sell, trade, do business, deal, bargain, barter, exchange

trafficker *n*
dealer, merchant, trader, seller, supplier, distributor, marketer, agent, broker, peddler, merchandizer, monger

tragedy *n*
adversity, misfortune, unhappiness, affliction, blow, calamity, disaster, catastrophe
F∃ success, triumph

tragic *adj*
calamitous, disastrous, catastrophic, deadly, fatal, sad, sorrowful, miserable, terrible, unhappy, wretched, unfortunate, unlucky, ill-fated, pitiable, pathetic, heartbreaking, shocking, appalling, dreadful, awful, deplorable, dire
F∃ happy, comic, successful

tragically *adv*
catastrophically, terribly, most unfortunately, awfully, dreadfully, appallingly, shockingly, wretchedly
F∃ happily, fortunately

trail *n, v*
♦ *n*
track, path, footpath, road, route, way, wake, piste, runway, footprints, footmarks, marks, scent, spoor, sign, trace
TECHNICAL abature
OLD sleuth; (*Spenser*) trade
♦ *v*
1 DRAG, pull, tow, haul, draw, droop, dangle, hang, extend, reach, stream, sweep, straggle, dawdle, lag, loiter, linger, fall, stream, sweep, draggle, ramble, traipse; *Scot* trauchle; *Irish* streel
OLD train
2 TRACK, stalk, hunt, follow, pursue, chase, dog, shadow, tail, tag along
■ **trail away**
decrease, die away, diminish, disappear, dwindle, fade (away), fall/melt away, lessen, peter out, shrink, sink, subside, tail/taper/trail off, weaken

trailblazer *n*
pioneer, ground-breaker, leader, pathfinder, developer, innovator, founder, discoverer

train *n, v*
♦ *n*
1 *a train of events*
sequence, succession, series, progression, order, set, suite,

string, chain, trail, line, path, track, stream, file, procession, column, convoy, cortège, caravan
FORMAL concatenation
2 RETINUE, entourage, attendants, court, household, staff, followers, following, cortège
♦ *v*
1 TEACH, instruct, coach, tutor, educate, improve, school, indoctrinate, discipline, prepare, drill, ground, exercise, work out, practise, rehearse, groom
FORMAL inculcate
2 LEARN, study, be trained, be taught, be prepared
3 POINT, direct, aim, focus, level

trainee *n*
probationer, apprentice, novice, beginner, learner, student, pupil, tiro

trainer *n*
teacher, instructor, coach, tutor, handler, educator

training *n*
teaching, instruction, coaching, tuition, tutoring, education, schooling, learning, lessons, discipline, preparation, grounding, drill, exercise, workout, working-out, practice, learning, apprenticeship

traipse *v, n*
♦ *v*
trudge, tramp, plod, slouch, trail
♦ *n*
trudge, trek, slog, plod, tramp

trait *n*
feature, attribute, quality, property, characteristic, idiosyncrasy, peculiarity, quirk

traitor *n*
betrayer, informer, deceiver, double-crosser, double-dealer, turncoat, renegade, deserter, defector, quisling, collaborator, fifth columnist, Judas, proditor
OLD traditor, treacher, treachetour, nithing
COLLOQ. backstabber, two-timer
F∃ loyalist, supporter, defender

traitorous *adj*
disloyal, unfaithful, faithless, false, untrue, treasonable, dishonourable, double-crossing, double-dealing, renegade, treacherous, apostate
FORMAL perfidious, seditious
F∃ faithful, loyal, patriotic

trajectory *n*
line, orbit, path, route, flight, flight path, course, track, trail

trammel *n, v*
♦ *n*
bar, block, bond, fetter, rein, shackle, check, clog, chain, hamper, curb, handicap, hindrance, impediment, restraint, obstacle, stumbling-block
♦ *v*
bar, block, clog, restrict, restrain, fetter, catch, check, tie, enmesh, ensnare, entrap, shackle, inhibit, impede, hinder, handicap, hamper, curb, capture, net

tramp *n, v*
♦ *n*
1 VAGRANT, vagabond, hobo, down-and-out, derelict, piker, *clochard*, floater, straggle, stroller; *dialect* walker; *Scot* caird, gangrel, hallan-shaker, landloper, rinthereout, (*derog*) tinkler; *Aust* sundowner
OLD cursitor, rogue, scatterling, truant, vagrom
OLD COLLOQ. Weary Willie
SLANG dosser, bum, toerag, knight of the road, gook; *Scot* jakey; *N Am* dingbat
2 TRUDGE, march, tread, step, walk, trek, hike, ramble
3 LOOSE WOMAN, prostitute, wench, trollop, whore, slattern, sloven
COLLOQ. hooker
SLANG floozie, slut, tart, scrubber, slag

♦ *v*

walk, march, tread, stamp, stomp, stump, plod, trudge, traipse, trail, trek, hike, ramble, roam, rove, footslog; *N Am* tromp

trample *v*

tread, stamp, crush, squash, flatten, tramp, poach, potch, override, ride down, hobnail; *Scot* stramp; *N Am* tromp
OLD foil

trance *n*

dream, reverie, daze, stupor, unconsciousness, catalepsy, spell, ecstasy, rapture

tranche *n*

part, piece, section, segment, length, cut, slice, wedge, instalment

tranquil *adj*

calm, peaceful, quiet, serene, composed, cool, imperturbable, unexcited, even-tempered, placid, sedate, relaxed, easy, restful, still, undisturbed, untroubled, hushed, silent, pacific, unimpassioned, disimpassioned
FORMAL reposeful
COLLOQ. laid-back, unflappable
E3 agitated, disturbed, troubled, noisy

tranquillity *n*

calm, peace, peacefulness, serenity, calmness, composure, quiet, quietness, rest, restfulness, stillness, hush, silence, imperturbability, coolness, equanimity, sedateness, placidity
TECHNICAL ataraxia, ataraxy
FORMAL quietude, repose
E3 disturbance, agitation, noise

tranquillize *v*

calm, quiet, pacify, relax, sedate, soothe, quell, lull, compose
TECHNICAL narcotize, opiate
E3 disturb, agitate, upset

tranquillizer *n*

sedative, calmative, sleeping pill, opiate, narcotic, barbiturate, depressant, quietive, bromide
COLLOQ. downer

transact *v*

carry out, conduct, do, perform, settle, handle, manage, carry on, accomplish, negotiate, conclude, dispatch, discharge, enact, execute
FORMAL prosecute

transaction *n*

1 *bank transactions*
deal, bargain, agreement, arrangement, negotiation, business, affair, matter, proceeding, enterprise, undertaking, deed, action, handling, settlement, enactment, execution, discharge
2 *the transactions of a learned society*
reports, proceedings, record, minutes, publications, concerns, annals, affairs, doings
COLLOQ. goings-on

transcend *v*

surpass, excel, outshine, eclipse, outdo, outstrip, leave behind, beat, surmount, exceed, go beyond, rise above, overstep

transcendence *n*

transcendency, superiority, supremacy, pre-eminence, predominance, incomparability, matchlessness, paramoun(t)cy, excellence, greatness
FORMAL ascendancy, sublimity

transcendent *adj*

1 SURPASSING, supreme, sublime, superlative, excelling, excellent, magnificent, incomparable, matchless, peerless, unparalleled, unsurpassable
2 SUPERHUMAN, supernatural, spiritual
FORMAL ineffable, numinous

transcendental *adj*

supernatural, spiritual, otherworldly, metaphysical, mystical, mysterious
FORMAL preternatural

transcribe *v*

write out, write up, copy out, copy up, reproduce, rewrite, transliterate, translate, render, take down, note, record

transcript *n*

transcription, copy, reproduction, duplicate, transliteration, translation, version, note, record, manuscript

transcription *n*

writing-out, reproduction, transliteration, translation, version

transfer *v, n*

♦ *v*
1 CHANGE, transpose, move, shift, remove, relocate, transplant, transport, carry, take, convey
2 *transfer land*
assign, convey, transmit, consign, grant, hand over
♦ *n*
change, changeover, transposition, move, movement, shift, removal, relocation, displacement, transmission, handover, assignment, transference
TECHNICAL conveyance

transfigure *v*

transform, change, alter, convert, exalt, glorify, idealize
FORMAL transmute, translate, metamorphose, apotheosize
COLLOQ. morph

transfix *v*

1 FASCINATE, spellbind, mesmerize, hypnotize, paralyse, stun, hold, engross, rivet, petrify
2 IMPALE, pierce, run through, spear, skewer, spike, stick

transform *v*

change, alter, adapt, convert, turn, remodel, rebuild, reform, resolve, reconstruct, renew, transfigure, revolutionize, transverse
TECHNICAL transmute, decentralize, absorb, receive
OLD disclose, trans-shape; (*Shakesp*) transpose
FORMAL commute, translate, metamorphose
COLLOQ. transmogrify, morph
E3 preserve, maintain

transformation *n*

change, alteration, conversion, transfiguration, revolution, turning, reformation
TECHNICAL metastasis, reaction, metaplasia, anthropomorphosis, theriomorphosis
FORMAL mutation, transmutation, metamorphosis
COLLOQ. sea change, transmogrification
E3 preservation, conservation

transfuse *v*

transfer, imbue, pervade, instil, permeate, suffuse

transgress *v*

break, offend, sin, contravene, disobey, misbehave, overstep, exceed, violate, breach, defy, infringe, encroach, lapse, err, trespass
E3 keep, obey

transgression *n*

wrong, wrongdoing, offence, infringement, lapse, trespass, crime, sin, violation, disobedience, fault, error, iniquity, misdeed, peccadillo, misbehaviour, misdemeanour, breach, contravention, encroachment, debt
FORMAL infraction

transgressor *n*

lawbreaker, offender, wrongdoer, evil-doer, criminal, culprit, delinquent, debtor, trespasser, miscreant, felon, sinner, villain
FORMAL malefactor

transience *n*
transitoriness, shortness, briefness, brevity, temporariness, impermanence, deciduousness
TECHNICAL caducity
FORMAL ephemerality, evanescence, fugacity, fugitiveness
COLLOQ. fleetingness
Fᴣ permanence

transient *adj*
transitory, passing, flying, fleeting, brief, short, momentary, short-lived, temporary, short-term, impermanent, volatile, bubble
OLD fleet; (*Shakesp*) summer-seeming
FORMAL ephemeral, evanescent, fugacious
COLLOQ. here today gone tomorrow
Fᴣ lasting, permanent

transit *n*
passage, journey, journeying, travel, crossing, route, movement, transfer, transportation, conveyance, carriage, haulage, shipment
■ **in transit**
en route, on the way, travelling, by road, by rail, by air, by sea

transition *n*
passage, passing, progress, progression, development, evolution, move, movement, flux, change, changeover, alteration, conversion, transformation, shift, switch, leap, rite of passage
TECHNICAL composition, metabasis, metastasis, transitional, unbecoming
FORMAL metamorphosis, transmutation

transitional *adj*
provisional, temporary, passing, intermediate, interim, developmental, evolutionary, changing, fluid, unsettled
Fᴣ initial, final

transitory *adj*
transient, passing, flying, fleeting, brief, short, momentary, short-lived, temporary, short-term, impermanent
OLD fleet
FORMAL ephemeral, evanescent, fugacious
COLLOQ. here today gone tomorrow
Fᴣ lasting, permanent

translate *v*
1 *translate into German*
put, render, paraphrase, reword, turn, explain, interpret, simplify, encode, decode, decipher, transliterate, transcribe, reduce
OLD traduce
FORMAL construe
2 CHANGE, alter, convert, turn, transform, improve, move, transfer, relocate, shift
FORMAL transmute
COLLOQ. transmogrify

translation *n*
1 *a translation from Spanish*
rendering, version, rendition, explanation, interpretation, gloss, crib, rewording, rephrasing, paraphrase, simplification, transliteration, transcription
OLD traduction
FORMAL metaphrasis
2 CHANGE, alteration, conversion, transformation, move, transfer, shift
FORMAL transmutation, metamorphosis
COLLOQ. transmogrification

translator *n*
linguist, polyglot, paraphraser, interpreter, glosser, dragoman
FORMAL exegete, exegetist, glossarist, glossator, metaphrast, paraphrast

translucent *adj*
transparent, clear, see-through, pellucid, translucid, limpid
FORMAL diaphanous
Fᴣ opaque

transmigration *n*
transformation, rebirth, reincarnation
FORMAL metempsychosis, Pythagoreanism

transmission *n*
1 BROADCASTING, diffusion, spread, communication, conveyance, carriage, transport, shipment, sending, dispatch, relaying, beaming, transfer, consignment, transference, imparting, trajection
FORMAL dissemination
2 *a live transmission*
broadcast, programme, show, performance, production, presentation, episode, simulcast, signal
Fᴣ **1** reception

transmit *v*
communicate, impart, convey, carry, bear, impart, transport, conduct, hand down/on, send, pass (on), dispatch, forward, consign, mediate, relay, beam, remit, transfer, broadcast, televise, telecast, radio, network, diffuse, spread, report, propagate, buzz, fax, message, modem, radiate, pipe, satellite
OLD traduce, traject
FORMAL disseminate, remit
Fᴣ receive

transmute *v*
transform, alter, change, convert, remake, transfigure, transverse
FORMAL metamorphose, translate
COLLOQ. transmogrify
Fᴣ retain

transparency *n*
1 CLEARNESS, clarity, translucence, translucency, sheerness, gauziness, filminess, pellucidity, pellucidness, perspicuousness, limpidity, limpidness, translucidity, water
FORMAL diaphanousness
2 PLAINNESS, clearness, clarity, obviousness, apparentness, distinctness, unambiguousness, straightforwardness, directness, openness, patentness, frankness, forthrightness, explicitness, candidness
3 *holiday transparencies*
slide, photograph, photo, picture
Fᴣ **1** opacity **2** ambiguity, unclearness

transparent *adj*
1 *transparent plastic*
clear, see-through, translucent, sheer, pellucid, diaphanous, gauzy, filmy
2 PLAIN, distinct, clear, lucid, explicit, unambiguous, unequivocal, unmistakable, apparent, visible, obvious, noticeable, discernible, perceptible, evident, patent, manifest, undisguised, open, direct, forthright, candid, straightforward
Fᴣ **1** opaque **2** unclear, ambiguous

transparently *adv*
plainly, clearly, distinctly, obviously, evidently, patently, explicitly, unambiguously, unequivocally, unmistakably, noticeably, perceptibly, discernibly
Fᴣ unclearly, ambiguously

transpire *v*
1 BECOME KNOWN, turn out, come to light, come out, be disclosed, become apparent, appear, prove
2 HAPPEN, occur, take place, ensue, arise, come about, come to pass
FORMAL befall

transplant *v*
move, shift, displace, remove, uproot, graft,

transfer, relocate, resettle, repot, replant
E3 leave

transport v, n
* v

1 CONVEY, carry, bear, take, fetch, bring, move, run, shift, transfer, ship, haul, remove, deport, exile
OLD traject
2 DELIGHT, enrapture, thrill, ravish, entrance, captivate, electrify, spellbind
COLLOQ. carry away
* n

1 CONVEYANCE, transit, vehicle, carriage, transfer, transportation, shipment, shipping, haulage, freight, removal
2 *transports of delight*
rapture, ecstasy, bliss, euphoria, elation, exhilaration, frenzy, fit
COLLOQ. seventh heaven

transportation n
conveyance, transit, carriage, transfer, shipment, shipping, haulage, freight

transpose v
swap, exchange, switch, interchange, transfer, shift, invert, rearrange, reorder, change, convert, alter, move, substitute

transverse adj
cross, crossways, crosswise, transversal, diagonal, oblique

trap n, v
* n

1 SNARE, net, mesh, noose, springe, gin, pit, hook, toils, booby-trap, pitfall, danger, hazard, ambush, trick, wile, ruse, stratagem, device, trickery, ploy, artifice, subterfuge, deception; *dialect* grin, weel
TECHNICAL mantrap, mouse-trap, rat-trap, dead-fall, fall-trap, flytrap, gin trap, pot, putcher
OLD snaphaunce
SLANG sting, plant
2 *Shut your trap!*
mouth
SLANG gob, traphole, cakehole, potato trap; *N Am* bazoo
* v

snare, net, entrap, ensnare, enmesh, confine, catch, capture, take, ambush, lure, beguile, corner, trick, deceive, dupe, decoy, tangle, gin, lime, dig a pit for; *dialect* grin
TECHNICAL mist-net
FORMAL inveigle

trapped adj
caught, beguiled, cornered, ensnared, ambushed, snared, stuck, netted, surrounded, tricked, deceived, duped
FORMAL inveigled
E3 free

trapper n
hunter, huntsman, backwoodsman, frontiersman, voyageur

trappings n
ornaments, accompaniments, clothes, adornments, dress, decorations, fripperies, accessories, equipment, paraphernalia, fixtures, fittings, furnishings, housings, finery, livery, gear, trimmings
FORMAL accoutrements, panoply, raiment
COLLOQ. things, bells and whistles

trash n, v
* n

1 RUBBISH, garbage, refuse, junk, waste, litter, sweepings, offscourings, scum, dregs, kitsch, trashery; *Scot* trashtrie
SLANG dreck; *N Am* grunge
2 NONSENSE, rubbish, garbage, junk, drivel, balderdash, gibberish, gobbledygook
COLLOQ. bunk, rot, tripe, bull, baloney, blah, bosh, eyewash, hogwash, rhubarb, guff, hooey, malarkey, moonshine

SLANG (*vulgar*) balls, bollocks, shit, bullshit
3 UNDESIRABLES, riff-raff, rabble, scum, dregs, *canaille*
* v

1 WRECK, destroy, ruin, demolish, devastate, shatter, smash, break, sink, spoil, mar, play havoc with, torpedo, ravage, write off
2 CRITICIZE, condemn, carp, snipe, disapprove of, find fault with, pass judgement on, denounce, attack, slate, run down, censure, blame
FORMAL disparage, excoriate, decry, denigrate, vituperate
COLLOQ. slam, knock, badmouth, rubbish, come down on, give someone some stick, go to town on, haul over the coals, pick holes in, pan, pull to pieces, tear to shreds, tear a strip off, do a hatchet job on, put the boot in
E3 1 build, repair 2 praise, commend

trashy adj
rubbishy, worthless, shabby, tawdry, tinsel, flimsy, third-rate, cheap, cheap-jack, kitschy, shoddy, inferior
FORMAL meretricious
SLANG naff, crappy
E3 first-rate

trauma n
injury, wound, hurt, lesion, damage, pain, suffering, grief, anguish, agony, torture, distress, ordeal, shock, disorder, jolt, upset, disturbance, upheaval, strain, stress
E3 healing

traumatic adj
painful, harmful, hurtful, injurious, wounding, shocking, agonizing, upsetting, distressing, disturbing, unpleasant, frightening, stressful
E3 healing, relaxing

traumatize v
shock, upset, distress, dismay, appal, outrage, horrify, startle, astound, stagger, amaze, stun, daze, stupefy, numb, paralyse, offend, hurt, grieve

travail n
1 TOIL, hardship, exertion, effort, drudgery, slog, strain, stress, suffering, distress, grind, tears, sweat
FORMAL tribulation
2 LABOUR PAINS, childbirth, birth-pangs, labour, throes
E3 rest

travel v, n
* v

journey, voyage, tour, make a trip, explore, go, go abroad/overseas, wend, make your way, move, advance, proceed, progress, wander, ramble, roam, rove, tour, cover, cross, traverse
OLD wayfare
COLLOQ. see the world
E3 stay, remain
* n

1 TRAVELLING, touring, journeying, tourism
OLD wayfare
COLLOQ. globetrotting
2 *travels abroad*
voyage, expedition, passage, journey, trip, excursion, sightseeing, tour, wanderings
COLLOQ. globetrotting
See panels on next page

traveller n
1 TOURIST, explorer, voyager, globetrotter, sightseer, holidaymaker, tourer, excursionist, passenger, commuter, wanderer, rambler, hiker, wayfarer, viator, seafarer, spacer
OLD roadster, peregrine
COLLOQ. tripper
2 WANDERER, wayfarer, migrant, nomad, Gypsy, itinerant, tinker, vagrant, tramp, drifter; *Aust & NZ* bushman
3 SALES REPRESENTATIVE, salesman, saleswoman, representative, commercial traveller, agent, commercial,

Methods of travel include:

aviate	cycle	hitch-hike	pilot	sail	trek
colloq. bike	drive	march	punt	shuttle	walk
bus	fly	motor	ramble	skate	
commute	freewheel	orienteer	ride	ski	
cruise	hike	paddle	row	steam	

Forms of travel include:

circumnavigation	exploration	journey	pilgrimage	tour	walk
cruise	flight	march	ramble	trek	
drive	hike	migration	ride	trip	
excursion	holiday	mission	safari	visit	
expedition	jaunt	outing	sail	voyage	

knight of the road; *N Am* drummer
OLD bagman, rider
COLLOQ. rep

travelling *adj*
touring, wandering, roaming, roving, wayfaring, migrating, migrant, migratory, nomadic, itinerant, mobile, moving, vagrant, homeless, unsettled
FORMAL peripatetic
E3 fixed, settled

travel-worn *adj*
weary, tired, jet-lagged, saddle-sore, travel-weary, footsore, waygone, wayworn
E3 fresh

traverse *v*
cross, pass over/through, go across/through, travel across/through, negotiate, bridge, span, ford, ply, range, roam, wander
FORMAL peregrinate

travesty *n*
mockery, parody, burlesque, farce, caricature, perversion, corruption, distortion, misrepresentation, sham, apology
COLLOQ. take-off, send-up, wind-up, spoof, tall story

trawl *v*
search, hunt, look for, investigate, sift, wade, comb

treacherous *adj*
1 TRAITOROUS, disloyal, unfaithful, faithless, unreliable, untrustworthy, false, untrue, deceitful
FORMAL duplicitous, perfidious
COLLOQ. double-crossing, backstabbing, two-timing
2 *treacherous roads*
dangerous, hazardous, risky, perilous, precarious, unsafe, icy, slippery
E3 1 loyal, faithful, dependable **2** safe, stable

treacherously *adv*
deceitfully, falsely, disloyally, faithlessly
FORMAL perfidiously
E3 loyally

treachery *n*
treason, betrayal, sabotage, unfaithfulness, faithlessness, disloyalty, infidelity, falseness, deceitfulness, double-dealing, double-crossing, traitorhood, bad faith, hollowness, Judas kiss, Punic faith, *fides Punica, trahison*
FORMAL duplicity, perfidity
COLLOQ. backstabbing, two-timing
E3 loyalty, dependability

tread *v, n*
◆ *v*
walk, step, pace, stride, march, go, hike, trek, tramp, trudge, plod, stamp, trample, walk on, press (down), crush, squash, flatten
◆ *n*
walk, footstep, step, pace, stride, tramp, gait, footprint, footmark, footfall

■ **tread on someone's toes**
offend, hurt, upset, vex, irk, annoy, infringe, injure, affront, bruise, inconvenience
FORMAL discommode
COLLOQ. disgruntle
E3 soothe

treason *n*
treachery, disloyalty, subversion, mutiny, rebellion, disaffection, lese-majesty, traitorhood, *trahison*
OLD perduellion
FORMAL perfidy, duplicity, sedition, *crimen laesae majestatis*
E3 loyalty

treasonable *adj*
traitorous, disloyal, false, unfaithful, faithless, subversive, seditious, mutinous, rebellious
FORMAL perfidious
E3 loyal

treasure *n, v*
◆ *n*
1 FORTUNE, wealth, valuables, riches, money, cash, gold, jewels, gems, hoard, cache
2 *she's a real treasure*
gem, prize, masterpiece, pride and joy, darling, *pièce de résistance*, crème de la crème
◆ *v*
prize, value, hold dear, cherish, revere, worship, love, adore, idolize, dote on, cherish, think highly of, preserve, guard, esteem
E3 belittle; *formal* disparage

treasurer *n*
bursar, cashier, purser

treasury *n*
bank, exchequer, repository, resources, revenues, finances, capital, money, funds, assets, coffers, cache, hoard, vault, store, storehouse, thesaurus, corpus

treat *n, v*
◆ *n*
indulgence, gratification, pleasure, delight, enjoyment, fun, entertainment, amusement, celebration, excursion, outing, party, celebration, feast, banquet, gift, present, surprise, thrill
◆ *v*
1 DEAL WITH, manage, handle, use, attend to, behave towards, view, regard, consider, study, discuss, cover, review
2 TEND, nurse, minister to, attend to, care for, look after, heal, cure, medicate
3 PAY FOR, buy, stand, give, pay/foot the bill, provide, take out, entertain, amuse, delight, regale, feast
4 *wood treated with creosote*
put on, apply, spread on, lay on, cover with, paint, smear, rub, prime

treatable adj
curable, remediable, operable, medicable, reparable, rectifiable, reformable
⟷ incurable

treatise n
essay, dissertation, thesis, monograph, paper, pamphlet, tract, study, discourse
FORMAL exposition, disquisition, prodrome

treatment n
1 HEALING, cure, remedy, medication, medicament, therapy, surgery, care, nursing, manipulation, therapeutics
2 MANAGEMENT, handling, dealing(s), use, usage, conduct, behaviour, action, discussion, coverage

treaty n
pact, convention, agreement, covenant, negotiation, bargain, contract, deal, pledge, bond, alliance, concord, peace, pacification
TECHNICAL protocol
OLD assiento, engagement
FORMAL concordat, compact
Related adjective: federal

treble adj
1 HIGH, high-pitched, shrill, sharp, piping
2 TRIPLE, threefold
⟷ **1** deep

tree n
bush, shrub, evergreen, conifer
Related adjective: arboreal
See panel on next page

trek v, n
♦ v
hike, journey, walk, march, tramp, traipse, trudge, plod, slog, journey, ramble, rove, roam
COLLOQ. yomp
♦ n
hike, walk, march, tramp, ramble, journey, trip, expedition, safari, odyssey

trellis n
framework, mesh, grid, net, network, lattice, latticework, grate, grating, grille
FORMAL reticulation

tremble v, n
♦ v
shake, vibrate, quake, shiver, shudder, judder, wobble, rock, quaver, quiver, dither, dodder; *Scot* hotter
♦ n
shake, vibration, quake, shiver, shudder, judder, quiver, tremor, wobble, dither, quaver; *dialect* wuther
⟷ steadiness

trembling n
shaking, vibration, quaking, quavering, quivering, shuddering, juddering, shivering, heart-quake, oscillation, rocking
COLLOQ. shakes
⟷ steadiness

tremendous adj
1 WONDERFUL, marvellous, stupendous, remarkable, sensational, spectacular, exceptional, extraordinary, great, amazing, incredible, impressive
COLLOQ. terrific, smashing, out of this world
SLANG wicked
2 HUGE, immense, vast, great, enormous, massive, colossal, gigantic, towering, formidable
⟷ **1** ordinary, unimpressive

tremendously adv
extremely, exceedingly, excessively, very, really, exceptionally, extraordinarily, intensely, thoroughly, remarkably, utterly, greatly, highly, unusually, unreasonably, immoderately, uncommonly, inordinately, acutely, severely, decidedly
COLLOQ. awfully, frightfully, terrifically

tremor n
shake, quiver, tremble, trembling, shiver, quake, quaver, wobble, vibration, agitation, thrill, shock, earthquake; *N Am* temblor
⟷ steadiness

tremulous adj
unsteady, shaky, shaking, wavering, vibrating, trembling, shivering, jumpy, jittery, quavering, quivering, quivery, agitated, trembly, afraid, scared, frightened, fearful, nervous, anxious, excited, timid
OLD aspen
⟷ steady, firm, calm

trench n
ditch, channel, excavation, trough, waterway, earthwork, furrow, gutter, pit, cut, drain, rill, sap, entrenchment, fosse

trenchant adj
1 INCISIVE, pungent, caustic, biting, scathing, acerbic, penetrating, acute, astute, sharp, clear, perceptive, effective, clear-cut
FORMAL mordant, perspicacious
2 FORTHRIGHT, vigorous, forceful, emphatic, blunt, terse, unequivocal, no-nonsense
⟷ woolly

trend n
1 TENDENCY, course, flow, current, drift, direction, bearing, inclination, leaning, tide, bent, rising tide, consensus
2 FASHION, craze, vogue, mode, style, look, mainstream, bandwagon
COLLOQ. rage, fad, latest, name of the game

trendsetter n
leader, model, pioneer, trailblazer, groundbreaker, innovator, modernist, new/modern man/woman, avant-gardist(e)

trendy adj
fashionable, latest, modish, stylish, up-to-the-minute, voguish
COLLOQ. all the rage, natty, hip, cool, funky, in, natty, snazzy, groovy, with it, now
⟷ unfashionable

trepidation n
fear, apprehension, alarm, dread, anxiety, worry, unease, qualms, disquiet, misgivings, dismay, uneasiness, excitement, emotion, trembling, nervousness, shaking, agitation, quivering, tremor, palpitation, fright
FORMAL consternation, perturbation
COLLOQ. butterflies (in your stomach), cold sweat, jitters, nerves
⟷ calm

trespass v, n
♦ v
invade, intrude, encroach, impinge, poach, infringe, violate, offend, sin, wrong
FORMAL obdurate, transgress
⟷ obey, keep to
♦ n
invasion, intrusion, encroachment, poaching, infringement, violation, wrong, wrongdoing, contravention, offence, sin, misdemeanour
FORMAL transgression

trespasser n
intruder, encroacher, burglar, poacher, offender, criminal, delinquent, evil-doer, sinner
FORMAL transgressor

tress n
hair, curl, lock, braid, bunch, plait, pigtail, ringlet, tail

Trees include:

					TYPES OF TREE:
acacia	cherry	hawthorn	mountain ash	sequoia	bonsai
acer	chestnut	hazel	oak	silver birch	conifer
alder	coconut palm	hickory	palm	silver maple	deciduous
almond	cottonwood	hornbeam	pear	spruce	evergreen
apple	cypress	horse chestnut	pine	sycamore	fruit
ash	date palm	jacaranda	plane	tamarisk	hardwood
aspen	dogwood	Japanese maple	plum	teak	ornamental
balsa	Dutch elm	larch	poplar	walnut	palm
bay	ebony	laurel	prunus	weeping willow	
beech	elder	lime	pussy willow	whitebeam	
birch	elm	linden	redwood	willow	
blackthorn	eucalyptus	mahogany	rowan	witch hazel	
blue gum	fig	maple	rubber tree	yew	
box	fir	melaleuca	sandalwood	yucca	
cedar	gum	monkey puzzle	sapele		

trial *n, adj, v*

♦ *n*

1 LITIGATION, case, lawsuit, hearing, inquiry, examination, tribunal, appeal, retrial

2 EXPERIMENT, test, examination, check, dummy run, try-out, practice, rehearsal, audition, contest, competition, selection, probation
FORMAL assay
COLLOQ. dry run

3 SUFFERING, grief, misery, distress, adversity, hardship, ordeal, trouble, nuisance, annoyance, burden, vexation, bother, bane, cross, cross to bear
FORMAL affliction, tribulation
COLLOQ. hassle, pest, pain in the neck, thorn in the flesh
EℲ 3 relief, happiness

♦ *adj*

experimental, test, testing, pilot, exploratory, provisional, probationary, dummy
COLLOQ. dry

♦ *v*

try out, pilot, experiment with, examine, assess, evaluate, check, investigate, study, analyse, screen, sample, put through its paces
FORMAL appraise, assay
COLLOQ. probe

triangle

Types of triangle include:

acute-angled	isosceles	scalene
congruent	obtuse-angled	similar
equilateral	right-angled	

triangular *adj*

triangle-shaped, three-sided, three-cornered, trilateral
TECHNICAL trigonous
FORMAL trigonal, trigonic

tribal *adj*

ethnic, family, native, indigenous, class, group, sectional

tribe *n*

race, nation, people, clan, sept, family, house, dynasty, blood, stock, group, ethnic group, caste, class, division, branch; *NZ* iwi

tribulation *n*

suffering, grief, pain, sorrow, vexation, ordeal, misery, unhappiness, misfortune, wretchedness, worry, care, anxiety, woe, burden, blow, distress, heartache, trial, reverse, adversity, hardship, trouble, curse
FORMAL affliction, travail
EℲ happiness, rest

tribunal *n*

court, committee, hearing, examination, inquisition, trial, bar, bench, kangaroo court

tributary *n*

stream, river, branch, feeder; *NAm* bogan
TECHNICAL head-stream
FORMAL confluent, influent

tribute *n*

1 PRAISE, commendation, compliment, high/good opinion, good word, accolade, present, gift, homage, respect, honour, applause, testimonial, credit, acknowledgement, evidence, proof, recognition, gratitude
FORMAL eulogy, paean, panegyric, enconium
2 PAYMENT, levy, charge, fee, toll, due, tax, tariff, duty, gift, offering, contribution
OLD pension, cain, gavel, scat, drift-land, Peter's pence, Rome-penny, Rome-scot

trice *n*

moment, minute, second, instant, flash, twinkling
COLLOQ. jiffy, sec, shake, tick, mo

trick *n, adj, v*

♦ *n*

1 FRAUD, swindle, deception, deceit, artifice, stratagem, ploy, ruse, dodge, subterfuge, trap, device, manoeuvre
COLLOQ. con, scam, diddle; *Aust & NZ* slinter
SLANG rip-off; *NAm* gold brick

2 HOAX, practical joke, joke, prank, antic, caper, frolic, gag, jape, feat, stunt
COLLOQ. leg-pull, frame-up, fast one, scam
SLANG *NAm* monkey shine

3 ILLUSION, apparition, mirage, fantasy, trick of light, sleight of hand, legerdemain

4 KNACK, gift, talent, technique, skill, art, flair, ability, capability, faculty, facility, capacity, secret, genius
COLLOQ. knowhow, hang

♦ *adj*

false, mock, artificial, imitation, ersatz, fake, forged, counterfeit, feigned, sham, bogus
EℲ real, genuine

♦ *v*

deceive, delude, dupe, fool, hoodwink, beguile, mislead, take in, bluff, hoax, cheat, swindle, diddle, defraud, trap, outwit, palter
COLLOQ. con, pull someone's leg, kid, fix, rook, have on, do, pull a fast one on, pull one over, lead up the garden path, pull the wool over someone's eyes; *NAm* pull/yank someone's chain
SLANG take for a ride

■ **trick out**

decorate, spruce up, ornament, adorn, dress up; *NAm* trick up
FORMAL array, attire, bedeck
COLLOQ. do up, doll up, tart up

trickery *n*
deception, deceit, cunning, illusion, sleight, sleight of hand, smoke and mirrors, pretence, contrivance, conveyance, dodgery, jugglery, legerdemain, practice, artifice, guile, wiliness, subterfuge, deceit, dishonesty, cheating, swindling, fraud, imposture, double-dealing, monkey business, chicanery, skulduggery; *Scot* joukery, joukery-pawkery, cantrip
OLD ropery
FORMAL duplicity
COLLOQ. funny business, hanky-panky, jiggery-pokery, hocus-pocus, shenanigans
SLANG trap
Ｅ３ straightforwardness, honesty

trickle *v, n*
 ◆ *v*
dribble, run, leak, seep, ooze, flow slowly, drizzle, exude, drip, drop, filter, percolate
Ｅ３ stream, gush
 ◆ *n*
dribble, drip, drop, leak, seepage
Ｅ３ stream, gush

trickster *n*
cheat, swindler, deceiver, fraud, fraudster, hoaxer, impostor, joker, pretender, tricker, cozener, rogue, rascal, charlatan, mountebank
OLD tregetour
FORMAL dissembler
COLLOQ. con man/woman, con artist, diddler, shark, rook, hustler, hood, hoodlum

tricky *adj*
1 *a tricky problem*
difficult, awkward, problematic, complicated, knotty, thorny, nasty, sensitive, delicate, ticklish
COLLOQ. dodgy
2 CRAFTY, artful, cunning, sly, wily, foxy, subtle, devious, slippery, scheming, deceitful, shifty
COLLOQ. dodgy
Ｅ３ **1** easy, simple **2** honest

tried *adj*
tested, proven, proved, reliable, dependable, trusted, trustworthy, established

trifle *n, v*
 ◆ *n*
1 LITTLE, bit, small amount, spot, drop, dash, touch, trace
2 TOY, plaything, trinket, bauble, knick-knack, gewgaw, geegaw, triviality, nothing, trivia, inessential, minor consideration

OLD flamflew
 ◆ *v*
toy, play, sport, flirt, treat frivolously, dally, dabble, fiddle, meddle, fool, potter
COLLOQ. mess about/around

trifling *adj*
small, paltry, slight, negligible, inconsiderable, unimportant, insignificant, minor, trivial, superficial, petty, silly, foolish, frivolous, idle, empty, shallow, worthless
OLD (*Shakesp*) baubling, immoment
FORMAL inconsequential
COLLOQ. piffling
Ｅ３ important, significant, serious

trigger *v, n*
 ◆ *v*
cause, start, initiate, activate, bring about, set off, spark off, touch off, provoke, prompt, elicit, generate, produce, set in motion/action
COLLOQ. set/start the ball rolling
 ◆ *n*
lever, catch, switch, spur, stimulus

trill *v*
sing, warble, flute, pipe, lilt

trim *adj, v, n*
 ◆ *adj*
1 NEAT, tidy, orderly, shipshape, in good order, spick-and-span, spruce, smart, well-turned-out, well-groomed, well-dressed, presentable, dapper; *Scot* snod
COLLOQ. natty, cool, snazzy
2 SLIM, slender, svelte, streamlined, fit, compact
Ｅ３ **1** untidy, scruffy
 ◆ *v*
1 CUT, clip, crop, dock, snip, prune, pare, shave, shear, chop
2 DECREASE, reduce, cut (down), cut back on, diminish, curtail, contract, scale down
3 DECORATE, ornament, embellish, garnish, adorn, festoon, dress, fringe, edge, adjust, arrange, order, neaten, tidy (up)
FORMAL array
 ◆ *n*
1 CONDITION, state, order, form, shape, fitness, health, fettle
2 TRIMMING, braid, border, edging, fringe, frill, decoration

trimming *n*
1 ADORNMENT, decoration, braid, border, edging, fringe, frill, embellishment, garnish, ornamentation, trim, extra, accompaniment, accessory, piping, falbala, frou-frou, passement, passementerie
TECHNICAL fimbriation
OLD furbelow
COLLOQ. bells and whistles
2 CUTTING, clipping, paring, end

trinket *n*
bauble, jewel, ornament, charm, knick-knack, trifle, gimcrack, gewgaw, geegaw, bagatelle, whim-wham, seal, trick, bijou, doodah, kickshaw(s); *Scot* whigmaleerie
OLD flamflew, trankum

trio *n*
threesome, triad, trinity, triune, triunity, triplet, triplicity, trilogy
FORMAL triumvirate, troika

trip *n, v*
 ◆ *n*
1 OUTING, excursion, tour, jaunt, ride, drive, spin, run, journey, voyage, expedition, sail, flip, whirl, foray; *Scot* hurl
COLLOQ. jolly, tootle
2 FALL, slip, stumble, tumble, false step
3 ERROR, blunder, mistake, inaccuracy, slip, gaffe, faux pas
COLLOQ. howler, bloomer, clanger, booboo
4 HALLUCINATION, illusion, vision, apparition, fantasy, dream, experience
COLLOQ. high, bummer

SLANG freak-out, buzz

♦ *v*

1 STUMBLE, slip, slide, fall, tumble, stagger, totter, lose your
footing
OLD spurn
2 DANCE, waltz, skip, gambol, hop, spring, caper, tiptoe;
Scot link
OLD kilt

■ **trip up**
catch (out), trap, disconcert, wrongfoot, throw off
balance, snare, ensnare, ambush, waylay, outsmart,
outwit, surprise, trick

tripe *n*
rubbish, nonsense, bunkum, drivel, garbage, inanity,
claptrap, trash
COLLOQ. balderdash, hogwash, twaddle, tosh, rot,
poppycock, blah, bosh, baloney, eyewash, rhubarb, guff,
hooey, malarkey, moonshine
SLANG (*vulgar*) balls, shit, bullshit, bollocks
F∃ sense

triple *adj, v, n*
♦ *adj*
treble, three times, triplicate, threefold, three-ply, three-
way, tripartite
♦ *v*
treble, triplicate
♦ *n*
trio, threesome, triad, trinity, triune, triunity, triplet,
triplicity, trilogy
FORMAL triumvirate, troika

tripper *n*
tourist, sightseer, traveller, voyager, holidaymaker, excursionist
COLLOQ. grockle

trite *adj*
banal, commonplace, common, ordinary, run-of-the-mill,
stale, tired, worn, well-worn, worn-out, threadbare,
unoriginal, uninspired, dull, routine, hackneyed, overdone,
overused, overworn, stock, stereotyped, cliché(e)d,
predictable, beaten, novelettish, truistic, tritical; *N Am*
cornball
FORMAL platitudinous
COLLOQ. corny, Mickey Mouse
SLANG *N Am* rinky-dink
F∃ original, new, fresh, imaginative, inspired

Synonym nuances
You can use the adjectives **banal** or **commonplace** to
suggest that something is without distinctive traits;
common, **ordinary** and **routine** are even more widely
used to describe something frequent and thereby
unremarkable.
 Stale, **tired**, **worn** and **well-worn** are more marked by
disapproval, and have further connotations of having
been seen or used too often: *the stale routines of life*;
tired old excuses, and **worn-out** and **threadbare**,
overdone, **overused** and **overworn** even more
markedly suggest this loss of effectiveness through
constant employment. **Hackneyed** and **clichéd** are
also highly critical, and applied particularly to verbal
expressions that have become meaningless or tedious
through excessive use: *clichéd phrases used every day in
the papers*.
 Unoriginal and **uninspired** are equally critical, but
make the accusation of a lack of new thinking, rather
than of overuse. **Stock** could describe something
conventionally used in certain situations: *he gave his
stock reply*, while **stereotyped** has more to do with fixed,
standardized images: *homeless people stereotyped as
drug addicts*. The word **predictable** puts the emphasis
on an inability to surprise: *a predictable plot where all the
usual events unfold*.

---

triumph *n, v*
♦ *n*
1 WIN, victory, conquest, success, mastery, achievement,
accomplishment, attainment, feat, coup, masterstroke, hit,
sensation, flying colours
COLLOQ. walkover
2 EXULTATION, jubilation, rejoicing, celebration, elation, joy,
happiness, glory, paean
F∃ 1 failure
♦ *v*
1 WIN, succeed, prosper, conquer, defeat, beat, overcome,
overwhelm, gain mastery, dominate
FORMAL vanquish, prevail
COLLOQ. win the day
2 CELEBRATE, rejoice, glory, gloat, exult, revel, swagger,
crow
OLD overcrow
FORMAL jubilate
F∃ 1 lose, fail

triumphant *adj*
winning, victorious, conquering, successful, prize-
winning, exultant, jubilant, rejoicing, celebratory, glorious,
elated, joyful, proud, boastful, gloating, swaggering,
crowing
COLLOQ. cock-a-hoop
F∃ defeated, humble

trivia *n*
details, trifles, trivialities, irrelevancies, technicalities,
minutiae
COLLOQ. pap
F∃ essentials

trivial *adj*
unimportant, insignificant, incidental, minor, petty, paltry,
trifling, flimsy, small, little, inconsiderable, negligible,
worthless, meaningless, frivolous, banal, trite,
commonplace, everyday, frothy, gimcrack, quibbling,
pettifogging, snippety, peppercorn
OLD bald
FORMAL inconsequential, of no consequence
COLLOQ. measly, piddling, piffling, no great shakes, cutting
no ice; *N Am* dinky
SLANG *N Am* rinky-dink
F∃ important, significant, profound, substantial

Synonym nuances
Unimportant can be used of anything that has a lack of
consequence, and **insignificant** of something not being
worthy of note, while **incidental** is more suggestive of
something, often unforeseen, accompanying a major
issue: *incidental expenses*. **Minor**, however, might be
used of anything inferior in size or importance: *the police
ignored the minor details of the incident*, whereas **petty**,
paltry and **trifling** are dismissive terms, suggesting
something is unworthy of consideration: *trifling details
are of no interest to me*. **Flimsy**, on the other hand, puts
the emphasis on a lack of substance: *flimsy evidence*.
 Inconsiderable suggests literally that something is
unworthy of notice, but is usually used in the negative to
mean the opposite: *using his not inconsiderable bulk*,
and **negligible** can be used in a less judgemental way of
something which can be safely ignored: *the hazards
were negligible*. **Worthless**, meanwhile, does suggest
more of a judgement that something has no inherent
value, and **frivolous** and **frothy** again imply a judgement,
suggesting an inappropriate lack of gravity, or excessive
concern with inconsequential things: *a frothy chat show*.
 To describe something, such as an opinion or phrase,
that has lost all significance through overuse, you might
use **banal** or **trite**, **commonplace** or **everyday**. The
terms **quibbling** and **pettifogging** have more to do with
an excessive concern for irrelevant detail.

triviality n

1 UNIMPORTANCE, insignificance, pettiness, smallness, worthlessness, meaninglessness, nonsense, nothingism, pretence, foolishness, frivolity, banality, frippery, puerility
2 TRIFLE, detail, technicality, nothing
F3 1 importance **2** essential

trivialize v

minimize, play down, underestimate, underplay, undervalue, devalue, belittle, depreciate, scoff at
F3 exalt

troll n

goblin, dwarf, elf, gnome, jinn; *Scot* trow, drow; *Irish* pooka

trollop n

prostitute, harlot, callgirl, rent-boy, woman of the streets, woman of the town, woman of ill repute, loose woman, fallen woman, scarlet woman, whore, street-walker, cocotte, courtesan, bawd, *fille de joie, fille des rues*, drab, grande cocotte, lorette, lady of the night, geisha, hetaera, hierodule, loose fish, magdalen, night-walker, vizard-mask
OLD bulker, convertite, trull, strumpet, cockatrice, public woman, wench, pug, punk, stew, stale; (*Shakesp*) quail, bona-roba, callet, polecat, road, venture
COLLOQ. hooker, hustler, moll, pro, hostess, fancy woman; *N Am* working girl
SLANG *poule de luxe*, quiff, rough trade, tart, tom, tramp, brass, floozie; *N Am* broad
OLD SLANG dell, mutton, dolly-mop, plover; (*Shakesp*) laced mutton

troop n, v

♦ n

1 *send in troops*
army, military, soldiers, armed forces, servicemen, servicewomen, fighters, cavalry, gunners, infantrymen, fusiliers, platoons, brigades, regiments, commandos, squadrons, paratroopers, paratroops, militia, convoys
OLD kern, turm
2 *a troop of soldiers/children*
contingent, squadron, unit, division, company, squad, team, crew, gang, band, bunch, group, body, pack, herd, flock, school, horde, crowd, throng, mob, gathering, multitude
FORMAL assemblage

♦ v

go, march, parade, walk, stream, flock, swarm, throng, traipse, trudge

trophy n

cup, prize, laurels, award, spoils, souvenir, memento, silverware

tropical adj

hot, very hot, torrid, sultry, boiling (hot), sweltering, stifling, steamy, humid
F3 arctic, cold, cool, temperate

trot v, n

♦ v

jog, canter, run, pace, scamper, scuttle, bustle, scurry; *S Afr* tripple

♦ n

jog, canter, run, dogtrot, jogtrot; *S Afr* tripple
TECHNICAL passage

■ **trot out**
bring out, bring up, drag up, relate, repeat, bring forward, exhibit, reiterate
FORMAL adduce, recite, rehearse

■ **on the trot**
in a row, consecutively, successively, sequentially, continuously, uninterruptedly, one after the other, in turn
COLLOQ. back to back

troubadour n

singer, minstrel, balladeer, cantabank, jongleur, poet, trouvère, trouveur, Minnesinger

trouble n, v

♦ n

1 PROBLEM, difficulty, struggle, annoyance, irritation, vexation, bother, nuisance, inconvenience, hardship, misfortune, adversity, trial, torment, burden, pain, suffering, distress, grief, woe, heartache, concern, unease, uneasiness, worry, anxiety, agitation
FORMAL tribulation, affliction, disquiet
COLLOQ. hassle, headache, hot water, mess, corner, fix, scrape, jam, pickle, tight spot
2 UNREST, strife, fighting, tumult, commotion, disturbance, disorder, bother, upheaval
3 *back trouble*
disorder, complaint, ailment, illness, disease, disability, defect
4 *engine trouble*
problem(s), failure, breakdown, cutting-out, shutdown, stopping, stalling
FORMAL malfunction
COLLOQ. packing-up
SLANG conking-out
5 EFFORT, exertion, pains, care, attention, thought, thoughtfulness, bother, fuss, ado, inconvenience
COLLOQ. hassle
F3 1 relief, calm **2** order, peace **3** health

♦ v

annoy, vex, harass, torment, bother, make the effort, inconvenience, disturb, upset, distress, sadden, pain, afflict, weigh (down), burden, worry, agitate, irritate, disconcert, perplex
FORMAL discommode, perturb
COLLOQ. put out, hassle
F3 reassure, help

troubled adj

worried, anxious, uneasy, ill at ease, apprehensive, concerned, bothered, upset, fearful, afraid, frightened, overwrought, tense, strained, nervous, disturbed, distraught, distracted, disquieted, dismayed, fretful, distressed, agonized
FORMAL perturbed
COLLOQ. on edge, uptight, (all) hot and bothered
F3 calm, unworried, unconcerned

troublemaker n

agitator, rabble-rouser, incendiary, instigator, inciter, ringleader, *agent provocateur*, mischief-maker
COLLOQ. stirrer, mixer
SLANG bovver boy; (*taboo*) shit-stirrer
F3 peacemaker

troublesome adj

1 ANNOYING, irritating, vexatious, irksome, bothersome, worrisome, disturbing, inconvenient, difficult, hard, awkward, tricky, thorny, taxing, demanding, exacting, laborious, tiresome, wearisome
FORMAL perturbing
2 UNRULY, mischievous, rowdy, turbulent, trying, unco-operative, insubordinate, rebellious
F3 1 easy, simple **2** helpful

trough n

1 MANGER, feeding trough, feeder, crib, watering-trough, sluice; *Scot* backet
2 GUTTER, conduit, drain, trench, ditch, gully, channel, chute, duct, groove, furrow, flume, hollow, valley, depression, trunk, hopper, launder; *N Am* gum
TECHNICAL sand table, tye, sheep-dip

trounce v

defeat, rout, beat, thrash, overwhelm, paste, punish, best, crush
COLLOQ. wallop, slaughter, hammer, clobber, lick, drub, wipe the floor with
SLANG take to the cleaners

troupe *n*
company, group, set, band, cast, troop

trouper *n*
actor, performer, player, theatrical, artiste, entertainer, veteran
FORMAL thespian
COLLOQ. old hand

trousers *n*
slacks, jeans, denims, Levis®, flannels, chinos, corduroys, cords, dungarees, breeches, shorts; *Scot* trews; *N Am* pants
OLD (*Shakesp*) strossers; *Irish* trouse
COLLOQ. *Aust* daks
SLANG *Irish* trouses

truancy *n*
absence, absenteeism, shirking, malingering, French leave
COLLOQ. skiving
F3 attendance

truant *n, adj, v*
♦ *n*
absentee, deserter, runaway, idler, shirker, dodger, malingerer
COLLOQ. skiver
♦ *adj*
absent, missing, runaway
♦ *v*
play truant, desert, dodge, shirk, malinger
COLLOQ. skive, skive off, play hooky
SLANG *N Am* goof off

truce *n*
ceasefire, peace, armistice, pacification, cessation, moratorium, suspension, stay, respite, lull, rest, break, interval, intermission; *dialect* barley
OLD (*Spenser*) treague
COLLOQ. let-up
F3 war, hostilities

truck¹ *n*
heavy trucks on the road
lorry, articulated lorry, heavy goods vehicle (HGV), juggernaut, van, wagon, float

truck² *n*
have no truck with someone
contact, communication, connection, assocation, relations, dealings, business, trade, commerce, traffic, exchange
FORMAL intercourse

truculence *n*
aggressiveness, belligerence, defiance, disobedience, quarrelsomeness, hostility, violence, rudeness, bad-temperedness, obstreperousness
FORMAL bellicosity, pugnacity

truculent *adj*
aggressive, belligerent, defiant, disobedient, quarrelsome, antagonistic, contentious, hostile, violent, savage, combative, fierce, argumentative, rude, bad-tempered, ill-tempered, sullen, cross, obstreperous, discourteous, disrespectful
FORMAL bellicose, pugnacious
F3 co-operative, good-natured

trudge *v, n*
♦ *v*
tramp, plod, clump, stump, lumber, traipse, slog, toil, labour, trek, hike, walk, march, shuffle
♦ *n*
tramp, traipse, slog, haul, trek, hike, walk, march

true *adj, adv*
♦ *adj*
1 REAL, genuine, authentic, actual, veritable, exact, precise, accurate, close, correct, right, factual, truthful, veracious, sincere, honest, legitimate, faithful, unerring, valid, rightful, proper
FORMAL veracious
2 FAITHFUL, loyal, constant, steadfast, fast, staunch, firm, dependable, reliable, true-hearted, trustworthy, trusty, honourable, sincere, dedicated, devoted
F3 1 false, wrong, untrue, incorrect, inaccurate **2** unfaithful, faithless
♦ *adv*
accurately, exactly, correctly, faithfully, honestly, precisely, rightly, truly, truthfully, unerringly, properly, perfectly, veritably
FORMAL veraciously
F3 falsely, inaccurately

true-blue *adj*
card-carrying, committed, confirmed, constant, dedicated, devoted, diehard, dyed-in-the-wool, faithful, loyal, orthodox, staunch, true, trusty, uncompromising, unwavering
F3 superficial, wavering

truism *n*
platitude, self-evident truth, truth, commonplace, cliché, bromide, axiom

truly *adv*
very, greatly, extremely, exceptionally, really, genuinely, sincerely, honestly, constantly, steadfastly, truthfully, on my word/honour, surely, definitely, certainly, undoubtedly, without a doubt, undeniably, indubitably, indeed, true, in fact, in reality, in truth, actually, exactly, precisely, correctly, rightly, properly, quite; *dialect* fegs
OLD certes; (*Spenser*) soothly, soothlich
F3 slightly, falsely, incorrectly

trump *v*
outdo, outshine, surpass, top, cap, eclipse, upstage
COLLOQ. knock spots off
▪ **trump up**
invent, fake, fabricate, falsify, create, devise, make up, concoct, contrive
COLLOQ. cook up

trumped-up *adj*
false, fabricated, fake, faked, falsified, invented, made-up, untrue, bogus, cooked-up, concocted, contrived, spurious
COLLOQ. phoney
F3 genuine, real, true

trumpery *adj*
worthless, useless, valueless, shabby, trifling, showy, cheap, flashy, nasty, rubbishy, shoddy, tawdry, trashy
FORMAL meretricious
F3 first-rate

trumpet *n, v*
♦ *n*
bugle, horn, cornet, trombone, ram's horn, clarion, clarino, shell, conch, blare, blast, roar, bellow, cry, call, clang, tantara, taratantara, tucket, last trump
OLD trump, tuba, alchemy, buccina, lituus, lure, salpinx, sennet
♦ *v*
blare, blast, roar, bellow, bay, shout, proclaim, announce, call, sound, herald, broadcast, advertise, taratantara, chide
OLD trump
COLLOQ. toot, parp
▪ **blow your own trumpet**
boast, crow, brag, show off, sing your own praises
COLLOQ. swank, talk big, loudmouth; *N Am* blow your own horn; *Aust* skite

truncate *v*
shorten, abbreviate, curtail, reduce, diminish, cut short, cut, lop, dock, prune, pare, clip, trim, crop
F3 lengthen, extend

truncheon n
baton, club, cudgel, cosh, stick, staff, shillelagh, knobkerrie; N Am billy, billystick

trundle v
roll, bowl, chug, cruise, freewheel

trunk n
1 STEM, shaft, stock, stalk
2 CASE, suitcase, chest, coffer, box, crate, portmanteau
3 SNOUT, nose
TECHNICAL proboscis
4 TORSO, body, frame

truss v, n
♦ v
tie, strap, bind, pinion, fasten, tether, secure, bundle, wrap, pack
ⓔ untie, loosen
♦ n
binding, bandage, pad, support, brace, prop, stay, shore, buttress, strut, joist; Scot dorlach

trust n, v
♦ n
1 FAITH, belief, credence, credit, hope, expectation, reliance, confidence, assurance, conviction, certainty
2 CARE, charge, custody, safekeeping, guardianship, trusteeship, protection, obligation, responsibility, duty, commitment
ⓔ **1** distrust, mistrust, scepticism, doubt
Related adjective: fiduciary
♦ v
1 RELY ON, depend on, put your confidence in, put your trust in, have confidence in, believe in, be sure of, count on, bank on, swear by
2 BELIEVE, imagine, assume, presume, suppose, hope, expect
FORMAL surmise
3 ENTRUST, commit, consign, confide, give, assign, turn over, delegate
ⓔ **2** distrust, mistrust, doubt, disbelieve

trustee n
keeper, administrator, agent, custodian, guardian, executor, executrix, fiduciary, depositary, assignee

trusting adj
trustful, credulous, gullible, naive, innocent, ingenuous, unquestioning, unsuspecting, unguarded, unwary
ⓔ distrustful, suspicious, cautious

trustworthiness n
honesty, integrity, consistency of character, honourableness, reliability, dependability, steadfastness, stability, commitment, devotion, faithfulness, loyalty, responsibility, sensibleness, level-headedness
ⓔ irresponsibility, unreliability

trustworthy adj
honest, upright, honourable, principled, ethical, dependable, reliable, steadfast, stable, staunch, true, safe, sound, committed, devoted, faithful, loyal, responsible, sensible, level-headed, creditable, authentic
COLLOQ. (as) good as your word
ⓔ untrustworthy, dishonest, unreliable, irresponsible

trusty adj
faithful, dependable, reliable, responsible, strong, supportive, firm, honest, loyal, staunch, trustworthy, true, solid, straightforward, steady, upright
ⓔ unreliable

truth n
1 TRUTHFULNESS, candour, frankness, honesty, sincerity, genuineness, authenticity, realism, exactness, precision, correctness, accuracy, validity, legitimacy, rightness, honour, honourableness, integrity, uprightness, faithfulness, loyalty, constancy

FORMAL verity, veracity, fidelity
2 tell the truth
facts, reality, actuality, fact, the gospel truth, axiom, maxim, principle, truism
OLD sooth
COLLOQ. home truth
ⓔ **1** deceit, dishonesty, falseness **2** lie, falsehood
■ in truth
in fact, indeed, really, in reality, surely, actually, as a matter of fact, in actual fact, in point of fact, to tell you the truth, truth to tell, if truth be told, to be honest
OLD forsooth, insooth, soothly, soothlich

truthful adj
frank, candid, straight, honest, open, forthright, true, sincere, veritable, exact, precise, right, factual, accurate, correct, valid, realistic, faithful, trustworthy, reliable
OLD sooth, soothfast
FORMAL veracious
ⓔ untruthful, deceitful, false, untrue

truthfully adv
honestly, openly, truly, sincerely, precisely, factually, accurately, correctly, faithfully, reliably
ⓔ falsely, deceitfully

truthfulness n
frankness, candour, honesty, openness, sincerity, straightness, uprightness, righteousness
FORMAL veracity
ⓔ untruthfulness

try v, n
♦ v
1 ATTEMPT, endeavour, venture, undertake, seek, strive, aim
FORMAL assay
COLLOQ. have a go, have a bash/crack/shot/stab, give something your best shot, give something a whirl
2 HEAR, judge
3 EXPERIMENT, test, try out, sample, taste, inspect, examine, investigate, evaluate
FORMAL appraise
4 try someone's patience
tax, make demands on, strain, stress, tire, wear out, weary, exhaust, drain, sap, weaken, stretch
♦ n
1 ATTEMPT, endeavour, effort
COLLOQ. go, bash, crack, shot, stab, whirl
2 EXPERIMENT, test, trial, evaluation, ample, taste
FORMAL appraisal
■ try out
test, evaluate, try on, check out, inspect, sample, taste
FORMAL appraise

trying adj
annoying, irritating, vexatious, exasperating, troublesome, tiresome, wearisome, bothersome, difficult, hard, tough, arduous, taxing, stressful, demanding, testing
COLLOQ. aggravating
ⓔ easy

tub n
bath, bathtub, washtub, basin, vat, tun, butt, cask, barrel, container, keg, hogshead, lucky dip, bran tub, stand, back, swill-tub, keeve, kid; dialect cowl, dan, kit
TECHNICAL kier
OLD bran-pie
COLLOQ. Aust bucket

tubby adj
chubby, plump, portly, podgy, paunchy, stout, pudgy, roly-poly, fat, overweight, obese, buxom, well-upholstered
FORMAL corpulent, rotund
ⓔ slim

tube n
hose, pipe, tubing, cylinder, duct, conduit, spout, channel, shaft, inlet, outlet

tubular adj
tubelike, pipelike, pipy
FORMAL tubulous, tubulate, tubiform, tubate, vasiform

tuck v, n
◆ v
1 INSERT, push, ease, thrust, stuff, cram, gird yourself
2 FOLD, pleat, gather, crease, ruffle, kilt
◆ n
1 FOLD, pleat, gather, pucker, crease
2 FOOD, comestibles, meals, snack(s)
COLLOQ. eats, scrab
SLANG grub, nosh, scoff, chow
■ **tuck away**
stash away, save (up), store, hide, conceal, hoard
■ **tuck in/into**
eat, eat up, eat heartily, gorge, devour, dine, feast
COLLOQ. gobble, scoff, wolf down
■ **tuck in/up**
put to bed, make comfortable, make snug, cover up, wrap up, fold in/under, truss

tuft n
crest, beard, tassel, truss, knot, clump, cluster, bunch, wisp
FORMAL flocculus

tug v, n
◆ v
pull, draw, tow, haul, drag, lug, heave, wrench, jerk, pluck
COLLOQ. yank
◆ n
pull, tow, haul, heave, wrench, jerk, pluck
COLLOQ. yank

tuition n
teaching, instruction, coaching, training, guidance, lessons, schooling, education

tumble v, n
◆ v
1 FALL, fall over, trip (up), topple, stumble, drop, flop, knock down, unseat, overthrow
2 PITCH, roll, toss, lurch, sway, reel, heave, welter
3 *prices are tumbling*
decrease, fall, decline, collapse, slide, plummet, dive, nosedive, plunge, fall headlong
4 TOUSLE, rumple, dishevel, disarrange, disorder
◆ n
1 FALL, stumble, trip, drop, roll, toss
2 DECREASE, fall, decline, collapse, slide, dive, nosedive
■ **tumble to**
understand, realize, grasp, perceive, become aware of, comprehend
COLLOQ. cotton on to, twig, suss, get, get the picture, latch on to; *N Am* savvy

tumbledown adj
broken-down, ramshackle, rickety, dilapidated, unstable, unsteady, shaky, unsafe, ruinous, ruined, crumbling, crumbly, disintegrating, decrepit, tottering
E3 well-kept

tumbler n
1 ACROBAT, gymnast, contortionist
2 DRINKING-GLASS, glass, beaker, cup, goblet, mug

tumid adj
1 SWOLLEN, enlarged, bulging, protuberant, bloated, puffed up, bulbous
FORMAL distended, tumescent
2 BOMBASTIC, pompous, affected, overblown, grandiose, high-flown, inflated, pretentious, fulsome, flowery, stilted, turgid
FORMAL euphuistic, grandiloquent, magniloquent
E3 **1** flat **2** simple

tummy n
stomach, gut, inside(s), belly, abdomen, paunch, pot-belly

COLLOQ. corporation
SLANG bread basket

tumour n
cancer, growth, malignancy, lump, swelling
TECHNICAL carcinoma, melanoma, lymphoma, myeloma, sarcoma, neoplasm

tumult n
commotion, turmoil, disturbance, upheaval, stir, agitation, unrest, disorder, confusion, chaos, pandemonium, bedlam, babel, noise, clamour, shouting, din, racket, hubbub, hullabaloo, row, rumpus, uproar, riot, fracas, brawl, affray, strife, mutiny, rout, bustle, hurricane, ferment, surge, whirl, pandemonium, hurly, hurly-burly, rabblement, ruffle, stour, williwaw; *Scot* brattle, stramash
OLD coil, deray, rore; (*Shakesp*) romage
FORMAL disarray
E3 peace, calm, composure

tumultuous adj
turbulent, stormy, raging, frenzied, fierce, violent, wild, vehement, fervent, hectic, boisterous, rowdy, noisy, loud, deafening, clamorous, disorderly, unruly, riotous, uncontrolled, restless, agitated, troubled, disturbed, excited
OLD troublous, tumultuary
E3 calm, peaceful, quiet

tune n, v
◆ n
melody, theme, motif, song, air, strain, serenade, chorus, dance, spring, lilt, round, folk-tune, signature, signature tune, theme song, jingle, port, rant, melisma
OLD ayre, dump, note, loure, hunt's-up, light-o'-love, maggot
◆ v
pitch, harmonize, set, regulate, adjust, adapt, temper, synchronize
FORMAL attune
■ **change your tune**
change your mind, change your attitude/opinions, change your approach
■ **in tune with**
in agreement with, in sympathy with, agreeing with, in harmony with, on the same wavelength as, true, *d'accord*
FORMAL in accord with
■ **out of tune**
jarring, false, disagreeing, at odds
TECHNICAL off-key, out of key, untuned, mistuned, scordato
OLD ajar, distuned

tuneful adj
melodious, melodic, catchy, musical, euphonious, harmonious, pleasant, agreeable, mellow, sonorous
FORMAL mellifluous
E3 tuneless, discordant

tuneless adj
unmelodic, unmelodious, unmusical, unpleasant, disagreeable, harsh, clashing, discordant, cacophonous, dissonant
FORMAL atonal, horrisonant
E3 tuneful

tunnel n, v
◆ n
passage, underground passage, passageway, gallery, subway, underpass, burrow, hole, mine, shaft, chimney
◆ v
burrow, dig, excavate, mine, bore, penetrate, undermine, sap

turbid adj
cloudy, clouded, hazy, dense, dim, foggy, fuzzy, muddy, murky, unclear, thick, muddled, opaque, confused, disordered, turbulent, unsettled, impure, incoherent, foul
FORMAL feculent
E3 clear

turbulence n

roughness, storm, unrest, boiling, upheaval, agitation, turmoil, tumult, confusion, commotion, chaos, disorder, disruption, instability, pandemonium
🖪 calm

turbulent adj

rough, choppy, foaming, stormy, blustery, tempestuous, raging, furious, violent, wild, tumultuous, unbridled, boisterous, noisy, rowdy, disorderly, unruly, undisciplined, obstreperous, rebellious, mutinous, riotous, agitated, in turmoil, unsettled, unstable, confused, disordered, outrageous, factious
OLD combustious
🖪 calm, composed

turf n, v

♦ *n*

grass, clod, sod, divot, sward, green, lawn, glebe

■ **turf out**

discharge, dismiss, eject, turn out, throw out, evict, banish, remove, fling out, expel, oust
FORMAL dispossess
COLLOQ. kick out, chuck out, elbow, fire, sack, give the elbow to

turgid adj

pompous, bombastic, flowery, fulsome, grandiose, high-flown, inflated, ostentatious, extravagant, overblown, pretentious, stilted, affected
FORMAL grandiloquent, magniloquent
🖪 simple

turmoil n

confusion, disorder, tumult, commotion, disturbance, trouble, disquiet, agitation, turbulence, stir, ferment, flurry, bustle, chaos, pandemonium, bedlam, noise, din, hubbub, row, uproar, upheaval
FORMAL disarray
🖪 calm, peace, quiet

turn v, n

♦ *v*

1 REVOLVE, circle, spin, go round (and round), go round in circles, twirl, whirl, spiral, wind, reel, twist, gyrate, pivot, hinge, swivel, rotate, roll, move, shift, invert, reverse, bend, veer, swing, swerve, pass, point, direct, aim, focus, divert
2 MAKE, transform, change, alter, modify, convert, develop, adapt, adjust, fit, mould, shape, cast, form, fashion, remodel
FORMAL mutate, transmute, metamorphose
3 *turn cold*
go, become, grow, come to be
4 RESORT, have recourse, apply, appeal, take up, become involved with, attend
5 SOUR, curdle, spoil, go off, go bad, make/become rancid
♦ *n*
1 REVOLUTION, cycle, round, circle, rotation, spin, twirl, whirl, twist, swivel, gyration, bend, curve, corner, loop, reversal
2 CHANGE, alteration, shift, variation, difference, deviation, divergence
3 *it's your turn*
go, chance, opportunity, occasion, time, stint, period, spell, say
COLLOQ. shot, crack, stab, bash
4 ACT, appearance, routine, performance, performer
5 TREND, tendency, inclination, direction, bias, leaning, heading, drift
FORMAL propensity
6 *he did me a good turn*
kindness, act of kindness, service, favour, good deed, courtesy, benefit
7 *gave her quite a turn*
illness, nervousness, faintness, shock, fright, scare, surprise, start

■ **turn against**

dislike, disapprove of, distrust, make/become hostile to
🖪 like, trust, support

■ **turn aside**

deviate, depart, diverge, deflect, ward off, fend off, parry, avert

■ **turn away**

reject, avert, deflect, refuse, deviate, depart, move away
COLLOQ. cold-shoulder
🖪 accept, help, receive

■ **turn back**

1 GO BACK, return, retreat, retrace your steps
2 *turned back by the border guards*
drive back, force back, repel

■ **turn down**

1 *turn down an offer*
reject, decline, refuse, spurn, rebuff, repudiate, veto
2 LOWER, decrease, reduce, lessen, make quieter, quieten, soften, mute, muffle
🖪 1 accept **2** turn up

■ **turn in**

1 GO TO BED, retire
COLLOQ. hit the hay, hit the sack; *N Am* sack out
2 HAND IN, give in, tender, submit, return, give back, hand over, give up, surrender, deliver
3 BETRAY, hand over, deliver, denounce, inform on, double-cross, turn traitor, be disloyal to, be unfaithful to, break faith with, go back on, renege on, let down
COLLOQ. tell on, rat on, sell (out), sell down the river, stab in the back, squeal on, blow the whistle on, walk out on, split on
SLANG shop, grass, rumble; *N Am* stool on
🖪 1 get up **2** keep

■ **turn of events**

incident, happening, occurrence, result, affair, outcome, phenomenon

■ **turn of phrase**

expression, idiom, saying, style, diction, metaphor, phraseology, manner of speaking
FORMAL locution

■ **turn off**

1 BRANCH OFF, leave, depart from, deviate, divert, go along a different road
COLLOQ. quit
2 SWITCH OFF, turn out, stop, shut down, shut off, unplug, disconnect, pull off
3 REPEL, sicken, nauseate, disgust, offend, displease, disenchant, alienate, bore, discourage, put off, turn against
🖪 1 join, meet **2** turn on, switch on, start up **3** *colloq.* turn on, excite, interest

■ **turn on**

1 SWITCH ON, put on, start (up), activate, plug (in), connect
2 AROUSE, stimulate, excite, thrill, please, attract
3 HINGE ON, depend on, rest on, hang on
FORMAL be contingent on
4 ATTACK, round on, fall on, set upon, lay into
🖪 1 turn off, disconnect **2** *colloq.* turn off, bore

■ **turn out**

1 HAPPEN, come about, ensue, result, end up, become, develop, emerge
FORMAL transpire
COLLOQ. pan out
2 SWITCH OFF, turn off, unplug, disconnect
3 APPEAR, present, dress, clothe
4 ATTEND, turn up, come, go, arrive, appear, be present
COLLOQ. show up
5 PRODUCE, make, manufacture, fabricate, assemble
COLLOQ. churn out
6 EVICT, throw out, expel, deport, banish, dismiss, discharge, drum out
COLLOQ. chuck out, kick out, turf out, sack, fire
7 *turn out the attic*
empty, clear (out), clean out
🖪 2 turn on, connect **6** admit, receive **7** fill

■ **turn over**
1 THINK OVER, think about, mull over, ponder, deliberate, reflect on, contemplate, consider, examine
FORMAL ruminate
2 HAND OVER, surrender, deliver, transfer, assign, consign
3 OVERTURN, upset, upend, turn turtle, invert, reverse, capsize, keel over

■ **turn up**
1 ATTEND, turn out, come, arrive, appear, be present
COLLOQ. show up
2 AMPLIFY, make louder, intensify, raise, increase
3 DISCOVER, find, uncover, unearth, dig up, expose, disclose, reveal, show, bring to light
E3 1 stay away **2** turn down

■ **to a turn**
perfectly, exactly, correctly, precisely, to perfection

Synonym nuances
verb sense 1
Spin suggests speedily going round: *he spun round when he heard a voice*, while **twirl** suggests a more graceful movement, and **whirl** a fast, but freer movement, as in a dance: *they whirled round the floor in a waltz.*
 Spiral implies a closer, tighter motion either up or down: *snowflakes spiralling earthwards*, while **wind** suggests following a somewhat snaking route: *the path wound up the hillside.* The verb **reel** has connotations of staggering or loss of balance, while **twist** can be used to suggest an unnatural or forced turn: *he twisted round awkwardly in his chair.* **Gyrate**, meanwhile, returns to the idea of more regular, smoother movement going round in circles: *she gyrated her hips to the slow music.*
 Pivot, **hinge**, **swivel** and **rotate** specifically describe remaining on a fixed point throughout making a turn: *he pivoted on one foot.* **Shift**, on the other hand, is more suggestive of a general, imprecise change of position: *he shifted round to face the other way*, while **invert** and **reverse** would refer more specifically to being moved in the opposite direction. **Veer** is suggestive of a more sudden change of course: *he veered to the left without warning*, while **swing** and **swerve** are again more appropriate for a fluid, swaying movement, although **swerve** has implications of last-minute avoidance: *she swerved when she noticed the oncoming car.*

---

turncoat *n*
traitor, defector, deserter, renegade, renegate, seceder, backslider, blackleg
FORMAL apostate, tergiversator
COLLOQ. fink, rat, scab

turning *n*
turn-off, junction, crossroads, fork, bend, curve, turn

turning-point *n*
crossroads, watershed, crux, crisis, critical/decisive moment, moment of truth

turnout *n*
1 ATTENDANCE, audience, gate, crowd, gathering, assembly, congregation, number
FORMAL assemblage
2 APPEARANCE, outfit, dress, clothes
FORMAL attire, array
COLLOQ. gear, clobber, togs, things, get-up

turnover *n*
income, profits, revenue, productivity, business, production, output, yield, volume, outturn, change, movement, flow, replacement

turpitude *n*
baseness, corruption, badness, corruptness, evil, criminality, immorality, vileness, wickedness, viciousness, depravity, degeneracy, foulness, sinfulness, villainy

FORMAL flagitiousness, nefariousness, iniquity
E3 honour

tussle *v, n*
♦ *v*
struggle, battle, wrestle, compete, vie, fight, contend, grapple, scrap, brawl, scuffle, scramble, touse
OLD *Scot* tuilyie, tuilzie
♦ *n*
struggle, battle, conflict, contest, scramble, fight, brawl, bout, fracas, fray, mêlée, punch-up, scuffle, scrum, competition, contention, scrimmage
COLLOQ. dust-up, set-to, scrap

tutelage *n*
guidance, charge, custody, care, protection, guardianship, wardship, patronage, vigilance, eye, teaching, instruction, education, schooling, tuition, preparation
FORMAL aegis

tutor *n, v*
♦ *n*
teacher, instructor, coach, educator, lecturer, supervisor, guide, mentor, guru, guardian, governess
♦ *v*
teach, instruct, train, drill, coach, educate, school, lecture, supervise, direct, guide

tutorial *n, adj*
♦ *n*
class, lesson, seminar, teach-in
♦ *adj*
coaching, didactic, educative, educatory, guiding, instructional, teaching

TV *n*
television, receiver, set, small screen
COLLOQ. telly, the box, goggle-box, idiot box, the tube, tele; *N Am* boob tube

twaddle *n*
drivel, rubbish, nonsense, trash, garbage, gabble, waffle, gossip, tattle, balderdash, bunk, bunkum, claptrap, inanity, gobbledygook, poppycock, stuff; *Scot* blethers; *dialect & N Am* blathers
COLLOQ. hogwash, hot air, piffle, rot, tosh, baloney, blah, bosh, eyewash, rhubarb, guff, hooey, malarkey, moonshine
SLANG (*vulgar*) balls, bollocks, shit, bullshit
E3 sense

tweak *v, n*
♦ *v*
1 TWIST, pinch, squeeze, nip, pull, tug, jerk, twitch
2 ADJUST, modify, change, adapt, fit, accommodate, suit, make adjustments
COLLOQ. fine-tune
♦ *n*
1 TWIST, pinch, squeeze, nip, pull, tug, jerk, twitch
2 ADJUSTMENT, modification, change, adaptation, alteration, conversion, remodelling, shaping, fitting, accommodation, amendment, revision, tuning, arranging, rearranging, rearrangement
COLLOQ. fine-tuning

twee *adj*
sweet, cute, pretty, dainty, quaint, sentimental, affected, precious

twiddle *v*
turn, twirl, swivel, twist, wiggle, adjust, fiddle, finger
■ **twiddle your thumbs**
have nothing to do, kick your heels, kill time, have time on your hands

twig¹ *n*
dried twigs
branch, sprig, spray, shoot, offshoot, stick, wattle, whip, withe, withy
FORMAL ramulus

twig² v

then I twigged
understand, see, realize, comprehend, grasp, fathom
COLLOQ. catch on, cotton on, get, tumble to, rumble

twilight n, adj

• n
dusk, half-light, dimness, sunset, evening, decline, ebb,
evenfall, demi-jour
OLD gloaming, gloom, owl-light, cockshut
FORMAL crepuscule
Related adjective: crepuscular
• adj
darkening, dim, declining, evening, shadowy, final, last,
ebbing, dying
FORMAL crepuscular

twin n, adj, v

• n
double, lookalike, likeness, duplicate, clone, match,
counterpart, equivalent, complement, fellow, mate,
couplet
OLD gemel
FORMAL corollary
COLLOQ. (dead) ringer
• adj
identical, matching, corresponding, symmetrical, parallel,
matched, paired, double, dual, duplicate, twofold
TECHNICAL didymous
• v
match, pair, couple, link, join, combine, yoke

Famous twins include:

MYTHOLOGICAL TWINS:
Castor and Pollux (Dioscuri)
Romulus and Remus
Otos and Ephialtes
  (Aloadae)
Apollo and Diana/Artemis
Hercules and Iphicles
Amphion and Zethus
Dylan and Llew Llaw Gyffes
Asvin twins
Navajo twins
Shachar and Shalim
BIBLICAL/RELIGIOUS TWINS:
Thomas the Apostle
Jacob and Esau
St. Cosmas and St. Damian
INVENTORS:
Jean-Felix and Auguste
  Piccard
Freelon and Francis Stanley
SPORTING TWINS:
Mario and Aldo Andreotti
Alec and Eric Bedser
Frank and Ronald de Boer
Tim and Tom Guliksen
Mark and Steve Waugh

LITERARY TWINS:
Sebastian and Viola (*Twelfth
Night*)
Antipholus of Syracuse and
Antipholus of Ephesus
(*Comedy of Errors*)
Dromio of Syracuse and
Dromio of Ephesus
(*Comedy of Errors*)
Tweedledum and
Tweedledee (*Alice in
Wonderland*)
King Louis XIV and Philippe
(*Man in the Iron Mask*)
Pat and Isabel O'Sullivan (*St
Clare's*)
Weasley twins (*Harry
Potter*)
Bobbsey Twins
Jessica and Elizabeth Wake-
field (*Sweet Valley High*)
OTHER FAMOUS TWINS:
Eng and Chang Bunker
Maurice and Robin Gibb
Ronnie and Reggie Kray
Norris and Ross McWhirter

---

twine n, v

• n
string, cord, thread, yarn, whipping, twist, intorsion
• v
wind, coil, spiral, loop, curl, bend, twist, tangle, wreathe,
wrap, surround, encircle, entwine, intertwine, plait, braid,
knit, weave

twinge n

pain, pang, throb, spasm, ache, throe, stab, stitch, cramp,
pinch, prick

twinkle v, n

• v
sparkle, glitter, shimmer, glisten, glimmer, flicker, wink,

flash, glint, gleam, shine, scintillate, twink
FORMAL coruscate
• n
sparkle, scintillation, glitter, shimmer, glisten, glimmer,
flicker, wink, flash, glint, shining, gleam, light
FORMAL coruscation

twinkling adj, n

• adj
bright, sparkling, glittering, shimmering, glistening,
glimmering, flickering, gleaming, flashing, blinking,
scintillating, shining, winking, polished
FORMAL coruscating, nitid
• n
moment, flash, short time, instant, minute, second
COLLOQ. sec, tick, jiff, jiffy, mo, trice, shake, wink, no time,
two shakes of a lamb's tail

twirl v, n

• v
spin, whirl, pirouette, wheel, rotate, revolve, swivel, pivot,
turn, curl, twist, gyrate, wind, coil, twiddle, twizzle, trill,
trundle
• n
spin, whirl, pirouette, rotation, revolution, turn, curl, twist,
gyration, convolution, spiral, coil, twiddle; *Scot* tirlie-wirlie

twirling adj

spinning, whirling, pirouetting, rotating, revolving,
pivoting, pivotal, gyratory, swivelling
FORMAL gyral, rotatory

twist v, n

• v
1 TURN, screw, wring, spin, rotate, revolve, swivel, wind,
zigzag, bend, coil, spiral, curl, wreathe, twirl, twine,
entwine, intertwine, weave, braid, plait, entangle, wriggle,
squirm, writhe, skew
2 *twist your ankle*
wrench, rick, sprain, strain
3 CHANGE, alter, garble, falsify, misquote, misrepresent,
misreport, distort, contort, warp, bend, misshape, deform,
pervert
• n
1 TURN, screw, spin, roll, bend, curve, arc, kink, curl, loop,
zigzag, coil, spiral, convolution, squiggle, tangle
2 WRENCH, rick, sprain, strain
3 CHANGE, variation, angle, slant, break, turn, surprise,
turnabout
4 PERVERSION, distortion, contortion, imperfection, defect,
flaw
FORMAL aberration
5 QUIRK, oddity, peculiarity, idiosyncrasy, foible, freak,
whim
■ **twist someone's arm**
persuade, force, intimidate, pressurize, bulldoze, bully,
coerce, dragoon
COLLOQ. lean on, put the screws on

twisted adj

winding, wavy, squiggly, warped, perverted, deviant,
unnatural, strange, peculiar, odd
FORMAL sinuous
E3 straight

twister n

1 SWINDLER, cheat, crook, fraud, rogue, deceiver, trickster,
scoundrel, blackguard
COLLOQ. con man/woman, con artist, phoney
2 TORNADO, storm, cyclone, gale, hurricane, whirlwind,
typhoon, monsoon, tempest, squall

twisty adj

winding, tortuous, meandering, curving, serpentine,
zigzag, circuitous, roundabout, indirect
FORMAL sinuous
E3 straight

twit *n*
idiot, fool, imbecile, simpleton, clown
COLLOQ. ass, ninny, halfwit, dope, twerp, nitwit, clot, nincompoop, chump, blockhead, knuckle-head, proper Charlie, dope, saphead
SLANG plonker, dork, geek, git, prat, goop, berk, nerk, nerd, airhead, dweeb, nig-nog; (*taboo*) dickhead

twitch *v, n*
♦ *v*
jerk, jump, start, blink, tremble, quiver, flutter, shake, pull, tug, tweak, snatch, pluck
♦ *n*
spasm, convulsion, tic, tremor, shiver, quiver, flutter, jerk, jump, start

twitchy *adj*
jumpy, nervous, anxious, agitated, apprehensive, uneasy, tense, panicky, fidgety, shaky, on edge
FORMAL restive
COLLOQ. edgy, nervy, het up, keyed up, wound up, jittery, uptight, with butterflies in your stomach, on pins and needles, shaking like a leaf/jelly, with your heart in your mouth, in a sweat, in a stew, in a tizzy

twitter *v, n*
♦ *v*
1 CHIRP, chirrup, tweet, cheep, sing, warble, whistle, chatter
2 PRATTLE, gabble, babble, jabber, chat, gossip, twaddle; *Scot* blether; *dialect & N Am* blather
COLLOQ. gab, witter
♦ *n*
chirping, chirruping, tweeting, song, cry, warble, chatter

two-faced *adj*
hypocritical, insincere, false, lying, deceitful, treacherous, double-dealing, devious, untrustworthy, Janus-faced
FORMAL perfidious, dissembling, duplicitous
E3 honest, candid, frank

twosome *n*
couple, pair, duo

tycoon *n*
industrialist, entrepreneur, captain of industry, magnate, mogul, baron, supremo, capitalist, financier
COLLOQ. fat cat, big noise, big cheese, moneybags, moneyspinner

type *n*
1 SORT, kind, form, set, style, variety, strain, species, breed, group, class, category, subdivision, classification, description, designation, stamp, mark, order, brand, model, make, standard
TECHNICAL genus
FORMAL genre
2 EMBODIMENT, prototype, original, model, pattern, specimen, example, epitome

FORMAL archetype, exemplar, quintessence
3 PRINT, printing, character(s), letter(s), number(s), symbol(s), lettering, typeface, face, fount, font

typhoon *n*
whirlwind, cyclone, tornado, hurricane, tempest, storm, squall
OLD typhon
COLLOQ. twister

typical *adj*
standard, normal, usual, average, ordinary, conventional, orthodox, classic, true, stereotype, stock, model, representative, illustrative, indicative, characteristic, distinctive
FORMAL archetypal, quintessential
COLLOQ. run-of-the-mill
E3 atypical, unusual

typically *adv*
usually, normally, ordinarily, characteristically, customarily, classically, routinely, habitually, as a rule
FORMAL quintessentially

typify *v*
embody, epitomize, encapsulate, personify, characterize, exemplify, symbolize, indicate, represent, illustrate, image, shadow, foreshadow

tyrannical *adj*
dictatorial, despotic, autocratic, absolute, totalitarian, arbitrary, authoritarian, domineering, overbearing, high-handed, imperious, magisterial, lordly, tyrannic, ruthless, harsh, severe, strict, cruel, oppressive, repressive, overpowering, unjust, unreasonable, Neronian, satrapal
FORMAL peremptory
E3 liberal, tolerant

tyrannize *v*
oppress, crush, intimidate, terrorize, coerce, repress, suppress, dictate, domineer, enslave, browbeat, bully, lord it over, tread on the neck of
FORMAL subjugate

tyranny *n*
dictatorship, despotism, autocracy, absolutism, authoritarianism, imperiousness, high-handedness, ruthlessness, harshness, severity, strictness, cruelty, oppression, injustice, domination
E3 democracy, freedom, liberty

tyrant *n*
dictator, despot, autocrat, absolutist, authoritarian, bully, oppressor, slave-driver, taskmaster, martinet
OLD tyranness

tyro *n*
see **tiro**.

U

ubiquitous adj
ever-present, everywhere, universal, global, pervasive, common, frequent
FORMAL omnipresent
≡ rare, scarce

ubiquity n
commonness, pervasiveness, universality, frequency, popularity, prevalence
FORMAL omnipresence
≡ rarity

ugliness n
1 UNATTRACTIVENESS, unloveliness, plainness, unsightliness, hideousness, monstrosity, deformity; *N Am* homeliness
2 UNPLEASANTNESS, repulsiveness, offensiveness, frightfulness, enormity, horridness, horror, vileness
FORMAL heinousness
3 DANGER, evil, nastiness, menace
≡ **1** beauty, charm, goodness **2** pleasantness, delightfulness

ugly adj
1 UNATTRACTIVE, unsightly, plain, unlovely, unprepossessing, hideous, revolting, repulsive, grotesque, monstrous, ogreish, misshapen, deformed, ill-favoured, evil-favoured, ill-faced, unfair, gorgon; *Scot* ill-faurd; *N Am* homely
OLD ouglie, oughly, loth; (*Shakesp*) foul; (*Spenser*) ill-faste
COLLOQ. ugly as sin; *N Am* plug-ugly
2 UNPLEASANT, disagreeable, nasty, horrid, hideous, objectionable, offensive, shocking, disgusting, loathsome, revolting, foul, repulsive, vile, frightful, obnoxious, terrible
COLLOQ. grotty
3 DANGEROUS, threatening, alarming, sinister, grave, nasty, hostile, evil
≡ **1** attractive, good-looking, beautiful, handsome, pretty **2** pleasant, delightful

---

Synonym nuances
sense 1
Unattractive and **unlovely**, although they put the emphasis on a lack of redeeming features, are not particularly euphemistic and point to a visible ugliness: *one of the unlovely suburbs of this city.* Less emphatic synonyms to use are **unprepossessing**, and **plain**, which suggests a lack of any distinguishing features rather than ugliness: *she was what could be described as a plain child.* **Unsightly**, however, implies that something is particularly unpleasant to look at, and is rather more uncomplimentary: *unsightly warts.*
   Far more emotive are the terms **hideous**, **revolting** and **repulsive**, which suggest something frightful or abhorrent, **grotesque**, which suggests an unsettlingly bizarre element: *grotesque puppets*, and **monstrous**, which goes further by implying an abnormal deviation: *a monstrous toad-like face.* **Misshapen** and **deformed** specifically suggest disfigurement, while **ill-favoured** and **evil-favoured** are rather more poetic terms which also suggest being unkindly served by nature.

---

ulcer n
sore, open sore, fester, abscess, boil, canker, ulceration, noma, bedsore, issue, plague-sore

TECHNICAL rupia, aphtha, fistula, peptic ulcer, varicose ulcer, decubitus ulcer
OLD impostume, sycosis
Related adjective: helcoid

ulterior adj
secondary, hidden, concealed, undisclosed, unexpressed, unrevealed, underlying, covert, secret, private, personal, selfish
≡ overt, declared

ultimate adj, n
  ◆ *adj*
1 FINAL, last, closing, concluding, eventual, terminal, furthest, end, remotest, extreme
2 RADICAL, basic, fundamental, primary
FORMAL elemental
3 BEST, utmost, greatest, topmost, highest, supreme, superlative, maximum, perfect, ideal
COLLOQ. the mostest
  ◆ *n*
best, greatest, peak, perfection, summit, culmination, greatest achievement, ideal, masterpiece, *chef d'oeuvre*, height, extreme
FORMAL consummation, epitome, *summum bonum*
COLLOQ. daddy of them all, last word

ultimately adv
1 FINALLY, eventually, at last, in the end, after all, sooner or later, in the last resort
COLLOQ. at the end of the day, when push comes to shove
2 BASICALLY, fundamentally, primarily

ultra- prefix
extremely, excessively, especially, exceptionally, unusually, extraordinarily, remarkably, extra

ululate v
howl, wail, screech, moan, lament, keen, mourn, cry, scream, weep, sob, holler, hoot

umbrage
  ■ **take umbrage**
take offence, resent, be angry, be annoyed, be exasperated, be hurt, be offended, be insulted, be upset, be/feel put out, take exception, take personally
COLLOQ. be miffed, get huffy, get your nose out of joint

umbrella n
1 *put up your umbrella*
parasol, sunshade, dumpy, en tout cas, chatta
COLLOQ. brolly, gamp; *N Am* bumbershoot
OLD COLLOQ. gingham
SLANG mushroom, mush
2 PROTECTION, cover, patronage, agency
FORMAL aegis, auspices

umpire n, v
  ◆ *n*
referee, linesman, judge, adjudicator, arbiter, arbitrator, mediator, moderator
COLLOQ. ref
  ◆ *v*
referee, judge, adjudicate, arbitrate, mediate, moderate, control

umpteen adj
numerous, very many, plenty, thousands, millions, countless, innumerable
COLLOQ. a good many
E3 few

unabashed adj
unashamed, unembarrassed, brazen, blatant, bold, confident, undaunted, unconcerned, undismayed
E3 abashed, sheepish

unable adj
incapable, powerless, impotent, unequipped, unqualified, unfit, incompetent, inadequate
FORMAL ineffectual
E3 able, capable; *colloq.* up to

unabridged adj
complete, entire, full-length, full, whole, uncondensed, unshortened, uncut, unexpurgated
E3 abridged, shortened

unacceptabie adj
intolerable, inadmissible, unsatisfactory, unsuitable, disappointing, undesirable, unwelcome, objectionable, disagreeable, offensive, unpleasant, obnoxious
COLLOQ. a bit off
E3 acceptable, satisfactory

unaccommodating adj
inflexible, uncompromising, unco-operative, unyielding, unbending, obstinate, stubborn, perverse, rigid, disobliging
FORMAL intransigent, uncomplaisant
E3 flexible, obliging

unaccompanied adj
alone, unescorted, unattended, by yourself, on your own, lone, solo, single, single-handed
E3 accompanied

unaccountable adj
1 INEXPLICABLE, unexplainable, unfathomable, impenetrable, insoluble, incomprehensible, baffling, puzzling, mysterious, astonishing, extraordinary, strange, odd, peculiar, singular, curious, bizarre, queer, unusual, uncommon, unheard-of
2 *unaccountable to the public*
not responsible, not answerable, free, immune
E3 1 explicable, explainable **2** accountable, bound

unaccountably adv
inexplicably, incomprehensibly, unexplainably, incredibly, strangely, mysteriously, mystifyingly, bafflingly, puzzlingly, miraculously
E3 explicably

unaccustomed adj
1 *unaccustomed to such luxury*
unused, unacquainted, unfamiliar, unpractised, inexperienced
FORMAL unwonted
2 STRANGE, unusual, uncommon, different, new, unexpected, surprising, extraordinary, remarkable, unfamiliar, uncharacteristic, unprecedented
E3 1 accustomed, familiar **2** customary

unacquainted adj
unfamiliar, unaccustomed, unused, inexperienced, strange, ignorant

unadorned adj
plain, simple, straightforward, undecorated, unornamented, unembellished, unvarnished, severe, stark, restrained
E3 decorated, embellished, ornate

unadulterated adj
1 *unadulterated gold*
pure, unalloyed, unmixed, undiluted, 100%, flawless, perfect, neat, straight, solid, simple, natural, real, authentic, genuine, true
2 *unadulterated bliss*
sheer, utter, pure, complete, total, thorough, absolute, perfect, unqualified, unmitigated, downright
E3 1 impure, adulterated

unaffected adj
1 UNMOVED, unconcerned, indifferent, impervious, untouched, unchanged, unaltered, immune
2 GENUINE, natural, unsophisticated, artless, naive, ingenuous, guileless, unspoilt, plain, simple, straightforward, unpretentious, unassuming, candid, true, honest, sincere
E3 1 moved, impressed, influenced **2** affected, pretentious, insincere

unafraid adj
fearless, confident, daring, undaunted, dauntless, brave, courageous, imperturbable, intrepid, unshak(e)able
E3 afraid, fearful, nervous

unalterable adj
unchangeable, invariable, unchanging, immutable, final, inflexible, unyielding, rigid, fixed, permanent
E3 alterable, flexible

unanimity n
consensus, unity, agreement, concurrence, like-mindedness, consistency, harmony, unison, concert
FORMAL accord, concord, congruence
E3 disagreement, disunity

unanimous adj
united, concerted, joint, common, as one, in agreement, like-minded, consistent, harmonious
FORMAL in accord, concordant
E3 disunited, divided

unanimously adv
unopposed, without opposition, without exception, as one, of one mind, with one voice, by common consent, in concert, *nem con*
FORMAL conjointly

unannounced adj
unexpected, unforeseen, unanticipated, unpredictable, unlooked-for, chance, accidental, sudden, abrupt, surprising, startling, amazing, astonishing, unusual
FORMAL fortuitous
E3 announced, expected, predictable

unanswerable adj
incontestable, incontrovertible, indisputable, unarguable, undeniable, absolute, final, conclusive, irrefutable
FORMAL irrefragable
E3 answerable, refutable

unanswered adj
undecided, unsettled, unresolved, open, in doubt, vexed
COLLOQ. up in the air
E3 decided, resolved, settled

unappetizing adj
unpleasant, tasteless, unpalatable, off-putting, distasteful, disagreeable, uninviting, unsavoury, insipid, unappealing, unattractive, unexciting, uninteresting
E3 appetizing

unapproachable adj
inaccessible, remote, distant, aloof, remote, standoffish, withdrawn, reserved, unsociable, unfriendly, unresponsive, uncommunicative, forbidding, cold, cool
E3 approachable, friendly

unapt adj
unsuitable, unfit, unfitted, unsuited, inappropriate, inapplicable, untimely, unseasonable, inapt
FORMAL inapposite, malapropos
E3 apt

unarmed *adj*
defenceless, unprotected, exposed, open, vulnerable, weak, helpless
E3 armed, protected

unashamed *adj*
shameless, unabashed, impenitent, unrepentant, unconcealed, undisguised, direct, open, honest, blatant
E3 ashamed, abashed

unasked *adj*
uninvited, unbidden, unrequested, unsought, unsolicited, unwanted, voluntary, spontaneous, unannounced
E3 invited, wanted

unassailable *adj*
invulnerable, incontestable, impregnable, incontrovertible, indisputable, secure, sound, positive, proven, absolute, conclusive, invincible, inviolable, undeniable, irrefutable, well-armed, well-fortified
E3 assailable

unassertive *adj*
self-effacing, unassuming, backward, bashful, quiet, retiring, shy, timid, meek, diffident, timorous
COLLOQ. mous(e)y
E3 assertive, bold

unassuming *adj*
unassertive, self-effacing, retiring, modest, shy, demure, humble, meek, quiet, reticent, unobtrusive, unpretentious, simple, natural, restrained
E3 presumptuous, assertive, pretentious

unattached *adj*
unmarried, unengaged, uncommitted, single, on your own, by yourself, free, available, footloose, fancy-free, independent, unaffiliated, with no ties, loose
E3 engaged, committed

unattended *adj*
ignored, disregarded, abandoned, neglected, forgotten, forsaken, unguarded, unwatched, unsupervised, unaccompanied, unescorted, alone
E3 attended, escorted, looked after

unattractive *adj*
unappealing, disagreeable, unlovely, plain, unpleasant, unprepossessing, uninviting, unexciting, unsightly, ugly, objectionable, offensive, disgusting, distasteful, off-putting, undesirable, ill-favoured, uncomely, unwelcome, unpalatable, unsavoury, repellent, unappetizing; *N Am* homely
E3 attractive

unauthorized *adj*
unofficial, unlicensed, unlawful, forbidden, prohibited, illegal, illicit, illegitimate, irregular, unapproved, unsanctioned, unwarranted
E3 authorized, legal; *formal* accredited

unavailing *adj*
unsuccessful, failed, abortive, vain, futile, useless, ineffective, fruitless, unproductive, unprofitable, sterile, luckless, unlucky, unfortunate, losing, beaten, defeated, frustrated, thwarted
E3 successful, effective

unavoidable *adj*
inevitable, inescapable, inexorable, certain, sure, fated, destined, predestined, obligatory, required, compulsory, necessary
FORMAL mandatory, ineluctable
E3 avoidable

unaware *adj*
oblivious, unconscious, ignorant, uninformed, unenlightened, in the dark, unknowing, unsuspecting, unmindful, heedless, blind, deaf, in the dark, with no idea
OLD wareless, witless

FORMAL insentient, incognizant
E3 aware, conscious

unawares *adv*
off guard, by surprise, accidentally, inadvertently, mistakenly, suddenly, unexpectedly, aback, abruptly, unintentionally, unconsciously, unknowingly, unprepared, unthinkingly, unwittingly, insidiously, in the dark, *à l'improviste*
OLD unwares
COLLOQ. on the hop, red-handed, with your trousers down

unbalanced *adj*
1 INSANE, mad, lunatic, deranged, disturbed, demented, irrational, unsound, unstable, mentally ill
COLLOQ. crazy, barmy, crackers, round the bend/twist, needing your head examining
2 *an unbalanced report*
biased, prejudiced, one-sided, partisan, unfair, unjust, unequal, uneven, asymmetrical, lopsided, unsteady, unstable
FORMAL inequitable
E3 1 sane, sound **2** unbiased, impartial

unbearable *adj*
intolerable, unacceptable, insupportable, insufferable, unendurable, excruciating
COLLOQ. too much, too bad, the limit, the last straw, the straw that broke the camel's back
E3 bearable, acceptable

unbeatable *adj*
invincible, unconquerable, unstoppable, unsurpassable, matchless, supreme, best, excellent
FORMAL indomitable

unbeaten *adj*
undefeated, unconquered, victorious, winning, supreme, triumphant, unsubdued, unsurpassed, unbowed
FORMAL unvanquished
E3 defeated; *formal* vanquished

unbecoming *adj*
unseemly, improper, unsuitable, inappropriate, unbefitting, indelicate, ungentlemanly, unladylike, unattractive, unsightly
OLD (*Shakesp*) ill-beseeming
FORMAL indecorous, unseemly
E3 suitable, attractive

unbeknown
▪ **unbeknown to**
unbeknownst to, unknown, unrealized, unperceived, unheard of
E3 known

unbelief *n*
atheism, agnosticism, scepticism, doubt, incredulity, disbelief
E3 belief, faith

unbelievable *adj*
incredible, inconceivable, unthinkable, unimaginable, amazing, astonishing, staggering, extraordinary, impossible, improbable, unlikely, implausible, unconvincing, far-fetched, preposterous, outlandish
E3 believable, credible

unbelievably *adv*
incredibly, amazingly, unimaginably, inconceivably, extraordinarily, outlandishly
E3 believably

unbeliever *n*
disbeliever, agnostic, atheist, doubter, doubting Thomas, sceptic, infidel
FORMAL nullifidian
E3 believer, supporter

unbelieving *adj*
sceptical, suspicious, disbelieving, distrustful, doubtful,

doubting, dubious, unconvinced, unpersuaded, incredulous
FORMAL nullifidian
☲ credulous, trustful

unbend v
loosen up, relax, become less formal/strict, thaw, unfreeze, unbutton, uncoil, uncurl, straighten
☲ stiffen, withdraw

unbending adj
rigid, inflexible, strict, tough, uncompromising, unyielding, resolute, firm, formal, formidable, stubborn, severe, stiff, stern, hardline, forbidding, aloof, distant, reserved
FORMAL intransigent
☲ approachable, friendly, relaxed

unbiased adj
impartial, unprejudiced, objective, just, fair, fair-minded, open-minded, independent, equitable, balanced, even-handed, disinterested, dispassionate, neutral, uninfluenced, uncoloured, candid
☲ biased

unbidden adj
spontaneous, unforced, free, voluntary, unsolicited, unprompted, uninvited, willing, unasked, unwanted, unwelcome
☲ invited, solicited

unbind v
untie, unfasten, unloose, unloosen, unchain, undo, unshackle, free, liberate, loose, loosen, release, unyoke, unfetter
☲ bind, restrain

unblemished adj
untarnished, unspotted, unstained, unsullied, unimpeachable, unflawed, pure, clear, perfect, spotless, immaculate, irreproachable, flawless
☲ blemished, flawed, imperfect

unblinking adj
steady, unfaltering, unflinching, unshrinking, unwavering, imperturbable, emotionless, unemotional, fearless, unafraid, assured, calm, impassive, cool, composed
☲ fearful, cowed

unblushing adj
shameless, brazen, blatant, bold, immodest, unabashed, unashamed, unembarrassed, amoral, conscience-proof
☲ abashed, ashamed

unborn adj
embryonic, *in utero*, expected, awaited, coming, to-come, future, subsequent, succeeding

unbosom v
unburden, confess, admit, reveal, tell, lay bare, divulge, disclose, confide, uncover, let out, pour out, bare
COLLOQ. tell all
☲ hide, conceal, suppress

unbounded adj
boundless, limitless, unlimited, unrestricted, unrestrained, uncontrolled, unchecked, unbridled, infinite, endless, immeasurable, vast
☲ limited, restrained

unbreakable adj
indestructible, shatterproof, toughened, resistant, durable, strong, tough, rugged, solid
FORMAL infrangible
☲ breakable, fragile

unbridled adj
immoderate, excessive, rampant, riotous, wild, uncontrolled, unrestrained, unconstrained, ungoverned, uncurbed, unchecked, intemperate, licentious, profligate

unbroken adj
1 INTACT, whole, entire, complete, solid, undivided, single

OLD unbroke
2 UNINTERRUPTED, continuous, seamless, endless, non-stop, ceaseless, incessant, unceasing, constant, perpetual, progressive, successive, in a row
OLD unbroke; (*Shakesp*) continuate
FORMAL unremitting
3 *an unbroken record*
unbeaten, unsurpassed, unrivalled, unequalled, unmatched
4 WILD, rough, untamed, undomesticated
OLD unbroke
☲ **1** broken, damaged **2** intermittent, fitful **4** broken, tamed, subdued

unburden v
confess, admit, reveal, tell, lay bare, divulge, offload, disclose, confide, uncover, let out, pour out, bare
COLLOQ. tell all
☲ hide, conceal, suppress

uncalled-for adj
unwarranted, gratuitous, unprovoked, unjustified, unasked, unsought, unsolicited, unprompted, undeserved, unwelcome, unnecessary, needless
☲ timely

uncannily adv
strangely, oddly, bizarrely, mysteriously, incredibly, remarkably, extraordinarily, unnaturally, supernaturally
COLLOQ. spookily

uncanny adj
weird, strange, queer, odd, bizarre, mysterious, unaccountable, incredible, remarkable, exceptional, extraordinary, fantastic, unnatural, unearthly, supernatural, eerie, creepy; *Scot* eldritch
FORMAL preternatural
COLLOQ. spooky

uncared-for adj
1 UNAPPRECIATED, neglected, disregarded, abandoned, undervalued, deserted, stranded, forsaken
2 *uncared-for waste ground*
neglected, derelict, overgrown, uncultivated, unmaintained, untended, untilled, unweeded, unhusbanded, dilapidated
COLLOQ. run-down
☲ **1** cared-for, cherished, treasured **2** cared-for, tended

uncaring adj
unconcerned, unmoved, unsympathetic, inconsiderate, unfeeling, cold, callous, indifferent, uninterested
☲ caring, concerned

unceasing adj
ceaseless, incessant, unending, endless, never-ending, non-stop, continuous, unbroken, constant, perpetual, continual, persistent, relentless, unrelenting, unremitting
☲ intermittent, spasmodic

unceremonious adj
1 INFORMAL, casual, easy-going, relaxed, unofficial
COLLOQ. laid-back
2 DIRECT, abrupt, sudden, impolite, rude, undignified, disrespectful, discourteous

uncertain adj
1 UNSURE, unconvinced, doubtful, dubious, undecided, unresolved, open, equivocating, ambivalent, hesitant, wavering, vacillating
COLLOQ. in two minds
2 INCONSTANT, changeable, variable, erratic, irregular, shaky, fitful, unsteady, unreliable
3 UNPREDICTABLE, unforeseeable, undetermined, unsettled, unresolved, unconfirmed, unknown, unclear, speculative, indefinite, vague, insecure, risky
COLLOQ. iffy, up in the air, touch-and-go, (hanging) in the balance, in the lap of the gods
☲ **1** certain, sure **2** steady **3** predictable

uncertainly *adv*
hesitantly, reluctantly, unwillingly, half-heartedly, doubtfully, sceptically, dubiously, indecisively, irresolutely, vacillatingly, delayingly, waveringly, tentatively, warily, shyly, timidly, haltingly, stammeringly, stutteringly
COLLOQ. in two minds
☒ confidently

uncertainty *n*
doubt, scepticism, irresolution, dilemma, ambiguity, ambivalence, hesitation, misgiving, qualm(s), uneasiness, confusion, vagueness, bewilderment, perplexity, puzzlement, unreliability, unpredictability, riskiness, insecurity
☒ certainty

unchallengeable *adj*
absolute, conclusive, incontestable, indisputable, incontrovertible, irrefutable, final, impregnable
FORMAL irrefragable, inappellable
☒ inconclusive

unchangeable *adj*
changeless, unchanging, invariable, irreversible, permanent, constant, fixed, stereotyped, final, eternal
FORMAL immutable, intransmutable
☒ changeable

unchanging *adj*
unvarying, changeless, same, invariable, steady, steadfast, constant, perpetual, lasting, enduring, abiding, eternal, permanent
☒ changing, changeable

uncharitable *adj*
unkind, cruel, hard-hearted, callous, hard, harsh, stern, severe, unfeeling, insensitive, unsympathetic, uncompassionate, unfriendly, mean, ungenerous, unforgiving
☒ kind, sensitive, charitable, generous

uncharted *adj*
unexplored, unsurveyed, undiscovered, unplumbed, foreign, alien, strange, unknown, unfamiliar, new, virgin
☒ familiar

unchaste *adj*
immoral, depraved, defiled, dissolute, dishonest, impure, immodest, promiscuous, fallen, loose, licentious, wanton, lewd
☒ chaste

unchecked *adj*
uncontrolled, unrestrained, unbridled, rampant, violent, wild, boisterous, riotous, unruly, uncurbed, undisciplined, unhindered
☒ controlled, restrained

uncivil *adj*
rude, impolite, discourteous, disrespectful, bad-mannered, ill-mannered, ill-bred, uncouth, unmannerly, ungracious, churlish, brusque, abrupt, gruff, curt, boorish, bearish, surly
☒ civil, polite

uncivilized *adj*
primitive, barbaric, barbarian, savage, wild, rough, boorish, brutish, untamed, uncultured, unrefined, unsophisticated, unenlightened, uneducated, illiterate, uncouth, antisocial
☒ civilized, cultured

unclassifiable *adj*
doubtful, indistinct, uncertain, undefinable, indescribable, unidentifiable, vague, elusive, ill-defined, indefinable, indefinite, indeterminate
☒ conformable, definable, identifiable

unclassified *adj*
1 *unclassified documents*
known, public, unrestricted, disclosed, published, revealed, official, on the record, for publication
2 *an unclassified country road*
general, basic, ungraded, minimum, minimal, lowest
☒ **1** secret, confidential **2** main

unclean *adj*
dirty, soiled, filthy, grimy, grubby, foul, polluted, contaminated, tainted, impure, unhygienic, unwholesome, corrupt, adulterated, defiled, sullied, profane, bad, evil, wicked
FORMAL ordurous
☒ clean, hygienic

unclear *adj*
indistinct, hazy, foggy, dim, obscure, vague, indefinite, ambiguous, equivocal, uncertain, undetermined, unsettled, unsure, doubtful, dubious
COLLOQ. iffy
☒ clear, evident

unclothed *adj*
naked, nude, stripped, undressed, disrobed, bare, stark-naked
FORMAL unclad
COLLOQ. in your birthday suit, in the altogether, in the buff, in the raw, starkers
☒ clothed, dressed

uncomfortable *adj*
1 CRAMPED, hard, cold, ill-fitting, irritating, painful, disagreeable
2 AWKWARD, embarrassed, self-conscious, nervous, uneasy, tense, on edge, troubled, worried, anxious, disturbed, distressed, disquieted, conscience-stricken
FORMAL discomfited
☒ **1** comfortable **2** relaxed

uncommitted *adj*
unattached, uninvolved, undecided, available, free, fancy-free, footloose, floating, non-aligned, non-partisan, neutral
☒ committed

uncommon *adj*
rare, scarce, infrequent, unusual, abnormal, atypical, unfamiliar, strange, odd, peculiar, queer, singular, curious, bizarre, extraordinary, remarkable, notable, outstanding, striking, exceptional, distinctive, special, out of the way
OLD seld
COLLOQ. thin on the ground, few and far between, like gold dust
☒ common, usual, normal

uncommonly *adv*
exceptionally, abnormally, peculiarly, remarkably, strangely, unusually, occasionally, singularly, rarely, seldom, infrequently, extremely, outstandingly, particularly, very
OLD seld
☒ commonly, frequently

uncommunicative *adj*
silent, taciturn, tight-lipped, close, secretive, unforthcoming, unresponsive, curt, brief, reticent, quiet, reserved, shy, retiring, diffident, withdrawn, aloof, unsociable
☒ communicative, forthcoming, talkative, conversational

uncomplicated *adj*
simple, easy, straightforward, direct, uninvolved, clear, undemanding
☒ complicated, complex, involved

uncompromising *adj*
unyielding, unbending, inflexible, unaccommodating, rigid, firm, stiff, strict, tough, hardline, hard-faced, immovable, inexorable, stubborn, obstinate, diehard
FORMAL obdurate, intransigent
☒ flexible, yielding

unconcealable *adj*
insuppressible, irrepressible, uncontrollable, indistinguishable, obvious, manifest, plain, clear, insistent

unconcealed *adj*
open, obvious, patent, evident, manifest, conspicuous, overt, undistinguished, admitted, visible, blatant, frank, apparent, noticeable, unashamed, ill-concealed, self-confessed
🗲 hidden, secret

unconcern *n*
aloofness, detachment, remoteness, apathy, nonchalance, indifference, disinterest, uninterestedness, negligence, callousness
FORMAL insouciance, pococurantism
🗲 concern

unconcerned *adj*
indifferent, apathetic, uninterested, nonchalant, carefree, relaxed, casual, complacent, cool, composed, untroubled, unworried, unruffled, unmoved, uncaring, unsympathetic, callous, aloof, remote, distant, detached, dispassionate, disinterested, uninvolved, oblivious
FORMAL unperturbed, insouciant, pococurante
🗲 concerned, worried, interested

unconditional *adj*
unqualified, unreserved, unrestricted, unlimited, absolute, utter, full, plenary, total, complete, entire, wholehearted, thoroughgoing, downright, outright, out-and-out, positive, definite, conclusive, categorical, unequivocal
🗲 conditional, qualified, limited

unconditionally *adv*
unreservedly, without qualifications, absolutely, completely, fully, totally, entirely, wholeheartedly, categorically, unequivocally
COLLOQ. with no strings attached
🗲 conditionally

unconfirmed *adj*
unproven, unproved, unratified, unverified, unauthenticated, unsubstantiated
FORMAL uncorroborated
🗲 confirmed

unconformity *n*
discontinuity, irregularity, unconformability
FORMAL disconformity
🗲 conformability

uncongenial *adj*
unfriendly, uninviting, unappealing, unattractive, unpleasant, displeasing, disagreeable, antagonistic, unsympathetic, incompatible, unsuited, unsavoury, discordant, distasteful
FORMAL antipathetic
🗲 congenial

unconnected *adj*
1 IRRELEVANT, unrelated, beside/off the point, inappropriate, unattached, detached, separate, independent
COLLOQ. neither here nor there
2 DISCONNECTED, incoherent, irrational, illogical, confused, unco-ordinated, disjointed
🗲 **1** connected, relevant **2** coherent, joined-up

unconquerable *adj*
irrepressible, enduring, ingrained, inveterate, undefeatable, unbeatable, invincible, unyielding, insuperable, insurmountable, irresistible, overpowering
FORMAL indomitable
🗲 weak, yielding

unconscionable *adj*
unprincipled, amoral, outrageous, unethical, unjustifiable, unscrupulous, unreasonable, unwarrantable, unpardonable, preposterous, criminal, exorbitant, extreme, extravagant, excessive, immoderate, inordinate

unconscious *adj*
1 STUNNED, knocked out, dazed, out, passed out, fainted, collapsed, lifeless, drugged, in a coma, concussed, blacked out, senseless, asleep
TECHNICAL comatose
FORMAL insensible
COLLOQ. out cold, out for the count, put out, zonked, dead to the world
2 UNAWARE, oblivious, blind, deaf, heedless, unmindful, ignorant
OLD inconscious, inconscient
FORMAL insensible, incognizant
3 *an unconscious reaction*
involuntary, automatic, reflex, instinctive, impulsive, innate, subconscious, subliminal, repressed, suppressed, latent, unthinking, unwitting, inadvertent, accidental, unintentional
COLLOQ. knee-jerk
🗲 **1** conscious **2** aware **3** intentional

unconsciously *adv*
1 OBLIVIOUSLY, heedlessly, unmindfully
FORMAL insensibly
2 INVOLUNTARILY, automatically, instinctively, impulsively, subliminally, unwittingly, unthinkingly, inadvertently, unintentionally, accidentally
🗲 **1** mindfully **2** intentionally

unconsciousness *n*
blackout, coma, faint, torpor, numbness, stupefaction, trance, sleep, doze, snooze, daydream
OLD inconscience
FORMAL insensibility

unconstraint *n*
unreserve, unrestraint, openness, freedom, liberality, relaxation, abandon, laissez-faire

uncontrollable *adj*
ungovernable, unmanageable, unruly, out of control, disorderly, wild, mad, furious, violent, strong, irrepressible
FORMAL intractable
🗲 controllable, manageable

uncontrolled *adj*
unrestrained, unbridled, unchecked, rampant, violent, wild, boisterous, riotous, unruly, uncurbed, undisciplined, unhindered
🗲 controlled, restrained

unconventional *adj*
unorthodox, alternative, different, offbeat, eccentric, bohemian, idiosyncratic, individual, original, odd, unusual, uncommon, rare, uncustomary, irregular, abnormal, bizarre, weird, radical, experimental, avant-garde, long-haired, Gypsy
COLLOQ. fringe, out of the ordinary, left-field, freaky, freakish, wacky, oddball, zany
SLANG way-out, far-out; *N Am* spacy
🗲 conventional, orthodox

Synonym nuances
While **unorthodox** is a straightforward synonym for diverging from the generally accepted way, both **alternative** and **different** imply that something is another option: *alternative medicine*. **Offbeat** and **eccentric**, however, are more suggestive of an endearing quirkiness, but **bohemian** has more to do with a rejection of the dominant social mores and lifestyle: *the bohemian atmosphere of the left bank is different from the rest of the city*. **Idiosyncratic** and **individual** suggest a singular approach to everything, and may be positive or negative depending on the context: *his highly idiosyncratic playing style can be irritating*.

The term **original**, on the other hand, can be used, usually in a positive way, to describe anything that is novel, unlike **odd**, which has less complimentary implications of strangeness. You can also use **uncustomary** to straightforwardly describe that something that is out of the ordinary: *uncustomary mealtimes*, whereas **irregular** implies something not conforming to accepted rules or norms in a way that is more disruptive: *this behaviour is most irregular*. **Abnormal**, meanwhile, suggests total deviation from the norm and tends to suggest disapproval: *this is not just a bad, but an abnormal habit*, and both **bizarre** and **weird** return to the suggestion of unsettling peculiarity: *bizarre, disturbing artworks*. **Radical**, **experimental** and **avant-garde**, however, imply something daringly new, and are far more approving in tone.

unconvincing *adj*
implausible, unlikely, improbable, questionable, doubtful, dubious, suspect, weak, feeble, flimsy, lame
COLLOQ. fishy
E3 convincing, plausible

unco-operative *adj*
unhelpful, awkward, obstinate, stubborn, rude, unpleasant, cubbish
COLLOQ. stroppy, bloody-minded
E3 co-operative, helpful, amenable, pleasant

unco-ordinated *adj*
clumsy, awkward, ungainly, ungraceful, bungling, bumbling, clodhopping, inept, disjointed
FORMAL maladroit
E3 graceful

uncork *v*
open, crack, broach, break/burst/slide/push/force/prise open, clear, expose, undo, uncover, unseal

uncouth *adj*
coarse, crude, vulgar, rude, bad-mannered, ill-mannered, impolite, improper, clumsy, rustic, ungainly, awkward, boorish, loutish, gauche, graceless, unrefined, uncultivated, unsophisticated, uncultured, uncivilized, rough, rough-hewn, rugged
OLD unrude
FORMAL unseemly
E3 polite, refined, urbane

uncover *v*
unveil, unmask, unwrap, strip, bare, lay bare, open, peel, expose, reveal, bring to light, show, disclose, divulge, make known, leak, unearth, dig up, exhume, discover, detect, rake, unrake, dismask, unlid, unsheathe
OLD (*Spenser*) unhele
COLLOQ. take the lid off
E3 cover, conceal, suppress

uncritical *adj*
undiscerning, undiscriminating, unselective, unquestioning, credulous, accepting, trusting, gullible, naive, non-judgemental, unfussy, superficial
E3 discerning, discriminating, sceptical

unctuous *adj*
1 INSINCERE, fawning, ingratiating, smooth, suave, sycophantic, gushing, slick, plausible, glib, sanctimonious, servile, pietistic
FORMAL obsequious
COLLOQ. smarmy
2 GREASY, oily, creamy

uncultivated *adj*
fallow, wild, rough, natural
E3 cultivated

uncultured *adj*
unsophisticated, unrefined, uncultivated, uncivilized, unintellectual, rough, uncouth, boorish, rustic, hick, coarse, crude, ill-bred
E3 cultured, sophisticated

undaunted *adj*
undeterred, undiscouraged, undismayed, unbowed, unflagging, resolute, steadfast, unafraid, brave, courageous, fearless, bold, brave, unalarmed, intrepid, dauntless, indomitable
E3 afraid, discouraged, timorous

undecided *adj*
uncertain, unsure, unknown, ambivalent, doubtful, hesitant, dithering, equivocating, wavering, irresolute, uncommitted, unestablished, indefinite, vague, dubious, debatable, moot, unresolved, unsettled, open
COLLOQ. in two minds, the jury is still out, up in the air
E3 decided, certain, definite

undecorated *adj*
plain, simple, severe, stark, austere, unadorned, unornamented, unembellished, functional, classical
FORMAL inornate
E3 decorated, ornate

undefeated *adj*
unbeaten, unconquered, victorious, winning, supreme, triumphant, unsubdued, unsurpassed, unbowed
FORMAL unvanquished
E3 defeated; *formal* vanquished

undefended *adj*
defenceless, exposed, vulnerable, unprotected, unguarded, open, unarmed, naked, pregnable
FORMAL unfortified
E3 armed, defended; *formal* fortified

undefiled *adj*
pure, spotless, unblemished, unsoiled, unspotted, immaculate, flawless, sinless, chaste, clean, clear, unstained, unsullied, intact, virginal
FORMAL inviolate

undefined *adj*
vague, hazy, ill-defined, indefinite, unclear, unexplained, unspecified, indistinct, inexact, imprecise, woolly, nebulous, formless, shadowy, tenuous
FORMAL indeterminate
E3 definite, precise

undemonstrative *adj*
aloof, distant, remote, withdrawn, reserved, reticent, uncommunicative, unresponsive, stiff, formal, cool, cold, unemotional, restrained, impassive, phlegmatic
E3 demonstrative, communicative

undeniable *adj*
indisputable, incontrovertible, unquestionable, sure, certain, undoubted, indubitable, beyond doubt, beyond question, definite, positive, proven, clear, obvious, manifest, patent, evident, unmistakable, irrefutable
E3 questionable

undeniably *adv*
incontrovertibly, indisputably, unquestionably, certainly, positively, definitely, unmistakably, undoubtedly, indubitably, beyond doubt, beyond question

undependable *adj*
unreliable, inconsistent, changeable, erratic, uncertain, fickle, capricious, irresponsible, inconstant, unpredictable, unstable, untrustworthy, variable, mercurial, treacherous, fair-weather
E3 dependable, reliable

under *prep, adv*
♦ *prep*
1 BELOW, underneath, beneath, lower than, less than
2 INFERIOR TO, secondary to, junior to, subordinate to, subservient to
E3 **1** over, above
♦ *adv*
below, underneath, beneath, down, downward, less, lower

underclothes n

underwear, underclothing, undergarments, underlinen, lingerie
COLLOQ. smalls, undies, unmentionables, frillies, scanties

undercover adj

secret, private, confidential, sly, intelligence, underground, surreptitious, stealthy, furtive, covert, hidden, concealed
FORMAL clandestine
COLLOQ. hush-hush
E3 open, unconcealed

undercurrent n

1 an undercurrent in the sea
undertow, underflow
2 FEELING, undertone, overtone, hint, suggestion, tinge, flavour, aura, atmosphere, sense, movement, tendency, trend, drift, undertow

undercut v

1 UNDERPRICE, undersell, undercharge, charge less than, underbid, undermine
2 EXCAVATE, hollow out, mine, gouge out, scoop out

underdog n

weaker party, outsider, loser, unfortunate, prey, victim, outcast, the exploited

underestimate v

underrate, undervalue, misjudge, miscalculate, fail to appreciate, minimize, belittle, dismiss, look down on, sell short, trivialize
FORMAL disparage
COLLOQ. play down
E3 overestimate, exaggerate

undergo v

experience, suffer, sustain, submit to, go through, put up with, tolerate, bear, stand, endure, weather, withstand

underground adj, n, adv

• adj
1 an underground passage
subterranean, buried, sunken, covered, hidden, concealed
2 SECRET, covert, furtive, surreptitious, undercover, revolutionary, subversive, radical, experimental, avant-garde, alternative, unorthodox, unofficial, illegal
FORMAL clandestine
• n
underground railway, subway, metro
COLLOQ. tube
• adv
below the surface, below ground level, below ground

undergrowth n

brush, brushwood, scrub, vegetation, shrubs, shrubbery, ground cover, bracken, thicket, bushes, brambles, briars

underhand adj

unscrupulous, unethical, immoral, improper, sly, crafty, sneaky, stealthy, secret, surreptitious, furtive, devious, dishonest, deceitful, deceptive, fraudulent, scheming
FORMAL clandestine
COLLOQ. crooked, shady
E3 honest, open; colloq. above board

underline v

mark, underscore, stress, emphasize, draw attention to, accentuate, italicize, highlight, foreground, point up
E3 play down; colloq. soft-pedal

underling n

minion, subordinate, inferior, lackey, menial, nonentity, flunkey, hireling, servant, slave, nobody
E3 boss, leader, master

underlying adj

basic, fundamental, essential, primary, elementary, root, intrinsic, inherent, latent, hidden, concealed, lurking, veiled
FORMAL basal

undermine v

1 WEAKEN, make less secure, destroy, erode, wear away, sap, damage, sabotage, subvert, injure, mar, impair, cripple, undercut
OLD underwork
FORMAL vitiate
COLLOQ. handbag
2 MINE, tunnel, dig, excavate
E3 **1** strengthen, fortify

undernourished adj

malnourished, underfed, starved, hungry, anorexic, anorectic

underprivileged adj

disadvantaged, deprived, poor, needy, in need, in distress, in want, impoverished, destitute, oppressed
FORMAL impecunious
E3 privileged, fortunate, affluent

underrate v

underestimate, undervalue, fail to appreciate, belittle, depreciate, dismiss, look down on, sell short
FORMAL disparage
E3 overrate, exaggerate

undersell v

undercharge, undercut, cut, mark down, reduce, slash, sell short, depreciate, play down, understate
FORMAL disparage

undersized adj

little, small, tiny, minute, miniature, pygmy, dwarf, stunted, underdeveloped, underweight, puny, runtish, atrophied; Scot wee
TECHNICAL achondroplastic
COLLOQ. pint-size(d), teeny, teensy
E3 oversized, big, overweight

understand v

1 I don't understand
grasp, take in, follow, fathom, comprehend, penetrate, make out, figure out, discern, perceive, see, realize, recognize, appreciate, accept, take, conceive, make of, penetrate, read, make sense of, catch; dialect gaum
OLD contrive
FORMAL apprehend
COLLOQ. get, get it, cotton on, click, twig, tumble to, latch onto, get the hang of, rumble, suss out, get the message, get the picture, get wise, get your head/mind round, know the ropes, the penny drops
SLANG savvy
OLD SLANG dig
2 SYMPATHIZE, empathize, commiserate, comfort, feel sorry for, feel for, identify with, support, appreciate, enter into
3 BELIEVE, think, know, hear, learn, gather, assume, presume, suppose, conclude
E3 **1** misunderstand

understandable adj

1 he reacted with understandable fury
natural, unsurprising, reasonable, acceptable, admissible, expected, comprehensible
2 COMPREHENSIBLE, intelligible, penetrable, straightforward, clear, plain, direct, unambiguous, transparent, lucid, accessible
E3 **1** surprising, unreasonable **2** impenetrable, deep, complex, abstruse

understanding n, adj

• n
1 GRASP, knowledge, wisdom, intelligence, intellect, sense, comprehension, judgement, discernment, insight, appreciation, awareness, impression, feeling, perception, view, belief, idea, notion, opinion, interpretation, hindsight
OLD conceit
FORMAL apprehension
2 AGREEMENT, arrangement, pact, bargain, harmony

FORMAL accord, compact, entente
3 SYMPATHY, empathy, compassion, comfort, support, consolation, commiseration, appreciation, trust
 • adj
sympathetic, compassionate, kind, considerate, supportive, sensitive, thoughtful, tender, loving, patient, lenient, tolerant, forbearing, forgiving
🖃 unsympathetic, insensitive, impatient, intolerant

understate v
underplay, play down, minimize, make light of, belittle, dismiss
COLLOQ. soft-pedal
🖃 exaggerate, emphasize

understated adj
subtle, implied, indirect, low-key, faint, indistinct, indefinite, mild, toned-down
🖃 exaggerated, overstated, emphasized

understatement n
minimization, restraint, underplaying, dismissal
TECHNICAL litotes, meiosis
🖃 overstatement, exaggeration

understood adj
accepted, assumed, presumed, implied, implicit, inferred, tacit, unstated, unspoken, unwritten

understudy n
stand-in, double, substitute, replacement, reserve, deputy, relief, locum
COLLOQ. fill-in

undertake v
1 BEGIN, embark on, tackle, set about, try, attempt, endeavour, take on, accept, assume, deal with, shoulder, put/set your hand to, apply yourself to, turn your hand to, get down to, get to grips with
OLD (Spenser) underfong
FORMAL commence
COLLOQ. grasp the nettle, get your teeth into, put your shoulder to the wheel, set your hand to the plough, take the bull by the horns
2 PLEDGE, promise, guarantee, agree, commit yourself, contract, covenant

undertaker n
funeral director, funeral furnisher; N Am mortician
OLD upholder

undertaking n
1 ENTERPRISE, venture, business, affair, task, project, operation, attempt, endeavour, effort, job, plan, campaign, scheme
OLD emprise
2 PLEDGE, commitment, promise, vow, word, assurance, guarantee, warrant

undertone n
hint, suggestion, whisper, murmur, intimation, trace, tinge, touch, flavour, feeling, aura, atmosphere, undercurrent
FORMAL connotation

undervalue v
underrate, underestimate, misjudge, minimize, depreciate, dismiss, look down on, sell short
FORMAL disparage
🖃 overrate, exaggerate

underwater adj
subaquatic, undersea, submarine, immersed, submerged, sunken
TECHNICAL demersed
FORMAL subaqueous, demersal

underwear n
underclothes, undergarments, lingerie
COLLOQ. undies, smalls, frillies, scanties, unmentionables

underweight adj
thin, undersized, underfed, undernourished, half-starved
🖃 overweight

underworld n
1 CRIMINAL WORLD, organized crime, gangland
SLANG the mob
2 NETHER WORLD, infernal regions, Hades, hell, inferno, lower regions, abyss, fire, fire and brimstone, bottomless pit, pit, Sheol, Acheron, Gehenna, Tophet, Abaddon, Tartarus, Malebolge, Erebus
FORMAL perdition, abode of the devil
COLLOQ. below, down there, other place
Related adjectives: chthonian, chthonic

underwrite v
endorse, authorize, sanction, approve, confirm, back, guarantee, insure, sponsor, support, fund, finance, subsidize, subscribe, write, sign, initial, countersign

undesirable adj
unwanted, unwelcome, unacceptable, unwished-for, disliked, unsuitable, unpleasant, disagreeable, distasteful, offensive, objectionable, foul, nasty, obnoxious, repugnant
🖃 desirable, pleasant

undeveloped adj
1 *undeveloped countries*
developing, underdeveloped, pre-industrialized, less advanced, Third World
2 UNFORMED, embryonic, potential, latent, immature, stunted, dwarfed
FORMAL inchoate, primordial
🖃 **1** advanced, industrialized **2** developed, mature

undignified adj
inelegant, ungainly, clumsy, foolish, improper, unsuitable, inappropriate, unbecoming
FORMAL unseemly, indecorous
🖃 dignified, elegant

undiluted adj
1 *undiluted praise*
strong, pure, heady, unspoilt, unalloyed, sheer, utter, unmitigated, unqualified
2 *an undiluted drink*
concentrated, neat, pure, straight, unmixed, unblended
🖃 **1** qualified, weak **2** diluted, mixed

undisciplined adj
wild, unrestrained, unruly, uncontrolled, wayward, disobedient, obstreperous, wilful, unpredictable, unreliable, unschooled, unsteady, untrained, disorganized, unsystematic
🖃 disciplined, self-controlled

undisguised adj
unconcealed, open, overt, explicit, frank, genuine, apparent, patent, obvious, evident, manifest, transparent, blatant, naked, unadorned, stark, utter, outright, thoroughgoing
🖃 secret, concealed, hidden

undisguisedly adv
overtly, outright, openly, obviously, transparently, patently, unreservedly, frankly, blatantly
🖃 secretly

undisputed adj
uncontested, unchallenged, unquestioned, irrefutable, undoubted, indisputable, incontrovertible, undeniable, indubitable, accepted, acknowledged, recognized, sure, certain, conclusive
OLD unargued
🖃 debatable, uncertain

undistinguished adj
unexceptional, unremarkable, unimpressive, ordinary, everyday, common, pedestrian, banal, indifferent, mediocre, inferior

COLLOQ. run-of-the-mill, so-so, not up to much, not all that it is cracked up to be, nothing to write home about, no great shakes, not much cop
☲ distinguished, exceptional, remarkable

undisturbed *adj*
untouched, calm, composed, equable, collected, even, quiet, placid, serene, tranquil, untroubled, motionless, unconcerned, unaffected, uninterrupted, unruffled
FORMAL unperturbed
☲ disturbed, interrupted

undivided *adj*
solid, unbroken, intact, whole, total, entire, one, single, individual, full, complete, combined, united, unanimous, unqualified, unreserved, concentrated, exclusive, wholehearted, serious, dedicated, sincere
TECHNICAL *pro indiviso*

undo *v*
1 UNFASTEN, untie, unbuckle, unbutton, unhook, unzip, unlock, unwrap, unwind, open, free, release, loose, loosen, separate, disentangle
2 ANNUL, invalidate, cancel, offset, neutralize, reverse, overturn, repeal, revoke, set aside, upset, quash, defeat, undermine, subvert, mar, spoil, ruin, wreck, crush, shatter, destroy, obliterate
OLD defeat
FORMAL nullify
☲ **1** fasten, do up

undoing *n*
downfall, ruin, ruination, collapse, destruction, defeat, overthrow, reversal, weakness, shame, disgrace

undomesticated *adj*
wild, untamed, uncivilized, natural, savage
FORMAL feral
☲ domesticated, tame

undone *adj*
1 UNACCOMPLISHED, unfulfilled, unfinished, uncompleted, incomplete, outstanding, left, omitted, neglected, ignored, forgotten, passed over
2 UNFASTENED, untied, unlaced, unbuttoned, unlocked, open, loose
3 RUINED, lost, destroyed, betrayed
☲ **1** done, accomplished, complete **2** fastened

undoubted *adj*
unchallenged, undisputed, acknowledged, uncontested, unquestionable, indisputable, incontrovertible, undesirable, sure, certain, definite, obvious, patent, indubitable, irrefutable

undoubtedly *adv*
certainly, definitely, doubtless, without doubt, without a shadow of a doubt, no doubt, beyond doubt, surely, of course, undeniably, unquestionably, unmistakably, assuredly, indubitably

undreamed-of *adj*
undreamt, inconceivable, unheard-of, unhoped-for, unimagined, unexpected, incredible, unforeseen, unsuspected, amazing, astonishing, miraculous

undress *v, n*
◆ *v*
strip, disrobe, divest, take off, remove, shed, unclothe
OLD make unready; (*Shakesp*) devest, discase, uncase; (*Spenser*) disattire
COLLOQ. peel off, streak, get your kit off
◆ *n*
nakedness, nudity, dishabille, *déshabillé*
OLD disarray

undressed *adj*
unclothed, disrobed, stripped, naked, stark-naked, nude, *en cueros*
COLLOQ. in the altogether, starkers, in your birthday suit, in

the raw, in the buff, not a stitch on, naked as the day you were born
☲ clothed

undue *adj*
unnecessary, needless, uncalled-for, unwarranted, undeserved, unjustified, unreasonable, disproportionate, excessive, immoderate, inordinate, extreme, superfluous, extravagant, exaggerated, obtrusive, improper, inappropriate
☲ reasonable, moderate, proper

undulate *v*
rise and fall, swell, roll, surge, wave, ripple, billow, heave

undulating *adj*
rolling, wavy, rippling, billowing, sinuous
FORMAL flexuose, flexuous, undate, undulant
☲ flat

unduly *adv*
too, over, excessively, immoderately, inordinately, disproportionately, out of all proportion, unreasonably, unjustifiably, unnecessarily, overmuch, exaggeratedly, obtrusively
COLLOQ. too ... by half
☲ moderately, reasonably

undutiful *adj*
negligent, neglectful, careless, disloyal, remiss, slack, defaulting, delinquent
FORMAL unfilial
☲ dutiful

undying *adj*
eternal, deathless, lasting, perpetual, everlasting, immortal, infinite, continuing, constant, perennial, permanent, unending, unfading, indestructible, inextinguishable, imperishable, undiminished
FORMAL abiding, sempiternal
☲ impermanent, inconstant

unearth *v*
dig up, exhume, disinter, excavate, uncover, expose, reveal, bring to light, find, discover, detect
☲ bury

unearthly *adj*
1 SUPERNATURAL, ghostly, phantom, eerie, uncanny, weird, strange, spine-chilling, otherworldly; *Scot* eldritch
FORMAL preternatural
COLLOQ. creepy
2 *at this unearthly hour*
unreasonable, preposterous, appalling, outrageous, ungodly, unheard-of
COLLOQ. horrendous
☲ **2** reasonable

unease *n*
uneasiness, anxiety, alarm, apprehension, apprehensiveness, worry, doubt, qualms, misgiving, nervousness, suspicion, disquiet, agitation
OLD dis-ease
FORMAL inquietude, perturbation
☲ calm, composure

uneasiness *n*
anxiety, alarm, apprehension, apprehensiveness, worry, doubt, qualms, unease, misgiving, nervousness, suspicion, disquiet, agitation
OLD dis-ease
FORMAL inquietude, perturbation
☲ calm, composure

uneasy *adj*
1 UNCOMFORTABLE, anxious, worried, alarmed, apprehensive, tense, strained, nervous, agitated, shaky, on edge, upset, troubled, disturbed, unsettled, restless, impatient, unsure, insecure, disquieted
FORMAL perturbed
COLLOQ. edgy, nervy, twitchy, keyed up, wound up, jittery

2 WORRYING, troubling, disturbing, unsettling, unnerving, disconcerting, disquieting
FORMAL perturbing
🖃 **1** calm, composed

uneconomic *adj*
unprofitable, uncommercial, loss-making, non-profit-making
🖃 economic, profitable, profit-making, remunerative

uneducated *adj*
unschooled, untaught, unread, ignorant, illiterate, uncultivated, uncultured, philistine, benighted
🖃 educated

unemotional *adj*
cool, cold, unfeeling, impassive, reserved, indifferent, apathetic, passionless, unresponsive, undemonstrative, unexcitable, phlegmatic, stolid, bland, bloodless, detached, objective, dispassionate
🖃 emotional, excitable

unemphatic *adj*
understated, unobtrusive, underplayed, played-down, unostentatious
COLLOQ. downbeat, soft-pedalled

unemployed *adj*
jobless, out of work, laid off, redundant, unwaged, idle, unoccupied
COLLOQ. on the dole
🖃 employed, occupied

unending *adj*
endless, never-ending, unceasing, ceaseless, incessant, interminable, continuous, uninterrupted, constant, continual, perpetual, everlasting, eternal, undying
FORMAL unremitting
🖃 transient, intermittent

unendurable *adj*
intolerable, unbearable, overwhelming, shattering, insufferable, insupportable
🖃 bearable, endurable

unenthusiastic *adj*
uninterested, unimpressed, cool, half-hearted, apathetic, bored, neutral, nonchalant, indifferent, unmoved, unresponsive, blasé, lukewarm, Laodicean
🖃 enthusiastic

unenviable *adj*
undesirable, unpleasant, disagreeable, uncongenial, uncomfortable, thankless, difficult, dangerous
🖃 enviable, desirable

unequal *adj*
1 DIFFERENT, varying, dissimilar, unlike, unfair, unjust, biased, inequitable, discriminatory
2 UNMATCHED, uneven, unbalanced, lopsided, disproportionate, asymmetrical, irregular
3 *unequal to a task*
incapable, unqualified, inadequate, unsuited, unfitted, incompetent
COLLOQ. not up to, not cut out for
🖃 **1, 2, 3** equal

unequalled *adj*
unmatched, unbeaten, unsurpassed, unrivalled, peerless, unique, paramount, matchless, incomparable, unparalleled, pre-eminent, surpassing, transcendent, supreme, exceptional, inimitable
FORMAL nonpareil

unequivocal *adj*
unambiguous, explicit, clear, plain, evident, distinct, unmistakable, express, direct, straight, straightforward, definite, positive, categorical, incontrovertible, absolute, outright, unqualified, unreserved
🖃 ambiguous, vague, qualified

unequivocally *adv*
unambiguously, unmistakably, clearly, directly, distinctly, explicitly, definitely, positively, firmly, unquestionably, incontrovertibly
🖃 ambiguously, vaguely

unerring *adj*
unfailing, perfect, impeccable, infallible, faultless, exact, certain, sure, accurate, uncanny
COLLOQ. dead
🖃 fallible

unerringly *adv*
unfailingly, infallibly, accurately
COLLOQ. bang, dead

unethical *adj*
unprofessional, immoral, improper, wrong, wicked, evil, unscrupulous, unprincipled, dishonourable, disreputable, illegal, illicit, dishonest, underhand
COLLOQ. shady
🖃 ethical

uneven *adj*
1 *uneven ground*
rough, bumpy, lumpy, stony, rugged, craggy, jagged, irregular, coarse, ruffled, rumpled, accidented
2 ODD, unequal, inequitable, unfair, unbalanced, one-sided, ill-matched, asymmetrical, lopsided, crooked
3 IRREGULAR, intermittent, spasmodic, fitful, jerky, unsteady, variable, changeable, fluctuating, erratic, inconsistent, patchy, streaky
OLD inequable
🖃 **1** even, flat, level **2** even, equal **3** regular, consistent

uneventful *adj*
uninteresting, unexciting, quiet, unvaried, boring, monotonous, tedious, dull, routine, humdrum, ordinary, everyday, commonplace, unremarkable, unexceptional, unmemorable
COLLOQ. run-of-the-mill
🖃 eventful, memorable, remarkable

unexampled *adj*
unprecedented, never before seen, incomparable, unequalled, unparalleled, unheard-of, unmatched, unique, novel

unexceptionable *adj*
inoffensive, harmless, innocuous, safe, innocent, unobjectionable, peaceable, mild, bland
🖃 exceptionable, offensive, objectionable

unexceptional *adj*
unremarkable, unmemorable, typical, average, normal, usual, ordinary, common, everyday, indifferent, mediocre, unimpressive, undistinguished
COLLOQ. run-of-the-mill, so-so, not up to much, not all that it is cracked up to be, nothing to write home about, no great shakes, not much cop
🖃 exceptional, impressive

unexcitable *adj*
self-possessed, cool, composed, relaxed, easy-going, serene, calm, contained, dispassionate, impassive, passionless, unimpassioned, phlegmatic
FORMAL imperturbable
COLLOQ. laid-back
🖃 excitable

unexpected *adj*
unforeseen, unanticipated, unpredictable, unlooked-for, chance, accidental, sudden, abrupt, surprising, startling, amazing, astonishing, unusual, emergent
OLD unhoped, inopinate, unware
FORMAL fortuitous
COLLOQ. snap, shock
🖃 expected, predictable

unexpectedly *adv*
suddenly, surprisingly, unpredictably, without warning, abruptly, by chance, fortuitously, unawares, accidentally, phenomenally, refreshingly, *ex improviso, à l'improviste*
OLD unware
COLLOQ. out of the blue, like a bolt from the blue

unexpressive *adj*
expressionless, emotionless, impassive, inexpressive, inscrutable, vacant, blank, deadpan, immobile
⧏ expressive, mobile

unfading *adj*
lasting, imperishable, durable, enduring, constant, undying, unfailing, fadeless, fast, evergreen
FORMAL abiding, immarcescible
⧏ changeable, transient

unfailing *adj*
constant, certain, dependable, reliable, sure, steady, true, steadfast, faithful, loyal, staunch, undying, unfading, inexhaustible, infallible, unerring
⧏ fickle, impermanent, transient

unfair *adj*
1 UNJUST, partial, biased, prejudiced, bigoted, discriminatory, unbalanced, weighted, one-sided, slanted, partisan, arbitrary, undeserved, unmerited, unwarranted, unreasonable, uncalled-for
FORMAL inequitable
COLLOQ. a bit off, thick
2 UNETHICAL, unscrupulous, unprincipled, wrongful, deceitful, dishonest, foul
COLLOQ. crooked, shady, bent, below the belt; *Aust & NZ* crook
⧏ 1 fair, just, unbiased, deserved **2** honest, ethical

unfairly *adv*
unjustly, wrongly, improperly, unreasonably, biasedly, partially, illegally, unlawfully, dishonestly
FORMAL inequitably
⧏ fairly, justly

unfairness *n*
injustice, inequity, one-sidedness, partiality, partisanship, prejudice, bigotry, bias, discrimination, misusage
FORMAL inequitableness
⧏ fairness, equity

unfaithful *adj*
disloyal, treacherous, false, untrue, insincere, deceitful, dishonest, untrustworthy, unreliable, fickle, inconstant, adulterous, double-dealing, faithless, unbelieving, godless
FORMAL duplicitous, perfidious
COLLOQ. cheating, two-timing
⧏ faithful, loyal, reliable

unfaltering *adj*
unfailing, unwavering, unyielding, unswerving, untiring, tireless, unflagging, unflinching, constant, firm, indefatigable, steady, steadfast, resolute, fixed
FORMAL pertinacious
⧏ faltering, uncertain, wavering

unfamiliar *adj*
1 STRANGE, unusual, uncommon, curious, alien, foreign, uncharted, unexplored, unknown, different, new, novel
2 UNACCUSTOMED, unacquainted, uninformed, inexperienced, unpractised, unskilled, unversed, unconversant
⧏ 1 familiar, customary **2** conversant, acquainted

unfashionable *adj*
outmoded, dated, out of date, out, passé, old-fashioned, *démodé*, antiquated, obsolete, unpopular
COLLOQ. old hat, square
⧏ fashionable

unfasten *v*
undo, untie, loosen, unwrap, unclasp, unlock, open, uncouple, disconnect, separate, detach
⧏ fasten, do up, bolt, lock

unfathomable *adj*
inexplicable, incomprehensible, impenetrable, baffling, fathomless, immeasurable, unknowable, mysterious, deep, profound, hidden, bottomless, unplumbed, unsounded, inscrutable, indecipherable
FORMAL abstruse, esoteric
⧏ comprehensible, explicable, penetrable

unfavourable *adj*
1 UNPROMISING, ominous, threatening, discouraging, inopportune, untimely, unseasonable, ill-suited, unfortunate, unlucky, in a bad light, disadvantageous, bad, foul, poor, adverse, contrary, negative
FORMAL inauspicious
2 HOSTILE, critical, adverse, negative, bad, poor, unfriendly, uncomplimentary, prejudiced
FORMAL inimical
⧏ 1 favourable, promising; *formal* auspicious **2** friendly, complimentary, good

unfavourably *adv*
badly, poorly, adversely, negatively, disadvantageously, unpromisingly, unfortunately
⧏ favourably, positively, well

unfeeling *adj*
insensitive, cold, hard, stony, callous, heartless, hard-hearted, harsh, cruel, inhuman, pitiless, uncaring, unsympathetic, iron-headed
⧏ sensitive, sympathetic

unfeigned *adj*
genuine, natural, pure, real, sincere, unaffected, frank, spontaneous, wholehearted, unforced, heartfelt
⧏ insincere, pretended, feigned

unfettered *adj*
unconstrained, free, unhampered, unrestrained, unhindered, unconfined, unchecked, unbridled, uninhibited, unshackled, untrammelled
⧏ constrained, fettered

unfinished *adj*
incomplete, uncompleted, half-done, sketchy, rough, crude, imperfect, lacking, wanting, deficient, undone, unaccomplished, unfulfilled
⧏ finished, perfect

unfit *adj*
1 UNSUITABLE, inappropriate, unsuited, inapt, ill-equipped, unqualified, disqualified, ineligible, untrained, unprepared, unequal, incapable, unable, incompetent, inadequate, ineffective, useless, condemned
2 UNHEALTHY, out of condition, out of shape, flabby, feeble, weak, decrepit, disabled, incapacitated, debilitated
⧏ 1 fit, suitable, competent **2** healthy, fit

unflagging *adj*
unfaltering, unfailing, untiring, tireless, unswerving, unceasing, undeviating, persevering, persistent, never-failing, indefatigable, constant, steady, fixed, single-minded, staunch
FORMAL unremitting
⧏ faltering, inconstant

unflappable *adj*
calm, collected, composed, level-headed, unworried, unexcitable, unruffled, equable, cool, impassive, easy-going, self-possessed, phlegmatic
FORMAL imperturbable
COLLOQ. laid-back
⧏ excitable, nervous, temperamental; *colloq.* panicky

unflattering *adj*
unbecoming, uncomplimentary, unattractive,

unfavourable, unprepossessing, critical, honest, blunt, candid, outspoken
🖃 complimentary, flattering

unflinching adj
steady, unfaltering, unwavering, unshaken, unshrinking, unswerving, firm, fixed, determined, constant, staunch, steadfast, sure, bold, resolute, stalwart, unblinking
🖃 unsteady, scared

unflinchingly adv
unfalteringly, unwaveringly, unshrinkingly, unswervingly, steadily, firmly, staunchly, steadfastly, boldly, resolutely
🖃 unsteadily, falteringly

unfold v
1 DEVELOP, evolve, grow, work out, come about, result, emerge
2 REVEAL, disclose, show, display, present, tell, relate, make known, describe, explain, clarify, elaborate, narrate, illustrate, interpret
OLD deploy
FORMAL explicate
3 *unfold a map*
open (out), spread (out), flatten, straighten (out), stretch out, undo, unfurl, unroll, uncoil, unravel, unwrap, uncover, extend, shake out, disenvelop, disinvolve, undouble, untuck
OLD unclew
🖃 **2** withhold, suppress **3** fold, wrap

unforeseen adj
unpredicted, unpredictable, unexpected, unanticipated, unlooked-for, surprising, amazing, astonishing, startling, sudden, unavoidable, unusual
🖃 expected, predictable

unforgettable adj
memorable, indelible, momentous, historic, noteworthy, notable, impressive, remarkable, significant, exceptional, extraordinary, striking, important, special, distinctive
🖃 unmemorable, unexceptional

unforgivable adj
unpardonable, inexcusable, unjustifiable, indefensible, intolerable, shameful, outrageous, disgraceful, deplorable, contemptible
FORMAL reprehensible
🖃 forgivable, venial

unforgiven adj
unredeemed, unabsolved, unregenerate, unrepentant
🖃 absolved, forgiven

unfortunate adj
1 UNLUCKY, luckless, unsuccessful, poor, wretched, unhappy, doomed, ill, ill-fated, hopeless, calamitous, disastrous, ruinous, adverse, unpleasant, disadvantageous, untoward
OLD evil, disadventurous, misfortuned; (*Shakesp*) misadventured; (*Spenser*) disaventrous
FORMAL hapless
COLLOQ. tough
2 REGRETTABLE, lamentable, deplorable, adverse, unfavourable, unsuitable, inappropriate, inopportune, untimely, ill-timed, ill-advised
FORMAL injudicious
🖃 **1** fortunate, happy **2** favourable, appropriate

unfortunately adv
regrettably, unhappily, unluckily, sadly, alas, sad to say, I am sorry to say, sad to relate
COLLOQ. worse luck
🖃 fortunately

unfounded adj
baseless, groundless, unsupported, unsubstantiated, unproven, unjustified, idle, false, spurious, trumped-up, fabricated, without foundation

FORMAL uncorroborated, conjectural
🖃 substantiated, justified

unfrequented adj
lonely, remote, secluded, uninhabited, unvisited, isolated, deserted, desolate, solitary, lone, god-forsaken
FORMAL sequestered
🖃 busy, crowded, populous

unfriendly adj
unsociable, standoffish, aloof, distant, unapproachable, inhospitable, uncongenial, unneighbourly, unwelcoming, unkind, cold, chilly, chill, cool, frosty, frozen, wintry, hostile, strained, aggressive, quarrelsome, antagonistic, ill-disposed, unpleasant, disagreeable, surly, sour; *Scot* fremd
FORMAL inimical, inauspicious
🖃 friendly, amiable, agreeable

Synonym nuances
The term **unsociable** could describe someone who does not enjoy company, but it tends to suggest disapproval: *although kind-hearted, he could be unsociable and stubborn*. **Standoffish**, however, is clearly suggestive of arrogance; similarly, **aloof** implies someone is behaving haughtily. **Distant**, on the other hand, is less judgemental and suggests reserve, but still has critical connotations, while **unapproachable** would imply that this reserve is discouraging or even frightening: *people feel banks are too unapproachable.*
   Inhospitable suggests an absence of comfort: *the inhospitable outback*, and **uncongenial** is similarly uninviting: *uncongenial surroundings.* **Unwelcoming** suggests a rather forbidding reception: *the unwelcoming look in his eyes.* **Unkind**, on the other hand, would suggest a degree of active cruelty: *she made an unkind comment the moment she met me.*
   Cold, **chilly**, **chill** and **cool** all share suggestions of remoteness, and the terms **frosty**, **frozen** and **wintry** suggest an even more marked display of unfriendliness: *he met me with a frosty glare.* **Hostile**, **aggressive**, **quarrelsome** and **antagonistic** go further by implying an openly confrontational disposition, unlike **ill-disposed**, which describes an internal attitude: *he felt ill-disposed towards her but hid his emotions well.*
   Surly and **sour** can be used to suggest moroseness or peevishness behind unfriendliness: *sour criticism*, while **strained** would be reserved for a situation or relationship that causes uneasiness: *her words were met with a strained silence.*

---

unfrock v
dismiss, depose, degrade, demote, suspend
🖃 restore, reinstate

unfruitful adj
unproductive, fruitless, barren, exhausted, impoverished, infertile, sterile, arid, unprofitable, unprolific, unrewarding
FORMAL infecund, infructuous
🖃 fruitful, productive

unfurl v
1 *unfurl a flag*
unfold, open (out), spread (out), flatten, straighten (out), stretch out, extend, undo, unroll, uncoil, unravel, unwrap, uncover
2 DEVELOP, unfold, evolve, grow, work out, come about, result, emerge

ungainly adj
clumsy, awkward, gauche, inelegant, ungraceful, gawky, unco-ordinated, lumbering, gangling, unwieldy, uncouth, loutish
FORMAL maladroit
🖃 graceful, elegant

ungodly adj
1 UNREASONABLE, outrageous, preposterous, intolerable,

unearthly, unsocial
COLLOQ. horrendous
2 IMPIOUS, irreligious, godless, blasphemous, profane, immoral, corrupt, depraved, sinful, wicked
FORMAL iniquitous

ungovernable *adj*
uncontrollable, wild, disorderly, unmanageable, unrestrainable, unruly, ungoverned, rebellious, masterless
FORMAL refractory

ungracious *adj*
discourteous, uncivil, impolite, rude, disrespectful, graceless, bad-mannered, ill-bred, unmannerly, offhand, boorish, churlish
E3 gracious, polite

ungrateful *adj*
unthankful, unappreciative, rude, impolite, uncivil, ill-mannered, ungracious, selfish, thankless, heedless
E3 grateful, thankful

unguarded *adj*
1 *in an unguarded moment*
unwary, careless, inattentive, off guard, incautious, indiscreet, undiplomatic, thoughtless, unthinking, heedless, foolish, foolhardy, rash, ill-considered, imprudent
FORMAL impolitic, uncircumspect
2 UNDEFENDED, unprotected, exposed, vulnerable, defenceless, unpatrolled
E3 1 guarded, cautious **2** defended, protected

unhappily *adv*
unfortunately, regrettably, unluckily, sadly, alas, sad to say, sad to relate
COLLOQ. worse luck
E3 fortunately

unhappy *adj*
1 SAD, sorrowful, miserable, melancholy, depressed, upset, dispirited, glum, despondent, dejected, downcast, crestfallen, long-faced, gloomy, mournful
FORMAL woebegone, disconsolate
COLLOQ. down, blue, fed up, low, down in the dumps
2 UNFORTUNATE, unlucky, ill-fated, ill-starred, luckless, unsuitable, inappropriate, inapt, ill-chosen, ill-advised, tactless, awkward, clumsy
FORMAL hapless, injudicious
E3 1 happy **2** fortunate, suitable

unharmed *adj*
undamaged, unhurt, uninjured, unscathed, untouched, whole, intact, safe, sound
E3 harmed, injured, hurt

unhealthy *adj*
1 UNWELL, sick, ill, poorly, ailing, sickly, infirm, invalid, weak, feeble, frail, debilitated, unsound, diseased, pasty
FORMAL indisposed
2 UNWHOLESOME, insanitary, unhygienic, harmful, injurious, detrimental, noxious, morbid, unnatural, unsanitary
FORMAL insalubrious, insalutary, epinosic
E3 1 healthy, fit **2** wholesome, hygienic, natural

unheard-of *adj*
1 UNTHINKABLE, inconceivable, unbelievable, unimaginable, undreamed-of, unprecedented, extraordinary, exceptional, unacceptable, offensive, shocking, outrageous, preposterous
2 UNKNOWN, unfamiliar, new, unusual, obscure, unsung, unheralded, undiscovered
E3 1 normal, acceptable **2** famous

unheeded *adj*
ignored, disregarded, disobeyed, unnoticed, unnoted, unobserved, unremarked, overlooked, neglected, forgotten
E3 noted, observed

unhelpful *adj*
awkward, obstructive, disobliging, troublesome, unaccommodating, unco-operative, obstinate, stubborn, irritable, touchy, prickly, oversensitive, rude, unpleasant, boorish, loutish, rustic, cubbish
COLLOQ. stroppy, bloody-minded
E3 helpful, accommodating, amenable, pleasant

unheralded *adj*
unsung, unrecognized, unproclaimed, unpublicized, unnoticed, surprise, unadvertised, unannounced, unexpected, unforeseen
E3 advertised, publicized, trumpeted, acclaimed

unhesitating *adj*
immediate, instant, instantaneous, prompt, ready, automatic, spontaneous, unquestioning, unwavering, unfaltering, wholehearted, confident, implicit
E3 hesitant, tentative

unhinge *v*
unbalance, unnerve, unsettle, upset, confuse, distract, disorder, drive mad, madden, craze, derange

unhinged *adj*
deranged, disordered, demented, crazy, mad, lunatic, insane, of unsound mind, *non compos mentis*, unbalanced, unsettled, disturbed, irrational, confused, frantic, delirious, distraught, berserk, out of your mind
COLLOQ. not all there, loopy, bonkers, barmy, potty, nuts, nutty, nutty as a fruitcake, round the bend, round the twist, out to lunch
SLANG loony, off your rocker, needing your head examined
E3 sane, calm

unholy *adj*
1 IMPIOUS, irreligious, godless, ungodly, blasphemous, sinful, immoral, corrupt, depraved, wicked, evil
FORMAL iniquitous
2 *an unholy mess*
unreasonable, shocking, outrageous, dreadful, terrible, ungodly, unearthly
COLLOQ. horrendous
E3 1 holy, pious, godly **2** reasonable

unhook *v*
undo, unfasten, untie, release, free, loose, loosen

unhoped-for *adj*
unexpected, unforeseen, unanticipated, unimaginable, unlooked-for, unbelievable, undreamed-of, incredible, surprising

unhurried *adj*
slow, leisurely, deliberate, easy, easy-going, relaxed, calm, sedate
COLLOQ. laid-back
E3 hurried, hasty, rushed

unhurt *adj*
unharmed, uninjured, unscathed, untouched, whole, intact, safe, sound
E3 hurt, injured

unhygienic *adj*
insanitary, unclean, impure, unhealthy, unsanitized, dirty, dirtied, contaminated, polluted, infected, disease-ridden, filthy, foul, infested
FORMAL unhealthful, noisome, noxious, insalubrious, feculent
E3 hygienic, sanitary, clean

unidentified *adj*
unknown, unrecognized, unmarked, unnamed, nameless, anonymous, incognito, unfamiliar, strange, mysterious, obscure, unclassified
E3 identified, known, named

unification *n*
union, uniting, merger, alliance, amalgamation,

combination, federation, fusion, incorporation, coalescence, coalition, confederation
FORMAL enosis
E3 separation, split, division

uniform *n, adj*
♦ *n*
outfit, costume, livery, insignia, regalia, robes, dress, suit, habit, regimentals
COLLOQ. garb, rig
♦ *adj*
same, identical, like, alike, similar, homogeneous, consistent, regular, equal, smooth, level, even, flat, monotonous, of a piece, unvarying, unchanging, constant, unbroken, steady, stable, invariable, undeviating
E3 different, varied, changing

uniformity *n*
sameness, constancy, invariability, regularity, similarity, evenness, flatness, monotony, drabness, dullness, tedium
FORMAL homogeneity, homomorphism, similitude
E3 difference, dissimilarity, variation

unify *v*
unite, bring/come together, join, bind, combine, integrate, mix, blend, merge, amalgamate, consolidate, coalesce, fuse, weld
E3 separate, divide, split

unifying *adj*
uniting, reconciling, combinatory, consolidative
TECHNICAL esemplastic
FORMAL unific, henotic
E3 divisive

unimaginable *adj*
inconceivable, unbelievable, incredible, amazing, astonishing, staggering, extraordinary, preposterous, impossible, fantastic, undreamed-of, unthinkable, unheard-of, implausible, unlikely, unconvincing, far-fetched, outlandish
COLLOQ. mind-boggling

unimaginative *adj*
uninspired, unoriginal, predictable, hackneyed, banal, mundane, pedestrian, ordinary, dull, boring, routine, usual, dry, barren, lifeless, stale, unexciting, tame
COLLOQ. matter-of-fact, samey
E3 imaginative, creative, original

unimpeachable *adj*
blameless, perfect, unblemished, spotless, faultless, immaculate, impeccable, irreproachable, unchallengeable, unquestionable, unassailable, reliable, dependable
E3 blameworthy, faulty

unimpeded *adj*
unrestrained, unconstrained, free, open, clear, unhindered, unblocked, unchecked, unhampered, uninhibited, untrammelled
COLLOQ. all-round
E3 hampered, impeded

unimportant *adj*
insignificant, irrelevant, immaterial, insubstantial, minor, secondary, incidental, marginal, peripheral, trivial, trifling, petty, slight, negligible, worthless, inconsiderable, light
FORMAL nugatory, inconsequential, of no consequence
COLLOQ. no great shakes, no big deal, not worth mentioning
E3 important, significant, relevant, vital

unimpressive *adj*
unspectacular, undistinguished, unexciting, unexceptional, unremarkable, uninteresting, dull, ordinary, common, average, commonplace, indifferent, mediocre
E3 impressive, memorable, notable, special

uninhabited *adj*
unoccupied, vacant, empty, deserted, abandoned, desolate, unpeopled, unpopulated, unsettled

uninhibited *adj*
unconstrained, unreserved, unself-conscious, liberated, free, unrestricted, uncontrolled, unrestrained, abandoned, natural, spontaneous, frank, outspoken, candid, open, relaxed, informal
E3 inhibited, repressed, constrained, restrained

uninspired *adj*
ordinary, boring, commonplace, dull, indifferent, stale, trite, stock, unexciting, unimaginative, uninspiring, uninteresting, undistinguished, unexceptional, unoriginal, pedestrian, prosaic, humdrum
COLLOQ. samey, dull as ditchwater
E3 original, inspired, exciting

uninspiring *adj*
boring, tedious, dull, monotonous, routine, repetitious, uninteresting, unexciting, uneventful, dreary, humdrum, tiring, tiresome, unvaried, commonplace, trite, unimaginative, dry, stale, flat, insipid, prosaic, long-winded
OLD stultifying, jejune
COLLOQ. samey, dull as ditchwater, soul-destroying, with the novelty worn off, ho-hum
E3 inspiring, interesting, exciting, stimulating, original

unintelligent *adj*
stupid, foolish, silly, slow, half-witted, empty-headed, fatuous, unreasoning, unthinking, dense, dull, obtuse, brainless
COLLOQ. thick, dumb, gormless
E3 intelligent

unintelligible *adj*
incomprehensible, incoherent, inarticulate, garbled, scrambled, jumbled, muddled, indecipherable, unreadable, illegible, impenetrable, unfathomable, puzzling, mysterious, obscure, complicated, complex, involved
COLLOQ. double Dutch
E3 intelligible, comprehensible, clear

unintentional *adj*
unintended, accidental, inadvertent, unplanned, unpremeditated, uncalculated, involuntary, unconscious, unwitting, careless
FORMAL fortuitous
E3 intentional, deliberate

uninterested *adj*
indifferent, unconcerned, uninvolved, bored, listless, apathetic, unenthusiastic, blasé, impassive, distant, unresponsive, incurious, *pococurante*
COLLOQ. not giving a hoot, not giving two hoots
SLANG not giving a monkey's, not giving a damn, not giving a toss, not giving a tinker's cuss
E3 interested, excited, enthusiastic, responsive, curious

> ⚠ **uninterested** or **disinterested**?
> *See panel at* **disinterested**.

uninteresting *adj*
boring, tedious, monotonous, humdrum, dull, drab, dreary, dry, flat, tame, stale, prosaic, pedestrian, uneventful, unexciting, uninspiring, unimpressive, tiresome, wearisome
COLLOQ. samey, dull as ditchwater
E3 interesting, exciting, entertaining

uninterrupted *adj*
unbroken, continuous, non-stop, unending, unceasing, ceaseless, endless, constant, continual, steady, sustained, undisturbed, peaceful
FORMAL unremitting
E3 broken, intermittent

uninvited adj
unasked, unsought, unsolicited, unwanted, unwelcome
🔁 invited

uninviting adj
unappealing, unattractive, undesirable, unpleasant, unwelcoming, repellent, repulsive, offensive, off-putting, unsavoury, disagreeable, distasteful, unappetizing
🔁 inviting, welcome

uninvolved adj
unattached, uncommitted, unengaged, free, independent, footloose, fancy-free, unhampered, unhindered, untrammelled
🔁 attached, committed

union n
1 FUSION, unification, unity, alliance, coalition, league, association, confederation, amalgamation, merger, combination, joining, juncture, consolidation, mixture, synthesis, blend, coalescence, cementation
TECHNICAL coadunation, conglutination, consubstantiation
2 ASSOCIATION, trade union, alliance, coalition, league, club, federation, confederacy, consortium
3 AGREEMENT, harmony, unity, unanimity
FORMAL accord, concurrence
4 MARRIAGE, wedding
OLD wedlock
FORMAL matrimony, nuptials, spousage, espousals
🔁 **1** separation, alienation; formal estrangement **4** divorce

unique adj
single, one-off, sole, only, one, one and only, one of a kind, lone, alone, solitary, unmatched, matchless, peerless, unequalled, unparalleled, unrivalled, incomparable, unprecedented, inimitable, singular
FORMAL nonpareil, idiographic, sui generis
🔁 common

uniquely adv
matchlessly, peerlessly, incomparably, inimitably, singly, solely, only, specially, distinctively, markedly, remarkably, peculiarly, idiosyncratically, singularly, by itself, in its own way

unison n
agreement, co-operation, harmony, unanimity, unity
FORMAL concert, accord, concord
▪ **in unison**
1 sing in unison
at the same time, simultaneously, at the same moment
2 work in unison
in agreement, in co-operation, in harmony

unit n
1 ITEM, part, element, constituent, piece, component, module, section, segment, portion, entity, whole, one, system, assembly
2 DETACHMENT, squad, force, corps, brigade, patrol, task force

unite v
join, connect, link, tie, couple, marry, wed, ally, co-operate, band, associate, federate, confederate, combine, join forces, pool, amalgamate, merge, blend, unify, consolidate, coalesce, weld, fuse, incorporate, make common cause, close, twist, knit, knot, lap, lock, splice, cement, consort, embody
TECHNICAL coadunate, conjugate, consubstantiate, synoecize
OLD concorporate, copulate, fay, ming
FORMAL accrete, cleave, conjoin, conglutinate
COLLOQ. pull together
🔁 separate, sever

united adj
allied, affiliated, corporate, unified, combined,

amalgamated, pooled, incorporated, collective, concerted, one, unanimous, agreed, in agreement, like-minded, co-operative
OLD concorporated
FORMAL in accord, conjoined, conjoint
🔁 disunited

unity n
1 AGREEMENT, harmony, peace, consensus, unanimity, solidarity
FORMAL accord, concord, concert
COLLOQ. togetherness
2 UNION, integrity, oneness, wholeness, amalgamation, unification
🔁 **1** disunity, disagreement, discord, strife

universal adj
worldwide, global, cosmic, all, all-embracing, all-inclusive, general, comprehensive, common, across-the-board, total, whole, entire, all-round, unlimited
TECHNICAL ecumenic(al)
FORMAL ubiquitous, omnipresent, catholic
COLLOQ. varsal
OLD COLLOQ. versal

universality n
commonness, comprehensiveness, all-inclusiveness, entirety, totality, completeness, generalization, generality, predominance, prevalence
FORMAL ubiquity

universally adv
always, everywhere, uniformly, invariably
FORMAL ubiquitously

universe n
cosmos, world, nature, creation, firmament, heavens
FORMAL macrocosm

university n
college, institute, varsity, academy
OLD polytechnic
FORMAL academia

unjust adj
unfair, wrong, partial, biased, prejudiced, one-sided, partisan, unreasonable, unjustified, undeserved
FORMAL inequitable
🔁 just, fair, reasonable

unjustifiable adj
indefensible, inexcusable, unforgivable, unpardonable, unreasonable, uncalled-for, unwarranted, immoderate, excessive, unacceptable, outrageous
🔁 justifiable, acceptable

unkempt adj
dishevelled, tousled, rumpled, uncombed, ungroomed, untidy, disordered, messy, sloppy, scruffy, shabby, shambolic, slovenly
COLLOQ. slobbish
🔁 well-groomed, tidy

unkind adj
cruel, harsh, inhuman, inhumane, callous, hard-hearted, cold-hearted, heartless, unfeeling, insensitive, thoughtless, inconsiderate, uncharitable, unkindly, pitiless, ruthless, nasty, malicious, malevolent, vicious, snide, spiteful, mean, unfriendly, uncaring, unsympathetic, disobliging
COLLOQ. shabby, bitchy
🔁 kind, kindly, considerate, generous, sympathetic

unkindness n
cruelty, harshness, uncharitableness, unfriendliness, inhumanity, callousness, hard-heartedness, insensitivity, maliciousness, meanness, spite
🔁 kindness, friendship

unknowable adj
unimaginable, unpredictable, untold, unascertainable, unfathomable, unforeseeable, incalculable, infinite
COLLOQ. in the lap of the gods

unknowing adj
unaware, unwitting, unsuspecting, unthinking, unconscious, involuntary, inadvertent, unplanned, accidental, chance, unintentional, unintended, unplanned
F3 knowing, conscious, deliberate

unknown adj
unfamiliar, unheard-of, strange, alien, foreign, mysterious, dark, obscure, hidden, concealed, undisclosed, secret, undivulged, untold, new, uncharted, unexplored, undiscovered, unrevealed, unidentified, unnamed, nameless, anonymous, incognito
F3 known, familiar

unlawful adj
illegal, criminal, illicit, illegitimate, against the law, unconstitutional, outlawed, banned, prohibited, forbidden, unauthorized, unlicensed, unsanctioned
F3 lawful, legal, allowed, permitted

unleash v
loose, let loose, (set) free, release, unloose, untie, untether
F3 restrain

unlettered adj
illiterate, ignorant, uneducated, unlearned, unschooled, untaught, untutored, unlessoned
F3 educated

unlike adj, prep
◆ adj
dissimilar, different, distinct, opposite, opposed, incompatible, contrasted, ill-matched, out of character, unrelated, unequal, divergent, diverse, various
OLD difform, unconform; (Spenser) unlich
FORMAL disparate, heterogeneous
F3 similar, related
◆ prep
dissimilar to, different from, in contrast to, as opposed to, as against
F3 like

unlikely adj
1 IMPROBABLE, implausible, far-fetched, unconvincing, unbelievable, incredible, inconceivable, fictional, unimaginable, unexpected, doubtful, dubious, questionable, suspect, suspicious, last
OLD (Shakesp & Spenser) unlike
COLLOQ. fishy
2 SLIGHT, faint, remote, distant, outside, slim, small, inconsiderable
F3 1 likely, plausible

unlimited adj
limitless, unrestricted, unbounded, boundless, inexhaustible, illimitable, infinite, endless, countless, incalculable, immeasurable, untold, vast, immense, extensive, great, indefinite, absolute, total, unconditional, unqualified, all-encompassing, total, complete, full, unconstrained, unhampered, unimpeded, uncontrolled, unchecked
F3 limited

unload v
unpack, empty, discharge, dump, offload, unburden, remove, relieve
F3 load

unlock v
unbolt, unlatch, unfasten, undo, unbar, open, free, release
F3 lock, fasten

unlooked-for adj
unexpected, unforeseen, unanticipated, unpredicted, unhoped-for, unthought-of, undreamed-of, surprising, surprise, fortunate, chance, lucky
FORMAL fortuitous
F3 expected, predictable

unloved adj
unpopular, disliked, hated, detested, unwanted, rejected, spurned, forsaken, loveless, uncared-for, neglected
COLLOQ. dumped
F3 loved

unluckily adv
regrettably, unhappily, unfortunately, sadly, alas, sad to say, I am sorry to say, sad to relate
COLLOQ. worse luck
F3 luckily, fortunately

unlucky adj
1 UNFORTUNATE, luckless, unsuccessful, poor, wretched, unhappy, miserable, ill-fated, ill-starred, star-crossed, jinxed, doomed, cursed, ill-omened; Aust stiff
OLD infaust
FORMAL hapless
COLLOQ. down on your luck, tough
2 UNFAVOURABLE, adverse, unfortunate, unpleasant, unpromising, doomed, ill-fated, ominous, disadvantageous, untoward, calamitous, disastrous, catastrophic, black, left-handed, sinister; Scot donsie, unchancy, wanchancy
OLD (Shakesp) wicked; Scot mischancy
FORMAL inauspicious, unpropitious
F3 1 fortunate, lucky 2 favourable, lucky

unmanageable adj
1 UNWIELDY, bulky, cumbersome, awkward, troublesome, inconvenient, unhandy
FORMAL incommodious
2 UNCONTROLLABLE, wild, unruly, disorderly, ungovernable, obstreperous, difficult
FORMAL recalcitrant, refractory
F3 1 manageable 2 controllable

unmanly adj
effeminate, dishonourable, feeble, weak, weak-kneed, soft, weedy, cowardly, chicken-hearted, lily-livered, craven, namby-pamby
FORMAL effete
COLLOQ. cissy, wet, yellow, wimpish
SLANG wussy
F3 manly

unmannerly adj
impolite, rude, uncivil, uncouth, discourteous, ill-mannered, badly-behaved, bad-mannered, disrespectful, graceless, ungracious, ill-bred, boorish, low-bred
F3 polite

unmarried adj
single, unwed, divorced, separated, celibate, unattached, free, partnerless, available, lone, on your own
COLLOQ. footloose and fancy-free
F3 married

unmask v
unveil, uncloak, uncover, bare, expose, reveal, show, disclose, discover, detect
F3 mask, conceal

unmatched adj
unrivalled, unique, unparalleled, unequalled, unsurpassed, incomparable, beyond compare, matchless, supreme, peerless, paramount, unexampled
FORMAL consummate, nonpareil

unmentionable adj
unspeakable, unutterable, forbidden, taboo, immodest, indecent, embarrassing, unpleasant, shocking, scandalous, shameful, disgraceful, abominable

unmerciful adj
merciless, pitiless, ruthless, cruel, brutal, hard, callous,

sadistic, heartless, implacable, relentless, remorseless, unrelenting, unsparing, uncaring, unfeeling
F3 merciful

unmethodical adj
unorganized, confused, muddled, disorderly, haphazard, illogical, irregular, unsystematic, unco-ordinated, random
FORMAL desultory
F3 methodical

unmindful adj
heedless, careless, negligent, remiss, unheeding, neglectful, lax, slack, indifferent, inattentive, unaware, unconscious, oblivious, forgetful, blind, deaf, regardless
F3 mindful, aware, heedful

unmistakable adj
clear, plain, distinct, pronounced, obvious, manifest, evident, patent, glaring, blatant, striking, explicit, conspicuous, clear-cut, well-defined, unambiguous, unequivocal, positive, definite, sure, certain, unquestionable, beyond question, indisputable, undeniable, indubitable
F3 unclear, ambiguous

unmistakably adv
clearly, plainly, manifestly, obviously, evidently, unquestionably, without question, without doubt, doubtlessly, definitely, surely, certainly, unambiguously, unequivocally, undeniably, indisputably, blatantly, conspicuously, indubitably
F3 unclearly, ambiguously

unmitigated adj
utter, absolute, complete, pure, rank, perfect, outright, downright, out-and-out, thorough, thoroughgoing, sheer, relentless, persistent, intense, unqualified, unalleviated, unrelieved, unbroken, unrelenting, unredeemed, unmodified, undiminished, harsh, grim
FORMAL arrant, consummate, unabated, unremitting

unmoved adj
unaffected, untouched, unshaken, unstirred, dry-eyed, unfeeling, cold, dispassionate, indifferent, impassive, unresponsive, unconcerned, unimpressed, firm, adamant, inflexible, unbending, undeviating, unwavering, steady, unchanged, resolute, resolved, determined
F3 moved, affected, shaken

unnatural adj
1 ABNORMAL, anomalous, freakish, irregular, against nature, unusual, strange, odd, peculiar, queer, bizarre, extraordinary, uncommon, uncanny, supernatural, inhuman, perverted, disnatured, monstrous
OLD absonant, cataphysical, unkindly; (Shakesp) kindless
2 AFFECTED, feigned, artificial, false, insincere, unspontaneous, contrived, laboured, stilted, forced, strained, staged, self-conscious, stiff, wooden, constrained, far-fetched, formal, stiff-necked, pompous, fustian
F3 1 natural, normal 2 sincere, fluent

unnaturally adv
strangely, unusually, oddly, peculiarly, uncommonly, extraordinarily, irregularly, abnormally
F3 naturally, normally

unnecessarily adv
needlessly, excessively, immoderately, superfluously

unnecessary adj
unneeded, needless, uncalled-for, unrequired, wasted, unwanted, gratuitous, non-essential, inessential, excessive, dispensable, expendable, superfluous, redundant, tautological
F3 necessary, essential, indispensable

unnerve v
daunt, intimidate, frighten, scare, alarm, discourage, deject, demoralize, dishearten, dismay, disconcert, put

out, disquiet, unsettle, upset, worry, shake, confound, fluster, unman
FORMAL perturb
COLLOQ. rattle
F3 nerve, brace, steel

unnoticed adj
unobserved, unremarked, unseen, unrecognized, undiscovered, overlooked, ignored, disregarded, neglected, unheeded
F3 noticed, noted

unobtrusive adj
inconspicuous, unnoticeable, unassertive, self-effacing, humble, modest, unassuming, unaggressive, unostentatious, unpretentious, restrained, low-key, subdued, quiet, retiring
F3 prominent, obtrusive, ostentatious

unobtrusively adv
inconspicuously, quietly, modestly, on the quiet, unostentatiously, surreptitiously, humbly, unpretentiously
F3 obtrusively, ostentatiously, showily, aggressively

unoccupied adj
1 UNINHABITED, unpopulated, vacant, empty, deserted, forsaken
2 JOBLESS, free, idle, inactive, workless, unemployed
F3 1 occupied 2 busy

unofficial adj
unauthorized, illegal, informal, off-the-record, personal, private, confidential, undeclared, unconfirmed, unauthenticated, unratified, alternative, fringe, black, kerb
F3 official, ratified; formal accredited, substantiated, corroborated

unoriginal adj
unimaginative, uninspired, hackneyed, stale, trite, copied, cliché-ridden, derivative, cribbed, second-hand, derived
F3 original, imaginative, creative, innovative, fresh

unorthodox adj
unconventional, nonconformist, heterodox, alternative, fringe, irregular, abnormal, unusual, eccentric, creative, cult, zany, innovative, new, novel, fresh
COLLOQ. left-field
SLANG way-out, off the wall
F3 orthodox, conventional

unpaid adj
1 *unpaid bills*
outstanding, overdue, unsettled, owing, due, payable, pending, uncollected, remaining
2 *unpaid work*
voluntary, honorary, unsalaried, unwaged, unremunerative, free
TECHNICAL pro bono (publico)
F3 1 paid

unpalatable adj
1 UNAPPETIZING, distasteful, insipid, bitter, uneatable, inedible, unsavoury, disgusting
2 UNPLEASANT, disagreeable, unattractive, distasteful, unsavoury, offensive, nasty, repellent, repugnant
F3 1 palatable 2 pleasant

unparalleled adj
unequalled, without equal, unmatched, matchless, peerless, beyond compare, incomparable, unrivalled, unsurpassed, supreme, superlative, rare, unique, exceptional, unprecedented

unpardonable adj
unforgivable, inexcusable, unjustifiable, indefensible, outrageous, deplorable, disgraceful, shocking, shameful, scandalous
FORMAL irremissible, reprehensible, unconscionable
F3 forgivable, understandable

unperturbed *adj*

calm, unexcited, unflustered, untroubled, unworried, undisturbed, unruffled, unflinching, self-possessed, composed, collected, tranquil, serene, placid, poised, cool, impassive
COLLOQ. unflappable
E3 anxious, perturbed

unpleasant *adj*

1 *an unpleasant smell*
disagreeable, nasty, objectionable, offensive, distasteful, unpalatable, unappetizing, unattractive, repulsive, repugnant, bad, foul, troublesome, disgusting, undesirable
FORMAL noisome
2 *an unpleasant person*
unfriendly, unkind, disagreeable, rude, impolite, discourteous, bad-tempered, ill-natured, nasty, objectionable, hostile, aggressive, quarrelsome, surly, sour, mean
E3 1, 2 pleasant, agreeable, nice

unpleasantness *n*

annoyance, nastiness, trouble, upset, bother, embarrassment, scandal, fuss, furore, ill-feeling, bad feeling/blood

unpolished *adj*

unfinished, unworked, rough and ready, sketchy, unrefined, unfashioned, unsophisticated, uncultivated, uncultured, uncivilized, coarse, crude, rough, home-bred, rude, uncouth, vulgar
E3 finished, polished, refined

unpopular *adj*

disliked, hated, detested, unloved, friendless, undesirable, unattractive, unsought-after, unfashionable, undesirable, unwelcome, unwanted, rejected, shunned, avoided, ignored, neglected
E3 popular, fashionable

unprecedented *adj*

new, original, revolutionary, unknown, unheard-of, exceptional, remarkable, extraordinary, abnormal, unusual, uncommon, freakish, unparalleled, unrivalled, unequalled, unexampled
E3 usual

unpredictable *adj*

unforeseeable, unexpected, changeable, variable, inconstant, unreliable, fickle, unstable, volatile, erratic, random, chance
FORMAL mercurial, capricious
E3 predictable, foreseeable, constant, reliable

Synonym nuances
You can use **unforeseeable** of something, especially a problem, that could not have been anticipated, while **unexpected** can describe any event that comes as a surprise.

Changeable, **variable** and **inconstant**, on the other hand, are appropriate for something which is unpredictable because it is moving between different states: *his changeable moods*; *changeable weather*. The term **unreliable** has a similar meaning but is more critical, and implies a lack of dependability. **Fickle** is similar in implication, and would be used of a propensity for changing your mind or opinion: *the fickle world of fashion*.

Unstable is also rather negative in tone, and can suggest emotional fluctuations, while **volatile**, although similar, is perhaps suggestive of more sudden and dramatic, and therefore more problematic, variations: *his volatile temperament meant he could become violent*; *the shares market has proved volatile*.

The term **erratic**, meanwhile, may be used to suggest an unwelcome irregularity or inconsistency: *the child's erratic behaviour became difficult for his parents to handle*, whereas both **random** and **chance** can be used fairly generally of something haphazard: *random searches*.

---

unprejudiced *adj*

unbiased, fair, fair-minded, impartial, just, objective, non-partisan, open-minded, even-handed, balanced, detached, uncoloured, dispassionate, enlightened
E3 prejudiced, narrow-minded

unpremeditated *adj*

spontaneous, unintentional, unplanned, unprepared, unrehearsed, offhand, impulsive, impromptu, extempore
FORMAL fortuitous
COLLOQ. off-the-cuff, spur-of-the-moment
E3 premeditated

unprepared *adj*

unready, surprised, unsuspecting, ill-equipped, unwilling, unfinished, incomplete, half-baked, raw, crude, unplanned, unrehearsed, spontaneous, improvised, ad-lib, napping, on the wrong foot; *N Am* flat-footed
COLLOQ. off-the-cuff
E3 prepared, ready

unprepossessing *adj*

plain, ordinary, uninteresting, unexciting, unappealing, unexceptional, unremarkable, indifferent, undistinguished, unattractive, unlovely, ugly; *N Am* homely
E3 attractive, good-looking

unpretentious *adj*

unaffected, natural, plain, simple, ordinary, unobtrusive, honest, straightforward, humble, modest, unassuming, unostentatious
E3 pretentious, showy, ostentatious

unprincipled *adj*

unscrupulous, unprofessional, unethical, dishonest, dishonourable, immoral, underhand, deceitful, devious, corrupt, discreditable
COLLOQ. crooked
E3 ethical, principled

unproductive *adj*

infertile, sterile, barren, dry, arid, unfruitful, fruitless, futile, vain, idle, worthless, useless, ineffective, unprofitable, unremunerative, unrewarding
FORMAL inefficacious, otiose
E3 productive, fertile

unprofessional *adj*

amateurish, inexpert, unskilled, incompetent, inexperienced, untrained, inefficient, casual, sloppy, negligent, lax, unethical, unprincipled, unscrupulous, improper, unacceptable, inadmissible
FORMAL unseemly, indecorous
E3 professional, skilful

unpromising *adj*

unfavourable, adverse, discouraging, gloomy, depressing, doubtful, dispiriting, ominous
FORMAL inauspicious, unpropitious
E3 promising, favourable, auspicious

unprotected *adj*

defenceless, unguarded, unattended, undefended, unfortified, unarmed, unshielded, unsheltered, uncovered, exposed, open, naked, vulnerable, liable, helpless
E3 protected, safe, immune

unprovable *adj*

unverifiable, indemonstrable, undemonstrable, indeterminable, unascertainable
E3 verifiable

unqualified *adj*

1 UNTRAINED, inexperienced, amateur, ineligible, unlicensed, unfit, unsuitable, incompetent, incapable, inapt, unprepared, ill-equipped
2 ABSOLUTE, categorical, utter, total, complete, perfect, positive, thorough, round, plenary, downright,

unmitigated, unreserved, wholehearted, outright, out-and-out, unconditional, unequivocal, unrestricted, unallayed
FORMAL consummate
F3 1 qualified, professional 2 conditional, tentative

unquestionable adj
unequivocal, beyond question, incontestable, faultless, flawless, indisputable, obvious, manifest, patent, clear, conclusive, definite, absolute, sure, certain, self-evident, unchallenged, undeniable, unmistakable, incontrovertible, indubitable, irrefutable
F3 dubious, questionable

unquestionably adv
unequivocally, unambiguously, unmistakably, clearly, manifestly, directly, distinctly, explicitly, definitely, positively, firmly, incontrovertibly, indubitably, irrefutably
F3 questionably, dubiously, vaguely

unquestioning adj
implicit, unhesitating, questionless, unconditional, unqualified, wholehearted
F3 doubtful

unravel v
unwind, undo, untangle, disentangle, free, extricate, separate, unknot, straighten out, resolve, sort out, clear up, solve, work out, figure out, puzzle out, penetrate, interpret, explain
F3 tangle, complicate

unreadable adj
unintelligible, too difficult to read, incomprehensible, incoherent, inarticulate, garbled, scrambled, jumbled, muddled, indecipherable, illegible, impenetrable, unfathomable, puzzling, mysterious, obscure, complicated, complex, involved
COLLOQ. double Dutch
F3 intelligible, comprehensible, clear

unreal adj
false, artificial, synthetic, mock, ersatz, fake, sham, faux, imaginary, visionary, fanciful, make-believe, fictitious, untrue, made-up, fairytale, legendary, mythical, fantastic, bizarre, illusory, illusive, immaterial, insubstantial, nebulous, hypothetical, non-existent, ungrounded, hollow, whimsical, notional, phantom, shadow, storybook, Alice-in-Wonderland, Disneyesque, moonshiny, aerial
FORMAL chimerical, phantasmagorical, aeriform
COLLOQ. pretend, phon(e)y
F3 real, genuine, authentic

unrealistic adj
impractical, idealistic, theoretical, romantic, quixotic, impracticable, unworkable, unreasonable, impossible, over-optimistic
F3 realistic, pragmatic

unreality n
irreality, artificiality, imaginariness, fancifulness, make-believe, bizarreness, insubstantiality, illusoriness, nebulousness, non-existence, hollowness
COLLOQ. phon(e)yness
F3 reality, genuineness, authenticity

unreasonable adj
1 UNFAIR, unjust, biased, unco-operative, unjustifiable, unjustified, unwarranted, unacceptable, undue, uncalled-for, unrealistic, exacting
COLLOQ. a bit much, unchristian
2 IRRATIONAL, illogical, inconsistent, arbitrary, absurd, nonsensical, ludicrous, far-fetched, outrageous, preposterous, mad, senseless, silly, foolish, stupid, headstrong, opinionated, perverse, froward
3 *unreasonable prices*
excessive, immoderate, extravagant, outrageous, expensive, exorbitant, extortionate, undue, s

candalous, iniquitous, obscene
COLLOQ. steep, over the top, OTT
F3 1 reasonable, fair 2 rational, sensible 3 moderate

unreasoning adj
irrational, unreasonable, unsound, illogical, inconsistent, invalid, groundless, implausible, arbitrary, ridiculous, absurd, crazy, wild, foolish, silly, senseless, beastlike, brute, brutish, nonsensical, unwise, beside yourself, taken leave of your senses
F3 reasoning, rational, reasonable

unrecognizable adj
unidentifiable, disguised, incognito, changed, altered, unknowable
FORMAL incognizable

unrecognized adj
unnoticed, unobserved, unremarked, unseen, undiscovered, overlooked, ignored, disregarded, neglected, unheeded
F3 recognized, noticed, noted

unrefined adj
raw, untreated, unprocessed, unpurified, unfinished, unpolished, crude, coarse, vulgar, unsophisticated, uncultivated, uncultured
F3 refined, finished

unregenerate adj
unconverted, hardened, impenitent, stubborn, obstinate, unreformed, unrepentant, persistent, abandoned, shameless, wicked, sinful
FORMAL intractable, obdurate, incorrigible, recalcitrant, refractory
F3 reformed, repentant

unrelated adj
unconnected, unassociated, irrelevant, beside/off the point, extraneous, different, dissimilar, unlike, distinct, foreign, separate, independent
FORMAL disparate
COLLOQ. neither here nor there
F3 related, similar

unrelenting adj
relentless, uncompromising, inexorable, unceasing, ceaseless, endless, unbroken, continuous, constant, continual, perpetual, steady, remorseless, ruthless, cruel, unmerciful, merciless, pitiless, unforgiving, unsparing, implacable
FORMAL unremitting, incessant, unabated, intransigent
F3 spasmodic, intermittent

unreliable adj
unsound, fallible, deceptive, false, mistaken, erroneous, inaccurate, doubtful, unconvincing, questionable, implausible, uncertain, undependable, untrustworthy, unstable, fickle, irresponsible
COLLOQ. iffy, slippery, dodgy, in-and-out
F3 reliable, dependable, trustworthy, sound

unremitting adj
unrelenting, unceasing, ceaseless, relentless, remorseless, tireless, constant, continual, continuous, perpetual, unbroken
FORMAL incessant, unabated
F3 spasmodic, intermittent

unrepentant adj
impenitent, unapologetic, unabashed, unashamed, shameless, confirmed, hardened, callous
FORMAL incorrigible, obdurate
F3 repentant, penitent, ashamed

unrequited adj
rejected, neglected, ignored, not returned, discarded, unacknowledged, unrecognized, unreciprocated, snubbed, spurned

unreserved *adj*
unqualified, unrestricted, unrestrained, unconditional, unhesitating, uninhibited, unlimited, complete, full, explicit, absolute, free, total, open, wholehearted, entire, frank, forthright, direct, candid, heart-to-heart, demonstrative, extrovert, outgoing, outspoken, talkative, communicative
COLLOQ. whole-footed
E3 inhibited, tentative, hesitant

unreservedly *adv*
completely, entirely, utterly, fully, absolutely, totally, wholeheartedly, outright, unhesitatingly, unconditionally

unresisting *adj*
submissive, docile, obedient, passive, meek
COLLOQ. like a lamb to the slaughter
E3 resisting, protesting

unresolved *adj*
undecided, unanswered, undetermined, unsettled, unsolved, vexed, vague, indefinite, doubtful, problematical, pending, moot
COLLOQ. up in the air
E3 definite, determined

unresponsive *adj*
unaffected, unmoved, unsympathetic, uninterested, indifferent, aloof, apathetic, cool
E3 responsive, sympathetic

unrest *n*
protest, rebellion, turmoil, agitation, disorder, restlessness, dissatisfaction, dissension, worry, turmoil, disquiet, discontent, unease, uneasiness, commotion
FORMAL disaffection, discord, perturbation
E3 peace, calm

unrestrained *adj*
unbridled, uncontrolled, unhindered, uninhibited, unrepressed, unreserved, unchecked, unconstrained, unbounded, irrepressible, inordinate, immoderate, intemperate, free, natural, rampant, abandoned, boisterous
E3 restrained, inhibited

unrestricted *adj*
unlimited, unbounded, unopposed, unhindered, unimpeded, unobstructed, clear, free, open, public, unconditional, absolute
COLLOQ. free-for-all
E3 restricted, limited

unripe *adj*
unripened, green, immature, undeveloped, unready
E3 ripe, mature

unrivalled *adj*
unequalled, unparalleled, unmatched, matchless, peerless, incomparable, unsurpassed, without equal, beyond compare, supreme, superlative
FORMAL inimitable, nonpareil

unruffled *adj*
undisturbed, untroubled, imperturbable, collected, composed, cool, calm, tranquil, serene, peaceful, smooth, level, even
FORMAL unperturbed
E3 troubled, anxious

unruly *adj*
uncontrollable, unmanageable, ungovernable, disorderly, wild, rowdy, riotous, rebellious, mutinous, lawless, insubordinate, disobedient, wayward, wilful, headstrong, obstreperous
FORMAL recalcitrant, refractory, intractable
E3 manageable, orderly

> ### Synonym nuances
> Naturally, the synonyms tend to be marked by disapproval. You can use **uncontrollable** and **unmanageable** to suggest an unruliness that has gone beyond restraint, while **ungovernable** and **lawless**, although similar, are generally used with regard to a place or a people: *the country had become ungovernable.*
>   **Disorderly** and **rowdy**, however, suggest a more temporary state of disruption and noisiness: *a disorderly crowd gathered in the square*, whereas **wild** has stronger suggestions of being uncivilized and uncontrollable. **Riotous**, likewise, implies unrestrained, destructive behaviour, but **rebellious** and **mutinous** would be reserved for where there is a defiance of authority: *mutinous troops.* **Insubordinate** is similar, but does not convey the same sense of resulting turbulence.
>   You can use **wayward** of a person to suggest an element of unpredictability in their nature, while both **wilful** and **headstrong** have implications of stubbornness. **Obstreperous** returns to the idea of being noisy and unrestrained: *the barman threw him out because he was getting too obstreperous.*

unsafe *adj*
dangerous, perilous, risky, high-risk, hazardous, treacherous, chancy, unreliable, uncertain, unsound, unstable, precarious, insecure, vulnerable, exposed, defenceless
COLLOQ. dicey, hairy
E3 safe, secure

unsaid *adj*
unspoken, unstated, unexpressed, unvoiced, unmentioned, undeclared, unuttered, unpronounced
E3 spoken

unsatisfactory *adj*
unacceptable, imperfect, defective, faulty, inferior, poor, mediocre, weak, empty, lame, tame, wrong, off-colour, inadequate, insufficient, deficient, unsuitable, displeasing, dissatisfying, unsatisfying, frustrating, disappointing
COLLOQ. leaving a lot to be desired, rop(e)y, lousy, rocky
E3 satisfactory, adequate, pleasing

unsavoury *adj*
distasteful, disagreeable, unpleasant, disgusting, nauseating, revolting, sickening, nasty, undesirable, repulsive, repugnant, objectionable, obnoxious, offensive, repellent, unattractive, sordid, squalid, unpalatable, unappetizing
E3 palatable, pleasant

unscathed *adj*
unhurt, uninjured, unharmed, undamaged, untouched, whole, intact, safe, sound
E3 hurt, injured, harmed

unscrupulous *adj*
unprincipled, ruthless, shameless, dishonourable, dishonest, corrupt, immoral, unethical, improper, unscrupled, unconscionable, villainous, Rottweiler
COLLOQ. crooked, stopping at nothing
E3 scrupulous, ethical, proper

unseasonable *adj*
seasonable, inappropriate, ill-timed, unsuitable, untimely, mistimed
FORMAL inopportune, intempestive, malapropos
E3 seasonable, timely

unseasoned *adj*
unprepared, unprimed, unmatured, untreated, untempered
COLLOQ. green

unseat *v*
remove, depose, dethrone, dismount, displace, dismiss,

discharge, oust, throw, overthrow, topple, unhorse, unsaddle, dishorse

unseemly *adj*
improper, indelicate, unbecoming, undignified, unrefined, disreputable, discreditable, undue, inappropriate, unsuitable, unbefitting
FORMAL indecorous
E3 seemly, decorous

unseen *adj*
unnoticed, unobserved, undetected, unobtrusive, invisible, hidden, concealed, veiled, obscure, lurking
E3 visible

unselfish *adj*
selfless, altruistic, self-denying, self-sacrificing, self-forgetting, disinterested, noble, kind, generous, open-handed, liberal, charitable, philanthropic, public-spirited, humanitarian
FORMAL magnanimous
E3 selfish

unsentimental *adj*
realistic, practical, pragmatic, hard-headed, hard-faced, tough, iron-headed, unemotional, unfeeling, unromantic, level-headed
E3 sentimental, idealistic

unsettle *v*
disturb, upset, trouble, bother, discompose, ruffle, fluster, unbalance, destabilize, shake, agitate, disconcert, confuse
FORMAL perturb, discomfit
COLLOQ. rattle, throw

unsettled *adj*
1 DISTURBED, upset, troubled, restless, unstable, agitated, anxious, uneasy, tense, on edge, fidgety, flustered, shaken, unnerved, disoriented, confused
OLD queasy
COLLOQ. edgy, fazed
2 UNRESOLVED, undetermined, indetermined, undecided, to be decided, open, uncertain, doubtful, in a state of flux
OLD undiscussed
COLLOQ. up in the air, in the balance
3 AIMLESS, directionless, pointless, purposeless, goalless, futile, unmotivated, irresolute, rambling, drifting, undirected, unguided, wandering, roving, vagabond, with no fixed abode
4 *unsettled weather*
changeable, variable, unpredictable, inconstant, unstable, uncertain, insecure, unsteady, shaky
5 UNPAID, outstanding, owing, in arrears, payable, overdue
6 UNINHABITED, unoccupied, deserted, abandoned, desolate, unpeopled, unpopulated
E3 1 composed, calm 2 decided, certain 3 purposeful 4 settled 5 paid 6 settled, peopled

unshakable, unshakeable *adj*
firm, well-founded, fixed, stable, immovable, unassailable, unswerving, unwavering, constant, steadfast, staunch, sure, resolute, determined
E3 insecure

unsightly *adj*
ugly, unattractive, unprepossessing, hideous, revolting, repulsive, repugnant, off-putting, unpleasant, disagreeable
E3 attractive

unskilful *adj*
unskilled, amateurish, inexperienced, unprofessional, unqualified, untaught, untrained, uneducated, untalented, unpractised, incompetent, awkward, clumsy, fumbling, bungling, inept, inexpert, gauche
FORMAL maladroit
E3 skilful, skilled

unskilled *adj*
untrained, unqualified, inexperienced, unpractised, inexpert, unprofessional, amateurish, incompetent
E3 skilled, professional

unsociable *adj*
unfriendly, aloof, distant, standoffish, withdrawn, introverted, uncompanionable, insociable, reclusive, solitary, retiring, reserved, taciturn, unforthcoming, uncommunicative, cold, chilly, cool, uncongenial, unneighbourly, inhospitable, hostile
E3 sociable, friendly, congenial

unsolicited *adj*
unrequested, unsought, uninvited, unasked, unwanted, unwelcome, uncalled-for, unasked-for, gratuitous, voluntary, spontaneous
E3 requested, invited

unsophisticated *adj*
1 *an unsophisticated person*
artless, guileless, innocent, ingenuous, naive, inexperienced, simple, unworldly, childlike, natural, unaffected, unpretentious
2 CRUDE, unrefined, plain, simple, basic, straightforward, rudimentary, undeveloped, uncomplicated, uninvolved
E3 1 sophisticated, worldly 2 complex, highly-developed

unsound *adj*
1 *unsound reasoning*
faulty, flawed, defective, ill-founded, unfounded, false, weak, erroneous, untenable, invalid, illogical, shaky
FORMAL fallacious
2 UNHEALTHY, unwell, ill, diseased, weak, ailing, delicate, frail, unbalanced, disordered, deranged, unhinged
3 UNSTABLE, unsteady, rickety, wobbly, shaky, insecure, broken, dangerous, unsafe, unreliable
E3 1 sound 2 well 3 stable

unsparing *adj*
1 GENEROUS, lavish, liberal, open-handed, ungrudging, unstinting, plenteous, abundant, bountiful, profuse
FORMAL munificent
2 HARSH, hard, merciless, unmerciful, ruthless, severe, stern, relentless, implacable, uncompromising, unforgiving
E3 forgiving, mean, sparing

unspeakable *adj*
unutterable, inexpressible, indescribable, unmentionable, awful, dreadful, frightful, terrible, horrible, shocking, appalling, monstrous, horrendous, inconceivable, unimaginable, unthinkable, unbelievable, nameless
FORMAL execrable, nefandous

unspeakably *adv*
indescribably, unutterably, inexpressibly, terribly, frightfully, awfully, appallingly, horrendously, inconceivably, unimaginably, unthinkably, unbelievably

unspecified *adj*
unknown, unnamed, uncertain, unidentified, undecided, indefinite, undefined, undetermined, obscure, mysterious, vague
E3 specified, known, certain

unspectacular *adj*
unremarkable, unimpressive, unexciting, uninteresting, dull, boring, ordinary, common, average, mediocre, plodding
E3 spectacular, impressive, memorable

unspoilt *adj*
preserved, unchanged, untouched, natural, unaffected, unsophisticated, unharmed, undamaged, unimpaired, unblemished, perfect
E3 spoilt, affected

unspoken *adj*
unstated, undeclared, unuttered, unexpressed, unsaid,

voiceless, wordless, silent, tacit, implicit, implied, inferred, understood, assumed
E3 stated, explicit

unstable *adj*
1 CHANGEABLE, variable, fluctuating, vacillating, wavering, fitful, erratic, moody, inconsistent, volatile, inconstant, unpredictable, unreliable, untrustworthy, unsettled, brittle, flighty, light-minded, labile, unballasted, slippery; *dialect* wankle; *Scot* bruckle
OLD unstable
FORMAL capricious, mercurial
COLLOQ. dodgy
2 UNSTEADY, wobbly, shaky, rickety, insecure, unsafe, weak, infirm, risky, precarious, tottering, unbalanced, shifting
OLD instable, tickle
3 *emotionally/mentally unstable*
deranged, insane, mad, disturbed, unsound, unhinged, off balance
OLD instable
COLLOQ. crazy, nuts, nutty, nutty as a fruitcake, barmy, bonkers, batty, crackers, dippy, daffy, loopy, off your head, wrong in the head, off the wall, out to lunch, round the bend, round the twist, having bats in the belfry
SLANG bananas, loony, off your rocker, off your trolley, needing your head examined, having a screw/tile loose, having lost your marbles, meshuga, mental
E3 1 stable **2** steady **3** stable, sane

unsteady *adj*
unstable, wobbly, shaky, rickety, doddery, insecure, unsafe, treacherous, precarious, tottering, unreliable, inconstant, irregular, flickering
COLLOQ. *Aust* warby
E3 steady, firm, stable

unstinting *adj*
abounding, abundant, ample, bountiful, full, generous, large, lavish, liberal, plentiful, profuse, ungrudging, unsparing
FORMAL munificent, prodigal
E3 grudging, mean

unstoppable *adj*
unrelenting, unremitting, unending, unceasing, undying, without a let-up, inevitable, unavoidable

unsubstantiated *adj*
unconfirmed, debatable, dubious, questionable, disputable, unestablished, unproved, unproven, unsupported, unverified
FORMAL unattested, uncorroborated
E3 proved, proven

unsuccessful *adj*
failed, lost, abortive, vain, futile, useless, ineffective, unavailing, miscarried, fruitless, unproductive, unprofitable, sterile, luckless, unlucky, unfortunate, losing, beaten, defeated, frustrated, thwarted, fumbled, bungled
FORMAL ineffectual
COLLOQ. going down like a lead balloon
E3 successful, effective, fortunate, winning

unsuitable *adj*
inappropriate, inapt, unsuited, unfit, unacceptable, out of place, improper, incompatible
FORMAL unseemly, unbecoming, incongruous, inapposite, infelicitous, malapropos
E3 suitable, appropriate

unsullied *adj*
untainted, unspotted, spotless, unstained, stainless, untarnished, unblemished, uncorrupted, undefiled, unspoiled, unsoiled, untouched, perfect, clean, pure, immaculate, intact, unblackened
FORMAL pristine
E3 dirty, stained

unsung *adj*
unhonoured, unpraised, unacknowledged, uncelebrated, unhailed, unacclaimed, unknown, unrecognized, overlooked, disregarded, neglected, forgotten, unknown, anonymous, obscure
E3 honoured, famous, renowned

unsure *adj*
1 *unsure of yourself*
uncertain, hesitant, insecure, lacking self-confidence, tentative, doubtful, dubious, suspicious, sceptical, unconvinced, unpersuaded, undecided
2 *unsure about what to do*
undecided, uncertain, unknown, ambivalent, doubtful, hesitant, dithering, equivocating, wavering, irresolute, uncommitted, indefinite, vague
COLLOQ. in two minds
E3 1 confident, sure, certain **2** sure, certain, decided

unsurpassed *adj*
surpassing, supreme, transcendent, unbeaten, unexcelled, unequalled, unparalleled, unrivalled, incomparable, unmatched, matchless, superlative, exceptional, second-to-none, state-of-the-art
E3 surpassed

unsurprising *adj*
expected, anticipated, promised, hoped-for, predicted, predictable, forecast, foreseen, forseeable, looked-for, wished-for
COLLOQ. just as you thought
E3 surprising, unexpected

unsuspecting *adj*
unwary, unaware, off guard, unconscious, trusting, trustful, unsuspicious, credulous, gullible, ingenuous, naive, innocent
E3 suspicious, knowing

unswerving *adj*
unflagging, unwavering, unfaltering, untiring, undeviating, staunch, steadfast, dedicated, devoted, steady, sure, true, firm, constant, fixed, immovable, resolute, single-minded, direct
E3 irresolute, tentative

unsympathetic *adj*
unpitying, unconcerned, uncaring, unmoved, unresponsive, indifferent, insensitive, unfeeling, cold, heartless, pitiless, soulless, hard-hearted, hard-faced, harsh, callous, cruel, inhuman, unkind, hard, stony, hostile, antagonistic
E3 sympathetic, compassionate

unsystematic *adj*
unmethodical, unco-ordinated, irregular, disorganized, unorganized, unstructured, unplanned, disorderly, untidy, haphazard, illogical, confused, muddled, jumbled, chaotic, indiscriminate, random, slapdash, sloppy, shambolic
E3 logical, systematic

untamed *adj*
wild, fierce, savage, undomesticated, unmellowed, untameable, barbarous
FORMAL feral
E3 domesticated, tame

untangle *v*
disentangle, extricate, unravel, undo, resolve, solve, work out, straighten out
E3 tangle, complicate

untarnished *adj*
unblemished, unstained, stainless, unspotted, spotless, unsullied, unsoiled, unspoilt, clean, immaculate, impeccable, intact, bright, pure, burnished, shining, glowing, polished, unimpeachable
FORMAL pristine
E3 tarnished, blemished

untenable adj

indefensible, unreasonable, unmaintainable, unsound, unjustifiable, inexcusable, insupportable, unsustainable, flawed, illogical, fallacious, rocky, shaky
OLD intenable
≠ tenable, sound

unthinkable adj

inconceivable, unimaginable, unheard-of, unbelievable, incredible, impossible, improbable, unlikely, implausible, unreasonable, illogical, absurd, preposterous, outrageous, shocking, staggering

unthinking adj

thoughtless, inconsiderate, insensitive, tactless, indiscreet, undiplomatic, unkind, rude, impolite, heedless, careless, negligent, rash, impulsive, instinctive, involuntary, unconscious, automatic, mechanical
COLLOQ. knee-jerk
≠ considerate, conscious

unthinkingly adv

thoughtlessly, inconsiderately, insensitively, unfeelingly, tactlessly, undiplomatically, indiscreetly, impolitely, rudely, inattentively, foolishly, stupidly, carelessly, recklessly, rashly
≠ thoughtfully, considerately, carefully

untidily adv

messily, disorderly, scruffily, dirtily, chaotically, unsystematically, shambolically, sluttishly, topsy-turvily
COLLOQ. sloppily, like a dog's breakfast/dinner
≠ tidily, neatly

untidy adj

messy, cluttered, disorderly, muddled, jumbled, unsystematic, chaotic, haywire, disorganized, shambolic, topsy-turvy, dirty, scruffy, bedraggled, rumpled, dishevelled, foul, unkempt, slovenly, slipshod, tatty, slatternly, sluttish
COLLOQ. sloppy, higgledy-piggledy, ratty, raunchy
≠ tidy, neat

untie v

undo, unfasten, unhitch, unknot, unbind, unwrap, free, release, loose, loosen
≠ tie, fasten

until

♦ *prep, conj*
1 *work until six o'clock*
till, to, up till, up to, up to the time, as late as
2 *not until the spring*
before, prior to, before the coming of, earlier than

untimely adj

early, premature, unseasonable, ill-timed, inopportune, inconvenient, awkward, unsuitable, inappropriate, unfortunate
FORMAL inauspicious, infelicitous, malapropos
≠ timely, opportune

untiring adj

unflagging, unfaltering, tireless, indefatigable, dogged, persevering, persistent, tenacious, determined, resolute, devoted, dedicated, constant, incessant, unceasing, steady, staunch, unfailing
FORMAL unremitting
≠ inconstant, wavering

untold adj

1 *cause untold damage*
indescribable, unimaginable, inconceivable, inexpressible, unutterable
2 COUNTLESS, uncounted, unnumbered, unreckoned, incalculable, innumerable, uncountable, infinite, measureless, immeasurable, boundless, inexhaustible, undreamed-of, unimaginable

untouched adj

unharmed, undamaged, unimpaired, unhurt, uninjured, unscathed, safe, intact, unchanged, unaltered, unaffected, unimpressed, unstirred
≠ damaged, affected

untoward adj

unfortunate, troublesome, inconvenient, annoying, adverse, unfavourable, unexpected, unsuitable, unfitting, untimely, vexatious, irritating, worrying, awkward, amiss, disastrous, improper, contrary, unlucky, inappropriate, ominous, ill-timed
FORMAL inauspicious, indecorous, inopportune, unbecoming, unpropitious, unseemly
≠ suitable, auspicious

untrained adj

unskilled, untaught, unschooled, uneducated, inexperienced, unpractised, unqualified, amateur, unprofessional, inexpert, incompetent
≠ trained, expert

untried adj

untested, unproved, unestablished, experimental, exploratory, new, novel, innovative, innovatory
≠ tried, tested, proven

untroubled adj

unworried, unconcerned, undisturbed, unexcited, unstirred, unflustered, unruffled, steady, calm, composed, peaceful, impassive, cool, placid, serene, tranquil
FORMAL unperturbed
COLLOQ. unflappable
≠ anxious, troubled

untrue adj

1 FALSE, fallacious, deceptive, misleading, wrong, incorrect, inaccurate, inexact, mistaken, erroneous, fabricated, inauthentic, unofficial, legendary, mythical
COLLOQ. made-up, trumped-up
2 UNFAITHFUL, disloyal, untrustworthy, dishonest, deceitful, fraudulent, untruthful
FORMAL perfidious
COLLOQ. two-faced, two-timing
≠ **1** true, correct **2** faithful, honest

untrustworthy adj

dishonest, deceitful, untruthful, disloyal, unfaithful, faithless, treacherous, false, untrue, dishonourable, capricious, fickle, fly-by-night, unreliable, untrusty
FORMAL duplicitous
COLLOQ. two-faced
≠ trustworthy, reliable

untruth n

lie, story, tale, fiction, invention, fabrication, falsehood, lying, untruthfulness, deceit, perjury
COLLOQ. fib, whopper, porky, tall story, made-up story, cock-and-bull story
SLANG (*vulgar*) bullshit, crap
≠ truth

untruthful adj

lying, deceitful, dishonest, hypocritical, insincere, false, untrue, fictional, fabricated, invented, erroneous, fallacious
FORMAL mendacious, unveracious
COLLOQ. crooked, two-faced
≠ truthful, honest

untutored adj

untrained, unschooled, unpractised, uneducated, unlearned, unversed, inexperienced, inexpert, illiterate, ignorant, unrefined, unsophisticated, simple, artless, unlessoned
≠ educated, trained

untwine v

unravel, uncoil, untwist, unwind, disentwine
≠ twine, wind

untwist v
uncoil, unravel, untwine, unwind
◨ twist

unused adj
1 LEFT OVER, remaining, surplus, extra, spare, available, new, fresh, blank, clean, untouched, unexploited, untapped, unemployed, idle
2 UNACCUSTOMED, unacquainted, unfamiliar, unpractised, inexperienced
FORMAL unwonted
◨ **1, 2** used

unusual adj
uncommon, rare, unfamiliar, strange, odd, curious, peculiar, queer, bizarre, weird, unconventional, unorthodox, irregular, abnormal, atypical, phenomenal, extraordinary, out of the ordinary, out of the way, remarkable, special, exceptional, different, anomalous, surprising, unexpected, unprecedented, eccentric, exotic; *Scot* unco
OLD (*Spenser*) unacquainted
FORMAL singular
COLLOQ. offbeat, freaky, freakish, kinky
◨ usual, normal, ordinary
See Synonym nuances panel at **strange**.

unutterable adj
unspeakable, indescribable, unimaginable, extreme, overwhelming, ineffable
FORMAL egregious, nefandous

unvarnished adj
unembellished, unadorned, straightforward, undisguised, simple, sincere, plain, candid, frank, bare, naked, honest, pure, sheer, stark
◨ disguised, embellished, exaggerated

unveil v
uncover, expose, lay open, bare, lay bare, unmask, betray, reveal, disclose, divulge, bring to light, bring out into the open, make known, discover
COLLOQ. take the lid off
◨ cover, hide

unwanted adj
undesired, uninvited, unwelcome, outcast, rejected, discarded, unrequired, unneeded, unnecessary, surplus, extra, superfluous, redundant, useless
TECHNICAL otiose
FORMAL unsolicited
◨ wanted, needed, necessary

unwarranted adj
unjustified, undeserved, unprovoked, uncalled-for, gratuitous, unnecessary, groundless, unreasonable, unjust, wrong, inexcusable, unjustifiable, indefensible
◨ warranted, justifiable, deserved

unwary adj
unguarded, off guard, incautious, imprudent, careless, indiscreet, thoughtless, unthinking, heedless, reckless, rash, hasty
◨ wary, cautious

unwashed adj
dirty, grubby, filthy, grimy, mucky, soiled, greasy, unclean, unhygienic, foul, messy, muddy, dusty, sooty, polluted, slimy, squalid, insanitary, miry, scruffy, shabby, sullied, stained, defiled, tarnished, clouded, cloudy, black, dark, dull, grungy; *dialect* clarty, grufted; *Aust & NZ* scungy
COLLOQ. grotty, yucky, flea-bitten, cruddy, manky; *Aust & NZ* chatty
◨ clean

▪ **the (great) unwashed**
the masses, the crowd(s), the herd, the mob, the lower/working class(es), the common people, the proletariat, the rabble, the hoi polloi, the rank and file, riff-raff
COLLOQ. plebs

unwavering adj
unswerving, unshak(e)able, unfaltering, undeviating, unshaken, untiring, unflagging, unquestioning, staunch, steadfast, steady, sturdy, dedicated, consistent, determined, resolute, single-minded, tenacious
◨ wavering, fickle

unwelcome adj
1 UNWANTED, undesirable, unpopular, uninvited, excluded, rejected
2 *unwelcome news*
unpleasant, disagreeable, upsetting, worrying, distasteful, unpalatable, unacceptable
◨ **1** welcome, desirable **2** pleasant

unwell adj
ill, sick, poorly, off-colour, ailing, sickly, unhealthy, unfit, rough, bad, queer
FORMAL indisposed
COLLOQ. in a bad way, dicky, out of sorts, under the weather, run down, rough, groggy, like death warmed up; *Aust* warby
◨ well, healthy

unwholesome adj
unhealthy, bad, harmful, demoralizing, evil, wicked, immoral, degrading, depraving, corrupting, perverting, sickly, tainted, unhygienic, poisonous, insanitary, innutritious, pasty, noxious, wan, pale, pallid, anaemic
FORMAL insalubrious, insalutary
COLLOQ. junk
◨ wholesome; *formal* salubrious

unwieldy adj
unmanageable, inconvenient, awkward, clumsy, ungainly, bulky, massive, hefty, hulking, weighty, ponderous, cumbersome
FORMAL incommodious
◨ handy, dainty

unwilling adj
reluctant, disinclined, indisposed, hesitant, resistant, opposed, averse, loath, slow, unenthusiastic, grudging, backward
OLD repugnant
FORMAL loathful
COLLOQ. not having any of
◨ willing, enthusiastic

unwillingness n
reluctance, disinclination, indisposition, hesitancy, slowness, lack of enthusiasm, backwardness
FORMAL loathfulness, nolition
◨ enthusiasm, willingness

unwind v
1 UNROLL, unreel, unwrap, undo, uncoil, untwist, unravel, disentangle
2 RELAX, wind down, calm down
COLLOQ. take it/things easy, let yourself go, make yourself at home, let your hair down, put your feet up, hang loose, cool it, chill (out), veg (out)
◨ **1** wind, roll

unwise adj
ill-advised, inadvisable, inexpedient, short-sighted, improvident, ill-considered, ill-judged, foolish, stupid, silly, senseless, thoughtless, indiscreet, imprudent, foolhardy, irresponsible, rash, reckless
FORMAL impolitic, injudicious
◨ wise, sensible, prudent

unwitting adj
1 UNAWARE, unknowing, unsuspecting, unthinking, unconscious, involuntary
2 INADVERTENT, accidental, chance, unintentional, unintended, unplanned
◨ **1** knowing **2** conscious, deliberate

unwonted *adj*
unusual, uncommon, unfamiliar, unexpected, unheard-of, strange, rare, peculiar, infrequent, exceptional, extraordinary, unaccustomed, uncustomary, atypical
FORMAL singular
🖃 wonted, usual

unworldly *adj*
1 NAIVE, visionary, idealistic, impractical, unsophisticated, inexperienced, innocent, gullible, ingenuous
COLLOQ. green
2 SPIRITUAL, transcendental, metaphysical, otherworldly, extra-terrestrial
🖃 **1** sophisticated, worldly **2** worldly, materialistic

unworried *adj*
untroubled, undismayed, unruffled, unabashed, composed, collected
FORMAL unperturbed
🖃 worried, anxious

unworthy *adj*
undeserving, inferior, ineligible, unsuitable, inappropriate, unfitting, improper, unprofessional, shameful, disgraceful, dishonourable, disreputable, discreditable, ignoble, base, contemptible, despicable
FORMAL unbecoming, unseemly, unbefitting, incongruous
🖃 worthy, commendable

unwritten *adj*
verbal, oral, word-of-mouth, unrecorded, unpenned, tacit, implicit, understood, accepted, recognized, traditional, customary, conventional
🖃 written, recorded

unyielding *adj*
unrelenting, uncompromising, relentless, unwavering, unbending, immovable, inflexible, hardline, adamant, steadfast, stubborn, obstinate, tough, firm, determined, resolute, staunch, rigid, solid
FORMAL implacable, inexorable, intractable, intransigent, obdurate
🖃 yielding, flexible

unzip *v*
undo, loosen, open, free, release, unhook, unwind, separate, detach

up-and-coming *adj*
promising, ambitious, eager, assertive, enterprising
COLLOQ. go-getting, pushing

upbeat *adj*
positive, buoyant, hopeful, optimistic, encouraging, favourable, promising, forward-looking, bright, cheerful, heartening, cheery, rosy
COLLOQ. bullish
🖃 downbeat, gloomy

upbraid *v*
reprimand, admonish, rebuke, reprove, reproach, scold, chide, criticize, censure
FORMAL castigate, berate
COLLOQ. *Aust & NZ* go crook on/at
🖃 praise, commend

upbringing *n*
bringing-up, raising, rearing, breeding, parenting, care, nurture, cultivation, tending, education, training, instruction, teaching

upcoming *adj*
imminent, impending, forthcoming, in the offing, (fast) approaching, coming, on the way, near, close, looming, in the air, at hand, about to happen, almost upon you, on the horizon
COLLOQ. round the corner
🖃 distant, remote, far-off

update *v*
modernize, revise, amend, correct, renew, renovate, revamp, upgrade

up-front *adj, adv*
♦ *adj*
1 FRANK, direct, open, honest, truthful, sincere, genuine, candid, blunt, free, plain, plain-spoken, forthright, straight, straightforward, downright, hard-hitting, outspoken, explicit, bluff
COLLOQ. straight from the shoulder
2 an up-front payment
advance, initial, first, introductory, primary
🖃 **1** insincere, evasive
♦ *adv*
in advance, initially, beforehand, early, earlier, sooner

upgrade *v*
improve, make better, better, modernize, enhance, promote, advance, elevate, raise
FORMAL ameliorate
🖃 downgrade, demote

upheaval *n*
disruption, disturbance, upset, chaos, confusion, disorder, turmoil, revolution, overthrow
COLLOQ. shake-up

uphill *adj*
hard, difficult, arduous, tough, taxing, strenuous, laborious, tiring, wearisome, exhausting, gruelling, punishing, burdensome, onerous
🖃 easy, downhill

uphold *v*
support, maintain, confirm, keep, hold to, stand by, defend, champion, advocate, promote, back, endorse, sustain, strengthen, justify, vindicate
FORMAL fortify
🖃 abandon, reject

upkeep *n*
1 MAINTENANCE, preservation, conservation, care, running, repair, support, sustenance, subsistence, keep
2 RUNNING COSTS, expenditure, outlay, overheads, operating costs, oncosts, expenses
🖃 **1** neglect

uplift *v, n*
♦ *v*
improve, better, boost, upgrade, advance, enlighten, exalt, inspire, elate, lift, elevate, raise, hoist, heave, refine, cultivate, edify, civilize
FORMAL ameliorate
♦ *n*
improvement, lift, enlightenment, enrichment, advancement, enhancement, refinement, edification, boost, cultivation
FORMAL betterment

up-market *adj*
expensive, high, good-quality, superior, prestige, prestigious, respectful, reputable, excellent, first-class, first-rate, high-class, exclusive, prime, quality, prize, choice, select, fine, de luxe, admirable, distinguished, exceptional, unrivalled, par excellence
COLLOQ. top-notch, top-flight
🖃 down-market, inferior, average

upper *adj*
higher, loftier, superior, greater, senior, top, topmost, uppermost, high, elevated, exalted, eminent, important
🖃 lower, inferior, junior

■ **upper hand**
advantage, dominance, control, sway, supremacy, superiority, mastery, domination, dominion
FORMAL ascendancy
COLLOQ. edge

upper-class *adj*
aristocratic, noble, well-bred, well-born, high-born, high-class, patrician, blue-blooded, exclusive, élite
COLLOQ. swanky, top-drawer
⊟ humble, working-class

uppermost *adj*
highest, loftiest, top, topmost, greatest, supreme, first, primary, foremost, leading, principal, main, major, chief, dominant, predominant, paramount, pre-eminent
⊟ lowest

uppity *adj*
arrogant, self-important, conceited, presumptuous, snobbish, supercilious, impertinent, affected, assuming, overweening, bumptious, cocky
COLLOQ. bigheaded, hoity-toity, stuck-up, swanky, toffee-nosed
⊟ unassertive, diffident

upright *adj*
1 VERTICAL, perpendicular, erect, straight, at right angles, sheer, steep
2 RIGHTEOUS, good, virtuous, upstanding, noble, worthy, decent, respectable, reputable, honourable, moral, ethical, principled, high-minded, incorruptible, honest, trustworthy
⊟ 1 horizontal, flat 2 dishonest

uprising *n*
rebellion, revolt, mutiny, rising, overthrow, insurgence, insurrection, revolution, coup d'état, putsch

uproar *n*
noise, din, racket, hubbub, hullabaloo, brouhaha, pandemonium, tumult, turmoil, turbulence, commotion, confusion, disorder, mayhem, bedlam, clamour, outcry, furore, riot, rumpus, fracas, ruction, hell, pandemonium, rough music, flaw, randan, *émeute; Scot* collieshangie, dirdum, rammy, reird; *N Am* katzenjammer
OLD garboil

uproarious *adj*
hilarious, riotous, rip-roaring, side-splitting, hysterical, boisterous, noisy, loud, rollicking, rowdy, confused, clamorous, deafening, wild, unrestrained
COLLOQ. killing, rib-tickling
⊟ quiet

uproot *v*
pull up, rip up, root out, weed out, remove, displace, eradicate, destroy, wipe out

upset *v, n, adj*
♦ *v*
1 DISTRESS, grieve, dismay, trouble, worry, agitate, disturb, hurt, bother, fluster, ruffle, sadden, discompose, shake (up), unnerve, disconcert, put out, confuse, disorganize, mess about, disrupt, disquiet, break up, take on, irritate, jangle, overset; *Scot* coup the cran
FORMAL perturb
COLLOQ. chew up, eat, play havoc with, ruffle someone's feathers, throw a spanner in the works
SLANG piss off; *N Am* discombobulate
2 TIP, spill, overturn, capsize, topple, knock over, tumble over, overthrow, destabilize, unsteady
OLD renverse
♦ *n*
1 TROUBLE, worry, agitation, distress, disturbance, bother, disruption, upheaval, reverse, surprise, shock, purl; *Scot* coup, upcast
FORMAL perturbation
COLLOQ. shake-up
2 *stomach upset*
disorder, complaint, illness, sickness, ailment
FORMAL malady
COLLOQ. bug

♦ *adj*
distressed, grieved, aggrieved, hurt, annoyed, dismayed, troubled, worried, agitated, disturbed, unsettled, discomposed, put out, flustered, bothered, shaken, disconcerted, confused, jealous, in a bad way
FORMAL perturbed
COLLOQ. in a state, het up, uptight, worked up, choked, gutted, shattered
SLANG pissed off

upsetting *adj*
distressing, worrying, alarming, disturbing, unsettling, off-putting, disconcerting, frightening, startling
FORMAL perturbing
⊟ comforting

upshot *n*
result, consequence, outcome, issue, end, conclusion, finish, culmination, dénouement
COLLOQ. pay-off

upside down
♦ *adj, adv*
inverted, upturned, up-ended, wrong way up, wrong side up, upset, overturned, disordered, in disarray, muddled, jumbled, confused, topsy-turvy, chaotic
COLLOQ. messed up
▪ **turn upside down**
disturb, upset, disorganize, make untidy, demolish, overthrow, turn inside out
COLLOQ. mess up

upstage *v*
outshine, outclass, outstrip, outdo, overshadow, transcend, eclipse, surpass, beat, best, excel, dwarf, outrank, top, put in the shade, put to shame

upstanding *adj*
upright, honest, honourable, strong, true, trustworthy, ethical, moral, principled, incorruptible, erect, good, virtuous, firm, four-square
⊟ untrustworthy

upstart *n*
social climber, arriviste, parvenu, *nouveau riche*, nobody

upsurge *n*
increase, rise, growth, surge, upturn, gain, boost, addition, increment, advance, step-up, build-up, intensification, heightening, development, enlargement, extension, expansion, spread, proliferation, escalation, mushrooming, snowballing, rocketing, skyrocketing
FORMAL augmentation
COLLOQ. hike
⊟ decrease, reduction, decline

uptight *adj*
on edge, tense, uneasy, anxious, hung-up, irritated, prickly, nervy
COLLOQ. edgy
⊟ calm, cool, relaxed

upturn *n*
revival, recovery, upsurge, upswing, rise, increase, boost, improvement, betterment
FORMAL amelioration
⊟ downturn, drop

upward *adj*
ascending, rising, going/moving up, uphill
⊟ downward
▪ **upwards of**
over, above, higher than, exceeding, more than, in excess of
⊟ less than

urban *adj*
town, city, inner-city, metropolitan, municipal, civic, built-up, megalopolitan
FORMAL oppidan
⊟ country, rural

urbane

⚠ **urban** or **urbane**?
Urban means 'of a town': *urban development; urban life; urban violence. Urbane* means 'cultured, elegant, refined': *urbane wit.*

urbane *adj*
cultivated, suave, sophisticated, refined, polished, mannerly, civilized, courteous, cultured, debonair, well-bred, well-mannered, civil, elegant, smooth
F3 gauche, uncouth, inurbane

⚠ **urbane** or **urban**?
See panel at **urban**.

urbanity *n*
refinement, cultivation, sophistication, suavity, mannerliness, polish, ease, smoothness, grace, elegance, culture, civility, courtesy, charm, worldliness
OLD eutrapelia
F3 awkwardness, gaucheness

urchin *n*
brat, rascal, rogue, imp, guttersnipe, ragamuffin, waif, gamin, street Arab, kid; *Scot* hurcheon
OLD townskip
OLD SLANG mudlark

urge *v, n*
♦ *v*
1 PERSUADE, encourage, press, push, incite, drive, impel, prod, goad, spur, constrain, compel, force, hasten, induce, instigate, stimulate
COLLOQ. egg on
2 BEG, entreat, appeal, implore, plead
FORMAL beseech
3 ADVISE, counsel, recommend, advocate, encourage
FORMAL exhort
F3 1 discourage, dissuade, deter, hinder
♦ *n*
desire, wish, inclination, fancy, longing, yearning, impulse, compulsion, need, impetus, drive, eagerness
COLLOQ. itch, yen
F3 disinclination

Synonym nuances
verb sense 1
You can use **persuade** of bringing someone round to a particular way of thinking, and **encourage** of inspiring someone to do something, but **press** and **push, compel** and **force** imply the exertion of strong pressure: *he was pushed into the business by parental desire.*
   Drive and **impel** are more suggestive of being firmly guided to a particular action: *driven by hunger, he went hunting,* while **prod** and **spur** imply arousal from inactivity: *he prodded me to start writing the show.*
Goad, however, suggests that an irritant is acting as a stimulus: *the crowd goaded the players with their chants.*
Incite also suggests rousing into action, but often a negative one: *emotive speakers incited people to riot.*
   You can use **constrain** to suggest that restrictions have a bearing: *decisions constrained by financial difficulty,* unlike **hasten**, which is more suggestive of increased momentum: *ill health hastened his retirement.* **Induce**, on the other hand, returns to the idea of providing an incentive, albeit a less forceful one, while **instigate** is appropriate where something is acting as a catalyst for a particular action or event: *the rise in violent crime instigated tougher jail sentences.* **Stimulate** has more to do with increasing interest: *the lowering of prices stimulated consumer demand.*

---

urgency *n*
hurry, haste, pressure, stress, priority, importance, seriousness, extremity, gravity, imperativeness, need, necessity

OLD instance
FORMAL exigency, importunity

urgent *adj*
1 PRESSING, immediate, instant, top-priority, emergency, important, critical, necessary, vital, essential, crucial, acute, imperative, prior
OLD importune
FORMAL exigent, emergent
COLLOQ. crying out for..., dire
2 COMPELLING, persuasive, earnest, serious, grave, eager, insistent, persistent, strident, strenuous
F3 1 unimportant

urinate *v*
pass water, make water, relieve yourself, answer the call of nature, be caught/taken short, wet, stale
OLD urine
FORMAL micturate
COLLOQ. leak, pee, piddle, spend a penny, tinkle, wee, tiddle, take a leak, widdle
OLD COLLOQ. ease yourself
SLANG (*vulgar*) piss, slash

usable *adj*
working, operational, serviceable, functional, fit to use, practical, exploitable, available, current, valid
F3 unusable, useless

usage *n*
1 TREATMENT, handling, management, control, running, operation, employment, application, use
2 TRADITION, custom, practice, habit, convention, etiquette, rule, regulation, form, routine, procedure, way, method, law, formalism, institution, usance
TECHNICAL practic
FORMAL mode, consuetude
3 *contemporary English usage*
style, form, meaning, way of speaking/writing, phraseology, expression, idiom, parlance, terminology
F3 1 abuse, mistreatment, maltreatment, misusage **3** abusage, misusage

use *v, n*
♦ *v*
1 UTILIZE, employ, make use of, exercise, service, practise, operate, work, apply, ply, wield, handle, deal with, treat, manoeuvre, enjoy, resort to, draw on, take advantage of, bring into play, put to use
2 EXPLOIT, manipulate, take advantage of, impose on, misuse, abuse, take liberties with
COLLOQ. cash in on, bleed, milk, wrap/twist someone round your little finger
3 CONSUME, exhaust, get through, go through, expend, spend, waste
♦ *n*
1 USAGE, application, employment, operation, exercise, utilization, manipulation, exploitation
2 USEFULNESS, value, worth, profit, service, advantage, benefit, good, avail, help, point, object, end, purpose
3 *have the use of the car*
right, permission, privilege, ability
4 EXPLOITATION, manipulation, imposition, mistreatment, misuse, abuse
5 NEED, cause, occasion, necessity, demand, call
▪ **use up**
finish, exhaust, drain, sap, deplete, consume, devour, absorb, waste, squander, fritter
▪ **used to**
accustomed to, adjusted to, in the habit of, familiar with, acclimatized to, given to, prone to, practised in
FORMAL habituated to, inured to, wont to
COLLOQ. at home with, no stranger to

used *adj*
second-hand, cast-off, hand-me-down, nearly-new, worn,

dog-eared, soiled; *N Am* pre-owned
🔁 unused, new, fresh

useful *adj*
1 CONVENIENT, handy, all-purpose, practical, effective, productive, fruitful, profitable, valuable, worthwhile, rewarding, advantageous, beneficial, helpful, functional, general-purpose
COLLOQ. nifty
2 SKILLED, proficient, practised, experienced, competent, expert, able, skilful, handy
🔁 **1** useless, ineffective, worthless

usefulness *n*
utility, use, value, worth, profit, advantage, benefit, good, help, avail, service, convenience, practicality, functionality, efficiency, fitness, serviceableness
FORMAL efficacy

useless *adj*
1 FUTILE, fruitless, unproductive, vain, idle, unavailing, to no avail, hopeless, unhelpful, pointless, worthless, unusable, unprofitable, broken-down, unworkable, impractical
FORMAL ineffectual, inefficacious
COLLOQ. clapped-out, kaput; *Aust* bung
2 INCOMPETENT, ineffective, incapable, inefficient, bad, weak
COLLOQ. hopeless, awful, terrible, botched, lousy, pathetic, rop(e)y, a load of rubbish/garbage
SLANG half-arsed
🔁 **1** useful, helpful, effective **2** good

uselessness *n*
futility, hopelessness, impracticality, incompetence, ineffectiveness, ineptitude, idleness
FORMAL ineffectuality, inutility
🔁 effectiveness, usefulness

usher *n, v*
◆ *n*
usherette, doorkeeper, attendant, escort, guide
◆ *v*
escort, accompany, conduct, lead, direct, guide, show, pilot, steer
▪ **usher in**
herald, inaugurate, initiate, introduce, launch, precede, announce, ring in, mark the start of, pave the way for

usual *adj*
normal, typical, stock, standard, regular, routine, habitual, customary, conventional, traditional, orthodox, accepted, recognized, accustomed, established, familiar, common, everyday, general, ordinary, average, unexceptional, expected, predictable
FORMAL wonted
🔁 unusual, strange, rare

usually *adv*
normally, generally, as a rule, ordinarily, typically, traditionally, regularly, routinely, habitually, commonly, by and large, on the whole, mainly, chiefly, mostly, for the most part, on average, in the main
COLLOQ. nine times out of ten
🔁 exceptionally

usurer *n*
extortionist, money-lender, Shylock; *Irish* gombeen-man; *N Am* note-shaver
COLLOQ. loan-shark
SLANG (*offensive*) Jew
OLD SLANG gripe

usurp *v*
take over, assume, arrogate, seize, take, take possession of, annex, appropriate, commandeer, steal

usury *n*
money-lending, extortion, interest; *Irish* gombeen
OLD (*Shakesp*) excess

utensil *n*
tool, implement, instrument, device, contrivance, gadget, apparatus, appliance
See also panels at **cutlery; domestic appliances; kitchen utensils.**

utilitarian *adj*
functional, practical, convenient, serviceable, sensible, useful, unpretentious, effective, efficient, pragmatic, down-to-earth, lowly
🔁 decorative, impractical

utility *n*
usefulness, use, value, worth, profit, advantage, benefit, good, help, avail, service, convenience, practicality, efficiency, fitness, serviceableness
FORMAL efficacy

utilize *v*
use, employ, make use of, put to use, resort to, take advantage of, turn to account, exploit, adapt

utmost *adj, n*
◆ *adj*
1 *with the utmost care*
extreme, maximum, most, greatest, highest, supreme, paramount
2 FARTHEST, furthest, furthermost, remotest, outermost, ultimate, final, last
◆ *n*
best, hardest, most, maximum, top, peak

Utopia *n*
paradise, Eden, Garden of Eden, bliss, Elysium, heaven, heaven on earth, Shangri-la
COLLOQ. seventh heaven
🔁 cacotopia, dystopia

Utopian *adj*
ideal, idealistic, illusory, imaginary, perfect, visionary, wishful, fanciful, fantastic, airy, dream, romantic, unworkable, impractical, Elysian
FORMAL chimerical
🔁 cacotopian, dystopian

utter¹ *v*
not utter a word
speak, say, voice, vocalize, verbalize, put into words, express, articulate, enunciate, sound, pronounce, deliver, state, declare, announce, proclaim, tell, reveal, divulge

utter² *adj*
to my utter amazement
absolute, complete, total, entire, thoroughgoing, thorough, out-and-out, downright, pure, sheer, stark, arrant, unmitigated, unqualified, positive, categorical, perfect, consummate

utterance *n*
statement, remark, comment, opinion, expression, word, articulation, delivery, speech, declaration, announcement, proclamation, pronouncement, enunciation

utterly *adv*
absolutely, completely, totally, fully, entirely, wholly, thoroughly, downright, perfectly, categorically, pure, stark, to the wide; *dialect* rank
OLD *N Am* plumb
COLLOQ. dead

U-turn *n*
about-turn, volte-face, reversal, backtrack

vacancy *n*
opportunity, opening, position, post, job, place, room, situation

vacant *adj*
1 EMPTY, unoccupied, unfilled, free, available, void, not in use, unused, deserted, abandoned, uninhabited
2 BLANK, expressionless, vacuous, inane, poker-faced, straight-faced, deadpan, impassive, inattentive, absent, absent-minded, unthinking, dreamy
⊟ 1 occupied, engaged, in use, busy

vacate *v*
leave, depart, evacuate, abandon, withdraw
COLLOQ. quit

vacation *n*
holiday, trip, leave, leave of absence, time off, break, rest, recess, furlough

vaccinate *v*
inoculate, immunize, protect, syringe
COLLOQ. jab; *Scot* jag

vaccination *n*
injection, inoculation, immunization, dose
COLLOQ. jab, shot

vacillate *v*
waver, hesitate, fluctuate, sway, oscillate, keep changing your mind, haver, temporize, teeter, wobble, dither, halt, back and fill, go back and forth, whiffle
OLD wave
FORMAL tergiversate
COLLOQ. shilly-shally, blow hot and cold, waffle

vacillating *adj*
wavering, hesitant, irresolute, uncertain, unresolved, shuffling, oscillating
COLLOQ. shilly-shallying, blowing hot and cold, waffling
⊟ resolute, unhesitating

vacillation *n*
wavering, inconstancy, hesitancy, hesitation, fluctuation, irresolution, indecision, indecisiveness, unsteadiness, temporization, teetering, wobbling, dithering
FORMAL tergiversation
COLLOQ. shilly-shallying, blowing hot and cold

vacuity *n*
emptiness, space, nothingness, blankness, vacuousness, vacuum, void, apathy, inanity, incomprehension, incuriosity
FORMAL incognizance

vacuous *adj*
empty, blank, vacant, void, unfilled, inane, unintelligent, stupid, uncomprehending, incurious, apathetic, idle

vacuum *n*
emptiness, void, nothingness, hollowness, vacuity, space, chasm, gap
FORMAL lacuna
⊟ *technical* plenum

vagabond *n*
vagrant, tramp, wanderer, wayfarer, down-and-out, hobo, rascal, beggar, rover, runabout, itinerant, migrant, outcast,

nomad, piker, clochard, floater, straggle, stroller; *dialect* walker; *Scot* caird, gangrel, hallan-shaker, landloper, rinthereout, (*derog*) tinkler; *N Am* hobo; *Aust* sundowner
OLD cursitor, rogue, scatterling, truant, vagrom
COLLOQ. loser, knight of the road, Weary Willie
SLANG bum, dosser, gook, toerag; *N Am* dingbat

vagary *n*
fancy, notion, prank, quirk, whim, whimsy, humour, crotchet; *Scot* megrim
FORMAL caprice

vagina *n*
TECHNICAL vulva, introitus
SLANG (*taboo*) cunt, pussy, fanny, box, hole, muff, crack, beaver, punani

vagrancy *n*
wandering, travelling, shiftlessness, rootlessness, unsettledness, nomadism, itinerancy, homelessness

vagrant *n, adj*
◆ *n*
tramp, wanderer, drifter, itinerant, stroller, hobo, beggar; *Scot* gangrel
COLLOQ. rolling stone
SLANG bum
◆ *adj*
wandering, vagabond, travelling, shiftless, rootless, unsettled, roaming, roving, nomadic, itinerant, homeless

vague *adj*
1 ILL-DEFINED, blurred, unfocused, out of focus, indistinct, hazy, dim, faint, shadowy, foggy, misty, fuzzy, woozy, nebulous, obscure
FORMAL amorphous, transcendental
2 INDEFINITE, imprecise, unclear, unsure, uncertain, undefined, undetermined, unspecific, unspecified, rough, sketchy, incomplete, approximate, generalized, general, inexact, ambiguous, evasive, loose, lax, woolly, woolly-minded; *dialect* yonderly
FORMAL indeterminate
⊟ 1 clear **2** definite, precise, specific

vaguely *adv*
slightly, imprecisely, faintly, dimly, inexactly, obscurely, vacantly, absent-mindedly, distantly

vagueness *n*
unclearness, fuzziness, haziness, uncertainty, dimness, faintness, impression, notion, obscurity, imprecision, looseness, ambiguity, generality, inexactitude, woolliness
FORMAL amorphousness
⊟ clarity, precision

vain *adj*
1 *a vain attempt*
useless, worthless, futile, fruitless, pointless, unproductive, unprofitable, unavailing, hollow, groundless, empty, idle, trivial, insubstantial, unimportant, insignificant
FORMAL abortive, nugatory
2 CONCEITED, proud, haughty, self-satisfied, arrogant, self-important, self-conceited, self-glorious, egotistical, affected, pretentious, ostentatious, swaggering, narcissistic, peacockish

COLLOQ. bigheaded, swell-headed, swollen-headed, stuck-up, snooty, high and mighty
E3 1 fruitful, successful **2** modest, self-effacing

■ **in vain**
for nothing, to no avail, unsuccessfully, uselessly, fruitlessly, to no end, vainly
OLD (*Shakesp*) for vain
FORMAL ineffectually
COLLOQ. no go
E3 successfully

vainglorious *adj*
boastful, proud, conceited, vain, puffed up, bragging, crowing, cocky, swaggering, arrogant, self-flattering, egotistical
COLLOQ. bigheaded, swollen-headed, swanky
E3 modest, self-effacing, humble

vainly *adv*
for nothing, to no avail, unsuccessfully, uselessly, fruitlessly, to no end
OLD (*Shakesp*) for vain
FORMAL ineffectually
COLLOQ. no go
E3 successfully

valediction *n*
goodbye, farewell, leave-taking, adieu
COLLOQ. send-off
E3 welcome, greeting

valedictory *adj*
farewell, parting, departing, final, last

valet *n*
manservant, man, gentleman's gentleman, body servant, *valet de chambre*

valetudinarian *adj*
sickly, invalid, infirm, weakly, feeble, frail, delicate, hypochondriac, neurotic

valiant *adj*
brave, courageous, gallant, fearless, intrepid, bold, dauntless, determined, audacious, heroic, plucky, staunch, stout-hearted, lion-hearted
FORMAL indomitable, valorous
E3 cowardly, fearful, dismayed

valiantly *adv*
bravely, courageously, gallantly, fearlessly, intrepidly, boldly, dauntlessly, audaciously, heroically, pluckily, staunchly, stout-heartedly
FORMAL indomitably
E3 cowardly, fearfully

valid *adj*
1 LOGICAL, well-founded, well-grounded, reasonable, justifiable, sound, good, convincing, telling, conclusive, credible, reliable, substantial, forceful, weighty, powerful, just, meaningful
FORMAL cogent
2 OFFICIAL, legal, lawful, legitimate, authentic, effective, bona fide, genuine, binding, contractual, proper, acknowledged, licensed, accredited, formalized, consummated
TECHNICAL available; *Scot* approbated
E3 1 false, weak **2** unofficial, invalid, null and void

validate *v*
confirm, authenticate, endorse, legalize, authorize, substantiate, underwrite, ratify, certify, accredit, formalize, consummate
FORMAL attest, corroborate

validation *n*
confirmation, authentication, endorsement, authorization, ratification, accreditation, formalization
FORMAL attestation, corroboration

validity *n*
soundness, legality, lawfulness, legitimacy, foundation, grounds, justifiability, strength, power, force, weight, substance, logic, point, authority
FORMAL cogency
E3 invalidity

valley *n*
dale, vale, dell, glen, hollow, depression, slade, gulch, coomb, dean, dene, ria, slade, dingle, gill; *dialect* griff, grike; *Scot* den, heuch, strath; *Welsh* cwm

valorous *adj*
brave, bold, heroic, courageous, fearless, plucky, lion-hearted, stout-hearted, valiant, intrepid, gallant, hardy, mettlesome, dauntless, doughty, stalwart
E3 cowardly, weak

valour *n*
boldness, courage, bravery, heroism, intrepidity, lion-heartedness, fearlessness, mettle, spirit, gallantry, hardiness, doughtiness
FORMAL fortitude
E3 cowardice, weakness

valuable *adj*
1 *a valuable necklace*
precious, prized, valued, costly, expensive, dear, high-priced, treasured, cherished, priceless, estimable
COLLOQ. worth a pretty penny, worth its weight in gold
2 *valuable suggestions*
helpful, worthwhile, useful, beneficial, invaluable, constructive, fruitful, profitable, advantageous, important, serviceable, worthy, handy
E3 1 worthless **2** useless

Synonym nuances
sense 1
You can use **precious** of something of great financial or emotional value, while **prized** further implies a degree of pride involved: *his prized trophies*. **Valued**, too, suggests that something is held in esteem, while the even more expressive **treasured** and **cherished** imply great love and care: *his treasured family photographs*. **Estimable** is more suggestive of being worthy of admiration rather than emotional attachment: *a surgeon of estimable skill*.
  Other synonyms, such as **costly**, **expensive**, **dear** and **high-priced** emphasize financial value. **Priceless** is rather more emotive in that it suggests being invaluable, and therefore irreplaceable.

---

valuation *n*
evaluation, value, assessment, estimate, computation, survey
FORMAL appraisement

value *n, v*
◆ *n*
1 COST, price, rate, worth
2 WORTH, use, usefulness, utility, merit, importance, desirability, benefit, advantage, significance, good, profit, gain, avail
3 *moral values*
morals, principles, moral principles, standards, ethics
◆ *v*
1 PRIZE, appreciate, treasure, hold dear, admire, respect, esteem, cherish, set great store by
2 EVALUATE, assess, estimate, price, put a price on, survey, rate
FORMAL appraise
E3 1 disregard, neglect **2** undervalue

valued *adj*
highly regarded, esteemed, cherished, treasured, prized, respected, dear, loved, beloved

valueless *adj*
worthless, useless, pointless, meaningless, futile, unavailing, unimportant, insignificant, trivial, unusable, cheap, poor, rubbishy, trashy, trifling, paltry
FORMAL ineffectual, nugatory
SLANG naff

vamp *n*
seductress, temptress, siren, *femme fatale*, Delilah, Lorelei, Circe, enchantress, flirt, coquette, charmer

van *n*
lorry, truck, wagon, trailer, carriage, pick-up, black Maria, prison van, box van, delivery van, mailvan, furniture van, pantechnicon, camper van, Dormobile®, caravan, mobile home; *N Am* motor home, recreational vehicle, RV, Winnebago®, guard's van, freight-car, railroad car
SLANG *N Am* meat wagon

vandal *n*
hooligan, ruffian, rowdy, hoodlum, mobster, thug, tough, rough, lout, delinquent, wrecker, annihilator, demolisher, desolater, despoiler, ransacker, ravager, locust
COLLOQ. mugger
SLANG bovver boy, yob

vandalize *v*
wreck, trash, destroy, ruin, demolish, devastate, shatter, smash, break, sink, torpedo, ravage, write off

vane *n*
fan, wing, blade, windsail, weathercock, plume, web
TECHNICAL dogvane
OLD fane

vanguard *n*
forefront, most advanced part, front, front line, firing line, spearhead, lead, fore, leading/foremost position

vanish *v*
disappear, fade, fade away/out, dissolve, evaporate, disperse, melt (away), die out, leave, depart, exit, fizzle out, peter out, ghost, end/go up in smoke
OLD evanish, faint
FORMAL evanesce, dematerialize
Ⓔ appear, materialize

vanity *n*
1 CONCEIT, conceitedness, pride, arrogance, haughtiness, self-conceit, self-love, self-satisfaction, self-glorification, narcissism, egotism, pretension, ostentation, affectation, airs
COLLOQ. bigheadedness, swollen-headedness, snootiness
2 WORTHLESSNESS, uselessness, emptiness, futility, pointlessness, unreality, unproductiveness, unprofitableness, hollowness, fruitlessness, triviality, idleness, unimportance, insignificance
OLD (*Spenser*) vainesse
Ⓔ **1** modesty, worth

vanquish *v*
defeat, conquer, beat, triumph over, overcome, overpower, overwhelm, subdue, humble, master, repress, quell, confound, crush, rout
FORMAL subjugate
COLLOQ. hammer, slaughter, clobber, thrash, lick, thump, trounce, drub, annihilate, smash, devastate, slaughter, make mincemeat (out) of, run rings round, paste, wipe the floor with
SLANG take to the cleaners

vapid *adj*
vacuous, uninteresting, lifeless, dead, banal, bland, boring, dull, tedious, flat, insipid, limp, stale, tame, flavourless, tasteless, watery, wishy-washy, colourless, tiresome, trite, weak, uninspiring
OLD jejune
Ⓔ interesting, vigorous

vaporous *adj*
1 STEAMY, misty, gaseous, fumy, fumous, foggy
2 FANCIFUL, flimsy, insubstantial, vain
FORMAL chimerical
Ⓔ 2 substantial

vapour *n*
steam, mist, fog, smoke, breath, fumes, haze, damp, dampness, exhalation

variable *adj, n*
• *adj*
changeable, inconstant, varying, shifting, mutable, unpredictable, fluctuating, fitful, unstable, unsteady, uneven, wavering, vacillating, temperamental, fickle, flexible
FORMAL chameleonic, Protean
Ⓔ fixed, invariable, stable
• *n*
factor, parameter

Synonym nuances
adjective
You can use **changeable** and **varying** fairly generally of anything continually altering: *changeable weather*, while **shifting** can also be used of a change of stance: *their shifting alliances*. **Mutable**, on the other hand, might be used of something that is subject to change: *truth is a mutable commodity*, whereas **inconstant** and **unpredictable** have negative overtones of a lack of dependability: *an inconstant friend*.
  While **fluctuating** suggests a strongly alternating movement: *the fluctuating tides*, **fitful** would describe something more intermittent and, often, unwelcome: *fitful sleep*.
  Wavering has connotations of a lack of resolve, and **vacillating**, while sharing this connotation, also echoes the image of moving back and forth: *the leaders vacillated between confrontation and compromise*.
Temperamental could be used, with negative overtones, of someone displaying mood swings, while **fickle** is equally uncomplimentary when applied to someone constantly changing his or her opinion.
Flexible is more suggestive of being accommodating, and therefore more positive in tone.

---

variance *n*
1 VARIATION, difference, discrepancy, divergence, inconsistency, disagreement
TECHNICAL covariance
2 DISAGREEMENT, disharmony, conflict, discord, division, dissent, dissension, quarrelling, opposition, strife, odds
Ⓔ 1 agreement **2** agreement, harmony
■ **at variance**
at odds, disagreeing, in disagreement, in conflict, conflicting, differing, clashing, quarrelling, arguing, at loggerheads, out of step; *N Am* at outs

variant *n, adj*
• *n*
alternative, variation, modification, development, deviant, rogue
• *adj*
alternative, different, divergent, modified, derived, deviant, exceptional
Ⓔ normal, standard, usual

variation *n*
diversity, variety, deviation, discrepancy, diversification, alteration, change, difference, vacillation, fluctuation, departure, modification, modulation, inflection, novelty, innovation
Ⓔ monotony, uniformity

varied *adj*
assorted, diverse, miscellaneous, mixed, various, sundry, motley, different, wide-ranging

FORMAL heterogeneous, multifarious
E3 standardized, uniform

variegated *adj*
multicoloured, many-coloured, parti-coloured,
varicoloured, speckled, mottled, dappled, pied, streaked,
marbled, jaspe, motley
TECHNICAL poikilitic
E3 monochrome, plain

variety *n*
1 ASSORTMENT, miscellany, mixture, collection, medley, potpourri, range
2 DIVERSITY, difference, dissimilarity, discrepancy, variation
FORMAL multiplicity, multifariousness
3 SORT, kind, class, category, species, type, breed, brand,
make, strain, classification
E3 2 uniformity; *formal* similitude

various *adj*
different, differing, dissimilar, unlike, diverse, varied,
varying, assorted, miscellaneous, distinct, diversified,
mixed, many, several, motley
FORMAL heterogeneous, disparate, variegated

varnish *n, v*
  ◆ *n*
lacquer, lac, glaze, enamel, shellac, resin, polish, gloss,
coating, veneer, japan
  ◆ *v*
lacquer, glaze, enamel, shellac, polish, gloss, coat, veneer,
japan

vary *v*
1 CHANGE, alter, modify, qualify, modulate, diversify, reorder, transform, alternate, permutate, waver, spice
FORMAL metamorphose, variate
2 DIFFER, diverge, disagree, depart, fluctuate, oscillate,
range, be dissimilar, clash, be in conflict, be at odds
TECHNICAL hunt

vase *n*
container, jar, jug, pitcher, urn, vessel, ewer, amphora,
hydria, flask, cornucopia, lustre, potiche
OLD diota, Canopus

vassal *n*
serf, slave, subject, thrall, man, vassaless, bond(s)man,
bondservant, retainer, villein, liege, liegeman, client

vassalage *n*
dependence, bondage, servitude, slavery, subjection,
serfdom, thraldom, villeinage
FORMAL subjugation

vast *adj*
huge, immense, massive, gigantic, enormous, great,
colossal, bulky, extensive, tremendous, sweeping,
unlimited, fathomless, limitless, boundless, immeasurable,
infinite, never-ending, teeming, monumental, monstrous,
far-flung, gargantuan, cyclopean
OLD vasty
FORMAL prodigious

vastly *adv*
hugely, immensely, greatly, massively, enormously,
extensively, boundlessly, limitlessly, without limits,
immeasurably, infinitely

vat *n*
barrel, tank, tub, container, kier, keeve, fat, back, stand,
case, cuvée, tan-pit; *Scot* girnel
OLD pressfat

vault[1] *v, n*
  ◆ *v*
vault over the wall
leap, spring, bound, clear, jump, hurdle, leap-frog
  ◆ *n*
leap, spring, jump, bound, hurdle, clearance

vault[2] *n*
1 CELLAR, crypt, strongroom, repository, cavern,
depository, wine-cellar, underground chamber,
basement, tomb, mausoleum
2 ARCH, roof, span, concave

vaunt *v*
boast, brag, exult in, flaunt, parade, trumpet, crow
COLLOQ. show off, swank, blow your own trumpet; *N Am*
blow your own horn
E3 belittle, minimize

veer *v*
swerve, swing, change, shift, diverge, deviate, wheel, turn,
sheer, tack

vegetable
See panels on next page

vegetate *v*
stagnate, degenerate, deteriorate, rusticate, go to seed,
idle, rust, languish, moulder, do nothing

vegetation *n*
plants, trees, flowers, flora, green plants, greenery
FORMAL herbage, verdure

vehemence *n*
passion, energy, enthusiasm, keenness, fervency,
eagerness, earnestness, emphasis, strength, power,
animation, intensity, zeal, verve, vigour, ardour, fervour,
force, forcefulness, urgency, impetuosity, violence,
warmth, heat, fire
E3 indifference

vehement *adj*
impassioned, passionate, ardent, fervent, intense,
forceful, emphatic, heated, hot, warm, strong, powerful,
spirited, vigorous, urgent, enthusiastic, animated,
eager, keen, earnest, forcible, fierce, violent, zealous,
thunderous
FORMAL fervid
E3 apathetic, indifferent

vehicle *n*
1 CONVEYANCE, transport
2 MEANS, agency, channel, medium, mechanism,
instrument, organ

Vehicles include:

S Afr bakkie	hackney-carriage	sled
barouche	hansom	sledge
bicycle	*N Am* Humvee®	sleeper
colloq. bike	*Aust* jinker	sleigh
boat	juggernaut	stagecoach
bobsleigh	landau	steam-roller
colloq.	litter	sulky
boneshaker	lorry	surrey
brougham	maglev	tandem
S Afr buck-wagon	minibus	tank
bus	minivan	taxi
cab	monorail	toboggan
camper	motorbike	tractor
S Afr Cape cart	motorcycle	trailer
car	omnibus	train
caravan	pantechnicon	tram
caravanette	penny-farthing	Transit®
charabanc	phaeton	trap
coach	plane	tricycle
cycle	post-chaise	troika
dog-cart	Pullman	trolleybus
double-decker	rickshaw	truck
dray	scooter	tube
fork-lift truck	*S Afr* Scotch cart	van
four-in-hand	sedan-chair	Vespa®
gig	*NZ* service car	wagon
golf cart	ship	wagon-lit

See also **aircraft; boat; car.**

Vegetables include:

artichoke	cabbage	courgette (or N	kale	parsnip	squash
asparagus	calabrese	Am & Aust	leek	pepper	swede
aubergine (or N	capsicum	zucchini)	lentil	potato	sweetcorn
Am eggplant)	carrot	cucumber	lettuce	colloq. spud	sweet potato
baby corn	cassava (or	daikon	lollo rosso	pumpkin	turnip
beetroot	manioc)	fennel	marrow	radish	water chestnut
bok choy (or pak	cauliflower	garlic	mooli	rocket	yam
choi)	celeriac	globe artichoke	mushroom	shallot	
broccoli	celery	Jerusalem	okra	spinach	
Brussels sprout	chicory	artichoke	onion	spring onion	

See also **food**.

Legumes and pulses include:

BEANS:	cannellini bean (or fasolia)	red kidney bean	German lentil
adzuki bean	carob bean (or locust bean)	runner bean	green lentil
asparagus bean (or yard-	chilli bean	scarlet runner bean	Puy lentil
long bean)	flageolet	N Am snap bean	red lentil
asparagus pea (or Goa	French bean (or green or	soy bean (or soya bean)	**PEAS:**
bean)	kidney or string bean)	tonka bean	chickpea (or garbanzo)
bean sprout	haricot bean	urd bean (or black gram)	d(h)al (or pigeon pea)
black bean	jicama	wax bean	mangetout (or snow pea or
black-eye(d) bean (or	lablab	winged bean	sugar pea)
cowpea)	lima bean (or sugar bean)	**LENTILS:**	petit pois
borlotti bean	mung bean	brown lentil	split pea
broad bean (or N Am fava	navy bean (or Yankee bean)	continental lentil	string pea
bean)	pinto bean	Egyptian lentil	sugar snap pea
butter bean			

See also **bean**.

Salad leaves include:

arugula (or rocket)	corn-salad (or	endive	radicchio	watercress
borage	lamb's lettuce)	iceberg lettuce	round lettuce	
chard	cos lettuce	lollo rosso		
chicory	cress	lovage	salad burnet	

veil v, n
♦ v
screen, cloak, cover (up), mask, mantle, blanket, shadow, shield, obscure, conceal, hide, shroud, disguise, shade, camouflage, mist, overveil, encurtain
E3 expose, uncover
♦ n
cover, covering, veiling, cloak, curtain, hood, mask, mantle, blanket, scarf, screen, disguise, film, blind, shade, canopy, shroud, purdah, chadar, yashmak, kalyptra, wimple, chrismal, lambrequin, mantilla, kiss-me, kiss-me-quick, weeper
OLD vail, caul, scene, volet; (*Spenser*) veale, vele

veiled adj
1 *veiled threats*
hidden, concealed, disguised, obscure, secret, masked, shrouded, cloaked, indirect, covert, surreptitious
2 COVERED, masked, shrouded, cloaked, disguised
E3 1 clear, open, obvious

vein n
1 STREAK, stripe, stratum, seam, lode, blood vessel
Related adjective: venous
2 MOOD, tendency, bent, strain, streak, temper, tenor, tone, frame of mind, humour, mode, style, disposition, temperament, attitude, inclination

Veins and arteries include:

aorta	hepatic	saphena
axillary	iliac	subclavian
brachial	jugular	superior
carotid	portal	temporal
femoral	pulmonary	tibial
frontal	radial	
gastric	renal	

veined adj
streaked, variegated, marbled, mottled, jaspe

velocity n
speed, rate, quickness, rapidity, pace, impetus, swiftness
OLD fleetness
FORMAL celerity

venal adj
corrupt, corruptible, bribable, mercenary, grafting, simoniacal
COLLOQ. bent, buyable
E3 incorruptible

vendetta n
feud, blood-feud, enmity, rivalry, quarrel, bad blood, bitterness

vendor n
seller, trader, salesperson, merchant, supplier, stockist
See panel at **seller**.

veneer n
1 FAÇADE, front, appearance, display, show, mask, gloss, camouflage, pretence, guise
2 LAYER, coating, surface, finish, gloss, covering, lamination

venerable adj
respected, esteemed, revered, honoured, venerated, dignified, grave, wise, august, aged, worshipped
FORMAL hallowed

venerate v
revere, respect, esteem, honour, worship, adore
FORMAL hallow
E3 despise, anathematize

veneration n
respect, esteem, reverence, deference, adoration, awe, worship, devotion

vengeance *n*
retribution, revenge, retaliation, reprisal, requital
OLD avengement, wrack; (*Spenser*) vengement
COLLOQ. tit for tat, an eye for an eye (and a tooth for a tooth)
ᴇᴈ forgiveness

■ **with a vengeance**
1 FORCEFULLY, violently, vigorously, powerfully, energetically, furiously, vehemently
OLD with a (wild) wanion, with a witness
COLLOQ. flat out, like crazy
2 TO A GREAT DEGREE, greatly, to a great extent, fully, to the full, thoroughly, to the utmost
COLLOQ. with no holds barred

vengeful *adj*
spiteful, rancorous, unforgiving, vindictive, avenging, revengeful, retaliatory, relentless, retributive, punitive, implacable
ᴇᴈ forgiving

venial *adj*
forgivable, excusable, pardonable, slight, minor, insignificant, trivial, trifling, negligible
ᴇᴈ mortal, unforgivable, unpardonable

venom *n*
1 POISON, toxin, virus
OLD swelter
2 RANCOUR, ill-will, malice, malevolence, acrimony, vindictiveness, spite, bitterness, resentment, hate, enmity, hostility, animosity, virulence, virus

venomous *adj*
1 POISONOUS, toxic, lethal, deadly, fatal, virulent, harmful
FORMAL noxious
2 MALICIOUS, spiteful, vicious, rancorous, vindictive, bitter, resentful, baleful, hostile, virulent, malignant, malevolent, baneful
ᴇᴈ **1** harmless

vent *n, v*
◆ *n*
opening, hole, aperture, outlet, gap, passage, orifice, duct, pipe, blowhole, breather, chimney, flue, vomitory
TECHNICAL mud volcano, solfatara, spiracle
◆ *v*
air, express, voice, utter, release, discharge, emit, let out, pour out, wreak, let off steam, take it out on, give vent to, give a loose to
OLD disclose

ventilate *v*
1 *ventilate a room*
air, aerate, freshen, cool
2 *ventilate your feelings*
express, air, broadcast, debate, discuss, bring out into the open

ventilation *n*
airing, cooling, freshening, aeration

venture *v, n*
◆ *v*
1 DARE, advance, go, make bold, be so bold as to, put forward, presume, suggest, volunteer, pretend, adventure, take the liberty, make so free as to; *Scot* mint
OLD venter, ventre
FORMAL assay
2 RISK, hazard, chance, endanger, imperil, jeopardize, put in jeopardy, speculate, gamble, wager, stake, come in on, invest, sink
OLD venter, ventre
◆ *n*
risk, chance, hazard, speculation, gamble, undertaking, project, adventure, exploit, endeavour, enterprise, operation, fling, promotion, foray
OLD venter, portage; (*Shakesp*) jump
COLLOQ. throw

venturesome *adj*
adventurous, enterprising, courageous, bold, brave, daring, fearless, intrepid, spirited, plucky, audacious, dauntless, doughty
COLLOQ. daredevil
ᴇᴈ unenterprising, cowardly

veracious *adj*
truthful, true, trustworthy, genuine, frank, honest, reliable, credible, dependable, straightforward, exact, factual, faithful, accurate
ᴇᴈ untruthful

veracity *n*
truthfulness, truth, trustworthiness, integrity, honesty, frankness, precision, accuracy, candour, credibility, exactitude
FORMAL probity, rectitude
ᴇᴈ untruthfulness

veranda *n*
terrace, decking, gallery, lanai; *N Am* piazza, porch; *S Afr* stoep
OLD viranda, virando

verbal *adj*
spoken, oral, said, uttered, vocal, linguistic, verbatim, unwritten, word-of-mouth
ᴇᴈ written

verbalize *v*
put in/into words, articulate, utter, voice, give voice to, say, speak, state, communicate, put/get over, pronounce, word, tell, announce, report, assert, declare, put across, formulate, point out, convey
FORMAL enunciate

verbatim *adv*
word for word, exactly, literally, to the letter, precisely, closely

verbiage *n*
repetition, verbosity, waffle
FORMAL circumlocution, pleonasm, periphrasis, prolixity
ᴇᴈ succinctness, briefness

verbose *adj*
long-winded, wordy, windy, garrulous, diffuse, voluble
OLD wordish
FORMAL prolix, loquacious, circumlocutory, periphrastic, pleonastic
ᴇᴈ succinct, brief

verbosity *n*
verboseness, windiness, wordiness, long-windedness, garrulity, logorrhoea, verbiage
FORMAL loquaciousness, loquacity, multiloquy, prolixity
ᴇᴈ economy, succinctness

verdant *adj*
lush, green, grassy, fresh, leafy
FORMAL viridescent, virid, graminaceous, gramineous

verdict *n*
decision, judgement, conclusion, finding, adjudication, assessment, opinion, ruling, sentence, rough justice
TECHNICAL recovery
OLD verdit, vardy

verdure *n*
grass, greenery, greenness, herbage, foliage, leafage, pasture, meadows
FORMAL verdancy, viridity, viridescence

verge *n, v*
◆ *n*
border, edge, margin, limit, rim, brim, brink, boundary, threshold, extreme, extremity, edging
■ **verge on**

approach, border on, come close to, near, tend towards, incline to

verification *n*
confirmation, checking, proof, substantiation, validation, authentication, ascertaining
TECHNICAL audit
FORMAL attestation, corroboration

verify *v*
confirm, substantiate, authenticate, bear out, prove, support, endorse, validate, testify, ascertain, check
TECHNICAL audit
FORMAL corroborate, attest, accredit
◼ invalidate, discredit

verisimilitude *n*
authenticity, credibility, resemblance, realism, likeliness, plausibility, semblance, colour
COLLOQ. ring of truth
◼ implausibility

veritable *adj*
positive, absolute, utter, sheer, complete, rank, perfect, unmitigated, outright, out-and-out, thorough
FORMAL consummate

verity *n*
truth, truthfulness, validity, factuality, actuality, authenticity, soundness
FORMAL veracity
◼ untruth

vernacular *adj, n*
◆ *adj*
indigenous, local, native, popular, vulgar, informal, colloquial, common
◆ *n*
language, speech, tongue, parlance, dialect, idiom, slang, cant, jargon
COLLOQ. lingo, patter

versatile *adj*
adaptable, flexible, all-round, all-purpose, multipurpose, multifaceted, adjustable, many-sided, general-purpose, functional, resourceful, handy, variable
◼ inflexible

verse *n*
poetry, rhyme, stanza, strophe, metre, doggerel, jingle;
Welsh pennill

Verse forms include:

ballad stanza	quatrain	Spenserian stanza
blank verse	rubai	tercet
cinquain	sapphic	terza rima
free verse	sestina	
Miltonic sonnet	Shakespearean	
ottava rima	sonnet	
Petrarchan (or	sicilian octave	
Italian) sonnet	sonnet	

See also **poem; prosody**.

---

versed *adj*
skilled, proficient, practised, experienced, familiar, acquainted, learned, read, knowledgeable, conversant, seasoned, qualified, competent, accomplished

versifier *n*
poet, poetess, poetaster, rhymer, rhymester, rhymist, verser, verse-maker, verse-monger, verse-smith, versificator, poeticule
OLD verse-man

version *n*
1 RENDERING, reading, interpretation, understanding, account, report, edition, translation, paraphrase, adaptation, portrayal

2 TYPE, kind, sort, variant, form, model, style, design, reproduction

versus *prep*
1 *Arsenal versus Manchester United*
against, v, playing, facing, opposing, in opposition to
2 *expense versus convenience*
as opposed to, rather than, instead of, in contrast to, as against

vertex *n*
peak, top, apex, summit, acme, apogee, zenith, height, highest point, pinnacle, culmination, crown, extremity
◼ nadir

vertical *adj*
upright, perpendicular, straight up, upstanding, sheer, plumb, erect, on end
◼ horizontal

vertigo *n*
dizziness, giddiness, light-headedness, sickness
COLLOQ. wooziness
Related adjective: dinic

verve *n*
vitality, vivacity, animation, energy, dash, élan, liveliness, sparkle, vigour, passion, fervour, enthusiasm, gusto, life, relish, spirit, force, brio
COLLOQ. pizzazz, zip
◼ apathy, lethargy

very *adv, adj*
◆ *adv*
extremely, greatly, highly, deeply, truly, remarkably, excessively, exceedingly, most exceptionally, acutely, particularly, really, quite, absolutely, noticeably, unbelievably, incredibly, unusually, uncommonly; *Scot* unco; *N Am* mighty
COLLOQ. pretty, terribly, dreadfully, awfully, ever so, real
SLANG majorly, mega
◼ slightly, scarcely
◆ *adj*
actual, real, same, selfsame, identical, true, genuine, simple, utter, sheer, pure, perfect, ideal, plain, mere, bare, exact, suitable, appropriate, fitting

---

Synonym nuances
adverb
You can use **extremely**, **greatly** and **highly** in many contexts to suggest a large extent: *highly critical*. **Deeply**, however, implies being emotionally affected: *deeply disturbing*, and **acutely** can also imply something is keenly felt: *acutely embarrassed*. **Truly** suggests something is irrefutable: *this is a truly momentous event*. **Remarkably**, however, might be used approvingly of something with a degree of distinction: *a remarkably clever novel*, and while **exceptionally** and **exceedingly** also convey this idea of standing out in a more neutral way, the word **excessively** implies it is too much: *an excessively clever novel that does not engage the emotions*.
  The term **particularly** sets up a comparison against other examples: *of all novels, this one is particularly bad*, while **really** is more informal in tone and tends to suggest strong feeling on the part of the speaker: *it was a really good day*, and **absolutely** would convey even less reservation: *an absolutely brilliant day*. **Quite**, on the other hand, is rather more formal in tone, and suggests a degree of qualification or restraint: *I was quite beside myself with anger*.
  The term **noticeably**, in its suggestion that something is simply apparent, does not give the same sense of intensity: *he was noticeably upset*, whereas both **unbelievably** and **incredibly**, in their suggestion of an unlikely degree, have far greater force: *you have been unbelievably stupid*.

vessel n
1 SHIP, boat, craft, barque
2 CONTAINER, bowl, receptacle, holder, jar, pot, pitcher, jug

vest v
give, endow, entrust, supply, grant, empower, authorize, sanction
FORMAL bestow, confer

vestibule n
foyer, hall, hallway, entrance, entrance hall, entranceway, lobby, porch, anteroom, portico

vestige n
trace, suspicion, touch, indication, sign, mark, track, impression, print, hint, evidence, inkling, glimmer, token, scrap, remains, remainder, remnant, residue, relics
COLLOQ. whiff

vestigial adj
remaining, surviving, rudimentary, undeveloped, imperfect, incomplete, reduced, functionless

vet v
investigate, examine, check (out), scrutinize, scan, examine, inspect, survey, review, screen, audit
FORMAL appraise

veteran n, adj
• n
master, pastmaster, old hand, old stager, old-timer, warhorse
COLLOQ. pro
≠ novice, recruit
• adj
experienced, practised, seasoned, long-serving, expert, adept, proficient, old, battle-scarred, case-hardened
≠ inexperienced

veto v, n
• v
reject, turn down, forbid, ban, prohibit, rule out, block, negate, blackball
FORMAL disallow, proscribe, interdict
COLLOQ. give the thumbs-down to
SLANG nix
≠ approve, sanction
• n
rejection, ban, embargo, prohibition
FORMAL proscription
COLLOQ. thumbs-down
≠ approval, assent

vex v
irritate, annoy, provoke, pester, trouble, upset, worry, bother, harass, disturb, distress, agitate, enrage, exasperate, torment, fret, rile
FORMAL perturb
COLLOQ. put out, hassle, aggravate, needle, bug, brass off, cheese off, get someone's blood up, get someone's back up, aggravate, bug, wind up, rub up the wrong way, wind up, get on someone's nerves, get up someone's nose, get under someone's skin, get someone's goat, get on someone's wick, get someone's back up, make someone's hackles rise; N Am tick/hack off
≠ calm, soothe

vexation n
annoyance, exasperation, displeasure, chagrin, anger, fury, pique, dissatisfaction, frustration, nuisance, misfortune, irritant, problem, trouble, upset, worry, bother, difficulty, bore
COLLOQ. headache, pain, bind, thorn in the flesh, aggravation
SLANG pain in the backside/arse; N Am pain in the ass/butt

vexatious adj
annoying, irritating, troublesome, upsetting, worrying, irksome, nagging, exasperating, infuriating, distressing, disappointing, bothersome, burdensome, disagreeable, unpleasant, trying, worrisome, provoking, teasing, tormenting, afflicting
FORMAL pestiferous
COLLOQ. aggravating, pesky
≠ pleasant, soothing

vexed adj
1 IRRITATED, annoyed, provoked, upset, troubled, worried, irate, incensed, infuriated, put out, exasperated, bothered, confused, perplexed, harassed, ruffled, riled, disturbed, flustered, distressed, displeased, agitated
COLLOQ. nettled, aggravated, hassled, peeved, miffed, narked
2 *a vexed question*
difficult, controversial, contested, disputed, in dispute, debated, awkward, tough, knotty, tricky, ticklish
FORMAL moot
COLLOQ. dicey, sticky

viability n
feasibility, practicability, achievability, workability, practicality, reasonableness, possibility, expedience

viable adj
feasible, practicable, possible, workable, usable, operable, achievable, sustainable, sound
≠ impossible, unworkable

vibes n
atmosphere, aura, ambience, feel, feelings, emotions, vibrations, reaction, response, emanation

vibrancy n
vitality, life, liveliness, animation, vigour, energy, vivacity, spirit, sparkle, exuberance, zest, strength, stamina
COLLOQ. go, get-up-and-go, oomph, pizzazz

vibrant adj
1 ANIMATED, vivacious, lively, energetic, vigorous, responsive, sparkling, spirited, sensitive, thrilling, dynamic, electrifying, electric
2 *vibrant colours*
vivid, bright, brilliant, colourful, striking

vibrate v
quiver, pulsate, shudder, shiver, resonate, reverberate, resound, throb, oscillate, tremble, undulate, sway, swing, shake, flutter, jar, quake, tingle, twinkle, warble, shimmy; dialect thirl; Scot dinnle, dirl, hotter
FORMAL pendulate

vibration n
quiver, pulsation, pulse, shudder, judder, juddering, resonance, reverberation, resounding, throb, throbbing, oscillation, trembling, tremor, shaking, flutter, jarring, quake, tingle, twinkle, frisson; Scot dirl, hotter

vicar n
minister, priest, chaplain, clergyman, clergywoman, parson, pastor, rector, curate, cleric, preacher
OLD arch-priest

vicarious adj
indirect, second-hand, substituted, surrogate, delegated, deputed, acting, commissioned
FORMAL empathetic

vice n
1 EVIL, evil-doing, wrongdoing, immorality, depravity, wickedness, sin, corruption, degeneracy
FORMAL iniquity, profligacy, transgression
2 FAULT, failing, defect, shortcoming, weakness, imperfection, foible, flaw, blemish, bad habit, besetting sin
≠ 1 virtue, morality

vice versa adv
conversely, reciprocally, oppositely, contrariwise, the other way round, inversely

vicinity _n_
neighbourhood, surroundings, surrounding district/area,
area, locality, district, precincts, environs, proximity
FORMAL propinquity

vicious _adj_
1 SAVAGE, wild, violent, fierce, barbarous, brutal, cruel,
ferocious, dangerous, lethal
2 MALICIOUS, spiteful, vindictive, virulent, cruel,
malevolent, mean, nasty, slanderous, venomous, caustic,
defamatory, brutal, Rottweiler
COLLOQ. bitchy, catty
3 WICKED, bad, wrong, immoral, depraved, unprincipled,
degenerate, diabolical, corrupt, debased, perverted, vile,
heinous
FORMAL profligate
E3 1 gentle **2** kind **3** virtuous

viciously _adv_
brutally, savagely, wildly, violently, fiercely, cruelly, lethally
E3 gently, kindly

viciousness _n_
savagery, brutality, cruelty, ferocity, virulence, spite,
spitefulness, venom, malice, wickedness, badness,
rancour, immorality, corruption, sinfulness, depravity
FORMAL profligacy, vitiosity, viciosity
COLLOQ. bitchiness
E3 goodness, gentleness, virtue

vicissitude _n_
change, variation, alteration, alternation, shift, turn,
revolution, deviation, divergence, fluctuation, twist
FORMAL mutation

victim _n_
sufferer, casualty, prey, quarry, scapegoat, fool, martyr,
sacrifice, fatality, murderee, nebbich
OLD host
COLLOQ. dupe, sucker, fall guy, sitting target, sitting duck,
sucker, muggee, angel, mark
SLANG _N Am_ patsy
E3 offender, attacker
■ **fall victim to**
succumb to, be overcome by, be attacked by, be stricken
with, catch, contract, develop, fall prey to, become a target
of, be deceived by, be taken in by
COLLOQ. fall for
SLANG be taken for a ride by

victimize _v_
1 OPPRESS, persecute, discriminate against, pick on, prey
on, bully, exploit, take (unfair) advantage of
COLLOQ. have it in for
2 CHEAT, deceive, trick, defraud, dupe, hoodwink, fleece,
fool
COLLOQ. swindle, frame, do, con, bamboozle, sting, rook,
stitch up, shaft, put one over on, pull the wool over
someone's eyes
SLANG rip off, take for a ride, take to the cleaners

victor _n_
winner, conqueror, champion, first, prize-winner
FORMAL subjugator, vanquisher, victor ludorum
COLLOQ. champ, top dog
E3 loser; _formal_ vanquished

victorious _adj_
conquering, champion, triumphant, winning, unbeaten,
successful, prize-winning, top, first
FORMAL vanquishing
E3 defeated, unsuccessful

victory _n_
conquest, win, triumph, success, superiority, mastery,
subjugation, overcoming, landslide; _dialect_ gree
FORMAL vanquishment
TECHNICAL triple crown

COLLOQ. walk-away, walkover
E3 defeat, loss, failure

victuals _n_
food, provisions, supplies, stores, edibles, bread, rations,
sustenance, comestibles
FORMAL aliment, viands
COLLOQ. eatables, eats, tuck, scran
SLANG grub, nosh, chow

vie _v_
strive, compete, contend, struggle, contest, fight, rival

view _n, v_
♦ _n_
1 OPINION, attitude, belief, judgement, point of view,
viewpoint, angle, thought, conviction, estimation, feeling,
sentiment, impression, idea, notion
2 SIGHT, scene, vision, range of vision, vista, spectacle,
outlook, prospect, perspective, panorama, landscape,
composition
3 SURVEY, inspection, examination, observation, study,
contemplation, scrutiny, scan, assessment, review
4 DESCRIPTION, account, impression, picture, portrait,
portrayal, sketch
5 GLIMPSE, look, sight, perception
♦ _v_
1 OBSERVE, watch, see, look at, examine, inspect, look at,
gaze at, scrutinize, scan, survey, witness, perceive
FORMAL descry, espy
2 CONSIDER, regard, contemplate, judge, reflect on, think
about, speculate
■ **in view of**
considering, bearing in mind, taking into account, taking
into consideration
■ **on view**
on show, showing, shown, on display, displayed, made
public, presented, exhibited

viewer _n_
spectator, watcher, observer, onlooker

viewpoint _n_
attitude, position, perspective, slant, standpoint, stance,
opinion, angle, feeling

vigil _n_
watch, wakefulness, wake, lookout, sleeplessness, stake-
out
FORMAL pernoctation

vigilance _n_
watchfulness, alertness, attentiveness, observation,
carefulness, caution, guardedness, wakefulness
FORMAL circumspection

vigilant _adj_
watchful, alert, attentive, observant, on your guard, on the
lookout, on the watch, on the qui vive, cautious, jealous,
aware, careful, wide-awake, awake, wakeful, waking,
sleepless, unsleeping
FORMAL circumspect
E3 careless

vigilante _n_
guard, neighbourhood watch, watch(man), watchperson,
security guard, armed guard, lookout, sentinel; _N Am_
Guardian Angel

vignette _n_
sketch, drawing, design, plan, diagram, outline, skeleton,
plan, abstract, draft, representation, scene, act, turn, cameo

vigorous _adj_
1 HEALTHY, energetic, active, lively, strong, strenuous,
tough, athletic, robust, lusty, sound, vital
2 DYNAMIC, forceful, forcible, powerful, stout, spirited, full-
blooded, effective, efficient, brisk, enterprising,
flourishing, lively, animated, sparkling, intense
E3 1, 2 weak, feeble

vigorously *adv*
briskly, hard, forcefully, energetically, eagerly, heartily, powerfully, strongly, strenuously, lustily
F3 feebly, weakly

vigour *n*
energy, vitality, liveliness, health, robustness, stamina, strength, resilience, sturdiness, toughness, soundness, spirit, verve, gusto, activity, animation, power, potency, force, forcefulness, might, dash, dynamism
FORMAL vivacity
COLLOQ. zip, oomph, pep, brio, pizzazz
F3 weakness

Synonym nuances
Energy is a widely applicable synonym for the body's capacity for physical and mental activity, while **vitality** and **liveliness** have connotations of a zest for life, and **health**, **robustness**, **soundness** and **strength** emphasize physical wellbeing and fortitude. **Stamina**, on the other hand, is more suggestive of the ability to last, whereas **sturdiness** and **toughness** suggest intractability, and **resilience** an ability to endure and recover from misfortune: *he fought his illness with characteristic resilience.*

While **activity** is widely used to suggest any movement, **animation** conveys the idea of spirit and feeling: *we knew by his animation that he was thrilled at the idea of a party.* **Spirit**, **verve** and **gusto** return to the idea of vibrancy and enthusiasm: *the sheer verve of his music makes you want to dance,* while **dash** also suggests a degree of swaggering.

Power, **potency** and **force** return to the idea of effectiveness, and **dynamism** has very positive implications of powerful drive: *I love the dynamism of contemporary jazz.* **Forcefulness**, although similar, has less positive overtones, and possible further implications of imposition: *the forcefulness with which he projected his views was disturbing,* while **might** suggests potential supremacy: *military might.*

---

vile *adj*
1 *vile weather; a vile meal*
disgusting, foul, nasty, unpleasant, disagreeable, horrible, horrid, nauseating, sickening, repulsive, repugnant, revolting, obnoxious, offensive, distasteful, loathsome
OLD vild, vilde
FORMAL noxious
COLLOQ. beastly
2 EVIL, base, contemptible, debased, low, depraved, degenerate, bad, wicked, wretched, worthless, sinful, detestable, miserable, mean, impure, corrupt, earthly, despicable, disgraceful, degrading, vicious, appalling, infamous, villainous, scurvy
OLD vild, vilde, scabbed
FORMAL iniquitous
F3 1 pleasant, lovely **2** pure, worthy

vileness *n*
foulness, nastiness, unpleasantness, dreadfulness, meanness, offensiveness, outrage, ugliness, wickedness, corruption, depravity, baseness, evil, profanity
FORMAL degeneracy, noxiousness

vilification *n*
criticism, defamation, abuse, denigration, scurrility
FORMAL aspersion, calumniation, calumny, contumely, disparagement, invective, revilement, vituperation
COLLOQ. mud-slinging

vilify *v*
criticize, snipe, slate, revile, denigrate, run down, denounce, slander, defame, stigmatize, abuse, smear, debase
FORMAL malign, disparage, asperse, berate, calumniate,

decry, traduce, vilipend, vituperate
COLLOQ. badmouth, slam, knock, rubbish
SLANG slag (off)
F3 praise, compliment, adore, eulogize, glorify

village *n*
hamlet, community, settlement, town
COLLOQ. one-horse town

villain *n*
evildoer, wrongdoer, scoundrel, rogue, criminal, reprobate, knave, rascal, wretch, devil, heavy, bravo
OLD scelerate
FORMAL miscreant, malefactor
COLLOQ. baddy
F3 hero, heroine; *colloq.* goody

villainous *adj*
wicked, bad, criminal, evil, sinful, vicious, notorious, cruel, inhuman, vile, depraved, debased, degenerate, disgraceful, terrible, fiendish
FORMAL heinous, nefarious, iniquitous, opprobrious
F3 good

villainy *n*
wickedness, viciousness, badness, crime, criminality, delinquency, atrocity, depravity, baseness, vice, sin, rascality, roguery, knavery
FORMAL iniquity, turpitude

vindicate *v*
1 CLEAR, acquit, excuse, absolve, rehabilitate
FORMAL exonerate, exculpate
2 JUSTIFY, right, uphold, support, back, maintain, sustain, champion, defend, establish, advocate, assert, verify, confirm, warrant
OLD darraign, salve
FORMAL corroborate

vindication *n*
justification, defence, plea, excuse, assertion, apology, support, maintenance, substantiation, verification, rehabilitation, extenuation
FORMAL exculpation, exoneration
F3 accusation, conviction

vindictive *adj*
spiteful, unforgiving, implacable, vengeful, relentless, unrelenting, revengeful, resentful, punitive, venomous, malicious, malevolent, rancorous
OLD (*Shakesp*) vindicative
F3 forgiving

vintage *n, adj*
♦ *n*
year, period, era, epoch, generation, time, origin, harvest, gathering, crop
♦ *adj*
1 CHOICE, best, fine, prime, quality, high-quality, select, superior, supreme, mature, ripe
2 *a vintage Beatles song*
classic, archetypal, ageless, timeless, enduring, old, veteran

violate *v*
1 CONTRAVENE, disobey, disregard, break, flout, offend, infringe, breach
OLD (*Shakesp*) fract
FORMAL transgress, infract
2 OUTRAGE, debauch, defile, abuse, rape, ravish, molest, dishonour, desecrate, profane, invade, disturb, interfere with, disrupt, invade, wreck
OLD stuprate, vitiate
FORMAL despoil
F3 1 observe

violation *n*
breach, contravention, offence, outrage, infringement, trespass, abuse, disruption, encroachment, profanation,

sacrilege, defilement, rape, abuse, desecration
OLD stupration, vitiation
FORMAL infraction, spoliation, transgression
E⅃ obedience, observance

violence n
1 FORCE, strength, power, forcefulness, vehemence, intensity, passion, ferocity, fierceness, severity, tumult, turbulence, wildness
FORMAL might
2 BRUTALITY, aggression, roughness, destructiveness, cruelty, bloodshed, murderousness, savagery, passion, wildness, fighting, frenzy, fury, hostilities

violent adj
1 CRUEL, brutal, aggressive, fierce, ferocious, bloodthirsty, impetuous, hot-headed, headstrong, murderous, savage, wild, vicious, unrestrained, uncontrollable, ungovernable, passionate, furious, intemperate, maddened, outrageous, riotous, fiery, destructive
2 INTENSE, strong, severe, sharp, acute, extreme, great, dramatic, harmful, destructive, devastating, injurious, powerful, painful, agonizing, excruciating, forceful, forcible, harsh, ruinous, rough, vehement, passionate, tumultuous, turbulent
E⅃ **1** peaceful, gentle **2** calm, moderate

violently adv
1 CRUELLY, brutally, aggressively, wildly, savagely, viciously, fiercely, ferociously, impetuously, hot-headedly, uncontrollably
2 INTENSELY, strongly, severely, sharply, extremely, greatly, powerfully, dramatically
E⅃ **1** gently, peacefully **2** moderately

VIP n
celebrity, luminary, magnate, somebody, notable, personage, dignitary, star, headliner, lion
COLLOQ. bigwig, big name, big noise, big shot, big cheese, heavyweight, top dog
E⅃ nobody, nonentity

virago n
shrew, termagant, vixen, tartar, scold, harridan, dragon, fury, gorgon, Xanthippe
COLLOQ. battle-axe

virgin n, adj
♦ n
girl, maiden, celibate, vestal
OLD maid, pucelle
♦ adj
virginal, chaste, intact, immaculate, maiden, maidenly, pure, modest, new, fresh, spotless, stainless, undefiled, unblemished, untainted, untouched, unspoilt, unsullied

virginal adj
pure, spotless, virgin, untouched, undefiled, uncorrupted, undisturbed, stainless, white, snowy, vestal, immaculate, chaste, fresh, celibate, maidenly
FORMAL pristine

virginity n
purity, chastity, chasteness, maidenhood, virtue, honour, innocence

virile adj
man-like, masculine, male, manly, robust, muscular, strapping, vigorous, potent, lusty, red-blooded, forceful, strong, rugged
COLLOQ. macho
E⅃ effeminate, impotent

virility n
manhood, manliness, masculinity, ruggedness, vigour, huskiness, potency, machismo
E⅃ effeminacy, impotence, weakness

virtual adj
effective, in effect, essential, practical, for all practical

purposes, in all but name, implied, implicit, potential, prospective

virtually adv
practically, effectively, in effect, almost, nearly, as good as, more or less, for all practical purposes, in all but name, in essence, conceivably, to all intents and purposes

virtue n
1 GOODNESS, morality, uprightness, worthiness, righteousness, integrity, honesty, honour, incorruptibility, justice, high-mindedness, excellence
FORMAL rectitude, probity
2 QUALITY, worth, merit, advantage, benefit, asset, credit, strength
COLLOQ. plus
E⅃ **1** vice
■ **by virtue of**
because of, on account of, by means of, owing to, with the help of, thanks to, by way of
FORMAL by dint of

virtuosity n
skill, mastery, expertise, artistry, brilliance, polish, finesse, flair, panache, éclat, finish, wizardry, bravura

virtuoso n, adj
♦ n
expert, master, maestro, prodigy, genius
♦ adj
skilful, masterly, expert, brilliant, excellent, dazzling

virtuous adj
good, moral, righteous, upright, upstanding, worthy, honourable, honest, irreproachable, incorruptible, exemplary, unimpeachable, ethical, high-principled, blameless, respectable, decent, clean-living, temperate, moderate, continent, innocent, excellent, angelic, above/beyond suspicion, keeping to the straight and narrow
OLD graced, virtual
COLLOQ. squeaky-clean
E⅃ immoral, vicious

virulence n
1 POISON, venom, toxicity, deadliness
2 HOSTILITY, bitterness, resentment, hurtfulness, harmfulness, spite, vindictiveness, viciousness, acrimony, antagonism, malevolence, malice, malignancy, spleen, vitriol, hatred
FORMAL rancour

virulent adj
1 POISONOUS, toxic, venomous, deadly, fatal, lethal, malignant, injurious, pernicious, severe, intense, extreme
2 HOSTILE, resentful, spiteful, acrimonious, bitter, blistering, vicious, vindictive, malicious, malevolent, rancorous, vitriolic, waspish
E⅃ **1** harmless **2** amicable, kind

visa n
permit, pass, passport, licence, warrant, authorization, sanction, permission, safe-conduct, docket, carnet, green card, laissez-passer, permis de séjour

vis-à-vis prep
in comparison with, as regards, in relation to, over against, opposite, facing

viscera n
innards, insides, intestines, vitals, bowels, entrails, gralloch

viscous adj
sticky, adhesive, gluey, thick, clammy, mucous, tacky, syrupy, treacly, gummy, tenacious, viscid
FORMAL gelatinous, glutinous, mucilaginous
COLLOQ. gooey
E⅃ runny, thin, watery

visible adj
perceptible, discernible, detectable, apparent, noticeable,

observable, perceivable, recognizable, distinguishable, discoverable, evident, in evidence, in sight, visual, unconcealed, undisguised, unmistakable, conspicuous, showing, clear, exposed, obvious, open, overt, palpable, plain, patent, manifest
OLD aspectable
≠ invisible, indiscernible, hidden

visibly *adv*
perceptibly, noticeably, evidently, clearly, obviously, manifestly, openly, overtly, plainly, conspicuously, patently
≠ invisibly, indiscernibly

vision *n*
1 SIGHT, seeing, eyesight, perception, discernment, far-sightedness, foresight, penetration
2 IDEA, ideal, conception, insight, perception, intuition, view, picture, image, mental image/picture, imagination, fantasy, dream, daydream; *Irish* aisling
3 APPARITION, hallucination, dream, illusion, optical illusion, delusion, mirage, phantom, ghost, chimera, spectre, wraith

visionary *adj, n*
♦ *adj*
idealistic, impractical, romantic, dreamy, unrealistic, utopian, quixotic, unreal, fanciful, prophetic, perceptive, discerning, far-sighted, speculative, unworkable, illusory, imaginary
COLLOQ. moonshiny, ivory-tower
♦ *n*
idealist, romantic, dreamer, daydreamer, fantasist, prophet, mystic, seer, utopian, Don Quixote, rainbow-chaser, theorist
≠ pragmatist

visit *v, n*
♦ *v*
1 *visit her brother*
call on, call in, call round, go and see, go round/over to, stay with, stay at, look in, look up, see, spend time with, stop off at/over at/in at, take, frequent, haunt; *dialect* mump; *N Am* come by, stop by
FORMAL wait on/upon
COLLOQ. drop in on, drop by, stop by, pop in, blow in
2 INFLICT, punish, trouble, afflict, curse, plague
OLD smite
♦ *n*
call, stay, stop, excursion, pop-visit
OLD salutation
FORMAL sojourn

visitation *n*
1 VISIT, inspection, examination
2 INFLICTION, punishment, retribution, catastrophe, disaster, calamity, bane, blight, scourge, ordeal, trial, cataclysm
3 APPEARANCE, manifestation

visitor *n*
caller, guest, company, tourist, traveller, holidaymaker

vista *n*
view, prospect, panorama, perspective, outlook, scene, vision

visual *adj*
visible, observable, discernible, perceptible, optical
FORMAL ocular, optic, specular

visualize *v*
picture, envisage, imagine, see, conceive (of), contemplate

vital *adj*
1 CRITICAL, crucial, important, imperative, key, significant, basic, fundamental, essential, necessary, indispensable, urgent, life-and-death, decisive, forceful
FORMAL requisite

2 LIVELY, alive, living, life-giving, invigorating, spirited, vivacious, vibrant, vigorous, forceful, dynamic, animated, energetic
FORMAL quickening
≠ 1 inessential, peripheral 2 dead

vitality *n*
life, liveliness, animation, vigour, energy, vivacity, spirit, sparkle, exuberance, zest, strength, stamina, juice; *Scot* foison, fushion, fizzen
OLD vivency
COLLOQ. go, get-up-and-go, oomph, pizzazz, bounce, zap, zing

vitally *adv*
crucially, critically, significantly, importantly, fundamentally, essentially, urgently, decisively

vitamin

Vitamins include:

aneurin (or thiamine)	cyanocobalamin	pantothenic acid
ascorbic acid	ergocalciferol	phylloquinone
bioflavonoid/	folic acid	pteroic acid
citrin	linoleic acid	pyridoxine (or
biotin	linolenic acid	adermin)
calciferol	menadione	retinol
cholecalciferol	nicotinic acid (or	riboflavin
	niacin)	tocopherol

vitiate *v*
spoil, mar, weaken, undermine, deteriorate, harm, injure, blemish, ruin, sully, taint, corrupt, pervert, pollute, debase, contaminate, blight, defile, invalidate, nullify, devalue, deprave, impair

vitriolic *adj*
bitter, abusive, virulent, vicious, venomous, malicious, acrimonious, caustic, biting, sardonic, scathing, destructive
FORMAL acerbic, mordant, trenchant, vituperative

vituperate *v*
blame, revile, slate, run down, reproach, censure, denounce, abuse
FORMAL berate, castigate, upbraid, vilify
COLLOQ. slam, nag, knock, rubbish
SLANG slag (off)
≠ praise, applaud, extol

vituperation *n*
censure, rebuke, reprimand, reproach, blame, abuse, fault-finding, scurrility
FORMAL castigation, invective, obloquy, revilement, contumely, diatribe, philippic, vilification, objurgation
COLLOQ. flak, stick, knocking, rubbishing
SLANG slagging(-off)
≠ acclaim, praise

vituperative *adj*
censorious, harsh, insulting, abusive, scornful, derogatory, defamatory, scurrilous, withering, belittling, sardonic
FORMAL calumniatory, denunciatory, fulminatory, opprobrious
≠ laudatory

vivacious *adj*
lively, animated, spirited, high-spirited, effervescent, cheerful, jolly, merry, sparkling, light-hearted
FORMAL ebullient
COLLOQ. bubbly, chirpy, bouncy

vivacity *n*
liveliness, spirit, animation, energy, quickness, vitality, dynamism, activity, élan, effervescence, light-heartedness, merriness
FORMAL ebullience

COLLOQ. brio, go, get-up-and-go, oomph, pizzazz, bounce, zap, zing

vivid *adj*
1 BRIGHT, colourful, intense, strong, rich, vibrant, brilliant, glowing, dazzling, glaring, lurid, vigorous, expressive, dramatic, flamboyant, animated, dynamic, lively, lifelike, spirited
2 MEMORABLE, powerful, graphic, clear, distinct, striking, dramatic, lively, sharp, realistic
E3 1 colourless, dull **2** vague

vividly *adv*
1 *vividly coloured*
brightly, intensely, strongly, richly, vibrantly, brilliantly, dramatically, flamboyantly
2 *I remember her vividly*
clearly, distinctly, powerfully, memorably, graphically
E3 1 dully **2** vaguely

vividness *n*
intensity, strength, glow, brilliancy, brightness, lucidity, radiance, realism, clarity, sharpness, immediacy, life, liveliness, distinctness
FORMAL refulgence, resplendence
E3 dullness, lifelessness

viz *adv*
namely, that is, ie, specifically, that is to say, in other words
FORMAL to wit

vocabulary *n*
language, words, glossary, lexicon, dictionary, wordbook, thesaurus, idiom, cant, pidgin, slang
TECHNICAL lexis, idioticon
OLD nomenclature
COLLOQ. vocab
Related adjective: vocabularian

vocal *adj*
1 SPOKEN, said, oral, uttered, expressed, voiced
2 ARTICULATE, eloquent, expressive, noisy, clamorous, shrill, strident, outspoken, frank, blunt, forthright, plain-spoken, vociferous
E3 1 unspoken **2** inarticulate

vocalize *v*
express, articulate, verbalize, put into words, utter, voice, give voice to, say, speak, state, communicate, put/get over, pronounce, word, tell, announce, report, assert, declare, put across, formulate, point out, intimate, convey, vent, ventilate, air
FORMAL enunciate

vocally *adv*
articulately, eloquently, expressively, stridently, forthrightly

vocation *n*
calling, pursuit, career, métier, mission, profession, occupation, trade, employment, work, craft, role, line, post, job, business, office

vociferous *adj*
noisy, vocal, clamorous, loud, obstreperous, strident, vehement, thundering, shouting, outspoken, frank, blunt, forthright
E3 quiet

vociferously *adv*
loudly, noisily, vocally, stridently, vehemently, bluntly, frankly, outspokenly
E3 quietly

vogue *n*
fashion, style, taste, craze, popularity, trend, prevalence, acceptance, custom
FORMAL mode
COLLOQ. fad, the latest, the rage, the thing
■ **in vogue**
fashionable, modish, popular, stylish, trendy, up-to-the-minute, voguish, current, prevalent
COLLOQ. in, with it

voice *n, v*
♦ *n*
1 SPEECH, utterance, articulation, language, words, sound, tone, intonation, inflection, expression, mouthpiece, agency, vehicle, medium, instrument, organ
Related adjective: vocal
2 SAY, vote, opinion, view, decision, option, will, desire, wish, airing
♦ *v*
express, say, utter, air, articulate, speak of, talk of, mention, verbalize, assert, convey, disclose, divulge, declare, enunciate

void *adj, n, v*
♦ *adj*
1 EMPTY, emptied, free, unfilled, unoccupied, vacant, clear, bare, blank, drained, lacking, devoid
2 ANNULLED, inoperative, invalid, cancelled, nullified, ineffective, futile, useless, vain, worthless, nugatory
E3 1 full **2** valid, binding
♦ *n*
emptiness, vacuity, vacuum, abyss, chasm, blank, blankness, space, lack, want, cavity, gap, hollow, opening
FORMAL lacuna
♦ *v*
1 NULLIFY, cancel, annul, invalidate, rescind
TECHNICAL avoid
FORMAL abnegate
2 DISCHARGE, eject, defecate, emit, empty, drain, evacuate
E3 1 validate **2** fill

volatile *adj*
changeable, inconstant, unstable, variable, erratic, irregular, temperamental, unsteady, unsettled, fickle, whimsical, unpredictable, fitful, restless, giddy, flighty, lively, volcanic, explosive, skittish, light-winged, rattle-brained, rattle-headed, rattle-pated
FORMAL mercurial, capricious
COLLOQ. up and down
E3 constant, steady

volatility *n*
instability, capriciousness, flightiness, fitfulness, fickleness, inconstancy, unsteadiness, shakiness, irresolution, uncertainty, changeableness, variability, fluctuation, unreliability, insecurity, precariousness
E3 constancy, stability

volcano *n*
Related adjective: volcanic

The world's active volcanoes include:

Etna (*Italy*)	Mauna Loa	Ruapehu (*New*
Hekla (*Iceland*)	(*Hawaii*)	*Zealand*)
Hudson (*Chile*)	Mayon	St Helens (*USA*)
Kilauea (*Hawaii*)	(*Philippines*)	Stromboli (*Italy*)
Klyuchevskoy	Nyamuragira	Taal (*Philippines*)
(*Russia*)	(*Zaire*)	Vesuvius (*Italy*)
Krakatoa	Pinatubo	Vulcano (*Italy*)
(*Sumatra*)	(*Philippines*)	

---

volition *n*
will, free will, choice, choosing, determination, option, election, preference, discretion, purpose, resolution
■ **of your own volition**
of your own free will, voluntarily, willingly, freely, intentionally, consciously, deliberately, purposely, spontaneously, by choice, on your own initiative, of your own accord
E3 involuntarily, unwillingly

volley *n*
barrage, salvo, bombardment, cannonade, fusillade, hail, shower, burst, blast, discharge, explosion

volte-face *n*
about-turn, about-face, (complete) reversal, turnabout
FORMAL enantiodromia
COLLOQ. U-turn

voluble *adj*
fluent, glib, articulate, talkative, forthcoming, garrulous
FORMAL loquacious
COLLOQ. chatty

volume *n*
1 BOOK, tome, publication
FORMAL omnibus
2 BULK, size, capacity, space, dimensions, amount, mass, quantity, aggregate, amplitude, body
3 LOUDNESS, sound, noise, amplification
TECHNICAL decibels

voluminous *adj*
roomy, big, ample, spacious, billowing, vast, full, bulky, huge, large
FORMAL capacious

voluntarily *adv*
willingly, freely, intentionally, consciously, deliberately, purposely, spontaneously, of your own free will, by choice, on your own initiative, of your own accord
█▄ involuntarily, unwillingly

voluntary *adj*
1 FREE, gratuitous, optional, spontaneous, unforced, willing, volunteer, unpaid, without pay, unsalaried, honorary
2 CONSCIOUS, deliberate, purposeful, intended, intentional, wilful, optional, of your own free will
FORMAL of your own volition
█▄ **1** compulsory, obligatory **2** involuntary

volunteer *v, n*
♦ *v*
offer, propose, put forward, come forward, present, suggest, step forward, advance, tender
OLD voluntary
FORMAL proffer
♦ *n*
voluntary worker, community-service worker, doer, activist, participant, recruit, helping hand
COLLOQ. do-gooder

voluptuary *n*
hedonist, sensualist, epicurean, pleasure-seeker, libertine, sybarite, debauchee, *bon vivant , bon viveur*
FORMAL profligate
COLLOQ. playboy
█▄ ascetic

voluptuous *adj*
1 SENSUAL, licentious, luxurious, self-indulgent, hedonistic, sensuous, opulent
2 EROTIC, shapely, buxom, full-figured, curvaceous, seductive, provocative, enticing
COLLOQ. sexy, beddable

vomit *v*
be sick, bring up, heave, retch, regurgitate
COLLOQ. throw up, puke, spew, sick up, chuck up, fetch up
SLANG *N Am* barf, upchuck; *Aust* chunder

vomiting *n*
sickness, retching, regurgitation, emission, ejection, chundering
TECHNICAL emesis
OLD parbreak
COLLOQ. puking, spewing
SLANG *N Am* barfing

voracious *adj*
insatiable, greedy, hungry, gluttonous, acquisitive, avid, devouring, ravenous, ravening, uncontrolled, unquenchable
FORMAL edacious, omnivorous, prodigious, rapacious

voracity *n*
greed, hunger, ravenousness, eagerness, acquisitiveness, avidity
FORMAL edacity, rapacity

vortex *n*
whirlpool, maelstrom, eddy, whirlwind, whirl

votary *n*
believer, follower, disciple, devotee, addict, adherent

vote *n, v*
♦ *n*
1 *to cast your vote*
ballot, poll, election, franchise, referendum, plebiscite, yes, no
OLD yea, nay
2 *give everyone the vote*
franchise, suffrage, enfranchisement
█▄ disenfranchisement
♦ *v*
elect, ballot, go to the polls, re-elect, choose, opt for, go for, plump for, suggest, put in, declare, return
■ **vote in**
elect, vote for, choose, pick, opt for, select, decide on, prefer, adopt, designate, appoint, determine, co-opt, return
OLD voice
COLLOQ. plump for
■ **vote out**
remove, oust, overthrow, dismiss, unseat, topple, displace, demote, dethrone
COLLOQ. boot out, turf out

voter *n*
vote, constituent, member of the electorate, franchiser, balloter, floating voter, no, yes, citizen, free person, burgher, outvoter
OLD yea, nay, faggot, ten-pounder; *N Am* colonist

vouch
■ **vouch for**
guarantee, assure, warrant, support, back, endorse, confirm, answer for, certify, affirm, verify, assert, speak for, swear to, uphold
FORMAL attest to, asseverate

voucher *n*
coupon, token, ticket, document, paper, chit, note, warrant, gift token/voucher, book token, luncheon voucher

vouchsafe *v*
give, grant, impart, deign, yield, cede
FORMAL bestow, confer, accord

vow *v, n*
♦ *v*
promise, pledge, swear, give your word, undertake, dedicate, devote, profess, consecrate, affirm; *Scot* hight
OLD behight, bename; (*Shakesp*) protest
FORMAL nuncupate
♦ *n*
promise, oath, pledge
OLD avow, hest; (*Spenser*) heast, heaste
FORMAL nuncupation
Related adjectives: votive

voyage *n, v*
♦ *n*
journey, travel(s), trip, passage, expedition, crossing, cruise, sail, tour, safari, course, rough passage
OLD navigation, shipping, traffic, middle passage

FORMAL odyssey
• v
journey, travel, go, cruise, sail, tour, go/put to sea

vulgar adj
1 INDECENT, obscene, coarse, improper, dirty, filthy, crude, suggestive, risqué, rude, indelicate, distasteful, offensive, off-colour, ribald, lewd, bawdy
COLLOQ. near the bone
2 UNREFINED, uncouth, coarse, rude, rough, common, crude, ill-bred, impolite, boorish
FORMAL indecorous
3 TASTELESS, flashy, showy, ostentatious, kitsch, garish, loud, gaudy, tawdry
COLLOQ. cheap and nasty, tacky, glitzy
4 ORDINARY, general, popular, vernacular, common, low, unsophisticated, uncultured
E3 1 decent **2** correct **3** tasteful, refined **4** sophisticated

vulgarity n
1 CRUDENESS, indecency, crudity, dirtiness, rudeness, suggestiveness, ribaldry, coarseness
2 TASTELESSNESS, tawdriness, gaudiness, showiness, ostentation, garishness
E3 1 decency, politeness **2** tastefulness

vulnerable adj
unprotected, exposed, unguarded, insecure, defenceless, in danger, exposed to danger, susceptible, weak, powerless, helpless, sensitive, open, open to attack, wide open
E3 protected, strong, safe

wacky *adj*
crazy, silly, wild, eccentric, offbeat, irrational, odd, unpredictable, zany, erratic, daft
COLLOQ. bonkers, goofy, loopy, nutty, screwy
SLANG loony
F3 sensible

wad *n*
chunk, plug, roll, bundle, ball, lump, hunk, mass, block
COLLOQ. wodge

wadding *n*
packing, padding, stuffing, filling, filler, lining, cotton wool

waddle *v*
toddle, totter, wobble, sway, rock, shuffle

wade *v*
cross, ford, loll, lie, wallow, roll, welter, lurch, flounder, splash
FORMAL traverse

■ **wade in**
pitch in, launch in, tear in, set to, get stuck in, wade through, trawl through, plough through

waffle *v, n*
◆ *v*
jabber, prattle, babble; *Scot* blether; *dialect & N Am* blather
COLLOQ. rabbit on, witter on
◆ *n*
prattle, wordiness, verbosity, padding, nonsense; *Scot* blethers; *dialect & N Am* blathers
COLLOQ. gobbledygook, hot air, guff, wittering

waft *v, n*
◆ *v*
drift, float, glide, blow, transport, carry, transmit
◆ *n*
breath, puff, draught, current, breeze, scent, whiff

wag *v, n*
◆ *v*
shake, waggle, wave, sway, swing, bob, nod, wiggle, oscillate, wobble, flutter, vibrate, quiver, rock
◆ *n*
wit, joker, humorist, jester, comic, comedian, clown, fool, droll, banterer, gagman

wage *n, v*
◆ *n*
pay, fee, earnings, salary, wage-packet, payment, stipend, remuneration, allowance, reward, hire, compensation, returns, recompense, pittance
OLD meed, pension, imprest, penny-fee
FORMAL emolument
SLANG screw
◆ *v*
carry on, conduct, engage in, undertake, execute, practise, pursue, levy, war

wager *v, n*
◆ *v*
bet, gamble, chance, risk, speculate, venture, stake, pledge, lay odds, hazard, punt
◆ *n*

bet, gamble, speculation, stake, venture, hazard, pledge, punt, flutter

waggish *adj*
amusing, mischievous, playful, sportive, funny, humorous, comical, droll, facetious, witty, impish, roguish, jesting, frolicsome, puckish, merry, bantering
FORMAL risible, jocular, jocose
F3 grave, serious, staid

waggle *v*
wiggle, wobble, shake, jiggle, wave, oscillate, wag, bobble, flutter

wagon *n*
cart, dray, carriage, truck, van, train, float, buggy

waif *n*
orphan, stray, ragamuffin, urchin, foundling

wail *v, n*
◆ *v*
moan, cry, howl, lament, weep, sob, complain, groan, keen
FORMAL ululate
COLLOQ. yowl
◆ *n*
moan, cry, howl, lament, complaint, groan, weeping, sob
FORMAL ululation

wait *v, n*
◆ *v*
delay, linger, hold back, hesitate, pause, remain, rest, stand, stand by, sit out, stay, await
OLD watch, expect, bide tryst
FORMAL abide, tarry, bide, bide your time
COLLOQ. hang around, hang on, hang fire, lick your chops
F3 proceed, go ahead
◆ *n*
hold-up, hesitation, delay, interval, pause, halt

■ **wait on**
serve, attend to, minister to, look after, take care of, tend, work for, see, dance attendance on

---

Colloquial ways of telling someone to wait include:

all in good time	hang on	just a minute
bear with me	hold on	just a moment
half a mo	hold your horses	just a second
half a moment	I'll be right with	just a tick
half a tick	you	wait a minute
hang in there	just a jiffy	wait a moment

---

waiter, waitress *n*
server, attendant, steward, stewardess, host, hostess, butler, *garçon, maître d'hôtel*, sommelier, commis; *N Am* waitron, busboy, busgirl
COLLOQ. pannier, maître d'

waive *v*
give up, do without, for(e)go, abandon, set aside, resign, surrender, yield, cede, postpone, defer
FORMAL renounce, relinquish
F3 enforce, claim, maintain

waiver *n*
disclaimer, postponement, resignation, surrender, abandonment
FORMAL abdication, deferral, relinquishment, remission, renunciation

wake¹ *v, n*
♦ *v*
1 RISE, get up, arise, waken, awake, awaken, rouse, stir, come to, bring round
2 STIMULATE, stir, activate, arouse, animate, excite, fire, galvanize, prod, goad, whet
COLLOQ. egg on
3 ALERT, notify, warn, signal, make/become aware of, make/become conscious of
E∃ 1 sleep
♦ *n*
funeral, death-watch, vigil, watch, lichwake; *Scot* lykewake

wake² *n*
in the wake of the ship
trail, track, path, aftermath, backwash, wash, rear, train, waves

wakeful *adj*
sleepless, restless, insomniac, unsleeping, watchful, vigilant, observant, heedful, attentive, alert, wary; *Scot* wakerife, waukrife
E∃ inattentive, sleepy, unwary

wakefulness *n*
sleeplessness, restlessness, insomnia, watchfulness, vigilance, attentiveness

waken *v*
wake, rise, get up, awake, awaken, arouse, rouse, stimulate, stir, whet, quicken, animate, activate, enliven, kindle, fire, ignite, galvanize

walk *v, n*
♦ *v*
1 GO ON FOOT
FORMAL perambulate
COLLOQ. hoof it, go on shanks's pony/mare, stretch your legs
2 ACCOMPANY, escort, guide, lead, conduct, usher, shepherd
♦ *n*
1 *he has an odd walk*
carriage, gait, step, pace, stride
2 *go for a walk*
stroll, amble, ramble, saunter, march, hike, tramp, promenade, trek, traipse, trudge, trail
3 *a tree-lined walk*
footpath, path, way, walkway, avenue, pathway, promenade, alley, esplanade, lane, drive, track, pavement, sidewalk
4 BEAT, round, rounds, circuit, way, path, route, trail
▪ **walk of life**
occupation, profession, trade, field, area, sphere, line, activity, arena, course, pursuit, career, vocation, calling, métier, background
▪ **walk off/away with**
go off with, make off with, run off with, steal, pocket
COLLOQ. pinch, nick, lift, filch, snaffle, knock up, nobble, knock off, swipe, whip, bag, nip, liberate, relieve of, help yourself to, have your fingers in the till; *Aust & NZ* duckshove, souvenir
▪ **walk out**
go on strike, strike, stop work, down tools, protest, mutiny, revolt, take industrial action
▪ **walk out on**
abandon, desert
FORMAL forsake
COLLOQ. run out on, jilt, dump, leave in the lurch, leave high and dry

▪ **walk over**
trample on, take advantage of, take liberties, misuse, abuse, profiteer, oppress, ill-treat, impose on, manipulate
COLLOQ. put something across someone, pull a fast one on, play off against
SLANG take for a ride

Ways of walking include:

amble	plod	strut
clump	potter	stumble
crawl	promenade	swagger
creep	prowl	tiptoe
dodder	ramble	*colloq.* toddle
expatiate	roam	totter
hike	sashay	traipse
Scot hirple	saunter	tramp
hobble	scuttle	trample
Scot lamp	shamble	tread
limp	shuffle	trek
lope	sleepwalk	trip
lurch	slink	troop
march	sneak	trot
mince	somnambulate	trudge
colloq. mooch	stagger	trundle
pace	stalk	waddle
pad	steal	wade
paddle	step	*colloq.* waltz
parade	stomp	wander
patter	*Scot* stot	*colloq.* yomp
formal	stride	
perambulate	stroll	

walker *n*
pedestrian, rambler, hiker

walk-out *n*
strike, stoppage, industrial action, protest, rebellion, revolt

walkover *n*
easy win/victory
COLLOQ. pushover, doddle, child's play, piece of cake, cakewalk, cinch

walkway *n*
path, pathway, passage, footpath, lane, pavement, promenade, esplanade; *N Am* sidewalk

wall
Related adjective: mural
▪ **wall in**
enclose, surround, encircle, encompass, ring, circle, fence, hedge, hem in, bound, envelop, confine, frame, cage, hold, shut in, close in, wrap, pen, corral
OLD (*Shakesp*) circummure
FORMAL circumscribe
▪ **go to the wall**
collapse, fail, founder, break down, fall through, finish, disintegrate, come to an end, come to nothing, slump
COLLOQ. go bust, fold, flop
See panels on next page

wallet *n*
pouch, purse, folder, holder, case, notecase, pochette; *N Am* bill-fold

wallop *v, n*
♦ *v*
beat, hit, smack, punch, pummel, buffet, swat, swipe, bash, strike, thrash, thump, pound, clout, batter, defeat, crush, trounce, rout, drub, hammer
FORMAL vanquish
COLLOQ. belt, lick, paste, clobber, whack, thwack, wallop, bonk, whop
SLANG *N Am* lam
♦ *n*
blow, kick, thump, clout, swat, swipe, smack, punch, bash
COLLOQ. whack, thwack, wallop, bonk

Types of wall include:

abutment	brick wall	dyke (or dike)	garden wall	paling	screen
bailey	bulkhead	divider	hedge	palisade	sea-wall
barricade	bulwark	embankment	inner wall	parapet	shield wall
barrier	buttress	enclosure wall	load-bearing wall	partition	stockade
block	cavity wall	fence	mural	party wall	stud partition
breeze-block	curtain wall	flying buttress	obstacle	rampart	wall of death
wall	dam	fortification	outer bailey	retaining wall	

Famous walls include:

Antonine Wall	Berlin Wall	Great Wall of China	Hadrian's Wall	Western Wall (or Wailing Wall)

wallow *v*
1 *wallow in mud*
loll, lie, roll, wade, welter, lurch, flounder, splash
2 *wallow in nostalgia*
indulge, relish, revel, bask, enjoy, glory, delight
FORMAL luxuriate

wan *adj*
pale, washed out, ashen, white, weak, discoloured, faint, colourless, anaemic, ghastly, feeble, whey-faced, waxen, pallid, pasty, sickly, bleak, mournful, weary

wand *n*
rod, baton, staff, stick, sprig, mace, sceptre, twig

wander *v, n*
♦ *v*
1 ROAM, rove, ramble, meander, saunter, stroll, prowl, drift, range, traipse, stray, straggle, cruise, gad, swan off, moon about/around, roll, walk the streets, maraud, maunder, vagabondize, pilgrim; *dialect* stroam; *Scot* ratch about, stravaig, taver; *Irish* streel
OLD expatiate, extravagate, forwander, squander, stooge around, wend, wilder; (*Shakesp*) wheel; *Scot* vague
FORMAL peregrinate
COLLOQ. kick about/around, mooch
SLANG bat around
2 DIGRESS, diverge, deviate, depart, go astray, stray, turn away, swerve, veer, err, lose your way, aberrate; *dialect* moider
FORMAL divagate
3 RAMBLE, rave, babble, gibber, talk nonsense
♦ *n*
excursion, ramble, amble, stroll, saunter, meander, prowl, cruise

---

Synonym nuances
verb sense 1
You can use **roam** to suggest a lack of purpose in one's wanderings, and **rove** and **ramble** are similarly directionless, but are more suggestive of wandering for recreation or pleasure. **Meander**, meanwhile, implies a slow, circuitous route: *the river meandered through the town*. Similarly, **saunter** and **stroll** imply walking at a slow pace, with connotations of being carefree, whereas **prowl** has rather furtive or sinister implications: *journalists prowled, on the lookout for a story*. **Drift**, on the other hand, implies the absence of a plan: *he drifted through life*, while **range** suggests covering a wide area: *the troops ranged hundreds of miles into the country*.
  Other terms have negative connotations. **Traipse** is suggestive of weariness. **Stray** implies deviating from the intended route, and **straggle** suggests falling behind. You can use **cruise** more narrowly to imply wandering in search of something, and this term is often associated with looking for a sexual partner, while **gad** also most often suggests the pursuit of pleasure: *gadding off on expensive holidays*. **Swan off** also suggests nonchalance but has a rather critical tone, while **roll** implies swagger: *what kind of time is this to roll in at?* **Maraud** is reserved for wandering with the aim of raiding or plundering.

---

wanderer *n*
itinerant, traveller, voyager, drifter, rover, rambler, stroller, stray, straggler, ranger, wayfarer, nomad, Gypsy, vagrant, vagabond, prodigal
COLLOQ. rolling stone

wandering *adj, n*
♦ *adj*
itinerant, travelling, rambling, wayfaring, roving, strolling, voyaging, rootless, homeless, unsettled, drifting, migratory, nomadic, vagabond, vagrant
FORMAL peripatetic
♦ *n*
1 TRAVELS, drift(ing), journey(ing), meander(ing), walkabout
FORMAL odyssey, peregrination
2 DIGRESSION, divergence, deviation, departure
FORMAL evagation

wane *v, n*
♦ *v*
diminish, decrease, decline, weaken, subside, fade (away), dwindle, ebb, lessen, sink, drop, taper off, peter out, dim, droop, contract, shrink, fail, wither, vanish
OLD welk, welke
FORMAL abate
▪ increase, wax
♦ *n*
fading, dwindling, decline, decrease, lessening, sinking, ebb, contraction, subsidence, weakening, decay, degeneration, failure, fall, drop, tapering off, atrophy
FORMAL abatement, diminution
▪ increase
■ **on the wane**
deteriorating, declining, degenerating, weakening, withering, fading, subsiding, dwindling, lessening, ebbing, tapering off, dropping, on the decline, obsolescent
FORMAL moribund
COLLOQ. on its last legs, on the way out

wangle *v*
manipulate, arrange, contrive, engineer, fix, scheme, manoeuvre, work, pull off, manage
COLLOQ. fiddle, wheel and deal

want *v, n*
♦ *v*
1 DESIRE, wish, like, feel like, crave, covet, fancy, hope for, long for, pine for, yearn for, hunger for, thirst for
2 NEED, require, demand, lack, miss, be without, be deficient in, call for
♦ *n*
1 DESIRE, demand, longing, pining, yearning, craving, coveting, hunger, thirst, requirement, wish, need, lust, appetite
2 LACK, dearth, insufficiency, absence, deficiency, shortage, inadequacy, scarcity, scantiness
FORMAL paucity
3 POVERTY, destitution
FORMAL privation, indigence, penury

wanting *adj*
1 ABSENT, missing, lacking, short, insufficient
2 INADEQUATE, imperfect, faulty, defective, substandard, poor, deficient, unsatisfactory, unacceptable, disappointing
COLLOQ. not up to scratch
1 sufficient **2** adequate

wanton *adj, n*
• *adj*
1 *a wanton action*
malicious, malevolent, arbitrary, unprovoked, unjustifiable, groundless, gratuitous, pointless, unrestrained, rash, reckless, wild, extravagant
2 *a wanton woman*
immoral, promiscuous, shameless, immodest, impure, abandoned, dissipated, dissolute, lewd, lecherous, lascivious, sportive; *Scot* cadgy
OLD cork-heeled, petulant, smicker, toyish, toysome; (*Shakesp*) nice, riggish
• *n*
slut, harlot, strumpet, trollop, prostitute, whore, voluptuary, debauchee, lecher, libertine, rake, roué, Don Juan, Casanova
SLANG tart

war *n, v*
• *n*
warfare, hostilities, fighting, fight, battle, combat, conflict, clash, skirmish, strife, struggle, bloodshed, contest, confrontation, campaign, contention, enmity, antagonism, ill-will
COLLOQ. *Aust & NZ* stoush
Related adjective: martial
■ peace, ceasefire
See panels on next page
• *v*
wage war, fight, take up arms, cross swords, make war, battle, clash, combat, strive, skirmish, struggle, contest, contend
■ **war cry**
rallying-cry, battle-cry, war song, slogan, watchword

warble *v, n*
• *v*
sing, chirrup, chirp, twitter, quaver, yodel, trill
• *n*
song, cry, call, chirp, chirrup, quaver, trill, twitter

ward *n, v*
• *n*
1 ROOM, apartment, compartment, cubicle, unit
2 DIVISION, area, district, quarter, precinct, zone
3 CHARGE, dependant, protégé(e), pupil, minor
■ **ward off**
avert, fend off, deflect, parry, repel, drive back, stave off, thwart, beat off, forestall, evade, turn aside, turn away, block, avoid
COLLOQ. dodge

warden *n*
keeper, custodian, guardian, protector, warder, caretaker, curator, ranger, steward, watchman, superintendent, supervisor, overseer, administrator, janitor, concierge, housekeeper, constable
COLLOQ. meter maid/man

warder *n*
jailer, keeper, prison officer, guard, wardress, custodian, warden
SLANG screw

wardrobe *n*
1 CUPBOARD, closet, locker, cabinet
2 CLOTHES, outfit, garments
FORMAL attire, apparel

warehouse *n*
store, storehouse, depot, depository, repository, stockroom, entrepôt, shed, goods shed, freight shed, bodega, godown, hong
COLLOQ. lock-up

wares *n*
goods, merchandise, commodities, stock, products, produce, stuff

warfare *n*
war, fighting, hostilities, battle, arms, combat, strife, struggle, passage of arms, contest, confrontation, campaign, conflict, contention, discord, blows
■ peace

warily *adv*
cautiously, carefully, with care, guardedly, watchfully, vigilantly, hesitantly, apprehensively, gingerly, cagily, charily, suspiciously, uneasily, distrustfully
FORMAL circumspectly
■ heedlessly, recklessly, thoughtlessly, unwarily

wariness *n*
caution, carefulness, attention, mindfulness, alertness, care, prudence, heedfulness, watchfulness, vigilance, foresight, discretion, caginess, apprehension, hesitancy, suspicion, distrust, unease
FORMAL circumspection
■ heedlessness, recklessness, thoughtlessness

warlike *adj*
martial, belligerent, aggressive, combative, bloodthirsty, warmongering, militaristic, militant, hostile, antagonistic, hawkish, unfriendly
OLD (*Spenser*) battailous
FORMAL bellicose, pugnacious
■ friendly, peaceable

warlock *n*
witch, wizard, sorcerer, enchanter, conjurer, magician, demon
FORMAL necromancer

warm *adj, v*
• *adj*
1 HEATED, hot, tepid, lukewarm
2 ARDENT, passionate, fervent, vehement, intense, earnest, eager, enthusiastic, heartfelt, sincere, zealous
3 *warm colours*
rich, intense, mellow, cheerful, relaxing
4 FRIENDLY, amiable, cordial, affable, kind, kindly, genial, hearty, hospitable, caring, sympathetic, loving, affectionate, tender
5 FINE, sunny, balmy, temperate, close
■ 1 cold, cool **2** indifferent **3** cold, cool **4** unfriendly, hostile **5** cool, chilly
• *v*
1 HEAT (UP), make warm, reheat, melt, thaw
2 ANIMATE, interest, please, delight, stimulate, liven up, enliven, put some life into, stir, rouse, excite, cheer up
■ 1 cool
■ **warm to**
begin to like, become enthusiastic about, become friendly towards
■ **warm up**
limber up, loosen up, exercise, prepare

warm-blooded *adj*
passionate, enthusiastic, excitable, fervent, hot-blooded, emotional, ardent, earnest, lively, spirited, vivacious, impetuous, rash

warm-hearted *adj*
kind, kind-hearted, kindly, affectionate, loving, sympathetic, tender, tender-hearted, compassionate, generous, cordial, ardent, genial
■ cold, unsympathetic

Types of war include:

ambush	biological warfare	counter-attack	invasion	resistance	war of attrition
armed conflict	blitz	engagement	jihad	skirmish	war of nerves
asymmetric(al)	blitzkrieg	germ warfare	jungle warfare	state of siege	world war
warfare	bombardment	guerrilla warfare	limited war	struggle	
assault	chemical warfare	holy war	manoeuvres	total war	
attack	civil war	hot war	nuclear war	trade war	
battle	cold war	intifada	private war	trench warfare	

Famous wars include:

American Civil War (or Second American Revolution)	Franco-Prussian War	Russo-Finnish War (or Winter War)	Thirty Years War
	Gulf War		Vietnam War
	Hundred Years War	Russo-Japanese War	War of 1812
American Revolution (or War of Independence)	Indian Wars	Russo-Turkish Wars	War of the Pacific
	Iran-Iraq War	Seven Years War	Wars of the Roses
Boer War	Iraq War	Six-Day War	World War I (or Great War)
Cod wars	Korean War	Spanish-American War	World War II
Crimean War	Mexican War	Spanish-American Wars of Independence	
Crusades	Napoleonic Wars		
English Civil War	Opium Wars	Spanish Civil War	
Falklands War	Peasants' War	Suez Crisis	

---

warmonger *n*
hawk, militarist, aggressor, sabre-rattler

warmth *n*
1 WARMNESS, heat, hotness, fire
2 FRIENDLINESS, affection, cordiality, tenderness, kindness, kindliness, care, love, compassion, sympathy, hospitality
3 ARDOUR, enthusiasm, passion, fervour, zeal, vehemence, intensity, eagerness, sincerity
Ⓕ3 1 coldness **2** unfriendliness **3** indifference

warn *v*
1 INFORM, notify, tell, let know, advise, alert, give (advance) notice, put on your guard, sound the alarm; *Scot* shore
OLD (*Spenser*) awarn
FORMAL forewarn, portend, presage
COLLOQ. tip off
2 ADVISE, counsel, urge, caution, exhort
TECHNICAL *N Am* factorize
3 REBUKE, caution, reprimand, reprove
OLD premonish
FORMAL admonish

warning *n, adj*
♦ *n*
1 CAUTION, alert, advice, notification, information, notice, advance notice, counsel, hint, lesson, alarm, threat
FORMAL admonition
COLLOQ. tip-off, shot across the bows, wake-up call
2 OMEN, threat, sign, premonition, signal
FORMAL augury, presage, portent
♦ *adj*
ominous, threatening, cautionary
FORMAL admonitory, premonitory, monitory

warp *v, n*
♦ *v*
twist, bend, contort, deform, distort, buckle, kink, misshape, pervert, corrupt, deviate
Ⓕ3 straighten
♦ *n*
twist, bend, contortion, deformation, distortion, bias, kink, irregularity, turn, bent, defect, deviation, quirk, perversion

warrant *n, v*
♦ *n*
authorization, authority, sanction, validation, permit, permission, consent, licence, guarantee, warranty, security, pledge, commission, voucher, assurance, pardon, death warrant, execution, search warrant, peace-warrant, bench-warrant; *Scot* fudgie-warrant

TECHNICAL detainer, diligence, precept, transire, fiat, mittimus, *lettre de cachet*
♦ *v*
1 GUARANTEE, pledge, swear, certify, assure, promise, declare, affirm, vouch for, answer for, underwrite, uphold, support, back, endorse, deserve
OLD vouchsafe, sepad; (*Shakesp*) able, warn; (*Spenser*) behight, behote
FORMAL avouch
2 AUTHORIZE, entitle, empower, sanction, permit, allow, consent to, license, justify, excuse, approve, support, call for, commission, require, necessitate

warrantable *adj*
permissible, allowable, defensible, excusable, justifiable, right, reasonable, proper, legal, lawful, accountable, necessary
Ⓕ3 indefensible, unjustifiable, unwarrantable

warranty *n*
guarantee, contract, certificate, bond, authorization, assurance, pledge, justification
FORMAL covenant

warring *adj*
fighting, hostile, opposing, opposed, conflicting, contending, combatant, embattled, belligerent, at war, at daggers drawn

warrior *n*
fighter, soldier, fighting man, combatant, champion, warhorse, wardog

wart *n*
growth, lump, protuberance, verruca, anbury, angleberry
OLD wen
FORMAL excrescence, keratosis, papilloma

wary *adj*
cautious, prudent, guarded, careful, chary, on your guard, on the lookout, distrustful, suspicious, heedful, attentive, (on the) alert, watchful, vigilant, wide-awake, leery; *Scot* tentie
OLD aware, ware
FORMAL circumspect
COLLOQ. cagey
Ⓕ3 unwary, careless, heedless

wash *v, n*
♦ *v*
1 CLEAN, cleanse, launder, shampoo, scrub, mop, swab down, sponge, wipe, rinse, soak, swill
2 BATHE, bath, freshen up, get cleaned up, have a wash, have a bath, (have a) shower, douche, shampoo
3 FLOW, sweep, wave, swell, stream, beat, splash, dash

4 *that excuse won't wash*
be believable, be plausible, be accepted, be convincing, hold, hold water, stand up, bear examination, bear scrutiny, carry weight, pass muster
COLLOQ. stick

◆ *n*

1 CLEANING, cleansing, bath, bathe, laundry, laundering, scrub, shower, shampoo, washing, rinse
2 FLOW, roll, sweep, wave, swell, surge
3 LAYER, coat, coating, rinse, stain

■ **wash your hands of**
abandon, give up on, have nothing to do with, leave to your own devices, abdicate responsibility

washed-out *adj*
pale, pallid, blanched, bleached, faded, wan, colourless, ashen, drained, drawn, exhausted, tired-out, fatigued, worn-out, weary, spent, flat, lacklustre, haggard
COLLOQ. all in, dead on your feet, dog-tired, knackered

washout *n*
failure, disaster, disappointment, fiasco, debacle, mess
COLLOQ. flop, lead balloon
E3 success, triumph

waspish *adj*
critical, irritable, bad-tempered, cross, ill-tempered, captious, irascible, peevish, petulant, prickly, snappish, testy, touchy
FORMAL cantankerous
COLLOQ. grumpy, bitchy, crabbed, crabby, crotchety, grouchy

wastage *n*
1 *wastage of scarce natural resources*
squandering, loss, exhausting, draining, frittering away, dissipation
2 DEGENERATION, atrophy, decay, emaciation
TECHNICAL marasmus

waste *v, n, adj*
◆ *v*
1 SQUANDER, misspend, misuse, fritter away, lavish, spend, throw away, get/go through
FORMAL dissipate
COLLOQ. blow, splurge
2 CONSUME, erode, exhaust, drain, destroy, spoil, devastate
3 WITHER, shrivel, shrink, become emaciated, atrophy
4 LAY WASTE, desolate, ravage, destroy, devastate, raze, ruin, sack, spoil, pillage, rape
FORMAL depredate, despoil
E3 **1** economize **2** preserve

◆ *n*
1 SQUANDERING, wastefulness, extravagance, loss
FORMAL dissipation, prodigality
2 MISAPPLICATION, misuse, abuse, neglect
3 RUBBISH, refuse, leftovers, debris, dregs, effluent, litter, scrap, slops, offscouring(s), dross; *NAm* trash, garbage
E3 **1** thriftiness

◆ *adj*
1 USELESS, worthless, unwanted, unused, left-over, superfluous, extra
FORMAL supernumerary
2 BARREN, desolate, empty, uninhabited, bare, devastated, uncultivated, unprofitable, unproductive, wild, dismal, bleak, dreary

Synonym nuances
verb sense 1
Many of the synonyms are, naturally, disapproving in tone. You can use **squander** of the profligate disposal of a resource: *he squandered his talent*, while the more restrained **misspend** and **misuse** suggest an inappropriate application: *the problems resulting from a misspent youth*. **Fritter away** could be used of using something up, bit by bit, in a worthless way: *I frittered away the morning*, while the stronger **throw away**, again,

implies lost opportunities: *he threw away his athletics career with his tendency for nights on the town.*
   Spend, on the other hand, is widely applied to any expenditure, and the terms **get through** and **go through** can be used similarly without suggesting an opinion: *he got through his salary very quickly.* **Lavish**, however, implies prodigious extravagance: *he lavished too much on fine food and wine.*

wasted *adj*
1 UNNECESSARY, needless, useless, unrequired
2 EMACIATED, withered, weak, weakened, shrivelled, shrunken, gaunt, washed-out, spent, atrophied
E3 **1** necessary **2** robust

wasteful *adj*
extravagant, spendthrift, prodigal, uneconomical, thriftless, unthrifty, ruinous, lavish, improvident; *Scot* wasterife, wastrife
OLD wastfull
FORMAL profligate
E3 economical, thrifty

wasteland *n*
wilderness, desert, barrenness, waste, wild(s), void, emptiness, barrenness

wasting *adj*
destroying, emaciating, enfeebling, devastating
TECHNICAL marasmic
E3 strengthening

wastrel *n*
good-for-nothing, idler, layabout, loafer, ne'er-do-well, malingerer, spendthrift
FORMAL profligate
COLLOQ. lounger, shirker, skiver, lazybones
SLANG *NAm* goof-off

watch *v, n*
◆ *v*
1 OBSERVE, see, look at, look on, regard, note, notice, mark, stare at, peer at, gape at, contemplate, scan, survey, gaze at, view
2 GUARD, look after, keep an eye on, mind, protect, superintend, inspect, take care of, keep
COLLOQ. keep tabs on, not take your eyes off
3 PAY ATTENTION, be careful, take care, take heed, look out
◆ *n*
1 TIMEPIECE, wristwatch, clock
FORMAL chronometer
See panel on next page
2 VIGILANCE, watchfulness, vigil, guard, observation, surveillance, notice, lookout, attention, heed, alertness, inspection, supervision

■ **watch out**
notice, be vigilant, look out, keep a lookout, keep your eyes open, keep a weather eye out
COLLOQ. keep your eyes peeled/skinned

■ **watch over**
guard, protect, stand guard over, keep an eye on, look after, take care of, mind, shield, defend, shelter, preserve

watchdog *n*
1 GUARD DOG, house-dog
2 MONITOR, inspector, scrutineer, vigilante, ombudsman, regulator, guardian, custodian, protector

watcher *n*
spectator, observer, onlooker, looker-on, viewer, (member of the) audience, lookout, spy, witness, eyewitness

watchful *adj*
vigilant, attentive, heedful, observant, alert, guarded, on your guard, wide awake, keeping your eyes open/peeled/skinned, on the lookout, on the qui vive, suspicious, wary, chary, cautious; *Scot* wakerife, waukrife

Types of watch include:

analogue watch	digital watch	hunter watch	pendant watch	ring watch	wristwatch
automatic watch	dive watch	kinetic watch	pocket watch	skeleton watch	
bracelet watch	fob watch	lever-watch	quartz watch	*N Am* stemwinder	
chronograph	half-hunter watch	nurse's watch	repeating watch	stopwatch	

OLD adviceful; (*Spenser*) avizefull; (*Shakesp*) open-eyed
FORMAL circumspect
F3 unobservant, inattentive

watchfulness *n*
vigilance, alertness, attention, attentiveness, heedfulness, caution, cautiousness, circumspection, suspicion, suspiciousness, wariness
OLD observance
F3 inattention

watchman *n*
guard, security guard, caretaker, custodian

watchword *n*
catchphrase, slogan, catchword, maxim, password, principle, motto, rallying-cry, battle-cry, signal, byword, buzz word, magic word, shibboleth

water *n, v*
• *n*
rain, sea, ocean, lake, river, current, stream, moisture, flooding, torrent
Related adjective: aqueous
• *v*
wet, moisten, dampen, soak, spray, sprinkle, irrigate, saturate, drench, flood, hose, douse
F3 dry out, parch
■ **water down**
dilute, thin, water, weaken, adulterate, mix, tone down, play down, soften, moderate, qualify
FORMAL mitigate
COLLOQ. soft-pedal
■ **hold water**
stand up, remain valid, cohere, hold (up), stand (up), be believable, be plausible, be accepted, be convincing, bear examination, bear scrutiny, carry weight
COLLOQ. wash, stick

watercourse *n*
river, stream, channel, ditch, canal, wadi, water-channel; *S Afr* spruit

waterfall *n*
fall, falls, cascade, chute, cataract, torrent, rapid(s), overfall, spout, force, foss, lasher, linn; *Can* sault, salt

Famous waterfalls include:

Angel (Venezuela)	Mtarazi (Zimbabwe)	Sutherland (New Zealand)
Cleve-Garth (New Zealand)	Niagara (USA & Canada)	Tugela (South Africa)
Cuquenan (Venezuela)	Ormeli (Norway)	Tyssetrengane (Norway)
Gavarnie (France)	Paulo Alfonso (Brazil)	Vestre Mardola (Norway)
Giessbach (Switzerland)	Ribbon (USA)	Victoria (Zambia & Zimbabwe)
Iguaçu (Brazil & Argentina)	Silver Strand (USA)	Yosemite (USA)
Itatinga (Brazil)	Stanley (Zaire)	
Kaieteur (Guyana)	Staubbach (Switzerland)	

waterproof *adj*
impervious, watertight, water-resistant, damp-proof, rubberized, impermeable, water-repellent, coated, proofed
F3 leaky

watertight *adj*
1 WATERPROOF, sound, sealed, hermetic
2 IMPREGNABLE, unassailable, airtight, flawless, foolproof, firm, sound, incontrovertible, indisputable
F3 1 leaky

watery *adj*
1 LIQUID, fluid, moist, wet, damp
TECHNICAL hydrous
FORMAL aqueous
2 WEAK, watered-down, diluted, adulterated, insipid, tasteless, thin, runny, soggy, squelchy, flavourless, washy
COLLOQ. wishy-washy
F3 1 dry

wave *v, n*
• *v*
1 BECKON, gesture, gesticulate, indicate, sign, signal, direct
2 BRANDISH, flourish, flap, flutter, stir, shake, sway, swing, waft, quiver, ripple, surge, move from side to side
FORMAL undulate
• *n*
1 BREAKER, roller, billow, ripple, comber, foam, froth, swell, surf, tidal wave, wavelet, undulation
COLLOQ. white horse
2 SURGE, sweep, swell, flow, upsurge, ground swell, current, drift, movement, rush, tendency, trend, stream, flood, outbreak, rash
■ **wave aside**
dismiss, brush aside, disregard, reject, set aside, shelve, spurn
COLLOQ. pour cold water on
■ **wave down**
flag down, signal to stop, summon
■ **make waves**
stir up/cause trouble, disturb things, cause a disturbance, challenge the status quo

waver *v*
1 VACILLATE, falter, hesitate, dither, fluctuate, vary, seesaw, equivocate, be undecided, haver, teeter
OLD wave
COLLOQ. shilly-shally, hum and haw, waffle, wobble
2 TREMBLE, oscillate, shake, sway, wobble, stagger, give way, reel, teeter, totter, rock
F3 1 decide

waverer *n*
ditherer, doubter, haverer, wobbler
COLLOQ. shilly-shallier

wavering *adj*
hesitant, doubting, doubtful, dithering, dithery, havering, in two minds
COLLOQ. shilly-shallying
F3 determined

wavy *adj*
undulating, rippled, curly, curling, curvy, curving, ridged, sinuous, winding, zigzag

wax *v*
1 GROW, increase, get bigger, rise, swell, develop, enlarge, expand, extend, spread, magnify, broaden, widen, mount, fill out, become
2 *wax lyrical*
speak, talk, say, state, declare, express, utter, voice, articulate, enunciate, pronounce, tell, communicate, address, hold forth
FORMAL converse, declaim
F3 1 decrease, wane

waxen *adj*
pale, colourless, ashen, wan, white, whitish, pallid, ghastly, anaemic, bloodless, livid
E₃ ruddy

waxy *adj*
soft, pallid, pasty, waxen, impressible, impressionable
FORMAL ceraceous, cereous

way *n*
1 METHOD, approach, manner, technique, process, plan, course of action, strategy, procedure, means, instrument, tool, system, style, fashion, lines
FORMAL mode, instrumentality
2 CUSTOM, practice, behaviour, manner, habit, usage, characteristic, idiosyncrasy, peculiarity, mannerism, personality, temper, temperament, disposition, trait, style, conduct, nature
FORMAL wont
3 ROAD, direction, course, route, path, pathway, channel, access, avenue, track, passage, highway, roadway, street, thoroughfare, lane
■ **way of life**
lifestyle, life, living conditions, position, situation, world
■ **ways and means**
methods, procedure, way, resources, wherewithal, capability, capacity, tools, cash, funds, reserves, capital
■ **by the way**
incidentally, in passing, secondarily, parenthetically, *en passant*
■ **give way**
1 COLLAPSE, break, fall in, sink, disintegrate, subside, cave in
2 GIVE IN, yield, surrender, capitulate, submit, concede
■ **under way**
in progress, moving, in motion, going, begun, started, in operation, afoot

wayfarer *n*
traveller, walker, wanderer, journeyer, globetrotter, rover, trekker, voyager, itinerant, nomad, Gypsy
E₃ resident, stay-at-home

wayfaring *adj*
journeying, walking, travelling, wandering, rambling, roving, drifting, itinerant, voyaging, nomadic
FORMAL peripatetic
E₃ resident, stay-at-home

waylay *v*
lie in wait for, ambush, attack, accost, set upon, surprise, catch, hold up, intercept, seize, buttonhole

way-out *adj*
weird, crazy, bizarre, outlandish, unusual, unorthodox, unconventional, fantastic, eccentric, wild, experimental, avant-garde, progressive
COLLOQ. far-out, freaky, off-beat, wacky, left-field
E₃ ordinary

wayward *adj*
wilful, perverse, contrary, changeable, fickle, unpredictable, stubborn, self-willed, unmanageable, ungovernable, headstrong, obstinate, disobedient, rebellious, insubordinate, unruly, incorrigible
FORMAL intractable, obdurate, contumacious, refractory, capricious
E₃ tractable, good-natured

waywardness *n*
unmanageableness, unruliness, stubbornness, obstinacy, wilfulness, perverseness, perversity, contrariness, disobedience, rebelliousness, insubordination
FORMAL obduracy, contumacy
E₃ tractableness

weak *adj*
1 FEEBLE, frail, infirm, shaky, unhealthy, sickly, puny, delicate, exhausted, worn out, fatigued, debilitated, fragile, flimsy

FORMAL enervated
COLLOQ. weedy
2 VULNERABLE, unprotected, unguarded, defenceless, exposed
3 POWERLESS, impotent, spineless, cowardly, indecisive, irresolute, poor, flimsy, feeble, lacking, lame, inadequate, faulty, imperfect, useless, defective, deficient, inconclusive, unconvincing, unsound, untenable
FORMAL ineffectual
4 FAINT, slight, dim, low, soft, muffled, stifled, dull, imperceptible, indistinct
5 INSIPID, tasteless, watery, thin, diluted, runny, adulterated
E₃ 1 strong, healthy **2** secure, protected **3** powerful, determined **4** strong, clear **5** strong

> **Synonym nuances**
> *sense 1*
> You can use **feeble** to suggest something rather pitiful and ineffective: *their feeble efforts*, while **frail** and **infirm** are more appropriate to describe an ailing physical condition. **Puny**, likewise, can suggest a deficient physique: *his puny chest*, but may also imply insignificance: *a puny gesture of defiance*. In both instances, the tone is more contemptuous.
>   A less critical and even slightly euphemistic synonym is **delicate**, which is more suggestive of something dainty or valuable. **Fragile** similarly suggests a lack of robustness, but has stronger connotations of a propensity for getting damaged: *a fragile unity*, whereas **flimsy** is rather more disapproving, and implies insubstantiality. **Shaky**, on the other hand, has connotations of a degree of uncertainty: *a shaky economy*.

weaken *v*
1 ENFEEBLE, tire, exhaust, sap, undermine, incapacitate, debilitate, disable, paralyse, cripple, impair, dilute, diminish, lower, lessen, reduce, moderate, mitigate, temper, soften (up), thin, water down, craze, effeminate, effeminize, kill, take the edge off, extenuate, taint, unnerve, disconcert
OLD disinvigorate, appal, pall, entender; (*Spenser*) deduct, delay
FORMAL enervate
2 TIRE, flag, fail, give way, droop, fade, ease up, dwindle
FORMAL abate
E₃ 1 strengthen

weakening *n*
fading, failing, flagging, reduction, diminishment, dwindling, easing, lessening, lowering, moderation, dilution, waning, undermining, impairment, extenuation, debilitation
FORMAL abatement, enervation
E₃ strengthening

weakling *n*
coward, underling, underdog, milksop, namby-pamby, mouse
OLD softling
COLLOQ. wimp, wet, wally, weed, drip, doormat, cissy
SLANG wuss; *Aust* tonk
E₃ hero, stalwart

weakly *adv*
1 *she sank weakly into the armchair*
feebly, frailly, faintly, slightly, powerlessly, helplessly, dispiritedly
2 *weakly argue a case*
ineffectively, indecisively, implausibly, tenuously, lamely
COLLOQ. pathetically
E₃ 1 strongly, powerfully **2** effectively, plausibly, convincingly

Weapons include:

GUNS:		BLADES:	BOMBS:	MISSILES:	
airgun	pistol	claymore	atom bomb	ballistic missile	cosh
air rifle	revolver	dagger	binary weapon	bolas	cudgel
anti-tank gun	rifle	dirk	(or munition)	boomerang	halberd
automatic	rocket-launcher	épée	bomb	Cruise missile	partisan
bazooka	shotgun	flick-knife	bomblet	Exocet®	poleaxe
blunderbuss	six-gun	foil	*colloq.* bunker	hand grenade	shillelagh
Bren gun	six-shooter	glaive	buster	rocket	taiaha
cannon	sten gun	knife	cluster-bomb	*colloq.* Scud	threshel
carbine	stun gun	lance	daisy-cutter	shuriken	tomboc
Colt®	submachine-gun	machete	depth-charge	torpedo	truncheon
elephant gun	taser	panga	H-bomb	PROJECTORS:	GASES:
field gun	tommy-gun	pike	incendiary bomb	ballista	Agent Orange
gatling-gun	turret-gun	poniard	landmine	blowpipe	CS gas
gun	Uzi	quarterstaff	Mills bomb	bow	*N Am* Mace®
howitzer	Winchester® rifle	rapier	mine	catapult	mustard gas
kalashnikov	BLADES:	sabre	nail bomb	crossbow	nerve gas
Luger®	arrow	scimitar	napalm bomb	flame-thrower	tear-gas
machine-gun	battleaxe	spear	smart bomb	harpoon	OTHER:
magnum	bayonet	stiletto	submunition	longbow	knuckleduster
Mauser	bowie knife	sword	thermobaric	sling	maurikigusari
mortar	broadsword	tomahawk	bomb	STICKS:	nunchaku
musket	caltrop	vouge	time-bomb	billy	

See also **bomb; gun.**

weak-minded *adj*
pliable, faint-hearted, irresolute, persuasible, submissive, compliant, weak-kneed, persuadable
FORMAL complaisant, pusillanimous
COLLOQ. spineless
🖃 strong-willed

weakness *n*
1 FEEBLENESS, infirmity, impotence, incapacity, debility, delicateness, frailty, powerlessness, vulnerability
FORMAL enervation
2 FAULT, failing, flaw, imperfection, shortcoming, blemish, defect, deficiency, foible, weak point, Achilles' heel
3 LIKING, inclination, fondness, passion
FORMAL penchant, predilection, proclivity, predisposition
COLLOQ. soft spot
4 *the weakness of the argument*
implausibility, improbability, uncertainty, flimsiness, ineffectiveness, tenuousness, unsoundness, doubt, doubtfulness, dubiousness, unlikelihood, unlikeliness, far-fetchedness
🖃 **1** strength **2** strength, virtue **3** dislike, distaste **4** effectiveness, plausibility

weal *n*
welt, stripe, streak, scar, ridge, mark, wound, contusion, cicatrice, cicatrix

wealth *n*
1 MONEY, cash, riches, assets, affluence, prosperity, funds, mammon, fortune, treasure, capital, finance, means, substance, resources, goods, possessions, property, estate
OLD lucre
FORMAL opulence
2 ABUNDANCE, plenty, mass, bounty, fullness, store, treasury, copiousness, profusion
FORMAL cornucopia, plenitude
🖃 **1** poverty

wealthy *adj*
rich, prosperous, affluent, well-off, moneyed, comfortable, well-heeled, well-to-do, solid, substantial
FORMAL opulent
COLLOQ. flush, rolling in it, made of money, fat-cat, posh
OLD COLLOQ. oofy
SLANG loaded, filthy rich, stinking rich
🖃 poor, impoverished

weapon
See panel above

wear *v, n*
◆ *v*
1 DRESS IN, be dressed in, have on, put on, be clothed in, don, sport, carry, bear, have, display, show, exhibit, assume
2 DETERIORATE, erode, corrode, consume, fray, become thinner/weaker/threadbare, rub, abrade, waste, grind
◆ *n*
1 CLOTHES, clothing, dress, garments, outfit, costume
FORMAL attire
2 DETERIORATION, erosion, corrosion, damage, wear and tear, friction, abrasion
3 USE, service, employment, usefulness, utility, durability
■ **wear down**
reduce, rub away, corrode, abrade, erode, grind down, chip away at, consume, undermine, diminish, lessen, overcome
FORMAL macerate
■ **wear off**
decrease, dwindle, diminish, subside, wane, weaken, fade, lessen, ebb, peter out, disappear
FORMAL abate
🖃 increase
■ **wear on**
go on, go by, pass, elapse
■ **wear out**
1 EXHAUST, consume, use up, fatigue, tire (out), strain, stress, drain, sap
FORMAL enervate
2 DETERIORATE, wear through, erode, impair, consume, fray

wearily *adv*
tiredly, lethargically, drowsily, sleepily, listlessly, unenthusiastically, unexcitedly
🖃 freshly, energetically

weariness *n*
fatigue, tiredness, exhaustion, lassitude, lethargy, ennui, drowsiness, sleepiness, listlessness, prostration
FORMAL enervation, languor
🖃 freshness, energy

wearing *adj*
exhausting, fatiguing, tiring, tiresome, wearisome, trying, taxing, oppressive, irksome, exasperating, erosive
🖃 refreshing

wearisome *adj*
tiresome, troublesome, wearing, fatiguing, exhausting, dreary, burdensome, bothersome, boring, monotonous,

humdrum, tedious, annoying, trying, exasperating, irksome, vexatious, dull
⊟ refreshing

weary *adj, v*
◆ *adj*
1 TIRED, exhausted, fatigued, sleepy, worn out, drained, drowsy, jaded, overweary, toil-worn
OLD aweary, awearied; (*Shakesp*) dog-weary
COLLOQ. all in, done in, fagged out, knackered, bushed, dead beat, whacked, dog-tired, zonked, half-dead, wiped out; *N Am* pooped (out), tuckered out
2 *weary of trying to please him*
bored, unenthusiastic, tired, uninterested, unexcited
COLLOQ. sick and tired, bored to tears, browned off, brassed off, cheesed off
⊟ 1 refreshed, energetic **2** excited, interested
◆ *v*
tire (out), exhaust, debilitate, wear out, fatigue, bore, fail, jade, sap, sicken, drain, burden, fade, annoy, irritate, exasperate, irk, tax, jade, bore, cloy; *Scot* ramfeezle, trauchle
OLD betoil, think long; (*Spenser*) forweary
FORMAL enervate, ennui
COLLOQ. bug, fag

wearying *adj*
tiring, fatiguing, exhausting, wearisome, wearing, taxing, draining, trying
⊟ refreshing

weather *n, v*
◆ *n*
climate, conditions, temperature, humidity, dryness, windiness, sunniness, cloudiness, meteorological reports, atmospheric conditions, forecast, outlook
◆ *v*
1 ENDURE, survive, live through, come through, get through, ride out, rise above, stick out, withstand, surmount, stand, brave, overcome, resist, pull through, suffer
2 EXPOSE, toughen, season, harden, dry
⊟ 1 succumb
▪ **under the weather**
ill, sick, poorly, queer, ailing, off-colour, the worse for wear, groggy, below par, squeamish, nauseous, hung over, out of sorts
FORMAL indisposed
COLLOQ. grotty, lousy, rough, rop(e)y, seedy

Types of weather include:

black ice	haze	smog
breeze	heatwave	snow
chinook	hoar frost	snowstorm
cloud	hurricane	squall
cyclone	ice	storm
deluge	lightning	sunshine
dew	mist	tempest
downpour	mistral	thaw
drizzle	monsoon	thunder
drought	rain	tornado
fog	rainbow	*colloq.* twister
frost	shower	typhoon
gale	sleet	whirlwind
hail	slush	wind

See also **precipitation; wind**.

---

weave *v*
1 INTERLACE, lace, plait, braid, intertwine, spin, knit, entwine, intercross, interweave, interwork, inweave, fuse, merge, unite, texture, tissue, twill, cane, damask
OLD plight; (*Spenser*) wind
2 CREATE, compose, construct, contrive, make up, put together, fabricate
3 WIND, twist, zigzag, criss-cross

web *n*
network, net, netting, lattice, latticework, lacework, mesh, mesh-work, complex, webbing, interlacing, weft, snare, knot, tangle, trap, mat, skein, tela
OLD texture

wed *v*
1 MARRY, get married, yoke
OLD take to wife
FORMAL espouse
COLLOQ. get hitched, splice, tie the knot, get spliced, take the plunge, lead to the altar, lead up the aisle, make an honest woman of
2 JOIN, unite, unify, coalesce, blend, ally, combine, link, interweave, fuse, merge
FORMAL commingle
⊟ 1 divorce **2** separate

wedded *adj*
married, marital, joined, husbandly, wifely
FORMAL conjugal, connubial, matrimonial, nuptial, spousal

wedding *n, adj*
◆ *n*
marriage, union, marriage service, marriage ceremony, celebration of marriage
OLD wedlock
FORMAL matrimony, nuptials, spousage, espousals
⊟ divorce
◆ *adj*
bridal, marriage
FORMAL matrimonial, nuptial, hymeneal, hymenean, epithalamic

wedge *n, v*
◆ *n*
lump, block, piece, doorstop, chunk, wodge, chock, triangle, trig, feather, key, scotch, cleat, cotter
TECHNICAL gad, quoin, whipstock
Related adjectives: cuneiform, cuneal, cuneatic, sphenic, sphenoid
◆ *v*
jam, cram, pack, ram, squeeze, stuff, push, lodge, fit, block, thrust, crowd, force, quoin

wedlock *n*
marriage, union
FORMAL holy matrimony, matrimony

wee *adj*
small, little, tiny, miniature, minute, negligible, insignificant, diminutive, minuscule, microscopic, midget, Lilliputian
COLLOQ. itsy-bitsy, teeny, teensy, teeny-weeny, weeny
⊟ big, large

weed
▪ **weed out**
get rid of, remove, root out, isolate, eradicate, eliminate, purge
FORMAL extirpate
⊟ add, fix, infiltrate
See panel on next page

weedy *adj*
thin, skinny, puny, scrawny, undersized, gangling, weak, feeble, frail, weak-kneed, insipid
COLLOQ. wet, wimpish
SLANG wussy
⊟ strong

weekly *adv, adj*
◆ *adv*
every week, by the week, once a week
FORMAL hebdomadally
◆ *adj*
FORMAL hebdomadal, hebdomadary

Weeds include:

annual nettle	common	duckweed	lesser celandine	petty spurge	spurge
bindweed	persicaria	fat hen	lesser yellow	pineapple weed	stemless thistle
birdsfoot trefoil	common plantain	field wood rush	trefoil	ragweed	sun spurge
bracken	common reed	greater (or rat-	liverwort	ribwort	thale cress
broad-leaved	couch grass	tailed) plantain	meadow grass	rosebay	vetch
dock	creeping	ground elder	mind your own	willowherb	white clover
burnet saxifrage	buttercup	ground ivy	business	rough hawkbit	yarrow
Canadian	creeping thistle	groundsel	moss	salad burnet	
pondweed	creeping yellow	hairy bittercress	mouse-ear	self-heal	
chickweed	cress	horsetail	chickweed	sheep's sorrel	
cinquefoil	curled dock	Japanese	oxalis	shepherd's-purse	
coltsfoot	daisy	knotgrass	pearlwort	small bindweed	
common burdock	dandelion	knapweed	perennial nettle	snakeweed	
common	deadnettle	knotgrass	perennial oat-	sow thistle	
chickweed	dock	large bindweed	grass	speedwell	

See also **wild flower**.

---

weep *v, n*

♦ *v*

cry, sob, be in/shed tears, moan, lament, wail, mourn, grieve, bawl, blubber, snivel, whine, whimper, outweep, pipe, pipe your eye, put a finger in the eye; *Scot* greet
OLD beweep
COLLOQ. blub, boo-hoo, turn on the waterworks
🔄 rejoice

♦ *n*

cry, sob, moan, snivel, blub, lament; *Scot* greet
COLLOQ. boo-hoo

weepy *adj, n*

♦ *adj*

crying, tearful, sobbing, blubbering, weeping, teary; *Scot* greeting
FORMAL labile, lachrymose

♦ *n*

melodrama, sob-stuff, tear-jerker

weigh *v*

1 *it weighs one kilogram*
have a weight of, tip the scales at
2 *weigh the apples*
measure the weight of, see/measure how heavy something is
3 BEAR DOWN, oppress, burden, depress, afflict, trouble, worry
COLLOQ. get down
4 CONSIDER, contemplate, evaluate, meditate on, mull over, ponder, think over, examine, reflect on, deliberate

■ **weigh down**
oppress, overload, load, burden, bear down, weigh upon, press down, depress, afflict, trouble, worry
COLLOQ. get down
🔄 lighten, hearten

■ **weigh up**
assess, examine, size up, evaluate, balance, compare, consider, contemplate, deliberate, mull over, ponder, think over, discuss
COLLOQ. chew over

weight *n, v*

♦ *n*

1 HEAVINESS, gravity, burden, load, pressure, mass, quantity, force, ballast, tonnage, poundage
FORMAL avoirdupois
2 IMPORTANCE, significance, substance, consequence, impact, moment, influence, force, value, authority, power, consideration
FORMAL preponderance
COLLOQ. clout
3 BURDEN, load, onus, responsibility, duty, worry, trouble, strain, encumbrance
🔄 **1** lightness

♦ *v*

1 LOAD, weigh down, burden, oppress, handicap
2 BIAS, unbalance, slant, prejudice, angle, load, twist, sway

weightless *adj*

light, insubstantial, airy
FORMAL imponderous
🔄 heavy

weighty *adj*

1 HEAVY, substantial, massive, bulky, hefty
2 IMPORTANT, significant, consequential, crucial, critical, momentous, vital, serious, influential, authoritative, grave, solemn
3 DEMANDING, burdensome, onerous, difficult, exacting, taxing
🔄 **1** light **2** unimportant, insignificant

weird *adj*

strange, uncanny, bizarre, eerie, creepy, supernatural, unnatural, ghostly, freakish, mysterious, queer, grotesque, unearthly, witching; *Scot* eldritch
OLD weyard, weyward
FORMAL preternatural
COLLOQ. spooky, far-out, way-out, left-field
🔄 normal, usual

weirdly *adv*

strangely, bizarrely, eerily, unnaturally, supernaturally, mysteriously
COLLOQ. spookily
🔄 normally, usually

weirdo *n*

eccentric, freak, crank
COLLOQ. case, character, card, crackpot, oddball, nut, nutter, nutcase, fruitcake, kook, queer fish, odd fish, square peg in a round hole, fish out of water; *N Am* flake
SLANG cure, geek, loony, loon; *N Am* dingbat, cupcake, wack; *Aust* dag

welcome *adj, n, v*

♦ *adj*

acceptable, desirable, popular, pleasing, pleasant, agreeable, gratifying, appreciated, delightful, refreshing
🔄 unwelcome

♦ *n*

reception, greeting, acceptance, hospitality, acclamation; *N Am* ticker-tape welcome, glad hand, salutatory
TECHNICAL the right hand of fellowship
COLLOQ. salutation, red carpet

♦ *v*

greet, hail, receive, salute, meet, accept, approve of, be pleased with, be satisfied with, embrace, acclaim
OLD gratulate
COLLOQ. roll out the red carpet for, kill the fatted calf for
🔄 reject, snub

welcoming *adj*

1 *a welcoming person*
friendly, cordial, amicable, affable, affectionate, agreeable, cheerful, genial, sociable, pleasant, heartfelt, warm, warm-hearted, wholehearted, earnest, hearty, stimulating, invigorating
2 *a welcoming room*
pleasant, comfortable, cosy, warm, friendly, relaxing, homelike, *gemütlich*
F3 1 hostile, aloof, cool **2** cold, unfriendly

weld *v, n*

♦ *v*
fuse, unite, bond, join, solder, bind, connect, seal, link, cement
F3 separate
♦ *n*
joint, bond, seal, seam

welfare *n*

1 WELLBEING, health, prosperity, happiness, comfort, soundness, security, benefit, good, fortune, advantage, interest, profit, success
2 *live off welfare*
benefit, income, allowance, pension, sick pay, payment, social security

well [1] *adv, adj*

♦ *adv*
1 *speak Czech well*
competently, skilfully, properly, ably, expertly, proficiently, effectively, adeptly, excellently, rightly, correctly
2 *everything turned out well*
satisfactorily, adequately, suitably, fittingly, sufficiently
3 *treat someone well*
kindly, genially, generously, hospitably, agreeably, fairly, decently, pleasantly, happily
4 *Did you know her well?*
thoroughly, properly, fully, deeply, profoundly, closely, intimately, completely, greatly, considerably
5 THOROUGHLY, completely, intensively, comprehensively, carefully, efficiently, rigorously, industriously
6 *live well*
successfully, prosperously, comfortably, splendidly, luckily, fortunately
7 *think/speak well of someone*
highly, approvingly, favourably, glowingly, admiringly, warmly
8 *well over a thousand people*
substantially, considerably, very much, to a great extent, far
9 *you may well be right*
conceivably, quite possibly, very likely, probably, certainly
F3 1 badly, inadequately, incompetently, wrongly **2, 3** badly **6** poorly **7** unfavourably
♦ *adj*
1 HEALTHY, in good health, fit, able-bodied, sound, robust, strong, thriving, flourishing, hale and hearty
2 SATISFACTORY, right, all right, good, pleasing, proper, agreeable, fine, lucky, fortunate
COLLOQ. OK
F3 1 ill **2** bad
▪ **as well**
too, also, in addition, furthermore, besides, moreover
COLLOQ. into the bargain
▪ **well done**
bravo, congratulations, hurrah, encore
▪ **as well as**
in addition to, together with, along with, including, over and above, not to mention, to say nothing of

well[2] *n, v*

♦ *n*
dig a well
spring, wellspring, fountain, fount, source, reservoir, pool, wellhead, water hole, supply; *Aust* Mickery

♦ *v*
flow, spring, surge, gush, stream, brim over, jet, spout, spurt, swell, issue, rush, pour, flood, ooze, run, trickle, rise, seep

Types of well include:

artesian well	hot spring	stairwell
borehole	inkwell	thermal spring
draw-well	lift-shaft	waterhole
gas well	mineral spring	wishing well
geyser	oil well	
gusher	pump-well	

well-advised *adj*
wise, reasonable, sensible, sound, far-sighted, long-sighted, shrewd, prudent, politic
FORMAL judicious, sagacious, circumspect

well-balanced *adj*
1 RATIONAL, reasonable, level-headed, well-adjusted, stable, sensible, sane, sound, sober
COLLOQ. together
2 SYMMETRICAL, even, harmonious, balanced, well-proportioned, well-ordered
F3 1 unbalanced, maladjusted **2** asymmetrical, disordered

well-behaved *adj*
well-mannered, good, polite, respectful, under control, obedient, compliant, considerate, co-operative
COLLOQ. good as gold
F3 disobedient, naughty

wellbeing *n*
welfare, good, happiness, comfort, (good) health

well-bred *adj*
well-mannered, polite, well-brought-up, mannerly, courteous, civil, refined, cultivated, cultured, genteel, gentlemanly, ladylike, aristocratic, blue-blooded, upper-crust, gallant, urbane
F3 ill-bred

well-built *adj*
strong, muscular, brawny, strapping, sturdy, burly, beefy, stout

well-deserved *adj*
deserved, due, just, justified, merited, rightful, appropriate
OLD meet
FORMAL condign
F3 undeserved

well-disposed *adj*
favourable, friendly, well-placed, sympathetic, agreeable, amicable, well-arranged, well-minded, well-aimed
F3 ill-disposed

well-dressed *adj*
smart, well-groomed, elegant, fashionable, chic, stylish, neat, trim, dapper, spruce, tidy
COLLOQ. natty
F3 badly-dressed, scruffy

well-founded *adj*
justifiable, reasonable, acceptable, warranted, sustainable, right, sensible, sound, proper, fit, valid, plausible

well-groomed *adj*
neat, tidy, smart, trim, spruce, dapper, well-turned-out, well-dressed

well-heeled *adj*
rich, wealthy, prosperous, affluent, well-off, moneyed, comfortable, well-to-do, solid, substantial
FORMAL opulent
COLLOQ. flush, rolling in it, made of money, fat-cat, posh
OLD COLLOQ. oofy
SLANG loaded, filthy rich, stinking rich

well-known *adj*

famous, renowned, celebrated, notorious, famed, eminent, notable, noted, illustrious, familiar, widely-known, usual, common
F3 unknown

well-mannered *adj*

well-bred, polite, well-brought-up, mannerly, courteous, civil, refined, cultivated, cultured, genteel, gentlemanly, ladylike, aristocratic, blue-blooded, upper-crust, gallant, urbane
F3 ill-mannered

well-nigh *adv*

almost, nearly, practically, virtually, all but, just about, to all intents and purposes

well-off *adj*

1 RICH, wealthy, affluent, prosperous, well-to-do, moneyed, thriving, successful, comfortable
COLLOQ. well-heeled, flush, rolling in it, made of money, in the money, with money to burn
SLANG loaded, filthy rich, stinking rich
2 FORTUNATE, lucky, prosperous, thriving, successful, comfortable
F3 1 poor, badly-off **2** unfortunate, unlucky

well-read *adj*

educated, literate, well-informed, knowledgeable, cultured, lettered

well-spoken *adj*

articulate, fluent, eloquent, clear, coherent, well-expressed

well-thought-of *adj*

respected, highly regarded, esteemed, venerated, admired, looked up to, honoured, revered
F3 despised, looked down on

well-to-do *adj*

rich, wealthy, affluent, moneyed, prosperous, well-off, comfortable
COLLOQ. flush, rolling in it, made of money, fat-cat, posh
OLD COLLOQ. oofy
SLANG loaded, filthy rich, stinking rich
F3 poor

well-versed *adj*

knowledgeable, familiar, acquainted, experienced, conversant, au fait, trained

well-wisher *n*

supporter, sympathizer, fan, well-willer

well-worn *adj*

1 *a well-worn phrase*
timeworn, stale, tired, trite, cliché(e)d, overused, unoriginal, hackneyed, commonplace, stock, stereotyped, threadbare
COLLOQ. corny
2 *well-worn clothing*
threadbare, worn, worn-out, frayed, ragged, scruffy, shabby
F3 1 original **2** new

welsh *v*

cheat, defraud, swindle
COLLOQ. diddle, do

welt *n*

weal, scar, mark, ridge, contusion, wound, streak, stripe, cicatrice, cicatrix

welter *v, n*

◆ *v*
roll, flounder, pitch, toss, wallow, splash, wade, lurch, heave
◆ *n*
mess, confusion, jumble, muddle, tangle, web, hotchpotch
COLLOQ. mish-mash

wend

■ **wend your way**
go, move, make your way, proceed, progress, travel, walk, hike, wander, trudge, plod, meander, amble
F3 stay

wet *adj, n, v*

◆ *adj*
1 DAMP, moist, soaked, soaking, sodden, saturated, soggy, sopping (wet), soppy, watery, waterlogged, drenched, dripping, dank, clammy, slippery, slippy, sloppy, sour, soused, spongy, squidgy, madid; *dialect* weet; *Scot* wat
2 RAINING, rainy, showery, teeming, pouring, drizzling, dank, damp, humid, clammy, muggy
3 WEAK, feeble, weedy, spineless, timorous, soft, namby-pamby, ineffective, irresolute
FORMAL ineffectual, effete
COLLOQ. pathetic, wimpish, weedy, cissy, drippy
F3 1, 2 dry **3** strong
◆ *n*
1 WETNESS, moisture, moistness, damp, dampness, liquid, water, clamminess, condensation, humidity, rain, drizzle; *dialect* weet
OLD imbruement, madefaction
2 *don't be such a wet*
fool, idiot, softy, weakling, namby-pamby, milksop
COLLOQ. wimp, wally, drip, cissy, weed
SLANG jerk, nerd, wuss
F3 1 dryness
◆ *v*
moisten, damp, dampen, wash, soak, saturate, drench, steep, flood, swamp, water, irrigate, spray, splash, sprinkle, imbue, douse, dip, sluice, sweat; *dialect* weet
OLD bedabble, bedrench, beweep, daggle, draggle, imbrue, madefy, moil; (*Shakesp*) bewet
F3 dry

■ **wet behind the ears**
new, untrained, inexperienced, immature, raw, innocent, naive, callow
COLLOQ. green
F3 experienced

Synonym nuances
adjective sense 1
You can use **damp** and **moist** of something showing traces of moisture, although **moist** in particular has positive connotations: *a moist sponge cake*. **Soggy** has more unwelcome connotations of something gone soft: *a disgusting breakfast of soggy corn flakes and warm milk*.
More tactile sensations are emphasized with the terms **spongy**, which might be used of something porous or springy, or **squidgy**, which suggests being soft and pulpy to the touch. **Sloppy** suggests a more nauseating excess of wetness: *sloppy kisses*.
Wet, humid atmospheres can be described using the terms **dank**, which suggests a somewhat unpleasant mustiness, and **clammy**, which suggests a disagreeable sticky warmth: *her heart raced and her skin felt clammy*.
Soaked, **soaking**, **drenched**, **sopping** and **sodden** can all be used to suggest being completely imbued with liquid: *she peeled off her sodden clothes*, while **saturated** and **dripping** suggest an excess of water running off: *her dripping hair and sodden dress*. The term **soused** would be used in the context of marinading or preserving food in liquid. **Waterlogged**, however, would be reserved for something rendered unusable by a surfeit of water: *a waterlogged pitch*.

---

wetness *n*

damp, dampness, moisture, wet, water, liquid, soddenness, sogginess, condensation, dankness, clamminess, humidity
F3 dryness

whack *v, n*

♦ *v*

hit, strike, smack, thrash, slap, beat, bang, clout, cuff, thump, box, buffet, rap

COLLOQ. bash, wallop, belt, clobber, biff, sock

♦ *n*

1 SMACK, slap, blow, hit, rap, stroke, thump, clout, cuff, box, bang

COLLOQ. bash, wallop

2 SHARE, portion, quota, allowance, allocation, lot, part, division, stint, proportion, percentage

COLLOQ. cut, rake-off, slice of the cake

whacking *adj*

enormous, huge, immense, vast, gigantic, massive, colossal, large-scale, gross, gargantuan, astronomic, monstrous, mammoth, considerable, tremendous, stupendous, prodigious, giant, Titanic

COLLOQ. jumbo, great big, whopping, walloping, whaling, plonking, ginormous, humongous, almighty, God-almighty

SLANG mega

F3 small, tiny

wharf *n*

dock, quay, quayside, jetty, landing-stage, dockyard, marina, pier; *dialect* staithe

what's-its-name *n*

thing

COLLOQ. thingummy, thingamy, thingy, thingummyjig, thingummybob, what-d'you-call-it, whatsit, doodah, doobrey, whatnot, gismo; *N Am* whatchamacallit, doodad, doofus, doohickey

wheedle *v*

cajole, coax, persuade, talk into, win over, charm, flatter, beguile, entice, induce, court, draw

FORMAL inveigle

COLLOQ. sweet-talk, butter up, soft-soap; *N Am* cozy up

F3 force

wheel *n, v*

♦ *n*

turn, revolution, circle, ring, hoop, rotation, gyration, pivot, roll, spin, twirl, whirl

♦ *v*

turn, rotate, circle, gyrate, orbit, spin, go round, pivot, twirl, whirl, swing, roll, revolve, swivel

■ **at the wheel**

1 DRIVING, steering, behind the wheel, in the driver's seat, turning

2 IN CHARGE, at the helm, in control, in command, responsible, directing

COLLOQ. heading up

Types of wheel include:

balance wheel	escape wheel	roulette wheel
big wheel	Ferris wheel	spinning jenny
buff-wheel	flywheel	spinning-wheel
cartwheel	gearwheel	sprocket
castor	idle wheel	spur gear
Catherine-wheel	mill wheel	steering wheel
charka	paddle wheel	wagon wheel
cogwheel	potter's wheel	water wheel
crown-wheel	prayer wheel	wheel of fortune
driving wheel	ratchet-wheel	worm wheel

---

wheeze *v, n*

♦ *v*

pant, gasp, cough, hiss, rasp, whistle

♦ *n*

1 RASP, gasp, cough, hiss, whistle

2 TRICK, joke, gag, crack, prank, ruse, practical joke, ploy, scheme, plan, stunt, idea, story, anecdote, catchphrase

COLLOQ. chestnut, one-liner, wrinkle

whereabouts *n*

location, position, place, situation, site, vicinity

wherewithal *n*

means, resources, supplies, money, cash, funds, capital, necessary

SLANG loot, readies, ready, megabucks, dough, dosh, bread, lolly, spondulicks, brass, loot, gravy, greens, shekels, moolah, greenies, scratch, smash, stumpy

whet *v*

1 SHARPEN, hone, file, grind, edge

OLD stroke

2 STIMULATE, stir, rouse, arouse, excite, provoke, kindle, quicken, incite, awaken, titillate, increase

OLD appetize

F3 **1** blunt **2** dampen

whiff *n*

1 *a whiff of fresh air*

breath, puff, hint, trace, blast, gust, draught, odour, smell, aroma, sniff, scent, reek, stink, stench

2 *a whiff of scandal/danger*

trace, hint, suspicion, suggestion, soupçon, touch

while *n, v*

♦ *n*

time, period, spell, stretch, season, span, interval

■ **while away**

spend, pass, occupy, use (up), devote

whim *n*

fancy, caprice, notion, idea, quirk, freak, humour, conceit, fad, craze, passion, vagary, urge, impulse

whimper *v, n*

♦ *v*

cry, sob, weep, snivel, sniffle, whine, grizzle, mewl, moan, groan

COLLOQ. whinge

♦ *n*

sob, cry, snivel, whine, moan, groan

whimsical *adj*

fanciful, quirky, playful, mischievous, impulsive, unpredictable, eccentric, funny, droll, curious, whimsy, queer, unusual, weird, odd, peculiar, quaint

FORMAL capricious

COLLOQ. dotty

whimsy *adj*

playful, whimsical, fanciful, quirky, unpredictable, eccentric, funny, droll, curious, unusual, weird, odd, peculiar, quaint

whine *v, n*

♦ *v*

1 CRY, sob, whimper, grizzle, moan, wail

2 COMPLAIN, carp, grumble, moan, groan, grouse

COLLOQ. gripe, whinge, grouch, beef, bellyache

♦ *n*

1 CRY, sob, whimper, moan, wail

2 COMPLAINT, moan, grumble, groan, grouse

COLLOQ. gripe, grouch, beef, bellyache

whinge *v, n*

♦ *v*

complain, grumble, moan, carp; *Scot* greet, peenge

COLLOQ. gripe, grouse, beef, bellyache; *Scot* wheenge; *Aust* winge

♦ *n*

complaint, grumble, moan, groan, grouse

COLLOQ. gripe, beef, bellyache

whip *v, n*

♦ *v*

1 BEAT, flog, lash, scourge, birch, cane, strap, thrash, punish, discipline, rawhide, cowhide, kurbash

OLD feague; (*Shakesp*) firk

FORMAL flagellate, chastise, castigate

COLLOQ. tan, belt, whack, wallop, hide, whop, whap, give someone a good hiding
2 PULL, jerk, snatch, whisk, flash
OLD braid
COLLOQ. yank
3 DASH, dart, rush, tear, flit, fly
4 *whip the cream*
stir, mix, whisk, beat, beat up, switch
5 GOAD, drive, spur, prod, push, urge, stir, rouse, agitate, incite, provoke, prompt, instigate
♦ *n*
lash, scourge, switch, birch, cane, horsewhip, crop, riding-crop, cat-o'-nine-tails, flagellum, thong, black snake, bullwhip, bullwhack, cowhide, hunting-crop, hunting-whip, stock whip, lunge whip, longe whip, lunging whip, coachwhip, kurbash, ash-plant; *S Afr* sjambok
OLD knout, taw
■ **whip up**
stimulate, stir up, work up, agitate, excite, arouse, incite, inflame, kindle, instigate, provoke, foment
COLLOQ. psych up
⊟ dampen, deter

whippersnapper *n*
scamp, scallywag, imp, rascal, nipper, upstart, pipsqueak, hobbledehoy

whipping *n*
beating, punishment, spanking, flogging, lashing, thrashing, birching, caning, hiding, scourging, knout; *Scot* laldie
FORMAL castigation, flagellation
COLLOQ. belting, tanning, walloping

whirl *v, n*
♦ *v*
spin, swirl, turn, twist, twirl, pivot, pirouette, swivel, wheel, rotate, revolve, turn round, eddy, reel, roll, gyrate, circle
♦ *n*
1 SPIN, twirl, twist, gyration, revolution, pirouette, swirl, turn, wheel, rotation, circle, reel, pivot, roll
2 BUSTLE, flurry, round, series, succession, merry-go-round, commotion, agitation, hubbub, hurly-burly, confusion, daze, muddle, jumble, giddiness, tumult, uproar
■ **give something a whirl**
try, attempt, strive, endeavour, venture
COLLOQ. have a go, have a bash/crack/shot/stab

whirlpool *n*
maelstrom, vortex, eddy, sea purse; *Scot* weel, weil, swelchie
OLD gulf, gurge
Related adjective: voraginous

whirlwind *n, adj*
♦ *n*
1 TORNADO, cyclone, vortex, typhoon, eddy, tourbillion, sand-devil, white squall
OLD typhon
2 BEDLAM, chaos, pandemonium, madhouse, commotion, confusion, furore, clamour, hubbub, hullabaloo, noise, tumult, turmoil, uproar, babel, anarchy
♦ *adj*
hasty, impulsive, quick, rapid, speedy, swift, lightning, headlong, impetuous, rash
⊟ deliberate, slow

whisk *v, n*
♦ *v*
1 WHIP, beat, stir, mix
2 DART, dash, rush, hurry, speed, fly, tear, bolt, hasten, race, shoot, dive, whip
COLLOQ. belt, bomb, pelt, scoot, zip, go like the clappers
3 BRUSH, sweep, flick, wipe, twitch
♦ *n*
beater, brush, swizzle-stick

whisky *n*
whiskey, Scotch, bourbon, malt, rye, usquebaugh, moonshine
COLLOQ. *Scot & Irish* the cratur

whisper *v, n*
♦ *v*
1 MURMUR, mutter, mumble, say/speak quietly, breathe, hiss, rustle, sigh, burr, buzz, sough; *dialect* tittle; *Scot* whittie-whattie
OLD susurrate, round
2 HINT, intimate, insinuate, gossip, divulge
⊟ **1** shout
♦ *n*
1 MURMUR, soft/quiet/low voice, undertone, sigh, hiss, rustle, breath, stage whisper, whisht, sough; *dialect* pig's whisper; *Scot* hark
OLD susurrus
2 HINT, suggestion, suspicion, breath, whiff, rumour, report, innuendo, insinuation, trace, tinge, soupçon, breath, buzz

whistle *v, n*
♦ *v*
pipe, sing, call, cheep, chirp, warble
♦ *n*
song, call, cheep, warble, chirp, siren, hooter

whit *n*
atom, little, drop, bit, scrap, shred, piece, fragment, particle, crumb, pinch, speck, trace, iota, jot, spot, grain, mite, modicum, dash, hoot
⊟ lot

white *adj*
1 PALE, light-skinned, pallid, wan, ashen, colourless, anaemic, pasty, waxen
2 LIGHT, snowy, milky, creamy, ivory, hoary, silver, grey
3 PURE, immaculate, spotless, stainless, undefiled, moral, virtuous, blameless
⊟ **1** black, dark, ruddy **2** dark **3** defiled

white-collar *adj*
executive, office, professional, salaried, clerical, non-manual
⊟ blue-collar, manual

whiten *v*
bleach, blanch, whitewash, pale, fade
OLD dealbate
FORMAL etiolate
⊟ blacken, darken

whitewash *n, v*
♦ *n*
cover-up, concealment, deception, camouflage, -gate
⊟ exposure
♦ *v*
1 COVER UP, conceal, hide, make light of, suppress, gloss over, camouflage
2 THRASH, beat, defeat utterly, crush, drub, best; *Scot* granny
COLLOQ. clobber, hammer, lick, paste, trounce
⊟ **1** expose

whittle *v*
1 CARVE, cut, scrape, shave, trim, pare, hew, shape
2 ERODE, eat away, wear away, diminish, consume, use (up), reduce, undermine

whole *adj, n*
♦ *adj*
1 COMPLETE, entire, integral, full, total, unabridged, uncut, undivided, unedited
2 INTACT, unharmed, undamaged, unbroken, perfect, sound, in one piece, mint, uninjured, unhurt
FORMAL inviolate
3 WELL, healthy, fit, sound, strong
⊟ **1** partial **2** damaged **3** ill

◆ *n*
total, aggregate, sum total, entirety, all, fullness, totality, ensemble, entity, unit, lot, piece, everything
COLLOQ. *Aust & NZ* the whole box and dice
☰ part

■ **on the whole**
generally, mostly, in general, generally speaking, in the main, as a rule, for the most part, all in all, all things considered, by and large, predominantly

wholehearted *adj*
enthusiastic, earnest, committed, dedicated, devoted, hearty, passionate, heartfelt, emphatic, warm, sincere, unfeigned, genuine, unreserved, unstinting, unqualified, complete, true, real, zealous
COLLOQ. *Aust & NZ* boots and all
☰ half-hearted

wholeheartedly *adv*
completely, enthusiastically, emphatically, warmly, heartily, passionately, sincerely, genuinely, unreservedly
☰ half-heartedly

wholesale *adj, adv*
◆ *adj*
comprehensive, far-reaching, extensive, sweeping, wide-ranging, mass, broad, all-inclusive, outright, total, massive, indiscriminate
☰ partial
◆ *adv*
indiscriminately, totally, extensively, comprehensively, massively, en bloc
☰ partially

wholesome *adj*
1 *wholesome food; a wholesome climate*
good, healthy, healthful, hygienic, sanitary, nutritious, nourishing, beneficial, salutary, refreshing, invigorating, bracing, sweet, healthsome; *Scot* healsome
FORMAL salubrious
2 *wholesome entertainment*
moral, decent, clean, proper, improving, edifying, uplifting, pure, virtuous, righteous, beneficial, helpful, ethical, honourable, respectable, sound
COLLOQ. squeaky-clean
☰ **1** unhealthy **2** unwholesome, immoral

wholly *adv*
completely, entirely, fully, purely, absolutely, totally, utterly, comprehensively, altogether, perfectly, thoroughly, all, exclusively, only, in every respect
COLLOQ. one hundred per cent
☰ partly

whoop *v, n*
shout, cry, yell, cheer, scream, shriek, roar, hoop, hoot, hurrah
COLLOQ. holler

whopper *n*
1 LIE, falsehood, fabrication, untruth, fable
COLLOQ. cracker, fairy story, tall story
2 GIANT, monster, mammoth, colossus, whale, hippopotamus, leviathan
OLD *NAm* scrouger
SLANG stonker, plumper, slapper
OLD SLANG swapper; *NAm* sockdologer

whopping *adj*
large, big, huge, massive, extraordinary, immense, vast, great, mammoth, tremendous, staggering, monumental, enormous, giant, gigantic
FORMAL prodigious
COLLOQ. jumbo, great big, walloping, whacking, whaling, plonking, ginormous, humongous, almighty, God-almighty
SLANG mega
☰ tiny

whore *n*
prostitute, harlot, callgirl, rent-boy, woman of the streets, woman of the town, woman of ill repute, loose woman, fallen woman, scarlet woman, trollop, street-walker, cocotte, courtesan, bawd, *fille de joie, fille des rues*, drab, grande cocotte, lorette, lady of the night, geisha, hetaera, hierodule, loose fish, magdalen, night-walker, vizard-mask
OLD bulker, convertite, trull, moll, strumpet, cockatrice, public woman, wench, pug, punk, stew, stale; (*Shakesp*) quail, bona-roba, callet, polecat, road, venture
COLLOQ. hooker, hustler, pro, hostess, fancy woman; *NAm* working girl
SLANG *poule de luxe*, quiff, rough trade, tart, tom, tramp, brass, floozie; *NAm* broad
OLD SLANG dell, mutton, dolly-mop, plover; (*Shakesp*) laced mutton

whorehouse *n*
brothel, bordello, bawdy-house, house of ill fame, house of ill repute, bagnio, disorderly house; *Irish* kip; *NAm* sporting house
OLD bordel, flash-house, stew, vaulting-house, Corinth; (*Shakesp*) hothouse, leaping-house
COLLOQ. red light
SLANG knocking-shop, crib; *NAm* cathouse

whorl *n*
spiral, twist, turn, coil, loop, helix, vortex, corkscrew
FORMAL convolution

wicked *adj*
1 EVIL, sinful, immoral, bad, depraved, corrupt, vicious, unprincipled, debased, abominable, ungodly, devilish, unrighteous, unholy, shameful, black-hearted, villainous, guilty, ill, perverse, abandoned, miscreant
OLD facinorous, felon, felonious, flagitious, scelerate, unkind, wick; (*Shakesp*) high-viced, naughty
FORMAL iniquitous, heinous, dissolute, egregious, nefarious
2 BAD, unpleasant, harmful, offensive, scandalous, vile, worthless, difficult, terrible, dreadful, distressing, awful, atrocious, severe, intense, nasty, injurious, troublesome, terrible, foul, fierce
3 NAUGHTY, mischievous, roguish, impish, rascally
4 EXCELLENT, admirable
COLLOQ. terrific, amazing, fantastic, brilliant, neat, ace, brill, boffo, out of this world, second to none, divine, heavenly, fabulous, sensational, not half bad
SLANG mega, cool, mean, the business, stonking, radical, rad, crucial, way-out, shit-hot, the dog's bollocks, groovy, clinking, def, fab
☰ **1** good, upright **2** harmless

wickedness *n*
evil, depravity, vileness, atrocity, abomination, corruption, ccrruptness, foulness, fiendishness, immorality, shamefulness, sin, sinfulness, impiety, unrighteousness, devilishness, enormity, amorality
FORMAL dissoluteness, heinousness, iniquity, reprobacy
☰ uprightness

wickerwork *n*
wicker, basket-work, wattle, wattle-work

wide *adj, adv*
◆ *adj*
1 BROAD, roomy, spacious, extensive, vast, immense, ample
2 DILATED, expanded, full
3 EXTENSIVE, wide-ranging, comprehensive, great, broad, vast, immense, far-reaching, general
4 LOOSE, baggy, full, roomy
FORMAL capacious
5 OFF-TARGET, off-course, off the mark, distant, remote
☰ **1** narrow **3** restricted **5** near
◆ *adv*
1 ASTRAY, off course, off target, off the mark

2 FULLY, completely, to the full extent, all the way
E3 1 on target

! wide or **broad**?
See panel at **broad**.

---

wide-awake *adj*
conscious, aware, fully awake, wakened, observant, watchful, vigilant, wary, sharp, alert, astute, roused, heedful, keen, quick-witted, on your toes, on the alert, on the qui vive
COLLOQ. on the ball
E3 asleep

wide-eyed *adj*
1 INEXPERIENCED, innocent, artless, guileless, ingenuous, naive, fresh, natural, simple, open, frank, unsophisticated, unworldly, childlike, angelic, credulous, gullible, trusting, trustful, dewy-eyed, unsuspecting
2 ASTONISHED, surprised, startled, amazed, astounded, stunned, dazed, staggered, dumbfounded, taken aback, shocked, confounded, bewildered, open-eyed, open-mouthed
COLLOQ. lost for words, knocked for six, bowled over, flabbergasted, gobsmacked, thunderstruck

widely *adv*
broadly, extensively, generally, comprehensively

widen *v*
broaden, expand, extend, spread, increase, stretch, enlarge
FORMAL distend, dilate
E3 narrow

wide-open *adj*
open, gaping, wide, outspread, outstretched, spread, unprotected, vulnerable, defenceless, exposed, susceptible
FORMAL unfortified
E3 closed, narrow

wide-ranging *adj*
far-reaching, broad, extensive, widespread, comprehensive, thorough, thoroughgoing, important, significant, momentous, sweeping

widespread *adj*
extensive, prevalent, rife, general, sweeping, universal, global, wholesale, far-reaching, unlimited, broad, common, pervasive, far-flung
E3 limited

widow *n*
feme sole, dowager, war widow, grass widow, hempen widow, suttee; *dialect* widdy
OLD relict
Related adjective: vidual

width *n*
breadth, broadness, diameter, wideness, compass, thickness, largeness, span, scope, range, measure, girth, beam, amplitude, extent, extensiveness, reach

wield *v*
1 *wield a weapon*
brandish, flourish, swing, wave, handle, ply, shake, play, manage, manipulate, apply
OLD weld, wild, sway, wind; (*Spenser*) sownd
2 *wield power*
have, hold, possess, employ, exert, exercise, use, utilize, control, maintain, command, manage, apply

wife *n*
partner, spouse, companion, mate, bride, woman, lady, married woman, *femme, frau*, consort, daughter-in-law, sister-in-law, stepmother, child-wife, concubine, first lady, helpmate, princess, queen
OLD helpmeet, dame; (*Shakesp*) kickie-wickie

COLLOQ. better half, other half, missus, old lady, rib
OLD COLLOQ. little woman
SLANG dutch, trouble and strife
Related adjective: uxorial

wig *n*
hairpiece, toupee, postiche, scratch-wig, spencer, bobwig, Brutus, buzz-wig, tie-wig; *Scot* gizz, jiz
OLD periwig, peruke, transformation, bagwig, caxon, major, Ramilie
OLD COLLOQ. jasey

wiggle *v, n*
jiggle, shake, jerk, wriggle, wag, waggle, twist, squirm, twitch, writhe

wild *adj*
1 UNTAMED, undomesticated, savage, barbarous, primitive, uncivilized, natural, unbroken, ferocious, fierce, brutish
FORMAL feral
2 UNCULTIVATED, natural, desolate, waste, barren, forsaken, unpopulated, uninhabited, unsettled, rugged, inhospitable
3 UNRESTRAINED, unruly, undisciplined, unmanageable, violent, turbulent, rowdy, lawless, out of control, uncontrollable, ungovernable, rampant, disorderly, riotous, boisterous
4 STORMY, tempestuous, raging, rough, furious, violent, blustery, choppy, turbulent
5 UNTIDY, unkempt, messy, dishevelled, tousled, uncombed
6 RECKLESS, rash, impulsive, foolish, foolhardy, impracticable, impractical, irrational, outrageous, preposterous, absurd, ridiculous, wayward, extravagant, fantastic, unwise, imprudent
7 MAD, frenzied, distraught, demented, berserk, frantic, beside yourself
COLLOQ. crazy, nuts, nutty, bonkers, bananas
8 ANGRY, furious, raging, enraged, infuriated, incensed, blazing, fuming
COLLOQ. crazy, mad, hopping mad, foaming at the mouth
9 ENTHUSIASTIC, keen, fervent, vehement, passionate, excited, fanatical
COLLOQ. crazy, mad, nuts, daft, potty
10 *a wild guess*
random, arbitrary, chance, casual, incidental, haphazard, irregular, accidental, aimless, purposeless, indiscriminate
FORMAL fortuitous, serendipitous
COLLOQ. hit-or-miss
E3 1 tame, civilized **2** cultivated **3** restrained **4** calm **5** tidy **6** sensible **7** sane

wilderness *n*
desert, wasteland, waste, wilds, jungle

wild flower
See panel on next page

wildlife *n*
animals, fauna

wildly *adv*
1 *behave wildly*
irresponsibly, rebelliously, anarchically, defiantly, recklessly, chaotically
2 *yell wildly*
unrestrainedly, uncontrollably, noisily, riotously, boisterously, angrily, furiously
3 *wildly impractical*
foolishly, outrageously, absurdly, preposterously, ridiculously, fantastically, extravagantly
4 *guess wildly*
arbitrarily, casually, haphazardly, aimlessly, indiscriminately, unmethodically, unsystematically
E3 1 responsibly **2** calmly **3** sensibly

wilds *n*
outback, remote areas, wasteland, wilderness, desert
COLLOQ. the back of beyond, the sticks, the middle of nowhere; *N Am* the boondocks, the boonies

Wild flowers include:

Aaron's rod	clary	crowfoot	horsetail	poppy	toadflax
ale hoof	clustered	cuckoo flower	lady's slipper	primrose	violet
bird's foot trefoil	bellflower	daisy	lady's smock	ragged robin	water lily
birth-wort	clover	edelweiss	lungwort	rock rose	white campion
bistort	columbine	field cow-wheat	marguerite	rough-fruited	wild chicory
black-eyed susan	comfrey	foxglove	masterwort	cinquefoil	wild endive
bladder campion	common	goatsbeard	moneywort	self-heal	wild gladiolus
bluebell	evening-	goldcup	multiflora rose	shepherd's club	wild iris
broomrape	primrose	goldenrod	New England	solomon's seal	wild orchid
butter-and-eggs	common mallow	great mullein	aster	stiff-haired	wild pansy
buttercup	common toadflax	harebell	oxeye daisy	sunflower	wood anemone
campion	cowslip	heartsease	oxslip	stonecrop	yarrow
celandine	crane's bill	heather	pennyroyal	teasel	yellow rocket

See also **weed**.

---

wiles *n*
tricks, stratagems, ruses, ploys, devices, contrivances, guile, manoeuvres, subterfuge, cunning, deceit, deception, cheating, trickery, fraud, craftiness, artfulness, chicanery
COLLOQ. dodges
F₃ guilelessness

wilful *adj*
1 DELIBERATE, conscious, intentional, voluntary, willing, calculated, planned, premeditated
2 SELF-WILLED, headstrong, obstinate, stubborn, pig-headed, mulish, inflexible, unyielding, uncompromising, perverse, wayward, contrary, determined, dogged; *Scot* willyard
FORMAL obdurate, refractory, intransigent, intractable
F₃ 1 unintentional, spontaneous **2** good-natured, easy-going

will *n, v*
◆ *n*
1 VOLITION, choice, option, prerogative, preference, decision, discretion
2 WISH, desire, inclination, feeling, fancy, disposition, mind, attitude
3 PURPOSE, resolve, resolution, determination, purposefulness, willpower, single-mindedness, aim, intention, command
◆ *v*
1 WANT, desire, wish, intend, choose, compel, direct, command, decree, order, ordain
2 BEQUEATH, leave, hand down, pass on, pass down, dispose of
FORMAL transfer, confer

willing *adj*
disposed, inclined, agreeable, ready, prepared, consenting, content, amenable, biddable, compliant, co-operative, pleased, well-disposed, so-minded, favourable, happy, glad, eager, enthusiastic, keen
COLLOQ. game, up for it
F₃ unwilling, disinclined, reluctant

willingly *adv*
readily, unhesitatingly, eagerly, freely, happily, cheerfully, by choice, voluntarily, gladly, nothing loath
F₃ unwillingly

willingness *n*
readiness, inclination, will, wish, consent, compliance, desire, favour, enthusiasm, agreeableness, agreement, disposition, volition
FORMAL complaisance
F₃ unwillingness

willowy *adj*
slender, slim, tall, graceful, svelte, sylph-like, limber, lissom, lithe, lithesome, supple
F₃ buxom

willpower *n*
determination, resolution, resolve, single-mindedness, commitment, will, strength of will, self-control, self-discipline, self-mastery, self-command, persistence, doggedness, drive
COLLOQ. grit

willy-nilly *adv*
1 WHETHER YOU LIKE IT OR NOT, necessarily, compulsorily, of necessity
FORMAL perforce
2 HAPHAZARDLY, randomly, by chance, arbitrarily, carelessly, indiscriminately, irregularly, unmethodically, unsystematically

wilt *v*
droop, sag, wither, shrivel, flop, flag, dwindle, weaken, faint, diminish, lessen, grow less, fail, fade, languish, taint, ebb, sink, wane
F₃ perk up

wily *adj*
shrewd, cunning, scheming, artful, sharp, crafty, foxy, intriguing, tricky, underhand, shifty, deceitful, cheating, deceptive, astute, sly, guileful, designing, crooked
COLLOQ. fly
F₃ guileless

wimp *n*
fool, softy, clown, milksop, weed, namby-pamby
COLLOQ. clot, drip, wally, wet
SLANG jerk, nerd, wuss; *Aust* tonk

wimpish *adj*
weak, feeble, weedy, spineless, timorous, soft, namby-pamby, ineffective, irresolute
FORMAL ineffectual, effete
COLLOQ. wet, pathetic, weedy, drippy, cissy
SLANG wussy

win *v, n*
◆ *v*
1 BE VICTORIOUS, triumph, succeed, achieve success, prevail, overcome, conquer, come (in) first, carry off, finish first
COLLOQ. win the day, win hands down, come out on top, turn up trumps, strike gold, hit the jackpot
2 GAIN, acquire, achieve, attain, accomplish, receive, secure, obtain, get, earn, collect, catch, net
FORMAL procure
F₃ 1 fail, lose
◆ *n*
victory, triumph, conquest, success, mastery
F₃ defeat

■ win over
persuade, convince, influence, convert, sway, win/talk/bring round, charm, allure, attract
FORMAL prevail upon

wince *v, n*
* *v*

start, jump, draw back, recoil, flinch, jerk, shrink, pull a face, cringe, blench, cower, quail
* *n*

start, cringe, flinch, jerk

wind¹ *n*

blowing in the wind

air, breeze, draught, gust, puff, breath, air-current, blast, current, bluster, gale, hurricane, tornado
Related adjective: aeolian

■ **get wind of**

hear about, learn of, find out about, discover, become aware of
COLLOQ. hear on the grapevine

■ **in the wind**

likely, probable, expected, about to happen
COLLOQ. on the cards

■ **put the wind up**

scare, frighten, discourage, alarm, unnerve, startle, panic, agitate, daunt, sound the alarm
FORMAL perturb
COLLOQ. rattle, spook, boggle, scare someone out of their wits, make someone's blood run cold, scare the living daylights out of, make someone's hair stand on end, make someone jump out of their skin, put the frighteners on
SLANG scare the shit out of

Types of wind include:

anticyclone	föhn	samiel
austral wind	gregale	simoom
berg wind	harmattan	sirocco
bise	helm wind	snow eater
bora	khamsin	southerly
Aust buster	levant	southerly buster
Cape doctor	libeccio	trade wind
chinook	meltemi	tramontana
cyclone	mistral	westerly
doctor	monsoon	wet chinook
east wind	north wind	williwaw
El Niño	nor'wester	willy-willy
etesian	pampero	zephyr
Favonian wind	prevailing wind	zonda

---

wind² *v, n*
* *v*

1 CURVE, bend, loop, spiral, zigzag, twine, turn, twist and turn, snake, deviate, meander, ramble
2 COIL, wrap, twist, turn, curl, twine, encircle, furl, wreathe, roll, reel
* *n*

bend, curve, turn, twist, zigzag, meander

■ **wind down**

1 SLOW (DOWN), slacken off, lessen, reduce, subside, diminish, dwindle, decline, stop, bring/come to an end
2 RELAX, unwind, quieten down, ease up, calm down
COLLOQ. take it/things easy, let yourself go, make yourself at home, let your hair down, put your feet up, hang loose, cool it, chill (out), lighten up
🖙 **1** increase

■ **wind up**

1 CLOSE (DOWN), end, finalize, finish, stop, bring to a close, bring to an end, liquidate
FORMAL conclude, terminate
2 END UP, finish up, find yourself, settle
3 ANNOY, irritate, disconcert, tease, fool, trick, make fun of
COLLOQ. kid, rib, pull someone's leg, rub someone up the wrong way, take the mickey out of

SLANG take the piss out of; *N Am* goof
🖙 **1** begin

windbag *n*

boaster, gossip, bore, braggart, blether
COLLOQ. gasbag, bigmouth

winded *adj*

puffed out, breathless, out of breath, panting, puffed, out of puff
🖙 fresh

windfall *n*

stroke of luck, bonanza, godsend, jackpot, treasure-trove, stroke of luck, find, manna, pennies from heaven

winding *adj*

curving, turning, twisting, twisting and turning, bending, crooked, tortuous, indirect, roundabout, spiral, twining, coiling, circuitous, meandering, serpentine
FORMAL sinuous, sinuate(d), flexuose, flexuous, anfractuous, convoluted
🖙 straight

window *n*

pane, light, opening

Types of window include:

astragal	French	rose window
bay	lancet	sash
bow	louvre window	secondary-glazed
bull's eye	lucarne	
casement	mullioned window	shop window
Catherine-wheel		skylight
compass	Norman	sliding window
decorated	oeil-de-boeuf	stained glass window
dormer	oriel	
double-glazed	patio door	ticket window
double-glazing	perpendicular	windscreen
early English	porthole	
fanlight	quarterlight	

---

windpipe *n*

throat, pharynx, larynx, pipes, throttle, thropple; *Scot* thrapple
OLD weasand, weasand-pipe
TECHNICAL trachea
Related adjective: tracheal

windswept *adj*

1 *a windswept mountainside*

windy, blowy, exposed, unprotected, unsheltered, open, barren, desolate, bleak
2 *windswept hair*

dishevelled, disordered, ruffled, tousled, unkempt, untidy, messy, in a mess

windy *adj*

1 *windy weather*

breezy, blowy, blustery, squally, windswept, stormy, wild, tempestuous, gusty
2 *windy speech*

long-winded, wordy, verbose, garrulous, rambling, turgid, pompous, bombastic
FORMAL prolix
3 NERVOUS, uneasy, on edge, anxious, stressed, afraid, frightened, scared, timid
COLLOQ. chicken, nervy
🖙 **1** calm, windless **3** fearless

wine *n*

SLANG vino
Related adjective: vinous
See panels on next page

Types of wine include:

alcohol-free	demi-sec	house white	port	sparkling	tonic wine
amontillado	dry	house wine	red wine	straw wine	vintage port
blush wine	dry sherry	medium sherry	rosé	sweet	vintage wine
Aust colloq.	fino	mulled wine	ruby port	sweet sherry	white port
bombo	fortified wine	oloroso	sec	table wine	
brut	house red	plonk	sherry	tawny port	

Varieties of wine include:

alicant	Cabernet	Douro	Madeira	Piesporter	Soave
Alsace	Sauvignon	Frascati	Malaga	Pinotage	Spätlese
Asti	canary	Gewürztraminer	Marcobrunner	Pinot Grigio	Steinberger
Auslese	Cava	Graves	Marsala	Pinot Noir	St Julien
bacharach	Chablis	Grenache (or	Médoc	retsina	Sylvaner
Bardolino	Chambertin	Garnacha)	Merlot	Rhine wine	Tarragona
Barolo	champagne	Hermitage	Minervois	Riesling	Tavel
Barsac	Chardonnay	hock	Montepulciano	Rioja	Tempranillo
Beaujolais	Chenin Blanc	jerepigo	d'Abruzzo	Rüdesheimer	Tokay
Beaujolais	Chianti	Johannisberg	Montilla	Sancerre	Valpolicella
Nouveau	claret	Kabinett	Moselle	Sauterne	vinho verde
Beaune	Constantia	lachryma Christi	Muscadet	Sauvignon Blanc	Viognier
Bordeaux	Côtes du Rhône	Lambrusco	muscatel	scuppernong	Vouvray
bucellas	Crémant d'Alsace	Langue d'oc	Niersteiner	Sekt	Zinfandel
Burgundy	Crémant de Loire	Liebfraumilch	Orvieto	Sémillon	
	Dao	Mâcon	Petite Sirah	Shiraz (or Syrah)	

wine bottle sizes

Sizes of wine bottles include:

magnum	jeroboam	salmanazar
flagon	methuselah	balthazar
Marie-Jeanne	rehoboam	nebuchadnezzar

wine glass *n*
glass, goblet, flute, schooner

wing *n, v*
♦ *n*
1 SECTION, branch, arm, faction, group, grouping, flank, circle, coterie, set, segment, side
2 ANNEXE, adjunct, extension, attachment, part, side
♦ *v*
fly, glide, flit, hurry, move, travel, pass, speed, race, soar, zoom
FORMAL hasten
■ **wing it**
extemporize, ad-lib, compose/perform without preparation, vamp
COLLOQ. say whatever comes into your head/mind, speak off the cuff, speak off the top of your head, play by ear

wink *v, n*
♦ *v*
blink, flutter, glimmer, glint, glitter, twinkle, gleam, sparkle, flicker, flash
FORMAL nictate, nictitate
♦ *n*
1 BLINK, flutter, sparkle, twinkle, glimmering, gleam, glitter, glint, flash
FORMAL nictation, nictitation
2 INSTANT, moment, second, split second, flash
■ **wink at**
ignore, disregard, overlook, neglect, pass over, condone, take no notice of
COLLOQ. turn a blind eye to

winkle *v*
extract, extricate, draw out, worm, force, prise, flush

winner *n*
champion, victor, prizewinner, medallist, title-holder, world-beater, conqueror
FORMAL vanquisher
COLLOQ. champ
Ｅ loser

winning *adj*
1 CONQUERING, triumphant, unbeaten, undefeated, victorious, successful
FORMAL vanquishing
2 WINSOME, charming, attractive, captivating, engaging, beguiling, bewitching, fetching, enchanting, endearing, delightful, amiable, alluring, lovely, pleasing, sweet
Ｅ **1** losing **2** unappealing

winnings *n*
jackpot, gains, proceeds, profits, takings, prize(s), prize money, booty, spoils
Ｅ losses

winnow *v*
sift, separate, screen, divide, cull, select, sort, part, comb, fan

winsome *adj*
charming, attractive, captivating, engaging, beguiling, bewitching, fetching, enchanting, endearing, appealing, cheerful, pleasant, delightful, amiable, alluring, lovely, pleasing, pretty, prepossessing, sweet
OLD comely
FORMAL delectable
Ｅ unattractive

wintry *adj*
1 *wintry weather*
cold, chilly, bleak, cheerless, biting, piercing, raw, desolate, dismal, harsh, snowy, arctic, frosty, freezing, frozen, icy, glacial
FORMAL hibernal, hiemal
2 UNFRIENDLY, hostile, bleak, cheerless, desolate, dismal, cold, frosty, icy, cool, harsh

wipe *v, n*
♦ *v*
1 RUB, clean, cleanse, dry, dust, brush, sweep, mop, swab, sponge, clear, dab; *Scot* dicht, dight
TECHNICAL absterge
FORMAL deterge
2 REMOVE, erase, take away, take off, get rid of
OLD expunct, null
FORMAL expunge, purge

♦ *n*

rub, clean, dry, dust, brush, mop, sponge, swab, dab

■ **wipe out**

eradicate, obliterate, destroy, massacre, exterminate, annihilate, erase, expunge, raze, abolish, blot out, demolish

FORMAL efface, extirpate

COLLOQ. liquidate, rub out, decimate, polish off, waste, blow away, zap

wire-pulling *n*

scheming, plotting, influence, intrigue, conspiring, manipulation, pull, Machiavellianism

COLLOQ. clout

wiry *adj*

1 SINEWY, muscular, lean, tough, strong

2 *wiry hair*

coarse, wavy, rough

F3 1 puny, flabby **2** soft

wisdom *n*

discernment, penetration, reason, sense, astuteness, comprehension, enlightenment, judgement, insight, common sense, prudence, understanding, knowledge, learning, intelligence, foresight, experience

OLD sapience

FORMAL sagacity, judiciousness, erudition, circumspection

Related adjective: Palladian

F3 folly, stupidity

wise *adj*

1 DISCERNING, perceptive, rational, informed, well-informed, understanding, enlightened, knowing, educated, knowledgeable, intelligent, clever, aware, experienced

OLD sapient

FORMAL sage, sagacious, erudite

2 WELL-ADVISED, reasonable, sensible, sound, far-sighted, long-sighted, shrewd, prudent, politic, common-sense

FORMAL judicious, sagacious, circumspect

F3 1 foolish, stupid **2** ill-advised, foolhardy

■ **put wise**

inform, notify, tip off, warn, tell, alert, fill in, intimate to, put in the picture, clue in

FORMAL apprise

COLLOQ. wise up

wiseacre *n*

wise guy, wiseling

COLLOQ. smart alec, smartypants, clever dick

wisecrack *n*

quip, joke, jest, funny, witticism, gag, barb, gibe, pun, in-joke

COLLOQ. one-liner

wisely *adv*

sensibly, soundly, shrewdly, perceptively, rationally, knowingly, intelligently, clearly

FORMAL sagely, sagaciously

F3 foolishly, stupidly

wish *v, n*

♦ *v*

1 DESIRE, want, yearn, long, hanker, pine, covet, crave, aspire, hope, fancy, hunger, thirst, prefer, need, lust

COLLOQ. yen

2 ASK, bid, require, order, instruct, direct, command

♦ *n*

1 DESIRE, want, hankering, aspiration, inclination, longing, craving, hunger, thirst, liking, fondness, preference, yearning, urge, whim, hope, fancy

COLLOQ. yen

2 REQUEST, desire, bidding, order, instruction, command, will

wishy-washy *adj*

feeble, weak, insipid, thin, watered-down, watery, flat, bland, ineffective, vapid, tasteless

FORMAL ineffectual

COLLOQ. namby-pamby, vanilla

F3 strong, firm

wisp *n*

shred, strand, thread, twist, piece, lock

wispy *adj*

thin, straggly, frail, fine, insubstantial, light, flimsy, fragile, delicate, ethereal, gossamer, faint

FORMAL attenuated

F3 substantial

wistful *adj*

1 THOUGHTFUL, pensive, musing, reflective, wishful, contemplative, dreamy, dreaming, meditative

2 MELANCHOLY, sad, forlorn, longing, yearning, mournful, regretful

FORMAL disconsolate

wistfully *adv*

thoughtfully, pensively, sadly, forlornly, longingly, mournfully, plaintively

wit *n*

1 HUMOUR, funniness, wittiness, repartee, facetiousness, drollery, banter, badinage, jocularity, levity, waggishness, liveliness, *esprit*, salt, sparkle

OLD eutrapelia

2 INTELLIGENCE, cleverness, sense, reason, common sense, wisdom, understanding, judgement, insight, shrewdness, astuteness, faculties, intellect, concetto, mother wit

FORMAL sagacity

COLLOQ. brains, gumption, nous, marbles

3 HUMORIST, comedian, comic, satirist, joker, gagman, wag, *bel esprit, homme d'esprit*

OLD wagha

F3 1 seriousness **2** stupidity

Synonym nuances

sense 1

You can use **humour** to suggest an inherent sense of delight in the ludicrous, while **funniness** implies the ability to cause laughter or smiles. **Wittiness**, on the other hand, is more redolent of sharp, intelligent humour which one admires, and **repartee** would be used likewise of sharp witty retorts. **Facetiousness**, however, is less approbatory, and implies an element of flippancy. **Drollery** suggests wry wit, unlike **banter**, which implies a degree of teasing, while **badinage** has implications of playfulness. You can use **jocularity** to suggest a propensity for joking, whereas **levity** has more to do with frivolity and being carefree. **Waggishness**, on the other hand, implies an element of mischievousness: *the waggishness of his cartoons satirizing politicians.*

---

witch *n*

sorceress, enchantress, occultist, magician, hex, hag, besom-rider, night-hag, pythoness, sibyl, weird, wise woman; *Scot* carline, gyre-carline

OLD *Scot* galdragon

FORMAL necromancer

witchcraft *n*

sorcery, magic, wizardry, occultism, the occult, the black art, black magic, enchantment, voodoo, spell, incantation, divination

FORMAL necromancy, conjuration

witch doctor *n*

magician, medicine man/woman, shaman, angekok, mganga; *S Afr* sangoma

witch hunt *n*

hounding, hue and cry, McCarthyism

with *prep*
accompanied by, in the company of, in association with, by, using, among, including, together

with it *adj*
fashionable, vogue, modern, contemporary, progressive, up-to-date, up-to-the-minute, modish
COLLOQ. cool, hip, in, trendy, groovy, all the rage, natty, glitzy, ritzy, snazzy, funky, hip
E3 out-of-date

withdraw *v*
1 REMOVE, take away, take out, pull back, draw back, draw out, pull out, extract
2 DEPART, go (away), absent yourself, retire, remove, leave, back out, draw back, fall back, recede, drop out, pull out, retreat, secede, scratch, opt out, contract out
3 RECANT, disclaim, take back, revoke, retract, cancel, annul, abolish, recall, take away
FORMAL rescind, abjure, nullify
4 RECOIL, shrink back, draw back, pull back

withdrawal *n*
1 REMOVAL, taking away, pulling back, drawing back/out, extraction, disengagement
2 DEPARTURE, exit, exodus, falling back, retirement, retreat, evacuation, disengagement
3 REPUDIATION, recantation, disclaimer, revocation, recall, secession
FORMAL disavowal, abjuration

withdrawn *adj*
1 RESERVED, unsociable, shy, introvert, introverted, quiet, retiring, retired, aloof, detached, shrinking, private, uncommunicative, unforthcoming, taciturn, silent
2 REMOTE, isolated, distant, secluded, out-of-the-way, private, hidden, solitary
E3 1 extrovert, outgoing, forthcoming

wither *v*
shrink, shrivel, dry (up), wilt, droop, weaken, decay, disintegrate, dwindle, wane, perish, die (off), disappear, fade (away), languish, decline, waste, taint, wilt, scorch, welt; *Scot* gizzen
OLD arefy, blast, welk
COLLOQ. miff off
E3 flourish, thrive

withering *adj*
scornful, contemptuous, scathing, snubbing, humiliating, mortifying, wounding, destructive, deadly, death-dealing, devastating
E3 encouraging, supportive

withhold *v*
keep back, retain, hold back, suppress, restrain, repress, control, curb, check, keep in check, reserve, deduct, refuse, hide, conceal
FORMAL decline
E3 give, accord

within *prep*
inside, not over, in reach of, inside the limits/bounds of, enclosed by, surrounded by

without *prep*
lacking, not having, in need of, needing, deprived of, free from

withstand *v*
resist, oppose, stand fast, stand your ground, stand, stand up to, stand firm/fast, fight, confront, brave, face, cope with, take on, thwart, defy, hold your ground, hold out, last out, hold off, endure, bear, tolerate, put up with, survive, weather
E3 give in, yield

witless *adj*
stupid, mindless, foolish, silly, senseless, unintelligent, inane, crazy, imbecilic, idiotic, moronic, gormless, dull,

empty-headed, half-witted, cretinous
COLLOQ. daft, loopy, barmy, potty, bonkers, nuts, nutty, nutty as a fruitcake, off the rails, cuckoo, mad as a hatter, raving, up the wall, wrong in the head
SLANG loony, off your chump, off your rocker, doolally, mental
E3 intelligent

witness *n, v*
♦ *n*
1 *witness in a court*
testifier, evidence, expert, vouchee; *Scot* man of skill
OLD compurgator
FORMAL attestant, deponent
2 ONLOOKER, eyewitness, looker-on, observer, spectator, viewer, watcher, bystander
3 TESTIMONY, evidence, authority
TECHNICAL teste
OLD (*Shakesp*) attest
♦ *v*
1 SEE, observe, notice, note, view, watch, look on, mark, perceive
2 TESTIFY, bear witness, give evidence, confirm, affirm, prove, verify, support, endorse, be evidence of, bear out, speak for
OLD obtest
FORMAL attest, depose, corroborate
3 ENDORSE, sign, countersign, validate
■ **bear witness**
record, testify, prove, confirm, corroborate, demonstrate, show, display, manifest, endorse, certify, affirm, assert, certify, declare, demonstrate, vouch for, verify
FORMAL attest, adjure, aver, asseverate, evince, evidence

witter *v*
chat, chatter, gabble, babble, jabber, rattle, twitter, twaddle, twattle, patter, drivel, gossip; *Scot* blether; *dialect & N Am* blather

witticism *n*
quip, riposte, pun, play on words, joke, repartee, pleasantry, *bon mot*, wisecrack, epigram
COLLOQ. one-liner

wittingly *adv*
knowingly, intentionally, willingly, on purpose, purposely, consciously, studiedly, wilfully, deliberately, designedly, by design, calculatedly
E3 unwittingly

witty *adj*
humorous, amusing, comic, sharp-witted, droll, whimsical, original, brilliant, clever, ingenious, lively, light, sparkling, funny, facetious, waggish, fanciful, jocular
FORMAL coruscating, lambent
E3 dull, unamusing

wizard *n, adj*
♦ *n*
1 SORCERER, magician, warlock, enchanter, occultist, witch, conjurer, hex; *dialect* wise man
OLD wisard
FORMAL necromancer, thaumaturge
2 EXPERT, adept, virtuoso, ace, master, maestro, prodigy, genius
COLLOQ. star, whiz, hotshot
♦ *adj*
wonderful, great, good, marvellous, brilliant, enjoyable, tremendous, super, superb, sensational
COLLOQ. fantastic, terrific, smashing

wizened *adj*
shrivelled, shrunken, dried up, withered, wrinkled, gnarled, thin, worn, lined

wobble *v, n*
♦ *v*
shake, oscillate, tremble, quake, sway, stagger, teeter,

totter, rock, seesaw, vibrate, waver, quiver, dodder, fluctuate, hesitate, dither, vacillate
COLLOQ. shilly-shally, wibble-wobble
• *n*
shake, unsteadiness, tremor, quaking, rock, tremble, vibration, oscillation

wobbly *adj*
unstable, shaky, rickety, unsteady, quavering, trembling, teetering, tottering, doddering, doddery, uneven, unbalanced, unsafe
COLLOQ. wonky
E3 stable, steady

woe *n*
misery, adversity, distress, sadness, sorrow, unhappiness, wretchedness, grief, melancholy, misfortune, suffering, hardship, trouble, pain, agony, anguish, gloom, curse, trial, depression, dejection, burden, disaster, calamity, heartache, heartbreak, tears
FORMAL affliction, tribulation
E3 joy

woebegone *adj*
miserable, wretched, sad, sorrowful, troubled, downcast, downhearted, gloomy, forlorn, grief-stricken, long-faced, dejected, crestfallen, mournful, doleful, dispirited, tearful, tear-stained
FORMAL disconsolate, lugubrious
COLLOQ. blue, down in the mouth
E3 joyful

woeful *adj*
1 SAD, miserable, wretched, mournful, sorry, unhappy, gloomy, grieving, grievous, heartbreaking, heart-rending
FORMAL disconsolate, doleful
2 DISTRESSING, disappointing, lamentable, pitiable, disgraceful, deplorable, shocking, sorrowful, tragic, cruel, hopeless, inadequate, mean, paltry, feeble, dreadful, appalling, awful, bad, terrible, poor, rotten, calamitous, catastrophic, disastrous
COLLOQ. lousy, pathetic
E3 **1** joyful

woefully *adv*
1 SADLY, unhappily, miserably, mournfully, gloomily, wretchedly, forlornly
FORMAL disconsolately, dolefully
2 *woefully inadequate*
lamentably, pitiably, disgracefully, deplorably, shockingly, tragically, hopelessly, appallingly, dreadfully, awfully, terribly, disastrously
COLLOQ. lousily, pathetically
E3 **1** joyfully

wolf *n, v*
• *n*
womanizer, seducer, ladies' man, lady-killer, lecher, philanderer, Casanova, Don Juan, Romeo
▪ **wolf down**
gobble, gulp, devour, cram, bolt, stuff, gorge, scoff
COLLOQ. put away, pack away
E3 nibble

woman *n*
1 FEMALE, lady, girl, maiden, maid, lass, madam, au pair, tomboy, hussy, *fille*, shiksa, geisha, belle, cutie, dolly, dolly bird, baby, beauty queen, Cinderella, bag lady, flirt, moppet, princess, nymphet; *Scot* lassie, gillet, jillet, cummer, kimmer, cutty, randy; *N Am* bachelorette
OLD damsel, wench, peat, popsy, blowze, quean
COLLOQ. puss, plain Jane, bobby-dazzler; *Aust* sheila
OLD COLLOQ. filly
SLANG bird, chick, biddy, bint, peach, Judy, bit, number, mystery, bit of stuff, tart, tottie
Related adjective: female

2 PARTNER, wife, lover, girlfriend, girl, lass, sweetheart, fiancée, mistress
SLANG bird, chick

womanhood *n*
1 ADULTHOOD, maturity
FORMAL muliebrity
2 WOMANKIND, woman, womenkind, womenfolk(s)

womanizer *n*
philanderer, seducer, wolf, lady-killer, ladies' man, lecher, Casanova, Don Juan, Romeo

womanly *adj*
feminine, female, ladylike, womanish, motherly, kind, warm, tender, effeminate, well-formed, shapely

wonder *n, v*
• *n*
1 AWE, amazement, astonishment, admiration, wonderment, fascination, surprise, pleasure, bewilderment
2 MARVEL, phenomenon, miracle, prodigy, sight, spectacle, rarity, curiosity; *Scot* ferly
FORMAL nonpareil
• *v*
1 ASK YOURSELF, meditate, speculate, ponder, question, puzzle, inquire, query, doubt, think, reflect
FORMAL conjecture
2 MARVEL, gape, be amazed, be surprised, be astonished, be astounded, stand in awe, be dumbfounded, be lost for words; *Scot* ferly
OLD admire, muse

The seven wonders of the world are:

Pyramids of Egypt	Mausoleum of
Hanging Gardens of	Halicarnassus
Babylon	Colossus of Rhodes
Statue of Zeus at Olympia	Pharos of Alexandria
Temple of Artemis at	
Ephesus	

---

wonderful *adj*
1 MARVELLOUS, magnificent, outstanding, excellent, superb, admirable, delightful, phenomenal, sensational, stupendous, tremendous
OLD (*Shakesp*) mirable
COLLOQ. super, terrific, brilliant, great, fabulous, fantastic, smashing, ace, top-notch, smashing, stunning, neat, brill, boffo, out of this world, second to none, divine, heavenly, sensational, not half bad, boss, bully, classic, crack, dilly, famous, jammy, knockout; *Aust & NZ* trimmer; *N Am* hunky, jim-dandy
OLD COLLOQ. capital, champion, spiffing
SLANG mega, cool, mean, wicked, stonking, radical, rad, crucial, way-out, shit-hot, groovy, clinking, def, fab, peachy, elegant, stellar, triff, triffic; *N Am* copacetic, dicty, righteous, socko; *Aust* beaut, castor
OLD SLANG lummy, ripping, tipping, topping
2 AMAZING, astonishing, astounding, startling, surprising, extraordinary, incredible, remarkable, staggering, awesome, strange
E3 **1** appalling, awful, dreadful **2** ordinary, unremarkable

wonderfully *adv*
fantastically, extremely, tremendously, terrifically, incredibly, unbelievably, amazingly, phenomenally

wonky *adj*
shaky, wobbly, weak, wrong, unsound, unsteady, crooked, askew, amiss
COLLOQ. skew-whiff
E3 stable, straight, balanced

wont adj, n
♦ adj
inclined, used, accustomed, given
FORMAL habituated
♦ n
habit, custom, routine, practice, rule, use, way

wonted adj
usual, customary, familiar, normal, regular, common, daily,
frequent, routine, accustomed, conventional
FORMAL habitual
🖃 unwonted

woo v
1 *woo a lover*
court, pay court to, chase, pursue, seek the hand of
OLD address, make love to; (*Spenser*) wow
2 *woo custom*
encourage, cultivate, attract, look for, seek, pursue

wood n
1 TIMBER, lumber, planks
Related adjective: ligneous
See also panel on next page
2 FOREST, woods, woodland, trees, plantation, thicket,
grove, coppice, copse, spinney
Related adjective: sylvan
■ **out of the wood(s)**
out of danger, safe, safe and sound, secure, in the clear, out
of difficulty, home and dry

wooded adj
forested, timbered, woody, tree-covered
FORMAL sylvan
🖃 open

wooden adj
1 TIMBER, woody
2 EMOTIONLESS, expressionless, awkward, clumsy, stilted,
stodgy, lifeless, spiritless, graceless, impassive,
unemotional, unresponsive, stiff, rigid, leaden, deadpan,
blank, empty, vacant, vacuous, slow
🖃 2 lively

woodland n
wood(s), forest, trees, plantation, thicket, grove, coppice,
copse, spinney
FORMAL boscage

woody adj
wooded, wooden, forested, tree-covered
FORMAL bosky, ligneous, sylvan, xyloid
🖃 open

wool n
fleece, down, hair, coat, floccus, yarn
Related adjective: lanate
See panel at **thread**.
■ **pull the wool over someone's eyes**
deceive, fool, trick, hoodwink, take in, bamboozle,
delude, dupe
COLLOQ. con, lead up the garden path, pull a fast one on,
put one over on

wool-gathering n
absent-mindedness, day-dreaming, forgetfulness,
distraction, inattention, preoccupation

woolly adj, n
♦ adj
1 WOOLLEN, fleecy, woolly-haired, hairy, downy, fluffy,
shaggy, fuzzy, frizzy
FORMAL flocculent
2 UNCLEAR, indistinct, ill-defined, hazy, fuzzy, blurred,
foggy, cloudy, confused, muddled, vague, indefinite,
nebulous
🖃 2 clear, distinct
♦ n
jumper, sweater, jersey, pullover, cardigan

woozy adj
dazed, dizzy, nauseated, light-headed, fuddled, confused,
blurred, wobbly, unsteady, rocky, befuddled, bemused,
tipsy
🖃 alert

word n, v
♦ n
1 NAME, term, expression, designation, utterance
FORMAL vocable
Related adjectives: verbal, lexical
2 CONVERSATION, chat, talk, discussion, consultation, tête-
à-tête
3 INFORMATION, news, report, communication, notice,
message, bulletin, communiqué, intelligence, statement,
utterance, dispatch, declaration, comment, assertion,
account, remark, advice, warning
FORMAL tidings
COLLOQ. gen, info, low-down, dope
4 PROMISE, pledge, oath, assurance, honour, vow,
guarantee, undertaking
5 COMMAND, instruction, signal, order, decree, will,
commandment, mandate
COLLOQ. go-ahead, green light, thumbs-up
6 RUMOUR, hearsay, gossip, talk, speculation, scandal,
whisper
7 *the words of a song*
lyrics, libretto, script, text, book
♦ v
phrase, express, couch, put, say, state, explain, write
■ **word for word**
verbatim, literally, exactly, precisely, accurately, closely
■ **have words**
argue, dispute, quarrel, disagree, row, squabble, bicker
■ **in a word**
briefly, in short, in brief, to be brief, to put it briefly,
concisely, succinctly, summarizing, to sum up
COLLOQ. in a nutshell, to cut a long story short

wordiness n
verboseness, verbosity, verbiage, wordage, long-
windedness, diffuseness, garrulity, garrulousness,
loquacity, logorrhoea
FORMAL prolixity, perissology
COLLOQ. waffle, verbal diarrhoea

wording n
words, choice of words, language, phrasing, expression,
phraseology, terminology, style, diction, wordage,
verbiage

word-perfect adj
accurate, faithful, exact, spot-on, letter-perfect
🖃 inaccurate

wordplay n
puns, punning, wit, witticisms, repartee
TECHNICAL paronomasia

wordy adj
verbose, long-winded, garrulous, rambling, diffuse,
discursive, phrasy, windy
FORMAL loquacious, prolix
🖃 concise

work n, v
♦ n
1 OCCUPATION, job, employment, profession, trade,
business, career, calling, vocation, pursuit, field, line, line
of business, métier, livelihood, craft, skill, art,
workmanship
2 TASK, assignment, undertaking, job, chore, responsibility,
duty, charge, mission, commission
3 TOIL, labour, drudgery, trouble, effort, exertion, industry
FORMAL travail
COLLOQ. slog, graft, elbow grease
4 CREATION, production, achievement, accomplishment,

Types of wood include:

acacia	camwood	hackmatack	olive	sissoo	**GENERAL CATEGORIES**:
afara	canary-wood	hazel	opepe	sneezewood	bitterwood
African mahogany	candlewood	hemlock	orange-wood	spruce	brushwood
	cedar	hickory	paddle-wood	stinkwood	chipboard
afrormosia	cheesewood	hornbeam	palay	sycamore	cordwood
alerce	cherry	iroko	palmyra wood	tallow wood	driftwood
Amboina-wood	chestnut	ironwood	Paraná pine	tamarack	firewood
apple	chittagong wood	jacaranda	partridge-wood	teak	fruitwood
arrowwood	citron wood	jatoba (or	peach-wood	thorn	green wood
ash	coachwood	Brazilian cherry)	pine	tigerwood	hardboard
balsa	coco-wood (or	kingwood (or	poon	toon	hardwood
bamboo	cocoa-wood)	violet-wood)	poplar	torchwood	heartwood
barwood	corkwood	kempass	porcupine wood	tulipwood	kindling
basswood	coromandel	kokra	purple heart (or	wagenboom	N Am lumber
beech	wood	lana	purple wood)	wallaba	matchwood
beefwood	cottonwood	lancewood	quassia	walnut	nutwood
black walnut	deal	larch	quebracho	wandoo	plywood
blackwood	deodar cedar	lignum vitae	rata	white cedar	pulpwood
bloodwood	Douglas fir	lima-wood	red sandalwood	willow	sapwood
boxwood	durmast	lime	redwood	yacca	seasoned wood
brazil (or brazil-wood or	eaglewood	mahogany	rosewood	yellowwood	softwood
sappanwood)	ebony	maple	rubberwood (or	yew	timber
	elm	meranti	hevea)	zante (or zante-wood)	whitewood
cabreuva	fiddlewood	myall	sandalwood		wood veneer
calamander	fir	nutwood	sapele	zebrawood	
campeachy wood	fustic	oak	satinwood		
	hackberry	obeche	sheesham		

See also **tree**.

---

composition, piece, poem, painting, book, play, writing, oeuvre, opus

5 *steel works*
factory, plant, workshop, mill, foundry, shop

6 *good works*
actions, acts, doings, deed

7 *the works of a clock*
machinery, mechanism, workings, action, movement, parts, working parts, installations
COLLOQ. innards, guts
F3 1 play, rest, hobby

♦ *v*

1 BE EMPLOYED, have a job, earn your living
2 LABOUR, toil, exert yourself, drudge, slave
COLLOQ. slog, graft, peg away, plug away, work your fingers to the bone, slog your guts out
3 FUNCTION, go, operate, perform, run, handle
4 OPERATE, run, handle, manage, use, drive, control
5 BRING ABOUT, accomplish, perform, execute, achieve, create, do, cause
FORMAL effect
COLLOQ. pull off
6 BE SUCCESSFUL, succeed, be effective, be satisfactory, have the desired effect, go well, prosper
7 MANIPULATE, manoeuvre, engineer, arrange, contrive
COLLOQ. fix, pull strings, fiddle, wangle
8 *work your way forward*
shift, guide, edge, move, make, penetrate, manoeuvre
9 CULTIVATE, farm, dig, till
10 MOULD, manipulate, knead, shape, form, fashion, model, make, process, squeeze
F3 1 be unemployed **2** play, rest **3** fail

■ **work out**
1 SOLVE, resolve, calculate, figure out, puzzle out, sort out, understand, clear up
COLLOQ. N Am dope (out)
2 DEVELOP, evolve, go well, succeed, be effective, prosper, turn out
COLLOQ. pan out
3 PLAN, devise, organize, arrange, contrive, invent, construct, formulate, develop, put together
4 ADD UP TO, amount to, total, come out, come to
5 EXERCISE, train, drill, practise, keep fit, warm up

■ **work up**
1 *work up a crowd*
excite, agitate, incite, arouse, stir up, move
2 *work something up*
incite, stir up, rouse, arouse, animate, move, stimulate, build up, inflame, spur, instigate, kindle, agitate, generate, whet

■ **the works**
everything, the lot, the whole lot, lock stock and barrel
COLLOQ. the whole caboodle, the whole kit and caboodle, the whole shooting-match, the whole shebang, the whole bag of tricks

---

Synonym nuances
noun sense 3
The term **labour** could be used of any arduous work, but you might use **toil** of something that is even more exhausting to do. **Drudgery**, on the other hand, is a very negative term suggestive of work that is habitual and repetitive: *the constant drudgery of housework*. **Effort**, however, returns to the idea of struggle: *with some effort and application, he passed the exam*; while **exertion** tends to suggest more strenuous physical activity: *breathing heavily from their exertions*. To suggest work involving steady application, then the word **industry** is appropriate.

---

workable *adj*
practicable, feasible, possible, practical, realistic, viable, doable
F3 unworkable

workaday *adj*
everyday, ordinary, routine, work-day, working, practical, mundane, average, humdrum, dull, common, commonplace, familiar, labouring, toiling
COLLOQ. run-of-the-mill
F3 exciting

worker *n*
employee, labourer, working man/woman, member of staff, artisan, workman/workwoman, craftsman/craftswoman, tradesman/tradeswoman, hand, operative, wage-earner, breadwinner, proletarian
COLLOQ. workhorse, workaholic

workforce n

workers, employees, personnel, labour force, staff, labour, human resources, manpower, workpeople, shop floor

working n, adj

♦ n

1 FUNCTIONING, operation, running, routine, manner, process, system, method, action

2 *mine workings*

mine, quarry, pit, shaft, diggings, excavations

3 *the workings of a clock*

works, machinery, mechanism, action, movement, parts, working parts, installations

COLLOQ. innards, guts

♦ adj

1 EMPLOYED, active, in work, in a job

2 FUNCTIONING, operational, running, operating, operative, going, in working order

COLLOQ. up and running

E3 1 unemployed, idle **2** inoperative, broken

workman, workwoman n

worker, employee, labourer, hand, artisan, craftsman/craftswoman, operative, manual worker, tradesperson, mechanic, journeyman, navvy, artificer

workmanlike adj

efficient, proficient, satisfactory, careful, adept, skilful, skilled, competent, thorough, painstaking, expert, professional, businesslike, masterly

E3 amateurish

workmanship n

skill, craft, craftsmanship, expertise, art, artistry, handicraft, handiwork, technique, execution, manufacture, work, finish

workmate n

colleague, associate, co-worker, fellow-worker, work-fellow, yoke-fellow

workout n

exercise, training, drill, practice, warm-up, limbering up, aerobics, gymnastics, isometrics, eurhythmics, callisthenics

workshop n

1 WORKS, workroom, atelier, studio, garage, factory, plant, mill, shop, machine-shop, forge, smithery, cooperage, rigging-loft, plumbery

2 STUDY GROUP, seminar, symposium, discussion group, class

work-shy adj

lazy, idle, slothful, slack, inactive, inert, slow, slow-moving, good-for-nothing, lethargic, sluggish

OLD laesie, lither, lusk, luskish

FORMAL indolent, torpid, languid, languorous, tardy, fainéant

COLLOQ. bone-idle

E3 busy, industrious, hard-working

world n

1 EARTH, globe, sphere, planet, star, heavenly body, universe, cosmos, creation, nature

2 EVERYBODY, everyone, people, population, human race, humankind, humanity, mankind, man

3 SPHERE, realm, field, area, domain, department, division, section, group, system, society, province, kingdom

4 TIMES, epoch, era, period, age, days, life

5 WAY OF LIFE, life, reality, existence, experience, situation

Related adjectives: terrestrial, global, mondial

■ **on top of the world**

overjoyed, delighted, elated, euphoric, ecstatic, in raptures, joyful, enraptured, rapturous, thrilled, jubilant, in transports of delight

COLLOQ. over the moon, tickled pink, on cloud nine, in seventh heaven, pleased as Punch, high as a kite

E3 sad, disappointed

■ **out of this world**

wonderful, excellent, incredible, marvellous, remarkable, great, fantastic, superb, unbelievable, phenomenal, indescribable

COLLOQ. smashing, stunning, terrific, neat, ace, brill, second to none, divine, heavenly, fabulous, sensational

SLANG mega, cool, mean, wicked, stonking, radical, rad, crucial, way-out, shit-hot

worldly adj

1 TEMPORAL, earthly, material, mundane, terrestrial, physical, secular, unspiritual, profane, carnal

FORMAL corporeal

2 WORLDLY-WISE, sophisticated, urbane, cosmopolitan, experienced, knowing

COLLOQ. streetwise

3 MATERIALISTIC, selfish, ambitious, grasping, greedy, covetous, avaricious

E3 1 spiritual, eternal **2** unsophisticated

worldly-wise adj

worldly, sophisticated, urbane, cosmopolitan, experienced, knowing, perceptive, shrewd, cultivated

COLLOQ. streetwise

worldwide adj

international, global, transglobal, general, universal, catholic

FORMAL mondial, ubiquitous

E3 local

worn adj

1 SHABBY, threadbare, worn-out, tatty, tattered, in tatters, frayed, ragged

2 EXHAUSTED, tired, weary, spent, fatigued, careworn, drawn, strained, haggard, jaded

COLLOQ. done in, all in, dog-tired, bushed, knackered

E3 1 new, unused **2** fresh, energetic

■ **worn out**

1 SHABBY, threadbare, useless, used, tatty, tattered, on its last legs, ragged, moth-eaten, frayed, decrepit

COLLOQ. tacky; *Aust* warby

2 TIRED OUT, exhausted, weary

COLLOQ. done in, all in, dog-tired, bushed, knackered, whacked, shattered, beat, dead-beat, zonked, clapped-out, rough, ready to drop, washed-out, hardly able to keep your eyes open; *N Am* pooped (out), tuckered out

SLANG (*taboo*) shagged out

3 HACKNEYED, stale, overworked, overused, tired, worn-out, time-worn, threadbare, wearing thin, unoriginal, cliché-ridden, cliché(e)d, stereotyped, stock, banal, trite, commonplace, common, pedestrian, uninspired, unimaginative

FORMAL platitudinous

COLLOQ. corny, run-of-the-mill, yawn-making

E3 1 new, unused **2** fresh, energetic **3** original, new, fresh

worried adj

anxious, troubled, uneasy, ill at ease, on edge, apprehensive, concerned, bothered, upset, fearful, afraid, frightened, overwrought, tense, strained, nervous, disturbed, distraught, distracted, disquieted, dismayed, fretful, distressed, agonized

FORMAL perturbed

COLLOQ. uptight, (all) hot and bothered, jittery, het up, beside yourself, in a stew, in a tizzy, having butterflies (in your stomach), tearing your hair out, with your knickers in a twist, a bundle of nerves

SLANG wired

E3 calm, unworried, unconcerned

worrisome adj

worrying, upsetting, troublesome, frightening, bothersome, agonizing, distressing, disturbing, insecure,

vexing, irksome, disquieting
FORMAL perturbing
COLLOQ. nail-biting, hairy, scary
F3 calm, reassuring

worry *v, n*
♦ *v*
1 BE ANXIOUS, be troubled, be distressed, agonize, fret,
stew; *dialect* worrit
COLLOQ. sweat, stress
2 IRRITATE, plague, pester, torment, upset, unsettle, agitate,
annoy, bother, disturb, trouble, concern, vex, tease, nag,
harass, harry, badger, dog, faze, niggle; *dialect* frab, worrit;
Scot deave, pingle
FORMAL perturb
COLLOQ. aggravate, bug, hassle, eat (up)
3 ATTACK, go for, tear at, bite, savage, touse
F3 1 be unconcerned **2** comfort
♦ *n*
1 PROBLEM, trouble, responsibility, burden, concern, care,
trial, annoyance, nuisance, pest, plague, irritation, vexation
COLLOQ. headache
2 ANXIETY, apprehension, trouble, distress, disquiet,
concern, unease, misgiving, fear, fearfulness, tension,
stress, strain, disturbance, agitation, torment, anguish,
misery, perplexity; *dialect* worrit
OLD tew
FORMAL perturbation
COLLOQ. hang-up, tizzy, tiz, stew
F3 2 comfort, reassurance

worrying *adj*
anxious, troublesome, trying, unsettling, upsetting,
niggling, disturbing, alarming, distressing, harassing,
disquieting, worrisome, uneasy, agonizing
FORMAL perturbing
COLLOQ. nail-biting, hairy, scary
F3 calm, reassuring

worsen *v*
1 AGGRAVATE, exacerbate, intensify, increase, heighten
2 GET WORSE, weaken, deteriorate, degenerate, decline,
slip, sink
COLLOQ. go from bad to worse, go down the tube(s), go to
pot, go downhill
F3 2 improve

worsening *n*
deterioration, decline, degeneration, decay, retrogression
FORMAL exacerbation, pejoration
F3 improvement

worship *v, n*
♦ *v*
revere, reverence, adore, exalt, glorify, honour, praise,
idolize, adulate, admire, love, be devoted to, extol,
respect, pray to, deify
FORMAL venerate, laud
F3 despise, hate
♦ *n*
reverence, adoration, devotion(s), homage, honour, glory,
glorification, exaltation, praise, prayer(s), respect, regard,
love, adulation, deification, idolatry
FORMAL veneration, laudation

Synonym nuances
verb
You can use **revere**, and the less common **reverence**, to
suggest regarding with high esteem, while **adore** implies
an element of passion. **Honour** and **praise**, on the other
hand, suggest expression and paying tribute: *he
honoured their achievements*. The stronger term **extol**,
however, suggests lavish approbation: *court singers
extolled the deeds of their princes*.
 Exalt could be used of according something with an
elevated status: *his exalted heroes*, whereas **glorify** goes

---

even further and suggests raising to an even higher level.
Deify is more strictly reserved for elevating to the status
of a god.
 Idolize implies an excessive, and perhaps even
unhealthy fixation: *he idolized and sought to imitate him*,
and **adulate** also suggests a degree of fawning. However,
the words **love**, **admire** and **respect** could be used
where a more restrained term is required, as can **be
devoted to**, although this has deeper implications of
dedication.

Places of worship include:

abbey	mandir	shul
bethel	masjid	synagogue
cathedral	meeting-house	tabernacle
chantry	minster	temple
church	mosque	wat
fane	pagoda	
kirk	shrine	

See also **religion**.

---

worshipful *adj*
reverential, respectful, admiring, deferential, humble, dutiful,
devoted, awed, solemn, pious, devout, adoring, loving
OLD obeisant
F3 irreverent, disrespectful

worst *v*
beat, defeat, get the better of, overcome, overpower,
overthrow, conquer, crush, master, subdue, drub,
whitewash, best
FORMAL subjugate, vanquish
COLLOQ. thrash, lick, hammer, thump, trounce, clobber,
annihilate, smash, devastate, slaughter, make mincemeat
(out) of, run rings round, paste
SLANG take to the cleaners

worth *n*
worthiness, merit, value, benefit, profit, gain, advantage,
importance, significance, eminence, use, usefulness,
utility, service, quality, good, virtue, excellence, credit,
desert(s), cost, rate, price, help, assistance, avail
F3 worthlessness

worthily *adv*
commendably, creditably, well, honourably, valuably,
admirably, reliably
FORMAL laudably

worthless *adj*
1 VALUELESS, useless, pointless, meaningless, futile,
unavailing, unimportant, insignificant, trivial, unusable,
cheap, poor, rubbishy, trashy, trifling, paltry
FORMAL ineffectual, nugatory
SLANG naff, cruddy
2 CONTEMPTIBLE, despicable, good-for-nothing, corrupt,
vile, low, useless
F3 1 valuable **2** worthy

worthlessness *n*
lack of worth, uselessness, futility, meaninglessness,
pointlessness, lack of importance/significance,
unusability, cheapness
FORMAL ineffectualness
F3 valuableness, worth, importance, significance

worthwhile *adj*
profitable, useful, valuable, of value, rewarding, worthy,
good, helpful, advantageous, beneficial, constructive,
gainful, justifiable, productive
F3 worthless

worthy *adj, n*
♦ *adj*
praiseworthy, creditable, commendable, valuable,

worthwhile, admirable, reliable, fit, deserving, appropriate, respectable, trustworthy, reputable, good, moral, honest, honourable, excellent, decent, upright, righteous, virtuous
FORMAL laudable, meritorious
Ⓔ unworthy, disreputable
♦ *n*
dignitary, personage, somebody, VIP, name, luminary, notable
COLLOQ. bigwig, big cheese/noise/shot/gun, top brass, top dog

would-be *adj*
aspiring, budding, striving, endeavouring, ambitious, enterprising, keen, eager, hopeful, optimistic, wishful, longing
COLLOQ. wannabe

wound *n, v*
♦ *n*
1 INJURY, trauma, hurt, cut, gash, graze, scratch, lesion, laceration, scar
2 HURT, distress, trauma, torment, heartbreak, blow, insult, harm, damage, pain, ache, anguish, grief, shock
♦ *v*
1 DAMAGE, harm, hurt, injure, hit, cut, gash, tear, graze, scratch, lacerate, slash, stab, puncture, pierce
2 DISTRESS, hurt, offend, shock, insult, pain, traumatize, mortify, upset, slight, grieve

wraith *n*
ghost, spirit, phantom, apparition, spectre, revenant, shade
COLLOQ. spook

wrangle *n, v*
♦ *n*
argument, quarrel, dispute, controversy, squabble, tussle, tiff, bickering, disagreement, clash, contest
FORMAL altercation
COLLOQ. row, slanging match, set-to, barney, scrap, spat, dust-up, punch-up, argy-bargy
Ⓔ agreement
♦ *v*
argue, quarrel, disagree, dispute, bicker, contend, have words, clash, row, squabble, fight, spar
FORMAL altercate
COLLOQ. be at each other's throats, be at loggerheads, fall out, hassle, have it out (with), have words, cross swords, scrap, have a bone to pick
Ⓔ agree

wrap *v, n*
♦ *v*
envelop, fold, enfold, enclose, cover, pack, shroud, wind, surround, package, parcel (up), gift-wrap, muffle, cocoon, encase, cloak, roll (up), bind, bundle up, swathe, immerse, lap, sheet, scarf, shawl, swaddle, enswathe, flannel, snug, wimple; *dialect* hap
OLD bemuffle, mail, wap; (*Spenser*) emboss
Ⓔ unwrap
♦ *n*
shawl, stole, cape, robe, cloak, mantle, rug, shroud, amice; *dialect* hap; *N Am* throw
OLD night-rail
■ **wrap up**
1 *wrap up well on a winter morning*
dress warmly, wear warm clothes, wear something warm, muffle up
2 *wrap up a present*
wrap, gift-wrap, pack up, package, parcel (up)
3 CONCLUDE, finish off, end, bring to a close, terminate, wind up, complete, round off
4 SHUT UP, be quiet
COLLOQ. dry up, belt up, pipe down, give it a rest, hold your tongue, put a sock in it, shut your mouth

wrapper *n*
wrapping, packaging, envelope, Jiffy bag®, cover, covering, jacket, dust jacket, sheath, casing, case, sleeve, paper

wrapping *n*
packaging, wrapper, envelope, Jiffy bag®, paper, case, carton, blister card, blister pack, bubble pack, Cellophane®, foil, tinfoil, silver paper

wrath *n*
anger, bitterness, rage, fury, exasperation, indignation, irritation, annoyance, temper, resentment, passion, displeasure, spleen, choler
FORMAL ire
Ⓔ calm, pleasure

wrathful *adj*
angry, furious, incensed, enraged, infuriated, raging, indignant, bitter, displeased, irate, ireful
OLD wroth
FORMAL furibund
COLLOQ. aggravated, cross, ratty, uptight, mad, hopping mad, raving mad, seeing red, in a lather, disgruntled, up in arms, hot under the collar, stroppy, choked, fit to be tied, on the warpath, in a paddy; *N Am* ticked off; *Aust* spewy, ropable; *Aust & NZ* crooked
SLANG pissed off, hairless; *N Am* burned up
Ⓔ calm, pleased

wreak *v*
inflict, exercise, create, cause, bring about, perpetrate, vent, unleash, express, execute, carry out
FORMAL bestow

wreath *n*
garland, coronet, chaplet, festoon, crown, band, loop, ring, circle, circlet

wreathe *v*
encircle, surround, enfold, entwine, twine, twist, wind, coil, wrap, envelop, crown, adorn, shroud, enwrap, festoon, intertwine, interweave

wreck *v, n*
♦ *v*
destroy, ruin, demolish, devastate, shatter, smash, break, split, sink, spoil, mar, play havoc with, torpedo, ravage, write off, shipwreck, cast away, crab; *Scot* stramash
COLLOQ. trash, handbag
SLANG gum up
Ⓔ conserve, repair
♦ *n*
1 RUIN, destruction, devastation, shattering, smashing, breaking, mess, demolition, ruination, write-off, disaster, loss, undoing, disruption, shipwreck, derelict, debris, remains, rubble, ruin, fragments, flotsam, pieces; *dialect* wrack; *Scot* stramash
2 *a nervous wreck*
neurotic, mouse, chicken
COLLOQ. bag/bundle of nerves
SLANG basket-case

wreckage *n*
debris, remains, rubble, ruin, fragments, flotsam, pieces, wrack
FORMAL detritus

wrench *v, n*
♦ *v*
yank, wrest, jerk, pull, tug, force, sprain, strain, rick, tear, twist, wring, rip, distort
♦ *n*
1 PULL, jerk, tear, twist, tug, sprain, pain, ache, pang
2 UPROOTING, upheaval, shock, sorrow, sadness, blow

wrest *v*
seize, force, extract, pull, take, win, wring, wrench, twist, strain

wrestle *v*
struggle, strive, fight, scuffle, grapple, tussle, combat, contend, contest, vie, battle

wretch *n*
scoundrel, rogue, villain, good-for-nothing, ruffian, rascal, vagabond, miscreant, outcast, devil, snake, miserable, pilgarlick
OLD cullion, rakeshame, recreant, scroyle; (*Shakesp*) vassal; (*Shakesp & Spenser*) miser
COLLOQ. rat, swine, worm, blighter, rapscallion, rascallion, insect

wretched *adj*
1 MISERABLE, sad, unhappy, sorry, melancholy, depressed, dejected, disconsolate, downcast, forlorn, gloomy, doleful, distressed, broken-hearted, crestfallen, woeful
OLD woe; (*Shakesp*) life-weary; (*Spenser*) wretch
2 PATHETIC, pitiable, pitiful, sad, unhappy, miserable, piteous, unfortunate, unlucky, sorry, hopeless, poor, woeful; *dialect* seely
OLD wretch
FORMAL hapless
3 CONTEMPTIBLE, despicable, vile, worthless, shameful, inferior, bad, low, base, mean, paltry, rascal
OLD wretch
4 ATROCIOUS, awful, miserable, deplorable, appalling, shocking, outrageous, dreadful, terrible, horrible, woeful, ratty
OLD wretch
5 *that wretched car*
damned, cursed, detestable, despicable, confounded, infernal, hateful, loathsome, odious, vile, fiendish, annoying, unpleasant
COLLOQ. blasted, blooming, flipping, darned, dashed, dratting, flaming, blinking
SLANG bloody, effing; (*taboo*) fucking, frigging
🖅 **1** happy **2** enviable **3** worthy **4** excellent

wretchedly *adv*
1 SADLY, woefully, unhappily, miserably, mournfully, gloomily, forlornly
FORMAL disconsolately, dolefully
2 *wretchedly small*
lamentably, pitiably, woefully, disgracefully, deplorably, shockingly, tragically, hopelessly, appallingly, dreadfully, awfully, terribly, disastrously
COLLOQ. lousily, pathetically

wriggle *v, n*
♦ *v*
1 SQUIRM, writhe, wiggle, worm, twist, snake, slink, crawl, edge, sidle, manoeuvre, squiggle, dodge, extricate, zigzag, waggle, turn
2 *wriggle out of a responsibility*
evade, stay/keep away from, elude, sidestep, escape, run away from, get out of, get round, shun, abstain from, steer clear of
FORMAL eschew, circumvent, refrain from, forbear
COLLOQ. hedge, duck, dodge, shirk, worm your way out of, give a miss, give a wide berth to, body-swerve
♦ *n*
wiggle, twist, squirm, writhe, jiggle, jerk, turn, twitch

wring *v*
1 SQUEEZE, twist, wrench, wrest, extract, mangle, screw
2 EXACT, extort, coerce, force
3 DISTRESS, pain, hurt, rack, tear, rend, pierce, torture, wound, lacerate, stab, tear

wrinkle *n, v*
♦ *n*
furrow, crease, corrugation, line, ridge, trench, fold, gather, pucker, crumple, wimple, crinkle, crankle, seam, ruck, ruckle, runkle, whelk; *Scot* lirk
OLD rumple, frounce

♦ *v*
crease, corrugate, furrow, line, fold, crinkle, crumple, shrivel, gather, pucker, ruck (up), ruckle, ruffle, unsmooth, frown, plough, ridge, crimple, runkle, shrivel; *dialect* frumple, rivel; *Scot* lirk
OLD rumple, frounce

wrinkled *adj*
crumpled, wrinkly, crinkled, creased, furrowed, furrowy, ridged, puckered, puckery, rivelled, rumpled, crinkly, crimpy, corrugated, ridged, rucked, ruffled, crankled; *dialect* rivelled
OLD frounced; (*Spenser*) wrizled
FORMAL rugose, rugate, rugous
🖅 smooth

writ *n*
court order, summons, decree, subpoena, warrant, brief, injunction, precept, extent, process, jury-process
TECHNICAL habeas corpus, replevin, ad inquievendum, audita querela, capias, certiorari, dedimus, devastavit, latitat, mandamus, mittimus, fiera facias, nisi prius, noverint, quare impedit, quo warranto, scire facias, supersedeas; *Scot* law-burrows
OLD inhibition, distringas, elegit, praemunire, supplicavit, tolt, venire facias; *Scot* letters of intercommuning

write *v*
pen, inscribe, record, register, jot down, note (down), set down, put down, take down, make a note of, transcribe, print, scribble, scrawl, correspond, communicate, draft, draw up, copy, compose, create
COLLOQ. dash off, put down in black and white
■ **write off**
1 DELETE, cancel, annul, cross out, wipe out, disregard, forget about
FORMAL nullify
2 WRECK, destroy, crash, demolish, smash (up), damage beyond repair

writer *n*
man/woman of letters

Writers include:

annalist	editor	penwoman
author	essayist	playwright
autobiographer	fabler	poet
bard	fiction writer	poet laureate
biographer	ghost writer	reporter
calligraphist	hack	rhymer
chronicler	historian	satirist
clerk	journalist	scribbler
columnist	leader-writer	scribe
composer	lexicographer	scriptwriter
contributor	librettist	short-story writer
copyist	lyricist	sonneteer
copywriter	novelist	stenographer
correspondent	pen-friend	*colloq.* storyteller
court reporter	penman	technical writer
diarist	pen-pal	web author
dramatist	*colloq.* penpusher	

write-up *n*
review, assessment, criticism, critique, evaluation, appraisal, judgement, report, commentary, examination, scrutiny, analysis, study, survey, rating, summing-up
FORMAL recension

writhe *v*
squirm, wriggle, thresh, thrash, twist, wiggle, jerk, toss, coil, contort, struggle
COLLOQ. twist and turn

writing *n*
1 HANDWRITING, calligraphy, script, penmanship, scrawl, scribble, hand, text, words, print

2 DOCUMENT, composition, work, opus, volume, publication
Related adjective: literary

Types of writing include:

account	drama	poem
advertising copy	editorial	profile
annals	epistle	propaganda
article	essay	record
autobiography	feature	report
biography	history	review
blog (or weblog)	journal	satire
book	legal document	scientific writing
chronicle	letter	script
commentary	life story	sketch
confessions	literature	sonnet
copywriting	lyric	statement
correspondence	memoir	story
criticism	monograph	study
critique	narrative	tale
curriculum vitae	news	thesis
diary	newspaper	travelogue
discourse	column	treatise
dissertation	paper	yearbook
documentary	parable	

See also **book; literature; poem; story; scripture.**

Writing instruments include:

ballpoint	dip pen	permanent
Biro®	eraser pen	marker
board marker	felt-tip pen	propelling pencil
brailler	fountain pen	quill
calligraphy pen	highlighter	reed
cane pen	ink pencil	Roman metal pen
cartridge pen	laundry marker	steel pen
CD marker	lead-pencil	stylus
chinagraph pencil	marker pen	typewriter
coloured pencil	pencil	writing brush
crayon		word-processor

---

written *adj*
set down, recorded, drawn up, transcribed, documented, documentary
FORMAL documental
🗲 unwritten, verbal

wrong *adj, adv, n, v*
♦ *adj*
1 INACCURATE, incorrect, mistaken, erroneous, false, in error, imprecise
FORMAL fallacious
COLLOQ. wide of the mark, off beam, off target
2 INAPPROPRIATE, unsuitable, improper, unconventional, unfitting, inapt
FORMAL unseemly, indecorous, incongruous, infelicitous, inapposite, malapropos
COLLOQ. hardly the place/time
3 UNJUST, unethical, unfair, unlawful, immoral, illegal, illicit, dishonourable, unjustified, dishonest, criminal, blameworthy, guilty, to blame, bad, wicked, sinful, evil
FORMAL reprehensible, iniquitous, felonious
COLLOQ. crooked; *Aust & NZ* crook
4 DEFECTIVE, faulty, out of order, amiss, awry
COLLOQ. up the spout
5 REVERSE, opposite, inside, inverse, inverted, back, contrary
🗲 **1** correct, right **2** suitable, right **3** good, moral **4** in order **5** right, front
♦ *adv*
amiss, astray, awry, inaccurately, incorrectly, inexactly, imprecisely, wrongly, mistakenly, faultily, badly,

erroneously, improperly
🗲 right
♦ *n*
sin, misdeed, offence, crime, trespass, immorality, sinfulness, wickedness, unlawfulness, wrongdoing, grievance, abuse, injustice, iniquity, inequity, infringement, unfairness, error
FORMAL transgression, injury
🗲 right
■ **in the wrong**
at fault, guilty, in error, mistaken, to blame, blameworthy
🗲 in the right
♦ *v*
abuse, ill-treat, mistreat, maltreat, injure, ill-use, hurt, harm, discredit, dishonour, misrepresent, malign, oppress, cheat
■ **go wrong**
1 BREAK DOWN, stop working, fail
FORMAL malfunction
COLLOQ. pack up, conk out, go phut, go on the blink, seize up; *N Am* go on the fritz
2 FAIL, be unsuccessful, collapse, come to grief, come to nothing, stray, go astray
COLLOQ. not make it, come a cropper, come unstuck, come unglued

wrongdoer *n*
offender, lawbreaker, criminal, delinquent, felon, miscreant, evildoer, sinner, trespasser, culprit
FORMAL transgressor, malefactor

wrongdoing *n*
crime, offence, lawbreaking, error, evil, misdeed, fault, felony, immorality, delinquency, sin, sinfulness, wickedness, mischief
FORMAL iniquity, maleficence, transgression

wrongful *adj*
immoral, improper, unfair, unethical, unjust, unlawful, illegal, illegitimate, illicit, dishonest, criminal, blameworthy, dishonourable, wrong, unjustified, unwarranted, reprehensible, wicked, evil
🗲 rightful

wrongfully *adv*
unjustly, unfairly, improperly, immorally, unethically, illegally, against the law, illicitly, illegitimately, dishonestly, criminally
🗲 justly, rightfully

wrongly *adv*
incorrectly, mistakenly, badly, by mistake, in error, inaccurately, erroneously
🗲 rightly

wrought *adj*
shaped, fashioned, hammered, beaten, made, manufactured, ornamental, ornate, decorative, ornamented
■ **wrought up**
agitated, worried, troubled, upset, disturbed, anxious, unsettled, flustered, ruffled, distraught, unnerved, disconcerted, nervous
COLLOQ. in a lather, in a tizzy
🗲 calm, composed

wry *adj*
1 *wry humour*
ironic, sardonic, dry, witty, sarcastic, mocking, scoffing, droll; *Scot* pawky, canny
2 TWISTED, distorted, deformed, contorted, warped, uneven, askew, crooked
🗲 **2** straight

X

xenophobia *n*
racism, ethnocentrism, racialism, xenophoby
 xenomania

xenophobic *adj*
racist, racialist, parochial, ethnocentrist

xerox *v*
photocopy, copy, duplicate, Photostat®, reproduce, print, run off

Xerox® *n*
photocopy, duplicate, facsimile, Photostat®

Xmas *n*
Christmas, Noel, Christmas-time, Christmas-tide, Nativity, Yule, Yuletide
COLLOQ. Chrissie, Crimbo

X-ray *n*
X-ray photograph, X-ray image, radiograph, radiogram, shadowgraph, angiogram, skiagram, skiagraph, röntgen ray
TECHNICAL encephalogram, encephalograph, mammogram, mammograph, pyelogram, sialogram

Y

yack *v, n*
- *v*

chatter, gossip, prattle, tattle, twattle, jabber, witter on, blather; *dialect & N Am* babble
COLLOQ. jaw, gab, yack-yack, yap
- *n*

chat, gossip, prattle, rant, harp on, twattle, jaw; *dialect & N Am* blather
COLLOQ. blah, chinwag, confab, hot air, yackety-yack

yank *v, n*
jerk, tug, pull, wrench, snatch, haul, heave

yap *v*
1 BARK, yelp
2 CHATTER, prattle, yatter, natter, witter on, jabber, babble
COLLOQ. jaw, gab

yard *n*
courtyard, court, garden, quadrangle
COLLOQ. quad

yardstick *n*
measure, gauge, criterion, standard, scale, guideline, benchmark, touchstone, comparison

yarn *n*
1 THREAD, fibre, strand, cotton
2 STORY, tale, anecdote, fable, fabrication
COLLOQ. tall story, cock-and-bull story

yawning *adj*
gaping, wide, wide-open, huge, vast, cavernous

year *n*
twelve-month period, calendar year
OLD twelvemonth
- **year in, year out**
regularly, repeatedly, again and again, time and (time) again, continually, endlessly, persistently, monotonously
Related adjective: annual

Special types of year include:

academic	Hebrew
anomalistic	Julian
astronomical (or equinoctial	leap
or natural or solar or	lunar
tropical)	Platonic (or great or perfect)
ecclesiastical	sabbatical
financial	sidereal
fiscal	Sothic (or canicular)
gap	

---

yearly *adj, adv*
- *adj*

annual, per year, per annum, perennial
- *adv*

annually, every year, once a year, perennially

yearn *v*
long, pine, desire, want, wish, sigh, crave, covet, hunger, thirst, hanker, ache, fancy, languish, itch, pant
OLD earn, think long; *Scot* green
COLLOQ. yen

yearning *n*
longing, pining, desire, wish, craving, hunger, thirst, hankering, fancy, panting
COLLOQ. yen

yell *v, n*
- *v*

shout, scream, cry (out), bellow, roar, bawl, shriek, squeal, howl, yelp, screech, squall, yelp, yowl, whoop
COLLOQ. holler
⊟ whisper
- *n*

shout, scream, cry, roar, bellow, shriek, howl, screech, squall, whoop
COLLOQ. holler
⊟ whisper

yellow *adj*
1 *yellow butter*
lemon, gold, golden, buff, tawny, light-brown, canary, primrose, saffron, flaxen
TECHNICAL xanthous, xanthic, xanthochroic, vitellary, vitelline
FORMAL flavescent, fulvous, fulvid
2 COWARDLY, faint-hearted, craven, fearful, timid, coward, dastardly, timorous, scared, unheroic, unmanly, chicken-hearted, chicken-livered, white-livered, lily-livered, spiritless, spineless, weak, weak-spirited, weak-kneed, soft, jittery; *dialect* mangy, nesh
OLD faint, cowish, milk-livered, nithing; (*Shakesp*) meacock
FORMAL pusillanimous
COLLOQ. chicken, gutless, wimpish, yellow-bellied, showing the white feather
⊟ 2 brave, courageous, bold

yelp *v, n*
- *v*

yap, bark, squeal, cry, yell, yowl, bay
- *n*

yap, bark, yip, squeal, cry, yell, yowl

yen *n*
longing, yearning, hunger, desire, craving, hankering, itch, passion, lust
COLLOQ. thing
⊟ dislike

yes *adv, interj*
right, quite, absolutely, certainly, agreed, of course, affirmative, very well, sure, indeed, all right, OK, definitely, by all means, rather, yah, aye, *ja wohl*; *Scot* ou ay
OLD yea
COLLOQ. yeah, yep, quite, sure, and how
⊟ no

yes-man *n*
sycophant, crawler, toady, lackey, minion, bootlicker
OLD toad-eater
SLANG (*vulgar*) arse-licker

yet *adv, conj*
- *adv*

1 UP TILL NOW, until now, up to this time, up till then, by now, by then, now, already, as yet, so far, still

OLD hitherto, heretofore
FORMAL thus far
2 IN ADDITION, still, even, too, also, further, furthermore, besides, moreover
COLLOQ. into the bargain
♦ *conj*
but, however, nevertheless, nonetheless, anyway, even so, all/just the same, for all that
FORMAL notwithstanding

yield *v, n*
♦ *v*
1 SURRENDER, give up, for(e)go, abandon, abdicate, cede, part with, give over
FORMAL relinquish, renounce
2 GIVE WAY, capitulate, surrender, concede, submit, succumb, give in, admit defeat, bow, cave in, knuckle under, resign yourself, go along with, permit, allow, accede, agree, comply, consent
FORMAL acquiesce
COLLOQ. throw in the towel/sponge
3 PRODUCE, bear, supply, provide, give, generate, bring in, bring forth, furnish, return, earn, fetch, pay, net, gross
FORMAL fructify, fructuate
1 hold **2** resist, withstand
♦ *n*
return, product, earnings, harvest, crop, produce, output, profit, revenue, takings, proceeds, income, haul

---

Synonym nuances
verb sense 2
Give way can be generally applied as a synonym of yield, while **surrender** suggests relinquishing any claims. **Capitulate**, however, has overtones of weakness: *he capitulated without any fight at all*, whereas **concede** makes the gentler suggestion of acknowledgement that you are defeated or wrong: *the ruling party conceded leadership to the democrats*. **Submit** also suggests admitting your opponent's superiority, although it implies that it has not been without a struggle, while **succumb** and **give in** would appropriately refer to being defeated in a struggle against difficulty: *she succumbed to weariness*.
  Bow, on the other hand, could be used of yielding to pressure: *they bowed to public opinion*, whereas **cave in** implies a rather sudden and ignominious collapse. The term **knuckle under** has more to do with acting in accordance with authority, but the tone suggests that this is not a desirable course of action. **Resign yourself** again implies acceptance, but **go along with** and **comply** have further implications of a lack of questioning.

---

yielding *adj*
1 FLEXIBLE, pliable, pliant, resilient, elastic, springy, soft, supple, spongy, quaggy
2 SUBMISSIVE, obedient, compliant, amenable, biddable, obliging, unresisting, accommodating, easy
FORMAL acquiescent, complaisant, tractable
1 solid **2** obstinate

yob *n*
lout, oaf, boor, dolt, barbarian, yahoo, gawk, lubber, calf, bull-calf, hob, lob, hallion, lumpkin, chuckle-head; *dialect* loblolly, swad; *Scot* coof, cuif; *N Am* jake
COLLOQ. clod, clodhopper, hick, hobbledehoy, slob, yobbo, bumpkin, oik; *N Am* roughneck; *Aust* hoon

yobbish *adj*
loutish, uncouth, oafish, boorish, doltish, ill-mannered, ill-bred, gawky, rude, coarse, rough, crude, vulgar, churlish, unmannerly, unrefined, uncivilized, gruff, impolite, rustic, uneducated, ignorant, bungling
COLLOQ. clodhopping
polite, refined, cultured, genteel

yoke *n, v*
♦ *n*
1 HARNESS, bond, link, tie, coupling, halter
OLD (*Shakesp*) bow
Related adjective: jugal
2 BURDEN, bondage, enslavement, slavery, tyranny, oppression, servility
FORMAL servitude, subjugation
♦ *v*
couple, link, join, tie, bond, harness, hitch, bracket, connect, unite, team, span; *S Afr* inspan

yokel *n*
country bumpkin, clodhopper, country cousin, hick, peasant, rustic, boor, bucolic
COLLOQ. hillbilly, hayseed
sophisticate, towny

young *adj, n*
♦ *adj*
1 YOUTHFUL, juvenile, childlike, baby, infant, junior, small, little, teenage, adolescent
COLLOQ. kid
2 IMMATURE, childish, early, new, recent, green, growing, fledgling, unfledged, inexperienced, undeveloped
1 adult, old **2** mature, old
♦ *n*
offspring, babies, little ones, issue, litter, brood, children, family
FORMAL progeny

Synonym nuances
adjective sense 2
The word **immature** can be used straightforwardly of a state of not being fully developed, but in certain contexts it can have critical overtones: *an immature way to behave for a 30-year-old*. The term **childish** is also suggestive of behaving in a manner that belies your more advanced years: *his childish petulance*.
  Early, on the other hand, simply suggests being in the initial stages: *it's still early days*. Similarly, **fledgling** could be used a venture in its infancy: *this fledgling democracy*, while **unfledged** suggests something that has yet to take its first steps and is, as a result, untried. **Undeveloped** suggests that some input is required before full potential can be achieved: *undeveloped countries*.
  Inexperienced and **green** can be used of people to suggest that they are unpractised in life, and have connotations of innocence: *the green child in me slipped out of the older woman, and I made a silly remark*.

---

youngster *n*
child, boy, lad, girl, lass, toddler, young person, young adult, young man, youth, young woman, teenager, adolescent; *Scot* bairn, wean, tyke, knave-bairn, gyte, smout; *N Am* subteen
COLLOQ. kid, young 'un, shaver, nipper, tot, tiny tot, brat, sprog; *N Am* hellion
SLANG ankle-biter; *N Am* rug rat

youth *n*
1 ADOLESCENT, teenager, youngster, juvenile, boy, lad, young man, young adult
COLLOQ. kid, teen
OLD COLLOQ. teeny-bopper
2 YOUNG PEOPLE, the young, younger generation
3 ADOLESCENCE, teenage years, teens, childhood, immaturity, inexperience, boyhood, girlhood
3 adulthood, maturity

youthful *adj*
young, boyish, girlish, childish, immature, juvenile, inexperienced, fresh, active, vigorous, lively, sprightly, spry, well-preserved
aged

youthfulness *n*

liveliness, vigour, spryness, sprightliness, vivaciousness, freshness, juvenileness, juvenility
FORMAL vivacity
⮏ agedness, languor

yowl *v, n*

◆ *v*
wail, yell, yelp, cry, howl, screech, squall, bay, yawl, caterwaul

FORMAL ululate

◆ *n*
wail, cry, howl, screech, yell, yelp, yawl

yucky *adj*

disgusting, revolting, horrible, unpleasant, messy, mucky, filthy, dirty, foul, sickly
COLLOQ. grotty, gross
SLANG grungy
⮏ nice

Z

zany *adj*
comical, funny, amusing, eccentric, odd, bizarre, absurd, ridiculous, droll, clownish
COLLOQ. crazy, daft, wacky; *N Am* kooky
serious

zap *v*
kill, destroy, hit, shoot, finish off
COLLOQ. do in, wipe out
SLANG bump off, rub out

zeal *n*
enthusiasm, ardour, fervour, passion, warmth, fire, devotion, spirit, energy, vigour, keenness, zest, eagerness, earnestness, dedication, commitment, wholeheartedness, vehemence, intensity, gusto, verve, study, bigotry, fanaticism, propagandism
OLD zelotypia
apathy, indifference, coolness, half-heartedness

zealot *n*
fanatic, radical, extremist, bigot, militant, partisan
FORMAL zealant
COLLOQ. eager beaver

zealous *adj*
ardent, fervent, impassioned, passionate, devoted, wholehearted, burning, fiery, enthusiastic, intense, warm, fanatical, militant, keen, committed, dedicated, eager, earnest, spirited, staunch, strenuous, diehard, bigoted
OLD true-devoted
FORMAL fervid
SLANG gung-ho
apathetic, indifferent, cold, half-hearted

zealously *adv*
ardently, fervently, enthusiastically, keenly, eagerly, earnestly, passionately, staunchly, fanatically
apathetically, indifferently, half-heartedly

zenith *n*
summit, peak, height, pinnacle, apex, high point, highest point, top, optimum, climax, culmination, meridian, acme, vertex, apogee
nadir

zero *n, v*
◆ *n*
nothing, nought, naught, nil, null, nadir, bottom, cipher, duck, love, duck's egg; *N Am* goose-egg
TECHNICAL absolute zero
COLLOQ. zilch
SLANG blob, zip, zippo
■ **zero in on**
aim for, concentrate on, converge on, home in on, direct at, level at, pinpoint, fix on, focus on, centre on, train on, head for

zest *n*
1 GUSTO, appetite, enthusiasm, enjoyment, relish, keenness, zeal, eagerness, liveliness, vigour, exuberance, interest, joie de vivre

COLLOQ. zing
2 FLAVOUR, taste, relish, savour, spice, tang, piquancy
3 RIND, peel, skin, husk, crust, shell
OLD rine
FORMAL epicarp, integument
1 apathy

zigzag *v, adj*
◆ *v*
meander, snake, wind, twist, curve
◆ *adj*
meandering, crooked, serpentine, sinuous, twisting, winding
straight

zing *n*
liveliness, life, energy, vitality, vigour, spirit, enthusiasm, animation, zest, sparkle, élan, joie de vivre
COLLOQ. go, get-up-and-go, oomph, pizzazz, zip, pep, punch, dash, brio
listlessness

zip *n, v*
◆ *n*
energy, verve, vitality, life, liveliness, enthusiasm, drive, sparkle, spirit, vigour, zest, gusto, élan
COLLOQ. go, get-up-and-go, oomph, pizzazz, pep, punch, zing
listlessness
◆ *v*
fly, dash, tear, rush, race, hurry, speed, shoot, flash, whisk, zoom
COLLOQ. pelt, belt, vroom, scoot, whiz, whoosh

zodiac *n*
baldric
OLD (*Spenser*) baudricke

The signs of the zodiac (with their symbols) are:

Aries (Ram)	Libra (Balance)	Aquarius (Water-
Taurus (Bull)	Scorpio	bearer)
Gemini (Twins)	(Scorpion)	Pisces (Fishes)
Cancer (Crab)	Sagittarius	
Leo (Lion)	(Archer)	
Virgo (Virgin)	Capricorn (Goat)	

---

zone *n*
region, area, district, territory, province, section, sector, belt, sphere, tract, stratum, zona

zoo *n*
zoological garden(s), zoological park, safari park, animal park, aquarium, aviary, menagerie

zoom *v*
race, rush, tear, dash, speed, fly, hurtle, streak, flash, shoot, whirl, dive, buzz, zip
COLLOQ. go all out, pelt, belt, vroom, whiz, zap